The Good Pub Guide
2000

The Good Pub Guide 2000

Edited by Alisdair Aird

Deputy Editor: Fiona Stapley

Editorial Research: Karen Fick
Research Officer: Tom Smith
Associate Editor: Robert Unsworth
Editorial Assistance: Fiona Wright
Additional Editorial Assistance: Elinor Breman

EBURY PRESS
LONDON

Please send reports on pubs to

The Good Pub Guide
FREEPOST TN1569
WADHURST
East Sussex
TN5 7BR

This edition first published in 1999 by Ebury Press,
Random House, 20 Vauxhall Bridge Road,
London SW1V 2SA

The Random House Group Limited Reg. No. 954009

www.randomhouse.co.uk

1 3 5 7 9 10 8 6 4 2

A CIP catalogue record for this book is available from the British Library.

ISBN 0 09 186792 4

Typeset from author's disks by Clive Dorman & Co.
Edited by Pat Taylor Chalmers
Printed and bound in Great Britain by Cox and Wyman Ltd, Reading, Berkshire

Contents

Introduction

The pub industry has seen several major structural changes this year. Swallow Group, formerly a major regional brewer, has closed its breweries (Vaux in Sunderland and Wards in Sheffield) and sold almost all its 664 pubs to Pubmaster, bringing its estate to over 2,000 pubs. After a fiercely resisted takeover battle, Marstons, the Burton on Trent regional brewer with nearly 900 pubs and the top-selling Pedigree beer, has been bought by its rival mainly Midlands super-regional brewer Banks's (the company is actually called Wolverhampton & Dudley, and includes Camerons of Hartlepool). This followed a deal Banks's made with yet another super-regional brewer, Greene King, to sell its 170 of the more southerly Marstons pubs. Greene King, expanding hungrily outside its East Anglian homeland, had previously been thought likely to bid for Marstons itself – and has since bought Morlands of Abingdon in Oxfordshire, bringing its estate up to nearly 1,700 pubs, and adding Old Speckled Hen and Ruddles to its beer brands. Banks's is selling some other pubs too, and is ending up with a combined estate of just under 1,500 pubs.

The biggest takeover battle involved the 3,600 pubs owned nationwide by Allied Domecq, including some 2,000 managed pubs (such as its Firkin and Big Steak chains) and 1,600 Vanguard tenanted pubs. Allied planned to sell to Whitbreads, which has some 2,000 managed pubs (including its Brewers Fayre, Beefeater and Hogshead chains), some 1,700 tenanted pubs, and the Boddingtons and Flowers beer brands. Of the national combines, Whitbreads pubs have always been the most likely to earn a place in this *Guide*, so on the whole, with this as a strong sign of good management at Whitbreads (at least from our point of view as customers), we hoped for good results from this planned sale. However, another bidder, Punch Taverns, eventually won a bitter fight with Whitbreads for the Allied pubs. Punch, a fairly new private company headed by a former Pizza Express executive, had bought Bass's tenanted estate in 1998. Its pubs' beer is supplied primarily by Bass, and a part of the Allied deal was that if Punch won Bass would put up over one-third of the total cost, and in return would cherry-pick around 600 of the most successful Allied managed pubs, as well as taking its fine London Nicholsons chain (places like the Black Friar). So Bass, whose entirely managed estate will now total over 3,000 pubs (including its Vintage Inns, Harvester, O'Neills and All Bar One chains), can be seen as the *éminence grise* in the Allied transaction. (The rest of Punch's backing is largely debt raised by an American investment bank, with some direct American investment.) Under supply contracts which last till 2007, the Allied pubs now passing into Punch's hands will continue to get beer from Carlsberg Tetleys, but there can be no doubt that in the long run the Punch/Allied takeover will strongly underpin Bass's ambition to replace Scottish Courage as Britain's main brewer. Bass's main beer brands (apart from Bass itself) are Worthington, Hancocks, Stones and M & B.

One consequence of the Punch/Allied takeover is that, because of the convoluted financing involved in such a relatively small new company making a major bid like this, the fees charged by the financial institutions involved are exceptionally high. These fees have been put at £140 million – which amounts to about 10% of the total annual sales in the pubs sold by Allied. It will be interesting to see what that surcharge boils down to, in terms of price per pint.

Punch has also now taken over another chain of some 700 tenanted pubs, Inn Business (which has some nice traditional locals), so in total will now own over 5,000 pubs. This makes it Britain's second-biggest pub landlord. The biggest is Nomura, the giant Japanese investment bank, with its tenanted chains such as Inntrepreneur, Unique Pub Co. and Grand Pub Co. Two other major non-brewing pub chains are the expansionist Enterprise Inns, which has some 2,500 tenanted pubs after its acquisition of Discovery Inns, Gibbs Mew and (in spring 1999) Century Inns, which included the Tap & Spile chain; and Greenalls, the former regional brewer, which also has over 2,000 pubs but in contrast now seems likely to slim down its estate, selling either its tenanted pubs to one of the more acquisitive non-brewing chains, or (more likely) its 750-plus managed pubs. At the right price, these would appeal to Whitbreads or to Scottish Courage – who would no doubt cherry-pick the 300 or so that fitted in best with its own branded chains, converting most of the others to tenancies and selling them on. Scottish Courage's pub-owning arm, Scottish & Newcastle, has some 2,600 pubs, including Chef & Brewers, and the John Barras, T & J Bernard and Rat & Parrot chains; its main beer brands are Theakstons, Courage and John Smiths.

This year we have taken a close look at exactly which real ale pubs have been selling as their cheapest beer – as well as what they have been charging for it. In the list that follows, we have included only those beers that we found cropping up more than once as a pub's cheapest offering. We also found some very cheap beers that were each stocked by only one of the 1,390 pubs in our sample, notably Holts (£1.16 a pint), Barnsley (£1.35), Bathams and Clarks (£1.40), Abbeydale and Watkins (£1.50), Hanby (£1.55), Daleside (£1.56) and Enville, Hexhamshire, Poole, Woodhampton and York (£1.60) – not to mention a special offer of only 99p we found on a beer called Wyre Piddle.

The list is in price order, starting with the cheapest, and shows in brackets after the beer names the number of pubs in which we found that beer offered as the cheapest. The prices should be taken as a guide only, as prices in individual pubs may vary quite widely around the average we found, depending on their area and style. (We have excluded one or two very high prices when these were clearly untypical of the beer concerned.) Obviously, the greater the number in brackets, the more reliable is our average price.

£/pint	
1.41	Sam Smiths (9)
1.53	Burton Bridge (2)
1.55	Lees (2)
1.57	Hobsons (10), Hardys & Hansons (2)
1.58	Berkeley (2), Cains (2)
1.60	Robinsons (9), Archers (6), Castle Rock, Wolf (2)
1.65	Burtonwood (8)
1.66	Yates (3), Moorhouses (2)
1.67	Greenalls (7)
1.68	Donnington (6), Summerskills (2)
1.69	Jennings (18)
1.70	Morrells (3), Dent, Old Forge, Teignworthy, Tolly (2)
1.71	St Austell (14), Smiles (6), Thwaites (3)
1.72	Batemans (10)
1.73	Branscombe Vale, Cottage, Oakham (3)
1.75	Banks's/Camerons/Marstons (35), Cotleigh (12), Hambleton, Reepham, Scotts (2)
1.76	Mansfield (11), Wye Valley (5), Blackawton (3)
1.77	Hook Norton (62), Black Sheep (19), Goachers (4), Timothy Taylor (4), Princetown (3)
1.78	Whitbreads group (97), West Berkshire (4), Hampshire (2), Scatter Rock (2)
1.80	Wadworths (23), Ushers (10), Palmers (8), Bunces, Freeminer, Moles (2)
1.81	Bass group (74) – **the national average price**
1.82	Sharps (17), Butcombe (12), Belhaven (9), Buckleys/Brains (6), Ridleys (3)
1.83	Scottish Courage group (153), Castle Eden (3)
1.85	Morlands/Ruddles (24), Shepherd Neame (16), Otter (13), Exmoor (9), Wickwar (3)
1.86	Greene King (86), Carlsberg Tetleys (75), Broughton (5)
1.87	Gales (9)
1.88	Ringwood (17), Everards (6), Cheriton (5)
1.89	Adnams (65), Woodfordes (8), Caledonian (3)
1.90	King & Barnes (4), Ballards, Hop Back (2)

1.92	Fullers (22), Hardy (7), Maclays (3)
1.93	Skinners (3)
1.95	Harveys (29), Charles Wells (5)
1.96	Youngs (12)
1.98	Vale (2)
1.99	Larkins (5)
2.00	Brakspears (36), Badger (18), Rebellion (2)
2.05	Arundel (2)
2.10	Nethergate (2)

Pubs brewing their own beers were in general very cheap, averaging £1.64 a pint, with £1.50 a pint a common price for them.

One of the most striking facts to emerge from this survey is how several quite small breweries, with very little advertising, have won a relatively large share of the market – at least among the good pubs covered by us. This says a great deal for their quality – and, for those in the upper part of the list, for their value for money. Hobsons, Jennings, St Austell, Batemans, Cotleigh, Black Sheep, Wadworths, Sharps and Butcombe all stand out in this way. But two small breweries, Hook Norton and Adnams, both show really massive support, and are now offered by more good pubs as their cheapest beer than Theakstons, Boddingtons, Tetleys, Courage, John Smiths or Bass, the biggest-selling brands from the four national brewers. Hook Norton, moreover, comes out at below average price even though it is a beer of choice in some of Britain's more expensive areas. With a visitor centre newly opened in September 1999 to celebrate the 150th anniversary of this most attractive and highly traditional small Oxfordshire brewery, Hook Norton is our **Brewer of the Year 2000**.

Which brings us to that millenary event – the Year 2000. How are pubs changing? And what future changes can we foresee? It's 20 years since we started research for the first edition of this *Guide*, and we have charted some massive changes in that time. Over those years we have inspected many thousands of pubs ourselves. In that time nearly 20,000 readers have been kind enough to write to us with their comments on pubs – thousands of them writing repeatedly, often on literally hundreds of places. We reckon this has given us some consumer-view information at one time or another on about one in three of all British pubs. Certainly, we could write volumes about trends and developments – and about what people want from pubs. But to keep things brisk, we will go out on a limb and sketch out ten predictions for the early years of the new millennium.

1   39% of the pubs in the *Guide* now have bedrooms – a big increase in the last couple of decades. This trend will continue, and standards of pub accommodation will also continue to improve. Pubs will soon be a major source of good low-priced accommodation.

2   Our readers are getting increasingly vocal in their criticisms of piped music in pubs where there's no call for it. More places are beginning to pay heed. We predict that thoughtless piped music will become a thing of the past – an outdated oddity that people remember from the last century.

3   There will be only two or three national brewers, instead of today's four. The trend for more pubs to brew their own beer will continue. The number of microbreweries, producing small quantities of beer for relatively few establishments, will also increase – but they will increasingly offer lager styles of beer, served cold, as well as or instead of the traditional British 'warm' beer.

4   The great growth in eating out in pubs will continue. In particular, more town and city pubs will start offering the good interesting individual food that so many country hostelries have already had to turn to, to gain customers in an era when drink-driving concerns have stopped alcohol being the main draw.

5   The trend towards special meal deals will accelerate markedly. Already quite a few country pubs which would otherwise be fairly empty on weekday lunchtimes are instead now filling with customers attracted by cheap OAP lunches. Many more will catch on to this. Town pubs will use similar food bargain offers to attract customers at off-peak times.

6   Children will be as readily accepted in pubs as in shops. As this comes to pass, it

will become more politically acceptable to frown on parents who let their children behave badly in pubs. Many more hostelries will go out of their way to attract families, with supervised play areas indoors and out to keep children out of their parents' hair, and even to look after children while parents shop.

7   Within ten years, it will become legally compulsory for pubs that wish to allow smoking on their premises to provide a separate smoking room, which is not part of their main bar. Smoking in the main bar will become illegal.

8   Licensing liberalisation will produce much more diversity in styles of pub, from true locals set up by individuals for their neighbours to elaborate hybrids with entirely different sorts of retail outlet. But the classic pub as we know it today, with its easy-going mix of good atmosphere, good drink and good food, will continue to go from strength to strength.

9   We've had Indian and Italian, then Tex-Mex and Thai; the next pub food trend will be Pacific Rim.

10 If the beer price rises we have charted over the last few years continue, by the end of this new century a pint will cost £383.57.

Awards

In the last decade pub wine has improved beyond recognition. In 1990 the *Guide* didn't even have Wine Awards – there would hardly have been any pubs to give them to. In our end-of-year roundups then, it was a question of noting the places which sold wine which was at least respectable. Now, virtually all pubs that pride themselves on their food also take care to keep a choice of enjoyable wines. Some places have gone much further, and either give a choice by the glass that would put many wine bars to shame, or track down some quite delicious offerings – or both. There are even pubs which have direct links with vineyards abroad, or which have their own retail wine business. Pubs which are now at the top of the league for wine are the Five Arrows in Waddesdon (Buckinghamshire), Trengilly Wartha near Constantine (Cornwall), Nobody Inn at Doddiscombsleigh (Devon), Fox at Lower Oddington (Gloucestershire), Wykeham Arms in Winchester (Hampshire), Crown at Colkirk (Norfolk), Blue Boar at Triscombe (Somerset), Crown in Southwold (Suffolk), General Tarleton at Ferrensby and Angel at Hetton (Yorkshire), and pubs in the small mainly Cambridgeshire Huntsbridge group (White Hart at Great Yeldham, Old Bridge in Huntingdon, Pheasant at Keyston, Three Horseshoes at Madingley and Falcon at Fotheringhay).

Of these, the Crown in Southwold and the Nobody Inn have been prominent standard-bearers in the revolution in pub wine. The Crown was perhaps the first pub to keep a really interesting changing range of very good wines by the glass, under vacuum for perfect freshness. The Nobody Inn's list has grown and grown in interest (and size – it now covers 850 wines). With helpful notes, tasting events and an expanding retail operation, it sets a magnificent example. The Nobody Inn at Doddiscombsleigh is our **Wine Pub of the Year 2000**.

Interest in malt whiskies has expanded considerably in the last decade. A good many pubs now have a fine choice – two or three dozen or more. Quite a few have a remarkable range, running into three figures, including real rarities: the Crown & Horns at East Ilsley (Berkshire), Nobody Inn at Doddiscombsleigh and Drake Manor at Buckland Monachorum (Devon), Hardwick Inn at Hardwick Hall (Derbyshire), Bulls Head at Clipston (Leicestershire), Angel at Larling (Norfolk), Victoria in Beeston (Nottinghamshire), White Horse at Pulverbatch (Shropshire), Sandpiper at Leyburn and Pack Horse at Widdop (Yorkshire), Bow Bar in Edinburgh, Cawdor Tavern at Cawdor, Crown at Portpatrick, Morefield Motel in Ullapool and Eilean Chraggan at Weem (Scotland), and Dinorben Arms at Bodfari and Old House at Llangynwyd (Wales). With a choice of well over 250 malts, the place to drink to the health of the new millennium in Scotland's own liquor must be the Crown at Portpatrick, which is our **Whisky Pub of the Year 2000**.

The life-blood of a good pub is its beer. Over 300 entries in the *Guide* now carry our Beer Award tankard symbol, showing exceptional merit in the choice or quality of the beer they keep. Here, we shortlist 15 pubs which combine real character (one is actually a boat) with a particularly interesting range – often quickly changing – of beers in top condition. They are Charters in Peterborough (Cambridgeshire),

Bhurtpore at Aston (Cheshire), Quayside Inn & Old Ale House in Falmouth and Old Ale House in Truro (Cornwall), Watermill at Ings (Cumbria), Brunswick in Derby (Derbyshire), Sun in Feering and Prince of Wales at Stow Maries (Essex), Lytton Arms in Knebworth (Hertfordshire), Swan in the Rushes in Loughborough (Leicestershire), Taps in Lytham (Lancashire), Fat Cat in Norwich (Norfolk), Lincolnshire Poacher in Nottingham, Halfway House at Pitney (Somerset) and the Fat Cat in Sheffield (Yorkshire). For its fine combination of over 20 well kept real ales, enjoyable food, and relaxed chatty atmosphere attracting a good mix of customers, we name the Old Ale House in Truro **Beer Pub of the Year 2000**.

Nearly 50 pubs in the *Guide* now brew their own beer. Usually, this is cheaper than mass-produced beers, almost always more distinctive, and sometimes a lot better. Pubs which stand out for the quality of their own brews include the Pot Kiln at Frilsham (Berkshire), Brewery Tap in Peterborough (Cambridgeshire), Black Bull in Coniston (Cumbria), Brunswick in Derby (Derbyshire), Flower Pots at Cheriton (Hampshire), Railway Tavern at Reedham (Norfolk), Three Tuns in Bishops Castle and Plough at Wistanstow (Shropshire), George in Eccleshall (Staffordshire), Gribble at Oving (Sussex), Beacon in Dudley (Warwickshire chapter – a delicious very strong dark Mild), Talbot at Knightwick (Worcestershire), Sair in Linthwaite and Brewers Arms in Snaith (Yorkshire), and Moulin in Pitlochry (Scotland). It's a new entry – and indeed a new pub – which gains the award of **Own Brew Pub of the Year 2000**: the Brewery Tap in Peterborough, for its fine range of Oakham beers, in surroundings that rather suit the start of the new millennium.

As we enter the 21st century, it's a double pleasure to find so many good pubs that would not have been out of place in the 19th. And they don't seem to be a dying breed, as some have feared: each year, we track down one or two more. From the many featured in the *Guide*, we have selected a couple of dozen classic unspoilt pubs to please the most demanding traditionalist: the Cock at Broom (Bedfordshire), Bell at Aldworth and Pot Kiln at Frilsham (Berkshire), Queens Head at Newton (Cambridgeshire), Quiet Woman at Earl Sterndale and Three Stags Heads at Wardlow (Derbyshire), Square & Compass at Worth Matravers (Dorset), Drake Manor at Buckland Monachorum, Rugglestone at Widecombe and Northmore Arms at Wonson (Devon), Boat at Ashleworth Quay (Gloucestershire), Harrow at Steep (Hampshire), Carpenters Arms at Walterstone (Herefordshire), Gate at Boyden Gate and Red Lion at Snargate (Kent), Tuckers Grave at Faulkland and Rose & Crown at Huish Episcopi (Somerset), Fleece at Bretforton and Monkey House at Defford (Worcestershire), Birch Hall at Beck Hole, White Horse in Beverley and Kings Arms at Heath (Yorkshire), Case is Altered at Five Ways and Beacon in Sedgley (Warwickshire chapter), Compton Arms in North London, and Blue Anchor at East Aberthaw (Wales). Licensed to sell beer for over three centuries, the unchanging and very welcoming Case is Altered at Five Ways is our **Unspoilt Pub of the Year 2000**.

For centuries, individual landlords have made their pubs famous for unusual collections. Plenty of them have their few dozen decorative plates, whisky-water jugs, chamber-pots, horsebrasses, cigarette cards. But a few go far beyond this, into the true collector's realm of almost obsessional hunting for that special find which will fill that last precious inch of space on his crowded walls. For sheer enjoyment, just try the King William IV at Heydon (Cambridgeshire), Railway in St Agnes and Eliot Arms at Tregadillett (Cornwall), Eagle & Child at Wharles (Lancashire), Allenheads Inn at Allenheads (Northumbria), Boot at Barnard Gate (Oxfordshire), George & Dragon in Much Wenlock (Shropshire), Old Station in Hallatrow (Somerset) and Yew Tree at Cauldon (Staffordshire). The Fleece at Bretforton (Worcestershire) has a remarkable collection of Jacobean furniture and pewter handed down with the pub through generations of the same family (the National Trust owns it now). The Highwayman at Sourton (Devon) is rather different from all of these, in that it's the pub itself that's really the collection – painstakingly put together piece by piece as a strangely compelling medley of make-believe. Alan East's quite remarkable series of collections, particularly of working music-making machinery of varying kinds, makes his Yew Tree at Cauldon the **Collector's Pub of the Year 2000**.

We no longer have to make a big song and dance about vegetarian food in pubs. A decade ago, few pubs offered it. Now, you can get something vegetarian virtually anywhere, and pubs putting any real thought into their food make non-meaty dishes an integral part of their menu. However, in a few pubs vegetarian cooking almost dominates: the King William IV at Heydon (Cambridgeshire), Masons Arms on Cartmel Fell (Cumbria), Snowdrop in Lewes (Sussex), Bryn Tyrch just outside Capel Curig (Wales) spring to mind. For the way it continues to add entertainingly to the vegetarian repertoire, we name the King William IV at Heydon **Vegetarian Pub of the Year 2000**.

As with vegetarian food, any pub however far inland which prides itself on cooking with fresh ingredients now tracks down a source of fresh fish, even if this means a weekly event. Some pubs have made fresh fish on a daily basis such a central part of their menu that they deserve special recognition: the Fish in Bray (Berkshire), Carrington Arms at Moulsoe (Buckinghamshire), Trinity Foot at Swavesey (Cambridgeshire), Drewe Arms at Broadhembury, Anchor at Cockwood and Start Bay at Torcross (Devon), Sussex Oak at Blackham, Dering Arms at Pluckley and Sankeys in Tunbridge Wells (Kent), Oddfellows Arms in Mellor (Lancashire chapter), Chequers at Gedney Dyke (Lincolnshire), Froize at Chillesford (Suffolk), Half Moon at Kirdford (Sussex), George & Dragon at Rowde (Wiltshire), Applecross Inn at Applecross, Loch Melfort Hotel at Arduaine, Crinan Hotel at Crinan, Cabin in St Monans, Tayvallich Inn at Tayvallich and Morefield Motel in Ullapool (Scotland), and Penhelig Arms in Aberdovey and Ferry in Pembroke Ferry (Wales). Kerstin and Nigel Burge have been setting standards for fish cooking in pubs throughout the last decade: their charming Drewe Arms at Broadhembury is our **Fish Pub of the Year 2000**.

Choosing a Dining Pub of the Year has been getting harder every year, with the competition really hotting up, throughout Great Britain. What we are looking for is first-rate food showing imaginative use of fresh ingredients, in surroundings which have the warmth of a pub and yet allow a sense of occasion for a special meal out. Places which more than live up to this are the Green Dragon in Haddenham and Rising Sun at Little Hampden (Buckinghamshire), Old Bridge in Huntingdon, Pheasant at Keyston and Three Horseshoes at Madingley (Cambridgeshire), Punch Bowl at Crosthwaite (Cumbria), White Hart at Great Yeldham (Essex), Riverside Inn at Aymestrey and Three Crowns at Ullingswick (Herefordshire), Falcon at Fotheringhay (Northamptonshire), Rose & Crown at Romaldkirk (Northumbria), Boars Head at Ardington (Oxfordshire), Blue Boar at Triscombe (Somerset), Griffin at Fletching, Halfway Bridge Inn at Lodsworth and Horse Guards at Tillington (Sussex), George & Dragon at Rowde and Seven Stars near Woodborough (Wiltshire), Angel at Hetton, Blue Lion at East Witton, Boars Head at Ripley and Three Acres in Shelley (Yorkshire), Wheatsheaf at Swinton (Scotland), and Walnut Tree at Llandewi Skirrid and Nantyffin Cider Mill near Crickhowell (Wales). The Three Acres at Shelley, which now has a delicatessen next door, is undeniably at the restaurant end of the dining pub spectrum, but has a really warm atmosphere (and a Beer Award) to go with its excellent imaginative food; it is our **Dining Pub of the Year 2000**.

Quite a few city pubs offer really cheap food, but usually it's more a question of filling a hole than titillating the tastebuds. Dotted about the country there is a handful of pubs which make a real effort to provide more thoughtful food at remarkably low prices: the Rugglestone at Widecombe (Devon), Elephant & Castle at Bloxham (Oxfordshire), Six Bells at Chiddingly (Sussex), and Fat Cat and New Barrack in Sheffield (Yorkshire). And in Derbyshire the Queens Head at Saddington does an excellent value OAP lunch. Our choice as **Bargain Pub of the Year 2000** is the Fat Cat in Sheffield: with interesting main courses at £2.50 and proper puddings at £1, how can you go wrong?

As we prepare the latest edition of the *Guide*, quite a few pubs stand out as exceptional all-rounders – very good atmosphere, food and drink, with first-class service, in interesting surroundings. In the top rank are the Bhurtpore at Aston (Cheshire), Trengilly Wartha near Constantine and Roseland at Philleigh (Cornwall), Masons Arms on Cartmel Fell, Britannia at Elterwater and Drunken Duck near Hawkshead (Cumbria), Nobody Inn at Doddiscombsleigh and Castle Inn at Lydford (Devon), Kings Head at Bledington (Gloucestershire), Flower Pots at Cheriton and Wykeham Arms in Winchester (Hampshire), Three Horseshoes at Warham (Norfolk), Feathers at Hedley on the Hill (Northumbria), Lamb in Burford

(Oxfordshire), Crown at Churchill (Somerset), Angel in Lavenham and De La Pole Arms at Wingfield (Suffolk), Griffin at Fletching (Sussex), Fiddle & Bone in Birmingham (Warwickshire chapter), Red Lion at Burnsall, Blue Lion at East Witton and Yorke Arms at Ramsgill (Yorkshire), Jerusalem Tavern (Central London) and Bear in Crickhowell (Wales). All of these are immensely enjoyable in their different ways, from the simplicity of the Flower Pots at Cheriton to the stylish comfort of the Yorke Arms at Ramsgill, from the beer-oriented good humour of the Bhurtpore at Aston to the foody sophistication of the Blue Lion at East Witton. For all-round appeal, though, it's very hard to beat the Bear at Crickhowell: it is **Pub of the Year 2000**.

Some pubs are great pubs purely because of the people who run them. The personalities of the landlord and landlady shine through so warmly that everyone – regular and visitor alike – feels special. On the basis of our own inspections and a tidal flow of enthusiastic reports from readers, a small number of licensees emerge this year as quite exceptional: Aubrey Sinclair Ball of the Millstone at Barnack (Cambridgeshire), John Pitchford of the Springer Spaniel at Treburley (Cornwall), Henry Lynch of the Dukes Head at Armathwaite (Cumbria), Jamie Stuart and Pippa Hutchinson of the Duke of York at Iddesleigh, Geoff and Clare Mann of the Manor Inn at Lower Ashton, David and Susan Grey of the Castle Inn at Lower Lydford and Sue and David Armstrong of the Church House at Marldon (Devon), Peter and Linda Stenson of the Allenheads Inn at Allenheads (Northumbria), Gordon and Diane Evans of the Nut Tree at Murcott and Colin Mead of the Red Lion at Steeple Aston (Oxfordshire), Stephen and Di Waring of the Wenlock Edge Inn on Wenlock Edge (Shropshire), Alistair and Sarah Cade of the Notley Arms at Monksilver (Somerset), Alan East of the Yew Tree at Cauldon (Staffordshire), and Michael and Margaret Fox of the Buck at Thornton Watlass (Yorkshire). Our **Licensees of the Year 2000** are Alistair and Sarah Cade of the Notley Arms at Monksilver.

What is a Good Pub?

The main entries in this book have been through a two-stage sifting process. First of all, some 2,000 regular correspondents keep in touch with us about the pubs they visit, and nearly double that number report occasionally. This keeps us up-to-date about places included in previous editions – it's their alarm signals that warn us when a pub's standards have dropped (after a change of management, say), and it's their continuing approval that reassures us about keeping a pub as a main entry for another year. Very important, though, are the reports they send us on pubs we don't know at all. It's from these new discoveries that we make up a shortlist, to be considered for possible inclusion as new main entries. The more people that report favourably on a new pub, the more likely it is to win a place on this shortlist – especially if some of the reporters belong to our hard core of about five hundred trusted correspondents whose judgement we have learned to rely on. These are people who have each given us detailed comments on dozens of pubs, and shown that (when we ourselves know some of those establishments too) their judgement is closely in line with our own.

This brings us to the acid test. Each pub, before inclusion as a main entry, is inspected anonymously by the Editor, the Deputy Editor, or both. They have to find some special quality that would make strangers enjoy visiting it. What often marks the pub out for special attention is fine value food (and that might mean anything from a well made sandwich, with good fresh ingredients at a low price, to imaginative cooking outclassing most restaurants in the area). Maybe the drinks are out of the ordinary (pubs with several hundred whiskies, with remarkable wine lists, with home-made country wines or good beer or cider made on the premises, with a wide range of well kept real ales or bottled beers from all over the world). Perhaps there's a special appeal about it as a place to stay, with good bedrooms and obliging service. Maybe it's the building itself (from centuries-old parts of monasteries to extravagant Victorian gin-palaces), or its surroundings (lovely countryside, attractive waterside, extensive well kept garden), or what's in it (charming furnishings, extraordinary collections of bric-a-brac).

Above all, though, what makes the good pub is its atmosphere – you should be able to feel at home there, and feel not just that *you're* glad you've come but that *they're* glad you've come.

It follows from this that a great many ordinary locals, perfectly good in their own right, don't earn a place in the book. What makes them attractive to their regular customers (an almost clubby chumminess) may even make strangers feel rather out-of-place.

Another important point is that there's not necessarily any link between charm and luxury – though we like our creature comforts as much as anyone. A basic unspoilt village tavern, with hard seats and a flagstone floor, may be worth travelling miles to find, while a deluxe pub-restaurant may not be worth crossing the street for. Landlords can't buy the Good Pub accolade by spending thousands on thickly padded banquettes, soft music and luxuriously shrimpy sauces for their steaks – they can only win it, by having a genuinely personal concern for both their customers and their pub.

Using the *Guide*

THE COUNTIES

England has been split alphabetically into counties, mainly to make it easier for people scanning through the book to find pubs near them. Each chapter starts by picking out the pubs that are currently doing best in the area, or specially attractive for one reason or another. Metropolitan areas have been included in the counties around them – for example, Merseyside in Lancashire. And occasionally we have grouped counties together – for example, Rutland with Leicestershire, and Durham with Northumberland to make Northumbria. When there's any risk of confusion, we have put a note about where to find a county at the place in the book where you'd probably look for it. But if in doubt, check the Contents.

Scotland and Wales have each been covered in single chapters, and London appears immediately before them at the end of England. Except in London (which is split into Central, North, South, West and East), pubs are listed alphabetically under the name of the town or village where they are. If the village is so small that you probably wouldn't find it on a road map, we've listed it under the name of the nearest sizeable village or town instead. The maps use the same town and village names, and additionally include a few big cities that don't have any listed pubs – for orientation.

We always list pubs in their true locations – so if a village is actually in Buckinghamshire that's where we list it, even if its postal address is via some town in Oxfordshire. Just once or twice, while the village itself is in one county the pub is just over the border in the next-door county. We then use the village county, not the pub one.

STARS ★

Specially good pubs are picked out with a star after their name. In a few cases, entries have two stars: these are the aristocrats among pubs, really worth going out of your way to find. The stars do NOT signify extra luxury or specially good food – in fact some of the pubs which appeal most distinctively and strongly of all are decidedly basic in terms of food and surroundings. The detailed description of each pub shows what its special appeal is, and it's that that the stars refer to.

FOOD AND STAY AWARDS: 🍴 🛏

The knife-and-fork rosette shows those pubs where food is quite outstanding. The bed symbol shows pubs which we know to be good as places to stay in – bearing in mind the price of the rooms (obviously you can't expect the same level of luxury at £30 a head as you'd get for £60 a head). Towns where there are pubs with bedrooms are marked on the maps as a square.

♀

This wine glass symbol marks out those pubs where wines are a cut above the usual run, and/or offer a good choice of wines by the glass.

◀

The beer tankard symbol shows pubs where the quality of the beer is quite exceptional, or pubs which keep a particularly interesting range of beers in good condition.

£

This symbol picks out pubs where we have found decent snacks at £2 or less, or worthwhile main dishes at £5 or less.

RECOMMENDERS

At the end of each main entry we include the names of readers who have recently recommended that pub (unless they've asked us not to).

Important note: the description of the pub and the comments on it are our own and not the recommenders'; they are based on our own personal inspections and on later verification of facts with each pub. As some recommenders' names appear quite often, you can get an extra idea of what a place is like by seeing which other pubs those recommenders have approved.

LUCKY DIPS

The Lucky Dip section at the end of each county chapter includes brief descriptions of pubs that have been recommended by readers, with the readers' names in brackets. As the flood of reports from readers has given so much solid information about so many pubs, we have been able to include only those which seem really worth trying. Where only one single reader has recommended a pub, we have now not included it in the list unless the recommender's description makes the nature of the pub quite clear, and gives us good grounds for trusting that other readers would be glad to know of it. So, with most, the descriptions reflect the balanced judgement of a number of different readers, increasingly backed up by similar reports on the same pubs from other readers in previous years (we do not name these readers). Many have been inspected by us. In these cases, LYM means the pub was in a previous edition of the *Guide*. The usual reason that it's no longer a main entry is that, although we've heard nothing really condemnatory about it, we've not had enough favourable reports to be sure that it's still ahead of the local competition. BB means that, although the pub has never been a main entry, we have inspected it, and found nothing against it. In both these cases, the description is our own; in others, it's based on the readers' reports. This year, we have deleted many previously highly rated pubs from the book simply because we have no very recent reports on them. This may well mean that we have left out some favourites – please tell us if we have!

Lucky Dip pubs marked with a ☆ are ones where the information we have (either from our own inspections or from trusted readers/reporters) suggests a firm recommendation. Roughly speaking, we'd say that these pubs are as much worth considering, at least for the virtues described for them, as many of the main entries themselves. Note that in the Dips we always commend food if we have information supporting a positive recommendation. So a bare mention that food is served shouldn't be taken to imply a recommendation of the food. The same is true of accommodation and so forth.

The Lucky Dips (particularly, of course, the starred ones) are under consideration for inspection for a future edition – so please let us have any comments you can make on them. You can use the report forms at the end of the book, the report card which should be included in it, or just write direct (no stamp needed if posted in the UK). Our address is *The Good Pub Guide*, FREEPOST TN1569, WADHURST, East Sussex TN5 7BR.

MAP REFERENCES

All pubs outside the big cities are given four-figure map references. On the main entries, it looks like this: SX5678 Map 1. Map 1 means that it's on the first map at the end of the book. SX means it's in the square labelled SX on that map. The first figure, 5, tells you to look along the grid at the top and bottom of the SX square for the figure 5. The third figure, 7, tells you to look down the grid at the side of the square to find the figure 7. Imaginary lines drawn down and across the square from these figures should intersect near the pub itself.

The second and fourth figures, the 6 and the 8, are for more precise pin-pointing, and are really for use with larger-scale maps such as road atlases or the Ordnance Survey 1:50,000 maps, which use exactly the same map reference system. On the relevant Ordnance Survey map, instead of finding the 5 marker on the top grid you'd find the 56 one; instead of the 7 on the side grid you'd look for the 78 marker. This makes it very easy to locate even the smallest village.

Where a pub is exceptionally difficult to find, we include a six-figure reference in the directions, such as OS Sheet 102 map reference 654783. This refers to Sheet 102 of the Ordnance Survey 1:50,000 maps, which explain how to use the six-figure references to pin-point a pub to the nearest 100 metres.

MOTORWAY PUBS
If a pub is within four or five miles of a motorway junction, and reaching it doesn't involve much slow traffic, we give special directions for finding it from the motorway. And the Special Interest Lists at the end of the book include a list of these pubs, motorway by motorway.

PRICES AND OTHER FACTUAL DETAILS
The *Guide* went to press during the summer of 1999. As late as possible, each pub was sent a checking sheet to get up-to-date food, drink and bedroom prices and other factual information. By the summer of 2000 prices are bound to have increased a little – to be prudent, you should probably allow around 5% extra by then. But if you find a significantly different price please let us know.

Breweries to which pubs are 'tied' are named at the beginning of the italic-print rubric after each main entry. That means the pub has to get most if not all of its drinks from that brewery. If the brewery is not an independent one but just part of a combine, we name the combine in brackets. Where a brewery no longer brews its own beers but gets them under contract from a different brewer, we name that brewer too. When the pub is tied, we have spelled out whether the landlord is a tenant, has the pub on a lease, or is a manager; tenants and leaseholders generally have considerably greater freedom to do things their own way, and in particular are allowed to buy drinks including a beer from sources other than their tied brewery.

Free houses are pubs not tied to a brewery, so in theory they can shop around to get the drinks their customers want, at the best prices they can find. But in practice many free houses have loans from the big brewers, on terms that bind them to sell those breweries' beers – indeed, about half of all the beer sold in free houses is supplied by the big national brewery combines to free houses that have these loan ties. So don't be too surprised to find that so-called free houses may be stocking a range of beers restricted to those from a single brewery.

Real ale is used by us to mean beer that has been maturing naturally in its cask. We do not count as real ale beer which has been pasteurised or filtered to remove its natural yeasts. If it is kept under a blanket of carbon dioxide to preserve it, we still generally mention it – as long as the pressure is too light for you to notice any extra fizz, it's hard to tell the difference. (For brevity, we use the expression 'under light blanket pressure' to cover such pubs; we do not include among them pubs where the blanket pressure is high enough to force the beer up from the cellar, as this does make it unnaturally fizzy.) If we say a pub has, for example, 'Whitbreads-related real ales', these may include not just beers brewed by the national company and its subsidiaries but also beers produced by independent breweries which the national company buys in bulk and distributes alongside its own.

Other drinks: we've also looked out particularly for pubs doing enterprising non-alcoholic drinks (including good tea or coffee), interesting spirits (especially malt whiskies), country wines (elderflower and the like), freshly squeezed juices, and good farm ciders. So many places now stock one of the main brands of draught cider that we normally mention cider only if the pub keeps quite a range, or one of the less common farm-made ciders.

Bar food refers to what is sold in the bar, not in any separate restaurant. It means a place serves anything from sandwiches and ploughman's to full meals, rather than pork scratchings or packets of crisps. We always mention sandwiches in the text if we know that a pub does them – if you don't see them mentioned, assume you can't get them.

The *food listed* in the description of each pub is an example of the sort of thing you'd find served in the bar on a normal day, and generally includes the dishes which are currently finding most favour with readers. We try to indicate any difference we know of between lunchtime and evening, and between summer and winter (on the whole stressing summer food more). In winter, many pubs tend to have a more restricted range, particularly of salads, and tend then to do more in the way of filled baked potatoes, casseroles and hot pies. We always mention barbecues if we know a pub does them. Food quality and variety may be affected by holidays – particularly in a small place, where the licensees do the cooking themselves (May and early June seem to be a popular time for licensees to take their holidays).

Any separate *restaurant* is mentioned. But in general all comments on the type of food served, and in particular all the other details about meals and snacks at the end of each entry, relate to the pub food and not to the restaurant food.

Children's Certificates exist, but in practice *Children* are allowed into at least some part of almost all the pubs included in this *Guide* (there is no legal restriction on the movement of children over 14 in any pub, though only people over 18 may get alcohol). As we went to press, we asked the main-entry pubs a series of detailed questions about their rules. *Children welcome* means the pub has told us that it simply lets them come in, with no special restrictions. In other cases we report exactly what arrangements places say they make for children. However, we have to note that in readers' experience some pubs make restrictions which they haven't told us about (children only if eating, for example), and very occasionally pubs which have previously allowed children change their policy altogether, virtually excluding them. If you come across this, please let us know, so that we can clarify the information for the pub concerned in the next edition. Beware that if children are confined to the restaurant, they may occasionally be expected to have a full restaurant meal. Also, please note that a welcome for children does not necessarily mean a welcome for breast-feeding in public. If we don't mention children at all assume that they are not welcome but it is still worth asking: one or two pubs told us frankly that they do welcome children but don't want to advertise the fact, for fear of being penalised. All but one or two pubs (we mention these in the text) allow children in their garden or on their terrace, if they have one. Note that in Scotland the law allows children more freely into pubs so long as they are eating (and with an adult). In the Lucky Dip entries we mention children only if readers have found either that they are allowed or that they are not allowed – the absence of any reference to children in a Dip entry means we don't know either way.

Dogs, cats and other animals are mentioned in the text if we know either that they are likely to be present or that they are specifically excluded – we depend chiefly on readers and partly on our own inspections for this information.

Parking is not mentioned if you should normally be able to park outside the pub, or in a private car park, without difficulty. But if we know that parking space is limited or metered, we say so.

Telephone numbers are given for all pubs that are not ex-directory.

Opening hours are for summer; we say if we know of differences in winter, or on particular days of the week. In the country, many pubs may open rather later and close earlier than their entries show unless there are plenty of customers around (if you come across this, please let us know – with details). Pubs are allowed to stay open all day Mondays to Saturdays from 11am (earlier, if the area's licensing magistrates have permitted) till 11pm. However, outside cities most English and Welsh pubs close during the afternoon. Scottish pubs are allowed to stay open until later at night, and the Government seems increasingly likely to allow later opening in England and Wales too. We'd be very grateful to hear of any differences from the hours we quote. You are allowed 20 minutes' drinking-up time after the quoted hours – half an hour if you've been having a meal in the pub.

Bedroom prices normally include full English breakfasts (if these are available, which they usually are), VAT and any automatic service charge that we know about. If we give just one price, it is the total price for two people sharing a double or twin-bedded room for one night. Otherwise, prices before the / are for single occupancy, prices after it for double. A capital B against the price means that it includes a private bathroom, a capital S a private shower. As all this coding packs in quite a lot of information, some examples may help to explain it:

£65 on its own means that's the total bill for two people sharing a twin or double room without private bath; the pub has no rooms with private bath; and a single person might have to pay that full price

£65B means exactly the same – but all the rooms have private bath

£60(£65B) means rooms with private baths cost £5 extra

£35/£60(£65B) means the same as the last example, but also shows that there are single rooms for £35, none of which have private bathrooms

If there's a choice of rooms at different prices, we normally give the cheapest. If there are seasonal price variations, we give the summer price (the highest). This winter (1999-2000) many inns, particularly in the country, will have special cheaper rates. And at other times, especially in holiday areas, you will often find prices cheaper if you stay for several nights. On weekends, inns that aren't in obvious weekending areas often have bargain rates for two- or three-night stays.

MEAL TIMES
Bar food is commonly served from 12-2 and 7-9, at least from Monday to Saturday (food service often stops a bit earlier on Sundays). If we don't give a time against the Meals and snacks note at the bottom of a main entry, that means that you should be able to get bar food at those times. However, we do spell out the times if we know that bar food service starts after 12.15 or after 7.15; if it stops before 2 or before 8.45; or if food is served for significantly longer than usual (say, till 2.30 or 9.45).

Though we note days when pubs have told us they don't do food, experience suggests that you should play safe on Sundays and check first with any pub before planning an expedition that depends on getting a meal there. Also, out-of-the-way pubs often cut down on cooking during the week, especially the early part of the week, if they're quiet – as they tend to be, except at holiday times. Please let us know if you find anything different from what we say!

NO SMOKING
We say in the text of each entry what if any provision a pub makes for non-smokers. Pubs setting aside at least some sort of no-smoking area are also listed county by county in the Special Interest Lists at the back of the book.

PLANNING ROUTES WITH THE GOOD PUB GUIDE
Computer users may like to know of two route-finding programmes which will show the location of *Good Pub Guide* pubs on detailed maps, work out the quickest routes for their journeys, add diversions to nearby pubs – and see our text entries for those pubs on screen. These programmes will also include material from *The Good Britain Guide*. The programmes are NextBase R Personal Navigator™ and Microsoft ® AutoRoute Express™ Great Britain 2000 Edition.

OUR NEW WEB SITE
Our new Internet web site is now open and combines material from *The Good Pub Guide* and its sister publication *The Good Britain Guide* in a way that gives people who do not yet know the books at least a taste of them. We also hope that we can use it to give readers of the books extra information (and allow them to report quickly to us), and hope to expand and improve the site significantly (for instance with pictures of the pubs) over the next year or two. You can try the site yourself at www.goodguides.com.

CHANGES DURING THE YEAR – PLEASE TELL US
Changes are inevitable, during the course of the year. Landlords change, and so do

their policies. And, as we've said, not all returned our fact-checking sheets. We very much hope that you will find everything just as we say. But if you find anything different, please let us know, using the tear-out card in the middle of the book (which doesn't need an envelope), the report forms here, or just a letter. You don't need a stamp: the address is *The Good Pub Guide*, FREEPOST TN1569, WADHURST, East Sussex TN5 7BR.

Author's Acknowledgements

We could not produce this book without the enormous help we have had from many thousands of readers, who have kindly reported to us on their good – and bad – experiences of pubs. This extremely generous help, all unpaid, gives us a marvellous continuing monitor of pubs' standards, as well as pointing us towards new discoveries.

For the outstanding assistance they have given us this year, I owe a special debt of gratitude to Richard Lewis, Ian Phillips, George Atkinson, CMW and JJW, Gwen and Peter Andrews, Jenny and Michael Back, the Didler, Peter and Audrey Dowsett, Ann and Colin Hunt, LM, Phyl and Jack Street, DWAJ, Gordon, Anthony Barnes, Jenny and Brian Seller, Lynn Sharpless and Bob Eardley, Martin and Karen Wake, Tracey and Stephen Groves, Tony and Wendy Hobden, Eric Larkham, Derek and Sylvia Stephenson, Roger Huggins, Dave Irving, Tom McLean, Ewan McCall, Marjorie and David Lamb, Pat and Tony Martin, Richard Houghton, Val and Alan Green, Alan and Paula McCully, Lyn and Geoff Hallchurch, Sue Holland and Dave Webster, Ted George, Dave Braisted, MDN, Maurice and Gill McMahon, E G Parish, Joan and Michel Hooper-Immins, Tom Evans, Tony and Louise Clarke, Dick Brown, Colin and Joyce Laffan, Nick and Alison Dowson, KC, Paul and Ursula Randall, Susan and John Douglas, Neil and Anita Christopher, Rona Murdoch, Kevin Thorpe, Stephen and Julie Brown, Jack and Philip Paxton, Joy and Peter Heatherley, JDM and KM, John Evans, R J Walden, Mark Percy and Lesley Mayoh, W W Burke, J F M and M West, David and Tina Woods-Taylor, Reg Nelson, Chris Glasson, M Joyner, M J Morgan, TRS and PAS, Tim Barrow and Sue Demont, Janet Pickles, Nick Lawless, Comus Elliott, Eddie Edwards, Karen and Graham Oddey, Mark and Rachael Baynham, Simon Collett-Jones, John and Joan Wyatt, Meg and Colin Hamilton, Sue and Bob Ward, Charles Bardswell, Eric J Locker, A D Marsh, Colin and Jan Roe, John Wooll, John and Joan Nash, TBB, Bruce Bird, David and Ruth Shillitoe, Malcolm Taylor, SLC, Mike and June Coleman, Mayur Shah, John C Baker, John Bowdler, Andy and Jill Kassube, Richard and Margaret Peers, Mike and Mary Carter, John Barker, B and K Hypher, J R Morris, N M Johns, Pete Baker, Howard Clutterbuck, David Carr, Neil Townend, David and Carole Chapman, Nigel Woolliscroft and James Nunns.

Particular thanks to Steve and Carolyn Harvey, our unofficial unpaid Channel Islands Inspectors; to John Holliday, who has patiently performed the remarkable and complex task of transforming our antiquated computer systems into something to be really proud of in this new century; and finally – and essentially – to the thousands of publicans and their staffs who work so warm-heartedly and for such long hours to give us so very many Good Pubs.

Alisdair Aird

England

Bedfordshire

At opposite ends of the scale here are the Knife & Cleaver at Houghton Conquest, a first-class dining pub, really more of a restaurant, and the Cock at Broom, a superb example of a little-changed country tavern. Another pub doing particularly well here these days is the Chequers at Keysoe – as so often, the quality here comes from licensees who clearly enjoy giving their customers outstanding personal attention; it gains a Food Award this year. Most of our main entries in this county are pretty foody, though there's plenty of character too, for example at the unpretentious Bell at Odell, at the Rose & Crown at Ridgmont (its hard-working licensees gaining it well earned promotion to the main entries), and the Globe at Linslade in its prime position near the canal, its current managers proving very popular for their huge helpings of good food. Another pub which earns its Food Award for the first time this year, the Red Lion at Milton Bryan – particularly popular with our older readers, and earning top marks for cleanliness – gains the title of Bedfordshire Dining Pub of the Year. It has not escaped a general current Bedfordshire trend towards higher pub food prices, but remains good value. There's value to be found at a good many of the recommended pubs in the Lucky Dip section at the end of the chapter, too, with the cream these days being the Black Horse at Ireland, Crown at Northill, Hare & Hounds at Old Warden, Swan at Radwell, Locomotive at Sandy, Lynmore at Sharpenhoe and Bell at Woburn. Beer prices are a little above the national average, with the Bedfordshire pint generally costing 10p more than it did this time last year – the cheapest we found, with the smallest price rise over the last 12 months, was Courage at the Three Cranes at Turvey, part of the Old English Pub Co. chain.

BIDDENHAM TL0249 Map 5

Three Tuns

57 Main Road; village signposted from A428 just W of Bedford

The bustling lounge of this friendly thatched village pub has low beams and country paintings, and its reasonably priced bar food is very popular at lunchtime. There are sandwiches (from £1.70), home-made soup (£2 – or with a choice of any sandwich £3), pâté (£2.40), ploughman's (£3), salads (from £3.50), quiche or chilli con carne (£5), seafood platter or home-made lasagne (£5.50), home-made steak and kidney pie or chicken casserole (£6), and 8oz sirloin steak (£8); children's menu (£2) and puddings (£2). Well kept Greene King IPA and Abbot on handpump; darts, skittle alley, dominoes and a fruit machine in the public bar; piped music. There are seats in the attractively sheltered spacious garden, and a big terrace has lots of picnic-sets and white doves in a dovecote; the very good children's play area has swings for all ages and a big wooden climbing frame. (Recommended by Nigel Williamson, Ian Phillips, JKW)

Greene King ~ Tenant Alan Wilkins ~ Real ale ~ Bar food (not Sun evening) ~ (01234) 354847 ~ Children in dining room ~ Open 11.30-2.30, 6-11; 12-3, 7-10.30 Sun

BROOM TL1743 Map 5

Cock ★

23 High Street; from A1 opposite northernmost Biggleswade turn-off follow Old Warden 3, Aerodrome 2 signpost, and take first left signposted Broom

Well worth going out of your way for, this friendly and delightfully unspoilt 17th-c inn is very much the focal point of its village with a strong local following. Visitors too like its four cosy rooms with simple latch doors, low ochre ceilings, stripped panelling and farmhouse-style tables and chairs on their antique tiles; winter log fires and table skittles. There's no counter, and the very well kept Greene King IPA, Abbot and Triumph are tapped straight from the cask. A central corridor runs down the middle of the building, with the sink for washing glasses on one side (pewter mugs hang over it) and on the other steps down to the cellar. Straightforward bar food includes sandwiches (from £2.55), home-made soup (£2.75), ploughman's (from £4.25), breaded mushrooms (£5.75), cajun chicken (£7.25), and 8oz sirloin steak (£7.95); children's helpings. There are picnic-sets on the terrace by the back lawn, and a fenced-off play area. *(Recommended by Ian Phillips, JP, PP, B A Lord, Pete Baker, Barry and Marie Males)*

Greene King ~ Tenants Gerry and Jean Lant ~ Real ale ~ Bar food (not Sun evening) ~ Restaurant ~ (01767) 314411 ~ Children welcome in eating area of bar ~ Open 12-3(4 Sat), 6-11; 12-4, 7-10.30 Sun

HOUGHTON CONQUEST TL0441 Map 5

Knife & Cleaver 🍴 🍷

Between B530 (old A418) and A6, S of Bedford

Dining pubs of the highest order are so scarce in this part of the world that we couldn't possibly exclude the Knife & Cleaver from the main entries even though our normal rule is to do so with places that are as close as this to being pure restaurants. The relaxed, comfortable bar has maps, drawings and old documents on the walls, panelling which is reputed to have come from nearby ruin Houghton House, and a blazing fire in winter; the airy conservatory no-smoking restaurant has rugs on the tiled floor, swagged curtains, cane furniture and lots of hanging plants. In the bar, as well as regular sandwiches (from £3), they offer ciabatta with chicken breasts, gruyère cheese and spinach (£5.95), and french bread with rib steak, bacon and mushrooms in balsamic vinegar (£6.25). Daily specials may include smoked haddock on marinated tomatoes with a welsh rarebit crust (£5.50), pan-fried squid and wild mushrooms with egg noodles in soy jus (£5.95), bolognese and gorgonzola stuffed pancakes with spicy tomato sauce, chicken and prawn risotto with deep-fried mussels or rabbit and bacon pasty with bacon and petit pois sauce (all £6.25) – and from a menu that changes regularly there might be home-made soup (£2.75), a small mixed hors d'oeuvre (£4.95; large £8.50), venison and stilton pancake with celery and port sauce (£5.95), thai style seafood noodles (£6.25), salmon and sorrell fishcake with creamy langoustine sauce or deep-fried aubergine and goat's cheese schnitzel (£6.50), scottish smoked salmon with scrambled eggs (£7.95); home-made puddings such as raspberry sorbet in a meringue vacherin, pear frangipane tart or frozen orange chocolate bombe (£3.25), and a good selection of cheeses (£3.50; you can enjoy these as a ploughman's £4). Beware, on Saturday evening if the restaurant is fully booked they may not serve bar meals. Well kept Adnams Extra and Batemans XB on handpump, Stowfod Press farm cider, 26 good wines by the glass, and a fine choice of up to 20 well aged malt whiskies; unobtrusive piped music. There are tables in the neatly kept garden. Well equipped bedrooms in a separate building. The church opposite is worth a look. *(Recommended by John Cooper, Andrew Clayton, Michael Sargent, Anthony Barnes, Mike and Mary Carter, Jackie Hammond, Maggie and Peter Shapland, Patricia and John White, E and K Leist, Marvadene B Eves, W A Evershed, John and Enid Morris, Eric Locker, Maysie Thompson, Gwen and Peter Andrews, Derek and Maggie Washington, Mr & Mrs R W Clark, M A & C R Starling, B M & P Kendall)*

Free house ~ Licensees David and Pauline Loom ~ Real ale ~ Bar food ~ Restaurant ~ (01234) 740387 ~ Children welcome in eating area of bar and restaurant ~ Open 12-

*2.30(2 Sat), 6.30-10.30(11 Sat); 12-3 (closed evening) Sun; closed 26-30 Dec ~
Bedrooms: £49B/£64B*

KEYSOE TL0762 Map 5

Chequers 🍺

Brook End (B660)

Pam and Jeff Kearns go to great lengths to make punters feel at home in this friendly
and unpretentious village local with its consistently good food. As well as
sandwiches (from £2), and daily specials such as home-made fish pie or tomato and
orange lamb casserole (£7), the bar menu includes home-made soup (£2.50), garlic
mushrooms on toast (£3.50), ploughman's (£4), chilli con carne (£5.50), home-made
steak and ale pie (£6.00), chicken breast stuffed with stilton in a chive sauce (£8),
steaks (from £9.25), and puddings like bread and butter pudding with Drambuie-
soaked raisins or banana ice cream with home-made butterscotch sauce (£2.25)
which are highly recommended by readers; children's menu (£3.25). Well kept
Fullers London Pride and Hook Norton Best on handpumps on the stone bar
counter; some malt whiskies. The leatherette seats lend an air of the 1960s to the
two neatly simple beamed rooms divided by an unusual stone-pillared fireplace; one
bar is no smoking; darts, shove-ha'penny, table skittles, dominoes; piped music. The
terrace at the back looks over the garden which has a wendy house, play tree, swings
and a sand-pit. *(Recommended by Michael and Jenny Back, Maysie Thompson, G Neighbour,
Margaret and Roy Randle)*

*Free house ~ Licensee Jeffrey Kearns ~ Real ale ~ Bar food (not Tues) ~ (01234)
708678 ~ Children welcome in eating area of bar ~ Open 11.30-2.30, 6.30-11; 12-
2.30, 7-10.30 Sun; closed Tues*

LINSLADE SP9225 Map 4

Globe

Globe Lane, off Stoke Rd (A4146) nr bridge; outside Linslade proper, just before you get to
the town sign

Popular 19th-c whitewashed pub idyllically set on its own alongside the Grand
Union Canal. While a perfect spot to laze away an afternoon watching life on the
water, it does get very busy in summer – but there are enough tables out here to
cope, most of them along the towpath, with others in a very well equipped fenced-
off play area with climbing forts and equipment, or in the garden under the trees
alongside the car park. In summer an outdoor bar serves ice creams as well as
drinks; it may be open in the afternoons when the pub itself is shut. Inside, a cosy
series of beamed and flagstoned rooms with intriguing quotations on the walls,
affords the same fine views from a warm environment. Vegetarians are well catered
for with a separate menu of about eight dishes such as avocado bake, vegetable tikka
masala or vegetable and cashew nut paella (all £7.25). Other bar food might include
home-made leek and potato soup (£2.50), filled baguettes (from £3.25),
ploughman's (from £5.45), steak and kidney pie (£6.25), gammon (£8.95), chicken
and pasta in a white wine and cream sauce (£9.95), 10oz rump (£10.75), grilled
halibut with prawns in lemon butter (£12.95) and three daily specials such as
sautéed lamb's liver and bacon (£7.95), a large bowl of moules marinières (£8.25) or
chicken breast in wild mushroom and brandy sauce (£9.95); puddings such as
spotted dick or fruits of the forest cheesecake (£2.95). Greene King IPA and up to
five weekly changing guests such as Adnams, Courage Directors, Marstons Pedigree,
Morlands Old Speckled Hen and Theakstons Old Peculier. To get to the pub you
come down a little private road that seems to take you further into the countryside
than you really are, and the Cross Bucks Way leads off from just along the canal.
*(Recommended by Jean and David Darby, Bill Sykes, George Atkinson, Paul Cleaver, Andrew
Scarr)*

*Old English Pub Co. ~ Manager Steve Dawson ~ Real ale ~ Bar food (till 10 Weds-
Sat) ~ Restaurant ~ (01525) 373338 ~ Children welcome ~ Open 11-3.30, 6-11; 12-4,
7-10.30 Sun*

MILTON BRYAN SP9730 Map 4
Red Lion 🍽
Toddington Rd, off B528 S of Woburn

Bedfordshire Dining Pub of the Year

Ray Scarbrow and his team of efficient and friendly staff continue to satisfy customers at this relaxed and comfortable pub close to Woburn Abbey and Safari Park. It's a well liked place for eating out, the weekday lunch menu for the over-55s remaining as popular as ever: three courses are a bargain £4.75. The full menu typically includes soup (£1.95), good chunky sandwiches (from £2.25), vegetable samosas (£3.25), moules marinières (£5.95), turkey and ham pie (£7.75), chicken tobago (£8.25) and half a dozen or so grilled fresh fish specials like haddock or trout (£9.25), a big whole plaice (£9.95), and dover sole (£15.50). Most of the tables are set for eating, and the smartly laid dining areas are all no smoking. The cool beamed bar area is spotlessly kept, with pristine white-painted walls, some exposed brickwork, big fading rugs on the part wood and part stone floors, a case of sporting cups, and fresh flowers on the round wooden tables; piped music. Well kept Bass, Greene King IPA and Abbot, Marstons Pedigree and a fortnightly changing guest on handpump. The lavatories are unusually well equipped, with shoe-shine kits and the like. In summer – when the pub is festooned with hanging baskets and plants – there's a separate bar outside, serving their own special pimms. Plenty of tables, chairs and picnic-sets out on the patio and lawn, which looks across to a delightfully thatched black and white timbered house; there's a climbing frame out here too.
(Recommended by Ian Phillips, Ted George, Elizabeth and Klaus Leist, CMW, JJW, George Atkinson, Steve and Stella Swepston, David & Ruth Shillitoe)

Marstons ~ Lease Ray Scarbrow ~ Real ale ~ Bar food ~ Restaurant ~ (01525) 210044 ~ Children welcome ~ Open 11-4, 6-11; 12-4, 6-10.30 Sun

ODELL SP9658 Map 4
Bell
Horsefair Lane; off A6 S of Rushden, via Sharnbrook

The outside of this popular thatched stone village pub is as pretty as the interior, where five small homely low-ceilinged rooms – some with shiny black beams – loop around a central servery and are furnished with quite a few handsome old oak settles, bentwood chairs and neat modern furniture; there's a log fire in one big stone fireplace and two coal fires elsewhere. Fairly priced bar food includes sandwiches (from £1.95), ploughman's (from £3.50), omelettes (from £3.85) ham, egg and chips (£4.25), home-made vegetable pie (£4.50), savoury pancakes (from £4.85), liver and bacon (£5.50), and daily specials from the board such as spicy pork sausages in onion gravy (£5.50), turkey and bacon pasta (£5.60) and beef, bacon and wine casserole (£6.50); usual children's dishes (from £2.30) and home-made puddings like boozy chocolate mousse or orange cheesecake shortbread (£2.20). Well kept Greene King IPA, Abbot, Triumph, and seasonal ales on handpump. There are picnic-sets on the flower-filled terrace overlooking the wooded garden that offers an attractive walk down through a wild area to a bridge over the Great Ouse. Golden pheasants, cockatiels, canaries, and an eight-year-old goose called Lucy roam the garden. Further along the road is a very pretty church; handy for the local country park.
(Recommended by Tom Saul, John McDonald, Ann Bond, G Neighbour, Ian Phillips, Maysie Thompson, John and Enid Morris, Andy and Jill Kassube, Ted George)

Greene King ~ Tenants Derek and Doreen Scott ~ Real ale ~ Bar food (not Sun evening Sept-May) ~ (01234) 720254 ~ Children welcome in eating area of bar ~ Open 11-2.30, 6-11; 12-2.30, 7-10.30 Sun

---

The details at the end of each main entry start by saying whether the pub is a free house, or if it's tied to a brewery or pub chain (which we name).

RIDGMONT SP9736 Map 4
Rose & Crown

2 miles from M1 junction 13: towards Woburn Sands, then left towards Ampthill on A418; in High Street

This civilised and attractive 17th-c brick house, formerly part of the Duke of Bedford's estate, has an eye-catching array of Rupert Bear annual covers and a collection of old English sheepdog china, besides a sofa and other comfortable chairs in its spick-and-span lounge, and a low-ceilinged traditional public bar – plenty of standing room – with brasses, prints of white geese and an open fire in its sizeable brick fireplace; a games area up a couple of steps has darts, pool, shove-ha'penny, dominoes, cribbage and a fruit machine. Consistently good sensible pub food served quickly even when busy includes sandwiches (from £1.95), cumberland sausage (£4.45), macaroni cheese (£4.95), steak and ale pie or lasagne (£5.85), vegetarian dishes such as vegetable tikka or avocado bake (£5.95) and steaks (from £7.25). Besides well kept Charles Wells Eagle and Bombardier on handpump, they stock over 50 whiskies and do good coffee; friendly service, maybe piped music. A big plus in summer is the long and attractive suntrap tree-lined garden behind, full of flowers and shrubs; there are also some picnic-sets out in front, below the pretty hanging baskets. Easy parking, good wheelchair access. *(Recommended by Nick Holmes, Dr Paul Khan, John Wooll, George Atkinson, Tracey and Stephen Groves)*

Charles Wells ~ Tenant Neil McGregor ~ Real ale ~ Bar food ~ (01525) 280245 ~ Children in family room ~ Open 10.30-2.30(3 Sat), 6-11; 12-3, 7-11 Sun

RISELEY TL0362 Map 5
Fox & Hounds

High St; village signposted off A6 and B660 N of Bedford

All refurbishments have been completed at this bustling pub run by the charismatic Zielinskis for almost a decade. A comfortable new lounge area with leather chesterfields, low tables and wing chairs, contrasts with the more traditional pub furniture spread among timber uprights under the heavy low beams; there's also a new terrace with outside heating and wooden tables and chairs, the car park and dining area have been expanded and the lavatories upgraded. The famous steaks remain as popular as ever: you choose which piece of meat you want and how you want it cooked, and you're then charged by the weight – £9.92 for 8oz rump, £10.64 for 8oz of sirloin and £12.48 for fillet. Other food includes home-made soups like tomato and sweet peppers or cream of mushroom (£2.25), salmon in a juniper sauce (£3.50), moules marinières (£5.95), steak and kidney pie (£7.25), beef stroganoff (£9.50), and a couple of vegetarian dishes. Well kept Charles Wells Eagle and Bombardier with regularly changing guests like Everards Tiger, Vaux Waggle Dance and Wadworths 6X on handpump, a decent collection of other drinks including a range of malts and cognacs; unobtrusive piped music. *(Recommended by S Markham, Michael Sargent)*

Charles Wells ~ Managers Jan and Lynne Zielinski ~ Real ale ~ Bar food (12-1.45, 7-10) ~ Restaurant ~ (01234) 708240 ~ Children welcome ~ Open 11.30-2.30, 6.30-11; 12-3, 7-10.30 Sun

TURVEY SP9452 Map 4
Three Cranes ◀

Just off A428 W of Bedford

Unchanging stone-built 17th-c inn owned by the Old English Pub Company. The airy two-level bar has a solid-fuel stove, a quiet decor including old photographs and Victorian style prints, and an array of stuffed owls and other birds in the main dining area; there are plenty of sensible tables with upright seats. Bar food includes lunchtime sandwiches (from £2.40), soup (£2.75), steak and ale pie (£6.95), lasagne (£6.95), trout (£8.75), medallions of chicken (£8.95), and steaks (from £9.95); readers enjoy the sausages (£5.95) which come from the butcher next door. Well kept Adnams, Courage Best and Directors, Hook Norton Best, Wadworths 6X, and guests on handpump. There are picnic-sets in a neatly kept garden with a climbing frame; in summer, the pub's front has been a mass of colour from carefully tended hanging baskets and window boxes. *(Recommended by Stephen Brown, David Toulson, Maysie Thompson, Gordon Tong, Nigel Williamson, Ian Phillips, Mike & Mary Carter, John & Phyllis Maloney)*

Old English Pub Co. ~ Managers Paul & Sheila Linehan ~ Real ale ~ Bar food ~ Restaurant ~ (01234) 881305 ~ Children welcome in eating area of bar ~ Live entertainment on St Patrick's Night ~ Open 11-2.30, 6-11; 12-3, 7-10.30 Sun; closed evening 25 Dec ~ Bedrooms: £35B/£45B

Lucky Dip

Besides the fully inspected pubs, you might like to try these Lucky Dips recommended to us and described by readers (if you do, please send us reports):

Biggleswade [TL1944]
Brown Bear: Enthusiastic and warmly welcoming new licensees with imaginative range of very well kept beer, good value food; live music Fri night; parking may be difficult *(Richard Houghton)*
Bletsoe [TL0258]
Falcon: Ex-coaching inn dating from 17th c, reopened as pub-restaurant with emphasis on fish, under same management as Fox & Hounds at Riseley (see main entries); clean and friendly, with red and blue banquettes and carpet, Charles Wells Bombardier and Eagle, piped Mozart; big riverside garden *(Ian Phillips)*
Bolnhurst [TL0859]
☆ *Olde Plough*: As we go to press it looks increasingly likely that this antiquated 15th-c pub in its lovely garden, long a favourite main entry in the Guide, will change hands – and therefore change from the idiosyncratic place we've so enjoyed in the hands of the Horridges; in the meantime, well worth a visit if you're passing, with enjoyable food, well kept beers, and a good choice of wines *(LYM, John Fahy, D A Norman)*
Bromham [TL0050]
Swan [nr A428, 2 miles W of Bedford]: Friendly and comfortable beamed village pub with lots of pictures, well kept Greene King IPA and Abbot, decent coffee, food from sandwiches or baked potatoes to steaks, quick service, evening log fire; quiet piped music; public bar with darts and fruit machine, provision for children, pleasant garden *(Ian Phillips)*
Chalton [TL0326]
Fancott Arms [B579 3 miles from M1 junction 12, via Toddington]: Steep-tiled cottagey pub with dining extension, Whitbreads and other ales, friendly staff, usual food (not that cheap), pleasant interior (though piped music may be loud); picnic-sets in front with lots of flowers, back garden with play area *(Ian Phillips)*
Clophill [TL0837]
Stone Jug [N on A6 from A507 roundabout, after 200 yds 2nd turn on right]: Secluded and very welcoming stone-built local with good range of reasonably priced food in

unpretentiously friendly pleasant front bar, comfortable side lounge and family area; B&T Bitter, Courage Directors and guest beers; couple of tables among flowers on small back terrace, roadside picnic-sets *(N Doolan)*
Great Barford [TL1352]
Anchor [off A421]: Fine spot by medieval bridge and church, tables out overlooking River Ouse; generous appetising food, spotless bright décor, Charles Wells Bombardier, Eagle and a guest such as Morlands Old Speckled Hen; piped music; bedrooms *(D C Poulton, Ian Phillips, Gordon Neighbour)*
Golden Cross: Thriving atmosphere in main-road pub with pretty back restaurant serving fine Chinese food; pristine tables, white linen cloths and napkins, very attentive service *(Sarah Markham)*
Harlington [TL0330]
White Hart: Large carefully redesigned Fullers dining pub, good atmosphere, well kept beers inc ESB *(Tom Evans)*
Ireland [TL1341]
☆ *Black Horse* [off A600 Shefford—Bedford]: Wide choice of good value plentiful piping hot food inc tasty puddings in busy and attractive dining pub's sizeable lounge or family dining area, well kept Bass and Worthington, good coffee, lots of very helpful friendly staff, lots of tables in lovely front garden with play area – peaceful rural setting *(Sidney and Erna Wells, Jenny and Michael Back, Maysie Thompson, BB)*
Leighton Buzzard [SP9225]
Stag: Cosy, clean and comfortable, with full Fullers range inc seasonal beer kept well, good bar food (not Sun) inc special evenings, friendly efficient service *(Bruce Bird)*
Luton [TL0921]
Duke of Clarence: Edwardian pub pastiche by Town Hall, very inexpensive usual lunchtime food, Boddingtons, Brakspears and Flowers *(Ian Phillips)*
Shannon: Former hat factory converted 1991 to resemble a Dublin hotel; bar darkly ornate and quieter than most locally, good bar snacks *(Ian Phillips)*
Maulden [TL0538]
White Hart [Ampthill end]: Thatched pub in

straggling village with large dining area split into more intimate sections inc no smoking; low beams, brick pillars, big fireplace dividing bar; ample helpings of freshly cooked good value food, Fullers London Pride, Marstons Pedigree, attentive friendly service; piped music *(George Atkinson, Barry and Marie Males)*

Northill [TL1546]

☆ *Crown* [signed from B658 W of Biggleswade]: Welcoming black and white thatched local in lovely tranquil village setting, low beams, huge open fire, small dining area, well kept Greene King IPA and Abbot and Marstons Pedigree, wines by the glass, good value bar food from sandwiches, ploughman's and baked potatoes to bargain three-course lunches, darts and cards in spartan public bar; seats by village pond at the front, play area in huge back garden; not far from the Shuttleworth Collection *(E A and D C T Frewer, Barry and Marie Males, D C Poulton, Pete Baker)*

Old Warden [TL1343]

☆ *Hare & Hounds*: Welcoming beamed pub in attractive thatched village, good helpings of enjoyable food, interesting menu, case of aircraft memorabilia, well kept Charles Wells Eagle and Bombardier with guests such as Adnams and Morlands Old Speckled Hen, friendly helpful landlord, simple but comfortable décor in four rambling rooms, open fire, dining room overlooking glorious garden stretching up to pine woods, play area; piped music; handy for Shuttleworth Collection, Swiss Garden and local walks (though mucky boots and sometimes children seem frowned on) *(BB, George Atkinson, M Brooks, Ian Phillips, Mark Brock, JKW, Michael Sargent)*

Radwell [TL0057]

☆ *Swan*: Charming beamed and thatched pub, two spacious rooms joined by narrow passage, woodburner, lots of prints, unobtrusive piped music, friendly service, wide choice of good food, well kept Charles Wells IPA and Eagle with a guest such as Camerons 80/-, decent coffee, popular evening restaurant (must book Fri/Sat); pleasant garden, attractive quiet village *(Stephen, Julie and Hayley Brown, Maysie Thompson)*

Sandy [TL2049]

☆ *Locomotive* [B1042 towards Potton and Cambridge]: Reliable pub nr RSPB HQ, packed with railway memorabilia inc lovely old signs; keenly priced food nicely prepared and presented, friendly staff, well kept Charles Wells ales with a guest such as Greene King Abbot, attractive and sizeable garden with views, barbecues and play area; piped radio; can be busy weekends, open all day Fri/Sat (food all day too); children allowed in no-smoking eating area *(Brian Robert, LYM, Ian Phillips, George Atkinson)*

Sharpenhoe [TL0630]

☆ *Lynmore*: Spacious and comfortable, with friendly beamy family lounge and back dining area (good views), huge helpings of quick consistently good value food inc children's dishes, good range of well kept ales, good

garden for children, big wendy house; popular with walkers *(Sidney and Erna Wells, Barry and Marie Males, Michael Sargent)*

Shillington [TL1234]

Musgrave Arms [towards Pegsdon and Hexton]: Friendly and civilised lounge with settles and tables, comfortable public bar, small dining room, wide choice of generous home-made food, Greene King IPA and Abbot tapped from the cask; big back garden with picnic-sets *(John and Esther Sprinkle)*

Souldrop [SP9861]

Bedford Arms [off A6 Rushden—Bedford]: Current tenants doing good choice of quality food in clean, bright and spacious bar with dining section and other areas off; Greene King ales, big stone fireplace, brasses, settles and prints; piped music; very peaceful village *(John Saul)*

Stanbridge [SP9623]

Five Bells [pub signed off A5 N of Dunstable]: Roomy and attractive old coaching inn, well run and very popular with business customers; emphasis on tasty food in bar and large restaurant overlooking pleasant grounds behind; Shepherd Neame Spitfire, attentive friendly service, lots of hanging baskets *(George Atkinson)*

Toddington [TL0028]

Angel: Tucked away by green, part 16th c but largely Victorian, lots of rooms, horsebrasses, pictures for sale, reasonable value food inc children's (not Sun-Tues evenings), real ales such as Banks's, Courage and Marstons, tea and coffee all day, restaurant; jazz Sun lunchtime; SkyTV; tables in garden *(Quentin Williamson, CMW, JJW)*

Sow & Pigs [handy for M1 junction 12; main street from junction into village]: Quaint 19th-c pub named after carving on church opp, mixed bag of furnishings inc pews, two armchairs and a retired chesterfield, bare boards, lots of old books and knick-knacks inc armless mannequin and amusing pig motifs, friendly landlord, particularly well kept Greene King ales, good coffee, wide choice of food (not Sun; back Victorian-style dining room can be booked for parties), two real fires, children allowed; picnic-sets in small garden, attractive village *(Ian Phillips)*

Upper Dean [TL0467]

Three Compasses: 17th-c beamed and thatched Charles Wells pub with good value food inc OAP special Mon (not bank hols) and children's dishes, well kept beer *(E Robinson, Michael Sargent)*

Wilstead [TL0643]

Woolpack [just off A6 S of Bedford]: 17th- or 18th-c village pub, well in no-smoking dining end, real fire, pewter mugs on beams, well kept ales such as Greene King Abbot, good choice of good food, friendly atmosphere; quiet piped music, darts, fruit machine, TV; picnic-sets in well kept garden *(CMW, JJW)*

Woburn [SP9433]

☆ *Bell*: Friendly and comfortable tastefully decorated hotel with long narrow bar/dining area, pleasantly furnished and cosy; well kept

Greene King ales, good coffee, generous helpings of reasonably priced bar food, evening restaurant; maybe piped radio, courteous staff; tables outside, handy for Woburn Park; bedrooms *(George Atkinson, Ted George)*

Fox & Hounds [A5 Bletchley—Hockcliffe]: Welcoming local with light, airy and clean bar, good choice of beers and wines by the glass, and very good, varied and reasonably priced food *(Mr and Mrs Wickens)*

Wootton [TL0045]

Chequers: Pretty 15th-c Charles Wells local, warm and cosy, with friendly licensees and cat, masses of brightly polished brass, woodburner, real ales inc a guest, very wide choice of wine by the glass, good food in bar and restaurant; nice quiet garden, attractive hamlet *(Ian Phillips)*

Bedroom prices normally include full English breakfast, VAT and any inclusive service charge that we know of. Prices before the '/' are for single rooms, after for two people in double or twin (B includes a private bath, S a private shower). If there is no '/', the prices are only for twin or double rooms (as far as we know there are no singles).

Berkshire

A new entry here goes right to the top of the class – the Water Rat at Marsh Benham, gaining our title of Berkshire Dining Pub of the Year. With the building works that were starting as we went to press, it looks like being even better. Other pubs doing very well on the food side here include the civilised Bell at Boxford, the restauranty Fish in Bray, the Thatched Tavern at Cheapside, the handsome old Bel & the Dragon in Cookham (back in these pages after a break), the Italian-run White Hart at Hamstead Marshall, the bustling Belgian Arms at Holyport (doing very well these days), the Swan at Inkpen (new owners using only organic produce), the distinctive Hare & Hounds near Lambourn, the Harrow at West Ilsley and the Winterbourne Arms at Winterbourne – new licensees since it was last in the Guide. Besides such pubs as these, often serving really imaginative if sometimes pricy food, Berkshire has a good few delightfully unspoilt taverns. The Bell up on the downs at Aldworth is a classic example, and other favourites are the Pot Kiln at Frilsham (brewing its own good beer – and gaining a Star Award this year) and the unaffected Queen Victoria at Hare Hatch. The first two stand out for low drinks prices, in a county where beer prices are generally much higher than the national average. In the Lucky Dip section at the end of the chapter, pubs showing very well these days are the Blackbird at Bagnor, Bunk at Curridge, Swan at East Ilsley, Pheasant at Great Shefford, Dundas Arms at Kintbury, Lock Stock & Barrel in Newbury, Fishermans Cottage in Reading, Old Boot at Stanford Dingley, George & Dragon in Swallowfield, Bull in Wargrave, Crooked Billet just outside Wokingham and Rose & Crown at Woodside.

ALDWORTH SU5579 Map 2
Bell ★ ♀ ◀ £
A329 Reading—Wallingford; left on to B4009 at Streatley

Happily, nothing changes at this unspoilt 14th-c country pub. It's much loved by both visitors and regulars and though it does get busy at weekends, you can be sure of a warm welcome from the charming licensees – whose family have been here for over 200 years. There's a woodburning stove, beams in the shiny ochre ceiling, a glass-panelled hatch rather than a bar counter for service, benches around the panelled walls, and an ancient one-handed clock. Exceptionally good value food is confined to hot crusty rolls (apart from winter home-made soup), filled with cheddar (£1.20), stilton or pâté (£1.40), ham or turkey (£1.50), smoked salmon, prawn or ox tongue (£1.90), and particularly good crab in season (£1.95). Very well kept and very cheap Arkells BBB and Kingsdown, Crouch Vale Bitter, and from the local West Berkshire Brewery, Old Tyler and Dark Mild on handpump (they won't stock draught lager); particularly good house wines. Darts, shove-ha'penny, dominoes, and cribbage. The quiet, old-fashioned garden is lovely in summer, and the pub is handy for the Ridgeway. Occasional Morris dancing; Christmas mummers. *(Recommended by Dick Brown, David Shillitoe, JP, PP, N Cobb, Martin Jennings, R Stamp, Ronald Harry, TBB, Brian Wadley, the Didler)*

Free house ~ Licensee H E Macaulay ~ Real ale ~ Bar food (11-2.45, 6-10.45; 12-2.45, 7-10.15 Sun) ~ (01635) 578272 ~ Children must be well behaved ~ Open 11-3, 6-11; 12-3, 7-10.30 Sun; closed Mon exc bank holidays, closed 25 Dec

BINFIELD SU8571 Map 2
Stag & Hounds 🍺
Forest Rd (B3034 towards Windsor)

This popular pub has lots of little rooms with interesting furnishings and pictures, log fires, extremely low black beams, soft lighting, and snugly intimate corners – the sort of place where it's easy to believe the tale that Queen Elizabeth I once watched Morris men dancing on the green outside. The walls in an airier end room on the right are hung with attractive sporting and other prints, including a fine group relating to 19th-c Royal Ascot; there's also a plusher high-ceilinged lounge on the left. One area is no smoking. Bar food includes lunchtime sandwiches (from £2.60), home-made soup (£2.65), ploughman's (£5.25), pies such as chicken and mushroom or steak and kidney (from £7.50), vegetable wellington (£7.95), daily specials such as chicken supreme (£7.75) or king prawns in garlic (£9.95), and puddings (£3.25). Best to book on Friday and Saturday evenings and Sunday lunch. Well kept Courage Best and Directors, and Theakstons XB on handpump, decent wines, daily papers, fruit machine, and piped music; tables outside on front terrace and in back garden. *(Recommended by M L Porter, Ian Phillips, Mr and Mrs T A Bryan, Stephen & Julie Brown, Phil & Sarah Kane)*

Eldridge Pope (Hardy) ~ Managers Mr & Mrs Brian Porter ~ Real ale ~ Bar food (not Sun evening) ~ Restaurant ~ (01344) 483553 ~ Children must be well behaved ~ Open 11.30-3, 5.30-11; 11.30-3, 6-11 Sat; 12-3, 7-10.30 Sun

BOXFORD SU4271 Map 2
Bell 🍷
Back road Newbury—Lambourn; village also signposted off B4000 between Speen and M4 junction 14

This civilised and neatly kept mock-Tudor inn is very popular for its enjoyable and imaginative food, though there is still some feel of a village pub with a country local atmosphere. The bar, round to the right, is quite long and snug, with a coal-effect fire at one end, a nice mix of racing pictures and smaller old advertisements (especially for Mercier champagne), red plush cushions for the mates' chairs, and some interesting bric-a-brac. From a changing choice, the food might include good sandwiches, Mongolian beef pancake, broccoli and salmon fishcake with lobster sauce or tomato and mozzarella salad with pesto dressing (£4.95), avocado and bacon (£5.25), pies such as steak in ale or pork and apricot (£7.25), and grilled duck on spicy and fruity rice with an orange and cranberry sauce or wild mushroom stroganoff (£12.95), and steaks (from £12.95); the summer lobster dishes are great favourites. The most serious eating takes place in the rather smart, partly no-smoking restaurant area on the left, and you can also dine on the covered and heated terrace. The well kept beers change daily and might include Courage Best, Greene King IPA, and Morrells Bitter on handpump, kept under light blanket pressure. All the wines and champagnes on their lists are available by the glass and there's a wide range of whiskies; pool, fruit machine, trivia, juke box, and piped music. A side courtyard has white cast-iron garden furniture; the lane is quiet enough for the main sound to be the nearby rookery. *(Recommended by Jenny and Brian Seller, Martin and Karen Wake, S Tait, S Lonie, B T Smith)*

Free house ~ Licensee Paul Lavis ~ Real ale ~ Bar food ~ (01488) 608721 ~ Children in eating area of bar and restaurant ~ Open 11-3, 6-11; 11-3, 6.30-11 Sat; 12-3, 7-10.30 Sun ~ Bedrooms: £60S/£70S

BRAY SU9079 Map 2
Fish 🍴 🍷
1¾ miles from M4 junction 8: A308(M), A308 towards Windsor, then first left into B3028 towards Bray; bear right into Old Mill Lane

It remains the really good fresh fish served in interesting ways that continues to draw customers to this handsome tucked-away Georgian pub, though locals and occasional walkers do drop in just for a drink and enjoy the casual relaxed atmosphere in the bar. The menu changes daily and offers half a dozen choices plus a popular and good value two-course lunch (£12). There might be smoked haddock and spinach fishcake (£5.50), tian of Cornish crab and avocado (£6.95), fresh Cornish oysters (£7.90 for 6), grilled swordfish on lemon grass with Thai dressing and coconut rice (£12.95), seared squid and king scallops on green lentils with a gremolata dressing (£13.95), and bass on fresh black pasta with white wine caviar sauce (£16.50); there are also some non-meaty dishes such as fresh herb pasta with rocket ricotta and tomato chilli concassé (£9.50), maize-fed chicken breast on a bed of spinach with bacon and gruyère sauce (£11.50), and fillet steak; vegetables are extra. The bar servery is very much part of the scenery, its two rooms linked by a broad row of arches; above the venetian red dado, reproduction Old Master drawings and details of paintings decorate the subtly off-white walls, and on the parquet floor are most attractive caucasian rugs, well spaced tables with little sprays of fresh flowers (candles at night), and a mix of continental-style rush-seat stained-wood dining chairs and country kitchen chairs; a no-smoking conservatory (with plenty of blinds) has more tables. Fullers London Pride on handpump, but the emphasis is on a fine range of mainly New World wines; very good service. *(Recommended by Stephen and Julie Brown, Roger Everett, Bob and Maggie Atherton, Mr Peter Saville, Nigel Wilkinson, Susan and John Douglas, Evelyn and Derek Walter, DHV, Cyril Brown, Penny Simpson)*

Free house ~ Licensee Jean Thaxter ~ Real ale ~ Bar food ~ Restaurant ~ (01628) 781111 ~ Children at lunchtime but must be over 12 in evening ~ Open 11-2.30, 6-11; 11.30-2.30, 6-11 Sat; 12-3 Sun; closed Sun evening, Mon

BURCHETTS GREEN SU8381 Map 2
Crown
Side rd from A4 after Knowl Green on left, linking to A404

With quite an emphasis on the generous helpings of very popular, interesting food it's best to book a table here at weekends. There's a good welcome from the licensees and their staff, and the civilised main bar is clean, warm and comfortable with a restaurant layout and unobtrusive piped music; the very small plain bar has two or three tables for casual customers. As well as the blackboard menu of half a dozen carefully presented starters and main courses that changes twice a day, the printed menu at lunchtime might include sandwiches (from £4.25), home-made soup, smoked trout with potato salad (£3.95), ploughman's (£4.95), cumberland sausages with mashed potatoes and onion gravy (£6.95), escalope of chicken milanese on a bed of spaghetti with tomato sauce (£7.95), and poached fillet of salmon with a prawn, dill and cream sauce (£8.95); evening dishes such as mushroom stroganoff (£7.95), calves' liver with bubble and squeak, crispy bacon and onion gravy (£10.95), and sautéed scallops with bacon and tomato glazed with cheese (£12.95). Well kept Ruddles Bitter and Charles Wells Bombardier on handpump, kept under light blanket pressure, and a good range of wines by the glass. There are tables out in a pleasant quiet garden. *(Recommended by Mark J Hydes, W K Wood, J and B Cressey, E J Locker, Bob and Ena Withers, Claire Drewer, KC, Nina Randall)*

Morlands ~ Lease: Ian Price and Alex Turner ~ Real ale ~ Bar food ~ Restaurant ~ (01628) 822844 ~ Children in restaurant ~ Open 12-2.30, 6-11

CHEAPSIDE SU9469 Map 2
Thatched Tavern
Off B383; village signed off A332/A329

The new licensees in this smartly civilised dining pub have worked hard to keep the good bustling atmosphere and have made minimal changes – the restaurant is now open on Sunday evenings and the bar is open all day on Saturday and Sunday serving bar food until 6pm. The building is not actually thatched but does have polished flagstones, very low gnarled and nibbled beams, small windows with cheerful cottagey curtains, and an old cast-iron range in a big inglenook with built-in wall benches snugly around it. There is still an area for drinkers (which fills up quickly at busy times, so best to get there early). At lunchtime the longish carpeted back dining area serves baguettes, home-made soup (£3.95), chicken liver salad (£6.25), mediterranean prawns with fresh herbs and garlic (£8.95), cumberland sausages with mustard mash and gravy (£9.95), home-made steak and kidney pudding (£11.50), and griddled tuna steak (£12.95); evening extras such as Thai crab cake (£7.95), smoked salmon (£8.95), noisettes of lamb (£13.95), and scallops with wild mushrooms (£17.95); 3-course Sunday roasts (£17.95, children £11). Well kept Brakspears Bitter, Fullers London Pride, and Greene King Abbot on handpump, an extensive wine list, and no games or piped music. Rustic seats and tables are grouped on the sheltered back lawn, around a big old apple tree; parking is not easy at busy times. Handy for walks around Virginia Water, with the Blacknest car park a mile or so down the road. *(Recommended by Mayur Shah, Martin and Karen Wake, George Atkinson, Derek Harvey-Piper)*

Free house ~ Licensees Tracey Coe and Graham Hodgson ~ Real ale ~ Bar food (12-3; not evenings; 12-6 Sat and Sun) ~ Restaurant ~ (01344) 620874 ~ Children in restaurant ~ Open 11-3, 6-11; 11-11 Sat; 12-10.30 Sun

CHIEVELEY SU4774 Map 2
Blue Boar

2 miles from M4 junction 13: A34 N towards Oxford, 200 yds left into Chieveley, then about 100 yds after Red Lion left into School Rd; at T-junction with B4494 turn right towards Wantage and pub is 500 yds on right; heading S on A34, don't take first sign to Chieveley

In 1644 on the eve of the Battle of Newbury, Oliver Cromwell stayed at this thatched inn. There are three rambling rooms furnished with high-backed settles, windsor chairs and polished tables, and decked out with a variety of heavy harness (including a massive collar); the left-hand room has a log fire and a seat built into the sunny bow window. Bar food includes soup (£2.35), sandwiches (from £2.50), ploughman's (£5.20), speciality sausages (£6.50), half chargrilled chicken (£8.45), and puddings; there's also a civilised oak-panelled restaurant. Well kept Fullers London Pride and Wadworths 6X on handpump; several malt whiskies; soft piped music. Tables are set among the tubs and flowerbeds on the rough front cobbles outside. *(Recommended by Gordon, Mr and Mrs I Brown, John and Christine Simpson, Cedric Leefe)*

Free house ~ Licensees Ann and Peter Ebsworth ~ Real ale ~ Bar food (12-1.45, 7-9.30; 12-1.45, 7-8.30 Sun) ~ (01635) 248236 ~ Children welcome ~ Open 11-3, 6-11; 12-3, 7-10.30 Sun ~ Bedrooms: £55B/£65B

COOKHAM SU8884 Map 2
Bel & the Dragon
High St; B4447 N of Maidenhead

Carefully refurbished, this fine old building has more emphasis on the food side now, and a gallery in the larger dining room has a big grill on one side. The three rooms have comfortable seats, heavy Tudor beams and open fires contrasting with the pastel walls and up-to-date low voltage lighting. From an interesting menu, there might be home-made soup (£3.95), warm duck liver salad with oyster mushrooms and garlic croutons (£4.95), minced lamb kebabs with a greek salad (£5.50, main course £10.50), dolcelatte risotto with a tomato and basil dressing or Thai green chicken curry (£10.95), chargrilled salmon fillet on oyster mushrooms and baby spinach with a prawn butter sauce (£11.95), and calves' liver and smoked bacon with chive mashed potatoes and onion gravy (£14.75); vegetables are £2.95 extra. From the low zinc-topped bar counter Brakspears PA, Courage Best, and Marstons Pedigree are well kept on handpump, and there's a good choice of wines, whiskies and liqueurs. Street parking can be very difficult. The Stanley Spencer Gallery is almost opposite. *(Recommended by David Peakall, Neil*

Beard, Piotr Chodzko-Zajko, Gordon, Comus Elliott, Charles Bardswell, Stephen and Julie Brown)

Free house ~ Licensee Michael Mortimer ~ Real ale ~ Bar food (12-2.30, 7-10) ~ Restaurant ~ (01628) 521263 ~ Children welcome ~ Open 11-3, 6-11

COOKHAM DEAN SU8785 Map 2
Uncle Toms Cabin

Hills Lane, Harding Green; village signposted off A308 Maidenhead—Marlow – keep on down past Post Office and village hall towards Cookham Rise and Cookham

Even when this pretty cream-washed cottage is busy – as it can be at the weekends and in the summer – the friendly series of 1930s-feeling mainly carpeted little rooms offer a degree of intimacy but still give a feeling of being part of everything. At the front are low beams and joists, lots of shiny dark brown woodwork, and old-fashioned plush-cushioned wall seats, stools and so forth; quite a lot of breweryana, and some interesting golden discs. Bar food includes soup (£3.25), thick-cut sandwiches with salad and crisps (£2.95), filled baked potatoes (from £3.95), home-made 6oz burgers, baltis or sausage and mash with onion gravy (£6.95), tuna and prawn pasta or spicy prawn stir fry (£7.25). Well kept Benskins Best, Fullers London Pride, and a regularly changing guest beer on handpump; shove-ha'penny, cribbage, and dominoes. Piped music, if on, is well chosen and well reproduced. The two cats – Jess (black-and-white) and Wilma (black) – enjoy the winter coal fire, and Oggie the busy black-and-white dog welcomes other dogs (who get a dog biscuit on arrival). There are picnic-sets and a climbing frame in an attractive and sheltered back garden. *(Recommended by Rev John D Morison, Gerald Barnett, Stephen and Julie Brown)*

Allied Domecq ~ Lease: Nick and Karen Ashman ~ Real ale ~ Bar food ~ Restaurant ~ (01628) 483339 ~ Children until 8pm ~ Open 11-3, 5.30-11; 12-3, 7-10.30 Sun

CRAZIES HILL SU7980 Map 2
Horns

From A4, take Warren Row Road at Cockpole Green signpost just E of Knowl Hill, then past Warren Row follow Crazies Hill signposts

Very much enjoyed by readers for its gentrified country atmosphere and friendly welcome, this tiled whitewashed cottage continues to have no juke box, fruit machine or piped music. The bars have rugby mementos on the walls, exposed beams, open fires and stripped wooden tables and chairs; the barn room is opened up to the roof like a medieval hall. Good bar food includes lunchtime baguettes (not Sunday), soup (£3.50), chicken liver and cointreau pâté with cumberland sauce (£4.95), pasta with a spicy tomato sauce (£6.95), chicken breast with a mild chilli and brie sauce (£8.95), daily specials such as lemon sole, crab and lemon grass ravioli with a saffron cream sauce (£5.95), ratatouille cooked on mozzarella in an aubergine skin topped with toasted almonds and béarnaise sauce (£7.95), and roast partridge on a lentil and bacon croûte with a plum sauce and whole bass with a fruits of the sea sauce (£11.95); Sunday roasts (£7.50). Fish comes daily from Billingsgate), and it is essential to book a table at weekends. Well kept Brakspears Bitter, Old, OBJ, Special, and seasonal ales on handpump, a thoughtful wine list, and several malt whiskies. There's plenty of space in the very large garden. *(Recommended by Mayur Shah, Ian and Marilyn McBeath, Martin and Karen Wake, Gerald Barnett, Simon Collett-Jones)*

Brakspears ~ Tenant A J Hearn ~ Real ale ~ Bar food ~ Restaurant ~ (0118) 940 1416 ~ Children until 7.30 in evening ~ Open 11.30-2.30, 6-11; 12-3, 7-10.30 Sun; closed 25 and 26 Dec, evening 1 Jan

---

Places with gardens or terraces usually let children sit there – we note in the text the very few exceptions that don't.

EAST ILSLEY SU4981 Map 2
Crown & Horns 🍺 🛏

A34

Very much in horse-training country and surrounded by plenty of tracks and walks, this busy old pub has a relaxed atmosphere in its warren of rooms and good mix of customers. The wide range of regularly changing real ales is reasonably priced and typically includes Adnams Broadside, Brakspears, Mansfield Bitter, Morlands Original, Ruddles County, Vaux Bitter, and Wadworths 6X on handpump. There is also an impressive collection of 160 whiskies from all over the world – Morocco, Korea, Japan, China, Spain and New Zealand. Good, interesting bar food includes sandwiches, toasties, french bread or baps (from £2.25), home-made soup (£2.95), lots of filled baked potatoes (from £3.75), ploughman's (from £4.50), steak and mushroom pie (£5.25), vegetable lasagne (£5.50), ham and egg (£5.75), pork with apple and cider (£8.75), chicken breast with stilton and mushroom sauce (£9.95), steaks (from £8.95), daily specials, and puddings (£3.25). The walls of the four interesting beamed rooms are hung with racing prints and photographs, and the side bar may have locals watching the races on TV. There is a no-smoking area. Skittle alley, pool, cribbage, and fruit machine. The pretty paved stable yard has tables under two chestnut trees. *(Recommended by K H Frostick, Phyl and Jack Street, Gordon, Martin and Penny Fletcher, Nigel Clifton, IHR, TBB, Michael Bourdeaux, MDN, R M Sparkes, Andrew Shore, Eddie Edwards, Michael & Jeanne Shillington)*

Free house ~ Licensees Chris and Jane Bexx ~ Real ale ~ Bar food (11-2.30, 6-10) ~ Restaurant ~ (01635) 281545 ~ Children in eating area of bar and restaurant ~ Open 11-11; 12-11 Sun; closed 25 Dec ~ Bedrooms: £48B/£58B

FRILSHAM SU5573 Map 2
Pot Kiln ★ 🍺

From Yattendon take turning S, opposite church, follow first Frilsham signpost, but just after crossing motorway go straight on towards Bucklebury ignoring Frilsham signposted right; pub on right after about half a mile

'An unspoilt gem' is how several readers describe this unpretentious cottagey pub. It is approached via single track roads which give quite a feeling of remoteness, and surrounded by plenty of walks – dogs are allowed in the public bar on a lead. The unchanging bar is not unsmart, with wooden floorboards and bare benches and pews, and there's a good winter log fire, too. Well kept Brick Kiln Bitter and Goldstar (from a microbrewery behind the pub) is served from a hatch in the panelled entrance lobby – which has room for just one bar stool – along with well kept Arkells BBB, and Morlands Original on handpump. Good, fairly simple food includes tasty filled hot rolls (from £1.30), home-made soup (£2.65); a decent ploughman's (from £3.85), very good salmon and broccoli fishcake (£6.25), parsnip and chestnut bake, steak and kidney pudding or chicken supreme in mild mustard sauce (£6.95), rich venison casserole (£7.55), and puddings (£2.65); no chips, and vegetables are fresh. Rolls only on Sundays. The public bar has darts, dominoes, shove-ha'penny, table skittles, and cribbage. The pink, candlelit back room/dining room is no smoking. There are picnic-sets in the big suntrap garden with good views of the woods and countryside. *(Recommended by Dick Brown, Tom Evans, Phyl and Jack Street, Susan and John Douglas, R Stamp, Gordon, TBB, TRS, Alan and Ros)*

Free house ~ Licensee Philip Gent ~ Real ale ~ Bar food (not Tues evening) ~ (01635) 201366 ~ Children in back room ~ Irish music first Sun evening of month ~ Open 12-2.30, 6.30-11; 12-3, 6.30-11 Sat; closed Tues lunchtimes

GREAT SHEFFORD SU3875 Map 2
Swan

2 miles from M4 junction 14 – A338 towards Wantage

After a walk, the tables on the terrace by big willows overhanging the River Lambourn are a fine place to enjoy a drink or meal. Inside, the low-ceilinged and newly refurbished rooms of the spacious bow-windowed bar are attractively and comfortably furnished and have magazines and newspapers, racing related and other sporting memorabilia and old photographs, and other bric-a-brac on the walls. What was the public side is now the Village Bar with a large open fire, a good mix of both locals and visitors, and a friendly welcome. Generous helpings of good food include filled home-baked french bread (from £2.75), home-made soups (£2.95), filled baked potatoes (from £3.95), ham and egg or moules marinières (£4.95), ploughman's (from £4.95), broccoli and cream cheese bake (£5.75), home-made pies or tuna steak (£6.95), steaks (from £9.95), daily specials such as fresh fish, vegetarian dishes and Italian or Indian dishes, and children's meals (from £3.25). Well kept Courage Best and guests like Bass and John Smiths on handpump; attentive service. The restaurant looks over the river. *(Recommended by John Fahy, George Atkinson, Trevor Owen, Lynn Sharpless, Bob Eardley, Dick Brown, Mark Brock, TBB, Hugh Spottiswoode)*

Eldridge Pope (Hardy) ~ Managers Kevin Maul and Sue Jacobs ~ Real ale ~ Bar food ~ Restaurant ~ (01488) 648271 ~ Children welcome away from bar ~ Open 11-3, 6-11; 12-3, 7-10.30 Sun

HAMSTEAD MARSHALL SU4165 Map 2
White Hart 🛏

Village signposted from A4 W of Newbury

It's unusual to find a pub specialising in Italian food, but this popular dining pub does just that. The good and imaginative (if a little pricy) daily specials are the best bet: home-made duck liver pâté (£4.50), potato and spinach gnocchi or home-made ravioli filled with wild mushroom and ricotta (£7.50), seafood spaghetti (£9.50), warm salad of marinated crispy fried lamb strips with pine nuts or organic meatballs with mozzarella in a wine sauce (£10.50), scallops wrapped in pancetta and grilled with sage and lemon juice (£12.50), dover sole poached in white wine with prawns and cream (£17.50), and puddings such as panettone pudding, tiramisu or profiteroles decorated with fresh fruit (£4.50); the food boards are attractively illustrated with Mrs Aromando's drawings, they grow many of their own herbs and some vegetables, the bread is home-made, and their beef is from a local organic farm. The restaurant is no smoking. Hardy Country and Wadworths 6X on handpump, decent Italian wines, and friendly, helpful service. The L-shaped bar has red plush seats built into the bow windows, cushioned chairs around oak and other tables, a copper-topped bar counter, and a log fire open on both sides; piped music. Their newfoundland-cross dog is called Sophie, and the pony, Solo. The interesting walled garden is lovely in summer, and the quiet and comfortable beamed bedrooms are in a converted barn across the courtyard. *(Recommended by LM, Mr and Mrs Peter Smith)*

Free house ~ Licensees Nicola and Dorothy Aromando ~ Real ale ~ Bar food ~ Restaurant ~ (01488) 658201 ~ Children welcome ~ Open 11.45-3, 6-11; closed Sun ~ Bedrooms: £55B/£80B

HARE HATCH SU8077 Map 2
Queen Victoria

Blakes Lane; just N of A4 Reading—Maidenhead

Diners and chatty locals are made equally welcome in this friendly pub. The two low-beamed rooms here have flowers on the tables, strong spindleback chairs, wall benches and window seats, and decorations such as a stuffed sparrowhawk and a delft shelf lined with beaujolais bottles; the tables on the right are no smoking. Popular bar food changes regularly and might include sandwiches, hot nutty brie with wholemeal toast (£3.75), sweet pepper, sun-dried tomato and basil sausages with herb sliced potatoes (£5.25), sizzling Thai pork curry (£5.95), barbecue spare ribs (£6.50), Sunday roast (£5.50), and puddings like home-baked fruit pies and crumbles; vegetables are fresh. Well kept Brakspears Bitter, Special and Old with a guest like Coniston Bluebird on handpump, a fair choice of wines by the glass, and obliging service. Dominoes, cribbage, fruit machine, and three dimensional noughts and crosses. There's a flower-filled covered terrace with tables and chairs, and a robust table or two in front by the car park. *(Recommended by Pat & Tony Martin, Richard Houghton)*

Brakspears ~ Tenant Ron Rossington ~ Real ale ~ Bar food (12-2.30, 6.30-10.30) ~ (0118) 940 2477 ~ Children welcome ~ Open 11-3, 5.30-11; 12-10.30 Sun

HOLYPORT SU8977 Map 2
Belgian Arms

1½ miles from M4 junction 8/9 via A308(M), A330; in village turn left on to big green, then left again at war memorial (which is more like a bus shelter)

At lunchtimes particularly, this homely pub is very popular with locals – though visitors are made just as welcome by the friendly staff. The L-shaped, low-ceilinged bar has interesting framed postcards of Belgian military uniform and other good military prints, and some cricketing memorabilia on the walls, a china cupboard in one corner, a variety of chairs around a few small tables, and a roaring log fire. Enjoyable bar food includes sandwiches (the toasted 'special' is very well liked, £2.75), a good ploughman's (£3.95), pizzas with different toppings (£4.95), home-cooked ham and eggs or lasagne (£5.95), Mexican chicken with sour cream (£8.95), and steaks (from £13.95); good Sunday lunch. You can also eat in the conservatory area. Well kept Brakspears Bitter and Special on handpump, and one or two good malts. In summer, sitting in the charming garden by the small lake with ducks and swans, it is hard to believe that you are so close to the M4. *(Recommended by Peter Saville, Gerald Barnett, Cyril S Brown, N Cobb, Paul and Sue Merrick, Peter Burton, Lynn Sharpless, Bob Eardley, Chris Glasson, Dick Brown, Stephen and Julie Brown, Ian Phillips, Chris and Ann Garnett, R Lake, James Morrell)*

Brakspears ~ Tenant Alfred Morgan ~ Real ale ~ Bar food (not Sun evening) ~ (01628) 634468 ~ Children in restaurant ~ Open 11-3, 5.30-11; 11-3, 6-11 Sat; 12-3, 7-10.30 Sun

HURLEY SU8283 Map 2
Dew Drop

Just W of Hurley on A423 turn left (if coming from Maidenhead) up Honey Lane and keep going till you get to a T-junction, then turn right – the pub is down a right-hand turn-off at the first cluster of little houses

Well run by hard-working licensees, this isolated brick and flint cottage has a warm and welcoming atmosphere. The simply furnished main bar has some rustic charm, a log fire in its fine old inglenook fireplace at one end of the room, and another log fire at the other – space is rather tight in the serving area; there's a homely little room at the back. Good popular bar food includes sandwiches or rolls (from £2.25; not Sunday), filled baked potatoes (from £3.50), and daily specials such as ham and egg, welsh pie or macaroni cheese (£5.95), steak in ale pie (£6.50), cajun chicken or Thai curry (£6.95), cod in batter (£7.95), steaks, and winter game dishes. Well kept Brakspears Bitter, Special and seasonal ales on handpump, and quite a few malt whiskies; darts, shove-ha'penny, backgammon and dominoes. The two cats are called R2 and D2, and the dog, Sparky. The sloping garden is attractive, there are new picnic-sets and gazebo seating, and a new barbecue; good surrounding walks. *(Recommended by D A Begley, Ian Phillips, Simon Collett-Jones, Roger & Debbie Stamp)*

Brakspears ~ Tenants Charles and Beattie Morley ~ Real ale ~ Bar food (not 25 or 26 Dec) ~ (01628) 824327 ~ Children in eating area of bar but must be well behaved ~ Tues evening quiz ~ Open 12-3, 6-11; 12-3, 7-10.30 Sun

INKPEN SU3564 Map 2
Swan

Lower Inkpen; coming from the A338 in Hungerford, take Park St (1st left after railway bridge coming from A4); Inkpen signposted from Hungerford Common

New licensees have taken over this beamed country pub and have made quite a few changes to the décor and food, and opened an organic farm shop next door selling gifts, books, vegetables and so forth. The rambling bar rooms are decorated in soft colours, with muted chintz, cosy corners, beams, fresh flowers, waxed furniture, and three open fires (there's a big old fireplace with an oak mantlebeam in the restaurant area). By the time this book is published, they hope to have opened a new restaurant. Good bar food includes sandwiches, leek and mushroom crumble or leek and bacon au gratin (£5.50), cottage pie or stilton, bacon and pasta bake with garlic bread (£5.75), beef stroganoff or curry (£6.25), and braised steak in a jumbo yorkshire pudding (£6.50); they do cream teas in summer. Well kept Butts Bitter and Blackguard, and Hook Norton Bitter and Mild on handpump; local Lambourn Valley cider. The games area has old paving slabs, bench seating and darts, shove-ha'penny, cribbage, and dominoes. There are flowers out in front by the picnic-sets, which are raised above the quiet village road on old brick terraces, and a small quiet garden. *(Recommended by Mark Brock, Klaus & Elizabeth Leist)*

Free house ~ Licensees Mary and Bernard Harris ~ Real ale ~ Bar food ~ Restaurant ~ (01488) 668326 ~ Children in lower bar area ~ occasional jazz or folk groups ~ Open 11-11; 12-3, 7-10.30 Sun; 11-3, 7-11 winter; closed 25 and 26 Dec ~ Bedrooms: £35S/£60S

LAMBOURN SU3175 Map 2
Hare & Hounds

Lambourn Woodlands – 2½ miles towards Newbury

Each of the rooms leading off the narrow bar in this stylish dining pub is decorated in a colourful and occasionally idiosyncratic way, and is of much interest to visitors. Instead of bar stools there are chairs that wouldn't be out of place in a cocktail lounge, and most of the pub is painted a cosy custard yellow, with the odd pinkish stripe, and equine prints and pictures serving as a reminder of the landlord's distinguished links with the racehorse training community. Perhaps the nicest area is the rather clubby pink-hued room off to the left as you head along the central passageway; there's a lovely fireplace, and some unusual red slatted chairs. The room next to that has a mix of simple wooden and marble-effect tables, a church-style pew, and neatly patterned curtains; one wall is almost entirely covered by an elaborately gilt-edged mirror, and there's a well worn rug on the red-tiled floor. Very good, daily changing bar food might include sandwiches, french onion soup (£3), smoked pigeon breast with orange vinaigrette (£4.50), crostini of roast goat's cheese (£5), scallops and bacon (£6), salmon fishcakes or ham and eggs (£6.50), generous seafood pancake with crisp matchstick chips and tasty honey dressing (£8.50), crispy duck salad (£9.50), swordfish with a citrus and caper sauce (£10), duck breast with raspberry and blackcurrant sauce (£12), steaks (from £14), and puddings (£3.50); they add a 10% service charge. On Saturday evening, you can eat only in the restaurant. Boddingtons Gold, Flowers IPA and Wadworths 6X on handpump, good wines and a choice of malt whiskies; helpful, friendly service, fresh flowers on the bar, piped music. There are a couple of benches in the garden behind. *(Recommended by Peter and Audrey Dowsett, Martin & Karen Wake, MDN, Dr M E Wilson)*

Free house ~ Licensee David Cecil ~ Real ale ~ Bar food ~ Restaurant ~ (01488) 71386 ~ Children welcome ~ Open 11-3.30, 6-11; 12-3.30 Sun; closed Sun evening, closed 25 and 26 Dec

MARSH BENHAM SU4267 Map 2
Water Rat 🍽 ♀

Village signposted from A4 W of Newbury

Berkshire Dining Pub of the Year

Carol Evans, now running this attractively extended old thatched pub, has an enviable record of hitting the bull's eye on the food side – as she did originally with her acclaimed Poppies restaurant at the Roebuck at Brimfield in Herefordshire, and more recently at the Three Horseshoes at Batcombe in Somerset. So it's no surprise that the emphasis is on food here, with care to interleave enterprising recipes that might add sparkle to a special meal out alongside other more familiar staples; in general, the watchword is careful, rather than fanciful, cooking of good ingredients. So besides interesting soups (£3), herby baked queen scallops or a zesty ham and mozzarella salad (£4.50), stuffed mushrooms with a herb and stilton crust (£5), crispy duck confit with orange cider sauce and red cabbage (£10.50) or chargrilled langoustines done with lemon grass and lime (£13.50), you might find black pudding and bacon (£6.50) or steak and kidney pie (£7.50). Puddings (£4) are delicious. As we went to press, work was starting on a new front orangery restaurant in addition to the present attractive no-smoking stripped-brick dining room, with other structural changes in hand, but the comfortable bar with its deeply carved Victorian gothick settles (and some older ones) and cheerful Wind in the Willows murals is unlikely to change much. Well kept Arkells 3Bs and Brakspears PA on handpump, good wines, lots of malt whiskies, and quite a few brandies and ports. There are seats on the terrace or on the long lawns that slope down to water meadows and the River Kennet. *(Recommended by John Milner, R M Sparkes, Dick Brown, A J Smith, John H Smith)*

Free house ~ Licensee Carol Evans ~ Real ale ~ Bar food ~ Restaurant ~ (01635) 582017 ~ Children welcome ~ Open 11.30-3, 6-11; 12-3 Sun; closed Sun and Mon evenings

PEASEMORE SU4577 Map 2
Fox & Hounds ♀
Village signposted from B4494 Newbury—Wantage

Tucked away in horse-training country, this is a cheerful pub with a good local atmosphere. The two bars have brocaded stripped wall settles, chairs and stools around shiny wooden tables, a log-effect gas fire (open to both rooms), and piped music. One wall has a full set of Somerville's entertaining Slipper's ABC of Fox-Hunting prints, and on a stripped-brick wall there's a row of flat-capped fox masks. Enjoyable bar food includes sandwiches, home-made soup (£1.95), basket meals (from £2.75), a home-made pie of the day (£5.50), pork tenderloin with mozzarella and tomatoes (£7.50), vegetarian dishes, steaks, daily specials (from £5.50), and home-made puddings such as lemon tart and fruit crumble (from £2.50); 3-course Sunday roast lunch (£8.50). The restaurant is no smoking. Well kept Greene King IPA and Abbot, and Marstons Pedigree on handpump, decent wines, and a good few malt whiskies. Darts, pool, dominoes, cribbage, fruit machine, discreet juke box, and football table. From the picnic-sets outside, there are views of rolling fields – and on a clear day you can look right across to the high hills which form the Berkshire/Hampshire border about 20 miles southward. *(Recommended by Julie Peters, Colin Blinkhorn, Dick Brown)*

Free house ~ Licensees David and Loretta Smith ~ Real ale ~ Bar food (12-2, 7-10) ~ Restaurant ~ (01635) 248252 ~ Children welcome ~ Irish band last Fri in month ~ Open 11.30-3, 6.30-11; 12-3, 6.30-11 Sat; 12-3.30, 7-10.30 Sun; closed Mon

READING SU7272 Map 2
Sweeney & Todd £
10 Castle Street; next to PO

From the street, this delightful oddity looks like a simple baker's shop and take-away, selling pies, soft drinks and even fresh eggs. But hidden away past the counter and down a few steps is a far more convivial cafe-cum-pub, almost like an illicit drinking den, with their unusually flavoured pies and good choice of beers vying for attention. There's a surprising number of tiny tables squeezed into the long thin room, most of them in rather conspiratorial railway-carriage-style booths separated by curtains, and each with a leather-bound menu to match the leather-cushioned pews. Old prints line the walls, and the colonial-style fans and bare-boards floor enhance the period feel. Efficient uniformed waitresses serve pies such as chicken, honey and mustard, hare and cherry, duck and apricot, goose and gooseberry or partridge and pear (all £3.30) as well as soup (£1.55), sandwiches (from £2.20) and casseroles; helpings are huge, and excellent value. The small bar has well kept Adnams, Hardy Royal Oak, Wadworths 6X and a changing guest on handpump, with various wines and a range of liqueurs and cigars. You can buy the pies in the shop to take away. *(Recommended by Richard Lewis, Stephanie Smith)*

Free house ~ Licensee Mrs C Hayward ~ Real ale ~ Bar food ~ Restaurant ~ (0118) 958 6466 ~ Children welcome as long as away from bar ~ Open 11-11; closed Sun; closed 25 and 26 Dec and bank holidays

SONNING SU7575 Map 2
Bull

Village signposted on A4 E of Reading; off B478, in village

The two old-fashioned bar rooms in this attractive and charming inn have low ceilings and heavy beams, cosy alcoves, cushioned antique settles and low wooden chairs, and inglenook fireplaces; the back dining area is no smoking. Popular, interesting (if pricy) bar food includes sandwiches, home-made soup (£4), ploughman's (from £7), lasagne (£9), braised lamb shank with root vegetables on garlic mash (£9.75), steak and kidney pie (£11), Thai crab cakes on lemon grass, coconut and cream sauce (£11.50), fish kebab (£12), roast pheasant in red wine (£13.95), and fillet steak flamed in brandy in a cream sauce (£15.95); good breakfasts. Well kept Gales Best, HSB and Butser Bitter on handpump, and lots of country wines; fruit machine. The courtyard is particularly attractive in summer with tubs of flowers and a rose pergola resting under its wisteria-covered, black and white timbered walls. If you bear left through the ivy-clad churchyard opposite, then turn left along the bank of the river Thames, you come to a very pretty lock. *(Recommended by Mrs J Burrows, M Borthwick, Simon Collett-Jones, Bill Sykes, Anne and John Peacock, Dr Peter Burnham, Julia Bryan, Roger and Valerie Hill, M L Porter, Mike & Jennifer Marsh)*

Gales ~ Manager Dennis Mason ~ Real ale ~ Bar food ~ (0118) 969 3901 ~ Children in eating area of bar and restaurant ~ Open 11-3, 5.30-11; 11-11 Sat; 12-10.30 Sun; 11-3, 6-11 Sat winter; 12-3, 7-10.30 Sun winter ~ Bedrooms: £70B/£70(£98B)

STANFORD DINGLEY SU5771 Map 2
Bull

From M4 junction 12, W on A4, then right at roundabout on to A340 towards Pangbourne; first left to Bradfield, and at crossroads on far edge of Bradfield (not in centre) turn left signposted Stanford Dingley; turn left in Stanford Dingley

The beamed tap room in this attractive 15th-c brick pub is firmly divided into two parts by standing timbers hung with horsebrasses. The main part has an old brick fireplace, red-cushioned seats carved out of barrels, a window settle, wheelback chairs on the red quarry tiles, and an old station clock; the other is similarly furnished but carpeted. There's also a half-panelled lounge bar with refectory-type tables, and a smaller room leading off with quite a few musical instruments. Bar food includes sandwiches, filled baked potatoes (from £2.55), soups (from £2.85; red pepper and sweet potato £3.25), garlic bacon and mushrooms on toast (£3.60), ploughman's (from £3.70), vegetable lasagne (£5.95), cottage pie (£6.55), and steaks (from £7.65), with daily specials such as grilled goat's cheese (£4.75), vegetable hotpot (£6.95), beef stew (£8.95), chicken breast with wild mushroom stuffing and a port sauce (£9.45), and puddings (£3.25). Well kept (and cheap for the area) Boddingtons Goldstar, Brakspears Bitter, and West Berkshire Good Old Boy and Skiff on handpump; friendly, helpful staff. Ring the bull, occasional classical or easy listening music. In front of the building are some big rustic tables and benches, and to the side is a small garden with a few more seats *(Recommended by Prof John and Mrs Patricia White, TRS, Neil and Karen Dignan, Lynn Sharpless, Bob Eardley)*

Free house ~ Licensees Pat and Trudi Langdon ~ Real ale ~ Bar food ~ (0118) 974 4409 ~ Children in eating area of bar till 8.30; not Sat evening ~ Open 12-3, 7-11; 12-3, 7-10.30 Sun; closed Mon lunchtimes exc bank holidays

WALTHAM ST LAWRENCE SU8276 Map 2
Bell

In village centre

The hanging baskets in front of this timbered black and white pub have won awards for the last three years, and there are seats in the garden and terrace behind – as well as rabbits and guinea pigs that are popular with children. Inside, the lounge bar has finely carved oak panelling, a log fire, and a pleasant atmosphere, and the public bar has heavy beams, an attractive seat in the deep window recess, and well kept Bass, Brakspears Bitter, Greene King Abbot, Marlow Rebellion, and Wadworths 6X on handpump; the small front room is no smoking. Bar food includes doorstep sandwiches or filled french bread (from £2.30), ploughman's, filled baked potatoes or sausage, bacon and egg (£5), chicken tikka masala or steak and kidney pie (£6), evening extras such as sesame and ginger prawns with chilli dip (£3.50), mushroom and nut fettucine (£6) or rack of lamb (£8), home-made puddings like raspberry riffin (£3), and children's menu (from £2). Darts.
(Recommended by David Price, Susan and John Douglas, Chris and Ann Garnett, Simon Collett-Jones, Nicholas Holmes, Mr and Mrs T A Bryan, M L Porter, Joan and Tony Walker)

Free house ~ Licensee Mrs Denise M Slater ~ Real ale ~ Bar food (not Sun or Mon evenings) ~ Restaurant ~ (0118) 934 1788 ~ Children in restaurant and small room ~ Open 11-3, 6-11; 12-3, 7-10.30 Sun

WEST ILSLEY SU4782 Map 2
Harrow 🍽 🍸

Signposted at East Ilsley slip road off A34 Newbury—Abingdon

To be sure of a seat, it's best to get to this bustling white-painted village pub in good time – but if it's just a drink you're after you can join the locals who gather around the bar for an early evening pint. The open-plan bar has dark terracotta walls hung with many mainly Victorian prints and other ornaments, big turkey rugs on the floor, and a mix of antique oak tables, unpretentious old chairs, and a couple of more stately long settles; there's also an unusual stripped twin-seated high-backed settle between the log fire and the bow window. Constantly changing, the very good home-made food might include interestingly filled french bread (from £3.50), roasted provençale vegetable terrine (£4.20), crostini of aubergine and goat's cheese or filled baked potatoes (£4.50), ploughman's (£5.20; the pickle is home-made), lamb's liver and bacon (£8.75), Cornish bass with artichoke mash and confit of tomato (£9.50), breast of guinea fowl with mushroom risotto (£10.50), and puddings like apple pie, sticky toffee pudding and warm orange tart with local cream (from £3.95). The dining room is no smoking. Well kept Morlands Original and Old Speckled Hen, and a guest like Flowers Original on handpump, and a good wine list with around 10 by the glass. This is a lovely spot with lots of nearby walks – the Ridgeway is just a mile away – and the big garden has picnic-sets and other tables under cocktail parasols looking out over the duck pond and cricket green.
(Recommended by D G Twyman, Dave Braisted, Dr R A L Leatherdale, G D Sharpe, Steve and Sarah de Mellow, TBB, I Maw, G W A Pearce, Gordon, K H Frostick, C G Mason, Julie Peters, Colin Blinkhorn, Mrs S Wharton, S J Edwards, Mr and Mrs R A Barton, P Collins, Stan Edwards)

Morlands ~ Tenants Emily Hawes and Scott Hunter ~ Real ale ~ Bar food (not winter Sun or Mon evenings) ~ Restaurant ~ (01635) 281260 ~ Children welcome but must be well behaved; not Fri/Sat evenings ~ Open 11-3, 6-11; 12-4, 7-10.30 Sun

WINTERBOURNE SU4572 Map 2
Winterbourne Arms

Not far from M4 junction 13; formerly the New Inn

Although this friendly country pub places much emphasis on its very good food – particularly in the evening – drinkers are still made welcome. There's a pleasant old-fashioned atmosphere and decorations such as hop swags over the archways and doors, a collection of old irons around the fireplace, brass fire extinguishers, early prints and old photographs of the village, pretty dried flower arrangements, and a log fire; you can see the original bakers' ovens in the restaurant area, which was once a bakery. Bar food includes interestingly filled sandwiches (from £4.25), a trio of sausages with red onion gravy (£6.25), cold poached salmon (£7.25), supreme of chicken on a basil cream (£9.95), and whole bass with a dill or chive beurre blanc or tournedos of beef topped with foie gras on a truffle sauce (£15.95). Well kept Bass, Brakspears, and West Berkshire Good Old Boy on handpump; juke box. The quiet road is slightly sunken between the pub's two lawns, and you can't actually see it from inside the bar – so the view from the big windows over the rolling fields is peaceful; there are picnic-sets among the pretty flowering tubs and hanging baskets, a big weeping willow, and a children's play area with swings; nearby walks to Snelsmore and Donnington. *(Recommended by D E Kent, Helen Spiller, Mark Brock, E W Roberts, Mrs S Wharton)*

Free house ~ Licensees Alan and Angela Hodge ~ Real ale ~ Bar food ~ Restaurant ~ (01635) 248200 ~ Well behaved children in restaurant ~ Open 11-3, 6-11; 12-3 Sun; closed Sun evening, Mon – exc bank holidays

YATTENDON SU5574 Map 2
Royal Oak ♀ 🛏

The Square; B4009 NE from Newbury; turn right at Hampstead Norreys, village signposted on left

The panelled and prettily decorated brasserie/bar is the place to head for in this elegantly handsome inn if you want to enjoy the very good food in an informal atmosphere – a marvellous log fire, lovely flowers, and Fullers London Pride and locally brewed West Berkshire Brewery's Good Old Boy, well kept on handpump. From a changing menu, bar food includes soup (£3.50), provençale vegetable terrine with goat's cheese (£5.50), marinated prawn salad with guacamole (£6.25), a plate of charcuterie (£6.75), caramelised skate wing with braised lettuce (£9.50), Jamaican jerk chicken with saffron risotto and bang bang sauce (£10.50), braised lamb shank with garlic mash and glazed carrots (£11.50), and puddings such as soupière of rhubarb with blood orange sorbet or cappuccino panacotta (£5.25); vegetables are extra. The restaurant is no smoking, and there's a good wine list. Best to book. In summer, you can eat at tables in the pleasant walled garden – and there are more in front on the village square. The attractive village is one of the few still owned privately *(Recommended by Phyl and Jack Street, Stephen Brown, Neil and Karen Dignan, Susan and John Douglas)*

Free house ~ Licensee Corinne Macrae ~ Real ale ~ Bar food (till 10pm Fri and Sat) ~ Restaurant ~ (01635) 201325 ~ Children welcome ~ Open 12-3, 6-11; 12-3, 6-10.30 Sun ~ Bedrooms: £104B/£134B

Lucky Dip

Besides the fully inspected pubs, you might like to try these Lucky Dips recommended to us and described by readers (if you do, please send us reports):

Ashmore Green [SU5069]
Sun in the Wood: Interesting choice of good food in pleasant flagstoned bar with adjoining restaurant area, friendly caring service; big garden with play area, surprisingly rural setting *(P Collins)*
Aston [SU7884]
Flower Pot [signed off A4130 Henley—Maidenhead]: Friendly but sophisticated pubby hotel handy for riverside strolls, with garden views over meadows to cottages and far side of Thames – busy with walkers and families w/e, when service can slow; well kept Brakspears inc Mild, reasonably priced food, bare-boards public bar with lots of stuffed fish in glass cases,

darts, unobtrusive piped music *(Nigel Wilkinson, Nigel and Amanda Thorp, Comus Elliott, J and B Cressey)*
Bagnor [SU4569]
☆ *Blackbird* [quickest approach is from Speen on edge of Newbury]: Chatty traditional pub in very peaceful setting nr Watermill Theatre – they do a pre-show menu; bar simple and unfussy with plates around walls, leaded lamps, plain wooden furnishings, old farm tools and firearms hanging from ceiling; more formal no-smoking eating area opens off; changing beers such as Brakspears, Shepherd Neame Spitfire, Ushers Best and brews from West Berkshire Brewery, friendly staff, well prepared

straightforward food, winter log fire; tables in side garden and on green in front; regular backgammon nights *(Peter and Audrey Dowsett, BB, Mrs Pat Crabb)*

Bisham [SU8485]

Bull: Spacious and well kept, with pleasant attentive service, well kept beer, interesting good value food from paella to Sun roasts in bar and restaurant *(Malcolm Clydesdale, Peter A Burnstone)*

Bray [SU9079]

☆ *Crown* [handy for M4 junction 9]: 14th-c pub with good mix of locals, walkers and well-off diners; three log fires, low beams, timbers and panelling, leather seats, good range of well cooked food in bar and restaurant (flying photographs in one dining area), well kept Courage Best and Theakstons XB, decent wines, friendly staff; well behaved children allowed, plenty of seating outside inc flagstoned vine arbour *(Chris Glasson, Piotr Chodzko-Zajko, Gill and Maurice McMahon, Margaret Dyke, LM, LYM)*
Hinds Head: Handsome, comfortable and civilised Tudor pub, panelling and beams, with good food (esp upstairs restaurant), well kept beers inc Courage, efficient service *(Gill and Maurice McMahon, J and B Cressey, LYM, A Hepburn, S Jenner)*

Chieveley [SU4773]

☆ *Olde Red Lion* [handy for M4 junction 13 via A34 N-bound]: Bustling local with good value straightforward food (Weds steak night, Thurs fish and chip night), helpful staff, well kept Arkells beers, comfortable low-beamed L-shaped bar with well worn furnishings, lots of brasses around walls, couple of old sewing machines, roaring log fire; piped music, fruit machine, pool, TV; parking immediately outside can be a squeeze – easier in overflow opp *(John and Christine Simpson, A and M Marriott, BB, Chris Sutton, Stephen & Julie Brown, Mr & Mrs W Morris)*

Cookham [SU8884]

Ferry: Splendid riverside position for modernised pub with upstairs Harvester restaurant, enjoyable bar food, cheerful courteous service; big terrace with views of the Thames *(LYM, Hugh Spottiswoode)*

Cookham Dean [SU8785]

☆ *Inn on the Green*: Inviting atmosphere, good solid furniture with attractive tables, unspoilt rambling layout with light and airy bar one side of double-faced log fire, sofa, easy chairs and daily papers the other, stripped beams, well kept ales inc Fullers London Pride, attractive rather smart two-room restaurant with conservatory, good genuine interesting if not cheap food (no snacks Sun), tables on terrace and in garden; bedrooms, attractive spot, good walks *(Martin & Karen Wake)*

☆ *Jolly Farmer* [off Hills Lane]: Owned by a village consortium and kept traditional, with small rooms, open fires, well kept Courage Best and a guest such as Old Codger, attractive dining room, unhurried feel, traditional games, no music or machines, good quiet garden with play area; well behaved children welcome away

from bar *(Gerald Barnett, Chris Glasson, LYM)*

Curridge [SU4871]

☆ *Bunk* [3 miles from M4 junction 13: A34 towards Newbury, then first left to Curridge, Hermitage, and left into Curridge at Village Only sign]: Worth booking for good interesting food (not cheap, not Sun evening) in stylish dining pub with smart stripped-wood tiled-floor bar on left, elegant stable-theme bistro on right with wooded-meadow views and conservatory; four well kept ales inc Fullers London Pride, good choice of wines, buoyant atmosphere, cheerful efficient service, tables in neat garden, fine woodland walks nearby *(Mrs D Rawlings, BB, Phyl and Jack Street)*

Datchet [SU9876]

Royal Stag [not far from M4 junction 5]: Above-average food and well kept Tetleys-related and guest beers in friendly and picturesque local; beautiful beams, ecclesiastical windows overlooking churchyard, attractively carved armchairs (and bar), one wall panelled in claret case lids, log fire, welcoming retriever; open all day, occasional juke box *(Bruce Braithwaite)*

East Ilsley [SU4981]

☆ *Swan*: Spacious, neat and well decorated, with a slightly formal look but pleasantly informal dining-pub feel; wide range of good bar food (busy with families Sun – best to book), friendly landlord, well kept Morlands Original and Charles Wells Bombardier, daily papers; no-smoking restaurant, tables in courtyard and walled garden with play area; excellent bedrooms, some in house down road *(Graham and Lynn Mason, Mr and Mrs T A Bryan, TBB, LYM, Val and Alan Green, Stan Edwards)*

Eastbury [SU3477]

Plough: Friendly service, good food; dogs and children allowed *(J M M Hill)*

Eton [SU9678]

☆ *Eton Wine Bar*: Hardly a pub, but well worth knowing for good food, nice house wines, friendly service; plain wood tables, some pews, tiled floor, bar stools; can be very busy if there's an event at the school *(Heather Martin, BB)*
Henry VI: Pleasantly refurbished, light and airy, with stripped brickwork, tasteful rugs on bare boards, comfortable sofas and high-backed settles on right; good value generous lunchtime food, very well kept changing ales such as Boddingtons, Fullers London Pride and Wadworths 6X, lots of old Eton photographs; unobtrusive piped music, a few tables outside *(BB, Sarah Smith)*
Hogshead: Good value bar food, splendid array of guest ales, draught and bottled Hoegaarden white beer; just over the bridge on the tourist trail to the College, and frequented by Eton masters in mufti *(Mr & Mrs Richard Osborne)*

☆ *Watermans Arms*: Friendly pub facing Eton College boat house, well kept Brakspears, Charles Wells Bombardier, Wadworths 6X and a guest, friendly efficient staff, good reasonably priced food (all day Fri/Sat, not Sun eve) inc good vegetarian choice, bright roomy restaurant, no-smoking area, lots of old boat photographs, conservatory full of H M Bateman cartoons, tables in plastic-roofed yard; parking can be very difficult *(Liz and Ian Phillips, LYM, Bruce Bird)*

Fifield [SU9076]

Fifield Inn: Old pub with eclectic décor, welcoming staff, generous good food esp Sun roasts; live jazz Sun evening; children welcome *(Brian Higgins, Ana Kolkowska)*

Great Shefford [SU3875]

☆ *Pheasant* [less than ½ mile N of M4 junction 14 – B4000, just off A338]: Good relaxing motorway break, four neat rooms, wide choice of good generous food inc Sun lunches, well kept Brakspears and Wadworths IPA and 6X, decent wines and coffee, log fires; public bar with games inc ring the bull; attractive views from garden *(LYM, J H Jones, Andrew & Eileen Abbess, Roger & Pauline Pearce)*

Holyport [SU8977]

☆ *George* [1½ miles from M4 junction 8/9, via A308(M)/A330]: Low-ceilinged open-plan bar with nice old fireplace, pictures and warming pans, friendly bustle, small dining area (usually booked Sun), Courage ales, enjoyable food inc fish and seafood; picnic-sets outside, lovely village green *(D J and P M Taylor, Paul and Sue Merrick, David Dimock, George Atkinson)*

Hungerford [SU3368]

Down Gate [by Hungerford Common, E edge of town]: Unspoilt friendly local, prettily placed and relaxing, with friendly efficient landlord, well kept Arkells, various bric-a-brac; two bars overlooking common, small lower room with open fire and a few tables for diners *(Anon)*

Hurley [SU8283]

Black Boy [A404]: Old-fashioned cottagey pub concentrating on wide-ranging food, but a few tables for drinkers, with very well kept Brakspears PA, Mild and SB, friendly service, open fire, attractive garden by paddock, picnic-sets looking over countryside rolling down to Thames *(Christopher Glasson, Simon Collett-Jones)*

☆ *Olde Bell*: Handsome and unusual old-fashioned timbered inn with some remarkable ancient features inc Norman doorway and window; small but comfortable bar with decent food, very friendly staff; good restaurant, fine gardens, very civilised gents'; keg beer, tolerable piped music; bedrooms *(Piotr Chodzko-Zajko, Mike and Heather Watson, LYM)*

Kintbury [SU3866]

☆ *Dundas Arms*: Consistently enjoyable, clean and tidy with comfortably upmarket feel, good fresh home-made food (not Mon evening or Sun) from sandwiches up, well kept real ales from smaller breweries, good coffee and wines by the glass, no piped music, remarkable range of clarets and burgundies in evening restaurant; tables out on deck above Kennet & Avon Canal, children welcome, pleasant walks; comfortable bedrooms with own secluded waterside terrace *(GLD, R M Sparkes, LYM, Tony Hobden, LM, Mrs J Lang)*

Knowl Hill [SU8279]

Old Devil: Roomy roadhouse under new management, keeping its cosy character; wide food choice, well kept ales, good view from pleasant verandah above attractive lawn with swings and slide; piped music, fruit machine *(Iain Robertson, Roger Stamp)*

Littlewick Green [SU8379]

☆ *Cricketers* [not far from M4 junction 9; A404(M) then left on to A4, from which village signed on left]: Charming spot opp cricket green, friendly service, well kept Fullers London Pride and ESB, freshly squeezed orange juice, decent food inc excellent free Sun bar nibbles, neat housekeeping, lots of cricketing pictures *(LM, Tom Evans, Chris Glasson, LYM, Gerald Barnett)*

Maidenhead [SU8783]

Brewers Tea House: Friendly down-to-earth pub with particularly well kept Courage Directors and good inexpensive food; can get smoky *(Christopher Glasson)*

Hand & Flowers: Tastefully refurbished but still a proper town pub, with no piped music, welcoming staff and well kept Brakspears *(Richard Houghton)*

Maidenhead [SU8582]

Stag & Hounds [just off A308 N]: Friendly refurbished pub with reasonably priced food in carpeted dining lounge, small side bar, well kept guest ales; pictures for sale, skittle alley *(Chris Glasson)*

Moneyrow Green [SU8977]

White Hart [between Holyport and B3024]: Morlands and regular guest ales in very welcoming and relaxed village local with lots of scientific trinkets from ex-headmaster landlord, bar billiards, dominoes, cribbage, food too; big garden, open all day Mon-Sat *(Richard Houghton)*

Newbury [SU4666]

☆ *Lock Stock & Barrel*: Modern pub standing out for canalside setting, with tables on suntrap terrace looking over a series of locks towards handsome church; clean and spacious wood-floored bar with antique-effect lights and fittings, and quite a sunny feel – lots of windows; efficient all-day food operation, well kept Fullers beers inc a seasonal one, plenty of newspapers, lots of tables and chairs, good mix of customers; no-smoking back bar; pop music may be loudish; canal walks *(C R L Savill, Warren Elliott, Peter and Audrey Dowsett, BB)*

Oakley Green [SU9276]

Olde Red Lion [B3024]: Cosy old low-beamed pub with good interesting reasonably bar food, welcoming helpful staff; restaurant, pleasant garden *(Ivan De Deken, M R Lewis)*

Old Windsor [SU9874]

☆ *Oxford Blue* [off B3021 – itself off A308/A328]: Very friendly and well placed extended pub, great with children, but keeping them sensibly away from other customers; packed with aeroplane memorabilia inc lots of suspended model aeroplanes, chintzy dining room in conservatory extension, food all day, Fullers London Pride and Wadworths 6X, decent wines by the glass, piped music; play fort and giant toadstool in garden, with picnic-sets, also sets on sheltered front terrace overlooking field *(Lin and Roger Lawrence, Piotr Chodzko-Zajko, Ian Phillips, Nigel Wilkinson, Andy and Jill Kassube, BB)*

☆ *Union* [off B3021 – itself off A308/A328]: Welcoming old pub with interesting collection of nostalgic show-business photographs, good bar food from sandwiches up, well kept ales such as Adnams and Fullers London Pride, consistently good friendly service, woodburner in big fireplace, fruit machine; good value attractive copper-decorated restaurant, white plastic tables under cocktail parasols on sunny front terrace (heated in cooler weather), country views; comfortable bedrooms *(BB, Mayur Shah, Ian Phillips)*

Reading [SU7272]

Blagrave Arms: Interesting pleasantly neo-Victorian town-centre pub with well kept Courage, good popular bar lunches *(Dr and Mrs A K Clarke)*

Brewery Tap: Refurbished under new owners, brewing own Tudor ales, with others such as Batemans XB and Shepherd Neame Spitfire and Early Bird; comfortable décor, good menu, friendly staff; open all day *(Richard Lewis)*

Broadwalk: Roomy, light and airy new Fullers café/bar, lots of light brown woodwork, parquet floor, well kept Chiswick, London Pride and ESB, bar food, no-smoking area; open all day *(Richard Lewis)*

Corn Exchange: Imaginative split-level conversion, lots of stone and wood, chandler's equipment, Fullers full range excellently kept (inc their bottled beers), friendly staff and locals, wheelchair access; open all day weekdays, cl Sun, no food Fri/Sat evening *(Richard Lewis)*

☆ *Fishermans Cottage* [easiest to walk from Orts Rd, off Kings Rd]: Good friendly backwater respite from Reading's bustle, by canal lock and towpath (shame about the gasometer), with lovely big back garden, modern furnishings of character, pleasant stone snug behind woodburning range, light and airy conservatory, waterside tables; good value lunches (very busy then but service quick), well kept Fullers ales, small choice of wines, small darts room, SkyTV; dogs allowed (not in back garden) *(D J and P M Taylor, C P Scott-Malden, Tony and Wendy Hobden)*

Griffin: Large food pub with good varied choice inc vegetarian, Courage-related beers, several separate areas; beautiful spot on Thames overlooking swan sanctuary *(J Harper, Tony Hobden)*

Hobgoblin: Popular and friendly, with four quickly changing well kept interesting guest beers (several hundred a year) and a couple of farm ciders as well as their well kept Wychwood ales, filled rolls and baps, lively landlord, bare boards, raised side area, alcovey panelled back rooms, hundreds of pumpclips on ceiling; open all day *(Richard Lewis, Dr and Mrs A K Clarke, Stephanie Smith)*

Hop Leaf [former Red Lion]: Friendly refurbished local tied to Hop Back of Wiltshire with their full beer range kept well, also occasional Reading Lion beers brewed on the

premises; nice atmosphere; parking close by difficult *(Richard Lewis, Stephanie Smith)*

Hope: Large comfortable open-plan Wetherspoons pub with lots of books and old Reading prints, no-smoking areas, good menu, good choice of well kept ales, friendly efficient service; open all day, good disabled facilities *(Richard Lewis)*

Lyndhurst: Bare-boards ale house with wooden furniture, good choice of real ales, pleasantly relaxed studenty atmosphere *(Bridget Griffin, David Hickson)*

Monks Retreat: Roomy L-shaped Wetherspoons pub, armchairs and settees at the back, upstairs gallery, nine well kept ales, Weston's farm cider, friendly efficient staff, plenty of seating inc no-smoking areas; open all day *(Richard Lewis, Stephanie Smith)*

Remenham [SU7683]

☆ *Little Angel* [A4130, just over bridge E of Henley]: Good atmosphere in low-beamed dining pub with panelling and darkly bistroish décor, good food – mainly restaurary, but snacks from sandwiches up too; friendly landlord, efficient servicee; splendid range of wines by the glass, well kept Brakspears, floodlit terrace *(LYM, Gordon, Chris Glasson)*

Slough [SU9779]

Moon & Spoon: Wetherspoons bringing a touch of refinement to the Slough pub scene; lots to do, excellent range of real ales *(Dr and Mrs A K Clarke)*

Stanford Dingley [SU5771]

☆ *Old Boot*: Stylish 18th-c beamed pub, well kept Brakspears SB and other ales such as Exmoor and Wadworths 6X, good measures of good wine, chatty landlord, two roaring log fires, one in an inglenook, assorted old country tables and chairs smelling nicely of furniture polish, stagecoach and hunting prints and attractive curtains; food from very generous sandwiches to fish and steaks, also vegetarian, children allowed in small public bar, dining room and conservatory; big suntrap back garden, lovely village *(Dr Wendy Holden, G C Hackemer, Lynn Sharpless, Bob Eardley, Dr M Ian Crichton, LYM)*

Streatley [SU5980]

Bull [A417/B4009]: Efficient staff in large friendly pub with emphasis on food; Hardy beers, friendly dog, tables outside – lovely setting; good walks *(Eddie Edwards)*

Swallowfield [SU7364]

☆ *George & Dragon* [towards Farley Hill]: Smart – even slightly trendy – dining pub, cosy and comfortable, with stripped beams, large log fire, rugs on flagstones, good generous seasonal food inc imaginative fish dishes, well kept ales inc Wadworths 6X, good wine choice (staff bring drinks to table), prompt service; piped music, can get very busy, best to book *(Bridget Griffin, David Hickson, David Prest, Simon Collett-Jones, John and Julia Hall)*

Three Mile Cross [SU7167]

Swan [A33 just S of M4 junction 11]: Warm welcome, reasonably priced home-made food, good sandwiches, good choice of well kept ales inc Brakspears and Gales *(Andy & Jill Kassube)*

Waltham St Lawrence [SU8376]

☆ *Star*: Clean and tidy old pub with good restaurant meals (a couple of tables straying into bar area, some no smoking), beams, brasses, newspapers on hangers, open fire, full range of Wadworths beers *(TRS)*

Warfield [SU8872]

Three Legged Cross [A3095]: Atmospheric Courage pub with a guest such as Marstons Pedigree, friendly welcome; limited food *(Chris Glasson)*

Wargrave [SU7878]

☆ *Bull* [off A321 Henley—Twyford]: Good friendly atmosphere in cottagey low-beamed pub popular for interesting selection of food esp good value lunchtime filled baguettes and hot dishes; well kept Brakspears, good log fires, tables on pretty covered terrace; bedrooms *(M L Porter, M Borthwick, LYM, the Didler)*

Windsor [SU9676]

Fort & Firkin: Worth knowing for large riverside terrace; pleasant lunchtime atmosphere, with this chain's usual food and beer range *(Stephen and Esther Sprinkle)*

Old Ticket Hall: Reasonably priced food, very friendly service, classy piped music giving wonderful atmosphere; keg beer *(Stephen and Julie Brown)*

☆ *Two Brewers* [off High St next to Mews]: Quaint snug three-roomed pub with pleasant relaxed atmosphere, good interesting home-made food (not Sat evening), well kept beers inc Courage, Wadworths 6X and Youngs Special, good choice of wines by the glass and bottle (and of Havana cigars), daily papers, bare boards and beams (covered with sayings and quotes), walls lined with corks; tables out on pavement of pretty Georgian street next to Windsor Park's Long Walk; has been open all day summer *(Val Stevenson, Rob Holmes, Ian Phillips, Chris Glasson, James Morrell)*

Vansittart Arms: Relaxed Victorian local, period decor in three rooms inc well stoked coal-fired range, cosy corners, good home-made food, well kept Fullers London Pride, ESB and Red Fox, interesting wines by the glass, good young NZ staff; children and dogs welcome, paved terrace, small play area *(Joy & Graham Eaton, Kaye Carver, Malcolm Kinross)*

Winkfield [SU9072]

☆ *White Hart*: Neatly modernised Tudor pub with ex-bakery bar and ex-courthouse restaurant, good varied food esp Sun lunch, relaxed atmosphere, real ales such as Brakspears and Fullers London Pride, good wine choice; sizeable attractive garden *(LYM, A Hepburn, S Jenner, Chris Glasson)*

Wokingham [SU8266]

☆ *Crooked Billet*: Really welcoming bustle in homely country pub with pews, tiles, brick serving counter, crooked black joists, big helpings of good value genuinely home-cooked lunchtime food, well kept Brakspears, small no-smoking restaurant area where children allowed; nice outside in summer, very busy weekends *(LYM, Mr and Mrs T A Bryan, Dr Philip Jackson, Patricia Heptinstall)*

Woodside [SU9270]

☆ *Rose & Crown* [just off A344]: Thriving dining pub with good (not cheap) really interesting meals inc fresh fish and vegetarian – best to book w/e; plenty of space for eating with most tables set for diners, wider choice in evenings; neatly painted low beams in long narrow bar, Charles Wells Bombardier, Marstons Best and Ruddles, big jugs of pimms, good service; tables and swing in side garden, attractive setting; bedrooms (not Sun) *(TAB, BB, S Lunn)*

Woolhampton [SU5767]

Rowbarge: Big canalside family dining place with beamed bar, panelled side room, small snug, bric-a-brac, candlelit tables, good choice of well kept ales; no-smoking back conservatory, tables in big garden with fish pond; maybe piped pop music *(Roger Byrne, DHV, LYM, R M Sparkes, B and C Clouting)*

Post Office address codings confusingly give the impression that some pubs are in Berkshire, when they're really in Oxfordshire or Hampshire (which is where we list them).

Buckinghamshire

This county gives a good choice between very foody pubs and nice little unspoilt places that it's a joy to discover. Newcomers to the Guide (or pubs back in these pages after a break) are the friendly Bell at Chearsley (great summer garden for families), the well run Red Lion at Chenies (imaginative food, but determined to stay a pub rather than an eating house), the cheerful Churchill Arms in Long Crendon (amazing range of sausages), and the Lone Tree strategically placed at Thornborough, with its fine choice of English beers and cheeses. More firmly in the dining pub image than any of these are the buoyant and attractively decorated Mole & Chicken at Easington, the restauranty rather upmarket Green Dragon at Haddenham, the Rising Sun at Little Hampden (consistently good imaginative cooking, in a nice spot), the Angel in Long Crendon (another restauranty place), the Carrington Arms at Moulsoe (have your choice of fish or meat weighed out for you before cooking), and the Five Arrows in Waddesdon (nice beers too, and first-class wines). The Walnut Tree at Fawley, long a favourite for food, is doing well after some refurbishment under new licensees. From among all these it's the Rising Sun at Little Hampden which we name as Buckinghamshire Dining Pub of the Year. Plenty of other pubs here do good food more informally, and among these are some favourite unpretentious haunts including the Prince Albert at Frieth and the Chequers at Wheeler End. Other pubs currently gaining really warm reports from readers are the Polecat at Prestwood (its garden is even better than before), the Frog at Skirmett (nice balance between eating and drinking), the pretty Bull & Butcher attractively placed at Turville, and the Chequers at Wooburn Common (a good traditional bar despite its success on the hotel/restaurant front). This county has many prizes in the Lucky Dip section at the end of the chapter, too, such as the Old Thatched Inn at Adstock, Bull & Butcher at Akeley, Bottle & Glass near Aylesbury, Ivy House in Chalfont St Giles, Ostrich in Colnbrook, Chequers at Fingest, Hampden Arms at Great Hampden, Red Lion at Great Kingshill (now entirely a restaurant, so no longer eligible for our main entries), Pink & Lily at Lacey Green, Kings Head at Little Marlow, Two Brewers in Marlow, Bull in Newport Pagnell, Black Boy at Oving, Hit or Miss at Penn Street, Old Hat at Preston Bissett, Red Lion above Princes Risborough and Red Lion in Wendover. We have already inspected most of these and can vouch for their quality.

AMERSHAM SU9597 Map 4

Queens Head ◖

Whielden Gate; pub in sight just off A404, 1½ miles towards High Wycombe at Winchmore Hill turn-off

Refreshingly unpretentious, this old brick and tile pub has a low-beamed, friendly bar with traditional furnishings, horsebrasses, and lots of brass spigots; flagstones surround the big inglenook fireplace (which still has the old-fashioned wooden built-in wall seat curving around right in beside the woodburning stove – with plenty of space under the seat for logs), and there's also a stuffed albino pheasant, old guns, and a good cigarette card collection. The family room is no smoking. Bar food includes sandwiches (£2), home-made soup (£2.50), omelettes or smoked salmon flan (£4.50), home-made pizzas (from £5), and pies such as steak in ale, pork and apricot or venison in red wine (£5.50), and puddings (£2.75). Well kept Adnams Bitter, Badger Golden Champion, and Rebellion Smuggler on handpump; darts, dominoes, cribbage, fruit machine, and piped music. The garden is quite a busy place with bantams running around, an aviary with barn owls, children's play equipment, a golden labrador called Tanner, and a jack russell called Ellie. *(Recommended by Tracey and Stephen Groves, Ian Phillips, Gerald Barnett, Mike Wells)*

Free house ~ Licensees Les and Mary Anne Robbins ~ Real ale ~ Bar food (12-2.15, 7-10; not Sun evening) ~ (01494) 725240 ~ Children in family room ~ Open 11-3, 5.30-11

BEACONSFIELD SU9490 Map 2
Greyhound
A mile from M40 junction 2, via A40; Windsor End, Old Town

With its rambling layout and warm welcome from the entertaining landlord and his staff, this pleasant and neatly kept two-bar former coaching inn is well liked locally. Food is quite a draw too: open baps (from £3.75), ploughman's (£4.95), huge burgers (from £6.25), aubergine bake (£6.95), shepherd's pie or smoked haddock with cream and spinach (£7.45), popular bubble and squeak with beef, ham, liver and bacon or sausages (from £7.45), and daily specials with a choice of pasta (from £5.25), lots of fresh fish, and home-made puddings (from £3.45); there's a partly no-smoking back bistro-like restaurant. Well kept Courage Best, Fullers London Pride, Wadworths 6X, and two guest beers on handpump; no piped music or games machines and no children. *(Recommended by George Atkinson, Geoff and Sylvia Donald, Gerald Barnett, Joan and Andrew Life, Mike Wells)*

Free house ~ Licensees Jamie and Wendy Godrich ~ Real ale ~ Bar food (not Sun evening) ~ Restaurant ~ (01494) 673823 ~ Open 11-3, 5.30-11; 12-3, 7-10.30 Sun

BLEDLOW SP7702 Map 4
Lions of Bledlow
From B4009 from Chinnor towards Princes Risborough, the first right turn about 1 mile outside Chinnor goes straight to the pub; from the second, wider right turn, turn right through village

A good place to relax after a walk in the nearby Chilterns, this 16th-c pub has fine views from the bay windows of the attractive low-beamed rooms over a small quiet green to the plain stretched out below. The inglenook bar has attractive oak stalls built into one partly panelled wall, more seats in a good bay window, and an antique settle resting on the deeply polished ancient tiles; log fires and a woodburning stove. Bar food includes sandwiches, pepper and mushroom lasagne (£4.95), jambalaya with garlic bread (£5.50), chicken breast with leeks and asparagus (£6.25), English lamb cutlets with redcurrant sauce (£6.50), prawns in garlic and white wine (£7.25), and sea bream with pesto and salad (£8.50); the restaurant is no smoking. Well kept Brakspears Bitter, Courage Best, Marstons Pedigree, Theakstons, and Wadworths 6X on handpump. One of the two cottagey side rooms has a video game and fruit machine. There are seats on the sheltered crazy-paved terrace and more on the series of neatly kept small sloping lawns. *(Recommended by Catherine and Richard Preston, JP, PP, B R Sparkes, Mike Wells, Greg Kilminster, Tim Brierly, Gerald Barnett, the Didler)*

Free house ~ Licensee Mark McKeown ~ Real ale ~ Bar food (not 25 Dec) ~ Restaurant ~ (01844) 343345 ~ Children must be well behaved ~ Open 11.30-3, 6-11; 11.30-3.30, 6-11 Sat; 12-4, 7-10.30 Sun

You can send us reports through our web site: www.goodguides.com

BOLTER END SU7992 Map 4
Peacock

Just over 4 miles from M40 junction 5 via A40 then B482

The brightly modernised bar in this bustling little pub has a cheerful atmosphere in its rambling series of alcoves, and a good log fire, and the Old Darts bar is no smoking. Good home-made bar food includes lunchtime sandwiches and ploughman's (not Sunday lunchtime or bank holidays), local butcher's sausages (£5.70), lasagne or cheesy pancakes (£6.10), home-made steak and kidney pie (£7.10), tiger prawns in filo pastry with a sweet and sour dip (£7.60), chicken stir fry with lime and ginger (£8.10), steaks (from £9), half a roast shoulder of lamb (£10.90), three changing daily specials such as mediterranean lamb, pork and lentil hotpot or bass fillet with asparagus sauce (£9.30), and puddings like home-made fruit crumble (£3). Well kept Adnams, Brakspears Bitter, Marstons Pedigree, and Tetleys Bitter on handpump, decent wines, and freshly squeezed orange juice; cribbage and dominoes. In summer there are seats around a low stone table and picnic-sets in the neatly kept garden. The 'no children' is strictly enforced here and there is no piped music. *(Recommended by Mr and Mrs T Bryan, Gerald Barnett, D Griffiths)*

Allied Domecq ~ Lease: Peter and Janet Hodges ~ Real ale ~ Bar food (not Sun evening) ~ (01494) 881417 ~ Open 11.45-2.30, 6-11; 12-3 Sun; closed Sun evening

BRILL SP6513 Map 4
Pheasant ♀

Windmill St; village signposted from B4011 Bicester—Long Crendon

From both the verandah and the garden here, you can look over the windmill opposite – it's one of the oldest post windmills still in working order. And on a fine day, you get a marvellous view of nine counties. The quietly modernised and neatly kept beamed bar has a friendly, unpretentious atmosphere, refectory tables and windsor chairs, a woodburning stove, and a step up to a dining area which is decorated with attractively framed prints. The views from both rooms are marvellous. Bar food includes avocado salad with shaved parmesan and pine nut kernels (£4.95), marinated chicken breast on mixed leaf salad (£5.60), venison steak with port and redcurrant jus (£8.95), and steaks. Well kept Marstons Pedigree and Tetleys on handpump, and seven good wines by the glass; piped music. No dogs (they have two golden retrievers themselves). Roald Dahl used to drink here, and some of the tales the locals told him were worked into his short stories. *(Recommended by Ted George, S J Hetherington, L Walker, K H Frostick, Piotr Chodzko-Zajko, Michael Sargent, Ian Phillips)*

Free house ~ Licensee Mike Carr ~ Real ale ~ Bar food ~ Restaurant (not 25 Dec) ~ (01844) 237104 ~ Children welcome ~ Open 11-3, 6-11; 11-11 Sat; 12-10.30 Sun; closed 25 Dec ~ Bedrooms: £40B/£70B

CADMORE END SU7892 Map 4
Old Ship ◖

B482 Stokenchurch—Marlow

New licensees have taken over this well liked country pub but reports from readers remain keen. The furnishings in the tiny low-beamed two-room bar are pretty basic – leatherette wall benches and stools in the carpeted room on the right, and on the left scrubbed country tables, bench seating (one still has a hole for a game called five-farthings), bare boards and darts, shove-ha'penny, cribbage, dominoes, and chess. Bar food includes baguettes (from £2.75; the steak sandwich is very popular £4.95), cod or sausage and egg (£4.50), and daily specials such as spicy parnsip or leek and potato soup (£2.20), warm greek salad (£2.95), and Thai chicken or Mongolian lamb (£6.75). Well kept Brakspears Bitter, Old, Special, seasonal and Mild tapped from the cask. There are seats on the terrace (with more in the sheltered garden), a large pergola with picnic-sets, boules, and do-it-yourself barbecues. Parking is on the other side of the road. No children. *(Recommended by Peter Plumridge, D Irving, E McCall, R Huggins, T McLean, Pete Baker, Simon Collett-Jones, JP, PP, Torrens Lyster, the Didler, Susan and John Douglas)*

Brakspears ~ Tenants Ray Court and Sue Hewitson ~ Real ale ~ Bar food (not Tues) ~ (01494) 883496 ~ Open 12-3, 6-11

CHEARSLEY SP7110 Map 4
Bell

The Green; minor rd NE of Long Crendon and N of Thame

Built from a clay found only in the surrounding area, this pretty thatched pub is a real haven for families on a sunny day – the spacious back garden is full of play equipment such as slides, a rope bridge, wendy house, climbing frames and the like, and on our early summer visit there were plenty of small children who looked to be in their element. In a corner are rabbits, ducks and chickens, and they sell ice pops and various drinks for children. There are plenty of tables out here, with more on a paved terrace, where there may be barbecues in summer. Inside, the pub has a quite different feel, cosy and traditional, with mugs and tankards hanging from the beams, and a collection of plates dominating one end of the room. There's an enormous fireplace, which several customers seemed almost to be sitting in. The handsome bar counter has piles of fresh local free range eggs for sale, as well as well kept Fullers Chiswick, London Pride and seasonal brews; there's a small but well chosen range of wines by the glass. Making good use of local ingredients, the simple well liked bar food might include lunchtime sandwiches, various omelettes, generously served ham, egg and chips (£5.45), cumberland sausage or lamb casseroled in a mint sauce (£5.95), and fried chicken breast in garlic and herbs (£6.95); lunchtime food service can stop promptly. You can't book tables, so best to get there early. On Friday evenings you might find the licensees or one of the locals coming round the bar with sausages. Prompt friendly service; cribbage, dominoes. A couple of tables in front overlook the very grassy village green. *(Recommended by B R Sparkes, Graham Parker, Marjorie and David Lamb)*

Fullers ~ Tenants Peter and Sue Grimsdell ~ Real ale ~ Bar food (not Sun evening or Mon) ~ (01844) 208077 ~ Children welcome in eating area of bar ~ Open 12-2.30, 6-11; 12-3, 7-10.30 Sun; closed Mon lunchtime

CHEDDINGTON SP9217 Map 4
Old Swan

58 High St

We are hoping that under the new licensees, the pretty tubs and hanging baskets outside this attractive thatched pub will remain and that the garden – much enjoyed by families – will keep its very good enclosed play area, furnished wendy house and child-size wooden bench and tables. Inside, the neatly kept and quietly civilised bar rooms on the right have quite a few horsebrasses and little hunting prints on the walls, old-fashioned plush dining chairs, a built-in wall bench, a few tables with nice country-style chairs on the bare boards, and a big inglenook with brass in glass cabinets on either side of it. On the other side of the main door is a room with housekeepers' chairs on the rugs and quarry tiles and country plates on the walls, and a step up to a carpeted part with stripey wallpaper and pine furniture. Decent bar food includes sandwiches (from £2.75; hot roast beef £3.95; baguettes £4.75), filled baked potatoes (from £3.25), home-made chicken and mushroom pie (£5.74), roast beef and yorkshire pudding or salmon steak with white wine and capers (£6.50), and steaks (from £8). The restaurant is partly no smoking. Well kept ABC Best, Fullers London Pride, Morlands Old Speckled Hen, and Vale Notley Ale on handpump. *(Recommended by Ted George, C A Hall, Ian Phillips, Mel Smith, Shirley Cannings)*

Allied Domecq ~ Lease: Gary Parker ~ Real ale ~ Bar food (12-2.30(4 Sat/Sun)), 7-9.30(10 Sat)) ~ Restaurant ~ (01296) 668226 ~ Children welcome ~ Occasional live entertainment ~ Open 11-11; 12-10.30 Sun

CHENIES TQ0198 Map 3
Red Lion ★

2 miles from M25 junction 18; A404 towards Amersham, then village signposted on r; Chesham Rd

The licensee tells us that he is very much running a pub that serves food and not a restaurant which serves beer – and the warmth of readers' comments testifies to that fact. Some refurbishment was taking place as we went to press, but the unpretentious L-shaped bar still has original photographs of the village and of traction engines, comfortable built-in wall benches by the front windows, and traditional seats and tables; there's also a small back snug and a dining room. Enjoyable bar food includes soup (£2.95), filled french bread and baps (from £2.75; the bacon and marshmallow is popular £3.65), baked potatoes with fillings such as crispy bacon, rocket and tomato or crayfish in a coconut curry sauce (from £3.50), pasta with bacon, olive oil, parsley and parmesan (£4.50, main course £5.95), home-made game pâté with cumberland sauce (£4.95), cumberland sausage hidden in a mash of cabbage, potato and mustard sauce (£6.25), venison burgers with a spicy tomato salsa (£6.50), home-made pies (from £7.25; the lamb is well liked), crispy duck legs on a bed of leeks with an aromatic plum sauce or lamb roulade stuffed with capers and mushrooms served with a port and orange sauce (£10.95), and puddings (from £2.35). Well kept Benskins Best, Rebellion Lion Pride (brewed for the pub), Vale Notley, and Wadworths 6X on handpump. The hanging baskets and window boxes are pretty in summer. No children, games machines or piped music. *(Recommended by Chris and Ann Garnett, Peter and Giff Bennett, Catherine and Richard Preston, Peter Burton, Mike Wells, Peter Saville, Tracey and Stephen Groves, BKA, Ian Phillips, Andrew Life)*

Free house ~ Licensee Mike Norris ~ Real ale ~ Bar food (12-2, 7-10) ~ (01923) 282722 ~ Open 11-2.30, 5.30-11; 12-3, 6.30-10.30 Sun; closed 25 Dec

DINTON SP7611 Map 4
Seven Stars

Stars Lane; follow Dinton signpost into New Road off A418 Aylesbury—Thame, near Gibraltar turn-off

You can be sure of a friendly welcome in this pretty white pub set in a quiet village. The characterful public bar (known as the Snug here) is notable for the two highly varnished ancient built-in settles facing each other across a table in front of the vast stone inglenook fireplace. The spotlessly kept lounge bar, with its beams, joists and growing numbers of old tools on the walls, is comfortably and simply modernised – and although these rooms are not large, there is a spacious and comfortable restaurant area. Popular, good value bar food includes sandwiches (from £1.75; toasties 25p extra), soup (£2.50), home-made chicken liver pâté (£3), filled baked potatoes (from £3.25), ploughman's or vegetable pasta bake (£4.25), home-made lasagne (£4.75), gammon and egg (£6), minted lamb chop (£5.75), steaks (from £9.25), and puddings (£2.50). Well kept ABC, and Vale Notley and Edgars on handpump. There are tables under cocktail parasols on the terrace, with more on the lawn of the pleasant sheltered garden. The pub is handy for the Quainton Steam Centre. *(Recommended by Marjorie and David Lamb, J Potter, Mike Wells, Ian Phillips, Michael Sargent, S J Sloan, Eric J Locker)*

Free house ~ Licensee Rainer Eccard ~ Real ale ~ Bar food ~ Restaurant ~ (01296) 748241 ~ Children welcome in eating area of bar and restaurant ~ Open 12-3, 6-11; closed Tues evening

---

People don't usually tip bar staff (different in a really smart hotel, say). If you want to thank them – for dealing with a really large party say, or special friendliness – offer them a drink.

EASINGTON SP6810 Map 4

Mole & Chicken 🍴 ♀

From B4011 in Long Crendon follow Chearsley, Waddesdon signpost into Carters Lane
opposite the Chandos Arms, then turn left into Chilton Road

One reader was happy to make a seventy mile round trip to enjoy lunch at this
deservedly popular dining pub – and indeed all the comments we have received over
the past year have been warmly enthusiastic. Although the inside is open-plan, it is
very well done, so that all the different parts seem quite snug and self-contained
without being cut off from what's going on, and the atmosphere is chatty and
relaxed. The beamed bar curves around the serving counter in a sort of S-shape –
unusual, as is the décor of designed-and-painted floor, pink walls with lots of big
antique prints, and even at lunchtime lit candles on the medley of tables to go with
the nice mix of old chairs; good winter log fires. Served by friendly staff, the
generous helpings of imaginative food might include starters such as chicken liver
and armagnac pâté, fresh ravioli stuffed with walnut and gorgonzola with a light
cream sauce or chicken satay with spicy peanut dip (all £5.95), and a plate of
antipasti with pickled mediterranean vegetables (£6.95), and main courses like
honey-glazed ham with two fried eggs (£6.95), steak and kidney pie (£7.95), chicken
curry or salad niçoise with chargrilled tuna steak with french beans (£8.95), half a
crispy norfolk duckling with an orange and kumquat sauce (£12.95), daily changing
fish and vegetarian dishes, and home-made puddings; it's best to book a table in
advance. Decent French house wines (and a good choice by the bottle), lots of malt
whiskies, and well kept Adnams Southwold, Morlands Old Speckled Hen, and
Notley Ale on handpump. There are quite a few seats and tables in the garden where
they sometimes hold summer barbecues and pig and lamb roasts. *(Recommended by S J
Hetherington, Maysie Thompson, Michael Sargent, B R Sparkes, James Chatfield, Marion Turner,
Graham and Karen Oddey, Bob and Maggie Atherton, Malcolm Clydesdale, Joan Yen, G R
Braithwaite, Liz Bell, Lesley Bass)*

*Free house ~ Licensee A Heather ~ Real ale ~ Bar food (12-2, 7-10; 12-9 Sun) ~
(01844) 208387 ~ Children welcome but not Thurs, Fri, Sat evenings ~ Live
entertainment on Burns night ~ Open 11-3, 6-11; 11-10.30 Sun; closed 25 Dec,
evenings 26 Dec and 1 Jan*

FAWLEY SU7586 Map 2

Walnut Tree ♀ 🛏

Village signposted off A4155 (then right at T-junction) and off B480, N of Henley

'Middle England at its most charming' is how one readers describes this very popular
pub. It's under new licensees this year who are keen to continue offering walkers and
diners the best quality food and ales in a relaxed, friendly atmosphere. You can
choose to eat in either of the two bars or the restaurant with its no-smoking
conservatory. From the monthly-changing menu, there are dishes like home-made
soup (£3), ploughman's (£4.25), marinated seafood salad (£4.95; main course
£7.25), chargrilled mediterranean vegetables with salsa and toasted bioche (£5.50),
Moroccan spiced fishcakes (£6.95), toulouse sausages on olive mash with rioja gravy
(£7.25), baked cod steak with grilled red peppers and buttered pasta (£9.95), and
roasted best end of spring lamb with a potato and redcurrant rosti and jus (£11.95),
with daily specials such as a pasta of the day (£5.95), home-made burger (£6.50),
and dressed crab salad (£6.50), and 3-course Sunday lunch (£13.95). Well kept
Brakspears Bitter and Special on handpump, and a good range of wines. The big
lawn around the front car park has some well spaced tables made from elm trees,
with some seats in a covered terrace extension – and a hitching rail for riders.
*(Recommended by George Little, Piotr Chodzko-Zajko, Gwen and Peter Andrews, Susan and
John Douglas, Mike and Mary Carter, Alan Morton, Gerald Barnett, Bob and Maggie Atherton,
Mrs L Imlah)*

*Brakspears ~ Lease: Adam and Michelle Dutton ~ Real ale ~ Bar food (12-2.30, 7-10)
~ Restaurant ~ (01491) 638360 ~ Children welcome ~ Open 12-3, 5.30-11; 12-11
Sat; 12-10.30 Sun ~ Bedrooms: £35B/£50B*

FORTY GREEN SU9292 Map 2

Royal Standard of England

3½ miles from M40 junction 2, via A40 to Beaconsfield, then follow sign to Forty Green, off B474 ¾ mile N of New Beaconsfield

Full of interest and atmosphere, this lovely old pub has rambling rooms with huge black ship's timbers, finely carved old oak panelling, roaring winter fires with handsomely decorated iron firebacks, and a massive settle apparently built to fit the curved transom of an Elizabethan ship; also, ancient pewter and pottery tankards, rifles, powder-flasks and bugles, lots of brass and copper, needlework samplers, and stained glass. Two areas are no smoking. Enjoyable bar food includes vegetable soup (£3.25), leek and mushroom tartlet (£3.75), garlic mushrooms with herbed sour cream (£4.25), chestnut, mushroom and sweet potato puff pie (£7.25), beer and herb battered cod (£7.65), beef in ale pie (£7.95), stir-fried lamb (£8.25), rib-eye steak (£9.45), and puddings such as spotted dick or toffee cheesecake. Well kept Brakspears Bitter, Marstons Pedigree and Owd Rodger, Morlands Old Speckled Hen, and Ruddles Best on handpump, and country wines. There are seats outside in a neatly hedged front rose garden, or in the shade of a tree. _(Recommended by JP, PP, Susan and John Douglas, Mark J Hydes, George Atkinson, Dr Gerald W Barnett, Michael Taylor-Waring, Greg Kilminster, L Granville, Mr S Lythgoe, the Didler)_

Free house ~ Licensees Cyril and Carol Cain ~ Real ale ~ Bar food ~ Restaurant ~ (01494) 673382 ~ Children until 9.30pm ~ Open 11-3, 5.30-11; 13-3, 7-10 Sun; closed evening 25 Dec

FRIETH SU7990 Map 2

Prince Albert ♀ ◀

Village signposted off B482 in Lane End; turn right towards Fingest just before village

This is a proper old-fashioned cottagey pub with a quietly chatty atmosphere undisturbed by noisy machines or piped music. On the left, there are hop bines on the mantlebeam and on the low black beams and joists, brocaded cushions on high-backed settles (one with its back panelled in neat squares), a big black stove in a brick inglenook with a bison's head looking out beside it, copper pots on top, and earthenware flagons in front, and a leaded-light built-in wall cabinet of miniature bottles. The slightly larger area on the right has more of a medley of chairs and a big log fire; magazines, books and local guides to read. Well kept Brakspears Bitter, Special, Mild, Old and OBJ on handpump, good wines, and decent whiskies on optic include Smiths Glenlivet and Jamesons. Bar food includes good home-made soup (£3.60), a fine choice of filled french bread (£4.25) such as cheese and onion, giant sausage, black pudding and bacon or pastrami and cucumber, ham and egg (£4.80), and daily specials such as steak and kidney pudding, fresh fish and chips, home-made curries and stews or boiled bacon with parsley sauce (£6.50); they now offer fish or moules and chips on Wednesday evenings – must book. Dominoes and cribbage. The lovely dog is called Leo. A nicely planted informal side garden has views of woods and fields, and there are plenty of nearby walks. Please note, children are not allowed inside. _(Recommended by Susan and John Douglas, S J Hetherington, Maureen Hobbs, Pete Baker, Ewan McCall, Tom McLean, Anthony Longden, Ron and Val Broom, Mike Wells, Roger and Jenny Huggins, Dave Irving, the Didler)_

Brakspears ~ Tenant Frank Reynolds ~ Real ale ~ Bar food (lunchtimes Mon-Sat, and Weds evening) ~ (01494) 881683 ~ Children welcome in eating area of bar and restaurant ~ Open 11-3, 5.30-11; 12-4, 7-10.30 Sun

GREAT MISSENDEN SP8901 Map 4

Cross Keys

High St

There's a good feel to this old-fashioned and friendly little town pub. The bar is divided into two by wooden standing timbers – one half has old sewing machines on the window sill, collectors' postcards, various brewery mirrors, lots of photographs,

and horse bits and spigots and pewter mugs on the beams by the bar counter, and
the other half has a bay window with a built-in seat overlooking the street, a couple
of housekeepers' chairs in front of the big open fire, and a high-backed settle. The
food is all Italian and at lunchtime in the bar, there is soup (£3.25), cold grilled
vegetables (£3.75), meatballs cooked in tomato sauce (£4.60), various pasta dishes
with sauces (from £4.60), and a selection of salami and cheeses (£4.95); more
elaborate food in the restaurant. Well kept Fullers Chiswick, London Pride, and ESB
on handpump, very cheap for the area. Cribbage, dominoes, fruit machine, and
piped music. The terrace at the back of the building has picnic-sets with umbrellas –
and you can eat out here, too. *(Recommended by Ian Phillips, Andy & Jill Kassube)*

*Fullers ~ Tenant Martin Ridler ~ Real ale ~ Bar food ~ Restaurant ~ (01494) 865373
~ Well behaved children in restaurant ~ Open 11-3, 5-11; 12-3, 7-10.30 Sun; closed
25 Dec*

HADDENHAM SP7408 Map 4
Green Dragon ★ ⑪ ♀
Village signposted off A418 and A4129, ENE of Thame; then follow Church End signs

Although there is still a respectable corner for people wanting just a drink, with a
few blond cast-iron-framed tables, some bar stools and well kept Fullers London
Pride and Vale Notley on handpump, the main reason for coming to this civilised
dining pub is to enjoy the imaginative food. The main area – two high-ceilinged
communicating rooms – is decorated in warm Tuscan blues and yellows, with
attractive still lifes and country pictures, pretty tablecloths, and a log fire on cool
days; piped music. At lunchtime, the very good food might include sandwiches
(from £1.75), home-made soup (£3.45), grilled pavé of fresh tuna blackened in
cajun spices on a chilled tropical fruit salsa or choux buns laced with cumin seeds
and filled with warm Indian vegetables on a mint and yoghurt sauce (£5.25),
terrine of grilled foie gras, veal shank and red onions (£5.95), omelettes (from
£6.50), fillet of Scottish salmon in sesame and aniseed with lightly tossed oriental
vegetables on a coconut and coriander pistou (£13.55), roast crown of English
lamb with an onion and bacon galette on a purée of new season's peas and fresh
sarriette jus (£14.25), with evening specials such as French goat's cheese
flavoured with tapenade and baked in a filo shell with chilled mediterranean
salad (£5.85), deep-fried nuggets of fresh crab with risotto rice and basil, a
julienne of cucumber, and a rich gazpacho sauce (£5.95), fried fillet of pork
wrapped in smoked bacon with diced cream potatoes and thyme on a cabernet
sauvignon sauce (£13.35), fillet of bass with home-made pasta and provençal
vegetables on a cherry tomato and basil coulis (£13.45), and puddings like crisp
strudel of banana and mace-infused raisins with crème fraîche and warm caramel
fudge sauce or bread and butter pudding (from £3.85). The wine list is well
chosen and sensibly priced, with a good choice by the glass. There are white
tables and picnic-sets under cocktail parasols on a big sheltered gravel terrace
behind, with more on the grass, and a good variety of plants; this part of the
village is very pretty, with a duck pond unusually close to the church.
*(Recommended by Ian Phillips, Cyril S Brown, Bob and Maggie Atherton, Dave Carter, Mike
Wells, Neil and Karen Dignan, Malcolm Clydesdale, Lesley Bass)*

*Whitbreads ~ Lease: Julian Ehlers ~ Real ale ~ Bar food (lunchtime only, not Sun) ~
Restaurant ~ (01844) 291403 ~ Children must be over 6 in evenings ~ Open 11.30-
2.30, 6.30-11; 12-2.30 Sun; closed Sun evening*

HAMBLEDEN SU7886 Map 2
Stag & Huntsman ◖
Turn off A4155 at Mill End. signposted to Hambleden; in a mile turn r into village centre

Just a field's walk from the river and set opposite the church in an especially
pretty village, this charming brick and flint pub is enjoyed by a good mix of
customers. The half-panelled, L-shaped lounge bar has low ceilings, a large
fireplace, upholstered seating and wooden chairs on the carpet, and a friendly

bustling atmosphere. The attractively simple public bar has darts, dominoes, cribbage, and piped music, and there's a cosy snug at the front, too. Good home-made bar food includes soup (£2.95), ploughman's (£5.25), vegetarian goulash (£6.25), home-cooked ham and egg (£6.75), liver and bacon (£6.95), fresh salmon fishcakes or marinated chargrilled chicken (£7.25), pork steak with a coarse-grain mustard and cream sauce (£8.75), steaks (from £11.25), and puddings like blackberry and apple crumble (£3); the dining room is pretty. Well kept Brakspears Bitter and Special, Wadworths 6X, and guest beers on handpump, farm ciders, and good wines served by cheerful staff. The spacious and neatly kept country garden is where they hold their popular big barbecues – cajun salmon, pork and apple burgers, pork and leek sausages, and various kebabs. The bedrooms are a little old-fashioned. (*Recommended by Peter and Giff Bennett, D Griffiths, Elizabeth and Klaus Leist, Gerald Barnett, Mike and Mary Carter, Gordon, Glen and Nola Armstrong, Christopher Glasson, Dave Carter, George Atkinson, Christine and Geoff Butler, Ken & Jenny Simmonds, Lesley Bass*)

Free house ~ Licensees Hon. Henry Smith and Andrew Fry ~ Real ale ~ Bar food ~ (01491) 571227 ~ Children welcome in eating area of bar ~ Open 11-2.30(3 Sat), 6-11; 12-3, 7-10.30 Sun ~ Bedrooms: £58B/£68B

IBSTONE SU7593 Map 4
Fox ★

1¾ miles from M40 junction 5: unclassified lane leading S from motorway exit roundabout; pub is on Ibstone Common

A popular place before a walk, this friendly 17th-c country inn has a comfortable low-beamed lounge bar with high-backed settles and country seats, old village photographs on the walls, and log fires. In the public bar – which has darts, dominoes, and fruit machine – the pine settles and tables match the woodblock floor; piped music. Decent bar food includes enjoyable sandwiches, ploughman's, and changing hot meals like crispy duck salad with raspberry dressing (£4.30 starter, £6.50 main course), beef and Guinness pie (£7.15), smoked haddock with mustard sauce (£7.60), lamb steak on ratatouille with a rosemary and red wine sauce (£9.35), and puddings such as plum crumble; efficient service. The small dining area is no smoking as is the smart restaurant. Well kept Brakspears Bitter and guest beers such as Fullers London Pride, Rebellion IPA or Wye Valley Dorothy Goodbody's Golden Springtime Ale on handpump. From the neat rose garden, you can overlook the common, with rolling fields and the Chilterns oak and beech woods beyond; the village cricket ground is close by. (*Recommended by Susan and John Douglas, Martin & Karen Wake, Catherine and Richard Preston, Peter Plumridge, S C Collett-Jones, Tracey and Stephen Groves, Mr S Lythgoe, Gerald Barnett, Mr M G Hart, Lesley Bass*)

Free house ~ Licensee Ann Banks ~ Real ale ~ Bar food ~ Restaurant ~ (01491) 638289/722 ~ Children welcome in eating area of bar and restaurant ~ Open 11-3, 6-11; 12-3, 7-10.30 Sun; closed evenings 25 and 26 Dec and evening 1 Jan ~ Bedrooms: £45S/£58S

LITTLE HAMPDEN SP8503 Map 4
Rising Sun ★ ⑪

Village signposted from back road (ie W of A413) Great Missenden—Stoke Mandeville; pub at end of village lane; OS Sheet 165 map reference 856040

Buckinghamshire Dining Pub of the Year

Much enjoyed by readers for its excellent and imaginative food, this smart dining pub firmly has no noisy games machines or piped music. One part of the interlinked bar rooms is no smoking, and there's also a separate no-smoking dining room (which enjoys the same food as the bar). From a constantly changing menu, there might be warm duck and bacon salad or asparagus and almond filo parcel (£4.95), poached fillet of halibut with a prawn and mushroom sauce (£9.45), roast breast of duck with a peach and passion fruit sauce (£9.95), and puddings like sticky toffee banana and walnut pudding (£3.50). Well kept Adnams, Brakspears Bitter,

Marstons Pedigree, and Morlands Old Speckled Hen on handpump, with home-made mulled wine and spiced cider in winter, Scrumpy Jack cider, and a short but decent wine list; efficient service. The secluded setting, with tracks leading through the woods in different directions, is delightful – walkers are welcome as long as they leave their muddy boots outside. There are some tables on the terrace by the sloping front grass. *(Recommended by Maysie Thompson, S J Hetherington, Peter and Giff Bennett, Stephen and Tracey Groves, Mike Wells, Peter Saville, David and Ruth Shillitoe, Cyril Brown, Peter and Christine Lea, B R Sparkes, Gerald Barnett, Sharon and Steven Baruch)*

Free house ~ Licensee Rory Dawson ~ Real ale ~ Bar food (not Sun evening, not Mon) ~ Restaurant ~ (01494) 488360 ~ Children welcome in eating area of bar ~ Occasional trad jazz winter Fri evenings ~ Open 11.30-3, 6.30-11; 12-3 Sun; closed Sun evening and all Mon (open bank hol Mon lunchtimes) ~ Bedrooms: £30B/£58B

LITTLE HORWOOD SP7930 Map 4
Shoulder of Mutton
Church St; back road 1 mile S of A421 Buckingham—Bletchley

The chatty licensees of this partly thatched and half-timbered old pub continue to offer a friendly welcome to all their customers. The rambling T-shaped bar is attractively but simply furnished with sturdy seats around chunky rustic tables on the quarry tiles, has a huge fireplace at one end with a woodburning stove, and a showcase of china swans; the friendly, well trained black labrador-cross (who loves children) is called Billy, and the black cat, Trouble. Well kept ABC Best and Marstons Pedigree on handpump; shove-ha'penny, cribbage, dominoes, and fruit machine in the games area. Much enjoyed, good value bar food includes home-made soup (£1.90), sandwiches (from £1.90), filled baked potatoes (from £2.50), mussels baked in garlic butter (£3.90), ploughman's (from £3.90), home-made dishes like chicken curry, large pork chop cooked in cider and orange, diced leg of lamb cooked in ale or steak and kidney pie (from £4.20), all-day breakfast (£4.30), home-made nut cutlet (£4.90), steaks, puddings like home-made fruit crumble (£2.50), and children's meals (from £1.60). French windows look out on the pleasant back garden where there are plenty of tables. From the north, the car park entrance is tricky. *(Recommended by Gordon Tong, Ted George, Nigel and Olga Wikeley, S Markham, Michael Bourdeaux, Klaus and Elizabeth Leist, Graham and Karen Oddey, Monica Shelley, John Branston)*

Pubmaster ~ Tenant June Fessey ~ Real ale ~ Bar food (not Sun evening, not Mon) ~ Restaurant ~ (01296) 712514 ~ Children until 8.30 ~ Open 11-2.30(3 Sat), 6-11; `12-3, 7-10.30 Sun; closed Mon lunchtime

LITTLE MISSENDEN SU9298 Map 4
Crown ★ ◀
Crown Lane, SE end of village, which is signposted off A413 W of Amersham

There's a good mix of customers and a chatty relaxed atmosphere in this bustling small brick cottage, run by the same family now for over 90 years. The bars are thoroughly traditional and sparkling clean, and have old red flooring tiles on the left, oak parquet on the right, built-in wall seats, studded red leatherette chairs, a few small tables, and a complete absence of music and machines. The Adnams Broadside, Hook Norton Best, and a guest such as Marstons Pedigree or Morrells Varsity on handpump are kept particularly well; they also have farm ciders and decent malt whiskies. Bar food is simple but all home-made, majoring on a wide choice of generous very reasonably priced sandwiches (from £2.20), as well as ploughman's, pasties, Buck's bite (a special home-made pizza-like dish £3.25), and steak and kidney pie (£4.25); darts, shove-ha'penny, cribbage, dominoes, and table skittles. There are picnic-sets and other tables in an attractive sheltered garden behind. The village is pretty, with an interesting church. No children. *(Recommended by Tracey & Stephen Groves, Catherine and Richard Preston, Peter and Christine Lea, Ian Phillips)*

Free house ~ Licensees Trevor and Carolyn How ~ Real ale ~ Bar food (lunchtime only; not Sun)) ~ (01494) 862571 ~ Open 11-2.30, 6-11; 12-2.30, 7-10.30 Sun

LONG CRENDON SP6808 Map 4

Angel ★

Bicester Rd (B4011)

It's the very good popular food that people come to this partly 17th-c civilised dining pub to enjoy. As well as light lunches such as crispy duck and bacon salad with hoisin vinaigrette (£4.50), Greek feta salad (£4.75), and hot seared pavé of smoked salmon on rocket with a lemon and chive vinaigrette (£6.75), there might be baguettes and sandwiches like ham and Cornish yarg with red onion confit or spicy sausage, bacon, mushroom and fried egg (from £4.50), chargrilled sausages (£6.95), chargrilled lamb's liver and crispy bacon with a shallot and sage sauce (£7.25), oriental chicken and vegetable stir fry with egg noodles (£10.75), herb risotto with shavings of parmesan and chargrilled vegetables (£10.25), and rib-eye steak with herb butter (£11.75); vegetables are extra. Well kept Hook Norton Old Hooky, Ridleys ESX Best, and Shepherd Neame Spitfire on handpump, quite a few malt whiskies and an extensive wine list. There are capacious sofas in a comfortable and pleasantly decorated lounge, sturdy tables and chairs in another area, and a no-smoking conservatory dining room at the back looking out on the garden; also, a terrace for summer eating out; piped music. *(Recommended by Francis and Deirdre Gevers, Joan Yen, G D Sharpe, Ian Phillips, Mr Peter Saville, Roger Braithwaite)*

Free house ~ Licensees Trevor Bosch and Angela Good ~ Real ale ~ Bar food (not Sun) ~ Restaurant ~ (01844) 208268 ~ Children welcome ~ Open 12-11; 12-3 Sun; closed Sun evening ~ Bedrooms: £55B/£65B

Churchill Arms

High St; B4011 NW of Thame

It's hard to imagine finding a bigger choice of sausages than that at this cheery village pub; they have over 50 different kinds, from smoked beer and beef or pineapple and ginger, through chicken and blue cheese or Moroccan lamb to duck and red cabbage or pheasant and whisky (all from £5.95). It's no use asking for a simple pork sausage – there are up to 20 of these, with traditional and more unusual flavourings (from £4.95). All served with mash, fried onions, baked beans and gravy, they're properly made without artificial ingredients, and the menu has hints on whether the sausage will be better accompanied by beer or wine. They also do sandwiches (from £3.25), ploughman's (£4.25), salads (£4.95) and steaks (from £6.95); some areas are no smoking. There's a good range of drinks too, with over 20 wines by the glass, and real ales such as Fullers London Pride, Greene King Abbot, Morlands Old Speckled Hen, Tetleys and Youngs Special on handpump; friendly service. The nicest part for eating is a neat well sized room to the left of the entrance, with wooden floors, red-painted walls, and a big fireplace; to the right is a comfortable drinking area with fresh flowers on the bar and newspapers to read, while beyond, the public bar has pool, fruit machine, and a TV. They may have jazz on summer Sunday afternoons; piped music at other times. Outside is a pleasant garden with half a dozen picnic-sets and a good view over the neighbouring sports field; it's a relaxing spot on a sunny day when the cricketers are out. *(Recommended by James Chatfield)*

Allied Domecq ~ Lease: Monique Knight and Paul Campion ~ Real ale ~ Bar food (till 10pm Fri/Sat, till 3 Sun, not Mon evening) ~ Restaurant ~ (01844) 208344 ~ Children welcome in eating area of bar and restaurant ~ Live jazz Sun afternoon in summer ~ Open 12-3, 6-11; 11-11 in summer Sat; 12-10.30 in summer Sun

MOULSOE SP9041 Map 4

Carrington Arms ★

1¼ miles from M1, junction 14: A509 N, first right signed Moulsoe; Cranfield Rd

The delicious meats and fresh fish are the highlight of any visit to this well refurbished old brick house and are interestingly displayed in a refrigerated glass case – friendly staff are particularly good at guiding you through what's on offer. As well as excellent rump, fillet and sirloin steaks (the bourbon-marinaded ones are popular), a typical choice might include local lamb and venison, duck breasts marinaded in gin with chillies, and fish and seafood such as Scottish salmon, bass, scallops, halibut, tuna, lobster, tiger prawns, and marlin. They're happy to let you try little bits of everything, and as the meat and fish are sold by weight (in pounds and ounces), you can have as much or as little as you like. Meals are cooked on an adjacent grill, rather like a sophisticated indoor barbecue. There are also bar snacks such as a good hot kipper fillet roll (£3.75), ploughman's (from £4.15), brie and apple omelette (£5.50), various Thai meals like green chicken (£6.50) or a spicy vegetable crumble (£7.25), and puddings like rice pudding with gin, treacle tart, and warm apple sponge with orange sauce. Furnishings are comfortable and traditional, with a mix of wooden chairs and cushioned banquettes around the tables and flame-effect fire, and up some steps a cosier seating area with hops hanging from the ceiling and a big mirror along the back wall; soft piped music. A separate oyster bar has caviar as well as oysters. Well kept Adnams Best, Boddingtons, Charles Wells Bombardier and Theakstons Old Peculier on handpump, good range of bottled wines, a choice of champagnes by the glass, and a very hot bloody mary. Behind the pub a long garden has a couple of tables, and there are bedrooms in a separate building alongside. The licensees also run the Fitzwilliam Arms at Castor in Cambridgeshire, with the same enjoyably distinctive culinary approach. *(Recommended by Mike and Mary Carter, George Atkinson, John Saul, Howard and Margaret Buchanan, Stephen, Julie and Hayley Brown, Cliff Blakemore, Ian Phillips, Dr A Sutton, Ian Stafford)*

Free house ~ Licensees Edwin and Trudy Cheeseman ~ Real ale ~ Bar food (12-2, 6.30-10) ~ (01908) 218050 ~ Children welcome ~ Open 11-2.30, 6-11; 12-3, 7-10.30 Sun ~ Bedrooms: £40.50B/£40.50B

NORTHEND SU7392 Map 4
White Hart

On back road up escarpment from Watlington, past Christmas Common; or valley road off A4155 Henley—Marlow at Mill End, past Hambleden, Skirmett and Turville, then sharp left in Northend

A good mix of customers fills the little bar of this friendly 16th-c pub – it is especially liked by ramblers as the surrounding countryside is excellent for walking. In summer, the garden is rather charming and full of flowers and fruit trees. The bar has good log fires (one in a vast fireplace), as well as very low handsomely carved oak beams, some panelling, and comfortable window seats. A small choice of food includes sandwiches, home-made soup with fresh baked bread or home-made pâté (£3.50), cumberland sausage with mash and onion gravy, various home-made pies, fresh salmon and steaks (£8.50), and weekend evening meals like home-made lasagne or chicken in a cheese and mustard sauce (£6.50), puddings (£2.95), and two Sunday roasts (and a home-made nut roast; fresh vegetables). Well kept Brakspears Bitter, Special and OBJ on handpump or tapped from the cask; darts, cribbage and dominoes; no piped *(Recommended by Catherine and Richard Preston, R V G Brown, Gordon, Mike Wells, Klaus & Elizabeth Leist)*

Brakspears ~ Tenants Derek and Susie Passey ~ Real ale ~ Bar food (lunchtimes; also Fri and Sat evenings) ~ (01491) 638353 ~ Children welcome in restaurant ~ Open 11-2.30, 6-11; 12-3, 7-10.30 Sun

PRESTON BISSETT SP6529 Map 4
White Hart

Pound Lane; village can be reached off A421 Buckingham bypass via Gawcott, or from A4421 via Chetwode or Barton Hartshorn

This friendly 18th-c thatched and timbered white-painted house is a tiny place of great charm. The three cosy little rooms have a genuinely traditional feel, with old lamps hanging from the low beams, captain's chairs, red banquettes and stools nestling around the tables, local prints and memorabilia from the local Tetleys-related Aylesbury Brewing Company around the walls, and a log fire with perhaps their golden retriever slumbering beside it. ABC Best and a guest like Morlands Tanners Jack on handpump, 8 wines by the glass, around a dozen malt whiskies, and country wines. The largest room (no smoking) has a well polished wooden floor and high-backed wooden settle, and is the nicest place to enjoy the tasty bar food which is listed on a big blackboard menu covering most of one wall. As well as nibbles such as marinated seafood or Greek olives (£1.75), dishes might include home-made soup (£2.75), chicken liver pâté (£4.25), warm roasted tomato and basil filo tartlet (£4.95), cod and chips served in the *Financial Times* (£5.50), sausage and mash with onion confit (£6.95), lamb, apricot and rosemary pie (£7.50), and prawns in garlic and lemon butter (£8.95), with lunchtime snacks like filled french bread (from £2.95), and Aga-baked potatoes (from £3.95). They recommend booking at busy times; service is chatty and helpful. There are tables behind in a yard and on a small grassy area. They occasionally have barbecues or wine tastings. So many dogs accompany their owners that they sell dog biscuits at the tiny central bar counter. No children. *(Recommended by Ray Crabtree, R C Watkins, George Atkinson)*

Pubmaster ~ Tenants Duncan Rowney and Lisa Chapman ~ Real ale ~ Bar food (not Mon evening, not Tues) ~ Restaurant ~ (01280) 847969 ~ Open 12-2.30, 6.30-11; 12-3, 7-10.30 Sun; closed Tues lunchtime

PRESTWOOD SP8700 Map 4
Polecat
170 Wycombe Rd (A4128 N of High Wycombe)

The garden here has been extended and hundreds of new herbaceous plants added, and there are picnic-sets on neat grass out in front beneath a big fairy-lit apple tree with more on a big well kept back lawn – as well as pretty hanging baskets and tubs. Inside, several smallish rooms open off the low-ceilinged bar, with a good medley of tables and chairs, all sorts of stuffed birds as well as the stuffed white polecats in one big cabinet, small country pictures, rugs on bare boards or red tiles, a couple of antique housekeeper's chairs by a good open fire in another; the Galley room is no smoking. At lunchtime there tend to be chatty crowds of middle-aged diners, with a broader mix of ages in the evening. A good choice of well presented bar food includes soup (£2.90), lunchtime sandwiches (from £2.70), filled baked potatoes (from £4), and ploughman's (£4.50), baked mushrooms with welsh rarebit and bacon on a garlic croûte (£4.20), roast parsnip and lentil bake (£6.50), lasagne (£6.90), home-made steak and kidney pie (£7.40), pork chop glazed with honey and ginger barbecue sauce or salmon fishcakes with watercress sauce (£7.90), pot-roast lamb shank on crushed butter beans (£8.90), daily specials like chilled cannelloni of smoked chicken and crisp vegetables with a sweet and sour chilli dressing (£4.20), lamb's liver and bacon casserole with bubble and squeak (£7.80), and magret of duck with caramelised apples and chestnuts (£10.20), and puddings such as raspberry shortcake, mango tart tatin with coconut ice cream or chocolate torte (£3.50). Well kept Marstons Pedigree, Morlands Old Speckled Hen, Ruddles County, Theakstons Best, and Wadworths 6X on handpump at the flint bar counter, a list on a board of wines by the glass, and at least 20 malt whiskies; quick friendly service. *(Recommended by Maysie Thompson, S J Hetherington, Tracey and Stephen Groves, Mike Wells, Peter Saville, B R Sparkes, Ian Phillips, Lesley Bass)*

Free house ~ Licensee John Gamble ~ Real ale ~ Bar food ~ (01494) 862253 ~ Children welcome in eating area of bar ~ Open 11.30-2.30, 6-11; 12-3 Sun; closed Sun evening

SKIRMETT SU7790 Map 2
Frog 🍺
From A4155 NE of Henley take Hambleden turn and keep on; or from B482 Stokenchurch—Marlow take Turville turn and keep on

They've managed to strike a good balance between eating and drinking in this brightly modernised country inn, and have kept something of the atmosphere of a smart rural local with leaflets and posters near the door advertising raffles and the like. The neatly kept beamed bar area has a mix of comfortable furnishings, a striking hooded fireplace with a bench around the edge (and a pile of logs sitting beside it), big rugs on the wooden floors, and sporting and local prints around the salmon painted walls. The function room leading off, with a fine-looking dresser, is sometimes used as a dining overflow. Good enjoyable bar food includes lunchtime dishes like an Irish fry-up (£6), omelettes (£6.25), a bagel with smoked salmon and cream cheese (£6.50), and seafood pasta in a tomato cream sauce (£7.25), as well as home-made soup (£2.95), glazed goat's cheese with chargrilled vegetables and pesto dressing (£5.50), braised shank of lamb (£8.95), roast fillet of cod (£9.75), breast of duck with a spicy plum sauce (£11.95), and puddings such as warm bakewell tart or orange and grand marnier pancakes stuffed with ice cream and an orange sauce (from £3.50); they offer a three-course meal with coffee and home-made shortbread for £16.50. Service stays slick even at busy times. The restaurant is no smoking; maybe piped music. Brakspears, Fullers London Pride and a weekly changing guest on handpump, a good range of wines, and various coffees. Through a gate at the side is a lovely garden, with a large tree in the middle, and unusual pentagon-shaped tables well placed for attractive valley views. The bedrooms are engaging, and it's a nice base for the area; Henley is close by, and just down the road the windmill at Ibstone is delightful. *(Recommended by Tracey & Stephen Groves, Peter Plumridge, Martin & Karen Wake, Dave Carter, Mr and Mrs B Thomas, Dick Brown, Anthony Longden, Ken & Jenny Simmonds, Gordon, W K Wood)*

Free house ~ Licensees Jim Crowe and Noelle Greene ~ Real ale ~ Bar food ~ Restaurant ~ (01491) 638996 ~ Children in eating area of bar, restaurant, and family room ~ Open 11-3, 6-11; 12-10.30 Sun; closed Sun evening Oct-May ~ Bedrooms: £48.50(£48.50B)/£58.50(£58.50B)

THORNBOROUGH SP7433 Map 4
Lone Tree
A421 4 miles E of Buckingham; pub named on Ordnance Survey Sheet 165

Though the tree that gives this nicely converted old house its name is long gone (knocked down by a lorry in 1918), the pub itself continues to stand alone beside the busy main road as it's thought to have done for centuries – even if recent road straightening has made it slightly more isolated. It's an agreeable stop for a carefully prepared meal, and particularly to try an unusual real ale or traditional English cheese – they're expert at tracking down obscure varieties of both. A blackboard on the wall of the single long room boasts that they've served over 915 different beers to date, most of them quite rare for the area; they usually have five cask-conditioned beers on handpump at a time (generally including a mild and a stout), such as Black Sheep, Chiltern Beechwood, Rebellion Smuggler, or York Stonewall. Over the same period they've stocked over 150 different cheeses; on our visit these included ticklemore (a goat's cheese from Devon), single gloucester, somerset rambler (made from ewe's milk), and the organic ashdown forsters. Many of the scrupulously polished tables are set for eating, with the choice of popular meals including a good range of sandwiches (from £2.60), filled baked potatoes (from £4.10), ploughman's (£4.95), blackboard specials such as tiger prawns with a ginger dip (£4.25), lamb korma (£6.95), steak and kidney pie (£7.25), black marlin steak (£8.95), and thai-style bass (£9.95), with a wide choice of puddings; children's helpings. The dining area is no smoking. Neatly carpeted and spotless, the beamed and panelled bar looks newer than it is, save for the handsome fireplace at one end, with a large dark hood and big piles of logs; there may be fresh flowers dotted around, and magazines such as *Horse and Hound* to read. It isn't huge and can fill up quickly, so booking is a good idea at busy times. There's a well chosen wine list, as well as farm cider, country wines, and various teas and coffee; shove-ha'penny, cribbage, dominoes, chess, scrabble, shut-the-box, unobtrusive piped music. You can buy locally made chutney and cheese. Outside are pleasantly positioned picnic-sets, though you can't quite escape the traffic noise. The adjacent thatched barn has at various times served as a stable, brewhouse and cycle repair shop; these days it houses a working post box for which the Post Office pay one shilling a year rent. *(Recommended by George*

Atkinson, Mr and Mrs D Lewis, Mr and Mrs B J P Edwards)

Free house ~ Licensee M Lister ~ Real ale ~ Bar food ~ (01280) 812334 ~ Children welcome in eating area of bar ~ Open 11.30-3, 6-11; 12-3, 6.30-10.30 Sun; closed 25 and 26 Dec

TURVILLE SU7690 Map 2
Bull & Butcher

Valley road off A4155 Henley—Marlow at Mill End, past Hambleden and Skirmett

After a walk, the seats on the lawn by fruit trees in the attractive garden here are a fine place to end up – especially in summer when they hold good barbecues. It's a pretty black-and-white timbered pub in a lovely Chilterns valley, and has a comfortable and atmospheric low-ceilinged and beamed bar (partly divided into two areas), cushioned wall settles, and an old-fashioned high-backed settle by one log fire; there's also an inglenook fireplace. A good choice of enjoyable bar food includes Thai fishcakes with a sweet chilli sauce (£5.95), steak in ale pudding or pie or beef and venison casserole (£8.95), and Thai green curry monkfish or rack of lamb (£11.95). Well kept Brakspears Bitter, Mild, Special, Old, and a guest beer such as Coniston Bluebird Bitter on handpump, and 39 wines by the glass; efficient service. Shove-ha'penny, dominoes, cribbage, and occasional piped music. Once a month (Tuesday evenings) the MG car club meet here. It does get crowded at weekends. *(Recommended by Richard Tredgett, Gerald Barnett, JP, PP, Dave Carter, Simon Collett-Jones, Jean Gustavson, Cyril Brown, Iain Robertson, Gordon, the Didler, Eddie Edwards)*

Brakspears ~ Tenant Nicholas Abbott ~ Real ale ~ Bar food (not Sun evening or Mon) ~ (01491) 638283 ~ Children welcome in eating area of bar ~ Open 11-3, 6(6.30 Sat)-11; 12-3, 7-10.30 Sun

WADDESDON SP7417 Map 4
Five Arrows ♀ ◖ 🛏

A41 NW of Aylesbury

Very much enjoyed by readers, this rather grand small hotel – part of the Rothschild Estate – offers a consistently friendly welcome, first-class bar food, and a good choice of drinks. The informally pubby bar is an open-plan series of light and airy high-ceilinged rooms with a relaxed but civilised atmosphere, and a handsome bar counter carved with the five arrows of the Rothschild crest which symbolise the dispersal of the five founding brothers of the international banking business. There are also family portrait engravings and lots of old estate-worker photographs on the leafy green wallpaper, heavy dark green velvet curtains on wooden rails, sturdy cushioned settles and good solid tables on parquet flooring (though one room has comfortably worn-in armchairs and settees), and newspapers and copies of *Country Life* in an antique magazine rack. As well as sandwiches (from £3.95) and ploughman's (from £4.95), the food might include soup such as watercress and potato (£3.95), aubergine stuffed with feta and sun-dried tomato (£4.95), roasted boned quail stuffed with wild rice and apricots with a balsamic dressing or baked scallops with spinach and vanilla butter (£5.95), chargrilled breast of chicken with a tomato and herb mayonnaise (£8.50), cajun blackened salmon with a mint and garlic mayonnaise (£10.75), roast loin of pork with apple purée and thyme jus (£10.95), and new season's lamb cutlets with a rich red wine jus (£14.95), with puddings like double chocolate fondant with a raspberry coulis, treacle tart or kiwi sorbet (£4.15). No sandwiches or snacks on Sundays. The country-house-style restaurant is no smoking; must book at busy times. The formidable wine list naturally runs to Rothschild first-growth clarets as well as less well known Rothschild estate wines. Well kept Adnams Bitter and Fullers London Pride on handpump; many malt whiskies, champagne by the glass, proper cocktails, and freshly squeezed orange juice; efficient service, unobtrusive piped music. The sheltered back garden has attractively grouped wood and metal furnishings. This is an ideal base for visiting Waddesdon Manor, the grounds, and aviary. *(Recommended by C R and M A Starling, Maysie Thompson, John Whitehead, W W Burke, Tom and Ruth Rees, Martin and Barbara Rantzen)*

Free house ~ Licensees J A Worster and F Bromovsky ~ Real ale ~ Bar food ~ Restaurant ~ (01296) 651727 ~ Children welcome ~ Open 11.30-3, 6-11; 12-3, 7-10.30 Sun ~ Bedrooms: £65B/£80B

WEST WYCOMBE SU8394 Map 4
George & Dragon
High St; A40 W of High Wycombe

The spacious and peaceful garden with picnic-sets and a fenced in play area is reached through the arched and cobbled coach entry behind this handsome Tudor inn; you can park through here too. The comfortable and colourfully decorated rambling main bar has massive beams, sloping walls, and a big log fire, and there's a no-smoking family bar; the magnificent oak staircase is said to be haunted by a wronged girl. Bar food includes lunchtime sandwiches, home-made soup (£2.25), potted stilton (£3.75), roast mediterranean vegetable parcel (£6.25), really good pies such as venison, beef and mushroom (£7.25), pork and prawn creole (£7.45), chargrilled tuna steak (£8.65), steaks (from £8.95), and home-made puddings like rich stout cake with chocolate sauce or treacle tart (from £2.65). Well kept Courage Best and Directors and guests like Greene King Abbot, Marstons Pedigree, Wadworths 6X, Charles Wells Bombardier, and Youngs Special on handpump, and quite a few malt whiskies; dominoes and cribbage. The inn does get crowded at weekends, so it's best to get there early then. Nearby you can visit West Wycombe Park with its fine furnishings and classical landscaped grounds (it is closed on winter Saturdays). *(Recommended by Chris Glasson, Gerald Barnett, Ian Phillips, Susan and John Douglas, Allan Engelhardt, Andy & Jill Kassube)*

Inntrepreneur ~ Lease: Philip Todd ~ Real ale ~ Bar food (12-2, 6-9.30) ~ (01494) 464414 ~ Children in family bar ~ Open 11-2.30(3 Sat), 5.30-11; 12-3, 7-10.30 Sun; closed evenings 25 and 26 Dec and evening 1 Jan ~ Bedrooms: £56B/£66B

WHEELER END SU8093 Map 4
Chequers ◀
Village signposted off B482 in Lane End NW of Marlow, then first left also signposted Wheeler End; or can be reached by very narrow Bullocks Farm Lane (sign may be defaced) from A40 lay-by just W of W Wycombe

You can be sure of a warm welcome from both the licensees and regulars at this small white-painted tiled house – which is steadfastly run as a good traditional village pub. Under its low ochre ceiling the bar has what might be called an inherently friendly layout: it's so small, and shaped in such a way, that you can't help but feel part of the general conversation. It angles back past a good inglenook log fire (that the black cat favours), and a little roomlet with a fruit machine, to a bigger back room with a couple of dart boards. Furniture is mainly scrubbed country-kitchen with a few board-backed wall benches, and the ochre walls have a liberal sprinkling of local notices alongside small hunting prints, cartoons and so forth; darts, shove-ha'penny, cribbage, dominoes, and fruit machine.Well kept Adnams, Brakspears PA, Fullers London Pride and Greene King IPA and Abbot on handpump, plus good malt whiskies and excellent coffee. Food includes very good hot and cold filled rolls (£2.50 for bacon and stilton and £3.40 for steak and onion, which will set you up nicely for a stroll on the nearby common), good soups, pesto pasta (£4.75), a late breakfast (£4.95), and bangers and mash or liver and bacon (£5). There are a few tables outside; no car park to speak of, but plenty of parking nearby. *(Recommended by Simon Collett-Jones, Susan and John Douglas, Mike Wells, Anthony Longden, Robert Turnham, George Atkinson)*

Free house ~ Licensees David and Patsy Robinson ~ Real ale ~ Bar food (not Sun or Mon) ~ (01494) 883070 ~ Children must leave before 8pm ~ Live blues/rock Tues evenings ~ Open 11-2.30, 5.30-11; 11-11 Sat; 12-10.30 Sun; closed Mon lunchtime

WOOBURN COMMON SU9187 Map

Chequers 🍴 🛏

From A4094 N of Maidenhead at junction with A4155 Marlow road keep on A4094 for another ¾ mile, then at roundabout turn off right towards Wooburn Common, and into Kiln Lane; if you find yourself in Honey Hill, Hedsor, turn left into Kiln Lane at the top of the hill; OS Sheet 175 map ref 910870

This is a most agreeable place in summer or winter and manages to keep an unchanging traditional atmosphere in its bar despite a lot of its custom from the flourishing hotel and restaurant side. The bar is low-beamed and partly stripped brick, and has standing timbers and alcoves to break it up, lived-in sofas on its bare boards, a bright log-effect gas fire, and various pictures, plates and tankards. There's an attractive brasserie on the left (they also have another more formal restaurant), and very good daily-changing food such as sandwiches (from £3.50), ploughman's (£4.95), home-made burger with bacon and cheese (£6.95), sautéed spicy chicken livers with lardons of bacon and raspberry dressing (£7.95), chargrilled pork with peppercorn and brandy sauce (£8.95), cold poached salmon with lemon mayonnaise or stir-fried vegetables and cashews on a bed of oriental noodles (£9.95), bass and bream with ginger and spring onion (£11.95), collops of monkfish and king scallops, kiwi mussels, king prawns and mixed herbs (£12.95), and puddings (£3.25). Well kept Fullers London Pride, Marstons Pedigree, Morlands Old Speckled Hen and Tanners Jack, and Ruddles County on handpump, a sizeable wine list (champagne and good wine by the glass), Scrumpy Jack cider, and a fair range of malt whiskies and brandies; spacious garden away from the road, with cast-iron tables. The attractive stripped-pine bedrooms are in a 20th-c mock-Tudor wing; breakfasts are good. *(Recommended by Peter and Giff Bennett, Bob and Maggie Atherton, Simon Collett-Jones, Susan and John Douglas, Terry Buckland, David and Helen Wilkins, Chris Glasson)*

Free house ~ Licensee Peter Roehrig ~ Real ale ~ Bar food (all day at weekends) ~ Restaurant ~ (01628) 529575 ~ Children welcome ~ Open 11-11; 12-10.30 Sun ~ Bedrooms: £92.50B/£97.50B

Lucky Dip

Besides the fully inspected pubs, you might like to try these Lucky Dips recommended to us and described by readers (if you do, please send us reports):

Adstock [SP7330]
☆ *Old Thatched Inn* [off A413]: Attractive beamed and flagstoned pub/restaurant, friendly and comfortable, with cosy corners and open fires, generous good food from baguettes up, well kept mainly Scottish Courage and guest ales (at a price), decent wines, friendly attentive staff; piped music; seats out in sheltered back garden, children in restaurant and eating area *(Karen & Graham Oddey, Gill and Keith Croxton, LYM, Chris Raisin)*
Akeley [SP7037]
☆ *Bull & Butcher* [just off A413]: Genuine village pub under helpful and obliging new landlady, three good fires in long open-plan beamed bar with red plush banquettes, bar food from sandwiches up, well kept Fullers London Pride, Marstons Pedigree, Morlands Original and a guest beer, decent house wines, traditional games; children allowed in eating area, tables in garden, handy for Stowe Gardens *(LYM, B J Smith, George Atkinson)*
Amersham [SU9597]
☆ *Eagle*: Pleasant and friendly low-beamed rambling pub with good helpings of tasty bar food inc rather more imaginative specials, well kept Benskins and guests such as Adnams and

Marstons Pedigree, quick cheerful service even on busy lunchtimes (worth booking), log fire; maybe soft piped music, fruit machine; more lively young person's pub evenings; back garden overlooking football pitch *(M J Dowdy, I D Barnett, TBB, David Clifton, Stan Edwards)*
☆ *Kings Arms*: Picture-postcard timbered building in charming street, lots of heavy beams and snug alcoves, big inglenook, high-backed antique settles and other quaint old furnishings among more standard stuff; low-priced bar food inc vegetarian, restaurant, pleasant service, well kept Tetleys-related and other ales, children in eating area; open all day, rather a young person's pub evening; nice garden *(LYM, Val Stevenson, Rob Holmes, Nina Randall)*
Asheridge [SP9404]
Blue Ball: Good atmosphere in small country local, busy and lively weekends, hearty home-made food, four changing well kept ales, good play area; piped music; good Chilterns walking country *(N Doolan)*
Ashley Green [SP9705]
Golden Eagle [A416 Chesham—Berkhamsted]: Friendly 17th-c beamed and timbered village pub doing well under present licensees, tasty

good value food, several real ales, tables in back garden and out in front *(Pat & Robert Watt)*

Aston Clinton [SP8712]
Bell: Short choice of good interesting food (good sandwiches, very good cheese choice) in small, civilised and welcoming hotel bar with solid dark tables on flagstones, well chosen wines; concentration on elegant restaurant, a comfortable place to stay *(M A & C R Starling)*

Aylesbury [SP7510]
☆ *Bottle & Glass* [A418 some miles towards Thame, beyond Stone]: Welcoming low-beamed thatched pub, tiled floor, rambling layout, wide choice of good imaginative (if not cheap) food inc good seafood range, lively atmosphere, helpful service, well kept Morrells Oxford and Varsity, good choice of wines, neat garden *(Michael Sargent, Marvadene B Eves, LYM, Marion Turner, Maysie Thompson)*

Aylesbury [SP8213]
Queens Head: Nice old corner pub on quiet and pretty square nr church and museum, spotless brass-topped tables, good range of reasonably priced food in bars and back dining area, very friendly welcome, Greenalls ales with a guest such as Exmoor Fox *(Ian Phillips)*

Beachampton [SP7737]
Bell: Large pub under new management, pleasant view from bar down attractive streamside village street, smartened-up dining area with well served if not cheap food, young staff, piped music, several real ales; terrace and play area in big garden *(Michael and Jenny Back, George Atkinson)*

Bellingdon [SP9405]
☆ *Bull* [about 1½ miles NW of Chesham]: Hard-working new tenants doing good home-made food, friendly welcoming atmosphere, pleasant furnishings, five real ales, decent wines by the glass; no piped music or machines *(LYM, Louise Kennedy-McGregor)*

Bennett End [SU7897]
Three Horseshoes: Unpretentious old beamed pub with antique range in small bar, separate lounge and dining area, good traditional and more exotic food, labrador called Kate; terrace overlooking lovely unspoilt valley *(Tim and Ann Newell)*

Bishopstone [SP8010]
Harrow: Welcoming country local with good food in bar and restaurant, steaks particularly good (butcher landlord), real ales inc Wadworths 6X; pub games, piped music; big well kept garden with barbecues, picturesque village *(Neil & Karen Dignan)*

Brill [SP6513]
Red Lion: Old and low-ceilinged, lively and friendly, with well kept ales and key-ring collection; pretty village *(Dr & Mrs A K Clarke)*

Buckingham [SP6933]
Whale: Simple Fullers pub with three of their real ales and a guest, usual food, old carved fireplace, pleasant staff; piped music or TV in front bar, often live music Sat *(Mrs Jess Cowley, George Atkinson)*

Butlers Cross [SP8406]
Russell Arms [off A4010 S of Aylesbury, at

Nash Lee roundabout; or off A413 in Wendover, passing stn]: Straightforward roadside pub with well kept ABC Best and Flowers Original and small sheltered garden, well placed for Chilterns walks; has been very popular for unusually good fresh fish, but tenant left in May 1999 and there was talk of a completely different style of food operation *(S J Hetherington, George Atkinson, LYM, Marion H Turner)*

Cadmore End [SU7892]
☆ *Blue Flag* [B482 towards Stokenchurch]: Smartened-up beamed village pub, comfortable and civilised, with separate modern hotel wing; well kept Fullers London Pride, Marlow Rebellion, Morlands Original and Wadworths 6X, decent wines, wide choice of good value generous food esp fish, expert unobtrusive service, lots of proper big dining tables; fascinating vintage MG pictures in side room; attractive little restaurant; bedrooms, good centre for walking *(Gerald Barnett, Simon Collett-Jones, T R and B C Jenkins, BB, Mr Peter Saville)*

Cadsden [SP8204]
Plough: Friendly little pub refurbished by new licensees, very popular with families and Chilterns ramblers, simple food inc reasonably priced sandwiches, Theakstons beers; lots of tables in delightful quiet front and back garden, pretty spot on Ridgeway Path *(A & S Hetherington, Tim and Ann Newell)*

Calverton [SP7939]
Shoulder of Mutton [just S of Stony Stratford]: Friendly old open-plan pub on edge of pretty village, big garden, wide range of cheap good food from sandwiches up in bar and restaurant, well kept ales inc Wadworths 6X and guests such as Batemans or Wye Valley, quick attentive service, attractive garden with pleasant view and play area; piped music, games machines; well equipped bedrooms *(George Atkinson)*

Chalfont St Giles [SU9893]
☆ *Ivy House* [A413 S]: Smart and attractively laid out 18th-c dining pub, comfortable armchairs by fire in elegantly cosy L-shaped tiled bar, lighter flagstoned no-smoking extension full of tables set for eating; wide range of good freshly cooked food from bangers and mash to wild boar steak with gooseberry sauce, not cheap but generous, well kept changing ales such as Brakspears and Everards Tiger, good wines by glass, espresso machine, good afternoon teas summer w/e; soft piped music; gravelled roadside terrace and sloping garden (can be traffic noise); watch out for the low beam in the gents' *(Cyril Brown, Simon Collett-Jones, P J Keen, Peter Saville, Mr and Mrs D Ayres-Regan, BB)*

White Hart: Clean well run pub with wide range of good generous food inc lots of fish and lovely puddings, well kept real ale, friendly owners and staff, cricketing décor, big garden; children welcome; bedrooms in barn at the back *(Michael Hill)*

Chenies [TQ0198]
Bedford Arms: Good pubby food lunchtime

and evening (as well as a main restaurant), efficient staff; tables in pleasant front garden; bedrooms *(Peter and Giff Bennett, Piotr Chodzko-Zajko)*

Clifton Reynes [SP9051]

Robin Hood [off back rd Emberton—Newton Blossomville; no through road]: Small local with two attractive bars, nice conservatory and very big garden leading to riverside walk to Olney, well kept Greene King and Charles Wells, good straightforward snacks and one or two more enterprising dishes (not Mon evening), very good service; old dark beams, brasses, horns, inglenook and newspapers in lounge, open fire, table skittles and juke box in public bar; no children inside *(George Atkinson)*

Colnbrook [TQ0277]

☆ *Ostrich* [1¼ miles from M4 junction 5 via A4/B3378, then 'village only' rd]: Striking Elizabethan pub, modernised but still signs of its long and entertaining history (and now even a life-sized stuffed ostrich); good log fire, Courage Best and Directors, Marstons Pedigree, prompt friendly service, though emphasis primarily on food side – good range of bar food, good upstairs restaurant; quiet piped music *(LYM, Ian Phillips, Simon Collett-Jones, D and M T Ayres-Regan, James House)*

Cublington [SP8322]

Unicorn: Relaxing and welcoming 16th-c beamed pub, supposedly haunted, with rickshaw, pictures and pine furniture, five interesting changing ales such as Vale Wychert, good reasonably priced food (not Sun evening) inc vegetarian, vegan and good puddings range, friendly attentive service, picnic-sets in garden behind with chickens and ducks *(Derek and Sylvia Stephenson)*

Denham [TQ0486]

Swan [¾ mile from M40 junction 1; follow Denham Village signs]: Pretty pub in lovely village, prints on timbered walls, picture windows overlooking splendid floodlit back garden with play area; comfortable seats, open fires, well kept Courage Best, John Smiths and Wadworths 6X, wide choice of food from lots of sandwiches up, prompt friendly service; games machine, piped pop may be obtrusive *(Ian Phillips, B Brewer, LYM)*

Dorney [SU9278]

☆ *Palmer Arms* [B3026, off A4, two miles from M4 junction 7]: Friendly renovated village pub with two small comfortable bars, dining room, wide choice of good if not cheap food, decent wine list, interesting well kept guest beers, friendly young staff; plenty of tables in pleasant garden behind *(Mr & Mrs Richard Osborne)*

Emberton [SP8849]

Bell & Bear [off A509 Olney—Newport Pagnell]: Jovial northern landlord, well priced food, Charles Wells Eagle and Websters Yorkshire, convivial homely atmosphere, comfortable lounge with two fireplace features and attractive flower displays, bar with darts, juke box and machines; big garden *(CMW, JJW)*

Farnham Common [SU9684]

Foresters Arms [A355]: Welcoming landlord

and locals in relaxed and civilised two-room dining pub popular for business lunches (set menu, many specials, Sun roasts), Bass, Fullers and Greene King IPA, prompt attentive service, rugs on woodblock floor, panelling, two log fires; soft piped music *(W K Wood)*

Farnham Royal [SU9583]

☆ *Emperor of India*: Small vine-covered dining pub with cosy corners, buoyant atmosphere, wide range of interesting food from good choice of sandwiches and baguettes to excellent fish, six or seven Whitbreads-related and guest ales, interesting licensees and super dog; back restaurant with barn as overflow, well kept garden *(B and K Hypher)*

Fingest [SU7791]

☆ *Chequers* [signed off B482 Marlow—Stokenchurch]: Civilised and relaxed, with several rooms around old-fashioned Tudor core, roaring fire in vast fireplace, sunny lounge by good-sized charming country garden, small no-smoking room, interesting furniture, well kept Brakspears PA, SB and Old, dominoes and cribbage, attractive restaurant; children in eating area; interesting church opp, good walks; family link to main entry White Hart at Northend *(Martin & Karen Wake, Gordon, JP, PP, LYM, Gerald Barnett, Eddie Edwards)*

Flackwell Heath [SU8889]

☆ *Crooked Billet* [A404 signed High Wycombe, 1st r Flackwell Heath, r Sheepridge Lane]: Cosy and comfortable old-fashioned 16th-c pub in lovely country setting, low beams, good choice of lunchtime food (not Sun), eating area spread pleasantly through alcoves, friendly prompt service, well kept Brakspears and Whitbreads-related ales, good open fire; juke box; delightful little front garden with quiet views *(G and M Stewart, BB, JP, PP, Gerald Barnett)*

Ford [SP7709]

☆ *Dinton Hermit* [signed between A418 and B4009, SW of Aylesbury]: Neat little stone cottage with snug and attractive furnishings and a woodburner in its huge inglenook, which has been a popular main entry for good value home-made food and well kept ABC Best, Adnams and Wadworths 6X, traditional games, a welcome for children, and an attractive sheltered country garden with play area; for sale as we go to press, reports please *(Peter and Jan Humphreys, S J Sloan, Michael Sargent, LYM, Ian Phillips, Graham Tayar, Catherine Raeburn, Lesley Bass)*

Frieth [SU7990]

☆ *Yew Tree* [signed off B482 N of Marlow]: Concentration on the food side (with quite a Greek flavour), but locals still dropping in for a drink – enjoyable atmosphere, exemplary service (now a family connection to the Highwayman at Exlade Street, Oxon), well kept ales such as Brakspears PA, Fullers London Pride and Gibbs Mew Bishops Tipple; unobtrusive piped music; walkers with dogs welcome *(Sheila Keene, Dr Gerald W Barnett, Dick Brown, LYM)*

Great Hampden [SP8401]

☆ *Hampden Arms* [signed off A4010 N and S of Princes Risborough]: Civilised dining pub in quiet spot opp village cricket pitch, good range of enjoyable food inc interesting dishes alongside familiar staples, more substantial evening choice, big sensible tables, quick pleasant service; has had well kept Greene King Abbot, Tetleys, and Wadworths 6X, and Addlestone's cider; peaceful tree-sheltered garden, good walks nearby. *(Gerald Barnett, B R Sparkes, Cyril Brown, S J Hetherington, LYM, Peter Saville, Greg Kilminster, Gill and Keith Croxton, John Roots)*

Great Horwood [SP7731]

☆ *Crown* [off B4033 N of Winslow]: Attractive and smartly welcoming two-room Georgian pub with good value fresh home-made food from unpretentious blackboard menu, popular hot lamb sandwiches and Sun lunches, chatty licensees, well kept Flowers IPA, Wadworths 6X and a weekly guest, farm ciders; fresh flowers in striking inglenook fireplace in summer, old-fashioned gramophone, parlour-like dining room with big wooden tables, board games; maybe soft piped music; quiz and theme nights inc jazz; tables on neat front lawn and more behind, very handy for Winslow Hall *(John Oddey, D Grace, Mrs B J P Edwards, Dr D E Granger, Graham and Karen Oddey, BB)*
Swan [B4033 N of Winslow]: Friendly front lounge with inglenook fires and dining area, small back bar with pool and darts, very wide choice of well prepared straightforward food using good ingredients, well kept Bass, Greene King IPA and Hook Norton Best; nice side garden; open all day w/e *(Graham and Karen Oddey)*

Great Kimble [SP8206]

☆ *Bernard Arms* [A4010]: Plush pub with some nice prints (and photographs of recent prime ministers dropping in for a drink – even Boris Yeltsin with the Majors), daily papers, good imaginative bar food, four changing Tetleys-related and other ales, decent wines, good range of malt whiskies and bottled beer, games room, attractive well kept fairy-lit gardens, interesting food in restaurant; well equipped bedrooms *(Mark Percy, Lesley Mayoh)*

Great Kingshill [SU8798]

☆ *Red Lion* [A4128 N of High Wycombe]: Now to all intents and purposes a small fish restaurant rather than the roadside local that it looks like – friendly staff, enjoyable fish and shellfish simply prepared; cl Sun evening, Mon *(Gerald Barnett, Alan & Eileen Bowker, Mark Girling, Mike Wells, M J Dowdy, Alan Knox, LYM)*

Great Missenden [SP8901]

George: Heavily beamed and timbered 15th-c pub with attractive alcoves, prints and china, inner snug with sofa and little settles, food in bar and no-smoking restaurant, real ales such as Adnams, Chiltern Beechwood, Fullers London Pride and Wadworths 6X; plenty of seats in the terrace and garden area; an interregnum as we went to press – reports on the new regime please *(Ian Phillips, LYM)*

Hanslope [SP7947]

Globe: Old cottage-type pub worth knowing for garden with excellent children's area; Banks's

and a guest ale, decent straightforward food in lounge (low tables) and no-smoking restaurant inc Sun lunch, games room *(CMW, JJW)*

Hawridge Common [SP9505]

☆ *Full Moon* [off A416 N of Chesham, then towards Cholesbury]: Welcoming little country local, clean and friendly, with snugly comfortable low-beamed rambling bar and spacious common-edge lawn, good friendly service by cheerful young staff, hot fresh well presented good value food, wide choice of changing well kept real ales; children and dogs welcome *(LYM, B Brewer)*

Hedgerley [SU9686]

☆ *White Horse* [towards Gerrards X]: Friendly old country local with enjoyable food inc sandwiches, bangers and mash, home-made fishcakes, particularly well kept Charles Wells Eagle, Greene King IPA and six unusual changing ales tapped from the cask, friendly service; relaxed atmosphere in charming small public bar, jugs, ball cocks and other bric-a-brac, log fire, larger lounge with cold food display cabinet, occasional barbecues in big pleasant back garden, lovely window boxes, occasional beer festivals; no dogs, can be very busy; attractive village, good walks nearby *(Iain Robertson, Dave Carter, Ron Gentry, the Didler)*

High Wycombe [SU8792]

Beech Tree: Cosy little red brick local, vastly expanded conservatory eating area at the back, well kept Courage Best and Wadworths 6X, friendly staff, good value generous food all day; quiet piped music; excellent big children's play area, lots of picnic-sets on grassy area, pleasant semi-rural setting *(Ian Phillips, A W Dickinson, Gerald Barnett)*

Iver [TQ0381]

☆ *Gurkha*: Gurkha paintings and trophies in pleasant bar, spacious yet cosy and individual – and very popular; good choice of reasonably priced imaginative home cooking, well kept beer, good atmosphere and service, big restaurant *(Nick Holmes)*

Ivinghoe [SP9416]

Kings Head: Comfortable, well organised pub with emphasis on food inc good set lunch, attentive polished service *(Maysie Thompson)*
Rose & Crown [off B489 opp church]: Limited choice of reasonably priced fresh food, well kept Adnams, Brains Reverend James, Greene King IPA and Morrells, friendly service, L-shaped bar with second room up a few steps; children welcome, quiet piped music, no muddy boots – nr one end of Ridgeway long-distance path; pleasant village *(Ian Phillips)*

Kingswood [SP6919]

Crooked Billet [A41]: Rambling white weatherboarded dining pub divided into several rooms, character stripped tables and mixed seats, large old fireplace, no-smoking dining area up a step or two, wide range of interesting food from baguettes up, well kept Adnams, Fullers London Pride and a guest such as Ansells, pleasant efficient service, piped classical music; can be busy; tables out on terrace and in back garden – attractive surroundings, handy

for Waddesdon Manor *(Mr W W Burke)*
Lacey Green [SP8201]

☆ *Pink & Lily* [from A4010 High Wycombe—
Princes Risboro follow Loosley sign, then Gt
Hampden, Gt Missenden one]: Charming old-
fashioned tap room (apostrophised sillily by
Rupert Brooke – poem framed here) in much-
extended Chilterns pub with airy and plush main
bar, food choice improved by welcoming newish
licensees with a fine track record; well kept ales
such as Boddingtons, Brakspears PA, Courage
Best and Glenny Hobgoblin, good wines,
friendly efficient service, open fire, dominoes,
cribbage, ring the bull; piped music, children
over 5 if eating; conservatory, big garden *(Mick
Hitchman, JP, PP, T R and B C Jenkins, Dave
Carter, B R Sparkes, LYM, the Didler)*
Lacey Green [SP8100]
Whip: Cheery pubby local welcoming walkers,
mix of simple traditional furnishings, reliable
food from good lunchtime soup and
sandwiches to Sun lunches, well kept beer,
copious coffee, friendly service; fruit machine,
TV; tables in sheltered garden, just below
windmill *(Maureen Hobbs, T R and B C
Jenkins, BB, Gerald Barnett)*
Lavendon [SP9153]
Horseshoe [A428 Bedford—Northampton]:
Friendly and comfortable beamed village pub
bright with hanging baskets and flower tubs;
bar and restaurant food, pleasant decor and
service, well kept Charles Wells and Morlands
Old Speckled Hen *(Dave Braisted)*
Little Marlow [SU8786]

☆ *Kings Head* [A4155 about 2 miles E of
Marlow]: Long, low flower-covered free house
with homely and cosy open-plan beamed bar,
very popular for wide choice of generous food
from unusual sandwiches to lots of steaks,
children's menu, smart red dining room (plenty
of reserved tables), good service, well kept beers
like Tetleys and Boddingtons, big garden
behind popular with families; piped music;
good farm shop opp, nice walk down to church
*(G and M Stewart, Kevin and Nina Thomas,
Don Mather, BB, Derek Harvey-Piper)*
Long Crendon [SP6808]

☆ *Chandos Arms* [B4011]: Handsome thatched
pub with pleasant low-beamed communicating
bars, good reasonably priced food from snacks
to steaks, separate restaurant menu, real ales
inc Brakspears, log fire, lots of brass and
copper, friendly efficient service *(Peter Lewis,
Marjorie and David Lamb)*
Ludgershall [SP6617]
Bull & Butcher [off A41 Aylesbury—Bicester]:
Quiet and cool little beamed country pub under
new management, reasonably priced freshly
made food, well kept Fullers London Pride and
Tetleys; children allowed in back dining room,
tables in nice front garden, attractive setting
(Marjorie & David Lamb)
Marlow [SU8586]
Clayton Arms: Refurbished but keeping its
simple bar unspoilt, bustling atmosphere, good
straightforward lunchtime bar food, well kept
Brakspears and seasonal guests, darts, no music
(the Didler)

Hand & Flowers [A4155 W]: Olde-worlde pub
with good well presented food from sandwiches
and baguettes up in big sympathetically lit
dining area leading off bar, pleasant staff, well
kept beers inc Bass and Marstons; boules pitch
for hire *(M L Porter)*
Hogshead: Recently built on site of old
brewery, basic feel with bare boards and
beams, big room divided on different levels, old
prints, good choice of real ale, wholesome food;
piped pop, SkyTV, very popular with young
people; tables and chairs out by pavement
*(Roger & Debbie Stamp, Susan and John
Douglas)*

☆ *Two Brewers* [first right off Station Rd from
double roundabout]: Low-beamed bar with
shiny black woodwork, nautical pictures,
gleaming brassware, new landlord putting
emphasis on well kept Brakspears, Flowers IPA,
Fullers London Pride, Wadworths 6X and a
guest like Rebellion, good food and wines
(unusual crypt-like dining area – may have to
book Sun lunch), considerate service, tables in
sheltered back courtyard, front seats with
glimpse of the Thames (pub right on Thames
Path); children in eating area *(Simon Collett-
Jones, T R and B C Jenkins, Val Stevenson,
Rob Holmes, David Shillitoe, LYM, Gordon,
the Didler)*
Marsh Gibbon [SP6423]
Greyhound: Traditional furnishings, stripped
beams and stonework, so a surprise to find
good Thai food, half-price for children (no
under-6s), in bar and two-room restaurant with
oriental statuary; Fullers London Pride, Greene
King Abbot and IPA, Hook Norton Best, and
McEwans 80/-, decent house wines, handsome
woodburner, dominoes, cribbage, and classical
piped music; tables outside with play area
(W M and J M Cottrell, LYM)
Medmenham [SU8084]

☆ *Dog & Badger*: Comfortably modernised low-
beamed bar with open fire, brasses and soft
lighting, usual food (not Sun evening) inc Fri
fish and chips and proper old-fashioned
puddings, well kept Brakspears PA and SB,
Flowers Original and local Rebellion IPA,
restaurant; children in eating area; piped music
*(M L Porter, DHV, Gordon, LYM, Gerald
Barnett)*
Milton Keynes [SP8335]
Old Beams [Paxton Crescent, Shenley Lodge]:
Lots of brick and wood in comfortably
extended sizeable pub, old photographs,
paintings and brass, candles on dining tables,
McMullens ales with a guest such as Courage
Directors, good choice of food, speciality
coffees; business faxes sent and received free,
very popular with local office staff; piped
music; big garden with two ponds *(E J and
M W Corrin, CMW, JJW)*
Newport Pagnell [SP8743]

☆ *Bull* [B526 2 miles from M1 junction 14]: Busy
and unspoilt town pub in welcoming 17th-c
coaching inn, up to eight properly kept
changing real ales inc rarities for the area, well
priced straightforward food (not Sun evening)
inc a fine vegetarian balti, friendly staff;

unpretentious but civilised and cosily lit low-ceilinged lounge with daily papers, bar with darts, juke box and pool; tables in pleasant courtyard; next to Aston Martin works, cars on show weekdays; bedrooms *(John C Baker, Nick Dowson, BB)*

Newton Longville [SP8430]

Crooked Billet [off A421 S of Milton Keynes]: Friendly new licensees in converted 17th-c thatched barn on edge of council estate, lounge and no-smoking dining room divided by log fires, four Marstons ales, reasonably priced bar food, fuller menu Fri/Sat evening and Sun lunch, lots of wood, tools, bric-a-brac, flowers and tiny aquarium; picnic-sets in nice garden *(CMW, JJW)*

Northall [SP9520]

Northall Inn [A4146 Hemel Hempstead—Leighton Buzzard]: 16th-c oak-beamed coaching inn, varied beautifully presented food in dining bar, cosy public bar, well kept beers, enthusiastic staff, big garden and courtyard; handy for Whipsnade and local walks *(Ken and Thelma Mitchell, Martin White)*

Olney [SP8851]

Two Brewers [A509]: Unpretentious, with several clean and tidy rooms, very wide choice of generous good value food inc good home-made pies and Sun lunches, big dining area with plenty of different-sized tables, well kept beer, good coffee, friendly prompt service, attractive courtyard interestingly decorated to show its brewery past, tables in small garden too *(Roger Braithwaite, Stephen Brown)*

Oving [SP7821]

☆ *Black Boy* [off A413 Winslow rd out of Whitchurch]: Friendly and interesting old pub nr church, more spacious inside than it looks; attractive old tables, magnificent collection of jugs, log fire, well kept Whitbreads-related beer, well presented generous food esp fish, cheerful service, superb views from extended back dining area over pleasant terrace and big sloping garden; TV in small bar; children welcome, good food choice for them *(JCW, Mr and Mrs B Edwards, Gill and Keith Croxton)*

Penn Street [SU9295]

☆ *Hit or Miss* [off A404 SW of Amersham]: Enormous range of good reasonably priced generous food from ploughman's to seafood in well laid out low-beamed three-room pub with own cricket ground, good cricket and chair-making memorabilia, friendly bustling atmosphere and welcoming service, well kept ales such as Brakspears, Fullers and Hook Norton, good wines, log fire, occasional live music; separate restaurant, picnic-sets out in front, pleasant setting *(Cyril Brown, Joan and John Fuller, Gerald Barnett, LYM, Brian White, Peter Saville, B Brewer, Howard Dell)*

Preston Bissett [SP6529]

☆ *Old Hat* [signed from A421, via Gawcott]: Cosy and cottagey thatched village pub, very peaceful atmosphere, excellent friendly service, well kept Hook Norton, good honest home-cooked lunchtime food (not Sun); comfortable carpeted area with high backed wooden settles around big stone fireplace, daily papers, darts

and dominoes in plainer room, tables on new lawn with pleasant farmland views *(Steve and Sarah De Mellow, Ray Crabtree, BB, Gill and Keith Croxton)*

Princes Risborough [SP8004]

☆ *Red Lion* [off A4010]: Very friendly and keen new management, redecorated bars with good log fire, good generous home-made food, well kept Brakspears PA, Hook Norton Best and Rebellion, traditional games, tables in garden; children in restaurant, good Chilterns walks; well refurbished bedrooms *(Tracey and Stephen Groves, Mark Percy, Lesley Mayoh, Tim and Ann Newell, Steve de Mellow, LYM, Mike Wells, A Barker)*

Shabbington [SP6607]

☆ *Old Fisherman* [off A418 Oxford—Thame]: Riverside pub with three roomy and attractive areas, good range of generous good food inc good fish choice and enjoyable steaks, particularly popular Sun lunch and w/e evenings; Morrells and guest ales, garden with play area, small camp site *(JA, GA, Kathryn & Mike Phillips)*

Skirmett [SU7790]

Old Crown [Fingest rd off B482 at Bolter End, then follow Skirmett sign]: Has been cosy and attractive dining pub, interesting decor in small pleasantly simple rooms, huge log fire, charming garden, good rich well presented but expensive food, well kept Brakspears, good house wines (not a place for just a drink); found closed Spring 1999 and no news since – reports please *(Peter Saville, Gerald Barnett, A & S Hetherington, JP, PP, Chris Glasson, Helen Pickering, James Owen, Mick Hitchman, Graham and Karen Oddey, Christine and Geoff Butler, LYM, Yavuz and Shirley Mutlu, the Didler)*

Slapton [SP9320]

Carpenters Arms: Small pub doubling as fascinating book shop, inside divided into four, inc a dining room; very friendly staff, ales inc Morlands Old Speckled Hen, attractively served good food (as the cat knows) *(Andrew Scarr)*

Speen [SU8399]

☆ *Old Plow* [road from village towards Lacey Green and Saunderton Stn]: Restaurant not pub (they won't serve drinks unless you're eating), but friendly, relaxing and charmingly cottagey, with good open fires, well kept Brakspears, good if not cheap food and wines (you can have just one course), fine service, log fires, children in eating area, pretty lawns, lovely countryside; cl Sun evening and Mon *(Mrs M Hobbs, Gwen and Peter Andrews, LYM)*

Stewkley [SP8526]

☆ *Carpenters Arms* [junction of Wing and Dunton rds]: Welcoming low-ceilinged village pub with generous reasonably priced fresh home-made food from sandwiches to imaginative main dishes, well kept ales inc Fullers London Pride and Marstons Pedigree, sociable alsatian called Boon; bookcases in extended dining lounge, darts in jolly little public bar, subdued piped music; garden with play area *(LYM, Nigel and Sue Foster, Frank and Annette Gesoff)*

Stony Stratford [SP7840]
Fox & Hounds: 17th-c, real ales inc guests, food inc special nights, hood skittles, darts, folk, blues or jazz Thurs and Sat; tables in walled garden *(Anon)*
Old George: Attractive and lively beamed and timbered inn, good value food, particularly hospitable staff and hard-working landlord, good coffee, dining room up at the back; piped music; tables in courtyard behind, bedrooms *(George Atkinson)*
Taplow [SU9082]
Feathers [opp Cliveden entrance]: Millers Kitchen much modified family dining pub, wide range of reasonably priced individually prepared food, efficient service, Greenalls ales; Wiveliscombe Gold cider, tables in courtyard, play area, dogs allowed only by front picnic-sets *(Ian Phillips)*
Twyford [SP6726]
☆ *Seven Stars* [Calvert—Gawcott rd E of village, just N of Twyford—Steeple Claydon one]: Rambling low-beamed country pub popular for reasonably priced food in lounge bar and dining room (not Sun evening; fish and meat from London markets daily), welcoming service, well kept Marstons ales, open fires, pictures, brasses and old farm tools; pool in games room, piped music may obtrude; tables in large pleasant garden with animals for children, live band Sun evening; handy for Claydon House *(Marjorie and David Lamb, George Atkinson)*
Waddesdon [SP7417]
☆ *Lion*: Busy village pub with three homely linked eating areas, nice wooden furniture, good generous French country food inc fish and vegetarian, quick very friendly service, good choice of beers inc guests, thriving local atmosphere *(Gill and Keith Croxton, Paul and Sarah Gayler)*
Wendover [SP8607]
☆ *Red Lion*: 17th-c inn with wide choice of good value changing food, generous and imaginative, inc fish specialities and Sun lunch in pleasant bustling refurbished oak-beamed bar and adjacent good value restaurant, well kept ales such as Brakspears, Courage Directors, Hancocks HB and one brewed for the pub, good wines, friendly efficient staff; can get smoky; walker-friendly – on Ridgeway Long Distance Path; comfortable bedrooms *(S J*

Hetherington, Catherine and Richard Preston, Kevin Thomas, Nina Randall)
West Wycombe [SU8394]
☆ *Old Plough* [A40]: Very small welcoming beamed bar with reasonably priced food from toasties to steaks, Friary Meux, Hardy and Youngs Special, huge corner log fire, pool table; upstairs lounge, restaurant, pretty little garden up behind *(Ian Phillips)*
Weston Underwood [SP8650]
☆ *Cowpers Oak* [off A509 at Olney]: Charming old creeper-clad pub, beams and stripped stone, five real ales such as Hook Norton Best and Tomintoul Scottish Bard, good value food inc good soup, back restaurant, chatty landlady, assorted furniture inc rocking chair, long school desk and piano, open fire, tropical fish tank, games area with darts and hood skittles; piped music; big attractive garden (no dogs) with play area, handy for Flamingo Gardens *(George Atkinson, Maysie Thompson, CMW, JJW)*
Wheelerend Common [SU8093]
☆ *Brickmakers Arms* [just off A40]: Homely pub with welcoming new licensees, inglenook log fire, some exposed flintwork, panelling, low beams, elderly settees, kitchen and other tables, shelves of china; good choice of good value bar food, upstairs no-smoking restaurant, decent range of beers and wines, good service; good play area in big garden, common opp for walks *(P Weedon)*
Wing [SP8822]
☆ *Cock*: Unusual range of consistently well kept changing ales, good value food (some buffet-style) inc uncommon dishes, good coffee, cottage armchairs and roaring fire, separate dining areas, friendly efficient service even when busy (as it is on their occasional beer festivals) *(John Poulter, Howard and Margaret Buchanan, Richard Houghton, Ted George)*
Worminghall [SP6308]
☆ *Clifden Arms*: Very picturesque 16th-c beamed and timbered thatched pub in pretty gardens, old-fashioned seats and rustic memorabilia in lounge bar with roaring log fire, another in public bar, well kept Adnams Broadside, Boddingtons, Fullers ESB and London Pride, Hook Norton and interesting guest beers, traditional games, children allowed; good play area, Aunt Sally; attractive village *(P A Legon, Ted George, LYM, Iain Robertson, Mrs Linda Jordan, Roger and Valerie Hill)*

Cambridgeshire

The standard for dining out in Cambridgeshire pubs is set by the small Huntsbridge group, with their excellent if restaurantish pubs each individually run by an imaginative chef-patron: the Old Bridge in Huntingdon, the Pheasant at Keyston and the Three Horseshoes at Madingley. The Chequers at Fowlmere, Crown & Punchbowl at Horningsea (a newcomer to the Guide) and Anchor at Sutton Gault are directly comparable with these civilised places, giving a similar sense of occasion; the White Hart at Bythorn is if anything even more restauranty. More thoroughly in line with the pub tradition of unpretentious informality are the idiosyncratic King William IV at Heydon (a very good vegetarian choice), the ebulliently run Woodmans Cottage at Gorefield (amazing puddings), the very friendly Queens Head at Kirtling, and the Trinity Foot so well placed on the A14 near Swavesey, with its great range of fresh fish. From all of these, it's the Pheasant at Keyston which wins our award of Cambridgeshire Dining Pub of the Year. If sheer value is what you're looking for, head for Cambridge itself – where all our main entries qualify for our increasingly hard-to-get Bargain Award (those students must be good for something, even if it's only keeping the prices there so competitive). One of our all-time favourites is the Queens Head at Newton, a very genuine pub, unspoilt and unpretentious. In that same vein we'd also highly recommend the hospitable Millstone at Barnack, and the basic but genteel Fountain in Ely. Three more newcomers are also well worth a visit: the informally stylish Crown & Punchbowl at Horningsea (good food), the remarkable new Brewery Tap in Peterborough (home of Oakham beers), and the intriguing Green Man at Thriplow (good beer here, too). Among the Lucky Dip entries at the end of the chapter, many of them already inspected and approved by us, we'd particularly pick out the Olde Mill at Brampton, Lion at Buckden, Castle and Mill in Cambridge, Leeds Arms at Eltisley, Golden Pheasant at Etton, White Pheasant at Fordham, Black Bull at Godmanchester, Blue Lion at Hardwick, Old Ferry Boat at Holywell, Plough & Fleece at Horningsea, Pike & Eel at Needingworth, Plough in Shepreth, Red Lion in Wisbech and Three Blackbirds at Woodditton.

BARNACK TF0704 Map 5
Millstone ♨

Millstone Lane; off B1443 SE Stamford; turn off School Lane near the Fox

Aubrey Sinclair Ball, the very hospitable landlord, has been at this friendly village local for fifteen years now. Readers continue to rave about his famous home-made pies (£6.75, same price as last year!) such as salmon and asparagus, minted lamb, or pork, cider and apple; other hearty food includes sandwiches (from £2.25 – or with a bowl of soup £3.25), crispy breaded mushrooms (£3.55), ploughman's (£4.95), roasted vegetable lasagne (£5.95), breaded haddock stuffed with cheese, prawns and mushrooms (£6.25), gammon steak and eggs (£6.75), sirloin steak (£8.95) and home-made puddings like sherry trifle and rhubarb crumble (from £2.95); smaller helpings for OAPs, and a straightforward children's menu. The Adnams, Everards

Old Original and Tiger and two guest beers on handpump are always well kept, and served along with 17 country wines in the traditional timbered bar, split into comfortably intimate areas, with cushioned wall benches on the patterned carpet and high beams weighed down with lots of heavy harness. A little snug displays the memorabilia (including medals from both world wars) of a former regular. The snug and dining room are no smoking. It's best to arrive early as seats fill up quickly, even midweek. *(Recommended by Jenny and Michael Back, Mike and Maggie Betton, B, M and P Kendall, P Stallard, Tony Gayfer, Ian Stafford, F J Robinson)*

Everards ~ Tenant Aubrey Sinclair Ball ~ Real ale ~ Bar food (not Sun evening) ~ Restaurant ~ (01780) 740296 ~ Children in snug and dining room ~ Open 11.30-2.30, 5.30(6 Sat)-11; 12-4, 7-10.30 Sun

BYTHORN TL0575 Map 5
White Hart 🍴 ♀

Village signposted just off A14 Kettering—Cambridge

This is now stretching our definition of a pub to the extreme limits, with White Hart now a sort of subtitle to 'Bennett's Bistro', and even a threat to the well kept Greene King IPA and Abbott on handpump. There is no doubting the emphasis on food, with some concentration on the restaurant; the bar menu might include home-made soup (£3.50), toasted asparagus and smoked salmon (£4.95, large £7.50), daily specials such as steak and mushroom pie, stuffed duck legs with sweet and sour sauce, Thai chicken curry, crispy loin of pork, or exotic fish dishes such as grilled marlin with olive oil and tomato (all £7.50), steaks (from £8.95), and tempting puddings such as coffee and rum roulade (£4.50); three-course Sunday lunch £15, more elaborate restaurant menu; good, affordable, well chosen wine list. There's a pleasant mix of furnishings in the homely main bar and several linked smallish rooms, such as a big leather chesterfield, lots of silver teapots and so forth on a carved dresser and in a built-in cabinet, and wing armchairs and attractive tables. One area with rugs on stripped boards has soft pale leather studded chairs and stools, and a cosy log fire in a huge brick fireplace; cookery books and plenty of magazines for reading. Cheerful landlord and helpful staff. *(Recommended by Joan and Michel Hooper-Immins, Prof Kenneth Surin, Ian Phillips, R C Wiles, Stephen and Julie Brown, Dr B H Hamilton, J F M West, Dr Andy Wilkinson, David & Mary Webb)*

Free house ~ Licensee Bill Bennett ~ Real ale ~ Bar food (Tues-Fri till 9.30, 12-3 Sat, set menu only Sun lunchtime) ~ Restaurant ~ (01832) 710226 ~ Children welcome ~ Open 11-2.30(3 Sat), 6-11; 12-3 Sun; closed Sun evening, all day Mon, 26 Dec, 1 Jan and bank holiday Mons

CAMBRIDGE TL4658 Map 5
Anchor 🍺 £

Silver St (where there are punts for hire – with a boatman if needed)

A lively student's forum during term-time, this cheery pub on the bank of the River Cam is perfectly situated for a lazy afternoon's punt-spotting in less frantic times – if you can drag yourself away from the delightfully placed suntrap terrace, you can even hire one here yourself. It's set on four levels with two bars, there's a cosy atmosphere among the nooks and crannies in the entrance area, and lots of bric-a-brac, church pews, and a brick fireplace at each end. The pubby upstairs bar with pews and wooden chairs (no smoking during food service times), commands good views over the river and Mill Pond. Downstairs, the café-bar has enamel signs on the walls and a mix of interesting tables, settles, farmhouse chairs, and hefty stools on the bare boards. More steps take you down to a simpler flagstoned room, and french windows lead out to the terrace (heated in the evenings). Most of the simple good value bar food remains the same price as last year, and includes home-made soup (£1.95), filled baked potatoes (from £2.95), ploughman's (£4.20), salads (£4.50), scampi (£5.25), four home-made daily specials such as aubergine and pasta bake, coq au vin, sweet and sour pork, or steak and vegetable pie (all £4.75), and puddings like sticky toffee pudding (£2.25); Sunday roasts (£5.50). Lots of well kept real ales might include Boddingtons Bitter, Castle Eden, Flowers Original, Fullers London Pride, Marstons Pedigree, Morlands Old Speckled Hen, Wadworths 6X, and Youngs Special tapped from the cask, and there's a good range of foreign bottled beers; friendly young service, and various trivia, video games and fruit machines, juke box and piped music; they open early on Sundays for soft drinks. *(Recommended by Jeff Davies, Roger Bellingham, Elizabeth and Alan Walker, Bill & Margaret Rogers)*

Whitbreads ~ Managers Alastair and Sandra Langton ~ Real ale ~ Bar food (12-8, till 4 Fri and Sat, 12-2.30 Sun) ~ (01223) 353554 ~ Children welcome during food service hours ~ Open 11-11; 12-10.30 Sun

Eagle ♀ £

Bene't Street

Ever-popular bustling old stone-fronted town centre coaching inn, once the headquarters of the notorious 18th-c Rutland Club headed by swindler extraordinaire John Mortlock; later, more honourable drinking alumni included the Nobel Prize winning scientists Crick and Watson, who discovered the structure of DNA. A relaxing atmosphere pervades the five rambling rooms (one no smoking), which retain many charming original architectural features. There are lovely worn wooden floors and plenty of original pine panelling, two fireplaces dating back to around 1600, two medieval mullioned windows, and the remains of two possibly medieval wall paintings. The high dark red ceiling has been left unpainted since the war to preserve the signatures of British and American airmen worked in with Zippo lighters, candle smoke and lipstick. The furniture is nicely old and creaky. Screened from the street by sturdy wooden gates is an attractive cobbled and galleried courtyard with heavy wooden seats and tables and pretty hanging baskets. The straightforward good value food, same price as last year and well liked by readers, is served from a counter in a small back room. At lunchtime, you can expect pastie, chips and beans (£3.95), ploughman's, quiche or ham and eggs (£4.25) and chilli, lasagne or roast chicken (£4.50), with evening burgers (from £4), barbecue chicken wings, fish and chips or breaded plaice (£4.95); daily specials, too. A neat little booklet lists up to 20 wines, sparkling wines and champagnes by the glass. Well kept Greene King IPA, Abbot, and seasonal ales on handpump. At Christmas, carols from King's College Choir are perfectly complemented by mulled wine. Friendly service from well dressed staff. *(Recommended by Rona Murdoch, Robert Gomme, John Wooll, John A Barker, A J Bowen, Dr Andy Wilkinson, Andy and Jill Kassube, A Hepburn, S Jenner, B T Smith, Anthony Barnes)*

Greene King ~ Managers Peter and Carol Hill ~ Real ale ~ Bar food (12-2.30, 5.30-8.45, not Fri, Sat and Sun evenings) ~ (01223) 505020 ~ Children in eating area of bar ~ Open 11-11; 12-10.30 Sun

Free Press £

Prospect Row

We'd agree with the reader who found this completely no-smoking pub everything a pub should be. Blissfully unspoilt and unpretentious, it has been run by the same friendly licensee for over 20 years. A collection of oars and rowing photographs in the sociable bare-board rooms reflects its status as a registered boat club. Good wholesome home-made bar food served in generous well priced helpings from a fairly short menu includes two vegetarian soups (£2.50), smoked mackerel or vegetarian pâté (£4.25), chilli con carne (£4.50), at least two meat and two vegetarian specials like minty lamb or pork and cider casserole, beef in beer, broccoli and butterbean or carrot and cumin bake (£4.25-£5), and puddings like fruit and almond slice, apple crumble, or lemon torte (£1.95). Well kept Greene King IPA, Abbot and Mild on handpump, with a good selection of malt whiskies and freshly squeezed orange juice; cribbage and dominoes behind the bar. The sheltered paved garden at the back might be rather tatty but is quite a suntrap; friendly cat. *(Recommended by Garth & Janet Wheeler, John Fahy, John Wooll, Andy and Jill Kassube, Ian Phillips, M A Buchanan, Rona Murdoch, Sharon Holmes, Tom Cherrett, Dr and Mrs Morley, A J*

Bowen, Michael and Hazel Duncombe, John A Barker, Mark J Hydes)

Greene King ~ Tenants Chris and Debbie Lloyd ~ Real ale ~ Bar food (12-2(2.30 Sat and Sun), 6(7 Sun)-9) ~ (01223) 368337 ~ Children welcome ~ Open 12-2.30(3 Sat), 6-11; 12-3, 7-10.30 Sun; closed evenings 25 and 26 Dec

Live & Let Live 🍺 £

40 Mawson Road; off Mill Road SE of centre

A recent fire has led to the seating area being extended and refurbished in this particularly friendly and welcoming unpretentious little backstreet local. The heavily timbered brickwork rooms have sturdy varnished pine tables with pale wood chairs on bare boards, and lots of interesting old country bric-a-brac and posters about local forthcoming events; cribbage and piped music. The eating area is no smoking, and basic but generous bar food includes big sandwiches (from £1.60, not Sunday), hot filled baguettes (from £2.60), filled yorkshire pudding (£3.75), ploughman's (from £3.85), vegetable curry or sausage casserole (£3.95) lasagne or goujons of plaice (£4.20), as well as daily specials; Sunday breakfast (£3.50). Well kept Adnams Southwold, Batemans Mild, Brunos Bitter (brewed for the pub by B&T, and named after the pub's boxer dog), Everards Tiger, Nethergate Umbel and a guest on handpump, and local cider and English wines; friendly service. On Sunday evenings they serve free snacks with the live music. Well behaved dogs are welcome. *(Recommended by Ian Phillips, Jeff Davies)*

Free house ~ Licensee Peter Gray ~ Real ale ~ Bar food ~ (01223) 460261 ~ Children in eating area of bar ~ Folk duo most Sun evenings ~ Open 11.30(12 Sat)-2.30, 5.30(6 Sat)-11; 12-2.30, 7-10.30 Sun

ELSWORTH TL3163 Map 5

George & Dragon

Off A604 NW of Cambridge, via Boxworth

Readers often comment on the exceptional friendly service from smartly dressed staff at this quiet brick-built pub, set back from the village street. They still offer a very good value three-course set menu on a Monday lunchtime (£8.50) – you will need to book. Other carefully prepared fresh food includes sandwiches from a light snack menu (from £2.50), good home-made soups (£3), half rack of baby pork ribs in a barbecue sauce (£4.50), ploughman's (from £4.50), chicken kiev or aubergine, tomato and mozzarella bake (£8), gammon (£8.50), salmon fillet topped with prawn and anchovy butter (£9), mixed grill (£12), 16oz scotch rump (£15.50) and home-made puddings (£3), and daily specials like roast scotch sirloin (£8), turkey stuffed with mozzarella cheese and bacon in a brandy, cream and mushroom sauce (£9), and swordfish steak topped with garlic prawns on a bed of horseradish and bacon mash (£10); weekly themed evening menus. A pleasant panelled main bar opens on the left to a slightly elevated no-smoking dining area with comfortable tables and a good woodburning stove. From here, steps lead down to another quiet no-smoking section behind, with tables overlooking the back garden. On the right is a more formal restaurant; soft piped music. Well kept Greene King IPA and Ruddles County on handpump, decent wines. There are attractive terraces and so forth in the back garden. *(Recommended by E A George, Anthony Barnes, Jenny and Michael Back, Gordon Theaker, Mr and Mrs D King, Ian Phillips, Stephen and Julie Brown, Margaret and Roy Randle, Maysie Thompson)*

Free house ~ Licensees Barrie and Marion Ashworth ~ Real ale ~ Bar food ~ Restaurant ~ (01954) 267236 ~ Children in eating area of bar and restaurant ~ Open 11-2.30, 6-11; 12-2.30 Sun; closed Sun evening and 25 Dec

---

If you enjoy your visit to a pub, please tell the publican. They work extraordinarily long hours, and when people show their appreciation it makes it all seem worth while.

ELY TL5380 Map 5
Fountain ◖

Corner of Barton Square and Silver Street

Spotless town corner pub, basic but genteel, with a very traditional approach: a good range of particularly well kept beers, no food, and a welcoming atmosphere that attracts a real mix of age groups. Though very close to the cathedral it escapes the tourists, and indeed on the lunchtimes when it's open you might have the place almost to yourself; it's delightfully peaceful then. Things get busier in the evenings, especially on Fridays and Saturdays, but even then this is the kind of place to come to for a chat rather than to shout over music or fruit machines. Old cartoons, local photographs, regional maps and mementoes of the neighbouring King's School punctuate the elegant dark pink walls, and neatly tied-back curtains hang from golden rails above the big windows. Above one fireplace is a stuffed pike in a case, and there are a few antlers dotted about – not to mention a duck at one end of the bar. Adnams Southwold and Broadside, Fullers London Pride, and a changing guest such as Everards Tiger on handpump; very efficient service. A couple of tables are squeezed on to a tiny back terrace. Note the limited opening times. *(Recommended by Dr Andy Wilkinson)*

Free house ~ Licensees John and Judith Borland ~ Real ale ~ (01353) 663122 ~ Children till 9pm ~ Open 5-11 (12-2 bank holidays); 12-2, 6-11 Sat; 12-2, 7-10.30 Sun

FEN DRAYTON TL3368 Map 5
Three Tuns

Village signposted off A14 NW of Cambridge

This well preserved ancient thatched building may once have housed the Guildhall of Fen Drayton. The splendidly atmospheric bar has two inglenook fireplaces, particularly interesting heavy-set moulded Tudor beams and timbers (the decorations on the central boss suggest a former link with the corn industry), comfortable cushioned settles and a nice variety of chairs. It's decorated with old local photographs, old song-sheets of local folk songs, big portraits, sparkling brass plates, fresh flowers, and old crockery in a corner dresser. Very welcoming licensees and staff serve generous helpings of good value bar food including sandwiches (from £1.75, not Sun), soup (£2.00), prawn cocktail (£2.75), ploughman's (£3.75), chicken curry, pie of the day, meat or vegetarian lasagne (£5.25), scampi (£6), 8oz rump steak (£8), specials like fisherman's crumble or cannelloni ricotta (£5.25), and puddings such as treacle and almond tart (from £1.80). Well kept Greene King IPA, Abbot, Triumph and a monthly guest on handpump as well as a range of malt whiskies. Sensibly placed darts, shove-ha'penny, cribbage, dominoes and fruit machine. A well tended lawn at the back has tables under cocktail parasols, apple and flowering cherry trees, and a good children's play area. It can get very crowded, so it's best to arrive early if you want to eat. *(Recommended by Ian Phillips, Eric Locker, Elizabeth and Klaus Leist, J I Davies, Jamie and Sarah Allan, F J Robinson)*

Greene King ~ Tenants Michael and Eileen Nugent ~ Real ale ~ Bar food ~ (01954) 230242 ~ Children in eating area of bar till 8pm ~ Open 11.30-2.30, 6.30-11; 12-2.30, 7-10.30 Sun

FOWLMERE TL4245 Map 5
Chequers ⑪ ♀

B1368

Civilised 16th-c country pub with a colourful history: it numbers Samuel Pepys and a squadron of Spitfire pilots among its past patrons. The menu (prices have changed little since last year), offers a high standard of imaginative cooking with starters including artichoke soup laced with chervil cream (£2.90), mushrooms creamed with white wine and tarragon with croutons (£3.90), smoked haddock, chive and tomato gratin (£4.80), confit of duck with toulouse pork sausages and white haricot beans served with a bitter leaf salad (£5.50, £8.80 large helping), and main courses like

grilled turkey escalope in a wild mushroom sauce (£7.90), roast salmon fillet on
tagliatelle with mussels, prawns and a creamed saffron sauce or lamb shank with
green flageolet beans in tomato and garlic sauce (£9.40), grilled Antarctic sea bass
spiced with pesto on a mint pea cream (£10.80), lightly peppered fillet steak on
white wine, brandy, tarragon, dijon mustard and cream sauce (£14.90). Sunday
lunch of roast beef (£10.50). Puddings include warm Jack Daniels chocolate and
pecan cake (£4), rhubarb crumble and custard or hot date sponge on a sticky toffee
sauce (£3.80), Irish farmhouse cheeses (£3.80). There's an excellent choice of very
well priced fine wines by the glass (including vintage and late-bottled ports), a very
good list of malt whiskies, well kept Adnams and a guest which might be Badgers
Tanglefoot, Bass, Fullers London Pride or Wards Waggle Dance on handpump,
freshly squeezed orange juice, and a good choice of brandies. Two warm and cosy
comfortably furnished communicating rooms downstairs have an open log fire –
look out for the priest's hole above the bar. Upstairs there are beams, wall timbering
and some interesting moulded plasterwork above the fireplace. The airy no-smoking
conservatory overlooks white tables under cocktail parasols among flowers and
shrub roses in a pleasant well tended floodlit garden. *(Recommended by George Little,
Tony Beaulah, Robert Turnham, Pat and Tony Hinkins, Dr Paul Khan, David and Diana
MacFadyen, Francis Johnston, Ian Phillips, Hilary Edwards, G Neighbour, Marvadene B Eves,
Tina and David Woods-Taylor, Gwen and Peter Andrews, R Wiles)*

*Free house ~ Licensee Norman Stephenson Rushton ~ Real ale ~ Bar food ~
Restaurant ~ (01763) 208369 ~ Children welcome ~ Open 11.30-2.30, 6-11; 12-2.30,
7-10.30 Sun; closed 25 Dec*

GOREFIELD TF4111 Map 8
Woodmans Cottage
Main St; off B1169 W of Wisbech

Readers continue to be entertained by Lucille, the ebullient ex-jazz singer landlady at
this friendly village local. Real care is taken to ensure customers enjoy the good food
(a full-time pudding girl is employed to make the amazing number of puddings (£3)
on offer – you can expect up to 50 at the weekend). Other bar food includes toasties
(from £1.50), omelettes or ploughman's (from £4), steak and kidney pie, gammon
and pineapple and about six vegetarian dishes such as vegetable curry (all £6.50),
cajun chicken (£7.25), mixed grill (£9), daily specials like beef stroganoff, lamb and
walnut casserole, tuna bake or chicken tikka masala (all £6.50), and children's dishes
(from £1.50); roast Sunday lunch (£6; children £4). The spacious modernised bar
rambles back around the bar counter, with leatherette stools and brocaded
banquettes around the tables on its carpet. There's a big collection of china plates in
a comfortable side eating area, as well as 1920s prints on its stripped brick walls.
The Cellar accommodates non-smoking diners, and has a display of Lucille's
paintings, some of which were recently hung at Westminster by the Society of
Botanical Artists. Beyond is an attractive pitched-ceiling restaurant – best to book
early. At the other end of the pub, a games area has darts, pool, cribbage, dominoes
and a juke box; Monday bridge nights, and piped music. Well kept Bass, Greene
King IPA and a guest such as Shepherd Neame Bishops Finger on handpump, and
quite a lot of Australian wines. There are tables out on a sheltered back terrace, with
a few more on a front verandah. *(Recommended by Michael and Jenny Back, David
Atkinson, Brian & Jean Hepworth, Miss S P Watkin, P A Taylor)*

*Free house ~ Licensees Barry and Lucille Carter ~ Real ale ~ Bar food (till 10) ~
Restaurant ~ (01945) 870669 ~ Children in eating area of bar ~ Open 11-3, 7-11; 12-
4, 7-10.30 Sun*

HEYDON TL4340 Map 5
King William IV
Off A505 W of M11 junction 10

Vegetarians are spoilt for choice at this charmingly atmospheric pub with food of a
consistently high standard. There are about a dozen meat-free dishes such as nutmeg,

spinach and cream cheese crispy pancakes with a tomato and chive sauce or field mushrooms and mediterranean fruits with Swiss gruyère, fettuccine with artichokes, mushrooms and roasted pine kernels and a fresh Italian tomato sauce or nutty and date curry with basmati wild rice and poppadums (from £7.75). Other good value bar food in generous helpings includes lunchtime sandwiches (from £2.45), filled french bread (from £3.55), soup (£3.50), deep-fried brie with cranberry chutney (£4.95), bangers and mash (£5.95), steak and kidney pie (£6.95), chicken and pistachio korma with a tarragon sauce (£7.75), salmon, prawns and asparagus on puff pastry (£7.95), beef and mushrooms in stout with herb dumplings or pork loin with sage and cider sauce (£8.65), 8oz sirloin (£10.95), and roast duck breast with port and cranberry sauce (£13.95); tempting puddings include spotted dick, pancakes with vanilla ice cream and syrup or fresh berries and fruit in a chocolate shell (from £3.95 to £4.55); part of the restaurant is no smoking. The nooks and crannies of the beamed rambling rooms, warmed in winter by a log fire, are crowded with a delightful jumble of rustic implements like ploughshares, yokes, iron tools, cowbells, beer steins, as well as samovars, cut-glass, brass or black wrought-iron lamps, copper-bound casks and milk ewers, harness, horsebrasses, smith's bellows, and decorative plates and china ornaments. Well kept Adnams Regatta, Boddingtons, and Greene King IPA and Abbot on handpump; friendly, efficient staff; fruit machine. There are seats in the pretty garden. *(Recommended by Barry and Marie Males, Zoe Morrell, Andrew Anderson, David and Diana MacFadyen, Sidney and Erna Wells, Sarah Markham, M A Buchanan)*

Free house ~ Licensee Elizabeth Nicholls ~ Real ale ~ Bar food (till 10) ~ Restaurant ~ (01763) 838773 ~ Children in snug bar ~ Open 12-3, 6-11; 12-3, 7-10.30 Sun

HINXTON TL4945 Map 5
Red Lion

Between junctions 9 and 10, M11; just off A1301 S of Gt Shefford

Pretty pink-washed twin-gabled old building not far from Duxford Aeroplane Museum. The bar menu includes reasonably priced home-made soup (£2.95), avocado and prawns (£4.95), mushroom rogan josh or Thai green vegetable curry (£6.25), lamb moussaka or smoked chicken and spinach lasagne (£6.50), pork, sage and onion pie (£6.95), toulouse sausages on a sun-dried tomato risotto (£7.95), lemon sole with roasted pepper and lime butter (£8.95), 8oz sirloin (£9.95), venison steak with port and wild berry glaze (£10.95) and puddings like banoffi pie, crème caramel and mango and peach cheesecake (£2.95); decent range of coffee liqueurs too. Smartly laid, partly no-smoking restaurant. The dark mainly open-plan bustling bar is filled with mirrors and pictures, grandfather and grandmother clocks, and a chatty amazon parrot called George. Well kept Adnams, Greene King IPA, Woodfordes Wherry and a guest on handpump, and Adnams wines, as well as trivia, cribbage and unobtrusive piped classical music. There are picnic-sets and a pleasant terrace in the tidy and attractive garden (the magnolia's nice in spring). *(Recommended by Joy and Peter Heatherley, Ian Phillips, John Vale, Mr and Mrs R Head, Bernard and Marjorie Parkin, Paul & Sandra Embleton)*

Free house ~ Licensees Jim and Lynda Crawford ~ Real ale ~ Bar food ~ Restaurant ~ (01799) 530601 ~ Children over 10 only ~ Open 11-2.30, 6-11; 12-2.30, 7-10.30 Sun; closed evenings 25 and 26 Dec

HORNINGSEA TL4962 Map 5
Crown & Punchbowl

Just NE of Cambridge; first slip-road off A14 heading E after A10, then left at T; or via B1047 Fen Ditton road off A1303

In the same small group as the Red Lion at Icklingham, and sharing its civilised atmosphere, this spacious low-beamed pub is darkly cosy: mostly bare boards, with some striking dark blue paintwork detailing, and stylish in its sparing use of big prints and mirrors, simple black iron wall candles, a blue and white flag and big stag's head on cream walls. Good solid stripped pine tables are well spaced throughout the four or five open-plan rooms which work their way round the central counter – which has some stained glass, and interestingly, a pulpit at one end. There are two little conservatory areas, and seats in the back garden. You can just catch a glimpse of the River Cam from the end of the car park. Two or three well kept real ales might include Hobsons Choice, Marstons Pedigree or Theakstons XB; English country wines and Scrumpy Jack. Very well cooked changing bar food from a shortish but varied and interesting menu might include soup of the day (£3.25), black pudding with apple salad and balsamic dressing (£4.95), Newmarket sausages with mash and gravy (£5.75), gnocchi with sun-dried tomatoes, olives and chilli (£7.45), and pork steaks with cider and cheese sauce (£8.95), all served by enthusiastic and friendly young staff; they'll also do sandwiches. *(Recommended by J F M West, Maysie Thompson, Dr Andy Wilkinson, David and Mandy Allen)*

Free house ~ Licensees Jonathan Gates and Ian Hubbert ~ Real ale ~ Bar food (till 10pm) ~ (01223) 860643 ~ Children welcome ~ Open 12-3, 6-11(7-10.30 Sun) ~ Bedrooms: £43.50B/£70B

HUNTINGDON TL2371 Map 5
Old Bridge ★ 🍽 ♀ 🛏

1 High St; just off B1043 entering town from the easternmost A604 slip-road

Stylish and well run hotel tucked away in a good spot by the River Great Ouse, with its own landing stage, and tables on the well kept garden's waterside terraces. The civilised – even rather sophisticated – bar has a quietly chatty atmosphere, and has been refurbished to reveal old polished floorboards in front of the counter; there's a new carpet around the good log fire. The airy restaurant, murals giving a summery open-air feel, is no smoking. A creative menu changes monthly, and might include pea and mint soup (£3.75), caesar salad (£4.75), honey-roast quail (£5.95), outstanding carpaccio (£6.50), red onion and parmesan tart with caramelised apple salad (£8.75), baked cod with a gruyère and herb crust and tomato and celery stew (£9.95), pot roast breast of chicken with tarragon butter sauce (£10.95), calves' liver with black pudding, mashed potato, crisp pancetta and onion gravy (£12.75), and saffron-roasted monkfish with wilted rocket and linguini pasta (£14.50); there's also a nice choice of extra vegetables like bubble and squeak (£1.50-£1.75), and puddings like warm rhubarb, lemon and polenta tart, bread and butter pudding, and iced honey and lavender parfait (from £3.95); they do small helpings for children, an unlimited-choice lunchtime cold table (£10.95), and Sunday roast lunch (£11.95). There's an excellent wine list including a really fine choice by the glass, and alongside Adnams Best and City of Cambridge Hobsons Choice, there's an annual rotation of about 250 guest beers; freshly squeezed orange juice and good coffee, too; very good waitress service. *(Recommended by Stephen Brown, R C Wiles, Michael Sargent, Gordon Theaker, C Smith, John Fahy, Ian Phillips, Derek Harvey-Piper)*

Free house ~ Licensee Nick Steiger ~ Real ale ~ Restaurant ~ (01480) 452681 ~ Children welcome ~ Live entertainment first Fri of month ~ Open 11-11; 12-10.30 Sun ~ Bedrooms: £79.50B/£89.50B

KEYSTON TL0475 Map 5
Pheasant 🍽 ♀

Village loop road; from A604 SE of Thrapston, right on to B663

Cambridgeshire Dining Pub of the Year

One reader thinks the food at this thoroughly enjoyable and civilised pub is as good as at any top London restaurant. Part of the same small group as the Old Bridge above, this exquisitely well run establishment is the place to treat yourself to a good meal. The same innovative menu is on offer throughout the building, with linen napkins and bigger tables in the no-smoking Red Room. Changing dishes might include celeriac soup with sautéed wild mushrooms (£3.95), spinach and ricotta ravioli with sage butter (£4.95, main course £9.50), salad of chargrilled tuna fish with confit of peppers and a chilli pepper dressing (£5.95), wild boar sausages with mash potato and a dijon mustard and onion sauce (£7.95), fresh tagliatelle with sun-dried tomatoes, roast red peppers, parmesan cheese and olive oil (£8.95), fillet of lemon sole with broccoli and parsley butter (£9.50), chargrilled sirloin steak with green beans, Sicilian pesto and chips (£12.95) and brill with steamed spinach, morel mushrooms and a vermouth and shallot sauce (£13.95); smaller helpings for children; extra vegetables (£1.50-£1.95); Sunday roast sirloin of beef (£11.25). Irresistible puddings might include amaretto brûlée with an almond biscuit, tarte tatin with double jersey cream, hot caramel soufflé with prune and armagnac ice cream or mango, raspberry and pink grapefruit sorbets with fresh fruit and lime sauce (£3.95-£5.95). The exceptionally good wine list has an interesting choice of reasonably priced bottles – though to make the most of their list requires quite a deep pocket – with around 14 by the glass, plus sweet wines and ports; freshly squeezed juices like carrot, orange and ginger; also well kept Adnams Bitter and a changing guest such as Adnams Broadside, Fenland Doctors Orders or Nethergate Old Growler; efficient courteous service. A friendly low-beamed room has old photographs, leather-slung stools and a heavily carved wooden armchair; another room, with high rafters, used to be the village smithy – hence the heavy-horse harness and old horse-drawn harrow there. Wooden tables are set in front of the pub. *(Recommended by Bob and Maggie Atherton, Michael Sargent, G Neighbour, Jane Kingsbury, Sarah Markham, R Gorick, O K Smyth, R Wiles, J F M and M West, Gordon Theaker, Chris and Liane Miller, Rita Horridge, John Fahy)*

Free house ~ Licensees Martin Lee and John Hoskins ~ Real ale ~ Bar food (till 10) ~ Restaurant ~ (01832) 710241 ~ Children welcome ~ Open 12-2, 6-10; 12-2, 7-9.30 Sun; closed evening 25 Dec, morning 31 Dec, all day 1 Jan

KIRTLING TL6857 Map 5
Queens Head

Village signposted off B1063 Newmarket—Stradishall, though pub reached more quickly from Newmarket on the Saxon Street road

This charming 16th-c building in a peaceful spot is believed to have connections with Elizabeth I, whose portrait hangs in the entrance to the lower bar. A particularly splendid blackboard listing daily changing bar food follows the pattern of its long-established sister pub, the Beehive in Horringer (just over the border in Suffolk), and might include cream of asparagus soup (£3.75), chicken, bacon and avocado or Thai prawn sandwiches (£4.75-£6.50), wild mushroom risotto with crème fraîche (£4.50), smoked haddock kedgeree with curried sauce (£4.75), and main courses such as casserole of wild mushrooms and tomatoes on a bed of horseradish cream and rice (£7), seared chicken breast on a bed of spicy peppers (£8.95), medallions of pork on onion marmalade with melted brie (£9.50), seared beef fillet in red wine, tomato, tarragon and balsamic vinegar (£13), and fresh lobster (£18.95, half £11.95), puddings (all £3.75) might include hot chocolate and coconut muffin or summer fruit and almond tart; well kept Greene King IPA, Triumph, and a guest like Marstons Pedigree under light blanket pressure, and a decent wine list plus almost twenty separate wines by the glass; very friendly staff. A timber footbridge leads over a stream from the car park to the meadow beyond. *(Recommended by MDN, Ian Phillips, Dr Andy Wilkinson, G and R Barber)*

Free house ~ Licensee Stuart Hopkinson ~ Real ale ~ Bar food ~ Restaurant ~ (01638) 731737 ~ Children welcome ~ Open 12-2, 7-11; 12-3 Sun; closed Sun evenings

MADINGLEY TL3960 Map 5
Three Horseshoes 🍽 ♀

Off A1303 W of Cambridge

The combination of stylishly imaginative food, exceptional wine and unfailing friendly courteous service has established this civilised thatched white pub as a favourite place to dine in the Cambridge area. Readers appreciate the sense of space in the airy restaurant, and in the pleasantly relaxed bar with open fire, recently refurbished with bare floorboards and Wedgwood green walls, you can enjoy tasty appetisers such as a large bowl of salted almonds (£1.25). In summer it's nice to sit out on the lawn, surrounded by flowering shrubs, roses and trees. Particularly well prepared sophisticated food from a daily changing menu might include a soup of borlotti beans, barley and spring greens with new season's Tuscan olive oil (£3.95), wild rocket, dandelion, raddichio and herb salad with cherry tomatoes, feta, aubergine toasts, olives and basil aioli (£4.75), seared salmon fillet with green papaya salad and flavoured fish sauce (£5.50), chargrilled chicken breast with wasabi mashed potato, stir fry of shi-itake mushrooms, sugar snap and sesame and a black bean, chilli, ginger and coriander salsa (£9.75), roast pigeon with rosti potato, morel mushrooms, roast whole garlics, butter onions, asparagus and gewurztraminer sauce (£10.95), turbot with olive oil, braised peas, leeks and broad beans with mustard and chive sauce and crispy bacon (£13.95), chargrilled beef fillet with grilled herb polenta, lemon-roasted fennel, cherry tomatoes, tarragon and tamari mustards (£15.75); and puddings such as pannacotta with warm rhubarb compote flavoured with ginger, pressed chocolate cake with Vin Santo ice cream and toffee and brioche pudding with hot chocolate sauce and jersey cream (£4.50-£5.50). The outstanding wine list includes about 17 wines by the glass, sweet wines and ports; four well kept real ales on handpump might be Adnams Southwold, Batemans XXXB, Elgoods Cambridge, Everards Tiger, Fullers London Pride or Morlands Old Speckled Hen, Shepherd Neame Spitfire or Wadworths 6X. *(Recommended by John Saul, Michael Sargent, C Smith, J F M West, Mr and Mrs Staples, Colin Barnes, David and Diana MacFadyen, Prof Kenneth Surin, R H Davies, Dr Phil Putwain, Mrs D Ball, Garth & Janet Wheeler, Charles Bardswell, B N F and M Parkin, MDN, Maysie Thompson, David Atkinson, A J Bowen, R Wiles, M Jean-Bernard Brisset)*

Free house ~ Licensee Richard Stokes ~ Real ale ~ Bar food ~ Restaurant ~ (01954) 210221 ~ Children welcome ~ Open 11.30-2.30, 6-11; 12-2.30, 7-10.30 Sun

NEWTON TL4349 Map 5

Queens Head ★ ◀▮

2½ miles from M11 junction 11; A10 towards Royston, then left on to B1368

Basic unspoilt gem of a pub run by the same licensee for more than quarter of a century. The well worn friendly main bar has a low ceiling and crooked beams, bare wooden benches and seats built into the walls and bow windows, a curved high-backed settle on the yellow tiled floor, a loudly ticking clock, paintings on the cream walls, and a lovely big log fire. The little carpeted saloon is similar but cosier. Satisfying simple food is limited to a range of very good value sandwiches (£1.90-£2.30) including very good roast beef ones and excellent beef dripping on toast (£1.80), mugs of lovely home-made soup and filled baked potatoes (both £2.10); in the evening and on Sunday lunchtime they serve plates of excellent cold meat, smoked salmon, cheeses and pâté (£2.90-£4). Adnams Bitter, Broadside and Extra are tapped straight from the barrel, with Regatta in summer, Old Ale in winter and Tally Ho at Christmas; country wines, Crone's and Cassells ciders and fresh orange and organic apple juice. Darts in a no-smoking side room, with shove-ha'penny, table skittles, dominoes, cribbage, and nine men's morris. There are seats in front of the pub, with its vine trellis and unusually tall chimney, or you can sit on the village green. Belinda the goose who used to patrol the car park now sits stuffed in a glass case, but lives on in the pub sign, painted by the licensee's father and son.

(Recommended by M A Buchanan, M A and C R Starling, Peter and Christine Lea, Tony Beaulah, Dr Andy Wilkinson, Anthony Barnes, Michael Sargent, R C Wiles, Chris and Liane Miller, Ian and Liz Phillips, Bob and Maggie Atherton, Barry and Marie Males)

Free house ~ Licensees David and Juliet Short ~ Real ale ~ Bar food ~ (01223) 870436 ~ Well behaved children in games room ~ Occasional poetry readings and art exhibitions ~ Open 11.30-2.30, 6-11; 12-2.30, 7-10.30 Sun; closed 25 Dec

---

We accept no free drinks or payment for inclusion. We take no advertising, and are not sponsored by the brewing industry – or by anyone else. So all reports are independent.

PETERBOROUGH TL1999 Map 5

Brewery Tap ◖

Opposite Queensgate car park

This striking conversion of an old labour exchange is not the usual housing of a microbrewery and pub – it's American in style and said to be one of the largest in Europe. A huge glass wall on one side gives an almost clinical view of the white-coated brewers and massive copper-banded stainless brewing vessels that produce the Oakham beers. Stylized industrial décor is continued throughout its vast open-plan areas, with blue-painted iron pillars holding up a steel-corded mezzanine level, light wood and stone floors, and hugely enlarged and framed newspaper cuttings on its light orange walls. It's stylishly lit by a giant suspended steel ring with bulbs running around the rim, and steel-meshed wall lights. A band of chequered floor tiles traces the path of the long sculpted light wood bar counter which is boldly backed by an impressive display of uniform wine bottles in a ceiling-high wall of wooden cubes. Largely Thai and entirely oriental bar food includes tempura vegetables (£2.75), spring rolls or wan ton (£2.90), chicken satay sandwich or dim sum (£3.50), green, red or yellow curries (£4.50), roast duck curry cooked in coconut milk, red curry with pineapple, tomato and basil (£5.50), stir-fried beef with oyster sauce, red and green peppers, mushroom and spring onions (£4.50), stir-fried noodles with sweet radish, tamarind sauce, bean sprouts, sping onions, peanuts, chillies, egg and tiger prawns (£5.95), and very good set menus. Of the six Oakham beers produced here, there were three on when we visited – Bishops Farewell, Old Tosspot and JHB, which were served alongside three or four guests such as Bass, Dent and Fullers London Pride. The staff are young and friendly, and there's a surprisingly mixed clientele – we're told it gets very busy at night; loud well reproduced techno and pop. It's owned by the same people as Charters. *(Recommended by Richard Lewis, Ian Stafford)*

Free house ~ Licensee Andrew Dorward ~ Real ale ~ Bar food (till 10pm) ~ (01733) 358500 ~ No children ~ Open 12-11; 12-10.30 Sun; closed 25, 26 Dec and 1 Jan

Charters ◖ £

Town Bridge, S side

This friendly bustling real ale flagship is a remarkable conversion of a sturdy 1907 commercial Dutch barge. The well timbered sizeable bar is housed below decks in the cargo holds, and above deck a glazed no-smoking restaurant replaces the tarpaulins that used to cover the hold. Twelve handpumps serve six quickly changing microbrewery guests alongside well kept Bass, Everards Tiger, Fullers London Pride and beers from the owner's own microbrewery: JHB (good value at £1.50), Bishops Farewell and one of their seasonal ales; good value bar food includes filled french bread (from £1.75), cumberland sausage (£3.95), steak sandwich (£4.25), chilli, steak and ale pie, vegetable or traditional lasagne, mushroom stroganoff or battered cod (all £4.95), barbecues in summer; friendly staff; piped music. Landlubbers can opt for tables in one of the biggest pub gardens in the city, often overrun with rabbits. *(Recommended by Ian Phillips, Richard Lewis, Stephen and Julie Brown, JP, PP, Andy and Jill Kassube)*

Free house ~ Licensee Paul Hook ~ Real ale ~ Bar food (lunchtime) ~ Restaurant (evening) ~ (01733) 315700 ~ Children in restaurant ~ Open 12-11; closed 25 and 26 Dec, 1 Jan

SPALDWICK TL1372 Map 5

George

Just off A14 W of Huntingdon

There's a chatty local atmosphere in the red-carpeted bar of this useful homely village pub. A mix of understated comfortable seats is grouped cosily around little tables, each with a posy of flowers in a vase on a lace doilie, and a candle. There are black beams hung with pewter mugs, some nice little prints, and some not-so-green

house plants; piped pop. Well kept real ales include Adnams Broadside and Charles Wells Bombardier. Besides sandwiches, bar food includes soup (£2.50), chicken liver and brandy pâté with cumberland sauce (£3.50), ploughman's (£4.50), New Zealand mussels with garlic (£4.95), deep-fried brie with gooseberry preserve (£3.95), chicken curry or spaghetti bolognese (£6.25), steak and kidney pie (£6.50), spinach and goat's cheese canelloni, battered haddock or fish pie (£6.95), chicken breast cooked with garlic, herbs and sun-dried tomatoes and topped with Italian cheese (£7.95), roast duck (£8.50) and fried bass with Pernod sauce (£12.95).
(Recommended by David and Mary Webb, P A Reynolds, Dr and Mrs Brian Hamilton, Margaret and Roy Randle, Michael Sargent, D and M T Ayres-Regan)

Charles Wells ~ Tenant Mr Watson ~ Real ale ~ Bar food ~ Restaurant ~ (01480) 890293 ~ Children in eating area of bar ~ Open 12-3, 6-11; 7-10.30 Sun

STILTON TL1689 Map 5
Bell ♀ 🛏

High Street; village signposted from A1 S of Peterborough

Elegant 16th-c old stone coaching inn, where Dick Turpin is alleged to have hidden from the law for nine weeks. A fine coach-arch opens on to tables in a lovely sheltered courtyard which sites a well, supposedly dating back to Roman times. The two neatly kept friendly bars have sturdy upright wooden seats on flagstone floors, plush-cushioned button-back banquettes built around the walls, bow windows, big prints of sailing and winter coaching scenes on the partly stripped walls, and a large warm log fire in a handsome stone fireplace; a giant pair of blacksmith's bellows hangs in the middle of the front bar. Seasonal bar food in generous helpings might include stilton and broccoli soup (£2.95), mussels with chilli, tomatoes and fresh herbs (£4.25, main course £6.95), spinach and ricotta gnocchi with tomato and herbs (£4.50), cod in beer batter or mushroom, aubergine and goat's cheese flan with herb salad (£7.50), chicken stuffed with stilton and pear on colcannon potatoes, stilton sausages with mash, onion and gravy or smoked haddock rarebit on warm potato salad (£7.95), seared salmon fillet on roasted fennel and artichoke bottom or lamb shank with mashed potato and redcurrant jus (£8.50), and 10oz rib-eye steak (£10.95); extra vegetables (£1.50); home-made puddings such as pan-fried peaches with brandy and vanilla seeds topped with crème fraîche or pear and almond tart (£2.95) or stilton cheese with plum bread (£3.95). The eating area of the bar and part of the restaurant are no smoking. Well kept Greene King Abbot and Marstons Pedigree with over 100 guests a year including Dent Bitter, Iceni Fine Soft Day, Oakham Jeffrey Hudson or Wychwoods Special on handpump, and a good choice of wines by the glass; good friendly service; dominoes, backgammon, cribbage and Scrabble; attractive chintzy bedrooms. *(Recommended by Paul and Diane Edwards, John and Esther Sprinkle, Joy and Peter Heatherley, Ian Phillips, Kevin Thorpe, P Rome, Alan and Heather Jacques, S F Parrinder, Paul and Sandra Embleton)*

Free house ~ Licensee Liam McGivern ~ Real ale ~ Bar food ~ Restaurant ~ (01733) 241066 ~ Well behaved children at lunchtime ~ Open 12-2.30(3 Sat), 6-11; 12-3, 7-10.30 Sun; closed evening 25 Dec ~ Bedrooms: £51.50B/£66.50B

SUTTON GAULT TL4279 Map 5
Anchor ★ 🍽 ♀ 🛏

Village signed off B1381 in Sutton

Although many readers now feel this is more of a restaurant, the snug atmosphere and good choice of ales ensure that this well run riverside inn remains as popular as ever. The imaginative menu might include carrot and coriander soup (£3.85), chicken, liver and brandy pâté with toast (£4.85), tian of crab with oven-dried tomatoes and an avocado salsa (£5.95), warm salad of tabouleh with grilled vegetables (£9.50), chicken, leek and bacon crumble, or steak, kidney and Guinness pie (£10.95), grilled salmon fillet with a lemon grass, ginger and chilli butter (£11.95), pan-fried breast of guinea fowl with puy lentils (£12.95), duck breast with a celeriac remoulade and red wine sauce (£13.50), venison steak with creamed spinach and sloe sauce (£14.95), puddings like steamed jam pudding and custard, nutty meringue with red fruits and cream or bread and butter pudding with honey and whiskey cream (£4.25), jersey ice creams (£3.95) and a particularly good changing British cheeseboard (£4.25). From Monday to Friday lunchtimes (not bank holidays), there's a very good value two-course menu (£7.50), and children can have most of their dishes in smaller helpings. On Sundays, if you arrive by 12pm and leave by 1.15pm, you can have two courses and a coffee from the three-course lunch menu (£15.50) for £8.95. There's a thoughtful wine list (including a wine of the month and 10 by the glass), winter mulled wine, freshly squeezed fruit juice. Well kept City of Cambridge Hobsons Choice, Elgoods Cambridge, Mauldons Bitter, Nethergate IPA, and Wolf Bitter tapped from the cask. Very friendly staff help to maintain a cosy intimate atmosphere in the four heavily timbered stylishly simple rooms, with three log fires, lighting by gas and candles, antique settles and well spaced scrubbed pine tables on the gently undulating old floors, and good lithographs and big prints on the walls; three quarters of the pub are now no smoking. In summer you can sit outside at the tables or watch the swans and house martins from the bank of the Old Bedford River; the river bank walks are lovely. No dogs. *(Recommended by R F Ballinger, M J Brooks, Steve and Sarah Pleasance, Gordon Theaker, Ian and Jane Irving, R C Wiles, A J Bowen, Joe and Mary Stachura, Michael Sargent, Betty Petheram, Anthony Barnes, Keith and Janet Morris, K F Mould, Gwen and Peter Andrews, NMF, DF, James Nunns, Ian Phillips, Pat and Tony Hinkins, Mrs C Archer, Anthony Longden, Ken and Jenny Simmonds, Malcolm Clydesdale, Chris Miller, Simon Reynolds, Mr and Mrs A Brooks)*

Free house ~ Licensee Robin Moore ~ Real ale ~ Bar food ~ (01353) 778537 ~ Children in eating area of bar till 8.30pm ~ Open 12-3, 7(6.30 Sat)-11; 12-3, 7-10.30 Sun; closed 26 Dec ~ Bedrooms: £50B/£62.50

SWAVESEY TL3668 Map 5
Trinity Foot

A14 eastbound, NW of Cambridge; from westbound carriageway take Swavesey, Fen Drayton turn

Prices have stayed more or less the same at this bustling pub, where an incredible range of fresh fish is delivered daily from the East Coast ports. Depending on the day's catch, there might be herring fillets in dill or soft herring roe on toast (£3.95), 6 oysters (£5), very good grilled mackerel, rock eel, haddock or cod (all £7.50), grilled skate wings (£8.25), fillet of plaice (£8.50), grilled lemon sole or tuna steak with garlic butter (£9.75), monkfish with cream and white wine sauce (£9.75), and fresh lobster (£13-£18.50); also, sandwiches (from £1.25), soup (£2.50), ploughman's (£4.25), omelettes (£6), mixed grill (£9.75), and generously served daily specials like cauliflower cheese with walnut or home-made beefburger and chips (£6.50), and grilled pork chops (£7.50); puddings (£3). Well kept Boddingtons and Flowers under light blanket pressure, decent wines, and freshly squeezed fruit juice. Service is cheerfully efficient, and there are well spaced tables, fresh flowers, and a light and airy flower-filled conservatory; no-smoking dining room. There are shrubs and trees in the big enclosed garden. The pub owns a fresh fish shop next door (open Tuesday-Fri 11-2.30, 6-7.30, Sat 11-2.30). *(Recommended by Gordon Theaker, Ian Phillips, Anthony Barnes, Mike and Mary Carter, P and D Carpenter, Ian Crichton, Jane Kingsbury, C J Darwent, Nigel Thompson, Michael Hyde)*

Whitbreads ~ Lease: H J Mole ~ Real ale ~ Bar food (till 10 Fri and Sat, 12-1.30 Sun) ~ Restaurant ~ (01954) 230315 ~ Children welcome ~ Open 11-3, 6-11; 12-3 Sun; closed Sun evenings

THRIPLOW TL4346 Map 5
Green Man ◖

3 miles from M11 junction 10; A505 towards Royston, then first right; Lower Street

The gregarious landlord of this welcoming Victorian pub, an ex-classical conductor, has amassed an incredible collection of curios. You can easily spend a happy half hour gazing at the bric-a-brac: teddy bears jostle on shelves with pewter mugs, decorated china, old scales and illustrated boy's annuals, while attractive dried flowers, hop bines and copper kettles lend a rustic theme. Equally striking is the blend of colours from the ochre ceiling to the green vertical planked panelling with a darker green Anaglypta wallpaper. The flowery red-carpeted bar rambles round a servery, and has a good mix of furniture, mostly sturdy stripped tables and attractive high-backed dining chairs and pews; there are unusual old Broads posters and comfortable armchairs and settees in the Memorial Lounge, a pleasantly cosy little place to congregate at the end of the bar on the right (unfortunately a little spoilt by a big fruit machine). Two arches lead through to a no-smoking dining area on the left, with red walls, a couple of old brocaded seats, lots more bric-a-brac and a mix of candlesticks on the tables. Simple bar food in big helpings includes soup (£3), hearty sandwiches and filled baguettes (from £3.25), ploughman's (£4), chilli con carne (£4.50), scampi (£6.90), steak, kidney and Guinness pie (£7.90) and 8oz rib-eye steak (£10.90), with good puddings (£3); there's a more elaborate evening menu. Well kept Timothy Taylors Landlord and four interesting changing guests such as Buckleys St Davids, Skinners Coastliner, Smiles Best and York Brewery Yorkshire Terrier; piped classical music. There are picnic-sets on the terrace, and globe lights throughout the newly landscaped garden, likely to be very attractive once it's matured. Very handy for Duxford. *(Recommended by M A C Rutherford)*

Free house ~ Licensee Roger Ward ~ Real ale ~ Bar food ~ (01763) 208855 ~ Well behaved children ~ Open 12-2.30, 6-11; 12-2.30, 7-10.30 Sun; closed Tues

WANSFORD TL0799 Map 5
Haycock ★ ♀ 🖃

Village clearly signposted from A1 W of Peterborough

Famous old coaching inn with very pleasant staff and handsome architecture. The fine flagstoned main entry hall has antique hunting prints, seats and a longcase clock. This leads into the panelled main bar with its dark terracotta walls, sturdy rail above a mulberry dado, and old settles. Through two comely stone arches is another attractive area, while the comfortable front sitting room has some squared oak panelling by the bar counter, a nice wall clock, and a big log fire. The airy stripped brick Orchard room by the garden has dark blue and light blue basketweave chairs around glass-topped basket tables, pretty flowery curtains and nice modern prints; doors open on to a big sheltered terrace with lots of tables and cream Italian umbrellas; piped music. As well as a very good range of around 11 well chosen house wines by the glass, there's an exceptional wine list, properly mature vintage ports by the glass and well kept Adnams Southwold, Bass, Ruddles Best, and a guest like Morlands Old Speckled Hen on handpump. They only serve ciabatta or bread sandwiches in the bar (£4.25), but you can have a full meal in the Orchard room: soup (£3.50), goose pâté (£5.75), seafood salad (£7.25), warm dolcellate, tomato and chive tart (£7.95), lamb and mint sausages with a whole-grain mustard and tomato coulis (£8.25), baked fillet of cod topped with a mozzarella and herb brioche crust and a lime and tarragon butter (£9.75), 8oz sirloin (£12.95). The spacious walled formal garden has boules and fishing as well as cricket (they have their own field). The restaurant is no smoking. *(Recommended by Heather Martin, James Curran, G Neighbour, Paul and Sandra Embleton, R C Wiles)*

Free house ~ Licensees Simon Morpuss and Louise Dunning ~ Real ale ~ Bar food (till 9.45) ~ Restaurant ~ (01780) 782223 ~ Children away from bar ~ Open 11-11; 12-10.30 Sun ~ Bedrooms: £75B/£95

Post Office address codings confusingly give the impression that some pubs are in Cambridgeshire, when they're really in the Leicestershire or Midlands groups of counties (which is where we list them).

Lucky Dip

Besides the fully inspected pubs, you might like to try these Lucky Dips recommended to us and described by readers (if you do, please send us reports):

Alconbury [TL1776]
White Hart [2 Vinegar Hill, Alconbury Weston; handy for A1, nr A14/M11 turn-offs]: Friendly and comfortable respite from trunk roads, spotlessly and extensively refurbished with plush dining room; good value generous food inc home-made chips, Courage-related beers and local Dons Dilemma, back bar with darts, very helpful licensees; charming village, ducks on stream *(Michael and Jenny Back)*

Babraham [TL5150]
George [just off A1307]: Beams and timbers, old pictures and artefacts, good imaginative food (not cheap) in bar and restaurant inc pudding club, well kept Greene King and unusual guest beers, no-smoking area, friendly efficient; staff; very quiet piped music; tables on front grass, attractive setting *(P and D Carpenter, Keith and Janet Morris)*

Barrington [ST3818]
☆ *Royal Oak* [from M11 junction 11 take A10 to Newton, turn right]: Rambling thatched Tudor pub with tables out overlooking charming village green, heavy low beams and timbers, lots of character, pleasant no-smoking dining conservatory, well kept Adnams, Courage Best and Directors and Greene King IPA, prompt service, food inc wide vegetarian range and good pasta; maybe piped music, children in one area *(T J Smith, LYM, James Nunns)*

Brampton [TL2170]
☆ *Olde Mill* [signed off A141 Huntingdon Rd opp Hinchingbrooke House]: Popular riverside Beefeater, idyllic summer setting – converted mill surrounded by water, with working wheel and mill race rushing under lounge's glass 'tables', fishy memorabilia, usual good value bar food inc nicely garnished sandwiches, upper restaurant, Whitbreads-related ales, quick pleasant service, tables out by water *(Charles and Pauline Stride, George Atkinson)*

Buckden [TL1967]
☆ *Lion*: Lovely partly 15th-c coaching inn, oak beams and carvings in small comfortable bar, good well presented food inc lots of fresh veg, attentive staff, roaring fire, good choice of wines, John Smiths and Ruddles on electric pump, no music or machines; bedrooms *(M R Lewis, Gordon Theaker, George Atkinson)*

Burrough Green [TL6355]
Bull [B1061 Newmarket—Sturmer]: Attractive pub with friendly landlord, well kept Greene King, interesting farm tools behind nice woodburner, separate dining area *(Gwen and Peter Andrews)*

Burwell [TL5866]
Anchor: Old-fashioned bar, dining area with wide choice inc vegetarian from soup and soda bread to poached salmon and seaweed, affable Irish landlord, good service; games room with big-screen sports TV, garden backing on to small river; handy for nearby camp site *(Mark Davenport)*

Cambridge [TL4658]
Bun Shop: Atmospheric studenty pub, popular food, Boddingtons and Marstons Pedigree *(Anthony Barnes)*
☆ *Castle*: Large, airy and well appointed, with full Adnams range kept well and guests such as Wadworths Farmers Glory, good value quickly served food inc burgers and vegetarian, no-smoking area with easy chairs upstairs, friendly staff; maybe piped pop music; picnic-sets in good garden *(Robert Gomme, Ian Hydes, Keith and Janet Morris)*
Champion of the Thames: Basic small and cosy local with welcoming atmosphere, wonderfully decorated windows, padded walls and seats, painted Anaglypta ceiling, lots of woodwork, no music, well kept Greene King IPA and Abbot *(Keith and Janet Morris, John Fahy)*
Clarendon Arms: Quaint partly flagstoned local with well kept Greene King and Rayments, friendly staff, wide choice of cheap but adventurous bar lunches inc giant crusty sandwiches; open all day; bedrooms simple but clean and comfortable *(G Coates)*
Flying Pig: Original small pub with great mix of people inc solicitors, journalists, students and locals, pig emblems everywhere, good variety of beers inc Bass, Boddingtons, Greene King Abbot and Wadworths 6X, young friendly staff, daily papers, piped music from great American blues to customers' occasionally very amateur tapes *(Shaun Noble)*
☆ *Mill*: Sturdily attractive bare-boards alehouse décor, eight changing ales inc Adnams and Nethergate Old Growler, farm ciders, country wines, simple lunchtime bar food from sandwiches up, fruit machine, piped pop; children in eating area, open all day; overlooks mill pond where punts can be hired, very popular waterside garden *(John Wooll, Bill & Margaret Rogers, Robert Lester)*
Mitre [opp St Johns Coll]: Dark and dim back-to-basics alehouse décor, friendly attentive service, good range of real ales, well priced wines, generous good value food from fine sandwiches and hot beef baps up, no-smoking area, log-effect fire *(Keith and Janet Morris, SLR, MLR)*

Chittering [TL4970]
Travellers Rest [A10]: Roomy open-plan roadside pub done up in comfortable chain-pub style, all very neat and clean, good generous straightforward food (real chips), well kept ales such as Greene King IPA and Marstons Pedigree, friendly efficient service, easy wheelchair access at back; piped music; children in family area, picnic-sets among fruit trees behind, camp site *(Michael and Jenny Back, BB)*

Coton [TL4058]
John Barleycorn: Cheerfully unpretentious local atmosphere, well kept sensibly priced Greene King IPA and Abbot, good food; garden with play area *(Mr and Mrs Staples)*

Dry Drayton [TL3862]

☆ *Black Horse* [signed off A428 (was A45) W of Cambridge; Park St, opp church]: Pleasant village local with very generous food inc wide vegetarian choice, well kept Greene King and other ales inc weekly changing guests, friendly prompt service, welcoming fire in central fireplace, games area, tables on pretty back terrace and neat lawn; camping/caravanning in meadow behind, maybe geese at end of car park *(BB, Keith and Janet Morris, E Robinson, R M Corlett)*

Duxford [TL4745]

☆ *John Barleycorn* [Moorfield Rd; village signed off A1301, pub at far end]: Thatched and shuttered early 17th-c cottage now open all day for food; tables out among flowers, softly lit relaxed bar with old prints, decorative plates and so forth, Greene King IPA and Abbot and a guest such as Bass, Mansfield Old Baily or Marstons Pedigree, decent wines; after successive recent management changes we'd like more reports, please *(M L Porter, LYM, M A Buchanan)*

Elm [TF4706]

Blacksmiths Arms [A1101]: Well kept Greene King beers, good value home-made food inc nice choice of generous puddings, friendly efficient service; tables outside *(R C Vincent)*

Eltisley [TL2659]

☆ *Leeds Arms* [signed off A428]: Knocked-through beamed bar overlooking peaceful village green, huge log fire, very friendly staff, plenty of dining tables, substantial usual food inc nicely presented sandwiches, well kept Greene King IPA and Hook Norton Best, Stowford Press cider, no-smoking restaurant; children in eating area, pleasant garden with play area; simple comfortable bedrooms in separate block *(AB, LYM, Keith and Janet Morris, Phil & Heidi Cook)*

Elton [TL0893]

☆ *Crown*: Carefully rebuilt old stone pub with interesting bar, well kept beers inc Greene King IPA and Marstons Pedigree, above-average varied food in bar, large dining conservatory and upstairs restaurant; opp green in beautiful small village *(Gordon Theaker)*

Ely [TL5380]

☆ *Cutter* [off A10 on outskirts]: Lovely riverside setting, with plenty of tables outside and a genuine welcome for children; friendly series of unpretentious bars, generous attractively priced food, Courage Directors, Greene King IPA, John Smiths and Morlands Old Speckled Hen, good house wines; piped music can be obtrusive; best to book Fri/Sat in boating season *(Frank Davidson, LYM, Michael and Jenny Back, Tim Smith)*

Etton [TF1406]

☆ *Golden Pheasant* [just off B1443 N of Peterborough, signed from nr N end of A15 bypass]: Looks like the 19th-c private house it once was, with strong local following for consistently well kept ales usually inc Adnams Broadside, Batemans XXXB, Cottage Goldrush, Greene King IPA, Kelham Island Pale Rider, Timothy Taylor Landlord and six weekly guests; homely plush bar, airy glass-walled no-smoking side room (children allowed here), tasty food in bar and restaurant, pub games; well reproduced piped music, friendly dogs; good-sized garden with soccer pitch, floodlit boules pitch, interesting aviary, adventure playground and marquee; bedrooms, open all day at least in summer *(John Fahy, BB, John C Baker)*

Fordham [TL6270]

☆ *White Pheasant*: Good choice of good food in well converted fresh-feeling dining pub (same management as Red Lion at Icklingham – Suffolk main entry – and Crown & Punchbowl at Horningsea), friendly helpful service, well kept beers, good wines, log fire, nice mix of mismatched furniture inc big farmhouse tables, rugs on bare boards, cheery log fire, Courage Directors, Morlands Old Speckled Hen and Theakstons Best, helpful service, maybe piped light jazz; opens noon *(Nicholas Law, BB, Bob and Maggie Atherton, J F M West)*

Glinton [TF1505]

Blue Bell [B1443 opp church]: Big rambling clean and tidy Greene King pub, lots of nooks and crannies, log fire; fairly priced bar food very popular with families w/e, extensive back garden with play area and plenty of room for children to run around *(Nick & Alison Dowson)*

Godmanchester [TL2470]

☆ *Black Bull* [signed off A14 (was A604) just E of Huntingdon]: Interesting heavily beamed old pub by church, big inglenook with roaring log fire, settles forming booths by leaded-light windows, glinting brassware, side room with lots of black rustic ironwork, no-smoking dining room, big courtyard, pretty garden; has been a popular main entry, well run and lively, with courteous staff, good value food and well kept Black Bull (brewed for the pub locally), Boddingtons, Flowers Original and Wadworths 6X under light blanket pressure; as we went to press a change of management and possibly of ownership was going ahead – reports on new regime please *(Charles and Pauline Stride, Howard and Sue Gascoyne, A J Bowen, Anthony Barnes, Mark O'Hanlon, LYM, Ian Phillips, Mrs P Forrest)*

Grantchester [TL4455]

Red Lion: Busy food pub, comfortable and spacious, with sheltered terrace and good-sized lawn (with animals to entertain the many children), Greene King IPA and Abbot *(LYM, Prof Kenneth Surin)*

Great Chishill [TL4239]

☆ *Pheasant* [follow Heydon signpost from B1039 in village]: Beamed split-level flagstoned and timbered bar with some elaborately carved though modern seats and settles, good choice of bar food, real ales such as Adnams, Courage Best and Directors and Theakstons, decent wine list, darts, cribbage, dominoes; piped music; children welcome, charming back garden with small play area *(LYM, Dave Braisted, M R D Foot, Mr and Mrs C Crichton, Enid and Henry Stephens)*

Hardwick [TL1968]

☆ *Blue Lion* [signed off A428 (was A45) W of Cambridge]: Enjoyably friendly local with lots of beams, open fire and woodburner, fairly priced good food from lunchtime sandwiches and baguettes to fresh Whitby fish (good value fish and chips Mon night), very extensive restaurant area (evening booking recommended), well kept Greene King IPA and Abbot tapped from the cask, old farm tools, two cats, conservatory; piped music; pretty roadside front garden, handy for Wimpole Way walkers *(Garth & Janet Wheeler, BB, Michael Sargent)*

Harston [TL4251]

Three Horseshoes [A10, nr M11 junction 11]: Friendly Greene King pub with well kept ales and wide choice of very reasonably priced lunchtime food inc children's; very quick service, large well kept garden with old apple trees and lots of play equipment *(R C Vincent)*

Hemingford Grey [TL2970]

Cock: Comfortable country pub, roomier than it looks from outside, with enjoyable well presented food, well kept Benskins, Shipstons and Tetleys, quick friendly service *(Peter and Anne Hollindale)*

Hildersham [TL5448]

Pear Tree [off A1307 N of Linton]: Busy straightforward village local with odd crazy-paved floor, generous genuine home cooking inc home-baked bread, vegetarian dishes, children's helpings; cheerful service, well kept Greene King IPA and Abbot, daily papers, board games, tables outside; children welcome *(BB)*

Histon [TL4363]

Red Lion: Popular local with basic public bar, comfortably well used lounge, real ales such as Benskins Best, Greene King, Marstons Pedigree and Morlands Old Speckled Hen (occasional beer festivals), good value pub food, friendly staff; big garden *(Keith and Janet Morris)*

Holywell [TL3370]

☆ *Old Ferry Boat* [signed off A1123]: Roomy old thatched low-beamed inn, now owned by Greene King, charmingly set with tables and cocktail parasols on front terrace and neat rose lawn by the Great Ouse; window seats overlook the river, with several open fires and some other hints of antiquity, real ales such as Greene King Abbot, Fullers London Pride, Marstons Pedigree, Morlands Old Speckled Hen and Timothy Taylor Landlord, food from sandwiches to full meals (all day in summer), pleasant service, good no-smoking areas; open all day w/e, can get very busy; children welcome, moorings, bedrooms *(M A Buchanan, Michael and Jenny Back, Ian Phillips, Mr & Mrs M Ashton, E Robinson, Paul and Pam Penrose, LYM, Ian Crichton)*

Horningsea [TL4962]

☆ *Plough & Fleece* [just NE of Cambridge: first slip-road off A14 heading E after A10, then left; or B1047 Fen Ditton road off A1303]: Rambling country pub, low black beams, comfortably worn high-backed settles and other sturdily old-fashioned wooden furnishings, dark cool recesses in summer, log fires in winter, more modern no-smoking back dining room and conservatory, generally enjoyable food and good service, well kept Greene King IPA and Abbot on handpump; dominoes and cribbage; garden with nice mix of wild and cultivated flowers; can be busy lunchtime, handy for Cambridge Science Park; cl Mon evening *(Mark J Hydes, M A Buchanan, Ian*

Phillips, Maysie Thompson, Sarah Markham, J F M West, Keith and Janet Morris, R C Morgan, LYM)

Houghton [TL2872]

Jolly Butchers: Beams and brasses, quiet family atmosphere, food inc good cheap generous specials and Sun lunches, well kept Greene King, Morlands Old Speckled Hen, Ruddles County and John Smiths, extensive gardens, play area and occasional barbecues; river moorings *(Rev John Hibberd)*

Huntingdon [TL2371]

Market Inn: Central town pub with pleasant service, well kept Ruddles Best, good well priced bar menu *(R T and J C Moggridge)*

Kimbolton [TL0968]

White Horse: Very hospitable olde-worlde beamed two-bar pub with log fire as well as central heating, attentive chatty landlord, good food from bar snacks to full restaurant meals inc three Sun roasts; nice small garden with sunny terrace, conservation village *(George Atkinson, Patrick and Melvynne Johnson)*

Linton [TL5646]

Crown: Friendly and well run village pub, good bar food, sizeable restaurant, well kept beers, decent wines *(M L Porter)*

Longstowe [TL3153]

Golden Miller: Well kept Adnams Bitter and Broadside and Hobsons Choice, wide range of generous reasonably priced well cooked food *(C M York)*

March [TL4195]

Plate & Porter: Pub/restaurant with good food and decent house wine; reasonable prices *(M J Brooks)*

Rose & Crown: Recently refurbished, with John Smiths, Tetleys and five well kept guest beers, very wide choice of whiskies, farm cider, basket meals Weds-Sun, no-smoking room *(F J Robinson, E Robinson)*

Needingworth [TL3472]

☆ *Pike & Eel* [pub signed from A1123]: Marvellous peaceful riverside location, with spacious lawns and marina; two separate eating areas, one a carvery, in extensively glass-walled block overlooking water, boats and swans; easy chairs, settees and big open fire in room off separate rather hotelish plush bar, well kept Adnams, Bass, and Greene King Abbot, good coffee, friendly and helpful staff, provision for children; clean simple bedrooms, good breakfasts *(LYM, D E Twitchett, Gordon Theaker)*

Odsey [TL2938]

Jester [A505 NE of Baldock, by Ashwell & Morden stn]: Attractive, roomy and comfortable open-plan pub with open fire, wide food choice from sandwiches and snacks to generous well prepared main dishes, friendly licensees, three real ales, large dining room, pleasant conservatory leading to well kept garden; rural spot by railway *(Sidney and Erna Wells)*

Perry [TL1467]

Wheatsheaf [nr Grafham Water sailing club]: Clean and pleasant, with good wide food choice, polite welcoming staff, plenty of tables in pleasant garden; bedrooms *(D J Nash)*

Peterborough [TL1999]

College Arms: Large open-plan recent Wetherspoons conversion with well kept real ales such as Courage Directors, Fullers London Pride, Marstons Pedigree and Nethergate Priory Mild, good value varied food inc bargains, friendly helpful staff, comfortable seating inc side alcoves and no-smoking areas; open all day *(John Wooll, Richard Lewis)*

Old Monk: Long and roomy relaxed open plan Wetherspoons pub on edge of the shopping area, nicely decorated, lots of comfortable seating inc cosy snugs on left, no-smoking areas, good steady cheap food, friendly staff, well kept ales such as Courage Directors, Fullers London Pride, Nethergate Golden Gate, Shepherd Neame Spitfire, Theakstons Best; open all day *(Richard Lewis, Ian Stafford)*

Palmerston Arms: Up to 12 well kept real ales, even organic lager (no gas!), tapped from the cask; no juke box or machines *(Mick Parr)*

Ramsey Forty Foot [TL3087]

George [B1096 NE of Ramsey]: Friendly softly lit beamed local, Grainstore Cooking and 1050 as well as more usual beers *(J and M Back)*

Ramsey St Marys [TL2588]

Lion [B1040 towards Whittlesey]: Attractive ivy-clad pub, real ales such as Butcombe, Ruddles County and Charles Wells Bombardier, food lunchtime and evening (all day weekends), helpful staff, lots of whisky-water jugs, small fish tank, nice restaurant, games room with pool etc; piped music; well kept garden with picnic-sets and play area *(JJW, CMW, Michael and Jenny Back)*

Shepreth [TL3947]

☆ *Plough* [just off A10 S of Cambridge]: Neatly kept bright and airy local, unfailingly welcoming, with popular well presented home-cooked food from excellent sandwiches and good home-made soup up, changing well kept ales such as Adnams, Greene King IPA, Tetleys and Wadworths 6X, decent wines, modern furnishings, family room, popular side dining room, piped music; well tended back garden with fairy-lit arbour and pond, summer barbecues and play area *(Catherine and Richard Preston, BB, Mrs S E Griffiths)*

Six Mile Bottom [TL5756]

Green Man [A1304 SW of Newmarket]: Very generous good reasonably priced food, good variety and frequent changes; polite staff, well kept ales such as Adnams, Thatchers and Theakstons *(K A Swatman, Roger Everett)*

Stapleford [TL4651]

Longbow: Welcoming bright local, comfortable and roomy, with pleasant staff, good wholesome sensibly priced food inc vegetarian and unusual specials, well kept ales such as Adnams, Buffys IPA, Courage Directors, Fenland and Theakstons, well chosen reasonably priced wines; pool table, some live music *(Keith and Janet Morris)*

Stow Cum Quy [TL5260]

White Swan [B1102]: Comfortable and cosy village pub, good value generous unusual food inc vegetarian cooked to order so may be a wait, no-smoking dining room with fresh flowers, four or five well kept real ales inc Adnams and Courage Directors; picnic-sets in garden, cl Mon *(P and D Carpenter, Dr Andy Wilkinson, Keith and Janet Morris)*

Stretham [TL5072]

☆ *Lazy Otter* [Elford Closes, off A10 S of Stretham roundabout]: Big rambling nicely furnished family pub in fine spot on the Great Ouse, with good views from waterside conservatory and tables in big garden with neat terrace; generous food inc good value children's meals, warm fire in bar, well kept Greene King IPA and Abbot and a guest such as Granny Wouldn't Like It, friendly attentive staff; piped music, can get busy w/e; open all day *(Hilary Edwards, Ted George, LYM, James Nunns, Raymond Hebson)*

Swaffham Prior [TL5764]

☆ *Red Lion* [B1102 NE of Cambridge]: Welcoming and attractive local in pleasant village, well kept Greene King ales, wide range of generous fresh food from sandwiches and baked potatoes to steaks, comfortably divided dining area, quick cheerful service; unusually plush gents' *(Dr Andy Wilkinson, Maysie Thompson)*

Trumpington [TL4454]

☆ *Coach & Horses* [A1309]: Roomy and tastefully restored, with simple but good fairly priced food from sandwiches to well presented meals, well kept beers, dining area, open fire, helpful friendly young staff, no piped music *(P and D Carpenter, T J Smith)*

Wansford [TL0799]

Cross Keys: Pleasant open-plan bar around central fireplace, generous food, Charles Wells Eagle and Bombardier, friendly licensees *(H Frank Smith)*

Waresley [TL2454]

Duncombe Arms [B1040, 5 miles S of A428]: Comfortable and welcoming old pub, long main bar, fire one end, good range of generous reasonably priced food inc imaginative main dishes, consistently well kept Greene King ales, good service, restaurant; picnic-sets in garden *(D H Heath, Rev John Hibberd)*

Wisbech [TF4609]

☆ *Red Lion*: Hospitable and civilised long front bar in lovely Georgian terrace on River Nene, closest Elgoods pub to the brewery with their beer kept well, decent wines, good range of good value home-cooked food inc interesting sandwiches, vegetarian and fish choice, Fri bargain salad bar; nr centre and NT Peckover House, very popular lunchtime *(K H Frostick, Frank Davidson, Sue and Bob Ward)*

Wooddition [TL6659]

☆ *Three Blackbirds* [village signed off B1063 at Cheveley]: A new tenant took over too late in 1999 for us to rate this pretty thatched two-bar village pub, which has till now been a popular main entry, with its old-fashioned furnishings on flagstone floors; he's doing some interesting food inc enterprising vegetarian dishes (as well as lunchtime sandwiches), with Adnams Broadside, Greene King IPA and Abbot, and quite a few malt whiskies; children welcome, pretty garden; cl first Tues of month; reports on the new regime please *(JG, Steve & Sue Griffiths, Steve Goodchild, Ian Phillips, David Shillitoe, LYM)*

Cheshire

Four interesting new entries here this year are the picturesque old Thatch at Faddiley, the traditional small-roomed and properly pubby Olde Park Gate at Over Peover, the extensively refurbished – and extensive – Windmill at Whiteley Green, and the beautifully sited Boot at Willington Corner. All these have enjoyable food; and all have that trademark of good Cheshire pubs – a genuinely welcoming atmosphere. Other pubs doing particularly well here these days are the stylish and civilised Grosvenor Arms at Aldford (provision for children now), the Bhurtpore at Aston (gaining a Star Award this year for its excellent combination of interesting well kept beers with good food, in interesting pubby surroundings), the Cholmondeley Arms near Bickley Moss (emphasis on imaginative food), the Dysart Arms at Bunbury (another imaginatively comtemporary dining pub), the fascinating Albion in Chester, the carefully run Dog at Peover Heath (earning a Stay Award for its comfortable new bedrooms), and the friendly and relaxed Boot & Slipper at Wettenhall. From among these, it's the Dysart Arms at Bunbury which this year gains the title of Cheshire Dining Pub of the Year. If it's a bargain you're after, it's well worth considering the timeless old White Lion at Barthomley, with its cheap daily roasts; and on the drinks side, the Olde Park Gate at Over Peover scores with its very attractively priced Sam Smiths beer. Interestingly, in our drinks price survey we found that two of the free houses had dropped their beer prices this year, while half the others had at least held their prices with no increase. By contrast, all but one of the pubs tied to a brewery or chain had increased their prices, often by about 10p a pint. The Lucky Dip section at the end of the chapter is full of engaging places. Among them, we'd particularly pick out the Blue Bell at Bell o' th' Hill, Boot, Falcon and Old Custom House in Chester, Badger at Church Minshull (particularly promising food here), Alvanley Arms at Cotebrook, Ring o' Bells at Daresbury, George & Dragon at Great Budworth, Swan With Two Nicks at Little Bollington, Lamb and Red Cow in Nantwich, Highwayman at Rainow, Bulls Head at Smallwood, Swettenham Arms at Swettenham, Swan in Tarporley and Swan at Wybunbury. As we have inspected almost all of these, we can firmly recommend them.

ALDFORD SJ4259 Map 7
Grosvenor Arms ★ 🍴 ♀ 🍺
B5130 Chester—Wrexham

Traditional decor at this well converted bustling pub is cleverly combined with a spacious open-plan layout; the best room is probably the huge panelled library with floor-to-ceiling book shelves along one wall. Buzzing with conversation, this also has long wooden floor boards, lots of well spaced substantial tables, and quite a cosmopolitan feel. Several quieter areas are well furnished with good individual pieces including a very comfortable parliamentary type leather settle. Throughout there are plenty of interesting pictures, and the lighting's exemplary. The airy terracotta-floored conservatory has lots of huge low hanging flowering baskets and chunky pale wood garden furniture, and opens on to a large elegant suntrap terrace and neat lawn with picnic-sets, young trees and a tractor. A very good range of drinks at the good solid bar counter includes well kept Batemans XB, Flowers IPA and a couple of more unusual beers on handpump, 40 malt whiskies, and each of the remarkable collection of wines – largely New World – served by the glass. The menu changes every day, but might include starters like home-made soup (£3.25), roasted pork belly marinated in Chinese spices on noodles with black bean sauce (£4.45), pan-fried lamb's kidneys in a warm pastry case with a grain mustard and tarragon sauce (£4.25), and main courses such as toasted open sandwich with avocado, and marinated warmed chicken or large tortilla with guacamole (£5.95), lasagne (£6.95), chicken breast marinated in grenadine, fresh chillies and lime on a Thai salad with hoisin dressing (£7.95), salmon fillet stuffed with coriander and lime mousse in puff pastry with creamed spinach and vermouth sauce (£9.95), 8oz fillet stuffed with dolcelatte wrapped in bacon with red wine sauce (£16.95). Two log fires, bar billiards, cribbage, dominoes and trivia machine. *(Recommended by E G Parish, Tim Harper, Mr & Mrs H Lambert, Mike and Wena Stevenson, Andrew Shore, Pat and Tony Hinkins, W K Wood, D Bryan, Raymond Hebson, Sue Holland, Dave Webster, F J Robinson, W Wood, W C M Jones, SLC)*

Free house ~ Licensees Gary Kidd and Jeremy Brunning ~ Real ale ~ Bar food (12-10(9 Sun)) ~ (01244) 620228 ~ Children till 6pm in library and conservatory ~ Open 11.30-11; 12-10.30 Sun

ASTON SJ6147 Map 7
Bhurtpore ★ ▰

Off A530 SW of Nantwich; in village follow Wrenbury signpost

This very welcoming real-ale enthusiast's pub (although there's lots more here that makes it a real favourite) has nine handpumps serving a rotating choice (between 900 and a thousand a year) of really unusual and very well kept beers like Backdykes Full Malky, Batemans Six Wives, Charles Wells Discovery, City of Cambridge Boathouse, Hanby Old Fools Gold, Whim Magic Mushroom Mild, Salopian Choir Porter and Snowdonia Gatheths Experimental Ale. They also have dozens of good bottled beers, fruit beers (and fruit-flavoured gins) and a changing farm cider or perry, and try to encourage people to try malt whiskies they've not had before (there's a choice of around 90). The wine list is interesting and attractively priced. The pub's unusual name comes from a town in India where local landowner Lord Combermere won a battle, and there's a slightly Indian theme to the décor and the menu. The carpeted lounge bar has a growing collection of Indian artefacts (one statue behind the bar proudly sports a pair of Ray-Bans), as well as good local period photographs, and some attractive furniture. As well as very good home-made curries and baltis on the specials board (from £6.25), enjoyable bar food includes soup (£1.95), hot filled baguettes (£3.25), mushrooms in creamy shropshire blue sauce wrapped in a herb pancake (£3.95), fresh scallops and creamed leeks in pastry tart (£4.25), quorn, mushroom and red wine casserole with herb dumplings (£6.50), chicken breast baked in a stilton and smoked bacon sauce or honeyed pork steak in a cider sauce (£7.95), rolled lemon sole fillets with asparagus sauce or venison casserole in damson wine with plums and topped with shortcrust pastry (£8.95) and puddings like chocolate brownie roulade or gooseberry and elderflower charlotte (£2.75). It can get extremely busy at weekends, but earlyish on a weekday evening or at lunchtime the atmosphere is cosy and civilised. Tables in the comfortable public bar are reserved for people not eating, snug area and dining room are non-smoking; darts, dominoes, cribbage, pool, fruit machine, and piped folk, jazz or blues; enthusiastic and friendly landlord and staff *(Recommended by E G Parish, Richard Lewis, Sue and Bob Ward, Comus Elliott, JP, PP, Nigel Woolliscroft, Sue Holland, Dave Webster, Rob Fowell, Paul Guest, Andy Chetwood, SLC, Derek and Sylvia Stephenson, M Joyner)*

Free house ~ Licensee Simon George ~ Real ale ~ Bar food ~ (01270) 780917 ~ Children till 8pm (preferably no babies or toddlers) ~ Folk third Tues of month ~ Open 12-2.30, 6.30-11; 12-3, 6.30-11 Sat; 12-3, 7-10.30 Sun; closed 25 Dec, 31 Dec 1999, 1 Jan

You can send us reports through our web site: www.goodguides.com

BARTHOMLEY SJ7752 Map 7

White Lion ★ £

A mile from M6 junction 16; take Alsager rd and is signposted at roundabout

The simply furnished and timeless feeling main bar at this delightfully unpretentious black and white thatched pub has a welcoming open fire, heavy oak beams dating back to Stuart times, attractively moulded black panelling, Cheshire watercolours and prints on the walls, latticed windows, and wobbly old tables. Up some steps, a second room has another open fire, more oak panelling, a high-backed winged settle, a paraffin lamp hinged to the wall, and shove-ha'penny, cribbage and dominoes; a third room is very well-liked by local societies. The straightforward lunchtime bar food fits very well with the overall style of the place: cheese and onion oatcakes with beans and tomato (£2), pie (£3), sausages with onion gravy (£3.50), a choice of four roasts (from £3.60) and very good ploughman's (£4.50). Very well kept Burtonwood Bitter, James Forshaws, Top Hat and a monthly guest on handpump; no noisy games machines or music. The cats are friendly. They provide very cheap hostel-type accommodation on a converted grain store for walkers and cyclists and there's a barbecue area in the back terrace. Seats and picnic-sets on the cobbles outside have a charming view of the very attractive village – the early 15th-c red sandstone church of St Bertiline across the road is worth a visit. *(Recommended by Graham & Lynn Mason, Andy and Jill Kassube, Sue Holland, Dave Webster, Chris and Ann Garnett, Jenny and Brian Seller, John Saul, Dr D J Walker, D Bryan, JP, PP, Nigel Woolliscroft)*

Burtonwood ~ Tenant Terence Cartwright ~ Real ale ~ Bar food (lunchtime) ~ (01270) 882242 ~ Children welcome away from public bar ~ Spontaneous folk music first Sun lunchtime of month ~ Open 11.30-11; 12-10.30 Sun; closed Thurs lunchtime

BICKLEY MOSS SJ5549 Map 7

Cholmondeley Arms ★ ⓌⒶ Ⓨ ⫞

Cholmondeley; A49 5½ miles N of Whitchurch; the owners would like us to list them under Cholmondeley Village, but as this is rarely located on maps we have mentioned the nearest village which appears more often

This imaginatively converted Victorian building, with its steeply pitched roof, gothic windows and huge old radiators, was the village school until 1982. The cross-shaped high-ceilinged bar is full of interesting things to look at such as old school desks above the bar on a gantry, masses of Victorian pictures (especially portraits and military subjects), and a great stag's head over one of the side arches; seats from cane and bentwood to pews and carved oak settles, patterned paper on the shutters to match the curtains. Imaginative very well cooked bar food from a daily changing menu is highly popular so you will need to book at weekends: stilton and watercress soup (£2.95), hot baked prawns in sour cream and garlic (£4.25), grilled peppers and courgettes with garlic and olive oil (£4.50), vegetable and bean cassoulet with salad (£7.75), salmon fishcakes with hollandaise sauce (£7.95), chicken breast in mushroom, mustard and cream sauce (£8.95) and duck breast grilled with raspberry vinegar, ginger and soy (£9.95), and rare lightly peppered rib-eye steak (£10.95). Very tempting puddings include home-made ice creams (£2.95), bread and butter pudding, chocolate hazelnut charlotte and iced soufflé Grand Marnier (£3.95). Despite the obvious concentration on food there is well kept Greene King Abbot, Marstons Pedigree and Weetwood Old Dog on handpump An old blackboard lists ten or so interesting and often uncommon wines by the glass; big (4 cup) cafetière of coffee, teas, and hot chocolate; friendly service but can be slow when busy. The bedrooms are across the old playground in the head master's house. There are seats out on a sizeable lawn, and Cholmondeley Castle and gardens are close by. *(Recommended by W K Wood, GLD, Derek and Margaret Underwood, Mike & Wena Stevenson, Mrs S Shanahan, Dr Peter Burnham, Julia Bryan, Richard and Margaret Peers, Mike and Karen England, Nigel Woolliscroft, Marvadene B Eves, C H Mauroy, Mike and Mary Carter, W C M Jones, Lorna and Howard Lambert)*

Free house ~ Licensees Guy and Carolyn Ross-Lowe ~ Real ale ~ Bar food (12-2.15, 7(6.30 Sat)-10) ~ (01829) 720300 ~ Children welcome ~ Occasional jazz ~ Open 11-3, 7(6.30 Sat)-11; closed 25 Dec ~ Bedrooms: £50/£65

BROXTON SJ4858 Map 7

Egerton Arms

A41/A534 S of Chester

This friendly family pub has a play area with a wendy house as well as picnic-sets in the garden, and lovely views over the surrounding sandstone countryside as far as the River Dee from the balcony terrace. Children are welcome in the roomy and attractive dark-panelled bar which has well polished old furniture, brasses, antique plates and prints; the neatly kept and recently extended no-smoking dining area opens off here. A good choice of bar food includes soup (£1.95), sandwiches (from £2), steak and ale pie (£5.25), lasagne (£5.95), half a roast chicken (£6.25), gammon and egg (£6.95), steaks (from £6.95), puddings (£2.45), children's menu and Sunday lunch (£5.75). Well kept Burtonwood Bitter, a second Burtonwood beer on handpump, decent wines by the glass; service is consistently friendly and efficient; piped music, fruit machine. We'd be interested to hear from readers about the refurbished bedrooms. *(Recommended by Paul and Maggie Baker, Graham and Lynn Mason, Andy Ransom, Dr Phil Putwain)*

Burtonwood ~ Manager Jim Monaghan ~ Real ale ~ Bar food (12-2.30, 6-9.30; 12-9.30 Sat; 12-9 Sun) ~ (01829) 782241 ~ Children in restaurant ~ Open 11-11; 12-10.30 Sun; closed 25 Dec ~ Bedrooms: £40.25B/£45.50B

BUNBURY SJ5758 Map 7

Dysart Arms ★ ♀

Bowes Gate Road; village signposted off A51 NW of Nantwich; and from A49 S of Tarporley – coming this way, coming in on northernmost village access road, bear left in village centre

Cheshire Dining Pub of the Year

Nicely laid out airy spaces ramble around the pleasantly lit central bar at this extended old farmhouse. The knocked through cream-walled rooms, under deep venetian red ceilings, might have fires, red and black tiles, some stripped boards and some carpet, a comfortable variety of well spaced big solid wooden tables and chairs, a couple of big bookcases, some carefully chosen bric-a-brac and properly lit pictures. One area is no smoking. The ceiling in the more restaurauty end room (with its book lined back wall) will be lowered this year, and lots of plants hung from the beams. Most people are here for the imaginative changing menu which, as well as sandwiches (from £3.25) might include carrot and orange soup (£2.95), chicken liver and pistachio (£3.75), ploughman's (£5.45), salmon and smoked haddock fishcakes with a spring onion and beef tomato garnish and lemon mayonnaise (£5.95), black pudding and chorizo sausage rissole on roasted red onion salad with balsamic vinegar dressing, topped with a poached egg (£6.75), gnocchi with roasted pepper and olive sauce topped with mozzarella and basil oil served with ciabatta bread (£7.50), spaghetti tossed in a garlic and smoked applewood cheese sauce (£7.95), chicken breast filled with brie and walnut pesto with a lemon and chive cream sauce (£8.95); vegetables or salad (£1.75), and puddings such as banoffi pie or fruits of the forest tartlets (£3.25) Well kept Boddingtons and Timothy Taylor Landlord, and a couple of guests on handpump, with good interesting wines by the glass and cider; friendly well trained young uniformed staff. There are tables out on the terrace and in the attractive and immaculate slightly elevated garden; a nice spot by the splendid church at the end of a picturesque village, with distant views of the Peckforton Hills. *(Recommended by Pat & Tony Hinkins, Joan Yen, MLR, E G Parish, Graham and Lynn Mason, Derek and Sylvia Stephenson, Rod and Moyra Davidson, Nigel Woolliscroft)*

Free house ~ Licensee Darren Snell ~ Real ale ~ Bar food (12-2.30, 5.30-9.30) ~ (01829) 260183 ~ Children in eating area of bar till 6pm ~ Open 11.30-11; 12-10.30 Sun; may close afternoons in winter

Waterside pubs are listed at the back of the book.

CHESTER SJ4166 Map 7

Albion ★ ◧

Park Street

Tucked away in a quiet part of town just below the Roman Wall you'll find this very individually run old-fashioned street corner pub. The bar atmosphere is friendly and chatty (no piped music), with maybe a serious game of cards in one corner. It's delightfully decorated throughout in a muted post-Edwardian style, with floral wallpaper, appropriate lamps, leatherette and hop-back chairs, period piano, cast-iron-framed tables. The landlord is devoted to his very interesting collection of World War I memorabilia. One room has big engravings of men leaving for war, another with similarly striking prints of wounded veterans, others with the more expected aspects – flags, advertisements and so on. Well kept Cains, Greenalls Bitter, Youngs Bitter and a weekly guest such as Titanic White Star on handpump, up to 30 malts and fresh orange juice. Service is very friendly (though they don't like people rushing in just before closing time – and won't serve crisps or nuts, let alone children). Food is above average, with proper robust home cooking including Staffordshire oatcakes filled with black pudding, smoked bacon and sliced potato, fresh garlic and herb pasta with blue cheese black olive sauce, chicken madras curry and basmati rice with mango chutney or lamb's liver and bacon with cider gravy (most at £5.60), and puddings such as caramelised rice pudding with jam or home-made ice cream (£3.20). The landlord is still hoping to add a couple of bedrooms and suggests readers enquire. *(Recommended by Mark Brock, Peg Cuskley, David and Kathy Holcroft, Nick & Meriel Cox, Sue Holland, Dave Webster, A J Barker)*

Inn Business ~ Lease: Michael Edward Mercer ~ Real ale ~ Bar food (not Mon evening) ~ Restaurant (evening only) ~ (01244) 340345 ~ Open 11.30-3, 5(6 Sat)-11; 12-2.30, 7-10.30 Sun

Old Harkers Arms ♀ ◧

1 Russell St, down steps off City Rd where it crosses canal – under Mike Melody antiques

The lofty ceiling and tall windows at this attractively converted early Victorian canal warehouse give a feeling of space and light. You can watch the canal and cruise boats drifting by outside from tables which are carefully arranged to allow a sense of privacy. The bar is decorated with attractive lamps, sepia nudes, an accordion, and a well stocked library at one end of the bar. The bar counter, apparently constructed from salvaged doors, dispenses well kept Boddingtons, Cottage Champflower, Hook Norton, Thwaites, and a guest on handpump; lots of malt whiskies and flavoured Polish vodkas, and decent well described wines. The good choice of well liked food might include sandwiches (from £2.95), soup (£3.25), warm ciabatta with tuna and melted cheese (£3.45), chicken and two pepper terrine with sesame dressing (£3.55), Chinese pork with five spice sauce and noodles (£4.95), chicken tikka (£5.55), battered cod (£7.95), steak, Guinness and mushroom pie (£8.95), and puddings like sticky fig and ginger pudding with ice cream or lemon tart with raspberry sauce (£2.95); Sunday roast (£6.95). Helpings are generous; friendly service; and high marks for housekeeping – often what lets city pubs down. *(Recommended by Mr and Mrs J K Clifton, Brad W Morley, SLC, Dr P A Sutton, Gill and Maurice McMahon, Pat and Tony Martin, D Bryan)*

Free house ~ Licensees Barbie Hill and Catryn Devaney ~ Real ale ~ Bar food (12-2.30, 5.30-9.30(9 Sun)) ~ Restaurant ~ (01244) 344525 ~ Children welcome till 7pm ~ Open 11.30-11; 12-10.30 Sun

COTEBROOK SJ5865 Map 7

Fox & Barrel

A49 NE of Tarporley

There's a good mix of tables and chairs in the cosy distinct areas of this well refurbished old pub. We liked the area with an oriental rug in front of the very big log fireplace, others might go for the comfortable banquette corner, or perhaps the part with shelves of rather nice ornaments and china jugs (or that good run of Jersey cattle annual registers). Silenced fruit machine, unobtrusive piped music. Beyond the bar, where friendly neatly uniformed staff serve decent wines, and (through a sparkler) Boddingtons, Marstons Pedigree, Tetleys and a guest such as Ash Vine Black Bess on handpump, a huge candlelit dining areas spreads away, with well spaced varying-sized tables, comfortable dining chairs, attractive rugs on bare boards, rustic pictures above the panelled dado, and one more extensively panelled section; part of the dining area is no smoking. Good food from a menu changed every six to eight weeks might include sandwiches (from £3.25), home-made soup (£2.45), ploughman's (£5.25), pie of the day (£7.50), 8oz home-made steak burger (£7.75), seafood lasagne (£8.45), pork with Chinese vegetables and soft noodles with plum sauce (£8.75), feta cheese salad with roasted mediterranean vegetables (£8.95), king prawn and fresh salmon kebab with orange and coriander butter (£11.75), and locally made puddings like almond and chocolate tart or raspberry and hazelnut meringue roll (£3.25); three-course Sunday roast (£10.50). *(Recommended by Graham & Lynn Mason, Mr and Mrs H Pearson)*

Inn Partnership (Nomura) ~ Tenant Martin Cocking ~ Real ale ~ Bar food (12-2.30, 6.30-9; 12-9.30 Sat, Sun; not Mon evening) ~ Restaurant ~ (01829) 760529 ~ Children in bar and restaurant ~ Open 12-3, 5.30-11; 11-11 Sat; 12-10.30 Sun

DELAMERE SJ5669 Map 7
Fishpool
A54/B5152

This attractive and well liked pub is well placed near the pike-haunted lake and Delamere Forest. This does mean it can be particularly busy at weekends so it's best to go early. There's a pleasant, relaxed atmosphere in its four comfortable small room areas which are bright with polished brasses and china, and have neatly polished tables, upholstered stools and wall settles. Greenalls Bitter, Mild and Original on handpump are very well kept, and simple but good bar food includes sandwiches, home-made steak pie (£5.50), chicken tikka (£5.95) and barnsley lamb chop (£6.95); no games or music; picnic-sets outside on the lawn. *(Recommended by Sue Holland, Dave Webster, John McDonald, Ann Bond, W C M Jones, Raymond Hebson, SLC, Gill and Maurice McMahon)*

Inn Partnership (Nomura) ~ Tenants Richard and Maureen Lamb ~ Real ale ~ Bar food ~ (01606) 883277 ~ Children welcome ~ Open 12-3, 6-11(10 Sun)

FADDILEY SJ5753 Map 7
Thatch
A534 Wrexham—Nantwich

Doing very well under its present landlord, this charming thatched and timbered 15th-c pub combines an engagingly homely feel with very good food – and service well above usual pub standards. On the right are low dark glossy beams, comfortable wall seats and other chairs, an open fire, and a snug inner room up a couple of steps. The left is more smartly laid out for dining, but also quite intimate in style, with a small area through an arch looking out over what's now a quietly pastoral scene with cows grazing peacefully, but was once the site of a fierce battle between the Mercians and the Welsh. It's the food which is the main draw here, generous and well presented, running from soup (£1.90), filled baguettes (from £2.95), and ploughman's (£3.95), to main dishes including steak and kidney pie or cheese and pasta bake (£5.50), chicken curry or vegetable moussaka (£5.95), gammon (£7.95), 8oz sirloin (£9.50), mixed grill (£10.95), and daily specials such as braised steak in red wine or poached salmon in pernod and fennel (£7.95) and duck in orange and Cointreau (£9.95); puddings include a range of tasty sponges, cheesecakes and fresh fruit gateaux (£2.95). Everything's kept immaculately – including the Courage Directors, Theakstons Best and Mild, Websters Yorkshire and a local guest such as Weetwoods Old Dog Bitter on handpump; cribbage and dominoes. The garden too is a delight: neat lawn, interesting and attractive plantings, solid rustic seats, and a couple of substantial yew trees guarding the gate in the white picket fence. *(Recommended by E G Parish, Sue Holland, Dave Webster, Graham & Lynn Mason, Bob Smith)*

Free house ~ Licensee Barry Ellis ~ Real ale ~ Bar food ~ (01270) 524223 ~ Children in eating area of bar ~ Open 12-3, 6.30-11(10.30 Sun)

HANDLEY SJ4758 Map 7
Calveley Arms
Village loop road, just off A41 Chester—Whitchurch

The changing menus at this attractive black and white country pub are bound in the covers of old children's annuals. Quite reasonably priced, dishes might include soup (£2.25), a good choice of sandwiches (from £2.50), battered squid rings (£3.75), hot avocado and stilton (£3.95), steak and kidney pie (£5.50), roasted seasonal vegetables (£5.85), pasta carbonara or curry (£5.95) or chicken supreme with mild creamy curried apricot sauce (£6.95); service is friendly and welcoming. They have well kept Boddingtons Bitter and Mild, Wadworths 6X, Whitbread Castle Eden, and ocassional guests such as Fullers London Pride or Greene King Abbot on handpump. The attractively furnished roomy beamed lounge has leaded windows, an open fire at one end and some cosy alcove seating; shove-ha'penny, dominoes, cribbage and bar skittles. Out in the secluded garden you can play boules in the summer and there are tables and a barbecue. *(Recommended by MLR, Mrs P J Carroll, Graham and Lynn Mason, Sue Holland, Dave Webster, Gill and Maurice McMahon, Joan Yen)*

Enterprise ~ Tenant Grant Wilson ~ Real ale ~ Bar food ~ (01829) 770619 ~ Children in eating area of bar ~ Open 12-3, 6-11; 12-3, 7-10.30 Sun; closed 25 Dec evening

HIGHER BURWARDSLEY SJ5256 Map 7
Pheasant 🛏️
Burwardsley signposted from Tattenhall (which itself is signposted off A41 S of Chester) and from Harthill (reached by turning off A534 Nantwich—Holt at the Copper Mine); follow pub's signpost on up hill from Post Office; OS Sheet 117 map reference 523566

A telescope on the terrace of this half-timbered and sandstone pub gives a fine view of the Pier Head and cathedrals in Liverpool. From inside, if you're prepared to share the window that affords the best view with Sailor the pub parrot (who does chicken and vacuum cleaner impressions) the views across the Cheshire plain are lovely too. The walls of the beamed and timbered bar are covered with pictures and rosettes of the licensees' own highland cattle (they guarantee their beef BSE free) from shows they've won prizes in, and there are plenty of reminders of the landlord's previous career as a ship's pilot, such as his Merchant Navy apprenticeship papers, some ship photographs, a brass ship's barometer and of course the parrot. Other decorations include a stuffed pheasant, a set of whimsical little cock-fighting pictures done in real feathers, and big colour engravings of Victorian officials of the North Cheshire Hunt. There are some plates above the high stone mantlepiece of the see-through fireplace (said to house the biggest log fire in the county), and around the fire is a tall leather-cushioned fender. Other seats include red leatherette or plush wall seats and one or two antique oak settles; there's a pleasant non-smoking conservatory. Bar food includes sandwiches (from £2.35), soup (£2.95), chicken liver parfait and toast (£4.25), mussels cooked in wine, cream and garlic (£4.50), ploughman's (£5.50), marinated vegetable and tofu kebab (£5.75) and home-made puddings (£2.80); they charge 50p for cheques or cards on transactions under £20. Well kept Bass, Hanbys, Jennings and Weetwood on handpump, and a choice of over 40 malts; friendly staff; cribbage. Picnic-sets on a big side lawn, and barbecues on some summer weekends. The very comfortable bedrooms are in an attractively converted sandstone-built barn, and all have views. The pub is well placed for the Sandstone Trail on the Peckforton Hills, and the nearby Candle Workshops are quite a draw in summer. *(Recommended by Sue Holland, Dave Webster, E G Parish, Michael and Jenny Back, D A Norman, Mark Brock, SLC, Sue & Bob Ward)*

Free house ~ Licensee David Greenhaugh ~ Real ale ~ Bar food ~ (01829) 770434 ~
Children in conservatory ~ Open 11-3, 6-11; 11-11 Sat; 12-10.30 Sun ~ Bedrooms:
£49.50B/£70B

LANGLEY SJ9569 Map 7

Hanging Gate

Meg Lane, Higher Sutton; follow Langley signpost from A54 beside Fourways Motel, and
that road passes the pub; from Macclesfield, heading S from centre on A523 turn left into
Byrons Lane at Langley, Wincle signpost; in Sutton (half-mile after going under canal bridge,
ie before Langley) fork right at Church House Inn, following Wildboarclough signpost, then
two miles later turning sharp right at steep hairpin bend; OS Sheet 118 map reference
952696

This very welcoming old drovers' pub is perched high on a ridge in the Peak District,
with stunning views over a patchwork of valley pastures to distant moors (and the
tall Sutton Common transmitter above them) from seats outside on a crazy-paved
terrace. Its three cosy low-beamed rambling rooms are spotlessly kept and simply
and traditionally furnished, with big coal fires and some attractive old prints of
Cheshire towns. There's an airy garden room down some stone steps. Simple but
well presented bar food (the licensees tell us prices haven't changed since the last
edition) includes sandwiches (from £2.50), soup, meat and potato pie (£4.95)
ploughman's (£4.75), gammon and egg (£5.75) and steaks from (£7.95); daily
specials include chicken and apricot curry (£4.95) and beef in Guinness casserole or
grilled local trout (£5.95). Well kept Cains, Marstons Bitter and Pedigree and a guest
on handpump; quite a few malt whiskies. The blue room is no smoking.
(Recommended by Jack Morley, Dr D J Walker, Jackie Lawler, Mike Ridgway, Sarah Miles, Gill
and Maurice McMahon, Nigel Woolliscroft, Stephen, Julie and Hayley Brown, W D Christian,
Mark J Hydes)

Free house ~ Licensee Carole Marshall ~ Real ale ~ Bar food ~ (01260) 252238 ~
Children in family area ~ Open 12-3, 7-11(10.30 Sun)

Leathers Smithy ◀

From Macclesfield, heading S from centre on A523 turn left into Byrons Lane at Langley,
Wincle signpost; in Langley follow main road forking left at church into Clarke Lane – keep
on towards the moors; OS Sheet 118 map reference 952715

There's lots of traditional pubby character in the lively, partly flagstoned right-hand
bar with its bow window seats or wheelback chairs, and roughcast cream walls hung
with motoring memorabilia at this nice old place. On the left, there are more
wheelback chairs around cast-iron-framed tables on a turkey carpet and a
locomotive name-plate curving over one of the two open fires. Very good value bar
food includes sandwiches (from £2), black pudding and apple sauce (£3), smoked
salmon and prawns (£4.50), spinach and ricotta canelloni, wild mushroom lasagne
or Thai red chicken curry (£5), steak pie (£5), roast or halibut (£6.50), steaks (from
£9). Alongside a more than decent collection of spirits, including well over 80 Irish
and malt whiskies they have Scrumpy Jack cider, gluhwein in winter from a copper
salamander and very well kept Morlands Old Speckled Hen, Morrells Oxford and
Timothy Taylor Golden Best and Landlord on handpump; faint piped music. The
pub is close to Macclesfield Forest and Teggs Nose country park and has fine views
across the Ridgegate Reservoir, not surprisingly it's a popular stop for walkers.
(Recommended by S W & L Shore, Gill and Maurice McMahon, P and M Rudlin, Mike & Wena
Stevenson, Stephen, Julie and Hayley Brown, Jackie Lawler)

Free house ~ Licensee Paul Hadfield ~ Real ale ~ Bar food (12-2, 7-9.30(8.30 Tues-
Thurs); not Mon evening) ~ (01260) 252313 ~ Open 12-3, 7-11; 12-10.30 Sun

---

Planning a day in the country? We list pubs in really attractive scenery at the
back of the book.

LOWER PEOVER SJ7474 Map 7

Bells of Peover ★

The Cobbles; from B5081 take short cobbled lane signposted to church

The interior of this delightful wisteria-covered pub is very neatly kept and full of character; the little tiled bar has side hatches for its serving counter, toby jugs, and comic Victorian prints, and the original lounge has antique settles, high-backed windsor armchairs and a spacious window seat, antique china in the dresser, pictures above the panelling, and two small coal fires. There's a second similar lounge. The emphasis is very firmly on the bar food which includes interesting daily specials, home-made soup (£2.25), sandwiches (from £2.90), vegetarian dishes (from £5.75), home-made pie of the day (£6.25), gammon and egg (£6.55), chicken in a tomato and basil sauce (£7.25), steaks (from £10.95), and puddings (£2.95); enjoyable Sunday lunch. Polite and efficient service even when busy; most people wear a jacket and tie in the restaurant. Well kept Boddingtons and Greenalls Bitter on handpump; dominoes. It's tucked away in a tranquil village and next to a lovely 14th-c black and white timbered church. A spacious lawn beyond the old coachyard at the side spreads down through trees and under rose pergolas to a little stream, and there are seats on the sheltered crazy-paved terrace in front. *(Recommended by RJH, P R and S A White, Colin Barnes, Dr Peter Burnham, Julia Bryan, M A Godfrey, Graham and Lynn Mason, JP, PP, W C M Jones, Mrs Caroline Cole, Sue Holland, Dave Webster, Mayur Shah, Peter & Audrey Dowsett, R Davies)*

Greenalls ~ Managers Ken and Wendy Brown ~ Real ale ~ Bar food (till 9.45 Sat) ~ Restaurant ~ (01565) 722269 ~ Children in restaurant ~ Open 11-3, 5.30-11; 11-11 Sat; 12-10.30 Sun

MACCLESFIELD SJ9271 Map 7

Sutton Hall Hotel ★ 🛏

Leaving Macclesfield southwards on A523, turn left into Byrons Lane signposted Langley, Wincle, then just before canal viaduct fork right into Bullocks Lane; OS Sheet 118 map reference 925715

Two peacocks strut on the lawn, and ducks and moorhens swim in the pond in front of this civilised but relaxing 16th-c baronial hall set in lovely grounds with tables on a tree-sheltered lawn. Inside there's a suit of armour by a big stone fireplace in the bar which is divided into separate areas by tall black oak timbers and also has some antique squared oak panelling, lightly patterned art nouveau stained-glass windows, broad flagstones around the bar counter (carpet elsewhere), and a raised open fire. It is furnished mainly with straightforward ladderback chairs around sturdy thick-topped cast-iron-framed tables, though there are a few unusual touches such as an enormous bronze bell for calling time, a brass cigar-lighting gas taper on the bar counter itself and a longcase clock. Readers find the atmosphere friendly and unpretentious. Home-made bar food includes soup (from £1.45), pâté (£3.25), lasagne (£4.95), steak and kidney pie or spinach pancakes filled with ratatouille with a sour cream dressing (£5.25), daily specials such as grilled smoked quail wrapped in bacon with warm redcurrant jelly (£4.25), beef in ale (£6.25), and lamb's liver and bacon (£6), and home-made puddings like apple and blackberry crumble or sticky toffee pudding (£3). Well kept Bass, Marstons, Worthington and a guest beer on handpump, 40 malt whiskies, decent wines, and a proper pimms. They can arrange clay shooting, golf or local fishing for residents, and there's access to new canal moorings at Gurnett Aqueduct on the Macclesfield Canal 200 yards away. *(Recommended by C P Knights, Bill Sykes, Brian and Anna Marsden, E G Parish, JP, PP, Dr Peter Burnham, Julia Bryan)*

Free house ~ Licensee Robert Bradshaw ~ Real ale ~ Bar food (till 10) ~ Restaurant ~ (01260) 253211 ~ Children in restaurant ~ Open 11-11; 12-4, 7-11 Sun ~ Bedrooms: £75B/£90B

Please let us know of any pubs where the wine is particularly good.

NANTWICH SJ6552 Map 7

Crown

High Street; in pedestrian-only centre, close to church; free public parking behind the inn

The overhanging upper galleries and uncertain black and white perpendiculars and horizontals of this striking three-storey timbered hotel have dominated the High Street here since 1583, when it was rebuilt from timbers donated by Queen Elizabeth I. The cosy rambling beamed and timbered bar is simply furnished with various antique tables and chairs on its sloping creaky floors. Lunchtime bar food includes a very good carvery, home-made soup (£1.95), sandwiches (from £2.25), filled baked potatoes (from £2.75), ploughman's (£3.50), cumberland sausage (£3.50), plaice (£3.95), steaks (£8.50) and puddings (£2.25); children's menu (£2.25); the lively evening restaurant specialises in Italian food. Boddingtons and Flowers Original on handpump; friendly service; very busy weekend evenings; piped music, and fruit machine. *(Recommended by E G Parish)*

Free house ~ Licensees Phillip and Susan Martin ~ Real ale ~ Bar food (lunchtime) ~ Restaurant (evening, all day Sat) ~ (01270) 625283 ~ Children welcome ~ Open 11-11; 12-10.30 Sun; closed 25 Dec ~ Bedrooms: £62.95B/£80.90B

OVER PEOVER SJ7674 Map 7

Olde Park Gate

Stocks Lane; off A50 N of Holmes Chapel at the Whipping Stock

A proper pub, this, with several small rooms, black beams and joists, and a good few striking Macclesfield oak seats in various sizes among more workaday chairs. Each immaculate room has its own character: flowery wallpaper and an oriental rug on parquet floor in one place, carpeting, coach horns, horse tack and guns in another, small hunting and other country prints in yet another. Most are quiet and civilised, and the back room with its darts and basic wall seats (and maybe *Coronation Street* on the television) is a real locals' haunt – much merriment after the serious business of the early August gooseberry competition. The current licensees are doing very well here, with warmly welcoming service, well kept Sam Smiths OB on handpump and good value food virtually all home-made such as soup (£2.20), sandwiches (£3.25), two proper pies like lamb and apricot or cheese and onion (£5.95-£7.95), ploughman's (£6.75), two roasts a day or curry (£6.95), and puddings like cheesecake or hot chocolate sponge (£2.50); no-smoking area, darts, television in the tap room, fruit machine, dominoes and piped music. There are picnic-sets under cocktail parasols among hawthorn trees on the pleasant lawn beyond the car park, behind the low ivy-clad dark brick building; no dogs allowed out here. *(Recommended by B Adams, Peter Marshall, Leo and Barbara Lionet, PACW)*

Sam Smiths ~ Manager Andrew Jordan ~ Real ale ~ Bar food (12-2, 6.30(7 Sun)-9) ~ (01625) 861455 ~ Open 11.30-11; 12-3.30, 7-10.30 Sun

OVERTON SJ5277 Map 7

Ring o' Bells £

Just over 2 miles from M56, junction 12; 2 Bellemonte Road – from A56 in Frodsham take B5152 and turn right (uphill) at Parish Church signpost

Unchanging over the years, this friendly early 17th-c pub is very much the sort of place where drinkers stand around the bar chatting. Filled with old-fashioned charm, a couple of its little rambling rooms give a view past the stone church to the Mersey far below. The room at the back has some antique settles, brass-and-leather fender seats by the log fire, and old hunting prints on its butter-coloured walls; a beamed room with antique dark oak panelling and stained glass leads through to a darts room (there's also dominoes, cribbage, shove-ha'penny and other board games). Good value waitress-served lunchtime bar food includes sandwiches and toasties (from £1.50), omelettes (£2.95), chicken tikka masala, cumberland sausage and mash, haddock and chips or home-made steak, mushroom and ale pie (£3.95). Greenalls Bitter and four or five guest ales a week on handpump, and about 80 different malt whiskies served from the old-fashioned hatch-like central servery. The cats are Tilly and Flora, and very friendly Ambrose. In summer the exterior is a mass of colourful hanging baskets, and a secluded garden at the back has tables and chairs, a pond, and lots of trees. *(Recommended by Gillian Jenkins)*

Greenalls ~ Tenant Shirley Wroughton-Craig ~ Real ale ~ Bar food (lunchtime) ~ Restaurant ~ (01928) 732068 ~ Children welcome away from bar ~ Open 11.30-3.30, 5.30-11; 11.30-4.30, 6-11 Sat; 12-4, 7-10.30 Sun

PEOVER HEATH SJ7973 Map 7
Dog 🛏

Off A50 N of Holmes Chapel at the Whipping Stocks, keep on past Parkgate into Wellbank Lane; OS Sheet 118 map reference 794735; note that this village is called Peover Heath on the OS map and shown under that name on many road maps, but the pub is often listed under Over Peover instead

Well equipped new bedrooms at this civilised old inn earn it a Stay Award for the first time. It's a carefully run place with friendly efficient service, and lots of attention to detail and customers' comfort. In the main bar – popular with locals and visitors alike – logs burn in one old-fashioned black grate, a coal fire opposite is flanked by two wood-backed built-in fireside seats, and there are comfortable easy chairs and wall seats (one built into a snug alcove around an oak table). Well liked bar food includes home-made soup (£2.50), a very good range of sandwiches (from £2.70), garlic mushrooms in a herb, cream and onion sauce, duck and port pâté, half a pint of prawns or rollmop herring (£4.50), ploughman's (£4.65), daily specials like roast beef with yorkshire pudding or rack of lamb with apricots and ginger (£6.95), and steak and mushroom pie, rabbit in herbs and mustard sauce, poached fresh salmon in a cream and cucumber sauce, leek, stilton and mushroom pancake topped with cheese sauce or roast pork with apricot and orange sauce (all £8.95), sirloin steak and sauce (£12.95), and puddings such as bread and butter pudding, sticky toffee meringue or fresh fruit pie. They serve well kept Moorhouses Black Cat, Flowers IPA, Tetley and Weetwood Old Dog on handpump, Addlestones cider, over 50 malt whiskies and freshly squeezed orange juice, and have a decent and expanding wine list; darts, pool, dominoes, cribbage, and piped music; no-smoking dining room. Advisable to book at weekends. There are picnic-sets out on the quiet lane, underneath the pub's pretty hanging baskets, and an attractive beer garden, nicely lit in the evenings. The licensees also run the Swettenham Arms, Swettenham. *(Recommended by Colin Barnes, J Roy Smylie, Bronwen and Steve Wrigley, Leo and Barbara Lionet, PACW)*

Free house ~ Licensees Frances and Jim Cunningham ~ Real ale ~ Restaurant ~ (01625) 861421 ~ Children welcome ~ Quiz night Thurs and Sun, pianist Tues ~ Open 11-3, 5.30-11 ~ Bedrooms: £50B/£65B

PLUMLEY SJ7175 Map 7
Smoker

2½ miles from M6 junction 19: A556 towards Northwich and Chester

This partly thatched old pub provides a reliable escape from the M6. Its three well decorated connecting rooms have dark panelling, open fires in impressive period fireplaces, some military prints, a collection of copper kettles, an Edwardian print on the wall capturing a hunt meeting outside (which shows how little the appearance of the pub has changed over the centuries) and a painting of the first Lord de Tabley mounted on Smoker; also, comfortable deep sofas, cushioned settles, windsor chairs, and some rush-seat dining chairs. A glass case contains an interesting remnant from the Houses of Parliament salvaged after it was hit by a bomb in World War II. The same menu covers both the bar and brasserie (though they will reserve tables and give full waitress service in the brasserie); this has created a relaxed atmosphere, with the brasserie becoming even more part of the pub. Enjoyable bar food includes home-made soup (£2.20), sandwiches (from £2.60), black pudding with a mustard and white wine sauce (£3.95), breaded mushrooms with garlic mayonnaise (£4.35), liver and onions (£6.65), vegetable curry, steak and kidney pie or home-made seafood bake (£6.95), gammon and egg (£7.35) and steaks (from £9.55). Well kept Robinsons Best, Hatters Mild and Old Stockport on handpump, 30 malt whiskies and a good choice of wines; friendly and helpful service; non-smoking areas in bar and brasserie; may be piped music. Outside there's a sizeable side lawn with roses and flower beds, and a children's play area in the extended garden. *(Recommended by J Roy Smylie, Bronwen and Steve Wrigley, SLC, Graham and Lynn Mason, M A Godfrey, Stan & Hazel Allen, M L Porter, P R and S A White, W C M Jones, Edward Leetham, Nancy Cleave, L Cherry, Roger Byrne)*

Robinsons ~ Tenants John and Diana Bailey ~ Real ale ~ Bar food (till 10pm; all day Sun) ~ Restaurant ~ (01565) 722338 ~ Children in eating area of bar and restaurant ~ Open 11-3, 6-11; 12-10.30 Sun

POTT SHRIGLEY SJ9479 Map 7
Cheshire Hunt

At end of B5091 in Bollington, where main road bends left at Turners Arms, fork straight ahead off it into Ingersley Road to follow Rainow signpost, then up hill take left turn signposted Pott Shrigley; OS Sheet 118 map reference 945782

It's well worth the effort to find this remote stone pub which easily retains its homely rustic atmosphere from the days when it was a farmhouse. There are several small rooms (one no smoking) that ramble up and down steps with spindleback and wheelback chairs, beams and black joists, hunting pictures and roaring log fires. Well kept Bass, Boddingtons, and Marstons Pedigree on handpump; friendly and efficient service even when busy. No games machines or piped music. As well as a good range of daily specials tasty bar food includes lunchtime sandwiches (from £2.50) and main courses like beef rogan josh, fried lamb's liver with smoked bacon, onions and a red wine sauce or steak and mushroom pie (£6.95), thai-style crab cakes (£7.95), escalope of pork with creamy diane sauce (£8.95), half a roast duckling with orange sauce (£10.95), fillet steak (£14.50), and puddings like apple pie (£2.95) and lemon brûlée (£3.95); it's best to book for the Sunday lunch carvery (£6.95). Outside, there are pleasant views from tables on three terraced areas. *(Recommended by Gill and Maurice McMahon, Bronwen and Steve Wrigley, R H Rowley, Nick Lawless, Dave and Deborah Irving)*

Free house ~ Licensee Alan J Harvey ~ Real ale ~ Bar food (till 10pm) ~ Restaurant ~ (01625) 573185 ~ Children welcome ~ Open 12-3, 5.30-11; closed Mon lunchtime except bank holidays

TARPORLEY SJ5563 Map 7
Rising Sun

High St; village signposted off A51 Nantwich—Chester

This cheery village pub is much enjoyed by locals and visitors alike, with any piped music probably drowned by conversation. Well chosen tables are surrounded by nice characterful old seats including creaky 19th-c mahogany and oak settles, and there's also an attractively blacked iron kitchen range (and three open fires), sporting and other old-fashioned prints on the walls, and a big oriental rug in the back room. Generously served lunchtime bar food includes sandwiches (from £2), filled baked potatoes (from £2.30), home-made cottage pie (5.25), home-made steak and kidney pie (£5.40), gammon and egg (£5.95), peppered pork or beef in ale (£6.30); more elaborate dishes in the evening from the restaurant menu. Well kept Robinsons Best and Mild on handpump; fruit machine. It's very pretty in summer with its mass of hanging baskets and flowering tubs. *(Recommended by Sue Holland, Dave Webster, W C M Jones, Dave Braisted, Janet Pickles)*

Robinsons ~ Tenant Alec Robertson ~ Real ale ~ Bar food (lunchtime) ~ Restaurant (evening) ~ (01829) 732423 ~ Children in eating area of bar at lunchtime ~ Open 11.30-3, 5.30-11; 11.30-11 Sat and bank holidays; 12-10.30 Sun

WESTON SJ7352 Map 7

White Lion 🛏

3½ miles from M6 junction 16; A500 towards Crewe, then village signposted on right

Originally a Tudor farmhouse, this pretty black and white timbered old inn has a busy low-beamed main room divided up into smaller areas by very gnarled black oak standing timbers. There's a varied mix of seats from cushioned modern settles to ancient oak ones, plenty of smaller chairs, and a friendly, relaxing atmosphere. In a smaller room on the left are three fine settles, well carved in 18th-c style. Bar food includes home-made soup (£1.95), sandwiches (£2.25), filled french bread (from £3.15), smoked salmon pâté (£3.50), vegetable lasagne (£4.50), roast of the day (£5.25), chilli (£5.50), poached local Dee salmon (£7.25), steak (£9.75), and home-made puddings (£2.75). You may need to book at the weekend, and it's worth noting that they stop serving lunch at 1.45 on Sunday. Well kept Bass and Boddingtons on handpump, and a sizeable wine list; dominoes, cribbage, trivia, and piped music. Two side rooms are no smoking. Picnic-sets shelter on neat grass behind, by the pub's own bowling green. *(Recommended by E G Parish, Rob Fowell, Colin Draper)*

Free house ~ Licensee Alison Davies ~ Real ale ~ Bar food ~ Restaurant ~ (01270) 587011 ~ Children in eating area of bar ~ Open 11-3, 5(6.30 Sat)-11; 12-3, 7-10.30 Sun ~ Bedrooms: £55B/£65B

WETTENHALL SJ6261 Map 7

Boot & Slipper 🛏

From B5074 on S edge of Winsford, turn into Darnhall School Lane, then right at Wettenhall signpost: keep on for 2 or 3 miles

Readers particularly enjoy the pleasant relaxed atmosphere at this welcoming old pub. The friendly licensee, who was new here for the last edition, has settled in well and mixes cheerily with customers. The knocked-through beamed main bar has three shiny old dark settles, more straightforward chairs, and a fishing rod above the deep low fireplace with its big log fire. The modern bar counter also serves the left-hand communicating beamed room with its shiny pale brown tiled floor, cast-iron-framed long table, panelled settle and bar stools; darts, dominoes, and piped music. An unusual trio of back-lit arched pseudo-fireplaces form one stripped-brick wall and there are two further areas on the right, as well as a back restaurant with big country pictures. Readers also praise the generous helpings of good value bar food which might include sandwiches (from £3.20), gravadlax (£4.75), breaded plaice (£6.50), peppered pork fillet (£6.95), gammon steak (£7.50) and shoulder of lamb (£8.95; friendly service. Well kept Marstons Pedigree and Tetleys on handpump, good selection of malt whiskies and a decent wine list. Outside there are picnic-sets on the cobbled front terrace by the big car park; children's play area. *(Recommended by John Cockell, Jim Bush, E G Parish, J Roy Smylie, John McIver, Norman & Sarah Keeping)*

Free house ~ Licensee Joan Jones ~ Real ale ~ Bar food ~ Restaurant ~ (01270) 528238 ~ Children in restaurant and in eating area of bar till 8.30 ~ Open 12-3, 5.30-11; 12-11(10.30 Sun) Sat ~ Bedrooms: £36B/£48B

WHITEGATE SJ6268 Map 7

Plough

Foxwist Green; along Beauty Bank, opp Methodist chapel – OS Sheet 118 map reference 624684; from A556 at W end roundabout of Northwich bypass take Whitegate road, bear right in village and then take Foxwist Green turn left; or from A54 W of Winsford turn off at Salterswell roundabout, then first left

They serve a wide range of very good value home-made food, often using fresh local produce, at this warmly welcoming old pub; soup (£1.95), sandwiches (from £2.95), filled jacket potatoes (from £4.85), chicken curry, steak pie or half a dozen vegetarian dishes like mushroom and sweetcorn stroganoff (£5.75), sirloin steak (£7.95), and daily specials like steak, mushroom and Guinness pie (£5.95), local chicken fillet in creamy orange sauce (£6.75), lamb in a mango and mint sauce or salmon poached in white wine and bay leaves served in a hollandaise sauce (£6.95) and half a honey roast duck with orange and Grand Marnier sauce (£8.75); two sittings for Sunday lunch. Its several cheerful rooms – including an intimate little dining room with just half a dozen tables – have straightforward but comfortable furnishings. Well kept Robinsons Best, Hatters Mild and Old Stockport; good considerate service; quiz night on Mondays; darts and piped music. The Whitegate Way – a former railway track – is one of several popular walks nearby. No children. *(Recommended by Sarah Jolley, Raymond Hebson, Miss I Nielsen)*

Robinsons ~ Tenant David Hughes ~ Real ale ~ Bar food (all day Sun in summer) ~ (01606) 889455 ~ Open 11.30-4, 5.30-11; 11-11 Fri-Sun; 11.30-3.30, 7-10.30 Sun winter

WHITELEY GREEN SJ9278 Map 7
Windmill

Hole House Lane; village signposted off A523 a mile N of B5091 Bollington turn-off

This large slate-roofed white house tucked away up a quiet country lane emerged last year from a £300,000 refit: good results, with the wood floored open-plan extensions from the original heavily beamed 16th-c core attractively integrated in a welcoming farmhouse country kitchen style, making for a roomy and pleasant pub/restaurant. What matters more is that the current Scots licensees have turned out to be good news; Mr Cunningham, in personal charge of the kitchen, does very good well prepared bar food such as soup (£2.45), chicken liver pâté with onion chutney (£3.25), spicy skewered chicken wings with sour cream (£3.95), stir-fried vegetables with noodles (£5.75), steak and mushroom suet pudding (£6.95), grilled tuna with red salsa or lamb meatballs on noodles with minted jus (£7.95); daily specials like warm salad of chorizo, potato and onion (£3.75), smoked salmon and dill tortellini with roast baby tomato sauce (£6.95), braised knuckle of lamb with root vegetables (£8.95), Thai green curry (£10.50) and monkfish, onions and green peppers in black bean sauce (£13.50). There may be a wait, but the quality makes up for it, and service is friendly. Most of the space is given over to dining, with well spaced tables and a good-sized no-smoking dining area; however, there's also room to sit over the daily papers with a pint of well kept Morlands Old Speckled Hen, Tetleys or guest Brakspears. Look out for the pegged wall draughts. The attractive four acre garden has pretty shrub borders around the lawn, plenty of picnic-sets, a summer bar and barbecues. There are smart wooden benches and green parasols at the front. Nearby, there are canal and other walks; the pub is close to the Middlewood Way, a sort of linear country park along former rail track. *(Recommended by R F Grieve, W D Christian, Philip and Ann Falkner, Brian and Anna Marsden, PACW)*

Allied Domecq ~ Lease: Ian Cunningham ~ Real ale ~ Bar food (12-2.30, 6.30-9.30) ~ Restaurant ~ (01625) 574222 ~ Irish folk second Mon in month, occasional jazz ~ Open 12-11(10.30 Sun); 12-3, 5-11(10.30 Sun) winter

WILLINGTON CORNER SJ5367 Map 7
Boot

Boothsdale, off A54 at Kelsall

This is one of those areas in the north-west which people sometimes call Little Switzerland. It's certainly picturesque, with good walks – and these converted sandstone cottages enjoy a prime spot on a wooded hillside looking out over the lush farmland and hedgerows of the Cheshire plain towards the Welsh hills. Inside has been carefully opened up, leaving small unpretentiously furnished room areas around the central bar with its woodburning stove. The restaurant extension is charming, with wheelback chairs around plenty of tables on its flagstones, and a good log fire. The enjoyable food includes soup (£1.95), sandwiches (from £3.20), home-smoked chicken with a herb vinaigrette (£4.95), nut-roasted brie with tangy cumberland sauce or mushrooms and bacon sautéed and served with blue cheese sauce (£5.50), ploughman's (£5.90), steak and kidney in ale pie (£6.50), steaks (from £7.95), breast of chicken wrapped in bacon and fried in honeyed lemon butter or smoked haddock with rarebit topping on a fresh tomato sauce (£8.50), daily specials (from around £4.95), and puddings such as rhubarb crumble, sticky toffee pudding or brûlées (£3.50). Well kept Bass, Greenalls Bitter, and a guest such as Cains Brewery Bitter or Flowers Original on handpump; 30 malt whiskies, and a decent wine list. The black labrador is called Floyd, the golden retriever Harvey, and the cat Monty. There are seats on the terrace and in the garden, and in the paddock are three donkeys and a pot-bellied pig, and children's dishes. There's a good relaxing atmosphere – a place that plenty of local well-heeled families come to for a meal out; service, too, is friendly as well as attentive. Bass, Flowers Original and a guest beer. Outside, the raised stone terrace with picnic-sets is a summer suntrap; the paddocks on either side have donkeys and a vietnamese pot-bellied pig. One reader recommends the fruit farm for its apples in October and November. *(Recommended by MLR, Mrs P J Carroll, Dr P D Putwain, Graham and Lynn Mason)*

Inn Partnership (Nomura) ~ Lease: Mike and Liz Gollings ~ Real ale ~ Bar food ~ Restaurant ~ (01829) 751375 ~ Children in restaurant and snug ~ Open 11-3, 6-11; 11-11 Sat; 12-10.30 Sun; closed evening 25 Dec

WINCLE SJ9666 Map 7
Ship ◗
Village signposted off A54 Congleton—Buxton

Two tap rooms at this quaint 16th-c pub mean that hikers can enjoy their refreshments without having to strip off muddy gear, while smarter visitors can dine apart in a completely separate area. The pub is said to be one of the oldest in Cheshire, and is tucked away in picturesque countryside with good walks all around. The old-fashioned and simple little tap rooms have thick stone walls, a coal fire, and two constantly rotating guest ales such as Derwent and Timothy Taylor Landlord; decent wines. Good value tasty bar food includes fresh fish on Wednesdays (you may need to book) such as local trout (£5.75), well liked gammon and eggs (£6.50), casseroles (£6.95), and home made puddings; Sunday roast (£6.25) The dining room is no smoking; no piped music or games machines; they may stay open all day on summer weekends. *(Recommended by E G Parish, Nigel Woolliscroft, James Nunns, Stephen, Julie and Hayley Brown, Colin Barnes)*

Free house ~ Licensee Steven Mark Simpson ~ Real ale ~ Bar food ~ Restaurant ~ (01260) 227217 ~ Children welcome ~ Open 12-3, 7-11(12 Sat, Sun); closed Mon Oct-Mar

WRENBURY SJ5948 Map 7
Dusty Miller
Village signposted from A530 Nantwich—Whitchurch

It's pleasantly relaxing entertainment watching the striking counter-weighted drawbridge going up and down outside this handsomely converted 19th-c mill which is perfectly positioned in a peaceful spot by the Llangollen branch of the Shropshire Union Canal. You can see all this from a series of tall glazed arches in the main area which is comfortably modern, with long low hunting prints on white walls, and varied seating including tapestried banquettes, an ornate church pew and wheelback chairs flanking rustic tables. Further in, there's a quarry-tiled standing-only part by the bar counter, which has well kept Robinsons Best, Frederics, Hartleys XB and Old Stockport Old Tom on handpump. Good generously served bar food includes home-made soup (£2.50), filled rolls (from £2.95), home stone-baked pizzas (from £4.75), wafers of smoked halibut with avocado salad or deep-fried feta cheese with cranberry sauce (£4.95), beef braised in ale with baby herb dumplings (£7.25), pork with coarse-grain mustard and cream sauce with garlic mashed potato (£7.50), chicken supreme on honeyed parsnips with cider and mushroom sauce or plaice fillet stuffed with prawns, mushrooms and lemon baked in cheese sauce (£7.95), baked bass with sauté potatoes, caramelised apple and warm tomato and watercress dressing (£10.25); vegetables (£1.50); the upstairs dining area is no smoking. Dominoes and piped music. In summer it's pleasant to sit outside at the picnic-sets on a gravel terrace among rose bushes by the water; they're reached either by the tow path or by a high wooden catwalk above the River Weaver. *(Recommended by Jim Bush, E G Parish, Sue and Bob Ward, Paul and Maggie Baker, Sheila McLardy, Comus Elliott)*

Robinsons ~ Tenant Mark Sumner ~ Restaurant ~ (01270) 780537 ~ Children in eating area of bar ~ Open 11-3, 6(6.30 winter)-11; 12-3.30, 7-10.30 Sun; closed Mon lunchtime Oct-Mar

---

Lucky Dip

Besides the fully inspected pubs, you might like to try these Lucky Dips recommended to us and described by readers (if you do, please send us reports):

Acton Bridge [SJ5975]
Hazel Pear [Hill Top Rd]: New chef doing good food (try the meringue with butterscotch sauce), obliging service – they go out of their way to help; children welcome *(Bruce Jamieson)*
☆ *Maypole* [Hill Top Rd; B5153 off A49 in Weaverham, then right towards Acton Cliff]: Civilised beamed dining pub very popular for wide choice of good varied generous food, roomy and pleasant dining area with lots of brass, copper and china, some antique settles as well as more modern furnishings, two coal fires, friendly staff, well kept Greenalls, gentle piped music; attractive outside with hanging baskets and tubs, seats in well kept garden with orchard behind *(Graham and Lynn Mason, A J Barker, LYM)*
Alderley Edge [SJ8478]
Drum & Monkey [past Royal Oak off Heyes Lane (which is off A34)]: Former Moss Rose, refurbished under new management, with excellent choice of imaginatively prepared reasonably priced food, good beer choice, large terrace overlooking bowling green *(Mrs E E Sanders)*
Oakwood [Brook Lane, nr golf course]: Well run Whitbreads pub with good range of beers, cosistently good value home-made food from lots of sandwiches up, pleasant decor and furnishings, no-smoking area, friendly staff; seats outside *(Mr and Mrs B Hobden)*
Royal Oak [Heyes Lane]: Large comfortable lounge bar, good range of reasonably priced hot bar food and sandwiches, well kept beers, good reasonably priced wine by the glass; back terrace with grassy play area *(Mrs E E Sanders)*
Allgreave [SU9767]
Rose & Crown: Small, very friendly, in great walking country – good views; small choice of good reasonably priced food (may be best to book w/e), excellent service *(John Brightley)*
Alpraham [SJ5959]
Tollemache Arms [Chester Rd (A51)]: Extended family pub with reasonably priced food all day, country décor, good service *(E G Parish, Graham and Lynn Mason)*
Travellers Rest [A51 Nantwich—Chester]: Particularly well kept Tetleys Bitter and Mild and McEwans 70/- in unchanging four-room country local in same family for three generations, leatherette, wicker and Formica,

some flock wallpaper, fine old brewery mirrors, darts, back bowling green; no food, cl weekday lunchtimes *(E G Parish, JP, PP)*
Alsager [SJ7956]
Lodge [Station Rd (B5077)]: Refurbished lounge with log fire, pool and games in busy little locals' bar with piped music (can get smoky, esp when the students are in), well kept ales such as Sam Allsopps, Everards, Greene King Abbot and Marstons Pedigree, reasonably priced bar food; happy hour Mon-Sat 5-6pm, picnic-sets in back garden *(E G Parish, Richard Lewis, Sue Holland, Dave Webster)*
Plough [Crewe Rd]: Spacious Big Steak family dining pub with big indoor play area, low beams and country decor, wide range of food inc children's favourites, helpful young staff, well kept Marstons Pedigree and Tetleys; open all day, good facilities for disabled *(Dave Braisted, Sue Holland, Dave Webster, Richard Lewis, E G Parish)*
Wilbraham Arms [Sandbach Rd N]: Large comfortable open-plan pub with well kept Hartleys XB and Robinsons Bitter and Hatters Mild from long bar, good choice of food, conservatory dining area, play area with pets corner; popular jazz Thurs *(Richard Lewis, Sue Holland, Dave Webster)*
Alvanley [SJ4974]
☆ *White Lion* [Manley Rd; handy for M56 junction 14]: Comfortable and civilised dining pub with good slightly upscale food inc children's dishes, friendly service, plush low-ceilinged lounge, busy restaurant extension (booking recommended), games in smaller public bar, Greenalls Mild, Bitter and Original; tables on new terrace, revamped play area, new pond for the ducks *(Graham & Lynn Mason, LYM)*
Anderton [SJ6575]
Stanley Arms [just NW of Northwich]: Busy friendly local overlooking Anderton boat lift, good value food all day from toasted sandwiches and baked potatoes to Sun lunch, well kept Greenalls Bitter and Mild and Tetleys, pleasant dining area, children welcome; tables in attractive yard with grassy play area; overnight mooring *(Bill and Kathy Cissna, Rita and Keith Pollard)*
Appleton [SJ6484]
Thorn [B5356 Stretton Rd, junction with Arley Rd; not far from M6 junction 20]: Cosy and

pleasant old inn, wide choice of unusually interesting home-made food, friendly staff, garden *(Joan Yen)*

Ashton [SJ5169]

Golden Lion [B5393, off A54 nr Tarvin]: Pleasant village pub with well furnished three-tier lounge, well kept Greenalls and a guest beer, good food from sandwiches hot and cold through huge salad bowls to steaks and Sun lunch, very friendly staff; children in eating areas, popular with walkers *(Graham and Lynn Mason)*

Astbury [SJ8461]

Egerton Arms [off A34 S of Congleton]: Big village local dating from 14th c, in nice spot on green opp interesting old church in pretty village (though busy main rd), wide choice of reasonably priced food with OAP bargains, log fires, well kept Robinsons ales, log fires, no-smoking lounge and part of restaurant, tables in back garden with play area; children welcome; bedrooms *(David Atkinson)*

Audlem [SJ6543]

☆ *Shroppie Fly*: Beautifully placed by Locks 12/13 of Shrops Union Canal, one bar shaped like a barge, good canal photographs, brightly painted bargees' china and bric-a-brac, usual food inc children's, well kept Boddingtons and Flowers IPA and Original, friendly staff, mainly modern furnishings, children in room off bar and restaurant; piped music; seats on waterside terrace, open almost all day summer, cl winter lunchtimes *(Bill and Kathy Cissna, LYM)*

Barbridge [SJ6156]

☆ *Barbridge Inn* [just off A51 N of Nantwich]: Well run and lively open-plan Greenalls family dining pub, replacing its Millers Kitchen theme with olde-worlde décor – tiled floors, hessian curtains, country prints and artefacts; pretty setting by lively marina at junction of Shropshire Union and Middlewich canals, with play area in busy riverside garden, flagstoned conservatory with washtub tables, no-smoking area, friendly staff, simple well cooked food, well kept Boddingtons, Cains and weekend guest beers, games room, quiet piped music; good disabled facilities, open all day, quiz Tues, jazz Thurs, barbecue *(E G Parish, Richard Lewis, LYM, Graham and Lynn Mason, Chris Glasson)*

Bell o' th' Hill [SJ5245]

☆ *Blue Bell* [just off A41 N of Whitchurch]: Cosy and attractive two-roomed heavily beamed 17th-c country local with decent food, Sun papers, interesting well kept ales such as Bearswood Bearskinful, Hanby Drawwell and Slaters, generous coffee, welcoming Californian landlord and Armenian wife, friendly dogs (other dogs allowed); piped music; nice garden, attractive surroundings *(Tim Harper, Andy Ransom, LYM, Sue Holland, Dave Webster, Nigel Woolliscroft)*

Bickerton [SJ5052]

Bickerton Poacher [A534 E of junction with A41]: Rambling old poacher-theme pub, very popular with families; good reasonably priced food, well kept Greenalls Bitter and Original, good choice of food, open fires, friendly staff,

copper-mining memorabilia, attractive barbecue extension around sheltered courtyard, play area and horseshoe quoits pitch *(Sue Holland, Dave Webster, E G Parish, LYM, Graham and Lynn Mason)*

Bollington [SJ9377]

☆ *Church House* [Church St]: Small friendly village pub with wide choice of good value quickly served lunchtime food, well kept Marstons and Tetleys, furnishings inc pews and working sewing-machine treadle tables, roaring fire, separate dining room; can book tables for busy lunchtimes *(Jack Morley)*

Bottom of the Oven [SJ9872]

☆ *Stanley Arms* [A537 Buxton—Macclesfield, 1st left past Cat & Fiddle]: Isolated moorland pub, small, friendly and cosy, lots of shiny black woodwork, plush seats, dimpled copper tables, open winter fires, dining room, small choice of generous well cooked traditional food, well kept Marstons and guest beers; children welcome, piped music; picnic-sets on grass behind, may close Mon in winter if weather bad *(Dave and Deborah Irving, John and Christine Lowe, LYM, Leo and Barbara Lionet)*

Bradfield Green [SJ6859]

Coach & Horses [A530 NW of Crewe]: Attractive and congenially if sedately cottagey, well kept Greenalls, good value food inc vegetarian and children's, horse pictures, friendly staff; discreet piped music *(E G Parish)*

Brereton Green [SJ7864]

Bears Head [handy for M6 junction 17; set back off A50 2 m S of Holmes Chapel]: Handsome old heavily timbered inn, open all day, refurbished along the lines of a comfortable chain dining pub, with good choice of well prepared fresh straightforward food, well kept Bass, Worthington BB and a guest such as Fullers London Pride, cheerful open fire, welcoming service; good value bedrooms in modern block *(LYM, E G Parish, Mike & Karen England)*

Broxton [SJ4754]

Shady Oak [A534 towards Bulkeley]: Attractive beamed old-world pub with well kept Theakstons and nice dining area *(Roy Smylie)*

Burleydam [SJ6143]

Combermere Arms [A525 Whitchurch—Audlem]: 16th-c beamed family-oriented pub with big indoor adventure play area, Bass, Worthington and guest beers from unusual circular bar, food from sandwiches to restaurant meals, jovial landlord, pub games; piped music; open all day *(LYM)*

Chester [SJ4166]

☆ *Boot* [Eastgate Row N]: Lovely 17th-c Rows building, heavy beams, lots of woodwork, oak flooring and flagstones, even some exposed Tudor wattle and daub, black-leaded kitchen range in lounge beyond good value food servery, no-smoking oak-panelled upper area, good atmosphere and service, cheap well kept Sam Smiths; piped music, children allowed *(Graham and Lynn Mason, SLC, Sue Holland, Dave Webster, Rona Murdoch, E G Parish)*

Dublin Packet [Northgate St]: Well done

reproduction of comfortable old-style town pub, etched windows, plenty of old-world prints, Greenalls Bitter and Original, Stones and a guest such as Ridleys, cheap food counter, cheery piped music, fruit machine; open all day *(BB, SLC)*

Falchion & Firkin [Watergate St]: Typical of the chain, polished wooden floors, several beers, usual food, machines, piped music, SkyTV *(SLC)*

☆ *Falcon* [Lower Bridge St]: Striking building with good bustling atmosphere, handsome beams and brickwork, well kept Sam Smiths, decent basic bar meals (not Sun), fruit machine, piped music; children allowed lunchtime (not Sat) in airy upstairs room; jazz Sat lunchtime, open all day Sat, interesting tours of the vaults; can get packed *(LYM, Sue Holland, Dave Webster, SLC)*

Oddfellows Arms [Frodsham St]: Corner pub, open all day Mon-Sat, well kept Greenalls Bitter and Mild, bar food; handy for canal visitors *(SLC)*

☆ *Old Custom House* [Watergate St]: Traditional bare-boards bar well furnished with settles, high chairs and leatherette wall seats, lounge with cosy corners, prints, etchings, panelling and coal-effect gas fire, well kept Banks's, Marstons Pedigree, Pedigree and Head Brewer's Choice, well reproduced piped music, fruit machine; open all day *(Stephen and Jean Curtis, BB)*

Olde Kings Head [Lower Bridge St]: Very welcoming softly lit Greenalls pub in ancient building, usual Henry's Table food, upstairs restaurant and hotel part; comfortable bedrooms *(Peg Cuskley, SLC, John T Ames)*

Olde Vaults [Bridge St]: Panelling and leaded lights, well kept Greenalls, upstairs lounge *(Sue Holland, Dave Webster)*

Temple Bar [Frodsham St]: Stone and board floors, rustic furniture, Greenalls and Cains ales, bar food *(SLC)*

Watergates [Watergate St]: Good choice of quickly served tasty food in rambling candlelit medieval crypt, good wines; late evenings fills with young people and loud well reproduced music *(BB, Rona Murdoch, Andy, Julie and Stuart Hawkins, SLC)*

Childer Thornton [SJ3678]

☆ *White Lion* [off A41 S of M53 junction 5]: Low two-room whitewashed pub with well kept Thwaites Mild and Bitter, good plain lunchtime food, open fire, framed matchbooks, welcoming staff, no music or machines; swings in nice quiet garden *(MLR)*

Christleton [SJ4466]

Plough [Plough Lane]: Friendly country local dating from 1700s, interlinked lounge areas with lots of old bottles and pictures, good generous well priced food from sandwiches up, well kept Greenalls and guest beers, wide choice of wines, good coffee, eager staff *(Mr and Mrs P A King)*

Church Lawton [SJ8155]

Red Bull [Congleton Rd S (A34), by Trent & Mersey Canal]: Large and comfortable, with several rooms inc upstairs lounge and eating

area, good value food inc children's, well kept Robinsons Bitter and Hatters Mild, friendly landlord, beaten brass table-tops; soft piped music *(Bill and Kathy Cissna)*

Church Minshull [SJ6661]

☆ *Badger* [B5074 Winsford—Nantwich; handy for Shrops Union Canal, Middlewich branch]: Small spotless pub in quiet village setting, new licensees with top-class catering credentials doing impressive food in popular restaurant, relaxed unpretentious atmosphere, good wines and beers, exceptional service; tables in garden behind *(E G Parish, Bill and Kathy Cissna, LYM)*

Congleton [SJ8663]

Heath Farm: Popular open-plan country-theme family dining pub in converted farmhouse, no-smoking and family areas inc attached indoor play area (but also a child-free dining area), usual food inc good vegetarian choice; well kept Marstons Pedigree, Slaters Premium and Tetleys, friendly staff, open all day *(Richard Lewis)*

Horseshoe [Fence Lane, Newbold Astbury, between A34 and A527 S]: Former farmhouse in peaceful countryside, farm tools, guns and decorative plates in the three rooms, some dimpled copper tables, well kept Robinsons, decent food all week, friendly staff and customers, no piped music; popular with farmers and in summer families – tables and good play area outside *(Rob Fowell)*

Coppenhall Moss [SJ7158]

White Lion [Warmington Rd]: Several original small rooms now combined into large comfortable lounge, wide choice of very reasonably priced no-nonsense food inc vegetarian here and in dining room, small helpings on request, rough-floored public bar, licensees who aim to please; by farmland just outside Crewe *(E G Parish)*

Cotebrook [SJ5765]

☆ *Alvanley Arms* [junction A49/B5152 N of Tarporley]: Handsome old creeper-covered Georgian inn with two clean comfortable rooms (one no smoking) off chintzy hall, tasty reasonably priced food from sandwiches to excellent fish, friendly landlord, well kept Robinsons Mild and Best, decent house wines, several malt whiskies, big open fire, neat high beams, interesting sporting and other prints; attractive fairy-lit pond-side garden; children in restaurant, good value bedrooms *(Raymond Hebson, LYM, A J Barker, John McDonald, Ann Bond, W C M Jones, SLC, Neil Ben)*

Crewe [SJ7053]

Albion [Pedley St]: Backstreet local in area awaiting redevelopment, well kept Tetleys Bitter and Dark Mild and ever-changing interesting guest beers, friendly staff, railway-theme lounge, lively bar with darts, dominoes, TV and pool room; piped music, quiz night Weds, open 7(4 Mon, 2 Fri, 12 Sat)-11, 12-3, 7-10.30 Sun *(E G Parish, Sue Holland, Dave Webster, JP, PP, Richard Lewis, Andy and Jill Kassube)*

Bank [Nantwich Rd]: Spacious converted bank popular with clubbers even midweek, karaoke thrice weekly, Fri/Sat party nights, but quieter lunchtime with Banks's Bitter and Mild, friendly staff; piped music *(E G Parish)*

British Lion [58 Nantwich Rd]: Snug local, genuine and friendly, with comfortable partly panelled bar, back snug, well kept Tetleys-related ales and a guest such as Fullers London Pride, friendly staff; known as the Pig *(E G Parish, Sue Holland, Dave Webster, Richard Lewis)*

Cheshire Cheese [Crewe Rd, Shavington (B5071)]: Comfortably refurbished Greenalls Millers Kitchen family dining pub, quiet alcoves, good friendly young staff, above-average bar food, OAP lunchtime bargains, less sedate evenings, well kept Boddingtons, Greenalls Original, Tetleys and a guest beer, good disabled access, high chairs, baby-changing; tables outside, play area *(E G Parish, Sue Holland, Dave Webster)*

Crewe Arms [Nantwich Rd (A534 nr rly stn)]: Victorian businessmen's hotel with obliging friendly service, comfortable lounge with marble-topped tables, alabaster figurines, period pictures, curtained alcoves, ornate ceiling; good pubby public bar with pool, well kept Ind Coope Burton or Tetleys, powerful heating, bar food, restaurant; open all day, bedrooms *(P A Legon, Richard Lewis)*

Crown [Earle St]: Sociable down-to-earth pub with busy main front bar, two lounges (service bell pushes), back games room with pool and juke box, drinking corridor; welcoming landlady and locals, well kept Robinsons, high ceilings, old-fashioned furnishings and wallpaper; handy for Railway Heritage Centre *(Pete Baker, E G Parish, Sue Holland, Dave Webster)*

Earl of Crewe [Nantwich Rd/Ruskin Rd]: Big mock-Tudor pub interestingly divided into small panelled areas, some curtained off with settles; lots of railway prints and beer memorabilia, good choice of changing real ales kept well, good service, reasonably priced lunchtime food popular with older people; evenings more young people, busy esp w/e with loud music then *(Sue Holland, Dave Webster, E G Parish)*

Kings Arms [Earle St]: Several friendly rooms, nice tiling and panelling, well kept Whitbreads-related ales, pool, darts, dominoes and cribbage; very busy lunchtime, no food *(Sue Holland, Dave Webster)*

Rookery Wood [Weston Gate, Duchy Rd; A5020 SE]: Plush and roomy Tom Cobleigh family pub with Grecian marble-effect lounge, big bar, lots of wood, prints and artefacts, their usual menu inc children's, vegetarian and early-evening bargains, good waitress service, well kept low-priced ales such as Bass, Boddingtons, Morlands Old Speckled Hen and Worthington, log fire; good indoor supervised play barn, lots of tables and another play area outside; open all day (but cl Sat if Crewe FC play at home), good disabled facilites *(Richard Lewis, E G Parish)*

Sydney Arms [Sydney Rd]: Very reasonably priced food inc bargain daily roast, well kept ales, fast friendly service; children's slides and swing in pleasant enclosed garden – where parents have been bringing their children for 70 years or more *(E G Parish)*

Three Lamps [Earle St, by town hall]: Very popular combination of good eating place with comfortably pubby bar, lots of woodwork and attractive prints, relaxed atmosphere, friendly staff; back food area, well kept Banks's ales inc Mild; piped music, games machines, live music some nights; open all day, overlooking Town Lawn and handy for Lyceum Theatre; very busy lunchtime, esp market days – Mon, Fri, Sat *(E G Parish, Sue Holland, Dave Webster)*

Croft [SJ6394]

Horseshoe [left just after the Noggin, right at next T-junction]: Comfortable and interesting village local, friendly and well run, with several separate rooms, wide choice of good home-made food inc fresh fish in bar and restaurant, helpful staff, well kept Tetleys *(N Revell)*

Daresbury [SJ5983]

☆ *Ring o' Bells*: Huge choice of reasonably priced good food inc vegetarian, well kept Greenalls Bitter, Original and Mild and a weekly guest beer, friendly efficient service, cosy homely feel, no-smoking rooms, no piped music; big garden and play area; short walk from canal; village church window shows all Alice in Wonderland characters; bedrooms *(Dave and Deborah Irving, Bryen Martin, Graham and Lynn Mason)*

Davenham [SJ6671]

Bulls Head [465 London Rd]: Recently revamped by Greenalls, with imaginative reasonably priced food in bar and informal no-smoking restaurant; interesting wines, friendly efficient staff, spotless housekeeping *(Mr and Mrs C Pearson)*

Dean Row [SJ8781]

☆ *Unicorn* [Adlington Rd]: Roomy bar with lower no-smoking dining area on right, rustic stripped brickwork and stripped pine furniture, generous good value food, prompt friendly young staff, Boddingtons, lots of tables in pleasant garden; children allowed, no dogs *(Dave and Deborah Irving, Mr and Mrs C Roberts)*

Disley [SJ9784]

White Lion [Buxton Rd (A6)]: Well kept Lees in relaxing refurbished pub with comfortable carpeted lounge areas off polished-floor bar area, glazed dark wood screens forming booths, pool in big new games room, friendly staff, bar food; bedrooms *(Richard Lewis)*

Dodleston [SJ3661]

Red Lion [turn right on A483 from Chester at Pulford – then 1½ miles]: Good choice of food in attractive listed building, good New World wines *(David and Mary Webb)*

Eaton [SJ8765]

☆ *Plough* [A536 Congleton—Macclesfield]: Smart and prettily extended 17th-c inn, cosy fires, friendly landlord, wide choice of food from sandwiches to imaginative reasonably priced French-influence food in raftered restaurant, carvery all day Sun, well kept Banks's, Marstons and a guest beer, decent wine; piped music; attractive newly built bedrooms in renovated barn annexe with own bathrooms *(E G Parish)*

Frodsham [SJ5278]

Helter Skelter: Wide range of excellent food inc speciality welsh rarebit and vegetarian choice, nice atmosphere, guest beers and ciders, upstairs restaurant Thurs-Sat *(Madeira Faye)*
Netherton Hall [Chester Rd (A56)]: Large converted town-edge farmhouse popular for good imaginative food all day, with well kept Tetleys and four interesting guest beers such as Cambrian Dominance or Rebellion Zebedee, good choice of wine by the glass, friendly attentive young staff, no-smoking area; well behaved children welcome *(Pat and Tony Hinkins, Sue and Glenn Crooks)*
☆ *Rowlands* [Church St]: American-style bar with well kept local Weetwood Best and quickly changing guest beers (well over 1,000 in last five years) such as Adnams Extra, Coach House Blunderbuss Porter and Mallard Duckling, also bottled wheat beers and good choice of wines by the glass; sensibly short choice of good value food inc vegetarian and fresh veg, open fire, upstairs bistro, children welcome, open all day *(Andy & Jill Kassube, G Coates)*

Fullers Moor [SJ4954]

☆ *Copper Mine* [A534]: Busy and comfortable dining pub, light and airy, with pine furnishings, interesting copper-mining memorabilia, pretty nooks and crannies, wide choice of well presented tasty food from big lunchtime sandwiches to good Sun lunches, well kept Bass and Burtonwood Best, friendly staff, children welcome; spacious garden with barbecues and lovely views; handy for Sandstone Trail *(LYM, Sue Holland, Dave Webster, Graham and Lynn Mason)*

Gawsworth [SJ8969]

☆ *Harrington Arms*: Farm pub's two traditional small rooms with bare boards, fine carved bar counter, well kept Robinsons Best and Hatters Mild served in big old enamelled jugs, friendly service, pickled eggs; benches on small front cobbled terrace *(JP, PP, LYM, I and E Rispin)*

Grappenhall [SJ6486]

Dog & Dart [Bradshaw Lane (A50)]: Useful Hungry Man chain food pub, big helpings *(Graham and Lynn Mason)*

Great Budworth [SJ6778]

☆ *George & Dragon* [signed off A559 NE of Northwich]: Attractive 17th-c building in delightful village, rambling panelled lounge, beams hung with copper jugs, red plush button-back banquettes and older settles, helpful service, sensibly priced bar food, well kept Tetleys and two weekly changing guest beers, farm cider, decent coffee, no-smoking area, games in public bar, upstairs restaurant; children welcome, open all day Sat/Sun *(I Maw, LYM, Dr Oscar Puls, D S and A R Hare, Dr Peter Burnham, Julia Bryan, Andy and Jill Kassube)*

Gurnett [SJ9271]

☆ *Olde Kings Head* [just S of Macclesfield]: Welcoming split-level local by Macclesfield Canal aqueduct (moorings), old-fashioned unlit kitchen range, well kept Banks's, Boddingtons and Camerons, very generous reasonably priced food, restaurant, great service *(S G Brown, Bill Sykes, Derek Stafford)*

Haslington [SJ7355]

Fox [Crewe Rd]: Roomy and very friendly village pub, good well presented food from fresh sandwiches to original hot dishes; real ale, good house wines, helpful service; lavatories for the disabled *(E G Parish, Sue Holland, Dave Webster)*

Haughton Moss [SJ5856]

☆ *Nags Head* [Long Lane, off A49 S of Tarporley]: Very friendly black and white pub with low beams, pristine furnishings, good food inc reasonably priced lunches, excellent welcoming service, real ales, big garden with unobtrusive play area, bowling green for hire; children welcome, no dogs *(Janet Pickles, E G Parish, Sue Holland, Dave Webster)*

Hooton [SJ3678]

Chimneys [A41 (Hooton crossroads)]: Gothic-style hotel refurbished as a Bass Vintage Inn, handsome bar counter, conservatory, consistently well kept beers, good wine choice, friendly staff, good well priced changing food; comfortable bedrooms *(Graham and Lynn Mason, S J Biggins)*

Hough [SJ7151]

White Hart [A500 3 miles from M6 junction 16]: Pleasant surroundings, good home cooking (all day w/e) inc children's helpings, local ales and guest beers, decent wines *(Mr and Mrs Meacock)*

Knutsford [SJ7578]

Leigh Arms [Chelford Rd]: Marstons pub with their beers and Ansells Mild at long bar quite busy with locals, good simple choice of good value food, waitress service *(Leo and Barbara Lionet)*
White Bear: Eye-catching black and white thatched coaching inn, immaculate inside with low beams, upscale but friendly atmosphere, comfortable chairs on thick carpet, speciality pies, well kept Greenalls *(Dr and Mrs A K Clarke)*

Little Bollington [SJ7286]

☆ *Swan With Two Nicks* [the one nr Altrincham, 2 miles from M56 junction 7 – A56 towards Lymm, then first right at Stamford Arms into Park Lane; use A556 to get back on to M56 westbound]: Busy and very welcoming refurbished beamed village pub full of brass, copper and bric-a-brac, cheerful atmosphere, snug alcoves, some antique settles, peaty-scented log fire, good choice of popular freshly made generous food served quickly, well kept ales inc Boddingtons, Morlands Old Speckled Hen and Timothy Taylor Landlord, tables outside; open all day, attractive hamlet by Dunham Hall deer park, walks by Bridgewater Canal *(E G Parish, Andy and Jill Kassube, Mrs E Sanders, Sue Holland, Dave Webster, LYM)*

Little Budworth [SJ5966]

Red Lion: Pleasant little pub in unspoilt spot, handy for country strolls; comfortable lounge bar, well kept beers, good food choice, quick service *(R Davies)*

Little Stanney [SJ4174]

Old Hall Farm [Cheshire Oaks factory outlet

village]: Useful Banks's Milestone chain pub with good pub food, very pleasant helpful young staff, Banks's and Marstons ales, decent house wines; very busy lunchtime *(SLC, J F M West)*

Lower Withington [SJ8169]
Black Swan: Excellent restaurant food, also bar with snacks *(PACW)*

Macclesfield [SJ9273]
Boar Hound [Brook St]: Very well kept Robinsons Best and Hatters Mild in big comfortable local, clean and tidy, with two lounge areas, bar and separate pool room, friendly welcome and busy landlord *(C P Knights, Richard Lewis)*
☆ *Castle* [Churchwallgate]: Deceptively big character local, with two lounges, small public bar, lots of nooks and crannies inc end glass-roofed area up steps, well kept Courage Directors and Theakstons Bitter and Mild, simple lunchtime food inc proper chips *(BB, JP, PP, Sue Holland, Dave Webster)*
Flower Pot [Congleton Rd, junction Pack Lane / Ivy Lane]: Useful Robinsons pub, comfortable and nicely decorated, good value food, friendly efficient staff, good 80s piped music, garden with play area; open all day *(Richard Lewis)*
Queens [Waters Green]: Two well restored high-ceilinged rooms, spacious and plush, with well kept Holts Bitter and Mild at wonderfully low prices; open all day *(Richard Lewis, Sue Holland, Dave Webster)*
Waters Green Tavern [Waters Green, opp stn]: Boddingtons and three well kept interesting quickly changing guest beers, basic layout with back and side lounges, lunchtime food (not Sun), friendly staff and locals; open all day *(Richard Lewis)*

Marbury [SJ5645]
☆ *Swan* [NNE of Whitchurch]: Creeper-covered dining pub with new licensees in summer 1999; neatly kept partly panelled lounge, upholstered easy chairs and other country furniture, good winter fire in copper-canopied fireplace (masses of greenery in summer), discreet lighting; simple bar food, chilled Greenalls Original, Hanbury Drawwell and Tetleys, up to 40 malt whiskies; darts, pool, cribbage and dominoes, no machines or piped music; delightful village, a half-mile's country walk from the Llangollen Canal, Bridges 23 and 24 *(E G Parish, Sue & Bob Ward, Sue Holland, Dave Webster, Joan Yen, LYM)*

Marton [SJ8568]
Davenport Arms [A34 N of Congleton]: Clean and spaciously modernised, with good value home-made food in bar and restaurant; vegetarian, popular Sun lunch, friendly service; well kept Courage Directors and Ruddles Best *(Dr D J Walker)*

Mickle Trafford [SJ4569]
Shrewsbury Arms [A56]: Large, with several rooms, good value traditional home cooking inc delicious ice creams and puddings, good friendly staff, guest beers such as Flowers IPA, Morlands Old Speckled Hen and Wadworths 6X; tables outside; children welcome *(Myke and Micky Crombleholme)*

Middlewich [SJ7066]

Kings Arms: Well kept games-oriented pub, exceptionally friendly service *(Dr and Mrs A K Clarke)*

Mobberley [SJ7879]
☆ *Bird in Hand* [Knolls Green; B5085 towards Alderley]: Cosy low-beamed rooms with comfortably cushioned heavy wooden seats, warm coal fires, small pictures on Victorian wallpaper, little panelled snug, no-smoking top dining area, promptly served food from sandwiches up, summer afternoon teas, helpful staff, well kept Sam Smiths, lots of malt whiskies, pub games; occasional piped music; children allowed, open all day *(LYM, James Nunns)*
Frozen Mop [Faulkners Lane]: Comfortable Brewers Fayre dining pub with reasonably priced good food, well kept Boddingtons, Marstons Pedigree and Whitbreads Fuggles Imperial, family area *(Mr and Mrs C Roberts)*
Plough & Flail [Paddock Hill; small sign off B5085 towards Wilmslow]: Friendly and comfortable three-room pub with big helpings of good food inc fish, well kept Boddingtons and Marstons Pedigree, log fire; restaurant, good garden with play area *(Brian and Anna Marsden)*
Railway [Station Rd]: Clean and comfortable, with wide choice of food from sandwiches up in large bar and side dining room, well kept Greenalls *(Mr and Mrs C Roberts)*
☆ *Roebuck* [Town Lane; down hill from sharp bend on B5085 at E edge of 30mph limit]: Spacious and pleasant open-plan bar with brasses, pews, polished boards, panelling and alcoves; well kept real ales, good food choice from lunchtime sandwiches up, good friendly service, upstairs restaurant, seats in cobbled courtyard and garden behind, play area; children welcome *(LYM)*

Nantwich [SJ6552]
Black Lion [Welsh Row]: Three rooms alongside main bar, old-fashioned nooks and crannies, beams and bare floors, small choice of bargain food served 12-7 (often with bubble and squeak), well kept local Weetwood ales, welcoming young licensees and friendly pub dogs; jazz or blues Fri/Sat *(Pete Baker)*
Frog & Ferret [Oatmarket]: Up to seven well kept real ales inc interesting guests and Beam Heath brewed for the pub, lunchtime food, friendly young staff, front terrace; piped music, games; open all day (Sun afternoon closure) *(SLC, Sue Holland, Dave Webster, Richard Lewis)*
☆ *Lamb* [Hospital St, by side passage to central church]: Warmly civilised hotel bar, quiet and relaxed, comfortable seats inc leather chesterfields, well kept Burtonwood, decent malt whiskies, good value nicely served generous home-cooked food inc outstanding fish and chips in bar and traditional upstairs dining room, welcoming attentive staff, unobtrusive piped music; bedrooms *(E G Parish, Sue Holland, Dave Webster, Ray Hebson, BB)*
Oddfellows Arms [Welsh Row]: Low ceilings, real fires, friendly service, Burtonwood ales, reasonably priced food inc vegetarian, garden;

lovely street, antique shops *(Sue Holland, Dave Webster)*

Peacock [Crewe Rd (A534)]: Very popular Greenalls Millers Kitchen family dining pub, roomy and comfortable, with good reasonably priced food, good friendly service, well kept ales inc a guest beer, big lawn with lots of picnic-sets and excellent play area; facilities for disabled, open all day; bedrooms behind *(Richard Lewis, Janet Pickles)*

☆ *Red Cow* [Beam St]: Well renovated former Tudor farmhouse, good relaxed atmosphere, smallish lounge and bar, no-smoking dining area, good range of good value home-made food esp vegetarian and vegan, also children's and weekday OAP bargain lunch, friendly staff, well kept Robinsons Best, Mild, Old Tom, Frederics and Hartleys XB, coal fire; back pool table *(Sue Holland, Dave Webster, E G Parish, Mrs J Pullan, SLC)*

Vine [Hospital St]: Friendly and popular 17th-c pub with quiet corners, good choice of food from hearty sandwiches up, Bass, Titanic and Worthington, pub games, friendly staff, dog and locals; children welcome *(Bill and Kathy Cissna, Richard Lewis)*

Neston [SJ2976]

Harp [Quayside, down track SW of Little Neston]: Marvellous spot by ruined quay looking out over the Dee marshes to Wales, glorious sunsets with wild calls of wading birds; cosy old beamed and tiled-floor bar with real fire (can get crowded and smoky), simple comfortable lounge, beers such as Chesters Mild, Flowers IPA, Whitbreads Trophy and Timothy Taylor Landlord, friendly landlord, straightforward food lunchtime and early evening inc Sun roast, mining memorabilia; plenty of seats outside with play area, open all day from noon *(Phil Putwain, Richard Lewis, MLR)*

No Mans Heath [SJ5148]

Wheatsheaf [A41 N of Whitchurch]: Civilised and chatty, with low beams, lots of pictures, brasses, wrought iron, comfortable seats, cosy fires, friendly staff, well kept Bass, Marstons Best and Pedigree and Worthington BB, proper food; piped music; play area in garden *(Sue and Bob Ward)*

Northwich [SJ6873]

Old Broken Cross [Broken Cross (B5082 E); byTrent & Mersey Canal, Bridge 184]: Highly decorated family pub/restaurant, food all day, Boddingtons and Greenalls; children welcome *(William D Cissna)*

Parkgate [SJ2878]

Red Lion [The Parade (B5135)]: Comfortable and welcoming Victorian-feel local on attractive waterfront with great view over silted grassy estuary to Wales, good value sandwiches and home-cooked main dishes, well kept Tetleys-related ales, friendly attentive staff, 19th-c paintings and beer-mug collection, open fire, darts and pool; chatty macaw called Nelson *(Phil Putwain, Gill and Maurice McMahon, Pete Yearsley)*

Poynton [SJ9483]

☆ *Boars Head* [Shrigley Rd, Higher Poynton, off A523]: Welcoming Victorian country pub next to Middlewood Way (ex-railway walk and cycle route) and Macclesfield Canal, well refurbished with button-back leather seats (and darts) in bar, good range of enjoyable food in lounge, reasonably priced Boddingtons and Wadworths 6X, coffee etc *(Brian and Anna Marsden, W D Christian)*

Prestbury [SJ9077]

Legh Arms: Striking long heavy-beamed 16th-c building with lots of woodwork, gallery, smart atmosphere, tables laid with cloths and cutlery in comfortable main dining bar, wide choice of food inc decent sandwiches, vegetarian and bargain three-course lunch, two smaller bars inc cosy lounge, well kept Robinsons Best and Frederics, good coffee, friendly service; open all day, children welcome *(E G Parish, Mr and Mrs C Robinson)*

Rainow [SJ9576]

☆ *Highwayman* [A5002 Whaley Bridge—Macclesfield, NE of village]: Timeless unchanging moorside pub with small rooms, low 17th-c beams, good winter fires (electric other times), plenty of atmosphere, lovely views; Thwaites real ales, bar food inc good sandwiches *(LYM, JP, PP)*

Rode Heath [SJ8057]

Royal Oak [A533; a walk from Trent & Mersey Canal, Bridge 141/142]: Wide menu inc smaller helpings and children's meals, good choice of beer inc Greene King Abbot, Tetleys and Titanic *(Bill and Kathy Cissna)*

Smallwood [SJ8160]

☆ *Bulls Head* [A50 N of Alsager]: Attractive interestingly decorated dining pub, neat and tidy, with lots of space inc two conservatories, and particularly good garden with play area; well kept Marstons Pedigree, decent wines, good choice of well presented generous food inc interesting salads and excellent puddings, welcoming service; piped music, children welcome; plants for sale, quite handy for Biddulph Grange (NT) *(Sue Holland, Dave Webster, R C Vincent, LYM)*

Spurstow [SJ5657]

Yew Tree [A49 S of Tarporley]: Newly furnished and extended, with good well presented meals inc children's, reasonable prices, Burtonwood, Greenalls and Tetleys, good service; unobtrusive piped music *(SLC, Mrs E Riley, G B Rimmer)*

Swettenham [SJ8067]

☆ *Swettenham Arms* [off A54 Congleton—Holmes Chapel or A535 Chelford—Holmes Chapel]: Attractive and prettily placed old country pub with wide choice of popular if not cheap food efficiently served in charming series of individually furnished rooms from sofas and easy chairs to no-smoking dining area (must book Sun), well spaced tables, well kept ales such as Bearskinful, Bearton and Jennings, farm cider, picnic-sets on quiet side lawn; children welcome, live music Weds *(JP, PP, LYM, S and L Shore, E G Parish)*

Tarporley [SJ5563]

☆ *Red Fox* [A49/A51, a mile S]: Sympathetically extended country pub with comfortable and spacious low-beamed bar, wide range of good reasonably priced interesting food, well kept Jennings and Theakstons, good service, pleasant conservatory; handy for Beeston and Peckforton castles, open all day Sun *(E G Parish, John Higgins)*

☆ *Swan* [High St, off A49]: Tastefully modernised Georgian inn with cosy little spaces, well kept Ruddles and three guests such as Adnams, Charles Wells Bombardier and Jennings, bottled Belgian beers, lots of malt whiskies, civilised informal brasserie with rather smart food inc superb goat cheeses (also lunchtime sandwiches and snacks), separate restaurant, polite service; tables outside, provision for children; comfortable well equipped bedrooms *(Derek and Sylvia Stephenson, LYM, Sue Holland, Dave Webster, E Parish)*

Tattenhall [SJ4959]
Letters: Traditional country pub with innovative as well as more familiar home-made food, good friendly service; in very attractive village *(E G Parish)*

Thelwall [SJ6587]
Little Manor [Bell Lane]: Friendly recently modernised pub/restaurant with good atmosphere in series of contrasting environments, good value food, fine range of beers, affordable wines, over-55 discounts *(Mr and Mrs Stuart Shore)*

Walgherton [SJ6949]
Boars Head [A51 between Bridgemere Gdn Centre and Stapeley Water Gdns]: Large Greenalls family pub with olde-worlde decor of prints and boar's head, small dining areas, nice conservatory, good choice of generous quick food all day from sandwiches up, Boddingtons and Greenalls, friendly young uniformed staff, games; big garden with picnic-sets and play area; bedrooms *(Roland Saussehod, E G Parish)*

Warmingham [SJ7161]
☆ *Bears Paw* [School Lane]: Interesting food inc lots of specials and enormous filled baguettes, plush seating around marble-top tables in raised areas, well kept Bass, Boddingtons and Worthington BB, relaxed atmosphere, friendly and helpful staff, charming restaurant, pool room, children very welcome; good spot by river and ancient church in small hamlet, seats in front garden, bedrooms *(E G Parish, Edward Leetham)*

Waverton [SJ4663]
Black Dog [A41 S of Chester]: Greenalls dining

pub with modern pine and light oak decor, good food choice, Boddingtons and Greenalls Bitter and Mild, cordial licensees, big tasteful lounge, small garden; occasional jazz evenings, piped music *(Graham and Lynn Mason, SLC)*

Wheelock [SJ7559]
Commercial [off new A534 bypass]: Old-fashioned unspoilt four-room local, one no smoking, high ceilings, Boddingtons, Thwaites and a guest beer, real fire, firmly efficient service; pool, occasional informal live music *(Sue Holland, Dave Webster)*

Wildboarclough [SJ9868]
☆ *Crag*: Welcoming old stonebuilt pub hidden in charming little sheltered valley below the moors, well kept beer, bar and restaurant food; plastic shoe covers in the entrance porch for ramblers, pretty terrace *(Richard C Morgan, Dave and Deborah Irving, LYM)*

Wilmslow [SJ8481]
King William [A34]: Robinsons pub with cosy alcoves opening off bar, well kept sensibly priced real ales, decent weekday lunchtime food, friendly atmosphere; children welcome *(Dave and Deborah Irving)*

Withington [SJ8169]
Red Lion [Trap St, Dicklow Cob, Lower Withington; off B5392]: Friendly and spacious two-bar pub on village green, good varied bar food from huge sandwiches up, well kept Robinsons Bitter and Hatters Mild and a guest beer, friendly efficient service, comfortable restaurant, children welcome; tables outside, handy for Jodrell Bank *(Ian & Nita Cooper)*

Wrenbury [SJ5948]
Cotton Arms: Beamed and timbered pub with good value food in two large dining areas, friendly staff, Greenalls Bitter and Mild and a guest beer, lots of brass, open fire, side games room *(Richard Lewis)*

Wybunbury [SJ6950]
☆ *Swan* [B5071]: Spotless bow-windowed pub with nooks and crannies in rambling lounge, snug dining areas inc no-smoking one, pleasant public bar, well kept Marstons, Boddingtons, Thwaites and two interesting guest beers, enjoyable reasonably priced home cooking, polite, efficient and helpful service, tasteful furnishings inc plenty of bric-a-brac – shop at the back; seats in garden by beautiful churchyard; bedrooms *(Sue Holland, Dave Webster, S and L Shore, E G Parish, Graham and Lynn Mason, SLC, M Dickinson, LYM)*

Post Office address codings confusingly give the impression that some pubs are in Cheshire, when they're really in Derbyshire (and therefore included in this book under that chapter) or in Greater Manchester (see the Lancashire chapter).

Cornwall

Cornwall has a good mix of interesting pubs, as well as some top-class landlords and landladies who run tight ships even under huge pressure at peak summer holiday times. Pubs currently doing particularly well here include the Trengilly Wartha near Constantine (cleverly combining an appeal to families and people wanting somewhere nice to stay, as well as those looking for good food and drink), the pretty Earl of St Vincent tucked away at Egloshayle (quite smart in the evening, with a fascinating clock collection), the Halzephron set back from the cliffs at Gunwalloe south of Helston, the very friendly Crown at Lanlivery, the ancient Miners Arms at Mithian (good newish licensees), the idyllically placed Pandora near Mylor Bridge, the delightful Roseland at Philleigh (a real charmer), the thriving harbourside Ship in Porthleven, the bustling waterside Sloop in St Ives with its St Ives School paintings (a newcomer to the Guide), the unaffected little Victory in St Mawes, the unpretentious White Hart in St Teath (back in these pages after an absence – a proper village pub of the best sort, with commendably cheap drinks), the Springer Spaniel at Treburley (enjoyable all round, particularly good food), the flourishing and very interesting Eliot Arms at Tregadillett, the eccentric Crooked Inn at Trematon (a new discovery for us), and the cheery Old Ale House in Truro (vast beer choice). Many of these have enjoyable food, but for a special meal out we name as Cornwall Dining Pub of the Year the Trengilly Wartha near Constantine. This year we found that in half the Cornish free houses the cheapest beer on offer was from Sharps of north Cornwall, which started only in 1994 – a real achievement to have penetrated the market so well, and a demonstration of their beers' quality (we always look forward to it on our Cornish inspection trips). The much longer-established St Austell brewery is the mainstay of the Cornish tied trade, and with its relatively low pricing policy helps to keep Cornish drinks prices below the national average; one St Austell tied pub, the Lugger in Polruan, was outstandingly cheap. In the Lucky Dip section at the end of the chapter, among a good choice (many inspected and firmly recommended by us) pubs which currently stand out are the Napoleon at Boscastle, Falcon in Bude, Chain Locker and Seven Stars in Falmouth, Gurnards Head Hotel on Gurnards Head, Red Lion at Mawnan Smith, Fountain in Mevagissey, Old Inn at Mullion, Royal Oak at Perranwell and Who'd Have Thought It at St Dominick.

BODINNICK SX1352 Map 1
Old Ferry ★
Across the water from Fowey

Reached by ferry from Fowey or down winding little lanes, this friendly old inn by the river is well worth finding. The three simply furnished little rooms have quite a few bits of nautical memorabilia, a couple of half model ships mounted on the wall, and several old photographs, as well as wheelback chairs, built-in plush pink wall seats, and an old high-backed settle. The games room at the back is actually hewn into the rock and has darts, dominoes, and piped music. Bar food includes home-made soup (£2.95), sandwiches (from £2.15; toasties 25p extra), ploughman's (from £4.95), quite a few dishes with chips (from £2.95; home-cooked ham and egg £3.95), home-made cream cheese and broccoli pasta bake (£5.95), curry of the day (£6.25), home-made steak and kidney pie (£6.50), fresh smoked haddock with scrambled egg (£7.95), puddings (from £2.75), good daily specials, and children's meals; the restaurant is no smoking. Well kept Sharps Own on handpump kept under light blanket pressure. Make sure your brakes work well if you park on the steep lane outside. Some of the bedrooms look out over the river. *(Recommended by Mr and Mrs D Humphries, A J Thomas, Caroline Jones, J and F Gowers, Mayur Shah)*

Free house ~ Licensees Royce and Patricia Smith ~ Real ale ~ Bar food (12-3, 6-9.30; 12-3, 6-8.30 in winter) ~ Restaurant ~ (01726) 870237 ~ Children in eating area of bar ~ Open 11-11; 12-10.30 Sun; 11-3, 6-11 Mon-Sat winter ~ Bedrooms: £30(£40B)/£40(£60B)

BOSCASTLE SX0990 Map 1
Cobweb

B3263, just E of harbour

One couple who stayed here on their honeymoon nearly 20 years ago were delighted to find that this bustling and friendly old pub had hardly changed at all. It's set in a pretty village close to the tiny steeply cut harbour, and has plenty of atmosphere in its lively public bar where hundreds of old bottles hang from the heavy beams; there are also two or three curved high-backed winged settles against the dark stone walls, a few leatherette dining chairs, and a cosy log fire. Well kept St Austell Tinners, HSD, and guest beers on handpump, and several malt whiskies. Bar food includes sandwiches (from £1.60; french bread from £2.30), filled baked potatoes (from £2), ploughman's or pizza (from £3.50), vegetarian dishes or a daily roast (£4.50), steaks (from £7.50), mixed grill (£10.50), and a home-made special (£5.50); the restaurant is no smoking. Darts, pool, dominoes, cribbage, video game, fruit machine, and juke box; the big communicating family room has an enormous armchair carved out of a tree trunk as well as its more conventional windsor armchairs, and another winter fire. Opening off this is a good-sized children's room and more machines. *(Recommended by the Didler, David Carr, Gwen and Peter Andrews, Keith Stevens, John and Vivienne Rice, JP, PP, Dr Peter Burnham, Julia Bryan, Barry and Anne, Mr and Mrs P Stubbs)*

Free house ~ Licensees Ivor and Adrian Bright ~ Real ale ~ Bar food (not 25 Dec) ~ (01840) 250278 ~ Children in eating area of bar and in own room ~ Open 11-11(11-2.30, 6-11 Mon-Thurs Jan/Feb; 12-10.30 Sun

CHAPEL AMBLE SW9975 Map 1
Maltsters Arms ★ ♀

Village signposted from A39 NE of Wadebridge, and from B3314

Run by friendly, hard-working licensees, this bustling pub is much enjoyed by readers. There's a pleasant, relaxed atmosphere in the attractively knocked-together rooms, black oak joists in the white ceiling, partly panelled stripped stone walls, heavy wooden tables on the partly carpeted big flagstones, and a large stone fireplace; the bar extension is hung with ship pictures and a growing collection of seafaring memorabilia. There's also a no-smoking side room with windsor chairs and a no-smoking upstairs family room. Popular bar food at lunchtime includes open sandwiches and ciabatta bread with fillings like rare beef and horseradish or avocado and prawns, ploughman's with good west country cheeses, home-made soup (£2.50), home-made pâté (£3.75), lamb hotpot (£4.95), and steak and kidney pudding or Cornish crab dishes like salad or au gratin (from £5.95); also, roasted sweet pepper with Cornish feta cheese (£4.75), seafood bisque (£5.25), wild mushroom tart (£10.25), shank of lamb braised with prunes, honey and almonds (£11.25), fishy daily specials such as sardines (£4.25), scallops with bacon and cream (£12.95) or whole bass baked with fennel and flamed in Pernod (£14.25), and puddings such as chocolate and banana bread and butter pudding; they also serve breakfasts between 9 and 11. The main restaurant is no smoking. Well kept Bass, Greene King Abbot, Sharps Cornish, and Malsters Special (brewed specially for the pub by Sharps) on handpump kept under light blanket pressure; 20 wines by the glass, 28 malt whiskies, a good range of brandies and armagnacs, and even milk shakes. Cribbage, dominoes, and piped music. Benches outside in a sheltered sunny corner, and pretty hanging baskets and tubs. *(Recommended by R and S Bentley, D R Eberlin, I H Baker, Juliet Winsor, M J Dowdy, M Borthwick, John Westlake, M G Hart, Roger Byrne, Peter Salmon, Jacquie and Jim Jones, the Didler, Mr and Mrs S Groves, Ted George, Graham Tayar, Catherine Raeburn, Mr and Mrs Ian Carrington, D B Jenkin, John A Barker, D Martin, C P Scott-Malden, Tim Barrow, Sue Demont, Rita Horridge, John and Jackie Chalcraft, Peter and Daphne Ross, David Carr)*

Free house ~ Licensees David & Marie Gray and David Coles ~ Real ale ~ Bar food (12-2, 6-9.30) ~ Restaurant ~ (01208) 812473 ~ Children in family room and, if over 8, in restaurant ~ Open 10.30-2.30, 6-11; 12-2.30, 7-10.30 Sun; closed evening 25 Dec

CONSTANTINE SW7229 Map 1
Trengilly Wartha ★ ⓦ ♀ ◣ 🛏

Constantine signposted from Penryn—Gweek rd (former B3291); in village turn right just before Minimarket (towards Gweek); in nearly a mile pub signposted left; at Nancenoy, OS sheet 204, map reference 731282

Cornwall Dining Pub of the Year

It's a real achievement to combine under one roof somewhere for a casual drink or very enjoyable meal, as well as a place where families feel genuinely welcomed and that offers thoughtfully furnished cottagey bedrooms. The hard-working licensees of this extremely well run inn, tucked away down narrow lanes, have done just that – as the continuing warm reports from many readers testify. The long low-beamed main bar has a woodburning stove and attractive built-in high-backed settles boxing in polished heavy wooden tables, and at one end, shelves of interesting wines with drink-in and take-out price labels (they run their own retail wine business, Cochonnet Wines). There's a bright no-smoking family conservatory with an area leading off that houses pool, fruit machine, video game, darts, shove-ha'penny, and cribbage. Super bar food includes specials like smoked mackerel and cheese pot (£3.50), king prawn kebabs (£4.50), wild mushroom pasta gratin (£5.80), cod baked on a bed of boulangère potatoes (£7.80) or Malaysian duck and chicken legs in a rich soy and fresh ginger sauce (£8.50), as well as home-made soup, meaty or vegetarian pasty (£3.50), Devon blue cheese and walnut pâté (£3.80), lunchtime ploughman's with their own pickled vegetables and chutneys (from £4.80), smoked chicken strudel (£6.80), Thai pork (£7.80); and home-made puddings such as chocolate and nut parfait, raspberry crème brûlée or sticky toffee pudding or a plate of 6 in miniature (from £2.60); they do a children's menu (from £2.40) but will give small helpings of adult food where possible and have marked the weekly specials with a smiley face to indicate dishes that are more appropriate to smaller appetites; good breakfasts with home-made jam and marmalade. They keep an unusually wide choice of drinks for the area, such as well kept Cotleigh, Keltek Golden Lance, Skinner's Best Bitter, and Sharps Cornish on handpump with regularly changing ales from smaller brewers tapped from the cask. Also, over 40 malt whiskies (including several extinct ones), 20 wines by the glass, and around 10 armagnacs. The pretty landscaped garden has some tables under large parasols, an international sized piste for boules, and a lake; lots of walks. *(Recommended by DJW, Marvadene B Eves, R and S Bentley, JP, PP, Walter and Susan Rinaldi-Butcher, RB, Mr and Mrs A Scrutton, W K Wood, N Cobb, George Atkinson, R and M Wallace, Gwen and Peter Andrews, Hazel R Morgan, Paul and Pam Penrose, Dave and Deborah Irving, John Woodward, John and Christine Lowe, Steve Willey, Dr and Mrs A J Newton, Tim Barrow, Sue Demont, W M and J M Cottrell, the Didler, Tim and Beryl Dawson, P and M Rudlin, Michael Sar; also in the Good Hotel Guide)*

Free house ~ Licensees Nigel Logan and Michael Maguire ~ Real ale ~ Bar food (12-2.15, 6.30-9.30) ~ Restaurant ~ (01326) 340332 ~ Children welcome ~ Open 11-3, 6.30-11; 12-3, 7-10.30 Sun ~ Bedrooms: £39(£45B)/£54(£68B)

CREMYLL SX4553 Map 1

Edgcumbe Arms

End of B3247, off A374 at Crafthole (coming from A38) or Antony (from Torpoint car ferry)

New licensees have taken over this bustling pub and are keen to make it a place for all the family. There are lots of old-fashioned small rooms with panelling, beam-and-plank ceilings, slate flagstones and bare boards, and furnishings to match – big stripped high-backed settles, pews, fireside sofa, housekeeper's chairs, pretty cushions and the like, with candles on tables and plenty of decorative china, copper, brass and old pictures; they plan to create an area for non smokers. At lunchtime, bar food includes sandwiches, ploughman's (£3.95), real ham and egg (£4.95), 12oz rump steak (£8.95), and half a roast duck or mixed grill (£10.95). Well kept St Austell HSD, Tinners, Trelawny's Pride , and Cousin Jack on handpump; darts, pool, fruit machine, video game, and juke box. The pub is in a super setting by the foot ferry from Plymouth, with good Tamar views from its bow-window seats and from waterside tables outside. There are splendid walks in nearby waterfront parkland. *(Recommended by Graham and Karen Oddey, Shirley Mackenzie, Miss A G Drake, Tim Jacobson, Ted George, June and Perry Dann, Betty Petheram, Andrea and Shirley Mackenzie, Dr and Mrs B D Smith, A Browne)*

St Austell ~ Managers David and Amanda Rowe ~ Real ale ~ Bar food ~ (01752) 822294 ~ Children welcome ~ Open 11-11; 12-10.30 Sun ~ Bedrooms: £32.50B/£50B

CROWS NEST SX2669 Map 1

Crows Nest £

Signposted off B3264 N of Liskeard; or pleasant drive from A30 by Siblyback/St Cleer rd from Bolventor, turning left at Common Moor, Siblyback signpost, then forking right to Darite; OS Sheet 201 map reference 263692

Handy for walks on the southern slopes of Bodmin Moor, this old-fashioned 17th-c pub used to be the pay office/company store where tin and copper miners were paid. There are lots of pictures and cards about the mines, stirrups, bits and spurs hanging from the bowed dark oak beams, an interesting table converted from a huge blacksmith's bellows (which still work), and an unusually long black wall settle by the big log fire as well as other more orthodox seats. On the right, and divided by a balustered partition, is a similar area with old local photographs. Good value bar food includes pasties (£1.55), baps (from £1.95), ploughman's (from £3.50), and daily specials such as a vegetarian dish or pies like beef in Guinness or chicken and mushroom (£5). Well kept St Austell Tinners and HSD on handpump, and decent wines; piped music. On the terrace by the quiet lane there are picnic-sets. *(Recommended by Miss A G Drake, JP, PP, Dr M W A Haward, Ted George, Ian Phillips)*

St Austell ~ Tenants Roy and Sue Hughes ~ Real ale ~ Bar food (not winter Sun evening) ~ (01579) 345930 ~ Children in eating area of bar ~ Open 11-3, 6-11; 12-3, 7-10.30 Sun

DULOE SX2358 Map 1

Olde Plough House

B3254 N of Looe

Very neatly kept, this bustling pub is well liked for its good, enjoyable food. As well as sandwiches and starters such as home-made soup (£1.95), salad niçoise (£3.85), local scallops in a creamy mushroom and basil sauce (£4.10), and home-made stilton pâté (£4.25), there might be tropical vegetable curry (£5.95), beef and stilton pie (£6.65), chicken breast filled with a walnut and mushroom stuffing wrapped in smoked bacon and served with a dijonnaise sauce (£7.95), tiger prawns in a chilli tomato sauce (£9.25), duck breast in blueberry sauce (£9.65), their speciality sizzler dishes (meat cooked on hot stones from £6.65), and home-made puddings. Both communicating rooms have a lovely dark polished Delabole slate floor, some turkey rugs, a mix of pews, modern high-backed settles and smaller chairs, foreign banknotes on the beams, three woodburning stoves, and a restrained decor – some prints of waterfowl and country scenes, a few copper jugs and a fat china pig perched on window sills. The public side (just as comfortable) has darts; cribbage and piped music. Bass, Butcome Bitter, and Sharps Doom Bar on handpump, sensibly priced wines, good attentive service. There is a small more modern carpeted dining room, and a few picnic-sets out by the road. The two friendly jack russells are called Jack and Spot, and the cat, Willow. *(Recommended by W W Burke, R Turnham, Ian Phillips, Martin Jones, John and Joan Calvert)*

Free house ~ Licensees Gary and Alison Toms ~ Real ale ~ Bar food ~ Restaurant ~ (01503) 262050 ~ Children in eating area of bar ~ Open 12-2.30, 6-11; 12-2.30, 7-10.30 Sun; closed evening 25 Dec

EDMONTON SW9672 Map 1
Quarryman
Village signposted off A39 just W of Wadebridge bypass

Just a good brisk walk from the Camel estuary, this relaxed pub is in a pleasant spot and is built around a carefully reconstructed slate-built courtyard of former quarrymen's quarters. The three beamed rooms (one is no smoking) have simple pleasant furnishings, fresh flowers on tables, a woodburner, and a couple of bow windows (one with a charming stained-glass quarryman panel) looking out to a distant wind farm; there's some interesting sporting memorabilia – particularly the Roy Ullyett menu cartoons for British Sportsman's Club Savoy lunches for visiting cricket and rugby international teams. Good bar food includes sandwiches (from £2.50; a bumper bacon butty £3), filled baked potatoes or ploughman's (from £3.50), meaty or vegetable lasagne or pies like minted lamb or sausage, cider and apple (£4.90), chargrilled sardines (£5.50), outstanding Aberdeen Angus sizzle steaks (from £9.50), fresh locally caught fish, daily specials like Moroccan lamb tagine, moussaka with greek salad or roast duck with plum and ginger sauce, and very tempting puddings (£2.50). They have four well kept beers on handpump such as Bass, Greene King Abbot, Sharps Doom Bar, and Skinners Coastliner, decent house wines and some interesting good value bottles, and 20 malt whiskies; pool and fruit machine. The dog's called Floyd. There's a cosy no-smoking bistro on the other side of the courtyard. This interesting pub forms part of an attractively understated small health and holiday complex. *(Recommended by S Stubbs, John Wood, Mr and Mrs B Hobden, P and M Rudlin)*

Free house ~ Licensees Terry and Wendy De Villiers Kuun ~ Real ale ~ Bar food ~ (01208) 816444 ~ Children in eating area of bar ~ Folk music Tues evenings ~ Open 12-11; 12-10.30 Sun ~ Bedrooms: /£50B

EGLOSHAYLE SX0172 Map 1
Earl of St Vincent
Off A389, just outside Wadebridge

Friendly and full of interest, this comfortable and civilised pretty pub is tucked away in a narrow quiet back street behind the church. There's a combination of rich furnishings and a fascinating collection of antique clocks (all in working order), golfing memorabilia and art deco ornaments; piped music. Well kept St Austell Tinners, HSD or Cousin Jacks, and good food such as home-made soup (£2), sandwiches (from £2), liver and bacon (£3.75), good salads (from £4; crab £6.50), steak and kidney pie (£4.50), chicken in leek and stilton (£8.50), fresh fish such as trout (£9), grilled dover sole (£12) or bass (£13), and puddings (£2.50); people do tend to dress smartly in the evening. The snug is no smoking. In summer, there are picnic-sets in the lovely garden here and marvellous flowering baskets and tubs. *(Recommended by David Carr, John Westlake, Christopher Darwent, C J Parsons, John A Barker, GS and EM Dorey, Mr and Mrs B Hobden, Pat and Tony Martin, Mike and Heather Watson, H J Gray, Mr and Mrs Cottrell, P and J Salmon, Nigel and Olga Wikeley, Chris Parsons, the Didler, Tim Barrow, Sue Demont, Hazel R Morgan)*

St Austell ~ Tenants Edward and Anne Connolly ~ Real ale ~ Bar food ~ (01208)

814807 ~ Children in eating area of bar lunchtime only; must be over 12 in evening ~ Open 11-3, 6.30-11; 12-3, 7-10.30 Sun

FALMOUTH SW8032 Map 1
Quayside Inn & Old Ale House 🍺 £
ArwenackSt/Fore St

As we went to press we heard that the licensee of this busy pub would shortly be leaving, so we are keeping our fingers crossed that the new people will carry on in the same tradition. It's the fine range of up to 20 real ales that the pub is known for: Bass, Courage Directors, Flowers Original, Sharps Special Ale, Doom Bar, and Own, and Tetleys on handpump, with up to another 14 tapped from the cask; they hold beer fesitvals during the Spring and Autumn half-terms. Scrumpy Jack cider and country wines. There are lots of beer mats on the panelled walls, book matches on the black ceiling, malt sacks tacked into the counter, a big white ensign, a mix of ordinary pub chairs on the bare boards, and a log-effect gas fire in the stripped stone fireplace; piped music. Upstairs is the lounge bar (which you enter from the attractively bustling shopping street) with comfortable armchairs and sofas at one end, more straightforward tables and chairs at the other, and picture windows overlooking the harbour. Bar food includes popular 'hot hands' (bloomer loaves filled with garlic butter, onions and cheese or bacon and mushrooms and baked in the oven from £1.95), filled baked potatoes (from £2.45), doorstep sandwiches (from £2.65), sausage and mash (£3.25), ploughman's (from £3.65), and sizzling beef with ginger and spring onion in oyster sauce, five spice chicken or cantonese prawns (from £4.95). There are picnic-sets on the tarmac by the Custom House Dock. *(Recommended by Ted George, John Wooll, Dr M E Wilson, Nigel Woolliscroft)*

Greenalls ~ Manager Raymond Thomas Gascoigne ~ Real ale ~ Bar food (served all day) ~ (01326) 312113 ~ Children welcome until 9pm ~ Live music Fri and Sat evenings ~ Open 11-11; 12-10.30 Sun

HELFORD SW7526 Map 1
Shipwrights Arms
Off B3293 SE of Helston, via Mawgan

In summer, this thatched pub is especially popular as the terraces outside are set above a lovely wooded creek, and in summer they hold barbecues in the evening with cajun pork chops, marinated lamb fillet or swordfish, steaks, and prawns in garlic or monkfish – all from around £8. Inside there's quite a nautical theme with navigation lamps, models of ships, sea pictures, drawings of lifeboat coxswains and shark fishing photographs – as well as a collection of foreign banknotes behind the bar counter. A dining area has oak settles and tables; winter open fire. Well kept Flowers IPA and Castle Eden on handpump, and bar food such as a starters (from £2.60), good ploughman's, summer salads including lobster and crab (from £7.50), winter stews such as steak and mushroom in ale, and home-made puddings (£3.75). It does get crowded at peak times and it is quite a walk from the nearest car park. *(Recommended by D P and J A Sweeney, JP, PP, C Robinson, John Woodward, Marvadene B Eves, Mike and Wena Stevenson, Ted George, George Atkinson, Trevor Owen)*

Greenalls ~ Lease: Charles Herbert ~ Real ale ~ Bar food (not winter Sun evenings) ~ (01326) 231235 ~ Children in eating area of bar ~ Open 11-2.30, 6-11; 12-2.30, 7-10.30 Sun; closed winter Sun evenings

HELSTON SW6527 Map 1
Blue Anchor 🍺 £
50 Coinagehall Street

It's the completely unchanging character that readers like so much about this old thatched pub. It remains a basic drinkers' tavern with its own very good Middle, Best, 'Spingo' Special, and Easter and Christmas Special ales from what is probably the oldest brewing house in the country; they also sell farm cider. A series of small, low-ceilinged rooms opens off the central corridor, with simple old-fashioned furniture on the flagstones, interesting old prints, some bared stone walls, and in one room a fine inglenook fireplace. A family room has darts; dominoes. Bar food includes rolls and sandwiches (from £1.30), home-made soup (£1.65), ham and egg (£3.45), ploughman's (from £3.50), liver and bacon hotpot (£3.55), steak and kidney pie or curry (£4.60), and daily specials. Past an old stone bench in the sheltered little terrace area is a skittle alley which you can hire. At lunchtimes you can usually go and look round the brewery and the cellar. *(Recommended by Mayur Shah, Dave and Deborah Irving, Jack and Gemima Valiant, JP, PP, Nick Lawless, George Atkinson, the Didler, Ewan and Moira McCall, Mark Brock, Hazel R Morgan, Reg Nelson, Roger Huggins)*

Free house ~ Licensee Mrs Kim Stone ~ Real ale ~ Bar food (12-4) ~ (01326) 562821 ~ Children in own room ~ Live jazz/folk ~ Open 11-11; 12-10.30 Sun

Halzephron ♀ ⇌

Gunwalloe, village about 4 miles S but not marked on many road maps; look for brown sign on A3083 alongside perimeter fence of RNAS *Culdrose*

It's such an enjoyable pub, that this former smugglers' haunt does get busy at peak times, but the friendly licensees remain unfailingly welcoming and helpful even at their busiest. The bustling and pleasant bar is spotlessly clean with comfortable seating, copper on the walls and mantelpiece, and the two cats (Humphrey the gentle black one and a lively marmalade one called Mr Chivers) much in evidence and usually sitting by the warm winter fire in the big hearth; there's also a quite a small no-smoking family room. Good bar food includes sandwiches (lunchtimes, from £2.40; crab £5.80), home-made soup (£3.20), ploughman's (from £4.20), grilled goat's cheese on garlic bread (£4.40), prawn or crab platters (from £9.80), tasty daily specials, evening extras such as chicken in a herb and dijon mustard marinade (£8.50) and sirloin steak (£10.40), and home-made puddings (£3.20); the restaurant and the snug are no smoking. Well kept Dartmoor Best and Sharps Own and Doom Bar on handpump, a good wine list, 40 malt whiskies, and around 35 liqueurs; darts, dominoes and cribbage. Small but comfortable and well equipped bedrooms – and huge breakfasts. There are lots of surrounding unspoilt walks with fine views of Mount's Bay, Gunwalloe fishing cove just 300 yards away, and a sandy beach one mile away at Gunwalloe Church Cove. *(Recommended by Freda Macnamara, Carolyn and Trevor Golds, D B Jenkin, Barry and Anne, P and J Salmon, W M and J M Cottrell, Mrs R Heaton, Hazel R Morgan, Cliff Blakemore, Nick Lawless, C Robinson, Michael Sargent, James Nunns, Tim Barrow, Sue Demont, Mark Brock, JMC, P Weedon, S Horsley)*

Free house ~ Licensees Angela Thomas ~ Real ale ~ Bar food ~ Restaurant ~ (01326) 240406 ~ Children in restaurant if over 8, and in family room ~ Open 11-2.30, 6(6.30 winter)-11; 12-2.30, 6.30-10.30 Sun; closed 25 Dec ~ Bedrooms: £35B/£64B

KINGSAND SX4350 Map 1
Halfway House ⇌

Fore St, towards Caws

There are marvellous walks surrounding this attractive old inn and after you've been blown about on the cliffs at Rame Head, the simply furnished but quite smart bar here is a good place to relax. It's mildly Victorian in style, neatly kept and cosy, and rambles around a huge central fireplace, with low ceilings, soft lighting, and plenty of locals – though there's a warm welcome for the many summer visitors. Bar food is good and enjoyable and includes daily specials such as fish soup with rouille and croutons (£3.50), grilled goat's cheese with onion marmalade (£3.95), venison casserole (£8.25), chicken supreme with sun-dried tomatoes and smoked sausage (£8.45), roast knuckle of lamb with wild mushrooms (£8.95), grilled duck breast with a port and orange sauce (£9.95), and bass with pimento and prawn butter (£11.95); they also offer soup (£2.75), filled french bread (from £2), filled baked potatoes (from £3.50), ploughman's (from £5), home-cooked ham and egg (£5.75), vegetable tikka masala (£6.50), a curry of the day (£7), and steaks (from £9.45); vegetables are fresh and carefully cooked. There are often attractive fresh flowers on the tables. Well kept Bass, Boddingtons, Sharps Doom Bar or Cornish on handpump kept under light blanket pressure, and decent wines. Service is quick and friendly, and the bar staff add a lot to the enjoyable atmosphere. The piped music is generally unobtrusive; cribbage, dominoes, backgammon, chess, and fruit machine. The village is well placed for visiting Mount Edgcumbe. *(Recommended by Dr and Mrs B D Smith, Ian Moore, R Turnham, Graham and Karen Oddey, Charles Gray, Jacquie and Jim Jones, Ted George)*

Free house ~ Licensees Sarah and David Riggs ~ Real ale ~ Bar food ~ Restaurant ~ (01752) 822279 ~ Children welcome ~ Quiz winter Thurs evenings; choirs Weds evenings ~ Open 12-4, 7-11; 12-4, 7-10.30 Sun ~ Bedrooms: £25S/£50S

LAMORNA SW4424 Map 1
Lamorna Wink
Off B3315 SW of Penzance

Just a short walk up a leafy lane from the attractive little cove (where there are bracing walks along the coastal path) this neatly kept local is a fine place for a lunchtime break. It's simply furnished, and has one of the best collections of warship mementoes, sea photographs and nautical brassware in the county. Bar food includes locally made pasty, sandwiches (from £1.50; fresh local crab £4.25), a choice of home-made quiche (£3.50), ploughman's (£4), and fresh local crab salad (in season, £10). Pool and fruit machine. There are front benches outside where you can just hear the sound of the sea and the burble of the stream behind. *(Recommended by Simon Williams, Michael and Lorna Bourdeaux, Jack and Gemima Valiant)*

Free house ~ Licensee Robert Drennan ~ Real ale ~ Bar food (not winter evenings) ~ (01736) 731566 ~ Children in games room ~ Open 11-11; 12-10.30 Sun; 11-4, 6-11 winter

LANLIVERY SX0759 Map 1
Crown 🍺
Signed off A390 Lostwithiel—St Austell

Genuinely helpful and friendly licensees run this popular little pub (acutally one of Cornwall's oldest inns), and the rambling series of rooms has no noisy games machines, music or pool tables – just a good chatty and relaxed atmosphere. The small, dimly lit public bar has heavy beams, a slate floor, and built-in wall settles and attractive alcove of seats in the dark former chimney; darts. A much lighter room leads off here with beams in the white boarded ceiling, some comfortable plush sofas in one corner, cushioned black settles, a small cabinet with wood turnings for sale, owl and badger pictures, and a little fireplace with an old-fashioned fire; there's another similar small room. Well liked bar food includes sandwiches (from £1.60), home-made soup (£2.60), ploughman's (from £3.50), home-made curries (from £5.95), and daily specials such as pasta neapolitan (£4.50), liver and bacon with onion gravy (£4.75), hake in green sauce or whiting in breadcrumbs (£5.95), and lemon sole bonne femme (£10.50); puddings (from £2.75) and children's meals (from £1.25). The restaurant is partly no smoking. Well kept Bass, Sharps Own and Doom Bar with guests like Sharps Cornish and Venton Wyn Old Pendeen on handpump; dominoes, cribbage, table skittles, darts, and shove-ha'penny. The slate-floored porch room has lots of succulents and a few cacti, and wood-and-stone seats. In the sheltered garden are some granite faced seats as well as white cast-iron furniture and picnic-sets, and a fruit and herb garden. *(Recommended by Klaus and Elizabeth Leist, Colin and Peggy Wilshire, Chris and Anna Rowley, George Atkinson, Martin Jones, R J Walden, Hazel R Morgan, Howard Clutterbuck, Mark Brock, Lorna and Michael Helyar, Ian Phillips, P P Salmon, J M Lefeaux, Brian Skelcher, D B Jenkin)*

Free house ~ Licensees Ros and Dave Williams ~ Real ale ~ Bar food ~ Restaurant ~ (01208) 872707 ~ Children welcome away from bar ~ Folk and trad jazz both once a month ~ Open 11-3, 6-11; 12-3, 6.30-10.30 Sun ~ Bedrooms: £27.50B/£45B

LOSTWITHIEL SX1059 Map 1
Royal Oak ◀

Duke St; pub just visible from A390 in centre

As long as this bustling, very well run pub has been in our Guide, we've always had consistently warm reports from readers. The staff are really friendly and welcoming and keep a fine range of real ales on handpump: Bass, Cotleigh Merlin Ale, Fullers London Pride, Hardy Royal Oak, Marstons Pedigree, and Sharps Own and Doom Bar – as well as lots of bottled beers from around the world. Good, popular bar food includes lunchtime sandwiches (from £1.35; toasties 20p extra) and ploughman's (from £3.45), as well as soup (£2.15), good stuffed mushrooms (£3.60), vegetarian crêpes (£6.35), scallops in garlic and butter (£8.50), steaks (from £8.55), daily specials such as a curry or steak and kidney in ale pie (£6.75), fresh salmon in a cucumber and cream sauce (£8.50), and garlic king prawns (£9.75), and puddings like cherry pie or treacle tart (£2). The neat lounge is spacious and comfortable, with captain's chairs and high-backed wall benches on its patterned carpet, and a couple of wooden armchairs by the log-effect gas fire; there's also a delft shelf, with a small dresser in one inner alcove. The flagstoned and beamed back public bar has darts, dominoes, cribbage, fruit machine and juke box, and is popular with younger customers. On a raised terrace by the car park are some picnic-sets. *(Recommended by Ted George, J Monk, I Blackwell, B, M, and P Kendall, John and Joan Calvert, A J Thomas)*

Free house ~ Licensees Malcolm and Eileen Hine ~ Real ale ~ Bar food ~ Restaurant ~ (01208) 872552 ~ Children in eating area of bar ~ Open 11-11; 12-10.30 Sun ~ Bedrooms: £35B/£58B

LUDGVAN SW5033 Map 1
White Hart

Churchtown; off A30 Penzance—Hayle at Crowlas – OS Sheet 203 map reference 505330

The cosy beamed rooms in this well run and marvellously unspoilt old place are full of interest: a fascinating mix of interesting old seats and tables, masses of mugs and jugs glinting in cottagey corners, bric-a-brac, pictures and photographs (including some good ones of Exmoor), soft oil-lamp-style lighting, and stripped boards with attractive rugs on them; the two big woodburning stoves run radiators too. One little area is no smoking. Simple bar food includes sandwiches and ploughman's, ham and egg or omelettes, and daily specials such as fresh cod (£4.50), and cider braised pork, steak and kidney pie or rabbit and bacon casserole (£5.25). Well kept Bass, Flowers IPA, and Marstons Pedigree tapped from the cask, and quite a few whiskies; cribbage, dominoes. *(Recommended by R J Walden, PP and J Salmon, Joan and Tony Walker, the Didler, P and M Rudlin, R and S Bentley, Brian Skelcher, Roger Byrne, Pat and Roger Fereday, Jack and Gemima Valiant)*

Inn Partnership (Nomura) ~ Tenant Denis Churchill ~ Real ale ~ Bar food (not Mon evenings Oct-Whitsun) ~ (01736) 740574 ~ Children in restaurant ~ Open 11-2.30(3 Sat), 6-11; 12-3, 7-10.30 Sun

MITHIAN SW7450 Map 1
Miners Arms

Just off B3285 E of St Agnes

Many original features remain in this friendly 16th-c pub – an upstairs room was used as a court and still has the original barrel ceiling, there's a passage behind the fireplace in the seating room that once led to a tunnel connecting it to the manor house, and there's an old well in the cellar bar. The small back bar has an irregular beam and plank ceiling, a wood block floor, and bulging squint walls (one with a fine old wall painting of Elizabeth I); another small room has a decorative low ceiling, lots of books and quite a few interesting ornaments, and there are warm winter fires. The Croust Room is no smoking. Bar food includes sandwiches, home-made soup (from £3), home-made pâté (£3.25), ploughman's (from £4.25), smoked pork sausage with fruit chutney (£5), curries (from £5.75), steak, kidney and oyster pie (£6), battered cod (£6.50), steaks (£8.50), and puddings (from £2.75); children's dishes (from £2.75).The dining room is no smoking. Sharps Doom Bar and Special and Ringwood Best on handpump. Shove-ha'penny, cribbage, dominoes, and piped music. There are seats on the back terrace, with more on the sheltered cobbled forecourt. *(Recommended by Miss E Murphy, Ted George, Patrick Hancock, James Nunns, Ian Wilson, Roger and Christine Mash)*

Inn Partnership (Nomura) ~ Lease: Richard Baylin ~ Real ale ~ (01872) 552375 ~ Children welcome away from bar ~ Open 12-3, 5.30(6 in winter)-11(10.30 Sun)

MOUSEHOLE SW4726 Map 1
Ship

Follow Newlyn coast rd out of Penzance; also signposted off B3315

There's always a cheerful, bustling atmosphere in this fisherman's local set right by the harbour in a lovely village. The friendly licensees welcome regulars and holiday-makers alike, and the opened-up main bar has black beams and panelling, built-in wooden wall benches and stools around the low tables, photographs of local events, sailors' fancy ropework, granite flagstones, and a cosy open fire. Bar food includes sandwiches (from £2.40; crab £4.80), ploughman's (£4.80), local mussels (£4.90), and local fish (from £8). On 23 December they bake Starry Gazy pie (£5.50) to celebrate Tom Bawcock's Eve, a tradition that recalls Tom's brave expedition out to sea in a fierce storm 200 years ago. He caught seven types of fish, which were then cooked in a pie with their heads and tails sticking out. Well kept St Austell BB, Tinners, HSD and Trelawny's Pride on handpump, and several malt whiskies; friendly staff. The elaborate harbour lights at Christmas are worth a visit; best to park at the top of the village and walk down. *(Recommended by Dr and Mrs Cottrell, Mayur Shah, James House, Tim Barrow, Sue Demont, Bronwen and Steve Wrigley, R J Walden, H Thomson)*

St Austell ~ Tenants Michael and Tracey Maddern ~ Real ale ~ Bar food ~ Restaurant ~ (01736) 731234 ~ Children welcome away from bar ~ Open 10.30-11; 12-10.30 Sun ~ Bedrooms: /£50B

MYLOR BRIDGE SW8137 Map 1
Pandora ★★ ♀

Restronguet Passage: from A39 in Penryn, take turning signposted Mylor Church, Mylor Bridge, Flushing and go straight through Mylor Bridge following Restronguet Passage signs; or from A39 further N, at or near Perranarworthal, take turning signposted Mylor, Restronguet, then follow Restronguet Weir signs, but turn left down hill at Restronguet Passage sign

You'd be hard pushed to find a position as lovely as that enjoyed by this charming medieval thatched pub. It's at its best at high tide when the sheltered waterfront is used by visiting boatmen (there are showers for yachtsmen) and you can sit on the long floating pontoon; there are also picnic-sets in front. Inside, the several rambling, interconnecting rooms are full of atmosphere and have low wooden ceilings (mind your head on some of the beams), beautifully polished big flagstones, cosy alcoves with leatherette benches built into the walls, a kitchen range, and a log fire in a high hearth (to protect it against tidal floods); half the bar area is no smoking – as is the restaurant. Bar food includes home-made soup (from £2.50), sandwiches or french bread (from £3.25, delicious local crab £6.50), home-made pâté (£3.50), sausages with onion rings (£4.95), filled savoury pancakes (from £5.25), mediterranean fish stew (£6.50), crab cakes (£7.50), puddings like home-made treacle tart or lemon meringue pie (from £2.75), and children's menu (from £3); Sunday roast (from £5.75). Bass, St Austell Tinners, HSD, and a guest like Cousin Jacks on handpump from a temperature controlled cellar, lots of good wines by the glass, and local cider; dominoes and winter pool. It does get very crowded in summer, and parking is difficult at peak times. *(Recommended by Tim Jacobson, Christopher Darwent, Ted George, Pat and Tony Martin, Michael Sargent, Mrs Maria Furness, JP, PP, Gwen and Peter Andrews, H and D Payne, Michael and Sally Colsell, Mr and Mrs B Hobden, the Didler, Patrick Hancock, Nick Lawless, J Henry, John and Christine Lowe, Ivan and Sarah Osborne, James House, Hazel R Morgan)*

*St Austell ~ Tenant Helen Hough ~ Real ale ~ Bar food ~ Restaurant ~ (01326)
372678 ~ Children in eating area of bar ~ Open 11(12 winter Sat)-11; 12-10.30 Sun;
12-2.30, 7-11 winter*

PELYNT SX2055 Map 1
Jubilee 🏠

B3359 NW of Looe

The name of this neatly kept 16th-c inn was changed in 1887 from the Axe to its
present name to celebrate the first fifty years of Queen Victoria's reign. The relaxed,
beamed lounge bar has mementoes of her, such as a tapestry portrait, old prints, and
Staffordshire figurines of the Queen and her consort, an early 18th-c Derbyshire oak
armchair, cushioned wall and window seats, windsor armchairs around oak tables,
and a good winter log fire in the stone fireplace; the Victorian bar has some carved
settles and more mementoes. The flagstoned entry is separated from the bar by an
attractively old-fangled glass-paned partition. Under the new licensee, bar food
includes sandwiches, home-made soup (£3.10), mushroom stroganoff (£5.50), local
scallops in garlic , home-cooked ham and eggs or spicy tomato pasta (all £5.90),
steaks (from £11.20), puddings (£3.50), and children's menu (from £3). Well kept
Bass and St Austell Dartmoor on handpump. The quite separate public bar has
sensibly placed darts, pool, fruit machine, and piped music. A crazy-paved central
courtyard has picnic-sets with red and white striped umbrellas and pretty tubs of
flowers, and there's a well equipped children's play area. *(Recommended by Bernard
Stradling, Michael Hill, Miss A G Drake, T Rowntree, June and Perry Dann, Mayur Shah)*

*Free house ~ Licensee Gary Rickard ~ Real ale ~ Bar food ~ Restaurant ~ (01503)
220312 ~ Children welcome ~ Open 11-3, 5-11; 11-11 Sat; 12-10.30 Sun ~
Bedrooms: £38.50B/£65B*

PENZANCE SW4730 Map 1
Turks Head

At top of main street, by big domed building (Lloyds Bank), turn left down Chapel Street

People enjoy relying on the unchanging atmosphere in this friendly little pub –
indeed, two of our readers have been coming here for 30 years. The bustling bar has
old flat irons, jugs and so forth hanging from the beams, pottery above the wood-
effect panelling, wall seats and tables, and a couple of elbow rests around central
pillars; piped music. A good choice of bar food includes soup (£2.10), sandwiches
(from £2.40), filled baked potatoes (from £3.65), ham and egg (£4), ratatouille
topped with cheese (£4.95), steak and kidney pie (£5.95), steaks (from £7.95), and
daily specials such as braised pigeon with cranberry and orange sauce (£6.75), fried
red snapper or pork tenderloin with cider and mustard sauce (£8.50) or a trio of
Cornish fish with prawn and lobster sauce (£9.75); roast Sunday lunch (£4.95). Well
kept Boddingtons, Sharps Doom Bar or Cornish, and Youngs Special with a guest
like Bass, Morlands Old Speckled Hen or Wadworths 6X on handpump; country
wines, and helpful service. The suntrap back garden has big urns of flowers. There
has been a Turks Head here for over 700 years – though most of the original building
was destroyed by a Spanish raiding party in the 16th-c. *(Recommended by P and M
Rudlin, James Flory, Brian Skelcher, G P Reeves, Simon Williams)*

*Inn Partnership (Nomura) ~ Tenant William Morris ~ Real ale ~ Bar food (11(12
Sun)-2.30, 6-10) ~ (01736) 363093 ~ Children in restaurant ~ Open 11-3, 5.30-11;
12-3, 5.30-10.30 Sun; closed 25 Dec*

PHILLEIGH SW8639 Map 1
Roseland ★ ♀

Between A3078 and B3289, just E of King Harry Ferry

Close to the King Harry ferry, this charming little pub has two bar rooms (one with
flagstones and the other carpeted) with wheelback chairs and built-in red-cushioned

seats, open fires, old photographs and some giant beetles and butterflies in glasses, and a relaxed chatty atmosphere; the little back bar is used by locals. Good, popular bar food includes cornish pasty (£2.50), sandwiches (from £3.25), ploughman's (from £4.95), a ciabatta roll or baked potato with fillings like chargrilled chicken, hummus, mint and tzatsiki or emmental and smoked bacon (from £5.95), skate with a Thai mayonnaise (£8.50), assorted mushrooms sautéed in brandy, french mustard and cream with chestnuts in a pastry case (£8.95), clams, cockles, mussels, langoustine and shrimp in pernod, cream and dill sauce (£9.95), and children's menu (from £3.25). The restaurant is in no smoking. Well kept Bass, Marstons Pedigree, Morlands Old Speckled Hen, and Sharps Cornish and Doom Bar on handpump, local cider, quite a few wines by the glass, and several malt whiskies; cribbage. The pretty paved front courtyard is a lovely place to sit in the lunchtime sunshine beneath the cherry blossom, and the back garden has been converted into a small outdoor children's play area. Handy for Trelissick Gardens. *(Recommended by B, M, and P Kendall, J Phillip, Michael Sargent, Mike and Mo Clifford, Charles Gysin, James House, William and Julie Ryan, Mr Parkes, W K Wood, D Martin, Mr and Mrs Peter Smith, Mike and Wena Stevenson, BB, Nick Lawless, JP, PP, Dennis Bishop, David Wallington, Colin Gooch, Ian and Deborah Carrington, Christopher Wright, R Inman, Mrs L E Phillips, Romey Heaton, the Didler, Miss E Murphy, Paul and Michelle Hancock, D P and J A Sweeney, Christine and Geoff Butler, Keith and Margaret Kettwell, Mr J Phil)*

Greenalls ~ Tenant Colin Philips ~ Real ale ~ Bar food ~ Restaurant ~ (01872) 580254 ~ Children welcome ~ Open 11-11; 12-3, 6-10.30 Sun

POLKERRIS SX0952 Map 1
Rashleigh
Signposted off A3082 Fowey—St Austell

Come rain or shine, this is a popular little pub. In good weather you can sit on the stone terrace and enjoy the views towards the far side of St Austell and Mevagissey bays (and the isolated beach with its restored jetty is just a few steps away), and on a wet and windy day, the bar is snug and cosy. The front part has comfortably cushioned seats and well kept Bass, St Austell HSD, Sharps Doom Bar and changing guest beers on handpump, decent wine list and several malt whiskies; the more simply furnished back area has local photographs on the brown panelling, a winter log fire and piped classical music. Good bar food includes sandwiches (from £1.85; open ones from £4.75), soup (£2.50), ploughman's (from £4), lentil shepherd's pie (£4.95), beef curry (£5.25), a lunchtime cold buffet (£6.50), fish pie (£6.75), daily specials such as sweet and sour pork or chicken lasagne in brandy sauce (£6.95), and lemon sole or sirloin steak (£9.95), puddings (£2.50), and children's menu (from £1.95). The restaurant is no smoking. Though parking space next to the pub is limited, there's a large village car park, and there are safe moorings for small yachts in the cove. This whole section of the Cornish Coast Path is renowned for its striking scenery. *(Recommended by Mrs C Stevens, Mayur Shah, B J Harding, R Turnham, the Didler, Peter Burton, JP, PP, Martin Jones, JDM, KM, Betty Petheram, Pete and Rosie Flower, Mr and Mrs A Scrutton, A J Thomas)*

Free house ~ Licensee Bernard Smith ~ Real ale ~ Bar food (12-2, 6-10 in summer; 12-2, 7-9 in winter) ~ Restaurant ~ (01726) 813991 ~ Children welcome ~ Pianist Sat evening ~ Open 11(12 Sun)-4.30, 5.30-11(10.30 Sun); 11.30-3, 6.30-11 winter

POLPERRO SX2051 Map 1
Old Mill House
Mill Hill; bear right approaching harbour

A little gem, popular locally, with a genuinely warm welcome and a nice civilised feel. There are polished boards, solid stripped pine furniture, dado and stall dividers, a couple of housekeeper's chairs and some hefty rustic implements by the big log fireplace, fishing-boat pictures, netting and some nautical hardware overhead. There are flagstones by the serving counter, which has well kept Bass, and St Austell Tinners and HSD on handpump, and farm cider. Service is very friendly, and lunchtime bar food includes sandwiches (from £1.85; fresh crab £3.30), home-made soup (£2.25), local cod and chips (£3.75), fishy ploughman's (£3.95), barbecued ribs (£4.20), vegetable lasagne (£4.95), fresh crab salad (£6.50), and daily specials with fresh fish straight from the boats in Looe; roast Sunday lunch. Round the corner is an area with darts and pool, shove-ha'penny, cribbage, dominoes, shut the box, and chess; piped music. A cosy little bistro opens off on the left, and down a long bright-painted corridor is a little children's room with seaside murals and a box of toys. There's a picnic-set by the very narrow lane in front of the pretty white cottage (hung with flowering baskets in summer), and more under parasols in a streamside garden with a terrace behind. We have not yet heard from readers using the bedrooms here, but the inn does have its own parking further up the village – a real boon. Dogs are welcomed with a dog biscuit. *(Recommended by Ted George, Mayur Shah)*

Free house ~ Licensees Jane Fletcher and Patricia Carroll ~ Real ale ~ Bar food ~ Restaurant ~ (01503) 272362 ~ Children in eating area of bar ~ Solo or duo singers Sat evenings ~ Open 11(12 in winter)-11; 12-10.30 Sun ~ Bedrooms: £37.50B/£55B

POLRUAN SX1251 Map 1
Lugger
Reached from A390 in Lostwithiel; nearby parking expensive and limited, or steep walk down from village-edge car park; passenger/bicycle ferry from Fowey

From the quay there's a flight of steep stone steps up to this friendly local, and once there, you can enjoy fine views of the little harbour. Inside, the two knocked-together bars have beams, high-backed wall settles, wheelback chairs, and a slightly nautical theme with big model boats and local boat photographs. Decent bar food includes lunchtime sandwiches (from £1.60) and ploughman's (from £3.40), filled baked potatoes (from £3.45), and home-made dishes such as stilton and leek bake (£4.75), chilli con carne (£4.85), chicken curry (£5.25), and chicken, ham and mushroom pie (£5.45); the restaurant is no smoking. St Austell BB, Tinners, HSD and XXXX Mild on handpump; darts and pool. Good surrounding walks. Self-catering cottage available. You can get here on the foot passenger ferry from Fowey. *(Recommended by Dr and Mrs B D Smith, Peter Salmon, A J Thomas, the Didler)*

St Austell ~ Managers Colin and Shelagh Dolphin ~ Real ale ~ Bar food ~ (01726) 870007 ~ Children welcome ~ Occasional duo singers ~ Open 11-11; 12-10.30 Sun

PORT ISAAC SX0080 Map 1
Golden Lion
Fore Street

The views over the harbour in this lovely steep village can be enjoyed from seats in the windows of the cosy rooms here – or you can sit out on the terrace. Inside, it's very much a friendly local and the bar has a fine antique settle among other comfortable seats, decorative ceiling plasterwork, and perhaps the pub dog Hollie. Bar food includes sandwiches (lunchtime only, from £2.25), ploughman's (£4.75), proper fish and chips (£5.95), and a pie of the day (from £5.95); during the summer, evening meals are served in the bistro. Well kept St Austell Tinners, HSD and Trelawny's Pride on handpump and several malt whiskies. Darts, shove-ha'penny, dominoes, a fruit machine in the public bar, and piped music. You can park at the top of the village unless you are luckily enough to park on the beach at low tide. The very steep narrow lanes of this working fishing village are most attractive. *(Recommended by Nick Lawless, Pat and Tony Martin, M Mason, D Thompson, Barry and Anne, Mr and Mrs P Stubbs, David Carr, Graham Tayar, Catherine Raeburn, Tim Barrow, Sue Demont, A J Thomas, Christopher Darwent, Ted George, Juliet Winsor, J Henry, the Didler)*

St Austell ~ Tenants Mike and Nikki Edkins ~ Real ale ~ Bar food ~ Restaurant (evening) ~ (01208) 880336 ~ Children in eating area of bar ~ Open 11.30-11; 12-10.30 Sun; may close in afternoon if quiet

---

It is illegal for bar staff to smoke while handling your drink.

nr PORT ISAAC SX0080 Map 1
Port Gaverne Hotel ♀ ⇐
Port Gaverne signposted from Port Isaac, and from B3314 E of Pendoggett

Close to splendid clifftop walks, this early 17th-c inn has big log fires and low beams in the neat bars, flagstones as well as carpeting, some exposed stone, and an enormous marine chronometer. In spring the lounge is filled with pictures from the local art society's annual exhibition, and at other times there are interesting antique local photographs. Bar food includes sandwiches (from £1.60; crab £4.25), home-made soup (£2.75), ham and egg (£3.25), ploughman's (from £3.25), cottage pie (£3.50), vegetarian lasagne (£3.75), and deep-fried local plaice (£5.95), and is served in the bar or 'Captain's Cabin' – a little room where everything except its antique admiral's hat is shrunk to scale (old oak chest, model sailing ship, even the prints on the white stone walls); the restaurant is no smoking. On Sunday lunchtime, they serve only a hot carvery in the restaurant – no bar meals then. Well kept Bass, Flowers IPA and Sharps Doom Bar on handpump, a good bin-end wine list with 60 wines, a very good choice of whiskies and other spirits. The Green Door Bar across the lane, which has a big diorama of Port Isaac, is open on summer afternoons. *(Recommended by Sue and Bob Ward, Graham Tayar, Catherine Raeburn, M J Dowdy, Brian and Jenny Seller, Freda Macnamara, Tim Barrow, Sue Demont, K Stevens, John Westlake)*

Free house ~ Licensee Marjorie Ross ~ Real ale ~ Bar food ~ Restaurant ~ (01208) 880244 ~ Children in captain's cabin or snug only ~ Open 11-11; 12-10.30 Sun; 11-2.30-6-11 weekdays in winter ~ Bedrooms: £51B/£102B

PORTHALLOW SW7923 Map 1
Five Pilchards
SE of Helston; B3293 to St Keverne, then village signposted

A new terrace with a waterfall is being constructed at this warmly friendly and sturdy stone-built pub, set just 20 yards from the beach. The walls and ceilings of the bars are hung with an abundance of salvaged nautical gear, lamps made from puffer fish, and interesting photographs and clippings about local shipwrecks. Good bar food includes sandwiches (from £2.50; good crab £4.50), home-made soup (£2.50), seafood chowder (£3.50), local crab ploughman's (£5.95), sirloin steak (£10.95), and fish dishes such as scallops in cream, wine and saffron or monkfish in garlic, mushrooms and cream (£11.95). Well kept Greene King Abbot and weekly guest beers like Sharps Doom Bar, Cornish and Special, and Skinners Knocker Ale on handpump, good wines, and there should be a juice extractor by the time this book is published; very nice staff. Tides and winds allowing, you can park on the foreshore. *(Recommended by Nigel Woolliscroft, Tim Barrow, Sue Demont, George Atkinson)*

Free house ~ Licensee Brandon Flynn ~ Real ale ~ Bar food ~ (01326) 280256 ~ Children in eating area of bar ~ Open 12-3, 6-11; 12-3, 6-11 Sun; closed winter Sun evening and all day Mon

PORTHLEVEN SW6225 Map 1
Ship ★
Village on B3304 SW of Helston; pub perched on edge of harbour

With a thriving atmosphere and full of both locals and visitors, this old fisherman's pub has marvellous views over the pretty working harbour and out to sea; there are seats in the terraced garden, and at night, the harbour is interestingly floodlit. The knocked-through bar has log fires in big stone fireplaces and some genuine character, and the family room is a conversion of an old smithy and has logs burning in the huge open fireplace. Popular bar food includes sandwiches (from £2.75; fine toasties from £3.25; excellent crusty loaf from £4.35), filled oven-baked potatoes (from £2.75), ploughman's (from £5.45), pot meals like vegetable curry, steak and kidney pudding or fish pie (from £6.85), interesting daily specials like fish and tomato bake or chicken tikka, sirloin steak (£10.95), puddings like home-made apple torte, evening extras, and children's meals; the candlelit dining room also enjoys the good view. Well kept Courage Best, Greene King Abbot, Morlands Old Speckled Hen, and Sharps Doom Bar on handpump, and several malt whiskies; dominoes, cribbage, fruit machine and piped music. To get to the pub you have to climb a flight of rough stone steps – it's actually built into the steep cliffs. *(Recommended by George Atkinson, Mr and Mrs Harris, JP, PP, the Didler, James Nunns, D B Jenkin, Cliff Blakemore, Paul and Pam Penrose, E A George, Bronwen and Steve Wrigley, W M and J M Cottrell, Barry and Anne, Michael and Lorna Bourdeaux, Marvadene B Eves, Dave and Deborah Irving, Jack and Gemima Valiant, Pete and Rosie Flower, Mr and Mrs Geoffrey Berrill, Tim Jacobson, P P Salmon)*

Free house ~ Licensee Colin Oakden ~ Real ale ~ Bar food ~ (01326) 572841 ~ Children in family room ~ Open 11.30-11; 12-10.30 Sun; 11.30-3.30, 6.30-11 in winter; 12-3, 7-10.30 Sun in winter

RUAN LANIHORNE SW8942 Map 1
Kings Head

Village signposted off A3078 St Mawes road

We're surprised not to get more reports on this attractive and neatly kept pub set opposite a fine old church in a pleasant out-of-the-way village. The beamed bar has a welcoming local atmosphere, and is decorated with hanging china and framed cigarette cards, and there's an attractive family room with lots of mirrors next door. Bar food includes home-made soup (£2.50), lunchtime open sandwiches or ploughman's (£4.50) and dishes like home-made lasagne or steak and mushroom pie (£5.25), as well as potted shrimps (£4.50), battered cod (£5.25), half a crispy duckling (£9.25), and fillet steak (£11.95), with daily specials such as garlicky mushroom toasts (£4.25), oriental prawns with plum sauce (£4.50), home-made vegetarian cannelloni (£5.25), moussaka (£5.95) or trout meunière (£6.95); good Sunday roasts. The dining room is no smoking. Well kept Hardy Country and Sharps Special on handpump with Worthington Best kept under light blanket pressure, a decent wine list with some by the carafe as well as glass, quick service, and unobtrusive radio; darts, cribbage, and dominoes, card and board games. There are seats in the suntrap sunken garden and views down over the pretty convolutions of the River Fal's tidal estuary. *(Recommended by Keith and Margaret Kettwell, Mayur Shah, Michael Sargent, Dennis Bishop, John and Jackie Chalcraft, Roger and Christine Hyde, Christopher Wright)*

Free house ~ Licensees Peter and Shirley Trenoweth-Farely ~ Real ale ~ Bar food ~ (01872) 501263 ~ Children welcome away from bar ~ Open 12-2.30, 7-11; 12-2.30, 7-10.30 Sun; closed Mon except bank holidays

ST AGNES SW7250 Map 1
Railway

10 Vicarage Rd; from centre follow B3277 signs for Porthtowan and Truro

In the older part of this little local is a remarkable collection of shoes – minute or giant, made of strange skins, fur, leather, wood, mother-of-pearl, or embroidered with gold and silver, from Turkey, Persia, China or Japan, and worn by ordinary people or famous men; also, some splendid brasswork that includes one of the finest original horsebrass collections in the country – and a notable collection of naval memorabilia from model sailing ships and rope fancywork to the texts of Admiralty messages at important historical moments, such as the announcement of the ceasefire at the end of the First World War. Decent bar food includes lunchtime sandwiches (from £2.50), as well as home-made soup (£2.25), filled baked potatoes (from £2.50), ploughman's (from £4.35), vegetable moussaka (£5.95), fisherman's platter with five different sorts of fish (£6.95), steaks (from £7.50), mixed grill (£8.50), and OAP specials (two courses with coffee £4.25). The restaurant is no smoking. Well kept Bass, Boddingtons and Flowers IPA on handpump under light blanket pressure; fruit machine and juke box. There are seats on the terrace. *(Recommended by Mayur Shah, Romey Heaton, John Woodward)*

Inn Partnership (Nomura) ~ Tenants Ian and Patsy Davey ~ Real ale ~ Bar food (maybe not on winter weekdays) ~ Restaurant ~ (01872) 552310 ~ Children in eating

area of bar ~ Open 11-11; 12-10.30 Sun; 11-3, 6-11; 12-3, 7-10.30 Sun winter ~ Bedrooms: £20/£40

ST AGNES (Isles of Scilly) SW7250 Map 1
Turks Head 🛏

The Quay

A super place to unwind, this little slate-roofed white cottage has wonderful views over the bay from the few tables on a patch of lawn across the sleepy lane from the pub, and there are steps down to the slipway so you can walk down with your drinks and food and sit right on the shore. Inside, the simply furnished but cosy and very friendly pine-panelled bar has quite a collection of flags, helmets and headwear and banknotes, as well as maritime photographs and model ships; the dining extension is no smoking, the cats are called Taggart and Lacey, and the collie, Tess. At lunchtime, the decent bar food includes legendary huge locally made pasties (though they do sell out; £3.50), open rolls (from £2.25; local crab £4.25), ploughman's (from £4.25), salads (from £5.25; local crab £6.95), cold roast beef with chips or vegetable pasta bake (£5.25), and puddings like sticky toffee pudding (£2.75), with evening gammon in port wine sauce (£6.25), fresh fish of the day, and sirloin steak (£9.45); children's meals (from £2.50). Ice cream and cakes are sold through the afternoon, and in good weather they may do evening barbecues. Remarkably, they also have real ale which arrives in St Agnes via a beer supplier in St Austell and two boat trips: Dartmoor Best, Flowers Original and IPA, Ind Coope Burton, and Sharps Doom Bar well kept on handpump, besides decent house wines, a good range of malt whiskies, and hot chocolate with brandy. Darts, cribbage, dominoes and piped music. In spring and autumn hours may be shorter, and winter opening is sporadic, given that only some 70 people live on the island; they do then try to open if people ask, and otherwise tend to open on Saturday night, Sunday lunchtime (bookings only, roast lunch), over Christmas and the New Year, and for a Wednesday quiz night. *(Recommended by Pete and Rosie Flower, Michael Sargent, R J Walden, John Saul)*

Free house ~ Licensees John and Pauline Dart ~ Real ale ~ Bar food ~ (01720) 422434 ~ Children welcome if well behaved ~ Open 11-11; 12-10.30 Sun; only open Weds and Sat evenings and Sun lunch in winter ~ Bedrooms: /£50B

ST BREWARD SX0977 Map 1
Old Inn

Old Town; village signposted off B3266 S of Camelford, also signed off A30 Bolventor— Bodmin

There's a lot of character in the two-roomed bar here, with fine broad slate flagstones, banknotes and horsebrasses hanging from the low oak joists that support the ochre upstairs floorboards, and plates on the stripped stonework. The outer room has fewer tables (old ones, of character), an open log fire in the big granite fireplace, a piano and sensibly placed darts. The inner room has cushioned wall benches and chairs around its tables, a good log fire, and a glass panel showing a separate no-smoking games room with darts, pool, juke box, video game, and fruit machine. Under the new licensee, bar food includes filled lunchtime baps or sandwiches (from £2.25) and ploughman's (from £4.25), as well as home-made soup (£2.50), filled baked potatoes (from £3.25), ham and eggs (£4.75), local plaice (£5.50), home-made chicken curry (£5.75), vegetable chilli or home-made pie of the day (£5.95), a huge mixed grill (£8.50 or £9.50), daily specials such as pork, cider and leek casserole, prawn madras or beef stroganoff, a Sunday roast, and children's menu ; the restaurant is no smoking. Well kept Bass and Sharps Doom Bar and Special Ale on handpump, decent wines, and a huge range of malt whiskies. Picnic-sets outside are protected by low stone walls. There's plenty of open moorland behind, and cattle and sheep wander freely into the village. In front of the building is a very worn carved stone; no-one knows exactly what it is but it may be part of a Saxon cross. *(Recommended by Ted George, the Didler, Howard Clutterbuck, Dr D J Walker, Anthony Barnes, M Mason, D Thompson)*

Free house ~ Licensee Darren Wills ~ Real ale ~ Bar food ~ Restaurant ~ (01208) 850711 ~ Children in eating area of bar ~ Live entertainment once a month ~ Open 11-11; 12-10.30 Sun; 11-3, 6-11 winter

ST EWE SW9746 Map 1

Crown

Village signposted from B3287; easy to find from Mevagissey

Very sadly, the long-standing licensee Mr Jeffery died, and while his widow was still running this popular unspoilt cottage as we went to press, there is the chance that things may change. Our strong hope is that any new tenant will follow the style that works so well here. The traditional bar has 16th-c flagstones, a very high-backed curved old settle with flowery cushions, long shiny wooden tables, an ancient weight-driven working spit, and a relaxed atmosphere. The eating area has cushioned old church pews and velvet curtains. Bar food has included sandwiches (from £1.95), soup (£2), very good fresh pasties made on the premises (£2.50), ploughman's or filled baked potatoes (from £3.95), gammon and egg or fresh seasonal crab salad (£8.25), tasty steaks (from £8.50), and daily specials such as lemon and pepper haddock (£5.60) or grilled lemon sole (£11.70; evenings only). Well kept St Austell Tinners and HSD on handpump, several malt whiskies, and local wine; fruit machine and piped music. Several picnic-sets on a raised back lawn. Handy for the Lost Gardens of Heligan. *(Recommended by Pete and Rosie Flower, Christopher Wright, Brian Skelcher, Gwen and Peter Andrews, Richard and Margaret Peers, Nick Lawless, MDN, R Inman, Keith and Norma Bloomfield, Peter and Daphne Ross, David Carr, Mrs Jo Williams, Roger Huggins, Ewan McCall, Ivan and Sarah Osborne, Maria Furness, John A Barker)*

St Austell ~ Tenant Ruth Jeffery ~ Real ale ~ Bar food ~ Restaurant ~ (01726) 843322 ~ Children in eating area of bar and restaurant ~ Open 11-3, 6-11; 12-3, 7-10.30 Sun

ST IVES SW5441 Map 1

Sloop 🍺

The Wharf

This quaint old waterside building must have been a lovely place in the days when its only customers were the fishermen and the St Ives School artists. Of course they've been largely replaced by us tourists, but there's still quite a bit of character here, especially in the front bar – and there are bright St Ives School paintings on the walls. To the right of the door is a tiny, simple public bar with two very long tables, and this is connected to the front part of the low-beamed lounge which has cushioned, built-in walls seats, cast-iron framed pub tables on the flagstones, and in both rooms, quite a few portrait drawings by Hyman Segal. At the back is the beamed Cellar Bar (which isn't actually downstairs) with plenty of booth seating against the brown panelled walls, a slate floor, and a bustling atmosphere. Well kept Bass, John Smiths, Morlands Old Speckled Hen on handpump, and good fresh coffee (you keep the mug); juke box and piped music. Well liked bar food includes home-made soup (£2.75; good home-made crab soup £3.95), sandwiches (from £2.75; the crab are excellent; filled french bread from £3.95), vegetarian or meaty pasty (from £3.25), ploughman's (£4.95), popular locally caught fresh fish such as mackerel simply cooked in seasoned flour (£4.94), cod in beer batter (£5.95) or a trio of monkfish, haddock and lemon sole in a prawn, cream and white wine sauce (£7.95), home-made chicken and bacon lasagne or ham and eggs (£5.95), home-made smoked salmon and crab fishcakes (£6.50), their speciality seafood chowder (£6.95), crab salad (£9.95), and sirloin steak (£9.95); staff are friendly and cope efficiently with the crowds. In front of the pub are some seats on a little cobbled area looking over the road to the harbour. *(Recommended by Dr and Mrs Cottrell, Liz and John Soden, Michael Sargent, Ted George, MDN, Tim Barrow, Sue Demont, Sue Holland, David Webster, Hazel R Morgan, the Didler, Peter and Gwyneth Eastwood)*

Courage (S & N) ~ Lease: Maurice and Sue Symons ~ Real ale ~ Bar food (12-3, 6-8.45) ~ (01736) 796584 ~ Children in eating area of bar until 9pm ~ Open 10.30-11; 12-10.30 Sun ~ Bedrooms: /£55B

ST KEVERNE SW7921 Map 1

White Hart

The Square; at the end of B3293 SE of Helston – the village is well signposted

New licensees have taken over this old coaching house – though Mr Travis is not new to the pub; he helped the previous licensee set up the Sports Bar and the popular restaurant. It's a bustling place with almost nightly events, a good chatty atmosphere, and new animals: Fred and Timmy the cats and Stella the labrador puppy. The black beams of the bar are hung with horsebrasses, there's a mix of wall seats, mate's chairs and some heavy rustic small wooden seats around sturdy tables on the bare boards, and an open fire. The Sports Bar has darts, juke box, pool, fruit machine, and SkyTV; piped music, euchre, and quiz evenings (Tuesdays); this room overlooks a partly covered raised terrace extension to the garden filled with herbs and creepers. Good bar food includes lunchtime snacks like sandwiches or french bread (from £3; hot french bread from £3.25) or filled baked potatoes (from £3.25), plus home-made soup (£2.50), garlic mushrooms (£3.95), salads (from £5.95), mushroom and stilton crumble (£6.50), fajitas (from £6.50), prawn curry (£6.95), a huge plate of spare ribs (£8), and children's menu (from £3; no children in the restaurant). Well kept Flowers Original, Morlands Old Speckled Hen, Wadworths 6X, and a summer guest beer on handpump, kept under light blanket pressure. Outside are some picnic-sets on a narrow front terrace, with more on a side lawn. *(Recommended by Mr and Mrs Geoffrey Berrill, Tim Barrow, Sue Demont, P J Hanson, George Atkinson, Paul and Pam Penrose, Peter Burton, Lyn and Geoff Hallchurch, John Wood, Mr and Mrs Harris, Marvadene B Eves)*

Inn Partnership (Nomura) ~ Tenants Steve Travis, Louise Tanswell ~ Real ale ~ Bar food ~ Restaurant ~ (01326) 280325 ~ Children welcome ~ Weekly live events ~ Open 11-11; 12-10.30 Sun; 11-2.30, 6-11in winter ~ Bedrooms: £35B/£50B

ST KEW SX0276 Map 1

St Kew Inn

Village signposted from A39 NE of Wadebridge

Run by a friendly landlord, this rather grand-looking old stone building has a neatly kept bar with winged high-backed settles and varnished rustic tables on the lovely dark Delabole flagstones, black wrought-iron rings for lamps or hams hanging from the high ceiling, a handsome window seat, and an open kitchen range under a high mantelpiece decorated with earthenware flagons. At lunchtime, bar food includes sandwiches, soup (£2.25), filled baked potatoes (from £3.75), ploughman's (£3.95), leeks and bacon in a cheese sauce (£4.95), plaice and chips (£5.95), vegetarian dishes, and sirloin steak (£9.95), with evening extras like oriental crab and vegetable parcels with a chilli and ginger dressing (£3.50), prawn and avocado salad with piquant sauce (£3.75), beef bourguignon (£6.95), fish of the day, fillet of lamb with a roquefort and mint stuffing and wrapped in puff pastry served with a rosemary and red wine sauce (£9.95), daily specials and puddings, and children's menu (from £3.50). Well kept St Austell Tinners and HSD tapped from wooden casks behind the counter (lots of tankards hang from the beams above it), a couple of farm ciders, a good wine list, and several malt whiskies; darts, cribbage, dominoes, and backgammon. The big garden has seats on the grass and picnic-sets on the front cobbles. Parking is in what must have been a really imposing stable yard. The church next door is lovely. *(Recommended by Ian Wilson, Graham Tayar, Catherine Raeburn, the Didler, Mike and Heather Watson, L Granville, Jacquie and Jim Jones, JP, PP, Peter Bell, Richard Cole, R and S Bentley, John A Barker, David Carr, Mike Gorton, Juliet Winsor)*

St Austell ~ Tenant Desmond Weston ~ Real ale ~ Bar food ~ (01208) 841259 ~ Children in eating area of bar ~ Open 11-11; 12-10.30 Sun; 11-3, 6-11in winter; 12-3, 7-10.30 Sun in winter; closed 25 Dec

---

Bedroom prices normally include full English breakfast, VAT and any inclusive service charge that we know of.

ST MAWES SW8533 Map 1
Victory
Victory Hill

Just up from the harbour and Falmouth ferry, this is an unpretentious and friendly little fisherman's local, well liked by both visitors and regulars. The simple but attractive bar is full of sailing and other sea photographs, and there's a carpeted back part with comfortable seats, an antique settle and old prints of Cornish scenes; piped music. Good bar food includes home-made soup (£2.75), sandwiches (from £2.90; crab £5.55), filled baked potatoes (from £3.30), local pasty (£3.50), cashew nut paella (£5.60), home-made lasagne (£5.75), home-made pie or chicken curry (£5.95), steaks (from £8.95), children's dishes (from £2.95), and daily specials; the restaurant is no smoking. Well kept Bass, Greenalls Original, and Morlands Old Speckled Hen on handpump. Benches outside on the cobbles give glimpses of the sea. They are kind to dogs. *(Recommended by Dr and Mrs M Wilson, Nigel Wikeley, Lyn and Geoff Hallchurch, R and S Bentley, D P and J A Sweeney, John Woodward, Ivan and Sarah Osborne)*

Inn Partnership (Nomura) ~ Lease: Philip and Bridget Savage ~ Real ale ~ Bar food (all day) ~ (01326) 270324 ~ Children welcome ~ Open 11-11; 12-10.30 Sun ~ Bedrooms: /£25(£30B)

ST MAWGAN SW8766 Map 1
Falcon
NE of Newquay, off B3276 or A3059

Close to a handsome church in a quiet village, this pretty wisteria-covered pub has a peaceful, pretty garden with plenty of seats, a wishing well, play equipment for children, and good views of the village; also, stone tables in a cobbled courtyard. The big friendly bar has a log fire, small modern settles and large antique coaching prints on the walls, and plenty of space for eating the enjoyable bar food, which might include lunchtime sandwiches such as smoked salmon and cottage cheese with chives (£3.55), fresh cod or plaice (£5.45), venison sausages in red wine and juniper berries (£6.30), prawns in garlic butter (£9.60), and steaks (from £9.85). The restaurant is no smoking. Well kept St Austell Tinners, HSD and Cousin Jacks on handpump; efficient service even when busy. *(Recommended by Mr and Mrs G R Parker, Klaus and Elizabeth Leist, David Carr, Brian Skelcher, Patrick Hancock, Mrs and Mrs Head, James House, D Stokes, D Eberlin)*

St Austell ~ Tenant Andy Banks ~ Real ale ~ Bar food ~ Restaurant ~ (01637) 860225 ~ Children in restaurant ~ Open 11-3, 6-11; 12-3, 7-10.30 Sun ~ Bedrooms: £17.50(£35S)/£45(£55B)

ST TEATH SX0680 Map 1
White Hart
B3267; signposted off A39 SW of Camelford

The rooms to head for in this friendly and unpretentious village pub are the main bar and lounge. There are sailor hat-ribands and ships' pennants from all over the world, swords and a cutlass, and a coin collection embedded in the ceiling over the serving counter in the main bar – which also has a fine Delabole flagstone floor. Between the counter and the coal fire is a snug little high-backed settle, and leading off is a carpeted room, mainly for eating, with modern chairs around neat tables, and brass and copper jugs on its stone mantelpiece; piped music. Straightforward popular bar food includes home-made soup (£2), sandwiches (from £2), ploughman's (from £4.50), various curries and steak and kidney or vegetarian pie (all £5.95), steaks (£9.95), and home-made puddings like treacle tart or bread and butter pudding (from £2.50); helpful, cheerful staff. The restaurant is partly no smoking. Well kept Bass, Ruddles County and Sharps Doom Bar on handpump. The games bar has darts, pool, cribbage, dominoes, fruit machine, and satellite TV. *(Recommended by Graham Tayar, Catherine Raeburn, Mr and Mrs Peter Smith, Jill Silversides, Barry Brown, Juliet Winsor)*

Free house ~ Licensees Barry and Rob Burton ~ Real ale ~ Bar food ~ Restaurant ~ (01208) 850281 ~ Children welcome ~ Singing duo in winter ~ Open 11-11; 12-10.30 Sun ~ Bedrooms: /£50B

TREBARWITH SX0585 Map 1
Port William
Trebarwith Strand

This busy place is probably at its best during the summer when you can make the most of the lovely setting – there are the picnic-sets across the road and on the covered terrace, with views over the beach, Gull Rock, and out to sea; the sunsets are marvellous. Inside, there's quite a nautical theme with fishing nets and maritime memorabilia decorating the walls, a separate gallery area with work by local artists, and the no-smoking 'marine room' which has three different fish tanks showing a live reef with corals, one with seahorses, and another with marine fish (popular with both adults and children). Bar food includes daily specials such as home-made celery and stilton soup (£2.95), good mussels in cider and cream (£4.75), vegetable and lentil bake (£6.45), steak and kidney pie (£6.95), halibut with mustard, cream and cheese sauce (£9.75), duck breast in green peppercorn sauce (£10.95), and whole grilled dover sole (£14.50); there's also a more standard menu with pasties and filled rolls. Bass, Flowers Original, and St Austell Tinners and HSD on handpump. Darts, pool, dominoes, fruit machine, and piped music. *(Recommended by R J Walden, Rita Horridge, Brian Skelcher, A A Whiting, Nigel Norman, Roger Byrne, Tim Barrow, Sue Demont, John Westlake, Mr and Mrs Archibald, Betty Petheram, Dennis Stevens, Mayur Shah)*

Free house ~ Licensee Peter Hale ~ Real ale ~ Bar food ~ Restaurant ~ (01840) 770230 ~ Children in eating area of bar ~ Folk Fri evenings ~ Open 11(12 in winter)11; 12-10.30 Sun ~ Bedrooms: £54.50B/£79B

TREBURLEY SX3477 Map 1
Springer Spaniel 🍴 ♀
A388 Callington—Launceston

Praise for this very well run and warmly friendly pub is as consistent as ever. Both the landlord (and his dogs) will make all customers welcome in the relaxed bar with its lovely, very high-backed settle by the woodburning stove in the big fireplace, high-backed farmhouse chairs and other seats, and pictures of olde-worlde stage-coach arrivals at inns; this leads into a room with chinzy-cushioned armchairs and sofa in one corner, and a big solid teak table; bagatelle. Up some steps from the main bar is the beamed, attractively furnished, no-smoking restaurant. Enjoyable food (which can be eaten in any part of the pub) includes snacks such as cockles (£1.50), a dozen different sandwiches or rolls, and ham and eggs (£4.50), as well as dishes like freshly made soup (£2.75), mushroom pots or a terrine of duck livers (£3.95), greek salad (£4.95), a fresh vegetable risotto (£5.95), scallops with bacon and shallots in balsamic vinegar (£6.50 starter, £10.95 main course), steak and kidney pie or chicken breast in a wine, mushroom and cream sauce (£6.50), smoked haddock and salmon fishcakes on a light mustard sauce (£8.95), steaks (from £9.50), Cornish crab pasty with leeks (£9.95), and puddings like fresh lemon tart with lemon marmalade and clotted cream, chocolate mousse served with a light and dark chocolate sauce or bread and butter pudding (from £2.95); some of the produce is home-grown. Well kept Dartmoor Best and St Austell HSD on handpump, a short but thoughtful wine list, several malt whiskies, and a good choice of spirits; very good service *(Recommended by Miss G Glen, John Kirk, Brian Skelcher, Richard and Margaret Peers, John and Vivienne Rice, J C Perry, Betty Petheram, Jacquie and Jim Jones, Marvadene B Eves, R J Walden, D B Jenkin, Mr and Mrs B Stamp)*

Free house ~ Licensee John Pitchford ~ Real ale ~ Bar food ~ Restaurant ~ (01579) 370424 ~ Children in eating area of bar ~ Open 11-3, 5.30-11; 12-3, 6.30-10.30 Sun; closed 4 days over Christmas

TREGADILLETT SX2984 Map 1
Eliot Arms ★★ ♀

Village signposted off A30 at junction with A395, W end of Launceston bypass

The charming series of little softly lit rooms in this creeper-covered house is full of interest. There are 72 antique clocks (including 7 grandfathers), 400 snuffs, hundreds of horsebrasses, old prints, old postcards or cigarette cards grouped in frames on the walls, a growing collection of barometers, and shelves of books and china. Also, a fine old mix of furniture on the Delabole slate floors, from high-backed built-in curved settles, through plush Victorian dining chairs, armed seats, chaise longues and mahogany housekeeper's chairs, to more modern seats, open fires, flowers on most tables, and a lovely ginger cat called Peewee; inoffensive piped music. Generous helpings of good home-made food include garlic egg mayonnaise (£2.95), open sandwiches (from £3.95; hot thick-cut rib of beef £4.50), ploughman's (from £4.75), vegetarian quiche (£5.25), steak, kidney and mushroom pie (£5.95), beef curry (£6.50), gammon and egg (£7.50), half a home-smoked chicken with barbecue sauce (£7.95), whole plaice with lemon and parsley butter (£8.95), steaks (from £8.95), daily specials such as Cornish crab soup (£3.50), honey beef casserole (£5.95), and cod steak topped with cheese and tomato (£6.95), and home-made puddings; enjoyable Sunday lunch. Well kept Dartmoor Best, St Austell HSD and XXXX Mile, and Marstons Pedigree on handpump, a fair choice of wines, several malt whiskies, farm cider, and friendly service from the long-standing licensee (who has been here 17 years now) and his staff; darts, shove-ha'penny, dominoes, and fruit machine. Sadly they've had to close the garden, but there are seats in front of the pub and at the back of the car park. By the time this book is published, they will have added a new family bedroom. *(Recommended by Graham Tayar, Catherine Raeburn, JP, PP, Nigel Wikeley, Roger and Christine Mash, David Carr, Peter Salmon, D B Jenkin, Mrs E Hayes, Chris and Anna Rowley, Paul and Judith Booth, John Gillett, Christopher Darwent, R J Walden, Hazel R Morgan, Chris and Margaret Southon, Mr and Mrs T Currell, J Roy Smylie, Brian Skelcher, M G Hart, J Henry)*

Free house ~ Licensees John Cook and Lesley Elliott ~ Real ale ~ Bar food (not 25 Dec) ~ (01566) 772051 ~ Children in eating area of bar ~ Open 11-3, 6-11; 12-3, 7-10.30 Sun ~ Bedrooms: £25(£30B)/£40(£50B)

TREMATON SX3959 Map 1
Crooked Inn

Off A38 just W of Saltash; 2nd (not first) turn signposted left to Trematon, then almost immediately right down bumpy drive with eccentric signs

As you wend your way past a small caravan site then down a long bumpy drive with slightly eccentric notices, you might start wondering what you've let yourself in for. The feeling grows when you get to the surprisingly isolated pub, to be met in the courtyard by a wandering sheep, pregnant goat or even pot-bellied or pink porkers. So it's almost a relief to find that it's actually all rather civilised, with a relaxed, friendly air and some interesting furnishings (though you might have to remove a couple of the six cats from the chair you want to sit on). The bar is more or less open plan, with lots of animal drawings and photographs, high bar chairs by the curved stone counter, mate's chairs and brocaded stools around a mix of tables on the blue patterned carpet, and a large sturdy elaborately turned standing timber with elbow table. Down a step is a bigger room with heavier stripped beams, wooden settles and some banquettes, quite a few brass and copper knick-knacks, a piano and fruit machine, and a stuffed alligator on the window sill looking out over the garden (which on our visit had a rather fine horse nibbling the lawn). Generous helpings of decent bar food (using local produce) include sandwiches, home-made pies such as steak and kidney and chicken and ham, cod and chips, ham and egg, curries or lasagne (all £4.75), steaks (from £7.75), and daily specials. Well kept Bass, Sharps Own, Skinners Who Put the Lights Out, St Austell HSD and Tetleys on handpump, and a decent wine list. As well as white metal seats and tables in the courtyard, there are more in the back garden with children's play equipment (including a really big slide built down a hill), and far-reaching country views. As we went to press, they were building a sizeable accommodation wing. *(Recommended by Ted George, P J Boyd, Bronwen and Steve Wrigley)*

Free house ~ Licensees Sandra and Tony Arnold ~ Real ale ~ Bar food (11-2.15, 6-9.30) ~ (01752) 848177 ~ Children in eating area of bar ~ Open 11-3, 6-11; 11-11 Sat; 12-10.30 Sun; not open all day weekends in winter ~ Bedrooms: £25(£39B)/£39(£60B)

TRESCO (ISLES OF SCILLY) SV8915 Map 1
New Inn ♀ ⚏

New Grimsby

It's pretty impressive to have five real ales well kept on handpump in this old island inn: Dartmoor Best, Ind Coope Burton, Skinners Betty Stogs Bitter, Spriggan Ale, and a beer brewed for the pub by Skinners called Tresco Tipple, as well as Hoegaarden wheat beer; interesting wines, 30 malt whiskies, and 12 vodkas. This was once a row of fishermen's cottages and has a good bustling atmosphere in its light and airy bars, attractively refurbished with lots of washed-up wood from a ship's cargo, as well as solid pine bar chairs, farmhouse chairs and tables, a collection of old telescopes, and a model yacht. Good bar food at lunchtime includes home-made soup with home-made bread (£2.70), filled french bread (from £4.60; white crab and citrus mayonnaise (£7.65), salad platters (£5.60), and fresh crispy cod in polenta batter with home-made tartar sauce (£6.70), daily specials, and puddings. The well regarded and cheerfully decorated no-smoking restaurant also has a separate children's menu. Darts, pool, juke box, cribbage, dominoes, and euchre. There are picnic-sets in the garden. Note that the price below is for dinner, bed and breakfast. *(Recommended by John and Jackie Chalcraft, Michael Sargent, Kevin Flack, Dr Alan Green, D J Walker, David Price, R J Walden)*

Free house ~ Licensees Graham and Sue Shone ~ Real ale ~ Bar food ~ Restaurant ~ (01720) 422844 ~ Children welcome until 9pm ~ Open 11-11; 12-10.30 Sun; 12-2.30, 6.30-11 in winter ~ Bedrooms: /£178B

TRURO SW8244 Map 1
Old Ale House ★ ⬛ £

7 Quay St/Princes St

The happy sound of contented customers eating and drinking fills this bustling, friendly pub that manages to appeal to quite a wide range of customers, despite its back-to-basics, old-fashioned style. It's probably down the the huge choice of constantly changing real ales on handpump or tapped from the cask (often over 20) that might include Bass, Fullers London Pride, Glentworth Dizzy Blonde, Phoenix Double Dagger, Sharps Own and Special Ale, Skinners Betty Stoggs Bitter, Timothy Taylor Landlord, Wadworths 6X , and so forth; also country wines. The highly enjoyable bar food is quite a pull too and is freshly prepared in a spotless kitchen in full view of the bar: doorstop sandwiches (from £2.65; delicious hot baked garlic bread with melted cheese from £2.70), filled oven-baked potatoes (from £2.65), ploughman's (from £3.65), very good hot meals served in a skillet pan like oriental chicken, sizzling beef or vegetable stir fry (small helpings from £4.65, big helpings from £5.95), lasagne or steak in ale pie (£4.65), daily specials, and puddings (£2.30). The dimly lit bar has an engaging diversity of furnishings, some interesting 1920s bric-a-brac, beer mats pinned everywhere, matchbox collections, newspapers and magazines to read, and a barrel full of monkey nuts whose crunchy discarded shells mix affably with the fresh sawdust on the floor; cribbage, dominoes, giant Jenga, trivia, and piped music. *(Recommended by JP, PP, Ted George, Klaus and Elizabeth Leist, Mr and Mrs B Hobden, W W Burke, J Davies, Stephen Horsley, B, M, and P Kendall, Sue Holland, David Webster, Jacquie and Jim Jones, the Didler, Barry and Anne, Pat and Tony Martin, George Atkinson, Dr and Mrs Cottrell, Mayur Shah, S Horsley, Tim Barrow, Sue Demont, John A Barker)*

Greenalls ~ Managers Howard Grave, Terry Wheatly ~ Real ale ~ Bar food (12-2.30, 6-7.45 weekdays; till 8.45 Sat) ~ (01872) 271122 ~ Children welcome until 8.30 ~ Live band Thurs, duo Sat ~ Open 11-11; 12-10.30 Sun

Lucky Dip

Besides the fully inspected pubs, you might like to try these Lucky Dips recommended to us and described by readers (if you do, please send us reports):

Altarnun [SX2182]
Rising Sun: Basic old local with very traditional flagstoned bar, six well kept ales inc some rare for the area, good value simple food, friendly staff, restaurant; attractive spot *(Mr and Mrs K A Treagust, Mrs C Stevens)*
Boscastle [SX0990]
☆ *Napoleon*: Appealing 16th-c pub, comfortable and welcoming little low-beamed rooms, interesting Napoleon prints, good generous bar food inc fresh veg and vegetarian, no-smoking restaurant, well kept Bass and St Austell tapped from the cask, decent wines, good coffee, friendly staff and locals, polished slate floor, big open fire, pool room, children allowed; piped music, maybe folk music; sheltered terrace, second larger family garden; may close early if quiet, steep climb up from harbour *(LYM, A Addington, Jeanne Cross, Paul Silvestri, Mr and Mrs K A Treagust, the Didler, John and Vivienne Rice)*
Breage [SW6128]
Queens Arms [3 miles W of Helston]: Popular expanding spotless pub with open fire, beams festooned with plates, no-smoking dining room, generous food inc sandwiches (sometimes hefty), vegetarian and children's dishes, Whitbreads-related ales, welcoming landlord, daily papers; tables and children's games room outside, another play area and garden over the lane; quiz night Weds; bedrooms, medieval wall paintings in church opp *(D B Jenkin, DC, P and M Rudlin)*
Bude [SS2005]
☆ *Falcon* [Falcon Terrace]: Bustling bar overlooking canal in impressive 19th-c hotel, lots of quick good value food inc crunchy veg, daily roast, local fish and good puddings, good value Sun lunch (must book), well kept Bass and St Austell Tinners and HSD, good coffee and herbal teas, attentive friendly staff; big family room with two pool tables, dogs welcome; bedrooms comfortable and well equipped, good breakfast *(Rita Horridge, Dr and Mrs N Holmes, R R Winn, David Carr, G Smale)*
Cadgwith [SW7214]
☆ *Cadgwith Cove*: Straightforward local with big front terrace overlooking fish sheds and bay, on Coast Path and open all day at least in summer; roomy and clean, local seascapes, well kept Sharps and a guest ale, bar food inc sandwiches, pasties and plain hot dishes, separate restaurant; dogs welcome, and children away from main bar, folk and jazz evenings *(Ewan and Moira McCall, George Atkinson, Paul and Pam Penrose, Barry and Anne)*

Camborne [SW6438]
☆ *Old Shire* [Pendarves; B3303 towards Helston]: Recently refurbished extended family dining pub with popular carvery, usual meals in dining area, friendly landlady, well organised staff, modern back part with lots of easy chairs and sofas, Bass and Dartmoor Best, decent wines, pictures for sale and great coal fire; picnic-sets on terrace, summer barbecues, five bedrooms *(Peter and Gwyneth Eastwood, Renee and Dennis Ball, Stephen Horsley, Dave and Deborah Irving, K H Frostick, P and M Rudlin)*
Canons Town [SW5335]
Lamb & Flag [A30 Hayle—Penzance]: Some concentration on good reasonably priced food, good choice inc vegetarian; well kept Bass and Boddingtons, warm welcome; tables in courtyard and garden *(James and Wendy Timms, Susan and Nigel Wilson)*
Cargreen [SX4362]
Crooked Spaniard [off A388 Callington—Saltash]: Big smart river-view dining area, small panelled bar, huge fireplace in another smallish room, well kept ales, good generous food; lovely spot, with waterside tables on terrace by Tamar – always some river activity, esp at high tide; under same management as Crooked Inn at Trematon *(Ted George)*
Cawsand [SX4350]
Devonport [The Cleave]: Proper pub with lovely bay views, good food inc very popular Sun roasts, well kept ales with lots of guest beers; bedrooms comfortable, good value *(Shirley Mackenzie)*
Charlestown [SX0351]
Harbour Inn [by Pier House Hotel]: Small well managed somewhat hotelish bar with good varied food, well kept Bass and Flowers Original, first-class location alongside and looking over the classic little harbour; interesting film-set conservation village with shipwreck museum *(Gwen and Peter Andrews, W W Burke)*
Rashleigh Arms: Large bar, very big lounge, good generous quick straightforward food inc fresh fish and popular puddings in cafeteria-style restaurant, seats out on terrace (dogs allowed there) and separate garden above little harbour and heritage centre; half a dozen well kept ales inc Sharps and Wadworths 6X, cheery quick service, good canalside family room; piped music may be loud, on the coach circuit; good value bedrooms *(D B Jenkin, George Atkinson)*
Crackington Haven [SX1396]
☆ *Coombe Barton*: Huge clean open-plan pub in tiny village, spectacular sea view from roomy lounge/dining area, good value food inc local

fish, well kept local and other ales, good coffee, back family room, tables on big terrace, games room with pool tables; bedrooms *(Barry and Anne, Jenny and Brian Seller, G Smale, Chris and Margaret Southon)*

Crafthole [SX3654]

☆ *Finnygook*: Clean and comfortable much-modernised lounge bar, good range of cheap bar food inc wholesome sandwiches, well kept St Austell beers, hospitable staff; piped music may be loud; pleasant restaurant, good sea views from residents' lounge, low-priced bedrooms; one car park is steep *(D B Jenkin, BB)*

Crantock [SW7960]

☆ *Old Albion* [Languroc Rd]: Pleasantly placed photogenic thatched village pub with old-fashioned tastefully decorated bar, low beams, brasses and open fires, friendly relaxed atmosphere, good range of generous home-made food inc giant ploughman's, up to five real ales; tables on terrace *(Colin Gooch, LYM)*

Cubert [SW7858]

☆ *Smugglers Den* [Trebellan, off A3075 S of Newquay]: 16th-c thatched stone pub doing well under current attentive efficient landlord, long bar with small barrel seats and tables, dining side with enormous inglenook woodburner and steps down to big family room, other side with armchairs, settees and pool; fresh generous quickly served food, well kept Morlands Old Speckled Hen and Whitbreads Fuggles, one or two guest beers tapped from the cask, no machines or juke box; tables in sheltered courtyard; cl winter Mon-Weds lunchtime *(Michael and Sally Colsell, P and M Rudlin, P Salmon, P T Lomas)*

Devoran [SW7939]

Old Quay: Old local doing well under friendly young licensees, steep newish garden to make the most of the idyllic spot – creekside village, lovely views; two unpretentious rooms, boating bric-a-brac, some interesting specials, well kept St Austell ales, quick service; no dogs, good value bedrooms *(Maria Furness, Ivan and Sarah Osborne)*

Falmouth [SW8032]

☆ *Chain Locker* [Custom House Quay]: Well placed overlooking inner harbour, with welcoming atmosphere and interesting strongly nautical decor, well kept Bass, Flowers Original, and Worthington Best, food majoring on good fresh local fish, good value sandwiches etc too, good separate darts alley; fruit machine, piped music; well behaved children welcome, open all day; self-catering accommodation *(Dr M E Wilson, R and T Kilby, LYM, W M and J M Cottrell)*

Grapes [Church St]: Spacious refurbished Greenalls pub with fine harbour view (beyond car park) from the back, beams, comfortable armchairs, sofas, lots of ships' crests and nautical memorabilia, plenty of tables, wide range of cheap food esp fish from adjoining servery, helpful friendly staff, John Smiths and Tetleys, games room; piped music, steep stairs to lavatories *(George Atkinson, Gwen and Peter Andrews)*

Jacobs Ladder [top of Jacobs Ladder steps]: Several rambling rooms, lively, casual and welcoming, with nice mix of ages, decent wine, food, live music inc Irish folk and dancing, weekly salsa *(John Wooll)*

☆ *Seven Stars* [The Moor]: Classic unchanging 17th-c local with wonderfully entertaining vicar-landlord, no gimmicks, warm welcome, well kept Bass and Sharps Own tapped from the cask, minimal food, quiet back snug, tables on roadside courtyard *(the Didler, BB, Hazel R Morgan)*

Flushing [SW8033]

Royal Standard [off A393 at Penryn (or foot ferry from Falmouth)]: Trim and traditional waterfront local, fabulous views from front terrace, neat bar with pink plush and copper, alcove with pool and darts, simple well done food inc good baked potatoes and home-made pasties, well kept Bass, Flowers IPA and local Sharps Doom Bar, very long-serving welcoming landlord, plenty of genuine characters; unreconstructed outside gents' *(the Didler)*

Fowey [SX1252]

Fowey Hotel: Comfortable hotel bar with estuary views, good lunchtime food in bar or on balcony; bedrooms good *(B Lake)*

King of Prussia [Town Quay]: Handsome building's upstairs bar, large, clean and neat, with bay windows looking over harbour to Polruan, well kept St Austell ales, good welcoming service, piped pop music (may obtrude), side family food bar with good value food inc fish and seafood, seats outside; open all day at least in summer, bedrooms *(Hazel R Morgan, LYM, Ted George)*

Lugger: Unpretentious locals' bar, comfortable small dining area popular with older people for good inexpensive food, cheap St Austell beers, friendly service, big waterfront mural, tables outside; bedrooms *(Ted George)*

☆ *Ship* [Fore St]: Friendly, clean and tidy local, good choice of good value generous food from sandwiches through local fish and good scallops to steak, lots of sea pictures, coal fire, pool/darts room, family dining room with big stained-glass window; well kept St Austell Tinners and HSD, juke box or piped music (may obtrude), dogs allowed; bedrooms old-fashioned, some oak-panelled *(G Washington, Caroline Jones, A J Thomas, Ted George, BB)*

Golant [SX1155]

☆ *Fishermans Arms* [B3269]: Plain but charming waterside local, nice garden, lovely views from terrace and window; warm welcome, good generous straightforward home-made food all day in summer (cl Sun afternoon), well kept Ushers Bitter, Founders and seasonal ales, log fire, interesting pictures, tropical fish *(the Didler)*

Gorran Churchtown [SW9942]

Barley Sheaf [follow Gorran Haven signs from Mevagissey]: Welcoming old pub, reputedly haunted but extensively modernised, central servery for three areas, back pool room, good food in bar and restaurant, real ales such as Sharps, Skinners, Ruddles and Wadworths 6X, good range of ciders; garden with summer barbecues; children welcome, facilities for disabled, nice village *(Nick Lawless)*

Gorran Haven [SX0141]

☆ *Llawnroc* [Chute Lane]: Comfortable family-friendly granite pub overlooking harbour and fishing village, good value home-made food inc imaginatively done local fish in bar and restaurant, wide range of well kept ales such as Sharps and Wadworths 6X, prompt service, very sunny tables out in front, barbecues; family/games room; good value bedroom block, handy for Lost Gardens of Heligan *(MDN, Keith and Norma Bloomfield)*

Grampound [SW9348]

☆ *Dolphin* [A390 St Austell—Truro]: Small village inn with buoyant atmosphere, welcoming landlord, good value generous straightforward food inc OAP lunches Weds and home-made pasties, well kept St Austell ales, decent house wines, two-level bar with comfortable chintzy settees and easy chairs, interesting prints; children allowed, pool, fruit machine, piped music; handy for Trewithen Gardens; bedrooms *(Dr and Mrs B D Smith, Howard Clutterbuck, Gwen and Peter Andrews)*

Gulval [SW4831]

☆ *Coldstreamer*: Busy but very clean and civilised local, caring service, comfortable dining atmosphere, attractive and popular hop-girt restaurant, very enjoyable food inc local fish and good Sun carvery, well kept Bass, Flowers IPA and Morlands Old Speckled Hen, friendly landlady and staff, unusual high ceilings; quiet pleasant village very handy for Trengwainton Gardens, and for Scillies heliport – turn right opp entrance *(John and Kathleen Potter, D Allen, Gwen and Peter Andrews)*

Gurnards Head [SW4338]

☆ *Gurnards Head Hotel* [B3306 Zennor—St Just]: Unspoilt flagstoned pubby bar, real fires each end, good food (not Mon evening) esp fish soup, real ales such as Bass, Flowers Original and Skinners, friendly service; plain family room, piped music may sometimes obtrude, live music twice weekly; bedrooms, glorious walks in outstanding NT scenery, inland and along the cliffy coast *(Gwen and Peter Andrews, Simon Williams, Bronwen and Steve Wrigley, Tim Barrow, Sue Demont, Brian Skelcher)*

Gweek [SW7027]

☆ *Gweek Inn* [back roads E of Helston]: Happy and comfortable family pub, large low-ceilinged bar with open fire, good reasonably priced home-made food, wide range of beers inc Cornish ones, good service, moderate prices, lots of motoring trophies (enthusiast licensees); separate restaurant Tues-Sat (summer); children welcome, tables on grass (safe for children), summer kiosk with all-day snacks, short walk from seal sanctuary *(Tim Barrow, Sue Demont, Ivan and Sarah Osborne)*

Gwithian [SW5841]

Pendarves Arms: Delightful village pub nr dunes, beach and coastal path; restaurant and children's room, lots of china mugs, varied food inc Sun roasts, reasonable prices; tables in garden across road *(Colin Gooch)*

Helford Passage [SW7627]

☆ *Ferry Boat* [signed from B3291]: Extensive modern bar in great – and popular – summer spot by sandy beach with swimming, small boat hire, fishing trips and summer ferry to Helford, full St Austell range kept well, wide choice of good generous food inc fresh fish and afternoon teas, comfortable no-smoking restaurant, prompt cheerful helpful service; maybe piped music, games area with juke box and SkyTV; suntrap waterside terrace, barbecues, usually open all day summer (with cream teas and frequent live entertainment); about a mile's walk from gate at bottom of Glendurgan Garden (NT); steep walk down from the overflow car park; we haven't yet had reports on the bedroom side – some emphasis on this now *(Gwen and Peter Andrews, George Atkinson, C and E M Watson, G L Carlisle, Ivan and Sarah Osborne, LYM, Tim Barrow, Sue Demont)*

Hessenford [SX3057]

Copley Arms [A387 Looe—Torpoint]: Spacious and attractive streamside garden and terrace, pleasant alcoves in modernised eating area (some emphasis on food), well kept St Austell ales; piped music, dogs allowed in one small area, big plain family room, play area; bedrooms *(Betty Petheram, D B Jenkin, John Wilson)*

Holywell [SW7659]

Treguth [signed from Cubert, SW of Newquay]: Comfortable and cosy thatched local nr big beach, several low-beamed rooms, real ales, home-cooked food inc vegetarian dishes and good value three course set menu, friendly service, real fire, darts; handy for camp sites *(Peter Salmon)*

Kuggar [SW7216]

Kennack Sands: Spotless, with dramatic coast views, light modern wood furniture, well kept ales such as Exmoor Gold and Sharps Doom Bar, satisfying bar food, welcoming service, restaurant; pool, darts, maybe piped music; bedrooms *(Gwen and Peter Andrews)*

Langdon [SX3089]

Countryman [B3254 N of Launceston]: Good choice of well kept beers, reasonably priced bar food inc good snacks, quick friendly service; very busy Sun lunchtime *(D B Jenkin, I S Wilson)*

Lanner [SW7240]

☆ *Fox & Hounds* [Comford; A393/B3298]: Relaxed rambling bar with very friendly helpful staff, black beams, stripped stone, dark panelling, high-backed settles and cottagey chairs, warm fires, good choice of generous reasonably priced food from sandwiches to duck or guineafowl inc plenty of vegetarian, well kept Bass and St Austell Tinners, HSD and Winter Warmer tapped from the cask, partly no-smoking restaurant, children in dining area; pub games, piped music (may be loud); great floral displays in front, neat back garden with pond and play area; open all day weekends *(C and E M Watson, Mr and Mrs G R Parker, J Davies, Mr and Mrs R C Robinson, LYM)*

Launceston [SX3384]

Cloisters: Friendly pub with good food in bar and downstairs cellar bistro (which has suit of armour), ample helpings, Irish beers *(Fiona Paxman)*

Lelant [SW5437]

☆ *Badger* [Fore St]: Dining pub with good range of food inc fresh fish, vegetarian and carvery, attractively softly lit modern L-shaped interior, partly no smoking, with panelled recesses, airy back conservatory, St Austell Tinners and other beers, friendly efficient service; bedrooms good value, prettily decorated; wonderful breakfast *(D Griffiths, Roger Byrne, Heather and Julie Louro)*

Lerryn [SX1457]

☆ *Ship* [signed off A390 in Lostwithiel]: Partly no smoking, with wide choice of reasonably priced popular bar food from sandwiches and good pasties to pheasant pie, well kept ales such as Bass, Courage Best, Morlands Old Speckled Hen and Sharps Doom Bar, local farm cider, fruit wines and malt whiskies, unrushed service, huge woodburner, games room with pool, dogs on leads and children welcome; pretty spot, with picnic-sets outside, play area; famous stepping-stones and three well signed waterside walks nearby; nice bedrooms in adjoining building, wonderful breakfast *(R Turnham, D B Jenkin, Ted George, A J Thomas, Nick Lawless, Dr and Mrs B D Smith, A J Barker, LYM)*

Linkinhorne [SX3173]

☆ *Church House* [off B3257 NW of Callington]: Neatly modernised bar, part rustic furniture and flagstones, part plush and carpet, with customer snapshots, some decorative china etc, woodburner, darts; well kept Sharps Doom Bar and Skinners Cornish Knocker, low mark-ups on wine, popular home-made food inc vegetarian and some bargains for children, also plush restaurant; piped pop music may be loudish; nice spot opp church, has been cl Mon *(BB, D J Meakin, JDM, KM, R A Cullingham, June Wilmers, J C Perry)*

Lizard [SW7012]

☆ *Top House*: Spotless well run pub particularly popular with older people; in same friendly family for 40 years, lots of interesting local sea pictures, fine shipwreck relics and serpentine craftwork in neat bar with generous good value bar food inc good local fish and seafood specials, interesting vegetarian dishes, well kept ales such as Banks's, Flowers IPA and Sharps Doom Bar and Special, roaring log fire, big no-smoking area, no piped music (occasional live); tucked-away fruit machine, darts, pool; tables on terrace, interesting nearby serpentine shop *(Tim Barrow, Sue Demont, E A George, Paul and Pam Penrose, Gwen and Peter Andrews, BB)*

Longrock [SW5031]

Mexico [old coast rd Penzance—Marazion]: Former office of Mexico Mine Company, with massive stone walls, cheerful local atmosphere, well kept Bass and Marstons Pedigree, comfortable surroundings, no-smoking dining extension *(Jack and Gemima Valiant)*

Looe [SX2553]

☆ *Olde Salutation* [Fore St, E Looe]: Big squarish beamed and tiled room with red leatherette seats and neat tables, nice old-fashioned fireplace, lots of local fishing photographs, side snug with olde-worlde harbour mural and fruit machine, step down to simple family room; consistently good simple food from new kitchen esp crab sandwiches or salads and Sun roasts, also vegetarian dishes, fast friendly service, well kept Ushers Best; piped music may be obtrusive, forget about parking; popular locally as The Sal – open all day, handy for coast path *(D P and J A Sweeney, BB, Erna and Sidney Wells, Dr and Mrs B D Smith, Michael Hill)*

Lostwithiel [SX1059]

Globe [North St]: Traditional pub with good food esp pies, pleasant landlady and staff, nice pubby atmosphere *(I Blackwell)*

Madron [SW4532]

King William IV: Friendly and well managed Ushers pub with imaginative food inc local specialities at competitive prices, good choice of beers, good fire; unusual building *(Charles Gysin)*

Malpas [SW8442]

☆ *Heron* [off A39 S of Truro]: Newly refurbished to a high standard, in stunning setting above wooded creek; good food choice, St Austell Tinners and HSD, log fire, lots of local photographs; pool, machines, piped music; suntrap slate-paved terrace; children welcome, can be very busy *(Mrs R Heaton, LYM, R Turnham, Lyn and Geoff Hallchurch)*

Manaccan [SW7625]

☆ *New Inn* [down hill signed to Gillan and St Keverne]: Attractive old thatched local, friendly and helpful landlady, well kept ales such as Flowers IPA and Wadworths 6X tapped from the cask, wide choice of food from lots of good sandwiches to local seafood and wonderful Sun lunch, traditional games – but modern tables and chairs; children welcome, sweet little terrier, winter darts and euchre nights, pleasant back garden with swing, pretty waterside village *(LYM, Adrian Hastings, David Crafts, George Atkinson, Peter and Gwyneth Eastwood, the Didler, Mrs R Heaton)*

Mawgan [SW7323]

Old Court House: Small comfortable open-plan pub, very welcoming, with well kept Whitbreads-related ales, dining area up a few steps, wide food choice from sandwiches to cheap Sun lunches, interesting plate collection, cat-loving landlord; pool in separate section, piped music; pleasant garden; bistro Thurs-Sat evenings and Sun lunchtime, children welcome *(Gwen and Peter Andrews, Mrs Maria Furness)*

Mawnan Smith [SW7728]

☆ *Red Lion* [W of Falmouth, off former B3291 Penryn—Gweek]: Big helpings of well cooked and presented food, lots of choice inc seafood (should book summer evening) in pleasantly furnished old thatched dining pub with open-view kitchen, welcoming helpful service, pictures, plates and bric-a-brac in cosy softly lit interconnected beamed rooms inc no-smoking room behind restaurant, lots of wines by the glass, well kept Bass, Greenalls, Worthington and a guest beer, good coffee; piped music, children welcome, handy for Glendurgan and Trebah Gardens *(LYM, Mrs Maria Furness, Mr and Mrs J Pitts, Linda and Julian Cooke, Maureen and Geoff Hall)*

Mevagissey [SX0145]

☆ *Fountain* [Fore St, down alley by Post Office]: Welcoming unpretentious beamed and slate-floored fishermen's local with good value tasty simple food inc fresh fish, well kept St Austell ales, lovely fire, obliging service, plenty of atmosphere, lots of old local prints and photographs, cosy back bar with glass-topped cellar; piano sing-song Fri, good fish in popular upstairs restaurant; SkyTV sports, pretty frontage *(Nick Lawless, Christopher Wright, JP, PP, Pete and Rosie Flower, the Didler, David Carr, George Atkinson)*

Ship [Fore St, nr harbour]: 16th-c pub with good generous quickly served food, full range of well kept St Austell beers, genial landlord, neat efficient staff; big comfortable room with small interesting areas, low ceilings, flagstones, nice nautical décor, open fire; fruit machines, juke box or piped music (may be loud), regular live music; bedrooms *(Nick Lawless, Pete and Rosie Flower, Tim Jacobson, M Rutherford, Christopher Wright, David Carr)*

Morwenstow [SS2015]

☆ *Bush* [signed off A39 N of Kilkhampton]: One of Britain's oldest pubs, take us as we are in style; part Saxon, with serpentine Celtic piscina in one wall, ancient built-in settles, beams and flagstones, and big stone fireplace, upper bar with interesting bric-a-brac, well kept St Austell HSD and Worthington BB tapped from the cask, Inch's cider, cheap malt whisky, basic lunchtime food (not Sun), darts; no piped music, children or dogs, seats out in yard; lovely setting, interesting village church with good nearby teashop, great cliff walks; cl Mon in winter *(James Nunns, Mike Gorton, Brian and Jenny Seller, Prof A N Black, Sam Samuells, Lynda Payton, Mike and Mary Carter, LYM, Sue and Bob Ward, JP, PP, Alan and Paula McCully)*

Mullion [SW6719]

Mounts Bay [B3296]: Pleasant and spacious genuine local, very welcoming, with well kept Courage Directors, Marstons Pedigree and Skinners, lounge bar, saloon, well integrated family room, restaurant, back bar with pool, good play area; bedrooms *(Roger and Jenny Huggins, Gwen and Peter Andrews, Dave and Deborah Irving)*

☆ *Old Inn*: Thatched and beamed Greenalls pub with central servery doing generous good value family food (all day Jul/Aug) from good doorstep sandwiches to pies and evening steaks, extensive eating areas, charming nooks and crannies, lots of brasses, nautical items and old wreck pictures, big inglenook fireplace, no-smoking room, well kept Bass, Sharps Doom Bar, John Smiths and Tetleys, friendly attentive staff; children welcome, open all day Sat/Sun and Aug; can be very busy (esp on live music nights), darts, fruit machine; picnic-sets in

pretty orchard garden; good bedrooms *(LYM, Gwen and Peter Andrews, Jenny and Roger Huggins, Paul and Pam Penrose, George Atkinson, Peter Salmon)*

Polurrian: Hotel bar, but outstanding staff and plenty of locals banish any stuffiness; plans to introduce a real ale; bedrooms *(Gwen and Peter Andrews)*

Newlyn East [SW8255]

Pheasant: Friendly traditional village inn in quiet back street, attractive window boxes and tubs, good home cooking and service; dogs welcome, not far from Trerice Gardens *(D J Nash, Michael and Sally Colsell)*

Notter [SX3861]

☆ *Notter Bridge* [signed just off A38 Saltash—Liskeard]: Lovely spot just off trunk road, tables in conservatory and fairy-lit garden looking down on sheltered stream, neatly kept open-plan dining lounge, wide choice of food esp particularly good home-made curries, good value children's meals and puddings inc delicious local farm ice creams, welcoming bustling atmosphere, well kept Bass, Courage Best and Greene King Abbot, helpful service, darts in public bar; children very welcome, friendly fat tortoiseshell cat, maybe unobtrusive piped music; open all day w/e, must book Fri/Sat, very handy for nearby holiday parks *(Bronwen and Steve Wrigley, June and Perry Dann, Ted George, BB, V Pitts)*

Padstow [SW9175]

☆ *Golden Lion* [Lanadwell St]: Friendly and cosy backstreet local with pleasant black-beamed front bar, high-raftered back lounge with plush banquettes against ancient white stone walls; reasonably priced simple lunches inc very promptly served good sandwiches, evening steaks and fresh seafood, well kept real ales, coal fire, good staff, pool in family area; piped music or juke box, fruit machines; bedrooms *(R R and J D Winn, Sue Holland, David Webster, Andrew Hodges, David Carr, Ted George, BB)*

☆ *London* [Llanadwell St]: Wonderfully unspoilt fishermen's local with lots of pictures and nautical memorabilia, good buzzing atmosphere (get there early for a table), St Austell beers, decent choice of malt whiskies, good choice of lunchtime bar food, more elaborate evening choice (small back dining area), great real fire; games machines but no piped music; open all day, bedrooms good value *(Ian Pendlebury, David Carr, Ted George, LYM, John and Christine Simpson, Paul and Sharon Sneller, Sue Holland, David Webster, Gwen and Peter Andrews)*

Old Custom House [South Quay]: Well organised large airy open-plan seaside bar with conservatory and big family area, decent unpretentious food inc fresh fish and vegetarian, evening restaurant, St Austell Tinners and HSD, quick service, pool; good spot by harbour, attractive sea-view bedrooms *(Sue Holland, David Webster, J F M West, Ted George, David Carr, BB, Mrs C Stevens, A J Barker, M L Hodge, Paul and Sharon Sneller, Bronwen and Steve Wrigley)*

Pendoggett [SX0279]
Cornish Arms: Big lively locals' bar with games and piped music, attractive more sedate front part with traditional oak settles on fine slate floor and small pleasant dining room, good varied food inc fresh fish, skilled friendly service; provision for children, open all day, terrace with distant sea view; bedrooms *(Mrs C Stevens, LYM, John Westlake)*

Penelewey [SW8240]
☆ *Punch Bowl & Ladle*: Much extended thatched pub in picturesque setting, cosy rooms, big settees and rustic artefacts, strong emphasis on plush and spreading dining side, with US-style hostess allocating seating and taking orders for the wide choice of good fresh generous food, inc good help-yourself salads, fish and vegetarian; Bass and Sharps Doom Bar, unobtrusive piped music, children and dogs on leads welcome, handy for Trelissick Gardens; open all day summer *(Hazel R Morgan, LYM, Romey Heaton, Ian Shorthouse, Nick J Lawless, Mrs Maria Furness, Ivan and Sarah Osborne)*

Penhallow [SW7651]
Plume of Feathers: Cosy 18th-c beamed pub full of pictures, jugs and bric-a-brac collected from Russia and beyond, good value bar food; nice garden, animals inc pot-bellied pig for children in back paddock *(Ivan and Sarah Osborne)*

Penzance [SW4730]
☆ *Dolphin* [The Barbican; Newlyn road, opp harbour after swing-bridge]: Busy welcoming local with attractive nautical décor, good harbour views, quick bar food inc good pasties, well kept St Austell ales, great fireplace, big pool room with juke box etc; children in room off main bar; no obvious nearby parking *(LYM, the Didler)*
☆ *Globe & Ale House* [Queens Sq]: Smaller sister pub to Old Ale House in Truro and Quayside in Falmouth, enthusiastic licensee, good local following, Bass, Sharps, Skinners and four changing guest beers *(P and M Rudlin)*
Mounts Bay [The Promenade, Wherry Town]: Great character in small and busy welcoming seafront free house, good choice of real ales inc Bass and Worthington *(the Didler)*

Perranarworthal [SW7839]
☆ *Norway* [A39 Truro—Penryn]: Large pub done up in traditional style, half a dozen areas, beams hung with farm tools, lots of prints and rustic bric-a-brac, old-style wooden seating, benches and big tables, tropical fish tank; big helpings of popular food inc vegetarian and under-5s bargains, well kept Sharps and Tetleys, decent wines, quick friendly service, attractive restaurant; games machine and piped music; tables outside, open all day *(BB, Ivan and Sarah Osborne)*

Perranwell []
☆ *Royal Oak* [off A393 Redruth—Falmouth and A39 Falmouth—Truro]: Clean and welcoming pub with large attractive old black-beamed bar, cosy seats, buoyant atmosphere, reliably good food from sandwiches to weekly lobster night in pretty check-clothed dining area, well kept

Bass and Flowers IPA and good wines by the glass, good log fire, provision for children, garden with picnic-sets *(Valerie Pitts, LYM, Gwen and Peter Andrews)*

Phillack [SW5638]
Bucket of Blood [Church Town Rd]: Welcoming busy village pub done out in stripped pine, generous attractive food, well kept St Austell Tinners and HSD, jolly gruesome ghost stories, tables outside *(Dave and Deborah Irving, LYM, JP, PP)*

Pillaton [SX3664]
☆ *Weary Friar* [off Callington—Landrake back road]: Pretty tucked-away 12th-c pub with four spotless and civilised knocked-together rooms (one no smoking), comfortable seats around sturdy tables, easy chairs one end, well kept Bass, Courage Directors, Morlands Old Speckled Hen and Wadworths 6X, farm cider, good wine choice, bar food inc lunchtime sandwiches, children's helpings and good puddings, quick service; big back restaurant (not Mon), children in eating area, helpful service; piped music; tables outside, Tues bell-ringing in church next door; comfortable bedrooms *(Ted George, W R Cunliffe, LYM, Bronwen and Steve Wrigley, P Salmon)*

Polgooth [SW9950]
Polgooth Inn [well signed off A390 W of St Austell]: Popular much modernised country local with good big family room and (up steep steps) outside play area, good value food servery, St Austell and guest ales, efficient service; garden with play area *(Peter Salmon, LYM)*

Polperro [SX2051]
☆ *Blue Peter*: Great setting up narrow steps above harbour, cosy and unpretentious little low-beamed wood-floored local with nautical memorabilia, well kept St Austell and guest beers such as Sharps Doom Bar, farm cider, quick service, log fire, traditional games, some seats outside, family area upstairs with video game; open all day, can get crowded, and piped music – often jazz or nostalgic pop – can be loudish; no food (you can bring in pasties) *(Bronwen and Steve Wrigley, Dr and Mrs B D Smith, Ted George, the Didler, LYM, Dean Riley, Michael Hill)*
☆ *Crumplehorn Mill* [top of village nr main car park]: Friendly service and good value generous food inc local fish in converted mill, dark cosy corners inc upper gallery, beams, stripped stone, flagstones, comfortable seats, well kept Bass and St Austell HSD and XXXX, farm cider; pool area, piped music; families welcome, good value bedrooms *(Michael Hill, BB, Ted George, Bronwen and Steve Wrigley)*
Manor: Friendly little wood and stone inn tucked away in back street, well kept beers, nice back eating room, tasty reasonably priced bar food *(Ted George)*
Noughts & Crosses [Llansallos St; bear right approaching harbour]: Steps down to cosy and cheerful beamed terraced pub with flagstoned woody servery, small food bar, more steps to bigger tiled-floor stripped-stone streamside bar, upstairs family room; Ushers seasonal ale, decent food inc local crab sandwiches, good

specials and cheap children's food, friendly young staff; children welcome, open all day w/e *(A J Thomas, Michael Hill, Ted George, I J and N K Buckmaster, BB, Bronwen and Steve Wrigley)*

☆ *Three Pilchards* [Quay]: Low-beamed fishermen's local high over harbour, lots of black woodwork, dim lighting, simple furnishings, food inc lots of seafood and good crab sandwiches, open fire in big stone fireplace, neat helpful and chatty staff, Ushers Best and Founders, tables on upper terrace up steep steps; piped music, open all day *(Miss A G Drake, Michael Hill, Ted George, Dennis Stevens, K Flack, BB)*

Polruan [SX1251]
Russell [West St]: Real no-frills local, friendly and lively, good simple food, full St Austell beer range kept well; maybe piped music *(Nick Lawless)*

Porthleven [SW6225]
☆ *Harbour Inn*: Large well looked-after pub/hotel in outstanding setting with tables out on big harbourside terrace, good value simple food in dining lounge and restaurant, separate bar, quick friendly service, well kept St Austell ales, comprehensive wine list; comfortable bedrooms *(Tim Barrow, Sue Demont, K Stevens, Ewan and Moira McCall)*

Portloe [SW9339]
☆ *Lugger*: Little hotel bar beautifully set in unspoilt village above cove; restaurant licence (so you can't go just for a drink), but bar lunches inc children's often excellent, simple easy chairs, two fires, evening restaurant, decent wines, pleasant service; tables on terrace, bedrooms (not all with sea view) *(LYM, MDN, J Hawkes)*
Ship: Simple unfussy local, well kept St Austell Tinners and HSD, small sensible choice of home-made food, chatty landlady, sheltered streamside garden over road; bedrooms, good breakfast, handy for coast path *(June and Perry Dann, Nick Lawless, Christopher Wright)*

Portmellon Cove [SX0144]
☆ *Rising Sun*: Fine spot overlooking sandy cove nr Mevagissey, flagstoned bar with unusual open fire, Birmingham City FC and nautical memorabilia, big upper family/games room and dining room, generous food inc children's, vegetarian and good value Sun roast, well kept Boddingtons, Marstons Pedigree and Wadworths 6X, good coffee and hot chocolate, seats outside; cl Oct-Easter *(BB, Pete and Rosie Flower, P P Salmon, Nick Lawless)*

Portscatho [SW8735]
Plume of Feathers: Friendly and comfortable, with good food freshly made by long-serving cook, side locals' bar, well kept St Austell and other ales, helpful smiling staff, new restaurant; pretty fishing village, very popular with summer visitors *(Kevin Macey, LYM)*

Poughill [SS2207]
☆ *Preston Gate*: Welcoming local with log fires, well kept Flowers and Tetleys, well cooked nicely presented good value food (evenings get there early or book), chatty landlord, back-to-back pews, darts, some seats outside; children

welcome, dogs looked after well; very busy in summer *(James Flory, LYM, Jenny and Brian Seller, Richard Cole)*

Redruth [SW6842]
☆ *Tricky Dickies*: Spotlessly converted isolated former tin-mine smithy, dark inside, with forge bellows, painting of how it might have looked; buoyant atmosphere, well kept beers, decent wines, good value food, exemplary service, a welcome for children; partly covered terrace with barbecues, aviary, adjoining squash and fitness centre; jazz Tues, other entertainment Thurs; new bedroom block *(P and M Rudlin, Dave and Deborah Irving)*

Rosudgeon [SW5529]
☆ *Coach & Horses* [A394 Penzance—Helston]: Roomy low-ceilinged stone dining pub with open fires in fine old fireplaces, wide changing food choice, well kept ales such as Sharps Doom Bar and Wadworths 6X, helpful service; piped music, juke box and pool table, separate family area – and big play area outside; bedrooms *(Gwen and Peter Andrews)*

Saltash [SX4258]
Boatman: Riverside pub beneath the road and rail bridges across to Tamar; limited space inside but tables outside in season; good choice of high quality food inc eight vegetarian dishes; well kept Fullers London Pride and Milligans Mist *(Peter Salmon)*

Scorrier [SW7244]
Fox & Hounds [B3298, off A30 just outside Redruth]: Long partly panelled well divided bar, two big log fires, comfortable furnishings, stripped stonework and creaky joists, large no-smoking area, wide choice of food inc lots oif vegetarian dishes, picnic-sets out in front *(Brian Skelcher, K Stevens, Mrs V Pitts, John and Christine Lowe, LYM)*

Sennen [SW3525]
First & Last: Comfortable and spacious roadhouse handy for Lands' End, well kept real ales (glass panel shows spring-cooled cellar), friendly local atmosphere, decent straightforward food; pool table, piped music can be intrusive, maybe lively, noisy and smoky in summer *(Colin and Peggy Wilshire)*

Sennen Cove [SW3526]
Old Success: 17th-c, radically modernised but lots of nooks and crannies, by clean beach with glorious view along Whitesand Bay; big bustling nautical-theme bar, perhaps best out of season, old photographs, well kept Bass and Sharps Doom Bar and Special, piped music, bar food, carvery restaurant; gents' past car park; children welcome, attractive bedrooms with good breakfasts in hotel part *(Gwen and Peter Andrews, Colin and Peggy Wilshire, Dave and Deborah Irving, G Kernan)*

St Austell [SX0152]
Carlyon Arms: Comfortable open-plan pub with reasonably priced hearty food, well kept St Austell Tinners, Tall Ships, Trelawnys Pride and HSD, friendly staff, lounge and games areas with pool, good juke box; open all day w/e *(Richard Lewis)*

St Blazey [SX0654]
Cornish Arms: Smartly refurbished and

carpeted, more dining pub than it used to be, but with well kept St Austell ales too and snacks from generous sandwiches up; bedrooms *(Gwen and Peter Andrews)*

St Dominick [SX3967]

☆ *Who'd Have Thought It* [a mile E of A388, S of Callington]: Spick and span, with interesting panelled bar, tasselled plush seats, Gothick tables, gleaming pottery and copper, two open fires; well kept Bass and St Austell HSD, decent wines, friendly staff, good generous food inc fresh fish, impeccable lavatories, superb Tamar views from roomy family conservatory; quiet countryside nr Cotehele *(Ted George, Alan and Paula McCully, Jacquie and Jim Jones, LYM, John and Vivienne Rice)*

St Erth [SW5535]

Star [Church St]: Deceptively spacious low-beamed 17th-c pub, lots of bric-a-brac, wide blackboard food choice, Bass, Banks's Mild and guest beers, good wine list; dogs welcome, open all day *(Ken Flawn)*

St Issey [SW9271]

Ring o' Bells [A389 Wadebridge—Padstow]: Neatly modernised cheerful and welcoming village local with consistently good home-made food inc children's helpings, well kept Bass and Courage Directors, open fire; darts, pool, some tables in flowery courtyard; can get packed in summer; bedrooms *(Mr and Mrs B Hobden, S Stubbs, LYM, David Carr)*

St Ive [SX3167]

Butchers Arms [A390 Liskeard—Callington]: 16th-c pub with huge helpings of good value food in cosy cottage-style dining lounge, prompt service, bar with pub games; lovely area *(Ted George, Mr and Mrs R C Robinson)*

St Ives [SW5441]

Castle [Fore St]: Cosy low-ceilinged local, lots of dark panelling, stained glass windows, old local photographs, maritime memorabilia, well priced bar food, Bass and Wadworths 6X, good value coffee, friendly staff; unobtrusive piped music; best out of season *(George Atkinson, B J Harding)*

Union: Small friendly pub with cosy dark interior, low beams, small fire, local photographs, decent sandwiches, Bass and John Smiths, coffee; piped music, can get very crowded *(George Atkinson)*

St Jidgey [SW9469]

Halfway House [A39 SW of Wadebridge]: Long narrow bar with current owners doing very good value generous food in eating area, good range of beers inc local brews, quick friendly service; pool, small back restaurant *(Gill and Keith Croxton)*

St Just in Penwith [SW3631]

Kings Arms: Friendly local, comfortable and clean, with good bar meals, St Austell ales, some tapped from the cask *(the Didler, G J Gibbs)*

☆ *Star* [Fore St]: Harking back to the 60s in customers, style and relaxed atmosphere, this interesting and informal dimly lit low-beamed local has appropriately old-fashioned furnishings, good value home-made food from sandwiches and pasties up, well kept St Austell

Tinners and HSD tapped from the cask and Mild and Trelawnys Pride on handpump; farm cider in summer, mulled wine in winter, and old-fashioned drinks-like rum shrub; traditional games inc bar billiards, nostalgic juke box, tables in attractive back yard; simple bedrooms, good breakfast *(David Howell, John McDonald, Ann Bond, Brian Skelcher, the Didler, Bronwen and Steve Wrigley, J Monk, LYM, Roger Byrne, Dave and Deborah Irving, Simon and Jane Williams, K Stevens)*

St Keverne [SW7921]

☆ *Three Tuns*: Relaxing local by church, lots of old photographs, good generous well presented food, well kept Sharps Doom Bar, quick friendly service; piped music; picnic-sets out by square, bedrooms *(BB, George Atkinson, Tim Barrow, Sue Demont)*

St Mabyn [SX0473]

St Mabyn Inn: Warm welcome, concentration on good choice of interesting rather upmarket food inc lots of good fish (not cheap), attractive décor, Sharps real ale; darts *(M Mason, D Thompson, J and F Gowers)*

St Mawes [SW8433]

☆ *Rising Sun*: Wide choice of food from triple-deck sandwiches up in big rather bare open-plan bar and restaurant, modern light wood, friendly new South African licensees, well kept St Austell ales and wines, good coffee; attractive conservatory, slate-topped tables on sunny terrace just across lane from harbour wall; open all day summer, pretty bedrooms *(Gwen and Peter Andrews, Tim Barrow, Sue Demont, John Crafts, LYM)*

St Merryn [SW8874]

☆ *Cornish Arms* [B3276 towards Padstow]: Well kept St Austell ales and usual bar food at reasonable prices inc good pasties in spotless local with fine slate floor and some 12th-c stonework; good games room, picnic-sets outside; children over 6 may be allowed in eating area *(Sue Holland, David Webster)*

Sticker [SW9750]

Hewas [just off A390]: Ivy-covered pub in pleasant village, lovely floral displays, genuinely warm welcome, popular reasonably priced food, St Austell beers *(Nick Lawless)*

Stratton [SS2406]

Kings Arms [A3072]: Well kept three-room 17th-c local with well kept Exmoor, Sharps and three or more guest beers, reasonably priced food; children welcome *(James Flory, P and M Rudlin, Mr and Mrs P Stubbs)*

☆ *Tree* [just E of Bude]: Cheerful young new management in rambling and interesting pub with seats alongside unusual old dovecot in attractive ancient coachyard, very friendly bar rooms, well kept St Austell Tinners and HSD, well priced food from good soup and sandwiches up, great log fires, character evening restaurant; children welcome in back bar, bedrooms *(Dr D E Granger, BB, Chris and Margaret Southon, Mike and Mary Carter)*

Tintagel [SX0588]

Olde Malt House: Warm welcome, good food *(Bernard Rousseau)*

Treen [SW3824]

☆ *Logan Rock* [just off B3315 Penzance—Lands End]: Relaxed local nr fine coast walks, low beams, high-backed modern oak settles, wall seats, inglenook seat by hot coal fire, popular food (all day in summer) from sandwiches and proper pasties up inc children's, local fish and cream teas, well kept St Austell ales, lots of games in family room, pub labrador; may be juke box or piped music, dogs allowed on leads; tables in small sheltered garden *(the Didler, Gwen and Peter Andrews, Keith Stevens, James Flory, Dr Phil Putwain, Simon and Jane Williams, Ewan and Moira McCall, LYM, Brian Skelcher)*

Tregony [SW9245]

Kings Arms [B3287]: Unpretentious old inn, two chatty bars, dining area, decent quickly served food at reasonable prices, well kept Flowers Original and guest beers; charming village *(Mr and Mrs Peter Smith, Christopher Wright, Colin and Peggy Wilshire)*

Truro [SW8244]

City: Small friendly local with particularly well kept Courage, genuine character, cosy atmosphere, attractive bric-a-brac *(Sue Holland, David Webster)*

☆ *Wig & Pen* [Frances St/Castle St]: Lots of well spaced comfortable tables around big horseshoe bar, good choice of good value well prepared and presented food inc vegetarian, several wines by the glass inc good New World ones, good range of beers, daily papers, good-humoured welcoming licensees and staff; unobtrusive piped music; tables out on busy street *(Sue Holland, Dave Webster, Richard and Janet Fleming, John Wooll, Ted George)*

Tywardreath [SX0854]

New Inn [off A3082]: Friendly, informal and busy conversion of private house in nice village setting, well kept Bass tapped from the cask and St Austell ales on handpump, food (till 8 evening), games and children's room; secluded garden, bedrooms *(the Didler, BB)*

Veryan [SW9139]

☆ *New Inn* [village signed off A3078]: Good value nourishing food with fresh veg in neat and homely one-bar beamed local, no-smoking dining area, leisurely atmosphere, genial landlord, well kept St Austell Tinners and HSD tapped from the cask, good value house wine, good coffee, two stone fireplaces, quiet garden behind the pretty house; bedrooms, interesting partly thatched village *(Julia and Richard Tredgett, Christopher Wright, Mr and Mrs Peter Smith, BB, A J Thomas, the Didler, I Blackwell)*

Wadebridge [SW9872]

Ship [towards Polzeath]: 16th-c, with wide range of enjoyable food in bar and restaurant, friendly staff and locals *(Michael and Sally Colsell)*

Zelah [SW8151]

Hawkins Arms [A30]: Cosy, with open fires, tempting food, pleasant service, good range of beers inc Skinners *(J Davies)*

Zennor [SW4538]

☆ *Tinners Arms* [B3306 W of St Ives]: Unaffected country local in lovely windswept setting by church nr coast path, limited food (all day in summer), well kept ales such as Sharps and Wadworths 6X from casks behind bar, Lane's farm cider, decent coffee, rather spartan feel with flagstones, lots of granite and stripped pine; real fires each end, back pool room (where children may be allowed), cats everywhere, friendly dogs, no music, tables and maybe chickens in small suntrap courtyard; limited parking *(Brian Skelcher, Russell Grimshaw, Kerry Purcell, the Didler, Tim Barrow, Sue Demont, Mark Brock, Simon Williams, LYM)*

Isles of Scilly

St Marys [SV9010]

Bishop & Wolf [Silver St, Hugh Town (A3110)]: Lively local atmosphere, interesting sea/boating decor with gallery above rd, nets, maritime bric-a-brac, lifeboat photographs, helpful staff, well kept St Austell Tinners and HSD, wide choice of generous food esp fish (should book, attractive upstairs restaurant); piped music, popular summer live music *(John Saul)*

'Children welcome' means the pubs says it lets children inside without any special restriction. If it allows them in, but to restricted areas such as an eating area or family room, we specify this. Places with separate restaurants usually let children use them, hotels usually let them into public areas such as lounges. Some pubs impose an evening time limit – let us know if you find this.

Cumbria

This is a very good county for pub-lovers, with lots of rewarding and well run pubs, some super food, interesting local beers (including own-brews in half a dozen main entries), and charming inns to stay in; the countryside is of course magnificent, so it's a bonus that so many of these good pubs welcome walkers. Pubs doing particularly well these days include the Dukes Head at Armathwaite (a fine all-rounder, now run by the son of the family – and very well, too), the Wheatsheaf at Beetham (hard-working licensees gaining their Food Award this year), the White Hart at Bouth (very friendly, run by two brothers who grew up in the village, and their wives), the Oddfellows Arms at Caldbeck (a hard-working team producing good value good food), the Cavendish Arms in Cartmel (another place now being run by the son), the Masons Arms on Cartmel Fell (a great favourite), the Sun at Crook (a newcomer to the Guide, stylish food), the Punch Bowl at Crosthwaite (on top form, with Steven Doherty its gifted landlord-chef back in day-to-day control), the Britannia so beautifully sited at Elterwater (another top favourite), the friendly Travellers Rest just outside Grasmere (its proper home cooking gains a Food Award this year), the Drunken Duck up above Hawkshead (good food and bedrooms – Awards for both this year), the welcoming Watermill at Ings (lots of interesting beers, but nice all round), the attractively redecorated Sun in Kirkby Lonsdale, the consistently enjoyable Kirkstile Inn at Loweswater, the charming and very well run Tower Bank Arms at Near Sawrey, the super old Queens Head at Troutbeck, the wonderfully placed Wasdale Head Inn (new to the main entries this year) and the Gate at Yanwath (surprisingly good imaginative food for such a happily unpretentious place). From among all these, so many of them doing good food, the Punch Bowl at Crosthwaite stands out for a special meal out, and is our Cumbria Dining Pub of the Year. Among quite a few new licensees we'd pick out the very friendly and cheerful people at the Mill Inn at Mungrisdale, and the couple now running the Burnmoor at Boot. The Lucky Dip section at the end of this chapter has a lot of gems, perhaps prime among them the New Inn at Blencogo (very good food), Trout in Cockermouth, Royal at Dockray and Howtown Hotel at Howtown. Drinks prices are generally low here – outstandingly so in the case of the Blue Bell at Heversham, tied to Sam Smiths. Of the national beers, Scottish Courage turns up most often as a pub's cheapest beer, under its Theakstons or Youngers brand names. Jennings of Cockermouth supplies its good beers to quite a lot of Lakeland free houses, but tends to be cheapest in pubs tied to the brewery. Yates, a smaller Cumbrian brewery, is well worth looking out for.

AMBLESIDE NY3804 Map 9
Golden Rule
Smithy Brow; follow Kirkstone Pass signpost from A591 on N side of town

This is a friendly and honest Lakeland local where the landlord welcomes walkers and their dogs and there are plenty of regulars to chat to. The bar has lots of local country pictures and a few fox masks decorating the butter-coloured walls, horsebrasses on the black beams, built-in leatherette wall seats, and cast-iron-framed tables; dominoes and cribbage. The room on the left has darts and a fruit machine, and the one down a few steps on the right is a quieter sitting room. Well kept Hartleys XB and Robinsons Best, Old Stockport, and Hatters Mild on handpump; pork pies (50p), and filled rolls (£1.50). There's a back yard with tables, and wonderfully colourful window boxes. The golden rule referred to in its name is a brass meausuring yard mounted over the bar counter. *(Recommended by John and Kay Morison, R J Bland, Mick Hitchman, Neil Spink)*

Robinsons ~ Tenant John Lockley ~ Real ale ~ Bar food ~ (0153394) 32257 ~ Children welcome until 9pm ~ Folk Weds evenings ~ Open 11-11; 12-10.30 Sun

APPLEBY NY6921 Map 10
Royal Oak
Bongate; B6542 on S edge of town

New licensees have taken over this old-fashioned coaching inn and although the Cheynes will be a hard act to follow, we are keeping our fingers crossed that what has been one of our favourite all-rounders remains just that. The oak-panelled public bar has a good open fire, and the beamed lounge has old pictures on the timbered walls, some armchairs and a carved settle, and a panelling-and-glass snug enclosing the bar counter; dominoes. Bar food now includes home-made soup with home-baked bread (£1.95), sandwiches (£2.95; open ones £4.95), prawns, mushrooms and onion in wine and cream, topped with cheddar (£3.95), little brown shrimps (£4.25), burrittos (from £4.50), lentil, red pepper and mushroom lasagne or cumberland sausage with chilli gravy (£5.95), home-made lasagne (£6.45), fillet of codling baked with a herb crust or Javanese curry (£7.95), pork fillet in madeira and cream (£9.95), steaks (from £11.75), and Sunday rare roast beef (£4.95). One of the dining rooms is no smoking. Well kept Black Sheep, Jennings Cumberland, John Smiths, and Yates Bitter on handpump, and a good range of wines and malt whiskies; dominoes and cribbage. In summer the outside is very colourful, with seats on the front terrace among masses of flowers in tubs, troughs and hanging baskets. You can get here on the scenic Leeds/Settle/Carlisle railway (best to check times and any possible delays to avoid missing lunch). *(Recommended by Michael and Hazel Duncombe, RB, Karen Eliot, Roger and Christine Mash, David Cooke, Anthony Barnes, Barry and Marie Males, Vann and Terry Prime, Susan and John Douglas, Liz Bell, JM, EM, Malcolm Taylor, John and Jackie Chalcraft, Janet Pickles, Gill and Maurice McMahon, Ann and Colin Hunt, Helen Pickering, James Owen)*

Free house ~ Licensee Ed McCauley ~ Real ale ~ Bar food (12-2,30, 6-9 weekdays; 12-9 weekends) ~ Restaurant ~ (01768) 351463 ~ Children in restaurant ~ Open 11-11; 12-10.30 Sun ~ Bedrooms: £35B/£76B

ARMATHWAITE NY5146 Map 10
Dukes Head ★ 🛏
Off A6 a few miles S of Carlisle

Now run by Mr Lynch's son, this smashing village pub continues to draw warm support from readers. It's an unpretentious place with a warm welcome for all and is an enjoyable place to stay with good, proper breakfasts. The civilised lounge bar has oak settles and little armchairs among more upright seats, oak and mahogany tables, antique hunting and other prints, and some brass and copper powder-flasks above its coal fire. Consistently good bar food includes sandwiches (from £2.20), home-made soups with croutons and cream (£2.40), black pudding and apple purée (£3), grilled goat's cheese, olives and croutons (£3.50), ploughman's (£5.85), baked cod on leeks or steak and kidney pie (£7), smoked salmon, and prawns on tossed salad (£7.95), and rib-eye steak (£8). The restaurant is no smoking. Well kept Boddingtons and a guest on handpump; piped music and dominoes; separate public bar with darts and pool. There are tables out on the lawn behind. You can now hire bicycles. *(Recommended by Canon David and Mrs Brenda Baxter, Mr and Mrs S Shore, John and Sylvia Harrop, Malcolm Taylor, Roy Morrison, Anthony Barnes, Mr and Mrs J Grayson, Mrs Frances Gray, Gill and Maurice McMahon, W Blachford, Jackie Moffat, P Cox, Chris and Ann Garnett, Lynn Sharpless, Simon and Amanda Southwell)*

Pubmaster ~ Tenant Henry Lynch ~ Real ale ~ Bar food ~ Restaurant ~ (016974) 72226 ~ Children welcome ~ Open 11-3, 6-11; 12-3, 6.30-11 Sun ~ Bedrooms: £28.50B/£48.50B

ASKHAM NY5123 Map 9
Punch Bowl
Village signposted on right from A6 4 miles S of Penrith

This attractive pub has a rambling bar with an antique settle by a log fire, interesting furnishings such as Chippendale dining chairs and rushwork ladder-back seats around sturdy wooden tables, and well cushioned window seats in the white-painted thick stone walls; there are coins stuck into the cracks of the dark wooden beams (periodically taken out and sent to charity), and local photographs and prints of Askham. The old-fashioned woodburning stove, with its gleaming stainless chimney in the big main fireplace, is largely decorative. Between the lounge and the games room is another log fire. Bar food includes lunchtime sandwiches (£2.70), home-made soup (£2.85), deep-fried mushrooms with herb and garlic butter (£2.95), cumberland sausage (£6.10), vegetarian lasagne (£6.50), beef in ale (£6.60), grilled salmon with a tangy lemon dressing (£6.80), stir-fry duck with plum sauce (£8.80), steaks (from £9.80), daily specials, and children's dishes (£3). Flowers IPA, Morlands Old Speckled Hen, Wadworths 6X, and Castle Eden on handpump; dominoes, cribbage, and piped pop music, and in the separate public bar darts and pool. There are tables out on a flower-filled terrace. *(Recommended by Paula Williams, Ian Jones, J Kirkham, Mick Hitchman)*

Whitbreads ~ Lease: David and Frances Riley ~ Real ale ~ Bar food ~ (01931) 712443 ~ Children welcome until 9pm ~ Open 11.30-3, 6-11; 12-11 Sat; 12-10.30 Sun ~ Bedrooms: £28.50B/£53B

BARBON SD6282 Map 10
Barbon Inn 🛏
Village signposted off A683 Kirkby Lonsdale—Sedbergh; OS Sheet 97, map reference 628826

Plenty of tracks and paths leading up to the fells start from this 17th-c coaching inn, and it is at the start of a beautiful drive to Dent. Several small rooms lead off the simple bar with its blackened range, each individually and comfortably furnished: carved 18th-c oak settles, deep chintzy sofas and armchairs, a Victorian fireplace. Decent bar food includes home-made soup (£2.25), sandwiches (from £2.25), Morecambe Bay potted shrimps (£4.75), cumberland sausage (£5.30), a vegetarian dish of the day (£5.75), home-made steak and kidney pie (£6.50), sirloin steak (£10.50), and daily specials such as cod in beer batter (£5.50) or Westmorland pie (£6.25). The restaurant is no smoking. Well kept Theakstons Best on handpump; dominoes, trivia and piped music. The lovely sheltered garden here is prettily planted and neatly kept. More reports please. *(Recommended by Alan J Morton)*

Free house ~ Licensee Lindsey MacDiarmid ~ Real ale ~ Bar food ~ Restaurant ~ (015242) 76233 ~ Children welcome ~ Open 12-3, 6.30-11; 12-3, 7-10.30 Sun ~ Bedrooms: £32(£35B)/£55(£60B)

By law pubs must show a price list of their drinks. Let us know if you are inconvenienced by any breach of this law.

BASSENTHWAITE LAKE NY1930 Map 9
Pheasant ★ 🛏

Follow Pheasant Inn sign at N end of dual carriageway stretch of A66 by Bassenthwaite Lake

From the garden of this civilised and rather smart hotel you can stroll into the very attractive surrounding woodlands – and there are plenty of walks in all directions. The little bars are pleasantly old-fashioned and pubby, and have persian rugs on the parquet floor, rush-seat chairs, library seats, and cushioned settles, hunting prints and photographs on the fine ochre walls, and well kept Bass, Jennings Cumberland, and Theakstons Best on handpump; quite a few malt whiskies, too. Enjoyable lunchtime bar food includes soup with home-made bread (£2.50), open sandwiches (from £4.75), ploughman's (£4.95), potted Silloth shrimps (£5.25), tasty venison sausages with smoked bacon and red onion gravy and sautéed potatoes or a hot dish of the day (£5.50), carrot, walnut and brie cheesecake with cumberland sauce and oatcakes (£5.50), local rainbow trout with roasted sweet peppers and balsamic vinaigrette (£5.60), and puddings (£2.95); the elegant restaurant is no smoking. If the bars are full, you might want to move to the large and airy beamed lounge at the back, which has easy chairs on its polished parquet floor and a big log fire on cool days; there are also some chintzy sitting rooms with antique furniture (one is no smoking). *(Recommended by P R and S A White, David and Kathy Holcroft, Christine and Geoff Butler, Nigel Woolliscroft, Andy, Julie and Stuart Hawkins, David Cooke, Paul S McPherson, H Thomson, Peter and Jennifer Sketch, Gill and Maurice McMahon, Maysie Thompson, Liz Bell)*

Free house ~ Licensee Christopher Curry ~ Real ale ~ Bar food (not in evening – restaurant only) ~ Restaurant ~ (017687) 76234 ~ Children welcome ~ Open 11.30-2.30, 5.30-10.30; 11.30-11(10.30 Sun) Sat; 11.30-2.30, 5.30-11 weekends winter; closed 24 and 25 Dec ~ Bedrooms: £59B/£90B

BEETHAM SD5079 Map 7
Wheatsheaf 🍴 🛏

Village (and inn) signposted just off A6 S of Milnthorpe

The friendly licensees of this fine 17th-c coaching inn work very hard to combine the relaxed, traditional atmosphere of the bar with its real ales, alongside very good food and carefully redecorated bedrooms, to create a thoroughly good all-rounder. The relaxed, partly no-smoking lounge bar has lots of exposed beams and joists, and well kept Jennings Bitter, Cumberland, and Sneck Lifter, and Theakstons on handpump, New World wines, and a good choice of whiskies, sherries, and liqueuers; daily newspapers and magazines to read. Changing regularly, the imaginative food includes lunchtime sandwiches, home-made soup (£2.25), a skewer of lamb's kidneys with a shallot and smoked bacon dressing (£3.95), terrine of corn-fed chicken with foie gras and new potato salad (£4.95), aubergine and parsnip crumble with beetroot bubble and squeak and yellow pepper sauce (£6.95), caramelised loin of pork with celeriac and apple roast (£8.50), seared Scottish salmon on a saffron and leek risotto with charred vegetables (£9.50), roast breast of duck marinated in ginger and soya sauce with an orange and passion fruit syrup (£9.75), and puddings such as steamed white chocolate pudding with dark chocolate sauce or almond and lemon curd tart with blackcurrant sorbet (from £3.50). The upstairs no-smoking restaurant (candlelit at night) is elegantly redecorated. You can fish in the River Bela. *(Recommended by Dr A McArthur Bennie, G Washington, A D Ryder, Gill and Maurice McMahon, M A Buchanan, Malcolm Taylor, Mr and Mrs C Frodsham, Neil Townend, Geoff and Angela Jaques)*

Free house ~ Licensees Diane and Donald Munro ~ Real ale ~ Bar food ~ Restaurant ~ (015393) 62123 ~ Children in eating area of bar ~ Open 11-3, 6-11; 12-3, 7-10.30 Sun ~ Bedrooms: £55B/£70B

If you report on a pub that's not a main entry, please tell us any lunchtimes or evenings when it doesn't serve bar food.

BOOT NY1701 Map 9

Burnmoor

Village signposted just off the Wrynose/Hardknott Pass road, OS Sheet 89 map reference 175010

If you are staying here, the new licensees have introduced an all-day breakfast, so that if you have exhausted yourself after one of the many surrounding walks, you could decide to have breakfast at 2pm; they also serve other food all day, with home-grown vegetables, and meat and fish coming from the local farms and lakes. Wines, too, are very good as one of the licensees is in the wine trade. The beamed and carpeted white-painted bar has an open fire (burning all day), comfortable seats, and Black Sheep, Jennings Bitter and Cumberland, and guest beers on handpump, quite a few malt whiskies (specialising in Islay malts), and good mulled wine all year; pool, cribbage, dominoes, and juke box. Bar food now includes sandwiches, home-made soup, and filled baked potaotes (from £1.60), deep-fried brie with cranberry sauce (£3.50; large £5.75), warm chicken and bacon salad (£4; large £6), home-roast ham and egg (£4; large £7), home-made vegetable crumble (£5.50), lamb hotpot with small chunks of black pudding and crunchy potatoes (£5.50; large £8.50), local game pie (£6; large £9), sirloin steak (£8.50), daily-made flans, fish and a roast, and children's meals (£2.50); they usefully serve morning coffee from 10am. The restaurant is no smoking. There are seats outside on the sheltered front lawn with a children's play area – slide, swings, and rope assault course. The inn is handy for the Ravenglass and Eskdale steam railway and for a restored watermill, said to be the oldest working example in the country. *(Recommended by Jenny and Brian Seller, Mike and Mary Carter, WAH, J H Bell, Tim Dobby, Brian Wainwright, H K Dyson, Derek Harvey-Piper, Mick Hitchman)*

Free house ~ Licensees Harry and Paddington Berger ~ Real ale ~ Bar food (all day) ~ Restaurant ~ (019467) 23224 ~ Children welcome ~ Open 10-11; 12-10.30 Sun ~ Bedrooms: £28B/£56B

BOUTH SD3386 Map 9

White Hart

Village signposted off A590 near Haverthwaite

The licensees – who run this small inn with their wives – are brothers and have grown up in the village; one is the chef and the other is the barman. It's a friendly place with a welcome for all ages, and readers are growing increasingly fond of it. The sloping ceilings and floors show the building's age, and there are lots of old local photographs and bric-a-brac – farm tools, stuffed animals, a collection of long-stemmed clay pipes – and two log fires, one in a fine old kitchen range. The games room has darts, pool, pinball, dominoes, cribbage, fruit machine, video game, and juke box; piped music. A fair choice of home-made food includes sandwiches, soups such as delicious tomato and carrot (£1.95), garlic mushrooms (£3.25), vegetarian bean burger (£5.95), chicken or vegetable balti (£6.50), pasta with a rich tomato and olive sauce (£6.95), halibut steak with garlic and parsley butter (£7.25), sirloin steak (£8.95), daily specials such as chicken breast stuffed with haggis in a smoked bacon sauce or lamb knuckle in redcurrant gravy, puddings (£2.75), and children's meals (£2.50). Well kept Black Sheep, Barnsley Bitter, Jennings Cumberland , Moorhouses Black Cat, and Tetleys on handpump, and 52 malt whiskies. The pub is well placed in good walking country, and there are tables out in the attractively planted and well kept garden. *(Recommended by Paul and Georgina Swinden, David Carr, JDM, KM, John and Kay Morison, Margaret and Roy Randle, Ron Gentry, Gill and Maurice McMahon, S and P Stubbs)*

Free house ~ Licensees Nigel and Peter Barton ~ Real ale ~ Bar food (12-2, 6-8.45; not Mon, not Tues lunchtime) ~ Restaurant ~ children in eating area of bar until 8.30 ~ Open 12-2, 6-11; 12-3, 7-11 Sun; closed Mon and Tues lunchtimes ~ Bedrooms: £28B/£38B

BOWNESS ON WINDERMERE SD4097 Map 9
Hole in t' Wall ◧

Lowside

Full of character and interest, this tucked away stone tavern has lots to look at in its beamed bar: giant smith's bellows, old farm implements and ploughshares, and jugs hanging from the ceiling, and a room upstairs has handsome plasterwork in its coffered ceiling; another long, narrow room has hops and chamber-pots, stuffed animals, and old pictures. On cool days a splendid log fire burns under a vast slate mantlebeam. The tiny flagstoned front courtyard (where there are sheltered seats) has an ancient outside flight of stone steps to the upper floor. Mrs Mitton decides what to cook each day once she gets into her kitchen. There might be sandwiches (from £2), vegetarian chilli or broccoli and cauliflower bake (£5.75), steak and kidney pudding or a hotpot (£5.95), whisky chicken (£6.50), fish pie (£6.95), sirloin steak (£7.95), popular whole roast pheasant with red wine sauce (£7.95), and puddings like home-made apple pie (£2.50). Hartleys XB and Robinsons Frederics and Best on handpump in excellent condition, home-made lemonade and very good mulled winter wine; darts, pool, fruit machine and juke box upstairs. If you'd rather catch it on a quiet day, it's better to visit out of season. *(Recommended by David Carr, Mike Gorton, P R and S A White, Neil Spink, SLC, Kerry Law, Smithy, Roy Bromell, Mrs S Miller, Roger Stamp, Karen Eliot)*

Robinsons ~ Tenants Audrey and Andrew Mitton ~ Real ale ~ Bar food ~ (015394) 43488 ~ Children in family room off tap room until 9pm ~ Open 11-11; 12-10.30 Sun

BRAITHWAITE NY2324 Map 9
Coledale Inn

Village signposted off A66 W of Keswick; pub then signed left off B5292

Walkers can start their hike straight from the door as this bustling inn is perfectly placed at the foot of Whinlatter Pass. The left-hand bar – liked by locals – has fine views of Skiddaw and the much closer bracken-covered hills from the window seats, a winter coal fire, and little 19th-c Lakeland engravings; the green-toned bar on the right, with a bigger bay window, is more of a dining bar. Bar food includes sandwiches, home-made soup (£1.95), filled baked potatoes (from £3.40), ploughman's or vegetarian sausage, gammon with egg or pineapple (£6.50), sirloin steak (from £8.95), daily specials, puddings like apple strudel (from £2.65), and children's meals (£2.40). Well kept Jennings Bitter, Theakstons XB, Yates Bitter, and Youngers on handpump; darts, dominoes, and piped music. The dining room is no smoking. The garden has tables and chairs on the slate terrace beyond the sheltered lawn, and a popular play area for children. *(Recommended by Lesley Bass, Maurice Thompson, David Yandle, Sheila Keene, Gill and Maurice McMahon, SLC, David J Cooke, H K Dyson)*

Free house ~ Licensees Geoffrey and Michael Mawdsley ~ Real ale ~ Bar food (12-2, 6-9) ~ (017687) 78272 ~ Children welcome ~ Open 11-11; 12-10.30 Sun; closed winter Mon-Thurs weekdays until 6.30 ~ Bedrooms: £23.50B/£57B

BRAMPTON NY6723 Map 10
New Inn

Note: this is the small Brampton near Appleby, not the bigger one up by Carlisle. Off A66 N of Appleby – follow Long Marton 1 signpost then turn right at church; village also signposted off B6542 at N end of Appleby

As we went to press, new licensees were poised to take over this attractively traditional inn. They plan to add bathrooms to the bedrooms and hope to make the atmosphere convivial to families and couples. The two cosy little rooms have nice stripped and polished old pine benches with upholstered cushions and old pine tables, and a good range of local pictures. The particularly interesting flagstoned dining room has horsebrasses on its low black beams, well spaced tables, and a splendid original black cooking range at one end, separated from the door by an immensely sturdy old oak built-in settle. Food examples had not been finalised but they were planning to offer traditional English pub dishes including sandwiches and ploughman's, a Yorkshire version of a Cornish pasty, gammon and egg, steaks, a big mixed grill, and 3-course Sunday lunch. Well kept Boddingtons, Theakstons Best, and Youngers Scotch on handpump, and a good choice of whiskies with some eminent malts; friendly service, darts, dominoes and piped music. There are seats on the lawn and a barbecue area. In June, the Appleby Horse Fair tends to use the pub as its base, so things tend to get crowded then. Incidentally, another Brampton near Chesterfield has a pub of the same name. *(Recommended by John and Enid Morris, Mr and Mrs A Bull, Patrick Herratt)*

Free house ~ Licensees Jack and Christine Goodwin ~ Real ale ~ Bar food ~ Restaurant ~ (017683) 51231 ~ Children welcome until 9pm ~ Open 12-11; 12-10.30 Sun; 12-2, 7-11 winter ~ Bedrooms: £20/£40B

BROUGHTON IN FURNESS SD2290 Map 9
Blacksmiths Arms
Broughton Mills; off A593

They believe in supporting the local community in this small, friendly pub. All produce comes from local suppliers, the local microbreweries are well represented, and they hold a marrow championship in September to raise money for the village charity. There are four simply but attractively refurbished little rooms with open fires in three of them, ancient slate floors, and well kept Dent Aviator, Barngates Brewery (from the Drunken Duck pub) Cracker Ale, Jennings Cumberland, and Theakstons on handpump, and farm cider. Enjoyable lunchtime food (not served in the bar) is cooked by the licensee and includes home-made soup (£1.95), open sandwiches (from £2.75), baked potatoes (from £3.25), a 6oz gammon steak (£4.75), daily specials such as haggis in cumberland sauce (£3.25), local cumberland sausage (£4.95), vegetarian Mexican crêpe (£5.75), chicken breast in stilton sauce (£6.25), tuna steak in mediterranean tomato sauce (£6.95), steaks (from £8.25), and puddings like peach crumble or sticky toffee pudding (£2.25); evening dishes are more elaborate. There are three smallish dining rooms (the back one is no smoking). Darts and dominoes. The hanging baskets and tubs of flowers in front are very pretty in summer, and the position is peaceful – tucked away in a charming hamlet in pretty countryside that's never too overrun with summer visitors. *(Recommended by Derek Harvey-Piper)*

Free house ~ Licensee Philip Blackburn ~ Real ale ~ Bar food (12-2, 6-9; not 25 Dec) ~ Restaurant ~ (01229) 716824 ~ Children welcome ~ Open 12-11; 12-10.30 Sun

BUTTERMERE NY1817 Map 9
Bridge Hotel 🛏
Just off B5289 SW of Keswick

The welcoming and relaxed atmosphere – plus the fact that it is surrounded by some of the best steep countryside in the county – makes this friendly inn a popular place with walkers. The flagstoned area in the beamed bar is good for walking boots, and has built-in wooden settles and farmhouse chairs around traditional tables, a panelled bar counter and a few horsebrasses, and there's a dining bar with brocaded armchairs around copper-topped tables, and brass ornaments hanging from the beams. Lunchtime snacks include a big soup (£3.25), filled baked potatoes (£4.10), ploughman's (£4.30), and battered chicken pieces with a honey and mustard dressing (£4.35); they also serve creamed garlic mushrooms (£2.90), butterbean casserole (£6.25), liver, bacon and onion casserole (£6.30), cumberland hotpot or steak and mushroom in ale pie (£7.10), salmon steak with chive butter (£7.75), and sirloin steak (from £10); the restaurant is no smoking. Well kept Black Sheep, Marstons Pedigree, Tetleys Bitter, and Theakstons Old Peculier on handpump, quite a few malt whiskies, and a decent wine list. Outside, a flagstoned terrace has white tables by a rose-covered sheltering stone wall. The views from the bedrooms are marvellous; self-catering, too. *(Recommended by Walter and Susan Rinaldi-Butcher, K F Mould, Gail Coskery, Elizabeth and Alan Walker, Carol and Jim Watson)*

Free house ~ Licensee Peter McGuire ~ Real ale ~ Bar food (maybe all day in summer) ~ Restaurant ~ (017687) 70252 ~ Children welcome but must be over 6 in evening restaurant ~ Open 10.30-11; 10.30-10.30 Sun ~ Bedrooms: £42B/£84B

CALDBECK NY3239 Map 9
Oddfellows Arms
B5299 SE of Wigton

The success of this comfortably extended pub is entirely due to to the hard-working and friendly young licensee and his staff. There's a good thriving atmosphere in the bar and attractively refurbished dining room, and a wide choice of particularly good, reasonably priced food: home-made soup (£1.95), sandwiches, open rustic rolls or filled baked potatoes (from £2.70), home-made pâté (£2.95), cumberland sausage with egg or apple butter (£4.50), steak in ale pie (£5.50), ploughman's or vegetable quiche (£5.95), honey-roast duck with orange gravy (£8.25), daily specials, and evening dishes like mushrooms in garlic sauce (£2.95), lamb on the bone marinated with mint, honey and spices and served with redcurrant and mint gravy or lovely grilled bass (£7.95), chicken fajitas (£8.25), and steaks (£10.95). The restaurant is no smoking. Well kept Jennings Bitter, Cumberland and a guest beer on handpump, good wines. Darts, pool, fruit machine, juke box and piped music. John Peel is buried in the village. *(Recommended by Neil and Claire Polley, Peter and Pat Frogley, Canon David and Mrs Brenda Baxter, Peter and Jan Humphreys, D and M Senior, Andy and Jill Kassube, Mike and Penny Sutton)*

Jennings ~ Manager Graham Davis ~ Real ale ~ (016974) 78227 ~ Children welcome until 9pm ~ Open 12-11; 12-10.30 Sun; 12-3, 6-11 winter ~ Bedrooms: £25S/£45S

CARTMEL SD3879 Map 7
Cavendish Arms 🍺 🛏
Off main sq

It's worth staying a night or two in this friendly little inn – Cartmel's oldest. There are plenty of good walks all round (and the local shop sells a simple map), the food is enjoyable, and the licensee is most helpful and welcoming. The relaxed bar has an open fire, farmhouse and other chairs and stools around traditional tables in the relaxed bar, well kept Bass, Jennings Cumberland, Mitchells Lancaster Bomber, Tetleys and changing weekly guest beers on handpump, a fair choice of malt whiskies, and quite a few wines by the glass. As well as sandwiches (from £3.45) and light lunches such as soup (£2.95), warm chicken, bacon and avocado salad (£5.95), and smoked fish platter (£6.25), there might be potted smoked mackerel pâté (£3.95), black and white puddings with a spiced apple compote and mustard sauce (£4.25), cumberland sausage and mash (£6.95), vegetable and cheese crumble (£7.25), stuffed baked cod with a tomato and fresh basil sauce (£8.95), chargrilled chicken breast on a sun-dried tomato, mushroom and basil cream (£9.95), and steaks (from £11.25). The restaurant is no smoking. There are tables in front of the pub, with more at the back by the stream, and their flower displays tend to win awards. *(Recommended by Peter and Jenny Quine, Margaret and Roy Randle, N Thomas, Gill and Maurice McMahon, David and Kathy Holcroft, SLC, Emma Collins, Vann and Terry Prime, Jane Taylor, David Dutton, P R and S A White, Andy, Julie and Stuart Hawkins, P H Roberts, Jenny and Brian Seller, David Heath, Miss A Godfrey)*

Free house ~ Licensee Tom Murray ~ Real ale ~ Bar food (12-2.15, 6-9.30) ~ Restaurant ~ (0153 95) 36240 ~ Children welcome ~ Open 11.30-11; 12-10.30 Sun ~ Bedrooms: £35(£35B)/£60(£72B)

'Children welcome' means the pubs says it lets children inside without any special restriction; readers have found that some may impose an evening time limit – please tell us if you find this.

CARTMEL FELL SD4288 Map 9

Masons Arms ★ ◖

Strawberry Bank, a few miles S of Windermere between A592 and A5074; perhaps the simplest way of finding the pub is to go uphill W from Bowland Bridge (which is signposted off A5074) towards Newby Bridge and keep right then left at the staggered crossroads – it's then on your right, below Gummer's How; OS Sheet 97 map reference 413895

Still one of the county's most popular pubs (perhaps best visited midweek when it's not so crowded), this beautifully set place remains the favourite of many of our readers. The main bar has plenty of character, low black beams in the bowed ceiling, country chairs and plain wooden tables on polished flagstones, and a grandly Gothick seat with snarling dogs as its arms. A small lounge has oak tables and settles to match its fine Jacobean panelling, and a plain little room beyond the serving counter has pictures and a fire in an open range; the family room has an old-parlourish atmosphere, and there's also an upstairs room which helps at peak times. A fine range of real ales includes their own Hoadstock Bitter (in summer only) and bottled Damson Ale, as well as Anchor Steam (from San Francisco), the rare Augustiner Maybock (from Munich), Barnsley Bitter, Blackpool Bitter from the Blackpool Brewery, Brains SA, Jennings Cumberland, Mitchells Original Bitter, and Morrells Oxford Bitter on handpump, a huge range of bottled beers, quite a few Belgian fruit beers, and Normandy cider; carefully chosen mainly New World wines, too. Wholesome food includes sandwiches (the hot roast local beef is good, £3.75), light meals such as cajun sausage and black pudding or lentil and hazelnut pâté (£5), and ploughman's (£6), plus specials such as red onion and wensleydale quiche, vegetable tikka or mediterranean roasted vegetable lasagne (all £6.95), local beef in Jennings Cumberland ale (£7.95), and puddings like apple, raspberry and scrumpy crumble or sticky toffee pudding (£2.95). They sell leaflets outlining local walks of varying lengths and difficulty. From the terrace in front, there are rustic benches and tables with an unrivalled view overlooking the Winster Valley to the woods below Whitbarrow Scar. *(Recommended by Peter and Audrey Dowsett, Bronwen and Steve Wrigley, Mick Hitchman, Phil and Heidi Cook, Nigel Woolliscroft, Tina and David Woods-Taylor, Ann and Colin Hunt, Barbara Wensworth, M E Ricketts, Paul S McPherson, J Phillips, Miss L Bruniges, Vicky and David Sarti, Colin and Sue Graham, Mrs S Kingsbury, Prof P A Reynolds, Suzy Miller, Liz Bell, Gill and Maurice McMahon, Ewan and Moira McCall, Steve Goodchild, Andy, Julie and Stuart Hawkins, Mr and Mrs Richard Osborne, Nick J Lawless)*

Free house ~ Licensee Helen Stevenson ~ Real ale ~ Bar food (12-2, 6-8.45) ~ (015395) 68486 ~ Children welcome until 9pm ~ Open 11.30-11; 12-10.30 Sun; 11-3, 6-11 winter; closed 25 Dec and evening 26 Dec

CASTERTON SD6279 Map 10

Pheasant ⓦ ♀ ⇌

A683 about a mile N of junction with A65, by Kirkby Lonsdale; OS sheet 97, map reference 633796

Some careful changes to this civilised inn this year include the turning of the residents' lounge into a super new bedroom, some refurbishment to the rest of the bedrooms, and the addition of a woodburning stove. The neatly kept and attractively modernised beamed rooms of the main bar have padded wheelback chairs, plush wall settles, newspapers and magazines to read, a woodburning stove surrounded by brass ornaments in a nicely arched bare stone fireplace with polished brass hood, and souvenir mugs on the mantlepiece; there's a further room (which is no smoking during meal times) across the passage with a piano. Good bar food includes home-made soup (£2.25), lunchtime sandwiches (from £2.50), freshly made greek salad (£4.25), steak and kidney pie (£6.25), tortellini ricotta in a neapolitan sauce topped with cheese (£6.95), steaks (from £11), and daily specials like fresh dressed crab with mango mayonnaise (£4.25), lamb curry with pickles (£7.95), chicken breast in a white wine and creamy asparagus sauce (£8.95), roast rack of lamb (£9.50), and fillet of red snapper grilled with butter and spring onions (£10.50); hearty breakfasts. The restaurant is no smoking. Well kept Theakstons

Best and a weekly changing guest beer such as Brakspears Special, Ridleys Rumpus or Wells Fargo on handpump, over 30 malt whiskies, and a good wine list offering 12 by the glass. Darts, dominoes, and piped music. There are some tables with cocktail parasols outside by the road, with more in the pleasant garden. The nearby church (built for the girls' school of Brontë fame here) has some attractive pre-Raphaelite stained glass and paintings. Dogs welcome. *(Recommended by Neil Townend, R Bouran, K H Richards, Michael A Butler, Karen Eliot, Alan J Morton)*

Free house ~ Licensees Melvin and May Mackie ~ Real ale ~ Bar food ~ Restaurant ~ (015242) 71230 ~ Children welcome ~ Quiz night winter Thurs evenings ~ Open 11-3, 6-11; 11-3, 6-10.30 Sun ~ Bedrooms: £37.50B/£68B

CHAPEL STILE NY3205 Map 9
Wainwrights
B5343

There's plenty of room in the characterful slate-floored bar of this traditional Lakeland pub and it is here that walkers and their dogs are welcomed. It's a charming fellside spot and there are picnic-sets on the terrace with fine views. Inside, there's a relaxed and friendly atmosphere; the bar has an old kitchen range, cushioned settles, and well kept Jennings Bitter, Cumberland Ale, and Sneck Lifter, and a guest beer on handpump. Bar food includes home-made soup (£1.95), sandwiches (from £2.90), filled baked potatoes (£3.95), ploughman's (£6), steak and kidney pudding or cannelloni filled with spinach and ricotta cheese (£6.75), lamb shoulder with honey and mint (£7.95), children's dishes (£3.50), and daily specials; they don't take bookings, so best to get there early; friendly service. The dining area is no smoking; darts, dominoes, cribbage, fruit machine, trivia, and piped music. This is part of the Langdale complex. *(Recommended by Roy Butler, John and Phyllis Maloney, SLC, V and E A Bolton, David J Cooke, Eddie Edwards)*

Free house ~ Licensees M Darbyshire and D Banks ~ Real ale ~ Bar food (12-2, 6-9) ~ (015394) 38088 ~ Children welcome until 9.30 ~ Quiz night Tues evening ~ Open 11.30-11; 12-10.30 Sun; 11.30-3, 6-11 weekdays winter

COCKERMOUTH NY1231 Map 9
Bitter End 🍺 £
15 Kirkgate

It's worth a wander around this interestingly refurbished place as the three main rooms have a different atmosphere in each – from quietly chatty to sporty, with the decor reflecting this such as unusual pictures of a Cockermouth that even Wordsworth might have recognised to more up-to-date sporting memorabilia. There's a tiny Victorian style shop window view of the little brewery behind the back room (some no-smoking tables here at lunchtime) where the landlord brews Cockersnoot and Skinners Old Strong – you can see the equipment without even getting up from your seat. He also keeps Jennings Bitter and Sneck Lifter, and four weekly changing guest beers on handpump, in good condition; quite a few bottled beers from around the world. At lunchtime, simple snacks (with prices as last year) include home-made soup (£1.50), filled rolls (from £1.65; spicy chicken £2.50), and filled baked potatoes (from £1.95), with a larger evening choice such as three-bean casserole (£4.75), home-made chicken tikka or lamb balti (£4.85), home-made steak and mushroom in ale pie (£4.95), puddings like home-made sticky toffee pudding (£1.95), children's meals (from £1.95), and roast Sunday lunch (£4.25). Service is very welcoming; piped music; the public car park round the back is free after 6. *(Recommended by Lester Edmonds, Gill and Maurice McMahon, Andy and Jill Kassube, Jane Taylor, David Dutton)*

Own brew ~ Licensee Susan Askey ~ Real ale ~ Bar food (12-2, 6-8.30) ~ (01900) 828993 ~ Children in eating area of bar ~ Quiz Tues evenings ~ Open 12-2.30, 6-11; 11.30-3, 6-11 Sat; 12-3, 7-10.30 Sun

CONISTON SD3098 Map 9

Black Bull 🍺 🛏️

Yewdale Rd (A593)

One of the beers brewed on site here is named after Donald Campbell's Bluebird, and there's quite a lot of memorabilia devoted to the attempting of the water speed records. Other own-brewed beers include Coniston Old Man, Opium, and Blacksmiths on handpump, plus guests such as Moorhouses Black Cat, Theakstons Old Peculier and Timothy Taylor Landlord. The cheerful back area has slate flagstones and is liked by walkers and their dogs, while the beamed and carpeted front part has cast-iron-framed tables, comfortable banquettes and stools, an open fire, and a relaxed, comfortable feel; part of the bar and all of the restaurant are no smoking. Bar food includes home-made soup (£1.95), sandwiches (from £2.95; toasties £3.25), filled baked potatoes (from £3.50), ploughman's or 10oz cumberland sausage (£5.95), spicy chilli (£6.80), leek and vegetable crumble (£7.45), local Esthwaite smoked trout (£7.95), gammon and eggs (£9.25), sirloin steak (£10.95), daily specials such as braised lamb shoulder in mint marinade, steak and kidney pie or fresh fish dishes, home-made apple pie (£2.50), and children's menu (£3.50). Good, prompt service even when busy; farm ciders, and quite a few bottled beers and malt whiskies. There are tables out in the former coachyard, and the inn is well placed at the foot of the Old Man of Coniston. Parking may not be easy at peak times. *(Recommended by Stan and Hazel Allen, Carol and Jim Watson, Neil Spink, G Coates, P R and S A White, Gill and Maurice McMahon, Maurice Thompson, D Braisted)*

Own brew ~ Licensee Ronald Edward Bradley ~ Real ale ~ Bar food (all day) ~ Restaurant ~ (015394) 41335/41668 ~ Children welcome till 9pm ~ Open 11-11; 12-10.30 Sun ~ Bedrooms: £37.50B/£70B

CROOK SD4795 Map 7

Sun

B5284 Kendal—Bowness

Away from the Windermere bustle and looking quietly out over rolling hills, this friendly and relaxed wayside pub still has something of the atmosphere of a village local, though its two rooms have been opened together so that the dining area now dominates; one area is no smoking. Among a wide choice of often unusual fresh food, recent high points have included smoked salmon and avocado timbale, crispy duck, and ragout of venison, pheasant and duck, as well as chicken done in all sorts of inventive ways: with smoked bacon and a fruity rocket salad, for instance, or with a plum and grape compote and wild mushrooms, or even with garlic prawns. Other dishes might include moules marinières (£4.50), honey and orange roasted duck breast with a citrus crème fraîche dressing or smoked shell-on prawns with aioli (£4.95), honey and rosemary roasted venison fillet with chestnut, prune and mixed berry confit (£5.50), home-made steak in ale pie (£6.95), garlic and herb tagliatelle or seared tuna with fresh fruit (£8.50), venison and red wine casserole (£8.95), warm smoked salmon steak with hollandaise and dauphinoise potatoes or fried lemon sole fillets with shallots, lemon, thyme and capers (£9.95), fried lamb fillet on an orange, apricot, strawberry and coriander salad (£10.50), and king scallops wrapped in smoked bacon and fried in lemon and garlic butter (£12.95); there are proper puddings such as spotted dick, apple and raspberry crumble or summer pudding (£2.95). Service by happy staff is briskly efficient; well kept Boddingtons, Jennings, Theakstons, and Wadworths 6X on handpump, an interesting choice of good value wines, welcoming fire; darts, dominoes, and piped music. *(Recommended by Mr and Mrs Noel Skelton, Paul and Sue Merrick, ALC, Bruce Braithwaite, V and E A Bolton, P H Roberts)*

Free house ~ Licensee Adrian Parr ~ Real ale ~ Bar food ~ Restaurant ~ (01539) 821351 ~ Children in eating area of bar and restaurant ~ Open 11-3, 5.30-11(10.30 Sun)

You can send us reports through our web site: www.goodguides.com

CROSTHWAITE SD4491 Map 9
Punch Bowl 🍴 ♟
Village signposted off A5074 SE of Windermere

Cumbria Dining Pub of the Year

Happily, Steven Doherty has returned to this idyllically placed 16th-c inn to take over the day-to-day running of things – though he continues to cook at the Spread Eagle at Sawley (Lancashire) which is run by his wife Marjorie. Of course most people do come here to eat (booking is strongly advised) but those wanting just a drink are welcomed, and it's an enjoyable place to stay, too. There are several separate areas carefully reworked to give a lot of space, and a high-raftered central part by the serving counter with an upper minstrel's gallery on either side; all dining areas are no smoking. Steps lead down into a couple of small dimly lit rooms on the right, and there's a doorway through into two more airy rooms on the left. It's all spick and span, with lots of tables and chairs, beams, pictures by local artist Derek Ferman, and an open fire. On weekday lunchtimes, they offer a set price lunch (2 courses £6.95, 3 courses £8.95) with starters such as fresh plum tomato bruschetta or baked garlic flatcap mushrooms, main courses like baked ham on forked crushed potatoes with vegetables and honey jus or seared fillet of salmon with a creamy lobster and basil sauce, and puddings like fresh apricot and apple crumble or half cantaloupe melon with fruit garnish, blackcurrant sorbet and fresh cherry sauce; there's also a full menu including pea and ham soup (£2.50), chicken and foie gras parfait with home-made chutney (£4.95), warm duck salad (£5.95), charcuterie plate (£6.75), chilled aubergine and polenta (£8.95), chargrilled breast of chicken with bacon, melted lancashire cheese on a bed of creamy leeks (£9.25), grilled lamb fillet on a bed of pilaff rice with fresh coriander and creamy curry sauce (£9.95), steaks (from £12.95), and puddings like chocolate nemesis or passion fruit crème brûlée. Popular Sunday lunch (2 courses £9.95, 3 courses £11.95). Well kept Black Sheep, Jennings Cumberland, Morlands Old Speckled Hen, Theakstons Best on handpump, a thoughtful wine list, and several malt whiskies. There are some tables on a terrace stepped into the hillside. *(Recommended by Karen Eliot, W K Wood, Elizabeth and Alex Rocke, Tina and David Woods-Taylor, David Carr, G Coates, JDM, KM, Pierre and Pat Richterich, Mike Gorton, Prof P A Reynolds, Mick Hitchman, Neil and Karen Dignan, Ann and Colin Hunt, David Hawkes, Peter Walker, Gwen and Peter Andrews, John and Christine Lowe, Andy, Julie and Stuart Hawkins, IHR, Brian Wardrobe, K F Mould, Sheelia Curtis, A Callister, Gill and Maurice McMahon)*

Free house ~ Licensee Steven Doherty ~ Real ale ~ Bar food (12-2, 6(6.30 Sat)-9(9.30 Sat) ~ Restaurant ~ (015395) 68237 ~ Children welcome ~ Open 11-11; 12-10.30 Sun; may close winter Mon; closed 2 wks mid Nov ~ Bedrooms: £37.50B/£55B

DENT SD7187 Map 10
Sun 🍺
Village signposted from Sedbergh; and from Barbon, off A683

Another own-brew pub in a pretty village is this attractive-looking little place. The Dent Brewery is actually a few miles up in the dale, and supplies them with Bitter, T'Owd Tup, Kamikaze, and Aviator Ale, kept well on handpump. The pub has a pleasant traditional atmosphere, simple furniture, a coal fire, some timbers and beams, and several local snapshots; one room to the left of the bar is no smoking. Straightforward bar food includes tasty home-made soup (£1.95), sandwiches (from £1.95), burgers (from £2.45), ploughman's (£4.45), home-made steak and kidney pie (£4.85), cumberland sausage or brie and courgette crumble (£4.95), steaks (from £6.75), daily specials such as chicken and ham lasagne, leek and mushroom pie, and sausages like pork and wensleydale cheese or lamb and rosemary, and children's helpings (£2.95). Darts, pool, dominoes, fruit machine, video game, and juke box (in the pool room). There are rustic seats and tables outside and the surrounding fells are popular with walkers. *(Recommended by Peter F Marshall, Paul and Sandra Embleton, Susan and Nigel Wilson, JP, PP, Joy and Peter Heatherley, Tracey Hamond)*

Own brew ~ Licensee Martin Stafford ~ Real ale ~ Bar food (no evening food Nov-

Feb) ~ (015396) 25208 ~ Children welcome until 9pm ~ Open 11-11; 12-10.30 Sun;
11-2, 7-11 winter ~ Bedrooms: £20/£37

ELTERWATER NY3305 Map 9
Britannia ★ 🍺 🛏

Off B5343

Of course the position at the heart of the Lake District is a huge draw to this well
loved pub, but what comes across strongly is the very relaxed, informal atmosphere
and the cheerful bustle from happy customers. There's a small and traditionally
furnished back bar, plus a front one with a couple of window seats looking across to
Elterwater itself, cosy coal fires, oak benches, settles, windsor chairs, a big old
rocking chair, and well kept Coniston Bluebird, Dent Aviator, Jennings Bitter, and
two guest beers on handpump, 24 malt whiskies, and a few country wines; the
lounge is comfortable. Good, popular bar food includes filled rolls and ploughman's,
home-made soup (£2.20), home-made pâté with cumberland sauce (£2.75), home-
made goulash (£6.50), home-made steak and mushroom pie , roast loin of pork with
mustard sauce or chicken tagine with apricots, almonds and honey (£6.95), puddings
such as very good bread and butter, fresh lemon tart with fresh fruits and fruit coulis
or sticky toffee pudding with toffee sauce (£2.95), and children's meals with activity
sheet and crayons (£3.25; they offer small helpings of daily specials, too); super
breakfasts and home-baked fruit scones for afternoon cream teas. The restaurant is
no smoking; dominoes and a Sunday evening quiz. In summer, people flock to watch
the Morris and Step and Garland dancers. *(Recommended by Tina and David Woods-
Taylor, Prof P A Reynolds, Eddie Edwards, Nick J Lawless, SLC, Roger Stamp, Jenny and Brian
Seller, Ewan and Moira McCall, Mrs R Heaton, Andy and Jill Kassube, Gill and Maurice
McMahon, P R and S A White, Nick Lawless, Mrs P Volkers, Ken and Jenny Simmonds, Peter
and Audrey Dowsett, V and E A Bolton, Mrs Frances Gray, Michael A Butler, Mr and Mrs
Staples, Peter and Giff Bennett)*

*Free house ~ Licensees Judith Fry and Christopher Jones ~ Real ale ~ Bar food ~
Restaurant ~ (015394) 37210 ~ Children welcome until 9pm ~ Quiz Sun evenings ~
Open 11-11; 12-10.30 Sun; closed 25 Dec and evening 26 Dec ~ Bedrooms:
£27/£54(£68B)*

ESKDALE GREEN NY1300 Map 9
Bower House 🛏

½ mile W of village towards Santon Bridge

A new licensee has taken over this old stone-built inn but happily there haven't been
any drastic changes. There's a good winter log fire in the lounge bar, as well as
cushioned settles and windsor chairs that blend in well with the original beamed and
alcoved nucleus around the serving counter, and a quietly relaxed atmosphere – no
noisy machines or piped music; also, a separate lounge with easy chairs and sofas.
Decent bar food includes sandwiches (from £2.50), ploughman's (from £4),
cumberland sausage, and daily specials such as roast beef and yorkshire pudding
(£5.50), nut roast or quorn tikka masala (£6.75), wild duck and cumberland sauce
or loin of lamb with mint and cucumber (£7.25), steaks (from £11.70), and
puddings such as sticky toffee pudding or home-made fruit crumble (£3.50). Well
kept Hartleys XB, Jennings Bitter and Sneck Lifter, Theakstons Best, and Youngers
Scotch on handpump. The restaurant is no smoking. The nicely tended sheltered
garden is a pleasant place to relax and on summer Sundays you can watch the
cricket on the field alongside the pub. Some of the comfortable bedrooms are in the
annexe across the garden. *(Recommended by Peter Smith, Gill and Maurice McMahon, Mrs S
Kingsbury, Tina and David Woods-Taylor, H K Dyson, P R and S A White)*

*Free house ~ Licensee Richard Anderson ~ Real ale ~ Bar food ~ Restaurant ~
(019467) 23244 ~ Children welcome ~ Open 11-11; 12-10.30 Sun; 11-3, 5.30-11
winter ~ Bedrooms: £51.50B/£74B*

GARRIGILL NY7441 Map 9
George & Dragon ◀

Village signposted off B6277 S of Alston

Walkers like this simple stone-built inn as the Pennine Way passes the door. Inside on the right, the bar has solid traditional furnishings on the very broad polished flagstones, a lovely stone fireplace with a really good log fire, and a friendly, relaxed atmosphere; there's a separate tartan-carpeted games room with sensibly placed darts, pool and dominoes. Good value straightforward bar food includes sandwiches (from £1.70), soup (£1.80), filled yorkshire pudding (from £2.20), filled baked potatoes (from £2.50), cumberland sausage and egg (£5.10), broccoli and cream cheese bake (£5.60), home-made steak pie (£5.95), sirloin steak (£8.95), daily specials, and children's dishes (from £1.20). The dining room is no smoking. Well kept Boddingtons, Marstons Pedigree, and Castle Eden on handpump. *(Recommended by Comus Elliott, K F Mould, M J Morgan, RT and JC Moggridge, Dr G Sanders, Gill and Maurice McMahon)*

Free house ~ Licensees Brian and Jean Holmes ~ Real ale ~ Bar food ~ Restaurant ~ (01434) 381293 ~ Children welcome ~ Open 11.30-4, 6-11; 11.30-11 Sat; 12-4, 7-10.30 Sun; 12-3, 7-11 winter ~ Bedrooms: £15/£30(£37B)

GRASMERE NY3406 Map 9
Travellers Rest 🍴

Just N of Grasmere on A591 Ambleside—Keswick; OS sheet 90, map ref 335089

After 10 years here, the particularly friendly and helpful licensees continue to offer customers a genuinely warm welcome, good enjoyable food, and a fair range of drinks. The comfortable, beamed lounge bar has a warming log fire, banquettes and cushioned wooden chairs around varnished wooden tables, local watercolours and suggested walks and coast-to-coast information on the walls, and a relaxed atmosphere; piped classical music. Well kept Jennings Bitter, Cumberland, Mild and Snecklifter, and Marstons Pedigree on handpump; at least a dozen malt whiskies, and friendly, efficient service. The games room is popular with families: darts, pool, dominoes, juke box, and fruit machine. There's quite an emphasis on the popular homely bar food (for which we have given them a Food Award this year) which includes home-made soup and sandwiches, honey-roast local ham (£4.95), cumberland sausage or tasty hock of bacon with parsley sauce (£5.95), home-made steak and kidney pie (£6.25), honey-peppered chicken or fresh fish of the day (£6.95), joint of lamb (£7.55), and daily specials (from £7.25; a good children's menu. The restaurant is no smoking. This is a lovely spot with wonderful surrounding scenery and good walks, and there are picnic-sets in the side garden from which you can admire the marvellous views. As well as the telephone number listed below, they have a freephone number – 0500 600725. *(Recommended by Ann and Colin Hunt, Susan and Nigel Wilson, Derek and Sylvia Stephenson, Ken and Norma Burgess, K F Mould, Elizabeth and Alan Walker, Nick Lawless, Sarah and Peter Gooderham, Mrs Sally Kingsbury, Vicky and David Sarti, Gill and Maurice McMahon, Tina and David Woods-Taylor, P R and S A White, Tim and Ann Newell, Dick Brown, SLC, Eddie Edwards, A E Brace)*

Free house ~ Licensees Lynne, Derek and Graham Sweeney ~ Real ale ~ Bar food (12-9.30; 12-3, 6-9.30 in winter) ~ (015394) 35604 ~ Children welcome ~ Open 11-11; 12-11 Sun ~ Bedrooms: £25(£31B)/£50(£62B)

HAWKSHEAD NY3501 Map 9
Drunken Duck ★ 🍴 ◀ 🛏

Barngates; the hamlet is signposted from B5286 Hawkshead—Ambleside, opposite the Outgate Inn; or it may be quicker to take the first right from B5286, after the wooded caravan site; OS Sheet 90 map reference 350013

Never one to rest on her laurels – even after 25 years here – Mrs Barton is still making improvements to this most attractive 17th-c Lakeland inn. The Bangates Brewery is proving so popular that this year they have expanded it and added viewing windows, and two more bedrooms suites have been created. It remains one of our best loved pubs in the Guide – as somewhere for a relaxing drink, for an excellent meal or as a very comfortable place to stay with little thoughtful extras in the bedrooms. The bar and snug are traditional pubby beamed rooms with good winter fires, cushioned old settles and a mix of chairs on the fitted turkey carpet, pictures, cartoons, cards, fox masks, and cases of fishing flies and lures, and maybe the multi-coloured cat. All of the pub is no smoking except the bar. At lunchtime, food is simpler and might include sandwiches (from £2.95; roast sirloin of beef with honey horseradish £4.10), soup (£3.50), stilton and port pâté (£4.20), ploughman's (£5.80), leek, potato and lancashire cheese bake (£6), smoked salmon and bacon salad with herb mayonnaise (£6.50), beef in their own ale casserole (£6.75), and puddings such as coconut and lime sponge pudding or fruit crumble tart (£3.25). In the evening, the choice is more elaborate: game and quail-egg terrine with a peppercorn and beetroot pickle (£4.95), strips of chicken breast marinated in ginger served on a hot mango and watercress salad (£5.80), roquefort and herb omelette with sautéed asparagus and roast potato discs, topped with a wholegrain mustard rarebit (£7.40), roasted cod fillet with a herb and honey crust with bouillabaisse and baby aubergine and carrots (£8), duck breast, cooked pink, served with bacon and butterbean cassoulet and a spring onion and cumin vinaigrette (£9.25), fried beef fillet served on mediterranean potato wedges with roast cherry tomatoes and topped with a watercress mousse (£14.60), and puddings such as eldererflower crème brûlée with caramelised poached pear or treacle and pecan tartlet with a fresh orange and Grand Marnier sorbet (from £3.95). As well as Chesters Strong and Ugly and Cracker brewed in their cellar, they now have Jennings Bitter, Theakstons Old Peculier, and Yates Bitter on handpump; over 50 malt whiskies. Dominoes and cribbage. There are seats on the front verandah with stunning views and quite a few rustic wooden chairs and tables at the side, sheltered by a stone wall with alpine plants along its top; the pub has fishing in a private tarn behind. *(Recommended by JP, PP, Larry and Karen House, Mick Hitchman, Alison McCarthy, Neil Townend, Derek and Sylvia Stephenson, Walter and Susan Rinaldi-Butcher, SLC, George Picton, John Wall, Mr and Mrs D W Mitchell, Roger and Christine Mash, Bronwen and Steve Wrigley, Dr J B Ainscough, Prof P A Reynolds, Ann and Colin Hunt, R W Tapsfield, David J Cooke, Lyn and Geoff Hallchurch, Phil and Heidi Cook, P R and S A White, Maurice Thompson, Tina and David Woods-Taylor, Nick Lawless, Mr and Mrs D Humphries, Paul Bailey, Liz B)*

Own brew ~ Stephanie Barton ~ Bar food (12-2.30, 6-9) ~ Restaurant ~ (015394) 36347 ~ Children welcome ~ Open 11.30-3, 6-11; 12-3, 6-10.30 Sun ~ Bedrooms: £60B/£85B

HEVERSHAM SD4983 Map 9
Blue Bell

A6 (now a relatively very quiet road here)

You can be sure of a warm welcome here – even if you turn up soaking wet with small children and dogs. It's a civilised and comfortable partly timbered old country inn with warm winter fires in the lounge bar, pewter platters hanging from the beams, an antique carved settle, cushioned windsor armchairs and upholstered stools, and small antique sporting prints and a display cabinet with two stuffed fighting cocks on the partly panelled walls; some redecoration will be taking place this year. One big bay-windowed area has been divided off as a children's room, and the long, tiled-floor public bar has darts, pool, cribbage, dominoes, fruit machine, and piped music. Decent bar food includes soup (£2.45), sandwiches (from £2.45), filled baked potatoes (from £3.45), lovely Morecambe Bay potted shrimps (£4.95), filled yorkshire puddings or pancakes (from £5.95), ploughman's (£6.25), gammon and pineapple (£6.95), sirloin steak (£10.95), and puddings (from £2.45); they also do morning coffee and afternoon tea. The restaurant is no smoking. Well kept Sam Smiths OB on handpump kept under light blanket pressure, quite a few malt whiskies, and a fair wine list; helpful staff. Crossing over the A6 into the village itself, you come to a picturesque church with a rambling little graveyard; if you walk through this and on to the hills beyond, there's a fine view across to the estuary of the River Kent. The estuary itself is a short walk from the pub down the country road that runs by its side. *(Recommended by Gill and Maurice McMahon, D Bryan, Roger and Christine Mash, Mr and Mrs C Roberts, Dr D E Granger)*

Sam Smiths ~ Managers Susan and Richard Cowie ~ Real ale ~ Bar food (12-9.30) ~ Restaurant ~ (015395) 62018 ~ Children welcome ~ Open 11-11; 12-10.30 Sun ~ Bedrooms: £47.50B/£64B

INGS SD4599 Map 9
Watermill 🍺 🛏

Just off A591 E of Windermere

This ivy-covered stone inn is such an enjoyable place and there's always a good mix of visitors and locals which creates a very friendly, bustling atmosphere – helped by no noisy machines or juke box. Of course, one of the draws is the marvellous range of up to 15 real ales perfectly kept on handpump: Black Sheep Special, Coniston Bluebird, Jennings Cumberland, Lees Moonraker, and Theakstons Best, Old Peculier and XB, with changing guests like Adnams Regatta, Batemans XXXB, Dent Ramsbottom and T'Owd Tup, Fullers London Pride, Hop Back Summer Lightning, Hughes Dark Ruby Mild, Isle of Skye Young Pretender, Jennings Sneck Lifter, Moorhouses Black Cat and Pendle Witches Brew, and Tomintoul Caillie; also, bottled beers, and up to 50 malt whiskies; thirsty dogs are kindly catered for, too, with a biscuit and bowl of water. The bars have a happy mix of chairs, padded benches and solid oak tables, bar counters made from old church wood, open fires, and amusing cartoons by a local artist on the wall. The spacious lounge bar, in much the same traditional style as the other rooms, has rocking chairs and a big open fire; two areas are no smoking. Well liked bar food includes lunchtime sandwiches, home-made soup (£2), filled savoury pancakes (£3.50), leek and grain mustard crumble on a horseradish mashed potato (£5.80), braised beef in ale or chicken, leek and smoked bacon pie (£6.20), local fish dishes (from £6.50), and puddings such as bramley apple pie or chocolate and praline truffle torte (£2.95). Darts, cribbage, dominoes, and Jenga. There are seats in the front garden. Lots of climbing, fell-walking, fishing, boating of all kinds, swimming and pony-trekking within easy reach. *(Recommended by P H Roberts, John and Kay Morison, Richard and Robyn Wain, R J Bland, Maurice Thompson, G Coates, K F Mould, Lesley Sones, Gill and Maurice McMahon, Neil Spink, David and Helen Wilkins, Roger Stamp, Sheila Keene, MLR, Tracey Hamond, Bronwen and Steve Wrigley, David and Kathy Holcroft, Ann and Colin Hunt, Dick Brown, David Carr, Nick J Lawless, Andy and Jill Kassube, SLC)*

Free house ~ Licensees Alan and Brian Coulthwaite ~ Real ale ~ Bar food (12-2, 6-9) ~ (01539) 821309 ~ Children in lounge bar only ~ 1st Tues of month story telling club; 3rd Tues acoustic guitar ~ Open 12-2.30, 6-11; 12-3, 6-10.30 Sun; closed 25 Dec ~ Bedrooms: £26S/£48S

KESWICK NY2624 Map 9
Dog & Gun

Lake Road; off top end of Market Square

Unpretentious and lively, this busy town pub – liked by walkers, hikers and climbers – has low beams, a partly slate floor (the rest are carpeted or bare boards), some high settles, a fine collection of striking mountain photograpahs by the local firm G P Abrahams, coins in beams and timbers by the fireplace, and log fires. Well kept Theakstons Best and Old Peculier on handpump, and decent food (they tell us prices are the same as last year) such as home-made soup (£2.25), filled french bread (from £2.25), baked trout in garlic butter with prawns, venison in red wine or the house speciality, goulash (all £5.95), and puddings such as sticky toffee pudding (£1.90); no grills or chips. 25 malt whiskies, piped music and fruit machine. *(Recommended by Neil Spink, Bob and Marg Griffiths, Paul and Sandra Embleton)*

Scottish Courage ~ Manager John Wiener ~ Real ale ~ Bar food (12-9.30) ~ (017687) 73463 ~ Children welcome until 9pm ~ Open 11-11; 12-10.30 Sun

KIRKBY LONSDALE SD6278 Map 7

Snooty Fox

Main Street (B6254)

As we went to press, new licensees were just taking over this rambling pub. The various rooms have kept their bustling atmosphere and their interesting decorations: mugs hang from beams, and the walls are full of eye-catching coloured engravings, stuffed wildfowl and falcons, mounted badger and fox masks, guns and a powder-flask, stage gladiator costumes, and horse-collars and stirrups. The bar counters are made from English oak, as is some panelling, and there are also country kitchen chairs, pews, one or two high-backed settles and marble-topped sewing-trestle tables on the flagstones, and two coal fires. Good interesting bar food now includes home-made soup (£2), filled baked potatoes (from £2.75), filled french bread (from £2.95), fried lamb kidneys flamed with sherry and served in a filo nest (£4.50), crispy duck pancakes with a sweet and sour tomatina sauce (£4.95), cumberland sausage with Irish champ and caramelised onion gravy (£5.95), savoury vegetarian tagine with minted yoghurt (£6.50), steak and kidney pudding (£6.95), supreme of sesame chicken with wild mushrooms and a creamy curry sauce (£9.25), pork tenderloin rolled in autumn fruits and air-dred ham with a rich scrumpy glaze (£10.95), and ragout of monkfish and scallops with Noilly Prat and baby vegetables (£12.25). The dining annexe is no smoking. Well kept Hartleys XB, Theakstons Best, and Timothy Taylor Landlord on handpump, several malt whiskies, and country wines; fruit machine in back bar only. There are tables out on a small terrace beside the biggish back cobbled stableyard, with more in a pretty garden. *(Recommended by Peter and Jenny Quine, Jenny and Brian Seller, Neil Townend, Roger and Lynda Goldstone, Paul S McPherson, JDM, KM, J F M West, Gill and Maurice McMahon, K H Frostick, Joy and Peter Heatherley)*

Free house ~ Licensee Kim Boleta ~ Real ale ~ Bar food ~ Restaurant ~ (01524) 271308 ~ Children welcome ~ Open 11-11; 12-10.30 Sun ~ Bedrooms: £35B/£55B

Sun 🏠

Market St (B6254)

The friendly and bustling bar of this little inn has a good mix of both visitors and regulars. It's been redecorated this year, and the rambling low-beamed rooms (one of which is no smoking) have window seats, cosy pews, and good winter fires, some banknotes above the bar, and Modigliani prints and objets d'art on the walls (some of which are stripped to bare stone or have panelled dados). Well kept Black Sheep Bitter, Boddingtons, and Dent Bitter on handpump, and 70 malt whiskies, bottled Belgian beers, a good choice of coffees, and Havana cigars; dominoes and piped music. Generous helpings of tasty bar food includes soup (£1.95), sandwiches or filled french bread (from £2.25), pizzas (from £4.95), and dishes priced at £3.75 for starter helpings or £5.75 for main course, such as bangers and mash with red wine and rosemary gravy, fresh salmon and dill fishcakes, sizzled chilli prawns, hungarian goulash, home-made steak and kidney pudding, and mediterranean vegetable tart; also, steaks (from £7.95) and puddings like milles feuilles of freshly caramelised apple and pineapple or sticky toffee pudding (£3.50), with evening dishes like rack of ribs, honey-roasted duck breast or grilled fillet of red snapper (£4.50 starter, £8.95 main course). Good personal service and super breakfasts. There's an unusual pillared porch; the steep cobbled alley is also attractive. Turner stayed here in 1818 while painting Ruskin's View and this is still a popular place to stay; some of the bedrooms are in a stone barn with lovely views across the Barbon Fells. *(Recommended by Barry and Marie Males, A Hepburn, S Jenner, MLR, Paul Cleaver, Dr Muriel Sawbridge, R J Walden, Mr and Mrs Leary, V and E A Bolton, Prof P A Reynolds, Mr and Mrs G S Thomas, Malcolm Taylor)*

Free house ~ Licensees Andrew and Belinda Wilkinson ~ Real ale ~ Bar food (12-2, 6-10) ~ Restaurant ~ (015242) 71965 ~ Children welcome ~ Open 11-11; 12-10.30 Sun ~ Bedrooms: £24.50(£29.50B)/£45.50(£49.50B)

LANGDALE NY2906 Map 9
Old Dungeon Ghyll 🛏

B5343

Down-to-earth and with a nice casual, bustling atmosphere, this simply furnished unchanging pub is in a marvellous position at the heart of the Great Langdale Valley and surrounded by fells including the Langdale Pikes flanking the Dungeon Ghyll Force waterfall; there are grand views of the Pike of Blisco rising behind Kettle Crag from the window seats cut into the thick stone walls of the bar. Straightforward food includes lunchtime sandwiches (£2.25), filled baked potatoes (£3.75), evening pizzas (from £4.40), cumberland sausage (£5.75), home-made chilli con carne (£6.35), puddings (£2.25), and children's meals (£3.50); if you are not a resident and want to eat in the no-smoking restaurant you must book ahead. Well kept Jennings Cumberland and Mild, Theakstons XB and Old Peculier, and Yates Bitter on handpump, and farm cider; darts, cribbage and dominoes. It can get really lively on a Saturday night (there's a popular National Trust camp site opposite). They usefully open at 9am for breakfast. *(Recommended by N Cobb, Nigel Woolliscroft, R J Bland, John and Phyllis Maloney, V and E A Bolton, Bronwen and Steve Wrigley, SLC, Vicky and David Sarti, H K Dyson, Roy Butler, Ewan and Moira McCall, Grant Thoburn, Tracey Hamond, Liz Bell)*

Free house ~ Licensee Neil Walmsley ~ Real ale ~ Bar food ~ Restaurant ~ (015394) 37272 ~ Children welcome ~ Open 11-11; 12-10.30 Sun; closed 23-26 Dec ~ Bedrooms: £32(£35B)/£64(£70B)

LITTLE LANGDALE NY3204 Map 9
Three Shires 🛏

From A593 3 miles W of Ambleside take small road signposted The Langdales, Wrynose Pass; then bear left at first fork

From seats on the terrace here there are lovely views over the valley to the partly wooded hills below Tilberthwaite Fells, with more seats on a well kept lawn behind the car park, backed by a small oak wood. Inside, the comfortably extended back bar has stripped timbers and a beam-and-joist stripped ceiling, antique oak carved settles, country kitchen chairs and stools on its big dark slate flagstones, Lakeland photographs lining the walls, and a warm winter fire in the modern stone fireplace with a couple of recesses for ornaments; an arch leads through to a small, additional area. Why not try counting all the notices. Decent bar food includes soup (£2.40), chicken, leek and wild mushroom terrine (£4.50), cumberland sausage (£6.50), beef in ale pie (£6.75), parsnip pie with a sage and onion salsa (£7.75), a tian of marinated pork fillet and crispy black pudding with honey and grain-mustard sauce finished with fresh fennel (£8.95), fried breast of guinea fowl on a bed of apple and baby leek mash with a calvados jus (£9.25), chargrilled tuna steak on oriental-style vegetables (£10.75), puddings such as luxurious bread and butter pudding on an apricot sauce topped with poached sultanas (£3.25), and children's dishes (£3; they can also have small helpings of most meals). The restaurant and snug are no smoking. Well kept Black Sheep Special, Jennings Bitter and Cumberland, Theakstons XB, and weekly guests on handpump, quite a few malt whiskies, and a decent wine list; darts, cribbage, and dominoes. The three shires are Cumberland, Westmorland and Lancashire, which used to meet at the top of the nearby Wrynose Pass. *(Recommended by Tina and David Woods-Taylor, V and E A Bolton, Gill and Maurice McMahon, K F Mould, Nigel Woolliscroft, W W Burke, David Cooke)*

Free house ~ Licensee Ian Stephenson ~ Real ale ~ Bar food (no evening meals Dec or Jan) ~ Restaurant ~ (015394) 37215 ~ Chidren welcome until 9pm ~ Open 11-11; 12-10.30 Sun; 12-3, 8-10.30 winter; closed 25 Dec ~ Bedrooms: £33B/£66B

We mention bottled beers and spirits only if there is something unusual about them – imported Belgian real ales, say, or dozens of malt whiskies; so do please let us know about them in your reports.

LOWESWATER NY1222 Map 9
Kirkstile Inn

From B5289 follow signs to Loweswater Lake; OS Sheet 89, map reference 140210

There's plenty of room for wet boots and gear in this friendly little country pub and plenty of marvellous surrounding walks. The bar is low-beamed and carpeted, with a roaring log fire, comfortably cushioned small settles and pews, and partly stripped stone walls; from the bow windows in one of the rooms off the bar are lovely views. Good, enjoyable bar food includes sandwiches or rolls (from £2.25), home-made soup and home-made roll (£2.50), home-made pâté (£3.25), ploughman's (from £4.95), cumberland sausage and fried egg (£5.95), fruit and vegetable curry (£6), tuna steak with herb butter, half roasted lemon and garlic chicken with sauce or steak in ale pie (all £6.75), sirloin steak (£9.75), and puddings such as toffee crunch pie or fruit crumble (£2.60); there's also a children's menu, and afternoon tea with home-made scones and cakes; big breakfasts. Well kept Derwent Mutineer, and Jennings Bitter and Cumberland on handpump, and several malt whiskies; darts, cribbage, dominoes, and a slate shove-ha'penny board; a side games room called the Little Barn has pool, fruit machine, and juke box. From picnic-sets on the lawn and from the very attractive covered verandah in front of the pub, there are views of the spectacular surrounding peaks and soaring fells. *(Recommended by Nick J Lawless, DC, Tina and David Woods-Taylor, Paul Bailey, Keith and Janet Eaton, H K Dyson, R Hebblethwaite, Roger and Christine Mash, John and Christine Lowe, Gill and Maurice McMahon, Mrs J Hinsliff, Pete Yearsley)*

Free house ~ Licensee Ken Gorley ~ Real ale ~ Bar food (12-9) ~ Restaurant ~ (01900) 85219 ~ Children welcome ~ Open 11-11; 12-10 Sun ~ Bedrooms: £39.50(£49.50B)/£49.50(£59.50B)

MELMERBY NY6237 Map 10
Shepherds ★ ♀

About half way along A686 Penrith—Alston

The impressive list of awards won by this pub over the years just proves how hard-working the warmly friendly licensees are here. It's got a good bustling atmosphere, and the bar is divided up into several areas; the heavy beamed no-smoking room to the left of the door is carpeted and comfortable with bottles on the mantlebeam over the warm open fire, sunny window seats, and sensible tables and chairs, and to the right is a stone-floored drinking part with a few plush bar stools and chairs. At the end is a spacious room with a high-raftered ceiling and pine tables and farmhouse chairs, a woodburning stove, and big wrought-iron candelabra, and steps up to a games area with pool; shove-ha'penny, dominoes, fruit machine and juke box. Enjoyable food includes weekly specials such as a vegetarian or meat-based soup (£2.20), garlic mushrooms (£4), cheese and onion and broccoli quiche (£4.20), various ploughman's (from £4.20, including their special one with home-made rolls and a choice of 3 cheeses from their award-winning array, £5.90), trout pâté (£4.60), shepherd's pie (£4.80), cumberland sausage hotpot (£5.80), home-cooked English ham with chips and pickles (£6.40), steak and kidney pie (£6.80), chicken Leoni (garlic chicken breast in parrmesan batter topped with cheese and asparagus £6.90), baked Ullswater trout (£7), venison and roquefort crumble (£7.90), and steaks (from £10.50); half helpings for children, and traditional Sunday roast. Much of the main eating area is no smoking. Well kept Jennings Cumberland and Hesket Newmarket Pigs Might Fly and guests like Black Sheep Special, Mansfield Bitter, and Morland Old Speckled Hen on handpump, as well as over 50 malt whiskies, a good wine list, country wines, and quite a few bottled continental beers. Hartside Nursery Garden, a noted alpine and primula plant specialist, is just over the Hartside Pass, and there are fine views across the green to the Pennines. *(Recommended by John Perry, Monica Shelley, Vicky and David Sarti, Mr and Mrs B Hobden, Gill and Maurice McMahon, D Braisted, Suzy Miller, Brian Wardrobe, K F Mould, Paul S McPherson)*

Free house ~ Licensee Martin Baucutt ~ Real ale ~ Bar food (11-2.30, 6-9.45; 12-2.30, 7-9.45 Sun) ~ Restaurant ~ (01768) 881217 ~ Children welcome until 9pm ~ Live entertainment monthly Fri evening ~ Open 10.30-3, 6-11; 12-3, 7-10.30 Sun; closed 25 Dec

MUNGRISDALE NY3630 Map 10
Mill Inn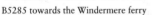

Village signposted off A66 Penrith—Keswick, a bit over a mile W of A5091 Ullswater turn-off

The new licensees here are making a good impression with customers and are helpful, very friendly people. The pub is in a lovely village in a high secluded valley and is, not surprisingly, popular with walkers. There's a warm fire in the stone fireplace in the simply furnished main bar, and the games room has darts, pool, board games, and carpet bowls; the pub is decorated with local artists' work and paragliding pictures; piped music; the separate restaurant is no smoking. Good bar food now includes home-made soup (£2.50), sandwiches (from £2.95), home-made hummus (£3.75), filled baked potatoes (from £3.95), black pudding and bacon with mustard sauce (£3.95), a medley of mushrooms in a creamy sauce (£4.95), grilled cumberland sausage (£6.65), ricotta cheese and spinach cannelloni (£6.95), good ploughman's (from £6.95), evening extras such as fruit and vegetable curry (£6.95), chicken breast wrapped in smoked bacon with a stilton sauce (£7.95), fresh fish of the day, and Aberdeen Angus sirloin steak (£10.95), and puddings such as home-made fruit crumble or cheesecake (£2.95). Well kept Jennings Bitter and Cumberland on handpump, quite a few malt whiskies, and a good wine list with 10 by the glass. There are seats on a gravel forecourt, and down on a neat and very sheltered lawn that slopes towards the little river. Some past guests here include Charles Dickens, Wilkie Collins, and John Peel (who is buried a few miles away). Note that there is a separate Mill Hotel in this same hamlet. *(Recommended by Peter and Pat Frogley, Tim Brierly, Lesley Bass, H K Dyson, Paul Bailey, Vicky and David Sarti, David Bennett, John Perry)*

Free house ~ Licensees Melissa Townson, John Mckeever ~ Real ale ~ Bar food (12-9 Mon-Sat, till 8.30 Sun) ~ Restaurant ~ (017687) 79632 ~ Children welcome ~ Open 11-11; 12-10.30 Sun; closed 25 Dec ~ Bedrooms: £26.50(£36B)/£49(£59B)

NEAR SAWREY SD3796 Map 9
Tower Bank Arms 🍺

B5285 towards the Windermere ferry

Despite its popularity – it was featured in *Jemima Puddle Duck* and backs on to Beatrix Potter's Hill Top Farm (owned by the National Trust) – this bustling pub is so well run that this doesn't seem to be an issue with readers. What comes across is the warmly friendly welcome from helpful staff and the generous helpings of good value food. The low-beamed main bar has a fine log fire in the big cooking range, high-backed settles on the rough slate floor, local hunting photographs and signed photographs of celebrities on the walls, a grandfather clock, and good traditional atmosphere. Good bar food includes home-made soup (£2.10), lunchtime filled rolls (from £2.75) or ploughman's (from £4.50), cumberland sausage (£5.50), wild boar and pheasant or game pies, a vegetarian dish or local venison in red wine (all £7.50), and duckling (£7.75). Well kept Theakstons Best, XB, and Old Peculier and weekly changing guest beers on handpump, as well as 24 malt whiskies, and Belgian fruit beers and other foreign beers; darts, shove-ha'penny, cribbage, dominoes, backgammon, and shut the box. Seats outside have pleasant views of the wooded Claife Heights. This is a good area for golf, sailing, birdwatching, fishing (they have a licence for two rods a day on selected waters in the area), and walking, but if you want to stay at the pub, you'll have to book well in advance. *(Recommended by Dr Rod Holcombe, Tina and David Woods-Taylor, P Thompson, DHV, Vicky and David Sarti, SLC, Nick J Lawless, P R and S A White)*

Free house ~ Licensee Philip Broadley ~ Real ale ~ Bar food (not 25 Dec) ~ Restaurant ~ (015394) 36334 ~ Children welcome at lunchtime but in restaurant only, in evenings ~ Open 11-3, 5.30(6 winter)-11; 11-3, 5.30-10.30 Sun; closed evening 25 Dec ~ Bedrooms: £35B/£50B

Pubs close to motorway junctions are listed at the back of the book.

PENRITH NY5130 Map 10
Agricultural 🍺

Castlegate; ¾ mile from M6 junction 40 – A592 into town, just off entrance roundabout

Carefully refurbished to retain much of its original charm and Victorian elegance, this market-town hotel has a comfortable L-shaped beamed lounge with partly glazed panelling, plenty of seating, a lovely log fire, curved sash windows over the bar, and a good down-to-earth local atmosphere with a thorough mix of customers. It can get extremely busy, staying cheerful and lively. Jennings Bitter, Dark Mild, Cumberland, Cocker Hoop, and Sneck Lifter on handpump are particularly well kept; prompt service, thoughtful and helpful, with a good chatty landlord; darts, piped music and fruit machine (in hall not in bar). A wide choice of reasonably priced food includes lunchtime dishes like sandwiches (from £1.90; toasties from £2.40), home-made soup (£2.80), filled baked potatoes (from £2.50), and french bread filled with things like home-cooked beef and onion or home-baked ham and tomato chutney (from £2.95), as well as home-made chicken liver pâté with cumberland sauce (£2.75), ploughman's (from £4.75), home-baked ham and egg or vegetarian lasagne (£4.95), home-made steak and kidney pie (£5.45), home-made minty lamb casserole (£5.75), chargrilled steaks (from £8.60), and specials such as Whitby haddock (£5.75), beef stroganoff (£6.50) or chargrilled fillet steak topped with a slice of haggis with a whisky sauce (£9.75). The restaurant is no smoking. There are good views from the picnic-sets out at the side. *(Recommended by Colin and Sue Graham, Richard Lewis)*

Jennings ~ Tenants Mr and Mrs J Hodge ~ Real ale ~ Bar food (12-2, 6-8.30; no evening snacks or Sun lunch) ~ Restaurant ~ (01768) 862622 ~ Children in eating area of bar and in restaurant until 9pm ~ Open 11-11; 12-10.30 Sun ~ Bedrooms: £25/£40

SEATHWAITE SD2396 Map 9
Newfield Inn

Duddon Valley, nr Ulpha (ie not Seathwaite in Borrowdale)

It's well worth the drive to get to this little 16th-c cottage and there are plenty of good surrounding walks. The slate-floored bar has a genuinely local and informal atmosphere and well kept real ales such as Dent Kamikaze, Hopback Salisbury and Summer Lightning, Kelham Island Pale Rider, Ringwood Old Thumper, Shepherd Neame Bishops Finger, and Theakstons Best on handpump; also, 24 malt whiskies, 16 Polish vodkas, and the occasional local perry. There's a comfortable side room and a games room with darts. Good value bar food includes filled granary french bread or proper home-made soup (£1.95), big cumberland sausages (£5.35), a vegetarian dish (£4.95), home-made steak pie (£5.30), huge gammon steaks with free-range organically fed eggs (£7.25), and good steaks; the restaurant is no smoking; good service. Tables out in the nice garden have good hill views. The pub owns and lets the next-door cottages and has self-catering flats. It is popular at weekends with climbers and walkers. *(Recommended by Dr E J C Parker, D Braisted, Gill and Maurice McMahon, David Cooke, Mike and Mary Carter, Jane Taylor, David Dutton)*

Free house ~ Licensee Chris Burgess ~ Real ale ~ Bar food (12-2, 6-9) ~ Restaurant ~ (01229) 716208 ~ Children welcome but must be well behaved ~ Occasional folk nights ~ Open 11-11; 11-10.30 Sun; 11-3, 6-11 Mon-Fri winter

SEDBERGH SD6692 Map 10
Dalesman 🛏

Main St

The Dales Way and Cumbrian Cycle Way pass the door of this nicely modernised pub, and there are lots of walks of varying difficulty all around. There's quite a mix of decorations and styles in the rooms – lots of stripped stone and beams, cushioned farmhouse chairs and stools around dimpled copper tables, and a raised stone hearth with a log-effect gas fire; also, horsebrasses and spigots, Vernon Stokes gundog pictures, various stuffed animals, tropical fish, and a blunderbuss. Through stone arches on the right a no-smoking buttery area serves tasty food such as home-made soup (£1.95), filled rolls (from £2.30; toasties from £2.40), lots of filled baked potatoes like grilled bacon and tomatoes or chargrilled chicken with tangy barbecue sauce (£4.90), big breakfast (£5.90), lasagne or home-made cumberland sausages (£5.95), steak and kidney pie (£6.50), 12oz gammon and egg (£6.95), spinach and ricotta chestnut parcel (£7.50), steaks (from £9.90), and specials such as salmon fishcakes (£4), chicken tikka masala or pheasant chasseur (£8), and ostrich fillet (£12); children's menu (from £2.90), and Sunday roast (£5.50). The restaurant is no smoking. Well kept Tetleys Bitter and one named for the pub on handpump, and 30 malt whiskies; dominoes and piped music. There are some picnic-sets out in front; small car park. *(Recommended by John and Enid Morris, Ann and Colin Hunt, Paul and Sandra Embleton, Brian Wardrobe, Paul S McPherson, K F Mould, Katherine Williams, Jenny and Brian Seller, Sheila Dunsire, Dick Brown, R F and M K Bishop, Paul Cowburn)*

Free house ~ Licensees Michael Garnett and Graham Smith ~ Real ale ~ Bar food (12-2.30, 6-9.30) ~ Restaurant ~ (015396) 21183 ~ Children welcome ~ Open 11-11; 12-10.30 Sun ~ Bedrooms: £30B/£60B

STAINTON NY4928 Map 10
Kings Arms

1¾ miles from M6 junction 40: village signposted from A66 towards Keswick, though quickest to fork left at A592 roundabout then turn first right

There's quite a cosy feel to the neatly kept open-plan bar in this pleasantly modernised pub – as well as leatherette wall banquettes, stools and armchairs around wood-effect tables, brasses on the black beams, and prints and paintings of the Lake District on the swirly cream walls; one room is no smoking during mealtimes. Enjoyable traditional bar food includes lunchtime snacks such as sandwiches (from £1.95; toasties from £2.25; open ones from £3.15), filled baked potatoes (from £3.40), and ploughman's (£3.95); also, home-made soup (£1.75), crispy mushrooms with garlic dip (£2.65), cumberland sausage with egg (£4.45), steak and kidney pie (£5.25), vegetarian lasagne (£6), sirloin steak (£9.85), and puddings (£2.55). Well kept Castle Eden and summer guests like Theakstons Old Peculier and Wadworths 6X on handpump, and 20 malt whiskies; friendly, welcoming staff. Sensibly placed darts, dominoes, cribbage, scrabble, mini Jenga, fruit machine, and piped music. There are tables outside on the side terrace and a small lawn. *(Recommended by John Morrow, Neil Townend, Basil J S Minson, Carol and Philip Seddon, Nick Lawless, W Blatchford, Linda Christison, Mrs B M Spurr, John and Cath Howard, Ann and Colin Hunt, Pete Yearsley)*

Whitbreads ~ Tenants James and Anne Downie ~ Real ale ~ Bar food (12-1.45, 7-8.30) ~ (01768) 862778 ~ Children welcome until 9pm ~ Open 11.30-3, 6.30(6 Sat)-11; 12-3, 7-10.30 Sun; evening opening 7 winter; closed Mon Nov-Easter exc bank holidays

THRELKELD NY3325 Map 9
Salutation

Old main rd, bypassed by A66 W of Penrith

The strength of this good old-fashioned Lakeland pub is its really welcoming atmosphere. The low-beamed connecting rooms have simple furnishings, a roaring log fire, and Courage Directors, Jennings Bitter, Theakstons Best and XB, Yates Lancaster Bomber, and Youngers Scotch on handpump; the tiled floor is used to muddy boots. Bar food includes sandwiches (from £2), soup (£2.25), basket meals (from £3.95), large ploughman's (from £4.95), meaty or vegetarian lasagne, steak and mushroom pie or hungarian goulash (all £5.85), steaks (from £10.85), daily specials, and puddings like sticky toffee pudding (£2.85). The spacious upstairs children's room has a pool table and juke box (oldies); also, darts, cribbage, dominoes, fruit machine, video game and piped music. The owners let a couple of holiday cottages in the village. *(Recommended by Keith and Janet Eaton, Tina and David*

Woods-Taylor, Jonathan and Ann Tross, Eddie Edwards, Nigel Woolliscroft)

Scottish Courage ~ Tenants Ken and Rose Burchill ~ Real ale ~ Bar food (12-2, 6.30-9; not 25 Dec) ~ Restaurant ~ (017687) 79614 ~ Children welcome ~ Open 11-3, 5.30-11; 11-11 Sat; 12-10.30 Sun; 12-2, 6.30-11 winter

TIRRIL NY5126 Map 10

Queens Head ★ 🍴 🛏

3½ miles from M6 junction 40; take A66 towards Brough, A6 towards Shap, then B5320 towards Ullswater

During their third Cumbrian Beer & Sausage Festival, the enterprising licensees officially opened their own little brewery in one of the old outhouses behind the pub. They will start off with John Bewshers Best, named after the landlord in the early 1800s who bought the inn off the Wordsworths and changed its name to the Queens Head in time for Victoria's coronation. Other well kept real ales on offer include Black Sheep, Boddingtons, Dent Aviator, and Jennings Cumberland on handpump; over 40 malt whiskies, fruit wines, and a carefully chosen wine list. The oldest parts of the bar have original flagstones and floorboards, low bare beams, black panelling, high-backed settles, and a roomy inglenook fireplace (once a cupboard for smoking hams); piped music. At lunchtime, bar snacks include filled french bread (from £2.50), filled baked potatoes (from £2.95), stuffed pitta breads (from £3.25), pasta dishes (£3 or £6), ploughman's (from £4.50), pasta dishes (£3 half helping, £6 main course), OAP lunches (£3.95), chilli (£5.95), home-made pie of the day (£6.50), and gammon and eggs (£7.50). Also, home-made soup (£2.25), home-made hummus (£2.75), lamb's liver and bacon (£6.75), cumberland lamb stew with mini dumplings (£6.75), Thai chicken curry (£6.95), Mexican mixed nut bake (£7.50), and daily specials such as tuna fishcakes on hollandaise sauce (£8.50), salmon and mango en croûte (£8.75), goose breast and orchard fruit jus (£9.50), and puddings like Tia Maria crème brûlée (£2.95); half of the restaurant is no smoking. Darts, pool, and dominoes in the back bar. The pub is very close to a number of interesting places, such as Dalemain House at Dacre. *(Recommended by Paul Cleaver, A Hepburn, S Jenner, Paul and Sue Merrick, Ian and Jane Irving, David and Ruth Shillitoe, P R and S A White, Yvonne and Mike Meadley, Dr B and Mrs P B Baker, Richard and Anne Hollingsworth, Ian Jones, Roger Byrne, D G Twyman, Mick Hitchman)*

Free house ~ Licensee Joanna Elizabeth Tomlinson ~ Real ale ~ Bar food (12-2, 6-9.30) ~ Restaurant ~ (01768) 863219 ~ Children welcome until 9.30pm ~ Open 12-3, 6-11; 12-11 Sat; 12-10.30 Sun ~ Bedrooms: £35B/£45B

TROUTBECK NY4103 Map 9

Mortal Man

Upper Rd, nr High Green; OS Sheet 90, map reference 411035

Surrounded by marvellous scenery and in a lovely village, this neatly kept place has new licensees this year. The partly panelled bar has a big roaring fire, a nice medley of seats including a cushioned settle and some farmhouse chairs around copper-topped tables, horsebrasses on the dark beams, and piped music; there's also a small, cosy room leading off, set for eating. Bar food now includes home-made soup (£2.25), sandwiches and filled french bread (from £2.50), home-made chicken liver pâté (£2.95), filled baked potatoes (from £3.50), steak and kidney pudding, Thai chicken curry or salmon and broccoli mornay (all £5.95), fresh vegetable stir fry (£5.75), grilled swordfish steak (£6.25), gammon and egg (£6.75), steaks (from £7.95), puddings (£3), and children's meals (£3.50). The restaurant, with its big picture windows, is no smoking. Well kept Marstons Pedigree, Theakstons Best, and a guest beer on handpump, and several malt whiskies; darts and dominoes. Walkers' boots must be left outside. *(Recommended by Peter and Audrey Dowsett, Pierre and Pat Richterich, IHR, Gill and Maurice McMahon, JDM, KM, W W Burke, P R and S A White, Tim and Ann Newell, David Carr, Sarah and Peter Gooderham, John Morrow, J H Bell, H K Dyson, Mr and Mrs Richard Osborne)*

Free house ~ Licensee Sam Eardley ~ Real ale ~ Bar food (12-9.30) ~ Restaurant ~ (015394) 33193 ~ Children welcome ~ Folk and blues Sun evening ~ Open 11-11; 12-10.30 Sun ~ Bedrooms: £60B/£90B

Queens Head 🍴 🍷 🍺 🛏

A592 N of Windermere

As well as offering very good, ambitious food, this popular gabled 17th-c coaching inn keeps a good range of real ales, and is a nice place to stay as well. The big rambling bar has some half dozen attractively decorated rooms, including an unusual lower gallery, a comfortable dining area, and lots of alcoves and heavy beams; two rooms are no smoking. A massive Elizabethan four-poster bed is the basis of the serving counter, and there's also some other fine antique carving, cushioned antique settles among more orthodox furniture, lots of musical instruments on the walls, and two roaring log fires in imposing fireplaces. Very good bar food includes lunchtime filled french bread, soup with home-made bread (£1.95), stilton, ricotta and red onion pudding with a coriander and apple salsa (£4.95), steak, mushroom and ale cobbler (£6.75), roast vegetables, goat's cheese and beef tomato mille feuille topped with a parmesan crumb (£8.75), chicken supreme marinated in lemon, soy and coriander set on crisp beansprouts with a liquor reduction (£8.95), whole shank of English lamb braised with red wine served on minted mash with a redcurrant and rosemary jus (£9.50), fillet of salmon topped with a basil crumb and served with creamy garlic noodles (£9.95), breast of barbury duck roasted onto a red cabbage sauerkraut with a kumquat and apricot syrup (£13.95), and good children's meals (from £3). Well kept Boddingtons, Coniston Old Man, Mitchells Lancaster Bomber, Tetleys and three guest beers on handpump; piped music. Plenty of seats outside have a fine view over the Trout valley to Applethwaite moors. *(Recommended by Elizabeth and Alan Walker, Tina and David Woods-Taylor, Helen Pickering, James Owen, Marvadene B Eves, P R and S A White, Mrs S Miller, Mr and Mrs Richard Osborne, Peter and Ruth Burnstone, Tracey Hamond, ALC, V and E A Bolton, W W Burke, Vann and Terry Prime, Gill and Maurice McMahon, Phil and Heidi Cook, Margaret and Jeff Graham, R F Gale, Mr and Mrs D W Mitchell, Charles and Claire Edmondson-Jones, A Callister, Maysie Thompson, RJH, Nick Lawless, Mrs Frances Gray, Maur)*

Free house ~ Licensees Mark Stewardson and Joanne Sherratt ~ Real ale ~ Bar food ~ (015394) 32174 ~ Children welcome ~ Open 11-11; 12-10.30 Sun; closed 25 Dec ~ Bedrooms: £45B/£65B

ULVERSTON SD2978 Map 7
Bay Horse 🍴 🍷

Canal Foot signposted off A590 and then you wend your way past the huge Glaxo factory

Although they keep a fair range of real ales in this civilised hotel, it remains the imaginative cooking that people come here to enjoy. In the bar, food is served at lunchtime only and might include sandwiches (from £1.85), home-made soup (£2.75), home-made herb and cheese pâté, savoury terrine or button mushrooms in a tomato, cream and brandy sauce on a peanut butter crouton (£5.75), cheese platter with home-made biscuits and soda bread (£5.95), smoked haddock and sweetcorn chowder served with hot garlic and paprika bread (£6.50), braised lamb, apricot and ginger puff pastry pie, layers of cooked ham, pear and stilton baked in a cheese and chive pastry or fried strips of chicken, leeks and button mushrooms on savoury rice with a sweet and sour sauce (all £8.50), fried medallions of pork, leek and lancashire cheese with a rich madeira sauce (£8.75), and home-made puddings (£4.50); it's essential to book for the restaurant. Well kept Everards Tiger, Mansfield Tavern Classic, Marstons Pedigree, and Timothy Taylor Landlord on handpump, a decent choice of spirits, and a carefully chosen and interesting wine list. The bar has a relaxed atmosphere and a huge stone horse's head, as well as attractive wooden armchairs, some pale green plush built-in wall banquettes, glossy hardwood traditional tables, blue plates on a delft shelf, and black beams and props with lots of horsebrasses. Magazines are dotted about, there's a handsomely marbled green granite fireplace, and decently reproduced piped music; darts, bar billiards, shove-ha'penny, cribbage, and dominoes. The no-smoking conservatory restaurant has fine views over Morecambe Bay (as do the bedrooms) and there are some seats out on the terrace. *(Recommended by Jenny and Chris Wilson, Gill and Maurice McMahon, Norman Stansfield, David Carr, Karen Eliot, Kim Maidment, Philip Vernon, John and Christine Lowe, Paul Bailey, A D Ryder, Tina and David Woods-Taylor; also in the Good Hotel Guide)*

Free house ~ Licensee Robert Lyons ~ Real ale ~ Bar food (lunchtime only; not Mon) ~ Restaurant ~ (01229) 583972 ~ Children in eating area of bar if over 12 ~ Open 11-11; 12-10.30 Sun ~ Bedrooms: £65B/£120B

WASDALE HEAD NY1808 Map 9
Wasdale Head Inn 🛏️

To NE of lake; long detour off A595 from Gosforth or Holmrook

This is a well run mountain hotel, three gabled storeys in beige and brown. Its marvellous steep fellside setting has the added advantage of being well away from the main Lakeland tourist areas; it makes an excellent base for walking and climbing. The high-ceilinged, spacious main bar has the feel of an old-fashioned country-house gunroom, with its shiny panelling, cushioned settles on the polished slate floor, great George Abraham early mountaineering photographs on the walls, and a log fire. It's named for the first landlord, Will Ritson, who by his death in 1890 had earned the reputation of being the World's Biggest Liar for his zany tall stories. There's a comfortably old-fashioned residents' bar and lounge, snug and restaurant. Popular bar food includes soup (£1.90), cumberland sausage and black pudding (£6.20) and steak and ale pie (£6.45). Lively, helpful staff; well kept real ales such as Dent, Derwent, Hesket Newmarket, Jennings Cumberland and Theakstons Best, Old Peculier and Yates XB on handpump, a decent choice of malt whiskies, and good wine list; dominoes, cribbage, quoits and croquet. The drive below the plunging majestic screes by the lake is quite awesome. Besides the comfortable bedrooms, there's well equipped self-catering accommodation. *(Recommended by Nigel Woolliscroft, Maurice Thompson, David Cooke, D Braisted)*

Free house ~ Licensee Howard Christie ~ Real ale ~ Bar food (11-2, 6-9) ~ Restaurant ~ (019467) 26229 ~ Children welcome ~ Open 11-11; 12-10.30 Sun; till 10 winter ~ Bedrooms: £39S(£39B)/£78B

YANWATH NY5128 Map 9
Gate Inn 🍽️

2¼ miles from M6 junction 40; A66 towards Brough, then right on A6, right on B5320, then follow village signpost

It's easy to miss this popular and unpretentious little pub on the one-way lane that leads through the village which would be a great shame since it is doing very well at the moment. As well as surprisingly imaginative food, there's a good atmosphere in the bar, very friendly and helpful service, and well kept real ales. The simple turkey-carpeted bar, full of chatting regulars, has a log fire in an attractive stone inglenook and one or two nice pieces of furniture and middle-eastern brassware among more orthodox seats; or you can go through to eat in a two-level no-smoking restaurant. Starters or light snacks might include sandwiches, home-made soup (£2.40), good 'black devils' (sliced black pudding with a wholgrain-mustard sauce laced with whisky, £3.20), tikka masala mushrooms (£3.30), fish pie, macaroni cheese and vegetable bake or good steak baguette (all £5.90), salmon fillet baked with ham and topped with mozzarrella cheese (£8.50), chicken paprika (£8.95), steaks (from £9.75), and puddings like fresh fruit crumble or sticky gingerbead pudding (£2.75). Well kept Theakstons Best and a local beer brewed for them called Creaking Gate Bitter on handpump, and a decent wine list; darts, shove-ha'penny, and unobtrusive piped music; the friendly border collie is called Domino and is good with children. The terrace and garden have been recently landscaped. *(Recommended by Dave Braisted, Neil Townend, R C Morgan, IHR, K F Mould, Jenny and Brian Seller, Steve Whalley, Gill and*

Maurice McMahon, Suzy Miller, Colin and Peggy Wilshire, Andrew and Eileen Abbess, John and Cath Howard)

Free house ~ Licensees Ian and Sue Rhind ~ Real ale ~ Bar food ~ Restaurant ~ (01768) 862386 ~ Children welcome ~ Open 12-3(2.30 winter), 6(7 winter)-11; 12-3, 7-11 Sun; closed 25 Dec

Lucky Dip

Besides the fully inspected pubs, you might like to try these Lucky Dips recommended to us and described by readers (if you do, please send us reports):

Alston [NY7246]
☆ *Turks Head* [Market Pl]: Convivial old-world local with low beams, log fires, cheerful landlord, well kept Boddingtons, Higsons and Theakstons, reasonably priced food inc vegetarian, spotless housekeeping; bar counter dividing big front room into two areas, cosy back lounge; at top of steep cobbled street *(J and H Coyle)*
Ambleside [NY4007]
Kirkstone Pass Inn [A592 N of Troutbeck]: Splendid position and surrounding scenery – Lakeland's highest inn, quaint inside, with lots of old photographs and bric-a-brac, good coffee, well kept Tetleys, open fire, lively amusements, tables outside; simple food, maybe piped radio; best out of season *(Jenny and Brian Seller, Ann and Colin Hunt, LYM, Eddie Edwards)*
Askham [NY5123]
☆ *Queens Head* [lower green; off A6 or B5320 S of Penrith]: Warmly welcoming two-room lounge, open fire, lots of beams, copper and brass, generous good home-made food from sandwiches to venison, steaks and fresh fish inc plenty of fresh veg and good pudding choice, well kept Wards Sheffield Best, wide choice of wines, friendly young local licensees; children welcome, pleasant garden; bedrooms comfortable with creaking floorboards, splendid breakfast *(David Cooke, LYM, Mrs B Couzens, J Kirkham)*
Bassenthwaite [NY2228]
☆ *Sun* [off A591 N of Keswick]: Rambling bar with low 17th-c beams, two big log fires, built-in wall seats and stools around heavy wooden tables, bar food inc some Italian dishes, Jennings Bitter; tables in pretty front yard looking up to the fells; no dogs. *(Mr and Mrs Richard Osborne, Eric and Shirley Briggs, LYM)*
Blencogo [NY1948]
☆ *New Inn* [signed off B5302 Wigton—Silloth]: Must book for fine choice of very good food – real serious cooking, yet at sensible prices – in bright and simply modernised former village local, log fire, real ale, decent wines and whiskies, a few big Cumbrian landscapes, pleasant service; cl Mon *(J M and G M Wilcock, BB)*
Boot [NY1700]
Brook House: Converted small Victorian hotel with wide choice of good generous home-cooked food on solid timber tables, small plush bar, comfortable hunting-theme lounge, log

fires, well kept Black Sheep and Theakstons, friendly newish owners, good views; handy for Ravenglass rly and great walks, good value bedrooms *(Eric and Shirley Briggs, H K Dyson, Eddie Edwards, Tim Dobby)*
Bowland Bridge [SD4289]
Hare & Hounds [village signed from A5074]: Handy for Sizergh Castle, this pleasantly set pub has been a very popular main entry, owing a lot to the personality of its landlord ex-footballer Peter Thompson; but it's now been sold, and we'd like more reports on the new regime; decent usual food, limited beer range, open fires in comfortably modernised carpeted bar, picnic-sets in spacious side garden, comfortable bedrooms *(J Phillips, Miss L Bruniges, LYM)*
Brampton [NY5361]
Nags Head [Market Pl; just off A69 E of Carlisle]: Roomy and friendly, with old-world decor, well kept Boddingtons and Castle Eden, smaller family room down a few steps, dogs; open afternoons; quiz Sun, bedrooms basic but good value *(Judith Hirst, Bob and Marg Griffiths)*
Burton [SD5376]
Dutton Arms [4 miles from M6 junction 35, via A6 N]: The Duttons who have been very popular for their food at the New Inn, Yealand Conyers have now opened this as a restaurantly dining pub; open all day Sun and summer weekdays *(anon)*
Carlisle [NY4056]
Woodrow Wilson [Botchergate]: Smart new Wetherspoons pub, no TV or music, well kept beers such as Courage Directors, Jennings and John Smiths, wide choice of good food, bargain prices, attractive terrace; no children *(Bob and Marg Griffiths)*
Cartmel [SD3879]
Royal Oak [The Square]: Tastefully refurbished, with low ceilings, cosy nooks, generous good value food from baguettes up, well kept real ales such as Wadworths 6X, friendly helpful service; nice big garden, bedrooms *(Nick J Lawless, David Heath, BB)*
Cockermouth [NY1231]
Tithebarn [Station St (A5086)]: Friendly town pub with well kept Jennings, good helpings of home-cooked food, low prices *(Andy and Jill Kassube, BB)*
☆ *Trout*: Solid old fishing hotel with pink plush sofas, captain's chairs and open fire in comfortable and friendly bar, good bar food from sandwiches up inc a vegetarian dish,

well kept Jennings Cumberland, Marstons Pedigree and Theakstons Best, over 50 malt whiskies, decent wines, freshly squeezed juices, attentive staff; coffee lounge and comfortable restaurant (best to book Sun lunch) both no smoking; piped music; nice gardens down to river; children welcome, good bedrooms *(RB, Gill and Maurice McMahon, LYM, Chris Rounthwaite)*

Coniston [SD3098]

Crown: Basic pub with friendly landlord, hot coal fire, quickly served bar food, well kept Hartleys; bedrooms, open all day *(Peter and Audrey Dowsett)*

☆ *Sun* [signed from centre]: Attractively placed below mountains (doubling as rescue post), with interesting Donald Campbell and other Lakeland photographs in basic walkers' and locals' back bar, friendly staff, good log fire, enjoyable home-made bar food with good fresh veg, Coniston Bluebird and Old Man (from back microbrewery), Jennings and Tetleys; children in carpeted no-smoking eating area and restaurant, darts, dominoes, piped music; open all day; comfortable bedrooms *(Ewan and Moira McCall, Tina and David Woods-Taylor, LYM)*

Culgaith [NY6129]

Black Swan [off A66 E of Penrith]: Well run clean and comfortable 17th-c inn in Eden Valley village, open fire, cheerful chatty landlord, well presented if not cheap food, real ales; bedrooms *(Malcolm Taylor, J and H Coyle)*

Dent [SD7187]

☆ *George & Dragon* [Main St]: Clean and comfortable pub/hotel, dark panelling, flagstones, partitioned tables, Dent Aviator, Bitter and Ramsbottom, also Scottish Courage ales, good generously served bar food, bargain Sun lunch, reasonably priced evening restaurant, no-smoking area, no piped music; pleasant staff and friendly locals, separate pool, TV and darts; bedrooms comfortable, lovely village *(G Coates, Paul S McPherson)*

Dockray [NY3921]

☆ *Royal* [A5091, off A66 W of Penrith]: Surprisingly plush and open-plan for the area, with wide choice of good food from lunchtime rolls and baked potatoes up, children's helpings, well kept Black Sheep, Boddingtons, Castle Eden, Jennings Cumberland, Theakstons and Timothy Taylor Landlord, good wines by the glass, prompt welcoming service, two dining areas (one no smoking), walkers' part with stripped settles on flagstones; darts, cribbage and dominoes; piped music; picnic-sets in garden; open all day, comfortable bedrooms *(Susan and Nigel Wilson, Monica Shelley, John C Baker, D S and J M Jackson, Vicky and David Sarti, RB, Mrs Holden, John and Enid Morris, Maurice Thompson, LYM, A E Brace, Dick Brown)*

Dovenby [NY0933]

Ship [A594 Cockermouth—Maryport]: Jennings country pub locally popular for good home-cooked food, well priced beers *(Andy and Jill Kassube)*

Ennerdale Bridge [NY0716]

Shepherds Arms: Friendly village inn with good food choice inc vegetarian and children's in spacious dining bar with polished wood floor, well kept Courage Directors, Jennings Cross Buttock, Theakstons Best and XB, decent coffee; weather forecast blackboard for walkers, bedrooms *(Neil and Anita Christopher)*

Eskdale Green [NY1400]

☆ *King George IV* [E of village]: Cheerful bustling beamed and flagstoned bar, comfortable lounge, back games room, wide choice of quickly served good generous food from sandwiches to steaks, well kept Bass, Jennings Cumberland and Theakstons Best, XB and Old Peculier, good collection of malt whiskies, restaurant; friendly staff, log fire, fine views from garden – idyllic spot, lots of good walks; children and dogs very welcome, open all day summer; good value bedrooms *(Bronwen and Steve Wrigley, H K Dyson, Jenny and Brian Seller, LYM, Nick J Lawless, Ann and Bob Westbrook)*

Glenridding [NY3917]

Travellers Rest [back of main car park, top of road]: Friendly unpretentious beamed and panelled two-bar pub with big helpings of food for hungry walkers, well kept Boddingtons and Castle Eden, simple décor; great views from seats on terrace with covered area *(H K Dyson, Neil and Anita Christopher)*

Grasmere [NY3406]

Red Lion [Red Lion Sq]: Plush wall seats and stools and cast-iron pub tables in hotel's Lamb bar, open fire in brick fireplace, well kept Theakstons, good range of malt whiskies, decent bar food, good friendly service, cane-chair conservatory, well priced restaurant; comfortable bedrooms, good breakfast, lovely views *(Eddie Edwards, Maurice and Gill McMahon)*

☆ *Swan* [A591]: Upmarket but relaxed and individual, with friendly service, lively little public bar, quieter old-fashioned lounge popular with older people (children allowed here), oak beams, armchairs, velvet curtains, prints and swords, inglenook log fires; well prepared bar food, keg Jennings Old Smoothie, good malt whiskies, tables in garden, picturesque surroundings, drying room for walkers; easy parking, comfortable bedrooms *(Eddie Edwards, LYM)*

Tweedies: Big square bar with settles, tartan panels and TV, family dining room, generous good food inc baguettes and vegetarian choice, well kept Coniston and Jennings, prompt friendly service; big pleasant hotel garden, bedrooms *(Eddie Edwards, Neil and Anita Christopher, David Cooke)*

Great Urswick [SD2674]

☆ *General Burgoyne* [Church Rd]: Small flagstoned early 18th-c village pub overlooking small tarn; bar and lounges with log fires, country atmosphere, Hartleys XB and Robinsons, friendly efficient service, good food; exemplary lavatories *(David Carr, W D Christian)*

Hallbankgate [NY5759]
Belted Will [A689 E of Brampton]: Cosy cheerful local with good value generous food, a well kept real ale, friendly new licensees, log fire, dining room, pool; busy w/e, open all day *(Bob and Marg Griffiths)*

Haverthwaite [SD3284]
☆ *Anglers Arms*: Busy and friendly refurbished two-bar local with generous fresh food inc tasty vegetarian dishes, quick welcoming service, Theakstons Best and Mild, overflow upstairs dining room – must book Fri/Sat night; small pool room *(S and P Stubbs)*
Rusland Pool: Good food, attractive décor, pleasant staff *(Paul Kitchener)*

Hawkshead [SD3598]
☆ *Kings Arms* [The Square]: Relaxed and chatty local with low-ceilinged bar, open fire, well priced food from sandwiches up, well kept Black Sheep, Coniston and other beers, summer cider, darts, dominoes, cribbage; no-smoking restaurant; fruit machine, piped pop music, tables on terrace overlooking little square of lovely Elizabethan village; well behaved children welcome, open all day, bedrooms (bar can be noisy till late), car park some way off *(Nick J Lawless, SLC, LYM)*
☆ *Queens Head*: Bustling red plush low-beamed and panelled bar and no-smoking snug and restaurant, food from usual pub things (but no nuts or crisps) to quite elaborate evening dishes; open fire, well kept Hartleys XB and Robinsons Bitter, Frederics and Mild, dominoes, cribbage; piped music, children in eating areas and snug, open all day; good bedrooms *(Gill and Maurice McMahon, Clive and Michele Platman, LYM, R W Tapsfield, SLC, Peter and Pat Frogley)*
Red Lion: Modernised local with some old-fashioned touches, good log fire, well kept Scottish Courage ales with guests such as Jennings, good range of usual food, friendly staff, piped music; open all day, bedrooms *(Andy, Julie and Stuart Hawkins, LYM, SLC)*
Sun: Lots of brass, brickwork and beams, reasonably priced bar food, sizeable restaurant with more exotic menu, well kept Bass; children and dogs welcome, tables out in front of small courtyard; bedrooms *(SLC, Leo and Barbara Lionet)*

Hesket Newmarket [NY3438]
☆ *Old Crown* [signed off B5299 in Caldbeck]: Relaxed and homely unfussy local in remote attractive village, decent reasonably priced food inc splendid range of curries, friendly landlord, six unusual beers brewed in back barn; outside lavatories, cl weekday lunchtimes exc school hols; bedrooms *(LYM, John Brightley, Andy and Jill Kassube, Peter and Pat Frogley)*

Howtown [NY4519]
☆ *Howtown Hotel*: Unrivalled position nr steamer pier on Ullswater's quieter shore, pre-war feel in both back walkers' bar (filling lunchtime sandwiches) and cosy very red hotel bar; restaurant (book for good Sun lunch), morning coffee and afternoon tea; welcoming very long-serving owners, Theakstons Best, decent wines by the glass, pleasant garden (maybe red squirrels); charming old-fashioned bedrooms, early morning tea ladies; can get very busy at peak holiday times *(Dick Brown, Dave Braisted, Christine and Geoff Butler, V and E A Bolton, Monica Shelley, Peter A Burnstone, Gill and Maurice McMahon)*

Hutton Roof [NY3734]
Horseshoe: Straightforward local, quiet and well placed, with lovely views, friendly welcome, good range of home-made food inc old-fashioned puddings and children's dishes, Jennings ales; children welcome, garden; bedrooms *(John Brightley)*

Ireby [NY2439]
Paddys Bar: Friendly pub in small village below Caldbeck Fells, wide range of beers; back post office and shop *(Gill and Maurice McMahon)*

Kendal [SD5293]
Olde Fleece [Highgate]: 17th-c but much refurbished, with pleasant atmosphere and service, well kept John Smiths and Theakstons, good helpings of reasonably priced usual food till 9.30, upstairs dining area; piped music and juke box, open all day *(Paul Mallett, Sue Rowland, SLC)*

Keswick [NY2624]
Bank [Main St]: Popular local welcoming visitors, clean and comfortable, full Jennings range kept well, professional service; bedrooms *(C J Fletcher, P and M Rudlin)*
Four in Hand [Lake Rd]: Recently neatly refurbished, cosy back lounge, stage-coach bric-a-brac, decent-sized tables in dining room, full Jennings range, varied food; very busy in summer *(David and Kathy Holcroft, Dick Brown, David Carr)*
George [St John St]: Attractive traditional black-panelled side room with interesting Wordsworth connection (and good log fire), open-plan main bar with old-fashioned settles and modern banquettes under Elizabethan beams; well kept Theakstons and Yates, bar food inc children's, restaurant; bedrooms comfortable *(David Carr, LYM, J Monk, P M Rudlin)*
Lake Road Inn [Lake Rd]: Old town pub with Victorian fireplace, panelling and prints in two communicating rooms, well kept Jennings Bitter, Cumberland and Snecklifter, keen young landlord, generous enjoyable food; tables on small terrace, open all day w/e and summer weekdays *(Andy and Jill Kassube, C J Fletcher, SLC, Dick Brown)*
Olde Golden Lion [Market St]: Long split-level central pub, interesting interior, plain wooden tables; popular food *(Eddie Edwards, SLC)*
☆ *Swinside* [Newlands Valley]: Hard-working new licensees in clean and friendly modernised pub in peaceful valley, stunning views of crags and fells, well kept Bass and Jennings, decent wines, good fires, welcoming service, good value generous freshly made bar food, restaurant; dogs allowed, tables outside with best view, open all day Sat and summer; bedrooms *(H K Dyson, LYM, DC, Sylvia and Tony Birbeck, Ewan and Moira McCall)*

Kirkby Stephen [NY7808]
Pennine: Good straightforward food in pleasant and airy pub with children's area, well kept

Lakeland and guest ales, upstairs restaurant, a few tables out overlooking attractive market place *(BB, Neil and Anita Christopher)*

Langdale [NY2906]

New Dungeon Ghyll [B5343]: Large dim-lit barn with solid tables on tiled floor, open fire, real ale, simple food all day in summer – popular with walkers down from the Langdale Pikes; restaurant in adjoining Victorian hotel with good views *(Sarah and Peter Gooderham, Keith and Norma Bloomfield)*

Stickle Barn [by car park for Stickle Ghyll]: Lovely views from café-style walkers' and climbers' bar, good choice of food inc packed lunches, well kept Scottish Courage beers, small no-smoking area, mountaineering photographs; fruit machines, TV, maybe loud piped music; big pleasant terrace, open all day; bunkhouse accommodation, live music in loft *(SLC, Eddie Edwards, Peter and Audrey Dowsett)*

Levens [SD4886]

☆ *Hare & Hounds* [off A590]: Welcoming village pub handy for Sizergh Castle, with partly panelled low-beamed lounge bar (part is no smoking), front tap room with coal fire and darts, cribbage and dominoes, pool room down steps with juke box and fruit machine, well kept Vaux Waggle Dance and Wards Darleys Thorne, friendly service, good simple food inc lunchtime sandwiches and a vegetarian dish, restaurant; children in eating area, good views from terrace *(Joy and Peter Heatherley, LYM, Ann and Colin Hunt, O K Smyth, Gill and Maurice McMahon, Mr and Mrs Richard Osborne, Mrs S Miller, Jenny and Brian Seller)*

☆ *Strickland Arms* [Sedgwick Rd, by Sizergh Castle gates]: Wide choice of generous imaginative well cooked food, friendly prompt service even when very busy, well kept Scottish Courage ales with a guest such as Masons Amazon, log fire; piped music, pool table; no-smoking upstairs restaurant, children allowed, good garden *(J H and Dr S A Harrop)*

Lorton [NY1525]

Wheat Sheaf [B5289 Buttermere—Cockermouth]: Bar and dining lounge, good generous food inc fresh local produce, very well kept Jennings, service highly efficient but still friendly; caravan park behind *(H K Dyson, Andy and Jill Kassube, BB, Vann and Terry Prime, DC)*

Lowick Bridge [SD2986]

☆ *Red Lion* [just off A5084]: Family food pub, warm, comfortable and clean, very busy in summer, with two spacious and attractive areas, well kept Hartleys XB and Robinsons, good choice of generous tasty bar food inc vegetarian and Sun roasts, half helpings if you want, good friendly service, open fire; tables outside, charming spot, open all day Sun and summer Sat, quiz night Thurs; smart reasonably priced bedrooms, good breakfast *(T M Dobby)*

Lowick Green [SD2985]

☆ *Farmers Arms* [A5092 SE of village]: Charming cosy public bar with heavy beams, huge slate flagstones, big open fire, cosy corners and pub games (also piped music, TV; this part may be

cl winter), some interesting furniture and pictures in plusher hotel lounge bar across yard, tasty well presented food in bar and restaurant inc two-person bargains, well kept John Smiths and Theakstons, friendly attentive staff; children welcome, open all day; unobtrusive piped music; comfortable bedrooms *(LYM, Sheila and Phil Stubbs)*

Nenthead [NY7843]

Miners Arms: Friendly relaxing family-run pub, basic decor, good genuine home cooking inc good chips, Brains, Jennings Cumberland, Marstons Pedigree and guest beers, no piped music; homely family bedrooms, filling breakfasts, also bunkhouse *(Phil Owens)*

Orton [NY6208]

George [2 miles from M6 junction 38; B6261 towards Penrith]: Roomy hunting-theme bar in attractive old inn, very friendly, wonderful peaceful setting, good reasonably priced food inc children's, well kept Black Sheep and Youngers, darts and pool room; bedrooms comfortable *(Neil and Anita Christopher)*

Outgate [SD3599]

Outgate Inn [B5286 Hawkshead—Ambleside]: Attractively placed warmly welcoming country pub with three pleasantly modernised rooms, well kept Hartleys XB and Robinsons Bitter and Frederics, usual food inc sandwiches; trad jazz Fri, open all day, comfortable bedrooms *(H K Dyson, BB, SLC, Mr and Mrs Staples)*

Patterdale [NY3916]

White Lion: Well kept Castle Eden and Theakstons Best, usual bar food, friendly service; busy with walkers in summer; bedrooms *(RT and JC Moggridge, H K Dyson)*

Penrith [NY5130]

Gloucester Arms [Cornmarket]: Cosy and very friendly low-beamed local, lots of wood and panelling, comfortable seats, big open fire, cheap filling food, well kept Castle Eden and Flowers IPA; open all day *(RT and JC Moggridge, John T Ames)*

Pooley Bridge [NY4724]

Sun: Panelled village pub with simple bar food inc sandwiches, well kept Jennings ales, small lounge bar, steps past servery to bigger bar with games and piped music (can obtrude), restaurant; tables in garden *(Nick Lawless, Andy and Jill Kassube)*

Ravenglass [SD0996]

Ratty Arms: Ex-railway bar in main line station (a bit of a trek from the narrow-gauge steam railway) with well kept real ales, interesting food, good value restaurant, service friendly and efficient even when busy; pool table in busy public bar; cl Sun *(John Baker, LYM, T M Dobby)*

Ravenstonedale [NY7204]

☆ *Black Swan* [just off A685 Kirkby Stephen to M6]: Hotel bar with open fire and some stripped stone, real ales such as Black Sheep, Jennings and Timothy Taylor Landlord, country wines, good set food inc some interesting dishes, friendly staff; dogs welcome, tables in pretty tree-sheltered streamside garden over road; comfortable bedrooms inc some for disabled, peaceful setting *(Pete Yearsley, Mrs*

Frances Gray, John Knighton, Ann and Colin
Hunt, John Saul, BB)

Fat Lamb [Crossbank; A683 Sedbergh—Kirkby
Stephen]: Remote inn with pews in brightly
modernised bar, log fire in traditional black
kitchen range, good local photographs and bird
plates; enjoyable food from sandwiches up inc
vegetarian, well kept Tetleys, maybe piped
classical music, restaurant, tables out by sheep
pastures; facilities for disabled, children really
welcome; comfortable bedrooms with own
bathrooms, good walks from inn *(T M Dobby,
Neil and Anita Christopher, John Saul, BB)*

Rosthwaite [NY2615]

☆ *Scafell* [B5289 S of Keswick]: Extended slate-
floored pubby back public bar in beautiful
tranquil spot with tables out overlooking beck,
well kept Theakstons Best and XB and a guest
beer, log fire, wide choice of good value food
inc vegetarian, children's helpings of most
dishes; prompt welcoming service even when
packed with walkers; afternoon teas, piped
music; hotel has cosy sun-lounge bar and dining
room; bedrooms not big but good *(H K Dyson,
Neil and Anita Christopher, Peter and Pat
Frogley, Andy and Jill Kassube, J H Bell)*

Rydal [NY3706]

Glen Rothay Hotel: Small hotel going up
market under new owners, armchairs around
fire in beamed hotel bar, well furnished back
bar with Bass and Hartleys XB and food (not
cheap) from baguettes up, tables in pretty
garden, boats for residents on nearby Rydal
Water; bedrooms comfortable *(LYM, Mrs
Dilys Unsworth)*

Sandside [SD4781]

☆ *Ship* [B5282]: Spacious modernised pub with
glorious view of estuary and mountains beyond;
good generous varied bar food inc unusual fresh
veg, cheerful service, well kept Scottish Courage
ales, decent wines, summer barbecues, tables out
on grass by good play area; children allowed,
high chairs *(LYM, D Rooke)*

Santon Bridge [NY1102]

Bridge: Relaxed traditional pub with good
choice of substantial meals inc children's in
cosy bar or small dining area, Jennings ales,
efficient friendly service; can get very busy in
summer; tables in garden, bedrooms, delightful
riverside spot with fell views *(Nick Lawless,
Mike Anderton)*

Scales [NY3427]

☆ *White Horse* [A66 W of Penrith]: Comfortable
beamed pub-restaurant, largely no smoking,
with cosy corners, interesting farmhouse-
kitchen memorabilia and good open fires,
Jennings real ales, decent food; well behaved
children welcome (over 5 evening), quiet piped
music, gets pubbier late evening when people
have stopped eating; open all day, lovely setting
below Blencathra *(Keith and Janet Eaton,
LYM, Mike and Penny Sutton)*

Sedbergh [SD6692]

Red Lion [Finkle St (A683)]: Cheerful beamed
Jennings local, comfortable and friendly, with
their full beer range kept well, good value food
all day (reduced menu late afternoon), good
service, coal fire *(MLR, BB)*

Skelwith Bridge [NY3503]

Talbot [part of Skelwith Bridge Hotel; A593 W
of Ambleside]: 17th-c Lakeland hotel nr River
Brathay, smart cheerful staff in oak-panelled
bar, Theakstons on handpump, good value
lunchtime bar food inc good big ploughman's
(choice of cheeses), good restaurant; bedrooms
(Roger Braithwaite)

Spark Bridge [SD3185]

☆ *Royal Oak* [off A5092 N of Ulverston]: Large
riverside food pub with good food (all day Sun)
inc wonderful steaks and fresh interestingly
prepared seafood, good children's menu,
raftered upper dining area, relaxed informal
atmosphere, friendly service, well kept
Boddingtons, Flowers Original and Wadworths
6X, decent house wines, open fire; large pool
room *(Clive Wheeler)*

Stainton [NY4928]

Brantwood [handy for M6 junction 40]: Large
country hotel but friendly and welcoming, bar
lunches inc nicely prepared sandwiches *(John
Cadman)*

Staveley [SD4798]

☆ *Eagle & Child* [off A591 Windermere—
Kendal]: Simple good low-priced home-made
food with fresh veg, friendly licensees, well kept
Theakstons and guest beers, lots of malt
whiskies, quick service, bright but comfortable
little modern front lounge and more spacious
carpeted bar; well kept, with small neat
riverside garden; good value bedrooms, good
breakfast *(BB, Paul Mallett, Sue Rowland, Dr
B and Mrs P B Baker)*

Railway [The Banks]: Friendly local with low-
priced generous blackboard food, well kept
Tetleys and Wadworths 6X; piped music,
SkyTV *(Paul Mallett, Sue Rowland)*

Stonethwaite [NY2613]

☆ *Langstrath* [Borrowdale]: Welcoming, neat and
clean, with decent food, well kept Black Sheep,
Jennings and Theakstons, lots of malt whiskies,
open fires and plenty of walkers and locals in
the bar; enthusiastic landlord, good service,
separate restaurant; delightful peaceful village,
pleasant good value bedrooms *(Jane Taylor,
David Dutton, Carol and Jim Watson)*

Thirlspot [NY3217]

☆ *Kings Head* [A591 Grasmere—Keswick]:
Attractively placed and well refurbished beamed
bar, long and low, with inglenook fires,
wide choice of usual food inc good puddings in
no-smoking eating area, well kept Jennings,
Theakstons Best, XB and Mild, Yates and a
guest ale, fast service, tables in garden, games
room with pool; piped music; children
welcome, with toy box; good value bedrooms
(the hotel part and restaurant are separate)
(Eddie Edwards, LYM, Mr and Mrs Dawes)

Threlkeld [NY3325]

Horse & Farrier: Formerly unspoiled 17th-c inn
now enlarged and refurbished by Jennings as
upmarket dining pub, roomy and pleasant, with
hunt cartoons, smallish helpings of rather
restauranty food, well kept beer, friendly
service; open all day, dogs allowed when
restaurant is closed *(Jonathan and Ann Tross,
A E Brace, Dick Brown, Eddie Edwards)*

Torver [SD2894]
☆ *Church House* [A593 S of Coniston]:
Welcoming and civilised low-beamed bar, keen
staff, splendid hill views, good log fire,
particularly well kept Castle Eden, reasonably
priced food, big garden; children welcome,
attractive evening restaurant; open all day at
least in summer; bedrooms *(Sarah and Peter
Gooderham)*

Troutbeck [NY3926]
Troutbeck Hotel [A5091/A66 – the 'other'
Troutbeck, nr Penrith]: Clean and bright, with
pleasant décor, good choice of well prepared
straightforward food, friendly service;
bedrooms *(Timothy Galligan)*

Ulverston [SD2978]
Farmers Arms [Market Sq]: Welcoming 17th-c
inn with warm inclusive atmosphere, good
food, good choice of guest ales, espresso
machine; attractive terrace overlooking market
and street entertainers *(H Johnson, C Killiner)*
Kings Head [Queen St]: Olde-worlde, low
ceilings, very welcoming, with particularly well
kept quickly changing real ales from far and
wide *(anon)*
Rose & Crown [King St]: Friendly and busy
open-plan local with good value varied home-
made food all day inc interesting vegetarian
dishes, well kept Hartleys XB, Robinsons Best
Mild and Bitter, quick service even when busy
on Sat market day, pleasant garden and
pavement tables *(David Carr)*

Underbarrow [SD4792]
Punchbowl: Small friendly open-plan village
local, smaller eating area, limited choice of
basic good value generous food inc lovely fish,
well kept Bass-related ales with a guest such as
Jennings Cumberland, quick helpful service
even when busy; unobtrusive piped music,
handy for walkers *(Jane Taylor, David Dutton,
Paul and Sue Merrick)*

Wetheral [NY4654]
Wheatsheaf [handy for M6 junctions 42/43]:
Easy motorway detour, food inc good
sandwich choice *(F Noble)*

Whitehaven [NX9718]
Distressed Sailor: Locally very popular for
enormous helpings of very good value food
(Kester Edmonds)

Winster [SD4293]
Brown Horse [A5074 S of Windermere]: Open-
plan dining place, light and comfortable, with
well spaced tables and good log fire; popular
especially among older people for attractively
priced food, prompt friendly service, well kept
Jennings Cumberland and Theakstons, decent
wines; children welcome (own menu, toys) *(Phil
and Heidi Cook, P R and S A White, LYM,
Mick Hitchman, Alison McCarthy)*

Winton [NY7810]
☆ *Bay Horse* [just off A685, N of Kirkby Stephen]:
Two low-key and low-ceilinged rooms with
Pennine photographs and local fly-tying, very
good generous home-cooked food inc fresh veg,
well kept Theakstons Best, Jennings and summer
guest beers, low prices, good young staff, pool in
games room; has been cl Mon/Tues lunchtimes
in winter; comfortable modestly priced
bedrooms, good breakfasts; peaceful moorland
hamlet *(LYM, Anthony Barnes)*

Real ale may be served from handpumps, electric pumps (not just the on-off
switches used for keg beer) or – common in Scotland – tall taps called founts
(pronounced 'fonts') where a separate pump pushes the beer up under air
pressure. The landlord can adjust the force of the flow – a tight spigot gives the
good creamy head that Yorkshire lads like.

Derbyshire

A fine area for people who like good beer, this, with plenty of good pubs notable for the quality of their real ales – particularly the Alexandra and the Brunswick in Derby, and out in the country the smart John Thompson brewing its own beers at Ingleby just outside Melbourne, and those very pubby establishments the quaint old Three Stags Heads at Wardlow, the idyllically rustic Quiet Woman at Earl Sterndale, and the very traditional Barley Mow at Kirk Ireton under its superlative landlady. And incidentally, did you know that Barley Mow should actually be pronounced Barley Mao? This favourite pub name has nothing to do with mowing the barley (nor of course with the late Chairman); the mow (as in ouch) is the old word for the place in which brewers' barley was heaped – or for the heap itself. On the food side, places that stand out are the inventive and stylish Waltzing Weasel at Birch Vale (a new Mediterranean emphasis in its cooking), the civilised Druid at Birchover (very restauranty, extremely wide choice), the Old Sun in Buxton (a good refurbishment by Marstons – and properly pubby, with good beer), the very friendly Navigation by the newly restored canal basin at Buxworth, the Chequers on Froggatt Edge (unusual food in attractive surroundings), the Red Lion at Hognaston (bistro food), the Monsal Head Hotel at Monsal Head (appetising seasonal menus at this attractively placed all-rounder, back in these pages after a break of some years), the Old Crown near Shardlow (interesting variations on good pub food) and the White Horse at Woolley Moor. From all these it's the Waltzing Weasel that lives up best to a special occasion, and is our Derbyshire Dining Pub of the Year. Other pubs here doing well all round include the cheerful Smiths Tavern in Ashbourne, the thriving Devonshire Arms at Beeley, the well refurbished Coach & Horses at Fenny Bentley, the enjoyably relaxed and very well run Cheshire Cheese at Hope (gains a Place to Stay Award this year), the comfortable Yorkshire Bridge just outside Bamford by the Ladybower Reservoir (another new Place to Stay Award), and the unspoilt and tranquilly placed Old Bulls Head at Little Hucklow. In the Lucky Dip section at the end of the chapter Derby itself has a good choice, and elsewhere we'd particularly pick out the Bulls Head at Ashford in the Water, Olde Nags Head in Castleton, Boat at Cromford, Barrel near Foolow, Plough in Hathersage, Lantern Pike at Hayfield, Colvile Arms at Lullington, Holly Bush at Makeney, Miners Arms at Milltown, Bulls Head at Monyash, Bell at Smalley, Three Horse Shoes at Spitewinter and George at Tideswell. Drink is considerably cheaper in Derbyshire than in most places: you can still easily find a pint for £1.50 or less – the Brunswick in Derby pricing its own brews particularly attractively.

Most of the big breweries now work through regional operating companies, with different names. If a pub is tied to one of these regional companies, we put the parent company's name in brackets, in the details at the end of each main entry.

ASHBOURNE SK1846 Map 7
Smiths Tavern £
St Johns St; bottom of market place

There's a choice of six newspapers to browse through in this nicely old-fashioned town tavern with a relaxed, chatty and cheerful atmosphere. The attractive bar has horsebrasses and tankards hanging from heavy black beams, a delft shelf of antique blue and white china, old cigarette and drinks advertisements, and a plush wall seat facing the bar counter. Steps lead up to a middle room with more plush seating around solid tables, a log-effect gas fire and piano, and beyond that a light and airy end dining room. Well kept Marstons Best and Pedigree and a guest on handpump, over 30 whiskies, and a range of vodkas. Popular and generously served bar food includes soup (£1.90), freshly cut sandwiches (from £1.75), ploughman's (£3.50) and daily specials like chilli (£4.50), steak and mushroom pie and several vegetarian dishes such as mushroom crumble or caribbean fruit and vegetable casserole (all £5.50), and 8oz rump steak (£7.95); home-made puddings might include strawberry and caramel cheesecake or lemon torte (£2.25); Sunday roast with good fresh vegetables (£5.50). Very friendly obliging service; darts, dominoes and cribbage.
(Recommended by Adrian and Sandra Pearson, Howard and Sue Gascoyne, JP, PP, David Carr, C J Fletcher, Dave and Deborah Irving, Joan and Andrew Life, Dr Peter Burnham, Julia Bryan, Darly Graton, Graeme Gulibert)

Marstons ~ Tenant David Gadsby ~ Real ale ~ Bar food ~ Restaurant ~ (01335) 342264 ~ Children welcome ~ Open 11-11; 12-10.30 Sun

BARLOW SK3375 Map 7
Trout
Valley Road, Common Side; B6051 NW of Chesterfield

This dining pub is surprisingly more inviting than you might have guessed from the road. The major part is given over to food service, and is carpeted, with neat good-sized tables, (candlelit at night), comfortable brocaded banquettes, old-world prints and beams; a second smaller dining room opens off. It's best to book at weekends. The other side of the bar has a good pubby atmosphere, with big stripped and scrubbed tables on bare boards, more banquettes and cushioned stools, and a big brick fireplace; you can eat the good home-made food round here among the drinkers too. The new lunchtime menu includes soup (£2.50), pâté (£2.95), hearty sandwiches (from £3.50), prawn and crab salad (£3.95), filled ciabatta bread (from £5.25), field mushrooms with asparagus risotto and stilton or fresh fish fillet of the day with herb crust, whole dressed crab or meat balls in a rich tomato sauce with spaghetti, or make up your own main course salad (all £5.95), and 10oz rump steak (£7.95); current pudding favourites include iced caramel pudding with toffee sauce and amaretti biscuits and baked vanilla cheesecake with raspberry coulis (£2.95). The evening menu has several additional dishes including fillet of smoked trout with a tomato and mustard dressing (£3.25) and chargrilled chicken breast with brie and fruits of the forest (£6.95); no-smoking restaurant. Service is very welcoming, quick and competent; well kept Bass, Boddingtons and Marstons Pedigree on handpump and good house wines; unobtrusive piped music. There are tables out on the terrace.
(Recommended by Joy and Peter Heatherley, Steve and Irene Law, Darly Graton, Graeme Gulibert, Steve Goodchild, Frank Gorman)

Free house ~ Licensee John Redfearn ~ Real ale ~ Restaurant ~ (0114) 2890893 ~ Children in restaurant ~ Open 12-3, 6.30-11; 12-3, 7-10.30 Sun

BEELEY SK2667 Map 7
Devonshire Arms
B6012, off A6 Matlock—Bakewell

Beautifully set in a pretty Peak District village, this very handsome old stone building, successfully re-converted from three early 18th-c cottages to a prosperous coaching inn in 1747, is rumoured to have been a tryst for Edward VII and his mistress Alice Keppel; Dickens was also a frequent visitor. Big warming log fires create a good pubby atmosphere in the black-beamed rooms which have comfortably cushioned stone seats along their stripped walls, and antique settles and simpler wooden chairs on the flagstoned floors; the restaurant and one area in the bar are no smoking. Very enjoyable bar food is served all day and might include home-made soup (£2.50), baguettes (from £3.95, toasted £4.50), smoked chicken and bacon salad (£4.25), shi-itake mushrooms in garlic (£4.95), a good value ploughman's, deep-fried haddock or haggis and neeps (£5.95), steak and ale pie or cumberland sausage (£6.25), chicken breast with stilton sauce, ham and eggs or roast vegetable and sun-dried tomato tarte (£6.95), and sirloin steak (£10.50); puddings (from £2.50). Friday night is fish night with butterfly king prawns or crab (£7.50), grilled halibut (£8.95), and seafood platter (£12.50). On Sundays they do a special Victorian breakfast with a glass of bucks fizz and the Sunday newspapers (£10.95). You will need to book for the fish night and Sunday breakfast, and probably at the weekends; efficient service. Well kept Black Sheep Special and Best, Theakstons XB and Old Peculier, and guest beers on handpump and about three dozen malt whiskies; shove-ha'penny. Handy for Chatsworth House. *(Recommended by Rita and Keith Pollard, JP, PP, Mike and Sue Loseby, John and Christine Lowe, David Carr, Dr S J Shepherd, Darly Graton, Graeme Gulibert, Joan and Andrew Life, Mike Green, Mrs J Hinsliff, Derek and Sylvia Stephenson, Peter Johnston, B M and P Kendall, Janet Pickles, K and B Forman, Paul and Maggie Baker, Christopher Turner)*

Free house ~ Licensee John A Grosvenor ~ Real ale ~ Bar food (12-9.30) ~ Restaurant ~ (01629) 733259 ~ Children welcome ~ Open 11-11; 12-10.30 Sun

BIRCH VALE SK0286 Map 7

Waltzing Weasel 🍽 ♇ 🛏

A6015 E of New Mills

Derbyshire Dining Pub of the Year

There are fine views of Kinder Scout and the Peak District from the charming back restaurant, pretty garden and terrace of this warmly welcoming civilised inn. The very comfortable, beautifully kept bar has cosy chatty areas, some handsome oak settles and tables among more usual furniture (the licensees are former antique dealers), plenty of houseplants on corner tables, lots of nicely framed mainly sporting Victorian prints, a good longcase clock, and a cheerful fire; there are daily papers on sticks, maybe classical piped music and a friendly old dog, Sam, pottering about. Although not cheap, bar food is really well liked by readers. As we went to press, the Atkinsons told us that they were encouraging country cooking in the bar with dishes such as lamb tagine, stifatho (Cypriot stew), Italian beef or wild boar casserole (all £9.50); other lunchtime food might include soup (£3), duck pâté (£4.75), vegetable tart (£6.75), home-baked ham or salt beef (£8.75), and seafood tart or meat pie (£8.95). Evening meals might comprise marinated anchovies, garlic mushrooms or mussels in wine (£4.75), leek and pasta mornay (£6.75), roast garlic lamb (£9.75), fish of the day (from £10.50) barnsley chop (£12.75), and lobster (£13.50); puddings (£3.50) and fine cheeses (£3.75); Well kept Marstons Best and Pedigree on handpump, and a good choice of decent wines and malt whiskies. Spacious comfortable bedrooms are well furnished and lovely breakfasts include home-made marmalade; friendly service. *(Recommended by Margaret and Roy Randle, Tim Brierly, Ian and Jane Irving, G Wheeler, Vann and Terry Prime, Tony and Joan Walker, David Hoult, Sue Holland, Dave Webster, Bronwen and Steve Wrigley, J F M West, Mike and Karen England, Stephen and Tracey Groves, RJH, A and S Hetherington, Ian and Jacqui Ross, M G Hart, Mrs Vanessa Brewer, Julie Peters, DAV, A N Dowling)*

Free house ~ Licensee Michael Atkinson ~ Real ale ~ Bar food ~ Restaurant ~ (01663) 743402 ~ Children welcome ~ Open 12-3, 5.30-11; 12-3, 5.30-10.30 Sun ~ Bedrooms: £58B/£78B

If you stay overnight in an inn or hotel, they are allowed to serve you an alcoholic drink at any hour of the day or night.

BIRCHOVER SK2462 Map 7
Druid 🍴

Village signposted off B5056

The emphasis is very much on dining at this civilised creeper-clad pub, so it's unlikely you'll be able to sit down if you only want a drink. An astonishing choice of imaginative dishes, written up on the blackboards that line the long fairly narrow bar, might include cold smoked duck breast with raspberry purée (£4.60), steak and mussel pie (£5.30), about a dozen vegetarian dishes such as fruit and vegetable lasagne or aubergine stuffed with rice, peppers, mushrooms, cheese and a peanut and garlic sauce (£6.90), Siam chicken with lime, lemon, ginger and banana or a casserole of venison, dark chocolate, red wine and herbs (£8.90), pan-fried swordfish steak (£9.40), and baked halibut with orange and garlic, black olives and water chestnuts (£10.70), puddings (£2.90); half-price helpings for children. It's best to book for evening and weekend meals. The spacious and airy two-storey dining extension, candlelit at night, is really the heart of the place, with pink plush seats on olive-green carpet, and pepper-grinders and sea salt on all the tables. The small plain bar has plush-upholstered wooden wall benches around straightforward tables, and a big coal fire; the Garden Room, tap room and part of the bar are no smoking. Well kept Mansfield Bitter, Marstons Pedigree, Morlands Old Speckled Hen and a guest on handpump, (Druid, brewed for the pub by nearby Leatherbritches, is often a summer fixture), good collection of malt whiskies; piped classical music. There are picnic-sets in front and good walks in the area. *(Recommended by JP, PP, Nigel Woolliscroft, Joan and Andrew Life, John and Christine Lowe, JDM, KM, Mr and Mrs C Pink, Ann Tross, Cameron, Joy and Peter Heatherley, B M and P Kendall)*

Free house ~ Licensee Brian Bunce ~ Real ale ~ Bar food ~ (01629) 650302 ~ Children in dining area till 8 ~ Open 12-3, 7-11; 12-3, 7-11 Sun; closed 25 Dec, evening 26 Dec

BRASSINGTON SK2354 Map 7
Olde Gate

Village signposted off B5056 and B5035 NE of Ashbourne

A fire struck this popular traditional old country pub last year, though you'd never know to look at it now. In the peaceful public bar, the gleaming copper pots are back on the lovely old kitchen range, pewter mugs hang once more from a beam, and the embossed Doulton stoneware flagons on a side shelf, ancient wall clock, and rush-seated old chairs and antique settles (one ancient, partly reframed, black oak solid one) are all back in their rightful place. Stone-mullioned windows look across lots of garden tables to small silvery-walled pastures. On the left of a small hatch-served lobby, another cosy beamed room has stripped panelled settles, tables with scrubbed tops, and a roaring fire under a huge mantelbeam. Promptly served good bar food includes very tasty grilled baguettes (£4.75), big open sandwiches (from £4.75), spinach and mushroom lasagne or three-cheese bake (£7.95), steak and mushroom pudding (£8.15), chicken balti (£10.95), crispy duck with plum and chilli (£12.95) and a popular summer barbecue, with lemon chicken, barnsley chop, swordfish and tuna (£8.95-£12.75); good puddings (£2.95). The dining room is no smoking. Well kept Marstons Pedigree and a guest on handpump, and a good selection of malt whiskies; cribbage and dominoes. The small front yard has a couple of benches. It's five minutes' drive from Carsington reservoir, ideal for water sports and activities. *(Recommended by the Didler, Mrs J Hinsliff, Peter Marshall, P Honour, JDM, KM, JP, PP, Patrick Hancock, Rob Fowell, Jason Caulkin, Derek and Sylvia Stephenson, Pat and Roger Fereday, Edmund Coan)*

Marstons ~ Paul Burlinson ~ Real ale ~ Bar food ~ (01629) 540448 ~ Children over 10 in bar ~ Open 12-2.30(3 Sat), 6-11; 12-3, 7-10.30 Sun; closed Mon lunchtime

BUXTON SK1266 Map 7
Bull i' th' Thorn

Ashbourne Road (A515) six miles S of Buxton, nr Hurdlow

Look out for the lively old carvings at the main entrance to this bizarre but fascinating amalgam of a medieval hall and straightforward roadside pub: one shows a bull caught in a thornbush, and others an eagle with a freshly caught hare, and some spaniels chasing a rabbit. In the hall dating from 1471, a massive central beam runs parallel with a forest of smaller ones, there are panelled window seats in the embrasures of the thick stone walls, handsome panelling, and old flagstones stepping gently down to a big open fire. It's furnished with fine long settles, an ornately carved hunting chair, a longcase clock, a powder-horn, and armour that includes 17th-c German helmets, swords, and blunderbusses and so forth. Served all day, bar food might include haddock or cod (£5), barnsley chop (£6.50), swordfish or shark (£7), 8oz rump steak, ostrich, crocodile or wild boar (£8.50); Sunday lunch (£5). An adjoining room has darts, pool, shove-ha'penny, dominoes and juke box; piped music. Robinsons Best on handpump. The three recently refurbished bedrooms have four-poster and rococo beds. A simple no-smoking family room opens on to a terrace and big lawn with swings, and there are more tables in a sheltered angle in front; medieval themed banquets. The pub is handy for the High Peak Trail. *(Recommended by Chris Raisin, John and Christine Lowe, David Hoult, Howard and Sue Gascoyne, Paul S McPherson, JP, PP, Tony and Wendy Hobden, the Didler, Maurice and Pauline Kean)*

Robinsons ~ Tenant Mrs Annette Maltby-Baker ~ Real ale ~ Bar food (9.30am-9pm) ~ Restaurant ~ (01298) 83348 ~ Children welcome ~ Open 9.30-11(10.30 Sun) ~ Bedrooms: /£60B

Old Sun ♀ ◖

33 High St

We'd agree with the reader who thought it was worth the uphill slog to reach this well furnished traditional Marstons-owned pub, the first to run virtually as a free house under a Union Taps flag. Several small cosy softly lit rooms lead off the central bar, with open fires, low beams, bare boards or terracotta tiles, comfortable leather armchairs and chesterfields, fresh flowers, stripped wood screens, old local photographs, and some carefully chosen bric-a-brac (such as the 19th-c Guinness bottles found during refurbishment of the cellar). Up to eight well kept real ales including Marstons Bitter and Pedigree and guest beers such as Timothy Taylor Landlord, Whim Hartington and Magic Mushroom Mild on handpump are served in lined oversized glasses; there's an impressive range of bottled beers and malt whiskies, with Bulmer's Old Hazy farm cider, and a good choice of wines, with about a dozen by the (huge!) glass. Tasty interesting bar food includes home-made soup (£1.80), sandwiches (from £3), black pudding in beer and mustard batter (£3.15), a daily pasta which dish might be tagliatelle with turkey and a leek and pepper sauce (£4.50), grilled local lamb cutlets with rosemary and onion (£7.15), daily specials such as roasted pepper croquette on a bed of stir-fried leeks and carrots (£6.85), daily salads like chargrilled chicken and pineapple (£7.90) or grilled lemon sole fillet with prawns, dill and lime butter (£9.95); puddings include grilled banana and chocolate (£1.90), bread and butter pudding (£2) and derbyshire cheese board (£2.75). Friendly staff; occasional beer festivals; cribbage; maybe food all day in summer. *(Recommended by Tim Barrow, Sue Demont, David Carr, Steve Godrich, Mike Ridgway, Sarah Miles, the Didler, R C Morgan, Paul Mason)*

Marstons ~ Manager Graham Taylor ~ Real ale ~ Bar food (12-2, 5.30-9; 12-9 Sat, Sun) ~ (01298) 23452 ~ Children in back bar till 8pm ~ Open 11.30(11 Sat)-11; 12-10.30 Sun

There are report forms at the back of the book.

BUXWORTH SK0282 Map 7

Navigation 🛏

Silkhill, off B6062, which itself leads off the A6 just NW of Whaley Bridge roundabout

With the canal basin restoration project now completed, the sight of barges on the water adds to the charms of this early 18th-c free house, whose car park was originally the site of the old Peak Forest Tramway (which connected the canal with limestone quarries in nearby Dove Holes). The cosy linked low-ceilinged rooms do have some canalia, but the bargees' days are brought back to life more vividly by the bright clutter of brassware, china and lacy curtains, all neat and shiny as a new pin. It's a smashing place to wander around at quiet times (some of the prints are particularly interesting), and when it's busy there are plenty of snug corners to tuck yourself into, with good coal and log fires and flagstone floors. Good value generous food includes soup (£1.95), sandwiches (from £2.50), ploughman's (£5.50), cheese and onion pie or lasagne (£5.75), bubble and squeak, chicken, leek and stilton pie or cumberland sausage (£6-£7), a huge grilled meat platter (£12.95), and puddings such as jam roly-poly or bread and butter pudding (£2.50), with vegetarian and children's dishes. Well kept and well priced Marstons Pedigree, Timothy Taylor Landlord, Websters Yorkshire and one or two guest beers on handpump, farm ciders in summer and mulled wine in winter; very friendly staff. A games room has pinball, pool, darts, dominoes, and TV; quiet piped music. There are tables out on a sunken flagstoned terrace, with a side play area and pets corner. The pub was once owned by the actress who played television's favourite landlady, Elsie Tanner. *(Recommended by Bill Sykes, John and Phyllis Maloney, Peter Marshall, B Adams, M A Buchanan, Jack Morley, Bernie Adams)*

Free house ~ Licensees Alan and Lynda Hall ~ Real ale ~ Bar food (12-9.30) ~ Restaurant ~ (01663) 732072 ~ Children away from bar area ~ Open 11-11; 12-10.30 Sun ~ Bedrooms: £29B/£48B

CASTLETON SK1583 Map 7

Castle Hotel 🛏

High Street at junction with Castle Street

At the last count, four ghosts were reputed to be haunting this historic hotel. The neatly kept atmospheric bar has stripped stone walls with built-in cabinets, an open fire, finely carved early 17th-c beams and, in one room, ancient flagstones. Good bar food in generous helpings includes soup (£1.95), bacon and cheddar melt (£2.95), lunchtime sandwiches served with chips and salad (from £3.25), gammon (£4.95), scampi or lemon chicken (£5.75) beef and Bass pie or cod and chips (£5.95), wild rice and spinach bake (£6.95), 8oz rump steak (£7.50), grilled peppered halibut with roasted mediterranean vegetables, and puddings such as chocolate and orange cake or vanilla bread and butter pudding (£2.25-£2.70); well kept Bass, Stones and Worthington on handpump; shove-ha'penny, cribbage, dominoes, fruit machine, trivia and piped music. There are seats in the pretty garden; friendly staff. A good day to visit is Saturday 29th May when the colourful Garland Ceremony procession, commemorating King Charles II's escape from the Roundheads, stops and dances outside. *(Recommended by K Stevens, JP, PP, Richard and Ann Higgs, David Carr, Lesley Bass, Sheila and Phil Stubbs, Katherine Williams)*

Bass ~ Lease: Paul Brady ~ Real ale ~ Bar food (11-10) ~ Restaurant ~ (01433) 620578 ~ Children welcome ~ Open 11-11; 12-10.30 Sun ~ Bedrooms: £40B/£50B

DERBY SK3435 Map 7

Alexandra 🍺 £

Siddals Rd, just up from station

Real ale fanatics say they are spoilt for choice at this friendly two-roomed Victorian town pub. The enthusiastic landlord will happily advise you about his half a dozen or so, often unusual, quickly changing guest beers which are particularly well kept alongside Batemans XB and Marstons Pedigree. Also, country wines, around two dozen malt whiskies, a good range of Belgian bottled beers, changing continental beers on draught, and farm cider tapped from the cask. The fairly basic but lively bar has good heavy traditional furnishings on dark-stained floorboards and shelves of bottles, while lots of railway prints and memorabilia signal the fact that it's just two minutes away from Derby station. Simple remarkably priced bar food includes filled hot or cold rolls (from £1.60), pie and peas (£1.80) and ploughman's, cod and chips or grilled liver and bacon (£3.50), Sunday lunch (£4.25); friendly service and locals; cribbage, dominoes and piped music. *(Recommended by Richard Lewis, Nigel Williamson, JP, PP, SLC, ALC, the Didler, Chris Raisin)*

Free house ~ Licensee Mark Robins ~ Real ale ~ Bar food ~ (01332) 293993 ~ Children in eating area of bar ~ Open 11-11; 12-3, 7-10.30 Sun ~ Bedrooms: £25B/£35B

Brunswick ◖ £

1 Railway Terrace; close to Derby Midland railway station

This traditional old railwaymen's pub is home to an incredible 17 constantly used handpumps. Seven of the beers – including Recession Ale, First Brew, Second Brew, the highly-praised Railway Porter, Triple Hop, Festival Ale, and Old Accidental – are from their own Brunswick Brewery (the workings of which are visible from a viewing area), with prices well below the average for the area. The other pumps serve guest beers which are sourced from independent brewers countrywide. They have beer festivals in February and the first week in October; draught farm cider. The very welcoming high-ceilinged serving bar has heavy, well padded leather seats, whisky-water jugs above the dado, and a dark blue ceiling and upper wall, with squared dark panelling below. The no-smoking room is decorated with little old-fashioned prints and swan's neck lamps, and has a high-backed wall settle and a coal fire; behind a curved glazed partition wall is a quietly chatty family parlour narrowing to the apex of the triangular building. Darts, cribbage, dominoes, fruit machine; good friendly service. Lunchtime bar food includes filled salad rolls with turkey, beef, ham, cheese and tuna and sweetcorn (£1.50), hot beef, hot turkey, cheese and bacon or hot traditional sausage beef cobs (£1.75), home-made leek soup (£1.95), ploughman's (£3.25), home-made chicken, leek, mushroom and celery pie (£3); changing specials might include salt beef or dry-cured ham (£2.95) and there's always a vegetarian dish such as mushroom stroganoff (£3.50); they do only rolls on Sunday. There are seats in the terrace area behind. *(Recommended by JP, PP, Richard Lewis, Derek and Sylvia Stephenson, David Carr, Sue Holland, Dave Webster, SLC, JDM, KM, the Didler, Kerry Law, Simon Smith, C J Fletcher, Chris Raisin)*

Own brew ~ Licensee Trevor Harris ~ Real ale ~ Bar food ~ (01332) 290677 ~ Children in family room and garden ~ Jazz Thurs evenings ~ Open 11-11; 12-10.30 Sun

Olde Dolphin £

6 Queen St; nearest car park King St/St Michaels Lane

This quaint little place which claims to be Derby's oldest pub (it dates from 1530), is perhaps best visited in the mid-afternoon, when you can quietly enjoy the snugly old-fashioned atmosphere. Its four cosy rooms – two with their own separate street doors – are traditionally decorated with varnished wall benches in the tiled-floor public bar and a brocaded seat in the little carpeted snug; there are big bowed black beams, shiny panelling, cast-iron-framed tables, a coal fire, lantern lights and opaque leaded windows; the atmosphere is friendly and quietly chatty, and they have daily papers and board games (no piped music). A good range of well kept real ales is served from an incredible twelve handpumps and includes Bass, Black Sheep, Fullers London Pride, Morlands Old Speckled Hen, Ruddles, Timothy Taylor Landlord, Woodfordes Wherry and Worthingtons, and a couple of guests; there's a beer festival in the last week in July. Cheap bar food includes soup (£1.50), filled baguettes (cold from £1.75, hot from £2.75), filled baked potatoes (from £2.25), sausages and mash, scampi or vegetarian dishes such as fruit curry or vegetable and pasta stir fry (£3.75), and 8oz rump steak (£4.25); three course Sunday lunch (£4.95). A new no-smoking restaurant upstairs serves good value steaks. *(Recommended by SLC, JDM, KM, Chris Raisin, JP, PP, David Carr)*

Bass ~ Manager Janina Holmes ~ Real ale ~ Bar food (11-9pm) ~ Restaurant (6-11pm) ~ (01332) 349115 ~ Children in eating area of bar, restaurant and garden till 7pm ~ Open 10.30-11; 12-10.30 Sun

EARL STERNDALE SK0967 Map 7
Quiet Woman 🍺 £
Village signposted off B4053 S of Buxton

A treasure for those who like their pubs really basic and old-fashioned, properly rooted in their locality, this stone cottage is one of those very rare places where you can buy free-range bantam and goose eggs, local cheese, local poetry books or even silage as easily as a pint of beer, and where the landlord may rush through in boots and overalls on his way to an emergency fencing job. There are hard seats, plain tables (we liked the sunken one for dominoes or cards), low beams, quarry tiles, lots of china ornaments and a good coal fire. When we went to press, the kitchen renovation was due to be completed later in the summer; the landlord promised that this was not part of a plan to turn the pub into a restaurant (he was also adamant that chips would not be on the menu!) but that a few extra snacks such as filled oat cakes will be added to the usual sandwiches (£1.30), home-made pork pies 70p (using their own pork), and maybe a winter hotpot. Particularly well kept Batemans Mild, Marstons Best, Pedigree and Owd Rodger and Timothy Taylor Landlord on handpump, cribbage, darts and pool in the family room. There are picnic-sets out in front, with various small animals to keep children amused. A classic. *(Recommended by JP, PP, the Didler, Derek and Sylvia Stephenson, John Beeken, Jenny and Roger Huggins)*

Free house ~ Licensee Kenneth Mellor ~ Real ale ~ (01298) 83211 ~ Children in family room till 10pm ~ Jamming sessions most Sun lunchtimes ~ Open 12-3(4 Sat), 7-11; 12-4.30, 7-10.30 Sun

EYAM SK2276 Map 7
Miners Arms 🛏
Signposted off A263 Chesterfield—Chapel-en-le-Frith

Well run little local – once a regular host of the Barmcote Court which legislated over mining matters – in a village which is a good base for exploring the Peak District. Historically however, Eyam has not always been a place to rush to: it's famous for the altruism of its villagers who, during the plague, isolated themselves to save the lives of others in the area. Well served by attentive staff, the reliable home-cooked food might include sandwiches (from £2.35), cumberland sausages (£3.95), ploughman's or sun-dried tomatoes and pesto pasta with a cheese sauce (£4.50), plaice mornay (£6.50), crispy roast duck (£7.25) and puddings like fresh fruit pavlova or bread and butter pudding (£2.35). There's an agreeably relaxed atmosphere in the three little plush beamed rooms, each of which has its own stone fireplace. In the evening (when they don't do bar food) it becomes a popular place when locals drop in for the well kept Stones and guest beer on handpump. Decent walks nearby, especially below Froggatt Edge. *(Recommended by JP, PP, Michael A Butler, Marvadene B Eves, IHR, Joy and Peter Heatherley, Julian and Linda Cooke, D Knott, Robert Gartery, DC)*

Free house ~ Licensee Nicholas Cook ~ Real ale ~ Bar food ~ Restaurant ~ (01433) 630853 ~ Children welcome ~ Open 12-3, 7-11; 12-7 Sun; closed Sun evening, Mon lunchtime and first two weeks Jan ~ Bedrooms: £27.50B/£55B

FENNY BENTLEY SK1750 Map 7

Coach & Horses

A515 N of Ashbourne

Landlord John Dawson has kept himself busy over the last year by refurbishing this charming friendly 17th-c rendered stone house himself. The little back room has been redecorated with a country cottage décor to reveal a lovely old fireplace, built-in wall banquettes and old prints on stained pine panelling. There are more prints in the friendly front bar, which has flowery-cushioned wall settles and library chairs around the dark tables on its carpet, waggonwheels hanging from the black beams, horsebrasses and pewter mugs. Reliable bar meals include soup (£2.50), lunchtime sandwiches (from £3.25), lunchtime ploughman's (from £4.95), steak and kidney pie or sweet and sour vegetable pasta (£5.95), chicken in leek and stilton sauce (£6.75), grilled salmon steak in a prawn and white wine sauce (£7.50), and 10oz sirloin (£11); puddings such as spotted dick or treacle sponge (£2.50), as well as several daily specials. The dining room and back bar are no smoking. Very well kept Mansfield Riding Bitter with four guests a week such as Abbeydale Moonshine, Adnams Broadside, Black Sheep and Timothy Taylor Landlord on handpump, and lots of malt whiskies; cribbage, dominoes and piped music. There are picnic-sets on the back grass by an elder tree, with rustic benches and white tables and chairs under cocktail parasols on the terrace in front. *(Recommended by Derek and Sylvia Stephenson, Colin Fisher, Jill Bickerton, Jack and Philip Paxton, Keith Berrett, George Atkinson, Mr and Mrs A J Woolstone, C J Fletcher, JP, PP, Derek and Margaret Underwood, Justin Hulford)*

Free house ~ Licensees John and Matthew Dawson ~ Real ale ~ Bar food ~ (01335) 350246 ~ Children in back bar, dining room and garden ~ Open 11-3, 5-11; 11-11 Sat; 11-10.30 Sun; closed 25 Dec

FROGGATT EDGE SK2477 Map 7

Chequers 🍴 ⇌

B6054, off A623 N of Bakewell

Beautifully situated busy country inn with Froggatt Edge just up through the woods behind. The fairly smart bar has library chairs or small high-backed winged settles on the well waxed floorboards, an attractive, richly varnished beam-and-board ceiling, antique prints on the white walls, partly stripped back to big dark stone blocks, and a big solid-fuel stove; one corner has a nicely carved oak cupboard. Tasty unusual bar food in the partly no-smoking dining area includes soup (£2.25), very enjoyable hearty sandwiches (from £3.25, smoked salmon £5.50), smoked duck with kumquat chutney or bresola with truffle oil and parmesan (£3.95), walnut and seared sweet pepper penne (£5.50), sausage of the day, liver stroganoff or Russian seafood pie (all £5.95), chicken, mushroom and tarragon pie (£6.50), baked salmon and leeks (£7.95), 8oz sirloin (£9.50) and daily specials such as chilli with rice and toasted tortilla (£6.95), minted lamb chops with sweet pepper cracked wheat (£8.95), whole baked grey mullet with vegetable pilau rice (£9.95), and pork fillet with poached pear and mustard sauce (£10.20); puddings might include chocolate and chestnut mousse and rhubarb puff pastry tart with greek yoghurt (£2.50-£4.95); pleasant efficient service. John Smiths and Tetleys on handpump, a good range of malt whiskies and a changing wine board; piped music. There are seats in the peaceful back garden; six nicely furnished comfortable bedrooms. *(Recommended by M G Hart, Mrs P Pearce, JP, PP, Sue Holland, Dave Webster, Leonard Robinson, Chris Flynn, Wendy Jones, David Carr, Carol and Steve Spence, Eric and Shirley Briggs, W K Wood, David and Mary Webb, Christopher Turner, Mike and Mary Carter, Peter Johnston, Mike and Karen England, Martin and Karen Wake)*

Wards ~ Tenants Tony Dipple and Mr R Graham ~ Real ale ~ Bar food (12-2, 6-9.30, wknds 12-(9 Sun)9.30) ~ (01433) 630231 ~ Children in eating area of bar and restaurant ~ Open 12-3, 5.30-11; 12-11 Sat; 12-10.30 Sun ~ Bedrooms: £46B/£58B

HARDWICK HALL SK4663 Map 7

Hardwick Inn

2¾ miles from M1 junction 29: at roundabout A6175 towards Clay Cross; after ½ mile turn left signed Stainsby and Hardwick Hall (ignore any further sign for Hardwick Hall); at Stainsby follow rd to left; after 2½ miles staggered rd junction, turn left

Owned by the National Trust, this busy 17th-c golden stone lodge is a particularly handy stop, being so close to the M1. Very generous helpings of popular bar food are served all day and might include soup (£1.50), sandwiches (from £2.50), ploughman's (from £4.20), lincolnshire sausage with egg (£4.50), home-made steak and kidney pie (£5.35), and daily specials such as wild mushroom lasagne or rabbit and cider casserole (£5.75), and poached halibut with lobster sauce (£6.95); children's menu (from £2.60), and afternoon teas (from £2.85). The carvery restaurant is no smoking. Its separate rooms have a relaxed homely atmosphere and stone-mullioned latticed windows – the most comfortable is the carpeted lounge with its upholstered wall settles, tub chairs and stools around varnished wooden tables; one room has an attractive 18th-c carved settle. Well kept Courage Directors, Morlands Old Speckled Hen, Ruddles County and Theakstons XB and Old Peculier on handpump, and over 115 malt whiskies. Tables in the garden offer a very nice view. The pub can get crowded, especially at weekends. *(Recommended by Jason Caulkin, John and Christine Lowe, Piotr Chodzko-Zajko, IHR, W W Burke, M A Buchanan, JP, PP, Darly Graton, Graeme Gulibert, George Little, Jack Morley, David and Gilly Wilkins, Ann and Bob Westbrook, Peter and Anne Hollinsdale, Martin, Jane and Laura Bailey, Don and Shirley Parrish, R M Macnaughton, O K Smyth, Jim Bush, David Carr, Richard Cole)*

Free house ~ Licensees Peter and Pauline Batty ~ Real ale ~ Bar food (11.30-9.30; 12-9 Sun) ~ Restaurant ~ (01246) 850245 ~ Children in eating area of bar and restaurant ~ Open 11.30-11; 12-10.30 Sun

HOGNASTON SK2350 Map 7

Red Lion

Village signposted off B5035 Ashbourne—Wirksworth

This friendly and welcoming open-plan oak-beamed dining pub has a good relaxed atmosphere and helpful attentive staff. There is an attractive mix of old tables (candlelit at night) on its ancient flagstones, with old-fashioned settles among other seats, and no less than three open fires. Among the bric-a-brac is a growing collection of teddy bears; dominoes, piped music. Good well presented food includes home-made soup (£2.95), home-made smoked salmon pâté (£3.95), filled baguettes (from £4.95), Thai chicken curry, fresh salmon and caper fishcakes or layers of puff pastry filled with cream cheese, spinach and oyster mushrooms on a creamy tarragon sauce (£8.95), medallions of pork in an apple and calvados sauce (£10.95), glazed duck breast with a rich plum sauce and Chinese pancake (£11.50), and steak or boeuf en croûte with a madeira and wild mushroom sauce (£11.95); booking is recommended for weekends. Despite the emphasis on food (with almost a bistro feel around the dining tables), this is still very much a pub where locals drop in for a drink, with well kept Marstons Pedigree, Morlands Old Speckled Hen and a guest on handpump; country wines. Handy for Carsington Reservoir. *(Recommended by Geoffrey and Karen Berrill, Mrs J Hinsliff, JDM, KM)*

Free house ~ Licensee Pip Price ~ Real ale ~ Bar food ~ (01335) 370396 ~ No children after 8pm ~ Open 12-3, 6-11; 12-3, 7-10.30 Sun; closed Mon lunchtime ~ Bedrooms: £45S/£75S

HOPE SK1783 Map 7

Cheshire Cheese 🛏

Edale Road – off A625 at W end of village

According to some readers, it's the attention to detail paid by the friendly licensees (he used to be an Aston Villa footballer) which perpetuates the popularity of this very friendly 16th-c village pub, set in fine walking country in the heart of the Peak

District. Three very snug oak-beamed rooms, up and down steps and divided by thick stone walls, are particularly cosy in cool weather as each has its own coal fire. The prices of the very tasty home-cooked bar food have changed little since last year with dishes including good soup (£2.25), lunchtime sandwiches (from £3), yorkshire puddings filled with vegetables or beef gravy (£4.95), ploughman's (£5.55), scampi or liver and bacon (£5.95), gammon or mixed grill (£7.95), and 8oz sirloin (£10.95); there are weekly deliveries of fresh haddock and cod, and in season, game dishes – often courtesy of the chef's own marksmanship – such as rabbit pie, pheasant casserole and jugged hare (£6.95-£9.95); puddings include apple pie or ginger pudding (£3); Sunday lunch (£6.95). The lower dining room is no smoking. Service is particularly efficient and cheerful, even when it gets busy, although parking can be a problem at such times. Well kept Wards Best and a couple of guests such as Black Sheep and Thwaites on handpump, a good choice of house wines and malt whiskies; beautifully furnished bedrooms. Guided walks are arranged from the pub in autumn and winter. *(Recommended by JP, PP, David Carr, Don and Shirley Parrish, M G Hart, Antonia Weeks, Christopher Turner, C J Fletcher, Audrey Preston, Graham Parker, Lawrence Bacon, Jean Scott, Richard Medhurst, Stephen and Tracey Groves)*

Free house ~ Licensees Mandy and Peter Eustace ~ Real ale ~ Bar food ~ (01433) 620381 ~ Children welcome ~ Open 12-3, 6.30-11; 12-11 Sat; 12-4, 6.30-10.30 Sun; closed winter Sun evening, all day Mon ~ Bedrooms: /£50S

KINGS NEWTON SK3826 Map 7
Hardinge Arms

5 miles from M1 junction 23A; follow signs to E Midlands airport; A453, in 3 miles (Isley) turn right signed Melbourne, Wilson; right turn in 2 miles to Kings Newton; pub is on left at end of village

As we went to press, Bass had just bought this attractive old inn from Whitbreads, and a new licensee was in the process of re-writing menus and reviewing real ales. Although no concrete decisions had been made, he planned to keep the fresh fish board – so popular with readers in the past – which lists four or five dishes a day, the well liked carvery and the two dozen or so puddings displayed in a cold counter. The French chef remains, and a new basic bar food menu (all prices are approximate), might include sandwiches (from £1.90), filled potatoes (from £5.25), and favourites such as fish and chips, lasagne or steak and kidney pie (all £6.50). The outgoing Whitbread beers will be replaced with Bass ales and a guest like Marstons Pedigree; several malt whiskies. No changes were intended for the friendly cosy rambling front bar with open fires, beams, a fine panelled and carved bar counter, and blue plush cushioned seats and stools – some in a pleasantly big bow window. The pub's frontage will undergo the inevitable brewery sign and advertising changes. There's a stately and spacious lounge at the back; very good service; piped music. The accommodation is in three chalets opposite the pub, and plans were under way to construct another by November. *(Recommended by Theo, Anne and Jane Gaskin, Ted George, B Adams)*

Free house ~ Licensee Mr Male ~ Real ale ~ Bar food ~ (01332) 863808 ~ Children in eating area of bar ~ Open 11-2.30. 6-11; 12-10.30 Sun ~ Bedrooms: £37B/£50B

KIRK IRETON SK2650 Map 7
Barley Mow ◖ ⇌

Village signed off B5023 S of Wirksworth

This tall gabled Jacobean building, with dimly lit passageways and narrow stairwells, has probably changed little since it first became an inn 200 years ago. The relaxing small main bar has a timeless pubby atmosphere: there are antique settles on the tiled floor or built into the panelling, a coal fire, a slate-topped table and shuttered mullioned windows. Hook Norton Best and Old Hooky, Marstons Pedigree and three or four guests from brewers such as Black Sheep, Burton Bridge, Cottage, Eccleshall and Leatherbritches are kept in their casks behind a modest wooden counter – refreshingly cheap; farm ciders. Another room has built-in cushioned pews on oak parquet flooring and a small woodburner, and a third has more pews, tiled floor, beams and joists, and big landscape prints. One room is no smoking. Popular inexpensive filled lunchtime rolls; good value imaginative evening meals for residents only. Civilised old-fashioned service, a couple of friendly pugs and a good-natured newfoundland. There's a good-sized garden, as well as a couple of benches out in front. The charming village is in good walking country. *(Recommended by Steve Whalley, David Hawkes, Dave and Deborah Irving, Mrs M A Stevenson, JP, PP, G Wheeler, Pete Baker, the Didler, Anthony Barnes, Steve Riches)*

Free house ~ Licensee Mary Short ~ Real ale ~ (01335) 370306 ~ Children at lunchtime, not in bar ~ Open 12-2, 7-11; 12-2, 7-10.30 Sun; closed 25 Dec, 1 Jan ~ Bedrooms: £25B/£45B

LADYBOWER RESERVOIR SK1986 Map 7
Yorkshire Bridge 🛏
A6013 N of Bamford

Bustling roadside hotel with a cheery atmosphere, attractively situated near the Ladybower, Derwent and Howden reservoirs immortalised by the WWII Dambusters. Popular bar food (you need to arrive early in summer) includes generous helpings of soup (£2.30), lunchtime sandwiches (from £2.75), filled baked potatoes (£2.95), ploughman's (£5.75), cracked wheat and walnut casserole (£5.95), very tasty steak and kidney pie or roast chicken breast (£6.25), filled yorkshire pudding (£6.50) and puddings like banana split and toffee apple pie (£2.75). Well kept Bass, Stones and Theakstons Best and Old Peculier on handpump, and good coffee with real cream; friendly efficient service. Floral wallpaper gives the rooms a cottagey feel. One area has sturdy cushioned wall settles, Staffordshire dogs and toby jugs on a big stone fireplace with a warm coal-effect gas fire, china on delft shelves, a panelled dado and so forth. Another extensive area with a fire is lighter and more airy, with pale wooden furniture, good big black and white photographs and lots of plates on the walls. All three dining rooms are no smoking: the new Bridge Room with coal-effect fire and oak tables and chairs, has created space for another forty diners, the small no-smoking conservatory has wicker chairs, and there are pleasant views across a valley to steep larch woods from the no-smoking Garden Room. Darts, cribbage, dominoes, fruit machine, and piped music; prettily decorated bedrooms, disabled lavatories. There are lots of pleasant walks nearby. *(Recommended by G Washington, N P Hodgson, Mr and Mrs G Turner, Norma and Keith Bloomfield, Darly Graton, Graeme Gulibert, David Carr, Pat and Tony Young, Ewan and Moira McCall, Eddie Edwards, Carol and Steve Spence)*

Free house ~ Licensee Trevelyan Illingworth ~ Real ale ~ Bar food ~ Restaurant ~ (01433) 651361 ~ Children in eating area of bar ~ Open 11-11; 12-10.30 Sun ~ Bedrooms: £40B/£60B

LITTLE HUCKLOW SK1678 Map 7
Old Bulls Head
Pub signposted from B6049

For years, a shaft in the cellar of this unspoilt friendly little country pub led down to a mine where the landlord would work during the day, while his wife took care of the pub. One day, an explosion in the shaft blew off a piece of the cellar roof to create the unusual little 'cave' room at the back of the pub. Two neatly kept main rooms have old oak beams, thickly cushioned built-in settles, antique brass and iron household tools, local photographs, and a coal fire in a neatly restored stone hearth. One room is served from a hatch, the other over a polished bar counter. Tasty bar food in generous helpings might include home-made vegetable soup (£2.25), hearty sandwiches including roast of the day (from £2.85, baguettes from £3.75), scampi, steak and kidney pie or vegetable lasagne (£6.25), seasonal salads (from £6.50), chicken with leek and stilton (£8.95), barnsley chop (£9.95), sirloin steak (£11.95), mixed grill (£12.95) and puddings like treacle sponge or fruit crumble (from £2.50); welcoming staff. Well kept John Smiths Magnet, Tetleys and Wards from carved handpumps, and several malt whiskies; darts, dominoes. There are tables in the neatly tended garden, which has lovely views over to the Peak District and is full of an unusual collection of well restored and attractively painted old farm machinery. Newly refurbished bedrooms with bathrooms. *(Recommended by JP, PP, David Hoult, R H Rowley, Jo and Richard Bamford, Bill and Kathy Cissna, Robin Smith, Stephen, Julie and Hayley Brown, George Atkinson)*

Free house ~ Licensee Julie Denton ~ Real ale ~ Bar food ~ (01298) 871097 ~ Children in eating area of bar ~ Open 12-3, 6(6.30 Sat)-11; 12-3, 6.30-10.30 Sun ~ Bedrooms: £35S/£50S

MELBOURNE SK3427 Map 7
John Thompson ♟

NW of village; turn off A514 at Swarkestone Bridge or in Stanton by Bridge; can also be reached from Ticknall (or from Repton on B5008)

The splendid own-brewed real ales – JTS, Summer Gold and winter Porter – are the real draw to this enthusiastically run enjoyable pub in a lovely setting above the River Trent; they are attractively priced, too. The big, pleasantly modernised lounge has ceiling joists, some old oak settles, button-back leather seats, sturdy oak tables, antique prints and paintings, and a log-effect gas fire; a couple of smaller cosier rooms open off, with pool, a fruit machine, video game, and a juke box in the children's room, and a no-smoking area in the lounge; piped music. Popular straightforward but good bar food is well priced and consists of sandwiches or rolls (from £1.30, nothing else on Sundays; the beef is excellent), home-made soup (£1.50), salads with cold ham or beef (£4), excellent roast beef with yorkshire puddings (£5, not Mondays) and well liked puddings such as bread and butter pudding or fruit crumble (£2). There are lots of tables by flowerbeds on the well kept lawns, and on a partly covered outside terrace with its own serving bar. *(Recommended by Ted George, Paul Robinshaw, Colin Buckle, JP, PP, Ian Phillips, JDM, KM, J and P Halfyard, Peter and Audrey Dowsett)*

Own brew ~ Licensee John Thompson ~ Real ale ~ Bar food (lunchtime) ~ (01332) 862469 ~ Children in garden and children's room ~ Open 10.30-2.30, 7-11; 12-2.30, 7-10.30 Sun

MONSAL HEAD Map 7
Monsal Head Hotel

B6465

This extended Victorian hotel, often full at weekends, offers dramatic views down over Monsal Dale from four of its eight bedrooms. The cosy side stable bar (which once housed the hapless horses that lugged people and their luggage up from the station deep down at the end of the valley viaduct) still has a bit of a horsey theme, with stripped timber horse-stalls, harness and brassware, as well as flagstones, a big warming woodburning stove in an inglenook, cushioned oak pews around tables, farm tools, and railway signs and lamps from the local disused station. Unpretentious very good bar food from seasonal menus might include soup (£2.20), sandwiches (from £2.75), salad niçoise (£4.75), steak and ale pie or wild mushroom pancakes (£5.95), lamb in honey and mint (£6.25), chicken fillet stuffed with goat's cheese in a sun-dried tomato sauce (£6.75), duo of salmon and sole (£7.25), rib-eye steak (£8.95) and an extensive choice of daily specials such as derbyshire oat cakes with sweet and sour sauce (£5.95), venison steak (£8.95) and chargrilled john dury (£9.95), Sunday roast (£5.95); more elaborate restaurant menu. Well kept Courage Directors, Hartington Bitter, Marstons Pedigree, Monsal Best Bitter, Theakstons Best and Old Peculier, and two guest beers such as Jennings Bitter and Coniston Bluebird on handpump, a very good choice of bottled German beers, and sensibly priced wines; friendly, helpful service. The boundary of the parishes of Little Longstone and Ashford run through the hotel – hence the spacious restaurant and bar (with fires at each end of the room), and smaller dining room are named according to which side of the line they fall on; beer garden. *(Recommended by Joy and Peter Heatherley, Mr M*

Joyner, P and M Rudlin, Hilary Dobbie, Dave and Deborah Irving, Phil and Heidi Cook, Paul and Sandra Embleton, Robert and Claire Andreoli, Paul and Maggie Baker, JP, PP, Dave Braisted, Kevin and Amanda Earl)

Free house ~ Licensees Christine O'Connell and Philip Smith ~ Real ale ~ Bar food (12-9.30pm) ~ Restaurant ~ (01629) 640250 ~ Children in eating area of bar and restaurant ~ Folk music alternate Fri eves and Sun afternoons ~ Open 10.30-11.30; 10.30-11 Sun; closed 25 Dec ~ Bedrooms: £40.55B/£45.60B

OVER HADDON SK2066 Map 7
Lathkil 🛏

Village and inn signposted from B5055 just SW of Bakewell

Comfortable hotel which makes the most of the stunning views at its location – the little hillside hamlet of Over Haddon, possibly Derbyshire's best situated village. Steeply down below is Lathkil Dale, one of the quieter dales, with an exceptionally harmonious spread of pastures and copses and plenty to interest the nature lover; paths from the village lead straight into this tempting landscape. Walkers will find a place for their muddy boots in the pub's lobby, and further in, some good civilised comforts. The airy room on the right has a warming fire in the attractively carved fireplace, old-fashioned settles with upholstered cushions or plain wooden chairs, black beams, a delft shelf of blue and white plates on one white wall, original prints and photographs, and big windows. On the left is the spacious and sunny family dining area – partly no smoking – which doubles as a restaurant in the evenings; it's not quite as pubby as the bar, but there isn't a problem with shorts or walking gear. At lunchtime the bar food is served here from a buffet and includes home-made soup (£2), salads (from £5), a vegetarian dish such as vegetable cheesy crumble bake (£5.50), lasagne or steak and kidney pie (£5.90), beef and peppercorn casserole (£5.95), venison, madeira and cranberry pie (£6.20) and a good range of tasty puddings like chocolate torte and strawberry and apple crumble (£2.50). As we went to press, Mr Grigor-Taylor was having to review his choice of ales due to changes at Wards brewery, but he was fairly certain that Timothy Taylor Landlord, Whim Hartington and a guest such as Marstons Pedigree on handpump would be offered in the future (samples of ales are offered in sherry glasses); select malt whiskies and a good range of new world wines; piped music, darts, bar billiards, shove-ha'penny, backgammon, dominoes, cribbage. It does get very busy so it's best to get here early in good weather. *(Recommended by Michael Sargent, JDM, KM, Richard Cole, Nigel Woolliscroft, M Joyner, Tim and Beryl Dawson, TBB, Richard W Marjoram, Carol and Steve Spence, Roger and Christine Mash, JP, PP, Mrs M A Stevenson)*

Free house ~ Licensee Robert Grigor-Taylor ~ Real ale ~ Bar food ~ Restaurant ~ (01629) 812501 ~ Children in eating area of bar and restaurant ~ Open 11.30-4(3 winter), 6.30(7 winter)-11; 11.30-11 Sat; 12-10.30 Sun; closed wknd lunchtimes winter ~ Bedrooms: /£70B

SHARDLOW SK4330 Map 7
Old Crown 🍺

Cavendish Bridge, off old A6 at Trent Bridge, actually just over Leics boundary

The bar at this friendly thriving 17th-c village pub is packed with bric-a-brac, including hundreds of jugs and mugs hanging from the beamed ceiling, brewery and railway memorabilia, and pictures and old brewery adverts covering the walls – even in the lavatories. Well kept real ales might include Bass, Burton Bridge Derby Triumph, Fullers London Pride, Marstons Pedigree, Shardlow Narrowboat and with the forthcoming birth of another grandchild of the landlord, a beer brewed for the pub such as last year's Taps Best Tipple; there's a nice choice of malt whiskies. If you fancy more than a sandwich (from £1.85), the very tasty popular home-made daily specials include beef, celery, mushroom and stilton pie or pan-fried liver with onions and bacon (£5.95), crespellini (pancakes filled with smoked haddock and spinach, topped with cheese sauce, £6.50), lamb chops with spring vegetables casseroled in ale (£6.75), fish pie or leg of pork stuffed with chopped liver, sausage meat, bacon and apples (£6.95) and rump steak (£7.50); shove-ha'penny, cribbage, dominoes and piped music. The pub is next to the River Trent and was once the deportation point for convicts bound for the colonies; handy for A6 and M1 J24. *(Recommended by JP, PP, Sue Holland, Dave Webster, John Fahy, M A Buchanan, Henry Paulinski, B T Smith, JDM, KM, Chris Raisin, Dr and Mrs B Baker, the Didler, Norma and Keith Bloomfield, B A Lord, John Robertson, Kevin Blake, R Inman, Michael Butler, Alistair Forsyth)*

Free house ~ Licensees Peter and Gillian Morton-Harrison ~ Real ale ~ Bar food ~ (01132) 792392 ~ Children in eating area of bar at lunchtime only ~ Open 11.30-3.30, 5-11; 12-5, 7-10.30 Sun; closed evenings 25/26 Dec

WARDLOW SK1875 Map 7
Three Stags Heads 🍺
Wardlow Mires; A623 by junction with B6465

This unspoilt little stone cottage is part of a dying breed of genuinely traditional pubs, and as such, is not for the faint-hearted. The readers who love the smoky fires, basic furnishings, very well kept beers and ample helpings of well cooked home-made food, are also those not offended by the sight of the odd dead hare on the bar, dogs taking a hopeful interest in your meal, or even the plain speaking of landlord Geoff Fuller. The tiny unassuming flagstoned parlour bar, warmed right through the winter by a cast-iron kitchen range, has old leathercloth seats, a couple of antique settles with flowery cushions, two high-backed windsor armchairs and simple oak tables – one curiosity is the petrified cat in a glass case; other antiques look elderly rather than venerable. The low-priced well kept beer here is pretty no-nonsense too, with Abbeydale Black Lurcher (brewed for the pub) at ABV 8%, Matins and Springhead, and a guest like Abbeydale Last Rites at ABV 10.5% on handpump, as well as lots of bottled continental and English beers. You can book the tables in the small no-smoking dining parlour with open fire. They try to vary the seasonal menu to suit the weather so dishes served on their hardy home-made plates (the barn is a pottery workshop) might include spinach and chickpea curry or tortelloni with tomato sauce (£6), popular lamb and spinach curry (£6.50), steak and kidney pie (£7), seasonal game such as woodpigeon breasts on toast (£5.50) or hare casserole (£8.50), and fillet steak (£12.50); the pub also does a roaring trade in mugs of tea. Cribbage and dominoes, nine men's morris and backgammon. Its damp location in a natural sink, and its popularity with walkers, mean that in wet weather, you can expect to find muddy floors and sopping dogs hogging the fire. The front terrace looks across the main road to the distant hills. The pub only opens on weekday evenings in high summer or when there's sufficient demand, so it's best to phone before visiting. *(Recommended by Nigel Woolliscroft, David Carr, Pete Baker, JP, PP, the Didler, Sue Holland, Dave Webster, Mrs J Hinsliff, Patrick Hancock)*

Free house ~ Licensees Geoff and Pat Fuller ~ Real ale ~ Bar food ~ (01298) 872268 ~ Children welcome away from bar room till 8.30pm ~ Folk music most Sat evenings ~ Open 7-11; 12-11 Sat; 12-10.30 Sun; closed Mon except bank holidays

WHITTINGTON MOOR SK3873 Map 7
Derby Tup 🍺 £
387 Sheffield Rd; B6057 just S of A61 roundabout

This unchanged corner house is a throwback to an earlier era of town pubs. The plain but sizeable rectangular bar, with frosted street windows and old dark brown linoleum, has simple furniture arranged around the walls (there's a tremendously long red plastic banquette) leaving lots of standing room. There are two more small no-smoking rooms; daily papers, possibly piped rock and blues, darts, dominoes and cribbage. An impressive ten real ales are kept on handpump, with regulars like Adnams Extra, Black Sheep Bitter, Greene King Abbot, Marstons Pedigree and Whim Hartington and five quickly changing guest beers such as Archers Golden, Fullers London Pride, Rudgate Ruby Mild, Timothy Taylor Landlord and Youngs Special. They also have lots of continental and bottle-conditioned beers and decent malt whiskies. Besides good sandwiches made with fresh bread from the neighbouring bakery (from £1.65), the daily changing bar food might include leek and sweetcorn soup (£2), corned beef hash (£3.60), vegetable chow mein (£3.95), liver and smoked-bacon casserole (£4), sweet chilli pork (£4.25), Thai minted lamb and home made pies (£4.50). Despite the remote-sounding name, Whittington Moor is on the northern edge of Chesterfield. It can get very busy on weekend evenings. *(Recommended by ALC, JP, PP, the Didler, David Carr)*

Free house ~ Licensee Peter Hayes ~ Real ale ~ Bar food (12-2, 5.30-9) ~ (01246) 454316 ~ Children in two side rooms ~ Folk/Blues most Thurs evenings ~ Open Mon/Tues 11.30-3, 5-11, Weds-Sat 11.30-11; 12-4, 7-10.30 Sun

WOOLLEY MOOR SK3661 Map 7
White Horse 🍺

Badger Lane, off B6014 Matlock—Clay Cross

There's a good balance between the dining areas and original tap room in this attractive, bustling old pub, very well run by friendly enthusiastic licensees: the former areas serve very good food (which readers continue to praise), while in the latter, cheerful locals gather to organise their various teams – darts, dominoes, and two each for football and boules (they have their own pitch and piste); cribbage. The bar food is prepared with fresh local produce and includes soup (£1.95), sandwiches (from £2.95), steak and kidney pie or ploughman's (£4.50), as well as several imaginative daily changing specials such as vegetable quiche of the day (£4.50), chicken, sage and wild mushroom pie (£5.95), honey-roasted pork butterflies (£6.75), lamb, cashew nut and apricot casserole (£6.95), salmon lasagne (£7.25), and puddings such as marmalade bread and butter pudding or blackberry and apple crumble (£2.30); good children's meals (£2) come with a puzzle sheet and crayons. Well kept Bass and four weekly changing guests on handpump such as Belvoir Star, Jennings Cocker Hoop and Snecklifter and Shepherd Neame Early Bird and a decent wine list. There is piped classical music in the lounge, and the new conservatory (no smoking, like the restaurant), looks over to nearby Ogston reservoir. Picnic-sets in the garden have lovely views across the Amber Valley, and there's a very good children's play area with wooden play train, climbing frame and swings. A booklet describes eight walks from the pub, and the landlord is a keen walker. *(Recommended by M A Buchanan, Darly Graton, Graeme Gulibert, JP, PP, Paul and Sandra Embleton, Jim Bush, Andy and Jill Kassube, Keith and Margaret Kettwell, John and Christine Lowe, JDM, KM, Mike and Mary Carter, Joy and Peter Heatherley, K and J Brooks, Geoffrey and Irene Lindley, Derek and Sylvia Stephenson, Don and Shirley Parrish, IHR)*

Free house ~ Licensees Bill and Jill Taylor ~ Real ale ~ Bar food (11.30-2, 6-9; 12-8.30 Sun) ~ Restaurant ~ (01246) 590319 ~ Children in eating area of bar and restaurant ~ Open 11.30-2.30, 6-11; 12-10.30 Sun; closed evening 25 and all day 26 Dec

Lucky Dip

Besides the fully inspected pubs, you might like to try these Lucky Dips recommended to us and described by readers (if you do, please send us reports):

Apperknowle [SK3878]
Yellow Lion [High St]: Welcoming 19th-c stonebuilt village local, comfortable banquettes in L-shaped lounge with TV, old organ, brass lamps, fruit machine, no-smoking dining room, wide choice of good value food from sandwiches and toasties up inc vegetarian, five real ales, good choice of wines by glass, caring licensees, garden with play area; Weds quiz night; children welcome, cheap bedrooms *(JP, PP, CMW, JJW)*
Ashbourne [SK1846]
White Hart [Church St]: Clean and comfortable, with friendly obliging staff, three well kept ales,

good value food in good-sized helpings *(John Foord)*
Ashford in the Water [SK1969]
☆ *Bulls Head*: Cosy and homely comfortable lounge, well kept Robinsons Best, enjoyable fresh home-made food from good soup and sandwiches up, reasonable prices, friendly service, no piped music; tables out in front *(Bill and Steph Brownson, JP, PP, David and Mary Webb, IHR, Rita and Keith Pollard, Peter F Marshall, Jeremy Burnside)*
Bakewell [SK2168]
Peacock [Market Pl]: Clean, bright and cheerful,

well kept Wards, interesting choice of good popular food (not Mon-Weds evenings), good prices and service *(Mrs C Dale, Darly Graton, Graeme Gulibert)*

Barlborough [SK4878]
Rose & Crown [handy for M1 junction 30]: Extended village pub with elegant dining room, lots of crimson plush, generous fair-priced food inc children's, Hardys & Hansons Bitter and Crowing Cock, good choice of soft drinks and wine; pool in games room, piped music, no dogs; picnic-sets and play area in side garden, rustic benches facing Norman cross in front *(CMW, JJW)*

Barlow [SK3474]
Peacock: Comfortable lounge and bars, views down valley, well kept Mansfield ales, good value food inc well filled rolls, friendly staff; bedrooms, good walks *(Richard Burton)*

Baslow [SK2572]
Cavendish [Church Lane]: Delightful upmarket hotel with very good interesting bar food in pleasant Garden Room with magnificent views over Chatsworth estate, comfortable lounge; bedrooms *(Mr and Mrs G R A Lomas)*
Robin Hood [just off A619]: Fairly modern, well decorated and comfortable, with tidy banquettes, soft piped music, well kept Mansfield ales, good reasonably priced food, brisk friendly service; big back uncarpeted bar for walkers and climbers (boots and dogs welcome); bedrooms, good walking country nr Baslow Edge *(James Nunns, Julia Cooper, Michael A Butler)*
Wheatsheaf: Reliable food inc good home-made meat pies *(John Wooll)*

Bonsall [SK2858]
Barley Mow [off A6012 Cromford—Hartington]: Friendly nicely furnished pub of character, with particularly well kept Whim and a guest beer, good if not cheap food made freshly – service can slow when busy, with no queue-jumping for simple dishes such as sandwiches; has cl weekday lunchtimes (may open Fri by arrangement) *(JP, PP, Derek and Sylvia Stephenson, Mrs J Hinsliff, the Didler)*

Bradley [SK2346]
Fox & Hounds [Belper Rd (A517)]: Lounge with lots of bric-a-brac and darts corner, Marstons Pedigree and occasional guest beers, fresh food, other rooms inc family room with pool and video games, garden with play area, duck pond, even peacock; dogs and children welcome, walks nearby *(CMW, JJW)*

Bradwell [SK1781]
Valley Lodge [B6049 S of Hope]: Half a dozen well kept changing ales in surprisingly red brick pub with foyer bar, comfortable lounge, big public bar with darts and pool, weekend food, friendly staff, seats outside; cl weekday lunchtimes, bedrooms *(JP, PP, Richard Lewis)*

Brassington [SK2354]
☆ *Miners Arms* [off B5035/B5056 NE of Ashbourne]: Very welcoming and pubby, with good choice of good value food from hot pork rolls up, well kept Marstons Pedigree and guest beers, good service, tables out among flower tubs; open all day, children welcome, live music some nights; bedrooms *(Martin and Caroline Page, David Carr)*

Breaston [SK4633]
Bulls Head [Wilsthorpe Rd (A6005)]: Open-plan Marstons Tavern Table dining pub with reliable food inc vegetarian and children's, swift friendly service, very low-beamed core, relaxed areas away from dining part (which is largely no smoking); good atmosphere *(Mike and Penny Sanders)*

Calver [SK2474]
Bridge [off A623 N of Baslow]: Cosy and clean unpretentious local, quick good value food, particularly well kept Hardys & Hansons Best and Classic, coal fire, pleasant landlord, old brass and local prints; tables in nice big garden by River Derwent *(David Shillitoe, JP, PP, Vann and Terry Prime, M Joyner, DC, Sue Holland, Dave Webster)*

Castleton [SK1583]
George [Castle St]: Good atmosphere and good value simple food, two roomy bars, one mainly for eating, with beams and stripped stone, friendly helpful staff, well kept Bass and Stones; tables on wide forecourt, lots of flower tubs; popular with young people – nr YHA; dogs welcome *(JP, PP, K Stevens, Jeremy Burnside, David Carr, Gill and Maurice McMahon)*
Olde Cheshire Cheese: Two communicating beamed areas, cosy and spotless, lots of photographs, cheery landlord, well kept Marstons Pedigree and Wards Waggle Dance tapped from the cask, friendly staff, wide choice of reasonably priced food, open fire, sensibly placed darts; bedrooms *(George Atkinson, BB)*
☆ *Olde Nags Head* [Cross St (A625)]: Small but solid hotel dating from 17th c, quiet and relaxed, with interesting antique furnishings in civilised turkey-carpeted main bar, coal fire, faint piped music, friendly staff, well kept Marstons Pedigree, good coffee, impressive bar food from sandwiches up inc vegetarian dishes, cosy Victorian restaurant; open all day, comfortable bedrooms *(Les Rowlands, Jeremy Burnside, Justin Hulford, Dr R Rowland, Stephen and Tracey Groves, JP, PP, LYM)*
Peak [How Lane, off A625]: Airy lounge, leather wall seats in smaller bar, dining room with high ceiling and picture-window hill view, wide choice of reasonably priced food inc vegetarian, huge helpings, well kept Marstons Pedigree, Richardsons Four Seasons and Tetleys, friendly service; bedrooms – a friendly place to stay *(Colin Roberts, Justin Hulford)*

Chesterfield [SK3871]
☆ *Royal Oak* [Chatsworth Rd]: Friendly pub, always a good atmosphere, fine choice of well kept beers, enthusiastic young landlord *(JP, PP)*

Chunal [SK0391]
☆ *Grouse* [A624 a mile S of Glossop]: Pleasant open-plan but cosy moorland pub, good generous food esp home-made pies, also lunchtime and early evening OAP bargains, good chips and interesting specials; well kept Thwaites, friendly service, spectacular views of Glossop, real fires, old photographs of surrounding countryside, traditional furnishings and candlelit tables; unobtrusive piped music, quiz night Thurs; children allowed in upstairs

restaurant *(J F M and M West)*

Church Broughton [SK2033]

Holly Bush [High St; off A50 E of Uttoxeter, via same exit as A511]: Neat and attractive village pub, popular for generous good value home cooking inc Sun lunch; well kept Marstons Pedigree, friendly labradors *(Chris Raisin)*

Crich [SK3554]

Cliff [Cromford Rd, Town End; nr National Tramway Museum]: Cosy two-room pub with real fire, Hardys & Hanson beers, bar food *(JP, PP)*

Cromford [SK2956]

☆ *Boat* [Scarthin, off Mkt Pl]: Spotless 18th-c traditional local in quaint village, long narrow low-beamed bar with stripped stone, bric-a-brac and books, charming service, friendly relaxed atmosphere, well priced inventive food from black pudding to wild boar inc good Sun lunch, log fire, real ales such as Bass, Leatherbritches Bespoke, Morlands Old Speckled Hen, Townes Muffin and one they brew for the pub; TV may be on for sports; children welcome, garden *(Graham Coates, John Foord, JP, PP)*

Crowdecote [SK1065]

Packhorse: 16th-c pub doing well under pleasant new licensees, good food from sandwiches up, Boddingtons and Ind Coope Burton, two refurbished bars and dining room, tables in back garden by shetland ponies, beautiful views; on popular walking route *(Doug Christian)*

Dale [SK4339]

☆ *Carpenters Arms* [Dale Abbey, off A6096 NE of Derby]: Ivy-clad pub with panelling, low beams, country prints, well kept Ansells, Black Sheep, Ind Coope Burton and Marstons Pedigree, good value food in bar, lounge (no dogs here) and restaurant, real fire, family room, darts, fruit machine; garden with play area (camping ground behind), good walking country – popular with walkers, can get very busy; pleasant village with Abbey ruins and unusual church attached to house *(John Beeken, JP, PP)*

Derby [SK3438]

☆ *Abbey Inn* [Darley St, Darley Abbey]: Interesting for including massive stonework remnants of 11th-c abbey; brick floor, studded oak doors, big stone inglenook, stone spiral stair to upper bar with handsome oak rafters; well kept cheap Sam Smiths, decent lunchtime bar food, children allowed; opp Derwent-side park, pleasant riverside walk out from centre *(JP, PP, LYM, Jeremy Burnside)*

Blessington Carriage [Chapel St]: Friendly town pub, long bar with well kept Courage Directors, Marstons Pedigree, Ruddles County, John Smiths and Theakstons Best and XB, popular freshly cooked food lunchtime and Tues evening, lots of memorabilia, walls panelled with old doors; children in eating area, big-screen TV, CD juke box, tables outside; open all day (cl Sun afternoon) *(SLC)*

Exeter Arms [Exeter Pl]: Super little snug with black-leaded and polished brass range, black and white tiled floor, two built-in curved settles, lots of wood and bare brick, HMS *Exeter* memorabilia; friendly staff, four well kept Marstons beers and a guest such as Whim,

lunchtime food, daily papers, well reproduced piped music *(Chris Raisin, Richard Lewis)*

☆ *Flowerpot* [King St]: Extended real-ale pub with excellent changing choice of well kept beers tapped from the cask – a dozen or more at a time, and regular beer festivals; friendly staff, comfortable back bar with lots of books and old Derby photographs, pub games, some good live bands; open all day, tables on terrace *(Richard Lewis, David Carr, SLC, Chris Raisin)*

Foal & Firkin [Morledge]: Popular Firkin, usual style, open all day for typical Firkin beers kept well, Addlestone's cider, friendly staff, reasonably priced food *(Richard Lewis)*

Friargate [Friargate]: Comfortable and relaxing, part carpeted, light green decor, heavily panelled central bar, bar food inc all-day rolls, good choice of well kept ales (some tapped from the cask), friendly landlady, disabled facilities; open all day; same ownership as Flower Pot *(Richard Lewis)*

New Zealand Arms [Peet St/Langley St; via Surrey St, off A52 N of centre]: Nicely refurbished corner pub, mix of furniture on bare boards, daily papers, several well kept changing ales, good lunchtime food (not Mon) inc huge sausage sandwiches; bar billiards, darts *(Chris Raisin)*

Old Silk Mill [Full St]: Good range of well kept beers such as Bass Museum Worthington and Offilers Mild, Boddingtons, Burton Bridge, Fullers London Pride and Marstons Pedigree, cheap sandwiches and basic hot dishes, life-size mural; open all day (may be cl Sun afternoon) *(SLC, Richard Lewis)*

Olde Spa [Abbey St]: Relaxed and sympathetically restored old local, well kept Marstons, tiled-floor bar, open fire, games room, garden with fountain *(Chris Raisin)*

Rowditch [Uttoxeter New Rd (A516)]: Well kept Mansfield Riding and Old Baily, Marstons Pedigree and guest beers, attractive small snug on right, quiz and food nights *(the Didler)*

Royal Standard [Exeter Pl/Derwent St]: Pleasant corner pub with up to six real ales such as Mansfield Bitter, Riding Mild and Old Baily, Marstons Pedigree, Morlands Old Speckled Hen and Woodfordes Wherry, lunchtime food; piped music *(SLC)*

Smithfield [Meadow Rd]: Friendly bow-fronted pub with big bar, two smaller rooms, up to a dozen very well kept changing ales such as Archers Golden, Bass, Enville Ginger Beer, Kelham Island Pale Rider, Marstons Pedigree, Whim Arbor, filled rolls and lunchtime meals, breweriana, pub games inc table skittles; open all day, children welcome, riverside garden; same family as Flower Pot *(Richard Lewis, JP, PP, the Didler, SLC)*

☆ *Standing Order* [Irongate]: Vast Wetherspoons conversion of imposing bank, central bar, booths down each side, elaborately painted plasterwork, pseudo-classical torsos, high portraits of mainly local notables; usual popular food all day, good range of well kept ales, reasonable prices, daily papers, neat efficient young staff, no-smoking area; rather daunting acoustics; disabled facilities

(Richard Lewis, Kevin Blake, JDM, KM, SLC, JP, PP, David Carr, the Didler, BB)

Station [Midland Rd]: Basic pub with good food lunchtime and early evening in bar and back room, Bass in jugs from cellar *(the Didler)*

Wardick [The Morlege]: Early 18th-c town pub recently refurbished as Tetleys Festival Alehouse, raised back lounge, lots of prints, wood and bare brickwork, big open fireplace, friendly staff, bar food, very well kept real ales; open all day *(Richard Lewis)*

Draycott [SK4433]

Coach & Horses: Cosy traditional village pub with extended dining area, friendly staff, good range of generous genuinely home-made food, well kept Marstons Pedigree and a quickly changing guest beer; tables in garden with occasional barbecues *(Gary Siddall)*

Duffield [SK3543]

Bridge [Duffield Bank, across River Derwent; off Holbrook rd]: Big modernised Mansfield family pub in lovely setting by River Derwent, superb play areas indoors (family area not very distinct from bar) and out, usual food, well kept ales, shelves of knick-knacks; riverside terrace *(JDM, KM)*

Pattenmakers Arms [Crown St, off King St]: Tall Victorian backstreet local with Bass and guest beers, piano *(the Didler)*

Edale [SK1285]

Old Nags Head [off A625 E of Chapel-en-le-Frith]: Popular walkers' pub at start of Pennine Way, recently refurbished for more comfort, food from basic hearty sustenance to more interesting dishes, open fire, Scottish Courage and other ales; room for muddy walkers, children in airy back family room, tables on front terrace and in garden – short path down to pretty streamside cottages *(Mrs C Dale, Tim Barrow, Sue Demont, LYM, David Hoult, JP, PP)*

Elton [SK2261]

☆ *Duke of York*: Unspoilt old-fashioned local, like stepping back in time, lovely little quarry-tiled back tap room with coal fire in massive fireplace, glazed bar and hatch to corridor, two front rooms – one like private parlour with dining table (no food, just crisps); Mansfield and occasional guest beer; open 8.30-11, and Sun lunchtime *(the Didler, JP, PP)*

Fenny Bentley [SK1750]

Bentley Brook [A515 N of Ashbourne]: Big open-plan bare-boards bar/dining room, log fire, communicating restaurant, one or two changing own-brewed Leatherbritches ales and several guest beers, marquee for beer festival spring bank hol, usual food (maybe free meals for children eating with adults early evening), well reproduced piped music, busy games machines; picnic-sets on terrace with proper barbecue area, skittles, kitchen shop; open all day, handy for Dovedale; bedrooms *(JP, PP, BB, Brian Abbott)*

Flagg [SK1368]

Plough [off A515 S of Buxton, at Duke of York]: Friendly refurbished local in beautiful Peak District village, lovely countryside; log fire, wide choice of good value food inc beautifully presented sandwiches, good service, separate

relaxed bar with pool, darts and cable TV, restaurant, play area; new bedrooms, camp site *(A M Pring, Miss W Wheeler)*

Foolow [SK2077]

☆ *Barrel* [Bretton, signed from Foolow]: Splendid site on ridge edge, seats on breezy front terrace, five-county views and good walks; cosy beamed bar with snug areas and log fire, sensibly short choice of good generous food from sandwiches up, attractive prices, well kept Black Sheep, Wards and guest beers, restaurant; cl Sun evening *(LYM, IHR, DC, JP, PP)*

Froggatt Edge [SK2577]

Grouse [B6054]: Plush front bar, open fire in back bar, big dining room, good home cooking, Wards beers; verandah and terrace popular with walkers *(L Davenport)*

Great Hucklow [SK1878]

Queen Anne: Comfortable beamed bar with home-cooked food inc fresh veg, well kept beer, good atmosphere, friendly staff, open fire, walkers' bar, small terrace and pleasant garden with lovely views; children welcome, handy for walks; two quiet bedrooms *(Mrs M A Stevenson, JP, PP)*

Hartington [SK1360]

Charles Cotton: Scottish Courage ales, good value food, roaring coal fires; bedrooms *(JP, PP)*

Devonshire Arms: Good choice of tasty food worth the price, well kept beer, good welcoming service even under pressure; bedrooms comfortable *(DC, Robert Gomme, Eric Locker)*

Hartshorne [SK3220]

Bulls Head [Woodville Rd]: Popular for excellent value generous bar food – booking advised; well kept Marstons, lots of beams and genuine bric-a-brac *(Chris Raisin)*

Hassop [SK2272]

☆ *Eyre Arms* [B6001 N of Bakewell]: Cosy 17th-c manorial pub with two unspoilt beamed rooms, grandfather clock, settles, open fires, good adventurous food in small dining area, John Smiths, Marstons Pedigree and an interesting guest beer, piped classical music; Peak views from garden tables, good walks nearby *(JP, PP, David and Ruth Hollands, Peter Johnston, Don and Shirley Parrish)*

Hathersage [SK2381]

☆ *George* [A625 W of Sheffield]: Substantial old inn, recently carefully and comfortably refurbished, with old-fashioned attentive service, good value well presented food from sandwiches with home-baked bread to interesting main dishes, calm atmosphere, well kept Boddingtons, decent wine, neat flagstoned back terrace by rose garden; a nice place to stay (the back bedrooms are the quiet ones) *(A Barker, Mr and Mrs G R A Lomas, LYM)*

Millstone [A625]: Cosy pub with lots of knick-knacks and antiques, many for sale, side brasserie, good bar meals and carvery; good choice of beers, wines and whiskies; tables outside with good views, bedrooms *(Andrew Staton)*

☆ *Plough* [A622 (ex B6001) towards Bakewell]: Beautifully placed ex-farm with Derwentside garden, very welcoming, with good helpings of good fresh varied food inc starters that would do as light main courses in bar and two restaurant areas (ex-butcher landlord), good atmosphere, prompt service even when very busy; well kept Tetleys and Wadworths 6X, good value wines *(Mr and Mrs R Head, IHR, Don and Shirley Parrish, Lesley Bass, A Barker, Mrs C M Smalley)*

☆ *Scotsmans Pack* [School Lane, off A625]: Big clean welcoming open-plan local very popular with walkers, huge choice of generous nicely presented good value food (best to book Sun lunch), reasonable prices, well kept Burtonwood, decent wines, good service; some seats on pleasant side terrace by trout stream; good bedrooms, huge breakfast *(DC, A Barker, Mr and Mrs R Head, Mrs E Haynes)*

Hatton [SK2130]
Kestrel: Hospitable and cosy, with lots of memorabilia, well kept Tetleys-related ales, good value food *(David Shillitoe)*

Hayfield [SK0388]
☆ *Lantern Pike* [A624 N of Hayfield]: Cosily unpretentious and welcoming, with plush seats, lots of brass, china and toby jugs, well kept Boddingtons, Flowers IPA and Timothy Taylor Landlord, good choice of malt whiskies, decent bar food from sandwiches up inc children's and OAP weekday lunches; no-smoking back dining room, darts, dominoes, maybe piped nostalgic music; back terrace looking up to Lantern Pike, great spot for walkers; children welcome, open all day w/e, good value bedrooms *(Martin and Caroline Page, Ewan and Moira McCall, Bill and Kathy Cissna, H K Dyson, Jenny and Roger Huggins, LYM, Stephen and Tracey Groves)*

Holbrook [SK3644]
☆ *Dead Poets* [Chapel St; off A6 S of Belper]: New venture connected to the Brunswick in Derby, with well kept ales from there and three guest beers; beams, settles, scrubbed tables, flagstones, big open fire; folk music every other Sun, bring your own instrument and join in; open all day Fri-Sun *(JP, PP, the Didler)*
Wheel [Chapel St]: Friendly beamed country local with well kept Courage Directors, Marstons Pedigree, Timothy Taylor Landlord and several guest beers maybe in jugs from the cellar, wide choice of good value home cooking, good log fire, cheerful helpful staff, snug, family room and dining room; tables on terrace and in pleasant secluded garden *(the Didler, JP, PP)*

Holmesfield [SK3277]
☆ *Robin Hood* [B6054 towards Hathersage]: Neatly extended moorland pub with wide choice of popular food (all day w/e) from sandwiches to steaks, half helpings for OAPs and children, well kept real ale, smart pleasant staff, good open fires, beams, partly carpeted flagstones, plush banquettes, high-raftered restaurant with big pictures; children in eating areas, piped music, stone tables out on cobbled front courtyard *(LYM, Stan and Hazel Allen)*

Holymoorside [SK3469]
Lamb [Loads Rd, just off Holymoor Rd]: Small cosy two-room village pub in leafy spot, Bass, Home, Theakstons XB and up to four guest beers inc one from Adnams, pub games, tables outside; cl l;unchtime Mon-Thurs *(the Didler, JP,*

PP)
Idridgehay [SK2848]
Black Swan: Attractive building given recent bistro-style makeover, very popular for good food; conservatory extension *(John and Christine Lowe)*

Ilkeston [SK4543]
Bridge [Bridge St, Cotmanhay; off A609/A6007]: Newish landlord in two-room local by Erewash Canal, popular with fishermen and boaters for early breakfast and sandwich lunches; extremely well priced well kept Hardys & Hansons Best and Best Mild; nice back garden with play area, well behaved children allowed, open all day *(the Didler)*
Dewdrop [Station St, Ilkeston Junction, off A6096]: Large three-room Victorian local by rly in old industrial area, friendly staff, good value bar snacks inc huge cheap sandwiches, Ind Coope Burton, Hook Norton Old Hooky, Kelham Island Pale Rider, Wards Kirby and guests, two coal fires, barbecue; cl Sat lunchtime, good value bedrooms *(JP, PP)*

Kniveton [SK1949]
Ketch [B5035 SW]: Former Greyhound, renovated by new licensees; excellent range of good value food inc oriental specialities and bargain lamb leg, well kept Marstons *(Richard and Ann Higgs)*

Little Longstone [SK1971]
☆ *Packhorse* [off A6 NW of Bakewell via Monsal Dale]: Snug 16th-c cottage with old-fashioned country furnishings in two cosy beamed rooms, well kept Marstons Best or Pedigree, decent food, pub games, terrace in steep little garden *(LYM, Mrs M A Stevenson, R H Rowley, JP, PP, David Carr, Jeremy Burnside, Joy and Peter Heatherley)*

Lullington [SK2513]
☆ *Colvile Arms* [Coton Rd; off A444 S of Burton]: Very well kept 18th-c village pub with basic panelled bar, cosy beamed lounge with soft seats and scatter cushions, pleasant atmosphere, friendly staff, piped music, four well kept ales inc Bass, Marstons Pedigree and a Mild, good value filled fresh cobs, picnic-sets on small sheltered back lawn overlooking bowling green; cl weekday lunchtimes *(CMW, JJW, LYM, C J Fletcher, John and Pat Raby)*

Makeney [SK3544]
☆ *Holly Bush* [A6 N, cross river Derwent, before Milford turn right, then left]: Unspoilt two-bar village pub, cosy and friendly, with five well kept ales brought from cellar in jugs, besides Ruddles County and one named for the pub – also annual beer festival; three roaring open fires (one by curved settle in snug's old-fashioned range), flagstones, beams, tiled floors; lunchtime rolls, basic evening food inc Thurs steak night, dining area; games machines in lobby; children allowed in back conservatory, dogs welcome, aviary on small terrace *(Derek and Sylvia Stephenson, Chris Raisin, JP, PP, the Didler)*

Mapleton [SK1648]
Okeover Arms [back rd just NW of Ashbourne]: Welcoming traditional two-room pub, small and comfortable, well kept Tetleys-related ales, good value bar food inc sandwiches, willing friendly

service, copper-topped tables, open fire and papers, magazines and books, restaurant; garden, pleasant village with interesting domed church, good riverside walks *(Paul Robinshaw, Colin Buckle, L Davenport)*

Matlock [SK2959]

Boat House [Dale Rd, Matlock Bridge – A6 S edge of town]: Friendly old-fashioned three-room riverside pub by River Derwent, between rd and cliff of old limestone quarry, very wide choice of good value food (not Sun evening) inc children's and good vegetarian dishes; well kept Hardys & Hansons ales, family room, pool, traditional games; can get smoky, old juke box may be loud; open all day – tea at teatime; some seats outside, interesting walks, bedrooms *(Jack and Philip Paxton, CMW, JJW)*

Thorn Tree [Jackson Rd, Matlock Bank]: Superb views over valley to Riber Castle from homely two-room 19th-c stonebuilt local, esp from front picnic-sets; well kept Bass, Mansfield Old Baily and Whim Hartington, pleasant quick service, chatty licensees, sensibly priced lunchtime food from sandwiches up (Weds-Sun), darts, dominoes; TV, piped nostalgic music, outside gents'; cl Mon/Tues lunchtime *(JP, PP, CMW, JJW, Kevin Blake, Derek and Sylvia Stephenson, the Didler)*

Matlock Bath [SK2958]

Midland [A6]: Picnic-sets in pleasant tiered riverside garden looking over Derwent to steep woods, wide choice of inexpensive food from sandwiches up, real ales, family-friendly back bar, light and airy conservatory, efficient welcoming service (outside too) by willing friendly staff even on a busy summer w/e *(Howard and Sue Gascoyne)*

Melbourne [SK3825]

Melbourne Arms [B4587 S]: Basic food inc good value sandwiches and fish and chips, well kept Theakstons Best, friendly service; also good if not cheap Indian restaurant with impressive menu *(the Reiterbunds)*

Railway [Station Rd; towards Kings Newton/Islay Walton]: Good old-fashioned chatty local, tiled and wooden floors, cast-iron gas fireplaces, good value simple fresh food, attractive dining room, well kept Marstons Pedigree, Timothy Taylor Landlord, Wards and guest beers mainly from very small breweries; well behaved children allowed; bedrooms good value, open all day Sun *(the Didler, JP, PP)*

Sir Francis Burdett [B587 N, between Stanton by Bridge and Kings Newton]: Wide range of real ales inc guests, good stock of whiskies, big food choice inc help-yourself veg from hot counter; basic bar, big family room off, American billiards room, tables outside *(Brian and Genie Smart, JP, PP)*

Mickleover [SK3034]

Great Northern [off Radbourne Lane, off A52 Ashbourne Lane]: Popular two-room local by disused railway line, lots of relevant prints in pleasant lounge, basic bar with pool, good helpings of reasonably priced food in eating area *(Chris Raisin)*

Middle Handley [SK4078]

Devonshire Arms [off B6052 NE of Chesterfield]: Friendly and picturesque three-room village local with Stones and weekly changing guest beer, sporting prints, darts, dominoes, cards etc, weekly quiz; no food *(anon)*

Millers Dale [SK1473]

Anglers Rest [Just down Litton Lane; pub is 'PH' on OS Sheet]: Friendly and comfortable creeper-clad pub with wonderful gorge views, good value food in cosy lounge, ramblers' bar and candlelit no-smoking dining room, Marstons Pedigree, Tetleys and changing guest beers such as Coach House Posthorn and Ruddles County, lots of toby jugs, plates and teapots, pool room; attractive village, good walks *(Michael and Jenny Back)*

Milltown [SK3561]

☆ *Miners Arms* [off B6036 SE of Ashover]: Comfortable dining pub with particularly good home-made food inc several unusual vegetarian dishes, main dishes with separate interesting veg, tempting puddings, attractive prices, well kept Mansfield and guest ales, good value wines, good friendly service, quiet piped classical music; lovely countryside, good walks right from the door; cl Mon/Tues, usually have to book a day or so ahead *(JDM, KM, Hugh Wood, A A R Wood, John and Christine Lowe)*

Monyash [SK1566]

☆ *Bulls Head* [B5055 W of Bakewell]: Homely and friendly high-ceilinged two-room bar with oak wall seats and panelled settle, horse pictures, shelf of china, roaring log fire, mullioned windows, impressive generous low-priced home-cooked food inc sandwiches, vegetarian and good salads, Black Sheep and Tetleys Mild and Bitter, efficient staff; nicely set tables in plush two-room dining area, pool in small back bar, maybe quiet piped music; long pews outside facing small green, friendly ginger cat, children and muddy dogs welcome; simple bedrooms, nice village *(Julia Hiscock, David Carr, BB, Mrs M A Stevenson)*

Morley [SK3940]

Rose & Crown: Bass pub in pleasant country setting, food; inc good ploughman's and mussels, well kept beer, wide choice of wines *(Dr S J Shepherd)*

Mugginton [SK2843]

☆ *Cock* [back rd N of Weston Underwood]: Clean, comfortable and relaxing, with tables and settles in L-shaped bar, big dining area, friendly efficient staff, well kept weekly changing ales such as Timothy Taylor Landlord and Wadworths 6X, sensibly priced wines, good value food from lunchtime sandwiches and snacks to more adventurous specials inc vegetarian, interesting fresh veg; tables outside, nice surroundings, good walks *(JDM, KM)*

New Mills [SJ9886]

Fox: Friendly and unspoilt old country pub cared for well by long-serving landlord, open fire, well kept Robinsons, straightforward food inc sandwiches, darts, pool; children welcome, handy for walkers; tucked-away hamlet down single-track lane *(David Hoult)*

Ockbrook [SK4236]

Royal Oak: Quiet 18th-c village local, small character rooms, well kept Bass, Worthington

Best and a guest beer, open fire, good lunches, evening rolls, traditional games; tables in charming cottage garden with play area, lovely hanging baskets; still has former (unused) brewhouse *(Jack and Philip Paxton, the Didler)*

Peak Forest [SK1179]

Devonshire Arms [A623]: Friendly, unpretentious and hospitable, beams and panelling, well kept Wards Best sensibly priced, good service, substantial well cooked food in Laura Ashleyesque restaurant (no evening bar snacks); tables on back lawn; piped music *(Peter F Marshall, George Atkinson)*

Pilsley [SK2471]

☆ *Devonshire Arms* [off A619 Bakewell—Baslow]: Welcoming tastefully refurbished local with good value generous home-made fresh food, carvery some evenings (may need to book), well kept Mansfield Riding and Old Baily and a guest such as Batemans, public bar area for walkers and children; lovely village handy for Chatsworth farm and craft shops *(IHR, Norma and Keith Bloomfield, M Joyner, DC)*

Ripley [SK3851]

☆ *Excavator* [Buckland Hollow; A610 towards Ambergate, junction B6013]: Welcoming open-plan Marstons Tavern Table with family dining area and no-smoking area, wide choice of good value food (all day Sun) inc vegetarian and good children's menu, friendly efficient staff, reasonable prices, well kept Pedigree and other ales *(Mary and David Richards)*

Rowarth [SK0189]

☆ *Little Mill* [off A626 in Marple Bridge at Mellor sign, sharp left at Rowarth sign, then pub signed]: Beautiful tucked-away setting, unusual features inc working waterwheel; cheap cheerful plentiful bar food all day (may be a wait), big open-plan bar with lots of little settees, armchairs and small tables, Banks's, Hansons, Robinsons Best Mild and Bitter and a guest beer, hospitable landlord, busy upstairs restaurant; can be smoky, pub games, juke box; children welcome, pretty garden dell across stream great for them, with good play area; vintage Pullman-carriage bedrooms *(JP, PP, Bronwen and Steve Wrigley, LYM)*

Rowsley [SK2566]

☆ *Grouse & Claret* [A6 Bakewell—Matlock]: Spacious and comfortable Mansfield Landlords Table family dining pub in well refurbished old stone building, good reasonably priced food (all day w/e) from carvery counter with appetising salad bar, friendly helpful efficient service, no-smoking area, decent wines, open fires; tap room popular with walkers, tables outside; good value bedrooms, small camp site behind nr river *(David and Mary Webb, Brian and Anna Marsden, Mr Cameron, David Carr, G Washington)*

Sawley [SK4731]

Bell [Tamworth Rd (B5640)]: Opulent local, very welcoming, with particularly well kept ales *(Dr and Mrs A K Clarke)*

Shardlow [SK4429]

Cavendish Arms [Cavendish Bridge; old A6 about ½ mile E, just over Leics border]: Well run old beamed pub with good food inc carvery, vegetarian, fresh veg and theme nights such as

tapas, well kept Bass and Marstons, friendly staff; open all day *(Dr B and Mrs P B Baker)*

Clock Warehouse [3½ miles from M6 junction 24; old A6 towards Derby]: Child-oriented Mansfield dining pub in handsome 18th-c brick-built warehouse with picture windows overlooking attractive canal basin, reasonably priced standard food, well kept ales, friendly efficient staff, play areas indoors and out, tables outside too *(GSB, LYM, M C and S Jeanes)*

☆ *Malt Shovel* [3½ miles from M1 junction 24, via A6 towards Derby; The Wharf]: Old pub in 18th-c former maltings attractively set by canal, interesting odd-angled layout, good cheap changing lunchtime food, well kept Marstons and guest ales, welcoming quick service, good open fire; no small children, seats out by water *(Alan Bowker, LYM, JP, PP)*

Sheen [SK1161]

Staffordshire Knot: Stonebuilt country pub, flagstones, two welcoming log fires, Marstons Pedigree and a guest beer, good value food from interesting oatcake snacks and home-made soups to Sun carvery, friendly landlord *(Dr and Mrs P Watson, A J Hutchins)*

Sheldon [SK1768]

Cock & Pullet: Fairly recent cottage conversion, good food, well kept beer, open fire and scrubbed oak tables, pool in adjacent room; welcomes ramblers *(L Davenport)*

Shottlegate [SK3247]

☆ *Hanging Gate* [A517 W of Belper]: Charming Bass dining pub, above-average food all day inc limited but interesting vegetarian choice, also pleasant bar with attractive settles, Bass and a guest ale, and decent choice of sensibly priced wines esp New World; polite helpful staff, garden *(JDM, KM)*

Smalley [SK4044]

☆ *Bell* [A608 Heanor—Derby]: Welcoming two-room village pub, dining area with good reasonably priced changing food, well kept ales such as Marstons Pedigree, Mallard Duckling and Waddlers Mild, Ruddles County and Whim Hartington, good choice of wines, smart efficient staff, post office annexe, tables out in front and on big relaxing lawn with play area, beautiful array of hanging baskets; attractive bedrooms behind *(JP, PP, Jack and Philip Paxton, Derek and Sylvia Stephenson, David and Kay Ross, the Didler)*

Snelston Common [SK1541]

☆ *Queen Adelaide* [B5033, about 1½ miles W of A515 – S of Ashbourne]: Delightfully unspoilt former Victorian farmhouse set back in tranquil spot, brick-effect wallpaper, stone-effect inglenook, Indian arch over little Formica serving counter, plastic-covered wooden tables, nice curved settle; second room has piano and huge case of stuffed birds and animals; outstanding Marstons Pedigree, darts, dominoes, cards, table skittles; muddy boots and dogs welcome; usually cl lunchtime exc Sun, no food but crisps *(Jack and Philip Paxton, the Didler, Pete Baker)*

Sparklow [SK1265]

Royal Oak [off A515 S of Buxton]: Two bars and dining area, with friendly country atmosphere, well kept Marstons Pedigree and

Tetleys, varied well cooked food inc vegetarian, log fire; children welcome, on Tissington Trail *(Terry King, Doug Christian)*

Spitewinter [SK3366]

☆ *Three Horse Shoes* [A632 SW of Chesterfield]: Doing well under same management as Greyhound at Warslow, similar food inc good curries and fresh fish sold in three sizes; Bass, Stones and Worthington, pleasant service, no-smoking restaurant; panoramic views of Chesterfield *(Derek and Sylvia Stephenson, Frank Gorman, Richard and Anne Hollingsworth)*

Stanton by Dale [SK4638]

☆ *Stanhope Arms* [off A6096 and B5010 E of Derby, not far from M1 junction 25]: Cosy and attractive unpretentious rambling local, friendly staff, well kept Tetleys-related ales, good value generous fresh food esp daily real pies, upstairs dining room converted from adjoining cottage; unspoilt village *(David and Gilly Wilkins, Dr and Mrs J H Hills, R Johnson)*

Stanton in Peak [SK2464]

Flying Childers [off A6 Matlock—Bakewell]: Cosy and unspoilt right-hand room with coal fire, Wards Sheffield Best and a guest beer, good value filled rolls, very welcoming landlord; in delightful steep stone village, overlooking verdant valley *(JP, PP, the Didler)*

Sudbury [SK1631]

Boars Head [Aston Bridge; A515, about 2 miles S]: Rambling pub/hotel handy for Sudbury Hall, lunchtime carvery and well presented bar food, very reasonable prices, well kept Bass and Ruddles County, cheerful efficient service despite the bustle; restaurant; bedrooms (motel-type) *(Norma and Keith Bloomfield, John and Christine Lowe)*

Taddington [SK1472]

Queens Arms: Attractively furnished and decorated, good generous honest pub food from sandwiches up inc good children's dishes (worth booking w/e), well kept Marstons Pedigree, John Smiths and Theakstons, jovial landlord, pleasant staff; quiet village in good high walking country *(Richard and Valerie Wright, Rita and Keith Pollard)*

Waterloo [off A6 Buxton—Bakewell; inn is 'PH' on OS Sheet]: Pleasant hotel bar and lounge, very friendly staff, reasonably priced food, Robinsons Best and Old Stockport; bedrooms *(Michael and Jenny Back)*

Tansley [SK3259]

Tavern [A615 Matlock—Mansfield]: Locally popular for excellent value very well prepared English cooking under present management, friendly relaxed atmosphere, well kept Marstons Pedigree, limited but reasonably priced wine list *(Mr and Mrs J K Miln)*

Ticknall [SK3423]

☆ *Chequers* [B5006 towards Ashby de la Zouch]: Small, friendly and full of atmosphere, with vast 16th-c inglenook fireplace, bright brass, old prints, well kept Marstons Pedigree and seasonal beers, Ruddles Best and County; nice garden, good walking area *(LYM, JP, PP, the Didler, Chris Raisin)*

Staff of Life [High St (Ashby Rd)]: Attractive

local, neat and friendly, with well kept beers such as Timothy Taylor Landlord (some tapped from the cask), good generous food at most attractive prices, very wide choice, meat cooked wonderfully; open fire, restaurant *(JP, PP, Chris Raisin, C A Hall)*

Tideswell [SK1575]

☆ *George* [B6049, between A623 and A6 E of Buxton]: Spacious and comfortable, with simple traditional decor and furnishings, separate room areas with nice balance between eating and drinking, varied good value generous food inc super rolls and ploughman's, well kept Hardys & Hansons, open fires, welcoming staff, pool room; by remarkable church, tables in front overlooking pretty village, sheltered back garden; children welcome; 60s music Fri, good value bedrooms, pleasant walks *(Pete Yearsley, BB, JP, PP, Mrs M A Stevenson, John Wooll, M G Hart, Sue Holland, Dave Webster, Tony and Wendy Hobden)*

Weston upon Trent [SK4028]

Coopers Arms [Weston Hall]: Tall and imposing early 17th-c manor house converted in early 1990s, massive stonework and ancient beams, comfortable carpeted bars in former rhubarb-forcing cellar, good food counter with changing menu from hot filled rolls and good home-made soup up, Bass, Worthington and a guest beer such as Fullers London Pride, huge log fire; conservatory, tables outside, fishing in lake; bedrooms *(JP, PP, JDM, KM)*

Whatstandwell [SK3354]

Derwent [A6/Crich rd]: Pleasant atmosphere, good bar food from sandwiches to good value Sun lunch, quick friendly service even when busy, well kept Hardys & Hansons *(Derek and Sylvia Stephenson)*

Winster [SK2460]

Bowling Green [East Bank, by NT Market House]: Refurbished free house with reliable plain home cooking inc good Sun lunch, friendly service, well kept beers *(Darly Graton, Graeme Gulibert)*

Miners Standard [B5056 above village]: Welcoming local, friendly family service, well kept Mansfield Mild and Bitter, Marstons Pedigree and Wadworths 6X, good value food inc huge pies, big open fires, lead-mining photographs and minerals, ancient well; children allowed away from bar; restaurant, attractive view from garden, interesting stone-built village below *(IHR, Norma and Keith Bloomfield, JP, PP, Alan and Heather Jacques)*

Wirksworth [SK2854]

Blacks Head [Market Pl]: Atmospheric local with Hardys & Hansons ales, good food range inc several soups *(L Davenport)*

Youlgreave [SK2164]

☆ *George* [Church St]: Handsome yet unpretentious stonebuilt local opp church, quick friendly service, good range of reasonably priced home-made food, comfortable banquettes, well kept Scottish Courage ales; flagstoned locals' and walkers' side room, games room, juke box; attractive village, roadside tables outside; handy for Lathkill Dale and Haddon Hall *(David Carr, JP, PP)*

Devon

With dozens of very good pubs right across this huge county, there's an embarrassment of riches to choose from: simple and unspoilt; ancient and lovely; or perhaps very foody. We've added several good pubs to the choice this year: the Watermans Arms with its pretty garden on the creek at Ashprington (helpful new licensees since it was last in these pages), the very friendly Drake Manor in the charming village of Buckland Monachorum (a hundred whiskies, nice food), the Hunters Lodge at Cornworthy (taken over by people who'd notched up a fine track record in their previous pubs, the Durant Arms at Ashprington and the Peter Tavy Inn), the Freebooter down in East Prawle (surprisingly good interesting food for such a simple and unspoilt place), the Globe opposite the creek at Frogmore (refreshingly open-air in mood), the interesting old Tower at Slapton (its Australian landladies, new since our last acquaintance with it, are a great success), the pretty 13th-c thatched Church House at Stokeinteignhead, the Cridford Inn at Trusham (another place to have changed hands since it last figured in these pages), the interesting Two Bridges Hotel beautifully placed up on Dartmoor (brewing its own beers), and the Westleigh Inn at Westleigh (thriving family atmosphere, super view). All these in their different ways have good food. Among the many other pubs here which offer really good food, two stand out: the Masons Arms at Branscombe (gaining a Food Award this year), and the Maltsters Arms at Tuckenhay. Of these, we choose the Maltsters Arms at Tuckenhay as Devonshire Dining Pub of the Year. Other pubs currently doing particularly well are the busy Sloop at Bantham (nice walks down to the sea), the intriguing Olde Globe at Berrynarbor (good for children), the civilised yet relaxed little Drewe Arms at Broadhembury (good fish and wines), the Five Bells at Clyst Hydon (friendly, neat and attractive), the Wild Goose at Combeinteignhead (a cracking good local, great jazz nights), the ancient and very friendly Cherub in Dartmouth, the Nobody Inn at Doddiscombsleigh (outstanding drinks choice), the Drewe Arms at Drewsteignton (managing to keep its unspoilt character, despite catering nowadays to a rather wider market), the Rock at Haytor Vale (good all round), the Duke of York tucked away at Iddesleigh, the Barn Owl at Kingskerswell (friendly new licensees), the Old Rydon at Kingsteignton (good food and service), the bustling Manor Inn at Lower Ashton (good ales, good food, super atmosphere), the attractive Church House at Marldon (very helpful landlady – and it gains a Food Award this year), the fine old Royal Oak at Meavy, the lovely restful Church House at Rattery, the Half Moon at Sheepwash (good mix of pub with fishing hotel), the Oxenham Arms at South Zeal (wonderful building), the Kings Arms at Stockland (a good locals' bar as well as its emphasis on fine food), the friendly and properly pubby Green Dragon at Stoke Fleming (imaginative home cooking), the Start Bay at Torcross (almost too famous for its good fresh fish – packed in summer), and the quaint old Northmore Arms at Wonson. With quite a few Devon pubs changing hands this year (and not always for the better), it's a pleasure to record that the Greys have now returned to their original stamping-ground, the Castle Inn at Lydford. The Lucky Dip at the end of the chapter has another 200 pubs well worth investigating: we'd

*particularly pick out the Church House at Churchstow, Ferry Boat at
Dittisham, New Inn at Fremington (bargain food), Hoops at Horns Cross,
Dartmoor Inn at Lydford (particularly good food), Globe at Lympstone and
Jack in the Green at Rockbeare. Devon drinks prices are close to the national
average. Pubs brewing their own beers are generally the cheapest here, though
cheapest of all in our survey was the Imperial in Exeter, a palatial
Wetherspoons pub. Pubs getting their beers from one of the small Devon
breweries such as Blackawton, Branscombe Vale, Exe Valley, Otter,
Princetown, Scatter Rock, Summerskills or Teignworthy also tend to have
lower prices than average. Rather confusingly, the Dartmoor Best often found
here is actually brewed over the border in Cornwall, for Carlsberg-Tetleys.*

ABBOTSKERSWELL SX8569 Map 1
Court Farm
Wilton Way; look for the church tower

For most of its life, this attractive 17th-c listed building was a farmhouse. The long
bar has a woodburning stove in a stripped red granite fireplace, a mix of seats on the
polished crazy flagstones, a nice big round table by an angled black oak screen, and
a turkey rug in one alcove formed by a low granite wall with timbers above; a
further small room is broadly similar with stripped kitchen tables and more
spindleback chairs; piped music. One area is no smoking. On the right of the
entrance is the two-roomed public bar with a woodburning stove, and fruit machine,
and a simple end room with darts and dominoes. Good bar food includes home-
made soup (£2.30), sandwiches (from £2.95; toasties from £2.60), home-made pâté
(£3.95), ploughman's (from £4.95), ham and egg or good vegetable and cashew nut
stir fry (£6.25), whole grilled fresh plaice (£6.75), home-made steak and kidney pie
(£7.45), steaks (from £7.95), roast rack of lamb with rich madeira sauce (£9.95),
and puddings (£2.95); half helpings for children. Well kept Bass, Boddingtons,
Flowers IPA, and Wadworths 6X on handpump from the long rough-boarded bar
counter, and helpful staff. The garden is pretty, and they have their own cricket
team. *(Recommended by Paul R White, Andrew Hodges, Bett and Brian Cox, Mr and Mrs A
Scrutton, Jeanne Cross, Paul Silvestri, Mrs Sylvia Elcoate)*

*Heavitree ~ Tenant Robin Roger Huggins ~ Real ale ~ Bar food (11.30-2.30, 5-10;
not 25 Dec) ~ (01626) 361866 ~ Children in eating area of bar ~ Open 11-11; 12-
10.30 Sun*

ASHPRINGTON SX8156 Map 1
Durant Arms
Village signposted off A381 S of Totnes; OS Sheet 202 map reference 819571

The name of this neatly kept and friendly inn comes from the mid-19th-c owner of
the Sharpham Estate, Richard Durant, who rebuilt many of the village and farm
buildings, including the pub, and built the school. The beamed open-plan bar has
several open fires, lamps and horsebrasses, fresh flowers, and a mix of seats and
tables on the red patterned carpet; there's a lower no-smoking carpeted lounge too,
with another open fire. There's quite an emphasis on the good bar food which
includes sandwiches and soup, lots of dishes at £5.75 such as leek, cheese and potato
pie, seafood flaky bake, avocado corn bake, ham and egg, and cottage pie, plus
chicken curry (£6.25), steak and kidney pie (£6.95), sirloin steak and puddings such
as rhubarb and apple crumble or bread and butter pudding; best to book if you want
to be sure of a table. Good, attentive service. Well kept Flowers Original and
Wadworths 6X on handpump, and local Pigsqueal cider; no games machines. There
is some wooden garden furniture on the terrace with more seats on the sheltered
back garden. They have a self-catering cottage in the grounds. The church is
opposite and this is a pretty village. *(Recommended by J H Bell, Mike Gorton, John Evans,*

P Haines, Dr and Mrs A J Newton, John Brightley)

Free house ~ Licensees Graham and Eileen Ellis ~ Real ale ~ Bar food (11.30-2, 6.30-9) ~ Restaurant ~ (01803) 732240 ~ Children in eating area of bar and restaurant ~ Open 11.30-2.30, 6(6.30 in winter)11; 12-2.30, 6-10.30 Sun ~ Bedrooms: £30B/£50B

Watermans Arms 🍺

Bow Bridge, on Tuckenhay road; OS Sheet 202 map reference 812565

Once a smithy and brewhouse, and a prison during the Napoleonic War, this bustling pub has a quarry-tiled and heavy-beamed bar area with a friendly atmosphere, and high-backed settles and built-in wall benches; the comfortable eating area has plenty of seats, more beams, and stripped stone walls; log fires. Decent bar food includes home-made soup (£2.75), filled ciabatta rolls (from £3.75), beef and mushroom in ale pie (£7.95), chicken breast filled with blue cheese (£8.95), really giant cod and chips (£9.60), lamb cutlets with red and green peppers, a red wine jus and garlic potatoes (£10.95), daily specials such as warm chicken liver salad (£7.95), aubergine, tomato and mozzarella bake (£8.20), and seafood platter (£13.95), and puddings such as two-tier toffee meringue gateau or chocolate and mandarin rousse with cointreau (£2.95), with home-made crumbles on Sunday lunchtime. Part of the restaurant is no smoking. Well kept Bass, Courage Directors, Flowers Original, and a beer named for the pub on handpump, local English wine, and Luscombe and Pigsqueal ciders. Darts, dominoes, cribbage and piped music. There are seats in the pretty flower-filled garden – or you can sit by the river across the road and watch the ducks (or even swans and kingfishers). *(Recommended by Pat and Robert Watt, John Evans, J Dwane, D Barlow, A J Goddard, Ian Shorthouse, Valerie Pitts, John Wilson)*

Jersey ~ Manager Steven Simmons ~ Real ale ~ Bar food (all day) ~ Restaurant ~ (01803) 732214 ~ Children in eating area of bar ~ Live jazz on various evenings – phone for details ~ Open 10.30-10.30; 12-10.30 Sun ~ Bedrooms: £49B/£69B

AVONWICK SX7157 Map 1
Avon

B3210, off A38 E of Plymouth, at South Brent

As Mr Velotti is from Italy, several of the enjoyable dishes on offer here are Italian – or have Italian leanings; to be sure of a table, it's best to book. Listed on boards in the small back bar, there might be sandwiches, home-made soup (£2.50), scallops in filo pastry or avocado, mozzarella and parma ham salad (£4.50), antipasto of chargrilled vegetables or smoked duck and chicken salad with tomato salsa (£4.75), pasta dishes such as cannelloni with spinach and ricotta, penne Siciliana or spaghetti genovese orecchiette (from £5.25), supreme of chicken fiorentina (£8.50), medallions of pork with a cider and stilton sauce (£10.50), duck stuffed with black olives and wild mushrooms and cooked in red wine (£11.50), and thai-style bass (£13); espresso coffee. Some decent Italian wines alongside the well kept Badger Best and Bass on handpump; fruit machine and piped music. Décor and furnishings are comfortable and pleasant in a fairly modern style. There are tables out in a pleasant garden by the River Avon. *(Recommended by John Evans, DJW, Mark Percy, Lesley Mayoh, John Braine)*

Free house ~ Licensees Mario and Marilyn Velotti ~ Bar food ~ Restaurant ~ (01364) 73475 ~ Children in restaurant ~ Open 11.30-2.30, 6-11; closed Sun and 1 week Jan

AXMOUTH SY2591 Map 1
Harbour Inn

B3172 Seaton—Axminster

Opposite the handsome church which has some fine stone gargoyles, this thatched and prettily set pub has a good local atmosphere. The Harbour Bar has black oak beams and joists, fat pots hanging from pot-irons in the huge inglenook fireplace, brass-bound cask seats, a high-backed oak settle, and an antique wall clock. A central lounge has more cask seats and settles, and over on the left another room is divided from the no-smoking dining room by a two-way log fireplace. At the back, a big flagstoned lobby with sturdy seats leads on to a very spacious and simply furnished family bar. Well kept Flowers IPA and Original, Otter Ale, and Wadworths 6X on handpump; pool, and winter skittle alley. Good bar food includes sandwiches (from £1.50), ploughman's (from £3.75), daily specials such as vegetarian homity pie (£5), lamb curry (£6; their lamb is home produced), plaice (£6.50) or lemon sole (£7.75), puddings (from £2.50), and children's menu (£2.50); cheerful service even when busy, and friendly cat. They have a lavatory for disabled people, and general access is good. There are some tables in the neat back flower garden. *(Recommended by Paul White, Basil Minson, Mr and Mrs McKay, Dr and Mrs Nigel Holmes)*

Free house ~ Licensees Dave and Pat Squire ~ Real ale ~ Bar food (not winter Sun evenings) ~ (01297) 20371 ~ Children in eating area of bar and in summer family room ~ Open 11-2.30, 6-11; 12-2.30, 7-10.30 Sun

BANTHAM SX6643 Map
Sloop ♀ ⇌
Off A379/B3197 NW of Kingsbridge

After a walk to the estuary and nearby lovely sandy beach, this is a fine place to end up for lunch. The black-beamed bar has a good bustling atmosphere, country chairs around wooden tables, stripped stone walls and flagstones, a woodburning stove, and easy chairs in a quieter side area with a nautical theme. Enjoyable bar food includes pasties (£2), sandwiches (from £2.45), tasty home-made soup (£2.45), basket meals (from £2.85), chargrilled gammon with pineapple (£7.95), steaks (from £8.95), and daily specials such as hot potted shrimps (£4.15), freshly picked local crab starter (£4.65), baked avocado with ratatouille and topped with melted cheese (£5.95), liver with caramelised onions and sage gravy (£5.25), roast cod on a bed of spinach glazed with smoked somerset cheese (£7.95), grilled local lamb with fresh rosemary sauce (£8.65), brochette of monfish and scallop wrapped in bacon on a red wine risotto (£10.75), and barbury duck breast with a creamy green peppercorn and apple brandy sauce (£10.75); home-made puddings; hearty breakfasts. Part of the dining room is no smoking. Well kept Bass, Flowers IPA, and a guest beer on handpump, Luscombe farm cider, 25 malt whiskies, 12 wines by the glass from a carefully chosen wine list (including some local ones), and a good choice of liqueurs and West Country drinks like rum and shrub or brandy and lovage. Darts, dominoes, cribbage, table skittles, and maybe piped music. There are some seats at the back. The bedrooms in the pub itself have the most character. *(Recommended by JDM, KM, Richard and Robyn Wain, Andrew Low, Nick Lawless, Paul R White, Jacquie and Jim Jones, John and Vivienne Rice, the Didler, Charles Eaton, M L Porter, Dr A J and Mrs P G Newton, Peter and Audrey Dowsett, Mrs Amanda Rudolf)*

Free house ~ Licensee Neil Girling ~ Real ale ~ Bar food ~ (01548) 560489/560215 ~ Children in eating area of bar ~ Open 11-2.30, 6-11; 12-2.30, 7-10.30 Sun; closed evenings 25 and 26 Dec

BERRYNARBOR SS5646 Map 1
Olde Globe ★ £
Village signposted from A399 E of Ilfracombe

Families are welcomed to this friendly, rambling 13th-c pub, but this doesn't spoilt the pubby feel. This year the size and equipment inside (which includes a children's ball pool) have been increased and the room has been made partly no smoking – there's also an activity house in the garden. The dimly lit homely rooms have low ceilings, curved deep-ochre walls, and floors of flagstones or of ancient lime-ash (with silver coins embedded in them). There are old high-backed oak settles (some carved) and plush-cushioned cask seats around antique tables, and lots of cutlasses, swords, shields and fine powder-flasks, a profusion of genuinely old pictures, priests (fish-coshes), thatcher's knives, sheep shears, gin-traps, pitchforks, antlers, and copper warming pans. Well kept Courage Directors, Ushers Best and a guest beer on handpump, and several country wines; sensibly placed darts, pool, skittle alley, dominoes, cribbage, fruit machine, and piped music. Bar food includes sandwiches (from £1.50), home-made soup (£1.75), ploughman's (£2.95), vegetable lasagne (£4.60), steak and kidney pie (£4.70), gammon (£5.90), steaks (from £7.20), daily specials, puddings (£2.15), children's dishes (£2.20), and popular main course Sunday lunch (£4.45); quick, friendly service. The gaslit restaurant is no smoking. The crazy-paved front terrace has some old-fashioned garden seats. *(Recommended by Gerald Barnett, Carole and John Smith, R V G Brown, Myke and Nicky Crombleholme, S Bobeldijk, Mr and Mrs M Clifford, Ian and Jane Irving, Maysie Thompson, Karen and Garry Fairclough, Paul and Jane Forrestal)*

Scottish Courage ~ Lease: Phil Bridle ~ Real ale ~ Bar food ~ Restaurant ~ (01271) 882465 ~ Children in own room ~ Open 11.30-2.30, 6(7 in winter)-11; 12-2.30, 7-11 Sun

BLACKAWTON SX8050 Map 1

George ◖

Main Street; village signposted off A3122 W of Dartmouth, and off A381 S of Halwell

They've now opened up bedrooms in this friendly local and reports from readers suggest that it is a nice place to stay in a quiet village, and that the breakfasts are hearty. The main bar has some timbering, a mix of cushioned wooden chairs, cushioned wall benches, and wheelbacks on the bare boards, mounted butterflies and a collection of beer mats and pump clips, and hop bines above the bar; another bar has train pictures and a big Loch Lomond station sign on the cream Anaglypta walls, and red Rexine-seated chairs on the dark blue and red patterned carpet. On one wall is a quaint old bow-windowed panel with little drawings of customers scratched on the black paint. There's also a cosy end lounge with an open fire and big bow window with a pleasant view. Good bar food includes lunchtime sandwiches (from £2.10), soup (£2.25), tagliatelle with creamed mushrooms or homity pie (£4.25), ploughman's (£5.25), giant yorkshire pudding filled with liver, bacon and onions (£6.25), beef stew with horseradish dumplings (£6.30), chicken balti (£6.45), sizzling steak, stilton and mushroom skillet (£7.25), and home-made puddings (£2.70). They keep a changing choice of three interesting beers from all over the country such as Clearwater Brewery Torrington Old Ale, Princetown Dartmoor IPA, Robinsons Best or Scatter Rock Summer Days on handpump, dozens of Belgian bottled beers, and quite a few whiskies; they hold a beer festival around the late May bank holiday with live bands. Darts and euchre, and an alsatian called Oscar. The garden, set below the pub, has several picnic-sets and nice views. *(Recommended by Mrs G Tuckey, J Dwane, Andrew Hodges)*

Free house ~ Licensee Stuart O'Dell ~ Real ale ~ Bar food ~ (01803) 712342 ~ Children in eating area of bar ~ Folk last Thurs evening of month – all players welcome ~ Open 12-3, 7-11; 12-3, 7-10.30 Sun; closed Mon-Thurs winter lunchtimes ~ Bedrooms: £20B/£40B

Normandy Arms 🛏

Signposted off A3122 W of Dartmouth; OS Sheet 202 map reference 807509

You may still be able to see some of the bullet scars here, as this whole village was commandeered as a training ground to prepare for the Normandy landings – hence the pub's name. The quaint main bar has an interesting display of World War II battle gear, a good log fire, and well kept Blackawton Bitter, 44 Special, Devon Gold, and Shepherd's Delight, Ind Coope Burton, and occasional guest beers on handpump. Good bar food includes home-made soup (£1.95), sandwiches (from £1.95), vegetable pancake (£3.60), ploughman's (£3.95), home-made chicken liver pâté (£4.50), steak and kidney pie (£4.95), whole lemon sole or pork in cider and cream (£8.95), steaks with quite a choice of sauces (from £8.95), and home-made puddings like tipsy cake or apple pie (£2.95); children's menu (from £2.50). The restaurant is no smoking. Sensibly placed darts, pool, shove-ha'penny, cribbage, dominoes, and piped music. Some tables out in the garden. *(Recommended by Mr and Mrs A Scrutton, JP, PP, D Marsh)*

Free house ~ Licensees Jonathan and Mark Gibson ~ Real ale ~ Bar food (no food winter Sun evening) ~ Restaurant ~ (01803) 712316 ~ Children in eating area of bar ~ Open 12-2.30, 7-11; 12-11 Sat; 12-3, 7-10.30 Sun; may close Sat if quiet winter; closed 25 Dec, 1 Jan ~ Bedrooms: £32B/£48B

BRANSCOMBE SY1988 Map 1
Fountain Head ◖

Upper village, above the robust old church; village signposted off A3052 Sidmouth—Seaton

By summer 2000, the friendly licensees here hope to be able to make some of the deliveries from their Branscombe Vale Brewery by Dolly, their shire horse; she was being broken to harness as we went to press. The own-brewed beers include Branoc, Jolly Geff (named after Mrs Luxton's father, the ex-licensee), summer Summa'that, winter Hells Belles, Christmas Yo Ho Ho, plus summer guest beers; their midsummer weekend beer festival comprises three days of spitroasts, barbecues, live music, Morris men, and over 30 real ales; farm cider, too. The room on the left – formerly a smithy – has forge tools and horseshoes on the high oak beams, a log fire in the original raised firebed with its tall central chimney, and cushioned pews and mate's chairs. On the right, an irregularly shaped, more orthodox snug room has a another log fire, white-painted plank ceiling with an unusual carved ceiling-rose, brown-varnished panelled walls, and rugs on its flagstone-and-lime-ash floor; the children's room is no smoking, the airedale is called Max, and the black and white cat, Casey Jones. Bar food such as home-made soup (£2.25), sandwiches (from £2.25), filled baked potatoes (£3.95), ploughman's (£4.25), home-made meaty or vegetarian lasagne or cottage pie (£4.75), home-made steak and kidney pie (£5.25), evening grills (from £6.75), daily specials like fresh battered cod (£5.25), lamb moussaka (£5.75), and pork steak with mustard sauce (£6.75), and children's meals (£from £1.75). Darts, shove-ha'penny, cribbage, dominoes. There are seats out on the front loggia and terrace, and a little stream rustling under the flagstoned path. They offer self-catering. *(Recommended by JP, PP, S Tait, S Lonie, Miss A G Drake, Comus Elliott, the Didler, Peter and Audrey Dowsett, Veronica Brown, Andy and Jill Kassube, Wendy Straker)*

Own brew ~ Licensee Mrs Catherine Luxton ~ Real ale ~ Bar food (may not do food winter Mon evening) ~ (01297) 680359 ~ Children in own room; must be over 10 in evening restaurant ~ Solo/duo guitar/folk summer Thurs ~ Open 11.30-3, 6-11; 12-3, 6(7 in winter)-10.30 Sun; 2.30 closing and 6.30 opening in winter

Masons Arms ⊕ ♀ ⇔

Main St; signed off A3052 Sidmouth—Seaton

New bedrooms have been created here in an extended row of thatched cottages that overlooks the roofs out to the sea beyond – and several have four-poster beds. The rooms across the road from the inn are now being refurbished and will soon be available for weekly lets as holiday cottages. Improvements continue with the choice of beers and wines, and with the selection and service of the very good food under the new chef. The no-smoking Old Worthies bar has a slate floor, a fireplace with a two-sided woodburning stove, and woodwork that has been stripped back to the original pine. The no-smoking restaurant (warmed by one side of the woodburning stove) is stripped back to dressed stone in parts, and is used as bar space on busy lunchtimes. The rambling low-beamed main bar has a massive central hearth in front of the roaring log fire (spit roasts on Tuesday and Sunday lunch and Friday evenings), windsor chairs and settles, and a good bustling atmosphere. As well as lunchtime sandwiches (from £2.50) and ploughman's (from £4.50), the imaginative dishes include mediterranean fish soup with rouille and croutons (£3.50), good deep-fried devilled whitebait, chicken and pistachio terrine with a crispy bacon and chicory salad (£3.95), rigatoni with courgettes, olives, tomatoes and basil with parmesan cheese, or cod in beer batter (£7.50), fried king prawns and baby squid in a garlic and lemon butter served on a greek salad (£8.50), baked duck breast with honey glazed summer vegetables and a redcurrant sauce (£9.50), daily specials like grilled goat's cheese topped with walnuts and glazed with stilton, cajun spiced pork risotto or tasty chargrilled red mullet fillets with stir-fried vegetables and an oyster sauce, and puddings such as white chocolate crème brûlée glazed with brown sugar or sticky toffee pudding with toffee sauce and crème fraîche; polite, attentive staff. Well kept Bass, Otter Bitter and Masons, and two guest beers like Hampshire 1066, Morlands Old Speckled Hen or Teignworthy Beachcomber on handpump or tapped from the cask; they hold a summer beer festival and keep 30 malt whiskies, 14 wines by the glass, and farm cider. Darts, shove-ha'penny, cribbage, dominoes, and skittle alley. Outside, the quiet flower-filled front terrace has tables with little thatched roofs, extending into a side garden. *(Recommended by John and Vivienne Rice, John Knighton, M Clifford, Revd A Nunnerley, Lawrence Bacon, P Legun, Mr and Mrs M Clifford, T P, Dave and Deborah Irving, M G Hart, Paul White, Gerald Barnett, Comus Elliott, Peter and Audrey Dowsett, Nick Lawless, A Hepburn, S Jenner, L H and S Ede)*

Free house ~ Licensees Murray Inglis and Mark Painter ~ Real ale ~ Bar food (12-2.15, 6-9.30; slightly shorter in winter) ~ Restaurant ~ (01297) 680300 ~ Children welcome until 9pm ~ Occasional live music but always during beer festival ~ Open 11-11; 12-10.30 Sun; 11-3, 6-11 in winter ~ Bedrooms: £22(£37B)/£44(£60B)

BROADCLYST SX9897 Map 1

Red Lion

B3121, by church

In early summer when the wistaria is out, this enjoyable old pub looks especially attractive. It's a peaceful place with no noisy machines or piped music, and a quietly relaxed atmosphere. The long red-carpeted bar has heavy beams, cushioned window seats, some nice chairs around a mix of oak and other tables, and a collection of carpenter's planes; a flagstoned area has cushioned pews and low tables by the fireplace, and at the end of the L-shaped room are big hunting prints and lots of team photographs. Good bar food includes home-made soup (£2.20), sandwiches (from £2.30), home-made chicken liver pâté (£3.85), lamb's kidneys in sherry (£4.30), ploughman's (from £5.30), vegetable lasagne (£5.45), steak and kidney pie or pork and apple in cider casserole (£6), rump steak (£9), daily specials, puddings (£3.30), children's meals (from £2.65), and roast Sunday lunch (£6). Well kept Bass, Fullers London Pride, and Hardy Royal Oak on handpump. There are picnic-sets on the front cobbles and more seats in a small enclosed garden across the quiet lane. *(Recommended by James Flory, Dr D J Walker, S Gregory, Barbara and Alan Mence, R T and J C Moggridge, Paul and Heather Bettesworth, Barry and Anne, Stan Edwards)*

Free house ~ Licensee Stephen Smith ~ Real ale ~ Bar food (12-2, 7-10) ~ Restaurant ~ (01392) 461271 ~ Children in eating area of bar and restaurant ~ Open 11-3, 5.30-11; 12-3, 7-10.30 Sun

BROADHEMBURY ST1004 Map 1

Drewe Arms ★ 🍴 🍷

Signposted off A373 Cullompton—Honiton

This is very much somewhere that people return to again and again – and can expect to enjoy consistently splendid fish dishes in a warmly friendly and chatty atmosphere. The bar has neatly carved beams in its high ceiling, and handsome stone-mullioned windows (one with a small carved roundabout horse), and on the left, a high-backed stripped settle separates off a little room with flowers on the three sturdy country tables, plank-panelled walls painted brown below and yellow above with attractive engravings and prints, and a big black-painted fireplace with bric-a-brac on a high mantlepiece; some wood carvings, walking sticks, and framed watercolours for sale. The flagstoned entry has a narrow corridor of a room by the servery with a couple of tables, and the cellar bar has simple pews on the stone floor. Locals are quite happy to drop in for just a chat and drink, but most people come to eat: spicy crab soup (£4), langoustines with garlic or crab thermidor (£5), whole griddled lemon sole (£10.50), whole crab salad (£11), and bass with orange and chilli or john dory with chartreuse (£14.50), as well as open sandwiches (from £5.25), fillet of brill (£10.50), half-crab salad (£11), and half-lobster salad (£12.50), as well as interesting soups (£4), open sandwiches (from £5.25), hot chicken and bacon salad (£7.50), fillet of beef with red pesto (£13.50), and puddings like St Emilion chocolate cake (£4); there's also a three-course menu (£22) which can be eaten anywhere in the pub – or in the flower-filled garden. Well kept Otter Bitter, Ale, Bright and Head tapped from the cask, and a very good wine list laid out extremely helpfully – including 10 by the glass. There are picnic-sets in the lovely garden which has a lawn stretching back under the shadow of chestnut trees towards a church with its singularly melodious hour-bell. Thatched and very pretty, the 15th-c pub is in a charming village of similar cream-coloured cottages. *(Recommended by JP, PP, Dr and Mrs Cottrell, Howard and Margaret Buchanan, Mrs Sylvia Elcoate, the Didler, Peter and Margaret Frost, John Askew, Marianne and Peter Stevens, Basil Minson, Ruth Warner, Jacquie and Jim Jones, L G Owen, Alan and Paula McCully, Comus Elliott, Marvadene B Eves, James Flory, Patrick Hancock, Andrew Hodges)*

Free house ~ Licensees Kerstin and Nigel Burge ~ Real ale ~ Bar food (12-2, 7-10) ~ Restaurant ~ (01404) 841267 ~ Children in eating area of bar and restaurant ~ Open 11-3, 6-11; 12-3, 7-10.30 Sun

BUCKLAND BREWER SS4220 Map 1
Coach & Horses ★ 🛏

Village signposted off A388 S of Bideford; OS Sheet 190, map reference 423206

The attractively furnished and heavily beamed bar in this friendly thatched house has a good mix of locals and visitors, as well as comfortable seats (including a handsome antique settle), and woodburning stove in the inglenook; a good log fire also burns in the big stone inglenook of the cosy lounge. A small back room serves as a children's room; Harding is the friendly cat. Good bar food includes sandwiches, home-made soup (£1.95), filled baked potatoes (from £2.50), home-made pasty (£2.60), quarter chicken (£4.95), five home-made curries (£6.50), fresh fish such as sole, skate, trout or bass, steaks (£8.95), puddings like sticky toffee pudding and butterscotch sauce (£2.50), and roast Sunday lunch (£4.95). Well kept Flowers Original, Fullers London Pride, and Wadworths 6X on handpump. Darts, pool, cribbage, fruit machine, video game, trivia, skittle alley, and piped music. There are tables on a terrace in front, and in the side garden. *(Recommended by D B Jenkin, Miss D Buckley, Rita Horridge, Betsy and Peter Little, Bett and Brian Cox, Jenny Cantle, R J Walden, R R Winn, Alan and Paula McCully, Steven M Gent, Richard and Robyn Wain, Lyn and Geoff Hallchurch, J and M de Nordwall, J Monk, Anthony Barnes, Piotr Chodzko-Zajko, Mike and Mary Carter, Myke and Nicky Crombleholme, Chris and Margaret Southon)*

Free house ~ Licensees Oliver Wolfe and Nicola Barrass ~ Real ale ~ Bar food (not 25 Dec) ~ Restaurant ~ (01237) 451395 ~ Children welcome until 9.30pm ~ Open 12-3, 6-11; 12-3, 7-10.30 Sun; closed evening 25 Dec ~ Bedrooms: £25B/£50B

BUCKLAND MONACHORUM SX4868 Map 1
Drake Manor

Off A386 via Crapstone, just S of Yelverton roundabout

In a charming village, this characterful little pub was originally built to house the masons constructing the church in the 12th c; it was rebuilt in the 16th c. The snug Drakes Bar has beams hung with tiny cups and big brass keys, a woodburning stove in an old stone fireplace hung with horsebrasses and stirrups, a fine stripped pine high-backed settle with a partly covered hood, and a mix of other seats around just four tables (the oval one is rather nice). On the right is a small, beamed dining room with Robin Armstrong wildlife prints and drawings, another woodburning stove, a big print of the Mallard locomotive, and a little high-backed stripped settle and wheelback chairs. The heavily beamed public bar on the left has a really big stone fireplace with yet another woodburning stove, horse tack and ship badges, red Rexine wall seats, and darts; a small door leads to a low-beamed cubbyhole where children are allowed. Shove-ha'penny, cribbage, dominoes, and fruit machine. Good, reasonably priced bar food includes lunchtime filled french bread and ploughman's (from £3.25), soup (£2.25), breaded camembert with lime, honey and tarragon sauce (£3.75), home-made lasagne or garlic mushrooms with chilli and prawns (£5.50), gammon and pineapple (£6.25), steaks (from £8.95), and fresh local fish. Particularly warmly friendly staff serve the well kept John Smiths and Ushers Best and Founders on handpump, and they keep nearly 100 malt whiskies, a decent wine list, and country wines; the siamese cat Pumpkin likes hanging around the bar, but the four other cats are not so gregarious. The prettily planted and sheltered back garden has a some picnic-sets. The pub is handy for Garden House. *(Recommended by F T and S M Simonds)*

Ushers ~ Lease: Mandy Fogwill ~ Real ale ~ Bar food (12-2, 7-10(9.30 Sun)) ~ Restaurant ~ (01822) 853892 ~ Children in eating area of bar and in restaurant ~ Open 11.30-2.30(3 Sat), 6.30-11; 12-3, 7-10.30 Sun

BUTTERLEIGH SS9708 Map 1
Butterleigh Inn

Village signposted off A396 in Bickleigh; or in Cullompton take turning by Manor House Hotel – it's the old Tiverton road, with the village eventually signposted off on the left

We're keeping our fingers crossed that the new licensee in this unspoilt and friendly village pub won't make any drastic changes. The little rooms are filled with pictures of birds and dogs, topographical prints and watercolours, a fine embroidery of the Devonshire Regiment's coat-of-arms, and plates hanging by one big fireplace. One room has a mix of Edwardian and Victorian dining chairs around country kitchen tables, another has an attractive elm trestle table and sensibly placed darts, and there are prettily upholstered settles around the three tables that just fit into the cosy back snug. Tasty bar food includes filled lunchtime rolls, ploughman's, chilli skins (£2.95), burger (£4.95), steaks (from £7.95), and puddings such as pancakes with hot toffee sauce or chocolate and brandy pot (£2.50); they always have a vegetarian dish. Well kept Cotleigh Tawny, Barn Owl and occasional Old Buzzard on handpump; darts, shove-ha'penny, cribbage, dominoes, and piped music; jars of snuff on the bar. Outside are tables on a sheltered terrace and neat small lawn, with a log cabin for children. *(Recommended by Sheila and Phil Stubbs, James Flory, B J Harding, R J Walden, Tom Gondris, Catherine Lloyd, Andy and Jill Kassube, Charles Gray)*

Free house ~ Licensee Jenny Hill ~ Real ale ~ Bar food ~ (01884) 855407 ~ Children welcome lunchtime only ~ Open 12-2.30, 6(5 Fri)-11; 12-3, 7-10.30 Sun

CHAGFORD SX7087 Map 1
Ring o' Bells

Off A382 Moretonhampstead—Whiddon Down

Over the years, this old pub has been many different things – a coroner's court and mortuary, a butcher, and even a holding prison. Today it's an altogether friendlier place with a relaxed atmosphere for visitors – who may like to borrow the daily papers while enjoying early morning coffee. The oak-panelled bar has black and white photographs of the village and local characters past and present on the walls, comfortable seats, a big fireplace full of copper and brass, and a log-effect gas fire; there's a small no-smoking candlelit dining room with another fireplace. Good value bar food includes sandwiches with a generous side salad and coleslaw (from £3), filled baked potatoes (from £4.50), home-cooked ham (£5.75), creamy mushroom risotto (£6.75), daily specials such as Indian spiced lamb soup (£3; they also do soup and a pudding £5.50), duck and orange pâté (£4), pork and apple griddle cakes with redcurrant gravy (£6.25), lamb's liver and bacon (£6.95), chicken breast with a creamy garlic muhroom sauce (£7.95), salmon with wine and herbs (£9.75), and home-made puddings such as rhubarb crumble, bread pudding with stout and black treacle or redcurrant and orange cheesecake (from £3.25); Sunday roasts (£6). Well kept Bass, and Butcombe Bitter and Gold on handpump, Addlestones cider, and quite a few malt whiskies. Shove-ha'penny, dominoes, and quiet piped music. The sunny walled garden behind the pub has seats on the lawn; dogs are welcome – the pub cat Coriander will keep them in control. Good moorland walks nearby. *(Recommended by Barbara and Alan Mence, John Wilson, John and Christine Vittoe, Mike Doupe, John and Christine Simpson, R J Walden)*

Free house ~ Licensee Mrs Judith Pool ~ Real ale ~ Bar food ~ Restaurant ~ (01647) 432466 ~ Children in eating area of bar ~ Open 11-3, 5-11; 12-3, 5-10.30 Sun; May close early on quiet evenings in winter ~ Bedrooms: £20(£22.50S)/£40(£45S)

CHARDSTOCK ST3004 Map 1
George 🛏

Village signposted off A358 S of Chard

Popular locally, this thatched 13th-c inn is under new ownership. The two-roomed original bar has stone-mullioned windows, massive beams, ancient oak partition walls, character furnishings, well converted old gas lamps, and two good log fires; there's also an interestingly laid out two-level back bar. The new menu was just being organised as we went to press, so these prices are more of a guideline: filled baps or french bread (from £2.65), home-made soup (£2.95), vegetarian sweet and sour stir fry, steak and kidney pie or cumberland sausage (£5.95), mixed pasta in a creamy carbonara sauce topped with sun-dried tomatoes or mixed seafood salad (£6.25), a choice of chicken tikka masala, vegetable curry or chicken korma (£6.50), a platter of garlic bread, battered lemon prawns, chicken wings, breaded mushrooms and several sauces (£6.95; this could also be a starter for two), and puddings (from £2.95). Well kept Courage Best and Fullers London Pride on handpump; skittle alley, darts, pool, fruit machine, video games, trivia, and piped music. There are some tables out in a back loggia by a flint-cobbled courtyard sheltered by the rather attractive modern extensions to the ancient inn, with more in a safely fenced grass area with a climber and swings. The bedrooms are in a well converted back stable block. Excellent walks nearby. *(Recommended by Pete and Rosie Flower, Nigel Clifton, Steve and Maggie Willey, Mr and Mrs S Barrington, Mr and Mrs R Hatfield)*

Old English Inns ~ Manager Andrina Morton ~ Real ale ~ Bar food ~ (01460) 220241 ~ Children in eating area of bar ~ Live music first Fri of month ~ Open 11.30-3, 6-11; 12-3, 7-10.30 Sun; closed evening 25 Dec ~ Bedrooms: £40B/£50B

CHERITON BISHOP SX7793 Map 1
Old Thatch Inn

Village signposted from A30

During the winter, they hold themed food evenings here which have proved very popular, and they continue to stage their May bank holiday weekend beer festival featuring only west country ales from small independent breweries. The rambling beamed bar is separated from the lounge by a large open stone fireplace (lit in the cooler months), and they keep Branscombe Vale Branoc, Sharps Own, and a changing guest beer on handpump; dominoes, cribbage, and piped music. Bar food includes sandwiches (from £2.30; toasties from £2.60; filled french bread from £3.50), home-made soup (£2.75), home-made chicken liver pâté (£3.25), ploughman's (from £4.05), butter bean stew (£5.25), fish and chips (£5.95), pasta with creamed smoked haddock (£6.50), pork with prunes and a cream sauce (£7.95), steaks (from £8.95), and daily specials such as skate wings in a white wine, onion and chive sauce (£8.95) or fried duck breast in an apple, walnut and calvados sauce (£10.95). *(Recommended by Lyn and Geoff Hallchurch, Mr and Mrs S Groves, P and M Rudlin, Gwen and Peter Andrews, Klaus and Elizabeth Leist, R Inman, R J Walden, Paul White, Andy and Jill Kassube, Kevin Flack, K Stevens)*

Free house ~ Licensee Stephen James Horn ~ Real ale ~ Bar food ~ (01647) 24204 ~ Children in eating area of bar ~ Open 11.30-3, 6-11; 12-3, 7-10.30 Sun; closed 25 Dec ~ Bedrooms: £34.50B/£46B

CHITTLEHAMHOLT SS6521 Map 1

Exeter Inn ⏛

Off A377 Barnstaple—Crediton, and B3226 SW of South Molton

The bars in this pleasant old inn are full of matchboxes, bottles and foreign banknotes, and there's an open woodburning stove in the huge stone fireplace, cushioned mate's chairs, settles and a couple of big cushioned cask armchairs. A side area has seats set out as booths around the tables under the sloping ceiling. Good bar food includes nice leek and mushroom soup (£1.95), sandwiches (from £2; filled french bread from £2.40), filled baked potatoes (from £2.95), home-made chicken liver pâté (£3.25), ploughman's and salads (from £4.10), vegetarian cheese and nut croquettes or hog (haggis-like) pudding (£4.95), local trout (£6.95), good local steaks (£9.95), daily specials, children's meals (from £2.95), and home-made puddings with clotted cream (£2.35); Sunday roast (£5.50; children £4.25). The restaurant is no smoking. Three well kept real ales from a choice of Dartmoor Best, Greene King Abbot, Marstons Pedigree, Morlands Old Speckled Hen and Tetleys Bitter on handpump or tapped from the cask, and farm ciders; darts, shove-ha'penny, dominoes, cribbage, fruit machine, trivia, and piped music. The dog is called Alice. The terrace has benches and flower baskets. The pub's cricket team play on Sundays. Exmoor National Park is almost on the doorstep so there are plenty of outdoor activities nearby. *(Recommended by R J Walden, J M Lefeaux, D J Tomlinson, Roger and Jenny Huggins, C P Scott-Malden)*

Free house ~ Licensees Norman and Margaret Glenister ~ Real ale ~ Bar food ~ Restaurant ~ (01769) 540281 ~ Children welcome ~ Open 11.30-2.30, 6-11; 12-3, 7-10.30 Sun ~ Bedrooms: £28S/£46S

CLYST HYDON ST0301 Map 1

Five Bells ⏥

West of the village and just off B3176 not far from M5 junction 28

'A thoroughly agreeable place' is a very apt description for this most attractive thatched pub with its reed pheasants on top. You can be sure of a warm welcome from the friendly and helpful licensees whether you are coming for just a drink or to enjoy their good, popular food. The bar is spotlessly kept and divided at one end into different seating areas by brick and timber pillars; china jugs hang from big horsebrass-studded beams, there are many plates lining the shelves, lots of sparkling copper and brass, and a nice mix of dining chairs around small tables (fresh flowers and evening candles in bottles), with some comfortable pink plush banquettes on a little raised area; the pretty no-smoking restaurant is up some steps to the left and has been redecorated this year in blue and gold. Past the inglenook fireplace is another big (but narrower) room they call the Long Barn with a pine dresser at one end and similar furnishings. Changing home-made daily specials such as mussels in cider and cream (£4.95), fresh scallops with bacon and coriander (£6.50), venison and apricot pie (£6.45), savoury vegetable crumble (£5.95), chicken curry with chutneys and poppadums (£6.25), cod fillet topped with tomato, onion and cheese in cider (£7.25), steak and kidney pudding (£7.45), hickory smoked salmon (£7.95), fish platter (£8.95), and puddings such as treacle tart, peach and honey sponge or raspberry and sloe gin mousse (£3.50); also, sandwiches (from £2), home-made soup (£2.75), ploughman's (from £4.50), smoked prawns with garlic mayonnaise (£4.25), cold rare roast beef with chips (£6.95), steaks (from £9.50), and children's menu (from £2.50); there may be a wait for food if they are busy. Well kept Cotleigh Tawny, Dartmoor Best, and Wadworths 6X on handpump, a thoughtful wine list, and several malt whiskies. The cottagey front garden is a fine sight with its thousands of spring and summer flowers, big window boxes and pretty hanging baskets; up some steps is a sizeable flat lawn with picnic-sets, a slide, and pleasant country views. *(Recommended by James Flory, R J Walden, John and Vivienne Rich, Mrs Sylvia Elcoate, Basil Minson, Catherine Pocock, Andrew Shore, M G Hart, Ian Phillips, Ewan and Moira McCall, Richard and Margaret Peers, G Washington, Andrew Hodges, Stan Edwards, Tony Beaulah, John and Sarah Perry)*

Free house ~ Licensees Robin Bean and Charles Hume Smith ~ Real ale ~ Bar food (till 10pm) ~ Restaurant ~ (01884) 277288 ~ Children in eating area of bar ~ Open 11.30-2.30, 6.30; 12-2.30, 7-10.30 Sun; winter weekday opening 7 winter

COCKWOOD SX9780 Map 1
Anchor 🍴

Off, but visible from, A379 Exeter—Torbay

Originally opened as a Seaman's Mission, this bustling pub is particularly popular for its wide choice of good fresh fish: 30 different ways of serving mussels (£5.95 normal size helping, £9.95 for a large one), 12 ways of serving scallops (from £5.25 for a starter, from £12.95 for a main course), and 10 ways of serving oysters (from £5.95 for starter, from £12.95 for main course); other fresh fish dishes might include tuna steak in tomato and garlic or locally caught cod (£5.95), whole grilled plaice (£6.50), salmon steak with ginger and lime (£11.95), and a shellfish selection (£14.95). Non-fishy dishes feature as well, such as home-made soup (£2.50), sandwiches (from £2.65), home-made chicken liver pâté (£3.85), ratatouille (£4.50), home-made steak and kidney pudding (£4.95), steaks (from £12.95), and children's dishes (£2.50). Well kept Bass, Hardy Royal Oak, Flowers Original, Marstons Pedigree, and two guests on handpump (under light blanket pressure) or tapped from the cask, with rather a good wine list (10 by the glass – they do monthly wine tasting evenings September-June), a good choice of brandies, 50 malt whiskies, and West Country cider; darts, dominoes, cribbage, fruit machine, and piped music. The small, low-ceilinged, rambling rooms have black panelling, good-sized tables in various alcoves, and a cheerful winter coal fire in the snug, and the cosy restaurant is no smoking From the tables on the sheltered verandah you can look across the road to the bobbing yachts and crabbing boats in the landlocked harbour. Nearby parking is difficult when the pub is busy – which it usually is. *(Recommended by Bruce Jamieson, John Beeken, John and Vivienne Rice, Michael Bordeaux, Mike Gorton, NMF, DF, Basil J S Minson, Mrs Sylvia Elcoate, Richard and Margaret Peers, Gordon, C F Nicholls, Peter Burton, Susan and Nigel Wilson, Keith Louden, Jeanne Cross, Paul Silvestri, John and Christine Simpson, Comus Elliott)*

Heavitree ~ Tenants Mr Morgan and Miss Sanders ~ Real ale ~ Bar food (12-3, 6.30-10) ~ Restaurant ~ (01626) 890203 ~ Children in eating area of bar ~ Open 11-11; 12-10.30 Sun; closed evening 25 Dec

COLEFORD SS7701 Map 1
New Inn 🍴 🍷 🛏

Just off A377 Crediton—Barnstaple

The friendly, hard-working licensees of this 600-year-old inn continue to keep up their high standards. As well as an extensive wine list, good real ales, and restaurant-quality food at pub prices, the fact that service remains quick and efficient even at the busiest times, very much pleases their many customers. Four interestingly furnished areas spiral around the central servery with ancient and modern settles, spindleback chairs, plush-cushioned stone wall seats, some character tables – a pheasant worked into the grain of one – and carved dressers and chests, as well as paraffin lamps, antique prints and old guns on the white walls, and landscape plates on one of the beams and pewter tankards on another; the resident parrot Captain is chatty and entertaining. The servery itself has settles forming stalls around tables on the russet carpet, and there's a winter log fire. From seasonally changing menus and using good local produce, there might be cream of local crab soup (£3.95), warm duck liver and smoked bacon salad (£4.25), Brixham fish pie, beef and venison in a rich sauce on a bed of pasta or wild mushroom in a dijon mustard sauce (all £6.95), a range of grills (from £6.95), seafood platter (£8.95), pork tenderloin with watercress sauce and deep-fried onion (£11.95), breast and confit of leg of Gressingham duck with mulled red wine sauce and caramelised onions (£13.95), and puddings such as chocolate cups filled with chocolate rum mousse with orange sauce, treacle tart with clotted cream or ginger steamed pudding (from £2.95); the restaurant is no smoking. Well kept Badger Best, Otter Ale, Wadworths 6X, and a guest beer on handpump, quite a range of malt whiskies, and ports and cognacs. Fruit machine (out of the way up by the door), darts, and piped music.There are some benches and seats outside by the stream; big car park. This is one of the oldest 'new' inns in the country. *(Recommended by R J Walden, J M Lefeaux, David and Ruth Shillitoe, Guy Vowles, Pat and Tony Martin, Barbara and Alan Mence, Richard and Margaret Peers, Andrew Shore, Tim Barrow, Sue Demont, G Smale)*

Free house ~ Licensees Paul and Irene Butt ~ Real ale ~ Bar food (till 10pm) ~ Restaurant ~ (01363) 84242 ~ Children welcome but must be well behaved ~ Open 12-3, 6-11; 12-3, 7-10.30 Sun; closed 25 and 26 Dec and 1 Jan ~ Bedrooms: £46B/£60B

COMBEINTEIGNHEAD SX9071 Map 1
Wild Goose

Just off unclassified coast road Newton Abbot—Shaldon, up hill in village

What a lucky village to have such a cracking good local on its doorstep. It is home to the local cricket club, the long-standing Monday evening jazz sessions are immensely popular, dogs are welcome, and there is no piped music or juke box – plus the fact that they keep a good range of real ales, and the food is most enjoyable. The spacious back beamed lounge has a mix of wheelbacks, red plush dining chairs, a decent mix of tables and french windows to the garden; the front bar has some red Rexine seats in the window embrasures of the thick walls, flagstones in a small area by the door, some beams and standing timbers, and a step down on the right at the end, with dining chairs around the tables and a big old fireplace with an open log fire. The main part has standard lamps in corners, a small carved oak dresser with a big white goose, and a fruit machine; darts, pool, cribbage, dominoes, backgammon, and shove-ha'penny; a cosy section on the left has an old settee and comfortably well used chairs. They have 30 well kept, monthly rotating beers on six handpumps: Exe Valley Bitter and Devon Glory, Dartmoor IPA, Otter Bright, Princetown Jail Ale, and Teignworthy Beachcomber; a good collection of 30 malt whiskies. Good bar food includes well liked daily specials such as fresh saddle of lamb with lemon and almonds (£8.50), caribbean chicken breast with bananas (£8.95), local wild boar haunch steak with juniper and cranberry sauce (£10.95), as well as home-made soup (£2.30), sandwiches (from £2.30), ploughman's (from £4.50), ham and egg or home-made vegetarian lasagne (£5.50), home-made steak and kidney pie or jumbo cod fillet (£5.75), steaks (from £8.95), home-made puddings, and Sunday roast lunch (£5.25); they've introduced a 'light bites' board with chilli salsa and yoghurt dip, chicken wings piri-piri, and spicy Mexican enchiladas (£1.75-£4.95). Some picnic-sets in the garden. *(Recommended by Dennis and Janet Johnson, the Didier, Robin and Sarah Constance, John Barker, Stan Edwards)*

Free house ~ Licensees Roland and Thelma Honeywill ~ Real ale ~ Bar food (till 10pm; 9.30 Sun) ~ Restaurant ~ (01626) 872241 ~ Well behaved children in restaurant – no babies ~ Trad jazz Mon evening ~ Open 11.30-2.30, 6.30-11; 12-2.30, 7-10.30 Sun

CORNWORTHY SX8255 Map 1
Hunters Lodge

Off A381 Totnes—Kingsbridge ½ mile S of Harbertonford, turning left at Washbourne; can also be reached direct from Totnes, on the Ashprington—Dittisham road

With such a strong track record – the warmly friendly and helpful licensees here previously ran the Durant Arms at Ashprington and the Peter Tavy Inn at Peter Tavy (both successful Devon main entries) – it's not surprising that this bustling inn is doing so well. Good, well presented food now includes home-made soup (£2.20), sandwiches (from £2.50), and ploughman's (from £3.50), with lunchtime dishes such as salmon fishcake with parsley sauce (£2.95), duck and orange pâté (£3.50), cumberland sausage and mash (£3.95), lamb and rosemary hotpot (£4.95), grilled gammon steak with two eggs or vegetable curry (£5.50), and large battered cod fillet

(£5.95); in the evening, there may be chicken satay with spicy sauce or avocado mousse with prawns (£3.75), paupiettes of plaice with salmon mousse (£7.50), supreme of chicken with fresh asparagus (£8.75), baked skate with peppered butter (£8.95), rack of lamb with plum and fresh mint sauce (£9.75), sirloin steak (£9.95), and puddings (£2.95); three-course Sunday roast (£5.25). Well kept Dartmoor IPA and Otter Ale on handpump, 10 malt whiskies, a decent wine list, and Luscombe cider. The two rooms of the little low-ceilinged bar have only around half a dozen red plush wall seats and captain's chairs around heavy elm tables, and there's also a small and pretty cottagey dining room with a good log fire in its big 17th-c stone fireplace. Dominoes, shove-ha'penny, Jenga, shut the box, children's games and puzzles, and piped music. In summer, there is plenty of room to sit outside – either at the picnic-sets on a big lawn stretching up behind the car park or on the flower-filled terrace closer to the pub; several walks start from here. They have a lovely black labrador, Henry. *(Recommended by B J Harding, Glenn and Gillian Miller, R J Walden, J Dwane)*

Free house ~ Licensees John and Jill Diprose ~ Real ale ~ Bar food ~ (01803) 732204 ~ Children in eating area of bar and in restaurant ~ Open 11-2.30(3 Sat), 6-11; 11-3, 6.30-10.30 Sun

DALWOOD ST2400 Map 1
Tuckers Arms
Village signposted off A35 Axminster—Honiton

This cream-washed thatched medieval longhouse has a fine flagstoned bar with lots of beams, a random mixture of dining chairs, window seats and wall settles (including a high-backed winged black one), a log fire in the inglenook fireplace, and a woodburning stove. A side lounge has shiny black woodwork and a couple of cushioned oak armchairs and other comfortable but unpretentious seats, and the back bar has an enormous collection of miniature bottles. You can choose to have a one-course (£9.95), two-course (£13.50 or £16.50) or three-course menu (£16.50 or £19.50), with starters such as celery and leek soup with stilton, terrine of duck with bacon served on a green and orange salad, warm salad of wild mushrooms and garlic prawns or kidneys in red wine, and main courses like red sea bream with oysters in cream, muscadet and dill, chicken with wild mushrooms, calvados and cream, rack of lamb with roasted shallots, steaks or sautéed king scallops with tarragon, cider, mustard and cream. Well kept Courage Directors and Otter Ale and Bitter on handpump kept under light blanket pressure; skittle alley and piped music. The flowering tubs, window boxes and hanging baskets are lovely in summer. *(Recommended by S G N Bennett, Pete and Rosie Flower, Mr and Mrs J Bishop, Mike Gorton, N M Johns, J C Barnes, M Clifford, Richard and Robyn Wain, Yavuz and Shirley Mutlu, Basil Minson, L H and S Ede, John and Vivienne Rice, Dr D E Granger)*

Free house ~ Licensees David and Kate Beck ~ Real ale ~ Bar food (till 10pm; not evenings 25 or 26 Dec) ~ Restaurant ~ (01404) 881342 ~ Children in eating area of bar, restaurant and skittle alley ~ Open 12-3, 6.30-11; 12-3, 7-10.30 Sun ~ Bedrooms: £32.50S/£45S

DARTINGTON SX7762 Map 1
Cott
In hamlet with the same name, signposted off A385 W of Totnes opposite A384 turn-off

Under new licensees, this lovely thatched 14th-c place has a traditional, heavy-beamed bar with several communicating rooms: big open fires, flagstones, and polished brass and horse-harnesses on the whitewashed walls; one area is no smoking. The chef has stayed on and so the food still changes daily and may include soups such as cream of broccoli and stilton or tomato, carrot and orange (£3.50), smoked venison salad (£4.95), king prawns and giant mussels in garlic (£5.50), lamb, leek, and apricot casserole or mushroom stroganoff (£7.95), cold fresh salmon (£8.50), braised pheasant in red wine and juniper (£8.95), tuna steak on stir-fried vegetables with a lobster sauce (£9.95), chargrilled fillet of lamb with a creamy oyster mushroom, mint and onion sauce (£12.25), sirloin steak (£12.50), Cornish scallops with smoked bacon, cream and garlic (£13.50), and puddings like pecan and whisky pie or chococlate mousse (£3.50). The restaurant is no smoking. Well kept Bass, and Courage Best and Directors on handpump, Inch's cider, an extensive wine list, and quite a few malt whiskies. Harvey the cat has stayed on and has been joined by 6 dogs (and visiting dogs are welcome). There are picnic-sets in the garden with more on the terrace amidst the attractive tubs of flowers. Good walks through the grounds of nearby Dartington Hall, and it's pleasant touring country – particularly for the popular Dartington craft centre, the Totnes—Buckfastleigh steam railway, and one of the prettiest towns in the West Country, Totnes. The Greys who formerly owned this pub can now be found at the Castle at Lydford. *(Recommended by John and Jean Frazier, Jacquie and Jim Jones, Kim and Nigel Spence, Mrs Mary Woods, R J Walden, John and Christine Simpson, W W Burke, Paul R White, John and Enid Morris, Colin and Ann Hunt, Aubrey Bourne, David and Nina Pugsley, Nigel Flook, Betsy Brown, Andrew Hodges, Dr B H Hamilton, Gethin Lewis, Bett and Brian Cox, J F M West, Richard and Robyn Wain, David and Natasha Toulson, Revd A Nunnerley, Nick Lawless, Mike Gorton, John Askew, Miss L Hodson, Chris and Margaret Southon, John Brightley)*

Free house ~ Licensee Julie Turner ~ Real ale ~ Bar food ~ Restaurant ~ (01803) 863777 ~ Children in restaurant ~ Live music Sun evenings ~ Open 11-2.30, 5.30-11; 12-3, 7-10.30 Sun ~ Bedrooms: £55B/£65B

DARTMOUTH SX8751 Map 1
Cherub

Higher St

Dating from 1380, this Grade II* listed pub is Dartmouth's oldest building, with each of the two heavily timbered upper floors jutting further out than the one below (and hung with pretty summer flowering baskets). Inside, the bustling bar has tapestried seats under creaky heavy beams, leaded-light windows, and a big stone fireplace; upstairs is the low-ceilinged no-smoking dining room. Well kept Morlands Old Speckled Hen, Wadworths 6X and a beer named for the pub on handpump, 20 malt whiskies, and Addlestones cider. Bar food includes sandwiches, ratatouille or smoked haddock baked in white wine and topped with cheese (£5), chilli con carne (£5.50), lamb curry (£6), smoked chicken, broccoli and ham bake or seafood pasta (£6.50), steak (£7.50). It does get packed in summer. *(Recommended by Colin and Ann Hunt, Michael Hill, John Askew, John Barker, Nick Lawless, I J and N K Buckmaster, Mr and Mrs C Roberts, Colin Thompson, Rob and Gill Weeks, John and Christine Simpson)*

Free house ~ Licensee Alan Jones ~ Real ale ~ Bar food (till 10pm) ~ Restaurant ~ (01803) 832571 ~ Children in restaurant if over 10 ~ Open 11-11; 12-10.30 Sun; 11-2.30, 5.30-11 in winter

Royal Castle Hotel 🛏

11 The quay

A good mix of both locals and visitors creates a bustling atmosphere in this rambling 17th-c hotel, overlooking the inner harbour. The left-hand local bar has navigation lanterns, glass net-floats and old local ship photographs, and a mix of furnishings from stripped pine kitchen chairs to some interesting old settles and mahogany tables; one wall is stripped to the original stonework and there's a big log fire. On the right in the more sedate, partly no-smoking carpeted bar, they may do winter spit-roast joints on some lunchtimes; there's also a Tudor fireplace with copper jugs and kettles (beside which are the remains of a spiral staircase), and plush furnishings, including some Jacobean-style chairs. One alcove has swords and heraldic shields on the wall. Well kept Blackawton Bitter, Courage Directors, Wadworths 6X, and guest beers on handpump, and a wide choice of malt whiskies; welcoming staff. Darts, fruit machine, and quiz nights (Monday). Enjoyable, good value bar food includes toasted sandwiches (from £2.95), home-made soup, pasties, deep-fried brie with gooseberry sauce, ploughman's, gammon and egg (£5.75), steak and kidney pie (£6.25), good seafood pie and nice prawn and crab salad, daily specials and steaks.

(Recommended by E G Parish, Peter and Audrey Dowsett, Mrs Mary Woods, Lawrence Pearse, Colin and Ann Hunt)

Free house ~ Licensees Nigel and Anne Way ~ Real ale ~ Bar food (all day from breakfast onwards) ~ Restaurant ~ (01803) 833033 ~ Children in restaurant ~ Jazz Sunday ~ Open 11-11; 12-10.30 Sun ~ Bedrooms: £66.95B/£103.90B

DODDISCOMBSLEIGH SX8586 Map 1
Nobody Inn ★★ ♀ ◖ ⇖

Village signposted off B3193, opposite northernmost Christow turn-off

This is very much somewhere people come back to year after year – it's that sort of marvellously unchanging place. The two rooms of the lounge bar have a relaxed, friendly atmosphere, handsomely carved antique settles, windsor and wheelback chairs, benches, carriage lanterns hanging from the beams, and guns and hunting prints in a snug area by one of the big inglenook fireplaces. They keep perhaps the best pub wine cellar in the country – 850 well cellared wines by the bottle and 20 by the glass kept oxidation-free; there's also properly mulled wine and twice-monthly tutored tastings (they also sell wine retail, and the good tasting-notes in their detailed list are worth the £3 it costs – anyway refunded if you buy more than £30-worth); also, a choice of 250 whiskies, local farm ciders, fresh orange juice, and well kept Bass, Nobody's (brewed by Branscombe), Scatter Rock Teign Valley Tipple, and a guest beer on handpump or tapped straight from the cask. Well liked bar food includes starters such as good home-made cream of pumpkin soup or local ostrich liver and juniper berry pâté (£3.50), mixed bean and vegetable casserole with cheese topping (£5.50), savoy cabbage parcels filled with minced lamb and rice with a fresh tomato sauce (£5.80), smoked haddock mornay (£6.20), breast of chicken in an orange marmalade and apricot and raisin sauce or home-made steak and kidney pudding (£6.80), and puddings such as raspberry and frangipane tart or caramel sponge with clotted cream fudge topping. They keep an incredible choice of around 50 West Country cheeses (half a dozen £4.80; you can buy them to take away as well). The restaurant is no smoking. There are picnic-sets on the terrace with views of the surrounding wooded hill pastures. The medieval stained glass in the local church is some of the best in the West Country. No children are allowed inside the pub. *(Recommended by Mike and Mary Carter, Peter Burton, Dr and Mrs G H Lewis, Steve Whalley, Guy Vowles, Andrew Low, John Evans, Nigel Flook, Betsy Brown, JP, PP, Mike Gorton, Gordon, Mrs Sylvia Elcoate, John Robertson, G Washington, Jasper Sabey, N P Bayliss, Dallas Seawright, Mr and Mrs P Eastwood, Richard and Margaret Peers, Nigel Cogger, John Askew, Basil Minson, Lynn Sharpless, Bob Eardley, Dr Rod Holcombe, the Didler, Martin Jennings, Richard and Robyn Wain, Catherine Lloyd, J Dwane, Jacqueline Orme, Dr R Price, J; also in the Good Hotel Guide)*

Free house ~ Licensee Nick Borst-Smith ~ Real ale ~ Bar food (till 10pm) ~ Restaurant ~ (01647) 252394 ~ Open 12-2.30, 6-11; 12-3, 7-10.30 Sun; closed 25 and 26 Dec ~ Bedrooms: £23(£38B)/£38(£64B)

DOLTON SS5712 Map 1
Union

B3217

This is a comfortable, quiet place to stay with particularly good, interesting food, a cheerful and relaxed atmosphere, and welcoming licensees. The little lounge bar has a comfortably cushioned window seat, a pink plush chesterfield, a nicely carved priest's table and some dark pine country chairs with brocaded cushions, and dagging shears, tack, country prints, and brass shell cases. On the right and served by the same stone bar counter, is another bar with a chatty, enjoyable atmosphere and liked by locals both eating or dropping in for just a drink: heavy black beams hung with brasses, an elegant panelled oak settle and antique housekeeper's chairs, a small settle snugged into the wall, and various dining chairs on the squared patterned carpet; the big stone fireplace has some brass around it, and on the walls are old guns, saws, antlers, some engravings, and a whip. As well as lunchtime snacks like baguettes filled with bacon and mushrooms or locally made sausages (from £2.50), and ploughman's or local cod in beer batter (£4.50), there might be sardines freshly grilled with olive oil and sea salt (£3.50), moules marinières (£4.25), tomato pasta filled with different cheeses and topped with tomato and herb sauce and parmesan (£5.50), escalope of pork with cream and marsala wine (£6.95), fish mixed grill (£8.50), rib-eye steak marinated in lemon juice and olive oil (£8.95), king scallops with a cream and vermouth reduction (£9.50), daily specials such as turkey, tomato and garam masala curry with rice (£5.95), tuna steak with roast tomato, onion and pepper sauce (£8) or herb crusted rack of local lamb (£9.50), and puddings such as hot summer fruits, mixed summer berries cooked in vodka and served with home-made meringues topped with clotted cream or chocolate truffle torte (£2.95). The restaurant is no smoking. Well kept Barum Original and BSE (from a small new Barnstaple brewery), Clearwater Bronze Bream (unknown to us), Sharps Doom Bar, and St Austell HSD, and decent wines. Out on a small patch of grass in front of the building are some rustic tables and chairs. *(Recommended by I Christie, DJW, Alan and Heather Jacques)*

Free house ~ Licensees Ian and Irene Fisher ~ Real ale ~ Bar food (not Weds lunchtime) ~ Restaurant ~ (01805) 804633 ~ Children in eating area of bar and in restaurant until 9.30pm ~ Open 12-2.30, 6-11; 12-2.30, 7-10.30 Sun; closed Weds lunchtime; no food or accomm last 2 wks Feb ~ Bedrooms: /£45B

DREWSTEIGNTON SX7390 Map 1
Drewe Arms
Signposted off A30 NW of Moretonhampstead

There's a lot of character in this unpretentious old thatched pub – and friendly licensees. The small room on the left changed hardly at all during the outstandingly long tenure of the former landlady, the late Mabel Mudge, and still has its serving hatch, basic seats, and huge fireplace yellowing its walls; the room on the right with its assorted tables and chairs and another log fire is not much bigger. Well kept Flowers IPA, a guest like Fullers London Pride, and Gray's cider kept on racks in the tap room behind. The back has however been opened up into a sizeable eating area, with food that really does mark a new departure for this ancient tavern – not just sandwiches, a good proper ploughman's, and pork and sage sausage with bubble and squeak (£4.95), but fresh crab and mushroom bake (£6.95), tasty duck breast, and steaks, with decent wines by the glass. Darts, shove-ha'penny, dominoes, and skittle alley. Castle Drogo nearby (open for visits) looks medieval, though it was actually built earlier this century. *(Recommended by Mrs Sylvia Elcoate, John Askew, Mike Gorton, John Barker, Kevin Thorpe, Philip Vernon, Kim Maidment, Guy Vowles, Alan and Paula McCully, John and Christine Vittoe, Sue and Bob Ward, Paul and Judith Booth, Robert Gomme, JP, PP)*

Whitbreads ~ Lease Janice and Colin Sparks ~ Real ale ~ Bar food ~ Restaurant ~ (01647) 281224 ~ Children in restaurant ~ Open 11-3, 6-11; 12-3, 7-10.30 Sun ~ Bedrooms: /£50B

EAST PRAWLE SX7836 Map 1
Freebooter
Village signposted off A379 E of Kingsbridge, at Frogmore and Chillington

In a pretty village close to the coastal path between Salcombe and Start Point and with stunning views, is this little 18th-c inn. It's a friendly, unspoilt place, and to the right of the door are wheelback chairs and brocaded wall seats on the parquet floor and a stone fireplace with its surround supposedly taken from a Spanish captain's cabin door, and on the left, another stone fireplace (which has holes in the huge granite block over it that were packed with explosives for blasting rock out of a nearby quarry), a couple of armchairs and a curved high-backed settle, flowers on chunky elm tables and more wheelback chairs; plenty of books on the area, shipping memorabilia, and a friendly, relaxed atmosphere; some tables are no smoking. Good, enjoyable food (using organic or additive free meat and poultry) includes sandwiches (from £1.80), home-made soups like parsnip and ginger (£2.50), home-made burgers or free-range three-egg omelettes (from £2.50), garlic mushrooms in cream and white wine (£3), grilled goat's cheese on walnut bread (£3.50), scallops in ginger or creamy leek croustade (£5.50), seafood au gratin (£7.50), various baltis (from £7.50), beef in ale (£8.50), steaks (from £9), and puddings such as gooseberry or plum pies or treacle sponge (£2.50). Well kept Greene King Abbot, St Austell Dartmoor Best, and a guest such as Princetown Jail Ale on handpump, kept under light blanket pressure, Heron Valley cider, and good wines by the glass; darts, shove-ha'penny, cribbage, dominoes, board games, and piped music. There are views of the sea from the walled garden and a couple of picnic-sets outside in front. The name Freebooter means pirate's ship. They hope to open bedrooms soon. *(Recommended by Sheila and Karen Stark, Caroline Raphael, Richard and Robyn Wain)*

Free house ~ Licensees John and Delphine Swaddle ~ Real ale ~ Bar food ~ (01548) 511208 ~ Children in eating area of bar ~ Occasional blues/swing ~ Open 11.30(12 winter)-3, 6-11; 12-3, 7-10.30 Sun

EXETER SX9190 Map 1
Double Locks ★ ◧

Canal Banks, Alphington; from A30 take main Exeter turn-off (A377/396) then next right into Marsh Barton Industrial Estate and follow Refuse Incinerator signs; when road bends round in front of the factory-like incinerator, take narrow dead end track over humpy bridge, cross narrow canal swing bridge and follow track along canal; much quicker than it sounds, and a very worthwhile diversion from the final M5 junction

With 10 real ales on handpump, jazz on Thursday evenings and live bands on Friday and Saturday, this remote old lockhouse is popular with the younger set. Tapped from the cask or on handpump, the beers might include Adnams Broadside, Badger Tanglefoot, Branscombe Branoc, Courage Directors, Fullers London Pride, Greene King Abbot, Smiles Best, Golden and Heritage, and Youngs Special; Grays farm cider. Bar food includes sandwiches (£2.70; garlic ciabatta with goat's cheese £3.40), mushrooms on toast (£4), filled baked potatoes (from £4.30), ham and eggs, chicken satay or ratatouille (all £4.95), ploughman's (£5), Wednesday evening curries (from £5), breakfast special (£5.95), and puddings like treacle tart (£3.15). There's quite a nautical theme in the bar – with ship's lamps and model ships – and friendly service; there have been a few comments from readers about housekeeping this year. Darts, shove-ha'penny, cribbage, trivia, and piped music. There are picnic-sets outside and cycle paths along the ship canal. *(Recommended by Mike Gorton, M A Buchanan, Mrs Sylvia Elcoate, Vivienne and John Rice, Dr and Mrs B D Smith, Barbara and Alan Mence, JP, PP, Paul White, the Didler, John Brightley, Andy and Jill Kassube, Hilary Dobbie)*

Smiles ~ Managers Tony Stearman & I G Williams ~ Real ale ~ Bar food (11-10.30; 12-10 Sun) ~ (01392) 256947 ~ Children welcome ~ Trad jazz Thurs evening, live bands Fri and Sat ~ Open 11-11; 12-10.30 Sun

Imperial ◧

Crediton/Tiverton rd nr St Davids Stn

Once past the gated lodge, you find this early 19th-c mansion in a 6-acre hillside park with plenty of picnic-sets in the grounds and elegant metal garden furniture in an attractive cobbled courtyard. Inside, there are all sorts of areas such as a couple of little clubby side bars and a great island bar looking into a light and airy former orangery – the huge glassy fan of its end wall is lightly mirrored – and a glorious ex-ballroom filled with elaborate plasterwork and gilding brought here in the 1920s from Haldon House (a Robert Adam stately home that was falling on hard times). One area is no smoking. The furnishings give Wetherspoons' usual solid well spaced comfort, and there are plenty of interesting pictures and other things to look at. Well kept and very cheap Bass, Courage Directors, Exmoor Stag, Theakstons Best, and a guest beer tapped from the cask. Good bar food includes soup (£1.95), filled baps (from £2.35; with soup as well £2.85), filled baked potatoes (from £2.75), quite a few burgers (from £3.15), ham and eggs (£3.65), bangers and mash (£4.30), mushroom stroganoff (£4.75), steak and mushroom pie (£4.95), rump steak (£7.95), puddings like blackberry and apple pie (£1.99), and Sunday roast (£4.55); between 2 and 10pm, two people can eat for £5.95. Silenced fruit machines and video game. No under-18s. *(Recommended by Jim and Maggie Cowell, Susan and John Douglas, Mike Gorton, Ian Phillips, Mike and Mary Carter, R J Walden, Andrew Hodges)*

Wetherspoons ~ Manager Jonathan Randall ~ Real ale ~ Bar food (11-10; 12-9.30 Sun) ~ (01392) 434050 ~ Open 11-11; 12-10.30 Sun

White Hart ★ ♀ ⇌

4 rather slow miles from M5 junction 30; follow City Centre signs via A379, B3182; straight towards centre if you're coming from A377 Topsham Road

The rambling atmospheric bar of this nicely old-fashioned 14th-c inn is full of character, a place where people have been meeting for centuries. There are heavy bowed beams in the dark ochre terracotta ceiling hung with big copper jugs, windsor armchairs and built-in winged settles with latticed glass tops to their high backs, oak tables on the bare oak floorboards (carpet in the quieter lower area) and a log fire in one great fireplace with long-barrelled rifles above it. In one of the bay windows is a set of fine old brass beer engines, the walls are decorated with pictorial plates, old copper and brass platters, and a wall cabinet holds some silver and copper. From the latticed windows, with their stained-glass coats-of-arms, one can look out on the cobbled courtyard – lovely when the wistaria is flowering in May. Bottlescreu Bill's (closed Sunday evening) is a dimly candlelit bar with bare stone walls and sawdust on the floor. Bar food includes rolls or sandwiches (from £2.75), a plate of toasted fingers (£3.75), home-made pork and chicken liver terrine (£3.95), steak and oyster pie or creamy leek pastry parcel (£6.95), barbecued dishes (cooked in another sheltered courtyard) like chicken breast (£7.95), butterfly lamb chops in honey and mint (£8.95) or 10oz rib-eye steak (£9.95), and puddings (£3.75). The restaurant is no smoking. Bass, Davy's Old Wallop (served in pewter tankards in Bottlescreu Bill's) and John Smiths on handpump, and a respectable range of Davy's wines. Bedrooms are in a separate modern block. *(Recommended by Ian Phillips, Susan and John Douglas, Reg Nelson, Mark Girling, Dr and Mrs B D Smith, D J and P M Taylor, Jacquie and Jim Jones, R J Walden, Mr and Mrs J Pitts, Paul R White)*

Free house ~ Licensee G F Stone ~ Real ale ~ Bar food (till 10pm) ~ Restaurant ~ (01392) 279897 ~ Children in eating area of bar ~ Open 11.30-3, 5-11; 11.30-11 Sat; 12-3, 7-10.30 Sun ~ Bedrooms: £61B/£94B

EXMINSTER SX9487 Map 1
Turf Hotel ★

Follow the signs to the Swan's Nest, signposted from A739 S of village, then continue to end of track, by gates; park, and walk right along canal towpath – nearly a mile; there's a fine seaview out to the mudflats at low tide.

To reach this isolated, friendly pub you can either walk (which takes about 20 minutes along the ship canal) or take a 40-minute ride from Countess Wear in the pub's own boat, the *Water Mongoose* (bar on board; £3 adult, £2 child return, charter for up to 56 people £140). They also operate a 12-seater and an 8-seater boat which bring people down the Exe estuary from Topsham quay (15 minute trip, adult £3, child £2). For those arriving in their own boat there is a large pontoon as well as several moorings. From the bay windows of the pleasantly airy bar there are views out to the mudflats – which are full of gulls and waders at low tide; polished bare floorboards, church pews, wooden chairs and alcove seats, big bright shorebird prints by John Tennent and pictures and old photographs of the pub and its characters over the years; woodburning stove and antique gas fire. From the new menu, bar food now includes ploughman's using only cheeses from Devon and Cornwall, brie, pesto and tomato toastie (£3.80), smoked haddock chowder (£4.85), garlic bread topped with melted goat's cheese (£5.25), leek and lentil lasagne (£5.95), and chargrilled fish and steaks on the deck area. The dining room is no smoking. Well kept Dartmoor Best, Marstons Pedigree, and Morlands Old Speckled

Hen on handpump, Green Valley farm cider, wines from the Loire Valley that they import themselves, and several gins; darts, shove-ha'penny, cribbage, dominoes, and piped music. The garden has a children's play area and they have built a new deck area by the water *(Recommended by Mike Gorton, James Flory, EML, Rick Glanvill)*

Free house ~ Licensees Clive and Ginny Redfern ~ Real ale ~ Bar food (not Sun evening) ~ Restaurant ~ (01392) 833128 ~ Children welcome ~ Open 11-11; 12-10.30 Sun; closed Nov-Mar (may open weekends) ~ Bedrooms: £22.50/£45

FROGMORE SX7742 Map 1
Globe
A379 E of Kingsbridge

This is a fine spot for exploring the South Hams with its birdwatching, sailing, diving, and many walks. The friendly lounge bar here has walls entirely papered with maritime charts and hung with ship and yacht paintings, some built-in settles creating a few booths in one corner, nicely old-fashioned pale blue plush chairs with wooden arms, a couple of wall settles, two attractive high-backed spindle farmhouse chairs, candles in bottles on the mix of simple tables, and an open fire. There's a simple flagstoned public bar with pool, darts, fruit machines, TV, a yellow cockatiel called Mr Pecker, and a rustic dining room. Well kept Exmoor Ale and Greene King Abbot on handpump, local scrumpy in summer, and country wines. Decent bar food includes sandwiches (from £1.75), home-made soup (£2.75), hot, crunchy nut brie (£3.50), battered cod (£4.25), ploughman's (from £4.50), home-made steak, kidney and Guinness pie or lasagne (£5.25), curry (£5.45), gammon and pineapple (£5.95), home-made pizzas (you can take them home as well), fresh fish dishes, rump steak (£9.95), puddings, and children's menu (£2.25). There are picnic-sets on the lower terrace, white garden furniture on the upper terrace, a children's play area, and views of the creek. *(Recommended by Roger Wain-Heapy, Lorna and Howard Lambert, Gilly and Frank Newman)*

Free house ~ Licensees Mr and Mrs D Johnston ~ Real ale ~ Bar food (12-2, 6-10) ~ Restaurant ~ (01548) 531351 ~ Children welcome away from bar ~ Occasional live bands ~ Open 11.30-3, 5.30-11; 12-3, 6.30-10.30 Sun ~ Bedrooms: £22(£27.50S)/£37(£42S)

HARBERTON SX7758 Map 1
Church House
Village signposted from A381 just S of Totnes

In a steep little twisting village, this ancient pub was probably used as chantry-house for monks connected with the church. The open-plan bar has some magnificent medieval oak panelling, and the latticed glass on the back wall is almost 700 years old and one of the earliest examples of non-ecclesiastical glass in the country. Furnishings include attractive 17th- and 18th-c pews and settles, candles, and a large inglenook fireplaces with a woodburning stove; one half of the room is set out for eating. The family room is no smoking. Bar food is most enjoyable and people tend to choose from the daily specials board: local mustard and herb sausages with onion gravy (£4.50), steak and kidney pudding or roasted red pepper and aubergine parmigiana (£6.95), various baltis using freshly ground spices (£7.95), chicken supreme filled with blue brie, apricots and almonds with a white wine and cheese sauce or local rabbit, pheasant, pigeon and venison pie (£8.95), and local scallops, prawn and monkfish kebabs (£9.95); from the standard menu there might be home-made soup (£2.40), sandwiches (from £2.50), ploughman's (from £3.95), a fry-up (£5.95), prawn curry (£7.50), grilled whole plaice (£7.95), steaks (from £7.95), puddings (from £2.50), and children's menu (from £1.95). Well kept Bass, Courage Best, and Charles Wells Bombardier and a guest beer on handpump, farm cider, and several malt whiskies; darts and dominoes. If you are staying, Tabitha the cat is keen to sleep on guest's beds. *(Recommended by Paul S McPherson, J H Bell, Bob Medland, R J Walden, Margaret and Roy Randle, Nigel and Amanda Thorp, John and Christine Lowe, Paul and Heather Bettesworth, Peter C B Craske)*

*Free house ~ Licensees David and Jennifer Wright ~ Real ale ~ Bar food ~ (01803)
863707 ~ Children in family room ~ Open 12-2.30, 6-11; 11.30-3, 6-11 Sat; 12-3, 7-
10.30 Sun; closed evenings 25 and 26 Dec and 1 Jan ~ Bedrooms: £25/£40*

HATHERLEIGH SS5404 Map 1
George ♀

A386 N of Okehampton

The courtyard around which this black and white timbered old pub is built has very
pretty summer window boxes and hanging baskets, and there are rustic wooden
seats and tables on the cobblestones; there's also a walled cobbled garden. The little
front bar in the original part of the building has huge oak beams, stone walls two or
three feet thick, an enormous fireplace, and easy chairs, sofas and antique cushioned
settles. The spacious L-shaped main bar was built from the wreck of the inn's old
brewhouse and coachmen's loft, and has more beams, a woodburning stove, and
antique settles around sewing-machine treadle tables; dominoes, piped music. The
right-hand bar, liked by younger customers, has darts, pool, juke box, and fruit
machine; the labrador is called Jessica. Well kept Bass, St Austell Dartmoor Best and
HSD and a guest beer on handpump, plus farm cider. Bar food includes sandwiches
(from £2), home-made soup (£2.25), filled baked potatoes (from £3.25),
ploughman's (£3.50), daily specials (around £3.95; delicious roast chicken and pork
fillet in a cider and sage sauce), steak and kidney pie (£6.50), steaks (from £8.95),
half a roast duck with black cherry and cassis sauce (£9.25), and hot seafood platter
(£9.50). Some of the bedrooms have four-poster beds. *(Recommended by David Carr, JP,
PP, John Askew, Dave Braisted, Rita Horridge, R J Walden)*

*Free house ~ Licensees David and Christine Jeffries ~ Real ale ~ Bar food ~ Restaurant
~ (01837) 810454 ~ Children welcome ~ Occasional jazz evenings ~ Open 11-3, 6-11;
12-3, 7-10.30 Sun ~ Bedrooms: £28.50(£48S)/£49.50(£69.50S)*

Tally Ho 🍺 ⛏

Market St (A386)

As well as enjoying this friendly pub's own-brewed ales here, you can take them
away in bottles or cartons: Potboiler, Jollop (winter only), Tarka Tipple, Thurgia
and Nutters; 20 malt whiskies, and Italian grappas. The opened-together rooms of
the bar have heavy beams, sturdy old oak and elm tables on the partly carpeted
wooden floor, decorative plates between the wall timbers, shelves of old bottles and
pottery, and two woodburning stoves. Bar food includes lunchtime sandwiches on a
fresh bagel or warm french bread (from £3), omelettes (from £3.55), and
ploughman's (from £3.75), as well as home-made soup, home-made game pâté
(£4.30), steaks (from £10.45), and daily specials like pasta with thai-style vegetables
(£5.50), steak and kidney in ale pie (£7.50), and chicken breast with herby
mozzarella and grilled vegetables (£8.70); pizzas on Wednesdays (from £4.35) and a
Swiss fondue on Thursdays (£22 per couple; not summer). The weekend restaurant
is no smoking. Darts, shove-ha'penny, dominoes, cribbage, trivia, and piped music.
There are tables in the sheltered garden. *(Recommended by R J Walden, Mr and Mrs Croall,
David Carr, JP, PP, John and Vivienne Rice, Jenny Cantle)*

*Own brew ~ Licensee Miss M J Leonard ~ Real ale ~ Bar food (till 10pm) ~
Restaurant ~ (01837) 810306 ~ Children in eating area of bar and in restaurant ~
Open 11-3, 6-11; 12-3, 7-11 Sun ~ Bedrooms: £30B/£50B*

HAYTOR VALE SX7677 Map 1
Rock ★ ⛏

Haytor signposted off B3387 just W of Bovey Tracey, on good moorland road to Widecombe

Readers enjoy staying here very much. It's a rather civilised inn with a peaceful
atmosphere, good, enjoyable food, well kept ales, and friendly, efficient staff. The
two communicating, partly panelled bar rooms have easy chairs, oak windsor

armchairs and high-backed settles, polished antique tables with candles and fresh flowers, old-fashioned prints and decorative plates on the walls, and good winter log fires (the main fireplace has a fine Stuart fireback); all rooms apart from the bar are no smoking. A wide choice of very good bar food includes home-made soup (£2.95), wild boar and apple sausages with garlic creamed potato (£4.95), lunchtime sandwiches (from £4.95; they come with julienne of french fries, salad leaves and olives), fresh mussels in garlic butter (£5.25), interesting salads such as scallops with hazelnut dressing, caramelised red onion tart or salmon fishcakes with a lemon caper dressing (from £5.95), pasta filled with ricotta and spinach with a leek sauce (£6.25), chicken curry (£6.95), steak and kidney pie (£7.50), shank of lamb in a minted rosemary and wine sauce (£9.95), steaks (from £10.95), puddings such as chocolate pot or lemon crème brûlée (from £3.45), and daily specials.Well kept Dartmoor Best and Hardy Royal Oak on handpump, and several malt whiskies. In summer, the pretty, well kept large garden opposite the inn is a popular place to sit and there are some tables and chairs on a small terrace next to the pub itself. The village is just inside the National Park, and golf, horse riding and fishing (and walking, of course) are nearby. *(Recommended by Mike Doupe, Martin Jennings, I Maw, R F Ballinger, J H Bell, NMF, DF, Paul and Maggie Baker, A de Montjoie, Andy and Jill Kassube, Revd John E Cooper, Richard and Valerie Wright, Alan and Paula McCully, Mr and Mrs C R Little, R J Walden, Tim and Beryl Dawson, Kim and Nigel Spence, B J Harding, John and Vivienne Rice)*

Free house ~ Licensee Christopher Graves ~ Real ale ~ Bar food ~ Restaurant ~ (01364) 661305 ~ Children in eating area of bar ~ Open 11-3, 6-11(10.30 winter wkdys); 11-11 Sat; 11-3, 6-10.30 Sun ~ Bedrooms: £57.50B/£69.95B

HOLBETON SX6150 Map 1
Mildmay Colours 🍺
Signposted off A379 W of A3121 junction

The own-brewed beers here (Mildmay SP and Colours) are still offered at a bargain price of £1.20 per pint during the 6-7pm 'happy hour'; Skinner's Cornish Knocker is a guest, and they keep local farm cider and 10 malt whiskies. The bar has various horse and racing pictures on the partly stripped stone and partly white walls, plenty of bar stools as well as cushioned wall seats and wheelback chairs on the turkey carpet, and a tile-sided woodburning stove; an arch leads to a smaller, similarly decorated family area. One area is no smoking. The separate plain back bar has pool, sensible darts, and fruit machine. Bar food (they tell us prices have hardly changed since last year) includes sandwiches (from £2.80), home-made soup (£2.75), home-made chicken liver pâté (£2.95), filled baked potatoes (from £2.75), ham and chips (£3.95), ploughman's (from £4.95), mushroom stroganoff (£5.40), Mexican chicken enchilada (£6.25), pork chops with apple sauce (£6.60), huge mixed grill or fresh scallops (£9.95), steaks (from £9.95), daily specials, puddings (£2.95), and children's meals (£2.70); Wednesday evening is curry night and there is a carvery in the restaurant on Saturday evening and Sunday lunch. The well kept back garden has picnic-sets, a swing, and an aviary, and there's a small front terrace. We've not yet heard from readers who have stayed here, but would expect it to be good. *(Recommended by Paul White, Alan and Paula McCully, David Lewis, Sarah Lart, JDM, KM)*

Own brew ~ Licensee Louise Price ~ Real ale ~ Bar food ~ Restaurant ~ (01752) 830248 ~ Children welcome ~ Open 11-3(2.30 in winter), 6-11; 12-3, 7-11 Sun ~ Bedrooms: £30B/£50B

HORNDON SX5280 Map 1
Elephants Nest ★ 🍺
If coming from Okehampton on A386 turn left at Mary Tavy Inn, then left after about ½ mile; pub signposted beside Mary Tavy Inn, then Horndon signposted; on the Ordnance Survey Outdoor Leisure Map it's named as the New Inn

In rather an untouched spot, this 400-year-old pub is on the edge of Dartmoor's lower slopes. There are wooden benches and tables on the spacious, flower-bordered lawn, you can walk from here straight onto the moor or Black Down, though a better start (army exercises permitting) might be to drive past Wapsworthy to the end of the lane, at OS Sheet 191 map reference 546805. Inside, there's a good log fire, large rugs and flagstones, a beams-and-board ceiling, and cushioned stone seats built into the windows, with captain's chairs around the tables; the name of the pub is written up on the beams in 60 languages; what was an old beer cellar is another bar with views over the garden and beyond to the moors. Enjoyable home-made bar food at lunchtime includes soup (£1.70), filled granary rolls (from £1.80), home-made crab or chive and cashew nut pâté (£3.50), chicken fillet burger (£3.70), ploughman's (from £3.80; the elephant's lunch £4 is good), steak and kidney pie (£5.50), and local game pie (£7), with evening dishes like deep-fried brie with gooseberry conserve or chicken satay (£3.50), beef curry (£5.50), chilli con carne (£4.60), and steaks (from £9.90); there are always 7 daily specials (2 or 3 are vegetarian), and puddings like treacle and walnut tart; small helpings for children. Well kept Boddingtons Bitter, Palmers IPA, St Austell HSD, and two changing guest beers on handpump; Harvest cider. Sensibly placed darts, cribbage, dominoes, and piped music. They have four dogs, one cat, ducks, chickens, rabbits, and horses; customers' dogs are allowed in on a lead. *(Recommended by Jeanne Cross, Paul Silvestri, Dr and Mrs N Holmes, JP, PP, Mrs Amanda Rudolf, Paul R White, P Taylor, Paul and Heather Bettesworth, Lynn Sharpless, Bob Eardley)*

Free house ~ Licensee Nick Hamer ~ Real ale ~ Bar food (till 10pm) ~ (01822) 810273 ~ Children welcome away from bar ~ Open 11.30-2.30, 6.30-11; 12-2.30, 7-10.30 Sun

HORSEBRIDGE SX3975 Map 1
Royal ◖

Village signposted off A384 Tavistock—Launceston

Sadly they've stopped brewing their own ale at this prettily-set pub, but they do keep Bass, Boddingtons, Sharps Doom Bar and Wadworths 6X on handpump. It's a quiet place with no music or fruit machines, and the simple slate-floored rooms haven't changed much since Turner slept on a settle in front of the fire so that he could slip out early to paint the nearby bridge, which marks the boundary with Cornwall; interesting bric-a-brac, and pictures of the local flood. The side room is no smoking, and what was the kitchen (a new one is being built into the disused brewery) will be used for extra eating space. Darts, bar billiards, and dominoes. Tasty bar food includes filled french bread (from £3.25), filled baked potatoes or ploughman's (from £3.50), ham and egg (£3.75), home-made lasagne (£4.50), pasta royal (£4.75), chilli cheese tortillas (£5), and sirloin steak (£8.95). There are seats in the big garden and on the back terrace. This was known as the Packhorse Inn until the Civil War when Charles I visited the pub and left his seal in the granite doorstep. No children in the evening. *(Recommended by Alan Kirkpatrick, Bruce Bird, Jacquie and Jim Jones, Paul and Heather Bettesworth, JP, PP, D B Jenkin, R J Walden, Betty Petheram, Chris and Margaret Southon, Alan and Paula McCully)*

Free house ~ Licensees Paul Eton and Catherine Bromidge ~ Real ale ~ Bar food ~ (01822) 870214 ~ Children in eating area of bar lunchtime only ~ Live duo monthly Sat ~ Open 12-3, 7-11(10.30 Sun)

IDDESLEIGH SS5708 Map 1
Duke of York

B3217 Exbourne—Dolton

There's a good mix of both locals and visitors in this friendly old thatched pub. The characterful bar has rocking chairs by the roaring log fire, cushioned wall benches built into the wall's black-painted wooden dado, stripped tables, and other homely country furnishings, and well kept Adnams Broadside, Cotleigh Tawny, Sharps Doom Bar, Smiles Golden, and Wye Valley Dorothy Goodbodys tapped from the cask; farm cider, Irish whiskies, local wine, and freshly squeezed orange and pink grapefruit juices. Good bar food includes sandwiches, home-made soup (£3.50), home-made port and stilton pâté, Thai spicy beef salad or fresh scallops wrapped in bacon (£4.50), duck parcel or liver and bacon (£6.50), good steak and kidney pudding (£7), fresh lemon sole (£7.50), and home-made puddings like sticky toffee pudding (£3.50); three-course menu in the dining room (£18.50), and hearty breakfasts. Darts, cribbage, and chess. Through a small coach arch is a little back garden with some picnic-sets. Good fishing nearby. *(Recommended by JP, PP, R J Walden, Mr and Mrs Croall, Richard and Ann Higgs, Tess Powderham, Bett and Brian Cox, Richard Fendick, Rachel Martin, Martin Jones, Stephen J Willmot)*

Free house ~ Licensees Jamie Stuart and Pippa Hutchinson ~ Real ale ~ Bar food (11-10; 12-9.30 Sun) ~ Restaurant ~ (01837) 810253 ~ Children welcome ~ Open 11-11; 12-10.30 Sun ~ Bedrooms: £25B/£50B

INSTOW SS4730 Map 1

Boat House

Just across the small road in front of this simple modern and friendly little pub is a huge sandy tidal beach – a big summer bonus. There's just one bar with high ceilings and an airy feel, black mate's chairs around black tables, red plush cushioned small settles against the wall and built into the high vertical-panelled dado, and big old-fashioned nautical paintings on wood hung on the stripped stone wall facing the long wooden bar counter (lined by green plush bar stools). Well kept Bass, Flowers IPA, and a guest beer on handpump, and good bar food such as sandwiches, home-made soup (£1.90), chicken liver pâté (£3.40), cumberland sausage (£3.50), broccoli and cream cheese bake or lasagne (£5.90), home-made steak and mushroom pie (£6.20), salmon with a cream and prawn sauce (£7.70), daily specials, steaks (from £10.90), and puddings (£2.60); they don't take bookings; good service, piped music. *(Recommended by Neil Townend, Roger and Pauline Pearce)*

Free house ~ Licensees Robert and Elizabeth Thompson ~ Real ale ~ Bar food ~ (01271) 861292 ~ Children welcome ~ Open 11.30-3, 6-11; 12-3, 7-10.30 Sun

KINGSKERSWELL SX8767 Map 1

Barn Owl 🖛

Aller Mills; just off A380 Newton Abbot—Torquay – inn-sign on main road opposite RAC post

Friendly new licensees have taken over this 16th-c converted farmhouse .The large bar has antique dark oak panelling, some grand furnishings such as a couple of carved oak settles and old-fashioned dining chairs around the handsome polished tables on its flowery carpet, an elaborate ornamental plaster ceiling, and a decorative wooden chimney piece; lots of pictures and artefacts, and old lamps and fresh flowers on the tables. The other rooms have low black oak beams, with polished flagstones and a kitchen range in one, and an inglenook fireplace in the other; part of the dining room is no smoking. Good popular bar food includes home-made soup (£2.95), sandwiches (from £3.50), filled baked potatoes (from £4.50), ploughman's (from £4.50), and daily specials such as Thai fishcakes (£4.95), fish and chicken paella (£6.95), tapenade-crusted salmon with ratatouille and tomato cream (£8.25), braised wood pigeon (£9.50), marinated pork fillet with crispy polenta and cider jus (£9.95), poached salmon with prawn sauce (£10.50), and puddings (£3). Well kept Bass and Flowers IPA on handpump, 9 wines by the glass, and several malt whiskies. There are picnic-sets in a small sheltered garden. *(Recommended by JP, PP, D I Baddeley, Mike Gorton, Gordon, Alan and Paula McCully, John Wilson, Mrs Sylvia Elcoate, JWGW, Mr and Mrs A Scrutton, Bett and Brian Cox, Andrew Hodges)*

Free house ~ Licensees Peter and Colleen Cook ~ Real ale ~ Bar food ~ (01803) 872130 ~ Children welcome ~ Open 11-11; 12-10.30 Sun ~ Bedrooms: £49B/£69B

Stars after the name of a pub show exceptional character and appeal. They don't mean extra comfort. And they are nothing to do with food quality, for which there's a separate knife-and-fork rosette. Even quite a basic pub can win stars, if it's individual enough.

Bickley Mill

Stoneycombe, on road from Abbotskerswell to Compton and Marldon; heading W towards Ipplepen, just over ½ mile after leaving Kingskerswell turn left at crossroads just after going under railway bridge

Cheerful new licensees have taken over this former flour mill and are building a restaurant and hope to add a games room. The main bar, one of a spreading series of beamed rooms, has lots of copper and brass implements, built-in cushioned wall benches and solid wooden chairs, candles on the tables, toby jugs on a shelf with plants on the window sills, and a log fire in the stone fireplace; a similarly furnished no-smoking room leads off this, and up some steps is another area with plates and pictures on the walls; piped music. Decent bar food now includes home-made soup (£2.50), sandwiches (from £2.75), ploughman's (£4.75), meaty or vegetarian lasagne (from £5.95), cajun chicken (£6.95), and steaks (from £8.95), with daily specials like Thai red chicken curry (£5.50), cold meat platter (£5.95), teriyaki fillet of salmon (£7.95), half a boned guinea fowl with a brandy apple sauce (£8.50), whole grilled lemon sole (£9.95), and puddings (£2.50). Well kept Bass, Fullers Summer Ale, and Marstons Pedigree on handpump; piped music. There are tables in a courtyard under a eucalyptus tree, and a series of sheltered hillside terraces creating a sub-tropical effect with dracaenas among the shrubs on this steep slope. *(Recommended by John Wilson, Gordon)*

Free house ~ Licensees Sarah Thomas and Ben Harding ~ Real ale ~ Bar food (till 10pm) ~ (01803) 873201 ~ Children in Top Room ~ Open 11-2.30, 6-11; 12-3, 7-10.30 Sun ~ Bedrooms: £22(£32B)/£64B

KINGSTEIGNTON SX8773 Map 1

Old Rydon ★ ⍟

Rydon Rd; from A381/A380 junction follow signs to Kingsteignton (B3193), taking first right turn (Longford Lane), go straight on to the bottom of the hill, then next right turn into Rydon Rd following Council Office signpost; pub is just past the school, OS Sheet 192 map reference 872739

Despite its rather surprising location in the middle of a residential area, this bustling pub is an enjoyable place for many of our readers. The small, cosy bar has a big winter log fire in a raised fireplace, cask seats and upholstered seats built against the white-painted stone walls, and lots of beer mugs hanging from the heavy beam-and-plank ceiling. There are a few more seats in an upper former cider loft facing the antlers and antelope horns on one high white wall; piped music. Very good bar food includes home-made soup (£2.50), filled baked potatoes or toasted muffins with various toppings (from £2.95), ploughman's (from £3.95), cashew and walnut roast with onion sauce or chargrilled chicken satay in pitta bread (£5.95), mixed leaf salad with fried potatoes and croutons and topped with grilled peppered Scotch salmon with crème fraîche, garlic prawns or 6oz sirloin steak (from £4.85), daily specials such as Thai lamb curry with lemon grass and coconut milk sauce or Brixham fish pie (£6.95), pork schnitzel (£7.40), and Exmoor venison steaks on bubble and squeak (£8.65), and children's meals (£2.95). The restaurant is no smoking (though you may smoke in the restaurant lounge). Well kept Bass, Fullers London Pride and a guest beer on handpump, and helpful, friendly service. The nice biggish sheltered garden has seats under parasols, with more on the terrace, and a much liked conservatory with its prolific shrubbery: two different sorts of bougainvillea, a vine with bunches of purple grapes, and lots of pretty geraniums and busy lizzies. *(Recommended by Robin and Sarah Constance, John and Christine Simpson, Gordon, L G Owen, Andrew Hodges, Richard and Margaret Peers, D I Baddeley, Basil Minson, Susan and Nigel Wilson)*

Free house ~ Licensees Hermann and Miranda Hruby ~ Real ale ~ Bar food ~ Restaurant ~ (01626) 54626 ~ Children in eating areas, conservatory; over 8 after 8pm ~ Open 11-2.30, 6-11; 12-3, 7-10.30 Sun

KINGSTON SX6347 Map 1

Dolphin 🛏️

Off B3392 S of Modbury (can also be reached from A379 W of Modbury)

Rather delightful, this quiet shuttered 16th-c inn has several knocked-through beamed rooms with a good mix of customers, a relaxed, welcoming atmosphere (no noisy games machines or piped music), amusing drawings and photographs on the walls, and rustic tables and cushioned seats and settles around the bared stone walls; one small area is no smoking. Good honest seasonally changing bar food includes sandwiches (from £2.25; crab £3.95), soup such as carrot and ginger (£2.25), ploughman's (£3.95), local sausages with apricot and dill relish (£4.25), crab bake (£4.50), spinach and stilton tart (£5.50), chicken in cider and sage sauce (£5.50), fish pie (£5.95), scallops and bacon fried in garlic butter (£8.95), steaks (from £8.95), plaice fillets stuffed with prawn and crab in a white wine and cream sauce (£9.95), and home-made puddings such as banoffee pie or treacle tart (£2.50).Well kept Courage Best and Ushers Founders and seasonal beers on handpump. Outside, there are tables and swings, plenty of nearby walks – which the friendly licensees can give you advice on – and half a dozen tracks leading down to the sea. *(Recommended by Paul White, Jacquie and Jim Jones, C C Jonas, B J Harding, Richard and Robyn Wain, Mark Percy, Lesley Mayoh, Mr and Mrs B Coad)*

Ushers ~ Lease: Neil and Annie Williams ~ Real ale ~ Bar food (till 10pm; not 25 Dec) ~ (01548) 810314 ~ Children in eating area of bar ~ Open 11-3(2.30 in winter), 6-11; 12-3, 6.30-10.30 Sun ~ Bedrooms: £37.50B/£49.50B

KNOWSTONE SS8223 Map 1

Masons Arms ★ ♀

Signposted from A361 Tiverton to South Molton road and B3227 Bampton to South Molton

One reader has been visiting this quiet 13th-c inn for 28 years and hopes it carries on with its unspoilt and unchanging charm. It does have a great deal of character and atmosphere and is run in a very casually personal way, which doesn't of course appeal to everyone – many customers, however, enjoy the difference. The simple little main bar has heavy medieval black beams hung with ancient bottles of all shapes and sizes, farm tools on the walls, substantial rustic furniture on the stone floor, and a fine open fireplace with a big log fire and side bread oven. A small lower sitting room has pinkish plush chairs around a low table in front of the fire, and bar billiards. Bar food can be very good: widely praised home-made soup and home-made pâté like cheese and walnut or smoked mackerel, ploughman's with proper local cheese and butter, cheese and leek pie or spaghetti with a gutsy tomato sauce (£4.95), curries or cassoulet (£5.95), fish pie (£6.25), and local lamb chops (£8.50); Sunday lunch. The restaurant is no smoking. They often sell home-made marmalades, fruit breads or hot gooseberry chutney over the counter. Well kept Cotleigh Tawny and Otter Ale tapped from the cask, farm cider, a small but well chosen wine list, and a fair choice of malt whiskies; several snuffs on the counter; darts, shove-ha'penny, dominoes, cribbage, and board games. *(Recommended by S G Bennett, JP, PP, Tim Barrow, Sue Demont, Dr B Lake, H Thomson, John A Barker, Jeremy Brittain-Long, Mr and Mrs Pyper, the Didler, S Tait, S Lonie, J F M West, Jenny Cantle, Colin and Peggy Wilshire, Julian Holland, Sarah Laver, C F Nicholls, Roger Byrne, N Cobb)*

Free house ~ Licensees David and Elizabeth Todd ~ Real ale ~ Bar food ~ (01398) 34123/341582 ~ Children welcome away from public bar ~ Open 11-3, 6(7 in winter)-11; 12-3, 7-11 Sun; closed evenings 25 and 26 Dec ~ Bedrooms: £21(£37.50B)/£42B

Please keep sending us reports. We rely on readers for news of new discoveries, and particularly for news of changes – however slight – at the fully described pubs. No stamp needed: The Good Pub Guide, FREEPOST TN1569, Wadhurst, E Sussex TN5 7BR.

LITTLEHEMPSTON SX8162 Map 1

Tally Ho!

Signposted off A381 NE of Totnes

Tucked away off a quiet road, this warmly welcoming little pub has neatly kept and cosy rooms with low beams and panelling, fresh flowers and candles on the tables, and bare stone walls covered with lots of porcelain, brass, copperware, mounted butterflies, stuffed wildlife, old swords, and shields and hunting horns and so forth; there's also an interesting mix of chairs and settles (many antique and with comfortable cushions), and two coal fires; no noisy machines or piped music. The new manager is also the chef, and the good bar food now includes sandwiches (from £2.95), home-made soup (£3.25), home-made chicken liver pâté (£3.95), ploughman's (£4.95), lasagne (£6.95), steak and kidney pie (£7.95), pork fillet with cider, almond, apple and cream sauce (£8.95), steaks (from £9.95), whole Torbay sole filled with prawns and mushrooms, topped with cheese, duckling breast in a lime and lemon sauce with fresh bananas (£10.95), tournedos rossini (£14.50), daily specials (from £5.95), seasonal game dishes, and home-made puddings with clotted cream (from £2.95). Well kept Dartmoor Best and Teignworthy Reel Ale on handpump from a temperature controlled cellar, and several malt whiskies. The three friendly cats are called Monica, Thomas and Ellwood. The terrace is a mass of flowers in summer. *(Recommended by Ruth Warner, Mike Gorton, Andrew Hodges)*

Free house ~ Licensees P Saint, A Greenwood, G Waterfield ~ Real ale ~ Bar food ~ (01803) 862316 ~ Children in eating area of bar ~ Open 12-2.30, 6(6.30 winter)-11; 12-3, 7-10.30 Sun; closed 25 Dec ~ Bedrooms: £48S/£55S

LOWER ASHTON SX8484 Map 1

Manor Inn 🍺

Ashton signposted off B3193 N of Chudleigh

It's a real pleasure to visit such a well run, bustling pub with caring, friendly licensees, good beer and enjoyable food. The left-hand room has beer mats and brewery advertisements on the walls and is more for locals enjoying the well kept Princetown Jail Ale, RCH Pitchfork, Teignworthy Reel Ale, Theakstons XB and a changing guest ale on handpump or tapped from the cask, or perhaps the local Grays farm cider. On the right, two rather more discreet rooms have a wider appeal, bolstered by the home-made food which might include soup (£1.85), sandwiches (from £1.85), lots of filled baked potatoes (from £2.95), home-made burgers with various toppings (from £3.40), ploughman's (from £4), vegetable bake (£4.70), home-cooked ham and egg (£5.50), steak, mushroom and ale pie (£5.75) and steaks (from £8.95), with a good choice of changing specials such as mixed bean chilli topped with cheese (£4.75), lamb goulash, pork with wine mushrooms and cream or hunters chicken (all £5.95), cauliflower and prawn au gratin (£6.25), and grilled lemon sole, tuna or swordfish steak or salmon (£7.35); service is quick. Shove-ha'penny, spoof. The garden has lots of picnic-sets under cocktail parasols (and a fine tall Scots pine). No children. *(Recommended by R J Walden, G Wall, the Didler, Mike Gorton, Edward Nicol, G Washington)*

Free house ~ Licensees Geoff and Clare Mann ~ Real ale ~ Bar food (12-1.30, 7-9.30) ~ (01647) 52304 ~ No children ~ Open 12-2.30, 6.30(7 Sat)-11; 12-2.30, 7-11 Sun; closed Mon (except bank holidays)

LUSTLEIGH SX7881 Map 1

Cleave

Village signposted off A382 Bovey Tracey—Moretonhampstead

In summer, the hanging baskets here are lovely and the neat sheltered garden is full of cottagey flowers (and has a wendy house). Inside this thatched old pub there is a low-ceilinged lounge bar with newly exposed granite walls, attractive antique high-backed settles, pale leatherette bucket chairs, cushioned wall seats, and wheelback chairs around the tables on its patterned carpet, and a roaring log fire. A second bar has similar furnishings, a large dresser, harmonium, an HMV gramophone, and prints, and the no-smoking family room has crayons, books and toys for children. Enjoyable bar food includes home-made soup (£2.95), sandwiches (from £3.25; hot sardines with pesto and cheese £4.50), ploughman's (from £3.95), home-made chicken liver pâté (£4.45), very good local sausages (£5.95), home-made steak, kidney and Guinness pie (£6.95), good Sunday roast pork with apple sauce or home-made nut roast with spicy tomato sauce (£7.50), daily specials, and children's menu (from £3.95). Well kept Bass, Flowers Original and Wadworths 6X on handpump kept under light blanket pressure, quite a few malt whiskies and several wines by the glass. *(Recommended by D B Jenkin, Edward Leetham, John and Christine Vittoe, Richard and Valerie Wright, Richard and Ann Higgs, R J Walden, B J Harding, John and Christine Lowe)*

Heavitree ~ Tenant A Perring ~ Real ale ~ Bar food (12-9 in summer) ~ Restaurant ~ (01647) 277223 ~ Children in family room ~ Open 11-11; 12-10.30 Sun; 11-3, 6.30-11 winter

LYDFORD SX5184 Map 1
Castle Inn ★ 🍽 🍷 🛏
Signposted off A386 Okehampton—Tavistock

Very occasionally there's something about a really good pub which lures back the licensees who put it in the top drawer to start with, but then moved away. This is one of them. The Greys, who made this so delightful before going on to great things at the Cott at Dartington, are back in place here – and so is Harvey the cat. They've brought with them all their enthusiasm, and have started by steering the pub back to its roots rather than following the country house hotel avenue. They've changed the bedroom pricing and anyone booking a standard room will receive a free upgrade if a better room is available, and they've introduced very good value winter breaks. The menu is very similar to the one they had at the Cott (and their second chef has come with them) which has been well received by customers, and the real ales have been put back into the cellar (and reduced in price). It is a charming pink-washed Tudor inn with country kitchen chairs, high-backed winged settles and old captain's chairs around mahogany tripod tables on big slate flagstones in the twin-roomed bar. One of the rooms has low lamp-lit beams, a sizeable open fire, masses of brightly decorated plates, some Hogarth prints, an attractive grandfather clock, and, near the serving-counter, seven Lydford pennies hammered out in the old Saxon mint in the reign of Ethelred the Unready, in the 11th c; the second room has an interesting collection of antique stallion posters; unusual stained-glass doors. The lounge area has stylishly old-fashioned sofas and attractive antique tables on the slate flagstoned floor, a Stuart oak dresser, a high backed settle, lots of pictures and plates on the walls, local oak beams supporting the bowed ceiling, and an open fire in the granite fireplace. At lunchtime, the good bar food includes soups (from £2.50), sandwiches (from £3.25), ploughman's (from £3.75), and a dozen changing daily specials (£5.95-£6.95). Also, Sharpham brie parcels with a basil and apple dressing (£4.50), baked avocado with a crab and herb filling (£4.95), spicy aubergine and mushroom stew flavoured with chilli and cumin (£7.50), super steak and kidney pie, chicken, spinach and mushroom lasagne, trout fishcakes with a leek and devon blue cheese sauce or cantonese pork (all £7.95), sirloin steak (£11.95), fillet of bass with queen scallops and white wine (£13.50), and puddings such as chocolate and brandy mousse, apple and rhubarb pie or sticky toffee pudding (£3.50). Well kept Butcombe, Fullers London Pride, and Summerskills Tamar Best Bitter on handpump, and an interesting, fairly priced and helpfully described wine list; sensibly placed darts. The pub is next to the village's daunting, ruined 12th-c castle and close to a beautiful river gorge (owned by the National Trust; closed Nov-Easter); the village itself was one of the four strong-points developed by Alfred the Great as a defence against the Danes. *(Recommended by JP, PP, Tony and Joan Walker, Kim and Nigel Spence, Graham and Karen Oddey, Gordon, Jacquie and Jim Jones, Mr and Mrs P M Board, John Moseley, Alan and Paula McCully, Ian and Jane Irving, John and Christine Simpson, Nigel Flook, Betsy Brown, Andy and Jill Kassube, John Askew, Catherine Lloyd, Brian Higgins and Ana Kolkowska, Jim Bush, David and Mandy Allen, Walter and Susan Rinaldi-Butcher, Peter and June Gregory, John and Vivienne Rice, Ted George, P Rome, Chris and Margaret Southon)*

Free house ~ Licensees David and Susan Grey ~ Real ale ~ Bar food (12-2.15, 6.30-9.30) ~ (01822) 820241 ~ Children in eating area of bar and restaurant; over 5 in bar ~ Open 11.30-3, 6-11.30; 12-3, 7-10.30 Sun; closed 25 Dec ~ Bedrooms: £45B/£65B

MARLDON SX8663 Map 1
Church House 🍴

Just W of Paignton

Run by really friendly, caring licensees, this charming and attractive inn is doing particularly well. There's a good relaxed atmosphere and a healthy mix of customers in the spreading bar that wraps itself around the big semicircular bar counter and divides into different areas. The main bar has interesting windows with swagged curtains, some beams, dark pine chairs around solid tables on the turkey carpet, and green plush-seated bar chairs; leading off here is a cosy little candlelit room with just four tables on the bare-board floor, a dark wood dado, and stone fireplace, and next to this is the attractive, dimly-lit, no-smoking restaurant with hops on the beams and dried flowers in the big stone fireplace. At the other end of the building is a characterful room split into two parts with a stone floor in one bit and a wooden floor in another (with a big woodburning stove). Good popular bar food includes lunchtime sandwiches (from £2.50; filled french bread from £3.25), home-made soup (£2.25), lunchtime filled baked potatoes (from £3.25), moules marinières (£3.45 starter, £5.50 main course), crock of Irish stew (£3.75), lunchtime omelettes (£4.25), crispy duck (enough for 2, £4.75), bangers and mash or stir frys (£5.25), vegetarian risotto or steak and kidney pudding (£6.50), steaks (from £8.95), salmon cakes finished with a lobster bisque (£9.45), daily specials such as wild mushroom pasta (£2.50), crab and red pepper cake (£3.45), chicken breast with a mustard and crumb coating served with a banana cream sauce and a bacon and sweetcorn crêpe (£7.25), Thai chicken (£7.75), braised leg of lamb (£8.25), and seared monkfish and salmon (£9.50), and puddings like blackberry and raspberry pie or bread and butter plum pudding (£2.50). Well kept Bass, Boddingtons, Flowers IPA and Original, and Fullers London Pride on handpump; fruit machine, skittle alley, and piped music. There are three grassy terraces with picnic-sets behind. *(Recommended by Margaret and Ian Taylor, Mr and Mrs C Roberts, Alan and Paula McCully, Dr A J and Mrs P G Newton, Mr and Mrs A Hedges, Mrs B Faulkner, Mr and Mrs Marsden Howell, Mr and Mrs K Rose, Gordon)*

Whitbreads ~ Lease: Sue and David Armstrong ~ Real ale ~ Bar food ~ Restaurant ~ (01803) 558279 ~ Children in restaurant but must be over 10 in evening ~ Open 11.30-2.30, 5-11; 12-3, 7-10.30 Sun ~ Bedrooms: £15B/£30B

MEAVY SX5467 Map 1
Royal Oak

Off B3212 E of Yelverton

On the edge of Dartmoor in a peaceful rustic village, this friendly traditional old pub is set by the green with picnic-sets there and more (benches, too) along the front of the building. The carpeted L-shaped bar has pews from the next door church, red plush banquettes and old agricultural prints and church pictures on the walls; a smaller bar – where the locals like to gather – has flagstones, a big fireplace and side bread oven. Bar food includes sandwiches (from £2.25), soup (£2.50), cheesy garlic mushrooms (£3.50), ploughman's or filled baked potato (£4.25), ham, egg and sauté potatoes (£5.50), roast beef and yorkshire pudding (£5.75), cheese and vegetable bake (£6.50), steak and kidney pie (£6.95), steaks (£7.95), and puddings like spotted dick or apple crumble (£2.25). Well kept Bass, Courage Best, and Meavy Valley Bitter on handpump kept under light blanket pressure, and three draught ciders. Dominoes, euchre, and piped music. No children. *(Recommended by Jacquie and Jim Jones, Neil Spink, Dr Rod Holcombe, Graham and Karen Oddey, Joan and Michel Hooper-Immins, B J Harding)*

Free house ~ Licensees Roger and Susan Barber ~ Real ale ~ Bar food (11.30-2.15, 6.30-9.15) ~ (01822) 852944 ~ Open 11.30-3, 6.30-11; 12-3, 7-10.30 Sun

NEWTON ST CYRES SX8798 Map 1
Beer Engine ◀

Sweetham; from Newton St Cyres on A377 follow St Cyres Station, Thorverton signpost

The own-brewed real ales in this friendly old station hotel are consistently excellent – you can take them home with you, too. Kept on handpump, there's Rail Ale, Piston Bitter, and the very strong Sleeper. The spacious main bar has partitioning alcoves, and windsor chairs and some cinnamon-coloured button-back banquettes around dark varnished tables on the brown carpet; the eating area is no smoking. Decent bar food includes speciality sausages (£4.50), vegetarian dishes (from £4.50), chicken in barbecue sauce (£5.50), steak in their own ale pie (£5.75), home-made steak and kidney pudding, and rump steak; roast Sunday lunch (£5.50 one course, £7.25 two courses). Darts, shove-ha'penny, dominoes and cribbage; fruit machine and video game in the downstairs lobby. The hanging baskets and window boxes are very pretty in summer, and there's lots of sheltered seating in the large sunny garden where they hold popular summer barbecues. *(Recommended by Andy and Jill Kassube, Alan and Paula McCully, John and Vivienne Rice, Stan Edwards, John and Bryony Coles, R J Walden)*

Own brew ~ Licensee Peter Hawksley ~ Real ale ~ Bar food (till 10pm) ~ (01392) 851282 ~ Children in eating area of bar ~ Open 11-11; 12-10.30 Sun

PETER TAVY SX5177 Map 1
Peter Tavy Inn

Off A386 nr Mary Tavy, N of Tavistock

From the picnic-sets in the pretty garden of this attractive old stone inn, there are peaceful views of the moor rising above nearby pastures. Inside, the low-beamed friendly bar has high-backed settles on the black flagstones by the big stone fireplace (a good log fire on cold days), smaller settles in stone-mullioned windows, a friendly atmosphere, and a snug no-smoking side dining area. Good bar food at lunchtime includes soup such as leek and stilton (£2.25), filled french bread (from £3.50), baked avocado and prawns (£3.95), ploughman's (£4.50), ham and egg or chicken tikka (£4.95), and steak and kidney pie or vegetable lasagne (£5.95), with evening dishes like seafood cocktail with citrus dressing (£3.75), poached pear with stilton-glazed prawns (£3.95), cannelloni ricotta (£5.95), pot roast pheasant with hunter's sauce (£8.95), monkfish with a creamy garlic sauce (£9.95), venison steak with juniper sauce (£10.95), and puddings such as apple charlotte or chocolate truffle torte (£2.95). Five well kept real ales on handpump, kept under light blanket pressure, such as Badger Best, Bass, Cotleigh Tawny, Princetown Jail Ale and Best, and Summerskills Tamar Best; 30 malt whiskies and Luscombe organic cider and pure apple juice; piped music. *(Recommended by Graham and Karen Oddey, Ewan and Moira McCall, R J Walden, Chris and Margaret Southon, Paul R White, Jacquie and Jim Jones, JP, PP, John Askew, D Hines, Rose Magrath)*

Free house ~ Licensees Graeme and Karen Sim ~ Real ale ~ Bar food ~ (01822) 810348 ~ Children in restaurant ~ Open 12-2.30(3 Sat), 6.30-11; 12-3, 6.30-10.30 Sun; Sun-Thurs evening opening 7 winter

PLYMOUTH SX4755 Map 1
China House ★

Marrowbone Slip, Sutton Harbour, via Sutton Road off Exeter Street (A374)

Cookworthy started his porcelain factory here in 1768 (hence the name) and this is the oldest warehouse in Plymouth. The views over Sutton Harbour and on to the Barbican are marvellous, and there are picnic-sets and benches on the heated verandah, so you can enjoy the view all year round. Inside, the bar is lofty and very spacious but cleverly partitioned into smaller booth-like areas, with great beams and flagstone floors, bare slate and stone walls, and lots of nets, kegs and fishing gear; there's even a clinker-built boat. On the left is the main bar with plain wooden seats around dark tables in front of a good log fire – all very comfortable and relaxed. Bar food includes sandwiches, home-made soup (£3.50), chicken livers and smoked bacon salad with raspberry vinaigrette (£4.25), moules marinières (£4.75), home-made cottage pie with leek and chive mash or beef stew and herb dumplings (£6.50), creamy mushroom stroganoff or bangers and rich onion gravy (£6.95), chicken breast with bacon, wine and leek sauce (£10.95), and duck with blackberry and port sauce (£11.95). Well kept Dartmoor Best, Marstons Pedigree, and Tetleys on handpump; fruit machine and piped music. *(Recommended by John Wilson, Mike Wells, Ted George, Ian Phillips, R J Walden, Andrew and Hazel Summerfield, Steve Whalley, Kim and Nigel Spence)*

Allied Domecq ~ Manager Nicole Quinne ~ Real ale ~ Bar food (12-3, 7-10) ~ Restaurant ~ (01752) 260930 ~ Children allowed only if eating ~ Live music monthly Fri evening ~ Open 11-11(12.30 Fri); 11-12.30 Sat; 12-10.30 Sun

POSTBRIDGE SX6780 Map 1
Warren House
B3212 1¾ miles NE of Postbridge

Despite its summer popularity, this friendly place has kept its character. It's a welcome oasis for walkers (muddy boots are welcome) and birdwatchers and is in a fine spot in the middle of Dartmoor. The cosy bar has a fireplace at either end (one is said to have been kept almost continuously alight since 1845), and is simply furnished with easy chairs and settles under a beamed ochre ceiling, wild animal pictures on the partly panelled stone walls, and dim lighting (fuelled by the pub's own generator); there's a family room (which could perhaps do with some brightening up). Good no-nonsense home cooking includes locally made meaty or vegetable pasties (£1.80), home-made soup (£2), sandwiches and filled baked potatoes (from £2.75), good ploughman's with local cheeses (£4.95), spinach and ricotta cannelloni (£5.50), home-made rabbit pie (£6), and home-made steak in ale pie (£6.50), with evening dishes such as Scottish salmon fillet with parsley sauce (£8.75), steaks (£10.50), and local wild boar in brandy and mushroom sauce (£11.50); daily specials, and puddings like home-made chocolate and brandy truffle torte or treacle tart with clotted cream (£2.80). Well kept Badger Tanglefoot, Butcombe Bitter, Gibbs Mew Bishops Tipple, and Scatter Rock Devonian on handpump, farm cider, and local country wines. Darts, pool, cribbage, dominoes, and piped music. *(Recommended by Canon and Mrs M A Michael Bourdeaux, Mayur Shah, W W Burke, Dick Brown, Neil Spink, JP, PP, Mrs Sylvia Elcoate, Vivienne and John Rice)*

Free house ~ Licensee Peter Parsons ~ Real ale ~ Bar food (all day summer and winter Sat and Sun) ~ (01822) 880208 ~ Children in family room ~ Open 11-11; 12-10.30 Sun; 11-2.30, 6-11 weekdays in winter

RACKENFORD SS8518 Map 1
Stag
Off A361 NW of Tiverton

There can be few bars reached along such a marvellous old cobbled entrance corridor between massive stone and cob walls as this little one. This thached inn is perhaps Devon's oldest and dates in part from 1196. A couple of very high-backed old settles face each other in front of the massive fireplace with its ancient bressumer beam (and good log fire), the shiny dark ochre ceiling is very low, and the bar counter is a grand piece of oak; there are some other interesting old pieces of furniture as well as more modern seats, a narrow sloping side area has darts, and a cottagey dining room leads off. Good bar food (they tell us prices have not changed) includes sandwiches (from £1.75), filled baked potatoes (from £2.95), ham and egg (£3.75), omelettes (£4.20), rump steak (£7.95), daily specials such as home-made lasagne or spinach and ricotta canelloni (£3.95), home-made pies like steak and kidney or lamb and apricot (£4.95), and salmon fillets with a mushroom and cream sauce (£6.50), puddings (£2.50), and children's menu (from £1.95). Well kept Adnams Broadside, Cotleigh Tawny and a guest beer on handpump, good house wines, Addlestones cider, very friendly service – a nice relaxed atmosphere; darts, pool, alley skittles, cribbage, dominoes, and piped music. The dog is called Spanner, and they now have a retired greyhound called Jacko who springs to life at the rustle of a crisp packet. *(Recommended by Mike Gorton, Gordon, Tony Gayfer)*

Free house ~ Licensees Norman and Jennie Foot ~ Real ale ~ Bar food ~ Restaurant ~ (01884) 881369 ~ Children welcome ~ Trad jazz every last Weds of month ~ Open 12-2.30, 6-11; 12-11 Sat; 12-10.30 Sun ~ Bedrooms: /£35(£37B)

RATTERY SX7461 Map 1
Church House

Village signposted from A385 W of Totnes, and A38 S of Buckfastleigh

The spiral stone steps behind a little stone doorway on your left as you come into this lovely old pub probably date from about 1030. It is one of the oldest pub buildings in Britain and has a fine restful atmosphere. There are massive oak beams and standing timbers in the homely open-plan bar, large fireplaces (one with a little cosy nook partitioned off around it), windsor armchairs, comfortable seats and window seats, and prints on the plain white walls; the dining room is separated from this room by heavy curtains; Shandy the golden labrador is very amiable. Good bar food includes generously filled rolls and ploughman's with local cheeses, and daily specials such as tasty chicken jambalaya, big lasagne, venison casserole and half roast guinea fowl with various fruit sauces (£7.95).Well kept Dartmoor Best, Greene King Abbot, and Marstons Pedigree on handpump, lots of malt whiskies, and a decent wine list. Outside, there are peaceful views of the partly wooded surrounding hills from picnic-sets on a hedged courtyard by the churchyard. *(Recommended by I J and N K Buckmaster, Steve and Maggie Willey, JP, PP, Mike and Karen England, David and Natasha Toulson, M L Porter, JKW, Richard and Margaret Peers, Alan and Paula McCully, B J Harding, Jacquie and Jim Jones)*

Free house ~ Licensees Brian and Jill Evans ~ Real ale ~ Bar food ~ Restaurant ~ (01364) 642220 ~ Children in eating area of bar and restaurant ~ Open 11-2.30, 6-11; 12-2.30, 7-10.30 Sun

SHEEPWASH SS4806 Map 1
Half Moon ♀ £ 🛏

Off A3072 Holidaysworthy—Hatherleigh at Highampton

This is an interesting combination of pub and hotel with a correspondingly mixed clientele – which creates a good bustling atmosphere. The white walls of the neatly-kept carpeted main bar are coverd in fishing pictures, there's solid old furniture under the beams, and a big log fire fronted by slate flagstones. Lunchtime bar snacks are traditionally simple and good and include sandwiches (£1.50, toasties £2.25), super home-made vegetable soup (£1.75), home-made pasties (£3), ploughman's (£3.50), home-cooked ham salad (£3.75), and home-made puddings (from £2). Well kept Courage Best, Jollyboat Mainbrace Bitter (brewed locally), and Marstons Pedigree on handpump (well kept in a temperature-controlled cellar), a fine choice of malt whiskies, and an extensive wine list; darts, fruit machine, and separate pool room. This is the place to stay if you love fishing as they have 10 miles of private fishing on the River Torridge (salmon, sea trout and brown trout) as well as a rod room, good drying facilities and a small shop stocking the basic things needed to catch fish. Since 1958, this civilised inn has been owned by the same friendly family. *(Recommended by Gordon, C P Scott-Malden, MB, Jenny Cantle, R J Walden, Mike Gorton, Dr AJ and Mrs PG Newton)*

Free house ~ Licensees Benjamin and Charles Inniss ~ Real ale ~ Bar food ~ Restaurant (evening only) ~ (01409) 231376 ~ Children at lunchtime and early evening ~ Open 11-2.30(3 Sat), 6-11; closed evening 25 Dec ~ Bedrooms: £37B/£60B

Planning a day in the country? We list pubs in really attractive scenery at the back of the book.

SIDFORD SY1390 Map 1
Blue Ball ★ ◧ ⛏

A3052 just N of Sidmouth

As we went to press, they were hoping to add to the bedrooms in this bustling thatched pub. It's a popular place to stay with an inviting residents' lounge and a roaring fire to eat breakfast in front of. The low, partly panelled and neatly kept lounge bar has heavy beams, upholstered wall benches and windsor chairs, three open fires, and lots of bric-a-brac; most of the eating areas are now no smoking. Quickly served bar food includes sandwiches (from £1.90; fresh crab £3.25), soup (£2.25), locally made sausages (£3.50, lots of ploughman's and salads (from £3.50), omelettes (£4.50), vegetable lasagne (£5.25), steak and mushroom pie (£5.95), chicken balti (£6.75), steaks (from £8.75), daily specials, children's dishes (£2.25), and puddings (£2.95); the two-course OAP lunches on Wednesdays are well attended, and they hold themed food evenings with appropriate music. Bass, Boddingtons, Flowers IPA, Otter Ale, and a guest beer on handpump, kept well in a temperature-controlled cellar; helpful staff. A plainer public bar has darts, dominoes, cribbage and a fruit machine; maybe piped music in the evening. Tables on a terrace look out over a colourful front flower garden, and there are more seats on a bigger back lawn – as well as in a covered area next to the barbecue; safe swing, see saw and play house for children. This inn has been owned by the same friendly family since 1912. *(Recommended by Pam Adsley, L H and S Ede, Mr and Mrs Cottrell, B T Smith, Geoffrey Lawrance, P and J Shapley, Dennis Bishop, M A Buchanan, Peter and Audrey Dowsett, M G Hart, Paul R White, Margaret and Richard Peers, Basil Minson, W W Burke, PP and J Salmon)*

Inn Partnership (Nomura) ~ Tenant Roger Newton ~ Real ale ~ Bar food (8.30-2, 6-9.30) ~ (01395) 514062 ~ Children in eating area of bar and in restaurant ~ Open 10.30-2.30(3 Sat), 5.30-11; 12-3, 6(7 in winter)-10.30 Sun ~ Bedrooms: £25/£42

SLAPTON SX8244 Map 1
Tower

Signposted off A379 Dartmouth—Kingsbridge

The two Australian landladies have introduced real warmth to this atmospheric old place. There are open log fires in the low-ceilinged bar, armchairs, low-backed settles on the flagstones, and candlelight. A good range of real ales might include Adnams Southwold, Badger Tanglefoot, Dartmoor Best, Gibbs Mew Bishops Tipple, Exmoor Bitter on handpump, Stancombe cider, Addlestones cider, and good Australian wines. Good bar food at lunchtime includes soup (£2.90), sandwiches (from £2.20; toasties from £2.30; filled french bread from £2.60), ploughman's (from £3.70), home-made meaty or vegetarian lasagne or steak in ale pie (£5.20), and gammon and pineapple or egg (£6.30), with evening dishes such as garlic mushrooms (£3.40), greek salad (£4.20), chicken breast slices with onions, tomatoes, fresh basil and a red wine sauce (£6.60), and sirloin steak (£9.50); puddings like home-made apple pie, and children's menu (from £2.40). There are picnic-sets on the neatly kept back lawn, which is overhung by the ivy-covered ruin of a 14th-c chantry. The lane up to the pub is very narrow. *(Recommended by Pat and Robert Watt, the Didler, Roger Wain-Heapy, I Buckmaster, J Dwane, D R Eberlin)*

Free house ~ Licensees Sandra Heskett and Helen Proudfoot ~ Real ale ~ Bar food (12-2.30, 6-9.30) ~ Restaurant ~ (01548) 580216 ~ Children in restaurant ~ Monthly jazz, folk, Irish music ~ Open 12-3, 6-11; 12-3, 7-10.30 Sun ~ Bedrooms: £25S/£40S

SOURTON SX5390 Map 1
Highwayman ★

A386, S of junction with A30

If you're on the long trek down to Cornwall, this fantastic place is a real tonic. For 40 years, the friendly owners have put great enthusiasm into this pub's remarkable design. The porch (a pastiche of a nobleman's carriage) leads into a warren of dimly lit stonework and flagstone-floored burrows and alcoves, richly fitted out with red plush seats discreetly cut into the higgledy-piggledy walls, elaborately carved pews, a leather porter's chair, Jacobean-style wicker chairs, and seats in quaintly bulging small-paned bow windows; the ceiling in one part, where there's an array of stuffed animals, gives the impression of being underneath a tree, roots and all. The separate Rita Jones' Locker is a make-believe sailing galleon, full of intricate woodwork and splendid timber baulks, with white antique-lace-clothed tables in the embrasures that might have held cannons. They only sell keg beer, but specialise in farm cider and organic wines, and food is confined to a range of meaty and vegetarian pasties (£1.50) or ploughman's with local and organic cheeses; service is warmly welcoming and full of character; old-fashioned penny fruit machine, and 40s piped music; no smoking at the bar counters. Outside, there's a play area in similar style for children with little black and white roundabouts like a Victorian fairground, a fairy-tale pumpkin house and an old-lady-who-lived-in-the-shoe house. You can take children in to look around the pub but they can't stay inside. The period bedrooms are attractive. A new cycle route which incorporates the disused railway line is to pass the inn this year. *(Recommended by Brian Websdale, JP, PP, Graham and Karen Oddey, Gordon)*

Free house ~ Licensees Buster and Rita Jones and S Thomson ~ Bar food ~ (01837) 861243 ~ No children inside ~ Open 11-2, 6-10.30; 12-2, 7-10.30 Sun; closed 25 and 26 Dec

SOUTH ZEAL SX6593 Map 1

Oxenham Arms ★ ♀ 🛏

Village signposted from A30 at A382 roundabout and B3260 Okehampton turn-off

A welcoming find in a pretty village, this very much liked, fine old place has friendly, attentive staff and a real sense of history. It was first licensed in 1477 and has grown up around the remains of a Norman monastery, built here to combat the pagan power of the neolithic standing stone that forms part of the wall in the family TV room behind the bar (there are actually twenty more feet of stone below the floor). It later became the Dower House of the Burgoynes, whose heiress carried it to the Oxenham family. And Charles Dickens, snowed up one winter, wrote a lot of *Pickwick Papers* here. The beamed and partly panelled front bar has elegant mullioned windows and Stuart fireplaces, and windsor armchairs around low oak tables and built-in wall seats. The small no-smoking family room has beams, wheelback chairs around polished tables, decorative plates, and another open fire. Popular bar food includes soup (£2.50), sandwiches (from £2.50), good ploughman's (£3.95), fish and chips (£5.25), home-made steak, kidney, Guinness and mushroom pie or a curry of the day (£6.25), fish and chips (£5.25), daily specials such as vegetable quiche (£5.25), lamb moussaka (£6.25), and smoked fish platter (£6.75), evening steaks (£9.25), and puddings (from £2.45). Well kept Princetown IPA and Jail Ale (brewed locally), and Sharps Doom Bar on handpump or tapped from the cask, and an extensive list of wines including good house claret; darts, shove-ha'penny, dominoes, and cribbage. Note the imposing curved stone steps leading up to the garden where there's a sloping spread of lawn. *(Recommended by Nigel Flook, Betsy Brown, Bernard Stradling, Basil Minson, George Atkinson, John and Christine Vittoe, Jacquie and Jim Jones, Catherine Lloyd, John Askew, the Didler, R F Ballinger, John McDonald, Ann Bond, Anne and Michael Corbett, A Hepburn, S Jenner, R R and J D Winn, Dallas Seawright, Mr and Mrs M Clifford, John and Christine Simpson, Graham and Karen Oddey, R J Walden, Mike and Heather Watson, JP, PP, W M and J M Cottrell, Colin Campbell)*

Free house ~ Licensee James Henry ~ Real ale ~ Bar food ~ Restaurant ~ (01837) 840244 ~ Children in eating area of bar ~ Open 11-2.30, 6-11; 12-2.30, 7-10.30 Sun ~ Bedrooms: £45B/£70B

STOCKLAND ST2404 Map 1

Kings Arms 🍴 ♀ ⛵

Village signposted from A30 Honiton—Chard

Although this busy 16th-c pub is somewhere to come and enjoy particularly good food in friendly surroundings, it has got a proper bar for locals which very much adds to the atmosphere. The dark beamed, elegant dining lounge has solid refectory tables and settles, attractive landscapes, a medieval oak screen (which divides the room into two), and a great stone fireplace across almost the whole width of one end; the cosy restaurant with its huge inglenook fireplace and bread oven has the same menu as the bar: lunchtime sandwiches, home-made soup (£3.50), smoked mackerel pâté or vegetable mousse (£4), smoked ostrich fillet or a terrine of three fishes (£5), pasta carbonara or royal rabbit (£7.50), supreme of chicken Jerez (£8.50), steaks (from £8.50), king prawn madras or baked bass (£9.50), lamb Siciliano (£10.50), breast of Quantock duck (£12.50), whole lemon sole meunière (£13.50), and puddings such as apple and treacle crumble, blueberry and raspberry cheesecake or Grand Marnier soufflé ice cream (£3.50); they don't serve bar snacks in the evening or on Sunday lunch. Booking is essential; good breakfasts. Well kept Courage Directors, Exmoor Ale, Otter Ale, and John Smiths on handpump, over 40 malt whiskies (including island and west coast ones; large spirit measures), a good wine list with house wines and special offers by the bottle or glass chalked up on a board, and farm ciders. At the back, a flagstoned bar has captain's-style tub chairs and cushioned stools around heavy wooden tables, and leads on to a carpeted darts room with two boards, another room with dark beige plush armchairs and settees (and a fruit machine), and a neat ten-pin skittle alley; table skittles, cribbage, dominoes, fruit machine, and quiet mainly classical piped music. There are tables under cocktail parasols on the terrace in front of the white-faced thatched pub and a lawn enclosed by trees and shrubs. *(Recommended by J H Jones, John and Sarah Perry, Gordon, Karen Jeal, G and P Dixon, Pete and Rosie Flower, Chris Raisin, Richard and Margaret Peers, Roger Price, Yavuz and Shirley Mutlu, Francis Johnston, Michael and Anne Corbett, Richard and Robyn Wain, John and Christine Simpson)*

Free house ~ Licensees Heinz Kiefer and Paul Diviani ~ Real ale ~ Bar food ~ Restaurant ~ (01404) 881361 ~ Children in eating area of bar; over 12 in restaurant ~ Piano Sat evening, various bands Sun evening ~ Open 12-3, 6.30-11.30; 12-3, 7-10.30 Sun; closed 25 Dec ~ Bedrooms: £25B/£40B

STOKE FLEMING SX8648 Map 1

Green Dragon ♀

Church Rd

Very much enjoyed for its friendly, relaxed atmosphere, this quietly set pub is opposite a church with an interesting tall tower. The main part of the flagstoned and beamed bar has two small settles, bay window seats, boat pictures, and maybe Electra or Maia the burmese cats or Rhea the relaxed german shepherd; down on the right is a wooden-floored snug with throws and cushions on battered sofas and armchairs, a few books (20p to RNLI), adult board games, a grandfather clock, and cuttings about the landlord (who is a long-distance yachtsman), and maps of his races on the walls. Down some steps is the Mess Deck decorated with old charts and lots of ensigns and flags, and there's a playbox of children's games; darts, shove-ha'penny, cribbage, and dominoes; piped music. Good home-made bar food includes lunchtime sandwiches such as home-cooked ham with apricot chutney or somerset brie and apple (£2.30) and ploughman's (£3.50), as well as soup (£2), baked crab and mushrooms in a creamy anchovy sauce (£3.90), strips of squid stir-fried with ginger, carrots, spring onions and dry sherry or pasta with a sauce of the day and parmesan cheese (£4), bangers and mash (£4.50), steak in ale or fish pie (£5.90), daily specials like crab cakes, venison pie or chicken basque (£5.90), and children's dishes (from £2). Well kept Bass, Hardy Royal Oak, and Wadworths 6X on handpump (all except Bass kept under light blanket pressure), big glasses of six good house wines from Australia, California, France and Germany, Addlestones cider,

Luscombes slightly alcoholic ginger beer and organic apple and pear juices, and a decent range of spirits; you can take the beer away with you. There's a back garden with swings, a climbing frame and picnic-sets and a front terrace with some white plastic garden tables and chairs. *(Recommended by Martin Jennings, Peter Cook, P R Graham, John Wilson, C P Scott-Malden, Charles Eaton)*

Heavitree ~ Tenants Peter and Alix Crowther ~ Real ale ~ Bar food (12-2.30, 6.30-9) ~ (01803) 770238 ~ Children welcome ~ Open 11-3, 5.30-11; 12-3, 6-10.30 Sun

STOKE GABRIEL SX8457 Map 1
Church House ★

Village signposted from A385 just W of junction with A3022, in Collaton St Mary; can also be reached from nearer Totnes; nearby parking not easy

There's a lot of unspoilt character in this enjoyable local, and a good mix of customers, too. The lounge bar has an exceptionally fine medieval beam-and-plank ceiling, a black oak partition wall, window seats cut into the thick butter-colour walls, decorative plates and vases of flowers on a dresser, and a huge fireplace still used in winter to cook the stew. The mummified cat in a case, probably about 200 years old, was found during restoration of the roof space in the verger's cottage three doors up the lane – one of a handful found in the West Country and believed to have been a talisman against evil spirits. Home-made bar food includes soup (£2.25), a big choice of sandwiches and toasties (from £2.25; good cheese and prawn toasties, lovely local river salmon £3.95, and local crab), ploughman's or pasties (£3.95), daily specials such as steak and kidney in ale pie, curries or good beef stew with herb dumplings (£5.75), and puddings (from £2.75). Well kept Bass, Worthington Best, and a weekly guest ale on handpump, and quite a few malt whiskies. Cribbage in the little public locals' bar. There are picnic-sets on the small terrace in front of the building. No children. *(Recommended by Mike and Mary Carter, Ian and Deborah Carrington, W W Burke, Rob and Gill Weeks, Paul R White)*

Free house ~ Licensee T G Patch ~ Real ale ~ Bar food (11-2.30, 6.30-10) ~ (01803) 782384 ~ No children ~ Open 11-11; 12-4, 7-10.30 Sun; 11-3, 6-11 winter

STOKEINTEIGNHEAD SX9170 Map 1
Church House

Village signposted (not clearly) in Combeinteignhead E of Newton Abbot; or off A379 N of Torquay

So carefully did local craftsmen restore this lovely old thatched inn after a roof fire in 1993, that you'd never know that the whole building didn't date back to the 13th c. Much of downstairs was luckily untouched, and the main bar to the right of the door has heavy beams, lots of copper and brass platters, kettles, and coffee pots in the inglenook fireplace and on the mantlepiece, a fine ornately carved huge settle and other smaller ones, rustic farmhouse chairs, a nice mix of tables including a big circular one, little lanterns, window seats, and a relaxed, informal atmosphere; a dining room leads off with an ancient stripped stone skeleton staircase with lots of little pictures around it; candles on the tables. Decent bar food includes home-made soup (£2.25), sandwiches (from £2.50; open ones £3.95), ploughman's (£4.60), lasagne, steak and kidney pie or vegetarian moussaka (£6.50), chargrilled chicken supreme with barbecue sauce (£6.95), seafood crêpes (£9.50), steaks (from £9.50), crispy breast of duck (£12.50), puddings such as spicy bread pudding or home-made fruit crumble (£2.50), and children's menu (£3.25). Well kept Bass, Flowers IPA, and Wadworths 6X on handpump, Churchward's cider, and a decent range of whiskies. There's a simple public bar with darts, shove-ha'penny, cribbage, dominoes, fruit machine, TV, and quiet piped music. The neat back garden with dracaenas is on the way to the car park. *(Recommended by Andrew Hodges, Stan Edwards, Gordon, John Wilson)*

Heavitree ~ Managers F and C Wilson, M Place ~ Real ale ~ Bar food (12-2.15, 6.30-9.30; 10 weekends) ~ (01626) 872475 ~ Children welcome away from bar ~ Open 11-11; 12-10.30 Sun; 11-3, 6-11 weekdays winter

STOKENHAM SX8042 Map 1

Tradesmans Arms

Just off A379 Dartmouth—Kingsbridge

Professional new licensees have taken over this charming thatched village cottage and have made a few changes. Apart from upgrading of the lavatories and cellar storage, the restaurant is being refurbished – and they tell us their aim is to offer restaurant food at pub prices in a pubby atmosphere. The little beamed bar has plenty of nice antique tables and neat dining chairs – with more up a step or two at the back, window seats looking across a field to the village church, and a big fireplace; the Tack Room is no smoking. Good bar food now includes home-made soup (£2.65; fish soup with garlic croutons £2.65), lunchtime filled french bread or home-made pâté (£3.50), prawns flamed in brandy with garlic dip (£3.75), chicken breast with sliced peppers and tarragon (£8.25), poached fillet of brill with a white wine sauce (£8.95), steaks or roast rack of lamb and redcurrant sauce (£9.95), daily specials such as scallops flamed in brandy with a light onion sauce (£4.75), vegetable goulash (£6.95) or baked cod with a fish jus (£8.50), and puddings such as apple charlotte with walnuts and coffee ice cream or iced Grand Marnier soufflé on a mango coulis (£2.95). Well kept Adnams Southwold and Broadside, and a guest beer on handpump, and quite a few malt whiskies. Dogs are welcome on a lead in the main bar area. There are some seats outside in the garden. *(Recommended by B J Harding, Richard and Robyn Wain, Lynn Sharpless, Bob Eardley)*

Free house ~ Licensees John and Elizabeth Sharman ~ Real ale ~ Bar food ~ (01548) 580313 ~ Children in back room ~ Open 12-2.30, 6-11; 12-3, 6.30-10.30 Sun; closed Sun evening, Mon, Tues and Sat lunch Sept-May

TORCROSS SX8241 Map 1

Start Bay

A379 S of Dartmouth

For 20 years Mr Stubbs has been running this immensely popular dining pub. It's the particularly good fresh fish and the fine position right on the beach that continues to pull in the crowds and in summer there may be queues before the doors open. Picnic-sets on the terrace look out over the three-mile pebble beach, and there are plenty of nearby walks. A local trawler catches the fish, a local crabber drops the crabs at the back door, and the landlord enjoys catching plaice, scallops, and bass: cod and haddock (medium £3.95; large £5.20; jumbo £6.50 – truly enormous), whole lemon sole (from £4.75), skate (£5.50), whole dover sole (in four sizes from £6.75), local scallops (£7.90), brill (from £8.50), and whole bass (small £9.25; medium £9.95; large £11.50). Other food includes sandwiches (from £1.95), ploughman's (from £3.20), vegetable lasagne (£4.75), gammon and pineapple (£5.95), steaks (from £7.95), puddings (£2.75), and children's meals (£3.25); they do warn of delays at peak times (and you will probably have to wait for a table); the sachets of tomato sauce or tartar sauce are not to everyone's taste. Well kept Bass and Flowers Original on handpump, Luscombe cider and fresh apple juice, and local wine. The unassuming main bar (which has a small no-smoking area) is very much set out for eating with wheelback chairs around plenty of dark tables or (round a corner) back-to-back settles forming booths; there are some photographs of storms buffeting the pub and country pictures on its cream walls, and a winter coal fire; a small chatty drinking area by the counter has a brass ship's clock and barometer. The children's room is no smoking. The good winter games room has pool, darts, shove-ha'penny, and juke box; there's more booth seating in a family room with sailing boat pictures. Fruit machine in the lobby. The freshwater wildlife lagoon of Slapton Ley is just behind the pub. *(Recommended by Bett and Brian Cox, Richard and Robyn Wain, Andrew Hodges, D Marsh, Peter Haines, June and Perry Dann, Martin Jennings, JDM, KM, N Hills, Chris and Margaret Southon, Pat and Robert Watt)*

Whitbreads ~ Tenant Paul Stubbs ~ Real ale ~ Bar food ~ (01548) 580553 ~ Children in restaurant ~ Open 11.30-11; 12-10.30 Sun; 11.30-2.30, 6-11 in winter; closed evening 25 Dec

TORRINGTON SS4919 Map 1
Black Horse
High St

Although the overhanging upper storeys of this pretty twin-gabled inn are dated 1616, the building actually goes back to the 15th c. The bar on the left has a couple of fat black beams hung with stirrups, a comfortable seat running right along its full-width window, chunky elm tables, and an oak bar counter; on the right, the no-smoking lounge has a striking ancient black oak partition wall, a couple of attractive oak seats, muted plush easy chairs, and a settee. The oak-panelled restaurant has an aquarium. Generously served, the good value bar food might include sandwiches (from £1.50; filled french bread from £2.75; triple decker toasties with chips from £2.95), filled baked potatoes (from £2.95), omelettes (£3.25), ploughman's (from £3.50), cod and prawn crumble (£4.10), vegetable curry (£4.25), steak and kidney pie (£4.40), gammon and egg (£4.75), rib-eye steak (£6.50), puddings (£2.10), and children's meals (from £1.95). Well kept Courage Best and Directors and John Smiths, with a changing guest beer on handpump; darts, shove-ha'penny, cribbage, dominoes, and well reproduced piped music; friendly cat and dogs. Both General Fairfax and Lord Hopton are thought to have stayed here during the Civil War. The inn is handy for the RHS Rosemoor garden and Dartington Crystal. *(Recommended by Karen and Garry Fairclough, G Washington, R J Walden, Mr and Mrs C R Little, Chris and Margaret Southon, K Flack, John A Barker)*

Scottish Courage ~ Lease: David and Val Sawyer ~ Real ale ~ Bar food ~ (01805) 622121 ~ Children in lounge or restaurant ~ Local 60s/70s singer 1st Sat of month ~ Open 11-3, 6-11; 11-11 Sat; 11-3.30, 7-10.30 Sun ~ Bedrooms: £18B/£32B

TRUSHAM SX8582 Map 1
Cridford Inn
Village and pub signposted from B3193 NW of Chudleigh, just N of big ARC works; 1½ very narrow miles

Tucked away in pretty countryside, this historic longhouse dates mainly from 1081 and in the dining room is a mosaic of the date stone with the initials of the then Abbot of Buckfastleigh. It became a farm in the early 1300s and the transept window in the bar is said to be the oldest domestic window in Britain and is Grade I listed. The bar has stout standing timbers, natural stone walls, flagstones, window seats, pews and chapel chairs around kitchen and pub tables, and a big woodburning stove in the stone fireplace; there is a no-smoking area. Mrs Farrell is Malaysian and some of the dishes on the menu hail from those parts. In generous helpings, the daily-changing bar food might include white onion and chive soup (£3), sandwiches (served with chips and garnish, £3.75), fried rice with curried vegetables or prawns or a vegetarian Lebanese curry with yoghurt (£5.50), ploughman's (from £5.50), terrine of venison with warm cumberland sauce, wild mushrooms and herb loaf (£5.95), steak and mushroom pie with cheese pastry (£6.50), wild boar with onion and marmalade, pork in cider or chicken in wine and mushrooms (all £7.50), perhaps nasi goreng or beef rendang, and home-made puddings such as toffee cheesecake with maple syrup and clotted cream, spotted dick or coffee walnut cake with fresh fruits (from £3.25). Well kept Courage Directors and Scatter Rock Teign Valley Tipple and Trusham Ale (brewed for them) on handpump; cribbage, dominoes, and a Wednesday evening quiz night; piped music. They have an alsatian called Lia, a noisy siamese cat called Holly, and a naughty malaysian cat called Sammy. The two ghosts are well behaved. *(Recommended by Mr and Mrs A Scrutton, John and Christine Simpson, Mr and Mrs Broadhurst, Dr and Mrs A K Clarke, Catherine Pocock, Richard and Margaret Peers, G Washington, Nigel Clifton, Basil Minson, Mike Gorton, Mark Brock)*

Free house ~ Licensee Bill Farrell ~ Real ale ~ Bar food (12-3, 7-9.30) ~ Restaurant ~ (01626) 853694/fax 853694 ~ Children in eating area of bar and in restaurant ~ Open 11.30-3, 6.30-11; 12-3, 7-10.30 Sun; closed evening 25 Dec ~ Bedrooms: £50B/£70B

TUCKENHAY SX8156 Map 1
Maltsters Arms 🍴 🍷 🛏️

Take Ashprington road out of Totnes (signed left off A381 on outskirts), keeping on past
Watermans Arms

Devonshire Dining Pub of the Year
The hard-working and enthusiastic licensees here continue to add little touches to
make this creekside inn even better. They hold barbecues every weekend and daily
during the school holidays, have live music on the quayside, have started their own
cricket team, and will be holding their second canoe regatta. The interesting food
continues to draw customers in, with lunchtime dishes such as spinach and
mushroom or local seafood soup (from £3.25), sandwiches (from £3.50), avocado,
marinated fig and brie salad (£4.75), ploughman's (from £4.75), smokehouse platter
of chicken, duck and air-dried ham (£5.75), sweet potato and banana red curry or
cottage pie (£6.95), roast leg of lamb with mint sauce and rosemary gravy (£7.25),
and tuna steak in lime and sambuca (£12.95); in the evening, there might be sauté of
lamb kidneys with bacon and red wine (£4.50), scrambled duck eggs with smoked
salmon (£4.95), whole dab grilled with lemon and parsley butter or flash-fried
pigeon breasts on a vegetable and nut stir fry (£8.50), medallions of pork with a
creamy apple sauce (£9.95), and fillet steak with a red wine and wild mushroom
sauce (£14.50); puddings such as pear and raspberry puff, marmalade and coconut
bread and butter pudding or spotted dick (£3.95), and a good children's menu
(£4.50). They've started doing little pots of home-made nibbles: home-roasted nuts
with peanut oil and sea salt (50p), marinated feta and garlic (£1.25), and seafood
salad (£1.75). Well kept Blackawton 44, Princetown Dartmoor IPA and two
changing guest beers on handpump, 15 good wines by the glass, local cider, a
wicked bloody mary, and drinks in the freezer like buffalo grass vodka and various
eau de vie. The long, narrow bar links two other rooms – a little snug one with an
open fire (where the big black dog likes to sit) and plenty of bric-a-brac, and another
with red-painted vertical seats and kitchen chairs on the wooden floor, and a second
open fire. Darts, shove-ha'penny, cribbage, dominoes, chess, Jenga, and
backgammon. This is a lovely spot by a peaceful wooded creek with tables by the
water and moorings for boats. The bedrooms in the next door Old Winery are pretty
special; plenty of bird life. They also run a mini shop. *(Recommended by Paul R White,
the Didler, Richard and Margaret Peers, Margaret and Roy Randle, John Evans, Andrew Hodges,
Glenn and Gillian Miller, Mike and Karen England, Bernard Stradling, John Wilson, Mrs Mary
Woods, John E Thomason)*

*Free house ~ Licensees Denise and Quentin Thwaites ~ Real ale ~ Bar food ~
Restaurant ~ (01803) 732350 ~ Children in rooms off bar and restaurant ~ Modern
jazz 1st Sun evening of month, trad jazz 3rd Fri evening of month ~ Open 11-11; 12-
10.30 Sun; 11-3, 6-11 weekdays winter ~ Bedrooms: /£75B*

TWO BRIDGES SX6175 Map 1
Two Bridges Hotel
B3357/B3212 across Dartmoor

In a fine spot in the middle of Dartmoor, this bustling inn had a really good mix of
customers of all ages on our inspection; this gave it a relaxed, chatty and friendly
atmosphere. The big L-shaped bar has brass-bound cask seats, brocaded built-in wall
seats and captain's chairs on the turkey carpet, with upholstered settles and
bentwood chairs in the longer area, black beams and joists with pewter mugs and
lots of horsebrasses, interesting old photographs and all sizes of Royal prints all over
the walls, a nice big butcher's mirror (Only the Best English Beef and Mutton Killed)
above the stone fireplace, a grandfather clock, some WWI-era photographs engraved
on some windows, one or two big engravings, and an old wall telephone by the bar
counter. To order your tasty food, you have to get a numbered table and pay first.
At lunchtime, this might include home-made soup (£2.25), chicken and pork or
mushroom and nut pâté (£3.75), filled baked potatoes (from £3.75), sandwiches
(from £3.95), local pasties (£4.50), pasta with a spicy mushroom, tomato and basil

sauce or curries (£5.95), and steak in ale pie, pork with a cider and grain mustard sauce, chicken casserole with local honey or Brixham cod fillet with a horseradish crust (£6.50); in the evening there might be extras such as green lip mussels (£4.50), oriental salmon (£6.95), and 8oz sirloin steak (£10.50). They brew their own real ales – Princetown IPA and Jail Ale well kept on handpump. A rather charming panelled corridor with a fine wall clock and lovely Chris Chapman photographs leads to an old-fashioned entrance lounge with comfortable button-back leather and other settees and armchairs in front of a big roaring log fire. Outside, there are some picnic-sets on grass with jackdaws hopping about; geese at the back. A fine old bridge (floodlit at night) leads away from the inn over a quiet river. *(Recommended by Bruce Bird)*

Free house ~ Licensee Lesley Davies ~ Real ale ~ Bar food ~ Restaurant ~ (01822) 890581 ~ Children welcome ~ Open 11-11; 12-10.30 Sun; 11-3, 6-11 but drinks still served in hotel lounge all day winter; closed 25 Dec ~ Bedrooms: £35B/£70B

UGBOROUGH SX6755 Map 1
Anchor

Off A3121 – signed from A38 W of South Brent

There's always a good mix of customers in the unchanging and pleasantly relaxed oak-beamed public bar here – as well as a log fire in the stone fireplace, and wall settles and seats around wooden tables on the polished woodblock floor; there are windsor armchairs in the comfortable restaurant (the lower area is no smoking). You can eat from either the bar or restaurant menus and sit anywhere in the pub (apart from Saturday night when there are no bar snacks in the restaurant). From the bar menu, there might be home-made soup (£2.95), good burgers (from £2.95, including ostrich, venison and vegetarian), omelettes (from £3.85), filled long rolls (from £4; crab £5.50), ploughman's (from £4), pizzas (from £4.35), pasta dishes (from £4.45), steak and kidney pie (£6.20), and gammon and pineapple (£6.50); the à la carte menu includes baby octopus (£4.50), crab and kiwi cocktail (£5.50), vegetarian creole (£8.75), chicken maryland (with bananas and sweetcorn, £11.75), steaks (from £12.50), veal in cream and mushrooms or duck breasts in honey, ginger and lemon (£13.50), and rack of lamb (£16.50); children's menu (£2.50); courteous service. Well kept Bass tapped from the cask and Sutton XSB and seasonal ales, and Wadworths 6X on handpump, and quite a few malt whiskies. Darts, dominoes, cribbage, video game, and fruit machine. There's a small outside seating area. *(Recommended by Colin and Ann Hunt, John Evans, Alan and Paula McCully, DJW, Tim Barrow, Sue Demont, Mick Hitchman, Ian Jones)*

Free house ~ Licensees Ken and Sheelagh Jeffreys-Simmons ~ Real ale ~ Bar food ~ Restaurant ~ (01752) 892283 ~ Children welcome ~ Open 11-11; 12-10.30 Sun ~ Bedrooms: £35B/£45B

UMBERLEIGH SS6023 Map 1
Rising Sun 🛏

A377 S of Barnstaple

New licensees have taken over this friendly, comfortable inn and are aiming to steer its appeal back towards locals and fishermen. It's set just across the road from the River Taw (they have five salmon and sea trout beats) and there are plenty of photographs in the bar of happy anglers holding enormous fish. A low stone wall with cushions on top divides the bar into two parts; at one end are some brocaded stools and spindleback chairs around traditional tables on the flowery carpet, a small stone fireplace with a log-effect fire and hops above the hunting horn on the bressumer beam, and a cushioned window seat; piped music and board games. The stone bar counter has a row of graded pewter tankards and lots of hops on the gantry, and serves well kept Bass, Courage Best, and Marstons Pedigree on handpump; thoughtful little wine list and several malt whiskies. The other end of the room has high bar stools on the flagstones, a pine built-in wall bench and long cushioned wall seat by a big mural of the river valley, and a woodburning stove with logs stacked on either side; the River Room is no smoking. Good bar food now includes sandwiches, home-made soups (£2.25), ploughman's (from £4.25), home-made pasty, bangers and mash with onion gravy or tagliatelle with fresh tomato and basil sauce (£4.95), warm salad of bacon and black pudding topped with a poached egg (£5.25), fish in beer batter (£5.95), steak and kidney pie or pudding (£6.25), fresh salmon with a mustard and herb crust (£8.95), and puddings such as warm flapjack with butterscotch sauce or summer pudding with clotted cream (£2.95). There are some green seats under parasols outside, and Umberleigh railway station is just a couple of hundred yards away, over the bridge. *(Recommended by Colin Thompson, Rita Horridge)*

Free house ~ Licensees Charles and Heather Manktelow ~ Real ale ~ Bar food ~ Restaurant ~ (01769) 560447 ~ Children in eating area of bar and in restaurant ~ Open 11-3, 6-11; 12-3, 7-10.30 Sun ~ Bedrooms: £40B/£77B

WESTLEIGH SS4628 Map 1
Westleigh Inn
½ mile off A39 Bideford—Instow

From the huge, neatly kept hillside garden here there are gorgeous views down over the Torridge estuary, and there's a particularly good children's play area; you can walk to the pub from Bideford along the Tarka Trail. Inside, it's warmly welcoming with a good mix of locals and visitors in the single room (split by the serving bar), old local pictures, dark ceiling joists, a log fire in the ingelnook fireplace, and a relaxed family atmosphere. Served by friendly, efficient staff, the good, reasonably priced bar food includes filled french bread (from £2.25, steak £3.95), filled baked potatoes or burgers (from £2.75), ploughman's (£3.45), garlic mushrooms (£3.75), half roast chicken (£4.25), breaded fish (from £4.95), home-cooked ham and eggs or sweet and sour chicken (£5.25), lasagne (£5.45), steak and Guinness pie (£5.95), evening steaks (from £8.25), puddings (from £1.95), and children's meals (from £2.25); enjoyable Sunday carvery (£5.25). Well kept Bass, Gales HSB, Ruddles County, and Ushers Best on handpump. The dog is named after the pub. *(Recommended by M Joyner, Piotr Chodzko-Zajko, James and Karen Davies)*

Free house ~ Licensee John Craze ~ Real ale ~ Bar food (11.30-2, 6-9) ~ (01271) 860867 ~ Children in one bar area only ~ Live music monthly Fri or Sat ~ Open 11.30-3, 6-11; 11.30-11 Sat; 12-11 Sun; 11.30-3, 6-11 winter Sat; 12-3, 6.30-10.30 Sun in winter; closed evening 25 Dec

WIDECOMBE SX7176 Map 1
Rugglestone £
Village at end of B3387; pub just S – turn left at church and NT church house, OS Sheet 191 map reference 720765

Tucked away down the lane from the bustling tourist village, this unspoilt local has a strong rural atmosphere. The small bar has just four small tables, a few window and wall seats, a one-person pew built into the corner by the nice old stone fireplace, and a rudimentary bar counter dispensing well kept Butcombe Bitter, Dartmoor Best, and a summer guest beer tapped from the cask; local farm cider and a decent little wine list. The room on the right is a bit bigger and lighter-feeling, and shy strangers may feel more at home here: another stone fireplace, beamed ceiling, stripped pine tables, a built-in wall bench, and winter darts. There's also a little no-smoking room; shove-ha'penny, cribbage, dominoes, and euchre. Good simple bar food includes home-made soup (£2.15), meaty or vegetarian pasties (from £2.25), ploughman's (£3.75), daily specials such as cheesy leek and potato bake or cottage pie (£3.45), chicken and broccoli bake (£3.70), roast mediterranean vegetable bake (£3.75), steak and kidney pie (£4.15), beef lean stew with dumplings (£4.45), and puddings such as treacle and walnut tart (£2.75); friendly service. The two cats are called Marbles (who is now 19) and Elbi, and the two terriers, Tinker and Belle. Outside across the little medieval leat bringing moor water down to the village is a field with lots of picnic-sets (and some geese and chickens); old-fashioned outside lavatories. No children inside (though they have constructed a large shelter with tables and chairs in the garden). *(Recommended by Mike Gorton, Andy and Jill Kassube, Richard and Valerie Wright, Colin and Ann Hunt, G and M Stewart, Mike Wells, JP, PP, I Maw, P and M Rudlin)*

Free house ~ Licensees Lorrie and Moira Ensor ~ Real ale ~ Bar food ~ (01364) 621327 ~ No children inside ~ Open 11-2.30(3 Sat), 6-11; 12-3, 6-10.30 Sun; winter evening opening 7

WONSON SX6789 Map 1
Northmore Arms ⚓ 🍺

Off A382 half mile from A30 at Whiddon Down; turn right down lane signposted Throwleigh/Gidleigh. Continue down lane over humpback bridge; turn left to Wonson; OS Sheet 191 map reference 674903

If you like simple, unspoilt locals, then this rustic, tucked away little cottage is well worth a visit. It's a friendly place with two small connected beamed rooms – modest and informal but civilised – with wall settles, a few elderly chairs, five tables in one room and just two in the other. There are two open fires (only one may be lit), and some attractive photographs on the stripped stone walls; darts, chess and cribbage. Besides well kept ales such as Adnams Broadside, Cotleigh Tawny and Exe Valley Dobs, they have good house wines, and food such as sandwiches, pâté (from £1.50; toasties from £1.95), garlic mushrooms (£2.45), ploughman's (£3.75), filled baked potatoes (from £3.75), ham and egg (£4.25), home-made steak and kidney pudding (£4.50), daily specials like liver and onions (£4.25) and roast lamb with garlic potatoes (£4.95), and home-made puddings such as treacle tart (£1.95). The ladies' lavatory is up steep steps. Tables and chairs sit precariously in the steep little garden – all very peaceful and rustic; excellent walking from the pub (or to it, perhaps from Chagford or Gidleigh Park). *(Recommended by Bett and Brian Cox, R J Walden, Dallas Seawright, Graham and Karen Oddey, Catherine Lloyd)*

Free house ~ Licensee Mrs Mo Miles ~ Real ale ~ Bar food (12-9; 12-2.30, 7-9 Sun) ~ (01647) 231428 ~ Well behaved children away from bar ~ Open 11-11; 12-10.30 Sun ~ Bedrooms: /£30

WOODBURY SALTERTON SY0189 Map 1
Diggers Rest

3½ miles from M5 junction 30: A3052 towards Sidmouth, village signposted on right about ½ mile after Clyst St Mary; also signposted from B3179 SE of Exeter

As this pleasant thatched village pub does fill up quickly at lunchtime, it's best to get there early. The heavy beamed bar has a log fire at one end with an ornate solid fuel stove at the other, comfortable old-fashioned country chairs and settles around polished antique tables set with fresh flowers, a dark oak Jacobean screen, a grandfather clock, and plates decorating the walls of one alcove. The big skittles alley can be used for families, and there's a games room with pool, fruit machine, pinball, and piped music.Well kept Bass and Dartmoor Best on ancient handpumps, and local farm ciders; sensibly placed darts and dominoes in the small brick-walled public bar. Decent bar food includes home-made soup (£1.95), sandwiches with home-cooked meats (from £2.95; good local crab £3.75), home-made pâté (£3.60), filled baked potatoes (from £3.95), ploughman's (from £4.05), cold roast beef with chips or vegetable curry (£4.95), liver and bacon with onion gravy (£5.75), steaks (from £9.85), puddings (from £1.95), and Sunday roasts (£5.55). The terrace garden has views of the countryside. *(Recommended by Alan and Paula McCully, Dr M E Wilson, Mr and Mrs J Bishop, John Askew, G Washington, B T Smith, Mrs Sylvia Elcoate)*

Free house ~ Licensee Sally Pratt ~ Real ale ~ Bar food (12-1.45, 7-9.45) ~ (01395) 232375 ~ Children in eating area of bar ~ Open 11-2.30, 6.30-11; 12-2.30, 7-10.30 Sun

Pubs with outstanding views are listed at the back of the book.

WOODLAND SX7968 Map 1
Rising Sun

Village signposted off A38 just NE of Ashburton – then keep eyes peeled for Rising Sun signposts

Surprisingly restauranty for this tucked-away countryside, but one reader finds it well worth the 90-mile round trip. There's an expanse of softly lit red plush button-back banquettes and matching studded chairs, partly divided by wooded bannister rails, masonry pillars and the odd high-backed settle. A forest of beams is hung with thousands of old doorkeys, and a nice part by the log fire has shelves of plates and books, and old pictures above the fireplace. Bar food is very good and includes sandwiches (from £2.75), home-made soup (£2.95), home-made pasties (£3), Thai fishcakes with vierge dressing (£3.95), ploughman's (from £5 with home-made chutney), local pork sausages with onion gravy, lamb and apricot pies or hazelnut and courgette bake with tomato sauce (£5.95), steak and kidney pudding with mustard mash (£6.95), roast cod fillet with green Thai curry and coconut sauce (£7.95), breast of Gressingham duck with black cherries and red wine sauce, local venison steak with prunes and port wine, and Scotch sirloin steak with caramelised onion compote (£10.95), and puddings such as chocolate marquise, sticky toffee pudding with butterscotch sauce or treacle tart (£2.95); children have home-breaded chicken breast, home-made fishcakes or local sausages (£2.50; they can also have small helpings of some adult dishes); super afternoon teas with home-made scones. You can have pies, cakes and pastries baked to order to take home, too, and there are regular themed food evenings. Well kept Princetown Jail Ale and weekly guests such as Butcombe Gold and Saddlers Highgate & Walsall on handpump; cheerful service. Two family areas include one up a couple of steps with various toys (and a collection of cookery books); the dining area is no smoking. There are some picnic-sets in the spacious garden, which has a play area including a redundant tractor. *(Recommended by Revd John E Cooper, Paul and Heather Bettesworth, Mrs M Webster, Pat and Robert Watt, Gordon, Dr A J and Mrs P G Newton)*

Free house ~ Licensee Heather Humphreys ~ Real ale ~ Bar food ~ Restaurant ~ (01364) 652544 ~ Children in eating area of bar and in restaurant ~ Open 11-3, 6-11; 12-3.30, 7-10.30 Sun; closed Mon morning except bank holidays and during July/Aug ~ Bedrooms: £25S/£40B

Lucky Dip

Besides the fully inspected pubs, you might like to try these Lucky Dips recommended to us and described by readers (if you do, please send us reports):

Abbotsham [SS4226]
Thatched House: Extensively refurbished family pub, mix of modern seats and older features, Bass, Butcombe, Courage Directors and John Smiths, attractive food inc good value Sun lunch, families welcome; tables outside; handy for the Big Sheep *(Chris and Margaret Southon)*
Appledore [SS4630]
☆ *Beaver* [Irsha St]: Great estuary views from raised area in light airy harbourside pub, good value food (esp fish), friendly staff, well kept changing ales such as Bass, Butcombe, Flowers, pool in smaller games room, views from outdoor tables; children really welcome, disabled access *(D M and M C Watkinson, Neil Townend, Eamonn and Natasha Skyrme)*
☆ *Royal George* [Irsha St]: Simple but good fresh food inc local fish in no-smoking dining room with superb estuary views, cosy and unspoilt front bar (where dogs allowed), well kept ales such as Bass, Ind Coope Burton, Morlands Old Speckled Hen, decent wines, good friendly

service, attractive pictures, fresh flowers; disabled access, picnic-sets outside, picturesque street sloping to sea *(Ursula and Paul Randall, D M and M C Watkinson)*
Aylesbeare [SY0392]
☆ *Halfway* [A3052 Exeter—Sidmouth, junction with B3180]: Spotless and comfortable, with lots of old wood, brasses and interesting sporting prints, good food esp fish and vegetarian, well kept ales inc changing guests, good very friendly service; high views over Dartmoor *(Dr M E Wilson, Alan and Paula McCully, Dr and Mrs D J Walker)*
Barbrook [SS7147]
Beggars Roost: Charming welcoming landlady, good cheap food *(Mrs S Mackenzie)*
Barnstaple [SS5533]
Rolle Quay [Rolle St]: Big Victorian pub with rather plush lounge, separate bar, skittle alley, well cooked bargain food from separate servery, well kept Cotleigh Tawny, Cottage Western Glory and uncommon guests such as

Barum and Dorothy Goodbodys, efficient service even when very busy; children welcome *(Ian and Nita Cooper, Carole and John Smith)*
Beer [ST2389]

Anchor [Fore St]: Nice old local photographs in simply furnished bow-windowed front public bar, sizeable no-smoking restaurant and back lounge bar; has been very popular for good fish fresh from the beach fishermen here, with efficient friendly service, local Otter beers, local cider and good wines, but has changed hands (and supply sources); comfortable bedrooms, delightful seaside village *(John and Sarah Perry, LYM)*

Barrel of Beer: Most favoured for beer, but also serves food; open all day, parking nearby *(Peter and Audrey Dowsett, Veronica Brown)*
Belstone [SX6293]

Tors [a mile off A30]: Imposing stone building, good choice of reasonably priced generous food inc good value soup and sandwich, well kept Butcombe and Otter ales, decent wines and malt whiskies, lovely woodburner mulling wine in winter; bedrooms, attractive village well placed for N Dartmoor walks *(John and Vivienne Rice, R J Walden)*
Bere Ferrers [SX4563]

Old Plough [long dead-end rd off B3257 S of Tavistock]: Welcoming and attractive, with stripped stone, low beam-and-plank ceilings, panelling, slate flagstones, old armchairs and other old-fashioned furniture, woodburner, steps down to cosy restaurant (home cooking, monster pies, plenty of fish), well kept real ales; garden overlooking estuary *(Betty Petheram)*
Berry Head [SX9456]

Berry Head Hotel: Large L-shaped pubby bar popular with Torquay businessmen, plenty of tables giving panoramic Torbay views, enjoyable food inc good carvery in room off, caring service, Dartmoor, Marstons Pedigree and Tetleys, unobtrusive piped music; children welcome *(D I Baddeley, Gwen and Peter Andrews)*
Bickington [SS5332]

Toby Jug: Full of toby jugs (one 3ft tall), good food, quick friendly service *(Paul and Heather Bettesworth)*
Bickleigh [SS9406]

☆ *Fishermans Cot*: Greatly extended thatched fishing inn with lots of tables on acres of turkey carpet attractively broken up with pillars, plants and some panelled parts, charming view over shallow rocky race below 1640 Exe bridge, more tables out on terrace and waterside lawn; good well served food inc popular reasonably priced carvery, well kept Bass and Wadworths 6X, friendly efficient service; piped pop music; comfortable bedrooms looking over own terrace to river *(Neil Townend, Dr and Mrs A Clarke, John and Vivienne Rice, BB)*

☆ *Trout* [A396, N of junction with A3072]: Recently refurbished thatched pub with comfortable easy chairs in huge bar and dining lounge, good choice of food from sandwiches to tempting puddings, well kept ales such as Cotleigh Tawny, Bass, Boddingtons, Exmoor

Gold, nice coffee, efficient friendly service; tables on pretty lawn, car park across rd; well equipped bedrooms, good breakfast *(LYM, G Washington, Veronica Brown)*
Bideford [SS4526]

Joiners Arms [Market Pl]: Good value food in eating area sectioned off by standing timbers, friendly helpful service, well kept Bass, Jollyboat Mainbrace and a guest beer, collection of joiner's tools and old Bideford pictures; live music Fri/Sat; bargain bedrooms, good breakfast *(Roger and Jenny Huggins)*

Kings Arms [The Quay]: Particularly well kept ales, decent food from good filled rolls up, cheerful atmosphere, Victorian harlequin floor tiles in alcovey front bar, back raised family area; pavement tables *(Karen and Garry Fairclough)*
Bishops Tawton [SS5630]

☆ *Chichester Arms* [signed off A377 outside Barnstaple]: Friendly 15th-c cob and thatch pub with low bowed beams, large stone fireplace, old local photographs, plush banquettes, open fire, well priced food from home-made soup and sandwiches up, well kept Dartmoor Best, Ind Coope Burton and Tetleys, games in family room, partly no-smoking restaurant; picnic-sets on front terrace and in back garden; open all day *(LYM, Colin and Peggy Wilshire, Rita Horridge)*
Bovey Tracey [SX8278]

King of Prussia [High St]: Traditional unpretentious pub with well kept Bass and farm cider, friendly landlady and son, amiable locals, darts, pool and fruit machine *(Dr and Mrs A K Clarke)*
Bradninch [SS9903]

White Lion: Warmly friendly open-plan bar with woodburner, helpful licensees, enjoyable traditional food, good lunchtime customer mix, Wadworths 6X, fresh flowers; two cats; pretty village *(Mrs B Williams)*
Bradworthy [SS3214]

Bradworthy Inn: Recently refurbished two-bar thatched local with comfortable bedrooms *(anon)*
Bratton Fleming [SS6437]

☆ *White Hart* [off A399 N of S Molton]: Welcoming service and big helpings of good value bar food (not Sun lunchtime) from concerned chef/landlord in village pub with big inglenook fire, lots of snug alcoves, Exmoor ale and farm cider, large tables, traditional games in one side area, small family room; some seats outside *(LYM, Mrs A Tilt)*
Braunton [SS4836]

Mariners Arms [South St]: Busy pleasantly untouristy local, friendly and comfortable, lots of nautical prints, cheerful service, dining area with good range of good value meals (not Mon), well kept Courage Best and Directors, Exmoor and Morlands Old Speckled Hen, unobtrusive piped music, skittle alley; back terrace safe for children *(Ian and Nita Cooper)*
Brendon [SS7547]

☆ *Rockford Inn* [Lynton—Simonsbath rd, off B2332]: Homely and friendly little inn well set for walkers (and fishermen) by East Lyn river, summer afternoon refreshments as well as usual bar food inc sandwiches, vegetarian and fish; well kept Cotleigh Barn Owl, Courage Best and a guest beer, darts, pool, shove-ha'penny, cribbage, dominoes; piped music; restaurant, children in eating areas, dogs welcome, folk night every 3rd Sat, bedrooms; open all day summer *(Ian and Jane Irving, Tim and Beryl Dawson, Piotr Chodzko-Zajko, Dick Brown, Steven M Gent, Paul and Jane Forrestal, R J Walden, Dr I Crichton, John Evans, Peter Meister, LYM, H and D Payne, Sandra and Chris Taylor)*

Brixham [SX9255]
Blue Anchor [King St]: Well kept Tetleys and guest beers such as Tapsters Flying Scotsman, friendly service, decent usual range of food inc local fish, nautical bar, two small dining rooms – one a former chapel, down some steps; open all day *(Erna and Sidney Wells, Colin Roberts)*
Maritime: Particularly well kept beer, pictures and bric-a-brac by the ton, hundreds of keyrings, chamber-pots and jugs, two coal fires, comfortable sofas in every window, cosy atmosphere *(Ted George)*

Buckfastleigh [SX7366]
☆ *Dartbridge* [Totnes Rd, handy for A38]: Big family pub, prettily placed opp Dart Valley Rly – very popular in summer; good food, well kept changing beers such as Butcombe and Hop Back Crop Circle, above-average house wines, friendly young staff; reasonable disabled access, tables in neatly kept roadside garden, ten letting chalets *(John Evans, John and Vivienne Rice)*

Budleigh Salterton [SY0682]
☆ *Salterton Arms*: Wide range of reasonably priced good food, well kept Bass, John Smiths and Theakstons Old Peculier, good choice of malts and Irish whiskeys, steam-train enthusiast landlord, lots of jazz musician and other prints, nautical mementoes, small open fires, neat uniformed staff, upper dining gallery; children and dogs welcome, can get very busy summer; jazz winter Sun evenings, open all day w/e *(LYM, Neil Spink, Paul White, Margaret and Richard Peers)*

Burgh Island [SX6443]
☆ *Pilchard* [300 yds across tidal sands from Bigbury on Sea; walk, or take summer Tractor – unique bus on stilts]: Great setting, high above sea on tidal island with unspoilt cliff walks; not at all smart, but atmospheric, with ancient beams and flagstones, lanterns, nets and blazing fire; Courage Best and Directors, basic food (all day summer, lunchtime only winter), piped music, children in downstairs bistro, dogs welcome, some tables down by beach *(the Didler, Neil Spink, Peter and Audrey Dowsett, JP, PP, LYM)*

Chillington [SX7942]
☆ *Open Arms* [A379 E of Kingsbridge]: Roomy modernised open-plan turkey-carpeted bar with well kept ales such as Badger Tanglefoot, Bass, Beer Engine Mild, Exmoor and Wadworths 6X, good wines and choice of spirits, good inexpensive home-made food, back games room with pool *(Roger Wain-Heapy, BB, Richard and Robyn Wain)*

Chittlehampton [SS6425]
Bell [signed off B3227 S Molton—Umberleigh]: Cheerful family-run village pub, sensibly priced food inc huge filled rolls, well kept Bass and guest beers, outstanding range of malt whiskies; children and dogs welcome, nice quiet garden *(David Horne)*

Chudleigh [SX8679]
Bishop Lacey [Fore St, just off A38]: Partly 14th-c church house with well kept Boddingtons, Flowers IPA, Fullers London Pride and Moor Merlins Magic or Princetown Jail, some tapped from casks in back bar, winter beer festival; good value food, no-smoking dining room, open all day *(the Didler, Mark Brock, JP, PP)*
Old Coaching House: Rambling bustling low-beamed bars, tables cosily separated by low partitions, good service, decent food, real ales inc Bass *(Gordon)*

Chudleigh Knighton [SX8477]
☆ *Claycutters Arms*: Attractive 17th-c thatched two-bar village pub with very wide choice of good food from sandwiches to local venison and all sorts of exotic dishes and speciality steamed puddings, well kept Marstons Pedigree, stripped stone, interesting nooks and crannies, pleasant restaurant; seats on side terrace and in orchard, under same management as Anchor at Cockwood *(John and Vivienne Rice, LYM, Richard and Margaret Peers)*

Chulmleigh [SS6814]
Old Court House [S Molton St]: 17th-c thatched inn doing well under newish landlord, good value food inc sandwiches, friendly staff, plenty of character, skittle alley, tables in cobbled courtyard; open all day, good value bedrooms, attractive unspoilt village *(Mrs Julia Rees, Mr and Mrs D Pither)*

Churchstow [SX7145]
☆ *Church House* [A379 NW of Kingsbridge]: Long character bar with heavy black beams, stripped stone, cushioned settles, back conservatory with floodlit well feature, seats outside; Bass, Fullers London Pride, Morlands Old Speckled Hen and changing guest ales, food from filled baps to mixed grill and popular carvery, pleasant waitresses, no piped music *(Peter and Audrey Dowsett, B J Harding, LYM, J H Bell, Paul R White, Andrew Hodges, JKW, M L Porter, Mark Percy, Lesley Mayoh)*

Churston Ferrers [SX9056]
Churston Court: Attractive Elizabethan former manor house in lovely setting next to village church nr Elbury Cove, nicely furnished bar, good food inc good fresh fish (the display counter doesn't seem quite right for the dining room); three big bull mastiffs add to the setting; bedrooms *(Dave and Sue Norgate, Andrew Hodges)*

Clovelly [SS3225]
Red Lion: Rambling building worth knowing for lovely position on curving quay, with character back bar, food from sandwiches up (may take ages); restaurant, simple attractive bedrooms *(M Joyner, Chris and Anna Rowley)*

Clyst St Mary [SX9790]

☆ *Half Moon* [nr M5 junction 30]: Attractive and genuine old pub next to multi-arched bridge over Clyst, well kept Bass and Wadworths 6X tapped from the cask, well priced home-made food inc some local dishes and local produce; wheelchair access, bedrooms *(Dr and Mrs A K Clarke, G Washington, Mrs Sally Britnell, Dr M E Wilson, Pat and Robert Watt)*

Cockington [SX8963]

Drum [Cockington Lane]: Busy and cheerful thatched and beamed tavern designed by Lutyens as olde-worlde pastiche to match the quaintly touristy Torquay-edge medieval village, Dartmoor Bitter and Legend, roomy bar (can be smoky) and two family eating areas, quick service, Weds summer barbecues, winter skittle evenings and live music; piped music; open all day, tables on terrace and in attractive back garden, by 500-acre park *(JP, PP, Nick Lawless, Dr A J and Mrs P G Newton, Erna and Sidney Wells, E G Parish, Andrew Hodges)*

Cockwood [SX9780]

☆ *Ship* [off A379 N of Dawlish]: Comfortable and welcoming 17th-c inn overlooking estuary and harbour, decorative plates and seafaring memorabilia, small no-smoking restaurant with large open fire, food from open crab sandwiches up inc imaginative evening fish dishes (freshly made so takes time), Ushers BB, Founders and a seasonal beer, reasonable prices; piped music may obtrude; good steep-sided garden *(John Beeken, Stan Edwards)*

Coffinswell [SX8968]

☆ *Linny* [just off A380 at Kingskerswell]: Very pretty partly 14th-c thatched country pub in same family for years, relaxed and cheerful big beamed bar, settles and other old seats, smaller areas off; some concentration on wide choice of good value bar food inc fine crab salad; well kept Bass, Morlands Old Speckled Hen and Tetleys, cosy log fires, lots of twinkling brass, neat friendly service, no-smoking area, children's room, upstairs restaurant extension, some tables outside; picturesque village *(Stan Edwards, John Barker, Andrew Hodges, John Wilson, Gordon, BB, Hugh and Carolyn Madge)*

Colyford [SY2492]

Wheelwright [A3052 Sidmouth—Lyme Regis]: Attractive 17th-c thatched pub, welcoming and civilised, with well kept Marstons Pedigree, Otter and Wadworths 6X, wide choice of good freshly cooked food inc outstanding veg, Thurs OAP lunch club, nicely decorated restaurant; said to have been haunted *(Gwen and Peter Andrews)*

Colyton [SY2493]

Kingfisher [Dolphin St – village signed off A35 and A3052 E of Sidmouth]: Village local with hearty popular food from good sandwiches and baked potatoes up, stripped stone, plush seats and elm settles, beams and big open fire, well kept Badger Best and Tanglefoot, Charles Wells Bombardier and changing guests, low-priced soft drinks; pub games, upstairs family room, skittle alley, tables out on terrace, garden with water feature, colourful inn sign *(LM, LYM)*

Combeinteignhead [SX9271]

☆ *Coombe Cellars* [Shaldon rd, off A380 opp main Newton Abbot roundabout]: Big bustling family Brewers Fayre open all day, with lots for children inc indoor play area, their own menu, baby-changing, fun days and parties with entertainment, outside play galleon and fenced-in playground; lovely estuary setting, tables on pontoons, jetties and big terraces, water-sports; roomy and comfortable bar with plenty of sporting and nautical bric-a-brac, usual food all day, well kept Whitbreads-related ales, lots of wines by the glass, friendly efficient staff, various events; good disabled facilities *(Andrew Hodges, Dr Rod Holcombe, LYM, JWGW)*

Countisbury [SS7449]

Exmoor Sandpiper [A39, E of Lynton]: Beautifully set rambling and friendly heavy-beamed pub with antique furniture, several good log fires, well kept Bass and two Exmoor ales tapped from the cask, pewter mugs on old beams, lots of stuffed animals (and two sandpipers); food in bar and restaurant, children in eating area, garden tables, open all day; comfortable bedrooms, good nearby cliff walks *(LYM, Nick Lawless, Richard Gibbs)*

Croyde [SS4439]

Billy Budds: Quite attractively opened up, with stripped brickwork and beams, old local photographs, Bass, Boddingtons and Flowers, bar food, cheerful helpful service, restaurant; sports TV; large gardens with picnic-sets and play area *(Ursula and Paul Randall)*

☆ *Thatch* [B3231 NW of Braunton]: Lively rambling thatched pub nr great surfing beaches, with cheerful efficient staff, laid-back feel and customers to match (can get packed in summer); wide choice of reasonably priced generous food, well kept Bass, St Austell HSD and Tetleys, cheerful young staff, tables outside; restaurant, children in eating area, open all day; piped music may be a bit loud, can be packed in summer; bedrooms simple but clean and comfortable *(Sue and John Woodward, LYM, Paul and Ursula Randall, I and N Buckmaster)*

Culmstock [ST1014]

Culm Valley: Ancient pub in lovely spot in small village by bridge, good tables out in front, friendly licensees and locals, good interesting food in bar and restaurant, well kept ales such as Bass, Bunces Pigswill, Shepherd Neame Bishops Finger, open fires, skittle alley; river walk to working wool museum *(James Flory)*

Dartington [SX7962]

White Hart Bar [Dartington Hall]: Simple modern décor and open fires in the college's bar (open to visitors), good low-priced food, very special atmosphere sitting out in the famously beautiful grounds *(John Brightley)*

Dartmouth [SX8751]

Dartmouth Arms [Lower St, Bayards Cove]: Thriving friendly local (popular with naval students evening) with well kept beer, good value efficiently served basic bar food inc lots of pizzas, log fire, panelling and boating memorabilia; tables out in prime spot overlooking Dart estuary *(I J and N K Buckmaster, Andrew Hodges)*

Dittisham [SX8654]

☆ *Ferry Boat* [best to park in village – steep but attractive walk down]: Very welcoming, with good low-priced food inc good range of baguettes and pies, and idyllic waterside setting – big windows making the most of it; nr little foot-ferry you call by bell, good walks *(Charles Eaton, I and N Buckmaster, LYM, John Brightley)*

Dolton [SS5712]

Royal Oak: Attractive bar and restaurant, very extensive bar menu inc fresh fish, good range of beers inc some local, good hospitable service; bedrooms *(R J Walden)* ·

Dousland [SX5368]

Burrator: Big Victorian pub with good value fresh food in bar and restaurant (jovial landlord is ex-Smithfields butcher and ex-farmer), real ales, pool room, lots of facilities (in and out) for children; live music some nights, good value bedrooms *(Paul Redgrave)*

Dunsford [SX8189]

Royal Oak [signed from Moretonhampstead]: Generous home-cooked food and well kept changing ales in relaxed village inn's light and airy lounge bar, local farm ciders, woodburner; steps down to games room, provision for children; quiz nights, piped music; Fri barbecues in sheltered tiered garden, good value bedrooms in converted barn *(Mr and Mrs C R Little, LYM)*

East Allington [SX7648]

Fortescue Arms [off A381 Totnes—Kingsbridge]: Friendly village pub doing well under new licensees, good food, racing memorabilia, comfortable dining room *(Dr J R Norman, MRSM)*

East Budleigh [SY0684]

☆ *Sir Walter Raleigh*: Small village inn, neat and clean, with faultless service, comsistently enjoyable food inc help-yourself salad bar and good Sun lunch, friendly staff and locals, cosy charming dining room, Flowers IPA and Marstons Pedigree; no children; nice village and church; bedrooms *(F J Willy, Richard and Margaret Peers, John Braine, LYM)*

East Down [SS5941]

☆ *Pyne Arms* [off A39 Barnstaple—Lynton nr Arlington]: Small and attractive, with spotless low-beamed bar, very wide choice of generous well cooked food till late evening, pleasant licensees, lots of nooks and crannies, individual furnishings inc high-backed curved settle, small no-smoking galleried loft (where children allowed), well kept Bass and Worthington, good value house wines, flagstoned games area with unobtrusive juke box and TV; handy for Arlington Court, good walks *(Richard and Ann Higgs, John A Barker, Ursula and Paul Randall, LYM)*

Ermington [SX6353]

First & Last: Beautifully set local, lots of well tended hanging baskets, friendly chatty landlord, limited choice of good cheap food with ample veg, Bass *(John Evans, A F Ford)*

Exeter [SX9292]

Cowick Barton [Cowick Lane, between A377 and B3212]: Friendly comfortable 17th-c red

sandstone former farmhouse, wide choice of good generous food, Bass, Courage Best and Ruddles County, lots of country wines, good service even though very busy, log fire, small back restaurant *(Barbara and Alan Mence)*

Duke of York [Sidwell St, nr bus stn]: Lively lunchtime crowd, not smart but atmospheric, with panelling and traditional atmosphere *(Reg Nelson)*

Exchange [Mary Arches St]: Lived-in bare-boards pub concentrating on good range of well kept Whitbreads-related and other ales; food inc good filled french bread, good attentive service *(Reg Nelson)*

Papermakers [Exe St, off Bonhay Rd]: Bistro pub with charming continental atmosphere, wide choice of good if not cheap unusual food running up to bass and venison, friendly efficient service, keg beers but good choice of wines; maybe piped music *(Mike Gorton, Ian Phillips)*

Port Royal [The Quay]: Chain pub worth knowing for the river views from its extensive bar and eating area; usual food from baguettes to scampi, real ales such as Flowers Original, Marstons Pedigree, Morlands Old Speckled Hen and Wadworths 6X *(Ian Phillips, D J and P M Taylor)*

Prospect [The Quay]: Good waterfront spot, with comfortable upper river-view dining area (food from good doorstep sandwiches up), well kept Bass, Boddingtons, Hardy Royal Oak and Wadworths 6X; lower bar with games machines, piped music – live some evenings *(Vivienne and John Rice, Ian Phillips, D J and P M Taylor)*

Ship [St Martins Lane]: Pretty 14th-c pub with substantial comfortable furniture in bustling heavy-beamed bar, well kept Boddingtons and Marstons Pedigree, farm cider, good service; sandwiches only down here, quieter upstairs restaurant *(G Washington, LYM, John and Vivienne Rice)*

☆ *Well House* [Cathedral Yard, attached to Royal Clarence Hotel]: Big windows looking across to cathedral in open-plan bar divided by inner walls and partitions; lots of interesting Victorian prints, well kept changing ales from good small breweries, popular bar lunches inc good salads, daily papers, good service; Roman well beneath (can be viewed when pub not busy); piped music *(Ian Phillips, BB, D J and P M Taylor, Reg Nelson)*

Exmouth [SY0080]

Beach [Victoria Rd]: Woody old quayside pub, one room covered with shipping and lifeboat photographs; real ales, food, welcoming service *(Reg Nelson)*

Bicton [Bicton St]: Classic character backstreet local, plenty of atmosphere without being clannish, real ales *(Reg Nelson)*

Grove [Esplanade]: Roomy panelled pub set back from beach with attractive seafront garden and play area, well kept Bass, Boddingtons, Brakspears, Flowers, Greene King Abbot and Wadworths 6X (more on guest beer nights), good reasonably priced food inc lots of local fish, friendly service, lots of pictures, attractive fireplace at back; live music some nights *(Chris Parsons, John Beeken)*

Heavitree Arms [High St]: Split-level town-centre pub for all ages, buzzing atmosphere, well kept ales, nice wood fittings, cosy corners *(Reg Nelson)*

Fairmile [SY0897]

Fairmile Inn [A30 Honiton—Exeter]: Refurbished after longish closure, food inc good value sandwiches, real ales inc Tetleys, no machines in bar *(John Kirk)*

Filleigh [SS6627]

☆ *Stags Head* [off A361, via B3226 N of S Molton]: Pretty 16th-c thatched pub with good varied home-made food, well kept Barum Original, Bass and Tetleys, reasonably priced wines, welcoming landlord, friendly local bar with crack darts team, banknotes on beams, Corgi toy collection, very high-backed settle, pleasantly cottagey dining room up a couple of steps; maybe piped nostalgic pop; old rustic tables out in fairy-lit honeysuckle arbour by big tree-sheltered pond with lots of ducks and fish; bedrooms comfortable and good value, good breakfast *(BB, Karen and Garry Fairclough, Lyn and Geoff Hallchurch)*

Folly Gate [SX5797]

Crossways [A386 Hatherleigh—Okehampton]: Welcoming atmosphere, wide range of good value interesting food inc fresh lobster and crab, well kept St Austell ales *(R J Walden, Brian and Bett Cox)*

Fremington [SS5132]

☆ *New Inn* [B3233 Barnstaple—Instow]: Good choice of great value generous home-cooked food inc three daily roasts with lots of veg in bar and restaurant, well kept Courage, John Smiths and Ushers, admirable service; attractive walled garden, bedrooms *(D S Beeson, Mrs A Adams, R J Walden)*

Georgeham [SS4639]

Rock [Rock Hill, above village]: Good value food in well restored oak-beamed pub, well kept ales such as Cotleigh, Theakstons, Ushers Best and Wadworths 6X, local farm cider, decent wines, old red quarry tiles, open fire, pleasant mix of rustic furniture, lots of bric-a-brac; children in pleasant back room, piped music, darts, fruit machine, pool room; tables under cocktail parasols on front terrace, pretty hanging baskets *(Richard and Ruth Dean, Paul Richards, BB)*

Goodrington [SX8958]

Inn on the Quay [Tanners Rd]: Huge comfortable Brewers Fayre family dining pub, good atmosphere and service, children's play room and outdoor equipment, baby-changing, disabled facilities; quiet TV and piped music; garden, handy for beach, Quaywest and Shipwreck Island; open all day *(Andrew Hodges)*

Hartland Quay [SS2224]

☆ *Hartland Quay* [off B3248 W of Bideford, down summer toll road]: Unpretentious old hotel in stunning cliff scenery, rugged coast walks, real maritime feel with fishing memorabilia and shipwreck pictures; good value generous basic food (dogs treat you as honoured guests if you're eating), maybe well kept Sharps Doom Bar (often keg beer only), Inch's cider, efficient friendly service, small no-smoking bar, lots of tables outside – very popular with holidaymakers; good value bedrooms, seawater swimming pool *(Jenny and Brian Seller, Jenny Cantle, C P Scott-Malden, Richard and Robyn Wain, Richard C Morgan)*

Hexworthy [SX6572]

Forest Inn [village signed off B3357 Tavistock—Ashburton, 3¾ m E of B3212]: Solid Dartmoor hotel in fine surroundings, doing well under current friendly management; comfortable and spacious open-plan bar and back walkers' bar, short choice of good bar food changing daily, perfect veg, good Sun roasts, well kept beer, prompt service; good-sized bedrooms, bunkhouse *(Lyn and Geoff Hallchurch, Mr and Mrs C R Little, LYM, Jacquie and Jim Jones, Dick Brown)*

Heybrook Bay [SX4948]

Eddystone [off A379 SW of Plymouth; follow HMS *Cambridge* signs]: Modern dining pub worth knowing for good views of sea, coast and shipping; friendly efficient staff, decent beer, good value food, restaurant with tables out on balcony *(anon)*

Holcombe [SX9574]

Smugglers: Pleasant modern-style pub with Bass and other real ales, carvery and children's menu, pool, bar billiards *(Susan and Nigel Wilson)*

Holne [SX7069]

Church House [signed off B3357 W of Ashburton]: Ancient country inn well placed for attractive walks, interesting building, log fires in both rooms, food from lunchtime sandwiches up, no-smoking restaurant, Dartmoor, Palmers and Wadworths 6X, Gray's farm cider, country wines, decent house wines, traditional games in public bar; well behaved children in eating area; bedrooms *(LYM, Miss L Hodson, Barbara and Alan Mence, John and Christine Simpson)*

Honiton [ST1500]

Heathfield [Walnut Rd]: Ancient and friendly, popular with older people *(R and S Bentley)*

☆ *Red Cow* [High St]: Welcoming local, very busy on Tues and Sat market days, scrubbed tables, pleasant alcoves, log fires, well kept Bass, Courage Directors and local Otter, decent wines and malt whiskies, wide choice of good value home-made food inc excellent sandwiches and good puddings, friendly Welsh licensees (may have Radio Wales), loads of chamber-pots and big mugs on beams, pavement tables; bedrooms *(JP, PP, BB, K R Harris, R Riccalton, John and Sylvia Harrop, Richard and Margaret Peers)*

Hope Cove [SX6640]

Hope & Anchor: Simple seaside inn, warm and comfortable, with good open fire, pleasant staff, good value food, Wadworths 6X, flagstone floor, no piped music, games room with pool; bedrooms *(LYM, Peter and Audrey Dowsett, Maxine Brazier)*

Horns Cross [SS3823]

☆ *Hoops* [A39 Clovelly—Bideford]: Attractive

and popular much-modernised thatched dining pub with wide choice of good if not cheap home-made food, well kept Whitbreads-related and other ales such as Bass and Morlands Old Speckled Hen, decent wines and coffee, friendly service, big inglenook log fire each end, cosy Civil War theme restaurant, tables in central courtyard, aircraft-minded landlord, provision for children and disabled; Easter beer festival; open all day, comfortable bedrooms *(JP, PP, R J Walden, H J Gray, Alan and Paula McCully, Mr and Mrs Ian Carrington, Roger and Jenny Huggins, LYM, Dr and Mrs Cottrell, C P Scott-Malden)*

Ideford [SX8977]

☆ *Royal Oak* [2 miles off A380]: Friendly, dark and cosy unspoilt thatched village local, vast and interesting collection of mainly marine memorabilia from Nelson to World War II, flagstones, well kept Bass and Flowers IPA, sandwiches, log fire; maybe a vociferous jack russell *(the Didler)*

Ilfracombe [SS5147]

☆ *George & Dragon* [Fore St]: Oldest pub here, handy for harbour, with plenty of olde-worlde character, soft lighting, lots of ornaments, china etc; very friendly, with good food inc Sun lunch and lots for vegetarians, well kept Courage and Ushers; piped music *(M Joyner, Kevin Blake)*

☆ *Royal Britannia* [Broad St, just by harbour]: Simple old-fashioned pub in attractive spot above harbour, terrace overlooking it; low seats, armchairs, copper tables and lots of prints in series of connecting rooms; wide choice of good value bar food inc local fish, well kept Scottish Courage beers, low drinks prices; bedrooms *(P Legon)*

Ilsington [SX7876]

Carpenters Arms: Friendly and pleasantly unspoilt 18th-c local next to church in quiet village, good food very reasonably priced, courteous service, log fire, well kept ales inc Morlands Old Speckled Hen; no music *(E G Parish, Dr Rod Holcombe)*

Instow [SS4730]

Quay Inn [Marine Parade]: Just above quay, tables looking out over estuary, pleasant open-plan interior, Whitbreads-related ales, friendly staff, good food inc afternoon teas; disabled access *(D M and M C Watkinson)*

Ipplepen [SX8366]

Wellington [off A381 Totnes—Newton Abbot]: Recently furnished two-bar village pub, good reasonably priced food, pool, darts, piped music; pleasant village *(Andrew Hodges)*

Ivybridge [SX6356]

Sportsmans [Exeter Rd]: Large open-plan bar with big dining area, lots of panelling, wide choice of food all day starting from breakfast, OAP and other bargains, children's menu, Boddingtons, Wadworths 6X and Whitbreads, entertainment Fri, Sat and Sun; bedrooms *(Barbara and Alan Mence)*

Kenn [SX9285]

☆ *Ley Arms* [signed off A380 just S of Exeter]: Extended thatched pub in quiet spot nr church, polished granite floor in attractive beamed public bar, plush black-panelled lounge with

striking fireplace, good wines, Bass and Flowers, bar food, efficient service, sizeable smartish restaurant side; piped music, no-smoking family room, games area *(Peter Salmon, LYM)*

Kennford [SX9186]

Gissons Arms [just off A38]: Busy dining pub, low beams, various levels, popular carvery; tables outside *(Dr and Mrs A K Clarke)*

Kenton [SX9583]

Dolphin: Local with old black range and carved oak counter in public bar, beams and settles in alcovey restaurant, generous food with fresh veg, well kept ales such as Charles Wells Eagle, Worthington Best and bargain Otter, reasonably priced wines; pretty village *(John Beeken)*

Kilmington [SY2797]

☆ *Old Inn* [A35]: Thatched pub with character front bar (dogs allowed here), back lounge with leather armchairs by inglenook fire, good value bar food and good Sun lunch, well kept Bass and Worthington BB, traditional games, small no-smoking restaurant; children welcome, two gardens *(D Marsh, Brian and Bett Cox, LYM)*

Kings Nympton [SS6819]

☆ *Grove* [off B3226 SW of S Molton]: Thriving thatched and beamed family local, well kept Ushers and farm cider, good value food (fish and chips Tues), welcoming landlord, two log fires; lots of games, skittle alley, picturesque village *(LYM, Simon and Karen Robinson, Garry and Karen Fairclough)*

Kingsbridge [SX7344]

☆ *Crabshell* [quayside, edge of town]: Lovely waterside position, charming when tide in, with big windows and tables out on the hard, wide choice of bar food inc lunchtime shrimp or crab sandwiches; hot food (ambitious, concentrating on very wide choice of local fish and shellfish) may be confined to upstairs restaurant, with good views; quick friendly staff, Bass and Charrington IPA, good farm cider, warm fire; can get a bit smoky *(Peter and Audrey Dowsett, BB, Colin and Ann Hunt)*

Kingskerswell [SX8767]

Sloop [A380 about halfway through town]: Modern pub with good value generous food in big bustling dining area, Sun carvery, quick cheerful helpful service, well kept beer; attractive hanging baskets, big terrace with splendid views *(Colin Roberts)*

Kingswear [SX8851]

Royal Dart: Friendly pub in fine setting by ferry and Dart Valley Railway terminal, Bass and Worthington, good restaurant food inc seafood upstairs *(Pat and Robert Watt, I J and N K Buckmaster)*

Ship [Higher St]: Tall and attractive old inn under new management, has had good quickly served food, well kept Bass, friendly efficient service; one table with Dart views, a couple outside *(C P Scott-Malden, I J and N K Buckmaster)*

Knowle [SS4938]

☆ *Ebrington Arms* [A361 2 miles N of Braunton]: Lots of bric-a-brac and relaxed olde-worlde atmosphere in comfortable main bar, good interesting food inc vegetarian in bar and attractive candlelit evening restaurant, theme nights *(LYM, David and Ruth Hollands, Frank and Kathy Mathison)*

Lamerton [SX4476]

Blacksmiths Arms [A384 Launceston—Tavistock]: Welcoming local with good value generous fresh food, friendly efficient service, well kept ales; children very welcome *(Paul and Heather Bettesworth)*

Landkey [SS5931]

Ring of Bells [Manor Rd, just off A361]: Small 14th-c local with good home cooking, Bass and Marstons Pedigree *(K R Harris)*

Lapford [SS7308]

Olde Malt Scoop: Cosy, old-fashioned and friendly, with huge log fire, good choice of good food *(Mr and Mrs K F Brame, Mr and Mrs W Toomath, Mr and Mrs J Lewis)*

Luppitt [ST1606]

Luppitt Inn [back roads N of Honiton]: Unspoilt little basic farmhouse pub, friendly chatty landlady who keeps it open because she (and her cats) like the company; one room with corner bar and one table, another with fireplace and not much else – maybe lots of locally made metal puzzles on trial, Otter (also local) tapped from the cask, no food or music, lavatories across the yard; a real throwback, may be cl some lunchtimes *(the Didler, Dave and Deborah Irving, Kevin Thorpe)*

Luton [SX9076]

☆ *Elizabethan* [Haldon Moor]: Friendly low-beamed pub with nice atmosphere, wide range of good well presented food inc lots of pies and fresh local fish, luscious puddings (esp toffee and vanilla cheesecake), good choice of well kept beer and of house wines *(John and Sonja Newberry)*

Lutton [SX5959]

Mountain [pub signed off Cornwood—Sparkwell rd]: Basic take-us-as-you-find-us beamed pub with simple furnishings, log fires, some stripped stone, a high-backed settle, log fires, dogs and cats (no visiting dogs), generous straightforward food, well kept Exmoor, Ind Coope Burton and Wadworths 6X, local farm cider; seats on verandah and vine-arbour terrace, children in eating area and small family room *(John Poulter, LYM, the Sandy family)*

Lydford [SX5184]

☆ *Dartmoor Inn* [A386]: New management doing notably good and creative food, beautifully presented, from good value ploughman's and well filled baguettes to limited but well planned choice of hot dishes (some rather expensive), in what is now essentially a fair-sized dining pub, several peaceful rooms, attractive Shaker-style décor, well kept Bass, Dartmoor and St Austell Tinners, good wines, helpful polite staff; bedrooms, track straight up on to moor *(Betty Petheram, Richard Harris, Dr and Mrs M Pemberton, John and Sarah Perry, Jacquie and Jim Jones)*

Lympstone [SX9984]

☆ *Globe* [The Strand; off A376 N of Exmouth]: Reopened under good new landlord (ex Passage House in Topsham), roomy and tasteful newly

extended dining area and bar, good menu from sandwiches to good fish, Bass, Flowers IPA and good house wines, welcoming staff – a strong recommendation *(Jacquie and Jim Jones, Chris Parsons)*

Swan [The Strand]: Olde-worlde decor, well priced food in bar and restaurant inc good fresh fish (booking advisable Thurs-Sun), Bass and Wadworths 6X; pool and fruit machine in pleasant public bar, piped music; pretty flower troughs and hanging baskets *(Chris Parsons)*

Lynmouth [SS7249]

☆ *Rising Sun* [by harbour]: Wonderful position overlooking harbour, good bedrooms in cottagey old thatched terrace stepped up hill; concentration on the hotel side and the attractive no-smoking restaurant, so people just dropping in to the small modernised bar can feel a bit left out, but they have well kept Courage Directors, Exmoor Gold, Theakstons XB and a beer brewed locally for them, decent lunchtime bar food and a nice dog called Sophie (and maybe piped music); charming gardens up behind, children may be allowed in eating areas *(Nigel Flook, Betsy Brown, Nick Lawless, Maysie Thompson, Ian and Jane Irving, Garth and Janet Wheeler, Tony Gayfer, LYM, I J and N K Buckmaster)*

Rock House [middle of harbour]: Stunning position for small relaxing bar popular with locals, friendly staff, good value simple food; restaurant, pleasant bedrooms with good breakfast *(Sue and John Woodward, Garth and Janet Wheeler)*

Maidencombe [SX9268]

☆ *Thatched Tavern* [Steep Hill]: Spotless hugely extended three-level thatched pub with lovely coastal views, good range of well priced food inc local fish and tasty puddings, well kept Bass, quick friendly service, big family room, no-smoking areas, restaurant; attractive garden with small thatched huts (dogs allowed out here but not in pub); children allowed; attractive bedrooms in annexe, good breakfast; small attractive village above small beach *(Pat and Robert Watt, P Rome, G M Regan)*

Malborough [SX7039]

Old Inn: Big refurbished open-plan dining pub with very wide choice of food majoring on fish; charming quick service, St Austell HSD and other beers on tap, good house wine, pleasant children's room; lovely village *(Nick Lawless, John A Barker, Mr and Mrs C R Little)*

Manaton [SX7581]

Kestor: Useful modern Dartmoor-edge inn in splendid spot nr Becky Falls, wide range of food, well kept Boddingtons and Marstons Pedigree, farm cider, helpful service, open fire; piped music; attractive bedrooms *(G and M Stewart, Graham and Karen Oddey)*

Marsh [ST2510]

☆ *Flintlock* [signed off A303 Ilminster—Honiton]: Comfortable and welcoming 17th-c inn popular for wide choice of good varied reasonably priced food inc vegetarian and well cooked Sun lunches; well kept beer and cider, armoury and horsebrasses *(Mel and Colin Hamilton, Mr and Mrs Peter Smith, Howard Clutterbuck)*

Mary Tavy [SX5079]

☆ *Mary Tavy* [A386 Tavistock—Okehampton]: Warmly welcoming unpretentious old pub, friendly locals, well kept Bass, St Austell HSD and Mild and two guest beers, woodburner, reasonably priced food inc vegetarian, weekend front carvery; good value bedrooms, big breakfast *(JP, PP)*

Meddon [SS2719]

Westcountry [A39 N of Welcombe Cross]: Large pub/hotel with well kept sensibly priced Wadworths 6X, good generous ploughman's, willing cheerful service even when busy *(Dr D E Granger)*

Miltoncombe [SX4865]

☆ *Who'd Have Thought It* [village signed off A386 S of Yelverton]: Attractive 16th-c black-panelled bar with interesting bric-a-brac, woodburner, barrel seats and high-backed winged settles, separate lounge, big dining conservatory with Plymouth Sound views, decent usual food, well kept Blackawton, Cornish Rebellion, Exmoor, Princetown Jail and Wadworths 6X; piped music, tables may be reserved for coach parties; children welcome, garden with water feature, more tables out in front; folk club Sun *(Jacquie and Jim Jones, Ted George, K R Harris, Mark Percy, Lesley Mayoh, LYM, Mr and Mrs J Brown)*

Morchard Bishop [SS7707]

London [signed off A377 Crediton—Barnstaple]: Done-up 15th-c coaching inn, big carpeted red plush bar with woodburner in big fireplace, generous reliable food in bar or small dining room, engaging service, real ales inc Fullers London Pride, pool, darts and skittles *(Barbara and Alan Mence, Peter Craske)*

Morchard Road [SS7707]

Sturt Arms [A377 NW of Crediton]: Friendly and popular, concentration on no-smoking restaurant with good value home-made food inc vegetarian and sizzling steaks, smallish bar with back darts area, three well kept ales inc one brewed for the pub by Branscombe Vale, log fires *(Ian and Nita Cooper)*

Moretonhampstead [SX7585]

☆ *White Hart* [A382 N of Bovey Tracey]: Oak settles and old clocks in cosy but lively carpeted back bar, more ordinary big lounge bar, attractive no-smoking restaurant, warmly welcoming atmosphere and helpful staff, well kept Bass, Butcombe and Princetown Jail, farm cider, wide choice of generous food from good fresh sandwiches up, cream teas; children welcome, open all day; well equipped bedrooms, well placed for Dartmoor, good walks *(C and E M Watson, LYM, Sam Samuells, Lynda Payton, R C Morgan, Mike Gorton)*

Mortehoe [SS4545]

Chichester Arms [off A361 Ilfracombe—Braunton]: Warmly welcoming young staff, lots of old village prints in busy plush and leatherette panelled lounge and restaurant area, wide choice of good value food inc local fish and good veg, Morlands Old Speckled Hen, Ruddles County and Ushers, reasonably priced wine, speedy service; pool, no piped music *(A Gibson)*

Newton Abbot [SX8671]

☆ *Olde Cider Bar* [East St]: Fat casks of interesting farm ciders and perries in unusual basic cider house, no-nonsense dark stools and wall benches, pre-war-style décor; good country wines, baguettes, hot pies, venison pasties etc, very low prices; small games room with machines *(JP, PP, the Didler)*

☆ *Two Mile Oak* [A381 2 miles S]: Atractively quiet and old-fashioned, with good log fire, black panelling, low beams, stripped stone, lots of brasses, comfortable candlelit alcoves, cushioned settles and chairs; wide choice of enjoyable generous food, well kept Bass, Flowers IPA, Hardy Royal Oak and guest beers (tapped from the cask if you ask), Taunton farm cider, friendly service; seats on back terrace, attractive garden; open all day in summer *(JP, PP, Jess and George Cowley, the Didler, LYM)*

North Bovey [SX7483]

☆ *Ring of Bells* [off A382/B3212 SW of Moretonhampstead]: Bulgy-walled 13th-c thatched inn, well kept Dartmoor Pride, Ind Coope Burton, Marstons Pedigree and Wadworths 6X, Gray's farm cider, games etc, good log fire, decent bar food from ploughman's and filled baguettes up, friendly if not always speedy service, restaurant; children welcome; seats outside by lovely tree-covered village green below Dartmoor; big bedrooms with four-posters *(LYM, Graham and Karen Oddey, John and Vivienne Rice)*

Noss Mayo [SX5447]

☆ *Old Ship* [off A379 via B3186, E of Plymouth]: Charming setting with tables on waterside terrace by own quay in picturesque village, two thick-walled friendly bars, generous food from sandwiches to steaks inc good local fish, well kept Bass, Dartmoor and a changing guest beer, swift helpful service; darts, fruit machine, piped music; children welcome, no-smoking restaurant upstairs with Sun carvery; watch the tide if you park on the slipway *(Ian Moore, Mick Hitchman, Lyn and Geoff Hallchurch, Jacquie and Jim Jones, LYM)*

Swan [off B3186 at Junket Corner]: Small pub with lovely waterside views, good range of bar food inc fresh fish, well kept Courage Best and Directors, old beams, open fire; can get crowded, with difficult parking; dogs on leads and children welcome, tables outside *(David Lewis, Sarah Lart)*

Okehampton [SX5895]

Plymouth Arms [West St]: Enterprising landlord proud of his range of mainly local ales, quality food *(R J Walden)*

White Hart [Fore St]: Rambling pub/hotel (quite a few steps) with St Austell Tinners, good value bar food *(Dave Braisted)*

Otterton [SY0885]

Kings Arms [Fore St]: Lively and comfortable open-plan pub in charming village by Ladram Bay, good value straightforward home-made food from sandwiches and baked potatoes up, good service, plenty of room, good skittle alley doubling as family room, beautiful evening view from picnic-sets in good-sized back garden

(David Hoult, Basil J S Minson)
Paignton [SX8960]
Isaac Merritt [Torquay Rd]: Well furnished
Wetherspoons conversion of former shopping
arcade, varied seating inc no-smoking area in
spacious open-plan bar, good reasonably priced
food and drink, no music *(Andrew Hodges)*
Ship [Manor Rd, Preston]: Large pub with
comfortable furnishings inc leather settees, very
long bar, good reasonably priced food (eating
area on three floors); a minute's walk from
Preston beach *(Andrew Hodges)*
Parracombe [SS6644]
☆ *Fox & Goose* [off A39 Blackmoor Gate—
Lynton]: Wide range of well priced freshly
made good food from sandwiches to barbecued
fish steaks; friendly unrushed service, well kept
Flowers IPA and plans for their own
microbrewery, interesting photographs *(Karen
and Graham Oddey)*
Petrockstowe [SS5109]
Laurels [signed off A386 N of Hatherleigh]:
Amiable and proficient licensees, good
reasonably priced food, well kept beers mainly
from small brewers *(R J Walden)*
Plymouth [SX4755]
Bank [Old George St, Derrys Cross, behind
Theatre Royal]: Smart and busy three-level pub
interestingly converted from former bank, dark
wood balustrades, conservatory area upstairs
(children allowed here), tables outside; cheerful
service (quickest on the top level, which is
quieter), good value food all day, Tetleys-
related ales; music nights, lively young evening
atmosphere *(Steve Whalley)*
Dolphin [Barbican]: Good lively unpretentious
atmosphere, good range of beers inc
particularly well kept Bass and Worthington
Dark tapped from the cask, coal fire; colourful
green and orange décor, Beryl Cook paintings
inc one of the landlord *(Steve Whalley, Sam
Samuells, Lynda Payton, John Poulter)*
Minerva [Looe St (nr Barbican)]: Lively
backstreet pub dating from 16th c, well kept
Ushers; quite small so can get packed *(Steve
Whalley)*
Mountbatten [Mountbatten]: Spacious new pub
with Whitbreads-related and other beers from
long counter (happy hour bargains), well
prepared competitively priced food, young
friendly efficient staff, daily papers; plans for
big motel extension *(John Wilson)*
Notte [Notte St]: Good atmospheric town pub,
single long bar (can get crowded), well kept
Bass, Fullers London Pride, Morlands Old
Speckled Hen and Wadworths 6X, wide range
of good value food, good service; free 50s/60s
juke box *(Colin and Peggy Wilshire, Steve
Whalley)*
Queens Arms [Southside St, Barbican]: Small
local, friendly and spotless, with comfortable
banquettes and excellent sandwiches inc fresh
crab *(Erna and Sidney Wells, Steve Whalley)*
Tap & Spile [Looe St]: Open-plan, with bare
bricks, panelling, breweriana, very well kept
changing interesting ales, good value food,
friendly landlady and locals, games area with
pool; open all day w/e, nr marina and quay

(Richard Lewis)
Thistle Park [Commercial Rd]: Friendly local nr
National Maritime Aquarium, good range of
well kept beers inc some from next-door Sutton
brewery, tasty well presented food, interesting
décor, friendly landlady; open all day, children
welcome, live music w/e *(the Didler)*
Postbridge [SX6579]
☆ *East Dart* [B3212]: Central Dartmoor hotel by
pretty river, roomy and cheerful open-plan bar
largely given over to promptly served good
value food from filled rolls up, hunting murals
and horse tack, well kept St Austell Tinners,
Gray's cider, good fire, pool room; children
welcome; bedrooms, some 30 miles of fishing
(John and Vivienne Rice, BB)
Poundsgate [SX7072]
Tavistock Inn [B3357 continuation]: 13th-c
Dartmoor-edge village local with narrow-
stepped granite spiral staircase, original
flagstones, ancient fireplaces and beams, well
kept Courage Best and Ushers Best and
Founders, local farm cider, bar food, pub
games, family room, tables outside *(LYM)*
Pusehill [SS4228]
☆ *Pig on the Hill* [off B3226 nr Westward Ho!]:
Newish family holiday dining pub on farm, pig
decorations, bar, raised gallery and adjacent
room through archways; decent food inc
children's, well kept Ind Coope Burton,
reasonable prices, children's TV room; good
views, huge playground, small swimming pool,
boules *(Piotr Chodzko-Zajko)*
Ringmore [SX6545]
☆ *Journeys End* [off B3392 at Pickwick Inn, St
Anns Chapel, nr Bigbury]: Atmospheric if
unsmart old village inn with character panelled
lounge, well kept real ales such as Adnams
Broadside, Badger Tanglefoot, Exmoor, Otter
and Wye Valley HPA, some tapped from casks
in back room, local farm cider, log fires; varied
interesting food inc good fresh fish, helpful
welcoming service, pleasant big terraced
garden, sunny back add-on conservatory;
provision for children, attractive setting nr
thatched cottages, not far from the sea;
bedrooms antique but comfortable and well
equipped *(Mick Hitchman, Mike Gorton, Ian
Jones, Paul R White, Alan and Paula McCully,
Peter and Audrey Dowsett, Mike and Wena
Stevenson, P and J Shapley, Lorna and Howard
Lambert, the Didler, LYM, Barbara and Alan
Mence, Richard and Robyn Wain, Dr Rod
Holcombe, David Lewis, Sarah Lart)*
Rockbeare [SY0295]
☆ *Jack in the Green* [off new A30 bypass]: Quiet
since the bypass, with log fire in snug bar, two
refurbished dining areas, good varied food, local
fish and game, delicious puddings, competitive
prices, well kept Bass, Cotleigh Tawny, Hardy
Country and Otter, plenty of good value wines
by the glass, welcoming staff, back restaurant;
tables out in courtyard, skittle alley *(Gwen and
Peter Andrews, Basil J S Minson, John and Sonja
Newberry, G P Reeves)*
Salcombe [SX7338]
Victoria [Fore St]: Well placed, friendly and
attractive, with bare-boards bar, comfortable

lounge, pleasant upstairs dining room, copious good food cooked to order, jovial landlord, Bass, Courage and Worthington; maybe unobtrusive piped music; segregated children's room, bedrooms (*B J Harding, John Barker, Peter and Audrey Dowsett, M L Porter*)

Sampford Peverell [ST0214]

☆ *Globe* [a mile from M5 junction 27, village signed from Tiverton turn-off]: Neat, spacious and comfortable, handy for good range of home-made dishes from sandwiches to steaks inc fish, vegetarian, children's and popular Sun lunch, well kept Otter and Wadworths 6X, piped music, games in public bar, pool room, skittle alley, tables in front; open all day; children allowed in eating area and family room (*K R Harris, LYM*)

Sandy Gate [SX9691]

Blue Ball [nr M5 junction 30, on Topsham rd]: Doing well under current tenants, with lovely settles, enjoyable food, good gardens inc good play area (*Dr and Mrs A K Clarke*)

Seaton [SY2490]

Fishermans [Marine Cres]: Cheap tasty food all day inc bargain appetising lunch from open kitchen, smiling welcome, open fire; basic décor, but sea view (*Brian Websdale*)

Hook & Parrot [East Walk]: Clean and tidy seafront Greenalls pub with friendly welcome and good choice of beer; open all day at least in summer (*Dave and Deborah Irving*)

Shaldon [SX9372]

☆ *Ferryboat* [Fore St]: Cosy and quaint little waterside pub, basic but comfortable, long low-ceilinged bar overlooking mouth of River Teign, welcoming landlord and staff, Courage Best and Directors and Youngs, big helpings of good value home-made food inc vegetarian, open fires; sunny terrace across narrow street overlooks the water, with Teignmouth ferry and lots of boats off sandy beach (*John Beeken, Jo Rees, Stan Edwards*)

Shebbear [SS4409]

☆ *Devils Stone Inn*: Village pub with big oak-beamed bar, three other rooms inc restaurant, warm welcome (for children and dogs too), good range of beers, sensible food at sensible prices with bargain OAP helpings, helpful service, large amiable pub dogs; handy for Tarka Trail; simple bedrooms (*C P Scott-Malden, Jenny Cantle, LYM*)

Shiphay [SX8865]

☆ *Devon Dumpling* [Shiphay Lane, off A380/A3022 NW edge of Torquay]: Open-plan farmhouse pub with atmospheric cosy corners, popular locally for good value generous straightforward food inc vegetarian served very quickly and cheerfully, pudding display by bar, well kept Boddingtons, Courage Best and Ruddles County; plenty of space in upper barn loft; aquarium, occasional live music, no dogs inside (*Mr and Mrs C Roberts, Reg Nelson, Andrew Hodges*)

Sidbury [SY1595]

☆ *Hare & Hounds* [A375 Sidbury—Honiton, crossroads with B3174]: Roomy and relaxed lounge bar, wood-and-tiles tap room, two fine old chesterfields and more usual furnishings,

stuffed birds, huge log fire; four or five well kept changing ales, very friendly staff, wide choice of quick inexpensive well cooked food in bars and restaurant with Sun carvery, pool in side room, another with giant sports TV; big garden, good views of valley below (*Peter and Audrey Dowsett, Sue and Adrian Upton*)

Sidford [SY1390]

Rising Sun: Simple, unpretentious and uncrowded, with friendly staff and small menu inc genuine home cooking (they pick local blackberries for the crumble) (*R C Fendick*)

Sidmouth [SY1089]

☆ *Bowd* [junction B3176/A3052]: Big thatched family dining pub with lovely garden, efficient food operation, well kept Bass and Flowers Original, indoor and separate outdoor play areas; open all day (*Pam Adsley, Basil Minson, LYM*)

☆ *Old Ship*: Partly 14th-c, with low beams, mellow black woodwork and panelling, ship pictures, wide choice of food (good but not cheap) inc vegetarian and local fish, well kept ales such as Boddingtons, Marstons Pedigree, Wadworths 6X, friendly atmosphere, good service even when busy; close-set tables but roomier raftered upstairs bar with family room, dogs allowed; just moments from the sea (note that around here parking is limited to 30 mins) (*E G Parish, Erna and Sidney Wells, Alan and Paula McCully, Jim and Maggie Cowell, John A Barker, BB*)

Slapton [SX8244]

Queens Arms: Old inn, modernised but with snug comfortable corners, good value food, well kept Bass, Exmoor and Palmers, friendly licensees, lovely suntrap back garden with plenty of tables (*J Dwane, Pat and Robert Watt, B J Harding*)

South Molton [SS7125]

Mill [off A361 at Bish Mill roundabout]: Neatly kept, with food in bar and restaurant inc vegetarian, evening casseroles and steaks, well kept Cotleigh and guest ales, big games room (children allowed there); pretty garden and terrace (*anon*)

South Pool [SX7740]

☆ *Millbrook* [off A379 E of Kingsbridge]: Spotless pub with two neat little bars, attractive front courtyard and streamside terrace with wandering ducks, both canopied, good home-made food from choice of soups and sandwiches to fresh fish inc very good puddings, well kept Bass, Ruddles Best, Wadworths 6X and a guest beer, local ciders; friendly staff, patient with children; can get very busy in summer; pretty creekside village (*Nick J Lawless, Richard and Robyn Wain, Mrs B Williams, LYM, Mrs Mary Woods, Peter and Audrey Dowsett*)

South Tawton [SX6594]

☆ *Seven Stars* [off A30 at Whiddon Down or Okehampton, then signed from Sticklepath]: Unpretentious beamed local in attractive village, good range of well prepared good value food (not Mon) inc seafood and children's dishes, cheerful landlord, well kept Bass, Boddingtons and a guest such as Fullers

London Pride, decent wines; pool and other bar games, large square restaurant (cl Sun and Mon evenings winter); children welcome; bedrooms *(LYM, Piotr Chodzko-Zajko, Brian and Genie Smart, George Atkinson, R J Walden)*

Sparkwell [SX5757]

Treby Arms: Warmly old-world atmosphere, helpful amusing landlord, usual food with some enterprising specials, good range of beers inc unusual guests and one brewed locally for the pub, small dining room, disabled facilities *(John Evans)*

Starcross [SX9781]

Atmospheric Railway: Named for Brunel's experimental 1830s vacuum-powered steam railway here, with lots of intriguing associated memorabilia, prints and signs; Bass and Boddingtons, good choice of home-made food (served in dining area), log fire, family room, skittle alley; garden with tables and play area *(BB, John Beeken, Comus Elliott)*

Courtenay Arms: 17th-c family pub, bar one end of big lounge, Bass and Greene King, good value well presented food inc enterprising specials (and Sun bar nibbles), enormous choice of Devon ice creams, welcoming log fires in double fireplace; service very efficient and friendly even when busy *(John Beeken, Mike and Mary Carter)*

Sticklepath [SX6494]

☆ *Devonshire* [off A30 at Whiddon Down or Okehampton]: Well used 16th-c thatched village inn next to foundry museum, easy-going low-beamed slate-floored bar, big log fire, friendly old furnishings, well kept Bass and St Austell Tinners and HSD tapped from the cask, farm cider, welcoming owners and locals, magazines to read, filling low-priced snacks, bookable Sun lunches and evening meals, hopeful pub dog; open all day Fri/Sat; bedrooms *(John Cockell, LYM, John A Barker, the Didler)*

Talaton [SY0699]

Talaton Inn [B3176 N of Ottery St Mary; off A30 at Fairmile]: Pretty outside, plainly modernised and spotless inside, busy at lunchtime with good food range from sandwiches and ploughman's up; friendly staff, Bass and local Otter Best *(Richard and Margaret Peers)*

Tavistock [SX4874]

Trout & Tipple [Okehampton Rd, outside]: Very good if not quick food (great emphasis on trout – it's under same ownership as nearby trout farm) *(Chris and Margaret Southon)*

Tedburn St Mary [SX8193]

☆ *Kings Arms* [village signed off A30 W of Exeter]: Good choice of sensibly priced food (all day Sun) inc unusual dishes in attractive old pub, open-plan but comfortable, with big log fire and lots of brass; well kept local real ales and cider, cheery landlord, end games area, children in eating area; bedrooms *(Pat and Robert Watt, LYM)*

Thelbridge Cross [SS7912]

Thelbridge Cross [B3042 W of Tiverton]: Welcoming lounge bar with log fire and plush settees, good generous food inc some unusual

dishes in extensive dining area and separate restaurant, pleasant service, particularly well kept Bass and Butcombe; reasonable disabled access, bedrooms *(G S B G Dudley, BB)*

Thorverton [SS9202]

Bell: Welcoming pub in beautiful village, good choice of tasty food from recently extended kitchen, Cotleigh Tawny, Marstons Pedigree and occasional guest ales; dogs on leads and children welcome *(Geoffrey Norwood)*

☆ *Thorverton Arms*: Nicely appointed pub with wide range of well prepared bar food inc sandwiches, vegetarian and children's, charming welcoming service, well kept Bass and Morlands Old Speckled Hen, good coffee, lots of country magazines, small restaurant; tables in flower-filled garden, pleasant village, enjoyable strolls by River Exe *(Richard and Margaret Peers, John and Bryony Coles, Dr Harding E Smith)*

Thurlestone [SX6743]

Village Inn: Much refurbished convivial pub emphasising food (cool cabinet, open kitchen behind servery, blackboards, etc) – wide good value choice inc vegetarian and lots of fish; well kept Marstons Pedigree, Palmers and Wadworths 6X, comfortable country-style furnishings, dividers forming alcoves, pleasant helpful staff; children and dogs catered for, darts, quiz nights, live music, handy for coast path *(Martin Jennings, Richard and Ann Higgs, Colin McKerrow)*

Topsham [SX9688]

☆ *Bridge* [handy for M5 junction 30; from centre head towards Exmouth via Elmgrove Rd]: Unchanging, unspoilt and very relaxing 16th-c pub, in same family for a century; fine old traditional furnishings in friendly little no-smoking lounge partitioned off from inner corridor by high-backed settle, log fire, bigger lower room open at busy times, cosy regulars inner sanctum with at least six or seven beers tapped from the cask, decent wine; lunchtime pasties, great sandwiches and huge ploughman's, no music or machines, children welcome *(JP, PP, Dr M E Wilson, the Didler, Catherine Lloyd, David Hoult, Dallas Seawright, G Washington, LYM, Alan and Paula McCully)*

Denleys [High St]: More bistro than pub, with well kept beer, entertaining decor – lots of knick-knacks *(Dr and Mrs A K Clarke)*

☆ *Globe* [Fore St; 2 miles from M5 junction 30]: Substantial traditional inn dating from 16th c, good solid furnishings and log fire in friendly heavy-beamed bow-windowed bar, good interesting home-cooked food, well kept Bass, Ushers Best and Worthington BB, decent reasonably priced wine, quick service, snug little dining lounge, separate restaurant, back extension; children in eating area, open all day; good value attractive bedrooms *(Alan and Paula McCully, Revd John E Cooper, LYM, the Didler, G Washington)*

☆ *Lighter*: Spacious and comfortably refurbished family pub, panelling and tall windows looking out over tidal flats, more intimate side room, well kept Badger Best, Tanglefoot and a beer brewed for the pub, good friendly staff, good quickly served bar food inc local fish, open fire; games machines, maybe loud piped music (they will turn it off if you ask); tables out on old quay, good value bedrooms *(R J Walden, Jacquie and Jim Jones, Alan and Paula McCully, James Nunns, BB)*

☆ *Passage House* [Ferry Rd]: Attractive waterside pub with seats on quiet shoreside terrace and in front courtyard (the concrete furniture is not a visual plus point), pews, big black beams, slate-floored no-smoking lower dining area, food from filled rolls and ploughman's to steaks and plenty of fresh fish, well kept Bass, Boddingtons, Flowers IPA and Wadworths 6X; friendly new management may now allow children; may be no nearby parking *(LYM, David Hoult)*

Steam Packet [Monmouth Hill]: Cheap bar food, several well kept ales, dark flagstones, scrubbed boards, panelling, stripped masonry, a lighter dining room; on boat-builders' quay *(the Didler, LYM)*

Torbryan [SX8266]

☆ *Old Church House* [most easily reached from A381 Newton Abbot—Totnes via Ipplepen]: Atmospheric early 15th-c inn by part-Saxon church, quaint bar on right with benches built into Tudor panelling, high-backed settle and big log fire, also series of comfortable and discreetly lit lounges, one with a splendid inglenook fireplace; helpful service, bar food from sandwiches to guinea fowl, well kept Bass, Flowers IPA and Original, Marstons Pedigree, Wadworths 6X and Worthington Best, good choice of malt whiskies, decent wines; piped music may distract; children welcome, well equipped bedrooms, roomy and immaculate *(Mike Wells, A J Barker, Mr and Mrs A Scrutton, LYM)*

Torquay [SX9175]

Crown & Sceptre [Petitor Rd, St Marychurch]: Friendly two-bar local in 18th-c stone coaching inn, eight real ales inc guests, bar food, interesting naval memorabilia and ceiling chamber-pot collection, good-humoured landlord, jazz Tues and Sun, folk first Thurs of month, bands Sat *(the Didler)*

☆ *Hole in the Wall* [Park Lane, opp clock tower]: Ancient unpretentious low-beamed two-bar local nr harbour, well kept Courage, Blackawton cider, friendly service, flagstones, lots of naval memorabilia, old local photographs, chamber-pots; open all day *(Reg Nelson, John Barker, Andrew Hodges)*

London [Strand]: Vast Wetherspoons conversion of former NatWest bank overlooking harbour and marina, no-smoking upper mezzanine bar, big local ship paintings and a couple of reproduction ships' figureheads, good value food, no piped music *(Andrew Hodges)*

Torrington [SS4919]

Puffing Billy [Old Station House]: Popular family pub in former station building done out in old Southern Railway colours, well kept ales, decent wines and food inc good value children's dishes, lots of train memorabilia and pictures,

garden with pets corner; on Tarka Trail walk/cycle route *(K Flack)*

Totnes [SX8060]

Dartmouth Inn [Warland]: Comfortable, with little balcony well suited to children, short choice of good value food from section of long lounge bar counter, well kept Courage Directors, good service *(Mr and Mrs C Roberts)*

☆ *Kingsbridge Inn* [Leechwell St]: Low-beamed rambling bar with timbering and some stripped stone, plush seats, small no-smoking area, home-made food from nicely presented sandwiches to steaks and local fish, well kept Badger Best and Tanglefoot, Bass, Courage Best, Dartmoor Best, and Theakstons Old Peculier, local farm cider, decent house wines, prompt service; children in eating area, some live music *(LYM, Mr and Mrs G Little, Gordon, Peter Craske, Paul White)*

☆ *Royal Seven Stars* [Fore St, The Plains]: Civilised old hotel with late 1960s decor in big rambling bar off flagstoned reception hall with imposing staircase and sunny skylight, well kept Bass and Courage Best, cheerful helpful service, cheap bar food, pretty pleasant; tables out in front – ideal on a Tues market day when the tradespeople wear Elizabethan dress; bedrooms, river on other side of busy main road *(Nick Lawless)*

Tytherleigh [ST3103]

Tytherleigh Arms [A358 Chard—Axminster]: Spacious and comfortable, with generous sandwiches and good freshly prepared hot dishes esp local fish, Hardy ales, small restaurant *(Roger Price, J H Jones)*

Ugborough [SX6755]

☆ *Ship* [off A3121 SE of Ivybridge]: Popular open-plan dining pub extended from cosy 16th-c flagstoned core, remarkably wide choice of good food inc lots of fresh fish, good fresh veg and tasty puddings, good sandwiches too; well kept Bass, tables outside *(John Evans, Brian White, Colin and Ann Hunt, John Murdoch)*

Welcombe [SS2217]

Old Smithy [signed off A39 S of Hartland]: Much modernised thatched pub in lovely setting by lane leading eventually to attractive rocky cove, rows of tables in relaxed if rather noisy open-plan family bar, functional modern decor, good value food, quick welcoming service, enthusiastic landlord, well kept Boddingtons and Butcombe; no dogs; plenty of seats in pretty terraced garden, handy for nearby campsite; may be cl winter Suns *(R J Walden, Nick Lawless, C P Scott-Malden, Chris and Margaret Southon, G Smale, LYM, John and Jean Frazier, Mr and Mrs P Stubbs, Roger and Jenny Huggins, Mike and Mary Carter)*

West Down [SS142]

☆ *Crown* [the one up nr Ilfracombe]: Friendly village pub with alcovey lounge, consistently good value generous home-made food inc children's and vegetarian, real ales such as Barum Gold, Butcombe and Marstons Pedigree, log fires, small red plush dining area, family room, back pool/darts room; pleasant garden behind with play areas and good shelter *(Ian and Nita Cooper)*

Weston [ST1400]
☆ *Otter* [signed off A30 at W end of Honiton bypass]: Very popular with families for relaxed atmosphere, good provision for children, and wide choice of food from sandwiches to steaks and duck, well kept Bass, Boddingtons and Hardy Country, good value wines, farm cider, good log fire, heavy low beams, interesting mix of furnishings and bric-a-brac, books and magazines; games room with bar billiards and pool, skittle alley; tables on lawn leading to River Otter and its ducks, play area; more reports on new regime please *(LYM)*

Whiddon Down [SX6992]
Post [Exeter rd, off A30]: Friendly local doing well under newish licensees, good relaxed atmosphere, wide choice of good value food inc vegetarian in bar and dining rooms, well kept beers, games bar with darts, pool and skittles, small garden *(Mrs C Baggaley)*

Whimple [SY0497]
☆ *New Fountain* [off A30 Exeter—Honiton]: Civilised and attractive beamed village pub with friendly landlord, good reasonably priced food inc interesting dishes and vegetarian, well kept beers inc Cotleigh and Teignworthy, woodburner *(LYM, Chris and Shirley Machin)*

Widecombe [SX7176]
☆ *Old Inn* [B3387 W of Bovey Tracey]: Friendly and comfortable, with stripped 14th-c stonework, big log fires in both bars, some concentration on wide choice of generous food (from well filled granary rolls up) and prominent restaurant area, well kept Courage and Ushers, local farm cider, decent wines, good friendly service, family room; in pretty moorland village, very popular with tourist coaches; room to dance on music nights, good big garden with pleasant terrace; great walks – the one to or from Grimspound gives spectacular views *(LYM, Richard and Valerie Wright, Revd John E Cooper, JP, PP, John Askew, Tim and Beryl Dawson)*

Winkleigh [SS6308]
☆ *Kings Arms* [off B3220 Crediton—Torrington]: Attractive and comfortable, with beams, flagstones, scrubbed pine tables, woodburner and big log fire, good range of good food, reasonable prices, well kept Princetown Jail and other ales, local Inch's farm cider, efficient service, well reproduced piped music, no-smoking restaurant (popular for Sun lunch); small sheltered side courtyard with pool *(LYM, Michael and Joan Melling, R J Walden, John Askew, John Evans)*

Woodbury [SY0187]
☆ *White Hart* [3½ miles from M5 junction 30; A376, then B3179]: Consistently good generous food all home-cooked in attractive and comfortable lounge bar or small homely restaurant, log fire, good friendly service, well kept Bass and Worthington BB, decent wines; good locals' bar, skittle alley with own buffet, peaceful village *(Jacquie and Jim Jones)*

Wrafton [SS4935]
Williams Arms [A361 just SE of Braunton]: Modernised thatched family dining pub giving children free rein, two big bars divided into several cosy areas, interesting wall hangings, wide choice of good value bar food, unlimited self-service from good carvery in attractive separate restaurant, quick friendly service, Bass; pool, darts, piped music, discreet TV; picnic-sets outside with play area and aviary *(M Joyner, DJW, K R Harris)*

Yarcombe [ST2408]
Yarcombe Inn [A30]: Attractive 14th-c thatched pub with welcoming local feel, good choice of food from tasty sandwiches and ploughman's up, cheerful licensee, separate dining room, nice little spotless front bar, well kept Dartmoor; quiet piped music *(D B Jenkin, R T and J C Moggridge)*

Bedroom prices normally include full English breakfast, VAT and any inclusive service charge that we know of. Prices before the '/' are for single rooms, after for two people in double or twin (B includes a private bath, S a private shower). If there is no '/', the prices are only for twin or double rooms (as far as we know there are no singles). If there is no B or S, as far as we know no rooms have private facilities.

Dorset

Pubs currently doing particularly well here include the Anchor in Burton Bradstock (a new entry, notable for its very good fresh fish and seafood), the New Inn at Cerne Abbas (a handsome old place, its current licensees bringing it back into the Guide after a break of some years), the Fox at Corscombe (notable food – yet determinedly remaining a pub rather than a dining-out place), the Countryman at East Knighton (a good all-rounder, gaining a Food Award this year), the attractively laid out Cock & Bottle at East Morden (another new Food Award here), the Acorn at Evershot (great improvements under its newish regime), the Stocks at Furzehill (another attractive new entry, very popular with older people at lunchtime), the friendly and attractive Elm Tree at Langton Herring (good food choice including imaginative specials), the unusual Bottle at Marshwood (especially good for vegetarian and organic food, or people with food allergies), the charming Brace of Pheasants at Plush, the warmly welcoming Marquis of Lorne at Nettlecombe, the attractive thatched Thimble at Piddlehinton, and the Three Horseshoes at Powerstock (back on form, with good fresh fish). From among these, the Fox at Corscombe stands out as our Dorset Dining Pub of the Year, as much for its individuality as for its good food. Some pubs that stand out at the moment among the Lucky Dip entries at the end of the chapter are the White Lion at Broadwindsor, Charlton Inn at Charlton Marshall, Kings Arms in Dorchester, Weld Arms at East Lulworth, Fiddleford Inn at Fiddleford, Hambro Arms at Milton Abbas, Ship in Distress at Mudeford, Poachers at Piddletrenthide, Inn in the Park in Poole, New Inn at Stoke Abbott, Springhead at Sutton Poyntz, Langton Arms at Tarrant Monkton, Crown at Uploders, Manor Hotel at West Bexington and Castle at West Lulworth. Drinks prices here are perhaps a shade higher than the national average, with Palmers of Bridport close to or a little below average, and Badger of Blandford noticeably more expensive. The cheapest pub in our survey was getting its beer from the little Poole brewery. An odd point we've noticed is that Dorset pubs are more likely than most to welcome dogs.

ABBOTSBURY SY5785 Map 2
Ilchester Arms 🛏
B3157

The cosy interior of this rambling stone inn is enthusiastically decked out as servants' quarters, with a cook's sitting room, a potting shed, a scullery and parlour, each area with themed decorations and bric-a-brac, an Aga and a couple of fireplaces. A nice mix of old pine furniture stands on wood and parquet floors. There's a collection of prints depicting the famous swans from the nearby abbey and prints of local scenes and characters. Changing bar food might include soup (£1.95), button mushrooms fried in creamy stilton sauce on granary toast or breaded brie with redcurrant jelly (£2.95), prawn cocktail (£3.75), cottage pie (£3.95), ploughman's (£4.50), four-cheese tagliatelle with sauté mushrooms or half tarragon and thyme roast chicken (£4.95), roast aubergine moussaka, battered cod or breaded scampi (£5.25), beef and ale pie (£5.95). Well kept Bass, Flowers Orginal and Ringwood; darts, winter pool, fruit machine, TV and piped music; sizeable and attractive no-smoking conservatory restaurant. *(Recommended by Richard Gibbs, Liz and Alistair Forsyth, Dr G Appleyard, Chris and Marianna Webb, J G Roberts, N M Johns, DAV, Neil Spink, Galen Strawson, Pat and Tony Martin, JKW, John and Vivienne Rice, Lee Melin, Karen Eliot, John Knighton)*

Greenalls ~ Managers Hugh McGill and Huw Williams ~ Real ale ~ Bar food ~ Restaurant ~ (01305) 871243 ~ Children in eating area of bar and restaurant ~ Open 11-11; 12-10.30 Sun ~ Bedrooms: /£45.50B

ASKERSWELL SY5292 Map 2
Spyway ★ ♀

Village signposted N of A35 Bridport—Dorchester; inn signposted locally; OS Sheet 194 map reference 529933

Locals say this simple country inn was once a smugglers' look-out post. These days its cosy little rooms are delightfully unspoilt, and decorated with old-fashioned high-backed settles, cushioned wall and window seats, a vast collection of china teacups, harness and a milkmaid's yoke, and a longcase clock; there's also a no-smoking dining area decorated with blue and white china, old oak beams and timber uprights. Promptly served reasonably priced bar food includes eight different ploughman's such as hot sausage and tomato pickle or home-cooked ham (from £3.50), breaded haddock (£4.25), 8oz rib-eye steak (£9.50) and daily specials such as quiche or chilli (£4.25) and chicken, game or steak pie (all £4.75). There's a fine choice of drinks including Adnams Southwold, Branscombe Vale Branoc and Morlands Old Speckled Hen on handpump, 24 reasonably priced decent wines by the glass, 20 country wines, around 40 whiskies and some unusual non-alcoholic drinks. Shove-ha'penny, table skittles, dominoes and cribbage. There are plenty of pleasant nearby walks along the paths and bridleways. Eggardon Hill, which the pub's steep lane leads up, is one of the highest in the region and there are marvellous views of the downs and to the coast from the back terrace and gardens (where you can eat on warm days). No children. *(Recommended by Geoffrey Lawrance, Pete and Rosie Flower, PP and J Salmon, Gethin Lewis, Mr and Mrs N Fuller, P R and S A White, C Robinson, Nigel Hyde, Nigel Flook, Betsy Brown, Anthony Barnes, Robert Flux, Karen Eliot, Mrs O Hardy, Chris and Marianna Webb, John and Vivienne Rice, Dr and Mrs G H Lewis, B and E Clements, S and R Preston, Galen Strawson)*

Free house ~ Licensees Don and Jackie Roderick ~ Real ale ~ Bar food ~ (01308) 485250 ~ Open 11-2.30(3 Sat), 6-11; 12-3, 7-10.30 Sun; closed Mon except bank holidays

BRIDPORT SY4692 Map 1
George

South St

Attracting an enjoyable mix of customers, and run by the same licensee for over twenty years, this delightful Georgian house happily manages the fairly rare achievement of being a jolly good town pub. Divided by a coloured tiled hallway, the two sizeable bars – one is served by a hatch from the main lounge – are full of friendly old-fashioned charm and atmosphere. There are nicely spaced old dining tables and country seats and wheelback chairs, big rugs on tiled floors, a mahogany bar counter, fresh flowers, and a winter log fire, along with an interesting pre-fruit machine ball game. Thursday night chess club – all welcome. Well kept Palmers Bridport, IPA and 200 on handpump, fresh orange, grapefruit and apple, several malts, decent wines, and hot toddies and proper pimms. Fairly straightforward but very tasty bar food includes home-made fishcakes with tomato sauce (£2.95), home-made chicken liver or smoked mackerel pâté (£3.30), kedgeree, fresh haddock or plaice or chicken and mushroom, rabbit or steak and kidney pie (£5.50); vegetables are extra (£1.65); puddings or English cheeses (£2.35); you can usually see the licensee at work preparing your meal. You need to make a reservation if you wish to eat in the evening out of season; piped classical radio or jazz *(Recommended by Galen Strawson, Karen Eliot, Mick and Hilary Stiffin)*

Palmers ~ Tenant John Mander ~ Real ale ~ Bar food (not Sun) ~ (01308) 423187 ~ Children welcome ~ Open 11-11(8.30 am for coffee); 12-10.30 Sun ~ Bedrooms: £25/£50

BURTON BRADSTOCK SY4889 Map 1
Anchor
B3157 SE of Bridport

An entire blackboard of fresh fish-filled french sticks (from £2.95, steak and mushroom £5.95), black pudding with cumberland sauce or game pâté (£3.95), fishcakes or clappidoo's – big Scottish mussels (£4.95), mushroom stroganoff or cod or mackerel fillet (£6.95), cajun-style stir-fried vegetables (£7.95), chicken cacciatore (£10.95), duck in redcurrant sauce (£12.95), red bream, skate wing, brill, stea bass, or scallops (bought from the diver; they are huge and served on a prawn rice with a spicy salad, very popular) (£14.95) and shellfish platter (£22); chocolate cheesecake, banoffee pie or steamed fruit pudding (£3.25); you will probably have to book a couple of weeks ahead for a table at the weekend. Well kept Ushers Best, Founders and Seasonal ales, and the Scottish landlord keeps a good selection of malts; darts, table skittles and bar billiards *(Recommended by David Newman, Sherry Rollinson, Pat and Robert Wyatt)*

Ushers ~ Tenant J R Plunkett ~ Real ale ~ Bar food (not Sun evening or Mon) ~ Restaurant ~ (01308) 897228 ~ Children in eating area of bar and restaurant ~ Open 11-3, 6-11; 12-3, 7-10.30 Sun

CERNE ABBAS ST6601 Map 2
New Inn
14 Long Street

Readers tell us that the new licensees at this 13th-c inn are bringing it back on form again – they've already refurbished the bedrooms – and as they've agreed a long contract any problems it's had in the past with too frequently changing licensees should now be resolved. It was built as a guest house for the nearby Benedictine abbey, and became a coaching inn in the mid 16th c. The comfortable L-shaped lounge bar has oak beams in its high ceiling, seats in the stone-mullioned windows with a fine view down the main street of the attractive stone-built village, and a warm atmosphere. You'll still find the old pump and mounting block in the old coachyard, and behind it there are tables on a big sheltered lawn. As well as daily specials like pint of prawns (£4.95), chicken curry (£5.95) and crab therimdor (£9.25) bar food includes soup (£2.50), pâté (£3.50), filled rolls (from £3.25), filled baked potatoes (from £3.50), cottage pie (£5.50), rabbit in cider (£5.75), stilton, walnut and leek pie or battered cod (£5.95), grilled lemon sole (£8.50), duck with orange and black cherry sauce (£9.40) and mixed grill (£10.95); puddings (£2.95). Well kept Eldridge Pope Hardy, Royal Oak and Three Valleys on handpump and several malt whiskies; piped music. A good track leads up on to the hills above the village, where the prehistoric Cerne Giant is cut into the chalk. *(Recommended by Anthony Barnes, Mr and Mrs N Fuller, G and T Edwards, Michel Hooper-Immins)*

Eldridge Pope (Hardy) ~ Tenants Dick and Ann Foad ~ Real ale ~ Bar food ~ Restaurant ~ (01300) 341274 ~ Children in eating area of bar and restaurant ~ Open 11-11; 12-10.30 Sun; closed 2.30-6 winter ~ Bedrooms: £25B/£50B

Red Lion ♀
Long Street

Parts of this neatly kept cottagey inn are a lot older than the unassuming mid-Victorian frontage suggests – the fine fireplace in the quietly relaxing bar for instance is 16th-c. There's also some rare Groves Brewery windows, a handsome wooden counter, wheelback chairs on the green patterned carpet, a good deal of china, plants on tables and two more little areas leading off the bar. The friendly white terrier

Gemma may sit waiting for titbits. Most of the popular meals are available in a reduced size for those with smaller appetites. Fairly straightforward but well cooked reliable bar food includes soup (£2), filled baked potatoes (from £3.40), prawn and seafood pancakes with béchamel sauce or chicken breast and chips (£5), cannelloni filled with spinach and ricotta (£6.20), several vegetarian pasta dishes (£5.45), scampi (£6.50), salmon steak (£7.50), sirloin steak (£9.95), puddings like crème brûlée or apple cake (from £1.85), and daily specials which might include greenlipped mussels (£4.25), braised lamb's kidneys or beef curry (£6.40) and halibut in white wine (£8.50). Some of the vegetables come from local gardeners and allotments. Well kept Bass and Wadworths Henrey's Original IPA and 6X, a decent wine list, with several available by the glass, and a fair choice of malt whiskies. Darts, skittle alley, shove-ha'penny, cribbage, and piped music. There's a secluded flower-filled garden. *(Recommended by the Didler, David Heath, Basil J S Minson, George Atkinson, P G Bardswell, Joan and Michel Hooper-Immins, Anthony Barnes, JP, PP, Ann and Colin Hunt, Mr and Mrs S Ballantyne, Lee Melin)*

Free house ~ Licensees Brian and Jane Cheeseman ~ Real ale ~ Bar food ~ Restaurant ~ (01300) 341441 ~ Children welcome ~ Open 11.30-2.30, 6.30-11; 12-3, 7-10.30 Sun

Royal Oak ♀

Long Street

The frontage of this creeper covered Tudor inn is so picturesque that one reader told us he had his picture taken by fifteen Japanese tourists while sitting outside – it's usually a delightfully quiet spot to sit and watch the world go by. Inside, an incredible range of small ornaments covers the stone walls and ceilings – local photographs, antique china, brasses and farm tools. Three flagstoned communicating rooms have sturdy oak beams, lots of shiny black panelling, an inglenook with an oven, warm winter log fires. The very friendly barmaid Jenny serves well kept Butcombe Bitter, Morlands Old Speckled Hen and Oakhill Bitter on handpump from the uncommonly long bar counter, as well as 16 wines by the glass, and a decent range of malt whiskies. Bar food includes sandwiches (from £2.30), soup (£2.60), whitebait (£3.95), ploughman's (from £4.25), breaded plaice (£5.50), 8oz sirloin (£10.75), as well as daily specials like moussaka (£5.95), venison casserole, honey and ginger chicken or steak and stilton pie (£6.95) and puddings like treacle tart, apple pie or raspberry and almond (£2.90); Sunday roast (from £6.50). There are also seats and tables in the enclosed back garden. *(Recommended by Simon Williams, Paul and Sue Merrick, Gordon, Joy and Peter Heatherley, Galen Strawson, JP, PP, Ann and Colin Hunt)*

Free house ~ Licensees Stuart and Noreen Race ~ Real ale ~ Bar food ~ (01300) 341797 ~ Children in eating area of bar ~ Open 11-3, 6-11; 12-3, 7-10.30 Sun

CHIDEOCK SY4292 Map 1
Anchor

Seatown signposted off A35 from Chideock

There's a marked change in the character of this well run old inn from winter to summer. It's splendidly situated, just a few steps from a nearly idyllic cove beach (they had quite bad problems with cliff falls last year) and nestling dramatically beneath the 617-foot Golden Cap pinnacle, almost straddling the Dorset Coast path. Seats and tables on the spacious front terrace are ideally placed for the stunning sea and cliff views. You'll have to get there pretty early in summer to bag a spot as it can get almost ridiculously busy. Out of season when the crowds have gone the cosy little bars seem especially snug with warming winter fires, some sea pictures and lots of interesting local photographs, a few fossils and shells, simple but comfortable seats around neat tables, and low white-planked ceilings; the family room and a further corner of the bar are no smoking, and there are friendly animals (especially the cats). Good bar food includes sandwiches (from £1.95), filled baked potatoes (from £3.45), ploughman's (£4.25), breaded plaice (£5.25), baked avocado filled with crabmeat topped with melted cheese (£6.45), and daily specials like cottage pie (£5.95), chicken curry or beef in Guinness (£7.25) and monkfish in Thai sauce (£8.25). Well kept Palmers 200, Bridport, IPA and Tally Ho on handpump, under light blanket pressure in winter only, freshly squeezed orange juice, and a decent little wine list. Darts, shove-ha'penny, table skittles, cribbage, dominoes, fruit machine (summer only), a carom board, and piped, mainly classical, music. There are fridges and toasters in the bedrooms where you can make your own breakfast and enjoy the sea views. The licensees also run the Ferry at Salcombe. *(Recommended by Paul and Judith Booth, Martyn and Helen Webb, Ian Phillips, Mark Matthewman, Miss A Drake, R J Walden, G and T Edwards, John Robertson, David Heath, N M Johns, R C Morgan, Marjorie and David Lamb, Peter and Pat Frogley, Pat and Tony Martin)*

Palmers ~ Tenants David and Sadie Miles ~ Real ale ~ Bar food ~ (01297) 489215 ~ Children welcome ~ Jazz, folk and blues Sat evening, and Weds evening in summer ~ Open 11-11; 12-10.30 Sun; 11(12 Sun)-2.30, 7-11 winter; closed 25 Dec evening ~ Bedrooms: £17.50B/£35B

CHRISTCHURCH SZ1696 Map 2
Fishermans Haunt
Winkton: B3347 Ringwood road nearly 3 miles N of Christchurch

This bustling cheerfully run hotel is a useful place to know for its friendly welcome and good value straightforward bar food: sandwiches (from £2.35; toasties from £2.85), filled baked potatoes (from £3.75), mushroom and nut fettucine, steak and kidney pie, scampi, lasagne or battered cod (£5.75). There are attractive views of the River Avon from the restaurant. The recently refurbished open-plan bar is very neat with tapestry upholstered chairs around new tables, stools at a pine panelled bar and a few pictures on brown wallpaper. At one end big windows look out on the neat front garden. Well kept Bass, Gales HSB, IPA and Ringwood Fortyniner on handpump, and lots of country wines. The quiet back garden has tables among the shrubs, roses and other flowers; disabled loos. *(Recommended by Mr and Mrs A P Reeves, Colin Fisher, R Moorehead, Andy and Jill Kassube, Tom and Joan Childs, Dr C C S Wilson, G P Reeves, Phyl and Jack Street, Paul Davies, D P and J A Sweeney, Mike Taylor, David and Jo Williams)*

Gales ~ Manager Kevin A Crowley ~ Real ale ~ Bar food ~ Restaurant ~ (01202) 477283 ~ Children in eating area of bar and restaurant ~ Open 10.30-2.30, 5-11; 10.30-11 Sat; 12-10.30 Sun ~ Bedrooms: £48B/£64B

CHURCH KNOWLE SY9481 Map 2
New Inn ♀
One of the main draws at this very attractive partly thatched 16th-c pub is the fresh fish which is delivered daily. Prices vary according to the market but there might be very tasty crab soup (£3.75), six grilled sardines (£5.50), mediterranean bouillabaisse, half pint prawns or moules marinières (£6), local trout (£6.65), fresh dressed crab (£8.25), haddock in beer batter (£9.35) and dover sole (£13.75). A fairly traditional menu includes sandwiches (from £3.10), much liked home-made blue vinney soup (£2.90), ploughman's (from £4.65), home-made steak and kidney pie (£6.55), broccoli and cream cheese bake (£7.15), game pie (£7.70), chicken tikka masala (£8.55) and 8oz fillet steak (£13.70), puddings like spotted dick or blackberry and apple pie and chidren's meals (£3.50). The two main bar areas are nicely furnished with farmhouse chairs and tables and lots of bric-a-brac on the walls, and there's a log fire at each end; the dining lounge has a good relaxed atmosphere. Well kept Flowers Original and Wadworths 6X and a changing guest beer on handpump, a dozen or so very reasonably priced wines all available in two sizes of glass, and around 20 malt whiskies and bourbons; skittle alley, darts, and piped music. When the local post office closed recently this became the first pub in the county to serve as local village post office and shop, and you can generally buy locally made cheese to take away. There are plenty of tables in the good-sized garden, which has fine views of the Purbeck hills. No dogs; camping in two fields at

the back but you need to book beforehand; good disabled facilities. *(Recommended by Simon Watkins, Mike and Heather Watson, Anthony Barnes, M G Hart, B H Sharpe, Keith and Margaret Kettell, Carol and John Fage, DAV, Joy and Peter Heatherley)*

Inn Partnership (Nomura) ~ Tenants Maurice and Rosemary Estop ~ Real ale ~ Bar food ~ (01929) 480357 ~ Children in eating area of bar ~ Open 11(12 Sun)-3, 6-11; closed Mon Jan to March

COLEHILL SU0302 Map 2
Barley Mow

From roundabout junction of A31 Ferndown bypass and B3073 Wimborne rd, follow Colehill signpost up Middlehill Rd, pass Post Office, and at church turn right into Colehill Lane; Ordnance Survey Sheet 195 map reference 032024

The cosy low-beamed main bar at this lovely old thatched 16th-c drover's cottage has a good warming fire in the huge brick inglenook fireplace, attractively moulded oak panelling, and some Hogarth prints. Attentive staff serve well kept Badger Best, Tanglefoot and a seasonal ale on handpump, and a dozen fruit wines; the cat is called Misty. Generous helpings of good bar food include open sandwiches (from £2.95), filled baked potatoes (from £3.75), a light pastry case filled with fresh mushrooms in a white wine, garlic, cream and parsley sauce (£3.95), ploughman's (£4.75), turkey, gammon and leek, steak and kidney pie (£6.25), lasagne (£6.50), chicken breast in creamy leek sauce (£7.75), tiger prawns (£8.75) and sirloin with creamy peppercorn sauce (£9.95); puddings like blackberry and apple pie (£2.95). There are two large no-smoking areas; piped music. It's particularly attractive in summer, when there are colourful tubs of flowers in front, and more flowers in hanging baskets set off vividly against the whitewash. At the back is a pleasant and enclosed big lawn sheltered by oak trees; boules; good nearby walks. *(Recommended by Betsy and Peter Little, Ian Phillips, G Coates, G Washington)*

Badger ~ Manager Bruce Cichocki ~ Real ale ~ Bar food ~ (01202) 882140 ~ Children in restaurant ~ Open 11-3, 5.30-11; 12-3, 7-10.30 Sun

CORFE CASTLE SY9681 Map 2
Fox 🍺

West Street, off A351; from town centre, follow dead-end Car Park sign behind church

Much of this characterful old pub is built from the same stone as Corfe Castle, the evocative ruins of which rise up behind the very pleasant suntrap garden here. There's some in an ancient fossil-dotted alcove, and in the pre-1300 stone fireplace. An ancient well in the lounge bar has been glassed over and lit from within. The tiny atmospheric front bar has closely set tables and chairs, a painting of the castle in its prime among other pictures above the panelling, old-fashioned iron lamps, and hatch service. Well kept Eldridge Pope Royal Oak, Gibbs Mew Bishops Tipple, Ind Coope Burton, Wadworths 6X and a guest are tapped straight from the cask. Bar food includes sandwiches (from £2.05), home-made soup (£2.30), ploughman's (£3.50), home-made steak and kidney pie or fresh cod (£5.45), and daily specials like pork in mustard or turkey Caribbean (£6.45), and puddings (from £2.45). The countryside surrounding this National Trust village is worth exploring, and there's a local museum opposite. No children. You reach the garden, which is divided into secluded areas by flowerbeds and has a nicely twisted old apple tree, through a pretty flower-hung side entrance. *(Recommended by Ian and Jacqui Ross, Mr and Mrs N A Spink, D P and J A Sweeney, R Moorehead, the Didler, Mark Percy, Lesley Mayoh, Alastair Tainsh, Pat and Robert Wyatt, David and Carole Chapman, Mike Green, Geoffrey Lawrance, Jeremy Burnside, Gordon, JP, PP)*

Free house ~ Licensees Graham White and Miss A L Brown ~ Real ale ~ Bar food (till 9.30) ~ (01929) 480449 ~ Open 11-3, 6.30-11; 12-3, 7-10.30 Sun; 2.30 lunchtime closing winter; closed 25, 26 Dec evening

We say if we know a pub has piped music.

Greyhound

A351

This bustling old pub, well positioned right next to the castle, was originally two early 16th-c cottages, and a stable at the back has some 12th-c timbers and stone. The garden borders the castle moat and has fine views of both the castle battlements and the surrounding Purbeck hills, and the courtyard (which opens onto the castle bridge) has lots of pretty climbing and flowering shrubs. The three pleasant small low-ceilinged areas of the main bar have mellowed oak panelling and lots of paintings, brasses, and old photographs of the town. Popular bar food includes filled rolls (from £1.65), filled baked potatoes (from £3.50; local crab £4.55), ploughman's (from £4.15), chilli (£5.25), fish pie (£5.95), cajun chicken (£6.25), steak in ale pie (£6.50), lobster (£17.50) and daily specials such as fried lamb's kidneys with crispy bacon and garlic mash (£6.95), pot roast shank of lamb with braised fennel and roast potato or confit of duck on sweet and sour vegetables with wild rice (£7.95). A new cellar means they're having a go at a better wine list to complement their well kept Flowers and Poole Dolphin on handpump. The May beer festival is timed to coincide with the Civil War re-enactment at the castle. Sensibly placed darts, winter pool, cribbage, dominoes, Purbeck shove-ha'penny on a 5ft mahogany board, TV, and piped music; the family room is no smoking although one reader found it smoky in there. *(Recommended by John and Vivienne Rice, the Didler, Ruth Lowbury, Chris Reeve, R Moorehead, Betsy and Peter Little, David and Carole Chapman, Mr and Mrs N A Spink, D P and J A Sweeney, Gordon, J and B Cressey)*

Whitbreads ~ Lease Mike and Louisa Barnard ~ Real ale ~ Bar food (all day summer, and winter Sat, Sun) ~ (01929) 480205 ~ Children in eating area of bar and restaurant ~ Open 11-11; 12-10.30 Sun

CORSCOMBE ST5105 Map 2

Fox

On outskirts, towards Halstock

Dorset Dining Pub of the Year

Although there is quite some emphasis on the very good food at this cosy thatched rural pub the licensees are determined to maintain a good atmosphere where you can pop in for a pint and a chat. Inspite of this it's hard not to begin a description of this place without first giving an account of the very good imaginative daily specials. Always using the best local produce where possible, these might include vegetable soup of the day (£3.25), wild mushroom risotto with parmesan shavings (£4.50), roast aubergines baked with mozzarella, garlic, tomato and cream (£4.75), fish soup (£4.95), fish pie (£7.75), venison braised in red wine or Moroccan lamb tagine with couscous (£8.95), grilled lemon sole (£9.50), breast of Barbary duck with red wine and cranberry sauce (£12.50), fillets of monkfish with red pepper salsa (£12.75), puddings such as treacle tart, sticky toffeee pudding and meringues with clotted cream (all £3.25, and an English cheeseboard (£4.25); the dining room is no smoking. The flagstoned room on the right has lots of beautifully polished copper pots, pans and teapots, harness hanging from the beams, small Leech hunting prints and Snaffles prints, Spy cartoons of foxhunting gentlemen, a long scrubbed pine table (a highly polished smaller one is tucked behind the door), and an open fire. In the left-hand room (partly no smoking) there are built-in wall benches, candles in champagne bottles on the cloth-covered or barrel tables, an assortment of chairs, lots of horse prints, antlers on the beams, two glass cabinets with a couple of stuffed owls in each, and an L-shaped wall settle by the inglenook fireplace; darts, dominoes and backgammon. Readers particularly enjoy the flower-filled conservatory which has a huge oak table. Well kept Exmoor Ale, Fullers London Pride and Shepherd Neame Spitfire on handpump, a very good thoughtful wine list, local cider and home-made elderflower coridal, damson vodka, and sloe gin. The labrador Bramble (who loves a bit of attention) now has a puppy friend called Cracker – unfortunately no other dogs are allowed. There are seats across the quiet village lane, on a lawn by the little stream. This is a nice area for walks. *(Recommended by J G Roberts, Jill Bickerton, Alistair Forsyth, David Gregory, Basil Minson, Ruth Lowbury, MDN, Mr and Mrs N*

Fuller, James House, M J Bastin, Colin Thompson, David and Ruth Shillitoe, Mr and Mrs N Heleine, Karen Eliot)

Free house ~ Licensees Martyn and Susie Lee ~ Real ale ~ Bar food ~ (01935) 891330 ~ Children in eating area of bar ~ Open 12-3, 7-11(10.30 Sun) ~ Bedrooms: £45B/£65.75B

CRANBORNE SU0513 Map 2
Fleur-de-Lys 🛏

B3078 N of Wimborne

Now practically swamped by rampant greenery, this 17th-c inn is full of reminders of its past. Its walls are lined with historical documents and mementoes of some of the people who have stayed here over the years, from Thomas Hardy while writing *Tess of the d'Urbervilles* to Rupert Brooke, whose wry poem about the pub takes pride of place above the fireplace. The oak-panelled lounge bar is attractively modernised, and there's a more simply furnished beamed public bar with well kept Badger Best and Tanglefoot on handpump, farm cider, and some good malt whiskies. Bar food includes soup (£2.25), sandwiches (from £2.35), pâté (£3.30), ploughman's (£4.25), nutty mushroom layer (£5.25), steak pie (£5.95), chicken breast with a sauce of the day (£6.95), local trout (£7.25), and daily specials such as gammon and venison pie (£7.95) and pork medallions with port and stilton sauce (£8.95). Puddings include chocolate pavlova or blackcurrant cheesecake (£2.95); one end of the restaurant is no smoking. It's best to arrive early for Sunday lunch. Darts, dominoes, cribbage, fruit machine, and piped music. A pair of ancient stone pillars in the car park are said to have come from the ruins of a nearby monastery, and there are swings and a slide on the lawn behind the car park. Bedrooms are comfortable, though one reader was disturbed by traffic noise. *(Recommended by Tom and Joan Childs, Gerald Barnett, Peter Meister, Colin Fisher, M Unwin, Jamie and Ruth Lyons, Phyl and Jack Street, Ann and Colin Hunt, B and K Hypher, R J Walden, D G Twyman, S G N Bennett)*

Badger ~ Tenant Charles Hancock ~ Real ale ~ Bar food ~ Restaurant ~ (01725) 517282 ~ Children over 5 welcome ~ Open 11-3, 6.30-11; 12-3, 7-10.30 Sun ~ Bedrooms: £27.50(£35B)/£45(£55B)

EAST CHALDON SY7983 Map 2
Sailors Return

Village signposted from A352 Wareham—Dorchester; from village green, follow Dorchester, Weymouth signpost; note that the village is also known as Chaldon Herring; Ordnance Survey sheet 194, map reference 790834

Although this well extended thatched pub is fairly isolated you will need to get here early for a table in summer, or on Sunday when the good value roast is popular. It's tucked away in a tranquil spot near Lulworth Cove, and benches, picnic-sets and log seats on the grass in front look down over cow pastures to the village. It's a good reliable welcoming place, and the bar food, although fairly straightforward, is dependable, good value and served in generous helpings. Even when busy, service remains as good as ever. The cheerful flagstoned bar still keeps much of its original character while the newer part of the building is uncompromisingly plain with unfussy furnishings, with old notices for decoration, and open beams showing the roof above. The dining area has solid old tables in nooks and crannies. The menu includes sandwiches (from £1.40), filled baked potatoes (from £4.25), and popular daily specials such as mushroom risotto or vegetable curry (£5.50), fisherman's pie (£6.25), whole gammon hock (£7.75), whole local crab (£8.25), and half a shoulder of lamb (£8.95). Half the restaurant is no smoking. Well kept Flowers IPA, Fullers London Pride, Quay Bombshell and three guests on handpump, country wines, and farm cider; darts, shove-ha'penny, cribbage, dominoes and piped music. From nearby West Chaldon a bridleway leads across to join the Dorset Coast Path by the National Trust cliffs above Ringstead Bay. *(Recommended by James Nunns, B and K Hypher, P G Bardswell, E A George, John and Vivienne Rice)*

Free house ~ Licensees Bob and Pat Hodson ~ Real ale ~ Bar food ~ Restaurant ~
(01305) 853847 ~ Children welcome ~ Open 11-11; 12-10.30 Sun; 11-2.30, 6.30-11
winter; 12-2.30, 7-10.30 Sun winter

EAST KNIGHTON SY8185 Map 2
Countryman 🍴 🍺 🛏️

Just off A352 Dorchester—Wareham; OS Sheet 194 map reference 811857

Doing really well at the moment, this lively free house hasn't generated a single word
of complaint from readers over the last two years. A good choice of well kept real
ales, good food, friendly welcome and comfortable bedrooms mean we can safely
call it a really good all-rounder. There's a relaxing atmosphere in the neatly
comfortable, long main bar with its mix of tables, wheelback chairs and relaxing
sofas, and fires at either end. This room opens into several other smaller areas,
including a no-smoking family room, a games bar with pool and darts, and a carvery
(£10.25 for a roast and pudding). Their five or six well kept real ales are Courage
Best and Directors, Morlands Old Speckled Hen, Ringwood Best and Old Thumper
and Theakstons XB on handpump, as well as farm cider and a good choice of wines.
There's been particularly high praise for the bar food this year, so we have given it a
new food award. Served in generous helpings, the menu includes sandwiches or filled
rolls (from £2.10), home-made soup (£2.20), ploughman's (from £4.95), chilli
potato tart with roasted tomatoes and garlic (£6.95), tomato and lentil lasagne
(£7.95), sardines in garlic or lemon and parsley butter (£6.95), gammon and
pineapple (£8.95) and steaks (from £12.25). A reassuringly shortish list of sensibly
imaginative daily specials might include steak and kidney pie (£6.25), creamy
chicken curry with banana and mango (£7.75), salmon supreme with creamy
watercress sauce (£8.95), and puddings like syrup and ginger steamed pudding or
lemon macaroon (from £2.50). There are tables and children's play equipment out in
the garden as well as some toys inside; dogs welcome. Breakfasts are nice if you're
staying, and the staff are well trained and courteous; piped music. *(Recommended by
John Hackett, Mick and Elizabeth Leyden, David Lamb, John and Joan Calvert, Jenny and Chris
Wilson, Ron and Sheila Corbett, Jane and John Dillon, Joy and Peter Heatherley, Simon Watkins)*

Free house ~ Licensees Jeremy and Nina Evans ~ Real ale ~ Bar food (till 9.30) ~
Restaurant ~ (01305) 852666 ~ Children welcome ~ Open 11-3, 6-11; 12-3, 6-10.30
Sun; closed 25 Dec ~ Bedrooms: £45B/£55B

EAST MORDEN SY9195 Map 2
Cock & Bottle 🍴 🍷 🍺

B3075 between A35 and A31 W of Poole

There's been warm praise from readers over the last year for the imaginative bar
food at this very attractive old red brick inn. The menu includes club sandwich
(£4.95), spicy chicken baguette or ploughman's (£5.50), grilled steak sandwich
(£6.25), home-made burger topped with smoked bacon and stilton (£6.95) and
Scotch sirloin steak (£10.95). In addition there's a very good choice of daily specials
like brie and pancetta tartlet with roasted mediterranean vegetable salad (£5.65),
spicy crab cakes with Thai dipping sauce (£5.75), baked aubergine filled with
mediterranean vegetables and olives (£7.25), Irish stew (£7.95), game in juniper
berry pudding with port wine sauce or lemon sole fillet with crab and asparagus
mousse with white wine sauce (£10.95), and home-made puddings like passion fruit
mousse, treacle suet pudding or fresh chocolate and strawberry roulade (£3.50);
most of the restaurant is no smoking. The handsome interior is divided into several
communicating areas, with a warmly rustic feel – heavy rough beams, some stripped
ceiling boards, some squared panelling, a nice mix of old furnishings in various sizes
and degrees of antiquity, small Victorian prints and some engaging bric-a-brac.
There's a good log fire, intimate corners each with just a couple of tables, and a
wood floored public bar (with piped music, dominoes, a fruit machine and a sensibly
placed darts alcove); this in turn leads on to yet another dining room, again with
plenty of character. They have well kept Badger Best, Tanglefoot and a Badger

seasonal ale on handpump and a good choice of decent house wines including several by the glass; cordial service (though when it's busy food can take time to come) and disabled facilities. There are a few picnic-sets outside, a garden area, and an adjoining field with a nice pastoral outlook. *(Recommended by Geoffrey and Joanne Camp, Howard and Margaret Buchanan, Betsy and Peter Little, Alastair Tainsh, Chris and Ann Garnett, James House, M J Harris, Basil Minson, Mike Green, Phyl and Jack Street, Miss A G Drake)*

Badger ~ Tenant Peter Meadley ~ Real ale ~ Bar food (12-2, 6-9) ~ Restaurant ~ (01929) 459238 ~ Children in restaurant ~ Open 11-3, 6-11; 12-3, 7-11 Sun

EVERSHOT ST5704 Map 2
Acorn ♀ ⇌
Village signposted from A37 8 miles S of Yeovil

Gentle improvements to this well run old coaching inn are steadily turning it into a more attractive traditional country style pub. Local craftsmen have worked oak panelling through some areas, and added brass coaching lamps, there are new roses on the front of the building, and a new cold room has improved the beer cellarage. Plans for the future include the conversion of the old stone walled and flagged cellar to a wine tasting room. All this was preceded by the exposure of a nice stone floor in the back bar last year. The comfortable L-shaped bar also has tapestry covered wooden benches, two fine old fireplaces, and copies of the inn's deeds going back to the 17th c on partly hessian covered stone walls; another lounge has a woodburning stove. Alongside a couple of bar food standards like fish and chips or chicken pie (£5.95), imaginative changing specials might include devilled kidneys (£3.95), mussels in white wine and stilton (£4.25), sliced cured haunch of venison with salsa verde (£4.50), sautéed squid scallops in lemon and vermouth (£5.50), green herb risotto (£6.25), squid in beer batter with orange mayonnaise or rabbit casserole with green cardamon (£7.25), loin of lamb stuffed with black pudding or wild boar sausages with red cabbage (£8.25), chicken escalopes with lemon and black pepper sauce (£8.95), lemon sole with parmesan crust (£9.25), sirloin steak with wild mushroom and red wine sauce (£11.50), and puddings like rhubarb and ginger crumble, chocolate brûlée or minted chocolate torte (£3.25). The front part of the bar, the dining room and the restaurant are no smoking. Well kept Exmoor, Fullers London Pride, Otter Bright and Shepherd Neame on handpump as well as farm cider, home-made elderflower cordial, damson vodka and sloe gin and a thoughtful wine list; pool, darts, shove-ha'penny, skittle alley, dominoes, and juke box. Outside, there's a terrace with dark oak furniture. It's a nice village to stay in and there are lots of good surrounding walks. *(Recommended by John Gillett, Stephen, Julie and Hayley Brown)*

Free house ~ Licensees Martyn and Susie Lee ~ Real ale ~ Bar food (11.30-3, 6.30-9) ~ Restaurant ~ (01935) 83228 ~ Children welcome ~ Open 11.30-2.30(3 Sat), 6.30-11; 12-3, 6.30-10.30 Sun ~ Bedrooms: £45B/£80B

FURZEHILL SU0101 Map 2
Stocks
Village signposted off B3078 N of Wimborne Minster

This welcoming and attractive thatched pub is on Stocks Corner where they used to hang people – hence the name. The oldest part has the most character, where two long rooms divided into rather snug sections each have an open fire – brick in one and stone in the other – plush wall and window seats and stools, and timbered ochre walls; a dining area leads off with lots of copper and earthenware, an area with nets and a crab pot, and a big wall mirror cleverly creating an illusion of even more space. There are other dining areas with more mirrors, solid farmhouse chairs and tables, low ceilings and soft lighting, and good New Forest black and white photographs, old prints, farm tools, hay sleds, and so forth – even a Rayburn range in one place. Popular bar food includes soup of the day (£2.25), crab and prawn cocktail or chicken satay (£3.95), scampi (£6.95), ratatouille and cheese suet pudding, beef and stilton stroganoff, filled yorkshire pudding or chicken and mushroom or steak and kidney pie (£7.95) and a couple of daily specials such as mango and brie filo parcels (£3.95), beef bourguignon or pork marinated with sage with a cream sauce (£8.95); plenty of older customers favour the good value two-course lunch (£4.50). Well kept Fullers London Pride and Ringwood Best and Fortyniner; the original cellar had a tunnel that came out in Smugglers Lane. Darts, fruit machine. Out in front are some green plastic seats, and under a fairy-lit arbour by the car park at the back, solid teak furniture. *(Recommended by John Hibberd, Gordon)*

Greenalls ~ Manager John Sheridan ~ Real ale ~ Bar food (12-2, 6.30-9.30(10 Fri, Sat)) ~ Restaurant ~ (01202) 882481 ~ Children in eating area of bar and restaurant ~ Open 11-2.30(3 Sat), 6-11; 11-3, 6-10.30 Sun

GODMANSTONE SY6697 Map 2
Smiths Arms
A352 N of Dorchester

As the characterful landlord here (a jockey in his former life) approaches retirement his concern is that he won't find anyone to buy this tiny 15th-c thatched building. It measures just 12 by 4 metres and claims to be one of the smallest in the country, so there isn't much scope in this for turning it into a slick dining operation. There are only six tables in the quaint little bar, as well as some antique waxed and polished small pews hugging the walls (there's also one elegant little high-backed settle), long wooden stools and chunky tables, National Hunt racing pictures and some brass plates on the walls, and an open fire. Very well kept Ringwood Best tapped from casks behind the bar; friendly, helpful staff; dominoes, trivia, cribbage and piped music. Simple but tasty home-made food might be sandwiches (from £1.70; the roast beef is lovely), giant sausage (£3.10), ploughman's (from £3.50), quiche or chilli (£4.55), a range of salads (from £4.35), home-cooked ham (£5.45), and daily specials such as curried prawn lasagne or topside of beef and steak and kidney pie (£5.45) and puddings (£2). There are seats and tables set outside on a crazy-paved terrace and on the grassy mound by the narrow River Cerne. A pleasant walk leads over Cowdon Hill to the River Piddle. No children. *(Recommended by the Didler, JP, PP, Dr and Mrs J H Hills)*

Free house ~ Licensees John and Linda Foster ~ Real ale ~ Bar food (till 9.45) ~ (01300) 341236 ~ Open 11-3, 6-11; 12-3, 7-10.30 Sun; closed Jan

KINGSTON SY9579 Map 2
Scott Arms
B3069

Even though this popular creeper-clad stone house is much bigger than you'd expect it does still get full in the summer season. Its rambling warren-like rooms have old panelling, stripped stone walls, beams, warming fires, some fine antique prints and a friendly, chatty feel; an attractive room overlooks the garden, and there's a decent extension which is well liked by families. Bar food in generous helpings includes crab sandwiches (£4.25), ploughman's (£5.25), steak and ale pie (£5.95), curry of the day (£7.95) and pork and stilton stroganoff (£8.95); no-smoking dining area; they do afternoon cream teas in summer. Well kept Greenalls Original and Ringwood Best on handpump, and lots of wines; darts, fruit machine, and piped music. There are wonderful views of Corfe Castle and the Purbeck Hills from the well kept garden. *(Recommended by John and Vivienne Rice, John and Joan Calvert, B and K Hypher, Mr and Mrs Sweeney, the Didler, Simon Williams, Keith and Margaret Kettell, Mr and Mrs A R Hawkins, Stephen and Wendy Flick, Simon Watkins, Mark Percy, Lesley Mayoh, David and Carole Chapman, K Stevens, D Marsh, Ian Jones, JP, PP, John Hayter, Martin and Caroline Page)*

Greenalls ~ Manager Bill Niddrie ~ Real ale ~ Bar food (12-2, 6.30-9) ~ (01929) 480270 ~ Children in restaurant ~ Open 11-3, 6-11; 12-3, 7-10.30 Sun ~ Bedrooms: /£60B

LANGTON HERRING SY6182 Map 2
Elm Tree 🍴
Village signposted off B3157

Readers really enjoy visiting this lovely old beamed pub for its friendly welcome, and more especially for its interesting well prepared daily specials. From an extensive range and served in generous helpings these might include creamed fennel and celery soup (£2.65), roasted red pepper and goat's cheese bruschetta (£4.95), pasta with fresh asparagus, leeks and pecorino cheese (£5.25), loin of pork with creamed shallot and rosemary sauce (£8.50), roasted red snapper fillet in a Moroccan marinade (£9.25), sirloin steak with a creamed oyster mushroom sauce (£9.75), and puddings such as treacle tart and clotted cream or hot banana fudge biscuit (from £2.95). More standard dishes from the bar menu include sandwiches (from £2), filled baked potatoes (from £2.50), ploughman's or ciabatta with goat's cheese and tomatoes (£3.75), hot garlic bread filled with hot roast beef (£3.45), lasagne (£6.50), steak and ale pie (£6.95), creamy cider, pork and apple casserole (£7.50) and baked crab mornay (£7.95), puddings including a very chocolate chocolate pudding (from £2.95) and the usual children's menu (from £2.25); good Sunday roasts. There may be a bit of a wait for food when they get busy in the summer. The Portland spy ring is said to have met in the main beamed and carpeted rooms, which have walls festooned with copper, brass and bellows, cushioned window seats, red leatherette stools, windsor chairs, and lots of tables; one has some old-fashioned settles and an inglenook. The traditionally furnished extension gives more room for diners. Greenalls Original and a guest such as Boddingtons under light blanket pressure; country wines. Outside in the pretty flower-filled sunken garden are colourful hanging baskets, flower tubs, and tables; a track leads down to the Dorset Coast Path, which here skirts the eight-mile lagoon enclosed by Chesil Beach. *(Recommended by Anthony Barnes, David Mead, Joy and Peter Heatherley, John and Joan Nash, Pete and Rosie Flower, John and Vivienne Rice, Richard and Margaret Peers, Galen Strawson, Karen Eliot, Basil Minson)*

Greenalls ~ Tenants L Horlock and Roberto D'Agostino ~ Real ale ~ Bar food ~ (01305) 871257 ~ Children in eating area of bar ~ Open 11-3, 6-11; 12-3, 6.30-10.30 Sun

LODERS SY4994 Map 2
Loders Arms 🛏
Off A3066 just N of Bridport; can also be reached off A35 E of Bridport, via Uploders

Still well used by a chatty bunch of locals, this relaxing place is situated in a pretty stonebuilt village of largely thatched cottages which is tucked into a sheltered fold of steep Dorset hills. The smallish long bar with a log fire, maybe piped classical music, and amiable dogs has Palmers Bridport, 200 and IPA on electric pump. Bar food is one draw here. The menu changes daily and might include huge filled french bread (from £3.25, smoked salmon and cream cheese £3.95) warm salad of pigeon breast, tiger prawns in garlic or fresh anchovies with tomato and basil salad (£4.25), lemon and ginger chicken or mushroom and aubergine risotto with fresh parmesan (£5.95), wild boar sausage, mash and onion gravy or rabbit in cider (£6.95), pork tenderloin with a cream and horseradish sauce (£8.95), venison steak with gin and juniper berry sauce (£10.95), and puddings like chocolate and brandy mousse, fruit crumbles or apricot pudding (£3); no-smoking dining room. There's a skittle alley and cribbage. Tables in the garden at the back have pleasant views. *(Recommended by Stephen, Julie and Hayley Brown, Mrs O Hardy, John and Joan Nash, Nigel Wikeley, Anthony Barnes, Basil Minson, Gethin Lewis, R Shelton, W W Burke, Galen Strawson, Stephen King)*

Palmers ~ Tenant Roger Flint ~ Real ale ~ Bar food (12.30-2, 7.30-9) ~ Restaurant ~ (01308) 422431 ~ Children in eating area of bar and restaurant ~ Open 11.30-3, 6-11; 12-10.30 Sun ~ Bedrooms: £25S(£25B)/£40S(£45B)

LYME REGIS SY3492 Map 1
Pilot Boat ♀ £

Bridge Street

Still the best pub in this well known little town, this simple airy seaside pub is decorated with lots of local pictures, navy and helicopter photographs, lobster-pot lamps, sharks' heads, an interesting collection of local fossils, a model of one of the last sailing ships to use the harbour, and a notable collection of sailors' hat ribands. At the back, there's a long and narrow lounge bar overlooking the little River Lym; you can sit outside on seats on the terrace. Just qualifying for a Bargain Award this year, fairly straightforward but generously served bar food includes soup of the day (£1.95), bouillabaisse (£4.75), ploughman's (£3.95), cod and chips (£4.25), vegetable pie (£4.75), lamb curry (£6.25), steak and kidney pie (£6.50) and local trout (£7.75). The dining area is no smoking. Well kept Palmers Bridport, IPA and 200 on handpump, although one reader reported only one of these on on a recent visit; skittle alley and piped music. The licensees run another Lyme Regis pub, the Cobb Arms, which has bedrooms. *(Recommended by Simon Williams, Pat and Tony Martin, Dr and Mrs Nigel Holmes, Peter and Pat Frogley, Ann and Colin Hunt, Mike Doupe, Dave and Deborah Irving, Joan and Michel Hooper-Immins, Keith and Janet Morris, M Brooks, Mr and Mrs J E Lockwood, Greg Kilminster, Mr M G Hart, Andy and Jill Kassube, Stephen King, Paul and Judith Booth, E G Parish)*

Palmers ~ Tenants Bill and Caroline Wiscombe ~ Real ale ~ Bar food ~ (01297) 443157 ~ Children welcome ~ Open 11-11; 12-10.30 Sun

MARNHULL ST7718 Map 2
Blackmore Vale

Burton Street; quiet side street

Well liked for its warmly welcoming atmosphere and affable staff and licensees, this old pub has a comfortably modernised lounge bar, which is decorated with fourteen guns and rifles, keys, a few horsebrasses and old brass spigots on the beams. There's a log fire and one bar is no smoking. As well as farm cider and a good wine list they have well kept Badger Best, Tanglefoot and a seasonal ale on handpump. Popular bar food includes soup (£2.25), sandwiches (£2.45), breaded brie with fruits of the forest sauce (£3.95), half a pint of prawns (£4.45), steak baguette (£4.75), ploughman's (£4.85), pork tenderloin with tarragon, cream, wine and mushroom sauce or chicken chasseur (£7.95) and 8oz sirloin (£9.45). They will bring your food to the garden, where one of the tables is thatched; cribbage and a skittle alley. No children. *(Recommended by W Burke, Charles and Pauline Stride, Mrs Laura Gustine, R H Rowley, Jill Bickerton, Michael Hill)*

Badger ~ Tenant Roger Hiron ~ Real ale ~ Bar food ~ (01258) 820701 ~ Open 11.30-3, 6.30-11; 12-3, 7-10.30 Sun

MARSHWOOD SY3799 Map 1
Bottle

B3165 Lyme Regis—Crewkerne

'Interesting and quite different' is how one reader described this thriving village local, which is reckoned to be pretty much the same as it was 30 years ago (so perhaps a little worn in places), and an enjoyable mix of customers from businessmen to bikers, and hikers to farmers seem to appreciate its genuinely friendly character. Its simple interior has down to earth furnishings including cushioned benches and one high-backed settle and there's an inglenook fireplace with a big log fire in winter. What really marks it out though is the particularly interesting range of unusual vegetarian and vegan dishes, international style dishes, organic wines, beers and ciders, and the enthusiastic licensees' ability to cater for people with food allergies. From a mainly locally sourced, organic menu and specials board they might be serving butterbean, garlic and parsley pâté (£2.95), filled baguettes (from £4.25), ploughman's or scrambled eggs with smoked salmon (£5.50), homity pie (£5.95), steak and mushroom pie (£6.95), spicy Indonesian chicken with coconut, chilli and lemon grass and stir-fried noodles (£7.25), Matar Paneer: an Indian dish of tofu, peas, tomatoes and warm spices served with aloo sag and pilau rice, mushroom stroganoff with wild organic rice, chicken balti or sweet potato, crème fraîche, lemon grass, chilli and garlic pie (£7.95), leg of lamb stuffed with rosemary and garlic or moussaka (£8.95), local wild boar casserole with red wine and juniper berries (£9.95), 8oz sirloin steak (£14.95), and organic ice creams (£3.65); well kept Branscombe Vale Branoc, Fullers London Pride and Otter Head on handpump; darts and pool in a smaller side room, also shove-ha'penny, dominoes and cribbage, a skittle alley and piped music. They have a craft shop with local wickerwork, pottery and paintings. A good big back garden has a well equipped play area, and beyond it a camp site. The pub is surrounded by pretty walking country and close to Lambert's Castle (a National Trust hill fort). *(Recommended by Mrs A K Davies, Pat and Tony Martin, Mrs J Ashdown, Dr and Mrs Nigel Holmes)*

Free house ~ Licensees Sim Pym and Chloe Fox-Lambert ~ Real ale ~ Bar food ~ (01297) 678254 ~ Children welcome ~ Open 12-3, 6.30-11(10.30 Sun); closed Mon lunchtime Nov-Easter

NETTLECOMBE SY5195 Map 2

Marquis of Lorne 🍴 🍺 🛏

Turn E off A3066 Bridport—Beaminster Road 1½ miles N of Bridport. Pass Mangerton Mill and 1m after West Milton go straight across give-way junction. Pub is on left 300 yards up the hill

Readers really do enjoy the warm welcome and lively atmosphere at this very well run pub which is tucked away in lovely peaceful countryside. The comfortable bustling main bar has a log fire, mahogany panelling and old prints and photographs around its neatly matching chairs and tables; two dining areas lead off, the smaller of which has another log fire and is no smoking. The wooden-floored snug has cribbage and table skittles, and piped music is mainly classical. Ed the chocolate labrador might be around performing his tricks in reward for a crisp or two. Notably good bar food might include curried parsnip and apple soup or sandwiches (from £2.50), avocado with curried chicken (£3.95), ploughman's (£4), cold leek, stilton and walnut pie (£5.50), spinach and walnut lasagne (£5.95), home-made steak, ale and mushroom pie or pudding (£6.95), lamb shank braised with vegetables or grilled plaice (£7.95), chcken breast with smoked bacon, mushroom and baby onion sauce (£8.25), roast duck breast with mango and blackcurrant sauce (£9.95) and seafood platter (£10.75), and puddings such as almond and apricot strudel or sticky toffee pudding (£3.25); good vegetables, and they may have locally-made chutneys and marmalade for sale. Well kept Palmers Bridport and IPA on handpump with 200 tapped straight from the cask, and good wine list that usually has around eight by the glass. A big garden has a rustic style play area among the picnic-sets under its apple trees. The earth-fort of Eggardon Hill is close by. They may ask you to leave your credit card behind the bar if you're eating outside and want to run a tab. *(Recommended by Jenny and Chris Wilson, Mrs M E Bell, Chris and Marianna Webb, Pete and Rosie Flower, M J Daly, David Heath, Stephen, Julie and Hayley Brown, Dr and Mrs Nigel Holmes, P J Hanson, John Robertson, Simon Williams, Dr and Mrs G H Lewis, Galen Strawson, Dr and Mrs J H Hills, Basil Minson)*

Palmers ~ Tenants Ian and Anne Barrett ~ Real ale ~ Bar food (till 9.30) ~ (01308) 485236 ~ Children in eating area of bar ~ Open 11-2.30, 6(6.30 winter)-11; 12-3, 7-10.30 Sun ~ Bedrooms: £40S/£60S

OSMINGTON MILLS SY7381 Map 2

Smugglers

Village signposted off A353 NE of Weymouth

The spacious interior of this partly thatched inn has shiny black panelling and woodwork dividing the relaxing bar into cosy, friendly areas. Soft red lantern-lights give an atmospheric hue to the stormy sea pictures and big wooden blocks and tackle on the walls, and there are logs burning in an open stove. Some seats are tucked into alcoves and window embrasures, with one forming part of an upended boat. Bar food includes filled baps (from £3.95), ploughman's or filled baked potatoes (£5.25), spinach and mushroom lasagne or fish and chips (£6.25), steak, kidney and mushroom pie or toasted goat's cheese and tomato salad, Thai coconut chicken curry (£6.95), roast shank of lamb with garlic and rosemary and port and redcurrant gravy (£8.95) and puddings like fruit crumble of the day and chocolate profiteroles (all £3.25). Service stays efficient and friendly even when they're busy. Part of the restaurant is no smoking. Well kept Bagder Dorset Best, Tanglefoot and a guest on handpump. Darts, pool and fruit machine are kept sensibly out of the way; piped music. There are picnic-sets out on crazy paving by a little stream, with a thatched summer bar where they have summer barbecues, and a good play area over on a steep lawn. It gets very busy in high season (there's a holiday settlement just up the lane). *(Recommended by John and Joan Calvert, David and Carole Chapman, the Didler, J and B Cressey, Mr and Mrs D E Powell, C Robinson, Tony Scott, Andy and Jill Kassube, Mr and Mrs N Fuller, Pat and Tony Martin, Kevin Thorpe)*

Badger ~ Manager David Southward ~ Real ale ~ Bar food (12-10 summer; 12-2, 6-9 winter) ~ Restaurant ~ (01305) 833125 ~ Children in eating area of bar and restaurant ~ Open 11-11; 12-10.30 Sun; 11-2.30, 6-11 winter; 12-2.30, 6-11 Sun winter ~ Bedrooms: £30B/£65B

PIDDLEHINTON SY7197 Map 1
Thimble
B3143

Readers speak highly of the very welcoming landlord at this beautifully kept thatched village pub which is prettily tucked away down winding lanes, and approached by a little footbridge over the River Piddle. Its flower-filled garden makes a charmingly restful place to enjoy lunch, and is attractively floodlit at night. Inside, the neatly kept and friendly low-beamed bar is simpler than the exterior suggests, although nicely spacious so that in spite of drawing quite a lot of people in the summer, it never feels too crowded – service doesn't falter when it's busy either. There's a handsome open stone fireplace, and a deep well. Good value tasty bar food includes fresh soup of the day (£2.50), sandwiches (from £2.95), ploughman's (from £3.65), well liked chilli (£5.30), fresh pasta with tomato, mushroom and pesto sauce and cheddar and mozzarella (£5.50), local sole (£5.95), chicken, ham and mushroom or game pie (£6.20), steak and oyster pudding (£8.05), mixed grill (£11.50) and mainly home-made puddings like spotted dick (from £3.25). Well kept Badger Best and Tanglefoot, Hardy Country and Popes Traditional and Ringwood Old Thumper on handpump, along with quite a few malt whiskies and farm cider; friendly service; darts, shove-ha'penny, dominoes, cribbage, trivia and piped music. *(Recommended by John and Vivienne Rice, Basil Minson, George Atkinson, G Neighbour, R J Walden, Bronwen and Steve Wrigley, John and Joan Nash, M J Harris, Mr and Mrs A R Hawkins, Richard and Jean Green, David Lamb, Simon Williams, FJW, M G Hart, Martin and Caroline Page, D B Jenkin, the Didler, J G Roberts)*

Free house ~ Licensees N R White and V J Lanfear ~ Real ale ~ Bar food ~ (01300) 348270 ~ Children in eating area of bar ~ Open 12-2.30, 7-11(10.30 Sun); closed 25 Dec, 26 Dec evening

PLUSH ST7102 Map 2
Brace of Pheasants 🍴
Village signposted from B3143 N of Dorchester at Piddletrenthide

This charming long low 16th-c thatched inn (once a row of cottages that included the village forge) in a pretty hamlet a little off the beaten track is a well known, popular place that attracts plenty of visitors and locals (including the local cricket team at times). Its unusual pub sign is a glass case containing two stuffed pheasants. Inside, the comfortably airy beamed bar has good solid tables, windsor chairs, fresh flowers, a huge heavy-beamed inglenook at one end with cosy seating inside, and a good warming log fire at the other. The friendly black labrador is called Bodger, and the golden retriever Molly. A wide choice of very well prepared imaginative bar food might include smoked salmon and crab pâté (£4.25), moules marinières (£3.75), venison sausages in red wine and onion gravy (£6.25), smoked haddock on spinach with poached egg and cheese sauce (£7.95), roast monkfish wrapped in bacon with rosemary, garlic and tomato (£12.25). The restaurant and family room are no smoking. Well kept Bass, Fullers London Pride and Smiles Golden straight from the cask. There's a decent-sized garden and terrace with an aviary, a rabbit cage and a lawn sloping up towards a rockery. The pub lies alongside Plush Brook, and an attractive bridleway behind goes to the left of the woods and over to Church Hill. *(Recommended by Mr and Mrs G Turner, Pat and Robert Watt, Chris and Ann Garnett, Joy and Peter Heatherley, Anthony Barnes, Dr and Mrs J H Hills, Mike Green, James House, Mr and Mrs S Ballantyne, Phyl and Jack Street, Mr and Mrs Broadhurst, Mr and Mrs N Fuller, the Didler, G and T Edwards, Karen Eliot, Miss E A Blease, John and Joan Nash)*

Free house ~ Licensees Jane and Geoffrey Knights ~ Real ale ~ Bar food (till 9.30) ~ Restaurant ~ (01300) 348357 ~ Children welcome in family room ~ Open 12-2.30, 7-11; 12-3, 7-10.30 Sun; closed 25 Dec

POWERSTOCK SY5196 Map 2
Three Horseshoes ★ ♀

Can be reached by taking Askerswell turn off A35 then keeping uphill past the Spyway Inn, and bearing left all the way round Eggardon Hill – a lovely drive, but steep narrow roads; a better road is signposted West Milton off the A3066 Beaminster—Bridport, then take Powerstock road

Doing really well under its new licensees, this busy stone-and-thatch pub is notable for a very good choice of well prepared fish, which is mostly cooked with fairly simple meditteranean-style ingredients. It's bought in from local boats so the weather is the mostly likely determinant of the day's selection. Listed on blackboards, the changing bar menu might include lunchtime baguettes and ploughman's (£4.50), leek and potato soup (£3.25), mussels cooked in wine and garlic (£4.95), wild boar sausages with mash and onion gravy, ratatouille gratin, sardines grilled with garlic and lemon juice or Thai green vegetable curry (£5.95), half a Lyme Bay crab (£6.95), squid stir fried with garlic, chilli and ginger (£9.95), hake with provençale sauce or seared tuna steak with salsa verde (£10.50), red mullet stuffed with sun-dried tomatos, anchovies and capers (£12.50) and bass with saffron and roasted pepper sauce (£14.95), and puddings like crème brûlée, bread and butter pudding and pears poached in red wine (from £3.25), local cheese board; no-smoking restaurant. Well kept Palmers Bridport and IPA on handpump, about 20 wines by the glass, and freshly squeezed fruit juice. The comfortable L-shaped bar has country-style chairs around the polished tables, pictures on the stripped panelled walls, and warm fires. Daisy and Jess, the friendly retrievers, or Charlie the springer spaniel may befriend you for titbits. There are lovely uninterrupted views towards the sea from the neat lawn rising steeply above the pub; swings and a climbing frame *(Recommended by Harold and Mary Smith, Mr and Mrs N Fuller, Nigel Hyde, Mr and Mrs R D Faram, Keith and Peggy Frew, M J Daly, Carole Smart, Andrew Jeeves)*

Palmers ~ Tenants Mark and Sue Johnson ~ Real ale ~ Bar food (12-2(2.30 Sat, 3 Sun), 7- 9.30(10 Sat)) ~ Restaurant ~ (01308) 485328 ~ Children welcome ~ Open 12-3, 6(6.30 winter)-11 ~ Bedrooms: /£40(£50B)

PUNCKNOWLE SY5388 Map 2
Crown 🛏

Church Street; village signposted off B3157 Bridport—Abbotsbury; or reached off A35 via Chilcombe

A most unpretentious down to earth village pub, this comfortable 16th-c thatched and flint inn is prettily set opposite a partly Norman church and its rookery. Its neat and welcoming rambling public bar has a pleasantly informal mix of furnishings, darts, table skittles and a comfortable family room opening off. The stripped stone lounge bar has red plush banquettes and stools; both rooms have heavy beams, and log fires in big stone fireplaces, and there are paintings by local artists for sale. There's a nice view from the partly paved back garden, which has tables under three venerable fairy-lit apple trees. Bar food includes sandwiches (from £1.45), soup (£2.25), ploughman's (from £4), pâté and toast (£2.60), bean and lentil curry (£4.95), steak and kidney pie or pork, spring onion and worcester sauce casserole cooked in cider (£5.80), breaded scampi (£6.25), salmon, broccoli and mascarpone casserole in tomato and white wine sauce (£6.50), mixed grill (£7.85) and rump steak (£9.05), and puddings like syrup sponge pudding, almond meringue with fruit filling or raspberry frozen yoghurt (£2.50); filling breakfasts. Well kept Palmers IPA, Bridport and 200 on handpump, Taunton Vale farm cider and country wines, good friendly service. The village name, incidentally, is pronounced Punnell. *(Recommended by Chris and Marianna Webb, Geoffrey Lawrance, H Frank Smith, WHBM)*

Palmers ~ Tenant Michael Lawless ~ Real ale ~ Bar food ~ (01308) 897711 ~ Children welcome in family room ~ Open 11-3, 6.30(7 in winter)-11; 12-3, 7-10.30 Sun; closed 25 Dec ~ Bedrooms: £22B/£40B

SHAVE CROSS SY4198 Map 1
Shave Cross Inn ★ £

On back lane Bridport—Marshwood, signposted locally; OS Sheet 193, map reference 415980

The licensees at this charming partly 14th-c flint and thatch inn are now into their second decade here, and one reader who's been coming every summer and winter for 22 years hasn't been disappointed yet. The original timbered bar is a lovely flagstoned room, surprisingly roomy and full of character, with one big table in the middle, a smaller one by the window seat, a row of chintz-cushioned windsor chairs, and an enormous inglenook fireplace with plates hanging from the chimney breast. The larger carpeted side lounge has a dresser at one end set with plates, and modern rustic light-coloured seats making booths around the tables, and is partly no smoking. They have Badger Best, Eldridge Pope Royal Oak and Otter well kept on handpump, and local cider in summer; darts, skittle alley, dominoes, cribbage, backgammon, chess and draughts. Served by friendly staff, bar food (with prices that time almost forgot) includes ploughman's or sausages and chips (£3.25), spinach and mushroom lasagne (£4.45), scampi and chips (£4.95), two sweet and sour pork and spicy lamb kebabs (£6.65), salmon steak (£7.75), sirloin steak (£8.45), and daily specials such as mushroom and nut fettucine or lasagne (£4.45), rack of ribs (£7.45), and puddings like black and redcurrant crumble or raspberry ice cream pavlova (£2.75). The very lovely pretty flower-filled sheltered garden has a thatched wishing-well and a goldfish pool. *(Recommended by JP, PP, Galen Strawson, Joy and Peter Heatherley, Yavuz and Shirley Mutlu, Dr and Mrs Nigel Holmes, Anthony Barnes, Mick and Elizabeth Leyden, Digby Linnett, Colin Thompson)*

Free house ~ Licensees Bill and Ruth Slade ~ Real ale ~ Bar food ~ (01308) 868358 ~ Children in lounge bar ~ Open 12-3(winter 2.30) 7-11(10.30 Sun); closed Mon except bank holidays

SHERBORNE ST6316 Map 2
Digby Tap ◄ £

Cooks Lane; park in Digby Road and walk round corner

An easy mix of customers enjoys the pleasant relaxed atmosphere in the stone-flagged main bar (which has plenty of bygone character and traditional seating) at this simple uncluttered old-fashioned town ale house. With four or five interesting real ales on handpump at a time, they work through about two dozen different ales a week from brewers like Brakspears, Cottage, Fullers, Oakhill, Quay and Teignworthy. Served only at lunchtime, huge helpings of very reasonably priced bar food include good sandwiches or filled french sticks (from £1.50; well liked bacon, lettuce and tomato £2.30), pasta with carbonara sauce (£3.50), filled yorkshire puddings or scampi and chips (£3.75), mixed grill (£4.95), and one or two daily specials. There are several small games rooms with pool, darts, cribbage, trivia, fruit machine and piped music; there are some seats outside. The pub is handy for the glorious golden stone abbey. *(Recommended by Tony and Wendy Hobden, Stephen Brown, Lynn Sharpless, Bob Eardley, R J Walden, Andy and Jill Kassube, Paul and Judith Booth, Gordon, Revd A Nunnerley, Pat and Tony Martin, Basil Minson)*

Free house ~ Licensees Peter Lefeure and Nick Whigham ~ Real ale ~ Bar food (not evenings, not Sun) ~ (01935) 813148 ~ Children welcome in eating area of bar at lunchtime ~ Open 11-2.30, 5.30-11; 11-3, 6-11 Sat; 12-2.30, 7-10.30 Sun; closed 25 Dec evening

UPWEY SY6684 Map 2
Old Ship
Ridgeway; turn left off A354 at bottom of Ridgeway Hill into old Roman Rd

We'd be very interested to hear reports on the new regime at this dining pub on the old Roman Road to Dorchester. Its several attractive interconnected beamed rooms have a peacefully welcoming atmosphere, as well as a mix of sturdy chairs, some built-in wooden wall settles, fresh flowers on the solid panelled wood bar counter and tables, china plates, copper pans and old clocks on the walls, a couple of comfortable armchairs, and an open fire with horsebrasses along the mantlebeam. Bar food includes soup (£2.50), sandwiches (£2.95), ploughman's (£4.25) and daily specials like medley of wild mushrooms (£4.75), curry of the day (£5.95), pie of the day (£6.95), whole roast poussin with venison stuffing and port or fresh fish of the day (£8.75), half a shoulder of lamb with redcurrant and mint sauce (£8.95), and puddings like chocolate pecan pie (£2.50); the restaurant is no smoking. Well kept Bass, Boddingtons, Greenalls Original and a couple of guests on handpump. There are colourful hanging baskets outside, and picnic-sets and umbrellas in the garden. *(Recommended by Jean and Michel Hooper-Immins, Pete and Rosie Flower, Simon Williams, Anthony Barnes, Keith and Janet Morris, P G Bardswell, Roger Price, J and B Cressey, Galen Strawson)*

Inn Partnership (Nomura) ~ Tenants David Wootton, Martin Boult and John Hana ~ Real ale ~ Bar food (lunchtime) ~ Restaurant (evening) ~ (01305) 812522 ~ Children welcome ~ Open 12-2.30, 6-11; 11-10.30 Sun

WORTH MATRAVERS SY9777 Map 2
Square & Compass ◀
At fork of both roads signposted to village from B3069

Thankfully there have been no changes in the last year at this basic but fascinatingly atmospheric little pub which has been run by the Newman family for over 90 years. In fact it hasn't changed much in that time either, except perhaps in the additon of a free little museum displaying local fossils and aretefacts, mostly collected by the current landlord and his father. The low-ceilinged old-fashioned main bar has simple wall benches around the elbow-polished old tables on the flagstones, interesting local pictures, and well kept Badger Tanglefoot, Quay Old Rott and Ringwood Best and Fortyniner tapped from a row of casks behind a couple of hatches in the flagstoned narrow passage which leads to a more conventional summer bar; farm cider. Bar food is limited to pork and chilli or cheese and onion pie or pasties (£1.40), served any time when they're open; cribbage, shove-ha'penny and dominoes. On a clear day the view from the peaceful hilltop is hard to beat, looking down over the village rooftops to the sea between the East Man and the West Man (the hills that guard the coastal approach), and on summer evenings the sun setting out beyond Portland Bill. There are benches in front of the pub with views over the countryside to the sea, and free-roaming hens, chickens and other birds may cluck happily around your feet. There are good walks from the pub. Perhaps best to park in the public car park 100 yards along the Corfe Castle road. *(Recommended by James Nunns, A C and E Johnson, John and Joan Nash, JP, PP, David and Carole Chapman, Jeremy Burnside, Kevin Thorpe, Nigel Flook, Betsy Brown, the Didler, Simon Williams, Mike and Sue Loseby, Anthony Barnes, Andy and Jill Kassube, Pat and Robert Watt)*

Free house ~ Licensee Charlie Newman ~ Real ale ~ Bar food ~ (01929) 439229 ~ Children welcome ~ Open 11-3, 6-11; 11-11 Sat; 12-3, 7-10.30 Sun

Lucky Dip

Besides the fully inspected pubs, you might like to try these Lucky Dips recommended to us and described by readers (if you do, please send us reports):

Abbotsbury [SY5785]
Swan [B3157]: Cosy pub in pretty village; good food and beer *(S P Bobeldijk)*
Almer [SY9097]
☆ *Worlds End* [B3075, just off A31 towards Wareham]: Roomily rebuilt open-plan thatched family dining pub, highest earner in the Badger chain, with their beers kept well, very wide choice of food (you can choose generous or smaller helpings), good service, panelled alcoves; open all day, picnic-sets out in front and behind, outstanding play area *(BB, WHBM, Dennis Stevens, Colin and Ann Hunt, Howard and Barbara Clutterbuck)*
Beaminster [ST4701]
Greyhound [A3066 N of Bridport]: Flagstones and simple furnishings on right, plusher on left, gas fires, well kept Palmers IPA and BB, wide choice of decent reasonably priced standard food, congenial service, small back family room; darts, piped music *(Glen and Nola Armstrong, Chris and Marianna Webb, Ian and Naomi Lancaster, Mark Matthewman, BB, James Currie)*
Bere Regis [SY8494]
Drax Arms [High St]: Comfortable village pub with helpful licensees), well kept Badger ales and farm cider, limited choice of good reasonably priced food esp home-made pies and casseroles, big open fire on left; good walking nearby *(John and Joan Nash, G Washington, R T and J C Moggridge)*
Bishops Caundle [ST6913]
☆ *White Hart* [A3030 SE of Sherborne]: Nicely moulded dark beams, ancient panelling, attractive furnishings, sizeable no-smoking family area with french windows to big prettily floodlit garden with fine play area and all sorts of games; friendly helpful service, Badger Best and Tanglefoot, food from sandwiches to steaks inc smaller and children's helpings; darts, skittle alley, fruit machine, piped pop music; reasonably priced bedrooms *(LYM, D B Jenkin, Marjorie and David Lamb, Anthony Barnes)*
Blandford Forum [ST8806]
Dolphin: Interesting and friendly town pub with bare boards, rugs and panelling, pews, fireside sofa, smallish menu of reasonably priced standard food, John Smiths, Theakstons Best, Wadworths 6X and guest beers, fruit wines; quiet fruit machine, music *(Lynn Sharpless, Bob Eardley, Dr and Mrs A K Clarke)*
Nelsons [Salisbury St]: Very old dim-lit bar, beams and flagstones, good value interesting food in big or small helpings, good Sun lunch, half a dozen well kept interesting beers, hospitable landlord, newspapers *(Dr and Mrs A K Clarke)*
Bournemouth [SZ0991]
Durley [Durley Chine]: Chain dining pub, but a model of its type, in great spot right on the beach, with tables outside; good service,

Boddingtons and Flowers, good choice of wines by the glass *(Mr and Mrs A P Reeves, Jill Bickerton, David and Carole Chapman, Nigel Flook, Betsy Brown)*
Goat & Tricycle [West Hill Rd]: Comfortable relaxed Wadworths pub with well kept beers inc guests such as Adnams Broadside and Archers Best, Cheddar Valley farm cider, lots of bric-a-brac hundreds of hats hung from ceiling; simple lunch menu from club sandwiches up *(Joan and Michel Hooper-Immins, Dr and Mrs A K Clarke)*
Lynton Court [Christchurch Rd]: Newly refurbished chain pub with varied food, Boddingtons and Flowers IPA, no-smoking area; children's play area *(Mr and Mrs A P Reeves)*
Neptune [seafront, by Boscombe Pier]: Popular chain dining pub with large no-smoking area, wide food choice, Boddingtons and Flowers IPA, outside area with glass canopy, play area *(Mr and Mrs A P Reeves)*
Yates's Wine Lodge: Plush and welcoming, with well kept beer and food all day *(Dr and Mrs A K Clarke)*
Bourton [ST7430]
White Lion [High St, off old A303 E of Wincanton]: Plushly refurbished stripped stone dining pub, nicely lit beamed bars with sporting equipment, well kept beers such as Bass, Courage Best and Fullers London Pride, well prepared food from generous sandwiches to steaks, friendly service, restaurant; dogs welcome, live music w/e *(LYM, Julie and Bill Ryan)*
Bridport [SY4692]
Boot [North Allington]: Friendly local, good all round *(Chris and Marianna Webb)*
Greyhound [East St]: Old pub converted by Wetherspoons, setting good new local standards for pricing with its cheap beers and food; open long hours *(Chris and Marianna Webb)*
Hope & Anchor [St Michaels Lane]: Friendly local with Somerset apple brandy *(Chris and Marianna Webb)*
Lord Nelson [East St]: Welcoming local, table skittles *(Chris and Marianna Webb)*
Broadmayne [SY7286]
Black Dog: Comfortably modernised village pub with reasonably priced popular food inc good sandwiches and Sun lunch, pleasant staff *(LYM, Geoffrey Lawrance)*
Broadwindsor [ST4302]
☆ *White Lion* [B3163/B3164]: Welcoming 17th-c stonebuilt pub/restaurant with pews and flagstones on left, pine booth seating and big inglenook with woodburner in carpeted area on right, a modicum of china, fresh and dried flowers, big woodburner; good choice of generous home-made food from good sandwiches to popular Sun roasts, using local produce, Palmers beers, darts, plenty of locals; disabled facilities, no machines, well behaved

dogs welcome, unobtrusive piped music *(Ray Williams, BB, KC, Mrs T A Bizat, Mrs O Hardy, Chris and Marianna Webb)*

Burton Bradstock [SY4889]

☆ *Three Horseshoes* [Mill St]: Attractive thatched inn in charming village, with comfortable and roomy carpeted lounge, Palmers real ales, good wines, unobtrusive piped music, no-smoking dining room, tables out on lawn, pleasant shingle beach a few minutes' drive away (with NT car park); has had friendly service and enjoyable food under previous long-serving tenant, but we've had no reports yet on the new regime; bedrooms *(LYM)*

Charlton Marshall [ST9003]

☆ *Charlton Inn* [A350 Poole—Blandford]: Comfortable country-style pub well extended by new licensees without losing local character, new chef doing wide choice of food from doorstep sandwiches and baked potatoes to enterprising main dishes with particularly good veg, Badger Best and Tanglefoot, quick friendly service, no-smoking area, unobtrusive piped music; small garden *(WHBM, DWAJ, W and J Cottrell, D B Jenkin)*

Charminster [SY6793]

Inn For All Seasons [North St]: Good value food inc fresh veg and good Sun lunch in bright airy back dining room, well kept Otter and Ringwood Fortyniner, attentive service; riverside garden with play area, bedrooms *(Joan and Michel Hooper-Immins)*

Charmouth [SY3693]

George: Very friendly, with big helpings of cheap food, well kept Palmers; dogs welcome *(K Stevens)*

Chickerell [SY6480]

Turks Head [East St]: Busy stonebuilt village pub with pleasant beamed bar and spacious eating area in former skittle alley, wide choice of good generous freshly cooked food inc children's and wonderful puddings, lots of old local photographs, pictures and decorative plates, cheerful service, restaurant; children welcome, comfortable bedrooms, good breakfast *(David Mead, Robert Flux)*

Chideock [SY4292]

Clock [A35 W of Bridport]: Friendly and attractive open-plan thatched village inn with Hardy Country, Morlands Old Speckled Hen and Wadworths 6X, food in bar and restaurant *(Val and Alan Green, BB)*

George [A35 Bridport—Lyme Regis]: Welcoming thatched 17th-c pub with neat rows of tables in simple front bar, plusher lounge, hundreds of banknotes on beams, various bric-a-brac, big log fire, well kept Palmers, efficient staff, big restaurant, no piped music; tables in back garden, bedrooms *(Pat and Tony Martin, Mark Matthewman, Galen Strawson, LYM)*

Child Okeford [ST8313]

☆ *Saxon* [Gold Hill; village signed off A350 Blandford—Shaftesbury and A357 Blandford—Sherborne]: Cosy and friendly old village meeting place, quietly clubby bar with log fire and more spacious side room (where children allowed), well kept Butcombe, Greene King Abbot and a guest such as Canterbury Jack,

country wines, traditional games, reasonably priced food (not Tues evening, not winter Sun evening) inc sandwiches and children's dishes; piped music, dry dogs on leads welcome; quite a menagerie in attractive back garden, also friendly golden retrievers and cats; good walks on neolithic Hambledon Hill *(LYM, Martin Sandercombe, WHBM)*

Christchurch [SZ2194]

Amberwood [Ringwood Rd, Walkford; just off A35 by Hants border]: Enjoyable food with imaginative homely touches in spacious bar and comfortable restaurant (booking advised), friendly staff; some live music, weekly trivia night, picnic-sets and play area; open all day, festooned with hanging baskets and flower tubs in summer; between coastal development and New Forest, paths to coast at Highcliffe Castle *(Phyl and Jack Street, D Marsh)*

Bailey Bridge: Very popular new chain pub/hotel with Boddingtons and Flowers IPA, varied food, no-smoking part, indoor play area *(Mr and Mrs A P Reeves)*

Ship [High St]: Dark and low-beamed Hogshead, with good choice of well kept ales and fine range of Belgian draught beers; good honest bar food, reasonably priced *(Andy and Jill Kassube, Mr and Mrs A P Reeves, W W Burke)*

Corfe Castle [SY9681]

Bankes Arms: Big and busy but welcoming, with flagstones and comfortable traditional décor, subtle lighting, well kept Wadworths 6X, generous food inc reasonable vegetarian choice, friendly service, restaurant; tables on terrace and in long garden with play area, running down to tourist railway; piped music, children and dogs welcome; bedrooms (no single-night bookings w/e), on attractive village square *(David and Carole Chapman, J and B Cressey, Betsy and Peter Little, Keith and Janet Morris)*

Mortons House [East St (A351)]: Good bar lunches beautifully served and lovely subdued peaceful atmosphere in renovated old stone building away from the bustle; terrace and gardens; also cream teas and restaurant, bedrooms *(B and K Hypher)*

Corfe Mullen [SY9798]

Coventry Arms [A31 W of Wimborne]: Nooks and crannies of reconstituted antiquity in two interconnecting bars separated by very open fire, Ringwood Best and three or four interesting guest ales tapped from the cask, decent clutch of malt whiskies, good food from filled baked potatoes and baguettes up, tables out by small stream; quiet lunchtime but busy evenings, with weekly live music and lots of special events *(Dr and Mrs A K Clarke, Paul R White)*

Dorchester [SY6890]

Blue Raddle: Compact and often busy sidestreet local with small menu of good value lunchtime food, well kept Greene King Abbot, Otter and two changing guest beers; maybe quiet piped jazz, can get busy *(the Didler, Simon House, John and Joan Nash)*

Junction [Gt Western Rd]: Much modernised

Eldridge Pope pub opp brewery, well kept Hardy Country, Popes and Royal Oak, unpretentious but interesting lunchtime food, smiling service; evening piped pop music may be loud; children allowed in skittle alley; well equipped bedrooms around courtyard *(Michel Hooper-Immins)*

☆ *Kings Arms* [High East St]: Hotel bar with comfortable armchairs, well kept Bass, Courage Directors, Flowers Original and Tetleys, decent wines (and large glasses really are large here), well presented food from sandwiches up, pleasant helpful service, open fire; close associations with Nelson and Hardy's *Mayor of Casterbridge*; bedrooms (the Lawrence of Arabia suite and the Tutenkhamen have to be seen to be believed) *(Greg Kilminster, John and Joan Nash, Gordon, LYM, John Hackett, Chris and Marianna Webb, B and K Hypher, the Didler, Chris and Ann Garnett, JP, PP, Colin and Janet Roe)*

Little Ship [High West St]: Unspoilt low-beamed down-to-earth local with Hardy ales, good value simple food, small back garden *(Joan and Michel Hooper-Immins)*

Old Ship [High West St]: Unspoilt low-ceilinged local, warm and cosy, with generous cheap food, well kept Hardy Country and Royal Oak, back dining room, friendly staff *(Chris and Marianna Webb)*

Royal Oak [High West St]: Comfortable two-level bar with well kept Hardy Country and Royal Oak, plentiful hot food esp steaks and Sun carvery, very friendly service; quiet piped music, back games room; bedrooms *(Michel Hooper-Immins)*

Station Masters House [Weymouth Ave, by Dorchester Sth Stn]: Spacious open-plan railway-theme pub with friendly service, well kept Hardy ales, full range straight from the handsome adjacent brewery; plush Victorian-style décor, courteous young staff, generous sensibly priced weekday food from filled warm baguettes and baked potatoes up; games area with darts, fruit machines and pool tables, quiet piped music; open all day Weds-Sat, busy Weds (market opp) *(Pat and Tony Martin, John and Joan Nash, Galen Strawson)*

Tom Browns [High East St]: Small basic and friendly town local with back microbrewery producing two or three well kept beers, lunchtime sandwiches, juke box *(Pat and Tony Martin)*

☆ *Trumpet Major* [A352 towards Wareham, just off bypass]: Bright and airy big-windowed modern lounge bar, empasis on food inc good help-yourself salad bar, vegetarian and children's helpings, speciality apple cake, peaceful conservatory restaurant, well kept Hardy Country and Royal Oak and a guest such as Bass, good choice of wines by the glass; handy for Max Gate (Thomas Hardy's house, now open to the public); garden, children welcome, very busy lunchtime *(Joan and Michel Hooper-Immins)*

East Lulworth [SY8581]

☆ *Weld Arms* [B3070 SW of Wareham]: Friendly, vivacious yet relaxed, with nice mix of individual furnishings, attractive little snug, good interesting food from well filled rolls up inc rabbit and good puddings, Wadworths 6X and Worthington, good service; faint piped music; tables out in big garden, good value bedrooms *(LYM, Keith and Janet Morris, PP and J Salmon, Paul S McPherson)*

East Stour [ST7922]

☆ *Kings Arms* [B3095, 3 miles W towards Shaftesbury]: Large bar with good eating area, good value fresh home-made food inc interesting specials and good puddings, wide range of well kept ales inc Bass, decent wines, good friendly service, local paintings and drawings, model railway locomotive collection, no piped music; public bar with darts and fruit machine, children welcome; lots of flowers in front, tables in big garden *(K H Frostick)*

Farnham [ST9515]

☆ *Museum Hotel* [signed off A354 Blandford Forum—Salisbury]: Wide changing range of well prepared and presented good food, attractive bar with inglenook and piped classical music, well kept Wadworths 6X and changing guests such as Butcombe, Fullers London Pride and Hook Norton, good choice of malt whiskies and wines, pretty dining conservatory, public bar with darts, pool, juke box; sheltered terrace, garden with swings and play tractor; service could sometimes be more obliging; bedrooms in former stables, pretty village with good walks (esp northwards) *(LYM, M J Daly, Stephen, Julie and Hayley Brown, Susan and Nigel Wilson, Brian Skelcher, Gwen and Peter Andrews, Pamela Turner, Phyl and Jack Street, Simon Williams, Roger White, Michael Hill, Ian Phillips)*

Ferndown [SU0700]

Old Thatch [Wimborne Rd, Uddens Cross (old A31)]: Much restored and extended pub/restaurant with plenty of thatch, beams and boards, nice secluded seating out at the back surrounded by woods, generous well cooked food inc fresh veg all day, well kept beers, decent wines inc interesting bin ends, pleasant helpful service, open fires, no-smoking area *(S H Godsell, John and Vivienne Rice, Michael Brookes, WHBM)*

Pure Drop [Wimborne Rd E]: Large Hardy Country pub (though not in fact the Pure Drop in *Tess of the D'Urbervilles* – that was the Crown at Marnhull), warm and friendly, with Hardy beers kept well, consistently good food, sizeable restaurant, good wines *(F Mundy)*

Fiddleford [ST8013]

☆ *Fiddleford Inn* [A357 Sturminster Newton—Blandford Forum]: Comfortable and spacious refurbished pub, ancient flagstones and some other nice touches, well kept Scottish Courage ales, friendly service, good quickly served food from sandwiches up in lounge bar, restaurant area and back family area, unobtrusive piped music; big garden with play area *(James House, LYM, Pat and Robert Watt, G Neighbour)*

Gussage All Saints [SU0010]

☆ *Drovers*: Sturdily furnished country dining pub with peaceful views, friendly staff, good freshly prepared food (so may be a wait) inc vegetarian and fresh veg, well kept Marstons Pedigree, Ringwood and Wadworths 6X, country wines, children in eating area; tables out on terrace, good play area, good walks *(LYM, B and K Hypher)*

Horton [SU0207]

Horton Inn [B3078 Wimborne—Cranborne]: Good range of well priced food inc popular Sun lunch in spaciously renovated bar and restaurant, well kept Courage Directors and Ringwood Best, friendly staff; dogs allowed on lead; tables in garden with good terrace, bedrooms *(Stephen and Jean Curtis)*

Hurn [SZ1497]

Avon Causeway [village signed off A338, then follow Avon, Sopley, Mutchams sign]: Roomy, civilised and comfortable, with partitioned areas inc no smoking, well kept Wadworths beers and guests such as Gales HSB, Highgate Old, Ringwood Old Thumper and Woodfordes Norfolk Nog, good range of bar food, good choice of wines and spirits, interesting railway decorations, good disabled access; Pullman-coach restaurant by former 1870s station platform; piped music, jazz Tues, open all day; sizeable bedrooms *(G Coates, D Marsh, Mr and Mrs A P Reeves, LYM)*

Little Canford [SZ0499]

Fox & Hounds [Fox Lane, off A31 Wimborne—Ferndown]: Extended thatched country pub under new management, big comfortable eating areas inc no smoking, wide choice of reasonably priced food, Whitbreads-related ales, good staff; spacious lawns with summer barbecues and pig roasts, good play area, pleasant walks *(Mr and Mrs A P Reeves)*

Longham [SZ0698]

☆ *Angel* [A348 Ferndown—Poole]: Spacious but cosy beamed roadside pub (big car park, can get very busy) with wide choice of food from sandwiches to steaks inc children's dishes, friendly prompt service, well kept Badger Best and Tanglefoot, unobtrusive piped music; separate children's room, big garden with lots of play facilities inc bouncy castle *(John and Vivienne Rice)*

☆ *White Hart* [A348 Ferndown—Poole]: Small traditional pub with pine furniture, quickly fills lunchtime for good food from sandwiches and baked potatoes up inc bargain midweek roasts with veg cooked to perfection, delicious puddings; well kept Badger Best and Tanglefoot with an interesting guest beer, friendly staff, bright log fire, old tools and newspapers, roomier dining room planned; soft piped music, dogs allowed *(Aleister Martin)*

Lower Burton [SY6894]

Sun [Old Sherborne Rd]: Comfortable 17th-c beamed dining pub well decorated with lots of pictures, wide choice of well kept ales, decent wines, good home-made food inc vegetarian, quick service, big well kept enclosed garden with limited play area, front terrace with summer live bands and good barbecues *(Simon House, Chris Reeve)*

Lyme Regis [SY3492]

Cobb Arms [Marine Parade, Monmouth Beach]: Spaciously refurbished and busy, under same management as Pilot Boat; interesting ship pictures, wide range of reasonably priced bar food, quick service even when busy, good value cream teas, well kept Palmers; next to harbour, beach and coastal walk, bedrooms *(David Lamb)*

☆ *Royal Standard* [Marine Parade, The Cobb]: Right on broadest part of beach, with suntrap courtyard (own servery and wendy house); bar serving area dominated by pool table and piped pop, but has some fine built-in stripped high settles, and there's a quieter no-smoking area with stripped brick and pine; well kept Palmers beers, good value food inc sensibly priced sandwiches, plenty of local crab and fish, good cream teas, darts; three bedrooms *(Pat and Tony Martin, Comus Elliott, BB)*

Victoria [Uplyme Rd]: Good value food in bar and restaurant, friendly owners *(D J and J Pilgrim)*

Volunteer [top of Broad St (A3052 towards Exeter)]: Unpretentious pub with wide food range inc lots of modestly priced fresh fish in cosy low-ceilinged bar and separate eating area *(Dr and Mrs R E S Tanner, LYM)*

Manston [ST8115]

Plough [B3091 Shaftesbury—Sturminster Newton, just N]: Richly decorated plasterwork, ceilings and bar front, quick helpful welcoming service, well kept changing ales such as Black Sheep, Butcombe and the hefty Clipper, good value food from sandwiches up inc vegetarian dishes; tables in garden, cl Sun evening *(Michael Hill, Pat and Robert Watt)*

Marnhull [ST7718]

☆ *Crown* [about 3 miles N of Sturminster Newton]: Part-thatched 17th-c inn with oak beams, huge flagstones, old settles and elm tables, window seats cut into thick stone walls, and logs burning in big stone hearth; small more modern lounge, friendly service, reasonably priced bar food inc good thick sandwiches, Badger Best and Tanglefoot, skittle alley and pub games, maybe piped music; restaurant, tables in peaceful enclosed garden, children welcome; good value bedrooms, good breakfast *(Dave Braisted, E A George, LYM)*

Martinstown [SY6488]

Brewers Arms: Friendly well kept and sensibly extended village pub, quite large, with good valuef food prepared to order inc well filled baguettes, vegetarian and even vegan, Flowers tapped from the cask, tables outside with barbecue area *(B and K Hypher, Dr G J Richards, Marjorie and David Lamb)*

Melplash [SY4898]

Half Moon [A3066 Bridport—Beaminster]: Transformed by current licensees, wide choice of well presented food, cheerful service, good choice of wines *(Galen Strawson)*

Milton Abbas [ST8001]

☆ *Hambro Arms* [signed off A354 SW of Blandford]: In beautiful late 18th-c thatched landscaped village, beams, bow window and good log fire, well kept Bass, Boddingtons and Tetleys, good generous food from sandwiches to steak inc fresh fish and some successfully inventive if not cheap dishes; darts in cosy back public bar, children in restaurant, tables out on terrace, comfortable bedrooms *(LYM, Richard and Maria Gillespie, Geoffrey Lawrance, NMF, DF, Lynda Katz)*

Moreton [SY7889]

Frampton Arms [B3390 nr stn]: Quiet, relaxed and very neatly kept, with good choice of good value food from sandwiches up inc good fish and seafood, Boddingtons and Flowers IPA, log fire, friendly landlord, steam railway pictures in lounge bar, Warmwell Aerodrome theme in public bar, bright and airy conservatory restaurant; comfortable bedrooms *(J S M Sheldon, Joan and Michel Hooper-Immins, F and A Parmenter)*

Mosterton [ST4505]

Admiral Hood [A3066 S of Crewkerne]: Civilised and popular dining pub with neatly furnished spacious L-shaped bar, well kept Courage-related ales, coal fire in handsome stone fireplace, quick welcoming service, simple skittle alley behind the thatched 18th-c stone building *(Michael Sargent, BB)*

Mudeford [SZ1892]

☆ *Ship in Distress*: Dining pub very popular for good fresh carefully cooked fish and seafood in restaurant (best to book) and bar – two rooms, one plain, one with hops, plants and nautical memorabilia; well kept Bass, Greenalls Original, Marstons Pedigree and Ringwood Best, good friendly service, cosy atmosphere *(John and Vivienne Rice, W Burke, D Marsh, John and Kathleen Potter, Nigel Flook, Betsy Brown)*

Norden Heath [SY9483]

☆ *Halfway* [A351 Wareham—Corfe Castle]: Thatched pub with Badger beers, pitched-ceiling back serving bar where the locals congregate, front rooms with flagstones, log fires, stripped stonework, snug little side area, picnic-sets outside with play area; can be quite a wait for the food; open all day *(David and Carole Chapman, BB, John and Joan Nash, Mr and Mrs Sweeney)*

North Wootton [ST6514]

Three Elms [A3030 SE of Sherborne]: Lively and welcoming, with enormous collection of Matchbox and other model cars and other vehicles, half a dozen well kept ales inc Fullers London Pride, Shepherd Neame Spitfire and an Ash Vine beer brewed for the pub, cheerful landlord, food from sandwiches up; seaside postcard collection in gents'; three comfortable bedrooms, shared bathrooms, good breakfast, big garden *(B J Shepard, Michael and Hazel Lyons)*

Piddletrenthide [SY7099]

European: Friendly and unpretentious traditional old oak-beamed pub locally popular for good generous reasonably priced food inc fine home-cooked ham; three well kept changing beers such as Fullers London Pride, log fire, willow-pattern china, stylish chairs; three bedrooms with own baths and good views *(Marianne and Peter Stevens, R G Glover, Richard Green)*

☆ *Piddle* [B3143 N of Dorchester]: Village and pub named after the river here, lots of chamber-pots hanging from ceiling, friendly atmosphere,

good food, real ale, children's room and pool room; spacious streamside garden with picnic-sets and play area; recently taken over by landlord who did so well at the Smugglers, Osmington Mills *(News please)*

☆ *Poachers* [B3143 N of Dorchester]: Welcoming family service, well kept Courage Best, Theakstons Best and Websters, generous tasty food, good atmosphere in recently extended bar, good value restaurant; piped music, good upstairs skittle alley, dogs welcome; garden with stream at bottom, comfortable good value chalet-style bedrooms around outside pool *(Martin and Caroline Page, Mark Seymour, Jackie Roberts, George Atkinson)*

Poole [SZ0190]

Brewhouse [High St]: Worth knowing as the home of Poole beer *(Roger and Jenny Huggins)*

☆ *Inn in the Park* [off A338 on edge of Poole, towards Branksome Chine – via The Avenue]: Pleasantly decorated and cheerful small hotel bar with well kept Adnams Broadside, Bass and Wadworths 6X, good value generous bar food (not Sun evening) from good sandwiches up, polite young staff, attractive dining room (children allowed), log fire, tables on small sunny terrace; comfortable bedrooms, quiet pine-filled residential area above sea *(Jill Bickerton, John and Vivienne Rice, LYM, JDM, KM)*

Shah of Persia [Longfleet Rd/Fernside Rd (A35)]: Spacious comfortably refurbished roadhouse, well kept Hardy Country, Popes and Royal Oak with a guest beer, wide choice of generous food inc vegetarian and outstanding mixed grill (occasional half-price bargains), big no-smoking area, friendly speedy service and pleasant atmosphere; quiet piped music *(B and K Hypher, Mr and Mrs A P Reeves, Joan and Michel Hooper-Immins)*

Portland [SY6971]

Mermaid [Wakeham]: Good food in pleasant newish back restaurant, light and clean; very friendly licensees *(Mr and Mrs T J Fincken)*

Sandford Orcas [ST6220]

☆ *Mitre* [off B3148 and B3145 N of Sherborne]: Good value attractively presented food (soups, puddings and steak and kidney pie praised by many) in tucked-away country local's opened-up dining area; flagstones and fresh flowers throughout, small bar with three changing well kept ales, country wines, welcoming service, two friendly dogs (not around when food's being served) *(LYM, Kenneth and June Strickson)*

Shaftesbury [ST8622]

Half Moon [Salisbury Rd (A30, by roundabout)]: Comfortably busy Badger pub with wide choice of well presented fairly priced generous food, quick service; garden with adventure playground *(Marjorie and David Lamb)*

Sherborne [ST6316]

☆ *Cross Keys* [Cheap St]: Comfortable and attractively refurbished local with lots of nooks and crannies, sensible choice of food, quick cheerful service, well kept Hardy Country and Royal Oak; pot plants on each table, interesting display of postal history, postbox in corridor; talking fruit machine; open all day Sun, bowls for dogs, some seats outside *(George Atkinson, Ann and Colin Hunt, Joan and Michel Hooper-Immins)*

Shroton [ST8512]

☆ *Cricketers* [off A350 N of Blandford (village also called Iwerne Courtney)]: Welcoming and popular with locals, visitors and their families, spacious bar with lots of cricket memorabilia, good home-made food inc game, plenty of fish and good puddings, ales such as Bass, Greene King IPA, Smiles and Wadworths 6X, pretty pink and blue restaurant; pool, discreet piped music *(Diana Brumfit, WHBM)*

Southbourne [SZ1591]

Commodore [Overcliff Dr, about 2 miles W of Hengistbury Head]: Clean and comfortably refurbished clifftop chain dining pub, separate areas for children and non-smokers, well kept Whitbreads-related beers, excellent service, good food range, lots of naval memorabilia; small terrace *(P Legon)*

Spetisbury [ST9102]

Drax Arms [A350 SE of Blandford]: Quiet comfortable local with innovative and sensibly priced blackboard food, well kept Badger, charming landlord; pleasant sheltered garden *(Dr D E Granger)*

Stoke Abbott [ST4500]

☆ *New Inn* [off B3162 and B3163 2 miles W of Beaminster]: 17th-c thatched pub with beams, brasses, stripped stone alcoves on either side of one big log fireplace, another with handsome panelling; friendly licensees and poodle, well kept Palmers ales, generous competitively priced food inc vegetarian and fish, no-smoking dining room, well kept attractive garden with play area, nice setting in unspoilt quiet thatched village; children welcome, bedrooms; cl Mon in July/Aug *(Basil Minson, Galen Strawson, Ian and Naomi Lancaster, John and Kay Grugeon, Anthony Barnes, LYM, Mark Matthewman, Chris and Marianna Webb)*

Studland [SZ0382]

☆ *Bankes Arms* [off B3351, Isle of Purbeck]: Very popular spot above fine beach, outstanding country, sea and cliff views from huge pleasant garden; comfortably basic, friendly and easy-going big bar with raised drinking area, substantial decent simple food (at a price) all day inc local fish, well kept beers such as Palmers, Poole, Wadworths 6X and recherché guest beers, attractive log fires, darts and pool in side games area; children welcome, just off Coast Path; can get very busily trippery at weekends and in summer, parking can be complicated or expensive if you're not a NT member; big comfortable bedrooms, has been cl winter *(Simon Williams, David and Carole Chapman, Anthony Barnes, D Marsh, Jeremy Burnside, John and Joan Calvert, P G Bardswell, Philip Vernon, Kim Maidment, IHR, D P and J A Sweeney, W W Burke, Pat and Robert Wyatt, G Coates)*

Sturminster Marshall [SY9499]

Red Lion [High St, opp church; off A350 Blandford—Poole]: Attractive and thriving

flower-decked old pub, open-plan, clean and pleasant inside, with good unusual food inc bargain OAP two-course lunch, friendly licensees, Badger ales, log fire, skittle alley doubling as family room *(Marianne and Peter Stevens, D M Brumfit)*

Sturminster Newton [ST7814]

Bull [A357 just W of bridge]: Low-beamed 16th-c country inn recently carefully refurbished to add character as well as space, with good home cooking from interesting sandwiches up, pleasant landlord, Badger beers, home-made walking sticks for sale; well behaved dogs welcome, pleasant garden *(WHBM)*

Swan [Market Pl]: Wide choice of well cooked and presented food inc good range of affordable specials, polite welcoming service; comfortable bedrooms *(Mrs S J Robson)*

Sutton Poyntz [SY7083]

☆ *Springhead* [off A353 NE of Weymouth]: Greenalls pub in lovely spot opp willow stream in quiet village, entertaining ducks, good play area in big garden, walks to White Horse Hill and Dorset Coastal Path; good quick friendly service, beams, dark décor, comfortable mix of furnishings, log fires, daily papers, well kept ales such as Bass, Flowers IPA and Wadworths 6X, good value wines, good range of malt whiskies, decent choice of freshly made food (not cheap) in bar and restaurant; bar billiards, well chosen piped music – often jazz; live music Sun lunchtime *(Liz and John Soden, Richard and Jean Phillips, Simon Williams)*

Swanage [SZ0278]

Black Swan [High St]: Small bar with lots of brass, changing real ales, good reasonably priced food *(David and Carole Chapman)*

Red Lion [High St]: Snug two-bar pub, beams densely hung with mugs and keys, lots of blow lamps, decent inexpensive food, well kept Ringwood and Whitbreads, friendly staff; children's annexe, partly covered back terrace *(the Didler, Jeremy Burnside)*

Symondsbury [SY4493]

☆ *Ilchester Arms* [village signposted from A35 just W of Bridport]: Attractive old thatched inn in peaceful village, cosy and welcoming open-plan low-ceilinged bar with high-backed settle built in by big inglenook, cosy no-smoking dining area with another fire, well kept Palmers beers, friendly service; pub games, skittle alley, piped music; tables by pretty brookside back garden; children welcome, good walks nearby *(Chris and Marianna Webb, LYM, Dr and Mrs J H Hills)*

Tarrant Monkton [ST9408]

☆ *Langton Arms* [off A354 Blandford—Salisbury]: 17th-c thatched pub with good range of interesting changing real ales inc ones from local Rington Brewery, beams, settles and inglenook, generous popular bar food, decent wines, no-smoking restaurant, games in public bar, skittle alley doubling as daytime no-smoking family room with play area; garden with another play area, good walks, modern chalet bedrooms *(LYM, Richard and Maria Gillespie, JDM, KM, Stephen, Julie and Hayley*

Brown, David Heath, Ian Phillips, J G Roberts, Dr C C S Wilson, Mr and Mrs A R Hawkins, Tom and Rosemary Hall)

Three Legged Cross [SU0904]

Old Barn Farm [Ringwood Rd]: Large thatched chain family pub with good value usual food, pleasant restaurant, efficient friendly service, Bass and Worthington; lots of seating outside, some children's amusements, enormous dovecote *(P L Jones, Ian Phillips)*

Tolpuddle [SY7994]

Martyrs: Well kept Badger beers, friendly staff, home-made food in bar and busy restaurant, nice garden with ducks, hens and rabbits *(Francis Johnston, KN-R)*

Trent [ST5918]

☆ *Rose & Crown*: Attractively sparse old-fashioned pub with log fire, flagstones, oak settles, nice pictures, fresh flowers, books, no piped music or machines; friendly licensees, well kept ales and wide choice of good food inc vegetarian and very popular Sun lunch; dining conservatory, no music, children and dogs welcome, picnic-sets behind – lovely peaceful surroundings *(Howard Clutterbuck, Mrs D Harwood)*

Uploders [SY5093]

☆ *Crown* [signed off A35 E of Bridport]: Friendly and homely brightly furnished low-beamed village pub, mainly no smoking, festooned with polished bric-a-brac, pictures by local artists, theatrical models; wide choice of simple but inventive good value home cooking (not Sun evening) inc Asian, vegetarian dishes and fine home-made puddings, well kept Palmers, good service, log fires, table skittles; tables in attractive two-tier garden, bedrooms *(Chris and Marianna Webb, Deborah and Ian Carrington, John and Joan Nash, Galen Strawson, BB, Dr J R Norman, Mrs M E Bell)*

Verwood [SU0808]

Albion [B3081]: Three pleasant rooms in a U shape, simple choice of well cooked food with proper chips, half a dozen well kept ales inc Gibbs Mew; pictures of former nearby railway *(Mr and Mrs T A Bryan)*

Wareham [SY9287]

Black Bear: Bow-windowed 18th-c hotel with old local prints in pleasant bar on right of through corridor, well kept Hardy Country and Royal Oak, good choice of good value food inc vegetarian and children's, decent coffee, back restaurant, picnic-sets in back yard; bedrooms *(J and B Cressey, Joan and Michel Hooper-Immins)*

☆ *Kings Arms* [North Street (A351, N end of town)]: Thriving traditional thatched town local, back serving counter and two bars off flagstoned central corridor, well kept Whitbreads-related ales, good value food (not Fri—Sun evenings), friendly staff; back garden *(LYM, B and K Hypher, R Moorehead)*

☆ *Quay* [South St]: Comfortable, light and airy stripped-stone bars, bar food from soup and sandwiches up, open fire, well kept Whitbreads-related and other ales, friendly staff, children allowed away from main bar; picnic-sets out on quay; parking nearby can be

difficult *(Anthony Barnes, Jeremy Burnside)*

Waytown [SY4697]

Hare & Hounds [between B3162 and A3066 N of Bridport]: Simply furnished traditional 17th-c pub, two rooms and dining room, good value well presented food inc OAP bargains, well kept Palmers tapped from the cask, helpful friendly service, simple garden with good play area *(Chris and Marianna Webb, R Shelton)*

West Bay [SY4590]

Bridport Arms: Thatched pub – recently filmed as the Bridehaven pub in *Harbour Lights* – on beach of Bridport's low-key holiday village, generous good value food esp fish, pleasant landlord, well kept Palmers BB, big fireplace in basic flagstoned back bar, no music *(Mr and Mrs J E Lockwood, P Legun)*

West Bexington [SY5387]

☆ *Manor Hotel* [signed off B3157 SE of Bridport]: Relaxing old stone hotel a short stroll from the sea, play area in sheltered garden outside bustling downstairs beamed cellar bar with log fire, smart no-smoking Victorian-style conservatory, good if not cheap bar food, well kept Hardy Country and Royal Oak, Smiles and Wadworths 6X, quite a few malt whiskies and several wines by the glass; children and dogs allowed, open all day, comfortable bedrooms *(LYM, Galen Strawson, Basil Minson, John and Vivienne Rice, Stephen, Julie and Hayley Brown, Kevin Thorpe, Roger Byrne, Chris Reeve, KC, James House)*

West Knighton [SY7387]

☆ *New Inn* [off A352 E of Dorchester]: Biggish neatly refurbished pub, very busy in summer, with interesting range of reasonably priced food, small restaurant, quick friendly staff, real ales, country wines, skittle alley, good provision for children; big colourful garden, pleasant setting in quiet village with wonderful views *(Geoffrey Lawrance)*

West Lulworth [SY8280]

☆ *Castle* [B3070 SW of Wareham]: Pretty thatched inn in lovely spot nr Lulworth Cove, good walks; flagstoned bar bustling with summer visitors, maze of booth seating, usual food inc children's, well kept Flowers Original and Marstons Pedigree, decent house wines, farm cider, piped music (may be loud), video and board games; cosy more modern-feeling lounge bar, helpful landlord, pleasant dining room, splendid ladies', popular garden with giant chess boards, boules, barbecues *(Mr and Mrs S Turner, LYM, P G Bardswell, David and Carole Chapman, Galen Strawson, Gordon)*

West Moors [SU0802]

Fryers Arms [Pinehurst Rd]: Very friendly Badger pub with good home-made food inc good specials such as chicken fillet on sautéed leeks or whiskied pheasant (must be booked Mon-Thurs), children eat free if adults eating; dogs welcome *(Rev J Hibberd, WHBM)*

West Stafford [SY7289]

☆ *Wise Man* [signed off A352 Dorchester—Wareham]: Comfortable 16th-c local nr Hardy's cottage, very busy in summer; thatch, beams and toby jugs, with wide choice of good value generous standard food (not Sun evening) inc fish from Poole, happy staff, well kept Greenalls, decent wines and country wines; piped light classics, public bar with darts; children not encouraged *(Geoffrey Lawrance, Howard Clutterbuck)*

Weymouth [SY6778]

Dorothy [Esplanade]: New bare-boards pub (and nightclub) in outstanding seafront spot, great views from outside tables; enthusiastic landlord keeps local Quay Dorothy, Old Rott and Summer Knight, also Cotleigh Tawny and Exmoor Gold, good value straightforward food inc crab sandwiches *(Joan and Michel Hooper-Immins)*

Dorset Brewers [Hope Sq]: Well kept beers such as Badger and local Quay and Summer Knight, quickly served simple meals from doorstep sandwiches up, bare boards, fishing stuff all over the ceiling, family atmosphere; plenty of tables outside, opp smart touristy Brewers Quay complex in former brewery *(Keith and Janet Morris, Joan and Michel Hooper-Immins, the Didler)*

George [Commercial Rd]: Sympathetically modernised and extended quayside pub, Badger Best and Tanglefoot, tasty good value bar food; bright with piped music etc in the evening *(Jean and Michel Hooper-Immins)*

Kings Arms [Trinity Rd]: Popular and friendly two-bar quayside pub, one local and lively, one more comfortable; well kept beer, considerable character *(P G Bardswell, the Didler)*

Lodmoor [A354, by Lodmoor Country Park]: New Brewers Fayre family pub, usual standards of service and food, by leisure park with plenty of family attractions *(S P Bobeldijk)*

Wimborne St Giles [SU0212]

Bull [off B3078 N of Wimborne]: Imaginative food inc fish fresh daily from Cornwall and vegan dishes in comfortable red-carpeted bar of converted private house, well kept Badger ales, farm cider; small pleasant garden *(G Washington, WHBM)*

Winkton [SZ1696]

Lamb [Bockhampton Rd, Holfleet; via Burley Rd, off B3347 Christchurch—Salisbury]: Popular country pub with good-sized helpings of nicely presented food in bar and restaurant, pleasant décor, good friendly service, well kept real ales; good garden for children with play area, nice setting *(DWAJ)*

Wool [SY8486]

Ship [Dorchester Rd]: Good reasonably priced food, friendly quick service *(anon)*

Post Office address codings confusingly give the impression that some pubs are in Dorset, when they're really in Somerset (which is where we list them).

Essex

A good variety of pubs here, with unchanged gems such as the Square & Compasses at Fuller Street or the Viper at Mill Green; pubs excelling in the range or quality of the beers they keep, such as the Hoop at Stock or the Prince of Wales at Stow Maries; pubs going out of their way to stock attractive wines – the Green Man at Toot Hill excels here; or pubs where the food is a main attraction, whether it's fish and chips at the Swan at Chappel (a pub that's doing really well all round these days) or the Jolly Sailor at Heybridge Basin, or more of a special meal out at the Green Man at Gosfield or the White Hart at Great Yeldham. This last pub really does give a sense of occasion: the White Hart at Great Yeldham is our Essex Dining Pub of the Year. Among a lot of changes here are new licensees at the charming little Flitch of Bacon at Little Dunmow and the Jolly Sailor at Heybridge Basin, a new chef at the Black Bull at Fyfield, and two new main entries, the most attractively decorated Crown at Little Walden, and the quietly welcoming Pheasant at Gestingthorpe – both doing enjoyable food. Other pubs currently gaining particularly warm reports from readers include the Bell at Castle Hedingham, the Sun at Feering, the Square & Compasses at Fuller Street and the bustling Rainbow & Dove at Hastingwood. Essex drinks prices are perhaps a shade higher than the national average, with the regional brewer Greene King rather dominating the beer scene, though beers from Ridleys and Crouch Vale are quite widely available here too. Some pubs to note particularly in the Lucky Dip section at the end of the chapter are the Queens Head in Boreham, Cricketers at Clavering, White Hart in Coggeshall, Three Horseshoes at Duton Hill, Cock in Hatfield Broad Oak, Sutton Arms at Little Hallingbury, Dog & Gun at Little Waltham, Station Buffet (yes, a real one) in Manningtree, Rose at Peldon, Bell at Purleigh, George at Shalford, Bell at Tolleshunt Major, Volunteer near Waltham Abbey, Black Buoy at Wivenhoe and (particularly good food) Royal Oak at Woodham Mortimer.

ARKESDEN TL4834 Map 5
Axe & Compasses ★ ♀

Village signposted from B1038 – but B1039 from Wendens Ambo, then forking left, is prettier

Rambling thatched country pub with a relaxed and cosy atmosphere, in one of the prettiest villages in the county. The carpeted lounge bar dating back to the 17th c is the oldest part with beautifully polished upholstered oak and elm seats, easy chairs and wooden tables, as well as a warm fire, lots of beautifully polished brasses on the walls, and a friendly well behaved cat called Spikey. There are darts and cribbage in the smaller quirky uncarpeted public bar, with cosy built-in settles. Bar food might include home-made soup (£2), sandwiches (from £2.50), grilled sardines (£3.50), deep-fried mushrooms with garlic dip (£3.95), home-made steak and kidney pie or chicken, leek and bacon crumble (£6.75), vegetarian cannelloni or pork loin with a stilton and mushroom sauce (£7.25), grilled sirloin steak (£9.50) and monkfish cooked on roasted pepper sauce (£10.95); impressive pudding trolly (£3); more elaborate restaurant menu, helpful and friendly service. Well kept Greene King IPA, Abbott and Triumph on handpump, a very good wine list and over 20 malt whiskies. There are seats outside on a side terrace with pretty hanging baskets; parking at the back. *(Recommended by A E Brace, A and M Marriott, George Little, Tony Beaulah, Tina and David Woods-Taylor, Richard Siebert)*

Greene King ~ Lease: Themis and Diane Christou ~ Real ale ~ Bar food ~ Restaurant ~ (01799) 550272 ~ Children in restaurant till 8.30pm ~ Open 11.30-2.30, 6-11; 12-3, 7-10.30 Sun; closed 25 Dec

BLACKMORE END TL7430 Map 5
Bull 🍴 ♈

Signposted via Beazley End from Bocking Church Street, itself signed off A131 just N of Braintree bypass; pub is on Wethersfield side of village

The enjoyable specials menu continues to draw people to this clean comfortable dining pub, now owned by Balls Brothers, the London based wine merchants – the new licensee is part of the clan himself. There's a good range of sandwiches (from £3.25, french sticks £3.75), and ploughman's (£4.75), and neatly written up on blackboards every four weeks or so, specials might include soup (£2.95), sweet-cured herrings on an apple, celery and walnut salad (£4.25), pan-fried lamb's liver and bacon (£7.95) chicken supreme in red wine sauce with shallots and herbs (£8.50), duck breast in a jus with a black cherry and kirsch compote (£10.95), mignons of fillet steak with stilton and port sauce (£11.95), and pork tenderloin in an apricot and kummel sauce with dried fruit and fresh orange stuffing (£12.50), all served in generous helpings with fresh vegetables in separate dishes. There are lots of tempting home-made puddings such as bread pudding with rum, whipped cream and toasted nuts, crushed meringue with fruit compote sundae and chocolate nut sundae (£3.50); from Tuesday to Saturday there are two- or three-course set lunches (£8.95 or £10.95, three-course Sunday lunch £10.95), and smaller helpings are offered at lower prices; friendly attentive staff. The flowery-carpeted dining bar has red plush built-in button-back banquettes, low black beams and lots of menu blackboards; maybe piped music. Beyond a massive brick chimneypiece is a pretty cosy cottagey restaurant area. Well kept Adnams, Greene King IPA, Mauldons White Adder and changing guest ales on handpump, extensive wine list with five or six wines by the glass; picnic-sets outside. *(Recommended by Tony Beaulah, Gwen and Peter Andrews, Richard Siebert, Richard and Robyn Wain, Paul and Sandra Embleton, B N F and M Parkin, Peter and Gwen Andrews, Adrian White)*

Free house ~ Licensee Geoffrey Balls ~ Real ale ~ Bar food ~ Restaurant ~ (01371) 851037 ~ Children in restaurant ~ Open 12-3, 6.30-11; 12-2.30, 7-10.30 Sun; closed Mon except bank holidays

BURNHAM ON CROUCH TQ9596 Map 5
White Harte £

The Quay

Some readers think this hearty old inn with its own private jetty and wonderful outlook over the yachting estuary of the River Crouch is at its most welcoming in winter when an enormous log fire burns in the bar. Popular with boaty types, it has a genuinely nautical atmosphere, and the decor in the partially carpeted bars reflects this: there are replicas of Royal Navy ships, a ship's wheel, a barometer, and a compass in the hearth; comfortably cushioned seats around oak tables. Other traditionally furnished, high-ceilinged rooms have sea pictures decorating the panelled or stripped brick walls. Straightforward but attractively priced bar food includes steak and kidney pie, barbecued pork, lasagne or toad in the hole (£4.80), pan-fried locally caught skate, plaice or cod (£6.80) and hot puddings such as jam sponge and stuffed apples (£2). Well kept Adnams, Crouch Vale Best and Tolly Cobbold Bitter on handpump; friendly service. The lively border collie is called Tilly. *(Recommended by Nigel and Olga Wikeley, John Wilmott, Gwen and Peter Andrews, A F Keary)*

Free house ~ Licensee G John Lewis ~ Real ale ~ Bar food ~ Restaurant ~ (01621) 782106 ~ Children in eating area of bar ~ Open 11-11; 12-10.30 Sun ~ Bedrooms: £38B/£55B

Post Office address codings confusingly give the impression that some pubs are in Suffolk, when they're really in Essex (which is where we list them).

CASTLE HEDINGHAM TL7835 Map 5
Bell

B1058 E of Sible Hedingham, towards Sudbury

Now in her fourth decade of running this historic old coaching inn, Sandra
Ferguson gives a welcome to visitors as warm as always, and her jolly character and
pleasant staff continue to sustain the pub's friendly convivial atmosphere. The
unchanging beamed and timbered saloon bar has Jacobean-style seats and windsor
chairs around sturdy oak tables, and beyond the standing timbers left from a
knocked-through wall, some steps lead up to an unusual little gallery. Behind the
traditionally furnished public bar, a games room has dominoes and cribbage. One
bar is no smoking, and each of the rooms has a good welcoming log fire; piped
music. Well liked bar food from a fixed menu includes tomato soup (£2.20), lamb
or beefburger (£3), ploughman's (£3.70), half pint of smoked prawns (£4), green-
lipped mussels (£4.50), chicken or vegetarian kebabs, steak and Guinness pie, or
Thai chicken curry (£6), salmon steak (£6.70), rainbow trout (£7), sirloin steak
(£8), and a few daily specials such as calamari (£4.50), ratatouille with garlic
yoghurt, warm bread and salad (£5.50) and citrus lamb casserole (£6.50); puddings
such as blackberry and apple crumble or banoffee pie (from £2.50); possibly no
food on Sunday evenings in winter. Greene King IPA and Abbot, Shepherd Neame
Spitfire and a guest beer tapped from the cask. The big walled garden behind the
pub – an acre or so of grass, trees and shrubs – is a pleasant place to sit in summer,
and there are more seats on a small terrace; Sunday evening quiz. The nearby 12th-c
castle keep is worth a visit. (Recommended by Richard and Valerie Wright, Paul and Sandra
Embleton, Lucie Miell, Gwen and Peter Andrews, G Neighbour, Ronald G Dodsworth)

Grays (Greene King, Ridleys) ~ Tenant Mrs Sandra Ferguson ~ Real ale ~ Bar food (till
10 Mon-Sat, no food Mon evenings) ~ (01787) 460350 ~ Children away from public
bar ~ Traditional jazz last Sun of month, acoustic guitar group Fri evening, bank hol
Sun evening ~ Open 11.30-3(3.30 Sat), 6-11; 12-3.30, 7-10.30 Sun; closed 25 Dec

CHAPPEL TL8927 Map 5
Swan

Wakes Colne; pub visible just off A1124 Colchester—Halstead

There's a warm welcome from the chatty attentive landlord at this fabulously set
timbered pub, parts of which date back to 1390. The River Colne runs through the
garden and on down to a splendid Victorian viaduct below, and gas heaters now
extend the use beyond summer of a sheltered suntrap cobbled courtyard, whose
parasols, big overflowing flower tubs and French street signs lend it a continental
feel. The spacious and low-beamed rambling bar has standing oak timbers dividing
off side areas, banquettes around lots of dark tables, one or two swan pictures and
plates on the white and partly panelled walls, and a few attractive tiles above the
very big fireplace which is filled with lots of plants in summer. Fresh fish is the
speciality here – one reader deems it the best place for fish and chips in Essex – and
as well as specials there might be rock eel (£5.45, large £7.45), plaice (£5.95, large
£7.95), haddock (£6.25, large £8.50) and trout grilled with almonds (£6.45). Other
good value and popular bar food (same price as last year) includes filled french rolls
or sandwiches (from £1.60, well liked rare roast beef £2.95), ploughman's (from
£3.50), home-made chicken and mushroom pie or gammon with pineapple (£4.95),
pork chops (£5.25, large £7.50), sirloin steak (£9.95), and good puddings (from
£2.50); simple children's menu; no-smoking area in restaurant. Well kept Greene
King IPA and Abbot and Mauldons on handpump, a good selection of wines by the
glass and just under two dozen malt whiskies served by cheery helpful staff;
cribbage. The nearby Railway Centre (a must for train buffs) is just a few minutes'
walk away. (Recommended by Gwen and Peter Andrews, Colin and Dot Savill, Ian Phillips, Dr
Oscar Puls, Margaret and Bill Rogers, Anthony Barnes, Nigel and Olga Wikeley, B N F and M
Parkin, Paul and Sandra Embleton, Malcolm and Jennifer Perry)

Free house ~ Licensees Terence Martin and Mark Hubbard ~ Real ale ~ Bar food (till
10.30pm) ~ Restaurant ~ (01787) 222353 ~ Children in eating area of bar ~ Open 11-
3, 6-11; 11-11 Sat; 12-3, 7-10.30 Sun

COGGESHALL TL8224 Map 5
Compasses

Pattiswick; signposted from A120 about 2 miles W of Coggeshall

There's a pleasant atmosphere in this neatly kept and spaciously attractive remote country pub with friendly welcoming staff and good straightforward bar food. The comfortable beamed bars have tiled floors and lots of brass ornaments. Greene King IPA, Abbot and Triumph on handpump under light blanket pressure; piped music. Generous helpings of home-made bar food such as sandwiches and filled baguettes (from £3.85), filled baked potatoes (from £4.95), ploughman's (£5.95), turkey curry or tagliatelle carbonara (£6.95), breaded plaice goujons or ham and eggs (£7.50), toad in the hole, scampi or steak and kidney pie (£8.95) and a good range of puddings including treacle sponge, coffee and chocolate cheesecake or apple flan (£3.25-£4.50). More elaborate dishes are served in the adjacent barn restaurant. Outside there are seats on the lawns, and an adventure playground. *(Recommended by Tony Beaulah, Peter Meister, Richard Siebert, Joan and Andrew Life, Richard and Robyn Wain, G Neighbour, A Hepburn, S Jenner, Ronald G Dodsworth)*

Free house ~ Licensees Chris and Gilbert Heap ~ Real ale ~ Bar food ~ Restaurant ~ (01376) 561322 ~ Children in eating area of bar ~ Open 11-3, 6.30-11; 11-3, 7-10.30 Sun

DEDHAM TM0533 Map 5
Marlborough Head 🛏

Mill Lane

This lovely old timbered pub in the heart of Constable's old town, having served as the local wool hall, and housed wool merchants and clothiers from the 15th to the late 17th c, gained its name and new status as an alehouse in 1704, the year in which the Duke of Marlborough conquered the French at the battle of Blenheim. Nowadays, its popularity with diners means that it's not a place to come to for a quiet drink: be warned, it can get very busy at weekends. The lovely central lounge has lots of beams and pictures, a wealth of finely carved woodwork, and a couple of roaring log fires. The beamed and timbered bar is set out for eating with lots of tables in wooden alcoves around its plum-coloured carpet. Bar food includes soup (£2.95), sandwiches (from £3.25), avocado filled with prawns (£3.95), deep-fried brie (£4.45), spicy vegetable casserole (£7.75), rabbit in mustard and anise sauce or paella (£8.95), beef stew (£9.45), chicken breast with prawns and lobster sauce or shank of lamb (£9.95), fillet steak with stilton (£11.95) half roast duckling in orange and cointreau sauce (£12.95), and specials such as halibut steak in lemon and dill sauce (£7.50) or shin of veal (£8.95). Adnams, Greene King IPA and Marstons Pedigree on handpump; young attentive staff; no-smoking family room; piped music. Seats on the terrace and in the garden at the back; very comfortable bedrooms. *(Recommended by Joan and Andrew Life, Anthony Barnes, Malcolm and Liz Holliday, Gwen and Peter Andrews, Ian Phillips, Jenny and Brian Seller, Chris and Ann Garnett, Janet and Colin Roe, J and P Maloney)*

Free house ~ Licensee Angela Coulwill ~ Real ale ~ Bar food ~ Restaurant ~ (01206) 323250 ~ Children in restaurant ~ Open 11-3, 6-11; 11-11 Sat; 12-10.30 Sun ~ Bedrooms: £45B/£55B

FEERING TL8720 Map 5
Sun 🍺

3 Feering Hill; before Feering proper, B1024 just NE of Kelvedon

This friendly gabled old inn, run by chatty licensees, was originally part of a 16th-c mansion. Good home cooking, well kept beer and a pleasant atmosphere ensure that it remains a favourite with readers. Standing timbers break up the several areas of the low-beamed bar which has plenty of neatly matching tables and chairs, and green-cushioned stools and banquettes around the walls. Carvings on the beams in the lounge are said to be linked with Catherine of Aragon, and there's a handsome canopy with a sun motif over the woodburning stove; newspapers, backgammon, cribbage, dominoes, fruit machine and piped music. Five very well kept real ales change virtually daily, with up to 20 different brews passing through the handpumps each week such as Adnams Best, Crouch Vale IPA, Exmoor Hart, Mighty Oak Burntwood Bitter and Nethergate Augustinian, also one or two weekly changing farm ciders, and 45 malt whiskies. Their Easter and August bank holiday beer festivals have a regional theme, when they'll stock ales from a particular county or area. The very big choice of enjoyable bar meals, written up on blackboards over the fireplace, includes sandwiches (from £1.55), home-made curried parsnip soup (£2.20), baked eggs in cheese sauce (£3.40), breaded plaice (£4.20), ploughman's (from £4.25), steak and kidney pudding or rabbit in red wine and caper sauce (£5.95), braised beef in honey and ginger (£6.20) and chicken and mushrooms in a spicy home-made sauce (£6.50), puddings such as poached pears, filled pancakes or banoffee pie (£2.70); children's menu; friendly and efficient service. On sunny weekends, there may be barbecues on the partly covered paved patio with quite a few seats and tables behind the pub; more tables are in an attractive garden beyond the car park. *(Recommended by Pete Yearsley, Val and Alan Green, Graham Simpson, Eddie Edwards, Ronald G Dodsworth, John Fahy, George Atkinson, Gwen and Peter Andrews, Ian Phillips)*

Free house ~ Licensees Charles and Kim Scicluna ~ Real ale ~ Bar food (12-2, 6-10, not 25-26 Dec and 1 Jan or evenings 24 and 31 Dec) ~ (01376) 570442 ~ Children welcome ~ Open 11-3, 6-11; 12-3, 6-10.30 Sun; closed evenings of 25/26 Dec and 1 Jan

FULLER STREET TL7416 Map 5
Square & Compasses

From A12 Chelmsford—Witham take Hatfield Peverel exit, and from B1137 there follow Terling signpost, keeping straight on past Terling towards Great Leighs; from A131 Chelmsford—Braintree turn off in Great Leighs towards Fairstead and Terling

As we went to press, the refurbishments were still in progress at this cheery civilised little country pub. The friendly landlord told us that the enlargement of the bar, kitchen and car park was nearly finished, and that work on a new private dining room extension (possibly to cater for the shooting parties who frequent the pub), was about to begin. Meanwhile, there is still the pleasant and quietly welcoming atmosphere in the open-plan L-shaped beamed bar, (comfortable and well lit), with a woodburner as well as a big log fire, and understated rural decor – stuffed birds including an albino pheasant above the mantlepiece, traps, old country photographs, brasses; shove-ha'penny, table skittles, cribbage, dominoes and piped music. With the opening of the new kitchen, the wait for the good food (all cooked to order) should decrease. A very extensive menu includes filled rolls and sandwiches (from £1.50), well liked tomato soup (£3.50), ploughman's (from £5.75), potted brown shrimps and toast (starter £5, main £6.75), smoked cod's roe with hot buttered toast, chicken leg stuffed with gammon, pork, sage and onion and topped with bacon or home-made mushroom and onion quiche (£5.75), ham and eggs (£6.75), local trout – caught and smoked by the landlord himself – or home-made steak and kidney pie (£7), venison sausages braised in red wine with red onions (£8.75), and wild smoked salmon salad (£11); main courses come with lots of fresh vegetables, and as the landlord shoots, there is usually game in season such as pheasant casserole in fresh orange juice and port (£8.50) and roast grouse (£14.50). Tables can be booked. Very well kept Ridleys IPA and Mauldons White Adder tapped from the cask, decent French regional wines, good coffee, attentive service; gentle country views from tables outside. *(Recommended by Gwen and Peter Andrews, John and Enid Morris, Adrian White, Colin and Dot Savill)*

Free house ~ Licensees Howard Potts and Ginny Austin ~ Real ale ~ Bar food ~ (01245) 361477 ~ Well behaved children welcome ~ Open 11.30-3, 6.30(7 in winter)-11; 11.30-3.30, 6-11 Sat; 12-3, 7-10.30 Sun

---

If we know a pub does summer barbecues, we say so.

FYFIELD TL5606 Map 5
Black Bull £

B184, N end of village

Good value daily specials continue to be the biggest draw to this comfortably welcoming 15th-c vine-covered pub, popular for its wide range and generous helpings of tasty bar food. They might include chicken curry or mushroom stroganoff, both with coriander rice, or home-made steak and mushroom pie (£4.25), pasta dish of the day or cold chicken and ham pie (£4.50), and a very generous helping of liver and bacon (£4.75). As we went to press, the landlord and his new chef were hoping to change the standard menu to introduce more spicy food such as chicken roasted with cider, mustard, ginger and spices (£7.15) and duck breast with orange, green ginger and red pepper sauce (£9.45), alongside old favourites such as soft roes (£3.25), well liked green-lipped mussels with black bean sauce (£3.65), excellent steak and kidney pudding (£7.50), skate wing (£8), and steaks (from £8.65); best to book at busy times. The communicating rooms have low ceilings, big black beams, standing timbers, and cushioned wheelback chairs and modern settles on the muted maroon carpet; fire in winter; no-smoking area in restaurant. Well kept Courage Best, Directors and Ruddles on handpump; darts, shove-ha'penny, cribbage, dominoes, fruit machine and piped music; efficient friendly service. There are lots of flower-filled barrels and white garden furniture outside, and picnic-sets on a nearby stretch of grass and to the side of the building; aviary with budgerigars and cockatiels by car park. (*Recommended by Joy and Peter Heatherley, Stephen Brown, R Wain, Beryl and Bill Farmer, Gwen and Peter Andrews, Tina and David Woods-Taylor, Dave Braisted, Stephen and Jean Curtis, W Ruxton*)

Free house ~ Licensees Alan Smith and Nicola Eldridge ~ Real ale ~ Bar food (till 10pm Fri and Sat) ~ (01277) 899225 ~ Open 11-2.30(3 Sat), 6.30-11; 12-3, 7-10.30 Sun

GESTINGTHORPE TL8138 Map 5
Pheasant

Village signposted from B1058

The lounge bar of this old-fashioned country pub with a quietly welcoming atmosphere has a big pheasant-print-cushioned bow window seat looking out over the quiet lane to gently rising fields, a raised log fire, and interesting old furnishings: a grandfather clock, arts-and-crafts oak settle, and a pew. The oak-beamed public bar, with more orthodox pub furniture, has another winter log fire. Simple bar food includes soup (£2.95), sandwiches (from £3), filled baked potatoes (from £4), and ploughman's (£4.50); from the restaurant menu, which is served throughout the pub, you can expect starters such as melon with cherry coulis (£3), deep-fried prawns with chilli and garlic (£4.50), and main courses including sautéed pork in cider and grain mustard (£8.95), rib-eye steak or pan-fried sea bass with polenta and lemon sauce (£9.95); home-made puddings include almond tart and chocolate pudding (£3.50). Well kept Adnams Southwold, Greene King IPA and Abbot and a guest beer, possibly from the York Brewery, on handpump. The garden has picnic-sets looking over the fine views of the countryside. (*Recommended by Gwen and Peter Andrews, Mrs Jenny Cantle*)

Free house ~ Licensee R Sullivan ~ Real ale ~ Bar food (till 10, no food Sun or Mon evenings) ~ Restaurant ~ (01787) 461196 ~ Children in eating area of bar and restaurant ~ Occasional live entertainment ~ Open 12-3, 6-11; 12-3, 7-10.30 Sun

GOSFIELD TL7829 Map 5
Green Man 🍴 ♈

3 m N of Braintree

Readers often comment about the particularly friendly helpful service at this smart well run dining pub. Apart from the warm welcome, one of the main attractions is the splendid lunchtime cold table which has a marvellous help-yourself choice of home cooked ham, tongue, beef and turkey, dressed salmon or crab in season, game pie, salads and home-made pickles (£6.95). The well cooked English-style menu includes soups like game with sherry (£3.10), home-made duck and brandy pâté (£3.25), fresh battered cod (£6.75), lamb's liver and bacon (£6.85), home-made steak and kidney pudding (£6.95), sweet and sour pork in batter (£7.25), chicken breast filled with cream cheese and prawns (£8.50), grilled whole lemon sole or venison in beer (£8.95) and half roast duck with orange sauce (£10.95); vegetarian dishes such as pancakes filled with vegetables are available on request (£5.95). A fabulous range of puddings might include fruit pies, pavlovas or home-made treacle tart (£3), vegetables are fresh and the chips home-made; advisable to book at busy times. The two little bars have a relaxed chatty atmosphere, Greene King IPA and Abbot on handpump, and decent nicely priced wines, many by the glass; darts, pool, dominoes, cribbage, fruit machine and juke box; friendly dog called Banjo. *(Recommended by Gwen and Peter Andrews, Ronald G Dodsworth, Malcolm and Jennifer Perry, R Wiles, Dr Oscar Puls, Colin and Dot Savill)*

Greene King ~ Lease: Mrs Janet Harrington ~ Real ale ~ Bar food (not Sunday evening) ~ Restaurant ~ (01787) 472746 ~ Well behaved children in restaurant and eating area of bar ~ Open 11-3, 6.30-11; 12-3, 7-10.30 Sun

GREAT YELDHAM TL7638 Map 5
White Hart ★ ⑪ ♀
Poole Street; A1017 Halstead—Haverhill

Essex Dining Pub of the Year
A couple of readers describe this black and white timbered building as a dining pub that still makes drinkers welcome, while retaining a pubby atmosphere in its no-smoking restaurant. Make no mistake however, most people come here for the exceptionally good and inventive food, and you can make your meal as smart or informal as you choose, as the same menu is available in the bar or restaurant. A very good value set lunch menu (two courses £8.50, third course £3.75, not Sundays) might include broccoli and blue cheese soup, prawn and pepper bruschetta with a pesto dressing, grilled sardines with lemon and parsley butter, thai-style chicken curry and poached figs with honey and home-made cardamom ice cream; a snack menu might offer baked aubergine with stir-fried vegetables and coriander pesto (£7.95) alongside more traditional dishes such as deep-fried cod with chips (£7.95) and lincolnshire sausages and mash (£5.95). The main menu might feature starters such as steamed mussels with spring onion, chilli and coriander (£3.75), smoked chicken, apricot and pecan risotto (£4.50), feta cheese and olive filos with a wilted rocket and cashew nut salad (£4.75), and main courses including mediterranean vegetable and mozzarella tart with warm new potato and chive salad (£7.95), chargrilled chicken breast with dauphinoise potatoes, braised leeks and a cranberry and apple tartlet (£10.50), seared salmon fillet with courgette tagliatelle and a rustic tomato and olive sauce (£11.75), duck breast with coconut and lime couscous and mango salsa (£12.95) rack of lamb with a potato and aubergine moussaka, warm fine bean salad and garlic dressing (£15.50) and chargrilled sirloin steak with a potato and mushroom cake, oven-dried tomatoes and red onion salsa (£16.75); irresistible puddings such as home-made ice cream (£3.95), pineapple and polenta cake with pineapple confit (£4.25), raspberry crème brûlée with home-made shortbread (£4.75) or a selection of unpasteurised cheeses (£5.50). There are smaller helpings for children. As well as an impressive list of about 100 well described wines there are up to 20 wines by the glass including a good selection of pudding wines. The well kept real ales on handpump change frequently but might include Adnams and Hook Norton Old Hooky. The main areas have stone and wood floors with some dark oak panelling especially around the fireplace; watch your head – the door into the bar is very low. There are pretty well kept garden seats among a variety of trees and shrubs on the lawns; strongly recommend booking. *(Recommended by Gwen and Peter Andrews, Quentin Williamson, MDN, Hazel R Morgan, B and M Parkin, Richard Siebert, Sommerville, G Neighbour, John Fahy, Mrs M Dixon, Michael Sargent, Lucie Miell, Margaret and Bill Rogers, R Wiles, C Smith, Paul and Ursula Randall, Paul and Sandra Embleton, Malcolm and Jennifer Perry, Peter and Giff Bennett, John Askew, R C Morgan)*

Free house ~ Licensees Roger Jones and John Hoskins ~ Real ale ~ Bar food (12-2, 6.30-9.30) ~ Restaurant ~ (01787) 237250 ~ Children welcome ~ Open 11-3, 6-11; 12-2, 7-10.30 Sun; closed evenings 25/26 Dec and 1 Jan

HASTINGWOOD TL4807 Map 5
Rainbow & Dove

¼ mile from M11, junction 7; Hastingwood signposted after Ongar signs at exit roundabout

Even when this friendly17th-c rose-covered cottage gets busy, the atmosphere still remains comfortable, thanks to the warm welcome offered by the father and son licensees. There are cosy fires in the three homely little low-beamed rooms which open off the main bar area; the one on the left is particularly snug and beamy, with the lower part of its wall stripped back to bare brick and decorated with brass pistols and plates. Among the choice of tasty sandwiches (from £2) are crab (£3.40) and steak and stilton (£4.50); other popular bar food includes ploughman's (from £3.25), steak and mushroom pie or kidneys and bacon (£5.25) and lots of fresh fish on a specials board such as skate wing, sea bream with mushroom sauce, pink trout with prawns and mushrooms, and fried cod (all around £5.75). Well kept Courage Directors, Greene King IPA and Morlands Old Speckled Hen; may be piped music. Picnic-sets under cocktail parasols, on a stretch of grass hedged off from the car park. A relaxing break from the nearby motorway. *(Recommended by Stephen Brown, Adrian White, Ian Phillips, Gwen and Peter Andrews, Tony Beaulah, Paul and Sandra Embleton, Francis Johnston)*

Inn Business ~ Tenants Jamie and Richard Keep ~ Real ale ~ Bar food (11.30-2.30, 7-9.30) ~ (01279) 415419 ~ Children in eating area of bar ~ Open 11.30-3, 6-11; 12-4, 7-10.30 Sun

HEYBRIDGE BASIN TL8707 Map 5
Jolly Sailor

Basin Rd (B1026 E of Maldon)

As well as looking for new licensees, the new manager was busy re-decorating this cheerful down-to-earth little pub as we went to press. Tucked in by the high sea wall of a popular boating estuary, it has seats out on a nice little terrace beside the wall. Flower baskets and new furniture were being added to the simple furnishings, with nautical charts and lots of boating and marine pictures on the freshly painted walls. Although a new chef had not been found when we spoke to the pub, from a straightforward good value menu you can expect soup (£1.80), filled baguettes (from £2.95, steak with mushrooms £3.95), ploughman's (£3.95), vegetable moussaka (£4.95), daily specials such as home-made pies and pasta dishes, and huge helpings of fresh fish and chips (from £6.95); well kept Courage Best, Greene King IPA with one or two guests such as Boddingtons or Morlands Old Speckled Hen on handpump, and mulled wine in winter; darts, dominoes, cribbage, games machines and piped music. There are shoreside walks from here, and this could make a good finish for longer walks by the Rivers Blackwater and Chelmer. Parking is limited, especially on summer weekends. *(Recommended by Gwen and Peter Andrews, John Wilmott, Roger and Pauline Pearce, Ursula and Paul Randall)*

Rainbow ~ Manager Mr Hardy ~ Real ale ~ Bar food ~ Restaurant ~ (01621) 854210 ~ Children in restaurant ~ Open 11-3, 6-11; 11-11 Sat; 12-10.30 Sun

HIGH ONGAR TL5603 Map 5
Wheatsheaf

King St, Nine Ashes; signposted Blackmore, Ingatestone off A414 just E of Ongar

The system adopted by the licensees at this cosy low-beamed pub – they take turns to perform the kitchen and front-of-house duties – obviously works, as readers often comment on the friendly welcome and cheerfulness of the efficient staff. On a fine day, the spacious back garden is practically irresistible, with a variety of well spaced tables and plenty of room for children to run around in, as well as a 'giant' play house and other play equipment. The most pleasant seats indoors are in the four unusual booths or stalls built into the big front bay window, each with an intimate little lamp and fresh flowers on its broad round-ended polished table. A wide choice of good home-made food includes sandwiches (from £1.70), soup (£2.50), ploughman's (from £3.50), smoked mackerel (£3.50), a good range of vegetarian dishes (mostly £6.90) such as vegetable lasagne, broccoli and cream cheese bake or creamy vegetable pie, and steaks (from £11.95); specials include garlic and lemon chicken on coriander mash or lamb steak in chinese plum sauce (£8.95), duck breast with a variety of sauces (£12.95), and lots of fresh fish with cod, haddock and skate most days (£6-£10.95), halibut steak with a stilton crust (£9.95) and whole sea bass with mange tout, onions and oyster sauce (£13.95); good vegetables and excellent chips (usually a choice of other types of potato too); small helpings on request. Well kept Flowers IPA and Original and a couple of guests on handpump such as Fullers London Pride or Mighty Oak. There's a log fire each end of the beamed bar; darts and cribbage. *(Recommended by Gwen and Peter Andrews, H O Dickinson, Rex Miller, Joy and Peter Heatherley)*

Free house ~ Licensees Tony and Sue Streeter ~ Real ale ~ Bar food ~ Restaurant ~ (01277) 822220 ~ Children in garden and eating area of bar till early evening ~ Open 11-3(4 Sat), 5.30(6 Sat)-11; 12-10.30 Sun; 12-5, 7-10.30 Sun winter; closed Mon lunchtime

HORNDON ON THE HILL TQ6683 Map 3

Bell 🍻 ☲ ⛵

M25 junction 30 into A13, then left into B1007 after 7 miles, village signposted from here

The heavily beamed bar at this flower-decked medieval inn has some antique high-backed settles and plush burgundy stools and benches, rugs on the flagstones or highly polished oak floorboards, and a curious collection of hot cross buns hanging from a beam. The menu, which is available in the bar and restaurant, changes twice a day and might include enjoyable spicy parsnip and apple soup (£3.60), ravioli of lamb sweetbreads with aubergine and almond pesto or wild mushroom and herb mash and roast tomato (£4.95), fishcakes with herb crust and spinach (£6.25), lamb and rosemary sausages with olive mash (£6.50), beef stovies with parsnip and oatcakes (£8.50), beef tomato and cheese tarte tatin (£9.50), calf's liver with mustard and honey mash (£10.95) and grilled salmon fillet with confit of fennel, olives and hazelnuts (£11.25); well liked puddings such as banana parfait mille feuille (£3.50), blueberry mousse (£4), and chocolate marquise (£4.50). There's a wine list of over 100 well chosen wines from all over the world with about 18 by the glass listed on a blackboard with suggestions on what to drink with your food; you can also buy them off-sales; Bass, Fullers London Pride, Greene King IPA, and a couple of guests such as Morlands Old Speckled Hen and Youngs Special on handpump. On the last weekend in June the High Road outside is closed (by Royal Charter) for period-costume festivities and a crafts fair and the pub holds a feast; they also host a beer festival in May. Very attractive beamed bedrooms. Longevity of service appears to be a theme here: the previous head chef recently left after 14 years, and the pub has been run by the same enthusiastic family for over 60 years. *(Recommended by Janet and Colin Roe, Dr S Pyle, John and Enid Morris, W Christian, G Neighbour, Joy and Peter Heatherley, Gwen and Peter Andrews, Sue and David Arnott, Caroline Wright, Ian Phillips, Michael and Hazel Duncombe, Dr Oscar Puls, H Dickinson, Richard Siebert, C Smith)*

Free house ~ Licensee John Vereker ~ Real ale ~ Bar food (12-2, 6.30-10, not 25/26 Dec) ~ Restaurant ~ (01375) 642463 ~ Children in eating area of bar and restaurant ~ Open 11-2.30(3 Sat), 6-11; 12-3, 7-10.30 Sun ~ Bedrooms: /£45B

People named as recommenders after the main entries have told us that the pub should be included. But they have not written the report – we have, after anonymous on-the-spot inspection.

LANGHAM TM0233 Map 5
Shepherd & Dog ♀

Moor Rd/High St; village signposted off A12 N of Colchester

In summer, this cheerful friendly inn has very pretty window boxes and a shaded bar in the enclosed side garden. The relatively straightforward popular menu, chalked on boards around the bar, changes daily and offers very generous helpings of enjoyable food, including a surprisingly decent range of fish dishes such as deep-fried cod (£5.95), skate or grilled red mullet (from £6.95), grilled tuna with chilli pesto, grilled halibut with anchovy sauce or undyed smoked haddock with poached egg (£7.95), and torbay sole (£8.95); other bar meals might be home-made tomato soup (£2.25), fresh asparagus with hollandaise or black pudding and lardons on a warm salad (£3.95), cumberland sausage (£4.95), vegetable and brie strudel (£5.50), home-made lasagne (£5.95), lamb with black olives and haricot beans or duck roasted with honey and sesame seeds on stir-fried vegetables (£6.95), and steaks (from £7.50), Sunday roasts (from £5.95); home-made puddings include lemon meringue or spotted dick (from £2.95). Well kept Greene King IPA, Abbot and Triumph with weekly changing guests from Mauldons and Nethergate on handpump, and a short but decent wine list. An engaging hotch potch of styles, the spick and span L-shaped bar has an interesting collection of continental bottled beers, and there's often a sale of books for charity. Tables outside. *(Recommended by Paul and Sandra Embleton, Margaret and Maurice Peterson, Mike and Mary Carter, A C Morrison, Gwen and Peter Andrews, Richard and Robyn Wain, IHR, Pete Yearsley)*

Free house ~ Licensees Paul Barnes and Jane Graham ~ Real ale ~ Bar food (till 10) ~ Restaurant ~ (01206) 272711 ~ Children welcome ~ Open 11-3, 5.30(6 Sat)-11; 12-3, 7-10.30 Sun

LITTLE BRAXTED TL8314 Map 5
Green Man

Kelvedon Road; village signposted off B1389 by NE end of A12 Witham bypass – keep on patiently

The cosy welcoming little lounge at this isolated pub, tucked away up a quiet lane, houses an interesting collection of bric-a-brac, including some 200 horsebrasses, some harness, mugs hanging from a beam, a lovely copper urn, and an open fire. In the tiled public bar friendly staff dispense well kept Ridleys IPA and Rumpus from handpumps in the form of 40mm brass cannon shells, also several malt whiskies; darts, shove-ha'penny, cribbage, dominoes and fruit machine. Good reasonably priced food includes sandwiches (from £2.10), filled french bread or filled baked potatoes (from £2.85), and daily specials such as fish pie or mushroom lasagne (£5.50), cheese and asparagus quiche (£5.75), diced pork with peppers in a cream and wine sauce or Jamaican chicken (£5.95), a colossal steak and ale pie (£6.95) and puddings such as bakewell or treacle tart, apple and coconut crumble and fresh strawberries – grown by the barman – in summer (£2.95). There are picnic-sets and a pretty pond in the delightfully sheltered garden behind. *(Recommended by Mrs M Dallisson, Tina and David Woods-Taylor, A E Brace, C Smith, Mike and Mary Carter, Gwen and Peter Andrews, Mike and Maggie Betton, Evelyn and Derek Walter)*

Ridleys ~ Tenant Tony Wiley ~ Real ale ~ Bar food ~ (01621) 891659 ~ Open 11.30-3, 6.30-11; 12-3, 7-10.30 Sun; closed evenings 25/26 Dec

LITTLE DUNMOW TL6521 Map 5
Flitch of Bacon ⇐

Village signposted off A120 E of Dunmow, then turn right on village loop road

As we went to press, the helpful new licensee David Caldwell had not yet moved in, but he maintained that he had no intention of changing the atmosphere of this unspoilt friendly country pub – so hopefully local characters will continue to rub shoulders with visiting businessmen. The small timbered bar is simply but attractively furnished, mainly with flowery-cushioned pews, and ochre walls. Quietly relaxing on weekday lunchtimes, it can be vibrantly cheerful in the evenings. Mr Caldwell had plans to create a more sophisticated menu, but unfortunately he was unable to give any examples of the types of meals readers could expect. Past bar food has included generous sandwiches (£2.20) – including excellent home-carved ham, soup (£2.50), ploughman's (£3.50), anchovies on toast (£3.50), local ham and eggs with a crusty roll (£4), Friday fish and chips (£4.50), smoked salmon and scrambled eggs (£5.50), and three or four changing hot dishes such as sausage hotpot (£4.95) game dishes, pork and apple or steak and kidney pie (£6.50), and a couple of puddings; good buffet lunch on Sunday. Greene King IPA will remain along with two guests such as Crouch Vale Best or Nethergate Umbel Magna on handpump. A keen guitarist himself, the new licensee hopes to set up a weekday folk evening with the help of the Morris dancers who frequent the pub. Cribbage, dominoes, no games machines or piped music; basic, but clean and comfortable bedrooms. The pub looks across the quiet lane to a broad expanse of green, and has a few picnic-sets on the edge; the nearby church of St Mary is well worth a visit (the pub has a key). *(Recommended by John Fahy, Tony Beaulah, Lucie Miell, Mrs Cynthia Archer, Mike and Karen England, Dr Oscar Puls, Stephen Brown)*

Free house ~ Licensee David Caldwell ~ Real ale ~ Bar food (not Sun evening) ~ Restaurant ~ (01371) 820323 ~ Children in restaurant until 7.30pm ~ Maybe folk sessions on weekday evenings ~ Open 12-3(3.30 Sat), 6-11; 12-3, 7-10.30 Sun ~ Bedrooms: £32.60B/£49.60B

LITTLE WALDEN TL5441 Map 5
Crown

B1052 N of Saffron Walden

This 18th-c low white cottage has been neatly and attractively renovated, with low beams, bookroom-red walls, flowery curtains and a mix of bare boards and navy carpeting giving a warm and cosy feel. Seats range from high-backed pews to little cushioned armchairs, around a good variety of tables, mostly big, some stripped. These are quite closely spaced, one next to a good log fire in a brick fireplace. Racked at the back of the very roomy servery are three to five changing real ales which might include well kept Greene King IPA and Abbot and Hobsons Choice, tapped straight from the cask. A small red tiled room on the right has two little tables, and darts. Generously served bar food might include sandwiches (from £2.25), soup (£2.95), filled baked potatoes (from £3.50), ploughman's (from £4.25), steak and ale pie (£6.50), and daily specials such as spare ribs (£4.25), garlic mushrooms and prawns (£4.95), cauliflower and broccoli mornay (£5.95), beef madras or very good fish and chips (£6.50), liver and bacon (£6.95), Caribbean seafood curry (£7.25), pork fillet dijon or skate wing (£8.95), grilled dover sole (£12.95), and puddings such as apple crumble or chocolate and almond pâté (£3.25); piped local radio. *(Recommended by Gwen and Peter Andrews, G Washington)*

Free house ~ Licensee Colin Hayling ~ Real ale ~ Bar food (not Sun evening) ~ (01799) 522475 ~ Children in eating area of bar and garden till 9pm ~ Open 11.30-2.30, 6-11; 12-10.30 Sun; closed evenings 25, 26 Dec

MILL GREEN TL6401 Map 5
Viper ✦

Mill Green Rd; from Fryerning (which is signposted off north-east bound A12 Ingatestone bypass) follow Writtle signposts

Readers appreciate the unchanging atmosphere at this cosy little pub, popular with walkers and almost hidden by overflowing hanging baskets and window boxes in summer. A quaint charm pervades the simple interior: two timeless little lounge rooms have spindleback seats, armed country kitchen chairs, and tapestried wall seats around neat little old tables, and a warming log fire. The fairly basic parquet-floored tap room (where booted walkers are directed), is more simply furnished with shiny wooden traditional wall seats, and beyond there's another room with country kitchen chairs and sensibly placed darts; shove-ha'penny, dominoes, cribbage and a fruit machine. Very well kept Ridleys IPA and three or four weekly changing guests from breweries such as Hook Norton, Mansfield, Mighty Oak, Charles Wells and Wolf on handpump are served from an oak-panelled counter. Simple lunchtime bar snacks include good sandwiches (from £1.75), soup (£2.50), chilli (£3.25), ploughman's (from £4), and home-made cold pies with pickles at weekends (£2); sweet toasted sandwiches such as banana and chocolate (£2.50). Pleasant service even when busy; no children in pub. Tables on the lawn overlook the marvellously cared for cottage garden. The pub may stay open for slightly longer on weekend afternoons (snacks are served until 2.30pm on Saturdays). *(Recommended by Joy and Peter Heatherley, Richard and Robyn Wain, Paul and Ursula Randall, John and Enid Morris, Mike and Karen England, Pete Baker, Ian Phillips)*

Free house ~ Licensees Roger and Fred Beard ~ Real ale ~ Bar food (12-2) ~ (01277) 352010 ~ Children in garden only ~ Open 12-3, 6-11; 12-3, 7-10.30 Sun

NORTH FAMBRIDGE TQ8597 Map 5

Ferry Boat

The quay; village signposted from B1012 E off S Woodham Ferrers; keep on past railway

The bar of this genuinely unpretentious 500-year-old weatherboarded pub is simply furnished with traditional wall benches, settles and chairs on its stone floor, nautical memorabilia, old-fashioned lamps, and a few historic boxing-gloves. There's a log fire at one end, and a woodburning stove at the other, although the fact that most of the buildings rest only on a bed of reeds allowing the old wood and plaster to move around according to the climate means that it can still be a bit draughty. Straightforward bar food includes soup (£1.80), sandwiches (from £2), filled baked potatoes, omelettes or ploughman's (from £3.50), deep-fried cod or plaice (£3.75), garlic chicken or country vegetable pie (£4.95), steak and kidney pie (£5.25), Essex skate or venison in port and red wine (£7.50). Well kept Flowers IPA, Morlands Old Speckled Hen and Wadworths 6X on handpump with a guest such as York Brewerys Bug; friendly chatty landlord; darts, shove-ha'penny, table skittles, cribbage, dominoes, fruit machine and piped music. There's a pond with ducks and carp, and seats in the garden. Six bedrooms in a barn-like building behind the pub were due to be completed by October. There are pleasant walks along the River Crouch which is nearer than you think – it sometimes creeps up the lane towards the car park. *(Recommended by Gwen and Peter Andrews, Paul and Sandra Embleton, Mike and Karen England)*

Free house ~ Licensee Roy Maltwood ~ Real ale ~ Bar food ~ Restaurant ~ (01621) 740208 ~ Children in family room and restaurant ~ Open 11-3, 6-11(7-11 winter); 12-10.30 Sun; 12-3, 7-10.30 Sun winter ~ Bedrooms: £25B/£40B

PAGLESHAM TQ9293 Map 3

Punchbowl

Church End; from the Paglesham road out of Rochford, Church End is signposted on the left

Beautifully kept, this pretty white weatherboarded pub has a very peaceful outlook over the fields – a reward for the long drive down country lanes. The cosy beamed bar and dining area has pews, barrel chairs and other seats, lots of bric-a-brac, and a most friendly feel – thanks to the particularly hospitable landlord. The tasty good value bar food includes sandwiches and filled baguettes, filled baked potatoes or soup (all from £1.95), cheese and ham toasties (from £2), jalapeno peppers filled with cream cheese (£2.90), ploughman's (from £3.25), southern-style fried chicken (£4.95), steak and kidney pudding (£5.50), steak (£8.95), daily specials such as steak in red wine or lamb casserole (£5.75), and good fresh fish including grilled plaice and salmon (£5.50), skate (£6.95), and lemon sole (£10.25); puddings such as blackberry and apple pie and ginger pudding (from £2.30). Well kept Adnams, Morlands Old Speckled Hen, a changing Ridleys ale and a guest such as Elgoods on handpump; piped music; music quiz some Friday evenings in winter. There are some tables in the small garden, with a couple out by the quiet road. *(Recommended by George Atkinson, Richard and Robyn Wain)*

Free house ~ Licensees Bernie and Pat Cardy ~ Real ale ~ Bar food ~ (01702) 258376 ~ Children in eating area of bar and restaurant ~ Open 12-3, 7-(10.30 Sun) 11; closed 25 Dec

RICKLING GREEN TL5029 Map 5
Cricketers Arms ♀

Just off B1383 N of Stansted Mountfichet

True to its name, this friendly family run pub which overlooks the cricket green where Essex CC play once a year is full of cricketing memorabilia including hundreds of cricket cigarette cards on the walls. The fairly plain Victorian facade veils a mass of Elizabethan timbering, and even more old beams were revealed during last year's refurbishments, in which the public bar was transformed to create a larger kitchen and bar area and the new no-smoking Lords dining room; the two bays of the softly lit and comfortable saloon bar are divided by standing timbers and in winter, chestnuts are roasted on the log fire. As well as sandwiches (from £1.50), the good bar food menu might include seafood soup (£2.95), ploughman's (£3.25), continental sausage platter (£3.95), deep-fried brie (£4.25), moules marinières (£4.95, large £8.95), liver and bacon (£5.50), nut roast (£5.95), steak and kidney pie (£6.95), espatada (beef or lamb shish kebab marinated in red wine, olive oil, garlic and herbs, £7.25), prawn balti (£8.50), chicken in apricot and cream sauce (£8.75), duck breast in orange sauce (£8.95), steaks (from £8.95), as well as daily fish specials (bought fresh from Billingsgate market) such as grilled tuna steak with tomato and basil sauce (£8.95) and chinese-style whole plaice with ginger and spring onion (£9.95); puddings include well liked fruit crumble (£2.30), blackcurrant cheesecake (£2.50) and spotted dick (£2.75); children's menu. Well kept Adnams Extra, Flowers IPA and Fullers ESB tapped from the cask, 12 wines by the glass and in summer about two dozen bottle conditioned beers from all over Britain; cribbage and dominoes. A sheltered front courtyard has picnic-sets. The Green Room overlooks the cricket pitch and has a four-poster bed and double jacuzzi; the other bedrooms are in a modern block behind and are handy for Stansted Airport, with a courtesy car for guests. *(Recommended by Gwen and Peter Andrews, A C Stone, G Neighbour, Quentin Williamson)*

Free house ~ Licensees Tim and Jo Proctor ~ Real ale ~ Bar food ~ (01799) 543210 ~ Children in eating area of bar ~ Live music every other Friday evening ~ Open 11-11; 12-10.30 Sun ~ Bedrooms: £55B/£70B

STOCK TQ6998 Map 5
Hoop ◖ £

B1007; from A12 Chelsford bypass take Galleywood, Billericay turn-off

Remaining happily unsophisticated and with a refreshingly mixed clientele, the little bar of this well-liked village local has a really friendly atmosphere. As well as a fine range of about six changing real ales from breweries such as Adnams, Crouch Vale, Fullers, Hop Back, Mighty Oak or Nethergate on handpump or tapped from the cask (during May they hold a popular beer festival when there might be around 150), there are changing farm ciders, perries and winter mulled wine. There's a coal-effect gas fire in the big brick fireplace, brocaded wall seats around dimpled copper tables on the left and a cluster of brocaded stools on the right; sensibly placed darts (the heavy black beams are studded with hundreds of wayward flights), dominoes and cribbage. The good value bar food remains virtually the same price as last year, and includes sandwiches (from £1.30), soup (£1.50), steak and kidney pie (£3.50), ploughman's (from £4), vegetable pie or well liked lancashire hotpot (£4), chicken curry (£4.50), and several daily specials such as moules marinières (£4.50), grilled skate or smoked haddock with poached egg (£5 – fresh fish is delivered daily), and breaded lamb steak (£5.50) – vegetables are charged in addition to these prices; home-made puddings such as apple pie or crème caramel (£1.50). The big sheltered back garden, prettily bordered with flowers, has picnic-sets, a covered seating area, and an outside bar and weekend barbecues when the weather is fine. Over 21s only in bar. *(Recommended by Gwen and Peter Andrews, Eddie Edwards, John and Enid Morris, David and Tina Woods-Taylor, Adrian White, Beryl and Bill Farmer, Dr Oscar Puls, Paul Barstow, John Wilmott, Karyn Taylor)*

Free house ~ Licensees Albert and David Kitchin ~ Real ale ~ Bar food (all day) ~ (01277) 841137 ~ Children in eating area of bar ~ Open 11-11; 12-10.30 Sun

STOW MARIES TQ8399 Map 5
Prince of Wales 🍺
B1012 between S Woodham Ferrers and Cold Norton Posters

Friendly unpretentious Essex marshland pub, run by a real-ale fanatic whose enthusiasm for beer has been rewarded with a monthly slot on a local radio station. Five or six very well kept real ales are changed weekly, and among the hundreds that pass through the handpumps every year, you might find Bank Top Fred's Cap, Harviestoun Bitter and Twisted, Hop Back, Otter Ale, Piddle in the Hole and Youngs Dirty Dick; they also have an impressive range of Belgian draught beers, and a particularly unusual range of continental bottled beers, Belgian fruit beers, farm cider, and a good choice of malt whiskies and vintage ports. Several readers have praised the careful restoration – in a genuinely traditional style – of the cosy and chatty low-ceilinged rooms, seemingly unchanged since the turn of the century; few have space for more than one or two tables or wall benches on the tiled or bare-boards floors, though the room in the middle squeezes in quite a jumble of chairs and stools. One room used to be the village bakery, and in winter the oven there is still used to make bread and pizzas. The chef is Greek, so that along with the usual bar food such as soup (£1.50, winter only), sandwiches (from £1.70), ploughman's (from £2.40), chicken with cheese and bacon (£4.95), and home smoked haddock with plum tomatoes and poached egg (£6.25), reasonably priced home-made meals might include blackboard specials such as mixed fish (tuna, swordfish and monkfish) kebabs (£5.45), greek-style lamb chops (£5.95), and puddings such as baklava (£2.25); Greek barbecues every Sunday in summer. There are seats and tables in the back garden and in summer the gap between the white picket fence and the pub's weatherboarded frontage is filled with beautiful dark red roses, with some scented pink ones at the side. Live entertainment ranges from magicians and jugglers to music. *(Recommended by TRS, George Atkinson, Gwen and Peter Andrews, Adrian White)*

Free house ~ Licensee Rob Walster ~ Real ale ~ Bar food ~ (01621) 828971 ~ Children in garden and family room ~ Open 11-11; 12-10.30 Sun; closed lunchtime 25 Dec

TOOT HILL TL5102 Map 5
Green Man 🍷
Village signposted from A113 in Stanford Rivers, S of Ongar; and from A414 W of Ongar

Busy country dining pub, exceptional for its tremendous choice and variety of wines: the list offers around 100 well chosen varieties, 20 half bottles and many by the glass; they also have occasional free tastings and talks by visiting merchants. The main emphasis is on the ambitious bar food served in the newly refurbished and now much more plush long dining lounge; in the evenings they take bookings for tables in here, but only for 7.30; after that, they put you on a queue for tables that come free. The ambitious bar food is freshly cooked to order (they warn of delays when busy), and daily changing blackboards might include starters such as kidneys in red wine and bacon (£3.95), avocado and strawberry salad with cider vinaigrette (£4.50), main dishes such as stuffed flat-top mushrooms with stilton sauce (£6.50), fresh cod with samphire, pork fillet with cider and grain mustard sauce or john dory with asparagus sauce (all £7.95), chicken breast in creamy pepper sauce (£8.95), and lamb cutlets glazed with honey and mint (£9.95); pleasant young staff. Well kept Crouch Vale IPA and a weekly changing guest such as Nethergate Umbel Ale on handpump; darts, shove-ha'penny, dominoes and cribbage; no-smoking area. In summer, the outside is a colourful haze of hanging baskets, window boxes and flower tubs, prettily set off by the curlicued white iron tables and chairs and wooden benches; more tables behind. A couple of miles through the attractive countryside at Greensted is St Andrews, the oldest wooden church in the world. *(Recommended by M A Starling, Gwen and Peter Andrews, J H Gracey, Martin and Jane Bailey, GL, A Hepburn, S Jenner)*

Free house ~ Licensee Peter Roads ~ Real ale ~ Bar food ~ Restaurant ~ (01992) 522255 ~ Children over 10 in restaurant ~ Open 11-3, 6-11; 12-3, 7-10.30 Sun; closed 25 Dec

WENDENS AMBO TL5136 Map 5
Bell ◗

B1039 just W of village

There is a veritable menagerie at this jolly little beamed village pub with Thug the friendly black cat, Kate the dog and in the garden Gertie and her pygmy counterparts, Reggie and Ronnie. Goats apart, the extensive back garden itself is quite special with a big tree-sheltered lawn, lots of flower borders and unusual plant-holders; the wooden wendy house, a proper tree swing, and a sort of mini nature-trail wandering off through the shrubs should keep children happily engaged. Inside, spotlessly kept small cottagey low ceilinged rooms are filled with interesting knick-knacks; as well as a welcoming open fire, there are brasses on ancient timbers, wheelback chairs around neat tables, comfortably cushioned seats worked into snug alcoves, and quite a few pictures on the cream walls. Bar food includes filled rolls (from £1.90), jalapeno peppers filled with cheese and prawns or tasty ploughman's (£3.75), vegetarian dishes (£5.50), chillies and curries (£5.95), beef and Guinness pie (£6.75), cajun chicken (£6.95), mixed grill (£7.75) and puddings such as spotted dick or treacle tart (£2.25); the dining room is no smoking. Four well kept real ales which might be from Adnams, Cambridge Brewery, Crouch Vale, Mighty Oak, Nethergate or Ridleys are well kept on handpump or tapped straight from the cask by the cheery landlord or motherly barmaid; darts, dominoes, cards, Monopoly and Scrabble; piped music. *(Recommended by Gwen and Peter Andrews, John Wooll, Richard and Robyn Wain, Joy and Peter Heatherley)*

Free house ~ Licensees Geoffrey and Bernie Bates ~ Real ale ~ Bar food (not Mon evening) ~ Restaurant ~ (01799) 540382 ~ Children in restaurant ~ Open 11.30-2.30(3 Sat), 6-11; 12-3, 7-10.30 Sun; closed evenings 25-26 Dec

WOODHAM WALTER TL8006 Map 5
Cats ◗

Back road to Curling Tye and Maldon, from N end of village

It would be easier to give a true impression of what this pleasantly relaxed timbered black and white country cottage sells and when it does so, if the landlord would deign to respond to our enquiries. As it is, we can't be too specific with factual information but can only tell you as much as we've been able to glean from readers' reports in the last year or so (in our defence we must say that letting licensees decide for us which pubs not to include would damage our independence almost as much as allowing other landlords to pay for their inclusion). Stone cats prowl across the roof and the feline theme is continued in the cosy interior with shelves of china cats in the rambling low-ceilinged bar; the low black beams and timbering are set off well by neat white paintwork, and there are interesting nooks and crannies as well as two log fires. Readers enjoy the well kept Greene King Abbot and IPA and a guest on handpump; good simple bar food; friendly service. No children or piped music. There are seats outside in the pretty garden with views across the surrounding farmland. *(Recommended by Lynn Sharpless, Bob Eardley, Mrs Jenny Cantle, Pete Yearsley, Mike and Karen England)*

Free house ~ Real ale ~ Open 11-2.30ish, 6ish-11; may close if not busy in winter; closed possibly Tues and Weds lunchtimes and all day Mon

YOUNGS END TL7319 Map 5
Green Dragon
A131 Braintree—Chelmsford, just N of Essex Showground

The very good bar food is extremely popular at this well run dining pub. Besides filled baguettes and ploughman's (from £3.50), the extensive bar menu might include home-made soup (£2.50), mushrooms d'amour (£3.95), ham and eggs (£5.95), bean, celery and coriander chilli or excellent steak and kidney pie (£6.50), chicken supreme stuffed with wild mushroom risotto (£7.75), kleftiko (£8.55), sirloin steak (£13.50) and fresh fish specials such as salmon fishcakes with tarragon (£7.50), baked rainbow trout stuffed with prawns and mushrooms (£7.95), salmon teriyaki with wild rice (£8.50) and whole lemon sole with lemon grass and ginger butter (£9.95); fresh vegetables; good puddings like strawberry cheesecake or spotted dick from a pudding cabinet (£3); fixed price set menu available. The restaurant area has an understated barn theme – stripped brick walls and a manger at one end; no-smoking 'hayloft' restaurant upstairs. The bar part has normal pub furnishings in its two rooms, with a little extra low-ceilinged snug just beside the serving counter. At lunchtime (not Sunday) you can have bar food in part of the restaurant, where the tables are a better size than in the bar; friendly service. Well kept Greene King IPA, Abbot and a guest such as Marstons Pedigree on handpump; unobtrusive piped jazz music. The neat back garden has lots of picnic-sets under cocktail parasols, a big green play dragon, climbing frame and budgerigar aviary. *(Recommended by Gwen and Peter Andrews, John Fahy, Paul and Ursula Randall, Colin and Dot Savill, Adrian White)*

Greene King ~ Bob and Mandy Greybrook ~ Real ale ~ Bar food (till 9.30, all day Sun) ~ Restaurant ~ (01245) 361030 ~ Children in the eating area till 8pm ~ Open 12-3, 6-11; 12-10.30 Sun

Lucky Dip

Besides the fully inspected pubs, you might like to try these Lucky Dips recommended to us and described by readers (if you do, please send us reports):

Althorne [TQ9199]
Black Lion [B1010 W of Burnham]: Pleasant atmosphere and varied reasonably priced food in pretty pub, fairly big and comfortably refurbished *(Rex Miller)*
☆ *Huntsman & Hounds* [B1010 E of S Woodham Ferrers]: Thatched rustic pub extended around low-beamed local-feel core, well kept Greene King ales, farm cider, good food and coffee, good friendly service; piped music; occasional barbecues in lovely big garden *(BB, Gwen and Peter Andrews, John Wilmott)*
Ashdon [TL5842]
Rose & Crown [back rd Saffron Walden—Haverhill, junction with back rd to Radwinter]: 17th-c, friendly locals in central bar with real fire and well kept Greene King Abbot and Ind Coope Burton, softly lit small beamed dining rooms, one with original gothic lettering and geometric patterns, simple choice of enjoyable food (fresh fish Fri), good service, no music; pool room *(Gwen and Peter Andrews)*
Barnston [TL6419]
Bushel & Sack [A130 SE of Dunmow]: Warm and welcoming 19th-c bar with comfortable restaurant beyond sitting room, another bare-boards bar with tables for eating, well kept Greene King IPA and a guest beer, friendly service, good usual food; quiet piped music *(Gwen and Peter Andrews)*

Battlesbridge [TQ7894]
☆ *Hawk* [Hawk Hill]: Recently attractively refurbished, with rugs, settles and oak tables on flagstones, hanging baskets, farm tools, dried hops, wide choice of food inc interesting light lunches and vegetarian, good wine list; packed w/e with antiques enthusiasts visiting the centre here; children welcome, small garden *(Paul and Diane Burrows, Mrs Jenny Cantle)*
Billericay [TQ6893]
Duke of York [Southend Rd, South Green]: Pleasant beamed local with real fire, longcase clock, local photographs, upholstered settles and wheelback chairs, good value food in bar and modern restaurant, long-serving licensees, Greene King and occasional guest beers, maybe unobtrusive piped 60s pop music *(David Twitchett)*
Birchanger [TL5022]
Three Willows [nr M11 junction 8 – right turn off A120 to Bishops Stortford]: Doing well under newish landlord, with wide choice of good reasonably priced food esp fish, well kept real ale; cricket memorabilia – pub's name refers to bats of 18th, 19th and 20th centuries *(Stephen and Jean Curtis, John Saul)*
Birdbrook [TL7041]
Plough: Pretty thatched pub under friendly new family, traditional two-room bar and more spacious dining room, good straightforward food, well kept Adnams, Fullers London Pride

and Greene King IPA, good coffee, nice open fire in public bar, no music *(Gwen and Peter Andrews, Richard and Valerie Wright)*

Blackmore [TL6001]

Bull [off A414 Chipping Ongar—Chelmsford]: Very hospitable old timbered dining pub, cosy and pleasantly decorated, with tempting choice of tasty if not cheap food, well kept ales such as Adnams Middle of the Wicket and Mauldons Whiteadder, brasses, maybe quiet piped music; fruit machine in public bar; nr church in quietly attractive village with big antique and craft shop *(George Atkinson)*

Boreham [TL7509]

☆ *Cock*: Concentration on good fresh fish in two partly curtained-off no-smoking restaurant areas off pleasant beamed central bar, other good value food from sandwiches up, cheerful young staff, well kept Ridleys, decent wines and coffee; piped music, some traffic/rail noise in family garden *(Adrian White)*

☆ *Queens Head* [Church Rd, off B1137 Chelmsford—Hatfield Peverel]: Homely and spotless traditional local with very welcoming licensees, well kept Greene King IPA and Abbot, decent wines, good value food (not Sun evening) inc Weds roast and Sun lunch; snug beams-and-brickwork saloon (fills quickly), more tables down one side of long public bar with darts at end; maybe piped music; small garden, pub tucked away by church *(Paul and Ursula Randall, Jan and Ken Keeble, R J Parsons, Gwen and Peter Andrews)*

Six Bells [B1137]: Comfortable bar in thriving good value dining pub, emphasis on substantial helpings of fresh fish, friendly efficient service even when busy, well kept Greene King and guest beers; play area in garden *(Paul and Ursula Randall)*

Braintree [TL7622]

Fowlers Farm [A120, by Wyevale garden centre]: Attractive farmhouse replica, floorboards and old farm equipment, well kept real ale, good value generous food from sandwiches up served quickly, plenty of seating inc no-smoking area, pleasant young staff; piped music not too obtrusive; rabbit run in attractive garden *(Paul and Sandra Embleton, Keith and Janet Morris)*

Broomfield [TL7010]

Angel [B1008 N of Chelmsford]: Busy main-road Big Steak pub, attractively restored (dates from 14th c), with well kept Tetleys-related ales and guests such as Adnams *(Paul and Ursula Randall)*

Broxted [TL5726]

Prince of Wales: Softly lit L-shaped dining pub, low beams, brick pillars, some settees, good choice of wines by the glass, Friary Meux and a guest such as Shepherd Neame, smiling service, food from hearty sandwiches up, family room; piped radio; conservatory, good garden with play area *(Gwen and Peter Andrews, John Fahy, Paul and Sandra Embleton)*

Bulmer Tye [TL8438]

Fox [A131 S of Sudbury]: More restaurant than pub, Spanish-run, with good welcoming service, well kept Batemans and Greene King IPA and

decent wine from small bar on left, good wines, popular lunchtime carvery, tapas and Italian dishes; tables out on terrace *(Gwen and Peter Andrews)*

Canfield End [TL5821]

Lion & Lamb [A120 Bishops Stortford—Dunmow]: Neat and comfortable, with friendly staff, wide choice of good value food inc children's in bar and spacious restaurant, well kept Ridleys, decent wines and coffee; piped music; back garden with barbecue and play area *(David and Mary Webb)*

Chelmsford [TL7006]

County Hotel [Rainsford Rd]: Smallish hotel bar, pubby but always civilised, well kept Adnams and Greene King IPA, good straightforward bar food inc sandwiches (can be a wait), friendly staff, no music; bedrooms *(Gwen and Peter Andrews, Paul and Ursula Randall)*

Chignall Smealy [TL6711]

Pig & Whistle: Charming building attractively restored and opened up, with beams, brasses and stripped brick, solid furniture and soft lighting, partly no-smoking restaurant, tables out on terrace with wide views; decent food (may be a wait), changing well kept ales such as Courage Best and Directors, Greene King IPA and Marstons Pedigree, good choice of house wines; children welcome away from bar, piped music may obtrude, drinks prices high for an out-of-the-way country pub *(Gwen and Peter Andrews)*

Chignall St James [TL6609]

Three Elms: Small open-plan country hideaway, food cooked to order inc good local ham and egg, two or three real ales, farm cider *(Paul and Ursula Randall)*

Clacton on Sea [TM1715]

Crab & Pumpkin [Jackson Rd]: Popular local with real ale and genuine atmosphere *(Reg Nelson)*

Tom Peppers [Marine Parade W, seafront]: Brash young décor, but fascinating – full of interesting photographs, bric-a-brac and other memorabilia *(Reg Nelson)*

Clavering [TL4731]

☆ *Cricketers* [B1038 Newport—Buntingford, Newport end of village]: Only a relative lack of recent reports keeps this nice low-beamed dining pub out of the main entries this year; wide choice of good imaginative home-made food, spacious yet cosy and attractive L-shaped bar with two open fires, well kept Adnams, Flowers IPA and a guest such as Tetleys, friendly service, restaurant; tables outside *(Maysie Thompson, Mrs D Ball, LYM, Charles and Pauline Stride)*

Coggeshall [TL8522]

Chapel Inn [Stoneham St, Market Pl]: Former 15th-c manor, roomy and recently comfortably renovated, with ancient beams, 19th-c woodwork, interesting prints, good value food, friendly efficient service *(Klaus and Elizabeth Leist, Mrs June Miller)*

☆ *Fleece* [West St, towards Braintree]: Handsome and friendly Tudor local, well kept Greene King IPA and Abbot, decent wines, reliable straightforward bar food (not Tues or Sun evenings) from sandwiches up, good coffee, cheery service, children welcome, open all day; spacious sheltered garden with play area, next to Paycocke's *(C L Kauffman, Gwen and Peter Andrews, LYM)*

☆ *White Hart*: Waiter-service dining pub with lots of low Tudor beams, antique settles among other more usual seats, prints and fishing trophies on cream walls, wide choice of food from sandwiches up, well kept Adnams, decent wines and coffee; bedrooms comfortable *(John Faby, Paul and Sandra Embleton, BB, Margaret and Bill Rogers, Janet and Colin Roe)*

Colchester [TM0025]
Firkin & Faunus: Typical Firkin, bright and breezy, with good range of real ales *(Reg Nelson)*

☆ *George Hotel* [High St]: Civilised country-town hotel carefully decorated in tune with its age and character, light and spacious entrance bar with locals popping in to read the paper, thriving lively atmosphere, good interesting food in restaurant with polished tables out alongside under wide parasols; open all day, bedrooms comfortable and good value, with good breakfast *(Chris and Ann Garnett, Margaret and Bill Rogers, R C Hopton)*
Goat & Boot [East Hill]: Character 17th-c pub with splendid old fireplace, real ales, tables on terrace *(Reg Nelson)*

☆ *Playhouse* [St John St]: Flamboyant Wetherspoons conversion of former theatre – good fun, on top of all the usual virtues, with the best features still preserved, inc gilded stage used as an eating area; good value food and drink *(John Faby, Reg Nelson, Rachael and Mark Baynham, Margaret and Bill Rogers)*

☆ *Rose & Crown* [East Gates]: Plush tastefully modernised Tudor inn, timbered and jettied, parts of a former gaol preserved in its rambling beamed bar, pew seats, decent food, nice afternoon teas, well kept Adnams Broadside, Tetleys and a beer brewed for them; comfortably functional bedrooms, many in modern extension, with good breakfast *(George Atkinson, Tony and Ann Allen, Reg Nelson, LYM, Tony and Wendy Hobden)*
Siege House [East St]: Amazing 16th-c timbered building, rambling olde-worlde interior; real ales *(Reg Nelson)*
Stockwell Arms [Stockwell St]: Relaxing timber-framed local in the old Dutch quarter – landlord organises local walks; good choice of well kept ales such as Marstons Pedigree, Morlands Old Speckled Hen, Nethergate, Ruddles County and Websters Yorkshire *(Reg Nelson)*

Coopersale Common [TL4702]
☆ *Theydon Oak* [off B172 E of Theydon Bois]: Attractive weatherboarded pub with lots of hanging baskets, tables in front garden with play area , welcoming beamed bar with lots of brass, copper and bric-a-brac, well kept Bass, Hancocks HB and Wadworths 6X, friendly service, ample cheap food in large eating area with interesting old maps; no piped music (not even the boss's), popular with all ages; tables in

garden with play area *(George Atkinson, A Hepburn, S Jenner, Tony Gayfer)*
Cressing [TL7920]
Three Ashes: Tidy and comfortable, with good value simple food, well kept Greene King ales, decent house wines, welcoming licensees; maybe piped music; tables in pleasantly informal garden *(Gwen and Peter Andrews)*
Danbury [TL7905]
☆ *Anchor* [N of A414, just beyond green]: Emphasis on generous food inc daily fresh Lowestoft fish, light dining conservatory and roomy bar, lots of carved beams, timbering, brickwork and brasses, two log fires, separate games bar, friendly licensees, well kept Ridleys, decent house wines *(LYM, Gwen and Peter Andrews, J H Bell)*
Griffin [A414, top of Danbury Hill]: Spaciously refurbished Chef & Brewer, 16th-c beams and some older carved woodwork, log fire, friendly service, wide choice of flavoursome food, well kept Theakstons; subdued piped music, high chairs *(Susan and Alan Dominey)*
Dedham [TM0533]
☆ *Sun* [High St]: Roomy and comfortably refurbished Tudor pub, cosy panelled rooms with log fires in huge brick fireplaces, handsomely carved beams, well kept ales, decent food, good food, cheerful staff; tables on back lawn, car park behind reached through medieval arch, wonderful wrought-iron inn sign; panelled bedrooms with four-posters, good walk to or from Flatford Mill *(LYM, Rex Miller)*
Doddinghurst [TQ5998]
Moat: Surprisingly pleasant tiny restaurant serving top quality food by a French chef *(Mr and Mrs B D O'Brien)*
Dunmow [TL6221]
Dunmow Hotel [High St]: Some armchairs and red plush, musical instruments and copper hanging from ceiling, reasonably priced food inc fresh fish, friendly atmosphere *(Diane and Paul Burrows)*
Duton Hill [TL6026]
☆ *Three Horseshoes* [off B184 Dunmow— Thaxted, 3 miles N of Dunmow]: Quiet traditional village pub (doubling as post office) with decent low-priced food inc good value big Lincs sausages with choice of mustards in wholemeal baps, well kept Elgoods Cambridge, Ridleys IPA and two guest beers, aged armchairs by fireplace in homely left-hand parlour, welcoming licensees, interesting theatrical memorabilia and enamel advertising signs; pool in small public bar, pleasant views from garden where local drama groups perform in summer *(Gwen and Peter Andrews, BB, M Creasy, John Faby)*
Epping [TL4602]
Thatched House [High St (B1393)]: Small and friendly, two bars, restaurant, low beams, Courage Best and Directors *(Robert Lester)*
Fiddlers Hamlet [TL4700]
☆ *Merry Fiddlers* [Stewards Green Rd, a mile SE of Epping]: Long low-beamed and timbered 17th-c country pub, lots of copper and brass, chamber-pots, beer mugs and plates, real ales

inc Adnams and Ind Coope Burton, good value food, attentive friendly staff, unobtrusive piped music, occasional live sessions; big garden with play area (can hear Mway) *(Robert Lester, A Hepburn, S Jenner)*

Finchingfield [TL6832]

Fox: Splendidly pargeted late 18th-c building (older in parts), straightforward dining pub inside, clean and spacious, with jugs and brass, well kept Courage Best, Morlands Old Speckled Hen and a beer brewed for the pub by Mauldons, pleasant service, good value food (not winter Sun evening); steps down to lavatories; open all day, tables in garden, very photogenic village *(A Hepburn, S Jenner, Gwen and Peter Andrews)*

Fingringhoe [TM0220]

☆ *Whalebone*: Doing well after reopening as dining pub, good imaginative well judged food, friendly service, good choice of wines; spacious garden – a former landlord built a bicycle-powered punt he used to pedal to Colchester *(J M Coumbe)*

Goldhanger [TL9009]

Chequers [B1026 E of Heybridge]: Friendly old village pub with good variety of food inc extremely fresh Friday fish, well kept Greene King and Ind Coope Burton; jazz and live music nights, good walks and birdwatching nearby *(Paul and Ursula Randall, Colin and Joyce Laffan, Pete Yearsley, G Neighbour)*

Great Bardfield [TL6730]

Vine: Simple pub with efficient staff, Adnams and Ridleys, wide range of good value bar food; children allowed if eating *(P and F Balaam)*

Great Easton [TL6126]

Green Man [Mill End Green; pub signed 2 miles N of Dunmow, off B184 towards Lindsell]: Dates from 15th c, cosy and interesting beamed bar, conservatory, reasonably priced food, well kept ales such as Adnams, Greene King IPA and Ridleys, decent wine; piped music may obtrude; children welcome, attractive garden in pleasant rural setting *(Gwen and Peter Andrews)*

Great Henny [TL8738]

☆ *Swan* [Henny Street; Sudbury—Lamarsh rd a mile or so E]: Cosy and friendly well furnished darkly timbered pub with well kept Greene King IPA and Abbot and Marstons Pedigree, decent wines, good coffee, partly no-smoking conservatory restaurant; children allowed, maybe unobtrusive piped music; tables on lawn by quiet river opp, some covered seating, w/e barbecues, friendly talking parrots and other birds *(LYM, Mrs P J Pearce, Gwen and Peter Andrews)*

Great Tey [TL8925]

Chequers [off A120 Coggeshall—Marks Tey]: Well kept comfortable old pub with good reasonably priced food, efficient courteous service, well kept real ale; children and dogs welcome, fine walled garden; quiet village, plenty of country walks *(June and Rex Miller)*

Great Waltham [TL6913]

☆ *Beehive* [old A130]: Neatly kept pub very popular with older people for lunch (freshly cooked, so there may be a wait), seafood nights Fri, well kept Ridleys, welcoming service, good log fire; tables outside, opp attractive church – pleasant village, peaceful countryside *(Adrian White, Gwen and Peter Andrews, Paul and Ursula Randall)*

Hatfield Broad Oak [TL5416]

☆ *Cock* [High St]: Character 15th-c beamed village pub with well kept Adnams Best, Nethergate IPA and changing guest beers, Easter beer festival, decent wines, friendly and attentive young staff, light sunny L-shaped bar with open fire, music hall song sheets and old advertisements, good choice of enjoyable fresh food (not Sun evening) from sandwiches to interesting hot dishes, restaurant; bar billiards; juke box and darts; children in eating area *(LYM, PACW, Joy and Peter Heatherley, A Nicholls)*

Hempstead [TL6337]

Bluebell [B1054 E of Saffron Walden]: Comfortable and attractive beamed bar with two small rooms off and restaurant, good generous changing food, friendly service, pleasantly arranged old pine tables and chairs, inglenook woodburner, good range of guest beers; outside seating; Dick Turpin was brought up in another pub here – the Rose & Crown, now a restaurant *(Pat and Bill Pemberton, DC)*

Herongate [TQ6391]

Green Man [Billericay Rd, A128 Brentwood—Grays]: Big bright beamed bar area with jug collection, cricket memorabilia, log fires each end, Adnams and Tetleys-related ales, decent wines, pleasant service; unobtrusive piped music; children allowed in back rooms, side garden *(R C Morgan)*

Old Dog [Billericay Rd, off A128 Brentwood—Grays at big sign for Boars Head]: Friendly and relaxed, with good choice of well kept ales and of lunchtime bar food inc good sandwiches in long traditional dark-raftered bar, open fire, comfortable back lounge; front terrace and neat sheltered side garden *(LYM, John and Enid Morris)*

Heybridge [TL8707]

Millbeach [Mill Beach, B1026 E]: Exceptional panoramic views over Blackwater estuary, machines in main bar, raised restaurant and family area, picnic-sets by sea wall which gives walks for miles; play equipment, flock of geese *(Howard and Sue Gascoyne)*

Heybridge Basin [TL8707]

Old Ship [Lockhill]: The smarter of the two pubs here, with good friendly service, lots of nautical bric-a-brac, well kept ales inc Adnams Broadside and Nethergate IPA, good value food inc help-yourself salad, blond wooden furniture, unobtrusive piped music; well behaved dogs welcome, no children; seats outside, some overlooking water by canal lock – lovely views of the saltings and across to Northey Island; can be very busy, esp in summer when parking nearby impossible (but public park five mins' walk) *(George Atkinson, Robert Turnham)*

Hockley [TQ8293]

Bull [Main Rd]: Attractive family local in nice

spot by ancient woods, so very popular with walkers; stable area with well kept beers, very hospitable; big garden with own servery, animals, pond and play area; vast car park *(Mrs Jenny Cantle)*

Howe Street [TL6914]

Green Man [just off A130 N of Chelmsford]: Spacious timbered two-bar pub dating from 14th c, not too modernised, with comfortably plush lounge, nice brass and prints, log fire, well kept Ridleys and a guest such as Adnams, cheerful friendly staff, wholesome unpretentious reasonably priced food, restaurant (very popular Sun lunch), separate public bar; unobtrusive piped music; big garden with play area *(Paul and Ursula Randall)*

Kelvedon Hatch [TQ5798]

Eagle [Ongar Rd (A128)]: Clean and friendly local with no-smoking dining area, good food inc fresh fish specials Thurs/Fri, all day Sun roasts, good choice of children's meals, well kept Fullers London Pride, large play area with children's tables; unobtrusive piped music, TV football, live music Thurs, Sat and Sun *(L C Rorke)*

Kirby le Soken [TM2222]

Ship [B1034 Thorpe—Walton]: Wide choice of generous good value food inc filled yorkshire puddings in tastefully refurbished old pink-washed beamed building with relaxing atmosphere, well kept Greene King IPA and Flowers IPA, good wine list, pleasant staff, rustic tables outside; unobtrusive piped music, children in eating area, has been open all day *(Pat and Robert Watt, Mrs June Miller)*

Knowl Green [TL7841]

Cherry Tree: Small thatched local on edge of pretty village, step down to rustic split-level bar, 15th-c beams, guns, brass trays, cricket photographs and vases, steps to back bar with darts and pool; garden with rustic seats and good play area; has had well kept Adnams, Greene King and guest ales and great value food, but genial licensees are talking of retirement – news please *(Richard and Valerie Wright)*

Lamarsh [TL8835]

☆ *Lion* [take Station Rd off B1508 Sudbury—Colchester – Lamarsh then signed]: Recently renovated attractive old pub with abundant beams and timbers, pews, big log fires, local pictures and mural one end, no-smoking area; limited choice of enjoyable food from refurbished kitchen (not Sun evening), well kept Greene King IPA and Nethergate, decent house wines, welcoming staff, restaurant; children in eating area, unobtrusive piped music, games area; sheltered sloping garden, quiet country views; bedrooms planned *(Gwen and Peter Andrews, LYM)*

Leigh on Sea [TQ8385]

Crooked Billet [High St]: Homely old pub with waterfront views from big bay windows, local fishing pictures and bric-a-brac, well kept Tetleys-related ales and a good choice of others, peaking at spring and autumn beer festivals, home-made lunchtime food (not Sun) inc vegetarian, friendly service; piped music, live

music nights; open all day, side garden and terrace *(LYM, John and Enid Morris, Pat and Baz Turvill)*

Little Baddow [TL7807]

☆ *Generals Arms* [minor rd Hatfield Peverel—Danbury]: Neatly kept, cheerful and pleasantly decorated, with well kept ales such as Adnams, Green Jacks Grasshopper and Shepherd Neame Spitfire, reasonably priced wines, enjoyable food inc lots of fish in long bar and modern restaurant, quiet piped music; big lawn with tables and play area, open all day Sun *(Gwen and Peter Andrews, LYM)*

Little Hallingbury [TL5017]

☆ *Sutton Arms* [Hall Green; A1060 Hatfield Heath—Bishops Stortford, E of village]: Pretty thatched rambling cottagey pub with lovely hanging baskets, low-beamed long bar with extension, interestingly varied home-made food, quick friendly service, well kept beers Banks's, B&T, Greene King Abbot, Ind Coope Burton, Timothy Taylor Landlord and Tetleys, daily papers; fruit machine; a bit of a detour off M11, but can get very busy *(Gwen and Peter Andrews, A Hepburn, S Jenner, Adrian White, Ian Phillips, Stephen and Jean Curtis)*

Little Walden [TL5441]

Plough [B1052 Saffron Walden—Linton]: Present owners doing good range of well kept ales tapped from the cask, interesting and enjoyable food too; unobtrusive piped music *(Gwen and Peter Andrews)*

Little Waltham [TL7012]

☆ *Dog & Gun* [E of village, back rd Great Leighs—Boreham]: Long L-shaped timbered dining lounge and suntrap conservatory, good varied generous food from sandwiches to steak inc good fresh veg, well kept Greene King IPA, Abbot and Rayments, decent wine, pleasant efficient smartly dressed staff, comfortable banquettes, piped radio; good-sized garden with elegant pondside willow, unobtrusive climbing frame and aviary *(Adrian White, Paul and Ursula Randall, Gwen and Peter Andrews)*

Littlebury [TL5139]

Queens Head [High St]: Unassuming pub with well kept Banks's and Marstons Bitter and Pedigree, decent wines, traditional games, partly no-smoking restaurant (current licensees concentrating on fish); maybe piped music; tables out in nicely planted walled garden with play area, open all day (Sun late afternoon closure) *(Richard Siebert, LYM, Mr and Mrs G Turner, Gwen and Peter Andrews, R Wiles, H Dickinson, Francis Johnston)*

Littley Green [TL6917]

Compasses [off A130 and B1417 SE of Felsted]: Unpretentiously quaint flagstoned country pub with well kept Ridleys (from nearby brewery) tapped from casks in back room, lots of malt whiskies, big huffers and ploughman's (also bookable evening meals); tables in big back garden, benches out in front *(Eddie Edwards, Tony Beaulah, Paul and Ursula Randall)*

Loughton [TQ4296]

Victoria [Smarts Lane]: Proper traditional pub with no machines, three well kept ales inc Greene King IPA, good range of malt whiskies, good value generous home-made food (not Sun evening, Mon or Tues), small separate dining area, maybe piped classical music; pleasant garden with aviary, rabbits and two newfoundlands *(Mrs A Chesher)*

Maldon [TL8506]

Blue Boar [Silver St]: Former largely 15th-c and later coaching inn, two bars one pubby one in separate coach house on left with beams, roaring log fire, Adnams tapped from the cask, helpful friendly staff, good bar food; bedrooms *(Tina and David Woods-Taylor, TRS, Janet and Colin Roe)*

Carpenters Arms [Gate St (behind Blue Boar)]: Convivial and welcoming, with well kept beer, inexpensive well cooked food for the hungry, friendly staff *(TRS)*

Royal Oak [Fambridge Rd (B1018 S)]: Two-bar local with Greene King IPA and Abbot, generous food inc cheap lunch, welcoming landlady; maybe piped radio *(Gwen and Peter Andrews)*

Manningtree [TM1031]

☆ *Station Buffet* [Manningtree Stn, out towards Lawford]: Clean and warm, with nostalgic early 1950s long marble-topped bar, three little tables and a handful of unassuming seats, interesting well kept ales such as Adnams, Mauldons and Shepherd Neame, good sandwiches and salads, traditional hot dishes, friendly helpful service, no piped music *(Dr Granger, Pat and Tony Martin)*

Margaretting [TL6701]

Red Lion [B1002 towards Mountnessing]: Friendly beamed Ridleys pub with good value food from good fish and chips to more elaborate dishes in non-smoking dining area, well kept beers, cat called Guinness, attractive floral displays; tables in front garden by road *(George Atkinson, Revd Graham E Wright, Sheila Robinson-Baker)*

Matching Green [TL5311]

Chequers: Friendly country local in quiet spot overlooking pretty cricket green, very helpful friendly landlord, good generous cheap food, well kept Adnams, Greene King IPA and Fullers London Pride, good choice of wines, lots of brass, barer bar on right with TV and aircraft pictures; garden *(Gwen and Peter Andrews, Michael and Jenny Back, A Hepburn, S Jenner)*

Matching Tye [TL5111]

Fox: Comfortable and attractive low-beamed 17th-c pub opp peaceful village green, huge choice of imaginative reasonably priced food inc vegetarian, fine choice of real ales, large garden *(Mrs A Chesher)*

Mill Green [TL6401]

☆ *Cricketers*: Cheerful and popular dining pub in picturesque setting, plenty of tables out in front, lots of cricketing memorabilia, some farm tools, well kept Greene King ales tapped from the cask, no-smoking area, friendly attentive service; children welcome, no music, cl winter Sun evenings *(Gwen and Peter Andrews, Neil Spink, Paul and Ursula Randall)*

Moreton [TL5307]

☆ *White Hart* [off A414 or B184 NW of Chipping Ongar]: Wide choice of enjoyable briskly served food inc enormous ploughman's,

good fish and veg and very popular Sun lunch (dining room should be booked then) in rambling multi-level local with small rather functional bars, sloping floor and ceilings, old local photographs, well kept ales such as Adnams, Courage Best and Directors and Ridleys, decent house wines, lovely log fire (with dogs), staff very friendly and helpful even when busy; pleasant circular walk from pub; bedrooms *(Joy and Peter Heatherley, Eddie Edwards, A Hepburn, S Jenner, Martin and Karen Wake)*

Mountnessing [TQ6297]

Prince of Wales [Roman Rd (B1002)]: Pleasant, popular rambling beamed pub opp windmill, modestly priced home-made food, well kept Ridleys IPA *(Paul and Ursula Randall)*

Mundon [TL8601]

Roundbush [B1018 S of Maldon]: Old wooden benches in one part, tables in carpeted part down stairs, no music, Greene King beers tapped from the cask with a guest such as Ushers, generous good value food (also now has café open 8.30-2; 10-1 Sun), helpful landlord *(John Wilmott, Gwen and Peter Andrews)*

Navestock [TQ5496]

Alma Arms [Horsemanside, off B175]: Generous good food inc Sun lunch (no bookings, cash only) *(J H Gracey, Dr Oscar Puls)*

☆ *Plough* [Sabines Rd, Navestock Heath (off main rd at Alma Arms)]: Friendly, unassuming and unsmart country local with half a dozen or more well kept ales and open fire in big divided room, good value usual food (just roasts Sun lunch, not Sun evening, not Mon), small no-smoking restaurant, traditional games; unobtrusive piped music; children welcome, good garden, open all day *(John Fahy, LYM, Beryl and Bill Farmer, Dr Oscar Puls, Kate Jenkins, Ian Brazil, Ted George)*

Newney Green [TL6507]

☆ *Duck* [off A1060 W of Chelmsford via Roxwell, or off A414 W of Writtle – take Cooksmill Green turn-off at Fox & Goose, then bear right]: Comfortable dining pub with attractive and tranquil rambling bar full of beams, timbering and panelling, well kept ales such as Courage Directors, Greene King IPA, Morlands Old Speckled Hen and Shepherd Neame Spitfire, good choice of wines by the glass, good food inc vegetarian, interesting bric-a-brac; attractive garden *(Gwen and Peter Andrews, LYM)*

Newport [TL5234]

Coach & Horses [Cambridge Rd (B1383)]: Great food, five real ales inc lots of guests *(M Creasy, Paul and Sandra Embleton)*

North Shoebury [TQ9485]

Angel [Parsons Corner]: Attractive conversion of timbered and partly thatched former post office, good bar food, Fullers London Pride, Greene King IPA and Abbot and a guest such as Ushers Winter Storm, restaurant popular for business lunches *(Richard and Robyn Wain)*

Nounsley [TL7910]

Sportsmans Arms [Sportsman Lane, back road between those from Hatfield Peverel to Little

Baddow]: Relaxing long open-plan bar with reliable food inc interesting range of unusual Filipino and Far Eastern dishes in small dining room at one end *(Philip Denton)*

Paglesham [TQ9293]

Plough & Sail [back road E of Hockley, Hawkwell and Rochford]: Beautifully kept 17th-c weatherboarded and low-beamed dining pub, recently refurbished with pine furniture, consistently good interesting bar food inc lots of seafood, warm and friendly atmosphere, two well kept beers (one changing weekly), quick helpful service even when busy, big open fires, good flower arrangements; pleasant garden with aviary, very popular on warm summer evenings, in pretty spot nr marshes *(Richard and Robyn Wain)*

Peldon [TL9916]

☆ *Rose* [junction unclassified Maldon road with B1025 Peldon—Mersea]: Cosy and very welcoming low-beamed bar with creaky close-set tables, some antique mahogany, chintz curtains and leaded lights, brass and copper, well kept Adnams, Flowers IPA and Wadworths 6X, decent wines, good food from separate counter (wide range from sandwiches up), no music; children welcome away from bar, restaurant Fri/Sat evening, big no-smoking conservatory, spacious relaxing garden with geese, ducks and nice pond with water voles, play area; bedrooms, good breakfast *(Gwen and Peter Andrews, Martin and Caroline Page, LYM, E A George, R T and J C Moggridge, Hazel R Morgan)*

Pleshey [TL6614]

☆ *White Horse*: Cheerful 15th-c pub with nooks and crannies, big dining-room extension (should book w/e), enjoyable bar food from good big hot filled baps up, welcoming licensees, well kept Ridleys and other real ales, local cider, decent wines, no music; children welcome, tables out on terrace and in garden with small safe play area; pretty village with ruined castle *(LYM, Paul and Ursula Randall, Gwen and Peter Andrews)*

Purleigh [TL8401]

☆ *Bell* [off B1010 E of Danbury, by church at top of hill]: Cosy rambling beamed and timbered pub with fine views over the marshes and Blackwater estuary; beams, nooks and crannies, big inglenook log fire, well kept Adnams, Benskins Best, Greene King IPA and Marstons Pedigree, decent house wines, good reasonably priced home-made lunchtime food, evening steaks, magazines to read, welcoming local atmosphere, Benares brass and other bric-a-brac; dogs welcome, picnic-sets on side grass *(Gwen and Peter Andrews, TRS, LYM)*

Radwinter [TL6137]

☆ *Plough* [B1053 E of Saffron Walden]: Neatly kept red plush open-plan black-timbered beamed bar under new management (central heating replacing the log fire and woodburner), more concentration on food inc good fresh fish, well kept Batemans, Greene King IPA and Ridleys, good coffee, friendly staff, no music; children and dogs on lead welcome, very attractive terrace and garden, open countryside;

bedrooms *(C S Stolings, Gwen and Peter Andrews, BB, Richard and Valerie Wright)*

Rowhedge [TM0021]

Anchor [Quay]: Cosily well used old-fashioned pub in wonderful spot overlooking River Colne with its swans, gulls and yachts; fishing bric-a-brac, good atmosphere, generous reasonably priced food inc fresh fish and cold counter, well kept Bass, cheerful staff; restaurant; gets very busy; picnic-sets on terrace *(Ursula and Paul Randall)*

Roydon [TL4109]

White Hart [High St (B181)]: Charming partly 15th-c pub, brasses on beams, good value generous food inc plenty of puddings and bargain Sun lunch, changing beers such as Greene King, Marstons and Tetleys; attractive village *(June and Perry Dann, G Neighbour)*

Saffron Walden [TL5438]

☆ *Eight Bells* [Bridge St; B184 towards Cambridge]: Large and handsomely timbered Tudor pub open all day for food in open-plan rambling bar and appealing partly no-smoking medieval theme tapestried restaurant, children allowed here and in family room with open fire, well kept real ales such as Adnams, Ind Coope Burton, Greene King Abbot and Tetleys, good wines; games machines; tables in garden, handy for Audley End, good walks *(LYM, A and M Marriott, Peter Smith, Gwen and Peter Andrews, Ian Phillips, Paul and Sandra Embleton, Mayur Shah, Ronald G Dodsworth, Jack Clarfelt, G Washington)*

Shalford [TL7229]

☆ *George* [B1053 N of Braintree]: Very friendly and amusing licensees and son, good attractively priced food inc sandwiches and vegetarian, well kept Adnams Broadside and Greene King IPA, well spaced tables, exposed beams and brickwork, decorative plates and brassware, good solid tables and chairs, log fire in enormous fireplace; lots of children at weekends, tables on terrace *(Anna Holmes, Gwen and Peter Andrews)*

South Hanningfield [TQ7497]

☆ *Old Windmill* [off A130 S of Chelmsford]: Attractive 18th-c beamed and timbered building opp reservoir, areas off spacious L-shaped bar, very friendly staff, good freshly cooked food, exceptional choice of wines by the glass, well kept Theakstons Best and XB, lots of hop bines; piped music turned down on request; tables on terrace and in garden *(Gwen and Peter Andrews)*

Southend [TQ8885]

Last Post [Weston Rd]: Wetherspoons pub in former post office, with all the usual features, no-smoking area, no music, food all day *(Tony Hobden)*

Stock [TQ6998]

Bear [just off B1007]: Civilised locals' front bar, well kept ales such as Adnams and Greene King Abbot, stained glass and bric-a-brac, cosy no-smoking restaurant, children's room; nice back garden overlooking pond *(BB, John and Enid Morris)*

Sturmer [TL6944]

☆ *Red Lion* [A1017 SE of Haverhill]: Warm and

welcoming thatched and beamed dining pub, good generous reasonably priced food (not Sun evening) inc interesting pasta and tasty puddings; well kept Greene King ales, attentive friendly staff, well spaced tables with solid cushioned chairs, convenient layout if you don't like steps, big fireplace; unobtrusive piped music, children in dining room and conservatory, pleasant garden *(MDN)*

Thaxted [TL6130]

Swan [Bullring]: Attractively renovated Tudor pub opp lovely church, well kept Adnams and Greene King, plenty of well spaced tables, polite service, no music, restaurant; open all day, bedrooms *(John Fahy, Gwen and Peter Andrews)*

Theydon Bois [TQ4599]

☆ *Queen Victoria* [Coppice Row (B172)]: Cosy beamed and carpeted lounge with roaring fire, local pictures, mug collection, McMullens ales, very friendly accommodating staff, well presented quick straightforward good value food, bright end dining area with interesting knick-knacks, smaller no-smoking front bar, pleasant bustle; tables on terrace *(Joy and Peter Heatherley, George Atkinson, Roger and Pauline Pearce)*

Thorpe le Soken [TM1922]

Bell: Nice cosy two-level pub with good service, generous food, real ale, reasonable prices; can be very quiet lunchtime *(Mr and Mrs Staples)*

Tillingham [TL9903]

Cap & Feathers [South St (B1021)]: Low-beamed and timbered 15th-c pub, attractive old-fashioned furniture, well kept Crouch Vale Best, IPA, Best Dark and an interesting guest beer, pleasant service, no-smoking family room with pool and table skittles; picnic-sets on side terrace; three bedrooms *(LYM, John Wilmott)*

Tolleshunt Major [TL9011]

☆ *Bell* [off B 1026 NE of Maldon]: Country pub with beams and studwork, comfortable banquettes and bay windows in L-shaped saloon with woodburner, good smiling service even when very busy, well kept Greene King with a guest such as Shepherd Neame Spitfire, good coffee, good value dining area (daily fresh fish), no music, public bar with fruit machine; children welcome, verandah and garden with big rustic pond, barbecue and play area, disabled facilities *(Gwen and Peter Andrews, Colin and Joyce Laffan)*

Upshire [TL4100]

Horseshoes [Horseshoe Hill, E of Waltham Abbey]: Friendly comfortable local dating back to 1800s, simple and clean, with pub food, McMullens beers; tidy garden overlooking Lea Valley, more tables out in front *(Eddie Edwards)*

Waltham Abbey [TL3800]

☆ *Volunteer* [Skillet Hill, Honey Lane, at junction with Claypit Hill, ½ mile from M25 junction 26]: Good genuine chow mein and big pancake rolls (unless Chinese landlady away Mar/Apr) and generous more usual food in well run roomy open-plan pub, swift service even when very busy, attractive conservatory, McMullens

Country and Mild; piped music; some tables on side terrace, pretty hanging baskets, nice spot by Epping Forest *(Robert Lester, Joy and Peter Heatherley, Francis Johnston, D and J Tapper, Sue and Mike Todd, BB)*

Wickham St Paul [TL8336]

Victory [SW of Sudbury]: Spacious pub with good food inc fresh veg, friendly efficient service, view of village cricket green with duck pond; unobtrusive piped music *(Margaret and David Watson)*

Witham [TL8214]

White Hart: Family local with good food, strong teams inc ladies' darts *(Sue Hewson)*

Wivenhoe [TM0321]

☆ *Black Buoy* [off A133]: Interesting 16th-c building, open-plan bar, cool, dark, roomy and convivial, well separated dining area with river view and wide choice of good generous food inc sandwiches, local fish and interesting vegetarian dishes, well kept Greene King and Flowers IPA, open fires; piped music; tucked away from water on steep photogenic street in lovely village, own parking *(Meg and Colin Hamilton, John Fahy, Ian Phillips)*

☆ *Rose & Crown* [Quayside]: Friendly unspoilt Georgian pub in delightful quayside position on River Colne, genuine nautical décor with low beams, scrubbed floors and log fire, well kept Adnams Broadside, Friary Meux Best and Shepherd Neame Spitfire, good baguettes, local and nautical books, no piped music, waterside seats (when the tide's in) *(Quentin Williamson, Rev J Hibberd, Mrs P J Pearce, John Fahy, Richard and Valerie Wright)*

Woodham Ferrers [TQ7999]

Bell: Friendly local with emphasis on usual food in bar and restaurant, real ales inc Adnams and Ridleys; pool; attractive garden with Crouch views *(Gwen and Peter Andrews, TRS)*

Woodham Mortimer [TL8104]

☆ *Royal Oak* [A414 Danbury—Maldon]: Wide choice of generous interestingly presented food esp fish (can take some time when it's busy, but worth the wait), sensibly attentive service, relaxed and friendly atmosphere, well kept Adnams, Flowers IPA and Tetleys from bar tucked away on left; film industry décor, no-smoking restaurant *(Adrian White, Julie King, Gwen and Peter Andrews, Sheila Robinson-Baker, Philip Denton)*

Woodham Walter [TL8006]

☆ *Bell* [signed off A414 E of Chelmsford]: Striking and well maintained 16th-c pub with beams and timbers, decorative plates and lots of brass, comfortable alcoves on various levels, log fire, wide choice of well presented enjoyable bar food (not Mon) from sandwiches to steaks, small dining area with partly panelled upper gallery, Adnams and Friary Meux Best; children in eating areas *(LYM, Paul and Ursula Randall, Gwen and Peter Andrews, Mike and Karen England, David Hanstead, R Turnham)*

Queen Victoria [village centre]: Doing well under current regime, with nice relaxed atmosphere, wide range of bar food, no piped music; Greene King *(Mike and Karen England)*

Gloucestershire

Quite a clutch of enjoyable new entries here this year includes the charmingly unspoilt Red Lion at Ampney St Peter, the civilised Queens Arms at Ashleworth (South African licensees doing imaginative food, in interesting surroundings), the Catherine Wheel in Bibury (back in these pages after a break – and some extensions), the handsome and well run Colesbourne Inn at Colesbourne, the attractively restored Kings Arms at Didmarton (good food, beer and wines), the interesting and very individual Old Spot in Dursley (particularly good beers), and the relaxed Farriers Arms tucked away at Todenham (some concentration on the dining room, but a delightful bar and good beers too). There are quite a lot of other changes in the county this year, too, with several new licensees making their mark. Other pubs currently on top form here include the Kings Head at Bledington (a hugely popular all-rounder), the civilised Crown at Blockley (emphasis on food, but a convivial bar too), the bustling Eight Bells in Chipping Campden, the charming New Inn at Coln St Aldwyns (top-notch food, but a welcome for walkers too), the carefully revived old Five Mile House at Duntisbourne Abbots, the Kilkeney Inn at Kilkenny (imaginative food and a very good wine list at this relaxed dining pub), the Fox at Lower Oddington (super food and wines here too), the friendly and pubby Masons Arms at Meysey Hampton, and the smartly refurbished Old Lodge on the common at Minchinhampton. Most of these have good food, and there are lots of other pubs in this county with really good food, so our choice of a county dining pub here has been particularly difficult this year. In the end our final choice as Gloucestershire Dining Pub of the Year is the New Inn at Coln St Aldwyns. The Lucky Dip at the end of the chapter also has plenty of stars here this year; we'd particularly pick out the Tunnel House at Coates, Dog & Muffler near Coleford, Glasshouse at Glasshouse, Hunters Hall at Kingscote, Golden Ball at Lower Swell, Weighbridge at Nailsworth, Black Horse at North Nibley, Royal Oak in Painswick, Berkeley Arms at Purton, Snowshill Arms in Snowshill, Eliot Arms at South Cerney, Swan at Southrop, Queens Head and Royalist in Stow on the Wold and Coach & Horses nearby, Plaisterers Arms at Winchcombe and Ram at Woodchester. For food, we'd note specially the Crown of Crucis at Ampney Crucis, Horse & Groom at Bourton on the Hill, Craven Arms at Brockhampton, attractively refurbished Green Dragon near Cowley, Churchill at Paxford, Ship at Upper Framilode and Old Fleece at Woodchester. Drinks prices are slightly below the national average here, with virtually no price increase over the last year in pubs here tied to the bigger national or regional combines. However, the cheapest beers tended to be from small more or less local breweries, such as Berkeley (very cheap at the Royal Oak at Woodchester), Archers, Wadworths, Cotleigh, Hook Norton, Donnington and Smiles; the Anchor at Oldbury on Severn stood out for selling a national beer at a very low price, and the Mill Inn at Withington, tied to Sam Smiths of Yorkshire, was also among the cheapest.

ALMONDSBURY ST6084 Map 2
Bowl 🛏

1¼ miles from M5, junction 16 (and therefore quite handy for M4, junction 20; from A38 towards Thornbury, turn first left signposted Lower Almondsbury, then first right down Sundays Hill, then at bottom right again into Church Road

As it is so close to the M5 (though you'd never know it), this attractive pub is popular at lunchtime for its wide choice of bar food. Some favourite dishes might include sandwiches (from £2.95; toasties £3.25; filled pitta bread £3.60), home-made soup (£3.25), leek, potato and aubergine au gratin (£6.95), black bean chilli (£7.95), steak and kidney pie, Mexican beef, hot chicken caesar salad or hungarian goulash (all £8.95), and puddings (from £3.15); service can slow down under pressure but remains pleasant. The long neatly kept beamed bar has blue plush-patterned modern settles, pink cushioned stools and mate's chairs around elm tables, quite a few horsebrasses, stripped bare stone walls, and a big winter log fire at one end, with a woodburning stove at the other; one area of the bar and another in the restaurant are no smoking. Well kept Bath Ales Gold, Coach House Dick Turpin, Courage Best, Moles Best, and Wadworths 6X on handpump; fruit machine, piped music. The brown spaniel is called Charlie, another dog Corrie, and there's a black and white cat. The flowering tubs, hanging baskets and window boxes are pretty, a back terrace overlooks a field, and there are some picnic-sets across the quiet road. *(Recommended by Pat and Tony Hinkins, Gwen and Peter Andrews, D Parkhurst, Mrs Heather March, John and Christine Simpson, Dave Braisted, N P Cox, Ian Phillips, Michael and Lorna Bourdeaux, Bill and Steph Brownson, Lawrence Pearse)*

Inntrepreneur ~ Lease: Mrs P Alley ~ Real ale ~ Bar food (12-2.30, 6-10) ~ Restaurant ~ (01454) 612757 ~ Children welcome ~ Open 11-3, 5(6 Sat)-11; 12-3, 7-11 Sun ~ Bedrooms: £35B/£58B

AMBERLEY SO8401 Map 4
Black Horse 🍺 £

Village signposted off A46 Stroud—Nailsworth; as you pass village name take first very sharp left turn (before Amberley Inn) then bear steeply right – pub on your left

After a walk in the Arun valley, coming here for one of their bargain midweek meals – most dishes are £4.50 then – makes a very pleasant day out. At other times, bar food includes soup (£1.95), ploughman's (from £4.25), sausages and chips (£3.95), steak in ale pie, gammon and egg, vegetable pie or lasagne (all £4.95), cajun chicken (£5.95), swordfish steak (£6.95), vegetable or chicken fajitas (£7.95), and steaks; fresh cod and chips on Friday (£4), and Sunday lunch (£4.95). The dining bar has wheelback chairs, green-cushioned window seats, newspapers to read, and a fire in a small stone fireplace, and there's a conservatory, and a family bar on the left which is no smoking; lovely photographs of old local pubs. A good range of well kept real ales on handpump such as Archers Best and Golden, Greene King Abbot, Ind Coope Burton, Marstons Pedigree, and guest beers; Black Rat scrumpy cider. A separate room (for younger customers) has darts, pool, pinball, fruit machine, and juke box. A back terrace has teak seats, picnic-sets, and a barbecue and spit roast area, and on the other side of the building, a lawn with pretty flowers and honeysuckle has more picnic-sets. There are remarkable views of the surrounding hills. *(Recommended by R Huggins, D Irving, E McCall, T McLean, Dave and Deborah Irving, Michael Gittins, Deborah and David Rees, Andy and Jill Kassube, D G King, Pete and Rosie Flower, Peter and Audrey Dowsett, Neil Porter)*

Free house ~ Licensees Patrick and Sharyn O'Flynn ~ Real ale ~ Bar food ~ (01453) 872556 ~ Children in eating area of bar ~ Open 12-3, 6-11; 12-11 Sat; 12-11 Sun; 12-3, 6-11 Sat and 12-3, 7-10.30 Sun in winter; closed evening 25 Dec

---

Post Office address codings confusingly give the impression that some pubs are in Gloucestershire, when they're really in the Midlands (which is where we list them).

AMPNEY ST PETER SP0801 Map 4
Red Lion ◖

A417, E of village

This little roadside pub is splendidly traditional – even staying closed at lunchtime during the week, saving its energies for the evening. A central stone corridor, served by a hatch, gives on to the little right-hand tile-floor public bar. Here, one long seat faces the small open fire, with just one table and a wall seat, and behind the long bench an open servery (no counter, just shelves of bottles and – by the corridor hatch – handpumps for the well kept Flowers IPA, and Hook Norton Best and summer Haymaker). There are old prints on the wall, but the main thing's the cheerful relaxed chatty atmosphere. On the other side of the corridor is a small saloon, with panelled wall seats around its single table, old local photographs, another open fire, and a print of Queen Victoria one could believe hasn't moved for a century – rather like the pub itself. The inn-sign is rather special – a bit like the MGM lion's face. There are seats in the side garden. *(Recommended by Giles Francis, R Huggins, D Irving, E McCall, T McLean, Mrs S Evans, Gordon, JP, PP)*

Free house ~ Licensee J Barnard ~ Real ale ~ (01285) 810280 ~ Children in the tiny games room ~ Open 6-11(till 10.30 if quiet); 12-2.30, 6-11 Sat; 12-2.30, 6-10.30 Sun

APPERLEY SO8627 Map 4
Farmers Arms ◖

Lower Apperley; nr Apperley on B4213, which is off A38 N of Gloucester

In the grounds of this extended friendly local is the little thatched, modern brick brewhouse where they brew their own very good and popular Mayhems Oddas Light and Sundowner Heavy; they also keep Wadworths 6X on handpump. The bar has guns lining the beams, old prints, horseshoes and stuffed pheasants dotted about, coal-effect gas fires, and plenty of room – though you'll generally find most people in the comfortable and spacious dining lounge; piped music. As well as enjoyable fresh fish, there's also good onion soup, open sandwiches (from £2.60), ploughman's (from £3.75), lasagne, lamb in rosemary and red wine, pork in cider and sage or beef in ale pie (all £5.95), mushroom stroganoff (£6.95), steaks (from £7.95), and puddings (£2.95); friendly service. The neat garden has picnic-sets by a thatched well, with a wendy house and play area. *(Recommended by John Teign, Iain Robertson, Joan and Michel Hooper-Immins, Tom Evans, Alan and Paula McCully, Simon Hulme, C R and M A Starling, Dave Braisted, Howard England)*

Own brew ~ Licensee Geoffrey Adams ~ Real ale ~ Bar food ~ Restaurant ~ (01452) 780307 ~ Children welcome ~ Open 11-3, 6-11; 12-3, 7-10.30 Sun

ASHLEWORTH SO8125 Map 4
Queens Arms ♀ ◖

Village signposted off A417 at Hartpury

Friendly new South African licensees at this attractive low-beamed country pub have brought in wines and dishes from there, as well as a couple of South African prints. There's good attention to detail with everything immaculately clean and lots of careful thought given to the civilised décor. The comfortably laid out main bar, softly lit by fringed wall lamps and candles at night, has faintly patterned earthy grey wallpaper and washed red ochre walls, big oak and mahogany tables and a nice mix of farmhouse and big brocaded dining chairs on a red carpet. Imaginative bar food is all home-made and includes pork and duck liver terrine (£2.95), lunchtime filled french bread (from £3), sherried kidneys (£3.50), mushroom, parsnip and nut terrine (£6.75), steak and kidney pie (£6.95), crispy duck with orange and Grand Marnier (£10.95), and specials like pork tenderloin medallions cooked in cider and apple sauce (£10.25), fried duck breast with creamy sherry and mushroom sauce (£11.50), monkfish on warmed lettuce with chilli, garlic and ginger dressing (£12.50), and puddings like orange and Cointreau trifle, walnut and fudge pudding and fresh strawberry tart (£3.25). Well kept Bass, Donningtons, Shepherd Neame Spitfire and a fourth guest ale in summer. Two perfectly clipped mushroom shaped yews dominate the front of the building, and there are a couple of tables and chairs and old-fashioned benches in the back courtyard. *(Recommended by S H Godsell, Jo Rees, P A Barnett)*

Free house ~ Licensees Tony and Gill Burreddu ~ Real ale ~ Bar food (till 10 Sun) ~ Restaurant ~ (01452) 700395 ~ Well behaved children welcome ~ Open 12-3, 7-11(10.30 Sun)

ASHLEWORTH QUAY SO8125 Map 4
Boat ★

Ashleworth signposted off A417 N of Gloucester; quay signed from village

This is the sort of delightful place where everyone talks to each other. It has been in the same family since it was originally granted a licence by Charles II, and the charming landladies work hard at preserving its unique, gentle character. Spotlessly kept, the little front parlour has a great built-in settle by a long scrubbed deal table that faces an old-fashioned open kitchen range with a side bread oven and a couple of elderly fireside chairs; there are rush mats on the scrubbed flagstones, houseplants in the window, fresh garden flowers, and old magazines to read; shove-ha'penny, dominoes and cribbage (the front room has darts and a game called Dobbers). A pair of flower-cushioned antique settles face each other in the back room where Arkells BBB, Oakhill Yeoman, and Smiles Best and guests like Batemans XXXB, Slaters Top Notch, and Wye Valley Bitter are tapped from the cask, along with a full range of Westons farm ciders. They usually do good lunchtime rolls (£1.60) or ploughman's with home made chutney during the week. This is a lovely spot on the banks of the River Severn and there's a front suntrap crazy-paved courtyard, bright with plant tubs in summer, with a couple of picnic-sets under cocktail parasols; more seats and tables under cover at the sides. The medieval tithe barn nearby is striking; some readers prefer to park here and walk to the pub. *(Recommended by Iain Robertson, JP, PP, Andy and Jill Kassube, Pete Baker, Derek and Sylvia Stephenson, R Michael Richards, the Didler, Kerry, Ian and Simon Smith, Howard England, P and S White, Mrs A Oakley)*

Free house ~ Licensees Irene Jelf and Jacquie Nicholls ~ Real ale ~ Bar food (lunchtime only) ~ (01452) 700272 ~ Children welcome until 8pm ~ Open 11-2.30(3 Sat), 6-11; 12-3, 7-10.30 Sun; closed Weds lunchtimes Oct-Apr

AUST ST5789 Map 2
Boars Head

½ mile from M4, junction 21; follow Avonmouth sign and keep eyes peeled for sign off on left

The neatly kept and comfortable main bar in this busy pub has well polished country kitchen tables and others made from old casks, old-fashioned high-backed winged settles in stripped pine, decorative plates hanging from one stout black beam, some walls stripped back to the dark stone, big rugs on dark lino, and a large log fire. Another room has a second log fire, while a third has more dining tables with lace tablecloths, fresh flowers and candles. Popular bar food includes sandwiches, soup (£2.95), fresh asparagus (£4.50), a help-yourself salad bar (£3.50), faggots and mash (£6.95), smoked salmon and scrambled eggs (£7.95), tasty half roast pheasant or haunch of venison (£8.50), fresh whole plaice or individual joints of lamb (£9.25), puddings like fruit crumble, and a choice of three Sunday roasts (£8.50). Part of the eating area is no smoking; piped music. Well kept Courage Best and Directors, and Hardy Royal Oak on handpump; quite a few malt whiskies. There's a medieval stone well in the pretty sheltered garden, which has an aviary and rabbits. Also a touring caravan site. *(Recommended by Dr and Mrs Morley, Christopher and Mary Thomas, Ian Phillips, S H Godsell, M Joyner, D G Clarke)*

Eldridge Pope (Hardy) ~ Manager Mary May ~ Real ale ~ Bar food ~ (01454) 632278 ~ Children welcome ~ Open 11-3, 6.30-11; 12-3, 7-10.30 Sun

AWRE SO7108 Map 4
Red Hart ◀

Village signposted off A48 S of Newnham

There's quite a choice of good, enjoyable food in this attractive and surprisingly tall country pub. As well as 2-course (£4.95) and 3-course (£6.25) lunches, there might be sandwiches and ploughman's, filled baked potatoes (from £3.95), spicy Thai crab cakes, curries or home-baked ham and egg (£6.25), steaks (from £9.75), daily specials such as home-made soup (£2.75), smoked trout pâté (£3.95), hot, spicy prawns (£4.50), mushroom stroganoff or guinea fowl (£6.25), cod in hollandaise and chilli sauce (£7.25), and lamb chops (£8.95), and puddings like profiteroles or banoffee pie (from £2.95). The neat L-shaped main part of the bar has a deep glass-covered illuminated well, an antique pine bookcase filled with cookery books, an antique pine display cabinet with Worcester china, and pine tables and chairs; there are plates on a delft shelf at the end, as well as a gun and a stuffed pheasant over the stone fireplace, and big prints on the walls; one area of the bar is no smoking, as is the restaurant. Well kept Bass, plus four changing guests like Freeminers Speculation, Fullers London Pride, Hampshire Pride of Romsey, and SP Sporting Ales Doves Delight on handpump, a growing collection of malt whiskies, and decent house wine; darts, dominoes, fruit machine, trivia, and piped music. In front of the building are some picnic-sets. *(Recommended by Neil Townend, Duncan Cloud, Julie and William H Ryan, Stuart and Alison Wallace, Paul and Heather Betterworth)*

Free house ~ Licensee Jeremy Bedwell ~ Real ale ~ Bar food ~ Restaurant ~ (01594) 510220 ~ Children in eating area of bar ~ Open 12-3, 6.30(6 Sat)-11; 12-3, 7-10.30 Sun ~ Bedrooms: /£55B

BARNSLEY SP0705 Map 4
Village Pub 🍴

A433 Cirencester—Burford

Enthusiastic new licensees had just taken over this popular pub as we went to press, and plan to refurbish the bars quite extensively. They've also brought a new chef with them who has introduced a menu that changes twice a day: sandwiches (from £2.95; smoked salmon, cream cheese and chives £4.75), vegetable soup with pesto (£3), ploughman's (£3.95), chicken liver parfait with onion marmalade or seared salmon salad with bacon and avocado (£4.75), black pudding stovie, poached egg and mustard sauce (£6.75), calf's liver, sage and sweet vinegar (£7.50), neck of lamb, couscous, pepper, tomato and parsley salsa (£8), fried scallops with spring cabbage, fresh peas and bacon (£9.50), fillet of beef with béarnaise sauce (£11.95), and puddings such as lemon tart or chocolate semifreddo (£3.95). Well kept Hook Norton Bitter,Wadworths 6X, and a guest beer on handpump, farm ciders, and malt whiskies. There are country pictures, gin-traps, scythes and other farm tools on the walls of the comfortable low-ceilinged communicating rooms, several winter log fires, and plush chairs, stools and window settles around the polished candlelit tables; one area is no smoking. Shove-ha'penny, cribbage, and dominoes. The sheltered back courtyard has plenty of tables, and its own outside servery. The pub is handy for Rosemary Verey's garden in the village. *(Recommended by John P W Bowdler, Simon Collett-Jones, R Huggins, D Irving, E McCall, T McLean, Paul S McPherson, Nigel and Elizabeth Holmes, Maysie Thompson, M Joyner, Sidney and Erna Wells, Gordon)*

Free house ~ Licensees Tim Haigh and Rupert Pendered ~ Real ale ~ Bar food (12-2.30(4 Sat/Sun), 7-9.30(10 Fri/Sat) ~ (01285) 740421 ~ Children in eating area of bar and restaurant ~ Open 11-3, 6-11; 11-11 Sat; 12-10.30 Sun ~ Bedrooms: £40S/£50S

BIBURY SP1106 Map 4
Catherine Wheel

Arlington; B4425 NE of Cirencester

In a pretty Cotswold village, this bustling low-beamed pub is a welcoming place with a series of rooms around a central bar. The main bar at the front dates back in part to the 15th c, and has lots of old-fashioned dark wood furniture, prints and photographs of old Bibury, and good log fires; there are also two smaller and quieter back rooms, and a dining room. Generous helpings of good food include home-made soup (£2.50), garlic mushrooms (£3.95), sandwiches and filled french bread (from £3.50), filled baked potatoes (from £4.25), ploughman's (from £4.25), home-cooked ham and egg (£5.75), chicken curry, vegetable or meaty lasagne or cottage pie (all £5.95), steak and mushroom pie (£6.25), fresh trout (£7.25), sirloin steak (£9.95), children's menu (£3.25), and roast Sunday lunch (£6.25). Well kept Hardy Country on handpump, fruit machine, TV, and piped music. There's a good sized, neat garden behind with picnic-sets among fruit trees, and some seats out in front. *(Recommended by Peter and Audrey Dowsett, Steve Whalley, Tracey Hamond, Tim and Ann Newell, Simon and Amanda Southwell)*

Free house ~ Licensees Cecil and Evelyn McComb ~ Real ale ~ Bar food (12-2, 6-9) ~ (01285) 740250 ~ Children welcome ~ Open 11-11; 12-3, 7-10.30 Sun ~ Bedrooms: /£50S

BISLEY SO9006 Map 4
Bear 🍺 ⇌
Village signposted off A419 just E of Stroud

To find this elegant rather gothic little village inn, just head for the church. The meandering L-shaped bar has an enormously wide low stone fireplace (not very high – the ochre ceiling's too low for that), a long shiny black built-in settle and a smaller but even sturdier oak settle by the front entrance, and a good relaxed atmosphere; a separate no-smoking stripped-stone area is used for families. Good home-made bar food includes soup (£2.50), tasty goat's cheese toasties (£3.25), lots of filled french bread like roasted ratatouille, black pudding, tomato and fried egg or prawns in lemon and garlic butter (from £3.95), sautéed potatoes and onions flavoured with smoked salmon and leek or chicken and bacon or burgers such as smoked haddock and caper with chilli and lime mayonnaise or sweet and sour pork (from £3.95), home-made pies and casseroles – rabbit and vegetable pie, potato, apple, leek and cheese wedge or steak, kidney and Guinness (from £5.95), and puddings; small helpings for children, and good breakfasts. Well kept Bass, Flowers IPA, Tetleys, Castle Eden, and Wadworths 6X on handpump; helpful, attentive service. Darts and table skittles. A small front colonnade supports the upper floor of the pub, and the sheltered little flagstoned courtyard made by this has a traditional bench; the garden is across the quiet road, and there's quite a collection of stone mounting-blocks. The steep stone-built village is attractive. *(Recommended by Mike and Heather Watson, Tim and Linda Collins, Peter and Audrey Dowsett, Mike and Mary Carter, P and S White, Bryen Martin, Lynn Sharpless, Bob Eardley, Richard Gibbs, Nick and Meriel Cox, Greg Kilminster, Lawrence Pearse, Simon Collett-Jones)*

Pubmaster ~ Tenants Nick and Vanessa Evans ~ Real ale ~ Bar food (not Sun evening) ~ (01452) 770265 ~ Children in restaurant area only ~ Occasional folk or Irish music ~ Open 11-3, 6-11; 12-3, 7-10.30 Sun ~ Bedrooms: £18.50/£37

BLAISDON SO7017 Map 4
Red Hart 🍺
Village signposted off A4136 just SW of junction with A40 W of Gloucester; OS Sheet 162 map reference 703169

A fine choice of real ales and enjoyable, interesting food continues to draw customers to this bustling pub. The flagstoned main bar has cushioned wall and window seats, traditional pub tables, a big sailing-ship painting above the good log fire, and a thoroughly relaxing atmosphere – helped along by well reproduced piped bluesy music, and maybe Spotty the perky young jack russell. There are always five real ales on handpump that change regularly from a list such as Cottage, Exe Valley, Goffs, RCH, Timothy Taylor, Uley, Woods and Wychwood, and so forth; a decent wine list. On the right, an attractive two-room no-smoking dining area with some interesting prints has good home-cooked specials such as ham, egg and bubble and

squeak (£4.75), smoked chicken and avocado salad or good salmon and coriander
fishcakes with hollandaise sauce (£3.75 starter, £5.95 main course), good curries,
steaks (from £8.50), roast monkfish with parma ham on a bed of spinach, bass on
noodles in a cream and white wine sauce or fillet of lamb with a port and cranberry
sauce (£9.50), and Sunday roast lunch (£5.25); sandwiches (from £3.25),
ploughman's (from £3.95), and children's menu. What was the games room is now
used as cosy extra eating space; piped music. There are some picnic-sets out beside
flowerbeds by the quiet road, and more in a pretty garden up behind where there's a
barbecue area; pot-bellied pigs and ponies. Dogs welcome on a lead. *(Recommended by
Mike and Mary Carter, E J Locker, S Godsell, Guy Vowles, Miss S P Watkin, P A Taylor, Ted
George, Neil and Anita Christopher, John Gillett, Tracey and Stephen Groves, F J and A
Parmenter, P G Topp, Howard England)*

*Free house ~ Licensee Guy Wilkins ~ Real ale ~ Bar food ~ Restaurant ~ Children
welcome ~ Open 12-3, 6-11; 12-3, 7-10.30 Sun*

BLEDINGTON SP2422 Map 4
Kings Head ★ ⑪ ♀ ◖ ⇦
B4450

When you find an inn that is enjoyable to stay at and also serves interesting,
reasonably priced food, it is a real bonus to discover that it also keeps a fine range of
real ales and has a really good pubby atmosphere, too. The spotlessly kept, smart
main bar is full of ancient beams and other atmospheric furnishings such as high-
backed wooden settles and gateleg or pedestal tables, and there's a warming log fire
in the stone inglenook (which has a big black kettle hanging in it); the lounge looks
on to the garden, and to the left of the bar is a carpeted sitting room with
comfortable new sofas, magazines to read, views of the village green from a small
window, and some attractive antiques and old gilt-edged paintings on the walls. At
lunchtime, bar food includes home-made soup (£2.25), super sandwiches served
with straw potatoes and salad (from £3.25 for pork and apple with crackling;
shredded duck, plum paste, cucumber and spring onion on tortilla or blackpudding,
apple and chive from £4.25), lasagne (£4.95), sautéed liver with calvados cream,
braised local rabbit in cider and mustard or noodles with various toppings (£5.95),
liver, parma ham, red onion and sage wrap on a skewer or roasted quail bruschetta
with sweet onion and black butter (£6.95), puddings like dark chocolate and prune
tart or fresh figs and caramelised mascarpone (from £2.50), and children's choice
(from £1.50); in the evening, there might be pork crackling and apple cider dip
(£1.95), pigeon and orange pâté (£2.95), smoked eel toasty with fresh watercress
and scrambled egg (£4.95), steak, mushroom and wine pie (£6.95), pork fillet
sautéed with stem ginger, spring onions, fresh sage and apple jus (£8.95), steaks
(from £10.95), half a crispy honey-roast duck with confit of orange peel, sloeberry
and cointreau (£12.95), specials like mussels with chilli and tomatoes or wine and
cream (£4.25), various pasta dishes (£6.95), and salmon, scallop and prawn pie
(£8.95); good value three-course meals (£10.95), and tasty breakfasts. An antique
bar counter dispenses well kept Hook Norton Best, Morlands Tanners Jack, Uley
Old Spot, Wadworths 6X, and Wychwood Fiddlers Elbow, an excellent extensive
wine list, with 10 by the glass, and 50 or so malt whiskies; efficient, friendly service.
Part of the restaurant area is no smoking; piped music. The public bar has darts,
table skittles, dominoes, trivia, and piped music. The back garden has tables that
look over to a little stream with lots of ducks. *(Recommended by Susan and John Douglas,
John Marshall, John P W Bowdler, Pam and David Bailey, John and Esther Sprinkle, Bob and
Maggie Atherton, Martin and Catherine Snelling, Marvadene B Eves, Sandra and Keith Abbley,
RJH, Maysie Thompson, Bett and Brian Cox, David and Anne Culley, Douglas Caiger, Martin
Jennings, Pam Adsley, Keith and Margaret Kettell, Steve Goodchild, Chris and Val Ramstedt, J H
Jones, Eddie Edwards, NWN, Susan and Nigel Wilson, Colin and Ann Hunt, Mrs C Fielder, Ted
George, D W Evans, Phil and Caroline Welch)*

*Free house ~ Licensees Michael and Annette Royce ~ Real ale ~ Bar food ~ Restaurant
~ (01608) 658365 ~ Children in Garden Room area ~ Open 11-2.30, 6-11; 12-2.30,
7-10.30 Sun; closed 24 and 25 Dec ~ Bedrooms: £45B/£65B*

BLOCKLEY SP1634 Map 4

Crown ★ ⏍ ♀ 🛏

High St

Of course many people come to this golden stone Elizabethan inn for the imaginative food, but there's a bustling convivial bar – especially popular during Happy Hour – and a good mix of customers. A long bar counter stretches from the front door through two interconnecting snug areas with comfortable padded green leather chairs and plush stools around pubby tables, padded window seats, various prints on the walls, and an open fire, into a larger atmospheric room with comfortable sofas and chairs, newspapers to read, and another open fire. There's a no-smoking upstairs restaurant and downstairs no-smoking brasserie with french windows overlooking terraces and gardens, with proper garden furniture; piped music. Good bar food includes home-made soup (£2.95), sandwiches (from £3.50), tasty fresh artichoke heart with vegetables cooked in white wine, saffron, basil and coriander or shredded skate wing on a red-skin potato and rocket salad with fresh herb dressing (£4.95), mixed vegetable strudel with fresh tomato sauce (£7.50), cod in beer batter (from £7.95), stir-fried chicken with chilli, egg noodles, and soya sauce (£8.95), pork medallions with an apple and rhubarb mash surrounded by a black grape and armagnac sauce (£9.95), lemon sole (£10.95), roast rack of lamb with garlic jus (£12.95), and puddings like chocolate and raspberry roulade or sticky toffee pudding with caramel sauce (£3.95). Well kept Fullers London Pride and Hook Norton Best on handpump, and a decent wine list; friendly staff. The terraced coachyard is surrounded by beautiful trees and shrubs, and there's a hatch to hand drinks down to people sitting out in front, by the lane. The inn is handy for Batsford Park Arboretum. *(Recommended by Chris and Val Ramstedt, Steve Whalley, Peter and Giff Bennett, John Bramley, Dorothy and Leslie Pilson, David and Nina Pugsley, LM, Joy and Peter Heatherley, Ted George, Mick and Jeanne Shillington, Peter and Janet Race, Rob Whittle, Martin Jones, Chris Miller, Liz Bell, SLC, IHR, Lawrence Pearse, David Edwards, Marvadene B Eves, N Christopher, R J Hebblethwaite)*

Free house ~ Licensee Peter Champion ~ Real ale ~ Bar food ~ Restaurant ~ (01386) 700245 ~ Well behaved children welcome ~ Open 11-12; 12-12 Sun ~ Bedrooms: £70B/£99B

BRIMPSFIELD SO9413 Map 4

Golden Heart ♀ ◖

Nettleton Bottom; A417 Birdlip—Cirencester, by start of new village bypass

This extended partly 16th-c pub has welcoming licensees and staff and a good pubby atmosphere. The main low-ceilinged bar is divided into three cosily distinct areas, with a roaring log fire in the huge stone inglenook fireplace in one, traditional built-in settles and other old-fashioned furnishings throughout, and quite a few brass items, typewriters, exposed stone, and wood panelling. A comfortable parlour on the right has another decorative fireplace, and leads into a further room that opens onto the terrace; two rooms are no smoking. It's the daily specials that draw attention here – though they do serve sandwiches and a more standard menu: hot bacon, chicken and avocado salad, grilled pollock with crab sauce or kangaroo and black cherry casserole (£8.25), rack of lamb (£8.95), and ostrich steak with coconut sauce (£10.95). Well kept Bass, Hook Norton, Marstons Pedigree and Timothy Taylor Landlord on handpump; decent wines.They hold beer festivals during the May and August bank holidays. There are pleasant views down over a valley from the rustic cask-supported tables on its suntrap gravel terrace; good nearby walks. *(Recommended by P and S White, Ian Phillips, JP, PP, R Huggins, D Irving, E McCall, T McLean, Chris and Ann Garnett, James Nunns, C R and M A Starling, Lawrence Pearse, N Christopher, Mrs Margaret Ross)*

Free house ~ Licensee Catherine Stevens ~ Real ale ~ Bar food (till 10pm) ~ Restaurant ~ (01242) 870261 ~ Children welcome ~ Open 11-3, 6-11; 11-11 Sat; 12-10.30 Sun ~ Bedrooms: £35B/£55B

BROAD CAMPDEN SP1637 Map 4
Bakers Arms ◀

Village signposted from B4081 in Chipping Campden

There are no noisy games machines, juke box or piped music in this traditional village pub.The biggish room is divided into two, and the tiny beamed bar has a pleasant mix of tables and seats around the walls (which are stripped back to bare stone), and an inglenook fireplace at one end. The oak bar counter is attractive, and there's a big framed rugwork picture of the pub. Bar food includes sandwiches, cottage pie, smoked haddock bake or chicken curry (£4.95), a pie of the day (£5.95), and daily specials such as liver and bacon, cauliflower cheese or pork and apricot (£5.95). Well kept Adnams Bitter and Marstons Pedigree with changing guests like Timothy Taylor Landlord on handpump. Darts, cribbage, dominoes. There are white tables under parasols by flower tubs on a couple of terraces and in the back garden some seats under an arbour, and a play area. The tranquil village is handy for the Barnfield cider mill. *(Recommended by Carol and David Harard, David and Nina Pugsley, Brian and Bett Cox, Ann and Bob Westbrook, Mrs G Connell, David Gregory, John Robertson, Jenny and Michael Back, Carol and Steve Spence, Ted George)*

Free house ~ Licensees Ray and Sally Mayo ~ Real ale ~ Bar food ~ (01386) 840515 ~ Children welcome away from bar ~ Folk music 3rd Tues evening of month ~ Open 11.30-3, 6-11; 12-3, 7-10.30 Sun; 11.30-2.30, 6.30-11 in winter; closed 25 Dec, evening 26 Dec

CHEDWORTH SP0511 Map 4
Seven Tuns

Upper Chedworth; village signposted off A429 NE of Cirencester; then take second signposted right turn and bear left towards church

Smiles Brewery have taken over this little 17th-c pub and are making improvements to the back garden so families, walkers and dogs will all be welcome. The cosy little lounge on the right has a good winter log fire in the big stone fireplace, comfortable seats and decent tables, sizeable antique prints, tankards hanging from the beam over the serving bar, a partly boarded ceiling, and a relaxed, quiet atmosphere. The basic public bar on the left is more lively, and opens into a games room with pool, cards, and juke box; there's also a skittle alley (which can be hired). Bar food changes daily and includes soup (£3.25), filled french bread (from £4.95), fish and chips (£6.50), brie baked with a herb crust (£6.95), calf's liver, smoked bacon and mushrooms or monkfish and king scallops with fresh rosemary and anchovy sauce (£8.95), Aberdeen Angus peppered steak (£11.95), and home-made puddings (£2.95). Well kept Smiles Best and Golden and guests like Adnams Broadside, Everards Old Original, Fullers London Pride, and Otter Ale on handpump. Across the road is a little walled raised terrace with a waterwheel and a stream, and there are plenty of tables both here and under cocktail parasols on a side terrace. Handy for the nearby famous Roman villa. *(Recommended by R Huggins, D Irving, E McCall, T McLean, Nick and Meriel Cox, JKW, A C Morrison, Neil and Anita Christopher, Paul and Judith Booth, Simon Collett-Jones, J Gibbs, J H Kane, Chris Raisin)*

Smiles ~ Manager N Jones ~ Real ale ~ Bar food ~ (01285) 720242 ~ Children in eating area of bar ~ Open 11-11; 12-10.30 Sun

CHIPPING CAMPDEN SP1539 Map 4
Eight Bells ♀ ◀ 🛏

Church Street (which is one way – entrance off B4035)

There's a friendly, bustling atmosphere in this handsome old inn and a good mix of locals and visitors. Heavy oak beams have massive timber supports, walls are of stripped stone and hung with caricatures of regulars and photographs of pub events), and there are cushioned pews and solid dark wood furniture on the broad flagstones, daily papers to read, and log fires in up to three restored stone fireplaces – an enormous one has a painting of the pub in summer; the bar extension has a fine rug on the wall and a glass inlet in the floor showing part of the passage from the church by which Roman Catholic priests could escape from the Roundheads. Several areas are no smoking. Good bar food includes tasty curried parsnip soup (£2.95), warm leek tart with parmesan crisps (£4.95), skate, leek and potato terrine with saffron vinaigrette (£5.25), pasta with tomato sauce and pesto (£6.50), sausage and mash with onion gravy (£7), sea bream with thai dipping sauce (£8), roast chicken breast in parma ham with mushroom sauce (£8.50), chargrilled hake with red wine and chorizo (£9), and loin of lamb with aubergine and basil cream (£10). Well kept Adnams, Marstons Pedigree, Exmoor Gold, Thwaites Bitter, and Vaux Waggledance on handpump on a striking oak bar counter, small or large glasses of wine from a decent list, and good cafetière coffee. A fine old courtyard surrounded by roses and climbers has picnic-sets. Handy for the Cotswold Way walk to Bath. *(Recommended by John P W Bowdler, Martin and Karen Wake, Nigel Clifton, Howard England, Peter and Anne Hollindale, Martin Jones, P and S White, Pat and Roger Fereday, Bett and Brian Cox, Richard and Robyn Wain, H Dickinson, Wendy Arnold, Tina and David Woods-Taylor, Gwen and Peter Andrews, Ann and David Blackadder, John Saul, Simon Collett-Jones, Paul S McPherson, Steve Goodchild)*

Free house ~ Licensee Kirstie Sykes ~ Real ale ~ Bar food ~ (01386) 840371 ~ Children welcome ~ Open 11-3, 5.30-11; 12-3, 6-10.30 Sun; closed 25 Dec ~ Bedrooms: £30B/£50B

Noel Arms ♀ 🛏

Carefully refurbished and under new licensees, this smart old place is where Charles II is reputed to have stayed after the Battle of Worcester in 1651. There are old oak settles and attractive old tables, seats and newer settles among the windsor chairs, armour, casks hanging from the beams, and farm tools, horseshoes and gin-traps on the bare stone walls; winter coal fire, and a back conservatory. The small lounge areas are comfortable and traditionally furnished with coach horns, lantern lighting, and some stripped stonework, and the reception area has its quota of pikes, halberds, swords, muskets, and breastplates. Well kept Bass, Hook Norton Best, and a guest beer on handpump kept under light blanket pressure, and quite a few malt whiskies; piped music. Decent bar food at lunchtime (not on Sunday) includes home-made soup (£2.50); sandwiches and soup £4.50), home-made pâté (£3.75), mussels in white wine and shallots with frites and garlic mayonnaise, vegetable curry or home-made chicken and mushroom pie (£5.95), gammon and pineapple or poached salmon (£6.25), and puddings (£2.75); afternoon tea. The restaurant is no smoking. The sunny enclosed courtyard has lots of pretty hanging baskets. *(Recommended by K and M Kettell, Pam Adsley, E A Froggatt, Mr and Mrs L Pilson)*

Free house ~ Licensee Eleanor Jobson ~ Real ale ~ Bar food ~ Restaurant ~ (01386) 840317 ~ Children welcome ~ Open 11-3, 6-11; 11-11 Sat; 12-3, 7-10.30 Sun ~ Bedrooms: £75B/£105B

COLD ASTON SP1219 Map 4
Plough

Village signposted from A436 and A429 SW of Stow on the Wold; beware that on some maps the village is called Aston Blank, and the A436 called the B4068

In a little village, this tiny 17th-c pub is cosy and welcoming with a good bustling atmosphere. The snug areas are divided up by standing timbers and have low black beams, a built-in white-painted traditional settle facing the stone fireplace, simple old-fashioned seats on the flagstone and lime-ash floor, and a happy mix of customers. Good bar food at lunchtime (they tell us prices have not changed since last year) includes filled rolls (from £2.75), ploughman's (£4.25), filled baked potatoes (from £4.50), tasty spinach and ricotta cannelloni (£5.25), steak in ale pie (£5.50), and scampi and king prawn platter (£6.96), with evening dishes such as fresh salmon on a bed of leeks with a dill sauce or calf's liver and bacon with garlic mash and onion gravy (£8.95), duck breast with an orange sauce (£9.50), pork with calvados sauce or enjoyable half shoulder of lamb (£9.95), and medallions of fillet steak with a dijon mustard sauce (£11.95); you must book for the no-smoking restaurant. Well kept Adnams, Hook Norton Best, and Theakstons Best on handpump; darts and piped music. The small side terraces have picnic-sets under parasols, and there may be Morris dancers out here in summer. *(Recommended by John and Joan Wyatt, Alison Keys, Stephen and Julie Brown, Chris Mawson, Neil and Anita Christopher, R Huggins, D Irving, E McCall, T McLean, Gwen and Peter Andrews, Ted George, Ian, Colin and Ann Hunt, Simon Collett-Jones)*

Free house ~ Licensees E A and C Goodwin ~ Real ale ~ Bar food ~ (01451) 821459 ~ Children in eating area of bar ~ Open 11-2.30, 6.30-11; 12-3, 7-11 Sun

COLESBOURNE SO9913 Map 4
Colesbourne Inn
A435 Cirencester—Cheltenham

The licensees at this quite noble-looking grey stone and gabled 18th-c coaching inn ran the Greyhound in Siddington until they came here a couple of year ago. They've refurbished the spacious bar with heavy dark wooden chairs, settles and tables on bare boards, ochre painted walls, soft lighting and a log fire; well kept Wadworths IPA, 6X and Farmers Glory; darts, shove-ha-penny, table skittles, dominoes and piped music. A room off to the left has chintzy sofas and armchairs by a cosy log fire in a big stripped stone fireplace and painted flint walls. Bar food includes soup of the day (£2.80), sandwiches (from £2.80), pâté (£3.95), garlic mushrooms in a vol au vent (£4.15), ploughman's (from £5.45), stilton and red onion quiche (£6.35), vegetable casserole with herb dumplings (£7.45), chicken and cashew nut curry (£7.55), steak and kidney pudding (£7.65), hotpot (£8.95), duck, bacon and brandy pie (£9.95), four or so daily specials like hot pork baguette (£3.95) and lasagne (£5.75) with more elaborate ones in the evening such as monkfish and queen scallops in tomato, basil and garlic sauce (£11.95) or pork tenderloin with stilton and horseradish sauce (£10.95), and puddings like banoffee pie or orange and ginger crunch (£3.15); Sunday lunch (£7.20); no-smoking restaurant. There are views of the Churn valley and wooded Cotswolds from the attractive back garden and terrace; well appointed bedrooms in converted stable block; no dogs. *(Recommended by John and Joan Wyatt)*

Wadworths ~ Tenant Robert Flaxman ~ Real ale ~ Bar food (12-2.30, 7-10 (9.30 Sun)) ~ Restaurant ~ (01242) 870376 ~ Children in restaurant ~ Open 11-3, 6.30-11; 12-3, 7-10.30 Sun; closed 25 and 26 Dec, I Jan ~ Bedrooms: £38B/£56B

COLN ST ALDWYNS SP1405 Map 4
New Inn 🍴 ♀ 🛏
On good back road between Bibury and Fairford
Gloucestershire Dining Pub of the Year

While most people do come to this civilised and welcoming creeper-clad inn to enjoy the very good food, there are plenty of surrounding country walks and walkers (not their muddy boots) are most welcome if a thirst-quenching drink is all they want. The two neatly kept main rooms are most attractively furnished and decorated, and divided by a central log fire in a neat stone fireplace with wooden mantlebeam and willow-pattern plates on the chimney breast; there are also low beams, some stripped stonework around the bar servery with hops above it, oriental rugs on the red tiles, and a mix of seating from library chairs to stripped pews. Down a slight slope, a further room has a log fire in an old kitchen range at one end, and a stuffed buzzard on the wall. From the bar menu, dishes might include soup (£3.25), sesame coated fishcakes with tomato and pepper salsa (£4.75; £9.25 main course), crab, ginger and coriander won tons with sweet chilli dipping sauce (£5; £9.25 main course), fish and chips (£8.50), steak and kidney pie with mustard mash (£10.50), slow roasted belly of pork with caramelised onions, pea and potato mash (£11), casserole of duck with olives, thyme and white wine (£12), grilled rib-eye steak with garlic butter (£13.50), and puddings such as spiced apple pudding with caramel cider sauce, rhubarb and ginger crumble or milk chocolate rice pudding served cold with orange sorbet, white chocolate and mint sauce (£4.25); vegetarian and child dishes available. The restaurant is no smoking. Well kept Butcombe Best Bitter, Hook Norton Best, Wadworths 6X, and Wychwood Shires XXX on handpump, 8 good wines by the glass, and several malt whiskies. The split-level terraced garden has plenty of seats. The peaceful Cotswold village is pretty, and the riverside walk to Bibury is not to be missed. They tell us they are now called The New Inn & Coln. *(Recommended by John Bowdler, Bronwen and Steve Wrigley, RJH, Bob and Maggie Atherton, Chris and Val Ramstedt, Tracey Hamond, W Burke, D Irving, E McCall, R Huggins, T McLean, Liz Bell, N J Worthington, S L Tracy, John Bramley, Chris Miller, Simon Collett-Jones, Mr and Mrs Broadhurst, D M and M C Watkinson, Neil and Anita Christopher, Peter and Giff Bennett, C R and M A Starling; also in the Good Hotel Guide)*

Free house ~ Licensee Brian Evans ~ Real ale ~ Bar food ~ Restaurant ~ (01285) 750651 ~ Children in eating area of bar; over 10 in restaurant ~ Open 11-11; 12-10.30 Sun ~ Bedrooms: £68B/£96B

CRANHAM SO8912 Map 4
Black Horse 🍺

Village signposted off A46 and B4070 N of Stroud; up side turning

Two bedrooms with their own bathrooms were just being opened up in this old-fashioned 17th-c pub as we went to press. A cosy little lounge has just three or four tables, and the main bar is quarry-tiled, with cushioned high-backed wall settles and window seats, and a good log fire. The food is good and popular, and it's best to book in the restaurant at weekends. As well as several themed food evenings during the year, the menu includes sandwiches (from £1.85; toasties £2.25), ploughman's (from £4), curried nut loaf with red pepper sauce (£6.50), Gloucester Old Spot pork chops (£7.25), beef and Guinness pie, sausage and bacon toad in the hole or breast of chicken with wine and mustard or stilton sauce (£7.50), haddock and prawn mornay (£8.25), kleftiko (£9.50), and home-made puddings like fruit crumble or sticky toffee pudding (£2.50); Sunday roast (£6.50). You can eat the same menu in the upstairs dining rooms (best to book at weekends). Very well kept Boddingtons, Flowers Original, Hook Norton Best, Marstons Pedigree, and Wickwar BOB on handpump, and country wines. Shove-ha'penny and piped music; Truffle the brittany spaniel is quite a character. Tables in the sizeable garden behind have a good view out over the steep village and wooded valley, and they keep chickens and rabbits. *(Recommended by Graham and Karen Oddey, Richard and Jean Phillips, Lawrence Pearse, James Nunns)*

Free house ~ Licensees David and Julie Job ~ Real ale ~ Bar food (not Sun evening) ~ Restaurant ~ (01452) 812217 ~ Children welcome ~ Occasional Irish music and Morris dancers ~ Open 11.30-2.30, 6.30-11; 12-3, 7-11 Sun ~ Bedrooms: £25B/£45B

DIDMARTON ST8187 Map 2
Kings Arms ♀ 🍺

A433 Tetbury rd

Working their way round a big central counter, the knocked-through rooms at this attractively restored and decorated 18th-c coaching inn have deep terracotta walls above a dark green dado, a pleasant mix of chairs on bare boards, quarry tiles and carpet, a big stone fireplace and a nice old upright piano. Everything is neat and tidy, with good attention to detail, and the particularly friendly welcome here attracts an appealing mix of customers. Well liked bar food includes soup (£2.95), filled french bread (from £3.50), chicken liver and oyster mushroom pâté with fig and ginger chutney (£4.35), moules marinières or thai spiced fishcakes with salad and lime mayonnaise (£5.95), local sausages with basil and potato mash (£6.20), haddock in beer batter (£6.25), beef, ale and vegetable casserole with baked potato or fisherman's pie (£6.95), and puddings like warm sticky toffee pudding with toffee sauce or dark chocolate fondant with Kahlua coffee sauce (£3.75). In the bar you can also have the more elaborate restaurant menu, with things like warm salad of pigeon breasts with pine kernels in balsamic and walnut dressing (£4.25) and seared

Scottish scallops with a concasse of tomato (£12.95). In addition to well kept John Smiths, Uley Hogshead and a couple of guests like Archers Golden and Theakstons Best on handpump there's quite a good wine list including some bin ends; darts, cribbage, dominoes, boules *(Recommended by Chas Wright, W J Williams, D Irving, E McCall, R Huggins, T McLean)*

Free house ~ Licensees Nigel and Jane Worrall ~ Real ale ~ Bar food (bar meals only Sun evening) ~ Restaurant ~ (01454) 238245 ~ Children in eating area of bar ~ Occasional live entertainment ~ Open 12-3, 6-11; 12-3, 7-10.30 Sun

DUNTISBOURNE ABBOTS SO9709 Map 4
Five Mile House ♣

Just off A417 5 miles N of Cirencester (newish bypass)

The friendly licensees have created a cheerful, bustling atmosphere in this 300-year-old coaching inn and reports from readers are most favourable. The front has a companionable bare-boards drinking bar on the right, with wall seats around the big table in its bow window and just one other table; on the left is a flagstoned hallway tap room snug formed from two ancient high-backed settles by a (new) woodburning stove in a tall carefully exposed old fireplace. The thoroughly old-fashioned feel of this part is preserved by the landlord's tactful insistence that if you want to eat even a sandwich you should move to one of the other areas, such as the lounge behind the left-hand snug. There's a small cellar bar (piped music on request down here – it's a perfect size for a group celebration), a back restaurant down steps, and a refurbished family room on the far side; cribbage and dominoes. The lounge and cellar bar are no smoking. Well kept Marstons Best, Timothy Taylor Landlord, and a changing guest on handpump (the cellar is temperature-controlled, interesting wines (strong on New World ones). Generous helpings of enjoyable bar food (cooked by the landlord and with virtually unchanged prices) includes, at lunchtime, home-made soup (£2.50), open sandwiches (from £2.50), ploughman's (£4.25), stilton, spinach and mushroom lasagne, 6oz rump steak baguette or home-cooked smoked ham with two eggs (£5.95), and whole local trout with prawn and lemon butter (£6.95); in the evening, there might be hot chicken-liver and bacon salad (£4.25), chicken breast stuffed with stilton and wrapped in bacon on a brandy and mushroom cream sauce (£7.95), shoulder of lamb stuffed with redcurrants and mint with a redcurrant and port gravy or fillet of red snapper with a white wine and chive cream sauce (£8.50), 12oz Aberdeen Angus rump steak with sauces (£9.95), and puddings such as home-made American chocolate cheesecake, good lime pie or fruit crumbles (£2.50); children's helpings where possible, and Sunday roast lunch (£5.95). Best to book at weekends. Service is thoughtful and friendly. There are front and back gardens with nice country views; quoits. This quiet country lane was once Ermine Street, the main Roman road from London to Wales. *(Recommended by Jenny and Roger Huggins, D Irving, E McCall, T McLean, Guy Vowles, Gordon, Mike and Mary Carter, JP, PP, Christopher Mobbs, DC, Neil and Anita Christopher, Kevin Thorpe, Giles Francis)*

Free house ~ Licensees John and Jo Carrier ~ Real ale ~ Bar food (12-2.30, 6-9.30) ~ Restaurant ~ (01285) 821432 ~ Children in restaurants ~ Open 12-3, 6-11; 12-3, 7-10.30 Sun

DURSLEY ST7598 Map 2
Old Spot ♣

By bus stn

Tucked away behind a car park and bus station this unassuming white-rendered old farmhouse is easily missed. Really popular with a lively bunch of locals, it's a good solid neatly restored pub with an interesting choice of very well kept ales including two from the small local brewer Uley (one of them, Old Ric, is named after the landlord and the brewer often drinks here), and changing favourites from brewers like Adnams, Bass, Hampshire, Marstons and Otter on handpump. The front door opens into a deep pink little room with stools on shiny quarry tiles along its pine boarded bar counter, and old enamel beer advertisements on the walls and ceiling.

Leading off here there's a little room on the left with a bar billiards table (also shove-ha'penny and cribbage), and the little dark-floored room to the right has a stone fireplace. From here a step takes you down to a no-smoking cosy Victorian tiled snug. Simple bar food includes doorstep sandwiches (£2.20), filled french sticks (£3) and a platter of English cheeses; pétanque in the attractive garden. *(Recommended by Chas Wright, Dr and Mrs A K Clarke, J R Jewitt, W J Williams)*

Free house ~ Licensee Ric Sainty ~ Real ale ~ Bar food (11-2.30) ~ (01453) 542870 ~ Children welcome in garden and separate meeting room ~ Folk club Wed ~ Open 11-3, 5-11; 11-11 Sat; 12-10.30 Sun

EBRINGTON SP1840 Map 4
Ebrington Arms
Signposted from B4035 E of Chipping Campden; and from A429 N of Moreton in Marsh

This is an unspoilt village local with plenty of regulars and walkers, and an unpretentious atmosphere. The little bar has some fine old low beams, stone walls, flagstoned floors and inglenook fireplaces (the one in the dining room still has the original iron work), plus sturdy traditional furnishings, some seats built into the airy bow window, and a slightly raised wood-floored area. A lower room, also beamed and flagstoned, has stripped country-kitchen furnishings. Decent simple bar food (chalked up on the beams) might include soup or egg and chips (£2.50), sausage and onion bap (£2.50; filled french bread £3.95), omelettes (from £3.75), ratatouille with garlic bread (£4.25), ploughman's (from £4.25), local sausages (£5.25), steak and mushroom pie or fresh cod (£5.95); decent breakfasts. Well kept Donnington SBA, Hook Norton Best and a guest beer on handpump; they have a pianola (absolutely no piped music or games machines). Trophies bear witness to the success of the pub's dominoes team, and you can also play cribbage, darts and shove-ha'penny. An arched stone wall shelters a terrace with picnic-sets under cocktail parasols. No dogs at least at mealtimes, when the licensees' friendly welsh springer is also kept out. Handy for Hidcote and Kiftsgate. *(Recommended by Ted George, John Brightley, A Y Drummond, Dr D E Granger, P and S White, Martin Jones, Simon Collett-Jones, NMF, DF, Marvadene B Eves, David Edwards, Mr and Mrs Richard Osborne, G Washington, Sandra and Chris Taylor)*

Free house ~ Licensee Gareth Richards ~ Real ale ~ Bar food (not Sun evening) ~ (01386) 593223 ~ Children welcome ~ Open 12-2.30, 7-11; 12-3, 7-10.30 Sun; closed evening 25 Dec ~ Bedrooms: /£40B

EWEN SU0097 Map 4
Wild Duck ★ ♀
Village signposted from A429 S of Cirencester

On the edge of a peaceful village, this civilised and popular 16th-c inn has a high-beamed main bar with a winter open fire, candles on tables, a nice mix of comfortable armchairs and other seats, paintings on the coral walls, crimson drapes, and magazines to read; another bar has a handsome Elizabethan fireplace and antique furnishings, and looks over the garden. Well liked bar food includes home-made soup, spicy chicken salad with warm ciabatta or deep-fried prawns with mustard and lime dip (all £4.95), ploughman's (£5.50), fish and chips or field mushroom and herb tagliatelle (£6.95), braised shank of lamb with a rosemary and lemon grass gravy (£7.95), chicken breast with a mushroom and tarragon sauce (£8.95), roast half duckling with a cherry and orange sauce (£10.95), fresh fish dishes, and puddings like honey and oat fruit crumble or bread and butter pudding (£3.50). As well as Duckpond Bitter, brewed especially for the pub, well kept beers might include Courage Directors, Smiles Best, and Theakstons Best and Old Peculier on handpump, kept under light blanket pressure. Good wines, several malt whiskies, and shove-ha'penny. There are attractive white painted cast-iron tables and seats in the neatly kept and sheltered garden. *(Recommended by Mrs Pat Crabb, Keith and Margaret Kettell, Ian, G Francis, RJH, Chris Raisin, D G King, Bernard Stradling, Andrew and Eileen Abbess, Paul S McPherson, H Spencer, Simon Collett-Jones, Mrs M Dyke, Ian Phillips, Maysie*

Thompson, Gordon, Tim and Linda Collins, M A and C R Starling, R Huggins, D Irving, E
McCall, T McLean, Marvadene B Eves, B Perfect, Howard England, Richard Fendick, Peter and
Janet Race, Louise Medcalf, Greg Kilminster, Stephen Brown)

Free house ~ Licensees Tina and Dino Mussell ~ Real ale ~ Bar food (till 10pm) ~
Restaurant ~ (01285) 770310 ~ Children welcome ~ Open 11-11; 12-10.30 Sun ~
Bedrooms: £55B/£69.50B

FORD SP0829 Map 4
Plough
B4077

The gallops for local stables are opposite, so there's quite a racing feel in this pretty
stone pub, and several customers are usually reading the *Racing Post*. Friendly new
licensees have taken over and there's always a good welcome and bustling
atmosphere in the beamed and stripped-stone bar; also, racing prints and photos on
the walls, old settles and benches around the big tables on its uneven flagstones, oak
tables in a snug alcove, and three welcoming log fires (one is log-effect gas).
Dominoes, cribbage, shove-ha'penny, fruit machine, and piped music. Enjoyable
home-made bar food includes lunchtime sandwiches (from £2.25; brunch baguette
£4.95) and ploughman's (£4.50), soup (£2.95), home-made chicken liver pâté or
stilton and mixed herb mushrooms (£3.95), ham and egg or cumberland sausage on
chive mash with red onion gravy (£6.50), 16oz cod fillet in beer batter (£6.95), pork
tenderloin on a bubble and squeak cake with mustard sauce (£8.95), fried duck
breast with oriental vegetables and black bean sauce (£9.95), and steaks (from
£9.95). They still have their traditional asparagus feasts every April-June, when the
first asparagus spears to be sold at auction in the Vale of Evesham usually end up
here. Well kept Donnington BB and SBA on handpump. There are benches in front,
with rustic tables and chairs on grass by white lilacs and fairy lights, and a play area
at the back. Look out for the llama farm between here and Kineton. *(Recommended by
Kevin Thorpe, JP, PP, Tim and Linda Collins, H Dickinson, Peter and Audrey Dowsett, Edward
and Richard Norris, Stan and Hazel Allen, Eddie Walder, Bill Wood, Nick J Lawless, Guy
Vowles, J Dwane, Marvadene B Eves, Martin Jones, Mrs C Fielder, R Huggins, D Irving, T
McLean, E McCall, Bernard and Becky Robinson, Stephen and Julie Brown, the Didler, Tom
Evans, Richard Gibbs)*

*Donnington ~ Tenant C Turner ~ Real ale ~ Bar food ~ (01386) 584215 ~ Children
welcome ~ Open 11-11; 12-10.30 Sun; closed 25 Dec ~ Bedrooms: £35S/£55S*

GREAT BARRINGTON SP2013 Map 4
Fox
Village signposted from A40 Burford—Northleach; pub between Little and Great Barrington

This is a very prettily set pub tucked away down a winding lane in a quiet little
village with the River Windrush beside the sizeable garden, and a landscaped pond
in the orchard; the terrace is heated so you can enjoy it all in cooler weather as well.
Inside, there's a new dining area with river views and the low-ceilinged small bar has
rustic wooden chairs, tables and window seats, stripped stone walls, and two roaring
log fires. Donnington BB and SBA on handpump, and Addlestones cider. The pub
dog is called Bruiser (though he's only little). Bar food includes sandwiches (not
Sundays), warm chicken, bacon and brie salad or portuguese sardines (£5.25), steak
in ale pie or lasagne (£7.50), stir-fried pork fillet with crispy vegetables in sweet and
sour sauce (£7.95), and fresh Bibury trout (£8.95). There's a skittles alley out beyond
the sheltered yard, and they have private fishing. *(Recommended by the Didler, Tim and
Linda Collins, George Atkinson, David Lamb, Jenny and Michael Back, R Huggins, D Irving, T
McLean, E McCall, Ted George, TBB)*

*Donnington ~ Tenant Paul Porter ~ Real ale ~ Bar food (12-2.30, 6.30-9.30; all day
Sun and summer Sat; not winter Mon evening) ~ Restaurant ~ (01451) 844385 ~
Children welcome ~ Open 11-11; 12-10.30 Sun ~ Bedrooms: £32.50S/£55S*

GREAT RISSINGTON SP1917 Map 4

Lamb ♀ 🛏

Overlooking the village and surrounding hills, this partly 17th-c inn has a rather civilised two-roomed bar. Wheelback and tub chairs with cushioned seats are grouped around polished tables on the light brown carpet, a table and settle are hidden in a nook under the stairs, and there's a log-effect gas fire in the stone fireplace; some interesting things to look at include part of a propeller from the Wellington bomber that crashed in the garden in October 1943, a collection of old cigarette and tobacco tins, photographs of the guide dogs the staff and customers have raised money to buy (over 20), a history of the village, and various plates and pictures. Good bar food such as home-made soup (£3), home-made chicken liver pâté (£3.95), home-made faggots with onion gravy (£8.25), lamb's liver and bacon (£8.95), grilled Bibury trout with apricot and caper stuffing (£9.50), chicken kiev (£9.85), half shoulder of lamb in wine gravy (£10.50), surf and turf fillet steak (£13.50), and home-made puddings (£4.50); you can also eat from the more extensive menu of the partly no-smoking restaurant. Well kept Fullers London Pride, Ruddles, and Wadworths 6X on handpump, a good wine list, and several malt whiskies; helpful service, piped classical music, and dominoes, cribbage, and trivia. You can sit out in the sheltered hillside garden or really take advantage of the scenery and walk (via gravel pits now used as a habitat for water birds) to Bourton on the Water. Bedroom prices are cheaper during the week. *(Recommended by Mike and Heather Watson, Bronwen and Steve Wrigley, John and Jackie Chalcraft, Alastair Campbell, Ted George, Walter Reid, Peter and Janet Race)*

Free house ~ Licensees Richard and Kate Cleverly ~ Real ale ~ Bar food ~ Restaurant ~ (01451) 820388 ~ Children in eating area of bar ~ Open 11.30-2.30, 6.30-11; 12-3, 7-10.30 Sun; closed 25 and 26 Dec ~ Bedrooms: /£90B

GREET SP0230 Map 4

Harvest Home

B4078 N of Winchcombe

It's well worth coming to this friendly pub if you're a senior citizen as they serve very good value two-course lunches (Monday-Thursday) for £4.95. Other food is good value too: home-made soup (£2.75), filled french bread (from £2.75), garlic mushrooms (£3.80), ploughman's (from £4.75), omelettes (£5.25), ham and egg (£6.25), home-made steak and mushroom pie (£6.45), seafood crêpes with mornay sauce (£6.55), chicken tikka (£6.50), pork schnitzel (£7.95), puddings like good apple strudel, and children's menu (from £2.75). The rooms are spotlessly kept, and the bar has a dozen or so well spaced tables, with seats built into the bay windows and other sturdy blue-cushioned seats; there are pretty flower prints and country scenes on the walls, and several dried-flower arrangements. The lounge bar is linked to the dining room by a servery with a bric-a-brac shelf, a big cartwheel centre light, and lots of hop bines to the exposed beams. Well kept Boddingtons, Fullers London Pride, Hook Norton Best, Tetleys, and Wadworths 6X on handpump, decent wines, and several malt whiskies; darts down at one end and a good open fire at the other; cribbage, dominoes, and general knowledge quizzes; helpful and pleasant young staff. There's a big beamed pitched-roof side restaurant (same food; no smoking). The sizeable garden has a play area and boules, a terrace with access to the restaurant, and a narrow-gauge GWR railway that passes it. The miniature schnauzers are called Oscar and Boris. The pub is not far from medieval Sudeley Castle. *(Recommended by H Wolstenholme, Martin Jones, Howard England, G R Williams, Sue and Steve Griffiths, Stephen and Julie Brown, Bernard and Majorie Parkin, C R and M A Starling, J H Kane, Nigel and Rita Cooke, Derek and Sylvia Stephenson, Steve Corrigan, Marvadene B Eves)*

Whitbreads ~ Lease: Karl-Heinz Stolzenberg ~ Real ale ~ Bar food ~ Restaurant ~ (01242) 602430 ~ Children welcome ~ Open 11-3, 6-11; 12-3, 6-10.30 Sun

---

If we know a pub has a no-smoking area, we say so.

GRETTON SP0131 Map 4
Royal Oak ◀

Village signposted off what is now officially B4077 (still often mapped and even signed as A438), E of Tewkesbury; keep on through village

Originally, this was a pair of old stone-built cottages, and the series of bare-boarded or flagstone rooms have a friendly bustle and candles in bottles on the mix of stripped oak and pine tables; also, dark ochre walls, beams (some hung with tankards, hop bines and chamber-pots), old prints, and a medley of pews and various chairs; the friendly setter is called George and there are two cats. The well liked no-smoking dining conservatory has stripped country furnishings, and a broad view over the countryside. Good bar food includes soup, ploughman's (£4.50), daily specials such as mustard and garlic baked leg of lamb or stilton stuffed chicken wrapped in bacon (both £7.95), steaks, and puddings. Well kept Goffs Jouster, John Smiths, Ruddles County, and Wickwar BOB on handpump, and a decent wine list; darts and shove-ha'penny. From seats on the flower-filled terrace you can enjoy the wonderful views over the village and across the valley to Dumbleton Hills and the Malverns. There are more seats under a giant pear tree, a neatly kept big lawn running down past a small hen-run to a play area (with an old tractor and see-saw), and even a bookable tennis court. *(Recommended by P and S White, Marvadene B Eves, Dr A Drummond, Gordon, Lawrence Pearse, Stephen and Julie Brown, George Atkinson, Derek and Sylvia Stephenson, Chris Raisin, Martin Jones, Nigel Clifton)*

Free house ~ Licensees Robert and Kathy Willison ~ Real ale ~ Bar food ~ Restaurant ~ (01242) 602477 ~ Children in eating area of bar and in restaurant ~ Folk music Weds evening ~ Open 11-3, 6-11; 12-3, 7-10.30 Sun; closed 25 and 26 Dec

GUITING POWER SP0924 Map 4
Hollow Bottom

Village signposted off B4068 SW of Stow on the Wold (still called A436 on many maps)

The comfortable beamed bar in this snug old cottage is full of racing memorabilia including racing silks, tunics and photographs (it is owned by a small syndicate that includes Peter Scudamore and two trainers), and there's a winter log fire in an unusual pillar-supported stone fireplace; the public bar has flagstones and stripped stone masonry and racing on TV. Bar food includes ploughman's (£4.50), steak and kidney or chicken and mushroom pies (£5.75), chicken kiev (£6.50), fresh beer battered cod (£7.50), 10oz rump steak (£9.50), various daily specials (£6-£9.50), and Sunday roasts (£7.50). Well kept Bass, Hook Norton, and Goffs Jouster on handpump; afternoon tea. From the pleasant garden behind are views towards the peaceful sloping fields. Decent walks nearby. *(Recommended by Gavin Smith, NWN, John and Esther Sprinkle, Lawrence Pearse, Pat and Roger Fereday, M L Berryman)*

Free house ~ Licensees Edward Rugge-Price and Marilyn Scudamore ~ Real ale ~ Bar food ~ Restaurant ~ (01451) 850392 ~ Children in eating area of bar and in restaurant ~ Irish duo occasionally ~ Open 11-11; 12-10.30 Sun; closed evening 25 Dec

HYDE SO8801 Map 4
Ragged Cot ♀ ◀ 🛏

Burnt Ash; Hyde signposted with Minchinhampton from A419 E of Stroud; or (better road) follow Minchinhampton, Aston Down signposted from A419 at Aston Down airfield; OS Sheet 162 map reference 886012

There's a good local atmosphere in this 17th-c Cotswold stone inn. The rambling bar has black beams and quite a bit of stripped stone, cushioned window seats, red cushioned wheelback chairs and bar stools, a stuffed owl, and at each end, a log fire – one has a traditional dark wood settle by it; there's also a no-smoking eating area. Good value bar food includes sandwiches and rolls (from £1.25; hot granary rolls from £3.75), home-made soup (£2), chicken liver pâté (£3.25), sausage, egg and chips (£3.35), filled baked potatoes (£3.95), pasta or pie of the day (£4.95), vegetarian dishes (£5.25), rump steak (£6.45), and daily specials such as greek salad (£2.95 starter, £4.95 main course), trout with three-herb butter or stuffed chicken breast with asparagus (£6.50), pork tenderloin with cider, cream and sage or duck with plum and ginger (£7.25), a huge mixed grill (£8.95), and fillet rossini (£11.95); at lunchtime, they also have cumberland sausage or faggots and onion gravy (£4.75), and home-baked ham and egg or liver and bacon (£4.95). Puddings such as toffee and banana crème brûlée, fruit crumbles, and apple and calvados sorbet (all £2.50). Well kept Bass, Theakstons Best, Uley Old Spot, Wadworths 6X, and a guest beer on handpump, a thoughtful wine list, 75 malt whiskies, and Westons cider; shove-ha'penny, cribbage, dominoes, backgammon, Scrabble, and dice. There are picnic-sets (and an interesting pavilion) in the garden, and bedrooms in an adjacent converted barn. *(Recommended by Simon Collett-Jones, R Huggins, D Irving, E McCall, T McLean, Neil and Anita Christopher, Peter and Audrey Dowsett, Simon Penny)*

Free house ~ Licensee Nicholas Winch ~ Real ale ~ Bar food (no food 25/26 Dec) ~ Restaurant ~ (01453) 884643 ~ Children in eating area of bar and in restaurant ~ Open 11-2.30, 6-11; 12-3, 7-10.30 Sun ~ Bedrooms: £40B/£58B

KILKENNY SP0018 Map 4
Kilkeney Inn 🍴 ♀

On A436, 1 mile W of Andoversford, nr Cheltenham – OS Sheet 163 map reference 007187

This is very much somewhere to come and enjoy reliably good imaginative food in a welcoming and relaxed atmosphere. There might be light lunch dishes such as filled french bread (from £3.20), ploughman's (£4.35), local pork sausage with onion gravy (£4.95), lasagne (£5.50), and fish pie (£6.25), as well as soup (£2.50), terrine of Gloucester Old Spot pork, red onion and mixed herbs served on brioche toast (£4.25), warm tartlet of ratatouille and wild mushrooms with a stilton dressing (£4.35), caramelised red onion and cherry tomato tart tatin with a sharp lemon sauce or steak and kidney pie (£7.25), fricassee of minted welsh lamb and butter beans (£7.95), deep-fried caribbean chicken with couscous and a tomato and apricot sauce (£9.25), grilled medallions of thai marinated beef fillet with king prawn stir-fry rice and a szechuan and coriander sauce (£11.95), steaks (from £11.25), and puddings such as honey, lemon and lime cheesecake, summer pudding, and chocolate délice (£3.25). Booking is recommended, especially at weekends. The extended and modernised bar, quite bright and airily spacious, has neatly alternated stripped Cotswold stone and white plasterwork, as well as gleaming dark wheelback chairs around the tables, and an open fire. Up at the other end of the same long bar is more of a drinking area, with well kept Ruddles Best and Tetleys on handpump, an excellent range of decent wines and lots of malt whiskies. It opens into a comfortable no-smoking dining conservatory. Attractive Cotswold views, and good parking. *(Recommended by Dr and Mrs Cottrell, Mr and Mrs C R Little, Michael Doswell, Paul and Yvonne Crispin, Mr and Mrs B J P Edwards, W M and J M Cottrell, Charles Gysin, Greg Kilminster, E A George, Dr and Mrs A Newton, Graham and Karen Oddey)*

Free house ~ Licensees John and Judy Fennell ~ Real ale ~ Bar food ~ Well behaved children in restaurant ~ Open 11.30-2.30, 6.30-11; 12-2.30, 7-10.30 Sun; closed Sun evenings Jan-Mar

LITTLE BARRINGTON SP2012 Map 4
Inn For All Seasons 🍴 ♀ 🍺 🛏

On the A40 3 miles W of Burford

To make the most of this friendly and civilised old inn, it's worth staying overnight – and the breakfasts are good. The attractively decorated mellow lounge bar has a relaxed atmosphere, low beams, stripped stone, and flagstones, old prints, leather-upholstered wing armchairs and other comfortable seats, country magazines to read, and a big log fire (with a big piece of World War II shrapnel above it); maybe quiet piped classical music. The licensee has a fish business in Brixham, so their half a dozen fresh fish dishes are particularly good: seared squid and chilli salad (£9.50), fresh Cornish crab or scallops, avocado and bacon with lime dressing (from £10), seared salmon with spinach on a bacon and vermouth sauce (£10.50), whole lemon sole (from £12), and fillet of bass with stir-fried vegetables on a ginger sauce (£14.50). Other good bar food might include home-made soup (£3.25), lunchtime sandwiches (from £3.25), pressed gammon and parsley terrine with a sweet red onion chutney (£4.25), fresh pasta cooked in a creamy port and wild mushroom sauce with parmesan shavings (£7.25), thai chicken curry (£7.95), slow roasted belly of pork with a braised savoy cabbage, black pudding and a rich peppercorn sauce (£8.75), crispy confit of Aylesbury duck with a spring onion and cucumber salad dressed in a ginger and hoi sin vinaigrette (£9.25), and Hereford rump steak (£11.95). Well kept Badger Best, Glenny Wychwood Shires XXX and St George's Ale, and Wadworths 6X on handpump, a good wine list, and over 60 malt whiskies; piped music. The pleasant garden has tables, and there are walks straight from the inn – if you're staying, you may be asked to take the owners' two well trained dogs along with you. It's very busy during Cheltenham Gold Cup Week – when the adjoining field is pressed into service as a helicopter pad. *(Recommended by J H Kane, Simon Collett-Jones, Peter and Audrey Dowsett, Bett and Brian Cox, Tom Evans, John and Joan Wyatt, Susan and John Douglas, Charles Gysin, Nick and Meriel Cox, Liz Bell, Nigel Williamson, Jenny and Chris Wilson)*

Free house ~ Licensees Matthew and Heather Sharp ~ Real ale ~ Bar food (11-2.30, 6-9.30) ~ Restaurant ~ (01451) 844324 ~ Children welcome ~ Open 11-2.30, 6-11; 12-2.30, 7-10.30 Sun ~ Bedrooms: £41.50B/£83B

LITTLE WASHBOURNE SO9933 Map 4
Hobnails

B4077 (though often mapped still as the A438) Tewkesbury—Stow on the Wold; 7½ miles E of M5 junction 9

Since 1743, the present landlord's family have been running this cheerful 15th-c pub – and you can still be sure of a friendly welcome. The snug little front bar has low sway-backed beams hung with pewter tankards, lots of old prints and horse brasses, and old wall benches by a couple of tables on its quarry-tiled floor; there's a more modern, carpeted back bar with comfortable button-back leatherette banquettes and newspaper cuttings about the pub and the family; open fire. Bar food (with prices unchanged since last year) includes their speciality baps (from £1.60; liver £3.10; steak in wine £5.25; you can build your bap with extras like fried banana, melted stilton, fried egg, and so forth), home-made soup (£2.75), ploughman's (£4.25), cashew nut and mushroom loaf (£6.60), lasagne or goulash (£6.75), daily specials, home-made puddings (£3.45), children's menu (from £1.25), and their special cider cake with cheese (£2.55); fresh vegetables (£2.55). Both dining rooms are no smoking. Well kept Boddingtons, Flowers Original, Hook Norton, and Wadworths 6X on handpump; darts, shove-ha'penny, quiet piped music. A separate skittle alley (with tables) can be hired weekday evenings. Between the two buildings, and beside a small lawn and flowerbed, there's a terrace with tables, and children's playground. *(Recommended by Mike and Mary Carter, Sheelia Curtis, Ron Fletcher, Sue and Steve Griffiths, Stephen and Julie Brown, Derek and Sylvia Stephenson, Tom Evans, Ted George, Chris Raisin, Nigel Clifton)*

Whitbreads ~ Lease: Stephen Farbrother ~ Real ale ~ Bar food (till 10pm) ~ Restaurant ~ (01242) 620237 ~ Children welcome ~ Open 11-2.30, 6-11; 12-2.30, 6-10.30 Sun; closed 25/26 Dec

LITTLETON UPON SEVERN ST5990 Map 4
White Hart ◗

3½ miles from M4 junction 21; B4461 towards Thornbury, then village signposted

Popular locally, this carefully restored and extended old farmhouse has three atmospheric main rooms. There are some fine furnishings that include long cushioned wooden settles, high-backed settles, oak and elm tables, and a loveseat in the big low inglenook fireplace; flagstones in the front, huge tiles at the back, and smaller tiles on the left, plus some old pots and pans, and a lovely old White Hart

Inn/Simonds Ale sign. By the black wooden staircase are some nice little alcove seats, there's a black-panelled big fireplace in the front room, and hops on beams. An excellent no-smoking family room, similarly furnished, has some sentimental engravings, plates on a delft shelf, and a couple of high chairs, and a back snug has pokerwork seats and table football; darts, cribbage, fruit machine, chess, backgammon and Jenga. Bar food includes sandwiches, home-made soup (£2.20), pork and chicken pâté (£3.95), scallop of fresh crab baked with mustard, cream and cheese or blue cheese and onion tart with red pepper relish (£4.95), smoked salmon flan or clam fries (£5.50), steaks (from £7.95), and sizzling chicken with garlic and prawns or pork steaks with mustard and mushrooms (£8.95). Well kept Smiles Best, Golden and Heritage, and a guest like Everards Tiger on handpump. Picnic-sets sit on the neat front lawn, intersected by interesting cottagey flowerbeds, and by the good big back car park are some attractive shrubs and teak furniture on a small brick terrace. Several walks from the pub itself. *(Recommended by D L Parkhurst, Alan Johnson, A Hughes, D Parkhurst, James Morrell, M J Carter, Joan and Michel Hooper-Immins, Steve Willey)*

Smiles ~ Managers Howard and Liz Turner ~ Real ale ~ Bar food ~ (01454) 412275 ~ Children in restaurant ~ Open 12-2.30, 6-11.30; 11-11 Sat; 12-10.30 Sun ~ Bedrooms: £34.50B/£44.50B

LOWER ODDINGTON SP2325 Map 4

Fox 🍽 ♟

Nr Stow on the Wold

This is a rather understatedly smart place with a good mix of customers, all of whom enjoy the relaxed atmosphere and warm welcome from the friendly staff. There are plenty of people dropping in for just a drink, but it seems a shame to miss out on the very popular, interesting food – best to get here early to be sure of a table, especially in the well liked Green Room. The simply and spotlessly furnished rooms have fresh flowers and flagstones, a woodburning stove, hunting scene figures above the mantlepiece, a display cabinet with pewter mugs and stone bottles, daily newspapers, and hops hanging from the ceiling; piped classical music, dominoes, backgammon, chess and cards. Efficiently served, the super food might include a quad of Cotswold sausages with meaux mustard (£2), watercress soup (£2.95), filled french bread (from £2.95), wild mushroom risotto (£3.50), spinach and mushroom lasagne with three-cheese sauce (£6.95), salmon fishcakes with parsley sauce, rich beef stew with parsley dumplings or warm chicken, bacon and avocado salad (£7.95), local trout baked in newspaper with fresh herb sauce (£8.95), rib-eye steak (£9.95), and puddings like lemon crunch, sticky chocolate pudding or treacle tart (£3.25); Sunday rare roast sirloin of beef (£8.95). The wine list is excellent and they keep good Badger Tanglefoot, Hook Norton Best, and a changing guest like Marstons Pedigree or Wadworths 6X on handpump. A good eight-mile walk starts from here (though a stroll around the pretty village might be less taxing after a fine meal). They hope to open bedrooms. *(Recommended by John P W Bowdler, Simon Collett-Jones, John Bramley, Mr and Mrs Hugh Spottiswoode, J H Kane, Tom Evans, Michael Sargent, R Crockett, Andrew Shore, Chris and Val Ramstedt, Liz Bell, Martin Jennings, George Atkinson, Hazel McCarthy, Tom and Joan Childs, Lawrence Pearse, RJH, Dr and Mrs C J Betts, Pat and Roger Fereday, Jackie Lawler, Mrs Jane Lowe, Marvadene B Eves, Guy Vowles, Michael Bourdeaux, G Neighbour, James Garvey, Susan and Nigel Wilson)*

Free house ~ Licensees John Corn and Vicky Elliot ~ Real ale ~ Bar food (till 10pm) ~ (01451) 870888 ~ Children in eating area of bar ~ Open 12-3, 6.30-11; 12-3, 7-10.30 Sun; closed 25 Dec, evenings 26 and 31 Dec

MEYSEY HAMPTON SU1199 Map 4

Masons Arms

High Street; just off A417 Cirencester—Lechlade

Run by friendly people, this popular 17th-c stonebuilt inn is pleasantly placed by the village green. There's a proper pubby atmosphere and the longish open-plan bar has painted brick walls, a good parquet floor, carefully stripped beams, solid part-upholstered built-in wall seats with some matching chairs, good sound tables, a big inglenook log fire at one end, daily newspapers, and a few steps up to the no-smoking restaurant. Well kept Hook Norton Best, Tetleys, Wadworths 6X and Wychwood Shires XXX, and guest beers on handpump, and decent wines including several ports; dominoes, cribbage, maybe piped music. Decent, reasonably priced bar food includes sandwiches (lunchtime, from £1.95; filled french bread from £3.95, hot bacon and mushroom £5.45), home-made soup (£2.45), filled baked potatoes (from £3.25), stilton, bacon and garlic mushrooms (£3.65), ploughman's (from £4.50), caesar salad with spicy chicken (£4.95), mushroom and mascarpone lasagne (£5.25), steak, kidney and ale pie or lamb balti (£6.35), lemon herb trout (£6.45), mixed grill (£10.90), and puddings (£2.35); Sunday roast, and good breakfasts. *(Recommended by Nigel and Elizabeth Holmes, MRSM, D M and M C Watkinson, Kevin Thorpe, A Wright, Mr and Mrs W R Martin)*

Free house ~ Licensees Andrew and Jane O'Dell ~ Real ale ~ Bar food (not Sun evening) ~ Restaurant ~ (01285) 850164 ~ Children in eating area of bar and in restaurant until 9pm ~ Open 11.30-2.30(3 Sat), 6-11; 12-4, 7-10.30 Sun; closed Sun evening Nov-Mar ~ Bedrooms: £36S/£54S

MINCHINHAMPTON SO8500 Map 4
Old Lodge 🍴

Nailsworth—Brimscombe – on common fork left at pub's sign

This smartly refurbished dining pub has a small and snug central bar with a relaxed, friendly atmosphere and substantial pine tables and chairs, and opens into a pleasant bare-brick-walled room; one area is no smoking and there are no noisy games or piped music; skittle alley. Good, interesting bar food includes lunchtime sandwiches (£2.75; toasted open sandwiches £4.95), and filled baked potatoes (£3.65), as well as soup (£2.95), fishcakes with a lemon and yellow pepper sauce (£4.75, main course £7.75), tiger prawns with noodles, oriental salad and sesame oyster sauce (£4.95, main course £7.75), big pork and chive sausage with spring onion mash and rich onion gravy (£7.50), baked goat's cheese in a walnut crust on braised celeriac and apples with red onion marmalade (£9.50), ragoût of wild mushrooms with potato and herb gnocchi (£9.95), seared teriyaki salmon with pickled ginger and lemon grass on chinese leaves, beansprouts and peppers (£10.45), 10oz porterhouse steak (£12.95), children's menu (£3), and puddings such as lemon tart with blackcurrant sauce and lemon sorbet basket, rich chocolate brûlée with caramel orange compote or sticky toffee sponge with toffee sauce (£3.75). Well kept Marstons Pedigree and Thwaites Bitter with a guest like Tetleys on handpump, and a good range of wines; friendly, helpful service. The pub stands in the middle of a common, and there are tables on a neat lawn by an attractive herbaceous border, looking over grey stone walls to the grazing cows and horses.They share car parking with the adjoining golf club, so lots of cars outside doesn't necessarily mean the pub is full. *(Recommended by D G King, Neil and Anita Christopher, P Hedges, Simon Collett-Jones, Christopher and Mary Thomas, R Huggins, D Irving, E McCall, T McLean, D and C Cosgrove, Michael Doswell)*

Free house ~ Licensees D Barnett-Roberts and E Halford ~ Real ale ~ Bar food (till 10pm; not Mon) ~ (01453) 832047 ~ Children welcome (no food for them after 8pm) ~ Open 11-3, 6.30-11; 12-3, 7-10.30 Sun; closed Mon except bank holidays

MISERDEN SO9308 Map 4
Carpenters Arms

Village signposted off B4070 NE of Stroud; also a pleasant drive off A417 via the Duntisbournes, or off A419 via Sapperton and Edgeworth; OS Sheet 163 map reference 936089

Both locals and visitors (including walkers) are made welcome in this pleasant local, beautifully placed in an idyllic Cotswold estate village. Its two open-plan bar areas have low beams, nice old wooden tables, seats with the original little brass name plates on the backs and some cushioned settles and spindlebacks on the bare boards, stripped stone walls with some interesting bric-a-brac, and two big log fires; there's also a small no-smoking dining room with dark traditional furniture. The sizeable collage (done with Laurie Lee) has lots of illustrations and book covers signed by him. Well kept ales on handpump such as Brakspears, Fullers London Pride and Wadworths 6X, country wines, darts, cribbage and dominoes. Good lunchtime food includes home-made soup (£2.25), filled rolls (from £3.50), tagliatelle with smoked salmon and avocado cream sauce (£3.95), filled baked potatoes (from £3.95), ploughman's (from £4.50), home-cooked honey roast ham and egg (£4.95), home-made beef and ale sausages cooked in a smoked bacon, shallot and mild mustard sauce (£6.50) and steaks (from £8.50), with evening dishes such as smoked breast of quail with hazelnut truffle dressing (£4.50), cajun pork chop with salsa (£6.95), and diced wild venison braised in red wine with pineapple, sage and field mushrooms (£7.95), and daily specials and fish dishes. There are tables out in the garden and occasional summer Morris men. The nearby gardens of Misarden Park, open midweek summer, are well worth visiting. *(Recommended by Neil and Louise Orchard, George Irvine, Sheila and Robert Robinson, Giles Francis, Dr and Mrs A K Clarke, Mrs G Connell)*

Free house ~ Licensee Johnny Johnston ~ Real ale ~ Bar food (not some winter Sun evenings) ~ Restaurant ~ (01285) 821283 ~ Children welcome until 9pm ~ Occasional folk music ~ Open 11-3.30, 6-11; 12-3.30, 7-11 Sun

NAILSWORTH ST8599 Map
Egypt Mill 🛏

Just off A46; heading N towards Stroud, first right after roundabout, then left

This is an attractively converted three-floor stonebuilt mill which still has working waterwheels and the millstream flowing through. The brick-and-stone-floored split-level bar gives good views of the wheels, and there are big pictures and lots of stripped beams in the comfortable carpeted lounge, along with some hefty yet elegant ironwork from the old mill machinery. Although it can get quite crowded on fine weekends, it's actually spacious enough to feel at its best when it's busy – with good service to cope, and the atmosphere is almost bistro-ish; piped music. There's a civilised upstairs restaurant, and a no-smoking area. Tetleys, Wadworths 6X, and a guest beer on handpump, and a wide choice of nicely presented good generous food such as lunchtime sandwiches and filled french bread (from £2.20), ploughman's (£4.70), and omelettes (£4.70), as well as soup (£2.50), chicken liver, pork and bacon terrine (£3.85), thai fishcakes (£3.95), home-made faggots (£6.50), cassoulet of beans (£6.95), seafood spaghetti (£7.20), home-made steak and mushroom pudding (£7.55), honey-roast pork hock (£8.95), supreme of duck with a confit of duck leg (£9.75), and steaks (from £9.95); Sunday roast lunch. The floodlit terrace garden by the millpond is most attractive, and there's a little bridge over from the car park; no dogs. *(Recommended by Keith and Margaret Kettell, Mr and Mrs J M Lefeaux)*

Free house ~ Licensee Stephen Webb ~ Real ale ~ Bar food ~ Restaurant ~ (01453) 833449 ~ Children welcome ~ Open 11-3, 6.30-11; 11-11 summer Sat; 11-3, 6.30-11 Sun

NAUNTON SP1123 Map 4
Black Horse ♀ 🛏

Village signposted from B4068 (shown as A436 on older maps) W of Stow on the Wold

Tucked away in an unspoilt little village, this friendly old inn has a comfortable, neatly kept bar with black beams, stripped stonework, simple country-kitchen chairs, built-in oak pews, polished elm cast-iron-framed tables, and a warming open fire. Decent bar food served by cheerfully efficient staff includes home-made soup (£2.75), ploughman's (£4.95), steak and kidney pudding or chicken breast in stilton sauce (£6.75), and puddings (£3.25); the restaurant is no smoking. Well kept and well priced Donnington BB and SBA on handpump, and sensibly placed darts, cribbage, dominoes, and piped music. Some tables outside, and enjoyable walks on the blowy hills. *(Recommended by James and Wendy Timms, Eddie Walder, Mr and Mrs Head,*

David and Anne Culley, D J and P M Taylor, Lawrence Pearse, Marjorie and David Lamb, E A Froggatt, Mr and Mrs J Brown, Stephen and Julie Brown, Andy and Jill Kassube, K Neville-Rolfe, Joan Morgan)

Donnington ~ Tenant Martin David Macklin ~ Real ale ~ Bar food ~ (01451) 850565 ~ Children in eating area of bar and in restaurant ~ Open 11.30-3, 6-11; 12-3, 7-10.30 Sun ~ Bedrooms: £25B/£45B

NORTH CERNEY SP0208 Map 2
Bathurst Arms ♀

A435 Cirencester—Cheltenham

After enjoying one of the many surrounding walks, head for this handsome old inn – just the place. It's warm and friendly with a good balance between diners and drinkers, and the beamed and panelled bar has a fireplace at each end (one quite huge and housing an open woodburner), a good mix of old tables and nicely faded chairs, old-fashioned window seats, and some pewter plates. There are country tables in a little carpeted room off the bar, as well as winged high-backed settles forming booths around other tables. A good choice of bar food might include sandwiches (from £2.20), home-made pâté (£3.65), warm cerney goat's cheese salad (£4.75), various pasta dishes (£5.50), home-made pies or home-made salmon fishcakes (£6.95), steaks with good sauces from (£8.50), duck with a sweet and sour sauce (£10.50), and monkfish in bacon and cream or ostrich with red wine sauce (£10.95). Well kept Hook Norton Best, Wadworths 6X and two guest beers on handpump, and good wines by the glass. The Stables Bar has darts, pool, cribbage, dominoes, and juke box; piped music. The attractive flower-filled front lawn runs down to the little River Churn, and there are picnic-sets sheltered by small trees and shrubs. The bedrooms have been refurbished this year. *(Recommended by Dr and Mrs B D Smith, MRSM, P and S White, John Fahy, John Robertson, Joan Olivier, RJH, Gwen and Peter Andrews, Nigel and Elizabeth Holmes, J Taylor, Dr and Mrs A K Clarke)*

Free house ~ Licensee Mike Costley-White ~ Real ale ~ Bar food ~ Restaurant ~ (01285) 831281 ~ Children in eating area of bar ~ Open 11-3, 6-11; 12-3, 7-10.30 Sun ~ Bedrooms: £35B/£50B

NORTH NIBLEY ST7596 Map 4
New Inn ◀

Waterley Bottom, which is quite well signposted from surrounding lanes; inn signposted from the Bottom itself; one route is from A4135 S of Dursley, via lane with red sign saying Steep Hill, 1 in 5 (just SE of Stinchcombe Golf Course turn-off), turning right when you get to the bottom; another is to follow Waterley Bottom signpost from previous main entry, keeping eyes skinned for small low signpost to inn; OS Sheet 162 map reference 758963; though this is the way we know best, one reader suggests the road is wider if you approach directly from North Nibley

New licensees were poised to take over this friendly country pub as we went to press. They plan to gently redecorated the place without changing its character, and Mrs Cartigny will do the cooking – as she has lived in France for the last 20 years with her French husband, perhaps locals are in for a treat. They hadn't organised the menu but will be offering daily specials alongside the standard menu. The lounge bar has cushioned windsor chairs and varnished high-backed settles against the partly stripped stone walls, and sensibly placed darts, dominoes, shove-ha'penny, cribbage, table skittles, and trivia in the simple public bar. Well kept Berkeley Dicky Pearce, Cotleigh Tawny and WB (a beer brewed specially for the pub), Greene King Abbot, and Theakstons Old Peculier are either dispensed from Barmaid's Delight (the name of one of the antique beer engines) or tapped from the cask. At the far end of the garden is a small orchard with swings, slides and a timber tree-house, and there's a neatly kept terrace. Please note, they no longer do bedrooms and plan to be more family friendly. More reports please. *(Recommended by JP, PP, Patrick Hancock, Peter and Jenny Quine, D Irving, E McCall, T McLean, Roger and Jenny Huggins, Mr and Mrs L Pilson, Gill Cathles)*

Free house ~ Licensees Jackie and Jacky Cartigny ~ Real ale ~ Bar food ~ (01453) 543659 ~ Open 11-11; 12-10.30 Sun; may close during afternoon in winter

OAKRIDGE LYNCH SO9103 Map 4
Butchers Arms

Village signposted off Eastcombe—Bisley road, E of Stroud, which is the easiest approach; with a good map you could brave the steep lanes via Frampton Mansell, which is signposted off A419 Stroud—Cirencester

It's lucky that this neatly kept pub's car park is up on the level top road or you'd have to plunge into the tortuous network of lanes in this particularly steep and twisty village. The spacious rambling bar has a few beams in its low ceiling, some walls stripped back to the bare stone, old photographs, comfortable, traditional furnishings like wheelback chairs around the neat tables on its patterned carpet, and three open fires. Bar food includes rolls, ploughman's, and tasty hot french sticks, cauliflower cheese (£4.50), moules marinières (£4.95), omelettes of steak (£5.50), seafood pasta (£5.95), and beef in stout pie (£6.50). Best to book at the weekend; the restaurant is no smoking. Well kept Archers Best, Berkeley Old Friend, Hook Norton Old Hooky, Tetleys Bitter and Timothy Taylor Landlord on handpump; a little room off the main bar has darts, and there's a skittle alley. In summer, the flowering tubs and hanging basket are very pretty, and picnic-sets on a stretch of lawn look down over the valley. There are good walks in the valley along the old Thames & Severn canal. *(Recommended by Tom and Ruth Rees, Mr and Mrs Spencer, Nick and Meriel Cox, M Joyner, Pete and Rosie Flower, Pat and John Millward)*

Free house ~ Licensees Peter and Brian Coupe ~ Real ale ~ Bar food ~ Restaurant ~ (01285) 760371 ~ Children welcome ~ Open 11-3, 6-11; 12-3, 7-10.30 Sun

ODDINGTON SP2225 Map 4
Horse & Groom

Upper Oddington; signposted from A436 E of Stow on the Wold

The Old English Pub Co. have taken over here and installed a couple of managers. The bar has pale polished flagstones, a handsome antique oak box settle among other more modern seats, some horsebrasses on the dark 16th-c oak beams in the ochre ceiling, stripped stone walls with some harness and a few brass platters, and an inglenook fireplace. Bar food now includes sandwiches, home-made soup (£3.50), sausage and mash or gammon and pineapple (£6.50), steak and kidney pudding or lasagne (£7.25), and salmon fishcake with parsley sauce or scampi (£7.95). The no-smoking candlelit dining room is pretty. Well kept Courage Directors and Hook Norton Best on handpump. The garden has a little water-garden beyond a rose hedge, picnic-sets on the neat lawn below the car park, and apple trees; there's a fine play area. *(Recommended by Minako Sato, Chris Mawson, John and Esther Sprinkle, Ted George, D G Clarke, Mrs J Webb, Dorothee and Dennis Glover, P Ridley)*

Old English Inns ~ Managers Mark Naylor, Trudi Kendall ~ Real ale ~ Bar food ~ Restaurant ~ (01451) 830584 ~ Children welcome ~ Live 60s/70s/80s music ~ Open 11-11; 12-10.30 Sun; 12(11.30 Sat)-3, 6.30-11 in winter ~ Bedrooms: £40S/£55S

OLD SODBURY ST7581 Map 2
Dog

Not far from M4 junction 18: A46 N, then A432 left towards Chipping Sodbury

The huge choice of good food is the reason so many people come to this busy pub – plus, it is a handy break from the M4. There are fresh fish dishes like sole, plaice, halibut, cod, trout, scallops, shark or tuna, and several different ways of serving mussels and squid, as well as sandwiches (from £1.75), ploughman's (£4.25), cheese and onion flan or lightly spiced crab meat baked in a shell (£4.95), ravioli or vegetarian moussaka (£5.25), Mexican tamales with chilli sauce (£6.25), sweet and sour chicken, barbecued spare ribs or prawn curry (£6.50), and steaks (from £6.95);

children's menu (from £1.95), and puddings like home-made fruit pie, rhubarb crumble or jam roly poly (from £2.25). The two-level bar and smaller no-smoking room both have areas of original bare stone walls, beams and timbering, low ceilings, wall benches and cushioned chairs, open fires, and a bustling atmosphere. Well kept Flowers Original, Marstons Pedigree, Wadworths 6X, and Wickwar BOB on handpump, and several malt whiskies; good service. Dominoes, fruit machine, video game, juke box, and skittle alley. Trophy, the border collie, likes playing football with customers. There's a large garden with lots of seating, a summer barbecue area and pets corner, climbing frames, swings, slides, football net, and see-saws, and a bouncy castle most bank holidays. Lots of good walks nearby. *(Recommended by Mayur Shah, John and Enid Morris, S Godsell, B J Harding, Pat Crabb, Simon and Amanda Southwell, Tina and David Woods-Taylor, Paul and Diane Burrows, Roy Sharman, Brian Abbott, John Weeks, Kim and Nigel Spence, Roy Smylie, KC, Carole Smart, Andrew Jeeves, Phyl and Jack Street, Meg and Colin Hamilton, Tom Evans, Christopher and Mary Thomas, Jane and David Raven, Dr and Mrs Cottrell, Lyn and Geoff Hallchurch)*

Whitbreads ~ Lease: John and Joan Harris ~ Real ale ~ (01454) 312006 ~ Children welcome ~ Open 11-11; 12-10.30 Sun ~ Bedrooms: £25/£40

OLDBURY ON SEVERN ST6292 Map 2
Anchor 🍺

Village signposted from B4061

Despite their 28 years here, the hard-working licensees continue to keep a keen eye on their high standards, and to ensure that customers – regulars or visitors – enjoy their visit. It remains as it always has, a traditional, friendly place with no music, games machines or chips. The lounge has modern beams and stone, a mix of tables including an attractive oval oak gateleg one, cushioned window seats, winged seats against the wall, pictures in gilt frames, and a big winter log fire. Diners can eat in the lounge or bar area or in the no-smoking dining room at the back of the building (good for larger groups) and the menu is the same in all rooms. All the food is home-made using local produce and although they don't do chips, they do offer dauphinois potatoes, new ones and baked, and Don Quizote (sliced and baked with cheese and onion): no sandwiches but wholemeal bread with cheeses, beef, home-baked ham, pâté or smoked mackerel (from £2.95), good salads (from £3.95; prawn £5.50), cashew nut paella (£5), fresh salmon in cream and white wine sauce, snorkers (charcoal grilled pork and garlic sausages with mushrooms) or beef with ginger (£5.95), minted lamb (£6.20), spiced butterfly breast of chicken (£6.75), sirloin steak (£8.50), and puddings like raspberry and brandy crème brûlée, Jamaican crumble (caramelised bananas and pineapple with an orange and coconut crumble topping) or chocolate doo-dah (macaroons, brandy and thick dark chocolate £2.95).Well kept Bass, Black Sheep, Butcombe Bitter, Theakstons Best and Old Peculier, and Worthington Best on handpump or tapped from the cask, all well priced for the area. Also over 75 malts, a decent choice of good quality wines (10 by the glass), and Inch's cider; darts, shove-ha'penny, dominoes and cribbage; they have wheelchair access and a disabled lavatory. There are seats in the pretty garden and lovely hanging baskets and window boxes, and the boules piste continues to draw in members – and spectators; plenty of walks to the River Severn and along the many footpaths and bridleways. St Arilda's church nearby is interesting, on its odd little knoll with wild flowers among the gravestones (the primroses and daffodils in spring are lovely). *(Recommended by Christopher and Mary Thomas, Andrew Shore, Tom Evans, James Morrell, R C Morgan, S H Godsell, Simon and Amanda Southwell, E A Froggatt, Meg and Colin Hamilton)*

Free house ~ Licensees Michael Dowdeswell, Alex de la Torre ~ Real ale ~ Bar food ~ Restaurant ~ (01454) 413331 ~ Children in restaurant ~ Open 11.30-2.30, 6.30-11; 11.30-11 Sat; 12-10.30 Sun; closed 25 Dec, evening 26 Dec

---

Looking for a pub with a really special garden, or in lovely countryside, or with an outstanding view, or right by the water? They are listed separately, at the back of the book.

REDBROOK SO5410 Map 4

Boat ◀

Pub's car park is now signed in village on A466 Chepstow—Monmouth; from here 100-yard footbridge crosses Wye (pub actually in Penallt in Wales – but much easier to find this way); OS Sheet 162 map reference 534097

They have a fine choice of around 8 well kept beers in this riverside pub – tapped straight from casks behind the bar counter: Adnams Broadside, Black Sheep Best, Butcombe Bitter, Freeminer Bitter, Fullers London Pride, Greene King IPA, Theakstons Old Peculier, and Wadworths 6X; a range of country wines and summer scrumpy, too. The unpretentious bar has lots of landscapes and pictures of the pub during floods, simple seating, and a woodburning stove on the tiled floor. Decent bar food includes filled baked potatoes (from £2.20), soup (£2.35), bacon and stilton melt (£2.85), tikka mushrooms (£3.15), ploughman's (£4.60), sweet and sour pork (£5.30), turkey and mushroom crumble or moussaka (£5.35), children's menu (from £1.35), and puddings (£2.40). Darts, cribbage, and dominoes. It does get very full at peak times, but you can sit on the sturdy home-built seats by the interestingly shaped tables in the garden and listen to the waters of the River Wye spilling down the waterfall cliffs into the duck pond below; it's a popular spot with walkers. *(Recommended by Miss S P Watkin, P A Taylor, David Lewis, Sarah Lart, Sidney and Erna Wells, J and F Gowers, Edward Leetham, JP, PP, Barry and Anne)*

Free house ~ Licensee Steffan Rowlands ~ Real ale ~ Bar food ~ (01600) 712615 ~ Children welcome ~ Easy listening live music Tues, rock and roll Thurs ~ Open 11.30-3, 6-11; 11.30-11 Sat; 12-10.30 Sun

SHEEPSCOMBE SO8910 Map 4

Butchers Arms ♀

Village signed off B4070 NE of Stroud, and A46 N of Painswick (narrow lanes)

As this friendly pub is Grade II listed, no major changes can take place here – which is a relief to their many customers. They still have no noisy games machines or piped music to spoil the chatty atmosphere and continue with their policy not to reserve tables in the bar so casual diners and locals have a welcoming area in which to enjoy their drinks. The bar has seats in big bay windows, flowery-cushioned chairs and rustic benches, log fires, and lots of interesting oddments like assorted blow lamps, irons, and plates. Good lunchtime bar food includes home-made soup (£2.50), filled rolls (from £3.25; 5oz rump steak £5), filled baked potatoes (from £4), smoked salmon pâté or spinach and feta cheese goujons with mint yoghurt dip (£4.50), ploughman's (from £5.25), stilton pasta bake (£5.95), home-cooked honey roast ham and egg (£6), home-made steak, mushroom and Guinness pie (£6.50), and roast quarter shoulder of lamb in honey and wholegrain mustard (£6.75), with evening dishes such as filo prawns with hot salsa dip (£4.50), barbecued spare ribs (£4.75), fresh local trout fillets in lemon and cracked black pepper (£6.75), New Zealand green-lipped mussels in white wine, garlic and cream (£8.50), whole scampi flambéed in pernod and finished with a dill and fresh cream sauce (£9.50), and steaks (from £9.50); daily specials like mixed game casserole (£6.95), grilled fresh monkfish medallions with redcurrant dressing (£8.50), and roast Barbary duck glazed with plum and ginger (£9.50). The restaurant and a small area in the bar are no smoking. Well kept Archers Best Bitter, Hook Norton Best, Uley Old Spot, and guest beers on handpump, decent wines, traditional ciders, and country wines; darts, cribbage, dominoes. The views are marvellous and there are teak seats below the building, tables on the steep grass behind, and a cricket ground behind on such a steep slope that the boundary fielders at one end can scarcely see the bowler. *(Recommended by T McLean, R Huggins, D Irving, E McCall, Neil and Anita Christopher, P and S White, Mrs G Connell, Martin Jones, Chris and Val Ramstedt, Pat and John Millward, Liz Bell)*

Free house ~ Licensees Johnny and Hilary Johnston ~ Real ale ~ Bar food (till 10pm) ~ Restaurant ~ (01452) 812113 ~ Children welcome until 9pm ~ Open 11-11; 12-10.30 Sun; 11-2.30, 6.30-11 winter

SIDDINGTON SU0399 Map 4
Greyhound

Ashton Rd; village signposted from A419 roundabout at Tesco

The two connecting rooms here have a friendly bustling atmosphere and are full of copper, brass and bric-a-brac. The biggish lounge bar has two big log fires, high-backed dining chairs and so forth on the old herringbone brick floor, and good tables – mainly stripped pine, but one fine circular mahogany one. The public bar with its slate floor has darts and cribbage. The newly extended function room doubles as a skittle alley and has an original stone well. Well liked bar food includes cheese and onion bread (£1.75), home-made soup (£2.50), sandwiches or filled baked potatoes (from £2.95), home-made chicken liver pâté (£3.50), chilli con carne (£5.50), chicken and mango curry or a pasta dish (£5.95), lamb chops with minted gravy (£7.50), mushroom stroganoff (£7.95), beef stroganoff (£9.95), home-made puddings such as bread and butter pudding or chocolate brandy crunch (£2.95), and popular 3-course Sunday carvery (£8.25). Well kept Badger Tanglefoot, and Wadworths IPA and seasonal beers on handpump. There are seats among lilacs, apple trees, flower borders and short stone walls behind the car park. *(Recommended by R Huggins, D Irving, E McCall, T McLean, G W A Pearce, Martin and Karen Wake, Simon Collett-Jones, Peter and Audrey Dowsett, P and S White)*

Wadworths ~ Managers Mike and Louise Grattan ~ Real ale ~ Bar food (till 10pm) ~ (01285) 653573 ~ Children in eating area of bar ~ Monthly live music and trivia quiz ~ Open 11.30-3, 6.30-11; 12-3, 7-10.30 Sun

ST BRIAVELS SO5605 Map 4
George 🛏

The 12th-c castle which this attractive little pub overlooks was once used by King John as a hunting lodge; there are seats on a flagstoned terrace at the back overlooking the grassy former moat, and more among roses and shrubs. Inside, the three rambling rooms have new carpets, old-fashioned built-in wall seats, some booth seating, cushioned small settles, toby jugs and antique bottles on black beams over the servery, and a large stone open fireplace; a Celtic coffin lid dating from 1070, discovered when a fireplace was removed, is now mounted next to the bar counter. Enjoyable home-made bar food includes home-made soup (£2.50), pâté or spicy chicken wings (£4.50), ploughman's (£4.50), smoked chicken and asparagus pancakes or curries (£7.95), fresh grilled tuna steak (£8.95), steaks (from £8.95), tenderloin of pork or scampi in pernod (£9.95), puddings such as banoffee pie, and Sunday roast lunch. The dining room is no smoking. Well kept Bass, Everards Tiger, Marstons Pedigree, and Shepherd Neame Spitfire on handpump, country wines, and quite a few malt whiskies; piped music. Lots of walks start nearby but muddy boots must be left outside. *(Recommended by Rona Murdoch, Mike and Sue Loseby, Ian Phillips, LM, Howard England, R T and J C Moggridge, Mike and Mary Carter, Donald Godden)*

Free house ~ Licensee Bruce Bennett ~ Real ale ~ Bar food ~ Restaurant ~ (01594) 530228 ~ Children welcome ~ Open 11-3, 6.30-11; 12-3, 7-10.30 Sun

STANTON SP0734 Map 4
Mount

Village signposted off B4632 (the old A46) SW of Broadway; Old Snowshill Road – take no-through road up hill and bear left

On a good day, you can see the Welsh mountains from seats on the pretty front terrace here – and the view back down over the lovely golden stone village is most attractive; boules. Inside, the original simple bar has black beams, cask seats on big flagstones, heavy-horse harness and racing photographs, cricket memorabilia, and a big fireplace. A spacious extension, with some big picture windows, has comfortable oak wall seats and cigarette cards of Derby and Grand National winners, and another extension (no smoking) is used in winter as a restaurant and in summer as a more informal eating bar. Donnington BB and SBA on handpump kept under light blanket pressure and farm cider; darts, shove-ha'penny, dominoes, cribbage, bar billiards, and piped music. Decent bar food includes sandwiches (£2.95; toasties £3.95), ploughman's (£4.50), tuna pasta bake, chicken balti or vegetables in a minted tomato sauce (£5.25), evening specials such as Gressingham duck in orange, and puddings (£2.95). *(Recommended by Tina and David Woods-Taylor, Paul S McPherson, Miss V Kavanagh, Mr and Mrs Richard Osborne, Pam Adsley, Colin and Ann Hunt, Martin Jones, D G Haines, David Walker)*

Donnington ~ Tenant Colin Johns ~ Real ale ~ Bar food (not Sun evening) ~ (01386) 584316 ~ Children welcome until 9pm ~ Open 11-3, 6-11; 11-11 Sat; 12-10.30 Sun; closed 25 Dec

TETBURY ST8394 Map 4
Gumstool

Part of Calcot Manor Hotel; A4135 W of town, just E of junction with A46

There are some concessions to those wanting just a drink, but this is a civilised dining bar where most emphasis is on the good, interesting food. The layout is well divided to give a feeling of intimacy without losing the overall sense of contented bustle, the lighting is attractive, and materials are old-fashioned (lots of stripped pine, flagstones, gingham curtains, hop bines) though the style is neatly modern. Beyond one screen, there are a couple of marble-topped pub tables and a leather armchair by the big log fire, daily papers, well kept Bass, Fullers London Pride, and Wickwar BOB and Coopers on handpump, and dominoes, shove-ha'penny, and cribbage. The changing menu has plenty of sensibly priced starters that for a little extra would do as a snack lunch – soups (£2.85; generous £4.35), local English cheeses with celery, grapes and crusty bread (£4.70; generous £7.20), thai spiced crab cakes with chilli, soy and coriander (£5.50; generous £7.50), and lightly curried mussels (£6; generous £8.50); also, steak ciabatta with crispy bacon, plum tomato and fried onions (£6), Swiss style rosti potatoes with smoked ham and gruyère topped with a poached egg (£8.20), braised chicken in red wine (£8.80), chargrilled swordfish steak with avocado, capers and cherry tomatoes (£9.75), chargrilled rib-eye steak with tarragon and shallot butter (£10.20), and puddings such as warm chocolate and cherry cake, sticky toffee pudding or home-made ice-creams and sorbets (from £3.80); extra vegetables (£1.50). Best to book. A very wide choice of interesting wines by the glass spans a wide price range; piped music. The neat side lawn has a couple of picnic-sets; Westonbirt Arboretum is not far. *(Recommended by Charles and Pauline Stride, Simon and Amanda Southwell, Howard England, W M and J M Cottrell, Dr and Mrs A Newton, Christopher and Mary Thomas, J Morrell, Pat and John Millward)*

Free house ~ Licensees Paul Sadler and Richard Bell ~ Real ale ~ Bar food ~ (01666) 890391 ~ Children welcome ~ Occasional jazz ~ Open 11.30-2.30, 6-11; 11.30-11 Sat; 11.30-10.30 Sun ~ Bedrooms: £105B/£120B

TEWKESBURY SO8932 Map 4
Olde Black Bear

High Street (N end, just before the bridge)

Careful refurbishments to this lovely timbered pub (said to be the county's oldest) have created a couple of little extra rooms, and a large room with plenty of extra seats has been added. But the fine, rambly ancient rooms are as atmospheric as ever: low heavy beams, lots of timbers, armchairs in front of open fires, bare wood and original tiled floors, plenty of pictures, bric-a-brac and photographs of Tewkesbury in the 1920s, a happy mix of tables and chairs, and fresh flowers. Fruit machine, darts, and TV in the public bar; piped music. Well kept Greenalls Bitter and Original, and guest beers such as Marstons Pedigree, Smiles and Wadworths 6X tapped on handpump or from casks behind the bar in the main front room; country wines; very friendly service. Enjoyable food includes filled french bread (from £1.80; open sandwiches from £3.50), home-made soup (£1.95), filled baked potatoes (from £3.25), creamy garlic mushrooms (£3.30), home-made steak and kidney pie (£6.70), cajun chicken or home-made lasagne (£6.95), thai seafood medley (£7.20), steaks (from £7.50), vegetarian dishes and daily specials, and puddings. Picnic-sets in the pleasant back garden overlook the River Avon; play area. *(Recommended by David E and Anne D Daniel, Gordon, Alan and Paula McCully, Sheila and Phil Stubbs, the Didler, Lynda Payton, Sam Samuells, Martyn and Helen Webb, Daren Haines, Ian Phillips)*

Greenalls ~ Managers Jean-Claude and Helen Bourgeois ~ Real ale ~ Bar food (12-2, 6-9) ~ Restaurant ~ (01684) 292202 ~ Children welcome away from bar ~ Open 11-11; 12-10.30 Sun; closed evening 25 Dec

TODENHAM SP2436 Map 4
Farriers Arms ♀ ◖

Between A34 and A429 N of Moreton in Marsh

It was the very cheery relaxed atmosphere on our early evening inspection, with the owner chef, his wife, a friendly young barmaid and a local all chatting enthusiastically round the bar, that really warmed us to this tucked away country pub. It's the only brick building in this otherwise stonebuilt part of the world, and was originally meant to house the men who built the church next door. The main bar has nice wonky white plastered walls, lovely old polished flagstones by the stone bar counter and a log burner in a huge inglenook fireplace. A tiny little room off to the side is full of old books and interesting old photographs. Very popular bar food includes soup (£2.75), sandwiches (from £3.65), ploughman's (£4.95), steak and kidney pie (£6.50), and daily specials like prawn cocktail (£4.25), avocado filled with prawns and chopped tomatoes and deep fried in filo pastry (£4.50), chicken breast poached in creamy mushroom sauce (£8.50), spinach and ricotta pasta (£8.85), provençale fish stew (£11.50), grilled brill (£12.50), fillet with mushrooms, bacon and pâté in pastry (£12.75). Exmoor Hounddog, Hook Norton Best and North Cotswold Genesis as well as good sensibly priced wines; darts, shove-ha'penny, dominoes, Aunt Sally and piped music. There are a couple of tables with views of the church on a small terrace by the quiet little road. *(Recommended by John Bowdler, Tim and Linda Collins, J H Kane, George Atkinson)*

Free house ~ Licensee William J Moore ~ Real ale ~ Bar food ~ Restaurant ~ (01608) 650901 ~ Children in eating area of bar ~ Occasional live entertainment ~ Open 12-3, 6.30-11; 12-3, 7-10.30 Sun ~ Bedrooms: £28B/£44B

WITHINGTON SP0315 Map 4
Mill Inn

Village signposted from A436, and from A40; from village centre follow sign towards Roman villa (but don't be tempted astray by villa signs before you reach the village!)

The bedrooms have been redecorated here this year, and one now has an open fire. The beamed and flagstoned bar and other wooden-floored rooms have little nooks and corners with antique high-backed settles, a bustling atmosphere, and large stone fireplaces; the old dining room is no smoking. Good bar food includes ploughman's, and daily specials such as fishcakes with a spicy tomato sauce (£3.75), popular chicken in a basket (£4.75), vegetarian lasagne or lamb chops with mint and rosemary (£5.75), roast beef and yorkshire pudding (£6.50), and puddings such as spotted dick or treacle sponge. Well kept Sam Smiths OB on handpump, a decent wine list, and quite a few malt whiskies; piped jazz and classical music. The setting for this mossy-roofed old stone inn is charming – it stands virtually alone in a little valley surrounded by beech and chestnut trees and a rookery. The pretty garden with the River Coln running through it is bridged, and there are seats and tables on the small island and on the main lawn. *(Recommended by Chris and Anna Rowley, Susan and Nigel Wilson, Dr Paul Kitchener, Ian, D Irving, E McCall, T McLean, Roger and Jenny Huggins, Rob Whittle, P J Hanson, Nick and Meriel Cox, G W A Pearce, Dr Ian Crichton, Howard England, J Dwane, David and Anne Culley)*

Sam Smiths ~ Managers Nathan Elvin and Robin Collyns ~ Real ale ~ Bar food ~ (01242) 890204 ~ Children in eating area of bar ~ Open 11.30-11; 12-10.30 Sun; 11-3, 7-11 winter ~ Bedrooms: £25B/£49.50B

WOODCHESTER SO8302 Map 4

Royal Oak ♀ ◀

Church Road, North Woodchester; signposted off A46 on S edge of Stroud

The small simple local-feeling bar in this plain stonebuilt pub has a few highly varnished tables in the rather bright and equally small eating area on the left, and a few more towards the back; the massive fireplace has a welcoming log fire. Well kept Archers Best, Berkeley Old Friend, Hook Norton Best, and Wychwood Special, good house wines and proper coffee; shove-ha'penny, cribbage, and dominoes. At best the food is way above what you'd expect from the surroundings: sandwiches, cream of tomato and basil soup (£3.25), goat's cheese pie (£4.50), fried pigeon breast with foie gras (£5.50), corned beef hash with poached eggs (£5.80), beef stroganoff or chicken and bacon club sandwich (£5.95), sausage and mash (£6.25), rib-eye steak (£8), best end of roast lamb niçoise (£11.95), and puddings like chocolate truffle cake or crème brûlée (£3.75). The restaurant is no smoking. They hold occasional themed food and music evenings. The jack russell is called Dylan, and the young black labrador puppy, Jasmine. *(Recommended by D Irving, R Huggins, T McLean, E McCall, Andrew Shore, Julie and William H Ryan, Bernard Stradling, Nigel Long, Tom and Ruth Rees, Peter Shaw, Kate Naylor, J H Kane, Hugh Pitt, D G King)*

Free house ~ Licensees Patrick Le Mesurier and Tony Croome ~ Real ale ~ Bar food ~ Restaurant ~ (01453) 872735 ~ Children welcome ~ Live music on themed evenings ~ Open 11-3, 5.30-11; 11-11 Sat; 12-10.30 Sun

Lucky Dip

Besides the fully inspected pubs, you might like to try these Lucky Dips recommended to us and described by readers (if you do, please send us reports):

Alderton [SP0033]
☆ *Gardeners Arms* [off B4077 Tewkesbury—Stow]: Civilised and attractive thatched Tudor pub with well kept Hook Norton Best, Theakstons Best and XB and Wadworths 6X, reasonably priced well presented lunchtime sandwiches, soup and good salads, above-average wines, log fire, good antique prints, high-backed settles among more usual seats; interesting restaurant food (evenings not Sun, and weekend lunchtimes; worth booking), extension keeping bar sensibly separate; swift friendly service, tables on sheltered terrace, well kept garden; children welcome *(LYM, B and J Shurmer, Marvadene B Eves)*

Aldsworth [SP1510]
☆ *Sherborne Arms* [B4425 Burford—Cirencester]: Very popular relaxing modernised dining pub – can be booked solid on Sun even though much extended; beams, bric-a-brac and spacious and attractive no-smoking conservatory dining area, wide choice of good fresh food from baked potatoes and ploughman's up esp fish, cheerful obliging service, well kept ales such as Archers, Bass, Boddingtons and Brakspears SB, log fire; darts, fruit machine; lovely garden, lavatory for disabled *(Neil and Anita Christopher, Marjorie and David Lamb, E G Peters, Simon Collett-Jones)*

Ampney Crucis [SP0602]
☆ *Crown of Crucis* [A417 E of Cirencester]: Bustling and flourishing rather hotelish food pub, open all day, with good popular choice from sandwiches and good ploughman's up inc nice puddings and fine display of cheeses, attractive split-level no-smoking restaurant, well

kept Archers Village, Theakstons XB and Wadworths 6X, lots of tables out on grass by car park; children welcome, disabled facilities, comfortable modern bedrooms around courtyard *(R C Watkins, LYM, Mike and Heather Watson, TRS, Mrs S Evans, Mr and Mrs J Brown)*

Andoversford [SP0219]
Royal Oak [signed just off A40]: Cosy and attractive beamed village pub reopened under new owners, lots of stripped stone, nice galleried dining room, big open fire, real ales inc Goffs Jouster, reasonably priced food, obliging service; tables in garden *(BB, Neil and Anita Christopher, John and Joan Wyatt)*

Apperley [SO8628]
☆ *Coal House* [village signed off B4213 S of Tewkesbury]: Airy bar notable for its splendid riverside position, with Bass, Wadworths 6X and a guest ale such as Fullers London Pride, decent food from good baguettes up, chatty landlord, red plush seats; front terrace with Severn views, play area *(Iain Robertson, James Skinner, BB)*

Arlingham [SO7111]
Old Passage: Roomy pub with french windows to big garden extending down to River Severn, reasonably priced simple food, Marstons and John Smiths, small restaurant, very friendly landlord; games machines, service can slow; popular with summer campers *(Tom Rees, BB, D G King)*

Berkeley [ST6899]
Bird in Hand [Marybrook St; handy for M5 junctions 13 and 14, via A38]: Pleasant restaurant (children allowed, large no-smoking

area) and bars, wide range of very reasonably priced snacks and meals inc OAP bargains, efficient friendly staff, attractive décor with beams, saddles, decorative plates and panelling, well kept Bass, local Berkeley beers and Worthington *(Christopher and Mary Thomas, James and Marjorie Hastie)*

Birdlip [SO9316]

Air Balloon [A417/A436 roundabout]: Useful much extended Whitbreads Wayside Inn dining pub, sound value for family groups, with good service, pubbier front bar with open fire, stone walls and flagstones, Boddingtons and Fullers London Pride; tables on terrace and in garden *(Ian Phillips, Neil and Anita Christopher)*

Bishops Cleeve [SO9527]

Crown & Harp [Cheltenham Rd]: Useful steak-oriented pub, relaxed and friendly, wide choice of Whitbreads-related ales with a guest such as Bunces, big garden and play area, good location; quiz night Thurs *(Mary and David Richards)*

Bisley [SO9006]

☆ *Stirrup Cup*: Spacious well furnished local, good modestly priced food from sandwiches up, well kept Flowers Original, Uley Hogs Back and Wadworths 6X, decent wines, friendly bustle, no music *(Tom and Ruth Rees)*

Blockley [SP1634]

☆ *Great Western Arms* [Station Rd]: Peaceful, comfortable and spacious modern-style lounge, wide choice of reasonably priced home-cooked food, well kept Flowers, Hook Norton and Marstons Pedigree, welcoming service, no piped music, busy public bar with games room; attractive village, lovely valley view *(G W A Pearce, David Gregory)*

Bourton on the Hill [SP1732]

☆ *Horse & Groom* [A44 W of Moreton in Marsh]: Attractively redecorated old Cotswold stone inn, good brasserie food at prices to match, pine furniture, flagstones and hessian in main bar, settees and easy chairs around log fire in lounge, attractive dining room, well kept Bass, Hook Norton Best and Morlands Old Speckled Hen; comfortable bedrooms *(Peter Danny, Ruth Levy, David and Ruth Hollands, NWN)*

Bourton on the Water [SP1620]

Duke of Wellington: Reasonably priced food in nicely furnished open-plan bar or back restaurant, friendly staff, beers and décor good; garden *(Ted George)*

Kingsbridge Arms [Riverside]: Former Parrot & Alligator, more mature feel since renaming, popular for wide choice of reasonably priced usual food; clean and tidy, with well kept Bass and guests such as Caledonian Deuchars IPA and 80/-, interesting old prints and cartoons; piped music may obtrude; pleasant village/river view from tables on terrace *(J Gibbs, Ted George)*

Mousetrap [Lansdown, W edge]: Small stone pub with well kept Hook Norton and Wadworths 6X in long narrow partly beamed bar, good food inc imaginative dishes in separate attractive kitchen-style dining area, attentive friendly service, welcoming fire;

picnic-sets out in front, bedrooms *(LM, Gill and Keith Croxton)*

Old Manse [Bridge End Walk]: Front garden and one end of long turkey-carpeted beamed bar overlooking River Windrush, big log fire, attractive old prints, bookshelves, some stripped stone, well kept Marstons Pedigree and Theakstons Best, good service, decent food from sandwiches up inc afternoon teas, pretty restaurant; piped music may obtrude; good bedrooms, open all day *(Ted George, BB, David Gregory, J Gibbs, George Atkinson, Mike and Heather Watson)*

Broadwell [SP2027]

☆ *Fox* [off A429 2 miles N of Stow on the Wold]: Attractive local opp broad green, generous food from good ploughman's up, well kept Donnington BB, SB and SBA, Addlestone's cider, friendly service, stripped stone and flagstones, beams hung with jugs, log fire, darts, dominoes and chess, plain public bar with pool room extension, separate restaurant, maybe piped jazz; good big back garden with Aunt Sally, field behind for Caravan Club members; bedrooms, nice village *(Derek and Sylvia Stephenson, Alastair Campbell, Rob Whittle, R Huggins, D Irving, E McCall, T McLean, A Y Drummond)*

Brockhampton [SP0322]

☆ *Craven Arms* [the one between Andoversford and Winchcombe, off A40 via Syreford, Whittington and Sevenhampton; or off A436 Andoversford—Naunton]: Stonebuilt 17th-c pub deservedly popular for lunch, particularly among retired people, with good value well presented food (not Sun evening; must book Sun lunch) in homely interlinked rooms inc restaurant, Hook Norton Best, Fullers London Pride and Wadworths 6X, low beams, sturdy stripped stone, pine furniture with some wall settles, captain's chairs and a log fire, darts, shove-ha'penny; wheelchair access, children welcome, swings in sizeable garden, attractive gentrified hillside village with lovely views *(David and Nina Pugsley, Mr and Mrs B J P Edwards, Dr and Mrs A K Clarke, Roger and Jenny Huggins, Michael Powell, DMT, P and S White, John and Joan Wyatt, BB)*

Brockweir [SO5401]

Brockweir Inn [signed just off A466 Chepstow—Monmouth]: Wye Valley walkers' pub with beams and stripped stonework, quarry tiles, sturdy settles, woodburner, snugger carpeted alcoves with brocaded seats, food inc sandwiches and vegetarian, well kept Adnams, Bass, Hook Norton Best, Whitbreads Best and Worthington BB, Stowford Press cider; upstairs restaurant, pool, machines and piped music in public bar, dogs allowed; covered courtyard, sheltered terrace, garden; open all day Sat, children in eating area; bedrooms *(David Lewis, Sarah Lart, Ian Phillips, LYM, Kevin Thorpe)*

Cambridge [SO7403]

George [3 miles from M5 junction 13 – A38 towards Bristol]: Big, busy and welcoming, with two spacious dining extensions, good value food, well kept Hook Norton Best and

Marstons Pedigree, helpful staff; garden with barbecues, aviaries and play area, also camp site; open all day Sun *(K R Harris, Alan and Paula McCully)*

Camp [SO9109]

Fostons Ash [B4070 Birdlip—Stroud, junction with Calf Way]: Welcoming open-plan refurbished Cotswold pub with good value ample home-made food inc OAP lunch, comfortable well spaced tables, open woodburners each end, well kept Ruddles and Theakstons, prompt friendly service; piped music; children and walkers welcome, garden with play area *(John and Joan Wyatt, A Y Drummond, Neil and Anita Christopher)*

Cerney Wick [SU0796]

Crown: Roomy modernised lounge bar, neat and clean, opening into comfortable semi-conservatory extension, popular straightforward food inc good Sun roasts, well kept Whitbreads-related ales, helpful service, coal-effect gas fires, unobtrusive piped music, public bar with pool, darts, fruit machine; children welcome, good-sized garden with swings, small motel-style bedroom extension *(Peter and Audrey Dowsett, BB)*

Chalford [SO9002]

Kings Head [France Lynch]: Friendly and attractive old country local, long room with brasses and jugs on beams, well kept beers, wide range of good bar food, no juke box or fruit machine, garden, great views *(R Huggins, D Irving, E McCall, T McLean)*

Charlton Kings [SO9620]

Little Owl [Cirencester Rd (A435)]: Concentration on carefully cooked food in much extended and smartened up open-plan neighbourhood pub, fresh ingredients inc carefully bred free-range pork from their own nearby farm, Boddingtons, Hook Norton and Wadworths 6X; piped music; bedrooms *(BB)*

Merry Fellow [School Rd/Church St]: Doing well under current regime, food (better than jokey menu suggests) served till 6 (4 Sun), real ales such as Marstons Pedigree, Smiles and Wadworths 6X; open all day, tables on terrace *(John and Joan Wyatt)*

Ryeworth Inn [Ryeworth Rd]: Friendly town-pub feel, low-priced food, Goffs Jouster as guest beer, good wine *(Guy Vowles)*

Chedworth [SP0511]

Hare & Hounds: Wide choice of good value food *(Lyn and Geoff Hallchurch)*

Cheltenham [SO9422]

Bath [Bath St]: Basic unspoilt 1920s layout, fire in locals' smoke room, bay window seats in tiny front room, Bass and Uley cared for much better than the décor and furnishings *(Roger Huggins, Pete Baker, JP, PP, the Didler)*

Suffolk Arms [Suffolk Rd]: Dark-décor local with comfortable wall seats, well kept beers such as Brakspears, Goffs Jouster and Wickwar BOB; food lunchtime and evening every day, sports TV, friendly *(Graham Coates)*

Tailors [Cambray Pl]: Friendly central pub with good basic lunchtime food inc plenty of ploughman's and baked potatoes, well kept Wadworths 6X and guest ales; lots of dark

wood, split-level main bar with two fireplaces and comfortable armchairs, cosy snug, cellar bar w/e evenings; piped music, some tables outside; can get crowded lunchtime – best to go early or late *(Steve Thomas, Trevor Owen, Tony and Wendy Hobden)*

Chipping Campden [SP1539]

Kings Arms [High St]: Useful small hotel with decent bar food, friendly staff and good log fire in comfortable old-fashioned bar; open all day Sat, bedrooms *(LYM, D H Gittins, Colin and Ann Hunt)*

Red Lion [Sheep St]: Attractive pleasantly cluttered left-hand bar, separate locals' back bar, upstairs dining room, good value generous food (not Mon/Tues evenings); open all day Sat *(Colin and Ann Hunt, Klaus and Elizabeth Leist, John A Foord)*

☆ *Volunteer* [Lower High St]: Early 18th-c pub with cosy little lounge, busy public bar, friendly family staff, good range of generous food from ploughman's up, well kept beers such as Marstons Pedigree and Theakstons, log fire, military memorabilia, books, lots of bric-a-brac, games room (children allowed here); tiny attractive courtyard with beautiful garden running down to river, well equipped bedrooms *(John Marshall, N Christopher)*

Chipping Sodbury [ST7282]

George [Broad St]: Lovely old coaching inn, recently renovated and reopened, interesting interior esp upstairs dining room, stimulatingg choice of food inc vegetarian and excellent soup, reasonably priced wine, enthusiastic and obliging young staff; attractive old town *(Mrs J Newton)*

Squire [Broad St]: Good home-cooked food inc fresh veg and popular lunchtime sandwiches, Bass, Courage, friendly staff *(K R Harris)*

Cirencester [SP0201]

☆ *Corinium Court* [Dollar St/Gloucester St]: Character building, warmly welcoming, cosy and soberly comfortable, with big log fire, attractive antique coaching prints, well kept Boddingtons, Hook Norton Best and Wadworths 6X, decent wine, food inc interesting specials in bar and nicely decorated restaurant, friendly landlord; no piped music; entrance through charming courtyard with tables, attractive back garden; bedrooms *(Peter and Audrey Dowsett, BB)*

☆ *Golden Cross* [Black Jack St, between church and Corinium Museum]: Honest backstreet 1920s local with long narrow bar, simple cheap generous food, three well kept Arkells ales, good friendly service, good beer mug collection; piped music; skittle alley, tables in back garden *(M Joyner, D Irving, R Huggins, T McLean, E McCall)*

Oddfellows Arms [Chester St]: Cosy backstreet local with Greene King and other ales, changing reasonably priced food, friendly service, tables out on good-sized terrace *(Alison and Nick Dowson)*

Slug & Lettuce [West Market Pl]: Flagstones, bare boards, lots of woodwork, wooden benches and chairs, good big tables, no-smoking area, big log fires; well kept Scottish

Courage ales and Marstons Pedigree, good coffee, wide choice of bar food inc good vegetarian, civilised atmosphere, children welcome; tables in inner courtyard; piped pop music, popular with young people evenings *(Lyn and Geoff Hallchurch, LYM, Mary and David Richards)*

Talbot [Victoria Rd]: Curious-looking homely 19th-c local with well kept Arkells 2B *(Giles Francis)*

☆ *Twelve Bells* [Lewis Lane]: Lively backstreet pub with small low-ceilinged bar, small dining area with sturdy pine tables and rugs on quarry tiles, two cosy back rooms, coal fires, pictures for sale, clay pipe collection, particularly well kept Archers Best, Uley and two or three very quickly changing guests, good food esp fish; small sheltered back garden with fountain *(R Huggins, D Irving, E McCall, T McLean, Dr and Mrs A K Clarke, Nick and Alison Dowson, BB)*

Wagon & Horses [London Rd]: Cosy and comfortable Gibbs Mew pub with snug narrow bar, lots of bric-a-brac *(G Coates)*

Clearwell [SO5708]

Butchers Arms: Attractive old stonebuilt pub with subdued red upholstery, dark woodwork, hops, big log fire, popular usual food, well kept Smiles; juke box; tables in neat back courtyard with pond and flowers *(Garth and Janet Wheeler)*

☆ *Wyndham Arms*: Primarily a hotel and restaurant, but with a smart bar awash with burgundy plush, decorative beams, sombre patchwork pictures on stripped stone walls, big open fireplace; well kept Bass, good wines, lots of malt whiskies, good food inc fresh veg from the garden; attractive countryside nr Wye and Forest of Dean, comfortable bedrooms *(Gwen and Peter Andrews, LYM, Stuart and Alison Wallace, Ian Phillips)*

Cleeve Hill [SO9826]

Rising Sun [B4632]: Worth knowing for the view over Cheltenham to the Malvern Hills from the terrace and lawn, esp as the evening lights come on; usual food, friendly staff, Greene King beers *(Dr Sharon Holmes, Dr Tom Cherrett)*

Cliffords Mesne [SO6922]

Yew Tree [out of Newent, past Falconry Centre]: Good value straightforward food (not Mon) in very red-plush place on slopes of May Hill (NT); well kept Scottish Courage ales and Wadworths 6X, cheery staff; restaurant, children welcome, pool table in separate area, tables out on sunny terrace *(DC)*

Coates [SO9600]

☆ *Tunnel House* [follow Tarleton signs (right then left) from village, pub up rough track on right after rly bridge; OS Sheet 163 map ref 965005]: Lots of character in idiosyncratic beamed country pub idyllically placed by interesting abandoned canal tunnel, very relaxed management style, mix of well worn armchairs, sofa, rustic benches, enamel advertising signs, stuffed mustelids, race tickets, real ales such as Archers Best, Morlands Old Speckled Hen, Smiles and Wadworths 6X, good simple food,

Sunday barbecues, log fire, pub games, big juke box much appreciated by Royal Agricultural College students; can be smoky; children welcome (plenty of room to run around outside, too), camping facilities *(Charles Turner, John Fahy, D Irving, R Huggins, T McLean, E McCall, Sheila and Robert Robinson, Pat Crabb, LYM)*

Codrington [ST7579]

Codrington Arms [handy for M4 junction 18, via B4465]: Child-friendly pub with several comfortable rooms, wide choice of interesting if not cheap food, quick friendly service, impressive housekeeping, good range of beers inc Hardy Country and Wadworths 6X, good house wines, big log fire, big garden with good views and play area; piped music *(T R and B C Jenkins, Peter and Audrey Dowsett)*

Coleford [SO5813]

☆ *Dog & Muffler* [Joyford, best approached from Christchurch 5-ways junction B4432/B4428, by church – B4432 towards Broadwell, then follow signpost; also signposted from the Berry Hill post office cross-roads; beyond the hamlet itself, bear right and keep your eyes skinned]: Very prettily set, with open-plan lounge, beamed and flagstoned back extension with games area (and juke box), pleasant back sun lounge dining room and verandah, well kept Sam Smiths and local Freeminer Speculation, cheerful helpful service, good value simple food from sandwiches to cheap Sun lunch; well spaced picnic-sets in attractive sheltered garden, play area, nice walks; children welcome, good bedrooms *(J Monk, Charles and Pauline Stride, Howard England, Gwyneth and Salvo Spadaro-Dutturi, LYM, E J Locker, Mrs M Hobbs)*

Compton Abdale [SP0616]

Puesdown Inn [A40 outside village]: Recently refurbished, with chesterfields, food from generous ploughman's up, well kept Hook Norton and guests such as Marstons Oyster Stout, no-smoking dining area; good base for walking *(J Gibbs)*

Cowley [SO9614]

☆ *Green Dragon* [off A435 S of Cheltenham at Elkstone signpost]: Done-up two-bar country dining pub in nice spot, good interesting if not cheap food (freshly cooked so may be a wait), Sun carvery, well kept ales such as Courage Directors, Hook Norton Best, Morlands Old Speckled Hen and Theakstons, good service, beams, pastel or stripped stone walls, log fires, tasteful oak fittings from Thompsons of Kilburn, pine boards or composition floor, jazz photographs (live jazz some nights); piped music, children allowed in public bar, restaurant; two terraces, one heated, bedrooms off courtyard *(LYM, NWN, Mike and Mary Carter, Neil and Anita Christopher, M J and C E Abbey, Guy Vowles, R Huggins, D Irving, E McCall, T McLean, Trevor Owen)*

Eastleach Turville [SP1905]

Victoria [off A361 S of Burford]: Unpretentious local brightened up under newish management, simple choice of reasonably priced food, pleasant back dining extension off small lounge, pool in big public bar, Arkells 3B and Kingsdown, no piped music, nice views; quiet midweek lunchtime, busy evenings; pleasant front garden overlooking picturesque buildings opp, delightful village esp at daffodil time *(Peter and Audrey Dowsett, Gordon, E McCall, R Huggins, T McLean, Dr A Y Drummond, G W A Pearce)*

Edge [SO8509]

☆ *Edgemoor:* Wide choice of well cooked good value food (lunchtime service stops 2) in tidy modernised dining pub with picture-window panoramic valley view, well kept Smiles, Uley Old Spot and Wickwar BOB; no-smoking area, children welcome, pretty terrace, good walks nearby; cl Sun evening *(Alan and Paula McCully, Barry and Anne, A E Brace, Martin and Karen Wake, LYM, John and Joan Wyatt, Peter Neate)*

Elkstone [SO9610]

☆ *Highwayman* [Beechpike; A417 6 miles N of Cirencester]: Good respite from this busy road, rambling 16th-c warren of low beams, stripped stone, alcoves, antique settles among more modern furnishings, big log fires, rustic decorations, well kept Arkells ales, good house wines, big back eating area (wide choice inc vegetarian), good friendly staff; quiet piped music; disabled access, good family room, outside play area *(the Didler, JP, PP, Margaret Ross, LYM)*

Fairford [SP1501]

Eight Bells: Comfortable, with big woodburner, friendly landlord, bar food, Arkells 3B, decent wine; no piped music *(Peter and Audrey Dowsett)*

Plough [London St]: Lively public bar, plusher yet homely lounge, good welcome, well kept Arkells *(Dr and Mrs A K Clarke)*

Fosse Cross [SP0609]

☆ *Hare & Hounds* [A429 N of Cirencester]: Barn-like roadside pub now under same management as Churchill at Paxford, good if not cheap food, Arkells ales, very good wines, good coffee, two big log fires, back restaurant with plans for enlargement and upgrading; nice area outside, good car park *(Guy Vowles)*

Fossebridge [SP0811]

☆ *Fossebridge Inn* [A429 Cirencester—Stow on the Wold]: Handsome Georgian inn with much older two-room bar at the back, attractively furnished in old-fashioned style with more modern side area, log fires, friendly welcome, popular food with Italian influence here or in dining area, well kept Bass; tables out on streamside terrace and spacious lawn; children welcome; comfortable bedrooms *(R Huggins, D Irving, E McCall, T McLean, Guy Vowles, LYM)*

Frampton Cotterell [ST6683]

Golden Lion [Beesmoor Rd]: Friendly, popular and good value family dining pub, handsome oak beams, lots of farm tools and old photographs, particularly well kept Marstons ales; no-smoking area *(Dr and Mrs A K Clarke)*

Frampton Mansell [SO9102]

☆ *Crown* [off A491 Cirencester—Stroud]: Quietly welcoming stripped stone lounge bar with dark beam-and-plank ceiling, flagstones, well kept ales such as Archers Village, Caledonian Deuchars, Wadworths 6X, public bar with darts, good food in bar and attractive restaurant; lovely views over village and steep wooded valley; children in eating area, teak seats outside; bedrooms *(Dr and Mrs A K Clarke, D Irving, R Huggins, T McLean, E McCall, LYM)*

Frampton on Severn [SO7407]

Bell [The Green]: Clean and welcoming Georgian dining pub by village green cricket pitch, good well priced innovative lunchtime food, log fire, pleasant staff, real ales inc interesting guests, separate locals' bar with pool *(Pete and Rosie Flower, Jo Rees)*

Glasshouse [SO7121]

☆ *Glasshouse* [first right turn off A40 going W from junction with A4136; OS Sheet 162 map ref 710213]: Carefully preserved small country tavern with well kept ales such as Bass and Butcombe tapped from the cask, flagstone floors, log fire in vast fireplace, widening range of generous straightforward food from good thick sandwiches up, interesting decorations, darts and quoits, lovely hanging baskets, seats on fenced lawn with big weeping willow loved by children; fine walks in nearby Newent Woods *(Mike and Mary Carter, LYM, Guy Vowles, P G Topp, the Didler)*

Gloucester [SO8318]

Linden Tree [Bristol Rd; A350 about 1½ miles S of centre, out past docks]: Lively unpretentious local with beams, stripped stone and new carpeting, particularly well kept ales – three Wadworths, three interesting guests, on unusual gravity dispense through wall from cellar; varied straightforward lunchtime food, refurbished back skittle alley; bedrooms *(Joan and Michel Hooper-Immins)*

New Inn [Westgate St]: Lovely medieval building with courtyard, recently reopened after renovation, four separate areas with local real ales in one welcoming bar; bedrooms *(Stephen and Jean Curtis)*

Guiting Power [SP0924]

Farmers Arms: Traditional local in lovely village, stripped stone, mix of carpet and flagstones, good log fire, well kept Donnington BB and SBA, decent home-made bar food; skittle alley, games area with darts, pool, cribbage, dominoes, fruit machine; piped music; seats (and quoits) in garden, good walks; children welcome, bedrooms *(Martin Jennings, Stephen and Julie Brown, the Didler, Lawrence Pearse, MRSM, LYM)*

Hanham [ST6472]

Elm Tree [Hanham Abbots; S, on back rd to Willsbridge and Oldland Common]: Cheerful, with friendly efficient service, well kept Courage and a guest beer such as Butcombe, good lunch menu from sandwiches to steaks inc good steak and kidney pie *(R T and J C Moggridge)*

Hawkesbury Upton [ST7786]

Beaufort Arms: Doing well under current very friendly landlord, with five well kept beers such as Bath, Fullers London Pride and local

Wickwar BOB, local farm cider, good basic food; seats outside, skittle alley; on Cotswold Way *(S Kimmins)*

Horsley [ST8397]

Tipputs [Tiltups End; A46 2 miles S of Nailsworth]: Spacious yet friendly refurbished pub, beams and stripped stone in L-shaped bar, big log fire, good range of well kept beers such as Berkeley Old Friend, tasty food, good prices *(Tom Evans)*

Huntley [SO7219]

☆ *Red Lion* [A40 Gloucester—Ross]: Roaring fires in comfortable lounge and public bar, wide choice of tasty interestingly cooked fresh food, friendly obliging service, nice atmosphere, Bass and Flowers beers *(Alec Hamilton, J Butler)*

Kemble [ST9897]

☆ *Thames Head* [A433 Cirencester—Tetbury]: Well served good food inc wide puddings choice, well kept Arkells Bitter, 2B and 3B, pleasant owners and staff, stripped stone, timberwork, cottage back area with pews and log-effect gas fire in big fireplace, country-look dining-room with another big gas fire, real fire in front area; seats outside, children welcome, bedrooms *(C and A Moncreiffe, LYM, Patrick Godfrey, B Perfect)*

Kineton [SP0926]

☆ *Halfway House* [signed from B4068 and B4077 W of Stow on the Wold]: Traditional unpretentious country local with attractive sheltered back garden, tables on narrow front terrace too, well kept cheap Donnington BB and SBA from nearby brewery, simple food inc sensibly priced hot dishes, friendly staff, pub games (and juke box), restaurant; children allowed lunchtime, no visiting dogs; simple comfortable bedrooms, good walks *(J Dwane, Gwen and Peter Andrews, R Huggins, D Irving, E McCall, T McLean, LYM)*

Kings Stanley [SO8103]

Kings Head: Comfortable lounge bar with wide menu, Flowers Original, attentive service, restaurant overlooking cricket pitch *(D G King)*

Kingscote [ST8196]

☆ *Hunters Hall* [A4135 Dursley—Tetbury]: Civilised Tudor dining pub with attractive layout – series of comfortable and relaxing individually furnished rooms on two floors, part no smoking, also cosy old flagstoned public bar with pool and other games; food inc sandwiches (not Sun lunch), buffet and various good hot dishes, friendly young staff, well kept Bass, Courage Directors and Theakstons Best, no piped music; children welcome, garden with ingenious play area, live music Sun evening, open all day; bedrooms *(Peter and Audrey Dowsett, LYM, Comus Elliott, Janet and Peter Race, Stephen Brown, Andy and Jill Kassube)*

Kingswood [ST7491]

Dinneywicks [The Chippings]: Smallish done-up village inn, two connected bars with good value home-made food in pleasant eating area, well kept ales inc Adnams Broadside, obliging service; open all day Sat; interesting village with some good architecture *(John and Joan Wyatt)*

Lechlade [SU2199]

☆ *Trout* [A417, a mile E]: Low-beamed three-room pub dating from 15th c, with some flagstones, stuffed fish and fishing prints, big Thamesside garden with boules, Aunt Sally and a simple summer family bar; Courage Directors and maybe related beers, popular well presented food from ploughman's through pizzas to steaks, no-smoking dining room; children in eating areas, jazz Tues and Sun, fishing rights; very busy in summer (open all day Sat then), service can be slow *(Gordon, R Huggins, D Irving, E McCall, T McLean, James Nunn, LYM, Dr and Mrs A K Clarke)*

Longborough [SP1729]

Coach & Horses [signed off A424]: Basic honest Donnington pub, plenty of character, welcoming landlady *(R Huggins, D Irving, E McCall, T McLean)*

Longford [SO8320]

Queens Head [Tewkesbury Rd]: Good lunches, slightly more upmarket evening meals – good value; well kept real ales such as Bass, Gales HSB, Hook Norton and Wadworths 6X *(Peter Williams)*

Longhope [SO6820]

☆ *Farmers Boy* [Boxbush, Ross Rd; A40 outside village]: Unpretentious and relaxing two-room country restaurant, good value wholesome food all day, curry specialities, good specials, OAP bargains Thurs; heavy beams, blazing fire, candles, fast friendly service, well kept ales such as Boddingtons, Smiles Best, Theakstons and Thwaites; piped music, separate public bar with big screen TV and electric organ; pleasant garden and terrace *(Alec Hamilton, BB)*

Lower Swell [SP1725]

☆ *Golden Ball* [B4068 W of Stow on the Wold]: Sprucely unspoilt local with well kept Donnington BB and SBA from the pretty nearby brewery, good range of ciders and perry, very friendly landlady, well presented generous home-made food, log fire, games area with fruit machine and juke box behind big chimneystack, small evening restaurant (not Sun evening), small garden with occasional barbecues, Aunt Sally and quoits; maybe piped classical music, no dogs or children; decent simple bedrooms; pretty village, good walks *(John and Joan Wyatt, R Huggins, D Irving, E McCall, T McLean, Walter Reid, the Didler, KN-R, John Fahy, LYM)*

Lower Wick [ST7196]

☆ *Pickwick* [signed off A38 Bristol—Gloucester just N of Newport]: Wide choice of attractively priced food (worth booking w/e evenings) in carpeted bar with woodburner and lots of wheelback chairs around shiny dark tables, brocaded small settles and more of the wheelbacks in dining room, some stripped stone, well kept Smiles Best and Golden with a guest such as Bass, traditional games inc antique table skittles; piped music may be loud; picnic-sets and play fort by back paddock – M'way noise out here; children welcome *(Peter and Audrey Dowsett, BB, Carol and Dono Leaman, Charles and Pauline Stride)*

Minsterworth [SO7716]

Apple Tree [A48 S of Gloucester]: Friendly and comfortable roadside Whitbreads family dining pub based on extended oak-beamed 17th-c farmhouse, decent standard food, open fires, prompt service, unobtrusive piped music, well kept ales, children's room with own bar; back dining room overlooking big garden with enclosed play area; open all day – lane beside leads down to the Severn, a good way of avoiding east bank crowds on a Bore weekend *(Mr and Mrs B Craig, June and Mike Coleman)*

Moreton in Marsh [SP2032]
Black Bear: Big comfortable blue-carpeted bar, beams, stripped stone with hanging rugs, full range of local Donnington ales kept well, bareboards separate dining room (not Sun evening), good range of home-made food inc lots of grilled fish, efficient welcoming service; TV and darts end *(N Christopher, BB, Joan and Michel Hooper-Immins, Ian and Nita Cooper)*
Inn on the Marsh [High St]: Good reasonably priced restaurant-style food in dining conservatory, well kept Banks's, friendly young staff, comfortable armchairs and sofa, pink walls giving bistro look; bedrooms *(R Huggins, D Irving, T McLean, E McCall)*
Swan [High St]: Comfortable lounge with flowered wallpaper and old photographs, good choice of low-priced food inc pies and children's, well kept Fullers London Pride and Wadworths 6X, decent wine, friendly staff, attractive restaurant *(Neil and Anita Christopher, Peter and Audrey Dowsett)*

Nailsworth [ST8599]
Cross: Big open-plan community pub, with stripped stone walls, wide mix of customers, several real ales, pool, darts, juke box, SkyTV *(D Irving, R Huggins, T McLean, E McCall)*
☆ *Weighbridge* [B4014 towards Tetbury]: Friendly new licensees, three stripped stone rooms with antique settles and country chairs, beams, rustic ironware, steps up to candlelit raftered loft, widening food choice (they still do the good two-in-one pies), well kept ales such as Marstons Pedigree, Smiles Best and John Smiths, good house wines, log fire; sheltered garden behind *(D Irving, R Huggins, T McLean, E McCall, S Godsell, Tom Rees, LYM, D G King)*

Nether Westcote [SP2120]
☆ *New Inn* [off A424 Burford—Stow]: Good freshly made food, well kept local real ales and charming helpful staff in unspoilt but cosy 17th-c pub, clean and comfortable; secondary dining area down a few steps; can get busy, piped pop music may be loud; sizeable adjoining campsite, pretty village *(Mrs N W Neill, A Y Drummond, Matthew and Sylvie Leggett)*

North Nibley [ST7496]
☆ *Black Horse*: Good straightforward village local with friendly helpful staff, wide range of generous good value home-made food inc vegetarian, well kept Flowers Original and Marstons Pedigree, good log fire, maybe piped music; popular restaurant Tues-Sat evenings, Sun lunchtime, tables in pretty garden; good value cottagey bedrooms, good breakfast, useful for Cotswold Way walkers *(D G King, Tina and David Woods-Taylor, Mary and David Richards, LYM)*

Northleach [SP1114]
Red Lion [Market Pl]: Handsome building in attractive village, good value generous food from good sandwiches to Sun roasts with thoroughly cooked veg and memorable puddings in straightforward bar with open fire, well kept Scottish Courage ales, decent house wine, good coffee, very friendly service, restaurant; unobtrusive piped music *(John T Ames, Mr and Mrs J Brown)*

Nympsfield [SO8000]
☆ *Rose & Crown* [signed off B4066 Stroud—Dursley]: Stonebuilt village inn with good value generous food inc Indian and vegetarian all day, well kept ales such as Bass, Boddingtons, Severn Boar, Smiles Best, Theakstons Old Peculier, Uley Old Spot, Wadworths 6X and Wickwar BOB, decent wines, pink plush banquettes and lots of brass in pubby beamed bar with log fire and fruit machine, dark pews around tables in back saloon opening into dining room; well behaved children allowed, picnic-sets in side yard and on sheltered lawn with good play area; bedrooms, handy for Cotswold walks *(Dave Braisted, J R Jewitt, BB, Peter Neate, Tom Evans, Andrew Hodges, Tom and Ruth Rees)*

Old Sodbury [ST7581]
Cross Hands [junction of A46 with A432; 1½ miles from M4 junction 18]: Popular and spacious recently refurbished pub/hotel, pleasant atmosphere, quick friendly service, subdued piped music, log-effect gas fire, real ales such as Bass, Theakstons Old Peculier and Wadworths 6X, good coffee; food in bar and restaurant, comfortable bedrooms *(Rob Holt, Peter and Audrey Dowsett, LYM)*

Painswick [SO8609]
☆ *Falcon* [New St]: Sizeable old stone inn opp churchyard famous for its 99 yews; open plan, largely panelled, with high ceilings, bare boards bar on right, mainly carpeted dining area with lots of prints on left, high bookshelves and shelves of ornaments by coal-effect fire, well kept Boddingtons, Brakspears, Greene King Abbot and Wadworths 6X, good coffee, wide range of home-made food from good baguettes and pies to more adventurous dishes, daily papers, carpeted L-shaped dining area; bedrooms *(D Irving, R Huggins, T McLean, E McCall, Tina and David Woods-Taylor, BB, B and K Hypher, John and Joan Wyatt, James Skinner)*
☆ *Royal Oak* [St Mary's St]: Lively bustle in old-fashioned partly 16th-c town local with interesting layout and furnishings inc some attractive old or antique seats, huge helpings of good reasonably priced food (bar nibbles only, Sun) from sandwiches up, well kept Whitbreads-related ales, friendly and efficient family service, open fire, small sun lounge by suntrap pretty courtyard; children in eating area; can get packed, nearby parking may be difficult *(R Huggins, D Irving, E McCall, T McLean, Tina and David Woods-Taylor, LYM, B and K Hypher)*

Parkend [SO6208]
Fountain [just off B4234]: Homely and

welcoming, with assorted chairs and settles, real fire, old local tools and photographs, good freshly made usual food inc good range of curries, efficient landlord, well kept local Freeminer and guest beers; children welcome *(Pete Baker)*

Paxford [SP1837]

☆ *Churchill*: Plenty of good reports on this busy dining pub, marrying unusually good interesting food, cooked with real flair, with a simply furnished flagstoned bar, low ceilings and log fire – also a newish restaurant extension; the wines are good value, too, and they have well kept Arkells 3Bs, Hook Norton Best and a guest beer; but a minority undercurrent of concern about the food price/quantity equation suggests that we were a little hasty in making this a main entry in last year's edition of what is after all a pub rather than a restaurant guide; some tables outside, well behaved children allowed away from bar; bedrooms *(John P W Bowdler, J H Kane, G R Braithwaite, H Dickinson, A M Phillips, Martin Jones, Ann and Bob Westbrook, John Bramley, Charles and Ann Moncreiffe, LYM)*

Prestbury [SO9624]

Royal Oak [The Burgage]: Small village local, friendly and comfortable, with well kept Flowers Original and Wadworths 6X, efficient service, freshly cooked wholesome food; no fruit machines or small children *(Mr and Mrs D Anderson)*

Pucklechurch [ST7077]

Rose & Crown [Parkfield Rd]: Pleasant old pub in quiet country setting, sensibly priced well kept Bass and Wadworths, decent food cooked to order inc Sun roasts and good choice of puddings, no-smoking dining room; seats outside *(K R Harris)*

Purton [SO6904]

☆ *Berkeley Arms* [just upstream from Sharpness village on left bank of Severn estuary]: Basic rustic Severnside local short walk from canal bridge, wonderful estuary view, two character flagstoned rooms with plain high-backed settles, well kept local Berkeley Dicky Pearce or Old Friend and a seasonal brew tapped from the cask, simple snacks till 1.30; nice garden, summer caravanning allowed when there's no risk of flooding *(John and Joan Wyatt, the Didler)*

Berkeley Hunt [just down bumpy lane from Berkeley Arms]: Basic ancient farmhouse local nr bridge over Sharpness—Gloucester canal, flagstoned rooms off central servery, coal fire in magnificent fireplace, guest beers, some tapped from the cask, inc local Berkeley microbrews *(the Didler)*

Quenington [SP1404]

Keepers Arms: Cosy and comfortable stripped-stone pub, traditional settles, bric-a-brac inc lots of mugs hanging from low beams, log fires, decent food in both bars and restaurant, Whitbreads-related ales, no piped music; bedrooms, tables in garden *(Bill Sykes, G W A Pearce)*

Redmarley [SO7631]

☆ *Rose & Crown* [Playley Green; A417 just off

M50 exit 2]: Generous helpings of good reasonably priced food from filled baps to Sun roasts in good-sized comfortable stripped stone lounge or big attractive restaurant (was skittle alley), well kept Flowers Original and Tapsters Fat Cat, quick cheerful service, darts and pool in public bar; tables in garden, beautiful countryside *(Neil and Anita Christopher, G W A Pearce)*

Rodborough [SO8404]

Prince Albert [Rodborough Hill]: Popular easy-going local, welcoming licensees, simple food, Bass and Flowers *(D G King)*

Ruardean [SO6117]

☆ *Malt Shovel*: Unusual, recently carefully restored so as still to seem in a time warp, stripped stone, oak and mahogany, central fire, good choice of home-made food, real ales and farm cider; attractively furnished well equipped bedrooms *(Jeremy Parkes, Jane Owen)*

Sapperton [SO9403]

☆ *Bell*: Neat village pub with games in big lively traditional public bar, extended stripped stone lounge, good log fire, sturdy pine tables, well kept Flowers Original, Tetleys and Wadworths 6X, consistently good value food from sandwiches to steaks, friendly service; skittle alley, tables outside; children welcome *(D Irving, E McCall, R Huggins, T McLean, Jenny Huggins, Laura and Stuart Ballantyne, LYM)*

☆ *Daneway* [signed off A419 Stroud—Cirencester]: Friendly local with amazing floor-to-ceiling carved oak fireplace, sporting prints, well kept Wadworths IPA, 6X and a guest such as Adnams, Weston's Old Rosie farm cider, food from filled baps (may be a wait), small no-smoking family room; traditional games in inglenook public bar, lovely sloping lawn in charming quiet wooded countryside alongside derelict canal with good walks and interesting tunnel *(Neil and Anita Christopher, Charles and Pauline Stride, Gordon, M G Hart, LYM)*

Slad [SO8707]

Woolpack [B4070 Stroud—Birdlip]: Small hillside village pub with lovely valley views; has had imaginative freshly cooked food such as duck and bacon pie, Weston's Old Rosie cider, well kept Bass and Uley Old Spot, but recently sold (to a local) – news please *(Pat and Jim Halfyard, Peter and Audrey Dowsett, R Huggins, D Irving, E McCall, T McLean)*

Slimbridge [SO7303]

Tudor Arms [Shepherds Patch]: Well kept Hook Norton Best, Tetleys, Wadworths 6X and a guest such as Buckleys, generous basic food from sandwiches and ploughman's up inc children's dishes, typical modernised lounge, bar with billiards and TV, skittle alley, family room, evening restaurant; handy for Wildfowl Trust and canal boat trips, snacks all day w/e; bedrooms in small annexe *(Alan Drummond, D G King, Steve Thomas)*

Snowshill [SP0934]

☆ *Snowshill Arms*: Handy for Snowshill Manor (which closes lunchtime) and for Cotswold Way walkers, with welcoming service, good popular inexpensive food served quickly, well kept Donnington BB and SBA, spruce and airy carpeted bar with neat array of tables, local photographs, stripped stone, log fire; skittle alley, charming village views from bow windows and from big back garden with little stream and good play area, friendly local feel midweek winter and evenings, can be very crowded other lunchtimes – get there early; children welcome if eating, nearby parking may be difficult *(LYM, Neil and Anita Christopher, Maysie Thompson, Neil Hardwick, David Walker, Mr and Mrs B Craig, D Irving, R Huggins, D Irving, T McLean, E McCall)*

South Cerney [SU0497]

☆ *Eliot Arms* [signed off A419 SE of Cirencester; Clarks Hay]: Smart pub/hotel, clean and tidy but full of relaxed and comfortable little rooms, interesting décor inc historic racing-car pictures; some emphasis on attractive choice of reasonably priced food, well kept Boddingtons, Flowers Original, Marstons Pedigree and Wadworths 6X, 120 malt whiskies, interesting foreign bottled beers, fast service; children welcome, restaurants, bedrooms *(P and S White, Mr and Mrs B Craig, D Irving, R Huggins, T McLean, E McCall, Neil and Anita Christopher, Phyl and Jack Street)*
Old George: Warmly pubby small rooms, log fire, food inc good sandwiches, Boddingtons, Courage and Hook Norton *(E B White-Atkins)*

Southrop [SP2003]

☆ *Swan*: Cottagey seats and log fire in extended low-ceilinged dining lounge with well spaced tables and good interesting food (former popular chef back at the stove), small no-smoking restaurant (not Sun evening), friendly helpful staff, Morlands Original and guests such as Marstons Pedigree, good wines; stripped stone skittle alley, public bar, children welcome; pretty village esp at daffodil time *(Peter and Audrey Dowsett, D M and M C Watkinson, Keith Symons, LYM, KN-R, John Hayter)*

Stonehouse [SO8005]

Woolpack [High St]: Very large old town pub with low ceilings, lots of interesting prints, well kept Uley Hogshead and Wadworths 6X, good choice of food, hard-working staff *(Tina and David Woods-Taylor)*

Stow on the Wold [SP1729]

☆ *Coach & Horses* [Ganborough (A424 N)]: Straightforward beamed and flagstoned roadside pub alone on former coaching road, central fire, steps up to carpeted dining area with high-backed settles; friendly staff, well kept Donnington BB and SBA, very wide choice of good sensibly priced food (all day summer Fri/Sat), friendly service; children welcome, tables in garden, open all day Sun too *(Peter and Audrey Dowsett, Walter Reid, Phil and Caroline Welch, Bob and Maggie Atherton, R Huggins, D Irving, E McCall, T McLean, E A Froggatt, John Fahy, Brian and Bett Cox, Paul and M-T Pumfrey, George Atkinson, Colin McKerrow, LYM, Joan and Michel Hooper-Immins)*
Farmers Arms [Fosseway (A429)]: Enjoyable food from sandwiches and baked potatoes to steaks and fruits de mer, inc vegetarian and

children's, in pub/hotel with good service and atmosphere *(P R Bevins)*
Fox: Old-fashioned, almost tea-shop atmosphere, friendly landlady who is a good listener, Hook Norton Old Hooky; long-haired pub dachshund *(Veronica Brown)*

☆ *Old Stocks* [The Square]: Well run simple hotel with civilised and welcoming small bar and dining room, decent food and wines, well kept real ale, friendly staff; subdued piped music; seats on pavement and in small sheltered garden; good value bedrooms *(George Atkinson)*

☆ *Queens Head* [The Square]: Welcoming old local with good chatty atmosphere, heavily beamed and flagstoned traditional back bar, high-backed settles, big log fire, horse prints, piped classical or opera; usual games, nice dogs; lots of tables in civilised stripped stone front lounge, good value straightforward fresh food (not Mon evening or Sun), well kept Donnington BB and SBA, mulled wine, quick helpful service; children welcome, tables outside, occasional jazz Sun lunchtime *(Klaus and Elizabeth Leist, R Huggins, D Irving, T McLean, E McCall, IHR, the Didler, TBB, Pam Adsley, John T Ames, Veronica Brown, Bill Sykes, Tim and Linda Collins, LYM)*

☆ *Royalist* [Digbeth St]: Behind the handsome 17th-c golden stonework this is one of Britain's most genuinely ancient inns, with interesting medieval features and parts of its timber frame around 1,000 years old; recently bought by licensees with a first-class GPG track record, now doing good promptly served bar food inc unusual dishes, well kept ales inc Adnams, well equipped bedrooms *(Miss Veronica Brown)*
Talbot [The Square]: Open-plan Wadworths pub, plain tables and chairs on bare boards, prints on magnolia walls, genteel relaxed atmosphere, continental-feel food, Farmers Glory, 6X and a seasonal beer, good friendly service even when busy; bedrooms, open all day *(R Huggins, D Irving, T McLean, E McCall, Joan and Michel Hooper-Immins)*
White Hart [The Square]: Something of the feel of an inn in the 1960s, with decent food and well kept beer in cheery and pleasant old front bar or plush back dining lounge; bedrooms *(Miss V Brown, BB)*

Stowe [SO5606]

Travellers Rest [between Clearwell and St Briavels, Forest of Dean]: Spacious lounge with well kept Bass, decent low-priced food inc vegetarian and generous Sun roasts, pleasant service, huge log fire, polished tables and chairs, some upholstered benches; bar billiards in public bar, tables out on front lawns *(Paul and Heather Bettesworth)*

Stroud [SO8504]

Golden Fleece [Nelson St, just E of centre]: Small old terrace pub, fairly dark inside, with daily papers, cheerfully musical decor, unobtrusive piped jazz, well kept beer, unspoilt feel, separate smaller upstairs room *(Dave and Deborah Irving)*
Lord John [Russell St]: Split-level conversion of formerly derelict PO sorting office, striking

decor (particularly the orange and turquoise nr entrance), tables in alcoves; usual Wetherspoons food *(W M and J M Cottrell)*
Retreat [top end of High St]: Pink walls, polished wooden floors and tables, well kept ales, imaginative lunchtime food, children welcome; can get crowded evenings, tiny courtyard now covered in as attractive extension *(Dave and Deborah Irving)*
Tetbury [ST8893]
Trouble House [A433 towards Cirencester, nr Cherington]: Pretty 17th-c two-bar pub with new emphasis on home-made food from sandwiches to duck, steaks and lobster, welcoming atmosphere, well kept Wadworths, open fire, garden with play area *(Mr and Mrs J Brown)*
Tewkesbury [SO8932]
☆ *Bell* [Church St]: Interesting hotel bar with black oak beams and timbers, neat 17th-c oak panelling, medieval leaf-and-fruit frescoes, tapestries, armchairs and small tables; good food in bar and attractive restaurant; well kept Smiles and Theakstons, good coffee, big log fire; garden above Severnside walk, nr abbey; bedrooms *(Joan and Michel Hooper-Immins, Peter and Audrey Dowsett, BB, Howard England, Mr and Mrs C West)*
Berkeley Arms [Church St]: Pleasant olde-worlde refurbishment in striking medieval timbered pub (the best part's down the side alley), with well kept Wadworths 6X, Farmers Glory and winter Old Timer with a summer guest beer, friendly staff, open fire, wide range of good value food inc succulent real chips; separate front public bar (can be smoky), raftered ancient back barn restaurant; open all day summer, bedrooms *(Howard England)*
Thornbury [ST6690]
White Horse [Buckover (A38, not far from M5 junction 14)]: Superb view of Severn and both bridges from bar, dining area and recently added garden room, food inc popular Sun lunch, friendly service *(Charles and Pauline Stride)*
Toddington [SP0432]
Pheasant [A46 Broadway—Winchcombe, junction with A438 and B4077]: Plenty of room inc no-smoking area, good choice of quickly served food with lots of veg, three or four real ales inc local Stanway; handy for nearby preserved Gloucestershire Warwickshire Railway *(John and Joan Wyatt, Martin Jones)*
Tolldown [ST7577]
☆ *Crown* [under a mile from M4 junction 18 – A46 towards Bath]: Tidy and largely unspoilt heavy-beamed stripped stone bar, usual food inc weekly OAP lunches, good steaks, fresh veg, interesting evening dishes; quick friendly service, well kept Wadworths, woodburner and coal fire, no-smoking area; dominoes, darts, fruit machine, piped music; children in eating area and restaurant, no dogs (friendly cat), good garden with play area; comfortable bedrooms *(Ian and Nita Cooper, LYM)*
Twyning [SO9036]
☆ *Fleet* [Fleet St, Twyning Green]: Superb setting at end of quiet lane, with good river views from

roomy high-ceilinged bar interestingly reworked in nautical style by new owners, snug styled as cosy kitchen with Aga, light and airy restaurant, good value tasty food, pleasant staff; tables on terrace and lawn; disabled access, boat shop *(Jo Rees, BB)*
Village Inn [Twyning Green]: Warmly welcoming village local with good atmosphere, helpful staff, good simple bar food (may be limited Mon and Tues), well kept Banks's, Flowers IPA and Wadworths 6X, decent wines, skittle alley; dogs allowed, pretty garden *(Francis Johnston)*
Tytherington [ST6688]
Swan: Big well furnished family food pub with good choice, no-smoking area, children's room; huge car park, very busy w/e *(Meg and Colin Hamilton, K R Harris)*
Uley [ST7898]
Old Crown: Prettily set by village green, long narrow lounge, usual food from baguettes to full meals inc vegetarian and children's, well kept Boddingtons, Hook Norton Best, Uley Bitter and Old Spot (the brewer is a regular) and guest beers, attractive garden; dogs welcome, darts and fruit machine, small pool room up spiral stairs, unobtrusive piped music; bedrooms good value with super breakfast, good base for walks *(anon)*
Upper Framilode [SO7510]
☆ *Ship* [Saul Rd; not far from M5 junction 13 via B4071]: Attractive family dining pub in relaxing setting by disused canalside offshoot from Severn with ducks and swans, surprisingly wide range of good food from sandwiches to steaks inc wide vegetarian choice, fresh fish and shellfish, plenty of puddings and lots for children, well kept Ansells and Bass, local farm cider; evening restaurant extension *(John Harris, D G King, Robert Moreland)*
Westbury on Severn [SO7114]
☆ *Red Lion* [A48, corner Bell Lane]: Substantial half-timbered building on busy road but by quiet church-side lane to river, welcoming and well managed; generous interesting home cooking in big dining room with old pews; cosy bar with button-back wall seats, velvet curtains, cotton cap collection on beams, coal stove, well kept ales such as Fullers and Wickwar, decent wine, very friendly service; evening opening 7; handy for Westbury Court gardens (NT) *(Mrs B Sugarman, BB, B Klinger)*
Westonbirt [ST8690]
☆ *Hare & Hounds* [A433 SW of Tetbury]: Well run turkey-carpeted bar, comfortable, relaxed and surprisingly pubby, with high-backed settles, food counter with decent reasonably priced lunches inc enterprising open sandwiches, Courage Best and Smiles Best, central log-effect gas fire, friendly efficient staff, sporting prints; games in public bar on left, small tweedy more central cocktail bar; pleasant gardens, handy for Arboretum; bedrooms *(Revd A Nunnerley, BB)*
Wick [ST7072]
Rose & Crown [High St (A420)]: One of the better Chef & Brewers, busy and roomy, with daily papers, plenty of character, good service,

very wide food range, well kept beers such as Theakstons Best and Wadworths 6X *(Andrew Shore, Mark and Heather Williamson, Tina and David Woods-Taylor)*

Willersey [SP1039]

Bell [B4632 Cheltenham—Stratford, nr Broadway]: Attractive 14th-c golden stone dining pub under new licensees, good carefully prepared food (may be a wait for an evening meal), well kept ales such as Boddingtons and Wadworths 6X; overlooks delightful village's green and duck pond, lots of tables in big garden *(Pam Adsley)*

Winchcombe [SP0228]

Corner Cupboard [High St]: Relaxed local atmosphere and traditional layout, with hatch-service lobby, small smoke room with woodburner, pleasant back lounge with heavy beams, stripped stone and good inglenook fireplace, attractive small back garden; well kept Flowers Original, Fullers London Pride and Goffs Jouster, friendly landlord, board games; home-made food from ploughman's to sizzler steaks (not Sun or Mon evenings), quiet piped music; bedrooms in self-contained wing, open all day Sun (happy hour 3-7) *(James Cooper, Giles Francis, BB)*

Old White Lion [North St]: Open, light and pleasant, with small bar, interesting food inc alternative genuine Chinese menu, Timothy Taylor Landlord, separate restaurant; bedrooms *(Guy Vowles)*

☆ *Plaisterers Arms* [Abbey Terr]: 18th-c pub with stripped stonework, beams, Hogarth prints and open fire, two front bars and steps down to dim-lit lower back dining area with tables in stalls; welcoming and helpful Irish landlord, well kept Goffs Jouster, short but interesting choice of good food, all freshly made, inc

sandwiches and enterprising specials; good play area in attractive garden, long and narrow; bedrooms comfortable and reasonably priced, handy for Sudeley Castle *(Michael Bourdeaux, Derek and Sylvia Stephenson, Chris Raisin, John Saul, Simon Collett-Jones, Rona Murdoch, BB)*

White Harte [High St (B4632)]: Comfortable stone-built beamed inn with cheerful service, good home-made usual food, real ales such as Boddingtons, Marstons Pedigree and Stanway Oatmeal Stout, pleasant staff; bedrooms spacious with good facilities *(KN-R, George Atkinson, Ann and Colin Hunt)*

Woodchester [SO8403]

☆ *Old Fleece* [A46 a mile S of Stroud]: Attractively informal bare-boards décor in two bars and bistro dining areas with well laid candlelit tables, wide choice of good interesting freshly made bar food with home-grown fruit puddings, particularly well kept Bass, Boddingtons and Greene King, good wines, local non-alcoholic drinks, smiling service, big log fire, daily papers, popular golden labrador *(J H Bescoby, Tim and Ann Newell, D G King, Sandra Childress)*

☆ *Ram* [South Woodchester]: Attractively priced real ales such as Archers Best, John Smiths, Theakstons Old Peculier, Uley Old Spot and several interesting guest beers, in relaxed L-shaped beamed bar with nice mix of traditional furnishings, stripped stonework, bare boards, three open fires, darts, food from sandwiches to steaks, restaurant; children welcome, open all day Sat/Sun, spectacular views from terrace tables *(Neil and Anita Christopher, R Huggins, D Irving, E McCall, T McLean, Susan and Nigel Wilson, Roger and Valerie Hill, J and P Halfyard, DC, Adrian White, LYM)*

Stars after the name of a pub show exceptional quality. One star means most people (after reading the report to see just why the star has been won) would think a special trip worth while. Two stars mean that the pub is really outstanding – one of just a handful in its region. The very very few with three stars are the real aristocrats – of their type, they could hardly be improved.

Hampshire

*Hampshire pubs doing particularly well in recent months include the Globe by
the ancient ponds in Alresford, the Milbury's up on the downs at Beauworth,
the cosy little Sun at Bentworth, the Red Lion at Boldre (good food, great
choice of wines by the glass), the Five Bells at Buriton (back in these pages
after a break), the White Hart in Cadnam (new licensees doing good
imaginative food), the unaffected Flower Pots at Cheriton (brewing their own
excellent beers), the attractively laid out White Horse at Droxford), the Royal
Oak at Fritham (friendly young new owners breathing new life into this
tucked-away New Forest pub), the Hawkley Inn at Hawkley (surprisingly
sophisticated food and good beers at this proper country local), the Yew Tree
at Lower Wield (a new entry, now a top-notch dining pub), the Old Horse &
Jockey on the edge of Romsey (good all round – another new entry), the
delightfully unspoilt Harrow at Steep, the friendly Brushmakers Arms at
Upham, the Wykeham Arms in Winchester (this old favourite on top form)
and yet another new entry, the Horse & Groom at Woodgreen (a proper New
Forest pub, yet – as one reader succinctly puts it – with the sort of food one
has come to expect). With the Wykeham Arms running it a very close second,
the White Hart at Cadnam is our Hampshire Dining Pub of the Year. Pubs
showing prominently in the Lucky Dip section at the end of the chapter are
the Oak at Bank, Hobler at Battramsley, Tally Ho at Broughton, White Buck
near Burley, Red Lion at Chalton, Hampshire Bowman at Dundridge, George
at East Meon, New Forest at Emery Down, Olde Whyte Harte in Hamble,
Chequers just outside Lymington, Gamekeepers at Mapledurwell (food), Red
Lion at Mortimer West End, Bush at Ovington, Trooper near Petersfield
(food), Rose & Thistle at Rockbourne, White Lion at Soberton, Rising Sun at
Swanmore (food), Cricketers Arms at Tangley and very ancient Royal Oak in
Winchester. Drinks prices here are rather higher than the national average.
Beers from Gales and Ringwood, the two main local brewers, quite often
cropped up as the cheapest beer a pub had to offer, and we occasionally found
other local brews at below-average prices – notably Cheriton (especially in its
own pub the Flower Pots at Cheriton), Hampshire, and Moondance Triple
FFF.*

ALRESFORD SU5832 Map 2
Globe ♀

The Soke, Broad Street (extreme lower end – B3046 towards Old Alresford); town signposted
off A31 bypass

A new Garden Room with a striped awning ceiling – which gives an attractive tented
effect – has been added to this popular pub. The comfortable bar has a bustling
atmosphere, big log fires at each end, and a clean and uncluttered décor – old local
photographs, information about the ponds, and so forth. Attentive, helpful staff
serve well presented and enjoyable home-made bar food such as filled french bread,
soup (£2.75), smoked mackerel or stilton and walnut pâté (£3.95), tasty potted
shrimps, home-made faggots with mash and onion gravy or cheese flan (£5.95),
enjoyable fish pie (£6), fresh fillet of cod in beer batter (£6.50), lasagne (£6.95), thai

chicken with noodles (£7.95), lovely seared salmon (£8.95), excellent whole plaice (£9.50), rib-eye steak au poivre (£10.75), and puddings like brownies with hot chocolate sauce or bakewell tart (£3.75); best to book. Part of the restaurant is no smoking. Well kept Cheriton Flower Pots and Courage Best with a guest such as Marstons Pedigree, John Smiths or Wadworths 6X on handpump, eight or so decent wines by the glass, winter mulled wine, and country wines; board games. There are terrace doors to the terrace and garden – and a good view over the Alresford Ponds, a sizeable stretch of water created in the 12th c and now a lovely haven for wildlife; some of the birds hope for scraps in the attractive garden, and in summer offer endless amusement for small children; no children inside. Nearby parking is rather limited; there's plenty about 100 metres away, at the bottom of truly named Broad St. The large village is full of charm and character. *(Recommended by Chris and Anna Rowersey, F Johnston, Dr Alan Green, P R and S A White, Chris and Ann Garnett, Tony Dickinson, Ann and Colin Hunt, Phyl and Jack Street, Mike Hayes, Lynn Sharpless, Bob Eardley, Neil Spink, M Inskip, Wendy Straker, Mrs J Warr)*

Inntrepreneur ~ Lease: Lyn O'Callaghan ~ Real ale ~ Bar food ~ Restaurant ~ (01962) 732294 ~ Open 11-3, 6-11; 12-3, 7-10.30 Sun

BEAUWORTH SU5624 Map 2
Milbury's ♟

Turn off A272 Winchester/Petersfield at Beauworth ¾, Bishops Waltham 6 signpost, then continue straight on past village

There's quite a cross section of customers in this popular pub who all come to enjoy the good food, well kept ales from local breweries, and friendly, bustling atmosphere. Another point of interest is the 600-year-old well with its massive 250-year-old treadmill – if you drop an ice cube into the spotlit shaft it take eight full seconds to reach the bottom, which apparently means it is 300 feet deep. Sturdy beams and panelling, stripped masonry, interesting old furnishings, and massive open fireplaces (with good winter log fires) offer other reminders of the building's age. Well kept Moondance Triple FFF, Dazed and Confused, Hampshire Brewery Pride of Romsey and King Alfred's, Tetleys, and a beer named for the pub on handpump, Addlestones cider, and country wines. Good bar food from an extensive menu includes home-made soup (£2.65), tasty filled french bread or baked potatoes (£4.20), home-made chilli (£5.25), good steak in ale pie (£6.25), well liked field mushrooms filled with cream cheese and spinach wrapped in puff pastry (£6.45), salads such as chicken, bacon and stilton (£6.65), thai green chicken curry (£7.25), lamb cutlets with a honey and rosemary sauce (£8.25), rib-eye steak (£10.45), daily specials, and children's meals (from £2.50); they serve Sunday brunch from 9.30am. Efficient, friendly service. The restaurant is no smoking. The two black and white cats are called Neville and Nancy, and there's a golden labrador; fruit machine, skittle alley. The name of this pub was at first only a nickname, coming from the Millbarrow, a Bronze Age cemetery surrounding it, briefly famous back in 1833 when a Norman hoard of 6,000 silver coins was found here. The South Downs Way passes the door and the Wayfarers Walk is nearby; the garden has fine views over rolling downland countryside. *(Recommended by Mr and Mrs Thomson, Simon Collett-Jones, Ron Shelton, Phyl and Jack Street, Martin and Karen Wake, TRS, PAS, Steve Power, Sheila and Robert Robinson, Eddie Edwards, Ann and Colin Hunt, Lynn Sharpless, Bob Eardley, Tony and Wendy Hobden, Catherine and Richard Preston, Danny Nicol)*

Free house ~ Licensee Lenny Larden ~ Real ale ~ Bar food ~ Restaurant ~ (01962) 771248 ~ Children in eating area of bar and in skittle room ~ Open 10.30-3.30, 6-11; 12-4, 7-10.30 Sun

---

Please tell us if the decor, atmosphere, food or drink at a pub is different from our description. We rely on readers' reports to keep us up to date. No stamp needed: The Good Pub Guide, FREEPOST TN1569, Wadhurst, E Sussex TN5 7BR.

BENTWORTH SU6740 Map 2
Sun 🍺

Sun Hill; from the A339 coming from Alton the first turning takes you there direct; or in village follow Shalden 2¼, Alton 4¼ signpost

This is a fine pub to visit at any time of the year. In winter, the open fires in the big fireplaces in both little traditional communicating rooms are lit, which makes it all very cosy (and the thoughtful Christmas decorations are pretty), and in summer there are seats out in front and in the back garden, and pleasant nearby walks. It's friendly and unspoilt, with high-backed antique settles, pews and schoolroom chairs, olde-worlde prints and blacksmith's tools on the walls, and bare boards and scrubbed deal tables. Tasty home-made bar food includes sandwiches, home-made soup (£2.25), ploughman's (£3.50), sausage and mash with onion gravy (£4.50), beef curry or stilton and mushroom pasta (£5.50), pies such as steak and kidney or chicken and apricot (£6.50), and puddings £2.50). They have around 8 real ales well kept on handpump such as Brakspears Bitter, Bunces Pigswill, Cheriton Pots Ale, Courage Best, Fullers London Pride, Hampshire Sun, and Ringwood Best and Old Thumper; several malt whiskies. *(Recommended by Lynn Sharpless, Bob Eardley, Howard Allen, Martin and Karen Wake, Jasper Sabey, John and Jean Frazier, David Peakall, Miss V Brown, Nigel Cogger, the Didler, Phyl and Jack Street)*

Free house ~ Licensee Mary Holmes ~ Real ale ~ Bar food ~ (01420) 562338 ~ Children in family room ~ Open 12-3, 6-11; 12-10.30 Sun

BOLDRE SZ3298 Map 2
Red Lion ★ 🍽 🍷

Village signposted from A337 N of Lymington

Although they place a lot of emphasis on the good, popular food here, this is by no means too restauranty, and you can eat anywhere in the pub. The four black-beamed rooms are filled with heavy urns, platters, needlework, rural landscapes, and so forth, taking in farm tools, heavy-horse harness, needlework, gin-traps and even ferocious-looking man traps along the way; the central room has a profusion of chamber-pots, and an end room has pews, wheelback chairs and tapestried stools, and a dainty collection of old bottles and glasses in the window by the counter; two rooms are no smoking. There's a fine old cooking range in the cosy little bar. Good, very popular bar food includes home-made soup (£2.90), sandwiches (£3.10), duck and peppercorn pâté with peach marmalade or smoked haddock fishcakes (£4.80), ploughman's (£5.50), good salads such as salmon and prawns with fresh coriander with a lime and chilli dressing or niçoise, warm goat's cheese on mediterranean vegetables or seafood pasta (all £6.50), calf's liver and bacon (£7.90), breast of chicken with a mustard mushroom sauce (£8.90), steak and kidney pie (£9.50), half a crispy duckling (£10.30), rump steak (£10.50), daily specials like freshly dressed crab or braised venison sausages with devilled sauce (£7.90), spring navarin of lamb (£8.90), half a pheasant in red wine sauce with a plum and pear compote (£9.90), and puddings such as summer pudding, sherry trifle, strawberry cheesecake or whisky bread and butter pudding (from £2.90); get there early to be sure of a seat. Well kept Bass, Hardy Royal Oak, and Websters Green Label on handpump, a range of malt whiskies, and up to 20 wines by the glass; prompt and friendly service. In summer, the flowering tubs and hanging baskets are lovely and there's a cart festooned with colour near the car park. This is a fine area for walking, with 1,000 acres of Raydon Wood Nature Reserve. No children. *(Recommended by John and Joan Calvert, Phyl and Jack Street, Vanessa Hatch, Dave Creech, Dr and Mrs A K Clarke, Howard G Allen, Martin and Karen Wake, Tim and Linda Collins, John and Christine Simpson, Maurice E Southon, Mrs B Williams, Susan and Philip Philcox, Nigel Cogger, Dave Braisted, Patrick Renouf, Ann and Colin Hunt, Roger J Trott, R Inman, J and P Halfyard, Mr and Mrs A R Hawkins, D Marsh, Lynn Sharpless, Bob Eardley, W Osborn-King, R H Rowley)*

Eldridge Pope (Hardy) ~ Lease: John and Penny Bicknell ~ Real ale ~ Bar food ~ Restaurant ~ (01590) 673177 ~ Open 11-11; 12-10.30 Sun; closed 25 Dec and evening 26 Dec

BRAMDEAN SU6127 Map 2

Fox

A272 Winchester—Petersfield

There's a rather relaxed, civilised atmosphere here, especially at lunchtime when the customers tend to be of a more mature age than they are in the evening. The open-plan and carefully modernised bar has black beams, tall stools with proper backrests around the L-shaped counter, and comfortably cushioned wall pews and wheelback chairs; the fox motif shows in a big painting over the fireplace, and on much of the decorative china. At least one area is no smoking. There's quite a firm emphasis on eating: sandwiches (from £2.50), soup (£2.95), pâté (£4.25), brandied mushrooms with bacon served on a crouton (£4.95), lunchtime dishes such as fresh whole trout with almonds (£7.95), fillet of fresh salmon with tarragon sauce (£8.95), and fillet of beef with peppercorn sauce (£9.95), and evening choices like chicken breast with parma ham in a boursin sauce (£11.50), roast rack of lamb with rosemary and garlic (£12.95), and half a roast duck with honey, ginger and grapefruit sauce (£13.95). Well kept Greene King Triumph on handpump. At the back of the building is a walled-in terraced area, and a spacious lawn spreading among the fruit trees, with a good play area – trampoline as well as swings and a seesaw. No children inside. *(Recommended by Phyl and Jack Street, Betty Laker, Mr and Mrs Thomson, Joy and Peter Heatherley, SLC, Mrs Margaret Ross, TRS, E A Froggatt, Michael Inskip)*

Greene King ~ Tenants Ian and Jane Inder ~ Real ale ~ Bar food (not winter Sun evenings) ~ (01962) 771363 ~ Open 11-3, 6(6.30 in winter)-11; 12-3, 7-10.30 Sun

BURITON SU7320 Map 2

Five Bells

Village signposted off A3 S of Petersfield

In a pretty village with a duck pond, this friendly country pub has several interesting rooms and a good bustling atmosphere. The low-beamed lounge on the left is dominated by a big log fire, and has period photographs on the partly stripped brick walls and a rather worn turkey carpet on oak parquet; the public side has some ancient stripped masonry, a woodburning stove, and old-fashioned tables; an end alcove has cushioned pews and board games. A good choice of popular bar food includes lunchtime filled french bread (£2.95), filled baked potatoes (£3.95), and ploughman's (£4.95), as well as cashew nut roast with spicy tomato sauce or asparagus, stilton and pasta bake (£6.45), speciality sausages and mash (£6.95), steak and mushroom in ale pie (£7.95), stuffed chicken breast with smoked stilton and bacon, venison casserole with Guinness, orange and juniper, Torbay sole with garlic and herb butter or golden trout with chive butter (all £8.95), salmon fillet with orange and tarragon (£9.95), and home-made puddings like pear and raspberry crumble, chocolate mousse or carrot cake (from £2.95). Well kept Badger Best, IPA, and Tanglefoot, Ballards Best, and Wadworths 6X on handpump, and decent wines. The three cats are called Trevor, Stan and Stells; darts, cribbage, dominoes, Trivial Pursuits, Scrabble, chess and backgammon. Piped music (in one bar only). There are a few tables on sheltered terraces just outside, with many more on an informal lawn stretching back above the pub. The converted stables are self-catering cottages. They are much involved in the village cricket club. *(Recommended by Dr Alan Green, Mr and Mrs Thomson, R T and J C Moggridge, Wendy Arnold, Lynn Sharpless, Bob Eardley, D Marsh, Brad W Morley, Val and Alan Green, Peter Bate, Phyl and Jack Street, Ann and Colin Hunt)*

Badger ~ Manager Bridget Slocombe ~ Real ale ~ Bar food (12-2(2.30 wknds), 6.30-10) ~ Restaurant (Fri/Sat evenings and Sun lunch) ~ (01730) 263584 ~ Children in eating area of bar (till 9pm) and in restaurant ~ Jazz last Mon of month, blues/rock Weds ~ Open 11-2.30(3 Sat), 5.30-11; 12-3, 7-10.30 Sun

---

The letters and figures after the name of each town are its Ordnance Survey map reference. 'Using the *Guide*' at the beginning of the book explains how it helps you find a pub, in road atlases or large-scale maps as well as in our own maps.

BURSLEDON SU4809 Map 2
Jolly Sailor ♀

2 miles from M27 junction 8; then A27 towards Sarisbury, then just before going under railway bridge turn right towards Bursledon Station; it's best to park round here and walk as the lane up from the station is now closed to cars

At weekends, this well liked pub is especially busy and the friendly staff can tell you about some of the fine yachts moored in the harbour. You can sit out at the tables under the big yew tree or on the wooden jetty or enjoy the same waterside view from the window seat inside. The airy front bar has ship pictures, nets and shells, as well as windsor chairs and settles on the floorboards. The atmospheric beamed and flagstoned back bar, with pews and settles by its huge fireplace, is a fair bit older. Bar food includes sandwiches, pasta with sun-dried tomato, pesto and mushrooms (£7.50), chargrilled cajun salad (£8.50), and bouillabaisse (£11.25). The dining area is no smoking. Well kept Badger Best, IPA, and Tanglefoot, Gales HSB, and Oving Bitter on handpump, and country wines; Jenga, Connect Four, and piped music. The path down to the pub (and of course back up again) from the lane is steep. *(Recommended by Roger and Pauline Pearce, Nigel and Amanda Thorp, Carolyn and Trevor Golds, Nigel Wilkinson, Bruce Bird, Jess and George Cowley, Ian Phillips, the Didler, John and Christine Simpson, Dave Braisted, Ann and Colin Hunt, Mrs A Chesher, JP, PP)*

Badger ~ Manager Adrian Jenkins ~ Real ale ~ Bar food (12-9.30) ~ (023) 8040 5557 ~ Children in no-smoking room ~ Open 11-11; 12-10.30 Sun

CADNAM SU2913 Map 2
White Hart ⑩

½ mile from M27 junction 1; A336 towards village, pub off village roundabout
Hampshire Dining Pub of the Year
On the edge of the New Forest and just off the M27, this comfortable pub is particularly popular for its good, imaginative food. Served by friendly, helpful staff, there might be soup (£3.25), open sandwiches (from £4.75), ploughman's (from £5.25), freshly battered cod or toulouse sausage with onion gravy (£7.25), a daily pasta dish (£8.25), steaks (from £9.95), fresh fish from Prawle like bass, whole lemon sole, scallops, monkfish or trout (from around £10.75), duck breast with orange and cranberry (£11.25), puddings like home-made apple or rhubarb crumble, banoffee pie or banana pancakes (£3.95), and Sunday roast such as beef with yorkshire pudding or half shoulder of lamb with mint gravy (£8.95). The spacious multi-level dining lounge has good solid furnishings, soft lighting, country prints and appropriate New Forest pictures and mementoes; well kept Flowers Original, Morlands Old Speckled Hen, Wadworths 6X, and Youngs Bitter on handpump, and decent wines; skittle alley, piped music. There are seats in the garden where there is a fish pond; horses in the next door paddock. *(Recommended by David Shillitoe, Mrs Pam Mattinson, Ian Phillips, M J Brooks, Ian and Jacqui Ross, Philip Vernon, Kim Maidment, Patrick Renouf, Martin & Karen Wake, Derek and Margaret Underwood, Eric and Charlotte Osgood, Lynn Sharpless, Bob Eardley, Paul White, Dennis Stevens, Brian Mills, J G Roberts, David Gregory, Phyl and Jack Street, D B Jenkin, John and Joan Nash, Steve Power, Dr C C S Wilson)*

Whitbreads ~ Lease: Peter and Shirley Palmer ~ Real ale ~ Bar food ~ (023) 8081 2277 ~ Children in eating area of bar ~ Open 11-3, 5.30-11; 12-3, 6-10.30 Sun

CHERITON SU5828 Map 2
Flower Pots ★ ◗

Pub just off B3046 (main village road) towards Beauworth and Winchester; OS Sheet 185 map reference 581282

For many people, this unspoilt bustling country pub is one of their favourites. The charming licensees continue to create a delightfully friendly atmosphere, and whatever time of year it is, there are always plenty of customers – particularly on Sunday lunchtime, when it's best to get there early for a seat. There are two little rooms and the one on the left feels almost like someone's front room, with pictures of hounds and ploughmen on its striped wallpaper, bunches of flowers, and a horse and foal and other ornaments on the mantlepiece over a small log fire; it can get smoky in here. Behind the servery there's disused copper filtering equipment, and lots of hanging gin-traps, drag-hooks, scaleyards and other ironwork. Good value straightforward bar food includes sandwiches (from £1.70, toasties from £1.90 or big baps from £2.40), ploughman's (from £3.30), and chilli con carne, lamb and apricot casserole or beef stew (from £4.40); the menu may be restricted at weekend lunchtimes, and on Wednesday evenings it is devoted to authentic Indian dishes. Their own-brewed beers from the Cheriton Brewhouse are very good indeed: Diggers Gold, Pots Ale and Cheriton Best Bitter. Darts in the neat extended plain public bar (where there's a covered well), also cribbage, shove-ha'penny and dominoes. On the pretty front and back lawns are some old-fashioned seats – very useful in fine weather as it can quickly fill up inside; they sometimes have Morris dancers out here in summer. Near the site of one of the final battles of the Civil War, the pub once belonged to the retired head gardener of nearby Avington Park, which explains the unusual name. *(Recommended by Susan and John Douglas, Richard and Valerie Wright, Mrs G Connell, Lynn Sharpless, Bob Eardley, JP, PP, Ann and Colin Hunt, Nigel Cogger, Ron Shelton, Martin and Penny Fletcher, the Didler, John and Christine Simpson, Eddie Edwards, Mr and Mrs Peter Smith, A R and B E Sayer, Michael Hasslacher, Howard Allen, Michael and Hazel Duncombe, Martin and Karen Wake, Wendy Straker, John Knighton, Francis Johnston, Mr and Mrs Thomson, M Unwin)*

Free house ~ Licensees Jo and Patricia Bartlett ~ Real ale ~ Bar food (not Sun evening or bank hol Mon evenings) ~ (01962) 771318 ~ Children in small sitting room off lounge bar ~ Open 12-2.30, 6-11; 12-3, 7-10.30 Sun ~ Bedrooms: £30B/£50B

DROXFORD SU6018 Map 2
White Horse 🍺 🛏

4 miles along A32 from Wickham

There's something for everyone in this rambling 16th-c inn – good reasonably priced food, well kept beers, decent bedrooms, and a relaxed and friendly atmosphere. The lounge bar is made up of several small cosy rooms – low beams, bow windows, alcoves, and log fires, while the public bar is larger and more straightforward: pool, table football, trivia, and CD juke box. Dishes on the menu might include lunchtime sandwiches (from £1.30), home-made soup (£2), ploughman's (from £3.50), locally smoked salmon pâté (£3.80), barbecued king ribs (£4), portuguese sardines in garlic butter (£5.50), mushroom stroganoff (£5.75), spicy cumberland sausage (£6.50), and steaks (from £8.50), with daily specials such as moules marinières (£4.50), mixed meat curry (£5.50), roast rib of beef, roast rabbit legs or roast leg of lamb (all £6.50), rich fish pie (£6.95), smoked fish platter, baked ham with cumberland sauce or half a braised guinea fowl (£7.50), steak, mushroom, and Guinness pie or stealmon steak on poached fennel with a pernod and cream sauce (£7.95), and grilled bass (£8.50); children's dishes (from £2.10). The restaurant is no smoking. Well kept Morlands IPA and Old Speckled Hen plus Flowers Original, Greene King Abbot, and Ruddles Best on handpump; several malt whiskies. One of the cubicles in the gents' overlooks an illuminated well. There are tables in a secluded flower-filled courtyard comfortably sheltered by the building's back wings. *(Recommended by W Burke, Brad W Morley, Brian Abbott, R Michael Richards, Ann and Colin Hunt, Mr and Mrs Thomson, A R and B E Sayer, Lynn Sharpless, Bob Eardley, Wendy Straker)*

Morlands ~ Tenant Paul Young ~ Real ale ~ Bar food (all day Sun; not 25 or 26 Dec) ~ Restaurant ~ (01489) 877490 ~ Children in eating area of bar and in family room ~ Open 11-11; 12-10.30 Sun ~ Bedrooms: £25(£40B)/£35(£50B)

DUMMER SU5846 Map 2
Queen

½ mile from M3 junction 7; take Dummer slip road

This tiled white cottage has an open-plan bar with a pleasantly alcovey feel, plenty of timbered brick and plaster partition walls, as well as beams and joists, and an open fire. There are built-in padded seats, cushioned spindleback chairs and stools around the tables on the dark blue patterned carpet, and pictures of queens, old photographs, small steeplechase prints and advertisements. Bar food includes sandwiches (from £3.50 with crisps and salad), filled baked potatoes (from £4.50), several types of burgers (from £6.50), cod in their own beer batter (£6.95 medium, £8.95 large), bangers and mash or lasagne (£6.95), steak and kidney pudding (£10.95), and steaks (from £10.95); the restaurant is no smoking. Well kept Courage Best, Fullers London Pride, and sometimes Morlands Old Speckled Hen on handpump; fruit machine in one corner, cribbage and piped music; picnic-sets under cocktail parasols on the terrace and in the extended back garden. *(Recommended by G C Wilkinson, Patrick Renouf, Martin and Karen Wake, P Weedon, KC, M C Girling, Phyl and Jack Street, Pete and Sue Robbins, Graham and June Ward, Ian Phillips, Howard Allen, Ann and Colin Hunt, Tony Gayfer)*

Scottish Courage ~ Managers John and Beverly Simm ~ Real ale ~ Bar food ~ Restaurant ~ (01256) 397367 ~ Children in eating area of bar until 9pm ~ Open 11-3, 5.30(6 Sat)-11; 12-3, 7-10.30 Sun

EAST TYTHERLEY SU2927 Map 2
Star

Off B3084 N of Romsey, via Lockerley – turn off by railway crossing nr Mottisfont Abbey

The atmosphere is so relaxed here that you almost feel as though you are dining in someone's house. The bar is pleasantly informal with an unassuming mix of comfortably homely furnishings, log fires in attractive fireplaces, a no-smoking lower lounge bar, and a cosy and pretty no-smoking restaurant; despite the very relaxed feel of the place, staff are smart and efficient – an excellent balance. Decent home-made food (with prices unchanged since last year) includes soup (£1.95), sandwiches (from £3.25), ploughman's (£4.25), steak and kidney pie, lasagne or chilli con carne (£5.95), daily specials such as game pie or mushrooms in stilton (£5.95), roast pheasant in red wine (£8.95), vegetarian dishes, and puddings such as apple and blackberry crumble, treacle sponge or spotted dick and custard (£2.95). Well kept Gales HSB and Ringwood Best on handpump, and country wines; shove-ha'penny and piped music. The garden has a play area, and there are picnic-sets on the forecourt; full size chess and draughts; skittle alley. *(Recommended by Dr and Mrs A K Clarke, D Marsh, A E Furley, Howard Allen, John and Joan Calvert, Ann and Colin Hunt, Ron and June Buckler, Phyl and Jack Street)*

Free house ~ Licensee Carol Mitchell ~ Real ale ~ Bar food ~ Restaurant ~ (01794) 340225 ~ Children welcome ~ Open 9-2.30, 6-11; 12-3, 7-10.30 Sun ~ Bedrooms: £40B/£60B

FRITHAM SU2314 Map 2
Royal Oak

Village signed from exit roundabout, M27 junction 1; quickest via B3078, then left and straight through village; head for Eyeworth Pond

At the end of a long no-through road deep in the New Forest sits this charming brick-built thatched pub. The friendly and welcoming young owners are working very hard to carefully restore the three bar rooms and are creating a civilised and relaxed atmosphere: antique wheelback, spindleback, and other old chairs and stools with colourful seats around solid tables on the new oak flooring, prints and pictures involving local characters on the white walls, restored panelling and black beams, and a roaring log fire. Simple lunchtime food consists of freshly made soup (£2.25) and ploughman's (£3.25), and they will do winter evening meals for parties by arrangement. Well kept Ringwood Best, Fortyniner and True Glory tapped from the cask; dominoes and cribbage – no noisy games or piped music; the back bar has quite a few books. There are new bench seats out in the well kept big garden, lovely views, and regular summer weekend barbecues (they have a marquee for bad weather); ponies on the green nearby and lovely surrounding walks. Dogs welcome. *(Recommended by Pete and Sue Robbins, Ann and Colin Hunt, Kevin Thorpe, Eddie Edwards, Pete Baker, JP, PP)*

Free house ~ Licensees Neil and Pauline McCulloch ~ Real ale ~ Bar food (lunchtime only) ~ (023) 8081 2606 ~ Children welcome ~ Open 11-3, 6-11; 11-11 Sat; 12-10.30 Sun

FROYLE SU7542 Map 2
Hen & Chicken
A31 Alton—Farnham

New licensees were taking over this old coaching inn as we went to press, and as far as we know, were planning no major changes. The three interconnecting rooms have beams hung with hops, candles on the tables, and a log fire in the inglenook fireplace; fruit machine, TV, and piped music. Bar food now includes sandwiches (from £3.50; toasties like chargrilled peppers on pesto or mushrooms in brandy cream sauce £4.95; filled french bread from £4.25), soup (£3.75), crêpes filled with garlic mushrooms and camembert cheese with a warm plum sauce (£5.25), ploughman's (£5.50), home-made burgers (from £5.50), omelettes (from £5.95), home-made beef and Guinness sausages or pasta with roasted red pepper, coriander and cream (£8.25), chargrilled liver and pancetta with a rich red wine and onion jus (£9.25), confit of duck with blackcurrants and pulses (£10.25), whole black bream poached with thai sauces and spices (£10.95), and steaks (from £11.95). Well kept Badger Best, Courage Best, Hop Back Summer Lightning, Hook Norton Old Hookey, and Timothy Taylor Landlord on handpump kept under light blanket pressure, and an enjoyable wine list. The big garden has picnic-sets and benches, and children's play equipment. (*Recommended by Lynn Sharpless, Bob Eardley, Ann and Colin Hunt, Chris and Ann Garnett, Guy Consterdine*)

Free house ~ Licensee Peter Atkinson ~ Real ale ~ Bar food (till 10pm) ~ Restaurant ~ (01420) 22115 ~ Children in eating area of bar and restaurant ~ Open 11-11; 12-10.30 Sun

HAWKLEY SU7429 Map 2
Hawkley Inn 🍺
Pococks Lane; village signposted off B3006, first turning left after leaving its junction with A325 in Greatham; OS Sheet 186 map reference 746292

Customers of all ages mix happily in this unpretentious country local, and there's a warm welcome and good chatty atmosphere, too. The opened-up bar and back dining room have simple décor – big pine tables, a moose head, dried flowers, and prints on the mellowing walls; parts of the bar can get a bit smoky when it's busy, but there is a no-smoking area to the left of the bar. A good choice of half a dozen well kept real ales changes all the time, but might inlcude Ash Vine Frying Tonight, Ballards Best Bitter, Brewery on Sea Spinnaker Bitter, Moondance Triple FFF, Hogs Back TEA, and RCH East Street Cream on handpump, and their own cider. Good, promptly served bar food includes various types of ploughman's (from £5.85), baked potato with garlic mushrooms and stilton (£7.85), scallops in a tarragon sauce, Tunisian fish tart, ham and leek pancakes or tarte provençale (all £8.45), beef stew (£9.25), and puddings like super bread and butter pudding and very good treacle tart (£3.50). Helpings are generous, and service is friendly. There are tables and a climbing frame in the pleasant garden behind, and the pub is on the Hangers Way Path. (*Recommended by Lynn Sharpless, Bob Eardley, Ann and Colin Hunt, Martin and Karen Wake, Diana Brumfit, Glen Armstrong, the Didler*)

Free house ~ Licensees E N Collins and A Stringer ~ Real ale ~ Bar food (not Sun evening) ~ (01730) 84205 ~ Children in eating area of bar until 8pm ~ Occasional blues ~ Open 12-2.30(3 Sat), 6-11; 12-3, 7-10.30 Sun

---

People don't usually tip bar staff (different in a really smart hotel, say). If you want to thank bar staff – for dealing with a really large party say, or special friendliness – offer them a drink. Common expressions are: 'And what's yours?' or 'And won't you have something for yourself?'

IBSLEY SU1509 Map 2
Old Beams

A338 Salisbury—Ringwood

At lunchtime particularly, this large black and white thatched pub fills up quickly with customers keen to enjoy the wide choice of food. The big main room is divided by wooden panelling and a canopied log-effect gas fire, and there are lots of varnished wooden tables and country-kitchen chairs under the appropriately aged oak beams; the small formal partly no-smoking restaurant has its own bar, and the buffet area and conservatory are no smoking. Under the new licensees, bar food might include home-made soup (£2), lunchtime sandwiches or baked potatoes (from £2.80), ploughman's (£4.50), vegetarian dishes (from £4.50), home-made steak and kidney pie or a roast of the day (£7.20), a popular cold buffet (from £7.50), steaks (from £10), and puddings. Well kept Ringwood Best and Old Thumper and guests such as Morlands Old Speckled Hen or Wadworths 6X on handpump, country wines, and a decent wine list. Fruit machine and piped music. *(Recommended by W W Burke, W Osborn-King, Mr and Mrs A R Hawkins, Phyl and Jack Street, Peter Meister, Jill Bickerton, N Cobb, Paul and Sue Merrick, Dr D Twyman, G C Wilkinson, JP, PP, Mr and Mrs B Hobden)*

Old English Inns ~ Manager Eddie Webber ~ Real ale ~ Bar food (12-9.30; 12-2, 6-9.30 in winter) ~ Restaurant ~ (01425) 473387 ~ Children in eating area of bar and restaurant ~ Open 11-11; 12-10.30 Sun; 11-3, 6-11 weekdays in winter

LANGSTONE SU7105 Map 2
Royal Oak

High Street (marked as cul-de-sac – actually stops short of the pub itself); village is last turn left off A3023 (confusingly called A324 on some signs) before Hayling Island bridge

On a summer evening when the tide is high, the seats on the terrace here are an ideal place to enjoy a drink; be careful you don't get marooned by the tide. Inside, the spacious and atmospheric flagstoned bar has windows from which you can see the ancient wadeway to Hayling Island, and simple furnishings like windsor chairs around old wooden tables on the wooden parquet and ancient flagstones, and two winter open fires. Bar food includes sandwiches, duck and port pâté (£3.95), ploughman's (£4.95), moules marinières (£5.95), various fish dishes (from £6), gammon (£6.95), and rump steak (£8.65); the dining area is no smoking. Well kept Boddingtons, Flowers Original, Gales HSB, Morlands Old Speckled Hen, and Wadworths 6X on handpump, decent wine, Bulmer's cider, and country wines; no noisy piped music or games machines. Morris dancers in summer; good coastal paths nearby. *(Recommended by J and P Halfyard, Val and Alan Green, Dennis Stevens, Ian Phillips, Lynn Sharpless, Bob Eardley, Ann and Colin Hunt)*

Whitbreads ~ Manager Chris Ford ~ Real ale ~ Bar food (12-2.30, 6-9 but snacks served all day) ~ Restaurant ~ (023) 9248 3125 ~ Children in eating area of bar ~ Open 11-11; 12-10.30 Sun

LONGPARISH SU4344 Map 2
Plough

B3048 off A303 just E of Andover

They regularly win awards for the lovely hanging baskets and flower tubs on the terrace and in the garden of this pretty creeper-covered village inn; plenty of seats here as well as guinea pigs, rabbits, and ducks for children. Inside, the dining lounge spreads through a series of low wide arches which gives a feeling of snugness: wheelbacks and built-in wall seats on the patterned carpet, fringed lamps, and a few farm tools, copper implements, and prints; there is a small pubby part with hops around the cream-painted walls, but the feel of the place is quite restaurChuanty. A large choice of quickly served bar food might include good home-made soup (£2.75), sandwiches (from £3.50 with chips; the crab is good), ploughman's (£3.95), good chilli (£5.50), gammon and pineapple or cod, chips and mushy peas (£5.95), steaks (from £7.25), vegetarian dishes like cream and mushroom pasta or vegetable bake (£7.50), daily specials like liver and bacon (£5.50) or cod provençale (£6.25), puddings such as home-made pineapple cheesecake or strawberry pavlova (£2.75), and children's menu (£3.25); the restaurant is partly no smoking; friendly service. Well kept Boddingtons, Flowers Original, Wadworths 6X and a guest such as Hampshire King Alfreds on handpump, and country wines; piped music. The two persian blue cats are called Chalis and Chardonnay, and the yellow labrador, Honey. *(Recommended by Lynn Sharpless, Bob Eardley, Val and Alan Green, Martin and Karen Wake, Graham and Lynn Mason, Phyl and Jack Street, John Branston, John and Vivienne Rice, Mike Gorton)*

Whitbreads ~ Lease Christopher and Pauline Dale ~ Real ale ~ Bar food ~ Restaurant ~ (01264) 720358 ~ Children in eating area of bar and restaurant ~ Occasional live entertainment ~ Open 11-3, 6-11; 12-3, 7-10.30 Sun ~ Bedrooms: £20/£40

LONGSTOCK SU3537 Map 2
Peat Spade

Village signposted off A30 on W edge of Stockbridge, and off A3057 Stockbridge—Andover

The River Test is only about 100 yards away from this popular dining pub, there are bacing downland walks up around the Danebury hillfort, and the attractive village is on the 44-mile Test Way long-distance path. As well as free range chickens, there are seats in the not large but pleasant garden, and three cats and Mollie the diabetic dog (who is not allowed to be fed). Inside, the roomy and attractive squarish main bar is airy and high-ceilinged, with pretty windows, well chosen furnishings and a nice show of toby-jugs and beer mats around its fireplace. A rather elegant smaller dining room leads off; one area is no smoking. Good, interesting food might include sandwiches, curried vegetable soup (£3.50), walnut and mushroom terrine with sun-dried tomato chutney (£4.25), smoked breast of duck with apple chutney (£4.50), home-made pork and bacon faggots (£6.25), local pork, chive and leek bangers and mash or madras chickpea, onion and sweet pepper curry (£6.50), bourride of salmon, halibut and mussels (£8.75), casserole of venison with garlic potato cake (£8.95), medallions of pork fillet with a meux mustard dressing (£9.95), Scottish sirloin steak (£10.95), Dorset scallops with lobster bisque (£11.25), and puddings like fresh orange and Cointreau tart, bread and butter pudding or chocolate and armagnac mousse (£3.75). Well kept Hampshire King Alfred, Ringwood Fortyniner, and a guest beer on handpump, and a decent wine list with 7 by the glass. *(Recommended by Val and Alan Green, Ron Shelton, Mrs Margaret Ross, Mrs J Taylar, Phyl and Jack Street)*

Free house ~ Licensees Bernie Startup and Sarah Hinman ~ Real ale ~ (01264) 810612 ~ Children welcome ~ Open 11.30-3, 6-10.30(11 Sat); 12-3 Sun; closed Sun evening, all Mon, 25 Dec, 1 Jan ~ Bedrooms: /£58.75B

LOWER WIELD SU6339 Map 2
Yew Tree 🍽

Off A339 NW of Alton, via Medstead or Bentworth; or off B3046 S of Basingstoke, signed from Preston Candover

Once you've tracked it down along the network of narrow lanes, this country pub opposite a village cricket pitch rewards with really good food. Recently taken over by its chef, it is decidedly a dining pub – they even meet you at the door expecting you'll be eating. There is a small cosy flagstoned bar, recently remodelled, with sofas and an open fire, and you can just have a drink here, but you won't find any locals propping up the bar – nor indeed even any real ale. Really, this serves as a waiting area for the comfortable carpeted restaurant: attractive, with fresh flowers, a central open fire, a dresser with blue and white china, rough-cast white walls, some stripped brickwork. The atmosphere is civilised and relaxed, not entirely formal. The food, beautifully presented on big plates, might include lunchtime sandwiches (from £2.75), filled baked potatoes (from £4.25), and ploughman's (from £4.95), dishes to be served in the bar, garden and terrace only such as oriental king prawns wrapped in filo pastry with a garlic mayonnaise dip (£4.75), warm tartlet of sweet peppers topped with goat's cheese and pesto (£5.75), crispy duck and plum sauce (£5.95), ratatouille and garlic bread (£6.50), venison and red wine sausages with onion gravy (£6.95), roast salmon salad (£7.50), and braised lamb shank with olive and chive mash (£7.95), and puddings like warm chocolate mousse with a Tia Maria ice cream, summer pudding with clotted cream or crème caramel with a rum and raisin sauce (£3.95). Service is friendly and helpful, and they keep decent wines. There are tables out on the front terrace and in the garden, and there are good walks nearby, particularly around Rushmoor Pond. *(Recommended by Phyl and Jack Street, Martin and Karen Wake, Miss U Brown, Mrs B Nickson)*

Free house ~ Licensee Chrisopher Richard ~ Bar food ~ Restaurant ~ (01256) 389224 ~ Children in restaurant ~ Open 11-3, 6.30-11; 11-11 Sat; 12-4 Sun; closed Sun evening, all Mon exc bank holidays

MATTINGLEY SU7357 Map 2
Leather Bottle

3 miles from M3, junction 5; in Hook, turn right-and-left on to B3349 Reading Road (former A32)

In early summer, the wisteria covering this brick and tiled pub is very pretty – as are the flowering baskets and tubs; seats in the tree-sheltered garden. Inside, there's a relaxed feel in the simple beamed main bar, with brocaded built-in wall seats, some sabres on the cream walls, and a ticking metal clock over one of the inglenook fireplaces (both have good winter log fires). At the back is the characterful cottagey second bar with lots of black beams, an antique clock, country pictures on the walls (some stripped to brick), lantern lighting, and sturdy inlaid tables with seats; newspapers to read. They hope to extend the restaurant area and add two covered terraces. Good popular bar food includes sandwiches (from £2.25; not Sunday lunchtime), home-made soup (£2.75), ploughman's (£4.50), sausage grill (£5.95), quite a few fresh fish dishes (from £6.50), steak and kidney pie (£7.50), chicken dijon (£8.75), steaks (from £10.95), and puddings like lemon brûlée or raspberry ruin (from £3.75). Well kept Courage Best (tapped from the cask) and Directors, and a guest such as Greene King Abbot on handpump; fruit machine and piped music. The flowering baskets and tubs are pretty in summer, and there are seats in the tree-sheltered garden. *(Recommended by Roger and Pauline Pearce, G D Sharpe, Ian Phillips, Mrs A Chesher, TBB, Peter Burton, KC, Comus Elliott, Susan and John Douglas)*

Scottish Courage ~ Managers David Meredith and Jane Evans ~ Real ale ~ Bar food (not Sun evening) ~ (01189) 326371 ~ Children in eating area of bar ~ Open 11-2.30, 6-11; 12-3, 6-10.30 Sun

MICHELDEVER SU5138 Map 2
Dever Arms

Village signposted off A33 N of Winchester

This is a friendly and pleasant country local with a good bustling atmosphere and helpful licensees. The simply decorated and beamed bar has heavy tables and good solid seats – a nice cushioned panelled oak settle and a couple of long dark pews as well as wheelback chairs – and a woodburning stove at each end; a no-smoking area with lighter-coloured furniture opens off. Quickly served tasty bar food includes sandwiches, mussels with cream and garlic (£4.95), steak in ale pie (£6.95), chicken boursin (£7.95), game casserole (£8.50), merlin steak with caper sauce or duck with blackberries (£9.50), and enjoyable (and very popular) Sunday lunch. Well kept Greene King Abbot, IPA, and Mild, and Marstons Pedigree on handpump, and country wines; darts, pool, dominoes, fruit machine, and piped music. The landlord plays the saxophone, and they have an alsatian called Brew, and four cats. There are seats on a small sheltered back terrace, and some more widely spaced picnic-sets and a play area on the edge of a big cricket green behind; also, rabbits and chickens and a pony. This is a good starting point for exploring the Dever Valley (there are lots of good walks nearby). *(Recommended by Ann and Colin Hunt, Adrian and Sandra Pearson,*

W W Burke, Jim and Janet, Stephen and Jean Curtis, J L Hall, Dr and Mrs A Marriott, Shirley Mackenzie, Phyl and Jack Street, R W Allan, Mike Gorton, Richard Fendick, Mrs Y M Lippett, Martin and Caroline Schimmer, P R and S A White, Charles Gysin, Pete and Sue Robbins, Jess and George Cowley)

Greene King ~ Tenants Ray Douglas and Belinda Boughtwood ~ Real ale ~ Bar food ~ Restaurant ~ (01962) 774339 ~ Children in eating area of bar and restaurant ~ Occasional live entertainment ~ Open 12-3, 6-11; 12-3, 7-10.30 Sun

NORTH GORLEY SU1611 Map 2
Royal Oak

Ringwood Rd; village signposted off A338 S of Fordingbridge

Across the road from this welcoming 17th-c thatched pub is a big pond with ducks and there are usually ponies roaming around. Inside on the left is a quiet, comfortable and neatly refurbished no-smoking lounge, though our own preference is for the busier main bar on the right: carpeted too, with pews, mate's chairs, a corner woodburning stove, old engravings and other pictures, with steps down to an attractive L-shaped eating area. This has a mix of dark pine tables and pleasant old-fashioned chairs, with big rugs on bare boards, and a further no-smoking part with pine booth seating. There are french windows to a neatly kept sheltered back garden, with a play area. Good, reasonably priced home-made food includes delicious soups such as chicken and bacon with croutons or vegetable and tomato (£2.50), doorstep toasties (£3.50), home-made spinach and mushroom bake, broccoli and stilton bake or curries (all £5.75), steak, kidney and ale pie (£5.95), puddings like treacle tart or apple pie (£2.75), and children's meals (£2.50). Well kept Fullers London Pride, Gales HSB, Ringwood Best, and Wadworths 6X on handpump, decent wines, quite a few malt whiskies, friendly and efficient young staff; sensibly placed darts, CD juke box, fruit machine, and skittle alley. *(Recommended by Mr and Mrs B W Twiddy, Diana Brumfit)*

Whitbreads ~ Lease Ron Newsham ~ Real ale ~ Bar food ~ (01425) 652244 ~ Children in family area ~ Open 11-2.30, 6-11; 12-10.30 Sun

OWSLEBURY SU5123 Map 2
Ship

Whites Hill; village signposted off B2177 between Fishers Pond and Lower Upham; can also be reached from M3 junction 10 via Morestead, or from A272 2½ miles SE of A31 junction

They've managed to retain the atmosphere of a village local here even though there's quite an emphasis on the very good food. The old bars on the right of the front entrance and the converted family room have a friendly bustling atmosphere, varnished black oak 17th-c ship's timbers as beams and wall props, sporting and naval mementoes, built-in cushioned wall seats and wheelback chairs around wooden tables, and a big central fireplace; on the left is a comfortable dining area. Good food includes sandwiches, home-made soup (£2.50), deep-fried goat's cheese with fruit coulis (£3.75), chicken satay (£4.50), prawn and crab cakes with hot chilli dip (£4.95), steak, orange and Guinness pie (£5.95), seared liver with shallot gravy (£6.95), wild mushroom and sweet pepper stroganoff or lamb curry (£7.95), chicken with lemon and tarragon, home-made Florida prawn and crab cakes or pork with apple and calvados (all £8.95), and lemon sole with champagne and prawns (£9.95). Well kept Greene King IPA, Abbot and Mild, and a guest beer on handpump; cribbage and piped music. As there are lots of good surrounding walks, the pub is naturally popular with walkers, especially at weekends. Both garden areas have fine views – one side looks right across the Solent to the Isle of Wight, the other gives a view down to Winchester, and there's now a pond area, as well as an aviary, sheep, a summer marquee, a children's play area, and a weekend bouncy castle. *(Recommended by Phyl and Jack Street, Lynn Sharpless, Bob Eardley, Jenny and Brian Seller, M Inskip, Stephen Harvey, D B Jenkin, P R and S A White, Danny Nicol, John and Christine Simpson, Ann and Colin Hunt, John and Joan Nash)*

Greene King ~ Lease: Clive Mansell and Alison Carter ~ Real ale ~ Bar food ~

(01962) 777358 ~ Children welcome ~ Open 11-3, 6-11; 11-11(11-3, 6-11 winter) Sat; 12-10.30 Sun

PETERSFIELD SU7129 Map 2
White Horse ★ ◀

Priors Dean – but don't follow Priors Dean signposts: simplest route is from Petersfield, leaving centre on A272 towards Winchester, take right turn at roundabout after level crossing, towards Steep, and keep on for four miles or so, up on to the downs, passing another pub on your right (and not turning off into Steep there); at last, at crossroads signposted East Tisted/Privett, turn right towards East Tisted, then almost at once turn right on to second gravel track (the first just goes into a field); there's no inn sign; alternatively, from A32 5 miles S of Alton, take road by bus lay-by signposted Steep, then, after 1¼ miles, turn off as above – though obviously left this time – at East Tisted/Privett crossroads; OS Sheet 197 coming from Petersfield (Sheet 186 is better the other way), map reference 715290; the Pub With No Name (as most of its regulars know it – there's no inn sign)

Several readers who had not visited this fine old farmhouse for some years were all delighted to find very little had changed, and thought the no-smoking dining room was a sympathetic addition; big open fire and nicely old-fashioned toys for children. The two charming and idiosyncratic parlour rooms (candlelit at night) have open fires, various old pictures, farm tools, drop-leaf tables, oak settles, rugs, stuffed antelope heads, a longcase clock, and a couple of fireside rocking-chairs, and so forth. A fine range of beers on handpump includes the very strong No Name Bitter, as well as Bass, Ballards Best, Bass, Fullers London Pride, Gales Best and HSB, Ringwood Fortyniner, and a couple of guests. Dominoes, cribbage, backgammon and Jenga. Under the new licensee, bar food includes home-made soup (£2.95), filled baked potatoes (from £3.25), sandwiches (from £3.50), vegetarian dishes (from £4.50), ploughman's or steak and kidney pie (£5.95), chicken with cream and thai spices (£6.50), liver and bacon (£6.95), steaks (from £8.95), and puddings like home-made bread and butter pudding (£3.50). Rustic seats (which include chunks of tree-trunk) and a terrace outside; as this is one of the highest spots in the county it can be quite breezy; boules. If trying to find it for the first time, keep your eyes skinned – not for nothing is this known as the Pub With No Name – though there are now boards as you approach. Dogs are welcome. *(Recommended by Ann and Colin Hunt, Lynn Sharpless, Bob Eardley, MCG, JP, PP, the Didler, Martin and Karen Wake, Elizabeth and Alan Walker, Dan Wilson, Dennis Stevens, David Cullen, Emma Stent)*

Gales ~ Manager Janet Egerton-Williams ~ Real ale ~ Bar food ~ Restaurant ~ (01420) 588387 ~ Children in restaurant ~ Open 11-2.30, 6-11; 11-11 Sat; 12-10.30 Sun; 11-3, 6-11 winter Sat; 12-3, 7-10.30 winter Sun

PILLEY SZ3298 Map 2
Fleur de Lys ⊮ ◀

Village signposted off A337 Brockenhurst—Lymington

There is some provision for drinkers, but most people do come here to eat and tables tend to be reserved in advance. The characterful lounge bar has heavy low beams, lots of bric-a-brac and a huge inglenook log fire. In the entrance-way is a list of landlords that goes back to 1498; a large part of the pub is no smoking. From a comprehensive menu, good bar food includes soup (£3.25), filled baked potatoes (from £3.65), mixed mushrooms in garlic and cream (£3.99), ploughman's (from £5.25), vegetable pasta (£6.25), steamed rabbit pudding (£7.99), fish duo (cod and salmon, £8.25), half shoulder of lamb (£9.99), and puddings such as home-made brûlée or fruit crumbles (from £3.75); in winter they cook over the log fire. A new thatched dining extension is to be added. Four well kept ales tapped from the cask such as Flowers Original, Gales HSB, Morlands Old Speckled Hen, and Ringwood Best, good wines, and farm ciders; courteous service. There are seats in the newly planted garden, a children's play area, and fine forest and heathland walks nearby. This is the oldest pub in the New Forest and was established as an inn in 1096. *(Recommended by Martin and Karen Wake, J and P Halfyard, Dr C C S Wilson, Sam Samuells,*

354 *Hampshire*

Lynda Payton, Ann and Colin Hunt, Neil Ben, Lynn Sharpless, Bob Eardley, Nigel Flook, Betsy Brown, D Marsh, Keith and Margaret Kettell, W Osborn-King, Nigel Cogger, David Gregory, Patrick Renouf, Gwen and Peter Andrews)

Free house ~ Licensee Craig Smallwood ~ Real ale ~ Bar food ~ (01590) 672158 ~ Children in eating area of bar and restaurant ~ Occasional live entertainment ~ Open 11.30-3, 6-11(10.30 winter weekdays); 12-3, 7-10.30 Sun; closed 25 Dec, 1 Jan ~ Bedrooms: /£50B

PORTSMOUTH SU6501 Map 2
Still & West

Bath Square; follow A3 and Isle of Wight Ferry signs to Old Portsmouth water's edge

You have to get here early for a seat on the terrace or in the upstairs restaurant to make the most of the marvellous position; there are wonderful views as far as the Isle of Wight, and the boats and ships fighting the strong tides in the very narrow mouth of Portsmouth harbour seem almost within touching distance. The bar is decorated in nautical style, with ship models, old cable, and photographs of famous ships entering the harbour, and they serve well kept Gales HSB, GB, IPA, and a guest beer on handpump, along with some aged whiskies and country wines; piped music, fruit machine. Bar food includes sandwiches, traditional fish and chips wrapped in newspaper, ploughman's, and home-made pies; there's a wider range of meals upstairs, with quite a few fresh fish dishes; part of the dining area is no smoking. The pub is not far from HMS *Victory*, and can get busy on fine days. Nearby parking can be difficult. *(Recommended by Derek Stafford, Simon and Amanda Southwell, Ann and Colin Hunt, David and Carole Chapman, TRS, Tony and Wendy Hobden, Chris and Ann Garnett, Mrs Mary Woods, R Nelson, Richard Dolphin)*

Gales ~ Managers Mick and Lynn Finnerty ~ Real ale ~ Bar food (12-9) ~ Restaurant ~ (023) 9282 1567 ~ Children welcome ~ Open 11-11; 12-10.30 Sun

ROMSEY SU3520 Map 2
Old Horse & Jockey

Mainstone, out over Middle Bridge

The Emberleys are no strangers to this book. In the last decade they have delighted readers with several pubs dotted around the New Forest. Here, you'll recognise the style: individually decorated little rooms around a brick-faced central servery, attractively simple light wood furnishings, careful lighting including standard lamps, and an agreeable atmosphere that owes a lot to attentive and welcoming service. Fresh fish is delivered daily and they do quite a few game dishes. The lunchtime snack board lists a good choice of enjoyable favourites such as soup (£3.50), open sandwiches (from £3.75), ploughman's (£4.25), continental ham and cheese platter (£5.25), salmon pancake with cheese sauce (£6.25) and sausage and mash (£6.75), alongside a daily specials board that might have grilled goat's cheese and fruit chutney (£4.25), moules marinières (£4.75), scallops with bacon and mushrooms (£5.25), cod and chips (£6.50), fried vegetables in a pancake with cheese sauce (£7.50), confit of duck with thai lentils, bacon and red wine sauce (£10.50), bass with black olives, pepper and pesto (£11.25), venison medallions with juniper and red wine (£11.50), and home-made puddings like pavlova, ginger and orange suet pudding or fruit crumble (£4.25). Well kept Courage Directors, John Smiths and Theakstons Old Peculier, decent house wines; piped music may obtrude a bit. There are tables out in a pleasant garden with terrace and lawn, and the Test Way long-distance path runs right past the pub, which is a little way outside the town centre. Before the Emberleys reworked it, it had been a veterinary surgery for some years (though a pub originally). They have plans to add two no-smoking dining rooms which will almost double the seating capacity. *(Recommended by Lynn Sharpless, Bob Eardley, Nigel Cogger, Tony Hobden, Phyl and Jack Street, G W Bernard, Joan and Dudley Payne)*

Free house ~ Licensees Nick and Sue Emberley ~ Real ale ~ Bar food (11.30-2, 6-9.30; 12-2, 6-9 Sun) ~ (01794) 519515 ~ Children welcome ~ Open 11-3, 6-11(10.30 Sun); closed 31 Dec, 1 Jan

ROTHERWICK SU7156 Map 2
Coach & Horses ◀

4 miles from M3, junction 5; follow Newnham signpost from exit roundabout, then
Rotherwick signpost, then turn right at Mattingley, Heckfield signpost; village also
signposted from B3349 N of Hook

Handy for the M3, this pleasant pub has a roaring fire in the stripped brick fireplace,
newspapers to read, oak chairs and other interesting furniture, attractive pictures,
and a relaxed, friendly atmosphere; one of the two small beamed front rooms is
tiled, the other flagstoned, and one is no smoking. Good bar food includes
sandwiches, a vegetarian choice (£6.25), hot, spicy chilli (£6.45), mediterranean
galette (£6.65), tasty game pie (£7.95), Thai curry (£8.25), and chicken sorrento
(£8.50), and as the landlord is from South Africa, a few specialities such as boerwors
(spicy sausage £6.65) and perhaps ostrich or crocodile; puddings such as home-made
banana and toffee pie or chocolate and nut brandy cake (£3.25). Well kept real ales,
on handpump at the servery in the parquet-floored inner area, include Badger Best,
IPA, and Tanglefoot, Gribble Black Adder II, and Oving Dick Turpin; South African
wines, and a few malt whiskies; piped music. The back garden has seats and pretty
summer tubs and hanging baskets. *(Recommended by Susan and John Douglas, Simon
Collett-Jones, Martin and Karen Wake, Hugh Roberts, Francis Johnston, J and B Cressey, G K
Smale, Ian Phillips)*

*Badger ~ Managers Lisa and Riaan de Wett ~ Real ale ~ Bar food ~ (01256) 762542 ~
Children in restaurant ~ Open 11-3, 5-11; 11-11 Sat; 12-10.30 Sun*

SOPLEY SZ1597 Map 2
Woolpack

B3347 N of Christchurch; can be reached off A338 N of Bournemouth, via B3073 Hurn exit
and minor road from Hurn roundabout

The rambling open-plan bar in this attractive pub has low beams, red leatherette
wall seats and simple wooden chairs around heavy rustic tables, a woodburning
stove, and a little black kitchen range; there's also a no-smoking conservatory. Bar
food includes soup (£2.95), open rolls (from £3.50), ploughman's (from £4.50),
avocado bake (£6.75), steak and kidney pudding, Thai curry or cod in beer (£6.95),
gammon steak (£9.95), steaks (from £11.95), puddings (£2.95), and Sunday roast
beef (£5.95). Well kept Flowers Original, Ringwood Best and Wadworths 6X on
handpump; piped music. In summer, there are seats in the garden from which you
can watch the ducks dabbling about on the little chalk stream under the weeping
willows, by the small bridge. *(Recommended by Mr and Mrs W G Turner, David Gregory,
Lynn Sharpless, Bob Eardley, Brian and Genie Smart, Neil Ben, JDM, KM)*

*Whitbreads ~ Lease: Chris and Christine Hankins ~ Real ale ~ Bar food ~ Restaurant
~ (01425) 672252 ~ Children in eating area of bar and restaurant ~ Open 11-11; 12-
10.30 Sun ~ Bedrooms: /£90B*

SOUTHSEA SZ6498 Map 2
Wine Vaults ◀

Albert Rd, opp Kings Theatre

Although this simple place is good for a relaxing lunchtime drink, many people come
on any night between Monday and Thursday as they have a double happy hour
between 5.30 and 7.30 when their three real ales are £1 a pint (in fact, on Monday
it's £1 all night), and if you are coming to eat on those days and arrive before 6.30,
you get a free drink: well kept Bass, Fullers London Pride, Hop Back Summer
Lightning, Ringwood Best, and Theakstons Old Peculier on handpump.The busy
straightforward bar has wood-panelled walls, a wooden floor, Wild West saloon-
type swing doors, and an easy-going, chatty feel; pool. Bar food is good value and
served in decent sized helpings, with sandwiches (from £1.55; not Sunday), filled
baked potatoes (from £2.40), specials such as minted lamb stew, beef in ale or
vegetable lasagne (all £4.95), and rack of ribs (£8.95); friendly staff. The one-eyed

black labrador is called Ziggy; other dogs are welcome. There are seats in the little garden, and a wooden gazebo. *(Recommended by Ann and Colin Hunt, Jess Cowley, Ian Phillips, Mr and Mrs D Lawson, Brad W Morley, Alan Green)*

Own brew ~ Licensees Mike Hughes and J Stevens ~ Real ale ~ Bar food (12-9.30) ~ (023) 9286 4712 ~ Children welcome if over 5 ~ Open 12-11; 12-10.30 Sun

SPARSHOLT SU4331 Map 2
Plough ♀

Village signposted off A272 a little W of Winchester

The food here is so popular, that you must either get here early or book a table in advance. It's a neatly kept and attractive pub, and the main bar has a good bustling atmosphere, an interesting mix of wooden tables and chairs, with farm tools, scythes and pitchforks attached to the ceiling; one area is no smoking. Good, popular bar food includes sandwiches, tomato, mushroom and vegetable pasta (£6.95), braised lamb with redcurrants and morello cherries (£8.50), tossed spicy beef fillet salad with ginger dressing (£8.95), supreme of chicken with ribboned vegetables and basil sauce (£10.95), whole grilled plaice glazed with brie and avocado (£11.95), breast of duck with ginger and rhubarb (£12.95), and good bass (£13.50). Well kept Wadworths IPA, 6X, Badger Tanglefoot, and a guest beer on handpump, and a good wine list. There's a children's play area, and plenty of seats outside on the lawn. *(Recommended by Prof A N Black, R J Walden, Howard Allen, Ann and Colin Hunt, Dr A Y Drummond, John and Joan Calvert, Mrs Margaret Ross, Lynn Sharpless, Bob Eardley, W W Burke, Nigel Cogger, Terry and Linda Moseley)*

Wadworths ~ Tenants R C and K J Crawford ~ Real ale ~ Bar food ~ (01962) 776353 ~ Children in eating area of bar ~ Murder mystery evenings: must book ~ Open 11-3, 6-11; 12-3, 6-10.30 Sun; closed 25 Dec

STEEP SU7425 Map 2
Harrow

Take Midhurst exit from Petersfield bypass, at exit roundabout first left towards Midhurst, then first turning on left opposite garage, and left again at Sheet church; follow over dual carriageway bridge to pub

This is everything a proper country local should be: friendly and quite charming in an old-fashioned way, with good home-made simple food, well kept ales, and a good mix of customers. It's been run by the same family for nearly 70 years, and happily, little has changed. The cosy public bar has hops and dried flowers hanging from the beams, built-in wall benches on the tiled floor, stripped pine wallboards, a good log fire in the big inglenook, and maybe wild flowers on the scrubbed deal tables (and on the tables outside); cribbage, dominoes. Generous helpings of enjoyable home-made bar food includes home-made scotch eggs (£2.20), sandwiches (from £2.50), excellent soups such as ham, split pea and vegetable (£3.30), huge ploughman's, home-made quiches or ham lasagne (£6.50), and puddings such as delicious treacle tart or seasonal fruit pies (£3.50). Well kept Ballards, Cheriton Diggers Gold and Best, and Ringwood Best tapped from casks behind the counter, country wines, and Bulmers cider; polite and friendly staff, even when under pressure. The big garden is left free-flowering so that goldfinches can collect thistle seeds from the grass. The Petersfield bypass doesn't intrude on this idyll, and you will need to follow the directions above to find it. No children inside. *(Recommended by JP, PP, Brad W Morley, Christopher Turner, Lynn Sharpless, Bob Eardley, S G N Bennett, Wendy Arnold, James Nunn, Mike and Mary Carter, David Cullen, Emma Stent, Ann and Colin Hunt, Dr Alan Green, the Didler)*

Free house ~ Licensee Ellen McCutcheon ~ Real ale ~ Bar food (limited Sun evening) ~ (01730) 262685 ~ Open 12-2.30, 6-11; 11-3, 6-11 Sat; 12-3, 7-10.30 Sun; closed evening 25 Dec

TICHBORNE SU5630 Map 2
Tichborne Arms
Village signed off B3047

New licensees had just taken over this neat and attractive thatched pub as we went to press and were introducing new wines and beers, and serving 5 types of freshly ground coffee and 3 teas. The comfortable, square-panelled room on the right has a log fire in an attractive stone fireplace, pictures and documents on the walls recalling the bizarre Tichborne Case (a mystery man from Australia claimed fraudulently to be the heir to this estate), wheelback chairs and settles (one very long), and latticed windows with flowery curtains. On the left, a larger and livelier room, partly panelled and also carpeted has been smartened up a bit and is now used for eating; sensibly placed darts, shove-ha'penny, cribbage, dominoes, shut the box, various board games, and trivia. Good bar food might include sandwiches such as watercress and cream cheese £3) or BLT (£4.50), chicken korma or home-made steak, ale and stilton pie (£6.75), chicken in Grand Marnier sauce (£6.95), and smoked salmon and scrambled eggs or home-made salmon fishcakes with watercress pesto (£7.50). Well kept Moondance Triple FFF, Burton Bridge, Stairway to Heaven, Itchen Valley Godfathers, Ringwood Best, Wadworths 6X, and Whitbread Fuggles IPA tapped from the cask, several wines by the glass or carafe, and country wines. There are picnic-sets outside in the big well kept garden, and plenty of surrounding walks. No children inside. *(Recommended by Lynn Sharpless, Bob Eardley, A R and B E Sayer, Prof A N Black, Neil Spink, Mrs G Connell, Sheila and Robert Robinson, Stephen and Jean Curtis, Ann and Colin Hunt, Brian Borwick, the Didler, Nigel Cogger, D P and J A Sweeney)*

Free house ~ Licensees Keith and Janie Day ~ Real ale ~ Bar food (12-1.45, 6.30-9.45) ~ (01962) 733 760 ~ Open 11.30-2.30, 6-11; 12-3, 7-10.30 Sun

UPHAM SU5320 Map 2
Brushmakers Arms
Shoe Lane; village signposted from Winchester—Bishops Waltham downs road, and from B2177 (former A333)

There's plenty of room for both drinkers and diners in this neatly attractive old village pub, and a warm welcome from the licensee and his friendly regulars. The comfortable L-shaped bar is divided into two by a central brick chimney with a woodburning stove in the raised two-way fireplace, and there are comfortably cushioned wall settles and chairs, a variety of tables including some in country-style stripped wood, a few beams in the low ceiling, and quite a collection of ethnic-looking brushes; also, a small snug. Well kept Bass, Gales HSB, Ringwood Best and a beer named for the pub on handpump, decent wines, Addlestones cider, and country wines. Reasonably priced bar food at lunchtime includes sandwiches (£3.25; toasties £3.75), filled baked potatoes (£3.75), ploughman's (£3.95), ham and egg (£4.95), chicken curry, vegetable chilli and tacos (£5.50), liver and bacon casserole (£6.50), plus more substantial dishes such as steaks (from £7.50), trout or salmon (£7.95), half shoulder of lamb or sole (£10.95), and home-made puddings such as delicious marmalade cheesecake (£2.95). Sensibly placed darts, shove-ha'penny, cribbage, fruit machine and piped music. The big garden is well stocked with mature shrubs and trees, and there are picnic-sets on a sheltered back terrace among lots of tubs of flowers, with more on the tidy tree-sheltered lawn. Good walks nearby – though not much parking. *(Recommended by Ann and Colin Hunt, Dennis Stevens, Lynn Sharpless, Bob Eardley, D G King, A R and B E Sayer, Phyl and Jack Street, Mrs G Connell, P R and S A White, Val and Alan Green)*

Free house ~ Licensee Tony Mottram ~ Real ale ~ Bar food (till 10pm Fri/Sat) ~ (01489) 860231 ~ Children in eating area of bar ~ Occasional Irish/folk/country music Thurs evenings ~ Open 11-2.30(3 Sat), 5.30-11; 12-3.30, 7-10.30 Sun

You can send us reports through our web site: www.goodguides.com

WELL SU7646 Map 2

Chequers

5 miles W of Farnham; off A287 via Crondall, or A31 via Froyle and Lower Froyle (easier if longer than via Bentley); from A32 S of Odiham, go via Long Sutton; OS Sheet 186 map reference 761467

Though the management seems to change fairly regularly here, it's still a popular pub with a welcoming atmosphere, and roaring winter log fire. The low-beamed cosy rooms have lots of alcoves, wooden pews, stools with new brocaded seats, and GWR carriage lamps, and the panelled walls are hung with 18th-c country-life prints and old sepia photographs of locals enjoying a drink. Bar food now includes sandwiches, smoked chicken and bacon salad (£5.45), oriental king prawns (£5.95), good salmon fishcakes (£6.95), chicken breast (£8.25), duck with a changing sauce (£9.95), and home-made puddings (from £3). Well kept Badger Best, Tanglefoot and IPA on handpump, and decent wines. In the back garden are some chunky picnic-sets, and at the front, there's a vine-covered front arbour. The pub can get busy at weekends. *(Recommended by Martin and Karen Wake, June and Malcolm Farmer, Roger and Valerie Hill, Lynn Sharpless, Bob Eardley, Chris and Ann Garnett, Dave Braisted, R M Sparkes, Mayur Shah)*

Badger ~ Manager Shawn Blakey ~ Real ale ~ Bar food (till 10pm; all day weekends and bank holidays) ~ Restaurant ~ (01256) 862605 ~ Children welcome ~ Open 11-3, 6-11; 11-11 Sat; 12-10.30 Sun

WHERWELL SU3839 Map 2

Mayfly ♀

Testcombe (i.e. not in Wherwell itself); A3057 SE of Andover, between B3420 turn-off and Leckford where road crosses River Test; OS Sheet 185 map reference 382390

The position here is quite a draw – especially on a sunny summer's day when there are lots of tables beside the River Test and plenty of swans, ducks and maybe plump trout to watch. Inside, the spacious, beamed and carpeted bar has been refurbished this year but still has fishing pictures and bric-a-brac on the cream walls above its dark wood dado, windsor chairs around lots of tables, two woodburning stoves, and bow windows overlooking the water; there's also a no-smoking conservatory. Bar food from a buffet-style servery includes a wide range of cheeses (around three dozen) or home-made quiche (£4.50), a good choice of cold meats such as rare topside of beef, pork or smoked chicken (from £4.50), smoked trout (£4.50), vegetable curry or macaroni cheese (£5.50), winter pies and casseroles (from £5.95), chicken tandoori (£6.60), winter steaks (from £9.95), and puddings (from £3); salads are an extra 70p a spoonful which can bump up prices a bit. You'll usually find queues at busy periods. Well kept Boddingtons, Flowers Original, Morlands Old Speckled Hen, and Wadworths 6X on handpump, a wide choice of wines, and country wines; fruit machine and piped music. *(Recommended by R J Walden, Ann and Colin Hunt, Brian and Jenny Seller, C Robinson, Dennis Stevens, A R and B E Sayer, Peter Burton, J L Hall, David and Ruth Shillitoe, Andy and Sarah Gillett, Joy and Peter Heatherley, John Hayter, G Neighbour, Mr and Mrs Thomson, Anthony Barnes)*

Whitbreads ~ Managers Barry and Julie Lane ~ Real ale ~ Bar food (11.30-9) ~ (01264) 860283 ~ Children in conservatory ~ Open 10-11; 12-10.30 Sun

White Lion

B3420, in village itself

The refurbishments here have been well received by customers, and the caring licensees feel they can now get on with running their pub. It's a friendly place, and the multi-level beamed bar has plates on delft shelves, sparkling brass, and fresh flowers, and well kept Adnams Best, Castle Eden, and Flowers Original on handpump; the Village bar has an open fire, and there are two dining rooms – the lower one is no smoking. Good bar food includes lunchtime sandwiches (from £2.20; not Sunday or bank holidays) and other straightforward bar snacks plus daily specials such as leek and stilton crumble (£5.50), liver and bacon with onion gravy (£5.80), minted lamb casserole or steak and mushroom pie (£5.90), breast of chicken with apricot sauce or smoked haddock and broccoli bake (£6.50), roast duck with black cherry sauce (£7.50), rib-eye steak with peppercorn sauce (£8.50), and puddings such as lemon meringue pie or treacle tart (£2.60); Sunday roasts (worth booking for these). The two friendly black labradors are called Sam and Guinness; shove-ha'penny, cribbage, dominoes, and piped music. There are plenty of seats in the courtyard and on the terrace. The village is well worth strolling through, and there's a nice walk over the River Test and meadows to Chilbolton. *(Recommended by Colin Laffan, Mr and Mrs R S Ray, Lynn Sharpless, Bob Eardley, R T and J C Moggridge, John Hayter, G W A Pearce, Joy and Peter Heatherley, Phyl and Jack Street, Colin and Ann Hunt)*

Free house ~ Licensees Adrian and Patsy Stent ~ Real ale ~ Bar food (not Sun evening) ~ (01264) 860317 ~ Children welcome ~ Irish folk Mon evening, trad folk 1st and 3rd Thurs of month ~ Open 10-2.30(3 Sat), 6(7 Mon/Tues)-11; 12-3, 7-10.30 Sun ~ Bedrooms: £27.50B/£40

WHITSBURY SU1219 Map 2
Cartwheel 🍺

Follow Rockbourne sign off A354 SW of Salisbury, turning left just before Rockbourne itself; or head W off A338 at S end of Breamore, or in Upper Burgate – we got mildly lost trying to find it direct from Fordingbridge!

Even when busy, this out-of-the-way pub keeps its friendly and cheerful village-local atmosphere. It's opened up inside, with pitched high rafters in one part, lower beams elsewhere, antlers, military prints, country pictures, what looks like a steam-engine's jockey wheel as a divider, and simple but comfortable cloth-cushioned wall seats and other chairs. There's a snug little room by the door, with a couple of tables either side of the fire; a small side room has darts, pool, fruit machine, dominoes, and cribbage, and dogs seem very welcome. Generous food includes good sandwiches, warm chicken liver salad (£4.50), sausages, mash and onion gravy (£5.50), and fried tuna steak (£6). Adnams Broadside, Brains Bitter, Exmoor Gold, Fullers London Pride, and Ringwood Best Bitter and 21 Not Out on handpump, in top condition, ciders, and beer festivals around the second week in August and in late October; efficient service. The garden, sheltered by a shrubby steep slope, has weekly summer barbecues and a particularly good play area that children really enjoy. It's good walking country. *(Recommended by John Moate, Ann and Colin Hunt, Miss K Bebbington, Jenny and Chris Wilson)*

Free house ~ Licensee Patrick James Lewis ~ Real ale ~ Bar food (not winter Tues evening) ~ Restaurant ~ (01725) 518362 ~ Children in eating area of bar and restaurant ~ Open 11-2.30(3 Sat), 6-11; 12-3, 7-10.30 Sun

WINCHESTER SU4829 Map 2
Wykeham Arms ★ 🍽 ♟ 🛏

75 Kingsgate Street (Kingsgate Arch and College Street are now closed to traffic; there is access via Canon Street)

There's a super atmosphere here – rather civilised but friendly and with plenty of life. A series of stylish bustling rooms radiating from the central bar has 19th-c oak desks retired from nearby Winchester College, a redundant pew from the same source, kitchen chairs and candlelit deal tables and big windows with swagged paisley curtains; all sorts of interesting collections are dotted around. A snug room at the back, known as the Watchmakers, is decorated with a set of Ronald Searle 'Winespeak' prints, a second one is panelled, and all of them have a log fire; several areas are no smoking. At lunchtime, the very good food might include sandwiches (from £2.60; toasties £2.95), rarebit with cheese, beer, English mustard and chives or seafood terrine (£4.95), curried mango chicken salad (£5.25), British cheese platter with home-made plum chutney and walnut bread or continental meat platter (£5.50), and Aberdeen Angus steaks (from £10.95); in the evening, there are daily specials such as leek and potato soup (£2.95), oriental duck confit or asparagus and salmon mousse (£4.95), caramelised onion and goat's cheese tart with a tomato and red onion salad and mustard dressing (£9.95), seared tuna steak with pasta and a spicy tomato and coriander salsa (£11.25), fillet of smoked haddock on cheesy mash with sweet grain mustard sauce (£11.50), and roast rack of lamb with dauphinois potatoes and rich redcurrant jus (£12.60); puddings like apricot and frangipane or bananas in butterscotch (£4.50). There's a fine choice of 20 wines by the glass, and quite a few brandies, armagnacs and liqueurs. Also, well kept Gales Bitter, Best, HSB, and Bass on handpump. There are tables on a covered back terrace, with more on a small but sheltered lawn. The lovely bedrooms in the pub are thoughtfully equipped, and the Saint George, a 16th-c annexe directly across the street (and overlooking Winchester College Chapel) has more bedrooms, a sitting room with open fire, a post office/general stores, and a Burgundian wine store; you can enjoy the good breakfasts either in your room there or at the pub. No children.

(Recommended by John Moate, Robert Gomme, Ann and Colin Hunt, J F Reay, Tony and Wendy Hobden, Karen Eliot, Michael and Hazel Duncombe, Martin and Karen Wake, David Dimock, the Didler, Dr and Mrs A K Clarke, Comus Elliott, Wendy Straker, Mr and Mrs A R Hawkins, Lynn Sharpless, Bob Eardley, George Little, Mr and Mrs Jon Corelis, P R and S A White, David Shillitoe, Tim Barrow, Sue Demont, David Cullen, Emma Stent, Peter Smith, Keith Louden, John Oates, Wendy Arnold; also in the Good Hotel Guide)

Gales ~ Manager Tim Manktelow-Gray ~ Real ale ~ Bar food (not Sun) ~ Restaurant ~ (01962) 853834 ~ Open 11-11; 12-10.30 Sun; closed 25 Dec ~ Bedrooms: £45S/£79.50B

WOODGREEN SU1717 Map 2
Horse & Groom

Off A338 N of Fordingbridge, signposted from Breamore

On the edge of a quiet New Forest village, this shuttered brick and flint house has picnic-sets out on a little fenced front terrace, and in a spreading sheltered back garden with lively and interesting aviaries. Inside there are local nature pictures in the set of smallish beamed rooms which ramble around the central servery. There's a warmly welcoming and properly pubby atmosphere, with games in the simple locals' bar on the left (but no piped music and the fruit machine is silenced), a log fire in a nice Victorian fireplace on the right, and a comfortable eating area. A good choice of good value home-cooked food includes sandwiches (from £2.20), home-made soup (£2.25), filled baked potatoes (from £2.50), ploughman's (from £3.75), daily specials such as steak and kidney pudding (£5.95), minted lamb casserole or chicken chasseur (£6.25), gammon (£7.45), lemon sole mornay (£8.95), steaks (from £8.95), and puddings such as raspberry crumble or apple pie (£2.50); good value Sunday roasts. Well kept Ringwood Best and Fortyniner and guests like Hampshire Lionheart and Tisbury Archibald Beckett on handpump; efficient service. The dining room is no smoking. *(Recommended by D M Riordan, Phyl and Jack Street, Lyn and Geoff Hallchurch, WHBM)*

Free house ~ Licensee Michael Whelan ~ Real ale ~ Bar food ~ Restaurant ~ (01725) 510739 ~ Children in restaurant ~ Open 11-3, 6-11; 12-3, 7-10.30 Sun

Lucky Dip

Besides the fully inspected pubs, you might like to try these Lucky Dips recommended to us and described by readers (if you do, please send us reports):

Alresford [SU5832]
Bell [West St]: Relaxing Georgian coaching inn under new management; extended bar, smallish dining room, quickly served good value food inc children's helpings, well kept beers, friendly service, daily papers, log fire, attractive back courtyard; comfortable bedrooms *(Ann and Colin Hunt, Ron Shelton, Neil Spink)*
☆ *Horse & Groom* [Broad St; town signed off A31 bypass]: Recently refurbished open-plan

bar with beams, timbers and some stripped brickwork, nice bow window seats, good friendly staff, well kept beers such as Fullers London Pride, good value food from sandwiches to steaks, coal-effect gas fire, unobtrusive piped music; children welcome, open all day at least in summer *(Susan and John Douglas, Ann and Colin Hunt, A R and B E Sayer, LYM, Neil Spink, John and Vivienne Rice)*

Ampfield [SU4023]

White Horse [A31 Winchester—Romsey]: Vastly extended open-plan Whitbreads dining pub, period-effect furniture, log fire, well kept ales (but served through sparkler), good choice of wines by the glass, Victorian prints and advertising posters in dining room; pub backs on to golf course and village cricket green; handy for Hillier arboretum, good walks in Ampfield Woods *(Phyl and Jack Street, Martin and Karen Wake, B M Baker, Douglas and Ann Hare)*

Arford [SU8336]

Crown: Tastefully refurbished local with good affordable food, lovely atmosphere and inc children's and vegetarian in big clean candlelit eating area, hospitable welcome, well kept Tetleys-related and guest beer, log fire, riverside garden *(G W Stevenson, E M Steinitz)*

Ashmansworth [SU4157]

Plough: Friendly no-frills pub in attractive village, Hampshire's highest; two rooms knocked together, simple home-cooked food with good attentive service, well kept Archers Village, Best and Golden and changing guest tapped from the cask; seats outside, good walks, handy for Highclere Castle *(the Didler)*

Avon [SZ1399]

New Queen [B3347 S of Ringwood]: Modern chain family dining pub with different areas and levels, low-pitched ceiling, good value traditional pub food, Badger ales, helpful staff; tables out on spacious covered terrace and lawn with play area, bedrooms *(Paul and Sue Merrick, John Hibberd)*

Axford [SU6043]

☆ *Crown*: Busy smartish pub with prints above dark panelling, very friendly prompt service, open fires, real ales such as Fullers London Pride and Billericay Dickie, good range of wines by the glass, good value generous food, separate dining area; juke box in public bar; seats in garden and on terrace, popular with walkers *(John and Vivienne Rice, John Vigar, Lynn Sharpless, Bob Eardley, Bob Deane)*

Bank [SU2807]

☆ *Oak* [signed off A35 S of Lyndhurst]: Cleanly refurbished 17th-c local in lovely New Forest spot, friendly staff, good choice of generous well prepared food inc real doorstep sandwiches and exceptional puddings, well kept chilled ales such as Flowers and Ringwood tapped from the cask, country wines; piped music, very busy evenings and weekends; good garden, village attractive and untouristy though within earshot of A35 (ponies stroll through) *(Jess Cowley, Mr and Mrs A Craig, Paul and Sue Merrick, M Joyner, Neil Ben, W W Burke)*

Battramsley [SZ3099]

☆ *Hobler* [A337 S of Brockenhurst]: Quirkily enjoyable bustling heavy-beamed pub with nice relaxed mix of furniture, lots of books and rustic bric-a-brac, matey atmosphere, good food from splendid bacon butties to bass, scallops and sizzle-your-own steaks, well kept Flowers IPA, Wadworths 6X and guest beers such as Ringwood Fortyniner, dozens of malt whiskies and country wines, traditional games; piped music; spacious lawn with summer bar, very good play area and paddock of livestock, good Forest walks; no children inside, jazz Tues, blues 2nd Thurs *(Dr D E Granger, Ann and Colin Hunt, Dr and Mrs A K Clarke, J and P Halfyard, LYM)*

Bighton [SU6134]

Three Horseshoes [off B3046 in Alresford just N of pond; or off A31 in Bishops Sutton]: Quiet old-fashioned village local with simple bare-boards stripped-stone public bar, solid fuel stove in its huge fireplace, small lounge with bright carpet, log fire in unusual thatched fireplace, collection of model cars and lorries and other transport-related decorations, well kept Gales HSB, BBB, winter 5X and Prize Old Ale, lots of country wines, basic food (not Weds evening), darts; children welcome, good walks nearby; cl Mon winter lunchtime *(J Sheldon, Ron Shelton, the Didler, Lynn Sharpless, Bob Eardley)*

Bishops Waltham [SU5517]

Bunch of Grapes [Church St]: Unspoilt simple two-room village local run by third family generation; well kept Ushers inc a seasonal beer, good chatty landlord, plenty of character *(Ann and Colin Hunt, Stephen and Jean Curtis)*

Bordon [SU7935]

Woodlands: Recently opened spacious pub with well kept Boddingtons, attractive grounds *(G B Lungden)*

Botley [SU5112]

Dolphin [High St]: Early Victorian, with beams, oak furniture, cream and red paint, Bass, Morlands Old Speckled Hen and Ruddles, bar food from baguettes to steak, back restaurant; quiet piped music and machines *(Val and Alan Green)*

Braishfield [SU3725]

Dog & Crook: Cottagey but spacious, with bar and two dining rooms inc one no smoking, imaginative changing freshly cooked food inc vegetarian, fish specialities, well kept Wadworths 6X, good house wine, friendly service; garden with play area *(Howard G Allen)*

☆ *Newport* [Newport Lane]: Popular very basic two-bar local, unspoilt inside – quite a time warp; simple good value food inc huge sandwiches and good value ploughman's, particularly well kept Gales HSB, Best and Butser, country wines, decent coffee, down-to-earth licensees, weekend singsongs; good garden with geese, ducks and chickens *(Lynn Sharpless, Bob Eardley, the Didler)*

Bransgore [SZ1897]

☆ *Three Tuns* [Ringwood Rd, off A35 N of Christchurch]: Pretty little thatched whitewashed pub, much restored inside with beamery etc, comfortable dining area popular with older people at lunchtime for wide range of good value food (same chef though new landlord), welcoming efficient service, well kept Ringwood Best and Fortyniner, tasteful bar, fresh flowers, small restaurant; pleasant back garden with play area and open country views, flower-decked front courtyard; bedrooms *(Ann and Alex Tolputt, Peter Walters, Sue and Mike Todd)*

Brockenhurst [SU3002]
Snakecatcher [Lyndhurst Rd]: Thriving well run pub with increasing concentration on good if not cheap food from baguettes to steaks cooked to order (so may be a wait), good Sat fish specials and children's food, interesting split-level bar and restaurant areas inc cosy part with log fire and easy chairs, well kept Hardy ales, good choice of wines by the glass, good service, candles at night; good walks nearby *(Jess and George Cowley, Phyl and Jack Street, WHBM, Lyn and Geoff Hallchurch, James Nunns)*

Brook [SU2714]
Bell: Really a hotel and restaurant (with thriving golf club), but does good interesting lunches in its quiet bar, with prompt friendly uniformed staff, well kept Ringwood and lovely log fire; big garden, delightful village; comfortable bedrooms *(B and K Hypher, John and Joan Calvert)*
Green Dragon [B3078 NW of Cadnam]: Big open-plan modernised New Forest pub with very wide quickly served food choice inc speciality game pie in dining area, big garden with good enclosed play area; picturesque spot *(Mrs Hilarie Taylor)*

Broughton [SU3032]
☆ *Tally Ho* [opp church; signed off A30 Stockbridge—Salisbury]: Sympathetically renovated local with a real welcome for visitors, big plain modern flagstoned bar with darts (they don't mind walking boots), comfortable hunting-print lounge, good value plain home cooking and good sandwiches, homely fire in each room, entertaining landlord, well kept Cheriton Pots and Ringwood Best and True Glory, decent wines in two glass sizes; children welcome, tables in secluded pretty back garden, good walks *(Martin and Karen Wake, Lynn Sharpless, Bob Eardley, Brian and Anna Marsden, Howard Allen, Tony Hobden)*

Burghclere [SU4660]
Carpenters Arms [Harts Lane, off A34]: Pleasantly furnished small pub with good country views from attractively laid-out dining conservatory, big helpings of bar food from well presented sandwiches up, well kept Arkells, unobtrusive piped music; garden; handy for Sandham Memorial Chapel (NT) *(F C Johnston)*

Buriton [SU7420]
Master Robert: Friendly welcome, well kept Flowers IPA and Fullers London Pride, popular food in low-ceilinged dining area, public bar with pool etc; bedrooms, good view from car park *(Val and Alan Green)*

Burley [SU2003]
☆ *White Buck* [Bisterne Close; ¾ mile E]: Lovely New Forest setting, superb walks towards Burley itself and over Mill Lawn, wide choice of reasonably priced good freshly made food, well kept Gales ales with guests such as Ringwood and Wadworths 6X, decent wines, elegant and spacious high-ceilinged plush bar/family eating area, smaller restaurant (should book), courteous efficient staff; dogs allowed, hitching posts, pleasant front terrace and spacious lawn; well equipped bedrooms

(Phyl and Jack Street, Joan and Dudley Payne, S H Godsell)

Bursledon [SU4809]
☆ *Fox & Hounds* [Hungerford Bottom; two miles from M27 junction 8]: Carefully refurbished rambling oak-beamed 16th-c Chef & Brewer, flagstones and carpet, log fires, piped music, nice young staff, newspapers, Courage Best and Directors, Theakstons XB and a seasonal guest, good value freshly made food from sandwiches to steak inc fish; linked by family conservatory area to ancient back barn with cheerful rustic atmosphere, immense refectory table, lantern-lit side stalls, lots of interesting and authentic farm equipment, wide choice from food bar; children allowed *(Val and Alan Green, LYM)*

Cadnam [SU3114]
Compass [Winsor; OS Sheet 195 map ref 317143]: Popular simply furnished pub off the beaten track, with good range of real ales inc occasional beer festivals, good cheapish food inc excellent bacon doorsteps, small side garden; Irish music Thurs *(Phyl and Jack Street)*
☆ *Sir John Barleycorn* [Old Romsey Rd; by M27, junction 1]: Low-slung thatched Whitbread Wayside Inn, attractive medieval bit on left with dim lighting, low beams and timbers, more of a chain-pub feel in extended part on right, Whitbreads-related ales with a guest such as Castle Eden, reasonably priced wines, big helpings of good value food running up to bass, helpful efficient service, two log fires, no-smoking restaurant end; can be very busy; suntrap benches in front, eye-catching flowers *(Dr and Mrs A K Clarke, W W Burke, Lynn Sharpless, Bob Eardley, John and Vivienne Rice, M Joyner, John Beeken, Eric and Charlotte Osgood, LYM)*

Chalton [SU7315]
☆ *Red Lion* [signed E of A3 Petersfield—Horndean]: Pretty timbered thatched pub, Hampshire's oldest, with high-backed settles, heavy beams, panelling and ancient inglenook fireplace in cosy original core, well kept Gales Buster, Best and HSB, good wines and a good choice of other drinks, hospitable staff, modern no-smoking family dining extension (no food Sun evening); piped music; pretty garden, nr Queen Elizabeth Country Park and Iron Age show farm and settlement, good downs walk to quaint St Hubert's Chapel, Idsworth *(Brad W Morley, Mr and Mrs Buckler, Ann and Colin Hunt, Richard Dolphin, D B Jenkin, J and P Halfyard, Phyl and Jack Street, Tony and Wendy Hobden, Dennis Stevens, LYM, P R and S A White, R and K Halsey)*

Charter Alley [SU5957]
White Hart [off A340 N of Basingstoke]: Friendly village local, woodburner and no-smoking area in lounge bar, skittle alley in simple public bar, wide choice of reasonably priced food in dining area, well priced real ales such as Bunces, Fullers London Pride, Greene King Abbot *(J V Dadswell)*

Chawton [SU7037]
Greyfriar: Well run village pub with low Tudor beams, standing timbers studded with foreign

coins, good reasonably priced generous food from very well filled home-baked bread sandwiches to fresh fish, Thai as well as traditional puddings, quick efficient service, well kept beer, good coffee, small garden behind with barbecue; opp Jane Austen's house, good walks *(A Cowell, B and K Hypher, Ann and Colin Hunt)*

Chilbolton [SU3939]

☆ *Abbots Mitre* [off A3051 S of Andover]: Busy and roomy, with good generous food inc very good value OAP special in bar and restaurant, well kept ales such as Boddingtons, Flowers Original, Greene King Abbot, Morlands Old Speckled Hen and Ringwood, friendly attentive smartly dressed staff, log fire, games room; garden with pleasant covered terrace, baskets and tubs of flowers, play area; attractive village *(Colin and Joyce Laffan, Jim and Janet, Michael Inskip, Ann and Colin Hunt)*

Chilworth [SU4118]

Clump [A27 Romsey Rd]: Useful extended dining pub, recently refurbished and open all day, warm homely décor, nice fireplaces, large bookshelves, sofas and spacious conservatory; good reasonably priced food, good range of well kept beer, efficient friendly service; unobtrusive piped music; large garden with barbecue *(Sharon Holmes, Tom Cherrett, Phyl and Jack Street, Howard G Allen)*

Church Crookham [SU8151]

Wyvern: Smartly refurbished suburban pub, some interesting food, well kept beer, pleasant lunchtime atmosphere, plenty of seats in tidy garden; handy for Basingstoke Canal *(Chris and Ann Garnett)*

Crawley [SU4234]

☆ *Fox & Hounds* [signed from A272 and B3420 NW of Winchester]: No longer a pub, though the attractive bar still survives; focus is now on the bistro restaurant – where we can recommend the good if pricy French cooking; bedrooms big and comfortable, good breakfast *(Howard Allen, D S Jackson, TRS, Dennis Stevens, LYM, Phyl and Jack Street, Pam Izzard, John and Joan Calvert, Tim Barrow, Sue Demont)*

Rack & Manger [A272 Stockbridge— Winchester, about 5 miles N of Winchester]: Comfortably extended Marstons pub with wide range of food inc interesting dishes, plenty of fish and good puddings, dining lounge, big no-smoking area, traditional public bar, good choice of beers, Sun bar nibbles, obliging service, quiet piped music; good-sized garden *(D M Brumfit, Ann and Colin Hunt)*

Crondall [SU7948]

Hampshire Arms: Unpretentious welcoming local, good choice of food from tasty baguettes to hearty main dishes, well kept Morlands Old Speckled Hen and Ruddles, pleasant service, cosy beamed main bar with huge fireplace, faded red velvet curtains, exposed brickwork, brasses, dining conservatory, rather bare public bar with traditional games; boules *(R T and J C Moggridge, KC, Martin and Karen Wake)*

Plume of Feathers [The Borough]: Cosy and attractive 15th-c village pub under new

landlord, beams and dark wood, prints on cream walls, open fire in big brick fireplace, Morlands and other ales, generous food from hot filled baguettes and double-decker sandwiches up, smarter restaurant end; no piped music or juke box, dogs and children welcome; two red telephone boxes in garden, picturesque village *(Simon Collett-Jones, Mrs B Nickson, Nigel and Sue Foster, Geoffrey Lawrance)*

Crookham [SU7852]

Black Horse: Friendly beamed village local with sturdy satisfying food, well kept beer, tables out on nice back and side areas with some amusements for children; pleasant Basingstoke Canal towpath walks *(Chris and Ann Garnett)*

Chequers [Crondall Rd]: Very welcoming new young couple in spaciously refurbished open-plan pub with appealing reasonably priced food and good range of beers, pleasant restaurant *(Chris and Ann Garnett, Iain Robertson)*

Curbridge [SU5211]

Horse & Jockey [Botley Rd (A3051)]: Beautiful setting by River Hamble tidal tributary at start of NT woodland trail, two neatly refurbished bars and dining area, cheerful waitress service, Gales ales and country wines; piped music may obtrude; lovely garden with small terrace, trees and fenced play area *(Gwen and Peter Andrews)*

Curdridge [SU5314]

Cricketers [Curdridge Lane (B3035, just off A334 Wickham—Botley)]: Open-plan low-ceilinged Victorian country pub with banquettes in refurbished lounge area, little-changed public part, good friendly service even when busy, Banks's Bitter and Mild and Marstons Pedigree, nice dining area; quiet piped music, tables on front lawn, pleasant footpaths *(Val and Alan Green, John and Christine Simpson, Phyl and Jack Street)*

Damerham [SU1016]

☆ *Compasses*: 16th-c, carefully refurbished, with good food inc tasty soups, shellfish, interesting cheeses, five changing ales, good choice of wines by the glass, over a hundred malt whiskies, very friendly staff, attractive dining room with booth seating (children allowed here), separate public bar; big pretty garden, well equipped bedrooms *(Joy Griffiths, Mrs J Josephson)*

Denmead [SU6611]

Harvest Home [Southwick Rd, Bunkers Hill]: Friendly and popular country pub with one long bar, separate eating area off, Gales ales, well priced straightforward food *(Ann and Colin Hunt)*

Dogmersfield [SU7853]

☆ *Queens Head* [Pilcot Lane]: Friendly 17th-c dining pub in attractive country setting, wide choice of tasty well priced food from filled baguettes through lots of salads to interesting restaurant main dishes; good choice of wines, real ales, faultless service; gets very busy, booking advised evenings, cl Mon *(Francis Johnston, Mrs Hilarie Taylor, M J Bastin)*

Downton [SZ2793]

☆ *Royal Oak* [A337]: Wide choice of good home

cooking inc some imaginative dishes in neat partly panelled family pub, half no smoking, with well kept Whitbreads-related ales, decent wines, jovial atmosphere, friendly landlady, unobtrusive piped music; huge well kept garden with good play area *(D Marsh, Neil Brown)*

Dunbridge [SU3126]

☆ *Mill Arms* [Barley Hill]: Friendly and cosy, with sofas, good well presented food inc fine Sunday beef, real ales such as Test Tickler and another brewed for the pub, open fire, conservatory, refurbished skittle alley; tables in pleasant two-level garden with wendy house, bedrooms planned *(Martin and Karen Wake, Mr and Mrs B Craig)*

Dundridge [SU5718]

☆ *Hampshire Bowman* [off B3035 towards Droxford, Swanmore, then right at Bishops W 3¾]: Friendly and cosy downland pub, not too smart, with remarkable mix of customers (children, dogs and walkers welcome, usually some classic cars or vintage motorcycles); well kept Archers Golden, King & Barnes Festive and Ringwood Best and Fortyniner tapped from the cask, decent house wines, country wines, good straightforward home cooking inc vegetarian, sensible prices, efficient staff, battered corner armchair for non-smokers; tables on spacious and attractive lawn *(Val and Alan Green, Howard G Allen, Ann and Colin Hunt, LYM, Wendy Straker)*

Durley [SU5217]

☆ *Robin Hood* [Durley Street, just off B2177 Bishops Waltham—Winchester]: Friendly and homely two-room dining pub, log fire, impressive food running up to kangaroo and crocodile, good cheerful service, Marstons ales, reasonably priced wines; darts and quiz evenings; back terrace and big pleasant garden with fine view and play area, good walks *(A R and B E Sayer, Val and Alan Green, Phyl and Jack Street)*

East End [SZ3697]

East End Arms [back road Lymington—Beaulieu, parallel to B3054]: Popular New Forest pub with Ringwood ales tapped from the cask, good value home cooking, log fire, curious tree trunk in lounge bar, tables in small garden *(D Marsh)*

East Meon [SU6822]

☆ *George* [Church St; signed off A272 W of Petersfield, and off A32 in West Meon]: Rambling country pub, heavy beams and inglenooks, four log fires, cosy areas around central bar counter, deal tables and horse tack; well kept Badger beers, decent wines, country wines, substantial straightforward food in bar and restaurant, summer cream teas, obliging service; children welcome, good outdoor seating arrangements, quiz night Sun; small but comfortable bedrooms, good breakfast; pretty village with fine church, good walks *(Susan and John Douglas, LYM, Phyl and Jack Street, Colin and Ann Hunt)*

Easton [SU5132]

☆ *Chestnut Horse*: Comfortable rambling beamed dining pub dating from 16th c, smartened up by new licensees, good food inc innovative

specials, Fullers London Pride, decent wines, efficient service, good log fire; small terrace with colourful flowers, lovely sleepy village, Itchen valley walks *(Lynn Sharpless, Bob Eardley, Ron Shelton, S A Edwards, TRS, Edgar Holmes)*

Cricketers [off B3047]: Friendly open-plan village local, small bright restaurant, wide choice of good interesting food, well kept ales such as Cottage Southern, local Moondance Triple FFF, Otter, Ringwood Best and Shepherd Neame Spitfire, good range of decent wines; darts and shove-ha'penny one end *(Lynn Sharpless, Bob Eardley, June and Peter Gregory, Ron Shelton, Ann and Colin Hunt)*

Ellisfield [SU6345]

Fox [Fox Green Lane, Upper Common]: Friendly and relaxed village local doing well under current regime, wide choice of good value generous standard food in two-level bar, good changing beers such as Badger Tanglefoot, Fullers London Pride, Gales HSB, Hampshire King Alfred, Ringwood Old Thumper and one brewed for the pub, decent wines and country wines, open fire, daily papers; pleasant garden, good walks (esp Bedlam Bottom to the W, lovely in spring) *(C P Baxter, Lynn Sharpless, Bob Eardley, P P Salmon, Phyl and Jack Street, Guy Consterdine)*

Emery Down [SU2808]

☆ *New Forest* [village signed off A35 just W of Lyndhurst]: Good position in one of the nicest parts of the Forest, with good walks nearby; attractive softly lit separate areas on varying levels, each with its own character, log fires, well kept ales such as Fullers London Pride and Marstons Pedigree, wide choice of house wines, proper coffee, generous good food, lively bustle, efficient service; children allowed, small but pleasant three-level garden *(Peter Mueller, John Fahy, Tim and Linda Collins, Lynn Sharpless, Bob Eardley, W W Burke, LYM, P G Bardswell)*

Emsworth [SU7406]

Coal Exchange [Ships Quay, South St]: Compact comfortable Victorian local, cheerful service, good lunchtime food, a real fire at each end, well kept Gales and a guest beer *(Ann and Colin Hunt)*

☆ *Kings Arms* [Havant Rd]: Comfortable friendly local popular for generous well priced interesting food inc vegetarian cooked by landlady, fresh veg, good choice of wines, friendly service, well kept Gales and a guest beer, small restaurant area; pleasant garden behind *(Ann and Colin Hunt, K and F Giles, David Coleman, J F Freay)*

Lord Raglan [Queen St]: Welcoming and relaxing little Gales pub with character landlord, log fire, good range of food esp fish, restaurant (must book summer w/e), live music Sun; children welcome if eating, garden behind nr water *(Ann and Colin Hunt)*

Eversley [SU7762]

Golden Pot [B3272]: Welcoming interlinked rooms, good food with German Swiss dishes alongside the usual cajun chicken etc (Mon is

Swiss rosti night with live music), a Swiss red house wine among others, well kept ales inc Flowers and Ruddles, restaurant; piped music, two friendly dogs *(KC)*

Eversley Cross [SU7861]

Chequers: Comfortably modernised (though in fact partly 14th-c) with quickly served food inc good long-running carvery, nice puddings *(Mrs J A Uthwatt)*

Toad & Stumps [The Green (B3272)]: Plain and old-fashioned, with dining tables on the left, Courage Directors, Gales HSB, Fullers London Pride and Marstons Pedigree, friendly service, food inc good baguettes; big attractive back garden, skittle alley *(Michael and Jenny Back)*

Exton [SU6120]

☆ *Shoe* [village signed from A32]: Now Wadworths, with friendly new licensees and their beers kept well, smart facade and bright decor, attractive panelled room off bar, good choice of generous food inc vegetarian in bar and cosy log-fire restaurant (may find all tables booked for Sun lunch – very popular with older people), efficient service; piped music; tables on lawn down to River Meon – pretty village, good walks *(Lynn Sharpless, Bob Eardley, Phyl and Jack Street, Ann and Colin Hunt)*

Fareham [SU5806]

Cob & Pen [Wallington Shore Rd, not far from M27 junction 11]: Pleasantly refurbished with pine furnishings, flagstones and carpets, Hook Norton Best and Ringwood ales tapped from the cask, wide choice of good value straightforward food; large garden *(Val and Alan Green, Ann and Colin Hunt)*

Delme Arms [Cams Hill, Porchester Rd (A27)]: Pleasant good value two-bar Victorian local with decent food, well kept Bass, Fullers London Pride, Worthington and a guest beer such as Badger, friendly service; opp splendidly restored Cams Hall *(Val and Alan Green)*

Fareham [Trinity St]: Greenalls Ale & Hearty pub with Bass, Boddingtons, Greenalls Original, Marstons Pedigree and several changing guest beers, food inc vegetarian and children's; piped music may obtrude *(Val and Alan Green)*

Lord Arthur Lee [West St]: New Wetherspoons pub/diner named for the local 1900s MP who presented Chequers to the nation, attractively priced beers inc Archers Porter and bargain Shepherd Neame Spitfire *(Val and Alan Green)*

White Horse [Wallington Shore Rd]: Smart two-bar pub with three real ales *(Ann and Colin Hunt)*

Farnborough [SU8753]

☆ *Prince of Wales* [Rectory Rd, nr Farnborough North stn]: Good range of well kept beers with interesting guests in friendly and lively local, Edwardian with stripped brickwork, open fire and antiquey touches in its three small connecting rooms, popular lunchtime food from sandwiches to imaginative specials, good service, decent malt whiskies *(Andy and Jill Kassube, R T and J C Moggridge)*

Fleet [SU8054]

Prince Arthur [High St]: Wetherspoons, with well kept cheap Courage Directors, Theakstons

and several guest beers, friendly efficient staff, good cheap food, no-smoking area; open all day *(Sharon Holmes, Tom Cherrett, Chris and Ann Garnett)*

Fordingbridge [SU1414]

George [Bridge St]: Superb position, terrace and conservatory bar (children welcome here) facing River Avon, pleasant interior with spacious no-smoking area, good value food, Flowers and Gales HSB, helpful service *(Eddie Edwards, JEB)*

Tudor Rose [A338]: Picturesque wisteria-covered pub with low beams, big fireplace, wide choice of very generous straightforward food, well kept Ringwood beers, friendly attentive service, back garden with play area; Avon Valley footpath passes the door, fine pedestrian suspension bridge *(Phyl and Jack Street, John Hackett)*

Freefolk [SU4848]

☆ *Watership Down* [N of B3400 – sharp lane uphill at W end of village]: Genuine unaffected compact village pub, partly brick-floored, nicely placed above grassy bank, friendly busy landlord, good choice of ale such as Archers Best, Brakspears PA and Mild, popular food inc good value Sun roasts, functional furnishings, games area with plenty of old-fashioned slot machines and table football; piped music, Sun quiz night; attractive garden with play area and rabbit pen, pleasant walks *(JCW, Jess and George Cowley, Phyl and Jack Street)*

Frogham [SU1712]

☆ *Foresters Arms* [Abbotswell Rd]: Busy extensively refurbished New Forest pub recently taken on again by former licensees, flagstones and small woodburner, well kept Wadworths and guest ales, decent wines, reasonably priced straightforward food inc very popular Sun lunch, extended dining room; children welcome, pleasant garden and front verandah; small camp site adjacent, good walks *(G Gibbs, Phyl and Jack Street, Lyn and Geoff Hallchurch, John and Joan Calvert, LYM)*

Godshill [SU1715]

Fighting Cocks: Generous good food inc beautifully cooked veg and good children's menu, well kept Flowers, Fullers London Pride, Gales HSB and Wadworths 6X, open fires, maps for walks; quiet piped music *(Rev J Hibberd)*

Gosport [SZ6199]

☆ *Clarence* [Mumby Rd (A32)]: Reopened as pub (after many years as club), Old Church from their own back brewery and changing guest beers, heavy furnishings, old books, prints and other pictures, no games or piped music; medieval evenings *(Ann and Colin Hunt)*

Queens [Queens Rd]: Bare-boards pub whose landlady keeps an incredible range of up to ten or more changing strong real ales with Badgers Tanglefoot as a regular fixture, three areas off bar with coal fire in interesting carved fireplace; very quick service, maybe huge filled rolls and other simple food; sensibly placed darts, family area with TV, no piped music, quiz night Thurs; bedrooms *(Ann and Colin Hunt, Val and Alan Green, Peter and Audrey Dowsett)*

Hamble [SU4806]
☆ *Olde Whyte Harte* [High St; 3 miles from M27 junction 8]: Friendly pub with low-beamed bar and well integrated flagstoned eating area, very helpful pleasant staff, blazing inglenook log fire, sensibly priced good home-made food inc plenty of fish, well kept Gales Best, BBB and HSB, lots of country wines, decent coffee, yachting memorabilia; children in eating area, some seats outside; handy for nature reserve *(Ann and Colin Hunt, Charles and Pauline Stride, LYM, Dr Alan Green)*
Hambledon [SU6414]
New Inn [West St]: Simple two-bar village local, friendly and chatty, with cheap Ringwood ales, pool room with darts *(Ann and Colin Hunt)*
☆ *Vine* [West St]: Particularly well cooked generous food (not Sun evening) in friendly beamed pub, open-plan but traditional, with panelling, old prints, china, ornaments, farm tools, high-backed settles, log fire – even a well in one of its four areas; good range of beers such as Charles Wells Bombardier, Fullers London Pride, Gales HSB and BBB, Hampshire Hare, country wines, long-serving landlord, welcoming helpful staff; shove-ha'penny, darts; pretty downland village *(Ann and Colin Hunt, Martin and Nicki Lampon, R M Corlett, G B Lungden)*
Hannington [SU5355]
Vine: Wide range of well kept real ales such as Badger Tanglefoot, Ringwood Old Thumper and Ruddles County, reliable reasonably priced food, attractive dining conservatory, billiards room, good friendly atmosphere – lively but not noisy, all ages; terrace, big garden, nice spot up on downs; Sun lunches, evening restaurant (not Sun/Mon) *(Dr and Mrs A K Clarke)*
Hatherden [SU3450]
Old Bell & Crown: Roomy, with reasonably priced tasty food from wide choice of sandwiches and baked potatoes to steaks, also vegetarian; Wadworths ales, restaurant with no-smoking section, pretty garden *(Ann and Colin Hunt, D M Brumfit)*
Havant [SU7106]
Old House At Home [South St]: Much modernised low-beamed Tudor pub, two fireplaces in lounge, well kept Gales BBB and HSB, welcoming licensees; piped music (live Sat – very popular with young people Fri/Sat night), back garden *(Ann and Colin Hunt, LYM, Tony and Wendy Hobden)*
Robin Hood [Homewell]: Cosy old pub with low ceilings in rambling open-plan bar, well kept Gales ales tapped from the cask, reasonably priced food, open fire; sensibly placed darts *(Ann and Colin Hunt)*
Headley [SU8235]
Hollybush [the one N of Liphook]: Welcoming and well appointed, good food and service, good choice of well kept beers *(John and Kathleen Potter)*
Heckfield [SU7260]
☆ *New Inn* [B3349 Hook—Reading (former A32)]: Big well run rambling open-plan dining pub, now tied to Badger with their beers kept

well, good choice of reliable food (waitress service now), some traditional furniture in original core, two good log fires, decent wines, no piped music; restaurant; bedrooms in comfortable and well equipped extension *(KC, LYM, Chris and Ann Garnett)*
Hill Head [SU5402]
☆ *Osborne View* [Hill Head Rd]: Roomy modern red plush clifftop pub with three stepped-back levels and picture windows for exceptional views to the Isle of Wight, generous bar food inc children's and Sun roasts (best to book then), well kept Badger Best, Tanglefoot and ales from the Gribble at Oving, efficient service, nautical prints and memorabilia, no music; evening restaurant; open all day, garden and beach access, nr Titchfield Haven bird reserve *(Ann and Colin Hunt, A R and B E Sayer, Eric and June Heley, Michael Inskip, Val and Alan Green, Phyl and Jack Street)*
Horndean [SU7013]
Ship & Bell [London Rd]: Big pub/hotel adjoining Gales brewery, full range of their beers kept well, good food and service, cosy relaxed local atmosphere in bar with deep well, comfortable snug lounge with steps up to dining room; bedrooms *(Ann and Colin Hunt)*
Horsebridge [SU3430]
☆ *John o' Gaunt* [off A3057 Romsey—Andover, just SW of Kings Somborne]: Friendly village pub very popular with walkers for good attractively priced food, simple L-shaped bar, well kept Palmers IPA, friendly service; picnic-sets out by mill on River Test; dogs welcome, no piped music *(Lynn Sharpless, Bob Eardley, John Hayter, Dr and Mrs N Holmes, John Fahy, Sheila and Robert Robinson)*
Houghton [SU3432]
Boot [S of Stockbridge]: Quiet country pub under newish owners, decent food in roomy dining bar on left, attentive service, regenerated garden running down to lovely stretch of River Test; good walks, and on Test Valley cycle way *(D Marsh, Phyl and Jack Street, John Fahy)*
Hursley [SU4225]
Dolphin [A3090 Winchester—Romsey]: Good relaxed country atmosphere, decent food, hard-working licensees, well kept Whitbreads and guest beer; tables in garden *(Ron Shelton)*
Kings Head [A3090 Winchester—Romsey]: Large open-plan food pub, rather elegant décor, with skittle alley in cellar bar, and bedrooms; has good value fresh interesting food inc vegetarian and sandwiches, and well kept ales such as Bass, Wadworths 6X and Youngs, but changing hands in 1999 *(Lynn Sharpless, Bob Eardley, Ron Shelton)*
Itchen Abbas [SU5332]
Trout [B3047]: Smallish plainly furnished country pub with friendly new tenant, low-key lounge bar (partly no smoking), chatty public bar with darts and bar billiards, well kept Marstons Bitter and Pedigree, decent wines, good reasonably priced food, no-smoking dining area; pretty side garden with good play area and pets corner; roomy comfortable bedrooms, pleasant village with good river and downland walks nearby *(Phyl and Jack Street,*

G B Lungden, Lynn Sharpless, Bob Eardley, BB)

Keyhaven [SZ3091]

☆ *Gun*: Busy 17th-c pub overlooking boatyard, popular at lunchtime particularly with older people for good choice of generous food using local produce; low beams, nautical memorabilia, well kept beers such as Flowers, Marstons Pedigree, Morlands Old Speckled Hen and Ringwood True Glory, well over a hundred malt whiskies; family room, garden with swings and fish pond *(Simon Mighall, Lyn and Geoff Hallchurch, W W Burke, D Marsh, WHBM, Phyl and Jack Street)*

Kingsclere [SU5258]

☆ *Crown*: Good reasonably priced food and Courage ales in long comfortable partly panelled lounge with central log fire; games in simpler public bar, children in family room, nearby downs walks *(Phyl and Jack Street, LYM)*

Langstone [SU7105]

☆ *Ship* [A3023]: Plenty of seats out on quiet quay by waterside pub with lovely view from roomy pleasantly decorated bar and upstairs restaurant, fast friendly service, full Gales range kept well, good choice of wines by the glass, country wines, log fire, generous food inc fish; children's room, long opening hours, good coast walks *(Ann and Colin Hunt, Dennis Stevens, John Saul, J F Freay, Gordon Neighbour)*

Lee on the Solent [SU5600]

Swordfish [Crofton Ave/Sea Lane, off Stubbington Lane]: Big comfortable pub notable for outstanding position with Solent views; big family room, usual pub food, Scottish Courage ales *(TRS)*

Linwood [SU1910]

☆ *High Corner* [signed from A338 via Moyles Court, and from A31; keep on]: Big rambling pub very popular for its splendid New Forest position, with extensive neatly kept lawn and sizeable play area; some character in original upper bar, lots of back extension for the summer crowds, large helpings of good value food from sandwiches to steaks inc Sun carvery (nicely partitioned restaurant open all day Sun), well kept Whitbreads-related and other ales such as Wadworths 6X, decent wine, no-smoking verandah lounge; children and dogs welcome in some parts, open all day Sat; bedrooms *(J A Snell, Neil Ben, John Fahy, D Marsh, Dennis Stevens, LYM, C A Hall)*

☆ *Red Shoot* [signed from A338 via Moyles Court, and from A31; go on up heath]: Nice New Forest setting, lots of space, some attractive old furniture and rugs on bare boards, large dining area with generous good value food inc good sandwiches and special sausage dishes, six well kept ales inc Wadworths and a beer brewed at the pub, friendly staff, children and dogs (and muddy boots) welcome; very touristy in summer (by big campsite and caravan park), can get smoky *(M Joyner, G J Gibbs, Mrs A Garrard, Wendy Straker, DAV)*

Little London [SU6359]

Plough [Silchester Rd, off A340 N of Basingstoke]: Cosy unspoilt local with tiled floor, low beams, friendly landlord, limited food inc lots of baguettes, well kept Ringwood and changing guest beers, log fire, darts, bar billiards; attractive garden, handy for Pamber Forest and Calleva Roman remains *(G Coates, J V Dadswell)*

Locks Heath [SU5006]

☆ *Jolly Farmer* [2½ miles from M27 junction 9; A27 towards Bursledon, left into Locks Rd, at end T-junction right into Warsash Rd then left at hire shop into Fleet End Rd]: Emphasis on wide choice of food from filled baps to steaks in extensive series of softly lit rooms with nice old scrubbed tables and a forest of interesting bric-a-brac and prints, coal-effect gas fires, no-smoking area, well kept Flowers Original, Gales HSB and Morlands Old Speckled Hen, country wines, neat friendly staff; piped music; two sheltered terraces, one with a play area; bedrooms. *(Bill and Steph Brownson, Mr and Mrs B Craig, Ann and Colin Hunt, John and Christine Simpson, LYM)*

Lower Froyle [SU7643]

Anchor [signed off A31]: Warm and attractive brightly lit traditional pub popular with older people lunchtime (esp Weds) for good straightforward food inc sandwiches and fish, cheerful service, well kept Hardy Royal Oak, decent malt whiskies; well in one of the two connecting bars, restaurant; piped music; seats outside *(Dr Robert Crail, Iain Robertson, KC)*

Lymington [SZ3295]

Bosuns Chair [Station St]: Light and airy high-ceilinged rooms, food inc fish cooked plainly or with options, well kept Wadworths ales; bedrooms *(Tony and Wendy Hobden, Tim Barrow, Sue Demont)*

☆ *Chequers* [Ridgeway Lane, Lower Woodside – dead end just S of A337 roundabout W of Lymington, by White Hart]: Stylishly simple young yachtsmen's local with polished boards and quarry tiles, attractive pictures, plain chairs and wall pews; good freshly cooked food inc fish and seafood, Marstons Pedigree and Wadworths 6X, good wines, fine rums; friendly landlord, well if not quietly reproduced piped pop music, TV, traditional games, tables in neat walled back family garden and on attractive front terrace; well behaved children allowed *(Nigel Cogger, Tim Barrow, Sue Demont, D Marsh, LYM, Mark Percy, Lesley Mayoh, Lydia Cahill)*

Fishermens Rest [All Saints Rd, Woodside]: Doing well under current licensees, wide choice of interesting reasonably priced food, well kept beers *(D Marsh)*

Kings Head [Quay Hill]: Unpretentiously upmarket attractive cottagey bar with comfortable settles, good food and atmosphere, tankards hanging from beams *(Dr and Mrs A K Clarke)*

Red Lion [High St]: Well run and comfortable, food inc good Sun roasts *(Lyn and Geoff Hallchurch)*

Wagon & Horses [Undershore Rd; rd to IOW ferry]: Wide range of reasonably priced food, partly no-smoking restaurant, well kept real ales inc Bass, good choice of sensibly priced wine, cheerful attentive staff *(D Marsh)*

Lyndhurst [SU2908]

Crown: Best Western hotel, log fire in traditional cosy bar, part-panelled walls, antlers, Bass and Ringwood Best, reasonably priced well served food; bedrooms *(Phyl and Jack Street)*

Crown Stirrup [Clay Hill; A337 ½ mile S]: 17th-c or older, extensive but cosy bar with two low-beamed rooms, reasonably priced food, well kept Boddingtons, Ringwood and Romsey ales, good friendly service, log fire; children welcome, covered back terrace, pleasant side garden with play area and gate to Forest *(Phyl and Jack Street, Neil Ben)*

Waterloo Arms [Pikes Hill]: 17th-c rambling thatched pub with low ceilings, pleasant furnishings, log fire, interesting beers tapped from the cask, good wine list, good food; some children's amusements in attractive back garden *(Phyl and Jack Street)*

Mapledurwell [SU6851]

☆ *Gamekeepers* [Tunworth Rd, off A30 Hook—Basingstoke]: Attractively laid-out Badger dining pub, candles, tablecloths and napkins, good choice of good food, well kept IPA, Tanglefoot and a guest beer, good house wines, glassed-over well in bar, family room behind, friendly efficient service, views from nice open garden, in lovely thatched village with duck pond, good walks *(Phyl and Jack Street, W W Burke, Kevin Macready, H H Hellin)*

Medstead [SU6537]

☆ *Castle of Comfort* [Castle St]: Genuinely traditional village pub, homely and old-fashioned, taken over 1999 by former long-serving licensees of Fox at Bix in Oxfordshire (popular main entry under them); Courage Best and Directors, simple pub food such as soup, rolls, sandwiches, toasties and ploughman's, play area, long sunny front verandah *(TBB)*

Meonstoke [SU6119]

☆ *Bucks Head* [just off A32 N of Wickham]: Good value substantial freshly cooked food inc local game and very good puddings in smallish dining lounge with dark red banquettes and good log fire, well kept Bass and Ruddles Best, country wines, friendly service, comfortable public bar (open all day Sun at least in spring and summer); pleasant walled garden, lovely village setting with ducks on pretty little River Meon, good walks *(A R and B E Sayer, JCW, Ann and Colin Hunt)*

Minstead [SU2811]

☆ *Trusty Servant* [just off A31 nr M21 junction 1]: In pretty New Forest village with wandering ponies, small bare-boards locals' bar, unsophisticated back lounge (also small), wide choice of good food from enormous sandwiches to fresh fish (nice seafood chowder) and imaginative main dishes, well kept changing ales such as Flowers Original, Fullers London Pride and Ringwood Best, Thatcher's farm cider, country wines; sizeable attractive restaurant, airy by day, candlelit by night; piped music, and rather a take-us-as-you-find-us feel; bedrooms simple, good breakfast *(Jasper Sabey,*

Neil Ben, Gwen and Peter Andrews, R T and J C Moggridge, Mike and Heather Watson, Lynn Sharpless, Bob Eardley, David Peakall, BB)

Mortimer West End [SU6363]

☆ *Red Lion* [Church Rd; Silchester turn off Mortimer—Aldermaston rd]: Country dining pub doing well under keen and friendly new young couple, good food, good range of Badger and other well kept ales, lots of beams, stripped masonry, timbers and panelling, good log fire; quiet piped music; plenty of seats in pleasant garden with climbing frame, and on small flower-filled front terrace; handy for Roman Silchester *(LYM, Phyl and Jack Street)*

Nether Wallop [SU3036]

Five Bells [signed from A30 or B2084 W of Stockbridge]: Simple village pub with long cushioned settles and good log fire in beamed bar, cheap food inc good Hawaiian melts, well kept Marstons Pedigree, chatty landlord, bar billiards and other traditional games in locals' bar with friendly labrador called Meg, small restaurant, seats outside, provision for children; pretty thatched village *(LYM, Jason Caulkin)*

New Cheriton [SU5828]

☆ *Hinton Arms* [A272 nr B3046 junction]: Roomy family-run pub with wide choice of good home-made food inc local hams and cheeses, good vegetarian choice, fresh fish, well kept real ales such as local Itchen Valley, dark décor with bric-a-brac; big garden, very handy for Hinton Ampner House (NT) *(Ron Shelton, Ann and Colin Hunt, Betty Laker, John and Joan Calvert, Richard Powell)*

North Warnborough [SU7351]

Swan [nr M3 junction 5]: Village local with cheapish usual food, well kept Courage, beams and stripped brickwork, cheapish usual food, TV and fruit machine, large well equipped play area beyond back courtyard *(Ian Phillips, Tony Dickinson)*

Odiham [SU7450]

☆ *George* [High St (A287)]: Civilised old-fashioned market-town hotel with well kept Scottish Courage ales, decent wines by the glass, good value food from rare beef sandwiches up, welcoming attentive staff, interesting old photographs, fish restaurant; comfortable little back locals' bar overlooking garden; soundproofed bedrooms, some in annexe *(LYM, Chris and Ann Garnett)*

Ovington [SU5531]

☆ *Bush* [signed from A31 on Winchester side of Alresford]: Charming spot with streamside garden and pergola dining terrace with a good-sized fountain pool, low-ceilinged bar with laid-back atmosphere and service, high-backed settles, pews and kitchen chairs, masses of old pictures, roaring fire, food from sandwiches to local trout and steaks, well kept Wadworths IPA, 6X and Farmers Glory and a guest such as Badgers Tanglefoot; nice walks *(J and B Cressey, Ann and Colin Hunt, Glen Armstrong, Pete and Sue Robbins, Howard Allen, Martin and Karen Wake, Nigel Cogger, Peter and Audrey Dowsett, Nigel Wikeley, D P and J A Sweeney, John Gillett, Lynn Sharpless, Margaret Fergusson, LYM, John and Christine*

Simpson, Ron Shelton, Marianne and Peter
Stevens, Gwen and Peter Andrews)

Pamber End [SU6158]

Queens College Arms [Aldermaston Rd
(A340)]: Varied good value well presented
food, friendly staff, good atmosphere *(anon)*

Pennington [SZ3194]

White Hart [Milford Rd]: Modernised
Whitbreads Wayside Inn with separate rooms
around central core, real ales such as Flowers
Original, Fullers London Pride, Gales HSB and
Wadworths 6X, popular food, friendly service;
terrace and garden *(W W Burke)*

Petersfield [SU7423]

☆ *Good Intent* [College St]: 16th-c core with low
oak beams and oak tables, four Gales ales, food
inc sandwiches, baguettes, lots of unusual
sausages, vegetarian choices, friendly staff;
children in cosy former restaurant area *(Val and
Alan Green, Derek and Margaret Underwood)*

☆ *Trooper* [old coach rd NW past Steep, OS Sheet
186 map ref 726273]: Civilised country pub
with scrubbed pine tables, fresh flowers,
candles and bare boards, log fire, good
generous rather upmarket food inc interesting
vegetarian dishes and bargain weekday lunches,
well kept Bass and Ringwood Fortyniner,
Czech lager on tap, decent wines by the glass,
watchfully friendly service; pretty new stables
restaurant with open range (may be used for
grilling), tables out on terrace, country views
*(Martin and Karen Wake, Wendy Arnold,
Terry Morgan)*

Portchester [SU6204]

Cormorant [next to Portchester Castle]:
Whitbreads dining pub with solid 1930s feel,
reasonably priced plentiful home-made food all
day, children in dining area; seats outside, in
pleasant close handy for castle and views over
Portsmouth harbour, plenty of parking *(Val
and Alan Green)*

Portsmouth [SU6501]

Bridge [The Wharf, Camber Dock]:
Comfortable, quiet and relaxing, with lots of
wood fittings, maritime theme, good water
views, bar food, upstairs fish bistro,
Boddingtons and Marstons Pedigree *(Colin and
Ann Hunt, Reg Nelson)*

Churchillian [Portsdown Hill Rd, Widley]:
Smallish open-plan dining pub, oak, cream and
red carpet, big windows overlooking
Portsmouth and Solent, usual food, Gibbs Mew
ales; quietish piped music; handy for Fort
Widley equestrian centre and nature trail *(Val
and Alan Green)*

Connaught Arms [Penhale Rd]: Attractive
Tudor corner pub with friendly long-serving
licensees, straightforward food inc lots of
pasties, well kept ales such as Bass, Cheriton
Pots and Fullers London Pride, sensibly placed
darts; terrace *(Ann and Colin Hunt)*

☆ *Dolphin* [High St, Old Portsmouth]: Spacious
and genteel old timber-framed inn with talk of
changes as we went to press; till now
they've had ten or more Whitbreads-related
and other ales, wide range of food, good log
fire, cosy snug; video games; open all day Sat,
children welcome in eating area, small terrace

(Ann and Colin Hunt, Reg Nelson)

Eastney Arms [Cromwell Rd]: Fairly large
tastefully refurbished dining pub, three or four
well kept ales (plenty of room for drinkers),
friendly service; handy for Royal Marines
Museum *(Colin and Ann Hunt)*

George [Queen St, nr dockyard entrance]:
Reopened after long closure, good sized pub,
with log fire, covered well and Nelson pictures,
separate food bar, real ales; handy for dockyard
and HMS *Victory (Colin and Ann Hunt)*

Mayflower Beer Engine [Highland Rd,
Eastney]: The cat's like the pub – good pedigree
but friendly; comfortable lounge, subdued
lighting, good prints, lots of original
woodwork, careful modern refurbishment,
engaging atmosphere, well kept Tetleys and
other ales, simple bar food; public bar with juke
box and games room off, garden *(Ann and
Colin Hunt, Reg Nelson)*

Sally Port [High St, Old Portsmouth]: Spick-
and-span hotel, sympathetically modernised
and still interesting, with good atmosphere,
leather chesterfields, soft lighting, reasonably
priced bar food esp fish, well kept chilled
Boddingtons and Marstons, decent coffee,
friendly staff, upstairs restaurant; comfortable
bedrooms *(Zoe Morrell, Andrew Anderson,
Derek Stafford, Reg Nelson, Ann and Colin
Hunt)*

Surrey Arms [Surrey St]: Comfortable two-bar
backstreet local popular lunchtime for good
food, good choice of well kept beer; bedrooms
(Ann and Colin Hunt, Reg Nelson)

Tap [London Rd, North End]: Ten or more
changing well kept ales, thriving atmosphere,
genuine service, straightforward weekday bar
food inc king-sized sandwiches *(Ann and Colin
Hunt)*

Wellington [High St, off Grand Parade, Old
Portsmouth]: Friendly and busy open-plan pub
nr seafront, good bar food inc fresh fish and
vegetarian, friendly landlord, relaxing
atmosphere, well kept beer *(Ann and Colin
Hunt)*

Preston Candover [SU6041]

☆ *Purefoy Arms* [Arlesford Rd]: Old village pub
with good range of sensibly priced generous
food inc speciality topped garlic breads,
interesting salads, vegetarian dishes, young
friendly landlord, well kept Ushers, games in
public bar; get there early for live jazz Thurs
and first Sun in month; big peaceful garden
with play area overlooking fields, nearby
snowdrop walks, open all day Sun *(John and
Vivienne Rice)*

Ringwood [SU1505]

White Hart [Mkt Pl]: Venerable old inn, lots of
panelling, big log fire, comfortable atmosphere,
helpful friendly staff, good varied menu in well
spaced eating areas and no-smoking area, well
kept Bass and Hardy beers; well equipped
recently refurbished bedrooms *(Mr and Mrs
A P Reeves)*

Rockbourne [SU1118]

☆ *Rose & Thistle* [signed off B3078
Fordingbridge—Cranborne]: Attractive
thatched 17th-c pub with good home-made

food inc vegetarian (can be a wait when busy, puddings rather pricy), well kept Courage Best, Marstons Pedigree, Ushers seasonal brews, Wadworths 6X and Youngers Scotch, good range of wines, pleasant service, civilised bar with booth seating, old engravings and good log fire, traditional games, no-smoking area, restaurant; maybe piped classical music; children welcome, tables by thatched dovecot in neat front garden, charming setting in lovely village, good walks *(Phyl and Jack Street, G Neighbour, Ann and Colin Hunt, D Marsh, Mrs Hilarie Taylor, Jamie and Ruth Lyons, Mike and Heather Watson, LYM)*
Romsey [SU3422]

☆ *Dukes Head* [Great Bridge Rd; A3057 towards Stockbridge]: Attractive six-room 16th-c dining pub festooned with flowering baskets in summer; smart helpful waitresses, well kept Bass, Hampshire and Hardy ales, decent house wines, good value well prepared food, inglenook eating places, log fires; maybe quiet piped music; charming back garden with old tractor and rabbits *(Pete and Sue Robbins, G W A Pearce, Paul Ransom, Ann and Colin Hunt)*

Luzborough House [Botley Rd; A27 towards N Baddesley – handy for M27 junction 3]: Extensive Whitbreads family dining pub with interesting smaller rooms leading off high-raftered rather sparsely furnished flagstoned main bar, generous food all day, well kept ales, big log fire, cheerful staff; piped music; children welcome away from bar, tables and play area in spacious walled garden *(Phyl and Jack Street, LYM, Dennis Stevens)*

Three Tuns [Middlebridge St; car park off A27 bypass]: Quaint old pub with bright fires in beamed bar; good reasonably priced generous food, good choice of real ales inc Flowers, Ringwood Best and Wadworths 6X, cheerful and attentive staff *(Phyl and Jack Street)*

White Horse [Mkt Pl]: Forte Heritage hotel, good value food in bar and small beamed dining room, very good service; bedrooms *(Basil Minson)*
Rowlands Castle [SU7310]

Castle [Finchdean Rd]: Enjoyable village pub, popular food, Gales beers, friendly young staff; children and dogs welcome, garden *(Mrs Val Worthington, Wendy Straker, Colin and Ann Hunt)*

Robin Hood [The Green]: Comfortable lounge bar with decent food inc wide choice of good value fish Thurs-Sun, three real ales; friendly landlord, dog and cats *(Ann and Colin Hunt)*
Selborne [SU7433]

Selborne Arms: Well kept real ales, good range of enjoyable food from ploughman's and baked potatoes up, twinkly landlord, old photographs, fresh flowers, log fire in fine inglenook, friendly staff cope very well even when very busy; tables in garden with good play area, right by walks up Hanger, and handy for Gilbert White museum *(Martin and Caroline Schimmer, Ian Phillips)*
Shawford [SU4624]

Bridge: Several large dining areas with decent

food range, well kept real ales, quietish piped music, silenced games machines, billiard room; garden with play area *(Val and Alan Green)*
Shedfield [SU5512]

Wheatsheaf [A334 Wickham—Botley]: Busy little family-run two-bar local, well kept ales such as Archers, Cheriton Pots, Hampshire and Hop Back, satisfying lunchtime food, reasonable prices; garden, handy for Wickham Vineyard *(Val and Alan Green)*
Sherfield on Loddon [SU6857]

☆ *White Hart*: Pleasant atmosphere, good friendly service, wide choice of generous fresh food, huge inglenook fireplace, well kept Courage and guest ales, good choice of wines, interesting coaching-era relics; soft piped music; tables outside, handy for The Vyne *(Mrs Bayliss, LYM)*
Shirrell Heath [SU5714]

Prince of Wales [High St (B2177)]: Pleasantly cluttered cheerful bar in red, green and brown with Victorian and Edwardian prints, three Marstons beers, wide menu from sandwiches to halibut inc children's and weekday OAP bargains, nice restaurant; piped radio; garden *(Val and Alan Green)*
Soberton [SU6116]

☆ *White Lion* [School Hill; signed off A32 S of Droxford]: Unaffected 16th-c country pub in nice spot by green, welcoming landlord, rambling no-smoking bistro area with enjoyable straightforward food, irregularly shaped public bar with built-in wooden wall seats and traditional games, well kept Gales HSB, Morlands Old Speckled Hen, Wadworths 6X and a beer brewed for them by Hampshire Brewery, decent house wine, sensible prices, no music, energetic beer mat retrieving collie called Spike; small sheltered pretty garden and suntrap fairy-lit terrace; children in eating areas, open all day *(Ann and Colin Hunt, LYM, Martin and Karen Wake, Barbara and Robert Sayer, P R and S A White, Howard G Allen, Ian Phillips, Wendy Straker, Simon Collett-Jones, Brad W Morley, Gareth Davies, Roy Grove)*
Soberton Heath [SU6014]

Bold Forester [Forester Rd]: Country pub with well kept Adnams Broadside, Morlands Original and Revival Mild and Ruddles County, plentiful straightforward food, daily papers, friendly licensees, dogs welcome; garden with fenced play area, field for camping behind, good walks *(Wendy Straker, Ian Phillips)*
Southampton [SU4212]

Cowherds [The Common]: Low beams and boards, numerous friendly alcoves, tables in nice little bay windows, lots of Victorian photographs, carpets on polished boards, log fires, Bass and Worthington, restaurant; pleasant spot on common, tables outside with tie-ups and water for dogs (50p deposit on glasses taken outside – just across from University) *(Dr and Mrs A K Clarke, Ian Phillips)*

Hedgehog & Hogshead [University Rd, Highfield]: Friendly open-plan bare-boards pub with real ales brewed in the bar, wide variety of home-cooked food, piano most evenings *(Dr and Mrs A K Clarke)*

Old Fat Cat [Above Bar St]: Large town dining pub with Greene King ales, modern cooking, young cheerful trained staff; piped radio may be rather loud *(Val and Alan Green)*

Platform [Town Quay Rd]: Good food and attentive service, Marstons beers, daily papers *(P A Legon)*

South Western Arms [Adelaide Rd, by St Denys stn]: A dozen or so real ales inc Badger, Gales and Wadworths, enthusiastic staff, basic food, bare boards, exposed brickwork, toby jugs and stag's head on beams, lots of woodwork, beer mats on ceiling, upper gallery where children allowed; popular with students, easy-going atmosphere, juke box; picnic-sets on terrace, live jazz Sun afternoon *(J Hibberd)*

Waterloo Arms [Waterloo Rd]: Small 1930s pub tied to Hop Back with their full beer range kept well, some lunchtime food, open fires, plenty of light-coloured wood, ochre walls with brewing awards, traditional games, back garden with boules, plans for conservatory; very busy w/e, Tues quiz night *(G Coates)*

Southsea [SZ6498]

☆ *Eldon Arms* [Eldon St/Norfolk St]: Roomy, comfortable and relaxing rambling bar with old pictures and advertisements, attractive mirrors, lots of enjoyable bric-a-brac; about a dozen Hardy and other changing well kept ales, decent wines, friendly manager, good changing range of promptly served food, sensibly placed darts; pool and fruit machine, restaurant, tables in back garden *(Ann and Colin Hunt, Reg Nelson)*

Fuzz & Firkin [Victoria St]: Good lively police-theme Firkin, usual bare boards and solid furnishings, friendly staff, good beer brewed at the pub; loud music and lots of young people Sat night *(Ann and Colin Hunt, Jess and George Cowley, Reg Nelson)*

Red White & Blue [Fawcett Rd]: Busy local, well kept Gales; games nights, live music *(the Didler)*

Stockbridge [SU3535]

☆ *Grosvenor* [High St]: Good atmosphere and quick cheerfully courteous service in pleasant and comfortable old country-town hotel's recently refurbished bar, decent food, Courage Directors and Whitbreads Best, country prints and log fire; big attractive garden behind; bedrooms good value *(Phyl and Jack Street, R J Walden, BB)*

Vine [High St]: Busy if not cheap pub/restaurant, old beams and woodwork, stripped bricks and purple wallpaper, delft shelf of china and pewter, bright floral curtains, Boddingtons, Brakspears and Flowers Original, good wine list, unobtrusive piped music, half helpings for children; open all day, tables in nice big garden, weekend barbecues *(John and Vivienne Rice, Anna and Martyn Carey, Stephen and Jane Curtis, LYM)*

☆ *White Hart* [High St; A272/A3057]: Cheerful and welcoming divided bar, oak pews and other seats, antique prints, shaving-mug collection, good reasonably priced home-made bar food, Sun lunches, well kept beers such as

Ringwood Fortyniner, country wines, nice licensees; children allowed in comfortable beamed restaurant with blazing log fire; bedrooms *(G B Lungden, Phyl and Jack Street, Mr and Mrs Thomson, Pat and Kay McCaffrey, LYM)*

Swanmore [SU5816]

Hunters [Hill Pound]: Plush much-extended low-beamed dining pub with big family room, wide choice of freshly made straightforward food inc vegetarian and children's, Charles Wells Bombardier and Eagle and Theakstons, good house wine, country wines, lots of boxer pictures, bank notes, carpentry and farm tools; plenty of picnic-sets, good big play area; very busy weekends *(A R and B E Sayer, Val and Alan Green)*

New Inn [Chapel Rd]: Friendly village pub with attentive licensees, Marstons ales, straightforward home cooking; games, darts, cricket team *(Val and Alan Green)*

☆ *Rising Sun* [Hill Pound Rd; off B2177 S of Bishops Waltham]: Welcoming and comfortable tile-hung pub, low beams, scrubbed pine, good log fires, good choice of food inc interesting dishes (booking advisable w/e), well kept Flowers, Greenalls, Marstons Pedigree and Tetleys, good reasonably priced wines, prompt courteous service, well separated extended dining area; pleasant garden with play area, handy for Kingsway long distance path *(Val and Alan Green, Phyl and Jack Street, Peter Tinker)*

Sway [SZ2898]

☆ *Hare & Hounds* [Durns Town – just off B3055 SW of Brockenhurst]: Airy and comfortable New Forest family dining pub, lots of children, good range of food inc vegetarian, well kept Flowers Original, Fullers London Pride and Ringwood Best, picnic-sets and play frame in sizeable neatly kept garden; open all day Sat *(Dr and Mrs A K Clarke, John and Joan Calvert, D Marsh, LYM)*

New Forest Hotel: Good interesting food in attractive French-managed bar and restaurant, boules in pretty garden with contemporary art gallery beyond; bedrooms *(Mrs B Williams)*

Tangley [SU3252]

☆ *Cricketers Arms* [towards the Chutes]: Small front bar with tiled floor, massive inglenook, roaring log fire, bar billiards and friendly labrador called Pots, bistroish back extension with green paint, woodwork, flagstones and a one-table alcove off, imaginative food inc fresh baguettes and mix-your-own evening pizzas, well kept Bass and Cheriton Pots tapped from the cask, some good cricketing prints; tables on neat terrace *(Ann and Colin Hunt, LYM, Mark Brock)*

Fox: Cosy but lively little beamed and timbered pub with generous good value imaginative food inc good puddings, well kept Courage and guest ales, good choice of wines, two big log fires, friendly chatty landlord and dog, prompt helpful service; two no-smoking dining rooms *(Mrs Margaret Ross, Mr and Mrs Thomson)*

Timsbury [SU3325]

☆ *Bear & Ragged Staff* [A3057 towards

Stockbridge; pub marked on OS Sheet 185 map ref 334254]: Very busy beamed Whitbreads country dining pub, much modernised, airy and comfortable, with wide choice of food all day inc good value ploughman's and good vegetarian dishes, quick service even when busy, several well kept ales, lots of wines by the glass, country wines, tables out in garden, good play area; children in eating area; handy for Mottisfont *(Ian and Deborah Carrington, LYM, Ann and Colin Hunt)*

Titchfield [SU5406]

☆ *Fishermans Rest* [Mill Lane, off A27 at Titchfield Abbey]: Comfortable Whitbreads pub/restaurant in pleasant spot opp Titchfield Abbey, food all day in mellow eating area off bar with no-smoking family area, good choice of well kept ales inc Gales HSB and Wadworths 6X, pleasant atmosphere, helpful service, two log fires, daily papers, fishing memorabilia; tables out behind overlooking river *(June and Eric Heley, John and Christine Simpson, Ann and Colin Hunt, LYM, Val and Alan Green)*

Totford [SU5738]

Woolpack [B3046 Basingstoke—Alresford]: Friendly, warm and cosy pub/restaurant with well kept Gales HSB, Palmers IPA and local Cheriton Pots, stripped-brick bar, large dining room, decent food inc vegetarian and good Sun roast, open fire; tables outside, lovely setting in good walking country; bedrooms *(Mike Hayes, Ann and Colin Hunt)*

Turgis Green [SU6959]

☆ *Jekyll & Hyde* [A33 Reading—Basingstoke]: Busy local feel in rambling black-beamed pub with eclectic mix of furniture, mezzanine dining area with wide range of good food from sandwiches up all day inc breakfast, children's helpings, well kept Badger and Wadworths 6X, prompt friendly service, some interesting prints particularly in back room; lots of picnic-sets in good sheltered garden (some traffic noise), play area and various games; lavatories for the disabled *(LYM, Dr and Mrs A K Clarke, KC)*

Twyford [SU4724]

Phoenix [High St]: Friendly open-plan local with lots of prints, bric-a-brac and big red inglenook log fire, wide choice of food from sandwiches through proper shortcrust pies to steaks, enthusiastic cheerful landlord, well kept Marstons, decent wines, quiet piped music, back room with skittle alley, garden; children allowed up one end *(Val and Alan Green, Lynn Sharpless, Bob Eardley)*

Upton [SU3555]

Crown [N of Hurstbourne Tarrant]: Unpretentious country local, genial, neat and clean, with pine and pink decor, comfortably worn-in furnishings, local paintings, obliging attentive service, well done food, well kept Bass, Courage, Marstons Best and John Smiths, good coffee; piped music in public bar; small garden and terrace *(HNJ, PEJ, John Hayter, Val and Alan Green, BB)*

Vernham Dean [SU3456]

☆ *George*: Relaxed and neatly kept rambling open-plan beamed and timbered bar, carefully refurbished, with some easy chairs, inglenook

log fire, good value bar food (not Sun evening) from imaginatively filled baguettes to steaks inc good home-made puddings and more elaborate evening dishes, well kept Marstons Best and Pedigree, farm cider; darts, shove-ha'penny, dominoes and cribbage; well behaved children allowed in no-smoking eating area, tables in pretty garden behind *(Penny and Peter Keevil, the Didler, LYM, JP, PP, Tim Barrow, Sue Demont)*

Waltham Chase [SU5616]

Chase [B2177]: Large house converted to bar and dining room, new young French licensees doing very good food from vast baguettes to fresh fish, real ales such as Marstons Bitter and Timothy Taylor Landlord *(Val and Alan Green)*

Warnford [SU6223]

George & Falcon [A32]: Spacious and comfortable softly lit country dining pub, all white wall panels and chintzy curtains, popular generous food in bar and restaurant inc Sun carvery, quick friendly service, well kept Hardy beers, maybe piped light classics *(Val and Alan Green, G B Lungden)*

Warsash [SU4806]

Rising Sun [Shore Rd; OS Sheet 196 map ref 489061]: Picture-window waterside pub, friendly and lively, open all day for well presented good value food inc seafood, efficient service, well kept Marstons and Whitbreads-related ales, decent wines, long bar part tiled-floor and part boards, nautical charts and wartime naval memorabilia, fine Hamble estuary views esp from summer restaurant up the spiral stairs; estuary walks, handy for Hook nature reserve *(Phyl and Jack Street, Vanessa Hatch, Dave Creech, M Inskip)*

West End [SU4614]

Master Builder [Swaythling Rd]: Simply furnished newish pub, good local atmosphere, good reasonably priced food in busy eating part (no-smoking area), good range of real ales; welcoming landlord, popular with pensioners at lunchtime *(Phyl and Jack Street)*

West Meon [SU6424]

☆ *Thomas Lord* [High St]: Attractive village pub with good value generous food inc fish and some Caribbean-style dishes, well kept Whitbreads-related ales, collection of cricket club ties in lounge, newly converted dining area off; tables in garden *(Ann and Colin Hunt)*

West Wellow [SU2919]

Rockingham Arms [off A36 Romsey—Ower at roundabout, signed Canada]: Plush beamed 19th-c pub down Forest-edge dead end, good choice of reasonably priced food in bar and restaurant, well kept real ales, good sensibly priced wine list, friendly atmosphere and service, open fire; children welcome, garden with play area *(D Marsh)*

Whitchurch [SU4648]

Bell [Bell St]: Friendly little two-bar pub in attractive country town, small cosy lounge bar with raised dining area, inglenook fireplace, Boddingtons, Courage and Wadworths 6X, good coffee; well equipped bedrooms; walled garden, open all day *(Ann and Colin Hunt)*

☆ *Red House* [London St]: Ancient flagstones under 14th-c beams by inglenook fireplace, good generous home-cooked food from home-baked rolls up, no-smoking restaurant, well kept ales inc Courage, efficient courteous service; marvellous terrace with play area *(LYM, D M Brumfit, Francis Johnston)*

White Hart [Newbury St]: Old hotel with plain public bar and comfortable lounge bar, good choice of bar meals inc bargain Sun roast, good service *(Ann and Colin Hunt)*

Wickham [SU5711]

Kings Head [The Square]: Pretty two-bar Gales pub with no-smoking restaurant up some steps, good log fire, decent food and coffee, friendly service; tables out on square and in back garden with play area *(Phyl and Jack Street, Ann and Colin Hunt)*

☆ *Roebuck* [Kingsmead; A32 towards Droxford]: Well appointed and very well run Gales pub, good food in bar and restaurant, library of books, even a white grand piano; conservatory *(S C J Fieldhouse, A R and B E Sayer)*

Winchester [SU4829]

Albion [Stockbridge Rd/Andover Rd]: Small imaginatively renovated traditional city pub, inexpensive simple lunchtime bar food, Bass, Worthington Best and Hook Norton, friendly landlord; open all day *(Lynn Sharpless, Bob Eardley)*

Black Boy [Wharf Hill]: Beamed L-shaped bar with all sorts of interesting bric-a-brac and memorabilia, pleasantly quirky atmosphere, unusual games in separate part, good food running up to tuna steaks, well kept beer and decent wines (good mulled wine in winter), welcoming licensees, dogs welcome, attractive secluded terrace with barbecues *(LYM, Anthony Bathurst, Tom Espley)*

Eclipse [The Square, between High St and cathedral]: Picturesque but unpretentious small partly 14th-c local, massive beams and timbers, well worn fittings, oak settles, well kept Flowers Original, Fullers London Pride and Ringwood Old Thumper, well done generous lunchtime bar food inc good value toasties; children in back room (no-smoking lunchtime – front room can get smoky), seats outside, very handy for cathedral *(Sue and Mike Todd, T R and B C Jenkins, Mr and Mrs Jon Corelis, Val and Alan*

Green, LYM, Brian and Anna Marsden)

King Alfred [Saxon Rd, Hyde]: Victorianised Marstons pub, unfussy decor, wood and opaque glass dividers, good standard food from lunchtime baguettes and baked potatoes up, helpful friendly new tenants, attentive staff; TV and piped music, and can get a bit smoky, but big enough to get away *(Lynn Sharpless, Bob Eardley)*

Old Gaol House: Good spacious Wetherspoons pub with large no-smoking area, food all day at competitive prices, courteous staff; no piped music *(Stephen Harvey)*

Queen [Kingsgate Rd]: Roomy refurbished pub in attractive setting opp College cricket ground, dark dado, cricketing prints on cream walls, friendly newish licensees, well kept Marstons, decent wines, food from good value sandwiches and baked potatoes up, disabled facilities; open all day Fri-Sun *(Paul McPherson, Dr and Mrs A K Clarke, the Didler)*

☆ *Royal Oak* [off upper end of pedestrian part of High St]: Cheerful well kept Hogshead real ale tavern with up to ten or so kept well, little rooms (some raised) off main bar, beams and bare boards, scrubbed tables, no-smoking areas, cheap quick straightforward food; piped music; the cellar bar (not always open) has massive 12th-c beams and a Saxon wall which gives it some claim to be the country's oldest drinking spot *(Val and Alan Green, Dr and Mrs A K Clarke, the Didler, Ann and Colin Hunt, LYM)*

Winchfield [SU7753]

Barley Mow [Winchfield Hurst]: Friendly two-bar local with light and airy dining extension, good value generous home-made food from sandwiches up, well kept Ushers inc a seasonal beer, decent wine, unobtrusive piped music; dogs welcome, nr Basingstoke canal – lots of good walks *(Ann and Colin Hunt, Chris and Ann Garnett)*

Wolverton [SU5558]

George & Dragon [Towns End; just N of A339 Newbury—Basingstoke]: Comfortable rambling open-plan oak-beamed pub, standing timbers, log fires, good choice of reasonably priced food, wide range of beers, decent wines, helpful service; no children in bar; pleasant large garden, skittle alley *(J V Dadswell, Martin Jennings)*

Herefordshire

This is the first time that Herefordshire has had a chapter to itself. It's been something of a revelation to us, in showing how much lower the county's drinks prices are than the national average, and how so many of the county's pubs offer really good food at sensible prices. Those which really stand out for their food are the Riverside Inn at Aymestrey (delightful bar, well prepared tasty food), the Roebuck at Brimfield (interesting and original), the Feathers at Ledbury (not cheap, but very satisfying), and the Three Crowns at Ullingswick (local produce, even home-grown veg); there's also good food to be had at the Ancient Camp at Ruckhall and the Lough Pool at Sellack. From among all these, it's the Three Crowns at Ullingswick which takes our award as Herefordshire Dining Pub of the Year – really interesting food at this tucked-away rustic pub. Other pubs doing particularly well here at the moment include the Pandy at Dorstone (friendly new South African licensees), the Cliffe Arms at Mathon (good value food, good beer and wines too – a newcomer to the Guide), the welcoming Slip Tavern at Much Marcle, the cosily traditional old Boot at Orleton (another new main entry), the remote old-fashioned Carpenters Arms at Walterstone (delightfully welcoming landlady) and the Salutation in Weobley. In our price survey, we found that the local Hobsons and Wye Valley beers often featured as the cheapest beers a pub here had to offer, with Hook Norton (all the way from Oxfordshire) also cropping up quite often. In the Lucky Dip section at the end of the chapter, pubs standing out strongly these days are the Bulls Head at Craswall, Olde Tavern in Kington, Royal George at Lingen, New Inn at Pembridge, Stagg at Titley (especially for its food), Farmers Arms at Wellington Heath and Rhydspence at Whitney on Wye.

AYMESTREY SO4265 Map 6
Riverside Inn 🍴 🍷

A4110; N off A44 at Mortimers Cross, W of Leominster

In summer, big overflowing flowerpots frame the entrances of this black and white timbered riverside inn, while in cooler weather, there's no shortage of warm log fires. There is a lovely laid back atmosphere in the rambling beamed bar with several cosy areas; décor drawn from a pleasant mix of periods and styles includes fine antique oak tables and chairs, stripped pine country kitchen tables, fresh flowers, hops strung from a ceiling waggon-wheel, horse tack, a Librairie Romantique poster for Victor Hugo's poems, and a cheerful modern print of a plump red toadstool. The French chef provides an eclectic mix of ambitious bar food too: reasonably priced and changing daily, it might include soups such as an excellent bouillabaisse (£3.25) or mushrooms with madeira (£2.95), lasagne or chicken korma (£5.95), tasty steak, kidney and own-brew ale pie or spinach and mushroom roulade with a fresh tomato coulis (£7.95), rack of lamb with a niçoise dressing (£10.95), Herefordshire duck breast marinated in coriander and honey (£11.95) and wild venison with summer fruit coulis or local beef fillet with an onion compote and sauce Arlette (£14.95); popular puddings such as lime and grape cheesecake, home-made gooseberry and elderflower sorbet or bread and butter pudding (£3.50); big restaurant area. Well kept own-brew ales on handpump include Kingfisher Ale, Jack Snipe, Raven's Head and Wagtail; local farm cider, decent house wines, and friendly obliging service; shove-ha'penny, table skittles, cribbage and dominoes but no machines. There are waterside picnic-sets, and rustic tables and benches up above in a steep tree-sheltered garden, and beyond that is a beautifully sheltered former bowling green. Residents of the comfortable well furnished bedrooms are offered fly-fishing (they have fishing rights on a mile of the River Lugg), and a free taxi service to the start of the Mortimer Trail. Busy at weekends, when booking would be wise. *(Recommended by Denys Gueroult, Mary and David Richards, Mike and Heather Watson, Kevin Thorpe, Brian Polhill, Margaret and Andrew Leach, Sue and Bob Ward, D Etheridge, A Caffyn, John and Esther Sprinkle, David Edwards, Mr and Mrs Head, Ian Jones, Sarah and Peter Gooderham)*

Free house ~ Licensees Steve and Val Bowen ~ Real ale ~ Bar food ~ Restaurant ~ (01568) 708440 ~ Children over 5 in eating area of bar ~ Open 12-3, 6-11; 12-3, 7-11 Sun ~ Bedrooms: £30B/£50B

BRIMFIELD SO5368 Map 4
Roebuck 🍴 ♀ 🛏

Village signposted just off A49 Shrewsbury—Leominster

The original and tasty food at this smart country dining pub, with its gentle relaxed atmosphere, continues to win the praise of readers. Alongside daily specials, the imaginative bar menu includes starters such as soup (£2.95), pumpkin, rocket and pine nut ravioli or spicy crab filo parcels (£5.25), while main courses might include steamed steak and mushroom suet pudding or fish pie (£7.95), pork tenderloin with apple, bacon and a mustard and calvados sauce or roast chicken breast on a shallot and thyme purée with a wild mushroom sauce (£11.95), griddled calf's livers (£13.95), and fillet steak stuffed with stilton, wrapped in bacon with a madeira sauce (£15.95). The interesting reasonably priced wine list is sourced from several merchants, and as well as the well kept Morland Old Speckled Hen and Tetleys, there's an occasional guest such as Greene King Abbot on handpump; local farmhouse cider. The quiet and old-fashioned locals' snug has an impressive inglenook fireplace, and the dark panelling in the two other quietly civilised bars with small open fires has been stripped to bare wood and polished to create a pleasant, more airy environment. Kind intelligent landlord and caring, pleasant staff; dominoes, cribbage and shove-ha'penny; the intimate dining room is no smoking. Seats outside on the enclosed terrace. *(Recommended by John Teign, Mr and Mrs William Moyle, Jill Bickerton, Mike and Wena Stevenson, Rob Whittle, Helen Pickering, James Owen, J H Jones, Mrs Blethyn Elliott, Marlene and Jim Godfrey, Kevin Thorpe, Simon G S Morton, Liz Bell, Arthur and Margaret Dickinson)*

Free house ~ Licensees David and Sue Willson-Lloyd ~ Real ale ~ Bar food ~ Restaurant ~ (01584) 711230 ~ Children in eating area of bar ~ Open 11.30-3, 6.30-11; 12-3, 7-10.30 Sun ~ Bedrooms: £45B/£60B

CAREY SO5631 Map 4
Cottage of Content ♀

Village signposted from good road through Hoarwithy

This very pretty and out-of-the-way medieval country cottage is a good place to unwind. Charmingly set, with a little lane running past by a stream, it has picnic-sets on the flower-filled front terrace and a couple more on a back terrace looking up a steep expanse of lawn. Inside, the atmospheric rooms have a pleasant mix of country furnishings – stripped pine, country kitchen chairs, long pews by one big table and a mix of other old-fashioned tables. One room has flagstones, another bare boards, and there are plenty of beams and prints; darts cribbage, dominoes and TV. Readers have found all tables laid for dining at weekends, when it is advisable to book. Good bar food includes soup (£2.25), ploughman's (£3.95) and daily specials such as vegetarian dishes (£5.95), pie of the day (£6.95), and fresh fish and game in season (£8.50-£13.50). Well kept Hook Norton Best on handpump, 120 wines by the bottle, 40 malt whiskies and farm cider; attractive beamed bedrooms with sloping floors. The samoyed dog is called Storm. *(Recommended by G Washington, Denys*

Gueroult, Joan and Michel Hooper-Immins, the Didler, Andy and Jill Kassube, David Edwards, J Goodrich, Ted George, Mrs G Connell)

Free house ~ Licensee Mike Wainford ~ Real ale ~ Bar food (till 10 pm Fri and Sat) ~ (01432) 840242 ~ Children welcome ~ Open 12-2.30, 7-11(10.30 Sun); closed 25 Dec ~ Bedrooms: £35B/£48B

DORSTONE SO3141 Map 6
Pandy
Pub signed off B4348 E of Hay on Wye

When they took over this ancient half-timbered pub at the end of 1998, the friendly South African licensees kept the original staff and added Oscar – their particularly prolix parrot – to the team. They have added new furniture and wall mountings to the bar and restaurant, taking care not to detract from the character of what is supposedly Herefordshire's oldest pub, built in 1185 by Richard de Brico to house workers constructing a chapel of atonement for his part in the murder of Thomas Becket. The neatly kept main room (on the right as you go in), is friendly and welcoming with heavy beams in the ochre ceiling, stout timbers, upright chairs on its broad worn flagstones and in its various alcoves, and a vast open fireplace with logs; no-smoking area; a side extension has been kept more or less in character. Meals are prepared by the landlady and may include South African dishes such as tomato bredie (a casserole of lamb, tomatoes and potatoes) and bobotie (curried minced beef – both £6.95). Other bar food includes soups such as stilton and vegetable or french onion (£2.25), filled baguettes (from £3.25), crispy whitebait or deep-fried mushrooms with garlic dip (£3.95), crêpes filled with broccoli and sunflower seeds in a mustard sauce or chicken, mushroom and orange casserole (£6.25), salmon or trout (£7.25), and local steaks (from £9.50). Well kept Bass and local brews Butty Bach and Dorothy Goodbodys on handpump, lots of malt whiskies, farm cider and chilled fruit juices; darts, quoits and piped music. Surrounded by pretty countryside, there are picnic-sets and a play area in the neat side garden. *(Recommended by Ted George, Mr Mann, SLC, N H E Lewis)*

Free house ~ Licensees Paul and Marja Gardner ~ Real ale ~ Bar food ~ Restaurant ~ (01981) 550273 ~ Well behaved children welcome ~ Open 12-3, 7-11(10.30 Sun); closed Monday lunchtime except bank holidays

LEDBURY SO7138 Map 4
Feathers 🍴 ♀ 🛏
High Street, Ledbury, A417

Elegant and striking Tudor timbered inn which increasingly styles itself more as a hotel than a pub. In spite of this, there is a congenial mix of drinkers and diners in the atmospheric and rather civilised Fuggles bar, with locals gathered at one end of the room or at stools by the bar counter, uninhibited by those enjoying the imaginative (if rather pricy) food and fine wines. There are some very snug and cosy tables with nicely upholstered seats with bays around them off to one side, as well as beams and timbers, hop bines, some country antiques, 19th-c caricatures and fowl prints on the stripped brick chimney breast (lovely winter fire), and fresh flowers on the tables. Very attractively presented good food might include home-made parsnip and apple soup or bruschetta of mushrooms in basil and garlic (£3.25), smoked chicken breast with roasted peppers and sun-dried tomato dressing (£4.25), mixed bean and artichoke ragout with rosemary, garlic and tomato (£4.95, large £8.50), duck and pistachio terrine with mixed leaves (£5.25), crab with chicory and orange salad (£5.50) and main courses such as home-made hamburgers or salmon and cumin fishcakes (£7.95), grilled pork cutlet with apple, cream and cider sauce (£8.25), stir-fried chicken breast with mange-tout, peppers, chilli, soy and egg noodles (£10.95), grilled minted lamb cutlets with watercress and fresh tomato sauce (£11.25), pork tenderloin with a herb and raisin stuffing and marsala jus (£13.50), fillet of beef escalopes with wild mushroom, brandy, grain mustard and cream sauce (£16.75), and home-made puddings such as baked warm cheesecake with raspberry and Pernod or apple and almond tarte tatin with clotted cream and calvados (£4.50); friendly, attentive service. They do excellent afternoon teas (again, not cheap) in the more formal quiet lounge by the reception area with comfortable high-sided armchairs and sofas in front of a big log fire, and newspapers to read. Well kept Bass, Everards Tiger, Fullers London Pride, Morlands Old Speckled Hen and Worthington Best on handpump, a fine wine list, various malt whiskies, and farm cider. Abundant pots and hanging baskets adorn the lawn at the back; pleasant bedrooms, and they have their own squash courts. *(Recommended by Mrs Fiona J and Paul H Meyrick, June and Mike Coleman, Stephen and Tracey Groves, Denys Gueroult, Paul and Sandra Embleton, Andy and Jill Kassube, Howard England, Joan and Tony Walker, D W Stokes, Fiona Jarman, Sue and Bob Ward, Alan and Paula McCully, P Lloyd, Ted George, Dr W J M Gissane, Tony Beaulah, Keith and Margaret Kettell, Tim and Linda Collins, Miss C Passmore, Liz Bell, NWN)*

Free house ~ Licensee David Elliston ~ Real ale ~ Bar food (till 10 Fri and Sat) ~ Restaurant ~ (01531) 635266 ~ Children in eating area of bar ~ Open 11-11; 12-10.30 Sun ~ Bedrooms: £69.50B/£89.50B

LUGWARDINE SO5541 Map 4
Crown & Anchor ♀

Cotts Lane; just off A438 E of Hereford

In the days when the Lugg flats – some of the oldest Lammas meadows in England – were farmed in strips by local farm tenants, meetings with the lord of the manor were held in this attractive old black and white timbered inn. A friendly and comfortable atmosphere pervades the several smallish charming rooms (one suitable for families), which have an interesting mix of furnishings and a big log fire. Good bar food might include a variety of sandwiches (from £1.90), home-made soup (£2.50), linguine with parmesan, basil and toasted pine nuts (£2.80), smoked salmon and sweet cucumber salad (£3.80), prawn and broccoli tartlets in a light cheese pastry (£3), ploughman's (£4), battered cod (£4.75), at least eight vegetarian and a couple of vegan dishes such as black-eye bean and seaweed casserole, lentil and ricotta moussaka or cheese and spinach lasagne (£5.50), grilled trout with almonds and herb stuffing (£6.50), chicken supreme with smoked oysters in saffron cream sauce (£6.90), chargrilled Herefordshire sirloin steak (£10) and a good choice of daily specials including game in season such as quails in blackcurrant and port sauce with wild rice and pine nut stuffing (£7.50) and venison steak (£10); puddings (£2.75), children's menu (£2.50); the main eating area is no smoking. Well kept Bass, Hobsons Best, Worthington Best and maybe a guest on handpump, decent wines, including a clutch of usefully priced bin ends, and lots of malts; service has sometimes been a bit vague. *(Recommended by Brian and Patricia Nichol, Denys Gueroult, Prof P A Reynolds, Mr and Mrs A Craig, David Gittins, David Edwards, Gary Benjamin, Simon G S Morton)*

Free house ~ Licensees Nick and Julie Squire ~ Real ale ~ Bar food (till 10) ~ (01432) 851303 ~ Children welcome ~ Live jazz first Wednesday evening of month ~ Open 11.30-11; 12-10.30 Sun

MATHON SO7345 Map 4
Cliffe Arms ♀ ◖

Signposted off B4220; or reached off A4103 via Cradley

This is a pretty old black and white building in a tucked away spot with white cast-iron seats and tables in the garden. Inside, there are several cosy little rooms with a good relaxed atmosphere, and a surprisingly large choice of food. A small bar to one side has just four seats and bar stools on the slate floor, a few big ceiling beams, and big pig naïve paintings; on the right is the dining area with a woodburning stove in one room, cushioned pews and nice dining chairs, a delft shelf over the window, hops on the beams, shelves of earthenware bottles, and white walls and crisp shiny black paintwork. Good food includes sandwiches (from £1.95), soup (£2.20), and daily specials like mussels or baked avocado (£3.50), ploughman's (from £3.95), mushroom and spinach balti (£5), steak in ale pie (£6.95), chicken in tequila, cream, chillis and peppers (£7.25), beer-battered cod (£7.50), 10oz sirloin steak (£12.95), and puddings like treacle sponge or summer pudding (£2.50). Well kept Frome Valley Bitter, Hobsons, and Teme Valley T'Other on handpump, and a good choice of wines. The simple public bar has a well lit pool table, cribbage, dominoes, fruit machine, TV, and juke box; piped music. *(Recommended by John Teign, PS, Dave Braisted)*

Free house ~ Licensee Phil Jenkins ~ Real ale ~ Bar food ~ (01886) 880782 ~ Children welcome ~ occasional live music ~ Open 12-3, 6.30(7 Mon and Sun)-11; closed Monday lunchtime

MUCH MARCLE SO6633 Map 4
Slip Tavern ♀

Off A449 SW of Ledbury; take Woolhope turning at village stores, then right at pub sign

The gardens overlooking cider orchards that stretch out behind this welcoming pub are really quite splendid and full of interesting plants; the hanging baskets and big urns in front are very pretty too. The cosy chatty bar is popular with older people at lunchtime with a more villagey local atmosphere in the evening. There are ladder-back and wheelback upholstered chairs around the black tables and little country prints on neat cream walls. Well kept Hook Norton Best and Wadworths 6X on handpump, and a decent range of wines; very friendly service. A good choice of straightforward bar food includes filled rolls (from £1.70), soup (£2.10), deep-fried camembert (£3.35), ploughman's (£4.75), faggots (£5.50), cauliflower cheese (£5.85), lemon sole or home-made steak pie (£6.45), beef in ale (£7.25) and chicken kiev (£7.75). There's more space for eating in the attractively planted conservatory, though it's best to book; fruit machine; well-separated play area. *(Recommended by Derek Stafford, M A and C R Starling, Mr and Mrs I Brown, R Michael Richards, Ian and Villy White, E A Froggatt)*

Free house ~ Licensee David Templeman ~ Real ale ~ Bar food ~ Restaurant ~ (01531) 660246 ~ Children welcome ~ Open 11.30-2.30, 6.30-11; 12-2.30, 7-10.30 Sun

ORLETON SO4967 Map 6
Boot

Just off B4362 W of Woofferton

Run by genuinely friendly licensees, this 16th-c partly black and white timbered place has a relaxed pubby atmosphere. The bar has a very high-backed settle, a mix of dining and cushioned armed wheelback chairs around a few old tables on the red tiles, hops over the counter and on some beams, and a big fireplace with horsebrasses along the bressumer beam; up a couple of steps is the lounge bar with green plush banquettes right the way round the walls, mullioned windows, an exposed section of wattle and daub, and standing timbers and heavy wall beams. The small, pretty partly no-smoking restaurant is on the left. Well kept Courage Directors and Hobsons Best and Town Crier or Old Henry on handpump. Enjoyable bar food includes lunchtime snacks such as sandwiches (from £2.25), sausages (£4.25), ploughman's (from £4.25), and ham and egg (£4.50), as well as home-made soup (£2.50), home-made pâté (£3.50), grilled plaice with a grape sauce (£7.25), stilton chicken or loin of pork with a honey and mustard or cider and apple sauce (£7.50), steaks (from £9.75), puddings like treacle tart or spotted dick (from £3.25), and daily specials such as cornet of smoked salmon filled with prawn or tiger prawns in garlic butter (£4.25), vegetable lasagne or moussaka (£5.50), lasagne (£5.75), strips of chicken with mushrooms and thyme (£6.25), cod mornay and poached egg with a parsley cake (£7.25), and fillet steak topped with garlic and served with a brandy cream sauce (£9.25). The garden has seats and a brick barbecue, a fenced-in children's play area with their own tables and chairs, a wooden wendy house, and swing, and a lawn with more seats under a huge ash tree. *(Recommended by Quentin Williamson, Rob Whittle)*

*Freehouse ~ Lease: Michael Whitehurst & Maureen Hanshaw ~ Real ale ~ Bar food
(not Sun evening) ~ Restaurant ~ (01568) 780228 ~ Children till 8.30pm ~ Occasional
Irish band ~ Open 12-2.30(3 Sat), 6-11; 12-3, 7-10.30 Sun; closed Monday lunchtime*

RUCKHALL SO4539 Map 4
Ancient Camp ♀ 🛏

Ruckhall signposted off A465 W of Hereford at Belmont Abbey; from Ruckhall pub signed
down private drive; can reach it too from Bridge Sollers, W of Hereford on A438 – cross
Wye, then after a mile or so take first left, then left again to Eaton Bishop, and left to
Ruckhall

Tucked down a quiet lane, this smart country dining pub has a very special setting:
among the roses on the long front terrace, tables and chairs look down sharply on a
picturesque landscape with the River Wye curling gently through the foreground –
sometimes you can see red kites circling above the valley. If you stay the night, ask
for the room at the front which shares this view. The damage caused by landslides
at Easter 1998 has been repaired, and the welcome remains as friendly as ever.
There's quite an emphasis on the stylish (not cheap) food which might include crab
bisque (£4.95), grilled goat's cheese salad (£5.25), baby leeks and asparagus
casserole (£5.95), tomato and red onion marmalade tart (£10.50), marinated corn-
fed chicken (£11.95), red snapper salad (£12.50), local lamb or roast pork with
honey and cider (£12.95), and puddings such as sticky lime pudding and spiced
crème brûlée (from £4.95); friendly efficient staff. The very civilised central beamed
and flagstone bar is simply but thoughtfully furnished with comfortably solid
green-upholstered settles and library chairs around nice old elm tables. On the left,
a green-carpeted room has matching sofas around the walls and kitchen chairs
around tripod tables. On the right, there are simple dining chairs around stripped
kitchen tables on a brown carpet, and stripped stonework; nice log fire. Well kept
Hook Norton Best and a guest every two or so weeks such as Wye Valley St
George's Bitter on handpump, fine wines and vintage port; piped classical music;
no-smoking restaurant. The licensee owns a stretch of the river so you could
combine your stay with some fishing. *(Recommended by Mike and Mary Carter, John
Branston, Jack and Gemima Valiant, Fiona Jarman, Denys Gueroult, Richard and Margaret
Peers, Richard and Julia Tredgett)*

*Free house ~ Licensees Ewart McKie and Lisa Eland ~ Real ale ~ Bar food ~
Restaurant ~ (01981) 250449 ~ Children over 12 in main dining room ~ Open 12-
2.30, 7-11; 12-2.30 Sun; closed Sun evening and all day Mon except bank holidays ~
Bedrooms: £45S/£70B*

SELLACK SO5627 Map 4
Lough Pool ★ ♀

Back road Hoarwithy—Ross on Wye

Readers enjoy the friendly service at this attractive black and white timbered country
cottage with plenty of picnic-sets on its neat front lawn and pretty hanging baskets.
The beamed central room has kitchen chairs and cushioned window seats around
plain wooden tables on the mainly flagstoned floor, sporting prints and bunches of
dried flowers, and a log fire at each end. Other rooms lead off, with attractive
individual furnishings and nice touches like the dresser of patterned plates. The well
liked and interesting bar menu includes soup (£2.45), country game pâté (£3.25),
filled baguettes (from £3.95), ploughman's (£4.35), home-made steak and kidney pie
(£5.95), deep-fried plaice (£6.35), turkey kiev (£7.25), welsh lamb and leek curry
(£7.95), local steaks (from £9.45), daily specials including a good vegetarian choice
such as smoked aubergine, vegetable and coconut curry or asparagus crêpes (£7.95),
fruited pork loin with port (£8.95), wild boar casserole (£9.25), and puddings such
as St Clements soufflé or french raspberry and bramble tart (from £2.95); the
restaurant is no smoking. Well kept Bass, John Smiths and Wye Valley Butty Bach
on handpump, as well as a good range of malt whiskies, local farm ciders and a well
chosen reasonably priced wine list; piped classical music. *(Recommended by Guy*

Vowles, Bernard Stradling, Christoper and Jo Barton, Mike and Sue Loseby, Richard and Jean Phillips, GSB, Neil and Anita Christopher, Ted George)

Free house ~ Licensees Malcolm and Janet Hall ~ Real ale ~ Bar food (not lunchtime 25 Dec) ~ Restaurant ~ (01989) 730236 ~ Children in restaurant, snug and garden ~ Open 11.30-2.30, 6.30-11; 12-3, 6.30(7 in winter)-10.30 Sun; closed evening 25 Dec

ST OWENS CROSS SO5425 Map 4
New Inn
Junction A4137 and B4521, W of Ross on Wye

Festooned with colourful hanging baskets in summer, this unspoilt old timbered black and white coaching inn has fine views over rolling countryside to the distant Black Mountains. Both the atmospheric lounge bar and no-smoking restaurant have huge inglenook fireplaces, intriguing nooks and crannies, settles, old pews, beams, and timbers. The good straightforward bar food includes soup (£2.75), sandwiches (from £2.95), deep-fried stuffed mushrooms (£4.25), omelettes (from £4.75), bean and vegetable goulash (£6.45), home-made steak and kidney pie (£6.75), trout and bacon (£8.95), supreme of duckling in a black cherry and kirsch sauce (£10.95), steaks (from £10.95), and specials such as chicken, stilton and apricot pie or smoked haddock and prawn bake (£8.95) and braised wood pigeon or venison (£9.95); Sunday lunch, children's meals; friendly efficient service. Bass, Tetleys Bitter, Wadworths 6X and guest beers such as Hartleys XB and Smiles Best on handpump, and a fair choice of malt whiskies; darts, shove-ha'penny, cribbage, dominoes, trivia and piped music. The three dobermans are called Baileys, Tia Maria and Ginnie. *(Recommended by Dr and Mrs A K Clarke, Mr and Mrs Head, TOH, Hugh and Shirley Mortimer, Tom Evans, K H Frostick, Jill Bickerton, Bill and Pam Baker)*

Free house ~ Licensee Nigel Donovan ~ Real ale ~ Bar food ~ Restaurant ~ (01989) 730274 ~ Children welcome ~ Open 12-2.30, 6-11; 12-3, 7-10.30 Sun ~ Bedrooms: £40B/£70B

STOCKTON CROSS SO5161 Map 4
Stockton Cross Inn
Kimbolton; A4112, off A49 just N of Leominster

The old-fashioned atmosphere in the long heavily beamed bar of this small beautifully kept black and white timbered pub is probably at its best on a cold winter's day when it's really snug at the top end. Here, a handsome antique settle faces an old black kitchen range, and old leather chairs and brocaded stools sit by the huge log fire in the broad stone fireplace. There's a woodburning stove at the far end too, with heavy cast-iron-framed tables and sturdy dining chairs; there are more tables and chairs up a step in a small no-smoking side area. Old-time prints, a couple of épées on one beam and lots of copper and brass complete the picture. The extensive blackboard menu comprises the landlady's enterprising and enjoyable recipes – some of which have been broadcast on local radio – and might include soup (£2.95), sandwiches (£3.25), mixed seafood pancakes in cheese sauce (£4.50), ploughman's (from £5.25), ham and eggs (£5.95), venison sausages (£7.95), rabbit casserole (£8.50), strudel of beansprouts, peppers and mushrooms in a creamy mushroom sauce (£8.75), chicken breast in a spicy tomato and mushroom sauce (£8.95), steaks (from £10.50), roast guinea fowl wrapped in smoked bacon (£10.95), pan-fried halibut in a lemon and tarragon sauce (£12.50) and half an aylesbury duck with orange sauce (£13.95). Well kept Castle Eden and Wye Valley Butty Bach and an occasional guest from a local brewery on handpump; good welcoming service; tables out in the garden, with maybe a fine summer show of sweet peas. It can get busy at weekends. *(Recommended by Denys Gueroult, Kevin Owen, Shirley Scott, June and Mike Coleman, Mr and Mrs Hugh Spottiswoode, Christopher and Jo Barton)*

Free house ~ Licensee Mr R Wood ~ Real ale ~ Bar food ~ (01568) 612509 ~ Well behaved children welcome in eating area (must be over 6 weekdays) ~ Open 12-3, 7-11; closed Mon evening except bank holidays

ULLINGSWICK SO5949 Map 4
Three Crowns 🍴 ♀

Village off A465 S of Bromyard (and just S of Stoke Lacy) and signposted off A417 N of A465 roundabout – keep straight on through village and past turn-off to church; pub at Bleak Acre, towards Little Cowarne

Herefordshire Dining Pub of the Year

One of the friendly landlords is also the chef at this happy mix of a pub and restaurant, so while he's busy preparing excellent food, his counterparts are dispensing beer to the local farmers. Each course on the extensive seasonally changing menu now has one fixed price; starters (£4.50) might include mussel and saffron soup, hot shellfish, or truffled chicken liver parfait, vegetarian dishes (£8) such as chickpea, mushroom and lovage pancakes or moroccan vegetable platter, while other main meals (£12.50) might be grilled pieces of shark and tuna, confit of duck with apple and gooseberry relish and crispy noodles, rack of lamb with buttered spinach and sweet bread sausages or rib-eye steak; puddings such as passion fruit tart or chocolate prune and armagnac soufflé (£3.75). From a smaller lunchtime choice you might expect grilled calf's livers, shellfish linguine or mackerel recheado with naan bread and tomato and onion salad (£6); they grow their own vegetables and other produce is purchased locally. The charmingly cosy traditional interior has hops strung along the low beams of its smallish bar, a couple of traditional settles besides more usual seats, a nice mix of big old wooden tables with small round ornamental cast-iron ones, open fires and one or two gently sophisticated touches such as candles on tables and napkins; half no-smoking. Service is very welcoming; well kept Hobsons Best, Tetleys and a stronger guest ale on handpump; farmhouse ciders and good house wines; cribbage. There are tables out on the attractively planted lawn, with good summer views. They still haven't started the planned extension. *(Recommended by Dave Braisted, Mr Mann, Christopher and Jo Barton, Denys Gueroult)*

Free house ~ Licensees Sue and Derrick Horwood and Brent Castle ~ Real ale ~ Bar food (12-2, 7-9.30(9 Sun)) ~ (01432) 820279 ~ Children welcome ~ Open 12-2.30, 7-11; 12-3, 7-10.30 Sun; closed earlier maybe if empty; closed Tues

UPTON BISHOP SO6527 Map 4
Moody Cow

2 miles from M50 junction 3 westbound (or junction 4 eastbound), via B4221; continue on B4221 to rejoin at next junction

This friendly bustling pub in a sleepy peaceful village has several snug separate areas angling in an L around the bar counter, a pleasant medley of stripped country furniture, stripped floorboards and stonework, a few cow ornaments and naïve cow paintings, and a big log fire. On the far right is a biggish no-smoking restaurant, rustic and candlelit, with hop-draped rafters and a fireside area with armchairs and sofas. The far left has a second smaller dining area, just five or six tables with rush seats, green-stained woodwork, shelves of country china; piped music. The large and changing choice of food might include sandwiches (from £3.95), starters such as soup (£3.65), caramelised onions and melted goat's cheese wrapped in filo pastry (£4.95), warm salad of king prawns and smoked bacon with a lemon and garlic chive dressing (£6.50), and main courses including lasagne (£4.95), chilli (£6.85), battered cod and chips in newspaper (£7.35), ratatouille strudel (£7.95), steak, kidney, sprouts, carrots, potatoes and gravy pie (£8.20), chicken breast stuffed with stilton and wrapped in bacon with a red wine sauce (£9.95), steaks (from £11.95) and duck breast with a fresh ginger and orange sauce (£11.95); puddings such as summer berry syllabub, chocolate and orange tart and home-made ice creams (£2.95). Boddingtons, Flowers IPA, Smiles Best and Wadworths 6X on handpump. *(Recommended by Neil and Anita Christopher, P Lloyd, LM, Mrs M A Watkins, Mike and Mary Carter, Christopher and Jo Barton, June and Mike Coleman, G C Kohn)*

Free house ~ Licensee James Lloyd ~ Real ale ~ Bar food (12-2, 6.30-9.30) ~ Restaurant ~ (01989) 780470 ~ Children welcome ~ Jazz first Thurs in month ~ Open

12-2.30, 6.30-11; 12-3, 7-10.30 Sun; closed Mon (Nov-Feb) winter; closed Mon lunch in summer

WALTERSTONE SO3425 Map 6
Carpenters Arms

Village signposted off A465 E of Abergavenny, beside Old Pandy Inn; follow village signs, and keep eyes skinned for sign to pub, off to right, by lane-side barn

This delightful little stone cottage run by a chatty friendly landlady is a firm favourite with readers. Set on the edge of the Black Mountains, this is the best sort of unspoilt country tavern with ancient settles against stripped stone walls, some pieces of carpet on broad polished flagstones, a roaring log fire in a gleaming black range (complete with pot-iron, hot water tap, bread oven and salt cupboard), pewter mugs hanging from beams, the slow tick of a clock, a big vase of flowers on the dresser in the snug dining room with its mahogany tables and oak corner cupboards, and the promising aroma of stock simmering in the kitchen. Food might include sandwiches (from £1.60), soup (£2.50), farmhouse pâté (£3), ploughman's (£3.50), vegetarian lasagne, lamb korma, beef and Guinness pie or scampi (£5), chicken supreme with brandy and mushroom sauce (£7.95), and pepper fillet steak (£10); home-made puddings (£2.50). Well kept Wadsworth 6X and one of their seasonal ales such as Summer Sault tapped from the cask; farm cider. There's a separate pool room with fruit machine and juke box; the outside lavatories are cold but in character. *(Recommended by John Cockell, GSB, Mrs V Rixon)*

Free house ~ Licensee Vera Watkins ~ Bar food ~ (01873) 890353 ~ Children welcome ~ Open 12-11

WEOBLEY SO4052 Map 6
Salutation 🍴 🍷 🛏

Village signposted from A4112 SW of Leominster; and from A44 NW of Hereford (there's also a good back road direct from Hereford – straight out past S side of racecourse)

This popular beautifully kept 500-year-old hotel is in a village so quaint, even the bus shelter is black and white timbered. The two areas of the quiet, comfortable lounge – separated by a few steps and standing timbers – have a relaxed, pubby feel, brocaded modern winged settles and smaller seats, a couple of big cut-away cask seats, wildlife decorations, a hop bine over the bar counter, and logs burning in a big stone fireplace; more standing timbers separate it from the neat no-smoking restaurant area, and there's a separate smaller parquet-floored public bar with sensibly placed darts, juke box, and a fruit machine; dominoes and cribbage. The good changing bar menu might include soup (£2.90), seafood gratin (£4.65), baked baguette or cheddar ploughman's (£4.95), pan-fried lamb's kidneys (£6.50), mushroom and pepper stroganoff (£6.80), roast loin of pork or steak and stout pie (£6.95), salmon fillet with mussel cream and a hint of star anise (£7.95), and sirloin steak (£10.95); home-made puddings include dark chocolate mousse with a compote of berries or bread and butter pudding with apricot purée (£3.95); well cooked and generous breakfasts; more elaborate restaurant menu; efficient service. Well kept Hook Norton Best, Fullers London Pride and a guest on handpump, an interesting extensive wine list and 25 malt whiskies. There are tables and chairs with parasols on a sheltered back terrace. One of the very comfortable and well equipped bedrooms was due to be refurbished as we went to press; residents' fitness room. *(Recommended by Mike and Mary Carter, Andrew Shore, Mr and Mrs McKay, Francis Johnson, June and Mike Coleman, Dorothee and Dennis Glover, Peter Shaw, Kate Naylor, P M Potter, John P W Bowdler, Steve Whalley, Dr Stephen Feast, Mrs G M Roberts, Mike and Wena Stevenson, Courtney and Elaine West, Denys Gueroult; also in the Good Hotel Guide)*

Free house ~ Licensee Christopher Anthony ~ Real ale ~ Bar food ~ Restaurant ~ (01544) 318443 ~ Children in eating area of bar ~ Open 11-11; 12-10.30 Sun ~ Bedrooms: £40B/£65B

WINFORTON SO2947 Map 6
Sun

A438 14 miles W of Hereford

As well as her tasty home-made cooking, you can now enjoy a range of the landlady's chutneys, vinegars and salad dressings (1lb jars £2.50-£3.50) at this neat and friendly well run little dining pub. The regularly changing menu of interesting tasty food might include seafood chowder (£3.20), smoked venison pâté with home-made chutneys (£3.95), asparagus with a parmesan crust (£4.95), red dragon pie – leeks, aduki beans, and spices baked under a mustard mash (£6.99), welsh lamb chops with leek sauce (£8.90), duck and apricot pie (£8.99), grilled tuna basquaise (£9.50) and rook pie (£8.99); as we went to press, they had recently started to smoke their own meat and fish at the pub, and hoped to be offering dishes such as smoked chicken breast salad and smoked trout fillets on future menus. The two friendly beamed areas on either side of the central servery have an individual assortment of comfortable country-kitchen chairs, high-backed settles and good solid wooden tables, heavy-horse harness, brasses and old farm tools on the mainly stripped stone walls, and two log-burning stoves; no-smoking area. Two changing well kept ales such as Adnams, Brains, Jennings or Woods Parish Bitter on handpump, several malt whiskies, and local cider; sensibly placed darts, cribbage, dominoes, maybe piped music; no-smoking area. As well as sheltered tables and a good play area, the garden has an 18-hole pitch-and-putt/crazy golf course. *(Recommended by M Kershaw, Mike and Mary Carter, Sarah and Peter Gooderham)*

Free house ~ Licensees Brian and Wendy Hibbard ~ Real ale ~ Bar food ~ (01544) 327677 ~ Children in eating area of bar ~ Open 11.30-3, 6-11; 11.30-3, 7-11 Sun; closed Tues winter ~ Bedrooms: £32B/£50B

WOOLHOPE SO6136 Map 4
Butchers Arms

Signposted from B4224 in Fownhope; carry straight on past Woolhope village

The atmosphere at this pub remains friendly and relaxed under the caring management of the Valleys. One of the spaciously welcoming bars has very low beams decorated with hops, old-fashioned well worn built-in seats with brocaded cushions, captain's chairs and stools around small tables and a brick fireplace filled with dried flowers. The other, broadly similar though with less beams, has a large built-in settle and another log fire; there are often fresh flowers. Good well presented bar food in generous helpings includes home-made soup (£2.95), deep-fried brie with fruits of the forest (£3.95), ploughman's (from £4.75), lasagne or well liked mushroom biriani (£5.95), venison sausages and mash (£6.75), steak and kidney pie or wild rabbit braised in cider (£6.95), fresh salmon fishcakes with creamy cheese sauce (£7.25), gammon steak (£7.50) and rump steak (£8.95); good breakfasts; the restaurant is no smoking. Well kept Hook Norton Best and Old Hookey and a guest such as Shepherd Neame Spitfire on handpump, local ciders, quite a few malt whiskies, and decent wines. Sliding french windows lead from the bar to a little terrace with teak furniture, a few parasols and cheerful flowering tubs; there's also a tiny willow-lined brook. The countryside around is really lovely – to enjoy some of the best of it, turn left as you come out of the pub and take the tiny left-hand road at the end of the car park; this turns into a track and then into a path; the view from the top of the hill is quite something. *(Recommended by Martin Wyss, Mr Mann, D A Norman, R and T Kilby, Lynn Sharpless, Bob Eardley, Tony Beaulah, J Goodrich, Mike and Mary Carter, D Bryan, Ursula Hofheinz, Andy and Jill Kassube, W and E Thomas, Ian and Villy White, David Gittins, Sarah and Peter Gooderham, Paul and Sue Merrick)*

Free house ~ Licensee Mr S L Valley ~ Real ale ~ Bar food (till 10 Fri and Sat) ~ Restaurant (Sat evening and Sun lunch) ~ (01432) 860281 ~ Children welcome ~ Open 11.30-3, 6.30-11.30; 12-3, 7-10.30 Sun; closed evening 25 Dec

---

Pubs brewing their own beers are listed at the back of the book.

Crown ♀

In village centre

In order to meet the demands wrought by the increasingly popular bar food at this carefully managed old pub, the charming licensees have enlarged the no-smoking dining area, using oak posts to support a thick stone wall. The neatly kept lounge bar has plush button-back built-in wall banquettes and dark wood tables and chairs. There's also an open fire, a timbered divider strung with hop bines, good wildlife photographs and little country pictures on the cream walls, and lots of attention to details such as flowers on tables. The very extensive bar menu includes a dozen or so vegetarian dishes such as chestnut casserole with dumplings or cheese and vegetable cutlets (£5.95), and cashew nut moussaka or courgette, mushroom and spinach lasagne (£6.45); you might also find home-made soup (£2.95), home-made crab cakes (£3.55), bacon and cheese crumpet (£4.50), ploughman's (lunchtime only, from £4.95), steak and kidney pie, lamb and cranberry casserole, chilli or chicken and asparagus lasagne (£6.70), home-made fish or rabbit pie (£6.95), grilled trout with almonds (£7.70), steaks (from £9.20) and mixed grill (£10.70); home-made puddings (£3.25) include plum and almond tart or apple and raspberry crunch; children's menu; booking is advisable. Well kept Bass, Smiles Best, Wye Valley Bitter and a guest beer in summer on handpump, decent wine list, and farm cider; darts, shove-ha'penny, and table skittles. In summer the pub is festooned with flowers, there are picnic-sets on the neat front lawn, and they play quoits in the garden. *(Recommended by D A Norman, E R Pearce, Andy and Jill Kassube, Sue and Bob Ward)*

Free house ~ Licensees Neil and Sally Gordon ~ Real ale ~ Bar food ~ (01432) 860468 ~ No children after 8 ~ Open 12-2.30, 6.30-11; 12-2.30, 6-11 Sat; 12-3, 6.30-10 Sun; opens half an hour later in evenings winter; closed evening 25 Dec

Lucky Dip

Besides the fully inspected pubs, you might like to try these Lucky Dips recommended to us and described by readers (if you do, please send us reports):

Bishops Frome [SO6648]
☆ *Chase* [B4214]: Large lounge bar with log fire, separate locals' bar, wide choice of good value home-made food inc interesting dishes, beers from local small breweries, attentive friendly staff; children welcome, seats on terrace, three newly furnished comfortable bedrooms *(DAV, Bill and Pam Baker)*
Bosbury [SO6943]
Bell [B4220 N of Ledbury]: Well kept Boddingtons and Hancocks HB, decent simple food *(Francis Johnston)*
Bromyard [SO6655]
Falcon: Attractive timbered hotel with good value food inc two-course carvery and popular Sun roast; comfortable bedrooms *(W H and E Thomas)*
Craswall [SO2736]
☆ *Bulls Head* [Hay on Wye—Llanfihangel Crucorney rd via Longtown]: Old and remote, bar like a Welsh farmhouse kitchen with many original features inc beams, flagstones, 19th-c prints; well kept Flowers and Wadworths 6X tapped from the cask and served through a hatch, friendly helpful landlord, surprisingly wide range of hearty food inc vast chunks of generously filled home-baked bread, even ginger ice cream made from ewe's milk *(Frank Davidson, John Hillman, John and Joan Nash)*
Ewyas Harold [SO3929]
Temple Bar: Bass and Hobsons, usual bar food

inc baltis and excellent steak baguette, engaging landlord, proper public bar, lace tablecloths in saloon *(Francis Johnston)*
Fownhope [SO5834]
☆ *Green Man*: Striking 15th-c black and white inn, often very busy (so the friendly service can slow), with big log fire, wall settles, window seats and armchairs in one beamed bar, standing timbers dividing another, popular well priced food from sandwiches to steak inc children's and Sun carvery (no-smoking main restaurant), well kept Courage Directors, Hook Norton Best, Marstons Pedigree, John Smiths and Sam Smiths OB, Weston's farm ciders, attractive prices; children welcome, quiet garden with play area; comfortable bedrooms, good breakfast *(LYM, Mr and Mrs P Stainsby, W Ruxton, Mrs Blethyn Elliott, DAV)*
Hereford [SO5139]
Barrels [St Owens St]: Lively two-bar local, far from plush, but well worth visiting for their four own-brewed Wye Valley real ales at prices to relish, also guest beers, farm ciders from Bulmer's, Stowford Press and Weston's; open all day, live music at beer festival end Aug *(Graham Brew)*
Bay Horse [Kings Acre Rd]: Attractive biggish pub with quick friendly service and wide choice of food on colourful plates, from enjoyable sandwiches and soup up, inc vegetarian; good range of beers, well chosen wines, relaxed

comfortable atmosphere, fresh flowers, good décor, pleasant piped music throughout *(Margaret and Andrew Leach, Mrs M Russell, R C Lacey)*

Lichfield Vaults [Church St]: Half-timbered traditional pub in picturesque pedestrianised street nr cathedral, eight quickly changing real ales, nice staff; pleasant outside drinking area behind *(Quentin Williamson)*

Hoarwithy [SO5429]

☆ *New Harp* [signed off A49 Hereford—Ross on Wye]: Well kept local with good simple well priced food, well kept Bass, decent wines, helpful friendly service, games area; children welcome, picnic-sets on yew-sheltered lawn beside pretty flower garden; bedrooms good value, in cottage across road, attractive village nr River Wye, unusual Italianate church *(BB)*

Howle Hill [SO6020]

☆ *Crown* [coming from Ross fork left off B4228 on sharp right bend, first right, then left at crossroads after a mile; OS Sheet 162 map ref 603204]: Interesting location, good range of well priced food with plenty of chips and exceptional value puddings (not Sun evening, Mon; no sandwiches), well kept beers inc Wadworths 6X, friendly labradors (no visiting dogs), very cheery staff, padded pews; bar skittles, piped radio may obtrude, winter opening may be limited; tables in garden *(John Goodrich, Guy Vowles)*

Kentchurch [SO4226]

Bridge: Good bar food, Hancocks HB, farm cider, big woodburner, pool in games area; small pretty restaurant overlooking river; they have two miles of trout fishing – very welcoming new landlord gives lessons; bedrooms *(Frank Smith)*

Kingsland [SO4561]

Angel: Timbered former coaching inn redeveloped by new owner as dining pub, very wide range of good value food from filled baguettes to venison etc, attractive restaurant, relaxed beamed bar, big stove, fresh flowers, prompt friendly service, well kept ales, decent sensibly priced wines; some tables outside *(DAV, Mrs V Rixon)*

Kington [SO3057]

☆ *Olde Tavern* [just off A44 opp B4355 – follow sign to Town Centre, Hospital, Cattle Mkt; pub on right opp Elizabeth Rd, no inn sign but Estd 1767 notice]: Wonderful time-warp old place, small plain often enjoyably crowded parlour and public bar, dark brown woodwork, big windows, old settles and other antique furniture, china, pewter and curios; well kept Ansells, gas fire, no music, machines or food; children welcome, though not a family pub; cl weekday lunchtimes, outside gents' *(BB, JP, PP, Pete Baker, the Didler, Kevin Thorpe)*

Ledbury [SO7138]

☆ *Olde Talbot* [New St]: Relaxed local atmosphere in 16th-c inn's black-beamed bar rambling around island servery, antique hunting prints, plush wall banquettes or more traditional seats, log fire in big stone fireplace, Hancocks HB, Marstons and local Ledbury Challenger or Northdown, quick friendly service, good usual bar food, smart no-smoking restaurant, tales of a friendly poltergeist; fruit machine, piped music; decent bedrooms sharing bath *(D W Stokes, Rona Murdoch, D Irving, R Huggins, T McLean, E McCall, BB)*

Prince of Wales [Church Lane; narrow passage from Town Hall]: Pleasant Banks's pub tucked nicely down narrow cobbled alley, low-beamed front bars, long back room, jovial landlord, well kept low-priced beers, good cheap sandwiches, couple of tables in yard crammed with lovely flower tubs and hanging baskets *(Sue and Bob Ward, D Irving, E McCall, R Huggins, T McLean)*

Royal Oak [Southend]: Brews its own Ledbury Best, Doghill and SB, good food inc Greek dishes, welcoming landlord; comfortable bedrooms *(Bill and Pam Baker)*

Leintwardine [SO4174]

☆ *Sun* [Rosemary Lane, just off A4113]: Treasure for lovers of basic unspoilt pubs, three benches by coal fire in decades-old red-tiled front parlour off hallway, venerable landlady brings you your pint (maybe Tetleys, Ansells or Woods, from casks in her kitchen), also small settee and a couple of chairs in her sitting room; no food *(Pete Baker, JP, PP, BB, Kevin Thorpe)*

Leominster [SO4959]

Grape Vaults [Broad St]: Welcoming and attractive old local with well kept Marstons Pedigree, Best and guests; wide range of simple freshly cooked food, open fire, no games machines or music *(Mary and David Richards)*

☆ *Talbot* [West St]: Comfortable and hospitable old coaching inn in charming town, heavy beams and standing timbers, antique carved settles, log fires with 18th-c oak-panelled chimneybreasts, sporting prints; decent straightforward home-made bar food inc good sandwiches, well kept Scottish Courage ales, good coffee, warmly friendly service; piped music; bedrooms *(LYM, Mary and David Richards, E G Parish)*

Three Horseshoes [Corn Sq]: Cosy Tudor pub with two real ales and two local farm ciders, very good value sandwiches, unspoilt beamed bar *(Quentin Williamson)*

Lingen [SO3767]

☆ *Royal George*: Charming archetypal English pub (with very friendly Australian licensees) combined with PO and shop, well kept Bass, Hook Norton and Morlands Old Speckled Hen, good cheap food (best to book for Sun lunch), coal fire, plenty of tables in big garden with good hill views, play area, fenced-off water garden; in beautiful country setting nr Kim Davis's alpine nursery and garden *(Dr Philip Jackson, Patricia Heptinstall, Mary and David Richards)*

Luntley [SO3956]

Cider House [off A44 in Pembridge at New Inn]: Airy country restaurant (not pub) but with an organic real ale and six excellent ciders and perries made on the premises; quite short menu inc cider/perry recipes, cooked to order (so may be a wait); can taste and buy from the cider farm *(BB, Mary and David Richards)*

Michaelchurch Escley [SO3134]

☆ *Bridge Inn* [off back rd SE of Hay on Wye, along Escley Brook valley]: Remote homely black-beamed riverside inn delightfully tucked away in attractive valley, several well kept ales and farm ciders, good simple food from sandwiches to steaks, obliging new owners, children welcome; seats out on waterside terrace, field for camping, good walks; has been open all day Sat (*LYM, John Brightley, Andrew Rogers, Amanda Milsom, M and A Leach, Kerry Law, Simon Smith*)

Mordiford [SO5737]

Moon [just off B4224 SE of Hereford]: Lounge with roaring fire, good value food from filled baked potatoes to unusual dishes of the day, front restaurant, friendly relaxed service, Bass, Boddingtons, Flowers IPA and Wye Valley Bitter, local farm ciders, reasonably priced wines; back bar popular with young locals (*Mr and Mrs R A Buckler, Fran and John Riley*)

Much Marcle [SO6633]

Walwyn Arms [A449 Ledbury—Ross on Wye]: Rambling former courthousedoing well under enthusiastic and friendly new landlord; chatty bustle, well kept Flowers IPA, Wadworths 6X and a guest beer, limited range of reasonably priced generous food inc popular Sun lunch; darts, pool room, long skittle alley – very child-friendly; grass for camping (*Ian and Nita Cooper*)

Westons Cider Factory [off A449]: Bar/restaurant in enjoyable cider factory with very good value generous home-made lunchtime food (not open Mon-Weds; open as restaurant Thurs-Sat evening), friendly service, two or three beers as well as good range of their own cider and perry (*Peter Lloyd*)

Norton Canon [SO3848]

Three Horseshoes [A480 Yazor—Eccles Green]: Basic two-bar country pub worth knowing for the Shoes ales it brews; log fire, old juke box, lunchtime food, children welcome, tables in orchard; one of the only two pubs we know of with an indoor shooting gallery (*Kevin Thorpe*)

Orcop Hill [SO4728]

Fountain [off A466 S of Hereford]: Small village pub run by three very friendly helpful sisters, locals' bar leading into small pleasant restaurant, wide range of carefully cooked well presented food esp excellent fish (*Mr and Mrs J T Grugeon*)

Pembridge [SO3958]

☆ *New Inn* [Market Sq (A44)]: Ancient inn overlooking small black and white town's church, comfortable and atmospheric three-room bar, antique settles, worn flagstones, substantial log fire, one room with sofas, pine furniture and books, good food from sandwiches up inc tender meat and interesting vegetarian dishes, attentive friendly staff, well kept Ruddles Best and County, Theakstons and a guest beer, farm cider, traditional games; quiet little family dining room (not Sun evening); outside lavatories, simple bedrooms (*LYM, A J Bowen, G W Bernard, Christoper and Jo Barton*)

Priors Frome [SO5739]

☆ *Yew Tree* [off A438 at Dormington, then second left and right at T; or off B4224 at Mordiford E of Hereford; OS Sheet 149 map ref 575390]: Country local with Tetleys-related ales, occasional guests such as Shepherd Neame or Smiles, surprisingly good imaginative generous food inc lunchtime carvery in simple bar and rather more ambitious downstairs restaurant, friendly service; terrace, fine views across Frome Valley to Black Mountains (*BB, Paul and Sue Merrick*)

Ross on Wye [SO6024]

☆ *Hope & Anchor* [Riverside; coming from A40 W side, 1st left after bridge]: Big-windowed family extension looking out on well kept flower-lined lawns leading down to river, plenty of tables out here (and summer ice-cream bar and barbecues), thoroughgoing boating theme in softly lit cheery main bar, cosy upstairs parlour bar and Victorian-style dining room, generous good value food inc good choice for children, well kept Banks's and Marstons Pedigree, farm cider, good house wine, attractive prices; open all day, can be crowded weekends (*LYM, E G Parish, Rachael and Mark Baynham, Michael and Gillian Ford, June and Mike Coleman, Steve Thomas, Tom L Rees*)

Kings Head [High St]: Comfortably old-fashioned beamed and panelled hotel bar, locally popular for generous good value lunchtime food inc home-made soup, good sandwiches (try their own ham), toasties and baked potatoes, swift friendly service, evening restaurant; open all day, bedrooms (*Peter Lloyd, Derek Bartlett*)

White Lion [Wilton]: Nice relaxing pub prettily placed in small hamlet just outside, garden sloping gently to banks of River Wye; well kept Hook Norton, good value food; outbuilding for children; bedrooms (*Dr I Crichton*)

Shobdon [SO4062]

Bateman Arms: Comfortable two-bar local with good interesting if not cheap food inc vegetarian choice and club sandwiches, good range of well kept ales, friendly father and son; restaurant, bedrooms (*Dorothy and Leslie Pilson, DAV*)

Staunton on Wye [SO3645]

New Inn: Pleasantly relaxed old-fashioned 16th-c village inn, congenial helpful landlord, roomy bar with cosy alcoves, good value generous home-cooked food in bar and restaurant inc vegetarian and local ingredients and cheeses, changing beers inc Wye Valley (*Dr Michael Smith, R J Richards*)

Symonds Yat [SO5615]

☆ *Saracens Head* [Symonds Yat E, by ferry, ie over on the Gloucs bank]: Riverside beauty spot next to ferry, busy down-to-earth flagstoned bar popular with canoeists, mountain bikers and hikers, cheerful staff, good range of well presented nourishing food inc vegetarian, Theakstons Best, XB and Old Peculier and Wye Valley, three farm ciders, settles and window seats; cosy carpeted restaurant, games bar with pool, piped jazz and blues, SkyTV, lots of waterside tables outside, live music Thurs; summer boat trips, parking

cheaper beyond Royal Hotel *(Giles Francis, Rona Murdoch, R Mann, Denys Gueroult, Stuart and Alison Wallace, Arthur and Margaret Dickinson)*
Titley [SO3360]

☆ *Stagg:* New owners doing outstanding food, all fresh, from cheese and pear chutney sandwich, crispy duck leg with cider sauce or unbeatable steak sandwich to local beef fillet with celeriac purée and wild mushrooms or duck breast with honey and ginger and teriyaki, fresh exotic salads and veg; tiny bar, good wines, Hobsons and a guest beer; tables in garden *(Hywel Jones, Gemma Tucker)*
Upper Colwall [SO7643]

Chase [Chase Rd, off B4218 Malvern—Colwall, 1st left after hilltop on bend going W]: Great views from attractive garden and refined and comfortable lounge of genteel rather clubby two-bar pub on Malvern Hills, well kept Donnington BB and SBA, Hobsons BB and Wye Valley Dorthy Goodbodys seasonal ales, limited choice of good bar food *(anon)*
Walton [SO3057]

Crown [A44 W of Kington]: Landlady cooks good food all day every day; no music *(Dorothy and Leslie Pilson)*
Wellington [SO4948]

Wellington [off A49 N of Hereford]: Recently plainly refurbished, with well kept beers such as Fullers London Pride, Hancocks HB, Highgate and Wallsall Fox Nob, log fire, generous good food in bar and candlelit restaurant, quiet classical piped music, good service; no machines *(Mr and Mrs M Wade, F C Johnston)*
Wellington Heath [SO7141]

☆ *Farmers Arms* [off B4214 just N of Ledbury – pub signed right, at top of village]: Big much modernised pub, doing well under new owners with a fine GPG track record, setting the same standards for good food and service as at their previous Hunters at Longdon; plenty of comfortable plush banquettes, flame-effect gas fire, soft lighting from Tiffany-style lamps, a few big country prints, Marstons Bitter, Pedigree and Oatmeal Stout *(BB, EML)*
Whitney on Wye [SO2747]

☆ *Rhydspence* [A438 Hereford—Brecon]: Very picturesque ancient black and white country inn right on Welsh border, with attractive old-fashioned furnishings, heavy beams and timbers in rambling spick-and-span rooms, good interesting food using local produce in bar and more expensive pretty dining room, Bass, Hook Norton Best and Robinsons Best, Dunkerton's farm cider, good wine choice, log fire, attentive service; children welcome, tables in attractive garden with fine views over Wye valley; comfortable bedrooms *(LYM, Paul Tindall, Stephanie Smith)*

Post Office address codings confusingly give the impression that some pubs are in Herefordshire, when they're really in Shropshire or even Wales (which is where we list them).

Hertfordshire

The county's pubs are going through something of a renaissance, with several newcomers to the main entries this year: the Gibraltar Castle at Batford with its warmly welcoming Irish landlord; the businesslike but attractively converted Moor Mill at Bricket Wood – a refuge from the motorways; the pristine and stylish Holly Bush at Potters Crouch; the Cabinet at Reed (welcoming new licensees since it was last in these pages – they've turned it into an attractive dining pub); and the cosy 17th-c Cock at Sarratt. Other places doing particularly well these days include the very welcoming Jolly Waggoner at Ardeley (good home cooking), the busy Lytton Arms at Knebworth (fine real ales), the Rose & Crown in St Albans (good atmosphere, great sandwiches), the civilised old George & Dragon at Watton at Stone, and the friendly Sword in Hand at Westmill. These last two both stand out for good food; the George & Dragon at Watton at Stone has rather more of the feel of a special occasion, and is our Hertfordshire Dining Pub of the Year. In the Lucky Dip section at the end of the chapter, current front-runners are the Valiant Trooper at Aldbury, Elephant & Castle at Amwell, Alford Arms at Frithsden, Rising Sun at Halls Green, Nags Head at Little Hadham, Garibaldi in St Albans and Sow & Pigs at Wadesmill. Drinks prices here are rather above the national average; Fullers pubs tend to be among the cheapest here, with Greene King becoming an increasingly dominant presence.

ALDBURY SP9612 Map 4
Greyhound

Stocks Road; village signposted from A4251 Tring—Berkhamsted, or reached directly from roundabout at E end of A41 Tring bypass

The combination of good food, friendly service and a warm welcome keeps this attractive country pub popular with readers. Prettily set below the Chilterns backdrop of the Ashridge Estate (National Trust), it has tables outside facing the village green, complete with stocks, duck pond – and plenty of vociferous ducks. The handsome Georgian frontage is especially so in autumn, when the virginia creeper is a brilliant counterpoint to the bronzing leaves of the beechwoods on the slopes behind. Inside, there are signs of an older building – around the copper-hooded inglenook, for example – and a thriving atmosphere pervades the two main rooms (with plenty of tables) that ramble off each side of the drinks and food serving areas. Good bar food in generous helpings includes sandwiches (from £2.20, with soup £4.25), soup (£3.45), ploughman's (from £4.50), baked potatoes (from £4.95), griddle cooked beef burger (£5.15), breaded plaice, game sausage casserole or sweet and sour mixed vegetables (£5.95), lasagne, ham and double egg or steak and ale pie (£6.95), grilled gammon or pork and apricot with dumplings (£7.50) and chicken breast topped with bacon and cheese in a barbecue sauce (£8.50). Well kept Aldbury Ale (brewed for the pub by Tring Brewery), Badgers Dorset Best and Tanglefoot and a guest on handpump. There's a weekday early evening happy hour (5-7pm), and service remains smiling and efficient even when under pressure. They don't mind well behaved dogs, and keep plastic bags by the entrance for muddy boots; no-smoking area. The garden is pleasant, and good walks abound nearby, for instance, around the monument to the canal mogul, the 3rd Duke of Bridgwater, up on the escarpment; for the more sedentarily inclined, the toll road through the Ashridge

Estate is very attractive. *(Recommended by David and Ruth Shillitoe, Klaus and Elizabeth Leist, Gwen and Peter Andrews, Catherine and Richard Preston)*

Badger ~ Manager Jo Coletta ~ Real ale ~ Bar food (12-2.30, 7-9.30 Mon-Sat; 12-8 Sun) ~ Restaurant ~ (01442) 851228 ~ Children away from bar ~ Open 11-11; 12-10.30 Sun ~ Bedrooms: £43.55S/£49.50B

ARDELEY TL3027 Map 5
Jolly Waggoner

Charming little pink-washed inn peacefully set in a pretty tucked-away village, handy for Cromer Windmill. The comfortable bar has lots of open woodwork and a relaxed and civilised atmosphere, while the restaurant (extended into the cottage next door) is decorated with modern prints. The well liked unpretentious bar food is carefully prepared using fresh local produce, and in addition to sandwiches (from £2.45) and soup (£4), might include tomato and mozzarella salad (£5.50), home-made burgers (from £5.50), vegetable and pasta bake (£5.95), fresh crab or mussels (£6), omelette Arnold Bennett (£6.95), chicken in wine, garlic and cream or salmon fillet on parmesan pasta (£9.95), calf's liver with sage and butter or roquefort cheese and horseradish (£11.50), sea bass (£15.95) and delicious puddings such as chocolate truffle torte, pineapple crème brûlée or lemon tart (£3.95); booking is essential for their Sunday lunch, and there's a £1 surcharge for credit cards. Well kept Greene King IPA tapped from the cask and Abbot on handpump, a good range of wines and freshly squeezed orange juice in summer; darts and maybe piped music. The landlord also runs a main entry pub at Cottered. *(Recommended by Peter and Joan Elbra, Amanda Hill, David Halliwell, Charles Bardswell, Eddie Edwards, Catherine and Richard Preston)*

Greene King ~ Lease: Darren Perkins ~ Real ale ~ Bar food (not Sun evenings) ~ Restaurant ~ (01438) 861350 ~ Well behaved children over seven welcome ~ Open 12-2.30(3 Sat), 6.30-11; 12-3, 7-10.30 Sun; closed Mon except bank holidays

ASHWELL TL2639 Map 5
Three Tuns

High St

The opulently Victorian lounge lends this flower-decked 18th-c inn the atmosphere of a pleasantly old-fashioned but unstuffy hotel. Alongside comfortable chairs and some big family tables, there are lots of pictures, stuffed pheasants and fish, and antiques. Well presented food includes sandwiches (from £2.25), soup (£2.95), ploughman's (from £3.95), blue cheese and broccoli quiche or vegetable pasta bake (£5.95), steak and kidney pie (£6.50), steaks (from £9.95), and daily specials such as grilled halibut with prawns and herb butter or grilled lamb chops with tomatoes and mushrooms (£9.95); home-made puddings (from £2.50). Well kept Greene King IPA, Abbot and a guest such as Marstons Pedigree under light blanket pressure, and a good choice of wines. It can get very busy, especially on summer weekends. The simpler more modern public bar has pool, darts, dominoes and a fruit machine; piped music, boules. The six bedrooms were refurbished in 1998, and include one with a four-poster bed, and another with its own dressing room. *(Recommended by Anthony Barnes, G Neighbour, Ian Phillips)*

Greene King ~ Tenants Claire and Darrell Stanley ~ Real ale ~ Bar food (12-2.30, 6-9.30; 12-9.30 wknds) ~ Restaurant ~ (01462) 742107 ~ Children in eating area of bar and restaurant ~ Occasional live entertainment ~ Open 11-11; 12-10.30 Sun ~ Bedrooms: £35B/£55B

Post Office address codings confusingly give the impression that some pubs are in Hertfordshire, when they're really in Bedfordshire or Cambridgeshire (which is where we list them).

AYOT ST LAWRENCE TL1916 Map 5
Brocket Arms

B651 N of St Albans for about 6 miles; village signposted on right after Wheathampstead and Mid Herts golf course; or B653 NE of Luton, then right on to B651

The pleasant mix of locals and visitors at this ancient pub mightn't always be corporeal – it's said to be haunted by the ghost of a Catholic priest who was tried and hanged here during the Reformation. The two very traditional low-ceilinged rooms have sturdy oak beams, a big inglenook fireplace (with a woodburning stove in the back room), old-fashioned furnishings and magazines to read; darts, dominoes and piped classical music. Adnams Broadside, Greene King IPA and Abbot, Wadworths 6X under light blanket pressure on handpump and two guests tapped from the cask; around a dozen wines by the glass. Straightforward lunchtime bar food includes sandwiches (from £2.50), soup (£3.50), filled baked potatoes (from £3.50), ploughman's (from £4.50), pasties (£4.75), macaroni cheese (£5), steak and kidney pie (£7.50), and 8oz sirloin steak (£12); no-smoking area in restaurant. It can get very crowded at weekends. The extensive south-facing suntrap walled garden has a summer bar and a children's play area. Tranquilly set in attractive countryside, it's handy for Shaw's Corner. *(Recommended by Mick and Hilary Stirrin, Ian Phillips, Barry and Marie Males, Elizabeth and Alan Walker, G D K Fraser)*

Free house ~ Licensee Toby Wingfield Digby ~ Bar food (reduced menu Sun and Mon evenings) ~ Restaurant ~ (01438) 820250 ~ Children welcome ~ Occasional live entertainment ~ Open 11-11; 12-11 Sun ~ Bedrooms: £45/£60(£65B)

BATFORD TL1415 Map 5
Gibraltar Castle

Lower Luton Rd; B653, S of B652 junction

The cheery Irish licensees at this cosy old roadside pub work hard to make visitors feel at home; the landlord is likely to sit and chat even if you've just popped in for a quick mineral water. There's an interesting collection of militaria, particularly at the end on the right as you go in, which has something of the feel of a hunting lodge; the low beams found elsewhere give way to soaring rafters, and glass cases show off pristinely kept uniforms, bullets, medals and rifles. Welcoming and friendly, the rest of the long carpeted bar has plenty to look at too, with a nice old fireplace, comfortably cushioned wall benches, and a couple of snugly intimate window alcoves, one with a fine old clock. The piano is put to good use on Tuesday evenings, when there's live Irish music; the pub can get busy then, but it's the kind of place that keeps its charm whether it's crowded or quiet. Well kept Fullers Chiswick, ESB, London Pride and seasonal brews on handpump, a good range of malt whiskies, well made Irish coffee, and a thoughtful choice of wines by the glass; piped music, cribbage, dominoes. The good honest bar food is popular with locals and passing businessmen, with a menu that might include club sandwiches (£2.50), soup (£2.95), steak and kidney pie or potato, leek and cheese bake (£5.95), sirloin steak with sautéed mushroom and onion (£8.95), sticky toffee pudding (£2.95), and specials such as smoked salmon soda bread with lemon and dill dressing (£5.95); booking is recommended for their good value Sunday roast (£5.95). There are a few tables in front by the road, and the hanging baskets and tubs out here have won a couple of local awards. They plan to improve the courtyard behind, and hope to open bedrooms some time this year. *(Recommended by N S Doolan, R A Buckler)*

Fullers ~ Tenant Derek Phelan ~ Real ale ~ Bar food ~ (01582) 460005 ~ Children welcome during food service ~ Live music Thurs evening ~ Open 11-3, 5-11; 12-3, 6-10.30 Sun; closed 25 Dec evening

BERKHAMSTED SP9807 Map 5
Boat
Gravel Path

Despite it being only 10 years old, readers are pleasantly surprised by the charming atmosphere at this beautifully set little canalside pub. Recent refurbishment has increased the dining area and besides sandwiches (from £2.65), soup (£2.95) and ploughman's (£4.95), changing bar food might include penne with sun-dried tomato and pesto (£5.95), steak and ale pie (£6.50), fresh cod in beer batter (£6.95), breaded turkey escalope topped with cheese and ham (£7.75), and fish specials such as salmon fillet on fettucine with white wine and cream sauce (£8.25). Friendly staff serve well kept and reasonably priced Fullers Chiswick, ESB, London Pride and a Fullers seasonal ale on handpump; good wine list. Fruit machine and piped music; no-smoking area at lunchtime. Over 21s only on Friday and Saturday nights when they don't serve food because it's so busy. A terrace overlooks the canal. *(Recommended by Pat and Tony Martin, Nigel and Amanda Thorp, Tracey and Stephen Groves, Quentin Williamson)*

Fullers ~ Manager Jane Bravey ~ Real ale ~ Bar food (12-3 daily, 6-9 Sun-Thurs) ~ (01422) 877152 ~ Children till 8pm ~ Open 11-11; 12-10.30 Sun

BRICKET WOOD TL1502 Map 5
Moor Mill
Off Smug Oak Lane; turn at the Gate pub and entrance is a little further on the left; 2 miles from M1 junction 6, but a bit of a maze getting through Bricket Wood; Smug Oak Lane is off Lye Lane, on the far side, towards Colney Street and the A5183

Best on a sunny day, this well converted 18th-c mill is hardly an undiscovered haven, but it's a useful and unexpected retreat from the M25 or M1. The current building dates from 1762, though a mill is thought to have stood on this site for around 1,000 years. Flour production stopped in 1939 and the mill fell into disrepair, until it was restored and developed by Whitbreads in 1992. Now it's a bustling little complex, with one of the company's Travel Inns immediately alongside, and a busy Beefeater restaurant upstairs in the mill itself. The pristine white-painted exterior looks much as it must have done in its prime, and ducks and other birds still potter happily around the millpond. There are masses of wooden picnic-sets out here, though the motorway noise is never far away. On very warm days they may have a separate outside servery, with sandwiches and a few hot dishes. Children have plenty of space to run around, as well as a massive fenced-off play area for under-9s, with quite a collection of slides, swings and so on. Inside many of the original features remain intact: behind glass, down a little corridor leading to the bar, you can still see one of the huge mill wheels churning determinedly through the water. Displays on the wall reveal interesting bits of history, including a detailed cross-section of exactly how the mill used to work. The smallish bar has beams, brick walls and a flagstone floor, with a few wooden tables and chairs; a passageway leads to a wood-floored room with more tables. There's further indoor seating at the opposite end of the building, as well as in a carpeted room upstairs with a real fire; some areas are no smoking. Beers such as Wadworths 6X on handpump, and bar snacks, served all day, include club sandwiches, baked potatoes, and changing hot dishes such as chicken tikka (all around £4); fruit machines, maybe loudish piped music. *(Recommended by CMW, JJW)*

Whitbreads ~ Manager T Bambury ~ Real ale ~ Bar food (12-10) ~ Restaurant ~ (01727) 875557 ~ Children in eating area of bar and restaurant ~ Open 12-11; 12-10.30 Sun ~ Bedrooms: /£39.95B

'Children welcome' means the pub says it lets children inside without any special restriction. If it allows them in, but to restricted areas such as an eating area or family room, we specify this. Some pubs may impose an evening time limit.

BURNHAM GREEN TL2516 Map 5
White Horse £

N of Welwyn, just E of railway bridge by Welwyn Station

This busy dining pub fills up quickly at lunchtime and readers suggest you should arrive in good time to secure a table. As we went to press, the Old Monk Pub Company had just taken it over, and they told us that a major refurbishment planned for the autumn would not interfere with the pub's décor. An original black-beamed area by the bar has solid traditional furnishings, hunting prints and corner china cupboards, and there are log-effect gas fires in two small communicating areas. A two-floor extension with pitched rafters in its upper gallery has many more tables; no-smoking downstairs. Well prepared reasonably priced food includes soup and sandwiches (from £2.95), potato skins with sour cream and bacon (£3.75), big baps (from £4.75), local sausages or ham, egg and chips (£4.95), ploughman's, roasted vegetable lasagne or 6oz beefburger (£5.25), half a roast chicken or lasagne (£5.50), battered cod (£6.25), steaks (from £10.50), fresh seafood specials such as crab and avocado salad (£5.95) and puddings including coffee and Tia Maria cheesecake or lemon meringue pie (£2.95). There's a more elaborate restaurant menu. Readers enjoy the gentle country view from the back brick terrace by a fountain, with neat green garden furniture, large umbrellas and outdoor heaters, so you can eat outside even on cooler evenings; rustic benches on grass by a pond beyond. Children under 16 are not allowed in this garden unless they stay seated as the water is deep, but there is lots of room to play on the broad green in front. Well kept Adnams, Brakspear, Greene King IPA and Abbot and Theakstons Old Peculier on handpump; piped music. The pub holds a ball every summer. *(Recommended by G Neighbour, Ian and Sandra Robey, Paul and Sandra Embleton, Phil and Heidi Cook, A C Morrison, Ian Phillips, Lynn Sharpless, Bob Eardley, Barry and Marie Males, George Atkinson, Greg Kilminster)*

Old Monk ~ Manager Victoria Harman ~ Real ale ~ Bar food ~ Restaurant ~ (01438) 798416 ~ Children in eating area of bar and restaurant ~ Open 11.30-3, 6-11; 12-4, 7-10.30 Sun

COTTERED TL3129 Map 5
Bull

A507 W of Buntingford

This old tree-surrounded inn, prettily placed opposite a row of thatched cottages, shares the same landlord as the Jolly Waggoner at Ardeley, and so consequently, bar food is of a similarly high standard: sandwiches (from £2.50), soup (£4), ploughman's (from £5.50), steak, Guinness and stilton pie or mushroom and sweet pepper stroganoff (£7.50), chicken in a creamy cheese and leek sauce in a corn crêpe (£10), pork fillet topped with cream, stilton and walnuts (£11), beef sirloin with red wine, tomato and fresh horseradish sauce (£12.50), and home-made puddings such as bread and brandy pudding, fruit crème brûlée or white chocolate cheesecake with a coffee and bitter orange sauce (£2.95); there's a £1 surcharge for credit cards. The roomy and comfortable low-beamed front lounge has antiques on a stripped wood floor, as well as lots of horsebrasses, and a good fire. A second bar has darts, a fruit machine, shove-ha'penny, cribbage and dominoes. Well kept Greene King IPA and Abbot on handpump, decent wines; prompt friendly service. There are benches and tables in the sizeable garden, a play area and maybe boules. *(Recommended by D Barlow, A J Goddard, Phil and Heidi Cook, Prof John and Patricia White, Charles Bardswell, Danny Nicol, B and M Kendall, E J Cutting)*

Greene King ~ Lease: Darren Perkins ~ Real ale ~ Bar food (not Tues evening) ~ Restaurant ~ (01763) 281243 ~ Well behaved children over seven welcome ~ Open 12-2.30(3 Sat), 6.30-11; 12-3, 7-10.30 Sun

> If you book a bedroom, you should ask for written confirmation – this last year or two a small but disturbing number of readers have found they've been double-booked, or the pub has denied all knowledge of their booking.

FLAUNDEN TL0100 Map 5
Bricklayers Arms

Village signposted from A41; Hogpits Bottom – from village centre follow Boxmoor, Bovingdon road and turn right at Belsize, Watford signpost

The model gorilla that once stood by the bar at this warmly decorated pub has been stolen. However, a friendly barmaid told us that a postcard from the errant primate revealed that he was being well looked after by his new owners – a giant frog now joins the life-size bronze dogs in his place. The low-beamed bar with roaring log fires has dark brown traditional wooden wall seats and stubs of knocked-through oak-timbered walls that maintain a feeling of intimacy in the three areas that used to be separate rooms. A very well kept range of half a dozen or so real ales on handpump might include Chiltern Beechwood, Fullers London Pride, Marstons Pedigree and four weekly changing guests such as Slaters Premium and Top Totty, and Titanic Captain Smiths and White Wash. Bar food includes sandwiches (from £3.25), ploughman's (from £4.45), stilton and leek pie or spaghetti carbonara (£5.95 with or without ham), filled yorkshire puddings (£5.95-£6.45), deep-fried cod (£6.25), and beef and ale pie (£6.95); puddings (from £2.75); a more elaborate restaurant menu can be eaten throughout the pub. In summer, tables in the old-fashioned garden are surrounded by foxgloves against sheltering hawthorn and ivy hedges. Just up the Belsize road there's a path on the left, through woods, to more forestry around Hollow Hedge. *(Recommended by Bob and Maggie Atherton, R C Morgan, Peter and Mavis Brigginshaw, Peter and Giff Bennett, Paul Coleman, Nigel and Amanda Thorp, BKA, Tracey and Stephen Groves, Peter Saville, David and Ruth Shillitoe, Comus Elliott)*

Free house ~ Licensees Rob Mitchell and P Frazer ~ Real ale ~ Bar food ~ Restaurant ~ (01442) 833322 ~ Children in restaurant ~ Open 11.30-2.30, 6-11; 11-11 Sat; 12-10.30 Sun; 11-3, 6-11 Sat winter; 12-4, 7-10.30 Sun winter

KNEBWORTH TL2320 Map 5
Lytton Arms ◖

Park Lane, Old Knebworth, 3 miles from A1(M) junction 7; A602 towards Stevenage, 2nd roundabout right on B197 towards Knebworth, then right into Old Knebworth Lane; at village T-junction, right towards Codicote

The real-ale total has now exceeded 3,000 over the past eleven years at this friendly Victorian brick pub, originally built for the long-defunct Hawkes & Company brewery of Bishop's Stortford. At any one time, besides nine guests such as Cottage Gold Rush, McMullens Country Bitter or Nethergates Umbel Ale, you should find well kept Bass, Fullers London Pride, own brew Millennium Ale and Woodfordes Wherry on handpump; also Stfrom beer from Prague on draught, 50 Belgian bottled beers and malt whiskies, country wines, up to four farm ciders, and hot chocolate and herb teas as well as coffee. The pub hosts beer festivals in spring and autumn, and in winter, they serve hot gluhwein by the log fire where chestnuts are roasted. Several solidly furnished simple big-windowed rooms, some panelled and each with a slightly different décor (railway memorabilia here, old Knebworth estate photographs there), ramble around the big central servery, ending in a newish no-smoking conservatory with orderly pale tables on its shiny brown tiles. Straightforward bar food includes soup (£2.60), sandwiches (from £2.90), deep-fried whitebait (£4.20), ham salad (£5.85), roast beef and yorkshire pudding (£6.40), well liked steak and kidney pie or lasagne, whole rack of pork ribs in barbecue sauce (£8.50), and daily specials such as mushroom stroganoff (£5.95) and chicken lasagne (£6.50); puddings (£2.60); possible delays when busy. There are picnic-sets and a giant chessboard on a terrace in front, and the back garden has a play area; dominoes and shove-ha'penny. The two cats are called Rumpole and Pitkin. *(Recommended by Peter Saville, George Atkinson, Ian Phillips, Enid and Henry Stephens, Pat and Tony Martin)*

Free house ~ Licensee Stephen Nye ~ Real ale ~ Bar food (12-2, 6.30-9.30) ~ (01438) 812312 ~ Well behaved children in eating area of bar till 9 ~ Open 11-3, 5-11 Mon-Weds, 11-11 Thurs-Sat; 12-10.30 Sun; closed evening 25 Dec and afternoons Mon-Thurs winter

POTTERS CROUCH TL1105 Map 5

Holly Bush ◀

Off A4147

A delight inside and out, this exquisitely kept pub has an elegantly timeless feel in its meticulously furnished bar. Everything is spotless and displays unusually dedicated attention to detail, and thoughtfully positioned fixtures create the illusion that there are lots of different rooms – some of which wouldn't be out of place in a smart country house. In the evenings neatly positioned candlesticks cast shadows over the mix of darkly gleaming varnished tables, all of which have fresh flowers, and, adding to the classy feel, china plates as ashtrays. There are quite a few antique dressers, several with plates on, as well as a number of comfortable cushioned settles, the odd plant, a stuffed fox's head, some antlers, a fine old clock, and carefully illuminated prints and pictures; a big fireplace is on the left as you go in. Needless to say, it's not the kind of place where you'll find fruit machines or piped music. The long, stepped bar counter has particularly well kept Fullers Chiswick, ESB and London Pride on handpump, and the sort of old-fashioned till you rarely see in this hi-tech age. Bar food is served lunchtimes only (not Sun), from a menu that includes sandwiches (from £2.20, toasted from £2.60), burgers (from £3.60) filled baked potatoes (from £4), ploughman's (from £4.80), and chilli (£5.30). Behind the very pretty wisteria-covered, white-painted cottagey building is a big fenced-off garden, with a nice lawn, some handsome trees, and good quality wooden tables and chairs. No dogs. Though the pub seems to stand alone on a quiet little road, it's only a few minutes from the centre of St Albans, and is very handy for the Gardens of the Rose. *(Recommended by Tracey and Stephen Groves, Peter and Giff Bennett, BKA, Mick and Hilary Stiffin)*

Fullers ~ Tenant R S Taylor ~ Real ale ~ Bar food (lunchtime) ~ (01727) 851792 ~ Open 11.30-2.30, 6-11; 12-2.30, 7-10.30 Sun

REED TL3636 Map 5

Cabinet

High Street; village signposted from A10

Having been an alehouse for centuries, this tiled and weatherboarded village house is now a civilised dining pub. The lounge bar has been converted into a no-smoking restaurant with stripped floors, a simple mix of wooden chairs and tables, a log fire in winter, and views over the sizeable back lawn. In the evenings, locals still gather in the cosy public bar, where there's a friendly relaxed atmosphere and comfortable seating by the inglenook fireplace; darts, dominoes and cribbage in the adjoining snug. A changing blackboard menu might include soup (£2.50), sandwiches (from £2.50), sausages with herb mash (£4.95), hearty baguettes filled with either chargrilled chicken or home smoked ham, with chips and salad (£5.25), pancakes filled with spinach and ricotta (£5.95), chilled poached salmon salad or steak, mushroom and ale pie (£6.95), and rib-eye steak (from £8.95); puddings (from £2.75); more elaborate restaurant menu. Well kept Abbot, Cabinet Ale (brewed for the pub by Greene King), and two guests on handpump. *(Recommended by Howard and Sue Gascoyne, Erna and Sidney Wells)*

Free house ~ Licensee Ross Moynihan ~ Real ale ~ Bar food ~ Restaurant ~ (01763) 848366 ~ Children welcome ~ Open 12-3, 6-11; 12-4, 7-10.30 Sun

SARRATT TQ0499 Map 5

Cock

Church End: a very pretty approach is via North Hill, a lane N off A404, just under a mile W of A405

Readers enjoy relaxing outside at this cosy white 17th-c country pub; benches in front look across a quiet lane towards the churchyard, while at the back there's an outside summer bar on a terrace, and tables under umbrellas on a pretty sheltered lawn with a children's play area and open country views. The latched door opens into a carpeted snug with a vaulted ceiling, original bread oven, bar stools and a television. Through an archway, the partly oak-panelled cream-walled lounge has a log fire in an inglenook, pretty Liberty-style curtains, pink plush chairs at dark oak tables, and lots of interesting artefacts. Well liked straightforward bar food in generous helpings includes sandwiches (from £2.95), ploughman's (from £4.25), wild boar sausages and mash or home-baked ham, egg and chips (£5.25), lasagne or roasted vegetable moussaka (£5.95), pan-fried lamb's liver and onion (£6.25), chicken and asparagus pie (£6.50), steak and ale pie (£6.75), daily specials such as warm cajun chicken salad (£8.95), salmon with hollandaise sauce (£9.50) or honey-glazed rack of lamb (£10.50), and puddings such as apple and blackberry pie and chocolate roulade (£3.25). Well kept Badger IPA, Dorset Best and Tanglefoot, with one or two guests from the Gribble brewery; darts, cribbage, dominoes, fruit machine and piped music. The restaurant is in a nicely restored thatched barn. *(Recommended by Peter Burton, S J Edwards, Joan and Andrew Life, Margaret and Roy Randle, Mike Wells, David and Ruth Shillitoe, M J Dowdy, Susan and Nigel Wilson, Peter and Giff Bennett, Minda Alexander, Derek Harvey-Piper, Cyril S Brown, LM, Penny and Dick Vardy, Ian Phillips)*

Badger ~ Manager Dale John Tozer ~ Real ale ~ Bar food (12-2.30, 6-9.30) ~ Restaurant ~ (01923) 282908 ~ Children welcome ~ Open 11-3, 5.30-11; 11-11 Sat; 12-10.30 Sun

ST ALBANS TL1507 Map 5
Rose & Crown

St Michaels Street; from town centre follow George Street down past the Abbey towards the Roman town

The friendly American landlord of this relaxed and civilised Victorian town pub takes inspiration for his unusual speciality sandwiches from the stars of stage and screen: for instance, among the Royalty sandwiches (served with potato salad, crisps and pickled cucumber on a granary or white loaf or bap) you can choose between Judy Garland's sweet peppers, mushroom, cucumber, tomato, lettuce and french dressing (£3.25), Benny Hill's ham, peanuts, American cheese, tomato and mayonnaise (£4.40) or Clarke Gable's roast beef, American cheese, onions, cucumber, tomato and horseradish (£4.95), while in a Flamingo Club toasted double decker, you'll find turkey, salami, Swiss cheese, lettuce, tomato and mayonnaise (£4.95); for the less star-struck, cheese (£2) and other usual sandwiches are also available. A few other dishes include soup (£2.50), chilli (£4.75) vegetable stroganoff or moussaka (£5.95). The very traditional beamed public bars – home to an impressive collection of sports tickets and other sporting memorabilia – have unevenly timbered walls, old-fashioned wall benches, chintzy curtains and cushions and black cauldrons in a deep fireplace which houses a big fire in winter; no-smoking area at lunchtime. Well kept Adnams, Tetleys, Wadworths 6X and a weekly guest on handpump; a dozen or so malt whiskies, country wines; efficient service. Darts (placed sensibly to one side), dominoes, cribbage. Lots of tables and benches along the side and at the back of the pub with shrubs and roses, flowerbeds and attractive hanging baskets. The approach from the town centre (down Fishpool Street) is especially pretty. *(Recommended by Tracey and Stephen Groves, Maggie and Peter Shapland, M A and R C Starling, Pat and Tony Martin, Roger and Pauline Pearce, Mrs G Bishop, Ian Phillips)*

Inn Partnership (Nomura) ~ Tenant Neil Dekker ~ Real ale ~ Bar food (lunchtime, not Sun) ~ (01727) 851903 ~ Children in eating area of bar ~ Blues, country and folk Mon evening, Irish folk Thurs evening ~ Open 11.30-3, 5.30(6 Sat)-11; 12-3, 7-10.30 Sun

WALKERN TL2826 Map 5
White Lion

B1037

This 17th-c brick pub is geared towards families: children will be happily occupied by the exciting wooden play area through conifers in the pleasant garden (which is fully enclosed so they can't wander off), with a bouncy castle, sand pit, football nets, and the satellite cartoon channel on the terrace in summer. Greene King IPA and Abbot under light blanket pressure are served in the comfortable open-plan bar. Bar food in generous helpings includes soup (£2.25), sandwiches (£2.95), Greek mezza of houmous, tsatziki and taramasalata (£3.75), moules marinières (£4.25), liver and bacon (£6.95), steak and kidney pie or fresh fish and chips (£7.25), Caribbean chicken or vegetarian pasta stir fry florentine (£7.50) and steaks (from £7.95); friendly staff; separate no-smoking restaurant. *(Recommended by Mr and Mrs Hayman)*

Greene King ~ Tenants Gerry Diaz and Helen Ward ~ Real ale ~ Bar food (12-2, 5-9.30) ~ Restaurant ~ (01438) 861251 ~ Children welcome ~ Open 11-3, 5-11; 11-11 Sat; 12-5 Sun; closed Sun evening, all day Mon except bank holidays, and for 10 days in Oct and Jan

WATTON AT STONE TL3019 Map 5
George & Dragon ★ ⑪

Village signposted off A602 about 5 miles S of Stevenage, on B1001; High St

Hertfordshire Dining Pub of the Year

The popularity of this civilised country dining pub stems from the good mix of excellent bar food, decent wines and friendly service (they do get busy so book or arrive early). Besides sandwiches (from £2.10), soup (£2.55) and ploughman's (£4.25), the imaginative bar food might include home-made beefburger (£4.55), deep-fried brie served with redcurrant and port sauce (£4.95), terrine of duck pâté with juniper berries and thyme (£5.75), fresh pasta with sun-dried tomato, yellow pepper and coriander topped with parmesan (£6.25), smoked salmon (£8.55), chicken breast with sautéed leeks in a creamy white wine and herb sauce served in a puff pastry shell (£8.95), pan-fried calf's liver with dijon mustard and red wine sauce (£10.25), Aberdeen Angus sirloin steak (from £11.45) and a wide range of changing daily specials such as chargrilled barnsley lamb chops with mint bitter (£8.75) or tiger prawns, whiting, cuttlefish and king prawns in ginger and garlic butter on a bed of samphire (£8.95); home-made puddings (£2.95). Service is friendly and attentive and the atmosphere is pleasantly sophisticated with kitchen armchairs around attractive old tables, dark blue cloth-upholstered seats in the bay windows, an interesting mix of antique and modern prints on the partly timbered ochre walls, and a big inglenook fireplace. A quieter room off the main bar has spindleback chairs and wall settles cushioned to match the green floral curtains, and a hunting print and old photographs of the village above its panelled dado. Proper napkins, antiques and daily newspapers add to the smart feel. As well as a very good wine list they have Greene King Abbot, IPA and a guest such as Marstons Pedigree on handpump, and several malt whiskies; the small dining room is no smoking; fruit machine, occasional Sunday quiz nights and boules in the pretty extended shrub-screened garden. The pub is handy for Benington Lordship Gardens. *(Recommended by Ian Phillips, Bob and Maggie Atherton, Dr and Mrs G H Lewis, Mrs Jo Williams, Peter Saville, Charles Bardswell, Maysie Thompson, J Sugarman, Peter Burton, Stephen and Jean Curtis, Gordon Tong)*

Greene King ~ Lease Kevin and Christine Dinnin ~ Real ale ~ Bar food (till 10pm) ~ Restaurant ~ (01920) 830285 ~ Children in garden and eating area of bar till 9pm ~ Open 11-2.30, 6-11; 11-11 Sat; 12-3, 7-10.30 Sun; closed evenings 25 and 26 Dec

WESTMILL TL3626 Map 5
Sword in Hand

Village signposted W off A10, about 1 mile S of Buntingford

Exposed beams, log fires and traditional furniture lend this 14th-c colour-washed listed building a very pleasant atmosphere. It is delightfully set in a picturesque village, and from the dining room (with no-smoking area) there are unspoilt views over the church, garden and fields beyond. Well cooked and tastefully presented bar food from a seasonally changing menu might include soup (£2.95) brioche filled with mushrooms in a cajun sauce (£3.95, large £5.95), smoked haddock topped with toasted welsh rarebit or warm salad of pigeon breast with crispy pancetta and pine nuts (£4.95, large £6.95), well liked sausage and mash (£6.95), spinach and mixed pepper tart with a mediterranean tomato sauce (£8.95), lobster and tiger prawn ravioli with a pesto sauce, Scotch beef rump with port, Guinness and pickled walnuts on a pesto mash, or herb and lemon crusted chicken breast on a lemon sauce (£9.95); tasty puddings might include lemon and sultana cheesecake with warm pecan toffee sauce, caramel oranges with Grand Marnier or apple and calvados sorbet with apple crisps (£3.50); Sunday roast (2 courses £12.95), 3 courses £15.50); as everything is made to order there may be delays at busy periods, but readers suggest that the quality of the food when it arrives far outweighs any wait. Well kept Greene King IPA and Abbot and Marstons Pedigree on handpump, and a changing range of wines; friendly service; piped music. There are seats on a terrace surrounded by climbing roses and clematis, and more in the partly crazy-paved side garden running down to the fields, where a play area has a log cabin, slide, and an old tractor to climb on; nice walks nearby. *(Recommended by Enid and Henry Stephens, Prof John and Patricia White, Peter Burton, Mr and Mrs J Richardson, Peter and Joan Elbra)*

Free house ~ Licensees David and Heather Hopperton ~ Real ale ~ Bar food ~ (01763) 271356 ~ No children in the restaurant after 8pm ~ Open 12-3, 5.30-11; 12-4 Sun; closed Sun evening and Mon except bank holidays

---

Lucky Dip

Besides the fully inspected pubs, you might like to try these Lucky Dips recommended to us and described by readers (if you do, please send us reports):

Aldbury [SP9612]
☆ *Valiant Trooper* [Trooper Rd, Aldbury Common; off B4506 N of Berkhamsted]: Lively beamed and tiled bar with woodburner in inglenook, some exposed brick in carpeted middle bar, good if not cheap food (not Sun or Mon evenings) inc good Sun lunch, well kept Bass, Fullers London Pride, John Smiths, Youngs Special and a guest beer, good friendly service; no-smoking dining area; traditional games, tables in pretty safely fenced garden – good walks nearby; children and dogs welcome (the pub's is called Alexander) *(S Lythgoe, LYM, Klaus and Elizabeth Leist)*
Amwell [TL1613]
☆ *Elephant & Castle* [village signed SW from Wheathampstead]: Secluded and spacious floodlit grass garden behind low-beamed ancient pub with relaxed and welcoming local feel, great inglenook log fire, panelling, stripped brickwork, 200-ft well shaft in bar; good value hearty bar food (not Sun), well kept Marstons, friendly locals, good service; restaurant, children in eating area, *(A and K Ward, Maggie and Peter Shapland, LYM)*
Ashwell [TL2639]
☆ *Bushel & Strike* [off A507 just E of A1(M) junction 10, N of Baldock, via Newnham; Gardiners Lane, opp church (car park down Swan Lane)]: Neat front dining bar with fresh flowers, hunting and coaching prints, local colour photographs, wide choice of food from nice sandwiches up, no-smoking restaurant with 'conservatory' murals, sofas in back area, well kept Charles Wells Bombardier and Eagle and a guest such as Adnams Broadside, freshly squeezed fruit juice, hot toddies, mulled wine and half a dozen wines by the glass; tables on lawn and small terrace, maybe summer barbecues

(LYM, Anthony Barnes, Minda and Stanley Alexander, Pat and Tony Martin)
Rose & Crown [High St]: Homely and comfortable open-plan local, 16th-c beams, lovely log fire, decent usual food, candlelit restaurant, well kept Greene King IPA and Abbot, pleasant staff, darts and machines at plainer public end of L-shaped bar; tables in big pretty country garden *(Nicholas Holmes, Barry and Marie Males)*
Berkhamsted [SP9807]
Crown [High St]: Recently refurbished as Wetherspoons, well kept cheap beer, good food, good quick service; no-smoking area *(Pat and Robert Watt)*
Old Mill [A4251, Hemel end]: Recently restored, with several rooms inc no smoking, lovely cosy décor, two wonderful fires, very friendly staff, very good wine, choice of super generous food from familiar to sophisticated; by Grand Union Canal *(Janet and Jean Nicolas)*
Bishops Stortford [TL4820]
Tap & Spile [North St]: Changing well kept beers such as Adnams Mild, Batemans XXXB, Gales Butser, Smiles Heritage and their own Premium, also Weston's Old Rosie farm cider, lots of country wines, helpful friendly staff, good lunchtime food, lovely old building with bare-boards rooms of different sizes and levels, décor tastefully in keeping; piped music may be loud *(Ian Phillips, Bruce Bird)*
Bourne End [TL0206]
White Horse [London Rd (A4251)]: Wide choice of food (all day Sun) from sandwiches up, well kept McMullens, decent wines, helpful welcoming staff; children welcome *(Roger Bellingham)*
Bricket Wood [TL1502]
Gate [Smug Oak Lane]: Very friendly, with

well kept beer and good country feel –
though only a couple of miles from M25 and
M1 *(Richard Houghton)*
Burnham Green [TL2516]
Duck [off B1000 N of Welwyn]: After
whetting our appetites with talk of really
good home cooking and well kept Adnams
and Hook Norton, readers told us in early
1999 of a threat of closure hanging over this
small old village pub, refurbished but
unspoiled; news please *(Charles Bardswell, G
Neighbour)*
Bushey [TQ1395]
Swan [Park Rd; turning off A411]: Homely
atmosphere in rare surviving example of
unspoilt single-room backstreet terraced pub,
reminiscent of 1920s *(Pete Baker, LYM)*
Chapmore End [TL3216]
Woodman [off B158 Hertford—Wadesmill]:
Tiny two-room village local by pond with
well kept Greene King IPA and Abbot, bare
boards, simple furnishings, big back garden,
small front one *(Mike and Karen England)*
Charlton [TL1727]
Windmill: Pleasant streamside setting in
small village, enjoyable food, well kept
Charles Wells and guest beers; garden with
ducks *(Peter Butterfield)*
Chipperfield [TL0400]
Plough [Denny Lane]: Rambling open-plan
timbered pub with two fires, well kept beers,
decent bar food choice, good-sized garden
(Stan Edwards)
☆ *Two Brewers* [The Common]: Country hotel
overlooking pretty tree-flanked cricket green,
reopened under Scottish & Newcastle, plenty
of space in four attractively laid out linked
rooms with bow windows and two log fires,
some emphasis on wide range of food from
sandwiches to quite sophisticated main
dishes, but drinkers welcome too – real ales,
but no bar stools or bar-propping; provision
for children, has been open all day Sat,
comfortable bedrooms *(Cyril S Brown, LYM,
Peter Saville)*
Chorleywood [TQ0295]
Land of Liberty Peace & Plenty [Long Lane,
Heronsgate; off M25 at junction 17]: Simply
decorated local with particularly well kept
real ales such as Brakspears SB, Courage Best
and Youngs Special, half a dozen Belgian
beers on tap, decent freshly made food,
friendly staff *(Ian Phillips, Mr and Mrs S
Groves)*
Rose & Crown [Common Rd, not far from
M25 junction 18]: In cottage terrace facing
common, cosy and friendly, with real ales
and decent snacks *(Quentin Williamson)*
Stag [Long Lane/Heronsgate Rd, The Swillet
– handy for M25 junction 17]: Clean and
friendly open-plan pub with new no-smoking
dining conservatory, well kept Courage
Directors, Fullers London Pride and
McMullens, good sensibly priced food inc
bargain suppers Weds, attentive staff; quiet
piped music, machines tucked around corner;
tables on back lawn, play area; good walking
area, busy w/e *(Richard Balkwill, Ian

*Phillips, E R Cowtan, Peter and Giff
Bennett)*
Coleman Green [TL1812]
John Bunyan: Quietly set family-run beamed
country local with well kept Bass, Courage
Directors and McMullens, good value home-
made food from good ploughman's up,
friendly service, good log fire, simple
furnishings, masses of decorative plates,
mugs, jugs and other china; big garden with
play area (no children in pub) and front
terrace; may close early on quiet weekday
evenings *(LM)*
Croxley Green [TQ0795]
Coach & Horses: Pleasant recent
refurbishment under new management, good
choice of beers inc guests, good value food
(John Branston)
Datchworth [TL2718]
☆ *Tilbury* [Watton Rd; off A602 SE of
Stevenage]: Attractively timbered two-room
pub with five or more well kept real ales inc
a popular own-brew in small drinking area,
some emphasis on enjoyable good value
home-made food from fish and chips to
paella inc vegetarian and a pie of the day
(lots of booked tables), big garden *(Mike
Ridgway, Sarah Miles, Erna and Sidney
Wells, R Turnham)*
Digswell [TL2314]
Red Lion [Digswell Hill]: Large and
attractive, with wide choice of very promptly
served good value home cooking; very
popular with business people from Welwyn
(Charles Bardswell)
Flamstead [TL0714]
Three Blackbirds [High St (just off A5)]:
Lively and friendly low-beamed partly Tudor
local, old dark wood and brickwork,
pictures, brass and copper, two real fires;
well kept Scottish Courage ales from central
bar, good value usual food from sandwiches
up, no-smoking area; pool, darts and fruit
machine in games area, piped music;
informal back garden, good walks nearby,
children welcome *(Valerie James, N A Fox,
Ian Phillips, David Shillitoe)*
Frithsden [TL0110]
☆ *Alford Arms* [from Berkhamsted take
unmarked rd towards Potten End, pass
Potten End turn on right, then take next left
towards Ashridge College]: Secluded country
local, sparkling fresh and clean, new chefs
doing good interesting food, pleasant old-
world atmosphere with helpful staff, step
down to nicely furnished eating area with
cosy alcoves, decent house wine; open all day
Sat; darts, bar billiards, fruit machine; in
attractive countryside, picnic-sets out in front
*(P and G Stephens, Beverley Campbell Stott,
LYM)*
Furneux Pelham [TL4327]
Brewery Tap [Bealey Croft End]: Welcoming
new licensees and enjoyable home-made food
in brightened-up dining area, well kept
Greene King IPA and Abbot; pool table,
piped music; children welcome, back garden
room and terrace overlooking neat attractive

garden *(Paul and Sandra Embleton, Gwen and Peter Andrews)*

Graveley [TL2327]

Waggon & Horses [High St]: Former coaching inn with above-average straightforward food inc children's and good Sun roast, friendly service, comfortable beamed and timbered lounge, big open fire, locals' snug by door, well kept Whitbreads-related ales; plenty of seats in secluded attractive streamside back garden with terrace and summer barbecues, duck pond over road *(Prof John and Mrs Patricia White, A W Dickinson)*

Great Amwell [TL3712]

☆ *George IV*: Clean and pleasant pub in pretty spot by church and river, generous good value home-made food inc fish, vegetarian and good puddings (restaurant gets booked ahead, Fri/Sat), friendly attentive staff, Adnams and other ales *(Mrs A Chesher, Mr and Mrs Williams)*

Great Offley [TL1427]

☆ *Green Man* [signed off A505 Luton—Hitchin]: Roomy Chef & Brewer family dining pub open all day, with wonderful country view from good seats on pleasant back terrace and garden, very wide choice of reliable food, good service, good choice of real ales, unobtrusive piped classical music; very busy w/e; conservatory, front play area, striking inn-sign *(James House, LYM, Mrs G Bishop, G Neighbour, Stephen and Jean Curtis, B, M, and P Kendall, Ian Phillips)*

Red Lion [towards Kings Walden]: Cosy and friendly, with low ceiling, stripped brickwork and brick floor, wide range of ales, log fire, reasonably priced food from sandwiches up, restaurant; piped music; picnic-sets in small back garden, bedrooms *(Stephen and Jean Curtis)*

Halls Green [TL2728]

☆ *Rising Sun* [NW of Stevenage; from A1(M) junction 9 follow Weston signs off B197, then left in village, right by duck pond]: Well restored and convivial 18th-c beamed country pub with reliable food in bar or pleasant conservatory restaurant inc special evenings (booking recommended w/e), well kept McMullens and a guest ale, big open fire in small lounge, good big garden with terrace, summer barbecues and play area *(Charles Bardswell, Gordon Tong)*

Harpenden [TL1015]

Fox [Luton Rd, Kinsbourne Green; 2¼ miles from M1 junction 10; A1081 (ex A6) towards town]: Beamed and panelled lounge, partly no smoking, with pews and plusher seats, lots of bric-a-brac and masses of prints, smaller tiled public bar, Benskins Best, Marstons Pedigree, Morlands Old Speckled Hen, maybe Ind Coope Burton, lots of wines by the glass, usual food from sandwiches up, log fires; piped music, some live music nights; children welcome, tables outside, play area *(BB, Ian Phillips, Phil and Heidi Cook)*

Oak Tree [Leyton Green]: Popular lunchtime with older people for good value plain

wholesome home-made food, well kept McMullens ales with good choice of guest beers *(N S Doolan)*

Hertford [TL3212]

Treacle Mine [St Martins St]: Very friendly local with well kept Banks's and guest beers at good prices, sports TV *(Graham Brew)*

☆ *White Horse* [Castle St]: Very friendly unpretentious 17th-c pub with good range of ales inc landlord's good own-brewed Dark Horse, Fallen Angel (brewed with ginger) and Sunrunner, open fire between the two bars, interesting furniture in three beamed and timbered no-smoking rooms upstairs, wide range of country wines, simple wholesome weekday lunchtime food from sandwiches up; popular with younger people evenings, opp Castle grounds *(Pat and Tony Martin)*

White Lion [Bengeo St]: Friendly local with good value food inc fresh fish and Sun roasts, well kept beers inc guests, decent wine, good range of unusual malt whiskies; children welcome *(Ken Dalley)*

Hertford Heath [TL3510]

Silver Fox [B1197, signed off A414 S edge of Hertford]: Bustling well kept local popular for wide choice of good value food inc vegetarian and lots of fish, Marstons beers, staff attentive and helpful; relaxing sheltered back terrace with fountain *(Nigel and Amanda Thorp, BB, Chris Mawson, Paul and Sandra Embleton, Stephen and Jean Curtis)*

Hexton [TL1230]

☆ *Raven* [signed off B655]: Neatly furnished plush 1920s pub with four bar areas inc long tidy public bar (open fire, pool one end), big no-smoking room, plenty of dining tables; wide range of good well presented food inc lots of starters, vegetarian and two children's menus, four well kept ales inc Greene King IPA and Morlands Old Speckled Hen, friendly efficient service; children welcome, big garden with terrace, barbecue, well segregated play area, pleasant village *(Barry and Marie Males, Ian Phillips, George Atkinson)*

High Wych [TL4614]

Hand & Crown [Hand Lane, just W of Sawbridgeworth]: Attractive bar and restaurant separated by open fire, wide choice of good value generous food from entertaining menu, inc interesting baguettes and well cooked fresh veg, Flowers IPA and Original, plenty of whiskies, quick friendly service even when busy; booking advised *(Paul and Sandra Embleton, Mrs A Chesher)*

Rising Sun [signed off A1184 S of Sawbridgeworth]: Simple, unspoilt and welcoming village local, three sparsely furnished rooms (children welcome in the games one), well kept Courage Best and a guest beer tapped from casks, woodburner in one room, log fire in the other, very friendly landlord and locals *(Pete Baker, Jack and Philip Paxton)*

Hinxworth [TL2340]
☆ *Three Horseshoes* [High St; just off A1(M)]:
Friendly and well run thatched, beamed and
timbered 18th-c pub with good value food
(not Sun evening, Mon) inc vegetarian and
children's, no-smoking high-ceilinged dining
area, well kept Greene King IPA and Abbot,
decent wines, woodburner in big brick
inglenook, soft lighting, no music; children
welcome, big garden with play area and
vietnamese pot-bellied pig called Kevin
(*Amanda Hill, David Halliwell, Anthony
Barnes*)

Langley [TL2122]
Farmers Boy [off B656 S of Hitchin]:
Enthusiastic new licensee doing good home-
made food in low-beamed and timbered
local, huge inglenook fire one end,
woodburner at the other, small public bar
behind; lots of brasses, old photographs and
prints, well kept Greene King IPA and
Abbot; garden behind; open all day, cl Mon
(*Erna and Sidney Wells*)

Lemsford [TL2112]
☆ *Crooked Chimney* [B653 towards
Wheathampstead]: Big well run open-plan
dining pub with good food inc children's
helpings and popular family Sun lunch;
central feature fireplace, good range of well
kept real ales, comfortable restaurant,
friendly helpful staff; pleasant garden by
fields, play area (*LYM, Hilary Edwards*)

Lilley [TL1126]
Lilley Arms [West St; off A505 NE of
Luton]: Friendly attractively placed village
pub with decent food in dining lounge, well
kept Greene King IPA and Abbot, public bar
with cats and dogs, tables in garden;
bedrooms (*A J Bowen*)

Little Berkamstead [TL2908]
Coach & Horses: Wide choice of good
interesting food in three rooms downstairs
and one small one up, 15 wines by the glass,
Theakstons (*Adrian White*)

Little Gaddesden [SP9913]
Bridgewater Arms [Nettleden Rd, off
B4506]: Upmarket dining pub with good if
pricy food, decent wines, well kept ales such
as Fullers London Pride and Marstons
Pedigree, good coffee; good walks straight
from the pub (*N A Fox, Gwen and Peter
Andrews, LYM, G Neighbour*)

Little Hadham [TL4322]
☆ *Nags Head* [just S of A120 W of Bishops
Stortford]: Cosy and relaxed 16th-c dining
pub with very wide choice of good fresh food
inc lots of fish, good steaks and al dente veg,
very generous helpings and sensible prices,
well kept Greene King IPA, Abbot and a
seasonal beer tapped from the cask, decent
wines, freshly squeezed orange juice, efficient
friendly staff; comfortable heavily black-
beamed interconnecting rooms, old local
photographs, guns, copper pans, no music;
restaurant down a couple of steps; must
book Sun lunch, children welcome, handy for
Hopleys nursery (*Michael Fullagar, Joy and
Peter Heatherley, LYM, Gwen and Peter*

*Andrews, B C Regan, Paul and Sandra
Embleton*)

Little Wymondley [TL2127]
Plume of Feathers [handy for A1(M) junction
8]: Spacious comfortably refurbished Greene
King pub with beams, inglenook, lots of bric-
a-brac, usual food, friendly chatty staff; piped
music; open all day (*George Atkinson*)

Much Hadham [TL4218]
☆ *Jolly Waggoners* [Widford Rd (B1004 S)]:
Busy mock-Tudor chintz and oak dining pub,
very family-oriented; beautiful lawn with
complex play equipment, also friendly
donkeys, horses, sheep, goats, ducks and
geese; good range of home-cooked food inc
vegetarian and children's, popular Sun lunch,
cheerful attentive service, McMullens AK and
IPA, good range of malt whiskies, small
lounge, nice window seats, dining room,
public bar with pool; attractive countryside
nr Hopleys nursery, some live jazz (*Carrie
Morley, Paul and Sandra Embleton, John
and Shirley Smith, Ted George, Val and Alan
Green*)

Northaw [TL2802]
Two Brewers [Judges Hill (B157)]: Snug and
friendly, nice light dining room and garden
with view of ancient parish church, good
range of well prepared and presented food
esp fish, well kept Adnams, Benskins and
Marstons Pedigree; lovely window boxes
(*Ian Phillips, David and Ruth Shillitoe*)

Perry Green [TL4317]
☆ *Hoops* [B1004 Widford—Much Hadham]:
Cosy and friendly, in small village opp the
Henry Moore Foundation (can be visited by
appt); good food from freshly baked
baguettes up, real ales, children allowed in
no-smoking dining area, tables in garden
(*Paul and Sandra Embleton*)

Pimlico [TL0905]
Swan [Bedmond Rd; just outside Hemel,
between Leverstock Green and Bedmond]:
Unpretentious pub, with friendly staff, good
choice of generous good value food; used to
have remarkable collection of militaria, but
no readers have mentioned this recently
(*Mark Aston, Lisa Hilton*)

Preston [TL1724]
Red Lion: Good lively village-owned pub,
good value food; local cricket HQ (*Barry and
Marie Males*)

Radlett [TL1600]
☆ *Cat & Fiddle* [Cobden Hill; A5183, opp
Tabard RUFC]: Cosy and attractive 18th-c
inn, three small rooms, fire in each, low red
banquettes, cat theme throughout inc lots
of china ones; five well kept ales, fairly
wide choice of good value lunchtime food
(one room no smoking then), picnic-sets in
small tree-sheltered garden; fruit machine,
darts, Sun quiz night (*CMW, JJW, Mrs G
Bishop*)

Rushden [TL3031]
Moon & Stars [Mill End; village signed off
A507 about a mile W of Cottered]: Unspoilt
cottagey beamed country pub with neatly
kept no-smoking lounge bar, inglenook log

fire, well kept Greene King ales, popular food, pleasant garden *(C Galloway, Charles Bardswell, LYM)*

Sarratt [TQ0499]

☆ *Boot* [The Green]: Friendly and attractive early 18th-c tiled pub in pleasant spot facing green, cosy rambling rooms, unusual inglenook fireplace, well kept Tetleys-related ales, good if not cheap bar food; handy for Chess Valley walks *(Peter and Giff Bennett, Ian Phillips, LYM)*

Sawbridgeworth [TL4814]

George IV [by stn]: Two bars and restaurant, good range of well priced food, friendly welcoming service, well kept McMullens, good value wines, photographs and bric-a-brac giving old-fashioned feel; tables out in front, handy for canal and barge trips; open all day w/e *(Eddie Edwards, Gwen and Peter Andrews)*

St Albans [TL1507]

Farmers Boy [London Rd]: Welcoming pub with two large friendly dogs and good own-brew beers *(Dr Simon Polovina)*

Fighting Cocks [Abbey Mill Lane; through abbey gateway — you can drive down]: Odd-shaped former abbey gatehouse with lots of potential, much modernised inside but still showing the sunken area which was a Stuart cockpit, some low and heavy beams, inglenook fires, daily papers, and pleasant nooks, corners and window alcoves; piped music and machines may obtrude, can get packed with summer visitors; children welcome, attractive public park beyond garden, open all day *(Allan Engelhardt, John Wooll, Ian Phillips, LYM)*

☆ *Garibaldi* [Albert St; left turn down Holywell Hill past White Hart — car park left at end]: Well run and friendly Fullers pub with Chiswick, London Pride and ESB and a guest such as Adnams, good low-priced lunchtime food (not Mon), good house wines in sensible measures; children welcome, piped nostalgic pop music, open all day *(David and Ruth Shillitoe, Kevin Macey, Ian and Joan Blackwell, LYM)*

Goat [Sopwell Lane, off Holywell Hill]: Old pews, bric-a-brac, books and prints in rambling areas around central servery, open fire, cheery atmosphere, Adnams, Courage Directors, Greene King IPA, Marstons Pedigree and Worthington Best, good range of malt whiskies, games machines, piped music, tables in neat back garden; children in eating area, jazz Sun lunchtime, open all day *(LYM)*

Lower Red Lion [Fishpool St]: Good atmosphere in old building's two cosy bars, interesting range of well kept beers, home-made food, log fire, red plush seats; tables in pleasant good-sized back garden; pleasant bedrooms *(Tracey and Stephen Groves)*

Portland Arms [Verulam Rd]: Relaxed local with all Fullers beers kept very well, big open fire *(Michael and Hilary Stiffin)*

Stevenage [TL2324]

Three Horseshoes [Hooks Cross (A602 S)]:

Large McMullens pub, old stable-style partitions, lots of tables for wide food choice, well kept ales, friendly welcome (for dogs too); open till 4 weekdays *(Eddie Edwards)*

Tewin [TL2714]

Rose & Crown: Smartly refurbished neatly kept low-beamed pub, cheerful and friendly, well kept Greene King ales, food in bar and restaurant; tables on attractive garden terrace *(Enid and Henry Stephens)*

Therfield [TL3336]

Fox & Duck [The Green; off A505 Baldock—Royston]: Pleasantly refurbished beamed village pub with rugs on old tiled floor, solid old-fashioned tables and chairs, dining room extension, real ales such as Adnams, Courage Directors, Greene King IPA and Ruddles, decent wines, courteous staff, unobtrusive piped music; good children's garden with climbing frames, swings and tree house *(Gwen and Peter Andrews)*

Tring [SP9313]

Grand Junction Arms [Bulbourne; B488 towards Dunstable, next to BWB works]: Very friendly open-plan canalside pub with real ales such as Jennings Cocker Hoop and Thwaites Daniels Hammer, reasonably priced food inc good curries in raised side eating area, canal photographs and memorabilia; play area in big garden overlooking canal, barbecues and Sat evening live music out here *(Ian Phillips, Pat and Robert Watt)*

Kings Arms [King St]: Unspoilt genuine backstreet local with no juke box or video screens, simple wholesome home-made food from hot beef sandwiches up, well kept Adnams, Rebellion and local Tring brews, green décor, friendly welcome *(Tracey and Stephen Groves, Andy and Jill Kassube)*

Robin Hood [Brook St]: Olde-worlde pub popular for fresh fish such as bass, brill or eels; well kept Fullers ales *(Andy and Jill Kassube)*

Rose & Crown [High St]: Roomy comfortable hotel lounge with ornate fireplace, Wadworths 6X and local Tring Crown Glory, decent coffee, pleasant staff; bedrooms *(George Atkinson)*

Wadesmill [TL3517]

☆ *Sow & Pigs* [Thundridge; A10, N of Ware]: Cheery dining pub, spacious pleasantly rustic beamed dining room off central bar with pig decor, very generous food from sandwiches up, Adnams, Shipstones, Wadworths 6X and one or two guest beers, coffee with frequent refills, log fire; no dogs, children in eating areas, tables outside; open all day *(Mike and Jennifer Marsh, Paul and Sandra Embleton, Ian Phillips, Bernard and Marjorie Parkin, LYM)*

Walkern [TL2826]

Yew Tree [B1036]: Wide choice of well cooked good food in cosily refurbished ancient pub, dark beams, pictures, flame-effect gas fires, McMullens ales, good unpretentious atmosphere, quiz nights *(Mr*

and Mrs Hayman, Peter and Judy Frost,
Sidney and Erna Wells, Charles
Bardswell)
Water End [TL2204]
Old Maypole [B197 N of Potters Bar]:
Attractive 16th-c split-level pub, low ceilings,
big inglenook fire, lots of brasses, miniatures
and bric-a-brac; good value basic food, well
kept Greene King IPA and Abbot, friendly
service, family room; outside tables *(Mrs G
Bishop)*
Welwyn Garden City [TL2312]
Cask & Glass [Howardsgate]: Well converted
bank, two well decorated floors; lively, with
well kept Boddingtons and other ales,
lunchtime food *(Dr and Mrs A K Clarke)*

Weston [TL2530]
Red Lion: Particularly good food cooked to
order *(Charles Bardswell)*
Wheathampstead [TL1716]
Tin Pot [Gustard Wood; off B651 1½ miles
N]: Small quiet 17th-c pub by rough common,
wide range of home-made food, well kept ales
such as Wadworths 6X and Youngs,
comfortable beamed lounge, tiled-floor public
bar; dogs welcome; good B&B *(Barry and
Marie Males, N S Doolan, Neil Fletcher)*
Wildhill [TL2606]
Woodman [off B158 Brookmans Pk—
Essendon]: Basic country local with open-plan
bar and small parlour, Greene King IPA, Abbot
and guest ales, darts; no food Sun *(anon)*

Isle of Wight

A couple of new entries here: the Blacksmiths Arms looking out over the Solent from Carisbrooke (welcoming Bavarian landlord, a touch of the exotic in both food and drink), and the Hare & Hounds up at Downend (a dependable family pub). Several other pubs here are well geared to children, notably the Clarendon at Chale and the Chequers at Rookley. The Fishermans Cottage on the beach at Shanklin could hardly have a more idyllic setting, and the Crown at Shorwell's garden is well worth tracking down in summer; both these pubs are doing particularly well these days. The Crab & Lobster at Bembridge has good food, especially its fresh local seafood, while the Seaview Hotel's food is consistently enjoyable: we name the Seaview Hotel in Seaview Isle of Wight Dining Pub of the Year. The Seaview also has the cheapest beer we found on the island this year. Beer prices here tend to be a bit higher than on the mainland, but the choice has been getting wider – including Goddards and Ventnor, both brewed here. The other island beer, Burts, has now been bought by Ushers, who seem to have been increasing their presence here recently. The Lucky Dip section at the end of the chapter includes quite a few extra pubs worth knowing, the Chine at Shanklin perhaps prime among them.

ARRETON SZ5486 Map 2
White Lion
A3056 Newport—Sandown

This cosy white village pub can get very busy due to its good, straightforward and reasonably priced food. Besides soup (£1.95), sandwiches (from £2.30) and filled baguettes (from £2.50), baked potatoes (from £3.65) and ploughman's (£3.75), the menu includes calamari (£3.75), four-cheese tagliatelle (£4.95), cod (£5.75), steak and kidney pie (£5.95), scampi (£6.25), gammon steak and egg or pineapple (£7.25), moules marinières (£7.95), steaks (from £6.95), and daily specials such as bangers and mash or ham, egg and chips (£4.95), chilli (£5.45), and home-made curry of the day (£5.95); children's menu (from £2.50). The pleasant beamed lounge bar has shining brass and horse-harnesses on the partly panelled walls, and cushioned wheelback chairs on the red carpet; darts and fruit machine; children's room. Well kept Bass and Wadworths 6X with a guest such as Badger Dorset Best tapped from casks behind the bar with an interesting cask-levelling device or on handpump (maybe under light blanket pressure). The pleasant garden has a small children's play area and aviary, and you can also sit out in front by the tubs of flowers.
(Recommended by David and Gilly Wilkins, Alan Skull, Mark and Victoria Andrew, Derek and Margaret Underwood, Jack Barnwell, Robert Flux)

Whitbreads ~ Lease: Paul and Kelly Haskett ~ Real ale ~ Bar food ~ (01983) 528479 ~ Children over seven in garden, restaurant and children's room ~ Open 11-3, 6-11; 12-3, 6-10.30 Sun; 12-3, 7-11 winter

BEMBRIDGE SZ6587 Map 2
Crab & Lobster
Foreland Fields Road, off Howgate Road (which is off B3395)

Among the many reports on the friendliness of the attentive staff at this cliff-top pub, perhaps the most bizarre is from the readers whose lucky dog had a sausage cooked for him to sate his appetite. Tucked away on a bluff above the shore, this looks past the Foreland coastguard station to the Channel, with great sea and shipping views from window seats and particularly from the many tables in its garden down towards the beach – an easy walk down – or from the new patio. It's attractively decorated in a civilised almost parlourish style, with lots of old local photographs and yachting memorabilia. There's more room inside than you'd expect from the frontage (prettily decked out with flower baskets), with a separate restaurant. Here and in the bar there is some emphasis on good local seafood (well liked by readers), such as crab and lobster soup (£3.50), half pint of Bembridge prawns (£4.25), stuffed mussels (£5.50), home-made crab cakes (£6.50), crab salad (£7.50) and lobster salad (£9.75); other bar food, served generously, includes sandwiches and baked potatoes (from £2), ploughman's (from £3.75) and daily specials such as vegetable lasagne (£5.75), gammon with egg (£5.95) and chicken breast with a herb and garlic sauce (£6.50); a better than average choice of puddings might include home-made plum crumble and crème brûlée (£2.50). Castle Eden, Flowers Original and Goddards Fuggledeedum on handpump, decent house wines, country wines from the barrel, good coffee; piped music (even in the lavatories), cribbage and fruit machine. It does get very popular, and is on coach trip itineraries, so best to get there early or late at lunchtime (the lunchtime coaches tend to leave at 2pm). *(Recommended by Lynda Bentley, D P and J A Sweeney, Martin and Karen Wake, Mark and Victoria Andrew, Phil and Heidi Cook, I R Goodwin)*

Whitbreads ~ Lease Keith Terrell ~ Real ale ~ Bar food ~ Restaurant (evening) ~ (01983) 872244 ~ Children in eating area of bar and restaurant ~ Open 11-3, 6-11; 11-11 Sat, Sun in summer holidays

BONCHURCH SZ5778 Map 2
Bonchurch Inn

Bonchurch Shute; from A3055 E of Ventnor turn down to Old Bonchurch opposite Leconfield Hotel

Once the stables for the nearby manor house, this old stone pub is made up of a separate bar, restaurant, rooms and kitchens all spread around a central courtyard. The friendly Italian landlord and locals offer a warm welcome in the furniture-packed Victorian bar, which conjures up an image of salvaged shipwrecks with its floor of narrow-planked ship's decking, and seats of the sort that old-fashioned steamers used to have. There's a separate entrance to the very simple no-smoking family room which is a bit separate from the congenial atmosphere of the public bar, making this not the best place on the island for families. Courage Best and Directors tapped from the cask, Italian wines by the glass, a few bottled French wines, and coffee; darts, bar billiards, shove-ha'penny, table tennis, dominoes and cribbage. Good bar food includes sandwiches (from £2.50, toasted 30p extra), soup (£2.75), ploughman's and pizzas (from £4), chicken and chips or mushroom provençale (£5), well liked Italian specials such as spaghetti bolognese, lasagne or tagliatelle carbonara (£5.50), seafood risotto (£6) grilled halibut steak (£7), duckling with orange sauce (£8) and steaks (from £7.25); puddings such as zabaglione (£3.50); a couple of children's meals (£2.50). They only open the restaurant across the courtyard for reservations in the evenings; bedrooms are simple but comfortable, and the pub owns a holiday flat for up to four people (children must be over 7 years old). *(Recommended by David Carr, Alan Skull, O and J Smith, G and J Wheeler, Richard Dolphin)*

Free house ~ Licensees Ulisse and Gillian Besozzi ~ Real ale ~ Bar food (11-2.15, 6.30-9) ~ Restaurant ~ (01983) 852611 ~ Children over 7 in eating area of bar ~ Open 11-3, 6.30-11; 12-3, 7-10.30 Sun; closed 25 Dec ~ Bedrooms: £30B/£50B

CARISBROOKE SZ4687 Map 2
Blacksmiths Arms

Park Cross, Calbourne Rd; B3401 1½ miles W – and pub signed off Tennyson Trail

On a quiet hillside, this commands great views over the Solent from its simply built and furnished dining extension, and from tables in the smallish back garden, which has a play area. Inside, there's a slightly old-fashioned feel about the neatly kept roadside front bars, and a homely and cosy upper bar, all kept spotless; table football. The surprise is the welcoming Bavarian landlord, who does varied and imaginative food (Bavarian-sized helpings, too) including continental dishes. His club sandwiches and platters of up to half a dozen cheeses, or of mixed cooked and smoked meats, are much enjoyed, and other dishes (all served with German-style potatoes and sauerkraut) might include frikadelle (mini burgers, £4.95), rinderrolade (beef stuffed with German mustard, olives, bacon and onions, £6.95), various schnitzels including wild mushroom (£7.25) and pork knuckles (£7.25); also sandwiches (from £1.95), soup (£2.25), ploughman's (from £3.95), stuffed mushrooms (£4.95), cajun chicken (£5.95), salmon with herb butter (£7.50), 8oz sirloin (£8.50) and puddings such as apple strudel and home-made cheesecake (from £2.50). Mr Nieghorn keeps German wines and beers on draught (he also has special deliveries from Munich every three or four months), as well as four (five in winter) changing real ales such as Archers, Batemans, Fullers London Pride and Ventnor Gold on handpump; helpful polite service. *(Recommended by Guy Vowles, HNJ, PEJ, D B Jenkin)*

Free house ~ Licensee Edgar Nieghorn ~ Real ale ~ Bar food (12-3, 6-10) ~ (01983) 529263 ~ Children welcome ~ Open 11-11; 11-10.30 Sun; 11-3, 6-11 Mon-Fri winter

CHALE SZ4877 Map 2
Clarendon (Wight Mouse) ♀ 🛏

In village, on B3399; also access road directly off A3055

One reader thinks this hugely popular rambling family pub is the best on the island – and when it comes to keeping children amused, it'd be hard to disagree with him. With a toddler play area, swings, slides, a bouncy castle, a junior adventure challenge, tricycles, shetland pony rides from Sid and Arthur, a pets corner and maybe even Punch and Judy shows in the spacious back garden, it offers good value fun to rival Blackgang Chine theme park across the road; and don't worry if it's raining, under 12s can let off steam in the indoor play area (admission £1). Considering how geared up to children it is, the original core of the pub is surprisingly traditional, with musical instruments, guns, pistols and so forth hanging over an open log fire. One end opens through sliding doors into a pool room with dark old pews, large antique tables, video game, juke box, darts, dominoes, fruit machine and pinball. At the other end there's a woody extension with more musical instruments, lots of china mice around a corner fireplace, decorative plates and other bric-a-brac, and even oars from old lifeboats hanging from its high-pitched ceiling; piped music; no-smoking area. A good range of well kept real ales includes Boddingtons, Gales HSB, Marstons Pedigree, Morlands Old Speckled Hen, Wadworths 6X and maybe a guest at Christmas on handpump, an outstanding choice of around 365 whiskies, over 50 wines, and some uncommon brandies, madeiras and country wines. Bar food includes soup (£2.10), sandwiches (from £2.30), baked potatoes (from £2.90), ploughman's (from £3.50), burgers (from £4.10), vegetable mornay (£4.80), chicken curry (£5.50) moules marinières (£6.20), mixed grill (£8.70) daily specials such as steak and kidney pie (£5.95), tempting puddings such as pecan strudel cheesecake with maple syrup or cherry crème brûlée pie (£2.75) and of course a children's menu (from £2.50). The landlord is very friendly and service is always efficient and smiling; no-smoking dining area. There's live music every evening and on Sunday lunchtimes; more restful souls can soak up the lovely views out towards the Needles and Tennyson Downs, where the poet was inspired to write 'Idylls of the King'. The bedrooms are beautifully decorated and include three luxury two-bedroom family suites, and ten en-suite bedrooms in the adjoining farm buildings. *(Recommended by David Carr, Mr and Mrs Philip Board, John Kirk, David and Carole Chapman, Michael Inskip, Peter and Audrey Dowsett, Derek and Margaret Underwood, C J Fletcher, Michael and Jeanne Shillington, Dennis Stevens, Phil and Heidi Cook)*

Free house ~ Licensees John and Jean Bradshaw ~ Real ale ~ Bar food (12-10) ~ Restaurant ~ (01983) 730431 ~ Children welcome ~ Live entertainment every night and Sun lunchtime ~ Open 11-12; 12-11 Sun ~ Bedrooms: £39B/£78B

COWES SZ5092 Map 2

Folly

Folly Lane – which is signposted off A3021 just S of Whippingham

This shipshape old pub on the bank of the estuary is a very handy and well known yachting stop, with moorings, a water taxi, long-term parking, and showers; they even keep an eye on weather forecasts and warnings. Popular with readers due to its delightful setting and nautical atmosphere, from its big windows and seats on a waterside terrace, you gain birds-eye views of the boats. Its maritime connections go back a long way; the original building was based around a beached sea-going barge and the roof still includes part of the deck. The nautically themed opened-out bar has a wind speed indicator, barometer and a chronometer around the old timbered walls, as well as venerable wooden chairs and refectory-type tables, shelves of old books and plates, railway bric-a-brac and farm tools, old pictures, and brass lights. It gets very busy at weekends during the summer. Straightforward reasonably priced bar food includes soup (£1.95), sandwiches (from £2.75), garlic mushrooms (£2.95), ploughman's (£4.75), battered haddock or chilli (£5.25), roast chicken (£5.65), steak and kidney pie (£5.85), 8oz sirloin steak (£9.25), and daily specials such as vegetable suet pudding (£5.50), pork chops (£5.65) and salmon steak (£8.25); children's menu (£2.25). Boddingtons, Flowers IPA and Original, Gales HSB and a guest in summer such as Morlands Old Speckled Hen on handpump; no-smoking area, pool, darts, fruit machine. There's a bouncy castle in the landscaped garden in summer, and it's not far to Osborne House. If you're coming by land, watch out for the sleeping policemen along the lane. *(Recommended by David Carr, D P and J A Sweeney, David and Gilly Wilkins, D Marsh, Mike and Robin Inskip, J F M West, Justin Pumfrey, Sarah Bee)*

Whitbreads ~ Managers Andy and Cheryl Greenwood ~ Real ale ~ Bar food (12-10) ~ (01983) 297171 ~ Children welcome ~ Live entertainment evenings Sat and summer Thurs and Sun ~ Open 11-11; 12-10.30 Sun

DOWNEND SZ5387 Map 2

Hare & Hounds

A3056, at the crossroads

Extended from its thatched original core as a family dining pub by the owners of the nearby Robin Hill Country Park (a great place for children), this has lots of beams, cream or stripped brick walls, civilised cosy alcoves in the original part, and more room in an airy barn-type extension. The rebuilding done five years or so ago has mellowed now. Good straightforward food, showing more thought than usual about what children would like, includes sandwiches and filled french bread (from £2 and £3.60 respectively, till 6pm only), home-made soup (£2.20), nachos (£3.25), filled baked potatoes (from £3.65), a hearty all day breakfast (£5.75), battered haddock or home-made lasagne (£5.95), ploughman's (from £6.30), pie of the day (£6.75), curry of the day, vegetable chilli or pasta napolitana (£6.95), gammon or scampi (£7.25), chicken breast in a creamy mushroom sauce (£7.65) and 8oz sirloin (£8.75), with a popular Sunday carvery and children's meals such as scampi and lasagne (from £2.25); puddings (£2.70). Friendly and well organised waitress service, well kept Courage Directors, Theakstons Best and a guest such as Gales HSB on handpump. One beam is said to come from the gibbet which hanged a 19th-c child killer on a nearby hilltop, and verses on the wall recount his exploits. Tables out on the terrace give wide views. *(Recommended by Mr and Mrs P Board, Michael Lang, Derek and Margaret Underwood)*

Free house ~ Licensee Tim Fradgley ~ Real ale ~ Bar food (12-9.30) ~ (01983) 523446 ~ Children away from bar ~ Open 11-11; 12-10.30 Sun; closed evenings 25, 26 Dec and 1 Jan

---

If you see cars parked in the lane outside a country pub have left their lights on at night, leave yours on too: it's a sign that the police check up there.

FRESHWATER SZ3487 Map 2
Red Lion 🍴

Church Place; from A3055 at E end of village by Freshwater Garage mini-roundabout follow Yarmouth signpost, then take first real right turn signed to Parish Church

This popular pub caters for holiday diners as well as thirsty locals and therefore can get extremely busy, so it's certainly a good idea to book – especially at weekends. Listed on a big blackboard behind the bar, a lengthy eclectic menu might include tomato and basil soup (£3), herring roes on toast (£4.25), smoked salmon terrine (£4.95), shepherd's pie (£5.75), fish pie, chicken curry, gammon steak with parsley sauce or pasta with basil and goat's cheese (£6.95), beef and Murphy's pie (£7.25), guinea fowl stuffed with mushrooms (£8.75), fresh lobster salad (half £8.95, whole £16.95), spicy moroccan lamb (£9.25), sirloin steak (£9.50), red sea bream with fresh pepper sauce (£10.25), fresh tuna steak with garlic butter (£10.75) and baby leg of lamb for two (£15.50); puddings include chocolate sponge pudding, citrus cheesecake or whisky and ginger trifle (£3). The comfortably furnished open-plan bar has open fires, low grey sofas and sturdy country-kitchen style furnishings on mainly flagstoned floors with bare boards at one end, and lots of local pictures and photographs and china platters on the walls. Flowers Original, Fullers London Pride, Wadworths 6X with a guest such as local Goddards Special Bitter under light blanket pressure, and a good choice of wines including 16 by the glass; fruit machine, darts, shove-ha'penny, dominoes, piped classical music. There are tables on a grassy area at the back (behind which is the kitchen's herb garden), and a couple of picnic-sets in a quiet tucked away square at the front, near the church; good walks nearby, especially around the River Yar. *(Recommended by Derek and Margaret Underwood, Robert Flux, Justin Pumfrey, Sarah Bee, Paul Latham, Peter and Audrey Dowsett, David and Gilly Wilkins, Guy Vowles, Michael Inskip, Mark Percy, Lesley Mayoh, Mrs S Quekett, Philip Vernon, Kim Maidment, Pamela Turner, Michael Hasslacher, Alan Skull)*

Whitbreads ~ Lease Michael Mence ~ Real ale ~ Bar food ~ (01983) 754925 ~ Children over 10 ~ Open 11.30-3, 5.30-11; 11-4, 6-11 Sat; 12-3, 7-10.30 Sun

ROOKLEY SZ5183 Map 2
Chequers

Niton Road; signposted S of village

Popular with holidaymakers from the local caravan site, this former customs and excise house has very good family facilities including a mother and baby room, a large no-smoking family room with Lego table, colouring competitions, a separate building behind with table tennis and a ball pool and a large play area, toboggan run and bouncy castle in the garden. It's all carefully designed so as to avoid the mayhem that large numbers of children can entail, and restricted to one area of the pub. The comfortable carpeted lounge bar is decorated with cottagey ornaments, and has a group of easy chairs and settees down at one end by the good winter log fire; inland views of rolling downland. The lively flagstoned public bar beyond retains its local character and is popular with young farmers; sensibly placed darts, cribbage, fruit machine, and maybe piped music. Courage Best and Directors, Gales HSB, John Smiths and Morlands Old Speckled Hen on handpump. The very extensive bar menu includes sandwiches (from £2.20), vegetable samosas with garlic mayonnaise (£3), jumbo sausage, bacon and cheese baguette (£3.25), thai seafood dim sum (£3.95), baked potatoes (from £4), ploughman's (£4.50), about half a dozen vegetarian dishes such as vegetable curry or lemon and cracked pepper tandoori schnitzel (£4.50-£5.25), battered cod (£4.95), home-made steak and ale pie (£5.45), chicken curry (£5.95), pint of prawns or open steak sandwich topped with fried onions and mushrooms (£6.25), grilled lamb steak (£6.50), rainbow trout fillet (£6.65), medallions of sautéed pork with onions, mushrooms and a white wine and mustard sauce (£7.25), grilled halibut steak mornay (£7.95), roast duckling with orange sauce (£8.35), 8oz rump steak (£9.45), mixed grill (£9.95) and a very good children's menu that includes steaks and baked potatoes besides the more usual sausages, fish fingers and chips; Sunday roasts and a weekday lunchtime carvery. *(Recommended by Michael and Jeanne Shillington, M Lockett, HNJ, PEJ, J Barnwell)*

*Free house ~ Licensees R G and S L Holmes ~ Real ale ~ Bar food (12-10) ~ (01983)
840314 ~ Children in family room and garden ~ Open 11-11; 12-10.30 Sun; closed
evening 25 Dec*

SEAVIEW SZ6291 Map 2

Seaview Hotel 🍴 🍷 🛏

High Street; off B3330 Ryde—Bembridge

Isle of Wight Dining Pub of the Year

Readers really enjoy the bustling atmosphere in the bars of this popular hotel, with
(as its name boasts), sea views from the continental-style terraces on either side of the
path to the front door. The nautical back bar is a lot more pubby than you might
expect from the hotel-like exterior, with traditional wooden furnishings on the bare
boards, plenty of seafaring paraphernalia around its softly lit ochre walls, and a log
fire; it can be busy with young locals and merry yachtsmen. The civilised airier bay-
windowed bar at the front has a splendid array of naval and merchant ship
photographs, as well as Spy nautical cartoons for *Vanity Fair*, original receipts for
Cunard's shipyard payments for the *Queen Mary* and the *Queen Elizabeth*, and a
line of close-set tables down each side on the turkey carpet. The very popular freshly
made bar food, imaginatively presented and generously served, includes soup
(£2.95), well liked crab with cream and spices grilled with cheese or chargrilled
tomato topped with goat's cheese and tomato salsa (£4.50), Italian seafood salad
(£4.95), roasted salmon with pea mash, mushroom and shallot stew or chicken, leek
and tarragon cream with fettuccine (£8.95), and steak (£11.95); interesting puddings
might include home-made spiced rice pudding with red berries, poached meringues
with hot chocolate sauce or frozen peach yoghurt (£2.95-£3.95); friendly landlord
and young staff. Goddards and Tetleys under light blanket pressure, good wine list
and a choice of malt whiskies; darts, cribbage, dominoes, shove-ha'penny and piped
music. Tables on the terraces at the front and in a sheltered inner courtyard; some of
the well furnished comfortable bedrooms also have sea views. *(Recommended by Mrs
Romey Heaton, Jack Barnwell, Alan Skull, Michael and Jeanne Shillington, David Carr, JFM and
M West, Mark and Victoria Andrew, P W Ross, D P and J A Sweeney, Geoffrey Kemp)*

*Free house ~ Licensee N W T Hayward ~ Real ale ~ Bar food ~ Restaurant ~ (01983)
612711 ~ Children in eating area of bar ~ Open 10.30-3, 6-11; 12-3, 7-10.30 Sun ~
Bedrooms: £55B/£70B*

SHANKLIN SZ5881 Map 2

Fishermans Cottage

Bottom of Shanklin Chine

It's easy to see why they chose to use this unchanging thatched cottage as the local in
a current TV drama series: although only a few minutes walk from busy Shanklin's
Esplanade, it enjoys one of the nicest and most unusual settings of any pub we
know, peacefully tucked into the cliffs and quite literally on Appley beach; it's a
lovely walk to here along the zigzagged path down the steep and sinuous chine, the
beautiful gorge that was the area's original tourist attraction. Tables on the terrace
soak up the sun by day and later moonlight romantically shimmers on the lapping
waves. Inside, the clean low-beamed and flagstoned rooms have photographs,
paintings and engravings on the stripped stone walls. Very simple bar food includes
sandwiches (from £2.50), ploughman's (from £3.80), filled baked potatoes (from
£3.20), and a few other dishes such as broccoli and stilton bake (£4.60), cod (from
£5), steak and ale or chicken and mushroom pie (£5.50), and a pint of prawns
(£7.50). Courage Directors under light blanket pressure, coffee all day, and a range
of local country wines; wheelchair access. Do remember before starting out that the
pub is closed out of season. *(Recommended by D P and J A Sweeney, David and Carole
Chapman, David Carr)*

*Free house ~ Licensees Mrs Springman and Mrs Barsdell ~ Real ale ~ Bar food ~
(01983) 863882 ~ Children welcome ~ Evening live entertainment Mon, Tues, Fri, Sat
~ Open 11-3, 7-11; 12-3, 7-10.30 Sun; closed Nov-early March*

SHORWELL SZ4582 Map 2
Crown
B3323 SW of Newport

In an attractive rural setting on the prettier south-eastern side of the island, this friendly popular old pub has a traditional atmosphere in the four friendly rooms that wander round its central bar. The warm and cosy beamed two-room lounge has blue and white china in an attractive carved dresser, old country prints on the stripped stone walls, other individual furnishings, a cabinet of model vintage cars, and a winter log fire with a fancy tilework surround. Black pews form bays around tables in a stripped-stone room off to the left, with another log fire; the stone window ledges are full of houseplants; several areas are no smoking. In summer, crowds are drawn to its peaceful tree-sheltered garden, where picnic-sets and white garden chairs and tables look over a little stream that broadens out into a wider trout-filled pool with prettily planted banks; a decent children's play area blends in comfortably. Well liked bar food includes sandwiches (from £2, crab or prawn £3.95), soup (£2.25), ploughman's (from £3.50), home-made steak and kidney pie (£4.95), spicy vegetable schnitzel (£5.75), liver and bacon casserole (£5.95), chicken breast in apricot and brandy sauce (£6.95), whole lemon sole with lemon and parsley butter (£7.95), steaks (from £8.95) and duck breast with cherry sauce (£9.50); puddings (from £2.25), children's meals. Well kept Badger Tanglefoot, Boddingtons, Flowers Original and Wadworths 6X on handpump; efficient service; darts, fruit machine, trivia, piped music. *(Recommended by Mark Percy, Lesley Mayoh, Mr and Mrs P Board, Phil and Heidi Cook, Jack Barnwell, I R Goodwin, Alan Skull, J F M West, Michael and Jeanne Shillington, David Carr)*

Whitbreads ~ Lease: Mike Grace ~ Real ale ~ Bar food (12-2.30, 6-9.30) ~ (01983) 740293 ~ Children welcome ~ Open 10.30-11; 10.30-3, 6-11 winter

VENTNOR SZ5677 Map 2
Spyglass
Esplanade, SW end; road down very steep and twisty, and parking can be difficult

There's a genuinely interesting jumble of memorabilia at this splendidly placed pub, perched on the top of a sea wall with wonderfully relaxing views out to sea. Among the bric-a-brac that fills the snug separate areas of the mostly quarry-tiled bar are wrecked rudders, ships' wheels, old local advertisements, rope makers' tools, stuffed seagulls, an Admiral Benbow barometer and an old brass telescope; pews around traditional pub tables; no-smoking area. Readers tell us that the spacious sunny terrace is a delightful place to enjoy the good bar food which includes sandwiches (from £2.25, including especially popular fresh local crab, £3.75), filled baguettes (from £3), ploughman's (from £3.95), burgers (from £4.25), creamy vegetable kiev (£4.95), seafood lasagne (£5.30), home-made cottage pie (£5.35), lemon and pepper butterfly chicken (£5.95), steaks (from £8.95) and daily specials such as lamb hotpot or beef or chicken curry (£5.95) and crab, prawn and broccoli tart (£6.25); efficient service. Well kept Badger Dorset Best and Tanglefoot and Ventnor Golden on handpump; on special occasions such as a lifeboat support week, there may be half a dozen or more guests tapped from the cask; fruit machine, piped music. They have no objection to dogs or muddy boots. *(Recommended by Lynn Sharpless, Bob Eardley, Pam Adsley, D P and J A Sweeney, David Carr, David and Carole Chapman, John Kirk, Alan Skull, J F M West, David and Gilly Wilkins, Derek and Margaret Underwood, Lynda Bentley, Mrs Mary Woods)*

Free house ~ Licensees Neil and Stephanie Gibbs ~ Real ale ~ Bar food ~ (01983) 855338 ~ Children in eating area of bar ~ Live entertainment every night in summer, six nights a week in winter ~ Open 10.30-11; 12-10.30 Sun; closed Mon-Fri 3-6.30 in winter ~ Bedrooms: /£45B

Pubs in outstandingly attractive surroundings are listed at the back of the book.

YARMOUTH SZ3589 Map 2

Wheatsheaf

Bridge Rd nearest pub to the ferry

Behind its slightly unprepossessing street frontage – this pub is comfortably relaxed, with four eating areas including a light and airy no-smoking conservatory. Reliably good and generous bar meals are now served all day and might include soup (£2), filled rolls (from £2.50), vegetable chilli or home-cooked ham (£5.95), chicken tikka masala (£6.95), ricotta pasta with salmon and prawns (£6.95), giant garlic and cheese crunch mussels (£7.45), half shoulder of roast lamb (£9.95), 16oz rump steak (£10.95), well liked whole lobster salad (£16) and daily fresh fish specials such as salmon fillet or grilled halibut steak (£7.95); friendly efficient service. Beers include Brakspear, Goddards Fuggle-Dee-Dum, Morlands Old Speckled Hen and Wadworths 6X on handpump or under light blanket pressure; pool (winter only) and juke box in the public bar; garden; the nearest pub to the ferry. *(Recommended by David Carr, Mike and Robin Inskip, D P and J A Sweeney, Mrs S Quekett, D P Wilcox, Sheila and Robert Robinson, D Marsh)*

Whitbreads ~ Lease Anthony and Suzanne Keen ~ Real ale ~ Bar food (11-9.30; 12-9.15 Sun) ~ (01983) 760456 ~ Children in the Harbour lounge, conservatory and garden ~ Open 11-11; 12-10.30 Sun

Lucky Dip

Besides the fully inspected pubs, you might like to try these Lucky Dips recommended to us and described by readers (if you do, please send us reports):

Brighstone [SZ4282]
Three Bishops [Main Rd]: Friendly bustling pub with good reasonably priced food inc weekday bargain OAP lunch, cheerful attentive service *(Sheila and Robert Robinson)*
Carisbrooke [SZ4888]
☆ *Eight Bells* [High St]: Plainly refurbished food pub, big and busy, well worth knowing for its good generous straightforward food with sparkling fresh veg, good vegetarian and puddings; reasonable prices, well kept Whitbreads-related and other beers, quiet piped music, children welcome; at foot of castle, with charming garden behind running down to lovely lake with lots of waterfowl, also play area *(P G Bardswell, Charles Bardswell, Lynda Bentley)*
Cowes [SZ5092]
Anchor [Shooters Hill]: Good value food, well kept ale *(D P and J A Sweeney)*
Union [Watchhouse Lane]: Small Gales local with good atmosphere, cosy side room, good choice of beers inc interesting guest beer, good value food from crab sandwiches to generous well cooked nicely presented hot dishes; bedrooms *(David Carr)*
Culver Down [SZ6385]
Culver Haven [seaward end, nr Yarborough Monument]: Isolated clifftop pub with superb Channel views, modern, clean and very friendly, with good home cooking inc fresh veg, fair prices, quick service, real ales, good coffee; big restaurant, piped music, children and pets welcome, small terrace, good walks *(Michael Lang)*
Freshwater Bay [SZ3386]
Albion: Big modern popular bar in great

seafront location, tables out on terrace, neat quick service, interesting local pictures, wide choice of reasonably priced food, well kept ales such as Fullers London Pride; piped music may obtrude; bedrooms comfortable, open all day *(Peter and Audrey Dowsett)*
Newport [SZ4988]
George [St James St]: Friendly staff, nice atmosphere, good food, garden *(David Carr)*
Niton [SZ5075]
☆ *Buddle* [St Catherines Rd, Undercliff; off A3055 just S of village, towards St Catherines Point]: Extended former smugglers' haunt, heavy black beams, big flagstones, broad stone fireplace, no-smoking areas, good range of Whitbreads-related and guest ales, some tapped from the cask, local farm cider, straightforward bar food inc seafood and griddled dishes, family dining room/games annexe, friendly dogs; well cared for sloping garden and terraces, good walks; open all day, some live jazz *(Lynda Bentley, D P and J A Sweeney, Robert Flux, LYM, Michael Inskip)*
Shalfleet [SZ4189]
New Inn [A3054 Newport—Yarmouth]: Popular pub with traditional beamed and panelled bar, carpeted dining lounge and restaurant, no-smoking family area, good food, Bass, log fire; piped music may be loud – but there may be good Weds lunchtime guitarists instead; open all day summer *(Guy Vowles, Paul and M-T Pumfrey, LYM)*
Shanklin [SZ5881]
☆ *Chine* [Chine Hill]: Great clifftop setting, tastefully refurbished, with flagstones, beams, good food (not Sun evening, Tues or Sat), well kept Bass and local Goddards; bright

family conservatory and small terrace overlooking beach and chine (which is illuminated at dusk) *(D P and J A Sweeney, David and Carole Chapman)*
Crab [High St; A3055 towards Ventnor]: Picturesque thatched pub with pleasant tables outside; modernised bar with Whitbreads-related ales, rows of tables in dining area, quickly served enjoyable family food, friendly service; open all day *(Michael Lang, LYM)*
Longshoreman [Esplanade]: Large comfortable low-beamed seafront pub with old island photographs, friendly staff, good food, garden overlooking Sandown Bay; entertainment some nights *(D P and J A Sweeney, David and Carole Chapman)*
Ventnor [SZ5677]
Mill Bay [Esplanade]: Seafront pub with light airy décor, large conservatory, good choice of reasonably priced generous food inc vegetarian, friendly service (and very friendly dog called Caffrey); play area outside *(Liz and John Soden, LYM)*
Wootton Bridge [SZ5492]
☆ *Sloop* [A3054 Ryde—Newport]: Reliable Whitbreads Brewers Fayre pub, very popular, with good value generous food inc tasty

puddings, lots of tables in huge spacious split-level bar, smart upmarket décor, friendly quick service, subdued piped music; nice setting, fine views over yacht moorings *(Michael Lang)*
Wroxall [SZ5579]
Worsley: Village local with new landlord stocking well kept local beers such as Burts Nipper and VPA and Ventnor Brewery Golden *(D P and J A Sweeney)*
Yarmouth [SZ3589]
☆ *Bugle* [St James Sq]: Civilised old inn with low-ceilinged panelled lounge, lively bar with counter like galleon stern, usual food from well filled sandwiches up, friendly staff, well kept Whitbreads-related ales, children very welcome; piped music can be rather loud; restaurant, games room with pool, sizeable garden, summer barbecues; good big airy bedrooms *(W W Burke, Mark Percy, Lesley Mayoh, LYM)*
Kings Head [Quay St]: Cosy low-ceilinged traditional pub opp car ferry, well kept ales, good food inc well prepared local fish, plush seats, friendly staff, open fires, children's eating area, unobtrusive piped music; can get crowded; bedrooms *(Paul Latham)*

Real ale to us means beer which has matured naturally in its cask – not pressurised or filtered. We name all real ales stocked. We usually name ales preserved under a light blanket of carbon dioxide too, though purists – pointing out that this stops the natural yeasts developing – would disagree (most people, including us, can't tell the difference!)

Kent

This county has some pubs of great character, in fine old buildings, with friendly staff. Several up-to-the-minute pubs here now have good modern cooking, too; but Kent also has a sprinkling of super genuinely unspoilt pubs, as well. On the food side, the current stars here are the Albion in Faversham (benefiting from its spacious new bar area), the civilised Hare at Langton Green, the Bottle House near Penshurst (it's opened up several cosy little rooms this year), the friendly old Spotted Dog also just outside Penshurst (wonderful views), the striking Dering Arms at Pluckley (good fresh fish), Sankeys in Tunbridge Wells (good fish here too) and a newcomer to the Guide, the Sussex Oak at Blackham. It's this last pub – run by an ex-chef from Sankeys, bringing his inventive fish cooking – which gains our award as Kent Dining Pub of the Year. Other newcomers to the Guide are the White Lion at East Farleigh (quite an emphasis on food), the ancient George & Dragon at Ightham, the Kentish Horse at Markbeech (surprisingly inventive Pacific Rim food gains this country local its place), the delightfully unspoilt Red Lion down at Snargate which goes straight in with a star (we wish we'd found it years ago) and the Crown at Stone in Oxney (very enjoyable food, but still a proper pub). Two 'old-stagers' doing particularly well these days are the lovely old Three Chimneys near Biddenden (very foody under its new licensees, with a new outside dining terrace), and the idiosyncratic old Gate Inn tucked away at Boyden Gate. There are some strong contenders in the Lucky Dip section at the end of the chapter, too: the Artichoke near Hadlow, Henry VIII at Hever, Plough at Ivy Hatch (very good food at this informal but very restauranty pub), Black Robin at Kingston and Brown Trout in Lamberhurst (food their main thing, too), Chequers at Smarden, Compasses at Sole Street, Red Lion at Stodmarsh, Padwell Arms at Stone Street, Tiger at Stowting, St Crispin at Worth and Bull at Wrotham. Drinks are still more expensive in Kent than the national average, though prices have held slightly steadier than elsewhere this last year (perhaps the moderating influence of cheap drink just across the Channel may even eventually bring Kent pub prices down to the national average). Shepherd Neame of Faversham supplies a lot of Kent pubs with the cheapest beer they offer, and its beer prices are lower than most here. Goachers, a much smaller brewery, also supplies quite a few Kent pubs with relatively cheap beer, and (though not so cheap) Larkins is another local beer well worth looking out for.

BIDDENDEN TQ8538 Map 3
Three Chimneys 🍺

A262, a mile W of village

New licensees have taken over this characterful old country pub and reports from readers have been warmly enthusiastic. The rambling and low-oak-beamed series of small, very traditional rooms have simple wooden furniture and old settles on flagstones and coir matting, some harness and sporting prints on the exposed brick walls, and good winter log fires. The simple public bar has darts, shove-ha'penny, dominoes and cribbage, and well kept Adnams Best, Marstons Pedigree, Morlands Old Speckled Hen, Shepherd Neame Master Brew, and an ale named for the pub tapped from the cask; local Biddenden cider and several malt whiskies. Bar food is totally home made and very good indeed: soup (£2.95), dijon kidneys (£4.25), ploughman's (£4.50), smoked salmon, capers and sun-dried tomatoes on toast or fresh crab cakes with a light thai dressing (£5.50), caramelised onion and goat's cheese tartlet (£6.75), fried chicken breast with roasted vegetables (£7.95), confit of duck (£8.50), leg of lamb with curried sweet roasted potato and wild rocket salad (£10.25), 10oz sirloin steak (£12.75), and puddings such as vanilla terrine with a strawberry coulis, chocolate and Baileys torte or sticky toffee pudding (£3.25). There's a new garden terrace area with plenty of tables for outside dining. Every 4th Sunday in summer, they have classic car meetings. Sissinghurst gardens are just down the road. The licensees also own the Bell at Smarden. *(Recommended by Tina and David Woods-Taylor, JP, PP, Mrs J Burrows, Nigel Wikeley, Paula Williams, R and S Bentley, Peter Burton, Kevin Thorpe, Ian Phillips, Janet & Colin Roe, Rachael and Mark Baynham, Niall and Jean Spears, Chris Brace, LM, Douglas and Ann Hare, the Didler, Peter Meister, Penny and Peter Keevil, Mr and Mrs P Eastwood, G Neighbour, S F Parrinder, Chris Rowley, TRS, Derek and Iris Martin, Joan and Andrew Life)*

Free house ~ Licensees Craig and Jackie Smith ~ Real ale ~ Bar food (12-2, 6.30-10) ~ Restaurant ~ (01580) 291472 ~ Children in Garden Room but not Fri/Sat evenings ~ Occasional light jazz ~ Open 11-2.30, 6-11; 12-3, 7-10.30 Sun; closed 25 Dec

BLACKHAM TQ4838 Map 3
Sussex Oak 🍴

A264 towards E Grinstead

Kent Dining Pub of the Year
The main draw at this relaxed little pub is the very good bar food, with real emphasis on the fresh fish cooked to order by the landlord (whose good track record includes several successful years as the chef at nearby Sankeys in Tunbridge Wells). As well as blackboard specials, the menu includes sandwiches (£3), filled french bread (£3.75), fish soup (£3.95), chicken liver pâté with red onion marmalade (£4.50), ploughman's (£5.75), fried calamari (£6.25), mussels and chips or cod and chips (£6.50), queen scallops with tagliolini and dry vermouth tarragon cream (£6.25), six whitstable rock oysters (£6.75), wild mushrooms on toast (£7.50), roast rack of lamb with green peppercorn sauce (£12.50), monkfish with tomatoes, oregano and mozzarella (£13.85), bass baked with spring onions, ginger and soy sauce (£16.75), dressed Cornish rock crab (£17.85), dover sole (£18.85) and Canadian lobster (from £20), with puddings like strawberries crème brûlée, pannacotta with summer fruits and coulis, sticky toffee pudding and toffee sauce or apple pie and custard (£3.65). Well kept real ales include Shepherd Neame Bitter and Spitfire and one of their seasonal beers. Most tables are taken by diners, and it's simply decorated with something of the feel of a little provincial French restaurant. *(Recommended by R and S Bentley, Comus Elliott, C and J Laffan)*

Shepherd Neame ~ Tenants Lou and Caroline Lizzi ~ Real ale ~ Bar food ~ Restaurant ~ (01892) 740273 ~ Children in eating area of bar and restaurant ~ Open 11-3, 6-11; 12-3, 7-10.30 Sun

BOUGH BEECH TQ4846 Map 3
Wheatsheaf 🍺

B2027, S of reservoir

A super place to have as your local, this lovely old pub is thought to have started life as a hunting lodge belonging to Henry V. There are thoughtful touches like piles of smart magazines to read, nice nibbles, chestnuts to roast in winter, summer pimms and mulled wine in winter. The neat central bar and the long bar (with an attractive old settle carved with wheatsheaves; shove-ha'penny, dominoes, and board games) have unusually high-ceilings with lofty oak timbers, a screen of standing timbers and a revealed king post. Divided from the central bar by two more rows of standing timbers – one formerly an outside wall to the building – is the snug, and another bar. Other similarly aged features include a piece of 1607 graffito, 'Foxy Galumpy', thought to have been a whimsical local squire. There are quite a few horns and heads, as well as a sword from Fiji, crocodiles, stuffed birds, swordfish spears, and the only matapee in the south of England on the walls and above the massive stone fireplaces. Popular bar food – served all day – includes field mushrooms on a garlic crostini with a roquette pesto (£4.95), grilled goat's cheese with oven-dried plum tomatoes and balsamic dressing (£5.25), tiger prawns in tempura batter with a sweet chilli dressing (£6.95), ploughman's with home-made piccalilli and chutney (£6.75), cod in beer batter or local pork and herb sausages with beer-battered onion rings and roasted garlic (£8.95), salad niçoise topped with seared fresh tuna loin (£9.25), crispy duck confit on a vegetable stir fry with pak choi and plum sauce (£9.95), and griddled sirloin steak (£15.95). Well kept Flowers Original, Fullers London Pride, Morlands Old Speckled Hen, Shepherd Neame Master Brew and Wadworths 6X on handpump, decent wines including local wine, and several malt whiskies. There's a rustic cottage in the garden, lovely garden furnitre and swings for children to play on, and flowerbeds and fruit trees fill the sheltered side and back gardens. *(Recommended by Timothy Galligan, Derek Harvey-Piper, Chris Rowley, R Michael Richards, Jilly Burrows, Howard England, LM, Brian Borwick, Paul and Sharon Sneller, Mr and Mrs D Mullett)*

Whitbreads ~ Lease: Elizabeth Currie ~ Real ale ~ Bar food (12-10) ~ (01732) 700254 ~ Children in eating area of bar ~ Folk and country Weds 8.30 ~ Open 11-11; 12-10.30 Sun

BOUGHTON ALUPH TR0247 Map 3
Flying Horse ⇔
Boughton Lees; just off A251 N of Ashford

Attractively set by the broad village green, this lovely old pub was probably built for the 'pilgrim traffic' and a few clues to the building's age still remain, mainly in the shiny old black panelling and the arched windows (though they are a later Gothic addition), and its two ancient glass-covered and illuminated spring-water wells. The open-plan bar has fresh flowers, hop bines around the serving area, horsebrasses, stone animals on either side of the blazing log fire, lots of standing room (as well as comfortable upholstered modern wall benches), and a friendly atmosphere; two more open fireplaces. From the no-smoking back room, big doors open out onto the spacious rose filled garden, where there are seats and tables; summer barbecues. Bar food includes sandwiches (from £1.90) mushroom or broccoli and stilton soup (£2.60), chicken and leek pie (£5.75), grilled plaice (£7.50), sirloin or entrecote steak (£10.95) and home-made puddings (£2.60). Well kept Courage Best, Fullers London Pride, Ruddles and Charles Wells Bombardier on handpump, and good wines. The Shuttle is only 8 miles away. *(Recommended by Klaus and Elizabeth Leist, Stephen Brown, James House, Ian Phillips, Mrs G Sharman, Janet & Colin Roe, Alan and Judith Gifford)*

Scottish Courage ~ Lease: Timothy Chandler ~ Real ale ~ Bar food ~ Restaurant ~ (01233) 620914 ~ Children in eating area of bar and restaurant ~ Open 12-3, 6-11; 12-11(10.30 Sun) Sat ~ Bedrooms: £25/£40

BOYDEN GATE TR2265 Map 3
Gate Inn ★ ◧
Off A299 Herne Bay—Ramsgate – follow Chislet, Upstreet signpost opposite Roman Gallery; Chislet also signposted off A28 Canterbury—Margate at Upstreet – after turning right into Chislet main street keep right on to Boyden; the pub gives its address as Marshside, though Boyden Gate seems more usual on maps

There's a good mix of customers in this splendidly welcoming old-style local – one reader found he and his wife had been beaten to the pub by several smartly dressed middle-aged ladies all arriving on equally smart bicycles. The good winter log fire serves both quarry-tiled rooms, and there are flowery-cushioned pews around tables of considerable character, hop bines hanging from the beam and attractively etched windows. Tasty bar food includes sandwiches (from £2), generous ploughman's (£3.95), coronation chicken salad (£4.95), spicy hotpots with toppings like grilled sausage chunks, gammon and pineapple or steak (£4.95), pasta with pesto (£5.20), and puddings; they use organically grown local produce where possible, and you can generally buy local honey and free-range eggs. The eating area is no smoking at lunchtime. Well kept Shepherd Neame Bitter, Spitfire, and seasonal ales tapped from the cask, with country wines and local apple juice. Shove-ha'penny, dominoes, trivia and cribbage. On a fine evening, it's marvellously relaxing to sit at the picnic-sets on the sheltered side lawn listening to the contented quacking of what seems like a million happy ducks and geese (they sell duck food inside - 10p a bag). *(Recommended by David Carr, Ian Phillips, Comus Elliott, Shaun Flook, N A Fox, Nigel and Olga Wikeley, David and Ruth Shillitoe, Kevin Thorpe)*

Shepherd Neame ~ Tenant Christopher Smith ~ Real ale ~ Bar food (12-2, 6-9) ~ (01227) 860498 ~ Well behaved children in eating area of bar and in family room ~ Occasional Morris dancers and mummers ~ Open 11-2.30(3 Sat), 6-11; 12-4, 7-10.30 Sun

BROOKLAND TQ9825 Map 3
Woolpack· £

On A259 from Rye, as you approach Brookland, take the first right turn just after the expanse of Walland Marsh

Once the Beacon Keeper's house, this crooked early 15th-c cottage has all the smuggling connections you'd expect and plenty of old-fashioned character and atmosphere. The ancient entrance lobby has an uneven brick floor and black painted pine panelled walls, and on the right, the simple but homely softly lit main bar has a good warming log fire and basic cushioned plank seats in the massive inglenook fireplace itself, a painted wood-effect bar counter hung with lots of water jugs, and some ships' timbers in the low-beamed ceiling that may date from the 12th c. On the quarry-tiled floor is a long elm table with shove-ha'penny carved into one end, other old and new wall benches, chairs at mixed tables, and characterful photos of the locals (and perhaps their award winning sheep) on the walls. To the left of the lobby there's a sparsely furnished little room, and an open-plan games room with central chimney stack, modern bar counter, and young locals playing darts or pool; dominoes, fruit machine, piped music. Well kept Shepherd Neame Master Brew and Spitfire on handpump. Generous helpings of good value, straightforward bar food include sandwiches (from £1.50), soup (£2.50), ploughman's (£3.95), cod and chips (£4.50), lasagne (£4.95), steak pie (£4.75), pork chops (£5.95), sirloin steak (£8.95) and daily specials. *(Recommended by Anthony Barnes, Kevin Thorpe, Jeremy Wallington, Jason Caulkin, Pat and Baz Turvill, D and J Tapper)*

Shepherd Neame ~ Tenants John and Pat Palmer ~ Real ale ~ Bar food ~ (01797) 344321 ~ Children in games bar ~ Open 11-2.30, 6-11; 12-3, 7-10.30 Sun

CHIDDINGSTONE TQ4944 Map 3
Castle ♀

Village signposted from B2027 Tonbridge—Edenbridge

An inn since 1730, this rambling old place has a handsome, carefully modernised beamed bar with well made settles forming booths around the tables, cushioned sturdy wall benches, an attractive mullioned window seat in one small alcove, and latticed windows. Well kept Harveys Best, Larkins Traditional (brewed in the village), and Youngs Ordinary on handpump, a good range of malt whiskies, and a very good wine list (the quality is reflected in the prices, though the house wines should suit all pockets). Darts, shove-ha'penny, dominoes and cribbage. Bar food (served all day) includes home-made soup (£3.15), prawn cocktail (£4.50), filled baguettes (from £4.95), half a pint of shell-on prawns (£5.65), open sandwiches (from £3.85), ploughman's (from £5.95), very hot chilli con carne or beef and vegetable curry (£4.35), local sausages (£5.75) and children's dishes (from £2.95). There are tables at the front opposite the church and in the pretty suntrap garden, and it's worth a walk around the village to look at the marvellously picturesque cluster of unspoilt Tudor houses; the countryside around here is lovely. *(Recommended by Anthony Longden, Peter Meister, Chris Rowley, Eddie Edwards, Nigel Wikeley, B and M Parkin, John and Phyllis Maloney, Colin and Alma Gent, R and S Bentley, Brian and Anna Marsden)*

Free house ~ Licensee Nigel Lucas ~ Real ale ~ Bar food ~ Restaurant ~ (01892) 870247 ~ Children welcome (not in public bar) ~ Open 11-11; 12-10.30 Sun

DARGATE TR0761 Map 3
Dove
Village signposted from A299

Unspoilt and charming, this bustling pub has plenty of happy customers served promptly by friendly staff. The rambling rooms have photographs of the pub and its licensees throughout the century on the walls, a good winter log fire, and plenty of seats on the bare boards; piped music. Changing daily, and using fresh seasonal local ingredients, the imaginative menu might include sandwiches, croque monsieur (£4.25), potted salmon and crab on a tomato and onion salad (£5), warm salad of marinated chicken scented with mint and lemon (£5.50), daily specials such as glazed onion and garlic soup (£3.25), grilled sardines with virgin olive oil and garlic (£4.50), avocado, bacon and baby spinach salad (£4.75), chargrilled breast of chicken with sauce tapenade (£10.75), whole grilled black bream with herbs (£11.75), and evening dishes like pork rillettes with tomato and apple chutney (£4.75), roast breast of duck scented with ginger and cinnamon (£13), and entrecote steak with wild mushrooms, shallots and lardons (£14). Well kept Shepherd Neame Bitter, and Spitfire in summer on handpump.The sheltered garden has roses, lilacs, paeonies and many other flowers, picnic-sets under pear trees, a dovecot with white doves, a rockery and pool, and a swing. A bridlepath leads up from the pub (along the charmingly named Plumpudding Lane) into Blean Wood. *(Recommended by Kevin Thorpe, Stephen Brown, Ian Phillips, David and Betty Gittins, David Gregory, Cyril S Brown, N A Fox)*

Shepherd Neame ~ Tenants Nigel and Bridget Morris ~ Real ale ~ Bar food (not Sun afternoon or all day Mon) ~ (01227) 751360 ~ Children in eating area of bar ~ Open 11.30-3, 6-11.30; 12-3, 7-11 Sun

DEAL TR3752 Map 3
Kings Head £
9 Beach Street, just off A258 seafront roundabout

This handsome three-storey Georgian inn is an exemplary seaside pub. It is particularly attractive in summer, when festooned with magnificent hanging baskets and window boxes; picnic-sets out on a broad front paved terrace area are just across the road from the promenade and sea. There's a good lively atmosphere in the four comfortable bar rooms around the central servery, with a couple of flame-effect gas fires. The walls, partly stripped masonry, are interestingly decorated with marine architectural drawings, other maritime and local pictures and charts, and other material underlining connections with the Royal and Merchant navies. A wide choice of enjoyable good value food includes soup (£1.85), sandwiches (from £1.90), pâté and toast (£2.75), filled baked potatoes (from £3.10), omelettes (from £3.65), ploughman's (from £3.95), cod and chips or home-made vegetable lasagne (£4.25), steak and kidney pie (£4.35), 6oz gammon steak (£6.75), and 8oz sirloin (£8.95), as well as a good value two-course lunch (£5.95). Well kept Courage Best, Shepherd Neame Early Bird and Master Brew and Wadworths 6X on handpump; helpful friendly staff. One room has darts and a fruit machine, and there may be quiet piped music. Beware that traffic wardens here are vigilant; there's pay-and-display parking nearby. Although we are still awaiting reports on the bedrooms, we imagine this is a good place to stay (you have to use pay-and-display parking even if you're staying). *(Recommended by Kevin Thorpe, E G Parish)*

Courage (S & N) ~ Lease Graham Stiles ~ Real ale ~ Bar food (11-2.30, 6-9) ~ (01304) 368194 ~ Open 11(12 Sun)-11 ~ Bedrooms: £38B/£50B

EAST FARLEIGH TQ7353 Map 3
White Lion
B2010 SW of Maidstone

The friendly licensees at this charming little white cottage used to run a restaurant, so it's not surprising that the emphasis here is decidedly on the imaginative and well cooked changing food. In the evening you might find all the tables laid for dining, but you are most welcome to enjoy a drink at the bar. There are cushioned wall seats and captain's chairs, photographs on the walls of sheep dipping, hop picking, and previous landlords (and a list of them from 1689 onwards), a growing collection of jugs hanging from beams, and an inglenook fireplace at one end with a few horsebrasses along the bressumer beam, with a little woodburning stove at the other end in an old brick fireplace. Food is simpler at lunchtime and might include sandwiches, ploughman's, omelettes and blackboard specials like liver and bacon (£5.25) or grilled fillet of red bream with tarragon butter or chicken supreme in cream and mushroom sauce (£6.25), with more elaborate evening dishes like leek and mussel soup with garlic croutons (£3), grilled sardines with garlic butter (£3.75), baked avocado with smoked chicken in herb and cheese crust (£3.95), monkfish and tiger prawn green curry (£4.25), duck breast in spiced plum sauce (£10.50), fillet medallions in green peppercorn sauce (£11.25), veal escalope with parma ham, sage and mozzarella (£11.50), seared scallops and crab risotto (£11.95), and puddings like crème brûlée, toffee apple tart and black cherry pancakes (£3.25). Well kept Fullers London Pride, Harveys Best and Larkins Traditional on handpump, and several wines by the glass. The lively chocolate labrador Ella is allowed into the bar only near closing time when she can't be a piggy; piped jazz or classical. The flowering baskets and tubs are very pretty in summer, and there are some seats under umbrellas on the terrace by the car park. (*Recommended by Peter Bethune, Pat and Baz Turvill*)

Free house ~ Licensees Sue and Allan Casey ~ Real ale ~ Bar food ~ (01622) 727395 ~ Open 12-3, 6.30-11; 7-11 Sat; 12-3 Sun; closed Mon, Sat lunchtime, Sun evening

FAVERSHAM TR0161 Map 3
Albion ♉

Follow road through town and in centre turn left into Keyland Road; just before Shepherd Neame Brewery walkway over road turn right over bridge, bear right, first right into public car park

Readers have welcomed the alterations to this cheerful creekside pub, which have allowed even more space for drinkers to perch comfortably on bar stools, in the light and airy open-plan bar, and take in the working waterside views through big french windows. Although there's quite a lot of emphasis on the popular food, there's still a good pubby atmosphere around the spacious bar area, with a simple but solid mix of old pine furniture on wood and sisal flooring, pale pea green walls with nautical paraphernalia and old pine mirrors; piped music. Very popular imaginative bar food prepared by the French chef/licensee Patrick, might include fresh smoked mackerel with mustard dressing (£4.25), excellent fish soup, aioli and croutons or goat's cheese tartlet with a mixed leaf and walnut salad (£4.35), mushrooms and prawns in a chilli and coriander sauce (£4.95), baked snail with tomato and black olive topped with melted goat's cheese (£5.75), local sausages and mash (£6.95), beef, mushroom and ale pie (£7.25), chana (a mild curry of tomato, okra and chickpea with coconut cream, £7.50), chicken breast baked with bacon, mushroom, tomato and wine (£8.95), pan-fried pork fillet with prunes marinated in calvados with a green peppercorn jus (£10.95), poached monkfish medallion with a white wine, tomato and basil sauce or 10oz chargrilled sirloin (£12.50) and puddings such as coffee and hazelnut roulade or fruit compote brûlée, mango, passion fruit and lemon grass syllabub pavlova or apricot tartlet with apricot and Cointreau sauce, (from £3.25); well kept Shepherd Neame Master Brew, Best Bitter, Bishops Finger, Spitfire and seasonal ales under light blanket pressure; a decent French wine list, too. There are picnic-sets out on the river walkway and you can stroll along the bank for about an hour; disabled lavatories. *(Recommended by June and Tony Baldwin, David Gittins, Mark Percy, Lesley Mayoh, Stephen Brown, T R Burden, JP, PP, Timothy Galligan, Douglas and Ann Hare)*

Shepherd Neame ~ Tenants Patrick and Josephine Coevoet ~ Real ale ~ Bar food (12-2, 7-9 Sun-Thurs, 6.45-10 Fri-Sat) ~ (01795) 591411 ~ Children in eating area of bar ~ Open 11-3, (6 Fri/Sat)6.30-11

FORDCOMBE TQ5240 Map 3
Chafford Arms

B2188, off A264 W of Langton Green

One reader told us that nothing appears to be too much trouble for the friendly and very attentive long-serving licensees and staff at this timeless tile-hung old pub. With a warm and relaxed atmosphere, it's been so carefully extended inside as to seem all of a piece, with plenty of room between the neat tables and comfortable seats; the uncluttered décor includes some show-jumping pictures and memorabilia. Popular food includes a good range of seafood (picked up from Hastings by the landlord) such as plaice and chips (£5.75), moules marinières (£5.95), local smoked trout with horseradish or home-made prawn provençale (£6.95), skate wing (£9.95) and a hot and cold seafood platter for two people (£25.95); other bar food such as sandwiches (from £2.25; fresh crab £3.75), sausage and chips (£3.95), ploughman's (£4.75), vegetarian quiche (£5.95), chicken kiev (£7.45) and 8oz fillet steak (£9.45); Sunday roast (£6.95). Tables can be booked. Unusually for a foody pub, it has a thriving local side, the pubby bar often getting busier towards the close of the evening while the dining side winds down. Well kept Gales HSB, Larkins and Youngs on handpump, local farm cider, and decent house wines. In summer it is festooned with flowers, with cascading creepers and carefully tended shrubs and perennials making it very inviting. Most of the flowers are in front; behind is a sheltered lawn, with plenty of shade from attractive shrubbery and arbours, and a fine big tree. The affable pets – four labradors, a dachshund and a cat – keep their natural interest in the food politely in check. Darts, shove-ha'penny, cribbage, dominoes and fruit machine. Just up the (steepish) lane is an archetypal village cricket green. *(Recommended by Colin Draper, Nigel and Olga Wikeley, Tina and David Woods-Taylor, George Atkinson, B J Harding, Geoffrey Lawrance, Chris Rowley, Mr and Mrs G Turner, Peter Meister)*

Whitbreads ~ Lease Barrie Leppard ~ Real ale ~ Bar food (not Sunday afternoon) ~ Restaurant ~ (01892) 740267 ~ Children welcome ~ Open 11.45(11 Sat)-3, 6.30-11; 12-4, 7-10.30 Sun

GROOMBRIDGE TQ5337 Map 3
Crown

B2110

Nearly every report this year has noted the excellent atmosphere at this quaint Elizabethan inn, which many readers regard as the perfect Kentish pub. It's very prettily set at the end of a row of attractive cottages overlooking a steep village green, where picnic-sets make it a very nice place to sit in summer; there are more tables on the sunny front brick terrace. In the several beamed snug rooms, a jumble of bric-a-brac includes old teapots, pewter tankards, and antique bottles, and in winter, large logs burn in the big brick inglenook; locals tend to crowd around the long copper-topped serving bar. The walls, mostly rough yellowing plaster with some squared panelling and timbering, are decorated with small topographical, game and sporting prints, and a circular large-scale map with the pub at its centre; a little no-smoking dining area leads off the main bar. The end room, normally for eaters, has fairly close-spaced tables with a variety of good solid chairs, and a log-effect gas fire in a big fireplace. At lunchtime, good value – particularly for this part of the world – tasty bar food includes home-made soup (£2.40), ploughman's (from £3), popular vegetable and bean crumble with nut and cheese topping (£5), chicken curry or steak and mushroom pie (£5.50), mixed game pie with suet crust (£7.50) and puddings (£2.50); a different evening menu includes poached egg florentine (£3), moules marinières (£5.50), pork schnitzel (£6.50), leg of lamb with red wine, honey and rosemary sauce or grilled red mullet with greek-style salad (£8) and 8oz sirloin steak with brandy and stilton sauce (£9). Well kept Courage Directors, Harveys IPA and a guest such as Spinnaker Classic from Brewery on Sea on handpump, and local farm cider; scrabble and word games on a blackboard. Across the road is a public footpath beside the small chapel which leads, across a field, to moated Groombridge Place and fields beyond. *(Recommended by Richard Gibbs, Jason Caulkin, Colin and Joyce Laffan, Brian Borwick, LM, Pat and Tony Martin, Conrad and Alison Freezer, G Francis, Peter Meister, G Simpson, Peter Rogers, Dave Braisted)*

Free house ~ Licensees Bill & Vivienne Rhodes ~ Real ale ~ Bar food (not Sun afternoon) ~ Restaurant ~ (01892) 864742 ~ Children in restaurant ~ Open 11-3, 6-11; 11-11 Sat; 12-10.30 Sun; 11-3, 6-11 Sat winter ~ Bedrooms: £25/£40

HERNHILL TR0660 Map 3
Red Lion

Off A299 at Highstreet roundabout via Dargate; or off A2 via Boughton Street and Staplestreet; follow Hernhill church signs

A few weeks after we went to press, new licensees were due to arrive. This is such a pretty Tudor inn ideally set next to the church and attractive village green that we are keeping our fingers crossed that all will be well. The narrow, characterfully beamed and flagstoned interior is often crowded with people gathering for the well liked bar food. This has included dishes such as soup, pâté of the day, fisherman's pie, mushroom stroganoff, beef in cream and peppercorn sauce, bass baked in foil with sliced mushrooms and tomatoes or duck breast with raspberry sauce on caramelised onions, and puddings. There is a restaurant upstairs. Well kept real ales have included Courage Directors, Fullers London Pride, Shepherd Neame Master Brew and Wadworths 6X, and country wines; log fires in winter; very good play area in garden; boules; darts. *(Recommended by David Gregory, Jeff Seaman, Dave Braisted, Stephen and Julie Brown, Kevin Thorpe, N A Fox)*

Free house ~ Real ale ~ Bar food ~ Restaurant ~ (01227) 751207 ~ Children in eating area of bar and restaurant ~ Open 12-3, 6-11; 12-11 Sat; 12-10.30 Sun

HODSOLL STREET TQ6263 Map 3
Green Man

Hodsoll Street and pub signposted off A227 S of Meopham; turn right in village

Next to the village green, this friendly village pub has lovely hanging baskets, tubs and window boxes in summer, and plenty of walks in the nearby North Downs. There's a peacefully relaxing atmosphere in the big airy carpeted rooms which work their way round a hop-draped central bar, with a turkey rug in front of a log fire at one end. Neat tables are spaced tidily around the walls, with interesting old local photographs and antique plates on the creamy walls above. A wide choice of good bar food might include filled rolls (from £2.75), filled baked potatoes (from £3.75), home-made steak and kidney or ham and mushroom pies (£5.95), oriental specialities such as Thai green and red, sweet and sour, and tom yam curries, Indonesian beef rendang, Malaysian satay and Szechuan chicken (all £7.50), fish dishes like halibut and bass (both £7.50), and mixed grills (from £8.50); a huge choice of puddings temptingly laid out in a big glass display cabinet (£2.95). Well kept Marstons Pedigree, Shepherd Neame Masterbrew, and Wadworths 6X plus guests such as Batemans XXB, Fullers London Pride, Greene King Abbot, and Larkins Chiddingstone on handpump, and a decent wine list; friendly staff; fruit machines and piped pop music; walkers are welcome but are asked to remove their boots. Behind the back car park are picnic-sets under parasols on a well tended lawn, as well as a play area, pets corner, and aviary. *(Recommended by Jenny and Brian Seller, Shirley Mackenzie, A E Brace, Dave Braisted, David and Ruth Shillitoe, Ian Phillips)*

Whitbreads ~ Lease: Mr and Mrs Colin Mcleod ~ Real ale ~ Bar food (not Sun evening) ~ Restaurant ~ (01732) 823575 ~ Children over 7 until 9.30pm ~ Open 11-2.30(3 Sat), 6.30-11; 12-3, 7-10.30 Sun

HOLLINGBOURNE TQ8455 Map 3
Dirty Habit
B2163, off A20

There's quite a bit of character in the various rooms of this early 15th-c inn, originally a monastic house. The main bar has a profusion of hops over the counter, four deeply comfortable old armchairs with tables on which to rest your drinks, some high bar chairs, and heavy beams, and a long, very low beam leading to a panelled, dimly lit room with candles on sizeable tables, a very high-backed plush red cusioned settle with rather grand arms set opposite a big brown sofa, and a mix of dining chairs. Another little area has long settles, some chunky dining chairs, a brick fireplace, and newspapers on racks; a door from here leads up steps to a brick-tiered terrace with stone slab tables, green plastic chairs, statues, chimney pots filled with flowers, and a pergola. At the other end of the bar is a lighter room with more panelling, a relaxed, chatty atmosphere, a mix of chairs and tables, and a woodburning stove. Well kept Bass, Fullers London Pride, Wadworths Farmers Glory and 6X on handpump kept under light blanket pressure, home-made country wines, and a red hot chilli vodka; piped music. A wide choice of good bar food includes home-made soup (£3.50), filled french bread (from £3.95), chicken satay (£4.50), warm salad of pigeon breast (£4.95), lasagne (£7.95), beef in ale pie (£9.25), pasta carbonara (£9.45), Scotch salmon fillets wrapped in filo pastry or Chinese roast pork (£11.95), rump steak (£13.95), daily specials, and puddings like lemon brûlée (£3.75). The pub is on the North Downs Way. *(Recommended by Mark Percy, Lesley Mayoh, Pat and Baz Turvill, Thomas and Audrey Nott)*

Free house ~ Licensees J and S I Brown ~ Real ale ~ Bar food (12-3, 6.30-10) ~ (01622) 880880 ~ Children welcome ~ Live band Mon evening ~ Open 11-3, 6.30-11; 12-3, 7-10.30 Sun

ICKHAM TR2257 Map 3
Duke William ♀
Village signposted off A257 E of Canterbury

Bigger than it looks from outside, this friendly and comfortable family-run pub has an open-plan carpeted bar that extends on either side of the serving counter; the front part has a comfortably lived-in feel, helped by the big inglenook, all the brasses, copper and other bric-a-brac, longcase clock, and even gas lighting. There's more formal seating behind, with a rather smart air-conditioned restaurant area, and a no-smoking well shaded Victorian-style conservatory. A wide choice of good home-made food includes sandwiches (from £1.90), filled french sticks (from £3.75), soup (£3), ploughman's (from £4.50), about a dozen pizzas (£4.95-£14), fajitas (£4.95-£6.25), about a dozen different pasta dishes including stir-fried squid (£5.45-7.95), steak and kidney pie or baked chicken breast with lemon, herbs and onion (£5.95), and puddings from a trolley (£3.50). Well kept beers such as Adnams, Fullers London Pride, Shepherd Neame Masterbrew and Youngs Special on handpump, as well as fifteen wines by the glass; darts, pool, shove-ha'penny, fruit machine and juke box. The attractive garden, overlooking fields, is very neatly kept; this is a picturesque village. *(Recommended by Derek Hayman, Kevin Thorpe)*

Free house ~ Licensees Mr and Mrs A R McNeill ~ Real ale ~ Bar food (12-2, 6-10 (not Sun evening unless bank hol)) ~ Restaurant ~ (01227) 721308 ~ Children in restaurant ~ Open 11-3, 6-11; 12-10.30 Sun; closed Mon lunchtime (except bank holidays)

IDEN GREEN TQ8031 Map 3
Woodcock
Iden Green is signposted off A268 E of Hawkhurst and B2086 at W edge of Benenden; in village at crossroads by bus shelter follow Standen Street signpost, then fork left at pub signpost – beware that there is an entirely different Iden Green just 10 miles away near Goudhurst

Bustling and friendly, this unaffected little country local has a snug, exposed brick bar with very low ceilings bearing down heavily on a couple of big timbers on its stone floor, as well as a comfy sofa and armchairs by a warming woodburner, and a couple of good sized old pine tables tucked snugly into little nooks. Real ales include well kept Greene King Abbot and IPA and three guests like Fullers London Pride, Harveys and Rother Valley Level Best on handpump. Fairly straightforward bar food served in generous helpings (with prices unchanged since last year) includes pâté (£2.95), prawn cocktail (£3.50), fried lamb's liver and bacon (£7), steak, kidney, mushroom and ale pie or grilled plaice with white wine and prawn sauce (£7.50) sirloin steak (£8.50), and puddings (from £2.95); darts, shove-ha'penny, cribbage, dominoes, fruit machine, and piped local radio. There are seats outside in the pretty garden. *(Recommended by Digby Linnett)*

Greene King ~ Lease: Frank Simmons ~ Real ale ~ Bar food ~ Restaurant ~ (01580) 240009 ~ Children welcome ~ Open 11-11

IGHTHAM TQ5956 Map 3
George & Dragon
The Street; A227 S of Borough Green

In 1515, this wonky black and white timbered pub was built for the Earl of Stafford. The long main bar has a stripped wooden floor, a circular table with tall farmhouse and mate's chairs by the fireplace (there's another fireplace at the other end with a woodburning stove), plenty of high bar stools, a cushioned settle and brocaded stools, hops in several areas, and a good chatty atmosphere; a very nice end room has heavy black beams, a big solid table with a long cushioned wall settle and quite a few church chairs, some big jugs in a corner display cupboard, dried flowers in the brick fireplace, and a rather civilised feel; piped Spanish guitar music. One area is no smoking. The Duke of Northumberland was imprisoned in the old restaurant (now an airy attractive room) after the Gunpowder Plot was discovered. Bar food includes tapas and mezze like tsatsiki, battered squid, three giant mussels soaked in vodka and tomato juice, tortilla, stuffed olives, white unsmoked anchovies (two dishes £4.25, additional dishes £1.25), tortilla sandwiches or filled french bread (from £2.75), ploughman's (from £4.25), fajitas (from £7.50), fried chicken breast in madeira sauce (£9.50), sirloin steak (£9.95), honey-roast rack of lamb (£12.50) with daily specials like home-made venison and red wine or lamb and apricot pie or spinach, mushroom and tomato lasagne (£5.75), with several fresh fish dishes like tuna steak (£7.95), Torbay sole (£8.50), skate (£10.50) or bass (£12.50), and puddings (£3); hog roast third Friday of month. Well kept Shepherd Neame Master Brew, Spitfire and seasonal ales, decent wines, and friendly staff. Seats out on the back terrace. *(Recommended by Mr and Mrs M Attlesey)*

Shepherd Neame ~ Manager Andrew Carr ~ Real ale ~ Bar food (12-2, 6.30-9(9.30 Fri, Sat); not Sun evening) ~ Restaurant ~ (01732) 882440 ~ Children in eating area of bar and restaurant ~ Open 11.30-3, 6-11; 12-3, 7-10.30 Sun

IGHTHAM COMMON TQ5755 Map 3
Harrow
Signposted off A25 just W of Ightham; pub sign may be hard to spot

You can be sure of a warm welcome from the friendly licensees and staff at this atmospheric creeper-covered country pub with a pleasant mix of customers. Assorted country furniture stands on nice old brick flooring in two unpretentious rooms, one cheerfully painted a sunny yellow above the dark green dado, both warmed by log fires in winter. Appealing attention to detail includes daily papers, and fresh flowers and candles on the tables. The good traditional local public bar (a big screen TV shows sports events only) has a relaxed feel. Flavoursome bar food includes popular soup such as vegetable and lentil, served in a tureen for four people (£3.95 each), calf's liver with bacon and mustard mash, chicken with tagliatelle or warm rich leek tart (£6.95), chunky smoked haddock pie with pastry top, cod and parsley fishcakes with piquant sauce, spicy hot chicken salad with chips (all £7.95), roast cod with ratatouille (£8.95) and puddings such as honey and lemon roulade, summer pudding or rhubarb crumble (£3.95). A decent sensibly priced wine list has plenty of good wines by the glass, and well kept ales include Greene King IPA, Abbot and Marstons Pedigree, and an occasional guest on handpump. A lush grapevine grows around the delightful little antiquated conservatory which leads off an attractive dining room; piped music; tables and chairs on a pretty little pergola-enclosed back lawn. Handy for Ightham Mote. *(Recommended by John and Phyllis Maloney, Catherine and Richard Preston, NMF, DF, Pat and Baz Turvill, B M and P Kendall, Pat and Tony Martin, Ian Phillips, Colin Draper)*

Free house ~ Licensees John Elton and Claire Butler ~ Real ale ~ Bar food (not Sun evening) ~ Restaurant ~ (01732) 885912 ~ Children in eating area of bar ~ Occasional jazz evenings ~ Open 12-3, 6-11, open longer for major sporting events

LANGTON GREEN TQ5538 Map 3
Hare ☏ ♀

A264 W of Tunbridge Wells

There's a pleasant feeling of space in this Victorian pub with lots of big windows and high ceilings in the knocked-through rooms, which have dark-painted dados below light walls, oak furniture and turkey carpets on stained wooden floors, old romantic pastels, and plenty of bric-a-brac (including a huge collection of chamber-pots). Old books, pictures and two big mahogany mirror-backed display cabinets crowd the walls of a big chatty room at the back which has lots of large tables (one big enough for at least 12) on a light brown carpet. From here french windows open on to a heated terrace with picnic-sets looking out on to a tree-ringed green (you don't see the main road). Good, popular interesting bar menu which might include sandwiches (from £3.50), home-made soup (£3.50), deep-fried aubergine in a parmesan crumb with tartare sauce (£3.95), gnocchi, salami and smoked ham topped with a tomato and basil sauce and mozzarella (£4.95), pasta and wild mushrooms sautéed in sesame oil and topped with blue cheese sauce (£6.95), steak burger with tomato, mozzarella and garlic mayonnaise (£7.95), chicken breast filled with a mushroom duxelle wrapped in smoked bacon with spinach gravy (£9.95), roast shoulder of lamb with herb crust and thyme and mustard sauce (£10.95), and puddings like sour cream and apple tart with vanilla ice cream, lemon cheesecake or spotted dick (£3.95). Well kept Greene King IPA, Abbot, Rayments and a guest like Marstons Pedigree on handpump,14 wines by the glass, and over 40 malt whiskies; piped pop music in the front bar area, shove-ha'penny, cribbage, dominoes, and board games. *(Recommended by R and S Bentley, Timothy Galligan, Mr and Mrs D M Hirst, J Sheldon, David Cullen, Emma Stent, Janet and Colin Roe, Kim and Nigel Spence, Tina and David Woods-Taylor, Ian Phillips)*

Greene King ~ Tenant Brian Whiting ~ Real ale ~ Bar food (no sandwiches on Sun) ~ Restaurant ~ (01892) 862419 ~ Children in restaurant ~ Open 12-11; 12-10.30 Sun

LINTON TQ7550 Map 3
Bull

A229 S of Maidstone

On a fine evening, this is just the place to enjoy a drink as there are marvellous views from the terrace in front of this country pub, down over farmland to the reservoir with its big fountains; plenty of picnic-sets, and an attractive sheltered side garden with more seats and the spire of the church peeking over the trees. Inside, the relaxed bar is divided into two rooms with brocaded stools, dining chairs and carved wooden settles on the stripped wooden floor, a few standing timbers with horsebrasses, guide dog photographs, and some guns and plates above the fine old fireplace; up a step, the second room has plenty of standing room, some big bar stools, one long table with a dark bench, and hops above the bar counter. Well kept Shepherd Neame Master Brew, Spitfire, and seasonal beers on handpump; fruit machine. Decent bar food includes soup (£1.95), sandwiches (£2.95), brie-stuffed mushrooms or mussels in garlic and white wine (£3.95), chicken breast stuffed with cheese and wrapped in bacon with a port and red wine sauce or half shoulder of lamb (£10.95), sirloin steak (£12.95), and puddings (£2.75); popular Sunday roasts; friendly staff. The sizeable attractive no-smoking restaurant is divided up by standing timbers and has its own bar; piped music. *(Recommended by Alan Caudell, Comus Elliott)*

Shepherd Neame ~ Tenants Graham and Lisa Gordon ~ Real ale ~ Bar food ~ Restaurant ~ (01622) 743612 ~ Children welcome ~ Live jazz Thurs ~ Open 11-3, 6-11; 11-11 Sat; 12-10.30 Sun; closed winter Sun evening

LUDDESDOWN TQ6667 Map 3
Cock

Henley Street, OS Sheet 177 map reference 664672; Luddesdown signposted with Cuxton off A227 in Meopham, and off A228 in Cuxton (first real turn-off S of M2 junction 2); Henley Street is off the N end of Luddesdown village

This tucked-away country pub has a traditional, relaxed atmosphere in its neat and tidy little red-carpeted lounge with copper- or wood-topped tables, and plenty of light from a huge bay window; well kept Adnams Southwold, Goachers, Greene King IPA and Abbot, O'Hanlons Blakeleys Best No 1, Welton Old Cocky and Youngs Special on handpump, and perhaps two farm ciders. The attractive quarry-tiled back bar has a conservatory leading off, as well as pews, an antique bar billiards table, shove-ha'penny, cribbage, dominoes, darts, sports photographs, and a glass case of model cars; the log fire has been knocked through so both rooms can enjoy it. Big helpings of well liked bar food include sandwiches (from £2), soup (£2.90), ploughman's (£3.50), sausage and mash (£3.90), chilli con carne, mushroom and nut fettucine or chicken curry (all £3.95), and rump steak (£6.95). There are some tables outside, and boules. *(Recommended by Alan Grahame, Ian Phillips, Pat and Baz Turvill, Robert Gomme)*

Free house ~ Licensee Andrew Turner ~ Real ale ~ Bar food (12-3; till 8 for cold food; not Sun) ~ (01474) 814208 ~ Open 12-11; 12-10.30 Sun

MARKBEECH TQ4742 Map 3
Kentish Horse

Off B2026 Hartfield—Edenbridge

It's the surprisingly good interesting food that draws customers to this partly white weatherboarded country pub. From a modern menu, there might be gazpacho soup (£3.50), lemon and vodka pasta (£4.50), good seared smoked salmon (£5.25), enjoyable seared beef on rocket and parmesan with pesto dressing (£7.20), tasty chargrilled breast of balsamic chicken with caramelised limes (£7.95), red mullet with sweet red pepper sauce (£8.95), and fried calf's liver with smoked bacon, basil mash and port jus (£9.95); also, filled french sticks (£4.50), ploughman's (£4.75), breaded brie with cumberland sauce (£5.50), thai crab cakes with chilli dip and rocket salad (£5.95), herb sausages and mash (£5.95), Spanish omelette (£6), Indonesian chicken, prawn and peanut stir fry with noodles (£6.95), sautéed black pudding and smoked bacon with garlic mash and mustard sauce (£7.50). Well kept Larkins Traditional and Wadworths 6X on handpump. The long bar has dark mint-green walls, a mix of straightforward seats around pub tables on the turkey carpet, and a small brick fireplace; at one end is a little flagstoned room with trophies in a cabinet and TV. On the way to the restaurant is an area with a fruit machine and sofa. The restaurant has a woodburning stove in a fine fireplace, pictures on the red walls, solid furniture, and french windows to the terrace and garden where there are picnic-sets, with more by the enclosed well equipped children's play area. *(Recommended by Pete and Mary Mustin)*

Free house ~ Lease: John Evanson and Maria O'Hara ~ Real ale ~ Bar food (12-3, 7-9) ~ Restaurant ~ (01342) 850493 ~ Children in eating area of bar and restaurant ~ Open 12-11; 12-10.30(8 winter) Sun; closed 26 Dec,

NEWNHAM TQ9557 Map 3
George
44 The Street; village signposted from A2 just W of Ospringe, outside Faversham

The spreading series of atmospheric rooms in this 16th-c pub have lots to look at: dressers with lots of teapots, prettily upholstered mahogany settles, dining chairs and leather carving chairs around candlelit tables, table lamps and gas-type chandeliers, and rugs on the waxed floorboards; hop bines hang from the beams and there are open fires and fresh flowers. Well liked bar food includes home-made soup (£2.50), filled french bread (from £3.25), oven-baked goat's cheese on a toasted brioche crouton with fresh raspberry and cranberry coulis (£3.95), cumin spiced chicken and avocado in a tortilla basket topped with cheddar and sour cream (£4.50), local sausages with rich onion gravy or home-made beef suet pudding (£5.95), beer-battered fresh cod (£7.25), and tagliatelle with ratouille (£7.50); three-course Sunday roast (£12.50). Well kept Shepherd Neame Master Brew, Spitfire and seasonal beers on handpump, and piped music. There are picnic-sets in a spacious sheltered garden with a fine spreading cobnut tree, below the slopes of the sheep pastures. Dogs allowed (drinking bowl in lobby). Good walks nearby. *(Recommended by June and Tony Baldwin, Tina and David Woods-Taylor, John E Thomason)*

Shepherd Neame ~ Tenants Tony and Jackie Richards ~ Real ale ~ Bar food ~ Restaurant ~ (01795) 890237 ~ Children in eating area of bar and restaurant ~ Jazz Mon, sixties music monthly ~ Open 11-3, 6.30-11; 12-3, 7-10.30 Sun

OARE TR0163 Map 3
Shipwrights Arms
Ham Road, Hollow Shore; from A2 just W of Faversham, follow Oare—Luddenham signpost; fork right at Oare—Harty Ferry signpost, drive straight through Oare (don't turn off to Harty Ferry), then left into Ham Street on the outskirts of Faversham, following pub signpost Pub ½ mile track off Faversham—Oare road, on E side of Oare Creek

To reach this unchanging and characterful 17th-c inn, some people choose to walk from the village through the tangle of boatyards or arrive by boat. The setting is quite striking as the surrounding salt marshes are designated areas of Special Scientific Interest and populated by rare birds; the small front and back gardens lead up a bank to the path above the creek where lots of boats are moored, and the Saxon Shore Way runs right past. Three unspoilt little bars are characterfully dark and cosy, and separated by standing timbers and wood semi-partitions or narrow door arches. There's a medley of seats from tapestry cushioned stools and chairs to black wood-panelled built-in settles forming little booths, pewter tankards hang over the bar counter, boating jumble and pictures, flags or boating pennants on the ceilings, several brick fireplaces, and a woodburning stove. Simple home-made but good value bar food such as doorstep sandwiches (from £2.20), soup (£2.20), filled baked potatoes (from £2.50), macaroni cheese (£4.25), ploughman's (£3.95), chilli (£4.25), steak and kidney or chicken and leek pudding (£5.95), and puddings like spotted dick (£2.50); part of the eating area is no smoking. Well kept Goachers Mild, Shepherd Neame Bitter and Spitfire, Shipwrecked (brewed for the pub), and guest beers tapped from the cask (they have a beer festival at the end of May), and strong local farm cider; table skittles, cribbage and dominoes. *(Recommended by JP, PP, the Didler, A de Montjoie, Ian Phillips, Howard Allen, Gordon Tong)*

Free house ~ Licensees Derek and Ruth Cole ~ Real ale ~ Bar food (11-3, 7-9) ~ (01795) 590088 ~ Children welcome ~ Folk music Mon ~ Open 11-11; 12-10.30 Sun

PENSHURST TQ5243 Map 3
Bottle House 🍷 🍽
Coldharbour Lane, Smarts Hill; leaving Penshurst SW on B2188 turn right at Smarts Hill signpost, then bear right towards Chiddingstone and Cowden; keep straight on

Several cosy little areas lead off the main bar in this friendly 15th-c pub which can all be booked for private parties and can be smoking or non smoking; one room is covered in sporting pictures – which extend to the ceiling. The neatly kept low-beamed front bar has a well worn brick floor that extends to behind the polished copper topped bar counter, and big windows look onto a terrace with climbing plants and hanging baskets around picnic-sets under cocktail parasols, and beyond to views of quiet fields and oak trees. The unpretentious main red-carpeted bar has massive hop-covered supporting beams, two large stone pillars with a small brick fireplace (with a stuffed turtle to one side), and old paintings and photographs on mainly plastered walls; quite a collection of china pot lids, which extend to the low-ceilinged dining room. Good bar food includes lots of fresh fish dishes such as dressed crab and prawn salad with new potatoes (£9.95), chargrilled marlin with ginger, spring onion and lime sauce (£10.50), chargrilled tuna or swordfish with sour cream, salsa and guacamole or skate wing with lemon, caper and butter sauce (£10.95), and giant king prawns (£14.50); also, fried whitebait (£3.95), duck liver pâté with port and orange sauce (£3.95), vegetarian samosas with jalapeno dip (£4.50), crispy duck with pancakes (£6.95), chilli con carne (£7.95), chicken tikka with naan bread (£8.95), calf's liver with onion mash (£13.95) and fillet of beef wellington with wild mushroom sauce (£12.95). Well kept Harveys Best and Larkins on handpump, cider from Chiddingstone, and local wine; unobtrusive piped music. Dogs welcome (they may offer them biscuits), and good surrounding walks. *(Recommended by John and Phyllis Maloney, Peter Meister, Tim and Pam Moorey, R and S Bentley, Chris Rowley, Derek Harvey-Piper, Tony Crafter)*

Free house ~ Licensees Gordon and Val Meer ~ Real ale ~ Bar food (till 10pm) ~ Restaurant ~ (01892) 870306 ~ Children welcome ~ Open 11-3, 6-11; 12-3, 7-10.30 Sun; closed 25 Dec

Spotted Dog 🍴

Smarts Hill; going S from village centre on B2188, fork right up hill at telephone box: in just under ½ mile the pub is on your left

Even when this quaint old tiled house is really busy, the licensee and his staff remain friendly and helpful. It is best to get here early on fine days as tables do fill up quickly – especially outside on the tiered garden slopes which enjoy a view of twenty miles of untouched countryside. The neatly kept, heavily beamed and timbered bar has some antique settles as well as wheelback chairs on its rugs and tiles, a fine brick inglenook fireplace, and attractive moulded panelling in one alcove. It's quite small, so there may be an overflow into the restaurant at busy times. Enjoyable and imaginative food listed on several blackboards might include sandwiches, lovely soups (£3.65), ploughman's (from £4.95), avocado and wild mushroom bake or spinach, cream cheese and green peppercorn roulade (£6.45), wild mushroom and cashew nut stroganoff (£6.45), steak and kidney pie (£7.45), Moroccan lamb on couscous (£7.95), chicken breast in lemon garlic (£8.25), good fresh fish dishes like golden trout (£6.95), flying fish (£7.25), tuna loin (£8.45) or marlin (£8.95), half a shoulder of lamb braised in red wine, garlic and rosemary (£10.25), and puddings such as sticky banana fudge pudding, blackberry cobbler or spotted dick (£3.65). Well kept Adnams, Greene King Abbot and King & Barnes Sussex on handpump, along with Old Spotty – a Best Bitter brewed specially for them; decent wine list. Shove-ha'penny, table skittles and piped music. Lots of room for children to play outside. *(Recommended by S F Parrinder, Colin and Janet Roe, R J Walden, Howard England, James House, Tina and David Woods-Taylor, Jules Akel, Conrad and Alison Freezer, Peter Meister, John and Phyllis Maloney)*

Free house ~ Licensees Andy and Nikki Tucker ~ Real ale ~ Bar food (not Mon evening) ~ Restaurant ~ (01892) 870253 ~ Children in restaurant ~ Open 11.45-3, 6-11; 11-3.30, 6-11 Sat; 12-4, 7-10.30 Sun; closed 25 and 26 Dec

---

Most pubs in the *Guide* sell draught cider. We mention it specifically only if they have unusual farm-produced 'scrumpy' or specialise in it. Do please let us know about any uncommon draught cider you find in a pub.

PLUCKLEY TQ9243 Map 3

Dering Arms 🍴 ♛ 🛏

Pluckley Station, which is signposted from B2077

Formerly part of the Dering estate, this striking old Dutch structure was originally built as a hunting lodge, and has massive grey stone blocked walls, dutch-gables outlined against the sky, and heavy studded oak doors. The stylishly plain high ceilinged bar has a variety of good solid wooden furniture on stone floors, and a roaring log fire in the great fireplace. It's popular with locals and there's a good pubby atmosphere; dominoes. A smaller panelled bar with wood floors has similar furnishings. There is quite some emphasis on very well cooked fresh fish such as half a dozen oysters, home-made salmon fishcakes with sorrel sauce, tuna steak with lemon and garlic butter, and bass with a champagne and chive sauce; also, home-made soup (£2.95), filled baguettes (£3.65), ploughman's (£3.75), chicken livers with bacon, onion and mushrooms (£3.95), ham, egg and chips (£4.75), and a home-made pie (£7.45); seasonal game dishes and winter 7-course black tie gourmet evenings (£25; must book as they are very popular). Well kept Goachers's Maidstone Porter and Dering ale (a beer brewed specially for them) on handpump, a very good extensive wine list, home-made lemonade, local cider and quite a few malt whiskies. There's a vintage car rally once a month, and maybe summer garden parties with barbecues and music; bedrooms are quite simple. *(Recommended by Rachael and Mark Baynham, Simon G S Morton, Kevin Thorpe, JP, PP, Tony Hobden, Peter Meister, Janet and Colin Roe, Hilary Dobbie, Ian Phillips)*

Free house ~ Licensee James Buss ~ Real ale ~ Bar food (not Sun evening or all day Mon) ~ Restaurant ~ (01223) 840371 ~ Children welcome ~ Open 11.30-3, 6-11; 12-3, 7-10.30 Sun; closed 26 and 27 Dec ~ Bedrooms: £30/£40

RINGLESTONE TQ8755 Map 3

Ringlestone ★ ♛ 🍺

M20 Junction 8 to Lenham/Leeds Castle; join B2163 heading N towards Sittingbourne via Hollingbourne; at water tower above Hollingbourne turn right towards Doddington (signposted), and straight ahead at next crossroads; OS Sheet 178 map reference 879558

This is a very comfortable place to stay with particularly good breakfasts, and by the time this book is published, a new garden cottage with self-catering facilities for a family of up to 6 should be open. It's surrounded by eight acres of land, including two acres of beautifully landscaped lawns, with shrubs, trees and rockeries, a water garden with four pretty ponds and cascading waterfalls, a delightful fountain, and troughs of pretty flowers along the pub walls; plenty of seats. The central bar room has farmhouse chairs, cushioned wall settles, and tables with candle lanterns on its worn brick floor, and old-fashioned brass and glass lamps on the exposed brick and flint walls; there's a woodburning stove and small bread oven in an inglenook fireplace. An arch from here through a wall – rather like the outside of a house, windows and all – opens into a long, quieter room with cushioned wall benches, tiny farmhouse chairs, three old carved settles (one rather fine and dated 1620), similar tables, and etchings of country folk on its walls (bare brick too). Regulars tend to sit at the wood-panelled bar counter, or liven up a little wood-floored side room; piped music. Bar food (served buffet style at lunchtime – there may be a queue) includes chicken, vegetable and bean soup with sherry and croutons (£3.85), coarse liver and apple pâté (£5.45), Kentish pork sausages (£5.95), chilli beef goulash (£6.95), cidered chicken casserole or spinach and cheese pancakes with a hot cream sauce (£7.95), lots of pies including steak, kidney and leek (£9.25), fish in elderflower wine (£9.65), and duck and damson wine (£10.25), grilled plaice fillets topped with mango chutney and bananas (£10.65), and rump steak (£11.75); vegetables are extra (£3.25). Puddings such as home-made cheesecake, treacle, orange and nut tart or fruit crumble (£3.95). Three or four changing well kept real ales (they list them on a blackboard) might include Bass, Boddingtons, Hook Norton, Marstons Pedigree, Shepherd Neame Spitfire, Theakstons Old Peculier, Wadworths 6X or a beer named after the pub on handpump or tapped from the cask; two dozen country wines (including sparkling ones), local cider and fresh fruit cordials. Well behaved dogs welcome *(Recommended by Mrs Maria Furness, Timothy Galligan, Peter Meister, Michelle Gallagher and Shaun Holley, David and Kay Ross, Gwen and Peter Andrews, June and Tony Baldwin, Brian Randall, S A Beele, D J Hayman, Tina and David Woods-Taylor, Roger and Lynda Goldstone, Richard Gibbs, Val and Alan Green, G Neighbour, Douglas and Ann Hare, Pat and Baz Turvill, Maria Furness; also in The Good Hotel Guide)*

Free house ~ Licensees M Millington Buck and M Stanley ~ Real ale ~ Bar food ~ Restaurant ~ (01622) 859900 ~ Children welcome ~ Open 12-3, 6-11; 12-11(10.30 Sun) Sat; evening opening time 7 winter; closed 25 Dec

SANDGATE TR2035 Map 3
Clarendon

Head W out of Sandgate on main road to Hythe; about 100m after you emerge onto the seafront park on the road across from a telephone box on the right; just back from the telephone box is an uphill track.

This very simple little local is set half way up a steep lane from the sea. Visitors will probably feel most comfortable in the big windowed lounge on the left – you can see the sea through one window, and occasionally, in the right conditions, the coast of France. There are a few impressions of the pub and a full display of the 1950s and 1970s Whitbread Inn-sign miniatures as well as some period advertising. There are coal fires in both bars in winter. There's a very simple chatty atmosphere in the straightforward right hand bar (popular with locals), and lots of old photographs of the pub and of Sandgate. Well kept Shepherd Neame Best, Bishops Finger, Spitfire and seasonal ales on handpump from a rather nice Victorian mahogany bar and mirrored gantry, as well as 16 wines by the glass, and 16 malts; shove-ha'penny, cribbage, dominoes, chess, backgammon, and draughts. Bar food includes sandwiches (from £1.85; crab in season £3), ploughman's (£3.75), and chicken or prawn curry, steak, kidney and ale pie or chicken in red wine (all £5.75). The hanging baskets and boxes are lovely. *(Recommended by Terry Buckland, David and Ruth Shillitoe, Ian Phillips)*

Shepherd Neame ~ Tenants Keith and Shirley Barber ~ Real ale ~ Bar food ~ (01303) 248684 ~ Well behaved children in dining area ~ Open 11.45-3, 6(7 winter Sat)-11; 12-3, 7-10.30 Sun

SELLING TR0456 Map 3
Rose & Crown

Signposted from exit roundabout of M2 junction 7: keep right on through village and follow Perry Wood signposts; or from A252 just W of junction with A28 at Chilham follow Shottenden signpost, then right turn signposted Selling, then right signposted Perry Wood

The flowering tubs and hanging baskets in front of this much enjoyed 16th-c pub are really lovely – but it's the award-winning back garden that readers like so much, and as well as being full of climbers and ramblers and colourful bedding plants, it also has a neatly kept children's play area, lots of picnic-sets, bat and trap, and a small aviary. The hard-working and genuinely welcoming licensees work just as hard inside, and there are pretty fresh flowers by each of the sturdy corner timbers in the relaxing central servery, hop bines strung from the beams, and an interesting variety of corn-dolly work – there's more of this in a wall cabinet in one cosy side alcove, and much more again down steps in the comfortably cottagey restaurant (which has been redecorated with stencils hand-made by Mrs Prebble of woodland animals). Apart from a couple of old-fashioned housekeeper's chairs by the huge log fire (replaced in summer by an enjoyably colourful mass of silk flowers interlaced with more corn dollies and so forth), the seats are very snugly cushioned. The Christmas decorations are marvellous. Good generously served bar food includes filled rolls (from £3.50), ploughman's (£4), steak and kidney pie (£5.75), chicken tikka masala or China Town platter (£7.50), fisherman's platter (£9), daily specials such as prawn creole, beef in red wine, and Jamaican chicken (£7.50), and a tremendous display of puddings on show in a cold cabinet down steps in a small family room, like toffee apple tart, pecan and maple pie with local honey ice cream and Italian white chocolate (£2.90). Well kept changing ales such as Adnams Southwold, Goacher's Maidstone, Harveys Best, and guests such as Adnams Broadside, Cottage Southern Bitter, and Timothy Taylor Landlord on handpump, local cider, a good range of malts and decent wines in good measures; informal, helpful service; cribbage, shove-ha'penny, dominoes and piped music; the local TVR club meets here on the first Sunday lunchtime of the month. *(Recommended by Kevin Thorpe, Revd Timothy Galligan, C J Hall, Dr Robert Perks, David Gittins, Douglas and Ann Hare)*

Free house ~ Licensees Richard and Jocelyn Prebble ~ Real ale ~ Bar food (Sun and Mon evenings) ~ Restaurant ~ (01227) 752214 ~ Children in eating area of bar and restaurant ~ Open 11-3, 6.30-11; 12-3, 7-10.30 Sun; closed evening 25 Dec

SMARDEN TQ8743 Map 3
Bell ★ ◖

From Smarden follow lane between church and The Chequers, then turn left at T-junction; or from A274 take unsignposted turn E a mile N of B2077 to Smarden

From the mid-17th c this pretty peg-tiled local doubled as both blacksmith's forge and pub until earlier this century. It's very pleasant sitting in the garden amongst the mature fruit trees and shrubs looking up at the attractive rose-covered building with its massive chimneys. Inside, the dimly lit snug little back rooms have low beams, ancient walls of bare brick or rough ochre plaster, brick or flagstone floors, pews and the like around simple tables, and warm fires in inglenook fireplaces; one room is no smoking. The larger white painted and green matchboarded bar has a beamed ceiling and quarry tiled floor, a woodburning stove in the big fireplace, and a games area with darts, pool, shove-ha'penny, cribbage, dominoes, fruit machine and juke box at one end; boules. Bar food includes vegetarian lasagne (£4.95), sausages and mash with onion gravy (£5.25), beer battered cod (£6.25), steak and kidney pudding or cheesy chicken (£6.95) and a mixed grill (£11.50). Well kept Boddingtons, Flowers Original, Fullers London Pride, Harveys Best, Marstons Pedigree, Morlands Old Speckled Hen, Rother Valley Level Best and Shepherd Neame Bitter on handpump, local cider, country wines, several malt whiskies, and winter mulled wine. The bedrooms are quite simple. *(Recommended by Peter and Joan Elbra, Janet and Colin Roe, John Steel, JP, PP, Pat and Baz Turvill, Bruce Bird, Rachael and Mark Baynham, R and M Bishop, G Neighbour, Ian Phillips)*

Free house ~ Licensees Mr and Mrs C J Smith ~ Real ale ~ Bar food (till 10pm) ~ Restaurant ~ (01233) 770283 ~ Children in eating area of bar ~ Open 11.30-2.30(3 Sat), 6-11; 12-3, 7-10.30 Sun; closed 25 Dec ~ Bedrooms: £35/£42

SNARGATE TQ9928 Map 3
Red Lion ★ ◖

B2080 Appledore—Brenzett

This totally unspoilt relaxing village local overcomes you with an almost irresistible desire to linger. In each of its three perfectly simple rooms a cheery group of regulars catch up on local news, play toad in the hole or sample the very palatable Double Vision cider (from nearby Staplehurst) or well kept small-brewery ales. As well as Goachers Light, there might be up to five guests from brewers like Batemans, Hart, Oakham or Swale tapped straight from casks on a low rack behind an unusual shop-like marble-topped counter, with little else behind to mark it as a bar other than a few glasses on two little shelves, some crisps and half a dozen spirit bottles. Its three rooms (and outdoor lavatories too), under the caring eye of the landlady and her friendly daughter, are delightfully frozen in the 1940s with original cream tongue and groove wall panelling, a couple of heavy beams in a sagging ceiling and dark pine Victorian farmhouse chairs on bare boards. One charming little room, with a frosted glass wall through to the bar and a sash window looking out to a delightful cottage garden, has only two dark pine pews beside two long tables, a couple more farmhouse chairs and a nice old piano stacked with books. They don't serve food. *(Recommended by Kevin Thorpe, Jeremy Wallington, JP, PP, the Didler)*

Free house ~ Licensee Mrs Jemison ~ Real ale ~ (01797) 344648 ~ Children away from bar ~ Open 11-3, 7-11; 12-3, 7-10.30 Sun

STONE IN OXNEY TQ9427 Map 3
Crown

Off B2082 Iden—Tenterden

A good balance between drinking and dining, and a nice homely cheeriness, mark out this very friendly welcoming tucked-away pub. Its unassuming exterior and lounge rather belie the very tasty, gently imaginative, good value food they serve. The three starters we chose as a meal between two of us proved to be more than ample and pleasingly fresh. Meaty king prawns were fried in a good garlic sauce (£4.95), fried black pudding with potato croutons and chutney dressing (£3.95) came with a nice selection of herb and salad leaves, and the dressed Scottish crab (£4.95) had enough prawns to make a starter in themselves. Main courses might include filled french bread (£2.50), warm salad of duck breast with plum vinaigrette (£6.25), cod and smoked haddock bake (£6.95), lamb pie or spiced pork kebab with a pepper and mushroom kebab (£7.95), strips of sirloin steak with mushroom sauce or confit of duck legs with blackcurrant sauce (£8.95), with puddings like lemon tart, banoffee pie or plum crème brûlée (£3.95). There's a big inglenook fireplace, two nice old dark wood pews and parquet flooring in the bar, and on the other side of the central servery the longish lounge has a red turkey carpet, well spaced dark wood pub tables, and two big bay windows with pretty views over a cornfield. More and more locals wandered in through the evening until there was quite a happy little group chatting to the friendly landlord. Keep an eye open for, and step over, Shelly, the well fed labrador who sleeps her way through opening times oblivious to the fact that she's lying in the middle of a thoroughfare; pool in a small side bar; pretty good disabled access to the lounge through the front door. *(Recommended by Janet and Colin Roe, E G Parish, Roy Agombar)*

Free house ~ Licensees Joe Cantor and Mandy Standen ~ Real ale ~ (01233) 758789 ~ Open 12-3, 6-11; 12-5 Sun; closed Mon, Sun evening

TOYS HILL TQ4751 Map 3
Fox & Hounds

Off A25 in Brasted, via Brasted Chart and The Chart

For 30 years, the fairly firm but kind Mrs Pelling has run this down-to-earth and slightly eccentric country local. It's the sort of place where bills are toted up on a piece of paper and change is given from a plastic box – and as several readers say, 'long may it stay exactly the same'. Mobile phones are banned, and there are little notices by the open fires warning against 'unofficial stoking'. When your eyes have adjusted to the dim lighting you'll see letters and press cuttings on the walls that describe the brewery campaign to upgrade the pub and Mrs Pelling's fight against it. Little has changed in the two homely rooms here since the 60s (including the service which isn't necessarily geared for a mid-summer tourist rush). You can sit comfortably on one of the well worn old sofas or armchairs which are scattered with cushions and throws, and read the latest *Country Life*, *Hello* or *Private Eye*. Lunchtime bar food is at an absolute minimum with pre-wrapped filled rolls (from £1.50) and one or two simple dishes like ploughman's, cauliflower cheese or sausage and tomato pie (£3.95), and well stocked chocolate shelves. Well kept Greene King IPA and Abbot on handpump; occasional sing-songs around the piano; darts, shove-ha'penny, cribbage and dominoes. The garden is lovely with picnic-sets on a good area of flat lawn surrounded by mature shrubs. As you approach this peaceful retreat from the pretty village (one of the highest in the county) you will catch glimpses through the trees of one of the most magnificent views in Kent. There are good walks nearby, and it's handy for Chartwell and for Emmetts garden. *(Recommended by Jules Akel, W Ruxton, Kevin Thorpe, Mike and Sue Loseby, Brian and Anna Marsden)*

Greene King ~ Tenant Hazel Pelling ~ Real ale ~ Bar food ~ (01732) 750328 ~

Children in snug end of bar lunchtime only ~ Open 11.30-2.30(3 Sat), 6-11; 12-3, 7-10.30 Sun; closed 25 Dec

TUNBRIDGE WELLS TQ5639 Map 3
Beacon ♀

Tea Garden Lane; leaving Tunbridge Wells westwards on A264, this is the left turn-off on Rusthall Common after Nevill Park

To make the most of the sweeping hillside views behind this airy Victorian pub, a new deck area has been built, a pergola added, and new furniture bought – there are quite a few seats on the terrace, too; volleyball, boules and rounders. Inside, the dining area and spreading bar run freely into each other with stripped panelling lovely wood floors, ornately built wall units and glowing lamps giving a solidly comfortable feel. There's usually a couple of business gents conversing at the sweeping bar counter with its ranks of shiny bottles and up to nine wines by the glass, ladies chatting on the comy sofas by the fire, with possibly a table of jovial old chaps lunching in the dining area. As well as their two-course 'food for a fiver' menu, there might be home-made soup (£3.25), filled french bread or filled potatoes (from £3.50; bacon, avocado and mayonnaise £3.95), game terrine with chicken and cranberries or spicy thai crab cakes with ginger and lemon grass sauce (£4.95), poached salmon salad, cod in beer batter or braised rabbit with mixed berries (£6.50), and more exotic (and pricy) dishes such as rocket and curly endive salad with parmesan, plum tomatoes, anchovies, scallions and pancetta bacon (£7), couscous and vegetable strudel on a mushroom and chive sauce (£9.50), pan-fried corn fed chicken breast with Drambuie, porcini mushroom and chervil sauce (£11.95), lightly grilled coriander-crusted calf's liver with smoked bacon on a sage and armagnac sauce (£12.25), and grilled kingfish with fennel and vine tomatoes with an apple balsamic jus (£12.75). Well kept Fullers London Pride, Harveys Best Bitter and Timothy Taylor's Landlord kept under light blanket pressure; shove-ha'penny, cribbage, dominoes and occasional piped music. *(Recommended by James House, Ian Phillips)*

Free house ~ Licensee John Cullen ~ Real ale ~ Bar food ~ Restaurant ~ (01892) 524252 ~ Children in eating area of bar ~ Open 11-11; 12-10.30 Sun

Sankeys ⊗ ♀

39 Mount Ephraim (A26 just N of junction with A267)

Not strictly a pub – more of a wine bar – this is downstairs from the popular seafood restaurant and has a good, friendly bustling atmosphere. It's furnished with lots of sturdy old pine tables on the york-stone floor, and decorated with old mirrors, prints, enamel advertising signs, antique beer engines and other bric-a-brac (most of which has been salvaged from local pub closures); french windows lead to a small suntrap terrace with white tables and chairs under cocktail parasols. Good, enjoyable food includes daily specials and fish soup (£4.50), chilli tiger prawns (£6.50), a plate of charcuterie, wild mushrooms, spinach and pine kernels or moules and frites (£7), smoked cod and prawn fishcakes (£8.50), lovely Cornish cock crab (£14.50), honey roast duck (£12.50), and a platter of fruits de mer (£19.50). Well kept Harveys IPA, King & Barnes, Larkins Traditional, and Shepherd Neame Masterbrew from an antique beer engine, though most people seem to be taking advantage of the superb wine list; they also have quite a choice of unusual teas. You need to get there very early for a table in the bar; the restaurant is no smoking. *(Recommended by Chris Rowley, Janet and Colin Roe, Tina and David Woods-Taylor, Ivan de Deken)*

Free house ~ Licensee Guy Sankey ~ Real ale ~ Bar food ~ Restaurant ~ (01892) 511422 ~ Children in eating area of bar ~ Open 11-11; 11-3, 6-11 Sat; closed Sun, bank hol Mon

ULCOMBE TQ8550 Map 3
Pepper Box ◖

Fairbourne Heath (signposted from A20 in Harrietsham; or follow Ulcombe signpost from A20, then turn left at crossroads with sign to pub

Views from the terrace outside this cosy old country inn stretch over a great plateau of rolling arable farmland, and if you're in the garden, with its small pond, swing and tables among trees, shrubs and flowerbeds, you may catch a glimpse of the deer that sometimes come up. Inside, the friendly, homely bar has standing timbers and low beams hung with hops, copper kettles and pans on window sills, some very low-seated windsor chairs and wing armchairs, and two armchairs and a sofa by the splendid inglenook fireplace with its warm log fire; the tabby tom is called Jones, and there are two more cats and a collie called Rosie. A side area is more functionally furnished for eating, and there's a very snug little no-smoking dining room. A short but good list of enjoyable daily specials includes sautéed devilled lamb kidneys laced with brandy (£4), fresh dressed crab with salad leaves and dill mayonnaise (£5.25), greenshell mussels with coconut and coriander pesto (£5.50), braised lamb shank with a redcurrant and mint sauce and sauté potatoes (£9), fried calf's liver with mash and sage butter sauce (£9.50), and Portuguese sizzling steak with garlic and red wine and sauté potatoes (£12.50); they also do lunchtime sandwiches, good puddings, and a Sunday roast. Very well kept Shepherd Neame Masterbrew, Bishops Finger and Spitfire tapped from the cask, and country wines; efficient, courteous service. The name of the pub refers to the pepperbox pistol – an early type of revolver with numerous barrels. No children inside. *(Recommended by Janet and Colin Roe, Comus Elliott, Mr and Mrs Peter Smith, Mr and Mrs Archibald)*

Shepherd Neame ~ Tenants Geoff and Sarah Pemble ~ Real ale ~ Bar food ~ Restaurant ~ (01622) 842558 ~ Open 11-3, 6.30-11; 12-3, 7-10.30 Sun

Lucky Dip

Besides the fully inspected pubs, you might like to try these Lucky Dips recommended to us and described by readers (if you do, please send us reports):

Aldington [TR0736]
☆ *Walnut Tree* [off B2067 SE of Ashford]: Friendly partly medieval smugglers' pub with ancient brick-floored kitchen bar, lounge bar and games room, decent food from sandwiches up, well kept Shepherd Neame, helpful landlady, sheltered garden with pool and summer barbecues; children allowed in eating areas, handy for Port Lympne zoo *(Michael and Jenny Back, LYM)*
Alkham [TR2542]
Marquis of Granby [back rd between Folkestone and Dover]: White Georgian house with beautiful garden in attractive old village, modernised inside, warm and pleasant; good food esp fish in bar and restaurant, well kept beers, welcoming staff *(Richard and Valerie Wright)*
Appledore [TQ9529]
Black Lion [The Street]: Friendly unpretentious pub locally popular for huge range of good value food served all day esp local fish, partitioned eating area, real ales inc Morlands Old Speckled Hen and John Smiths *(Colin and Janet Roe, R E Swainson, Roy Agombar, Rev John Hibberd)*
Ashurst [TQ5038]
Bald Faced Stag [High St (A264 by stn)]: Friendly family-run local, good value food, well kept Larkins Bitter; small garden with

picnic-sets *(LM)*
Barfrestone [TR2650]
Yew Tree [off A256 N of Dover; or off A2 at Barham]: This friendly, attractive and unpretentious inn, a popular main entry in last year's edition, closed in spring 1999; we hope it may reopen *(LYM)*
Biddenden [TQ8538]
Red Lion [High St]: Plush but friendly Tudor-style inn in lovely village, good straightforward food and service, well kept Whitbreads-related ales *(Janet and Colin Roe)*
Bishopsbourne [TR1852]
Mermaid [signed off A2]: Traditional welcoming unpretentious country local in same family for many years, in lovely unspoilt Kentish village; simple food (not Sun) inc good filled rolls, well kept Shepherd Neame beers, coal fire, darts, no music or machines *(Kevin Thorpe)*
Bodsham [TR1045]
Timber Batts: Attractive, busy and welcoming, with good service, unspoilt country setting, usual food *(Joan and Andrew Life)*
Borden [TQ8862]
Tudor Rose [just off A249]: Well refurbished village pub with well kept Boddingtons, Flowers IPA and Wadworths 6X, wide

choice of reasonably priced food, big
conservatory restaurant, good service,
upstairs evening carvery (Tues-Sat), garden
behind for children, ample parking; open all
day *(Ian Phillips)*

Boughton Street [TR0559]

White Horse [nr M2 junction 7]: Carefully
restored dark-beamed bars and timbered
dining room, well prepared food all day inc
early breakfast and good value carvery
Thurs, Fri, Sat, well kept Shepherd Neame
beers, decent wines, good tea and coffee,
friendly service; tables in garden, children
allowed; good value bedrooms (back ones
quieter), good breakfast *(N A Fox, Stephen
Brown, LYM)*

Boxley [TQ7758]

Kings Arms [1¾ miles from M20 junction 7;
opp church]: Friendly recently refurbished
Whitbreads Wayside Inn, largely 16th or
17th c, low beams, red chesterfields by huge
fireplace, Boddingtons, Fullers London Pride,
Gales HSB, Swale Kentish Pride and
Wadworths 6X, good choice of sensibly
priced straightforward food (all day Sun)
from good sandwiches to Sun roasts,
secondhand books for sale; piped music;
good garden for children, open all day, pretty
village, pleasant walks *(Mark Percy, Lesley
Mayoh)*

Brasted [TQ4654]

☆ *White Hart*: Spacious dining lounge and
extension sun lounge with large no-smoking
area, substantial food inc very generous ice-
cream concoctions and good sponge
puddings, pleasant staff, Bass and Hancocks
HB served through chiller, Battle of Britain
bar with signatures and mementoes of Biggin
Hill fighter pilots; children welcome, big
neatly kept garden with well spaced tables
and play area; bedrooms, pretty village with
several antique shops *(Brian Borwick, LYM,
E G Parish, Catherine and Richard Preston,
Tina and David Woods-Taylor)*

Bridge [TR1854]

Plough & Harrow [High St]: Particularly
well kept Shepherd Neame in small 17th-c
two-bar pub, coal fire and lots of sporting
prints (giant young landlord played rugby for
Canterbury), good lunchtime sandwiches (no
food evenings or Sun), darts and games in public bar; good wine
choice; open all day Sat *(Kevin Thorpe)*

☆ *White Horse* [High St]: Good fresh food
from doorstep sandwiches up and friendly
service in smartly comfortable good value old
dining pub with huge fireplace in main bar,
second bar, dining area and civilised
restaurant, well kept Bass and guest ales,
interesting wines; attractive village *(Norman
Fox, Mr and Mrs T A Bryan)*

Broadstairs [TR3967]

Tartar Frigate [Harbour St, by quay]: Huge
helpings of seafood in busy upstairs
restaurant with good harbour view,
Victorian tile-and-plush style, well kept beer,
fishing memorabilia, pool *(Margaret and Bill
Rogers, Sue Holland, Dave Webster)*

Broomfield [TR1966]

Huntsman & Horn [Margate Rd]:
Sympathetically refurbished (even lime
mortar for fireplace), with Tetleys-related
beers, excellent welcome, super log fire, food
inc very good home-made soup *(David
Gittins)*

Canterbury [TR1557]

☆ *Canterbury Tales* [The Friars, just off main St
Peters St pedestrian area]: Popular
pub/bistro, clean and airy, with well kept
Shepherd Neame and guests such as Adnams,
Batemans and Goachers, enjoyable food inc
good sandwiches, vegetarian and Mexican
tapas, books, games and chess table,
theatrical memorabilia (they serve you
quickly if you're going to a play or concert),
more noise from conversation than the piped
jazz, cheerful young well trained staff;
peaceful at lunchtime, busier with young
people evening; live music Mon, jazz some
Sun afternoons *(David Carr, Rachael and
Mark Baynham, Ian and Nita Cooper, Tim
Barrow, Sue Demont, Janet and Colin Roe,
Kevin Thorpe, Martin, Pat and Hilary
Forrest, Howard England)*

Millers Arms: Welcoming pub prettily set in
quiet street nr river (no drinking outside
though), several rooms, well kept beers inc
Boddingtons and Morlands Old Speckled
Hen, bar food *(Mrs D Hibberd)*

New Inn [Havelock St]: Traditional unspoilt
Victorian alehouse, elderly furnishings, bare
boards, gas fire, good beermat collection,
Greene King and several changing real ales,
simple food; modern conservatory (and juke
box) *(Kevin Thorpe)*

Olde Beverlie [St Stephens Green; A290 from
centre, then R at Tyler Hill/Univ sign]: Built
1570 with adjoining almshouses, beam and
wattle open-plan rooms with flagstones, old
prints, brasses, jugs etc, varied food,
Shepherd Neame ales, small restaurant, nice
walled garden with bat and trap; piped music
(Kevin Thorpe)

Pilgrims [The Friars]: Partly 18th-c hotel
handy for theatre, busy bar with Ind Coope
Burton and Wadworths 6X, well presented
food, good service; bedrooms *(R F and M K
Bishop)*

Thomas Becket [Best Lane]: Cheerful beamed
city pub with rustic furnishings, hanging hop
bines, tankards and farm tools, good
generous food inc sandwiches and
vegetarian, real ales *(Joan and Andrew Life)*

Thomas Ingoldsby [Burgate]: Big, wide and
handsome Wetherspoons pub with good
range of beer inc bargain Shepherd Neame,
good food choice, lots of local interest
around the walls, very friendly staff; popular
with young people *(Rev John Hibberd, Dick
Brown)*

Three Compasses [High St]: Whitbreads pub,
with Shepherd Neame beer too; SkyTV
sports, piped music *(Rev John Hibberd)*

Capel [TQ6344]

☆ *Dovecote* [Alders Rd; SE of Tonbridge]:
Attractive pub in pleasant tucked-away

hamlet, doves and big thatched dovecote in back garden, bare bricks, beams and brasses, good choice of food from baguettes up, good range of beers tapped from the cask *(Ian Phillips)*

Chiddingstone Causeway [TQ5146]

Little Brown Jug [B2027]: Spacious, clean and comfortable even when busy, olde-brick-and-beam style décor, well kept Harveys and other ales, decent wines, friendly welcome, wide range of promptly served food (no sandwiches), restaurant, no-smoking area; children welcome if eating, attractive garden with play area; bedrooms *(Peter Meister, Chris Rowley, Robert Gomme)*

Chilham [TR0753]

☆ *Woolpack* [High St; off A28/A252]: Good value food inc vegetarian and good sandwiches, cheerful service, pews, sofa, little armchairs, inglenook fires, well kept Shepherd Neame ales; restaurant (children allowed till early evening); bedrooms, delightful village *(Ivan de Deken, Janet and Colin Roe, LYM)*

Chipstead [TQ4956]

Bricklayers Arms [Chevening Rd]: Attractive old local overlooking lake and green, heavily beamed bar with open fire, larger back restaurant, good choice of appetising food (not Sun evening), full range of Harveys beers tapped from casks behind long counter, good atmosphere *(Mike Gorton, A E Brace)*

Cobham [TQ6768]

Inn on the Lake [Silvermere Golf Club, Redhill Rd]: Newish pub, effectively golf club restaurant but open to all, Hardys Royal Oak and Tetleys, friendly staff, wide choice of good food inc tasty seafood platters *(R B Crail)*

☆ *Leather Bottle* [handy for M2 junction 1]: Ancient beamed and timbered pub with interesting woodwork and masses of Dickens prints reflecting his connections with the pub; much modernised inside, decent food in bar and restaurant, well kept Courage and a guest beer, friendly service; tables on big back lawn with play area, summer tuck shop and fish pond; quiet, pretty village; bedrooms *(Dave Braisted)*

Cowden [TQ4642]

☆ *Queens Arms* [Cowden Pound; junction B2026 with Markbeech rd]: Unspoilt two-room country pub like something from the 1930s, with splendid landlady, well kept Brakspears, darts; strangers quickly feel like regulars *(the Didler, Pete Baker, JP, PP)*

Cranbrook [TQ7735]

Crown: Friendly small town local, well kept real ales, good value lunchtime specials *(Comus Elliott)*

George [Stone St]: Civilised and friendly small-town pub *(Comus Elliott)*

Darenth [TQ5671]

Chequers [down unsigned lane between A225 and B260 S of Dartford]: Traditional local with good choice of generous food (not Sun-Tues evening) inc good value Sun roast, well kept Courage Best and a guest beer,

friendly staff, cheap drinks and crisps for children; can book tables in pleasant dining room, good view from sizeable back garden with small terrace *(Kevin Flack, LM)*

Dungeness [TR0916]

Britannia [by old lighthouse]: Don't be put off by blockhouse appearance: friendly and spotless inside, with good range of modestly priced food inc fresh local fish, several well kept real ales inc local Swale; handy for Romney Hythe & Dymchurch railway, RSPB reserve *(Tony Hobden, R F and M K Bishop)*

Dunton Green [TQ5157]

Bullfinch [London Rd]: Country Carvery family dining pub, friendly service, slide in garden *(A M Pring)*

East Malling [TQ7057]

King & Queen [N of stn, back rd between A20 at Larkfield and A26]: 14th-c but much altered, with big low-ceilinged dark plum rooms, some handsome panelling, wide choice of food, not cheap but imaginative, inc lots of fish, Brakspears, Charles Wells Bombardier and Hopback Summer Lightning; can get smoky; tables in smallish garden *(BB)*

East Sutton [TQ8349]

Shant Hotel [aka Prince of Wales]: Good pub atmosphere in big bar/restaurant facing cricket green, vast choice of good value food, courteous staff, real ales; bedrooms *(B R and M J Cooper)*

Egerton [TQ9047]

George: Friendly two-bar village pub with welcoming licensee brothers, well presented if not speedy bar food, wide range of well kept ales, attractive restaurant Weds-Sat; pretty setting, pleasant country view *(Janet and Colin Roe)*

Elham [TR1743]

Kings Arms [St Marys Rd]: Good interesting reasonably priced food, relaxing attractive lounge bar, good open fire, unobtrusively attentive friendly service, steps down to big dining area (booking advised); pool table in public bar; opp church in square of charming village *(Janet and Colin Roe)*

Eynsford [TQ5365]

Malt Shovel: Neatly kept spacious old-fashioned dining pub handy for castles and Roman villa, generous bar food inc lots of good value fish and seafood (lobster tank), well kept Fullers, friendly attentive service, nice atmosphere; car park across busy road *(David Peakall, Robert Gomme, B J Harding, LM)*

Faversham [TR0161]

Anchor [Abbey St]: Smallish friendly two-room local nr quay, well kept Shepherd Neame Bitter and winter Porter, good quiet relaxed atmosphere, bare boards and individual furniture, hall with bench seats, a couple of picnic-sets outside, attractive old street *(David Gittins, the Didler)*

Elephant [The Mall]: Picturesque flower-decked terrace town pub with very good choice of well kept changing ales, thoughtful staff, simple but attractive furnishings on stripped boards, home-made food inc vegetarian and summer barbecues *(the Didler, Judy Tolman)*

Sun [West St]: Roomy and rambling old-world 15th-c weatherboarded town pub with good unpretentious atmosphere, tasty reasonably priced lunchtime food, well kept Shepherd Neame, good service; tables in pleasant back courtyard, interesting street *(David Gittins)*

Goudhurst [TQ7037]

Green Cross [Station Rd (A262 W)]: Popular with older people for good interesting home-made food from sandwiches to Sat carvery, well kept Harveys and more distant beers (though atmosphere not really very pubby, despite the dog); beamed dining room for residents; bedrooms light and airy, good value *(Colin and Janet Roe, TRS)*

☆ *Star & Eagle* [High St]: Striking medieval inn with settles and Jacobean-style seats in heavily beamed open-plan bar, well kept Whitbreads-related ales, wide choice of decent food, polite service, tables behind with pretty views; children welcome; lovely character bedrooms, well furnished and comfortable; open all day *(Gwen and Peter Andrews, LYM, Ivan de Deken)*

Hadlow [TQ6252]

☆ *Artichoke* [Hamptons, 4 miles SE of Plaxtol; OS Sheet 188 map ref 627524]: Dating from 13th c, with ancient low beams, high-backed wooden settles, some unusual wrought-iron glass-topped tables, huge welcoming inglenook log fire, gleaming brass, country pictures and bric-a-brac, bar food inc good home-made pies, no-smoking restaurant, well kept Adnams, Fullers London Pride, Greene King Abbot and Youngs Special, good range of spirits; children in eating area, seats outside inc pews in shower-proof arbour, quiet rural setting; may keep credit card if you're running a tab; cl winter Sun evenings *(Tim Barrow, Sue Demont, Peter Meister, Martin, Pat and Hilary Forrest, BB)*

Hawkhurst [TQ7730]

☆ *Oak & Ivy* [Pipsden; A268 towards Rye]: Immaculately refurbished and extended, heavy low beams and timbers, quarry tiles, dark brown terracotta bar, bright dining area, roaring log fires (one in massive inglenook), well kept Whitbreads-related ales, friendly efficient staff, generous reasonably priced food inc popular Sun roasts, cheerful service; piped music, fruit machine; tables outside, good play area *(B R Sparkes, G S B G Dudley, BB)*

Wellington Arms [Gills Green; just off A229 N]: Basic well used pub dating from 16th c, wide choice of good value well prepared food from sandwiches up, well kept Batemans, Harveys and Tetleys, restaurant *(Janet and Colin Roe)*

Hever [TQ4744]

☆ *Henry VIII* [outside gates of Hever Castle]: Comfortable Shepherd Neame pub dating from 14th c, some fine oak panelling and heavy beams, inglenook fireplace, Henry VIII

décor, friendly staff, usual bar food (all day Mar-Nov) inc good ploughman's and half-helpings for children, restaurant; tables out on terrace and pondside lawn *(Jenny and Brian Seller, Derek Harvey-Piper, Mrs S Miller, Wendy Arnold, B, M and P Kendall)*

Hollingbourne [TQ8454]

Sugar Loaves [High St]: Two bars, beams and alcoves, good local and visiting mix, good choice of home-made food inc imaginative vegetarian, real ales inc Flowers IPA *(Rev John Hibberd)*

Horton Kirby [TQ5668]

Fighting Cocks: Country pub with comfortable saloon, good food inc take-away pizzas Mon, big riverside garden with goats, ducks, bat and trap, boules, ping-pong in marquee *(Kevin Flack)*

Ide Hill [TQ4851]

Cock [off B2042 SW of Sevenoaks]: Pretty village-green pub with well kept Greene King, fine log fire, bar billiards, straightforward bar food (not Sun evening, only clingfilm-wrapped sandwiches Sun lunchtime), piped music, some seats out in front; handy for Chartwell and nearby walks – so gets busy, with nearby parking sometimes out of the question; no children *(LYM, Robert Gomme, W Ruxton, Matthew Cooper)*

Ivy Hatch [TQ5854]

☆ *Plough* [off A227 N of Tonbridge]: More restaurant than pub, often fully booked, with wide choice of good food at a price, fastidious French cooking, impressive range of reasonably priced wines (and well kept Greene King IPA), attractive candlelit surroundings – upmarket in a friendly informal style; very efficient well turned out staff, delightful conservatory and garden *(Mr and Mrs Powell, M J Dowdy, F C Johnston, Comus Elliott, Maysie Thompson, LYM, Chris Rowley, Jason Caulkin)*

Kemsing [TQ5558]

Wheatsheaf: Limited choice of carefully cooked food, prompt pleasant service *(DMT)*

Kennington [TR0245]

Golden Ball [Canterbury Rd; A28 NE of Ashford]: Welcoming Shepherd Neame pub with well kept beer, decent food inc Sun roast; pool, darts *(Rev John Hibberd)*

Kingsdown [TR3748]

Rising Sun [Cliffe Rd]: Attractive 17th-c clapboard pub by shingle beach, mainly modern inside but keeping some old brickwork and beams; Whitbreads-related ales with a guest such as Fullers London Pride, log fire, decent straightforward food, darts in back bar, quiet piped music; small cottage garden, good walks *(Kevin Thorpe)*

Kingston [TR1951]

☆ *Black Robin* [Valley Rd; off A2 Canterbury—Dover at Barham sign]: Good unusual food inc enterprising starters, gorgeous puddings and enjoyable Sun lunch in friendly unpretentious pub with Shepherd Neame and maybe a guest beer, cheerful staff, wooden floors, stripped brick, chunky old pine tables and assorted chairs, old prints and paintings for sale, flowers, lots of hop bines around bar, low lighting inc candles; maybe piped radio; tables in garden; cl Sun evenings and Mon until Easter *(Chris and Anna Rowley, Michael and Jenny Back, Kevin Thorpe)*

Laddingford [TQ6948]

Chequers: Friendly village local with well kept ales such as Adnams, Boddingtons and Whitbreads, good food cooked by landlord, plenty for children; big garden, reasonably priced bedroom, Medway walks nearby *(Simon and Sally Small)*

Lamberhurst [TQ6735]

☆ *Brown Trout* [B2169, off A21 nr entrance to Scotney Castle]: Popular dining pub specialising in briskly served fish, sauce and vinegar bottles on lots of tables in biggish extension off small beamed bar, well kept Fullers London Pride and Marstons Pedigree, fair choice of decent wines, friendly staff, picnic-sets in large safe garden with play area; children in eating areas, open all day Sun and summer, can be very busy w/e *(Brian Skelcher, Ian Phillips, Jules Akel, G Simpson, Conrad and Alison Freezer, Jilly Burrows, James House, BB, Tom and Ruth Rees, Brenda and Stuart Naylor, Derek and Iris Martin)*

☆ *Elephants Head* [Hook Green; B2169 towards T Wells]: Ancient rambling timber-framed country pub under new tenants, well kept Harveys inc seasonal brews, heavy beams, brick or oak flooring, log fire and woodburner, plush-cushioned pews etc; darts and fruit machine in small side area, quiet piped music, bar food, picnic-sets in big back garden with terrace and impressive play area (peaceful view), and by front green; nr Bayham Abbey and Owl House, popular with families w/e, quiz nights etc *(Ian Phillips, James House, Peter Meister)*

George & Dragon [High St]: Large rambling pub with well kept Harveys, Greene King Abbot and Ruddles, good choice of food from baguettes up, genial licensees, side restaurant; bedrooms, quieter behind *(Colin and Janet Roe)*

Leigh [TQ5446]

Bat & Ball [High St]: Two-bar village pub, good generous food, Shepherd Neame beers, no music; busy w/e *(Rev John Hibberd)*

Lenham [TQ8952]

Dog & Bear [The Square]: Friendly inn with decent choice of food from sandwiches up inc OAP bargains, Shepherd Neame ales, no-smoking bar, restaurant, rare authentic Queen Anne coat of arms; good value bedrooms, pretty village *(Janet and Colin Roe)*

Leybourne [TQ6958]

Castle Lake: Usefully placed Whitbreads Brewers Fayre with usual reasonably priced food and excellent friendly service; bedrooms in adjoining Travel Inn *(R C Vincent)*

Littlebourne [TR2057]

Evenhill House [The Hill (A257)]: Former

roadhouse now a smart split-level bare-boards bar and restaurant, stripped pine furniture, dining areas inc upper gallery, good food and service, well kept Shepherd Neame, friendly staff *(Bill Rogers, Comus Elliott)*

Loose [TQ7552]

Chequers [Old Loose Hill]: Attractive neatly kept riverside pub with unusual range of good freshly made food, good choice of Whitbreads-related ales, warmly welcoming efficient service *(Mr and Mrs J Gallaher)*

Luddesdown [TQ6766]

Golden Lion: Friendly traditional pub in peaceful valley for walkers, with big woodburning stove as well as open fire, well kept ales inc Marstons Pedigree, good value well presented simple bar lunches, prompt service *(A E Brace)*

Maidstone [TQ7757]

Chiltern Hundreds [Penenden Heath Rd; ¼ mile from M20, junction 7, towards Maidstone]: Upmarket Chef & Brewer dining pub popular with families, restrained decor, wide choice of food all day, Scottish Courage ales, obliging staff; conservatory, terrace *(Alan M Pring, BB, Thomas and Audrey Nott)*

Pilot [Upper Stone St (A229)]: Busy roadside inn, bar food (not Sun), well kept Harveys Bitter, Mild and seasonal ales; listed building *(the Didler)*

Marden Thorn [TQ7842]

☆ *Wild Duck* [Pagehurst Lane; off A229 in Staplehurst or B2079 in Marden]: Neat and very welcoming country pub concentrating on wide choice of interesting well presented food, not over-priced, in attractive bar and big smart dining room, four well kept ales inc Fullers London Pride and Harveys, good range of wines, good landlord and staff, plenty of atmosphere *(Comus Elliott, Pat and Baz Turvill, BB, RDK)*

Margate [TR3571]

Spread Eagle [Victoria Rd]: Traditional corner pub with bar and lounge eating area, popular blackboard food, good range of well kept ales such as Courage Directors, Kent Swifty and Delight, Wychwood *(Ian Phillips)*

Marsh Green [TQ4345]

Wheatsheaf [B2028 SW of Edenbridge]: Cosy and attractively renovated village pub, up to ten or so well kept ales inc Fullers, Harveys and local Larkins, farm cider, wide-ranging good value freshly made food inc tasty lunchtime sandwiches, fresh fish and popular Sun lunch, friendly landlord and staff, roomy conservatory, tables on small terrace and in garden *(R and S Bentley, Brian Borwick, Andy and Jill Kassube, Jenny and Brian Seller)*

Marshside [TR2265]

Hog & Donkey: Idiosyncratic small pub with Flowers tapped from the cask, no food, cottagey front room with unsmart mix of tables, chairs, sofas and bright cushions strewn around, coal fire, maybe 1960s radiogram playing; car park may be full of cars even if pub empty – landlord collects them; handy for Stour Valley and Saxon Shore walks *(Kevin Thorpe)*

Mersham [TR0438]

☆ *Farriers Arms* [Flood St]: Smart and attractive three-room local based on early 17th-c forge, wide choice of good straightforward food inc good value Sun lunch, well kept Tetleys-related ales, good friendly service; tranquil well kept streamside garden behind, pleasant country views; bedrooms *(R F and M K Bishop)*

Minster [TR3164]

Mortons Fork [Station Rd; the one nr Ramsgate]: Attractive country-style small bar and linked dining area in well kept small hotel, settles and sewing-machine tables, log fire, helpful friendly staff, good choice of varied good value unusual bar food inc exotic puddings, decent wine, good housekeeping; restaurant, tables outside; three luxurious bedrooms *(A Cowell)*

Otford [TQ5359]

☆ *Bull*: 15th-c, with several spacious rooms, log fires in two enormous fireplaces; now a new-style Chef & Brewer with very wide choice of good food all day *(Brian Borwick)*

Pembury [TQ6240]

Black Horse [High St]: Small pleasantly modernised low-beamed local with well kept ales inc Harveys and one brewed locally for the pub, friendly staff, log fire, wide choice of generous quickly served food, fish restaurant in separate building behind; children's garden neat and well kept *(Michael and Hazel Duncombe)*

Penshurst [TQ5243]

Leicester Arms: Busy pub in charming village by Penshurst Place, cosy old bars and original dining room up steps, with country views, plainer back extension eating area, good choice of generous reasonably priced food, well kept Fullers London Pride, Larkins and Wadworths 6X, willing young staff; children welcome, tables in back garden, economical bedrooms *(Colin and Joyce Laffan, A M Pring, Robert Gomme)*

Pett Bottom [TR1652]

☆ *Duck* [off B2068 S of Canterbury, via Lower Hardres]: Remote tile-hung cottage with two small bars, big 17th-c fireplace, plain furnishings – can get packed out for wide choice of good food inc interesting pies and pasta; well kept Greene King ales, decent wines by the glass, local cider; restaurant, children allowed in smaller room; tables in sizeable garden *(Kevin Thorpe)*

Plaxtol [TQ6054]

Golding Hop [Sheet Hill]: Secluded country pub, good in summer with suntrap streamside lawn; small and simple inside, with well kept Adnams and Youngs tapped from the cask, farm ciders (sometimes even their own), limited bar food (not Mon evening), woodburner, pool, game machine, good friendly service *(LM, Hugh Roberts)*

Pluckley [TQ9245]

Black Horse: Open-plan bar with roomy back dining area in attractive old house, hops on beams, vast inglenook, usual furnishings and food, cheery atmosphere, Whitbreads-related beers with Brakspears and Wadworths 6X; piped music, fruit machine; children allowed if eating; picnic-sets in spacious informal garden by tall sycamores, good walks, open all day Fri-Sun *(Rachael and Mark Baynham, JP, PP, Pat and Baz Turvill)*

☆ *Rose & Crown* [Mundy Bois – spelled Monday Boys on some maps]: Welcoming little pub with very popular nicely furnished dining room, good varied food esp fresh fish, soups, puddings and Sun lunch, interesting sensibly priced wines and country wines, well kept Hook Norton Best and Shepherd Neame, farm cider, plenty of malt whiskies, reasonable prices, helpful service; friendly dog *(Dominic Dunlop, Colin and Janet Roe, Pat and Baz Turvill)*

Reculver [TR2269]

King Ethelbert: Very welcoming, usual bar food with good specials, well kept Flowers Original; by surviving towers of Saxon church within a Roman encampment *(R T and J C Moggridge)*

Rochester [TQ7467]

Coopers Arms [St Margarets St]: Jettied Tudor building behind cathedral, cosy and quaint inside, bustling local atmosphere, friendly staff, comfortable seating, generous low-priced bar lunches, well kept Scottish Courage ales *(Tony Hobden, Quentin Williamson, A E Brace)*

Queen Charlotte [High St]: Very welcoming spotless traditional pub, good choice of sensibly priced early evening weekday food, well kept beers inc Morlands Old Speckled Hen; jazz Thurs *(J Hibberd)*

Sandgate [TR2035]

Ship [High St]: Old-fashioned, not smart but cosy and welcoming, barrel seats and tables, well kept Harveys and good choice of other changing beers tapped from the cask, good reasonably priced food, good service, seafaring theme, great atmosphere, friendly landlord; seats out behind overlooking beach *(Janet and Colin Roe)*

Sandling [TQ7558]

Yew Tree [nestling under M20 just N of Maidstone]: Comfortable and peaceful old local, a relaxing break from junction 6; limited choice of decent lunchtime food, well kept Shepherd Neame, pretty village with attractive church *(Comus Elliott)*

Sandwich [TR3358]

Bell [The Quay]: Comfortable carpeted lounge, soft pleasant piped music, usual bar food inc sandwiches, ploughman's and main dishes, with extra choice from restaurant, unobtrusive piped music; bedrooms *(Margaret and Bill Rogers)*

George & Dragon [Fisher St]: Cheerful attractively refurbished old building in centre, well cooked food inc pizzas from woodburning oven, four well kept local ales *(Derek Hayman)*

Kings Arms [Strand St]: So simple and unpretentious that the striking Elizabethan carving (inside and out) comes as a surprise; warm welcome, good well cooked food, well kept Flowers IPA; traditional games and pool in public bar, children in restaurant *(David Gittins)*

Red Cow [Moat Sole; 100 yds from Guildhall, towards Woodnesborough]: Two carefully refurbished open-plan bars and eating area, old beams and pictures, changing ales such as Boddingtons, Fullers London Pride, Greene King Abbot, King & Barnes, Morlands Old Speckled Hen and Whitbreads, good value food, good atmosphere, friendly staff, lovely log fire; soft piped music; guide dogs only, garden bar, hanging baskets *(Kevin Thorpe, Margaret and Bill Rogers, F C Johnston)*

Sarre [TR2565]

☆ *Crown* [A28 Canterbury—Margate]: Carefully restored pub making much of its long history as the Cherry Brandy House, two attractive beamed bars, pictures of celebrity guests, good choice of reasonably priced home-cooked food, well kept Shepherd Neame beers, log fires, quiet restaurant; garden, open all day; comfortable spacious bedrooms *(Stephen and Julie Brown, Margaret and Bill Rogers, Kevin Thorpe)*

Selling [TR0456]

☆ *White Lion* [E of A251; Selling signed from exit roundabout, M2 junction 7]: 17th-c pub with friendly helpful staff, wide choice of popular food, well kept Shepherd Neame Bitter and Spitfire, decent wines, comfortable bar with two big log fires (one with a spit), pews on stripped boards, unusual semicircular bar counter, nice dog, back restaurant; children welcome; rustic picnic-sets in attractive garden, colourful hanging baskets *(Kevin Thorpe, LYM, Paul and Sharon Sneller, Michelle Gallagher, Ivan de Deken, Chris and Sue Bax)*

Shipbourne [TQ5952]

Chaser [Stumble Hill]: Fairly sophisticated food from ploughman's up, bistro-like end part with candles and stripped pine, cheerful public bar welcoming walkers, friendly efficient service, well kept Harveys, decent wines, high-vaulted restaurant, tables outside; comfortable bedrooms – lovely spot by village church and green *(R C Morgan)*

Smarden [TQ8842]

☆ *Chequers*: Cosy and relaxed beamed local in lovely village, one small eating area with a good deal of rustic character off main turkey-carpeted bar, another at the back more orthodox; second parquet-floored bar largely laid for diners; good generous freshly made food from a fine filled baguette to quite exotic main dishes inc vegetarian, Bass, Morlands Old Speckled Hen, Ruddles County, Worthington and Youngs Special, decent wines and spirits, log fire, local-interest books, no music or machines; pleasant tables outside; bedrooms simple

(and some within earshot of bar) but good value, with huge breakfast *(R F and M K Bishop, Valerie James, Janet and Colin Roe, Pam and Tim Moorey, Mark Baynham, Rachael Ward, BB)*

Sole Street [TR0949]

☆ *Compasses* [note – this is the Sole Street near Wye]: Unspoilt 15th-c country pub, easy-going low-ceilinged rambling bars with bare boards or flagstones, antique or reclaimed furnishings, massive brick bread oven, enamel advertisements, well kept Fullers ESB, London Pride, Shepherd Neame and Stour Valley Kentish Pride, Biddenden farm cider, fruit wines, well presented hearty food, loudly cheery landlord; children welcome in extended garden room; bar billiards, piped music; big neatly kept garden with rustic tables, play area and various pets, good walks *(Kim Hollingshead, John and Elizabeth Thomason, Mark Percy, Lesley Mayoh)*

Southfleet [TQ6171]

☆ *Wheatsheaf* [High Cross Rd, Westwood; from A2, keep straight on through Southfleet itself, past The Ship]: Unpretentious thatched and beamed Tudor country pub with ornamental pheasants and fowl on big lawn above car park, tables around sizeable softly floodlit carp pond, aviaries with parakeets and owls; heavy beams and partitions inside, padded barrel chairs, traditional high-backed settles, inglenook with big woodburner; well kept ales such as Courage Best, Wadworths 6X and Whitbreads Fuggles Imperial, good value food, resident african grey parrot *(BB, Michael and Jenny Back)*

Speldhurst [TQ5541]

George & Dragon [signed from A264 W of T Wells]: Fine timbered building, partly 13th c, panelling, massive beams and flagstones, huge log fire, high-backed settles, sofa, banquettes, handsome upstairs restaurant; well kept Harveys PA and Best and a guest such as M&B Brew XI, lots of malt whiskies, good wines; bar food (not Sun evening), pub games, piped music; provision for children, tables in garden; blues Sun evening, open all day (not Mon-Thurs in winter) *(Pat and Tony Martin, E and K Leist, Thomas Nott, Jill Bickerton, LYM, John and Elspeth Howell, Peter Meister)*

St Margarets Bay [TR3844]

Coastguard: Tremendous views to France from cheery modernised seaside pub, hefty helpings of fish and chips, open all day in summer; children welcome, lots of tables on balcony below NT cliff *(Catherine and Richard Preston, Ms S Bodell, LYM)*

St Mary in the Marsh [TR0627]

Star [opp church]: Relaxed and remote down-to-earth pub, Tudor but very much modernised; friendly family service, well kept Shepherd Neame inc Mild tapped from the cask, good value competent food; good value attractive bedrooms with Romney Marsh views *(Jeremy Wallington)*

St Nicholas at Wade [TR2666]
Bell [just off A299]: 16th-c, with four olde-worlde beamed rooms, friendly staff, open fires, good well priced seafood and other food, well kept Shepherd Neame *(Paul and Sharon Sneller, R F and M K Bishop)*
Stalisfield Green [TQ9553]
Plough [off A252 in Charing]: Well presented food from filled baguettes up, friendly service, peaceful atmosphere, four real ales, farm cider, big but tasteful side extension, tables in big pleasant garden, attractive village green setting, good view and walks *(Mr and Mrs McKay)*
Stansted [TQ6062]
Black Horse [Tumblefield Rd]: Friendly recently refurbished pub, pretty location and views, with Greene King Abbot, Larkins, Youngs and a seasonal ale, good range of reasonably priced food *(T Neate)*
Staplehurst [TQ7847]
Lord Raglan [Chart Hill Rd]: Sympathetically refurbished traditional country pub, almost a 1930s feel, friendly staff and locals, well kept Goachers and Rother Valley, imaginative well presented food inc wide choice for Sun lunch, decent wine list, coal fires; reasonable wheelchair access, good-sized garden *(Sylvia Law, Colin and Janet Roe, Alan Caudell)*
Stodmarsh [TR2160]
☆ *Red Lion* [High St; off A257 just E of Canterbury]: Well rebuilt, with hops on beams, flagstones and bare boards, log fires, pine furniture, pictures and rustic bric-a-brac, good food inc chargrills, duck and game, friendly helpful landlord, well kept Greene King IPA and occasional guest beers such as Stour Valley Kentish Pride tapped from the cask, farm cider, winter mulled wine, pub games; open all day, can get busy w/e, some live music, garden with bat and trap; bedrooms, handy for bird sanctuary *(Kevin Thorpe, I Pritchard, David Gregory)*
Stone Street [TQ5754]
☆ *Padwell Arms* [by-road Seal—Plaxtol]: Small relaxed local with long tables on front terrace overlooking orchards, more in nice back garden, good choice of genuinely home-cooked food using local produce, sensible prices, friendly staff, well kept Badger, Hook Norton Old Hooky and changing guest ales, farm ciders, open fires; dogs welcome, occasional live music and other events; good walks *(S A Beele, Catherine and Richard Preston, Hugh Roberts)*
Stowting [TR1242]
☆ *Tiger* [off B2068 N of M20 junction 11]: Recently saved from closure, unspoilt partly 17th-c pub with attractive unpretentious furniture, candles on tables, faded rugs on bare boards, well prepared changing food usually inc local trout, venison and beef (booking advised), well kept Everards Tiger, Fullers London Pride, Theakstons Best and Old Peculier and guest beers, good log fire, tables outside with occasional barbecues; well behaved children allowed, good jazz

Mon (cl Mon lunchtime) *(Mrs Anne-Marie Logan, Kevin Thorpe, LYM)*
Tenterden [TQ8833]
White Lion [High St]: Sizeable hotel's clean and tidy beamed bar, dark panelling, books and fishing memorabilia, log fire, good service, generous popular food inc huge fish and chips in front bars or back restaurant, Bass, Courage Directors, Harveys and a guest beer; jazz Thurs, bedrooms, open all day *(Kevin Thorpe, Janet and Colin Roe)*
William Caxton [West Cross; top of High St]: Cosy and friendly 15th-c oak-beamed local, big inglenook log fire, wide choice of home-made food inc vegetarian in bar or pleasant restaurant, Shepherd Neame beers; tables in garden, open all day; children welcome; bedrooms *(Pat and Baz Turvill, Kevin Thorpe)*
☆ *Woolpack* [High St]: Striking 15th-c inn with several oak-beamed rooms inc family dining room, inglenook log fires, pleasant modest atmosphere, good generous home-cooked food, friendly quick service, well kept Whitbreads-related and other ales, decent coffee; open all day; comfortable bedrooms *(Joan and Andrew Life)*
Tunbridge Wells [TQ5839]
Brokers Arms [Mount Ephraim; A264]: Pubby downstairs bar with city accent, upstairs restaurant, well kept Harveys and guest beers, welcoming owners, cosy log fires, good mix of ages and genuine locals, giant helpings of good value interesting food inc particularly good grills and fish *(John and Phyllis Maloney)*
Chaplins [Pantiles/Fish Market]: Former Duke of York, now more of a wine bar, but still has draught beers as well as half a dozen wines by the glass, pleasant staff *(John A Barker)*
Crystal Palace [Camden Rd/Victoria Rd]: Well kept Harveys, pleasant service, entertaining customers *(John A Barker)*
Hooden on the Stage [St Johns Rd]: Another pub in the Hooden Horse chain, similar food with heavy Mexican slant, lots of wines by the glass inc New World. *(Hilary Dobbie)*
Mount Edgcumbe [The Common]: Small bar with lots of bricks, hops and wood, well kept beer, good choice of food from ploughman's and good baguettes up, obliging service, tables outside – pleasant setting with Common views; bedrooms *(Janet and Colin Roe, LYM, John and Phyllis Maloney)*
Royal Wells [Mount Ephraim]: Well lit hotel bar with comfortable settees and chairs, cosy corners, views over T Wells, well kept Courage Directors, Harveys Best and Wadworths 6X, good value enterprising lunchtime brasserie menu, friendly efficient staff; bedrooms *(John and Phyllis Maloney, John Beeken)*
Under River [TQ5551]
White Rock [SE of Sevenoaks, off B245]: Comfortable bars, friendly service, good food inc ploughman's, steak sandwich and vegetarian dishes, well kept real ales, no

piped music; handy for walkers on Greensand Way *(Robert Gomme, Martin, Pat and Hilary Forrest)*

Warehorne [TQ9832]

Woolpack [Church Rd; off B2067 nr Hamstreet]: Big very neatly kept heavy-beamed 16th-c dining pub with very wide choice of good value food in rambling bar and big restaurant; popular carvery Weds evening (booking essential), elaborate puddings, well kept Greene King ales, decent wines, friendly staff, huge inglenook; picnic-sets out overlooking quiet lane and meadow with lovely big beech trees, lots of flower tubs and little fountain *(BB, Pat and Baz Turvill)*

West Farleigh [TQ7152]

Tickled Trout [B2010 SW of Maidstone]: Pleasant bar and attractive dining room, well kept Whitbreads-related ales, decent food (can be slow if very busy), friendly staff; colourful flowers and hanging baskets outside, Medway views (esp from big garden with play area), path down to river with good walks *(David and Betty Gittins, Simon Small)*

West Malling [TQ6857]

Five Pointed Star [High St]: Greene King pub, part very old, small and cosy at the back, good food choice, log fire *(Wendy Reynolds)*

Westerham [TQ4454]

General Wolfe [High St]: Unspoilt unchanging country pub, well kept Greene King, good inexpensive food, nice licensees *(David Twitchett)*

Whitstable [TR1166]

Four Horseshoes [Borstal Hill (A290)]: Jolly three-bar pub with comfortable atmosphere, well kept Shepherd Neame; can get crowded, popular with coach parties *(Robert Lester)*

☆ *Pearsons* [Sea Wall]: What makes this special is the good fresh fish and seafood in the cheerful little upstairs seaview restaurant; bar (no view) has more usual pub food inc some seaside lunchtime snacks, nautical décor, well kept Whitbreads-related ales with guests such as Fullers London Pride and Youngs, decent wines, and a huge lobster tank in its lower flagstoned part; piped music, children welcome in eating areas, open all day w/e *(LYM, Ian Phillips, Tim Barrow, Sue Demont, Kevin Flack, A Cowell)*

Rose in Bloom [Joy Lane]: Friendly and consistent, with modestly priced bar food in large conservatory, guest beers; main feature is the garden with sea views to Isle of Sheppey *(Norman Fox)*

Royal Naval Reserve [High St]: Friendly, comfortable and cosy, with well kept Shepherd Neame, good reasonably priced fresh local fish, steps up to spotless and

attractive dining room *(Ian Goodwin, Mr and Mrs T A Bryan)*

Wingham [TR2457]

☆ *Dog* [Canterbury Rd]: Medieval beams, lots of character, good range of Whitbreads-related ales, good-sized wine glasses, reliable food, friendly service *(Geoff Bichard)*

Woodchurch [TQ9434]

Bonny Cravat [Front Rd; off B2067 E of Tenterden]: Old village pub next to church; wide variety of good value food from sandwiches up, jovial efficient landlord, Shepherd Neame beers, small restaurant; pool in games room, side garden *(Alan J Vere)*

Wormshill [TQ8757]

Blacksmiths Arms [handy for M20 junction 8]: Comfortably old-fashioned and relaxed renovation of isolated low-beamed country cottage, small cosy rooms, tiled or wood floors, open fire, friendly staff, well kept Shepherd Neame and changing ales such as Goachers Dark and Greene King IPA, good varied freshly made food (not Tues evening) inc vegetarian and doorstep sandwiches, end dining area; Fri nostalgic 60s music (same man, same records for 25 yrs), large pretty garden with country views *(Eric Blackham)*

Worth [TR3356]

☆ *St Crispin* [signed off A258 S of Sandwich]: Stripped brickwork, bare boards, low beams, central log fire, real paraffin lamps, simple but interesting good food from sandwiches up, well kept changing ales such as Brakspears SB, Gales HSB, Marstons Pedigree, Shepherd Neame and Charles Wells Bombardier, local farm cider, welcoming service, piped satellite music, restaurant; charming big garden with barbecue, lovely village position not far from beach; bedrooms *(Kevin Thorpe, David Gittins)*

Wrotham [TQ6159]

☆ *Bull* [1¾ miles from M20, junction 2 – Wrotham signposted]: Welcoming helpful service in attractive 14th-c inn with good food, log fires, well kept Whitbreads-related ales, decent wines; children welcome, separate restaurant; comfortable bedrooms, huge breakfasts, attractive village *(LYM, C H Jobson)*

Yalding [TQ7050]

☆ *Walnut Tree* [B2010 SW of Maidstone]: Pleasant brightly lit beamed bar on several levels with inglenook and interesting pictures, friendly efficient staff, food inc good fresh fish and bargain OAP weekday lunch, wide restaurant choice, well kept Harveys and Wadworths 6X; piped music not over-intrusive, live music Sun evening; bedrooms, attractive village, handy for Organic Garden *(TRS, Mr and Mrs M Brooks, Joy and Peter Heatherley)*

Lancashire

Very customer-friendly, this part of the world, with plenty of pub bargains in both food and drink. There's also a great variety of really enjoyable pubs, from the best sort of old-fashioned city tavern to unspoilt country pubs and rewarding dining pubs. Several country pubs here now stay open all day for food service: the friendly Black Dog at Belmont (exceptionally cheap beer), the relaxed Stork at Conder Green (delicious potted local shrimps) and the Old Rosins up above Darwen (now owned by the flourishing Lake District brewer, Jennings). In Manchester, the Mark Addy and the Royal Oak have a great selection of cheeses. For a fuller meal, pubs that stand out include the ambitious Eagle & Child at Bispham Green, the Cavendish Arms at Brindle (new licensees turning out very well), the Stork mentioned above, the beautifully set Assheton Arms at Downham, the Forest at Fence (all fresh), the Bushells Arms at Goosnargh (very much a dining pub, good wines too), the Parkers Arms at Newton, the Inn at Whitewell (using a lot of local produce) and the New Inn at Yealand Conyers (but the Duttons will be leaving around the time this edition is published). From this wide choice, the Bushells Arms and Inn at Whitewell stand out as having particularly good food; with the added charm of its surroundings and special atmosphere, it's the Inn at Whitewell which we name Lancashire Dining Pub of the Year. Other pubs here doing really well these days include the warmly welcoming White House at Blackstone Edge, the Black Horse in Croston (cheap food, good beer), the Strawbury Duck at Entwistle (back in these pages on fine form, after a break of several years), the Baltic Fleet in Liverpool (a handsome new entry on the waterfront, with an excellent landlord), the very relaxed Taps in Lytham (great beer, good value food too), the charming Britons Protection in Manchester (another new entry, with the highest old-fashioned standards of service), and the Oddfellows Arms in Mellor (good all round). The Lucky Dip section at the end of the chapter includes plenty of classic old-fashioned multi-roomed pubs with cheap beer – perhaps not quite main entry material, but excellent all the same. Pubs in that section that do look like nudging the main entries these days include the Irby Mill at Irby, Cains Brewery Tap in Liverpool, Peveril of the Peak in Manchester, Freemasons Arms at Wiswell, and – particularly for their good food – the Red Pump at Bashall Eaves, Lord Raglan up above Bury, Royal Oak in Garstang, Saddle at Lea Town and Spread Eagle at Sawley. As we've said, this is a bargain part of the world for pubs. Drinks prices are nearly 25p a pint below the prevailing national average, with Holts standing out as an extraordinarily low-priced brewer. Interestingly, it's otherwise the big national brewers which most often supply a pub's cheapest beer here in this very cheap area – showing how competitive their pricing has become, now that the anti-monopoly beer regulations have had a few years to take real effect. A good few good local beers such as Cains, Moorhouses and Passageway are well worth looking out for – but don't waste your time looking for Mitchells, who stopped brewing in 1999.

BELMONT SD6716 Map 7
Black Dog £ 🛏
A675

Jim and Helen Pilkington, the friendly licensees of this 18th-c farmhouse, are proud to be appearing in the Guide for the fifteenth time, and readers' reports testify that the welcome they offer to customers remains as warm as ever. The original cheery and traditional small rooms are packed with antiques and bric-a-brac, from railwaymen's lamps, bedpans and chamber-pots to landscape paintings, as well as service bells for the sturdy built-in curved seats, rush-seated mahogany chairs, and coal fires. The atmosphere is perhaps best on a winter evening, especially if you're tucked away in one of the various snug alcoves, one of which used to house the village court. Very popular, generously served bar food includes home-made soup (£1.30), sandwiches (from £2, toasted from £2.20), local black pudding or pâté (£2.80), quiche (£4), ploughman's (from £4), breaded cod (£4.20), vegetarian or chicken rogan josh (£4.80), 8oz sirloin (£6.20), well liked salads (with various fruits including grape, banana and strawberry) including the mighty 'landlord's' mix of chicken, ham, beef, pastrami, ox tongue and a pork pie (£6), and daily specials such as melon in port (£2.50) or deep-fried brie (£2.90), twelve-bean chilli (£5), salmon fillet in lemon and herb butter (£6.50), pork valentine in cumberland sauce (£7), duck breast in plum sauce (£8), and pigeon stuffed with venison with port and cranberries (£8.50); well kept Holts Bitter and Mild. Despite their admirable policy of not taking bookings, it does tend to fill up quickly so get there early for a table. An airy extension lounge with a picture window has more modern furnishings; morning coffee, darts, pool, shove-ha'penny, dominoes, cribbage, and fruit machine; softly piped classical music. A small orchestra plays Viennese music on New Year's Day at lunchtime, and on several other evenings throughout the year. From two long benches on the sheltered sunny side of the pub, there are delightful views of the moors above the nearby trees and houses; there's a track from the village up Winter Hill and (from the lane to Rivington) on to Anglezarke Moor, and paths from the dam of the nearby Belmont Reservoir. *(Recommended by Vicky and David Sarti, Dr Muriel Sawbridge, M A Buchanan, Brian Wainwright, Willie Bell, P Abbott, Mrs Dilys Unsworth, Gordon Tong)*

Holts ~ Tenant James Pilkington ~ Real ale ~ Bar food (till 8pm Sun; for residents only Mon and Tues evenings) ~ (01204) 811218 ~ Children welcome ~ Open 12-4, 7-11; 12-4, 6.30-10.30 Sun ~ Bedrooms: £32B/£42B

BISPHAM GREEN SD4914 Map 7
Eagle & Child 🍽 🍺
Maltkiln Lane (Parbold—Croston rd, off B5246)

The brood of oxford sandy and black pigs continues to grow at this striking red brick pub. Attractively refurbished in an understated old-fashioned way, the stylishly simple interior consists of a civilised largely open-plan bar, well divided by stubs of walls. There are fine old stone fireplaces, oriental rugs and some coir matting on flagstones, old hunting prints and engravings, and a mix of individual furnishings including small oak chairs around tables in corners, several handsomely carved antique oak settles – the finest apparently made partly from a 16th-c wedding bed-head, and an oak coffer. The snug area is no smoking. The owner's family farm much of the land around Parbold, so there may be well hung meat from their various herds. As well as sandwiches (from £2.20), ambitious bar food from a daily changing blackboard might include soups such as celery, herb and cheese or continental vegetable (£2.50), smoked salmon with pine nuts and basil dressing (£5), garlic vegetable goujere (£6), warm crispy duck salad with chorizo, lardons and croutons or roast local veal (£7.50), Singapore chicken and beef stir-fry (£8), tuna niçoise (£9), salmon and asparagus lattice (£10), duck breast and apricots (£11), Aberdeen Angus fillet steak bordelaise (£12.50), baked whole sea bass with chilli, orange and lime butter (£13), and puddings such as indian-style yoghurt or blackcurrant brûlée (£3). A particularly good range of well kept beers on handpump includes Moorhouses Black Cat Mild, Theakstons Best, and Thwaites, with three or four changing guest ales such as Coach House Gunpowder Dark Mild and one from their own-brew pub, the Liverpool Brewing Co. in the centre of Liverpool; also farm cider, decent wines, some country wines and about 25 malt whiskies. Friendly and interested service and personable landlady; maybe piped pop radio. The pub holds a beer festival over the second bank holiday in May, with live music in the evenings. There is a neat bowling green behind (with croquet in summer), and the pub garden has a lovely wild section with crested newts and nesting moorhens; we hear that Harry the dog is as lively as ever. *(Recommended by Paul and Sandra Embleton, M A Buchanan, Phil and Dilys Unsworth, ALC, David and Kathy Holcroft, Vicky and David Sarti, J H Kane, Mr and Mrs C Frodsham, Steve Whalley, RJH, Gill and Maurice McMahon, John Fazakerley)*

Free house ~ Licensee Monica Evans ~ Real ale ~ Bar food (12-2, 5.30-8.30(9 Fri and Sat)) ~ (01257) 462297 ~ Children away from bar area ~ Open 12-3, 5.30-11; 12-10.30 Sun; closed evening 25 Dec

BLACKSTONE EDGE SD9716 Map 7
White House £

A58 Ripponden—Littleborough, just W of B6138

This very popular 17th-c pub, spectacularly set 1,300 feet above sea level on the Pennine Way, has impressive views over the moors from its lounge. The busy, welcoming and cheery main bar has a turkey carpet in front of a blazing coal fire and a large-scale map of the area (windswept walkers hardly know whether to head for the map or the fire first). The snug Pennine Room opens off here, with brightly coloured antimacassars on its small soft settees; there's also a recent dining extension. A spacious room on the left has comfortable seating and a big horseshoe window looking over the moors. Generous helpings of good value homely bar food served with well cooked vegetables include soup (£1.50), sandwiches (from £2.50), cumberland sausage with egg (£3.75), steak and kidney pie, roast chicken breast or vegetarian quiche (£4.25), chilli, beef curry or lasagne (£4.95), daily specials such as grilled halibut steak or greek-style lamb steak (£6.50), and home-made apple pie (£1.50); children's meals (from £1.60). Prompt friendly service. Well kept real ales on handpump include Theakstons Best and one or two guests such as Exmoor Gold and Moorhouses Pendle Witches Brew; also farm cider, and malt whiskies; fruit machine. Muddy boots can be left in the long, enclosed porch. *(Recommended by Graham and Lynn Mason, Norman Stansfield, Chris Smith, R T and J C Moggridge, M A Buchanan, Derek and Sylvia Stephenson, Bronwen and Steve Wrigley, Ian and Nita Cooper)*

Free house ~ Licensee Neville Marney ~ Real ale ~ Bar food ~ (01706) 378456 ~ Children welcome ~ Open 12-3, 6.30(6 Fri and Sat)-11

BRINDLE SD6024 Map 7
Cavendish Arms

3 miles from M6 junction 29; A6 towards Whittle le Woods then left on B5256

As we went to press, the builders were just about to begin work on extending this snug old building into the cottage next door. Although the new landlady could not give many specific details (she had only just received confirmation of the refurbishment herself), she told us that the new space would be used for diners and drinkers, that it would be furnished in harmony with the décor of the rest of the pub, and that as part of the enlargement, the bar would be moved to the back wall. Hopefully the cosy atmosphere will still prevail in the several quaint little rooms which ramble round the central servery. Certain to be left untouched are the woodwork partitions containing fascinating stained-glass scenes with lively depictions of medieval warriors and minstrels. Many of them commemorate the bloody battle of Brundenburg, a nasty skirmish between the Vikings and Anglo-Saxons on the Ribble estuary. We assume the numerous pictorial plates and Devonshire heraldic devices in plaster on the walls, as well as comfortable seats and discreet flowery curtains will also stay. Once the refurbishment is finished, the menu will also be reviewed, with a view to adding dishes such as ploughman's and a few more specials to the usual food. In the past, simple bar meals have included soup (£2), well liked open sandwiches (from £3.95) home-made pies such as beef (£4.95), or fish (£5.25), and daily specials such as vegetarian tagliatelle carbonara (£4.95) and chicken stuffed with mushrooms and ham in a cream sauce (£5.25); puddings (£2.50). Burtonwood Bitter and a guest on handpump, and a good choice of malt whiskies; darts, cribbage, dominoes and fruit machine. There are white metal and plastic tables and chairs on a terrace by a rockery with a small water cascade, with another table on a small lawn behind. It's nicely set in a tranquil little village, and there's a handsome stone church across the road. *(Recommended by G Armstrong, M A Buchanan, Miss J E Winsor, Janet Pickles, Mr and Mrs D Price, Dave Braisted, Roger and Jenny Huggins)*

Burtonwood ~ Tenant Sandra Doyle ~ Real ale ~ Bar food (except all day Mon and Tues, and Weds and Sun evenings) ~ Restaurant ~ (01254) 852912 ~ Children welcome ~ Open 12-3, 5.30-11; 12-11 Sat; 12-10.30 Sun

CHIPPING SD6243 Map 7
Dog & Partridge ♀

Hesketh Lane; crossroads Chipping—Longridge with Inglewhite—Clitheroe

Comfortably relaxed and spotlessly kept dining pub offering good straightforward food. At lunchtime this includes soup (£2.25), sandwiches (from £3.25, prawn £4.50), prawn cocktail (£4.25), mushroom stroganoff or curried nut roast with tomato chutney (£6.50), steak and kidney pie (£7.25), grilled pork chop with apple sauce and stuffing or poached salmon with prawn sauce (£8), and 10oz sirloin steak (£10.25). The evening menu contains more starters such as deep-fried garlic mushrooms (£4), and avocado with prawns (£5.50), and a couple more main dishes such as broccoli and stilton pancakes (£6.50) and jumbo scampi (£10.25); the home-made chips are particularly well liked and they do various fish and game specials; puddings include home-made fruit pavlova or hot sticky toffee pudding (£2.80). Parts of the building date back to 1515, though it's been much modernised since, with the eating space now spreading over into a nearby stable. The main lounge is comfortably furnished with small armchairs around fairly close-set low wood-effect tables on a blue patterned carpet, brown-painted beams, a good winter log fire, and multi-coloured lanterns; service is friendly and helpful. Tetley Bitter and Mild and a weekly changing guest such as Moorhouses Pride of Pendle on handpump, over 40 wines, and a good range of malt whiskies; piped music. Smart casual dress is preferred in the restaurant; dining areas are no smoking. *(Recommended by J F M West, Roger and Christine Mash, Gillian Jenkins)*

Free house ~ Licensee Peter Barr ~ Real ale ~ Bar food (12-1.45, 7-9; 12-9 Sun) ~ Restaurant ~ (01995) 61201 ~ Children welcome ~ Open 12-3, 7-11; 12-10.30 Sun

CONDER GREEN SD4556 Map 7
Stork £ 🍺

3 miles from M6 junction 33: A6 towards Lancaster, first left, then fork left; just off A588

There is a marked contrast between the surrounding bleak marshes (made all the more eerie by the cries of waterfowl when the wind and tides are right), and the warm bustle inside this rambling white-painted ancient inn. Set in a fine spot, where the River Conder joins the Lune estuary, it has tables outside looking out over the watery wastes, and provides a handy quiet retreat from Lancaster. Several unspoilt cosy panelled rooms (one has a list of licensees going back to 1660), and a good fire. Although it's a place where people come to eat out, the atmosphere is pleasantly informal and relaxed, with service that stays cheerful (and efficient) even on a busy Saturday night. Food served in the bar and separate dining room includes soup (£1.75), good value sandwiches (£1.75, good toasties from £2.25), excellent potted shrimps or smoked duck and cranberry platter (£2.75), with good generous home cooking including stilton, wild mushroom and courgette lasagne (£4.50), cumberland sausage with fried egg, ploughman's or steak and mushroom pie

(£4.95), game casserole or fresh fish of the day (£5.50), chicken breast stuffed with cheese and wrapped in bacon (£6.50) and sirloin steak (£9.95); children's menu (from £1.95). Hot dishes are served with a choice of potatoes and of salad or vegetables; puddings (£1.95). Well kept Boddingtons, Stork (brewed for the pub by Whitbreads), Timothy Taylor Landlord and interesting guest ales such as Hardys & Hansons Guzzling Goose and Jennings Snecklifter on handpump; good coffee; darts, pool, fruit machine, video game and a juke box; dogs welcome. The inn is just a mile from Glasson Dock. *(Recommended by Jacqueline Morley, David Cooke, B, M and P Kendall, P J Rowland)*

Free house ~ Licensee Tony Cragg ~ Real ale ~ Bar food (12-2.30, 6.30-9; 12-9 Sun) ~ Restaurant ~ (01524) 751234 ~ Children welcome ~ Open 11-11; 12-10.30 Sun; closed 25 Dec ~ Bedrooms: £24B/£38B

CROSTON SD4818 Map 7
Black Horse ♠ £

Westhead Road; A581 Chorley—Southport

Readers report a pleasant range of ages at this very friendly Victorian village free house, furnished (almost exaggeratedly) in keeping with that period. The neatly kept bar has patterned carpets, attractive wallpaper, solid upholstered wall settles and cast-iron-framed pub tables, a fireplace tiled in the Victorian manner and reproduction prints of that time (also a couple of nice 1950s street-scene prints by M Grimshaw), as well as darts, pool, cribbage, dominoes, fruit machine, satellite TV and piped music. The lounge extension with a log-burning stove is decorated in a quietly comfortable style, in sympathy with the rest of the building. Very reasonably priced reliable home-cooking is generously served and includes home-made soup (£1.65), sandwiches (from £2), ploughman's (£3.75), lasagne, steak and kidney pie or vegetable curry (£3.95), 6oz sirloin (£4.95), puddings (£1.90) and daily specials such as chicken casserole (£3) and fisherman's pie (£3.50); children's meals (£2) and senior citizens' specials (£2.95); no-smoking dining area. A surprising seven well kept real ales might include Black Sheep, Courage Directors, Jennings Bitter, Hancocks HB, Moorhouses Pendle Witches Brew, and Theakstons Bitter and Mild. There are picnic-sets outside, and a good solid safely railed-off play area; the pub has its own crown bowls green and boules pitch (boules available from the bar). *(Recommended by Carl Reid, C P Knights, John Fazakerley, B Kneale, Ellis Heaton)*

Free house ~ Licensee Graeme Conroy ~ Real ale ~ Bar food (12-2.30, 5.30-8.30; 12-7 Sun) ~ Restaurant ~ (01772) 600338 ~ Children welcome ~ Quiz Thurs evening ~ Open 11-11; 12-10.30 Sun

DARWEN SD7222 Map 7
Old Rosins

Pickup Bank, Hoddlesden; from B6232 Haslingden—Belthorn, turn off towards Edgeworth opposite the Grey Mare – pub then signposted off to the right

On clear days there are lovely views over the moors and down into the wooded valley from the spacious crazy-paved terrace of this remotely set but popular friendly pub, bought by Jennings last summer. The brewery were planning to renew the furniture in the open-plan bar in the autumn, and hopefully this will not detract from the good pubby atmosphere. As we went to press, no changes had yet been made, and the comfortable red plush built-in button-back banquettes, stools and small wooden chairs around dark cast-iron-framed tables, remained. Lots of mugs, whisky-water jugs and so forth hang from the high joists, while the walls are decorated with small prints, plates and old farm tools; there's also a good log fire. Parts of the bar and restaurant are no smoking. Served all day, the good value bar food includes soup (£1.60), club sandwich (£2.95), hearty hot loafers with fillings such as cajun pork or steak and onion gravy (from £4.95), home-made pies (from £4.15), broccoli and walnut potato cakes (£4.25), cod and chips, lasagne, chicken curry or cumberland sausage (£4.45), marinated pork in garlic and thyme or beef in Jennings Snecklifter (£5.25), sirloin steak (£7.50), mixed grill (£7.65) and puddings (from £2.25). Well kept Jennings ales including Bitter, Cumberland, Cocker Hoop, Snecklifter and an occasional guest on handpump, plenty of malt whiskies, and coffee; fruit machine and maybe piped music; there are picnic-sets on the terrace. *(Recommended by M A Buchanan, GLD, Gillian Jenkins, Bronwen and Steve Wrigley, Pat and Tony Martin, Ian Phillips, Lynda Katz)*

Jennings ~ Manager Michael Connell ~ Real ale ~ Bar food (11.30(12 Sun)-10pm) ~ Restaurant ~ (01254) 771264 ~ Children welcome ~ Open 11.30-11; 12-10.30 Sun ~ Bedrooms: £37.50B/£45B

DOWNHAM SD7844 Map 7
Assheton Arms
From A59 NE of Clitheroe turn off into Chatburn (signposted); in Chatburn follow Downham signpost

Charmingly set in a delightful stone-built village, this dining pub can get very cosy in winter when there's a roaring fire in the massive stone fireplace that helps to divide the separate areas of the rambling, beamed and red-carpeted bar. Furnishings include olive plush-cushioned winged settles around attractive grainy oak tables, some cushioned window seats, and two grenadier busts on the mantelpiece over the fire; part of the bar is no smoking. Popular (if not cheap) bar food includes ham and vegetable broth (£2.50), sandwiches (from £3.25, not Saturday evening or Sunday lunchtime), stilton pâté or ploughman's (£3.95), cauliflower and mushroom provençale (£5.95), chilli (£6.25), steak and kidney pie (£6.50), venison, bacon and cranberry casserole (£7.95), ham and eggs (£8.50), halibut steak with cream cheese sauce (£8.95), pan-fried beef sirloin with brandy, cream and mushrooms (£10.95), as well as specials including a couple of Asian dishes such as chicken dopiaza and vegetable balti (£7.95) and seasonal fish specialities including oysters, salmon, scallops and lobster. Well kept Boddingtons and Castle Eden under light blanket pressure; decent wines by the glass or bottle; piped music. The pub takes its name from the family who bought the village in 1558 and have preserved it in a traditional style ever since. Window seats and picnic-sets outside look across to the church. *(Recommended by Ken and Joan Bemrose, Bronwen and Steve Wrigley, N Thomas, Vicky and David Sarti, Mrs Ursula Hofheinz, Malcolm Taylor)*

Whitbreads ~ Tenant David Busby ~ Real ale ~ Bar food (till 10pm) ~ (01200) 441227 ~ Children welcome ~ Open 12-3, 7-(10.30 Sun)11

ENTWISTLE SD7217 Map 7
Strawbury Duck 🍺 🛏
Overshores Rd, by stn; village signposted down narrow lane from Blackburn Rd N of Edgworth; or take Batridge Rd off B6391 N of Chapeltown and take pretty ¾ mile walk from park at Entwistle reservoir; OS Sheet 109 map reference 726177

Tucked into a sheltered fold of the moors, this traditional beamed and flagstoned country pub is a popular base for Pennine walks (leave muddy boots in the porch). The cosy dimly lit L-shaped bar has Victorian pictures on its partly timbered, partly rough-stone walls, a variety of seats, stools, little settees and pews, a mounted gun, and one table made from an old church organ bellows. Bar food includes soup (£1.50), sandwiches (from £1.50, steak £3.95), filled french bread (from £2.95), ploughman's (from £3.50), deep-fried cod (£4.95), popular beef and ale casserole (£5.50), various daily pies such as steak and kidney or chicken and asparagus (£5.95) and 8oz sirloin steak (£9.95), with specials including three or four different types of sausage and mash per week such as pork and tomato bangers with black pudding and spring onion mash (£5.50), roasted balsamic vegetables with couscous and sour cream (£5.95), and roasted cod fillet with olive oil crusted potatoes and herb beurre blanc (£6.75); puddings (from £2.50); also children's dishes (and, if you're staying, big sizzling breakfasts). Well kept ales include Moorhouses Pendle Witches Brew and Timothy Taylor Landlord with four changing guests such as Coniston Bluebird, Dent Barber of Seville, Ridleys Bitter and Ruddles County on handpump; friendly service, satellite TV and good unobtrusive piped music. A games room has darts, a fruit machine and a pool table. Outside, tables are perched high over the cutting of the little railway line which brings occasional trains (and customers) from Blackburn or Bolton. *(Recommended by Vicky and David Sarti, P Abbott, Peter Cropper)*

Free house ~ Licensee Keith Graham ~ Real ale ~ Bar food (12-2.30(3 Fri), 6.30-9.30(10 Fri); 12-8 Sun (10 Sat)) ~ (01204) 852013 ~ Well behaved children away from bar till 9pm ~ Live music every Thurs evening ~ Open 11-11; 12-10.30 Sun ~ Bedrooms: /£38B

FENCE SD8237 Map 7
Forest
Cuckstool Lane; B6248 Brierfield road off A6068

They use as much fresh local produce as possible when cooking the creative well liked meals at this smartly attractive dining pub. Along with daily specials such as chicken supreme with garlic, lemon and mint sauce (£10.50) and grilled halibut steak with oven-dried leeks (£10.95), the good varied menu includes soup of the day (£2.45), sandwiches (from £3.95), watercress and spinach salad with parmesan shavings and cider and vinegar dressing (£3.95), king prawns in filo pastry with marinated cucumber and a coriander and mint dressing (£4.95), mediterranean vegetable ragoût with garlic and fresh herb-stuffed field mushrooms (£7.50), tagliatelle with fresh mussels, chorizo and tomato sauce with fresh herbs (£7.95), Indonesian chicken satay (£8.95), 8oz rump steak or pavé of Scottish salmon with a spring onion and dill velouté (£9.95), rack of lamb with potato purée, confit of root vegetables and rich mint lamb jus or sea bass steak with provençale vegetables (£11.50); home-made puddings might include fresh strawberries with home-made cinnamon ice cream, warm lemon tart or dark chocolate marquise (from £3.95); there is no children's menu but they will do small helpings of suitable dishes; you will need to book at the weekend. The ceilings are painted a striking red, and there's heavy panelling, lots of paintings, vases, plates and books, and a cosy comfortable feel, thanks to its big open fire and subdued lighting. The open-plan bar has two rooms opening off it, and a side restaurant; no-smoking area in conservatory dining room; quiet piped music. Ruddles and Theakstons Best on handpump as well as a couple of guests such as Marstons Pedigree or Morlands Old Speckled Hen, a good choice of wines, friendly helpful service. *(Recommended by Norman Stansfield, M A Buchanan, Barry and Anne, P Abbott)*

Free house ~ Licensee Clive Seedall ~ Real ale ~ Bar food ~ Restaurant ~ (01282) 613641 ~ Children away from bar ~ Open 12-11; 12-10.30 Sun; closed evening 25 Dec

GARSTANG SD4845 Map 7
Th'Owd Tithebarn ★
Signposted off Church Street; turn left off one-way system at Farmers Arms

We're told that only the York Museum has a bigger collection of antique farming equipment than the one displayed at this unique converted tithe barn, creeper-covered, and prettily set by a canal. To some extent, this fascinating old building is a bit like a simple old-fashioned farmhouse kitchen parlour, with an antique kitchen range, agricultural equipment on the walls, stuffed animals and birds, and pews and glossy tables spaced out on the flagstones under the very high rafters – waitresses in period costume with mob-caps complete the vintage flavour. A new 30 foot dining table in the middle of the restaurant caters for parties. There are lots of benches on the big flagstoned terrace that overlooks ducks and boats wending their way along the Lancaster Canal. Simple bar food includes soup (£1.95), black pudding (£2.50), filled cottage bloomers (from £3.25, lunchtime only), broccoli quiche (£4.95), trio of sausages (£5.25), steak and kidney pudding or tuna pasta bake (£5.75), steaks (from £7.95), and specials such as seafood platter (£5.25), roast of the day or minted lamb casserole (£5.50); puddings might include toffee pavlova and fudge cake (£2.50). They do afternoon teas in summer. As we went to press, Mitchells were just about to stop brewing altogether, but a brewery spokesman told us that Bass, Boddingtons and a possible guest could be expected on the handpumps in the future; lots of country wines, dominoes and piped music. As it's something of a tourist attraction, it can get very busy. *(Recommended by Andy and Jill Kassube, Gill and Maurice McMahon, Mrs S Kingsbury)*

Mitchells ~ Manager Gordon Hutchinson ~ Real ale ~ Bar food (12-2.30, 6-9; all day Sunday) ~ Restaurant ~ (01995) 604486 ~ Children in eating area of bar and restaurant ~ Open 11-11; 11-10.30 Sun; 11-3, 6-11 winter; 12-10.30 Sun winter

GOOSNARGH SD5537 Map 7
Bushells Arms 🍴 ♀

4 miles from M6 junction 32; A6 towards Garstang, turn right at Broughton traffic lights (the first ones you come to), then left at Goosnargh Village signpost (it's pretty insignificant – the turn's more or less opposite Whittingham Post Office)

At this rather special and very good value dining pub not far from haunted Chingle Hall, the signal for opening the doors at lunchtime is the tolling of the church clock. The interesting menu comprises Eurasian influences, with daily specials determined by the availability of good fresh ingredients and fresh Fleetwood fish. Recently, such dishes have included greek-style lentil soup (£1.50), smoked trout fillet (£2), hot and spicy chicken wings (£3), sweet and sour pork chop or chicken in red wine with raisins (from a medieval recipe, £6) and lamb cooked with pasta, olives, tomatoes, garlic, herbs, mediterranean vegetables and red wine or fresh salmon marinated in red wine, balsamic vinegar and mint (£6.50). Nowadays, sandwiches (from £2) are usually available every day and other bar food includes spring rolls, samosas or falafel (£2), steak and kidney pie (£5.50), boeuf bourguignon (£6) and salmon and hollandaise puff pastry parcel or well liked chicken fillet filled with smoked bacon, asparagus and grated cheese in hollandaise sauce and wrapped in puff pastry (£6). Crisp and fresh vegetables include tasty potatoes done with garlic, cream, peppers and parmesan, and there's a good range of puddings such as lemon roulade or blackcurrant pie (£2.50). The spacious, modernised bar has lots of snug bays, each holding not more than two or three tables and often faced with big chunks of sandstone (plastic plants and spot-lit bare boughs heighten the rockery effect); also soft red plush button-back banquettes, with flagstones by the bar. Two areas are no smoking. The landlord (a wine writer himself), has replaced his wine list with a continually changing blackboard of about half a dozen well chosen wines, including house wines by the glass. Also well kept Timothy Taylor Best on handpump, and a good choice of malt whiskies that reflects the landlord's knowledge on the subject. Tables in a little back garden, and hanging baskets at the front. Beware – they may close early on Sunday lunchtimes if it's quiet. *(Recommended by Neil Townend, Ian Phillips, Steve Whalley, Pete Yearsley, Brian and Anna Marsden, Jamie and Ruth Lyons, Wendy Fairbank, N Stansfield, Mr and Mrs J E Murphy, Vicky and David Sarti, Margaret and Roy Randle, N Thomas, J Perry, Canon David Baxter, Colin and Peggy Wilshire)*

Whitbreads ~ Lease: David and Glynis Best ~ Real ale ~ Bar food ~ (01772) 865235 ~ Well behaved children in eating area of bar and garden ~ Open 11ish-3, 6-11; 12-3, 6.30-10.30 Sun; closed occasional Mons and 25 Dec

Horns ♀

Pub signed from village, about 2 miles towards Chipping below Beacon Fell

Readers enjoy the food, atmosphere and friendly service from the welcoming licensees and staff at this pleasantly positioned old coaching inn. A number of colourful flower displays are dotted around its neatly kept snug rooms, all of which have log fires in winter. Beyond the lobby, the pleasant front bar opens into attractively decorated middle rooms with antique and other period furnishings. At lunchtime there's popular tasty bar food such as beef and vegetable soup (£2.95), well presented sandwiches (from £3.10), ploughman's (£4.95), steak and kidney pie (£6.95), plaice or roast chicken (£6.95), roast local pheasant or grilled gammon and egg (£7.75), sirloin steak with mushrooms (£9.95), and daily specials such as tuna and pasta bake (£5.50) and mushroom stroganoff (£6.50) all nicely served with freshly cooked, piping hot chips; home-made puddings might include home-made fruit pies or an excellent sticky toffee pudding (£3.75). A very good range of up to ten or so wines by the glass, an extensive wine list and a fine choice of malt whiskies; cheerful and helpful young staff, piped music. *(Recommended by Malcolm Taylor, W W Burke, Dr Michael Allen, RJH)*

Free house ~ Licensee Mark Woods ~ Bar food (not Sat evening or Sun lunch) ~ Restaurant ~ (01772) 865230 ~ Children welcome ~ Open 11.30-3, 6-11; 12-3, 6-10.30 Sun; closed Monday lunchtime ~ Bedrooms: £49B/£75B

LIVERPOOL SJ4395 Map 7

Baltic Fleet 🍺 £

Wapping

Reopened a decade or so ago as part of the waterfront rejuvenation, this impressive Victorian dockside pub stands majestically across from the Albert Dock complex. It's a fairly unique building, brightly painted green, burgundy and white, and shaped in a triangle with pavements on all sides and more entrances (eight) than any other pub in Liverpool. Recently refurbished and doing well under its very nice landlord, it has lots of woodwork from the stout mahogany board floors up, a good mix of old school furniture and dark wood tables and nice big arched windows. Simon Holts' family have lived in this part of the world since the mid 19th c. His father was involved in the shipping trade to West Africa and you can spot pictures of him amongst the interesting old Mersey shipping prints. Particularly well kept reasonably priced beers on handpump include Cains and a Cains guest, Baltic Fleet Extra or Summer Baltic, both brewed locally just for the pub by Passageway, a guest from Passageway, and possibly another northern guest, all served through a sparkler, as well as about eight wines by the glass. During summer lunchtimes there's a shortish list of home-made bar food including soup (£2.75), sandwiches (from £2.95) and filled french sticks (from £3.95). In the winter the fairly priced menu expands to include generous helpings of maybe sausage and mash or fishcakes (£4.75), vegetarian lasagne (£4.95). The year-round evening menu departs from the completely ordinary a little with dishes like aubergine and rosemary bake or beef in ale (£4.95), salmon steak with lemon butter and dill sauce or chicken and sun-dried tomatoes with couscous (£6.75), and puddings like cheesecake, bakewell tart or chocolate mousse (from £2.50); one room is no smoking; the pub has its own car park. *(Recommended by Mark A Brock, Grant Thoburn)*

Free house ~ Licensees Simon Holt and Julie Broome ~ Bar food (12-2.30, 6-9.30(9 Tues, Wed), 12-4 Sun, not Sun or Mon evening) ~ (0151) 709 3116 ~ Children in eating area of bar ~ Open 11.30-11; 12-10.30 Sun

Philharmonic Dining Rooms ★ 🍺 £

36 Hope Street; corner of Hardman Street

'Marvellous', is how one enamoured reader described this magnificent old Victorian gin palace. The wonderfully opulent rooms are still exquisitely decorated in their original style, and bustle happily with theatre-goers, students, locals and tourists. The heart of the building is a mosaic-faced serving counter, from which heavily carved and polished mahogany partitions radiate under the intricate plasterwork high ceiling. The echoing main hall is decorated with stained glass including contemporary portraits of Boer War heroes such as Baden-Powell and Lord Roberts, rich panelling, a huge mosaic floor, and copper panels of musicians in an alcove above the fireplace. More stained glass in one of the little lounges declares 'Music is the universal language of mankind', and backs this up with illustrations of musical instruments; there are two plushly comfortable sitting rooms. Lavatory devotees may be interested to know that the famous gents' are original 1890s Rouge Royale by Twyfords: all red marble and glinting mosaics; some readers have long felt these alone earn the pub its star. Well kept Marstons Pedigree, and Tetleys Bitter and Mild on handpump, some malt whiskies and cask cider; pool, TV and piped music. Good value simple bar food includes sandwiches (from £1.25), soup (£1.65), and various well priced dishes including vegetable lasagne (£3.50), chilli or battered cod (£3.95), steak and kidney pie or half a roast chicken (£4.25) and puddings (£1.50); no-smoking area in restaurant. Friendly service. *(Recommended by Olive and Ray Hebson, Gillian Jenkins, the Didler, Dave Braisted, Alan and Paula McCully, G Dunstan, Tim Barrow, Sue Demont, JP, PP, Chris Raisin)*

Allied Domecq ~ Manager John Sullivan ~ Real ale ~ Bar food ~ (0151) 7091163 ~ Children in eating area of bar and restaurant ~ Open 11.30-11; 7-10.30 Sun

LYTHAM SD3627 Map 7
Taps ◖ £
A584 S of Blackpool; Henry Street – in centre, one street in from West Beach

The enthusiastic landlord at this cheery alehouse told us that if a beer is available, he will endeavour to get it. Unsurprisingly perhaps, he has now dispensed some 2,000 real ales through the 12 handpumps. Changing weekly, up to ten well kept guest beers have included Brakspears Bitter, Caledonian Deuchars IPA, Coniston Bluebird, Everards Tiger, Harveys Best, Jennings Snecklifter, Moorhouses Black Cat Dark Mild and Pendle Witches Brew, Nethergate Umbel Ale and Timothy Taylor Landlord. Boddingtons is more or less a regular fixture, and anyone who's been a little over-zealous in sampling the beers will appreciate the seat belts on the bar stools and the headrest in the gents'; a view-in cellar allows you the chance to admire the choice of beers on offer, and there are usually some country wines and a farm cider. The Victorian-style bare-boarded bar has a really friendly and unassuming atmosphere, as well as plenty of stained-glass decoration in the windows, with depictions of fish and gulls reflecting the pub's proximity to the beach; also captain's chairs in bays around the sides, open fires, and a coal-effect gas fire between two built-in bookcases at one end. There's also a bit of a rugby theme, with old photographs and portraits of rugby stars on the walls; piped music, shove-ha'penny, dominoes, fruit machine and juke box. The home-made bar food is simple but good value (prices have not risen since last year), with the most popular dishes including well liked soups such as chicken and mushroom or pea and ham (95p), sandwiches (from £1, hot roast beef £2.35), beer sausages and mash or chilli (£2.95) and chicken curry or ploughman's (£3.25); the ham and beef is home-cooked. There are no meals on Sunday, but instead they have free platters of food laid out, with tasty morsels such as black pudding, chicken wings or minted lamb. There are a few seats outside. Parking is difficult near the pub – it's probably best to park at the West Beach car park on the seafront (it's free on Sunday), and walk. *(Recommended by Steve Whalley, Arthur and Margaret Dickinson, ALC)*

Whitbreads ~ Manager Ian Rigg ~ Real ale ~ Bar food (lunchtime) ~ (01253) 736226 ~ Open 11-11; 12-10.30 Sun

MANCHESTER SJ7796 Map 7
Britons Protection ♀
Great Bridgewater St, corner of Lower Mosley St

Chatty, genuine and well run by long-serving licensees, this city pub has a fine chequered tile floor and some glossy brown and russet wall tiles, solid woodwork and elaborate plastering in its rather plush little front bar. In tribute to Manchester's notorious climate, the massive bar counter has a pair of heating pipes as its footrail. A tiled passage lined with battle murals leads to two inner lounges, one served by hatch, with attractive brass and etched glass wall lamps, a mirror above the coal-effect gas fire in the simple art nouveau fireplace, and again good solidly comfortable furnishings. Besides well kept Jennings, Robinsons and Tetleys on handpump, they have good wines, a great collection of malt whiskies (over 150) and other interesting spirits – and proper career barmen. Good reasonably priced home-cooked bar lunches might include home-made soup (£1.75), sandwiches (from £1.90), ploughman's (£3.75), ham and egg (£3.95), pies such as kangaroo, wild boar and ostrich (£4.75), and home-made daily specials such as chicken curry or finnan haddock (£3.65), shepherd's pie (£3.75), and wild mushroom lasagne (£4.75). There may be piped music, but no juke box or machines. Busy at lunchtime, it's usually quiet and relaxed in the evenings, and handy for the GMEX centre and Bridgewater Hall (to the delight of many orchestral players). There are tables out behind, *(Recommended by Ian Phillips, Tim Barrow, Sue Demont, Doug Christian, GLD, Peter Plumridge)*

Allied Domecq ~ Tenant Peter Barnett ~ Real ale ~ Bar food (lunchtime only) ~ (0161) 236 5895 ~ Separate room for children lunchtime only ~ Open 11-11; 12-10.30 Sun; closed 25 Dec

Dukes 92   £

Castle Street, below the bottom end of Deansgate

In a superbly atmospheric setting by locks and under railway arches in the rejuvenated heart of old industrial Manchester, this cavernous old building was once a stable for canal hoses. Although it has been significantly enlarged (there is now twice as much drinking room downstairs), the tasteful décor remains unchanged: black wrought-iron work contrasts boldly with whitewashed bare plaster walls, there's a handsome marble-topped bar, and an elegant spiral staircase leads to an upper room and balcony. Down in the main room the fine mix of furnishings is mainly rather Edwardian in mood, with one particularly massive table, elegantly comfortable chaises-longues and deep armchairs. It's under the same ownership as the well established Mark Addy (see below), and has a similar excellent choice of over three dozen cheeses and several pâtés – some quite unusual – served in huge helpings with granary bread (£3.50). Soup (£2.50), ciabatta sandwiches such as chargrilled spiced chicken with mayonnaise or grilled bacon with melted jarlsberg cheese (from £4.75), daily pasta dishes (from £4.95), mixed mezze (£7.95) and oriental platter (£9.95). Well kept Boddingtons and a guest such as Timothy Taylor Landlord on handpump, along with the Belgian wheat beer Hoegarden, and quite a few Belgian fruit beers; decent wines and a large selection of malts, friendly staff; piped classical music. There are tables out by the canal basin which opens into the bottom lock of the Rochdale Canal. On bank holiday weekends events in the forecourt may include jazz and children's theatre, and there's a permanent theatre in the function room. *(Recommended by John McDonald, Ann Bond, R C Morgan, ALC, David Carr, Liz and Ian Phillips, John Fazakerley, Pete Yearsley)*

Free house ~ Licensee Barry Lavin ~ Real ale ~ Bar food (12-3, 5-8.30) ~ (0161) 839 8642 ~ Children welcome ~ DJs on Fri and Sat evenings ~ Open 11-11(12 Sat); 12-10.30 Sun

Lass o' Gowrie ■ £

36 Charles Street; off Oxford Street at BBC

At weekends during term time, this tiled Victorian pub is so alive with good-natured university students, that you might have to drink your own-brew pint on the pavement outside, in true city-centre pub style. Seats around a sort of glass cage give a view of the brewing process in the cellar microbrewery where they produce the lightly flavoured LOG35 and the meatier LOG42. Eight other well kept real ales on handpump change weekly but might include Castle Eden, Fullers London Pride, Marstons Pedigree, Morlands Old Speckled Hen, Timothy Taylor Landlord and Wadworths 6X, also Inch's Stonehouse cask cider; it might take some while to get served at busy periods. The simple but characterful long bar has gas lighting and bare floorboards and lots of exposed brick work. Hop sacks are draped from the ceiling, and the bar has big windows in its richly tiled arched brown facade. Good value bar food includes soup (£2.10), sandwiches (from £2.20), bacon bap (£2.35), baked potatoes (from £2.50), ploughman's (£3.10), cheese and onion pasty (£3.65), fish and chips or sausage and mash (£3.70), and steak and ale pie (£4.25); efficient cheery service. The volume of the piped pop music really depends on the youth of the customers at the time; fruit machine and satellite TV; the snug is no smoking at lunchtime; no children. *(Recommended by Sue Holland, Dave Webster, David Carr, Gill and*

Maurice McMahon, John McDonald, Ann Bond)

Whitbreads ~ Manager David McGrath ~ Real ale ~ Bar food (11.30-3) ~ (0161) 273 6932 ~ Children in eating area of bar, family room and garden till 7pm ~ Open 11.30-11; 12-10.30 Sun; closed 25 Dec

Marble Arch 🍺 £

73 Rochdale Rd (A664), Ancoats; corner of Gould St, just E of Victoria Station

Behind the rather ordinary façade of this city alehouse lies a beautifully preserved Victorian pub with a magnificently restored lightly barrel-vaulted high ceiling and extensive marble and tiling, amongst which the frieze advertising various spirits and the chimney breast above the carved wooden mantelpiece particularly stand out. A mosaic floor slopes down to the bar, and some of the walls are partly stripped back to the glazed brick; there are armchairs by a fire in the back bar. They now brew over half a dozen of their own real ales including Dades, Dobber Strong, Chorlton, Liberty IPA, McKenna's Revenge Porter, Marble, IPA, Totally Marbelled, all well kept alongside seasonal beers such as Ginger Marble and a good choice of bottled beers (including Belgian Trappist beers) with a selection of country wines. Served in the lounge extension at the back, remarkably low-priced bar food includes sandwiches (£1), soup (£1.50), lasagne and various curries (from £3). A plethora of games includes Manchester darts (played on a board without trebles), bar billiards, cribbage, dominoes, table skittles, fruit machine, pinball, juke box and lively piped music. The Laurel and Hardy Preservation Society meet here on the third Wednesday of the month and show old films. *(Recommended by David Carr, Richard Lewis, the Didler, JP, PP, Karen Eliot, Ian Phillips)*

Free house ~ Licensee Mark E Dade ~ Real ale ~ Bar food (12-4) ~ (0161) 832 5914 ~ Open 12-11; closed Sunday

Mark Addy 🍷 £

Stanley Street, Salford, Manchester 3 (if it's not on your street map head for New Bailey St); look out not for a pub but for what looks like a smoked glass modernist subway entrance

If you have an appetite for cheese, this atmospheric riverside pub is the place for you. It comes in huge helpings with granary bread, and you choose from a list of almost 50 different cheeses and 9 pâtés from all over Britain and Europe (all carefully described on the menu, along with suggested alcoholic accompaniments). It's £3.40 for a helping and they automatically give you a doggy bag. There are also toasted sandwiches (from £2.50), and a small choice of puddings (£1.75). Well converted from waiting rooms for boat passengers, the pub has quite a civilised and trendy feel, especially in the flower-filled waterside courtyard from where you can watch the home-bred ducks. Inside, the series of barrel-vaulted red sandstone bays is furnished with russet or dove plush seats and upholstered stalls, wide glassed-in brick arches, cast-iron pillars, and a flagstone floor. Well kept Boddingtons and two weekly changing guests such as Marstons Pedigree or Timothy Taylor Landlord kept under light blanket pressure; quite a few wines too. They get very busy, so it is worth getting there early, and they prefer smart dress. The pub is run by the same people as another Manchester main entry, Dukes 92 (see above). *(Recommended by David Carr, Ian Phillips)*

Free house ~ Licensee Thomas Joyce ~ Real ale ~ Bar food (till 8.30/9pm) ~ (0161) 832 4080 ~ Children welcome ~ Open 11.30-11; 12-10.30 Sun; closed 25/26 Dec, 1 Jan

Royal Oak £

729 Wilmslow Road, Didsbury

Similar to the Mark Addy (see above), this bustling end-of-terrace pub is famous for its incredibly vast array of cheeses, rarely served in less than a pound helping and with a substantial chunk of bread and extras such as olives and pickled onions

(£3.50 for a choice of two cheeses); take-away bags are provided. Well kept Bateman's Mild, Marstons Bitter and Pedigree and a fortnightly changing guest beer such as Gales Trafalgar on handpump, and some sherries and ports from the wood; efficient, friendly service. Antique theatre bills and so forth cover the walls of the busy bar which has a cosy atmosphere and is very popular with local drinkers. There are some tables and chairs outside, and lots of hanging baskets cheer up its simple exterior. *(Recommended by Ian Phillips, Brian Wainwright)*

Marstons ~ Manager Norma Hall ~ Real ale ~ Bar food (12-2.30, not weekends or bank holidays) ~ (0161) 434 4788 ~ Children over 14 at lunchtime ~ Open 11-11; 12-10.30 Sun

MELLOR SJ9888 Map 7
Oddfellows Arms

73 Moor End Road; follow Mellor signpost off A626 Marple—Glossop and keep further on up hill – this is the Mellor near Stockport

Fine old country pub which, with no piped music or games, has a pleasantly civilised buzz of conversation in its two flagstoned bars with low ceilings and open fires. While there is a significant emphasis on food, readers tell us they feel perfectly welcome just having a drink. Among the daily specials, there's a particularly good choice of fish with up to nine dishes such as wild sea bass steamed cantonese style with ginger and soy, whole lemon sole, turbot fillet grilled with herbed olive oil and served with a sauce Vierge of olives, anchovy, garlic, tomato and parsley or duo of silver snapper fillets poached with vermouth, prawns, and capers (£10.95). Other well liked bar food includes three or four soups (from £1.90), sandwiches (from £1.95), hot rump steak baguette (£3.95), ploughman's (from £4.95), roast of the day (£5.95), pasta with pesto (£6.25), various curries such as lamb rogan josh or Senegalese eggs (£6.50), Italian pork and smoked pork cassoulet (£7.25), yoghurt-marinated garlic chicken (£7.95), steaks (from £9.75), and puddings such as passion fruit cheesecake or orange and ginger sponge (£2.75); three-course Sunday lunch (£8.50). Well kept Adnams, Marstons Pedigree and a weekly changing guest such as Badger Dorset Best on handpump. There's a small no-smoking restaurant upstairs, and a few tables out by the road. *(Recommended by Mrs B Ormrod, Richard and Ruth Dean, David Hoult)*

Free house ~ Licensee Robert Cloughley ~ Real ale ~ Bar food ~ Restaurant ~ (0161) 449 7826 ~ Children welcome ~ Open 12-3, 5.30-11; 12-3, 7-10.30 Sun

NEWTON SD6950 Map 7
Parkers Arms

B6478 7 miles N of Clitheroe

There's a very friendly welcome from the licensees and their menagerie at this delightfully set timbered pub: pygmy goats, rabbits, guinea pigs, hens, pheasants, parrots and a lot more birds keep children entertained, while their parents take in the view from well spaced picnic-sets on the big lawn looking down towards the river, and beyond to the hills. There's also a play area, and two playful black labradors. Inside there are paintings and plenty of the pets' stuffed counterparts, as well as red plush button-back banquettes, a mix of new chairs and tables, and an open fire. Beyond an arch is a similar area with sensibly placed darts, pool, cribbage, dominoes, table skittles, fruit machine, TV and discreet piped music. Well kept Boddingtons, Flowers IPA, Greene King Abbot, own-brew Parkers Ale and a guest on handpump, a good range of malt whiskies, and a choice of around 50 wines. Generous helpings of enjoyable bar food might include soup (£2.50), hearty sandwiches (from £2.75), deep-fried camembert (£2.95), baked potatoes (from £3.50), moules marinières (£4.25), big ploughman's (£5.95), steak and kidney pie (£5.75), mushroom stroganoff (£6.25), mango-glazed chicken (£7.95), sirloin steak (£9.50), and a shellfish platter (£11.95); puddings such as home-made banoffee pie, jam rolypoly or summer pudding (£2.95); generous well prepared breakfasts; no-smoking restaurant. *(Recommended by Geoffrey and Brenda Wilson, Linda Christison, David J Cooke)*

Whitbreads ~ Lease: Barbara Clayton ~ Real ale ~ Bar food (12-9 summer, 12-2.30, 6-9 winter; 12-9 wknds in winter) ~ Restaurant ~ (01200) 446236 ~ Well behaved children in restaurant and eating area of bar till 9pm ~ Open 11-11; 12-10.30 Sun; 11-2.30, 5-11 Mon-Fri in winter ~ Bedrooms: £35B/£50B

RABY SJ3180 Map 7
Wheatsheaf 🏆

The Green, Rabymere Road; off A540 S of Heswall

Known locally as the Thatch, this half-timbered and whitewashed country cottage is not easy for strangers to find. The splendidly atmospheric rooms are simply furnished, with an old wall clock and homely black kitchen shelves in the cosy central bar, and a nice snug formed by antique settles built in around its fine old fireplace. A second, more spacious room has upholstered wall seats around the tables, small hunting prints on the cream walls, and a smaller coal fire. Straightforward but tasty bar food includes soup (£2), a very good range of toasted sandwiches (from £2.40), ploughman's (£4.35), battered cod (£5.30), chicken breast with garlic and herbs (£5.45), steak and ale pie (£5.50), braised knuckle of lamb (£6.25), gammon steak (£6.40), and 8oz sirloin (£8.50). The spacious restaurant (with more elaborate evening menu) is in a converted cowshed that leads into a larger no-smoking conservatory. Along with a couple of guests, well kept beers on handpump include Morlands Old Speckled Hen, Theakstons Best, Old Peculier and XB, Tetleys, Thwaites Best, Wadworths 6X and Youngers Scotch; a good choice of malt whiskies. There's a patio area with picnic-sets behind. *(Recommended by Gill and Maurice McMahon, E G Parish, Olive and Ray Hebson, Graham and Lynn Mason, Ian Phillips, Sue and Bob Ward, Tom and Joan Childs)*

Free house ~ Licensee Thomas Charlesworth ~ Real ale ~ Bar food (lunchtime) ~ Restaurant (Evenings Tues-Sat) ~ (0151) 336 3416 ~ Children in lounge, conservatory and restaurant at lunchtime ~ Open 11.30-11; 12-10.30 Sun

RIBCHESTER SD6435 Map 7
White Bull

Church Street; turn off B6245 at sharp corner by Black Bull

Situated as it is in a former Roman town, there's no shortage of ancient history in and around this early 18th-c stone dining pub. The pillars of the entrance porch are Tuscan, and have stood here or nearby for nearly 2,000 years, there's the remains of a Roman bath house behind the pub, and a small Roman museum nearby. Inside, the decorations in the spacious and attractively refurbished main bar, with comfortable old settles, take their influence from a more recent era, with Victorian advertisements and various prints, as well as a stuffed fox in two halves that looks as if it's jumping through the wall; most areas are set up for eating during the day, and you can also eat out in the garden behind. Half the dining area is no smoking. Service is friendly and attentive, even during busy periods, and children are made particularly welcome. Good value bar meals include soup (£1.75), open sandwiches (from £2.85), mushrooms stuffed with cheese and peppers (£3), steak and kidney pie, meat or vegetable lasagne (£5.50), ploughman's (£5.75), grilled lamb chops (£7.25), various steaks with a choice of toppings (from £8), and changing specials such as pan-fried chicken supreme diane (£7.50) and chargrilled snapper on a bed of spinach mash (£8.15); children's menu. Well kept Boddingtons, Flowers IPA, Marstons Pedigree and Theakstons on handpump, a good range of malt whiskies, and a blackboard list of several wines by the glass or bottle; they also do coffees, tea, and hot chocolate. It can get busy, so it's worth arriving early for a table. Darts, TV, pool, juke box, dominoes and fruit machine in the games room; piped music. *(Recommended by Gill and Maurice McMahon, Bronwen and Steve Wrigley, M A Buchanan, Brian and Anna Marsden)*

Whitbreads ~ Lease: Neil Sandiford ~ Real ale ~ Bar food (11.30-2, 6.30-9.30; 12-8 Sun; not Mon evenings) ~ Restaurant ~ (01254) 878303 ~ Children welcome ~ Open 11.30-3, 6.30-11; 12-10.30 Sun ~ Bedrooms: £32.50B/£45B

STALYBRIDGE SJ9698 Map 7
Station Buffet ◧ £

Classic Victorian platform bar much loved by readers. Not smart but comfortably nostalgic, it has a marble-topped bar counter, roaring fire below an etched-glass mirror, newspapers and magazines to read, old photographs of the station in its heyday and other railway memorabilia – there's even a little conservatory. An extension along the platform leads into what was the ladies' waiting room and part of the station-master's quarters, with original ornate ceilings and a dining/function room with Victorian-style wallpaper; dominoes, cribbage, draughts. On a sunny day you can sit out on the platform. As well as good coffee and tea made freshly by the pot, there are cheap old-fashioned snacks such as black peas (40p), sandwiches (from £1.30), and three or four daily specials such as an all day breakfast, bacon casserole and a home-made pie with peas (£1.75-£2.50). A very good range of well kept beers includes Boddingtons, Flowers IPA, Wadworths 6X and five interesting changing guest beers such as City of Cambridge Boathouse Bitter, Columbus Outlaw Bitter and Lloyds Blooming July on handpump, as well as farm cider, Belgian and other foreign bottled beers. They hold beer festivals in early May and late November; Monday night quiz. *(Recommended by Mr J and Dr S Harrop, Pat and Tony Martin, JP, PP, Richard Lewis, Ian Phillips, Stephen Brown, the Didler)*

Free house ~ Licensees John Hesketh and Sylvia Wood ~ Real ale ~ Bar food ~ (0161) 303 0007 ~ Children till 9pm ~ Folk music on Sat evenings ~ Open 11-11; 12-10.30 Sun; closed 25/26 Dec

WHARLES SD4435 Map 7
Eagle & Child

Church Road; from B5269 W of Broughton turn left into Higham Side Road at HMS Inskip sign

A tranquil atmosphere pervades this delightfully timeless thatched ale house, which certain readers regard as the perfect antidote to a busy day in nearby Blackpool. Dotted throughout the neatly kept rooms is the landlord's marvellous collection of lovely antique furnishings. The most interesting are in the L-shaped bar, where a beamed area round the corner past the counter has a whole cluster of them. One of the highlights is a magnificent, elaborately carved Jacobean settle which originally came from Aston Hall in Birmingham, carrying the motto exaltavit humiles. There's also a carved oak chimneypiece, and a couple of fine longcase clocks, one from Chester, and another with a nicely painted face and an almost silent movement from Manchester. The plain cream walls are hung with modern advertising mirrors and some older mirrors, and there are a few exotic knives, carpentry tools and so forth on the plastered structural beams; even when it's not particularly cold, there should be a good fire burning in the intricate cast-iron stove. Well kept Boddingtons and three regularly changing guests such as Clarks Festival, Mansfield Bitter and Wadworths 6X on handpump; darts in a sensible side area, pool, dominoes, friendly cat. One or two picnic-sets outside. *(Recommended by Ian and Nita Cooper, Pete and Josephine Cropper)*

Free house ~ Licensee Brian Tatham ~ Real ale ~ (01772) 690312 ~ Children over 14 ~ Open 7-11; 12-4, 7-10.30 Sun

WHITEWELL SD6546 Map 7
Inn at Whitewell ★★ ⓦ ♀ ⇔

Most easily reached by B6246 from Whalley; road through Dunsop Bridge from B6478 is also good

Lancashire Dining Pub of the Year

This civilised country house hotel has a legion of fans among our readers. Beautifully set deep in the Forest of Bowland and surrounded by well wooded rolling hills set off against higher moors, it is perhaps most dramatically approached from Abbeystead. It houses a wine merchant (hence the unusually wide range of around 180 wines available – the claret is recommended) and an art gallery, and owns several miles of trout, salmon and sea trout fishing on the Hodder; with notice they'll arrange shooting. Although it gets very busy, it's very spacious inside and out, so usually remains tranquil and relaxing. The old-fashioned pubby bar has antique settles, oak gateleg tables, sonorous clocks, old cricketing and sporting prints, log fires (the lounge has a very attractive stone fireplace), and heavy curtains on sturdy wooden rails; one area has a selection of newspapers, dominoes, local maps and guide books; there's a piano for anyone who wants to play. Reached via a corridor with objects like a stuffed fox disappearing into the wall is the pleasant suntrap garden, with wonderful views down to the valley. Very highly praised bar food includes soup (£3.20), open sandwiches (from £3.90), grilled lamb in breadcrumbs with aubergine pickle (£4.80), marinated trout fillets (£5.50), grilled norfolk kipper (£6.50), salad of roast wood pigeon (£7), very well liked sausage and mash (£7.20), fish pie (£8.20), warm roquefort cheesecake (£9.50), lamb's kidneys (£10), 10oz sirloin (£11.80), home-made puddings such as sticky toffee pudding and redcurrant cheesecake (£3.50) and hand-made farmhouse cheeses (from £3.50); the evening menu is just slightly different; they serve coffee and cream teas all day; very polite service. Well kept Boddingtons and Marstons Pedigree on handpump. So far we have had no reports on the four new spacious bedrooms in the 'Coach House' (all with their own CD players), but the licensee joked that they were so popular that regulars now refuse any other rooms! *(Recommended by M Meadley, Paul S McPherson, Roger and Christine Mash, W W Burke, Guy Vowles, Jean and Peter Walker, Karen Eliot, GLD, HLD, Steve Whalley, Norman Stansfield, Dorothee and Dennis Glover, Brian Higgins and Ana Kolkowska, Nigel Woolliscroft, Linda Christison, David J Cooke, Vicky and David Sarti)*

Free house ~ Licensee Richard Bowman ~ Real ale ~ Bar food ~ Restaurant ~ (01200) 448222 ~ Children welcome ~ Open 11-3, 6-11; 12-3, 7-11 Sun ~ Bedrooms: £55B/£78B

YEALAND CONYERS SD5074 Map 7
New Inn 🍴

3 miles from M6 junction 35; village signposted off A6

This simple ivy-coloured stone pub has been a popular dining establishment under several successive regimes. As we went to press, the Duttons told us they would probably be leaving around the time that this edition is published, so although the pub is likely to remain under the management of Robinsons, there's no guarantee that the meals they produce will continue to be served after their departure. In the past, well prepared food has included filled baguettes (from £4.50), starters such as soup (£2.95) and mushroom and cheese pyramids with a date chutney crouton (£4.50), main courses such as cumberland sausage with smoky onion and apricot stuffing or courgette, cream cheese and hazelnut roulade with tomato and cheese sauce (£8.50), Scotch salmon fillet with a rich mature cheddar sauce (£9.50), and braised gammon with scrumpy apple and sultana (£9.95), and puddings including boozy bread and butter pudding or caramelised apple meringue (from £3.50). Despite the emphasis on dining, there's still a cosy village atmosphere. On the left is a simply furnished little beamed bar with a log fire in the big stone fireplace, and on the right are two communicating cottagey dining rooms (one no smoking) with black furniture to match the shiny beams, an attractive kitchen range and another winter fire. Beers on handpump might include Robinsons Best and Frederics, Hartleys XB, Hatters Mild and Old Tom. Under the Duttons there was a good choice of around 30 malt whiskies and mulled wine in winter; piped music. A sheltered lawn at the side has picnic-sets among roses and flowering shrubs. More reports please. *(Recommended by John Voos)*

Robinsons ~ Tenants Ian and Annette Dutton ~ Real ale ~ Bar food ~ Restaurant ~ (01524) 732938 ~ Children welcome ~ Open 11-3, 5.30-11; 11-11 Sat; 12-10.30 Sun

Ideas for a country day out? We list pubs in really attractive scenery at the back of the book – and there are separate lists for waterside pubs, ones with really good gardens, and ones with lovely views.

Lucky Dip

Besides the fully inspected pubs, you might like to try these Lucky Dips recommended to us and described by readers (if you do, please send us reports):

Abbey Village [SD6422]
Hare & Hounds: Popular well kept chatty family-run local with big beamed main bar, toby jugs, plates, brasses and animal heads, food inc good cheeses and Indian dishes, quick friendly service; machines, juke box, pool room, can be smoky; seats outside, good views of Darwen tower; live music and quiz nights *(Mrs Dilys Unsworth)*
Arkholme [SD5872]
Bay Horse [B6254 Carnforth—Kirkby Lonsdale]: Attractive neatly kept old country pub, lovely inglenook, good pictures of long-lost London pubs, popular food inc good value sandwiches; has had Mitchells beers; own bowling green, charming valley handy for Lune Valley walks *(Jenny and Brian Seller)*
Balderstone [SD6332]
☆ *Myerscough Hotel* [Whalley Rd, Samlesbury; A59 Preston—Skipton, just over 2 miles from M6 junction 31]: Reliable refuge, with solid furnishings in cosy and relaxed softly lit beamed bar, well kept Robinsons Best and Mild, maybe Hartleys XB, traditional games, good basic bome-made food from sandwiches up, no-smoking front room (children allowed there, mealtimes); picnic-sets, bantams and rabbits outside, Weds quiz night, bedrooms *(Alyson and Andrew Jackson, Andy and Jill Kassube, Gill and Maurice McMahon, LYM)*
Barnston [SJ2883]
☆ *Fox & Hounds* [A551]: Very neatly kept partly flagstoned long lounge bar with blacked range, copper kettles, china on delft shelf, intriguing hat collection, plush wall banquettes, good value quickly served straightforward food from ploughman's up inc very popular Sun lunch, well kept Scottish Courage and guest ales, lots of malt whiskies, comfortable restaurant area, well groomed staff, efficient booking system; pretty summer courtyard and garden with outside bar; by farm and lovely wooded dell *(Gill and Maurice McMahon)*
Bashall Eaves [SD6943]
☆ *Red Pump* [NW of Clitheroe, off B6478 or B6243]: Tucked-away partly 18th-c country pub increasingly popular for good varied food inc good value Sun lunch; well refurbished and expanded, with very relaxed unpretentious atmosphere, two roaring log fires, roomy smartly decorated restaurant, friendly service, Whitbreads-related ales, no piped music; two bedrooms, good breakfast, own fishing on River Hodder *(M and A Dickinson, J A Boucher)*
Bilsborrow [SD5139]
☆ *Owd Nells* [off A6 N of Preston; at S end of village take Myerscough Coll of Agriculture turn]: Purpose-built pub in busy expanding thatched canalside tourist complex inc hotel, craft and teashops and so forth, best for

families; easy-going rustic feel, high pitched rafters at either end, lower beams (and flagstones) by the bar counter in the middle, a big welcome for children (maybe bread for feeding the ducks), wide choice of generous bar food inc two-for-one bargains (can take a while when really busy), half a dozen Whitbreads-related and other ales such as Timothy Taylor Landlord, good value wines, malt whiskies, tea and coffee, popcorn machine, plenty of games, adjacent restaurant; good play area outside (even cricket and bowls); open all day, live music Thurs/Fri, comfortable bedrooms *(Stan and Hazel Allen, Ian Phillips, W W Burke, LYM)*
Birkenhead [SJ3289]
Chester Arms [Chester St]: Friendly Cains local with good choice of guest beers as well as their own, pleasant service, big screen TV, games machine; handy for Woodside ferry terminal, open all day *(Richard Lewis)*
Commodore [Lord St]: Changing real ales such as Morlands Old Speckled Hen, Phoenix Wobbly Bob and Plassey Dragons Breath in friendly bare-boards backstreet local with pool, live music nights and good basic food; open all day *(Richard Lewis)*
Crown [Conway St]: Multi-roomed town centre alehouse with interesting tilework, a dozen changing real ales, Weston's farm cider, good basic food, low prices; open all day, cl Sun lunchtime *(Richard Lewis)*
Old Colonial [Bridge St]: Refurbished by Cains, Liverpool maps and prints, attractive bare-boards eating areas with wide range of cheap food, good range of well kept beers inc Dark Mild, Bitter, FA and Sundowner, friendly staff and locals; open all day *(Richard Lewis)*
Shrewsbury Arms [Claughton Firs – look out for Oxton sign]: Lots of cosy snug areas in spacious lounge and matching extension, good value standard food, good choice of particularly well kept beers inc Cains Formidable and Titanic, Higsons and Theakstons, friendly bustling atmosphere; terrace *(Ian Phillips)*
Blacko [SD8541]
☆ *Moorcock* [A682 towards Gisburn]: Beautifully placed moorland pub with spaciously comfortable bar, big picture windows for breathtaking views, tables set close for the huge range of popular and often enterprising food inc lamb from their own flock, excellent beef and some German dishes, decent wine but nitrokeg beers, hillside garden with various animals; open all day for food Sun, children welcome, bedrooms *(Gwen and Peter Andrews, Karen Eliot, Paul S McPherson, N Thomas, Dr G Sanders, LYM)*
Blackpool [SD3035]
Bispham [Red Bank Rd]: Large very comfortable lounge area, lively atmosphere,

simple good value bar food lunchtime and early evening, well kept very well priced Sam Smiths bitter *(John and Audrey Butterfield, Andy and Jill Kassube)*
George [General Drive]: Well updated, with well kept Boddingtons very competitively priced *(Dr and Mrs A K Clarke)*
Blackrod [SD6110]
Gallaghers [Little Scotland]: Consistently well kept ales, good food in bar and restaurant esp fish, bargain weekday early suppers *(Graham and Norma Field)*
Bolton [SD7108]
Clifton Arms [Newport St]: Striking green tiled entrance, pleasantly dated flowery wallpaper décor, quiet front snug, good local feel, reasonably priced lunchtime food (not Sun), well kept ales inc Jennings and Marstons Pedigree; folk night Mon eve, quiz Weds, regular mini beer festivals; open all day, easy wheelchair access *(G Coates)*
Howcroft [Pool St]: Friendly backstreet local with well preserved period interior – lots of small screened-off rooms around central servery with fine glass and woodwork, cosy snug with coal fire, good value lunches in lounge, well kept Tetleys-related ales with guests such as local Bank Top, Addlestone's cider, plenty of games inc pinball, darts, bar billiards; bowling green, occasional live music *(C J Fletcher)*
Lord Clyde [Folds Rd (A676 NE)]: Traditionally laid out local, sympathetically refurbished and very welcoming to visitors, with well kept Hydes on electric pump; good value home-cooked lunches Fri *(Pete Baker)*
Bolton by Bowland [SD7849]
Coach & Horses: Untouristy traditional décor, good fresh food with crunchy veg, well kept Whitbreads-related beers, coal fires, restaurant (where children may be allowed); get there early weekends for a table, lovely streamside village with interesting church *(Mr and Mrs Pink)*
Bury [SD8115]
☆ *Lord Raglan* [Nangreaves; off A56/A666 N under a mile E of M66 junction 1, down cobbled track]: Ivy-covered cottage row in lonely moorside location, with great views; carefully made food from sandwiches to good meals using fresh ingredients, welcoming efficient service, well kept Theakstons, interesting foreign bottled beers, lots of bric-a-brac in traditional front bar, big open fire in cosy back room, plainer blond-panelled dining room (where children allowed); crudités as you wait to go in) *(Bronwen and Steve Wrigley, LYM, John and Sylvia Harrop, Ian Phillips)*
Chadderton [SD9005]
Hunt Lane [Hunt Lane]: Decent food inc well cooked steak pies and veg *(Tony Hobden)*
Cheadle Hulme [SJ8787]
Hesketh [Hulme Hall Lane]: Comfortable carpeted open-plan room with raised area one end, food servery the other end with good value piping hot food; well kept

Theakstons Best and Old Peculier, friendly attentive service *(Mr and Mrs C Roberts)*
Old Mill [Mill Lane]: Newly refurbished 1980s mill-look streamside building, high roof, lots of rustic timber and stonework, quite a range of well kept ales such as Ind Coope Burton, Jennings Snecklifter, Moorhouses Premium, friendly staff, steaks and so forth *(Richard Lewis)*
Churchtown [SD3618]
☆ *Hesketh Arms* [Botanic Rd; off A565 from Preston, taking B5244 at Southport]: Spacious Victorian-style family dining pub with good value fresh food from chip butties to roast beef inc children's helpings; Tetleys Bitter and Mild from central servery, open fires, lively atmosphere, Weds jazz; pleasant tables outside, attractive partly thatched village nr Botanic Gardens *(BB, Mrs Dilys Unsworth)*
Clitheroe [SD7241]
Edisford Bridge [B6243 W]: Several quiet rooms with separate dining area, well priced food, full range of Jennings ales; back garden, open all day Sat, handy for walks by River Ribble *(Pete and Josephine Cropper)*
Diggle [SE0008]
Diggle Hotel [village signed off A670 just N of Dobcross]: Welcoming bustle in modernised three-room hillside pub popular lunchtime and early evening for good value food (can be a wait) from sandwiches up inc generous Sun roasts and children's dishes; well kept Timothy Taylor Golden Best and Landlord, decent wines, good choice of malt whiskies, good coffee, friendly service, soft piped music, rustic fairy-lit tables among the trees, quiet spot just below the moors; children welcome, opens noon; bedrooms *(Bruce Drew, BB, Bronwen and Steve Wrigley)*
Eccles [SJ7698]
Crown & Volunteer [Liverpool Rd]: Popular local with cheap Holts Bitter and Mild in unfussy panelled bar and good compact lounge *(JP, PP, the Didler)*
Golden Cross [Liverpool Rd]: Open-plan lounge, popular plain bar, well kept low-priced Holts Bitter and Mild; live music nights *(the Didler, JP, PP)*
Grapes [Liverpool Rd, Peel Green; A57 ½ mile from M63 junction 2]: Classic Edwardian local with superb glass and tiling, lots of mahogany, brilliant staircase, cheap Holts Bitter and Mild, fairly quiet roomy lounge and smoke room, pool room, vault with Manchester darts (can get quite loud and smoky), drinking corridor; open all day *(JP, PP, the Didler, Pete Baker)*
Lamb [Regent St (A57)]: Untouched Edwardian three-room Holts local with splendid etched windows, fine woodwork, tiling and furnishings, admirable trophies in display case; cheap well kept Bitter and Mild, full-size snooker table; popular with older people *(the Didler, JP, PP)*
Euxton [SD5519]
Euxton Mills [A49, 3 miles from M6

junction 28]: Popular traditional roasts with good choice of veg, other food inc good sandwiches and black pudding, well kept Burtonwood ales *(Andy and Jill Kassube)*

Fleetwood [SD3247]
North Euston [Esplanade, nr tram terminus]: Big comfortably refurbished bar in architecturally interesting Victorian hotel overlooking seafront, long railway connections; decent lunchtime food, wide range of well kept mainstream real ales, well organised staff, no-smoking family area (till 7), seats outside; bedrooms *(Arthur and Margaret Dickinson)*

Garstang [SD4845]
Flag [A6, nr Knott End signs]: Huge, plush and relaxing, well done in old-fashioned style, with good value tasty food from good filled baguettes to appetising puddings, Marstons Pedigree, friendly attentive staff; open all day, large conservatory, seats outside, disabled facilities *(Bronwen and Steve Wrigley, Arthur and Margaret Dickinson)*

☆ *Royal Oak* [Market Pl]: Ancient pub, cosy yet roomy and comfortably refurbished, with attractive panelling, several eating areas inc charming snug, generous food (all day Sun) inc good range of home-cooked meats, imaginatively presented specials, children's helpings of any dish, efficient pleasant staff, Hartleys and Robinsons beers, good value coffee; restaurant, disabled access, comfortable bedrooms, open all day Sun *(Dr B and Mrs P B Baker, Arthur and Margaret Dickinson)*

Goosnargh [SD5537]
Grapes: Welcoming local with two low-beamed areas separated by coal fire, lots of brass around this, collection of whisky-water jugs and old telephones, reasonably priced generous standard food inc sandwiches and good Sun roast, pleasant landlord, well kept Tetleys and guest beers; pool room *(Andy and Jill Kassube)*

Greenfield [SD9904]
Railway Hotel [Shaw Hall Bank Rd, opp stn]: Friendly straightforward two-bar pub, well kept beers *(Richard Houghton)*

Heskin Green [SD5214]
Brook House [Barmskin Lane]: Stylish low 17th-c stonebuilt pub in Wigan Alps area, roses on wall, bright window boxes and baskets, two smallish rooms with low beams, plates, pictures and maps, imaginative well cooked food (popular with older lunchers), friendly efficient staff, soft piped music; opens noon *(Ian and Nita Cooper)*

Hest Bank [SD4666]
Hest Bank Hotel [Hest Bank Lane]: Picturesque and welcoming coaching inn, good range of good freshly made generous food all day inc fresh fish, well kept Boddingtons and guest beers, friendly efficient service; canalside garden *(Denise Dowd, P A Legon, Karen Eliot)*

Heswall [SJ2781]
Devon Doorway [Telegraph Rd (A540)]:

Large thatched and low-beamed Bass dining pub, inglenook log fire, pine tables on flagstones, carpeted restaurant area, good choice of wines by the glass and bin ends, good coffee, courteous staff, newspapers, no music or machines; quize nights, back and front gardens *(John T Ames, Graham and Lynn Mason)*

Hurst Green [SD6838]
☆ *Bayley Arms* [off B6243 Longridge—Clitheroe, towards Stoneyhurst Coll]: Sympathetically renovated carpeted bar with attractive mix of old furniture, sporting and music memorabilia, brasses, log fire; enjoyable good value bar food inc children's, several mainly Whitbreads-related ales, more formal restaurant, friendly licensees, smart staff; comfortable bedrooms, attractive Ribble valley village *(Gill and Maurice McMahon)*

Inglewhite [SD5440]
Green Man [Silk Mill Lane; 3 miles from A6 – turn off nr Owd Nells, Bilsborrow]: Red plush bar and dining room, sparklingly clean and well polished, with good generous food served piping hot at attractive prices (children's menu and small helpings available), wide choice of good sandwiches, well kept Greenalls, staff pleasant and attentive even when busy, log fire, pool, darts, games machines; garden with unspoilt views nr Beacon Fell country park; bedrooms with own bathrooms, camp site behind *(Ken and Joan Bemrose, J F M and M West)*

Irby [SJ2684]
☆ *Irby Mill* [Irby Mill Hill, off Greasby rd]: Well kept Bass, Boddingtons, Cains Bitter and Dark Mild, Jennings and interesting guest beers, good house wines and decent well cooked lunchtime food (not Sun) in four low-beamed largely flagstoned rooms, comfortable pub furniture, coal-effect gas fire, relaxed local atmosphere, interesting old photographs and history of the former mill, a few tables outside *(Sue and Bob Ward, Gill and Maurice McMahon, BB)*

Knott End on Sea [SD3548]
Bourne Arms: Large helpings of reasonably priced food, Boddingtons and Flowers IPA, interesting pictures and model boat; open all day, passenger ferry to Fleetwood *(Dr B and Mrs P B Baker)*

Lancaster [SD4862]
Lancastrian [Scale Hall Farm, Morecambe Rd]: Good food, friendly service, wide range of reasonably priced food, no-smoking area *(Anne and David Robinson)*

Lea Town [SD4832]
☆ *Saddle* [Sidgreaves Lane, N towards Woodplumpton]: Neatly refurbished and well run country pub with wide choice of very good home-made food cooked to order from sandwiches up, inc vegetarian and children's, five real ales, sensibly priced wines, good service, restaurant; tables outside, play area; bedrooms *(H F Rowe)*

Leyland [SD5422]
Eagle & Child [Church Rd]: Well renovated,

stone floors, friendly atmosphere *(Dr and Mrs A K Clarke)*

Little Eccleston [SD4139]

☆ *Cartford* [Cartford Lane, off A586 Garstang—Blackpool, by toll bridge]: In scenic countryside by toll bridge on River Wyre, brewing its own interesting Hart beers; well kept Theakstons too, oak beams, plenty of atmosphere, pleasant service, two of its three floors set with tables for good choice of reasonably priced generous food inc sandwiches, vegetarian and children's; quiet juke box, pool, tables outside (not by water), play area; very busy esp weekends; well equipped bedrooms, fishing rights *(Andy and Jill Kassube, R T and J C Moggridge)*

Liverpool [SJ4395]

Beluga [Wood St]: More wine bar than pub, in basement of refurbished warehouse; bare boards, spartan decoration, very imaginative lunchtime food such as stir-fried squid, decent choice of wine and beers; rather more lively in the evening, with clubbing types; *(Tim Barrow, Sue Demont)*

☆ *Cains Brewery Tap* [Stanhope St]: Splendidly restored Victorian architecture with nicely understated décor, wooden floors, plush raised side snug, lots of old prints and breweriana, wonderful bar, flame-effect gas fire, newspapers; cosy relaxing atmosphere, friendly efficient staff, good well priced food, and above all four well kept attractively priced Cains ales with four guest beers from other small breweries; popular brewery tour ending here with buffet and singing; sports TV *(Gill and Maurice McMahon, JP, PP, Richard Lewis)*

Carnarvon Castle [Tarleton St]: Neat and welcoming city-centre pub next to main shopping area; long and narrow, with one main bar and back lounge; cabinet of Dinky toys, well kept Bass, Cains Mild and Bitter, lunchtime bar snacks; open all day, cl Sun *(the Didler)*

Cracke [Rice St]: Attractively basic, bare boards, walls covered with posters for local events and pictures of local buildings, unusual Beatles diorama in largest room, juke box and TV, very cheap lunchtime food, well kept Marstons Pedigree; popular mainly with young people; sizeable garden *(JP, PP, the Didler)*

Dispensary [Renshaw St; formerly the Grapes]: Well refurbished by Cains in unpretentious Victorian style, marvellous etched windows, full range of their ales and four guest beers, bare boards, comfortable raised back bar, Victorian medicine bottles and instruments; good food 12-7, friendly staff, open all day *(Richard Lewis, the Didler)*

Everyman Bistro [Hope St]: Not a traditional pub, but has well kept Marstons Pedigree and often guest beers, European ones too, good well priced wholefood inc amazing puddings; canteen/student bar atmosphere *(Tony Huish)*

Flanagans Apple [Mathew St]: One of the first Irish pubs here, good atmosphere, Guinness of course, live music most nights usually with trad Irish flavour, limited lunchtime menu *(Tony Huish)*

Globe [Cases St]: Welcoming traditional local, good service, well kept Bass, Cains Bitter and Dark Mild, good port, tiny sloping-floor back lounge, friendly licensees, lots of prints of old Liverpool; lunchtime filled baps *(the Didler, JP, PP, Roy Moorehead)*

Grapes [Matthew St]: Lively and friendly, with well kept Boddingtons and Cains, good value lunchtime bar food, open-plan but cottagey décor (flagstones, old range, wall settles, gas-effect lamps); open all day, can get crowded Fri/Sat, cl Sun *(Chris Raisin, JP, PP, the Didler)*

Midland [Ranelagh St]: Attractive Victorian pub with ornate lounge, long corner bar, nice etched glass and mirrors; Tetleys *(the Didler)*

White Horse [Acrefield Rd, Woolton]: Pretty Victorian pub, small and cosy, in conservation area, traditional décor, panelling, friendly staff and regulars, well kept Cains, basic cheap and plentiful lunchtime food *(Dr P Burnham, J Bryan)*

Longridge [SD6037]

New Drop [Higher Rd, Longridge Fell, parallel to B6243 Longridge—Clitheroe]: In lovely moors-edge country overlooking Ribble Valley, spacious room with attentive family service, relaxed atmosphere, good reasonably priced food in bar and restaurant, real ales such as Boddingtons, Timothy Taylor Landlord and Wild Boar *(K C and B Forman)*

Manchester [SJ8284]

Ape & Apple [John Dalton St]: Smart newish Holts pub with their fantastic value beer kept well, comfortable seats in bare-boards bar with nice lighting and lots of old prints and posters, armchairs in upstairs lounge; good mix on busy weekend evenings (unusually for city centre, over-25s won't feel out of place), quieter lunchtime or midweek *(Richard Lewis, Brian Wainwright, the Didler, Paul Mason)*

Bar Fringe [Swan St]: Friendly sawdust-floor café-style bar with appropriate glasses for Belgian beers, well kept real ales inc Bank Top, farm cider, food till 8, cartoons and bank notes; open all day *(Richard Lewis)*

Barleycorn [Barlow Moor Rd]: Rather opulent, very friendly; well kept beer, amazingly cheap *(Dr and Mrs A K Clarke)*

☆ *Beer House* [Angel St, off Rochdale Rd]: Lively basic open-plan real-ale pub with splendid well kept range, mainly unusual, farm ciders and perry, several Belgian beers on tap, good range of bottled foreign beers, country wines, cheap spirits doubles (wide choice); bare boards, lots of seating, friendly helpful staff and dog, old local prints, good CD juke box (may be loud), bar billiards, darts, robust cheap bar food lunchtime and Thurs/Fri evening inc vegetarian and lots of cheeses; tables outside, frequent beer festivals, ceilidh band Tues, open all day *(Richard Lewis, the Didler, Stephen Brown, Ian Phillips, JP, PP)*

Castle [Oldham St, about 200 yards from Piccadilly, on right]: Unspoilt traditional front bar, small snug, back games room, full Robinsons range kept well from fine bank of handpumps, nice tilework outside; children's room till 7, blues Thurs, open all day (Sun afternoon closure) *(Alex Koval, the Didler, Michael and Jenny Back)*

Circus [Portland St]: Two tiny rooms, back one panelled with leatherette banquettes, very well kept Tetleys from minute corridor bar, friendly landlord, no music or machines; often looks closed but normally open all day weekdays (you have to knock) *(the Didler, Peter Plumridge)*

City Arms [Kennedy St, off St Peters Sq]: Well kept changing beers such as Robinsons, Tetleys, Wadworths Old Timer and a seasonal Ushers ale, Belgian bottled beers, occasional beer festivals, popular bar lunches, quiet evenings; bare boards, wheelchair access but steps down to back lounge, open all day (cl Sat lunchtime, Sun) *(Richard Lewis, Peter Plumridge, Michael and Jenny Back)*

Coach & Horses [Old Bury Rd, Whitefield; A665 nr Besses o' the Barn Stn]: Multi-room coaching inn built around 1830, little changed, very popular and friendly, with well kept Holts, table service, darts, cards *(the Didler)*

Coach & Horses [Belle Vue St, Gorton (A57)]: Warm, welcoming two-room local with fine tiled bar, well kept Robinsons Bitter and Hatters Mild, darts, cards, juke box in lounge, TV in vault; open all day weekends, cl weekday lunchtimes *(the Didler)*

☆ *Copper Face Jacks* [Oxford Rd/Whitworth St, basement of Palace Hotel]: Stylish basement bar full of copper inc huge carefully lit dome over island serving counter; calls itself Irish, but the Celtic references are pleasantly understated (soda bread, Irish smoked salmon); friendly service, interesting food all day; live music (late licence) *(GLD)*

Crown [Wilmslow Rd, Didsbury]: Lively and friendly, several separate areas, well kept ales, good food *(Dr and Mrs A K Clarke)*

Didsbury [Wilmslow Rd, Didsbury]: Attractively reworked Chef & Brewer, roomy yet surprisingly intimate, with mixed oak and pine furniture, old oak beams, stone fireplaces, old Didsbury prints, and log fires, alcoves, soft lighting inc candles; Scottish Courage ales with a guest such as Shepherd Neame, interesting hot dishes, also sandwiches, baked potatoes, topped ciabatta etc, Sun coffee and croissants; quiet piped jazz *(Dr and Mrs A K Clarke, Ian Phillips, Mrs J Hinsliff)*

Dock & Pulpit [Encombe Pl, Salford; off A6 nr cathedral]: Unspoilt gaslit pub with lots of character and several real ales; open all day Sat *(the Didler)*

Eagle [Collier St, off Greengate, Salford]: Old-fashioned backstreet local, absolutely no frills, well kept Holts Bitter and Mild at old-fashioned prices, bar servery to tap and passage with two smoke rooms (can indeed get smoky), old Salford pictures, very friendly manager, cheap filled rolls *(the Didler)*

Eagle & Child [Higher Lane, Whitefield]: Black and white pub set back from rd, with Holts Bitter and Mild; open all day *(the Didler)*

Egerton Arms [Gore St, Salford; A6 by stn]: Several rooms, chandeliers, art nouveau lamps, excellent value Holts Bitter and Mild, also Boddingtons and Marstons *(the Didler)*

Friendship [Hyde Rd, Gorton; A57 nr B6167 junction]: Well named pub with four rooms inc lobby, Marstons Bitter and two Milds – Banks's and Batemans; singalong three nights a week *(the Didler)*

Goose on Piccadilly [Piccadilly]: Roomy and comfortable faux-wetherspoons Bass pub, panelling, books and prints, friendly helpful staff, good choice of reasonably priced food, even a bargain beer; open all day *(Richard Lewis)*

Grey Horse [Portland St, nr Piccadilly]: Cosy traditional Hydes local, welcoming and busy, with timbering, pictures and plates, well kept Bitter and Mild, some unusual malt whiskies, popular lunchtime food; no juke box or machines, open all day *(the Didler, Richard Lewis)*

Hare & Hounds [Shudehill, behind Arndale]: Three rooms served by central bar, notable tile work, wooden panels and stained glass, Tetleys beers and a guest – usually Holts; open all day *(the Didler)*

Hogshead [High St]: Popular bare-boards Whitbreads ale house with good choice of very well kept beers inc plenty of Belgian and American ones, lots of drinking areas, barrel tables, interesting prints and breweriana, pool, juke box, games machines, friendly staff, good food; open all day, cl Sun evening *(Richard Lewis)*

Hogshead [Deansgate]: Spacious and well furnished, with wide choice of food and of well kept beers, flagons, barrels, books, bric-a-brac and bare brick, friendly staff. no-smoking area, good piped music; open all day *(Richard Lewis)*

☆ *Jacksons Wharf* [Castlefield, across bridge from Barca]: New pub with masses of carved oak in amazing cathedral-like interior, pulpits on upper level, lovely views over canal quay, good range of beers and food *(Doug Christian)*

Jolly Angler [Ducie St]: Unpretentious backstreet local, small and friendly, with well kept Hydes Bitter and Strong, coal fire, darts, pool and TV; informal folk singing Mon *(the Didler, JP, PP, BB, Pete Baker, Richard Lewis, Peter Plumridge)*

Kings Arms [Bloom St, Salford]: Big busy old local, small snug with a deep corridor and pinball machines, ten or more real ales, open all day *(the Didler)*

Metropolitan [Lapwing Lane, Didsbury]:
Huge welcoming recently adapted pub,
gabled roof, open fires, separate areas,
popular food inc Sun lunch, lively w/e
evenings *(Dr and Mrs A K Clarke)*
Moon Under Water [Deansgate]: Britain's
biggest pub, well done Wetherspoons cinema
conversion, beautifully fitted and decorated,
with superb ceiling, lovely plasterwork, very
long bar, balcony seating, no-smoking area;
good range of real ales inc bargain pints,
bustling atmosphere, friendly efficient staff,
good choice of popular food all day *(Ian
Phillips, John Wood, Sue Holland, Dave
Webster, Richard Lewis)*
New Grove [Bury New Rd, Whitefield]: Busy
two-bar 1920s local with particularly well
kept Holts Bitter and Mild; open all day *(the
Didler)*
Old Monkey [Portland St]: Traditional Holts
pub, built 1993 but you'd never guess from
the etched glass and mosaic tiling; interesting
memorabilia, well kept cheap Bitter and Mild,
low-priced food, upstairs lounge, warm
hospitality, wide mix of customers *(JP, PP)*
Olde Nelson [Chapel St; A6 opp cathedral]:
Lots of brewery and whisky mirrors in
drinking corridor linking front sliding-door
snug and back lounge – more mirrors and
brass here; Boddingtons and Chesters *(the
Didler)*
☆ *Peveril of the Peak* [Gt Bridgewater St]:
Three traditional rooms around central
servery, lots of mahogany, mirrors and
stained or frosted glass, splendidly lurid green
external tilework; busy lunchtime but
welcoming and homely evenings, with cheap
basic lunchtime food (not Sun), very
welcoming family service, log fire, well kept
Scottish Courage ales, sturdy furnishings on
bare boards, interesting pictures, pub games
inc pool, table football, juke box; seats
outside, children welcome, cl weekend
lunchtimes *(JP, PP, Peter Plumridge, Ian
Phillips, the Didler, LYM)*
Pot of Beer [New Mount St]: Small
refurbished two-bar pub with bare boards,
stripped bricks and timber, interesting
changing guest beers some tapped from the
cask in unusual stillage system (cask fronts
projecting from temperature-controlled
chamber), Thatcher's farm cider, continental
beers inc Polish – food (weekday lunchtimes)
from there too; open all day, cl Sun *(Richard
Lewis, JP, PP, the Didler)*
☆ *Queens Arms* [Honey St, Cheetham; off Red
Bank, nr Victoria Stn]: Well preserved
Empress Brewery tiled facade, well kept
Phoenix Bantam, Timothy Taylor Landlord
and guest beers from small British and Belgian
breweries, Weston's farm cider, food simple
but often all day, coal fire, bar billiards,
backgammon, chess, good juke box; children
welcome, quiz night Tues; unexpected views
of Manchester across the Irk Valley and its
railway lines from large back garden with
good play area, worth penetrating the
surrounding viaducts, scrapyards and

industrial premises *(the Didler)*
Rising Sun [Queen St, off Deansgate]: 18th-c
Greene King pub, recently refurbished but
keeping character; IPA and Abbot, Bass and
John Smiths, good choice of low-priced food,
old pictures, pleasant atmosphere *(Doug
Christian)*
Smithfield [Swan St]: Open-plan pub with
unusual well kept changing beers such as
Briscoes Badger Stone, Hanby Drawwell,
Highgate Dark, Ceredigion Golden and
Hampshire Vickery, good April beer festival,
cheap food in back eating area from open
kitchen servery, friendly family service, pool
on front dais; open all day, cl Sun lunchtime,
bedrooms in nearby building *(Richard Lewis,
BB)*
Wetherspoons [Piccadilly]: Good range of
beers and wines, friendly efficient service and
pleasant décor, good lunchtime menu with
special offers; open all day *(P A Legon,
Richard Lewis)*
Mellor [SJ9888]
Devonshire Arms [Longhurst Lane; this is the
Mellor near Marple, S of Manchester]:
Cheerful front bar with old leather-seated
settles among other seats, lots of old local
photographs, a couple of small period back
rooms (one no smoking), Victorian fireplaces
all round, well kept Robinsons Best and
Mild, usual lunchtime food, cribbage, shove-
ha'penny and dominoes; picnic-sets out in
front and in back garden, well behaved
children in eating area *(LYM, Marvadene B
Eves)*
Morecambe [SD4665]
Dog & Partridge [Bare Lane, Bare]:
Traditional bare-boards layout, lively buzz,
ten real ales inc Boddingtons and Timothy
Taylor, freshly cooked standardised food,
friendly staff; can get crowded weekends
(Andy and Jill Kassube, Karen Eliot)
Mottram [SJ9995]
Pack Horse: Large, welcoming and
comfortable, low beams in back room, coal-
effect fire in two-way stone fireplace, friendly
efficient staff; generous helpings of above-
average food, reasonable prices, good coffee;
pleasant sitting area outside *(J H and Dr S A
Harrop)*
Oldham [SD9606]
Roebuck [Roebuck Low, Strinesdale; A62
NE]: Welcoming moorland pub with good
value generous food, mostly pies, beers from
Boddingtons and Lees, central bar with
through room to both sides, the far one with
hillside views *(Brian A Haywood)*
Ramsbottom [SD7916]
Fishermans Retreat [Twine Valley Park, Bye
Rd; signed off A56 N of Bury at
Shuttleworth]: Surrounded by well stocked
trout lakes, good interesting well presented
reasonably priced food with proper chips,
generous helpings, good choice of changing
beers (and of whiskies), busy restaurant,
games room with two pool tables and games
machines; open all day from 8am *(M A
Buchanan)*

462 Lancashire

Rimington [SD8045]
☆ *Black Bull* [off A59 NW of Clitheroe]:
Spotless popular dining pub, tasteful dining
area (bar tables may be booked too), flower
arrangements and other nice touches, very
friendly good service, comfortable furniture,
real fire, lots of wildlife paintings, railway
memorabilia, impressive model trains; good
food from sandwiches with real chips
through duck, pheasant etc to three-course
Sun lunch, well kept Theakstons, well chosen
piped music; cl Mon exc bank hols, no food
Sun evening *(Margaret and Arthur
Dickinson, Mr and Mrs Pink, J A Boucher)*
Sale [SJ7992]
Kings Ransom [Britannia Rd]: Large well
furnished pub on Bridgewater Canal,
individual seating areas inc BIG no-smoking
one, roaring fires, antique oil paintings,
candlelight, well kept Boddingtons, Courage
Directors and Ruddles County, lots of malt
whiskies, food inc carvery and interesting
salads, also served Sun 4-7; open all day
(Alex Koval, F and A Parmenter)
Sawley [SD7746]
☆ *Spread Eagle*: Quiet upmarket 16th-c
establishment, perhaps rather too restauranty
for the main entries of what is after all a pub
guide, despite the high quality of its food –
very good cooking, beautiful puddings, good
value weekday set lunches and bargain early
suppers; comfortable and sophisticated feel in
light and airy lounge bar with well kept
Black Sheep and Morlands Old Speckled
Hen, well chosen wines, coal fire, cosy
banquettes, lots of small round tables; food
orders taken here for the soothing back no-
smoking dining room with big picture
windows overlooking a pretty stretch of the
River Ribble; bedrooms *(K F Mould,
Norman Stansfield, Warwick and Jillian
Green, David Hawkes, Steve Whalley, P
Abbott)*
Scarisbrick [SD3813]
Master McGraths [Southport Rd]: Single-
storey modern pub-restaurant with
imaginative impressive interior – beams,
leaded lights, soft piped music, good hot food
inc good choice of children's dishes, efficient
service, Burtonwood beers *(M J Bourke)*
Slaidburn [SD7152]
☆ *Hark to Bounty* [B6478 N of Clitheroe]: Old
stone inn in charming Forest of Bowland
village, straightforwardly comfortable rather
modern décor inside though some older
chairs by open fire, wide choice of good
value bar food (lots of tables) inc children's
and old-fashioned puddings, full Theakstons
range kept well, decent wines; bedrooms,
open all day, pleasant garden behind, good
walks *(LYM, Margaret and Arthur
Dickinson, Linda Christison)*
Southport [SD3316]
Coronation [King St]: Well preserved biggish
late Victorian pub, now a Whitbreads
Hogshead with very wide choice of very well
kept ales, friendly staff, good choice of food;
open all day, children till 3 *(Richard Lewis)*

Stockport [SJ8889]
Alexandra [Northgate Rd]: Large backstreet
pub with listed interior, reputedly haunted;
Robinsons beers, pool room *(the Didler)*
Arden Arms [Millgate St, behind Asda]:
Traditional and welcoming, with several
room areas inc old-fashioned snug through
servery, 1920s décor, fine old vault, brighter
lounge area, great collection of working
grandfather clocks, also Dinky toys; good
value limited lunchtime bar food, well kept
Robinsons *(Pete Baker, the Didler)*
Florist [Shaw Heath]: Classic local, some
alterations but still several separate rooms;
Robinsons Best and Hatters Mild *(the Didler)*
Strines [SJ9786]
Sportsmans Arms [B6101Marple—New
Mills]: Pleasant roadside pub with copper-
topped bar tables, hand-painted artefacts,
generous good value food from snacks to Sun
roasts, real ales inc Bass, Boddingtons, Cains
Bitter and Dark Mild, smart dining room,
good piped music *(Michael and Jenny Back)*
Swinton [SD7701]
Moorside Farm [Moorside Rd (A580)]: Old
farmhouse converted into biggish pub,
Banks's ales, simple hot food; pool and
machines on different level at back *(Ian
Phillips)*
Morning Star [Manchester Rd, Wardley
(A6)]: Busy Holts local, well kept ales, good
value basic food weekday lunchtime, lively
games-oriented bar, usually some Sat
entertainment in lounge *(Pete Baker)*
Thingwall [SJ2784]
Basset Hound: Bass Vintage Inn dining pub
with huge helpings, excellent wine list
(Graham and Lynn Mason)
Tyldesley [SD6802]
Mort Arms [Elliott St]: Two-room pub
popular with older locals, mahogany bar,
etched glass and panels, comfortable lounge,
very reasonably priced Holts Bitter and Mild,
friendly landlord, crowds huddled around
TV for Sat horseracing; open all day *(the
Didler)*
Uppermill [SD9905]
Hare & Hounds [High St]: Large helpings of
very cheap food in nicely laid out pub,
various beers, and friendly staff; can arrange
breakfast *(Chris Johnson)*
Waddington [SD7243]
Higher Buck: Pleasant pub in picturesque
village, good value food inc good beef
sandwiches, well kept Thwaites, welcoming
service; open all day Sun *(John and Joan
Wyatt)*
Waddington Arms: Prettily kept, with neat
dining extension, imaginative well prepared
food (not Mon) using fresh local produce,
friendly efficient staff, well kept Morlands
Old Speckled Hen, Theakstons Mild and
Bitter and a beer brewed for the pub, two
airy rooms with woodburners, no-smoking
area, well chosen piped music; children
welcome; bedrooms – where the church bells
either will or won't lull you to sleep *(J A
Boucher, T M Dobby)*

Weeton [SD3834]
Eagle & Child [Singleton Rd (B5260)]:
Greenalls Millers Kitchen refurbished as very
well kept rustic dining pub in byre-like style,
low brick walls with old curved standing
timbers, plenty of bric-a-brac, log fires;
attractively served food from sandwiches and
soup in tureens to imaginative main dishes,
Greenalls and Tetleys ales, cafetière coffee,
good wine list, 1950s nostalgic music, caring
staff *(Arthur and Margaret Dickinson)*

Wiswell [SD7437]
☆ *Freemasons Arms* [just NE of Whalley]: Cosy
and friendly Victorian terraced pub (don't be
put off by dour exterior) with small bar and
overflow upstairs dining room, friendly
efficient service, several well kept real ales,
lots of malt whiskies, and excellent meals
cooked by the landlady (must book
restaurant Fri/Sat evening); lovely village
below Pendle Hill; cl Mon/Tues evening
(Janet Foster, Marjorie Carr)

Incidentally, please note that we include in this chapter the metropolitan areas of
Manchester and Merseyside (and therefore those places around Stockport and on
the Wirral which have for the last couple of decades been absorbed into them –
though everyone knows that they are really in Cheshire).

Leicestershire (with Rutland)

Pubs on top form here these days include the Sun at Cottesmore (good food under its French landlord brings this new entry into the Guide), the Bell at East Langton (imaginative food and nice bedrooms in this cosy country pub), the Old White Hart at Lyddington (good value generous interesting food), the interesting old Nevill Arms at Medbourne (only just misses one of our Bargain Awards), the Peacock at Redmile (new licensee, very imaginative modern food), the Queens Head at Saddington (good bargain OAP lunches – a newcomer to the Guide), the Stilton Cheese at Somerby (good all round – another newcomer) and the Kings Arms at Wing (down to earth pricing for good food in nice surroundings). Besides places we've already picked out for good food, the Old Plough at Braunston is popular for imaginative food, and new licensees at the Finches Arms at upper Hambleton are doing interesting restauranty food there. And it's good news that the new people at the Old Barn at Glooston are opening it at lunchtimes now (and keeping the same popular chef). From all these places, we choose the Old White Hart at Lyddington as Leicestershire Dining Pub of the Year. Places featuring prominently in the Lucky Dip section at the end of the chapter are the Barnsdale Lodge at Barnsdale, Blue Ball at Braunston, Anne of Cleves in Melton Mowbray, Old Brewery at Somerby, Ram Jam Inn at Stretton, Pear Tree in Woodhouse Eaves, and, particularly for their food, the Nags Head in Castle Donington, Welford Place in Leicester and Black Bull in Market Overton. Drinks prices here are close to the national average.

BRAUNSTON SK8306 Map 4
Old Plough ♀
Village signposted off A606 in Oakham

Set in a pretty village in the heart of Rutland, this cosy country pub is well known locally for its nicely presented enjoyably imaginative food. The menu changes seasonally and might include soup of the day (£2.35), grilled ciabatta bread with pesto and mozzarella (£2.95), home-made pork and brandy pâté with onion bread (£3.95), filled granary rolls (from £3.50), lasagne (£6.95), stir-fry vegetables (£7.50), fried liver and bacon with port wine jus (£8.25), fried salmon with roast fennel and olive jus (£8.95), chicken breast filled with goat's cheese and basil with tarragon sauce (£9.25), 8oz fillet (£13.75), and puddings (from £3.65). The cosily traditional low-beamed lounge with upholstered seats around cast-iron-framed tables has plenty of brass ornaments on the mantelpiece (over a huge warming fire in winter) and leads into a modern no-smoking dining conservatory with a false ceiling made from parasols. The carpeted public bar has darts in winter; maybe piped music.Very well kept real ales are likely to include Courage Directors, Hook Norton, John Smiths and Marstons Pedigree. There's also a well noted wine list, fruit punches in summer, Scrumpy Jack cider, and a choice of teas and coffees. In the garden picnic-sets shelter among fruit trees, there's a boules pitch, children's play area and a small children's animal farm. *(Recommended by Jenny and Michael Back, Derek and Margaret Underwood, Derek and Sylvia Stephenson, Ian Stafford, L Walker, David and Anne Culley, Richard Lewis, D Goodger, David and Brenda Tew)*

Free house ~ Licensees Andrew and Amanda Reid ~ Real ale ~ Bar food (till 10pm;

9.30 Sun) ~ Restaurant ~ (01572) 722714 ~ Children in restaurant ~ Open 11-3, 6-11(11-11 bank holidays); 12-2.30, 6(winter 6.45)-10.30 Sun ~ Bedrooms: £45B/£60B

COTTESMORE SK9013 Map 7
Sun ♀ 🍺

B668 NE of Oakham

Doing well under its newish licensees, this 17th-c stonebuilt thatched village pub now concentrates on imaginative food, not cheap but good. It includes a few snacks such as imaginatively filled french bread (from £2.95) and good local sausages, but the dishes people have enjoyed most recently have been more in the line of meals: pissaladière (a compote of mediterranean vegetables with puff pastry) or king prawn and scallop salad (£5.95), grilled salmon on niçoise salad (£7.95), pork fillet with stir-fry vegetables and potato gratin (£8.95) and puddings such as summer berry and lemon crème brûlée or rhubarb crumble (from £2.95) have all come in for particular praise. Other meals on the menu include soup (£2.95), lasagne or cod and salmon cannelloni (£3.95; £5.95 large helping), moules marinières (£4.20; £6.95 large helping) and 9oz fillet steak (£13.95), with specials such as sea bream fillet with roasted peppers and prawns (£7.95), sautéed veal with courgettes and roasted pepper (£11.95) and monkfish wrapped in bacon in a vermouth sauce (£12.95). There are not many tables in the rooms off the bar, so it pays to get there early, or even book. There's a hot fire in the stone inglenook, sunny yellow walls with some nice sporting prints and other pictures, and stripped pine furnishings. Besides Adnams and Everards Tiger they have a guest beer on handpump, and also decent wines. Service is friendly and helpful. There are tables out in the garden; boules. *(Recommended by Mike and Sue Loseby, Mike and Maggie Betton, Nigel and Caroline Aston, Chris and Susie Cammack, Chris Mawson)*

Everards ~ Tenants Franck and Sylvie Garbez ~ Real ale ~ Bar food (12-2, 7-10; not Sun evenings) ~ Restaurant ~ (01572) 812321 ~ Children welcome ~ Open 11-3, 6-11; 12-3, 7-10.30 Sun; closed evening 25 Dec

EAST LANGTON SP7292 Map 4
Bell 🛏

The Langtons signposted from A6 N of Market Harborough; East Langton signposted from B6047

Going from strength to strength, this welcoming creeper-covered country pub serves good imaginative home-cooked food at plain wooden tables in its long stripped-stone beamed bar which is cosy in winter with a good log fire. The menu changes seasonally but might include generous helpings of soup of the day (£2.75), open lemon chicken sandwich (£3.45), coarse chicken liver and garlic pâté with home-made date and orange chutney (£3.95), steak sandwich (£5.35), lamb madras (£7.75), beef, mange tout and black bean stir or toad in the hole (£7.95), wild mushroom filo parcels (£8.25), poached salmon with lemon and parsley butter (£8.50), chicken breast stuffed with broccoli, bacon and cheese and a cheese sauce (£9.50), game and port casserole (£9.95), 8oz sirloin (£10.95); puddings (£2.95); Sunday carvery and weekday senior citizens' lunches; booking is advised at busy times. Well kept Greene King IPA and Abbot and Jennings Cumberland under light blanket pressure and a couple of guests tapped from the cask (there's a £1 discount on a four pint pitcher); friendly and efficient service; no-smoking green-hued dining room. This is a nice place to stay as the bedrooms are very well appointed and service is particularly friendly. There are tables out in the garden, and the village is attractive and set in peaceful countryside. *(Recommended by Rona Murdoch, Jim Farmer, Barbara and James Woods, O K Smyth, JP, PP, E J Locker, David G and Mrs Miriam Peck, Pat and Roger Fereday, George Atkinson, Joan and Michel Hooper-Immins, Stephen and Julie Brown, Bernard and Becky Robinson, Duncan Cloud, B Adams, Anthony Barnes)*

Free house ~ Licensee Alastair Chapman ~ Real ale ~ Bar food (till 10; 9.30 Sun) ~ Restaurant ~ (01858) 545278 ~ Seated children away from bar ~ Open 11.30-2.30, 7(6 Fri, Sat)-11; 12-3.30, 7-10.30 Sun; closed 25 Dec ~ Bedrooms: £37.50B/£49.50B

EMPINGHAM SK9408 Map 4
White Horse 🛏

Main Street; A606 Stamford—Oakham

A very useful place to know, this attractive and bustling old inn is close to the edge of Rutland Water (Europe's largest man-made lake) and is a particulary nice place to stay. Some of the bedrooms are in a delightfully converted stable block, the breakfasts are very good and they offer deep freezing facilities for lucky anglers. The open-plan carpeted lounge bar has a big log fire below an unusual free-standing chimney-funnel, lots of fresh flowers, and a very relaxed and comfortable atmosphere. Very popular well cooked bar food includes filled french bread, soup (£2.35), seafood crêpe (£4.25), garlic king prawns (£4.85), filled yorkshire puddings (from £6.45), fish crumble (£6.95), lasagne (£7.35), scampi or blue cheese and vegetable tartlets (£7.45), daily specials like chicken, ham and mushroom pie (£6.65), steak and kidney pie (£6.95), local trout with spring onions and tomatoes (£7.25), sautéed lamb's liver, bacon and onions in red wine sauce (£7.45) and baked salmon supreme with creamy seafood sauce (£7.85), and puddings like summer pudding, bakewell tart or pineapple cheesecake (£2.95); they also do morning coffee and afternoon tea. The restaurant and the Orange Room are no smoking. Well kept Courage Best and Directors, Grainstore Triple B, John Smiths and Ruddles County on handpump; fruit machine and piped music; friendly service. Outside are some rustic tables among urns of flowers. *(Recommended by Mrs M Dixon, Keith and Margaret Kettell, Barry and Marie Males, R and M Bishop, Michael Butler, Julie Dunne, Andrew Potts, Gwen and Peter Andrews, R Inman, George Atkinson, David and Anne Culley, Joy and Peter Heatherley, Anthony Barnes, JDM, KM, Mr Bewley, Brian Horner, Brenda Arthur)*

Courage (S & N) ~ Lease Roger Bourne ~ Real ale ~ Bar food (12-2.30, 7-9.45) ~ Restaurant ~ (01780) 460221 ~ Children in eating area of bar, and till 8.30 in restaurant ~ Open 10.30-11; 11-10.30 Sun ~ Bedrooms: £50B/£63B

EXTON SK9211 Map 7
Fox & Hounds

Signposted off A606 Stamford—Oakham

This rather grand old coaching inn is a striking reminder of the days when this now quiet and characterful village was part of the main coach route to Oakham. The comfortable high-ceilinged lounge bar has some dark red plush easy chairs as well as wheelback seats around lots of dark tables, maps and hunting and military prints on the walls, brass and copper ornaments, and a winter log fire in a large stone fireplace; piped music. Bar food includes, lasagne or lamb chops with mint and apple sauce (£6.95) liver, bacon and onions or seafood pasta (£7.25), plaice and prawns, sautéed chicken with sherry, cream and mushroom sauce or steak and kidney pie (£7.75), and honey roasted local trout (£9.25); maybe Sunday roast. The lively and quite separate public bar has darts, pool, cribbage, dominoes. One well kept real ale such as Fullers London Pride. There are seats among large rose beds on the well kept back lawn, overlooking paddocks. Rutland Water is only a couple of miles away and it's very handy for walkers on the Viking Way. *(Recommended by Derek and Margaret Underwood, David and Anne Culley, Chris Raisin, Michael Butler, Marion Turner, L Walker, Paul and Sandra Embleton, M J Morgan, F J Robinson, Norma and Keith Bloomfield, Steven M Gent)*

Free house ~ Licensees David and Jennifer Hillier ~ Real ale ~ Bar food ~ Restaurant ~ (01572) 812403 ~ Children welcome ~ Open 11-3, 6.30-11; 12-3, 6.30-10.30 Sun ~ Bedrooms: £32/£36

GLASTON SK8900 Map 4
Monckton Arms 🍷 🛏

A47 Leicester—Peterborough, E of Uppingham

The three interconnecting rooms at this stone roadside inn originally formed a 16th-c farmhouse. It's now owned by the Old English Pub Company and has a sizeable modern extension. The nicest seats are by a big woodburner in an inglenook fireplace.

The seasonally changing bar menu might include sandwiches (from £2.45), soup (£2.75), ploughman's (£5.95), steak and ale pie (£6.95), ostrich stir fry (£9.95) and shank of lamb or fried duck breast (£10.95), as well as daily specials like liver and bacon in onion gravy, minted lamb steak or cod in lemon and beer batter (£6.95); puddings like summer pudding or spotted dick (£2.50); the restaurant is no smoking. As well as ten wines by the glass they also have Courage Directors, John Smiths, Marstons Pedigree, Ruddles Best and a guest like Moles Tap under light blanket pressure; dominoes, cribbage and piped music. There are picnic-sets on a sheltered terrace, and Rutland Water is ten minutes' drive away. It's also handy for Burghley House and Rockingham Castle. *(Recommended by K and E Leist, D Sinclair, J Dawson, John Wooll)*

Free house ~ Licensee Natasha Walker ~ Real ale ~ Bar food (12-9; 12-2, 7-9 Sun) ~ Restaurant ~ (01572) 822326 ~ Children welcome ~ Jazz barbecues monthly ~ Open 11-11; 12-3, 7-10.30 Sun; closed 25 Dec ~ Bedrooms: £40B/£55B

GLOOSTON SP7595 Map 4
Old Barn ★ 🍽 🍷 🍺 🛏

From B6047 in Tur Langton follow Hallaton signpost, then fork left following Glooston signpost

Good news here is that the new licensee is now opening this carefully restored 16th-c pub at lunchtimes as well as in the evening during the week. The old chef has stayed on so we're hoping that the imaginative very well cooked food will continue to be as good as ever. The monthly changing menu might include roasted red and green pepper and courgette soup (£3.50), bacon and brie baguette (£3.95), steak and Guinness pie (£8.50), pork fillets in cider and clove sauce (£9.50) and roast guinea fowl in beetroot and orange sauce (£9.95), as well as daily specials like roasted stuffed red peppers (£6.50), pork in apricot, brandy and cream sauce (£9.95), scallops in ginger and lemon (£11.50), sliced duck breast in mango and mint dressing (£11.95), and puddings like sticky toffee or summer pudding (£3.50). The warmly welcoming lower beamed main bar has stripped kitchen tables and country chairs, pewter plates, Players cricketer cigarette cards, and an open fire; dominoes. Four well kept real ales on handpump are rotated from a wide choice of beers like Adnams Broadside, Buttcombe Bitter, Fullers London Pride, Wadworths 6X; good wine list (with half a dozen by the glass), champagne by the glass. The dining area is no smoking. There are a few old-fashioned teak seats and picnic-sets in front. Breakfasts are good and the bedrooms are comfortable with French-style shower-and-wash cabinets that please most readers, but might perhaps suit best those with at least a modest degree of mobility; no dogs. *(Recommended by Dr G Martin, JP, PP, Eric Locker, Mike and Sue Loseby, M Borthwick, Barbara and James Woods, Ed Miller, Duncan Cloud, Peter Smith, Anthony Longdon, Joyce McKimm, Bob and Maggie Atherton, Alan J Morton, Stephen, Julie and Hayley Brown, D Goodger, Patrick Hancock, Ted George, David Child)*

Free house ~ Licensee Andrew Mark Price ~ Real ale ~ Bar food (not Sun evening) ~ Restaurant ~ (01858) 545215 ~ Children in eating area of bar ~ Open 12-2, 6-11; 12-2, 7-10.30 Sun ~ Bedrooms: £37.50S/£49.50S

HALLATON SP7896 Map 4
Bewicke Arms ★

On good fast back road across open rolling countryside between Uppingham and Kibworth; village signposted from B6047 in Tur Langton and from B664 SW of Uppingham

Easter Monday in Hallaton brings the ancient tradition of bottle kicking with its associated parades and celebrations. You can watch all this in safety from the front windows of this ancient thatched inn which is prettily set on the edge of the village green (they quite often have Morris dancing here too). The unpretentious beamed main bar has two small oddly shaped rooms with farming implements and deer heads on the walls, pokerwork seats, old-fashioned settles (including some with high backs and wings), wall benches, and stripped oak tables, and four copper kettles gleaming over one of the log fires. Well kept Marstons Pedigree, Ruddles Best and County and a guest beer; darts; piped music. Bar food includes sandwiches (from

£1.50), home-made soup (£2.70), ploughman's (£4.20), breaded plaice (£5.60), scampi (£6.20), 10oz rump steak (£9.20), puddings like treacle sponge or lemon cheesecake (£2.90), as well as weekly changing specials such as fried brie and cranberry dip (£4.45), lasagne or courgette stuffed with tomato, peppers, mushrooms and celery topped with cheese and breadcrumbs (£6.80), salmon fillet with honey and mustard sauce or beef and beer casserole (£7.20) and chicken breast filled with stilton, wrapped in bacon and cooked in red wine (£8.20); no dogs. Across the courtyard a converted stable houses a tea room and gift shop, with a big terrace overlooking the animal paddock and lake. *(Recommended by John Wooll, George Atkinson, JP, PP, Duncan Cloud, Eric Locker, Jim Farmer, CMJ, JJW, Ted George)*

Free house ~ Licensee Neil Spiers ~ Real ale ~ Bar food (till 9.45) ~ (01858) 555217 ~ Children welcome ~ Open 12-3, 6(7 Sun)-11

HOSE SK7329 Map 7
Rose & Crown ◖

Bolton Lane

As we went to press there was a chance that this straightforward old free house would change hands; until now its excellence on the beers side has depended on the keen enthusiasm of Carl Routh who's quite happy to drive to a small brewer to pick up his own barrel, and keeps up to eight regularly changing and well kept real ales on at a time. If he is still here when you visit there might be beers from Archers, Belvoir, Brewster, B&T, Cannon, Greene King, Hook Norton, Jennings and Taylor, and around a dozen malt whiskies. There's a relaxed lighthearted atmosphere in the more-or-less open-plan bar which has pool, dominoes, cribbage, a fruit machine and juke box. Bar food includes filled rolls (from £1.60), garlic mushrooms (£1.80), home-made soup (£2.25), ploughman's (from £3.75), home-made chicken and ham or steak and ale pie (£5.50), grilled trout (£6.75) and blackboard specials like garlic mushrooms in shropshire blue cream sauce (£2.50) and rack of lamb with mint gravy (£7.95); no-smoking areas in restaurant and lounge bar. There are tables on a fairy-lit sheltered terrace behind the building, and a fenced family area at the rear of the car park. *(Recommended by Norma and Keith Bloomfield, the Didler, Stephen Brown, R M Taylor, JP, PP, June and Malcolm Farmer, P Stallard, Chris Raisin)*

Free house ~ Licensees Carl and Carmel Routh ~ Real ale ~ Bar food ~ Restaurant ~ (01949) 860424 ~ Children welcome in eating area of bar and restaurant till 9pm ~ Open 12-2.30, 7-11; 12-3, 7-10.30 Sun; closed 25 Dec

KEGWORTH SK4826 Map 7
Cap & Stocking ★ ◖ £

Under a mile from M1 junction 24: follow A6 towards Loughborough; in village, turn left at chemists' down one-way Dragwall opposite High Street, then left and left again, into Borough Street

Quite a rare thing now, they still serve Bass from the jug, at this old-fashioned small town local which makes a handy welcoming stop just off the M1. They also have Hancocks HB and maybe a guest on handpump. Each of the two determinedly simple but cosy front rooms has its own coal fire, and a friendly and easy-going feel; on the right there's lots of etched glass, big cases of stuffed birds and locally caught fish, fabric-covered wall benches and heavy cast-iron-framed tables, and a cast-iron range; cribbage, dominoes, trivia and piped music. The back room has french windows to the pleasant garden where there maybe floodlit boules. Good value bar food includes filled rolls (from £1.20, hot sausage and onion (£1.35), soup (£1.80), burgers (from £2.35), ploughman's (from £4.40), pizzas (from £4.40), chilli or vegetable curry (£4.75), hungarian goulash (£5.95), beef stroganoff (£6.25) and daily specials such as minty lamb, chicken curry (£5.95) and beef in Guinness (£6.25). *(Recommended by Nigel and Sue Foster, Joan and Michel Hooper-Immins, the Didler, Dr B H Hamilton, D E Twitchett, Vicky and David Sarti, Pete Baker, JP, PP, M G Hart, Lynn Sharpless, Bob Eardley, G P Kernan, Susan and Nigel Wilson, Duncan Cloud, Jason Caulkin, Roger and Abigail Huggins, Patrick Hancock)*

Punch Taverns ~ Tenants Graham and Mary Walsh ~ Real ale ~ Bar food (11.30-2.15, 6.30-8.45) ~ (01509) 674814 ~ Children in eating area of bar ~ Open 11.30-2.30(3 Sat), 6.30-11; 12-3, 7-10.30 Sun; closed 25 Dec evening

LOUGHBOROUGH SK5319 Map 7
Swan in the Rushes ◖ £
The Rushes (A6)

A fine choice of beers, an enjoyable cross section of society, and a good friendly welcome are the main attractions at this rather spartan but well liked bare-boarded town pub. There are interesting German, Belgian and other bottled beers well kept Archers Golden, Marstons Pedigree and Tetley and up to seven guests like Castle Rock Hemlock, a farm cider and a good range of malt whiskies and fruit wines. The several neatly kept and simply furnished room areas all have their own style – the most comfortable seats are in the left-hand bay-windowed bar (which has an open fire) and in the snug no-smoking back dining room. It can get very crowded, but service is good. Very reasonably priced home-made bar food includes filled rolls (from £1.30) jacket potatoes (from £2.25), a choice of ploughman's (from £4.25), chilli (£3.95), and specials such as chicken curry or spicy vegetables (£3.95) and grilled trout (£4.95). Shove-ha'penny, cribbage, dominoes, juke box. The simple bedrooms are clean and cosy; generous breakfasts. There are tables in an outside drinking area. *(Recommended by Joan and Michel Hooper-Immins, Rona Murdoch, JP, PP, Bruce Bird, the Didler, Tim Barrow, Sue Demont, Ian Phillips, Barry and Anne, John Voos)*

Free house ~ Licensee Peter Thomson ~ Real ale ~ Bar food ~ Restaurant ~ (01509) 217014 ~ Children in restaurant ~ Open 11-11; 12-10.30 Sun; closed 25 Dec ~ Bedrooms: £20(£25B)/£40(£50B)

LYDDINGTON SP8797 Map 4
Old White Hart ⑭
Village signposted off A6003 N of Corby

Leicestershire Dining Pub of the Year

There's a warm and cosy welcome at this 17th-c village inn. The cosy softly lit bar has just three close-set tables in front of the warm log fire, with heavy bowed beams and lots of attractive dried flower arrangements. The bar opens into an attractive restaurant with corn dollies and a big oak dresser, and on the other side is a tiled-floor room with some stripped stone, cushioned wall seats and mate's chairs, a woodburning stove; a thriving dominoes school, and piped music. Very popular imaginative bar food served in very generous helpings includes home-made soup (£2.95), warm tomato tarte tatin with basil oil (£3.95), pork and pistachio terrine (£4.25), seafood salad (£5.25), fried chicken breast on spinach with beetroot sauce (£9.75), pork fillet with raspberry and sage sauce (£11.25), madeira-glazed duck with black cherry and Cointreau sauce (£12.95), and daily specials like beef stir fry (£4.25), home-made sausages and mediterranean potatoes (£6.95) and macaroni with parmesan, gruyère and balsamic sauce (£7.95); one of the restaurants is no smoking. Well kept, Greene King IPA and Abbot and a guest such as Bass, Black Sheep or Timothy Taylor Landlord on handpump. There are picnic-sets in the safe and pretty walled garden which has twelve floodlit boules pitches – on Thursday you can listen to the church bell ringers. Good nearby walks; handy for the Bede House. *(Recommended by M J Morgan, RB, Tracey and Stephen Groves, Mike and Sue Loseby, Eric Locker, David and Anne Culley, Pat and Roger Fereday, Jim Farmer, George Atkinson, Rona Murdoch, June and Malcolm Farmer)*

Free house ~ Licensee Stuart East ~ Real ale ~ Bar food (12-2, 6.30-9.30) ~ Restaurant ~ (01572) 821703 ~ Children welcome ~ Open 12-3, 6-11; 12-3, 6.30-10.30 Sun

Post Office address codings confusingly give the impression that some pubs are in Leicestershire, when they are really in Cambridgeshire (which is where we list them).

MEDBOURNE SP7993 Map 4
Nevill Arms 🛏
B664 Market Harborough—Uppingham

You reach this handsome old mullion-windowed pub via a footbridge over the duck-filled River Welland. It's a particularly nice place to stay, with rooms in two neighbouring cottages and good breakfasts in the sunny conservatory. The appealing main bar has a cheerful atmosphere, as well as two winter log fires, chairs and small wall settles around its tables, a lofty, dark-joisted ceiling and maybe a couple of dogs or a cat; piped music. A spacious back room by the former coachyard has pews around more tables (much needed at busy times), and some toys to amuse the children. In summer most people prefer eating at the tables outside on the grass by the dovecote. Well kept Adnams, Ruddles Best and County and two changing guests; about two dozen country wines. Good value bar food includes home-made soups like carrot and orange or cauliflower and stilton (£2.65), sandwiches (from £3.50) and ploughman's (£3.80), blackboard specials (£5.50) might include smoked haddock and spinach bake, chicken in lime and mango, pork in white wine and mushrooms, lamb in honey and ginger or beef in Guinness and orange. Darts, shove-ha'penny, cribbage, table skittles, hood skittles, dominoes and other board games on request. The church over the bridge is worth a visit. *(Recommended by Jim Farmer, Eric Locker, Mike and Sue Loseby, Joan and Michel Hooper-Immins, Jeff Davies, Dorsan Baker, M Morgan, Alan J Morton, D Goodger, Barbara and James Woods, Rona Murdoch, CMW, JJW, JP, PP)*

Free house ~ Licensee Elaine Hall ~ Real ale ~ Bar food ~ (01858) 565288 ~ Children welcome ~ Open 12-2.30, 6-11; 12-3, 7-10.30 Sun; closed 25 Dec evening ~ Bedrooms: £32.50B/£39.95B

OLD DALBY SK6723 Map 7
Crown
By school in village centre turn into Longcliff Hill

This smart creeper-covered farmhouse has been popular for its imaginative if not cheap contemporary food, but as we go to press a new licensee is taking over. So we can't promise that you will still find the sort of thing which up to now has appealed so much to readers – such as soup of the day (£2.50), sandwiches (£2.95), iced plum tomato soup with baby mozzarella and basil (£3.50), ciabatta sandwiches (from £5.95), warm chicken, avocado and spring onion salad with grain mustard dressing or sautéed field mushrooms on toast with truffle oil (£5.95), ploughman's (£7.95), roast red onion and grilled goat's cheese tartlets (£8.95), smoked chicken, mushroom and tarragon linguine (£7.95), daube of beef with parsley mash potatoes and madeira sauce (£11.95), seared salmon with tomato and basil purée and confit of plum tomatoes (£12.95), roast spiced breast of duck with sweet potato purée and red onion marmalade (£14.95), and puddings like chocolate and raspberry mousse with orange coulis or bakewell tart with crème chantilly (£4.50). The atmosphere is fairly formal. Three or four intimate little rooms have black beams, one or two antique oak settles, William Morris style armchairs and easy chairs, hunting and other rustic prints, fresh flowers, and open fires; the snug and one dining area are no smoking; cribbage and dominoes. Half a dozen or so real ales tapped from the cask might include Adnams, Black Sheep, Fullers London Pride, Greene King Abbot, Marstons Pedigree and Morlands Old Speckled Hen; there's been an interesting wine list, quite a few malt whiskies, and several brandies and Italian liqueurs. There are rustic tables and chairs on a terrace, with a big, sheltered lawn sloping down among roses and fruit trees; you can play boules. *(Recommended by The Reiterbunds, Roger Bellingham, Mike and Sue Loseby, David Peakall, Alan J Morton, JP, PP, Stephen and Julie Brown, G Neighbour, GL, J H Kane, John Poulter, Andrew Tiplady, Julie Sage, George Green, P and S Merrick, Simon G S Morton, Mike and Mary Carter, Ted George)*

Free house ~ Licensee Lynn Busby ~ Real ale ~ Bar food (till 10pm; not Sun evening) ~ Restaurant ~ (01664) 823134 ~ Children in eating area of bar and games room ~ Open 12-3, 6-11; 12-3, 7-10.30 Sun; 2.30 lunchtime close winter

PEATLING MAGNA SP5992 Map 4

Cock £

Village signposted off A50 S of Leicester

There's a cheery start to the evening at this chatty little village local with discounted beers and spirits and free cut-your-own sandwiches, from loaves of good crusty bread and hunks of excellent stilton or red leicester on the bar (weekdays 5.30-7). During the evening the friendly and energetic landlord likes the kitchen to send out little snacks like free baked potatoes. The narrow main bar has horsey pictures and plates above the coal-effect gas fire and on some beams, cushioned wall benches and plush stools; there's a neat country dining area in the right-hand room; well kept Courage Directors and John Smiths on handpump, and decent house wines. Good straightforward bar food includes home-made soup (£2.05), sandwiches such as local ham and cheese with a salad garnish and chips (£3.30) and home-made specials such as curry, chilli, lasagne or haddock and chips (£5). The very popular Sunday lunch has three bookable sittings; maybe piped pop music. *(Recommended by Ed Miller)*

Free house ~ Licensee Max Brown ~ Real ale ~ Bar food (not Sun, Mon evenings) ~ Restaurant ~ (0116) 247 8308 ~ Children welcome ~ Open 5.30-11; 10-2.30, 6-11 Sat; 12-4, 7-10.30 Sun; closed weekday lunchtimes

REDMILE SK7935 Map 7

Peacock 🍴 🍷

Off A52 W of Grantham; at crossroads follow sign for Belvoir Castle, Harlby, and Melton

New licensees at this lovely stone dining pub plan to make fairly major improvements to the bar and restaurant this year. They will make its four beamed pubby rooms more open plan, add new carpets, and smarten up some of the furnishings. The open fires, pews, stripped country tables and chairs, the odd sofa and easy chair, some stripped golden stone, old prints, chintzy curtains for the small windows, and a variety of wall and table lamps will remain; we'd be very interested to hear what readers think of the changes; no-smoking area; dominoes, piped music, and tables outside. A new chef trained at Gary Rhodes in Manchester, so we have high hopes for the very freshly prepared bar food from the imaginative menu: soup (£2.95), fresh crab bavarois and citrus fruit salad or fried goat's cheese and spinach in filo on a plum tomato fondue (£4.95), grilled chicken breast with wild mushroom, tarragon and grain mustard sauce (£9.95), medallions of pork loin ville fuille with creamed leeks, roast shallots and lemon jus (£10), seafood panache with squid ink risotto timbale (£11.95), beef wrapped in pancetta with sun-dried tomato, roast garlic jus and parmesan crackling (£13.95) and puddings like iced lemon parfait with caramelised melba toast and steamed orange sponge with quenelles of cream and sweet orange sauce (£3.95), and cheese with french bread (£4.50). Booking is advised. Well kept real ales on handpump include Boddingtons, Flowers IPA, Timothy Taylor Landlord and Whitbreads on handpump, and they have an interesting wine list including fairly priced bottles and some by the glass. Spacious, nicely decorated bedrooms; good breakfasts. The pub is in an extremely pleasant tranquil setting near Belvoir Castle. *(Recommended by John Fahy, Stephen Brown, Mr and Mrs P Johnson, David and Helen Wilkins, Alan Caudell, M A Buchanan, RB)*

Free house ~ Licensee Mark Fairburn ~ Real ale ~ Bar food (12-2, 7-9.30; 12-3, 7-9 Sun) ~ Restaurant ~ (01949) 842554 ~ Children in eating area of bar ~ Open 11-11; 12-10.30 Sun ~ Bedrooms: £75B/£90B

SADDINGTON SP6591 Map 4

Queens Head

S of Leicester between A50 and A6

Welcoming and very well run, this dining pub is hugely popular at lunchtime for its bargain quickly served two-course meals (£3.50) for OAPs from Monday to Saturday. Other dishes include sandwiches (from £1.85), soup (£2.75), filled french bread (from £2.95), sausage and mash (£4.95), ham, egg and chips or lasagne

(£5.50), fillet steak sandwich or steak and Guinness pie (£5.95), and puddings like
spotted dick or pancakes with ice cream and hot cherries (£2.50). People like the
fresh mussels in season. The main dining room, built on just a few years ago as part
of a general refurbishment, is no smoking, and looks across the valley to the
reservoir. There's a small second dining room at the back for smokers. The brothers
who run the pub keep a buoyantly friendly and informal atmosphere going – helped
along by the well kept Everards Beacon and Tiger and a couple of guests such as
Adnams or Greene King Abbot; good wine list, daily papers. The bar's very
comfortable and civilised – a different world from how it was before the
refurbishment, when young farmers would leave their wellies outside the back door
to come in and play darts; piped music. Tables in the long sloping garden also have
lovely country views. *(Recommended by Mrs Lynn Hornsby, Steve Hornsby, P Tailyour, Jean
Cloud, George Atkinson, John Saul)*

*Everards ~ Tenants Steve and Malcolm Cross ~ Bar food (12-2, 7-10) ~ Restaurant ~
(0116) 240 2536 ~ Open 11-3, 5.30-11; 12-3.30, 7-10.30 Sun*

SIBSON SK3500 Map 4
Cock
A444 N of Nuneaton

This quaint thatched pub dates back to the 13th c, and there was a cock pit here
until 1870; though it's changed a fair bit over the years, proof of its age can still be
seen in the unusually low doorways, ancient wall timbers, heavy black beams, and
genuine latticed windows. An atmospheric room on the right has comfortable seats
around cast-iron tables, and more seats built in to what was once an immense
fireplace where Dick Turpin is rumoured to have hidden. The room on the left has
country kitchen chairs around wooden tables, and there's a no-smoking dining area.
Well kept Bass and M & B Brew XI on handpump; fruit machine and piped music.
Good value bar food in generous helpings includes home-made soup (£2),
sandwiches (from £2.30), home-made pâté (£2.35), steak and kidney pie, lasagne,
chilli or beef curry (£6.50), steaks (from £8.75), and one or two similar daily
specials; on Sunday the only food is a three-course roast £9.95) in the restaurant (in
a former stable block). A little garden and courtyard area has tables and maybe
summer barbecues; summer hanging baskets and a flower filled dray cart in front.
They have a caravan field (certified with the Caravan Club). *(Recommended by G
Braithwaite, Eric Locker, Tim Phillips, Paul and Sandra Embleton, JP, PP, Joan and Andrew Life,
Ian Blackwell, Simon Hulme, R W Allan, Ted George, Sam Samuells, Lynda Payton, Paul R
White)*

*Punch Taverns ~ Lease Graham Lindsay ~ Real ale ~ Bar food (11.30-2, 6.30(6 Sat)-
9.45) ~ Restaurant ~ (01827) 880357 ~ Children in eating area of bar and restaurant
~ Open 11.30-2.30, 6.30(6 Sat)-11; 12-3, 7-10.30 Sun*

SOMERBY SK7710 Map 7
Stilton Cheese 🍺
High Street; off A606 Oakham—Melton Mowbray, via Cold Overton, or Leesthorpe and
Pickwell; can also be reached direct from Oakham via Knossington

In a peaceful setting on the edge of a pretty Rutland village, this 16th-c pub is
comfortable and friendly, with a thriving relaxed atmosphere. The hop-strung
beamed bar/lounge has lots of country prints on its stripped stone walls, a collection
of copper pots, and plenty of comfortable seats; board games. There's a no-smoking
side restaurant up steps. With three chefs in the family, food is consistently good
value with sandwiches (from £1.85), stilton and onion soup (£1.95), sausage and
mash (£4.95), chicken chasseur (£5.25), steak and kidney pie (£5.45) on the menu,
and daily specials that might include whitebait or warm salad with mushrooms,
bacon and stilton (£2.95), penne and vegetable bolognese (£4.50), turkey stroganoff
(£5.25), duck in blackcurrent liqueur (£5.95), grilled rolls of plaice fillet stuffed with
prawns and lobster (£6.95), and puddings like baked almond tart, ginger and walnut
tart and butterscotch mousse (£2.35). They have well kept local Grainstore 1050,

Marstons Pedigree and Tetleys and guests such as Castle Rock NPA and Shepherd Neame Spitfire on handpump, and a good choice of wines and about two dozen malt whiskies; good unruffled service. *(Recommended by Joan and Michel Hooper-Immins, Sue and Bob Ward, Richard Lewis, Denise and Quentin Thwaites)*

Free house ~ Licensees Carol and Jeff Evans ~ Real ale ~ Bar food (12-2, 6(7 Sun)-9) ~ (01664) 454394 ~ Children welcome ~ Open 12-3, 6-11; 12-3, 7-10.30 Sun

THORPE LANGTON SP7492 Map 4
Bakers Arms 🍴

Village signposted off B6047 N of Market Harborough

Made with fresh ingredients, well presented good bar food at this popular dining pub might include leek and potato soup (£2.95), goat's cheese en croûte with tapenade (£4.85), seared scallops with beurre blanc (£5.95), fried lamb's liver and bacon (£8.95), chicken breast with bacon, leek and barley risotto (£9.95), halibut supreme on grain mustard noodles or chump of lamb with roast parsnips (£10.95) and sea bass with parmesan crust and roast vegetables (£12.95); puddings like pancakes with orange and brandy sauce or hot chocolate fudge cake (£3.50). Fairly simple but attractive furnishings include straightforward seating and stripped pine tables (you'll probably find most given over to eating) in lots of nooks and crannies. Booking is advisable and it's worth checking their opening times below carefully. Well kept Tetleys on handpump, and an extensive wine list with five by the glass; good friendly service, and no games or piped music. There are picnic-sets in the garden. *(Recommended by G Neighbour, Simon G S Morton, Stephen Brown, Jim Farmer, Mike and Sue Loseby, Duncan Cloud, Patrick Tailyour)*

Allied Domecq ~ Lease Kate Hubbard ~ Real ale ~ Bar food (till 9.30) ~ (01858) 545201 ~ Children over 12 ~ Pianist Fri evening ~ Open 6.30-11; 12-3, 6.30-11 Sat; 12-3 Sun; closed Mon, lunchtime Mon-Fri, Sun evening

UPPER HAMBLETON SK9007 Map 4
Finches Arms 🍴

Village signposted from A606 on E edge of Oakham

The new licensees at this delightfully positioned stone pub – with fine views over Rutland Water – are well known to us for their successful work at the Peacock at Redmile. There will be more emphasis on freshly prepared imaginative food from a changing menu which might include sandwiches (£4.25), soup (£2.95), toasted mozzarella and ciabatta (£2.75), wild mushroom risotto with poached egg (£5.25), dressed crab salad (£6.95), lasagne of oyster mushrooms, asparagus and chervil cream, tagliatelle with roasted peppers, black olives and capers with pesto or lamb shank with celeriac mash (£7.95) and 8oz sirloin topped with shallots, shi-itake mushrooms and roquefort (£13.50), and puddings like chocolate and pine nut brûlée with passionfruit or armagnac parfait with prunes and Earl Grey syrup. The bar and modern no-smoking restaurant both have stylish cane furniture on wooden floors. Greene King Abbot, Marstons Pedigree and Theakstons on handpump. The twin village of Lower Hambleton is now somewhere below the expanse of Rutland Water. *(Recommended by M J Morgan)*

Free house ~ Licensees Celia and Colin Crawford ~ Real ale ~ Restaurant ~ (01572) 756575 ~ Classical guitarist Fri, jazz Sun evenings and bank holidays ~ Open 10.30-3, 5.30-11; 10.30-11 Sat; 10.30-10.30 Sun ~ Bedrooms: /£65B

WING SK8903 Map 4
Kings Arms

Top Street, signed off A6003 S of Oakham

Readers really do like this genuinely friendly and relaxing early 17th-c inn , with particular praise for the impressively courteous and efficient service. The bar has a traditional feel with wooden beams and a flagstone floor, as well as two large log fires, captain's chairs around pine and darker wood tables, old local photgraphs and a collection of tankards and old-fashioned whisky measuring pots; in the snug there are fishing rods and tackle. There are no complaints at all about the good, very fairly priced bar food which includes soup (£2.25), filled french rolls (£2.95), grilled trio of sausages (£4.95), steak and kidney pudding (£5.50), ploughman's or fish stew (£5.95), pasta of the day (£6.95), salmon fillet with ginger hollandaise sauce (£8.95), grilled lamb steak with fresh redcurrant and port sauce (£9.50) and seafood platter (£12.50); they add a 10% service charge. Beers from Batemans and Grainstore and a guest are kept under light blanket pressure, the restaurant (and bedrooms) are no smoking, and there are seats, swings and slides in the sheltered garden. There's a medieval turf maze some 17 yards across just up the road. *(Recommended by Stephen and Julie Brown, Roger Brady, Kathy Burke, Mike and Sue Loseby, JP, PP, Derek and Margaret Underwood, R P and P F Edwards)*

Free house ~ Licensees Neil and Karen Hornsby ~ Real ale ~ Restaurant ~ (01572) 737634 ~ Children welcome ~ Open 12-11(6-11 only Mon); 12-11 Sat; 12-10.30 Sun; closed Sun evening winter ~ Bedrooms: £40B/£50B

Lucky Dip

Besides the fully inspected pubs, you might like to try these Lucky Dips recommended to us and described by readers (if you do, please send us reports):

Ashby Folville [SK7011]
Carrington Arms: Simple, welcoming and comfortable Tudor-style country pub, generous plain cooking with local ham and sausages, good chips, well kept Adnams, Everards Tiger and Beacon, fair choice of malt whiskies; children welcome, nice garden, maybe calves or horses in back paddock, live music w/e, monthly veteran car rally *(O K Smyth)*

Barkby [SK6309]
Brookside [Brookside, towards Beeby; off A607 6 miles NE of Leicester]: Warmly welcoming unpretentious pub in pretty village with a brook running past the front door, homely, welcoming and cosy, real ales inc interesting guest beer; lounge, bar and extended dining area, lots of toby jugs, brass and copper *(Duncan Cloud)*

Barnsdale [SK9008]
☆ *Barnsdale Lodge* [just off A606 Oakham—Stamford]: Extensive conservatory dining bar with good choice of generous if not cheap attractively presented food, charming décor, comfortable sitting-roomish coffee lounge, real ales such as Morlands Old Speckled Hen, Ruddles County and Tetleys, cream teas, friendly attentive staff; bedrooms comfortable and attractive, with good breakfast, adjacent antiques centre and handy for Barnsdale Gardens *(Janet Pickles, BB, M J Morgan, R C Watkins, John Knighton)*

Barrowden [SK9400]
☆ *Exeter Arms* [just off A47 Uppingham—Peterborough]: Beautiful rambling pub built with local stone in super setting with front terrace overlooking big village green, distant duck pond and Welland Valley; now brews its own distinctive beers, long lounge/dining area, limited but good lunchtime food from doorstep sandwiches up inc vegetarian choice, prompt cheery service, lively public bar, restaurant; folk club, good R&B nights *(RB, George Atkinson, Mr Ellis)*

Belmesthorpe [TF0410]
Blue Bell [Shepherds Walk]: Quaint and friendly olde-worlde village pub with good fire, well kept Marstons Pedigree and Ruddles County, good traditional home cooking (not Sun evening), generous and sensibly priced, inc game, poultry and fresh fish; open all day w/e *(Anna Blowers, Judith Overton, Nina Blowes, M J Morgan)*

Billesdon [SK7202]
Queens Head [Church St]: Beamed and partly thatched pub with wide range of good well priced home cooking, Everards and a guest ale such as Adnams, decent wines, comfortable lounge bar with warm log fire, unspoilt public bar, small conservatory eating area and upstairs restaurant, friendly efficient staff; children welcome, pretty stone village *(John Wooll, Ted George)*

Bottesford [SK8038]
Red Lion: Friendly two-room village pub with well kept Hardys & Hansons beers inc Mild, simple food choice inc good home-made specials, helpful staff *(Richard Lewis, Francis Johnston)*

Braunston [SK8306]
☆ *Blue Ball* [Cedar Street; off A606 in Oakham]: Relaxed and informal feel in thatched dining pub's long series of individually furnished separate rooms, beams, woodburner and country pine, food from sandwiches to interesting hot dishes inc children's helpings, good friendly service even when busy, well kept beers such as Courage Directors, John Smiths, Ruddles Best and Theakstons Best, good choice of wines, no-smoking areas inc restaurant; dominoes, shove-ha'penny, piped music; children welcome, conservatory, open all day Sun *(Anthony Barnes, Helen Rendell, David and Anne Culley, Pat and Roger Fereday, Chris Raisin, George Atkinson, LYM)*

Breedon on the Hill [SK4022]
☆ *Holly Bush* [A453 Ashby—Castle Donington]: Comfortably plush, with low black beams, lots of brass, sporting plates etc, well kept Marstons Pedigree and Tetleys, bar food (stops early lunchtime; not Sun), restaurant (may be fully booked Sat, cl Sun), no-smoking area, friendly efficient staff; piped music; some tables outside, nice bedrooms; interesting village with Anglo-Saxon carvings in hilltop church above huge limestone face *(BB, JP, PP)*

Burbage [SP4294]
Cross Keys: Two-bar Marstons pub with central servery, snug with open fire, wide food range; long garden with children's room and cricket pitch *(L Davenport)*

Caldecott [SP8693]
Castle: Attractively refitted, good helpings of very affordable excellent fresh food, pleasant staff *(Doug and June Miles, Mrs Harvey)*

Castle Donington [SK4427]
☆ *Nags Head* [Hill Top; A453, S end]: Good atmosphere in dining pub with linked rooms from cosy low-beamed bar to busy and interesting Mediterranean-feel separate no-smoking dining rooms, beautifully cooked and presented food inc imaginative dishes, well kept beer, decent wine, coal fire, friendly service *(JP, PP, Sue Holland, Dave Webster, S J and B S Highmore, Melville Summerfield, M Kershaw, G Washington, the Didler)*

Catthorpe [SP5578]
Cherry Tree [just off A5 S of M1/M6/A14 interchange]: Welcoming and attractive country local, cosy, clean and warm, with good value generous mainly traditional food from heavily garnished sandwiches up (even take-away curries), well kept Bass, Hook Norton Best and a guest such as Greene King, attentive service, dark panelling, lots of plates and pictures, coal-effect fire; hood skittles, no juke box, machines or pool table, but maybe piped radio; cl Mon/Tues lunchtimes *(John C Baker, Rona Murdoch, Andy and Jill Kassube)*

Coalville [SK4313]
Birch Tree [Bardon Rd (A50)]: Friendly local with well kept Marstons, excellent reasonably priced food inc OAP lunchtime bargains *(Janet Box)*

Coleorton [SK4017]
Angel [The Moor]: Friendly modernised old inn with attractive oak beams, coal fires, well kept Marstons Pedigree, good bar food from sandwiches up, hospitable attentive staff, lots of Laurel and Hardy photographs, nostalgic piped pop music; tables outside *(Ian Irving)*

Dadlington [SP4097]
Dog & Hedgehog [The Green]: Comfortably extended modernised dining pub with minstrel's gallery in upstairs room, Hobsons and M&B Brew XI, very wide choice of food inc fish and enormous grills, great views over Bosworth Field *(Joan and Michel Hooper-Immins)*

Fleckney [SP6493]
Old Crown [High St]: Welcoming and very clean, with decent home-cooked food inc bargains Tues, Weds and Fri, Everards ales with a guest such as Adnams, lots of polished wood, cricket memorabilia; delightful views from back garden *(Patrick Tailyour)*

Foxton [SP7090]
Shoulder of Mutton [off A6 N of Market Harborough]: Friendly service, big log fire, lots of pine tables and chairs, well kept Ruddles and Tetleys, wide choice of food, well kept beers, small restaurant; pleasant big garden *(Jim Farmer)*

Great Glen [SP6597]
Yews: Newly refurbished and revitalised, getting popular for enjoyable food and well kept beers; young helpful staff *(Anthony Barnes, O K Smyth)*

Greetham [SK9214]
☆ *Wheatsheaf* [B668 Stretton—Cottesmore]: Wide choice of good value generous food served till 11 inc lots of chargrills, nicely decorated welcoming L-shaped communicating rooms, country prints and plates on dining room walls, odd pivoted clock, roaring woodburner, well kept Boddingtons and Tetleys, welcoming service, soft piped music; pool and other games in end room, restaurant, picnic-sets in streamside garden; bedrooms in annexe *(Michael and Jenny Back, BB)*

Grimston [SK6821]
☆ *Black Horse* [off A6006 W of Melton Mowbray]: Clean and firmly upmarket, with good imaginatively presented straightforward bar food – all freshly cooked, so takes time; remarkable collection of cricket memorabilia (landlord happy to talk about it), well kept Marstons Pedigree, open fire, discreet piped music; no food Sun, cl Sun evening and Mon exc bank hols; attractive village with stocks and 13th-c church *(LYM, J H Gracey)*

Gumley [SP6790]
Bell: Bustling little country local with good food inc fish night every other Fri, Boddingtons, Mansfield and Charles Wells Bombardier, friendly service *(Stephen and Julie Brown)*

Halstead [SK7405]
Salisbury Arms [Oakham Rd]: Roomy village pub with lovely country views from restaurant conservatory, good varied food esp roast duck, good choice of well kept beers inc local brew *(Jim Farmer)*

Heath End [SK3621]
Saracens Head [follow Calke Abbey coach signs from main rd]: Basic unspoiled two-room farm pub by Staunton Harold Reservoir visitor centre, handy for Calke Abbey; well kept Bass served by jug from the cask, great value filled rolls and toasties, cosy coal fires, picnic-sets on nice grass area *(JP, PP, John Beeken)*

Hemington [SK4528]
Jolly Sailor: Very welcoming village local with well kept Bass, Mansfield, Marstons Pedigree and two guest ales, farm cider, good range of malt whiskies and other spirits, good big fresh rolls; good open fire each end, big country

pictures, brasses, blow-torches and bric-a-brac, table skittles; beautiful hanging baskets and tables outside *(JP, PP, the Didler)*

Hose [SK7329]

Black Horse [Bolton Lane]: Friendly local with well kept real ale, quarry tiles, darts, open fire *(JP, PP, the Didler)*

Houghton on the Hill [SK6703]

Old Black Horse: Extensively refurbished Everards dining pub with their beers and a guest such as Adnams, good value well presented food (no hot food Mon lunchtime) inc vegetarian, friendly helpful staff, separate restaurant; big attractive garden with boules *(Eric Locker, Rona Murdoch)*

Illston on the Hill [SP7099]

☆ *Fox & Goose* [off B6047 Mkt Harboro—Melton]: Welcoming and idiosyncratic unspoilt local full of interesting decorations, well kept Everards Mild, Beacon, Old Original and Tiger, good coal fires; no food *(LYM, Jim Farmer)*

Kegworth [SK4826]

Red Lion [High St]: Four small character rooms in busy village local with very cheap beers such as Bass, Batemans XB, Marstons Pedigree, Theakstons Best and guest beers inc a Mild, wholesome food, big garden with play area; open all day *(the Didler, JP, PP)*

☆ *Station* [towards West Leake, actually just over the Notts border]: Busy well refurbished pub with bare brick and woodwork, coal fires, two rooms off small bar area, well kept Bass, Courage Directors, Worthington and guest beers, upstairs restaurant with good home cooking; big back lawn, play area; simple good bedrooms, sharing bathroom *(JP, PP, the Didler)*

Kibworth Beauchamp [SP6893]

Coach & Horses [Leicester Rd]: Friendly efficient service, welcoming relaxed atmosphere, good home-made food in lounge or lovely candlelit restaurant inc beautifully done mussels (best in a long time) and mushroom stroganoff with lots of flavour, and reasonably priced (about £6); thatched cottage with lots of beams, log fire in lounge, well kept Ansells and Marstons Pedigree, decent wines *(Rona Murdoch, Eric Locker, Jim Farmer)*

Old Swan [High St]: Friendly pub/restaurant with wide range of good value food inc popular Mon/Tues curry nights and fish and chip suppers Weds, well kept Marstons Pedigree and John Smiths *(Jim Farmer, Rona Murdoch)*

Kibworth Harcourt [SP6894]

☆ *Three Horseshoes:* Village pub doing well under very friendly new landlord, good choice of food running up to steaks, well kept Marstons Best and Pedigree with a guest such as Everards Tiger, comfortable and spacious plush seating, side eating areas; piped music, children welcome; tables on attractive back terrace *(LYM, Duncan Cloud, Nigel Thompson)*

Leicester [SK5804]

Cafe Bruxelles [High St]: Former bank with tall Victorian bar gantry, ornate domed ceiling with painted scenes between gold filigree plasterwork, back area done out as Belgian café with more plasterwork, check oilcloth tablecloths, old labels and coloured tiles on walls, good service, short choice of well presented food inc Belgian snacks (Sun limited to roast, filled baguettes and ciabattas), lots of bottled beers and several continentals on draught, coffees, good budget wines, small downstairs bar; jazz Mon night, may have bouncer *(Ted George, Anthony Barnes, Rona Murdoch, John A Barker)*

Craddock Arms [Knighton Rd/Newmarket St]: Substantial friendly Everards pub with raised eating area in spacious back lounge, good food, guest beers, open fires, good crowd of locals; the large but unobtrusive TV screen in main bar for Leicester Tigers' rugby matches *(Veronica Brown)*

Edwards [Granby St]: Very light and airy, polished wood floors, good modern prints, real ales such as Bass, good house wines, cappuccino etc from long bar, good value generous food, pleasant efficient service *(John Wooll)*

Fourpence & Firkin [Loseby Lane]: Small Firkin pub with a great atmosphere; wooden tables and settles, good value food, Firkin beers inc Dogbolter and Fourpenny; juke box loudish, but good choice *(John A Barker)*

Globe [Silver St]: Comfortable three-room local with lots of woodwork, gas lighting, coal-effect gas fire, good value simple generous lunchtime food from sandwiches up, more peaceful upstairs dining room with friendly service; full Everards range and guest beers kept well, juke box in back room, children allowed in some parts *(John A Barker, John Wooll, LYM, Ted George)*

Hogshead [Market St]: New Whitbreads alehouse, smarter than some in the chain; bare boards and flagstones, panelling, old local photographs, up to 14 real ales with free tasters, bottled beers, good value food, no-smoking area, friendly helpful young staff, daily papers; open all day *(Joan and Michel Hooper-Immins, Stephen, Julie and Hayley Brown, Tony and Wendy Hobden, the Didler)*

Last Plantagenet [Granby St]: Welcoming Wetherspoons pub with the usual comfortable seats inc no-smoking area and some booths at the back; occasional beer festivals, a couple of guest beers, and good cheap food; disabled facilities *(G Coates)*

Mollie O'Gradys [Hotel St/Market Pl S]: Quite large, with low ceiling, dim lighting, a great atmosphere, well kept Everards Tiger and Beacon, friendly staff *(John A Barker)*

☆ *Tom Hoskins* [Beaumanor Rd; off Abbey Lane (A5131), right fork S from A6 at Red Hill Circle]: Tap for Hoskins small brewery – group brewhouse tours can be arranged; flagstones, floorboards, panelling, varnished pews, brewery memorabilia; well kept cheap Hoskins and guest ales, limited but good value lunchtime food (not Sun), friendly prompt service, traditional games, sports TV *(LYM, Rona Murdoch)*

Vaults [Wellington St]: Very basic concrete-floored cellar bar linked to Leatherbritches Brewery of Fenny Bentley, with their and other interesting quickly changing microbrews, some tapped from the cask; friendly staff, filled rolls, Sunday cheeses, low ceiling with iron pillars (can get smoky), tall settles forming booths, stripped brick walls with old signs rather reminiscent of a railway station; open all day Fri-Sun, cl Mon-Thurs lunchtime, may be entrance fee for Sun live bands *(the Didler, Graham Coates, JP, PP, Joan and Michel Hooper-Immins, Rona Murdoch)*

☆ *Welford Place* [corner Newarke St/Welford Rd]: Spacious former Constitutional Club, up impressive flight of stone steps and appealing to older readers; quiet, comfortable and clubby semicircular Victorian bar with emphasis on imaginative changing food 8am-11pm, well kept Adnams and Marstons Pedigree, good choice of Italian wines and other drinks, fresh orange juice, good coffee, obliging management, friendly service even under pressure, attractive dining room (children allowed here), daily papers, no piped music, jazz Weds; same management as Wig & Mitre, Lincoln *(Ian Phillips, O K Smyth, P Stallard, J Middis, Duncan Cloud)*

Wilkies [Market St]: Has been bare yet cheerful (no reports since spring 1999 closure for refurbishment), with imaginative lunchtime food inc German and Spanish, well kept Adnams, Boddingtons and other ales, up to three German or Belgian beers, farm cider, lots of continental bottled beers, friendly service; open all day, cl Sun *(the Didler, Stephen, Julie and Hayley Brown)*

Little Bowden [SP7487]

☆ *Cherry Tree* [Church Walk; edge of Mkt Harboro, nr Sainsburys]: Attractive low-beamed thatched and timbered pub with two sitting rooms, lots of prints, well kept Everards Beacon, Tiger and Old Original with a guest beer, friendly staff, good value food (not Sun evening) from filled baked potatoes up inc some vegetarian, no-smoking dining room on left, games room; children welcome, garden with picnic-sets and play area, open all day Sat/Sun, nr 12th-c church *(George Atkinson, Rona Murdoch, Stephen, Julie and Hayley Brown)*

Long Whatton [SK4723]

Falcon [not far from M1 junction 24]: Spacious and relaxing, with good choice of food in comfortable restaurant stepped up from lounge, and upstairs coffee lounge with fish tanks; well kept Everards Old Original and Tiger, friendly efficient Portuguese licensees; bedrooms planned *(B Adams)*

Loughborough [SK5319]

Tap & Mallet [Nottingham Rd]: Fairly plain pub distinguished by five or six changing microbrews, farm cider, occasional beer festivals; back garden, open all day Sat/Sun *(the Didler, JP, PP)*

Market Harborough [SP7388]

Red Cow [High St]: Greene King, with well kept Marstons Pedigree as a guest; bedrooms planned *(Stephen and Julie Brown)*

Sugar Loaf [High St]: Popular new Wetherspoons, many guest beers, good value food, no piped music – just a silenced juke box *(Patrick Tailyour)*

☆ *Three Swans* [High St]: Comfortable and handsome Best Western coaching inn with good range of food from well priced sandwiches to well cooked main dishes, plush and peaceful panelled bar with old local prints, fine conservatory and attractive suntrap courtyard, decent wines, Courage Directors and Theakstons Best, good coffee, efficient service, upstairs restaurant; bedrooms *(Joan and Michel Hooper-Immins, George Atkinson)*

Market Overton [SK8816]

☆ *Black Bull* [Teigh Rd, nr church]: Attractive thatched pub with thriving lounge bar, good helpings of well cooked reasonably priced food from baguettes to good fresh fish and Sun roasts here and in small back restaurant, very prompt welcoming service, well kept Ruddles Best, Theakstons and a guest such as Hook Norton, artificial pool and waterfall by entrance, nice atmosphere combining village pub and eating house; get there early Sun and in summer; pretty village, some tables out in front; bedrooms *(G P Stancey, Anne and David Robinson, Anthony Barnes, Bill and Sheila McLardy)*

Medbourne [SP7993]

Horse & Trumpet [Old Green; B664 Uppingham—Mkt Harboro]: Unspoilt and unchanging, in same family for 60 years, very welcoming; well kept Batemans XB and Greene King IPA, no music or machines, two rooms, scrubbed tables, coal fire, traditional games, piano; cl lunchtime exc Sun *(Pete Baker, the Didler)*

Melton Mowbray [SK7518]

☆ *Anne of Cleves* [Burton St, by St Mary's Church]: Medieval stonebuilt pub recently stripped back to beams and stonework, nice fireplace, scrubbed tables – even unobtrusive Tudor piped music; plenty of atmosphere, enjoyable food inc good local sausages in long no-smoking bar with small end restaurant, friendly staff, separate snug (smoking allowed), well kept Everards Tiger and Nutcracker, daily papers; no under-7s *(Dr and Mrs D E Awbery, Meg and Colin Hamilton, Andrew Clayton, Duncan Cloud)*

Mountsorrel [SK5714]

☆ *Swan* [Loughborough Rd, off A6]: Two small busy whitewashed bars with warm log fires, old flagstones and red banquettes, well kept Batemans XXXB, Theakstons Best, XB and Old Peculier, wide choice of bottled beers and of good wines by the glass, good value home cooking inc vegetarian (freshly made so can be slow), courteous staff; small walled back garden leading down to canalised River Soar; bedrooms *(Sue Eland, Jim Farmer)*

Mowsley [SP6489]

Staff of Life [off A50 S of Leicester]:

Refurbished village pub, clean and attractive, with comfortable lounge bar, big back dining conservatory, good range of enjoyable freshly cooked food inc fresh fish and chargrills, well kept Bass, Boddingtons and Marstons Bitter and Pedigree; lovely back garden with terrace *(Dorsan Baker, Eric Locker, Stephen, Julie and Hayley Brown)*

Muston [SK8237]

Muston Gap [Church Lane; just off A52 W of Grantham]: Thriving Brewers Fayre with comfortable extension in style of old barn, reliable reasonably priced family food, helpful friendly staff, well kept beers, play area outside (and a small one inside); good disabled facilities *(R C Vincent, Janet Box, Richard Lewis)*

Newton Burgoland [SK3708]

☆ *Belper Arms* [Main St, off B586 W of Ibstock]: Ancient rambling pub said to date from 13th c, friendly and interesting, with good reasonably priced food esp fish, also vegetarian, in roomy lounge and low-beamed areas off, masses of bric-a-brac, well kept Adnams, Marstons Pedigree and a guest beer, farm cider, good choice of malt whiskies, beer festivals (with live music), chatty landlord and staff, restaurant; children and locals' dogs welcome, resident ghost, big garden with play area and boules *(Rona Murdoch, the Didler, JP, PP, Janet Box)*

Oadby [SK6200]

Cow & Plough [Stoughton Farm Pk, Stoughton Rd – follow Farmworld signs off A6]: Pub in working farm open to the public 5-9, 7-9 Sun (and to farm patrons 12-2), up to seven real ales such as Belvoir Star, Fullers London Pride and Steamin' Billy, good choice of bottled beers or wines by the glass, Weston's cider, three rooms filled with brewing memorabilia, enamel signs, old church pews – no food; can watch milking and so forth *(JP, PP, the Didler, Duncan Cloud)*

Oakham [SK8508]

Grainstore [Station Yard]: Converted grainstore, bare brick and boards, cast-iron pillars and pews, ex-Ruddles brewer producing his own Cooking, Triple B, Tom Cribb Winter Ale and Ten Fifty here; filled rolls, good service *(Chris Raisin, JP, PP, the Didler)*

Normanton Park [off A606 E, S of Rutland Water nr Empingham]: Refreshingly informal waterside hotel's Sailing Bar with good choice of food, well kept Morlands Old Speckled Hen, Ruddles Best and County and Tetleys; bedrooms, fine views *(M J Morgan)*

Wheatsheaf [Northgate]: Neat and friendly unspoilt three-room 17th-c local nr church, Everards and guest ales, decent usual food, open fire; back garden *(Rona Murdoch)*

Peggs Green [SK4117]

New Inn [nr junction A512/B587, just N of Swannington]: Masses of bric-a-brac and farming memorabilia in two main rooms, snug and even the lavatories, particularly well kept ales, friendly licensees with interesting

Irish background; food limited to rolls *(Bernie Adams, the Didler, JP, PP)*

Pinwall [SP3099]

Red Lion: Very friendly landlord, well kept guest beers, good reasonably priced bar food, restaurant with good fish choice *(Graham and Elizabeth Hargreaves)*

Redmile [SK8036]

Olde Windmill [off A52 Grantham—Nottingham]: Comfortable lounge and dining room, well kept Boddingtons and Ruddles Best, good house wines, good value food esp Sun lunch, friendly landlord; tables outside *(K H Frostick, Norma and Keith Bloomfield)*

Shawell [SP5480]

White Swan [village signed off A5/A427 roundabout – turn right in village; not far from M6 junct 1]: 17th-c beams, open fire, good bar food inc home-made pies, good hot beef baguettes and some unusual specialities, four well kept real ales, service cheerful and helpful even when busy; some emphasis on good no-smoking panelled restaurant, cl lunchtime exc Sun *(M J Brooks, Dr Alan Sutton)*

Shearsby [SP6290]

☆ *Chandlers Arms* [off A50 Leicester—Northampton]: Comfortable village pub with brocaded wall seats, wheelback chairs, flowers on tables, house plants, swagged curtains, dog pictures for sale, good food, well kept Marstons Bitter and Pedigree and Fullers London Pride, good service, no-smoking bar on left; piped pop music may be intrusive; tables in secluded raised garden *(Peter Smith, Jim Farmer, P Tailyour, BB)*

Sileby [SK6015]

☆ *White Swan* [Swan St]: Good choice of food (not Sun evening or Mon) from filled home-made rolls and baked potatoes to interesting restaurant dishes, speciality steaks, fresh fish and tasty puddings, inc exceptional value weekday bargains, in friendly recently redecorated pub with comfortable and welcoming dining lounge, well kept Bass and Marstons Pedigree, good house wines, entertaining boxer dogs, small tasteful book-lined restaurant (booking needed) *(Jim Farmer, Stan and Hazel Allen)*

Somerby [SK7710]

☆ *Old Brewery* [off A606 Oakham—Melton Mowbray; or back road from Oakham via Knossington]: Roomy modernised pub with new licensees from John o' Gaunt brewery in Melton Mowbray, still also interesting cheap Parish ales brewed in pub yard (and the popular group brewery tours); roaring open fires, cheery relaxed atmosphere, thriving bar, cosy lounge, cheap food; piped music; open all day, children very welcome, tables in garden, boules and play area *(Anthony Barnes, JP, PP, Stephen Brown, Ed Miller, LYM, Dr and Mrs J H Hills, Norma and Keith Bloomfield, Richard Lewis, CMW, JJW)*

South Croxton [SK6810]

Golden Fleece: Large pleasant pub/restaurant, clean and friendly, with good value all-fresh food from tasty baguettes up, good service, ales such as Ansells Mild and Marstons Pedigree; lovely area *(S Lewis, Anthony Barnes, Duncan Cloud, James Osborne)*

Stretton [SK9416]

Jackson Stops: Thatched pub in quiet village, well kept Ruddles and Theakstons, decent wines, good range of generous freshly cooked standard food inc good ploughman's and puddings, log fire, old farm tools, pleasant staff, cosy bar on left kept for drinkers; local for three-nation fighter squadron at RAF Cottesmore with lots of relevant memorabilia *(Eric J Locker, LYM)*

☆ *Ram Jam Inn* [just by A1]: Not a pub, but a good A1 stand-in – a civilised and relaxing modern version of a Great North Road coaching stop: mix of sofas and neat contemporary seating in airy modern upmarket café-restaurant, open fire, good stylish food from light snacks up, efficient service, good wines, freshly squeezed orange juice, fresh-ground coffee and so forth, daily papers, no-smoking area; children welcome, comfortable bedrooms, open all day, food 7am-10pm *(Francis Johnson, M and J Godfrey, John C Baker, John Fahy, BB)*

Thornton [SK4607]

Typsy Fisherman: Great choice of generous very reasonably priced food inc daily fresh fish and veg, friendly staff, good range of well kept beers inc Ansells, Bass and Marstons Pedigree *(D E Piggott)*

Tilton on the Hill [SK7405]

Rose & Crown [B6047]: Friendly old place with genuine pub atmosphere, good reasonably priced freshly made food, well kept Tetleys-related beers, great coffee; unobtrusive piped traditional jazz *(Mrs Y Beaumont)*

Tur Langton [SP7194]

Bulls Head [Shangton Rd]: Very welcoming landlady, well kept Marstons Bitter and Pedigree and Timothy Taylor Landlord, eating area off lounge, unspoilt bar with open fire and darts, good choice of freshly made food from doorstep sandwiches up, unobtrusive piped music; cl weekday lunchtime *(Jim Farmer)*

Ullesthorpe [SP5087]

Chequers: Big country inn popular with lunchtime businessmen, beamed and flagstoned bar and most of lounge areas with emphasis on very wide choice of reasonably priced food from large servery (pay as you order), real ales such as Batemans XXXB, Gales HSB and Theakstons Old Peculier, faint semi-classical music, no-smoking areas; children welcome, family room and play area; comfortable bedrooms *(P Tailyour)*

Uppingham [SP8699]

White Hart [High Street W]: Wide choice of good value simple tasty food using local produce, inglenook fire in panelled front lounge, quite a warren of passages and rooms, three well kept real ales, reasonably priced wines, good service, back restaurant; bedrooms *(Michael Hyde, E J Locker)*

Whitwell [SK9208]

☆ *Noel Arms*: Wide choice of good food (till 10) from good value ploughman's and bacon baguette to fish and delicious puddings, in spaciously extended light pine restaurant and smart new carpeted bar with lower side room, well kept Courage and Marstons Pedigree, charming quick service, suntrap tables outside with play area, occasional barbecues; piped music, can get busy; handy for Rutland Water, children welcome; bedrooms *(Mr and Mrs C Roberts, LYM, Mr and Mrs M Reeve, Jim Farmer)*

Whitwick [SK4514]

Bulls Head [former B587 towards Copt Oak; quite handy for M1 junction 22]: Busy but welcoming L-shaped plush beamed bar with splendid views over Charnwood Forest – highest pub in Leics; well kept Tetleys-related ales, quickly served home-made food (lunchtime, not Sun) using good ingredients, friendly efficient service, back games room with piped music, big garden with menagerie of farm animals; children very welcome away from bar *(Janet Box)*

Wigston [SK5900]

Royal Oak [Leicester Rd]: Recently pleasantly refitted John Barras pub, well priced food inc good Sun lunch, Courage beers *(Veronica Brown)*

Woodhouse Eaves [SK5214]

☆ *Pear Tree* [Church Hill; main street, off B591 W of Quorndon]: Attractive upper flagstoned food area with pitched roof and pews forming booths, open kitchen doing enjoyable food (not Sun Night) from sandwiches up; sympathetically refurbished lower pub part with conservatory, log fire, Ansells, Bass, Ind Coope Burton and Marstons Pedigree, good choice of malt whiskies, decent wines; children welcome, open all day bank hol w/e, picnic-sets and summer bar outside, good nearby walks *(Michael and Jenny Back, JP, PP, David and Helen Wilkins, Barry and Anne, LYM)*

☆ *Wheatsheaf* [Brand Hill; beyond Main St, off B591 S of Loughborough]: Plush and busy open-plan beamed country pub, smart customers, pleasant service, good home-cooked food inc sandwiches and vegetarian, Bass, Ruddles County, Timothy Taylor Landlord and several well kept weekly changing guest ales, decent wines, log fires, upstairs restaurant; floodlit tables outside, dogs welcome but no motorcyclists or children *(Alan Johnson, Joan and Michel Hooper-Immins, the Didler, Duncan Cloud, LYM, JP, PP)*

Wymeswold [SK6023]

Hammer & Pincers [A6006]: Clean, bright and spaciously extended country dining pub with pine furniture in four or five rooms on several levels, good value generous home-cooked food inc vegetarian, well kept Bass, Ruddles County, Marstons Pedigree, Theakstons Best and XB and guest beers, friendly service; tables on terrace and in neat garden *(Jim Farmer)*

Lincolnshire

Pubs on top form here these days include the Chequers at Gedney Dyke (new licensees doing imaginative food), the Black Horse at Grimsthorpe (this comfortable dining pub gains its Guide entry for the first time), the Victoria in Lincoln (a classic Victorian real-ale pub), the Wig & Mitre there (imaginative food and substantial improvements and enlargements after a management buy-out), the handsome and very civilised old George of Stamford, and the well preserved Mermaid at Surfleet (another newcomer to the Guide. For a special meal out, we name the Chequers at Gedney Dyke Lincolnshire Dining Pub of the Year. For drinks, the aptly named Cider Centre at Brandy Wharf stands out in its special field – an unrivalled choice (and decent food, too). Some pubs coming to prominence in the Lucky Dip section at the end of the chapter include the Castle at Castle Bytham, Five Bells at Edenham, Bell at Halton Holegate, Bull in Market Deeping, Vine in Skegness, and, especially for their food, the Ship at Barnoldby le Beck, Browns Pie Shop in Lincoln, Pyewipe just outside and Vine at South Thoresby. Though a hotel, the Angel & Royal in Grantham has a fascinating pair of ancient bars. Drinks prices in the area are generally close to the national average, but the local family brewer Batemans supplies many pubs here with good beer at below-average prices. A smaller local brewer worth looking out for too is Highwood, with its Tom Wood and Bomber Command beers cropping up increasingly often; you may also find Oldershaws beers here and there, and Adnams of Suffolk is now making some inroads into the county.

ALLINGTON SK8540 Map 7
Welby Arms 🍺

The Green; off A1 N of Grantham, or A52 W of Grantham

This friendly village local makes a pleasant respite from the A1. A stone archway divides the two rooms of the bar; there are comfortable burgundy button-back wall banquettes and stools, black beams and joists, red velvet curtains, a coal fire in one stone fireplace and logs burning in an attractive arched brick fireplace; piped music, cribbage and dominoes. Tasty home-cooked food might include home-made soup (£2.65), garlic mushrooms (£3.25), chicken and broccoli bake (£6.25), fish pie (£6.95), brie and bacon chicken (£7.95), steak and kidney pudding (£9.25); the fresh Grimsby haddock in beer batter (£6.45, Tues-Fri) is especially well liked by readers, and puddings like bread and butter pudding and cheesecake (£2.95); advisable to book especially at weekends. Bass, John Smiths, Timothy Taylor Landlord and up two guests served through a sparkler but kept well, decent wines and a good range of country wines. The no-smoking candlelit dining lounge round to the back has been extended this year and looks out onto tables on the sheltered walled courtyard with its pretty hanging baskets in summer. There are picnic-sets on the lawn in front. *(Recommended by Dr and Mrs J H Hills, Steven M Gent, John Fahy, Mike and Penny Sanders, John C Baker, JP, PP, Michael Hyde, Christopher Turner, the Didler, Sue Rowland and Paul Mallett, D S and A R Hare, Gordon Tong, Jenny and Michael Back, Nigel and Anne Cox, DC, Derek and Sylvia Stephenson, Anthony Barnes, H Bramwell, Tony Gayfer, P Stallard, P W Taylor, John and Enid Morris, Joy and Peter Heatherley, Kevin Thorpe, Bill and Sheila McLardy)*

Free house ~ Licensee Bob Dyer ~ Real ale ~ Restaurant ~ (01400) 281361 ~ Children in eating area of bar and restaurant ~ Open 12-2.30(3 Sat), 6-11; 12-3, 7-10.30 Sun ~ Bedrooms: £48B/£60B

ASWARBY TF0639 Map 8
Tally Ho ♀ 🏠

A15 S of Sleaford (but N of village turn-off)

There's a gently civilised atmosphere at this handsome 17th-c stone-built inn. The country-style bar has dark oak beams and cast-iron-framed tables, a big log fire, some stripped masonry and country prints; maybe piped music. Well kept Bass, Batemans XB and a guest on handpump and good house wines; daily papers. Besides soup (£2.50), lincolnshire sausage (£3.75), ploughman's or filled french bread (£4.20), blackboard specials might include four-cheese tartlet or smoked mackerel pâté (£3.85), warm duck leg salad (£4.10), mediterranean vegetable lasagne (£6.25), chicken pieces in pepper and orange sauce (£7.15), salmon fillet with pesto or lamb kebabs and rice (£5.50) Spanish pork with olives (£7) and steak (£9.50); they take great care and attention with the home-made puddings which might include German cheesecake or plum pie (£2.75). You may need to book for the attractive pine-furnished restaurant. There are tables out behind among fruit trees, and usually sheep in the meadow beyond. The bedrooms are in a neatly converted back block, formerly the dairy and a barn. Over the road, the pretty estate church, glimpsed through the stately oaks of the park, is worth a visit. *(Recommended by Sue and Bob Ward, Tracey and Stephen Groves, M J Morgan, R T and J C Moggridge, June and Malcolm Farmer, J and D Ginger, Graham and Lynn Mason, Dr G Sanders, Paul and Sandra Embleton, JCW, Simon and Angela Taylor)*

Free house ~ Licensees Peter and Christine Robertson ~ Real ale ~ Bar food (12-2.30, 6.30-10) ~ Restaurant ~ (01529) 455205 ~ Children in eating area of bar ~ Open 12-3, 6-11; 12-3, 7-10.30 Sun ~ Bedrooms: £33B/£48B

BRANDY WHARF TF0197 Map 8
Cider Centre

B1205 SE of Scunthorpe (off A15 about 16 miles N of Lincoln)

The friendly landlord here knows all about cider, and this unusual pub is his shrine to it. As well as Addlestone's, Scrumpy Jack and Weston's Old Rosie on handpump, he keeps some five dozen other farm ciders and perries – up to 8 tapped from casks, the rest from stacks of intriguing bottles and small plastic or earthenware kegs on shelves behind the bar; they also keep country wines and mead. The landlord's very happy to talk cider, and will on request show you his extraordinary collection of hundreds of different cider flagons, jugs and bottles. The main bar is a simple room with wheelback chairs and brown plush wall banquettes, cheery customer photographs and a good little coal fire. The dim-lit lounge bar has all sorts of cider memorabilia and good-humoured sidelights on cider-making and drinking (not to mention the foot of 'Cyril the Plumber' poking down through the ceiling); there is also a small museum. Good value generous bar food includes sandwiches (£3), ploughman's (from £3.20), pork and cider sausage (from £4.20), steak and vegetable pie, chicken curry or chilli (£5.50) with wonderful real chips; piped British folk music. The pub is set in four acres of orchard and meadow, and a simple glazed verandah overlooks the river where there are moorings and a slipway. There's also a caravan site; quite a few appropriate special events. No children. *(Recommended by J and D Ginger, M J Morgan, James Nunns, JP, PP, CMW, JJW, Alison Keys)*

Free house ~ Licensee Ian N Horsley ~ Bar food (12-2, 7-9.45; not Tues lunchtime, or Mon Nov-Easter) ~ (01652) 678364 ~ Open 12-3, 7-11; 12-4(winter 3), 7-10.30 Sun; closed Mon lunchtime winter; closed Fri before Christmas-early Jan

---

Pubs with particularly interesting histories, or in unusually interesting buildings, are listed at the back of the book.

DYKE TF1022 Map 8

Wishing Well ◖

21 Main Street; village signposted off A15 N of Bourne

There's a friendly bustling atmosphere at this very welcoming big black and white village inn. There's a wishing well at the dining end of the long, rambling bustling front bar – as well as lots of heavy beams, dark stone, brasswork, candlelight and a cavern of an open fireplace. The carpeted lounge area has green plush button-back low settles and wheelback chairs around individual wooden tables. The quite separate public bar, smaller and plainer, has sensibly placed darts, pool, fruit machine, video game, juke box and piped music. There's a small conservatory, and tables and a play area in the garden. The landlord is a real-ale fan, and as well as hosting a beer festival in August, he keeps a running tally over the bar of the number of different real ales he's served (they were up to 1,500 as we went to press). He keeps five well kept changing real ales such as Adnams Broadside, Exmoor Beast, Greene King Abbot, Everards Tiger and Titanic Anniversary all on handpump. Well liked and good value food includes home-made soup (£2.10), sandwiches (from £2.30), jacket potatoes (from £3.10), ploughman's (from £4.75), lincolnshire sausages with chips, egg and peas (£4.75), home-made pies, home-made meat or vegetarian lasagne, seafood platter, gammon and egg, or chicken tikka (£5.95), steak (£6.95), children's meals (£2.50) and a wide range of daily specials; popular Sunday lunch (£8.50; children £5.50; must book). The no-smoking restaurant has been extended, and they've added some bedrooms this year. *(Recommended by Gordon Thornton, Jenny and Michael Back, JP, PP, M J Morgan, Ian and Nita Cooper, Eric Locker, Paul and Ursula Randall, Mr and Mrs Peter Smith, Paul and Sandra Embleton, Mark J Hydes, Norma and Keith Bloomfield)*

Free house ~ Licensee Barrie Creaser ~ Real ale ~ Bar food (12-2, 7-9.30) ~ Restaurant ~ (01778) 422970 ~ Children in eating area of bar and restaurant (no infants in restaurant) ~ Open 11-2.30, 6-11; 12-3, 7-10.30 Sun ~ Bedrooms: £25B/£45B

GEDNEY DYKE TF4125 Map 8

Chequers ⑭

Village signposted off A17 Holbeach—Kings Lynn

Lincolnshire Dining Pub of the Year

Very well known for particularly good imaginative food, this stylish but friendly and informal Fenland pub is spotlessly kept, with an open fire in the bar, a small rather old-fashioned restaurant area at one end, and an elegant no-smoking dining conservatory at the other, overlooking a garden with picnic-sets. A speciality here is the really fresh fish and seafood specials such as cromer crab salad, seared monkfish with herb crumb and coriander relish and seabass fillet with beurre blanc sauce. There's a wide choice of other well cooked and attractively presented food, including home-made soup (£2.95), open sandwiches (from £3.95), ploughman's, pâté or warm goat's cheese salad (£4.50), chestnut and vegetable roast (£6.50), cajun chicken breast (£7.50), smoked pork fillet with pickled pears and creamy sage polenta (£9.95), Gressingham duck breast with orange sauce (£11.95), good home-made puddings; roast Sunday lunch and a two-course lunch (£7.50) Monday to Friday; service is friendly and professional. Well kept Adnams Bitter, Bass Elgood Pageant on handpump, about ten decent wines by the glass, elderflower pressé and apple juice; piped music. *(Recommended by Nigel and Amanda Thorp, Roger Everett, Geoffrey Lawrance, JDM, KM, David and Helen Wilkins, Paul Mallett, Sue Rowland, JP, PP, Alan Morton, Dr G Martin, R Macnaughton, Mike and Maggie Betton, R C Wiles, W K Wood, Anthony Barnes, Ian Stafford)*

Free house ~ Licensees Simon and Linda Rattray ~ Real ale ~ Bar food ~ (01406) 362666 ~ Children welcome ~ Open 12-2.30, 7-11; 12-3, 7-10.30 Sun; closed 25, 26 Dec

---

We say if we or readers have seen dogs or cats in a pub.

GRANTHAM SK9135 Map 7
Beehive £

Castlegate; from main street turn down Finkin Street opposite St Peter's Place

The comfortably straightforward bar at this simple no-frills pub has a bustling, friendly atmosphere, scrubbed tables on bare board floors, and Batemans XB, and two guests like Kelham Island Easy Rider and Shepherd Neame Spitfire on handpump. It's popular with students. Very good value bar food includes home-made soup (£1), sandwiches (from £1.50), ploughman's (£1.80), battered cod (£2.50) and scampi, mixed grill or 8oz rump (£3), cheerful service. Fruit machine, pinball, darts, trivia, lots of board games, video game and piped music. Generally known as the pub with the living sign, its real claim to fame here is its remarkable pub sign – a hive full of living bees, mounted in a lime tree. It's been here since at least 1830, and probably the eighteenth century, making this one of the oldest populations of bees in the world and if the landlord is not behind the bar he is probably up a ladder checking them out. *(Recommended by Shirley Mackenzie, Stephen Brown, the Didler, JP, PP)*

Free house ~ Licensee Wayne Welbourne ~ Real ale ~ Bar food (11-8 Mon-Thurs, 11-5 Fri, 12-3.30 Sat, Sun) ~ (01476) 404554 ~ Well behaved children till 7 ~ Open 11-11; 12-10.30 Sun; closed 25 Dec, 1 Jan, bank hol evenings

GRIMSTHORPE TF0422 Map 8
Black Horse ♀

A151 W of Bourne

The main draw at this attractive grey stone coaching inn is the fashionably presented bar food (and their more elaborate restaurant menu) which is all home-made, and of a standard and style that are quite unusual for this part of the world. The changing bar menu might include soup of the day (£2.25), sandwiches (from £2.50), game terrine (£3.45), warm avocado, bacon and walnut salad (£3.55), toasted bagel with smoked salmon and mascarpone cheese (£4.50), lasagne (£5.95), steak and kidney pie or Lincoln red beef casserole (£6.25), salmon fishcakes with salsa and cream sauce (£6.50), chicken breast with chasseur sauce (£6.95), poached salmon with broccoli mash and shellfish sauce (£7.25), duck breast with red cabbage and sultanas and red wine sauce (£7.85), sirloin steak (£9.95) and puddings like baked caramel and vanilla cheesecake and warm toffee apple pie (£3.45). The neatly kept narrow bar, with seagrass flooring and homely wallpaper, has stools along a black timbered counter (with a little tiled roof) on one side, and intimate tables in red velvet curtained booths on the other. There's also a cosy window seat, a nice round oak table, a coal fire in a stripped stone fireplace, lamps and dried flowers. Alongside an astonishly good wine list, with over a dozen by the glass, they serve well kept Black Horse Bitter and Grimsthorpe Castle (both brewed for the pub by Oldershaws), and usually Batemans XXXB. Bedrooms look very pretty, though we've not yet had reports from readers on them. *(Recommended by M J Morgan, V and E A Bolton, Gordon Thornton, Mike and Heather Watson)*

Free house ~ Licensees Brian and Elaine Ray ~ Real ale ~ Bar food ~ Restaurant ~ (01778) 591247 ~ Children in bar till 8pm ~ Open 11.30-3, 6.30-11; 12-3, 7-10.30 Sun ~ Bedrooms: £50B/£69B

HECKINGTON TF1444 Map 8
Nags Head

High Street; village signposted from A17 Sleaford—Boston

Apart from decorating the interior of this low white 17th-c village inn with soft warm colours new licensees have made very few other changes, and plan to try and keep its very friendly atmosphere going. The snug two-roomed bar has a comfortable lived-in feel. The left-hand part has a coal fire below a shiny black wooden chimney-piece in what must once have been a great inglenook, curving into the corner and taking up the whole of one end of the small room – it now houses three tables, one of them of beaten brass. On the right there are red plush button-back built-in wall banquettes, small spindleback chairs, and an attractive bronze statuette-lamp on the mantelpiece of its coal fire; also, a lively watercolour of a horse-race finish (the horses racing straight towards you), and a modern sporting print of a problematic gun dog. Traditional home-made bar food might include soup (£1.95), sandwiches (£2.95), ploughman's (£3.75), steak, Guinness and mushroom pie (£5.25), liver, bacon and onions (£5.95), pork in brandy and cream sauce (£6.95) and comfy home-made puddings like hot chocolate fudge cake or treacle tart with home-made ice cream (£2.95). Well kept Stones, Tetleys and Worthington on handpump; darts, pool, shove-ha'penny, fruit machine, juke box and piped music. The garden behind has picnic-sets and a play area, and it's not far to an unusual eight-sailed windmill. *(Recommended by David Rule, R T and J C Moggridge, Don and Shirley Parrish, Anthony Barnes, John Watt, Stephen Brown, Tony and Wendy Hobden, Paul and Sandra Embleton)*

Pubmaster ~ Lease: John James Clark ~ Real ale ~ Bar food ~ (01529) 460218 ~ Children welcome ~ Live entertainment twice a month Fri or Sat night ~ Open 11-11; 12-10.30 Sun ~ Bedrooms: £20B/£40B

LINCOLN SK9771 Map 8
Victoria ◖ £
6 Union Road

A visit to this classic quaint early Victorian local, tucked away in a back street behind the castle is like going back in time. It's a proper ale house with no airs and graces, and few concessions to comfort. The atmosphere is really buoyant – homely, warm and chatty. The plainly furnished little front lounge has a coal fire and some good Queen Victoria pictures. It's always bustling, and can get very crowded at lunchtime and in the later part of the evening – especially when the city's Christmas Fair is on, when you can scarcely squeeze in; darts. A remarkable range of excellently kept real ales includes Batemans XB, Everards Old Original, Oldershaws Regal Blonde and Timothy Taylor Landlord as well as half a dozen or possibly more very interesting changing guest beers, also foreign draught and bottled beers, and country wines; there are beer festivals the third week in June and the last week in November. Lunchtime food includes well filled cobs (from £1.20, the bacon ones, £2.50, are a meal in themselves), ploughman's (£3.25), all-day breakfast and basic home-made hot dishes such as beef stew, steak and kidney pie, chilli or curry (£3.50); Sunday roast (£4.50); friendly staff; no children *(Recommended by B Shiner, the Didler, JP, PP, Derek and Sylvia Stephenson, Mark J Hydes)*

Free house ~ Licensee Neil Renshaw ~ Real ale ~ Bar food (lunchtime) ~ Restaurant (Sun lunchtime only) ~ (01522) 536048 ~ Children in conservatory ~ Open 11-11; 12-10.30 Sun; closed 25 Dec

Wig & Mitre ★ ⊕ ⦿
30-32 Steep Hill; just below cathedral

Having run it for thirty years, the licensees here have bought this business from Sam Smiths and moved the whole operation into an even more attractive building next door to the original site of this pub. It's another ancient building with plenty of period features, and they've decked it out in a similar style, with improvements. The simpler beamed downstairs bar has exposed stone walls, and pews and Gothic furniture on oak floor boards, and comfy sofas in small carpeted areas. Upstairs, the civilised dining room is light and airy with views of the castle walls and cathedral (Thursday evening is a nice time to visit when they leave the windows open for bell ringing practice), shelves of old books, and an open fire, and is decorated with antique prints and more modern caricatures of lawyers and clerics, with plenty of newspapers and periodicals lying about. They serve an incredible range of very well prepared food from several different menus – including a full breakfast menu (English breakfast £7.50) – from 8 o'clock in the morning to closing, and even when busy the service is always cordial and efficient. With prices approaching restaurant levels, dishes might include sandwiches (from £3.95), wild mushroom and celeriac soup, warm salad of smoked chicken with crispy bacon in mustard seed dressing (£6), bangers and mash (£7), wild mushroom risotto with olive oil and parmesan (£9), squid in beer batter with guacamole (£10), fillet of john dory with broccoli purée, lemon and chives (£14.75), roast duck breast with buttered spinach and balsamic sauce (£14.95), and puddings like sticky toffee pudding with crème Anglaise or baked apricot cheesecake with walnut biscuits (£4). As well as an excellent selection of over 95 wines, many of them available by the glass, they have Marstons Pedigree and Timothy Taylor Landlord on handpump, lots of liqueurs and spirits, freshly squeezed orange juice, and a bean to cup espresso machine. *(Recommended by David and Ruth Hollands, M Kershaw, Peter Burton, R Wiles, V and E A Bolton, Francis Johnson, Shirley Mackenzie, Karen Eliot, JP, PP, Christopher Beadle, Peter and Pat Frogley, John Honnor, Meg and Colin Hamilton, Robert Gomme, Bill and Pam Baker, Maysie Thompson, David Rule, W W Burke, Neil Glover, John Fazakerley)*

Free house ~ Licensees Paul Vidic and Valerie Hope ~ Real ale ~ Bar food (8-11) ~ Restaurant ~ (01522) 535190 ~ Children in eating area of bar and restaurant ~ Open 8-12

NEWTON TF0436 Map 8
Red Lion ★

Village signposted from A52 E of Grantham; pub itself also discreetly signed off A52

The comfortably welcoming rooms at this impeccably kept civilised old place have fresh flowers, old-fashioned oak and elm seats and cream-rendered or bare stone walls covered with farm tools, malters' wooden shovels, a stuffed fox, stag's head and green woodpecker, pictures made from pressed flowers, and hunting and coaching prints. Besides blackboard specials such as vegetarian pasta and ratatouille (£6), steak pie, hotpot, liver and onions or chicken curry (£7.25), fisherman's hotpot (£8.50), lamb cutlets in cranberry, gammon and egg, or pork chops in garlic and mushrooms (£8.50), they offer an impressive cold buffet with a splendid choice of meats (the licensee used to be a butcher), fish and salads – you help yourself to as much as you like, a small helping is £8.95, normal £9.95, and large £12.95, with children's helpings £4.50. On Saturday evening and Sunday lunchtime there are also four roasts; no-smoking area in dining room; well kept Bass and Batemans XXXB on handpump; friendly service, piped music, a fruit machine, and a nice dog called Charlie. During the day and at weekends two squash courts run by the pub can be used by non-members. A neat, well sheltered back garden has some seats on the grass and on a terrace, and a good play area. The countryside nearby is ideal for walking, and acccording to local tradition this village is the highest point between Grantham and the Urals. *(Recommended by Gordon Thornton, R C Vincent, JP, PP, M J Morgan, R Wiles, G Neighbour, Mike and Maggie Betton, Mike and Penny Sanders)*

Free house ~ Licensee Graham Watkin ~ Real ale ~ Bar food ~ (01529) 497256 ~ Children welcome ~ Open 12-3, 6-11; 12-2, 7-10.30 Sun; closed 25 Dec

STAMFORD Map 8
George of Stamford ★ ⑭ ♀ 🛏

1 High St, St Martins

Built in 1597 for Lord Burghley (though there are surviving parts of a much older Norman pilgrims' hospice – and a crypt under the cocktail bar that may be 1,000 years old) this very civilized old coaching inn has retained its character despite now having every modern comfort. There's a medley of seats in its smart, but relaxed rooms ranging from sturdy bar settles through leather, cane and antique wicker to soft settees and easy chairs, while the central lounge has sturdy timbers, broad flagstones, heavy beams, and massive stonework; some claim that you can see a ghostly girl's face in the wooden panelling in the London room. The Garden Lounge has well spaced white cast-iron furniture on herringbone glazed bricks around a central tropical grove. There's a continental lean to the not cheap but very good bar food which might include soup of the day with Italian bread (£4.25), chicken liver pâté with orange and redcurrant sauce (£5.95), a choice of seven very Italian pasta, risotto and gnocchi dishes (£9.45), fish and chips or chargrilled lamb's liver with tomato, flat grilled mushrooms and smoky bacon (£9.95), lamb cutlets coated in breadcrumbs on mediterranean vegetables (£11.95) and sea bream fillet on spring onions and beansprouts with thai orange sauce (£12.95). Well kept Adnams Broadside, Ruddles Best and a guest on handpump, but the best drinks are the Italian wines, many of which are good value and sold by the glass; also freshly squeezed orange juice, filter, espresso or cappuccino coffee; friendly and very professional staff. There's waiter drinks service in the cobbled courtyard at the back which is lovely in summer, with comfortable chairs and tables among attractive plant tubs and colourful hanging baskets; there's also a neatly maintained walled garden, with a sunken lawn where croquet is often played. *(Recommended by Charles Gysin, JP, PP, John Fahy, Brian Wainwright, R C Wiles, Jason Caulkin, Gordon B Thornton, Walter and Susan Rinaldi-Butcher, Paul and Pam Penrose, J F M West, Mike and Sue Loseby, Christine and Geoff Butler, D W Stokes; also in the Good Hotel Guide)*

Free house ~ Licensees Chris Pitman and Ivo Vannocci ~ Real ale ~ Bar food (all day) ~ Restaurant ~ (01780) 750750 ~ Children welcome ~ Open 11-11; 12-10.30 Sun ~ Bedrooms: £78B/£103B

SURFLEET TF2528 Map 8
Mermaid

A16 N of Spalding at bridge over River Glen

It was the genuinely old-fashioned atmosphere we enjoyed at this time-frozen dining pub: much of it looks unchanged since the 70s, but kept absolutely pristine. A small central counter, with memories of Babycham, serves two high-ceilinged rooms, which have huge netted sash windows, green patterned carpets, beige Anaglypta dado, brass platters, navigation lanterns and horse tack on cream textured walls, and green leatherette banquettes and stools. To our delight the piped music was even Hot Chocolate. Well kept Adnams Broadside and a couple of guests like Badger Tanglefoot and Hook Norton Old Hooky. Two steps down, the restaurant is decorated in a similar style. Readers really enjoy the big helpings of good value bar food, and you may need to book. The very traditional menu includes soup (£1.90), prawn cocktail (£3.25), lasagne, fillet of plaice, steak pie or liver and bacon (£5.50) and a couple of daily specials like minted lamb casserole, roast beef salad or lemon chicken (£5.50), double lamb or pork chop (£5.95), puddings like cheesecake (£2.50), and Sunday lunch (£8.50). Service is friendly and attentive. There's a pretty garden which is safely walled from the river which runs beside the pub. *(Recommended by Mike and Penny Sanders, N Doolan, Michael and Jenny Back, Ian and Nita Cooper, Bill and Sheila McLardy, R F and M K Bishop)*

Free house ~ Licensee C D Wilcox ~ Real ale ~ Bar food (11.30-2, 6.30-9.30; 12-2, 7-9 Sun) ~ Restaurant ~ (01775) 680275 ~ Children over 5 in restaurant ~ Open 11.30-3, 6.30-11; 12-3, 7-10.30 Sun; closed 26 Dec, 1 Jan

WOODHALL SPA TF1963 Map 8
Abbey Lodge

Tattersall Rd (B1192 Woodhall Spa—Coningsby)

The discreetly decorated bar at this solidly reliable roadside inn has Victorian and older furnishings, as well as pictures showing its World War II connections with RAF Coningsby – Squadron 617 which is based at the former airfield opposite and still holds reunion dinners here. There's a friendly welcome from the affable licensee and his wife who cook all the blackboard specials which are served alongside a menu that includes sandwiches (from £1.50), soup (£2.25), prawn cocktail (£4.95), generous ploughman's (£4.50), lasagne (£4.95), chicken curry (£5.95), scampi (£6.75), poached salmon fillet (£7.25) and 8oz sirloin (£9.75), and a wide selection of puddings like banana split, peach melba and treacle sponge (£2.50). Well kept Bass, Worthington and a guest on handpump; piped music; no children in bar; they may close for holidays in January and October so it's worth ringing to check.

(Recommended by Bill and Sheila McLardy, W W Burke, J and D Ginger, JP, PP, Richard Cole, Mark J Hydes, Geoffrey Lawrance)

Free house ~ Licensee Annette Inglis ~ Real ale ~ Bar food (till 10pm Fri, Sat) ~ Restaurant ~ (01526) 352538 ~ Children over 5 in restaurant ~ Open 11-2.30, 6.30-11; 12-2.30, 7-11 Sun; closed Sun winter

Lucky Dip

Besides the fully inspected pubs, you might like to try these Lucky Dips recommended to us and described by readers (if you do, please send us reports):

Alford [TF4576]
White Hart: Two small welcoming nicely decorated rooms, one with pool; very well kept Batemans *(Judith Hirst)*
White Horse [West St (A1004)]: Comfortably plush low-ceilinged pub, well kept Mansfield and guest beers, good value fresh-cooked food in bar and restaurant, polite staff; clean bedrooms, good breakfast *(LYM, Judith Hirst)*
Althorpe [SE8309]
Dolphin: Friendly, clean and tidy, with comfortable banquettes in dining area, pictures, plates and bric-a-brac, wide choice of good value home cooking (not Sun/Mon evenings), three real ales; piped pop music may be loud; tables and play area outside *(Geoffrey Lawrance, Tony Hobden)*
Ancaster [SK9843]
Ermine Way [High St (B6403)]: Well kept Ansells Mild, Ind Coope Burton, Marstons Best and Pedigree and John Smiths, good value food inc generous Sun lunch in bar and back lounge/restaurant, friendly landlord; open all day, bedrooms *(Richard Lewis, Mrs J Nuttall)*
Barholm [TF0810]
☆ *Five Horseshoes*: Old-fashioned relaxed village local, clean, cosy and friendly, with well kept Adnams, Batemans and interesting guest beers, mini beer festivals, decent wines, comfortable seats, rustic bric-a-brac; tables out under shady arbour, w/e barbecues, paddocks behind *(LYM, M J Morgan)*
Barkston [SK9341]
Stag [Church St]: Beamed pub with good home-made food in left-hand dining bar with mixed tables and chairs, well kept Everards Tiger and Beacon and a guest beer, friendly atmosphere, pool in second bar *(Gill and Keith Croxton)*
Barnoldby le Beck [TA2303]
☆ *Ship* [SW of Grimsby]: Warm well furnished country pub with antiques and horse-racing memorabilia in immaculate main lounge, good sensibly priced home cooking inc game, vegetarian, fresh Grimsby fish and two daily roasts, friendly attentive service, good range of wines, comfortable dining room, pleasant village setting; bedrooms *(John Cooper, Brian A Haywood)*
Belchford [TF2975]
Blue Bell [E of A153 Horncastle—Louth]: Three well kept interesting guest beers, simple food inc delicious home-made pies, good local trout and good value Sun lunch,

nicely refurbished bar, pleasant atmosphere *(JP, PP, M J Morgan)*
Boston [TF3244]
Burton House [Wainfleet Rd (A52)]: Big comfortable country-theme Brewers Fayre family dining pub on outskirts, children's play areas inside and out with games machines, well kept ales such as Bass, Boddingtons, Marstons Pedigree and Whitbreads Fuggles, bar food inc good specials with fresh veg, efficient helpful staff; open all day, good disabled facilities, bedrooms *(Richard Lewis)*
☆ *Carpenters Arms* [Witham St]: Lively traditional bare-boards local, well kept Bass, Batemans Mild and XB and guest beers, enterprising home-cooked lunchtime food inc good cheap rolls; bedrooms reasonably priced *(the Didler)*
☆ *Eagle* [West St, towards stn]: Basic cheery local now owned by Tynemill, with well kept Batemans, Castle Rock, Timothy Taylor Landlord and three guest beers at low prices, cheap food, children in eating area lunchtime; Mon folk club, live music Sat, open all day Sat *(BB, JP, PP, the Didler)*
☆ *Goodbarns Yard* [Wormgate]: Wide choice of good value home-made food from filled French bread and baked potatoes to steaks inc interesting snacks in popular and comfortable place, well kept Theakstons and guest ales, old beams in original core (former riverside cottages looking up to Boston Stump), modern but matching back extension, plenty of alcoves, terrace overlooking river *(V and E A Bolton, Tony Albert, O K Smyth)*
Mill [Spilsby Rd (A16)]: Clean roadside pub with restaurant feel, usual bar food with three-course bargains, plush dining rooms (one no smoking), friendly efficient service, Batemans, quiet piped music; seats out in front *(Jenny and Michael Back)*
Ropers Arms [Horncastle Rd]: Batemans corner local in nice spot by river and windmill, quiet and unassuming – gets lively for big screen TV football Sun; some live entertainment; open 2-11, all day w/e and summer *(the Didler)*
Brant Broughton [SK9154]
Generous Briton [just off A17 Leadenham—Newark]: Unspoilt family-run two-bar local, good choice of food inc vegetarian; pretty village *(John Wooll)*
Burton upon Stather [SE8717]
Sheffield Arms [N of Scunthorpe]: Good

choice of well kept ales and of generous food in attractively furnished old-fashioned stonebuilt country pub, elegant, roomy and well run, with old photographs *(Geoffrey Lawrance)*

Carlton le Moorland [SK9058]

White Hart [Church St]: Comfortable beamed village pub with good choice of good reasonably priced freshly made food inc Sun lunch, welcomijng licensees, well kept Worthington; children welcome, Thurs quiz night; fruit machine, TV, piped pop music; garden with play area, pleasant village *(Bill and Sheila McLardy, CMW, JJW, Richard Hyde)*

Castle Bytham [SK9818]

☆ *Castle* [High St; off B1176 N of Stamford; or off A1 at Stretton]: Warm welcome, consistently good generous well presented food (not Mon evening) inc imaginative dishes, efficient service, real ales such as Ansells Mild, Boddingtons, Mansfield, Shepherd Neame Bishops Finger, Tetleys and Charles Wells Bombardier, roaring log fire, no-smoking dining room with huge pig collection; soft piped music, no children at the bar; tables in back garden, CCTV for parked cars, attractive village *(Michael and Jenny Back, E J Locker)*

Caythorpe [SK9348]

Red Lion: Homely 16th-c pub in pleasant surroundings, considerate service, wide choice of fair-priced food from sandwiches to good fresh Grimsby fish and Whitby scampi, well kept ales inc Boddingtons, Greene King Abbot, Timothy Taylor Landlord and Youngs Special, no piped music *(Peter Burton)*

Chapel St Leonards [TF5572]

Ship [Sea Rd]: Friendly old comfortable local just outside Skegness, well kept Batemans Mild, XB, XXXB and a seasonal beer, traditional games, tables outside *(Jack and Philip Paxton)*

Cleethorpes [TA3008]

No 2 Refreshment Room [Station Approach]: Tiny basic 60s-throwback bar almost on platform, Mansfield Mild, John Smiths Magnet and usually a good guest beer from a small brewery, no food; open all day *(Jack and Philip Paxton, the Didler)*

Willys [High Cliff Rd; south promenade]: Refurbished modern open-plan bistro-style seafront pub with café tables, tiled floor and painted brick walls; brews its own good beers, also well kept Batemans and guest beers and good value basic lunchtime home cooking; friendly staff, quiet juke box, Humber estuary views; popular November beer festival, open all day *(JP, PP, R M Taylor, D J Walker, the Didler)*

Coleby [SK9760]

Bell [village signed off A607 S of Lincoln; turn right and right into Far Lane at church]: Dining pub with three linked rooms each with a log fire and low black joists, well kept Bass, Flowers Original, and Tetleys, new tenants doing wide choice of food, picnic-sets

outside, handy for Viking Way walks; open all day, comfortable bedrooms; the tenants who made this a popular main entry are now to be found at the Pyewipe just outside Lincoln *(Janet and Peter Race, LYM, Paul and Sandra Embleton)*

Tempest Arms [Hill Rise]: Roomy, friendly and comfortable local, with well kept Batemans XB, nicely presented interesting food Thurs-Sat, good service, friendly spaniel, lots of hanging baskets, wonderful view from pretty garden; on Viking Way *(M Kershaw, M J Morgan, JP, PP)*

Coningsby [TF2458]

☆ *Leagate* [Boston Rd (B1192), ¾ mile NW)]: Dark old heavy-beamed fenland local with three linked areas, ageing medley of furnishings inc great high-backed settles around the biggest of the three log fires, ancient oak panelling, even a priest hole; friendly licensees, prompt good value home-made food, well kept Batemans XB and Marstons Pedigree; piped jazz or pop music (not at lunchtime), fruit machine; rustic garden with play area; children if eating *(N Doolan, LYM, Bill and Sheila McLardy, JP, PP, M J Morgan, Mr and Mrs B James)*

Corby Glen [SK9924]

Woodhouse Arms [Bourne Rd (A151)]: Victorian stone inn tastefully reworked as smart restaurant and comfortable bar area with open fire and leather chesterfields, well kept beers inc Ruddles, Theakstons Best and XB, good food inc Sardinian specialities and well priced 3-course lunch; three bedrooms inc converted stable block *(M J Morgan, Doug Spivey)*

Donington on Bain [TF2382]

☆ *Black Horse* [between A153 and A157, SW of Louth]: Relaxed atmosphere and pleasant layout, with low-beamed snug back bar and softly lit inner room (with murals of carousing Vikings) off main village bar, log fires, bar food from filled baked potatoes to steaks, Ruddles Best and John Smiths; no-smoking restaurant, games room off public bar, juke box or piped music; children very welcome, picnic-sets in back garden, on Viking Way *(Mike and Maggie Betton, Geoffrey Lawrance, LYM)*

Dunston [TF0663]

Red Lion [½ mile off B1188 SE of Lincoln]: Pleasant tucked-away village pub, big beamed lounge and restaurant, good simple home cooking inc very good puddings, good choice of well kept beers *(Mr and Mrs J Brown)*

East Barkwith [TF1781]

Crossroads [Lincoln Rd (A157)]: Popular new owners doing good range of food in bar and restaurant, very pleasant atmosphere, John Smiths and Tom Woods real ales; cl Mon *(Maureen and Arnold East)*

East Kirkby [TF3362]

Red Lion: Lots of chiming clocks, old tools and breweriana, Batemans XB, John Smiths and changing Highwood beers, lunchtime and evening meals, welcoming landlord, real fire, family room, traditional games; wheelchair access, tables outside, camping; handy for Air Museum *(Jack and Philip Paxton, the Didler)*

Edenham [TF0621]

☆ *Five Bells* [A151]: Welcoming family service, wide choice of reliable generous food in neat busy comfortable dining lounge, well kept Bass and Tetleys, two log fires, dominoes, piped music, lots of foreign banknotes, soft lighting; back restaurant/function room, tables in garden with good play area; children and walkers welcome *(M J Morgan, Peter Burton, LYM, Francis Johnson)*

Ewerby [TF1247]

☆ *Finch Hatton Arms*: Handsomely built and plushly furnished well decorated mock-Tudor pub with good home-made food esp fresh fish, well kept beers, coal fire, decent bar food, smart restaurant, comfortable back locals' bar; bedrooms *(BB, F J and A Parmenter, Richard Cole)*

Folkingham [TF0733]

Greyhound [Market Pl]: Enormous 17th-c coaching inn with Georgian facade, now more showroom (12 rooms brimming with antiques, crafts and collectables) than pub, but still does excellent bar lunches and may have real ales such as Bass; open 9.30-5 *(Mrs A K Davies, Mr and Mrs A Lumley-Wood, M J Morgan)*

Freiston [TF3743]

Castle [off A52 NE of Boston]: Busy and lively, with very good value food, well kept local beers *(Christine and Geoff Butler)*

Frognall [TF1610]

Goat [Spalding Rd (B1525, off A16 NE of Mkt Deeping)]: Cheap straightforward food (all day Sun) inc fish and vegetarian, with Adnams, Batemans XB and interesting guest beers, low beams, stripped stonework, two dining lounges, restaurant, helpful landlord, no piped music; big garden with play equipment (no children inside) *(R F and M K Bishop, Michael and Jenny Back)*

Gainsborough [SK8189]

Eight Jolly Brewers [Ships Ct, Caskgate Lane]: Bustling unpretentious pub with half a dozen well kept well priced changing ales and one brewed for them by Highwood, simple weekday lunchtime food; folk club, open all day *(Mr and Mrs A Turk, JP, PP, the Didler)*

Grantham [SK9135]

☆ *Angel & Royal* [High St]: Hotel with remarkable worn medieval carved stone facade, ancient oriel window seat in upstairs plush bar on left, massive inglenook in friendly high-beamed main bar opp, tapestries, well kept Camerons Strongarm and two guest beers, bar food; open all day Fri/Sat, bedrooms in comfortable back extension *(JP, PP, the Didler, LYM, Richard Hyde)*

Blue Bull [Westgate]: Refurbished local with two cosy bars, lots of brass, ornaments, pictures and stuffed fox, well kept Marstons Pedigree and quickly changing guest beers such as Batemans Dark Mild and Valiant,

Brewsters Hophead, Fenland FBB and Oldershaws Regal Blonde, Belgian bottled beers, quite a few ciders, papers and beers magazines, friendly licensees, partly no-smoking dining room with good reasonably priced home-cooked food (not Sun or Mon evenings), traditional games, juke box; handy for stn *(Richard Lewis, Tony Hobden, the Didler)*

Blue Pig [Vine St]: One of only three buildings here to survive the great fire of 1660, beams, character, well kept beer, welcoming service, simple lunchtime bar food, Whitbreads beers with a guest such as Timothy Taylor Landlord or Wadworths 6X, open fire, friendly service; three rooms, piped music, games machine *(Richard Lewis, the Didler, JP, PP)*

Hogshead [Market Pl]: Recent addition to this chain, usual bare boards, barrels and brick, light and airy, eight well kept ales and Belgian bottled beers, good menu; open all day *(Richard Lewis)*

Muddle Go Nowhere [W edge, nr A1/A52]: Large comfortable newish Tom Cobleigh family pub, lots of beams and woodwork, country décor with range fireplaces, good choice of generous food and of well kept mainstream ales, friendly efficient staff; outside and inside play areas, disabled facilities, open all day *(Richard Lewis)*

Nobody Inn [Watergate]: Friendly bare-boards pub with three changing well kept ales from the region, pool, table footer and TV at back; open all day *(Richard Lewis)*

Porters [Market Pl]: Popular and interesting bare-boards ale house, some comfortable carpeted sitting areas, lots of wood, very well kept Bass, Greenalls Porters Bitter and Mild and a couple of other beers, good friendly staff, pool; open all day *(Richard Lewis)*

Tollemache [St Peters Hill]: Roomy and popular L-shaped Wetherspoons, interesting choice of well kept ales, good food choice, bargains, usual high standard décor with no-smoking areas and old local pictures, efficient friendly service, attractive garden; open all day *(Richard Lewis)*

Grimsby [TA2609]

Corporation [Freeman St]: Well kept Bass and Worthington in traditional town pub with nice back lounge – original panelling, leather seats, old Grimsby shipping photographs; second lounge, lively public bar with games and TV *(Pete Baker)*

Hope & Anchor [Victoria St]: Basic relaxing traditional bar and lounge off central servery, friendly staff and locals, reasonably priced lunchtime food inc hot filled rolls, well kept real ales with ambitious two-week beer festival *(R M Taylor)*

Tap & Spile: Stone floors, heavy wooden chairs and tables, good choice of ales, decent food inc unusual light snacks *(R M Taylor)*

Halton Holegate [TF4165]

☆ *Bell* [Frisby Rd; B1195 E of Spilsby]: Pretty village local, simple but comfortable and consistently friendly, with wide choice of decent home-made food inc outstanding fish and chips, vegetarian dishes and Sun lunches, well kept Bass, Batemans and Mansfield Old Baily, aircraft pictures, pub games, maybe piped music; children in eating area and restaurant *(JP, PP, the Didler, LYM)*

Harmston [SK9762]

Thorold Arms [High St; off A607 Lincoln—Grantham]: Very friendly and comfortable 18th-c country pub with own post office and occasional microbrewery, generous food (fresh produce only) in recently refurbished dining room, well kept Bass, Greene King IPA and Youngs, real fire, pool table, table skittles, other pub games; tables outside *(J H Lewis, Richard Lewis)*

Hemingby [TF2374]

Coach & Horses [off A158/B1225 N of Horncastle]: Unpretentious welcoming village local, long, low and attractive, with comfortable pews, sewing-machine tables, oak beams, reasonably priced food from sandwiches to steaks inc vegetarian and children's, well kept Batemans and Highwood ales, interesting collection of beer mats and pump clips, friendly licensees and cat; pool and darts tucked away on left of central dividing fireplace, Sun quiz night, cl Mon/Tues lunchtimes *(Jenny and Michael Back, N Doolan)*

Horncastle [TF2669]

Old Nicks [North St]: Pleasant, warm and friendly, with very good value lunchtime roasts, no-smoking dining area *(Gordon Thornton)*

Keal Cotes [TF3661]

Coach House [Main Rd (A16)]: Small bar and lounge area with nice dining conservatory; reasonably priced bar food, Everards ales *(M J Morgan)*

Kirkby on Bain [TF2462]

Ebrington Arms: Five or more well kept changing ales from small breweries far and wide, low 16th-c beams, two open fires, nicely set out dining areas each side, copper-topped tables, wall banquettes, jet fighter and racing car pictures; prompt welcoming service, good choice of sensibly priced food all day in summer inc generous cheap Sun lunch, daily papers, games area with darts, maybe piped Irish music; beer festivals Easter and Aug bank hols, tables out in front, wheelchair access, camp site behind *(JP, PP, Derek and Sylvia Stephenson, Richard Lewis, the Didler)*

Leadenham [SK9552]

George [A17 Newark—Sleaford]: Remarkable range of several hundred whiskies, good choice of wines by the glass inc their own direct German imports, well kept ales inc Boddingtons, fair-priced quickly served food from sandwiches to steaks in unassuming bar, side games room, piped music, restaurant; bedrooms plain but good value, good breakfast *(LYM, Gordon Thornton)*

Lincoln [SK9872]

☆ *Browns Pie Shop* [Steep Hill]: Wide choice of

good food inc popular chunky pies; restaurant licence only, but does have a beer such as Charles Wells as well as decent wines, attractive prices, comfortable seats, smiling helpful waitresses, pleasant traditional atmosphere *(MDN, V and E A Bolton, Francis Johnson)*

Cornhill Vaults [Exchange Arcade]: Unusual vaulted underground pub with cheap well kept Sam Smiths, freshly made bar lunches inc unusual sandwiches, pool table in separate area, friendly service; juke box after 3, live music evenings *(M Kershaw, the Didler, JP, Bill and Pam Baker)*

Golden Eagle [High St]: Cheerfully busy basic two-bar town pub now owned by Tynemill, wide choice of well kept changing ales such as Batemans, Everards, Fullers and Timothy Taylor, good choice of country wines, good value lunchtime food inc vegetarian; beers; open all day Fri/Sat *(the Didler, John C Baker, JP, PP)*

☆ *Lincolnshire Poacher* [Bunkers Hill]: Roomy and comfortably modernised family flagship, with old chairs and books, Lincolnshire memorabilia inc interesting prints, big dining part with no-smoking areas, good range of food inc local dishes, well kept Mansfield Riding and Old Baily, cheerful attentive service; play areas inside and (with video surveillance) outside; open all day Sun *(Ian and Nita Cooper)*

Morning Star [Greetwellgate]: Unpretentious well scrubbed local handy for cathedral, friendly atmosphere, good value lunches esp Fri specials, well kept reasonably priced Bass, Ruddles Best and a guest such as Charles Wells Bombardier, coal fire, aircraft paintings, nice outside area; piano night Sat, open all day exc Sun *(the Didler, MDN, Bill and Pam Baker, JP, PP)*

Portland Arms [Portland St]: Lively bar, quieter back lounge, Bass, Batemans, Courage and half a dozen guest beers inc a Mild, also changing farm cider; open all day *(the Didler)*

☆ *Pyewipe* [Saxilby Rd; off A57 just S of bypass]: 18th-c pub doing very well under the team which made the Bell at Coleby a popular main entry for food in previous editions, good food here now inc good fish choice, well kept real ales; on Roman Fossdyke Canal, pleasant walk out from centre *(David and Ruth Hollands)*

☆ *Queen in the West* [Moor St; off A57 nr racecourse]: Well kept Marstons Pedigree, Theakstons XB and Old Peculier and Timothy Taylor Landlord, reasonably priced simple home cooking in busy and welcoming old backstreet pub below cathedral; military prints and miniatures in well decorated lounge, interesting sporting prints in public bar with TV, darts, games; open all day Fri *(the Didler)*

Sippers [Melville St, opp bus stn]: Popular lunchtime pub with good food (not w/e evenings), Courage Directors, Marstons Pedigree, Morlands Old Speckled Hen and guest beers, very friendly licensees; quieter evenings, cl Sun lunchtime *(the Didler)*

Long Sutton [TF4222]

Crown & Woolpack [off bypass A17 Kings Lynn—Holbeach]: Good generous cheap home cooking (well filled baguettes only, Mon-Weds) in basic lively local with panelled back dining room, good Sun lunch (must book), Bass and Worthington BB, roaring fire, dominoes; may be smoky, piped music may be rather loud, outside lavatories *(Michael and Jenny Back)*

Louth [TF3387]

Kings Head [Mercer Row]: Large unfussy bar, well kept beer, good range of good value bar food inc roasts and traditional puddings *(the Didler, Mike and Maggie Betton)*

Malt Shovel [Northgate]: Fine early 17th-c inn, real fires in all three bars, Bass, Boddingtons and Flowers; open all day Sat *(the Didler)*

Masons Arms [Cornmarket]: Edwardian reworking of 18th-c posting inn, light and airy, with well restored woodwork and fancy glass, friendly landlord and family, well kept full Batemans range, Bass, Marstons Pedigree and a guest beer, good home-made food inc vegetarian and big sandwiches, good upstairs dining room (remarkable art deco former masonic lodge meeting room); good bedrooms, open all day Sun *(MDN, the Didler, Stephen and Julie Brown, N Doolan, Derek and Sylvia Stephenson)*

Olde White Swan: Reopened after refurbishment – popular and friendly, with ancient low beams, Bass and guest beers *(the Didler)*

Wheatsheaf [Westgate]: Well kept early 17th-c inn, real fires in all three bars, Bass, Boddingtons and Flowers, decent food, cheerful atmosphere; can be crowded, open all day Sat *(the Didler)*

Woolpack [Riverhead]: 18th-c wool merchant's house popular for good home cooking and Batemans, Marstons Pedigree and guest ales; bar, lounge, snug, two real fires *(the Didler)*

Maltby le Marsh [TF4782]

Crown [A1104]: Picturesque brick-built creeper-covered village inn with china jugs, sauceboats and other ornaments packing the beams and walls, mix of old tables and chairs, soft lighting, enthusiastic friendly landlord, well kept Batemans and Marstons Pedigree, good bar food from sandwiches up *(James Nunns)*

Mareham le Fen [TF2861]

Royal Oak [A115]: Pretty partly thatched 14th-c building with well kept Batemans XB and guest ales and limited good value food in pleasant friendly bar – TV too; small attractive unpubby dining area *(M J Morgan, Dorothy and Leslie Pilson)*

Market Deeping [TF1310]

☆ *Bull* [Market Pl]: Bustling local with cosy low-ceilinged alcoves, little corridors, interesting heavy-beamed medieval Dugout Bar; well kept Everards Tiger and Old

Original and a guest such as Adnams, very friendly efficient service, well priced standard food (not Sun or Mon evening), attractive eating area, restaurant (booking advised); no piped music lunchtime, seats in pretty coachyard; children in eating areas; open all day Fri, Sat *(M J Morgan, R T and J C Moggridge, Gordon Thornton, LYM)*

Morton [TF0123]

Lord Nelson [off A15 N of Bourne]: Village pub with good value generous basic food inc good children's choice, well kept beers inc Mansfield Riding and Old Baily, friendly staff, pool, games machine, good piped music; open all day *(Richard Lewis)*

Navenby [SK9858]

☆ *Kings Head* [High St (A607 S of Lincoln); car park behind off East Rd]: Small village pub with appetising reasonably priced food esp good varied puddings in pleasant no-smoking area off bar, interesting knick-knacks, books, quick friendly service, well kept Bass, unobtrusive piped music *(Donald and Margaret Wood, Paul McPherson)*

Nettleham [TF0075]

☆ *Brown Cow* [A46 N of Lincoln]: Comfortable civilised lounge bar, kept spotless, with wide range of good value generous food inc two-course bargain lunch, pleasant helpful staff; Sun lunch very popular; pleasant village *(Gordon Thornton, B P White, M J Morgan)*

North Kelsey [TA0401]

☆ *Butchers Arms* [Middle St; off B1434 S of Brigg]: Busy reopened village local, tastefully refurbished and opened up but not too modern, low ceilings, flagstones, bare boards, dim lighting, with five well kept Highwood beers (brewed by owner on his farm), good sensibly priced cold lunchtime food, enthusiastic cheerful service, woodburner; pub games, no juke box, tables outside, open all day *(the Didler, JP, PP, John C Baker)*

North Thoresby [TF2998]

Granby [A16/B1201]: Traditional two-bar pub with Bass, Worthington and weekly guest beers, good food inc Sun lunch in lounge bar and no-smoking restaurant, attractive prices, good service; tables out on terrace *(Geoffrey Lawrance)*

Norton Disney [SK8859]

☆ *St Vincent Arms* [off A46 Newark—Lincoln]: Attractive and welcoming village pub with well kept Batemans Mild and XXXB, Marstons Pedigree, three guest beers, open fire, good cheap generous plain food from sandwiches up inc beautifully cooked veg, pleasant landlord; tables and big adventure playground out behind *(JP, PP, D J and P M Taylor, the Didler)*

Oasby [TF0039]

Houblon Arms: Large and rambling, with lots of low beams, panelling and stonework, well kept Batemans and a guest ale, good interesting food, friendly service; four bedrooms *(Mr and Mrs J Brown)*

Rothwell [TF1599]

☆ *Nickerson Arms* [off B1225 S of Caistor]:

Cheerful open-plan bar divided by arches and good coal fire, attractive wildlife prints, heavy beams, spacious dining area, well presented food (either sandwiches and basic snacks or much more expensive things like steaks and fresh fish), well kept Batemans XB, XXXB and a seasonal beer, Courage Directors, Fullers London Pride and Marstons Pedigree, plenty of malt whiskies, pleasant small dining room, friendly service; piped music, darts and dominoes; children welcome, tables outside *(JP, PP, Michael Butler, M J Morgan, LYM, Mike and Sue Walton, Mr and Mrs D J Watkins)*

Sandilands [TF5280]

Grange & Links [off A52 nr Sutton on Sea]: A hotel, but good bar food inc good summer salads served in the ballroom, well kept beer; fine gardens, some 200 yds from good beach; bedrooms *(Gordon Thornton)*

Scawby [SE9605]

Sutton Arms [West St]: Popular local, good food (book ahead for Sun), real ales inc Flowers IPA, friendly efficient staff *(Alison Keys)*

Scunthorpe [SE9011]

Honest Lawyer [Oswald Rd]: Quaint two-floor pub with cheap food and half a dozen beers inc a Batemans seasonal one *(Tom Evans)*

Skegness [TF5660]

Red Lion [Lumley Rd/Roman Bank]: Usual Wetherspoons features inc no-smoking areas, food all day, no music; bargain offers on both food and beer, good value coffee too *(Tony Hobden)*

☆ *Vine* [Vine Rd, off Drummond Rd, Seacroft]: Charming extended hotel based on late 18th-c country house, calm and comfortable well run bar overlooking drive and own bowling green, imposing antique seats and grandfather clock in inner oak-panelled room; three well kept Batemans ales, good value food in bar and restaurant, friendly staff, tables on big back sheltered lawn with swings; good reasonably priced bedrooms, peaceful suburban setting not far from beach and birdwatching *(the Didler, JP, PP, BB, Joan and Michel Hooper-Immins, Andy and Jill Kassube, Christine and Geoff Butler, Geoffrey Lawrance)*

Skendleby [TF4369]

☆ *Blacksmiths Arms* [Spilsby Rd; off A158 about 10 miles NW of Skegness]: Some concentration on good imaginative generous food in big busy back restaurant, also old-fashioned bar, cosy and quaint, with view of cellar, deep 17th-c well, well kept Batemans XB and XXXB tapped from the cask, open fire *(Gordon Thornton, JP, PP, the Didler)*

Sleaford [TF0645]

Carre Arms [Mareham Lane]: Hotel with pub part, good generous enterprising food in brasserie and good value restaurant, decent wines, helpful landlady; bar can be smoky; bedrooms *(June and Malcolm Farmer, MDN)*

Nags Head [Southgate]: Comfortably

refurbished, with nostalgic atmosphere, well kept Batemans, friendly staff, lunchtime food; seats outside, open all day – till late Thurs-Sat *(Richard Lewis)*

South Thoresby [TF4077]

☆ *Vine* [about a mile off A16 N of Ulceby Cross]: Large village inn with small pub part – tiny passageway servery, steps up to three-table lounge, wide choice of good food from Thai fishcakes to Aberdeen Angus steaks in nicely panelled no-smoking dining room, well kept Batemans XB and a guest such as Fullers London Pride, first-class choice of malt whiskies, good value wines, separate pool room; bedrooms, tables in pleasant garden *(M J Morgan, the Didler)*

South Witham [SK9219]

☆ *Blue Cow* [High St; off A1 S of Colsterworth]: Fine unspoilt pub brewing its own good Cuddy and Best behind, flagstoned lounge bar with low beams, woodwork, old fireplace and riding memorabilia, restaurant area off and a carvery room, first-class service, friendly staff and locals; open all day *(Anthony Barnes, Richard Houghton, Richard Lewis, JP, PP)*

Spalding [TF2422]

Red Lion [Market Pl]: Bass, Greene King and Marstons ales, good filled rolls and daily specials in bar and no-smoking restaurant; jazz and blues nights *(John and Lesley Honner)*

Springthorpe [SK8789]

New Inn [Hill Rd]: Good home cooking (evening and Sun lunch) in basic village local with particularly well kept Batemans XXXB, Marstons Pedigree and guest beers, real fire; tables outside, cl Mon lunchtime *(Jack and Philip Paxton)*

Stamford [TF0207]

Daniel Lambert [St Leonards St]: Friendly open-plan town local with big picture of the eponymous giant in clean comfortable bar, cheerful landlord, several well kept changing beers such as Timothy Taylor Best and Landlord, restaurant; evening meals Tues-Sat, open all day Fri *(the Didler)*

St Peters [St Peters St]: 18th-c, with upstairs, cloisters and downstairs bars, well kept Marstons Best and Pedigree and several guest beers tapped from the cask, good bistro food inc pasta, oriental and vegetarian, quiet music, friendly staff; open all day Fri/Sat, cl weekday lunchtimes, parking some way off *(the Didler, P Stallard, Tony and Wendy Hobden)*

Surfleet Seas End [TF2728]

Ship [Reservoir Rd; off A16 N of Spalding]: Unspoilt 17th-c riverside pub, flagstone bar, open fires, well kept Marstons Bitter and Pedigree and guests such as Fullers London Pride, good home-cooked meals inc interesting recipes (delicious seafood platter needs 24 hrs' notice), no-smoking dining room; bedrooms *(M J Morgan)*

Swineshead Bridge [TF2142]

Barge [A17, nr A1121 junction]: Welcoming lunch stop, relaxing uncrowded front room, good value food inc bargain fish, friendly staff, lots of interesting knick-knacks and old beer bottles, pool table in public bar, quiet garden with swing; children given puzzle and picture to colour *(Bronwen and Steve Wrigley, John T Ames)*

Tallington [TF0908]

Whistle Stop [A16 E of Stamford]: U-shaped bar with settles on pine boards, simple but interesting food, well kept Bass, Everards, John Smiths and two guest beers, good atmosphere; pool, large garden, caravan camp facilities *(Mike Simpson)*

Tealby [TF1590]

Kings Head [Kingsway, off B1203]: 14th-c thatched and beamed pub in quiet and attractive Wolds village, handy for Viking Way walk; generous food freshly prepared to order inc sandwiches, vegetarian and meaty home-made pies, well kept ales inc Bass, farm cider, pleasant service, restaurant *(John Ringrose, the Didler, JP, PP, Geoffrey Lawrance, M J Morgan, Bill and Sheila McLardy)*

Olde Barn [Cow Lane]: Pleasant pub handy for Viking Way, cheerfully served good straightforward food inc fresh fish in bar and restaurant, well kept Everards Old Original and Tiger, guest beers, big attractive back garden with lawn *(M J Morgan)*

Tetford [TF3374]

☆ *White Hart* [off A158 E of Horncastle]: Early 16th-c, with good atmosphere, well kept Mansfield Riding and a guest beer, wide choice of food from good value sandwiches to popular Sun lunches; old-fashioned settles, slabby elm tables and red tiled floor in pleasant quiet inglenook bar, no-smoking snug, basic games room; seats and swings on sheltered back lawn, simple bedrooms *(JP, PP, LYM, M J Morgan, the Didler)*

Timberland [TF1258]

Penny Farthing [Station Rd; off B1191 and B1189 NW of Billinghay]: Pleasant and spacious stripped-stone beamed lounge, current chef/landlord doing wide choice of good generous food in bar and restaurant, puddings cabinet, good range of real ales, neat uniformed staff, unobtrusive piped music, local paintings for sale; comfortable bedrooms *(Maureen and Arnold East)*

Uffington [TF0607]

Bertie Arms [Bertie Lane]: Beautifully kept thatched pub with good food, excellent landlord *(M J Morgan)*

Ulceby [TA1014]

Open Gates: Small welcoming pub with emphasis on attractive no-smoking dining room, good reasonably priced food cooked by landlord inc OAP bargains Tues, real ales such as Marstons Pedigree, Shepherd Neame, Tetleys and local Woods Bomber Command, friendly service; children's garden, great Wolds views *(M J Morgan, Christine and Geoff Butler)*

West Deeping [TF1109]

Red Lion [King St]: Long low bar with plenty of tables, roaring coal fires each end, old stonework and beams, well kept ales such as Adnams Broadside, Ansells, Black Sheep and Tetleys, good coffee, wide choice of generous food from appetising bacon baps to piping hot dishes inc vegetarian, puddings from cold cabinet, prompt cheerful service, friendly alsatian called Prince; big pool room, open all day, tables in back garden with attractive play area *(Michael and Jenny Back)*

Woolsthorpe [SK8435]

Chequers [the one nr Belvoir, signed off A52 Grantham—Nottingham]: Attractively refurbished and extended village pub within sight of Belvoir Castle, with good food in bar and restaurant, well kept ale, friendly service, lots of events esp Fri in big entertainments area, own cricket ground; tables outside, boules; bedrooms *(BB, Geoffrey Lawrance)*

'Children welcome' means the pubs says it lets children inside without any special restriction. If it allows them in, but to restricted areas such as an eating area or family room, we specify this. Places with separate restaurants usually let children use them, hotels usually let them into public areas such as lounges. Some pubs impose an evening time limit – let us know if you find this.

Norfolk

*A good crop of new entries here consists of the White Horse at Brancaster
Staithe (good food in a recent bistro-style conversion), the rambling Fox at
Garboldisham (nice mix of pubby food and good beers), the Walpole Arms at
Itteringham (a very popular country dining pub), the friendly Railway Tavern
at Reedham (very good beers, some brewed on the spot) and the Old Brewery
House in Reepham (nice bar, good drinks, enjoyable food – and open all day).
Other pubs currently doing particularly well here are the White Horse in
Blakeney, the civilised Buckinghamshire Arms in its lovely setting at Blickling,
the Hoste Arms in Burnham Market (informally smart, imaginative modern
cooking), the quaint Lord Nelson at Burnham Thorpe, the Crown at Colkirk
(up to 50 wines by the glass), the welcoming Angel at Larling (bargain prices),
the Crown at Mundford (a nice place to stay in), the Fat Cat in Norwich
(colossal range of real ales – and children are now allowed in the
conservatory), the Rose & Crown at Snettisham (good newish chef, new no-
smoking dining area), the nicely decorated Red Lion at Stiffkey (fresh local
fish), the very cheerful Darbys at Swanton Morley, the Three Horseshoes at
Warham (a special favourite, good all round), and the Fishermans Return
close to the beach at Winterton on Sea. All these in their different way have
decent food – some of them, as we've said, very good indeed. The place that
stands out most prominently for a special meal out is the Hoste Arms in
Burnham Market; for the second year running, it is our Norfolk Dining Pub
of the Year. The Lucky Dip section at the end of the chapter has a very wide
choice of good pubs; we'd note particularly the Great Danes Head at
Beachamwell, Jolly Sailors at Brancaster Staithe, Ratcatchers at Cawston,
Jenyns Arms at Denver Sluice, Locks at Geldeston, Ferry at Reedham, Scole
Inn at Scole, Crown at Stanhoe, Coldham Hall at Surlingham, Chequers at
Thompson, Dukes Head at West Rudham, Bell at Wiveton and Bird in Hand
at Wreningham. The Village Inn at West Runton looks very promising under
its new landlord. Drinks prices are perhaps a trifle above the national average
here, but have been keeping more stable than in most places. Formerly the
preserve of the big national brewing combines, Norfolk is now well supplied
by a lot of smaller breweries, who do seem to be competing quite hard on
price with Greene King, the dominant regional brewer; Woodfordes is now
available very widely. Other local beers we've noted particularly here this year
have come from Reepham, Wolf, Buffys and Iceni, with Adnams from Suffolk
now gaining a great deal of ground in Norfolk. An incidental point worth
noting is that pubs here seem more likely than in most places to have provision
for camping.*

Post Office address codings confusingly give the impression that some pubs are in
Norfolk when they're really in Suffolk (which is where we list them).

BAWBURGH TG1508 Map 5
Kings Head
Pub signposted down Harts Lane off B1108, which leads off A47 just W of Norwich

The four linked rooms at this old pub have low beams, some standing timbers, a log fire in a large knocked-through canopied fireplace, a woodburner and dried flowers in the attractive inglenook in the end room, and comfortable green or rust plush banquettes. Ample helpings of attractively presented food include home-made soup (£2.50), sandwiches or filled french bread (from £3), spicy fresh chicken fillet burger (£5.50), tagliatelle carbonara (£5.60), sausage and mash (£6.25), beef pie (£6.95), honey glazed ham on creamy mash with cream mustard sauce (£7.50) and honey and lime or pesto and parmesan chicken (£7.60). Helpings are generous; no-smoking restaurant. Three well kept real ales on handpump such as Adnams Bitter, Greene King IPA and Woodfordes Wherry on handpump; good quick service; cribbage, dominoes and piped music. There are rustic tables and benches on the gravel outside. *(Recommended by Sue Rowland, Paul Mallett, MDN, Tina and David Woods-Taylor, Frank Davidson, Bob Arnett, Judy Wayman, Lesley Kant, Tony Albert, Stephen Horsley, Mr and Mrs L P Lesbirel, Anthony Barnes, John McDonald, Ann Bond, Paul Maccett)*

Free house ~ Licensee Anton Wimmer ~ Real ale ~ Bar food (12-2, 7-10 (12.30-2.30 only Sun)) ~ Restaurant ~ (01603) 744977 ~ Children welcome ~ Live entertainment alternate Mon ~ Open 11-11; 12-10.30 Sun; closed 25 Dec evening

BLAKENEY TG0243 Map 8
Kings Arms ⬤
West Gate St

Probably at its most enjoyable out of the main holiday seasons, this popular white thatched house can get very busy and the atmosphere and service suffer a little as a result at peak times. Its three simply furnished, knocked-together rooms have some interesting photographs of the licensees' theatrical careers, other pictures including work by local artists, and what's said to be the smallest cartoon gallery in England in a former telephone kiosk; two small rooms are no smoking; the airy extension is liked by families and diners. Bar food includes sandwiches (from £1.65), soup (£2.25), filled baked potatoes (from £3.75), ploughman's (from £4), vegetable curry (£4.95), local cod or haddock (£5.75) and 10oz sirloin (£11.50); enjoyable breakfasts. Woodfordes Wherry tapped from the cask and very well kept Marstons Pedigree, Morlands Old Speckled Hen, Websters Yorkshire and a guest on handpump; darts, shove-ha'penny, dominoes, and fruit machine. The large garden has lots of tables and chairs and a separate, equipped children's area; there are baby-changing facilities. *(Recommended by M Morgan, Kevin Macey, Peter Plumridge, Mrs D Rathbone, Mary and David Richards, Ken and Jenny Simmonds, John Wooll, Chris and Val Ramstedt, Bernard and Marjorie Parkin, Klaus and Elizabeth Leist, Jeremy Burnside, Nigel Woolliscroft, NMF, DF, Tracey and Stephen Groves, A C Curry, J Monk, Peter and Anne Hollindale, K H Frostick)*

Free house ~ Licensees John Howard and Marjorie Davies ~ Real ale ~ Bar food (12-9.30(9 Sun)) ~ Restaurant ~ (01263) 740341 ~ Children welcome ~ Open 10.30-11; 11-10.30 Sun ~ Bedrooms: £35B/£55B

White Horse ♀ 🛏
4 High Street; off A149 W of Sheringham

Doing well at the moment, this small hotel is an enjoyable place with a warmly comfortable atmosphere and friendly efficient service. The chatty long main bar has a good mix of visitors and locals, and is predominantly green (despite the Venetian red ceiling), with a restrained but attractive décor – including two big reproductions of Audubon waterfowl prints up at the far end; well kept Adnams and Bass on handpump, and a wide choice of reasonably priced wines (wine tastings in spring and winter); cribbage. There's wheelchair access, though a short flight of steps to the back part of the bar. Good bar food includes soup (£2.75), mediterranean vegetable and brie flan (£5.95), crab flan (£6.25), thai green chicken curry (£6.75) and grilled salmon fillet with salsa verde (£6.95); no-smoking area. The attractive conservatory restaurant is much liked by readers (as is the food there). Tables out in a suntrap courtyard. The bedrooms are well equipped, if small. *(Recommended by Eric Locker, Mr and Mrs A H Young, Keith and Janet Morris, MDN, Lesley Kant, Minda and Stanley Alexander, M J Morgan, D Blackford, Mark O'Hanlon, Peter and Anne Hollindale, Charles Bardswell, K H Frostick, David and Anne Culley, O K Smyth, George Atkinson)*

Free house ~ Licensees Daniel Rees and Dan Goff ~ Real ale ~ Bar food (12-2, 6-9) ~ Restaurant ~ (01263) 740574 ~ Children in garden room ~ Open 11-3, 6(5.30 Sat)-11; 12-3, 6-10.30 Sun ~ Bedrooms: £35B/£70B

BLICKLING TG1728 Map 8
Buckinghamshire Arms
B1354 NW of Aylsham

There's plenty of praise for this bustling and handsome Jacobean inn, attractively placed at the gates to Blickling Hall and owned by the National Trust. The small front snug is simply furnished with fabric-cushioned banquettes, while the bigger lounge has neatly built-in pews, stripped deal tables, and Spy pictures. Well liked by readers, lunchtime bar food includes home-made soup (£2.75), filled french bread (from £2.95), ratatouille (£4.95), chilli (£5.25), home-made steak and kidney pie (£5.95), scampi (£6.25), with evening dishes such as fried puy lentils with chorizo and salad (£4.50) and salmon steak (£8.25). and puddings (£2.95). Adnams Best, Woodfordes Wherry and Blickling (brewed for the pub) on handpump, and a good range of wines; cribbage, shove-ha'penny and board games. There are lots of tables on the big lawn, and they serve food from an out-building here in summer; they may stay open all day in summer if it's busy or there's an event on at the Hall. *(Recommended by Mike Wells, Dr Andy Wilkinson, Jean Gustavson, D E Twitchett, S Lythgoe, R C Vincent, Anthony Barnes, R M Macnaughton, Steve and Sarah Pleasance, M Theodorou, Ian Phillips, P A Legon, A Bowen, Kevin Thomas)*

Free house ~ Licensee Marc Stubley ~ Real ale ~ Bar food ~ Restaurant ~ (01263) 732133 ~ Children in restaurant ~ Open 12-3, 6-11(10.30) Sun ~ Bedrooms: /£60

BRANCASTER STAITHE TF7743 Map 8
White Horse
A149 E of Hunstanton

Very recently converted, this spacious open-plan bistro-style free house has mainly stripped wood floors, big windows, solid stripped tables with country chairs, pews, and cream walls packed with interesting local black and white photographs; don't be put off by the very plain exterior. Stools line a handsome counter manned by friendly young staff; there's a particularly easy-going relaxed atmosphere here. Round to the side and back, tables are laid for dining, and picture windows give lovely views over saltings and the sea channel. Well kept Greene King IPA and Abbot, Woodfordes Wherry and a guest on handpump. Bar food includes soup (from £2.50), antipasti (£4.25), pork and leek sausages with mash and shallot sauce (£5.50), fish pie (£5.95), chicken fajitas (£7.25), and a more elaborate evening menu that might include baked salmon on fennel braised in orange (£9.95), fillets of lemon sole on couscous with lemon parsley butter (£10.50), roast guinea fowl on confit of its own leg and wild mushroom reduction (£12.95) and puddings like summer pudding (£3.25) and warm banana sponge with caramel sauce or chocolate tart with warm caramel sauce and fresh cream (£3.50). We'd be very interested to hear from readers about the new bedrooms – this should be a nice place to stay in. *(Recommended by Paul Munton, J D Hodgson, M J Morgan, Mrs D Rawlings, Louise Medcalf)*

Free house ~ Licensees Cliff Nye and Kevin Nobes ~ Real ale ~ Bar food (no snacks Sat evening) ~ Restaurant ~ (01485) 210262 ~ Children welcome ~ Live entertainment monthly Sun ~ Open 11.30-11; 12-10.30 Sun; 11.30-3, 6-11 winter; 12-2.30, 7-10.30 Sun winter ~ Bedrooms: /£52B

BURNHAM MARKET TF8342 Map 8
Hoste Arms ⑪ ⇨
The Green (B1155)

Norfolk Dining Pub of the Year
You'll probably need to book even a midweek table at this handsome 17th-c civilised but informally smart hotel, which is very popular for its imaginative contemporary cooking. Well presented lunchtime food is served in the no-smoking conservatory and might include soup (£3.25), game terrine scented with juniper, caramelised onion chutney (£4.95), roast pigeon with sautéed chicken livers, bubble and squeak (£5.50), charred tuna served rare with egg noodle and pickled ginger or dim sum (£5.75), seared king scallops with black pasta and sweet lemon dressing (£7.50) and main courses like roast cod and fennel with herb dresssing (£8.95), fried monkfish with steamed spinach, asparagus and borlotti beans (£11.75), crisply fried bass on risotto with coriander, spring onion and smoked salmon (£12.95) and roast saddle of venison, cassoulet of rabbit, button onions and wild mushrooms (£15.95). The boldly decorated bars have massive log fires, and a good mix of people, especially at the weekend. The panelled bar on the right has a series of watercolours showing scenes from local walks, there's a bow-windowed bar on the left, a nice sitting room, a little art gallery in the staircase area, and well kept Adnams Broadside, Greene King IPA and Woodfordes Wherry on handpump, a good wine list including champagne by the glass, a decent choice of malt whiskies, and freshly squeezed orange juice. A pleasant walled garden at the back has tables on a terrace. *(Recommended by M J Morgan, Nigel Woolliscroft, Eric Locker, Bernard and Marjorie Parkin, Anthony Barnes, David and Helen Wilkins, Mrs Jill Silversides, Barry Brown, Dr Andy Wilkinson, Tracey and Stephen Groves, Mr and Mrs A H Young, Steve and Sarah Pleasance, R J Bland, Pat and Tony Martin, MDN, JP, PP, David and Diana MacFadyen, Ken and Jenny Simmonds, Peter Shaw, Kate Naylor; also in the Good Hotel Guide)*

Free house ~ Licensees Paul and Jean Whittome and Rebecca Mackenzie ~ Real ale ~ Restaurant ~ (01328) 738777 ~ Children welcome ~ Jazz pianist Fri Oct-Mar ~ Open 11-11; 12-10.30 Sun ~ Bedrooms: £60B/£76B

BURNHAM THORPE TF8541 Map 8
Lord Nelson ◖
Village signposted from B1155 and B1355, near Burnham Market

A very good allrounder, this delightful little place is unusual in that it doesn't have a bar counter. You order your pint of well kept Greene King IPA, Abbot and Mild or Woodfordes Nelsons Revenge at the table, and they are then tapped from the cask in a back stillroom and brought to you by the very friendly staff. Nelson was born in this village, so it's no surprise to find lots of pictures and memorabilia of him lining the walls, and they have an unusual rum concoction called Nelson's Blood. The characterful little bar has well waxed antique settles on the worn red flooring tiles and smoke ovens in the original fireplace, and an eating room has flagstones, an open fire, and more pictures of the celebrated sailor; there's one no-smoking room. We've recently had very good feedback about the tasty bar food which includes sandwiches (from £2.10), garlic mushrooms (£2.95), breakfast (£3.95), ploughman's or breaded plaice (£4.95), grilled lamb chops with red wine and rosemary sauce (£8.75), and daily specials like fresh crab (£4.15), steak and kidney pie (£6.45) and baked cod fillet or roasted boar and apple sausages (£8.25), and puddings like spicy orange cheesecake (£2.80); friendly staff, shove-ha'penny, dominoes, draughts, cards, and children's toys. They have baby changing facilities and a disabled lavatory. There's a play area with basketball and a climbing frame in the very big garden. *(Recommended by David and Helen Wilkins, Mick Hitchman, Bill Pemberton, John Wooll, R J Bland, Paul Kitchener, Pat and Tony Martin, JP, PP, John Beeken, R C Vincent, Tracey and Stephen Groves, Nigel Woolliscroft)*

Greene King ~ Lease: Lucy Stafford ~ Real ale ~ Bar food ~ (01328) 738241 ~ Children welcome at lunchtime, in restaurant only evenings ~ Jazz and blues first and third Fri of month Oct-May ~ Open 11-3, 6-11; 12-3, 7-10.30 Sun

COLKIRK TF9126 Map 8

Crown ♀

Village signposted off B1146 S of Fakenham; and off A1065

'As good as ever' is the description used by one reader to describe this bustling village pub, with its particularly friendly staff, and very warmly welcoming atmosphere. The public bar and small lounge both have open fires, solid straightforward country furniture, rugs and flooring tiles, and sympathetic lighting; the no-smoking dining room leading off is pleasantly informal. Well kept Greene King IPA, Abbot, Mild, and a guest like Marstons Pedigree; several malt whiskies, and 50 wines (all are available by the glass). Well presented bar food in good sized helpings includes home-made soup (£2.50), pâté (£3.75), tiger prawns with ginger sauce (£4.50), spinach and ricotta cannelloni (£6.50), scampi (£6.75), chicken supreme with blue cheese sauce (£7.45), and daily specials such as roast peppers with goat's cheese topping (£6.50), steak and kidney pie (£6.75), fresh crab salad (£6.95), salmon fillet with creamy lemon sauce (£7.95), roast duck breast with cumberland sauce (£9.75), and puddings like triple chocolate cheesecake and pecan and maple pie (£2.75); the dining room is no smoking. Darts, bar billiards, shove-ha'penny, cribbage, dominoes, and fruit machine. There's a garden and suntrap terrace with picnic-sets. *(Recommended by Maurice and Jean George, Frank Davidson, John Wooll, Steve and Sarah Pleasance)*

Greene King ~ Tenant Patrick Whitmore ~ Real ale ~ Bar food (12-1.45, 7-9.30(9 Sun)) ~ Restaurant ~ (01328) 862172 ~ Children welcome ~ Open 11-2.30, 6-11; 12-3, 7-10.30 Sun

ERPINGHAM TG1732 Map 8

Saracens Head ⊕ ♀ ⇌

At Wolterton – not shown on many maps; Erpingham signed off A140 N of Aylsham, keep on through Calthorpe, then where road bends right take the straight-ahead turn-off signposted Wolterton

Comfortably bold décor marks out the interior of this civilised remotely situated pub. The two-room bar is simple and stylish, with high ceilings, terracotta walls and red and white striped curtains at its tall windows all lending a feeling of space, though it's not actually large. There's a mix of seats from built-in leather wall settles to wicker fireside chairs as well as log fires and flowers on the mantelpieces. It looks out on a charming old-fashioned gravel stableyard with picnic-sets. There's a pretty little four-table parlour on the right – cheerful nursery colours, and another big log fire. Well kept Adnams and Woodfordes Blickling on handpump; decent malt whiskies. The wine list is really quite interesting, with some shipped direct from a French chateau. It's almost essential to book for the imaginative bar food, served in a relaxed and informal atmosphere, which might include soup (£2.95), fresh Cromer crab salad or grilled goat's cheese and marinated mediterranean vegetables, mussels cooked in cider and cream (£4.95), pasta with wild mushrooms and cream (£7.50), baked whole mackerel with white wine and apple (£7.95), halibut steak with orange (£8.95), and evening dishes like baked avocado with sweet pear, apple and mozzarella (£7.50), fried monkfish with orange and ginger (£9.50), roast breast of barbary duck and red fruit sauce (£9.55), stir-fried julienne of sirloin, olives and tomatoes (£10.25); very good value two-course weekday lunch (£5.50). *(Recommended by Ken and Jeni Black, Peter and Pat Frogley, Ralph and Jane Doyle, Marion H Turner, Ken and Jenny Simmonds, Mick Hitchman, K F Mould, David and Diana MacFadyen, Anthony Barnes, D E Twitchett, John Beeken, Ian Phillips, Charles Bardswell, Miss M Hamilton, Mr and Mrs G Turner, Mr and Mrs P J Frogley, G Neighbour; also in the Good Hotel Guide)*

Free house ~ Licensee Robert Dawson-Smith ~ Real ale ~ Bar food (12.30-2.15, 7.30-9.30) ~ Restaurant ~ (01263) 768909 ~ Children welcome ~ Occasional summer live entertainment ~ Open 11.30-3, 6-11; 12-3, 7-10.30 Sun ~ Bedrooms: £40B/£60B

Prices of main dishes usually include vegetables or a side salad.

FAKENHAM TF9229 Map 8
Wensum Lodge 🛏
Bridge St (B1146 S of centre)

The conversion work here has been carefully built round the original mill which, quite surprisingly, was still in operation in the 1970s. The very roomy and relaxing civilised bar is in what was the grain store. A multitude of artefacts and pictures fill every nook and cranny, and there are mate's chairs grouped around polished tables. Two beamed dining areas (one is no smoking) lead off, with more dark tables and chairs, prints and houseplants; fruit machine and piped music. As well as sandwiches (from £2.10) and filled french bread (from £3.60), generous helpings of bar food include soup (£3.25), creamy garlic mushrooms on toast (£4.25), smoked fish platter (£5.75), pancakes with various fillings like chilli or mushrooms in madeira sauce (£5.95), pasta with chicken and asparagus (£7.25), filled yorkshire pudding or chilli (£7.25), swordfish marinated in lime, coriander and ginger on tagliatelle rosti with spicy salsa or local spare ribs (£9.50), fried venison steak on a balsamic vinegar crouton with malt whisky and redcurrant sauce and pink and green peppercorns or steamed bass on a tomato and onion concassé with fresh fennel butter sauce (£11.95), and puddings like warm apricot and almond tart or bread and butter pudding (£3.50); attentive service; Theakstons Best and XB on handpump, kept under light blanket pressure. There's a lounge area with a conservatory leading to a new bedrooms development, and tables outside, with grass running down to the river, weeping willows along its banks. *(Recommended by David and Anne Culley)*

Free house ~ Licensees Dawn Woods and P and G Hobday ~ Real ale ~ Bar food (11.30-3, 6.30-10) ~ Restaurant ~ (01328) 862100 ~ Children welcome ~ Open 11-11; 12-10.30 Sun ~ Bedrooms: £45B/£60B

GARBOLDISHAM TM0081 Map 5
Fox
A1066 Thetford—Diss, junction with B1111

This long low pink roadside inn is worth knowing for its useful bar menu, which includes good soup (£2), a very interesting choice of sandwiches like chicken with mango and mayonnaise (from £2.50), hot steak sandwich (£4.25), a good choice of sausages like venison sausage in red wine sauce (£5.50), scampi, cod in beer batter, steak and kidney pie or salmon, prawn and pasta bake (£6.65). Rambling around under dark beams in low shiny ochre ceilings, its knocked-through rooms have stripped chapel pews and tables by a logburner, dark pub tables and chairs and a couple of wing armchairs on clattery red tile floors. There are a couple of prints on its mainly bare heavy cream walls. Five real ales include well kept Adnams Best, Broadside, possibly Regatta, Greene King IPA and a guest like Black Sheep; piped light classics. The public bar has pool, darts a fruit machine and trivia; no-smoking restaurant. *(Recommended by Ian Phillips)*

Free house ~ Licensees Leigh Parkes and Mark Smith ~ Real ale ~ Bar food ~ Restaurant ~ (01953) 688151 ~ Children welcome ~ Open 11.30-2.30, 5-11; 11.30-11 Sat; 12-10.30 Sun

GREAT BIRCHAM TF7632 Map 8
Kings Head ♀ 🛏
B1155, S end of village (which is called and signposted Bircham locally)

Unchanging and going on steadily this rather grand looking place is brought to life by its friendly Italian licensee. The unassuming lounge bar (two room areas) has a pleasantly quiet and relaxed atmosphere and a mix of high and low tables suiting both diners and drinkers, with a good hot fire in a third more homely bit round behind. Reliably good bar food includes lunchtime sandwiches (from £2.70), ploughman's (£4.80), cod fillet in ale batter (£6.90), chicken breast filled with cheese and wrapped in bacon and served with fresh spaghetti, steak and kidney pudding, smoked haddock mornay or home-made fishcakes with crab sauce (£7.90), and quite a few Italian specialities such as fresh spaghetti or tortelline (£5.90); tempting home-made puddings (£3.30). The dining area is no smoking. Besides well kept Adnams, Bass and Greene King IPA there's a good choice of malt whiskies, and decent wines; maybe unobtrusive piped music, dominoes. The somnolent alsatian is called Brandy. The big side lawn, with a well kept herbaceous border, has picnic-sets and play things. The attractive village has a decent art gallery, Houghton Hall is not far off and there's a very striking windmill in this long village. *(Recommended by Diana Brumfit, John Wooll, Prof Kenneth Surin, Alison and Richard Bedford, E A Froggatt)*

Free house ~ Licensees Isidoro and Iris Verrando ~ Real ale ~ Bar food ~ Restaurant ~ (01485) 578265 ~ Children welcome ~ Open 11-2.30, 6.30-11; 11-2.30, 7-11 Sun ~ Bedrooms: £38B/£59B

HEMPSTEAD TG1137 Map 8
Hare & Hounds

Towards Baconsthorpe – and actually closer to that village, though just inside the Hempstead parish boundary; village signposted from A148 in Holt; OS Sheet 133 map reference 115372

This unspoilt and relaxed pantiled flint cottage isn't the easiest pub to find but it's well worth tracking down. Two simple bars (the charming no-smoking snug is down a step) have a mix of old-fashioned furnishings, lots of pine, beams, newspapers to read, and a log fire in the broad low-beamed fireplace, with well kept Greene King, Elgoods and Wolf Golden Jackal on handpump as well as Belgian beers; darts, cribbage, dominoes, TV and shut the box. Enjoyable bar food under the new licensee includes soup (£2.50), sandwiches (from £2.95), ploughman's (from £3.50), steak and kidney pie (£5.95), and daily specials like thai prawn balls (£3.95), fresh Cromer crab or chicken in grape and white wine (£6.95), duck (£7.95), ostrich (£8.95) and venison (£9.95), with puddings like brandysnap baskets and bread and butter pudding (£3). There are some picnic-sets on the side grass facing a pond and rockery, and a children's play area. *(Recommended by Bryan Osborne, Ian Phillips, Ken and Jeni Black, Charles Gysin)*

Free house ~ Licensee Tim Stone ~ Real ale ~ Bar food (12-2.30, 6.30-9) ~ (01263) 712340 ~ Children in eating area of bar ~ Live music Thurs evening ~ Open 11-11; 12-10.30 Sun; 11-3, 6-11 Mon-Sat winter, 12-3, 7-10.30 Sun winter; closed 25 Dec evening

HEYDON TG1127 Map 8
Earle Arms

Village signposted from B1149 about midway between Norwich and Holt

Easily described as idyllic, this very special little village has hardly changed since the 1630s. Its simple but pretty green is lined with charming cottages and houses, and this imposing yellow-painted brick pub. Inside, two carpeted rooms, one with hatch service, open off a small lobby with a handsomely carved longcase clock, and are individually furnished and decorated, with pretty rosehip wallpaper over a stripped dado, china on shelves, deep tiled-floor cupboards with interesting bric-a-brac, attractive prints and good log fires; dominoes, darts, cribbage and piped music. There's a tiny homely dining room, and a simple but well heated no-smoking conservatory beyond; booking is advised for weekends. Bar food under the new licensee might include soup or sandwiches (£2.25), home-made pigeon pâté (£3.25), vegetable madras (£5.50), cajun chicken (£6.25), fresh cod delivered daily (£6.85), lamb fillet with butter bean stew (£7.25), gammon steak with apricot sauce (£7.75), and puddings like summer pudding (£2.75). Well kept Adnams Bitter and Broadside, Bass and Tollys Original on handpump. There are picnic-sets in a small and prettily cottagey back garden, and on the front wall above the colourful front flower borders is what looks like a figurehead of possibly Ceres the Mother Earth symbol. *(Recommended by David and Anne Culley, Sue and Mike Loseby, Mick Hitchman, Tracey and Stephen Groves, Paul Tindall, John Wooll, Ken and Jenny Simmonds, Peter and Pat Frogley, Ralph and Jane Doyle, David and Diana MacFadyen)*

Free house ~ Licensee Andrew Harrison-Taylor ~ Real ale ~ Bar food ~ Restaurant ~ (01263) 587376 ~ Children welcome ~ Open 12-3, 6-11; 12-10.30 Sun; 12-3, 6-10.30 Sun winter

HORSEY TG4522 Map 8
Nelson Head

Signposted off B1159 (in series of S-bends) N of Gt Yarmouth

The two unpretentious rooms at this simple country pub are divided by a slung-back red velvet curtain, have simple but comfortable seats (including four tractor-seat bar stools), lots of shiny bric-a-brac and small local pictures for sale, geraniums on the window sill and a relaxed cottagey feel. Besides usual dishes such as ploughman's (£4.25), vegetarian tagliatelle (£5.25), ham and egg or breaded cod (£5.50) and 8oz sirloin £8.75), the Austrian managers do several good specialities such as znaimer goulash with noodles (£7.50), wiener schnitzel (£7.75), sacher torte and apple strudel (£2.95), and a couple of daily specials like venison in red wine or roast Norfolk duckling (£7.25). Woodfordes Wherry and (of course) Nelsons Revenge on handpump, good fire; piped music. There's a homely family dining room, the garden has picnic-sets and an outside marquee, and dogs on leads are allowed. The beach is just down the road *(Recommended by JDM, KM, Alan and Paula McCully, Minda and Stanley Alexander, Martin and Caroline Page, Anthony Barnes, Bronwen and Steve Wrigley, John McDonald, Ann Bond)*

Free house ~ Licensee Reg C Parsons ~ Real ale ~ Bar food ~ (01493) 393378 ~ Children in eating area of bar ~ Open 11-2.30, 6(7 winter)-11; 12-3, 7-10.30 Sun

HUNWORTH TG0635 Map 8
Blue Bell

Village signposted off B roads S of Holt

This village local has a pleasantly welcoming L-shaped bar with windsor chairs around dark wooden tables, comfortable settees (some of which are grouped around the log fire) and Norfolk watercolours and pictures for sale hanging above the panelling dado; the dining room is no smoking. Well kept Adnams Best and Greene King Abbot on handpump, quite a few malt whiskies, and decent wines. Bar food under the new chef includes sandwiches (from £2.50), soup (£3), filled french sticks (from £3.50), ploughman's (£4), steak and ale pie or leek and potato bake or fish pie (£5.50), lasagne (£5.75), scampi (£5.95), lamb cutlets (£6.75), and daily specials like thai chicken curry or spicy chickpea and lentil bake (£5.50), pork cutlets with stilton sauce (£5.95), and puddings like gooseberry pie (£2.50); darts, dominoes, and cribbage. In summer, the garden is very pleasant and there's bar service to the tables on the lawn; children's play area. *(Recommended by Tracey and Stephen Groves, Ian Phillips)*

Free house ~ Licensees Thomas and Sally King ~ Real ale ~ Bar food ~ Restaurant ~ (01263) 712300 ~ Children welcome during food serving hours ~ Open 11-3, 5.30-11; 11-11 Sat; 12-10.30 Sun

ITTERINGHAM TG1430 Map 8
Walpole Arms 🍺

Village signposted off B1354 NW of Aylsham

This quietly set brick dining pub is very popular for its solid yet imaginative home cooking. As well as sausages (£6.50) and salmon smoked in their own smoke house, bar food from a daily changing menu might include tomato and tarragon soup or stilton and cheese pâté (£3.25), pasta with pesto topped with parmesan shavings (£5.75), ploughman's (£5.95), very tasty stilton tart (£6.25), their own smoked sausages and mash or very fresh scampi (£6.75), local game, red wine and tarragon casserole (£7.95) thai-style chicken stir fry or roast cod with dolcelatte and herb dressing on black spaghetti (£8.25), and puddings like chocolate fudge cake and treacle and walnut tart (£3.25). The biggish open-plan bar has little windows, a dark navy carpet, heavy timber props for the stripped beam and plank ceiling, well spaced heavy unstripped tables including two long glossy planked dark ones, and stripped brick walls. You probably won't hear the faint piped music over the sound of contented chat. As well as Adnams Bitter and Broadside, Bass, Morlands Old Speckled Hen and Woodfordes they have decent wines by the glass, a reasonable wine list and some Belgian bottled beers; cribbage, fruit machine; picnic-sets on an area of grass at the back and side. *(Recommended by Mr and Mrs M A Steane, Ken and Jeni Black, Anthony Quinsee, John Wooll, Susan and Philip Philcox)*

Free house ~ Licensee Paul Simmons ~ Real ale ~ Bar food ~ Restaurant ~ (01263) 587258 ~ Children welcome ~ Open 12-3, 6-11; 12-3, 7-10.30 Sun

KINGS LYNN TF6220 Map 8

Tudor Rose ◖ £ ⇔

St Nicholas St (just off Tuesday Market Place – main square)

Refurbished and increasingly popular, the separate back bar in this bustling half-timbered pub now has panelling, old-style furniture, and medieval-style tapestries. The old-fashioned snug little front bar has high beams, reproduction squared panelling, a big wrought-iron wheel-rim chandelier, newspapers to read, and a really warm welcome from the friendly staff; fruit machine, dominoes and piped music. Good food includes cheap home-made food such as sandwiches (from £1.35), home-made soup (£2.35), garlic mushrooms with smoked bacon (£3.95), scambled egg with smoked salmon and chives or ploughman's (£4.50), local pork sausages (£3.99), crispy vegetables in a sweet and sour sauce (£3.75), stilton and leek bake (£4.50), hot chicken sandwich (£5.99), chilli (£4.95), chicken tikka masala (£6.95), mediterranean lamb (£8.95), venison casserole (£9.75) Well kept Bass, Batemans XB, Timothy Taylor Landlord, and a guest beer on handpump, a fine choice of whiskies, and decent wines. The upstairs raftered restaurant and a small area of the lounge are no smoking. There are seats and flowerbeds in the courtyard garden. Bedrooms are simple and modern but comfortable, and some have a pretty view of St Nicholas's Chapel. *(Recommended by John Wooll, Margaret and Allen Marsden, Anthony Barnes, R C Vincent, Pat and Tony Martin)*

Free house ~ Licensees John and Andrea Bull ~ Real ale ~ Bar food (not Sun) ~ Restaurant ~ (01553) 762824 ~ Children in eating area of bar ~ Open 11-11; 7-10.30 only Sun ~ Bedrooms: £35(£45B)/£60B

LARLING TL9889 Map 5

Angel ◖ ⇔

A11 S of Attleborough

There's always a genuinely friendly welcome from the very pleasant licensees and helpful staff at this neatly kept pub which has been in the same family since 1913: readers tell us it's a particularly nice place to stay. The comfortable 1930s-style lounge on the right has cushioned wheelback chairs, a nice long cushioned panelled corner settle, some good solid tables for eating off and some lower ones, squared panelling, a collection of whisky-water jugs on the delft shelf over the big brick fireplace which houses a big woodburner, a couple of copper kettles, and some hunting prints; there are two dining rooms (one of which is no smoking). Reliable bar food includes sandwiches and toasties (from £2.25; the bacon and banana toastie is popular), soup (£2.50), breaded brie with cranberry and port sauce (£3.75), steak sandwich (£4.25), ploughman's (£4.95), home-made burgers (from £4.95), stilton, mushroom and leek bake (£6.25), lamb balti, fresh cod fillet or steak and kidney pie (£6.95), salmon and asparagus crêpes (£7.50), pork and mushroom stroganoff (£8.25), and puddings like hot fudge cake or crêpes filled with black cherries soaked in kirsch (£2.95). Well kept Adnams Best and changing guests from local brewers like Cottage Atlantic, Iceni Celtic Queen and Sarah Hughes Pale on handpump, and over 100 malt whiskies; friendly helpful service. The quarry-tiled black-beamed public bar has a good local atmosphere, with darts, dominoes, cribbage, juke box and fruit machine; piped music. A neat grass area behind the car park has picnic-sets around a big fairy-lit apple tree, and a safely fenced play area. Peter Beale's old-fashioned rose nursery is nearby. *(Recommended by K H Frostick, Ian Phillips, Beryl and Bill Farmer, Richard and Sharon Spencer, Bill and Sheila McLardy, A N Ellis, Stuart Ballantyne, Mr and Mrs Stiffin, Richard Houghton, M and D Beard, B and M Parkin, Sue Holland, Dave Webster, M and C Starling, James and Pam Benton)*

Free house ~ Licensee Andrew Stammers ~ Real ale ~ Bar food (12-2.30, 6.30-9.30(10 Fri, Sat)) ~ Restaurant ~ (01953) 717963 ~ Children welcome ~ Live music Thurs ~ Open 10-11; 12-10.30 Sun ~ Bedrooms: £30B/£50B

MUNDFORD TL8093 Map 5
Crown ◖ £

Crown Street; village signposted off A1065 Thetford—Swaffham

Contented readers have been delighted with this attractive 17th-c posting inn, which is very handy for Thetford Forest; it has a warmly friendly atmosphere, good tasty food and well kept beer. The beamed lounge bar has a huge open fireplace in a flint wall, captain's chairs around highly polished tables, interesting local advertisements and other memorabilia, and a friendly bustling atmosphere. If the pub is full, a spiral iron staircase with *Vanity Fair* cartoons beside it leads up to the club room, an elegant restaurant and the garden. There are more heavy beams in the separate red-tiled locals' bar on the left, which has cast-iron-framed tables, another smaller brick fireplace with a copper hood, sensibly placed darts, cribbage, dominoes, fruit machine, a juke box and a screened-off pool table. Well kept Courage Directors, Iceni Gold, Marstons Pedigree, and Woodfordes Wherry on handpump, and over 50 malt whiskies. Kind staff serve bar snacks such as sandwiches (from £1.75), home-made soup (£2.25), burgers (from £3.50), filled french sticks (from £3.95), chicken nuggets (£4.75), breaded prawns with hoi sin (£4.95), pasta parcels with tomato and pesto sauce (£5.50), ploughman's or scampi (£5.75), sirloin steak (£9.95), and puddings like treacle and nut tart, Belgian lattice apple pie or chocolate fudge cake (from £2.95); children's helpings of most meals. *(Recommended by Sue and Bob Ward, Colin Fisher, Muriel and Peter Gleave, Adrian White, June and Malcolm Farmer, MDN, James Nunns, B and M Parkin, Anthony Barnes, Ian Phillips, Lesley Kant)*

Free house ~ Licensee Barry Walker ~ Real ale ~ Bar food (12-3, 7-10) ~ Restaurant ~ (01842) 878233 ~ Children welcome ~ Open 11-11; 12-10.30 Sun ~ Bedrooms: £35B/£55B

NORWICH TG2308 Map 5
Adam & Eve ♀ £

Bishopgate; follow Palace St from Tombland, N of cathedral

It's nice to find such a cottagey atmosphere and genuinely friendly welcome in a pub so near to the city centre. This is Norwich's oldest pub and is thought to date back to at least 1249 – though the striking Dutch gables were added in the 14th and 15th c. Closely set tables in the little old-fashioned characterful bars quickly fill at lunchtime with a good mixed crowd of people who happily adjust to the close confines. There are antique high-backed settles (one handsomely carved), cushioned benches built into partly panelled walls, and tiled or parquet floors; the snug room is no smoking. Enjoyable, good value food (with a new Bargain Award this year) includes sandwiches, granary baps or filled french bread (from £2.55), cheese and ale soup with pastry top (£3.45), ratatouille (£3.75), sausage casserole in a yorkshire pudding (£3.95), ploughman's (from £4.05), chilli or chicken curry (£4.65), beef and mushroom pie (£4.80), game pie (£4.90), roast of the day (£4.95), and puddings like home-made spicy bread and butter pudding (from £2.50). Well kept Adnams Bitter, Greene King IPA, Theakstons Old Peculier, and guest beers on handpump, a wide range of malt whiskies, about a dozen decent wines by the glass or bottle, and Addlestone's cider. There are table-clothed picnic-sets in front of the pub and very pretty summer tubs and hanging baskets. *(Recommended by Ian Phillips, John McDonald, Ann Bond, John Honnor, Tracey and Stephen Groves, Anthony Barnes, Conrad and Alison*

Freezer, Tina and David Woods-Taylor, Mike and Mary Carter, John T Ames, Sue Holland, Dave Webster, Prof Kenneth Surin, Muriel and Peter Gleave, R J Bland, John Wooll, Mick Hitchman)

Free house ~ Licensee Colin Burgess ~ Real ale ~ Bar food (12-7; till 2.30 only Sun) ~ (01603) 667423 ~ Children welcome in snug ~ Open 11-11; 12-10.30 Sun

Fat Cat 🍺

West End St

They keep a quite astonishing range of drinks at this award winning traditional alehouse, and not even we could believe that they've actually increased the range since we made them our Beer Pub last year. It's certainly enough to get customers chatting to each other about it, and trying a half of this and a half of that. To begin with they keep a fantastic range of around 27 changing well kept ales from all sorts of brewers like Adnams, Batemans, Greene King, Fullers, Hop Back, Iceni, Kelham Island, Reepham and so forth. About half are on handpump, while the rest are tapped from the cask in a still room behind the bar – big windows reveal all. They also keep four draught Belgian beers (two of them fruit), draught lagers from Germany and the Czech Republic, up to 15 bottled Belgian beers, fifteen country wines, and local Norfolk cider. And this is more than just a real-ale pub with a good mix of customers enjoying its good lively bustling atmosphere at some times in the day, or tranquil lulls in the middle of the afternoon. The no-nonsense furnishings include plain scrubbed pine tables and simple solid seats, lots of brewery memorabilia, bric-a-brac and stained glass. Bar food consists of a dozen or so rolls at lunchtime (60p; not Sunday). There are tables outside. *(Recommended by David Twitchett, Sue Holland, Dave Webster, Tracey and Stephen Groves, Ian Phillips, Mark J Hydes, Rev John Hibberd)*

Free house ~ Licensee Colin Keatley ~ Real ale ~ (01603) 457883 ~ Children in conservatory till 9pm ~ Open 12(11 Sat)-11; 12-10.30 Sun

REEDHAM TG4101 Map 5
Railway Tavern 🍺

Just off B1140 Beccles—Acle; in the Beccles direction the little chain ferry stops at 10pm

You can easily imagine the costumed bustle of travel at this attractive listed Victorian brick building, quite imposing just above the railway station, in years gone by. It's a jolly nice relaxing place these days, well worth visiting for its good atmosphere and food, and most notably for its own well kept real ales. The cheerily friendly landlord here is also the brewer of Humpty Dumpty beers, and of the six brews he produces there are usually two on in the pub, served alongside four interesting microbrewery guests. This is one of very few own-brew pubs to be awarded a Casque Marque certificate. In mid April and mid September he hosts a beer festival with up to 90 beers on in a week – it's such a popular event they put on extra trains. The fairly simple but nicely pubby lounge has a high ceiling, dark wood tables and chairs on a turkey carpet, high netted and swagged windows, and red leatherette stools and a couple of tractor seats at the red velvet studded bar, behind which an impressive range of about 80 malt whiskies make a mouth-watering sight. The much simpler very pubby public bar has bare boards, darts, pool, shove-ha'penny, cribbage, dominoes, a TV and trivia. Very tasty bar food includes sandwiches (from £1.90), soup (£2.35), hummous or taramasalata with pitta bread fingers (£2.55), breaded whitebait (£3.75), chilli or vegetarian nut roast (£4.95), roast of the day or steak in a french stick (£5.25), steak and kidney pudding or chicken and stilton strudel (£6.95), and mostly home-made puddings like cheesecake and sponges with custard (£3.25). There's a pretty gravelled courtyard at the back, and white metal chairs on a terrace at the front overlook the station. *(Recommended by David Carr, Keith Berrett, Anthony Barnes, A J Thomas)*

Free house ~ Licensee Ivor Cuders ~ Real ale ~ Bar food (12-2.30, 6.30-9) ~ Restaurant ~ (01493) 700340 ~ Jazz at weekends and during April and Sept beer festivals ~ Open 11-3, 6-11; 11-11 Sat; 12-10.30 Sun ~ Bedrooms: £30B/£50B

REEPHAM TG0922 Map 8
Old Brewery House
Market Square; B1145 W of Aylsham

The big high-ceilinged bar of this old-fashioned town square hotel is thoroughly pubby, with a nice mix of oldish pub tables, lots of farming and fishing bric-a-brac and old enamel advertisements on its pale ochre walls, a piano and a dark green dado. A step down from this main seating area takes you to a tiled-floor serving area with well kept Adnams, Green King Abbot, Morlands Old Speckled Hen and local Reepham, and up to eighteen malt whiskies. There's also a red-carpeted lounge leading off, with dark panelling and sturdy brocaded armchairs. Bar food includes soup (£3.25), mushroom and stilton pot (£4.10), salmon and prawn mousse (£4.25), chicken breast with asparagus sauce (£8.95), pork medallions topped with parma ham and marsala cream (£9.95), baked bream and saffron sauce (£9.95), fried beef and king prawns with thai spices and stir-fried vegetables (£10.50), roast duck breast with strawberry and green peppercorn sauce (£10.95), and puddings like chocolate terrine or sticky toffee pudding (£3.50). *(Recommended by Les Rowlands, Mrs Mandy Littler, R C Vincent, Paul and Ursula Randall)*

Free house ~ Licensee Sarah Gardner ~ Bar food (12-2, 6.30-9.30) ~ Restaurant ~ (01603) 870881 ~ Children welcome ~ Open 11-11; 11-10.30 Sun ~ Bedrooms: £39.95S/£67.50S

RINGSTEAD TF7040 Map 8
Gin Trap £
Village signposted off A149 near Hunstanton; OS Sheet 132 map reference 707403

Perhaps unsurprisingly, this very sound village local is adorned with a huge collection of gin-traps. There are also copper kettles, carpenter's tools, cartwheels, and bottles hanging from the beams in the lower part of the well kept chatty bar, toasting forks above the woodburning stove, a couple of gin-traps ingeniously converted to electric candle-effect wall lights, and captain's chairs and cast-iron-framed tables on the green-and-white patterned motif carpet; part of this bar is no smoking. It does get busy at times but it's still a relaxing place to be. A small no-smoking dining room has quite a few chamber-pots suspended from the ceiling, and high-backed pine settles; you can book a table in here. Well kept Adnams Bitter, Woodfordes Nog, and Gin Trap Bitter brewed by Woodfordes for the pub, and a guest on handpump. Good bar food includes lunchtime sandwiches (£2.25) and ploughman's (from £3.50), as well as scampi (£4.75), nut cutlet (£5), lasagne (£5.75), steak and kidney pie (£6), steaks (from £8.75), daily specials like cod (£5.50), trout (£7) and chicken in filo pastry with cream cheese and leeks (£7), and home-made puddings like lemon meringue pie or chocolate brandy crunch cake. A handsome spreading chestnut tree shelters the car park, and the back garden has seats on the grass or small paved area and pretty flowering tubs. The pub is close to the Peddar's Way; hikers and walkers are welcome, but not their muddy boots. There's an art gallery next door, and boules in the back car park. *(Recommended by John Beeken, R M Corlett, John Wooll, Chris Mawson, Pat and Clive Sherriff, Brian Horner and Brenda Arthur, Paul Craddock, Tracey and Stephen Groves, M J Morgan, JKW, Bob Arnett, Judy Wayman)*

Free house ~ Licensees Brian and Margaret Harmes ~ Real ale ~ Bar food (12-2(1.45 Sun), 7-9) ~ (01485) 525264 ~ Children in eating area of bar ~ Open 11.30-2.30, 6.30-11; 11.45-2.30, 6.30-10.30 Sun; 7 evening opening winter; closed 25 Dec

SCULTHORPE TF8930 Map 8
Sculthorpe Mill
Pub signed off A148 W of Fakenham, opposite village

This 18th-c converted watermill is delightfully set in a quiet and pretty spot, with the River Wensum emerging from the bridge just in front, and plenty of tables outside – including one virtually out on an island among the mallards. Inside, the three small genteel rooms of the bar have soberly attractive furnishings, with good well polished tables, sensible chairs for diners (food is the main thing here), black beams and joists, and generous open fires in winter. The reception desk on the left of the bar and the neatly uniformed staff add a touch of dignity. Bar food includes sandwiches or filled french bread (from £3.25), ploughman's, filled baked potatoes (from £5.25), cajun chicken or game pie (£7.95), rump steak (£8.95), puddings (£2.75) and blackboard specials like tomato and basil soup (£2.50), spicy battered mushroooms with mint and yoghurt dip (£3.25), cottage pie (£5.95), cumberland sausage ring and mash (£6.25), lasagne (£6.95) and walnut lattice tart or trout with almond and parsley sauce (£8.95). Real ales change every now and then and might include very well kept Adnams Southwold, Charles Wells Bombardier, Greene King IPA and Theakstons XB on handpump; decent wines; piped music. *(Recommended by M J Morgan, John Wooll, Mark, Amanda, Luke and Jake Sheard, John Beeken, PM Sheard, George Atkinson, T R Burden, R C Vincent)*

Old English Inns ~ Managers Ben Brown and Debbie Grant ~ Real ale ~ Bar food ~ Restaurant ~ (01328) 856161 ~ Children welcome in rooms off main bar ~ Open 11-11; 12-10.30 Sun; 11-3, 6-11 Mon-Fri winter ~ Bedrooms: £50B/£60B

SNETTISHAM TF6834 Map 8

Rose & Crown 🍽 ♇ 🛏

Village signposted from A149 King's Lynn—Hunstanton Rd, just N of Sandringham

On-going improvements at this pretty white pub will include the addition of a new bedroom and reception area for overnight guests, and a new informal no-smoking dining area (the cellar bar) which it's hoped will be as enjoyable but perhaps not as bustling as the adjoining Back Bar. The garden room will be improved with a lower ceiling, new lighting, and sofas and armchairs around a large new fireplace. The unchanged Back Bar still has cushioned seats on the dark wooden floor, the landlord's sporting trophies, old racquets and real tennis racquets, golf clubs and fishing rods, and a big log fire. A small no-smoking bar has a fine collection of prints of local interest, including Queen Victoria leaning from her window at Sandringham to acknowledge the gentlemen of the Snettisham hunt, and a newspaper rack; this room is popular with eaters. Some lovely old pews and other interesting furniture sit on the wooden floor of the dining room, and there are shelves with old bottles and books, and old prints and watercolours. The old-fashioned beamed front bar has lots of carpentry and farm tools, cushioned black settles on the red tiled floor, and a great pile of logs by the fire in the vast fireplace (which has a gleaming black japanned side oven). A new chef last year has brought real improvements to the bar food here, which is now listed on a sensibly shortish and nicely up-to-date weekly changing menu. There might be home-made soup (£2.75), game pâté with home-made plum and onion compote (£4), stir-fried tiger prawns with thai spices and peppers (£5.50), creamy smoked haddock and leek risotto or warm spinach, mozzarella and omelette bake (£6.95), sautéed lamb's kidneys with creamy mash and madeira sauce, steak and kidney or sausage, onion and mushroom casserole (£8.75), baked honey and lemon marinated salmon with noodles (£9.15), well kept Adnams Bitter, Bass, Fullers and Hancocks, lots of wines by the glass and freshly squeezed orange juice. The colourful garden is particularly attractive, with picnic-sets among the flowering shrubs, and two spectacular willow trees; summer barbecues. There's a good adjoining fort adventure playground, guinea pigs and chipmunks. *(Recommended by Pat and Tony Martin, Brenda Crossley, John Wooll, John Sleigh, NMF, DF, Steve and Sarah Pleasance, G Neighbour, David and Anne Culley, R C Vincent, M Morgan, D and M Senior, Graham and Lynn Mason, Mr and Mrs G Turner, Mr and Mrs A H Young, Rita and Keith Pollard, Mike and Wena Stevenson)*

Free house ~ Licensee Anthony Goodrich ~ Real ale ~ Bar food (12-2, 6.30-9) ~ Restaurant ~ (01485) 541382 ~ Children in restaurant, in bar at quieter times ~ Open 11-11; 12-10.30 Sun ~ Bedrooms: £40B/£60B

Food details, prices, timing etc refer to bar food – not to a separate restaurant if there is one.

STIFFKEY TF9743 Map 8

Red Lion

A149 Wells—Blakeney

The very best kind of country pub this, with lots of unspoilt traditional atmosphere in the three fairly spartan interestingly shadowy bars, the smallest now painted red. The oldest parts have a few beams, aged flooring tiles or bare floorboards, open fires, a mix of pews, small settles and a couple of stripped high-backed settles, a nice old long deal table among quite a few others, and oil-type or lantern wall lamps. Well liked by readers, good varied bar food, with a good range of fresh local fish (£5.95–£7.95), includes whitebait, crab and delicious mussels in season (from £4.50), goat's cheese salad (£4.95), steak and kidney pie or game casserole (£6.50), rump steak (£7.25), and roast Sunday lunch (from £6.50); they may ask to hold your credit card behind the bar if you are running a tab. Well kept Adnams Bitter, Greene King Abbot, Woodfordes Great Eastern Ale and a guest on handpump, with Woodfordes Wherry tapped from the cask, Adnams wines, and Stowford Press cider; darts, dominoes, cribbage, board games and paper and crayons for children. The back restaurant leads into a no-smoking conservatory, and there are wooden seats and tables out on a back gravel terrace, with more on grass further up beyond. There's a pretty stream with ducks and swans across the road, and some pleasant walks from this unspoilt village. New bedrooms will be completed by summer 2000 and we'd be really interested to hear from readers who stay here. *(Recommended by Anthony Barnes, JP, PP, Charles Bardswell, Dr and Mrs D E Awbery, Tony Albert, Kevin Macey, O K Smyth, Frank Davidson, Peter and Pat Frogley, Mary and David Richards, John Wooll, Charles Gysin, NMF, DF, Keith and Janet Morris, M J Morgan, Tracey and Stephen Groves, Fiona Wynn, Pete Stroud, Chris and Shirley Machin, Dr Andy Wilkinson, MDN, Miss S P Watkin, P A Taylor)*

Free house ~ Licensee Matthew Rees ~ Real ale ~ Bar food ~ (01328) 830552 ~ Children away from main bar ~ Live bands Fri fortnightly ~ Open 11-2.30(3 Sat, Sun), 6.30-11(10.30 Sun); 7 evening opening winter

STOW BARDOLPH TF6205 Map 5

Hare Arms ♀

Just off A10 N of Downham Market

There's a good bustling atmosphere in the welcoming bar at this pretty creeper-covered pub. It's decorated with old advertising signs and fresh flowers, has plenty of tables around its central servery, and a good log fire; maybe two friendly ginger cats and a sort of tabby. This bar opens into a spacious heated and well planted no-smoking conservatory, and that in turn opens into a pretty garden with picnic-sets under cocktail parasols and wandering peacocks, turkeys and chickens. Bar food includes sandwiches (from £1.95), filled baked potatoes (from £3.95), ploughman's (from £5.95), mushroom stroganoff or steak sandwich (£6.25), chilli or curry (£6.50), lasagne or spinach and ricotta canellonni (£6.75), 8oz fillet steak (from £12.95), and daily specials like stilton and bacon soup (£2.95), cod and chips (£5.25), ratatouille pancake (£6.75), pork steak with stilton and mustard sauce or beef and ale pie (£7.25), swordfish steak with tomato and basil dressing (£8.45), lamb steak with rosemary sauce or salmon fillet in lemon and tarragon sauce (£8.95), and puddings (£2.95); efficient staff, even when pushed. Well kept Greene King IPA, Abbot, and their seasonal ales on handpump a good range of wines, and quite a few malt whiskies; maybe cockles and whelks on the bar counter; fruit machine. *(Recommended by V and E A Bolton, Basil J S Minson, Mr and Mrs Staples, John Wooll, Lesley Kant, June and Malcolm Farmer, R Wiles, M Morgan, P M Millikin, Anthony Barnes, Charles Bardswell, Dr Andy Wilkinson, Jenny and Michael Back, Ian Phillips)*

Greene King ~ Tenants David and Trish McManus ~ Real ale ~ Bar food (12-2, 7-10) ~ Restaurant ~ (01366) 382229 ~ Children in conservatory and Old Coach House on Sun and bank holidays only ~ Open 11-2.30, 6-11; 12-2.30, 7-10.30 Sun; closed 25, 26 Dec

SWANTON MORLEY TG0117 Map 8

Darbys ◀

B1147 NE of Dereham

A genuinely happy pub this, with a cheery farmer landlord, perhaps wandering around, glass in hand. A cheery bunch of village locals gather at the bar for the good range of well kept real ales, diners arrive for the tasty Thai menu and specials, and families are attracted by the cheery welcome for children. This creeper-covered brick building is a careful conversion of two derelict farm cottages, its long bare boarded country style bar has a comfortable lived in feel. There are lots of gin-traps and farming memorabilia, a good log fire (with the original bread oven alongside), tractor seats with folded sacks lining the long, attractive serving counter, and fresh flowers on the big stripped pine tables; maybe papers to read. A step up through a little doorway by the fireplace takes you through to the no-smoking dining room. The children's room has a toy box and a glassed-over well. Enjoyable bar food includes a range of Thai dishes such as tempura vegetables with sweet chilli sauce (£2.95), tom yum soup (£4.25), spare ribs with coriander and garlic sauce (£5.85), stir-fried pork in plum sauce (£6.50), stir-fried beef in oyster sauce (£6.75), green chicken curry (£7.25), stir-fried chicken and cashews in oyster sauce (£7.50), as well as more traditional things like soup (£2.15), ploughman's (£3.75), vegetable lasagne (£5.65), beef and ale pie (£6.50), chicken and mushroom pie (£6.95), 8oz sirloin (£9.50) and honey glazed duckling (£10.95). Well kept Adnams Bitter, Badger Tanglefoot, Woodfordes Wherry and four guests – one at bargain price – on handpump. A labrador and border collie might be around; darts, dominoes, cribbage, piped music. The garden has a really good play area, and in summer they have cook-your-own barbecues out here (beware, they may ask to impound your credit card if you're eating outside). The bedrooms are in carefully converted farm buildings a few minutes away (they usually run a free taxi service to and from the pub for residents), and there's plenty to do if you're staying as the family also own the adjoining 720-acre estate, and can arrange clay pigeon shooting, golf, fishing, nature trails, and craft instruction. *(Recommended by Mrs Hilarie Taylor, Mike Wells, Jenny and Michael Back, Muriel and Peter Gleave, John Wooll, Chris Miller, Anthony Barnes, Chris and Shirley Machin, Lesley Kant, Brenda Crossley)*

Free house ~ Licensees John Carrick and Louise Battle ~ Real ale ~ Bar food ~ Restaurant ~ (01362) 637457 ~ Children welcome ~ Occasional live music ~ Open 11-2.30, 6-11; 11-11 Sat; 12-3, 7-10.30 Sun; closed evening 25 Dec ~ Bedrooms: £23(£27B)/£38(£45B)

THORNHAM TF7343 Map 8

Lifeboat

Turn off A149 by Kings Head, then take first left turn

You will need to get to this rambling old white-painted stone pub early for a table as it is very popular, but service does seem to cope well with the rush. It's tempting to say that it's more enjoyable out of season but it seems to be just as bustling then. The genuinely characterful main bar is dimly lit with antique paraffin lamps, has low settles, window seats, pews, and carved oak tables on the rugs on the tiled floor, great oak beams hung with traps and yokes, and masses of guns, swords, black metal mattocks, reed-slashers and other antique farm tools; there are a couple of little rooms leading off here, five open fires and no noisy games machines or piped music, though they still play the ancient game of 'pennies', outlawed in the late 1700s, and dominoes. Bar food includes soup (£2.95), whitebait (£4.50), filled french sticks (£4.95), ploughman's (£5.50), six oysters (£5.95), very good fresh fish and chips (£6.95), fish pie (£7.95), daily specials like pigeon and chicken terrine layered with chargrilled vegetables with tomato chutney or grilled feta on an aubergine crouton with dijon mustard dressing (£4.95), penne with mushrooms and cherry tomatoes in a cream pesto sauce (£8.50), grilled lamb's liver with smoked bacon and red onion jus (£8.95), fried duck breast with caramelised orange and juniper sauce (£9.50) and grilled tuna steak flavoured with ginger, garlic and herbs on red pepper chutney

(£10.95) and puddings like fruit crumble and lemon tart (£3.50). As well as well kept Adnams, Bass, Greene King IPA and Abbot, and Woodfordes Wherry on handpump they have freshly squeezed orange juice and farm ciders. Up some steps from the smart conservatory is a sunny terrace with picnic-sets, and further back is a children's playground with fort and slide. The pub faces half a mile of coastal sea flats – plenty of surrounding walks. *(Recommended by NMF, DF, Colin McKerrow, Anthony Barnes, Dr Andy Wilkinson, Martin Chambers, JP, PP, MDN, Paul Kitchener, Tracey and Stephen Groves, O K Smyth, John Wooll, Sue and Bob Ward, G Neighbour, Nigel Woolliscroft, Arthur Williams, M J Morgan, Charles Bardswell, Steve and Sarah Pleasance, N Cobb, Kevin Blake, A C Curry, Eric Locker, Ken and Jenny Simmonds)*

Free house ~ Licensee Charles Coker ~ Real ale ~ Bar food (12-2.30, 6-10) ~ Restaurant ~ (01485) 512236 ~ Children welcome ~ Live entertainment Fri fortnightly ~ Open 11-11; 12-10.30 Sun ~ Bedrooms: £57B/£74B

TITCHWELL TF7543 Map 8
Manor Hotel 🛏

A149 E of Hunstanton

One reader when telling us about the good birdwatching near here said he'd never seen so many telescopes – it's not surprising as this comfortable well run hotel overlooks the Titchwell RSPB reserve with lots of good walks and footpaths all round. From the end bar there are wonderful views over the salt marshes to the sea from the seats by the picture windows. The tranquil lounge has magazines, an open fire, and a good naturalists' record of the wildlife in the reserve. The pretty no-smoking restaurant leads into a conservatory which opens onto the sheltered neatly kept walled gardens. Bar food from a menu with a mix of international styles is good but certainly not cheap. There might be local oysters (£1 each), pea and ham soup or malaysian-style crab and coconut chowder (£3.50), seared king scallops with sun-dried tomato and basil relish (£5.95), hock of ham with bubble and squeak (£7.50), battered cod (£8.50), grilled red mullet on linguini pasta in a tomato and herb sauce (£9.50), chargrilled neck of lamb with marinated vegetables and red wine jus (£11.50), black bream on stir-fry oriental vegetables and sweet chilli dressing (£11.75), duck breast on chorizo sausage risotto (£12) and lobster thermidor (£19.90). Greene King IPA and Abbot on handpump. There's a championship golf course only moments away. *(Recommended by M Morgan, Peter and Pat Frogley, E A Froggatt, Charles Bardswell, Arthur Williams, Paul Craddock)*

Free house ~ Licensees Ian and Margaret Snaith ~ Real ale ~ Bar food ~ Restaurant ~ (01485) 210221 ~ Children welcome ~ Open 12-2, 6.30-11(10.30 Sun); closed 18 to 31 Jan ~ Bedrooms: £45B/£90B

TIVETSHALL ST MARY TM1686 Map 5
Old Ram 🍷 🛏

A140 15 miles S of Norwich, outside village

This much extended carefully run place is popular throughout its rambling brick-floored rooms from almost the crack of dawn for tasty bar food. Service starts with breakfast (£6.50) from 7.30 to 11.30, and goes on throughout the day with dishes like salmon bisque or griddled chicken breast with sour cream and coriander dressing (£3.95), calamari with garlic butter (£4.95), ploughman's (£6.50), steak and mushroom pie, scampi or chicken curry (£7.95), chicken supreme with lemon and sage sauce (£8.95), salmon en croûte with cheese and prawns on dill sauce or grilled skake with black butter or roast loin of lamb with mint and mild mustard sauce (£9.95), and puddings like summer pudding, chocolate and orange pudding and Belgian apple pie (from £3). They also offer an Over Sixty Club Menu with main courses at £5.95. Well kept Adnams, Boddingtons, Fullers London Pride, Woodfordes Wherry, and Worthingtons on handpump, 13 wines including champagne by the glass, and freshly squeezed orange juice; unobtrusive fruit machine and piped music. With lots of stripped beam and standing timbers, the country kitchen styled spacious main room has a turkey rug on rosy brick floors, a longcase clock, antique craftsmen's tools on the ceiling, and a huge log fire in the brick hearth. It's ringed by cosier side areas, one with bright red walls, and a no-smoking dining room with an open woodburning stove and black walls and ceiling. This leads to a second comfortable no-smoking dining room and gallery. The sheltered flower-filled terrace has outdoor heaters and big green parasols. They gain a Stay Award this year for nicely decorated, comfortably furnished bedrooms, some of them attractively beamed; no dogs. *(Recommended by Beryl and Bill Farmer, Mike and Mary Carter, Andy and Sarah Gillett, Keith Berrett, Mrs D P Dick, Tina and David Woods-Taylor, Stephen and Julie Brown, Brian Horner and Brenda Arthur, Roy and Valerie Taylor)*

Free house ~ Licensee John Trafford ~ Real ale ~ Bar food (7.30am-10pm) ~ (01379) 676794 ~ Children in eating area of bar (under sevens till 8pm) ~ Open 11(12 Sun)-11; closed 25, 26 Dec ~ Bedrooms: £51.50B/£70B

UPPER SHERINGHAM TG1441 Map 8
Red Lion

B1157; village signposted off A148 Cromer—Holt, and the A149 just W of Sheringham

This delightfully simple, relaxing little flint cottage is popular for its interesting well cooked bar food which might include home-made soup (£2.95), home-made pâté (£3.50), stilton-stuffed mushrooms (£3.50), mushroom stroganoff or vegetable curry (£5.95), fried liver and onion (£6.25), thai chicken in oyster sauce (£6.50), pigeon braised in port, orange and cranberries or drunken thumper – rabbit in real ale, wine and a spirit (£6.95), steak and kidney pie – described by one reader as superb (£7.50), up to eight fresh fish dishes like crab salad (£5.50), shark steak (£6.95), cod fillet with stilton and mushroom sauce (£7.95) and lobster thermidor (£8.95), and puddings like chocolate fudge gateau and port and lemon syllabum (£2.50). Well kept Greene King IPA, and Woodfordes Wherry on handpump, with over 60 malt whiskies and decent wines. The two quiet small bars have stripped high-backed settles and country-kitchen chairs on the red tiles or bare boards, plain off-white walls and ceiling, a big woodburning stove, and newspapers to read; the snug is no smoking. Dominoes and cribbage, and maybe some cats. *(Recommended by David and Anne Culley, Peter and Pat Frogley, Marion H Turner, R C Vincent, A J and M A Seaman, Anthony Barnes, D Twitchett)*

Free house ~ Licensee I Bryson ~ Real ale ~ Bar food (12-2, 6.30-9) ~ (01263) 825408 ~ Children welcome ~ Open 10.30(11 Sat, 11.30 Sun)-11; 11.30-3, 7-11(10.30 Sun) winter ~ Bedrooms: £18/£36

WARHAM TF9441 Map 8
Three Horseshoes 🍺 🛏

Warham All Saints; village signposted from A149 Wells next the Sea—Blakeney, and from B1105 S of Wells

This unspoilt, old-fashioned country pub with its great beer, very good bar food and genuine atmosphere is a real favourite so you will need to get here early for a table (they don't take bookings, we're happy to say). It's very well run and neatly kept by the friendly licensees, and even when really busy, service remains cheerful and efficient. Parts of the building date back to the 1720s, and the simple interior with its gas lighting looks little changed since the 1920s. Its three rooms have stripped deal or mahogany tables (one marked for shove-ha'penny) on a stone floor, red leatherette settles built around the partly panelled walls of the public bar, and open fires in Victorian fireplaces; an antique American Mills one-arm bandit is still in working order (it takes 5p pieces; there's a 1960s one that takes 1p pieces), there's a big longcase clock with a clear piping strike, and a twister on the ceiling to point out who gets the next round. That would be from a choice of well kept Greene King IPA, Woodfordes Wherry, and a weekly guest like Buffys Norwich Terrier on handpump or tapped from the cask, good home-made lemonade, and local cider. The very enjoyable bar food includes sandwiches (from £2.50, not served at weekends), two sausages and bacon in a roll (£2.90), filled baked potatoes (from £3), game, pork and liver terrine (£3.50), ploughman's (from £5.20), mushroom, nut and elderberry pie (£6.50), chicken and ham pie or cheesy fish bake (£6.80), game pie (£7.90), and daily specials like mussels (£4.50), parsnip and tomato bake (£4.80), lamb hotpot (£5.80) and pot roast pheasant (£7.20). The dining room is no smoking. Fruit machine, darts, cribbage, shove-ha'penny, dominoes, and one of the outbuildings houses a wind-up gramophone museum – opened on request. There are rustic tables out on the side grass. One area is no smoking. *(Recommended by John Beeken, Dr Andy Wilkinson, Andrew Turnbull, John Honnor, Ken and Jenny Simmonds, Sue and Bob Ward, Anthony Longden, John Wooll, Paul Craddock, Charles Bardswell, Susan and Philip Philcox, Tracey and Stephen Groves, David and Anne Culley, David and Helen Wilkins, M Morgan, Mrs B Williams)*

Free house ~ Licensee Iain Salmon ~ Bar food (12-2, 7-8.30) ~ (01328) 710547 ~ Children in eating area of bar ~ Open 11.30-2.30, 6-11; 12-3, 6-10.30 Sun ~ Bedrooms: £24/£48(£52B)

WELLS NEXT THE SEA TF9143 Map 8
Crown £
The Buttlands

This cosy little hotel is unspoilt by refurbishments – except perhaps those done some years ago by the Georgians who added a black and white frontage that's belied by the pubby front bar whose bowed beams show that it's a fair bit older than its frontage suggests – it's still quite attractive really inspite of their meddling. Two quieter back rooms have some interesting pictures on the wall over the roaring log fire, including several big Nelson prints and maps showing the town in the 18th and 19th centuries. Tasty waitress-served bar food includes sandwiches (from £1.60), soup (£2.25), vegetable curry (£4.75), tagliatelle with Italian meat sauce (£4.95), steak in ale cobbler (£5.75), choux pastry filled with prawns, tomato and onion and baked with cheese on top (£5.55), scampi (£5.95), sirloin steak (£10.50), and daily specials like cauliflower soup (£2.25), pasta with Scottish salmon with a dill, onion, mushroom, white wine and cream sauce (£6.50), grilled lamb fillet marinated in garlic, mint and lamb (£7.50) and sea trout fried with tomato sauce (£8.95), and puddings like red and white grape ice-cream sundae or steamed marmalade pudding with Grand Marnier sauce and cinnamon crème fraîche (£2.95). Adnams, Bass, and a guest beer on handpump, and several malt whiskies; piped music. A neat conservatory has small modern settles around the tables. The central square of quiet Georgian houses is most attractive, and archers used to practise on the tranquil village green opposite. *(Recommended by M J Morgan, Charles Bardswell, John Wooll, NMF, DF, Mary and David Richards)*

Free house ~ Licensee Wilfred Foyers ~ Real ale ~ Bar food ~ Restaurant ~ (01328) 710209 ~ Children in eating area of bar ~ Open 11-2.30, 6-11; 12-2.30, 7-10.30 Sun ~ Bedrooms: £35(£55B)/£59(£69B)

WEST BECKHAM TG1339 Map 8
Wheatsheaf ◀
Church Road; village signposted off A148 Holt—Cromer

There's a pleasantly homely feel in the gently renovated separate beamed areas of this attractive village inn with its flint walls and cottagey doors. There's a roaring feature log fire in one part, a smaller coal one in another, comfortable chairs and banquettes, and an enormous black cat. Well kept Bass, Woodfordes Wherry, Nelsons Revenge, Norfolk Nog, Headcracker and possibly others, a good choice of wines in generous measures, and over a dozen locally produced country wines. Big helpings of bar food include sandwiches (from £1.75), soup (£2.50), chicken liver pâté and redcurrant jelly or fried herring roes on toast with lemon butter (£3.50), ploughman's (from £4.75), lasagne (£5.25), roast mediterranean vegetables in tomato sauce on tagliatelle or steak and kidney pudding or pie (£5.95), scampi (£6.25), tuna steak with a sweet and sour sauce (£6.95), sirloin (£9.95), and puddings (£2.95). The two dining rooms are no smoking. Darts, bar billiards, shove-ha'penny, dominoes and piped music. There are tables out in the partly terraced

front garden, which may have wandering chickens; behind is a small craft centre.
(Recommended by Anthony Barnes, Derek Field)

Free house ~ Licensee B Fletcher ~ Real ale ~ Bar food (not Sun evening) ~ Restaurant ~ (01263) 822110 ~ Children welcome ~ Jazz and shanty music in summer ~ Open 11-3, 6-11; 12-3, 7-10.30 Sun

WINTERTON ON SEA TG4919 Map 8
Fishermans Return 🍺 🛏️

From B1159 turn into village at church on bend, then turn right into The Lane

This traditional brick and flint pub, in a beautiful secluded spot near a lovely sandy beach, is run by friendly people and has a pleasantly relaxing atmosphere. The attractive and cosy white-painted panelled lounge bar with its vases of fresh flowers has neat brass-studded red leatherette seats and a winter log fire. The panelled public bar has low ceilings and a glossily varnished nautical air. Well liked bar food includes sandwiches (from £1.75), ploughman's (£4), fish pie (£4.75), chilli (£5.50), nice unusual omlettes (from £5.75), scampi (£6.50), sirloin steak (£9.75), and daily specials like lentil and vegetable moussaka or aubergine and mushroom stroganoff (£5.50), thai pork or chicken in lime and coriander with tagliatelle (£6.75), lamb in rhubarb and ginger sauce (£7.50), tuna on niçoise salad (£7.75), monkfish on spinach and wild rice (£8.75), and some home-made puddings like lemon and lime cheesecake on a ginger base or bread and butter pudding (£2.50). Well kept real ales include Buffys Pollys Folly and Mild, Woodfordes Wherry and Nog and two guests like Burton Bridge and Maldons Cuckoo on handpump, decent wines, around 30 malt whiskies, and James White cider; darts, dominoes, cribbage, pool, fruit machine, video game, and juke box. The characterful bedrooms, up the steep curving stairs, have low doors and uneven floors; two rooms are no smoking. Attractive wrought-iron and wooden benches on a pretty front terrace have nice views, as do the sheltered garden and terrace, which open out from the back bar; there's a pond and pets corner with ornamental chickens and bantams. *(Recommended by Mike and Sue Loseby, Alan Kilpatrick, Klaus and Elizabeth Leist, John Kirk, David and Anne Culley, Alan and Paula McCully, Dr C A Brace)*

Free house ~ Licensees John and Kate Findlay ~ Real ale ~ Bar food ~ (01493) 393305 ~ Children away from bar ~ Open 11-2.30, 6.30-11; 11-11 Sat; 12.10.30 Sun ~ Bedrooms: £30/£50

WOODBASTWICK TG3315 Map 8
Fur & Feather 🍺

Off B1140 E of Norwich

The entire range of eight Woodfordes beers are tapped from the cask at this converted thatched cottage which serves as the tap for Woodfordes brewery which is right next door; you can even take some home with you. Bar food is pretty good here too, with the rooms set out in the style of a dining pub. There might be soup (£2.30), sandwiches (from £2.75), home-made chicken liver pâté (£3.75), ploughman's or burgers (£5.95), chilli or red onion and apple casserole (£6.25), meatloaf with brandy and pepper sauce (£6.50), sweet and sour chicken, ham and mushroom tagliatelle, spare ribs or filled yorkshire puddings (£6.95), beef stroganoff (£11.95), puddings (from £2.50), and children's meals (£3.15); friendly, helpful staff. The restaurant and part of the bar are no smoking; piped music and cribbage. There are tables out in the very pleasant garden, and the pub forms part of a very attractive estate village; no dogs. *(Recommended by Alan and Paula McCully, Sue Holland, Dave Webster, Martin and Caroline Page, Lesley Kant, JP, PP, Mike Gorton, K and E Leist, Andrew Barker, Claire Jenkins, D Bryan, Mick Hitchman, Alison McCarthy, James House, Martin and Karen Wade, James Nunn, Tracey Hamond)*

Woodfordes ~ Tenants John and Jean Marjoram ~ Real ale ~ Bar food (12-2, 6.30-9) ~ Restaurant ~ (01603) 720003 ~ Children in eating area of bar and restaurant ~ Open 11.30(12 winter)-3, 6-11; 12-3, 7-10.30 Sun

Lucky Dip

Besides the fully inspected pubs, you might like to try these Lucky Dips recommended to us and described by readers (if you do, please send us reports):

Aylmerton [TG1840]
Roman Camp [Holt Rd (A148)]: Refurbished Victorian pub attached to hotel, comfortable bar with balustraded partitioned dining area, sitting room and conservatory, interesting food from sandwiches to nouvelle cuisine dishes, well kept Adnams and other beers, tables in garden behind, smiling service even when busy; bedrooms *(Pat and Bill Pemberton)*

Banningham [TG2129]
Crown [Colby Rd]: Consistently friendly welcome and well kept beer, decent food and wines *(Ken and Jeni Black)*

Barton Bendish [TF7105]
Spread Eagle: Attractive bar with good range of sandwiches, filled baguettes and potatoes as well as excellent soup and straightforward main dishes, good friendly service, curios for sale; tables outside *(Mr and Mrs W G Beeson, Anthony Barnes)*

Beachamwell [TF7505]
☆ *Great Danes Head* [off A1122 Swaffham—Downham Mkt]: Cosy and friendly genuine village pub, with good varied food using local produce inc game, helpful licensees, Greene King Abbot and Marstons Pedigree, good house red; children and dogs welcome, small separate public bar with pool, restaurant; by green of tiny village *(David and Brenda Tew, Philip and Caroline Pennant-Jones)*

Binham [TF9839]
☆ *Chequers* [B1388 SW of Blakeney]: Long beamed bar with coal fires each end, one in inglenook, sturdy plush seats, ales such as Adnams, Greene King IPA, Abbot and Triumph, Woodfordes Wherry, enterprising promptly served home-made food from good rolls and sandwiches up using local produce (Sun lunch very popular), reasonable prices, small no-smoking dining area, efficient cheerful staff, no piped music; picnic-sets on grass behind, open all day, interesting village with huge priory church *(John Beeken, BB, R Vincent, George Atkinson, K H Frostick)*

Blakeney [TG0243]
Manor: Small attractive hotel in own grounds with civilised, comfortable and peaceful pub part, popular with older people for good generous waitress-served bar food from well filled crab sandwiches up, not expensive; decent house wines; sunny tables outside, bedrooms; opp wildfowl reserve and sea inlet *(Minda and Stanley Alexander, MDN, Frank Davidson)*

Bramerton [TG2904]
Woods End: Much modernised high-ceilinged lounge, big windows overlooking bend of River Yare, roomy L-shaped extension with pool table, restaurant, terrace tables by the grassy river banks (and hordes of ducks); wide choice of food up to chargrills, well kept Bass and Woodfordes *(Alan and Paula McCully)*

Brancaster Staithe [TF7743]
☆ *Jolly Sailors*: Good freshly cooked specials and good range of home-made puddings in simple but stylish and rather upmarket old-fashioned pub, popular with yachtsmen and the local gentry; prompt cheerful service even when busy, well kept Bass and Greene King, good wines, provision for children (dogs allowed, too), log fire, attractive restaurant, sheltered tables in nice garden with terrace, enclosed play area and tennis court, open all Sun in summer *(E J Locker, Pat and Clive Sherriff, JJW, CMW, LYM)*

Brandon Creek [TL6091]
☆ *Ship* [A10 Ely—Downham Market]: Good summer pub, in lovely spot on confluence of Great and Little Ouse, tables out by the moorings; spacious bar with massive stone masonry in sunken area that used to be a forge, big log fire one end, woodburner the other, friendly staff, interesting old photographs and ales such as Burton Bridge XL, Dark Horse Fallen Angel and Sam Smiths, usual bar food priced reasonably from sandwiches up, two labradors, evening restaurant *(Ian Phillips, LYM)*

Bressingham [TM0781]
Old Garden House [A1066 Thetford—Diss]: Thatch, beams and timbering, good choice of good affordable food inc vegetarian in attractive dining area, well kept ales; handy for Bressingham Garden and steam museum, tables in garden *(D and H Parberry)*

Briston [TG0532]
☆ *John H Stracey* [B1354, Aylsham end of village]: Welcoming, clean and well run country dining pub, wide choice of good reasonably priced quickly served food inc fresh fish Tues and other good value speciality nights, well kept Greene King Abbot, decent house wines, comfortable seats, log fire, long-serving landlord, friendly obliging staff, dog and cat; popular pleasant restaurant, a few tables in small well kept garden; good value bedrooms with good breakfast - nice for people who like being part of family *(John and Julia Hall, John Wooll)*

Burnham Overy Staithe [TF8442]
Hero [A149]: Pleasant service, generous usual food inc very fresh sandwiches, friendly atmosphere, interesting bygones *(M J Morgan)*

Caister on Sea [TG5211]
Ship [Victoria St, off Tan Lane]: Busy local notable for its magnificent hanging baskets and spectacular floral displays on front terrace and small back garden; modern furnishings, well kept Greene King IPA and Morlands Old Speckled Hen, decent house wines, good value satisfying food inc cheap fresh local fish, coal fire; nostalgic piped pop music, pool, big screen TV and games machines in side areas, no dogs; not far from long sandy beach *(Mr and Mrs T Drake, John Kirk, Eddie Edwards, Mr and Mrs Rout, BB)*

Castle Acre [TF8115]
☆ *Ostrich* [Stocks Green]: Interesting

ungentrified pub prettily placed overlooking a tree-lined green, odd mix of utilitarian furnishings and fittings with some ancient beams, masonry and huge fireplace, well kept Greene King ales; at best the food's very enjoyable and good value (with plenty of vegetarian dishes), and service individual and welcoming; dominoes, cribbage, fruit machine, piped music, family room, picnic-sets in sheltered garden; jazz 2nd and 3rd Weds of month, folk last Weds of month, attractive village with castle and monastery remains *(Charles Bardswell, LYM, R J Bland)*

Castle Rising [TF6624]

Black Horse: Comfortable and spotless Beefeater family dining pub by church and almshouses in pleasant unspoilt village, good furnishings inc sofas, usual reliable food, mainly Whitbreads-related ales, friendly unhurried service, long hours; children welcome, own menu and play packs; no dogs, pleasant tables out under cocktail parasols, play area *(R C Vincent, John Wooll)*

Cawston [TG1422]

☆ *Ratcatchers* [Eastgate, S of village – on B1149 from Norwich turn left towards Haveringland at crossroads ½ mile before the B1145 Cawston turn]: Bustling pub-restaurant under new licensees, good interesting freshly made food from sandwiches up inc good fish and vegetarian choice, well kept Adnams Extra, Bass, Hancocks HB and a guest, good range of wines, L-shaped beamed bar with open fire, no-smoking candlelit dining room (not Sun evening); children welcome; bedrooms *(Anthony Barnes, Mr and Mrs L Lesbirel, Ken and Jeni Black, LYM, B and C Clouting, G D Cove, David and Diana MacFadyen)*

Cley next the Sea [TG0443]

☆ *George & Dragon* [Holt Rd, off A149 W of Sheringham]: Comfortably Edwardian, popular with salt-marsh birdwatchers, cosy locals' bar, lounge and dining area, St George artefacts, wide choice of good generous food inc good vegetarian choice, well kept Greene King IPA, Abbot and a seasonal ale; sizeable garden over road, with boules pitch; bedrooms *(Rita and Keith Pollard, G Staple, Eric Locker, Peter Frogley, LYM, Kevin Macey, NMF, DF, Charles Bardswell)*

☆ *Three Swallows* [Holt Rd, Newgate Green; nr church]: Plain take-us-as-you-find-us village local on quiet lane facing green, banquettes around long high leathered tables, roaring fire, steps up to second simple eating area, separate no-smoking dining room with good log fire, good value generous quickly served home-made food from sandwiches (good crab) to fresh fish, well kept Greene King IPA and Wadworths 6X from unusual richly carved bar, decent wines; dogs welcome, wandering tabbies; barbecues in big attractive garden with croquet, aviary, surprisingly grandiose fountain, wooden climbing frame, goat pen and close-up view of lovely church tower; bedrooms simple but clean and comfortable, handy for the salt marshes *(Mr and Mrs A H Young, M J Morgan, Patrick Renouf, BB,*

Miss S P Watkin, P A Taylor, Andrew Turnbull, Eric Locker, George Atkinson, Mrs B Williams, Charles Bardswell, G Staple, Anthony Barnes)

Cockley Cley [TF7904]

☆ *Twenty Churchwardens* [off A1065 S of Swaffham]: Straightforward no-frills village pub in converted former school, small, clean and welcoming, with well kept Adnams, courteous landlord, helpful waitresses, limited but good bar food, beams, darts alcove *(Colin Fisher)*

Coltishall [TG2719]

Kings Head [Church St (B1354)]: Refurbished pub largely laid out for eating, good choice of tasty food inc cheap set-price lunches, well kept Adnams, Marstons Pedigree, Woodfordes Wherry and guest beers, decent wines, personable landlord, open fire, several stuffed fish inc a 50lb pike; cheap comfortable bedrooms, moorings nearby *(Martin and Caroline Page, Stephen and Julie Brown)*

☆ *Red Lion* [Church St (B1354)]: Friendly modernised family pub under new ownership, decent straightforward generous food inc good puddings, good range of well kept beers inc Weasel brewed for them by Woodfordes, several attractive split-level rooms esp the attractive cellar bar, restaurant; away from water but pleasant setting, tables out under cocktail parasols by fountain, good play area *(Stephen and Julie Brown, M A Buchanan, Ian Phillips)*

Colton [TG1009]

Ugly Bug [well signed once off A47]: Surprisingly big recently done largely open-plan pub out in the country, built-in banquettes, turkey carpet, red velvet curtains, pleasant décor with old enamel advertisements, well kept changing ales such as Buffys, Greene King Abbot, Hancocks HB, Timothy Taylor Landlord and one brewed locally for them by Iceni, good if not cheap food with particularly good chips in bar and restaurant, evening choice wider, sensible choice of wines, good atmosphere and service; piped music, children in conservatory with bar billiards, big garden, lake fishing; two comfortable bedrooms *(Bill and Sheila McLardy, BB)*

Cromer [TG2142]

Dolphin [clifftop, overlooking pier]: Good pier and sea views, with most tables right by windows; decent food from good home-made soup and sandwiches up, friendly staff, well kept Morlands Old Speckled Hen and Theakstons Best and Old Peculier *(JDM, KM)*

Denver Sluice [TF6101]

☆ *Jenyns Arms* [signed via B1507 off A1122 Downham Mkt bypass]: Extensive and well laid out roadhouse-style pub in fine spot by the massive hydraulic sluices which control the Great Ouse, tables out by the waterside with strutting peacocks, well kept ales such as Adnams, Greene King IPA, Morlands Old Speckled Hen and Woodfordes Wherry, generous usual food (not Sun evening) from sandwiches to roasts inc vegetarian and tempting puddings, helpful efficient staff; children welcome, big light and airy games area, piped music; bedrooms, handy for Welney wildfowl reserve *(BB, Bruce Bird, Charles Bardswell)*

Dereham [TF9913]

☆ *George* [Swaffham Rd]: Clean and comfortable, with good value home cooking and carvery, good range of well kept beers, friendly attentive service; bedrooms good *(Mike Baldwin)*

Kings Head [Norwich St]: Decent value bar food – can eat in dining room if bar full *(V and E A Bolton, Frank Davidson)*

Dersingham [TF6830]

☆ *Feathers* [B1440 towards Sandringham]: Solid Jacobean sandstone inn with relaxed modernised dark-panelled bars opening on to attractive garden with elaborate play area and secluded pond; well kept Adnams, Bass and a quickly changing guest beer, log fires, generous bar food from sandwiches up, restaurant (not Sun evening), separate games room; children welcome, can get very busy in season; some live music in bar; comfortable well furnished bedrooms *(John McDonald, Ann Bond, LYM, R C Vincent, Muriel and Peter Gleave, E A Froggatt)*

Diss [TM1179]

☆ *Saracens Head* [Mount St]: 17th-c jettied building with thriving local atmosphere in handsome beamed and timbered lounge, well kept Bass and Greene King IPA from oak corner bar, jovial welcoming landlord, good choice of generous bar food, separate small dining room (often fully booked); a splendid small-town pub, some picnic-sets out by back car park *(BB, Rita and Keith Pollard, Alan and Paula McCully)*

Docking [TF7637]

Hare Arms [B1153 towards Brancaster]: This attractive and individually decorated pub was closed in 1999; we hope it will reopen *(LYM)*

Pilgrims Reach [High St]: Warm and comfortable small bar (can be busy), well kept Adnams Bitter and Broadside and their good wines, friendly new chef/landlord, quiet restaurant, children's room; tables on attractive sheltered back terrace *(O K Smyth, Alan and Judith Gifford)*

Downham Market [TF6103]

Castle [High St]: Very comfortable, with reasonably priced bar food inc roast of the day, Bass, helpful staff, interesting things on wall inc old cuttings *(R C Vincent)*

☆ *Crown* [Bridge St]: 17th-c coaching inn, all steps, nooks and crannies, with log fire in small homely oak-panelled bar, 635 Pathfinder bomber squadron WWII photographs, well kept Theakstons, speedy service, good food Thurs-Sun (stops sharply at 2) inc attractively presented veg, can be eaten in restaurant; picnic-sets in coach yard, comfortable bedrooms cantilevered out over it, big breakfast *(Richard Phillips, Ian Phillips, R C Vincent)*

East Barsham [TF9133]

White Horse [B1105 3 miles N of Fakenham]: Pleasantly refurbished and extended, reasonably priced food in long main bar with big log fire and in two small attractive restaurants, well kept Greene King ales, decent wine, good coffee, efficient service; piped music, darts; children welcome; bedrooms – a pleasant quiet place to stay *(Derek and Sylvia Stephenson, John Wooll, JKW)*

Edgefield [TG0934]

Three Pigs: Unpretentious pub with 18th-c smuggling connections, friendly landlord, chatty atmosphere, well kept ales, limited but sensible choice of generous food; attractive and secluded site for a few caravan tourers at the back *(Ken and Jeni Black)*

Elsing [TG0516]

Mermaid: Welcoming local, bright clean L-shaped bar, good value usual food inc Sun lunch, well kept Adnams, Woodfordes and a guest ale, friendly helpful landlord, pool table one end; nice garden, church opp with interesting brasses, small quiet village *(John Wooll, Perry and June Dann)*

Fakenham [TF9229]

Henry IV [Greenway Lane]: Extensively refurbished as Hungry Horse dining pub, useful for reasonably priced food, Greene King ales, friendly if not always speedy service; local and RAF pictures *(R C Vincent)*

Framingham Earl [TG2702]

Railway [Norwich Rd (B1332)]: Modern food pub under friendly new management, with good choice of beers, generous home-cooked food from sandwiches to good vegetarian dishes and steaks *(Martin and Caroline Page)*

Framingham Pigot [TG2703]

Old Feathers [Loddon Rd (A146)]: Comfortable well laid-out dining pub, friendly staff, airy conservatory restaurant, wide choice of good value very generous food inc good well priced Sun lunch *(Sue Rowland, Paul Mallett)*

Geldeston [TM3991]

☆ *Locks* [off A143/A146 NW of Beccles; off Station Rd S of village, obscurely signed down long rough track]: Remote drinking pub alone at the navigable head of the River Waveney, virtually unchanged in several decades (and certainly in the more than 40 years your editor has known it), ancient candlelit core with brick walls, tile floor, big log fire, well worn assorted chairs and tables, Woodfordes ales tapped from casks, friendly informal service; big extension for summer crowds and w/e reggae nights, summer evening barbecues, meadow camping; may be cl winter weekdays *(LYM, Howard and Sue Gascoyne, S Pyle)*

Gooderstone [TF7601]

Swan: Neat and unassuming village pub doubling as PO, notable for huge picturesque back garden with big play area; good value generous food, well kept local Celtic and Elgoods, conservatory with pool and TV; opp historic church, handy for nearby water gardens *(Ted George)*

Great Cressingham [TF8401]

☆ *Windmill* [Water End, just off A1064 Swaffham—Brandon; OS Sheet 144 map ref 849016]: Roomy family pub with three beamed bars, cosy nooks and crannies, huge log fireplace, lots of farm tools, conservatory, games room, SkyTV; good value generous food, friendly prompt service, well kept Adnams, Batemans, Bass, Sam Smiths and guest beers, decent wines; well kept big garden, dogs allowed *(Anthony Barnes, Minda and Stanley Alexander, Charles and Pauline Stride, K H Frostick)*

Great Ellingham [TM0196]

☆ *Crown* [pub signed off B1077, which is off A11 SW of Norwich]: Neatly kept open-plan bar well divided into quiet alcoves, comfortable plush and other seats, soft lighting, relaxed atmosphere, enjoyable food inc good fresh fish and seafood, home-made bread and pickles, bargain lunches, three small attractive dining rooms (one for families), well kept Adnams, John Smiths, Woodfordes Wherry and local Wolf, good friendly service, tables in garden; no dogs *(Gwen and Peter Andrews, BB, Adrian White, Bill and Sheila McLardy)*

Great Yarmouth [TG5207]

Star [Hall Quay]: Smart hotel's oak-panelled lounge bar with chandeliers, cosy armchairs, military bric-a-brac and quay view, Woodfordes and other real ales, some straight from the barrel; bedrooms *(Kevin Blake)*

Haddiscoe [TM4497]

Crown [A143 SW of Gt Yarmouth]: Spacious and comfortable former coaching inn, interesting bric-a-brac, good home-made food from baguettes, burgers and Fri fish and chip suppers to restaurant meals inc Sun lunch, well kept Courage Directors and Greene King IPA, good service *(Sue Rowland, Paul Mallett, M and C Starling)*

Hainford [TG2218]

Chequers [Stratton Rd]: Comfortable and friendly rebuilt thatched cottage in charming setting, well prepared food from filled baguettes up, real ales such as Courage Directors, Fullers ESB and John Smiths, big airy bar area and rooms off, pleasant staff, well arranged gardens with play area; piped music; children welcome *(B and C Clouting, Ian Phillips)*

Happisburgh [TG3830]

Pebbles [the village is pronounced Hazeboro]: Good value food from hot filled rolls to Sun roast, beers inc Adnams, Greene King IPA and Shepherd Neame Spitfire, friendly landlord; heavily refurbished *(Derek and Sylvia Stephenson)*

Harpley [TF7825]

Rose & Crown [off A148 Fakenham—Kings Lynn]: Good home-made food inc fresh veg, unusual vegetarian dishes and good children's meals in small comfortable lounge, well kept Greene King IPA and Tetleys, decent wine, helpful efficient service; high chairs provided; lovely garden with play equipment inc an unusual tyre arrangement, quietly attractive village *(John Wooll, R C Vincent)*

Hethersett [TG1404]

☆ *Kings Head* [Old Norwich Rd (B1172)]: Cheerful and homely traditional pub with well kept Courage Directors, Marstons Pedigree,

Morlands Old Speckled Hen and Woodfordes Wherry, substantial good value food (very popular weekdays with older people), comfortable carpeted lounge, obliging staff, old chairs and tables, big log-burning stove in inglenook, traditional games in cosy public bar, attractive and spacious back lawn, good play area *(Ian Phillips, Brian Horner and Brenda Arthur, LYM)*

Hevingham [TG1921]

☆ *Marsham Arms* [B1149 N of Norwich]: Roomy modern-feeling roadside pub with wide range of good generous straightforward food inc fresh seafood and vegetarian, self-serve salads and children's helpings, well kept ales inc Adnams and Fullers London Pride, good wines and country wines, friendly helpful staff; double family room on right, tables in garden behind; well appointed roomy chalet bedrooms behind, good wheelchair access *(BB, John Wooll)*

Holkham [TF8943]

☆ *Victoria* [A149 near Holkham Hall]: Relaxed and simply furnished brick-and-flint inn with open-plan communicating areas, interesting pictures, well kept Adnams, Greene King IPA and Tetleys, decent house wine, log fire, good service; dominoes, cribbage, piped music; children allowed in restaurant, tables outside; bedrooms, handy for coastal nature reserves, open all day Sat *(C J Machin, P Sheard, LYM)*

Holme next the Sea [TF7043]

White Horse [Kirkgate St]: Good value generous food inc tasty fish and chips as well as more adventurous dishes, welcoming licensees and locals, useful two-glass wine bottles, big garden; cl Mon lunchtime *(John Wooll, Anthony Barnes, Pat and Clive Sherriff)*

Holt [TG0738]

☆ *Feathers* [Market Pl]: Interesting locals' bar comfortably extended around original panelled area with open fire, busy on Sat market day, attractive entrance/reception area with antiques, friendly staff, good value promptly served generous food, well kept Greene King IPA and Abbot, decent wines; bedrooms spacious and comfortable *(Keith and Janet Morris, Prof Kenneth Surin)*

Honingham [TG1011]

Buck [just off A47]: Beamed pub with very good range of enjoyable food inc huge sandwiches, vegetarian dishes, lunchtime bargains and nice puddings, well kept ales inc Flowers Original, welcoming licensees *(Don and Shirley Parrish, B and P Lamb)*

Horstead [TG2619]

Recruiting Sergeant [B1150 just S of Coltishall]: Spacious village pub, friendly landlady, generous good value food, Bass, John Smiths and Theakstons, big open fire, brasses and muskets on walls, small separate dining room *(R J Davey, J Mansfield)*

Hunstanton [TF6842]

Marine Bar [part of Marine Hotel, St Edmunds Terr]: Small bar packed with tables (and sometimes with people), prompt welcoming service, wide range of good value quick food all day, Stones and Worthington, lots of china, bric-a-brac and 50s advertisements; tables out on attractive lower fairy-lit terrace, live entertainment summer; bedrooms *(Kevin Blake)*

Kings Lynn [TF6220]

Olde Maydens Heade [Tuesday Mkt Pl]: Large popular recently refurbished Scottish Courage pub doing well under present experienced management, increasing emphasis on food inc good value lunchtime carvery (special OAP price), efficient service; all ages at lunchtime and a younger set in the evening *(R C Vincent, Tony Hobden, Charles Bardswell)*

Wildfowler [Gayton Rd, Gaywood]: Useful Big Steak pub, smart but comfortable and relaxed even when busy, popular food inc children's menu (fun packs for them), good choice of wines in big glasses, fast friendly service, maybe a guest beer such as Morlands Old Speckled Hen, separate non-food adult area *(R C Vincent)*

Langley Street [TG3601]

Wherry: Simple comfort, good range of Woodfordes, bar food and pretty cottagey dining area; well placed for nice walks *(Alan and Paula McCully)*

Letheringsett [TG0538]

☆ *Kings Head* [A148 just W of Holt]: Set well back from the road like a private house, with plenty of tables on spacious lawn, informally furnished but (not smart) with sepia prints of Norfolk life, friendly staff, well kept Adnams, Greene King IPA and Abbot and Woodfordes Wherry, usual food from sandwiches to steaks inc children's, log fire, small lounge, games room with darts, pool, shove ha'penny, dominoes, cribbage, fruit machines; piped music, occasional live, children and dogs welcome, open all day *(Martin and Caroline Page, Bernard and Marjorie Parkin, M J Morgan, LYM)*

Loddon [TM3698]

Swan [just off A146 Norwich—Lowestoft]: 17th-c coaching inn in attractive village not far from the water, long bar with lounge at one end and upstairs bar with pool table and video games, good choice of generous home-made food, good range of real ales, friendly service, simple décor, separate dining room; seats in yard outside *(A J Thomas, Val and Alan Green)*

Needham [TM2281]

Red Lion: Popular dining pub with wide food choice, Greene King IPA and Theakstons; large back garden with caravan park *(Nick and Alison Dowson)*

North Elmham [TF9820]

☆ *Kings Head* [B1110/B1145 N of E Dereham]: Welcoming inn with wide choice of good value basic home-cooked food in log-fire lounge or lovely small dining room; friendly efficient service even when busy, Scottish Courage ales and Greene King IPA, good coffee, unusual hat collection and coaching prints, no-smoking room, restaurant, games room with pool and darts; children welcome, quiet piped music; garden with play area; big character old-

fashioned bedrooms, pleasant walks *(JJW, CMW, Graham and Lynn Mason)*

North Wootton [TF6424]

House on the Green [Ling Common Rd]: Doing well under present owners, roomy lounge with reasonably priced Sun roasts, wide range of food on other days inc good vegetarian, pleasant back garden with lots of tables, bowling green and some play equipment *(R C Vincent)*

Northrepps [TG2439]

Parsons Pleasure: Converted tithe barn with well kept Greene King IPA and Abbot and good food in lively and friendly bar and restaurant; bedrooms *(D E Twitchett)*

Norwich [TG2308]

Bedfords [Old Post Office Yard]: Wine bar not pub, with keg or nitrokeg beers, but worth knowing for good reasonably priced food in beamed upstairs room; good choice of good wines *(John Wooll)*

Bell [Timber Hill]: Wetherspoons – good value, no music, pleasant furnishings and atmosphere, well kept ales inc Adnams Extra and Woodfordes Wherry; open all day *(Anthony Barnes)*

Eaton Cottage [Mount Pleasant, off A11]: Very tidy and well run, with comfortable lounge and nice atmosphere *(Richard Houghton)*

Pickwick [Earlham Rd]: Comfortably converted spacious 1830s town house, raised lounge on right, darts and pool on left, recently extended restaurant, well kept Boddingtons, Greene King Abbot and Tetleys, good coffee, wide choice of good value generous standard food from doorstep sandwiches up, Sun carvery, usual pub memorabilia *(Chris Mawson, Ian Phillips, Paul Maccett, Sue Rowland)*

Take Five [St Andrews Hill, next to Cinema City]: Not a pub (in the evenings you can get in only through Cinema City for which it serves as the cafeteria), but very pleasant relaxed atmosphere, with well kept Woodfordes ales with a guest such as Shepherd Neame, also two farm ciders and very good choice of wines by the glass; good value vegetarian-oriented food, changing local art, piped classical music; can get a bit smoky, but some no-smoking tables; tables in nice old courtyard *(Peter and Pat Frogley, Tim Barrow, Sue Demont, J Middis)*

Pulham Market [TM1986]

Crown: Beautiful low thatched white pub by church overlooking green, heavy beams, unusual mix of pictures, very welcoming landlady, plentiful well cooked food, well kept beer, well behaved dog and a couple of cats, good service even when very busy *(Helen Winter, Keith Berrett, Mike and Mary Carter)*

Reedham [TG4101]

☆ *Ferry Inn* [B1140 Beccles—Acle; two-car ferry till 10pm]: Popular with boaters (free mooring and showers if you eat here), with well spaced tables on waterside terrace, long modern front conservatory bar (part no smoking), secluded dimly lit back bar with antique rifles, copper

and brass, and fine log fire, well kept Adnams, Greene King Abbot, and Woodfordes Wherry, nice country wines; food service, usually quick and friendly, may slow in summer; good arrangements for families, piped music; interesting wood-turner's shop next door *(David Carr, Tim Barrow, Sue Demont, Paul and Sandra Embleton, Alan and Paula McCully, Ian Phillips, Mike and Mary Carter, Tina and David Woods-Taylor, M A Buchanan, LYM, June and Perry Dann, John Wooll, Bronwen and Steve Wrigley)*
Ship: Nice atmosphere, reasonably priced food, well kept beer, good range of games in family room; fascinating swing bridge for railway *(Keith Berrett)*

Rockland St Mary [TG3104]
New Inn: Over rd from staithe, views from attractive barn-style restaurant extension, well kept Bass, friendly obliging staff, reasonably priced generous food, daily papers for sale from 8.30; front terrace tables, back garden, good walks to Rockland Broad and bird hides *(Alan and Paula McCully)*

Roydon [TM0980]
White Hart [A1066 just W of Diss]: New landlord settling well into roomy and attractive partly 15th-c pub, brasses on beams, good value generous well cooked food, changing beers such as Marstons, restaurant *(June and Perry Dann, G Neighbour)*

Rushall [TM1982]
Half Moon: Spotless extended 16th-c coaching inn popular for wide choice of competitively priced food inc lots of fish and imaginative puddings; Adnams, Woodfordes and other real ales; bedrooms in adjacent chalets *(Ian and Nita Cooper)*

Salthouse [TG0743]
Dun Cow [A149 Blakeney—Sheringham]: Extensively refurbished pub looking over salt marshes, good bar food, well kept Greene King and other ales, open fires, stripped beams and cob walls; children welcome, blues nights, big attractive walled garden with figs, apples and play area, good walks and birdwatching nearby (also seafood/samphire shack) *(Miss S P Watkin, P A Taylor)*

Scole [TM1579]
☆ *Scole Inn* [off A140 bypass just N of A143]: Stately old coaching inn of outstanding architectural interest, with a real sense of history, antique settles, old oak chairs and tables, huge inglenook log fires, old prints and collectables and other old-fashioned features in lounge and bare-boards public bar; decent bar food from baguettes up, more elaborate menu in large no-smoking restaurant, well kept Adnams, Courage Directors and summer guest beers on handpump or tapped from the cask, friendly staff; cribbage, dominoes, piped music; children welcome, open all day, comfortable bedrooms *(Dr B Lake, Ian Phillips, Pat and Bill Pemberton, LYM, Neil Spink)*

Sedgeford [TF7136]
☆ *King William IV* [B1454, off A149 Kings Lynn—Hunstanton]: Relaxed and friendly local with energetic landlord, consistently

good straightforward food inc Sun roast with good veg, warm woodburner, fast service, well kept Bass and Worthington, decent wine, restaurant; children allowed in lounge if eating, weekly music and quiz nights *(John Wooll, Ted George)*

Sheringham [TG1543]
Two Lifeboats [on promenade]: Lovely sea view from comfortable lounge and terrace tables, no-smoking restaurant and cosier rooms behind, big helpings of good value usual food inc fresh fish, well kept Greene King ales, helpful friendly service; bedrooms reasonably priced *(R C Vincent, Anthony Barnes, Catherine and Richard Preston)*

South Wootton [TF6422]
Farmers Arms [part of Knights Hill Hotel, Grimston Rd (A148/A149)]: Olde-worlde conversion of barn and stables, wide choice of tasty reasonably priced food all day in bar and restaurant inc vegetarian, Scottish Courage ales with a guest such as Marstons Pedigree, good wines, abundant coffee, friendly service; children welcome, open all day; comfortable motel bedrooms, health club *(John Wooll, R C Vincent)*
Swan [Nursery Lane]: Good value home cooking in small old-fashioned two-bar pub overlooking village green, duckpond and bowling green; conservatory dining area, well kept Scottish Courage ales and Greene King IPA, small enclosed garden with play area *(John Wooll, Ted George)*

Stanhoe [TF8036]
☆ *Crown* [B1155 towards Burnham Mkt]: Cosy and friendly Elgoods local, popular good value home cooking inc excellent game (food may stop early on quiet evenings), well kept Elgoods Cambridge, decent wine and coffee, convivial licensees, small bright bar, central log fire, one beam studded with hundreds of coins; well behaved children welcome; tables on side lawn, lots of fancy fowl (and chicks) outside; caravan site, s/c cottage available *(Charles Bardswell, R C Vincent, Ted George, BB, John Wooll)*

Surlingham [TG3206]
☆ *Coldham Hall* [signed off A146 just SE of A47 Norwich ring rd, then Coldham Hall s]: Lovely position, with picnic-sets by big well kept waterside lawn with shrubs, weeping willows and moorings, plenty of walks; well kept Courage Directors, Greene King Abbot and Marstons Pedigree, wide choice of enjoyable generous food, comfortable high-backed settles, friendly service, woodburner, pool in games area, Broads-view dining area, sensible dress code, well reproduced piped music (also juke box); children in family room, open all day in summer *(A J Thomas, BB, Alan and Paula McCully)*

Thetford [TL8783]
☆ *Bell* [King St]: Attractive beamed and timbered bar with Adnams and Greene King ales, obliging staff and generously served bar food; part of otherwise spaciously modern Forte hotel; tables out behind, bedrooms *(Pam Adsley, BB)*

Thompson [TL9296]

☆ *Chequers* [Griston Rd, off A1075 S of Watton]: Long, low and picturesque 15th-c thatched house with interesting good food inc vegetarian in series of olde-worlde quaint rooms, well kept Adnams, Fullers London Pride, Greene King IPA and local Wolf, good modestly priced wine list, friendly service, low beams, inglenooks, some stripped brickwork, antique tools and traps; games machines; tables outside (*Anthony Barnes, Maurice E Southon, Mick Hitchman, LYM, Pam and David Bailey, G F Tomlinson, Mr and Mrs Peter Chance, Adrian White*)

Thornham [TF7343]

☆ *Kings Head* [Church St/A149]: Pretty old pub with lots of hanging baskets, roomy low-beamed bars with banquettes in well lit bays, decent food inc vegetarian and fresh fish, Greene King IPA and Abbot, Marstons Pedigree and Tetleys, friendly service, open fire, no-smoking area; dogs allowed; well spaced tables on back lawn with barbecues, three homely and comfortable bedrooms, pleasant walks (*Paul Kitchener, MDN, O K Smyth*)

Thorpe Market [TG2335]

Green Farm [A149 N Walsham—Cromer]: Hotel based on 16th-c farmhouse, good value original food inc vegetarian in big pine-furnished lounge bar and smart restaurant, log fire, friendly attentive service, local Buffys and Wolf real ales; children welcome, attractive bedrooms (*Mr and Mrs L Lesbirel*)

Titchwell [TF7543]

Three Horseshoes [A149]: Good range of generous bar food, well kept Adnams and Woodfordes Wherry and friendly service in refurbished bar with rough walls, exposed wood, beams and struts, log fires; family room, restaurant, play area in garden overlooking RSPB reserve; peaceful pleasantly furnished bedrooms, handy for beach (*Charles Bardswell*)

Wells next the Sea [TF9143]

☆ *Robert Catesby* [Staithe St]: Very small bar serving three very different attractive rooms, one pink and carpeted, others more pubby; new owners doing good food using only fresh local produce, reasonable prices, well kept Adnams and Woodfordes Wherry, quick friendly service; picnic-sets in lovely walled yard (*M Lickert, Pat and Tony Martin*)

West Rudham [TF8127]

☆ *Dukes Head* [A148 Fakenham—Kings Lynn]: 17th-c, with three attractively homely rooms, relaxed mix of locals and visitors, short choice of good generous home-made food from sandwiches to local fish and game, well kept Adnams, Woodfordes Wherry and Shepherd Neame, decent wines, good coffee, friendly landlord, polite service, log fires, newspapers and plenty of books, interesting cricketing prints; no dogs (*John Wooll, Derek and Sylvia Stephenson, BB*)

West Runton [TG1842]

Village Inn: Large pub reopened and renovated by landlord of Saracens Head nr Erpingham,

so should be good though no reports yet; bar snacks, big back room doing food all day from breakfast on, restaurant, large garden area with separate snack counter (*anon*)

Weybourne [TG1042]

Maltings: Cosy and comfortable, with good reasonably priced food inc good choice of fresh vegetarian and local fish, well kept local Wolf beer, helpful staff (*Miss S P Watkin, P A Taylor*)

Wiveton [TG0342]

☆ *Bell*: Big welcoming open-plan local with lots of Jaguar and other motoring mementoes (even an engine in the fireplace), dozens of model planes, good usual food with interesting specials, well kept beers such as Morlands Old Speckled Hen, Wolf BB, Woodfordes Wherry and ones brewed for them in Suffolk and given Jaguar-related names, daily papers, piped music (may be loud); more automania in carpeted no-smoking conservatory, picnic-sets on lawn and small garden behind with personal hibachi-substitutes apparently made from car bits; dogs welcome; bedrooms (*BB, Charles Bardswell, Tracey and Stephen Groves*)

Wreningham [TM1598]

☆ *Bird in Hand* [outside village, just off B1113 E of Wymondham]: Roomy tastefully refurbished dining pub with wide choice of decent reasonably priced food from sandwiches up inc unusual vegetarian dishes, well presented Sun lunch and OAP midweek lunches; well kept Whitbreads-related and Woodfordes ales, good friendly service, local bygones and Lotus car photographs, Victorian-style panelled restaurant; quiet piped pop music; picnic-sets in neatly kept garden (*BB, Paul Mallett, Sue Rowland, Martin and Caroline Page*)

Wroxham [TG2814]

☆ *Green Man* [Rackheath; A1151 towards Norwich]: Well kept and comfortable, with easy chairs, plush banquettes and other seats in open-plan bar, log fires, interesting WWII memorabilia (nearby air base), good value popular food (two small dining areas can get crowded) inc generous Sun lunch, friendly landlord, well kept ales such as Greene King Triumph and Woodfordes Wherry and Nelsons Revenge; children in eating areas, beautifully kept bowling green (*LYM, R J Davey, J Mansfield*)

Hotel Wroxham [Bridge Precinct]: Modern building with large bar and dining area, picture windows and terrace overlooking River Bure, waterfowl hoping for food, good value generous carvery with help-yourself veg and children's prices, well kept ales such as Adnams, Woodfordes Wherry and Nog, maybe a bargain guest (*JDM, KM*)

Wymondham [TG1101]

Cross Keys [Market Pl]: Attractive old pub with friendly staff and locals, relaxed atmosphere, well kept Sam Smiths, usual food from sandwiches up; piped music; bedrooms simple but clean and reasonably priced (*Ian Phillips*)

Northamptonshire

A good range of attractive pubs here, many with good food (and often usefully placed for motorways or major roads). Places which have been earning more than their due share of praise from readers recently are the busy Windmill at Badby (good all round – food, service and accommodation), the George & Dragon at Chacombe (great atmosphere, well kept beers, and a Food Award granted this year for its good fish, pasta and vegetarian dishes), the Red Lion at Crick (good food and beer), the very welcoming and relaxed Eastcote Arms at Eastcote, the Falcon at Fotheringhay (particular praise for the interesting food), the interesting Fox & Hounds at Great Brington, the White Swan at Harringworth (new licensees), the friendly old Ship in Oundle, the Three Conies at Thorpe Mandeville (back in these pages after a break of quite a few years) and the welcoming Kings Head at Wadenhoe. From among all these the Falcon at Fotheringhay wins the accolade of Northamptonshire Dining Pub of the Year. Some stars in the Lucky Dip section at the end of the chapter include the New Inn at Abthorpe, Olde Coach House at Ashby St Ledgers, Maltsters Arms at Badby, Red Lion at Hellidon, Marston Inn at Marston St Lawrence, Sun at Marston Trussell, White Horse at Old and Vane Arms at Sudborough. Drinks prices here are generally just a very few pence higher than the national average; we often found Hook Norton beer here at below-average prices.

BADBY SP5559 Map 4
Windmill 🍽 🛏
Village signposted off A361 Daventry—Banbury

Over the year, there have been several glowing reports on the warm friendly service at this attractive old thatched inn, set in a peaceful village. A gentle balance is struck between traditional, unsophisticated pubby charm and efficient management, and this is reflected by the comfortable mix of locals and businessmen in the two chatty beamed and flagstoned bars with cricketing and rugby pictures and appropriately simple country furnishings in good solid wood. There's an enormous inglenook fireplace in one area, a cosy and comfortable lounge and pleasant modern hotel facilities for staying guests – an unobtrusive modern extension is well hidden at the back. Good popular bar food is served promptly and in generous helpings and might include home-made sandwiches (from £2.25 to triple-decker £5.25), soup (£2.75), crispy whitebait, goat's cheese on garlic bread with basil and tomato or ploughman's (£4.25), lasagne or chilli (£6.50), deep-fried jalapeno chillies and cream cheese (£6.95), home-made pie of the day (£7.25), venison burgers or scampi (£7.50), chicken breast with a white wine and stilton sauce (£8.50), 8oz sirloin steak (£9.50) and roast barbary duck with orange and port sauce (£10.50); daily specials; puddings (from £3.25), and children's meals (from £2.95). There's a pleasant restaurant and marquee in summer. Well kept Bass, Boddingtons, Flowers Original, Highgate Dark Mild and Wadworths 6X on handpump; dominoes, piped music. *(Recommended by Ray Roberts, Anthony Barnes, JKW, Eric Locker, G Braithwaite, Howard and Margaret Buchanan, Susan and John Douglas, Basil and Suzy Wynbergen, John Brightley, George Little, George Atkinson, Mr and Mrs C J Pulman, K H Frostick)*

Free house ~ Licensees John Freestone and Carol Sutton ~ Real ale ~ Bar food ~ Restaurant ~ (01327) 702363 ~ Children welcome ~ Jazz one Sat every month ~ Open 11.30-3(4.30 Sat), 5.30-11; 12-4.30, 6-10.30 Sun ~ Bedrooms: £49B/£65B

CHACOMBE SP4943 Map 4
George & Dragon 🍴

2½ miles from M40 junction 11: A361 towards Daventry, then village signposted on right; Silver Street

Genuinely relaxing, this charming village pub is an extremely welcome break to drivers on the nearby M40. The tidy spacious bar has comfortable seats, beams, flagstones, and logs burning in a massive fireplace, and Courage Directors, Theakstons XB and Best on handpump; fruit wines. A wide range of good imaginative food from a changing blackboard might include sandwiches (from £3.50), pears poached in ginger with a passion fruit sorbet (£3.95), baguettes with fillings such as coronation chicken or roasted vegetables and pesto (£4.95), good vegetarian meals such as baked cauliflower and broccoli in a mustard and herb sauce (£7.25) or fennel sautéed with mushrooms and courgettes in a brandy cream sauce (£7.95), artichoke ravioli with prawn sauce (£7.50), chicken breast wrapped in smoked bacon with a cheese sauce (£9.25), roasted red snapper with chilli and samphire or seafood medley with tarragon and rice (£10.45), and 8oz sirloin (£11.95); puddings such as chocolate marble cheesecake or hot ginger pudding (£3.25). The friendly and attentive service copes with people who need to get back on the road fairly quickly yet doesn't hurry those who have more time to spare. Afternoon teas and snacks; no-smoking area in restaurant; darts, dominoes and piped music. The friendly black and white cats are called Sooty and Elliot. One of the bedrooms has a sunken bath and built-in Breton bed. *(Recommended by Ted George, Ian Phillips, Howard and Margaret Buchanan, R J Frearson, George Atkinson, Mr and Mrs C Moncreiffe, John Bramley, Stephen, Julie and Hayley Brown, K H Frostick, Dr and Mrs Cottrell)*

Free house ~ Licensee Ray Bennett ~ Real ale ~ Bar food (12-9.30) ~ Restaurant ~ (01295) 711500 ~ Children welcome ~ Open 12-11(10.30 Sun) ~ Bedrooms: £39.50B/£56B

CHAPEL BRAMPTON SP7266 Map 4
Brampton Halt

Pitsford Road; off A50 N of Northampton

Roger Thom, the chatty licensee who left the pub a year ago, is back with his daughter Caroline at this attractive Victorian station master's house standing alone by the little Northampton & Lamport Railway. A stop here makes part of a terrific day out for the family. There are train rides at weekends with additional bank holiday and Santa specials, and the Nene Valley Way – a 14 mile walk and cycle-way – runs along an adjacent converted old track through pretty countryside. Inside, one low-ceilinged area with a woodburning stove has wash drawings of steam trains; by the bar counter, a high-raftered dining area has dagging shears and other agricultural bygones; there's Victorian-style floral wallpaper throughout, with matching swagged curtains, and furnishings are sturdily comfortable. There are a few tables in a small sun lounge. Bar food includes soup (£2.50), filled french bread (from £3.95), ham and eggs or various burgers such as chicken, beef or spicy bean (£5.50), warm chicken and bacon salad (£5.95) and sirloin steak (£8.95); puddings (£2.95). Well kept Adnams, Everards Old Original and Tiger, Fullers London Pride and a guest such as Boddingtons on handpump; decent wines; friendly service; trivia, maybe piped music. They may stay open all day at weekends when the weather's fine. *(Recommended by Ted George, George Atkinson, Stephen Brown, Penny and Martin Fletcher)*

Free house ~ Licensees Roger and Caroline Thom ~ Real ale ~ Bar food (not Sunday) ~ (01604) 842676 ~ Children in eating area of bar ~ Open 11.30-2.30, 5.30-11

All main entries have been inspected anonymously by the Editor or Assistant Editor. We accept no payment for inclusion, no advertising, and no sponsorship from the drinks industry – or from anyone else.

CLIPSTON SP7181 Map 4

Bulls Head ◧

B4036 S of Market Harborough

The story behind the hundreds of coins that glisten from the black beams of this delightful atmospheric village inn, lies in an odd tradition started by US airmen based nearby during World War II – they used to wedge the money in cracks and crannies of the ancient woodwork while waiting for their next drink. Readers report a warm welcome from the friendly licensees, their staff and the two white west highland terriers, Rags and Daisy. The convivial bar is divided into three cosily dim and snug areas leading down from the servery, with comfortable seats, sturdy small settles and stools upholstered in red plush, a grandmother clock, some harness and tools, and a log fire. Well kept Batemans, Flowers, Hook Norton, Morlands Old Speckled Hen, Stones Bitter and Timothy Taylor Landlord on handpump, and an incredible choice of 556 malt whiskies. There's a dining area in the room at the back with oak settles, high-back chairs and a grandfather clock keeping time; the walls are hung with china meat plates. Good food includes sandwiches (from £1.85), soup (£2.20), ploughman's (from £3.95), drunken bull pie (steak, kidney and mushrooms in a Guinness gravy), home-made minced beef pie or home-baked ham and eggs as well as a good choice of vegetarian dishes from the menu and specials board such as spinach and mushroom lasagne or provençale nut wellington (£6.50), hawaiian gammon with pineapple and cheese or chicken filled with stilton wrapped in bacon with mustard and wine sauce (£7.95), steak with onions, mushrooms and bacon (£9.50), and fresh fish specials on Thursday and Friday such as cod and chips (£5.95) and Greenland halibut or red sea bream (£7.95). Among the puddings (£2.25), home-made fruit pies are a speciality, with the landlord using his experience of 19 years as a greengrocer to create suitable seasonal fillings. Table skittles, fruit machine, dominoes and piped music. Slightly saucy pin-ups decorate the gents', and indeed the ladies'. Outside, a terrace has a few white tables under cocktail parasols. *(Recommended by Sue and Mike Loseby, Ted George, Mr and Mrs A Bull, Chris Gabbitas, Hugh McPhail, B Adams, Charles and Pauline Stride, Greg Kilminster, Rona Murdoch, George Atkinson)*

Free house ~ Licensees Jenny and Colin Smith ~ Real ale ~ Bar food (11.30-2.30, 6.30-9.30; not Mon) ~ Restaurant ~ (01858) 525268 ~ Children in eating area of bar ~ Open 11.30-2.30, 6.30-11; 12-3, 7-10.30 Sun; closed Monday lunchtime and 25 Dec ~ Bedrooms: £29.50B/£39.50B

CRICK SP5872 Map 4

Red Lion ◧ £

A mile from M1 junction 18; A428

Hearty good value food, friendly service, well kept ales and the added bonus of it being only a mile from the M1, keep this dark sandstone old thatched pub popular with readers. With a relaxed and welcoming atmosphere, it's quietest and snuggest in the inner part of the low-ceilinged bar. No noisy games machines or piped music, and lots of comfortable seating. Four changing beers might include Marstons Pedigree, Morlands Old Speckled Hen, Theakstons Best and Websters Yorkshire on handpump. Lunchtime snacks include sandwiches (from £1.45), ploughman's (from £2.60), and main courses such as chicken and mushroom pie, leek and smoky bacon bake, plaice or vegetable pancake rolls (all £3.90); in the evening they offer a wider range of dishes including gammon or rainbow trout (£6.50), lamb cutlets (£7), steaks (from £9) and a more extensive choice of vegetarian meals. There are a few picnic-sets under cocktail parasols on grass by the car park, and in summer you can eat on the terrace in the old coach yard which is sheltered by a Perspex roof; lots of pretty hanging baskets. *(Recommended by Ted George, Val and Alan Green, Janet Box, Rona Murdoch, Ian Phillips, J M Hoare, CMW, JJW, K Stevens, P J Keen, Mr and Mrs Staples)*

Free house ~ Licensees Tom and Paul Marks ~ Real ale ~ Bar food (not Sun evening) ~ (01788) 822342 ~ Under 14s in snug at lunchtime only ~ Open 11-2.30, 6.15-11; 12-3, 7-10.30 Sun

EAST HADDON SP6668 Map 4

Red Lion 🍺 🛏

High St; village signposted off A428 (turn right in village) and off A50 N of Northampton

The well appointed neat lounge bar of this rather elegant substantially-built golden stone hotel will appeal to antiques lovers. Along with oak panelled settles, white-painted panelling, library chairs, soft modern dining chairs, and a mix of oak, mahogany and cast-iron-framed tables are recessed china cabinets, old prints and pewter, and little kegs, brass pots, swords and so forth hung sparingly on a couple of beams. The small public bar has sturdy old-fashioned red leather seats. Very well kept real ales such as Adnams Broadside, Charles Wells Eagle and Bombardier on handpump, and decent wines; piped music. Popular (if not cheap) bar food from a daily changing menu might include soups (£3), sandwiches (from £3.75), chicken liver pâté (£6.95), cheese platter with fruit and crunchy bread (£7.95), Loch Fyne kippers with scrambled eggs, lincolnshire sausage and red wine casserole with a cheese and mustard yorkshire pudding or mushroom and cashew nut roast with tomato sauce (£8.95), chicken chasseur or pie of the day (£9.95), roasted lamb shank with port sauce (£10.95) and sirloin steak topped with mushrooms, onions and melted cheese (£13.95); puddings such as apple pie, bakewell tart or chocolate roulade (£3.50). It's worth booking for their three-course set Sunday lunch (£19.95) and there's a more elaborate menu in the pretty restaurant; good breakfasts. The walled side garden is a pleasant place to enjoy coffee after a meal, with lilac, fruit trees, roses and neat little flowerbeds; it leads back to the bigger lawn, which has well spaced picnic-sets. There are more tables under cocktail parasols on a small side terrace, and a big copper beech shades the gravel car park. *(Recommended by Ian Phillips, Martin and Penny Fletcher, Maysie Thompson, Susan and John Douglas, B A Lord, David Rule, Ted George, Anthony Barnes)*

Charles Wells ~ Tenant Ian Kennedy ~ Real ale ~ Bar food (not Sun evening) ~ Restaurant ~ (01604) 770223 ~ Children in eating area of bar and restaurant (over 14s only in evenings) ~ Open 11.30-2.30, 6-11; 12-2.30, 7-10.30 Sun; closed 25 Dec ~ Bedrooms: £60B/£75B

EASTCOTE SP6753 Map 4

Eastcote Arms

Gayton Rd; village signposted from A5 3 miles N of Towcester

Despite last year's redecorations and the recent emphasis on more sophisticated evening food, this friendly village pub remains reassuringly unpretentious – on one occasion some readers spotted a barn owl perched on a table by his master. A relaxed atmosphere prevails in the bar with lots of rugby prints above the maroon dado, as well as traditional furnishings with two imitation log fires, cottagey curtains, fresh flowers; dominoes, cribbage, and unobtrusive piped music. Well-liked lunchtime snacks include sandwiches (from £2), filled baguettes (from £2.50), filled baked potatoes (from £3), double egg and chips (£3.25), ploughman's (from £3.75), fish and chips (£3.95) and steak and ale pie (£5.45); puddings (£2.75). On Friday and Saturday evenings there are more adventurous specials such as wild mushroom risotto with parmesan shavings (£2.75), seafood salad with feta, crispy parma ham and balsamic vinegar (£3.75), 8oz sirloin or spinach and ricotta pasta with a white wine and herb sauce (£7.95), poached salmon with spinach, cheese and mustard velouté (£8.95) and chicken breast stuffed with woodland mushrooms (£9.95); Sunday lunchtime roasts; no-smoking dining room. Well kept Adnams Bitter, Fullers London Pride, Hook Norton Best and a guest on handpump. There are picnic-sets and other tables in an attractive back garden, with roses, geraniums and so forth around the neat lawn. When we went to press, the landlord was seeking permission to build five bedrooms. *(Recommended by K H Frostick, CMW, JJW, Bruce Bird, George Atkinson, Anthony Barnes)*

Free house ~ Licensees John and Wendy Hadley ~ Real ale ~ Bar food (not Mon lunchtime or evenings Sun-Thurs) ~ Restaurant ~ (01327) 830731 ~ Children in restaurant ~ Open 12-2.30, 6-11; 12-3, 7-10.30 Sun; closed Monday lunchtime except bank hols

FARTHINGSTONE SP6155 Map 4

Kings Arms ♈ ◀

Off A5 SE of Daventry; village signposted from Litchborough on former B4525 (now declassified)

Having been unable to find a suitable replacement chef, the friendly licensees of this handsome 18th-c stone pub now only serve food at weekend lunchtimes. However readers' reports show that the new changing menu of interesting bar food is popular, with dishes such as home-made soup (£2.55), filled baguettes (from £3.75), macaroni and lentil bake (£6.55), thai-style chicken or salmon fillet in a fennel and whole-grain mustard sauce (£6.65), mandarin pork steak (£6.75), lamb and rosemary cassoulet (£6.90), duck in plum and ginger sauce (£7.55), game casserole (£7.85), and highly praised puddings including Tunisian lemon pudding or raspberry meringue (£2.75). They also have plans to introduce interesting cheeses at lunchtimes in the future. The former dining area is now the Egertons' private lounge, but the local crafts (once displayed there) can still be bought along with wines and even olive oil at the counter. There's a huge log fire in the small atmospheric flagstoned bar, with comfortably homely sofas and armchairs near the entrance; whisky-water jugs hang from oak beams, and there are lots of pictures and decorative plates on the walls; a games room at the far end of the bar has darts, dominoes, cribbage, table skittles and board games. Four or five well kept real ales might include Adnams, Black Sheep Bitter, Brakspear, Hook Norton Best and Smiles; decent wines and fruit wines, and good informal service; no credit cards. There are some tables in the neatly kept sheltered garden, and the outside gents' has an interesting newspaper-influenced décor. It's a pretty village, with good walks nearby (including the Knightley Way). *(Recommended by George Atkinson, Simon Collett-Jones, R M Corlett, Joan and Andrew Life, Stephen, Julie and Hayley Brown, Rona Murdoch, Pete Baker, Mrs Mary Walters, David Mead, Bob and Maggie Atherton, John and Shirley Smith, Mike and Jennifer Marsh)*

Free house ~ Licensees Paul and Denise Egerton ~ Real ale ~ Bar food (Sat, Sun lunchtimes only) ~ (01327) 361604 ~ Children in eating area of bar and games room ~ Folk music on first Weds of month ~ Open 6.30(7 in winter)-11; 12-3, 6.30(7 Sun)-11 Sat/Sun

FOTHERINGHAY TL0593 Map 5

Falcon ★ ♈

Village signposted off A605 on Peterborough side of Oundle

Northamptonshire Dining Pub of the Year

A relaxed atmosphere pervades this sophisticated dining pub in the village where Richard III was born; Fotheringhay Castle, where Mary Queen of Scots was executed, is not far away. Many readers have commended the interesting and varied food – now almost a trademark of the Huntsbridge group, to which this pub belongs. Other than lunchtime sandwiches (from £2.95) and ploughman's (from £4.95), the seasonally changing menu might include spicy roast aubergine soup with fresh coriander oil (£3.95), warm salad of chickpeas, feta, chilli and garlic (£4.50), potato and goat's cheese tart with a tomato salsa and goat's cheese fondue or lamb's liver with mashed potato, spinach, bacon, caramelised onions and rosemary gravy (£7.95), grilled smoked haddock with a mustard butter sauce or spicy oriental pork belly hotpot with soft noodles and coriander (£9.75), seared salmon with a tomato, onion and saffron compote or roasted chicken breast with Thai spices, rosti potatoes, Chinese greens and a mushroom Thai sauce (£10.95) and rump steak (£11.50); tasty puddings include plums soaked in Zinfandel with mascarpone cream and cantuccini biscuits or coconut cream with chilli and Malibu-flavoured pineapple (from £3.95); very good value two-course lunch (£9.50); as it can get very busy, it's a good idea to book. The comfortable lounge has cushioned slatback armchairs and bucket chairs, winter log fires in stone fireplaces at each end, fresh flower arrangements, and a hum of quiet conversation; the pleasant conservatory is popular for Sunday lunch and in summer, the terrace is a particularly nice place for an al fresco meal. Locals gather in the much smaller tap bar with darts, cribbage and dominoes; the dining room and conservatory are no-smoking. Well kept Adnams Bitter and Extra, Greene King IPA, and a guest on handpump, and decent wines including a champagne by the glass; helpful staff. The vast church behind is worth a visit. *(Recommended by Ted George, Mike and Sue Loseby, David and Mary Webb, P Vigano, R Inman, Ian Phillips, Michael Sargent, George Atkinson, M and J Back, Tina and David Woods-Taylor, O K Smyth, John Bowdler, M J Morgan, R Wiles, John and Shirley Smith, Eric Locker, Andy and Jill Kassube, A Sutton, Jim Farmer, Maysie Thompson, Derek and Margaret Underwood)*

Free house ~ Licensees Ray Smikle and John Hoskins ~ Real ale ~ Bar food ~ Restaurant ~ (01832) 226254 ~ Children welcome ~ Open 11.30-3, 6-11; 12-3, 7-10.30 Sun; closed Mondays except bank hols

GREAT BRINGTON SP6664 Map 4
Fox & Hounds ★ ◖

Signposted off A428 NW of Northampton, near Althorp Hall; can also be reached via Little Brington, off A45 (heading W from M1 junction 16 it's the first right turn, signed The Bringtons)

You can combine lunch with a horse and carriage ride in summer at this carefully restored golden stone thatched village inn. Inside, the bar has a lovely relaxed atmosphere with lots of old beams and saggy joists, an attractive mix of country tables and chairs on its broad flagstones and bare boards, plenty of snug alcoves, some stripped pine shutters and panelling, two fine log fires, and an eclectic medley of bric-a-brac including an old typewriter and country pictures. There's a good changing range of around a dozen well kept real ales such as Beowulf Heroes Bitter, Brakspear, Fullers London Pride, Greene King IPA and Abbot, Hook Norton Old Hooky, Lloyds Country Gold, Marstons Fever Pitch, Robinsons Old Tom, Summerskills Whistle Belly Vengeance, Timothy Taylor Landlord and Wadworths 6X; country wines. Bar food includes soup (winter only, £3.95), filled baguettes (from £3.95), vegetable bake (£5.95), steak and kidney pie or moules marinières (£6.95), fresh crab salad or Whitby haddock (£7.95), venison casserole (£8.95), steaks (from £8.95) and puddings (£3.95); friendly service. A cellarish games room down steps has pool, darts and table skittles. They hold a quiz on Monday evenings, and as we went to press, they were planning to introduce afternoon teas with a quiz in the autumn. A coach entry goes through to an attractive paved courtyard with sheltered tables, and there are more, with a play area, in the side garden. *(Recommended by Ted George, Simon G S Morton, Brian and Anna Marsden, Dorothee and Dennis Glover, George Atkinson, Simon Collett-Jones, John C Baker, Martin and Penny Fletcher, Francis Johnson, L Granville, J W G Nunns, Susan and John Douglas, P J Robbins, Maysie Thompson, Rona Murdoch)*

Free house ~ Licensee Peter Krempelf ~ Real ale ~ Bar food (lunchtime 12-3) ~ (01604) 770651 ~ Children welcome ~ Live country and blues Tues, jazz Sun ~ Open 11.30-11; 12-10.30 Sun

HARRINGWORTH SP9298 Map 4
White Swan ⇔

Seaton Road; village SE of Uppingham, signposted from A6003, A47 and A43

This limestone-built Tudor inn fills up with a mix of diners and staff from the local stables at lunchtime. The blocked-in traces of its central carriage-entry arch point to its earlier days as a coaching house. Inside the spotless central bar area there are good solid tables, a hand-crafted oak bar counter with a mirror base and handsome swan carving emblazoned on its front, an open fire, and a display of the WWII airfield at nearby Spanhoe among a collection of old village photographs (in which many of the present buildings are clearly recognisable). The roomy and welcoming lounge/eating area has comfortable settles, while a quieter no-smoking dining room hosts a collection of old jugs, craft tools, dried flower arrangements and locally painted watercolours. From a changing blackboard, reasonably priced home-made bar food might include sandwiches (from £2, salmon £3.95), home-made soup

(£2.50), cumberland sausage with bubble and squeak, asparagus au gratin or tuna and prawn pasta (£6.50), chicken breast stuffed with mushrooms, onions and melted stilton (£6.95), salmon with watercress sauce (£7.95), fillet steak topped with stilton (£10.95) and puddings such as lemon crunch, rhubarb crumble or treacle tart (£2.95). Well kept Greene King IPA and Abbot, Marstons Pedigree and maybe a guest such as Batemans XXXB on handpump. Darts, dominoes, cribbage and piped music; tables outside on a little terrace. The attractive village is dominated by the famous 82-arch railway viaduct. *(Recommended by Ian and Nita Cooper, M J Brooks, O K Smyth, Anthony Barnes, Joan and Michel Hooper-Immins)*

Free house ~ Licensees John and Carol Harding ~ Real ale ~ Bar food (12-2, 7-10) ~ Restaurant ~ (01572) 747543 ~ Children in eating area of bar and restaurant ~ Open 11.30-2.30, 6.30-11; 12-3, 7-10.30 Sun ~ Bedrooms: £38.50B/£52B

LOWICK SP9780 Map 4
Snooty Fox 🍴
Village signposted off A6116 Corby—Raunds

This imposing 16th-c inn was once home to the Countess of Peterborough. Nowadays, its atmospheric rooms are filled with customers enjoying the wide choice of food and well kept ales. On cooler days there will be a roaring log fire in the huge stone fireplace in the two-roomed lounge with handsomely moulded dark oak beams and stripped stone walls decorated with a series of prints by Terry Thomas of Guinness advert fame entitled 'A Day in the Life of the Snooty Fox'; neat and attractive dining chairs are set around tables and there's a formidable monumentally carved bar counter. Good bar food from the blackboards above the fireplace might include filled baguettes (from £2.95), soup (£2.95), jalapeno peppers with herb and cream cheese dip (£3.95), stuffed peppers or steak and ale pie (£5.95), fresh plaice or cod (£6.95), grilled tuna steak in a parmesan sauce (£7.95), marinated Nile perch (£8.95) and steaks (from £7.95); puddings such as apple crumble, chocolate fudge cake or sticky toffee pudding (£3.95). Up to six well kept ales might include Adnams Best, Banks Bitter, Bateman Valiant, Everards Beacon and Tiger, and Wards Waggledance on handpump; fruit machine and piped music. The softly floodlit picnic-sets on the grass in front are very inviting on a warm evening. *(Recommended by Joan Morgan, Miss J Torte, Michael and Jenny Back)*

Free house ~ Licensee Geoff Monks ~ Real ale ~ Bar food (12-2, 7-10(9 Sun)) ~ Restaurant ~ (01832) 733434 ~ Children welcome ~ Open 12-3, 6.30-11; 12-3, 7-10.30 Sun

OUNDLE TL0487 Map 5
Mill
Barnwell Rd out of town; or follow Barnwell Country Park signs off A605 bypass

The new licensees have extended the range of ales on handpump at this splendidly restored old mill building: changing weekly, they might include beers from Elgoods, Greene King, Mauldons and Nethergate. The Doomsday Book records a mill on this site, and although it stopped turning in 1930, the waterwheel dates from the early 17th c. Today, customers can watch the stream race below the building through a big glass panel by the entrance. Bar food is available in the upstairs Trattoria that has stalls around tables with more banquettes in bays, stripped masonry and beams, and a millstone feature; its small windows look down over the lower millpond and the River Nene; large no-smoking area. The extensive (not cheap) menu might include soup (£2.95), filled baguettes (from £3), ploughman's (from £3.75), snails in garlic and herb butter (£4.35), roast chicken (£7.95), steak and mushroom pie or haddock fishcakes (£8.55), swordfish (£8.95), vegetable fajitas (£9.95), 8oz rump steak (from £10.55), daily specials such as chicken marinated in cumin, coriander, garlic and coconut milk (£9.95) and mixed grill (£10.95); puddings such as home-made pavlovas, profiteroles and bread and butter pudding (£3.50); large selection of liqueur coffees. A ground floor bar (only open at weekends and from Wednesday to Sunday in summer) has red leatherette button-back built-in wall banquettes against its stripped-stone walls; the beamed top-floor no-smoking restaurant houses the corn hoist; piped music. There are picnic-sets under cocktail parasols among willow trees by the mill pond, with more on the side grass, and some white cast-iron tables on a flagstoned terrace. *(Recommended by Dorothee and Dennis Glover, T R and B C Jenkins, Paul and Sandra Embleton, Ian Phillips)*

Free house ~ Licensees Julia Galligan and Peter Bossard ~ Real ale ~ Bar food ~ Restaurant ~ (01832) 272621 ~ Children in eating area of bar and restaurant ~ Open 11-3, 6.30-11; 11-11 Sat; 12-10.30 Sun

Ship ◖ £

Barnwell Rd out of town; or follow Barnwell Country Park signs off A605 bypass

This cheerful and unpretentious local can get busy with a lively young crowd in the evenings, but has a pleasant mix of customers at lunchtime. A bustling yet friendly and genuinely welcoming atmosphere fills the heavily beamed lounge bar made up of three rooms that lead off the central corridor on the left: up by the street there's a mix of leather and other seats including a very flowery piano stool (and its piano), with sturdy tables and a log fire in a stone inglenook, and down one end a panelled snug has button-back leather seats built in around it; no-smoking snug. Well kept Bass, Fullers London Pride, Hopback Summer Lightning and Tetleys on handpump, a good range of malt whiskies, cappuccino and espressos. Very good value bar food might include sandwiches (from £1.85), soup (£2.25), chicken liver pâté (£3.25), ham, egg and chips (£4), steak and ale pie (£5.50) and lunchtime specials such as barnsley lamb chop or home-made seafood pie (£4.50); puddings might include hot fudge sundae, raspberry meringue or home-made fruit crumble (£2.25). Smiling, efficient service; maybe free Sunday nuts and crisps on the bar. The tiled-floor public side has darts, dominoes, pinball, fruit machine, juke box and piped music. The wooden tables and chairs outside on the series of small sheltered terraces, are lit at night. Several of the clean and comfortable bedrooms are in a recent extension. *(Recommended by Anthony Barnes, Michael and Jenny Back, Michael Sargent, Peter Plumridge)*

Free house ~ Licensees Andrew and Robert Langridge ~ Real ale ~ Bar food ~ (01832) 273918 ~ Children welcome ~ Open 11-11; 12-10.30 Sun ~ Bedrooms: £30B/£50B

SULGRAVE SP5545 Map 4

Star ⇐

E of Banbury, signposted off B4525; Manor Road

One of the more quirky ornaments amassed in the bar of this creeper-covered former farmhouse is the stuffed backside of a fox, seeming to leap into the wall. Plenty of other curios catch one's attention: newspaper front pages recording events such as Kennedy's assassination, the death of Churchill and the first successful hole in the heart operation, other (equally bizarre) stuffed animals such as a hare's head fitted with little antlers to make it resemble a miniature stag and a kangaroo with an Ozzie hanging-corks hat, miners' lamps and various other tools; a blackboard displays an obscure fact of the day. The part by the big inglenook fireplace (with a paper skeleton on its side bench) has polished flagstones, the other part a red carpet, and furnishings are mainly small pews, cushioned window seats and wall benches, kitchen chairs and cast-iron-framed tables. Generous helpings of tasty seasonal dishes from the changing blackboard menu might include very good double-decker sandwiches (from £2.75), soup (£3.50), smoked mackerel and apple mousse (£3.75), ploughman's (£5.75), steak and Hook Norton pie or well liked daily tarts such as watercress and wensleydale or spinach and ricotta (£7.50), lamb and chilli fry (£9), Thai chicken curry, smoked salmon with coriander butter or local trout with gooseberry and dill relish (£9.50), fillet steak with gorgonzola and cream sauce (£11.50) and home-made puddings such as white chocolate torte, cappuccino syllabub or raspberry sorbet (£3.50). Well kept Hook Norton Best, Old Hooky and Double Stout and a monthly changing guest beer on handpump; no-smoking back restaurant; piped music. There's a warm welcome from the friendly staff and one or two very regular locals; some tables outside. Clean and comfortable bedrooms. The pub is on the road to George Washington's ancestral home. *(Recommended by Ted George, R Macnaughton, W M and J M Cottrell, George Atkinson, Dr A Sutton, Anne P Heaton, Patrick Hancock, Richard and Valerie Wright, Mike and Mary Carter, Anthony Barnes, Mr and Mrs J E Lockwood, R M Corlett, Penny and Martin Fletcher)*

Hook Norton ~ Tenant Andrew Willerton ~ Real ale ~ Bar food ~ Restaurant ~ (01295) 760389 ~ Well behaved children in garden ~ Open 11-2.30, 6-11; 12-3, 7-10.30 Sun; closed Sun eves in winter ~ Bedrooms: £35B/£55B

THORPE MANDEVILLE SP5344 Map 4
Three Conies
Village signposted off B4525 E of Banbury

The licensee here ran the Butchers Arms in Farnborough in its heyday back in the mid-1980s (when we awarded it a star and dining award), and is now serving good food at this friendly stone-built 17th-c dining pub with a fine wall-mounted sundial. The main emphasis is on fresh fish, with deliveries from several markets ensuring that more than 10 specials are available every day. Alongside dishes such as mixed seafood salad (£4.50), salmon in cream and tarragon sauce (£7.95), pan-fried marlin and swordfish (£10.50) and whole lobster (£18), the popular platter of the day feeds two people with fish ranging from red snapper and bream to yellow grunter and parrot fish. Other bar food includes soup (£2.95), filled baguettes (from £3.25), steak and kidney pie (£6.50), pasta pillows stuffed with artichoke and cream cheese in a sun-dried tomato sauce (£7.50), 8oz sirloin steak (£8.50) and puddings such as treacle tart, bread and butter pudding and fresh meringue filled with vanilla cream and strawberries (£3.25). Two Hook Norton beers and a guest such as Wadworths 6X on handpump. Inside, modern furnishings contrast pleasantly with the original building: there's a good mix of old and new tables on the flagstone floor, modern art and sculpture complement the striking blue walls of the open plan bar, and the dining room, with similarly striking red and yellow walls, leads on to an outside terrace. There are tables on the spacious back lawn. Three cats, Webb, Milly and Spider, live happily alongside Boris, the scruffy cocker spaniel. Close to Sulgrave Manor (George Washington's ancestral home) and Canons Ashby House (the Dryden family home). *(Recommended by W Ruxton, George Atkinson, Ted George, Carol and David Havard)*

Hook Norton ~ Tenant Sue Hilton ~ Real ale ~ Bar food ~ Restaurant ~ (01295) 711025 ~ Children welcome till 8.30pm ~ Open 11-3, 6-11; 11-3, 7-10.30 Sun

WADENHOE TL0083 Map 5
Kings Head 🏠
Church Street; village signposted (in small print) off A605 S of Oundle

The licensees offer a civilised and friendly welcome at this country inn, which one reader referred to as a pub of uncluttered simplicity. Set in a picturesque village of thatched stone cottages, it has picnic-sets among willows and aspens on a rough swathe of grass sloping down to boat moorings on the River Nene. The welcoming and atmospheric partly stripped-stone main bar has pleasant old worn quarry tiles, solid pale pine furniture with a couple of cushioned wall seats, and a leather-upholstered chair by the woodburning stove in the fine inglenook. The bare-boards public bar has similar furnishings and another fire; steps lead down to a games room with darts, dominoes and hood skittles, and there's yet more of the pale pine furniture in an attractive little beamed dining room. In the summer, lunchtime bar food is limited to soup (£2.50), sandwiches (from £2.75), filled french bread (from £3.25), welsh rarebit (£3.50) and ploughman's (£5), but in the evening and at lunchtime in winter, there's a sensible choice of imaginative well cooked dishes such as chicken liver pâté with onion confit (£3.75), goat's cheese in filo pastry with red pepper sauce (£4.50), smoked salmon mousse (£5.25), popular steak and kidney casserole with herb dumplings (£8), roasted vegetables with polenta and tomato sauce (£8.50), lamb cutlets on herb salad with a casserole of beans (£8.75), salmon in filo pastry with a herb cream sauce and roast chicken breast with leeks and a

The Good Pub Guide

The Good Pub Guide
FREEPOST TN1569
WADHURST
E. SUSSEX
TN5 7BR

Please use this card to tell us which pubs *you* think should or should not be included in the next edition of *The Good Pub Guide*. Just fill it in and return it to us – no stamp or envelope needed. And don't forget you can also use the report forms at the end of the *Guide*.

ALISDAIR AIRD

YOUR NAME AND ADDRESS (BLOCK CAPITALS PLEASE)

☐ *Please tick this box if you would like extra report forms*

REPORT ON *(pub's name)*

Pub's address

☐ **YES MAIN ENTRY**　　☐ **YES** *Lucky Dip*　　☐ NO don't include
Please tick one of these boxes to show your verdict, and give reasons and descriptive comments, prices etc

☐ Deserves FOOD award　　☐ Deserves PLACE-TO-STAY award

REPORT ON *(pub's name)*

Pub's address

☐ **YES MAIN ENTRY**　　☐ **YES** *Lucky Dip*　　☐ NO don't include
Please tick one of these boxes to show your verdict, and give reasons and descriptive comments, prices etc

☐ Deserves FOOD award　　☐ Deserves PLACE-TO-STAY award

chive butter sauce (£10.25), puddings (£2.75); they do good winter Sunday roasts; pleasant service. Well kept Adnams Southwold, Regatta and Broadside, and Marstons Pedigree on handpump, freshly squeezed orange juice, home-made lemonade and an extensive wine list; magazines to read, no piped music; no-smoking restaurant. Well equipped bedrooms look out over the garden. *(Recommended by E J Locker, Charles and Pauline Stride, Michael Hawkins, John Bowdler, Ian Stafford, G Noel, Peter Plumridge, Ted George, Francis Johnson, B T Smith)*

Free house ~ Licensees Alasdair and Catherine Belton ~ Real ale ~ Bar food (not Sun evening or all day Mon) ~ Restaurant ~ (01832) 720024 ~ Children welcome ~ Open 12-3, 6-11; 12-3, 7-11 Mon-Thurs in winter; closed Mon lunchtime ~ Bedrooms: £35B/£50B

WOODNEWTON TL0394 Map 5

White Swan

Main Street; back roads N of Oundle, easily reached from A1/A47 (via Nassington) and A605 (via Fotheringhay)

Careful attention to detail is paid throughout this friendly country dining pub. An unremarkable frontage hides a welcoming and surprisingly capacious inside where the main focus is on the attractively set-out dining area, with double tablecloths and fresh flowers on all the tables. The blackboard changes daily, and displays an interesting range of good food cooked by a French chef, including meals such as soup (£2.95), filled baguettes (£3.25), asparagus and prawn salad with a herb dressing (£4.75), ploughman's (from £4.95), mushroom and edam pie (£7.50), steak and kidney pie (£7.95), chicken supreme with mushrooms and brandy (£8.95), cod with a creamy leek sauce (£9.20), duck with a honey and lemon sauce (£13), monkfish fillet with a bacon sauce (£13.75) and fillet steak with a shallot and red wine sauce (£14.75); main courses are served with lots of freshly cooked vegetables. Tempting puddings include sticky toffee pudding with pecan sauce, Grand Marnier mousse and home-made ice creams and sorbets. Cheerful waitresses, obviously well trained by the friendly licensees, offer attentive service. Despite the concentration on food, the other end has a flame-effect fire and space for drinkers, with well kept Fullers London Pride, Oakham JHB and a guest on handpump; maybe local radio. It's best to book in the evening or at weekends. There are tables and a boules pitch on the back lawn (league matches on Tuesday evenings). *(Recommended by John Bowdler, Rev J E Cooper, Dr and Mrs B Baker, Mike and Sue Loseby)*

Free house ~ Licensee Anne Dubbin ~ Real ale ~ Bar food ~ Restaurant ~ (01780) 470381 ~ Children welcome ~ Open 12-4, 6.45(6.30 Sat, 7 Sun)-11

Lucky Dip

Besides the fully inspected pubs, you might like to try these Lucky Dips recommended to us and described by readers (if you do, please send us reports):

Abthorpe [SP6446]
☆ *New Inn* [signed from A43 at 1st roundabout S of A5; Silver St]: Tucked-away partly thatched real country local, rambling take-us-as-you-find-us dim-lit bars, beams, stripped stone, inglenook log fire, masses of pictures and old family photographs, attractively priced home cooking (not Sun/Mon) inc good cheap crab sandwiches, well kept Hook Norton Best, Old Hooky and Double Stout, good choice of malt whiskies, hospitable landlord, lots of old family photographs etc; big garden with goldfish pool, rabbits and aviary, quiet village *(Mr and Mrs A Bull, BB, George Atkinson)*
Apethorpe [TL0295]
Kings Head [Kings Cliffe Rd]: Roomy stonebuilt pub bought by residents of attractive

conservation village, comfortable lounge with real fire, ales such as Fullers London Pride, Marstons Bitter and Pedigree and Wadworths 6X, obliging landlord and staff, arch to big dining area with wide choice of good food inc fish, separate bar food menu (not Mon); cosy bar with pool; children welcome, picnic-sets in small enclosed garden *(David and Mary Webb)*
Arthingworth [SP7581]
☆ *Bulls Head* [Kelmarsh Rd; just above A14 by A508 junction]: Refurbished pub, with good value freshly cooked food in bar and restaurant inc vegetarian and popular Sun lunch, jovial landlord, well kept ales such as Courage Directors, Marstons Pedigree and Everards Tiger, decent small-bottle wines; open all day summer *(Frank Davidson, Stephen and Julie*

Brown, John and Moira Watson)

Ashby St Ledgers [SP5768]

☆ *Olde Coach House* [4 miles from M1 junction 18; A5 S to Kilsby, then A361 S towards Daventry; village also signed off A5 N of Weedon]: Rambling softly lit rooms with high-backed winged settles on polished black and red tiles, old kitchen tables, harness and hunting pictures (often of the Pytchley, which sometimes meets outside), big log fire, well kept Everards Old Original, Flowers Original, Marstons Pedigree and a couple of guest beers, good choice of decent wines and other drinks, front games room, decent food, normally inoffensive piped music; seats out among fruit trees and under a fairy-lit arbour, barbecues, play area, disabled access, interesting church nearby; comfortable bedrooms, open all day w/e *(John Wooll, John Bowdler, LYM, Christopher Turner, Anthony Barnes, Jim Bush, JP, PP)*

Badby [SP5559]

☆ *Maltsters Arms*: Friendly village pub much improved by current licensees, single long room refurbished with light wood furniture, roaring fire each end, good reasonably priced food, hood skittles; piped music; garden with terrace and new seats, well placed for walks on nearby Knightley Way; bedrooms *(George Atkinson, John Brightley)*

Barnwell [TL0484]

☆ *Montagu Arms* [off A605 S of Oundle – 2nd left off village rd]: Attractive unspoilt stonebuilt pub in lovely village setting, two bars with low beams, flagstones or tile and brick floors, warm, cosy, welcoming and old-fashioned; four well kept changing ales such as Adnams, Batemans XXB, Flowers and Oakham, good choice of interesting food running up to swordfish with good puddings; games room off yard, big garden with barbecue and camping; open all day w/e, comfortable bedrooms in separate block *(George Atkinson, Dr and Mrs B Baker)*

Blakesley [SP6250]

Bartholomew Arms [High St (Woodend rd)]: Cosy and attractive beamed pub with lots of dark panelling in bar and lounge, stuffed birds and bric-a-brac, decent food, friendly service, well kept Flowers and Marstons Pedigree, soft lighting; piped music, children welcoming in dining area; fine tranquil sheltered garden set some way back with summer house *(George Atkinson, Michael Jones)*

Blisworth [SP7253]

Royal Oak [High St; former A43 S of Northampton]: 17th-c beamed pub, long and narrowish, with open fire, hospitable licensees, well kept reasonably priced real ales, limited choice of well cooked and presented food; pool table, piped music; garden, nr Grand Union canal *(Mr and Mrs T Martin)*

Boughton [SP7566]

Whyte-Melville [Church St; off A508 N of Northampton]: Pleasantly renovated, with wide range of food from good open sandwiches up, three or four real ales inc local Frog Island Shoemaker, bare boards, coal fire, beams, Victorian pictures, friendly attentive service, piped music; spacious, but can get very busy

lunchtime *(George Atkinson)*

Braunston [SP5466]

Admiral Nelson [Dark Lane, Little Braunston, overlooking Lock 3 just N of canal tunnel]: Popular 18th-c ex-farmhouse in peaceful setting by Grand Union Canal Lock 3 and hump bridge, with pleasant waterside garden and towpath walks; well kept Courage Directors, good friendly service, good quick reasonably priced food inc children's and sandwiches, restaurant; bedroom overlooking lock *(George Atkinson)*

Brigstock [SP9485]

Green Dragon [Hall Hill, off A6116]: Long stone building with narrow bar, window tables, friendly staff, Everards Tiger, Morlands Old Speckled Hen and Mansfield, back games room; thorough-going Indian restaurant on left styled as garden with miniature fountains, sizzling authentic food *(Jenny and Michael Back, David and Mary Webb)*

Brixworth [SP7470]

Coach & Horses [just off A508 N of Northampton]: Pleasant old village inn nr Pitsford reservoir, good staff, reasonably priced food, decent house wine; no-smoking restaurant *(Roy Bromell)*

George [Northampton Rd]: Old stonebuilt pub with dark beams, inglenook, brasses, copper, pictures, plates and shaving mugs in big open-plan carpeted bar and dining area, Charles Wells ales with a guest such as Everards Tiger, good value food from filled baked potatoes up, good friendly service; quiet piped music; seats in flower-filled courtyard, handy for Saxon church and Pitsford reservoir *(George Atkinson, Alan J Vere)*

Broughton [SP8375]

Red Lion [High St]: Spotless polished dining pub, lounge/restaurant laid out for eating, varied menu inc lots of vegetarian and grills, lunchtime and early evening meal bargains for two, real ales such as Fullers London Pride, Marstons Pedigree, Ruddles and John Smiths; pleasant staff, areas for smokers and non-smokers, large plain separate bar with pool, darts etc, pleasant garden with play area *(Ian Phillips, David and Mary Webb)*

Bulwick [SP9694]

Queens Head [just off A43 Kettering—Duddington]: Good interesting beautifully served food inc imaginative puddings and popular Sun roasts in long neatly kept partly beamed bar with small fire each end, well kept real ales *(BB, Michael and Julie Underdown)*

Chapel Brampton [SP7266]

Spencer Arms: Very big beamed Chef & Brewer family dining pub, well presented food, welcoming staff, Theakstons XB and Old Peculier; piped music *(George Atkinson)*

Collingtree [SP7555]

Wooden Walls of Old England [High St; 1¼ miles from M1 junction 15]: Tidy thatched pub run well by friendly new landlord, stripped stonework, low black beams, model galleon and some other nautical memorabilia (underlining the meaning of the name), well kept Mansfield ales, freshly cooked food, open fire; children welcome, lots of picnic-sets and play area in nice back garden *(Kevin Macey, BB)*

Cranford St John [SP9277]

Red Lion [High St; 3 miles E of Kettering just off A14]: Good range of good value generous food inc bargain OAP lunches in welcoming and attractive two-bar stone pub, well kept Ind Coope and Tetleys, decent house wine, good-humoured service; pleasant garden, quiet village *(Anthony Barnes, Pete Yearsley)*

Croughton [SP5433]

Blackbird [B4031 SW of Brackley]: Friendly old L-shaped bar with beams and ironstone walls, wide choice of good value generous food from sandwiches up, cheap Sun lunch, well kept Ruddles, games end, maybe piped music *(John and Joan Wyatt)*

Daventry [SP5762]

Dun Cow [Brook St]: Interesting former coaching inn, log fire and lots of old local photographs in down-to-earth cosy character bar (no piped music), roomier more peaceful rare Elizabethan gallery bar, cheap lunchtime food (not Sun) inc home-made steak and kidney pie, back family eating room, attentive service, well kept Bass, Davenports and a guest such as Elgoods *(Pete Baker)*

Duddington [SK9800]

☆ *Royal Oak* [A43 just S of A47]: Attractive stone hotel with strong emphasis on wide choice of good value popular food; spotless and comfortable, with plush banquettes, fresh flowers, gleaming brass inc wartime shell cases, lots of pictures, open fire, Ruddles County and Theakstons Old Peculier, very friendly and efficient Portuguese family (Portuguese wines strong on the list); nice garden and terrace; good bedrooms, nice village *(W W Burke, Dorothy and Leslie Pilson)*

Duston [SP7161]

Longboat [Eastfield Rd]: Decent modern estate pub, two large rooms, limited choice of very good value food (not Sun), well kept M&B Brew XI; fruit machine, quiet piped music, quiz night Thurs *(CMW, JJW)*

Evenley [SP5834]

Red Lion [The Green]: Small friendly local opp attractive village green, tables out on lawn; beams, inglenook, some flagstones, Banks's and Marstons Pedigree, decent coffee and jugs of wines, very wide choice of good usual food inc good sandwiches and Sun lunch, books and magazines with cricket emphasis; piped music *(George Atkinson)*

Great Billing [SP8162]

Elwes Arms [High St]: Thatched stonebuilt 16th-c village pub, good value food inc good vegetarian choice and tempting Sun lunch, four well kept real ales; darts, fruit machine, maybe piped music; children welcome, no dogs, wheelchair access, seats outside *(CMW, JJW)*

Great Everdon [SP5857]

Plough: Friendly and spotless pub dating from 16th c, two coal fires, pictures and jugs in lounge/dining area, three well kept ales inc Banks's, wide choice of good food, games room, juke box; spacious garden with shrubs, fruit trees and barbecue, good walks nearby *(CMW, JJW)*

Great Houghton [SP7958]

Old Cherry Tree [Cherry Tree Lane; a No Through Road off A428 just before the White Hart]: Cosy old pub in quiet village spot, several rooms, stone, low beams and dark panelling, limited range of good value lunchtime bar food, well kept Charles Wells Eagle and Bombardier, good friendly service, no music, no dogs; picnic-sets in good back garden *(CMW, JJW, George Atkinson)*

Great Oxendon [SP7383]

☆ *George* [Harborough Rd (A508)]: Very friendly helpful staff, civilised L-shaped bar/lounge, pleasant no-smoking conservatory overlooking big pretty garden and terrace, well kept Adnams and Bass, good house wines, good reasonably priced food inc good assorted cheese ploughman's, restaurant; comfortable bedrooms *(Shirley Fletcher, Anthony Barnes, Stephen and Julie Brown)*

Greatworth [SP5542]

Inn [Chapel Rd, off B4525]: Epitome of simple friendly village pub, Hook Norton ales inc Mild, log fire, limited food maybe inc home-made organic dishes, cairn terrier, very welcoming licensees, small no-smoking family room; open all day w/e, cl Mon lunchtime *(George Atkinson)*

Hackleton [SP8055]

White Hart [B526 SE of Northampton]: Comfortable country pub with split-level flagstoned open-plan bar/dining area down corridor, stripped stone and brickwork, illuminated well, brasses and artefacts, soft lighting, fresh flowers, good choice of reasonably priced fresh food inc local produce, three real ales, bar with fruit machine and pool; piped music; garden with picnic-sets, open all day *(CMW, JJW)*

Hardingstone [SP7657]

Crown [High St]: Two-bar pub with good value food inc sizzlers lunchtime and Thurs evening, well kept Courage Directors, games room with pool and darts; piped music; children welcome, picnic-sets in sizeable garden with play area, dovecot and pets corner *(CMW, JJW)*

Sun [High St]: Newly refurbished, with stripped stone, tankards and jugs hanging from 18th-c beams, nice wooden furniture, friendly atmosphere, wide choice of good value generous basic food (not Sun evening or Mon) from baguettes and sandwiches up, bargain OAP lunch Thurs, real ales such as Courage Directors, Theakstons and Youngers, daily papers, quiet piped music, log fire and flame-effect gas one, games room, tables on attractive back terrace with play area *(CMW, JJW, Gill and Keith Croxton)*

Harlestone [SP7064]

Fox & Hounds [A428]: Comfortable and spick and span old beamed pub with long-serving landlord, two rooms off central bar, nice wooden furniture, stripped masonry, lots of brasses, decent moderately priced lunchtime food from baguettes up, biggish no-smoking area, Scottish Courage ales and Tetleys; piped pop music, machines, TV, Diana paintings and local postcards for sale; lots of tables in garden with terrace and summer house, attractive village nr

Althorp House, pleasant walks; tricky exit from car park (*David and Mary Webb, George Atkinson*)

Harrington [SP7779]

☆ *Tollemache Arms* [High St; off A508 S of Mkt Harboro]: Good home-cooked fresh food in civilised beamed Tudor pub, friendly and obliging service, well kept Charles Wells Eagle and Bombardier, cheap house wines, open fires, small back garden with country views; children welcome, clean and attractive bedrooms, quiet stonebuilt village (*Eric Locker, K H Frostick, M J Morgan, Pete Yearsley*)

Hellidon [SP5158]

☆ *Red Lion* [off A425 W of Daventry]: Small wisteria-covered inn in beautiful setting by green of unspoilt village, clean, cosy and comfortable, good value food inc good Tues/Weds OAP lunch, well kept Bass, Hook Norton and Worthington, two farm ciders, very helpful chatty staff, two friendly retrievers, two lounges, woodburner in bar, games room, skittles area, small dining area and restaurant; tables outside, good bedrooms, pleasant walks nearby (*M C and S Jeanes, Mr and Mrs A Bull, George Atkinson*)

Higham Ferrers [SP9668]

Green Dragon [4 College St (no inn sign – look for 'Dragon' lettering over door)]: 17th-c stone pub with good range of well kept interesting ales inc one brewed for them, main bar with bare boards and piped music, restaurant bar with good value food, good friendly service; big garden with dovecote in walls, bedrooms (*Joan and Michel Hooper-Immins, Stephen Brown, Ian Phillips*)

Holcot [SP7969]

☆ *White Swan* [Main St; nr Pitsford Water, N of Northampton]: Attractive partly thatched two-bar village local with hospitable series of rooms, good choice of well kept ales from thatched servery such as Fullers London Pride, Greene King IPA, Hook Norton, Morlands Old Speckled Hen and Tetleys, efficient smiling service even when very busy, good reasonably priced food (not Sun-Weds evenings) from baked pots up inc good value Sun lunch, games room with darts, skittles and pool; open all day Sun and summer, children welcome; bedrooms (*George Atkinson, Eric Locker*)

Islip [SP9879]

Woolpack [just off A14, by bridge into Thrapston]: Comfortable old inn, friendly licensees, armchairs and prints in spacious beamed and stripped-stone lounge, Adnams, Bass, Greene King IPA and Abbot and Marstons Pedigree, enjoyable food usual and less familiar, woodburner, Sun restaurant lunch; bedrooms (*Anthony Barnes, David and Mary Webb, George Atkinson*)

Kislingbury [SP6959]

Sun [Mill Rd; off A45 W of Northampton]: Thatched stone village local, four small cosy linked rooms with beams, lots of brasses and pictures, Mansfield ales with guests such as Adnams and Morlands Old Speckled Hen, decent food till 8 (not Sun); service can slow when busy, real and gas fire, attentive welcoming licensees, charity book swap; darts,

SkyTV, fruit machine, unobtrusive piped music, no dogs; back terrace and small garden with waterfall and fish pond, barbecues; river walks nearby (*George Atkinson, CMW, JJW*)

Little Brington [SP6663]

☆ *Saracens Head* [4½ miles from M1 junction 16, first right off A45 to Daventry; also signed off A428]: Fine old pub with alcoves in roomy lounge, lots of pictures, books and odds and ends, even a red telephone box, lovely log fire, games bar, extended no-smoking restaurant area, well kept local Frog Island Best, Fullers London Pride and Hook Norton Best, good choice of food (not cheap but generally good); maybe piped music; tables in neat back garden, handy for Althorp House and Holdenby House (*Ted George, Bruce Bird, BB, James Nunns, Dr A Sutton*)

Little Harrowden [SP8771]

☆ *Lamb* [Orlingbury Rd/Kings Lane – off A509 or A43 S of Kettering]: Spotlessly refurbished 17th-c pub, cosy three-level lounge with log fire, brasses on beams, intimate no-smoking dining area, hard-working jovial landlord, good nicely presented food (not Sun evening) inc good Sun lunch, game and vegetarian dishes, veg extra, well kept Charles Wells Eagle and Bombardier and a guest beer, decent coffee, quiet piped music; small public bar, games room with darts and hood skittles, theme and quiz nights; children welcome, small terrace and garden, delightful village (*George Atkinson, David and Mary Webb*)

Little Houghton [SP8059]

Red Lion [Bedford Rd, off A428 E of Northampton]: Large comfortable village pub with shelves of bric-a-brac, no-smoking room, big helpings of reasonably priced food inc OAP lunches, Everards Tiger and Websters, skittles and games machine; weekly quiz night, picnic-sets outside (*CMW, JJW*)

Marston St Lawrence [SP5342]

☆ *Marston Inn* [off A422 Banbury—Brackley]: Small, cosy and welcoming end-of-terrace local, laid back atmosphere in cottagey lounge littered with books and maps, good reasonably priced simple lunchtime and more extensive evening food in restaurant, well kept Hook Norton ales inc Mild, very friendly landlord; pleasant garden with aunt sally and play area (*LYM, George Atkinson, Mr and Mrs Goodman*)

Marston Trussell [SP6985]

☆ *Sun* [Main St; just off A4304 W of Mkt Harboro]: Wide choice of beautifully presented home-made food in bar, lounge/dining area and restaurant, well kept Bass, decent house wines, unusual malt whiskies, helpful uniformed staff; good bedrooms, pleasant village (*M J Morgan, Stephen and Julie Brown, DC*)

Mears Ashby [SP8466]

Griffins Head [Wilby Rd]: Quiet pleasantly refurbished country pub with smart front lounge and cosy back locals' bar, courteous service, good food from sandwiches to good value Sun roasts, generous OAP lunches Mon-Fri, attractive views and hunting prints, Everards ales inc Mild with a guest such as Marstons Pedigree, huge fireplace; games room with darts, skittles and machine, piped music; children welcome, seats out in small garden, on edge of attractive thatched village *(CMW, JJW, K H Frostick, Eric Locker, George Atkinson, Peter and Pat Frogley, Ted George)*

Middleton [SP8390]

Red Lion [B670, off A427 Corby—Mkt Harboro]: Village local doing well under newish licensees, reasonably priced food in bars and restaurant (cl Sun/Mon evenings) inc good Sun carvery, Hancocks HB and Stones, pool and skittles in public bar; big garden, open all day Fri-Sun and bank hols, cl Mon lunchtime *(Mike and Sue Loseby)*

Milton Malsor [SP7355]

☆ *Greyhound* [former A43 S of Northampton]: Big busy old-fashioned Chef & Brewer, very popular locally for imaginative choice of good generous food all day from wide range of filled rolls and hot cobs to steak, fish, Thai and vegetarian; well refurbished in olde-worlde mode, 15th-c beams, old paintings and china, pewter-filled dresser etc; quick cheery service, John Smiths, Theakstons Best and XB, good choice of wines, candlelit tables, good log fire, piped classical music; open all day, spreading front lawn with duck pond *(Gill and Keith Croxton, George Atkinson, Kevin Macey, Meg and Colin Hamilton)*

Moreton Pinkney [SP5749]

Englands Rose [Upper Green]: 17th-c beamed stone pub now filled with Diana, Princess of Wales memorabilia (some for sale), also big clock collection; settees and armchairs in lounge, woodburner between small bar and one of two dining areas, Bass and Morrells, good food inc Sun lunch; pool and hood skittles in separate room, unobtrusive piped music, back garden *(CMW, JJW)*

Nassington [TL0696]

Black Horse [Fotheringhay Rd – 2½ miles S of A1/A47 interchange W of Peterboro]: Civilised 17th-c beamed and panelled dining pub in nice village, friendly staff, splendid big stone fireplace, panelling, easy chairs and small settees in two rooms linked by bar servery, well kept Scottish Courage ales, good varied wine list; attractive garden, open all day summer w/e *(Maysie Thompson, David and Mary Webb, LYM, Gordon Theaker)*

Nether Heyford [SP6558]

Olde Sun [pub signed off A45 just W of M1 junction 16; Middle Lane]: Friendly old stone pub packed with brassware, railway memorabilia and other bric-a-brac; three beamed bars, rugs on parquet, red tiles or flagstones, big log fire, homely restaurant, good cheap sandwiches, rolls and simple lunchtime food, more choice evenings and Sun, Banks's, Ruddles Best and a guest such as Buckleys, hood skittles; picnic-sets in yard with dovecote, flowers and shrubs among old farm equipment *(George Atkinson)*

Newnham [SP5859]

Romer Arms [The Green]: Light and airy pub on green, cheerful landlord, lots of stripped pine, mix of flagstones, quarry tiles and carpet, open fire, back conservatory, cheerful landlord, good generous home cooking inc Mon bargain for two and popular Sun lunch (no snacks then), real ales such as Batemans, Greene King IPA,

Jennings and Mansfield Old Baily, conservative papers; games room, piped music, opens noon or so, picnic-sets in front garden *(George Atkinson, CMW, JJW)*

Northampton [SP7962]

Bold Dragoon [High St, Weston Favell]: Worth knowing for wide range of well kept reasonably priced beers; conservatory restaurant, terrace and garden *(JJW, CMW)*

Fish [Fish St]: Bustling atmosphere, eight real ales inc unusual ones (not cheap), farm cider, pies and other food, mainly bare boards, newspapers; games machines, piped pop music, busy and loud with young people evenings; disabled access, bedrooms, open all day *(Richard Lewis, CMW, JJW)*

Fitchet & Firkin [Kingswell St]: Large friendly Firkin, usual bare boards, barrels and breweriana, well kept Firkin beers, reasonably priced food, juke box, machines, some live music; open all day *(Richard Lewis)*

Hogshead [Drapery/Bridge St]: Recent open-plan shop conversion extending way back to a conservatory, bare boards and tiles, alcove seating, lots of wood and panelling, shelves of old books, shoe industry memorabilia, small no-smoking area (smoke may drift in from main eating area); usual pub food inc vegetarian, very good choice of well kept beers and farm ciders, daily papers, friendly staff; piped music, games machines; disabled facilities, open all day *(CMW, JJW, Richard Lewis, George Atkinson)*

☆ *Malt Shovel* [Bridge St; approach rd from M1 junction 15; best parking in Morrisons opp back entrance]: Long pine and brick bar opp Carlsberg Brewery, up to ten changing well kept beers, many from small breweries, Belgian bottled beers, lots of whiskies, farm cider, country wines, occasional beer festivals, friendly enthusiastic landlord, daily papers, good home-made usual food lunchtime (can take a while), expanding collection of breweriana, open fire; piped music, darts, weekly live music; picnic-sets on small back terrace *(CMW, JJW, George Atkinson, Richard Lewis, Bruce Bird)*

Moon on the Square [Market Pl]: Popular Wetherspoons, with pews and masses of books, good range of real ales from long bar, interesting good value food all day, good coffee, quiet back no-smoking conservatory; no music, good disabled facilities, open all day *(Anthony Barnes, Richard Lewis, George Atkinson)*

Old Black Lion [Black Lion Hill]: Five changing beers from interesting small breweries such as Frog Island Natterjack, Marston Moor Brewers Pride and Yorks Yorkshire Terrier in bar and split-level lounge, cigarette lighter collection, pool, darts and hood skittles, tables outside; TV, juke box; Fri disco *(Richard Lewis)*

Rat & Parrot [St Giles Sq]: Spacious Scottish Courage two-level bank conversion open for usual food all day from breakfast, Courage Directors and Theakstons, comfortable settees and armchairs, friendly neat staff, back terrace with tubs and statuary; fruit machines, piped pop music (may be loud), more young people evening; disabled facilities *(George Atkinson, CMW, JJW)*

Old [SP7873]

☆ *White Horse* [Walgrave Rd, N of Northampton between A43 and A508]: Wide choice of enjoyable sensibly priced food from good low-priced baguettes to interesting main dishes, cosy and comfortable lounge with thriving atmosphere, welcoming log fire, lots of pictures and plates, friendly service, well kept Banks's and Marstons Pedigree, decent wines, good coffee, restaurant, unusual theme nights; piped radio; lovely garden overlooking 13th-c church *(Eric Locker, Roy Bromell, K H Frostick)*

Orlingbury [SP8572]

Queens Arms [signed off A43 Northampton—Kettering, A509 Wellingborough—Kettering]: Large airy lounge with side no-smoking area, wide choice of good fresh reasonably priced food, evening restaurant, well kept guest beers, stylish furnishings, good atmosphere; nice garden with play area *(Leo Eadon, David and Mary Webb)*

Oundle [TL0388]

Black Horse [Benefield Rd; A427 towards Corby]: This roadside local, previously popular for good value food and well kept beers, has now closed *(BB)*

Polebrook [TL0687]

Kings Arms [just SE of Oundle]: Welcoming young licensees, good friendly atmosphere in big partly divided open-plan lounge, very good sandwiches and good choice of other food, real ales such as Adnams, Bass and Greene King, excellent value food, separate dining room, spotless lavatories; piped music can be rather loud *(Peter Plumridge)*

Ravensthorpe [SP6670]

Chequers [Church Lane]: Spotless refurbished pub worth knowing for wide range of good value bar food inc good well priced Sun lunch (worth booking this), well kept Fullers London Pride, Mansfield and interesting guest beers, good service, restaurant (Weds-Sat); TV, fruit machine, piped music, monthly quiz night; quiet garden with play area *(Ted George, Derek and Sylvia Stephenson)*

Shutlanger [SP7250]

Plough [off A43 N of Towcester]: Good value food inc vegetarian, children's and take-away pizzas (not Weds), log fire, lots of hanging mugs and tankards, stuffed animals, horse pictures and brasses, Charles Wells Eagle and Bombardier, couple of dogs, bar with darts and hood skittles, piped music; garden with picnic-sets, play area and boules *(CMW, JJW)*

Sibbertoft [SP6782]

☆ *Red Lion* [Welland Rise, off A4303 or A508 SW of Mkt Harboro']: Cosy and civilised dining pub, lounge tables set for generous standard food inc vegetarian; big tables and comfortably cushioned wall seats, well kept Everards IPA and Tiger, decent wines, good friendly service, piano, magazines; lovely beamed restaurant, covered tables outside; cl Mon/Tues lunchtimes *(Stephen and Julie Brown, George Atkinson, Dorsan Baker)*

Southwick [TL0192]

Shuckburgh Arms: Small cosy genuinely old stone pub reopened a few years ago, substantial tasty well priced food, friendly welcome, well

kept Fullers London Pride; tables and play area in garden *(David and Mary Webb, Eric Locker)*

Stoke Bruerne [SP7450]

Boat [3½ miles from M1 junction 15 – A508 towards Stony Stratford then signed on right]: Busy pub in nice spot by beautifully restored lock opp British Waterways Museum and shop; little character flagstoned bar by canal, more ordinary back lounge without the views (children allowed in this bit), tables by towpath; well kept ales such as Marstons Best and Pedigree, Sam Smiths OB, Theakstons XB, Wadworths 6X and guests; skittle alley; bar snacks, no-smoking restaurant (not Mon lunchtime) and all-day tearooms, pub open all day summer Sats, canal boat trips *(Anthony Barnes, Charles and Pauline Stride, LYM)*

Stoke Doyle [TL0286]

Shuckburgh Arms [S of Oundle]: Unpretentious 17th-c stonebuilt pub, chesterfields by fire, big helping of well cooked food inc some interesting dishes and children's helpings (no evening snacks, only meals then), daily papers, four real ales, friendly service, no piped music; skittles and hood skittles in separate room, garden with play area *(CMW, JJW, Anthony Barnes)*

Sudborough [SP9682]

☆ *Vane Arms* [High St, off A6116]: Cheerily take-us-as-you-find-us thatched pub notable for its fine choice of well kept ales mostly from interesting small breweries and often strong, friendly helpful service from enthusiastic landlord and daughter; also Belgian fruit beers, farm cider, country wines; stripped stonework, inglenook fires, games in public bar (can be noisy), food (not Sun evening, Mon lunch) from sandwiches to steaks; piped music, and Nelson the dog gets around; plush lounge, dining area and upstairs restaurant (not Sun evening) all no smoking; children in eating area, bedrooms in purpose-built block, nice country setting; sometimes live music Sun lunchtime with bargain beers, cl Mon lunchtime *(Christopher Beadle, Joan and Michel Hooper-Immins, Roger and Pauline Pearce, JP, PP, Brian Horner, LYM, Stephen and Julie Brown, Rona Murdoch, CMW, JJW, David and Mary Webb, John McDonald, Ann Bond)*

Sutton Bassett [SP7790]

Queens Head [B664; village signed off A6 Mkt Harboro bypass]: Peaceful village pub, new licensees but same chef doing enjoyable family food, upstairs restaurant, Marstons Pedigree and Timothy Taylor Landlord; some seats out beyond car park *(Stephen, Julie and Hayley Brown)*

Thornby [SP6775]

☆ *Red Lion* [Welford Rd; A50 Northampton—Leicester]: Friendly old bar with decorative china, pews, leather settee and armchairs, log fire, well kept Greene King IPA and a seasonal beer, good range of traditional games, food from sandwiches to steaks inc Sun roasts and children's helpings; piped radio, no dogs; open all day w/e, children welcome *(LYM, M J Morgan, George Atkinson)*

Thorpe Waterville [TL0281]

Fox [A605 Thrapston—Oundle]: Pleasantly

extended old pub with lots of fox pictures, wide range of decent food, well kept Charles Wells ales with a guest such as Morlands Old Speckled Hen, log-effect fire, no-smoking dining area; piped music, children allowed, no dogs, small garden with play area *(George Atkinson, Dave Braisted)*

Titchmarsh [TL0279]

Wheatsheaf [signed from A14 and A605, just E of Thrapston]: Welcoming village local popular for good value straightforward food, well kept ales inc Greene King IPA, lots of stripped stone, golfing memorabilia, pool room, restaurant, cat and dogs, piped music; children allowed in eating areas; cl Mon evening, weekday lunchtimes *(Francis Johnston, Stephen and Julie Brown, LYM)*

Towcester [SP6948]

Saracens Head [Watling St West]: Substantially modernised coaching inn with interesting *Pickwick Papers* connections, steps up from cobbled entrance to panelled bar on right with carpets on pine boards, comfortable lounge, Victorian dining room, bar food inc good sandwiches, Charles Wells Eagle and Bombardier with a guest such as Courage Directors, neat staff; gents' down steep steps; well equipped bedrooms *(LYM, George Atkinson)*

Wakerley [SP9599]

Exeter Arms [off A43 nr Harringworth]: 17th-c stone pub with L-shaped bar, comfortable lounge end, welcoming atmosphere, friendly staff, reasonably priced home-made food (not Mon), real ales such as Adnams Bitter and Broadside, Batemans XXXB, Marstons Pedigree and guests, woodburner, local photographs; piped music, fruit machine, occasional live music; good views, garden with swings, wheelchair access, Welland Valley walks *(David and Mary Webb, Ian and Nita Cooper)*

Weedon [SP6259]

Crossroads [3 miles from M1 junction 16; A45 towards Daventry; on A5 junction]: Plush and spacious dark wood Boddingtons Henry's Table dining pub with useful food, light and airy separate all-day coffee bar, attractive gardens down to river; recently extended comfortable bedroom block *(George Atkinson)*

Globe [junction A5/A45]: Atractive, tidy and roomy family-run country hotel with plentiful good value fresh food all day inc good filled rolls, vegetarian and take-aways, small helpings for children or OAPs, quick friendly service, well kept beers such as Fullers London Pride and Greene King, log fire, restaurant – open for coffee from breakfast on; piped radio; picnic-sets outside, bedrooms *(George Atkinson, P A Evans, Ted George, Pat and Robert Watt)*

Heart of England [A45; handy for M1 junction 16]: Big pub much extended from 18th-c core, partly no-smoking panelled eating area, busy attractively refurbished lounge bar with small areas off, three Mansfield real ales, wide choice of food inc children's and good vegetarian dishes, restaurant with conservatory, lively family room; piped pop music; big garden leading down to Grand Union Canal, good value pine-furnished bedrooms *(CMW, JJW, G Braithwaite)*

Plume of Feathers [Bridge St/West St, Weedon Bec, off A5/A45]: Recently refurbished, beams, stripped brickwork, pine furniture, candles and old books, generous food cooked to order, largely no-smoking dining area, well kept real ales inc Greene King IPA; piped music; picnic-sets and play area in garden, canal and walks nearby *(CMW, JJW)*

Wheatsheaf [High St]: Village pub with well kept Banks's beer, black beams, pine panelling, lace curtains, cases of brass and bric-a-brac, lots of enamel advertising signs; quiet piped music *(Sam Samuells, Lynda Payton)*

Welford [SP6480]

Shoulder of Mutton [High St (A50)]: Neat and tidy low-ceilinged pub nr canal marina, partly divided by standing timbers and arches, plenty of tables and wheelback chairs, copper and brass, usual food inc children's, real ales such as Bass, Fullers London Pride and Ruddles Best, good house wines and coffee, friendly service; piped music; skittle room, exemplary lavatories, good back garden with play area; cl Thurs *(E J Cutting, BB, Ted George)*

Wellingborough [SP8968]

Cannon [Cannon St]: Up to six real ales from their own back microbrewery, several well kept guest beers, real fire, 1980s décor, rare beer bottle collection in pillared and partitioned lounge, pleasant service; piped music can be loud, fruit machine, games room with bar billiards; open all day *(Richard Houghton, CMW, JJW, Richard Lewis)*

Welton [SP5866]

White Horse [High St; off A361/B4036 N of Daventry]: Friendly little old pub rejuvenated by young energetic chef and wife, two beamed bars, cosy dining areas, small but imaginative choice of good value food, real ales inc guests such as Morlands Tanners Jack, attentive service, big open fire; attractively lit garden with play area, terrace and barbecue *(George Atkinson)*

West Haddon [SP6272]

Sheaf [about 3 miles from M1 junction 18; A428 towards Northampton]: Cosy upstairs lounge and restaurant, beams and log fire, Bass and Worthington; friendly service, reasonably priced straightforward food *(George Atkinson)*

Weston [SP5846]

☆ *Crown* [Helmdon Rd; the one N of Brackley]: Good promptly served simple food (not Sun evening or Mon lunch) in spacious and very welcoming no-frills 17th-c stonebuilt ex-farmhouse, log fires, beams and flagstones, lots of agricultural bric-a-brac, pictures and sporting trophies, four well kept ales inc Judges Barristers and Grey Wig, good coffee, unusual long room (former skittle alley) with cubicle seating; pool room, darts alcove; bedrooms, handy for NT Canons Ashby and Sulgrave *(George Atkinson, Jim Bush, JJW, CMW)*

Yardley Hastings [SP8656]

Red Lion [just off A428 Bedford—Northampton]: Attractive stonebuilt pub with particularly well kept Charles Wells, interesting brass bric-a-brac, new management doing good value food *(B A Lord)*

Northumbria

This chapter includes Northumberland, County Durham, and the Tyneside conurbations. It's had a bit of an infusion of new blood this year: the Morritt Arms at Greta Bridge, an interesting old inn, back in these pages with a popular change of management since its last appearance in the Guide; the Carts Bog Inn up on the hills near Langley on Tyne, a welcoming retreat with good food); and the Seven Stars at Shincliffe, a good traditional inn just outside Durham. Othe pubs currently doing specially well here include the cheerful and extraordinary Allenheads Inn up at Allenheads, the Manor House Inn at Carterway Heads (good food, continuing careful refurbishments), the unpretentious Jolly Fisherman above the harbour at Craster (try that crab soup!), the Dipton Mill Inn in its charming location at Diptonmill (with good value beers from the small Hexhamshire family brewery), the friendly Feathers at Hedley on the Hill (imaginative food including lots of vegetarian dishes), and the Rose & Crown at Romaldkirk (very good all round – gaining a Star this year). This last pub really stands out for a good meal out, so for the third year running we name the Rose & Crown at Romaldkirk Northumbria Dining Pub of the Year. The Lucky Dip section at the end of the chapter has quite a few pubs worth a special mention: the Sun in the excellent Beamish open-air museum, Highlander at Belsay, High Force Hotel at High Force, Black Bull at Matfen, Keelman in Newburn, Cooperage in Newcastle, Tynemouth Lodge in Tynemouth, Hermitage at Warkworth and (particularly for food) the County at Aycliffe. Drinks prices are a bit lower than the national average. Scottish Courage tend to dominate the beer scene here, mainly with their Theakstons brand, but there are quite a few good value local small breweries such as Hexhamshire and Four Rivers, and we found pubs quite often bringing in good beers from further afield at fairly low prices, such as Jennings, Black Sheep and Batemans. The 1999 closure of the Vaux brewery in Sunderland has carved a big gap in the region's brewing panoply, though as we went to press it seemed certain that the beers themselves would survive at least in name, brewed elsewhere.

ALLENDALE NY8355 Map 10
Kings Head 🛏
Market Place (B6295)

A fine choice of real ales in this old coaching inn set in the rambling town square, includes Greene King Abbot, Jennings Cumberland, Tetleys, Theakstons Best, and three guest ales on handpump, all kept well in a temperature-controlled cellar; 75 malt whiskies. The spacious bar/lounge has a big log fire, straightforward pub furnishings, and decent bar food such as sandwiches, venison sausage (£5.50), beef in ale or jester chicken (£5.95), venison in wine and herbs (£7.95), steaks, and puddings. Darts, dominoes, and piped pop music; quoits on clay pitches in the back garden. There are good walks in the area, and the road through the valley is a fine scenic drive. (Recommended by M A Buchanan, Paul S McPherson, Andy and Jill Kassube, M P and K T Guy)

Free house ~ Licensee Margaret Taylor ~ Real ale ~ Bar food ~ (01434) 683681 ~

Children welcome ~ Folk/blues most Fri evenings and some Sat ~ Open 11-11; 12-10.30 Sun ~ Bedrooms: £23B/£45B

ALLENHEADS NY8545 Map 10
Allenheads Inn £ 🛏
Just off B6295

Every available space on the walls, ceilings, and bar in this cheerfully run pub is covered by more than 5,000 collectibles, and in the loosely themed rooms you can find stuffed animals, mangles, old radios, typewriters, long silenced musical intruments, a ship's wheel and engine-room telegraph, brass and copper bygones, a plastic lobster, a four-foot wooden chicken, brooms, birdcages and even shoes – the list is endless and it's all clean and enthusiastically well cared for. The games room (with darts, pool, and antique juke box) has perhaps the most effervescent collection, and the car club discs and number plates on the panelling are a symptom of the fact that members of a classic car club try to persuade their vehicles to wend their way up here every other Tuesday; the naval room is no smoking. They do huge helpings of good value straightforward food such as sandwiches (from £1.50), vegetarian chilli (£4.50), cod (£4.75), beef or chicken curry (£5.25), minced lamb or steak pie (£5.50), and puddings (from £1.50); also maybe special offer of two steaks and a bottle of wine (£12); one room no smoking. Well kept Ind Coope Burton, Tetleys, and two guest beers on handpump; decent coffee, real fire, piped music, friendly alsatian, very warm-hearted service from the friendly, eccentric licensees. Readers report the bedrooms to be warm and comfortable. There are tables outside, flanked by more hardware – the sorts of machinery that wouldn't fit inside, including a Vintage Rolls-Royce parked in front; it's on the Sustrans C2C cycle route.
(Recommended by D J Carter, James and Clare Hand, Byron and June Etherington, Dennis Stevens, Mr and Mrs W Donworth, Mrs Gillian Wild, Jonathan Rowe, Louise Ezzard, Mr and Mrs D W Mitchell)

Free house ~ Licensees Peter and Linda Stenson ~ Real ale ~ Bar food (till 10pm) ~ Restaurant ~ (01434) 685200 ~ Children in pool room ~ Open 12-3(4 Sat), 7-11; 12-4, 7-10.30 Sun; closed Mon and Tues lunchtimes ~ Bedrooms: £25S/£43S

ALNMOUTH NU2511 Map 10
Saddle 🛏
Northumberland Street (B1338)

In a village with attractive beaches and good surrounding coastal walks, this unpretentious stonebuilt hotel is bigger than you'd expect from the outside, and rambles through several areas including a spacious dining part. All are clean, friendly and attractively decorated, with a seascape over the tiled fireplace in the bar, brocaded stools, built-in wall benches and neat shiny dark tables. A wide choice of food includes soup (£1.95), sandwiches (from £2.50), Craster kipper (£3.25), savoury mushrooms (£3.75), northumberland sausage (£3.95), vegetable curry (£5.50), steak and kidney pie (£5.75), huge ploughman's (£5.95), gammon with peach, pineapple or egg (£8.50) and steak (£10.25); good puddings (from £2.40) or fine cheese board (£3.75). Ruddles Best, Theakstons Best, and Wadworths 6X on handpump, decent wines, friendly helpful staff; darts, pool, dominoes, and table tennis; unobtrusive piped music. The restaurant is no smoking. *(Recommended by W K Wood, J and H Coyle, Andy and Jill Kassube, Fiona, Robert W Tapsfield, Neil Ben)*

Free house ~ Licensee Michael McMonagle ~ Real ale ~ Bar food ~ Restaurant ~ (01665) 830476 ~ Children welcome ~ Open 11-3, 6-11; 12-3, 6-10.30 Sun ~ Bedrooms: £33B/£56B

People named as recommenders after the main entries have told us that the pub should be included. But they have not written the report – we have, after anonymous on-the-spot inspection.

BELFORD NU1134 Map 10
Blue Bell
Market Place; village signed off A1 S of Berwick

A welcome refuge from the busy A1, this is an attractive and substantial old coaching inn. In the comfortable lounge bar there are upholstered seats standing on the turkey carpet, coaching prints on the walls and a log fire; the bar counter itself was taken from the Theatre Royal in Newcastle; piped music. Good bar food includes sandwiches and soup, warm salad of goat's cheese with tomato salsa and pine kernels (£3.95), home-made steak and kidney pie, baked salmon fillet with braised rice (£6.95), fillet of beef en croûte with roasted shallots (£11.95), and home-made puddings; the restaurant is no smoking. Well kept Marstons Pedigree, Morlands Old Speckled Hen, Northumberland Secret Kingdom, Theakstons XB and Wadworths 6X on handpump; darts, pool, table skittles, hood skittles, cribbage, dominoes, juke box and fruit machine; large garden. *(Recommended by W K Wood, Comus Elliott, Martin and Helen Hickes, M J Morgan)*

Free house ~ Licensee Paul Shirley ~ Real ale ~ Bar food ~ Restaurant ~ (01668) 213543 ~ Children welcome ~ Live bands/comedians ~ Open 11-2, 6.30-12; 12-2.30, 7-11 Sun ~ Bedrooms: £42B/£84B

BLANCHLAND NY9750 Map 10
Lord Crewe Arms
Before it became home for several distinguished families after the dissolution in 1536, this fine old inn was part of the 13th-c guest-house of a Premonstratensian monastery; the attractive walled garden (where you can eat) was formerly the cloisters. There are some unique original features such as the unusual barrel-vaulted crypt bar which has plush bar stools, built-in wall benches, ancient flagstones, and stone and brick walls that are eight feet thick in some places; Vaux Samson on handpump; darts. Upstairs, the quietly welcoming Derwent Room has low beams, old settles, and sepia photographs on its walls, and the Hilyard Room has a massive 13th-c fireplace once used as a hiding place by the Jacobite Tom Forster (part of the family who had owned the building before it was sold to the formidable Lord Crewe, Bishop of Durham). Lunchtime bar food includes soup (£2), filled rolls (from £3.25), broccoli, tomato and mushroom quiche (£4.60), ploughman's (from £4.60), pork and apple burgers (£5.40), and grilled fillet of cod with herb butter (£5.60); evening dishes like sautéed breast of chicken with tarragon sauce (£8.25), grilled lamb cutlets (£9.50), and sirloin steak (£10.50); puddings (£3.50), and children's dishes (£1.99). *(Recommended by Bill Wood, Kevin Thorpe, M Morgan)*

Free house ~ Licensees A Todd, Peter Gingell and Ian Press, Lindsey Sands ~ Real ale ~ Bar food ~ Restaurant ~ (01434) 675251 ~ Children welcome ~ Open 11-3, 6-11.30; 12-2.30, 7-11 Sun ~ Bedrooms: £80B/£110B

CARTERWAY HEADS NZ0552 Map 10
Manor House Inn 🍽 ♀ 🍺
A68 just N of B6278, near Derwent Reservoir

The careful refurbishments continue at this popular stone house, and the restaurant now has a huge collection of jugs. Picture windows have fine southerly views over moorland pastures and there's a woodburning stove in the comfortable lounge bar. The locals' bar has an original wooden-boarded ceiling, pine tables, chairs and stools, old oak pews, and a mahogany counter. Well kept Courage Directors, Ruddles County, Theakstons Best, and guest beers from local breweries like Border, Butterknowle, Durham, Mordue, and Northumberland on handpump, draught scrumpy, over 60 malt whiskies, and decent wines; darts, dominoes and piped music (only in the bar). Good, well liked home-made food from a wide and changing menu might include sandwiches (from £1.90), soup such as mint and tomato (£1.95), mushrooms in chilli and coriander (£2.90), dill herrings with crème fraîche (£3.80), ploughman's (£4.75), cumberland sausage (£4.75), vegetable stir fry (£9.95), popular duck breast with chilli and ginger or salmon sauce with crayfish, lime and dill sauce (£10.50), and puddings such as sticky toffee pudding or fig and almond cake with butterscotch and Baileys sauce (£2.95); part of the restaurant is no smoking. Rustic tables out on a small side terrace and lawn. Clean and comfortable bedrooms and good breakfasts. *(Recommended by John Prescott, M J Morgan, John Poulter, E J Locker, R Macnaughton, Andy and Jill Kassube, R Stanley, Jack Morley, M Borthwick, Walter and Susan Rinaldi-Butcher, Colin Ferguson, Brenda and Stuart Naylor, Eric Larkham, B, M and P Kendall, H Frank Smith, John Oddey, Paul S McPherson, Jack and Heather Coyle, Chris Rounthwaite, Alistair Forsyth)*

Free house ~ Licensees Moira and Chris Brown ~ Real ale ~ Bar food ~ Restaurant ~ (01207) 255268 ~ Children in lounge and restaurant until 8.30pm ~ Open 11-3, 5.30-11; 11-11 Sat; 12-10.30 Sun; 11-3, 5.30-11 Sat, 12-3, 7-10.30 Sun in winter; closed evening 25 Dec ~ Bedrooms: £24.50/£43

CHATTON NU0628 Map 10
Percy Arms

B6348 E of Wooller

Even when this stone pub is at its busiest, service remains friendly and efficient. The attractively lit and neatly kept bar has horse bits and brasses on beams, maps and country pictures on the walls, green stripy upholstered wooden wall seats, and cushioned farmhouse chairs and stools. Through a stone arch is a similar room with a woodburning stove. The panelled dining room with its pretty plates on a delft shelf is most attractive. Generously served bar food includes good filled french bread, home-made soup (£1.95), grilled goat's cheese or smoked chicken with a lemon and herb mayonnaise (£3.45), fresh local haddock in batter, steak and kidney pie or vegetable pasta bake (all £5.75), luxury chicken kiev (£6.25), cold mixed seafood platter (£7.95), half roast duckling with a cranberry and orange sauce (£9.25), Aberdeen Angus steaks (from £10.45), puddings like home-made sherry trifle (£1.95), and children's meals (£2.95). Well kept Theakstons XB or Morlands Old Speckled Hen on handpump, a wine of the month plus blackboard specials, and 20 malt whiskies; unobtrusive piped music; public bar with darts, pool, dominoes, fruit machine, video game and juke box. There are picnic-sets on the small front lawn above the village road; bedrooms and a holiday cottage. No dogs in public areas. Residents have the use of a sauna, sunbed, keep fit equipment and 12 miles of private fishing, where there may be salmon, sea trout or stocked rainbow trout. *(Recommended by JKW, Iain Patton, Chris Rounthwaite, Mr and Mrs A Bull, Richard and Anne Hollingsworth, Kevin Thorpe, W K Wood, K McManus, Mr and Mrs F Carroll)*

Free house ~ Licensees Pam and Kenny Topham ~ Real ale ~ Bar food (12-1.30, 6.30-9.30) ~ Restaurant ~ (01668) 215244 ~ Children welcome ~ Open 11-3, 6-11; 12-3, 7-10.30 Sun ~ Bedrooms: £25B/£50B

COTHERSTONE NZ0119 Map 10
Fox & Hounds 🍽

B6277 – incidentally a good quiet route to Scotland, through interesting scenery

Run by accommodating licensees, this simple 200-year-old country inn is liked by a good cross-section of customers. The beamed bar has a peaceful atmosphere and a warming winter log fire, various alcoves and recesses, with comfortable furnishings such as thickly cushioned wall seats, and local photographs and country pictures on the walls. Well liked home-made bar food – served in the L-shaped lounge – includes soup (£1.95), creamed mushrooms in red wine sauce (£3.95), tiger prawns in filo pastry or warm bacon salad with garlic croutons sprinkled with wensleydale cheese or omelette (£4.95), gammon and egg (£5.95), vegetarian sausage and yorkshire pudding (£6.95), steak and kidney pie (£7.95), and breast of chicken in dill sauce (£9.95); coffee (95p) is served with home-made fudge; you can also eat from the more adventurous (and pricy) restaurant menu in the bar; one of the restaurants is no smoking. Well kept Black Sheep Best and Special on handpump kept under light blanket pressure, and quite a few banknotes on the ceiling above the bar; cheerful, friendly service. This is a pretty spot overlooking the village green; good nearby walks. *(Recommended by P Abbott, H Frank Smith, M J Morgan, Kevin Thorpe, Ian and Nita Cooper, Stephen and Tracey Groves, Maurice Thompson)*

Free house ~ Licensees Michael and May Carlisle ~ Real ale ~ Bar food (12-3, 6-10) ~ Restaurant ~ (01833) 650241 ~ Children welcome ~ Open 11(12 Sun)-3, 6-11; closed 25 Dec ~ Bedrooms: £37.50B/£55B

CRASTER NU2620 Map 10
Jolly Fisherman £
Off B1339, NE of Alnwick

It's worth coming to this unpretentious local just for their marvellous crabmeat soup with whiskey and cream (£2.50); the well filled crab sandwiches (£2.20) are also highly praised and other simple but popular bar snacks include sandwiches (from £1.75) and home-made craster kipper pâté (£2.50). From the big picture windows or the little garden there are lovely views over the harbour and out to sea and there's a nice mix of locals and visitors in the atmospheric bar: the snug by the entrance is popular with workers from the harbour or the kippering shed opposite. Well kept Marstons Pedigree, Tetleys, and Wards Thorne Best Bitter on handpump, and a range of malt whiskies; friendly service. Darts, pool, dominoes, cribbage, fruit machine and juke box. The pub can get crowded on sunny days, but unlike places in similar settings never begins to feel like a tourist attraction. There's a lovely clifftop walk to Dunstanburgh Castle. *(Recommended by Kevin Thomas, Nina Randall, Chris Rounthwaite, Peter Meister, Roy Morrison, C A Hall, J and H Coyle, Arthur Williams, Robert W Tapsfield, JP, PP, Comus Elliott, GLD, M A Buchanan, W K Wood, Alison Keys, Mr and Mrs F Carroll, Pat and Tony Martin, the Didler)*

Vaux ~ Lease: W P Silk ~ Real ale ~ Bar food (11-8 summer) ~ (01665) 576218 ~ Children in eating area of bar until 9pm ~ Open 11-11; 12-10.30 Sun; 11-3, 6-11 winter

DIPTONMILL NY9261 Map 10
Dipton Mill Inn ◀
Dipton Mill Road; off B6306 S of Hexham at Slaley, Blanchland and Dye House, Whitley Chapel signposts and HGV route sign

This is a lovely spot in a peaceful wooded valley and you can sit at seats on the sunken crazy-paved terrace by the restored mill stream, or in the attractively planted garden with its aviary; plenty of easy-walking footpaths nearby. Inside, the snug little bar has a very relaxed and friendly atmosphere, dark ply panelling, red furnishings and open fires. The friendly landlord really knows his ales and is a brewer in the family-owned Hexhamshire Brewery, hence the good choice of their well kept beers: Hexhamshire Shire Bitter, Devil's Water, Devil's Elbow and Whapweasel; they also keep Tetleys Bitter, two dozen malt whiskies and Westons Old Rosie cider. Good wholesome bar food includes soup such as spiced parsnip or carrot and celery (£1.60), filled rolls (from £1.60), ploughman's (£3.50), cheese and broccoli flan or tomato, bean and vegetable casserole (£4.50), steak and kidney pie or haddock baked with tomato, onion and basil (£5), lamb steak in a wine and mustard sauce or bacon chop in cider sauce (£5.80) and puddings like syrup sponge and custard or apple and pear crumble (£1.60); home-made cakes and coffee (£1.65); pleasantly brisk service. Darts, bar billiards, shove-ha'penny and dominoes. *(Recommended by Dr B and Mrs P B Baker, Andy and Jill Kassube, D and J Wheeler, Mr and Mrs A Bull, M J Morgan, Eric Larkham, Nigel and Amanda Thorp, John and Esther Sprinkle, John A Foord, GSB)*

Free house ~ Licensee Geoff Brooker ~ Real ale ~ (01434) 606577 ~ Children welcome until 9pm ~ Open 12-2.30, 6-11; 12-4.30, 7-10.30 Sun; closed 25 Dec

---

Credit card companies frown on pubs keeping your credit card behind the bar; please let us know of any that do.

EGLINGHAM NU1019 Map 10
Tankerville Arms
B6346 Alnwick—Wooler

New licensees again this year for this pleasant village pub. The long stone building has coal fires at each end, black joists, some walls stripped to bare stone and hung with brassware, and plush banquettes and captain's chairs around cast-iron-framed tables on the turkey carpet; there's a snug no-smoking lounge. Bar food includes soups such as celeriac or smoked salmon (from £1.95), sandwiches (£2.75), chestnut and pork sausage (£4), oak smoked duck with baked vegetables (£4.50), sautéed lamb's kidneys, steak in ale pie or stuffed aubergine (£5.95), baked gammon with caramelised apples (£7.50), steaks (from £9.50), puddings (£3.50), and Sunday roast lunch. Well kept Bass, Batemans, Courage Directors, Morlands Old Speckled Hen, and Theakstons on handpump; decent selection of wines and malt whiskies; dominoes and piped music. There are seats in the garden. *(Recommended by Mr and Mrs F Carroll, K McManus, Mr and Mrs Justin Beament, Michael Doswell)*

Free house ~ Licensee J E Blackmore ~ Real ale ~ Bar food ~ Restaurant ~ (01665) 578444 ~ Children welcome ~ Open 11(12 winter)-3, 6(7 winter)-11; 12-3, 6(7 winter)-10.30 Sun

ETAL NT9339 Map 10
Black Bull
Off B6354 SW of Berwick

This white-painted cottage is the only thatched pub in Northumberland. The spacious open-plan lounge bar has windsor chairs around the tables on its carpet, and glossily varnished beams. Enjoyable food includes sandwiches (from £1.40), home-made soup (£1.75), filled baked potatoes (from £1.80), deep-fried camembert with mango chutney (£3.95), ploughman's (£4.95), steak and kidney pie (£5.25), cumberland sausage (£5.75), vegetable lasagne (£5.95), yorkshire pudding filled with roast beef (£6.95), steaks (from £11.95), and puddings like fruit pies (£2.25); children's menu (£2.65). Well kept Stones, John Smiths, and Tetleys on handpump, 30 malt whiskies, and farm cider. Darts, dominoes, pool, TV, juke box and piped music in the pool room. There are a few picnic-sets in front. A three-mile light railway runs between Heatherslaw (where there's a working watermill from which you can buy flour ground on the premises) and the bare ruins of Etal Castle on the banks of the River Till at the far end of this particularly picturesque village. *(Recommended by Kevin Thorpe, Andy and Jill Kassube)*

Pubmaster ~ Lease: Mr Gott ~ Real ale ~ Bar food ~ (01890) 820200 ~ Children in eating area of bar until 9.30pm ~ Open 11-11; 12-10.30 Sun; 12-3, 6.30-11 winter

GREAT WHITTINGTON NZ0171 Map 10
Queens Head 🍴 🍷
Village signposted off A68 and B6018 just N of Corbridge

The food here is very good indeed, but this simple stone inn has kept its pubby atmosphere. The two beamed rooms are comfortably furnished and neatly decorated with some handsome carved oak settles among other more modern furnishings, a mural over the fireplace near the bar counter, old prints and a collection of keys, and log fires. The wide choice of good bar food might include sandwiches, soup (£2.95), terrine of chicken fillets layered with oyster mushrooms and spinach mousse, wrapped in bacon and sprinkled with a tomato and herb dressing (£4.75), sautéed duck livers in a filo pastry case glazed with a blue cheese sabayon (£5.75), steamed leek pudding surrounded by a turret of mushrooms and roasted shallots (£8.95), poached Scotch salmon on tagliatelle with a light herb cream (£9.95), steaks (from £11.95), pot roasted guinea fowl with baby onions and mushrooms (£12.95), and home-made puddings (£3.50); the restaurant is no smoking. Well kept Queens Head Bitter (brewed for them by Hambleton Brewery), Hambleton Bitter and Black Sheep Best on handpump, 30 malt whiskies, and decent wines; friendly attentive service, maybe unobtrusive piped music. There are six picnic-sets on the small front lawn, and the surrounding partly wooded countryside is pretty. *(Recommended by Andy and Jill Kassube, John Prescott, Paul and Ursula Randall, A Denniss, Chris Rounthwaite, Nigel and Amanda Thorp)*

Free house ~ Licensee Ian Scott ~ Real ale ~ Bar food ~ Restaurant ~ (01434) 672267 ~ Children in eating area of bar and restaurant ~ Open 12-2.30, 6-11; 12-3, 7-10.30 Sun; closed Mon except bank hols

GRETA BRIDGE NZ0813 Map 10
Morritt Arms ♀
Hotel signposted off A66 W of Scotch Corner

The delightfully pubby bar at this characterfully civilised old coaching inn is named after Charles Dickens, who stayed here in 1838 on his way to start his research for *Nicholas Nickleby*. Running all the way round the walls is a rather jolly Dickensian mural painted in 1946 by J V Gilroy, more famous for his old Guinness advertisements – six of which are displayed on the wall. There are also big windsor armchairs and sturdy plush-seated oak settles clustered around traditional cast-iron-framed tables, and big windows that look out on the extensive lawn. The adjacent no-smoking green room has wall seats, a stag's head and a big case of stuffed black game. Flowers brighten up the rooms, and there are open fires. Well kept Black Sheep, Butterknowle Conciliation, Tetleys and Timothy Taylor Landlord on handpump, quite a few malt whiskies, a very extensive wine list with about two dozen by the glass; friendly staff. There's a proper old shove-ha'penny board, with raisable brass rails to check the lie of the coins, and darts, pool, cribbage, dominoes and a juke box in the separate public bar. Freshly cooked bar food includes sandwiches (from £2.50), soup (£2.95), chicken liver pâté (£3.25), fresh peeled prawns with spicy tomato mayonnaise (£3.95), grilled lamb's liver with thyme bubble and squeak, bacon and onion rings (£6.25), braised lamb shank with baby onions and rosemary sauce or baked cod chunk with saffron mash and pickled sauce (£6.50), ploughman's (£6.95), and several changing daily specials like broccoli and five-cheese cream soup (£3.25), prawn and crab salad (£3.95), vegetable stir fry (£6.95), salmon and balsamic sauce (£7.50), roast beef with garlic and mushroom sauce or pork with cider cream sauce (£7.95) and puddings like sticky toffee pudding, summer pudding or lemon and lime cheesecake (£3.95); the restaurant is no smoking. There are some picnic-sets in the nice garden, teak tables in a pretty side area looking along to the graceful old bridge by the stately gates to Rokeby Park, and swings, slide and rope ladder at the far end. *(Recommended by James Nunns, Neil and Anita Christopher, P Abbott)*

Free house ~ Licensees Peter Phillips and Barbara Johnson ~ Bar food (12-2.30, 6-9.30) ~ Restaurant ~ (01833) 627232 ~ Children welcome ~ Open 11-12; 12-10.30 Sun ~ Bedrooms: £59.50B/£75B

HALTWHISTLE NY7166 Map 10
Milecastle Inn ◀
Military Rd; B6318 NE – OS Sheet 86 map reference 715660

Despite the remote situation – on a moorland road running alongside Hadrian's Wall – this little 17th-c pub does get very busy at peak times. The snug little rooms of the beamed bar are decorated mainly with brasses, horsey and local landscape prints and attractive dried flowers, and two winter log fires; at lunchtime the small comfortable restaurant is used as an overflow. Popular bar food might include lunchtime sandwiches (from £2.40) and ploughman's (£4.75), home-made soup (£1.90), smoked duck breast on an apricot coulis (£4.35), vegetable curry (£5.25), pies such as steak and kidney or turkey, ham and chestnut (from £5.95), tasty venison sausage (£6.25), gammon and egg (£7.20), sirloin steak (£9.50), and daily specials such as wild boar and duckling pie (£6.95) or venison casserole (£7.25); home-made puddings (from £2.50). The local meat is well hung and the fresh local vegetables are good. Well kept Derwent Bitter, Northumberland Castles Bitter and

Tetleys on handpump, a fair collection of malt whiskies, and a good wine list. Walkers welcome (but no rucksacks allowed). No games or music. There are some white plastic seats and tables outside in a sheltered walled garden with a dovecote. *(Recommended by Penny and Martin Fletcher, Martin, Jane and Laura Bailey, Justin Hulford, E A Thwaite, Elizabeth and Alan Walker, Ian Phillips, Bob and Marg Griffiths, Dr and Mrs B Baker, John A Foord, GSB)*

Free house ~ Licensees Ralph and Margaret Payne ~ Real ale ~ Bar food ~ Restaurant ~ (01434) 321372/320682 ~ Children in eating area of bar and in restaurant if over 5 and must be eating ~ Open 12-3, 6.30-11

Wallace Arms

Rowfoot, Featherstone Park – OS Sheet 86 map reference 683607

There are five interlinked rooms in this rambling former farmhouse with simple furnishings and unpretentious decorations. The small beamed main bar has dark oak woodwork, some stripped stone, comfortable seats, and a good log fire; the side games room has another fire (also pool, shove-ha'penny, table skittles, dominoes, trivia, and juke box), and there's a third in the middle of the big no-smoking dining room (a former barn), which has its own interesting menu. Good value bar food includes soup (£1.95), lunchtime sandwiches (from £2.65), filled baked potatoes (from £2.95), three-egg omelette or trout fish cakes (£4.95), pasta bake or cumberland sausage (£5.25), Whitby haddies (crumbed haddock pieces, £5.95), and children's menu (£2.75). Good Sunday roasts. Well kept ales from Four Rivers on handpump, and 36 malt whiskies; quizzes every second Wednesday. Genuinely friendly licensee, nice old english sheepdog called Molly, and a good bustling atmosphere. Access for disabled people is fairly easy. Picnic-sets outside on both sides of the quiet lane have lovely fell views; one good walk from the pub is along the former Alston railway line; there's a play area at the back and quoits. *(Recommended by R and K Halsey, Ian Phillips, John Oddey, Eric Larkham, Mrs M Wood)*

Free house ~ Licensees John and Mary Stenhouse ~ Real ale ~ Bar food (not Mon/Tues or Sun evening) ~ Restaurant ~ (01434) 321872 ~ Children in snug and pool room until 9.30pm ~ Occasional small bands ~ Open 11.30-2.30, 4-11; 12-11 Fri; 11.30-11 Sat; 12-3.30, 7-10.30 Sun; closed Mon/Tues lunchtime

HEDLEY ON THE HILL NZ0859 Map 10
Feathers

Village signposted from New Ridley, which is signposted from B6309 N of Consett; OS Sheet 88 map reference 078592

An old favourite for its many regulars, this genuinely friendly and attractive little stone pub is just as welcoming to visitors, too. There's a chatty, relaxed atmosphere in the three well kept turkey-carpeted traditional bars, with beams, woodburning stoves, stripped stonework, solid brown leatherette settles and old black and white photographs of local places and country folk working the land. Well kept Boddingtons, Mordue Workie Ticket and two guest beers such as Big Lamp Prince Bishop, Fullers London Pride or Northumberland Castles Bitter on handpump; they hold a mini beer festival around Easter with thirteen real ales on at any one time, which ends with a barrel race on Easter Monday; decent wines, and around 30 malt whiskies. The range of good imaginative food changes twice a week and might include leek and parsnip soup (£2.25), Bywell smoked duck breast with redcurrant jelly (£3.75), mushroom pâté with toasted pine nuts (£3.95), cumberland sausage with grainy mustard sauce, feta and spinach filled pancake or lentil and vegetable hotpot with herby dumpling (all £4.95), Thai crab cakes with tomato and coriander salsa (£5.75), salmon steak with lemon butter (£6.25), beef in red wine or home-cooked ham with mango chutney (£6.50), and puddings like rich brandy chocolate, walnut and cherry cake with chocolate sauce or home-made ice creams such as mango and ginger (£2.85). Darts, shove-ha'penny, table skittles, cribbage, and dominoes. From picnic-sets in front you can watch the world drift by. *(Recommended by M Doswell, S Hesketh, GSB, Andy and Jill Kassube, Iris Penny, Graham and Karen Oddey)*

Free house ~ Licensee Marina Atkinson ~ Real ale ~ Bar food (not Mon) ~ (01661) 843607 ~ Children in small lounge and pleasant back room until 9pm ~ Open 6-11; 12-3, 6-11 Sat; 12-3, 7-10.30 Sun; closed weekday lunchtimes and 25 Dec

LANGLEY ON TYNE NY8160 Map 10

Carts Bog Inn

A686 S, junction B6305

The clean and tidy main black-beamed bar of this isolated moorside pub is a welcoming place, with a big log fire in the central stone fireplace, local photographs and horsebrasses, and windsor chairs and comfortably cushioned wall settles around the tables. It rambles about, with flagstones here, carpet there, mainly white walls with some stripped stone. Good freshly made food includes sandwiches (from £2.25), soup (£2.35), ploughman's or battered cod and a good choice of daily specials such as Caribbean fruit and vegetable curry, peppercorn pork, chicken breast in lemon and tarragon sauce, local lamb and apricot casserole or beef teriyaki (all £5.85); tasty puddings include chocolate fudge cake and apple crumble (£2.10). Well-kept Marstons Pedigree, Theakstons Best and a weekly guest such as Charles Well Bombardier on handpump, and around 30 malt whiskies; good friendly service. A side lounge (once a cow byre) with more wall banquettes has pool, darts, dominoes and a fruit machine; piped music. There are tables outside, with summer barbecues and a quoits pitch; it's a nice spot, out among the silvery drystone walls of these high sheep pastures. *(Recommended by Dr and Mrs D Spencer, John Oddey, Andy and Jill Kassube)*

Free house ~ Licensees Neil and Alison Wishart ~ Real ale ~ Bar food ~ (01434) 684338 ~ Children welcome ~ Open 12-3(4 Sat), 7-11(10.30 Sun)

NEW YORK NZ3370 Map 10

Shiremoor Farm ★

Middle Engine Lane/Norham Road; from A19 going N from Tyne Tunnel, right into A1058 then next left signposted New York, then left at end of speed limit (pub signed); or at W end of New York A191 bypass turn S into Norham Road, then first right (pub signed)

This smartly relaxed place – cleverly transformed from derelict farm buildings – has a bustling, chatty atmosphere, and a good mix of customers (it's well liked by businessmen at lunchtime). There's a charming mix of interesting and extremely comfortable furniture, a big kelim on the broad flagstones, warmly colourful farmhouse paintwork on the bar counter and several other tables, conical rafters of the former gin-gan, a few farm tools, and good rustic pictures such as mid-West prints, big crisp black and white photographs of country people and modern Greek bull sketches. Gentle lighting in several well divided spacious areas cleverly picks up the surface modelling of the pale stone and beam ends. Besides Stones and Theakstons Old Peculier well kept real ales might include Mordue Workie Ticket, and Timothy Taylor Landlord; decent wines by the glass. Bar food includes sandwiches (£1.50), pork balti (£4.95), scampi or ricotta and spinach cannelloni with a rustic tomato sauce and mozzarella (£5.45), flash roasted salmon fillet on creamed ginger leeks (£5.95), fried chicken breast coated with stilton, garlic and prawn sauce (£7.95), medallions of beef fillet with pepper sauce (£8.45), and puddings like pecan pie or sticky toffee pudding (£2.25). The no-smoking granary extension is good for families; no games or piped music. There are picnic-sets on neat grass at the edge of the flagstoned farm courtyard, by tubs and a manger filled with flowers. *(Recommended by Valerie Pitts, D and J Wheeler, Eric Larkham, Ian Phillips, Andy and Jill Kassube, Roger A Bellingham, Bill and Sheila McLardy)*

Free house ~ Licensees M W Garrett and C W Kerridge ~ Real ale ~ Bar food (12-9) ~ Restaurant ~ (0191) 257 6302 ~ Children in eating area of bar and restaurant ~ Open 11-11; 12-10.30 Sun

NEWCASTLE UPON TYNE NZ2563 Map 10
Crown Posada ◗ £

31 The Side; off Dean Street, between and below the two high central bridges (A6125 and A6127)

'A gem' is one way of describing this marvellously unspoilt old pub. It's the second oldest in the city and the golden crown adds grandeur to an already imposing carved stone façade – as do the pre-Raphaelite stained-glass windows. Inside there's a lot of architectural charm such as an elaborate coffered ceiling (which is apparently best viewed by lying on your back so one reader tells us, though the manager might frown on this), stained glass in the counter screens, a line of gilt mirrors each with a tulip lamp on a curly brass mount which match the great ceiling candelabra, and Victorian flowered wallpaper above the brown dado; below this are fat heating pipes – a popular footrest when the east wind brings the rain off the North Sea. It's a very long and narrow room (the front snug was once the preserve of ships' masters and chief engineers), making quite a bottleneck by the serving counter, and beyond that, a long soft green built-in leather wall seat is flanked by narrow tables. Well kept Bass, Boddingtons, Butterknowle Conciliation, Jennings, Theakstons Best and a guest on handpump; lunchtime sandwiches (£1). Friendly barmen, chatty customers; fruit machine and an old record player that provides background music when the place is quiet. Best to visit during the week when regulars sit reading the papers put out in the front snug; at the weekend it's usually packed. No children. A few minutes' stroll to the castle. *(Recommended by Eric Larkham, the Didler)*

Free house ~ Licensee Malcolm MacPherson ~ Real ale ~ Bar food (lunchtime) ~ (0191) 232 1269 ~ Open 11-11; 12-3, 7-10.30 Sun

NEWTON ON THE MOOR NU1605 Map 10
Cook & Barker Arms ⑪ ⇔

Village signposted from A1 Alnwick—Felton

It's the beautifully prepared, imaginative food that draws customers to this busy long stone pub. From the bar menu, there might be sandwiches, mozzarella with avocado, sun-dried tomato and olive oil (£4.25), venison and red wine sausage with roasted shallots and a rosemary and thyme jus (£7.25), roast fillet of bass on a rocket and watercress panache with basil pesto (£7.50), scallops on a niçoise of vegetables with swiss gruyère (£7.95), and lovely puddings. The unfussy, long beamed bar has stripped, partly panelled walls, brocade-seated settles around oak-topped tables, framed banknotes and paintings by local artists on the walls, brasses, a highly polished oak servery, and a coal fire at one end with a coal-effect gas fire at the other; another room has tables, chairs, an old settle, and darts (popular with locals), and the games room has scrubbed pine furniture and french windows leading onto the terrace; the top bar area is no smoking. Well kept rotating ales on handpump include Batemans XXXB, Black Sheep, Fullers London Pride, Theakstons Best, and Timothy Taylor Landlord, quite a few malt whiskies, and six red wines and six white wines by the glass. *(Recommended by Richard and Anne Hollingsworth, Simon G S Morton, Anthony Barnes, GLD, Penny and Martin Fletcher, Alison Keys, G Neighbour, M Borthwick, Christine and Malcolm Ingram)*

Free house ~ Licensees Phil and Lynn Farmer ~ Real ale ~ Bar food ~ Restaurant ~ (01665) 575234 ~ Children welcome ~ Open 11-3, 6-11; 12-3, 6-10.30 Sun ~ Bedrooms: £37.50B/£70B

RENNINGTON NU2119 Map 10
Masons Arms ⇔

Stamford Cott; B1340 NE of Alnwick

The comfortable, spotlessly clean bedrooms in the adjacent stable block here are just the place from which to explore the nearby Northumbrian coast. It's a friendly place and the comfortably modernised beamed lounge bar has wheelback and mate's chairs around solid wooden tables on the patterned carpet, plush bar stools, lots of brass, pictures and photographs on the walls, and a relaxed atmosphere; the dining rooms (one is no smoking) have pine panelling and wrought-iron wall lights. Quickly served good value food includes sandwiches, home-made soup (£1.95), Orkney dill herrings (£3.75), home-made craster kipper pâté (£3.95), fried haddock (£4.95), hickory smoked sausage (£5.45), mediterranean vegetable crumble (£5.95), gammon and pineapple or lamb cutlets (£6.55), game casserole (£6.75), steaks (from £11.95), and puddings (£2.30); Sunday lunch is popular. Courage Directors and Ruddles Best on handpump; shove-ha'penny, dominoes and piped music. There are sturdy rustic tables on the little front terrace, surrounded by lavender. Please note, children are not allowed to stay overnight. *(Recommended by Neil Townend, Barry and Marie Males, Peter Meister, Gerald Barnett, GSB, Martin and Helen Hickes, Chris Rounthwaite, Peter Guy, Richard and Anne Hollingsworth, Sarah and Peter Gooderham, Willie Bell, Jack and Heather Coyle, Jackie Moffat)*

Free house ~ Licensees Frank and Dee Sloan ~ Real ale ~ Bar food ~ Restaurant ~ (01665) 577275 ~ Children in restaurant but must be over 5 in evening ~ Open 12-2, 6.30-11; 12-2.30, 7-10.30 Sun ~ Bedrooms: /£52B

ROMALDKIRK NY9922 Map 10

Rose & Crown ★ 🍽 ♀ 🛏

Just off B6277

Northumbria Dining Pub of the Year

The refurbishment of the bedrooms here is nearly completed and all rooms now have fresh flowers, hair dryers, and trouser presses – and on the top floor are three rooms (two are suites and one has a sitting area) with hi-fi systems. The bar menu now changes weekly and they have extended their range (the fixed price restaurant menu changes daily), wines by the glass change every three months and are kept vacuum-fresh, and the kitchen has started making marmalades, jams and chutneys to sell over the bar. The beamed traditional bar has old-fashioned seats facing the log fire, a Jacobean oak settle, lots of brass and copper, a grandfather clock, and gin-traps, old farm tools, and black and white pictures of Romaldkirk on the walls. The smart Crown Room, where bar food is served, has more brass and copper, original etchings of game shooting scenes and farm implements. The hall is hung with wine maps and other interesting prints and a photograph of the Hale Bopp comet over Romaldkirk church that was taken by a guest; no-smoking oak-panelled restaurant. As well as lunchtime baps (from £3.35) and ploughman's with three home-made pickles and their own bread (£5.50), the excellent food might include home-made soup (£2.95), three-cheese soufflé with chive cream sauce (£3.95), roquefort, roasted walnut and sweet pear salad (£4.50), creamed scrambled eggs with ribbons of smoked salmon (£4.85), queenie scallops with braised leeks and oyster mushrooms or hot chive and potato pancake with smoked salmon and sour cream (£5.95), steak, kidney and mushroom in ale pie (£7.75), grilled venison sausage with red onion gravy and butter bean purée (£8.75), crispy confit of duck leg with hot pickled red cabbage and sweet red wine jus (£9.25), sautéed rosettes of pork with green peppercorns and creamed gnocchi (£9.75), fried strips of beef fillet with mushrooms and brandy cream sauce (£12.95), and puddings like dark chocolate terrine, hot sticky toffee pudding or crème caramel with compote of rhubarb (£3.25); good three-course Sunday lunch (£12.95). Well kept Marstons Pedigree and Theakstons Best on handpump; good, friendly service. Tables outside look out over the village green, still with its original stocks and water pump. The village is close to the superb Bowes Museum and the High Force waterfall, and has an interesting old church. *(Recommended by Ian Phillips, DJW, K F Mould, John Read, Chris Brace, Dr T Hothersall, David Hawkes, P Abbott, Mark Percy, Lesley Mayoh, M J Morgan, E Thwaite, H H Liesner, David Philcox, T M Dobby, Janet and Peter Race, Mrs V Pitts; also in the Good Hotel Guide)*

Free house ~ Licensees Christopher and Alison Davy ~ Real ale ~ Bar food (12-1.30, 7-9) ~ Restaurant ~ (01833) 650213 ~ Children welcome ~ Open 11-3, 5.30-11; 12-3, 7-10.30 Sun; closed 24-26 Dec ~ Bedrooms: £62B/£84B

Tipping is not normal for bar meals, and not usually expected.

SEAHOUSES NU2232 Map 10
Olde Ship ★ ◼ 🛏

Just off B1340, towards harbour

The long-awaited sun lounge extension to the function room has been completed here and has a sprung dance floor, and the little back no-smoking Locker Room has been refurbished. But this is still a treasure-trove of seafaring memorabilia: shiny brass fittings, sea pictures and model ships (including a fine one of the North Sunderland lifeboat and a model of Seahouses' lifeboat *The Grace Darling*), as well as ship's instruments and equipment, and a knotted anchor made by local fishermen; all the items are genuine. Even the floor of the saloon bar, with its open fire, is scrubbed ship's decking. The one clear window (the others have stained-glass sea pictures) looks out across the harbour to the Farne Islands, and as dusk falls you can watch the Lonstones lighthouse shine across the fading evening sky; there's another low-beamed snug bar. Bar food includes soup (£2.50), liver and onion casserole, a vegetarian dish or daily roast (£5.95), and puddings such as chocolate trifle or apple pie (£2.95). A good choice of real ales takes in Bass, Courage Directors, Marstons Pedigree, McEwans 80/-, Morlands Old Speckled Hen, Ruddles Best, John Smiths, and Theakstons Best on handpump, and several malt whiskies; dominoes and piped music. Pews surround barrel tables in the back courtyard, and a battlemented side terrace with a sun lounge looks out on the harbour; putting and quoits. An anemometer is connected to the top of the chimney. You can book boat trips to the Farne Islands Bird Sanctuary at the harbour, and there are bracing coastal walks, particularly to Bamburgh, Grace Darling's birthplace. The pub is not really suitable for children. *(Recommended by M A Buchanan, Roy Morrison, Lynn Sharpless, Bob Eardley, Chris Brace, Alison Keys, Mrs J Truesdale, Andy and Jill Kassube, Comus Elliott, JP, PP, the Didler)*

Free house ~ Licensees Alan and Jean Glen ~ Real ale ~ Bar food ~ (01665) 720200 ~ Open 11-4, 6-11; 12-4, 7-10.30 Sun

SEATON SLUICE NZ3477 Map 10
Waterford Arms

A193 N of Whitley Bay

Enjoyable food – especially the fresh fish – is the main reason for coming to this very restauranty pub. Double doors open from the restaurant into the comfortable and homely bar, where it is likely that all the tables will be laid for dining. The same menu covers both areas and might include fish and chips (from £5.50), Mexican chicken (£6.15), sole stuffed with crab (£8.30), and peppered fillet steak (£13.75); two no-smoking areas, friendly and efficient service. Marstons Pedigree, Stones, Tetleys and Worthingtons on handpump. More reports please. *(Recommended by Dr L H Groves)*

Pubmaster ~ Lease: Michael Naylor ~ Real ale ~ Bar food ~ Restaurant ~ (0191) 237 0450 ~ Children welcome until 9pm ~ Open 12-2, 5-10; 12-10 Sun and Sat ~ Bedrooms: £25S/£50S

SHINCLIFFE NZ2941 Map 10
Seven Stars 🛏

High Street North; A177 a mile or so S of Durham

Just ten minutes' or so drive from central Durham, with fairly frequent buses passing the door, this early 18th-c village inn is a very handy outpost – and a pretty one, too, with its window boxes, creepers, and seats out at the end of the attractive village street. Inside, it's largely unspoilt: relaxed, comfortable and welcoming. The lounge bar has a coal fire in its handsome Victorian fireplace, with a pair of big Staffordshire dogs on the mantelpiece below a big mirror, old brewery advertisements, copper kettles hanging from the beams, and cushioned wall banquettes and stools around cast-iron-framed tables. Enjoyable bar food from a changing menu runs from home-made soups such as beef and vegetable (£2.95 –

almost a meal in itself, in a big bowl with plenty of fresh bread) to sandwiches (from £2.95), grilled vegetable tart (£4.50), Mexican-style chicken with tortilla, guacamole, salsa and sour cream (£5.50), steak and ale pie (£6.50), charred chicken breast with wild mushroom sauce and herb mash or roasted halibut with spinach, tomato and fennel salad and home-made sun-dried tomato pesto (£10.25), 10oz sirloin steak with bacon and black pudding salad and red wine sauce (£10.95) and daily specials such as Mexican pork casserole (£6.50), pan-fried sea bass with Chinese cabbage and mushroom stir-fry (£10.50) and roast duck breast with plum and beetroot chutney (£10.95); home-made puddings might include chocolate fudge cake, lemon and lime tart with strawberry coulis or raspberry brûlée with shortbread (£3.75). Well kept Stones, Tetleys and two guests such as Fullers London Pride or Marstons Pedigree on handpump, 25 malt whiskies, friendly staff; chess, draughts, dominoes and piped music. The candlelit dining room is no smoking. Parking can be a problem. *(Recommended by Margaret and Allen Marsden, Mr and Mrs W Cunliffe, Robert Gartery, Dr Muriel Sawbridge)*

Swallow Group ~ Lease: Nigel and Deborah Gadd ~ Real ale ~ Bar food (12-2.30, 6-9.30(9 Sun)) ~ Restaurant ~ (0191) 384 8454 ~ Children in restaurant and eating area of bar till 8.30pm ~ Open 11-11; 11.30-10.30 Sun ~ Bedrooms: £40S/£50S

STANNERSBURN NY7286 Map 10
Pheasant 🛏️

Kielder Water road signposted off B6320 in Bellingham

As well as being newly painted outside, this unpretentious old inn has redecorated bar and dining areas and several of the bedrooms have been refurbished. The traditional and comfortable lounge is partly stripped stone and partly panelled, and the separate public bar, similar but simpler, opens into a games room with darts, pool, and dominoes. A good mix of visitors and locals in the evening when the small no-smoking dining room can get crowded; friendly, helpful landlord, and cheerful staff. Bar food includes sandwiches, lasagne, garlic chicken breast or crisp haddock fillet (£5.95), and game pie or smoked salmon salad (£6.95); good breakfasts. Well kept Marstons Pedigree, Theakstons Best, and Timothy Taylor Landlord on handpump, and 34 malt whiskies. It's in a peaceful valley with picnic-sets in the streamside garden, a pony paddock behind, and quiet forests all around. *(Recommended by John and Kathleen Potter, John Poulter, Richard and Anne Hollingsworth, Paul and Ursula Randall, Derek Stafford)*

Free house ~ Licensees Walter and Irene Kershaw ~ Real ale ~ Bar food ~ Restaurant ~ (01434) 240382 ~ Children in eating area of bar and in restaurant until 9pm ~ Open 11-3, 6-11; 12-3, 7-10.30 Sun; 12-2, 7-10.30 Nov-Mar winter ~ Bedrooms: £40B/£60B

THROPTON NU0302 Map 10
Three Wheat Heads 🛏️

B6341

From the attractive garden of this stonebuilt 17th-c village inn – set in the heart of Coquetdale – there are lovely views towards the Simonside Hills; play area and dovecot. Inside, the refurbished carpeted bar on the right and the pleasant and roomy dining area have good fires (there's a fine tall stone fireplace), wheelback chairs around neat rows of dark tables, more heavily cushioned brocaded seats, comfortable bar stools with backrests, and an elaborate longcase clock; darts and dominoes. Good home-made food, served in huge helpings with copious vegetables includes sandwiches, home-made soup (£2.25), garlic mushrooms (£3.25), fresh battered cod (£4.95), home-made lasagne (£5.95), steak and kidney pudding (£6.50), lamb and apricot casserole (£6.95), supreme of pheasant with orange and ginger sauce (£7.50), steaks (from £9.50), and children's dishes (from £3.25); the restaurant is no smoking. Batemans XXXB, McEwans 80/-, and a seasonal beer on handpump, 10 malt whiskies, and welcoming obliging service; piped music. *(Recommended by Mr and Mrs T A Bryan, J Wheeler)*

Pubmaster ~ Lease: Gordon Young ~ Real ale ~ Bar food ~ Restaurant ~ (01669) 620262 ~ Children welcome ~ Open 11-3, 5-11; 11-11 Sat; 12-10.30 Sun ~ Bedrooms: £35B/£55B

WARENFORD NU1429 Map 10
Warenford Lodge
Off A1 3 or 4 miles S of Belford

It would be easy to drive straight past this stone house as there's no pub sign outside. But that would be a pity as it's well worth seeking out for the attractively presented and interesting home-made food. The menu includes home-made soup (£2.25), ham and cheese risotto or crispy crab parcels (£3.20), Northumberland sausages (£4.50), Singapore noodles with vegetables in a savoury broth (£6.40), beef in ale pie with garlic crust (£6.90), salmon smoky fish pie (£7.95), Northumbrian fish soup (£8.90), sirloin steak (£10.65), excellent stincotto (Italian pork shank for two people £15.70), and puddings such as their special baked lemon pudding or steamed marmalade pudding (£2.90); and they have an impressive range of local cheese. A decent selection of wines and malt whiskies, and a good choice of teas. The bar looks modern but is actually quite old, with cushioned wooden seats around pine tables, some stripped stone walls, and a warm fire in the big stone fireplace; steps lead up to an extension which now has comfortable dining tables and chairs, and a big woodburning stove. *(Recommended by Roy Morrison, V and E A Bolton, Richard and Anne Hollingsworth, Martin and Helen Hickes)*

Free house ~ Licensee Raymond Matthewman ~ Bar food (not lunchtimes except wknds when lunchtime service stops 1.30, or all day Mon) ~ Restaurant (evening) ~ (01668) 213453 ~ Children in restaurant ~ Open 7-11; 12-2, 7-11 Sat and Sun; closed weekday lunchtimes and all day Mon except bank hols

---

Lucky Dip
Besides the fully inspected pubs, you might like to try these Lucky Dips recommended to us and described by readers (if you do, please send us reports):

Acomb [NY9366]
Miners Arms: Charming small 18th-c pub, up to seven real ales, good coffee, comfortable settles, huge fire in stone fireplace, advertising mirrors, brass plates, children in dining room; garden behind *(Nick and Alison Dowson)*
Allendale [NY8456]
Golden Lion: Friendly and well worn in, with well kept Boddingtons, John Smiths and Timothy Taylor Landlord, good value food (not Mon) inc vegetarian, partly no-smoking dining area with more room upstairs, two real fires, pictures, old bottles, willow-pattern plates; games area with pool and darts, piped music; children welcome; bedrooms *(Andy and Jill Kassube)*
Alnmouth [NU2511]
Schooner: Georgian coaching inn with one busy bar, another quieter with red plush seats, interesting local and nautical pictures, good choice of well kept beers, cheerful service, pleasant conservatory, candlelit Italian restaurant; comfortable good value bedrooms *(John Bateman, Richard and Anne Hollingsworth)*
Anick [NY9665]
☆ *Rat* [signed NE of A69/A695 Hexham junction]: Quaint little pub, warm and cosy with coal fire in old-fashioned kitchen range, chamber-pots hanging from beams, brocaded

chairs, three eating areas and conservatory, lovely north Tyne views, good service, good value food inc plenty of fish and vegetarian, well kept ales inc one brewed for the pub; children welcome, pretty garden with dovecote and statues *(Bill and Sheila McLardy, John and Lynn Busenbark, John Foord)*
Ashington [NZ2787]
Black Diamond [South View]: Former CWS dairy, food in roomy and comfortable dining lounge (not Sun evening) with piped music, bar with good collection of mining pictures and memorabilia, cheap house beer brewed by Northumberland, pool, juke box, fruit machine and large TV *(Eric Larkham)*
Bubbles [Station Rd]: Well kept beers usually inc local Northumberland, tasty lunchtime home cooking, tables (and lavatories) in back yard; weekly live music, juke box, machines *(Eric Larkham)*
Elephant: Imposing corner pub, now tied to Batemans with their beers kept well, original features inc stained glass and decorated windows, bar food lunchtime and evening, obliging licensees; disabled facilities, bedrooms *(Eric Larkham)*
Aycliffe [NZ2722]
☆ *County* [The Green; just off A1(M) junction 59, by A167]: Bistro-style pub-restaurant with friendly bar, good food from bar lunches (not

Sun) inc sandwiches, sausages and mash or black pudding to tempting and interesting restaurant dishes (not Sun/Mon evenings), well kept Raby beer, good choice of wines by the glass; harder to get a table since it's been on the BBC's *Food & Drink* programme *(M Borthwick)*

Bamburgh [NU1835]
Lord Crewe Arms: Small hotel under new management, prettily set in charming coastal village dominated by Norman castle; back hotel bar with log fire, more modern side bar with hunting murals (children and dogs allowed here), Bass and Stones under light blanket pressure, usual food from lunchtime sandwiches to steaks, no-smoking restaurant (not always open); short walk from splendid sandy beach, bedrooms comfortable, good breakfasts esp kippers; winter opening may be restricted *(LYM, W K Wood, Kevin Thorpe)*
Victoria [Front St]: Done up with style and panache, caring young staff, good bar food, well kept beer inc Morlands Old Speckled Hen, interesting brasserie; comfortable bedrooms – very cheap in winter *(Kevin Thomas, Nina Randall, Neil Hunter)*

Barnard Castle [NZ0617]
Old Well [The Bank]: Emphasis on pleasantly atmospheric no-smoking dining room (well behaved children allowed here), big helpings of good food cooked by daughter from sandwiches, baked potatoes and extremely good chips to gourmet evenings, friendly landlady, good atmosphere, well kept Courage and Tetleys, decent wines; terrace over town walls, comfortable bedrooms *(D and M Senior, M Smith)*

Barrasford [NY9274]
☆ *Barrasford Arms*: Friendly country local with blazing fires in compact bar, lounge across hall, usual food in big high-ceilinged dining room, cheery regulars, children's room; lovely sandstone building with pretty yard and wonderful views, good value bedrooms handy for Hadrian's Wall, good breakfast (but early-morning quarry traffic passes) *(John and Esther Sprinkle)*

Beamish [NZ2254]
☆ *Sun* [far side of Beamish Open Air Museum – paid entry]: Turn-of-the-century pub moved from Bishop Auckland as part of the lively and excellent museum; very basic real period feel at quieter times, with well kept McEwans 80/-, Theakstons Best and Youngers No 3, filled rolls *(Penny and Martin Fletcher, LYM, Paul S McPherson, Nick and Alison Dowson)*

Belsay [NZ1079]
☆ *Highlander* [A696]: Efficiently run dining pub with good range of food in extensively refurbished side bar and open-plan dining area, nice plain wood tables, reasonable prices, good welcoming service, well kept Scottish Courage ales, good log fires, unobtrusive piped music, separate locals' bar; open all day *(Christopher Turner, Bill and Sheila McLardy)*

Berwick upon Tweed [NT9552]
☆ *Cantys Brig* [B6461 towards Paxton]: Rather modern attractive bar with yachting décor, real

ales, good reasonably priced enterprisingly cooked fresh food inc local fish and haggis, efficient friendly service, open fire, upstairs dining room overlooking River Whiteadder, tables out on lawn running down to it *(L Fraser)*
Foxtons: Two-floor bar with slightly wine bar/bistro atmosphere, good range of wines and whiskies, changing ales such as Caledonian Deuchars and Timothy Taylor Landlord, wide choice of reasonably priced food, dedicated locals, side restaurant *(Alison Keys)*
☆ *Rob Roy* [Dock View Rd/Dock Rd, Spittal (Tweedmouth)]: Local fish a speciality, not cheap but very fresh, in quiet and cosy seaview pub, dark fishing-theme traditional bar (can be smoky) with roaring fire and polished wood floor, pleasant dining room, friendly landlord; keg beers but decent wines and good fresh coffee; bedrooms *(A and B Jones, Paul S McPherson)*

Birtley [NZ2756]
Moulders Arms [Peareth Terr]: Pleasantly refurbished local by church in old part of village, substantial reasonably priced straightforward food (till 10 evenings) inc children's, quick service; very popular lunchtime and Sat evening, must book Sun; garden *(M Borthwick)*

Corbridge [NY9964]
Angel [Newcastle Rd]: Small hotel with welcoming and attentive neat staff and good value bar food in plushly comfortable lounge; locals' back bar, restaurant, Scottish Courage ales; bedrooms *(LYM, Eric Locker)*
☆ *Black Bull* [Middle St]: Roomy unpretentious pub, old-fashioned and low-ceilinged, with good choice of generous well priced pub food, well kept Whitbreads-related and guest ales, reasonably priced wines, large no-smoking restaurant; stone-floored bar with traditional settles, mix of comfortable chairs, roaring fire, efficient staff, friendly atmosphere even on crowded Fri/Sat night; open all day *(A Denniss, R and K Halsey, Liz and John Soden)*
Dyvels [Station Rd]: Unassuming but pleasant and friendly, with particularly well kept Bass, Black Sheep and a guest such as Batemans, reasonably priced food, tables in pleasant area outside; good value well equipped bedrooms, open all day Sat and summer Sun, cl winter weekday lunchtimes *(Andy and Jill Kassube, Dr and Mrs B Baker)*
Golden Lion [Hill St]: Refurbished but keeping character and old fireplaces in large rambling lounge with no-smoking area, old local photographs, cheap lunchtime food inc vegetarian *(J and H Coyle)*
☆ *Robin Hood* [East Wallhouses, Military Rd (B6318 5 miles NE)]: Unpretentious pub popular for good generous plain food (choice widest in restaurant); two or three real ales, blazing real fires, friendly staff, interesting carved settles in saloon; piped music *(Blaise Vyner, John Oddey, John Prescott)*

Cornhill on Tweed [NT8639]
Collingwood Arms: Very busy, with well kept Caledonian, Tetleys and a guest beer, good

coffee, food all hours inc good scampi and roast beef, willing friendly service *(N K Campbell)*

Dunstan [NU2520]

Cottage: Long low cottage-row conversion, low beams, panelling, stripped brickwork, banquettes, copper-topped tables and soft lighting, with smart and helpful young staff, pleasant well planted back conservatory, good value food, comfortable beamed medieval-theme restaurant; partly covered sheltered arbour full of flowers, huge lawn; modern bedrooms *(B and C Clouting)*

Durham [NZ2742]

Court [Court Lane]: Well kept Bass and a guest beer, good cheap generous food inc fine chips all day (not Sun), helpful outside price list, big L-shaped room with seats outside; good mix from students to academics and prison officers, very busy during University term time *(John Fazakerley, Eric Larkham, Dr Muriel Sawbridge)*

Dun Cow [Old Elvet]: Unsmart but very welcoming traditional town pub in pretty black and white timbered cottage, tiny front bar with wall benches (unusual sliding door gives it a homely parlour feel), larger back bar with machines etc, particularly well kept Boddingtons, Castle Eden and a guest ale, cheap soup and sandwiches etc; children welcome, open all day *(LYM, Eric Larkham, Peter Plumridge, Karen Eliot)*

Old Elm Tree [Crossgate]: Big pub with three linked rooms on steep hill opp castle; unpretentious but warm welcoming atmosphere, prompt cheerful service, open fires, impressive beer choice, farm cider, seats outside; TV, machines, juke box; regulars can clock in and out *(Bruce Drew, Eric Larkham)*

Victoria [Hallgarth St; A177 nr Dunelm House]: Down-to-earth cosy unpretentious local, three small and attractive unspoilt rooms packed with Victoriana, well kept Marstons Pedigree, McEwans 80/- and Theakstons Best, lots of malt whiskies, welcoming landlord, wonderful crisps, no juke box or TV, coal fires in bar and back room; bedrooms *(the Didler, P Vigano, Eric Larkham)*

Elwick [NZ4533]

Spotted Cow [¼ mile off A19 W of Hartlepool]: Nicely refurbished old building facing village green, Camerons ales, good food inc fresh fish from Hartlepool Fish Quay in pleasantly plush lounge and dining room *(Norma and Keith Bloomfield)*

Embleton [NU2323]

Sportsman: Large pub converted from two guest-houses, big terrace, stunning views to Dunstanburgh Castle, good food esp curry; bedrooms *(Richard and Anne Hollingsworth)*

Falstone [NY7287]

Blackcock: Cosy and old-fashioned friendly local, well run, with open fires, usual food inc baguettes, baked potatoes and big filled yorkshire puddings, well kept changing ales such as Boddingtons, Castle Eden and their own cheap Blackcock; dogs welcome, children allowed in pool room, quiet juke box;

bedrooms, handy for Kielder Water *(John and Kathleen Potter, Mr and Mrs F Carroll)*

Framwellgate Moor [NZ2644]

Marquis of Granby [Front St]: Classic small roadside village pub, well kept very cheap Sam Smiths OB *(Eric Larkham)*

☆ *Tap & Spile* [Front St; B6532 just N of Durham]: Fine range of rapidly changing well kept beers inc local ones like Big Lamp, Butterknowle and Mordue, two farm ciders, decent food at low prices, warm and comfortable atmosphere, daily papers, tourist guides, free Sun nibbles; child-friendly, no-smoking lounge, one room with board games, another with bar billiards and fruit machine *(Andy and Jill Kassube, Eric Larkham)*

Gateshead [NZ2657]

Angel View [Low Eighton; A167, just off A1]: Named for exceptional view of controversial nearby Angel of the North, sympathetically refurbished hotel, several small attractively furnished areas, good value bar food from sandwiches to steaks, helpful friendly staff; restaurant; more bedrooms this year *(M Borthwick, Brian Abbott)*

Green [White Mare Pool, Wardley; W of roundabout at end of A194(M)]: Large nicely decorated modern lounge, light and airy, separate bar, restaurant area, Bass, Theakstons Best and XB with interesting guest beers and regular beer festivals, huge helpings of freshly prepared food inc unusual dishes; light piped music *(Brian Abbott, Andrew Jefferies)*

Ship [Eighton Banks, quite handy for A1(M)]: Recently extended open-plan pub popular at lunchtime for good choice of food inc unusually good side salads, Sun lunch, large pleasantly decorated no-smoking dining room, model ships and marine artefacts, well kept real ale; south-facing garden with play area, great moor views inc interesting animals opp *(Brian Abbott, M Borthwick, Andrew Jefferies)*

Great Stainton [NZ3422]

Kings Arms: Friendly atmosphere, good choice of good value generous food, well kept Whitbreads-related and guest ales, good service, spotless and comfortable; restaurant; lovely spot *(Roy Morrison)*

Hexham [NY9464]

☆ *Royal* [Priestpopple]: Being refurbished by the Pellys, who scored such a hit at the Manor House, Carterway Heads; tasteful décor in handsome stylish bar, three real ales and two ciders, shortish choice of delicious unusual bar food *(John Oddey)*

Tap & Spile [Battle Hill/Eastgate]: Two bars, up to ten real ales, country wines, cheap but limited weekday lunchtime food, good service; no dogs *(Andy and Jill Kassube)*

High Force [NY8728]

☆ *High Force Hotel* [B6277 about 4 miles NW of Middleton in Teesdale]: Beautifully placed high-moors hotel, named for England's highest waterfall nearby and doubling as mountain rescue post, with basic décor to suit; brews its own good value hoppy Teesdale Bitter, Cauldron Snout and Forest, also Theakstons and good choice of bar food (and of malt whiskies), helpful service, friendly atmosphere, quiz night Fri; children very welcome, comfortable bedrooms, pleasant garden *(LYM, Ian and Nita Cooper, Nick and Alison Dowson, John and Joan Wyatt, Mark Percy, Lesley Mayoh, M Borthwick)*

Holwick [NY9027]

Strathmore Arms [back rd up Teesdale from Middleton]: Quiet and cosy unspoilt country pub in beautiful scenery just off Pennine Way, maybe beseiged by ducks; landlady's husband cooking good Polish-influenced food such as chicken breast stuffed with home-smoked salmon and smoked cheese sauce, well kept Scottish Courage and a guest ale, friendly staff and locals, log fire, lovely dog called Bisto, games, books etc; bedrooms, camp site *(J and H Coyle)*

Holy Island [NU1343]

☆ *Ship* [Marygate; former Northumberland Arms]: Cosy bar with eating area off, beamery, wooden furniture, bare boards, panelling, maritime/fishing memorabilia and pictures; good value food inc vegetarian, good open sandwiches and local seafood, quick chatty service, well kept real ales in summer such as Border Blessed, Holy Island and Sacred Kingdom, good choice of whiskies; children welcome, nice setting; three comfortable Victorian-décor bedrooms, may close for a while Jan/Feb *(Comus Elliott, Paul S McPherson, Anthony Barnes)*

Holystone [NT9503]

Salmon: Comfortably furnished Coquet Valley local, very welcoming landlady, good value simple food from sandwiches up, well kept real ale, roaring fire, pool; in attractive countryside close to venerable Lady's Well, good nearby walks *(LYM, John Allen)*

Horsley [NZ0966]

☆ *Lion & Lamb* [B6528, just off A69 Newcastle—Hexham]: Well converted back to a pub a couple of years ago after almost 20 years as a restaurant; two main rooms, small smart restaurant, stripped stone, flagstones, panelling, untreated tables and chairs; good well presented food (not Sun evening) inc bargain specials, four well kept changing ales such as Hartleys, Higsons, Timothy Taylor, friendly efficient staff, attractive garden *(T M Dobby, John Foord, Graham and Karen Oddey, John Oddey)*

Matfen [NZ0372]

☆ *Black Bull* [off B6318 NE of Corbridge]: Striking stone building, a mass of hanging baskets and flowerbeds; local eating-out atmosphere in extended turkey-carpeted bar with plush banquettes, comfortable restaurant (no smoking at lunchtime), nicely presented good food from sandwiches up inc good fresh veg, 1940s *Picture Post* photographs, well kept Morlands Old Speckled Hen, Theakstons Best and Black Bull and guest beers, log fires; children in eating area, separate games bar, juke box; picnic-sets on terrace overlooking green of interesting out-of-the-way estate village; bedrooms, open all day w/e *(Chris Rounthwaite, Andy and Jill Kassube, Canon*

David Baxter, LYM, K F Mould, Anthony Barnes)

Mickley [NZ0761]

Blue Bell [Mount Pleasant, off A695 Prudhoe—Stocksfield]: Cosy little pub with rural feel (though on edge of built-up area), very popular locally for good home-cooked food cooked to order – may have to book; Courage Directors and Marstons Pedigree, friendly staff *(J and H Coyle)*

Middleton in Teesdale [NY9526]

Kings Head [Market Pl]: Tastefully refurbished pub/bistro with imaginative varied food inc plate of local cheeses, Theakstons Best and XB *(Mark Percy, Lesley Mayoh)*

Milbourne [NZ1275]

Waggon [A696 NW of Ponteland]: Open-plan, with huge fire each end, cheerful welcome, five or six well kept ales, good choice of tasty food inc interesting dishes *(John Oddey)*

Morpeth [NZ2086]

☆ *Tap & Spile* [Manchester St]: Consistently welcoming, with up to ten well kept ales and farm cider in cosy and easy-going two-room pub with limited choice of good value food made by excellent landlady, fair prices, stripped pine furniture, interesting old photographs, folk music Sun afternoons, Mon quiz night, board games, dominoes, cards, darts, fruit machine; unobtrusive piped music, children welcome, open all day *(John Allen)*

Newburn [NZ1665]

☆ *Keelman* [Grange Rd, by Tyne Riverside Country Park]: Shares attractive granite-built former 19th-c pumping station with Big Lamp Brewery, their full range at attractive prices; high ceiling, wooden gallery, no-smoking area, lofty windows; limited but good waitress-served bar food (not Sun evening) inc vegetarian, children's and early evening specials; brewery open to visitors; fruit machine, piped pop music; open all day, tables outside; bedrooms in new block, handy for country park walks *(Eric Larkham, John Oddey, GSB, Andy and Jill Kassube)*

Newcastle upon Tyne [NZ2464]

Bacchus [High Bridge East, between Pilgrim St and Grey St]: Two beautifully fitted rooms with lovely old mirrors, panelling and solid furnishings, six well kept ales inc local Mordue and two guests, one at bargain price, cheap hot lunches (not Sun); piped music, machines; cosy and comfortable when not too busy, open all day (cl Sun lunchtime unless Newcastle United playing at home) *(John A Foord, Eric Larkham)*

Bodega [Westgate Rd]: Beautifully refurbished partly divided Edwardian drinking hall, bare boards, colourful walls and ceiling, two magnificent original stained-glass domes; good value lunchtime food inc sandwiches and interesting vegetarian, well kept Mordue Geordie Pride (sold here as No 9) and other mainly local beers tapped from the cask, friendly staff; juke box or piped music may be loudish, machines, TV, Tues quiz night, busy evenings (and if Newcastle Utd at home or on TV); open all day, next to Tyne Theatre *(Andy*

and Jill Kassube, Eric Larkham)
Bridge Hotel [Castle Sq, next to high level bridge]: Big high-ceilinged room divided into several areas leaving plenty of space by the bar with replica slatted snob screens, six well kept ales, decent lunchtime food inc vegetarian, welcoming staff, magnificent fireplace, great views of river and bridges from back windows; sports TV, piped music, fruit machines, very long-standing Mon folk club upstairs; tables on flagstoned back terrace overlooking section of old town wall; open all day *(Eric Larkham, LYM)*
Chillingham [Chillingham Rd, Heaton]: Two big impressive rooms, fine panelling and furnishings, six well kept ales inc guests, occasional beer festivals, good cheap food lunchtime and (not w/e) early evening; piped music, pool tables in room off, board games, juke box, TV, machines; children in lounge (cl afternoon – rest open all day) *(Eric Larkham)*
☆ *Cooperage* [The Close, Quayside]: One of city's oldest buildings in good waterfront setting, all bare stone and wooden beams; a Bass managed pub with a good range of other ales such as Ind Coope Burton, Marstons Owd Rodger, Stones, Timothy Taylor Landlord and Tetleys, with Addlestone's cider and a good choice of good well presented hearty fresh food, sensible prices; pool, juke box, machines; restaurant, night club *(LYM, Bob and Marg Griffiths)*
Duke of Wellington [High Bridge West, between Grey St and Bigg Mkt]: Often crowded L-shaped Victorian-style pub lined with pictures commemorating the Iron Duke, well kept Tetleys-related beers and a good choice of guests, occasional beer festivals, hot and cold lunchtime sandwiches and baked potatoes (not Sun); juke box, machines, TV; open all day (cl Sun afternoon) *(Eric Larkham)*
Fighting Cocks [Albion Rd]: Basic friendly pub tied to local Four Rivers with their beers kept well, farm cider, hot and cold sandwiches, good bridge views, keen staff, free juke box, fruit machine, original space game; Thurs quiz night, occasional live music; couple of steps down to bar, open all day (cl Sun afternoon) *(Eric Larkham)*
Fitzgeralds [Grey St]: Beautifully refurbished Victorian pub in elegant street on fringe of Bigg Market, lots of alcoves, discreet lighting, red mahogany and polished brass, real ales inc interesting guests, wide range of good value lunchtime food inc freshly baked baguettes; can get very busy, piped music, machines; cl Sun am *(Michael Doswell)*
Free Trade [St Lawrence Rd, off Walker Rd (A186)]: Great atmosphere in artfully basic split-level pub with awesome river and bridge views, three or four local Mordue beers inc Radgie Gadgie and Workie Ticket and a couple from Scottish Courage, weekday lunchtime sandwiches, real fire, cricket radio, interesting free juke box; high-standard gents' graffiti, tables outside, open all day *(Eric Larkham)*
Hotspur [Percy St]: Light and airy open-plan Victorian pub, big front windows and decorated mirrors, four Scottish Courage and

up to four guest beers, farm cider, lots of bottled Belgian beers, good value wine; machines, big-screen sports TV (refurbishment means people out in the new seating area in the side lane can watch too), piped music; open all day, sandwiches and hot snacks all day till 9; can get packed, esp pre-match *(Eric Larkham, Ted George)*
New Bridge [Argyle St]: Large bar, comfortably refurbished and welcoming with separate areas and alcoves, home-made lunchtime food (just snacks such as hot beef sandwiches Sat), two changing ales – usually local; piped music, TV, machines, open all day *(Eric Larkham)*
Newcastle Arms [St Andrews St]: Open-plan pub on fringe of China Town, good range of well kept Tetleys-related and other real ales with occasional mini beer festivals, friendly staff, lunchtime sandwiches etc, juke box, fruit machine; open all day (cl Sun afternoon), can get very busy esp on football match days *(Eric Larkham, Lester Edmonds, Andy and Jill Kassube)*
☆ *Ouseburn Tavern* [Shields Rd, Byker; formerly Tap & Spile]: The well run original Tap & Spile, renamed when the namesake chain of pubs was sold off; nine interesting well kept real ales, three farm ciders, decent lunchtime bar food inc sandwiches, quiet and solidly comfortable back lounge, front bar with pool, machines and TV; jazz Mon, quiz Tues, maybe folk/blues Sun afternoon; open all day *(Eric Larkham, LYM)*
Ship [Stepney Bank]: Traditional local beside Byker city farm, Whitbreads-related beers, unusua sandwiches (normally all day), pin table, pool, juke box, fruit machine, TV; seats outside and picnic-sets on green opp, open all day; popular with craft, drama and music workers from nearby arts centre *(Eric Larkham)*
Tilleys [Westgate Rd]: Next to Tyne Theatre and nr performing arts college, so interesting mix of customers; large bar with scores of classic film stills, snug mirrored lounge; lunchtime soup, ploughman's with up to 16 cheeses and six pâtés, sole outlet around Newcastle for full Jennings beer range; big TV, juke box, fruit machines; open all day (evening only, Sun) *(Andy and Jill Kassube, Eric Larkham)*
Tyne [Maling St]: Single-room pub at confluence of Ouseburn and Tyne, local Mordue and Whitbreads-related ales, unusual lunchtime hot or cold sandwiches, décor of band posters, free CD juke box, fruit machine, sports TV; tables out under arch of Glasshouse Bridge, barbecue Sun lunch, early Fri evening; fairy-lit garden (loudspeakers out here too) under an arch of Glasshouse Bridge, some barbecues; open all day, can get very full *(Eric Larkham)*
Newton by the Sea [NU2424]
☆ *Ship* [The Square, Low Newton]: Good genuine local quaintly tucked into top corner of courtyard of old cottages facing beach and sea, efficient service even when busy (as it can be on a hot day), good reasonably priced crab

sandwiches and ploughman's, coffee, tea, real ale in summer, pool table, ices served outside in summer; children welcome, tables out on green *(Richard and Anne Hollingsworth, Iain Patton, Chris Wrigley)*

North Bitchburn [NZ1733]

Red Lion: 17th-c beams, log fires, welcoming staff, good food, well kept beers inc guests, thriving atmosphere *(C A Hall)*

North Hylton [NZ4057]

Shipwrights [Ferryboat Lane; N bank of River Wear almost under the A19 bridge]: Friendly landlord, wide choice of good food running to alligator, ostrich and kangaroo steaks, chamber-pots and copper pans hanging from beams, open fires, cosy bedrooms *(B Adams)*

North Shields [NZ3468]

Chain Locker [Duke St, New Quay]: Simple nautical-theme Victorian pub nr pedestrian ferry, half a dozen or more well kept ales inc unusual local ones, farm cider, open fire; food (not Sun evening) from lunchtime sandwiches up; piped music, fruit machine; children welcome, open all day Thurs-Sun, Fri folk night *(Graham and Karen Oddey, LYM)*

Colonel Linskill [Charlotte St]: Happy comfortable atmosphere, up to six beers such as Harviestoun Schiehallion kept well by keen manager (his father was world haggis-eating champion), TV, fruit machine, darts in back room; open all day, cheap beer 4-7 *(Eric Larkham)*

☆ *Magnesia Bank* [Camden St]: Big brightly lit bar in well run Victorian pub overlooking Tyne, well kept Mordue, Durham and guest beers, vast choice of cheerful home-made lunchtime food, friendly staff, open fire, quiet piped pop music, TV, fruit machines; children welcome, tables outside, open all day, live music Thurs and Sun often featuring members of Lindisfarne *(Eric Larkham)*

Prince of Wales [Bell St; former Old Wooden Dolly]: Well refurbished, quiet pleasant sitting/dining area, back lounge with black and red tiled floor and pool table, small front bar with TV and juke box; cheap well kept Sam Smiths OB and Museum, good value usual food, dark red leather settle, stained wood, polished brass, lots of photographs of the late Duke of Windsor and of Tyne ships, coal fire *(Eric Larkham)*

Tap & Spile [Tynemouth Rd]: Recently reconverted to two rooms, quiet comfortable lounge on right, bar with TV, darts and occasionally live music, constantly changing beers, two or three ciders, good home-cooked food, excellent company; open all day *(Eric Larkham)*

☆ *Wooden Doll* [Hudson St]: Under good new management, with high view of fish quay and outer harbour, informal mix of furnishings in bare-boards bar, up to nine well kept changing ales, helpful staff, tasty food lunchtime and early evening, largely no-smoking eating area, lots of paintings by local artists for sale; children welcome till 8, occasional live music, open all day Sat *(Eric Larkham, LYM)*

Piercebridge [NZ2116]

George [B6275 just S of village, over bridge]:

Attractive old inn under new licensees, wide choice of enjoyable food, three comfortably worn-in bars with five open fires between them, Scottish Courage ales, decent wines, the famous clock that stopped short never to go again, river-view restaurant, fine waterside garden; perhaps too rambling for disabled people; children in eating areas, piped music; open all day, good value bedrooms *(Eddie Edwards, John Poulter, Louise Jaive Stephenson, Jim Bush, LYM)*

Pity Me [NZ2645]

Lambton Hounds [Front St]: Three real ales, proper public bar, lounge and snug, food lunchtime and evening, tables in garden; usually open all day Mon-Sat *(Eric Larkham)*

Plawsworth [NZ2748]

Red Lion [A167 S of Chester le Street]: Recently attractively refurbished, with well kept Courage Directors, Morlands Old Speckled Hen and Nimmos, varied good value food inc lunchtime bargain *(Brian Abbott)*

Ponteland [NZ1871]

☆ *Badger* [Street Houses; A696 SE]: Well done rustic conversion of 18th-c house by main road garden centre, relaxing well furnished rooms and alcoves, flagstones, carpet or bare wood, timbered ceilings, stripped stone, brick and timbering, real fires, three Bass-related ales, good-sized food helpings (most people here for this), helpful efficient uniformed staff, quiet piped music; good disabled access and facilities *(John Oddey, Beryl and Bill Farmer, GSB)*

Riding Mill [NZ0262]

☆ *Wellington* [A695 just W of A68 roundabout]: Large 17th-c chain dining pub carefully refurbished in tune with its age, beams, two big log fires and mix of tables and chairs, some upholstered, some not; wide range of interesting food cooked to order running up to bass and lobster, four well kept Scottish Courage ales, good wine choice, friendly welcome and service, disabled access; piped classical music, children welcome, play area and picnic-sets outside, pretty village with nearby walks and river *(Richad Tebay, Isabel Izzett, John Oddey)*

Rothbury [NU0602]

Newcastle Hotel: Small solid Victorian hotel, comfortably refurbished lounge with separate dining area, second bar, Tetleys and two guest ales, friendly service and entertaining locals, good carefully prepared food inc high teas 3.30-5.30 Apr-Oct; comfortable bedrooms, imposing spot at end of green; bedrooms, open all day, handy for Cragside (NT) *(Lynn Sharpless, Bob Eardley, John Foord, Kevin Thomas, Nina Randall)*

Seaton Sluice [NZ3477]

Kings Arms [West Terr]: Reasonably priced home-made food all day, usual Scottish Courage beers *(M W Robinson)*

Shildon [NZ2326]

Flag & Whistle [Strand St]: By what was the world's first railway, and handy for the museum; good food cooked by landlord, good value New World wine *(Sue and Jim Sargeant)*

Shoreswood [NT9447]

Salutation [A698 Berwick—Cornhill]:

Welcoming inn with roaring coal fire, good value food all sessions, prompt friendly service; space for caravans *(A and B Jones)*

Slaley [NY9858]

Travellers Rest [B6306 S of Hexham]: Early 18th-c pub reopened after total refurbishment by warmly welcoming new owners, now open-plan, a bit spartan but still attractive, beams, flagstones and polished wood floors, comfortable high-backed settles forming discrete areas; lunchtime bar food, evening restaurant, slick service; very well equipped adventure play area behind *(John Oddey)*

Stanley [NZ1953]

Harperley Inn [Harperley Country Park, 1½ m W of Stanley]: Recently refurbished, straightforward home cooking inc bargain three-course lunch with help-yourself tea and coffee, well kept Courage Directors and Jennings or Ruddles County *(M W Robinson, Anne and David Robinson)*

Sunderland [NZ4057]

Fitzgeralds [Green Terr]: Busy city pub with two bars, one rather trendy (nr University), friendly atmosphere, generous basic cheap food, eight real ales *(MLR)*

Tudhoe [NZ2636]

Green Tree: Good home-cooked food, friendly family service, elegant dining room, very reasonable prices *(Dr M Sawbuck)*

Tynemouth [NZ3669]

Cumberland Arms [Front St]: Small nautical-theme bar, more seats in upper bar (lunchtime food here, not Sun), Scottish Courage and guest beers, back terrace with barbecues *(Eric Larkham)*

Fitzpatricks [Front St]: Well refurbished in mahogany, red leather and cast iron, cosily divided open-plan rooms on split levels, good mix of low and tall tables, settles, armchairs and so forth; six well kept ales, huge helpings of usual bar food lunchtime and early evening (not Fri-Sun nights), friendly helpful staff, children welcome – high chairs; piped music, back room with machines and big-screen sports TV, live music Tues, open all day, picnic-sets outside (but you can't take glasses out) *(Eric Larkham)*

Percy Arms [Front St]: Part of Celebration Ale House chain with house beer brewed by Hull, others inc guests, table footer, big screen sports TV, piped music; jazz Tues *(Eric Larkham)*

Salutation [Front St]: Single long bar in handsome former coaching inn's big split-level lounge, lots of mahogany and brass rails, comfortable settles along walls, six beautifully kept Whitbreads-related ales, friendly staff, good range of standard food *(Stephen and Jean Curtis)*

Turks Head [Front St]: Scottish Courage pub with good beer choice, two small bars, quite comfortable and friendly; TV, fruit machine, even a stuffed border collie *(Eric Larkham)*

☆ *Tynemouth Lodge* [Tynemouth Rd (A193), ½ mile W of Tynemouth Metro stn]: Genuine-feeling friendly little Victorian-style pub (actually older), very popular for particularly well kept Bass, Belhaven, Black Sheep, a local guest beer and farm ciders, quiet on weekday

afternoons, can be packed evenings; cheap lunchtime filled rolls, coal fire, keen and friendly landlord, no music or machines, no dogs or children; open all day, tables outside *(Eric Larkham, LYM)*

Waldridge [NZ2550]

Waldridge [off A167]: Comfortable and well laid out dining pub with wide choice of good value food inc Chinese and Indian buffet in lounge and restaurant, good service, real ales, soft piped music but no machines; by Waldridge Fell, one of the last surviving low-level moors *(J and H Coyle)*

Wall [NY9269]

☆ *Hadrian*: Solidly comfortable two-room beamed lounge with wide choice of good generous well presented food inc fresh fish and local cheeses, well kept real ales, good house wine, interesting reconstructions of Romano-British life, woodburner, smart efficient staff, unobtrusive piped music, games in public bar, no-smoking Victorian dining room; children welcome, neat garden; roomy comfortable bedrooms – back ones quieter, with good views *(Phil and Heidi Cook, BB)*

Warkworth [NU2506]

Black Bull [Bridge St]: Very individual, with well kept Lambtons, Northumbria Castle, Theakstons Best and a guest such as Adnams, interested welcoming service, huge choice of good food esp Italian and seafood, small helpings for children, no music *(Rev J Hibberd, Robert W Tapsfield)*

☆ *Hermitage* [Castle St]: Rambling pub with interesting quaint décor, old range for heating, well kept Jennings and John Smiths, generous reasonably priced food from sandwiches to good fresh local fish and vegetarian, good service, friendly dry-humoured landlord and staff, dining area and small plush upstairs restaurant; bedrooms *(BB, Jack and Heather Coyle, Richard Tebay, Isabel Izzett)*

Masons Arms [Dial Pl]: Welcoming and comfortable thriving local, quick friendly service, good generous food inc good fish choice, well kept Courage Directors, Newcastle Exhibition and Youngers, good coffee, local pictures, dogs allowed; attractive back flagstoned courtyard *(Comus Elliott, GLD, Richard and Anne Hollingsworth, Kevin Thorpe)*

Sun [Castle Terr]: 17th-c hotel below castle in attractive village not far from sea, friendly helpful staff, well kept S&N ales, wide choice of reasonably priced good food inc local fish in homely comfortable bar; children welcome, bedrooms with good views *(Richard and Anne Hollingsworth, G B Lungden)*

Weldon Bridge [NZ1399]

Anglers Arms [signed just off B6344 nr A397 junction]: Welcoming pub in splendid location, traditional furnishings, old prints, grandfather clock, old china and stuffed fish; good generous bar food inc lunchtime sandwiches, hot beef baguettes and memorable cheese platter, more upmarket restaurant, changing guest beers such as Everards Tiger, Mordue and Ridleys Rumpus; bedrooms *(Michael Doswell)*

West Boldon [NZ3561]
Black Horse [Rectory Bank, just off A184]: Locally popular dining pub with good range of tasty food in bar and big restaurant inc three-course lunches, Whitbreads-related ales with a local guest such as Mordues Radgie Gadgie, friendly attentive staff; parking can be a problem *(Maurice Thompson)*

West Mains [NU0542]
Plough [A1 at Holy Island exit]: Friendly and clean, with good usual food, Scottish Courage beers; Chester the newfoundland/golden retriever welcomes other dogs; bedrooms *(Richard and Anne Hollingsworth)*

West Sleekburn [NZ2985]
Foresters: Welcoming, with good range of generous food, and has had well kept Vaux Sampson, Double Maxim and Wards *(John Allen)*

West Woodburn [NY8987]
Bay Horse [A68]: Well worn in open-plan bar with open fire, well kept Theakstons XB, good coffee, straightforward bar food inc home-made pizzas, vegetarian, children's and Sun roasts; airy dining room, games room, children welcome, riverside garden, play area; cl Mon/Tues lunchtime in winter; bedrooms *(T M Dobby, Sue and Ken Ruskin, LYM)*

Whittonstall [NZ0857]
☆ *Anchor* [B6309 N of Consett]: Attractively refurbished stonebuilt beamed village pub, comfortable banquettes in L-shaped lounge and dining area with high-raftered pitched roof, well kept Scottish Courage ales, huge choice of good generous food from sandwiches through interesting hot dishes to popular Sun lunch, service efficient and friendly even under pressure; piped music; pool, darts and fruit machine in public bar; nice countryside *(GSB, Bob and Marg Griffiths)*

Wylam [NZ1265]
Boathouse [Station Rd; across Tyne from village]: Eight well kept ales inc Timothy Taylor Landlord, good choice of malt whiskies, good cheap generous food inc take-aways, warm welcome *(Andy and Jill Kassube, John A Foord)*

Real ale to us means beer which has matured naturally in its cask – not pressurised or filtered. We name all real ales stocked. We usually name ales preserved under a light blanket of carbon dioxide too, though purists – pointing out that this stops the natural yeasts developing – would disagree (most people, including us, can't tell the difference!).

Nottinghamshire

Pubs here stand out both for friendliness and for much lower drinks prices than the national average. We found beers at below-average prices from a good spread of breweries, including the regional Mansfield, the more local Hardys & Hansons (with their Kimberley beer) and – much smaller and newer – Castle Rock, though the cheapest beer of all was in a Whitbreads pub, the Fellows Morton & Clayton in Nottingham. Other small local breweries worth keeping an eye open for include Mallard and Springhead. Nottingham city, with its deep sandstone cellars, has plenty of fine beer and a good choice of pubs: the Lincolnshire Poacher (very well kept real ales) and the Olde Trip to Jerusalem both doing particularly well these days, the latter after some good restoration work that makes this interesting building more than ever worth a visit. The Lincolnshire Poacher is part of the small Tynemill group: their pubs, here and in neighbouring counties, are all good, with some concentration on interesting real ales, but generally good individual food too, traditional bare-boards furnishings, and a relaxed chatty atmosphere. Other pubs on fine form are the Victoria in Beeston (good value food, splendid beer choice), the Caunton Beck at Caunton and the Martins Arms at Colston Bassett (both have excellent food), and the friendly Nelson & Railway in Kimberley (good value food, well kept beers). The Caunton Beck and Martins Arms are the county's front-runners in the pub food stakes, both memorable places for a meal out: it's the Martins Arms at Colston Bassett which is our choice as Nottinghamshire Dining Pub of the Year. We must mention the spectacular floral displays at the Three Horse Shoes at Walkeringham: a very well run pub in a part of the county where good pubs are spread very thin. The Lucky Dip section at the end of the chapter also has several pubs well worth a special mention: the Beehive at Maplebeck, Vat & Fiddle in Nottingham, Market Hotel in Retford and Bramley Apple in Southwell.

BEESTON SK5338 Map 7
Victoria 🍴 ◧
Dovecote Lane, backing on to railway station

Ideally situated for the beer-loving train buff, the lounge and bar of this friendly roomy pub back on to the railway station, and picnic-sets in a pleasant area outside overlook the platform – trains pass just feet below. Among the 12 changing well kept real ales on handpump there might be Adnams Broadside, Batemans XB, Burton Bridge Summer Ale, Caledonian IPA, Castle Rock Hemlock Ale, Dark Star Cascade, Enville White, Hook Norton Best Bitter and Roosters Yankee; also, two traditional ciders, 105 malt whiskies, 20 Irish whiskeys, and half a dozen wines by the glass. The three downstairs rooms in their original long narrow layout have simple solid traditional furnishings, very unfussy décor, stained-glass windows, stripped woodwork and floorboards (woodblock in some rooms), newspapers to read, and a good chatty atmosphere; dominoes, cribbage, piped music. Popular imaginative food is served in the no-smoking dining area, and a daily changing menu includes around ten vegetarian dishes such as stuffed vine leaves with buffalo mozzarella and peppers or asparagus, taleggio and chive tart (£4.95), pasta with herb, tomato and fresh rocket pesto or baked field mushrooms with garlic, parmesan and fresh herbs (£5.50); as well as sandwiches (from £1.40), the rest of the menu might consist of lincolnshire sausages and mash (£4.95), portuguese-style pork (£5.95), beef in ale (£6.50), seared salmon fillet with cajun spices or chargrilled marinated lamb kebabs (£7.95) and grilled monkfish and pancetta parcels (£10.50); puddings (£2.95-£3.50) such as apple crumble, plum tart with amaretto ice cream or hot bananas with dark rum and ice cream. *(Recommended by Martin Wyss, Dave Braisted, JP, PP, Darly Graton, Graeme Gulibert, the Didler, Roger Everett, Andrew Scarr, Derek and Iris Martin, Marianne and Peter Stevens, Mark and Heather Williamson, Mike and Wena Stevenson, R M Taylor)*

Free house ~ Licensees Neil Kelso and Neil Trafford ~ Real ale ~ Bar food (12-9pm) ~ (01159) 254049 ~ Children in eating area of bar till 8pm ~ Alternate jazz and folk every 2nd Sunday ~ Open 11-11; 12-10.30 Sun

CAUNTON SK7460 Map 7
Caunton Beck 🍴 ♀
Main Street; village signposted off A616 Newark—Ollerton

Despite the emphasis on very good food at this popular establishment, an informal atmosphere and well kept ales define its pubbiness. Virtually new (but not new-looking), the pub was reconstructed, using original timbers and reclaimed oak, around the bones of the old Hole Arms. Scrubbed pine tables and country-kitchen chairs, low beams and rag-finished paintwork create a pleasant relaxed environment, and more atmosphere is bound to develop as it all wears in. There are tables out on delightful terraces with lots of flowers and plants. It is run by part of the team that manages the Wig & Mitre in Lincoln, and consequently, offers similarly well prepared meals from 8am to 11pm – they change what's available to suit the time of day. Lunchtime and evening food includes soup (£3.50), sandwiches (from £3.95), chicken breast terrine with spinach, bacon and sage (£5.25), mince and onion pie, sautéed lamb's kidney with mustard sauce and jasmine rice or bangers and mash with yorkshire pudding (£6.95), deep-fried tiger prawns with a mustard seed mash and butter sauce or wild mushroom and truffle cappelletti with a slow-cooked tomato and herb sauce (£8.50), sirloin steak with a stilton sauce (£12.50) and pan-fried lemon sole with lemon, prawns and nut brown butter (£12.95); puddings such as marinated oranges, strawberries and raspberries with ice cream, lemon cream tart or tiramisu (£3.50); good value set meal for two. Well kept Adnams, Marstons Pedigree and Timothy Taylor Landlord on handpump, good house wines and usually a fine choice of half bottles, freshly squeezed orange juice; welcoming service, daily papers and magazines, no music or games. *(Recommended by June and Malcolm Farmer, Jack Morley, Dr G Martin, John Fahy)*

Free house ~ Licensees Adam Morgan and Paul Vidic ~ Real ale ~ Bar food (8am-11pm) ~ Restaurant ~ (01636) 636793 ~ Children welcome ~ Open 8am-12am

COLSTON BASSETT SK7033 Map 7
Martins Arms 🍴 ♀ 🍺
Signposted off A46 E of Nottingham

Nottinghamshire Dining Pub of the Year

In summer, you can play croquet in the sizeable attractive garden of this pleasant dining pub, set in estate parkland. There's a comfortable atmosphere in the attractively decorated bars – one has two open fires, and proper snug. The decorous and smart restaurant is well laid out with sensibly spaced tables, and smart uniformed staff serve very good (if not cheap) food, carefully prepared to order from fresh, daily-delivered produce. There may be delays when it's busy, but readers assure us that it's worth the wait. The extensive bar menu might include home-made soup (£2.95), sandwiches (from £2.95; on fresh ciabatta bread from £5.95), tasty grilled black pudding with marinated new potatoes and roasted peppers or baked goat's cheese with roasted beetroot and chive cream dressing (£5.95), pickled trout fillets with tomato compote, chervil and olive oil (£6.95), hearty ploughman's, potato cake filled with local stilton or cheddar with mango chutney or penne with mushrooms, pesto and asparagus (£7.95), grilled plaice fillet with roasted leeks and a chive beurre blanc (£11.95), roast pork fillet with parsnip purée and mustard jus, roast chicken breast with pearl barley, red onion and chilli jam or seared salmon with tomato and basil purée (£12.95) and roast loin of lamb with spicy couscous and redcurrant jus, beef rump with basil pesto and ratatouille or roast spiced duck breast with sweet potato purée and red onion marmalade (£14.95); home-made puddings include bakewell tart with crème chantilly, chocolate and raspberry mousse with an orange coulis and poached pears with chilli and ginger syrup and vanilla ice cream (£4.50). A good choice of well kept real ales on handpump might include Adnams, Bass, Black Sheep Bitter, Castle Rock, Greene King Abbot, Marstons Best and Pedigree, Morlands Old Speckled Hen and Timothy Taylor Landlord; a good range of malt whiskies and cognacs, and an interesting wine list; cribbage and dominoes. *(Recommended by Ian Phillips, Stephen Brown, Joan and Michel Hooper-Immins, Mike Brearley, M A Buchanan, JP, PP, J H Kane, Richard Butler)*

Free house ~ Licensees Lynne Strafford Bryan and Salvatore Inguanta ~ Real ale ~ Bar food (12-2, 6-10; not Sun evenings) ~ Restaurant ~ (01949) 81361 ~ Children over 14 in restaurant and garden ~ Open 12-(2.30 Mon-Fri in winter)3, 6-11; 12-3, 7-10.30 Sun

ELKESLEY SK6975 Map 7
Robin Hood
High Street; village well signposted just off A1 Newark—Blyth

This friendly village local provides a handy stop for the A1, offering weary travellers enjoyable bar food. Changing seasonally, a varied menu might include tasty hot filled rolls (from £1.90) such as good local pork and sage sausages, home-made soup (£2.60), courgette, mushroom and cheddar bake (£4, large £7), spaghetti and crab with red chilli (£4.60), smoked salmon with celeriac remoulade (£5.70), excellent gammon steak (£7.80), chargrilled chicken breast on mediterranean vegetables (£8.20), roast cod fillet topped with crispy leeks on a casserole of mushrooms (£8.30), pan-fried duck breast on potato rosti with port wine and cherry sauce (£9.30), roast rack of lamb on a minted caper sauce with ratatouille tartlet (£10.50), sirloin steak (£11.50), daily specials including a good range of fish dishes from sea bass (£8.50) to whole dover sole (£11.50), and home-made puddings such as crème brûlée or lemon tart (£3). The roomy and comfortably furnished carpeted family dining lounge has pictures, some copper pans and a small collection of horse bits. There's also a plain but neatly kept public bar, with pool, dominoes, cribbage and trivia machines; unobtrusive piped music. Boddingtons on handpump and a guest such as Flowers IPA under light blanket pressure; friendly and efficient service. The garden is moderately well screened from the A1 and has picnic-sets and a play area. *(Recommended by Tony Gayfer, Derek and Sylvia Stephenson, Richard Cole, Jonathan Oxley, Michelle Gallagher and Shaun Holley, Kevin Thorpe)*

Whitbreads ~ Lease: Alan Draper and Leanda Roberts ~ Real ale ~ Bar food ~ Restaurant ~ (01777) 838259 ~ Children welcome ~ Open 11.30-3, 6.30-11; 11.30-11 Sat; 12-3, 7-10.30 Sun; closed evening 25 Dec

KIMBERLEY SK5044 Map 7
Nelson & Railway ◖ £
3 miles from M1 junction 26; at exit roundabout take A610 to Ripley, then signposted Kimberley, pub in Station Rd, on right from centre

One reader described this splendid two-roomed Victorian building as the epitome of a good pub, while another enthused about the friendly relaxed atmosphere, and with such accolades, it's no wonder it can get very busy. The pub used to stand between two competing railway stations and gains its unusual name from a shortening of its original title, the Lord Nelson, Railway Hotel. A real hub of village life, the pub even has its own amateur dramatic society, and they put on a pantomime for charity every year. There's an attractive mix of Edwardian-looking furniture in the beamed bar and lounge, with interesting brewery prints and railway signs on the walls. With the Hardys & Hansons brewery directly opposite, the Kimberley Bitter, Classic and seasonal ales on handpump are particularly well kept; several malt whiskies. Good value straightforward bar food includes soup (£1.30), sandwiches (from £1.30; hot rolls from £1.60), baked potatoes (£2.45), cottage pie (£2.95), cod in batter, lasagne or steak and kidney pie (£4.45), ploughman's (£4.55), chicken tikka masala or deep-fried vegetables with cheese and garlic sauce (£4.85), gammon and egg (£4.95), sirloin steak (£5.95), daily specials including home-made pie of the day (£4.95, readers recommend the rabbit), and seafood dishes such as sweet and sour prawn stir fry or moules marinières (£5-£6), puddings (£1.85) and children's meals (£1.65); Sunday lunch (£3.95 adults, £2.95 children); the dining room is no smoking at meal times. Darts, alley and table skittles, dominoes, chess, cribbage, Scrabble, fruit machine and juke box. There are tables and swings out in a good-sized cottagey garden. *(Recommended by Tom Evans, JP, PP, RT and JC Moggridge, Dr and Mrs B Baker, Derek and Sylvia Stephenson, Robert Gartery, John and Elspeth Howell, John Honnor, Jenny and Roger Huggins, D Parkhurst, George Atkinson, William Foster)*

Hardys & Hansons ~ Tenants Harry and Pat Burton ~ Real ale ~ Bar food (12-2.30, 5.30-9; 12-6 Sun) ~ (0115) 938 2177 ~ Children in eating area of bar ~ Open 11.30-3 Mon-Weds, 11-11 Thurs-Sat; 12-10.30 Sun ~ Bedrooms: £22B/£37B

LAXTON SK7267 Map 7
Dovecote
Signposted off A6075 E of Ollerton

This popular redbrick house is set in a village which is a model of living history: Laxton is one of the few places in the country still farmed using the open field system and the pub stands next to the three huge medieval fields. A former stable block behind the pub has a visitor centre explaining it all and as part of this ancient farming system the grass is auctioned for haymaking in the third week of June, and anyone who lives in the parish is entitled to a bid – as well as to a drink. The central room has brocaded button-back built-in corner seats, stools and chairs, and a coal-effect gas fire, and opens through a small bay (which was the original entry) into another similar room. Around the other side, a simpler room with some entertaining Lawson Wood 1930s tourist cartoons leads through to a pool room with darts, fruit machine, pool, dominoes and piped music; no-smoking area. Straightforward but popular good value food includes home-made soup (£1.90), sandwiches (from £2.50), ratatouille or broccoli and cauliflower mornay (£5.25), steak and kidney or beef and Guinness pie (£5.40) and occasional specials such as chicken and ham or steak and mushroom pie (£5.60), fresh cod or haddock (£5.75), mixed grill (£7.25) and 10oz fillet steak (£8.90); friendly and efficient service. Mansfield Bitter and two guest ales, (one changing weekly) such as Charles Wells Bombardier or Flowers IPA. There are white tables and chairs on a small front terrace by a sloping garden with a disused white dovecote, and a children's play area; also, a site for six caravans with lavatories and showers. *(Recommended by Bill Flisher, Geoffrey Lawrance, Derek and Iris Martin)*

Free house ~ Licensees Stephen and Betty Shepherd ~ Real ale ~ Bar food ~ (01777) 871586 ~ Children in eating area of bar and restaurant ~ Open 12-3.30, 6-11(7-10.30 Sun)

NOTTINGHAM SK5640 Map 7
Fellows Morton & Clayton 🍺 £
54 Canal Street (part of inner ring road)

Although it can get very busy at weekend lunchtimes, this carefully converted old canal building is the kind of place you feel comfortable in from the moment you cross the door. Buzzing with businessmen and lawyers at lunchtime, it's popular with a younger crowd in the evening. The pub brews its own beers, Fellows and Post Haste (which are very reasonably priced for the area), and from a big window in the quarry tiled glassed-in area at the back you can see the little brewery: Samuel Fellows

and Matthew Claytons. They also have well kept Boddingtons, Burtonwood Top Hat, Castle Eden, Tetleys, Timothy Taylor Landlord and Wadworths 6X on handpump. As we went to press, the licensees had plans to change the menu, but were unable to give us any further ideas as to what a future one might include. Popular good value lunchtime bar food has included home-made soup (£1.75), filled french bread (from £3), cheeses with bread (£3.65), broccoli and cheese pasta (£4.25), half roast chicken (£4.45), steak and kidney pie (£4.95), battered haddock (£5.25), 8oz rump steak (£5.95), daily specials such as vegetable lasagne (£3.95) or seafood platter (£4.75) and puddings (£1.75-£2.50); prompt, friendly service. The softly lit bar has dark red plush seats built into alcoves, wooden tables, some seats up two or three steps in a side gallery, and bric-a-brac on the shelf just below the glossy dark green high ceiling; a sympathetic extension provides extra seating. Piped pop music, trivia, fruit machine and daily newspapers on a rack. Outside there's a terrace with seats and tables; Nottingham station is just a short walk away.
(Recommended by Derek and Sylvia Stephenson, Dr and Mrs J H Hills, David Carr, Patrick Hancock, Ian Phillips, Norma and Keith Bloomfield, Rona Murdoch, JP, PP, D Parkhurst, Roger and Jenny Huggins)

Whitbreads ~ Lease: Les Howard and Keely Willans ~ Real ale ~ Bar food (12-2, 6-9) ~ Restaurant ~ (0115) 950 6795 ~ Children in restaurant ~ Open 11-11; 12-10.30 Sun

Lincolnshire Poacher ◖

Mansfield Rd; up hill from Victoria Centre

Impeccably kept real ales are well complemented by friendly obliging service at this bustling and homely town pub. Twelve handpumps mean that alongside Batemans XB and XXXB, Marstons Pedigree and Timothy Taylor Landlord, you can expect up to eight changing guest ales on offer such as Springhead Roaring Meg and Clarks Festival; also good ciders, and around 70 malt whiskies and 10 Irish ones. The traditional big wood-floored front bar has wall settles and plain wooden tables, and is decorated with breweriana; it opens on to a plain but lively room on the left, from where a corridor takes you down to the chatty panelled back snug – newspapers to read; cribbage, dominoes, cards, backgammon, piped music; no-smoking area at lunchtime. Sandwiches aside (from £1.40, served all day), good reasonably priced daily specials might include goat's cheese ravioli (£4.75), Lincolnshire sausages and mash, home-made steak and kidney pie or spaghetti and meat balls with tomato sauce (£4.95); no chips. It can get busy in the evenings when it's popular with a younger crowd. A conservatory overlooks tables on a large terrace behind.
(Recommended by Ian Phillips, Roger and Jenny Huggins, JP, PP, the Didler, John Robertson, R M Taylor, David Carr)

Batemans ~ Lease: Paul Montgomery ~ Real ale ~ Bar food (12-3, 5-8) ~ (0115) 9411584 ~ Children in eating area of bar ~ Open 11-11; 12-10.30 Sun; closed 25 Dec

Olde Trip to Jerusalem ★

Brewhouse Yard; from inner ring road follow The North, A6005 Long Eaton signpost until you are in Castle Boulevard then almost at once turn right into Castle Road; pub is up on the left

Deceptively normal-looking from the outside, this popular pub is built onto caverns burrowing into the sandstone rock below the castle, and the panelled walls of the unique upstairs bar – thought to have served as cellarage for an early medieval brewhouse which stood here – soar narrowly into the dark rent above. The name refers to a tradition that 12th-c crusaders used to meet on this site on the way to the Holy Land. The friendly downstairs bar is also mainly carved from the rock, with leatherette-cushioned settles built into the dark panelling, tables on tiles or flagstones, and more low-ceilinged rock alcoves; also a parlour/snug and two more caves open to the public. Well kept real ales include Hardys & Hansons Kimberley Best, Best Mild, Classic and their cellarman's cask (brewed every two months or so), and Marstons Pedigree on handpump. Bar food includes sandwiches (from £2.29), filled french bread and baked potatoes or burgers (from £2.79), giant yorkshire pudding filled with vegetables, roast beef, pork, lamb or sausages, steak and kidney pudding, courgette and mushroom lasagne or liver and onions (£4.99), fisherman's medley (£5.99), and puddings (from £1.99). Cribbage, fruit machine; seats outside. Children in garden only. *(Recommended by R M Taylor, Ian Phillips, JP, PP, Tim Barrow, Sue Demont, Derek and Sylvia Stephenson, David Carr, Brad W Morley, Chris Raisin, Sidney and Erna Wells)*

Hardys & Hansons ~ Manager Patrick Dare ~ Real ale ~ Bar food (11.30-3(6 Sat, Sun)) ~ (0115) 9473171 ~ Open 11-11; 12-10.30 Sun

UPTON SK7354 Map 7
French Horn
A612

Readers are impressed by the particularly warm welcome at this friendly and popular dining pub which has attractive flower displays in summer. Most of the tables are laid for eating, even on weekday lunchtimes, and a good range of well cooked and presented food might include soup (£2.25), sandwiches (from £2.95), smoked salmon and scrambled eggs or scallops with bacon and garlic sauce (£3.65), steak and ale pie (£5.50), and enjoyable specials such as well liked nut cutlet with red and green pepper cream sauce (£6.25), roasted monkfish tail wrapped in parma ham with dijon mustard and tomato cream (£8.50), tuna loin steak in a rich mussel and prawn ragoût with olives and anchovies (£8.75), pork fillet stuffed with bramley apple and wrapped in smoked bacon with a rosemary and calvados cream (£8.85), crab thermidor (£9.25) and beef sirloin provençale topped with cheese (£10.50); puddings (£2.95). Usefully they also do a range of sandwiches and hot snacks all afternoon; helpful and efficient staff even when busy. There's a nicely relaxed atmosphere in the neat and comfortable open-plan bar with cushioned captain's chairs, wall banquettes around glossy tables, and watercolours by local artists on the walls (some maybe for sale). As we went to press, the landlady was hoping to increase and diversify the range of ales on handpump beyond the well kept Marstons Pedigree, Tetleys and Worthingtons already on offer; several wines by the glass; piped music. Picnic-sets on the big sloping back paddock look out over farmland. *(Recommended by JP, PP, Keith Berrett, Phyl and Jack Street, Ian Phillips, David and Helen Wilkins, Joy and Peter Heatherley, Darly Graton, Graeme Gulibert, G Neighbour, Irene and Geoffrey Lindley, J H Kane)*

Pubmaster ~ Tenant Joyce Carter ~ Real ale ~ Bar food (12-2, 6-9.30; light snacks 2-6) ~ Restaurant ~ (01636) 812394 ~ Children welcome ~ Jazz every 2nd Sun evening ~ Open 10.30-11; 12-10.30 Sun; closed evening 25 Dec

WALKERINGHAM SK7792 Map 7
Three Horse Shoes
High Street; just off A161, off A631 W of Gainsborough

This pleasant village pub is at its best in summer, when the rather ordinary frontage is transformed into a blaze of colour by the licensees' award wining hanging baskets and flower displays. Using 9,000 plants, they are quite astonishing and combine attractively with the slight austerity of the simple old-fashioned décor inside. As we went to press, plans were being made to start a Japanese style millennium garden beside the top car park, hopefully to be completed by next summer. Of the two brothers who run it, John keeps the bar, while Ray is responsible for the wide choice of good value food which might include lunchtime sandwiches (from £1.25), home-made soup (£1.50), home-made pâté or chicken wings with garlic dip (£3.25), haddock or plaice (£5.50), tortellini with tomatoes, peppers and cream, home-cooked ham and chips or liver, bacon and sausage casserole (£5.75), home-made steak and kidney pie, prawn salad or curry of the day (£6.25), gammon and pineapple (£6.50), chicken supreme in a creamy stilton, leek, mushroom and white wine sauce or medallions of pork in a white wine, herb, mustard and cream sauce (£7.75), steaks (from £8.95) and possibly game, monkfish, brill or dover sole specials; vegetables are fresh and lightly cooked. Well kept Bass, Stones, Worthington Best and a guest beer are served from handpumps in the warmly welcoming bar. Darts, dominoes, fruit machine, video game, and piped music. There are seats on a lawned area. (Recommended by Richard Cole, Alan and Judith Gifford, Peter Marshall, Marlene and Jim Godfrey, David Twitchett, JP, PP)

Free house ~ Licensee John Turner ~ Real ale ~ Bar food (not Sun evening or all day Mon) ~ Restaurant ~ (01427) 890959 ~ Children in restaurant ~ Open 11.30-3, 7-11; 12-3, 7-10.30 Sun

Lucky Dip

Besides the fully inspected pubs, you might like to try these Lucky Dips recommended to us and described by readers (if you do, please send us reports):

Awsworth [SK4844]
Gate [via A6096 off A610 Nuthall—Eastwood bypass]: Fine old two-bar traditional pub with Hardys & Hansons Best and Mild, coal fire, small pool room; nr site of once-famous 40 railway bridges – photographs in passage (the Didler)
Bagthorpe [SK4751]
Red Lion [Church Lane; off B600, nr M1 junction 27]: Comfortable and spacious open-plan split-level refurbishment of 17th-c village pub, Boddingtons, Marstons Pedigree and guest beers, some tables set aside for reasonably priced usual food inc vegetarian, children's and OAP lunches, cushioned settles, open fire, pictures, penny arcade machine, no piped music; picnic-sets and big play area in big garden with terrace, attractive setting; open all day Fri-Sat (CMW, JJW, JP, PP, Alan Bowker)
Shepherds Rest [Lower Bagthorpe; 2 miles from M1 junction 27, via A608 towards Eastwood, then off B600]: Extensively refurbished but keeping character, cheerfully enterprising landlord, very pleasant staff, well kept Theakstons and guest beers, wide choice of good home-made food inc OAP lunches, early evening bargains, monthly theme nights; occasional live music; pretty surroundings (Bernard Stradling, Alan Bowker)
Barnby in the Willows [SK8652]
☆ *Willow Tree* [Front St; off A17 E of Newark]: Tastefully extended 17th-c village local with original features in open-plan L-shaped bar, friendly chatty licensees, good reasonably priced freshly cooked food in bar and restaurant, well kept Batemans, Marstons Pedigree, Rudgate Viking and guest beers, log fires throughout; children welcome, games room, tables outside; bedrooms, cl Mon lunchtime (Jack and Philip Paxton)
Beeston [SK5338]
Hop Pole [Chilwell Rd]: Well kept Bass, Marstons Pedigree and two or three guest beers, bare-boards stripped-brick bar, games machine; limited evening food (Darly Graton, Graeme Gulibert)
Bleasby [SK7149]
Waggon & Horses [Gypsy Lane]: Comfortable banquettes in carpeted lounge, open fire in character bar, Banks's and Marstons Pedigree, reasonably priced fresh lunchtime food from snacks up, Fri fish and chips night, chatty landlord, tables outside, back lobby with play

area and comfortable chairs to watch over it; piped music; small camping area behind (CMW, JJW, JP, PP, Jeremy Burnside)
Burton Joyce [SK6443]
Wheatsheaf: Recently refurbished, several individual dimly lit rooms around a central bar, lots of interesting antiques, grandfather clock, lots of wine bottles scattered around; very wide choice of good food, well kept real ales with two or three guests and mini beer festivals; one of very few pubs to have a paddock for visiting horses (Kevin Blake)
Carlton on Trent [SK7964]
Great Northern [Ossington Rd; signed just off A1 N of Newark]: Large busy local next to railway line, comfortable and welcoming, with lots of railway memorabilia, toys in large family room; Mansfield Riding, local Springhead and guest ales, decent food inc good fish and chips, small dining area, good service; play area in garden (JP, PP)
Caythorpe [SK6845]
Black Horse [off A6097 NE of Nottingham]: Unspoilt uncluttered country pub well run by same friendly family for many years, good food inc imaginative sandwiches, good fresh fish Weds-Fri, Mon curry night, microbrewery producing its own good Dover Beck ales, guests such as Adnams and Black Sheep, modest prices, small bar, larger tap room across yard; opp pottery, handy for Trent walks (Jeremy Burnside, Dr and Mrs J H Hills, Derek and Sylvia Stephenson)
Clarborough [SK7383]
Gate [Smeath Lane]: Welcoming open-plan pub in attractive canalside setting, good value food esp fish and chips, all freshly cooked (so will be a wait), Adnams, Mansfield and Stones, open fire, friendly service, restaurant, Sun lunches; can get busy, moorings available (Mike and Sue Losebey)
Costock [SK5726]
Generous Briton [off A60 Nottingham—Loughborough]: Old village local with comfortable lounge, traditional old-fashioned bar, good value food from filled baps up inc OAP bargain lunches Mon-Weds, couple of no-smoking tables up two steps, Mansfield Riding, Best and Old Baily, good choice of soft drinks, friendly chatty landlady, children allowed if eating, very quiet piped music (the Didler, JJW, CMW)

Cotgrave [SK6435]

Manvers Arms [off A46 SE of Nottingham]:
Assorted comfortable furniture in various areas,
brick and beams, pictures, bric-a-brac up high,
friendly service; wide choice of good cheap
lunchtime food inc vegetarian, real ales, quiet
piped music; well behaved children welcome,
small attractive garden with picnic-sets; open all
day *(B and C Clouting)*

Rose & Crown [off A46 SE of Nottingham]:
Recently refurbished, with Boddingtons and
guest beers such as Greene King Abbot and
Morlands Old Speckled Hen, good simple food
(Richard Butler)

Cuckney [SK5671]

Greendale Oak [High Croft]: Good range of
reasonably priced well cooked and served food
(not w/e evenings) from sandwiches up, helpful
licensees, swift service even when very busy
midweek lunchtime, roomy but cosy and
friendly L-shaped bar, good coffee, popular
evening restaurant; bedrooms *(Brenda and
David Tew)*

Drakeholes [SK7090]

Black Swan [signed off A631 Bawtry—
Gainsborough]: Former Griff Inn sorting itself
out under new management, friendly efficient
staff, civilised plush lounge bar, partly no
smoking, attractively redone airy brasserie-style
restaurant, real ales, children in eating area,
piped music; neat landscaped gardens with
pretty view above Chesterfield Canal, quiet
bedrooms being comfortably refurbished, good
breakfast *(Roger and Pauline Pearce, Mike and
Mary Carter, LYM)*

Dunham [SK8174]

Bridge: Nr toll bridge, with good food, real fire,
Springhead and three guest beers inc a bargain
on handpump, tables outside; wheelchair
access, open all day Sun *(Jack and Philip
Paxton)*

Eastwood [SK4846]

Foresters Arms [Main St, Newthorpe]: Cosy
and chatty two-room village local, clean and
well run, with Hardys & Hansons on electric
pump, relaxing lounge, TV and old local
photographs in bar, piano sing-alongs w/e; nice
garden, occasional barbecues *(the Didler)*

Farnsfield [SK6456]

Red Lion [Main St, off A614]: Roomy
refurbished village pub, comfortable
banquettes, pictures and brass, four Mansfield
ales, friendly obliging service, popular food inc
children's and (Mon-Sat) OAP roast lunches,
fair prices; restaurant (not Sun/Mon evenings),
picnic-sets and swings in garden *(JJW, CMW)*

Gateford [SK5781]

Three Legged Stool: Wood and bare stone in
Mansfield dining pub based on former dairy,
brass and books etc in large galleried lounge
with children's room off, decent food inc
children's helpings, Mansfield Riding; piped
music *(CMW, JJW)*

Gotham [SK5330]

Cuckoo Bush: Cosy 19th-c L-shaped lounge
bar with pictures, plates etc, quiet piped music,
limited good value food, well kept Bass, very
friendly staff, sensibly segregated darts and TV

(with sofa); picnic-sets and barbecue in small
garden *(Dr and Mrs J H Hills)*

Gringley on the Hill [SK7391]

Blue Bell [just off A361 Bawtry—Gainsboro]:
Very friendly, with well kept ales such as
Barnsley, Marstons Pedigree and Tetleys,
dinners Thurs-Sat evening, Sun lunch – small
pleasant dining room, must book *(Peter
Marshall)*

Hickling [SK6929]

Plough: Interesting old pub recently refurbished
by friendly new licensee, nice spot by Grantham
Canal basin (locally navigable), two levels and
several rooms extended around old cottage,
armchairs and settees in largest room, very cosy
snug, four real ales, inexpensive food, pool and
TV, quiet piped local radio; handy for towpath
walks, children welcome *(Norma and Keith
Bloomfield, CMW, JJW)*

Hoveringham [SK6946]

Reindeer [Main St]: Open fires in bar and
lounge, lots of beams, some antiques; friendly
and unpretentious, with popular bar food, well
kept Marstons Pedigree *(JP, PP)*

Kimberley [SK5044]

Stag [Nottingham Rd]: Relaxing 16th-c pub
with low beams, dark panelling and settles,
impressive bank of handpumps with Greenalls,
Marstons Pedigree, Shipstones Mild and Bitter
and a guest beer; attractive back garden with
play area; cl weekday lunchtime, open from 2
Sat *(the Didler)*

Kirkby in Ashfield [SK5056]

Countryman [Park Lane (B6018 S)]: Great
traditional atmosphere in upgraded former
miners' local, attractive bas relief murals of
shooting scenes, mining memorabilia, well kept
Theakstons and guest beers, beer festivals,
generous bar food (not Sun evening), low
prices; popular with walkers, music nights *(the
Didler, Peter and Audrey Dowsett, JP, PP,
Kevin Blake)*

Linby [SK5351]

Horse & Groom: Theakstons XB, bar food
(just good choice of hot and cold filled rolls
Tues); in attractive village nr Newstead Abbey
(JP, PP)

Mansfield [SK5561]

Rufford Arms [Chesterfield Rd]: Good-sized
cheerful pub, well presented reasonably priced
food, quick service, good range of real ales and
wines *(Peter and Audrey Dowsett)*

Maplebeck [SK7160]

☆ *Beehive* [signed down pretty country lanes from
A616 Newark—Ollerton and from A617
Newark—Mansfield]: Cosy and unspoiled
beamed country tavern, excellent landlady, tiny
front bar, rather bigger side room, traditional
furnishings, open fire, free antique juke box,
well kept Mansfield Riding and Old Baily,
cheese or ham rolls, tables on small terrace with
flower tubs and grassy bank running down to
little stream, play area with swings; may be cl
Mon lunchtime, delightfully peaceful spot
weekday lunchtimes, very busy w/e and bank
hols *(LYM, JP, PP, the Didler, B Adams)*

Moorgreen [SK4847]

Horse & Groom: Good choice of food inc OAP

bargains, well kept Hardys & Hansons *(JP, PP)*
Morton [SK7251]
Full Moon [back rd SE of Southwell]: 16th-c
local with wide choice of good value standard
food inc lots of puddings, lots of Theakstons
and guest beers, energetic congenial landlord,
comfortable L-shaped lounge; children
welcome, pool and TV in separate games room,
no piped music or dogs, lots of events; big
garden with terrace, picnic-sets, play area;
delightfully out-of-the-way hamlet not far from
River Trent *(JP, PP, Jack Morley)*
Newark [SK8054]
Fox & Crown [Applegate]: Friendly and
comfortable Tynemill refurbishment with
various nooks and corners inc no-smoking
family areas, stone or wood floors, six well kept
ales mainly from small breweries, farm cider
and perry, dozens of malt whiskies, continental
draught and bottled beers, flavoured vodkas,
good choice of wines, good food from
sandwiches up inc vegetarian, good wheelchair
access; open all day *(Richard Lewis)*
Lord Ted [off A46 SW]: Useful Tom Cobleigh
pub, with enjoyable food from their usual menu
inc children's and vegetarian, good décor, very
pleasant efficient service, wide choice of well
kept beers such as Boddingtons and Courage
Directors; open all day *(Kevin Blake, Bill and
Sheila McLardy)*
☆ *Mail Coach* [London Rd, nr Beaumond Cross]:
Friendly Georgian pub, dimly lit, with tasteful
décor, three separate areas, lots of pictures, big
fire, well kept ales such as Boddingtons,
Flowers IPA and Original, Springhead Bitter
and Leveller, home-made lunchtime food,
pleasant staff; pub games, jazz, blues or folk
Thurs; tables outside *(Richard Lewis, Kevin
Blake)*
Navigation Waterfront [Millgate]: Converted
warehouse rising out of canalised River Trent,
bare bricks and flagstones, iron pillars, well
kept Everards Tiger, friendly staff, good
atmosphere, lunchtime food; live music twice a
week *(David and Ruth Hollands)*
Newcastle Arms [George St]: Quiet traditional
two-bar Victorian local with well kept Brains
Dylans, Home Bitter and Mild and Charles
Wells Bombardier, several bottled beers,
welcoming landlord, pub games; cl Tues
lunchtime *(Richard Lewis)*
Old Malt Shovel [North Gate]: Welcoming and
comfortably opened-up local with good
doorstep sandwiches and lunchtime hot dishes
inc fresh veg, well kept Adnams Broadside,
Greene King Abbot, Theakstons XB, Timothy
Taylor Landlord and one brewed for them by
Rudgate, open fire, choice of teas, lots of books
and bottles on shelves, cheerfully laid-back
atmosphere and service; evening restaurant
Weds–Sun; pub games, wheelchair access;
*(Richard Lewis, John C Baker, Derek and
Sylvia Stephenson)*
Roman Way [Lincoln Rd]: Big popular rustic-
theme Brewers Fayre family dining pub, lots of
bric-a-brac, wide choice of good food, well kept
Whitbreads-related ales and Wadworths 6X,
indoor play area and soft play area, friendly

efficient staff, garden; disabled facilities, open
all day; bedrooms *(Richard Lewis)*
Normanton on Trent [SK7969]
Square & Compass [Eastgate; signed off B1164
S of Tuxford]: Has been very much enjoyed as
cosy no-frills village pub with friendly licensees,
good value straightforward bar food from
sandwiches to game, and well kept changing
ales such as Adnams and Brewsters; but in
summer 1999 seemed to be becoming much
more of a family eatery, under new licensees,
and as we went to press it was not yet clear
quite how this would turn out; children
welcome in eating areas, piped music, open all
day Fri-Sun *(LYM, Derek and Sylvia
Stephenson)*
Nottingham [SK5640]
Bell [Angel Row, off Market Sq]: Quaint low-
beamed 15th-c pub with Bass, Black Sheep,
Jennings Mild and Bitter, Mansfield Bitter,
Ruddles County and guest beers kept well in
extraordinarily deep sandstone cellar, three
bustling timbered and panelled bars (very
crowded and maybe smoky), ancient stairs to
attractive calmer raftered room with nice
window seats used as lunchtime family
restaurant for good value simple well presented
lunchtime food; good value wines; trad jazz Sun
lunchtime (rolls only then), Mon and Tues
evenings; open all day weekdays *(R M Taylor,
JP, PP, LYM, the Didler, David Carr)*
☆ *Bunkers Hill* [Hockley]: Outstanding choice of
up to a dozen well kept real ales from small
breweries far and wide in former bank, effective
and unusual green décor, beams, comfortable
traditional feel, good value wholesome food inc
speciality curries and generous Sun lunch,
recently opened upstairs room; quiz nights, no
machines or juke box *(R M Taylor, Kevin
Blake, JP, PP, the Didler, Alan Bowker)*
Coopers Arms [Porchester Rd, Thornywood]:
Superb solid old Victorian local with three
unspoilt rooms, Home Mild and Bitter,
Theakstons XB; small family room in skittle
alley; cl Weds lunchtime *(the Didler, JP, PP)*
Hogshead [Pelham St]: Wide range of English
and Belgian beers, good value food, pleasant
staff, two very large open bars *(Doug Christian)*
Hole in the Wall [North Sherwood St]:
Mansfield Bitter and Old Baily and three guest
beers, long room with scrubbed tables and bare
wood, good value usual food (not after 7) inc
Sun lunch, SkyTV sports; popular with
students, open all day (cl Sun afternoon) *(JP,
PP, the Didler)*
Horse & Groom [Radford Rd, New Basford]:
Partly divided open-plan pub next to former
Shipstones brewery, with their name over door
and other memorabilia; well kept ales such as
Bass, Belvoir Star, Courage Directors, Marstons
Pedigree, Ruddles County and guest beers,
good value fresh food from sandwiches to
restaurant meals, new back room for jazz, folk,
blues or skiffle nights Fri; open all day *(JP, PP,
Alan Bowker, the Didler)*
Lily Langtry [opp Royal Concert Hall]: Lots of
character, unchanging feel, basic furniture on
bare boards, wide range of real ales, old

theatrical posters and photographs of Lily Langtry *(Peter and Audrey Dowsett)*
Limelight [Wellington Circus, nr Playhouse]: Extended convivial bar and restaurant attached to Playhouse theatre and run by Tynemill, well kept Adnams, Batemans XB, Courage Directors, Marstons Pedigree, Theakstons XB and guests inc a Mild, reasonably priced food from rolls to full meals (not Sun lunchtime), pleasant efficient staff, theatre pictures, occasional modern jazz, attractive continental-style outside seating area; open all day, live blues and jazz *(R M Taylor, the Didler, JP, PP, Kevin Blake)*
Lion [Lower Mosley St, New Basford]: Doing well under former landlord of Derby Tup at Whittington Moor, wide choice of well kept ales inc local Mallard from one of city's deepest cellars (glass viewing panel – and can be visited at quiet times), tasty food inc doorstep sandwiches, open-plan bare bricks and boards, live jazz and blues Fri-Sun; summer barbecues, open all day *(R M Taylor, the Didler, JP, PP)*
Navigation [Wilford St; end of A453 into city, at canal bridge]: Good value simple food and Banks's real ales with a weekly guest such as Camerons Strongarm, big two-level pub with pool and a couple of TVs; popular with students *(Roger and Jenny Huggins)*
☆ *New Market Hotel* [Broad St, corner of Lower Parliament St, on inner ring rd]: Austerely neo-classical facade, well kept Scottish Courage ales, interesting array of gins from magnificent engraved bottles, comfortable back bar with carved fittings, open fire in snug, occasional Victorian or Edwardian themed entertainment, efficient staff, good value food inc some interesting dishes *(David Carr, LYM)*
Pitcher & Piano [Lace Market]: Remarkable converted church with well kept Marstons; the windows show best in daylight (and it's very busy at night) *(D J Atkinson)*
Salutation [Maid Marion Way]: Ancient back part with beams, flagstones and cosy corners, plusher modern front, good range of nicely presented food, up to a dozen or more changing ales, sensible prices and good atmosphere – can get a bit noisy *(BB, Derek and Sylvia Stephenson, R M Taylor, JP, PP)*
☆ *Sir John Borlase Warren* [Ilkeston Rd/Canning Circus (A52 towards Derby)]: Several connecting traditional rooms, lots of old prints, interesting Victorian decorations and fittings, enjoyable lunchtime food, no-smoking eating area, very friendly staff, well kept Greenalls Original, Shipstones, Tetleys, also guests tapped from the cask; tables in back garden with barbecues; children welcome (not Fri/Sat evenings) *(JP, PP, LYM, Roger and Jenny Huggins)*
☆ *Vat & Fiddle* [Queensbridge Rd]: Tynemill pub beside Castle Rock brewery, with their Daze, Hemlock, Nottingham, Reaper 39 and Black Jack Stout kept well, guests such as Archers Golden, Batemans Dark Mild, Caledonian Murrayfield, Everards Tiger, Fullers London Pride and Gales Winter Brew, dozens of malt

whiskies; small semicircular character bar with tiled floor, scrubbed tables, old local pictures, daily papers, upstairs function room used for lunches; open all day *(Richard Lewis, JP, PP, R M Taylor, Steve Godrich, the Didler, C J Fletcher)*
Via Fossa [Canal St]: Recently opened maze of rooms and alcoves in different themes – olde-worlde, romanesque, art deco; upstairs bars, restaurant, Tetleys-related beers; lots of canalside tables with winter heating *(Kevin Blake)*

Nuthall [SK5144]
Three Ponds [Nottingham Rd (B600), away from city), off A610 nr M1 junction 26]: Friendly and tastefully refurbished Hardys & Hansons roadhouse with wide range of good value food inc OAP bargains, well kept Best, Best Mild and Classic, good coffee, good staff; piped music; big back garden with play area *(JJW, CMW, JP, PP)*
Orston [SK7741]
Durham Ox [Church St]: Welcoming local opp church, well kept Home and Theakstons ales, good value beef, ham and other rolls (no hot food); comfortable split-level open-plan bar with interesting RAF/USAF memorabilia, collection of whisky bottles; tables outside (and hitching rail for ferrets as well as for horses) *(R M Taylor, the Didler, Norma and Keith Bloomfield, Dr and Mrs J H Hills)*
Ranby [SK6580]
Chequers [Old Blyth Rd, just off A1 by A620 Worksop—E Retford]: Nice building in superb canalside spot, delightful waterside terrace, some mooring, weekend boat trips; three well kept beers, popular tea and coffee, cheerful service, several attractive and comfortable areas off bar inc dining room with farm tools and bric-a-brac, games area with darts, pool and machines; children very welcome, open all day, food all day w/e *(Mike and Grete Turner, CMW, JJW, D Parkhurst, P and R Baker)*
Retford [SK6980]
☆ *Market Hotel* [off West Carr Rd, Ordsall; follow Leisure Centre signs from A620, then just after industrial estate sign keep eyes skinned for pub sign on left]: Good choice of well kept ales, comfortable plush banquettes, splendid range of good value generous home cooking inc great fresh haddock, friendly helpful service; very busy Fri/Sat night, jazz 3rd Sun in month *(Richard Lewis, JP, PP, LYM, D Parkhurst, John C Baker, Mike and Sue Loseby, Derek and Sylvia Stephenson)*
Turks Head [Grove St]: Cosy oak-panelled town pub with good value lunches (not Sun), real fire, traditional games; has had Vaux Sampson, Wards Best and related beers *(Jack and Philip Paxton)*
South Leverton [SK7881]
Plough [Town St]: Tiny pub doubling as PO, basic trestle tables and benches, real fire, Ruddles Best and a guest beer, traditional games, tables outside; open 2-11 (all day Sat, 12-4, 7-10.30 Sun) *(Jack and Philip Paxton)*
Southwell [SK6953]
☆ *Bramley Apple* [Church St (A612)]: Friendly

prompt service, good value food inc fresh fish and vegetarian, very crisp veg, generous Sun lunch, well kept Mansfield and a good guest beer, good atmosphere, attractively worked Bramley apple theme, eating area screened off by stained glass; comfortable bedrooms *(Derek and Sylvia Stephenson, Bill and Sheila McLardy, BB)*

Strelley [SK5141]
Broad Oak [off A6002 nr M1 junction 26]: Good value dining pub, Hardys & Hansons Bitter, Classic and Mild, lots of partitioned areas, comfortable banquettes, OAP specials, no piped music, picnic-sets outside, play area in back garden; no dogs *(JP, PP)*

Thurgarton [SK6949]
Red Lion [Southwell Rd (A612)]: Pleasant, bright and cheery old inn with good food inc fresh fish in roomy bars and restaurant, well kept ales, lovely fire; children welcome, big garden *(RJH, Paul McPherson)*

Toton [SK5034]
Manor [Nottingham Rd (A6005)]: Good value friendly Tom Cobleigh dining pub with big no-smoking area, well kept Boddingtons and Marstons Pedigree with guests such as Courage Directors, Morlands Old Speckled Hen and Timothy Taylor Landlord, several cheap wines by bottle; handy for Attenborough Nature Reserve – good birdwatching, fine walks *(Mike and Penny Sanders)*

Underwood [SK4750]
Dixies Arms [School Rd]: 18th-c beamed village local, Home Bitter and Mild and a guest beer, real fire, tables outside; own football team and pigeon, gun and Morris dancing clubs; open 2-11, all day w/e *(Jack and Philip Paxton)*
Hole in the Wall [nr M1 junction 27 via A608 towards Eastwood]: Open-plan Brewers Fayre in mining village – comfortable, with good bar food, well kept Boddingtons and Marstons Pedigree, coal fires in winter, friendly staff, family area, lovely valley view on one side; piped music; small garden, bedrooms *(Richard Lewis)*

Upton [SK7354]
☆ *Cross Keys* [A612]: Rambling heavy-beamed bar with lots of alcoves, central log fire, masses to look at, interesting medley of furnishings, well kept real ales, decent wines; unobtrusive piped music, Sun folk night; children in back extension with carved pews or upstairs restaurant *(JP, PP, Dr S J Shepherd, LYM)*

Watnall Chaworth [SK5046]
☆ *Queens Head* [3 miles from M1 junction 26: A610 towards Nottingham, left on B600, then keep right]: Tastefully extended old pub with wide range of good value food, well kept Home Bitter and Mild, Theakstons XB and Old Peculier and a guest beer, efficient friendly service; intimate snug, dining area, beams and stripped pine, coal fires; fruit machine, piped music; picnic-sets in spacious and attractive back garden with big play area; open all day Fri/Sat *(the Didler, JP, PP, Mike and Penny Sanders)*

Wellow [SK6766]
☆ *Olde Red Lion* [Eakring Rd, just off A616 E of

Ollerton]: Low-beamed and panelled 16th-c pub by green with towering maypole which gives its name to the local brewery that brews Lions Pride for the pub, alongside well kept changing beers such as Robinsons Old Stockport, Ruddles Best and Shepherd Neame Spitfire; friendly staff, reasonably priced food from sandwiches up inc vegetarian and Sun roasts, no-smoking restaurant and dining area, no piped music; children welcome, picnic-sets outside *(LYM, D Parkhurst, Alan Bowker, J W G Nunns, Michael and Jenny Back, Peter and Audrey Dowsett)*

West Bridgford [SK5837]
Southbank [Trent Bridge]: Now under same ownership as Fellows Morton & Clayton; bright and airy refurbishment, polished wood floors, up to four real ales usually inc local Mallard; handy for cricket ground and Nottingham Forest FC *(the Didler)*
Stratford Haven [Stratford Ave, Trent Bridge]: Comfortable new Tynemill pub in former pet shop, long back area, beer boards, lots of brewery pictures, cosy no-smoking snug, good atmosphere, well kept changing ales such as Batemans XB and XXXB, Belvoir Star, Castle Rock Hemlock, Marstons Pedigree, Woodfordes Wherry and a Mild such as Moorhouses Black Cat, farm ciders, good choice of whiskies and wines, good home-cooked food inc vegetarian, daily papers, tables outside; handy for cricket ground and Nottingham Forest FC, open all day *(the Didler)*

West Leake [SK5226]
☆ *Star* [off A6006]: Traditional beamed and quarry-tiled country pub with a good deal of character, hunting trophies, wall settles, comfortable partly oak-panelled lounge with good log fire, short choice of good value simple weekday lunchtime food, well kept Bass and Marstons Pedigree; children in eating area *(JP, PP, LYM, Richard Green)*

West Markham [SK7272]
Royal Oak [Sibthorpe Hill; B1164 nr A1/A57/A638 roundabout N of Tuxford]: Mansfield Landlords Table dining pub with wide choice of good specials, modern bar and dining areas; open all day, real ales inc Dark Mild, decent wines, friendly staff; civilised journey respite, views over wheatfields, play area outside *(P Meoney)*

West Stockwith [SK7995]
☆ *Waterfront* [Canal Lane; opp marina, off A161]: Extended two-bar pub in excellent waterside spot on basin between River Trent and Chesterfield Canal, very friendly landlord, well kept Marstons, John Smiths and two or three guests such as Robinsons and Shepherd Neame Spitfire, big dining area with good value food inc Sun lunch; TV, fruit machine, piped music; garden with barbecue and tyre swings, open all day w/e, crowded summer evenings with jolly boating types; caravan park behind *(JJW, CMW, Derek and Sylvia Stephenson)*

Wilford [SK5637]
Ferry [off B679 S of Nottingham]: Good

lunchtime pub, with good bar meals, low beams and bare boards, bays of comfortable banquettes, chesterfield, pictures, two snugs, four well kept sensibly priced ales, restaurant with pitched roof and imposing fireplace; piped pop music; tidy back terrace, garden with play area, view over River Trent to Nottingham Castle *(JJW, CMW, Mike and Penny Sanders)*

Willoughby on the Wolds [SK6325]
Three Horseshoes [just off A46, Leics border]: Comfortable modern pub with well kept Barnsley Bitter and Old Tom, fair food choice inc children's, Sun lunch and OAP Mon lunch, restaurant with real fire, lots of brass and copper and teapot collection; disabled access, play area in small garden *(CMW, JJW)*

Worksop [SK5879]
Mallard [Station, Carlton Rd]: Listed station building with quickly changing beers from small breweries, wide range of foreign bottled beers, coal fire, traditional games; open all day (Sun afternoon closure), wheelchair access, seats outside *(Jack and Philip Paxton)*

Wysall [SK6027]
Plough [off A60 at Costock, or A6006 at Wymeswold]: Lively and attractive 17th-c beamed country local, well kept Bass and guest ales, welcoming staff, nice mix of furnishings, soft lighting, big log fire, french doors to newly reworked terrace and good compact garden with barbecues Fri night, Sun afternoon; no cooked lunches Sun *(Chris Raisin, Frank Palethorpe)*

If you have to cancel a reservation for a bedroom or restaurant, please telephone or write to warn them. A small place – and its customers – will suffer if you don't. And recently people who failed to cancel have been taken to court for breach of contract.

Oxfordshire

The county has a large and increasing number of smart restauranty pubs: it's not a cheap place for pub food, and drinks prices are higher than the national average, too. Of course there are exceptions: three or four pubs here qualify for our bargain food symbol, and these also tended to have relatively cheap drinks. The Oxfordshire brewer that stands out for value is Hook Norton. We found it the most likely beer to be the cheapest on offer in a pub, and the pubs that sold it almost all had lower-than-average prices – particularly pubs tied to the brewer by tenancy. An invader from Wiltshire, Archers, tended to be very cheap in the pubs where we found it. Morlands of Abingdon (who also brew Ruddles) was also generally good value, not usually quite so low-priced but always cheaper than average. By contrast, Brakspears of Henley, another common supplier of Oxfordshire pubs, was by contrast almost always more expensive than average; nice pubs, though. Morrells, the venerable Oxford brewery, closed in 1999; we have left references to it in the text of this edition not so much as a memorial as some indication of the style or range of beers that a pub stocks – the closure was too recent for Morrells pubs to have settled into a firm new pattern by the time we went to press with this chapter in August. To turn to happier thoughts, pubs doing particularly well here these days include the Boars Head at Ardington (imaginative new chef), the smart and civilised old Lamb in Burford, the delightfully pubby Chequers in Chipping Norton (a newcomer to the Guide: good food here too), another properly traditional old place, the Eight Bells at Eaton (also a newcomer), the Sun in Hook Norton (particularly warm reports from readers this year propel it too into the main entries for the first time), the friendly Plough near the Thames at Kelmscot, the Machine Man at Long Wittenham (our final newcomer – and yet another place that's a proper pub rather than just another eatery), the friendly Five Horseshoes at Maidensgrove (good imaginative food, and some extension to give more tables the fine view), the bustling Kings Arms in Oxford, the friendly and civilised Lamb at Shipton under Wychwood (popular carvery), the redecorated Star at Stanton St John, and the Red Lion at Steeple Aston (a real favourite, with a first-class landlord). Other places with very good food are the Perch & Pike at South Stoke (new licensees adding bedrooms), the Kings Head at Wootton, and, at a price, the Feathers in Woodstock; our choice as Oxfordshire Dining Pub of the Year rests with the Boars Head at Ardington. The Lucky Dip at the end of the chapter is a store of further riches: Oxfordshire has too many good pubs to squeeze them all into the main entries. We'd mention particularly the Maytime at Asthall, Barley Mow at Clifton Hampden, Red Lion at Cropredy, Deddington Arms at Deddington, White Horse at Duns Tew, Trout at Godstow, Crown at Pishill, Rose & Crown at Shilton, Swan at Swinbrook, Six Bells at Warborough, North Arms at Wroxton, and, especially for food, the Bull in Charlbury, Hand & Shears at Church Hanborough, Three Horseshoes at Garsington, Roebuck at North Newington, Crooked Billet at Stoke Row and Hare at West Hendred.

ARDINGTON SU4388 Map 2
Boars Head 🍴 ♀

Village signposted off A417 Didcot—Wantage, signed two miles E of Wantage

Oxfordshire Dining Pub of the Year

The emphasis in this civilised place is very much on the good, ambitious food, and under the new chef this might include poached egg and toulouse sausage salad (£4.50), crab, gruyère and ginger tart (£5.50), proper cornish pasty (£6), lamb shank with minted mash (£7), tranche of foie gras with apple and muscat chutney (£8), parsleyed cod with mustard hollandaise (£13), roast rack of English lamb with rosti and deuxelle (£13.50), rare breast of duck with plum tatin (£14), whole roast baby monkfish, sun-dried tomato and chickpea salad (£14.50), feuillete of bass with mussels and spinach (£15), puddings like lemon tart with lemon curd ice cream, banana cheesecake with chocolate sorbet or pink grapefruit gratin with passionfruit sorbet (£4), and interesting cheeses (£4). The restaurant is no smoking. Well kept Brakspears, Butts Jester, and Mansfield Original on handpump under light blanket pressure, and a good wine list with three different wine glass sizes. The three simply furnished but smart interconnecting rooms have low beams and timbers, lots of pictures on the walls, oil lamps on the tables, fresh flowers, and rugs on the light-coloured wood block floor. One room is primarily for eating, with pine settles and well spaced big pine tables, the others have smaller country tables and chairs – still with room for drinkers. Darts, shove-ha'penny, cribbage, dominoes, and piped music. In a peaceful and attractive village, the pub is part of the Ardington estate; good walks nearby. *(Recommended by R C Watkins, Dick Brown, Dr D Twyman)*

Free house ~ Licensee Mark Stott ~ Real ale ~ Bar food ~ Restaurant ~ (01235) 833254 ~ Children welcome ~ Open 12-2(3 Sat, 4 Sun), 6.30-11; closed Sun evening

BAMPTON SP3103 Map 4
Romany ◧ £

Bridge St; off A4095 SW of Witney

This 17th-c pub is a hospitable place with a friendly licensee and good value food and drink. The comfortable bars have plush cushioned windsor chairs and stools around wooden tables, foreign currency notes from all over the world, plates and prints on the partly stripped stone walls, and a winter open fire. Bar food includes sandwiches, soup or mushroom provençale (£2.25), baked potato with cheese and broccoli (£3.95), vegetable lasagne or spanish omelette (£4.50), spaghetti carbonara (£4.95), Thai chicken curry or steak in ale pie (£5.50), lemon sole (£5.95), and magret of duckling with port and redcurrant sauce (£8.50). The restaurant is no smoking. Well kept Archers Village, Wychwood Hobgoblin and Special, and guest beers handpumped from the Saxon cellars below the bar; darts, cribbage, fruit machine, and piped music. The big garden has picnic-sets, Aunt Sally, and a children's play area with tree house, see-saw, and mushroom slide and house. *(Recommended by Peg Cuskley, Patrick Hancock, Anthony Barnes, Alan and Ros, Stephen Brown, John Higgins, Brian A Haywood, Marjorie and David Lamb)*

Free house ~ Licensees Robert and Tessa Smith ~ Real ale ~ Bar food (11-2.30, 6.30-9.30) ~ Restaurant ~ (01993) 850237 ~ Children welcome ~ Open 11-11; 12-10.30 Sun ~ Bedrooms: £22(£26.50B)/£42.50B

BANBURY SP4540 Map 4
Reindeer £

47 Parsons Street, off Market Place

Refreshingly old-fashioned town centre pub with friendly licensees, good honest food, and a chatty atmosphere. The long front room has heavy 16th-c beams, very broad polished oak floorboards scattered with rugs, a magnificent carved overmantle for one of the two roaring log fires, and traditional solid furnishings. Ask to be shown the Globe Room – a beautifully proportioned room, where Cromwell held court before the Battle of Edgehill, with original gloriously carved 17th-c panelling.

Well kept Hook Norton Best, Old, Mild, and Generation and a guest ale on handpump, country wines, 30 Irish whiskies, good coffee, and even snuffs and clay pipes for the more adventurous. Lunchtime bar food includes doorstep or hot sandwiches (from £2), home-made chicken liver pâté (£2.85), filled baked potatoes (from £3.10), bubble and squeak with ham, egg and baked beans or pasta with tomato sauce (£3.20), ploughman's (from £3.40), shepherd's pie (£3.50), steak in ale pie (£4.70), and daily specials. A smaller back room up steps is no smoking at lunchtime. The grey fluffy cat is called Cromwell and the tabby, Oliver. Small back courtyard with picnic-sets under parasols, Aunt Sally, and pretty flowering baskets; no under-21s (but see below). *(Recommended by Ted George, David Campbell, Vicki McLean, E and D Frewer, Klaus and Elizabeth Leist)*

Hook Norton ~ Tenants John and Hazel Milligan ~ Real ale ~ Bar food (lunchtime) ~ (01295) 264031 ~ Children in Globe Room lunchtime only if eating ~ Open 11-11; closed Sun; 25 Dec; bank hol Mon

BARNARD GATE SP4010 Map 4
Boot
Village signposted off A40 E of Witney

As the name suggests, there's quite a collection of celebrities' boots in this attractive neatly kept pub. A new licensee has taken over this year but few changes have been made. There are stout standing timbers and stub walls with latticed glass breaking up the main area, a huge log fire, a civilised atmosphere, and good solid country tables and chairs on bare boards. Good, if not cheap, food might include soup (£3.25), sandwiches (from £3.75), grilled king prawns with dip and garlic bread (£3.95; main course £11.75), winter steak and kidney pie, vegetable tangine (£11.25), pasta with scallops and smoked salmon (£11.75), sea bream or dover sole (£12.95), daily specials, and puddings like sticky toffee pudding (£3.50); part of the restaurant is no smoking. Well kept Hook Norton Best and a guest beer on handpump, and decent wines. There are tables out in front of the stone-tiled stone pub, which despite being so handy for the A40 is out of earshot. *(Recommended by Stephen and Julie Brown, Maureen Hobbs, H W Clayton, GL, TRS, TBB, Francis Johnston, Carl and Jackie Cranmer, Peter and Audrey Dowsett, Simon Collett-Jones, Michael Sargent)*

Free house ~ Licensee Annabelle Dailey ~ Real ale ~ Bar food ~ Restaurant ~ (01865) 881231 ~ Children welcome ~ Piano Mon and Fri evening and Sun lunch ~ Open 11-3, 6-11; 12-3, 7-10.30 Sun

BINFIELD HEATH SU7478 Map 2
Bottle & Glass ★
Village signposted off A4155 at Shiplake; in village centre fork right immediately after Post Office (signposted Harpsden) and keep on for half mile

Happily, little changes at this very pretty thatched and black and white timbered pub – once three farm cottages before its conversion in the 15th c. The neatly kept low-beamed bar has a fine fireplace, scrubbed ancient tables, a bench built into black squared panelling, and spindleback chairs on the attractive flagstones, and a window with diamond-scratched family records of earlier landlords. The smaller, relaxed side room is similarly decorated. Written up on blackboards, the range of promptly served bar food might include lunchtime sandwiches (£3.25; not Sunday) and a good ploughman's (£4.95), potted shrimps (£4.95), rollmop herrings in a sherry and almond marinade (£5.50), beef and apricots in red wine (£8.25), boned half guinea fowl (£8.95), pork tenderloin with wine and mustard sauce (£9.50), breast of duck with a black cherry sauce (£9.75), and steaks (£10.75); friendly staff. Well kept Brakspears Bitter, and seasonal Old or Special on handpump, and quite a few malt whiskies. The lovely big garden has old-fashioned wooden seats and tables under little thatched roofs (and an open-sided shed like a rustic pavilion). No children or dogs. *(Recommended by Richard and Stephanie Foskett, Mike Wells, Roger and Valerie Hill, Mike and Heather Watson, Chris Glasson, the Didler)*

Brakspears ~ Tenants Mike and Anne Robinson ~ Real ale ~ Bar food (12-1.45, 7-

9.30; *not Sun evening*) ~ *Restaurant* ~ *(01491) 575755* ~ *Open 11-4, 6-11; 12-4, 7-10.30 Sun*

BLEWBURY SU5385 Map 2
Red Lion
Nottingham Fee – narrow turning N from A417

Quietly relaxed with no noisy games machines or music, this pleasant village pub has a beamed bar with upholstered wall benches and armed seats on its scrubbed quarry tiles, cupboards and miniature cabinets filled with ornaments, and foreign banknotes on the beams; in winter you can maybe roast chestnuts over the big open fire. Bar food includes sandwiches (from £3), moules (£4.50), salmon fillet with a herb crust and peppercorn sauce (£7.50), steaks (from £7.50), chicken stuffed with smoked cheddar with a mushrooms and tarragon sauce (£8.50), puddings like sticky toffee pudding or crème caramel (from £3), and children's dishes (£3); the restaurant is no smoking. Well kept Brakspears Bitter, Old Ale and Special on handpump; dominoes. The extended garden has a terrace with quite a few seats and tables. *(Recommended by Col A Reade, Richard Gibbs, Dick Brown)*

Brakspears ~ Tenant Roger Smith ~ Real ale ~ Bar food ~ Restaurant ~ (01235) 850403 ~ Children in restaurant; cannot stay overnight ~ Open 11-2.30(3 Sat), 6-11; 12-3, 7-10.30 Sun ~ Bedrooms: £25/£35

BLOXHAM SP4235 Map 4
Elephant & Castle £
Humber Street; off A361, fairly hndy for M40 junction 11

The elegantly simple public bar here has a striking 17th-c stone fireplace, a strip wood floor, and a relaxed, unchanging feel; the comfortable lounge is divided into two by a very thick wall, and has a good winter log fire in its massive fireplace, too; sensibly placed darts, bar billiards, dominoes, cribbage, fruit machine, and shove-ha'penny on a hardy board they have been using for over a century. Good value straightforward lunchtime bar food includes sandwiches or filled french bread (from £1.70), sausage, eggs and beans (£3), steak and kidney or minty lamb pies or vegetable or meaty lasagne (£3.50), and daily specials (from £2.50). Well kept and cheap Hook Norton Best, Old Hooky, Generation, summer Haymaker, Twelve Days, a monthly guest, and Bulmers cider (guest ciders in summer), and around 30 malt whiskies. The flower-filled extended yard has Aunt Sally in summer and maybe weekend barbecues. This is an imposing Cotswold village. *(Recommended by Tom Evans, Jenny and Roger Huggins, Martin Jones, Ted George)*

Hook Norton ~ Tenants Charles and Simon Finch ~ Real ale ~ Bar food (lunchtime) ~ Restaurant ~ (01295) 720383 ~ Children welcome ~ Open 10-3, 6(5 Sat)-11; 12-10.30 Sun

BROADWELL SP2504 Map 4
Five Bells
Village signposted off A361 N of Lechlade, and off B4020 S of Carterton

The neatly kept garden here is especially worth a visit – particularly in summer when it is a blaze of colour; the hanging baskets and flower tubs in front of the stone building are also very pretty. Inside, there's a restful atmosphere, and the neatly kept series of well furnished rooms have a pleasant mix of flagstones and carpeting, low beams, antique pistols, and plates and rural pictures on the walls; big warming log fires. The sizeable dining room to the right of the lounge, and the small conservatory (both no smoking), overlook the spacious garden – where they play Aunt Sally, and grow some of the vegetables used in the kitchen. Enjoyable bar food includes sandwiches (from £1.50), soup (£2.25), garlic mushrooms (£3.50), cajun prawns (£3.95), ham, egg and chips (£4.25), somerset pork (£5.75), chicken breast in stilton sauce (£5.95), steak and kidney pudding (£6.25), almond nut roast or honey-glazed lamb steak (£6.50), steaks (from £8.95), and puddings (£2.50); good vegetables in separate tureens. Well kept Wadworths 6X with two guest beers such as Archers Village and Brakspears Bitter on handpump, and decent house wine. The public bar has darts, shove-ha'penny, dominoes, trivia, and Aunt Sally. Wheelchair access. *(Recommended by Marjorie and David Lamb, Joan Olivier, Peter and Audrey Dowsett, Ted George, P and S White, Mr and Mrs Peter Smith)*

Free house ~ Licensees Trevor and Ann Cooper ~ Real ale ~ Bar food (not Sun evening, not Mon) ~ Restaurant ~ (01367) 860076 ~ Children in small restaurant; must be over 10 Sat evening ~ Open 11.30-2.30, 6.30-11; 12-3, 7-10.30 Sun; closed Mon except bank hols ~ Bedrooms: /£45B

BUCKLAND SU3497 Map 4
Lamb ♀ ⇌
Village signposted off A420 NE of Faringdon

Opening off a hallway, and divided in two by dark painted timbers, the neatly civilised little bar in this smartly refurbished stone inn has plush blue furnishings, potted plants around the windows, and a few carefully chosen sheep and lamb pictures and models around the cream-painted walls. On a piano are newspapers to read, and examples of their own chutneys and jams. The good food (restaurant quality as well as prices) might include weekday sandwiches, soups such as curried apple or spiced Italian bean and tomato soup (£3.50), confit of duck (£4.95), rabbit and guinea fowl terrine (£5.50), scrambled eggs with smoked salmon and prawns (£5.95), warm crab and spinach tart with fresh herb sauce (£6.25), bangers and mash (£6.95), daube of lamb or green Thai chicken curry (£9.95), steak and kidney pie (£10.95), salmon fishcakes with a spicy tomato and prawn sauce (£11.95), baked bass with a light Pernod sauce (£17.50), and puddings such as roast pear with butterscotch sauce, chocolate pecan pie or sticky toffee and date pudding (from £3.95); 3-course Sunday lunch – with coffee and petits fours – is £19.95. Three well kept real ales such as Adnams Broadside, Hook Norton Best, and Wadworths 6X, a dozen or so wines by the glass, and carefully mixed pimms or bucks fizz; very friendly service; piped music. There are a couple of white plastic tables on a terrace, and a good few wooden picnic-sets in the very pleasant tree-shaded garden. The village is pretty, with good walks nearby. *(Recommended by W K Wood, Hugh Spottiswoode, Dr Irvine Loudon, GL, TBB, D R Ellis)*

Free house ~ Licensees Paul and Peta Barnard ~ Real ale ~ Bar food ~ Restaurant ~ (01367) 870484 ~ Children welcome ~ Open 11-3, 5.30-11; 12-3, 7-11 Sun; closed 25 and 26 Dec ~ Bedrooms: £37.50B/£55B

BURCOT SU5695 Map 4
Chequers
A415 Dorchester—Abingdon

In summer, this attractive thatched pub is just the place to be. There are seats on the terrace (lit at night), lots of pretty pots, hanging baskets, and bedding plants, tables and chairs among roses and fruit trees on the neatly kept roadside lawn, and a vegetable patch at the lower end of the garden to grow their own salad and herb produce. Inside, the smartly comfortable and surprisingly spacious lounge has beams, an open fire, a very relaxed and friendly atmosphere, and well kept Brakspears, Flowers IPA, and Wadworths 6X on handpump, with some good whiskies, unusual liqueurs, and a large collection of miniatures in display cabinets. Good enjoyable food is all home-made (they also bake all their own bread) and includes home-made soup (£2.95), sandwiches (£3.75, with fries), ploughman's (£4.75), lasagne or spicy five-bean crumble (£5.95), steak and kidney pudding or Thai green chicken curry (£6.35), fish pie (£6.95), gammon and egg (£8.25), sirloin steak (£8.95), and puddings. They have their own decent little no-smoking art gallery. *(Recommended by Nick Holmes, Iain Robertson, Mike Wells, Jim Bush, Ian Phillips, Brad W Morley, TBB, Marjorie and David Lamb)*

Scottish Courage ~ Lease: Michael and Mary Weeks ~ Real ale ~ Bar food (not Sun evening) ~ (01865) 407771 ~ Children in eating area of bar and no-smoking gallery ~ Grand piano Sat evenings ~ Open 11-2.30, 6-11; 12-3, 7-10.30 Sun; closed evenings 25/26 Dec

BURFORD SP2512 Map 4
Lamb ★★ 🍺 🍷 🍴 🛏

Sheep Street; A40 W of Oxford

There's a timeless character to this lovely 15th-c Cotswold stone inn. The spacious beamed main lounge has a civilised atmosphere, distinguished old seats including a chintzy high winged settle, ancient cushioned wooden armchairs, and seats built into its stone-mullioned windows, bunches of flowers on polished oak and elm tables, oriental rugs on the wide flagstones and polished oak floorboards, and a winter log fire under its fine mantelpiece. Also, a writing desk and grandfather clock, and attractive pictures, shelves of plates and other antique decorations. The public bar has high-backed settles and old chairs on flagstones in front of its fire.There may be nibbles on the bar counter, as well as good bar lunches such as sandwiches or filled french bread (from £2.50; bacon and avocado £3.95), home-made soups like cream of broccoli and blue cheese soup with toasted almonds (£3.25), ploughman's (£5.25), coarse venison and cranberry pâté with apricot relish (£5.95), sautéed chicken livers with crispy bacon (£6.95), tagliatelle with smoked haddock in a grain mustard and parmesan cream sauce (£7.50), salmon and lemon grass fishcakes on a tomato and garlic sauce, roast saddle of lamb with spinach and sage stuffing or steak, mustard and stilton pie (£8.50), and puddings such as ginger sponge or redcurrant cheesecake (£3.25); on Sundays there are proper roasts but no bar meals; the restful formal restaurant is no smoking. Well kept Adnams Best, Hook Norton Best and Wadworths 6X are dispensed from an antique handpump beer engine in a glassed-in cubicle; good wines. A pretty terrace leads down to small neatly kept lawns surrounded by flowers, flowering shrubs and small trees, and the garden itself can be really sunny, enclosed as it is by the warm stone of the surrounding buildings. *(Recommended by Peter Saville, Basil J S Minson, Nick J Lawless, Maysie Thompson, Adam and Elizabeth Duff, Lynn Sharpless, Bob Eardley, TBB, Simon Collett-Jones, C M F Redlich, Dick Brown, Mike Wells, Colin and Ann Hunt, J H Jones, Stephen Brown, Peter Neate, Bob and Maggie Atherton, Marvadene B Eves, Gordon, John and Esther Sprinkle, E A and D C Frewer, Bernard Stradling, Mr and Mrs M F Norton, Walter Reid, Paul Cleaver, James and Wendy Timms, John Robertson, Gillian Jenkins, Jackie Hammond, Nigel Woolliscroft)*

Free house ~ Licensee Richard de Wolf ~ Real ale ~ Bar food (lunchtime; not Sun) ~ Restaurant ~ (01993) 823155 ~ Children welcome ~ Open 11-2.30, 6-11; 12-3, 7-10.30 Sun; closed 25/26 Dec ~ Bedrooms: £60B/£105B

Mermaid
High St

The handsome Tudor façade of this bustling pub is slightly set back behind the higgledy-piggledy terraces of the surrounding buildings that wend their way up the quaint High Street. Mullioned bay windows invite you into the attractive long and narrow bar with its beams, polished flagstones, brocaded seats in bays around the single row of tables down one side, and pretty dried flowers. The inner end, with a figurehead over the fireplace and toby jugs hanging from the beams, is panelled, the rest has stripped stonework; there's an airy dining room and a no-smoking upstairs restaurant. Bar food (usefully served all day by helpful staff) might at lunchtime include sandwiches or filled french bread (from £2.95; chicken, avocado, mayonnaise and crispy bacon £3.25), and filled baked potatoes or ploughman's (£4.95); also, soup (£3.50), hot garlic bread filled with cheese (£3.95), omelettes (£5.95), large fish and chips (£6.95), steak and kidney pie (£7.95), steaks (from £12.95), evening smoked duck breast with an orange and pine nut salad (£4.95), chargrilled tuna steak in lemon sauce (£10.95), and noisettes of lamb with garlic and mint in port gravy (£12.95). Well kept Bass, Morlands Original and Old Speckled Hen, and Ruddles on handpump; pool and fruit machine. There are picnic-sets under cocktail parasols. *(Recommended by Steve Whalley, Simon Collett-Jones, B Brewer, Rona Murdoch, David and Nina Pugsley, Gordon, Stephen Brown)*

Morlands ~ Lease: John and Lynda Titcombe ~ Real ale ~ Bar food (all day; 12-3, 6-9.45 in winter) ~ Restaurant ~ (01993) 822193 ~ Children in restaurant ~ Open 10.30(11 in winter)-11; 12-10.30 Sun

CHALGROVE SU6396 Map 4
Red Lion
High St (B480 Watlington—Stadhampton)

The landlord of this charming pub will go out of his way to make you feel welcome, whether you are a visitor or regular. The décor is smartly modern and attractive with all the walls painted a crisp white which contrasts sharply with the simple dark furnishings, the windows have neatly chequered green curtains and fresh flowers, and there's an old woodburner and a log fire. Across from the fireplace is a painting of the landlady's aunt, and there are a few carefully collected prints and period cartoons; piped music, cribbage, dominoes, and darts in the tiled public bar. There's quite an emphasis on the imaginative and very well presented bar food: soup such as carrot and coriander (£3.20), fishcakes with raw vegetable and chilli salsa and aioli (£3.25; £6 main course), tortellini with pesto, wild mushrooms and cream sauce (£3.50; main course £5.95), filled french bread (from £3.50; club sandwich with chips £6.50), pork sausages roasted in honey and grainy mustard with mash and gravy (£5.95), lamb stew with dumplings (£8.50), calf's liver with mustard mash and shallot jus (£9.50), and puddings like steamed treacle pudding (£3.50); two-course set meal (£12.50) and three courses (£15.50). They will generally open a bottle of wine and buy back the remainder if you don't finish it. Well kept Brakspears, and Fullers London Pride and Summer Ale on handpump, and a decent wine list; attentive service. The back dining room (sometimes used for functions) is no smoking. The local church (which has some notable medieval wall paintings) has owned this since it first appeared in written records in 1637, and probably a good deal longer: some of the timbers date back to the 11th c. There's a good big garden behind with a pergola, quite a few seats, and play equipment, and picnic-sets in front, attractively floodlit at night. *(Recommended by E A and D C T Frewer, TBB, Rona Murdoch, Kevin Thorpe, Dick and Jan Chenery, D B Jenkin)*

Free house ~ Licensees Jonathan and Maggi Hewitt ~ Real ale ~ Bar food (not Sun evening) ~ Restaurant ~ (01865) 890625 ~ Children in eating area of bar and in restaurant ~ Open 12-3, 5.30(6 Sat)-11; 12-3, 7-10.30 Sun; closed evening 25 Dec

CHECKENDON SU6684 Map 2
Black Horse
Village signposted off A4074 Reading—Wallingford; coming from that direction, go straight through village towards Stoke Row, then turn left (the second turn left after the village church); OS Sheet 175 map reference 666841

For many decades this unpretentious and tucked away country local has been in the same family and there's a splendidly relaxed atmosphere – plus well kept Brakspears and a few local guests like Rebellion IPA and West Berkshire Good Old Boy tapped from casks in a back still room. The room with the bar counter has some tent pegs ranged above the fireplace, a reminder that they used to be made here; a homely side room has some splendidly unfashionable 1950s-look armchairs, and beyond that there's a third room. They'll usually do fresh filled rolls (from £1.35), and keep pickled eggs. There are seats out on a verandah and in the garden *(Recommended by Pete Baker, JP, PP, the Didler)*

Free house ~ Licensees Margaret and Martin Morgan ~ Real ale ~ Bar food ~ (01491) 680418 ~ Children welcome ~ Open 12-2(3 Sat), 7-11(10.30 Sun); closed evening 25 Dec

CHINNOR SU7698 Map 4
Sir Charles Napier ♀

Spriggs Alley; from B4009 follow Bledlow Ridge sign from Chinnor; then, up beech wood hill, fork right (signposted Radnage and Sprigg Alley) then on right; OS Sheet 165 ref 763983

At quiet moments during the week, you'll generally feel quite welcome coming to this decidedly civilised place for just a drink in the cosy and simply furnished little front bar. At other times you may find the whole place is virtually dedicated to the stylish back partly no-smoking restaurant, and there's little point coming at weekends unless you want to eat. This is definitely somewhere to come for a treat, and a typical day's bar menu might include chargrilled mediterranean vegetable salad (£5.75), noodles with crab, chilli and ginger (£6), parfait of foie gras with toasted brioche (£6.90), confit of rabbit with white beans and mustard seed (£12.50), baked sea bream with aubergine, peppers and tapenade (£13.50), saddle of lamb with couscous and rosemary jus (£14.50), chargrilled rib-eye of beef with bubble and squeak (£15.50), and puddings (£5.50); service is not included. Two-course set lunch (£15.50), and Sunday lunch is distinctly fashionable – in summer it's served in the crazy-paved back courtyard with rustic tables by an arbour of vines, honeysuckle and wisteria (lit at night by candles in terracotta lamps). An excellent range of drinks takes in well kept Wadworths 6X, IPA and Summersault tapped from the cask, champagne on draught, an enormous list of exceptionally well chosen wines by the bottle (and a good few half-bottles), freshly squeezed juice, Russian vodkas and quite a few malt whiskies. Piped music is well reproduced by the huge loudspeakers, and there's a good winter log fire. The croquet lawn and paddocks by the beech woods drop steeply away to the Chilterns, and there's a boules court out here too. *(Recommended by Dave Carter, B R Sparkes, Lesley Bass)*

Free house ~ Licensee Julie Griffiths ~ Real ale ~ Bar food (lunchtime; not Sat or Sun) ~ Restaurant ~ (01494) 483011 ~ Children in evening if over 7 ~ Open 12-2.30, 6.30-12; 12-3.30 Sun; closed Sun evening, all day Mon

CHIPPING NORTON SP3127 Map 4
Chequers ◀

Goddards Lane

The Chequers is living proof that it's entirely possible for a pub to offer good food from a kitchen that aims high, while at the same time keeping a totally unpretentious genuinely pubby atmosphere. Its three softly lit beamed rooms, with log fires and low ochre ceilings, are nicely old-fashioned – no frills, but clean and comfortable, with plenty of character, friendly efficient service, and a lively evening atmosphere. Besides lovingly kept Fullers Chiswick, London Pride, ESB and seasonal brews on handpump (rare to have the full Fullers range around here), they have nice house wines and good espresso and cappuccino coffee; cribbage, dominoes, shove-ha'penny, and board games. The good generously served food includes home-made soup (£2.50), lunchtime sandwiches (from £2.50), ploughman's (from £4.50), three or four Thai dishes such as mixed bean mussamen or green chicken curry (from £5.50), vegetable lasagne (£5.65; they always have three vegetarian dishes), popular home-cooked ham and egg (£5.95), pork loin steaks marinated in soy sauce and honey (£6.95), duck stir fry with noodles (£7.45), changing fish dishes such as shark steaks (£7.50), whole plaice (£8), and turbot (£9), and puddings like home-made bread and butter pudding or double baked chocolate cheesecake (from £2.95). Besides the no-smoking back restaurant (quiet piped music), they have a new garden room, and tables in the old courtyard. It's very handy for the town's Victorian theatre. *(Recommended by P and M Rudlin, David Campbell, Vicki McLean, Peter and Audrey Dowsett)*

Fullers ~ Tenant Josh Reid ~ Real ale ~ Bar food (12-2.30, 6-9) ~ Restaurant ~ (01608) 644717 ~ Children in restaurant ~ Open 11-11; 12-10.30 Sun; closed 25 Dec

---

If we know a pub has an outdoor play area for children, we mention it.

CLANFIELD SP2802 Map 4
Clanfield Tavern
A4095 S of Witney

The bustling main bar in this pretty village inn has several flagstoned, heavy-beamed and stone-walled small rooms leading off it, with a good mix of seats, brass platters, hunting prints, and a handsome open stone fireplace crowned with a 17th-c plasterwork panel; there's a no-smoking conservatory that links the pub to a barn with a courtyard and fountain just outside it. Bar food (cooked by the chef who has now been here 10 years) includes lunchtimes sandwiches (from £3; steak £5.75) and ploughman's (£4.95), home-made smoked mackerel pâté (£3.25), stilton filled mushrooms (£3.50), burgers with different toppings (£6.75), pasta in a tomato and garlic sauce with smoked ham, mushrooms, onions and cream (£7.50), steaks (£7.75), and trout with flaked almonds (£7.95); the ices and sorbets are home-made. Well kept Courage Best, Hook Norton Best and a guest beer on handpump. It's attractive in summer, with tiny windows peeping from the heavy stone-slabbed roof and tables on a flower-bordered small lawn that look across to the village green and pond. *(Recommended by Peter and Audrey Dowsett, P J Kimber, Tim Barrow, Sue Demont, TRS, Mike and Mary Carter, Andrew Shore)*

Free house ~ Licensees Richard Mills Roberts, Andron Ingle ~ Real ale ~ Bar food (12-2, 6-9.30) ~ Restaurant ~ (01367) 810223 ~ Children welcome ~ Open 11.30-3, 6-11; 12-3, 7-10.30 Sun

CLIFTON SP4831 Map 4
Duke of Cumberlands Head ♀ ⇐
B4031 Deddington—Aynho

The building works are now completed at this friendly pub and readers report that the excellent standards have not suffered. It's a stylish and reliable place with a spacious, simply furnished lounge with a lovely log fireplace and well kept Adnams Southwold, Hook Norton Best, and Wadworths 6X on handpump, a good wine list, and 30 malt whiskies. Enjoyable bar food now has several dishes that are served in smaller helpings for the not-so-hungry: lunchtime sandwiches (not Sun), soup such as cream of mushroom (£3.50), chicken liver pâté (£4.50), deep-fried camembert with cranberry dip (£4.75), wild mushroom stroganoff, venison in port and orange sauce, deep-fried haddock and shepherd's pie (all £5 smaller helping, £7.50 or £8 large helping), spinach and ricotta cannelloni (£8), fresh fillet of plaice (£9), and puddings such as cherry and almond tart or raspberry and apple crumble (£3.50); decent breakfasts. The restaurant is no smoking. There are tables out in the garden, and the canal is a short walk away. *(Recommended by Mrs J Hinsliff, Keith and Margaret Kettell, Penny and Martin Fletcher, Prof P A Reynolds, John and Joan Wyatt, Richard Gibbs, E A and D C Frewer, Sir Nigel Foulkes)*

Free house ~ Licensee Nick Huntington ~ Real ale ~ Bar food (not Sun evening) ~ Restaurant ~ (01869) 338534 ~ Children welcome ~ Open 12-2.30(3 Sat), 6.30-10.30; 12-3 Sun; closed Sun evening ~ Bedrooms: £30/£60S

CLIFTON HAMPDEN SU5495 Map 4
Plough ♀ ⇐
On A415 at junction with Long Wittenham turn-off

There are only a handful of pubs in the country that are totally no smoking, and this friendly place is one of them; they also have no piped music or games machines which appeals to quite a few people, too. The licensee and his wife are helpful and charming, and the opened-up bar area has beams and panelling, black and red floor tiles, antique furniture, attractive pictures, and a relaxed atmosphere. It is very much a place people come to for a meal, with sandwiches (from £3.50), ploughman's or home-made soup (£3.75), a pastry case filled with sautéed oyster mushrooms with a courgette salsa or crisp salad with asparagus, smoked duck breast, quail eggs, sautéed potatoes with a balsamic vinaigrette (£4.75), Cornish scallops with spring onion, ginger and mint (£5.25), breast of maize-fed chicken with risotto and a tomato salsa (£8.50), pasta with chargrilled vegetables and a walnut oil dressing (£9.50), fillet of beef with shi-itake mushrooms and beetroot sauce (£12), and puddings such as traditional sherry trifle or summer pudding (£3.50); the restaurant has an engaging portrait of the licensee. Well kept Courage Best and Directors, and John Smiths on handpump, plenty of good wines, and a dozen malt whiskies. Some tables and seats outside. Several of the bedrooms in the converted building across the courtyard have 4-poster beds. *(Recommended by R Huggins, D Irving, E McCall, T McLean, Ian Phillips, E and D Frewer, TBB, W K Wood, Dr and Mrs A Newton, Anni Cittern, John Suddaby, Kim Darnes, Mrs J Burrows, Susan and John Douglas, JP, PP, the Didler)*

Free house ~ Licensee Yuksel Bektas ~ Real ale ~ Bar food (all day) ~ Restaurant ~ (01865) 407811 ~ Children in eating area of bar and restaurant ~ Open 11-11; 12-10.30 Sun ~ Bedrooms: £62.50B/£82.50B

CUDDESDON SP5903 Map 4
Bat & Ball 🍺

S of Wheatley; if coming from M40 junction 7 via Gt Milton, turn towards Little Milton past church, then look out for signpost

Every inch of wall-space here is covered with cricketing programmes, photographs, porcelain models in well lit cases, score books, cigarette cards, pads, gloves and hats, and signed bats, bails and balls. The immaculately kept L-shaped bar has beams and low ceilings, comfortable furnishings, a partly flagstoned floor, and a relaxed, friendly atmosphere. Bar food includes filled french bread, mushroom brioche (£4.45), prawns (£4.75), smoked salmon platter (£5.95), west country pork (£9.25), fillet of salmon (£9.75), and grilled lamb steak on rosemary and garlic mash (£9.95). The restaurant is no smoking. Well kept Marstons Pedigree and a changing guest beer on handpump, and a decent wine list; fruit machine. A very pleasant terrace at the back has seats, Aunt Sally, and good views over the Oxfordshire plain. *(Recommended by John Wilson, Mrs J Burrows, Carl and Jackie Cranmer, Miss A Aronica, P Weedon, S J Hetherington, Giles Francis, TBB, Dr T F. Hothersall, Nigel Clifton, James Chatfield)*

Hardys & Hansons ~ Tenant Tony Viney ~ Real ale ~ Bar food (12-2.45, 6.30-9.45) ~ Restaurant ~ (01865) 874379 ~ Children welcome ~ Open 11-11; 12-10.30 Sun

CUMNOR SP4603 Map 4
Bear & Ragged Staff

19 Appleton Road; village signposted from A420: follow one-way system into village, bear left into High St then left again into Appleton Road – signposted Eaton, Appleton

New licensees were just taking over this smart old place as we went to press and were about to shut the pub for up to a month for a refit. They aim to make it more of a dining pub but will keep the comfortably rambling, softly lit bar with its roaring log fires, easy chairs, sofas and more orthodox cushioned seats and wall banquettes. They had not finalised the menus but were hoping to include sandwiches, ploughman's, light pubby snacks and traditional dishes such as steak and kidney pie, as well as plenty of vegetarian and fish dishes, and daily specials. Well kept Morrells Oxford Bitter, Graduate, and Varsity, and a changing guest beer on handpump, plus lots of wines by the glass from a good wine list. The building is named for the three-foot model of a Warwick heraldic bear which guards the large open fire. More reports please. *(Recommended by E A and D C Frewer, Gordon, Dr D Twyman, TBB, Dick Brown, Steve and Sarah De Mellow)*

Morrells ~ Nigel and Carol Myles ~ Real ale ~ Bar food ~ Restaurant ~ (01865) 862329 ~ Children in eating area of bar and restaurant ~ Open 11.30-11(11.30-3, 5.30-11 winter); 12-10.30(12-3, 7-10.30 winter) Sun

---

Real ale to us means beer which has matured naturally in its cask – not pressurised or filtered.

CUXHAM SU6695 Map 2
Half Moon
4 miles from M40, junction 6; S on B4009, then right on to B480 at Watlington

New licensees again for this thatched, rather cottagey village pub. Each of the three comfortable low-beamed bar areas has an open fire, country-style furnishings, and books and prints, and they keep Brakspears Bitter and Special on handpump. Cheerfully served bar food now includes winter home-made soup (£3.25), filled french bread (from £4.25, with salad and chips), half pint of prawns with garlic mayonnaise (£4.95), ploughman's (£5.75), home-made quiche (£5.95), bangers and mash, lamb and apricot pie or chicken supreme stuffed with olives, feta and garlic (£6.95), duck breast with honey glaze or venison and ginger casserole (£7.25), and puddings such as toffee apple riffin (from an 18th-c recipe, £3.25). Darts, dominoes, trivia, and piped music. There are seats sheltered by an oak tree on the back lawn, and a climbing frame. Across the road, a stream runs through this quiet village. *(Recommended by TBB, Derek Harvey-Piper, Kevin Thorpe, Mike Wells, Ron Gentry, John and Kathleen Potter)*

Brakspears ~ Tenant Judith Bishop ~ Real ale ~ Bar food (not Sun evening) ~ (01491) 614110/613939 ~ Children in eating area of bar ~ Open 12-2.30(3.30 Sat), 6-11; 12-10.30 Sun

DORCHESTER SU5794 Map 4
George ♀ 🛏
High St; village signposted just off A4074 Maidenhead—Oxford

Before it was a flourishing coaching inn, this lovely timber and tile house was used as a brewhouse for the Norman abbey which still stands opposite. There's lots of old-fashioned charm in the civilised beamed bar with its fresh flowers on the tables, roaring winter log fire, comfortable seats and fine old furniture (including cushioned settles and leather chairs), and copies of *Country Life*. Good bar food includes sandwiches, watercress and pistou soup with a poached egg (£4.50), roll of aromatic duck confit with mango and lime leaf chutney, cucumber salad and soy dressing (£5.50), home-smoked guinea fowl salad (£6), salmon and lemon grass kebabs, crispy noodles, stir-fried greens and a chilli broth (£12), calf's liver on smoked bacon and sage risotto with baby spinach and madeira sauce (£13), and bass fillet with a spicy tomato confit (£14); potatoes and vegetables are extra; on Sunday lunchtime they serve sandwiches and a roast only. Well kept Brakspears Bitter and a guest beer on handpump, good wine by the glass from a quite exceptional wine list, and a range of malt whiskies. Pleasant and welcoming service. *(Recommended by John Hayter, Peter Burton, Gordon, Susan and John Douglas)*

Free house ~ Licensees Brian Griffin and M C Pinder ~ Real ale ~ Bar food ~ Restaurant ~ (01865) 340404 ~ Children in restaurant ~ Open 11-11; 12-10.30 Sun ~ Bedrooms: £62.50B/£80B

EAST HENDRED SU4588 Map 2
Wheatsheaf ♀
Chapel Square; village signposted from A417

Standing amongst thatched brick buildings, this attractive black and white timbered 16th-c village pub has a comfortable bar with high-backed settles and stools around tables on quarry tiles by an inglenook fireplace, some wall panelling, and a tiny parquet-floored triangular platform by the bar; low, stripped deal settles form booths around tables in a carpeted area up some broad steps. Good bar food includes sandwiches (from £2), home-made soup, ham and egg, home-made vegetarian dishes (£5.25), steak in ale or chicken and leek pies (£5.95), and fresh fish (Thursday-Saturday from £5.50 to £10). Well kept Morlands Original and Old Speckled Hen, and Ruddles County on handpump, and a decent wine list. Dominoes, shove-ha'penny. The black labrador is called Bob and the springer spaniel, Harry. The garden behind (where they play Aunt Sally) is colourful with roses and other flowers beneath conifers and silver birch. The nearby church is interesting – its Tudor clock has elaborate chimes but no hands. *(Recommended by John E Vigar, Ron and Barbara Watkins, Justin Hulford)*

Morlands ~ Tenant Neil Haywood ~ Real ale ~ Bar food (not Sun evening) ~ (01235) 833229 ~ Children welcome ~ Jazz and swing monthly ~ Open 11-11; 12-10.30 Sun; 11-3, 5.30-11 in winter

EATON SP4403 Map 4
Eight Bells

Village signposted off B4017 SW of Oxford; can also be reached direct from A420 via Bessels Leigh or Appleton

Not too prettified, this quietly placed friendly and unspoilt Tudor village pub is a nice find. There are pleasant walks nearby: it's only a short way from Bablock Hythe, where Matthew Arnold's scholar-gypsy crossed the stripling Thames. The two small low-beamed bars have a cosy atmosphere, with their open fires, sensibly straightforward furnishings, farm tools, horse tack and brasses; a dining area leads off the cosy lounge; open fires. Well kept Morlands IPA and Original and a guest like Adnams Broadside on handpump, welcoming helpful licensees; no dogs. The kitchen was refurbished fairly recently, and they now do a wide range of good value food, cooked to order (so there may be a wait), such as home-made soup (£2.55), sandwiches (from £2.95), caesar salad (£3.15), smoked mackerel and horseradish mousse (£4.15), ham and egg (£5.45), spinach and mushroom lasagne (£6.15), steak and mushroom in ale pie (£6.45), 6oz rump steak (£6.75), gammon with a creamed grain mustard sauce (£7.95), smoked haddock with bacon rarebit sauce (£8.25), chicken stuffed with tarragon butter (£9.85), and puddings like home-made chocolate fudge cake, sticky toffee pudding or rice pudding with jam (£2.95). The cat is called Sybil and the dog, Eric. There are tables out in the garden; the stunted but thriving yew tree in front is the result of a lightning strike some years ago, which catapulted its upper part on to the roof of the pub. The car park has a tethering rail for horses. *(Recommended by Marjorie and David Lamb, Gordon, Maureen Hobbs, Joan Olivier)*

Morlands ~ Tenant Nicholas Semenenko ~ Real ale ~ Bar food ~ Restaurant ~ (01865) 862983 ~ Children in eating area of bar ~ Acoustic/jazz 1st Weds of month ~ Open 12-2.30, 6-11; 12-3, 7-10.30 Sun; closed evening 25 Dec

EXLADE STREET SU6582 Map 2
Highwayman ♀ ◨ ⇌

Signposted just off A4074 Reading—Wallingford

Surrounded by lovely wooded countryside, this rambling inn is mostly 17th c, though some parts date back to the 14th c. The two beamed rooms of the bar have quite an unusual layout, with an interesting variety of seats around old tables and even recessed into a central sunken inglenook; an airy no-smoking conservatory dining room has more seats (mainly for eating) and overlooks the garden. Good bar food includes sandwiches, home-made soup (£3.75), garlic mushrooms with bacon (£5.45), bacon and rabbit terrine with tarragon vinaigrette (£5.95), wild mushroom linguini (£8.95), fillet of pork with a mustard sauce (£11.50), liver and bacon or chilli prawns (£13.95), steaks (from £13.95), whole bass (£15.95), and roast Sunday lunch; home-made crisps on the bar, and well kept Brakspears Bitter, Fullers London Pride, Gibbs Mew Bishops Tipple, and a guest beer on handpump, several malt whiskies, decent wines, freshly squeezed orange juice, winter mulled wine and summer pimms, and champagne and kirs. The friendly mongrel is called Gurty and the black and white spaniel, Saigon. The attractive garden has tables and fine views. *(Recommended by Dick Brown, Nicholas Holmes, Roger and Valerie Hill, JP, PP, G Neighbour, the Didler)*

Free house ~ Licensees Carole and Roger Shippey ~ Real ale ~ Bar food (12-2.30, 6-10.30) ~ Restaurant ~ (01491) 682020 ~ Children in eating area of bar ~ Open 11-11; 12-10.30 Sun ~ Bedrooms: £50B/£60B

FINSTOCK SP3616 Map 4
Plough ♀ ⇌

The Bottom; just off B4022 N of Witney

Friendly and neatly kept, this thatched pub has a long low-beamed rambling bar that is comfortable and relaxed and nicely split up by partitions and alcoves, with an armchair by the open logburning stove in the massive stone inglenook, tiles up at the end by the servery (elsewhere is carpeted), and walls decorated with rosettes the licensees have won at Crufts and other doggy-related paraphernalia. Their llasl apso is called Jumbo, and other dogs are welcome in the garden (on a lead) and in the public bar. Good bar food includes sandwiches, and specials such as teriyaki salmon with egg noodles (£8.95), steak, stout, stilton and mushroom pie (£9.95), and herb-crusted rack of lamb with port and redcurrant gravy (£10.25). A comfortable low-beamed stripped-stone dining room is on the right. Brakspears Special, Fullers London Pride, Greene King Abbot, Hook Norton Best, and Timothy Taylor Landlord on handpump or tapped from the cask, and a special bloody mary. A separate games area has bar billiards, cribbage, and dominoes. There are tables (and Aunt Sally) in the good, sizeable garden and several rare specimen roses (heavily scented); plenty of good walks in the attractive surrounding countryside.
(Recommended by John Robertson, N Cobb, H W Clayton, Joe and Mary Stachura, Sandra Childress, D Bryan, Mrs S Evans)

Free house ~ Licensees Keith and Nigel Ewers ~ Real ale ~ Bar food ~ Restaurant ~ (01993) 868333 ~ Children welcome away from bar ~ Occasional bands ~ Open 12-2.30, 6-11; 12-11 Sat; 12-3.30, 7-11 Sun; 12-2.30, 6-11 Sat in winter; closed evening 1 Jan ~ Bedrooms: /£50S

FYFIELD SU4298 Map 4
White Hart

In village, off A420 8 miles SW of Oxford

The impressive medieval interior in this rather humble-looking building comes as quite a surprise – soaring eaves and huge stone-flanked window embrasures, and an attractive carpeted upper gallery making up the main room – a grand hall rather than a traditional bar, though the atmosphere is informal and relaxed. A low-ceilinged side bar has an inglenook fireplace with a huge black urn hanging over the grate, and a framed history of the pub on the wall. The priests' room and barrel-vaulted cellar are no-smoking dining areas. Well kept Boddingtons, Fullers London Pride, Hook Norton Best, Theakstons Old Peculier, and Wadworths 6X on handpump or tapped from the cask, and country wines. Good bar food includes lunchtime sandwiches, home-made soup (£2.95), fried portuguese sardines or caesar salad (£4.25; main course £7.25), king prawns in garlic butter (£6.50; main course £8.75), steak, mushroom and Guinness pie (£7.25), pork steaks coated with an orange, prune and brandy sauce with wild rice or baked trout (£8.50), grilled chicken breast topped with sliced mushrooms and melted stilton cheese (£8.95), steaks (from £9.95), vegetarian dishes, and children's meals (from £3); friendly, attentive service. Darts, shove-ha'penny, dominoes, cribbage, and piped music. A heavy wooden door leads out to the rambling, sheltered and flowery back lawn, which has a children's playground.
(Recommended by Tony and Joan Walker, TBB, Graham Parker, Ted George, Lynda Payton, Gordon, Sandra Childress, Jim Bush, Andy and Sarah Gillett)

Free house ~ Licensees John and Sherry Howard ~ Real ale ~ Bar food (until 10pm) ~ Restaurant ~ (01865) 390585 ~ Children in eating area of bar ~ Open 11-3, 6-11; 12-3, 7-10.30 Sun; closed 25 and 26 Dec

HOOK NORTON SP3533 Map 4
Gate Hangs High ♀

Banbury Rd; a mile N of village towards Sibford, at Banbury—Rollright crossroads

Even though this welcoming country pub is rather tucked away, it does tend to fill up quickly and has long been a handy find for travellers in the area, as indicated by the sign outside: 'The gate hangs high, and hinders none, Refresh and pay, and travel on'. There's quite an emphasis on the popular bar food with changing dishes such as honey-baked ham and eggs (£6.95), mild creamy chicken curry or cold poached salmon salad (£7.95), local asparagus with ham and cheese sauce (£8.25), barbary duck breast with cranberry and orange sauce (£9.25), medallions of venison with port and stilton sauce (£9.95), monkfish cooked in lemon and parsley butter (£10.50), and home-made puddings (£2.95). The bar has joists in the long, low ceiling, a brick bar counter, stools and assorted chairs on the carpet, and a gleaming copper hood over the hearth in the inglenook fireplace. Well kept Hook Norton Best, Old Hooky, Generation, and Twelve Days on handpump, a good wine list, and a range of malt whiskies; dominoes. The pub is quite a sight in summer with spectacular flowering tubs and wall baskets around the picnic-sets in front; at the back, the broad lawn with holly and apple trees, has swings for children to play on and fine views. Five miles south-west of the pub are the Bronze Age Rollright Stones – said to be a king and his army who were turned to stone by a witch. *(Recommended by Hugh Spottiswoode, Sir Nigel Foulkes, Sue and Steve Griffiths, Martin Jones, John Bowdler, Mrs N W Neill, E A George, Marjorie and David Lamb, John H Kane, John Robertson, Dick Brown, M & C Starling)*

Hook Norton ~ Tenant Stuart Rust ~ Real ale ~ Bar food (not Sun evening) ~ Restaurant ~ (01608) 737387 ~ Children in eating area of bar and restaurant ~ Open 11.30-3, 6.30-11; 12-3, 7-11 Sun

Pear Tree ◖

Village signposted off A361 SW of Banbury

This unspoilt, friendly little pub is barely 100 yards from the Hook Norton brewery and has the full range of their ales on handpump: Hook Norton Best, Old Hooky, Generation, and Mild along with a guest ale; country wines. The knocked together bar area has country-kitchen furniture on the nicely timbered floor, some long tables, a well stocked magazine rack, and open fires; maybe locals drifting in with their dogs; dominoes, chess (outside also), and Jenga. Good bar food includes generous sandwiches (£2.50), cottage pie (£4.95), beef in ale casserole (£5.50), sweet and sour chicken or Thai chicken curry (£5.75), and puddings such as a proper ice-cream sundae (£2.50). The attractive, sizeable garden has plenty of seats, and Aunt Sally. *(Recommended by Gwyneth and Salvo Spadaro-Dutturi, JP, PP, Penny and Martin Fletcher, John Bowdler, Colin and Ann Hunt, Helen Pickering, James Owen, Tom Evans, the Didler)*

Hook Norton ~ Tenant J Sivyer ~ Real ale ~ Bar food ~ (01608) 737482 ~ Children in eating area of bar ~ Open 11.30-3(4 Sat), 6-11; 12-4, 7-10.30 Sun ~ Bedrooms: /£45S

Sun ◖ ⇨

High Street

Enlarged in 1991by the incorporation of the next door Red Lion, this has been improved still further in the last couple of years by its present friendly tenants. It has a buoyant and relaxed local atmosphere, particularly in the flagstoned front bar, with its huge log fire, hop-strung beams, and one table reserved for dominoes. Beyond this another room has sensibly placed darts, while behind the central servery is a snug carpeted room with comfortable banquettes and other seats, leading into the attractive partly no-smoking green-walled restaurant. A wide choice of good bar snacks includes a good range of excellent triple decker sandwiches (from £2.25), soup (£2.95), ploughman's (from £4.50), ciabatta bread topped with chorizo, olives, basil and mozzarella (£5.45), steak and ale pie (£6.50), cajun chicken with avocado, salad and french stick (£6.95), mild chicken curry with mango (£7.85) and duck confit with red wine sauce (£8.50), all served with a good selection of vegetables; also, terrine of wild boar with a sweet fruit chutney (£3.85), king prawns in garlic butter (£5.50), roasted mediterranean vegetables and mozzarella on couscous and finished with sun-dried tomato and basil pesto dressing (£7.75), crab cakes (£10.50), and bass on a stir fry of spinach, bean sprouts and mushrooms cooked in sesame oil and soy sauce or noisettes of lamb with a redcurrant and red wine sauce (£11.95). Well kept Hook

Norton Best, Best Mild, Generation, Old Hooky and Twelve Days on handpump, good value wines, efficient service. Facing the church, the pub has a prime site in this pretty village; with tables out on a back terrace. Good wheelchair access and disabled facilities. *(Recommended by Steve and Irene Law, R E Syrett, Sue and Jim Sargeant, E G Peters, D M and M C Watkinson, Pete Baker, Liz and Paul Wisniewski, Paul and Linda Thomson)*

Hook Norton ~ Tenants Richard and Jane Hancock ~ Bar food ~ Restaurant ~ (01608) 737570 ~ Well behaved children welcome ~ Open 11.30-3, 6-11; 12-3, 7-10.30 Sun ~ Bedrooms: £30B/£50B

KELMSCOT SU2499 Map 4
Plough 🛏

NW of Faringdon, off A417 or A4095

Run by friendly, charming licensees, this pretty pub is minutes from the Thames, and Mr Pardoe is happy to offer advice on local walks. The small traditional front bar has ancient flagstones and stripped stone walls, and a relaxed chatty atmosphere, and there's also a larger cheerfully carpeted lounge bar with interesting prints on the walls, and a second lounge (which had been the restaurant); dogs are allowed in the public bar (where there is satellite TV for sport). A wide choice of enjoyable popular food includes sandwiches and filled french bread (from £2.25; toasties 25p extra; smoked salmon and cream cheese french bread £5.25), soup (£2.50), garlic mushrooms (£3.75), filled baked potatoes (from £4.25), home-cooked ham and egg (£5.25), ploughman's (from £5.25), filled pancakes (from £5.95), vegetable bake (£6.50), grilled trout (£7.95), steaks (from £8.95), daily specials like spiced chicken with yoghurt dressing (£7.75) or pork loin in prune and calvados sauce (£7.95), and puddings such as apple crumble or bread and butter pudding (£3.25); children's dishes (£2.95). Well kept Bass, Flowers Original, Morlands Original and Wadworths 6X on handpump; darts, shove-ha'penny, cribbage, dominoes, fruit machine, trivia, and piped music. The Thames Path is close by as is the Oxfordshire cycleway, and there is both fresh and coarse fishing available locally; moorings for boats, too, and the attractive garden has seats amongst the unusual flowers. *(Recommended by Edward Leetham, Ted George, Peter and Audrey Dowsett, Kay Neville-Rolfe, K and E Leist, K H Frostick)*

Free house ~ Licensees Trevor and Anne Pardoe ~ Real ale ~ Bar food ~ (01367) 253543 ~ Children in eating area of bar until 9pm ~ Solo guitar/keyboard Sat evening ~ Open 11-11; 12-10.30 Sun; 12-3.30, 7-10.30 Sun in winter; closed Sun evenings Jan/Feb ~ Bedrooms: £30B/£50B

KINGSTON LISLE SU3287 Map 4
Blowing Stone ♀

Village signposted off B4507 W of Wantage

The new licensees of this comfortable brick-built dining pub were highly thought of hoteliers before coming here, so we have confidence that all will be well. The brightly modernised bar has quite a light, fresh feel, as well as simple wooden tables and red-cushioned chairs on the neatly polished red-tiled floor, newspapers to read, and an open fire. A little room leading off is filled by its pool table, while over towards the no-smoking restaurant and conservatory there's a comfortable lounge, and a small area with a piano. Bar food includes a hearty home-made soup (£3.50), generous open sandwiches (£4.50), bangers and mash (£5.75), home-cooked ham and eggs with sautéed potatoes (£6.50), stir-fried beef with a julienne of vegetables and noodles in a black bean sauce (£8.50), grilled fresh fish of the day, seasonal game, and evening dishes such as vegetable terrine on tossed spinach (£3.75), deep-fried goat's cheese with crispy bacon (£5), noisettes of lamb with a redcurrant and brandy jus (£11.50), and 10oz fillet steak (£14.50); two-course Sunday lunch (£10), three courses (£12.75). Bass, Morlands Original and Wadworths 6X on handpump, and a good choice of wines. A few tables behind look over a pond with koi and goldfish. The pub takes its name from a stone pierced with holes on the edge of the village, said to have been used by King Alfred as a horn to summon his troops. Handy for Uffington Castle hill fort and the other ancient sites up on the downs above the village. *(Recommended by Peter and Audrey Dowsett, Dr Irvine Loudon, Mr and Mrs J Chaffe, Michael Sargent, HNJ, PEJ, Robert Tapsfield)*

Free house ~ Licensees Geoffrey and Amanda Snelson ~ Real ale ~ Bar food ~ Restaurant ~ (01367) 820288 ~ Children welcome ~ Open 11.30-2.30, 6.30-11; 12-3, 7-10.30 Sun ~ Bedrooms: £20/£40B

LEWKNOR SU7198 Map 4
Olde Leathern Bottel
Under a mile from M40 junction 6; just off B4009 towards Watlington

Readers are really fond of this friendly, bustling little pub set in a charming village. The two rooms of the bar have heavy beams in the low ceilings, rustic furnishings, open fires, and an understated décor of old beer taps and the like; the no-smoking family room is separated only by standing timbers, so you don't feel cut off from the rest of the pub. Popular and generously served bar food includes lunchtime sandwiches (from £1.95), ploughman's (£4.10), prawns in filo pastry with a dip or spare ribs in barbecue sauce (£3.95), home-made beef in ale pie or chicken balti (£5.95), pasta with mozzarella and tomatoes (£6.95), and puddings like toffee crunch (£2.50); quick, obliging service. Well kept Brakspears Bitter, SB and winter Old on handpump; dominoes and piped music. There are tables on the sizeable lawn alongside the car park, and a children's play area with climbing frame, swing and slide. *(Recommended by Elizabeth and Klaus Leist, Marjorie and David Lamb, B R Sparkes, Mr and Mrs C Moncreiffe, Kevin Thorpe, Gordon, M Mason, D Thompson, P Weedon, Mrs J Hilditch, NMF, DF, Paula Williams, Roger Huggins, TBB, Karen Eliot)*

Brakspears ~ Tenant Mr L S Gordon ~ Real ale ~ Bar food ~ (01844) 351482 ~ Children in restaurant ~ Open 11-2.30(3 Sat), 5.30(6 Sat)-11; 12-3, 7-10.30 Sun

LONG WITTENHAM SU5493 Map 4
Machine Man 🛏️
Fieldside; back lane parallel to main road, off A415 SE of Abingdon

From the road this plain largely 19th-c building looks mildly forbidding – a highly misleading impression, as inside the single bar has a buoyant and very welcoming atmosphere. There's a great mix of customers, from thirsty farmers straight in from hedge-cutting to elderly couples out for a lunchtime treat with the weekly pension money. It's the sort of place that happily takes dogs and muddy shoes in its stride: sensibly unpretentious furnishings, and helpful landlords. Good generous fresh food includes sandwiches (from £1.80), soup (£2.50), ploughman's (£3.75), smoked salmon and prawns (£5.25), spicy bean hotpot (£5.25), steak and kidney pudding (£6.95), chicken topped with ham and cheese (£7.95), fillet steak (from £10.50), sensibly priced game (you may meet the man who shot your partridge in the bar), generous Sunday roasts (£5.95), maybe fresh fish specials, and puddings like pecan and toffee pie or plum crumble (£2.50); no-smoking restaurant. Eight well kept beers include Black Sheep, Greene King Triumph, Rebellion Smuggler, West Berkshire Good Old Boy, alongside four changing guests such as Eccleshall Slaters, Greene King Abbot, Shepherd Neame Spitfire and York Yorkshire Terrier, decent malt whiskies and wines (half a dozen by the glass); darts (which they take seriously here), fruit machine and piped music. They still play Aunt Sally outside. *(Recommended by Cliff Blakemore, Stephanie Smith, Gareth Price, E R Pearce, Iain Robertson, Marjorie and David Lamb, B Adams)*

Free house ~ Licensees Gordon and Chris Lindsay ~ Bar food ~ (0186 730) 7835 ~ Children welcome ~ Open 11.30-3, 6-11; 12-4, 7-10.30 Sun; closed 25 Dec evening ~ Bedrooms: £35B/£48B

MAIDENSGROVE SU7288 Map 2
Five Horseshoes 🍴 🍷
W of village, which is signposted from B480 and B481; OS Sheet 175, map reference 711890

High up in the Chiltern beechwoods on a lovely common, this popular 17th-c brick pub has fine views from several tables in the newly extended restaurant and from the sheltered back garden (which also has a rockery and some interesting water features); maybe summer barbecues. The rambling bar is furnished with mostly modern wheelback chairs around stripped wooden tables (though there are some attractive older seats and a big baluster-leg table), and has a good log fire in winter; the low ceiling in the main area is covered in bank notes from all over the world, mainly donated by customers. There's also a separate bar for walkers where boots are welcome – plenty of surrounding walks. Good, imaginative food includes lunchtime dishes such as home-made soup (£3.50; well liked stilton soup £3.95), ploughman's (£4.95), filled baked potatoes (from £5.95), pancakes with fillings such as spicy Thai vegetables or prawns in a creamy cheese sauce (from £6.75), warm chicken salad (£7.50), steak and kidney pie (£7.95), and daily specials; also, there's an à la carte menu which can be taken at any time: chargrilled vegetables (£5.50), prawn and crab mornay (£5.95), salmon and crab cakes with a piquant tomato sauce (£9.50), corn fed chicken breast with spicy fruit chutney (£10.95), roast rack of lamb with a mustard and herb crust (£12), calf's livers with sage butter (£12.50), steaks (from £14), and puddings like dark chocolate brûlée with crisp caramel topping or rich lemon and lime posset with wafer cigarettes (from £3.95); they also do a set menu – two courses £16.50, three courses £19.50. Well kept Brakspears Bitter, Special and seasonal ales on handpump, and a dozen wines by the glass, including champagne. *(Recommended by Miss Mary Imlay, Michael Sargent, Graham and Karen Oddey, Gerald Barnett, Miss C Passmore, Gordon, R C Morgan, Pat and Robert Watt)*

Brakspears ~ Tenants Graham and Mary Cromack ~ Real ale ~ Bar food ~ Restaurant ~ (01491) 641282 ~ Children in eating area of bar and in restaurant; over 5 in evening ~ Open 11.30-2.30, 6-11; 12-3, 7-10.30 Sun; closed evenings 25 and 26 Dec and 1 Jan

MURCOTT SP5815 Map 4
Nut Tree ♀

Off B4027 NE of Oxford, via Islip and Charlton on Otmoor

For over 20 years, Mr and Mrs Evans have carefully run this neatly thatched, warmly welcoming pub. They've refurbished inside this year which gives more room for diners but keeps a quiet section for those only wanting a drink.The civilised beamed lounge has a long polished bar with brasses, antiques and pictures all round, fresh flowers on its tables (set for food), and a winter log fire; there's also a small back partly no-smoking conservatory-style restaurant. Good bar food includes soup (£2.95), sandwiches (from £3.50), egg mayonnaise with strips of smoked salmon (using free-range eggs £3.95), stilton mushrooms (£4.50), ham and egg (£4.95), ploughman's (£5.50), mushroom stroganoff (£6.50), fresh cod mornay or dijon chicken pasta (£7.50), cajun chicken (£8.50), calf's liver and bacon (£9.50), rack of lamb (£10.95), steaks (from £10.20), puddings (£3.50), and good cheeses (£4.50). Well kept Wadworths IPA and 6X and a guest beer on handpump, a fair number of malt whiskies, and a decent range of wines with several by the glass. There are usually ducks on a front pond, pretty hanging baskets and tubs, and plenty of animals such as donkeys, peacocks and rabbits; also Aunt Sally, and an unusual collection of ten gargoyles, each loosely modelled on one of the local characters, and carved into a magnificently grotesque form from a different wood. Nine of them hang in the walnut tree and one from a pillar overlooking the well. The pub is handy for walks through the boggy Otmoor wilderness. Roundhead soldiers came here extensively when Cromwell had his headquarters at nearby Boarstall. *(Recommended by Gordon, Michael Sargent, Mark Johnson, Derek and Sylvia Stephenson, TBB, D S and A R Hare, Ted George, Paul Edgington, John McDonald, Ann Bond, P J Kimber, Steve and Sarah de Mellow, Mr and Mrs T A Bryan, Keith and Margaret Kettwell, NWN, Susan and John Douglas)*

Free house ~ Licensees Gordon and Diane Evans ~ Real ale ~ Bar food (not Sun) ~ (01865) 331253 ~ Children in restaurant ~ Open 11-3, 6.30-11; 12-4, 7-10.30 Sun

Pubs with attractive or unusually big gardens are listed at the back of the book.

OXFORD SP5106 Map 4
Kings Arms   £
40 Holywell St

Quite a few readers have known this pub for over 30 years and feel it's as good today as it ever was – still with a bustling atmosphere and a good mix of customers. There's a big rather bare main room, with a no-smoking coffee room just inside the Parks Road entrance, and several cosy and comfortably worn-in side and back rooms, each with a different character and customers. An extra back room has a sofa and more tables and there's a tiny room behind that. They still keep a dictionary for the crossword buffs in the Dons Bar, with its elderly furnishings and tiled floor; fruit machine and video game; a mix of old prints and photographs of customers, and sympathetic lighting. Well kept Youngs Bitter, Special and seasonal ales and Wadworths 6X on handpump, a fine choice of wines with 21 by the glass, up to 20 malt whiskies, and decent bar food such as sandwiches (from £1.50), home-made soup (£1.95), filled baked potatoes (from £2.95), burgers (from £3.95), spinach and mushroom lasagne or chicken curry (£4.75), beef and mushroom in ale pie (£5.45), and sirloin steak (£6.45); on Sundays they open at 10.30 for breakfast and coffee; daily papers, tables out on the pavement. *(Recommended by Pat and Roger Fereday, Anthony Barnes, Stephanie Smith, Gareth Price, Walter Reid, Stephen and Julie Brown, Gordon, Keith and Janet Eaton, Dick Brown, R Huggins, D Irving, E McCall, T McLean)*

Youngs ~ Manager David Kyffin ~ Real ale ~ Bar food (11.30-9.30) ~ (01865) 242369 ~ Children in eating area of bar until 9pm ~ Open 10.30-11; 12-10.30 Sun; closed 24-26 and 31 Dec

Turf Tavern
Tavern Bath Place; via St Helen's Passage, between Holywell Street and New College Lane

The two atmospheric little rooms with their dark beams and low ceilings in this busy pub are much as Hardy described them when Jude the Obscure discovered that Arabella the barmaid was the wife who'd left him years before; there's also a bar in one of the courtyards. They keep a changing range of real ales such as Archers Golden, Boddingtons, Morlands Old Speckled Hen, Whitbreads The Abroad Cooper, and eight guest beers on handpump; also, Belgian beers, a few country wines and a couple of farm ciders; video game. Food is straightforward and includes sandwiches (from £2.95), filled baked potatoes, burgers (£3.25), ploughman's (£4.55), and steak in ale pie (£5.25); the top food area is no smoking. This is a pretty place – especially in summer, when there are tables in the three attractive walled-in flagstoned or gravelled courtyards around the old-fashioned building; in winter you can huddle around the braziers in the courtyard. *(Recommended by Liz, Wendy and Ian Phillips, Gordon, TBB, SLC, Brad W Morley, S Lythgoe, Simon Pyle, Graham and Karen Oddey, Martin and Karen Wake, Stephen and Julie Brown, Brian and Anna Marsden, Giles Francis, Stephanie Smith, Gareth Price, Lawrence Pearse, R Huggins, D Irving, E McCall, T McLean, R J Bland, Nigel Woolliscroft, Tony Scott, the Didler)*

Whitbreads ~ Manager Trevor Walter ~ Real ale ~ Bar food (12-8) ~ (01865) 243235 ~ Children in eating area of bar ~ Open 11-11; 12-10.30 Sun

RAMSDEN SP3515 Map 4
Royal Oak ♀ 🍴
Village signposted off B4022 Witney—Charlbury

To find this popular village inn, look out for the church which is opposite. They keep a fine choice of well kept real ales on handpump here: Adnams Broadside, Archers Golden, Fullers ESB, Goffs White Knight, and Hook Norton Best and Old Hooky; enjoyable house wines. Served by helpful staff, the well liked bar food might include home-made soup (£2.95), chicken, liver and Cointreau pâté (£3.50), lunchtime sandwiches (not Sunday; club sandwich £4.75), ploughman's (£4.50), lunchtime sausages with thick onion gravy (£6.25), burgers (from £6.25), cream cheese, spinach and garlic pancakes topped with melted cheese (£7.25), chilli con carne (£7.95), mediterranean-style lamb casserole with couscous (£8.95), steaks (from £9.50), smoked salmon and fresh crab fishcakes with a piquant tomato and sweet pepper sauce (£10.95), and English lamb leg steak with a port and redcurrant sauce (£11.95); on Thursday evenings they do rump steak, a glass of wine and home-made pudding (£11.50); roast Sunday lunch (no snacks then). The traditional beamed bar is simply furnished and decorated but comfortable, and has fresh flowers, and a cheery winter log fire. The evening dining room is no smoking. The cosy bedrooms are in separate cottages. *(Recommended by M G Hart, Guy Vowles, Derek and Sylvia Stephenson, Ronald Harry, Mike and Mary Carter, Peter and Audrey Dowsett, George Atkinson, Paul and Ursula Randall, Sandra Childress)*

Free house ~ Licensee Jon Oldham ~ Real ale ~ Bar food (till 10pm) ~ Restaurant ~ (01993) 868213/(01993) 868864 fax ~ Children in eating area of bar and restaurant ~ Open 11.30-3, 6.30-11; 12-3, 7-10.30 Sun

ROKE SU6293 Map 2
Home Sweet Home
Village signposted off B4009 Benson—Watlington

Even when this pleasantly old-fashioned, rather smart pub is busy – which it often is – service remains friendly and efficient. The two smallish rooms of the bar have a relaxed, welcoming atmosphere, heavy stripped beams, leather armed chairs on the bare boards, a great high-backed settle with a hefty slab of a rustic table in front of it, a few horsey or game pictures such as a nice Thorburn print of snipe on the stone walls, and a big log fire. On the right, a carpeted room with low settees and armchairs and an attractive corner glass cupboard, leads through to the restaurant. A wide choice of enjoyable bar food includes sandwiches, toasties, and club sandwiches (from £2.55; savoury crab and mushroom toastie £4.25, smoked duck breast £4.50, smoked salmon club sandwich £5), home-made soup (£2.75), filled baked potatoes (from £4.25), lots of ploughman's (from £4), home-made burgers (from £4.65), omelettes (£5.75), ham and eggs (£6.45), scallops provençale or smoked haddock and egg pancakes (£6.75), vegetable stroganoff, and daily specials like fresh cod in light beer batter (£6.25), warm crab and saffron tart (£6.95), steak and kidney pudding (£7.25), and chicken breast with gorgonzola cheese, sun-dried tomatoes and spring onions (£8.95). Well kept Hardy Royal Oak on handpump, and a good choice of malt whiskies. The low-walled front garden is ideal for eating on a sunny day; there are lots of flowers around the tables out by the well. *(Recommended by Marjorie and David Lamb, Mike Wells, B R Sparkes, Adam and Elizabeth Duff, Kevin Thorpe)*

Free house ~ Licensees Jill Madle, Peter & Irene Mountford ~ Real ale ~ Bar food ~ (01491) 38249 ~ Children in eating area of bar and restaurant ~ Open 11-3, 6-11; 12-3 Sun; closed Sun evening

SHENINGTON SP3742 Map 4
Bell
Village signposted from A422 W of Banbury

In a quiet village with good surrounding walks, this 300-year-old pub is part of a row of golden stone cottages. The heavy-beamed and carpeted lounge has cushioned wall and window seats, vases of flowers on the tables, and horsebrasses and an old document on the cream walls; the wall in the flagstoned area on the left is stripped to stone and decorated with heavy-horse harness, and the right side opens into a little pine-panelled room (popular with locals) with decorated plates; cribbage, dominoes, coal fire. Decent bar food includes sandwiches and dishes such as walnut, stilton and green bean lasagne (£6.50), salmon in watercress sauce (£7.95), and duck in port and black cherries (£9.95). Well kept Hook Norton Best on handpump. There's a west highland terrier, Lucy, and a labrador, Daisy. The tables at the front look across to the green, and there are seats in the small attractive back garden. *(Recommended by J H Kane, Colin and Ann Hunt, Marlene and Jim Godfrey, M and C Starling, John Brightley, Maysie Thompson, Brian Borwick, John Robertson, John Bowdler, John Bramley, Martin Jones)*

*Free house ~ Licensee Jennifer Dixon ~ Real ale ~ Bar food ~ (01295) 670274 ~
Children welcome ~ Open 12-3, 6.30-11(10.30 Sun) ~ Bedrooms: £20B/£40B*

SHIPTON UNDER WYCHWOOD SP2717 Map 4
Lamb ♀ 🛏

Off A361 to Burford

As this friendly and civilised old place is nicely positioned to many of the Cotswold
attractions, it makes sense to use this as a base and enjoy the comfortable bedrooms
and super breakfasts. The relaxed beamed bar has a fine oak-panelled settle, a nice mix
of solid old farmhouse-style and captain's chairs on the wood-block floor, polished
tables, cushioned bar stools, an oak bar counter, pictures on old partly bared stone
walls, newspapers on rods to read, and an open fire. Good bar food includes a popular
lunchtime carvery (£5.95-£8.95), soup (£2.95), smoked haddock tartlets (£4.25),
chicken liver parfait with cumberland sauce (£4.75), spinach, pine nut and cream
cheese samosas and tomato and basil sauce (£7.95), venison sausages, saffron mash
and redcurrant gravy (£9.50), sirloin steak with black peppercorn sauce (£11.95),
crispy duck with orange sauce (£12.50), and daily specials such as chargrilled tuna
(£8.95) or roast halibut with lime and coriander (£10.95); three-course roast Sunday
lunch (£16.95). The restaurant is no smoking; best to reserve a table at weekends. Well
kept Hook Norton Best and Marstons Pedigree on handpump, several malt whiskies,
and a good wine list (champagne by the glass). There are seats in the garden.
*(Recommended by J H Kane, Brian Borwick, S H Godsell, Tracey and Stephen Groves, Maysie
Thompson, Walter Reid, Catherine Pocock, Jackie Hammond, John Bowdler, Mr and Mrs M F
Norton, D M and M C Watkinson, Howard and Margaret Buchanan, Keith and Janet Eaton, A
Sutton, Sandra Childress, Nick Lawless, David and Nina Pugsley)*

*Old English Inns ~ Manager Marnie Frith ~ Real ale ~ Bar food ~ Restaurant ~
(01993) 830465 ~ Children in restaurant ~ Open 11-3, 6-11; 12-3, 7-10.30 Sun ~
Bedrooms: £65B/£75B*

Shaven Crown 🛏

Elizabeth I is said to have used parts of this grand old place as a hunting lodge, and
earlier it was a hospice for the monastery of Bruern in the 14th c. There's a magnificent
double-collar braced hall roof, lofty beams and a sweeping double stairway down the
stone wall, and the beamed bar has a relief of the 1146 Battle of Evesham, as well as
seats forming little stalls around the tables and upholstered benches built into the walls.
Bar food includes sandwiches, soup (£2.95), warm mushrooms with stilton and walnut
sauce (£3.50), ploughman's (£4.75), vegetable and bean gratin (£5.75), poached
salmon with white wine sauce, venison sausages in red wine or liver and bacon (all
£6.95), lamb cutlets (£7.50), sirloin steak (£8.95), and puddings like syrup and ginger
sponge or dark chocolate and rum mousse (£2.90); children's helpings, and Sunday
lunch.Well kept Greene King Abbot, Hook Norton Best, and Youngs Special on
handpump, and several wines by the glass; shove-ha'penny, dominoes and cribbage.
There are old-fashioned seats set out on the stone cobbles and crazy paving, with a
view of the lily pool and roses; the pub has its own bowling green *(Recommended by
NMF, DF, LM, Sidney and Erna Wells, Marjorie and David Lamb, Gordon, Brian Borwick, Sue and
Steve Griffiths, D M and M C Watkinson, Simon Collett-Jones)*

*Free house ~ Licensees Robert and Jane Burpitt ~ Real ale ~ Bar food ~ Restaurant ~
(01993) 830330 ~ Children welcome ~ Open 12-2.30, 5-11; 12-2.30, 6-10.30 Sun ~
Bedrooms: £45(£55B)/£85B*

SOUTH STOKE SU5983 Map 2
Perch & Pike ♀

Off B4009 2 miles N of Goring

New licensees have taken over this little brick and flint pub and are hoping to add
three bedrooms and a restaurant. The relaxing bar has comfortable seats, open fires,
a nice assortment of tables, well kept Brakspears Bitter on handpump, and a good

wine list with quite a few by the glass served from the old oak bar counter. Good bar food now includes moules marinières (£4.50; main course £6.50), squid ink risotto with fried squids and lemon, served with aioli (£4.50; main course £8.75), coriander tiger prawn brochettes with honey and sesame bok choi (£5.50; main course £10.50), soft polenta with gorgonzola and mascarpone or wild boar sausages with mustard mash and onion gravy (£8.50), Thai green chicken curry with jasmine rice and charred limes (£8.75), naturally smoked haddock on wilted spinach (£10.50), French trimmed lamb cutlets with pea, baby broad bean and crushed potato salad with mint oil (£12.50), and chargrilled Scotch fillet steak with a herbed potato gallet, a selection of mushrooms, and red wine jus (£15.50). The window boxes are pretty, there are seats out on the large flower-bordered lawn, and more on a new Cotswold stone terrace. The Thames is just a field away. *(Recommended by JP, PP, T R and B C Jenkins, G S Dudley, TBB, Robert Turnham)*

Brakspears ~ Tenants Peter and Pat Gully ~ Real ale ~ Bar food ~ (01491) 872 415 ~ Children in eating area of bar ~ Open 12-2.30, 6-11; 12-3, 7-10.30 Sun; closed 25 Dec

STANTON ST JOHN SP5709 Map 4
Star

Pub signposted off B4027; village is signposted off A40 heading E of Oxford (heading W, you have to go to the Oxford ring-road roundabout and take unclassified road signposted to Stanton St John, Forest Hill etc); bear right at church in village centre

Well worth the effort it takes to get here, this is a friendly place with enjoyable food. It's been redecorated this year – but just smartened up rather than changed. There's an attractive extension on a level with the car park which has rugs on flagstones, pairs of bookshelves on each side of an attractive inglenook fireplace, old-fashioned dining chairs, an interesting mix of dark oak and elm tables, shelves of good pewter, terracotta-coloured walls with a portrait in oils, and a stuffed ermine; down a flight of stairs are little low-beamed rooms – one has ancient brick flooring tiles and the other quite close-set tables. Good bar food includes sandwiches (£2.20), filled baked potatoes (from £2.95), ploughman's (£3.95), steak and kidney pie (£6.75), spinach and mushroom strudel (£6.95), fresh salmon, Thai chicken curry or half shoulder of lamb with a rosemary and redcurrant sauce (£8.50), and puddings (£2.95). Well kept Wadworths IPA, Farmers Glory, 6X and Summersault, and a guest such as Badger Tanglefoot on handpump, and country wines. The family room is no smoking. The walled garden has seats among the rockeries, and children's play equipment. *(Recommended by TBB, David Lamb, Ted George, Mr and Mrs J Brown, Paul and Sarah Gayler, Martin Jones, R T and J C Moggridge, Robert Gomme)*

Wadworths ~ Manager Michael Urwin ~ Real ale ~ Bar food (not Sun evening) ~ (01865) 351277 ~ Children in restaurant and family room ~ Open 11-2.30, 6.30-11; 12-2.30, 7-10.30 Sun

Talk House ♀ 🍺
Wheatley Road (B4027 just outside village)

Most of the tables in this capacious series of linked areas are set for dining, but there's plenty of room for those wanting just a drink and a chat. The various rooms have lots of oak beams, flagstoned and tiled floors, stripped 17th-c stonework, simple but solid rustic furnishings, and attractive pictures and other individual and often light-hearted decorations. Good bar food (with prices unchanged since last year) includes sandwiches, home-made soup (£2.95), grilled goat's cheese toasts (£4.95), skewers of chicken satay and prawns (£5.95), pesto pasta (£6.95), ham and eggs (£7.95), chicken curry or steak and kidney pie (£8.95), Scotch salmon steak (£9.95), Scotch sirloin steak (£11.95), a half shoulder of lamb with rosemary and honey (£10.95), half a Gressingham duck with orange suace (£11.95), and puddings (£3.50). Well kept Morlands Original and Old Speckled Hen, Vale Notely Ale, and Wychwood Owzat on handpump, good house wines, and several malt whiskies. The sheltered courtyard has tables around an impressive fountain. *(Recommended by Ian Jones, Mark and Heather Williamson, P A Reynolds, Mike and Mary Carter, Prof Kenneth Surin, Maggie and Peter Shapland)*

Free house ~ Licensees Shane Ellis and Alan Heather ~ Real ale ~ Bar food ~ (01865) 351648 ~ Children welcome ~ Open 11-3, 5.30-11; 12-10.30 Sun ~ Bedrooms: £40B/£49.50B

STEEPLE ASTON SP4725 Map 4
Red Lion ♀
Off A4260 12 miles N of Oxford

It's a tricky thing to do, but Mr Mead manages to convey genuine warmth and friendliness to all his customers without being too much 'mine host'. This is a civilised little village pub with a steady stream of regulars dropping in for a drink, a chat, or just to read the newspapers. The comfortable partly panelled bar has beams, an antique settle and other good furnishings, and under the window a collection of interesting language and philosophy books that crossword fans find compelling. Enjoyable lunchtime bar food might include tasty stockpot soup (£2.60), sandwiches (from £2.75, the rare beef is good), excellent ploughman's with nicely ripe stilton (£4), home-made pâté, winter game hotpots and so forth (from £4.50), and summer salads (from £5.50; tasty crab); the evening no-smoking restaurant is more elaborate with a good three-course meal. Well kept (and reasonably priced) Hook Norton Best and guest beers on handpump, a choice of sixty or so malt whiskies, and a fine wine list of over 140 different bottles. The suntrap front terrace with its lovely flowers is a marvellous place to relax in summer. *(Recommended by Ian Phillips, E A and D C Frewer, D and J Tapper, Dave Braisted, Tim Barrow, Sue Demont, Michael Sargent, Simon Collett-Jones, Hugh Spottiswoode, Gordon, Rona Murdoch, John Bowdler, Eric Locker)*

Free house ~ Licensee Colin Mead ~ Real ale ~ Bar food (12-2; not evenings) ~ Restaurant ~ (01869) 340225 ~ Children in restaurant ~ Open 11-3, 6-11; 12-3, 7-10.30 Sun

TADPOLE BRIDGE SP3300 Map 4
Trout
Back road Bampton—Buckland, 4 miles NE of Faringdon

They are hoping to add six letting bedrooms and a restaurant to this busy Thames-side pub over the next year. The small L-shaped original bar with plenty of seats on the flagstones is dedicated only to enjoying the Archers Village and Fullers London Pride and a couple of guest beers on handpump; comprehensive little wine list, several malt whiskies, and darts, dominoes, and cribbage. Tasty bar food includes lunchtime snacks such as filled french bread (£3.50), ploughman's (£4.75), fish pie or spicy Moroccan meatballs in tomato sauce (£6.50), and steak and kidney pudding (£6.95), as well as home-made soup (£2.65), roasted English goat's cheese encasing a pickled walnut on deep-fried celery (£4.75), fresh poached Cornish scallops on pasta in an oriental sauce (£4.95; main course £9.75), mushroom roast (£7.75), salad of chargrilled venison and rabbit loin and baby spinach and fresh summer berries dressed with a sharp redcurrant vinaigrette (£9.85), thai-style red snapper with crispy coconut, carrot and ginger (£9.95), and chargrilled Scottish sirloin steak (£11.75); piped music. The garden (with Aunt Sally) is pretty in summer with small fruit trees, attractive hanging baskets, and flower troughs, and you can fish on a two-mile stretch of the river (the pub sells day tickets); moorings for boaters, too. *(Recommended by Joan Olivier, TBB, Anthony Barnes, Dr and Mrs Morley, Calum and Jane Maclean, Elizabeth and Alan Walker)*

Free house ~ Licensee Christopher J Green ~ Real ale ~ Bar food (not Sun evening except bank hol weekends) ~ (01367) 870382 ~ Children in eating area of bar and restaurant ~ Open 11.30-3, 6-11; 12-3, 7-10.30 Sun; closed Sun evening Nov-Easter

TOOT BALDON SP5600 Map 4
Crown
Village signed off A4074 at Nuneham Courtenay, and B480; past green

A super little pub with no pretensions, a warm, welcoming atmosphere, and good, honest, accomplished cooking. Unchanged from last year, there might be sandwiches and ploughman's, good home-made soup, pork chop with stilton sauce (£7.50), venison in wine sauce, chicken supreme with fresh herbs or halibut in cream and mustard sauce (all £8.50), nice mixed grill and chicken breast stuffed with garlic and mushrooms, puddings like super apple and blackberry pie, and Sunday roast lunch; they use home-grown herbs and other produce whenever possible. Best to book, especially at weekends. The simple beamed bar has a log fire, solid furnishings on the tiled floor, and a pleasant atmosphere. Well kept Mansfield Bitter, Ruddles County, and a guest beer on handpump; darts, shove-ha'penny, and dominoes. Aunt Sally, summer barbecues, and tables on the terrace. *(Recommended by Keith and Margaret Kettell, Glen and Nola Armstrong, Robert Turnham, Ian Jones, TBB, Peter Brueton)*

Free house ~ Licensees Liz and Neil Kennedy ~ Real ale ~ Bar food (not Sun or Mon evenings) ~ Restaurant ~ (01865) 343240 ~ Children in eating area of bar and restaurant ~ Open 11-3, 6.30-11; 12-3, 7-10.30 Sun

WATLINGTON SU6894 Map 4
Chequers
3 miles from M40, junction 6; Take B4009 towards Watlington, and on outskirts of village turn right into residential rd Love Lane which leads to pub

After the bustle of the main street, the notably pretty garden of this tucked away pub is quite refreshing, and there are picnic-sets under apple and pear trees, and sweet peas, roses, geraniums, begonias, and rabbits. The relaxed rambling bar has a low panelled oak settle and character chairs such as a big spiral-legged carving chair around a few good antique oak tables, a low oak beamed ceiling darkened to a deep ochre by the candles which they still use, and red and black shiny tiles in one corner with rugs and red carpeting elsewhere; steps on the right lead down to an area with more tables. A conservatory with very low hanging vines looks out over the garden. Popular bar food includes toasties (from £2.50), deep-fried camembert (£4.50), ploughman's (£4.90), filled baked potatoes, aubergine and lentil moussaka (£5.80), steak and kidney pie (£7.20), lasagne (£7.50), cajun chicken (£8.50), steaks (from £9.90), calf's liver and bacon (£10.50), half a duck with orange sauce (£12.80), and puddings like chocolate fudge cake or lemon tart (£3.50); good Sunday lunch. Well kept Brakspears Bitter, Special, and OBJ and seasonal ales on handpump, a decent little wine list, and friendly staff. The cheese shop in Watlington itself is recommended. No children inside. *(Recommended by P J Keen, Sidney and Erna Wells, Michael Sargent, Gordon)*

Brakspears ~ Tenants John and Anna Valentine ~ Real ale ~ Bar food (not Sun evening) ~ (01491) 612874 ~ Open 11.30-2.30, 6-11; 12-3, 7-10.30 Sun; closed 25 and 26 Dec

WESTCOTT BARTON SP4325 Map 4
Fox
Enstone Road; B4030 off A44 NW of Woodstock

The charming Italian licensees have now opened bedrooms in this lovely stone-built village pub, redecorated the restaurant, and added a stream and a pets corner to the very pleasant back garden – where there's also a wooden play fort for children and quite a few trees. They like to call themselves 'a pasta and ale house', and the good enjoyable bar food is a mix of Italian and English dishes: filled ciabatta bread or rolls (from £2.25), filled baked potatoes (£2.95), omelettes (£3.95), ploughman's (£4.75), steak in ale pie (£5.95), eleven pasta dishes (from £4.50; a favourite is with mussels, calamari, clams and king prawns £5.95), baked chicken with bacon, mixed herbs, and cheese sauce and served with garlic bread (£5.95), various fresh fish dishes (from

£6.95), steaks (from £7.95), puddings such as treacle sponge or tiramisu (from £2.25), Sunday roast (£5.95), and children's meals (£2.25). Hops hang from the low beams in the deceptively small and very relaxed bar, above snug little window seats, high-backed settles and pews around tables on flagstones, and the odd trap or horsebrass on the stone walls; open fires, juke box. A narrow corridor leads to a tucked-away back room with a faded tapestry and an old coach wheel, and an elegant restaurant. They have five well kept real ales on handpump: Hook Norton plus guests such as Brakspears Special, Cottage Goldrush, Fullers ESB, Mansfield Old Baily, and Theakstons XB; espresso and cappucinno. Watch your head as you go inside – the porch is very low. *(Recommended by David Campbell, Vicki McLean, K and M Kettell, George Atkinson, Tim Barrow, Sue Demont, Alan and Paula McCully)*

Free house ~ Licensee Vito Logozzi ~ Real ale ~ Bar food ~ Restaurant ~ Children welcome ~ Open 12-3, 5-11; 12-3, 7-10.30 Sun ~ Bedrooms: £25B/£40B

WOODSTOCK SP4416 Map 4
Feathers 🍴 🛏

Market St

This is, of course, a civilised Cotswold stone hotel with food and drinks prices to match. But the Garden Bar at the back is quietly relaxed and old-fashioned, with oils and watercolours on its walls, stuffed fish and birds (a marvellous live parrot, too), and a central open fire, and opens on to a splendid sunny courtyard with a small water feature, and attractive tables and chairs among geraniums and trees. Good, imaginative food from a short but thoughtful menu might include chicken liver parfait or risotto of spinach, smoked bacon and nutmeg (£5.75), collar of bacon with split peas and parsnips or smoked haddock with poached egg and hollandaise (£8.50), and puddings such as crème brûlée with ginger biscuits or chocolate and hazelnut pudding with chocolate sauce (£4.15); the restaurant is no smoking. Well kept (rather pricy) Wadworths 6X on handpump, a good choice of malt whiskies, summer home-made lemonade and pimms, and freshly squeezed orange juice; excellent service; piped music. Get there early for a table. *(Recommended by Adam and Elizabeth Duff, David and Anne Culley, M Borthwick, Steve Power, Alan and Paula McCully, R T and J C Moggridge)*

Free house ~ Licensees Messrs Godward, Malin and Leeman ~ Real ale ~ Bar food (not Sat or Sun evenings) ~ Restaurant ~ (01993) 812291 ~ Children welcome ~ Open 11-3, 6-11; 12-3, 7-10.30 Sun; closed to non-residents evening 25 Dec ~ Bedrooms: £95B/£105B

WOOTTON SP4419 Map 4
Kings Head 🍴

Chapel Hill; off B4027 N of Woodstock

There's no doubt that this pretty 17th-c Cotswold stone house is very much somewhere to come and enjoy the particularly good, imaginative food, but they do have Marstons Pedigree, Ruddles Best and Wadworths 6X well kept on handpump, and you can eat in either the bar, no-smoking restaurant or garden which creates a more relaxed, informal atmosphere. Best to book to be sure of a table. Carefully redecorated this year, the civilised and relaxing beamed no-smoking lounge bar has a nice mix of old oak settles and chairs around wooden tables, comfortable armchairs and chintzy sofas, an open log fire, and old prints and ceramics on the pale pink walls. At lunchtime, the good food might include home-made soup (£3.95), muscovado and lime cured Scottish salmon (£4.95), charred ceviche of plump scallops (£5.95), pork medallions with a crust of mascarpone cheese blended with fresh herbs and pink peppercorns with a red pimento coulis (£6.95), cantonese braised leg of duckling or wild mushroom risotto (£8.95), and collops of Scotch fillet steak (£9.95), with evening dishes such as szechuan seared breast of pigeon (£5.95), parfait of foie gras (£6.95), pink bream marinated in creamed coconut and miso paste and rolled in nori seaweed and steamed (£14.95), and roasted cutlets of English lamb with five peppers (£17.95); extra vegetables or salad leaves (£3.95).

Lovely puddings like delice of white chocolate, hand-made ice creams or caramelised citrus tart (£4.95). A good wine list with quite a few by the glass. *(Recommended by E A and D C Frewer, Tim Brierly, G V Holmes, J H Kane, Sir Nigel Foulkes, Audrey and Peter Dowsett, The Rev A D H and Mrs Duff, Dr C C S Wilson)*

Free house ~ Licensees Tony & Amanda Fay ~ Real ale ~ Bar food ~ Restaurant ~ (01993) 811340 ~ Children over 12 in restaurant but must be well behaved ~ Open 11-11; 12-3 Sun; may close Sun evening Nov-Mar ~ Bedrooms: £65B/£70B

WYTHAM SP4708 Map 4
White Hart
Village signposted from A34 ring road W of Oxford

New licensees were poised to take over here as we went to press, but we are hoping that little will change in this charmingly placed pub. The partly panelled, flagstoned bar has high-backed black settles built almost the whole way round the cream walls, a shelf of blue and white plates, and a winter log fire with a fine relief of a hart on the iron fireback; there's also another log fire, and a small no-smoking area. Well kept Adnams Best, Morlands Old Speckled Hen and a guest beer on handpump, and a fair choice of malt whiskies. Bar food has included cheese or pâté with bread (£2.50), filled baked potatoes (from £2.95), vegetable kiev (£7.25), fresh fish like plaice, trout or salmon, swordfish and tuna (from £8), steaks (from £9.45), daily specials such as beef in ale pie (£6.95) and grilled chicken breast (£8.45), and puddings; it does get busy on weekday lunchtimes. There are seats in the pretty garden. The pub's name is said to have come from a badge granted to the troops of Richard II after the Battle of Radcot Bridge in 1390. This is an unspoilt village with houses owned and preserved by Oxford University. *(Recommended by Gordon, Pat and Roger Fereday, TBB, Peter Hoare, Caroline Wright, Mike and Mary Carter, R T and J C Moggridge, Peter and Audrey Dowsett, Ian Jones, Alan Green, Tony and Wendy Hobden, Roger Byrne)*

Allied Domecq ~ Real ale ~ Bar food ~ (01865) 244372 ~ Children in eating area of bar ~ Open 11.30-2.30, 6-11; 12-3, 7-10.30 Sun

Lucky Dip
Besides the fully inspected pubs, you might like to try these Lucky Dips recommended to us and described by readers (if you do, please send us reports):

Abingdon [SU4997]
Old Anchor [St Helens Wharf]: Well kept Morlands in little front bar looking across Thames, flagstoned back bar with shoulder-height serving hatch, roomy lounge, panelled dining room overlooking neat almshouse gardens; warm fire, some comfortable leather armchairs, wide choice of decent food inc children's, friendly service, good wine choice; piped music may be loud; plenty of tables outside, summer barbecues *(Elizabeth and Alan Walker)*
Punchbowl [Market Pl]: Small low-ceilinged dimly lit oak-panelled lounge off side door (W St Helens St), Morlands Original and Ruddles County; also plain front bar *(Stephanie Smith, Gareth Price)*
Adderbury [SP4635]
☆ *Red Lion* [The Green]: Smartly civilised, with big inglenook, panelling, high stripped beams and stonework, cosy dining area on left, no-smoking back dining room, well kept Hook Norton Best, Marstons Pedigree and Theakstons Best, several wines by the glass, daily papers; piped music, food not cheap but good range; comfortable bedrooms, children in eating area,

tables out on well kept terrace; open all day summer *(D C T and E A Frewer, Dr T E Hothersall, Kevin Thorpe, John Bramley, George Atkinson, TRS, Mrs H Davis, LYM)*
Alvescot [SP2704]
Plough [B4020 Carterton—Clanfield]: Partly 17th-c beamed village pub with wide choice of good value food inc vegetarian and Sun lunch (must book), friendly licensees, well kept beers such as Adnams Broadside and Wadworths 6X and a seasonal beer, decent wines, good coffee, end dining area, old maps and plates, log fire (but cool and pleasant on hot days), quiet piped music, separate public bar; colourful flowers out in front *(Marjorie and David Lamb, G W A Pearce)*
Appleford [SU5293]
Carpenters Arms [B4016 Abingdon—Didcot]: Open-plan renovation with distinct areas for eating and drinking, nostalgic décor, well kept Morlands, traditional food from sandwiches up, no-smoking dining area *(Trevor Owen)*
Appleton [SP4401]
Thatched [Eaton Rd]: Attractive two-room Brakspears pub (actually tiled now), enjoyable food from sandwiches up, dining area with

woodburner, soft piped music, very friendly licensees – she`s Canadian; small garden *(Joan Olivier)*

Ardley [SP5427]
Fox & Hounds [B430 (old A43), just SW of M40 junction 10]: Old stone pub with small cosy lounge bar, snug beyond, and long opened-up dining area, low beams, lots of horsebrasses, pictures and old glassware, flowers on tables, open fires, well kept Banks's, Marstons Pedigree and Wadworths 6X, good Australian wines by the glass, food inc Sun roasts and old-fashioned puddings; keen and very friendly new young licensees; piped music, Sun evening singalong *(Marjorie and David Lamb, Val and Alan Green)*

Ashbury [SU2685]
Rose & Crown [B4507/B4000]: Big comfortable open-plan beamed bar, part of hotel, with highly polished woodwork, settees, pews and oak tables and chairs, traditional pictures, good choice of unpretentious sensibly priced food, well kept Arkells, friendly helpful staff, neat lavatories; bedrooms, nr Ridgeway *(Robert Tapsfield, Marjorie and David Lamb)*

Asthall [SP2811]
☆ *Maytime* [off A40 at W end of Witney bypass, then 1st left]: Genteel and comfortable dining pub with very wide choice of good value well served meals inc plenty for vegetarians, some bar snacks, slightly raised plush dining lounge neatly set with tables (best ones down by fire may be booked for overnight guests), airy conservatory restaurant (children allowed behind screen), Morrells and Wadworths 6X, decent wines, prompt service, interesting pictures, small locals' bar; piped music; in tiny hamlet, nice views of Asthall Manor and watermeadows from garden, big car park; quiet comfortable bedrooms around charming back courtyard, attractive walks *(BB, Paul McPherson, Brian Borwick, P and J Shapley)*

Bampton [SP3103]
Jubilee [Market Sq]: Friendly unassuming local in attractive village, civilised bar with well kept Wadworths beers, darts, cards, bar billiards; super little garden behind *(Pete Baker)*
Talbot [Market Sq]: Quaint, welcoming and comfortable, with low beams, good-sized log fire, well kept real ales such as Archers, Courage Best and Wadworths 6X, decent choice of food inc children's, attractive prices, small dining area; quiet piped music; clean old-fashioned bedrooms, lovely village *(Peter and Audrey Dowsett)*

Banbury [SP4540]
Wine Vaults [Parsons Lane]: Nicely altered, with bare boards, cushioned wall seats and unusual lamps in two snugs past small bar on right, small eating area beyond, another room on left leading to comfortable front lounge, good range of well kept beers, cheap wholesome food; walled garden *(Ted George)*

Begbroke [SP4613]
Royal Sun [A44 Oxford—Woodstock]: Busy much refurbished open-plan stripped-stone pub with emphasis on prompt good value food from baguettes to Sun roasts, inc vegetarian; Tetleys-related and guest ales such as Adnams, friendly

young staff, piped music and machines, tables on terrace and in small garden *(P and S White, LM)*

Benson [SU6191]
Crown: Doing well under current regime, good choice of reasonably priced food, good bar, thriving atmosphere; reasonably priced bedrooms *(Nick Holmes)*

Bicester [SP5822]
Penny Black [Sheep St]: Spacious and attractive Wetherspoons conversion of former 1920s main post office, comfortable screened-off sections and raised area, usual food such as slow-roasted lamb, four competitively priced ales, good cheap coffee, good choice of wines (not so cheap), books and newspapers *(George Atkinson, E A and D C T Frewer)*

Bix [SU7285]
Fox [A4130]: Brakspears have sold this unassuming little pub to Bass, who plan to extend it as a family dining pub; the tradition-minded long-serving former tenants can now be found at the Castle of Content at Medstead down in Hampshire *(BB)*

Bladon [SP4515]
White Horse [A4095]: Atmospheric and friendly, with good value traditional food; handy for back gate of Blenheim Park (beautiful walks), in village where Churchill is buried *(Tim Brierly)*

Bletchingdon [SP5017]
Blacks Head [Station Rd; B4027 N of Oxford]: Traditional village pub settling down under current tenant, locals' bar with darts, cards and dominoes, cosy stripped-stone lounge with woodburner, dining area and newish conservatory behind; good choice of home-cooked food from sandwiches to steaks inc Fri fish night, well kept Flowers IPA, Marstons Pedigree and Wadworths 6X; pleasant garden with aunt sally, long-standing Thurs folk nights *(Pete Baker)*

Bloxham [SP4235]
Red Lion [High St (A361)]: Friendly beamed dining pub with decent food, good service, Adnams and Wadworths 6X, good coffee, lots of flowers, dozens of whisky-water jugs, open fire *(George Atkinson, Hugh Spottiswoode)*

Boars Hill [SP4802]
Fox [between A34 and B4017]: Clean and attractive refurbished family-friendly pub in pretty countryside, rambling rooms on different levels, huge log fireplaces, poems on the wall, food inc vegetarian, well kept ales inc Greenalls, decent wine, polite service; maybe piped music; restaurant, pleasant raised verandah, big well designed sloping garden with play area *(E A and D C Frewer, Tim and Ann Newell, Dick Brown)*

Bodicote [SP4537]
Plough [Goose Lane/High St; off A4260 S of Banbury]: Quaint and dark 14th-c pub with well kept Archers Best, Theakstons XB and Old Peculier and guest beers, country wines, wide choice of well cooked straightforward food, good friendly service; old beams, pictures and brasses, dining area *(the Didler)*

Brightwell [SU5790]
Red Lion [signed off A4130 2 miles W of Wallingford]: Small friendly unspoilt local in

peaceful village, helpful staff, comfortable lounge, simple public bar with bar billiards in end games area, log fires, good menu, unobtrusive dining extension, four well kept guest beers from far and wide; dogs welcome, tables outside *(Dick Brown)*

Brightwell Baldwin [SU6595]

☆ *Lord Nelson* [off B480 Chalgrove—Watlington, or B4009 Benson—Watlington]: Civilised and friendly turkey-carpet pub with dining chairs around country-kitchen tables, most laid for the food (not cheap but worth it; may be a delay when busy), real ales such as Courage Best, Ruddles Best and Charles Wells Bombardier, decent house wines, no-smoking restaurant, simple décor with some maritime pictures; piped music, well behaved children allowed; front verandah, back terrace and attractive garden *(G S B G Dudley, TBB, M A and C R Starling, DHV, LYM)*

Britwell Salome [SU6793]

Goose [B4009 Watlington—Benson]: Former Red Lion, emphasis now on limited choice of good plainly cooked food in two small back dining rooms, worth the high prices; sandwiches served in the bar *(Rufus Isaacs)*

Bucknell [SP5525]

Trigger Pond [handy for M40 junction 10]: Neat stone-built pub opp the pond, newish owners working hard to please, good home cooking inc old-fashioned puddings, nice atmosphere, well kept changing ales such as Adnams, Badger Best and Tanglefoot and Hook Norton Best; piped music; pleasant terrace and garden *(D W Frostick, E A and D C Frewer)*

Burford [SP2512]

Angel [Witney St]: This former dining pub, in an attractive ancient building, has now closed *(LYM)*

☆ *Bull* [High St]: Well kept Wychwood ales and good choice of wines by the glass in proper chatty small front bar up a few steps, big comfortable beamed and panelled dining area with wide choice of food inc sandwiches and lunchtime buffet, three big log fires, attractive restaurant; piped music; children welcome, open all day, seats out in old coach entry; comfortable bedrooms *(Nick Lawless, LYM, Gordon, John and Esther Sprinkle)*

Cotswold Gateway [The Hill]: A hotel, but pleasant separate bar for non-residents – good welcoming service and atmosphere, good value food *(Bett and Brian Cox)*

Golden Pheasant [High St]: Warm atmosphere, well kept Scottish Courage beers such as Theakstons, interesting flavoured coffees, appealing food in main bar and side eating area; big woodburner one end; bedrooms *(David and Nina Pugsley)*

☆ *Royal Oak* [Witney St]: Neat and chatty 17th-c local tucked away from summer crowds, beams and stripped stone, great collection of beer tankards and steins, pine tables and chairs, well kept Wadworths beers, wide range of good simple food, bar billiards, friendly staff; tables out on terrace; sensibly priced bedrooms behind, off garden *(Ron and Barbara Watkins, Ted George, E J Cutting, George Atkinson, Quentin Williamson)*

Caulcott [SP5024]

Horse & Groom [Lower Heyford Rd (B4030)]: Part-thatched creeper-covered 16th-c cottage, cosy and homely L-shaped beamed bar and dining room, blazing coal fire in stone fireplace with unduly long bressummer beam, popular food from sandwiches up, friendly landlady, Brakspears, Morlands Old Speckled Hen and Charles Wells Bombardier, snug popular with families at w/e; front sun lounge, pretty garden with picnic-sets under cocktail parasols *(D C T and E A Frewer, Ian Phillips, Gordon)*

Chadlington [SP3222]

☆ *Tite* [Mill End; off A361 S of Chipping Norton, and B4437 W of Charlbury]: Comfortable rambling food-oriented local with well kept ales such as Archers and Wychwood, good house wines, friendly efficient service, log fire in huge fireplace, settles, wooden chairs, prints, rack of guidebooks; good if not cheap food inc lovely puddings, vine-covered restaurant evenings and Sun lunchtime, superb garden full of shrubs, some quite unusual, with stream running under pub – lovely views, pretty Cotswold village, good walks nearby; children welcome, cl Mon exc bank hols, car park right beyond garden *(George Atkinson, Peter and Audrey Dowsett, P and M Rudlin, Guy Vowles)*

Charlbury [SP3519]

☆ *Bull* [Sheep St]: Very good bistro-style atmosphere and surroundings, restaurant on left and freshly furnished dining bar on right with armchairs and magazines, good range of well presented good food in generous helpings, well kept Greene King IPA, good wines, jovial landlord – but not really a place for just a drink; cl Mon *(GL, BB, Giles Francis)*

Charney Bassett [SU3794]

Chequers: Popular 18th-c two-room village-green local run by very friendly family, wide choice of freshly made food, well kept ales such as Morlands, Ruddles Best and Wadworths 6X; some singalongs, pool, piped music; small garden, children welcome, cl Mon *(Pete Baker, Dick Brown)*

Chazey Heath [SU6977]

Pack Horse [Woodcote Rd (A4074 Wallingford—Reading)]: Well kept and attractive 17th-c pub with big log fire in simply furnished lounge bar, well kept Gales ales and country wines, good value food inc Thai dishes, sizeable back garden with play area and fairy-lit barbecue terrace, family room *(P Weedon, BB)*

Checkendon [SU6682]

Four Horseshoes [off A4074 Reading—Wallingford]: Attractive partly thatched local, friendly landlord happy to serve his well kept Brakspears and good pub food Sun lunchtime (unlike some other pubs in the area), music-free stripped-floor dining lounge (where children allowed), locals' bar with pool and piped music; big garden with picnic-sets, super hanging baskets *(JP, PP, Margaret Dyke, Mrs M Hobbs)*

Chipping Norton [SP3127]

Blue Boar [High St]: Spacious and cheery well worn-in stone-built pub divided by arches and pillars, wide choice of food from separate servery, Courage Directors, Marstons Pedigree, John Smiths and a guest such as Wychwood, good value coffee; juke box or piped music, fruit machines, TV, piano, separate beamed back restaurant, light and airy long flagstoned conservatory; open all day Sat *(Colin and Ann Hunt, Joan and Michel Hooper-Immins)*

Christmas Common [SU7193]

☆ *Fox & Hounds* [signed from B480/B481]: Basic no-frills cottage nr Chilterns viewpoint of Watlington Hill, Alberic Barbier rose around the door, cosy beamed bar with wall benches, bow-window seats, floor tiles and big inglenook log fire, locals' side bar, darts in third room (children allowed here), well kept Brakspears Bitter, Special and winter Old tapped from the cask in a back still room, friendly landlady, good home-made soup, wrapped sandwiches, tables outside *(JP, PP, Pete Baker, Gordon, Joan Olivier, the Didler, LYM)*

Church Enstone [SP3724]

☆ *Crown* [Mill Lane; from A44 take B4030 turn-off at Enstone]: Spotless pub with wide choice of food from filled baguettes up in cottagey bar, good sized restaurant and conservatory, log fire in brass-fitted stone fireplace, beams and stripped stone, real ales such as Hampshire King Alfred, Hook Norton Best and Wadworths 6X; new regime since our last edition, so we'd be glad of more reports on it; bedrooms *(Sir Nigel Foulkes, Dr W J M Gissane, Mr and Mrs Richard Osborne, NWN, LYM)*

Church Hanborough [SP4212]

☆ *Hand & Shears* [opp church; signed off A4095 at Long Hanborough, or off A40 at Eynsham roundabout]: Attractively done pub/restaurant, long gleaming bar, steps down into spacious back eating area, another small dining room, wide choice of good brasserie-style food from simple bar dishes to fish and grills inc good Thai curries, attentive Australian staff, Adnams Broadside, Fullers London Pride and Morlands Original, decent wines, open fires, good atmosphere, soft piped music *(Tim Barrow, Sue Demont, Mr and Mrs D Shier, Joan Olivier, BB, G P Stonhill)*

Clifton Hampden [SU5495]

☆ *Barley Mow* [towards Long Wittenham, S of A415]: Interesting and attractively refurbished thatched Chef & Brewer, very low ancient beams, oak-panelled family room, Scottish Courage ales, food inc good range of fish, log fire, piped music, restaurant, new kitchen; tables on pleasant terrace and in well tended waterside garden with doves and fancy fowls, short stroll from the Thames; bedrooms *(LYM, JP, PP, TBB, Susan and John Douglas)*

Cothill [SU4699]

Merry Miller: Large popular rather upmarket olde-worlde pub/restaurant contrived from 17th-c granary, stripped stone and flagstones, friendly efficient staff, wide choice of good food from expensive sandwiches up inc children's helpings, vegetarian and some interesting dishes, well kept Timothy Taylor and a beer brewed for the pub, good choice of wines; disabled access *(Mrs B Kingley, Alison James, Joan Olivier)*

Crawley [SP3412]

☆ *Lamb*: 17th-c stonebuilt village pub on several

levels with unspoilt old beamed bar, log fire in big fireplace, good food immaculately served inc tasty soup and puddings, welcoming young licensees, well kept Adnams Broadside and Hook Norton Best, decent wines, small family area, restaurant, piped Irish music; views from tables on terraced lawn *(Graham and Belinda Stapleburst)*

Plough: Very popular under new licensees (same as Bat & Ball, Cuddesdon – see main entries) for good value food, friendly quick service, good wine, well kept Marstons Pedigree, typical Cotswold interior with open fires and cricket theme throughout; quiet piped music, pretty village *(Peter and Audrey Dowsett)*

Cropredy [SP4646]

☆ *Red Lion* [off A423 N of Banbury]: Old thatched stone pub charmingly placed opp churchyard, low beams, inglenook log fire, high-backed settles, brass, plates and pictures; generous good value home-made food from baguettes up (two rooms set for eating, children allowed in restaurant part), well kept Scottish Courage ales, pub games; piped music, small back garden *(G B Lungden, Ted George, Colin and Ann Hunt, NMF, DF, LYM)*

Crowell [SU7499]

Shepherds Crook [B4009, 2 miles from M40 junction 6]: Traditional pub tastefully refurbished with stripped brick, timber and flagstones, good value filling home-made food inc good fresh fish, carpeted raftered dining area, well kept beers inc Bathams, Batemans, Hook Norton and a guest ale, decent wines, friendly landlord, no music; views from tables out on green *(Torrens Lyster)*

Cumnor [SP4603]

☆ *Vine* [Abingdon Rd]: Busy and restauranty modernised pub with remarkably wide choice of enjoyable fresh food from baguettes up, extended back dining area, no-smoking area in conservatory, quick polite service, three well kept guest ales, good range of malt whiskies and wines, picnic-sets in attractive back garden *(Dick Brown)*

Curbridge [SP3308]

Lord Kitchener [Bampton Rd (A4095)]: Well organised new licensees settling in well, good value food, old local photographs, big log fire, end dining area, well kept real ales, friendly efficient service; garden with play area *(Marjorie and David Lamb)*

Deddington [SP4631]

☆ *Deddington Arms* [off A4260 (B4031) Banbury—Oxford]: Welcoming 16th-c hotel with pubby unfussy bar, black beams and timbers, mullioned windows, attractive settles, leather armchairs by fine log fire, nooks and crannies, small end games area, TV sports; good imaginative food, well kept ales inc Wadworths 6X, good choice of wines by the glass, prompt service; open all day, children in eating area, busy spacious restaurant, comfortable chalet bedrooms around courtyard, attractive village with lots of antique shops *(Hugh Spottiswoode, Ted George, W M and J M Cottrell, Mrs K I Burvill, Dr and Mrs J R C Wallace, Dr P Wallace, Prof R M Shackleton, LYM, Alan and

Paula McCully, Lesley Bass)
Unicorn [Market Pl]: Friendly 17th-c inn with inglenook bar, usual food inc inexpensive set lunch in oak-beamed restaurant, pleasant service – quick without making you feel rushed; family room with separate games area, terrace, attractive walled back garden; bedrooms *(George Atkinson, Dr P Wallace, Prof R M Shackleton)*

Denchworth [SU3791]
☆ *Fox* [off A338 or A417 N of Wantage]: Picturesque old thatched pub with two good log fires in low-ceilinged comfortable connecting areas, friendly prompt service, good ample food from sandwiches up, Morlands ales, good house wines and coffee, reasonable prices, carvery in small beamed restaurant; nostalgic piped music; pleasant sheltered garden, peaceful village *(Marjorie and David Lamb)*

Dorchester [SU5794]
Plough: Small friendly one-man pub, particularly good English home cooking by the landlord, good atmosphere, pub games inc aunt sally, pictures and prints for sale, well kept Morlands; piped Radio 2 *(Bruce Pennell)*

Ducklington [SP3507]
☆ *Bell* [Standlake Rd; off A415, a mile SE of Witney]: Thatched pub by village pond, scrubbed tables, woodburner (and glass-covered well), old local photographs, farm tools, stripped stonework and flagstones in big bar, hatch-served public bar, very well laid out restaurant (its beams festooned with hundreds of bells – these dominate the pub's décor); well kept Morlands and Ruddles, good house wines, wide choice of reasonably priced fresh food all home-made, friendly service, cards and dominoes, no piped music, folk night 1st Sun of month; garden behind with side play area; bedrooms *(Peter and Audrey Dowsett, Pete Baker)*
Strickland Arms [off A415 SE of Witney]: Welcoming and cosy, smart bar (half for dining), limited choice of well prepared and presented good value food inc vegetarian and fish, well kept Adnams and Wadworths, decent wine; small no-smoking restaurant; small garden *(Martin Walsh)*

Duns Tew [SP4528]
☆ *White Horse* [off A4260 N of Kidlington]: 16th-c beamed pub in pretty village, seems back on form after a blip in 1998; roomy bar and pretty dining extension, stripped bricks and stonework, rugs on flagstones, oak timbers and panelling, enormous inglenook, settles and homely stripped tables, daily papers, smaller quieter room, well kept beers inc Hook Norton Best and Wadworths 6X, decent food, friendly young staff; disabled access, bedrooms in former stables *(Martin Jones, LYM, Adam and Elizabeth Duff, Charles and Pauline Stride, Phyl and Jack Street, John Bowdler, John Bramley, Gordon, Brian Smart, J V Dadswell, Martin and Patricia Forest, Alan and Paula McCully)*

East Hagbourne [SU5288]
Fleur de Lys: Clean and tidy black and white timbered building, half drinking place (well kept Morlands) and half pubby dining room – quite

a bit of emphasis on the unusual good value food; good service, tables out behind *(Karen Hogarth)*

East Hendred [SU4588]
☆ *Plough* [Orchard Lane]: Good range of enjoyable food in family-run beamed village pub's attractive and airy main bar, Morlands ales with a guest such as Charles Wells Bombardier, attentive friendly service, farm tools; booking advised for Sun lunch, walking groups welcome with prior notice, occasional folk nights, pleasant garden with good play area; attractive village *(D C T and E A Frewer, Dick Brown, BB)*

Ewelme [SU6491]
Shepherds Hut [off B4009 about 5 miles SW of M40 junction 6]: Simple extended local, good value freshly made food (worth booking w/e), quick cheerful service, well kept Morlands Bitter and Old Masters, decent coffee, pot plants, darts, small restaurant; piped pop music, fruit machine; children welcome, tables and swing in small pleasant side garden *(Nick Holmes, Marjorie and David Lamb)*

Faringdon [SU2895]
Bell [Market Pl]: Relaxing well worn in bar with red leather settles, inglenook fireplace with 17th-c carved oak chimneypiece, interesting faded mural in inner bar, well kept Wadworths 6X, good value food inc vegetarian, restaurant; piped music; children and dogs allowed, tables out among flowers in attractive cobbled back coachyard; bedrooms *(Stephen Newell, Tim and Ann Newell, LYM, D Irving, R Huggins, E McCall, T McLean, Gordon)*
Crown [Market Pl]: Civilised old inn, flagstones, beams, panelling, leaded lights, huge woodburner, two bars and tiny comfortable hidden-away snugs, popular reasonably priced well presented food, friendly current management, well kept ales; children welcome, piped music; good big quiet bedrooms overlooking lovely cobbled summer courtyard *(LYM, D Irving, R Huggins, E McCall, T McLean, Peter and Audrey Dowsett, Gordon)*

Filkins [SP2304]
Five Alls [signed off A361 Lechlade—Burford]: Cotswold stone pub nicely refurbished and furnished by new licensees, imaginative choice of good food in bar and restaurant inc lots of specials, well chosen house wines, real ales, good coffee; reasonably priced well equipped bedrooms *(Brian and Pat Wardrobe)*
Lamb [A361 Burford—Lechlade]: Generous food all home-cooked (limited Sun), well kept Morlands and John Smiths, decent house wines in two-bar stonebuilt local, part Elizabethan, warm, friendly and comfortable; no piped music, good big garden, peaceful village (when the RAF aren't flying), pleasant bedrooms; cl Mon *(TBB)*

Finmere [SP6432]
Kings Head: Landlord's good value home cooking inc cured hams in plain 18th-c two-bar pub, well kept Morrells, good choice of wines by the glass, no music *(E A and D C T Frewer)*

Gallowstree Common [SU7081]
☆ *Greyhound* [Gallowstree Common Rd, Shiplake

Bottom; off B481 at N end of Sonning Common]: Low-beamed 17th-c pub in lovely setting nr green, big fireplace in spotless attractive bar with walking stick collection, dog prints, horsebrasses, wide choice of good home-made food from baguettes and sandwiches to sizzlers (tables may be reserved), Bass and Morlands Old Speckled Hen, pine-furnished barn restaurant; tables out in front and at side, charming garden with terrace, arbour and boules *(TRS, Susan and John Douglas, Maysie Thompson, M L Porter)*

Garsington [SP5702]

☆ *Three Horseshoes* [The Green]: Spotless lounge and restaurant area, prompt cheerful service by welcoming French licensees, well kept Morrells ales, wide range of good food from delicious omelettes to bass and steak, separate public bar; lovely views *(TBB, P J Keen)*

Godstow [SP4809]

☆ *Trout* [off A34 Oxford bypass northbound, via Wytham, or A40/A44 roundabout via Wolvercote]: Creeper-covered medieval pub, much extended and commercialised as big tourist draw – can sometimes get swamped by visitors, nicely done, with fires in three huge hearths, beams and shiny ancient flagstones, furnishings to suit, attractive pictures, roomy extended dining area, back extension with *Inspector Morse* memorabilia and children's area; decent food all day inc good big pies, Bass and Worthington, good New World wines, winter mulled wine, charming in summer with lovely flagstoned terrace by a stream full of greedily plump perch, peacocks in the grounds *(JWGW, LYM, P and J Shapley, Lawrence Bacon, Jean Scott, Gordon, TBB, D C T and E A Frewer)*

Goring [SU6080]

Catherine Wheel [Station Rd]: Good value food, well kept Brakspears, good informal atmosphere, very friendly staff, two cosy bars, good log fire; notable door to gents` *(TRS, Christine and Geoff Butler)*

☆ *John Barleycorn* [Manor Rd]: Endearing and well run low-beamed cottage local in pretty Thames village, prints in cosy little lounge bar, good choice of well priced home-made food in adjoining eating area, well kept Brakspears, pool in end room, friendly helpful service; bedrooms clean and simple *(Paul Weedon, JP, PP, the Didler)*

Goring Heath [SU6678]

☆ *King Charles Head* [off A4074 NW of Reading – OS Sheet 175 map ref 664788]: Charming small-roomed rambling country pub with lovely big garden and idyllic woodland setting, good walks nearby, good value generous home-made food, well kept beers, log fire, relaxed atmosphere, friendly staff, big restaurant; furnishings and decor more modern than you'd expect from cottagey appearance *(Tina and Andy Stanford, LYM)*

Great Milton [SP6202]

Kings Head [Lower End; a mile from M40 junction 7]: Picturesque village pub, clean and neat, with wide food choice, reasonable prices, separate small dining room, well kept beers *(David Gregory)*

Great Tew [SP3929]

☆ *Falkland Arms* [off B4022 about 5 miles E of Chipping Norton]: Idyllic setting of untouched golden-stone thatched cottages; high-backed settles, stripped tables, flagstones and bare boards, shuttered stone-mullioned latticed windows, fine inglenook fireplace, panelling, nice old-fashioned touches, well kept Wadworths ales with guests such as Adnams Broadside or Theakstons Old Peculier (not cheap), farm cider, lots of malt whiskies and country wines, no-smoking dining room, tables outside; small bedrooms, open all day w/e and summer weekdays *(E A and D C Frewer, Colin and Ann Hunt, Eamonn and Natasha Skyrme, JP, PP, Jenny and Michael Back, Kerry Law, Kevin Blake, Elizabeth and Alan Walker, Graham and Karen Oddey, Peter and Giff Bennett, M and C Starling, the Didler)*

Hailey [SP3414]

Bird in Hand [Whiteoak Green; B4022 Witney—Charlbury]: Greatly extended old Cotswold pub, smart rather than pubby, popular for wide range of reasonably priced food inc good fish in lounge or attractive restaurant, quick friendly service, well kept Boddingtons, Courage Directors and Marstons Pedigree, lots of wood, well chosen pictures and subdued lighting (inc candles on tables), nice views, unobtrusive piped music; comfortable cottage-style bedrooms, huge car park *(Peter and Audrey Dowsett, Gordon, Mike and Mary Carter)*

Hailey [entirely different village from previous entry – SU6485]

☆ *King William IV* [leave Wallingford on A4130, turn left to Hailey 2 miles on]: Attractive and relaxing 16th-c pub in charming peaceful countryside, friendly newish tenants settling in well, beams, bare bricks and tiled floor, big log fire, well kept traditional furnishings and fittings, full Brakspears range, wide choice of good generous food (not cheap) inc vegetarian in extended dining room, nice views from front terrace *(M L Porter, Sheila Keene, A H N Reade, D Griffiths, LYM)*

Lamb & Flag [B4022 a mile N of Witney]: Friendly little pub, good range of reliable low-priced food prepared to order (so can be a wait if busy), attentive service, well kept Morlands Original and Old Speckled Hen *(Marjorie and David Lamb)*

Hampton Poyle [SP5015]

Gone Fish Inn [Oxford Rd]: Emphasis on simply cooked good fresh fish in pretty and spotless 18th-c cottage with small bar and beamed dining extension with attractively set old oak tables, Adnams, Arkells and another ale tapped from the cask, good choice of French wines by the glass, settee and big log fire, welcoming and obliging licensees, no piped music, bar billiards *(E A and D C T Frewer, Steve and Sarah de Mellow)*

Hanwell [SP4343]

Moon & Sixpence: Rather more restaurant than pub, comfortable bar and dining area, friendly efficient service, wide food choice; popular with business people; small terrace, pretty location *(A Goodman, J H Kane, Mr and Mrs Goodman)*

Henley [SU7882]

Anchor [Friday St]: Cosy and relaxing informally run Brakspears local not far from Thames, homely country furniture and bric-a-brac in softly lit parlourish beamed front bar, huge helpings of reasonably priced food, well kept beers, friendly and obliging landlady; darts, bar billiards, piano and TV in room on right, back dining room; charming back terrace surrounded by lush vegetation and hanging vines *(Gerald Barnett, the Didler)*

Old Bell [Bell St]: Well kept Brakspears PA, Old and Mild in homely and attractive heavily beamed front bar with wall-length window filled with pot plants, back dining room *(the Didler)*

Three Tuns [Market Pl]: Heavy beams and panelling, two rooms opened together around old-fashioned central servery with well kept Brakspears, straightforward generous home-cooked food all day, floodlit back terrace and separate games bar with juke box and fruit machine; no children *(JP, PP, LYM, the Didler)*

Highmoor [SU6984]

☆ *Dog & Duck* [B481 N of Reading, off A4130 Henley—Oxford]: Cosy and cottagey low-beamed country pub with chintzy curtains, floral cushions, lots of pictures; relaxing bar on left, dining room on right, log fire in each, smaller dining room behind, fine choice of good generous food inc good vegetarian dishes, hard-working young licensees, well kept Brakspears PA, SB and Old; tables in garden *(D W Chesterman, John Roots, the Didler)*

Kidmore End [SU6979]

☆ *New Inn* [Chalkhouse Green Rd; signed from B481 in Sonning Common]: Attractive and immaculate black and white pub by church, polished hallway with fruit and flowers, beams, big fires, smart comfortable feel, pleasant restaurant with good sophisticated food, nicely presented (may be fully booked Sun), lighter bar meals, well kept Brakspears PA, SB and Old, good range of wines; public bar; tables in attractive large sheltered garden with pond *(Richard Douglas, Canon and Mrs J Y Crowe, Roy and Judy Tudor Hughes, Isabel and Robert Hatcher)*

Kirtlington [SP4919]

Oxford Arms [Troy Lane]: Old-fashioned oak-beamed village pub with pews and woodburner in relaxed lounge popular with families, good interesting freshly made food, real ales inc changing guest, good value French house wines, friendly landlord, daily papers, wide mix of customers; separate dining area, games room with pool, small sunny back garden with barbecues *(David Campbell, Vicki McLean, D C T and E A Frewer, Sue and Jim Sargeant)*

Langford [SP2402]

☆ *Bell*: Friendly restaurant/pub with two rooms off tiny bar, pleasantly low-key simple but smart décor, big log fire, books and magazines, fresh flowers, evening candles, sensibly short choice of enjoyable food inc some stylish dishes and good veg, Hook Norton and Marstons Pedigree, good wines, proper coffee; no piped music *(Peter and Audrey Dowsett, Mrs L Ferstendik, P R and S A White, Sandra Childress)*

Letcombe Regis [SU3784]

Greyhound: Genuine welcoming two-bar village local doing well under new management, all sorts of community event, good range of food inc steaks and huge mixed grill, Morlands inc Old Speckled Hen; handy for Ridgeway walks *(Dick and Madeleine Brown)*

Littleworth [SU3197]

Fox & Hounds [A420 NE of Faringdon]: Straightforward pub with good value simple food, well kept Hook Norton and Morlands, friendly service, big log fire, small no-smoking restaurant; public bar with pool room and piped music; garden with play area and apple trees, small caravan site *(Peter and Audrey Dowsett)*

Long Wittenham [SU5493]

Vine: Cosy and friendly beamed village local with comfortable two-level bar, plenty of pictures and bric-a-brac, wide choice of food cooked to order, well kept Morlands *(Marjorie and David Lamb)*

Lower Assendon [SU7484]

Golden Ball [B480]: Attractive 16th-c beamed pub with good food and atmosphere, log fire, well kept Brakspears, decent house wines; garden behind *(TBB)*

Middle Assendon [SU7385]

Rainbow [B480]: Pretty and cottagey Brakspears local, unspoilt friendly low-beamed bar split into two areas, well kept beers, short choice of unpretentious but tasty food, tables on front lawn *(C J Bromage, Gordon, John Roots)*

Middleton Stoney [SP5323]

☆ *Jersey Arms* [B430/B4030]: Small 19th-c stonebuilt hotel, low and rambling, with cosily upmarket traditional bar, friendly efficient service, beams and panelling, dark tables and chairs, good log fire in big fireplace, good range of interesting home-made food from well filled baguettes up, well kept Tetleys, Theakstons and Wadworths 6X, good wine list and coffee; piped music; restaurant popular for business lunches; garden; bedrooms comfortable *(G Braithwaite, Mrs J K Edwards, E A and D C Frewer)*

Milton [SP4535]

Black Boy [off Bloxham Rd; the one nr Adderbury]: Old-world oak-beamed bar in former coaching inn, inglenook, woodburner, flagstones and bare boards, stripped stonework, plenty of brasses; well kept Bass and Worthington, food using local produce with creole and other exotic dishes, candlelit restaurant very popular Thurs-Sat nights; piped music *(TRS)*

Minster Lovell [SP3111]

Old Swan [just N of B4047 Witney—Burford]: Old inn, interesting and atmospheric despite being rather geared to well heeled visitors and conference people, popular lunchtime for good if not cheap snacks and light meals (no sandwiches, asked to pay in advance, no puddings served in bar), Marstons ales, log fire, deep armchairs, rugs on flagstones, restaurant, tables in lovely garden; bedrooms *(Mike and Heather Thomas, LYM, Paul S McPherson)*

White Hart [B4047 Witney—Burford]: Welcoming 17th-c former coaching inn, big pleasant lounge, well kept changing ales, wide choice of reasonably priced bar food from sandwiches up, good log fire, big separate restaurant; quiet piped music; open all day *(Peter and Audrey Dowsett)*

Moreton [SP6904]

☆ *Royal Oak* [off A329 SW of Thame]: Small bar with French landlord doing excellent food, several well kept ales inc Hook Norton, low beams, old candlelit pine tables on stripped boards, some stripped brickwork, open fire, small pink dining room, good wine list; country views from big terrace *(Neil Dury)*

Nettlebed [SU6986]

Sun [Watlington Rd]: Friendly landlord, good atmosphere, enjoyable food, well kept Brakspears, interesting small bar with lots of jugs hanging from old beams, dining room; sheltered attractive garden with climbing frame, swing and barbecue *(Mr and Mrs D Lewis, Paul McPherson)*

☆ *White Hart* [High St (A4130)]: Civilised rambling two-level beamed bar, handsome old-fashioned furnishings inc fine grandfather clock, discreet atmosphere, good log fires, well kept Brakspears, spacious restaurant; children welcome, bedrooms *(LYM, Tim and Ann Newell)*

North Moreton [SU5589]

Boar [off A4130 Didcot—Wallingford]: Enjoyable food, Hook Norton, John Smiths and Theakstons ales, old snuggery one end, conservatory the other *(R C Watkins)*

North Newington [SP4139]

☆ *Roebuck* [off B4035 (or A422 via Wroxton) just W of Banbury]: Attractive and welcoming bistro-style dining bar, very wide range of good value interesting food all freshly made here, crisp fresh veg, well kept Morlands, good wines and country wines, attentive service, open fires, individual furnishings, piped classical music; open fire in traditional public bar, children very welcome, good garden with play area; quiet village nr Broughton Castle *(Michael and Jeanne Shillington, John Bowdler)*

Northmoor [SP4202]

Red Lion [B4449 SE of Stanton Harcourt]: Refurbished 15th-c stonebuilt village pub, heavily beamed bar and small dining room off, welcoming log fire, good choice of very reasonably priced food inc good value Sun lunch, well kept Morlands Original, garden; no dogs *(Marjorie and David Lamb, Miss M Oakeley)*

Oxford [SP5106]

☆ *Bear* [Alfred St/Wheatsheaf Alley]: Friendly little low-ceilinged and partly panelled rooms, not over-smart and often packed with students; thousands of vintage ties on walls and ceiling, simple food most days inc sandwiches (kitchen may be closed Weds), well kept Badger Tanglefoot, Ind Coope Burton, Tetleys and Wadworths 6X from centenarian handpumps on rare pewter bar counter, no games machines, tables outside; open all day summer *(R Huggins, D Irving, E McCall, T McLean, TBB, Gordon, Margaret and Bill Rogers, LYM, SLC)*

Eagle & Child [St Giles]: Busy rather touristy pub (tiny mid-bars full of actors' and Tolkien/

C S Lewis memorabilia), but students too; nice panelled front snugs, tasteful stripped-brick modern back extension with no-smoking conservatory, well kept Greene King Abbot, Marstons Pedigree, Morlands Old Speckled Hen and Tetleys, plentiful quickly served food, newspapers, events posters; piped music *(Eric Locker, Christopher Glasson, BB, SLC)*

Folly Bridge [Abingdon Rd]: Friendly open-plan Wadworths pub with five real ales (more 1st Thurs in month), jolly atmosphere, straightforward food; landlord can suggest nearby B&Bs; children welcome if eating, short walk from Thames *(SLC)*

Kings [Banbury Rd, Summertown]: Bright, light and airy bar popular with young people, plenty of exposed wood and cosy corners, good generous food esp hot and cold salads, speedy well drilled service, well kept real ales such as Adnams, tables outside *(David Campbell, Vicki McLean)*

Lamb & Flag [St Giles/Banbury Rd]: Reopened early 1999, with big windows over street, well kept Scottish Courage ales, good value well served food; can be packed with students, piped pop music may be loud, back rooms with exposed stonework and panelled ceilings have more atmosphere *(TBB)*

Radcliffe Arms [Cranham St, Jericho]: Good value generous food inc lots of pizzas; popular with younger crowd *(J Potter)*

Seacourt Bridge [West Way (B4044 just off ring rd)]: Recently refurbished, lively and friendly with well kept ales *(Dr and Mrs A K Clarke)*

Three Goats Heads [Friars Entry, St Michael St]: Two friendly, individual and attractive bars, relaxed downstairs (with bare boards, TV, fruit machine and piped music – can be loud), more formal up; well kept cheap Sam Smiths, good choice of quick generous food, dark wood, booths and political prints *(SLC, Kevin Blake, TBB)*

Wheatsheaf [High St]: Extending some way down alley off High St, comfortable, friendly and relaxed, with several well kept ales inc Marstons Pedigree and a guest beer tapped from the cask, simple reasonably priced food, bare boards, plain wooden seats (if you can get one); back dining room *(Gordon, R Huggins, D Irving, E McCall, T McLean)*

White Horse [Botley Rd]: Good well presented food, well kept Greene King Abbot, Tetleys and Wadworths 6X, good friendly service *(P J Kimber)*

☆ *White Horse* [Broad St]: Bustling and studenty, sandwiched between bits of Blackwells bookshop; single small narrow bar with snug one-table raised back alcove, mellow oak beams and timbers, ochre ceiling, beautiful view of the Clarendon building and Sheldonian, good lunchtime food (the few tables reserved for this), well kept Tetleys-related ales and Wadworths 6X, Addlestone's cider, friendly licensees *(TBB, Giles Francis)*

Pishill [SU7389]

☆ *Crown* [B480 Nettlebed—Watlington]: Lovely wisteria-covered ancient building with black beams and timbers, log fires and candlelight, relaxed atmosphere, tasty home-cooked food (not Sun or Mon evenings) from sandwiches to steaks, separate restaurant, well kept Brakspears, Flowers Original and a guest beer, friendly service, picnic-sets on attractive side lawn, pretty country setting – lots of walks; bedroom in separate cottage; children allowed Sun lunchtime in restaurant *(JP, PP, Mark Percy, Lesley Mayoh, M L Porter, Lesley Bass, Susan and John Douglas, M Borthwick, LYM, the Didler)*

Rotherfield Peppard [SU7181]

Dog [Peppard Common]: Low-beamed 17th-c pub nr green, big fireplace, horsebrasses, dog prints, Bass and Morlands Old Speckled Hen, very quickly served food from sandwiches, baguettes and generous filled baked potatoes through pies and pasta to Thai specials and sizzlers, pleasant staff, golden retriever called Oliver, small restaurant, tables out in front and in side garden; maybe piped music *(TBB, John Roots, Mark Percy, Lesley Mayoh)*

Salford Hill [SP2628]

Cross Hands [junction A44/A436]: Pleasant stonebuilt beamed country pub open all day Sat and summer Fri, with usual food inc nice sandwiches and good value ploughman's, Bass, Hook Norton Best, Wadworths 6X and Worthington; games room, camping area behind *(John and Elspeth Howell, LYM)*

Shilton [SP2608]

☆ *Rose & Crown* [off B4020 S of Burford]: Mellow and attractive 17th-c low-beamed stonebuilt village local opp pond in pretty village, small beamed bar with tiled floor, woodburner and inglenook, small carpeted dining area, reasonably priced home-made food from sandwiches and toasties up (should book for Sun roasts), well kept Morlands Old Speckled Hen, Ruddles Best and County, friendly staff; soft piped music, darts *(George Atkinson, Marjorie and David Lamb, G W A Pearce, Joan Olivier)*

Shiplake Row [SU7578]

White Hart [off A4155 W of Shiplake]: Relaxed and friendly, with good choice of good food inc Sun roast, well kept Brakspears, decent house wines, log fires; interestingly planted garden, nice location, fine views, good walks *(B A Haywood, A J Bowen)*

Shrivenham [SU2488]

Prince of Wales [High St; off A420 or B4000 NE of Swindon]: Ancient stone pub with spotless low-beamed carpeted lounge, pictures, lots of brasses, log fire, wholesome plain food, small dining area, cheerful thoughtful landlord, Wadworths ales, big L-shaped public bar with fruit machine, no piped music or dogs; garden *(CMW, JJW, Gwen and Peter Andrews)*

Victoria [B4000 S]: Recently tastefully refurbished, with new landlord, Arkells 2B and 3B, large open fire, wide choice of good value food, no piped music, charming no-smoking conservatory restaurant, picnic-sets in garden with play area *(Peter and Audrey Dowsett)*

Sibford Gower [SP3537]

Bishop Blaize [Burdrop]: Friendly small pub, very old and nicely kept, with good value food inc lots of home-made pies, well kept Hook

Norton, efficient service; play area in big garden, good views *(Simon Pyle)*

☆ *Wykham Arms* [signed off B4035 Banbury—Shipston on Stour]: Pretty thatched cottage with comfortable open-plan low-beamed stripped-stone lounge, nice pictures, table made from glass-topped well, inglenook tap room, good service, well kept Banks's, Hook Norton and a guest ale, good coffee, decent wines, dominoes, wide food choice from sandwiches up, attractive partly no-smoking restaurant; children welcome; country views from big well planted garden, lovely manor house opp; cl Mon lunchtime *(Tim Brierly, Tim and Linda Collins, Dave Braisted, Ted George, LYM)*

South Leigh [SP3908]

Mason Arms [3 miles S of A40 Witney—Eynsham]: Very restauranty upmarket dining pub, by no means cheap, but good food, two big log fires, pictures on dusky red walls, candlelight and flagstones, sturdy antique furnishings, nice table linen in the main dining room; no children in bar, no no-smoking area, tables outside, cl Mon *(RJH, Terry Morgan, LYM)*

Sparsholt [SU3487]

Star: Good choice of good if not cheap freshly made food worth waiting for in comfortable and relaxed old local, Morlands Original, Worthington BB and a guest beer, good atmosphere with horse-racing talk, log fire, attractive pictures, daily papers, subdued piped music, back garden; pretty village *(Marjorie and David Lamb)*

Standlake [SP3902]

Bell [High St]: Quiet Morlands pub with good original if not cheap food (no bar lunches Sun/Mon), well kept beers inc a guest, good value wine, plush back restaurant (evening, also Sun lunch) *(Judith Madley)*

Steventon [SU4691]

☆ *Cherry Tree* [B4017 S of Abingdon]: Good value generous well priced food inc sophisticated dishes and good vegetarian choice in spacious and relaxing interconnecting rooms, dark green walls, two or three old settles among more modern furnishings, interesting bric-a-brac; full Wadworths range kept well with guest beers too, decent wines, friendly and courteous licensees and staff, log-effect gas fires; unobtrusive piped music in public bar, tables on newly extended terrace *(Dick Brown, Stephanie Smith, Gareth Price)*

☆ *North Star* [The Causeway, central westward turn off main rd; village signed off A34]: Tiled passage leading to unchanging unspoilt main bar with built-in settles forming snug, steam-engine pictures, interesting local horse brasses and other brassware; open fire in parlourish lounge, simple dining room; Morlands Mild, Bitter and Best tapped from casks in a side room, cheap weekday lunchtime bar food, cribbage; tables on grass by side grass, front gateway through living yew tree *(Pete Baker, Iain Robertson, Gordon, JP, PP, LYM, the Didler)*

Stoke Lyne [SP5628]

☆ *Peyton Arms* [off B4100]: Largely unspoilt stonebuilt pub with well kept Hook Norton beers (full range) tapped from casks behind small corner bar in sparsely decorated front snug, very friendly landlord and locals, real fire, hops hanging from beam, bigger refurbished bar with traditional games, charity book store; dogs welcome, pleasant garden with aunt sally; cl Mon lunchtime (Pete Baker, CMW, JJW, JP, PP, Kevin Thorpe, the Didler)

Stoke Row [SU6784]

Cherry Tree [off B481 at Highmoor]: Friendly low-beamed village local, one room like someone's parlour, another with pool; friendly licensees and locals, Brakspears BB, SB and Mild tapped from casks in back stillage room (the Didler)

☆ *Crooked Billet* [Newlands Lane, off B491 N of Reading – OS Sheet 175 map ref 684844]: Opened-up rustic beamed country pub/restaurant with wide choice of good interesting meals inc full vegetarian menu, relaxed homely atmosphere – like a French country restaurant; well kept Brakspears tapped from the cask, decent wines, good log fires, children welcome; big garden, by Chilterns beech woods (JP, PP, Bob and Ena Withers, J W G Nunns, LYM, Mrs M Hobbs, the Didler)

Stoke Talmage [SU6799]

Red Lion [signed from A40 at Tetsworth]: Basic old-fashioned country local, very friendly and cheerful, bare-boards public bar with Hook Norton and lots of changing guest beers from small corner servery, open fire, prints, posters, darts, shove-ha'penny and other games, chatty landlord, carpeted modern lounge; tables under cocktail parasols in pleasant garden, cl lunchtime Mon/Tues (JP, PP, Pete Baker, Torrens Lyster, Kevin Thorpe, Iain Robertson, the Didler)

Stratton Audley [SP6026]

Red Lion [off A421 NE of Bicester]: Welcoming thatched local with four or five real ales inc Hook Norton, good choice of good well priced food inc three Sun roasts (not Sun evening), freshly made so may be a wait – but attentive chatty service even when busy; inglenook log fire, stripped stone and low beams, antique sale posters, suitably old varnished wooden furniture; piped music may obtrude; small garden, pretty village (CMW, JJW, Ian Phillips, Marjorie and David Lamb, Steve de Mellow, George Atkinson)

Sutton Courtenay [SU5093]

George & Dragon: Friendly and chatty 16th-c pub, attractive mix of furnishings, nice log fire, good choice of fair-priced home-made food from thick sandwiches up inc popular Sun lunch, well kept Bass and Morlands Original and Old Speckled Hen, good range of decent wines, candles on tables, pewter mugs hanging from low beam; restaurant, big back terrace overlooking graveyard where Orwell is buried; no dogs (Chris Glasson, TBB)

Swerford [SP3731]

Masons Arms [A361 Banbury—Chipping Norton]: Wide range of enjoyable food, plenty of room to eat, wonderful country views; bedrooms comfortable, play area (David Gregory, H D Spottiswoode)

Swinbrook [SP2811]

☆ *Swan* [back rd a mile N of A40, 2 miles E of Burford]: Softly lit little beamed and flagstoned 16th-c pub prettily set by a bridge over the Windrush, gently smartened up, with antique settles, sporting prints and woodburner in friendly flagstoned tap room and back bar, carpeted dining room; good attractively presented food (all day w/e) inc interesting specials, traditional games, Flowers and Morlands Original, farm ciders, no piped music; seats by the lane and in small side garden; the nearby churchyard has the graves of Nancy, Unity and Pamela Mitford (Graham Parker, John Saul, Miss C Passmore, G W A Pearce, Ian Irving, LYM)

Swinford [SP4309]

Talbot [B4044 just S of Eynsham]: Oldish beamed building under new landlord with good track record, good value fresh food, well kept Arkells, friendly staff, long bar with naval memorabilia; pleasant walk along Thames towpath (A Kilpatrick)

Tackley [SP4720]

☆ *Gardeners Arms* [Medcroft Rd, off A4260]: 17th-c village pub, comfortable spick and span lounge bar with beams, brasses and coal-effect gas fire in inglenook, well presented good value food from sandwiches up inc good vegetarian choice, charming Dickensian landlord, quick attentive service, well kept ales (have been Morrells, with a guest such as Adnams), good coffee, prints, brasses, old photographs and cigarette cards; separate public bar with darts, TV and fruit machine, piped music, bookable skittle alley, picnic-sets on sunny terrace; handy for Rousham House (E A and D C T Frewer, JJW, CMW)

Kings Arms [Nethercote Rd]: Convivial unpretentious village local, welcoming to strangers, conversation, darts and dominoes on left, pool on right, good monthly folk nights (Pete Baker)

Tetsworth [SP6802]

Lion on the Green [A40, not far from M40 junction 7]: Welcoming local, good choice of food in bar and small restaurant, Brakspears and Ruddles, real fire, no dogs; bedrooms (Stan Edwards)

Swan [A40, not far from M40 junction 7]: Busy and popular bar and restaurant as part of antiques centre in rambling 15th-c coaching inn, well kept Brakspears, good upmarket food inc lots of fish (Stan Edwards)

Thame [SP7005]

Rising Sun [High St]: Flagstones, bare boards and nice settees in three linked rooms, good value generous food inc vegetarian and good range of sandwiches, well kept Brakspears with guests such as Boddingtons and Theakstons, real fire, pleasant atmosphere, decent piped music; can get busy evenings (Tim and Ann Newell, Giles Francis)

Thrupp [SP4815]

Boat [off A4260 just N of Kidlington]: Unpretentious and relaxing bare-boards stonebuilt local in lovely surroundings close to canal, decent food, quick friendly service, well

kept Morrells, coal fire, old canal pictures and artefacts, no piped music; restaurant, nice garden behind with plenty of tables, some in shade *(George Atkinson, Pete Baker, TBB)*
Jolly Boatman [Banbury Rd]: Extended basic pub with enjoyable cheap food, real ales, eating area and conservatory overlooking canal; children allowed *(TBB)*
Upper Wardington [SP4945]
Plough [off A361 NE of Banbury and M40 Junct 11]: Sociable partly 16th-c L-shaped local in attractive village, beams and brasses, plates and pictures, two stone fireplaces, darts, dominoes; Adnams and Hook Norton, several wines and country wines, wide choice of food inc Sun roast, no-smoking dining area, no music or machines; no dogs *(Richard Houghton)*
Upton [SU5186]
George & Dragon [A417 Harwell—Blewbury]: Welcoming little pub with well presented good food prepared to order, reasonable prices, Morlands Original, small end dining area *(Marjorie and David Lamb)*
Wantage [SU4087]
Royal Oak: Very friendly two-bar local with lots of ship photographs and naval hatbands, several well kept ales such as Badger Best, Wadworths and beers brewed for the pub by West Berkshire; table football, darts, cribbage *(BB)*
Warborough [SU5993]
☆ *Six Bells* [The Green S; just E of A329, 4 miles N of Wallingford]: Low-ceilinged thatched pub facing cricket green, particularly welcoming licensees, attractive country furnishings in interconnecting seating areas off bar, wide choice of good value interesting well cooked food, well kept Brakspears and a guest beer, decent wines, big log fire, antique photographs and pictures; tables in back orchard *(LYM, Marjorie and David Lamb, D C T and E A Frewer, Kathryn and Mike Phillips)*
West Hendred [SU4489]
☆ *Hare* [A417]: Civilised pub recently gutted and refurbished, doubling the space without losing the welcoming atmosphere; very popular for generous good interesting food served till late evening, decent wine, Morlands ale, pleasant garden *(Ron and Barbara Watkins, Sue Mandelbaum)*
Witney [SP3510]
Angel [Church Green]: Friendly extended 17th-c local, little changed in 40 years, cheap Hook Norton Old Hooky, wide choice of attractively priced food, hot coal fire, nice pubby atmosphere, very quick service even when packed; pool room, coffee bar *(Peter and Audrey Dowsett)*
Wolvercote [SP5009]
Plough [First Turn]: Convivial and comfortably pubby, armchairs and Victorian-style carpeted bays in main lounge, flagstoned dining room, traditional snug, good-sized public bar with pool and machines; good varied food esp soups and fresh seafood, well kept Morrells, decent wines; children welcome, tables outside looking over rough meadow to canal and woods *(Dr and Mrs J H Hills)*
Red Lion: Good value food in clean and spacious pleasant pub *(TBB)*
Woodstock [SP4416]
☆ *Bear* [Park St]: Handsome old THF inn with relaxing heavy-beamed bar on right, cosy alcoves, tastefully casual mix of well worn wooden antique oak, mahogany and leather furniture, tartan curtains, chintz cushions, paintings, sporting trophies, blazing inglenook log fire, well kept Morrells, good fresh sandwiches, bar lunches, morning coffee, afternoon tea, helpful service; restaurant; good bedrooms *(Kevin Blake, George Atkinson, BB)*
Queens Own [Oxford St (A44)]: Small attractive stone building dating from 17th c, friendly and unpretentious long narrow bar done up with bare boards, stripped stone, beamery, antique settles, elderly tables, hops on beams and candles; well kept Ushers Best and Founders, country wines, wide range of homely food inc Italian (all day Sat/Sun), reasonable prices, daily papers, discreet piped music; small back courtyard, lively Mon quiz night *(Kevin Blake, LM)*
Wootton [SP4320]
☆ *Killingworth Castle* [Glympton Rd; B4027 N of Woodstock]: Striking three-storey 17th-c inn, good local atmosphere, well kept Morlands Original and a guest beer, generous freshly made food, friendly licensees, long narrow main bar with candles and log fire, bar billiards, darts and shove-ha'penny in smaller games end, pleasant garden; jazz Weds, folk Fri; bedrooms *(Gordon, Pete Baker, Michael Hyde)*
Wroxton [SP4142]
☆ *North Arms* [Church St; off A422 at hotel, pub at back of village]: Pretty thatched stone pub with good bar food from soup and sandwiches to interesting main dishes and super salads, well kept Morrells, cheerful efficient service, log fire, eclectic furnishings, lots of beer mugs; character restaurant (not Mon); piped music, darts, dominoes, fruit machine; attractive quiet garden, lovely village *(Keith Sheppard, Dave Braisted, LYM, Gill and Keith Croxton)*

Shropshire

Pubs on particularly good form here in recent months have been the Three Tuns in Bishops Castle (new emphasis on good food, alongside beers brewed in its classic Victorian tower brewery), the Burlton Inn at Burlton (newish licensees really hitting it off, imaginative food), the Crown at Hopton Wafers (new licensees bringing it back into the main entries after quite a long absence), the Armoury in Shrewsbury (good imaginative food in nice surroundings – it gains our title of Shropshire Dining Pub of the Year), the consistently very welcoming Wenlock Edge Inn on Wenlock Edge (good food here too), and the cheerful Willey Moor Lock near Whitchurch (bargain real food). The Castle in Bishops Castle gains a Stay Award this year, and the Crown at Munslow now have letting bedrooms. New licensees in the Longville Arms at Longville are proving popular, stripping it down to beams and old stonework; there are also new people at the Crown at Wentnor. In the Lucky Dip section at the end of the chapter, we'd particularly note the Bear in Bridgnorth, Stokesay Castle Hotel in Craven Arms, Coalbrookdale Inn in Coalbrookdale, Lion at Hampton Loade, Bear in Hodnet, Queens Head at Queens Head, entirely no smoking Three Fishes in Shrewsbury and (for food) Falcon at Woore. Drinks prices here are significantly lower than the national average – especially so in the growing number of pubs getting beer from Hobsons of Cleobury Mortimer, and in the Plough at Wistanstow and Three Tuns in Bishops Castle (brewing their own). The Woods beers brewed behind the Plough are also sold quite widely elsewhere in the area.

BISHOPS CASTLE SO3289 Map 6

Castle 🛏

The Square; just off B4385

The very spacious and characterful bedrooms at this substantial Georgian stone coaching inn are very attractively decorated with antique furniture. Readers' feedback over the last twelve months has confirmed our hopes that we would be able to give them a Stay Award this year. Set in a commanding position at the top of the town it dates from 1719 and was first used as a hotel in the 19th c. On the right is a clubby small beamed and panelled room glazed off from the entrance, with old local prints and sturdy leather chairs on its muted carpet; on the left a bigger room with maroon plush wall seats and stools, big Victorian engravings, a coal fire and nice table-lamps. Service too is old-fashioned, in the best sense – friendly and pains-taking – Wellington the basset hound is very welcoming too. Besides good sandwiches (from £2.20) and ploughman's (£4.50), the landlady cooks tasty and generous food such as soup (£2.50), fish and chips (£5.95), cheese, leek and mushroom sausages (£6.50), roasted vegetable tart (£7.50), steak and ale pie (£7.75) and chicken breast in creamy apricot and coriander sauce (£8.25); there is a dining room which is no smoking in the evening and Sunday lunchtime. Well kept Bass, Hobsons Best and Town Crier and Worthington Best on handpump, and over 50 malt whiskies; darts, shove-ha'penny, cribbage and dominoes; a couple of picnic-sets out by flower tubs in front, with more in the sizeable back garden. *(Recommended by SLC, Chris and Shirley Machin, Sue Holland, Dave Webster)*

Free house ~ Licensees David and Nicky Simpson ~ Real ale ~ Bar food (12-1.45,

6.30-9) ~ Restaurant ~ (01588) 638403 ~ Children welcome ~ Open 12-2.30, 6.30-11; 12-2.30, 7-10.30 Sun ~ Bedrooms: £35B/£60B

Three Tuns ◀

Salop Street

Readers are enthusiastic about this well converted pub which is slowly developing into a more sophisticated, but still lively and friendly, operation – it's now much more than just a tap for the very good beers that are produced in the many-storied Victorian brewhouse across the yard. Each stage of the brewing process descends from floor to floor within the unique tower layout (it's a Grade 1 listed building) and there are brewery tours by appointment. Well kept Three Tuns XXX, Offa and Sexton on old-fashioned handpump, with bottled Clerics Cure, Little Tun and Bellringer; they do home brew kits and carry-out kegs, sales by the barrel or cases of Clerics Cure – phone Steve Dunn the brewer on (01588) 638023. They hold an annual beer festival in July with Morris dancers in the yard; decent wine list. The simply furnished no frills beamed rooms are bustling and friendly, with low backed settles, heavy walnut tables and newspapers to read, and a good mix of customers. There's a growing emphasis on the good home-made bar food which is listed on the blackboard and might include fish soup (£3.25), pâté (£3.50), liver and onions or sausage and mash (£5.50), beef and ale pie or venison casserole (£7), quite a range of fresh fish, and puddings like summer pudding or rhubarb crumble (from £2.75). Darts, dominoes, backgammon and cards. There's a small garden and terrace. We'd like to hear about the new suites that have opened in a converted stable block which has it's own peaceful garden. *(Recommended by Pat and Tony Martin, Christoper and Jo Barton, Jill Bickerton, SLC, John and Esther Sprinkle, Tony and Wendy Hobden, Nigel Woolliscroft, Andrew Rogers, Amanda Milsom, Derek and Sylvia Stephenson, Sue Holland, Dave Webster, D Etheridge, the Didler)*

Free house ~ Licensee Margaret Anthony ~ Real ale ~ Bar food (12-2, 7-9.30) ~ (01588) 638797 ~ Children welcome ~ Occasional jazz Sun evening ~ Open 12-3.30, 5-11; 12-11.30 Sat; 12-10.30 Sun ~ Bedrooms: £55B/£75B

BRIDGES SO3996 Map 6

Horseshoe £ ◀

Near Ratlinghope, below the W flank of the Long Mynd

This attractive old-fashioned local is charmingly set in good walking country, and is run by the second generation of the Muller family. There's a genuinely unpretentious atmosphere in the comfortable bar which has interesting windows, a good log fire, Adnams Regatta and Southwold and Shepherd Neame Spitfire on handpump, as well as several bottled beers, and a small no-smoking dining room leading off. Good value lunchtime bar food includes sandwiches and filled rolls (from £1.50), home-made soup (£1.95), a good traditional ploughman's (from £3.25), home-made vegetable lasagne (£3.75) and chilli (£4), good ham salad (£3.95), and home-made puddings. Darts, cribbage and dominoes. There are very pleasantly positioned tables outside by the little River Onny, and the pub's particularly handy for walks on the Long Mynd itself and on Stiperstones – despite its isolation, it can get very busy in summer, but is lovely and cosy in winter. *(Recommended by John Brightley, Nigel Woolliscroft, Gwen and Peter Andrews, Rob and Gill Weeks, Catherine and Richard Preston, SLC, Derek and Sylvia Stephenson)*

Free house ~ Licensee Simon John Muller ~ Real ale ~ Bar food (lunchtime only) ~ (01588) 650260 ~ Open 12-2.30, 6-11; 12-3, 6-11 Sat; 12-3, 7-10.30 Sun; closed Mon lunchtime, winter lunchtimes

BROCKTON SO5894 Map 4

Feathers

B4378

Popular for its imaginative restauranty food, this stylish stone-built pub has charmingly beamed rooms very attractively decorated with stencilling on the terracotta or yellow colour wash walls; there are comfortable seats, and a delightful conservatory. The seasonally changing menu might include soup (£2.75), stilton and crispy bacon salad (£4.25), pâté stuffed mushrooms, sautéed kidneys in cream, sherry and tarragon or crispy duck and mango salad with mango and chilli dressing (£4.75), lemon sole fillet filled with crabmeat and spinach with vermouth sauce, grilled salmon fillet on warm potato and asparagus salad with lemon butter or chicken fillet stuffed with shropshire blue, wrapped in smoked bacon and baked on a bed of leeks in white wine sauce (£10.95), half roast duck with traditional gravy or half shoulder of lamb with red wine and rosemary jus (£12.95), good Sunday lunch, and efficient, friendly waitress service. Two rooms are no smoking, and they have a policy not to sell cigarettes; piped music. Banks's Bitter and Morrells Varsity kept under light blanket pressure. *(Recommended by W Ruxton, John and Shirley Smith, Catherine and Richard Preston, Ian and Jacqui Ross, Mike and Mary Carter, Chris Gabbitas, Hugh McPhail, Alan and Paula McCully)*

Free house ~ Licensee Martin Hayward ~ Real ale ~ Bar food ~ Restaurant ~ (01746) 785202 ~ Children welcome ~ Open 6.30-11; 12-3, 6.30-11(10.30 Sun) Sat; closed Mon

BURLTON SJ4626 Map 6
Burlton Inn 🍴

A528 Shrewsbury—Ellesmere, near junction with B4397

Even on the licensees' night off things go smoothly, with the neatly uniformed staff at this very well run, attractively restored old pub efficient and eager to please. It's done so well since the Beans took over a couple of years ago that we're pleased to say we're now able to give them a Food Award for the beautifully prepared bar meals served from a menu that changes about four times a year. There might be soup (£2.95), glazed chicken wings with spicy relish (£3.95), sardine and mushroom pâté (£4.50), goat's cheese and tomato salad (£4.75), steak, kidney and beer pie (£6.75), filo and feta roulade (£7.95), grilled salmon fillet with mustard and dill mayonnaise (£8.50), cod with goat's cheese and coriander crust (£8.95), half shoulder of braised lamb with redcurrant and mint sauce (£9.50), and puddings like coffee pavlova with Baileys and hazelnut cream, sticky toffee pudding with toffee sauce and lime and lemon cheesecake (£2.95). Everything in the three fresh-feeling cottagey connecting rooms seems meticulously arranged and cared for, from the flower displays in the brick fireplace or beside the neatly curtained windows, to the piles of *Country Living* and interior design magazines left seemingly casually in the corner. There are a few racing prints, spurs and brasses on the walls, and open fires in winter; dominoes, cribbage. Well kept Banks's and up to six guests from all over the country on handpump. There are tables on a small lawn behind, with more on a strip of grass beyond the car park; there's a climbing frame here too, and a new terrace has smart wooden furniture. The pub sign is a reminder of the days when this was known as the Cross Keys; dogs welcome. *(Recommended by Sue and Bob Ward, Rita and Keith Pollard, Miss S P Watkin, P A Taylor, SLC, Mr and Mrs F Carroll, Jill Bickerton)*

Free house ~ Licensee Gerald Bean ~ Real ale ~ Bar food (12-2, 6.30-9.45(7-9.30 Sun); limited menu Mon lunchtime) ~ (01939) 270284 ~ Children in eating area of bar, over 5 evenings ~ Open 11-3, 6-11; 12-3, 7-10.30 Sun; closed bank hol Mon lunchtimes

CARDINGTON SO5095 Map 4
Royal Oak

Village signposted off B4371 Church Stretton—Much Wenlock, pub behind church; also reached via narrow lanes from A49

The friendly, rambling, low-beamed bar at this lovely old wisteria-covered white stone inn is has a roaring winter log fire, cauldron, black kettle and pewter jugs in its vast inglenook fireplace, old standing timbers of a knocked-through wall and red and green tapestry seats solidly capped in elm. You may have to book for the very tasty home-made bar food which might include cauliflower cheese (£3.30), cottage pie or very tasty fidget pie (£5.50), meat or vegetable lasagne (£4.95) and fish and chips (£5.90), seafood lasagne (£6.10). Bass, Hobsons, Marstons Pedigree and Woods Shropshire Lad kept under light blanket pressure; dominoes and cribbage in the main bar. A comfortable no-smoking dining area has exposed old beams and studwork. Tables in the rose-filled front courtyard have lovely views over hilly fields, and a mile or so away – from the track past Willstone (ask for directions at the pub) – you can walk up Caer Caradoc Hill which looks over scenic countryside. *(Recommended by E A Froggatt, Nigel Woolliscroft, Sue and Bob Ward, John Whitehead, DAV, John Teign, Alan and Paula McCully, John Cockell, David and Kathy Holcroft, A G P Pounder, Patrick Hancock, TOH, Graham Parker)*

Free house ~ Licensee Dave Baugh ~ Real ale ~ Bar food (12-2, 7-8.30; not Sun evening) ~ (01694) 771266 ~ Children in eating area of bar during meal times ~ Open 12-2.30, 7-11; closed Mon except bank holidays

CLEOBURY MORTIMER SO6775 Map 4
Kings Arms ♜

Church Street (A4117 Bewdley—Ludlow)

This friendly welcoming inn is centuries older than its Georgian frontage suggests. It's open-plan inside but has kept lots of character, with an interesting mix of furnishings including various-sized pews on its broad floorboards, well spaced bar tables, a good log fire, an attractive longcase clock, pleasant lighting and lots of local pictures and Victorian music posters; big shuttered windows look across to the church. A step down through a snug little central heavily-beamed area takes you into the main back dining part, carpeted, and more low beams liberally hung with whisky water jugs and teapots. Bar food includes soup (£2.25), warm bacon and avocado salad (£4.40), steak and kidney pie, blue cheese and sage fusilli with leeks or green Thai vegetable curry (£6.99), chicken breast with leeks and stilton (£7.99), crispy barbary duck breast with spicy plum sauce (£8.50), and daily specials like chicken curry or beef in orange and Guinness (£5.99), trout (£7.25), or salmon fillet (£7.50); friendly attentive staff, well kept Hobsons Best on handpump; maybe piped classical or operatic music. A simpler area on the right has a fruit machine. The bedrooms are well decorated, comfortable and good value, with a good breakfast (you may be asked to order the night before), but some walls could be thicker, and the floor of the front ones is the ceiling of the bar. *(Recommended by John Whitehead, Jim Bush, DAV, Derek and Sylvia Stephenson)*

Free house ~ Licensee Michael Purnell ~ Real ale ~ Bar food ~ Restaurant ~ (01299) 270252 ~ Children in eating area of bar ~ Open 11.30-11; 12-10.30 Sun ~ Bedrooms: £28B/£50B

CRESSAGE SJ5904 Map 6
Cholmondeley Riverside ♀

Off A458 SE of Shrewsbury, slightly before Cressage itself if coming from Shrewsbury

At its best the food at this neatly converted white riverside hotel can be very good. Cooking is fairly traditional English, and dishes might include lunchtime baguettes (£3.95), smoked salmon blini (£4.95), devilled lamb's kidneys (£7.50), beef curry or fish and chips (£7.75), with daily specials like tomato soup (£2.95), grilled goat's cheese on tomatoes (£4.50), home-cured gravadlax with mustard and dill sauce (£4.95), ratatouille (£7.95), chicken and mushroom pie (£7.50), cassoulet or chicken breast in mushroom, dijon mustard and cream sauce (£8.95) and fillet steak with pepper, cream and brandy sauce (£13.95), with puddings like bakewell tart, hot chocolate sponge and chocolate sauce or blackcurrant ripple ice cream (from £3.50); booking is advised at weekends. The spaciously civilised bar has a variety of stripped pine and oak church pews, cushioned settles and tables dotted around the central servery, with a mix of country prints, plates and tapestries on the walls. Marstons Best on handpump, along with a couple of weekly changing guests; there's an excellent choice of interesting wines, as well as tea and coffee. French windows lead out to tables perfectly positioned in a garden overlooking a very pretty stretch of the

Severn – in less amenable conditions you can have the same idyllic view down to the water from the big new conservatory. Coarse fishing on the river costs £4 a day, though it's free if you're staying. *(Recommended by June and Mike Coleman, Graham and Liz Bell, W C M Jones, M Joyner, TOH, Nigel and Olga Wikeley, Phil Revell, E A Froggatt, Steve Whalley, SLC, John Whitehead, Nigel Woolliscroft)*

Free house ~ Licensees John Radford and John P Wrigley ~ Real ale ~ Bar food (12-2.15, 7-10.30) ~ (01952) 510900 ~ Children in eating area of bar and restaurant ~ Open 10.30-3, 6.30-11(10.30 Sun); closed 25 Dec ~ Bedrooms: £50S(£50B)/£65S(£65B)

HOPTON WAFERS SO6476 Map 6
Crown
A4117 Kidderminster—Ludlow

New licensees have made great efforts to restore this attractive welcoming creeper-covered stone inn to its previous high standards. The cosy cream painted beamed bar with its large inglenook fireplace has been smartened up and has new purpose-built dark wood furniture, oil paintings, and maybe fresh flowers. Outside the terrace areas, with tables under cocktail parasols, have been extended, with the streamside garden, tubs of bright flowers and duck pond as pretty as ever. Good bar food now includes plenty of fresh seafood dishes: there might be soup (£3.25), fried calamari with lemon and spicy tomato dip (£3.85), sardines with garlic mayonnaise (£3.75), venison sausages with onion and redcurrant sauce and garlic mash (£7.45), fried chicken breast with garlic and herb cream glazed with stilton (£8.45), plaice stuffed with crab, coriander, red onion and ginger (£8.95), barbary duck breast with ginger and plum sauce (£9.95), poached halibut steak with orange and chervil butter (£10.50), and puddings like summer pudding, champagne and white chocolate truffle and tangy lemon bavarois (£3.50); no-smoking restaurant. Alongside well kept Marstons Best and Pedigree and two guests like Crown Glory (brewed for the pub by Woods) and another local ale on handpump there's an improved wine list with about half a dozen wines by the glass; pretty, timbered bedrooms, one with lovely oak floor, another with woodburning stove. *(Recommended by M Downes, Mr and Mrs Donald Anderson, Barbara and Alan Mence, George Atkinson, John Whitehead)*

Free house ~ Licensees Liz and Alan Matthews ~ Real ale ~ Bar food (12-2.30, 6-9.30(7-9 Sun)) ~ Restaurant ~ (01299) 270372 ~ Well behaved children away from bar ~ Open 12-3, 6-11(7-10.30 Sun) ~ Bedrooms: £45B/£75B

LLANYBLODWEL SJ2423 Map 6
Horseshoe
Village and pub signposted from B4936

This wonky old black and white timbered Tudor inn is in a lovely spot by the River Tanat. There are plenty of outside seats and a you can buy a day ticket (£7.50) for a mile of fly-fishing. The simple low-beamed front bar has an old black range in the inglenook fireplace, traditional black built-in settles alongside more modern chairs around oak tables on a reclaimed maple floor, and lots of brass and china. In the rambling rooms leading off you'll find darts, pool, cribbage, dominoes, fruit machine, and piped music. Bar food includes good lunchtime baguettes (from £3), soup (£2.25), king prawns fried in garlic butter (£4.95), mediterranean bean casserole (£5.50), steak and kidney pie (£5.95), grilled fresh fish of the day with lemon and dill butter (£6.50), roast poussin with sherry and brandy sauce or chicken supreme in a mushroom, cream and white wine sauce (£8.95) and venison steak with dijon and redcurrant sauce (£10.50). The dining room is oak panelled. Well kept Banks's Mild and Bitter and a range of malt whiskies. *(Recommended by David Edwards, Pete Yearsley, Nigel Woolliscroft, Miss V Kavanagh, Rob Whittle, R J Bland, Mr and Mrs Archibald)*

Free house ~ Licensee Dennis John William Plant ~ Real ale ~ Bar food ~ (01691) 828969 ~ Children at landlord's discretion ~ Open 11.30-3, 6.30-11; 12-3, 7-11 Sun; closed Mon lunchtime

LONGVILLE SO5393 Map 4
Longville Arms 🛏
B4371 Church Stretton—Much Wenlock

New welcoming owners have put in lots of effort transforming the two spacious bars at this once modest-looking inn. They've stripped sections of plasterwork back to the original stone walls, stripped beams, and generally smartened up the décor. The bar on the left has sturdy elm or cast-iron-framed tables, covered banquettes, and a woodburning stove at each end. The right-hand lounge has dark plush wall banquettes and cushioned chairs, with some nice old tables. New oak panelling gives the dining room a cosy library feel. There's a wide range of good-value homely bar food, including sandwiches, soup (£1.95), whitebait with yoghurt dressing (£2.95), deep-fried camembert with cranberry sauce (£3.25), mushroom stroganoff or tagliatelle with creamy tomato, basil and garlic sauce (£4.95), lasagne (£5.95), breaded plaice stuffed with prawns, mushroom and white wine sauce (£7.95), lamb steak fried with rosemary with mint and red wine sauce (£8.95), and 8oz sirloin (£9.95). Well kept Courage Directors on handpump with maybe a guest in summer, and several malt and Irish whiskies; darts, dominoes. There are picnic-sets under cocktail parasols in a neat terraced side garden, with a good play area and trampoline. The pub is delightfully set in really beautiful countryside and well placed near to an excellent range of local attractions. Bedrooms in a converted stable block are comfortable and private. *(Recommended by Roger Byrne, Mr and Mrs P Eastwood, Nigel Woolliscroft, TOH, Bruce Howells, John Whitehead, Jill Bickerton, John and Shirley Smith, Philip Champness, E A Froggatt, Alan and Paula McCully, DC, Mike Gorton, Mike and Mary Carter)*

Free house ~ Licensees Chris and Wendy Davis ~ Real ale ~ Restaurant ~ (01694) 771206 ~ Children welcome away from the bar ~ Live entertainment some Fridays ~ Open 12-3, 7(6 Sat)-11; 12-4, 7-10.30 Sun ~ Bedrooms: £28B/£42B

LUDLOW SO5175 Map 4
Unicorn 🍴
Lower Corve St, off Shrewsbury Rd

Splendidly set on the edge of a picturesque town, this very much enjoyed 17th-c inn, built in a row of black and white houses, has a pretty little terrace with tables sheltering pleasantly among willow trees right next to the modest river Corve. Inside, the warmly atmospheric solidly beamed and partly panelled bar has a bustling atmosphere, a good mix of friendly locals and visitors, and a huge log fire in a big stone fireplace. There's also a timbered, candlelit no-smoking restaurant. Good, tasty, properly home-made bar food might include soup (£2.50), mussels in pesto butter or chicken liver pâté (£3.95), sesame prawn toasts (£4), bacon, mushroom and cauliflower bake (£5.50), home-cooked ham in parsley sauce or nut roast or garlic mushroom pancake (£6.25), penne with chargrilled sweet pepper sauce (£7.25), cod mornay (£8.25), chicken wrapped in bacon with creamy mushroom sauce (£8.95), roast duck with orange and Grand Marnier sauce (£11.25), rack of lamb with cumberland sauce (£11.50), swordfish steak with crab bisque (£11.95). Service is attentive, cheerful and willing. Well kept Bass and Hancocks HB on handpump; dominoes. *(Recommended by Mike and Heather Watson, Janet Lee, Steve Whalley, R F Grieve, John and Esther Sprinkle, Ian Jones, Keith Sheppard, Jack and Rosalin Forrester, Karen Hands, John Whitehead, W W Burke, Ann Williams, Tony Hughes, Neil and Anita Christopher, Gillian Jenkins, Graham and Liz Bell, Stan and Hazel Allen, Judith Coley)*

Free house ~ Licensees Alan and Elisabeth Ditchburn ~ Real ale ~ Bar food (12-2.15, 6(7 Sun)-9.15) ~ (01584) 873555 ~ Children in eating area of bar and restaurant ~ Open 12-2.30(3 Sat), 6-11; 12-3.30, 7-10.30 Sun ~ Bedrooms: £18(£25B)/£36(£50B)

Cribbage is a card game using a block of wood with holes for matchsticks or special pins to score with; regulars in cribbage pubs are usually happy to teach strangers how to play.

MUCH WENLOCK SO6299 Map 4

George & Dragon ◀

High St

This unpretentious town local has an impressive collection of old brewery and cigarette advertisements, bottle labels and beer trays, George-and-the-Dragon pictures, and over five hundred water jugs hanging from the beams in the cosily atmospheric rooms. It has a few antique settles as well as conventional furnishings, and a couple of attractive Victorian fireplaces (with coal-effect gas fires). At the back, the quieter snug old-fashioned rooms have black beams and timbering, little decorative plaster panels, tiled floors, a big mural as well as lots of smaller pictures (painted by local artists), and a little stove in an inglenook. Very well liked bar food in generous helpings might include sandwiches (from £1.95), lasagne, leek and mushroom bake or battered cod (£4.95), steak and kidney pie (£5.25), and daily specials like stilton and walnut pâté (£3.95), chicken breast in apricot and Shropshire mead sauce (£7.50) and home-baked ham with parsley sauce (£7.75), with puddings like bread and butter pudding (£2.75); no-smoking restaurant. Well kept Hook Norton Best and up to four guest beers from brewers like Everards, Hobsons, Lichfield or Woods on handpump, as well as fruit and country wines, elderflower, and ginger and lemon grass pressé; piped music may be intrusive. *(Recommended by John Whitehead, Peter King, M Joyner, John Andrew, Nigel Woolliscroft, Paul Tindall, Sam Samuells, Lynda Payton, Mr and Mrs P Eastwood, Tony and Wendy Hobden, JP, PP, CMJ, JJW, John and Shirley Smith)*

Free house ~ Licensee Barry Blakeman ~ Real ale ~ Bar food ~ Restaurant ~ (01952) 727312 ~ Children in restaurant ~ Open 12-2.30, 6-11; 12-2.30, 7-10.30 Sun

Talbot 🛏

High Street

The other main entry in this fine market town is this partly 14th-c civilised coaching inn, with its delightful little coach entry leading off the high street to white seats and tables in an attractive sheltered courtyard, and the entrance to the bar. Inside there are several neatly kept areas with comfortable green plush button-back wall banquettes around highly polished tables, low ceilings, and two big log fires (one in an inglenook); the walls are decorated with prints of fish and brewery paraphernalia; piped music. Generous helpings of bar food might include sandwiches or soup (£2.95), ploughman's (£3.75), broccoli and stilton quiche (£5.95), rabbit casserole with prunes and apricot (£6.50), pork, leek, apple and cider stew or steak and kidney pie (£6.95), and puddings like sticky toffee pudding or strawberry pavlova (£3.50). The restaurant is no smoking. Well kept Courage Directors and a guest like Morlands Old Speckled Hen on handpump, and several malt whiskies; piped music. *(Recommended by David and Kathy Holcroft, Janet and Peter Race, E A Froggatt, John Whitehead, Mr and Mrs Donald Anderson, Paul Tindall)*

Free house ~ Licensee Cheryl Brennan ~ Real ale ~ Bar food (12-2, 7-9.30; not Sat evening) ~ Restaurant ~ (01952) 727077 ~ Children in restaurant ~ Open 10.30-3, 6-11; 12-3, 7-10.30 Sun ~ Bedrooms: £45B/£90B

MUNSLOW SO5287 Map 2

Crown ◀

B4368 Much Wenlock—Craven Arms

They now have accommodation at this big old brewhouse which is notable for its lovely friendly welcome which encompasses children, and very praiseworthily even one reader's muddy dogs. They have their own friendly dog Tosh, the cat is Sarge and there's a donkey in the back yard. Behind its imposing Georgian facade, there's a cosy Tudor interior with oak beams, nooks, and crannies. The warm and friendly split-level lounge bar has a pleasantly old-fashioned mix of furnishings on its broad flagstones, a collection of old bottles, country pictures, a bread oven by its good log fire, seats in a traditional snug with its own fire; the eating area has tables around a central oven chimney, stripped stone walls, more beams and flagstones. From their own microbrewery they produce Munslow Boys Pale Ale and Munslow Hundred, and have a guest like Shepherd Neame Spitfire on handpump. A wide choice of generously served home-made food includes filled french bread (from £1.75), ploughman's (£3.50), chicken liver terrine (£3.75), ratatouille and cheese or grilled haddock (£5.95), lamb with sherry and rosemary sauce (£8.50) sliced pork steak on a prosciutto and pimento sauce or salmon fillet with cream and mushroom sauce (£8.95) and tiger prawns in lemon sauce (£10.95). Relaxed and friendly family service; games room with darts, table skittles, cribbage and dominoes; piped music. Tables outside. *(Recommended by TOH, John Whitehead, A W and K J Randle, G Coates, Chris Gabbitas, Hugh McPhail, E A Froggatt, Mike and Mary Carter, Roger Tame, John and Esther Sprinkle, Tracey Hamond, Dr B and Mrs P Baker)*

Own brew ~ Vic, Mike and Zoe Pocock ~ Real ale ~ Bar food (12-2, 7-9.30) ~ Restaurant ~ (01584) 841205 ~ Children welcome ~ Open 12-2.30, 7-11; 12-3, 7-10.30 Sun ~ Bedrooms: £30B/£45B

NESSCLIFFE SJ3819 Map 6
Old Three Pigeons
A5 Shrewsbury—Oswestry

An amusing assortment of diversions in the two acres of ground at this busy dining pub ranges from ducks and swans on the new lake, to a very well stocked bird garden to military hardware which they often lend to museums or shows. There are a few tables out here too. The long low building (parts of which are thought to be 14th-c) looks quite big from the outside, with the restaurant taking up much of the space, leaving two traditional bar areas separated by a brick pillar mostly covered by the food blackboard. These have brown cushioned sofas along the walls, a mix of plain wooden chairs and tables, log fires, and quite a few brasses on the walls or hanging from the ceiling; the juke box by here isn't always switched on. Four changing real ales might include Boddingtons, Courage Directors, John Smiths and Wadworths 6X kept under light blanket pressure. Food here is very popular. As well as the more usual lunchtime (not Sunday) bar snacks like ploughman's (£4.95), lamb curry (£5.95) and scampi (£6.95), the licensees hang and butcher their own meat, and feature fresh fish heavily on the huge chalkboard menu, with might include pork crumble, beef stroganoff, chicken breast wrapped in bacon and topped with a cream and cheese sauce, cajun Scottish salmon, oak smoked haddock in a grain mustard sauce or swordfish in olive oil with garlic and herbs (£9.95), silver hake and roasted almonds (£10.95), whole oven baked bass (£13.95), and puddings (£2.75); Sunday roast £7. There may be a wait at busy times; friendly service. It's handy for Kynaston Cave, and some good cliff walks. *(Recommended by Mr and Mrs F Carroll, June and Mike Coleman, William Cunliffe, Jack and Rosalin Forrester, Karen Hands, E A Froggatt, Miss S P Watkin, P A Taylor)*

Free house ~ Licensee Dillon Brooks ~ Real ale ~ Bar food ~ Restaurant ~ (01743) 741279 ~ Children welcome ~ Open 11.30-3, 6.30-11; closed Mon, Sun evening

NORTON SJ7200 Map 4
Hundred House 🍴 ♀ 🛏
A442 Telford—Bridgnorth

A genuine family business this, with tremendous attention to detail, and some emphasis on the bar food. The very neatly kept interior, prettied up with lots of dried and fresh flowers, herbs and hops, is divided into several separate areas, with old quarry tiles at either end and modern hexagonal ones in the main central high-beamed part. Steps lead up past a little balustrade to a partly panelled eating area where stripped brickwork looks older than that elsewhere. Handsome fireplaces have log fires or working Coalbrookdale ranges (one has a great Jacobean arch with fine old black cooking pots), and around sewing-machine tables are a variety of interesting chairs and settles with some long colourful patchwork leather cushions.

Bar food includes soup (£3.50), greek salad (£4.50), duck liver pâté (£4.95), local sausage and mash (£5.95), steak and kidney pie (£6.95), hot potato cakes with aioli, tempura onion rings, mushroom sauce and rocket (£7.95), warm Thai salad of roast beef with spiced shallots, pak choi, coriander and rice (£8.95), and 10oz sirloin (£12.95). Well kept Charles Wells Bombardier, Heritage Bitter (brewed for them by a small brewery: light and refreshing and not too bitter), Woods Shropshire Lad and a guest on handpump, an extensive wine list with house wines by the carafe, half carafe, and big or small glass, and lots of malt whiskies; dominoes, piped music; pretty bedrooms. The very well established cottagey gardens are worth a visit in themselves, with old-fashioned roses, trees, and herbaceous plants, and a very big working herb garden that supplies the kitchen. (*Recommended by David and Kathy Holcroft, Tony Walker, Mike and Mary Carter, R Gorick, Dick Brown, Anthony Longden, Joyce McKimm, E A Froggatt, John Robertson, Tracey Hamond, JCW, John Teign, Michael and Gillian Ford, SLC*)

Free house ~ Licensees The Phillips Family ~ Real ale ~ Bar food (12-2.30, 7-9.30) ~ Restaurant ~ (01952) 730353 ~ Children welcome ~ Open 11-11; 12-3, 7-10.30 Sun ~ Bedrooms: £69B/£95B

PULVERBATCH SJ4202 Map 6
White Horse

From A49 at N end of Dorrington follow Pulverbatch/Church Pulverbatch signposts, and turn left at eventual T-junction (which is sometimes signposted Church Pulverbatch); OS Sheet 126 map reference 424023

Masses of gleaming brass and copper fill the friendly rambling rooms at this bustling country pub. A collection of antique insurance plaques, big brass sets of scales, willow-pattern plates, and pewter mugs hang over the serving counter, and an open coalburning range has gleaming copper kettles. There are black beams and heavy timbering, as well as unusual fabric-covered high-backed settles and brocaded banquettes on a turkey carpet, sturdy elm or cast-iron-framed tables, and even a good Thorburn print of a grouse among the other country pictures. Good bar food includes soup (£1.50), sandwiches (from £1.75), liver pâté (£2.50), burgers (from £3.10), steak sandwich (£3.95), macaroni cheese (£3.95), lasagne (£4.75), beef curry (£5.75), prawn and chicken curry (£6.25), sirloin steak (£7.50), and puddings like apple pie (£1.95), and lots of sundaes (£2.75). Well kept Boddingtons, Flowers Original, Tetleys and Whitbread Trophy on handpump, several decent wines by the glass, and over 100 malt whiskies; friendly efficient service. The quarry-tiled front loggia with its sturdy old green leatherette seat is a nice touch. The entrance is around the back of the pub. (*Recommended by John and Shirley Smith, M Joyner, Betty Petheram, John Whitehead, Chris Gabbitas, Hugh McPhail, G Neighbour*)

Whitbreads ~ Lease: Hamish MacGregor ~ Real ale ~ Bar food (12-2, 7-9.30) ~ (01743) 718247 ~ Children welcome ~ Open 11.30-3, 7-11; 12-3, 7-10.30 Sun

SHREWSBURY SJ4912 Map 6
Armoury 🍽 ♀

Victoria Quay, Victoria Avenue

Shropshire Dining Pub of the Year

Interesting bistro-style food at this smartly converted warehouse might include soup (£2.95), sandwiches (from £3.25), ploughman's (£3.95), warm chorizo sausage with soy and balsamic dressing (£4.95), salmon and smoked haddock fishcakes with lemon mayonnaise (£5.95), Thai marinated chicken breast with minted yoghurt (£6.25), wild mushroom and risotto cakes with broad bean and spinach sauce (£6.75), chicken supreme with blue cheese and herb sauce on cauliflower and broccoli with crispy fried potatoes(£8.45), steamed salmon fillet on noodles and roasted peppers with warm lemon and coriander dressing (£9.25), grilled tuna steak with warm green bean and olive salad (£9.25), roast duck breast on vegetable terrine with raspberry and ginger jus (£11.25), and puddings like vanilla crème brûlée with crispy biscuits or lemon cheesecake(£3.75). Big arched windows overlooking the river light up the single airy room which is packed with old prints, documents and other neatly framed ephemera, has glass cabinets showing off collections of explosives and shells as well as corks and bottle openers, and one entire wall covered with copiously filled bookshelves. There's a mix of good heavy wooden tables, chairs and high-backed settles, interspersed by the occasional green-painted standing timber, and colonial fans whirring away on the ceiling. Tables at one end are laid out for eating, with a grand stone fireplace at the other end; backgammon and draughts. An eyecatchingly huge range of varied drinks served from behind the long bar counter includes well kept Boddingtons, Wadsworths 6X, Woods Shropshire Lad and two guests on handpump, as well as a good wine list that includes around 15 by the glass, 70 or so malt whiskies, a dozen different gins, lots of rums and vodkas, a wide choice of brandies, and some unusual liqueurs. The place can get busy in the evenings, particularly at weekends. You can paddle boats along the Severn outside, escorted past rows of weeping willows by swans and gently quacking ducks. The pub doesn't have its own parking but they sell vouchers for parking on the road. *(Recommended by R J Bland, M Joyner, W W Burke, Peg Cuskley, Rita and Keith Pollard)*

Free house ~ Licensees Jill Mitchell and Eugene Millea ~ Real ale ~ Bar food (12-2.30, 6-9.30; 12-9.30 Sat(9 Sun)) ~ (01743) 340525 ~ Children till 9pm ~ Open 12-11(10.30 Sun)

WENLOCK EDGE SO5796 Map 4

Wenlock Edge Inn ★ 🍴 🛏

Hilltop; B4371 Much Wenlock—Church Stretton, OS Sheet 137 map reference 570962

Once again there are floods of enthusiastic reports from readers telling us about the genuinely warm welcome extended by the friendly landlord and his family at this cheerful old place. What makes it really special is the way visitors are immediately involved in the bar room chat, with the cosy feel perhaps at its best on story telling night (the second Monday in the month at 8pm) when the right hand bar is packed with locals telling tales, some true and others somewhat taller. Bar food is very popular too, with perhaps tomato and sweet red pepper soup (£2.75), orkney herrings marinated in dill (£3.85), cheese, leek and tomato flan (£6.40), steak and mushroom pie (£6.50), cod fillet with parsley sauce (£7), chicken breast with creamy apple and cider sauce or hot smoked salmon (£7.20), venison pie (£7.25) and sirloin steak (£9.90), and puddings like lemon pudding or chocolate and orange mousse cake (from £3.20) from a changing menu, and you'll get a good breakfast if you stay. There's a big woodburning stove in an inglenook and a high shelf of plates in the right hand bar which leads into a little dining room.The room on the left has pews that came from a Methodist chapel in Liverpool, a fine oak bar counter, and an open fire. The dining room is no smoking. Well kept local Hobsons Best and Wadsworths 6X on handpump, interesting whiskies, decent wines by both glass and bottle, and lots of non-alcoholic drinks like old-fashioned lemonade, ginger beer, raspberry and ginger brew, fruit cordials and cappuccino, and no music – unless you count the deep-throated chimes of Big Bertha the fusee clock. Water comes from their own 190 foot well. There are some tables on a front terrace and the side grass, a herb garden and a wildlife pond. The building is in a fine position just by the Ippikins Rock viewpoint and there are lots of walks through the National Trust land that runs along the Edge. *(Recommended by Mike and Mary Carter, Gillian Jenkins, M Kershaw, John and Shirley Smith, Joy and Peter Heatherley, Gwen and Peter Andrews, Nigel Woolliscroft, Mr and Mrs G Lloyd, TOH, John Vale, Alan and Paula McCully, John Whitehead, Paul and Margaret Baker, Dr Stephen Feast, John Teign, Mike and Wena Stevenson, Catherine and Richard Preston, M Joyner, E A Froggatt, Mike Gorton, R and M Wallace, Chris and Ann Garnett, Chris Brace, SLC)*

Free house ~ Licensees Stephen and Di Waring ~ Real ale~ Bar food ~ (01746) 785678 ~ Children in eating area of bar and restaurant ~ Open 11.30-2.30, 6.30-11; 12-2.30, 6.30-10.30 Sun; closed 24-26 Dec ~ Bedrooms: £45S/£70S

WENTNOR SO3893 Map 6
Crown

Village and pub signposted (not very clearly) off A489 a few miles NW of junction with A49

Do persevere in finding this out-of-the-way 16th-c dining pub which is tucked away in a quiet village down the lanes. One end has a snug area with two elderly sofas, pictures and a dresser filled with Portmeirion 'Botanic Garden' china, but the main bar area, with beams, standing timbers, a good log fire, some nice big prints and a collection of china and cut glass, is filled with a variety of tables set for food. Under new licensees this might include sandwiches (from £1.75), soup (£2.30), spinach timbale (£3.25), oriental prawns (£3.50), ploughman's (£5.25), local sausages (£5.50), scampi (£6.50), baked vegetables in a creamy cheese sauce (£7.50), kidneys in sherry (£7.95), seafood crumble (£9.20) and Shrewsbury lamb with mint gravy (£10.20). There's also a cosy beamed no-smoking restaurant. Well kept Hobsons Best, Morlands Old Speckled Hen, Woods Shropshire Lad and Worthington on handpump, decent wines, very friendly helpful staff (the little spaniel's friendly, too); piped music. Booking is suggested for Sunday lunch – and the bedrooms tend to get booked quite a way ahead. There's a fine view of the Long Mynd from picnic-sets and old-fashioned teak garden seats on its neat back lawn. *(Recommended by S Phillips, John Whitehead, SLC, S W Ramin, TOH, Dr Phil Putwain, John Brightley)*

Free house ~ Licensees Simon and Joanna Beadman ~ Real ale ~ Bar food (lunchtimes only) ~ Restaurant ~ (01588) 650613 ~ Children in eating area of bar and restaurant till 9pm if eating ~ Open 12-3, 7(6.30 summer Sat)-11; 12-3, 7-10.30 Sun ~ Bedrooms: £27.50B/£53B

WHITCHURCH SJ5345 Map 7
Willey Moor Lock ◖ £

Actually just over the Cheshire border, the pub is signposted off A49 just under two miles N of Whitchurch

A jolly good and well liked pub this old lock keeper's cottage, with an interesting choice of well kept real ales, very welcoming landlady, a good mix of customers of all types and ages, and incredibly good value food. It's in an idyllic setting across a little footbridge over the Llangollen Canal and its rushing sidestream. Several neatly decorated low-beamed rooms have brick-based brocaded wall seats, stools and small chairs around dimpled copper and other tables, a large teapot collection and a decorative longcase clock, and two winter log fires. In addition to well kept Theakstons Best there are four guest beers like Abbeydale Archangel, Coach House Squires Gold, Hanby All Seasons and Weetwood Oast House Gold on handpump, and about 30 malt whiskies. Gaining a Bargain Award this year, bar food comes in generous helpings and includes sandwiches (from £1.75), filled baked potatoes (from £2.95), minced beef and onion pie (£3.75), ratatouille (£3.95), vegetable curry (£4.25), chicken curry (£4.50), battered cod (£4.95), lasagne or steak pie (£5), sirloin steak (£8), with puddings like chocolate fudge cake or spotted dick (from £1.70). Fruit machine, piped music, and several dogs and cats. There are tables under cocktail parasols on a terrace, and a children's play area with swings and slides in the garden. *(Recommended by Graham and Lynn Mason, SLC, Mr and Mrs F Carroll, Nigel Woolliscroft, David and Kathy Holcroft, Chris Gabbitas, Hugh McPhail, Mike and Wena Stevenson, John Cockell)*

Free house ~ Licensee Elsie Gilkes ~ Real ale ~ Bar food (12-2, 6(7 Sun)-9) ~ (01948) 663274 ~ Children away from bar ~ Open 12-2.30(2 winter), 6-11; 12-3(2.30 winter), 7-10.30 Sun

WISTANSTOW SO4385 Map 6
Plough ♀ ◖

Village signposted off A49 and A489 N of Craven Arms

The simple, light and airy interior of this brick built Woods Brewery tap has high rafters, cream walls and mahogany furniture on a russet turkey carpet. The delicious

Woods beers, Shropshire Lad, Special and some seasonal ones are produced in a separate building behind. They are kept here in perfect condition alongside a guest on handpump, as well as farm ciders, about 16 wines by the glass, and a fine display cabinet of bottled beers. Very well cooked home-made bar meals might include soup (£2.25), breaded hot peppers stuffed with cream cheese (£3.25), cheese spinach slice or chicken fillet marinated in lemon juice and peppercorns or steak and kidney pie (£5.95), venison sausage (£6.25), pork stroganoff (£8.25) and 10oz sirloin (£8.95). The games area has darts, pool, juke box and piped music. There are some tables under cocktail parasols outside. *(Recommended by Nigel Woolliscroft, Chris Gabbitas, Hugh McPhail, TOH, Derek and Sylvia Stephenson, John Whitehead, Stan and Hazel Allen, John and Esther Sprinkle, Gwen and Peter Andrews, KC, Jenny and Michael Back)*

Own brew ~ Tenant Kay Louise Edwards ~ Real ale ~ Bar food ~ (01588) 673251 ~ Children welcome ~ Open 12-3, 7-11(10.30 Sun)

Lucky Dip

Besides the fully inspected pubs, you might like to try these Lucky Dips recommended to us and described by readers (if you do, please send us reports):

All Stretton [SO4595]
Yew Tree [Shrewsbury Rd (B4370)]: Comfortable beamed bars and dining room, food inc interesting vegetarian choice, well kept Bass and Worthington BB, quiet piped music, bookable dining room; children welcome, friendly animals; can get busy, small village handy for Long Mynd *(John Brightley, Mr and Mrs R S Ray, TOH)*
Astley [SJ5319]
Dog in the Lane [A53 Shrewsbury—Shawbury]: Greenalls pub with Tetleys-related ales, reasonably priced good straightforward food, pleasantly relaxed beamed lounge with good brass, copper and china décor inc toby and whisky-water jugs; piped music; tables outside *(SLC)*
Bishops Castle [SO3289]
Six Bells [Church St]: Re-opened after closure in the early 90s, cosy bar with simple wooden benches, lounge with settles and comfortable armchairs, back brewery producing Big Nevs, Cloud Nine, Spring Forward, Castle Ruin and Old Recumbent, good food such as chicken pie, curry and fish served till it's finished; tables in nice outdoor area *(John and Esther Sprinkle, Sue Holland, Dave Webster, Pat and Tony Martin, the Didler)*
Boningale [SJ8102]
Horns [A464 NW of W'hampton]: Three friendly bars with changing ales such as Bass, Hook Norton and Old Hooky, wholesome nicely presented food inc good quickly served Sun lunch, panelled dining room *(E A Froggatt)*
Bridgnorth [SO7293]
☆ *Bear* [Northgate]: Well run busy two-room pub with low beams, mix of wall banquettes, padded chairs and one or two pews and settles, old notices and local pictures, french windows to small sheltered lawn with picnic-sets, good attractively priced food inc sandwiches, interesting specials, good fish and must-book Thurs gourmet nights, well kept changing ales such as Bathams Best, Greene King Abbot, Theakstons XB and Worfield JLK, good choice of wines; juke box; dogs welcome, disabled access, bedrooms *(SLC, CMW, JJW, BB,*

Graham Coates)
Black Boy [Cartway]: Good helpings of fairly priced good straightforward food inc Sun lunch, Banks's Bitter and Mild and Marstons Pedigree, real fire, daily paper, maybe quiet piped music, separate bar with darts and TV; seats out in small back yard with plants and canopy; live music nights *(CMW, JJW)*
Friars [St Marys St, Central Ct]: Small town pub in quaint location off courtyard, well kept beers, reasonably priced food, three real ales, good coffee; piped music; bedrooms *(CMW, JJW)*
Kings Head [Whitburn St]: 17th-c timbered coaching inn with pretty unusually patterned windows, good value food from cheap sandwiches and baked potatoes up, well kept Bass and Worthington, lounge with lots of brass, bar with machines and piped music; bedrooms *(CMW, JJW)*
Poachers Pocket: Surprising amount of decorations inc naughty (but not crude) jokes in family pub with excellent food, good young staff, well kept beer *(Bernie Adams)*
☆ *Punch Bowl* [B4364 towards Ludlow]: Recently refurbished beamed and panelled 17th-c country pub, friendly and comfortable, with good generous bar food inc fresh veg, good Sun carvery (best to book), beers inc Marstons Pedigree; piped music; bedrooms, superb views *(E A Froggatt, Eric and Shirley Briggs)*
☆ *Railwaymans Arms* [Severn Valley Stn, Hollybush Rd (off A458 towards Stourbridge)]: Good interesting real ales inc a Mild in converted waiting-room at Severn Valley steam railway terminus, bustling on summer days; simple summer snacks, coal fire, station nameplates, superb mirror over fireplace, seats out on platform; children welcome; the train to Kidderminster (another bar there) has an all-day bar and bookable Sun lunches *(Gwen and Peter Andrews, LYM, Nigel Woolliscroft)*
Bucknell [SO3574]
Baron of Beef [Chapel Lawn Rd; just off B4367 Knighton Rd]: Pleasant lounge with big open fire, rustic memorabilia inc grindstone and cider press, welcoming newish owners, good bar

food inc some interesting and vegetarian dishes, largish upstairs restaurant with own bar and popular w/e carvery, well kept beer such as Hobsons, decent house wines *(June and Mike Coleman)*

Burwarton [SO6285]

Boyne Arms [B4364 Bridgnorth—Ludlow]: Unassuming country local inside imposing Georgian building, generous good value home-made food, changing well kept ales such as Bass, Ind Coope Burton and Woods, cheery atmosphere; tables in garden *(E A Froggatt)*

Calverhall [SJ6037]

Old Jack [New St Lane]: Thriving village pub with friendly staff, good range of food in bar and separate dining area, beams and button-back banquettes *(M Joyner, B and M Robins)*

Chelmarsh [SO7288]

Bulls Head: Well restored group of buildings with good choice of good bar food, well kept beer esp cheap Banks's Mild, very friendly helpful staff; simple pretty bedrooms, lovely views, good walking country *(M G Lavery)*

Clun [SO3081]

☆ *Sun* [High St]: Friendly Tudor pub, timbers and beams, some sturdy antique furnishings, enormous open fire in flagstoned public bar, good food, well kept ales inc Banks's Bitter and Mild, Marstons Pedigree and Woods Special; children allowed in eating area, tables on sheltered back terrace; bedrooms, lovely village *(John Teign, E A Froggatt, BB, the Didler)*

Coalbrookdale [SJ6704]

☆ *Coalbrookdale Inn* [Wellington Rd, opp Museum of Iron]: Long flight of steps up to handsome dark brick 18th-c pub, simple, cheerful and bustling tiled-floor bar with local pictures, six or seven well kept changing ales such as Courage Directors, Enville, Everards Tiger, Freeminer Celestial Steam and Theakstons XB from square counter also serving rather smaller room set more for the good value often imaginative food (not Sun); good log fire, farm cider, country wines, good mix of people, piano, no piped music; dogs welcome, opens noon *(M Joyner, SLC, CMW, JJW, BB, Sam Samuells, Lynda Payton, Tracey Hamond, the Didler)*

Grove [Wellington Rd]: Large pub next to Museum of Iron, light and airy twin bars, one with sofas, other with green furniture, downstairs restaurant, good menu, fast friendly service, Marstons, Morlands Old Speckled Hen and a guest beer, friendly helpful landlord; piped music; back garden *(SLC)*

Coalport [SJ6903]

☆ *Boat* [Salthouse Rd, Jackfield; nr Mawes Craft Centre, over footbridge by chinaworks museum]: Cosy 18th-c quarry-tiled bar close enough to the river sometimes to have had floods, coal fire in lovely range, good food inc local free-range pork, game and cheeses and good value Sun lunch, well kept, Banks's Bitter and Mild, Camerons and Marstons, Weston's farm cider, darts; summer barbecues on big tree-shaded lawn, in delightful part of Severn Gorge *(BB, Dr Steve Hugh, the Didler, N L Jones, B J Harding)*

Corfton [SO4985]

Sun [B4368 Much Wenlock—Craven Arms]: Country local with reasonably priced food inc children's, lots of vegetarian, fish and bargain Sun lunch, well kept Flowers, pleasant lounge with interesting prints and a covered well, lively bar, dining room; tables on terrace and in good-sized garden with good play area; piped music; open all day, disabled access throughout *(Dr B and Mrs P B Baker)*

Coton [SJ5234]

Bull & Dog [Tilstock Rd; B5476 Wem—Whitchurch]: Black and white open-plan Greenalls pub with screened-off dining area, good value food running up to bass and mixed grills, Boddingtons and Greenalls, pleasant service; piped music *(Sue and Bob Ward, SLC)*

Craven Arms [SO4383]

☆ *Stokesay Castle Hotel* [School Rd (B4368, just off A49)]: Cheerful bar and small cosy panelled restaurant, very clean and well cared for under friendly new management (who have an excellent GPG track record), with good imaginative modern cooking, well kept beer, good wines; attractive comfortable bedrooms with lots of little extras, nice big garden *(Michael Walsh, Margaret Measures and family, Alan and Sheila Hart)*

Ellerdine Heath [SJ6122]

Royal Oak: Happy atmosphere (maybe lots of children), well priced ales such as Brains SA, Hanby Drawwell, Hobsons Best and Woods Shropshire Lad, simple choice of good value food (not Tues) from sandwiches up; pool room, TV, piped music; play area, open all day Sat *(SLC)*

Ellesmere [SJ4035]

☆ *Black Lion* [Scotland St; back car park on A495]: Good value simple cheap substantial food all day inc bargains for children and OAPs, pleasantly relaxed and well run bar off tiled entrance corridor, interesting décor and some nice unusual features, quiet and comfortable roomy dining room, cheery service, well kept Marstons Bitter, Pedigree and Head Brewers Choice; piped music; bedrooms, not far from canal wharf *(BB, Mr and Mrs C Gibson)*

Halfway House [SJ3411]

Seven Stars [A458 Shrewsbury—Welshpool]: Spotless and unspoilt, like a private house; very small bar, Burtonwood Best and Mild tapped from casks in the friendly licensees' kitchen area *(the Didler)*

Hampton Loade [SO7586]

☆ *Lion*: Warm and welcoming 17th-c stripped-stone inn tucked away down pot-holed lane, in very attractive spot overlooking River Severn; open fires, friendly efficient staff, good unusual food inc generous Sun lunch, well kept Hook Norton Best and one or two guest beers usually inc local Enville, country wines, two bars, lounge, two dining rooms behind smaller bar with log fire, restaurant for booked meals; if anything the well worn-in interior adds to the cosy feel; very busy in summer or when Severn Valley Rly has weekend steam spectaculars (quaint ferry crossing to stn), quiet otherwise;

well behaved children welcome if eating lunchtime (or if booked to dine evening), dogs welcome, picnic-sets outside, good day-ticket fishing; cl Mon exc bank hols, cl weekday lunchtimes Oct-Apr exc Christmas *(Tracey Hamond, David and Kathy Holcroft, John Cumberland, Nigel Woolliscroft)*

Harley [SJ5901]
Plume of Feathers [A458 NW of Much Wenlock]: Spacious and popular beamed pub with big open fire, reasonably priced food inc particularly good steak and kidney pie, well kept Scottish Courage and guest ales, good welcoming service even when busy, darts, piped music (Sun evening live); dining room, tables outside; bedrooms with own baths *(June and Mike Coleman, E A Froggatt)*

Hodnet [SJ6128]
☆ *Bear* [Drayton Rd (A53)]: Busy but relaxed 16th-c pub with good range of reasonably priced well presented food from sandwiches up inc vegetarian, Scottish Courage ales, friendly helpful service; sofas and easy chairs in foyer, roomy refurbished bar with good solid furnishings and log fire, restaurant with corner alcove with glass-tile floor over unusual sunken garden in former bear pit; open all day, children welcome (high chairs and child-size cutlery), six good value comfortable bedrooms, opp Hodnet Hall gardens and handy for Hawkstone Park *(G Washington, Neil and Anita Christopher, Olive and Ray Hebson, SLC, Mr and Mrs F Carroll)*

Hopton Wafers [SO6476]
☆ *Crown* [A4117 Kidderminster—Ludlow]: Newish management doing well in friendly and attractive old creeper-covered inn with thriving relaxed atmosphere in warmly decorated beamed dining bar with big inglenook fire and woodburner, nice mix of individually chosen tables and chairs, short but interesting choice of good generous well prepared good food, well kept real ales inc Marstons Pedigree and one brewed for the pub, good house wines, welcoming efficient service, restaurant with no-smoking area; tables out on terraces and in garden running down to pond and stream with geese and ducks, provision for children (and they'll open a door at the back for wheelchair access), comfortable and pretty timbered bedrooms *(LYM, M Downes, Mr and Mrs Donald Anderson, Barbara and Alan Mence, George Atkinson, John Whitehead)*

Ironbridge [SJ6704]
Bird in Hand [Waterloo St]: Lovely position above wooded gorge, older than the iron bridge; friendly landlord, good choice of food including vegetarian; comfortable bedrooms *(Mrs P Pearce)*
Golden Ball [Wesley Rd, off Madeley Hill]: Friendly partly Elizabethan local with helpful landlord, well kept Courage Directors, Marstons Pedigree, Ruddles and a guest beer, competitively priced food inc good vegetarian choice, real fire, pleasant terraced walk down to river; children welcome, comfortable bedrooms *(Christopher Glasson, Neil and Anita Christopher, MLR)*

☆ *Malthouse* [Wharfage]: Clean, comfortable and relaxed, with refreshing blue, yellow and aubergine décor, welcoming attentive young licensees and staff, well kept beer, creative food (not Sun evening) from sandwiches up using fresh produce in bar and restaurant, reasonable prices; bedrooms planned *(M Joyner, Peter and Janice Blackstaffe)*
Meadow [Buildwas Rd]: Popular and welcoming Severnside dining pub done up with old-fashioned beamery, cigarette cards, tasteful prints and brasses; wide choice of good value generous freshly prepared food in lounge and downstairs restaurant, quick service, well kept Scottish Courage ales and Marstons Pedigree, decent wines; pretty waterside garden *(SLC, E A Froggatt)*
☆ *New Inn* [Blists Hill Open Air Museum – follow brown museum sign from M54 exit 4, or A442]: Rebuilt Victorian pub in this good heritage museum's re-created working Victorian community (shares its opening hours); informative licensees and friendly staff in period dress, well kept Banks's Bitter and Mild, pewter measure of mother's ruin for 2½d (money from nearby bank), good pasties, gas lighting, traditional games, good generous home cooking in upstairs tearoom; back yard with hens, pigeon coop, maybe children in costume playing hopscotch and skipping; children welcome *(CMJ, JJW, LYM, Sam Samuells, Lynda Payton, John and Esther Sprinkle)*

Kemberton [SJ7204]
Masons Arms: Popular village local with super views, Greenalls and guest beers, good value food, friendly staff, tables in garden; busy weekday lunchtimes with Telford businessmen *(M Joyner)*

Leebotwood [SO4798]
☆ *Pound* [A49 Church Stretton—Shrewsbury]: Attractive and comfortable beamed and thatched 16th-c pub, good choice of well presented good value food inc fresh fish, lots of specials and separately served veg in bar and big well laid-out no-smoking restaurant, well kept ales inc Morlands Old Speckled Hen and Woods Shropshire Lad, friendly efficient staff, tables in garden *(TOH, Mrs M A Watkins, David and Ann Knowles)*

Little Stretton [SO4392]
Green Dragon [village well signed off A49]: Well kept Tetleys, Wadworths 6X, Woods Shropshire Lad and quickly changing guest beers, reasonably priced straightforward food from good baguettes up, cheap house wine, malt whiskies, children in eating area and restaurant; tables outside, handy for Cardingmill Valley (NT) and Long Mynd *(Clive Petts, R J Bland)*
Ragleth [village well signed off A49]: Neatly kept bay-windowed lounge, walkers and dogs welcome in brick-and-tile-floored bar with huge inglenook, wide range of reasonably priced home-made food from sandwiches to steaks, quick service, well kept ales such as Morlands Old Speckled Hen and Charles Wells Bombardier, farm cider, tables on lawn by tulip

tree; children welcome, restaurant *(Tony and Wendy Hobden, LYM)*

Llanfair Waterdine [SO2476]

Red Lion [signed from B4355; turn left after bridge]: Old inn nicely set nr good stretch of Offa's Dyke, heavy-beamed turkey-carpeted rambling lounge bar with cosy alcoves and woodburner, small black-beamed and flagstoned tap room with traditional games, usual food from lunchtime sandwiches up, Marstons Pedigree and Wye Valley Dorothy Goodbody under light blanket pressure, good wine list, comfortable back restaurant looking down to River Teme (the Wales border); children in eating area, comfortable bedrooms, cl Tues *(LYM, TOH)*

Loppington [SJ4729]

Dickin Arms [B4397]: Straightforward two-bar country local in pretty village, open fire, Bass, Wadworths and Youngers, usual food inc Sun lunch, dining room; babies and dogs welcome, play area outside; pretty village *(Mr and Mrs F Carroll, Lorna and Howard Lambert)*

Ludlow [SO5175]

Feathers [Bull Ring]: Superb timbered building, striking inside too with Jacobean panelling and carving, fine period furnishings; sadly you'll probably be diverted to a less distinguished more modern side bar for the good sandwiches and other decent bar food, or a casual drink – well kept Flowers Original and Wadworths 6X; pleasant service, restaurant, good parking; comfortable bedrooms, not cheap *(Basil Minson, G Washington, JP, PP, E A Froggatt, LYM)*

Rose & Crown [Church St, behind Buttercross]: Small brightly lit Greenalls pub with its own beers, standard reasonably priced food, smart friendly staff *(Tony and Wendy Hobden)*

Wheatsheaf [Lower Broad St]: Traditional 17th-c beamed pub spectacularly built into medieval town gate, Bass, M&B Brew XI and Ruddles County, choice of farm ciders, restaurant; attractive bedrooms, warm and comfortable *(W W Burke)*

Madeley [SJ6904]

All Nations [Coalport Rd]: Spartan but friendly one-bar pub brewing its own distinctive well priced pale ale since the 1930s; good value lunchtime sandwiches, handy for Blists Hill *(Pete Baker, JP, PP, the Didler)*

Market Drayton [SJ6734]

Gingerbread Man [northern outskirts]: Recently opened large Tom Cobleigh family pub with old-fashioned country-style décor, lots of beams and wood, no-smoking areas, decent food inc bargains and good children's menu, friendly efficient staff, well kept Bass, Boddingtons and Marstons Pedigree, disabled access; play areas indoors and out, open all day *(Richard Lewis, SLC)*

Morville [SO6794]

Acton Arms [A458 Bridgnorth—Shrewsbury]: Good home-made food in dining lounge, well kept Banks's and sensibly priced wines, big attractive garden *(E A Froggatt)*

Newcastle [SO2582]

☆ *Crown* [B4368 Clun—Newtown]: Friendly and

pretty village pub with good mix of locals and campers, good value usual food in quiet and quite spacious lounge bar with log fire and piped music, lively locals' bar with darts, pool and so forth in games room, well kept Tetleys, good coffee, decent wines, efficient service, friendly great dane called Bruno; tables outside; charming well equipped bedrooms, good breakfast, attractive walks *(M and A Leach, LYM, Philip and Katherine Carpenter)*

Oswestry [SJ2929]

Wynnstay [Church St]: Friendly welcome, good food from interesting baguettes up, very spacious and comfortable rather Home Counties-feel bar, Marstons Pedigree; children's area, tables outside, nice bedrooms, camp site – a comfortable secluded respite from Offa's Dyke Path; cl Tues *(Richard C Morgan)*

Picklescott [SO4399]

☆ *Bottle & Glass* [off A49 N of Church Stretton]: Warmly welcoming unspoilt early 17th-c country local tucked away in delightful spot below N end of Long Mynd, pleasant quarry-tiled bar and lounge/restaurant, two log fires, well kept Bass, Worthington and Hook Norton Best, good value food esp home-made pies; quiet in winter, busy summer – wise to book for food then, esp Sun lunch; bedrooms *(Janet and Peter Race, TOH, David and Kathy Holcroft, SLC)*

Queens Head [SJ3427]

☆ *Queens Head* [just off A5 SE of Oswestry, towards Nesscliffe]: Emphasis on good value food (all day Fri and w/e) from speciality sandwiches to lots of fish and steaks, well kept Theakstons Best, XB and Old Peculier with a guest such as Woods, friendly very efficient staff, two dining areas with roaring coal fires, pleasant conservatory; garden by restored Montgomery Canal, country walks *(Mr and Mrs F Carroll, SLC, David and Kathy Holcroft)*

Shrewsbury [SJ4912]

Beaten Track [Old Potts Way]: New Tom Cobleigh family dining pub complete with play barn, decent food and service *(SLC)*

☆ *Boathouse* [New St/Quarry Park; leaving centre via Welsh Bridge/A488 turn into Port Hill Rd]: Comfortably modernised Whitbreads Hogshead in lovely position by footbridge to Severn park, river views from long lounge bar, tables out on sheltered terrace and rose lawn; well kept changing ales such as Black Sheep, Boddingtons, Castle Eden, Fullers London Pride and Whitbreads Fuggles, friendly helpful staff, good range of standard food, bare boards, low ceilings, darts in smaller bar; children welcome, summer barbecues, popular with young people evening; open all day *(R J Bland, John and Esther Sprinkle, Richard Lewis, G Coates, J A Barker, M Joyner, LYM)*

Castle Vaults [Castle Gates]: After the landlord's retirement in spring 1999 this friendly old timbered local with its interesting food and drinks has sadly turned into yet another faux-Irish theme bar called Bradys *(Richard Lewis, SLC)*

Coach & Horses [Swan Hill/Cross Hill]: Small unspoilt Victorian pub brewing its own

Goodalls ale, also well kept Bass and an interesting guest beer; pine-panelled bar, two comfortable lounge areas, good home-made lunchtime food, attentive service, back restaurant with carvery; pretty flower boxes outside *(Mr and Mrs B Craig, J A Barker, SLC, David and Kathy Holcroft)*

Cromwells [Dogpole]: Smallish dim-lit pubby bar attached to hotel, Marstons, Ruddles and an interesting guest such as Hanby All Seasons, good value food from baguettes up through bangers and mash or game pie, pleasant staff, decent wines, raised garden and terrace behind; piped music; open all day Sat; nice bedrooms sharing bathrooms *(R J Bland, SLC, Betty Petheram, J A Barker, Peg Cuskley)*

Golden Cross [Princess St]: Attractive partly Tudor hotel with two bars, one with a comfortable no-smoking area, short choice of good cheap lunchtime food inc very good steak sandwich and a vegetarian dish, three well kept beers, pleasant helpful staff; four reasonably priced and good value bedrooms *(J A Barker)*

Loggerheads [Church St]: Small pub refurbished in old style by Banks's, back panelled smoke room with scrubbed-top tables, high-backed settles and real fire, three other rooms with lots of prints, flagstones and bare boards, quaint linking corridors, food all day Mon-Sat till 6, friendly staff and locals, well kept Bitter, Mild, Camerons Strongarm and a guest such as Bass, darts, dominoes, poetry society *(SLC, Richard Lewis, J A Barker, the Didler)*

☆ *M A D O'Rourkes Dun Cow Pie Shop* [Abbey Foregate]: Zany but homely décor, good range of good value food, friendly helpful staff, lots of jugs hanging from ceiling and enjoyably silly meat-pie and pig's-head memorabilia on walls, well kept Tetleys-related ales and Lumphammer, sharply trained attentive staff; attractive timber-framed building with enormous antique model cow on porch *(SLC, M Joyner, BB)*

Old Post Office [off Milk St almost opp Wheatsheaf, nr St Julians Craft Centre]: Big split-level pub with plenty of bric-a-brac and brass, good atmosphere, good value food from heated counter, Marstons ales; piped music *(Marjorie and David Lamb, J A Barker)*

Ruby Red Tap House [St Juliens]: A Banks's all-wood chain ale house, L-shaped bar with raised end drinking area, tile and wood floors, panelled dado, beamery, mix of barrel and ordinary tables, one alcove with cinema seats, big mirror and curtain; a guest beer such as Wychwood Rugby Special, good value food (not Sat evening); disabled access possible *(G Coates)*

Shrewsbury [Bridge Pl, Old Welsh Bridge]: First Wetherspoons conversion to have bedrooms, otherwise typical – part open plan, some cubicles, no-smoking area, no music, food all day, good choice of well kept beer, good service; quiet at lunchtime, busy evening *(SLC)*

☆ *Three Fishes* [Fish St]: Extensively refurbished heavy-beamed timbered pub, no smoking throughout – very clean and fresh; well kept

changing ales such as Bass, Batemans XB, Fullers London Pride, Marstons Pedigree and Pridewood, Salopian Minsterley and Timothy Taylor Landlord, lunchtime food, lots of interesting photographs, prints and bric-a-brac, friendly quick service; open all day, cl Sun *(SLC, John and Joan Wyatt, LYM, Richard Lewis, M Joyner, David and Kathy Holcroft, John Whitehead)*

Wheatsheaf [High St]: Comfortable open-plan beamed lounge, bar food, well kept Banks's, pleasant helpful staff; games machine, TV, juke box; open all day Mon-Sat *(J A Barker)*

Stanton upon Hine Heath [SJ5724]

Stanton Arms: Plain pub with stools around small bar tables, Boddingtons, friendly cheerful service, surprisingly wide choice of good food in comfortable dining room; children welcome, tables out on terrace and lawn *(Mr and Mrs C Roberts)*

Stiperstones [SJ3600]

☆ *Stiperstones Inn* [signed off A488 S of Minsterley; OS Sheet 126 map ref 364005]: Very good value simple food served all day, inc vegetarian and their famous local whinberry pie, in welcoming little modernised lounge bar with comfortable leatherette wall banquettes, lots of brassware on ply-panelled walls, well kept Boddingtons, Flowers IPA and Woods Parish, good service, darts in plainer public bar, maybe unobtrusive piped music; restaurant, tables outside; clean basic cheap bedrooms, good breakfast, open all day; good walking *(BB, E A Froggatt, SLC)*

Stottesdon [SO6783]

Fox & Hounds: Classic plain village local which brews its own beer inc Fox & Hounds Bostin Bitter, Gobstopper and Wust Bitter; pork pies; cl weekday lunchtimes *(anon)*

Telford [SJ6710]

Bridge Builder [Wrekin Retail Park]: Big split-level Tom Cobleigh family dining pub, bridge-theme bric-a-brac, decent food, good service, Boddingtons, Marstons Pedigree and Worthington BB, play barn; piped music throughout *(SLC)*

Euston Way: Useful and comfortable new Brewers Way dining pub, well kept Wadworths 6X, reliable food, friendly young helpful staff, tolerable piped music; good bedrooms in adjacent Travel Inn *(Mr and Mrs C Roberts)*

Uckington [SJ5810]

Horseshoes [B5061 E of Atcham]: Food all day and good friendly service in big Brewers Fayre family dining pub with Whitbreads-related ales, children's eating area and play area *(M Joyner)*

Wall under Heywood [SO5093]

Plough: Popular for good helpings of standard food in large, clean and comfortable bar and dining extension, good range of well kept beers inc Marstons Pedigree, tables in garden *(TOH)*

Welsh Frankton [SJ3732]

Narrow Boat [A495 Ellesmere—Oswestry; by Shrops Union Canal]: Well kept Tetleys and three changing guest beers, cheap cheerful food, pleasant small waterside garden; much used by owners of boats moored nearby *(Margaret Mason, David Thompson)*

Weston Heath [SJ7713]
Countess's Arms: Large two-level pub with well kept Banks's Original, Boddingtons, Marstons Pedigree and Morlands Old Speckled Hen, 30 wines by the glass, wide choice of good interesting largely modern food, children's area, barbecue, disabled facilities; open all day till midnight *(Russell J Allen)*

Whitchurch [SJ5842]
Horse & Jockey [Church St]: Three or four cosy and comfortable dining areas with good value carefully prepared food from interesting starters and light dishes to wide choice of main dishes running up to duck and bass *(Sue and Bob Ward)*

Whittington [SJ3331]
Olde Boot [A495 Ellesmcrc rd, just off A5]: Panelled lounge with copper-topped tables and lots of brass, well kept Robinsons Best, Hatters Mild and a guest such as Hartleys XB, good value food inc popular Sun roast and OAP specials Mon and Tues night, friendly staff, small restaurant area, TV and games in popular friendly bar; bedrooms, attractive spot opp 13th-c castle *(Albert and Margaret Horton)*

Woore [SJ7342]
Coopers Arms [Nantwich Rd]: Wide variety of traditional country food inc house speciality steak and kidney pie in long room with coopering memorabilia *(Jennie Aldren)*

☆ *Falcon* [London Rd (A51)]: Particularly hospitable licensees and polite young staff, wide choice of tasty nicely presented home-made food inc lots of fish (best to book restaurant, esp weekends), well kept Ansells Mild and Marstons Bitter and Pedigree, two comfortable cottagey bars, pristine copper-topped tables, interesting prints; colourful hanging baskets, bookmakers' in grounds, nr Bridgemere Garden World *(Sue Holland, Dave Webster, Richard Gibbs, E G Parish, Paul and Maggie Baker)*

Swan [London Rd (A51)]: Increasingly popular locally for good food inc immaculate veg; smart efficient service, neat public bar *(Sue Holland, Dave Webster)*

Yorton [SJ5023]
Railway: Same family for over 60 years, friendly and chatty mother and daughter, unchanging atmosphere, simple cosy bar with coal fire, big comfortable lounge with fishing trophies, well kept Wadworths 6X, Woods Parish, Special and Shropshire Lad on handpump, a guest beer tapped from the cask, pub games – no piped music or machines, no food *(the Didler)*

Please keep sending us reports. We rely on readers for news of new discoveries, and particularly for news of changes – however slight – at the fully described pubs. No stamp needed: The Good Pub Guide, FREEPOST TN1569, Wadhurst, E Sussex TN5 7BR.

Somerset

Lovely old buildings in unspoilt countryside, skittle alleys, farm ciders, glowingly friendly licensees – all these things spring to mind when we think of Somerset pubs, perhaps coming gloriously together in a proper local that at the same time does good food and has a genuine welcome for passing visitors. Somerset pubs currently on top form include the Globe at Appley (nice mix of good food with unspoilt country-pub atmosphere) the Three Horseshoes at Batcombe (a thriving mix of eaters and drinkers, in charming surroundings – a new entry this year), the civilised and relaxing George in Castle Cary (good new licensee), the tucked-away Crown at Catcott (this quiet country local is another newcomer to the Guide), the Crown at Churchill (an unspoilt country drinking pub, good simple food too), the nicely individual Black Horse at Clapton in Gordano, the Ring o' Bells at Compton Martin (a good family pub), the Strode Arms at Cranmore (very popular for food), the friendly and very well run New Inn at Dowlish Wake (good food), the cheerful and relaxed Hungerford Arms at Farleigh Hungerford (yet another new entry), the Inn at Freshford (back in these pages after a break of several years), the Kingsdon Inn at Kingsdon (popular new licensees since it was last in the Guide, really good food these days), the welcoming and attractive Kings Arms at Litton, the bustling and enjoyable Royal Oak at Luxborough, the superbly run Notley Arms at Monksilver (good imaginative reasonably priced food; near the top of our very short private list of Pubs We Wish Were Just Down Our Road), the George at Norton St Philip (a magnificent restoration by Wadworths of this remarkable old building; one of our finds of the year and a good place to stay in), the Rose & Crown at Stoke St Gregory (in the same good hands for 20 years now), the Blue Ball at Triscombe (made over by a new landlord since it was last in the Guide, foody as well as friendly now), the Cotley at Wambrook (an excellent country inn), and yet another new entry, the comfortable and unusual 16th-c City Arms in Wells (good interesting food). With so many really strong new entries here this year, it's perhaps not entirely surprising that one of them, the Blue Ball at Triscombe, carries off our award of Somerset Dining Pub of the Year. The Lucky Dip section at the end of the chapter has so many starred entries this year that it's worth picking out some specially notable pubs: the Ring o' Bells at Ashcott, Square & Compass at Ashill, Princes Motto at Barrow Gurney, Star in Bath, Brewery Tap and Hope & Anchor in Bristol, Pony & Trap at Chew Magna, Manor House at Ditcheat, Crown at Exford, Bull at Hardway, Wheelwrights Arms at Monkton Combe, Lord Nelson at Norton sub Hamdon, Royal Oak at Over Stratton, Swan at Rowberrow, Montague at Shepton Montague, Globe in Somerton, White Hart at Trudoxhill, Fountain in Wells and Crossways at West Huntspill. Drinks prices in Somerset are close to the national average. Often, we found the cheapest beer a pub could offer came from Butcombe, a small local brewery, with Exmoor and Cotleigh (also local) making a significant contribution, and Otter (from Devon) turning up increasingly. Other interesting local brews include Smiles, Cottage, RCH and Oakhill; all these could be found at or below average prices.

APPLEY ST0621 Map 1
Globe

Hamlet signposted from the network of back roads between A361 and A38, W of B3187 and W of Milverton and Wellington; OS sheet 181 map reference 072215

This is a thoroughly good pub – nicely unimproved with a relaxed, chatty atmosphere, and a good mix of customers. The simple beamed front room has benches and a built-in settle, bare wood tables on the brick floor, and pictures of magpies, and there's a further room with easy chairs and other more traditional ones, open fires, a collection of model cars, and *Titanic* pictures; alley skittles. Generous helpings of cheerfully served, good bar food include sandwiches, home-made soup (£2.50), mushrooms in cream, garlic and horseradish (£3.50), a light cold egg pancake filled with prawns, celery and pineapple in marie rose sauce (£5), home-made steak and kidney pie in stout or savoury vegetable crumble (£6.25), steaks (from (£8.25), fresh salmon with chive, white wine and cream sauce (£8.50), chicken breast with pine nuts, bacon, raisins and apricots with a madeira sauce (£9.25), garlic king prawns (£11.75), children's dishes (from £3.25; some adult dishes can be served as half-helpings), and roast Sunday beef (£5.75). The restaurant is no smoking. A stone-flagged entry corridor leads to a serving hatch from where Cotleigh Tawny and guests like Butcombe Bitter, Cotleigh Barn Owl, and Teignworthy Reel Ale and Spring Tide are kept on handpump; summer farm cider. Seats, climbing frame and swings outside in the garden; the path opposite leads eventually to the River Tone. *(Recommended by S G N Bennett, Adrian and Jane Tierney-Jones, R D and C M Hillman, S Richardson, James Flory, JP, PP, Richard and Margaret Peers, the Didler, John and Fiona McIlwain)*

Free house ~ Licensees A W and E J Burt, R and J Morris ~ Real ale ~ Bar food (till 10pm) ~ Restaurant ~ (01823) 672327 ~ Children welcome ~ Open 11-3, 6.30-11; 12-3, 7-10.30 Sun; closed Mon lunchtime except bank hols

ASHCOTT ST4336 Map 1
Ashcott Inn

A39 about 6 miles W of Glastonbury

This pleasant old pub has an attractive bar with stripped stone walls and beams, some interesting old-fashioned seats among more conventional ones, a mix of oak and elm and other tables, and a log-effect gas fire in its sturdy chimney. Bar food includes home-made soup (£2.25), home-made chicken liver pâté (£3.45), mushrooms and bacon au gratin (£3.75), filled french bread (from £3.95), ploughman's (£4.25), cider baked ham with two eggs (£5.45), oriental vegetable stir fry (£6.25), beef in ale pie (£6.50), steaks (from £6.95), grilled plaice (£7.50), lamb steak with rosemary and redcurrant sauce (£9.25), and daily specials; the restaurant is mostly no smoking. Butcombe Bitter and guest beers like Flowers Original or Wadworths 6X on handpump kept under light blanket pressure; cribbage, dominoes, shove-ha'penny, fruit machine, alley skittles, and piped music. Seats on the terrace, and a pretty walled garden with children's adventure play areas. *(Recommended by K H Frostick, Christopher and Mary Thomas, Dr and Mrs B D Smith, Martyn and Anna Carey, Lyn and Geoff Hallchurch)*

Heavitree ~ Managers Jon and Helen Endacott ~ Real ale ~ Bar food ~ Restaurant ~ (01458) 210282 ~ Children in restaurant ~ Open 11-11; 12-10.30 Sun; 11-3, 5-11 in winter

BATCOMBE ST6838 Map 2
Three Horseshoes ♦ ♀

Village signposted off A359 Bruton—Frome

By 7.30pm on our inspection visit, this honey stone, slate-roofed pub was almost full, with many people already enjoying the very good food – though there were several people drinking at the bar who obviously did not feel out of place. The longish narrow main room has cream-painted beams and planks, ivy-stencils and

attractive artificial ivy, fruit and flowers decorations, a few naïve cow and farm
animal paintings on the lightly ragged dark pink walls, some built-in cushioned
window seats and stripy-cushioned solid chairs around a nice mix of old tables,
candles in black spiral holders, two clocking-in clocks, and a woodburning stove at
one end with a big open fire at the other; there's a plain tiled room at the back on
the left with more straightforward furniture. Good, popular bar food includes baked
goat's cheese salad with pine nuts and pesto (£3.95), mussels cooked with bacon,
onion, garlic and cream (£4.25), pork and wild mushroom sausages with mash and
apple and sage gravy (£6.95), salmon fishcakes with a chive cream sauce (£7.95),
and puddings like crème brûlée or sticky toffee pudding (£3.50). The stripped stone
dining room is pretty. Well kept Adnams, Butcombe Bitter, and Wadworths 6X, and
a good choice of wines by the glass. The back terrace has picnic-sets with more on
the grass, and a big well equipped play area. The pub is on a quiet village lane by the
church which has a very striking tower. *(Recommended by Jill Bickerton)*

*Free house ~ Licensees Mr and Mrs Lethbridge ~ Real ale ~ Bar food (till 10pm at
weekends) ~ Restaurant ~ (01749) 850359 ~ Open 12-3, 6.30-11; 12-3, 7-10.30 Sun*

BATH ST7464 Map 2
Old Green Tree

12 Green St

The three little oak-panelled rooms in this genuinely unspoilt, friendly pub include a
comfortable lounge on the left as you go in, its walls decorated with wartime aircraft
pictures, and a no-smoking back bar; it can get pretty packed at peak times. The big
skylight lightens things up attractively. Lunchtime bar food includes soup (£3),
popular smoked trout open sandwich, tasty salads or bangers and mash (£4.80), and
daily specials such as steak and kidney pie, rabbit terrine, scrambled eggs with
prawns, vegetable gratin, and Spanish meatballs. There are usually five well kept
beers on handpump such as Bath SPA, Oakhill Black Magic, RCH Pitchfork, Uley
Hogshead, and Wickwar Brand Oak Bitter, several few malt whiskies, a nice little
wine list with helpful notes and 12 wines by the glass, a perry on draught, winter hot
toddies, a proper pimms, and good coffee; chess, backgammon, shut the box, Jenga.
The gents', though good, are down steep steps. No children. *(Recommended by Val
Stevenson, Rob Holmes, D Irving, R Huggins, E McCall, T McLean, J Sheldon, Jack and Philip
Paxton, Colin and Peggy Wilshire, Dr and Mrs A K Clarke, Nick J Lawless, Stephen, Julie and
Hayley Brown, Matt Natton, Douglas Caiger, JP, PP, David Wood, Richard and Ann Higgs,
Simon and Amanda Southwell, Susan and Nigel Wilson, Rob Holt)*

*Free house ~ Licensees Nick Luke and Sarah Le Feure ~ Real ale ~ Bar food
(lunchtime) ~ (01225) 448259 ~ Open 11-11; 7-10.30 Sun; closed Sun lunchtime;
25/26 Dec, 1 Jan*

BECKINGTON ST8051 Map 2
Woolpack

Off A36 Bath Rd/Warminster Rd

This old stone building has a rather modern interior – spacious and light and rather
appropriate. The attractive no-smoking lounge has antique furnishings and pictures,
a lively flagstoned public bar has stripped pine tables and a good log fire, and there's
also a cosy no-smoking dining room. Good, if pricy bar food under another new
licensee includes soup (from £3), sandwiches (from £4), ploughman's (£6.50), steak
and kidney pie (£6.50), and daily specials such as a salad of warm artichoke with
marinated tuna loin glazed with goat's cheese (£4.95), pâté campagne with red onion
confit (£5.50), ragoût of lamb sweetbreads and prawns with a sesame seed crust
(£5.95), stuffed saddle of young rabbit with green lentils and rosemary jus (£11.50),
savarin of pink trout with caramelised scallops and braised asparagus (£14.75), fillet
of venison, sweet red cabbage, cassis and blueberry sauce (£15.95), roasted fillet of
turbot on dried fennel, ginger and caper beurre blanc (£16.95), and puddings like
snow eggs with roasted apples or chocolate terrine with a duo of sauces (£4.95).
Well kept Courage Directors, Greene King IPA, and Wadworths 6X on handpump.

(Recommended by Edward Leetham, Nancy Cleave, Mrs S Evans, Dr R H Hardwick, Dr and Mrs A K Clarke, Ian Phillips)

Old English Inns ~ Managers Neil and Alison Ferguson ~ Real ale ~ Bar food ~ Restaurant ~ (01373) 831244 ~ Children in conservatory ~ Open 11-11; 12-10.30 Sun ~ Bedrooms: £55B/£65B

BRADLEY GREEN ST2538 Map 1

Malt Shovel

Pub signposted from A39 W of Bridgwater, near Cannington; though Bradley Green is shown on road maps, if you're booking the postal address is Blackmoor Lane, Cannington, BRIDGWATER, Somerset TA5 2NE; note that there is another different Malt Shovel on this main road, three miles nearer Bridgwater

Nicely tucked away in a remote hamlet, this pleasant and friendly pub has a homely no-frills main bar with window seats, some functional modern elm country chairs and sturdy modern winged high-backed settles around wooden tables, various boating photographs, and a black kettle standing on a giant fossil by the woodburning stove. There's also a tiny snug with white walls and black beams, a solid oak bar counter with a natural stone front, and red tiled floor. Decent bar food includes lunchtime sandwiches (£1.95, crusty rolls £2.45) and ploughman's (from £3.60), as well as home-made smoked haddock cheesy bake (£4.60), filled baked potatoes (£4.80), mushroom stroganoff (£4.95), home-made steak and kidney pie (£5.75), chicken breast in lemon and tarragon with a white wine and cream sauce (£7.95), and steaks (from £9.25). Well kept Butcombe Bitter, Exmoor Fox, and two guest beers on handpump, farm cider, and a fair choice of wines by the glass; sizeable skittle alley, dominoes, cribbage, and piped music. The family room opens on to the garden, where there are picnic-sets and a fish pond. No dogs inside. West of the pub, Blackmore Farm is a striking medieval building. *(Recommended by Richard Gibbs, JCW, Maysie Thompson, B and K Hypher, S H Godsell, H Beck, G W A Pearce)*

Free house ~ Licensees R and F Beverley & P and S Monger ~ Real ale ~ Bar food ~ Restaurant ~ (01278) 653432 ~ Children in restaurant and family room ~ Open 11.30-2.30(3 Sat), 6.30-11; 12-3, 7-10.30 Sun; closed winter Sun evenings ~ Bedrooms: £26.50B/£38B

BRISTOL ST5872 Map 2

Highbury Vaults £

St Michaels Hill, Cotham; main road out to Cotham from inner ring dual carriageway

At busy times, this town pub has a fine buoyant atmosphere with lots of chatty customers. The bustling little front bar with the corridor beside it leads through to a long series of little rooms – wooden floors, green and cream paintwork, and old-fashioned furniture and prints, including lots of period Royal Family engravings and lithographs in the front room. It's one of the handful of pubs tied to the local Smiles brewery, so has all their beers on handpump at attractive prices, plus changing guests such as Fullers London Pride, Hampshire Pendragon, and Youngs Special. Incredibly cheap bar food includes filled rolls, and hot dishes such as pork in mustard, chilli con carne, vegetable chilli, lamb hotpot or beef in beer (all £3), and meaty or vegetable lasagne (£3.50). Bar billiards, dominoes, and cribbage. The attractive back terrace has tables built into a partly covered flowery arbour that is heated on winter evenings. In early Georgian days, this was used as the gaol where condemned men ate their last meal – the bars can still be seen on some windows. *(Recommended by J Gowers, Simon and Amanda Southwell, Ian Phillips, Tony Hinkins, Susan and Nigel Wilson, Tony and Wendy Hobden, Dr and Mrs Morley, the Didier)*

Smiles ~ Manager Bradd Francis ~ Real ale ~ Bar food (not Sat or Sun evenings) ~ (0117) 973 3203 ~ Children allowed until 9pm ~ Open 12-11; 12-10.30 Sun; closed evening 25 Dec, lunchtime 26 Dec, lunchtime 1 Jan

BUCKLAND DINHAM ST7551 Map 2
Bell

High St

The friendly licensees in this attractive old pub work hard to look after their customers. There's a good bustling atmosphere throughout, and the narrow main bar has solid pine pink-cushioned country chairs, pine tables, a flowery cushioned window seat, and beams covered with beer mats, whisky bottle boxes, and hats; to the right is a huge stone fireplace with a woodburning stove, stripped modern pine high-backed settles creating booths, and wooden skis and golf clubs on the ceiling. Good bar food includes sandwiches and filled french bread (lunchtime only, from £2.95), filled baked potatoes (from £3.95), ploughman's (lunchtime only, from £4.50), omelettes (£4.85), home-cooked ham and egg (£4.95), vegetable tikka masala (£5.50), steak, kidney and Guinness pie (£5.95), steaks (from £9.95), puddings, and children's dishes (from £3.50). Well kept Courage Best, Marstons Pedigree, and John Smiths on handpump, a decent wine list, quite a few malt whiskies, a good choice of sherries and ports, freshly squeezed orange juice, and lots of different teas and coffees; cribbage, dominoes, and piped music, a news letter with listed forthcoming events, and a chalkboard with daily news. The comfortable partly no-smoking two-level dining room leads to the back garden: several small areas divided by low stone walls with a variety of seats (a couple of little stone ones for children), two side terraces with a few tables tucked into small secluded walled sections, and pretty flowers planted in a bicycle and a barrow; the two-acre field has a small wendy house and play area; boules. *(Recommended by Elizabeth John, Susan and Nigel Wilson, Kenneth and Sarah McNaught, Dr M E Wilson, MRSM)*

Enterprise ~ Lease: Mr and Mrs M Filsell ~ Real ale ~ Bar food ~ Restaurant ~ (01373) 462956 ~ Children in restaurant ~ Open 12-3, 6-11; 12-3, 6-10.30 Sun

CASTLE CARY ST6332 Map 2
George 🛏

Market Place; just off A371 Shepton Mallet—Wincanton

Quieter during the week (it does get pretty busy at weekends), this lovely thatched coaching inn is a good all-rounder – as somewhere pleasant to stay, and as a place to enjoy a good meal or relaxing drink. The cosy beamed front bar has a massive black elm mantlebeam over the log fire that is said to be over 1,000 years old, as well as a bow window seat, a cushioned high-backed settle by the fire, just six or seven tables, and a civilised and relaxed atmosphere (despite the piped pop music). An inner no-smoking bar, separated by a glazed partition from the inn's central reception area, has a couple of big landscapes, some pictures made from butterfly wings, and a similarly decorous but busy feel. Under the new licensee, enjoyable bar food includes sandwiches (from £2.25), home-made soup (£2.80), a medley of game on a brioche bun (£4.25), smoked salmon pâté or duck terrine with pistachio nuts and sweet peppers (£4.95), steak and kidney pie or lamb casserole (£7.95), wild boar sausages (£8.95), chicken layered with potato pancake, bacon and tomatoes and a sweet basil dressing (£9.25), fillet of salmon with samphire and lemon butter sauce (£9.95), and puddings such as hot chocolate pudding with vanilla ice cream, sticky toffee pudding or lime cream crunch (£3.25). Well kept Morlands Old Speckled Hen and Otter Bitter on handpump, decent house wines with several by the glass, and a fair range of malt whiskies and other spirits; pleasant staff. Cribbage, dominoes, and trivia *(Recommended by Christopher and Mary Thomas, Ruth Warner, Richard Gibbs, Stephen G Brown, Gordon, Charles Gysin, Janet Pickles)*

Free house ~ Licensee Guillaume Lesage ~ Real ale ~ Bar food ~ Restaurant ~ (01963) 350761 ~ Children in eating area of bar and restaurant ~ Open 10-3, 6-11; 12-3, 7-10.30 Sun ~ Bedrooms: £45B/£85B

You can send us reports through our web site: www.goodguides.com

CATCOTT ST3939 Map 1
Crown ◀

Village signposted off A39 W of Street; at war memorial turn off northwards into Brook Lane and keep on

On a quiet country lane in a farming community, this friendly pub was once a cider house. To the left of the main door is a pubby little room with built-in brocade-cushioned settle, a church pew and red leatherette stools around just four rustic pine tables, a tall black-painted brick fireplace with dried flowers and a large cauldron, and working horse plaques; around the corner is a small alcove with a really big pine table on its stripped stone floor. Most of the pub is taken up with the roomy, more straightforward dining area with lots of wheelback chairs around tables, and small 19th-c fashion plates on the cream walls – and it's obviously here that people come to enjoy the good, popular food. From the specials lists, there might be brie fritters with hot cherry sauce (£2.95), a crêpe filled with chicken and spinach in a parmesan cheese sauce (£3.75), chicken, broccoli and tarragon crumble (£5.95), fillet of cod topped with ratatouille and cheese sauce (£7.15), and pork tenderloin stuffed with mushrooms and wrapped in bacon with a blue cheese sauce, and fillet steak with a brandy, cream and green peppercorn sauce (£12.45); from the menu, bar food includes sandwiches and toasties (from £1.50), filled baked potatoes (from £3.35), ploughman's (from £3.65), ham and mushroom quiche (£3.85), parsnip and tomato bake (£5.45), and children's dishes (from £1.50); three-course Sunday lunch (£6.95). Well kept Butcombe, Hardy Royal Oak, and Smiles Best on handpump or tapped from the cask, piped old-fashioned pop music on our visit; fruit machine. There's a back skittle alley with tables and chairs. Out behind are picnic-sets and a play area for children with wooden equipment. *(Recommended by Richard Fendick)*

Free house ~ Licensees C R D Johnston and D Lee ~ Real ale ~ Bar food (11.30-2, 6-10) ~ (01278) 722288 ~ Children welcome ~ Open 11.30-2.30, 6-11; 12-3, 7-10.30 Sun

King William

Village signed off A39 Street—Bridgwater

New licensees have taken this neatly kept cottagey pub in hand. The spacious bar has traditional furnishings such as kitchen and other assorted chairs, brown-painted built-in and other settles, window seats, Victorian fashion plates and other old prints, and one or two rugs on the stone floors; big stone fireplaces. Decent bar food includes sandwiches (from £2.20), home-made soup (£2.50), ploughman's (from £2.90), spinach and ricotta cheese cannelloni (£4.85), steak and kidney pie, curry or haddock in cider sauce (£5.25), Somerset pork (£6.95), steaks (from £8.65), duckling with orange and Grand Marnier sauce (£10.95), daily specials, and puddings. Well kept Palmers Bridport, IPA, and 200 on handpump, and a good range of malt whiskies; darts, cribbage, dominoes, and piped music. A large extension at the back includes a skittle-alley and a glass-topped well. *(Recommended by Paul and Judith Booth, A C and J M Curry, Theo, Anne and Jane Gaskin, Jane and Adrian Tierney-Jones)*

Palmers ~ Tenants M Finch and L Miles ~ Real ale ~ Bar food (till 10pm) ~ Restaurant ~ (01278) 722374 ~ Children welcome ~ Open 11.30-3, 6-11; 12-3, 7-10.30 Sun

CHURCHILL ST4560 Map 1
Crown ◀

Skinners Lane; in village, turn off A368 at Nelson Arms

For those who really enjoy a proper unspoilt drinkers' pub, then this is the place to come. The small and local stone-floored and cross-beamed room on the right has a wooden window seat, an unusually sturdy settle, and built-in wall benches; the left-hand room has a slate floor, and some steps past the big log fire in a big stone fireplace lead to more sitting space. Well kept Bass, Otter Ale, RCH Hewish IPA and

P G Steam, Smiles Golden Brew, and guest beers such as Greene King Abbot or Robinsons Best all tapped from casks at the back, and country wines. Good value bar food includes tasty home-made soups like minestrone or stilton and celery (from £2.20), good rare beef sandwich (£2.50), ploughman's, chilli con carne or faggots (£3.95), and various casseroles (from £4.95); some of the meat comes from their own farm. They can be busy at weekends, especially in summer. There are garden tables on the front and a smallish but pretty back lawn with hill views; the Mendip Morris Men come in summer. Good walks nearby. *(Recommended by M G Hart, Alan and Paula McCully, Tom Evans, Jenny and Roger Huggins, Michael Halsted, Comus Elliott, Mrs A Oakley, Mike and Mary Carter, Stephen G Brown, JP, PP, the Didler)*

Free house ~ Licensee Tim Rogers ~ Real ale ~ Bar food ~ Restaurant ~ (01934) 852995 ~ Children in eating area of bar ~ Open 11.30-3, 5.30-11; 11-11 Fri and Sat; 12-10.30 Sun

CLAPTON IN GORDANO ST4773 Map 2
Black Horse

4 miles from M5 junction 19; A369 towards Portishead, then B3124 towards Clevedon; in N Weston opp school turn left signposted Clapton, then in village take second right, maybe signed Clevedon, Clapton Wick

'Bursting with character' is how one reader described this characterful pub – and there are plenty who would agree with him. There's a good mix of locals and visitors in the partly flagstoned and partly red-tiled main room – as well as winged settles and built-in wall benches around narrow, dark wooden tables, pleasant window seats, a big log fire with stirrups and bits on the mantlebeam, and amusing cartoons and photographs of the pub. A window in an inner snug is still barred from the days when this room was the petty-sessions gaol; high-backed settles – one a marvellous carved and canopied creature, another with an art nouveau copper insert reading East, West, Hame's Best – lots of mugs hanging from its black beams, and plenty of little prints and photographs. There's also a simply furnished room just off the bar (where children can go), with high-backed corner settles and a gas fire; darts, dominoes, cribbage, and piped music. Good, simple bar food includes filled baps (£1.70; sausage baguette £2.50) or ploughman's, and hot dishes like chilli con carne or lasagne (£4.50), and beef in ale or steak and kidney pie (£4.95). Well kept Bass, Courage Best, Smiles Best, and Websters Green Label on handpump or tapped from the cask, and Thatchers farm cider. The little flagstoned front garden is exceptionally pretty in summer with a mass of flowers in tubs, hanging baskets and flowerbeds; there are some old rustic tables and benches, with more to one side of the car park and in the secluded children's play area with its sturdy wooden climber, slide, rope ladder and rope swing. Paths from here lead up Naish Hill or along to Cadbury Camp. *(Recommended by Comus Elliott, Ian Phillips, Howard Clutterbuck, Tom Evans, Dr and Mrs Brian Hamilton, JP, PP, Jack Morley, R Winn, Susan and John Douglas, the Didler)*

Inntrepreneur ~ Tenants Nicholas Evans and A Prieto Garcia ~ Real ale ~ Bar food (not evenings, not Sun lunchtime) ~ (01272) 842105 ~ Children in family room ~ Live music Mon evening ~ Open 11-3, 6-11; all day Fri and Sat; 12-3,7-10.30 Sun

COMBE HAY ST7359 Map 2
Wheatsheaf

Village signposted from A367 or B3110 S of Bath

The setting here – on the edge of a steep wooded valley with good nearby walks – is very pretty, and there are three dovecotes built into the walls, and plenty of tables on the spacious terraced lawn looking down to the church and ancient manor stables. Inside, the pleasantly old-fashioned rooms have low ceilings, brown-painted settles, pews and rustic tables, a very high-backed winged settle facing one big log fire, old sporting and other prints, and earthenware jugs on the shelf of the little shuttered windows. Popular bar food includes home-made soup (£2), ploughman's (from £4.95), game terrine (£5.70), hot baked ham (£6.30), quiche (£6.55), seasonal pheasant (£9.60), fresh trout (£9.80), daily specials like deep-fried brie in an apricot and almond coating, chicken livers (£6.30), tagliatelle with wild mushrooms and peppers (£6.50), good pigeon, tasty steak and kidney pie, sautéed tiger prawns with garlic and whisky (£9), and home-made puddings like apple and fruit pie or tiramisu (£3.25). Well kept Courage Best and a guest like Morlands Old Speckled Hen tapped from the cask, several malt whiskies, and decent wines; shove-ha'penny and cribbage. *(Recommended by Paul and Judith Booth, Lawrence Pearse, David and Valerie Hooley, D S and J M Jackson, Alan Morton, Dr and Mrs A K Clarke, Howard and Barbara Clutterbuck, Catherine and Richard Preston, P and M Rudlin, Lyn and Geoff Hallchurch, Edward Leetham)*

Free house ~ Licensee Michael Graham Taylor ~ Real ale ~ Bar food ~ (01225) 833504 ~ Children in restaurant ~ Open 11-2.30, 6(6.30 in winter)-10.30(11 Sat); 12-2.30, 7-10.30 Sun; closed 25 and 26 Dec ~ Bedrooms: /£68B

COMPTON MARTIN ST5457 Map 2
Ring o' Bells
A368 Bath—Weston

They are good to families here – the family room is no smoking, has blackboards and chalks, a Brio track, and a rocking horse, and they have baby changing and nursing facilities; children have their own menu but can have small helpings of adult dishes (and are given a chocolate bar if they eat all their food), and the big garden has swings, a slide, and a climbing frame. The snugly traditional front part of the bar has rugs on the flagstones, inglenook seats right by the log fire, and a warmly cosy atmosphere; up a step is a spacious carpeted back part with largely stripped stone walls and pine tables. Popular, reasonably priced bar food includes sandwiches (from £1.35; toasties from £2.15; BLT in french bread £2.75), soup (£1.85), filled baked potatoes (from £2.95), good omelettes (from £2.95; not Sundays), stilton mushrooms (£3.25), ploughman's (from £3.25), ham and eggs (small £3.50, large £4.20), lasagne or mushroom, broccoli and almond tagliatelle (£4.75), beef in ale (£4.95), generous mixed grill (£9.35), daily specials like moussaka, good chicken curry, smoked roast salmon, and Somerset pork, and children's meals (from £1). Well kept Butcombe Bitter and Gold, Wadworths 6X and a weekly guest beer on handpump or tapped from the cask, and local ciders, and malt whiskies. The public bar has darts, cribbage, and shove-ha'penny; table skittles. The pub is not far from Blagdon Lake and Chew Valley Lake, and is overlooked by the Mendip Hills. *(Recommended by John A Barker, Tom Evans, M Borthwick, Ruth Warner, Hugh Roberts, Dr and Mrs A K Clarke, Susan and Nigel Wilson, D Godden)*

Free house ~ Licensee Roger Owen ~ Real ale ~ Bar food (till 10pm) ~ Restaurant ~ (01761) 221284 ~ Children in family room ~ Open 11.30-3, 6.30-11; 12-3, 7-10.30 Sun

CRANMORE ST6643 Map 2
Strode Arms ★ ⑪ ♀
West Cranmore; signposted with pub off A361 Frome—Shepton Mallet

There's no doubt that most people do come to this early 15th-c former farmhouse to enjoy the reliably good food – though drinkers are made just as welcome. It's in an attractive setting by the village duck pond, and the rooms have charming country furnishings, fresh flowers (and pretty dried ones), pot plants, a grandfather clock on the flagstones, remarkable old locomotive engineering drawings and big black and white steam train murals in a central lobby, good bird prints, newspapers to read, and lovely log fires in handsome fireplaces. The same menu is used in both the bar and restaurant: sandwiches, soup (£2.85), good crispy mushrooms with a mild curry mayonnaise (£2.95), Italian salami platter (£3.85), duck liver terrine (£4.25), scallops and bacon (£5.75), ham and eggs with sauté potatoes or pheasant, venison and wild boar sausages with onion gravy and bubble and squeak (£6.25), home-made steak and kidney or chicken, ham, and leek pies (£7.25), good smoked haddock and cod fishcakes or roast vegetable parcel (£7.75), breast of pheasant en croûte with a rich game sauce (£9.50), steaks (from £9.50), and puddings such as fresh orange and chocolate mousse, sticky toffee pudding or treacle tart (from £2.65); also, daily specials and Sunday roasts; friendly service. Well kept Flowers IPA, Fullers London Pride, Marstons Pedigree, and a guest such as Batemans Hill Billy on handpump, an interesting choice of wines by the glass from a thoughtful menu, and lots more by the bottle, and quite a few liqueurs and ports. The pub is an attractive sight in summer with its neat stonework, cartwheels on the walls, pretty tubs and hanging baskets, and seats under umbrellas on the front terrace; more seats in the back garden. On the first Tuesday of each month, there's a vintage car meeting, and the pub is handy for the East Somerset Light Railway. *(Recommended by Bett and Brian Cox, Peter and Margaret Frost, Gethin Lewis, Revd A Nunnerley, Lyn and Geoff Hallchurch, Colin Thompson, Tom Evans, M G Hart, Meg and Colin Hamilton, Howard Clutterbuck, Susan and Nigel Wilson, A C and J M Curry, Mike Green, Michael Doswell, Andrew Shore)*

Free house ~ Licensees Rodney and Dora Phelps ~ Real ale ~ Bar food (till 10pm Fri and Sat) ~ Restaurant ~ (01749) 880450 ~ Children in restaurant ~ Open 11.30-2.30, 6.30-11; 12-3, 7-10.30 Sun; closed Sun evening Oct-Mar

DOULTING ST6445 Map 2
Waggon & Horses ♀

Doulting Beacon; eastwards turn off A37 on Mendip ridge N of Shepton Mallet, just S of A367 junction; the pub is also signed from the A37 at the Beacon Hill crossroads and from the A361 at the Doulting and Cranmore crossroads

There can be few pubs where the piano is a carefully tuned Steinway grand, but then this attractive 18th-c inn is quite special in that the flower-lined imposing external flight of stone steps leads to a big raftered upper gallery where they hold regular classical music and other events (perhaps including gypsy music, jazz, and art shows); they often theme the food to match the music. The rambling bar has studded red leatherette seats and other chairs, a homely mix of tables including antiques, and paintings and drawings everywhere – not just for sale (as in so many pubs these days), but ones you actually want to buy. Two rooms are no smoking. As well as good fresh fish dishes, they regularly cook Chinese dishes as their assistant cook hails from Hong Kong. From the menu, enjoyable, robustly flavoured food cooked by Mr Pajan (who comes from Austria) might include interesting daily specials plus dishes from the menu such as sandwiches (from £1.90), soup (small £2.90, large £4.20, hearty winter pheasant and lentil £4.50), duck liver pâté (£3.90), Thai prawns in filo pastry with garlic dip (£3.90; large £8.50), spicy bean casserole or omelettes using their own free-range eggs (£5.90), ham and eggs or lasagne (£6.20), steaks (from £9), chicken breast topped with ham, cheese and tomato (£9.90), and puddings such as steamed ginger and lemon pudding, crème brûlée or treacle tart (from £3.20). Well kept Ushers Best and Founders and seasonal ales on handpump, a good choice of decent house wines, cocktails; cheerful service; chess and skittle alley. The big walled garden (with summer barbecues) is one of our favourites. Elderly tables and chairs stand on informal terracing, with picnic-sets out on the grass, and perennials and flowering shrubs intersperse themselves in a pretty and pleasantly informal way. There's a wildlife pond, and a climber for children. Off to one side is a rough paddock with a horse (horses are one passion of Mr Cardona, who comes from Colombia) and a goat called Dennis, and various fancy fowl, with pens further down holding many more in small breeding groups – there are some really quite remarkable birds among them, and the cluckings and crowings make a splendidly contented background to a sunny summer lunch. They often sell the eggs, too. *(Recommended by Susan and Nigel Wilson, MRSM)*

Ushers ~ Lease: Francisco Cardona and Richard Pajan ~ Real ale ~ Bar food ~ Restaurant ~ (01749) 880302 ~ Children welcome but must be well behaved ~ Classical concerts and some jazz ~ Open 11-3, 6-11; 12-3, 7-10.30 Sun; closed 25 Dec

There are report forms at the back of the book.

DOWLISH WAKE ST3713 Map 1
New Inn 🍴

Village signposted from Kingstone – which is signposted from old A303 on E side of Ilminster, and from A3037 just S of Ilminster; keep on past church – pub at far end of village

Readers are fond of this very neatly kept village pub, and the licensees and their staff offer a genuinely warm welcome to all their customers. The bar has dark beams liberally strung with hop bines, old-fashioned furnishings that include a mixture of chairs, high-backed settles, and attractive sturdy tables, and a woodburning stove in the stone inglenook fireplace. Tasty, enjoyable bar food includes sandwiches (from £1.90), soup (£2), sausage and rosti (£3.65), pasta dishes (£3.75), warm duck salad, soft toes on toast or ploughman's (£3.85), omelettes (£4.10), all day breakfast (£4.95), liver with onion, bacon and mushrooms in wine sauce (£5.45), nut and lentil roast (£5.55), steaks (from £8.75), rack of lamb (£11.80), some Swiss specialities like raclette (£5.75) or charbonnade (£9), and small meals (from £1.90). Well kept Butcombe Bitter and two guests such as Theakstons Old Peculier and Wadworths 6X on handpump, a decent choice of whiskies, and Perry's cider. This comes from just down the road, and the thatched 16th-c stone cider mill is well worth a visit for its collection of wooden bygones and its liberal free tastings (you can buy the half-dozen different ciders in old-fashioned earthenware flagons as well as more modern containers; it's closed on Sunday afternoons). In a separate area they have darts, shove-ha'penny, dominoes, cribbage, bar billiards, table skittles as well as alley skittles and a fruit machine. The family room is no smoking. In front of the stone pub there's a rustic bench, tubs of flowers and a sprawl of clematis; the pleasant back garden has flowerbeds and a children's climbing frame. *(Recommended by Galen Strawson, C P Scott-Malden, Pete and Rosie Flower, Revd A Nunnerley, Joan and Michel Hooper-Immins, Douglas Allen, Helen Flaherty, Peter and Audrey Dowsett, Mr and Mrs H Quick, Theo, Anne and Jane Gaskin, Jeanne and George Barnwell, J M Lefeaux, Howard Clutterbuck, Mr and Mrs N Fuller, Sandra and Chris Taylor, Stephen G Brown, MDN, Lynn Sharpless, Bob Eardley, Roger Price, Jane and Adrian Tierney-Jones)*

Free house ~ Licensees Therese Boosey and David Smith ~ Real ale ~ Bar food (not winter Sun evening) ~ Children in family room ~ Open 11-3, 6-11; 12-3, 7-10.30 Sun

EAST LYNG ST3328 Map 1
Rose & Crown

A361about 4 miles W of Othery

The open-plan beamed lounge bar in this popular pub has a winter log fire (or a big embroidered fire screen) in a stone fireplace, a corner cabinet of glass, china and silver, a court cabinet, a bow window seat by an oak drop-leaf table, copies of *Country Life*, and impressive large dried flower arrangements. Good bar food includes sandwiches (from £1.85), soup (£2.20), ploughman's (from £3.65), ham and egg (£4.25), omelettes (from £4.75), vegetable chilli or mushroom stroganoff (£5.75), trout (£6.45), steaks (from £9.95), roast duckling with orange sauce (£11.75), and puddings like home-made treacle tart or sherry trifle (£2.85); Mr Mason is quite a character, and waitress service is pleasant. Well kept Butcombe Bitter and Gold, and Royal Oak on handpump; skittle alley and piped music. The back garden (largely hedged off from the car park) is prettily planted and has plenty of seats. *(Recommended by Douglas Allen, Ann and Colin Hunt, Bett and Brian Cox, Alan and Paula McCully)*

Free house ~ Licensee Derek Mason ~ Real ale ~ Bar food ~ Restaurant ~ (01823) 698235 ~ Children in restaurant ~ Open 11-2.30, 6.30-11; 12-3, 7-10.30 Sun ~ Bedrooms: £28B/£46B

EAST WOODLANDS ST7944 Map 2
Horse & Groom 🍴 ♀ 🍷

Off A361/B3092 junction

On the edge of the Longleat estate, this is a small civilised pub serving particularly good food – though there's also a fine choice of real ales in the small pleasant bar on the left with its stripped pine pews and settles on dark flagstones: Brakspears, Butcombe, Greene King IPA, Uley Bitter, and Wadworths 6X tapped from the cask; good wines by the glass. The comfortable little lounge has a relaxed atmosphere, an easy chair and settee around a coffee table, two small solid dining tables with chairs, and a big stone hearth with a small raised grate. Well presented food includes home-made filled rolls (from £1.10) and french bread (from £2.20), home-made soup (£2.50), prawn dumplings with a white wine sauce or niçoise salad (£4.25), broccoli and mushroom chow mein (£5), liver, bacon and onion (£5.50), cod fillet with lovage and prawn sauce (£6.90), sautéed scallops with bacon and Pernod dressing (£7.20), chicken with apricots and brandy (£7.50), Brixham seafood casserole (£8.50), steaks (from £8.95), and puddings such as home-made summer pudding or lemon and sultana cheesecake (£3.25); helpful service. Shove-ha'penny, cribbage and dominoes. There are picnic-sets in the nice front garden by five severely pollarded limes and attractive troughs and mini wheelbarrows filled with flowers; more seats behind the big no-smoking dining conservatory. *(Recommended by Stephen, Julie and Hayley Brown, Lyn and Geoff Hallchurch, A C and J M Curry, S G N Bennett, J and E Gladston, M Joyner, Dr D E Granger)*

Free house ~ Licensees Mr and Mrs Gould ~ Real ale ~ Bar food (12-1.45, 6.30-9; not Sun evening, not Mon) ~ Restaurant ~ (01373) 462802 ~ Children in eating area of bar and restaurant ~ Open 11.30-2.30(3 Sat), 6.30-11; 12-3, 7-10.30 Sun; closed Mon lunchtime

FARLEIGH HUNGERFORD ST8057 Map 2
Hungerford Arms
A366 Trowbridge—Norton St Philip

The back terrace here has fine country views across sheep fields, rolling countryside, and the ruins of Hungerford Castle which can be enjoyed from picnic-sets under umbrellas on the terrace – pretty hanging baskets, flower tubs, vines, and roses – and from the lower grass area with more seats. Inside, there's a relaxed atmosphere and a friendly welcome from the licensees, maybe some jolly locals at the bar, and well kept Bass, Courage Best, Otter Bitter and Bright, and Wadworths 6X on handpump on the linenfold panelled counter; perhaps Thatchers cider, too. The bar has stone-mullioned leaded lights, dark wood and stained glass and pink plaster stub walls making snug booths for some solid cast-iron framed tables with cushioned built in seats and library chairs, hunting prints on one pink end wall, heavy dark beams (some nicely moulded), and a carved stone fireplace at each end. Steps lead down to the no-smoking restaurant which has a picture window overlooking the ruins. Home-made bar food includes soup (£1.95), sandwiches (from £2.75), ploughman's (from £4.25), spaghetti bolognese or ham and egg (£4.75), meaty or vegetable lasagne (£4.95), steaks (from £8.95), daily specials such as various curries and steak and kidney or turkey and mushroom pies (from £4.75), fresh local trout with wine and cream (£7.95), fresh salmon with a prawn and butter cream (£9.95), and puddings like treacle sponge or sticky toffee pudding with local clotted cream (£2.75); roast Sunday lunch £4.95). The neat carpeted lobby has a sturdy long table, darts and fruit machine. Dogs are allowed in on a lead. *(Recommended by S E Pauley, Mr and Mrs R G Ewen, Ted George)*

Free house ~ Licensee Nigel Day ~ Real ale ~ Bar food ~ Restaurant ~ (01225) 752411 ~ Children in restaurant and family room ~ Open 11.30-3, 5.30-11; 11-11 Sat; 12-10.30 Sun

FAULKLAND ST7354 Map 2
Tuckers Grave £
A366 E of village

An old favourite with many people, this marvellously atmospheric and warmly friendly basic cider house has for many years claimed the title of Smallest Pub in the Guide. The flagstoned entry opens into a teeny unspoilt room with casks of well kept Bass and Butcombe Bitter on tap and Thatchers Cheddar Valley cider in an alcove

632 *Somerset*

on the left. Two old cream-painted high-backed settles face each other across a single table on the right, and a side room has shove-ha'penny. There's a skittle alley and tables and chairs on the back lawn, as well as winter fires and maybe newspapers to read. Food is limited to sandwiches and ploughman's at lunchtime. *(Recommended by Pete Baker, John Poulter, JP, PP, the Didler)*

Free house ~ Licensees Ivan and Glenda Swift ~ Real ale ~ Bar food ~ (01373) 834230 ~ Children in eating area of bar ~ Open 11.30-3, 6-11; 12-3, 7-10.30 Sun

FRESHFORD ST7960 Map 2
Inn at Freshford
Village signposted off B3108 – OS Sheet 172 map reference 790600

This picturesque stonebuilt pub has seats in pretty gardens and is in a nice spot by the River Frome, with walks to the Kennet & Avon Canal. It's well run and comfortably modernised and the atmospheric bar is interestingly decorated: well kept Courage Best, Marstons Pedigree, and Wadworths 6X on handpump. Bar food includes home-made soup (£2.45), sandwiches (£2.95), ploughman's (£4.25), steak in ale pie (£5.95), spinach and cheese parcels (£6.45), half a dozen fresh fish specials such as salmon (£8.95), or whole lemon sole (£9.85). The restaurant is partly no smoking; friendly, helpful staff and occasional piped music. *(Recommended by Meg and Colin Hamilton, Andrew Shore)*

Free house ~ Licensee John Williams ~ Real ale ~ Bar food (12-2, 6-9.30) ~ Restaurant ~ (01225) 722250 ~ Children welcome ~ Open 11-3, 6-11; 12-3, 7-11 Sun

HALLATROW ST6357 Map 2
Old Station
Old Station Wells Road (A39, close to junction with A37 S of Bristol)

An entertaining and formidable collection of bric-a-brac fills this pub to the brim. The forest of clutter hanging from the ceiling includes anything from sombreros and peaked caps to kites, from flags to fishnets, from ceramic charcoal stoves to sailing boats, from parasols to post boxes. Entertaining nonsenses abound, like the kilted dummy girl, the wall of car grills. The rather handsome island bar counter has well kept Ash Vine Challenger, Bass, Moles Best, Otter and Wickwar Brand Oak on handpump, and a mix of furnishings includes a sofa, high chairs around big cask tables, and small settles and dining or library chairs around more orthodox tables. Given the style of the place, it's quite a surprise to find such a wide range of enjoyable food: home-made soup (£1.95), home-made chicken liver pâté (£3), sweet melon and honey baked ham roulade (£4.25), deep-fried prawn and crab fritters (£4.65), beef curry (£5.50), Thai vegetable curry (£5.60), home-made steak and kidney pie or lasagne (£5.80), rack of lamb with a rosemary and redcurrant sauce, chicken breast sautéed with bacon, onions, mushrooms and madeira sauce or duck breast with a sweet and sour cherry sauce (all £7.95), and home-made puddings (£2.60). Piped radio, fruit machine. Behind is a no-smoking railway carriage restaurant (photographs in the bar show the hair-raising difficulty of getting it here). The garden alongside has picnic-sets under cocktail parasols, and spreads back to a well equipped play area, with a recreation ground beyond. *(Recommended by Tom Evans, M G Hart, Chris Plumb, DB, MK, Dr Oscar Puls, Andrew Shore)*

Free house ~ Licensee Miles Redwood-Davies ~ Real ale ~ Bar food (not 25 Dec) ~ (01761) 452228 ~ Children in eating area of bar ~ Open 11-3, 5(6 Sat)-11; 12-3, 7-10.30 Sun ~ Bedrooms: £31B/£45B

HUISH EPISCOPI ST4326 Map 1
Rose & Crown
A372 E of Langport

Very much a focus for the area, this unspoilt thatched pub has been run by Mrs Pittard's family for well over 130 years – it's known locally as 'Eli's' after the friendly landlady's father. The atmosphere and character are determinedly unpretentious and welcoming, and there's no bar as such – to get a drink, you just walk into the central flagstoned still room and choose from the casks of well kept Bass and couple of local guest beers such as Branscombe Vale Summa That, Butcombe Bitter, and Teignworthy Reel Ale; farm cider (and local cider brandy) and country wines which stand on ranks of shelves all around (prices are very low); this servery is the only thoroughfare between the casual little front parlours with their unusual pointed-arch windows; genuinely friendly locals. Food is home-made, simple and cheap: generously filled sandwiches (from £1.70), a good choice of soups (£2.40), good filled baked potatoes (from £2.50), stilton and broccoli quiche (£5.25), spinach lasagne (£5.45), and pork, apple and cider casserole, steak and Guinness pie or cottage pie (£5.75); good helpful service. Shove-ha'penny, dominoes and cribbage; a much more orthodox big back extension family room has pool, darts, fruit machine, trivia, and juke box; skittle alley and popular quiz nights. There are tables in a garden outside, and a second enclosed garden with a children's play area. George the dog will welcome a bitch but can't abide other dogs, though Bonny the welsh collie is not so fussy. A beer and music festival is held in the adjoining field every September, the local folk singers visit regularly, and on some summer weekends you might find the pub's cricket team playing out here (who always welcome a challenge); good nearby walks, and the site of the Battle of Langport (1645) is close by. *(Recommended by Pete Baker, Christopher Darwent, Mr and Mrs N Fuller, Gordon, R J Walden, Adrian and Jane Tierney-Jones, M Gardner, JP, PP, the Didler)*

Free house ~ Licensee Mrs Eileen Pittard ~ Real ale ~ Bar food ~ (01458) 250494 ~ Regular live music ~ Open 11.30-2.30, 5.30-11; 11.30-11 Fri and Sat; 12-10.30 Sun

KINGSDON ST5126 Map 2
Kingsdon Inn

At Podimore roundabout junction of A303, A372 and A37 take A372, then turn right on to B3151, right into village, and right again opp post office

The three charmingly decorated, low-ceilinged rooms in this pretty little thatched cottage are relaxed and friendly, and on the right are some very nice old stripped pine tables with attractive cushioned farmhouse chairs, more seats in what was a small inglenook fireplace, a few low sagging beams, and an open woodburning stove with colourful dried and artificial fruits and flowers on the overmantle; down three steps through balustrading to a light, airy room with cushions on stripped pine built-in wall seats, curtains matching the scatter cushions, more stripped pine tables, and a winter open fire. Another similarly decorated room has more tables and another fireplace. From a changing blackboard menu and served by helpful staff, lunchtime bar food includes soup (£2.60), ploughman's (£3.90), filled baguettes (from £3.20), tomato, onion and basil quiche (£4.90), a popular walnut, leek and stilton pie (£4.90), steak and kidney or chicken and cider pie (£5.50), baked haddock and prawn mornay (£5.50), poached salmon (£5.90); the evening menu is slightly more expensive and can include leek, potato and goat's cheese bake (£7.40), lemon sole, sea bass and cod, sole and salmon with a shrimp sauce (all around £9.90), and nice steaks (from £10.90); desserts include sticky ginger pudding with chunky ginger ice cream (£2.90). Well kept Cottage Golden Arrow, Fullers London Pride, Cotleigh Tawny and guests on handpump, local cider, wine list and 20 malt whiskies. Darts and quiet piped music. Picnic-sets on the grass. *(Recommended by S Stubbs, Luke Worthington, NMF, DF, Andrew Scarr, Jill Silversides, Barry Brown, R J Walden, Michael Hill, Tom Evans, John and Vivienne Rice, Mike and Heather Watson, Janet Pickles, Mrs Mary Woods)*

Free house ~ Licensees Leslie and Anna-Marie Hood ~ Real ale ~ Bar food (12-2, 7-9.30; not Sun) ~ Restaurant ~ (01935) 840543 ~ Well behaved children away from main bar ~ Open 11-3, 6-11; 12-3, 7-10.30 Sun

---

Most pubs in this book sell wine by the glass. We mention wines only if they are a cut above the – generally low – average. Please let us know of any good pubs for wine.

KNAPP ST3025 Map 1

Rising Sun 🍴 ☒

Lower Knapp – OS Sheet 182 map reference 304257; off A38/A358/A378 E of Taunton

It's well worth the effort it takes to find this rather smart 15th-c longhouse, and you can be sure of a good meal and a warm welcome from the genteel landlord once you get here. From the bar menu, there might be home-made soup (£3.10), welsh rarebit (£3.40), ploughman's (£4.50), open sandwiches (from £4.70), lamb's liver and bacon or smoked salmon and prawn bake (£4.85), and home-cooked ham and egg with sauté potatoes (£5); also moules marinières (£4.50; large helping £8), spicy crab and prawn (£6.50), nut roast with provençale sauce (£9.50), chicken breast with a mushroom sauce (£11), steaks (from £11), scallops poached in a vermouth and cream sauce (£12.75), john dory with mussels and prawns (£15), and puddings like trealce tart or chocolate and hazelnut slice with a raspberry coulis (£3.50). Sunday roast rib of English beef (£6.50); part of the restaurant is no smoking. The big single room has two inglenook fireplaces (one with an old bread oven and range), well moulded beams, woodwork, and some stonework in its massive rather tilting walls, and a relaxed atmosphere. Well kept Bass, Boddingtons and Exmoor Ale on handpump, farm ciders, and a decent wine list. The staff (and dogs – Pepi the poodle and Pompey, who weighs in at nine stone) are very welcoming. The terrace is a sun-trap in summer. *(Recommended by Ian Phillips, Dave Braisted, Nigel Cogger, Alan and Paula McCully, Mr and Mrs J M Lefeaux, Mr and Mrs N Fuller, J Monk, Ken Flawn, Comus Elliott, Gethin Lewis, Sam Samuells, Lynda Payton)*

Free house ~ Licensee Tony Atkinson ~ Real ale ~ Bar food ~ Restaurant ~ (01823) 490436 ~ Children in eating area of bar and restaurant ~ Open 11.30-2.30, 6.30-11; 12-3, 7-10.30 Sun ~ Bedrooms: £25/£36

LANGLEY MARSH ST0729 Map 1

Three Horseshoes ★ 🍺

Village signposted off B3227 from Wiveliscombe

Surrounded by farmland, this is a friendly little country pub. The back bar has low modern settles and polished wooden tables, dark red wallpaper, planes hanging from the ceiling, banknotes papering the wall behind the bar counter, a piano, and a local stone fireplace. Well kept Butcombe Bitter, Fullers London Pride, Otter Best, Palmers IPA, and Wadworths 6X tapped from the cask, and Sheppeys farm cider; polite staff. Genuinely home-made food includes filled rolls (from £1.95), soup (£2.20), pizzas (from £3.95; can take away as well), chilli and chickpea hotpot or butterbean bourguignon (£3.95), lamb in Pernod (£5.25), good steak and kidney pie or pigeon breasts in cider and cream (£5.50), enjoyable fish pie (£5.95), popular steaks (from £8.95), daily fresh fish dishes like mussels in wine and cream or lemon sole (£7.95), and lovely puddings such as apple-filled pancake or lemon mousse (£2.50); no chips or fried food and some vegetables come from the garden. The no-smoking dining area has antique settles and tables and benches, and the lively front room has sensibly placed darts, shove-ha'penny, table skittles, dominoes, and cribbage; separate skittle alley, and piped music. You can sit on rustic seats on the verandah or in the sloping back garden, with a fully equipped children's play area; in fine weather there are usually vintage cars outside. *(Recommended by the Didler, David Lewis, Sarah Lart, Christopher Darwent)*

Free house ~ Licensee John Hopkins ~ Real ale ~ Bar food ~ (01984) 623763 ~ Well behaved children in eating area of bar ~ Open 12-2.30, 7-11(10.30 Sun); closed winter Mon

LITTON ST5954 Map 2

Kings Arms

Off A39 Bath—Wells

Doing particularly well, this enjoyable pub is popular for its good food served by friendly staff. There's a big entrance hall with polished flagstones, and bars lead off to the left with low heavy beams and more flagstones; a nice bit on the right beyond the huge fireplace has a big old-fashioned settle and a mix of other settles and wheelback chairs; a full suit of armour stands in one alcove and the rooms are divided up into areas by standing timbers. From the menu, there might be sandwiches (from £2.95), garlic mushrooms (£3.50), mini chicken satay (£3.95), lots of platters and salads (from £3.95; marinated pork ribs and potato skins with sour cream and barbecue sauces £7.50), daily vegetarian and pasta dishes, battered cod (£4.95), chilli (£6.95), lamb cutlets (£7.25), chicken and broccoli bake (£7.50), king prawns in garlic butter (£9.95), and steaks; children's colouring sheet menu with crayons. Well kept Bass, Courage Best, and Wadworths 6X on handpump. Children enjoy the excellent heavy wooden play equipment in the neat gardens, including a commando climbing net, slides, and baby swings; the River Chew runs through the bottom of the garden. *(Recommended by M Borthwick, Bett and Brian Cox, Jacquie and Jim Jones, J P Harris, M Joyner, J H Bescoby)*

Free house ~ Licensee Neil Sinclair ~ Real ale ~ Bar food (12-2.30, 6.30-10) ~ (01761) 241301 ~ Children in large family room ~ Open 11-2.30, 6-11; 12-3, 6(7 in winter)-10.30 Sun

LONG SUTTON ST4625 Map 1
Devonshire Arms

B3165 Somerton—Martock, just off A372 E of Langport

This is another pub taken over by Old English Inns who were installing new managers as we went to press. It's a tall gabled and solid stone inn with a cosily old-fashioned front bar separated from the rather smart restaurant area on the left by not much more than a sideboard – which makes for a very relaxed atmosphere. The built-in green plush corner seat is the prime spot, and there's a charming décor – deep green ceiling, lighter green walls, and good sporting and country prints. There's also a flagstoned back bar with shelves of china, seats with lots of scatter cushions, and darts, fruit machine, and TV. Bar food now includes sandwiches (from £2.95), ploughman's (from £3.95), steak and kidney pie (£6.25), daily specials like moules marinières or squid in light beer batter with a chilli dip (£5.95), chicken breast stuffed with ham topped with mozzarella and served with a tomato and basil sauce (£10.25), skate wing grilled with lemon butter and capers (£12.95), and rack of lamb with rosemary juice (£13.95), and puddings (£3.25). Well kept Courage Directors on handpump, and decent wines. *(Recommended by Ian Phillips, Frank Willy, G Smale, Janet Pickles, John Weeks, John Evans, Stephen Brown, Douglas Allen, Jane and Adrian Tierney-Jones)*

Old English Inns ~ Managers Barbara and Chris Callaghan ~ Real ale ~ Bar food ~ (01458) 241271 ~ Children in eating area of bar and restaurant ~ Open 12-3, 6-11; 12-3, 7-10.30 Sun; closed evening 24 Dec ~ Bedrooms: /£55S

LUXBOROUGH SS9837 Map 1
Royal Oak ★ ◖ ⇌

Kingsbridge; S of Dunster on minor rds into Brendon Hills – OS Sheet 181 map reference 983378

This is a marvellous place to relax – and to make the most of the surrounding area with its good walks it might be best to stay overnight. The bedrooms (if not huge) are thoughtfully furnished and comfortable and have their own teddy, and the breakfasts are first class. The atmospheric bar rooms have beams and inglenooks, good log fires, flagstones in the front public bar, a fishing theme in one room, a real medley of furniture, and a friendly, thriving atmosphere; two characterful dining rooms (one is no smoking). Well kept real ales such as Cotleigh Tawny, Exmoor Gold, Flowers IPA, and weekly guest beers on handpump, local farm cider, 20 malt whiskies, and a decent wine list. Good bar food includes home-made soup (£2.25), sandwiches (from £2.50), filled baked potatoes (from £3.95), home-made port and stilton pâté (£4.25), ploughman's (from £4.45), various salads (from £4.95), spinach and nut lasagne (£5.75), chicken curry or steak in ale pie (£5.95), and evening dishes such as fresh local trout pâté (£4.25), smoked duck (£5.95), vegetarian curry (£6.95), daily fresh fish and seasonal game dishes, pork fillet with apricots and a brandy cream sauce (£9.95), venison casserole in a plum and cranberry sauce (£10.95), steaks (from £10.95), and home-made puddings (£2.95), and children's meals (from £2.50). Pool, dominoes, cribbage, board game, and shove-ha'penny – no machines or music.Tables outside *(Recommended by David Lewis, Sarah Lart, Lynn Sharpless, Bob Eardley, Paul Watt, Frank Davidson, Sarah Bond, Murray and Jackie Hynd, Rose Magrath, Andrew Scarr, Colin and Peggy Wilshire, Richard Gibbs, JP, PP, Tamsin Turnbull, Keith Moore, Darly Graton, Graeme Gulibert, Adrian and Jane Tierney-Jones, Dave Braisted, Mr and Mrs M Tarrant, S A Beele, G Grant, Nigel Woolliscroft)*

Free house ~ Licensees Kevin and Rose Draper ~ Real ale ~ Bar food (till 10pm; 9.30 Sun) ~ (01984) 640319 ~ Children in restaurant and back bar ~ Open 11-2.30, 6-11(10.30 in winter); 12-3, 6-11 Sun ~ Bedrooms: £45B/£50B

MELLS ST7249 Map 2
Talbot 🍺 🛏

W of Frome; off A362 W of Buckland Dinham, or A361 via Nunney and Whatley

The 15th-c tythe barn opposite the restaurant entrance here has been transformed into a bar for locals with a high-beamed ceiling, and Butcombe and Fullers London Pride tapped from the cask. What was the two-roomed public bar is now a comfortable dining bar, and the old derelict room above the original bar/restaurant is a luxurious 4-poster bedroom. This is a popular old coaching inn with a friendly licensee, and the attractive main room has stripped pews, mate's and wheelback chairs, fresh flowers and candles in bottles on the mix of tables, and sporting and riding pictures on the walls, which are partly stripped above a broad panelled dado, and partly rough terracotta colour. A small corridor leads to a nice little room with an open fire; piped music. Good bar food includes home-made soup (£2.95), a light mousse of fresh Cornish crab and Pernod with a lemon and herb mayonnaise (£4.50), macaroni cheese (£4.85), spaghetti bolognese (£5.25), ploughman's, hot cheese and ratatouille flan or cold duck and cherry pie (all £5.50), steak and kidney in ale pie (£8.95), breast of duck with plum sauce and caramelised poached pear (£11.50), roast saddle of Somerset roe deer with tagliatelle and cranberry sauce (£12.50), Sunday roast, and nice breakfasts; good wines, and well chosen staff. There are seats in an informally planted cobbled courtyard. The village was purchased by the Horner family of the 'Little Jack Horner' nursery rhyme and the direct descendants still live in the manor house next door. The inn is surrounded by lovely countryside and good walks. *(Recommended by Susan and Nigel Wilson, Walter Reid, S G N Bennett, Roger Wain-Heapy, Jill Bickerton, S G Bennett, Paul S McPherson, Edward Leetham, Nancy Cleave, John Hayter, Geoffrey Kemp, Jane and Adrian Tierney-Jones)*

Free house ~ Licensee Roger Stanley Elliott ~ Real ale ~ Bar food ~ Restaurant ~ (01373) 812254 ~ Children in eating area of bar and restaurant ~ Open 12-2.30, 6-11; 12-3, 7-10.30 Sun ~ Bedrooms: £39.50B/£65B

MONKSILVER ST0737 Map 1
Notley Arms ★ 🍽

B3188

One reader was so taken with this friendly, bustling pub that he bought a house in the same village. Whilst the many other customers aren't perhaps quite as keen as that, this is an immensely well liked place and as they don't take reservations, you do have to get there pretty promptly – there are usually people waiting for the doors to open. The characterful beamed and L-shaped bar has small settles and kitchen chairs around the plain country wooden and candlelit tables, original paintings on the black-timbered white walls, fresh flowers, a couple of woodburning stoves, and maybe a pair of cats. Reasonably priced very good food includes home-made soup (£2.50), sandwiches (from £2.50), very good ploughman's (from £3.50), home-made tagliatelle with ham, mushrooms, cream and parmesan cheese (£4.25), potato cakes with leeks in a three mustard sauce (£4.95), roasted vegetable and goat's cheese feuillete or fresh salmon fishcakes with piquant crème fraîche sauce (£5.75), lamb curry with spinach and tomato (£6.75), teriyaki chicken with stir-fried vegetables (£7.75), fresh cod fillet with mash and caper butter (£7.95), sirloin steak (£8.95), puddings such as pear and almond tart or treacle tart (from £2.50), and winter roast Sunday lunch (£5.50); very good cheerful staff. Well kept Exmoor Ale, Smiles Best, Wadworths 6X, and Youngs Special on handpump, and country wines; cribbage, dominoes and alley skittles. Families are well looked after, with colouring books and toys in the bright no-smoking little family room. There are more toys outside in the immaculate garden, running down to a swift clear stream. *(Recommended by Dr Rod Holcombe, Russell Sunderland, H O Dickinson, Clive Steed, John and Christine Vittoe, Lesley Sones, Christopher Darwent, Hugh Roberts, Ian Phillips, Jan and Steve Nash, J M and L M Lefeaux, Peter and Audrey Dowsett)*

Inn Partnership (Nomura) ~ Lease Alistair and Sarah Cade ~ Real ale ~ Bar food ~ (01984) 656217 ~ Children in eating area of bar and in family room ~ Open 11.30-2.30, 6.30-11; 12-2.30, 7-11(10.30 in winter) Sun; closed last week Jan, first week Feb

NORTH CURRY ST3225 Map 1
Bird in Hand 🍺

Queens Square; off A378 (or A358) E of Taunton

A good range of live music – pop, rock, modern jazz and so forth – appeals to a wide mix of customers here. They also run cricket and skittle teams, and hold quiz nights. The bar has pews, settles, benches, and old yew tables (candlelit at night) on the flagstones, original beams and timbers, and log fires in inglenook fireplaces (the two big sofas next to these are coveted). The public bar has darts, pool, cribbage, and piped music. Using fresh local produce and organic vegetables, the weekly changing dishes might include soups such as tomato and lentil or wild mushroom (£3.25), deep-fried lemon sole with lemon mayonnaise (£4.75), ploughman's (£4.95), ham and egg (£5.95), pork, apple and leek sausages with onion gravy (£6.75), grilled cod with bacon, beer and cabbage (£8.25), chargrilled sirloin steak (£10.95), and puddings such as tarte tatin with crème fraîche or apple and cinnamon pie (£3.25); children's helpings; only the main menu is available on Friday-Sunday. Sunday roast beef (£7.50). More formal dining is available in the separate restaurant area with conservatory. Well kept Badger Tanglefoot, Bass, Cotleigh Tawny, Exmoor Ale, Otter Ale, and a guests beer such as RCH Pitchfork on handpump or tapped from the cask, a thoughtful choice of wines including a local one, and Rich's farm cider; skittle alley and piped music. Summer barbecues on the terrace. *(Recommended by Susan and Nigel Wilson, Adrian and Jane Tierney-Jones, Mark Howard, James Flory, Dinks, the Haworth family)*

Free house ~ Licensees Tom Cosgrove and Michael Gage ~ Real ale ~ Bar food ~ (01823) 490248 ~ Well behaved children welcome until 9pm ~ Regular rock, modern jazz, solo artists Fri/Sat evenings ~ Open 12-3(4 Sat, 5 Sun), 7-11(10.30 Sun); closed Mon lunchtime; also winter Tues/Thurs lunchtimes

NORTON ST PHILIP ST7755 Map 2
George ★ 🛏

A366

After careful restoration, this exceptional building is once again offering hospitaility to locals and travellers – as it has been doing for nearly 700 years. Several rare features were uncovered during the restoration, including beautiful 16th-c wall paintings of flowers and leaves; and bedrooms have now been created – some reached by the external Norman stone stair-turret, and some across the cobbled and flagstoned courtyard and up into the fine half-timbered upper gallery (where there's a lovely 18th-c carved oak settle); these rooms are very atmospheric with a nice mix of good reproduction and antique oak furniture. The Charterhouse Bar has a wonderful pitched ceiling with trusses and timbering, heraldic shields and standards, jousting lances, and swords on the walls, a carved oak mirror above the fine old stone fireplace, a stripped pine box settle in one corner, high backed cushioned heraldic-fabric dining chairs, an oak dresser with some pewter, heavy brocaded curtains in mullioned windows, and a big central rug on the plank floor. The Norton Room, which was the original bar, has really heavy beams, an oak panelled settle and solid dining chairs on the narrow strip wooden floor, a variety of 18th-c pictures, an open fire in the handsome stone fireplace, and a low wooden bar counter. Well kept Wadworths IPA, Farmers Glory, and 6X on handpump, decent wines with a good choice by the glass, and good, organised, friendly service. Lunchtime bar food includes home-made soup (£3.95), sandwiches (from £4.95), filled baked potatoes and ploughman's (from £5.25), and daily specials like hot beef baguette or caesar salad (£5.25), moules (£5.95), and roasted garlic vegetables (£7.95), with evening dishes such as chicken liver, pork and spinach terrine (£5.75), wild mushroom stroganoff or tiger prawns in filo pastry (£8.95), cajun chicken (£9.25), salmon and prawn fishcakes with tarragon sauce (£9.95), and roasted rack of English lamb with a redcurrant and rosemary jus (£13.95). There's yet another room as you enter the building, with high dark beams, squared dark half-panelling, a broad carved stone fireplace with an old iron fireback and pewter plates on the mantlepiece, a big mullioned window with leaded lights, and a round oak 17th-c table reputed to have been used by the Duke of Monmouth who stayed here before the Battle of Sedgemoor – after their defeat, his men were imprisoned in what is now the Monmouth Bar. The dining room – a restored barn with original oak ceiling beams, a pleasant if haphazard mix of early 19th-c portraits and hunting prints, and the same mix of vaguely old-looking furnishings, has a good relaxing, chatty atmosphere. A stroll over the meadow behind the pub (past the picnic-sets on the narrow grass pub garden) leads to an attractive churchyard around the medieval church whose bells struck Pepys (here on 12 June 1668) as 'mighty tuneable'. *(Recommended by Andy Lewcock, Maggie Cumberland, Colin McKerrow, Simon and Amanda Southwell, Ian and Jacqui Ross, M Joyner, Ian Phillips, Andrew Shore)*

Wadworths ~ Managers Les and Bunty Morgan ~ Real ale ~ Bar food ~ Restaurant ~ (01373) 834224 ~ Children in eating area of bar and restaurant ~ Open 11-11; 12-10.30 Sun; closed evening 25 Dec ~ Bedrooms: £65B/£110B

PITNEY ST4428 Map 1
Halfway House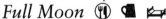

Just off B3153 W of Somerton

There's a good chatty atmosphere in this friendly old-fashioned pub with plenty of customers enjoying the fine real ales. They keep six regulars tapped from the cask – Butcombe Bitter, Cotleigh Tawny, Hop Back Summer Lightning, Otter Bitter and Bright, and Teignworthy Reel Ale, with around another four as changing guests. They also have 20 or so bottled beers from Belgium and other countries, Wilkins farm cider, and quite a few malt whiskies. The three rooms all have good log fires, and the homely feel is underlined by a profusion of books, maps and newspapers; cards and chess. Good simple filling food includes sandwiches (from £2; the smoked salmon one is popular), filled baked potatoes (from £2.25), soup (£2.50), and a fine ploughman's with home-made pickle (from £3.95). In the evening they do about half a dozen home-made curries (from £7.50). There are tables outside. *(Recommended by Hugh Roberts, P and M Rudlin, Adrian and Jane Tierney-Jones, Theo, Anne and Jane Gaskin, Veronica Brown, Robin and Sarah Constance, the Didler)*

Free house ~ Licensees Julian and Judy Lichfield ~ Real ale ~ Bar food (not Sun) ~ (01458) 252513 ~ Well behaved children welcome ~ Open 11.30-2.30, 5.30-11; 12-3, 7-10.30 Sun; closed 25 Dec

RUDGE ST8251 Map 2
Full Moon

Off A36 Bath—Warminster

At lunchtime, this is more of a local – in the evening and at weekends, there is far more emphasis on dining, with a more elaborate menu.The differently shaped rooms have a lot of character, and a gently upmarket but friendly atmosphere. The two rooms on the right have low white ceilings with a few black beams, a built-in settle by the bar, wheelbacks and slatback chairs around mainly cast-iron-framed tables, a woodburning stove in a big stone fireplace with riding boots on the mantlebeam, and big shutters by the red velvet-cushioned window seats. Other rooms are similarly furnished except the smallish flagstoned dining room with stripped pine tables and high traditional settles; there's also a small plush restaurant and a big back carpeted extension alongside the skittle alley; shove-ha'penny and cribbage. Reasonably priced tasty bar food includes home-made soup (£2.50), greek salad (£4.20), ploughman's (from £4.20), filled baked potatoes (from £4.25), open sandwiches (from £4.50; minute steak and caramelised onions £5.95), home-made fishcakes with a mango and prawn salsa (£4.95), spicy balti curry (£5.75), and tomato and spinach risotto (£5.95); also, roasted pigeon breast (£4.75), red onion and goat's cheese tart topped with parma ham (£5.25), pasta with courgettes and pesto (£8.50), chicken goujons coated in parmesan on pasta in a light tomato sauce (£9.50), fresh fish dishes, and fillet of beef with beetroot crisps (£14.50); Sunday roast lunch (they don't offer full bar food then). Several dining areas are no smoking. Well kept Bass, Butcombe Bitter, and Fullers London Pride on handpump, local ciders, and several malt whiskies. Opposite the village green, this charming pub has fine views across the valley to Salisbury Plain and Westbury White Horse. *(Recommended by Ian Phillips, Dr and Mrs J H Hills, Tom Evans, Derek and Sylvia Stephenson, Susan and Nigel Wilson, Peter and Audrey Dowsett, Edward Leetham, Bett and Brian Cox)*

Free house ~ Licensees Chris and Patrick Gifford ~ Real ale ~ Bar food ~ (01373) 830936 ~ Children welcome ~ Open 12-3, 6-11; 12-11 Sat; 12-10.30 Sun ~ Bedrooms: £40B/£60B

SOUTH STOKE ST7461 Map 2
Pack Horse

Village signposted opposite the Cross Keys off B3110, leaving Bath southwards – just before end of speed limit

For over 91 years, the same family has run this unpretentious 500-year-old pub. It was built by the local priory as a hostelry for travellers, and the entrance alleyway that runs through the middle of the building is still a public right of way to the church, and used to be the route along which the dead were carried to the cemetery. It pauses along the way at a central space by the serving bar with its well kept Courage Best, and Ushers Best and Founders on handpump or tapped from the cask, and farm cider. The ancient main room has a good local atmosphere, a log fire in the handsome stone inglenook, antique oak settles (two well carved) and cushioned captain's chairs on the quarry-tiled floor, some Royalty pictures, a chiming wall-clock, a heavy black beam-and-plank ceiling, and rough black shutters for the stone-mullioned windows (put up in World War I); the cupboard in the fireplace used to be where they kept drunks until they sobered up. There's another room down to the left (with less atmosphere). Good value bar food includes sandwiches, filled baked potatoes (from £2.50), lots of dishes at £5.85 such as pork in apple and dijon mustard sauce, chicken in stilton, lamb shank, steak and kidney pie, game suet pudding, braised steak provençale, and camembert and bacon with lyonnaise potatoes, and rump steak (£6.25). Rather fine shove-ha'penny slates are set into two of the tables, and there's dominoes. The spacious back garden has seats and pretty roses, and they keep chickens. *(Recommended by Dr Martin and Mrs Pat Forrest, Colin and Peggy Wilshire, Roger and Jenny Huggins, Susan and Nigel Wilson, Michael Doswell)*

Ushers ~ Tenant Michael Tibble ~ Real ale ~ Bar food (all day until 10pm; till 9pm Sun) ~ (01225) 832 060 ~ Children welcome ~ Open 11-11(10.30 Sun)

SPARKFORD ST6026 Map 2
Sparkford Inn

High Street; just off A303 bypass W of Wincanton

Handy for the A303, this homely old coaching inn is run by friendly people. A rambling series of rather low-beamed rooms has a nice mix of old tables in varying sizes, good dining chairs, a colour scheme leaning towards plummy browns and dusky pinks, and plenty of worthwhile prints and other things to look at – including an intricate old-fashioned scrapbook screen; no-smoking areas. There's an indoor play room for children, open on Sunday lunchtimes. Decent bar food includes sandwiches (from £2.40, prawns in lemon mayonnaise £3.40), home-made soup (£2.50), ploughman's (£4.65), and salads (from £5.50), as well as cheese and chilli scrunchies or creamy garlic mushrooms (£3.85), filled baked potatoes (from £3.95), home-cooked ham and egg (£5.50), beef and Guinness casserole, smoked haddock and bacon or vegetable pie (£5.95), steaks (from £8), and home-made puddings; the restaurant is no smoking. Well kept Butcombe Bitter, Church End What the Fox's Hat, Moor Peat Porter, Otter Bitter, and Tisbury Stonehenge on handpump, country wines, and local cider. Tables outside, with a good play area, and pretty tubs of flowers. *(Recommended by Peter and Audrey Dowsett, Mr and Mrs S R Bonfield, Stephen G Brown, Guy Consterdine, Ian Phillips, Mayur Shah, Lynn Sharpless, Bob Eardley)*

Free house ~ Licensees Nigel Tucker and Paul Clayton ~ Real ale ~ Bar food ~ Restaurant ~ (01963) 440218 ~ Children in eating area of bar ~ Open 11-11; 12-10.30 Sun; 11-2.30, 6-11 in winter ~ Bedrooms: £29.50B/£39.50B

STANTON WICK ST6162 Map 2
Carpenters Arms ♀ ⇐

Village signposted off A368, just W of junction with A37 S of Bristol

A cheerful new licensee has taken over this enjoyable pub and has decorated the bars. The Coopers Parlour on the right has one or two beams, seats around heavy tables with fresh flowers, and attractive curtains and plants in the windows; on the angle between here and the bar area there's a fat woodburning stove in an opened-through corner fireplace. The bar has wood-backed built-in wall seats and some red fabric-cushioned stools, stripped stone walls, and a big log fire. Diners are encouraged to step down into a snug inner room (lightened by mirrors in arched 'windows'), or to go round to the sturdy tables angling off on the right; most of these tables get booked at weekends. Good bar food now includes home-made soup (£2.75), filled french bread (from £3.95; steak, onion and mushroom £6.25), macaroni cheese or grilled goat's cheese with roasted peppers on a bed of aubergines and tomato (£4.25), home-made game terrine (£4.55), devilled kidneys with red onions, mushrooms and a red wine sauce (£5.65), chargrilled ham and eggs (£6.75), roast cod with a chilli lime crust and spicy salsa (£7.75), cumberland sausage with onion gravy and garlic mash (£7.95), home-made pies, chicken breast stuffed with wild mushrooms and spinach with a mustard sauce (£8.25), and steaks (from £10.25). Well kept Bass and Butcombe Bitter on handpump, a decent wine list, and quite a few malt whiskies; cribbage and fruit machine. There are picnic-sets on the front terrace and pretty flowerbeds. *(Recommended by Howard Clutterbuck, JCW, Susan and Nigel Wilson, Iain Robertson, Julian Holland, Sarah Laver, John Knighton, Robin and Sarah Constance)*

Free house ~ Licensee Simon Pledge ~ Real ale ~ Bar food ~ Restaurant ~ (01761) 490202 ~ Children welcome ~ Pianist at weekends ~ Open 11-11; 12-10.30 Sun ~ Bedrooms: £52.50B/£69.50B

STOGUMBER ST0937 Map 1
White Horse £

From A358 Taunton—Williton, village signposted on left at Crowcombe

In a quiet village, this pleasant whitewashed pub has been taken over by new licensees who will be carrying out some renovation work to the bars, skittle alley, and the cellar – but aim to retain the friendly community atmosphere. The neatly kept long bar room has old-fashioned built-in settles, other settles and cushioned captain's chairs around the heavy rustic tables, nice old photographs, a warm winter coal fire, and unobtrusive piped jazz, celtic folk or classical music. Reasonably priced bar food includes sandwiches (from £1.20), home-made soup (£1.80), sausage and beans (£2.20), filled baked potatoes (£2.80), ham and egg or omelettes (£3.30), ploughman's (£3.50), lasagne (£4.10), chicken curry (£4.80), steak and kidney pudding or fish pie (£5.80), steaks (from £6.50), and puddings (from £1.80). Well kept Cotleigh Tawny and Otter Ale on handpump, and farm cider in summer. A side room has sensibly placed darts and fruit machine; cribbage and separate skittle alley. The garden is quiet except for rooks and sheep in the surrounding low hills. *(Recommended by F J Willy, K R Harris, Bill and Steph Brownson, Ian Phillips, H Dickinson, Jean and Michel Hooper-Immins, Frank Davidson)*

Free house ~ Licensees Graham Roy, Edith Broada ~ Real ale ~ Bar food (11-2, 7-10) ~ Restaurant ~ (01984) 656277 ~ Children in eating area of bar and restaurant ~ Open 11-2.30, 6-11; 12-3, 7-10.30 Sun ~ Bedrooms: £27B/£40B

STOKE ST GREGORY ST3527 Map 1
Rose & Crown 🍴 🍷 🛏

Woodhill; follow North Curry signpost off A378 by junction with A358 – keep on to Stoke, bearing right in centre

Mr and Mrs Browning have now been running this popular country cottage for 20 years – and it remains a genuinely friendly pub with particularly good food cooked by the Brownings' two sons, and a comfortable place to stay. The neatly kept bar is decorated in a cosy and pleasantly romanticised stable theme: dark wooden loose-box partitions for some of the interestingly angled nooks and alcoves, lots of brasses and bits on the low beams and joists, stripped stonework, and appropriate pictures including a highland pony carrying a stag; many of the wildlife paintings on the walls are the work of the landlady, and there's an 18th-c glass-covered well in one corner. Using fresh local produce, fresh fish from Brixham, and their own eggs, the bar food at lunchtime might include sandwiches in home-made granary bread, grilled liver and bacon (£6.75), scrumpy chicken or gammon and pineapple (£6.95), grilled skate wings (£7.75), vegetarian dishes such as nut roast chasseur or stir-fried vegetables, steaks (from £8.95), and puddings (£2.75); in the evening, they offer a three-course meal for £13.25 with more elaborate dishes like stuffed Burgundy snails, lobster soup, roast duckling with orange or roast rack of lamb. Plentiful breakfasts, and a good three-course Sunday lunch (£7.95). One small dining area is no smoking. Well kept Exmoor Ale, Hardy Country and Royal Oak, and a guest beer on handpump, Thatchers farm cider, and a good wine list; unobtrusive piped classical music, dominoes, and skittle alley. Under cocktail parasols by an apple tree on the sheltered front terrace are some picnic-sets; summer barbecues and a pets corner for children. In summer, residents have use of a heated swimming pool. The pub is in an interesting Somerset Levels village with willow beds still supplying the two basket works. *(Recommended by Paul S McPherson, Lyn and Geoff Hallchurch, Roy Smylie, Barbara and Brian Greenhaf, M G Hart, Mr and Mrs Broadhurst, Mr and Mrs R Banks, Pat and John Millward, R D and C M Hillman, Mrs Y Richardson, Theo, Anne and Jane Gaskin, Mike and Wena Stevenson, Mr and Mrs N Fuller, Roger and Jenny Huggins, Karen Eliot, John and June Hayward)*

Free house ~ Licensees Ron and Irene Browning ~ Real ale ~ Bar food ~ Restaurant ~ (01823) 490296 ~ Children welcome ~ Open 11-3, 6.30-11; 12-3, 7-10.30 Sun ~ Bedrooms: £25(£35B)/£38(£50B)

TRISCOMBE ST1535 Map 1
Blue Ball 🍴 🍷

Village signposted off A358 Crowcombe—Bagborough; OS Sheet 181 map reference 155355

Somerset Dining Pub of the Year

Tucked away into the Quantocks, this snug little unspoilt pub has quite a reputation for its popular, imaginative food with an emphasis on fresh fish dishes. It's run by a friendly, cheerful landlord who has carefully improved the beamed bar and former conservatory by careful reworking with panelling and rough-sawn oak partitions, and added attractive sporting prints, memorabilia and lanterns, and a woodburner in the opened up inglenook fireplace. The menu changes weekly, but at lunchtime might include home-made soup (£2.25), filled french bread (£3.95), moules marinières (£4.95), baked clams (£5.25), broccoli and stilton quiche or seafood crumble (£5.50), indonesian-style beef curry or fresh shrimps (£5.95), fresh Cornish crab (£7.95), and fresh lobster salad (£10.95); evening dishes such as smoked chicken and avocado in a blue cheese sauce (£3.50), chicken liver terrine (£3.95), crevettes with chilli and garlic (£5.50), baked fennel with ginger and orange (£7.95), open ravioli of feta and sun-dried tomatoes with olive tapenade (£9.25), roast duck breast with spring onion and port sauce (£10.95), fillet steak with horseradish mash and red wine coulis (£12.50), seared scallops and warm potato salad, seafood medley in a thick chowder sauce or tempura-fried monkfish with lemon couscous (£12.95), and puddings like chocolate and orange truffle or mango cheesecake with Benedictine and sweet potato and tiramisu (from £3.25). Well kept Cotleigh Tawny and two weekly changing guest beers, a marvellous wine list (they will open any bottle under £20 if you want only a glass), a dozen malt whiskies, and farm cider. They have two tortoiseshell cats, tables outside in the colourful woodside terraced garden with peaceful hill views, and a holiday cottage next door. *(Recommended by James Flory, G W A Pearce, Dr P F A Watkins, Veronica Brown, Mr and Mrs J M Lefeaux, Christopher Darwent, David Lewis, Sarah Lart, D Godden, D S and T M Beeson)*

Free house ~ Licensee Patrick Groves ~ Real ale ~ Bar food ~ Restaurant ~ (01984) 618242 ~ Well behaved children welcome ~ Open 12-2.30, 7-11(10.30 Sun); closed 25 Dec

WAMBROOK ST2907 Map 1
Cotley 🍴 🛏

Village signposted off A30 W of Chard; don't follow the small signs to Cotley itself

No matter how busy this popular stone-built pub is, the friendly licensees always offer a warm welcome. It's in a quiet spot reached down country lanes, has plenty of surrounding walks, and is a fine place to stay – with lovely breakfasts. There is a smart but unpretentious local atmosphere and the simple flagstoned entrance bar opens on one side into a small plush bar, with beyond that a two-room no-smoking dining area; several open fires. An extension is often used for painting sessions, and the results (complete with price-tags in case you see something you like) can be seen around the walls of the various rooms. Generous helpings of enjoyable food include sandwiches, home-made soup (£2.50), devilled mushrooms on toast (£3.50), lamb's kidneys with port and cream (£3.75), lasagne or vegetable and stilton crumble (£6.95), gammon and egg (£7.50), chicken with ginger and cream sauce (£7.95), whole trout stuffed with apple and celery (£8.95), steaks (from £7.95), three lamb chops with rosemary and garlic (£8.50), and whole king prawns (£9.95) . The restaurant is no smoking. Otter Ale and Wadworths 6X on handpump kept under light blanket pressure, and a good choice of wines; pool, piped music, and skittle alley. Out in the garden below are some picnic-sets, with a play area and goldfish pool. *(Recommended by Joyce and Geoff Robson, Mick Hitchman, Mr and Mrs Broadhurst, J M Lefeaux, Richard and Margaret Peers, Chris Raisin, Mr and Mrs J Bishop, Anthony Barnes, John and Christine Simpson, Basil J S Minson, Ann and Colin Hunt)*

Free house ~ Licensee David Rex Livingstone ~ Real ale ~ Bar food ~ Restaurant ~ (01460) 62348 ~ Children welcome ~ Open 12-3, 7-11 ~ Bedrooms: £29B/£41B

WELLS ST5545 Map 2
City Arms

High St

Just off the High Street and through a charming cobbled couryard with white metal seats and tables, virginia-creepered walls, an attractive side verandah, and trees and flowers in pots, is this characterful 16th-c pub. It's rather like a cellar bar with arched doorways with double baluster-shaped pillars, green-cushioned mate's chairs, a nice old black settle, a Regency-style settee and a couple of well worn, homely sofas, a plush pink sturdy wall settle, and a really relaxed, friendly atmosphere – the sort of place where single women feel perfectly comfortable; up a step is a similar room with pictures and Wills Grand National cigarette cards on the walls, big tables and solid chairs, and beyond that, a separate bar with neat sturdy brocaded settles forming booths around tables; plenty of Victorian and Victorian-style engravings. Served by neat, cheerful staff, the interesting bar food might include soup (£2.25), sandwiches (from £3.35; chargrilled chicken breast and bacon baguette £3.95), ploughman's (from £4.25), home-cooked ham and eggs (£4.35), beef and ale sausage with rich onion gravy (£4.60), home-made salmon and spinach fishcakes (£4.70), vegetable pilaf (£5.35), steak and kidney in ale pie (£5.95), steaks (from £8.95), and evening extras like Thai chicken (£8.25), baked salmon with broccoli and prawns in a light pastry case with a white wine and tarragon sauce (£9.25), and supreme of duck with a rich red wine sauce and roasted shallots (£9.50); the chutneys and preserves are home-made. They keep four real ales on handpump such as Butcombe Bitter, Dartmoor Bitter, Hardy Country and Marstons Pedigree, with a guest such as Black Sheep or Timothy Taylor Landlord; piped pop music. There's a a fine open-beamed upstairs restaurant. *(Recommended by B T Smith, Meg and Colin Hamilton, Howard Clutterbuck, Peter Smith)*

Free house ~ Licensees Brian and Sue Marshall ~ Real ale ~ Bar food (snacks all day; main meals 12-3, 6-10) ~ Restaurant ~ (01749) 673916 ~ Children in eating area of bar and restaurant ~ Open 11-11; 12-10.30 Sun

WINSFORD SS9034 Map 1
Royal Oak ♀ 🛏

In Exmoor National Park, village signposted from A396 about 10 miles S of Dunster

Set in a lovely valley, this immaculate and very pretty thatched inn is enjoyed by quite a mix of customers. It remains popular locally (always a good sign) but also has plenty of diners and residents, too – which all creates a relaxed, chatty atmosphere. The attractively furnished and cosy lounge bar has a cushioned big bay-window seat from which you can look across the road towards the village green and foot and packhorse bridges over the River Winn, tartan-cushioned bar stools by the panelled counter (above which hang horsebrasses and pewter tankards), the same cushions on the armed windsor chairs set around little wooden tables, and a splendid iron fireback in the big stone hearth (with a log fire in winter). Another similar bar offers more eating space with built-in wood-panelled seats creating booths, fresh flowers, and country prints; there are several pretty and comfortable lounges. Well liked bar food includes good home-made soup such as asparagus and lovage or brown onion (£2.50), sandwiches (with salad and crisps, from £3.35; steak sandwich with mushrooms and tomatoes £5.25), home-made chicken liver pâté (£3.95), ploughman's (£4.95), chargrilled chicken fillet with tomato butter (£6.65), steak and kidney pudding (£8.25; the chicken and leek pie is very good), lamb pasty (£7.95), sirloin steak (£10.95), daily specials such as bacon and onion quiche (£3.95), escalope of pork with a creamy cider sauce (£6.95), seared tuna steak with capers (£7.50), and venison steak with provençale sauce or roast leg of Exmoor lamb (£7.95), and home-made puddings like honey and drambuie cheesecake, bakewell tart or strawberry charlotte (£2.95). Well kept Exmoor Ale and a changing guest beer on handpump; shove-ha'penny, cribbage, and dominoes. They do a useful guide to Exmoor National Park identifying places to visit and there are good nearby walks – up Winsford Hill for magnificent views, or over to Exford. *(Recommended by David and Anne Culley, Nigel Woolliscroft, Mrs J Murphy, Peter and Audrey Dowsett, Christopher Darwent, Pauline Starley, R J Walden, E A Froggatt, P A Legon, Howard and Barbara Clutterbuck, Yavuz and Shirley Mutlu, Adrian and Jane Tierney-Jones, Darly Graton, Graeme Gulibert, John and Christine Vittoe, Gordon)*

Free house ~ Licensee Charles Steven ~ Real ale ~ Bar food ~ Restaurant ~ (01643) 851455 ~ Children in eating area of bar and restaurant ~ Open 11-3, 6-11; 12-3, 7-10.30 Sun ~ Bedrooms: £45B/£65B

Most pubs in the *Guide* sell draught cider. We mention it specifically only if they have unusual farm-produced 'scrumpy' or even specialise in it.

644 *Somerset*

WITHYPOOL SS8435 Map 1
Royal Oak ♀ ⇔
Village signposted off B3233

Set in the middle of Exmoor National Park, this bustling and friendly country village inn has plenty of fine riverside or moorland walks – and should you decide to stay overnight, the licensees arrange riding, hunting, fishing, shooting, and Exmoor safaris; breakfasts are good, and can be enjoyed by non residents, too. The smart cosy beamed lounge bar has a fine raised log fireplace, comfortably cushioned wall seating and slat-backed chairs, and stags' heads, stuffed fish, several fox masks, sporting prints and paintings and various copper and brass ornaments (including a warship's binnacle) on its walls. The locals' bar (named after the barman Jake who has been here for 25 years) has some fine old oak tables, and plenty of character. Good bar food includes sandwiches (from £2; sirloin steak and onions in a big roll £3.80), ploughman's (from £3.80), filled baked potatoes (from £3.90), mixed cheese and broccoli pasta bake (£5), sausages such as pork and garlic or venison and bacon (from £6), home-cooked ham and eggs (£6.25), steaks (from £6.50 for 4oz minute), daily specials such as curried parsnip or Italian tomato soup (£2.20), country terrine with nuts (£3.75), tiger prawns (£4.25), seafood pancakes (£4.75), steak and kidney pie (£6), game pie or sweet and sour pork (£6.50), and skate wing (£7.50). Well kept Exmoor Ale on handpump, over 25 malt whiskies, a decent wine list, and farm cider. It can get very busy (especially on Sunday lunchtimes), and is popular with the local hunting and shooting types; cribbage, dominoes, and shove-ha'penny; piped music in the restaurant only. There are wooden benches on the terrace, and just up the road, some grand views from Winsford Hill. The River Barle runs through the village itself, with pretty bridleways following it through a wooded combe further upstream. R D Blackmore stayed here while writing *Lorna Doone*. *(Recommended by Richard Gibbs, Graham and Karen Oddey, Harry and Doreen Payne, Ray Ryan, Peter and Audrey Dowsett, Dr Rod Holcombe, P A Legon, Sarah and Peter Gooderham, Mrs H Forrest, JKW, Lesley Sones, Colin and Peggy Wilshire, Jane and Adrian Tierney-Jones)*

Free house ~ Licensees Richard and Jo-Anne Howard ~ Real ale ~ Bar food ~ Restaurant ~ (01643) 831506 ~ Children in eating area of bar ~ Open 11.30-11; 12-11 Sun ~ Bedrooms: £33B/£74B

WOOKEY ST5145 Map 2
Burcott
B3139 W of Wells

The two simply furnished small front bar rooms in this neatly kept and friendly little roadside pub are connected but different in character, with a square corner bar counter in the lounge, fresh flowers at either end of the mantlepiece above the tiny stone fireplace, Parker-Knollish brocaded chairs around a couple of tables, and high bar stools; the other bar has beams (some willow pattern plates on one), a solid settle by the window and a high backed old pine settle by one wall, cushioned mate's chairs and fresh flowers on the mix of nice old pine tables, dried flowers in a brass coal scuttle, old-fashioned oil-type wall lamps, and a hunting horn on the bressumer above the fireplace. A little room on the right has darts, shove-ha'penny, cribbage and dominoes, neat built-in wall seats, and small framed advertisements for Schweppes, Coke, Jennings and Oakhill, and there's a roomy back restaurant with black joists, stripped stone walls and sea-green check tablecloths. Tasty bar food includes home-made soup (£2.25), sandwiches (1½ rounds, from £2.25; toasties from £2.15; open french sticks £3.40), filled baked potatoes (from £3.45), stuffed mushrooms (£3.60), ploughman's (from £4.45), home-cooked ham and eggs (£5.25), 8 pasta dishes like meaty or vegetarian lasagne (£6.15), home-made steak and kidney pie (£6.25), chicken with a wine and orange sauce (£8.95), salmon fillet topped with prawn and parsley sauce (£10.45), steaks (from £10.50), and daily specials. Well kept Cotleigh Barn Owl, Cottage Southern Bitter, and Timothy Taylor Landlord on handpump, and several wines by the glass. The sizeable garden is well spread and has picnic-sets and plenty of small trees and shrubs, and there's a paddock beyond. The window boxes and tubs at the front are pretty in summer. *(Recommended by Evelyn and Derek Walter, Mr and Mrs J M Lefeaux)*

Free house ~ Licensees Ian and Anne Stead ~ Real ale ~ Bar food (not Sun evenings) ~ Restaurant ~ (01749) 673874 ~ Children in eating area of bar and restaurant ~ Open 11.30-2.30(3 Sat), 6-11; 12-3, 7-10.30 Sun; closed 25 Dec, 1 Jan

---

Lucky Dip

Besides the fully inspected pubs, you might like to try these Lucky Dips recommended to us and described by readers (if you do, please send us reports):

Abbots Leigh [ST5473]
George [A369, between M5 junction 19 and Bristol]: Friendly main-road dining pub with huge choice of attractively presented food from snacks up, real ales inc Marstons Pedigree; no children, good-sized enclosed garden *(LYM, J Osborn-Clarke, Simon and Amanda Southwell)*
Ashcott [ST4436]
☆ *Pipers* [A39/A361, SE of village]: Large cosy welcoming lounge, wide choice of good reasonably priced food from sandwiches to steaks inc vegetarian and children's in prettily set no-smoking beamed dining area, well kept ales such as Butcombe, Cotleigh, Courage Best and John Smiths; prompt service, log fire, pleasant roadside garden *(Christopher and Mary Thomas, F J and A Parmenter, Dr and Mrs A K Clarke, Mrs Lynda Matthews)*
☆ *Ring o' Bells* [follow Church and Village Hall signs off A39 W of Street]: Neatly kept comfortably modernised local, steps up and down making snug areas, well kept local Moors Avalon Springtime, Merlins Magic or Withy Cutter with two interesting guest beers such as Moondance Triple FFF or Humpty Dumpty Butt Jumper (all the way from Reedham – see Norfolk main entries), Wilkins' farm cider, wide choice of good value well presented food inc some unusual dishes, vegetarian and build-you-up puddings, separate no-smoking stripy pink dining room, decent wines, chatty landlord and helpful service, inglenook woodburner; piped pop music; skittle alley, fruit machines; very nicely planted back garden with play area *(Veronica Brown, Adrian and Jane Tierney-Jones, BB, Mr and Mrs K H Burton, Robert and Sarah Sibson)*
Ashill [ST3116]
☆ *Square & Compass* [Windmill Hill; turn off A358 at Stewley Cross Garage]: A strong recommendation - unassuming tucked-away country pub with sweeping views, simple comfortable furnishings, open fire, enjoyable and enterprising freshly made food from sandwiches through interesting snacks to carefully cooked main dishes, well kept Exmoor, Greene King Abbot, Marstons Pedigree, Morlands Old Speckled Hen and local guest beers, chatty friendly service, traditional games, restaurant; children in eating areas, tables outside, good play area *(LYM, Richard Percival, Colin Roberts, Roger Price)*
Axbridge [ST4255]
☆ *Lamb* [The Square; off A371 Cheddar—Winscombe]: Welcoming old inn in attractive square, dark beams, rambling odd corners,

good value generous food (not Sun evening) inc good vegetarian choice and lots of puddings, well kept ales such as Bass, Butcombe and Wadworths 6X, Thatcher's farm cider, huge log fire, staff cheerful even when busy, pub games inc table skittles, pretty little garden, skittle alley; children in eating area; old-world spacious bedrooms, huge breakfast *(Comus Elliott, LYM, Alan and Paula McCully, JCW)*
Backwell [ST4968]
George [Farleigh Rd; A370 W of Bristol]: Pleasantly modernised old coaching inn with soft lighting, well kept Ushers, well priced food inc good fresh fish in bar and separate restaurant, good choice of wines, good service; children welcome, pleasant terrace and garden with play area *(Gwen and Peter Andrews, Alan and Paula McCully)*
Rising Sun [Weston Rd (A370)]: Wide range of home-cooked food inc great choice of self-serve veg and excellent bargain weekday OAP lunches; Courage, Fullers, Marstons Pedigree *(K R Harris)*
Banwell [ST3959]
Brewers Arms [Church St]: Very old genuine local with friendly landlord, cheap food, two well kept Ushers beers and farm cider; shame that the huge inglenook fireplace has a giant TV screen instead of a roaring log fire; good outside area inc ducks on little stream *(Dr and Mrs A K Clarke, Comus Elliott)*
Barrow Gurney [ST5367]
☆ *Princes Motto* [B3130, just off A370/A38]: Very welcoming cosy unpretentious local, long refurbished lounge/dining area up behind snug traditional tap room, well kept Bass and other ales such as Butcombe, Wadworths IPA and 6X, cheap wholesome lunchtime snacks, cricket team photographs, jugs and china, pleasant garden *(LYM, Tom Evans, Simon and Amanda Southwell, Steve and Carolyn Harvey, Alan and Paula McCully)*
Bath [ST7565]
Bell [Walcot St]: Musicians' pub, with well kept Butcombe, Wadworths 6X and guest beers, good cheap rolls, friendly efficient service; frequent free music *(Dr and Mrs A K Clarke, LM, JP, PP)*
Coeur de Lion [Northumberland Pl; off High St by W H Smith]: Tiny single-room pub in charming flower-filled flagstoned pedestrian alley, cosy and friendly little bar, well kept mainly Whitbreads-related ales, good mulled wine at Christmas, log-effect gas fire, lunchtime filled rolls in summer – perhaps Bath's prettiest pub, esp in summer *(LYM, Dr and Mrs A K*

Clarke, Giles Francis, Veronica Brown, the Didler)

☆ *Cross Keys* [Midford Rd]: Well refurbished dining lounge with smarter end restaurant (best to book, high chairs for children), good cheap food cooked to order from home-made burgers and sausages through popular pies to duck with cherry sauce, good chips and veg, great choice of puddings, Courage Directors, Ushers Bitter and Founders, friendly service, locals' bar; big garden with prettily populated aviary – great attraction for children *(Meg and Colin Hamilton)*

Curfew [Clevedon Pl W]: Busy and friendly low-ceilinged bar, big table on landing down stairs, Bass and Wadworths IPA, no music *(R Huggins, D Irving, E McCall, T McLean, Dr and Mrs A K Clarke)*

Farm House [Lansdown Rd]: Pleasant setting on hill overlooking Bath, good choice of food and well kept beer, jazz some evenings *(Dr and Mrs A K Clarke, the Didler)*

☆ *George I* [Mill Lane, Bathampton (off A36 towards Warminster or A4 towards Chippenham)]: Attractive creeper-covered canalside pub, wide choice of well presented usual food inc fish and vegetarian, good log fires, Bass, Courage Directors and Wadworths 6X, quick friendly service even when busy; dining room by towpath, no-smoking family room, tables on quiet safe spacious back terrace with garden bar (interesting seats on front yard, but traffic noise then); can get crowded, esp weekends *(GSB, H and D Payne, LM, R C Fendick)*

Hacketts [Queen St, off Queen Sq]: Daily-changing beers such as Batemans XXXB and Hook Norton at below-average prices, lunchtime food (not Sun); steps up to pub, and to lavatories; can get very busy Sat night *(G Coates, the Didler)*

Mulligans [Westgate Rd]: Small simple Irish bar, good lunchtime snacks, traditional music, impressive choice of whiskeys, pleasant staff *(anon)*

Pig & Fiddle [Saracen St]: Small busy pub with good unusual choice of real ales from island bar, friendly service, two big open fires, clocks set to different time zones, relaxed daytime, very lively at night (lots of students), good piped music, seats on big front terrace; home-cooked food here and in upper restaurant area, takeaways too *(Dr and Mrs A K Clarke, D Irving, E McCall, R Huggins, T McLean)*

Pulteney Arms [Daniel St]: Very small, with well kept Bass, Oakhill and Wadworths 6X, good chip baps and other fine food, jugs around walls; popular with Bath rugby players, unobtrusive piped music or juke box; pavement tables *(Dr and Mrs A K Clarke)*

Richmond Arms [Richmond Pl, off Lansdown Rd]: Small 18th-c two-room local off the tourist track, good simple food on scrubbed pine tables, well kept beer, friendly staff, interesting décor; tables in front garden *(Miss A G Drake)*

Rising Sun [Grove St]: Friendly and relaxed small pub doing well under newish landlord, Ushers Best, Founders, a seasonal and guest ale,

attractively priced food *(Colin Wilshire)*

Sam Weller [Upper Borough Walls]: Well kept Bass and Wadworths 6X, good food cooked to order inc all-day breakfast, no-smoking area, friendly young staff, lively mixed clientele *(Dr and Mrs A K Clarke)*

☆ *Star* [The Paragon, junction with Guinea Lane]: Four small friendly and unspoilt interconnecting rooms separated by glass and panelling, particularly well kept Bass and Wadworths 6X in jugs from the cask, Wickwar BOB on handpump, low prices, basic old-fashioned furnishings, card-playing regulars in snug, dim lighting (famously bricked-in windows), no piped music; open all day Sat, cl lunchtime Mon-Thurs *(Pete Baker, BB, JP, PP, D Irving, R Huggins, E McCall, T McLean, Dr and Mrs A K Clarke, the Didler)*

Bathford [ST7966]

Crown [Bathford Hill, towards Bradford on Avon, by Batheaston roundabout and bridge]: Spacious and attractively laid out, several distinct but linked areas inc no-smoking garden room, good log fire, wide choice of food inc bargain deals (otherwise not that cheap), well kept Worthington Best and other ales, decent wines; families welcome, with children's entertainment Sun, tables on terrace, nice garden *(Meg and Colin Hamilton, LYM)*

Bilbrook [ST0340]

Dragon House: Very good atmosphere, food and service under new landlord *(R C Watkins)*

Bishops Lydeard [ST1629]

Bird in Hand [Mount St]: Comfortable village local with young and pleasant staff, real ales such as Brakspears and Butcombe, maybe sandwiches and freshly baked pizzas; garden, cl Thurs lunchtime *(Veronica Brown)*

☆ *Kingfisher* [A358 towards Taunton]: Two neat communicating rooms, cottagey and relaxing, with quick cheerful service and concentration on food, from good beef sandwiches up; well kept local real ale, comfortably shaded tables outside *(Frank Davidson, LYM, Howard Clutterbuck)*

Blagdon [ST5059]

New Inn [Church St]: Good reasonably priced food, ancient beams, two big inglenook log fires, interesting antique settles among comfortable more modern furniture, well kept Bass and Wadworths ales, a couple of dogs, well behaved children in eating area, nice view down to lake from picnic-sets on back grass; piped music, pub games *(LYM, Comus Elliott)*

Seymour Arms [Bath Rd (A368)]: Pleasant family pub with wholesome food inc OAP weekday lunchtime bargains, Tetleys-related ales and one brewed for the pub by Churchill on handpump, solid furnishings, raised balustraded areas, good décor; good car park, steps down to pub *(Tom Evans)*

Blagdon Hill [ST2217]

☆ *Lamb & Flag* [4 miles S of Taunton]: Cosy, clean and welcoming, tastefully and simply decorated in homely and relaxing country style keeping beams, settles etc; friendly licensees, good fair-priced food, well kept Otter ales, log fire; entertainment evenings *(David and Benita*

Moores, David and Jean Hall, Rex Miller)
Bradford on Tone [ST1722]
White Horse: Welcoming stonebuilt local in quiet village, pleasant décor, varied reasonably priced good food (worth the wait) in bar and restaurant, Cotleigh Tawny and decent wines, well laid out side garden, skittle alley *(Neil Townend)*
Brent Knoll [ST3350]
☆ *Red Cow* [2 miles from M5 junction 22; right on to A38, then first left]: Sensibly short choice of good value food inc proper veg and Sun lunch in warmly welcoming spotless dining lounge where children allowed, with well spaced tables, quick pleasant service even on crowded bank hols, well kept beers such as Fullers London Pride, skittle alley, sheltered gardens *(BB, M G Hart, Margaret and Bill Rogers, Michael Hill, Mark J Hydes)*
Bristol [ST5773]
Alma [Alma Vale Rd, Clifton]: Cheerful town pub well refurbished without losing character, real ales such as Greene King Abbot, Theakstons XB and Wadworths 6X, good plain cheap food, friendly service, no music; popular upstairs theatre Tues-Sat – best to book *(Simon and Amanda Southwell)*
Bag o' Nails [St Georges Rd, Hotwells]: Small shop front for cosy room with small tables along its length, wooden floor, inglenook seat by gas fire, glazed peepholes into cellar, old local pictures, real ales such as Adnams Oyster Stout, Butts Barbus Barbus and Smiles Best *(G Coates)*
☆ *Brewery Tap* [Upper Maudlin St/Colston St]: Tap for Smiles brewery, small and busy – get there early for a seat; their beers kept well and sensibly priced, also unusual continental bottled ones, interesting unpretentious décor, good chatty atmosphere even when packed, log fire in no-smoking room, food inc filled rolls and vegetarian, no piped music; cl Sun *(Simon and Amanda Southwell, Dr and Mrs A K Clarke)*
Bridge [Passage St]: Neat tiny one-bar city pub close to Courage Brewery, popular lunchtime snacks, good friendly service, lots of film stills, well kept beers; nr floating harbour *(Dr and Mrs A K Clarke)*
Chateau [Park St]: Big busy Smiles pub with their ales kept well, Victorian feel, lots of pictures, open fires, roomy back conservatory, good home-made lunchtime food (many tables reserved Sat), more limited evening *(Simon and Amanda Southwell, Veronica Brown)*
Commercial Rooms [Corn St]: Vast Wetherspoons establishment in impressive building, lofty ceiling, snug cubicles along one side, can get smoky – comfortable quieter back room should be better; reasonable prices, wide changing choice of good real ales, food all day; good location, very busy w/e evenings *(Simon and Amanda Southwell, Val Stevenson, Rob Holmes, Dr and Mrs A K Clarke)*
Coronation Tap [Sion Pl, Clifton; off Portland St]: Friendly bustling old-fashioned low-ceilinged tavern with fat casks of interesting farm ciders, Courage Best and Directors, simple lunchtime food *(LYM, Margaret and Bill Rogers)*

Cottage [Baltic Wharf, Cumberland Rd]: Converted customs house on southern bank of floating harbour, access through sailing club; Boddingtons, Flowers IPA and Wadworths 6X, reasonable range of lunchtime food, plenty of space; piped music may be loud, pub can get smoky; open all day, fine views of Bath landmarks from terrace, handy for SS *Great Britain* and Maritime Heritage Centre *(Richard and Margaret Peers)*
Fleece & Firkin [St Thomas St, off Redcliff St and Victoria St]: Lively atmosphere in lofty dim-lit 18th-c hall stripped back to original stonework and flagstones, basic furniture, well kept Smiles, lunchtime food (not Sun) inc gigantic filled baps, pleasant staff, live music Weds-Sat, children weekends *(LYM)*
☆ *Hope & Anchor* [Jacobs Wells Rd, Clifton]: Character bare-boards 18th-c pub with plenty of atmosphere, hop bines, various sizes of old pine table, good choice of particularly well kept ales such as Adnams Broadside, Badger Tanglefoot, Bath SPA, Fullers London Pride and Shepherd Neame Spitfire, fast efficient service by pleasant studenty staff, good generous food inc interesting dishes – very popular lunchtime; summer evening barbecues on good back terrace with interesting niches, occasional live music *(Hugh Roberts, Dr and Mrs B D Smith)*
Lion [Church Lane, Clifton]: Two unspoilt bare-boards bars, friendly welcome, well kept beer *(Dr and Mrs A K Clarke)*
Llandoger Trow [off King St/Welsh Back]: By docks, interesting as the last timber-framed building built here, and making the most of its picturesque past in very cosy collection of small alcoves and rooms with original fireplaces and carvings; some concentration on food, draught sherries, eclectic array of liqueur coffees *(Val Stevenson, Rob Holmes, Chris Raisin)*
Masons Arms [Park Rd, Stapleton]: Unspoilt and traditional, good range of real ales inc some local ones, spectacular views from good terrace *(Dr and Mrs A K Clarke)*
Micawbers Ale House [St Michaels Hill]: Friendly two-bar pub, former Colston Arms, with quiet garden *(Dr and Mrs A K Clarke)*
Old Fish Market [Baldwin St]: Ground floor of imposing red and cream brick building converted to Fullers pub, good mural showing it in 1790s along one wall, lots of wood inc rather ornate counter, parquet floor, lunchtime food inc sandwiches and home-baked pies, Fullers ales, good coffee, daily papers, quiet piped music *(Ian Phillips, Dr and Mrs A K Clarke)*
Penny Farthing [Whiteladies Rd, Clifton]: Panelled pub with late Victorian bric-a-brac inc penny farthing, armchairs opp bar, lots of table seating, at least five real ales such as Butcombe and Wadworths 6X racked behind bar, home-made food lunchtime and evening, friendly helpful staff; can get very busy evenings *(Simon and Amanda Southwell)*
Plume of Feathers [Hotwell Rd]: Under new management, Marstons beers, wide range of food, open all day, pool table *(P B Godfrey)*

Rhubarb [Queen Ann Rd, Barton Hill]: Tastefully restored, with lots of old photographs, well kept beer, separate drinking areas, pool, nice people *(Dr and Mrs A K Clarke)*

Shakespeare [Lower Redland Rd]: Pleasant atmosphere and décor, friendly service, plenty of choice of genuinely home-made food *(Mrs Lesley Chiles)*

Ship [Lower Park Row]: Low-ceilinged long narrow bar with fascinating nautical memorabilia, dimly lit back balcony, spiral stairs down to lower area with pool table, small lounge, several well kept ales such as Smiles and Wadworths 6X, reasonably priced food; small sunny terrace, well reproduced piped music esp evening, open all day *(Lyn and Geoff Hallchurch)*

Watershed [Canons Rd]: Particularly well kept Bitter in this large multi-media art centre's lively café-bar *(Dr and Mrs A K Clarke)*

Burnham on Sea [ST3049]

Railway [High St]: Seaside pub nr front, good range of ales inc Boddingtons, decent wine, wide choice of low-priced food, friendly efficient service, no piped music; discos *(Peter and Audrey Dowsett)*

Burrington [ST4759]

Burrington Inn: Large restaurant-pub in beautiful surroundings, next to well laid-out garden centre; extensive menu, several real ales, attractive décor, no piped music *(Peter and Audrey Dowsett)*

Chard [ST3208]

Choughs [High St]: Attractive 16th-c building (supposedly haunted by Judge Jeffreys) with friendly family service, farm cider, cheap usual food *(Howard Clutterbuck, R T and J C Moggridge)*

Hornsbury Mill [Hornsbury Hill (A358 N)]: Well run restaurant with rooms rather than pub, but also does snacks in comfortable bar (tidy dress); charming setting by big pond with ducks, natural fountains and turning mill wheel – good for children; bedrooms *(Howard Clutterbuck)*

Lord Leeze [well signed on outskirts]: Interesting and unusual food in bar or dining conservatory, Boddingtons, choice of wine *(Janet Pickles)*

Charlton Musgrove [ST7229]

☆ *Smithy* [B3081, 5 miles SE of Bruton; about a mile off A303]: Quiet open-plan 18th-c pub, roomy and sparkling clean, with stripped stone, heavy beams, log fires, plenty of pleasantly secluded corners, good range of cheap tasty home-cooked food inc Sun lunch and good vegetarian choice, well kept Bass and Smiles, cheerful landlord, good service, walking sticks for sale; arch to small restaurant overlooking garden full of cottagey flower tubs; skittle alley and pool table *(Brian Chambers, K R Harris, WHBM, Alan and Paula McCully)*

Chew Magna [ST5861]

☆ *Pony & Trap* [New Town; back rd to Bishop Sutton]: Attractively refurbished Ushers pub in delightfully rural hillside setting, relaxing atmosphere, flagstones and antiques, well kept

ales inc seasonal, good coffee, good value generous food inc vegetarian, friendly efficient staff, daily papers (ballpoint pens for crosswords); quiet piped music, children's room, good views at the back; good walks *(K Boreland, G Thomas, Dr and Mrs B D Smith, Tom Evans, Martyn and Katie Alderton)*

Chew Stoke [ST5661]

Stoke Inn: Large straightforward welcoming family pub with good carefully cooked food from sandwiches to wonderful steaks, well kept Bass, local Butcombe, Courage, Smiles and Youngers, good fresh coffee, helpful smartly dressed staff, no-smoking restaurant; piped music, jazz Sun lunchtime in back room, side garden *(MRSM, Jenny and Michael Back, A C and J M Curry, J W G Nunns)*

Churchill [ST4560]

Nelson Arms [Skinners Lane; A368, just off A38 SW of Bristol]: Roomy and atmospheric bar with lots of dining tables, small rustic dining room, very popular bargain weekday roasts in huge helpings, other cheap food, Ushers ales, several ciders; piped music, pool room; tables outside *(Michael Doswell)*

Clevedon [ST4071]

Campbells Landing [The Beach]: Good position opp restored Victorian pier, done up like old Campbells steamer with nautical items inc coastal charts and old local photographs, good choice of well kept beers inc Bass, Courage and guests, wide range of food; bedrooms *(Alan and Paula McCully)*

Combe St Nicholas [ST3011]

Green Dragon [2½ miles N of Chard]: Pleasantly refurbished, good value food (should book even midweek), welcoming service, well kept ales, decent wines, open fire; well behaved children allowed; open all day Sat, bedrooms *(Howard Clutterbuck)*

Congresbury [ST4363]

Old Inn [St Pauls Causeway, off main rd]: Low-beamed tucked-away family local doing well under current licensees, smartened up without being spoilt, deep-set windows with pretty curtains, huge fireplaces, one with ancient stove opening to both bar and dining area, well kept Bass, Smiles and other ales tapped from the cask, tasty cheap food, some no-smoking tables; tables in back garden *(anon)*

☆ *White Hart* [signed from A38 Bristol—Bridgwater; Wrington Rd]: Modernised pub with fires each end of cosy lounge, solidly furnished long narrow bar, conservatory extension, some concentration on wide choice of generous tasty home-made food inc vegetarian and good puddings, full range of Badger beers kept well, welcoming landlady, good service, children's room, no piped music; good-sized garden with terrace, Mendip views, big play area and aviary *(K R Harris, Dr and Mrs A K Clarke, Tom Evans, Dr and Mrs B D Smith, Alan and Paula McCully)*

Corfe [ST2319]

☆ *White Hart* [B3170]: Welcoming licensees, son cooks good food inc vegetarian (worth the wait), priced in snack or full meal size, also sandwiches, ploughman's and unusual home-made ice creams; lounge with small stools, attractive small no-smoking dining room, good choice of real ales (not cheap); children welcome *(Sarah Armitage, Howard Clutterbuck)*

Crewkerne [ST4409]

George [Market Sq]: Former coaching inn (the coach entry now opens into a shopping precinct); long bar, lounge and dining room, good standard food inc very cheap, tasty and filling baguettes, good service; comfortable bedrooms *(Frank R Joyce, Janet Pickles)*

White Hart [Market Sq, opp Post Office]: 15th-c, cosy, quiet and peaceful, comfortable plain wooden furniture, fresh food and veg, wide choice of beers and spirits, efficient jolly staff *(Howard Clutterbuck)*

Crowcombe [ST1336]

Carew Arms: Village inn dating back several centuries, friendly, unspoilt and original, sensibly priced home-made food, Butcombe, Exmoor and Wilmots, Lane's farm cider; good refurbished bedrooms, nice spot at foot of Quantocks *(JP, PP, S P A Child, the Didler)*

Culbone Hill [SS8247]

Culbone [Culbone Hill; A39 W of Porlock, opp Porlock Weir toll rd]: Low building, spotless, with friendly service, Bass and other real ales, wide range of reasonably priced straightforward food *(Lyn and Geoff Hallchurch)*

Ditcheat [ST6236]

☆ *Manor House* [signed off A37 and A371 S of Shepton Mallet]: Pretty village pub recently taken over and carefully refurbished by licensees of Talbot at Mells (see main entries), unusual arched doorways connecting big flagstoned bar to comfortably relaxed lounge and dining area, ales inc Butcombe, Courage Directors and Wadworths 6X tapped from the cask, open fires, skittle alley, tables on back grass *(BB)*

Doulting [ST6443]

☆ *Poachers Pocket* [Chelynch Rd, off A361]: Popular modernised black-beamed bar with log fire in stripped-stone end wall, gundog pictures, welcoming efficient staff, good generous reasonably priced food from sandwiches up, well kept Butcombe, Oakhill Best, Wadworths 6X and a guest beer, local farm cider, pub games, children in eating area, friendly but well behaved cat and dog, back garden with country views *(LYM, Tim Schofield)*

Dulverton [SS9127]

Bridge: Wide choice of reasonably priced food from gorgeous sandwiches up, quick service, well kept beers such as Morlands Old Speckled Hen, friendly landlord, no piped music *(Peter and Audrey Dowsett)*

Lion [Bank Sq]: Rambling and comfortably old-fashioned country-town hotel, large bar popular with locals from surrounding villages, big log fire, well kept Exmoor and Ushers, decent wine and coffee, helpful service, no music; pub food; children allowed in room off, bedrooms, pleasant setting *(Jenny Cantle, Dorothy and Leslie Pilson, Peter and Audrey Dowsett)*

Dunster [SS9943]

Dunster Castle Hotel [High St]: Popular well run hotel with friendly staff, wide choice of sensibly priced food in bar eating area and dining room from good sandwiches to Sun lunch, Bass and other real ales; bedrooms with own bathrooms *(E A Froggatt, P A Legon)*

☆ *Luttrell Arms* [High St; A396]: Forte hotel in interesting 15th-c timber-framed abbey building, back bar with high beams hung with bottles, clogs and horseshoes, stag's head and rifles on walls above old settles and more modern furniture, big log fires, ancient glazed partition dividing off small galleried and flagstoned courtyard, garden with Civil War cannon emplacements; well kept Bass and Exmoor Gold, bar food from sandwiches to steak, no-smoking restaurants; food and service have not recently been consistent enough for the main entries, but a nice old place well worth knowing; bedrooms *(Richard Gibbs, LYM, Mrs Mary Woods, Darly Graton, Graeme Gulibert, Dick Brown, Ken Flawn)*

East Coker [ST5412]

☆ *Helyar Arms* [off A37 or A30 SW of Yeovil]: Well decorated spotless and roomy open-plan lounge and restaurant, oak beams, woodburner, lots of brass and pictures, world map with pushpins for visitors; good atmosphere despite considerable extensions, good generous food, well kept beer, friendly helpful staff; attractive setting, *(D B Jenkin, Ray Watson)*

Edington Burtle [ST4043]

Olde Burtle [off B3151 W of Glastonbury, then Catcott Rd; or off A39 via Catcott]: Character bar, much refurbished lounge and comfortable restaurant, lovely log fire, well kept if not cheap Fullers London Pride, Wadworths 6X and an interesting guest beer, good wine, attentive service, reasonably priced food inc fresh fish and steak sold by ounce, local veg and good Sun lunch; skittle alley *(E H and R F Warner, Tom Evans, P H Roberts)*

Exebridge [SS9224]

☆ *Anchor* [B3222 S of Dulverton; pub itself actually over the river, in Devon]: Well furnished, clean and comfortable rather hotelish pub in idyllic Exmoor-edge spot, big riverside garden with plenty of tables and play area; wide food choice from sandwiches up, well kept Courage Directors, Morlands Old Speckled Hen, Ushers Best and Wadworths 6X, local farm cider, above-average wines, some attractive furnishings and pictures; open all day summer w/e, children welcome, restaurant, smaller back games bar, skittle alley; comfortable bedrooms, good breakfast, fishing rights *(R J Walden, John and Vivienne Rice, Neil Townend, LYM)*

Exford [SS8538]

☆ *Crown* [The Green (B3224)]: Civilised country hotel's small intimate bar popular with farmers and smart local couples, generous food from good ploughman's to beautifully presented imaginative main dishes with lots of veg, well kept Brakspears, Exmoor and Wadworths 6X, decent wines, big log fire, welcoming helpful service, no piped music; attractive streamside garden, comfortable bedrooms *(Jane and Adrian Tierney-Jones, Alistair and Carol Tindle, Peter and Audrey Dowsett)*

☆ White Horse: Exmoor hotel in lovely riverside village, rustic-style open-plan Dalesman bar, hunting prints and trophies, pine tables and settles, very wide choice of food from filled baguettes to venison pie etc, generous Sun carvery, ales such as Bass, Cotleigh Tawny, Exmoor and Worthington, log fire; children in eating area, dogs allowed, safe waterside garden; open all day summer, stabling available *(Richard Gibbs, Adrian and Jane Tierney-Jones, Dick Brown, LYM)*

Fitzhead [ST1128]
Fitzhead Inn [off B3227 W of Taunton]: Decorative tucked-away country pub, clean and compact, with Cotleigh Tawny, Fullers London Pride, Hook Norton, Tisbury Natterjack and two guests, farm cider, decent wines, some emphasis on good food from bar food to more elaborate evening dishes; casual service, piped music can obtrude *(LYM, James Flory, Richard and Margaret Peers)*

Frome [ST7747]
Packhorse [Christchurch St W]: Small and friendly, with cosy settles and well kept Ushers *(Dr and Mrs A K Clarke)*

Glastonbury [ST5039]
Mitre [Benedict St]: Good value food inc fresh fish and veg, home-made pies and big puddings, well kept Ushers Founders and other ales *(Evelyn and Derek Walter)*

☆ Who'd A Thought It [Northload St]: Friendly town pub, light and airy, with no-smoking dining area, interesting bric-a-brac and memorabilia, good range of good value food, well kept ales such as Bass, Hardy Country and Palmers, decent wines, stripped brickwork, flagstones and polished pine, coal fires, pleasant staff, entertaining decorations in lavatories; bedrooms cosy and comfortable, good breakfast *(Peter Beever, Adrian and Jane Tierney-Jones)*

Hardway [ST7134]
☆ Bull [towards Alfreds Tower, off B3081 Bruton—Wincanton at Redlynch; pub named on OS Sheet]: Pretty and welcoming beamed country dining pub, popular locally esp with older people weekday lunchtimes for wide choice of good generous food with fresh veg, obliging service, warm comfortable bar, character dining rooms, log fire, well kept Butcombe and Wadworths 6X, farm cider; unobtrusive piped music, sell paintings and meringues; tables and barbecue in rose garden over road; bedrooms *(Mr and Mrs Gordon Turner, Dr M E Wilson, David A Ellis)*

Haselbury Plucknett [ST4611]
☆ Old Mill [Merriott Rd; off A30 E of Crewkerne towards Merriott, away from village]: Very modernised country dining pub in quiet spot, going strong under new owners; big picture windows looking over duck pond, good enjoyable food inc carvery, well spaced tables in comfortable light and airy dining lounge, snug

low-ceilinged bar on right, tables out on informal lawn by pretty stream, new play area beyond car park; open all day exc Sun afternoon *(BB, Howard Clutterbuck)*

Henstridge [ST7119]
Virginia Ash [A30 Shaftesbury—Sherborne, junction with A357]: Big popular rambling renovated pub, wide choice of food in large restaurant, particularly good puddings and ices, friendly staff, well kept beer, family area, no-smoking area; tables outside with play area *(John A Barker)*

Hewish [ST4064]
Full Quart [nr M5 junction 21; A370 towards Congresbury]: Friendly roadside pub, civilised décor and layout, lots of beams and brasses, wide range of real ales, good food generously and stylishly served *(Dr and Mrs A K Clarke)*

Hillfarance [ST1624]
Anchor: Clean and comfortable modernised pub with lots of flower tubs outside, good usual food inc children's in eating areas off attractive two-part bar, good value evening carvery, well kept Butcombe and Exmoor, friendly prompt service, family room with wendy house, garden with play area; bedrooms, caravan site, holiday apartments *(Mr and Mrs C Roberts)*

Hinton Charterhouse [ST7758]
☆ Rose & Crown [B3110 about 4 miles S of Bath]: Roomy open-plan partly divided nicely panelled bar with well kept Bass, Butcombe and Smiles tapped from casks, wide choice of good value generous home-made food inc plenty of fish and vegetarian, hard-working and amiable young owners, rugby memorabilia, ornate recently carved stone fireplace, magazines to read, restaurant, skittle alley; open all day Sat *(BB, Meg and Colin Hamilton, Howard Clutterbuck, Mr and Mrs N Abraham)*

Hinton St George [ST4212]
Lord Poulett [signed off A30 W of Crewkerne, and off Merriott road (declassified – former A356, off B3165) N of Crewkerne]: Current licensees running this 17th-c pub looking very much as a restaurant (good food esp fish, though little in the way of bar snacks; not Sun evening), but still has well kept Butcombe, Fullers London Pride, Otter and Wadworths 6X tapped from the cask, farm cider, traditional games, also skittle alley with darts; seats in prettily planted back garden, rare very old surviving fives court, children welcome; may not open till 12.30 *(Dr and Mrs A J Newton, LYM, Galen Strawson, Dr Martin and Mrs Pat Forrest)*

Holcombe [ST6649]
Ring o' Roses [A367 S of Radstock]: !7th-c inn extensively renovated by welcoming current owners, good food in comfortable bar and large beamed restaurant, real ale, log fire, daily papers, afternoon teas; children and dogs welcome, comfortable bedrooms, good breakfast *(Philip Crawford)*

Holton [ST6827]
☆ Old Inn [off A303 W of Wincanton]: Charming rustic 16th-c pub, unassuming and friendly, with beams, ancient flagstones, log fire, hundreds of key fobs, nice bric-a-brac, big

open woodburner, plump cat; pleasant service, Butcombe, Wilmots and Wadworths 6X, good interesting attractively priced food in bar and restaurant (must book Sun lunch); walking sticks for sale, tables outside, sheltered garden up steps *(BB, James Nunns)*

Horsington [ST7023]

Half Moon [signed off A357 S of Wincanton]: Pleasant knocked-through bars with beams and stripped stone, oak floors, inglenook log fires; good value home-made food, well kept ales, decent wines, quick service, evening restaurant; big back garden with play area, comfortable chalet bedrooms *(Rene Huiveneers, LYM, Mr and Mrs Slingo, M Beever)*

Ilminster [ST3614]

Lord Nelson [B3168 W; from A303 take Ilminster exit – ¼ mile on left]: Unpretentious village local, quiet, pleasant and friendly, good value bar food, good service, well kept Courage beers inc Georges; good garden, bedrooms *(Sue and Mike Todd, Howard Clutterbuck)*

Kelston [ST7067]

Old Crown [Bitton Rd; A431 W of Bath]: Four small traditional rooms with hops on beams, carved settles and cask tables on polished flagstones, logs burning in an ancient open range, two more coal-effect fires, well kept Butcombe (it's tied to them) and other beers tapped from the cask, Thatcher's cider, low-priced generous bar food (not Sun or Mon evenings), small restaurant (not Sun); children in eating areas, open all day w/e, picnic-sets under apple trees in sheltered back garden *(LYM, Gwen and Peter Andrews, Colin and Peggy Wilshire)*

Keynsham [ST6568]

New Inn [Bath Hill]: Well placed local with well kept Bass, prompt friendly service, simple but decent good value food, river-view lounge *(Lyn and Geoff Hallchurch)*

Kilve [ST1442]

Hood Arms [A39 E of Williton]: Woodburner in bar, cosy little plush lounge, no-smoking restaurant, wide choice of popular bar food (no sandwiches), friendly service, well kept Ushers Founders; skittle alley, tables on sheltered back terrace by garden; nice bedrooms – back are quietest *(LYM, Bett and Brian Cox)*

Langford Budville [ST1022]

Martlet [off B3187 NW of Wellington]: Welcoming old pub sensitively done up keeping character features, open fires, inglenook, beams and flagstones, central woodburner, steps up to carpeted lounge with another woodburner, well kept ales inc Cotleigh Barn Owl and Tawny, good choice of good value food; skittle alley *(James Flory)*

Langport [ST4226]

Kelway: Not long opened but getting very popular for well kept beers and good food; spacious bar and two upstairs restaurants in converted Victorian warehouse of Kelways nursery company *(Douglas Allen)*

Limington [ST5322]

Lamb & Lark [off A37 from S end of Ilchester]: Homely old two-room village pub with good range of well cooked interesting very

reasonably priced food inc vegetarian, entertaining landlord, well kept real ale; tables outside, pub ram in field over road *(Beverley Bottle, Janet Pickles)*

Long Ashton [ST5570]

Angel [Long Ashton Rd]: Welcoming, with log fire, good choice of reasonably priced home-made food from baked potatoes and baguettes up inc vegetarian, well kept Bass, Courage Best and Smiles Best, children's rooms, small courtyard; tolerable piped music *(Simon and Amanda Southwell)*

Mark [ST3747]

White Horse: Spacious and well maintained 17th-c pub, attractively old-world, with wide choice of home-made food (and of coffees), well kept Flowers and guest beers, good friendly service, some decent malt whiskies; good garden with play area *(John A Barker, H Beck, Norman Revell)*

Midford [ST7560]

☆ *Hope & Anchor* [Bath Rd (B3110)]: Cosy and clean, with welcoming service, particularly good interesting food in bar and flagstone restaurant end, well kept Bass, Butcombe and Smiles, good Spanish wines, good friendly service, log fire; tables outside, pretty walks along River Frome *(Lyn and Geoff Hallchurch)*

Monkton Combe [ST7762]

☆ *Wheelwrights Arms* [just off A36 S of Bath]: Small country inn with attractively laid-out bar, wheelwright and railway memorabilia, friendly service, wide choice of good reasonably priced home-made food, well kept ales such as Adnams, Butcombe and Wadworths 6X, big open fire, tiny darts room at end, fruit machine, quiet piped music; garden with valley view, well equipped small bedrooms in separate block *(LYM, Christopher Wickens, Anthony Hoyle, Paul Wickens)*

Montacute [ST4916]

☆ *Phelips Arms* [The Borough; off A3088 W of Yeovil]: Roomy and airy, with good wide range of freshly cooked food inc sandwiches and interesting specials, friendly efficient service even when busy, well kept Palmers; skittle alley, tables in appealing garden, delightful village, handy for Montacute House; well kept bedrooms *(Richard and Margaret Peers, Richard Long)*

Nailsea [ST4670]

Blue Flame [West End]: Small traditional local, Bass, Fullers London Pride, Oakhill Best, Smiths Best and guest beers tapped from the cask, farm cider, cosy open fires, pub games, children's room, sizeable informal garden; bar snacks *(the Didler)*

Nettlebridge [ST6548]

Nettlebridge Inn [A367 SW of Radstock]: Good value food, enormous helpings; local Oakhill Best, Mendip Gold, Stout and seasonal ale *(Susan and Nigel Wilson)*

North Perrott [ST4709]

☆ *Manor Arms* [A3066 W of Crewkerne]: Attractively modernised 16th-c pub on pretty village green, inglenook, beams and mellow stripped stone, no-smoking area, good value imaginative freshly made food from sandwiches up inc plenty of fish and fresh veg in clean and tidy bar and cosy restaurant, well kept Boddingtons and Smiles, decent wines, good coffee, attentive service, cheerful atmosphere, pleasant garden with adventure play area *(Basil Minson, Ian and Naomi Lancaster, I C Malcolmson)*

North Petherton [ST2932]

Walnut Tree [High St; handy for M5 junction 24]: Big hotel's plush bar, well kept Courage Directors, Exmoor and Wadworths 6X, good bar food; bedrooms spacious and well equipped *(W W Burke)*

Norton Fitzwarren [ST1925]

Cross Keys: Well refurbished and extended local, with wide choice of good value food inc original dishes, well kept Theakstons *(Ben and Sheila Walker)*

Langford Inn [Langford; just off A358]: Roomy pub doing well under present witty landlord, good if not cheap food choice, well kept Courage Directors, country wines, family areas, restaurant, plenty of fresh flowers, bird prints; pretty courtyard, barbecues *(Alan and Paula McCully)*

Norton St Philip [ST7755]

Fleur de Lys: 13th-c stone cottages joined centuries ago for many-roomed black-beamed flagstoned village local, huge fireplace, good value home-made food inc good fresh veg, well kept Bass, Oakhill, Wadworths 6X and Worthington, friendly staff; children very welcome, skittle alley *(Colin and Peggy Wilshire, Veronica Brown, JP, PP, Brad W Morley, the Didler)*

Norton sub Hamdon [ST4615]

☆ *Lord Nelson* [off A356 S of Martock]: Doing well under current licensees, carefully restored to recover a proper country-pub style, thriving civilised welcoming atmosphere, good choice of well served imaginative food at reasonable prices inc two-person bargains Sun and Tues, four well kept real ales such as Teignworthy, farm cider; may be cl Mon w/e, cl Mon lunchtime *(Paul and Judith Booth, C J T Coombs, Douglas Allen, Mr and Mrs N Fuller)*

Nunney [ST7345]

George [Church St; signed off A361 Shepton Mallet—Frome]: Rambling much modernised open-plan bar with stripped stone walls, log fire, four well kept changing ales such as Exmoor and Wadworths 6X, good food choice (no sandwiches) in bar and restaurant, afternoon teas; piped music; rare gallows inn-sign spanning road, in quaint village with stream and ruined castle; children allowed in side room; bedrooms *(Edward Leetham, BB)*

Oake [ST1426]

Royal Oak [Hillcommon, N; off B3227 W of Taunton]: Good value food, friendly local atmosphere, good beer choice, efficient service; skittle alley, big garden *(S J C Hill, Nikki Hamwee)*

Over Stratton [ST4315]

☆ *Royal Oak*: Attractive and welcoming family dining pub, flagstones, prettily stencilled beams, scrubbed pine kitchen tables, pews, settles etc, log fires and rustic décor; impressive choice of

competitively priced food, no-smoking restaurant, well kept Badger ales, good service; open all day Aug, tables outside with barbecues and good play areas for toddlers and older children *(Guy Consterdine, LYM, Mike Gorton, Mr and Mrs Painter, Mr and Mrs A Floyd-Jewell)*

Panborough [ST4745]

Panborough Inn [B3139 Wedmore—Wells]: New management in large genteel 17th-c inn, several clean, comfortable and attractive rooms, inglenook, beams, brass and copper; good range of generous and imaginative if not cheap food, helpful service, real ales; skittle alley, small restaurant, tables in front terraced garden; bedrooms comfortable *(Allen and Margaret Marshall, BB)*

Pitminster [ST2219]

☆ *Queens Arms* [off B3170 S of Taunton (or reached direct); nr church]: Peaceful village pub, cosy and unspoilt, with smiling service, log fire, seven well kept ales, interesting wines, good bar food from fine crab sandwiches up, wonderful fish restaurant in pleasant dining room; no music, dogs allowed, bedrooms with own bathrooms *(Howard Clutterbuck)*

Porlock [SS8846]

Ship [High St]: Picturesque thatched partly 13th-c pub, chimney as big as a lighthouse, welcoming low-beamed locals' front bar with flagstones, inglenooks each end, hunting prints, well kept Bass, Cotleigh, Courage Best and a local guest beer, good country wines, simple bar food, pub games and pool table, no piped music; back restaurant (children welcome), garden *(Darly Graton, Graeme Gulibert, LYM, Veronica Brown, JP, PP, Adrian and Jane Tierney-Jones, Peter and Audrey Dowsett)*

Porlock Weir [SS8547]

☆ *Ship* [separate from but run in tandem with neighbouring Anchor Hotel]: Prettily restored old inn included for its wonderful setting by peaceful harbour, with tables in terraced rose garden and good walks (but no views to speak of from bars); usual bar food inc sandwiches, friendly staff, well kept ales such as Bass and Exmoor in straightforward Mariners Bar with family room, roaring fire; attractive bedrooms *(Roy and Claire Head, LYM, H O Dickinson, John and Joan Calvert)*

Portishead [ST4777]

Albion [Old Bristol Rd]: Expanding choice of food inc good filling sandwiches, well kept Marstons Pedigree and changing guest beers *(Dr A Sutton)*

Phoenix [just off High St]: Former wine bar, now a thriving pub open all day; bar food, well kept Marstons Pedigree, friendly locals *(Tom Evans)*

Poacher [High St]: Popular with older lunchers for wide range of good reasonably priced freshly cooked food with real veg – get there early as many things sell out by 1ish, though they'll do the good trout much later; well kept Courage, Smiles Best and a guest such as Wychwood (may be chosen by customer ballot), friendly helpful staff; evening restaurant, cl Sun pm *(Tom Evans, K R Harris)*

Priddy [ST5250]
New Inn [off B3135]: Bustling low-beamed pub, modernised but still traditional, with good log fire, spacious conservatory, good value food inc interesting dishes, well kept Fullers London Pride and Wadworths 6X, good local cider and house wines, skittle alley; motorcyclists made welcome; bedrooms comfortable and homely, tables outside facing quiet village green with famous hurdles (*LM, Alan and Paula McCully*)
Puriton [ST3241]
Puriton Inn [Puriton Hill]: Friendly character pub with good value food, good service even when busy (*anon*)
Ridgehill [ST5462]
Crown [Crown Hill; off B3130 2 miles S of Winford]: Deep in the country, pleasantly redone in rustic style with new beams, delightful old fireplace and attractive furniture inc upholstered settles; good food from good sandwiches up, well kept Wadworths, family area, lovely views from window tables and tables outside (*S E Paulley, Tom Evans*)
Rode [ST8153]
Mill: Tastefully refurbished mill in lovely setting, more restaurant than pub, with wide choice of good value food (*Lyn and Geoff Hallchurch*)
Roundham [ST4209]
Travellers Rest [A30 Crewkerne—Chard]: Pleasant and quiet, well run by friendly ex-Navy landlord and wife, good choice of food all day cooked to order, ales such as Butcombe and Worthington BB, good wine choice; garden (*Howard Clutterbuck*)
Rowberrow [ST4558]
☆ *Swan* [about ½ mile off A38 at Churchill]: Spacious olde-worlde pub, low beams, some stripped stone, warm red décor, comic hunting prints and ancient longcase clock, good chatty atmosphere, good freshly cooked food (not Sun evening) from fine sandwiches to good pudding choice, well kept Butcombe and Wadworths 6X, careful well managed service, huge log fires; children in smaller room on right, attractive garden with picnic-sets by pond and tethering post, quiet village (*MRSM, M Borthwick, Alan and Paula McCully, Bett and Brian Cox, Gethin Lewis, JCW, GL*)
Rumwell [ST1923]
Rumwell Inn [A38 Taunton—Wellington, just past Stonegallows]: Welcoming and comfortable, with old beams, lots of tables in several areas, very wide choice of well presented good value food inc children's, well kept changing ales such as Bass, Worthington and Wadworths 6X, friendly efficient service, restaurant, family room; tables outside, handy for Sheppy's Cider (*P J Robbins, Dr and Mrs A K Clarke, Mel and Mick Smith*)
Shepton Montague [ST6731]
☆ *Montague* [off A359 Bruton—Castle Cary]: Tastefully furnished old-fashioned deep-country pub with stripped wooden chairs, kitchen chairs and log fire in attractive inglenook fireplace, slightly upmarket in a laid back way; friendly atmosphere, well kept beers such as Butcombe and Marstons Pedigree, fine wines, good

interesting food, small elegant candlelit dining rooms (one no smoking), no machines or music, pretty back garden and terrace with good views; three attractive bedrooms with own bathrooms (*Gordon*)
Simonsbath [SS7739]
Exmoor Forest Hotel [B3223]: Exmoor inn with several bar rooms inc games room, good local atmosphere with a welcome for wet tourists, straightforward furnishings, log fires, lots of whiskies, well kept local ales, good lunches from ploughman's up; bedrooms – nine miles of good trout fishing for residents (*LYM, Dick Brown*)
Somerton [ST4828]
☆ *Globe* [Market Pl]: Chatty old two-bar stonebuilt local with log fire, wide choice of good home-made bar food inc interesting ice-creams, well kept ales inc Bass, good choice of wine, friendly efficient staff, spacious bars, dining conservatory, back pool room; no music, skittle alley, tables in garden (*Janet Pickles, Joyce and Geoff Robson, K R Harris*)
Staple Fitzpaine [ST2618]
☆ *Greyhound* [off A358 or B3170 S of Taunton]: Relaxing sophisticated atmosphere in interesting rambling country pub with antique layout, flagstones and inglenooks, welcoming log fires throughout, pleasant mix of settles and chairs; well kept changing ales such as Badger Tanglefoot, Exmoor, Fullers London Pride and Otter, good food from soup and substantial fresh filled rolls up inc beautifully cooked fresh fish (*Mr and Mrs C Roberts, Paul and Judith Booth, LYM*)
Star [ST4358]
Star [A38 NE of Winscombe]: Unpretentious roadside pub, good mix of tables, huge inglenook fireplace, big fish tank, well kept Bass, decent food inc good fish and chips, enthusiastic Sun lunchtime raffle (bar nibbles then) (*Alan and Paula McCully*)
Stoke St Mary [ST2622]
Half Moon [from M5 junction 25 take A358 towards Ilminster, 1st right, right in Henlade]: Roomy much-modernised village pub, five neat open-plan main areas, food from sandwiches to steaks inc vegetarian, one no-smoking restaurant, pleasant staff, well kept Whitbreads-related beers and Wadworths 6X, quite a few malt whiskies; bar billiards, maybe piped radio, children welcome, picnic-sets in well tended garden (*D B Jenkin, LYM, Anneke D'Arcy, John Watt, Caroline Jones, Mr and Mrs C Roberts*)
Stoke sub Hamdon [ST4717]
Fleur de Lis [West St, off A303/A3088 W of Yeovil]: Golden stone inn dating from 14th c, spacious rambling part-flagstoned bar with homely mix of furnishings, wide changing choice of good value food inc vegetarian here and in simple dining room, well kept Hardy and other beers and local ciders, log fires; good value bedrooms, charming village (*LYM, Howard Clutterbuck*)
Stone Allerton [ST4051]
Wheatsheaf: Good honest food inc nursery puddings with proper custard in cosy pub with

log fires and friendly staff *(Mr and Mrs G R A Lomas)*

Tarr [SS8632]

· *Tarr Farm* [Tarr Steps]: Nicely set for river walks, lovely views from gardens front and back, cosy inside with huge tables made from slabs of wood, Flowers ale, good choice of appealing bar food, cream teas (log fires in tea room), no piped music; open all day *(Peter and Audrey Dowsett, Dave Braisted)*

Taunton [ST2525]

☆ *Hankridge Arms* [Hankridge Way, Deane Gate (nr Sainsbury)]: very handy for M5 junction 25]: Old-style new pub in modern shopping complex, well appointed, with good atmosphere, welcoming staff, good choice of reasonably priced generous good food inc some interesting dishes in bar and restaurant, Badger Best, Tanglefoot and two beers brewed for the pub, big log fire; plenty of tables outside *(Dr and Mrs A K Clarke, Cherry Garland, Ian Phillips, Gill and Keith Croxton)*

☆ *Masons Arms* [Magdalene St]: Fine friendly town pub, often very busy, with good changing range of particularly well kept ales, good reasonably priced quick food (not Sun but served late other evenings) inc succulent sizzler steaks and interesting soups, no chips, comfortably basic furnishings, no music or pool tables; good bedrooms *(Howard Clutterbuck, Adrian and Jane Tierney-Jones)*

Pen & Quill [Shuttern]: Cosy and relaxing, with good value food, efficient friendly service, well kept ales inc Butcombe, decent wines, friendly staff, comfortably unhurried atmosphere *(Mr and Mrs D W Thomson, Robert Gartery, Veronica Brown)*

Vivary Arms [Middleway, Wilton; across Vivary Park from centre]: Pretty pub with good range of distinctive freshly made lunchtime food esp good soup, fish and garlic prawns, in snug plush lounge and small dining room; prompt friendly service, relaxed atmosphere, no music; bedrooms with own bathrooms in Georgian house next door, easy street parking *(Robert Gartery, Howard Clutterbuck)*

White Lodge [Bridgwater Rd]: Very pleasant well upgraded Beefeater, well kept ales *(Dr and Mrs A K Clarke)*

Tickenham [ST4571]

Star [B3130 Clevedon—Nailsea]: Dining pub with good range of food (can be a wait) inc early-eater bargains and fresh fish Weds evening, good choice of beers such as Bass, Morlands Old Speckled Hen and Wadworths 6X, decent wines, friendly landlord, log fire, big family room, no-smoking conservatory; piped music, high chairs; garden with good play area *(Alan and Paula McCully, Dave Braisted, Bryan Osborne)*

Trudoxhill [ST7443]

☆ *White Hart* [off A361 SW of Frome]: Beams, stripped stone, friendly atmosphere, mainly table seating with a couple of easy chairs by one of the two log fires; main attraction the fine range of Ash Vine ales brewed here (you can usually visit the brewery), also Thatcher's farm cider and country wines; wide choice of good

bar food inc off-peak bargains, children in eating area, restaurant, picnic-sets in flower-filled sheltered side garden *(LYM, Stephen, Julie and Hayley Brown, JP, PP, the Didler)*

Upton Noble [ST7139]

☆ *Lamb* [Church St; off A359 SW of Frome]: Small 17th-c stripped-stone village local with well kept Butcombe, Flowers, Morlands Old Speckled Hen and Wadworths 6X, good home-made food, friendly efficient staff; comfortable bars, one with darts, pool etc, no-smoking restaurant, two dogs, lovely views; big garden, cl Mon lunchtime *(Susan and Nigel Wilson, K J Thurstans)*

Vobster [ST7049]

Vobster Inn [Lower Vobster]: Spacious and comfortable old village pub, good food choice from sandwiches up in bar and restaurant, well kept beers; tables on side lawn with boules, adventure playground behind *(Edward Leetham)*

Watchet [ST0743]

Star [Mill Lane]: Old low-beamed cottagey pub nr seafront, wooden furniture, cheerful efficient service, good log fire, straightforward food from sandwiches up inc good fish and chips, well kept Bass, Worthington and a guest such as Oakhill *(S Richardson, P Legon)*

Wells [ST5545]

☆ *Fountain* [St Thomas St]: Decidedly a dining pub, friendly, good value and original, inc good lunchtime salads, fresh fish and seafood and interesting ice creams in unpretentious downstairs bar with roaring log fire and popular upstairs restaurant (worth booking w/e, good Sun lunch); friendly quick staff, well kept Courage Best, Ushers Best and Founders, farm cider, good choice of wines with Spanish emphasis, good coffee, though not really a place just for a drink; piped music; right by cathedral – popular with choir, and you may even be served by a Vicar Choral; children welcome *(P H Roberts, Veronica Brown, Sylvia and Tony Birbeck, Hugh Roberts, A R Blackburn, Peter Smith)*

West Camel [ST5724]

Walnut Tree [off A303 W of Wincanton]: Smart extended dining pub, comfortable grey plush banquettes and red plush cushioned wicker chairs, enjoyable food esp fresh fish and puddings, courteous efficient staff (nicely flexible over menus), well kept Bass and Butcombe; neatly kept garden, good bedrooms *(Ursula and Paul Randall, Mr and Mrs Peter Smith, Beryl Morris, J M M Hill)*

West Huntspill [ST3044]

☆ *Crossways* [A38 (between M5 exits 22 and 23)]: Very relaxed and friendly, and very popular with many readers; an interesting variety of places to sit inc a family room, good decorations and log fires, good sensibly priced food, well kept beers such as Banks's, Butcombe, Flowers IPA and Original, Moor Merlins Magic and Smiles Best, farm cider, decent wines, quick service, no piped music; skittle alley and pub games, picnic-sets among fruit trees in quite a big garden; this last year the housekeeping has not kept everyone happy, but as we go to press it looks as if things have tightened up again *(Christopher Darwent, John A Barker, Steve Whalley, LYM, R R Winn, Mike and Karen England, C J Parsons, Tom Evans, Martin Jones, Sue and Bob Ward, Pat Crabb, Nigel Flook, Betsy Brown, Ted George, Bronwen and Steve Wrigley, Adrian and Jane Tierney-Jones, Howard Clutterbuck, Roger and Jenny Huggins, Alan and Paula McCully)*

West Pennard [ST5438]

Apple Tree [A361 towards Pilton]: Well renovated good value food pub, good choice inc proper pies, thoroughly cooked veg and good Sun lunch; flagstones, exposed brickwork, beams, good woodburner, comfortable seats, thatch above main bar, second bar and two eating areas; well kept Bass, Cotleigh and Worthington BB, good coffee, friendly service; can get crowded lunchtime; tables on terrace *(MRSM, C and E M Watson, Lyn and Geoff Hallchurch, Bett and Brian Cox)*

☆ *Lion* [A361 E of Glastonbury]: Good quickly served food using local ingredients in three neat dining areas opening off small flagstoned and black-beamed core with settles and woodburner in big stone inglenook, log fire in stripped-stone family area, well kept Ushers ales, reasonable prices, pool in back room; tables on big forecourt, bedrooms comfortable and well equipped, in neatly converted side barn *(Susan and Nigel Wilson, Peter Beever, BB, Walter Reid, Peter and Audrey Dowsett)*

Weston Super Mare [ST3261]

Claremont Vaults [seafront, N end]: Large plush dining pub with wonderful views down the beach or across the bay, helped by floor being raised about a foot; good choice of good value food inc lots of fish, Tetleys, decent wine, friendly obliging service; quiet piped music *(Peter and Audrey Dowsett)*

☆ *Woolpack* [St Georges, just off M5, junction 21]: Olde-worlde 17th-c coaching inn with lively but relaxing local atmosphere, pleasant window seats and library-theme area, well kept and attractively priced Oakhill with other changing beers such as Timothy Taylor Landlord, good well priced bar food inc home-made pies and some less usual dishes inc good fish choice, keen efficient service, small but attractive restaurant; skittle alley *(Comus Elliott, P and M Rudlin)*

Wheddon Cross [SS9238]

☆ *Rest & Be Thankful* [junction A396/B3224, S of Minehead]: Spotless comfortably modern two-room bar with buffet bar and no-smoking restaurant, wide range of generous home-cooked food inc children's, friendly speedy service even when busy, well kept ales such as Bass, Morlands Old Speckled Hen, Theakstons XB, Ushers Best, two good log fires, huge jug collection, aquarium and piped music; communicating games area, skittle alley, public lavatory for the disabled; bedrooms *(LYM, Lyn and Geoff Hallchurch, W H and E Thomas, Richard Gibbs)*

Winscombe [ST4157]

Woodborough: Recently extensively refurbished as dining pub, popular for good range of reasonably priced food *(R C Fendick)*

Winsley [ST7961]

Seven Stars [B3108 W of Bradford on Avon (pub just over Wilts border)]: Big stripped-stone open-plan dining place with good food, snug alcoves, log-effect gas fires, Ushers ales; picnic-sets out on terrace, attractive village *(Lyn and Geoff Hallchurch, MRSM)*

Witham Friary [ST7440]

Seymour Arms [signed from B3092 S of Frome]: Welcoming unspoilt local, two rooms served from central hatch, well kept Ushers Best and a guest beer, Rich's local farm cider; darts, cards, dominoes – no juke box or machines; attractive garden *(the Didler)*

Wiveliscombe [ST0827]

Bear [North St]: Friendly, with home-cooked food, well kept local beers, local beer festival with music and Morris dancers *(Adrian and Jane Tierney-Jones, JP, PP, the Didler)*

Woolverton [ST7954]

☆ *Red Lion* [set back from A36 N of village]: Roomy beamed pub, panelling, flagstones and rugs on parquet, smart Regency chairs and chandeliers, well kept Bass and Wadworths 6X, wide choice of decent wines by the glass, good straightforward food inc popular filled baked potatoes, friendly attentive service; open all day, plenty of tables outside *(Colin McKerrow, LYM, Meg and Colin Hamilton)*

Wraxall [ST4872]

Old Barn [just off Bristol Rd (B3128)]: Traditionally refurbished, with oak beams, flagstones, fresh flowers on scrubbed tables, real ales such as Moles, Smiles and Wickwar tapped from the cask, pretty terrace with DIY barbecue (bring your own food or buy here) *(Alan and Paula McCully)*

Yatton [ST4365]

Bridge [B3133 Clevedon—Congresbury]: More road-house restaurant than pub, but good value food served quickly, plenty of seating inc baby chairs, a real ale; children's play room and outside playground *(Richard Fendick)*

Bedroom prices are for high summer. Even then you may get reductions for more than one night, or (outside tourist areas) weekends. Winter special rates are common, and many inns cut bedroom prices if you have a full evening meal.

Staffordshire

The distinctive Yew Tree at Cauldon, long a special favourite of ours and our readers, has now found fame on Channel 4's TV programme Collector's Lot. Other pubs doing particularly well here these days include the appealingly simple George at Alstonefield, the Black Lion at Butterton (another old inn with a strong appeal to walkers, back in these pages after a bit of a gap), the Burton Bridge Inn in Burton on Trent (making more space in which to enjoy the good beers it brews), the George in Eccleshall (a good all-rounder – also brewing its own good beers, with brewery tours now), the Swan With Two Necks at Longdon (nice combination of good food with particularly well kept real ales), the attractive old Holly Bush at Salt (its consistently good food earns it our title of Staffordshire Dining Pub of the Year), and the warmly welcoming Greyhound at Warslow (another good well placed all-rounder, with nice bedrooms). The Moat House at Acton Trussell has expanded into a hotel/conference extension, and though this has made the pub more impersonal there's no doubting its convenience. Pubs that shine brightly in the Lucky Dip section at the end of the chapter include the Boat at Cheddleton, Three Horseshoes up above Leek, Scales in Lichfield, Bulls Head at Shenstone, Crown at Wrinehill, and, for food, the Plough at Huddlesford, Wolseley Arms near Rugeley and Olde Dog & Partridge in Tutbury. Drinks prices in the county are significantly cheaper than in most other areas – even in the most expensive pub we found here, beer costs less than the national average, and in the cheapest pub we found (the Yew Tree at Cauldon) drinks are a real bargain.

ACTON TRUSSELL SJ9318 Map 7
Moat House

Village signposted from A449 just S of Stafford; the right turn off A449 is only 2 miles (heading N) from M6 junction 13 – go through the village to find the pub on the W side, by the canal

The new hotel and conference centre extension at this busy canalside pub makes a marked contrast with the adjacent timbered building, parts of which date back to 1320. It can get quite busy in the charmingly civilised oak-beamed bar which has a big open fireplace and comfortable armchairs. Fresh produce from the family's 400-acre farm constitutes some of the sophisticated bar menu which might include sandwiches (lunchtime only), home-made soup (£2.50), toasted panini (from £3.95), warm roast vegetables and sun-dried tomato tart with melted mascarpone (£4.25), baked potatoes (from £4.25), wild mushroom and potato wedge gratin (£6.50), tagliatelle with smoked bacon, crème fraîche and pecorino (£6.95), salad of chicken, feta and bacon with caesar salad and warm foccacia or penne with smoked salmon, broccoli, ricotta, parmesan and lemon grass oil (£7.95), oriental fishcakes with cumin and ginger ketchup (£8.50), 8oz sirloin steak (£10.95) and daily specials such as home-made pie of the day (£5.95) or roast of the day (£6.25); two course set lunch (£10). Well kept Banks's Mild and a guest changing every month or so such as Marstons Pedigree on handpump, a good wine list with about ten by the glass, and a decent range of spirits; efficient service. No-smoking restaurant; fruit machine, piped music. It's attractively set in six acres of lovely landscaped grounds, and from waterside picnic-sets in front of the pub you can watch ducks and narrowboats cruise along the Staffordshire & Worcestershire canal. Although it's a handy stop for the A6, readers have noted that the wind sometimes carries noise from the nearby traffic. *(Recommended by David and Kathy Holcroft, Ian Phillips, Brian and Anna Marsden, Graham and Elizabeth Hargreaves, Roy Butler, Gill and Maurice McMahon, Paul and Diane Edwards, R T and J C Moggridge)*

Free house ~ Licensee Mr G R J Lewis ~ Real ale ~ Restaurant ~ (01785) 712217 ~ Children welcome ~ Open 11.30-3, 5.30-11; 11.30-11 Sat; 12-10.30 Sun ~ Bedrooms: £65B/£80B

ALSTONEFIELD SK1355 Map 7
George
Village signposted from A515 Ashbourne—Buxton

A good mix of locals, campers and hikers gather by the fire of this appealingly simple stone pub, charmingly placed by the village green in the middle of a peaceful farming hamlet. In the unchanging straightforward low-beamed bar there's a collection of old photographs and pictures of the Peak District, and pewter tankards hanging by the copper-topped bar counter. A spacious no-smoking family room has plenty of tables and wheelback chairs. You order the generous helpings of good value straightforward bar food at the kitchen door: a printed menu includes sandwiches (£1.95), soup (£2.05), ploughman's (from £4.10), meat and potato pie or smoked trout (£5.25), Spanish quiche (£5.85), lasagne, breaded plaice or chicken (£5.95), local fillet steak (£9.95) and a couple of daily specials; home-made puddings such as fudge and walnut pie, pineapple upside down pudding or meringue glace (£1.50-£2.50). Well kept Burtonwood Bitter, Forshaws and a guest such as Ushers Best on handpump; darts, dominoes and piped music. The big sheltered stableyard behind the pub has a pretty rockery with picnic-sets. You can arrange with the landlord to camp on the croft; no dogs or muddy boots. The stone seats beneath the pub sign are a nice place to sit and soak up the tranquil village atmosphere. *(Recommended by David Hoult, the Didler, Barry and Anne, Hilary Dobbie, Nigel Woolliscroft, John and Christine Lowe, JP, PP)*

Burtonwood ~ Richard and Sue Grandjean ~ Real ale ~ Bar food (12-2, 7-9 Mon-Fri, all day Sat-Sun, not 25 Dec) ~ Restaurant ~ (01335) 310205 ~ Children in restaurant ~ Open 11-3, 6-11; 11-11 Sat; 12-10.30 Sun

Watts Russell Arms
Hopedale

Given the location of this solid 18th-c stone pub, gloriously set down a quiet lane outside the village in a deep valley of the Peak District National Park, it's no wonder that it's popular with walkers. The cheerful beamed bar has brocaded wall banquettes and wheelback chairs and carvers, an open fire below a copper hood, a collection of blue and white china jugs hanging from the ceiling, bric-a-brac around the roughcast walls, and an interesting bar counter made from copper-bound oak barrels; no-smoking area. Be warned - it can get busy at weekends. Good value bar food in generous helpings includes filled baps (from £1.95, hot bacon and tomato £3.50), soup (£2.35), filled baked potatoes (from £3.25), English breakfast (£4.95), ploughman's, home-cooked ham and eggs, omelettes, vegetable or beef lasagne, breaded plaice or sausage and eggs (£5.25), scampi (£6.50), gammon and egg (£7.50), 8oz sirloin steak (£9.50) and daily specials such as cod and parsley potato bake (£5.75) or chicken breast in stilton and leek sauce (£6.95); puddings (£2.75); children's meals (£2.95). Well kept Mansfield Best and Old Baily and a guest such as Morlands Old Speckled Hen under light blanket pressure, and about a dozen malts; darts, table skittles, dominoes and piped music. Outside there are picnic-sets under red parasols on the sheltered tiered little terrace, and garden; close to Dovedale and the Manifold. *(Recommended by Jason Caulkin, JP, PP, M Joyner)*

Free house ~ Licensees Sara and Frank Lipp ~ Real ale ~ Bar food (not Sun and Mon evenings in winter) ~ (01335) 310271 ~ Children over 5 yrs in garden and bar area

*only if eating ~ Open 12-2.30(3 Sat), 7-11; 12-3, 7-10.30 Sun; closed Mon lunchtime
except school holidays*

BURTON ON TRENT SK2423 Map 7
Burton Bridge Inn ◀ £

24 Bridge St (A50)

There were changes afoot at this decidedly unpretentious and friendly brick local as
we went to press: the simple little front bar is to be knocked into an adjacent room to
provide a new bar area and oak panelled lounge. While the bar counter will be moved
to separate the two areas, the décor will remain the same with wooden pews, plain
walls hung with notices and awards and brewery memorabilia; the new lounge will
have a gas effect fireplace and old oak tables and chairs. The well kept Burton Bridge
ales brewed on the premises are the biggest attraction here and might include Bitter,
XL, Porter, Festival, Old Expensive, Knot Brown Ale, Battle Brew and a monthly
changing guest on handpump; they also have about a dozen malt whiskies and
country wines. Basic but good bar snacks include filled cobs (from £1, hot roast pork
or beef £2), oatcakes (from £2.60), faggots with mushy peas and chips (£2.70) and
filled giant yorkshire puddings (ratatouille £2.70, pork or beef £3.20); the panelled
upstairs dining room is open at lunchtime only. They are also building a blue-brick
patio which will overlook the brewery in the long old-fashioned yard at the back –
you can tour the building on Tuesdays provided you book in advance. There's also a
skittle alley (booked well in advance) and dominoes. *(Recommended by JP, PP, John Fahy,
David Carr, David Shillitoe, C J Fletcher, Bronwen and Steve Wrigley, ALC, the Didler)*

*Own brew ~ Tenant Kevin McDonald ~ Real ale ~ Bar food (12-2, not Sun) ~
(01283) 536596 ~ Open 11.30-2.15, 5.30-11; 12-2, 7-10.30 Sun; closed Bank holiday
Mons till 7*

BUTTERTON SK0756 Map 7
Black Lion

Village signposted from B5053

There's a cheerily warm welcome at this homely 18th-c stone inn, and readers have
told us that if you wear something green on St Patrick's day you'll be rewarded with
a pint of stout and a meal. There are plenty of interesting things to look at in the
neat and tidy rambling rooms. One welcoming bar has a low black beam-and-board
ceiling, lots of brassware and china, a fine old red leatherette settle curling around
the walls, well polished mahogany tables, and a good log fire. Off to the left are red
plush button-back banquettes around sewing-machine tables and Victorian prints,
while an inner room has a fine old kitchen range. Well liked bar food served in
generous helpings from a changing blackboard might include soup (£2), sandwiches
(from £1.95), ploughman's (£4.50), greek salad (£5), vegetable and stilton crumble
or leek, cheese and onion hotpot (£5.50), steak and stout casserole, chicken, bacon
and mushroom pie or halibut steak (£6), venison in red wine (£7), 8oz sirloin with
cheese, white wine and mushroom sauce (£9.25), and puddings like bread and butter
pudding or gateaux (£2.35). In addition to well kept Marstons Pedigree and
Theakstons they have two or three guests like Charles Wells Bombardier and
Courage Directors on handpump; several malt whiskies; a cocktail bar is open
weekend evenings. Darts, bar billiards, shove-ha'penny, dominoes, cribbage, table
football, table skittles, and separate well lit pool room; piped music and television.
Outside picnic-sets and rustic seats on a prettily planted terrace look up to the tall
and elegant spire of the local church of this pretty conservation village; pleasant
views over the Peak National Park; bedrooms have just been refurbished.
*(Recommended by Andy and Jill Kassube, Vicky and David Sarti, Mr and Mrs Hayman, Jason
Caulkin, Andrew and Carol Walker, B Adams, JP, PP, Mr and Mrs Paice, the Didler, Pete
Yearsley, Sue and Bob Ward)*

*Free house ~ Licensees Tim and Lynn Lowes ~ Real ale ~ Bar food ~ (01538) 304232
~ Children in family room ~ Open 12-3, 7-11(10.30 Sun); closed Mon lunchtime ~
Bedrooms: £35B/£55B*

CAULDON SK0749 Map 7
Yew Tree ★★ £
Village signposted from A523 and A52 about 8 miles W of Ashbourne

By the time this edition is published, Alan East, the landlord of this gem of a pub, will have revealed an Aladdin's cave of treasures to the nation on Channel 4's *Collectors Lot*. Tucked inpropitiously between enormous cement works and quarries and almost hidden by an enormous yew tree, this plain roadside local doesn't from the outside suggest any reason for stopping. Inside however, is a veritable museum's worth of curiosities all lovingly collected by the lively landlord himself. The most impressive pieces are perhaps the working Polyphons and Symphonions – 19th-c developments of the musical box, often taller than a person, each with quite a repertoire of tunes and elaborate sound-effects; go with plenty of 2p pieces to work them. But there are also two pairs of queen Victoria's stockings, ancient guns and pistols, several penny-farthings, an old sit-and-stride boneshaker, a rocking horse, swordfish blades, and even a fine marquetry cabinet crammed with notable early Staffordshire pottery. Soggily sprung sofas mingle with 18th-c settles, plenty of little wooden tables and a four-person oak church choir seat with carved heads which came from St Mary's church in Stafford; above the bar is an odd iron dog-carrier (don't ask how it works!). As well as all this there's an expanding set of fine tuneful longcase clocks in the gallery just above the entrance, a collection of six pianolas (one of which is played most nights), with an excellent repertoire of piano rolls, a working vintage valve radio set, a crank-handle telephone, a sinuous medieval wind instrument made of leather, and a Jacobean four-poster which was once owned by Josiah Wedgwood and still has the original wig hook on the headboard. Remarkably cheap simple snacks, well liked by readers, include hot pork pies (70p), meat and potato pies, chicken and mushroom or steak pies (85p), hot big filled baps and sandwiches (from 85p), quiche, smoked mackerel or ham salad (£3.40) and home-made puddings (£1-£1.50). Well kept beers – also very reasonably priced – include Bass, Burton Bridge and Mansfield Riding Mild on handpump or tapped from the cask, and there are some interesting malt whiskies such as overproof Glenfarclas; spirits prices are very low here, too. Darts, shove-ha'penny, table skittles (taken very seriously here), dominoes and cribbage. Dovedale and the Manifold Valley are not far away. *(Recommended by Sue Holland, Dave Webster, Richard Gibbs, Chris Raisin, Kerry Law, Simon Smith, B Adams, Ewan and Moira McCall, JP, PP, James Nunns, John and Christine Lowe, Justin Hulford, the Didler, Pete Yearsley, Nigel Woolliscroft, Lynn Sharpless, Bob Eardley)*

Free house ~ Licensee Alan East ~ Real ale ~ Bar food (11-3, 6-9.30) ~ (01538) 308348 ~ Children in Polyphon room ~ Occasional folk music ~ Open 10-3, 6-11; 12-3, 7-10.30 Sun

ECCLESHALL SJ8329 Map 7
George ♀ 🍺 🛏
Castle Street; A519 S of Newcastle under Lyme, by junction with B5026

The very friendly bar staff will give you a personal tour of the brewery at this 18th-c inn. Among the good Slaters beers that it currently brews are Bitter, Original, Top Totty, Organ Grinder and Premium (head brewer is the owners' son Andrew); good wines by the glass, 30 malt whiskies and occasional beer festivals with a massive choice. The cosy beamed bar has a genuinely pubby atmosphere with a part-carpeted, part-York stone floor, brocaded seats, and an open fire in a big brick inglenook with a handsomely carved oak bressumer beam. A wide choice of enjoyable hearty home-made food includes sandwiches (from £1.90), filled french bread (from £2.95), soup (£3.25), vegetarian sausages with a stilton cream sauce, stir-fried squid in black bean sauce with egg noodles and peppers, wholemeal pancakes filled with roasted mediterranean vegetables in a tomato and basil sauce or boiled bacon with mustard, parsley or onion sauces (£6.50), chicken, peppers, mushroom and ham tossed with pasta in tomato and basil sauce, roasted cod topped with a salsa verde crust, chargrilled pork chop with caramelised apple and hazelnut butter or deep-fried salmon and cod fishcakes (£6.95), 10oz gammon steak (£10.25) and 8oz sirloin steak (£12.50). There is a pleasant bistro restaurant; good service, friendly landlord; cribbage and piped music. *(Recommended by Jenny and Brian Seller, Ian Phillips, Richard Lewis, Sue Holland, Dave Webster, Rob Fowell, David and Ruth Shillitoe, Maurice and Gill McMahon, MLR, John Whitehead)*

Own brew ~ Gerard and Moyra Slater ~ Real ale ~ Bar food ~ Restaurant ~ (01785) 850300 ~ Children in eating area of bar ~ Open 11-11; 12-10.30 Sun ~ Bedrooms: £49B/£80B

LONGDON SK0714 Map 7
Swan With Two Necks 🍺
Brook Road; just off A51 Rugeley—Stafford

There's a pleasant chatty atmosphere at this neatly kept pub, set in an attractive village. Fresh food is well cooked by the French licensee, and readers particularly enjoy the superb fish and chips – cod in home-made batter (small £5, large £6). Other food on the good value menu includes soup (£1.70), lunchtime sandwiches (from £1.90), sausage and egg or lunchtime ploughman's (£4.10), ham and chips (£5), seafood platter or pies such as beef, ale and mushroom or chicken, ham and leek (£5.40), stuffed chicken breast (£5.60), beef stroganoff, venison steak or fresh salmon and asparagus (£5.90), rack of spring lamb (£6.90) and half a large duck with orange sauce (£7.50). The long quarry-tiled bar is divided into three room areas, with low beams (very low at one end), a restrained décor, five cosy warm coal fires and house plants in the windows; there's a two-room carpeted restaurant. Particularly well kept ales on handpump include Ansells, Burton Bridge Bitter, Ind Coope Burton, Greene King Abbot, changing guests such as Batham Best Bitter or Exmoor Gold; decent wines and kir, friendly helpful service; piped music. The garden, with an outdoor summer servery, has picnic-sets and swings. No children. *(Recommended by Colin Fisher, Martin Jones)*

Allied Domecq ~ Lease Jacques and Margaret Rogue ~ Real ale ~ Bar food ~ Restaurant ~ (01543) 490251 ~ Open 12-2.30(3 Sat), 7-11; 12-3, 7-10.30 Sun; closed 25 Dec evening

ONECOTE SK0555 Map 7
Jervis Arms
B5053, off A523 Leek—Ashbourne

This cheerful and lively 17th-c pub caters well for families: there's a pets corner with pigmy goats, slides and swings, two family rooms (one no smoking) with high chairs, and a mother and baby room. In summer it's pleasant to sit outside in the gardens which run right down to the banks of the River Hamps, with picnic-sets under cocktail parasols on the tree-sheltered lawn, a little shrubby rockery and a footbridge leading to the car park. The irregularly shaped cosy main bar has white planks over shiny black beams, window seats, wheelback chairs, two or three unusually low plush chairs, little hunting prints on the walls, and toby jugs and decorative plates on the high mantlepiece of its big stone fireplace. Marstons Pedigree and four weekly changing guests such as Greene King IPA, Shepherd Neame Bishops Finger, Titanic Best Bitter and Whim Old Izaak on handpump and maybe under light blanket pressure, and a fair range of malt whiskies. A changing choice of food might include soup (£1.45), sandwiches (from £1.80), breaded baked lobster (£2.95), filled baked potatoes (from £3.95), ploughman's (from £4.75), hot pork bap with stuffing (£4.95), steak and kidney pie (£5), salmon and broccoli pasta (£5.25) minted lamb (£7.25) and puddings (£2.30); children's menu (from £2.30); one of the dining rooms is no smoking. Darts, dominoes, cribbage, fruit machine piped music and TV on special occasions. A spacious converted barn behind the pub has self-catering accommodation. *(Recommended by Jenny and Michael Back, Nigel Woolliscroft, JP, PP)*

Free house ~ Licensee Pete Hill ~ Real ale ~ Bar food ~ (01538) 304206 ~ Children in eating area of bar ~ Open 12-3, 7(6 Sat)-11; 11-10.30 Sun

SALT SJ9527 Map 7
Holly Bush

Village signposted off A51 S of Stone (and A518 NE of Stafford)

Staffordshire Dining Pub of the Year

Although this thatched white-painted house fills up quickly for its very popular bar food, the welcome stays friendly and the speedy service copes well with the rush – be warned however, you may have to arrive early to be sure of a table. Changing menus are prepared from as much fresh local produce as possible, and at lunchtime you might find very generous sandwiches (from £2, triple deckers £3.25), filled baked potatoes (from £2.50) and lunchtime specials such as pork, apple and fresh ginger sausages with garlic-infused mash and white onion sauce (£5.25) or deep-fried haddock in beer batter with mushy peas (£6.50). The evening menu might include soup (£2.35), prawn cocktail (£3.50), gammon steak or Greek lamb (£6.25), chicken piri piri (£6.70), mixed grill (£7), and particularly good dishes of the day such as salmon steak with lemon butter (£6.75), whole braised ham hock with a creamy horseradish sauce (£6.95), tuna loin seared with fajita spices and served with caramelised red onions (£8.95) or roast duck breast in green peppercorn sauce (£9.50); home-made puddings (£2.75); Sunday roasts. The oldest part dates back to the 14th c, and has a heavy beamed and planked ceiling (some of the beams are attractively carved), a salt cupboard built in by the coal fire, and other nice old-fashioned touches such as an antique pair of clothes brushes hanging by the door, attractive sporting prints and watercolours, and an ancient pair of riding boots on the mantlepiece. Around the standing-room serving section several cosy areas spread off, including a modern back extension which blends in well, with beams, stripped brick work and a small coal fire; there are comfortable settees as well as more orthodox seats. Well kept Bass, Burtonwood Bitter and Forshaws on handpump, friendly and efficient service, maybe piped nostalgic pop music; darts, shove-ha'penny, cribbage, backgammon, jenga, fruit machine. The big back lawn, where they may have traditional jazz and a hog roast in summer and a fireworks display on 5 November, has rustic picnic-sets, a rope swing and a busy dovecote. It's in a pretty village, and in summer there are hanging baskets at the front. *(Recommended by Gill and Maurice McMahon, Graham and Lynn Mason, Janet Pickles, Peter and Jenny Quine, DAV, Sue Holland, Dave Webster, Dave Braisted, David Cooke, Pete Yearsley)*

Free house ~ Licensee Geoffrey Holland ~ Real ale ~ Bar food (12-2, 6-9.30) ~ (01889) 508234 ~ Children in eating area till 8.30 ~ Open 12-3, 6-11; 12-11 Sat; 12-10.30 Sun

WARSLOW SK0858 Map 7
Greyhound 🛏

B5053 S of Buxton

The landlord of this slated stone pub, surrounded by pretty countryside, is renowned for the warm and friendly welcome he offers his customers. There are long cushioned oak antique settles (some quite elegant), a log fire, and houseplants in the windows of the long beamed bar. The pool room has darts, dominoes, cribbage, and fruit machine; piped music. Big helpings of good home-made bar food include sandwiches (from £2), soup (£2.75), burgers or sausages in baps (£2.50), filo prawns with a plum and ginger dip (£3), filled baked potatoes (from £3.50), ploughman's (from £5), cheesy leek and potato bake, scampi, lasagne, battered cod or caribbean vegetable hotpot (all £6), steak, mushroom and ale pie, chicken and smoked bacon in asparagus sauce, minted lamb casserole, pork and peaches in peppercorn sauce or venison casserole (all £6.50); puddings such as treacle sponge, chocolate fudge cake or bread and butter pudding (£2.50). Well kept Marstons Pedigree, Worthingtons and a guest beer such as Charles Wells Bombardier or Jennings Cumberland on handpump. There are picnic-sets under ash trees in the side garden, with rustic seats out in front where window boxes are a riot of colour in summer. The simple bedrooms are comfortable and clean, and breakfasts good. Handy for the Manifold Valley, Dovedale and Alton Towers. The licensees also run the Devonshire Arms in

Hartington. *(Recommended by Mr and Mrs D Lawson, B M and P Kendall, Derek and Sylvia Stephenson, Anne and Phil Keeble, Paul and Maggie Baker, Nigel Woolliscroft, Cameron Watson)*

Free house ~ Licensees David and Dale Mullarkey ~ Real ale ~ Bar food ~ (01298) 84249 ~ Children in tap room and garden ~ Live music Sat evenings ~ Open 12-2.30(3 Sun), 7-11(10.30 Sun); closed Mon and Tues lunchtime ~ Bedrooms: £16.50/£33

WETTON SK1055 Map 7
Olde Royal Oak

Believe it or not, this white-painted and shuttered stone village pub is the international centre of the sport of toe wrestling – the official world championships are held here every summer. The rest of the year local enthusiasts are happy to explain the intricacies of the sport and you can taste Anklecracker, an ale brewed especially for them by Titanic as a tribute to the importance of the event. There's also well kept Ruddles County and Rutland, Theakstons XB and a weekly guest beer on handpump, about 18 malt whiskies. There's a good mix of locals and visitors, and a timelessly relaxed atmosphere in the bar which has black beams – hung with golf clubs – supporting the white ceiling boards, small dining chairs sitting around rustic tables, a piano surrounded by old sheet music covers, an oak corner cupboard, and a coal fire in the stone fireplace; this room extends into a more modern-feeling area which in turn leads to a carpeted sun lounge looking out on to the small garden. Under new licensees bar food includes soup (£1.90), prawn cocktail (£2.95), ploughman's (£4.75), battered cod (£4.95), scampi (£5.25), lasagne or leek and stilton bake (£5.45) and puddings like chocolate sponge pudding or cherry cheesecake (from £1.95). Darts, dominoes. Wetton Mill and the Manifold Valley are nearby, and behind the pub is a croft suitable for caravans and tents. *(Recommended by Dorothee and Dennis Glover, Nigel Woolliscroft, JP, PP, C J Fletcher, John Brightley)*

Free house ~ Licensees Kath and Brian Rowbotham ~ Real ale ~ Bar food ~ (01335) 310287 ~ Children in sun lounge ~ Open 12-3, 7-11(10.30 Sun) ~ Bedrooms: /£38B

Lucky Dip

Besides the fully inspected pubs, you might like to try these Lucky Dips recommended to us and described by readers (if you do, please send us reports):

Appleby Parva [SK3109]
Appleby Inn [Atherstone Rd; A444 half mile from M42 junction 11]: Large busy roadhouse, plenty of tables in well divided areas around central bar, quick efficient friendly service, good value usual food all day, well cooked and presented, Bass beers; separate restaurant evening and Sun lunch; motel bedrooms, six suited to disabled; handy for Twycross Zoo *(M Borthwick)*
Ashley [SJ7636]
☆ *Peel Arms* [signed from A53 NE of Mkt Drayton]: Immaculate plush local with good atmosphere, olde-worlde touches such as warming old kitchen range, friendly licensees, well kept Marstons; no food Sun; lovely big garden with swings *(Nigel Woolliscroft, G Washington)*
Audley [SJ7951]
Plough [Bignall End; B5500 just E]: Good value straightforward food (not Sun evening) and good choice of beers inc Banks's, Marstons and interesting guests from small breweries; pleasant friendly service, dining area off lounge, lots of flowers outside *(Sue Holland, Dave Webster, Derek and Sylvia Stephenson)*
Potters Lodge [Nantwich Rd]: Big busy

extended open-plan Brewers Fayre family pub with indoor Lego play area, games machine for under-10s, wide choice of food, friendly service, Marstons Pedigree and Morlands Old Speckled Hen, no-smoking area; outside play area too; good disabled access, open all day *(Richard Lewis, Sue Holland, Dave Webster)*
Balterley [SJ7650]
Broughton Arms [A531/B5500, Balterley Heath]: Busy well run Greenalls family pub, clean and airy, with comfortable low-ceilinged lounge, nice décor, prints, real fire; wide choice of generous home-made food, back restaurant, friendly staff, well kept beers *(Graham and Lynn Mason)*
Burton on Trent [SK2423]
Alfred [Derby St]: Tied to local small Burton Bridge brewery, their full range kept well from central bar serving two spartan rooms, good beer-oriented food too; pool in back, friendly landlord, lots of country wines; cheap bedrooms *(C J Fletcher)*
☆ *Coopers Tavern* [Cross St]: Traditional counterless back tap room with notably well kept Bass, Hardys & Hansons Classic and Best and Marstons Pedigree straight from imposing row of casks, barrel tables, cheap nourishing

lunchtime hot filled cobs, pie and chips etc (not Sun), comfortable front lounge with piano and coal fire, very friendly staff; tap room can get smoky; impromptu folk nights Tues *(the Didler, LYM, David Carr, C J Fletcher, JP, PP)*

Derby [Derby Rd]: Unspoilt friendly local with cosy panelled lounge, great collection of railway memorabilia in long narrow bar, Marstons Pedigree, local veg, eggs and cheese for sale; sports TV, open all day Fri/Sat *(the Didler)*

Roebuck [Station St]: Comfortable Victorian-style alehouse opp Bass and former Ind Coope breweries, lots of their beers and interesting changing guests inc a bargain pint, good value food, friendly staff, prints and artefacts; piped music, open all day weekdays; decent bedrooms *(John Fahy, Richard Lewis, David Carr)*

Thomas Sykes [Anglesey Rd]: In former stables and waggon shed of ex-Everards brewery (latterly Heritage Brewery Museum), two high-ceilinged rooms with stable fittings and breweriana, wood benches, cobbled floors, well kept Bass and Marstons Pedigree on handpump and guest beers tapped from the cask, fine pumpclip collection, good cheap basic food; outside gents' *(the Didler)*

Cauldon Lowe [SK0748]

Cross [Waterhouses, A52 Stoke—Ashbourne]: Neatly set out tables in bar and beamed dining room with US registration plates, decent reasonably priced food inc vegetarian, occasional carvery and exotic ice creams, well kept ales such as Marstons Pedigree, Morlands Old Speckled Hen, Shipstones and St Austells; pleasant bedrooms, scenic setting *(Michael and Jenny Back)*

Cheddleton [SJ9651]

☆ *Boat* [Basford Bridge Lane, off A520]: Cheerful local with neat long bar, low plank ceilings, particularly well kept Marstons Bitter and Pedigree, good value simple food, interesting pictures, attractive dining room with polished floor, black-leaded range and brass fittings; handy for flint mill, steam museum and country park; children welcome, fairy-lit tables outside overlooking canal *(Bill Sykes, LYM)*

Consall [SJ9748]

☆ *Black Lion* [Consall Forge, OS Sheet 118 map ref 000491; best approach from Nature Park, off A522, using car park ½ mile past Nature Centre]: Country tavern tucked away in rustic old-fashioned canalside settlement, by newly opened steam railway; smartened up but still traditional, with good generous cheap food from sandwiches up, good coal fire, well kept Marstons Best and Pedigree, friendly landlady, traditional games, piped music; children (but not muddy boots) welcome; busy w/e, good walking area *(L Davenport, LYM, Pete Yearsley)*

Copmere End [SJ8029]

☆ *Star* [W of Eccleshall]: Classic simple two-room country local, Bass and guest ale, beautifully presented freshly made food from sandwiches up inc fine puddings and popular Sun lunch, very friendly service, children welcome; picnic-sets in beautiful back garden full of trees and shrubs, overlooking mere – good walks *(Nigel Woolliscroft)*

Cresswell [SJ9739]

Izaak Walton [off A50 Stoke—Uttoxeter]: This has been a popular main-entry dining pub for some years, but it was sold in spring 1999 to a local company who planned major rebuilding and a reopening in late 1999; we'd be glad of reports on the new regime *(LYM)*

Dovedale [SK1452]

☆ *Izaak Walton* [follow Ilam sign off A52, or Thorpe off A515, NW of Ashbourne]: Relaxing, informal and pleasantly individual low-beamed bar in sizeable hotel, some distinctive antique oak settles and chairs, good log fire in massive central stone chimney; Ind Coope Burton and two guest ales (hotel prices), efficient courteous service, ample nicely presented food in bar and restaurant, morning coffee and afternoon tea; very tranquil spot – seats on two spacious well kept lawns by sheep pastures, superb views; bedrooms comfortable *(LYM, DC, JP, PP, George Atkinson)*

Eccleshall [SJ8329]

Royal Oak [High St]: Ancient black and white local with friendly staff and good value meals; very popular and lively *(Sue Holland, Dave Webster)*

Enville [SO8286]

Cat [A458 W of Stourbridge]: Mainly 17th-c, with four friendly bar areas, cheerful fire, landlord helpful with the very wide choice of ales inc local Enville, mulled wine, decent quickly served food inc unusual specials, popular upstairs restaurant; cl Sun, popular with walkers – on Staffordshire Way *(Ivan and Sarah Osborne)*

Foxt [SK0348]

Fox & Goose: Welcoming three-room pub with pre-film *Titanic* memorabilia and lots of sewing machines, four well kept ales inc one brewed for the pub, Addlestone's cider, short choice of well cooked generous bar food (no puddings), wider choice in upmarket restaurant, friendly chatty service *(Pete Yearsley)*

Fradley [SK1414]

☆ *Swan* [Fradley Junction]: Perfect canalside location, very popular summer w/e; wide choice of quickly served food from sandwiches to Sun lunch inc vegetarian, friendly service, well kept Tetleys-related ales inc Mild, cheery traditional public bar, quieter plusher lounge and lower vaulted back bar (where children allowed), lots of malt whiskies, real fire, cribbage, dominoes; can get busy with boaters; waterside tables, good canal walks *(LYM, CMW, JJW, Roger and Pauline Pearce, Charles and Pauline Stride)*

Froghall [SK0247]

Railway: Cheerful new landlord, well kept Boddingtons, Marstons and Tetleys, well presented standard food inc good fish; bedrooms, plans for tea room, handy for Caldon Canal and Churnet Valley steam railway *(Pete Yearsley)*

Gnosall [SJ8221]

Boat [Gnosall Heath, by Shrops Union Canal, Bridge 34]: Charming small canalside pub with well kept Marstons Bitter and Pedigree in first-floor bar, wide range of good value evening meals, small waterside seating area; friendly

landlord a former pro footballer *(Bill and Kathy Cissna)*
Navigation: Pleasant two-bar pub overlooking Shrops Union Canal, reasonably priced usual food, well kept beers, good friendly service, dining conservatory *(Gill and Maurice McMahon)*
Grindon [SK0854]
☆ *Cavalier* [signed off B5033 N of A523]: 16th-c character pub with well kept real ale, decent straightforward food, pleasant service; smallish front bar with larger room behind and separate games room, good mix of locals and visitors; pleasant informal garden, attractive countryside; often closed – sure to be open Fri night, w/e and bank hol Mons *(LYM, Nigel Woolliscroft, JP, PP)*
Hanley [SJ8747]
Coachmakers Arms [Lichfield St]: Unpretentious friendly town local, three small rooms and drinking corridor, well kept Bass and Worthington, well filled cobs, popular darts, cards and dominoes, skittles *(Pete Baker, the Didler, Sue Holland, Dave Webster)*
Golden Cup [Old Town Rd]: Friendly local with imposing Edwardian facade, Bass and Ruddles County; can be busy w/e, nice garden *(the Didler)*
Reginald Mitchell: Typical Wetherspoons shopping-arcade conversion, well kept Theakstons Best, XB and Mild with early evening bargains, pleasant quick staff; handy for newly reopened Victoria Theatre *(Pete Yearsley)*
Hartshill [SJ8545]
Jolly Potters [Hartshill Rd (A52)]: Outstanding Bass in four-room local, gently smartened-up but largely unspoilt, with classic central bar, corridor to public bar (with TV) and three small homely lounges; very welcoming to strangers *(Pete Baker, the Didler, Nigel Woolliscroft, Sue Holland, Dave Webster)*
High Offley [SJ7826]
☆ *Anchor* [off A519 Eccleshall—Newport; towards High Lea, by Shrops Union Canal, Bridge 42]: Unspoilt homely canal pub in same family for over a century, very basic, bar with two plain rooms behind partition, well kept Marstons Pedigree and Owd Rodger and Wadworths 6X from jugs, Weston's farm ciders, lunchtime sandwiches; outbuilding with small shop and semi-open lavatories, seats outside, cl Mon-Weds winter; caravan/campsite *(Nigel Woolliscroft, Bill and Kathy Cissna)*
Huddlesford [SK1509]
☆ *Plough* [off A38 2 miles E of Lichfield, by Coventry Canal]: Extended and refurbished Greenalls canalside dining pub with wide choice of good value generous food from very interesting sandwiches through wild boar sausages to seafood and Sun roasts in four neat and pleasant eating areas, well kept Bass, Greenalls Original and guest beers tapped from the cask, good range of wines, attentive young staff, games area; attractive hanging baskets, waterside tables, hitching posts *(Dave Braisted, David R Shillitoe)*
Hulme End [SK1059]
Manifold Valley Hotel [B5054 Warslow—

Hartington]: Comfortable 18th-c country pub nr river, spacious lounge bar with open fire, four well kept real ales, wide choice of generous popular food from superb stilton sandwiches to Sun lunch, separate dining room; children and cyclists welcome; bedrooms in recently converted stone smithy in secluded back courtyard, disabled facilities *(C Fisher, BB, JP, PP)*
Ipstones [SK0249]
Linden Tree [Froghall Rd]: Well kept Bass, Worthington and a quickly changing interesting guest beer, home-made food from cheap sandwiches to steaks, prompt friendly service, good atmosphere, dining room; garden with play area *(Pete Yearsley)*
Ivetsey Bank [SJ8311]
Bradford Arms [A5 Telford—Cannock, 5 miles from M6 junction 12]: Large locally popular dining pub, well kept Banks's ales, good reasonably priced food inc midweek bargains, local steaks, wide vegetarian choice, children's menu; old car prints, interesting specialist magazines, friendly staff, disabled access; big garden with play area and animals; caravan/campsite *(Chris Gabbitas, Hugh McPhail, William Robert Cunliffe)*
Keele [SJ8045]
Sneyd Arms [A525 W of Newcastle under Lyme]: Solid 19th-c stonebuilt former court, a refuge for students and conference delegates; Tetleys-related ales, wide choice of lunchtime food inc fish, friendly staff, good landlord; cribbage, pool *(Sue Holland, Dave Webster)*
Kidsgrove [SJ8354]
Blue Bell [Hardingswood Rd]: Recently reopened traditional ale house with two bar areas, real ales such as Butcombe Wilmots, Burton Bridge Porter, Jennings Snecklifter, RCH Pitchfork and Thwaites, friendly landlord and customers; quiet piped music *(Richard Lewis)*
Kinver [SO8483]
Plough & Harrow: Popular old split-level pub, one of a handful tied to Black Country brewers Bathams, with their Best, Mild and XXX kept well, good choice of ciders and malt whiskies, bar food, film star pictures, SkyTV and fruit machine in lounge; children allowed in some parts, tables outside *(G Coates)*
Leek [SJ9856]
☆ *Swan* [St Edward St]: Comfortable old three-room pub with good reasonably priced lunchtime food, pleasant helpful staff, no-smoking lounge, well kept Bass and guest ales, occasional beer festivals, lots of malt whiskies, choice of coffees; downstairs wine bar; folk club, seats in courtyard *(the Didler, Sue Holland, Dave Webster)*
☆ *Three Horseshoes* [A53 NNE, on Blackshaw Moor]: Friendly and homely family-run inn, lots of nooks and crannies, open fire, no-smoking area, good service, good generous food inc self-service veg, good puddings, good range of real ales, sensible prices, children's area, candlelit beamed restaurant – Sat dinner-dance; bedrooms *(B Adams, JP, PP, E G Parish)*
Valiant [off St Edward St]: Comfortable Marstons local, also well kept Bass and

Timothy Taylor Landlord, friendly staff *(David Carr)*

White Swan: Very friendly and comfortable, good cheap food *(David Carr)*

Wilkes Head [St Edward St]: Basic three-room local dating from 18th c (still has back coaching stables), tap for well kept Whim ales and tied to them, also interesting guest ales; welcoming regulars and dogs, lunchtime rolls, good choice of whiskies, farm cider, pub games; children allowed in one room (but not really a family pub), tables outside, open all day *(Sue Holland, Dave Webster, JP, PP, David Carr, Richard Lewis, Pete Baker, the Didler)*

Lichfield [SK1109]

☆ *Scales* [Market St, one of the central pedestrian-only streets]: Cosy traditional oak-panelled bar with wooden flooring, screens, gas lights, sepia photographs of old Lichfield; welcoming service, reasonably priced food, well kept Bass (great value happy hour price), related ales and interesting guest beers, daily papers, darts; piped music, machines; suntrap back courtyard *(Chris Raisin, LYM, David R Shillitoe)*

Long Compton [SJ8522]

☆ *Yew Tree*: Recent tasteful conversion based on 17th-c cottage, smart and friendly, interesting range of restaurant-quality bar food, well kept Greene King Abbot and Marstons Pedigree *(Paul and Maggie Baker)*

Longnor [SK0965]

☆ *Olde Cheshire Cheese*: 14th-c building, a pub for 250 years, some emphasis on the two attractive dining rooms full of steam railway models and bric-a-brac with their own separate bar and cosy after-dinner lounge, wide choice of good attractively priced home-made food here and in traditionally furnished main bar, well kept Robinsons ales inc Best and Hartleys Dark Mild, friendly staff; hikers welcome, bedrooms *(Doug Christian, Dr D J Walker)*

Meerbrook [SJ9861]

Lazy Trout: Cosy character local with basic décor, well kept Banks's and cheap food in small bar and connecting rooms, tables in garden, good walking *(John Brightley)*

Newcastle under Lyme [SJ8445]

Boat & Horses [Stubbs Gate]: Recently reopened after comfortable refit, mellow chintz, Bass and Marstons Pedigree, bar meals, no-smoking area, garden *(Nigel Woolliscroft)*

Holy Inadequate [Liverpool Rd/High St]: Rock/heavy metal/motorcyclists' pub with unusual murals and décor – Triumph Bonneville on wall; seven well kept ales, logs burning in old range, pleasant staff, new extension for food and good live music *(Nigel Woolliscroft)*

Ironmarket [Ironmarket]: Three-storey Hogshead alehouse with stairs up from entrance seating to long bar with bare boards and brick, up to 18 real ales inc some tapped by gravity from windowed still room, good range of wines, country wines and bottled Belgian beers, wide food choice, daily papers, friendly staff and locals, prints and artefacts, old stove; open all day *(Nigel Woolliscroft, Richard Lewis, Sue Holland, Dave Webster)*

Penkhull [SJ8644]

☆ *Greyhound*: Relaxed traditional two-room pub in surprisingly villagey hilltop setting, particularly good value filling snacks, well kept Marstons Pedigree and Tetleys; children in eating area, picnic-sets on back terrace *(LYM, Sue Holland, Dave Webster)*

Penkridge [SJ9214]

Boat [Penkridge Lock, Cannock Rd (B5012), by Staffs & Worcs Canal, Bridge 86]: Particularly friendly landlady in bustling comfortably old-fashioned pub by canal (not very scenic here), pleasant layout, real ales such as Ansells, Greene King IPA and Marstons Pedigree, good usual food (not Sun) inc sandwiches and vegetarian; piped music; picnic-sets out by car park *(Kate and Robert Hodkinson, Bill and Kathy Cissna)*

Reaps Moor [SK0861]

Butchers Arms [Reaps Moor, off B5053 S of Longnor]: Isolated moorland pub, lots of atmosphere in several distinct areas, good value food inc Sun lunch, Marstons Pedigree and a guest beer; free camping for customers *(the Didler)*

Rolleston on Dove [SK2427]

Spread Eagle [Church Rd]: Attractive old village pub with good range of well kept Bass-related ales, good value food all day, small restaurant with fresh fish, popular Sun carvery; pleasant garden, nice village *(John and Christine Lowe)*

Rugeley [SK0220]

☆ *Wolseley Arms* [Wolseley Bridge, A51/A513 NW]: Large pleasantly modernised L-shaped bar with alcoves and raised dining area, wide choice of reasonably priced good straightforward food all day every day esp fish, good range of well kept ales, Czech draught lager, first-class attentive service even when busy, prints and farm tools, smart lavatories; no bar stools, you really have to sit at a table; garden runs down to Trent & Mersey Canal, handy for Shugborough and Cannock Chase (not to mention local arts, crafts, antiques and garden centres) *(Derek and Margaret Underwood, G R Braithwaite, SLC, Derek Stafford, S M Cutler)*

Shenstone [SK1004]

☆ *Bulls Head* [Birmingham Rd; A5127 Lichfield—Sutton Coldfield]: Roomy rambling 18th-c coaching inn, smartly refurbished, with low beams, flagstones, bare bricks, panelling, close-set old pine tables and mixed chairs in narrow rooms, good value well presented home-made food inc fish and chips and more unusual dishes, welcoming quick food service even when busy, well kept Bass, M&B Brew XI and a changing guest beer; children welcome, disabled facilities *(G Coates, Dr S J Shepherd, Paul and Maggie Baker)*

Highwayman [off A5127 Lichfield—Sutton Coldfield]: Recently substantially refurbished, doing well under current manager – good service, enjoyable food all day in bar and restaurant, Bass-related beers *(Cliff Blakemore)*

Shraleybrook [SJ7850]

☆ *Rising Sun* [3 miles from M6 junction 16; from

A500 towards Stoke take first right turn signposted Alsager, Audley; in Audley turn right on the road still shown on many maps as A52, but now in fact a B, signposted Balterley, Nantwich]: Relaxed and well worn in, with well kept changing ales such as Cottage Golden Arrow, Courage Directors, Morlands Old Speckled Hen and Tomintoul Scottish Bard, occasional beers brewed at the pub, good collection of malt whiskies, other spirits and foreign beers, simple generous cheap food inc pizzas, omelettes and plenty of vegetarian dishes; beams, timbering, shiny black panelling, two log fires; children and well behaved dogs welcome, piped music (may be loud), TV room, folk nights 2nd and 4th Thurs; open all day Fri-Sun and bank hols, cl winter lunchtimes Mon-Thurs, play area, camping in two paddocks. *(LYM, Rob Fowell, Richard Lewis)*

Stafford [SJ9223]

Bird in Hand [Mill St, Victoria Sq end]: Very well kept Courage Best and Directors, John Smiths and a Bass beer, annual beer festival, friendly staff, good menu, two bars, snug, back pool room, open fire, back terrace; open all day, can get very busy – nr university *(Richard Lewis, Dr and Mrs A K Clarke)*

Forester & Firkin [Eastgate St]: Good simple food all day exc Sun, good beers brewed on the premises inc a Mild, friendly staff and atmosphere, usual bare boards, lots of barrels, print and brewery artefacts, framed beer mats on panelled walls, daily papers; open all day, machines, music evenings *(Richard Lewis, Chris Raisin, Derek and Sylvia Stephenson)*

Hogshead: Bare-boards Whitbreads pub with good choice of well kept real ales and bottled beers, Inch's cider, breweriana and bric-a-brac, friendly staff, good food choice; open all day *(Richard Lewis)*

Lord Nelson [Eastgate St]: Big bustling local in attractive building, well kept ales such as Bass, Boddingtons, Theakstons Best and XB and Youngers No 3, farm ciders, open fires, friendly staff, limited well priced food; open all day weekdays *(Richard Lewis, Chris Raisin)*

Picture House [Bridge St/Lichfield St]: Grade II listed art deco cinema well converted by Wetherspoons keeping ornate ceiling plasterwork and stained glass name sign, bar on stage with well kept Courage Directors, Marstons Pedigree, Theakstons Best and XB, Wadworths 6X and guests such as Lichfield Steeplejack, farm cider, seating in stalls, circle and upper circle, no-smoking areas, good choice of food all day, friendly efficient staff (and Peter Cushing mannequin in preserved ticket box), film posters; good disabled facilities, spacious terrace, open all day *(Chris Raisin, G Coates, Richard Lewis, John and Christine Simpson)*

☆ *Stafford Arms* [Railway St; turn right at main entrance outside station, 100 yards down]: Full range of Titanic beers (and namesake memorabilia) kept well in busy and unpretentious beamed real-ale pub, two or three changing guest beers, farm cider, cheap simple food (all day weekdays; not Sun evening or Sat), chatty staff, daily papers, wide range of customers (no under-21s – exc babies); pool, bar billiards, table skittles, juke box; barbecues and live bands during summer beer festivals; bedrooms with own bathrooms, open all day exc Sun afternoon *(Richard Lewis, Derek and Sylvia Stephenson, Sue Holland, Dave Webster)*

Tap & Spile [Peel Terr, just off B5066 Sandon Rd]: Good choice of changing well kept ales such as Mordue Workie Ticket, Jennings and Wadworths, farm cider and perry, country wines, sensibly priced food, friendly landlord, bare boards and bricks with lots of prints and framed beermats, no-smoking room, free bar billiards; quiz night Tues, meat raffle Fri, occasional live music Thurs, tables outside; open all day Fri-Sun *(Richard Lewis)*

Stoke on Trent [SJ8745]

Crown [Chapel St/Butt Lane]: Very friendly, with wide choice of generous cheap food, good atmosphere generated by pleasant staff *(E G Parish)*

Staff of Life [Hill St]: Character Bass city local, welcoming even when packed, unchanging layout of three rooms and small drinking corridor; well kept ales *(the Didler, Pete Baker, Sue Holland, Dave Webster)*

Stone [SJ9034]

Crown [High St]: Popular and friendly, with bargain meals inc vegetarian – booking recommended evenings *(E G Parish)*

Tatenhill [SK2021]

☆ *Horseshoe* [off A38 W of Burton]: Civilised tiled-floor bar, cosy no-smoking side snug with woodburner, two-level restaurant and back family area, good value food (all day Sat) from sandwiches to steaks inc vegetarian and children's, well kept Marstons Pedigree and Owd Rodger, good wine range, quick polite service; pleasant garden, good play area *(LYM, Stan and Hazel Allen, Jenny and Michael Back)*

Tutbury [SK2028]

☆ *Olde Dog & Partridge* [High St; off A50 N of Burton]: Handsome and well managed Tudor timbered inn, now too entirely a restaurant to qualify any more for the main entries (the former bar is now a second restaurant, alongside the big popular carvery); early-eater bargains, friendly service, well kept Marstons Pedigree and a guest beer; comfortable bedrooms in separate block *(John and Christine Lowe, LYM, Eric Locker, Dr S J Shepherd, Liz Picken, A Williams, Derek and Margaret Underwood, Alan and Eileen Bowker, Ian Phillips, David Green)*

Uttoxeter [SK0933]

Vaults [Market Pl]: Bass and Worthington in unpretentious three-room local, handy for stn; large bottle collection *(the Didler)*

Waterhouses [SK0850]

Olde Crown: Welcoming pub with good value standard food and good Sun lunch, well kept Ind Coope Burton and Tetleys; bedrooms with bathrooms *(Dr D J Walker)*

Wheaton Aston [SJ8412]

Hartley Arms [Canalside, Tavern Bridge]: Spacious and restful pub in pleasant setting just above canal, decent food inc interesting dishes,

Banks's beers, quick courteous service; seats outside, nice long view to the church tower in the next village *(A J Bowen)*

Whitmore [SJ8141]

☆ *Mainwaring Arms* [3 miles from M6 junction 15 – A53 towards Mkt Drayton]: Popular old place of great character, rambling interconnected oak-beamed rooms, stone walls, four open fires, antique settles among more modern seats; well kept Bass, Boddingtons, Marstons Pedigree, wide range of foreign bottled beers and ciders, friendly service, seats outside, children in eating area, no piped music; open all day Fri/Sat, picturesque village *(Nigel Woolliscroft, E G Parish)*

Wrinehill [SJ7547]

☆ *Crown* [pub signed up Den Lane just off A531

Newcastle—Nantwich]: Well kept beers such as Bass, Fullers London Pride, Marstons Best and Pedigree and Timothy Taylor Landlord, wide choice of good generous food inc vegetarian, in busy but cosy neatly refurbished beamed pub with friendly long-serving landlord and staff, plush seats but olde-worlde feel, interesting pictures, two big log fires, good house wines, well reproduced pop music; children allowed lunchtime, early evening; cl weekday lunchtimes exc bank hols; tables in garden, lovely floral displays *(E G Parish, LYM, Richard Lewis)*

Yoxall [SK1319]

Golden Cup [Main St]: Refurbished Victorian village pub with good bar food from sandwiches up, well kept Marstons ales *(Pat and Robert Watt)*

Bedroom prices normally include full English breakfast, VAT and any inclusive service charge that we know of. Prices before the '/' are for single rooms, after for two people in double or twin (B includes a private bath, S a private shower). If there is no '/', the prices are only for twin or double rooms (as far as we know there are no singles). If there is no B or S, as far as we know no rooms have private facilities.

Suffolk

A lot of good pubs here, with plenty of unassuming charm as well as the growing concentration on good food that's becoming so much a mark of this county's pubs. Choosing our county dining pub of the year has been particularly hard for this reason, with at least eight very strong candidates, but in the end it's the stylishly elegant yet very friendly Angel at Stoke by Nayland which gains the title of Suffolk Dining Pub of the Year. Other pubs doing particularly well here this year are the Queens Head at Bramfield (gaining a Food Award – and very fairly priced), the bustling Bull at Cavendish (good balance between local atmosphere and the dining side), the Froize at Chillesford (quite outstanding for fresh fish, excellent drinks too), the welcoming and pleasantly pubby Ship at Dunwich, the attractively refurbished Crown at Great Glemham (brought back into the Guide by good newish licensees), the Red Lion at Icklingham (a civilised dining pub), the Angel in Lavenham (a great favourite, good all round), the Star at Lidgate (excellent combination of rather continental food with buoyant pubby atmosphere), the Crown in Southwold (imaginative food, good beer, terrific wines by the glass), the Moon & Mushroom at Swilland (a delightful new entry), the Bell in Walberswick (sensibly extended from its old-fashioned core by newish licensees, bringing it back into the Guide after a long absence), and the De La Pole Arms at Wingfield. This last pub, like the smarter Cornwallis Arms at Brome, is tied to the enterprising newish little St Peters Brewery up towards Bungay. Pubs that stand out in the Lucky Dip section at the end of the chapter span the gamut from the cheerfully local Lord Nelson in Southwold to the rather grand and impressive Bull in Long Melford, with food quality often a major reason for people's pleasure. Other notable pubs in that section are the Cross Keys in Aldeburgh, Old Chequers at Friston, Kings Arms at Haughley, Pykkerel at Ixworth, Cock at Polstead, Cherry Tree at Stradishall, Rose at Thorington Street and Crown at Westleton. Adnams of Southwold dominate the beer scene in Suffolk (and many Suffolk drinkers say their beers always taste best on this their home ground). We found Adnams now supply more than half the pubs in our sample with the cheapest beer they offer. Other good local brews do crop up, including St Peters, Scotts, Nethergate, Mauldons, Tolly and Harwich, and of course the regional brewer Greene King has a strong presence.

BILDESTON TL9949 Map 5
Crown 🛏
104 High St (B1115 SW of Stowmarket)

Plenty of readers' praise confirms this lovely old black and white timbered pub as a warmly welcoming main entry with good value tasty bar food. Meals are all home-made and might include sandwiches (from £2.50), ploughman's (£4.25), omelettes or roast leg of cajun-spiced chicken (£4.95), fillet steak (£10.95), and daily specials like leek and potato soup (£2.50), black olive pâté or mushroom baked with stilton (£3.95), cod in beer batter (£4.95), battered cod, chicken curry or turkey, ham and leek pie (£5.95), steak and kidney pie (£6.25), chicken breast with white wine, tarragon and thyme (£6.95), and puddings like apple charlotte or orange and lemon cheesecake (from £2.95); part of the dining room is no smoking. The pleasantly comfortable bar has dark beams, dark wood tables with armchairs and wall banquettes upholstered to match the floral curtains, latticed windows, an inglenook fireplace (and a smaller more modern one with dried flowers). Well kept Adnams and a weekly changing guest like Everards Perfick tapped straight from the cask, several malt whiskies and fresh fruit juices. Darts, bar billiards, table skittles, shove-ha'penny, cribbage, dominoes, fruit machine and piped music. A nice surprise at this high street pub is the big, attractive back garden which has well spaced picnic-sets sheltering among shrubs and trees. Quiet and comfortable bedrooms. *(Recommended by Penny and Martin Fletcher, J H Bell, Charles and Pauline Stride, Prof Kenneth Surin, Gwen and Peter Andrews, Bill Pemberton, Paul and Sandra Embleton, Quentin Williamson)*

Free house ~ Licensees Dinah and Ted Henderson ~ Real ale ~ Bar food ~ Restaurant ~ (01449) 740510 ~ Children in eating area of bar ~ Open 11-2.30, 6-11; 12-3, 7-10.30 Sun; closed 25 Dec evening ~ Bedrooms: £39B/£59B

BRAMFIELD TM4073 Map 5
Queens Head 🍴
Church Farm Road (A144 S of Halesworth)

The imaginative restaurant-style meals at this friendly old pub are notable too for their very reasonable prices. As well as a couple of bar standards like sandwiches with home-made crisps and ploughman's the landlord prepares carefully flavoured starters like cream of courgette and smoked brie soup (£2.95), grilled dates wrapped in bacon on a mild mushroom sauce (£3.75), Suffolk potted herring slowly cooked and marinated in cider vinegar and spices (£3.95), smoked chicken breast, mango and deep-fried brie salad (£5.50), and main courses like vegetable lasagne or spinach and potato gnocchi in tomato sauce (£4.95), fried chicken supreme marinated in olive oil, herbs, lemon and garlic (£6.95), steak, kidney and ale pie (£6.95), wild rabbit braised in cider and mustard (£8.50), roasted Gressingham duck breast with five-spice sauce (£10.50) and venison steak with port, orange and redcurrants (£12.95). The especially tempting puddings are all made by the landlady and might include crème brûlée, chocolate and brandy pot and warm bakewell tart with custard (£3.25). Hot dishes come piping hot, and pies have proper shortcrust pastry. They keep a good English cheeseboard, and good bread comes with nice unsalted butter. There's a pleasantly relaxed atmosphere in the high-raftered lounge bar, which has scrubbed pine tables, a good log fire in its impressive fireplace, and a sprinkling of farm tools on the walls; a separate no-smoking side bar has light wood furnishings. Good friendly service (real linen napkins), well kept Adnams Bitter, Broadside and seasonal ales, half a dozen good wines by the glass and local apple juices and organic cider. The former back games bar is now a cosy family room. *(Recommended by Gwen and Peter Andrews, Mrs P Sarson, MDN, Perry and June Dann, Tom Gondris)*

Adnams ~ Tenants Mark and Amanda Corcoran ~ Real ale ~ Bar food (12-2, 6.30-10(7-9.30 Sun)) ~ (01986) 784214 ~ Children in no-smoking and garden view rooms ~ Open 11.45-2.30, 6.30-11; 12-3, 7-10.30 Sun; closed 25, 26 Dec evenings

BRANDESTON TM2460 Map 5
Queens Head £
Towards Earl Soham

One reader told us that the landlord at this unpretentious country local has 'the knack of keeping several conversations going at once without anyone feeling neglected'. Even without those impressive social skills in action we'd still agree that this is a cheery welcoming place with efficient friendly service. The simply decorated open-plan bar is divided into separate bays by the stubs of surviving walls, and has some panelling, brown leather banquettes and old pews. Well kept Adnams Broadside and an Adnams seasonal ale; shove-ha'penny, cribbage, dominoes, backgammon and faint piped music. Straightforward very reasonably priced bar food includes sandwiches (from £1.50), home-made soup (£2.50), ploughman's (£4.25), kedgeree (£4.50), macaroni cheese (£4.75), braised liver and bacon (£4.95), steak and ale pie or sausages in yorkshire pudding (£5.75), and puddings (£2.75); Sunday roast beef (£5.75). In the big rolling garden there are plenty of tables on the neatly kept grass among large flowerbeds; also, a play tree, climbing frame, and slide. There's a caravan and camping club site at the back. *(Recommended by Pat and Tony Martin, Michael Owens)*

Adnams ~ Tenant Anthony Paul Smith ~ Real ale ~ Bar food (not Sun evenings) ~ (01728) 685307 ~ Children in family room ~ Open 11.30-2.30, 6-11; 12-3, 7-10.30 Sun ~ Bedrooms: £18/£36

BROME TM1376 Map 5
Cornwallis Arms
Rectory Road; after turning off A140 S of Diss into B1077, take first left turn

A splendid driveway leads you through impressive 17th-c grounds with magnificent topiary and wandering ducks, to this largely 19th-c country building. Although a hotel, the stylish and comfortable bar has emerged with all the virtues that you'd want in a civilised country pub since it was taken over a year or two ago by the award winning local St Peters Brewery. The bar – with St Peters Best, Stong and Golden Ale tapped straight from the cask and a large range of St Peters bottled ales – includes parts of the building's beamed and timbered 16th-c core; a step up from the tiled-floor serving area, through heavy timber uprights, takes you into a relaxed carpeted area, attractively furnished with a good mix of old and antique tables, some oak settles alongside cushioned library chairs, a glazed-over well, and a handsome woodburning stove. A well planted Victorian-style side conservatory has coffee-lounge cane furniture, and there's an elegant restaurant. Imaginative well prepared bar food from a not over long but very well balanced menu includes soup (£3.45), filled french sticks (from £4.25), game terrine with red onion marmalade (£4.50), grilled slivers of salmon marinated in olive oil with capers, parsley and shallots (£4.75), local sausages with St Peters ale, onion gravy and mashed potatoes (£6.50), sun-dried tomato, artichoke and black olive risotto topped with parmesan shavings (£6.95), fishcakes on mixed leaves with sweet chilli dressing (£8.95), steak and kidney pudding (£8.50), chicken and vegetable stir fry with ginger and black bean sauce and noodles (£9.25), skate wing with lemon and caper butter (£11.25) and 10oz rump steak with brandy and green peppercorn sauce (£11.25); puddings like summer pudding or apple and sultana crumble (£3.45). *(Recommended by Mr and Mrs L P Lesbirel, D Twitchett, Pamela Goodwyn)*

St Peters ~ Manager Mr G Wortley ~ Real ale ~ Bar food ~ Restaurant ~ (01379) 870326 ~ Children in eating area of bar ~ Open 11-3, 6-11; 12-3, 6-10.30 Sun ~ Bedrooms: £67.50B/£87.50B

BUTLEY TM3651 Map 5
Oyster
B1084 E of Woodbridge

Virtually unchanged over the many years we've known it, this cheerful little old country pub stands alone on the road, rather outside the village itself. There's still a pair of good coal fires burning in fine Victorian fireplaces, a medley of stripped pine tables, stripped pews, high-backed settles and more orthodox seats, and a spinning dial hanging below one of the very heavy beams for deciding who'll buy the next round – the Adnams Bitter, Broadside Extra and their seasonal beers on handpump are well kept; darts and dominoes. A good selection of generously served food might include sandwiches (from £2.20), soup (£2.50), New Zealand mussels (£4.50), ploughman's (£4.95), cumberland sausage or steak and kidney pie (£5.95), cod and chips (£6.25), lobster or seafood platter (£12.95), puddings (£2.95), and Sunday roast (£6.25). The back garden has picnic-sets and solid wooden tables and chairs, with budgerigars and rabbits in an aviary. *(Recommended by June and Malcolm Farmer,*

Ronald Dodsworth, Mike and Mary Carter, Mike and Karen England, Mrs P Goodwyn)

Adnams ~ Tenant Mr Hanlon ~ Real ale ~ Bar food (not Sun evening) ~ Restaurant ~ (01394) 450790 ~ Children in restaurant ~ Impromptu folk Sun evening ~ Open 11.30-3, 6-11; 11.30-11 Sat; 12-3, 7-10.30 Sun

CAVENDISH TL8046 Map 5
Bull

High Street (A1092 Long Melford—Clare)

There's a lively bustling atmosphere in the attractive 16th-c beamed interior of this cheerful pub which is charmingly set in a famously pretty village. It can get quite crowded at lunchtime, but service stays smiling, attentive and efficient, and there's a good balance between the dining (tables can be booked) and local side of things. It's open-plan, but laid out well, with heavy standing timbers and attractive fireplaces; one room is no smoking. Besides sandwiches (from £1.85) and ploughman's (from £3.50), a very big choice of daily specials chalked up all round the pub on blackboards might include crispy duck with chinese pancakes (£3.95), smoked salmon stuffed with prawns or tiger prawns in filo with a dip (£4.25), various curries or pasta and fennel bake (£5.95), baked lamb shank with herbs and red wine served with a tasty greek salad (£8.95), breaded veal escalope topped with ham and mozzarella with a tomato and oregano sauce, a good mixed grill (£10.95) and steak (from £10.95); fish is delivered fresh daily, and might include fresh squid with garlic and chillies (£4.95), grilled haddock, skate or cod (around £6.25), and lemon sole or scampi provençale (£8.95). Puddings are home-made too, from (£2.95). In addition to well kept Adnams Bitter, Broadside and a seasonal ale they have a good choice of wines by the glass. There are tables in the garden and they have summer barbecues. *(Recommended by Marion Turner, Gwen and Peter Andrews, Nick Holmes, Richard and Valerie Wright, Nicholas Stuart Holmes, Mrs M Dixon, John Fahy, Dr Andy Wilkinson)*

Adnams ~ Tenant Gavin Crocker ~ Real ale ~ Bar food (not Mon) ~ Restaurant ~ (01787) 280245 ~ Children welcome ~ Open 10.30-3, 6(6.30 winter)-11; 12-3, 6.30-10.30 Sun ~ Bedrooms: £30B/£45B

CHELMONDISTON TM2038 Map 5
Butt & Oyster

Pin Mill – signposted from B1456 SE of Ipswich

This very simple old bargeman's pub is in a superb spot next to the River Orwell, with a fine view of ships coming down the river from Ipswich, lines of moored black sailing barges, and woods beyond. The same views can be had from the bay window inside, where there's quite a nautical theme to match the surroundings. The half-panelled timeless little smoke room is pleasantly worn and unfussy, with model sailing ships around the walls and high-backed and other old-fashioned settles on the tiled floor; the most unusual carving of a man with a woman over the mantelpiece is worth a glance. Straightforward but good value bar food includes lunchtime sandwiches (from £1.40), ploughman's (£3.25), ravioli (£3.75), tiger prawns in garlic butter (£5.65), honey-roast half duck (£6.95), daily specials like tuna and mushroom crumble, steak and kidney pudding, seafood provençale or Normandy pork (£4.50-£5), and popular hot and cold buffet on weekend lunchtimes (£4.95). Tolly Cobbolds Bitter, IPA, Original, Shooter, and Mild, and occasional guest beers on handpump or tapped from the cask, and decent wines; shove-ha'penny, shut-the-box, cribbage and dominoes. Readers especially enjoy visits here during the annual Thames Barge Race (end June/beginning July). *(Recommended by Mr and Mrs Staples, Ian Phillips, Jenny and Brian Seller, Penny and Martin Fletcher, MDN, Mr and Mrs Head, Mrs P Goodwyn, Richard and Valerie Wright, the Didler)*

Pubmaster ~ Tenants Dick and Brenda Mainwaring ~ Real ale ~ Bar food (12-2, 7-9.30) ~ (01473) 780764 ~ Children in eating area of bar ~ Open 11-11; 12-10.30 Sun; 11-3, 7-11 Mon-Fri winter; closed 25 Dec evening

CHILLESFORD TM3852 Map 5

Froize 🍴 ♔ 🍺 🛏

B1084 E of Woodbridge

Once again there is tremendous praise from readers for the big helpings of restaurant-y food they serve at this very well run welcoming country pub. Licensee Alistair Shaw is in charge of the kitchen (popping out, apron and all, to see that everything's going well), while Joy Shaw runs the comfortable open-plan dining lounge (with gentle good humour, and help from the latest in a long succession of courteous young men from one particular village in the Loire valley). An incredible range of fresh fish predominates on a menu that might include cobblers (from £3.35) and ploughman's (£5.50), starters like soup (£4.15), Thai squid with lemon grass, chilli and oriental vegetables on rice noodles (£7.25), fried wild mushrooms in madeira and cream sauce with pastry topping, baked scallops wrapped in bacon or baked clams with spaghetti, tomato and garlic (£7.95), main courses like smoked haddock fishcake with basil and leek sauce (£6.95), vegetarian filled pancake (£7.95), cod wrapped in parma ham on garlic potatoes with tomato and olive ragoût (£10.95), grilled skate with orange, pink peppercorn and Cinzano sauce, fish pie or seafood pancake (£10.95), wok-fried grey mullet with pak choi, ginger and lemon grass or roast breast and stuffed leg of guinea fowl with red wine, tarragon and morrel sauce (£11.95), a good choice of puddings, and Sunday roasts (£8.95). Besides well kept Adnams and Woodfordes they have up to five local guests on handpump from brewers like Brettvale, Buffys, Mighty Oak, Old Chimneys and St Peters; also a good range of wines by the glass. The beamed bar has a turkey carpet, a mix of mate's chairs and red-cushioned stripped pews around the dark tables, and a couple of housekeeper's chairs by the open stove in the big arched brick fireplace, with a huge stuffed pike over it; new no-smoking dining room; darts (league winter Wed), dominoes, shove-ha'penny and fruit machine. There are tables outside on a terrace and a play area, disabled loos and baby changing facilities. It's a very welcoming place to stay with gargantuan breakfasts. *(Recommended by D J Hayman, Helen Pickering, James Owen, John Wooll, Pat and Tony Martin, Mrs P M Dale, C P Grimes, C Smith, Charles and Pauline Stride, John Faby, Mr and Mrs R A Bradbrook, Ron Baden Hellard, Dave Carter, Anthony Barnes, Evelyn and Derek Walter, P Whight, Mr and Mrs J Heron, John Richmond, Jim Bush, Bill Pemberton, Roy Oughton, George Little, R and M Cudmore, Tim and Linda Collins, Brenda Crossley, MDN, C Fowler, Mike and Mary Carter, K Arthur, Derek and Sylvia Stephenson, Paul S McPhee)*

Free house ~ Licensees Alistair and Joy Shaw ~ Real ale ~ Bar food ~ (01394) 450282 ~ Children in restaurant ~ Open 12-3, 6-11; 12-11 Sat; 12-10.30 Sun; closed Mons (except bank holidays), last week Feb, first two weeks March, last week Sept ~ Bedrooms: £30B/£50B

COTTON TM0766 Map 5

Trowel & Hammer ♔

Mill Rd; take B1113 N of Stowmarket, then turn right into Blacksmiths Lane just N of Bacton

You will probably need to book a table at this thatched cottage as there's quite an emphasis on the enjoyable fairly priced bar food: the daily-changing menu might include cream of tomato and basil soup (£2.25), greek salad in pitta bread (£3.95), baked goat's cheese in filo pastry (£4.25), smoked salmon and seafood terrine (£4.75), with main courses like cumberland sausage with braised cabbage and tomato sauce, pork steak with stilton and walnut sauce or spinach and mushroom lasagne (£6.25), steak, kidney and ale pie (£6.75), crispy duck salad with honey and ginger (£6.95), crab cakes with mango salsa (£7.25), breaded haddock with pesto crust and tomato sauce (£7.95), sirloin steak with parsley butter (£9.75) and casserole of king scallops, langoustines, salmon, mussels and cod (£10.95). The large spreading lounge has wheelbacks and one or two older chairs and settles around a variety of tables, lots of dark beamery and timber baulks, fresh flowers, a big log fire, and at the back an ornate woodburning stove. Well kept Adnams, Greene King IPA and Abbot, and maybe Nethergate Bitter and a local guest on handpump or tapped from the cask, an interesting wine list and lots of unusual spirits; pool, fruit machine and piped music. A pretty back garden has lots of roses and hollyhocks, neat climbers on trellises, picnic-sets and a fine swimming pool. *(Recommended by Pat and Tony Martin, Peter Meister, Ronald Dodsworth, Mrs P Goodwyn, Ian Phillips, Ian and Nita Cooper, Howard and Sue Gascoyne)*

Free house ~ Licensees Julie Huff and Simon Piers-Hall ~ Real ale ~ Bar food (12-2, 6-10) ~ Restaurant ~ (01449) 781234 ~ Children in eating area of bar ~ Open 11.30-3, 6-11; 11.30-11 Sat; 12-10.30 Sun

DENNINGTON TM2867 Map 5
Queens Head £
A1120

You can be sure of a cheerfully friendly welcome from the helpful staff and chatty landlord, and a jolly good value tasty meal at this very neatly kept Tudor inn. It was owned for centuries by a church charity and the arched rafters in the steeeply roofed part of the bar are reminiscent of a chapel. The main L-shaped room has carefully stripped wall timbers and beams, a handsomely carved bressumer beam, comfortable padded wall seats on the partly carpeted and partly tiled floor and well kept Adnams Bitter, Morlands Old Speckled Hen and Wadworths 6X on handpump served from the brick bar counter; piped classical music. Bar food includes sandwiches (from £1.85) ploughman's (from £4.25), as well as soup (£2.35), tiger prawns in filo pastry and garlic dip (£3.65), vegetable curry (£4.25), lasagne (£4.75), chicken curry (£4.95), braised sausages in red wine (£5.50), steak and kidney pie or layered sausage pie (£5.95), chicken and creamy asparagus sauce or salmon and prawn au gratin (£6.75), steaks (from £8.95), lots of puddings like apricot sponge pudding with butterscotch, pistachio and apricot sauce or treacle tart (£2.60); Sunday roast (£5.75); vegetables and chips might be extra. The pub is prettily set by the church and the side lawn, attractively planted with flowers, is sheltered by some noble lime trees and has picnic-sets; this backs onto Dennington Park where there are swings and so forth for children. *(Recommended by Mrs Romey Heaton, Tony Gayfer, Martin and Caroline Page, Gwen and Peter Andrews, Perry and June Dann, Jane Carroll, Ian Phillips, Mr and Mrs L P Lesbirel, MDN, J F M and M West)*

Free house ~ Licensees Ray and Myra Bumstead ~ Real ale ~ Bar food (12-2, 6.30-9) ~ Restaurant ~ (01728) 638241 ~ Children in restaurant, over seven Sat evening ~ Open 11.30-2.30, 6.30-11; 12-3, 6.30-10.30 Sun

DUNWICH TM4770 Map 5
Ship ★ ◼ 🛏
St James Street

The cosy main bar at this delightful old brick pub is traditionally furnished with benches, pews, captain's chairs and wooden tables on its tiled floor, a wood-burning stove (left open in cold weather) and lots of nautical memorabilia; darts, dominoes and cribbage. There's a good bustling atmosphere, especially at lunchtime, but the friendly, helpful staff and licensee manage to cheerfully cope with the crowds and make everyone feel welcome. Very well kept Adnams Bitter, Broadside, Extra and seasonal ales on handpump at the handsomely panelled bar counter. There's a conservatory, an attractive sunny back terrace, and a large garden with well spaced picnic-sets and an enormous fig tree. Comfortable bedrooms and generous breakfasts. They serve deliciously simple fresh fish and home-made chips, with the fish straight from boats on the beach (£5.45 lunchtime, from £6.75 in the evening). The lunchtime menu is quite simple with dishes like home-made soup (£1.80), ploughman's (£4.50), potato and onion bake (£4.95), lasagne or beef pie (£5.25) and salad platter (£5.95), with one or two extras in the evening like marinated sardines in a lime and dill dressing (£4.25), stilton and port cheesecake (£4.75), spinach and mushroom lasagne (£6.85), leg of lamb with redurrant gravy (£7.50), fish pie or steak and stout vol au vent (£8.25) and sirloin steak (£8.95); scrumptious home-made puddings (£3.25). Dunwich today is such a charming little place it's hard to imagine that centuries ago it was one of England's busiest ports. Since then fairly rapid coastal erosion has put most of the village under the sea, and there are those who claim that on still nights you can sometimes hear the old church bells tolling under the water. The pub is handy for the RSPB reserve at Minsmere. *(Recommended by Peter Plumridge, Jeff Davies, Jonathan and Ann Tross, Anthony Barnes, K and E Leist, MJVK, William Foster, David Carr, Peter Cutler, Conrad and Alison Freezer, S A Edwards, Tim and Linda Collins, Eric Locker, Ronald Dodsworth, Paul and Sandra Embleton, Malcolm and Liz Holliday, Dr J P Cullen, Pat and John Millward, Mr R Styles, MDN, David and Margaret Nicholls, Prof Kenneth Surin, Neil Powell, Tina and David Woods-Taylor, CMW, JJW, Mr and Mrs McKay, John Wooll, Nigel Woolliscroft, Helen Crookston)*

Free house ~ Licensees Stephen and Ann Marshlain ~ Real ale ~ Bar food ~ Restaurant ~ (01728) 648219 ~ Children in restaurant ~ Open 11-3(3.30 Sat), 6-11; 12-3.30, 6.30-10.30 Sun; closed 25 Dec evening ~ Bedrooms: £38S/£52S

EARL SOHAM TM2363 Map 5
Victoria ◖

A1120 Yoxford—Stowmarket

This delightfully unpretentious and popular village pub is now leased from the previous licensees who still operate the microbrewery that produces the Victoria Bitter, a mild called Gannet, and a stronger ale called Albert that are all well kept and served on handpump here. The relaxed bar has kitchen chairs and pews, plank-topped trestle sewing-machine tables and other simple country tables with candles, tiled or board floors, stripped panelling, an interesting range of pictures of Queen Victoria and her reign, and open fires. Bar food includes sandwiches (from £1.75), soup (£2), ploughman's (from £3.25), corned beef hash (£3.50), vegetarian pasta dishes (£4.25), avocado and prawns (£4.95), beef in Guinness (£5.25), moules marinières (£5) and a winter Sunday roast (£5.50). Shove-ha'penny, cribbage and dominoes; seats out in front and on a raised back lawn. The pub is close to a wild fritillary meadow at Framlingham and a working windmill at Saxtead. *(Recommended by Pat and Tony Martin, J F M and M West, CMW, JJW, Mr and Mrs Staples, Ian Phillips, Tony Gayfer, Tom Gondris)*

Own brew ~ Lease: Paul Hooper ~ Real ale ~ Bar food (12-2, 5.30-10) ~ (01728) 685758 ~ Children welcome ~ Folk music Tues ~ Open 11.30-2.30, 5.30-11; 12-3, 7-10.30 Sun

ERWARTON TM2134 Map 5
Queens Head ♀ ◖

Village signposted off B1456 Ipswich—Shotley Gate; pub beyond the attractive church and the manor with its unusual gate (like an upturned salt-cellar)

The sunny welcoming bar at this unassuming and relaxed 16th-c pub has bowed black oak beams in the shiny low yellowing ceiling, comfortable furnishings, a cosy coal fire, several sea paintings and photographs and fine views over the fields to the Stour estuary. Adnams Bitter, Broadside and seasonal beer, and Greene King IPA are very well kept on handpump, and they have a decent wine list with several half bottles, and a wide choice of malt whiskies. Good value tasty bar food includes soup (£2.50), ploughman's (£4.25), moussaka or beef and ale casserole (£6.50), chicken breast in pernod and prawn sauce (£6.95), breaded prawns with lemon and cajun dip (£7.50), steak, kidney and mushroom pudding (£7.95), daily specials like chestnut casserole (£6.50), venison and cranberry tart (£6.95), pheasant casserole or sole fillet with prawn sauce (£7.35), and lots of puddings like lemon meringue pie or treacle and nut tart (£3.50); no-smoking area in restaurant. Darts, bar billiards, shove-ha'penny, cribbage, dominoes and piped music. The gents' has a fascinating collection of navigational maps. There are picnic-sets under summer hanging baskets in front. Handy for Erwarton Hall. *(Recommended by Mr and Mrs Albert, Mike and Mary Carter, Stephen Rudge, Ian Phillips, Pamela Goodwyn)*

Free house ~ Licensees Julia Crisp and B K Buckle ~ Real ale ~ Bar food ~ Restaurant ~ (01473) 787550 ~ Children in restaurant ~ Open 11-3, 6.30-11; 12-3, 7-10.30 Sun; closed 25 Dec

FRAMSDEN TM1959 Map 5
Dobermann ◀ 🛏

The Street; pub signposted off B1077 just S of its junction with A1120 Stowmarket—Earl Soham

There's a friendly relaxed atmosphere at this charmingly restored thatched pub. Two spotlessly kept bar areas have very low pale stripped beams, a big comfy sofa, a couple of chintz wing armchairs, and a mix of other chairs, and plush-seated stools and winged settles around polished rustic tables; there's a wonderful twin-facing fireplace, photographs of show rosettes won by the owner's dogs on the white walls, and maybe Puss Puss the cat. Well kept Adnams Bitter and Broadside, Dobermann which is brewed for the pub by Woodfordes and guests such as Bass, Mauldons or Morrels on handpump; efficient service. Shove-ha'penny, table skittles, cribbage, dominoes, and piped radio. Good bar food in generous helpings includes sandwiches (from £1.95), soup (£3.25), ploughman's (from £4.75), steak (from £7.95) and daily specials like chicken liver pâté (£3.45), venison and beer pie or duck leg stuffed with rosemary and apple (£9.95) and puddings like raspberry and apple crumble or summer pudding (£2.95). They play boules outside, where there are picnic-sets by trees and a fairy-lit trellis, and in summer there are lots of pretty hanging baskets and colourful window boxes; no children. *(Recommended by H Frank Smith, Mike and Mary Carter, Mr and Mrs L P Lesbirel, JKW, David Gregory, J F M and M West, Ronald Dodsworth)*

Free house ~ Licensee Susan Frankland ~ Real ale ~ Bar food ~ (01473) 890461 ~ Open 12-3, 7-11(10.30 Sun); closed 25, 26 Dec ~ Bedrooms: £25B/£40B

GREAT GLEMHAM TM3361 Map 5
Crown

Between A12 Wickham Market—Saxmundham and B1119 Saxmundham—Framlingham

This quietly set pub has been attractively and sensitively refurbished by its friendly newish licensees – not overdone or suburbanised, though the central heating's a welcome addition. There are sofas on rush matting in the big entrance hall. The open-plan beamed lounge has wooden pews and captain's chairs around stripped and waxed kitchen tables, local photographs and paintings on cream walls, and fresh flowers, pot plants and some brass ornaments. There may be log fires too, in the two big fireplaces. Well kept Greene King IPA and Abbot and a guest beer are served from old brass handpumps, and the coffee's good. Freshly made good food using good ingredients includes sandwiches (from £2.50), soup (£2.75), ploughman's (£4.25) and blackboard specials like greek salad (£3.50), grilled goat's cheese and tomatoes (£3.75), salmon fishcakes with spicy thai sauce or half a pint of prawns (£4.25), three-cheese fritters, beef rissoles or onion tart (£5.95), lasagne (£6.25), trout or cod and chips (£6.95), with puddings such as trifle, baked chocolate mousse and an excellent spicy apple and raisin crumble. There's a no-smoking restaurant. Shove-ha'penny, dominoes, and cribbage. A tidy, flower-fringed lawn, raised above the corner of the quiet village lane by a retaining wall, has some seats and tables under cocktail parasols; disabled access and baby changing. *(Recommended by P Devitt, Charles Gysin, Charles and Pauline Stride, Keith and Jill Wright, Mrs R Heaton, Mrs P Goodwyn, Neil Powell)*

Free house ~ Licensees Barry and Susie Coote ~ Real ale ~ Bar food ~ (01728) 663693 ~ Children welcome ~ Open 11.30-3, 6.30-11; 12-3, 7-10.30 Sun; closed Monday

HARTEST TL8352 Map 5
Crown

B1066 S of Bury St Edmunds

Tucked away to one side of the village and church (bell-ringing practice Thurs evening), there is a relaxed and chatty atmosphere at this neatly kept pink-washed dining pub. There's plenty of space for its many regular dark wood tables, and besides two no-smoking dining areas there's a family conservatory. Reliable, reasonably priced home cooking includes sandwiches (from £2.25), soup (£2.50), whitebait (£3.95), filled french sticks or ploughman's (from £4.50), pork fillet with port and wild mushroom sauce (£8.50), sole fillet or lamb chump chops with garlic and rosemary (£9), skate wing with garlic and prawn butter (£10.50), puddings like rice pudding, apple and walnut cheesecake or damson and maple syrup tart (£3.25), a very good value Friday two course fresh fish meal (£6.95) and summer Sunday barbecues if the weather is nice. Well kept Greene King IPA and Abbot under light blanket pressure, decent house wines, quick and friendly black-tie staff; quiet piped music. The big back lawn has picnic-sets among shrubs and trees, and there are more under cocktail parasols in a sheltered side courtyard, by a plastic play treehouse. *(Recommended by Gwen and Peter Andrews, Ronald Dodsworth, Allen and Margaret Marshall, JKW, Richard and Valerie Wright, Ian Phillips, George Atkinson)*

Greene King ~ Tenants Paul and Karen Beer ~ Real ale ~ Bar food ~ Restaurant ~ (01284) 830250 ~ Children in bar and restaurant till 9pm ~ Open 11-2, 6-11; 12-3, 7-10.30 Sun; closed winter Sun evenings

HORRINGER TL8261 Map 5
Beehive ♀

A143

There are some very low beams in some of the rambling little rooms that radiate from the central servery of this little cottage, as well as carefully chosen dining and country kitchen chairs on coir or flagstones, one or two wall settles around solid tables, picture-lights over lots of 19th-c prints, stripped panelling or brickwork, and a woodburning stove. The gent's has an amusing frieze depicting villagers fleeing from stinging bees. Changing blackboard specials might include tomato and sweet potato soup (£3.50), chicken liver and sun-dried tomato pâté (£4.50), toasted salt beef sandwich (£5.50), cheese platter (£5.95), asparagus tart (£6.95), haddock fillet with creamed leeks and tagliatelle (£8.95), lamb brochettes with minted couscous and cucumber yoghurt dressing or cold roast Gressingham duck on citrus salad with mild chilli dressing (£9.50) and baked halibut with crayfish tails and lemon tomato salsa (£11.50), with puddings like orange bread and butter pudding or baked banana cheesecake with toffee sauce (£3.75). Well kept Greene King IPA and Greene King Abbot on handpump and decent changing wines with half a dozen by the glass. An attractively planted back terrace has picnic-sets and more seats on a raised lawn. Their dog Muffin is very good at making friends, although other dogs are not really welcome. Keep your eyes skinned on your journey here as the pub is easily missed with its small low sign standing in the front garden. *(Recommended by Simon Cottrell, Mrs P Goodwyn, Simon Reynolds, Paul and Sandra Embleton, Ian Phillips, Dr M Owton)*

Greene King ~ Tenants Gary and Dianne Kingshott ~ Real ale ~ Bar food (12-2, 7-9.30; not Sun evening) ~ (01284) 735260 ~ Children welcome ~ Open 11.30(12 Sun)-2.30, 7-11

HUNDON TL7348 Map 5
Plough 🍽

Brockley Green – nearly 2 miles SW of village, towards Kedington

This remotely set pub is nicely positioned on top of one of the few hills in the area, with fine views of the Stour valley. Its five acres of landscaped gardens have a trout lake, a pleasant terrace with a pergola and ornamental pool, croquet and putting. The neatly kept knocked-through carpeted bar has plenty of old standing timbers, low side settles with Liberty-print cushions, pine kitchen chairs and sturdy low tables on the patterned carpet, lots of horsebrasses on the beams, and striking gladiatorial designs for Covent Garden by Leslie Hurry, who lived nearby. Home-made bar food includes sandwiches (from £2.50), soup (£2.95), pâté (£3.25), asparagus bake, ploughman's or mackerel salad (£3.75), sweet and sour prawn potato skins (£5.75), chilli beef crèpes with melted cheese (£6.50), steak or lamb pie (£6.95), seafood crumble (£7.50) or pot roasted minted lamb (£7.95) and puddings like apple pie, jam roly poly or strawberry tiramisu (£3.25). Well kept Greene King IPA, Woodfordes Wherry and maybe a guest beer; quite a few wines and malt whiskies, and freshly squeezed orange juice; piped music. Parts of the bar and restaurant are no smoking. It's a certified location for the Caravan Club, with a sheltered site to the rear for tourers, and if you stay in the pub the comfortable understated bedrooms have good views. There are two friendly resident retrievers. *(Recommended by Ian Phillips, G Neighbour, Richard and Valerie Wright, Pamela Goodwyn)*

Free house ~ Licensees David and Marion Rowlinson ~ Real ale ~ Bar food ~ Restaurant ~ (01440) 786789 ~ Children in restaurant and eating area of bar, no under fives in bar Sat evening ~ Open 11(12 winter)-2.30, 5(6 Sat)-11; 12-3, 7-10.30 Sun ~ Bedrooms: £45B/£65B

ICKLINGHAM TL7772 Map 5
Red Lion 🍴
A1101 Mildenhall—Bury St Edmunds

There's a gently relaxing atmosphere at this very civilised 16th-c thatched dining pub. Although the emphasis is mainly on the very tasty food there's still plenty of standing at the bar by the big inglenook fireplace for a pre-meal drink. Get there a bit earlier (or book) for a table in the nicer beamed open-plan bar which is attractively furnished with a nice mixture of wooden chairs and big candlelit tables and turkey rugs on the polished wood floor. A simpler area behind a knocked through fireplace has dark wood pub tables on carpets; piped classical music. From a changing blackboard menu, very popular bar food includes soup (£3.55), pâté (£3.65), pork satay with a coriander and peanut dip (£4.75), Newmarket sausages and mash (£5.35), lamb's liver with bacon and onion gravy (£7.25), warm chicken fillet with crispy pasta salad (£8.95), pork chops with maple syrup and barbecue sauce (£8.95), lamb's liver and kidneys in Dijon mustard and bacon sauce (£10.95), chicken breast with mild curry and mango sauce (£11.65) and Gressingham duck breast with plum sauce (£12.75). Well kept Greene King IPA and Abbot and occasional guest beers on handpump, lots of country wines and elderflower and citrus pressé, and mulled wine in winter. In front (the pub is well set back from the road) old-fashioned white seats overlook the car park and a flower lawn, and at the back picnic-sets on a raised back terrace face the fields – including an acre of the pub's running down to the River Lark, with Cavenham Heath nature reserve beyond. Handy for West Stow Country Park and the Anglo-Saxon Village. *(Recommended by M and C Starling, Jean Gustavson, Bill Pemberton, June and Malcolm Farmer, Paul and Sandra Embleton, Ronald Dodsworth, R Wiles, Jill Bickerton, Ian Phillips, Gwen and Peter Andrews, DAV, John Fahy, Raymond Hebson, Pamela Goodwyn)*

Greene King ~ Lease Jonathan Gates and Ian Hubbert ~ Real ale ~ Restaurant ~ (01638) 717802 ~ Children welcome ~ Open 12-3, 6-11; 12-3, 7-10.30 Sun

LAVENHAM TL9149 Map 5
Angel ★ 🍴 ♀ 🍷 🛏
Market Pl

This carefully renovated Tudor inn still generates more enthusiastic reports than any other pub in this county, with readers consistently delighted by the excellent friendly service, good bar atmosphere and imaginative food. The long bar area, facing on to the charming former market square, is light and airy, with plenty of polished dark tables and a buoyant pubby atmosphere. There's a big inglenook log fire under a heavy mantlebeam, and some attractive 16th-c ceiling plasterwork (even more elaborate pargeting in the residents' sitting room upstairs). Round towards the back on the right of the central servery is a no-smoking family dining area with heavy stripped pine country furnishings. Very popular bar food from a changing menu might include cream of mushroom soup (£2.95), chicken liver pâté, mussels in white wine and cream or grilled sardines (£4.25), ploughman's (£4.75), half a dozen oysters, game or fish pie (£5.25), fennel and sweet potato gratin (£7.25), lamb and apricot casserole (£8.25), chicken breast with orange and lemon (£8.50), pork escalope with pear and orange (£9.25), sirloin steak with red wine and mushroom sauce (£9.95), and puddings like plum and almond tart or sticky toffee pudding

(£3.25). Well kept Adnams Bitter, Greene King IPA, Mauldons White Adder and Nethergate Bitter on handpump, quite a few malt whiskies, and several decent wines by the glass or part bottle (you get charged for what you drink). They have shelves of books, dominoes, cribbage and trivia; piped music. There are picnic-sets out in front overlooking the square, and white plastic tables under cocktail parasols in a sizeable sheltered back garden; it's worth asking if they've time to show you the interesting Tudor cellar. Comfortable bedrooms and enjoyable breakfasts. *(Recommended by Dr M Owton, Gwen and Peter Andrews, Anthony Barnes, Mrs O Hardy, Mrs P Goodwyn, Mr and Mrs J Roberts, Paul and Ursula Randall, Peter and Giff Bennett, Rachael and Mark Baynham, John Robertson, C Smith, Ronald Dodsworth, Penny and Martin Fletcher, Richard and Margaret Peers, Maysie Thompson, JP, PP, Andrew Barker, Claire Jenkins, Hugh O'Neill, David and Kay Ross, Mike Wells, Ian Phillips, David Heath, R Wiles, Helen Pickering, James Owen, Bill Pemberton, Mr R Styles, D E Twitchett, Mr and Mrs Richard)*

Free house ~ Licensees Roy Whitworth & John Barry ~ Real ale ~ Bar food ~ Restaurant ~ (01787) 247388 ~ Children welcome ~ Open 11-11; 12-10.30 Sun; closed 25, 26 Dec ~ Bedrooms: £42.50B/£69B

Swan ★ 🛏

High St

This lovely timbered Elizabethan inn is one of the buildings which gives this once-prosperous wool town its great charm. It actually incorporates several lovely half-timbered buildings, including an Elizabethan house and the former Wool Hall. It's quite smart, but ideal for an atmospheric afternoon tea or for those who need that extra bit of luxury as it does have all the trimmings of a well equipped hotel (and not a cheap one). The peaceful little tiled-floor bar, buried in its heart, has leather chairs, a set of handbells that used to be employed by the local church bell ringers for practice, and memorabilia of the days when this was the local for the US 48th Bomber Group in the Second World War (many Americans still come to re-visit old haunts). From here armchairs and settees spread engagingly through a network of beamed and timbered alcoves and more open areas. Overlooking the well kept and sheltered courtyard garden is an airy Garden Bar. Well kept Adnams and Greene King IPA; darts, cribbage, dominoes and piped music. A fairly short bar food menu includes soup (£3.25), open sandwiches (from £5.95), ploughman's (£6.50), toasted brioche with scambled egg, also morning coffee and good afternoon tea. There is a lavishly timbered no-smoking restaurant with a minstrel's gallery. *(Recommended by Kevin Blake, Maysie Thompson, David Heath, Paul and Sandra Embleton, JP, PP, Ronald Dodsworth)*

Free house ~ Manager Elizabeth Combridge ~ Real ale ~ Bar food ~ Restaurant ~ (01787) 247477 ~ Children welcome ~ Pianist Tues-Sun evening, Sun lunchtime ~ Open 11-2, 6-11; 12-2, 7-10.30 Sun ~ Bedrooms: £75B/£120B

LAXFIELD TM2972 Map 5

Kings Head 🍺

Behind church, off road toward Banyards Green

The delightfully old-fashioned front room at this thatched Tudor House is charmingly furnished with a high-backed built-in settle on the tiled floor, and an open fire. A couple of other rooms have pews, old seats, scrubbed deal tables, and some interesting wall prints. Well kept Adnams Bitter, Broadside, Extra and winter Old and Tally Ho, and Greene King IPA are tapped from the cask, and they keep good James White cider; shove ha'penny and dominoes. As well as sandwiches (£2, hot roast beef £2.75) and ploughman's (£4.25), changing blackboard specials might include tomato soup (£2.50), cauliflower cheese (£4.75), tagliatelle with roast pepper and pesto sauce, Norfolk dumpling filled with pork and thyme, dressed crab salad, paprika beef, lamb casserole or grilled plaice (£5.75), 8oz steak (£8.50), and puddings like sticky toffee pudding or rice pudding with toasted almonds (£2.95). Going out past the casks in the back serving room, you find benches and a trestle table in a small yard. From here a honeysuckle arch leads into a sheltered little garden and a well kept secluded bowling, badminton and croquet green. *(Recommended by Gwen and Peter Andrews, Mike and Mary Carter, Tony Gayfer, CMW, JJW, JP, PP, A Ridgway, Martin and Caroline Page, the Didler)*

Free house ~ Licensees Adrian and Sylvia Read ~ Real ale ~ Bar food ~ (01986) 798395 ~ Children in eating area of bar ~ Open 11-11; 12-11 Sun

LEVINGTON TM2339 Map 5
Ship

Gun Hill; village signposted from A45, then follow Stratton Hall sign

The interior of this charmingly traditional inn has quite a nautical theme with lots of ship prints and photos of sailing barges, and a marine compass set under the serving counter in the middle room, which also has a fishing net slung over it. As well as benches built into the walls, there are a number of comfortably upholstered small settles, some of them grouped round tables as booths, and a big black round stove. The dining room has more nautical bric-a-brac, beams taken from an old barn, and flagstones; two no-smoking areas. Tasty home-made bar food is solidly reliable, and might include winter soup (£3.25), very good ploughman's (£4.25), asparagus quiche (£5.50), sausages in mustard sauce (£6.25), steak and kidney pudding, poached salmon, braised lamb knuckle, mediterranean lamb or chicken with pesto and tomato sauce (£6.50), and puddings like banana cream pie or lemon and ginger flan (£2.95). Four or five real ales on handpump or tapped from the cask might include well kept Greene King Abbot and IPA, Flowers IPA and Tetleys; country wines. If you look carefully enough, there's a distant sea view from the picnic-sets in front. *(Recommended by Ronald Dodsworth, Ian and Nita Cooper, Charles and Pauline Stride, MDN, Maggie and Derek Washington, J F M and Dr M West)*

Pubmaster ~ Tenants William and Shirley Waite ~ Real ale ~ Bar food (not Sun-Tues evenings) ~ Restaurant ~ (01473) 659573 ~ Open 11.30-3, 6-11; 12-3, 7-10.30 Sun

LIDGATE TL7257 Map 5
Star 🍽 ♟

B1063 SE of Newmarket

Going from strength to strength, this very attractive little village pub under the cheery guidance of its friendly Spanish landlady is a delightful mix of traditional English and Mediterranean influences. The small main room has lots of English pubby character, with handsomely moulded heavy beams, a good big log fire, candles in iron candelabra on good polished oak or stripped pine tables, bar billiards, dominoes, darts and ring the bull, and just some antique Catalan plates over the bar to give a hint of the Mediterranean. Besides a second similar room on the right, there's a cosy simple dining room on the left. The easy going atmosphere, and the changing bar menu with crisp and positive seasonings in some dishes, speak more openly of the South. There might be mediterranean fish soup or tomato and goat's cheese salad (£4.50), warm chicken liver salad (£5.90), roast lamb in garlic and wine, paella, home-made lasagne, monkfish marinière or lamb's kidney in sherry (£10.50), baked bass, scallops santiago, wild boar in cranberry sauce or sirloin steak in stilton sauce (£12.50). Greene King IPA, Abbot, and a guest on handpump, enjoyable house wines; darts, bar billiards, dominoes, ring the bull and maybe unobtrusive background music. There are tables on the raised lawn in front and in a pretty little rustic back garden. *(Recommended by Brian Gallen, Gwen and Peter Andrews, David and Diana MacFadyen, Jean Gustavson, Ronald Dodsworth, Richard and Valerie Wright, MDN, Richard and Robyn Wain, R C Wiles, A Albert, John Fahy, Sue Grossey, A J Bowen, Charles and Pauline Stride, Jules Akel, Ian Phillips, Dr Andy Wilkinson)*

Greene King ~ Lease: Maria Teresa Axon ~ Real ale ~ Bar food (12-2, 7-10) ~ Restaurant ~ (01638) 500275 ~ Children welcome ~ Open 11-3, 5(6 Sat)-11; 12-3, 7-11 Sun; closed 26 Dec, 1 Jan

---

Soup prices usually include a roll and butter.

LINDSEY TL9744 Map 5
White Rose

Rose Green, which is SW of village centre; off A1141 NW of Hadleigh (and signposted from Kersey)

There is quite some emphasis on the very imaginative menu at this civilised thatched and timbered dining pub which is tucked away in a quiet rural spot, well away from housing. The long beamed main bar has a good log fire in the inglenook, country chairs and pine tables. Attractively presented bar food from a changing menu might include vichyssoise soup or roasted pepper and zucchini salad with basil oil (£3.25), filled french sticks (£3.50), smoked haddock on toasted muffin with parsley and lemon sauce (£4.95), penne with spinach, wild mushroom and plum tomato sauce (£6.75), savoury bread and butter pudding with provençal sauce (£6.95), moules marinières (£7.95), lamb's liver with crispy bacon on mushroom cassoulet with red wine jus (£8.25), thai-style sweet and sour pork with snow peas and lemon scented rice (£8.95), peppered sirloin steak with whisky and honey sauce (£9.95) and puddings like forest fruits crème brûlée or raspberry tart with sauce anglais (£3.95). A cosy and comfortable second bar opens into a restaurant in a raftered former barn, with slightly higher prices and a wider choice; no smoking area. Well kept Adnams and Greene King IPA and Abbot on handpump or tapped from the cask, good wines, welcoming service; bar billiards and piped music. *(Recommended by Bill and Pat Pemberton, Tom Gondris, Gwen and Peter Andrews, Pamela Goodwyn)*

Free house ~ Licensee Richard May ~ Real ale ~ Bar food (12-2.30, 6.30-9.30) ~ Restaurant ~ (01787) 210664 ~ Children in family area and restaurant if eating ~ Open 12-3, 6-11(10.30 Sun); closed 25 Dec

ORFORD TM4250 Map 5
Jolly Sailor £

Quay Street

This unspoilt old favourite is well placed in a lovely area for coastal walks, and several picnic-sets on grass at the back have views over the marshes. It was built in the 17th c mainly from wrecked ships' timbers and had a reputation as a smugglers' inn. The several snugly traditional rooms are served from counters and hatches in an old-fashioned central cubicle. There's an unusual spiral staircase in the corner of the flagstoned main bar – which also has 13 brass door knockers and other brassware, local photographs, and a good solid-fuel stove; a small room is popular with the dominoes and shove-ha'penny players, and has draughts, chess and cribbage. Chatty and friendly staff serve well kept Adnams Bitter and Broadside on handpump and good straightforward bar food such as local fish and chips, home-made steak pie or lasagne, home-cooked ham and egg, and daily roasts (all £4.75); the dining room is no smoking. No children or credit cards. *(Recommended by Yavuz and Shirley Mutlu, Chris Mawson, Paul Hathaway, James Nunns, Gwen and Peter Andrews, Richard and Valerie Wright, Jill Bickerton, Pamela Goodwyn)*

Adnams ~ Tenant Philip Attwood ~ Real ale ~ Bar food (Not Mon evening or Tues-Thur evenings Nov-Easter) ~ (01394) 450243 ~ Open 11.30-2.30, 7-11; 12-2.45, 7-10.30 Sun; closed 25 Dec evening ~ Bedrooms: /£35B

RATTLESDEN TL9758 Map 5
Brewers Arms 🍴

Signposted on minor roads W of Stowmarket, off B1115 via Buxhall or off A45 via Woolpit

There's a jolly friendly atmosphere at this solidly built 16th-c village local, with a particularly warm smile from the sociable welcoming landlady. There's a small but lively public bar, and on the left, the pleasantly simple beamed lounge bar has booklined walls, individually chosen pictures and bric-a-brac. It winds back through standing timbers to the main eating area, which is partly flint-walled, has a magnificent old bread oven and new more comfortable seating. The imaginative bar menu changes constantly but might include cream of asparagus soup (£2.50), stuffed garlic mushrooms (£3.75), tomato and mozzarella with a garlic and balsamic vinegar dressing (£3.95), prawn risotto or stir-fried vegetables in a filo basket with garlic and tomato sauce (£7.95), salmon fishcakes with lobster, brandy and cream sauce or steak and Guinness casserole with puff pastry leaves (£8.95), sandwich of plaice and prawns with warm salsa verde (£9.95), stuffed noisettes of lamb with port and mint gravy or duck breast with light cherry sauce (£10.95), and puddings like pecan nut and golden syrup bread and butter pudding, chilled coffee mousse with almond praline or apple pie (from £3.50). The restaurant and part of the bar are no smoking. Very welcoming and friendly service, and well kept Greene King Abbot and IPA and a monthly changing guest like Bass or Morlands Old Speckled Hen under light blanket pressure; decent wines. French windows open on to a garden edged with bourbon roses, with a boules pitch. *(Recommended by Gwen and Peter Andrews, Bill and Pat Pemberton, J Pickett, P Green, Peter Dodd, J F M and M West, Mrs R Talbot, Charles and Pauline Stride, Ian Phillips, David Gregory, Pamela Goodwyn)*

Greene King ~ Lease: Jeffrey Chamberlain ~ Real ale ~ Bar food (12-2, 7-9.30 (not Sun evening)) ~ Restaurant ~ (01449) 736377 ~ Children in eating area of bar, over 5 in restaurant, no babies ~ Jazz and light music Thurs evening ~ Open 12-2.30(3 Sat), 6.30-11; 12-3, 7-10.30 Sun; closed Mon

REDE TL8055 Map 5
Plough 🍴 🍷

Village signposted off A143 Bury St Edmunds—Haverhill

There's a genuinely friendly welcome from the cheery licensees and helpful staff at this lovely old thatched pub. The traditionally simple and cosy bar has copper measures and pewter tankards hanging from low black beams, decorative plates on a delft shelf and surrounding the solid-fuel stove in its brick fireplace, and red plush button-back wall banquettes; maybe piped pop music. Readers really enjoy the consistently good and interesting food here which usually includes game and lots of fresh fish dishes on its changing quite reasonably priced menu. Served in generous helpings, there might be bobotie (£7.50), Moroccan lamb tagine with couscous or local rabbit braised in cider and mustard cream (£7.95), hock of venison in red wine sauce on a bed of red cabbage (£8.95), bass with white wine and ginger sauce (£10.95) and puddings like lemon gateau (£2.95); decent wines, and Greene King IPA on electric pump. This is a lovely spot, sometimes the only sound is birdsong from the aviary or surrounding trees, or perhaps the cooing from the dovecote. There are picnic-sets in front and pheasants strutting across the lawn in the sheltered cottagey garden at the back. *(Recommended by Richard and Valerie Wright, Ronald Dodsworth, Gwen and Peter Andrews, MDN)*

Greene King ~ Tenant Brian Desborough ~ Real ale ~ Bar food (not Sun evening) ~ Restaurant ~ (01284) 789208 ~ Children in eating area of bar and restaurant ~ Open 11-3, 6.30-11; 12-3, 7-10.30 Sun

SNAPE TM3959 Map 5
Crown 🍴 🍷 🛏

B1069

Beautifully presented freshly cooked food forms the focus of this homely unspoilt smugglers' inn. The sensibly imaginative changing menu might include coconut, vegetable and chilli soup (£2.95), asparagus roulade (£4.50), wild mushroom risotto (£4.95), Thai prawn balls with soy chilli dip (£5.50), crayfish tails spiced with mango, served with poppadums (£5.95), salmon and dill fishcakes with lime tartare, spaghetti with asparagus, chilli and garlic sauce or warm spinach and parmesan tart (£7.95), steak and kidney pudding (£8.95), calf's liver with mash, sage and port sauce (£9.50), and puddings like fresh figs with ricotta cream, sticky toffee pudding or lemon tart (£3.75). Its attractive rooms are furnished with striking horseshoe-shaped high-backed settles around the big brick inglenook, spindleback and country kitchen chairs, nice old tables on some old brick flooring. An exposed panel shows how the ancient walls were constructed, and there are lots of beams in the various small side rooms. Well kept Adnams Bitter, Broadside and a seasonal ale on handpump, and a good thoughtful wine list with about a dozen by the glass (including champagne). There are tables and cocktail parasols in the pretty roadside garden. The clean and comfortable bedrooms are full of character with beamed ceilings, sloping floors and doorways that you may have to stoop through; good generous breakfasts. Handy for Snape Maltings. *(Recommended by Neil and Anita Christopher, T R and B C Jenkins, R Wiles, Jenny and Brian Seller, Mrs P Goodwyn, G Neighbour, Gwen and Peter Andrews, Comus Elliott, George Little, J F M and M West, Neil Powell, W K Wood, John Akerman, MDN, Phil and Heidi Cook, Tracey and Stephen Groves, Martin Howard Pritchard, Jill Hallpike, Carl Upsall, David and Kay Ross, Penny and Martin Fletcher)*

Adnams ~ Lease: Diane Maylott ~ Real ale ~ Bar food (not Sat evening) ~ Restaurant ~ (01728) 688324 ~ Open 12-3, 6-11; 12-3, 7-10.30 Sun; closed 25 Dec, 26 Dec evening ~ Bedrooms: £35B/£50B

Golden Key ★

Priory Lane

By extending into the next door cottage they've added a dining room and another bedroom at this quietly elegant and rather civilised inn. The low-beamed stylish lounge has an old-fashioned settle curving around a couple of venerable stripped tables on the tiled floor, a winter open fire, and at the other end, some stripped modern settles around heavy Habitat-style wooden tables on a turkey carpet, and a solid-fuel stove in the big fireplace. The cream walls are hung with pencil sketches of customers, a Henry Wilkinson spaniel and so forth; a brick-floored side room has sofas and more tables. They have the full range of well kept Adnams beers on handpump including the seasonal ones, as well as a good wine list, and about a dozen malt whiskies. Unfussy but well executed home-cooking might include fish chowder (£3.50), ploughman's (£4.95), sausage, egg and onion pie or smoked haddock quiche (£6.25), beef, Guinness and mushroom pie (£6.95), fillet steak (£11.95). There are plenty of white tables and chairs on a terrace at the front near the small sheltered and flower-filled garden. *(Recommended by Derek Hayman, Jill Hallpike, Carl Upsall, Derek and Sylvia Stephenson, Phil and Heidi Cook, Anthony Barnes, Neil Powell, Ian Phillips, Peter Meister)*

Adnams ~ Tenants Max and Suzie Kissick-Jones ~ Real ale ~ Bar food (12-2.30, 6-9.30) ~ (01728) 688510 ~ Children in restaurant ~ Open 11-3, 6-11; 12-3, 7-10.30 Sun ~ Bedrooms: £45B/£60B

Plough & Sail 🍴 ♈

Snape Maltings Riverside Centre

When the malting business here finally ground to a halt in 1965 a local farmer and relative of the present licensee bought the buildings, which are still known collectively as Snape Maltings, and set them up to house this pub, a famous concert hall, an art gallery and shops. The pub itself is a buff-coloured long narrow building with the bar facing you as you walk through the door; beyond this on the right is a raised airy eating room with attractive pine furniture and – to one side – a settle in front of the open fire. To the left of the bar and down some steps is a quarry-tiled room with dark traditional furniture; also a busy little restaurant. There's a nice mix of customers and the atmosphere is relaxed and friendly; the dining room is no smoking. A shortish lunchtime menu might offer sandwiches (from £2.40), a choice of three home-made soups (£3.75), ploughman's or pâté (from £3.95) and a couple of daily specials like aubergine and tomato focaccia with shaved parmesan (£4.60) and smoked halibut and scrambled eggs (£5.60). A much more comprehensive very good contemporary style evening menu offers more choice, such as spring salad of herb-baked ricotta and plum tomatoes (£4.50), smoked fish platter (£5.95), roasted vegetables on focaccia with balsamic dressing (£6.75), shell-on tiger prawns with sesame ginger vinaigrette or fish pie (£6.95), Thai green chicken curry with cardamom rice (£7.95), Suffolk pork loin on polenta with duxelle and parsley sauce (£8.75), scallop and monkfish fettucine with mascarpone, tomato and chilli jam or fried sirloin steak with forest mushrooms (£9.95), and puddings like white chocolate tart with chocolate sauce or apple and almond galette with apricot sauce (£3.50). Well kept Adnams and Wooodfordes on handpump, and a fine wine list with a few by the glass; darts, shove-ha'penny, cribbage and dominoes. The big enclosed back terrace has lots of picnic-sets. *(Recommended by David and Kay Ross, Maggie and Derek Washington, Andy and Sarah Gillett, Ian Phillips, Tony Gayfer, S A Edwards, Mrs Romey Heaton, John C Baker, Jonathan and Ann Tross, Perry and June Dann, Tracey and Stephen Groves)*

Free house ~ Licensees G J C and G E Gooderham ~ Real ale ~ Bar food (12-2.30, 7-9) ~ Restaurant ~ (01728) 688413 ~ Children in restaurant ~ Open 11-3, 5.30-11; 12-3, 7-10.30 Sun

SOUTHWOLD TM5076 Map 5
Crown ★ ⑪ ☐ ◧ ⇌
High Street

You do need to arrive at this rather smart old hotel in good time for a table as it is very popular. It's not surprising as it's very much Adnam's flagship so they do tend to do things quite well here. The elegant beamed main bar has a stripped curved high-backed settle and other dark varnished settles, kitchen chairs and some bar stools, pretty, fresh flowers on the mix of kitchen pine tables, newspapers to read, a carefully restored and rather fine carved wooden fireplace, and a relaxed atmosphere; the small no-smoking restaurant with its white cloths and pale cane chairs leads off. The smaller back oak-panelled locals' bar has more of a traditional pubby atmosphere, red leatherette wall benches and a red carpet; the little parlour on the left is also no smoking; shove ha'penny, dominoes and cribbage. There's a particularly carefully chosen wine list (they have the full Adnams range, well over 300), with a monthly changing choice of 20 interesting varieties by the glass or bottle kept perfectly on a cruover machine, as well as the full range of Adnams beers which are perfectly kept on handpump; also a good choice of malt whiskies, tea, coffee and herbal infusions. Beautifully cooked stylish bar food includes green pea and mint soup (£3.20), seared roulade of vegetables and goat's cheese with endive and parsley salad (£4.25), gravadlax with chicory, rocket and olive salad and pesto dressing (£4.60), smoked chicken with tarragon and oakleaf salad (£4.75), baked cod fillet with sweet tomatoes and crushed potatoes (£8.75), home-made fettucine with plum tomatoes, baby spinach, parmesan and hazelnut dressing, braised brisket of beef with roasted peppers, olives, tomatoes and sour cream dressing or roast salmon in cumin, potato and lentil broth (£9), and puddings like glazed lemon tart, meringue with tropical fruit and vanilla cream or chocolate and orange mousse layered with orange coulis (£3.75). There are a few tables in a sunny sheltered corner outside. *(Recommended by Peter and Giff Bennett, David and Anne Culley, Richard Siebert, Helen Pickering, James Owen, J Monk, Tina and David Woods-Taylor, Paul and Sandra Embleton, Mr and Mrs McKay, D H Ford, John and Shirley Smith, Malcolm and Liz Holliday, W Park Weir, Evelyn and Derek Walter, R C Wiles, Nigel Woolliscroft, Ronald Dodsworth, Pat and John Millward, Simon Cottrell, J and P Maloney, P A Legon, M Clifford, Gwen and Peter Andrews, David Peakall, Jane Carroll, J F M West, Mrs D P Dick, Pat and Tony Hinkins)*

Adnams ~ Tenant Angela Brown ~ Real ale ~ Bar food (12.15-2, 7-9(6.30-9.30 summer)) ~ Restaurant ~ (01502) 722275 ~ Children in eating area of bar and restaurant ~ Open 10.30-3, 6-11; 12-3, 6(7 winter)-10.30 Sun; closed first two weeks Jan ~ Bedrooms: £47B/£68(£72B)

STOKE BY NAYLAND TL9836 Map 5
Angel ⑪ ☐ ⇌
B1068 Sudbury—East Bergholt; also signposted via Nayland off A134 Colchester—Sudbury
Suffolk Dining Pub of the Year

For many readers this stylishly elegant dining place is the best pub in Suffolk – which means you do need to get there early or book a table. There's a very friendly and quite pubby atmosphere here, but the main source of its incredible popularity is the excellent attractively presented food from a changing menu that might include home-made soup (£2.75), griddled fresh sardines in oregano (£4.25), fresh dressed crab with home-made mayonnaise (£5.50), sautéed liver and bacon with madeira sauce (£6.75), steak and kidney pudding or vegetable filo parcels with fresh tomato coulis (£6.95), chicken and king prawn brochette with yoghurt and mint dip (£9.50), steamed fillets of salmon and halibut with dill sauce (£9.95), brochette of scallops wrapped in bacon (£10.95) and honey glazed roast rack of lamb (£11.25); home-made puddings might include tuille basket of brown bread ice cream or steamed apple pudding with vanilla sauce (£3.50). The comfortable main bar area has handsome Elizabethan beams, some stripped brickwork and timbers, a mixture of furnishings including wing armchairs, mahogany dining chairs, and pale library chairs, local watercolours and older prints, attractive table lamps, and a huge log fire. Round the corner is a little tiled-floor stand-and-chat bar – with well kept Adnams, Greene King IPA and Abbot and a guest beer on handpump, and a thoughtful wine list. One no-smoking room has a low sofa and wing armchairs around its woodburning stove, and Victorian paintings on the dark green walls. There are cast-iron seats and tables on a sheltered terrace. Spacious well equipped rooms and good breakfasts. *(Recommended by Richard and Robyn Wain, J M Waller, Richard and Margaret Peers, Tom Gondris, Bob and Maggie Atherton, Mrs P Goodwyn, D E Twitchett, Gwen and Peter Andrews, Ivan de Deken, Jasper Sabey, Ronald Dodsworth, MDN, David Gregory, R Wiles, C L Kauffmann, John and Enid Morris, V and E A Bolton, Derek Stafford)*

Free house ~ Licensee Peter Smith ~ Real ale ~ Bar food (12-2, 6.30-9) ~ Restaurant ~ (01206) 263245 ~ Open 11-2.30, 6-11; 12-3, 6-10.30 Sun; closed 25, 26 Dec, 1 Jan ~ Bedrooms: £47B/£61B

SWILLAND TM1852 Map 5
Moon & Mushroom
Village signposted off B1078 Needham Market—Wickham Market, and off B1077

An unusual touch at this cosy little place is the four hearty hotpots like coq au vin, pork with peppers, minted lamb, pheasant au vin (all £5.95), all served to you from Le Creuset dishes on a warming counter. You then help yourself to a choice of half a dozen or so tasty vegetables. Another couple of dishes might include ploughman's (£3.25), halibut mornay and stilton and pasta bake (£5.95), with proper home-made puddings like raspberry and apple crumble, bread and butter pudding and toffee and ginger pudding with butterscotch sauce (£2.25). There's a relaxed and friendly atmosphere in the smallish beamed bar, with the jovial licensee serving only well kept independent East Anglian beers such as Adnams, Buffys IPA, Nethergates Umbel, Scotts Hopleaf and Blues & Bloater and Woodfordes Norfolk Nog and Wherry, straight from casks racked up behing the long counter; there are about eight decent wines by the glass too. The pub is owned by a group of locals who bought it in 1996 and renamed it in a competition, with the Moon coming from its old name (the Half Moon) and the Mushroom from the licensees' enthusiasm for exotic mushrooms (which they include on the menu wherever possible). The homely interior is mainly quarry tiled with a small coal fire in a brick fireplace, old tables (with lots of board games in the drawers) arranged in little booths made by pine pews, and cushioned stools along the bar – this is still a real local, with food service ending quite early. A small doorway takes you into the no-smoking dark green and brown painted cottagey dining room. A little terrace in front has flower containers, trellis and green plastic furniture under parasols. *(Recommended by J F M and M West, Pat and Bill Pemberton, Anna Gough)*

Free house ~ Licensees Clive and Adrienne Goodall ~ Real ale ~ Bar food (12-2, 6.30-8.15; not Sun, Mon) ~ (01473) 785320 ~ Open 11-2.30, 6-11; 12-3, 7-10.30 Sun; closed Mon lunchtime

THORNHAM MAGNA TM1070 Map 5
Four Horseshoes 🛏
Off A140 S of Diss; follow Finningham 3¼ signpost, by White Horse pub

Said to date back to the 12th c, this handsome thatched pub with its dimly lit interior is full of charm and character, and because it rambles round so much is deceptively spacious. The extensive bar is well divided into alcoves and distinct areas, with very low and heavy black beams, some tall windsor chairs as well as the golden plush banquettes and stools on its spread of fitted turkey carpet, country pictures and farm tools on the black-timbered white walls, and logs burning in big fireplaces; the area with the inside well is no smoking, as is the restaurant. Bar food includes soup (£2.75), filled baps (from £2.95), roast turkey (£6.50), battered cod, scampi or mushroom and almond tagliatelle (£6.95), chicken and ham or game pie (£7.25), whole roast chicken (£7.95) or mixed grill (£8.25), daily specials like rib-eye steak (£7.95) and fish casserole with mushroom and garlic sauce (£10.25), and puddings like pecan pie (£2.95). Well kept Adnams Southwold, Courage Directors, Marstons Pedigree, Nethergate, and Theakstons Old Peculier on handpump; piped music. In summer, you can sit at the picnic-sets beside the flowerbeds on a sheltered lawn. Nearby, Thornham Walks consists of nearly 12 miles of permissive footpaths on the beautiful and privately owned Thornham Estate and there is a half mile hard-surfaced path through the parkland, woodland and farmland which is suitable for wheelchairs and pushchairs as well as those with walking difficulties. The thatched church at Thornham Parva is famous for its ancient wall paintings. *(Recommended by Michael and Hazel Duncombe, Charles and Pauline Stride, B K and R S Levy, Trevor Moore, Peter Plumridge, Gwen and Peter Andrews, Mr and Mrs L P Lesbirel, Conrad and Alison Freezer, Mrs P Goodwyn, Grahame McNulty)*

Old English Inns ~ Manager Sharon Palmer ~ Real ale ~ Bar food (12-2, 7-9(9.30 Fri, Sat)) ~ (01379) 678777 ~ Children welcome but only in Country bar at weekends ~ Open 12-2.30(3 Sat), 7-11; 12-3, 7-10.30 Sun ~ Bedrooms: £45S/£55S

TOSTOCK TL9563 Map 5
Gardeners Arms ◀

Village signposted from A14 (former A45) and A1088

You can be sure of a cheery welcome from the friendly licensees at this charmingly unspoilt pub. It's a popular local with a bustling villagey atmosphere in the smart lounge bar, as well as heavy low black beams, lots of carving chairs around black tables, and in the lively tiled public bar there's darts, pool, shove-ha'penny, dominoes, cribbage, juke box, and an unobtrusive fruit machine. Very well kept Greene King Abbot, IPA and seasonal beers on handpump. Enjoyable and good value bar food includes sandwiches (from £1.60), ploughman's (from £3.75), burgers (from £4.25), and daily specials such as soup (£2.15), paw paw with curried prawns (£3.75), mediterranean seafood cocktail (£3.50), vegetable and brown rice risotto (£5.75), Moroccan lamb tagine (£6.25), tuna fried in garlic butter or Thai king prawn green curry on rice (£7.50), and sirloin steak with brandy and mushroom sauce (£10.25). There's a pleasantly sheltered lawn with picnic-sets among roses and other flowers. *(Recommended by C Smith, Bill and Sheila McLardy, Mr and Mrs Staples, Conrad and Alison Freezer, Mrs P Goodwyn, D R A Field, Ian Phillips, T R Burden, Gwen and Peter Andrews, J F M and M West, Peter Meister)*

Greene King ~ Tenant Reg Ransome ~ Real ale ~ Bar food (not Mon, Tues evening, Sun lunchtime) ~ Restaurant ~ (01359) 270460 ~ Children in eating area of bar ~ Open 11.30-2.30, 7-11; 12-3, 7-10.30 Sun

WALBERSWICK TM4974 Map 5
Bell

Just off B1387

This unpretentious old place has the same brick floors, well worn flagstones and oak beams that were here 400 years ago when the sleepy little village was a flourishing port. The characterful, rambling bar is traditionally decorated with curved high-backed settles, tankards hanging from oars above the bar counter, and a woodburning stove in the big fireplace; a second bar has a very large open fire. Home-made bar food includes sandwiches (from £1.50), soup (£2.50), ploughman's (£4.75), fish and chips (£5.50), and blackboard specials like duck, orange and Grand Marnier pâté (£3.95), Thai crab cakes with chilli dip (£4.24), pasta with lentils and fresh herbs (£6.25), steak and kidney pie (£6.95), fishcakes (£7.90), and puddings like strawberry shortcake or sticky toffee pudding (£3). Four well kept Adnams beers on handpump, darts, and boules outside. This is a nice spot close to the beach, with a well placed hedge sheltering the seats and tables on the sizeable flower-filled lawn from the worst of the sea winds. To really make the most of the setting, it's worth taking the little ferry from Southwold, and then enjoying the short walk along to the pub. There are two resident boxer dogs, and other dogs are welcome. Most of the bedrooms look over the sea or the river. *(Recommended by John Wooll, Richard Gibbs, Yavuz and Shirley Mutlu, A and M Seaman, David and Anne Culley, D H Ford, Conrad and Alison Freezer, Hugh O'Neill, J McDougal, Dr J P Cullen)*

Adnams ~ Tenant Sue Ireland Cutting ~ Real ale ~ Bar food (12-2, 6(7 Sun)-9; not Sun evening end Oct-Easter) ~ (01502) 723109 ~ Children in family area ~ Open summer school holidays 11-11; 12-10.30 Sun; 11-3, 6-11 Mon-Fri; 11-4, 6-11 Sat, 12-4, 7-9 Sun winter; closed 25, 26 Dec evening ~ Bedrooms: £40B/£70B

WANGFORD TM4679 Map 5
Angel 🛏

High St; village signposted just off A12 at junction of B1126 to Southwold

New licensees here don't have the most traditional background – they've come from New York where they practised law – so it will be very interesting to hear how they get on at this neatly kept handsome cream-painted 17th-c village inn. There's a feeling of relaxed solidity about the light and airy bar with its well spaced, simple but substantial furniture which includes some sturdy elm tables, cushioned winged wall benches, and a splendid old bar counter, as well as old local photographs on the cream walls. Bar food might include soup (£2), sandwiches (from £2.75), hot filled french bread (£3.75), ploughman's or battered cod (£5.25), two course Sunday lunch (£4.95), fish pie (£5.60), potato and lentil pie (£5.95), beef stroganoff (£6.75) and sirloin steak (£8.75). The restaurant is no smoking. Well kept Adnams, Charles Wells Bombardier and Wolf on handpump, decent house wines from the Adnams list, good generous coffee; pleasant staff, maybe piped music; cribbage and a weekly quiz. The garden behind has picnic-sets under cocktail parasols. Comfortable, spotlessly clean bedrooms. *(Recommended by D and M Senior, June and Perry Dann, David Carr, Mr and Mrs P Bastable, Anthony Barnes, Mrs P Goodwyn, Paul and Sandra Embleton)*

Free house ~ Licensee Susan Dibella Harvey ~ Real ale ~ Bar food ~ Restaurant ~ (01502) 578636 ~ Children in restaurant and away from main bar ~ Open 11-11; 12-10.30 Sun ~ Bedrooms: £40B/£53B

WINGFIELD TM2277 Map 5
De La Pole Arms 🍺

Church Road; village signposted off B1118 N of Stradbroke

This beautifully restored village inn is owned by St Peters, a newish small brewery at South Elmham, some 11 or 12 miles to the NE of here, which although only a small operation was the winner of our Pub Group of the Year Award last year – this well run place is typical of its three civilised yet characterful pubs. Deliberately simple yet elegant décor is very traditional with interesting bric-a-brac, comfortable traditional seating, and no distraction by juke boxes, machines or flashing lights. Good bar food, with some emphasis on local fish and seafood, includes soup (£3.95), green-lipped mussels with pesto (£4.25), smoked duck salad (£4.95), beef carpaccio (£5.25), fishcakes (£6.50), smoked salmon salad or game pie (£7.25), fish and chips (£7.50), mixed seafood bowl (£8.25), halibut with green peppercorn sauce (£11.25), monkfish in honey glaze wrapped in parma ham (£12.50), and puddings like rhubarb fool and brandy snap biscuits or ginger and orange pudding with vanilla (£3.35). They stock the entire range of St Peters beers on handpump. *(Recommended by Mr and Mrs J B A Aldridge, Charles and Pauline Stride, D Twitchett, Roger Everett, Bob Arnett, Judy Wayman, Pat and Robert Watt, Tom and Rosemary Hall, Pamela Goodwyn)*

St Peters ~ Manager George Wortley ~ Real ale ~ Bar food ~ Restaurant ~ (01379) 384545 ~ Children welcome ~ Open 11-2.30, 6.30-11; 11-3, 6-11 Sat; 12-3, 6.30-11 Sun; closed Mon winter

Lucky Dip

Besides the fully inspected pubs, you might like to try these Lucky Dips recommended to us and described by readers (if you do, please send us reports):

Aldeburgh [TM4656]

☆ *Cross Keys* [Crabbe St]: Busy 16th-c pub newly extended from low-ceilinged core with antique settles, Victorian prints, woodburners, food from new kitchen from open sandwiches to fresh local fish (shame about the loudspeaker announcements), Adnams ales (the full range) and wines; can get smoky, fruit machine; open all day July/Aug, children in eating areas, tables in back yard which opens on to promenade and beach; elegant new bedrooms with own bathrooms *(Dr I Crichton, Maggie and Derek Washington, J F M and M West, LYM, George Little, Neil Powell)*

Mill [Market Cross Pl, opp Moot Hall]: Friendly, with good value food cooked to order inc local fish; good service, well kept Adnams ales, decent coffee, locals' bar, cosy no-smoking beamed dining room with *Gypsy Queen* model, sea view; cream teas July/Aug; fruit machine, can get rather full in summer; bedrooms *(David Peakall, CMW, JJW)*

Bardwell [TL9473]

☆ *Six Bells* [village signed off A143 NE of Bury; keep straight through village, then fork right into Daveys Lane off top green]: Comfortably modernised low-beamed pub dating from 16th c, good atmosphere, well kept Adnams and Marstons Pedigree, decent wines, pleasant décor, coal-effect fire in big fireplace; wide choice of bar meals with more elaborate evening dishes, restaurant with no-smoking conservatory, children welcome, garden with play area and wendy house; attractive pine-furnished bedrooms, cl Mon-Weds lunchtimes exc bank hols *(Ian Phillips, Bernard Stradling, David Gregory, Ronald Dodsworth, J F M and M West, George Atkinson, LYM)*

Barham [TM1451]

Sorrel Horse [Old Norwich Rd]: Cheerful and attractive pink-washed pantiled 17th-c country pub, nicely refurbished bar with magnificent log fire, lots of beams, lounge and two dining areas off, particularly well kept Tolly ales, decent food inc interesting specials, prompt friendly service; good garden with big play area and barbecue, timber stables opp; well placed for walks *(J F M and M West, John Baker)*

Beccles [TM4290]

Swan House [town centre]: Dining pub with short choice of imaginative well prepared food (worth booking), several comfortable rooms, good attentive service, Adnams and St Peters ales, chilled glass for unusual bottled beers from around the world, bar nibbles; tables in courtyard *(June and Malcolm Farmer, Lee Melin)*

Waveney House [Puddingmoor, off old mkt]: Hotel with pleasant bar overlooking river, good choice of food inc Sun roasts and home-made puddings; bedrooms *(Perry and June Dann)*

Blaxhall [TM3657]

☆ *Ship* [off B1069 S of Snape; can be reached from A12 via Little Glemham]: Welcoming and helpful landlord in spotless low-beamed traditional country local, log fire, generous home cooking with fresh veg in unassuming dining lounge, well kept Tolly and Marstons Pedigree, piped music, pool in public bar; children in eating area; self-catering cabins available, attractive setting; cl Mon lunchtime *(Perry and June Dann, LYM, Derek and Maggie Washington)*

Blyford [TM4277]

☆ *Queens Head* [B1123 Blythburgh—Halesworth]: Thatch, very low beams, a well they still use, some antique settles alongside more modern conventional furnishings, huge fireplace, popular generous food inc bargain lunches (but no sandwiches), well kept Adnams Bitter, Mild, and Broadside; children allowed in no-smoking restaurant, tables outside with good play area, bedrooms *(June and Malcolm Farmer, Trevor Williams, John Wooll, LYM, Perry and June Dann, David Carr, Chris Mawson)*

Blythburgh [TM4575]

☆ *White Hart* [A12]: Experienced new licensees in welcoming open-plan family dining pub with fine ancient beams, woodwork and staircase, good fish, well kept Adnams Bitter, Old and Broadside, decent wines; children in eating area and restaurant, open all day Fri/Sat; spacious lawns looking down on tidal marshes, magnificent church over road *(Derek and Maggie Washington, Peter Plumridge, Anthony Barnes, LYM, Perry and June Dann)*

Brandon [TL7886]

Ram [High St (A1065)]: Sizeable pub in interesting old building, well kept Flowers, interesting good value food inc vegetarian and proper home-made pies, good-sized helpings, friendly cheerful staff, comfortable seats, separate dining room and restaurant *(Keith and Janet Morris)*

Brent Eleigh [TL9447]

Cock [Lavenham Rd (A1141)]: Two bars, one very cosy and one more general, lots of old photographs of local villages, Adnams and Greene King IPA and Abbot; nice garden *(Nick and Alison Dowson)*

Bromeswell [TM3050]

Cherry Tree [Bromeswell Heath]: Good value honest food inc good vegetarian range and friendly staff in comfortably modernised neat beamed lounge with open fire and velvet curtains; seats outside, charming inn sign *(BB, Pamela Goodwyn)*

Bury St Edmunds [TL8564]

Nutshell [Traverse, Abbeygate St]: Quaint and attractive corner pub, perhaps the country's smallest inside, with particularly well kept Greene King IPA and Abbot, friendly landlord, lots of odd bric-a-brac inc mummified cat; cl Sun and Holy Days *(Richard and Valerie Wright, Kevin Blake, the Didler)*

Buxhall [TM0057]

Crown [signed off B1115 W of Stowmarket, then left at Rattlesden sign; Mill Rd]: Tucked-away genuine country local, family run and very welcoming, with snug and unassuming little bar and side room, good choice of bar food, well kept Greene King ales inc XX Mild, open fires, games in separate public bar, restaurant; children allowed if eating, pleasant garden *(Simon Reynolds, LYM)*

Clare [TL7645]

☆ *Bell* [Market Hill]: Large timbered inn with comfortably rambling lounge bar, splendidly carved black beams, old panelling and woodwork around the open fire, side rooms (one with lots of canal and other prints), well kept Nethergate ales inc Mild, also others such as Courage Directors, decent wines, friendly helpful staff, food inc children's dishes in dining conservatory opening on to terrace; darts, pool, fruit machine; bedrooms off back courtyard, open all day, interesting village *(Gwen and Peter Andrews, C J Fletcher, Prof Kenneth Surin, Pat and Tony Martin, LYM, Richard and Valerie Wright, Dr Andy Wilkinson)*

☆ *Swan* [High St]: Straightforward village local, early 17th-c but much modernised, lots of copper and brass and huge log fire, public bar with WWII memorabilia and another fire (dogs allowed here), friendly landlord, reasonably priced food from huge bargain huffers up, lovely flower tubs out behind; very special village, lovely church *(Nick Holmes, Richard and Valerie Wright, Prof Kenneth Surin, Patrick Hancock, BB, Mrs M Dixon, Dr Andy Wilkinson)*

East Bergholt [TM0734]

☆ *Kings Head* [Burnt Oak, towards Flatford Mill]: Well kept attractive beamed lounge with comfortable sofas, interesting decorations, quick pleasant service, good value home-made bar food inc several vegetarian dishes, good starters and curry, well kept Tolly and guest beers, decent wines and coffee, piped classical music (juke box in plain public bar); lots of room in pretty garden, flower-decked haywain, baskets and tubs of flowers in front *(Mike and Mary Carter, Pamela Goodwyn)*

Eastbridge [TM4566]

☆ *Eels Foot* [off B1122 N of Leiston]: Light modern furnishings in friendly country pub with wide choice of generous cheap food, well kept Adnams and other ales, darts in side area, neat back dining room; walkers, children and dogs welcome, tables and swings outside, pretty village handy for Minsmere bird reserve and heathland walks; open all day in summer for coffee and cream teas, live music some Sats, impromptu music Thurs *(CMW, JJW, LYM, Gwen and Peter Andrews, Maggie and Derek Washington, G Neighbour, J Middis, Helen Pickering, James Owen, Perry and June Dann, Jonathan and Ann Tross)*

Felixstowe Ferry [TM3337]

Ferry Boat: 17th-c pub tucked between golf links and dunes nr harbour and Martello tower, extended and much modernised as family pub; decent choice of food, busy summer w/e – can be very quiet other times *(Conrad and Alison Freezer, LYM)*

Victoria: Child-friendly riverside pub hoping to extend, good food emphasising local seafood, competitively priced Adnams and guest beers,

welcoming service *(Howard and Sue Gascoyne, Pamela Goodwyn)*

Finningham [TM0669]

White Horse [B1113]: Pleasant olde-worlde bar and dining areas, friendly licensees, well kept Flowers and Tolly, very big menu changing daily inc good vegetarian choice; handy for walkers *(Michael and Hazel Duncombe, Grahame McNulty)*

Framlingham [TM2863]

Castle [Castle St]: Friendly young staff in old small pub with well kept Whitbreads and other ales, wide range of decent food inc good soups, baguettes and omelettes; children welcome *(Helen Winter, Mr and Mrs Staples)*

☆ *Crown* [Market Hill]: Old-fashioned heavy-beamed public bar opening into hall and comfortable character lounge with armchairs by log fire, pleasant staff, bar and limited restaurant food, real ales inc Adnams, decent wines, lively atmosphere on Sat market day; comfortable period bedrooms *(LYM, Pamela Goodwyn)*

Freckenham [TL6671]

Golden Boar [B1102 Fordham—Mildenhall]: Very friendly, handy for Newmarket *(Racing Post* available), good choice of drinks, good if not cheap freshly made food *(Mike and Jennifer Marsh)*

Friston [TM4160]

☆ *Old Chequers* [just off A1094 Aldeburgh—Snape]: Welcoming dining pub with simple but stylish country pine furnishings, light and airy décor, good if not cheap interesting food (no wait, served from bain-marie) inc fish, game, vegetarian, Sun carvery, good puddings, well kept Adnams, good wines and whiskies; good walk from Aldeburgh *(MDN, Maggie and Derek Washington, Mrs Romey Heaton, Peter Smith, Mrs P Goodwyn, LYM, P F Whight)*

Grundisburgh [TM2250]

Dog: Good bar food inc bargain OAP Mon lunches in well run carefully extended elegant period village pub with restaurant, good range of well kept beers *(J F M and M West)*

Hadleigh [TM0242]

Ram [Market Pl]: Pleasantly unassuming, very friendly, with good reasonably priced food, well kept Greene King IPA and quick service *(C L Kauffmann, Mike and Mary Carter)*

Halesworth [TM3877]

Angel [Thoroughfare]: 16th-c coaching inn with obliging service, bar food from soup and sandwiches up, well kept ales, decent wines, good Italian restaurant; interesting interior courtyard with 18th-c clock and vines trained round the walls; seven well equipped bedrooms, open all day *(Perry and June Dann)*

White Hart [Thoroughfare]: Roomy and well restored open-plan local, well arranged and nicely furnished; comfortable welcoming atmosphere, well kept beers inc Adnams and Bass, good home-cooked food with fresh fish and excellent local veg, attentive friendly service *(Perry and June Dann, Neil Powell)*

Haughley [TM0262]

☆ *Kings Arms* [off A45/B1113 N of Stowmarket]: Good atmosphere with nice mix of pub and dining, wide choice of good value home-made food inc interesting fish, Greek dishes (landlady's mother comes from Cyprus) and puddings, airy beamed dining lounge with lots of shiny dark tables, restaurant area on left, busy public bar with games, log fire, well kept Greene King IPA and Abbot, decent wines, friendly helpful staff; piped music; tables and play house in colourful back garden *(John and Elizabeth Thomason, BB, Charles and Pauline Stride, Conrad and Alison Freezer)*

Hintlesham [TM0843]
George [George St]: Village pub with large refurbished flagstoned bar, comfortable eating area extending to roomy conservatory restaurant, a real welcome for children, good value food inc big filled baguettes and yorkshire puddings, friendly landlord, Tetleys; garden with play area and animals *(Mike and Maggie Betton)*

Holbrook [TM1636]
Compasses [Ipswich Rd]: Clean and tidy, recently spaciously renovated, with good value food inc interesting dishes in bar and restaurant, welcoming staff, big log fire, well kept ales inc Flowers and Tolly, garden with play area *(Rex Miller)*

Hoxne [TM1777]
☆ *Swan* [off B1118; signed off A140 S of Diss]: Striking late 15th-c pub, handsomely restored by previous owners, with broad oak floorboards, armchairs by deep-set inglenook fireplace, no-smoking snug, another fireplace in dining room, food from sandwiches to steaks, Adnams, Courage Directors and IPA and Marstons Pedigree, piped music; pool, cribbage, dominoes; children welcome, sizeable attractive garden behind *(Gwen and Peter Andrews, Mike and Mary Carter, Ronald Dodsworth, Muriel and Peter Gleave, LYM, Paul and Sandra Embleton)*

Ipswich [TM1744]
☆ *Fat Cat* [Spring Rd]: Reconstruction of basic genuine pub outstanding for around 20 well kept ales such as Adnams Bitter and Broadside, Charles Wells Bombardier, Gales HSB, Hampshire Pendragon, Lees Ruff Yeo, Mauldons Mid Autumn Gold, Roosters Cream and Shepherd Neame Spitfire; farm ciders, friendly first-rate staff, snacks such as scotch eggs and filled rolls, lots of old advertisements; pleasant garden *(John Baker, Ian Phillips)*

Ixworth [TL9370]
☆ *Pykkerel* [High St; just off A143 Bury—Diss]: Several rooms off central servery, Elizabethan beams, attractive brickwork, big fireplaces, antique tables and chairs, persian rugs on gleaming boards, small back sun lounge; food (not Sun evening) concentrating on good fresh fish, friendly staff, well kept Greene King IPA and Abbot and a guest beer under light carbon dioxide blanket, restaurant; children welcome *(J F M West, LYM, J and P Maloney, Ronald Dodsworth, Paul Tudge)*

Kersey [TL9944]
☆ *Bell* [signed off A1141 N of Hadleigh]: Quaint flower-decked Tudor building in picturesque village, low-beamed public side with tiled floor and log fire divided from lounge by brick and timber screen, good service, wide choice of bar food inc lots of fresh fish, well kept local ales,

decent house wines, restaurant, sheltered back terrace with fairy-lit side canopy; open all day (afternoon teas), children allowed, small caravan site *(A Jennings, Mrs P Goodwyn, D and J Tapper, C L Kauffmann, LYM)*

Knodishall [TM4261]
Butchers Arms: Recently renovated local with good reasonably priced home-made food inc Sun roasts, well kept Adnams, pleasant airy dining room; darts, cribbage etc, garden with terrace *(Norman Smith)*

Lavenham [TL9149]
Cock [Church St]: Attractive thatched village pub, quiet at lunchtimes, with Adnams and Greene King XX Mild and IPA on handpump, Abbot tapped from the cask *(the Didler)*
Great House: Good food in a lovely seting, excellent service, fine choice of wines *(Nick Holmes)*

Layham [TM0240]
☆ *Marquis of Cornwallis* [Upper Layham; B1070 E of Hadleigh]: Beamed 16th-c pub with plush lounge bar, nicely prepared generous food inc good ploughman's and fresh veg, popular lunchtime with businessmen and retired locals, friendly atmosphere, well kept beers such as Marstons Pedigree, good wines and coffee; good valley views, popular bird table and picnic-sets in extensive riverside garden, open all day Sat in summer; bedrooms handy for Harwich ferries *(Rex Miller, C L Kauffmann)*

Little Glemham [TM3458]
Lion [The Street (A12)]: Well kept Adnams, wide choice of attractively priced food, garden with animals and aviary *(Perry and June Dann)*

Long Melford [TL8645]
☆ *Bull* [B1064]: Medieval former manorial great hall, now a hotel, with beautifully carved beams in old-fashioned timbered front lounge, log fire in huge fireplace, antique furnishings, daily papers; more spacious back bar with sporting prints; good range of bar food from sandwiches to one-price hot dishes inc imaginative salads and fresh fish, no-smoking restaurant, well kept Adnams Best, Greene King IPA and Nethergate, good wines; children welcome, tables in courtyard, open all day Sat/Sun; comfortable if pricy bedrooms *(LYM, David Heath, JP, PP, Ian Phillips, Ronald Dodsworth, Maysie Thompson, Helen Winter, Dr Andy Wilkinson, Pamela Goodwyn)*
Cock & Bell [Hall St]: Attractive cream-washed pub recently open-planned to give spacious carpeted bar and dining area, well kept Courage Best and Directors and Greene King IPA, attentive pleasant jolly staff, decent wine, tasty food, unobtrusive piped music *(Gwen and Peter Andrews)*
☆ *Crown*: Dark green ceiling and walls show off carefully chosen prints and nicely placed furniture, dusky pink banquettes on one side, big log fire, reasonably priced generous food cooked to order, well kept Melford Antique (brewed by the pub) and guests such as Bass, Greene King IPA, Morlands Old Speckled Hen, good open fire; quiet and pleasant piped music; well equipped bedrooms, huge breakfast *(Ian Phillips, John Fahy, LYM)*
George & Dragon [Hall St]: Good choice of

reasonably priced food in refurbished bar and dining room, roaring log fires, no-smoking area, Greene King real ales, decent wines, good polite service, bar billiards; sheltered garden and courtyard; open all day exc Sun, five comfortable bedrooms *(John and Shirley Smith)*

Lound [TM5099]

Village Maid [Yarmouth Rd]: Friendly service, good choice of good food quickly served, good view of village pond with friendly ducks; handy for Somerleyton Hall *(R E Perry)*

Lowestoft [TM5490]

Jolly Sailors [Pakefield St/Wilson Rd, off A12]: Generous well prepared food esp fish in big busy partly no-smoking bar and much-booked restaurant; popular all-day Sun carvery, sweeping sea view from front part, no-smoking family garden room, uniformed staff; handy for beach and quaint Pakefield church *(Howard and Sue Gascoyne, Albert and Margaret Horton)*

Oak [just off Somerleyton Rd]: Two-bar pub with fair choice of well kept beers *(Richard Houghton)*

Middleton [TM4367]

Bell [The Street]: Welcoming new landlord in charming little pub, part thatched and beamed, in pretty village; woodburner in comfortable lounge, Adnams ales tapped from the cask, good simple food inc children's; darts and open fire in public bar (dogs allowed), small back dining room, picnic-sets in garden, camping; maybe piped radio, some folk nights *(CMW, JJW, Derek and Maggie Washington, Richard Gibbs, Perry and June Dann, Jonathan and Ann Tross)*

Monks Eleigh [TL9647]

☆ *Swan* [B1115 Sudbury—Stowmarket]: Clean and comfortably modernised lounge bar, current landlord doing innovative fresh home-cooked food inc good vegetarian dishes, real ales inc Adnams and Greene King, good wine list, friendly efficient service, open fire, pleasant dining extension; bedrooms *(A Jennings)*

Nayland [TL9734]

White Hart [B1087, just off A134 Sudbury—Colchester]: This carefully renovated inn, 16th-c behind its 17th-c coaching frontage, is now determinedly enforcing its former pubby atmosphere by barring non-dining drinkers; good upmarket country food inc good value Sun supper, scrubbed tables on partly glass floor looking down into cellar, cosy back bar with big comfortable settee by blazing log fire, friendly service, Adnams and Greene King IPA, good value wines; bedrooms *(Charles and Pauline Stride)*

Newbourne [TM2643]

Fox: Good atmosphere in 17th-c pub with straightforward home cooking using fresh local produce, well kept Tolly tapped from the cask, cosy unspoilt oak-beamed drinking area around log fire, separate family room, recent dining room extension; pretty hanging baskets, lots of tables out in attractive garden with pond, musical evenings *(Pamela Goodwyn, Richard and Valerie Wright)*

Norton [TL9565]

☆ *Tickled Trout* [Ixworth Rd (A1088)]: Modern brick pub, former Plumbers Arms, refurbished as single bar with restaurant – good interesting

generous food esp fish; cheerful and spotless, with faultless service, particularly well kept Hook Norton Best and guest ales, good choice of wines *(C W Dix, Derek Field, John Baker)*

Orford [TM4250]

Kings Head [Front St]: Bright cheerful feel in cleanly refurbished beamed lounge bar overlooking churchyard, well kept Adnams ales, good coffee, food inc lunchtime snacks from sandwiches up, decent wines, friendly staff and locals, attractive restaurant; live music Fri, attractive character bedrooms with own bathrooms *(John Prescott, David Child, Tim and Linda Collins, Tony and Shirley Albery, CMW, JJW, LYM, Gwen and Peter Andrews, P and J Banks)*

Pettistree [TM2954]

Three Tuns [off A12 just S of Wickham Mkt]: Comfortable easy chairs, civilised food *(Pamela Goodwyn)*

Polstead [TL9938]

☆ *Cock* [signed off B1068 and A1071 E of Sudbury, then pub signed; Polstead Green]: Friendly and unspoiled, with very civilised landlord, interesting reasonably priced food (not Sun evening) from good value imaginatively filled lunchtime big rolls and real soups through honest rewarding main courses to imaginative puddings, inc superb Sun lunch and their own smoked meats; relaxed atmosphere, black beams and timbers, dark pink walls, woodburner and open fire, random mix of unassuming furniture, nice prints, lit candles, well kept ales such as Adnams Broadside, Greene King IPA and Woodfordes Wherry, good coffee (with warmed shortbread), good choice of wines, evening barn restaurant; piped music not too obtrusive, picnic-sets out overlooking quiet green, side play area; children welcome, cl Mon *(BB, John Prescott, V J Parry, Deborah Cox, Michael Ellis, Keith and Janet Morris, Pamela Goodwyn)*

Ramsholt [TM3041]

Ramsholt Arms [Dock Rd, off B1083]: Worth knowing for the lovely isolated spot, with picture-window nautical bars overlooking River Deben; good log fire, good but pricey beer choice such as Adnams, Batemans XB and Flowers Original, several wines by the glass, no-smoking restaurant, summer afternoon terrace bar (not Sun); longish steep walk down from car park; children welcome, comfortable spacious bedrooms, yacht moorings nearby; busy on summer w/e *(LYM, Richard and Valerie Wright, J A Middis, Mr and Mrs M Ashley Miller, Gwen and Peter Andrews, Pamela Goodwyn)*

Reydon [TM4978]

Cricketers [Wangford Rd]: Relaxed local atmosphere, very friendly helpful staff, good choice of good generous food inc plenty of fish and vegetarian and interesting puddings, Adnams beers and wines, light and airy bar with pleasant cricketing décor, tables in garden; comfortable bedrooms, bath across landing *(D Field, V and E A Bolton, Perry and June Dann)*

Saxtead Green [TM2665]

☆ *Old Mill House* [B1119]: Roomy dining pub across green from working windmill, beamed carpeted bar, neat country-look flagstoned restaurant, brick servery, wooden tables and chairs, pretty curtains, popular reasonably priced freshly made food inc good puddings and nightly carvery, well kept Adnams, Courage Best and Directors and Shepherd Neame Spitfire, decent wines; children very welcome, discreet piped music; sizeable garden, pretty back terrace, good play area *(Mrs Sandford, Mrs P Goodwyn, Ian and Nita Cooper, Gwen and Peter Andrews, Mr and Mrs Staples, LYM)*

Shotley Gate [TM2434]

Bristol Arms [end of B1456]: Good spot by river with real ales inc local Harwich, food inc tempting fresh fish; most unusual wine shop in pub selling cut-price drinks inc uncommon whiskies and liqueurs, also cuddly toys in bar for sale *(Jenny and Brian Seller)*

Shottisham [TM3144]

Sorrel Horse: Simple thatched two-bar pub in tucked-away village, well kept Tolly ales tapped from the cask, reasonably priced straightforward food lunchtime and early evening, friendly service, good fire; quiz nights some Sats, tables on green in front *(JP, PP, Richard and Valerie Wright, Pat and Tony Martin)*

Sibton [TM3669]

White Horse [Halesworth Rd]: Comfortable and attractively laid out former 16th-c farmhouse with interesting furnishings, well kept Adnams Bitter and Broadside, pleasant owners, attractive big garden with play area *(LYM, Richard Houghton, Pamela Goodwyn)*

South Elmham [TM3389]

☆ *St Peters Brewery* [St Peter S Elmham; off B1062 SW of Bungay]: Bar and restaurant attached to tucked-away brewery in medieval buildings, interesting brewery tour: imaginative range of ales, using water from 200-ft bore hole, hand capping and labelling *(Rachael and Mark Baynham)*

Southwold [TM5076]

Harbour Inn [Blackshore; from A1095, right at Kings Head – pass golf course and water tower]: New landlord and restaurant extension, tiny low-beamed front bar, upper back bar with lots of nautical bric-a-brac – even ship-to-shore telephone and wind speed indicator; varied food (not Sun evening, just fish and chips in newspaper Fri evening/Sat lunch), well kept Adnams Bitter and Broadside, coal fires, solid old furnishings; darts, table skittles, themed evenings and music nights; tables outside with play area and ducks – can be a bit untidy out here *(LYM, Klaus and Elizabeth Leist, Conrad and Alison Freezer, John and Phyllis Maloney, Jeff Davies, MJVK)*

Kings Head [High St]: Spacious dining pub popular with family parties, lots of maroon and pink plush, very wide choice of decent food from filled rolls up inc fish and vegetarian, well kept Adnams, good house wines, no-smoking area; comfortable family/games room with well lit pool table; jazz Sun night, decent bedrooms *(MJVK, John Wooll, Mrs Romey Heaton, BB, MLR)*

☆ *Lord Nelson* [East St]: Bustling cheerful easy-going seaside local with cool Adnams Mild, Bitter, Extra, Broadside and Old, decent wines, good generous basic lunchtime food freshly made from sandwiches up, low prices, attentive service; low ceilings, panelling and tiled floor, spotless light wood furniture, lamps in nice nooks and crannies, Lord Nelson memorabilia and super soda-syphon collection, no music, sheltered back garden; open all day, children and shirtless trippers welcome *(John Wooll, Gwen and Peter Andrews, Nigel Woolliscroft, Tony Gayfer, Ted George, J F M West, J and P Maloney, A J Thomas, Tim and Linda Collins, P J Keen, C R L Savill, BB, Jeff Davies, Dr Andy Wilkinson, the Didler)*

Red Lion [South Green]: Tidy, comfortable and relatively quiet, with big windows looking over green to sea, ship pictures, brassware and copper, elm-slab barrel tables, pale panelling; well kept Adnams Bitter, Broadside and Mild, good range of good value basic food inc vegetarian and good fish, family room and summer buffet room, tables outside; right by the Adnams retail shop; bedrooms small but comfortable *(BB, MDN, John Wooll)*

☆ *Sole Bay* [East Green]: Homely Victorian local moments from sea, opp brewery (and the Sole Bay lighthouse), light wood furnishings, particularly good value simple lunchtime food (not Sun in winter) esp local smoked sprats, well kept full Adnams range, good house wines, friendly dogs, lots of polished seafaring memorabilia, unobtrusive piped music, caged birds; conservatory with cockatoos, tables on side terrace *(John Wooll, Tony Gayfer, June and Perry Dann, LYM, Jeff Davies, Gwen and Peter Andrews, Dr Andy Wilkinson)*

☆ *Swan* [Market Pl]: Hotel not pub, but has well kept Adnams and Broadside with the full range of their bottled beers as well as decent wines and malt whiskies in the relaxed comfortable back bar, also bar food (not cheap) inc generous open sandwiches; friendly helpful staff, chintzy and airy front lounge, good bedrooms inc garden rooms where (by arrangement) dogs can stay too *(J H Bell, J F M West, Gwen and Peter Andrews, Tina and David Woods-Taylor, LYM, John Wooll)*

Stanton [TL5673]

Rose & Crown: Tidy and comfortable dining pub open all day, with good service, wide range of well priced food esp fresh fish, scottie and west highland white pictures, parrot; smart conservatory restaurant, booking advised; children welcome *(Maria Beane)*

Stonham Aspal [TM1359]

Ten Bells: Old but extensively modernised, popular food inc children's and local produce in bar and restaurant, well kept beers, welcoming staff, small locals' bar; tables out on terrace *(Ian and Nita Cooper)*

Stowmarket [TM0457]

Magpie [Combs Ford]: Friendly local, lots of old beams, good range of generous traditional food, well kept Greene King; new conservatory fits in well *(Paul and Maggie Baker)*

Stradbroke [TM2374]

Ivy House [Wilby Rd]: Busy and full of character, with well kept beer and good food inc bargain lunches *(J F M and M West)*

Stradishall [TL7452]
☆ *Cherry Tree* [A143]: Two small traditional beamed bars, consistently good value home cooking inc vegetarian, pleasant atmosphere, open fires, Greene King beers under light pressure, cheerful expert licensees; friendly ducks and pond in huge rustic garden (dogs allowed here); outside gents' (*BB, Pam and David Bailey*)

Stratford St Mary [TM0434]
Swan: Cosy and interesting olde-worlde beamed pub with good choice of generous food cooked to order (so may be a wait), well kept Tolly, log fire in big fireplace; children welcome, some tables over road by River Stour (*C L Kauffmann, Meg and Colin Hamilton*)

Theberton [TM4365]
Lion [B1122]: Good atmosphere in cosy lounge with comfortable banquettes, lots of old photographs, pictures, copper, brass and plates, fresh flowers, good value freshly made food inc children's, welcoming licensees, Adnams and interesting guest beers; piped radio, cribbage, separate part with darts, pool and TV; garden with picnic-sets, small terrace and camp site (*Sarah Phillips and Phil Kane, CMW, JJW*)

Thorington Street [TM0035]
☆ *Rose* [B1068 Higham—Stoke by Nayland]: Partly Tudor, with old beams and pine furniture in long pleasantly decorated divided bar/dining area, good home-made food esp very wide choice of fresh fish and seafood, interesting vegetarian choice and good value puddings; welcoming landlady, well kept Adnams, modestly priced decent house wines, big garden with view of Box valley (*MDN*)

Thorpeness [TM4759]
Dolphin: Reopened after refurbishment and restoration following the fire damage which closed it some years ago, attractive décor, good food; dogs welcome in public bar; comfortable bedrooms (*Pamela Goodwyn*)

Ufford [TM2953]
White Lion [Lower St]: Good reasonably priced home-cooked food and well kept Tolly in clean, small and friendly pub nicely placed on village edge not far from quiet section of River Deben; open central fireplace (*Pamela Goodwyn*)

Waldringfield [TM2844]
Maybush [The Quay; nr Woodbridge]: Riverside pub with sailing memorabilia inc Giles cartoons, wide range of generous well priced and well cooked food, very friendly quick service, sizeable verandah with good views over River Deben and its bird-haunted sandbanks (*B Lord, Joan and Andrew Life, Pamela Goodwyn*)

Westleton [TM4469]
☆ *Crown* [B1125 Blythburgh—Leiston]: Extended beamed inn with country chairs, attractive stripped tables, good local photographs and farm tools in genteelly lit bar area, six interesting real ales, lots of malt whiskies, good wines, farm cider, log fires, pleasant service, piped classical music; wide range of home-made food inc good vegetarian choice in big dining area opening off on left (children allowed) and in roomy no-smoking conservatory, pretty garden with aviary and floodlit terrace, beautiful setting, good walks nearby; 19 comfortable bedrooms, good breakfast (*LYM, Mrs Romey Heaton, June and Perry Dann, Gwen and Peter Andrews, Pamela Goodwyn*)

Weybread [TM2480]
Crown [B1116]: Reopened under new management, busy local feel, good cheap food (special nights such as curry nights), well kept beers such as Morlands Old Speckled Hen (*Revd John Hibberd*)

Wickham Market [TM3056]
George [High St]: Spotless local with good log fire, well kept Tolly and a guest beer, amenable landlord, simple food (*Neil Powell*)

Wissett [TM3679]
Plough [The Street]: Popular open-plan 17th-c local, lounge area one end, well kept Adnams Bitter and Broadside, good food inc good value lunches; live music some Sats, buskers Thurs (*Perry and June Dann, N S Doolan*)

Witnesham [TM1851]
Barley Mow: Pleasant old pub with home-made food inc good Fri fish and chips in separate dining room, well kept Greene King (*J F M and M West, David and Mary Webb*)

Woodbridge [TM2749]
☆ *Anchor* [opp quay]: High-ceilinged plainly furnished bar with lots of nautical character and paintings by a local artist for sale, separate eating area, good value usual food inc sandwiches, vegetarian, good pies, well priced fresh local fish, well kept Greene King IPA and Abbot, friendly new owners (*Pat and Tony Martin, M Mason, D Thompson, J F M and M West*)
Angel [Theatre St]: Attractive Tudor pub, cosy inside, open fires, beams, well kept Flowers Original, meals inc beef stew in huge yorkshire pudding (*Quentin Williamson*)
Cross Quays: Food inc good Lowestoft cod and mussels, well kept Adnams, friendly staff; busy local bar, restaurant, back terrace; piped music (*Rupert Cutler*)
Kings Head [Market Hill]: Large character bar with lots of flagstones and timbering, blazing inglenook log fire, big tables, back conservatory, good if not cheap choice of generous food from sandwiches up inc lots of fish, service efficient and cheery even during busiest lunchtime bustle, full Adnams range kept well, no loud music (*Richard and Valerie Wright, Pat and Tony Martin, Peter Plumridge*)

Yoxford [TM3968]
Griffin [High St]: 14th-c pub with good atmosphere, bar food inc children's, friendly staff, medieval feasts in restaurant decorated to match; quiz night Thurs; beamed bedrooms (*John Cooke, Alison and Richard Bedford*)

Post Office address codings confusingly give the impression that some pubs are in Suffolk when they're really in Norfolk or Cambridgeshire (which is where we list them).

Surrey

Drinks prices are very high indeed here, much higher than the national average. In most Surrey pubs beer now costs £2 a pint or more – the first county to have smashed through the £2 barrier so convincingly. In even the cheapest pub we found here beer cost as much as it did in another county (such as Staffordshire's) most expensive pub of all. Such high prices mean that it's doubly important to track down the county's better pubs, for a better chance of getting value for money. Pubs on peak form here these days include the Abinger Hatch in a lovely setting at Abinger Common (a new main entry, under licensees who formerly made their mark at the Stephan Langton at Friday Street), the Woolpack at Elstead (a good all-rounder – good beer, imaginative food), the King William IV clinging to the hillside at Mickleham (cosier and pubbier than most, with good food and beer), the Surrey Oaks at Newdigate (individualistic and nicely furnished, with a good garden – another newcomer to the Guide), the Royal Oak in Pirbright (good atmosphere, lots of real ales), and the quaint White Lion in Warlingham (showing that decent food can be cheap, even in Surrey. The best food this year has been at the King William IV and the Woolpack; it's the latter pub that has the wider choice of food, including more dishes that might suit a special meal out, so the Woolpack at Elstead is out choice as Surrey Dining Pub of the Year. The Lucky Dip section at the end of the chapter has a very good choice of pubs: we'd particularly pick out the William IV at Albury Heath, Crown at Chiddingfold, Villagers at Chilworth, Plough in Effingham, Ram in Farncombe, Parrot at Forest Green, Jolly Farmer in Guildford, Three Horseshoes in Laleham, Kings Arms at Ockley, Red Lion in Shepperton, Volunteer at Sutton and, for food, Botley Hill Farmhouse near Warlingham, Brickmakers Arms in Windlesham and Jolly Farmer at Worplesdon.

ABINGER COMMON TQ1145 Map 3
Abinger Hatch

Off A25 W of Dorking; follow Abinger signpost, then turn right towards Abinger Hammer

Beautifully placed, this friendly pub sits in a village clearing in the marvellous mixed woodland that covers these rolling hills, with the church just across the green. Wisteria tumbles over its tiled roof, and picnic-sets under fir trees on a neat stretch of side grass sheltered by beech and rose hedges tempt out patrols of friendly ducks; a big fig tree grows in front. Inside is quiet on weekday lunchtimes, but has a happy crowd of families at the weekend. There's plenty of cosy character, with heavy beams, flagstones, big log fires, and simple homely furnishings, including pews forming booths around oak tables in a side carpeted part. A very wide range of straightforward good food is cooked by the landlord who intends to introduce a range of Mexican dishes at about the time this book comes out. Bar food runs from a good range of filled petits pains and sandwiches (from £2.45) to luscious puddings (£2.75), and might include soup (£2.45), ploughman's (from £4.25), half a dozen vegetarian meals such as vegetable chilli, pasta or kiev (from £4.95), chicken curry (£5.25), pork loin or poached salmon with hollandaise sauce (£7.95) and 8oz sirloin steak (£9.75); children's meals (from £1.75); the restaurant is no smoking. A good range of real ales includes Abinger Hatch Best (brewed for the pub by local Weltons

Brewery) along with Badger Best and Tanglefoot, Fullers London Pride, Harveys
Best, Hogs Back TEA and a guest such as Hop Back Summer Lightning on
handpump; winter mulled wine. Darts, shove-ha'penny, table skittles, cribbage,
dominoes and piped music; friendly efficient service. *(Recommended by Sue and Mike
Todd, JEB, C J Bromage)*

*Free house ~ Licensees Jan and Maria Walaszkowski ~ Real ale ~ Bar food (not Sun
or Mon evenings) ~ Restaurant ~ (01306) 730737 ~ Children welcome ~ Jazz Fri
evening once a month ~ Open 11-3, 5-11; 11-11 Sat; 12-10.30 Sun*

BETCHWORTH TQ2149 Map 3
Dolphin
The Street

Although this friendly village local can get very busy, readers report that service
remains cheerful and efficient throughout. The homely front room has kitchen chairs
and plain tables on the 400-year-old scrubbed flagstones, and the carpeted back
saloon bar is black-panelled with robust old-fashioned elm or oak tables. There are
three warming fires, and a nice chiming longcase clock. Good value bar food
includes stilton and chestnut pâté (£2.95), cheese and bacon waffles (£3.35), prawns
in garlic (£3.95), penne with chilli tomato sauce (£5.45), chicken curry (£5.85),
smoked haddock or steak and mushroom pie (£5.95), and puddings like spotted dick
or apple pie (£2.25). Well kept Youngs Bitter, Pale Ale, Special and seasonal brews
on handpump; up to 18 wines by the glass; efficient service; darts, dominoes,
cribbage, and fruit machine. There are some seats in the small laurel-shaded front
courtyard and picnic-sets on a lawn by the car park, opposite the church and on the
back garden terrace. No children inside. *(Recommended by G Simpson, D WAJ, David and
Carole Chapman, Martin and Karen Wake, James Nunns, Klaus and Elizabeth Leist, Don Mather,
John Pettit, John Evans, G S Dudley, Susan and John Douglas, Dick and Madeleine Brown,
Catherine and Richard Preston)*

*Youngs ~ Managers George and Rose Campbell ~ Real ale ~ Bar food ~ (01737)
842288 ~ Open 11-3, 5.30-11; 11-11 Sat; 12-10.30 Sun; 11-3, 5.30-11 Sat, 12-3, 7-
10.30 Sun winter; closed 25 Dec evening*

BLACKBROOK TQ1846 Map 3
Plough ♀
On byroad E of A24, parallel to it, between Dorking and Newdigate, just N of the turn E to
Leigh

Carefully run by attentive friendly licensees and friendly smartly dressed staff, this
neatly kept white pub is beautifully decorated with marvellous hanging baskets and
window boxes in summer. There are fresh flowers on the tables and sills of the large
linen-curtained windows in the partly no-smoking saloon bar, and down some steps,
the public bar has brass-topped treadle tables, a formidable collection of ties as well
as old saws on the ceiling, and bottles and flat irons; piped music. There are a good
few tables, and children can play in the prettily painted Swiss playhouse furnished
with tiny tables and chairs, in the secluded garden. As well as the lunchtime snack
menu with sausage and chips (£3.95), ploughman's (from £4.75), toasted bagels
(from £4.95) and scampi (£5.75), good blackboard specials might include chicken,
prune and armagnac pâté with cranberry sauce (£3.75), clam chowder (£3.95),
ratatouille niçoise (£5.95), prawn curry, chicken, ginger and lime curry or brioche
with mushrooms in creamy white wine garlic sauce (£6.45), pork fillets in dijon
mustard sauce (£7.45), smoked haddock on spring onion mash with grain mustard,
egg and lemon sauce (£8.50) and fillet steak (£12.45), with puddings like almond
tart, Italian nougat ice cream or crème caramel (£3.45). Well kept King & Barnes
Sussex, Broadwood, Festive, and seasonal beers on handpump, about 15 wines by
the glass, freshly squeezed juice and several malt whiskies and port. The countryside
around here is a particularly good area for colourful spring and summer walks
through the oak woods. They usually have an atmospheric carol concert the Sunday
before Christmas. No children inside. *(Recommended by Colin Draper, Comus Elliott,*

Derek and Maggie Washington, Mrs G Sharman, John Pettit, Maggie and Derek Washington, Tina and David Woods-Taylor)

King & Barnes ~ Tenants Chris and Robin Squire ~ Real ale ~ Bar food (not Mon evening) ~ (01306) 886603 ~ Open 11-2.30(3 Sat), 6-11; 12-3, 7-10.30 Sun; closed 25, 26, 31 Dec, open 1 Jan 2000 for brunch

COBHAM TQ1060 Map 3
Cricketers

Downside Common; 3¾ miles from M25 junction 10; A3 towards Cobham, 1st right on to A245, right at Downside signpost into Downside Bridge Rd, follow road into its right fork – away from Cobham Park – at second turn after bridge, then take next left turn into the pub's own lane

A lovely place to find yourself in summer, the delightful front terrace of this bustling old pub has white iron furniture, parasols and lots of flowers in containers and a charming view across to the attractive village green. The attractively neat back garden is pretty too with standard roses, dahlias, bedding plants, urns and hanging baskets. In winter head for the spacious open-plan interior with its good log fire and crooked standing timbers – creating comfortably atmospheric spaces – supporting heavy oak beams so low they have crash-pads on them. In places you can see the wide oak ceiling boards and ancient plastering laths. Furnishings are quite simple, and there are horsebrasses and big brass platters on the walls; the stable bar is no smoking. At lunchtime most people are here to eat, with dishes listed on the blackboards including soup (£2.50), sandwiches (from £3.25), ploughman's (£3.95), vegetable and nut wellington (£5.50), chicken, ham and leek pie (£5.95), pork and leek sausages with onion gravy (£5.75), sugar baked ham (£6.25), steak, ale and mushroom pie (£6.50), grilled salmon with tarragon butter sauce (£6.75) and puddings like pear and almond brownie or treacle tart (£2.95). It's worth arriving early to be sure of a table – especially on Sunday. Well kept Morlands Old Speckled Hen, Theakstons Best, Wadworths 6X and Websters Yorkshire on handpump, and several wines by the glass. Dogs welcome. *(Recommended by Colin Draper, JEB, Jenny and Brian Seller, Piotr Chodzko-Zajko, Anthony Barnes, John and Patricia White, Dave Braisted, Ian Phillips, Mrs Jane Basso, John and Enid Morris, Martin and Karen Wake)*

Scottish Courage ~ Tenant Wendy Luxford ~ Real ale ~ Bar food (12-2, 7-10) ~ Restaurant (not Sun evening, Mon) ~ (01932) 862105 ~ Children in Stable bar ~ Open 11-2.30, 6-11; 12-3, 6(7 winter)-10.30 Sun

COLDHARBOUR TQ1543 Map 3
Plough

Village signposted in the network of small roads around Abinger and Leith Hill, off A24 and A29

Children are now welcome in the newly converted barn at this well placed inn. In the main pub, the two bars have stripped light beams and timbering in the warm-coloured dark ochre walls, with quite unusual little chairs around the tables in the snug red-carpeted games room on the left (with darts and pool), and little decorative plates on the walls and a big open fire in the one on the right – which leads through to the no-smoking restaurant. As well as a fine range of eight or nine real ales on handpump, such as Badger Tanglefoot, Black Sheep, Hogs Back TEA, Ringwood Old Thumper and Fortyniner, Sharps and Shepherd Neame Master Brew, the friendly licensees now brew two of their own beers – Crooked Furrow and Tallywhacker; they also keep country wines and Biddenden farm cider on handpump. Bar food includes filled rolls (from £2.75), ploughman's or filled baked potatoes (£4.50), lamb's liver, smoked bacon and onion gravy, baby spinach leaf salad with smoked bacon, avocado and chicken breast, filled beer pancake with spinach, ricotta and mushrooms, grilled garlic and herb chicken breast with caesar salad or steak, onion and ale pie (£7). Outside there are picnic-sets by the tubs of flowers in front and in the the terraced garden with fish pond and waterlilies. Good walks all around. *(Recommended by Mr and Mrs G Stonehouse, Richard and Catherine Preston, Peter Meister, Gwen and Peter Andrews, NMF, DF, Minda and Stanley Alexander,*

Stephanie Smith, Gareth Price, C Bromage, Dick Brown, Nick and Fiona Andrews-Faulkner, Tom and Rosemary Hall, Tim Barrow, Sue Demont, Ian Jones)

Free house ~ Licensees Richard and Anna Abrehart ~ Real ale ~ Bar food (12-2.30, 7-9.30) ~ (01306) 711793 ~ Children in barn ~ Open 11.30-3, 6-11; 11.30-11 Sat; 12-10.30 Sun; closed 25, 26 Dec, 1 Jan evenings ~ Bedrooms: /£60S

COMPTON SU9546 Map 2
Withies

Withies Lane; pub signposted from B3000

There's quite some emphasis on food at this smartly atmospheric 16th-c dining pub although there's still a genuinely pubby atmosphere in the little bar with its low beams, massive inglenook fireplace with a roaring log fire in winter, some attractive 17th-c carved panels between the windows, and a splendidly art nouveau settle among the old sewing machine tables (it can get smoky in winter). A short and straightforward choice of bar food includes soup (£3), sandwiches (from £3.50), a choice of pâté (£3.75), good ploughman's (from £3.90), cumberland sausages (£4.75), filled baked potatoes (from £4) and seafood platter (£7.50), and is supplemented by a more elaborate not so cheap restaurant menu which is popular with business people during the week. Well kept Bass, Fullers London Pride, King & Barnes Sussex and Marstons Pedigree on handpump. The immaculate garden, overhung with weeping willows, has tables under an arbour of creeper-hung trellises, more on a crazy-paved terrace and yet more under old apple trees. The neat lawn in front of the steeply tiled white house is bordered by masses of flowers. *(Recommended by B Lake, Derek Harvey-Piper, John Evans, James and Wendy Timms, Ian Phillips, C J Machin, Elizabeth and Alan Walker, Michael Sargent)*

Free house ~ Licensees Brian and Hugh Thomas ~ Real ale ~ Bar food (12-2.30, 7-10) ~ Restaurant ~ (01483) 421158 ~ Children welcome ~ Open 11-3, 6-11; 12-4 Sun; closed Sun evening

DUNSFOLD TQ0036 Map 3
Sun

Off B2130 S of Godalming

The rather nice sign at this elegantly built brick-fronted 18th-c pub depicts a farmer walking into the sunset. There are seats outside overlooking a quiet village green, symmetrical arched double porches and neat twin bottle-glass bow windows. The old but basic interior has a friendly old-fashioned atmosphere, scrubbed pine furniture, a log fire in an inglenook, and Friary Meux Best, Hogsback Hair of the Hog and Marstons Pedigree on handpump – along with country wines and a decent wine list. Quickly served in generous helpings, the good popular home-made bar food includes sandwiches (from £2.20), soup (£3.50), ploughman's (from £5.25), steak and kidney pie (£6.95) and daily specials like spinach and bacon salad or salmon terrine (£4.95), venison sausage or chicken in wine and tarragon (£6.95), fresh fish at the weekend (from £8), steak (from £11.95), and puddings like treacle tart or hazelnut and raspberry roulade (£3.50); cottagey restaurant. Darts, table skittles, dominoes, and trivia. *(Recommended by Susan and John Douglas, Wendy Arnold)*

Allied Domecq ~ Lease: Ian Greaves ~ Real ale ~ Bar food (12-2.15, 7-10) ~ (01483) 200242) ~ Well behaved children in restaurant and eating area of bar ~ Open 11-3, 6-11; 12-4, 7-10.30 Sun

EFFINGHAM TQ1253 Map 3
Sir Douglas Haig

The Street; off A246 W of Leatherhead

The well used spacious interior of this large open-plan pub has a 1940s feel with its ochre wood floors, beams, shelves and bar, and creamy floral wallpaper. At the lounge end of its single long room there are armchairs and a sofa by the coal fire, and books and a TV on wood shelves. The other end of the room also has a coal fire, as well as mixed new and old chairs and tables on a small turkey carpet. Bar food includes soup (£2.75), sandwiches (from £3.25), ploughman's (£4.50), and daily specials like cumberland sausage (£4.95), ham, egg and chips (£5.50), plaice or cod (£6.75), roast beef, lasagne or chilli (£6.95), half a shoulder of lamb (£7.50) and fillet steak (£11.95). They serve a good choice of coffees including cappuccino. Well kept Bass, Gales Best and HSB and a changing guest on handpump, with jugs of pimms in summer. There's a back lawn and an attractive terraced area with seats and tables; fruit machine, piped music and a TV in the corner of the lounge. *(Recommended by Brian and Anna Marsden, John Pettit, DWAJ, D P and J A Sweeney, Mrs G Sharman, Joy and Peter Heatherley)*

Free house ~ Licensee Adam Smart ~ Real ale ~ Bar food (12-2.30, 6.30-9.30(10 Fri, Sat), 12-4 Sun; not Sun evening) ~ Restaurant ~ (01372) 456886 ~ Children in eating area of bar and restaurant ~ 60s and 70s music most Sun evenings ~ Open 11-11; 12-10.30 Sun; closed 25 Dec evening ~ Bedrooms: £60B/£70B

ELSTEAD SU9143 Map 2
Woolpack
The Green; B3001 Milford—Farnham

Surrey Dining Pub of the Year
Doing well in all respects, this bustling friendly pub is popular for its imaginative generously served bar food, well kept Greene King Abbot and Fullers London Pride tapped from the cask, and its cheery atmosphere. The nicely informal long airy main bar has fireplaces at each end, window seats and spindleback chairs around plain wooden tables, and a fair amount of wool industry memorabilia, such as the weaving shuttles and cones of wool that hang above the high-backed settles. Leading off here is a big room decorated with lots of country prints, a weaving loom, scales, and brass measuring jugs; the fireplace with its wooden pillars lace frill is unusual. A changing choice of bar food might include mushrooms in stilton and port sauce or turkey strips in almond, mustard breadcrumbs with orange and cranberry sauce (£4.95), monkfish in Pernod and fennel sauce (£10.25), salmon in lemon, lime and coriander butter (£10.95) and calf's liver in orange, sage and red Martini (£11.95); Sunday lunch is popular; decent wine list. Dominoes and cribbage. A family room leads to the garden with picnic-sets and a children's play area. *(Recommended by R B Crail, G C Hackemer, I S Wilson, Colin Draper, Miss J Broadhead, Roger and Valerie Hill, Derek and Margaret Underwood, Elizabeth and Alan Walker, Nigel Wikeley, Miss J F Reay, James and Wendy Timms, Mr and Mrs N Heleine)*

Ind Coope (Allied Domecq) ~ Lease: J A Morris and S A Askew ~ Real ale ~ Bar food (12-2, 7-9.45) ~ Restaurant ~ (01252) 703106 ~ Children away from bar area ~ Open 11-2.30, 6-11; 12-3, 7-10.30 Sun; closed 25 Dec evening, 26 Dec

FRIDAY STREET TQ1245 Map 3
Stephan Langton
Village signed off B2126, or from A25 Westcott—Guildford

New licensees at this busy country local have painted the comfortable bar and parlour-like lounge poppy red. There are some handsome brass vases in front of the fireplace, and a mix of pub furnishings. Bar food is listed on boards above the bar and might include soup (£2.95), filled baguettes (from £3.95), ploughman's (from £4.45), curry (£4.50), vegetable quiche (£4.75), sausage and egg (£4.95), steak (£9.50), and children's meals (from £2.85); Sunday lunch (£6.50); the restaurant has a no-smoking area. Well kept Bass, Fullers London Pride, Harveys Sussex and Youngs Special on handpump, and half a dozen wines by the glass; darts, shove-ha'penny, cribbage and piped music. There are plenty of tables in a front courtyard, with more on a back tree-surrounded steam-side terrace. It's in a beautifully peaceful spot, surrounded by good walks – Leith Hill is particularly rewarding, and the village is so unspoilt they prefer you to leave your car in a free car park just outside, but if you don't fancy the lovely stroll there are a few spaces in front of the pub itself. *(Recommended by L Granville, Mr and Mrs Phillip Board, Mayur Shah, Dick Brown)*

Bass ~ Tenants Chris and Sharon Thorn ~ Real ale ~ Bar food (12-3.30, 6-9.30) ~
Restaurant ~ (01306) 730775 ~ Children in snug and restaurant ~ Open 11-11; 12-10
Sun; 11-3.30, 6-11; 12-3.30, 7-10 Sun winter

GOMSHALL TQ0847 Map 3
Compasses
Station Road (A25)

The main focus here is the neat no-smoking dining area, which takes up most of the
space, with primrose yellow tablecloths toning with the soft yellow patterned
wallpaper and new burgundy carpet. Good value generous well presented food
includes sandwiches (from £2.45), filled french sticks (from £3.25), ploughman's
(from £3.95), battered cod and mushy peas (£6), fried lamb's liver with onions and
bacon (£6.25), spinach and ricotta tortellini with tomato and aubergine sauce
(£6.50), steak and kidney pie or chicken and mushroom pie (£7.25), grilled
swordfish steak with tomato and chilli chutney (£8.75), and sirloin steak (£9.95),
and a very good children's menu. The carpeted bar is relatively plain, with some
farm tools on the high ceiling, simple pub furniture and some architectural drawings
of historic sailing ships. Well kept Courage Best, Fullers London Pride, Whitbread
Castle Eden and a guest like Youngs Special on handpump from a modern servery,
good value house wines; pleasant efficient service; dominoes, cribbage. Though it's
beside a main road, this has a pretty garden, with picnic-sets under cocktail parasols
on a neat lawn sloping down to the mill stream that runs along beside the road,
below three big weeping willows. Take care to park in the pub's spaces – other
tempting places nearby risk clamping. (Recommended by Don Mather, Mayur Shah, Tony
Scott, Gwen and Peter Andrews, Anna and Martyn Carey)

Enterprise ~ Lease Nicky Tullett ~ Real ale ~ Bar food (12-9) ~ Restaurant ~ (01483)
202506 ~ Children welcome ~ Blues Fri ~ Open 11-11; 12-10.30 Sun ~ Bedrooms:
/£55B

HASCOMBE TQ0039 Map 3
White Horse
B2130 S of Godalming

This picturesque old rose-draped inn is tucked away in a pretty village among lovely
rolling wooded country lanes on the Greensand Way and is popular with walkers.
Its simple but characterful rooms have a bustling, friendly atmosphere. The cosy
inner beamed area has a woodburning stove and quiet small-windowed alcoves that
look out onto the garden; there's also a conservatory with light bentwood chairs and
peach coloured décor. Generous helpings of good, quickly served bar food include
sandwiches (from £3.25), good proper ploughman's (from £4.75), steak burgers (£6)
and fish pie (£7.95), half roast guinea fowl (£8.95), grilled steak (£10.50); best to get
there early for a table at lunchtime, especially at weekends; quick cheerful service.
Well kept Badger Best, Marstons Pedigree and Youngs on handpump; quite a few
wines. Darts, shove-ha'penny, dominoes, and fruit machine. There are quite a few
tables on the spacious sloping back lawn, with more on a little terrace by the front
porch. The village is pretty, and the National Trust's Winkworth Arboretum, with
its walks among beautiful trees and shrubs, is nearby. (Recommended by Elizabeth and
Alan Walker, Susan and John Douglas, LM, John Evans, Catherine and Richard Preston, Michael
Sargent, Ian, Liz and Wendy Phillips, Mick Hitchman, Gordon Stevenson)

Allied Domecq ~ Lease: Susan Barnett ~ Real ale ~ Bar food (12-2.20, 7-10) ~
Restaurant ~ (01483) 208258 ~ Children in eating area of bar ~ Open 11-3, 5.30-11,
11-11 summer Fri; 11-11 Sat; 12-10.30 Sun; closed 25 Dec

LEIGH TQ2246 Map 3
Plough
3 miles S of A25 Dorking—Reigate, signposted from Betchworth (which itself is signposted
off the main road); also signposted from South Park area of Reigate; on village green

There's still a good pubby atmosphere in the bar at this pretty tiled and weatherboarded cottage which is handy for Gatwick airport, and popular at lunchtime for its nicely presented bar food: a huge range of sandwiches (from £2.50), soup (£2.75), ploughman's (£4.75), lasagne or vegetable lasagne (£5.95), grilled tuna steak (£8.50), 8oz sirloin (£10.50), venison steak with port and mushroom sauce (£12.75), daily specials like turkey curry (£5.75) and smoked haddock in cheese and egg sauce (£6.55), and puddings like hot chocolate fudge cake (from £3.25). Well kept King & Barnes Bitter, Broadwood, Festive and seasonal ales on handpump, most kept under light blanket pressure, and a decent wine list (all bottles are available by the glass as well). On the right is a very low beamed cosy white walled and timbered dining lounge and on the left, a simple, more local pubby bar with a good bow-window seat and an extensive choice of games that takes in darts, shove-ha'penny, dominoes, table skittles, cribbage, trivia, a fruit machine and video game, Jenga, backgammon, chess and Scrabble; piped music. It's very attractively placed overlooking the village green, and has picnic-sets under cocktail parasols in a pretty side garden, fairy lights in the evening, and pretty hanging baskets. Parking nearby is limited. *(Recommended by D and J Tapper, DWAJ, G W Stevenson, Terry Buckland, Colin and Janet Roe, Jules Akel, David and Carole Chapman, Chris Rowley)*

King & Barnes ~ Tenant Sarah Bloomfield ~ Real ale ~ Bar food (12-2(2.30 Sat), 7-10, 12-10.30 Sun) ~ Restaurant ~ (01306) 611348 ~ Well behaved children welcome ~ Open 11-11; 12-10.30 Sun

MICKLEHAM TQ1753 Map 3
King William IV 🍴 ◗

Byttom Hill; short but narrow steep track up hill just off A24 Leatherhead—Dorking by partly green-painted restaurant – public car park down here is best place to park; OS Sheet 187 map reference 173538

Doing particularly well at the moment, this friendly bustling pub is probably readers' favourite in this county. It's unusually cut into a steep hillside, with panoramic views down from the snug plank-panelled front bar. The more spacious back bar is quite brightly lit, with kitchen-type chairs around its cast-iron-framed tables, log fires, fresh flowers on all the tables, and a serviceable grandfather clock. At the back, the lovely terraced garden is neatly filled with sweet peas, climbing roses and honeysuckle and plenty of tables (some in an open-sided wooden shelter); a path leads straight up through woods where it's nice to walk after lunch – quite a few walkers do come here. Very tasty bar food might include ploughman's (from £4.50), baked spinach and oyster mushroom pancake, seafood pie or steak and kidney pie (£7.50), tandoori chicken salad with minted yoghurt (£8.95), poached Scottish salmon with prawn and lobster sauce (£9.25), peppered rump steak with brandy cream sauce (£10.95), and puddings like fruit crumble, hot chocolate fudge cake or treacle tart (£3.25); the choice is more limited on Sundays and bank holidays. Well kept Adnams, Badger Best, Hogs Back TEA, Hop Garden Gold and a guest on handpump; quick and friendly service. Dominoes, and light piped music. *(Recommended by Barry and Marie Males, C Smith, Tina and David Woods-Taylor, Tom and Rosemary Hall, Joy and Peter Heatherley, B and M Parkin, LM, Martin and Karen Wake, Mr and Mrs B Hobden, Kevin Flack, D P and J A Sweeney, Catherine and Richard Preston, Anthony Hughes, J and D Ginger, Tony Scott)*

Free house ~ Licensees Chris and Jenny Grist ~ Real ale ~ Bar food (12-2, 7-9.30) ~ (01372) 372590 ~ Open 11-3, 6-11; 12-3, 7-10.30 Sun; closed 25, 31 Dec

NEWDIGATE TQ2042 Map 3
Surrey Oaks

Parkgate Road; A24 S of Dorking, then left on to unmarked road signposted for Beare Green – go through that village and take first left fork

The menagerie at this cheerful country pub includes a goat, an aviary of budgerigars, and a flock of pure white doves. The very pleasant and quite elaborate garden has a large terrace and a rockery with pools, fountains and a waterfall. The pub itself is quite small: the old part has a little snug beamed room by a coal-effect gas fire, with a woodburning fire in a standing area with unusually large flagstones, while rustic tables are dotted around the light and airy main lounge. A separate games room has a pool table, dominoes, cribbage, pinball, a fruit machine, video game, and juke box. Decent reasonably priced bar food includes sandwiches (from £2.50), home-made soup (£2.95), ploughman's (£4.25), ham, egg and chips (£5.25), fish and chips, steak and kidney pudding or various sausages with bubble and squeak (£5.95), scampi (£6.95) and daily specials such as chicken supreme with ginger and coriander or red mullet in Pernod and cream (£6.95), and half shoulder of lamb with mint gravy (£8.95); puddings such as home-made apple pie or bread and butter pudding (£2.95); children's meals (from £3.25). Well kept Adnams, Fullers London Pride and a couple of guests such as Timothy Taylor Landlord and Tolly Cobbold Sunshine on handpump; friendly service. *(Recommended by Jenny and Brian Seller, C J Bromage)*

Allied Domecq ~ Lease: Ken Proctor ~ Real ale ~ Bar food (not Sun and Mon evenings) ~ (01306) 631200 ~ Children welcome ~ Open 11.30-2.30(3 Sat), 5.30(6 Sat)-11; 12-3, 7-10.30 Sun

PIRBRIGHT SU9454 Map 2
Royal Oak 🍺
Aldershot Rd; A324S of village

There's a good country pub atmosphere at this lovely old cottage which runs its own cask ale club, has up to nine changing real ales on handpump, serves over 100 beers a year and holds regular festivals. There might be well kept Flowers IPA and Original, Hogs Back TEA or Hop Garden Gold and half a dozen guests from brewers like Black Sheep, Elgoods, Gales, Eccleshall and Youngs on handpump; they also have around 15 wines by the glass and bottle. A bar extension overlooks the pretty flower filled back garden and is joined onto the existing dining area. A rambling series of snug side alcoves has heavy beams and timbers, ancient stripped brickwork, and gleaming brasses set around the three real fires, and furnishings include wheelback chairs, tapestried wall seats, and little dark church-like pews around the trim tables; one area is no smoking. No noisy games machines or piped music. Good value tasty bar food includes soup (£2.45), stilton mushrooms (£3.45), sausage and mash (£4.95), ploughman's (from £5.45), fish and chips (£5.55), steak and ale pie or scampi (£5.95), lamb casserole pudding (£6.95), chicken in red wine, bacon and shallot sauce (£7.45), moules frites salmon in white wine and dill sauce (£7.95), steak (£9.95) and bass fillet with red pepper sauce on roasted vegetables (£10.95); Sunday roast (£6.95). Children may be allowed to sit at limited tables in the dining area to eat with their parents. The front gardens are very colourful and look particularly attractive on fine evenings when the fairy lights are switched on. The big back garden leads down to a stream, and is less affected by noise from passing traffic; there may be barbecues and spit-roasts out here in summer. Good walks lead off in all directions, and the licensees are usually happy to let walkers leave their cars in the car park – if they ask first. *(Recommended by S F Parrinder, Andy and Jill Kassube, KC, Mr and Mrs G Stonehouse, Colin Draper)*

Whitbreads ~ Manager John Lay ~ Real ale ~ Bar food (12-2, 6.30-9.30 Mon-Fri, 12-9 Sat, Sun) ~ (01483) 232466 ~ Children in no-smoking area if eating ~ Open 11-11; 12-10.30 Sun

REIGATE HEATH TQ2349 Map 3
Skimmington Castle
3 miles from M25 junction 8: through Reigate take A25 Dorking (West), then on edge of Reigate turn left past Black Horse into Flanchford Road; after ¼ mile turn left into Bonny's Road (unmade, very bumpy track); after crossing golf course fork right up hill

There's a very friendly welcome at this quaint old country local – although it does get very busy so you do need to get there early for a table. The bright main front bar leads off a small central serving counter with dark simple panelling. There's a miscellany of chairs and tables, shiny brown vertical panelling, a brown plank ceiling, and well kept Flowers IPA, Greene King, Youngs Special and Wadworths 6X on handpump, as well as around nine wines by the glass and cask conditioned cider. The cosy back rooms are partly panelled too, with old-fashioned settles and windsor chairs; one has a big brick fireplace with its bread-oven still beside it – the chimney is said to have been used as a highwayman's look-out. A small room down steps at the back has shove-ha'penny, cribbage, dominoes, board games and trivia; piped music. Popular bar food includes sandwiches (£3.10), ploughman's (£3.95), stir fry (£5.95), steak and kidney pie (£6.50), fish pie (£6.75), Thai chicken curry (£7.50), rack of lamb (£7.95), duck breast (£8.95) and puddings like sticky toffee or bread and butter pudding (£2.95). There are nice views from the crazy-paved front terrace and tables on the grass by lilac bushes, with more tables at the back overlooking the meadows and the hillocks. There's a hitching rail outside for horses, and the pub is handy for ramblers on the North Downs. *(Recommended by David and Carole Chapman, John Bell, Tony Scott, Dave Cupwell, LM, Derek Harvey-Piper, Mr and Mrs Staples, Mike Gorton)*

Pubmaster ~ Tenants Anthony Pugh and John Davidson ~ Real ale ~ Bar food (12-2.15, 7-9.30; 12-2.30, 7-9 Sun) ~ (01737) 243100 ~ Children in no-smoking area ~ Folk second Sun of month ~ Open 11-3, 5.30(6 Sat)-11; 12-10.30 Sun

SOUTH GODSTONE TQ3648 Map 3
Fox & Hounds

Tilburstow Hill Rd; just outside village, turn off A22 into Harts Lane, pub is at the end; handy for M25 junction 6

Parts of this pretty old-fashioned place were built in 1368 though most of what you see today is 17th-c, with even some of the high-back settles in the cosy low-beamed bar thought to date back at least that far. It's bigger than its dark furniture, low beams and raised levels make it seem, with lots of little nooks and crannies to sit in. The fine antique high-backed settles are in the cosy low-beamed bar which also has some more modern ones, cushioned wall-benches, a window seat and a few low tables, as well as racing prints on the walls, prettily arranged dried hops, and a big kettle on the woodburning stove; there are a couple more seats and tables around the tiny bar counter, up a step and beyond some standing timbers. Lunchtime bar food, which isn't cheap, might include sandwiches or soup (from £4), soft roes on toast (£5), ploughman's (£5.50), smoked haddock mornay (£6.50), prawn or smoked salmon salad or scampi (£7) and steak, ale and mushroom pie (£7.50). You can reserve tables in the restaurant which is the only part of the pub where they serve the more elaborate evening food (but check food times below). Well kept Greene King IPA and Abbot on handpump, and a very extensive wine list; piped classical music. It's in a pleasant spot on Tilburstow Ridge with views from a good few picnic-sets out in the garden. *(Recommended by James House, Dick Brown, Maggie and Derek Washington, J Sheldon, Mrs Hilarie Taylor, Paul and Pam Penrose, Gill and Maurice McMahon, Mrs Sara Varey)*

Greene King ~ Tenant David McKie ~ Real ale ~ Bar food (not Sun-Tues evening) ~ Restaurant ~ (01342) 893474 ~ Children in eating area of bar and restaurant lunchtime only ~ Open 11-3, 6-11; 12-3, 7-10.30 Sun

WALLISWOOD TQ1238 Map 3
Scarlett Arms

Village signposted from Ewhurst—Rowhook back road; or follow Oakwoodhill signpost from A29 S of Ockley, then follow Walliswood signpost into Walliswood Green Road

The charmingly unspoilt straightforward small-roomed layout is the main delight at this little red-tiled country cottage which is perhaps best enjoyed if you pop in for a drink. Its three neatly kept communicating rooms have low black oak beams, deeply polished flagstones, simple but perfectly comfortable benches, high bar stools with backrests, trestle tables, country prints, and two roaring winter log fires, one in a huge inglenook. Well kept King & Barnes beers on handpump. Darts, cribbage, shove-ha'penny, table skittles, dominoes and a fruit machine in the small room at the end. Straightforward bar food includes sandwiches (from £2.75), ploughman's (£4.25), plaice (£5.25), leek, bacon and cheese bake, (£5.95), curry or steak and kidney pie (£6.25), half shoulder of lamb (£9.95) and 12oz rib-eye steak (£10.95); puddings (£2.95). There are old-fashioned seats and tables with umbrellas in the pretty well tended garden, and lots of walks nearby. No children. *(Recommended by Colin Draper, DWAJ, Maggie and Derek Washington)*

King & Barnes ~ Tenant Jess Mannino ~ Real ale ~ Bar food ~ (01306) 627243 ~ Open 11-2.30, 5.30-11; 12-3, 7-10.30 Sun; closed 25 Dec evening

WARLINGHAM TQ3658 Map 3
White Lion £
B269

Readers have been delighted with the genuinely pubby atmosphere – so expect locals drinking at the bar – at this unspoilt old place. It's based on two 15th-c cottages with a fine Tudor fireplace enclosed by high-backed settles at its heart, and a warren of friendly dark-panelled rooms with nooks and crannies, wood-block floors, very low beams, and deeply aged plasterwork. A side room decorated with amusing early 19th-c cartoons has darts, cribbage, trivia and fruit machine. Incredibly good value, simple but tasty bar food is served in the bigger brighter no-smoking room at the end of the building, from a range including soup (£1.95), filled baked potatoes (from £2.45), filled french sticks (£3.45), tagliatelle carbonara (£3.95), lasagne (£4.35), fish and chips (£4.40), steak and ale pie (£4.85) and mixed grill (£4.95), chips and peas (£1.35) are extra, and puddings (from £1.95); quick service. Well kept Bass, Fullers London Pride, Hancocks HB, and guests like Gales Anniversary or Morlands Old Speckled Hen on handpump. Piped music in the eating area. The well kept back lawn, with its rockery, is surrounded by a herbaceous border; there may be outside service here in summer. *(Recommended by Christopher Wright, Roger and Jenny Huggins, Anna and Martyn Carey, Michael and Hazel Duncombe, James House, D and J Tapper, Kevin Flack)*

Bass ~ Manager Charlie Evans ~ Real ale ~ Bar food (12-2, 6-9) ~ (01883) 629011 ~ Children in eating area of bar until 8 ~ Open 11-11; 12-10.30 Sun

WOTTON TQ1247 Map 3
Wotton Hatch
A25 Dorking—Guildford; coming from Dorking, start slowing as soon as you see the Wotton village sign – the pub's round the first bend

Although this is part of a family dining pub chain it is nevertheless a carefully run place with a very friendly smiling welcome in a nice rambling old 17-c building. The low-ceilinged rooms have cushioned wheelback chairs and rugs on timber, slate or carpeted floors, and to one side a handsome cocktail bar has medieval-style settles ranked around its panelled walls under a high frieze of plates; gentle piped classical or older style music. Bar food changes four times a year but might include asparagus and mushroom soup (£1.95) sandwiches (from £3.60), spiced chicken fillets and red chilli relish (£3.95), ploughman's (£4.50) and beef pie or fish and chips (£5.95). The evening menu is more extensive with things like chicken breast stuffed with cheese and bacon and cheese sauce or salmon pasta salad (£6.95), rump steak (£7.95) and puddings like caramel apple pie with vanilla biscuit base and toffee topping (£2.50). Well kept Bass and Fullers London Pride and a guest like Hancocks HB on handpump, and about ten wines by the glass; more than half the pub is no smoking. There are impressive views from the neatly kept garden; no dogs. *(Recommended by Gwen and Peter Andrews, Dick Brown, Ian, Wendy and Liz Phillips, Mayur Shah, Neale and Sandra Dewar)*

Bass ~ Manager Phil Conisbee ~ Real ale ~ Bar food (Mon-Wed 12-3, 6-10; Thurs-Sun 12-10(9.30 Sun)) ~ (01306) 732931 ~ Children in eating area of bar ~ Open 11-11; 12-10.30 Sun

Post Office address codings confusingly give the impression that some pubs are in Surrey when they're really in Hampshire or London (which is where we list them). And there's further confusion from the way the Post Office still talks about Middlesex – which disappeared in 1965 local government reorganisation.

Lucky Dip

Besides the fully inspected pubs, you might like to try these Lucky Dips recommended to us and described by readers (if you do, please send us reports):

Albury [TQ0547]
☆ *Drummond Arms* [off A248 SE of Guildford]: Comfortable and civilised panelled alcovey bar, conservatory (children allowed here) overlooking pretty streamside back garden with fountain and covered terrace; popular with older people lunchtime for food from sandwiches to steaks, well kept Courage Best and Directors, King & Barnes Broadwood, Festive and Sussex, and Youngs; piped music; bedrooms, attractive village, pleasant walks nearby *(P J Keen, Mr and Mrs Sheppard, Wendy Arnold, James Nunns, LYM, Evelyn and Derek Walter, Ian S Morley, John Pettit, Martin and Karen Wake)*
Albury Heath [TQ0646]
☆ *William IV* [Little London, off A25 Guildford—Dorking – OS Sheet 187 map ref 065468]: Bustling take-us-as-you-find-us country pub in good walking area, old-fashioned character low-beamed flagstoned bar with big log fire, simple café-style dining area, close-packed tables in upstairs restaurant; home-made food from sandwiches up (good hot salt beef ones), monthly seafood nights and spitroasts, well kept ales such as Boddingtons, Fullers London Pride, Greene King Abbot, Wadworths 6X and local Hogs Back, quick service; shove-ha'penny and cards, children welcome, attractive front garden with long wall seat *(Jenny and Brian Seller, Mrs Hilarie Taylor, Ian S Morley, LYM, James Nunns)*
Ash Vale [SU8952]
Swan [Hutton Rd, off Ash Vale Rd]: Large homely dining pub with good food – very popular w/e; well kept Scottish Courage beers, friendly efficient staff, piped classical music; garden, well kept terraces and window boxes, open all day; on the workaday Basingstoke Canal *(Sharon Holmes, Tom Cherrett)*
Betchworth [TQ2049]
Red Lion [Old Reigate Rd]: Friendly new licensees doing wide choice of good generous food inc unusual dishes, fish specials and good Sun lunches; friendly old pub with smallish fairy-lit bar, good service and well kept ales; plenty of tables in rose-trellised garden with play area, squash court *(DWAJ, Simon Pickup)*
Bletchingley [TQ3250]
☆ *Prince Albert* [Outwood Lane]: Good sensibly priced food esp fish in attractive cosy beamed pub, several nooks and corners, well kept beer, plenty of character, smallish restaurant, attentive and welcoming Irish licensees; tables on terrace and in small pretty garden *(Mr and Mrs A Burge, James Nunns, W A F Ruxton)*
☆ *William IV* [3 miles from M25 junction 6; Little Common Lane, off A25 on Redhill side of village]: Quaint quiet old country pub down pretty lane, tile-hung and weatherboarded, with comfortable little back dining room, good choice of good food and of well kept ales inc Fullers London Pride, Harveys Best, Pilgrims Progress and Youngs Special, good wines, good

atmosphere, lots of bric-a-brac, helpful friendly service; seats in nice two-level garden with summer barbecues *(LYM, Jane and Richard Doe, Bruce Bird, James and Lynne House)*
Brockham [TQ1949]
☆ *Royal Oak* [Brockham Green]: Attractively refurbished with comfortable lounge/dining area, bare boards and log fire on other side, good range of well kept beers such as Adnams, Gales HSB, Harveys, Morlands Old Speckled Hen and Wadworths 6X (Aug beer festival), reasonably priced interesting food inc good value sandwiches, local pictures for sale; good garden with play area, nice spot on green nr River Mole, below N Downs; children and dogs welcome, open all day *(Tony Scott, Jenny and Brian Seller, David and Carole Chapman, Catherine and Richard Preston)*
Brook [SU9338]
☆ *Dog & Pheasant* [A286 N of Haslemere]: Big busy low-beamed roadside pub in attractive spot opp cricket green nr Witley Common, quick friendly service by helpful staff, good range of well kept ales, good choice of reasonably priced home-made food inc daily fresh Shoreham fish, big fire, shove-ha'penny, small restaurant with upstairs overflow, children's eating area; small pretty garden *(David and Brenda Tew, Mike and Sue Todd, Derek and Margaret Underwood, Mr and Mrs B W Twiddy)*
Capel [TQ1740]
Crown [signed off A24 at Beare Green roundabout]: Pleasantly rustic old beamed village pub with cosy and comfortable lounge bar and restaurant area, partly no smoking, well kept Friary Meux Best and Marstons Pedigree, good varied menu, friendly staff; pool in two-level public bar, dogs welcome; by interesting church *(Eddie Edwards)*
Charleshill [SU8944]
☆ *Donkey* [signed off B3001 Milford—Farnham nr Tilford]: Old-fashioned beamed cottage pub in same family for three generations, very friendly service, simple home-made food (not Sun evening) from sandwiches up, well kept Morlands IPA and Old Speckled Hen with a guest such as Charles Wells Bombardier, country wines, traditional games, maybe quiet piped music; children allowed in no smoking conservatory, attractive garden with play area, good walks *(J Sheldon, LYM, A E Brace)*
Charlwood [TQ2441]
Greyhound: Comfortable and popular Greene King pub, good atmosphere, nets hanging from ceiling, lots of bric-a-brac and fishing lanterns, good mix of customers; good value Hungry Horse menu served all day; piped music at times, big screen sports TV Sat *(David and Carole Chapman, Tony Scott)*
Chertsey [TQ0466]
Crown [London St (B375)]: Friendly and relaxed Youngs pub with button-back banquettes in traditionally renovated high-

ceilinged bar, very tall chiming longcase clock, well kept ales, nicely presented food from doorstep sandwiches up, courteous attentive staff; neatly placed darts, discreet fruit machines; garden bar with conservatory, tables in courtyard and garden with pond; children welcome; smart 30-bedroom annexe *(Margaret and Peter Brierley)*

Golden Grove [Ruxbury Rd, St Anns Hill (nr Lyne)]: Busy local with low beams, bare boards and stripped wood, cheap straightforward home-made food from sandwiches up (not Sat-Mon evenings) in pine-tabled eating area, well kept ales inc Ind Coope Burton, Fullers London Pride and Theakstons, cheerful service, coal-effect gas fire; piped music, fruit and games machines; big garden with friendly dogs and goat, play area, wooded pond *(Ian Phillips)*

Chiddingfold [SU9635]

☆ *Crown* [The Green (A283)]: Picturesque old inn in attractive surroundings, worth a visit for its fine carving, Elizabethan plaster ceilings, massive beams, lovely inglenook log fire and tapestried panelled restaurant; imaginative food in simpler side bar, friendly attentive service, three Badger beers, tables out on verandah; children allowed, has been open all day; good bedrooms *(Douglas Caiger, Val and Alan Green, M Kershaw, LYM, Simon Penny, A Hepburn, S Jenner, Elizabeth and Alan Walker)*

Rams Nest [Petworth Rd (A283 S)]: 18th-c inn, recently well restored in traditional style, hops on beams, big log fires, relaxing atmosphere, cosy reading area with easy chairs, books and magazines; lots of antique furnishings, well rounded choice of well presented reasonably priced food, good value wines, friendly service, pool, seemly piped music; children allowed in restaurant, garden with covered terrace, wendy house and play area; good newish bedrooms in separate block *(anon)*

Chilworth [TQ0346]

☆ *Villagers* [Blackheath; off A248 across the level crossing, SE of Guildford]: Attractive woodland pub, good walks all around (shown on table-mats); small flagstoned room with big fireplace suiting walkers and dogs, main carpeted bar with beams, timbers and pews, neat little adjoining dining room, well kept Courage Best, Fullers London Pride, Hogs Back TEA, Morlands Old Speckled Hen, decent wines, pleasant young staff, food from big sandwiches up, unobtrusive piped music; sheltered back terrace, steps up to good-sized lawn, short path through trees to cricket green; newly decorated good value simple bedrooms; children in eating areas, open all day w/e *(Mark Percy, Lesley Mayoh, Marianne and Peter Stevens, Gordon Stevenson, Jamie Allan, S F Parrinder, Mr and Mrs Phillip Board, Mayur Shah, LYM)*

Chipstead [TQ2757]

☆ *Ramblers Rest* [Outwood Lane (B2032)]: Picturesque collection of partly 14th-c buildings, extensive range of different drinking areas with different atmospheres, panelling, flagstones and low beams, wide range of well kept ales inc Fullers London Pride, Marstons Pedigree and Wadworths 6X, good generous

well presented freshly made food worth waiting for, family restaurant; big pleasant garden behind, decent walks nearby; piped music; open all day inc Sun, no dogs *(David and Carole Chapman, Tony Scott, G W Stevenson, BB)*

☆ *Well House* [Chipstead Lane, off A23 just W of Coulsdon; nearer Mugswell or Kingswood]: Well run partly 14th-c pub, cottagey and comfortable, with lots of atmosphere, good straightforward lunchtime food (not Sun) from sandwiches up, friendly staff, log fires in all three rooms, well kept Fullers ales; dogs allowed; attractive garden with well reputed to be mentioned in Doomsday Book, loudspeaker food announcements, delightful setting *(W Ruxton, G W Stevenson, LYM)*

Cobham [TQ1059]

☆ *Plough* [Plough Lane, towards Downside]: Cheerful black-shuttered local with comfortably modernised low-beamed lounge bar, well kept Scottish Courage ales, helpful staff, pine-panelled snug with darts, lunchtime food from sandwiches up inc plenty of cold snacks and a few hot dishes (with French leanings); seats outside *(LYM, Shirley Mackenzie, Gordon Prince)*

Snail [A245 Pains Hill/Byfleet Rd, by Sainsburys]: Cottagey, attractive and comfortable dining pub, with panelling, soft music, well kept ales, efficient friendly staff, good food in bar and restaurant; handy for Painshill Park *(James Nunns)*

Compton [SU9546]

☆ *Harrow* [The Street; B3000 towards Godalming off A3]: Food expensive, but varied, home-made and good, from sandwiches and filled baked potatoes up; good welcoming atmosphere, well kept Greene King IPA and Abbot and Harveys Best; children welcome, open all day, cl Sun evening; bedrooms *(Francis Johnston, Mrs Hilarie Taylor, Chris and Ann Garnett, LYM, Derek and Margaret Underwood)*

Dorking [TQ1649]

Bush [Horsham Rd]: Simple Victorian local, quiet and cosy, with well kept ales such as Boddingtons, Brakspears, Fullers and Thwaites, good value lunches, friendly unobtrusive service, polished woodwork and red wallpaper; partly covered terrace, small garden *(Val and Alan Green)*

Olde House At Home [West St]: Well furnished Youngs pub with pleasant atmosphere, tables on concrete back terrace, food; parking limited *(Tony Scott)*

Surrey Yeoman [High St]: Pleasant refurbished local, well kept ales such as Bass, Brakspears, King & Barnes *(James Nunns)*

Eashing [SU9443]

Stag [Eashing Lane]: Attractive 17th-c beamed riverside pub, several cosy traditional interconnecting rooms, good food, attentive service, log fire; waterside tables *(P N Randell)*

East Clandon [TQ0651]

☆ *Queens Head* [just off A246 Guildford—Leatherhead]: Small rambling connecting rooms, big inglenook log fire, fine old elm bar counter, bookcases, pictures, copperware; wide choice of sensibly priced food inc lots of fish, friendly service, well kept ales inc Morlands Old Speckled Hen, no lunchtime piped music; children welcome, tables in quiet garden, handy for two NT properties *(LYM, John Evans, Shirley Mackenzie, KC, J Sheldon, Mrs T Bizat, Mrs Hilarie Taylor)*

Effingham [TQ1253]

☆ *Plough* [Orestan Lane]: Characteristic commuter-belt Youngs local with friendly efficient staff, consistently well kept ales, honest home cooking (fresh veg and potatoes may be extra) inc enjoyable Sun lunch, two coal-effect gas fires, beamery, panelling, old plates and brassware in long lounge, no-smoking extension; popular with older people – no dogs, children or sleeveless T-shirts inside, no music or machines, attractive garden with play area; convenient for Polesdon Lacey (NT) *(Ray Roberts, John Pettit, Annie and Will Dennis, J Sheldon, Tom and Rosemary Hall)*

Egham [TQ0171]

☆ *Beehive* [Middle Hill]: Small friendly pub doing well under present landlord, several well kept Gales ales and others such as Brakspears and Fullers London Pride, beer festivals, good quick reasonably priced home-made food, polite service, nice garden *(Ian Phillips)*

Crown [High St]: Busy simply furnished local with warm-hearted landlord, good reasonably priced promptly served basic food, half a dozen changing ales such as Adnams, Fullers and Gales, coal fires, TV, juke box or piped music; pool in public bar; mellow back walled garden with lively aviary and pretty pond *(Ian Phillips, JJW, CMW)*

Englefield Green [SU9970]

Barley Mow [Northcroft Rd]: Stereotyped refurbished pub overlooking cricket green, reasonably priced food inc children's and vegetarian, back dining area with no-smoking section, well kept Scottish Courage ales with a guest such as Marstons Pedigree, darts, quiet piped machine; tables on front terrace, pleasant back garden with play area *(A Hepburn, S Jenner, CMW, JJW)*

☆ *Fox & Hounds* [Bishopsgate Road; off A328 N of Egham]: Popular pub recently taken over by Old Monk, good setting backing on to riding stables on edge of Windsor Great Park, short walk from Savile Garden, tables on pleasant front lawn and back terrace; good log fire, Brakspears, Courage Directors and Fullers London Pride, bar food inc baguettes (only these w/e), pricier meals in candlelit dining room; children no longer welcome, open all day w/e and July-Sept *(Mayur Shah, Susan and John Douglas, Ian Phillips, NMF, DF, Peter Saville, LYM)*

Sun [Wick Lane, Bishopgate]: Unassuming welcoming local, well kept Courage Best, Greene King Abbot and Wychwood, decent wines, good value home-cooked food inc lots of sandwiches and good Sun lunch, reasonable prices, daily papers, roaring log fire in back conservatory, biscuit and water for dogs; pleasant garden with aviary, handy for Savile Garden and Windsor Park *(Ian Phillips, Simon Collett-Jones, John Robertson)*

Epsom [TQ2160]

Tattenham Corner [opp racecourse]: Big Beefeater worth knowing for food all day inc summer barbecues, garden with play fort; does get busy, esp on race days *(J Sheldon)*

Esher [TQ1464]

Bear [High St]: Two landmark life-size bears behind roof parapet of smartly renovated Youngs pub with their full range kept well, bar food from cauliflower cheese to fillet steak *(Ian Phillips, James Nunns)*

☆ *Prince of Wales* [West End Lane; off A244 towards Hersham, by Princess Alice Hospice]: Very well managed Victorian Chef & Brewer attractively refurbished in period style, cosy corners, open fires, turkish carpets, old furniture, prints and photographs, candlelight; massive choice of generous reasonably priced food, at least four well kept Scottish Courage ales, good wine choice, quick friendly staff, daily papers, family area; big garden, nr green and pond *(Susan and John Douglas)*

Farncombe [SU9844]

☆ *Ram* [off A3100 in Godalming; Catteshall Rd opp Leathern Bottle, into Catteshall Lane; after Farncombe Boathouse take second left, then right, then left]: 30 ciders, also cider cocktails, country wines, Fullers London Pride and ESB and a guest such as Batemans XB in attractive 16th-c timbered white pub in unexpectedly charming setting beyond industrial estate, basic food from sandwiches up, three simply furnished small heavy-beamed rooms, talking parrot in public bar (which can be smoky), dominoes and shove-ha'penny; very popular with younger people late evening; big back family garden with covered terrace, barbecue, small play area, and big carved wooden ram *(Lynn Sharpless, Bob Eardley, Pete and Sue Robbins, CMW, JJW, Pat and Tony Martin, Elizabeth and Alan Walker, Nigel Wikeley, LYM)*

Farnham [SU8544]

☆ *Spotted Cow* [Bourne Grove, Lower Bourne (towards Tilford)]: Welcoming rural local with wide choice of consistently appetising home-made food inc lots of reasonably priced good fresh fish and vegetarian dishes, well kept Adnams, Courage and Hogs Back TEA, decent wine, witty landlord, attentive friendly service, reasonable prices; play area in big garden *(G B Lungden, Mrs J A Blanks, Lisa Adam, Ruth Gardner)*

Forest Green [TQ1240]

☆ *Parrot* [nr B2126/B2127 junction]: Rambling country pub recently upgraded under new licensees, more upmarket furnishings and extended restaurant, well kept Courage Directors, Fullers London Pride, Hogs Back TEA, John Smiths and Wadworths 6X, good often interesting food, end locals' bar with open fire, pool and interesting bric-a-brac, good cheerful service even when crowded; children welcome, open all day; plenty of tables in newly landscaped garden by cricket pitch, good walks nearby *(Steve Goodchild, LYM, Mike and Sue Todd)*

Frensham [SU8341]

Holly Bush: Bright and friendly pub nr

Frensham Ponds, Charles Wells Bombardier and Morlands, good value generous home-made food from toasted sandwiches to daily roast inc vegetarian dishes *(Mrs C Stevens)*

Frimley Green [SU8856]

Old Wheatsheaf [Frimley Green Rd]: Good busy lunchtime pub with bargain generous food then, hard-working landlord, cheerful prompt servicef, well kept Morlands ales and a guest such as Marstons Pedigree, good malt whiskies *(Sheila and Robert Robinson, R B Crail)*

Godalming [SU9743]

Red Lion [Mill Lane, High St S end]: Lively pub formed from several old properties inc mayor's lodging and courthouse (cellar was gaol); two big bars (one with games), well presented food, real ales, good coffees inc cappuccino, good friendly service; open all day weekdays *(Tony Hobden)*

Grayswood [SU9234]

Wheatsheaf [A286 NE of Haslemere]: Much modernised pub under newish management, well kept Badger beers, helpful service, food in bar and restaurant; conference/bedroom extension *(Mrs J A Blanks, C J Bromage)*

Guildford [SU9949]

Hogshead [High St]: Good range of beers, pleasant garden behind *(P A Legon)*

☆ *Jolly Farmer* [Shalford Rd, Millbrook; across car park from Yvonne Arnaud Theatre, beyond boat yard]: Big popular two-level pub, recently tastefully and plushly refurbished, with good choice of well kept Whitbreads-related and guest beers, decent wines, good food in bar and restaurant, friendly young staff, good atmosphere – no music or games; pleasant conservatory, lots of picnic-sets in big garden with moorings and terrace by River Wey, good walks; open all day *(Tony Scott, Julia and Tony Gerhold, David and Carole Chapman)*

Hale [SU8448]

Cricketers: Good recent refurbishment, good menu – emphasis on restaurant *(Iain Robertson)*

Hersham [TQ1164]

Barley Mow [Molesey Rd]: S&N Country Carvery chain dining pub, but cottagey and largely unspoilt with beams, timbers and comfortable modern kitchen chairs; welcoming staff, quiet bar, decent food, well kept Theakstons *(DWAJ)*

Holmbury St Mary [TQ1144]

Royal Oak: Well run warm and cheery 17th-c beamed coaching inn in pleasant spot by green and church, good helpings of standard fresh food, Friary Meux Best and a guest such as Tapsters Gimbleys, log fire, some tables outside; bedrooms, good walks *(G W Stevenson, Martin and Karen Wake)*

Horley [TQ2842]

Air Balloon [Brighton Rd]: Big Steak pub with exceptionally speedy friendly service even when busy, good value changing food, good big adjoining children's indoor play barn, small outdoor play area; handy for Gatwick *(R C Vincent)*

Chequers [Brighton Rd]: Hotel handy for Gatwick, with good value food in surprisingly

friendly bar; bedrooms *(Dave Braisted)*

Olde Six Bells [quite handy for M23 junction 9, off Horley turn from A23; Church Rd – head for the church spire]: Ancient Bass pub – part of heavy-beamed open-plan bar was probably a medieval chapel, and some masonry may date from 9th c; local atmosphere, reasonably priced food, Bass and Hancocks HB, log fires, upstairs raftered dining room, conservatory, tables out by bend in River Mole; open all day weekdays *(David and Carole Chapman, LYM, John and Phyllis Maloney, Tony Scott)*

Horsell [SU9859]

Cricketers [Horsell Birch]: Friendly local with neatly kept bar and extended eating area, carpet and shiny boards, good choice of good straightforward food inc vegetarian and very good veg, Brakspears and Wadworths 6X; children well catered for; big well kept garden, and seats out in front overlooking overgrown village green *(Gill and Keith Croxton, Ian Phillips)*

Plough [Cheapside]: Small friendly pub set back from road, warm in winter; good service, good choice of well cooked food at reasonable prices, Adnams, Marstons Pedigree, Greene King IPA and Youngs Special, several malt whiskies *(R B Crail)*

Horsell Common [SU9959]

Bleak House [Chertsey Rd, The Anthonys; A320 Woking—Ottershaw]: Welcoming and cheerful, with wide choice of generous standard food, Tetleys-related ales with a guest such as Morlands Old Speckled Hen, comfortable seats; picnic-sets and barbecues in pleasant back garden which merges into woods with good shortish walks to the sandpits which inspired H G Wells's *War of the Worlds*; weekly jazz *(R B Crail, Ian Phillips)*

Irons Bottom [TQ2546]

☆ *Three Horseshoes* [Sidlow Bridge, off A217]: Friendly unassuming country local, enjoyable carefully made lunchtime food, good range of excellently kept real ales inc Fullers London Pride and interesting guest beers such as Hook Norton, quiz or darts night Tues, summer barbecues *(Derek and Maggie Washington, Don Mather, Stephen Wand)*

Kingswood [TQ2455]

Kingswood Arms [Waterhouse Lane]: Big and busy, with wide variety of reasonably priced popular food, cheerful quick service (announcements when orders are ready), Scottish Courage ales, conservatory dining extension; spacious rolling garden with play area *(Mrs G Sharman, Tony and Wendy Hobden)*

Laleham [TQ0568]

☆ *Three Horseshoes* [Shepperton Rd; B376, off A308 W of M3 junction 1]: Popular and plushly modernised, but dating from 13th c, with flagstones, heavy beams, log-effect fires, cosy areas off central serving area, interesting history, lots of tables in enjoyable garden, and easy stroll to Thameside lawns; generous reasonably priced usual food from sandwiches and big ploughman's to restaurant dishes, well kept ales such as Courage Best, Greene King

Abbot, Fullers London Pride and Charles Wells Bombardier, decent wines, efficient service, piped music, restaurant; children in no-smoking conservatory, open all day *(LYM, Ian Phillips, G S Dudley, Mayur Shah, Martin and Karen Wake, D P and J A Sweeney)*

Limpsfield Chart [TQ4251]

Carpenters Arms: Much modernised open-plan pub in delightful setting by village common, lovely walks, easy reach of Chartwell; well kept Friary Meux Best and Tetleys, good coffee, efficient friendly service, well worn-in furnishings, darts one end, eating area the other *(Robert Gomme, R T and J C Moggridge)*

Little Bookham [TQ1254]

Windsor Castle: Pleasant dining area in lounge bar of well extended family dining pub, good choice of food from bar snacks to main meals inc some interesting dishes and children's helpings, friendly staff, tables in huge garden with terrace and popular children's play area *(DWAJ)*

Martyrs Green [TQ0957]

Black Swan [handy for M25 junction 10; off A3 S-bound, but return N of junction]: Extensively enlarged, open all day, with simple furnishings, well worn back bar, SkyTV, fine range of a dozen or more well kept ales, usual food (queue to order), log fires, restaurant; can get crowded with young people evenings, piped pop music may be loud then, maybe karaoke or live entertainment; plenty of tables in big woodside garden with barbecues and good play area – bouncy castle, playground-quality frames, roundabouts etc; handy for RHS Wisley Garden *(Dr M Owton)*

Mogador [TQ2452]

Sportsman [from M25 up A217 past 2nd roundabout, then Mogador signed; edge of Banstead Heath]: Interesting and welcoming low-ceilinged local, quietly placed on Walton Heath, a magnet for walkers and riders; well kept ales, popular food, darts, bar billiards; dogs welcome if not wet or muddy; tables out on common, on back lawn, and some under cover – shame about the loudspeaker food announcements *(Tony Scott)*

Normandy [SU9351]

Duke of Normandy [Guildford Rd E (A323)]: Well run and friendly Greene King pub with their ales inc seasonal brews, sensibly priced food quickly served, good choice of malt whiskies *(R B Crail)*

Norwood Hill [TQ2343]

☆ *Fox Revived* [Leigh—Charlwood back rd]: Good food in spacious bare-boards country pub's large and attractive double dining conservatory, cottagey old-fashioned furnishings, well kept Marstons Pedigree and Morlands Old Speckled Hen, good vintage port, daily papers and magazines, shelves of books, pleasant atmosphere, spreading garden *(James Nunns, Jules Akel, LYM)*

Ockham [TQ0756]

☆ *Hautboy* [Ockham Lane – towards Cobham]: Red stone small hotel, a Gothick folly on a grand scale; crypt bar with good bar food, also pubby-feeling character upstairs brasserie bar,

darkly panelled and high-raftered, with oil paintings and minstrels' gallery; keg beer, friendly service, table on cricket-view terrace and in secluded orchard garden with upmarket play area; chintzy bedrooms *(LYM, Liz and Ian Phillips)*

Ockley [TQ1439]

☆ *Cricketers* [Stane St (A29)]: Pretty 15th-c stonebuilt village local with Horsham slab roof, flagstones, low beams, inglenook log fires, farm tools, shiny pine furniture, good simple generous bar food from sandwiches to good value Sun roast, well kept ales such as Fullers London Pride and Ringwood Best, country wines, maybe piped radio, darts area, small attractive dining room with cricketing memorabilia; seats in delightful back garden with duck pond and play area *(Tony Scott, LYM, David and Carole Chapman, Don Mather)*

☆ *Kings Arms* [Stane St (A29)]: Old-fashioned 17th-c beamed country inn with inglenook log fire, imaginative fresh food in bar and small restaurant, real ales inc a seasonal beer, good welcoming service; discreetly placed picnic-sets in immaculate big back garden; bedrooms with beautifully fitted bathrooms *(S Nelkin, Derek Harvey-Piper)*

☆ *Punch Bowl* [Oakwood Hill, signed off A29 S]: Friendly, welcoming and cosy country pub with huge inglenook log fire, polished flagstones, lots of beams, well kept Badger Best and Tanglefoot and Wadworths 6X, wide choice of good value bar food, traditional games; children allowed in dining area, tables outside with flower tubs and maybe w/e barbecues *(LYM, Peta Keeley)*

Ottershaw [TQ0263]

Castle [Brox Rd, signed off A320 S]: Comfortable and friendly local dated 1905, lots of farm tools etc, stripped brick and beamery, log fire; wide range of good home-made food inc interesting dishes (no-smoking dining area), well kept changing ales such as Adnams, Fullers London Pride, Greene King Abbot, Tetleys, Wadworths 6X and Youngs Special, Addlestone's cider; tables on front terrace and in pleasant creeper-hung arbour at side and back *(George Atkinson, Ian Phillips, J W G Nunns, Tony Scott)*

Outwood [TQ3245]

☆ *Bell* [Outwood Common, just E of village; off A23 S of Redhill]: Attractive extended 17th-c country dining pub, olde-worlde beamed bar and sparser restaurant area, good choice of well kept ales such as Harveys and Youngs, quick friendly service, log fires; children and dogs welcome, summer barbecues and cream teas, has been open all day; pretty fairy-lit garden with country views, handy for windmill *(Jenny and Brian Seller, Michael and Jenny Back, LYM, Tony Scott, Klaus and Elizabeth Leist)*

☆ *Dog & Duck* [Prince of Wales Rd; turn off A23 at Station sign in Salfords, S of Redhill – OS Sheet 187 map ref 312460]: Welcoming rambling beamed country cottage, open all day, with good mix of furnishings, huge log fires, half a dozen well kept Badger and guest ales, popular food all day, lots of board games etc;

children in restaurant, tables outside *(Jules Akel, LYM, G Simpson, Tony Scott)*
Oxshott [TQ1460]
Bear [Leatherhead Rd (A244)]: Busy yet relaxed Youngs pub with well kept beer, their usual wide choice of wines by the glass, big conservatory dining room, friendly courteous staff, usual decent pub food with fresh veg, good log fire, teddy bear collection, occasional barbecues in small garden *(J Sheldon, Martin and Karen Wake, James House)*
Oxted [TQ3852]
George [High St, Old Oxted; off A25 not far from M25 junction 6]: Neat and tidy, with chatty atmosphere, attractive prints, pleasant restaurant area, generous food all day from sandwiches to steaks, well kept Badger Best and Tanglefoot and guest beers, decent wines and coffee, welcoming fire; children welcome over 10 *(Joan and Andrew Life, Dick Brown, R T and J C Moggridge, D and J Tapper, Michael Bastin, LYM)*
Haycutter [Tanhouse Rd, Broadham Green; off High St opp Old Bell]: Very welcoming and happy pub well run by long-serving witty landlord, lots of pictures esp haywains, well kept Marstons Pedigree, good straightforward food from sandwiches to Sun lunch, seafood Sun bar nibbles, skittle alley, huge garden; handy for Greensand Way *(Jenny and Brian Seller, Mr and Mrs D Mapp, James House)*
Royal Oak [Caterfield Lane, Staffhurst Wood, S of town]: Good dining room with well presented French-style food *(R and S Bentley)*
Peaslake [TQ0845]
Hurtwood [off A25 S of Gomshall]: Small prewar country hotel in fine spot for walkers (no muddy boots inside, though), worth knowing for well kept Courage Best, Fullers London Pride and local Hogs Back, also good coffee and malt whiskies; reasonably priced bar food, no piped music, sizeable restaurant *(BB, Mrs A M Arnold, R B Crail, Gwen and Peter Andrews)*
Puttenham [SU9347]
Good Intent [Seale Lane]: Friendly and atmospheric country local, good range of attractively presented reasonably priced food, constantly changing range of well kept ales, Inch's farm cider, roaring log fire, pool; dogs allowed, no children *(John Davis, Gordon Prince)*
Ranmore Common [TQ1451]
Ranmore Arms [towards Effingham Forest, past Dogkennel Green; nr Dunley Hill Farm]: Useful for walkers, bungalow-style building by farmyard, with cheap food inc particularly tasty freshly baked brown bread, informal service, variable real ales inc Greene King IPA and Abbot and local Dorking, front picnic-sets, large play area *(Jenny and Brian Seller)*
Reigate [TQ2550]
Market [High St]: Smartish recently opened pub with good food inc good steak sandwiches, interesting choice of regularly changing real ales; open all day *(Tony Scott)*
Rowledge [SU8243]
Hare & Hounds: Clean and welcoming, with

well kept Morlands, good food; children welcome, prize-winning garden *(Iain Robertson)*
Runfold [SU8747]
Princess Royal [off A31 just NE of Farnham]: Large comfortable 1920s pub with good value straightforward food, good range of beers and house wine, friendly service, inglenooks, dining conservatory – very busy with families Sun lunchtime; picnic-sets and play area behind *(D Marsh, Iain Robertson)*
Send [TQ0155]
New Inn [Cartbridge]: Nice spot by canal with appropriate memorabilia, good value generous food, Tetleys-related and other ales, cheerful staff; piped music; picnic-sets in garden *(Ian Phillips)*
Sendmarsh [TQ0455]
☆ *Saddlers Arms* [Marsh Rd]: Low-beamed local very popular with older people lunchtime for consistently good value straightforward food from sandwiches up inc vegetarian and Sun lunch; friendly staff and dog, well kept Tetleys-related ales with a guest such as Wadworths 6X, open fire, no-smoking area, toby jugs, brassware etc, quiet piped music, machines in separate bar; tables outside *(Shirley Mackenzie, D WAJ, Ian Phillips)*
Shackleford [SU9345]
Cyder House [Pepperharrow Lane]: Wide choice of good food, friendly atmosphere, good range of well kept ales such as Badger Tanglefoot and Hogs Back TEA, farm ciders, log fires, interesting bric-a-brac, families welcome; prices on the high side, piped pop music; picnic-sets on back lawn, nice village setting *(Robert Crail, J S M Sheldon, Peta Keeley)*
Shamley Green [TQ0343]
☆ *Red Lion*: Attractively furnished dining pub, rows of books, local cricketing photographs, enjoyable if pricy food from sandwiches to steaks inc children's helpings, well kept Courage Best, Greene King Abbot and Flowers, good choice of wines; open all day, children welcome, sturdy tables outside; bedrooms *(LYM, J S M Sheldon, D P and J A Sweeney)*
Shepperton [TQ0867]
Goat [Upper Haliford Rd]: Large chain dining pub with brisk professional service, good self-service starters and generous carvery – a bargain for OAPs *(Mr and Mrs D Ayres-Regan)*
☆ *Kings Head* [Church Sq, off B375]: Immaculate old pub in quiet and attractive square, coal fire in inglenook, neat panelling, oak beams, highly polished floors and furnishings, various discreet little rooms, big conservatory extension; good value unpretentious home-made food (not Sun), well kept Scottish Courage ales, attentive service, sheltered back terrace; children welcome, open all day Sat *(LYM, M D Jeffries)*
☆ *Red Lion* [Russell Rd]: Roomy, quiet and welcoming old wisteria-covered two-bar local across rd from Thames, plenty of tables on terrace among fine displays of shrubs and flowers, more on lawn over road (traffic noise) with lovely river views and well run moorings; ever-wider choice of generous food in bars and

restaurant, well kept Scottish Courage ales with guests such as Fullers London Pride, quick service, interesting prints, red-cushioned seating, restaurant *(D P and J A Sweeney, Mayur Shah, D and M T Ayres-Regan)*
Thames Court [Shepperton Lock, Ferry Lane; turn left off B375 towards Chertsey, 100yds from Square]: Huge recently rebuilt pub well placed by Thames, generous tasty usual food from snacks upwards all day (ordering can sometimes take time), well kept Bass and Fullers London Pride, galleried central atrium with separate attractive panelled areas up and down stairs, two good log fires, daily papers, friendly service; children welcome, attractive riverside tree-shaded terrace with big gas radiant heaters *(Mayur Shah)*
Shere [TQ0747]
☆ *White Horse* [signed off A25 3 miles E of Guildford; Middle St]: Striking half-timbered medieval Chef & Brewer recently significantly enlarged but still full of character, with several rooms off the small busy bar, uneven floors, massive beams, Tudor stonework, oak wall seats, two log fires, one in a huge inglenook; good choice of well kept beers such as Courage Best and Theakstons, lots of wines by the glass, food all day; tables outside, children in eating areas – beautiful village, park if you can *(John Evans, MDN, Nigel Roper, John Pettit, Steve Goodchild, Mrs G Sharman, LYM)*
Shottermill [SU8732]
Mill [Liphook Rd, S of Haslemere]: 17th-c pub with a rustic feel, three bar areas, lots of beams, pews, log fire, good choice of daily specials, generous helpings, well kept Greene King Abbot, Marstons Pedigree, Ringwood Best and two guests usually from small local breweries, good choice of wines, service quick and friendly even when busy; small restaurant, pleasant sloping garden with play area and wendy house *(Bruce Bird)*
Staines [TQ0471]
Angel [High St]: Venerable coaching inn with picnic-sets on tranquil small terrace among flowers and trees, beers such as Brakspears, Everards Tiger, Robinsons Frederics, Charles Wells Bombardier and Eagle, decent food, daily papers, restaurant; maybe loudish piped music *(Ian Phillips)*
Jolly Farmers [Farmers Rd, The Hythe]: Long busy bar with a few dining tables at one end, huge helpings of reasonably priced food, Ushers Founders and a seasonal beer, pretty terrace with cocktail parasols and mellow brick walls *(Ian Phillips, CMW, JJW)*
Old Red Lion [Leacroft]: Popular and happy, crowded lunchtime with all ages; good value food, dedicated landlord, quick service, real ales inc Courage Best, Fullers London Pride and Morlands Old Speckled Hen, seats out on terrace opp small green *(Ian Phillips)*
☆ *Swan* [The Hythe; south bank, over Staines Bridge]: Splendid Thameside setting, with moorings, tables on riverside verandah, big conservatory, two pleasant bars, newly refurbished upstairs restaurant; promising new menu with emphasis on English food, cheerful

service, well kept Fullers ales, soft piped music; can be very busy Sun lunchtime and summer evenings; comfortable bedrooms *(Ian Phillips, Shirley Lunn, LYM)*
Swan on the Moor [Moor Lane]: Cosy central fire, beams, panelling, exposed bricks, ornamental books, decent food inc choice of Sun roasts (and bar nibbles then), Courage Best, daily papers, quiet piped music; conservatory restaurant *(CMW, JJW)*
Wheatsheaf & Pigeon [Penton Rd]: Welcoming 1920s local with indelicate local nick-name, well kept Scottish Courage ales, good fresh food in largish bar/lounge and small dining area – quickly fills up even midweek; also fish and chips to go, and Tues quiz night *(Shirley Lunn)*
Sunbury [TQ1068]
Magpie [Thames St]: Lovely spot, with river views from upper bar and small terrace by boat club, good food from ploughman's up, well kept Bass and Boddingtons, decent wines, efficient antipodean service; bedrooms *(D P and J A Sweeney, Martin and Karen Wake)*
Sutton [TQ1046]
☆ *Volunteer* [Water Lane; just off B2126 via Raikes Lane, 1½ miles S of Abinger Hammer]: Three well modernised low-ceilinged linked traditional rooms, antique military prints, big rugs on bare boards or red tiles, usual food from baguettes to fresh fish (loudspeaker announcements outside), no-smoking area, Badger IPA, Best, Tanglefoot and a seasonal beer, decent wines, pleasant staff, small coal fire, well reproduced piped music; restaurant, children welcome away from bar; tables out on flowery terrace and suntrap lawns stepped up behind, good walks, comfortable bedrooms, open all day summer w/e *(Liz and Ian Phillips, J H Bell, B Lake, Mr and Mrs C Fraser, Mayur Shah, Nigel and Olga Wikeley, Mrs Hilarie Taylor, LYM, James Nunns)*
Tadworth [TQ2354]
Blue Anchor [Dorking Rd (B2032)]: Busy, warm and homely, with log fire and candles, cheerful helpful staff, well kept Bass, Fullers London Pride and Worthington, decent wine, vast helpings of food; piped music may obtrude *(Mrs G R Sharman)*
Tandridge [TQ3750]
Barley Mow [Tandridge Lane, off A25 W of Oxted]: Well run with Badger IPA and other real ales, generous well cooked reasonably priced food in bar and restaurant, friendly efficient staff, big garden *(C J Bromage)*
Brickmakers Arms [Tandridge Lane, off A25 W of Oxted]: Friendly and popular country dining pub, dating from 15th c but much extended and modernised, with good range of freshly made food inc their own smoked dishes and lots of fish, well kept Whitbreads-related ales, decent wines inc local ones, restaurant with good log fires, prompt service *(James House, C C S Reeves, Mrs O Hardy)*
Thames Ditton [TQ1567]
Fox on the River [Queens Rd, signed off Summer Rd]: Delightful spot, tables on terrace looking across Thames to Hampton Court, food such as sandwiches, ploughman's, seafood

salad, beef and ale pie, well kept reasonably priced ales inc Bass and Fullers London Pride, friendly helpful staf; moorings *(Martin and Karen Wake, D Marsh)*

Greyhound [Hampton Court Way, Weston Green]: Food-oriented Wayside Inn, with good range of Whitbreads-related and guest ales, very popular Sun lunch, pleasant atmosphere, big pine tables in airy rooms; very busy after Twickenham internationals *(Christopher Wright)*

Thorpe [TQ0268]

Rose & Crown [Sandhills Lane, Thorpe Green]: Good roomy Chef & Brewer, sympathetically renovated without faux-rustic antiquity; good changing home-made food, good atmosphere, real ales such as Courage Best and Directors, Morlands Old Speckled Hen and Theakstons XB, good choice of wines by the glass, daily papers, piped classical music; can get crowded; good outdoor children's area *(RBC, Nigel & Sue Foster, Ian Phillips, Tom and Ruth Rees)*

Thursley [SU9039]

Three Horseshoes [just off A3 SW of Godalming]: Neat and cosy beamed country pub with log fires, well kept Gales HSB and BBB, country wines, good malt whiskies, welcoming landlord, good beer in bar and restaurant, no piped music; seats out in front and in lovely big back garden with barbecues; no dogs; has been open all day *(R B Crail, Derek Harvey-Piper, LYM, Susan and John Douglas, J W G Nunns)*

Tilford [SU8743]

☆ *Barley Mow* [The Green, off B3001 SE of Farnham]: Good food esp vegetarian, well kept Scottish Courage ales, good log fire in big inglenook, comfortable traditional seats around scrubbed tables, interesting prints; small back eating area, weekend afternoon teas; darts, table skittles, no children; pretty setting between river and geese-cropped cricket green nr ancient oak, with waterside garden – village gets busy in summer *(G and M Stewart, Martin and Karen Wake)*

Walton on Thames [TQ1066]

Anglers Tavern [Riverside, off Manor Rd]: Riverside setting distinguishes this chain pub tucked away on Thames towpath, generous bar food from filled baguettes to good fish and steaks, oilcloth tablecloths, Courage-related beers and Wadworths 6X, plenty of bare-boards floor area, large first-floor river-view family room, some peaceful tables out by the boats, moorings, boat hire next door *(D P and J A Sweeney, Mayur Shah)*

Weir [Sunbury Lane]: Wide range of good food, Badger Best and Tanglefoot, traditional all-wood décor, lots of pictures, big terrace with picnic-sets and superb view over river and weir; lovely towpath walks *(D P and J A Sweeney)*

Warlingham [TQ3759]

☆ *Botley Hill Farmhouse* [B269 towards Limpsfield]: Very busy more or less open-plan dining pub, lots of low-ceilinged interlinked rooms up and down steps, soft lighting, spreading turkey carpet, quite closely set tables, big fireplace with copper and blacked pans

above the log fire in one attractive flagstoned room, restaurant with overhead fishing net and seashells, no-smoking area; good food inc lots of fish and seafood, well kept if not cheap ales such as Greene King IPA and Abbot, Pilgrims and Shepherd Neame Spitfire, good house wines, quick service; children welcome, with attractions for them, cream teas, tables on terrace, w/e entertainments *(G Simpson, Carol Bulled, Mrs Hilarie Taylor, Michael and Hazel Duncombe, BB, Chris and Anna Rowley)*

West Clandon [TQ0452]

☆ *Bulls Head* [A247 SE of Woking]: Friendly and comfortably modernised 16th-c country local, very popular esp with older people lunchtime for good value straightforward home-made food from sandwiches, ploughman's and baked potatoes to steak, small lantern-lit front bar with open fire and some stripped brick, old local prints, raised rather canteenish back inglenook dining area, efficient service, Courage Best, Marstons Pedigree and Morlands Old Speckled Hen, good coffee, no piped music, games room with darts and pool; lots of tables and good play area in garden, convenient for Clandon Park, good walking country *(James Nunns, DWAJ, S Mackenzie, John Pettit)*

☆ *Onslow Arms* [A247 SE of Woking]: Partly 17th-c rambling country pub, pricy but good and convivial; dark nooks and corners, heavy beams, flagstones, warm seats nr inglenook log fires, soft lighting, lots of brass and copper; eight well kept ales, decent wines, nicely presented sandwiches, carvery-style hot-lamp bar food servery (not Sun evening), partly no-smoking dining room (popular Sun lunches), great well lit garden; children welcome, open all day *(LYM, Joy and Peter Heatherley, B Lake, Iain Robertson, Susan and John Douglas)*

West Horsley [TQ0753]

King William IV [The Street]: Comfortable red plush banquettes in neatly secluded areas, very low beams, Courage Best and Directors and Youngs Special, decent coffee, log fire, good disabled access; darts area, piped radio, small garden *(Mr and Mrs Phillip Board, J Sheldon, J E and L J Roth, Ian Phillips)*

Weybridge [TQ0764]

Hogshead [Church St]: Attractive and spacious, with interesting range of well kept ales, though done to a format *(James Nunns)*

Jolly Farmer [Princes Rd]: Relaxed and cosy small local opp picturesque cricket ground, tied to Hop Back the small Wiltshire brewer, with their beers kept well and a guest such as Fullers London Pride, good interesting reasonably priced simple food esp sandwiches and snacks; SkyTV; lovely garden with terrace, marquee extension and barbecue *(Ian Phillips)*

Old Crown [Thames St]: Friendly and well run old-fashioned three-bar pub, warm and comfortable, very popular lunchtime for reasonably priced generous straightforward food from sandwiches up esp fresh Grimsby fish (served evening too), freshly made so may be a wait; real ales such as Brakspears, Courage Best and Directors and John Smiths, no music or machines but may be sports TV in back bar;

children welcome, suntrap streamside garden *(R B Crail, Judith Hirst, D WAJ, Ian Phillips)*

Windlesham [SU9264]

☆ *Brickmakers Arms* [Chertsey Rd]: Popular well run dining pub with concentration on good interesting freshly made food esp ciabatta sandwiches and fish, not cheap but good value; cheerfully basic busy bar, well kept Brakspears, Courage Best and Fullers London Pride, wide choice of wines inc interesting bin-ends, log fire, splendid service, daily papers, no music; well behaved children allowed in restaurant, attractive garden with boules and barbecues, lovely hanging baskets *(Shirley Mackenzie, Guy Consterdine, Ian Phillips, A Hepburn, S Jenner, Dr M Owton)*

Windmill [A30/B3020 junction]: Completely refurbished Bass pub, decent low-priced food, various small areas off main bar; handy for Ascot racecourse, some seats outside *(Mayur Shah)*

Witley [SU9439]

White Hart [Petworth Rd]: Tudor beams, good oak furniture, log fire in cosy panelled inglenook snug where George Eliot drank; Shepherd Neame ales with a guest such as Marstons Pedigree, public bar with usual games, restaurant; piped music; seats outside, lots of pretty hanging baskets etc, play area *(Robert Crail, LYM)*

Woking [TQ0159]

Bridge Barn [Bridge Barn Rd; right off Goldsworth Rd towards St Johns]: Large Beefeater worth knowing for position by Basingstoke Canal (lots of waterside tables) and interesting layout – restaurant up in barn rafters, lots of nooks and crannies in flagstoned bars below; very welcoming, with well fenced play area, and comfortable new bedrooms *(George Atkinson)*

Wood Street [SU9550]

Royal Oak: Brightly lit pub with well kept beers such as Batemans, Brecknock, Harveys, Hogs Back and Milligans, moderately priced food with lots of fresh veg and good home-made puddings, friendly service *(R B Crail)*

White Hart [White Hart Lane; off A323 just W of Guildford]: Country local dating from 16th c, now tied to Gibbs Mew with their beers kept well, also guests such as Bass, Morlands Old Speckled Hen and Theakstons, good range of malt whiskies, helpful young landlord, good range of food from snacks up in big dining area *(R B Crail, Miss J Broadhead)*

Worplesdon [SU9854]

☆ *Jolly Farmer* [Burdenshott Rd, Whitmore Common; off A320 Guildford—Woking, not in village]: Smart and roomy beamed country dining pub recently refurbished and extended with bare bricks and natural materials, good if not cheap food inc unusual dishes, plenty of fish and super puddings, good choice of beers inc Fullers London Pride, a seasonal ale and Hogs Back, warmly attentive service, log fire, restaurant; big sheltered garden *(Betty Laker, Michael Hasslacher, James Nunns, LYM, Mrs Hilarie Taylor, Guy Consterdine)*

Wrecclesham [SU8245]

☆ *Bat & Ball* [approach from Sandrock Hill and unmade Upper Bourne Lane, or park in Short Heath Rd and walk down unmade Bat & Ball Lane]: Cosy old pub with well kept Fullers, Youngs and local beers, good choice of good English and Indian food inc home-made baltis, pasta and generous sandwiches, Sun bar nibbles, polite welcoming service, good atmosphere; family extension, dogs welcome, spacious terrace and gardens *(Andy and Jill Kassube, Iain Robertson, W Ruxton)*

Sussex

New entries here this year are the Fox Goes Free at Charlton, an attractively placed and individual pub doing well under new licensees; the Jolly Sportsman at East Chiltington, concentrating on good food; the old-fashioned Horse & Groom at Rushlake Green, now flourishing under the people who own the Star at Old Heathfield just outside Heathfield; the Giants Rest at Wilmington (good mix of well kept beers and enjoyable food in attractive unpretentious surroundings); and the nicely opened-up Cricketers Arms at Wisborough Green (good food, under the family that has the Halfway Bridge Inn near Lodsworth). Other pubs on top form here include the Fountain at Ashurst (lots of careful improvements, and they grow their own fruit, veg and herbs), the friendly and bustling Blackboys Inn at Blackboys (good all round), the George & Dragon at Burpham (another good all-rounder), the chatty and relaxed Bell in Burwash, the Merrie Harriers at Cowbeech (popular food and beer, nice licensees), the cheerful Cricketers at Duncton, the cheerfully simple and atmospheric Elsted Inn at Elsted (good imaginative food, good beers), the Griffin at Fletching (service, food, wines and beer all come in for high praise this year – and they have a good sensible attitude to children), the low-beamed nicely placed Woodmans Arms at Hammerpot, the well run Queens Head at Icklesham (friendly, fine choice of beers, good food), the welcoming Juggs at Kingston Near Lewes, the civilised Halfway Bridge Inn near Lodsworth (very good food, good drinks choice), the Blacksmiths Arms at Offham (good dining pub), the friendly Ypres Castle in Rye (the food's getting very good now), the remarkably busy Golden Galleon near Seaford, and the charming Horse Guards at Tillington (good food and wines, a nice place to stay in). For a special meal out, the Jolly Sportsman, Elsted Inn, Griffin, Halfway Bridge Inn and Horse Guards all give a sense of occasion with cooking to match; our choice as Sussex Dining Pub of the Year is the Halfway Bridge Inn at Lodsworth. We can't leave the subject of food without a special mention for the Six Bells at Chiddingly: remarkably cheap enjoyable food (and good jazz) at this individualistic country pub. In a high proportion of pubs here, the cheapest beer on offer comes from Harveys of Lewes. Other local beers worth looking out for, from this county or over the Hampshire border, include Old Forge, Cheriton, Ballards, Brewery on Sea, Arundel and King & Barnes – and Plumpton, brewed by the village parson. The cheapest beer we found was the own brew in the Blacksmiths Arms at Donnington; the Gribble at Oving also brews its own beers, which can often now be found in other pubs tied to Badger. From the very wide choice of good pubs in the Lucky Dip section at the end of the chapter, we'd mention particularly the Gardeners Arms at Ardingly, Old Oak and Yew Tree at Arlington, Black Horse at Binsted, Cricketers and Greys in Brighton, Crown & Anchor at Dell Quay, Royal Oak at East Lavant, George at Eartham, Rose & Crown at Fletching, Gun at Gun Hill, Anglesey Arms at Halnaker, George & Dragon at Houghton, Crabtree at Lower Beeding, Onslow Arms at Loxwood, Cock at Ringmer, Wyndham

Arms at Rogate, White Hart at South Harting, White Horse at Sutton, Best Beech near Wadhurst, Greets at Warnham and New Inn at Winchelsea. In most of these food is a prime consideration.

ALCISTON TQ5005 Map 3
Rose Cottage
Village signposted off A27 Polegate—Lewes

Whatever time of year it is, this charming country cottage is an enjoyable place to visit. There are seats under cover outside (and they now have outdoor heaters for chillier evenings), and warm log fires inside – and if you're staying, there is nearby fishing and shooting. The friendly little cosy bar soon fills up, so get there early for one of the half-dozen tables with their cushioned pews – under quite a forest of harness, traps, a thatcher's blade and lots of other black ironware, with more bric-a-brac on the shelves above the stripped pine dado or in the etched glass windows; in the mornings you may also find Jasper, the talking parrot (it can get a little smoky for him in the evenings). There's a lunchtime overflow into the no-smoking restaurant area. They take great care over their food, using fresh fish from a local fisherman at Eastbourne, eggs from their own chickens, a lot of locally grown organic vegetables, pheasants shot by the landlord, and venison from the landlord's brother-in-law. Not surprisingly, the bar food remains quite a draw, and daily specials might include cheesy topped mussels (£3.50; main course £6.95), very popular thai-style tiger prawns with a hot soy dip (£3.65; main course £6.95), rabbit and bacon or chicken and ham pies (£5.95), barbecue ribs (£6.75), winter steak and kidney pudding (£6.25), chicken in tomato and basil topped with mozzarella (£6.95), chargrilled lamb cutlets with a honey and mint glaze (£7.50), thai-style curries or barbecued spare ribs (£6.25), chicken in tomato and basil topped with mozzarella (£6.50), venison braised in port and Guinness (£7.95), and roast Sunday lunch (£6.95; the lamb marinated in red wine, rosemary and garlic is good); from the lunchtime bar menu there is ploughman's (from £4.50), Lincolnshire sausages (£4.75), honey-roast ham and egg (£4.95), and steaks (from £9.50), with evening scampi (£6.95) and half roast duckling with orange and green peppercorns (£10.95). Well kept Harveys Best and Rother Valley Level Best on handpump, decent wines including a 'country' of the month and six by the glass (or half litre), and Biddenden farm cider; darts, dominoes, cribbage, and maybe piped classical music. Yet again, the house martins and swallows returned to nest above the porch, seemingly unperturbed by the people going in and out beneath them. The small paddock in the garden has ducks and chickens. *(Recommended by Colin and Joyce Laffan, Jules Akel, Glen and Nola Armstrong, Jan Collings, R and S Bentley, Mrs M A Stevenson, RDK, Tony and Rachel Schendel, R J Walden, Dave Carter, Dr and Mrs J H Hills, Mr and Mrs C Moncreiffe, Anthony Bowen, Tim and Pam Moorey, Peter Meister, Marjorie and Bernard Parkin, Timothy Galligan, Mike Wells, Tony Scott, B M and P Kendall)*

Free house ~ Licensee Ian Lewis ~ Real ale ~ Bar food ~ Restaurant ~ (01323) 870377 ~ Children welcome but must be over 6 in evening ~ Open 11.30-3, 6.30-11; 12-3, 7-10.30 Sun; closed 25 and 26 Dec

AMBERLEY SO8401 Map 3
Black Horse
Off B2139

Handy for walking in the Arun Valley, this very pretty village pub has high-backed settles on the flagstones, beams over the serving counter festooned with sheep and cow bells, traps and shepherd's tools, and walls decorated with lots of old local prints and engravings; there are plenty of pictures too and some unusual teapots in the similar but more comfortable saloon bar; log fires at either end of the main bar and one in the lounge. Bar food includes sandwiches (from £2.25), ploughman's (£4.95), home-made pies (£5.50), various fish dishes, children's dishes, puddings

(£2.50), Sunday roast, and a Tuesday three-course lunch (£5); the restaurant is no smoking. Well kept Friary Meux, Ind Coope Burton, Wadworths 6X, and a guest beer on handpump; friendly, welcoming staff. Darts, cribbage, dominoes, fruit machine, and piped music; two big dogs and a sleepy cat. There are seats in the garden. The attractive village is close to the River Arun, with a castle, and the pub is handy for the South Downs Way and Amberley Industrial Museum. *(Recommended by Ian Wilson, Bruce Bird, David and Carole Chapman, Tim Barrow, Sue Demont, Neil Porter)*

Pubmaster ~ Tenant Chris Acteson ~ Real ale ~ Bar food ~ Restaurant ~ (01798) 831552 ~ Children in eating area of bar and restaurant ~ Open 11-3, 6-11; 11-11 (11-3, 7-10.30 winter) Sat; 12-3, 7-10.30 Sun

Bridge

B2139

As well as being a charming pub, this attractive old white painted place with its pretty hanging baskets is very well liked for its good food. The friendly and relaxed narrow bar has a couple of cushioned window seats and a mix of old wooden chairs by a few tables along one side, a group of brown velveteen bucket seats around a table at one end with a button-backed brown sofa beside them, candles in bottles creating a soft light, and a tiled bar gantry with fairy lights along it; a cosy small room with similar seats leads off the bar, and a delft shelf and beam with brass, copper, and lots of bottles lead to the attractively furnished two-roomed dining part; the walls throughout are covered with modern portrait art and impressionist-style paintings by the owner. Generous helpings of totally home-made changing bar food includes a huge bowl of good soup like french onion or crab bisque (£4), smoked salmon or salt beef open sandwiches or ploughman's (£4.25), popular mussels (£6.50), steak and kidney pudding, vegetarian pasta bake or asparagus and mushroom quiche (£7.25), whole bacon hock or half shoulder of lamb (£8.25), a proper paella (£9.25), lots of fresh dishes such as red snapper, monkfish medallions, tuna steak, golden trout, and fresh dressed crab salad (£10.50), puddings such as toffee, raspberry and marshmallow pie, steamed treacle pudding or oranges marinated in brandy (£3), and roast Sunday lunch (£7.75). Well kept Flowers Original, Gales Best and HSB, Harveys Best, King & Barnes Sussex, and Morlands Old Speckled Hen on handpump, and lots of cocktails; good, friendly service, and piped music. There are white plastic seats and tables in front of the pub, with more in a little side garden. Children are not allowed inside. *(Recommended by Tracey and Stephen Groves, K and J Morris, Tony and Wendy Hobden, Bruce Bird, David Holloway)*

Free house ~ Licensee Stephen Chandler ~ Real ale ~ Bar food ~ Restaurant ~ (01798) 831619 ~ Open 11-3, 6-11.30; 12-3, 7-10.30 Sun

Sportsmans

Crossgates; Rackham Rd, off B2139

The panoramic views from the tables on the decked terrace, the little conservatory and bars at this unassuming village local are quite special. Its two friendly and chatty little lounge bars are simply decorated in a homely way with well used brocaded chairs on its light brown patterned carpet, and lots of little notices and pictures, and postcards from locals to the pub. As well as Miserable Old Bugger – brewed for the pub by Brewery on Sea, and named after a club that's based here – three well kept guests might be Fullers London Pride and Youngs Bitter and Special; scrumpy cider and country wines. The brick floored public bar has a hexagonal pool table and darts, cribbage, dominoes and giant Jenga, and the pretty little red-tiled conservatory is engagingly decorated with old local bric-a-brac. Home-made bar food includes toasties (from £2.50), soup (£2.75), local sausage in a french stick (£3.50), ploughman's (from £3.75), home-made steak and kidney pie (£5.90), half roast chicken (£6.75), halibut steak with tartare butter (£7.50), steaks (from £9.25), and daily specials; piped music. *(Recommended by D S Jenkin, Malcolm Taylor)*

Free house ~ Licensees Jenny and Chris Shanahan ~ Real ale ~ Bar food ~ (01798) 831787 ~ Children in eating area of bar ~ Open 11-2.30, 6-11; 12-3, 7-10.30 Sun

ASHURST TQ1716 Map 3
Fountain ◀

B2135 S of Partridge Green

A lot of work has gone into the garden of this 16th-c country pub. A new orchard has been planted to one side, kitchen gardens with herbs, fruit and vegetables have been established, the duck pond cleaned out, and wooden decking with tables and chairs built to one side with access to the skittle alley. Inside, the newly opened snug has flagstones, heavy beams, simple furniture, and an inglenook fireplace. The charmingly rustic tap room on the right has a couple of high-backed wooden cottage armchairs by the log fire in its brick inglenook, two antique polished trestle tables, fine old flagstones, and Fullers London Pride, Harveys Sussex and Shepherd Neame Masterbrew with two guests like Adnams and Gales HSB on handpump, plus changing guests like Flowers Original and Gales HSB tapped from the cask; decent wines. A bigger carpeted room with its orginal beams and woodburning stove is where most of the good bar food is served. This might include at lunchtime, sandwiches (from £2.95), ploughman's (from £4.95), lasagne or home-cooked ham with a free-range egg (£5.95), steak, mushroom and ale pie (£6.95), and goat's cheese, sun-dried tomato and sweet pepper tartlets or chicken piri-piri (£8.95), with evening steaks (from £11.50), and daily specials such as fish pie, fresh dressed crab salad, breast of pheasant wrapped in bacon and stuffed with apricots, or rabbit casserole; puddings like blackberry and apple pie (£3.25). Shove-ha'penny, cribbage, dominoes, table skittles, and oak-beamed skittle alley. No children. *(Recommended by Malcolm Taylor, Don Scarff, Bruce Bird, Jenny and Brian Seller, David Holloway)*

Free house ~ Licensees Mark and Christopher White ~ Real ale ~ Bar food (11.30-2, 6.30-9.30; not Sun or Mon evenings) ~ (01403) 710219 ~ Open 11.30-2.30(3 Sat), 6-11; 12-3, 7-10.30 Sun; closed evening 25 Dec

BARCOMBE TQ4114 Map 3
Anchor

From village follow Newick, Piltdown sign, then turn right at Boast Lane leading to Anchor Lane, marked with a No Through Rd sign, then first left (by post box)

It's during the summer that this cheerful little pub really comes into its own. It's set by the River Ouse with neatly kept waterside lawns and a fairy-lit terrace with plenty of picnic-sets and white metal seats and tables, and you can hire boats on an unspoilt three-mile stretch of the river as it winds through the meadows (£3.20 per adult per hour, half price for children) – reckon on about two hours if you're going all the way to the fish ladder Falls near Sutton Hall and back. A riverside kiosk serves cream teas and cold drinks, and there are barbecues most summer weekends; plenty of surrounding walks, too. In winter the approach road can flood and cut the pub off – they leave out a boat or two then. Inside, there are two tiny bars decorated with a good few motor racing trophies won by the landlord's late father, along with some car models, and other racing and RAF memorabilia – meetings of the Jaguar Owners Club, Vintage Sports Car Club, and MG Club are held here. Bar food includes home-made soup (£2.60), sandwiches (from £2.25; filled french bread from £4.50), filled baked potatoes (from £3.95), ploughman's (from £4.75), home-baked ham and eggs (£5.25), local pork sausages with onion gravy (£5.50), daily specials like smooth chicken liver pâté (£4.25), turkey and pepper stroganoff (£8.95), barnsley chop with rosemary jus (£9.25), and ostrich steak with a pink peppercorn sauce (£11.95). There's an intimate no-smoking candlelit restaurant. Well kept Badger Best and Tanglefoot, and Harveys Best on handpump, and a decent wine list including some local English ones. Good friendly service; dominoes, shut the box, and scrabble. The no-smoking family room has toys and children's videos. *(Recommended by Betsy and Peter Little, Gill and Maurice McMahon, John Saul, Bruce Bird, John Knighton, A J Bowen, Colin and Ann Hunt, Colin and Janet Roe, Tony Scott)*

Free house ~ Licensees Graham and Jaci Bovet-White ~ Real ale ~ Bar food ~ Restaurant ~ (01273) 400414 ~ Children welcome ~ Open 10.30-11; 12-10.30 Sun; closed maybe winter 1999 until Mar ~ Bedrooms: £32/£55

BARNHAM SU9604 Map 3
Murrell Arms ◗
Yapton Rd

To reach this charming unspoilt pub you walk from the car park through a pretty flower-filled courtyard with a large cider press on one side, and fine ancient wooden benches and tables under a leafy grape vine on the other – note the huge bellows on the wall; there are picnic-sets on a cottagey little enclosed garden up some steps. Inside, the two bar rooms are packed with mementoes collected by the licensees over the 35 years they have been here. The saloon bar has some nice old farmhouse chairs, a very high-backed settle by the piano, and a mix of tables (including a fine circular Georgian one) on the partly turkey carpeted very old dark wood parquet floor, candles in bottles, hundreds of jugs, mugs, china plates and old bottles crammed along delft shelves, walls completely covered with little prints and pictures, agricultural artefacts hanging from the ceiling, an elderly grandfather clock, a collection of old soda syphons, and a huge polished half-barrel bar counter. To get to the cheerful public bar, you walk past the stillage room where the barrels of well kept Gales Bitter, Best, HSB, BBB and a changing guest are stored; ring-the-bull – they have no noisy machines or piped music; two open fires, lots of farming tools, old photographs and more pictures, an interesting Cox's change machine and Crystal Palace clock by the bar, and some old horsebrasses; a simple tiny snug over a half wall (the only place where really well behaved children are tolerated) has an enormous bell wheel from the church on the ceiling. Straightforward bar food includes ploughman's (£1.50), local sausages, and a couple of changing daily specials such as suet bacon pudding or liver and bacon casserole (£2.95). *(Recommended by David and Carole Chapman, John Donnelly, Tony Scott)*

Gales ~ Tenant Mervyn Cutten ~ Real ale ~ Bar food (not Thurs evening) ~ (01243) 553320 ~ Well behaved children in snug ~ Folk Thurs evening and last Sun of month ~ Open 11-2.30, 6-11; 11-11 Sat; 12-10.30 Sun

BERWICK TQ5105 Map 3
Cricketers Arms
Lower Rd, S of A27

After a walk on the downs, the old-fashioned garden of this peaceful and unspoilt old flint cottage is just the place to quench your thirst – it's lovely on a sunny day with little brick paths, mature flowering shrubs and plants, and lots of picnic-sets in front of and behind the building. Inside, the three little similarly furnished rooms have simple benches against the half-panelled walls, a happy mix of old country tables and chairs, burgundy velvet curtains on poles, a few bar stools, and some country prints; quarry tiles on the floors (nice worn ones in the middle room), two log fires in little brick fireplaces, a huge black supporting beam in each of the low ochre ceilings, and (in the end room) some attractive cricketing pastels; helpful, friendly staff – even when really busy. Sound bar food includes home-made soup (£2.95), creamy garlic mushrooms (£4.25), home-cooked honey ham and egg (£4.75), platters or filled baked potatoes (from £4.75), a vegetarian dish, fresh local cod in batter (£5.75), sirloin steak (£8.50), daily specials, and puddings like home-made fruit crumble (£2.95); they hold winter themed food evenings. Well kept Harveys Best, PA and seasonal ales tapped from the cask, and decent wine; darts, cribbage, and an old Sussex game called toad in the hole. The wall paintings in the nearby church done by the Bloomsbury group during WWII are worth a look. *(Recommended by Comus Elliott, Lesley Sones, Tony and Wendy Hobden, R D and S R Knight, P Rome, Peter Meister, Anthony Bowen, David and Carole Chapman, Tony Scott, Gwen and Peter Andrews, Amanda Ariss, the Didler)*

Harveys ~ Tenant Peter Brown ~ Real ale ~ Bar food (all day on Sun) ~ (01323) 870469 ~ Children in eating area of bar ~ Open 11-3, 6-11; 11-11 Sat; 12-10.30 Sun; 11-3, 6-11 Sat in winter; closed 25 Dec

BILLINGSHURST TQ0830 Map 3
Blue Ship ◧

The Haven; hamlet signposted off A29 just N of junction with A264, then follow signpost left towards Garlands and Okehurst

Pleasantly remote, this genuinely unpretentious little country pub has a blazing fire in the inglenook fireplace of the cosy beamed and brick-floored front bar, and hatch service dispensing well kept King & Barnes Broadwood, Sussex and seasonal beers tapped from the cask; a corridor leads to a couple of similar small rooms. A games room has darts, bar billiards, shove-ha'penny, cribbage and dominoes. It can get crowded with a pleasant mix of customers, particularly at weekends; there may be a playful cat. Straightforward but enjoyable bar food includes sandwiches (from £2), winter soup (£3.25), ploughman's (from £3.80), macaroni cheese (£4.35), cottage pie (£4.55), and steak and kidney pie or scampi (£6.10). It's very nice in summer, when you can relax at the tree-shaded side tables or by the tangle of honeysuckle around the front door, and there's a play area for children. *(Recommended by Brad W Morley, John Robertson, David and Carole Chapman, James Nunn, Tony Scott, Dave Cupwell, the Didler)*

King & Barnes ~ Tenant J R Davie ~ Real ale ~ Bar food (not Sun or Mon evenings) ~ (01403) 722709 ~ Children in two rooms without bar ~ Open 11-3, 6-11; closed evening 25 Dec

BLACKBOYS TQ5220 Map 3
Blackboys Inn

B2192, S edge of village

Vibrant and friendly, this 14th-c weatherboarded house has a good log fire in the inglenook fireplace, antique prints and masses of bric-a-brac (including a collection of keys above the bar) in its string of old-fashioned and unpretentious little rooms, dark oak beams, and bare boards or parquet. Good waitress-served bar food includes home-made soup (£2.50), ploughman's (from £3.75), home-smoked ham and egg (£4.95), vegetable curry (£5.50), tagliatelle napolitana or chicken curry (£5.95), steak and kidney pie (£6.50), well liked seafood pancake (£6.75), entrecote steak (from £7.50), and puddings such as treacle sponge pudding or marquis de chocolat (from £3.25); friendly, efficient staff even when busy. The restaurants are no smoking. Well kept Harveys Best, Pale Ale, Old, Mild and seasonal brews on handpump; darts, dominoes, cribbage, fruit machine, and juke box. Outside, there's masses of space, with rustic tables overlooking the pond and on the front lawn under the chestnut trees; good Woodland Trust walks opposite the pub and handy for the Vanguard Way footpath. *(Recommended by Kevin Thorpe, John Beeken, Ian and Carol McPherson, Tessa Burnett, Jenny and Brian Seller)*

Harveys ~ Tenant Nicola Russell ~ Real ale ~ Bar food ~ Restaurant ~ (01825) 890283 ~ Children in eating area of bar ~ Open 11-3, 6-11; 12-3, 7-11 Sun

BROWNBREAD STREET TQ6715 Map 3
Ash Tree ◧

Village signposted off the old coach road between the Swan E of Dallington on B2096 Battle—Heathfield and the B2204 W of Battle, nr Ashburnham

Not easy to find as it is hidden away in a charmingly isolated hamlet, this tranquil country local has cosy beamed bars with nice old settles and chairs, stripped brickwork, two inglenook fireplaces, and evening candlelight. Good bar food includes sandwiches or ploughman's, home-made soup (£3.25), home-made smoked salmon mousse (£4.25), cottage pie (£5.25), liver and bacon (£6.75), chicken in tarragon and cream (£7.50), with evening dishes such as braised oxtail in wine (£7.50), grilled halibut (£8.25) or duck breast (£11.25). They may only do full meals at some of their busiest times. Very well kept Harveys Best and a guest such as Fullers London Pride, Morlands Old Speckled Hen or Wadworths 6X on handpump; cheerful, friendly service, and darts, pool, fruit machine, juke box, and piped music in the simple games room on the left. There's a pretty garden with picnic-sets. *(Recommended by Christopher Turner, Peter and Joan Elbra, B and M Parkin, Ray Watson)*

Free house ~ Licensees Malcolm and Jennifer Baker ~ Real ale ~ Bar food ~ Restaurant ~ (01424) 892104 ~ Children in eating area of bar ~ Open 12-11(10.30 Sun)

BURPHAM TQ0308 Map 3
George & Dragon ◀

Warningcamp turn off A27 outside Arundel: follow road up and up

There are splendid views down to Arundel Castle and the river just a short walk away from this popular pub; plenty of surrounding walks. Inside, there's a genuine welcome from the friendly licensees in the neatly kept and spacious open-plan bar, good strong wooden furnishings, lots of interesting prints, and well kept Arundel ASB, Cotleigh Tawny, Cottage Brewery Southern Bitter, Harveys Best, Timothy Taylor Landlord, and Woodfordes Wherry on handpump, and a decent wine list; piped music. Bar food continues to draw in customers, and it's the daily specials that really stand out: excellent home-made soup, smoked chicken and raspberry salad (£5.90), beef and horseradish pie or pork, apple and cider casserole (£6.20), duck breast with plum sauce (£8.50), red bream fillet and caper sauce (£8.90), skate wing (£9.50), halibut fillet with orange sauce (£9.70), and puddings such as white chocolate mousse, strawberry shortcake or sticky toffee pudding (£3.75); from the menu, there might be sandwiches (from £3.25; chicken, bacon and salad toastie £5.25), home-made pâté (£4.25), filled baked potatoes (from £4.95), ploughman's (£5), and steaks (from £11.75). Many of the tables get booked up in advance. The nearby partly Norman church has some unusual decoration. *(Recommended by Comus Elliott, Anna and Martyn Carey, Mrs J A Powell, Tony and Wendy Hobden, Ian Phillips, Tim and Pam Moorey, David and Carole Chapman, Nigel Wilkinson, Alan Skull, R T and J C Moggridge, Chris and Anna Rowley, B J Harding, Tony Scott, Penny and Martin Fletcher, T R and B C Jenkins, Derek and Maggie Washington, Martin and Karen Wake, Mrs P Goodwyn, Malcolm Taylor, David Gould, Nigel Cogger, Bruce Bird, Mrs Romey Heaton)*

Scottish Courage ~ Tenants James Rose and Kate Holle ~ Real ale ~ Bar food ~ Restaurant ~ (01903) 883131 ~ Well behaved children (preferably over 8) in eating area of bar and in restaurant ~ Occasional jazz/cajun live music ~ Open 11-2.30, 6-11; 12-3, 7-10.30 Sun; closed Sun eveening Oct-Easter; 25 Dec

BURWASH TQ6724 Map 3
Bell

A265 E of Heathfield

There's always a good quietly chatty atmosphere in this village pub and usually a couple of cheerful locals sitting at the high-backed bar stools by the counter. The relaxed L-shaped bar to the right of the main door has built-in pews and a mix of seats with brocaded cushions, all sorts of ironwork, bells and barometers on its ochre Anaglypta ceiling and dark terracotta walls, and a good winter log fire. Well kept Arundel Footslogger, Batemans XB, Greene King IPA, and Harveys Best on handpump, and a range of malt whiskies and wines. Darts, bar billiards, shove-ha'penny, ring the bull and toad in the hole, table skittles, cribbage, dominoes, and unobtrusive piped music. Generous helpings of decent bar food include sandwiches and 3-cheese ploughman's, egg and chips (£4.50), spinach and ricotta cannelloni (£4.95), hot, sweet and sour chicken or fresh cod (£5.50), smoked salmon and smoked mackerel platter (£6.95), half duck with home-made plum sauce or fillet steak in a creamy peppercorn sauce (£9.95), and puddings such as bananas in butterscotch sauce (£2.50). The restaurant is no smoking. Car park at the back. In summer, the hanging baskets and tubs in front are a marvellous sight, and there are seats that look across the busy road to the church. This is a pretty village. *(Recommended by Janet and Colin Roe, Val and Alan Green, G W Stevenson, Joan and Andrew Life, Mick and Hazel Duncombe, Comus Elliott)*

Greene King ~ Lease: Colin and Gillian Barrett ~ Real ale ~ Bar food (not Sun evenings) ~ Restaurant ~ (01435) 882304 ~ Children welcome ~ Open 11.30-3.30, 6-11; 11-11 Sat; 12-10.30 Sun; closed evenings 25 and 26 Dec ~ Bedrooms: £25/£40

BYWORTH SU9820 Map 2
Black Horse
Signposted from A283

The garden of this unspoilt old pub is lovely – and not surprisingly can get busy in summer. There are tables on a steep series of grassy terraces, sheltered by banks of flowering shrubs, that look across a drowsy valley to swelling woodland, and a small stream runs along under an old willow by the more spacious lawn at the bottom; dogs are welcome on a lead. Inside, there's a nice relaxed atmosphere in the simply furnished though smart bar with its pews and scrubbed wooden tables on the bare floorboards, and open fires; the no-smoking back dining room has lots of nooks and crannies and a tented curtain to keep out the draughts. Bar food includes sandwiches (from £3.25), good ploughman's (from £4.25), daily specials (from £4.95), puddings, and Sunday roasts. Well kept Arundel Gold, Fullers London Pride and guest beers on handpump kept under light blanket pressure. Darts, bar billiards, cribbage, dominoes, and piped music. *(Recommended by David Gould, Juliet Winsor, Graham and Karen Oddey, Tom and Rosemary Hall, Bruce Bird, MCG, Ann and Colin Hunt, Charles Turner)*

Free house ~ Licensees Rob Wilson and Teri Figg ~ Real ale ~ Bar food (not evening 24 Dec) ~ Restaurant ~ (01798) 342424 ~ Children in restaurant ~ Open 11-2.30(3 Sat), 6-11; 12-3, 7-10.30 Sun

CHARLTON SU8812 Map 3
Fox Goes Free
Village signposted off A286 Chichester—Midhurst in Singleton, also from Chichester—Petworth via East Dean

Now under new licensees, this characterful old place has been a pub for nearly 500 years. The first of its cosy series of separate rooms is a small, carpeted bar with one table, a few very mixed chairs and an open fireplace. Standing timbers divide a larger beamed bar which has some new and some old elm furniture, a huge brick fireplace with woodburning stove, a couple of elderly armchairs, red tiles and carpet and brasses and old pictures of the pub and village on the yellowed walls. A plaque and memorabilia explain that this was where the very first Women's Institute meeting in England was held in 1915. A dining area has hunting prints on the walls, and views over the garden and South Downs. The no-smoking family extension is a clever conversion from horse boxes and the stables where the 1926 Goodwood winner was housed; darts, cribbage, cards and piped music in some areas. Four (possibly five in summer) well kept real ales include Ballards Best, Fox Goes Free (brewed for the pub by Tetleys), Marstons Pedigree and a guest like Hop Back Summer Lightning on handpump, and eight wines by the glass. Bar food includes soup (£3), sandwiches or avocado and stilton bake (£3.50), duck liver, port and hazelnut pâté or charcuterie (£4.50), ratatouille and goat's cheese bake (£6), steak and kidney pie (£6.50), sea bream with prawns and capers (£9), venison steak with port, redcurrant and juniper (£9.50) duck breast with roquefort and red wine (£10.50), and home-made puddings like pear and chocolate tart or crème brûlée (£3). There's a very pleasant secluded back garden, with tables among fruit trees, one with seats built into its trunk, a notable downland view, and a safe children's play area with sandpit. The barbecue area can be booked. The pub is handy for the Weald and downland Open Air Museum, and this normally quiet village is busy on race days. *(Recommended by Bruce Bird, Martin and Karen Wake, Ann and Colin Hunt)*

Free house ~ Licensee Oliver Ligertwood ~ Real ale ~ Bar food (12-2.30, 6.30-10.30(10 Sun)) ~ Restaurant (Sat evening, Sun lunch only) ~ (01243) 811461 ~ Live music one Wed a month ~ Open 11-3, 6-11; 12-4, 7-10.30 Sun ~ Bedrooms: £35(£40B)/£50(£55B)

CHIDDINGLY TQ5414 Map 3
Six Bells ★ £

Village signed off A22 Uckfield—Hailsham

There's such a diverse mix of customers at this old-fashioned pub, but the friendly, chatty landlord has a good welcome for all, and it's a firm favourite with quite a few readers who enjoy the bustling, informal atmosphere – and of course, the regular jazz. The characterful beamed rooms have solid old wood furnishings including some pews and antique seats, log fires, lots of fusty artefacts and interesting bric-a-brac, and plenty of local pictures and posters. A sensitive extension provides some much needed family space; dominoes and cribbage. It can get quite lively. A big draw is the remarkably low-priced bar food, straightforward but tasty, with dishes such as french onion soup (£1.25), the landlord's special cheesy garlic bread (£2.25), filled baked potatoes (from £2.30), green-lipped mussels, buttered crab, ham or cheese with french bread (from £3.50), shepherd's pie (£2.30), steak and kidney pie (£2.50), tuna pasta bake (£3.50), stilton and walnut pie (£3.75), rack of ribs (£4.95), and puddings like treacle tart, banoffee pie or raspberry pavlova (£2.50). Well kept Courage Best and Directors and Harveys Best on handpump or tapped from the cask. Outside at the back, there are some tables beyond a big raised goldfish pond, and a boules pitch; the church opposite has an interesting Jeffrey monument. Vintage and Kit car meetings outside the pub every week. This is a pleasant area for walks. *(Recommended by Ann and Colin Hunt, Jason Caulkin, David Cullen, Emma Stent, Janet and Colin Roe, Kevin Thorpe, Peter Meister, David Lamb, Dave Carter)*

Free house ~ Licensee Paul Newman ~ Real ale ~ Bar food (till 10pm) ~ (01825) 872227 ~ Children in family room ~ Jazz Sun lunchtime, blues and other live music in barn, Tues, Fri, Sat and Sun evenings ~ Open 11-3, 6-11; 12-10.30 Sun

CHIDHAM SU7804 Map 2
Old House At Home

Off A259 at Barleycorn pub

Over the years, this charming country pub has remained a consistently enjoyable place for either a meal or a drink. The homely bar has timbering and low beams, windsor chairs around the tables, long seats against the walls, and a welcoming log fire. At lunchtime, the good bar food might include filled french bread (from £2.95), soup (£3.25), ploughman's (from £4.95), home-made bangers and mash (£5.95), fresh cod (£6.50), lamb's liver (£7.25), rib-eye steak (£8.50), and a weekday special (£4.50); in the evening (best to book), there is table service and plenty of fresh fish, on Sunday lunchtime they have two roasts (£6.25), and hold monthly seafood nights. Food can be served in both front and back gardens. The eating area is no smoking. Well kept real ales such as a beer named for the pub (Old House), Badger Best, Ringwood Best and Old Thumper, and a weekly changing guest beer on handpump, as well as a good selection of country wines and several malt whiskies; there's a large friendly german shepherd. *(Recommended by E A Froggatt, Guy Lockton, Mr and Mrs D E Powell, J F Reay, Nigel Wilkinson, Derek Stafford, June and Eric Heley, Colin and Ann Hunt, Peter Meister, Tony Scott, Charles Turner, Richard Dolphin)*

Free house ~ Licensees Cliff Parry and Terry Brewer ~ Real ale ~ Bar food ~ (01243) 572477 ~ Children in eating area of bar until 8pm ~ Open 11.30-2.30(3 Sat), 6-11; 12-4, 7-10.30 Sun

COOLHAM TQ1423 Map 3
George & Dragon

Dragons Green; pub signposted off A272 between Coolham and A24

At lunchtime particularly, this old tile-hung cottage does get pretty busy with people keen to enjoy the good food. The bustling bar has unusually massive beams (see if you can decide whether the date cut into one is 1577 or 1677), unpretentious furnishings, and an enormous inglenook fireplace – as well as more modern features such as a fruit machine, darts, bar billiards, table skittles, shove-ha'penny, cribbage, dominoes, and TV. Totally home-made, the bar food might include sandwiches (not Sunday), soup such as tomato and coriander (£2.95), hot tiger prawns in filo pastry (£5.50), battered cod, bacon and onion quiche or lasagne (£5.95), pasta bake with broccoli and mushrooms in a stilton and garlic sauce (£6.25), minted lamb and leek pie or roast loin of pork with apple sauce (£6.50), half shoulder of English roast lamb (£9.95), peppered rib-eye steak (£11.25), and puddings such as tangy lemon sponge, treacle and walnut tart or chocolate sponge with white chocolate sauce (£2.95). Well kept King & Barnes Broadwood, Festive, Sussex and seasonal ales on handpump. Stretching away behind the pub, the big grassy garden is beautifully kept, with lots of rustic tables and chairs well spaced among fruit trees, shrubs and lovely flowers; the little front garden has a sad 19th-c memorial to the son of a previous innkeeper. *(Recommended by Bruce Bird)*

King & Barnes ~ Tenant Roger Nash ~ Real ale ~ Bar food ~ Restaurant ~ (01403) 741320 ~ Children in eating area of bar and restaurant ~ Open 11-3, 6-11; 11-11 Sat; 12-10.30 Sun; evening opening 6.30 in winter

COWBEECH TQ6114 Map 3
Merrie Harriers
Village signposted from A271

'A thoroughly pleasant pub' is how several readers have described this white-clapboarded village inn. The friendly bar is beamed and panelled, and has a traditional high-backed settle by the brick inglenook, as well as other tables and chairs, and darts; piped music. There's quite an emphasis on the popular bar food which includes sandwiches, home-made soup (£2.80), home-made salmon mousse (£3.95), almond-coated brie with redcurrant jelly (£4.95), deep-fried butterfly prawns with garlic dip (£5.65), nut roast with tomato sauce (£5.75), home-made steak and kidney in ale pie (£7.75), salmon steak with hollandaise sauce (£9.15), grilled breast of duck with a changing home-made sauce (£10.25), steaks (from £10.25), daily specials, and puddings like home-made fruit cheesecake (£2.95); on Mondays to Saturdays they offer a two-course lunch for £6.50, and on Monday to Thursday evenings, they have a two-course meal for £9.95; two-course Sunday lunch (£9.95). Well kept Harveys Best and a monthly guest beer on handpump; charming, professional service. The brick-walled and oak-ceilinged back restaurant is no smoking. Rustic seats in the terraced garden. *(Recommended by Colin and Joyce Laffan, J H Bell, Janet and Colin Roe)*

Free house ~ Licensees J H and C P Conroy ~ Real ale ~ Bar food ~ Restaurant ~ (01323) 833108 ~ Children in restaurant ~ Open 11-2.30(3 Sat), 6-11; 12-3, 7-10.30 Sun

CUCKFIELD TQ3025 Map 3
White Harte ◖ £
South Street; off A272 W of Haywards Heath

By 12.30 on a weekday lunchtime, most of the tables in this bustling cheerful pub will already have been snapped up. The popular, straightforward meals include ploughman's (from £3.60), sausage and egg, and salads, but most people tend to go for the five or so very good value home-cooked specials: pies like chicken and mushroom, fish, or steak and kidney, turkey breast in mushroom sauce, smoked haddock bake, or stilton and celery quiche (all £4.20). The comfortable beamed lounge has a mix of polished floorboards, parquet and ancient brick flooring tiles, standing timbers, a few local photographs, padded seats on a slightly raised area, and some fairly modern light oak tables and copper-topped tables. Furnishings in the public bar are sturdy and comfortable with a roaring log fire in the inglenook, maybe the friendly cat, and sensibly placed darts. Well kept King & Barnes Bitter and Broadwood and a guest beer on handpump; fruit machine, shove-ha'penny. The village is attractive. *(Recommended by B and M Kendall, DWAJ, Terry Buckland, Steve Willey, Elizabeth and Klaus Leist)*

King & Barnes ~ Tenant Ted Murphy ~ Real ale ~ Bar food (lunchtime; not Sun) ~ (01444) 413454 ~ Children in eating area of bar lunchtime only ~ Open 11-3, 6-11; 12-3, 7-10.30 Sun

DONNINGTON SU8502 Map 2

Blacksmiths Arms

Left of A27 on to A286 signed Selsey, almost immediate left on to B2201

New licensees have taken over this little white roadside cottage and are working to create a happy combination of real local and dining pub. The small redecorated rooms have low ceilings, quite a few Victorian prints on the walls, solid and comfortable furnishings, and four well kept real ales including their own-brewed Buckland Brewery Wholehearted and Old Anvil and guests such as Hampshire Bees Knees on handpump. Good, totally home-made bar food cooked by the landlord might include soup (£2.50), sandwiches (from £2.50), ploughman's (from £3.95), ham and egg (£5.95), whole roast poussin, roast vegetables topped with goat's cheese in an Italian tomato sauce, lamb balti or fresh whole Selsey plaice (all £7.95), Selsey crab (£8.95), steaks (from £8.95), half a lobster americaine (£9.95), bass with fresh herbs (£11.95), and puddings such as steamed rum and raisin pudding or hot chocolate fudge sundae (from £3.95). The restaurant is partly no smoking. The big garden has been opened up and has a play area with a bouncy castle, plenty of picnic-sets, and a summer dining marquee. The pub is now owned by the Winchester Ale House company. *(Recommended by E A Froggatt, Prof and Mrs S Barnett, D S and J M Jackson, John Donnelly, Mrs Mary Woods, J Snell, Lawrence Pearse, Michael Sargent)*

Free house ~ Licensee David Reed ~ Real ale ~ Bar food ~ Restaurant ~ (01243) 783999 ~ Children in eating area of bar ~ Open 11-3, 6-11; 11-11 Fri and Sat; 12-10.30 Sun; 11-3, 6-11 Fri and Sat, 12-3, 7-10.30 Sun in winter

DUNCTON SU9617 Map 3

Cricketers

Set back from A285

There's always a rather jolly atmosphere in this pretty little white pub – helped by the cheerful licensee and his staff. The bar has a few standing timbers giving the room an open-plan feel, there's an inglenook fireplace at one end with a large summer dried flower arrangement and some brass pots and warming pans on either side of the grate, local photographs on the mantlepiece, half a dozen bar stools and a mix of country tables and chairs, and green-cushioned settles; wildlife pictures, and a cartoon of the licensees. Down a couple of steps a similarly furnished room is set for eating and is decorated with farming implements, pictures, and cricketer cigarette cards. Good, popular bar food includes soup (£3.50), tasty garlic mushrooms (£3.95), ploughman's, open granary sandwiches (from £4.25), oven-roasted vegetables and mozzarella cheese (£4.50), chicken liver pâté with onion confit (£4.75), fish terrine with prawn sauce (£4.95), vegetable pasta bake (£5.50), steak and kidney pudding (£7.25), chicken with oven-roasted tomatoes and rosemary (£7.95), oven-roasted salmon fillet with tomato and chives or sliced magret duck breast with orange and lemon sauce (£8.95), and puddings (£3). Well kept Archers Golden, Friary Meux Bitter, Gales HSB, Ind Coope Burton, Youngs, and guest beers on handpump, lots of malt whiskies, decent wines; cribbage. The charming garden behind the building has a proper barbecue (maybe summer Sunday lunchtime barbecues and jazz), picnic-sets, and an attractive little creeper-covered seating area. There's a separate skittle alley at the front to one side of the building, lovely flowering baskets and tubs, and a rope swing for children. *(Recommended by Colin and Ann Hunt, John Fahy, Miss J F Reay, Nigel Cogger, E A Froggatt, Ron Gentry, Nigel and Olga Wikeley)*

Free house ~ Licensee Philip Edgington ~ Real ale ~ Bar food (not Sun or Mon winter evenings) ~ Restaurant ~ (01798) 342473 ~ Well behaved children in restaurant only ~ Open 11-2.30, 6-11; closed winter Sun evenings

---

Please tell us if any Lucky Dips deserve to be upgraded to a main entry – and why. No stamp needed: The Good Pub Guide, FREEPOST TN1569, Wadhurst, E Sussex TN5 7BR.

EAST CHILTINGTON TQ3715 Map 3

Jolly Sportsman 🍷

2 miles N of B2116; Chapel Lane

Recently opened by Bruce Wass of Thackerays in Tunbridge Wells fame, this tucked away Victorian conversion has been simply but effectively decked out with stripped wood floors, one or two groups of mixed tables and chairs, and a fireplace in the chatty little bar, and contemporary light wood furniture and modern landscapes on pale yellow painted brick walls in the informally civilized restaurant. You can drop in for a drink – well kept Harveys and a couple of beers from Rectory who are just down the road and a remarkably good wine list – but the main draw is the imaginative (though by no means cheap) cooking from a changing menu that might include basil risotto (£4.50), duck liver parfait with onion marmalade or grilled mediterranean vegetables and couscous salad (£4.75), haggis, neaps and tatties (£6.90), crispy duck confit with plums and ginger or cod fillet with pine nut and coriander crust (£9.85), herb roasted free range chicken breast (£11.75), and puddings like apricot, walnut, ginger and toffee pudding or chocolate espresso block with coffee sauce (£4.85). There are rustic tables and benches under gnarled trees in a pretty cottagey front garden. *(Recommended by David Reekie, Tim Locke)*

Free house ~ Licensee Bruce Wass ~ Real ale ~ Bar food ~ Restaurant ~ (01273) 890400 ~ Children welcome ~ Open 12-3, 6-11; 12-4 Sun; closed Mon, Sun evening

EAST DEAN TV5597 Map 3

Tiger 🍷

Pub (with village centre) signposted – not vividly – from A259 Eastbourne—Seaford

Popular with walkers – the pub is on the South Downs Way – this old-fashioned local is in a lovely spot on the edge of a secluded sloping village green lined with low cottages (like the pub itself) bright with flowering climbers and window boxes; there are rustic seats and tables on the brick front terrace. Inside, the smallish rooms have low beams hung with pewter and china, traditional furnishings including polished rustic tables and distinctive antique settles, and old prints and so forth. Well kept Adnams Best, Flowers Original, and Harveys Best on handpump, and a fair choice of wines with several interesting vintage bin-ends and 7 good wines by the glass; cribbage and dominoes. A short but good choice of home-made bar meals, listed on a blackboard, might include 20 different ploughman's (£4.50; they keep 10 different cheeses), fresh haddock and chips or mediterranean vegetable casserole topped with goat's cheese (£5.95), whole local crab (£7.95), and whole local lobster (£11.95); their meat comes from the very good local butcher who wins awards for his sausages. The upstairs family room is no smoking. Morris dancers visit every bank holiday. The lane leads on down to a fine stretch of coast culminating in Beachy Head. No children inside. *(Recommended by Mike Wells, Edward Froggatt, David and Carole Chapman, R J Bland, Tony Scott, Michael and Hazel Duncombe, G W Stevenson)*

Free house ~ Licensee Nicholas Denyer ~ Real ale ~ Bar food ~ (01323) 423209 ~ Open 11-11; 12-10.30 Sun; 11-3, 6-11 weekdays in winter

ELSTED SU8119 Map 2

Elsted Inn ★ 🍴 🍺 🛏

Elsted Marsh; from Midhurst left off A272 Petersfield Rd at Elsted and Harting sign; from Petersfield left off B2146 Nursted Rd at South Harting, keep on past Elsted itself

There's a great atmosphere and a warm welcome from the staff (and from the two big friendly dogs Sam and Truffle) in this simple and unpretentious village pub. The two small bars have country furniture on wooden floors, original shutters, old railway photographs (the pub was built to serve the railway when there was a station next door), and three open log fires; no piped music or noisy games machines but plenty of local chat, and darts, shove-ha'penny, dominoes, cribbage, backgammon, and cards. The small restaurant (candlelit at night) has patchwork curtains, an old oak dresser, and restored old polished tables and chairs. They use the best ingredients for their very good cooking: local game, Jersey cream from a local farm, hand-made bread from the National Trust bakery at Slindon, free-range eggs, mainly free-range chicken and duck, and local vegetables and fruit. The menu sometimes changes twice a day and might include sandwiches (from £3), filled baked potatoes or ploughman's (£4.95), macaroni cheese (£5.50), good mussels baked with garlic and cheese (£6.50), king prawns in garlic butter (£6.25), good local sausages, roast vegetables with couscous (£7.50), Sussex bacon pudding (£7.75), fish pie (£8), local rabbit in mustard sauce or scrumptious pheasant (£8.50), and puddings like little dark chocolate mousse, apple and cinnamon crumble or raspberry brûlée (£4); Sunday roasts (£7.50). As there isn't much space, they reluctantly advise booking for meals. Well kept Ballards Trotton Bitter, Best, Wassail, summer Nyewood Gold, and winter Wild, Fullers London Pride, Gales GB, and guest beers from small local independent breweries on handpump. The lovely enclosed garden has a big terrace, plenty of wooden garden furniture, a good view of the South Downs, and boules; summer barbecues. The bedrooms are in the old brewery building next door. The vintage sports car club meets every second Friday of the month with a big rally on New Year's Day. *(Recommended by Dr B H Hamilton, Mrs S E Griffiths, D Marsh, Mike and Mary Carter, Peter Meister, Derek Harvey-Piper, William and Julie Ryan, David Cullen, Emma Stent, Lynn Sharpless, Bob Eardley, Jerry and Alison Oakes, R D Knight, Mrs Val Worthington, Dave Braisted)*

Free house ~ Licensees Theresa Jones and Barry Horton ~ Real ale ~ Bar food ~ Restaurant ~ (01730) 813662 ~ Children in eating area of bar and restaurant ~ Folk 1st Sun of month ~ Open 11.30-3, 5.30(6 Sat)-11; 12-3, 6-10.30 Sun; closed evening 25 Dec ~ Bedrooms: £35B/£50B

Three Horseshoes 🍺

Village signposted from B2141 Chichester—Petersfield; also reached easily from A272 about 2 miles W of Midhurst, turning left heading W

From the lovely garden here there are marvellous views over the South Downs – and free-roaming bantams. The snug little rooms in this 16th-c pub are full of rustic charm, with ancient beams and flooring, enormous log fires, antique furnishings, attractive prints and photographs, and night-time candlelight. Good bar food includes home-made soup (£3.95), a generous ploughman's with a good choice of cheeses (£5.50), avocado with stilton and mushroom sauce topped with bacon (£6.50), steak, kidney and ale pie or braised lamb with apples and apricots in a tomato chutney sauce (£8.95), fresh seasonal crab and lobster, and home-made treacle tart or Grand Marnier cheesecake (£3.95). Well kept changing ales racked on a stillage behind the bar counter might include Ballards Best, Cheriton Pots, Hop Back Summer Lightning, Otter Bitter and changing guests; summer cider; friendly service; dominoes. *(Recommended by David Cullen, Emma Stent, Paul and Penny Dawson, Charles Turner, Ann and Colin Hunt, Lynn Sharpless, Bob Eardley, John H Davis)*

Free house ~ Licensees Andrew and Sue Beavis ~ Real ale ~ Bar food ~ Restaurant ~ (01730) 825746 ~ Well behaved children in eating area of bar and in restaurant ~ Open 11-2.30(3 Sat), 6-11; 12-3, 7-10.30 Sun; closed Sun evening

FAIRWARP TQ4626 Map 3
Foresters Arms

Set back from B2026, N of northern Maresfield roundabout exit from A22

The setting for this bustling, pleasant local is pretty – right on a small green among oak trees; the Vanguard Way and Weald Way at the south end of Ashdown Forest are nearby. Inside, it's homely and welcoming, with a comfortable lounge bar, a public bar with a big aquarium, a woodburning stove in a big stripped stone fireplace, and well kept King & Barnes Bitter, Broadwood, Festive, Mild, and a guest beer on handpump, and Westons cider. Decent bar food includes sandwiches (from £2.50), home-made soup (£2.75), home-made curries (from £5.95), home-made pies (from £6.50), and roasts (£6.75); children's meals, good popular Sunday lunch, and efficient service. Darts, pool, dominoes, fruit machine, video game, trivia, and piped music. There are tables and benches outside in the garden, a children's play area, and pretty award-winning hanging baskets. *(Recommended by W Ruxton, John Bell, John Steel, R J Walden, J Bell, Colin and Joyce Laffan, R D and S R Knight)*

King & Barnes ~ Tenants Melanie and Lloyd West ~ Real ale ~ Bar food (not winter Sun evenings) ~ Restaurant ~ (01825) 712808 ~ Children welcome ~ Open 11-3, 6-11; 12-3, 7-10.30 Sun

FIRLE TQ4607 Map 3
Ram
Village signposted off A27 Lewes—Polegate

Delightfully unspoilt (and perhaps a bit too well worn in the eyes of some) this simple 17th-c village pub is handy for exploring a particularly fine stretch of the South Downs. There's a good friendly atmosphere in its unspoilt bars with winter log fires, comfortable seating, soft lighting, and a relaxed atmosphere; the snug is no smoking. Well kept Harveys and a couple of guests like Cotleigh Harrier and RCH Pitchfork on handpump; darts, shove-ha'penny, dominoes, cribbage and toad in the hole. The gents' has a chalk board for graffiti, and there are tables in a spacious walled garden behind. They have a fine ginger cat called Orange, and two comical geese. Bar food includes soup (£3), ploughman's (£6), cheese and onion tart (£7.50), sausage in a puff pastry plait (£8), spicy chicken (£8.50), salmon steak (£9), steak and mushroom pie (£10), local ice creams (£3) and puddings like blackberry and apple crumble or bakewell tart (£3.50). Nearby Firle Place is worth visiting for its collections and furnishings. *(Recommended by Simon Cottrell, Kevin Thorpe, John Robertson, Martin Wright)*

Free house ~ Licensee Michael Wooller ~ Real ale ~ Bar food (12-9) ~ (01273) 858222 ~ Children welcome away from the bar ~ Folk music second Mon and first Wed of month ~ Open 11.30-11; 12-10.30 Sun

FLETCHING TQ4223 Map 3
Griffin ★ ⑪ ☖ ⛌

Village signposted off A272 W of Uckfield

'One of our favourites' is how several readers describe this civilised old inn. It's a popular place with a good bustling atmosphere, a warm welcome from the friendly, efficient licensees and their staff, enjoyable beers and wines, and especially interesting food. The beamed and quaintly panelled bar rooms have blazing log fires, old photographs and hunting prints, straightforward furniture including some captain's chairs, china on a delft shelf, and a small bare-boarded serving area off to one side. A separate public bar has darts and pool. They use only fresh seasonal ingredients and local organic vegetables and meat wherever possible in the food: soups such as carrot, honey and ginger (£3.95), hot ciabatta sandwiches with fillings like roast mediterranean vegetables or salami, tomatoes and mozzarella (£4.95), confit of pork and mungbean terrine with plum chutney (£4.95), deep-fried crab wontons with chilli sauce (£5.50), chargrilled sausage with grain mustard mash and onion gravy (£6.50), good moules frites with mayonnaise, summer salad of broad beans, Jersey Royals, croutons and quail's eggs or penne with piperade and mozzarella, basil and parmesan (all £6.95), steak in ale pie or fishcakes of salmon, smoked haddock and coriander with lemon mayonnaise (£7.50), game pie of venison, pigeon and pheasant with juniper berries (£8.25), home-made sweet potato gnocchi, roasted plum tomato and basil (£8.50), chargrilled rib-eye steak (£9.50), and puddings such as rhubarb and ginger crumble, seasonal fruit brûlée or chocolate and cognac flan (£3.95); 2-course children's menu (£4.50); enjoyable breakfasts. Well kept Badger Tanglefoot, Hardy Country and Royal Oak, and Harveys Best on handpump, amd a fine wine list with a dozen wines (including champagne) by the glass. There are tables in the beautifully arranged back garden with lovely rolling Sussex views, with more on a sheltered gravel terrace, and they now have a spit roast for suckling pig, spring lamb and marinated chickens; trees for children to climb, banks to roll down, and a couple of acres to wander around. The converted coach house now has extra bedrooms including new 4-poster ones. The pub is in a pretty spot just on the edge of Sheffield Park. *(Recommended by Dr Paul Khan, Richard Siebert, G Simpson, Colin and Ann Hunt, Paul Tindall, Colin and Joyce Laffan, Pierre and Pat Richterich, Ian and Carol McPherson, Jules Akel, Cyril Brown, Bernard and Marjorie Parkin, B K and R S Levy, Martin and Karen Wake, Evelyn and Derek Walter, Sue and David Arnott, Peter Meister, John and Joan Calvert, Colin Draper, Mr and Mrs R J Salter, J H Bell, A Cowell, David Cullen, Emma Stent, R D and S R Knight, P Rome, Paula Williams, Mr and Mrs B H Robinson, David and Betty Gitti)*

Free house ~ Licensees N Pullan, J Pullan and John Gatti ~ Real ale ~ Bar food ~ Restaurant ~ (01825) 722890 ~ Children welcome ~ Open 12-3, 6-11; 12-3, 7-10.30 Sun; closed 25 Dec ~ Bedrooms: £55B/£70B

HAMMERPOT TQ0605 Map 3
Woodmans Arms
Pub visible and well signposted on N (eastbound) side of A27 just under 4 miles E of A284 Arundel; heading W on A27 the turn is about ½ mile beyond the pub

The garden here – despite some road noise – is delightful, with picnic-sets and tables on a terrace (they now have mobile outside heaters for chillier weather), under a fairy-lit arbour and on small lawns among lots of roses and tubs of bright annuals. This is good walking country and several readers have enjoyed the free map of a good circular walk from the pub – best to phone ahead if you are a sizeable party. Inside this delightful 16th-c thatched pub, some of the beams are so low they are strung with fairy lights as a warning. The brick-floored entrance area has a chatty atmosphere, a cosy armchair by the inglenook's big log fire, lots of brass, pictures by local artists for sale, and genuine old photographs of regulars. On the right a carpeted dining area with candles on the tables has wheelback chairs around its tables, and cheerfully cottagey decorations; on the left is a small no-smoking room with a few more tables. Good, well presented home-made food in generous helpings includes sandwiches (from £2.45), and maybe home-made macaroni cheese (£5.50), poached fresh cod fillet or home-made creamed celery and mushroom stroganoff on tagliatelle (£5.95), home-made steak and kidney pie (£6.50), home-made chicken curry (£6.95), fresh dressed Selsey crab salad (£7.25), grilled chicken fillet with tomato and basil sauce (£8.95), and duck breast with a port and cumberland sauce (£9.25). Well kept Gales Best, HSB and a guest such as Fullers London Pride or Timothy Taylor Landlord on handpump, country wines, and good friendly service. Cribbage, dominoes and maybe some piped music. The yellow labrador is called Tikka. *(Recommended by John Beeken, Colin Draper, John Donnelly, George Little, Joy and Peter Heatherley, Judith Reay, B and M Kendall, E A Froggatt, Ann and Colin Hunt, Bruce Bird)*

Gales ~ Tenants Malcolm and Ann Green ~ Real ale ~ Bar food (not Sun evening) ~ Restaurant ~ (01903) 871240 ~ Well behaved children in eating area of bar ~ Folk every 2nd Sun evening ~ Open 11-3(3.30 Sat), 6-11; 12-4(3 in winter), 7-10.30 Sun

HARTFIELD TQ4735 Map 3
Anchor 🍺
Church Street

The original bar in this late 15th-c pub has heavy beams, old advertisements and little country pictures on the walls above the brown-painted dado, houseplants in the brown-curtained small-paned windows, and a woodburning stove. Another bar has flagstones, more old beams, a dining area with good tables and chairs, and huge logs burning in an old inglenook fireplace. Well kept Bass, Flowers IPA and Original, Fullers London Pride, and Harveys Best on handpump. Decent bar food includes sandwiches or toasties (from £1.75; avocado and prawn £3), home-made soup (£2.75), filled baked potatoes or ploughman's (from £4), moules marinières or vegetable stir fry (£4.50), home-made pork and walnut pâté with cumberland sauce, local sausages or home-cooked ham and egg (all £4.75), prawn and crab curry (£6), lamb kebab with yoghurt and mint (£8.75), sirloin steak (£11), good value daily specials, and puddings (from £2.75); children's meals (from £2.50); quick friendly

service. Darts in a separate lower room; shove-ha'penny, cribbage, dominoes, and
piped music. The front verandah soon gets busy on a warm summer evening. There's
a play area in the popular garden. *(Recommended by Brian and Anna Marsden, Pierre and
Pat Richterich, LM, Colin and Joyce Laffan, W Ruxton, Ms S Bodell, Michael and Hazel
Duncombe)*

*Free house ~ Licensee Ken Thompson ~ Real ale ~ Bar food (12-2, 6-10) ~ Restaurant
~ (01892) 770424 ~ Children welcome ~ Open 11-11; 12-10.30 Sun; closed evening
25 Dec*

HEATHFIELD TQ5920 Map 3
Star

Old Heathfield – head east out of Heathfield itself on A265, then fork right on to B2096;
turn right at signpost to Heathfield Church then keep bearing right; pub on left immediately
after church

There's a lot of character in the L-shaped beamed bar of this 14th-c inn. Reached up
some well worn brick steps, it has a relaxed, chatty atmosphere, a log fire in the
inglenook fireplace, panelling, built-in wall settles and window seats, and just four or
five tables; a doorway leads into a similarly furnished smaller room. A fair range of
bar food is chalked up on a board (they tell us prices again remain virtually
unchanged) and includes ploughman's (£4.75), fresh mussels or cold meats with
bubble and squeak (£6.25), good local cod with chips, fresh crab (£7.95), half a free-
range duckling (£11.95), fresh lobster (£15), and winter game dishes; efficient,
courteous service. Well kept Harveys Best and Greene King IPA and a guest such as
Bass, Greene King Abbot or Hop Back Summer Lightning on handpump, some malt
whiskies and farm cider; bar billiards and shove-ha'penny. The prettily planted
sloping garden with its rustic furniture has views of rolling oak-lined sheep pastures
– Turner thought it fine enough to paint. The neighbouring church is rather
interesting, with its handsome Early English tower. *(Recommended by B R and M J
Cooper, Kevin Thorpe, John Gillett, Heather Simpson, Peter Meister, Comus Elliott)*

*Free house ~ Licensees Mike and Sue Chappell ~ Real ale ~ Bar food ~ Restaurant ~
(01435) 863570 ~ Children in eating area of bar and restaurant ~ Open 11.30-3,
5.30-11; 12-4, 7-10.30 Sun*

HORSHAM TQ1730 Map 3
Black Jug

31 North St

As well as good, interesting bar food, this bustling town pub has a friendly, chatty
atmosphere and a fair choice of well kept beers. The airy open-plan turn-of-the-
century-style room has a large central bar, a nice collection of heavy sizeable dark
wood tables, comfortable chairs on a stripped wood floor, dark wood panelled dado
above which are cream walls crammed with interesting old prints and photographs,
and a warm terracotta ceiling. A spacious dark wood conservatory has similar
furniture and lots of hanging baskets; dominoes and trivia. Well kept Boddingtons,
Charles Wells Bombardier, Courage Directors, Marstons Pedigree, and Wadworths
6X on handpump, two dozen malt whiskies, and eight chilled vodkas from Poland
and Russia. The changing bar menu, densely written on a blackboard, includes
sandwiches, soup (£2.95), chicken liver and wild mushroom pâté (£3.75), roast
tomato, artichoke and mozzarella tartlet on a spring onion salad (£4.25),
cumberland sausages with mustard mash and onion gravy (£5.50), Thai salmon and
crab fishcakes with chilli dressing (£5.95), hot, spicy lamb koftas in pitta bread with
a minted yoghurt and cucumber dressing (£6.25), mixed tagliatelle with a creamy
mushroom and garlic sauce topped with melted halloumi cheese (£7.25), pork steaks
with a sweet chilli, pine nut and tarragon sauce (£9.75), rib-eye steak with a green
peppercorn sauce (£10.25), and whole grilled plaice filled with mushrooms and
prawns and topped with a lime and chilli butter (£11.25). There are quite a few
tables shelted under a pagoda outside on a back flower-filled terrace. *(Recommended
by G Simpson, R Cooper, David and Carole Chapman, Ron Gentry, Tony Scott)*

Scottish Courage ~ Manager Neil Stickland ~ Real ale ~ Bar food (all day Sun) ~ Restaurant ~ (01403) 253526 ~ Children in conservatory weekends only until 6pm ~ Open 11-11; 12-10.30 Sun

ICKLESHAM TQ8716 Map 3
Queens Head ♀ ◖

Just off A259 Rye—Hastings

No matter how deservedly busy this comfortably relaxed pub is, you can be sure of a warm welcome from the very friendly licensees. The open-plan areas work round a very big serving counter, which stands under a vaulted beamed roof; the high beamed walls and ceiling of the easy-going bar are covered with lots of farming implements and animal traps, and there are well used pub tables and old pews on the brown patterned carpet. Other areas (two are no smoking) are popular with diners – the bar food is very reasonably priced – and have big inglenook fireplaces. The generous helpings of food quickly served by friendly efficient staff include sandwiches (from £1.95; steak in french bread), home-made soup (£2.50), soft herring roes on toast (£3.95), ploughman's (£4.10), home-cooked ham and egg (£4.75), home-made pâté (£4.95), cheesy ratatouille (£5.50), a curry of the day or steak and mushroom in ale pie (£6.50), steaks (from £9.50), and home-made daily specials such as ham and leek crumble (£5.75), courgette and lentil gratin (£6.25), chicken breast with stilton and mushroom sauce (£6.75), and fresh fish such as skate, cod, plaice, halibut or lemon sole (£6-£9). From a constantly changing choice of at least four, the very well kept real ales might include Courage Directors, Greene King Abbot, Harts Siren, Hogs Back TEA, Old Forge Brothers Best, Ringwood Old Thumper, Rother Valley Level Best, Swale Kentish Pride, and Woodfordes Wherry; a good choice of wines by the glass, Biddenden cider, and sparking elderflower cordial; shove-ha'penny, dominoes, fruit machine, and piped music. There are broad views over the vast gently sloping plain of the Brede valley from wooden picnic-sets in the little garden, and a children's play area; boules. Good walks. *(Recommended by Joan and Tony Walker, Karina Spero, Bruce Bird, E G Parish, Janet and Colin Roe, Mrs J Clarke, Brian and Jenny Seller, Joan and Andrew Life, D Buckley, Mike Gorton, J H Bell, Peter and Joan Elbra, Kevin Thorpe)*

Free house ~ Licensee Ian Mitchell ~ Real ale ~ Bar food (12-2.45(3 Sun), 6.15(7 Sun)-9.45) ~ (01424) 814552 ~ Well behaved children welcome away from bar, until 8.30pm ~ Open 11-11; 12-5, 7-10.30 Sun; closed evening 25 Dec

KINGSTON NEAR LEWES TQ3908 Map 3
Juggs ◖

The Street; Kingston signed off A27 by roundabout W of Lewes, and off Lewes—Newhaven road; look out for the pub's sign – may be hidden by hawthorn in summer

Quaint inside and out, this tile-hung, rose-covered cottage has a welcoming, informal atmosphere. The rambling beamed bar has an interesting mix of furnishings that ranges from an attractive little carved box settle, Jacobean-style dining chairs and brocaded seats and other settles to the more neatly orthodox tables and chairs of the small no-smoking dining area under the low-pitched eaves on the right. The cream or stripped brick walls are hung with flower pictures, battle prints, a patriotic assembly of postcards of the Lloyd George era, posters, and some harness and brass. Popular bar food includes home-made soup or ploughman's (£3.95), open sandwiches (from £3.95), sausages (£4.50), haddock and chips (£5.75), vegetable savoury or pitta bread with chicken tikka (£5.95), home-made steak and kidney pudding (£8.95), steaks (from £8.95), daily specials, and home-made puddings (£2.95). On Sunday lunchtime food is limited to a cold buffet. One of the family rooms is no smoking. Service remains speedy and efficient (aided by a rather effective electronic bleeper system to let you know when meals are ready) even when the pub is very busy. Well kept Harveys Best, King & Barnes Festive, and a guest on handpump. Log fires and shove-ha'penny. There are a good many close-set rustic teak tables on the sunny brick terrace; a neatly hedged inner yard has more tables under cocktail parasols, and there are two or three out on grass by a timber climber and commando net. The pub was named for the fish-carriers who passed through on their way between Newhaven and Lewes. *(Recommended by Mike Wells, A Bowen, Colin and Janet Roe, Gill and Maurice McMahon, JEB, R J Walden, Mayur Shah, Mrs Jenny Cantle, Jason Caulkin, Derek Harvey-Piper, Bruce Bird, R and S Bentley, Tony Scott)*

Free house ~ Licensees Andrew and Peta Browne ~ Real ale ~ Bar food ~ Restaurant ~ (01273) 472523 ~ Children welcome away from bar area ~ Open 11-11; 12-10.30 Sun; 11-3, 6-10.45 winter; closed evening 25 Dec, 26 Dec, evenings 31 Dec and 1 Jan

KIRDFORD TQ0126 Map 3
Half Moon

Opposite church; off A272 Petworth—Billingshurst

Apart from the pretty village setting, one of the main reasons for coming to this sizeable tile-hung cottage is to enjoy the interesting fresh fish. The Morans have had links with Billingsgate for over 130 years, and there might be such rarities as tile fish, porgy, parrot fish, soft shell crabs, Morton Bay bugs, scabbard fish, razor shells, mahi-mahi, and baramundi. But as fresh fish is seasonal, there may be times when the range isn't as big as you might hope: potted shrimps (£5.10), moules marinières (£5.25), deep-fried crab claws with chutney (£5.50), filo-wrapped prawns with sweet and sour dip (£5.75), swordfish steak with herb sauce (£11), mahi-mahi cajun style (£11.95), and whole baked bass with fresh coriander and peppers (£15.95). Also, non-fishy things like filled french bread (from £3.95), ploughman's (from £3.80), baked mushrooms stuffed with three cheeses and almonds (£4.95), spare ribs with barbecue sauce (£5.75), steaks (from £10.95), and duck with peach and mango (£14.20). The friendly licensees have now opened their own fish shop close by – so you can order your fish, have lunch and go back to collect it to take home. Well kept Arundel Best, Ballards Wassail, Greene King Abbot, and King & Barnes Sussex on handpump, and local cider. The simple partly quarry-tiled bars are kept ship-shape and very clean, and there's a beamed eating area with an open fire; darts, cribbage, dominoes, and piped classical radio. The restaurant is partly no smoking. There's a back garden with swings, barbecue area, tables, and big boules pitch, and more tables in front facing the church. *(Recommended by Rod and Moyra Davidson, Marianne and Peter Stevens, Guy Consterdine, Elizabeth and Alan Walker, Mr and Mrs D Powell, Peter Meister, Dr Paul Khan, Richard Tosswill)*

Whitbreads ~ Lease Anne Moran ~ Real ale ~ Bar food (not winter Sun evening) ~ Restaurant ~ (01403) 820223 ~ Children welcome until 9pm ~ Open 11-3, 7(6 Sat)-11; 12-3, 7-10.30 Sun; closed evening 25 Dec ~ Bedrooms: £30(£45B)/£45(£55B)

LEWES TQ4110 Map 3
Snowdrop

South Street; off Cliffe High Street, opp S end of Malling Street just S of A26 roundabout

Eccentric and certainly unique, this basic pub has a positively laid-back atmosphere, but is enjoyed by an extraordinarily mixed bunch of people of all ages. The interior is unusual to say the least with a glorious profusion of cast-iron tables, bric-a-brac and outlandish paraphernalia that no doubt owes much to the next-door antique shop. Unfolding the rather dreamlike maritime theme, downstairs there are three ships' figureheads dotted around, walls covered with rough sawn woodplank and upstairs a huge star chart painted on a dark blue ceiling, and a sunset sea mural with waves in relief. The pub is quiet at lunchtime but a young people's preserve, and lively to match, in the evenings, when the loudish juke box plays anything from Bob Dylan or Ella Fitzgerald to Indian chants. They serve no red meat, and the good value light hearted menu includes sandwiches, burritos or large home-made pizzas (from £2.50, margherita pizza £4.75), paella (£6.50), fresh fish, and lots of well priced vegan and vegetarian dishes like delicious hearty home-made soup or hummus in pitta bread (£2.50), spicy stuffed peppers (£4.50); also Mexican seafood (£6.50); children's helpings. Five well kept real ales such as Fullers ESB, Harveys Best, Hop Back Summer Lightning, and changing guests on handpump, good coffee, friendly licensees and staff; pool and juke box. There are a few tables in the garden. *(Recommended by Colin and Ann Hunt, Pat and Tony Martin, K and J Morris, Kevin Thorpe, R J Walden, Anthony Bowen, Dan Wilson, Brad W Morley, Mike and Mary Carter)*

Free house ~ Licensees Tim and Sue May ~ Real ale ~ Bar food (12-3(2.30 Sun), 6(7Sun)-9) ~ (01273) 471018 ~ Children in eating area of bar ~ Live jazz Mon evening and other live music some weekends ~ Open 11-11; 12-10.30 Sun

LODSWORTH SU9223 Map 2
Halfway Bridge Inn ★ ⑪ ♀ ◪

Just before village, on A272 Midhurst—Petworth

Sussex Dining Pub of the Year

The food here is so very good that it remains the strongest reason for coming to this smartly civilised family-run pub, but many people do drop in solely to enjoy the well kept real ales and relaxed, friendly atmosphere – and are made just as welcome. The three or four comfortable rooms have good oak chairs and an individual mix of tables (many of them set for dining), and use attractive fabrics for the wood-railed curtains and pew cushions. Down some steps the charming no-smoking country dining room has a dresser and longcase clock. Log fires include one in a well polished kitchen range, and paintings by a local artist line the walls. Changing regularly, the interesting food at lunchtime includes open sandwiches (from £4.50; croque monsieur £4.95), crabcakes with spicy salsa (£4.95), salad of guinea fowl with fresh figs (£6.50), spring onion and parmesan risotto with rocket salad (£7.25), home-salted cod with a sweet and sour cucumber salad (£8.50), and confit of duck with a plum purée sauce (£8.95); also, roquefort soufflé with pear and walnuts (£4.50), mediterranean king prawns with garlic butter (£6.50), walnut and mushroom strudel with crème fraîche and chives or Moroccan tagine of chicken with preserved lemon, prunes and couscous (£8.50), half shoulder of roast lamb (£9.50), calf's liver, bubble and squeak with bacon snippets (£10.50), 10oz rib-eye steak with onion marmalade (£11.50), and puddings like chocolate tart with orange crème anglaise, glazed poached pear with green apple sorbet or banana toffee pie (£3); popular Sunday roasts; polite service. A good range of well kept beers includes Cheriton Pots Ale, Fullers London Pride, Gales HSB, and guests from breweries such as Brewery on Sea, Hampshire Brewery, Harveys, Hogs Back or Pilgrim; farm ciders, and a thoughtful little wine list with a changing choice by the glass. Dominoes, shove-ha'penny, cribbage, backgammon, and other games like Jenga, bagatelle, and mah jong. Ralph the jack russell is looking much trimmer these days. At the back there are attractive blue wood tables and chairs on a terrace with a pergola. They also own another pub, the Cricketers Arms at Wisborough Green. *(Recommended by J H Bell, David Crafts, John Evans, Martin and Karen Wake, Mike and Heather Watson, Tony and Wendy Hobden, Ron Shelton, E A Froggatt, Dennis Stevens, C P Baxter, Joy and Peter Heatherley, Dodie Buchanan)*

Free house ~ Licensees Sheila, Simon, Edric & James Hawkins ~ Real ale ~ Bar food (till 10pm) ~ Restaurant ~ (01798) 861281 ~ Children over 10 in restaurant ~ Jazz every 2nd Sun evening in summer ~ Open 11-3, 6-11; 12-3, 7-10.30 Sun; closed winter Sun evenings

LURGASHALL SU9327 Map 2
Noahs Ark

Village signposted from A283 N of Petworth; OS Sheet 186 map reference 936272

In summer or winter, this 16th-c local is a relaxing place to be. It's charmingly set overlooking the village green – tables on the grass in front are ideal for watching summer cricket matches – and has splendid summer flowering baskets. Inside, the two neatly furnished bars have fresh flowers or warm log fires (one in a capacious inglenook), depending on the season, well kept Greene King Abbot and IPA on handpump, and a friendly welcome from the licensees; darts, pool, shove-ha'penny, table skittles, dominoes, and cribbage. Bar food includes sandwiches (from £3.95, toasties such as bacon and mushroom £4.25), ploughman's (from £4.50), tomato and vegetable tagliatelle (£5.95), steak and kidney pudding (£6.15), lamb cutlets (£7.95), calf's liver and bacon (£8.25), smoked salmon salad (£8.75), and fillet steak (£12.75). *(Recommended by Charles Turner, J Sheldon, Wendy Arnold, Martin and Karen Wake, Elizabeth and Alan Walker)*

Greene King ~ Lease: Kathleen Grace Kennedy ~ Real ale ~ Bar food ~ Restaurant ~ (01428) 707346 ~ Children welcome ~ Open theatre annually, dances in garden in summer, in function room in winter ~ Open 11.30-3, 6-11; 12-3, 7-10.30 Sun; weekday opening half an hour later in winter

NUTHURST TQ1926 Map 3
Black Horse 🍺

Village signposted from A281 at Monks Gate 2 miles SE of Horsham

The main bar in this old-fashioned, pleasant pub has big Horsham flagstones in front of the inglenook fireplace, interesting pictures on the walls, and magazines to read. At one end it opens out into other carpeted areas including a dining room. Well kept Fullers London Pride, Greene King IPA, Harveys Sussex Best, Hop Back Summer Lightning, and Shepherd Neame Spitfire on handpump, and they hold beer festivals twice a year; Belgian fruit beers and country wines. Bar food includes sandwiches, soup (£2.95), filled baked potatoes (£4.25), lasagne (£6.95), curries (£8.25), and ostrich steaks (£9.95); the restaurant is no smoking; cribbage, Jenga, and piped music. There are seats on the front terrace with more in the back woodland streamside garden; plenty of surrounding walks *(Recommended by Mrs Jenny Cantle, John and Elizabeth Cox, Simon Collett-Jones, John Fahy, David and Carole Chapman, R and S Bentley, Eamonn and Natasha Skyrme, Susan and John Douglas, Tony Scott)*

Free house ~ Licensee Karen Jones ~ Real ale ~ Bar food ~ Restaurant ~ (01403) 891272 ~ Children welcome ~ Live jazz monthly Sun ~ Open 11-3, 6-11; 11-11 Sat; 12-10.30 Sun; 11-3, 6-11 Sat and 12-3, 7-10.30 Sun in winter

OFFHAM TQ4012 Map 3
Blacksmiths Arms

A275 N of Lewes

Most of the close-set tables in this attractive, very neatly kept red brick dining pub are ready for customers to enjoy the imaginative, consistently good food. At one end of the gleaming central counter in the open-plan bar is a huge inglenook fireplace with logs stacked at one side, and at the other is the airy dining area. Nice old prints of London, some Spy prints and several old sporting prints decorate the walls above shiny black wainscoting. Bar snacks include ploughman's (from £4.25), filled baked potatoes (£5.25), and ham and eggs (£5.75), plus soups such as creamed tomato and vegetable (£2.95), smoked chicken and chicken liver pâté with onion, apple, cranberry and port compôte (£4.50), mussel, bacon and goat's cheese tartlet with basil vinaigrette (£4.75), various curries (from £6.75), steak and kidney pie (£7.50), turkey steak filled with smoked ham and gruyère cheese with a garlic and parsley cream sauce (£8.50), lamb steak on a bed of minted creamed leeks with a port sauce or chicken and pine-nut sizzler with lemon and ginger (£8.75), grilled halibut steak with saffron and vegetable nage sauce (£8.95), steaks (from £10.75), a vegetarian special, and puddings like coconut torte with chocolate sponge and rum sauce, redcurrant brûlée or Cointreau, cappuccino, dark chocolate and brandy mousse with whipped cream flavoured with orange liqueur (£3.50); careful efficient service. Well kept Harveys Best on handpump. French windows open onto a tiny little brick and paved terrace with a couple of flowering tubs and picnic-sets with umbrellas and the car park; beware of the dangerous bend when leaving the car park; spotless disabled lavatories. *(Recommended by Ian and Carol McPherson, Mayur Shah, Patrick Renouf, Evert Haasdijk, Tony and Wendy Hobden, LM, P Rome)*

Free house ~ Licensee Jean Large ~ Real ale ~ Bar food ~ Restaurant ~ (01273) 472971 ~ Children in eating areas if over 5 ~ Open 11-3, 6.30-11; 12-3 Sun; closed Sun evening, 25 and 26 Dec

OVING SU9005 Map 2
Gribble Inn 🍺

Between A27 and A259 just E of Chichester, then should be signposted just off village road; OS Sheet 197 map reference 900050

With eight own-brewed beers, it's not surprising that this charming rose-covered thatched cottage is so well liked: Black Adder II, Ewe Brew, Fursty Ferret, Gribble Ale, Oving Bitter, Pigs Ear, Reg's Tipple, and winter Wobbler on handpump; country wines, and farm cider. But there's also a good friendly atmosphere and well presented food, and the bar has lots of heavy beams and timbering, and old country-kitchen furnishings and pews. On the left, there's a no-smoking family/dining room with pews which provides one of the biggest no-smoking areas we've so far found in a Sussex pub. Home-made bar food at lunchtime includes open sandwiches (from £3.50), platters (£4.95), three sausages with egg and beans (£5.50), and burgers (from £5.95), plus home-made soup (£2.25), creamy garlic mushrooms (£3.95), broccoli and cream cheese pasta (£5.25; larger helping £6.25), steak and mushroom pie or scrumpy chicken (£6.25), tuna steak with an asparagus and cheese mornay sauce (£7.95), steaks (from £7.25), pork steaks topped with mozzarella and sage with a mild dijon mustard and brandy cream sauce (£7.50), and home-made pies and crumbles (£3.50); children's meals (£3.25). Darts, shove-ha'penny, cribbage, dominoes, fruit machine and a separate skittle alley. There are seats in the pretty garden and a covered seating area. *(Recommended by Ann and Colin Hunt, Miss J F Reay, Brad W Morley, Peter and Audrey Dowsett, D Marsh, Tony and Wendy Hobden, Lawrence Pearse, Dr Alan Green, David Gould, David Dimock, John Donnelly, Jean-Bernard Brisset)*

Badger ~ Managers Brian and Cynthia Elderfield ~ Real ale ~ Bar food ~ (01243) 786893 ~ Children in family dining room ~ Trad jazz 1st Tues of month ~ Open 11-3, 5.30-11; 11-11 Sat; 12-10.30 Sun; 1-3, 5.30-11 Sat, 12-3, 7-10.30 Sun in winter

PETT TQ8714 Map 3
Two Sawyers 🍺

Pett Rd; off A259

Next door to this genuine and rather characterful old country pub is the Old Forge brewery which brews the Bitter and Pett Progress sold here – also, Flowers IPA, Fullers London Pride, Gales HSB, and Greene King Abbot on handpump; half a dozen wines by the glass. The meandering low-beamed rooms are simply but genuinely put together, with black band saws on cream walls, handsome iron wall lamps and stripped tables on bare boards in its two simple bars, and dark wood pub tables and cushioned banquettes in a tiny low-ceilinged snug, with a very old painted flint wall on one side; a sloping old stone floor leads down to a low-beamed restaurant. Big helpings of bar food, cooked by the easy going young landlord, include filled french bread (from £2), soup (£2.50), pâté and ploughman's, smoked cod and leek mornay or lasagne (£5.95), beef and mushroom in ale pie (£6.25), home-made chicken curry (£6.75), steak (£9), and puddings (£2.50); friendly service. An iron gate leads from a pretty suntrap front brick courtyard to a quiet back garden with shady trees, a few well spaced picnic-sets and children's play area; pétanque, darts, fruit machine, shove-ha'penny. *(Recommended by E G Parish, Jenny and Brian Seller, the Didler)*

Free house ~ Licensees Peter Neumark-Payne and Julie Payne ~ Real ale ~ Bar food ~ Restaurant ~ (01424) 812255 ~ Children in eating area of bar and restaurant ~ Blues/jazz/funk/folk Fri evenings and occasional Sun afternoons ~ Open 11-3, 6-11(maybe longer in summer); 11-11 Fri and Sat; 12-10.30 Sun ~ Bedrooms: £20/£36

PETWORTH SU9719 Map 2
Badgers 🍷

Coultershaw Bridge; just off A285 1½ miles S

Although there is a small chatty drinking area by the entrance of this stylish dining pub, with a couple of tables (and an attractive antique oak monk's chair) and some bar stools – and locals drop in regularly for a pint – this is very much somewhere to come and enjoy the particularly good food. All the rest of the space around the island bar servery is devoted to dining tables – well spaced, and an attractive mix of chairs and of tables, from old mahogany to waxed stripped pine. White walls, the deep maroon colour of the high ceiling, charming wrought-iron lamps, winter log fires, stripped shutters for the big Victorian windows, and a modicum of carefully chosen decorations including a few houseplants and dried flower arrangements induce a feeling of contented relaxation in the several linked areas; this is underlined by informal yet punctilious service. Besides the good if not cheap restaurant menu, the imaginative changing choice of attractively presented bar dishes might include tiger prawns in sherry and ginger sauce (£5.95), tapas (£6.95), pigeon breast with cabbage and bacon potato cake (£7.95), pheasant with rosti (£10.95), and a good choice of shellfish. Please do record for us the price and details of any other dishes you particularly enjoy here. Well kept Badger Best, Hop Back Summer Lightning and Theakstons Best on handpump, with a good range of well chosen house wines and a fine list by the bottle; maybe faint piped music (the dominant sound is quiet conversation). A terrace by a waterlily pool has stylish metal garden furniture under parasols, and some solid old-fashioned wooden seats. No motorcyclists. *(Recommended by Martin and Karen Wake, M Campbell, David Cullen, Emma Stent, Michael Hill, Dodie Buchanan)*

Free house ~ Licensee Mr Arlette ~ Real ale ~ Bar food ~ Restaurant ~ (01798) 342651 ~ Children over 5 may be allowed away from bar

PLAYDEN TQ9121 Map 3
Peace & Plenty
A268/B2082

Popular for its good, enjoyable food, this cottagey dining pub has a cosy bar with pot plants and dried flowers, deep pink walls and shelves attractively crowded with lots of china, little pictures, brass implements, and cat paraphernalia, small lamps creating a warm glow, a good mix of tables, and a woodburning stove in a big inglenook at one end with comfortable armchairs either side; gentle classical piped radio. There are two similarly cosy cottagey dining areas. Bar food might include home-made soup (£2.95), ham and egg (£4.95), well liked roast beef in a giant yorkshire pudding (£7.75), lamb curry or salmon fishcakes with a light lemon sauce (£7.95), steak and kidney pudding (£8.25), chicken wellington (£9.25), seafood parcel (£9.40), mediterranean avocado bake with corn on the cob and garlic bread (£11.95), and puddings such as treacle pudding or chocolate ice-cream sundae (£2.95); they will add a 10% service charge unless you ask them not to. Well kept Greene King IPA, Abbot and Triumph on handpump from a small counter; attentive service. The friendly little children's room has a comfy sofa, Sega games, toys, and books; cards, trivial pursuit, and mind trap on each table. There are seats in the pretty flowery garden though there is traffic noise. *(Recommended by B and M Parkin, Brenda and Stuart Naylor, D Buckley, S Cutier, Ray Watson, Pat and Baz Turvill, Paula Williams, Mr and Mrs P Eastwood, G Washington)*

Free house ~ Licensee Mrs Yvonne Thomas ~ Real ale ~ Bar food (11-9.30) ~ Restaurant ~ (01797) 280342 ~ Children welcome ~ Open 11-11; 12-10.30 Sun; closed 25 and 26 Dec

PUNNETTS TOWN TQ6220 Map 3
Three Cups 🍺
B2096 towards Battle

On either side of this high ridge of the Weald are plenty of good walks – and this unspoilt traditional local is just the place to head for afterwards; the pub dogs Monty and Lettie and the cat Hattie welcome other dogs (on a lead). The peaceful and friendly long low-beamed bar has attractive panelling, comfortable seats including some in big bay windows overlooking a small green, and a log fire in the big fireplace under a black mantlebeam dated 1696. A partly no-smoking back dining room leads out to a small covered terrace with seats in the garden beyond. Decent bar food includes sandwiches (from £2), soup (£2.50), ham and eggs (£4), ploughman's (£4.25), meaty or vegetarian lasagne or steak in ale pie (£5.50), chicken in a mushroom and red wine sauce (£6), grilled trout with almonds (£7), sirloin steak (£8.50), several home-made daily specials like moussaka, quiche, and devilled kidneys, and puddings such as fruit crumble or banoffee pie (£2.50); children's meals (from £3), and Sunday roast (£5.25). Well kept Greene King IPA and Abbot, Harveys, and two weekly guest beers on handpump; darts, shove-ha'penny, cribbage, and dominoes. *(Recommended by David and Betty Gittings, Pat and Clive Sherriff)*

Greene King ~ Tenants Colin and Barbara Wood ~ Real ale ~ Bar food ~ (01435) 830252 ~ Children welcome ~ Open 11.30-3, 6.30-11; 11.30-11 Sat; 12-10.30 Sun

RUSHLAKE GREEN TQ6218 Map 3
Horse & Groom
Village signposted off B2096 Heathfield—Battle

Opposite the large village green, this country local has pretty flowering tubs, rustic picnic-sets on either side of the main door, and more in the garden among newly planted flowerbeds. Inside on the right is the heavily beamed dining room with guns and hunting trophies on the walls, plenty of wheelback chairs around pubby tables, and a log fire. The little L-shaped bar (more low beams – watch your head) is simply furnished with high bar stools and bar chairs where there are usually a few regulars chatting, red plush cushioned wall seats and a few brocaded cushioned stools, and a little brick fireplace with some brass items on the mantlepiece; horsebrasses and photographs of the pub and local scenes on the walls, and fresh flowers. A little room down a step has jockeys' colours and jockey photographs and watercolours of the pub, and hops on the ceiling. Bar food includes sandwiches, fresh tuna (£5.50), kedgeree (£6.25), braised lamb fillet in blackcurrant sauce (£7.95), fresh marlin (£8.50), and fried smoked salmon fillet in a piquant mayonnaise or goujons of salmon stir fried with chillies (£9.50). Well kept Greene King IPA, Harveys Sussex, and a guest beer on handpump. The licensees also own the Star in Old Heathfield. *(Recommended by Gavin May)*

Free house ~ Licensees Mike and Sue Chappel ~ Real ale ~ Bar food ~ Restaurant ~ (01435) 830320 ~ Children in eating area of bar and restaurant ~ Maybe live music Sun ~ Open 11.30-3, 6-11; 12-4, 7-10.30 Sun

RYE TQ9220 Map 3
Mermaid ♀ 🛏
Mermaid Street

It would be a shame not to include this lovely hotel with its striking black and white timbered façade dating back mainly to the 15th and 16th centuries on the grounds that it is not a pub, because it does have a small unchanging back bar with well kept if not cheap Marstons Pedigree and Morlands Old Speckled Hen – kept in cellars that date back seven centuries. A mix of quite closely set furnishings includes Victorian gothic carved oak chairs, older but plainer oak seats and more modern ones in character, and a massive deeply polished bressumer beam across one wall for the huge inglenook fireplace; three antique but not ancient wall paintings show old English scenes. Bar food includes soup (£3.50), filled french bread (£5), vegetarian dish (£6.50), local codling (£7.50), cold roast beef or ham salad (£10), entrecote steak (£10.70), and puddings like pear and almond tart (£5); there's a smart restaurant. Good wine list, piped music, chess and cards. Seats on a small back terrace overlook the car park – where Morris dancing teams may vie with each other on some bank holiday weekends. *(Recommended by Pat and Baz Turvill, J Sheldon, Paul S McPherson, David and Nina Pugsley, Sharon Berry, Elizabeth and Alan Walker, Kerry Law, Simon Smith, the Didler)*

Free house ~ Licensees Robert Pinwill and Mrs J Blincow ~ Real ale ~ Bar food (11-6 in summer) ~ Restaurant ~ (01797) 223065 ~ Well behaved children welcome ~ Open 11-11; 12-10.30 Sun

Ypres Castle ♀ ◖

Gun Garden; steps up from A259, or down past Ypres Tower from Church Square

Given that this simple pub has the feel of a good local, it's quite a surprise to find that they serve particularly enjoyable, interesting food. It's fairly spartan, with basic furnishings, local events posters and so forth – what transforms it is the friendly atmosphere, which seems particularly warm and embracing on a blustery winter's night; and the three friendly labradors do their bit to help. The nicest place to eat is in a quieter room beyond the bar with simple but comfortable wall seats and local pictures; the dining room is no smoking. What's on the menu depends on what the landlord's found in the markets – not just the fresh local fish and seafood, but the products of his weekly trips to London. Besides good value filled baguettes (from £2), there might be soup (£2.50), ploughman's (from £4.50), good spinach and ricotta filled crêpes (£6.65), roast fillet of cod (£7.70), moules marinières (£7.95), excellent scallops in garlic butter (£10.95), and daily specials such as stir-fried pasta with tomato and garlic sauce (£5.85), grilled Biscay sardines (£6.85), chicken, bacon and mushrooms in a white wine sauce (£7.95), duck with morello cherry and brandy sauce (£9.40), tasty rack of Marsh lamb with a mint and redcurrant glaze (£9.60), monkfish in a creamy garlic sauce (£9.95), lovely grilled bass or sirloin steak (£10.95), and puddings (£2.75); good fresh vegetables. Well kept Badger Tanglefoot, Bass, Charles Wells Bombardier, Harveys Best, and Youngs on handpump, good value wine (especially by the bottle) with lots by the glass, and farm cider; maybe old yachting magazines to leaf through. Darts, shove-ha'penny, dominoes, cribbage, and piped jazz or classical music. In summer, there's the big bonus of a sizeable lawn; picnic-sets out here have a fine view out over the River Rother winding its way through the shore marshes. Ypres, pub and tower, is pronounced WWI-style, as Wipers. *(Recommended by Ian and Carol McPherson, Val and Alan Green, Kerry Law, Simon Smith, Pat and Baz Turvill, Joan and Andrew Life, Nigel and Olga Wikeley)*

Free house ~ Licensee R J Pearce ~ Real ale ~ Bar food (12-5.30, 6.30-10 in summer; 12-2.30, 7-10 in winter) ~ Restaurant ~ (01797) 223248 ~ Children welcome until 9pm ~ Blues Sun evening ~ Open 12-11(10.30 Sun)

SALEHURST TQ7424 Map 3
Salehurst Halt ♀

Village signposted from Robertsbridge bypass on A21 Tunbridge Wells—Battle Rd

With a chatty and friendly atmosphere, this little village local is a very pleasant place for a drink or enjoyable meal. The L-shaped bar has good plain wooden tables and chairs on flagstones at one end, a cushioned window seat, beams, a little open brick fireplace, a time punch clock and olde worlde pictures; lots of hops on a big beam divide this from the beamed carpeted area with its mix of tables, wheelback and farmhouse chairs, and a half wall leads to a dining area. Nice home-made food includes lunchtime sandwiches (from £2.50), winter soup (£2.95), burgers (from £5.50), cod and prawn bake or lasagne £5.95), cider chicken or beef in ale pie (£7.95), fish parcel (£8.95), steaks (from £8.95), and monkfish in mediterranean-style sauce (£9.95). There are fresh flowers on the bar, well kept Harveys Best on handpump, and good wines. The little garden has terraces and picnic-sets, the window boxes and tubs are very pretty, and there's an attractive 14th-c church almost next door. *(Recommended by Peter Meister, Sinclair Robieson, Comus Elliott, Tony and Rachel Schendel, Janet and Colin Roe, Jason Caulkin)*

Free house ~ Licensees Vicky and Ozker Hassan ~ Real ale ~ Bar food ~ (01580) 880620 ~ Children welcome ~ Open 12-3, 7(6 Fri)-11; closed Mon

SCAYNES HILL TQ3623 Map 3
Sloop

Freshfield Lock; at top of Scaynes Hill by petrol station turn N off A272 into Church Rd, keep on for 1½ miles and then follow Freshfield signpost

After a visit to the nearby lakeside gardens of Sheffield Park or a ride on the Bluebell Line steam railway, this country pub is a popular place to come for a meal. The long saloon bar has wheelbacks and other chairs around pubby tables, a warmly friendly atmosphere, and well kept Greene King IPA and Harveys Best on handpump, and a decent wine list; maybe piped music; there are benches in the old-fashioned brick porch. Good home-made bar food might include soup (£3.75), filled french sticks (from £3.75), green-lip mussels grilled with a cider, cream and stilton sauce (£4.50), crab cake with courgette and pepper chutney (£4.95), sausages and mash with onion gravy (£6.95), home-made fish pie (£7.25), home-made chicken curry (£7.95), calf's liver and bacon with a sauce diable (£10.50), 10oz rib-eye steak (£11.95), and puddings such as brûléed lemon tart with a blackcurrant coulis, sticky toffee pudding or chocolate nemesis (£3.75); best to book. The basic but airy public bar has stripped woodwork, settles and cushioned stools on the bare boards, and a small room leading off is used for extra dining. This is a lovely spot beside what used to be the Ouse canal with a sheltered garden and lots of tables to enjoy the sunshine and birdsong. *(Recommended by Sara Riley, P W Taylor, Mayur Shah, John Knighton, Charles Parry, Mr Payne, Lisa Day)*

Greene King ~ Tenant Ian Philpots ~ Real ale ~ Bar food (not Sun evening) ~ (01444) 831219 ~ Well behaved children welcome ~ Open 11.30-3, 6-11; 12 3, 7-10.30 Sun; closed evenings 25 and 26 Dec and 1 Jan

SEAFORD TV4899 Map 3
Golden Galleon 🍴 ♟ 🍺

Exceat Bridge; A259 Seaford—Eastbourne, near Cuckmere

By the time this book is published, a new bar and food servery will have been added to this immensely popular pub, new ladies' lavatories with baby changing facilities and a disabled lavatory will have been opened, the gents' will have been refurbished, and extra car parking built. It does get very busy, particularly on sunny weekends, but the efficient staff remain cheerful despite the crowds. Two thirds of the premises are no smoking – there's a conservatory and river room, and a spreading main bar with high trussed and pitched rafters which create quite an airy feel. A fine choice of real ales includes their own from the little microbrewery on site. Brewed by the landlord's brother-in-law, they might include Cuckmere Haven Best, Guv'nor, Golden Peace, an old-fashioned cask conditioned stout, Saxon King, and seasonal beers; they also brew their own keg conditioned lager, as well as keeping other ales like Bass, Greene King Abbot and IPA, Hardy Royal Oak, Hart Ambassador and Squirrels Hoard, Old Forge Summer Eclipse and Bitter, and Shepherd Neame Bishops Finger on handpump or tapped from the cask, and hold occasional beer festivals; farm ciders, good wines by the glass, a decent selection of malts, continental brandies, Italian liqueurs, and cappuccino or espresso coffee. Most people, however, come to enjoy the good food which might include home-made soups (£3), bruschetta romana (a chunk of garlic bread topped with warm plum tomatoes, garlic, onion, finely chopped celery, and fennel, £3.60), ploughman's (from £4.30), filled baked potatoes (from £5.20), Sardinian sardines or smoked salmon from their own smokery (£5.40), daily fresh local fish (from £6.80), meaty, vegetarian or seafood lasagne (£7.90), a medley of Italian sausages with spicy mediterranean beans (£8.25), an Italian platter (£9), steaks (from £10.70), stincotto (£10.95), fresh local bass with seasoned breadcrumb stuffing and fresh herbs or fresh ostrich steak with a wild mushroom, sweet pepper, cream and wine sauce (£13), and puddings such as tiramisu made by the landlord's mother or summer pudding (£3); cold snacks and a few hot dishes are sold all day, and they are hoping to start a Sunday carvery. There are plenty of walks – along the river, down to the sea or inland to Friston Forest and the downs; children's play area and plenty of tables in the sloping garden with views towards the Cuckmere estuary and Seven Sisters Country Park. *(Recommended by Tony and Wendy Hobden, Joy and Peter Heatherley, Lawrence Pearse, John Beeken, Tim and Pam Moorey, Mike Wells, Tony Scott, Simon Collett-Jones, David and Carole Chapman, P Rome, N B Thompson, Anthony Bowen, Janet and Colin Roe)*

Own brew ~ Licensee Stefano Diella ~ Real ale ~ Bar food ~ (01323) 892247 ~ Children in eating area of bar ~ Open 11-11; 12-4 Sun; closed Sun evenings except over bank holidays

TILLINGTON SU9621 Map 2
Horse Guards 🍽 🍷 🛏

Village signed off A272 Midhurst—Petworth

As well as being a fine place to come for a meal, this neatly kept 300-year-old inn is also enjoyed by readers as somewhere to spend the weekend – and the breakfasts are first class. It's run by warmly friendly and experienced licensees who do a marvellous job in very busy conditions, but still have time to show you to your table. The setting is pretty with a lovely view beyond the village to the Rother Valley from the seat in the big black-panelled bow window of the cosy beamed front bar – which also has some good country furniture and a log fire. A wide choice of good, interesting food includes lunchtime bar snacks such as sandwiches (from £3.40), ploughman's (£5.80), good caesar salad (from £5.55), and seafood pie or mushroom and bacon risotto with a poached egg and shaved parmesan (£7.95), as well as spicy crab linguine (£5.50), moules marinières (£5.95), warm salad of calf's liver goujons rolled in oatmeal with dijon mustard, croutons and vinaigrette (£6.25), thai-style stir fry of mixed vegetables on wild rice or casserole of rabbit in a rich port and cranberry sauce (£7.75), beef, mushroom and ale pie (£8.25), and sirloin steak (£12.95), with evening specials like chilled pear and watercress soup (£4.15), herrings in sour cream with salad and sauerkraut (£5.25), scallop and monkfish warm salad (£13.95), fresh Selsey lobster (from £12.50), and roast rack of lamb with herb jus (£14.25); excellent Sunday roast beef with yorkshire pudding (£9.45) or roast partridge with game chips (£13.95); when you book a table, you will be asked whether you wish a smoking or no-smoking area. The good wine list usually has a dozen by the glass; well kept Badger Best and Wadworths 6X on handpump, and good espresso and cappuccino coffee. Darts, and cribbage. There's a terrace outside, and more tables and chairs in a sheltered garden behind. The church opposite is 800 years old. *(Recommended by W Ruxton, J H Bell, L Granville, B and M Kendall, Mr and Mrs D E Powell, R E Syrett, Martin and Karen Wake, Mike and Heather Watson, G D Sharpe, Evelyn and Derek Walter, Ian and Jane Irving, Wendy Arnold, John Evans, Brian Mills, John Knighton)*

Free house ~ Licensees Lesley and Aidan Nugent ~ Real ale ~ Bar food ~ Restaurant ~ (01798) 342332 ~ Children in eating area of bar; must be over 8 in evening ~ Open 11-3, 6-11; 12-3, 6-10.30 Sun ~ Bedrooms: /£70B

WEST ASHLING SU8107 Map 2
Richmond Arms 🍺

Mill Lane; from B2146 in village follow Hambrook signpost

With a good choice of real ales on handpump, this out-of-the-way village pub is a pleasant place for a quiet midweek drink. Well kept on handpump, there might be Adnams Southwold, Greene King IPA and Abbot, Harveys Sussex, Hop Back Summer Lightning, and Timothy Taylor Landlord. The main bar, dominated by the central servery, has a 1930s feel with its long wall benches, library chairs and black tables; there's a dark wooden dado with a cream wall in one part and wallpaper in the other, wooden ducks on the picture rails and pictures on the walls, and an open fire in the stripped brick fireplace; piped music. Bar food includes toasties (from £1.95), filled french bread (£2.95), cheesy chips and chilli (£4.45), home-cooked ham and eggs (£5.95), and home-made steak and kidney pudding (£6.45). Darts, pool, bar billiards, table skittles, dominoes, cribbage, fruit machine, and skittle alley. There's a pergola, and some picnic-sets by the car park. *(Recommended by Ann and Colin Hunt)*

Greene King ~ Tenants Alan and Dianne Gurney ~ Real ale ~ Bar food ~ (01243) 575730 ~ Children welcome ~ Open 11-2.30(3 Sat), 5.30-11; 12-10.30 Sun

WILMINGTON TQ5404 Map 3
Giants Rest

Just off A27

New licensees have brought a cheery lease of life to this Victorian pub at the foot of the South Downs and quite literally at the foot of the impressive chalk-carved Long

Man of Wilmington. The long wood floored bar and three adjacent open areas are simply furnished with old pews and pine tables with period pictures and local paintings dotted around. Well presented and very reasonably priced bar food from a changing blackboard includes soup (£2.50), garlic mushrooms (£3), smoked salmon pâté (£3.50), avocado and prawns (£4), several vegetarian dishes like goat's cheese tart with olives and onion (£5) and asparagus and sweetcorn crêpes (£7.50), salmon fishcakes with lemon mayonnaise or rabbit and bacon pie (£7), chicken breast in creamy leek and stilton sauce (£7.50), plaice or skate (£9) and puddings like gooseberry crumble or chocolate pudding with chocolate sauce (£3). As well as orange juice and grapefruit juice squeezed in front of you on the bar, their three well kept real ales are Harveys Best, Hop Back Summer Lightning, and a guest like Hook Norton on handpump. There are a couple of rustic tables and chairs on the front lawn. *(Recommended by Darly Graton, Graeme Gulibert, Catherine and Richard Preston, Alan Skull, John Beeken)*

Free house ~ Licensees Adrian and Rebecca Hillman ~ Real ale ~ Bar food ~ (01323) 870207 ~ Children in family areas ~ Open 11-3, 6-11; 12-3, 7-10.30 Sun

WINEHAM TQ2320 Map 3
Royal Oak
Village signposted from A272 and B2116

One reader was delighted to find this old-fashioned pub had not changed since he last visited it fifteen years earlier. There are logs burning in an enormous inglenook fireplace with its cast-iron Royal Oak fireback, a stuffed ferret and lizard, a collection of jugs, ancient corkscrews decorating the very low beams above the serving counter, racing plates, tools and a coach horn on the walls, maybe a nice young tabby cat, and simple furnishings. Well kept beers tapped from the cask in a still room include Harveys Best and Wadworths 6X, and the back parlour has views of quiet countryside; darts, shove-ha'penny, dominoes, cribbage. There's a limited range of bar snacks such as home-made winter soup (£2), fresh-cut or toasted sandwiches (from £2, home-cooked roast beef £2.25 or lovely smoked salmon £2.50), and ploughman's (from £3.95); courteous service – the pub has been in the same family for over 50 years. It can get very busy at weekends and on summer evenings. The charming frontage has a lawn with wooden tables by a well. On a clear day sharp-eyed male readers may be able to catch a glimpse of Chanctonbury Ring from the window in the gents'. No children inside. *(Recommended by Tim Locke)*

Inn Business ~ Tenant Tim Peacock ~ Real ale ~ Bar food ~ (01444) 881252 ~ Open 11-2.30, 5.30(6 Sat)-11; 12-3, 7-10.30 Sun

WISBOROUGH GREEN TQ0526 Map 3
Cricketers Arms ♀
Loxwood Road; just off A272 Billingshurst—Petworth

Right on the green, this attractive old pub has tables out by the cricket field. On still summer days hot-air balloons may set off from here, and in autumn the chestnut trees furnish ammunition for the pub's conker competition, the winner gaining a crown spiked with chestnuts – and the title William the Conkerer. The pub, which has a lovely outlook over the green, has recently been taken over by the Hawkinses, who have made such a success of the Halfway Bridge Inn over at Lodsworth Bridge. They've opened up the low-beamed bar, but there's still a good local feel in the area by the counter near the entrance, with the bare-boards public area over on the right dominated by a huge double-sided woodburning stove in the central chimney breast. The other side, with another woodburning stove, is largely given over to food, with stripped brick walls and low beams, panelled dado, rugs on its parquet flooor, and a variety of chairs and pews around its miscellaneous stripped tables; there are some cricketing prints. Good food includes soup (£3.25), sandwiches (from £3.95), avocado, goats cheese and tomato (£4.95), mushroom and celeriac curry (£7.25), grilled tuna steak with nicoise salad or poached chicken breast with dijon mustard sauce (£8.95), duck breast with brandy and peach sauce (£11.50) with puddings such as apple pie, lemon tart with raspberry coulis and a zesty bread and butter pudding (£3.50). Well kept Cheriton Potts, Fullers London Pride, Wadworths 6X and a gust like Tetleys on handpump, a good choice of wines by the glass, cheerful competent service. *(Recommended by Joy and Peter Heatherley, Margaret Ross, David and Carole Chapman)*

Whitbreads ~ Lease: Sheila, Edric, Simon and James Hawkins; Manageress Julie Mander ~ Bar food (12-2, 7-10) ~ Restaurant ~ (01403) 700369 ~ Jazz Sun lunchtimes ~ Open 11-2.30, 5.30-11; 12-3, 7-10.30 Sun

WITHYHAM TQ4935 Map 3
Dorset Arms
B2110

In pleasant countryside, this bustling 16th-c inn is well liked for its good food, so it's usually best to book a table. The bar has a traditional welcoming atmosphere, sturdy tables and simple country seats on the wide oak floorboards, quite a few silk flower decorations, and a good log fire in the stone Tudor fireplace. The good bar food includes home-made soup (£2.35), quite a few sandwiches (from £2.35; toasties from £2.45), ploughman's (from £3.95), filled baked potatoes (from £4.50), spinach and feta cheese goujons (£4.95), omelettes (£5.25), home-roasted ham and egg (£5.65), crispy cod and chips (£5.75), baked trout (£6.95), rump steak (£7.95), and home-made daily specials such as cheesy topped ratatouille (£5.25), chicken curry (£5.50), lamb's liver with bacon and onions (£5.75), crispy duck breast or filo topped salmon and prawn pie (£6.25), popular half-shoulder of lamb (£7.50), and puddings such as deep lemon tart, white chocolate cheesecake with Baileys, and rhubarb fool (£3.50); the pretty restaurant is no smoking. Well kept Harveys Best, Pale Ale, Mild and seasonal beers on handpump, and a reasonable wine list including some local ones. Darts, dominoes, shove-ha'penny, cribbage, fruit machine, and piped music. There are white tables on a brick terrace by the small green. The countryside around here is nice, and the nearby church has a memorial to Vita Sackville-West. *(Recommended by John and Phyllis Maloney, R and S Bentley, Peter Meister, Alan Kilpatrick, Tony Scott, Martin Wright, Jason Caulkin)*

Harveys ~ Tenants John and Sue Pryor ~ Real ale ~ Bar food (not Sun or Mon evenings) ~ Restaurant ~ (01892) 770278 ~ Children in restaurant ~ Open 11.30-3, 5.30(6 Sat)-11; 12-3, 7-10.30 Sun

---

Lucky Dip

Besides the fully inspected pubs, you might like to try these Lucky Dips recommended to us and described by readers (if you do, please send us reports):

Alfriston [TQ5203]
☆ *George* [High St]: Welcoming 14th-c timbered inn, ancient low beams, huge inglenook, jovial landlord, hard-working staff, popular home-made bar food inc lots of good fish and fresh veg in lively public bar, intimate candlelit restaurant or garden dining room, beers such as Courage Best, Fullers London Pride, Harveys, Marstons and Morlands Old Speckled Hen; comfortable attractive bedrooms, lovely village, fine riverside walks down to Cuckmere Haven *(Tony and Shirley Albert, G Hallett, Phyl and Jack Street)*
☆ *Star* [High St]: Fascinating frontage decorated with fine medieval carvings, striking figurehead red lion on the corner; stolid quiet heavy-beamed bar with medieval sanctuary post, fine antique furnishings, big log fire in Tudor fireplace, some no-smoking areas; limited choice of simple though not cheap bar food, Badger Tanglefoot and Bass, restaurant,

comfortable bedrooms in up-to-date part behind, open all day summer *(Paul and Sandra Embleton, LYM, Mike Wells, Janet and Colin Roe, Liz Bell, the Didler)*
Angmering [TQ0704]
Spotted Cow [High St]: Well kept Fullers London Pride, Harveys, King & Barnes Sussex, Morlands Old Speckled Hen and a beer brewed locally for the pub, good bar food from imaginative sandwiches up (very popular weekday lunchtimes with older people), friendly efficient service, smuggling history; restaurant, roomy garden, good play area; open all day summer w/e (very busy then), lovely walk to Highdown hill fort *(Bruce Bird, R T and J C Moggridge)*
Ardingly [TQ3429]
☆ *Gardeners Arms* [B2028 2 miles N]: Immaculately refurbished olde-worlde dining pub very popular for consistently good if not cheap fresh home-made food esp fresh fish, big

inglenook log fire, service pleasant and efficient even when crowded, well kept Boddingtons, Harveys and Theakstons, morning coffee and tea, attractive decorations, maybe soft piped music, no children; well spaced tables out among small trees, handy for Borde Hill and Wakehurst Place *(Martin and Karen Wake, Ian and Carol McPherson, Tony Scott, G Simpson, John Pettit, D Wilcox, R and S Bentley, Derek and Maggie Washington)*

Arlington [TQ5407]

☆ *Old Oak* [Caneheath, off A22 or A27]: 17th-c former almshouses, with relaxing and spacious open-plan L-shaped heavily beamed bar, dining room, good reasonably priced promptly served home-made food, well kept Badger, Harveys and usually a guest beer tapped from the cask, friendly helpful landlord, log fires, no music, peaceful garden; children allowed, handy for Abbotswood nature reserve *(J H Bell, Alan Skull, John Beeken, Mr and Mrs A Albert, BB)*

☆ *Yew Tree* [off A22 nr Hailsham, or A27 W of Polegate]: Very generous helpings of wholesome home cooking inc delicious puddings in neatly modernised two-bar village local with new conservatory, well kept Fullers London Pride, Harveys, Morlands Old Speckled Hen and Worthington BB, log fires, efficient cheery service, subdued piped music, darts, maybe eggs for sale; good big garden and play area, by paddock with farm animals *(BB, John Beeken, Enid and Henry Stephens, H Orchard, LM, Tony Scott, R D and S R Knight, John Boyle)*

Arundel [TQ0107]

☆ *Black Rabbit* [Mill Rd, Offham; keep on and don't give up!]: Big touristy riverside pub, plenty of provision for families, best on a quiet day – lovely spot, with lots of tables out looking across to bird-reserve water-meadows and castle; Badger IPA, Best and Tanglefoot and guest ales, log fires, wide range of generous food inc good salad bar, restaurant, open all day, doubling as summer tea shop; summer boat trips, good walks *(John Beeken, David and Carole Chapman, Mr and Mrs Sweeney, David Gould, Eamonn and Natasha Skyrme, Roger and Pauline Pearce, LM, Tony Scott)*

Kings Arms [Kings Arms Hill]: Cosy two-bar local with good fire in quiet lounge, well kept Harveys and Hopback Summer Lightning or Crop Circle, guests such as Fullers London Pride and Gales HSB, food inc lunchtime sandwiches and huge ploughman's, Sun bar nibbles, friendly staff; darts and piped music in public bar, third small room up a step, large dog; small back yard, open all day *(Tony Scott, John Donnelly, David and Carole Chapman)*

Norfolk Arms [High St]: Comfortable genuinely old hotel with hearty good value food, well kept Whitbreads and guest beers such as Greene King Abbot, town bar and separate hotel bar and lounge; restaurant, ample parking under coach arch, bedrooms *(R T and J C Moggridge)*

Swan [High St]: Smartly refurbished open-plan L-shaped bar with beatiful woodwork and attractive matching fittings, beaten brass former inn-sign hanging on wall, good value food inc vegetarian, full range of Arundel beers and a couple of guest beers, all well kept, friendly young staff; piped music can get loud – small side room a bit quieter; restaurant, good bedrooms *(LYM, Bruce Bird, David and Carole Chapman, Mark Matthewman)*

White Swan [Chichester Rd (A27)]: Spotless, with smart staff, well kept Arundel ales, afternoon tea *(Colin and Ann Hunt)*

Balcombe [TQ3033]

Cowdray Arms [London Rd (B2036/B2110 N of village)]: Roomy country pub filling quickly at lunchtime for good choice of well prepared and presented food inc some interesting dishes, good helpings, attentive welcoming service, well kept Beards, Harveys and guest such as Adnams, Buckleys or Thwaites Mild, occasional beer festivals, spacious no-smoking restaurant; children welcome, garden with good play area *(DWAJ, Tony Scott, Bruce Bird, Dr and Mrs D J Walker)*

Barcombe [TQ4214]

Anglers Rest [Barcombe Mills; off A26 N of Lewes]: Homely welcoming Victorian brick pub in quiet spot nr River Ouse, changing ales such as Adnams Broadside, Batemans Valiant, Harveys Best and Mansfield Old Baily; extensive imaginative menu (no sandwiches) inc good puddings, big collection of miniatures and prints of surrounding area; large tree-sheltered garden with verandah, play house; good walks *(John Beeken)*

Beckley [TQ8523]

Rose & Crown [B2088 towards Northiam]: Character coaching inn with friendly and unspoilt local feel, simple choice of very generous good freshly prepared food, Adnams Broadside, Harveys and at least three guest beers changing weekly basis; garden with swing *(Conrad and Alison Freezer)*

Bepton [SU8618]

Country Inn [Severals Rd]: Properly old-fashioned, with real fire, darts-playing locals, sensible but not over-priced, welcoming landlord *(Jill Silversides, Barry Brown)*

Bexhill [TQ7107]

Sovereign [part of Cooden Beach Hotel]: Comfortable hotel bar with good choice of lunchtime bar food, well kept Bass and Harveys, spacious no-smoking area; big-screen TV; open all day, cream teas, bedrooms *(Richard Lewis)*

Billingshurst [TQ0925]

Olde Six Bells [High St (A29)]: Picturesque partly 14th-c flagstoned and timbered pub with well kept King & Barnes, cheerful landlord, inglenook fireplace, pretty roadside garden *(Colin and Janet Roe, Tony and Wendy Hobden, LYM)*

Binsted [SU9806]

☆ *Black Horse* [Binsted Lane; about 2 miles W of Arundel, turn S off A27 towards Binsted]: Cheery and pretty 17th-c pub with ochre walls and open fire in big comfortable bar, seven or eight well kept ales, darts and bar billiards one end, warmly welcoming licensees, bar food inc generous sandwiches and well presented freshly cooked specials, wider range in back conservatory restaurant, Courage Directors, Gales HSB, Harveys Best, Hop Back Summer Lightning and King & Barnes, shelf of sweetie jars, greyhound racing trophies; piped music; tables on terrace, idyllic garden, views over valley; bedrooms *(John Donnelly, Mrs Romey Heaton, JDM, KM, BB)*

Birdham [SU8200]

Bell [A286 SW of Chichester]: Open-plan, with Bass, Fullers London Pride and Worthington BB, dining area, relaxing atmosphere; garden *(SLC)*

Bolney [TQ2623]

Eight Bells [The Street]: Friendly, clean and comfortable, well kept Harveys and Flowers Original, good promptly served food, local paintings, open fires; occasional live music, garden *(Bruce Bird)*

Bosham [SU8003]

Anchor Bleu [High St]: Lovely waterside position in attractive village, sea and boat views, little terrace outside massive wheel-operated bulkhead door to ward off high tides (cars parked on seaward side often submerged); low beams and flagstones, log-effect gas fire, cosy feel out of season, Courage Best and Directors, Ind Coope Burton, Theakstons, Scottish Courage beers, open all day *(Betsy and Peter Little, Tony Scott, JDM, KM, LYM, David and Carole Chapman, Ian Phillips, Ann and Colin Hunt)*

Brighton [TQ3105]

Basketmakers Arms [Gloucester Rd]: Busy corner pub with good food choice, Gales and guest beers *(the Didler)*

Cobblers Thumb [New England Rd]: Friendly happy local, surprisingly large and grand, obliging service, well kept Badger Tanglefoot, Fullers London Pride and Harveys, basic food; separate rooms for music, pool and conversation *(Dan Wilson)*

☆ *Colonnade* [New Rd, off North St; by Theatre Royal]: Small but beautifully kept, with velvet, shining brass, gleaming mirrors, interesting pre-war playbills and lots of signed theatrical photographs, good friendly service even when very busy, some snacks esp salt beef sandwiches (free seafood nibbles Sun lunchtime instead), particularly well kept Boddingtons, Flowers and Harveys (early-evening weekday happy hour), good choice of house wines, tiny front terrace; next to Theatre Royal, they take interval orders *(Tim Barrow, Sue Demont)*

☆ *Cricketers* [Black Lion St]: Bustling down-to-earth town pub, very well run, with ageing Victorian furnishings and lots of interesting bric-a-brac – even a stuffed bear; well kept Courage Directors, Morlands Old Speckled Hen and Wadworths 6X tapped from the cask, friendly staff, usual well priced lunchtime bar food inc vegetarian and fresh veg in upstairs bar, restaurant (where children allowed) and covered ex-stables courtyard bar; piped music; open all day *(Tony Scott, Tony and Wendy Hobden, Ann and Colin Hunt, Tom Espley, LYM, Jean-Bernard Brisset)*

Evening Star [Surrey St]: Very popular for half a dozen or more well kept interesting changing ales inc their own Skinners brews; enthusiastic landlord, changing farm ciders, good lunchtime food (not Sun), old-fashioned atmosphere, bare boards, simple furnishings, good mix of customers, railway memorabilia; live music nights *(Bruce Bird)*

Font & Firkin [Union St, The Lanes]: Clever circular church refurbishment (still has pulpit and bell pulls, alongside Sunday comedians and other live entertainment), sturdy old furnishings, some tables up on narrow balcony around cupola base, pleasant service, good choice of well kept ales inc some brewed here, decent food inc good value Sun roasts; good loud music, can be packed with young people at night *(Tim Barrow, Sue Demont, Pat and Tony Martin, R Cooper, BB)*

☆ *Greys* [Southover St, Kemp Town]: Buoyant atmosphere in very small basic single-room corner local with two or three rough and ready tables for eating – must book, strongly recommended for limited choice of good food lunchtime and Tues-Thurs evenings, Belgian chef with some adventurous original recipes; very friendly staff, well kept Flowers, Fullers London Pride, guest beers and Belgian bottled beers, well chosen and reproduced piped music, interesting live music Sun lunchtime (more during Brighton Festival) *(R T and J C Moggridge, Tim Barrow, Sue Demont, BB)*

King & Queen [Marlborough Pl]: Medieval-style lofty main hall with well kept Theakstons Best and XB from long bar, generous good value food, friendly service, pool table, flagstoned courtyard; good free jazz most evenings (when parking tends to be difficult) and Sun lunchtime; open all day Sun, good roasts *(LYM, Ann and Colin Hunt, Tony Scott)*

Prince Arthur [Dean St]: Well run town centre local, unspoilt décor with real air of well preserved antiquity, well kept Courage Directors, Gales HSB and Harveys, good food *(Tom Espley)*

Sir Charles Napier [Southover St]: Warmly welcoming cosy and busy Gales pub with well kept ales, plenty of food, friendly staff and locals, lots of interesting local memorabilia, quaint terrace; some live music, quiz nights, Morris dancing *(Dan Wilson)*

Sussex [East St]: Busy and well run, with traditional L-shaped pubby bar, good basic food from sandwiches up, good choice of wines by the glass, pleasant staff; piped music; open all day, tables out in the square *(Colin and Janet Roe)*

Broad Oak [TQ8220]

☆ *Rainbow Trout* [A28/B2089, N of Brede]: Wide range of well cooked food esp fish served by pleasant waitresses in attractive bustling low-beamed bar and big adjacent restaurant extension; gets very crowded but plenty of room for drinkers, with wide range of well kept beers, wines and spirits *(E G Parish)*

Bucks Green [TQ0732]

Fox [A281 Horsham—Guildford]: Ancient open-plan pub with wide choice of good bar food, well kept King & Barnes (full range), inglenook, friendly helpful staff, wide choice of good value food, play area *(M Whybrow)*

Burwash [TQ6724]

Bear [A265]: Friendly and spacious comfortably modernised bar with relaxing atmosphere, popular bar food, well kept real ales, obliging service, cosy seats around good log fire; open all day, quiet views from attractive back garden; restaurant, bedrooms *(Eddie Edwards, BB)*

Rose & Crown [pub signed just off A265]: Timbered and low-beamed local tucked away down lane in pretty village, well kept Harveys, decent wines, good log fire, good value varied food in bar and pleasant restaurant; tables out in small quiet garden *(BB)*

Burwash Weald [TQ6624]

Wheel [A265 two miles W of Burwash]: Enjoyable food all day in friendly and well run open-plan pub with good inglenook log fire, comfortable banquettes, nicely framed old local photographs, well kept Harveys and other ales, games bar up a step or two behind, recently built dining room leading out to garden; tables on sunny front terrace too, lovely walks in valley opp *(BB, Jason Caulkin)*

Bury [TQ0113]

☆ *White Horse* [A29 Fontwell—Pulborough]: Some concentration on wide changing range of good food inc superb tournedos in big sectioned dining area, friendly service, well kept ales inc Fullers London Pride; tables in pretty outside area, cl Sun evening, Mon *(Malcolm and Ann Grant, John Evans)*

Chichester [SU8605]

Coach & Horses [St Pancras]: Comfortably refurbished open-plan pub, clean and friendly, well kept Banks's and King & Barnes, good lunchtime bar food, back garden *(Tony and Wendy Hobden, Bruce Bird)*

Sluping Toad [West St]: Recent conversion of redundant church nr cathedral, good lunchtime food and coffee, Hardy beers; very popular with young people at night *(J A Snell)*

Chilgrove [SU8116]

☆ *Royal Oak* [off B2141 Petersfield—Chichester, signed Hooksway down steep hill]: Welcoming and smartly simple country tavern in very peaceful spot, beams, brick floors, country-kitchen furnishings, huge log fires; sensibly priced home-made standard food inc vegetarian, well kept real ales inc Arundel Best, games, attractive seats outside; provision for children, has been cl winter Mons, good walks *(Colin and Ann Hunt, David Cullen, Emma Stent, LYM)*

White Horse [off B2141, Petersfield—Chichester]: More smart restaurant than pub, lunches cheaper than evening, good food in bar too; remarkable list of outstanding wines, idyllic downland setting with small flower-filled terrace and big pretty garden *(E A Froggatt, J Sheldon, Dennis Stevens)*

Colemans Hatch [TQ4533]

☆ *Hatch* [signed off B2026, or off B2110 opp church]: Attractive old weatherboarded Ashdown Forest pub with big log fire in beamed bar, small back restaurant with another log fire, good interesting food from baked potatoes, giant ploughman's and filled ciabatta bread to bass and steak, two Harveys beers, Larkins and guest beers, freshly pressed local apple juice, good friendly mix of customers inc families; front terrace and beautifully kept big garden *(Colin and Joyce Laffan, LYM, James Shepherd)*

Compton [SU7714]

☆ *Coach & Horses* [B2146 S of Petersfield]: Spick and span 15th-c former coaching inn, good atmosphere, well kept ales such as Cheriton Diggers Gold and King & Barnes Best, roomy walkers' bar with log fire, charming little plush beamed lounge bar with attractive restaurant, well presented appetising food, friendly Flemish landlady, attentive staff; tables out in front, small secluded back garden, attractive village; fine wooded hilly walking country *(G B Longden, Ann and Colin Hunt, Phyl and Jack Street)*

Cousley Wood [TQ6533]

☆ *Old Vine* [B2100 Wadhurst—Lamberhurst]: Attractive tastefully redecorated dining pub with lots of old timbers and beams, wide range of generously served modestly priced decent food inc good fish, good house wines, four well kept ales, pleasant waitresses and barmaids; rustic pretty restaurant on right, pubbier bare-boards or brick-floored area with woodburner by bar; credit cards impounded if you run a bar bill; a few tables out behind *(Mr and Mrs R D Knight, BB, Comus Elliott)*

Crawley [TQ2636]

Hawth Park [Haslett Ave, Paymaster General roundabout]: Roomy child-friendly family Brewers Fayre, some character though new; good value generous food, flexible service *(Eamonn and Natasha Skyrme)*

Heathy Farm [Balcombe Rd; B2036 2 miles N of Pound Hill]: Smart ex-farmhouse family pub with good choice of well kept beers and of wholesome food inc original puddings, efficient staff, children well catered for *(Eamonn and Natasha Skyrme, Terry Buckland)*

White Hart [High St]: Two-bar Harveys local with their full range, lunchtime food, friendly staff, comfortable saloon, pool and darts teams; open all day, busy market days (Thurs-Sat); jazz or Irish music w/e *(Tony Scott, Dave Cupwell)*

Crowborough [TQ5130]

Half Moon [Groombridge Rd, Lye Green, Friars Gate]: Small pretty refurbished country pub on edge of Ashdown Forest, tables out in front and in extensive back area with play area, boules and room for caravans, good reasonably priced food inc Sun lunch, Harveys and full Shepherd Neame range, good service *(Colin and Joyce Laffan)*

Danehill [TQ4128]

☆ *Coach & Horses* [School Lane, Chelwood Common; off A275]: Consistently good home-cooked food inc vegetarian in cottagey local with two small bars and roomy ex-stables dining extension, well kept Harveys, Greene King and guest beers, decent house wine, friendly service, good atmosphere, pews in bar, two big dogs; attractive big garden (Mr and Mrs R D Knight, Ron Gentry, Geoffrey Lawrance, Ian and Carol McPherson)

Dell Quay [SU8302]

☆ *Crown & Anchor* [off A286 S of Chichester]: Modernised 15th-c pub in splendid spot overlooking Chichester Harbour on site of Roman quay, good home-made food from sandwiches up esp plenty of fresh local fish, well kept Courage Best and Directors and Theakstons XB, smartly dressed staff; marina views from garden and comfortable bow-windowed lounge bar, panelled public bar with unspoilt fireplace (dogs welcome), restaurant *(Tony and Wendy Hobden, JEB, JDM, KM, BB, Miss P M Stevenson, Keith Stevens, Mrs Jenny Cantle, J Snell)*

Ditchling [TQ3215]

Bull [High St (B2112)]: Beamed 14th-c inn with attractive antique furnishings in main bar (can be smoky), old pictures, inglenook fireplace, well kept Whitbreads-related ales, good choice of malt whiskies, comfortable family room, restaurant, fairly good wheelchair access; picnic-sets in garden and on suntrap concrete terrace, charming old village just below downs *(Peter Meister, LYM, Simon Collett-Jones, Tony Scott)*

White Horse [West St]: Popular local, very busy weekends, with well kept Harveys and changing guest beers, unpretentious food from sandwiches up, quick service, log fire, bar billiards, live ha'penny etc, unobtrusive piped jazz, live alternate Thurs/Fri *(Tony Scott)*

Eartham [SU9409]

☆ *George* [signed off A285 Chichester—Petworth, from Fontwell off A27, from Slindon off A29]: Big popular pub smartly refurbished in light wood, comfortable lounge opening on to new terrace and pleasant garden, attractive pubbier public bar with games, old farm tools and photographs, popular food from baguettes and baked potatoes to vegetarian, fish, steaks and interesting pies, well kept Gales Best, Butser, HSB, and maybe a guest beer, log fire, cheerful welcome, no-smoking restaurant; piped music; children welcome in eating areas, open all day summer w/e *(A G Drake, R T and J C Moggridge, Gwen and Peter Andrews, Ann and Colin Hunt, Barry and Marie Males, Sue and Bob Ward, E A Froggatt, Elizabeth and Klaus Leist, LYM)*

Easebourne [SU8922]

☆ *Olde White Horse* [off A272 just NE of Midhurst]: Cosy unpretentious pub with promptly served generous home-made food inc good sandwiches and fresh veg, reasonable prices, welcoming licensees, Greene King IPA and Abbot, small log fire, traditional games in tap room, tables on back grass and in courtyard *(Paul and Penny Dawson, LYM, G C Hackemer)*

East Dean [SU9012]

☆ *Hurdlemakers* [signed off A286 and A285 N of Chichester – OS Sheet 197 map ref 904129]: Charmingly placed by peaceful green of quiet village, with rustic seats and swing in pretty walled garden; good value food inc vegetarian

in softly lit L-shaped bar, friendly efficient staff, well kept ales such as Adnams, Ballards, Boddingtons and Gales HSB, pleasant atmosphere and staff; comfortable bedrooms, self-serve breakfast; a helpful welcome for wet walkers (South Downs Way) and children *(E A Froggatt, Gwen and Peter Andrews, LYM, H Orchard)*

East Lavant [SU8608]

☆ *Royal Oak* [signed off A286 N of Chichester]: Peaceful village pub doing well under friendly newish licensees, three well kept Gales ales, country wines, good food from interesting sandwiches up, pleasant simple furnishings, rugs on bare boards and flooring tiles, two open fires and a woodburner; children welcome if eating, dogs welcome, attractively planted gardens inc secluded new terrace with bookable tables, good walks *(D B Jenkin, LYM, Martin and Penny Fletcher, J Snell, Jill Silversides, Barry Brown, Keith Stevens)*

Eastbourne [TV5895]

Beachy Head Hotel [Beachy Head]: Brewers Fayre in excellent position, nice bars, well kept Bass, Boddingtons, Harveys, King & Barnes, Wadworths 6X and Youngs Special, decent food from good sandwiches to restaurant meals and lunchtime carvery, no-smoking areas, friendly efficient staff, tables outside, play area, great views; handy for walks, open all day *(Colin Laffan, Richard Lewis)*

Pilot [Holywell Rd, Meads; just off front below approach from Beachy Head]: Bustling, comfortable and friendly, prompt ample food, pleasant service, well kept real ales, good ship photographs; garden *(TRS, B and M Parkin)*

Port Hole [Cornfield Terr]: Small pub with very friendly Dutch landlord with an interesting line in lighters, comfortable wooden seats and tables, imaginative home-made food, well kept beer, upstairs dining room open some days *(S J Hetherington)*

Eastergate [SU9305]

Wilkes Head [signed off A29 Fontwell—Bognor; Church Lane]: Small friendly local with flagstones and big open fire; well kept beers with a guest such as Greene King IPA, good food choice, pleasant service *(R T and J C Moggridge)*

Felpham [SZ9599]

Southdowns [A259]: Well run Big Steak dining pub, wide range of other well priced food too, Morlands Old Speckled Hen and Tetleys-related beers, good value house wine *(R T and J C Moggridge)*

Fernhurst [SU9028]

Kings Arms [A286 towards Midhurst]: Refined and attractive 17th-c dining pub in pleasant setting, low beams, open fires, dark oak settles and heavy dining tables in three connected bars, decent choice of food from sandwiches to steaks, good choice of ales such as Hook Norton Old Hooky, Otter Bright and one brewed for the pub, attentive staff, daily papers; small car park *(Simon Hillcox, Sam Samuells, Lynda Paton)*

☆ *Red Lion* [The Green; off A286, 3 miles S of Haslemere]: Heavy-beamed old pub tucked quietly away by green nr church, friendly staff, good value food inc interesting specials, attractive layout and furnishings, well kept King & Barnes and other ales, good wines, no-smoking area, good relaxed atmosphere; children welcome, pretty garden *(G B Longden, BB, Wendy Arnold)*

Ferring [TQ0902]

Tudor Close [Ferringham Lane, S Ferring]: Thatched former barn, restaurant rather than pub, with big fireplace, high rafters, small upper gallery and no-smoking room, good choice of reasonably priced home-made pubby food (not Sun evening or Mon), well kept Courage, Gales BB and Wadworths 6X, good-natured helpful if not swift service, no piped music, peaceful seats outside *(Tony and Wendy Hobden, Howard Dell)*

Findon [TQ1208]

☆ *Village House* [High St; off A24 N of Worthing]: Good food inc fish and local game in quiet and attractive converted 16th-c coach house, oak tables, panelling, pictures, racing silks from local stables, big open fire, well kept ales inc Courage and King & Barnes, good service, restaurant popular for Sun lunch, small attractive walled garden with terrace and fish pond; comfortable bedrooms, handy for Cissbury Ring and downland walks *(Nigel Williamson, Tony and Wendy Hobden, John Beeken)*

Fishbourne [SU8404]

Bulls Head [Fishbourne Rd; just off A27 Chichester—Emsworth]: Interesting old building with fair-sized main bar, full Gales range kept well, unusual guest beers, friendly landlord and locals, good choice of food (not cheap but good value, not Sun evening), log fires, no-smoking area, children's area, skittle alley, boules pitch, restaurant *(K and J Morris)*

Woolpack [Fishbourne Rd W; just off A27 Chichester—Emsworth]: Big comfortably refurbished pub with good food inc Sun roast, lots of very well kept real ales inc guests such as Black Sheep Best, Greene King IPA and Youngs Bitter and Special, good friendly service, no-smoking area; dogs welcome, garden with summer barbecues *(J Snell, Keith Stevens, Bruce Bird)*

Fletching [TQ4223]

☆ *Rose & Crown* [High St]: Well run unpretentious 16th-c village pub locally popular for good home-made food with fresh veg in bar and small restaurant, friendly attentive service, real ales, beams, inglenooks and log fires, tables in pretty garden *(Eddie Edwards, Derek and Maggie Washington, Mr and Mrs R D Knight, John Knighton, Colin and Joyce Laffan, Comus Elliott)*

Frant [TQ5835]

Abergavenny Arms [A267 S of Tunbridge Wells]: Main-road pub useful for wide choice of reasonably priced popular food inc ploughman's, up to a dozen changing ales tapped from casks in unusual climate-controlled glass-fronted chamber, log fire, bar billiards, children welcome *(Mr and Mrs A Albert)*

☆ *George* [High St, off A267]: Tucked down charming quiet village st by ancient church and cottages, bar with several rooms rambling round servery, low ceiling, mix of seats inc pews, high-backed settles and a sofa, coal-effect gas fire in big inglenook, well kept Boddingtons, Fullers London Pride, Greene King Abbot and Harveys, lots of wines by the glass, decent food inc bargain lunches, good coffee, darts in public bar; busy w/e, pleasant restaurant, picnic-sets in walled garden *(Michael and Hazel Duncombe, Pat and Tony Martin, Colin and Janet Roe, BB)*

Fulking [TQ2411]

☆ *Shepherd & Dog*: Charming partly panelled country pub with antique or stoutly rustic furnishings around log fire, attractive bow windows, generous food from sandwiches and lots of cheeses to fresh fish and steaks inc vegetarian choice, well kept Harveys Best, Flowers Original and changing guest beers, good farm cider, welcoming staff, downs views from pretty streamside garden with upper play lawn (loudspeaker food announcements out here); open all day, food 12-6 w/e, can be packed out, dogs welcome, no children in bar *(LYM, M R Lewis, Anna and Martyn Carey, R J Walden, A Sutton, Martin and Karen Wake, Gerald Karn, David Holloway, Tony Scott)*

Gun Hill [TQ5614]

☆ *Gun* [off A22 NW of Hailsham, or off A267]: Big welcoming country dining pub, close-set tables in several interesting rambling rooms, log fires (and an Aga on which they've done some of the cooking), good straightforward food, well kept Adnams Extra, Flowers Original, Harveys Best and Wadworths, good wines, efficient pleasant service; children allowed in two no-smoking rooms, lovely garden with big play area, right on Wealden Way *(LYM, B and M Parkin, Peter Meister, Mr and Mrs A Albert, Janet and Colin Roe, Colin and Joyce Laffan)*

Hadlow Down [TQ5324]

New Inn [A272 E of Uckfield]: 1950s feel in basic unspoilt roadside bar with snacks on shelves, Harveys beers inc Mild, pool room, very friendly family with plenty of stories to tell; houses the post office *(the Didler)*

Halnaker [SU9008]

☆ *Anglesey Arms* [A285 Chichester—Petworth]: Welcoming service and quickly cooked genuine food esp steaks, fish and occasional interesting Spanish specialities in bar with traditional games, well kept King & Barnes and Tetleys-related ales, good wines (some direct Spanish imports); simple but smart candlelit dining room with stripped pine and flagstones (children allowed), tables in garden *(B and C Clouting, John H Davis, LYM)*

Hastings [TQ8109]

Hastings Arms [George St]: Good atmosphere, good value imaginative food, all home-made, inc fish, vegetarian and unusual puddings and ice creams, friendly staff *(L Elliot)*

Haywards Heath [TQ3324]

Dolphin [Butley Green Rd]: Good standard food – a Bass Vintage Inn, with their beers *(Ian Phillips, Tony Scott)*

Hermitage [SU7505]

☆ *Sussex Brewery* [A259, by Thorney Island turn]: Pleasant stripped-brick bar with immense log fire, sawdust on boards and flagstoned alcove (this bit food-free Fri/Sat night), well kept ales such as Badger Best, Shepherd Neame Spitfire, Timothy Taylor Dark Mild and Youngs Special, good local fish and vast choice of sausages inc vegetarian, no-smoking red plush dining room up a few steps; no machines or piped music, small walled garden; can get very busy, open all day Sat, busy w/e *(Bruce Bird, Ian Phillips, Ann and Colin Hunt)*

Herstmonceux [TQ6312]

Welcome Stranger: Unspoilt country pub in same family for nearly a century, well kept Harveys Bitter and Old and a guest beer from small serving hatch; cl weekday lunchtimes *(Jack and Philip Paxton, the Didler)*

Holtye [TQ4539]

☆ *White Horse* [Holtye Common; A264 East Grinstead—Tunbridge Wells]: Huge choice of good value if not cheap food inc lots of fish, good vegetarian dishes and popular carvery in unpretentiously refurbished ancient village pub with pleasant brisk service, well kept ales inc Brakspears, illuminated aquarium set into floor; good facilities for the disabled, marvellous view from back lawn; bedrooms *(R and S Bentley, Elizabeth and Klaus Leist, Barry Perfect, P J Heaps)*

Hooe [TQ6809]

☆ *Lamb* [A259 E of Pevensey]: Prettily placed dining pub, extensively refurbished with arches and lots of stripped brick and flintwork, one snug area around huge log fire and lots of other seats, big tables, very wide choice of generous popular food inc good sandwiches and vegetarian, children's dishes, well kept Bass and Harveys, quick friendly service *(Brian Skelcher, Angela Gibson, B and M Parkin, Jenny and Brian Seller)*

Horsham [TQ1730]

Dog & Bacon [North Parade, Warnham Rd (A24)]: Cosy and cottagey two-bar King & Barnes pub, pleasant local feel; no food Sat/Sun evening *(Tony Scott, Tony Hobden)*

Royal Oak [Great Benhams/Langhurst; back rd N, E of A24 between Warnham and Rusper]: Very rural spot on Sussex Border Path, King & Barnes beer, some picnic-sets *(G B Longden)*

Horsted Keynes [TQ3828]

Green Man [The Green]: Traditional village inn in attractive spot facing green, spotless but not too modernised, with welcoming and obliging service, well kept Adnams and Harveys, good usual home-made food in bistro dining room, reasonable prices; handy for Bluebell Line *(John C Baker, DEE, Tony Hobden)*

Houghton [TQ0111]

☆ *George & Dragon* [B2139 W of Storrington]: Fine old timbered pub with pretty views from terraces of charming sloping garden, occasional summer barbecues with live music; civilised rambling heavy-beamed bar, nice comfortable mix of furnishings inc some antiques, wide choice of enjoyable reasonably priced food from ploughman's and baked potatoes up,

Mon-Thurs over-50s bargain lunch, cheerful prompt service even when busy, well kept Courage Best and Directors and Morlands Old Speckled Hen, log fire, no-smoking room; children welcome, with lots of games; handy for South Downs Way *(Mrs D Bromley-Martin, Martin and Karen Wake, M J Dowdy, D Marsh, Mrs Jenny Cantle, N B Thompson, LYM, David and Carole Chapman)*

Hunston [SU8501]

Spotted Cow [B2145 Chichester—Sidlesham]: Small and unpretentiously attractive, with flagstones and comfortable sofas, big fires, well kept Gales and guest ales, good value interesting food from lunchtime sandwiches to Chinese take-aways and more elaborate evening restaurant meals; skittles, big garden; handy for towpath walkers *(K Stevens, Prof and Mrs S Barnett)*

Ifield [TQ2437]

Plough: Ancient local in pleasant spot nr 13th-c church, full King & Barnes range kept well, traditional food, good atmosphere, friendly staff, comfortably refurbished saloon with lots of brass and wood, games in small public bar; tables out in front, handy for local Barn Theatre *(Tony Scott, David and Carole Chapman)*

Isfield [TQ4516]

Halfway House [Rose Hill (A26)]: Low beamed rambling roadside house, dark pub furniture on turkey carpet, well kept Harveys Bitter and Old, good home cooking, good service; picnic-sets in small back garden *(Colin and Joyce Laffan, Tony Scott, BB)*

Lavant [SU8508]

☆ *Earl of March* [Lavant Rd (A286)]: Roomy village pub with well kept Bass, Cottage Golden Arrow, Ringwood Old Thumper and changing guest beers from small breweries, Weston's Old Rosie cider, good generous home-cooked food inc vegetarian, no-smoking area by servery, efficient service even when busy, naval memorabilia, bric-a-brac and prints, games and puzzles, no piped music; dogs welcome, live music Thurs; good views from garden, good local walks *(Bruce Bird, David Gould)*

Lewes [TQ4110]

Black Horse [Western Rd]: Nice two-bar local with well kept Harveys and other ales such as Brakspears, Fullers and Wadworths 6X, bar food, friendly service *(Tony Scott)*

Gardeners Arms [Cliffe High St]: Light and airy simple bar, small and quiet, with good value food and ever-changing range of eight or so real ales, good friendly service (with helpful opinions on the ales) *(Dan Wilson)*

John Harvey [Harveys Brewery]: New tap adjoining Harveys brewery, all their beers tapped from the cask kept perfectly, nice snacks, interestingly different crisps *(Comus Elliott)*

Litlington [TQ5201]

Plough & Harrow [between A27 Lewes—Polegate and A259 E of Seaford]: Cosy beamed front bar in attractively extended flint local, six well kept real ales, decent wines by the glass, good home cooking, dining area done up as railway dining car (children allowed here); back lawn with children's bar, aviary and pretty views; live music Fri *(Gwen and Peter Andrews, LYM)*

Littlehampton [TQ0202]

☆ *Arun View* [Wharf Rd; W towards Chichester, opp railway stn]: Roomy and comfortable 18th-c inn right on harbour with river directly below windows, well kept Boddingtons and other ales, wide choice of reasonably priced well cooked bar food, restaurant strong on local fish (wise to book), flower-filled terrace overlooking busy waterway; summer barbecues evenings and w/e; bright good value bedrooms *(David and Carole Chapman, Tony and Wendy Hobden, Dennis D'Vigne)*

Littleworth [TQ1920]

☆ *Windmill* [pub sign on B2135; village signed off A272 southbound, W of Cowfold]: Small spotless local with log fires in compact but cosy beamed lounge and panelled flagstoned public bar; simple but good bar food (not Sun eve winter) inc vegetarian, well kept King & Barnes beers inc Mild and a guest such as Arundel, friendly truly helpful service, bric-a-brac large and small inside and out, darts, dominoes, cards and bar billiards, no music; children welcome, peaceful side garden *(C J Bromage, Bruce Bird)*

Lodsworth [SU9223]

☆ *Hollist Arms* [off A272 Midhurst—Petworth]: Cosy bars inc lovely little snug, welcoming staff and locals, big cheerful dining room, good well priced home-made food, well kept Ballards and Arundel beers, two log fires, snug with darts, shove ha'penny etc; nice garden, whole lamb barbecues, attractive village spot *(Ann and Colin Hunt, E M Steinitz)*

Lower Beeding [TQ2225]

☆ *Crabtree* [Brighton Rd]: 16th-c pub with fine inglenook log fire in character beamed back bar and genuine public bar with cribbage and dominoes, well kept King & Barnes Sussex, Festive and seasonal ales, impressive choice of bottled beers; the food side (the main thing here) is best thought of as a quite separate restaurant, and therefore not really suited to the main entries of a pub guide, but the quality is very high, quite transcending the dining room's décor and atmosphere *(Terry Buckland, Peter and Giff Bennett, G Simpson, George Little, John and Enid Morris, John Fahy, John Davis, David and Ruth Shillitoe, B and M Kendall, Colin McKerrow, Ian and Carol McPherson, BB)*

Loxwood [TQ0431]

☆ *Onslow Arms* [B2133 NW of Billingshurst]: Well refurbished, with lively young staff, well kept full King & Barnes range, good house wines, big helpings of good value simple food inc notable pizzas, lovely old fireplaces, picnic-sets in garden sloping to river and nearby newly restored canal, good walks and boat trips *(Prof and Mrs S Barnett, Elizabeth and Alan Walker)*

Maplehurst [TQ1924]

White Horse: Quiet friendly family-run beamed country local, four seating areas inc sun lounge (no smoking at lunchtime), well kept Harveys,

King & Barnes and guest beers from small brewers, good value basic food, efficient staff, no music or machines; children welcome, garden, car enthusiasts' evenings *(Bruce Bird)*

Mayfield [TQ5827]

Carpenters Arms [Fletching St]: Comfortably unpretentious, pleasant décor and atmosphere, no music, good food esp fresh-grilled fish, well kept beer, good landlord, traditional games *(DC)*

☆ *Middle House* [High St]: Handsome 16th-c timbered inn in pretty village, L-shaped beamed bar with massive fireplace, well kept Fullers London Pride, Greene King Abbot, Harveys Best and a guest beer, local cider, decent wines, quiet lounge with leather chesterfields around log fire in ornate carved fireplace, generous if not cheap food from home-made sausages and mash to 3-course Weds jazz menu, panelled no-smoking restaurant; piped music; afternoon tea in terraced back garden with lovely views, slide and play house; children welcome, open all day *(David and Betty Gittings, LYM, Peter and Christine Lead, Ivan de Deken, John Saul, Jules Akel, J Burnham, S Litchfield, Comus Elliott)*

Midhurst [SU8822]

Bricklayers Arms [West St]: Warm welcome in two cosy and relaxing olde-worlde bars, good value generous home-made food inc Sun roast, well kept Greene King IPA and Abbot, friendly helpful service, sturdy old oak furniture, 17th-c beams, old photographs and bric-a-brac *(Teresa Gess)*

☆ *Spread Eagle* [South St]: Handsome and atmospheric old hotel, not a pub, mainly 17th-c but partly much older; friendly lounge bar (waiter service), welcoming staff, restaurant; children welcome, bedrooms *(J A Snell, J H Bell, LYM)*

Wheatsheaf [corner Wool Lane and A272]: Attractive and welcoming unpretentious low-beamed half-timbered 16th-c local with good value generous food inc very good sandwich choice, very friendly staff, well kept King & Barnes beers *(Michael and Hazel Duncombe)*

Netherfield [TQ7118]

☆ *Netherfield Arms* [just off B2096 Heathfield—Battle]: Friendly low-ceilinged country pub with newish licensees doing well, wide choice of food and of well kept ales and wines, inglenook log fire, no-smoking area, cosy restaurant, no music; lovely back garden *(BB, Desmond Barker)*

Newick [TQ4121]

☆ *Bull* [A272 Uckfield—Haywards Heath]: Attractive old rambling pub, welcoming, comfortable and peaceful for a midweek lunch, lots of beams and character, good value generous food inc interesting cooking and fresh Newhaven fish in sizeable eating area, inglenook log fires, welcoming attentive service, well kept ales such as Courage Directors, Harveys, Marstons Pedigree and Theakstons; no music, booking advised w/e *(Colin and Joyce Laffan, G Simpson, Renee and Dennis Ball, Ann and Colin Hunt, BB)*

Newpound Common [TQ0627]

Bat & Ball [just off B2133 Loxwood Rd]:

Open-plan country pub with lots of beams and pillars, good range of tasty bar food, well kept King & Barnes ales inc seasonal beers, open fires; big pleasant garden with fruit trees, aviaries and play area, campsite *(G B Lungden, Bruce Bird)*

Ninfield [TQ7012]

Kings Arms [Bexhill Rd]: Comfortable and popular Brewers Fayre with wide choice of food, well kept Whitbreads ales with a guest such as Harveys, garden with play area, friendly staff; open all day, good disabled access *(Richard Lewis)*

Northchapel [SU9529]

☆ *Half Moon* [A285 Guildford—Petworth]: Nice décor with beams, lots of farm tools, warm lighting, well kept ales such as Friary Meux, Hampshire Uncle Sam, King & Barnes and Ringwood Old Thumper, food inc choice of ploughman's; garden with tame goose, big red tractor, even old buses; live music last Mon of month *(J W G Nunns, James Nunns)*

Northiam [TQ8224]

Hayes Arms [The Green]: Civilised Georgian-fronted hotel overlooking village green, comfortable back heavy-beamed Tudor bar; Adnams and Goachers tapped from the cask, friendly staff, log fire in big brick inglenook, lunchtime bar food inc rare beef sandwiches and hot dishes, eating area and small back restaurant; bedrooms *(Conrad and Alison Freezer, Colin and Janet Roe)*

Nutbourne [TQ0718]

Rising Sun [the one nr Pulborough]: Simple and clean old local with friendly service, Badger and other ales, generous good value food from well garnished ploughman's up; children and dogs allowed, some live music; tables on small back terrace under apple tree *(LM)*

Oxleys Green [TQ6921]

Jack Fullers [Oxleys Green; from village follow Robertsbridge sign]: Tucked-away restauranty country dining pub, two charming old rustic rooms with huge log fire, candlelit tables, good mix of old-fashioned furnishings, well kept Brakspears PA, Harveys and a guest beer, particularly good wines by the glass esp English ones, robust home cooking esp individual pies and meat puddings with interesting veg and old-fashioned steamed puddings, very attractive garden with unspoilt views; children welcome, cl Sun evening, Mon/Tues lunchtimes *(LYM, K Arthur)*

Patching [TQ0806]

Coach & Horses [signed off A27 Worthing—Arundel]: Large roadside pub with Badger beers, good value bar food, evening restaurant; popular with walkers *(Tony and Wendy Hobden)*

Fox [off A27 Worthing—Arundel]: Friendly enthusiastic landlord, well kept King & Barnes inc seasonal brews, good reasonably priced home-made food, lots of panelling, nice tree-shaded garden; occasional live music *(Bruce Bird, Tony and Wendy Hobden)*

Horse & Groom [off A27 Worthing—Arundel]: Large and attractive, with open fire, well kept Badger, good value restaurant with

imaginative choice, good fresh veg, succulent steaks and children's menu *(Tony and Wendy Hobden)*

Petworth [SU9721]

☆ *Well Diggers* [Low Heath; A283 towards Pulborough]: Picturesquely cluttered low-ceilinged stripped stone bar, long tables in stylishly simple dining room, good if not cheap food esp fish, friendly landlord, well kept Ballards and Youngs, decent wines, no music or machines; plenty of tables on attractive lawns and terraces, lovely views *(Charles Turner, LYM)*

Portslade [TQ2505]

Stanley Arms [Wolseley Rd]: Homely backstreet pub, very friendly and welcoming, with well kept changing beers, often unusual *(Dan Wilson, Richard Houghton)*

Poynings [TQ2612]

Royal Oak: Well kept Scottish Courage ales and King & Barnes, good generous food inc vegetarian and fish, service efficient even when very busy, large but cosy bar around central servery, no-smoking area, big attractive garden with barbecue and summer marquee *(Bruce Bird, James Nunns)*

Pyecombe [TQ2813]

Plough [A23]: Handy for South Downs Way walks, with warm welcome, well kept Wadworths 6X and decent food inc excellent ploughman's in spacious bar and dining area *(Catherine and Richard Preston)*

Rake [SU8027]

Sun [Portsmouth Rd (A3 S of Liphook)]: Comfortable dining pub with wide choice of generous home-made food inc good Sun lunches, quick friendly service, log fires, Bass, Gales BBB and HSB *(G B Longden)*

Ringmer [TQ4412]

☆ *Cock* [Uckfield Rd – blocked-off section of rd off A26 N of village turn-off]: Very welcoming country pub, heavy 16th-c beams and flagstones in main bar with big inglenook log fire, pleasant modernised rooms off inc no-smoking lounge, back restaurant, well kept Harveys Best and a seasonal beer, Fullers London Pride and a guest such as Rother Valley, huge blackboard choice of enjoyable food, good service, lovely flower arrangements; children allowed in overflow eating area; quiet piped music; tables on small terrace and in big sloping fairy-lit garden with shrubs, fruit trees and lots of spring flowers *(John Beeken, LYM, A M Atkinson, Kevin Thorpe, Colin and Joyce Laffan)*

☆ *Stewards Enquiry* [A26 Lewes—Uckfield, outside village S of Isfield turnoff]: Affable newish landlord, good varied food inc good vegetarian and reasonably priced Sun roasts and well kept Harveys in tastefully refurbished olde-worlde beamed pub; children welcome, some outside tables, play area *(Colin and Joyce Laffan)*

Ripe [TQ5010]

Lamb [signed off A22 Uckfield—Hailsham, or off A27 Lewes—Polegate via Chalvington; Church Lane]: Interestingly furnished rooms around central servery, masses of attractive antique prints and pictures, nostalgic song-sheet covers, Victorian pin-ups in gents'; wide choice of generous food inc fish, vegetarian and children's, well kept Scottish Courage ales and a guest such as Harveys, good range of reasonably priced wines, several open fires; pub games, pleasant sheltered back garden with play area and barbecues *(BB, D Everest)*

Robertsbridge [TQ7323]

Seven Stars [High St; off A21 N of Hastings]: Good local said to date from 11th c, wide range of beers, good value generous food, welcoming service, lively chatter; restaurant area, garden *(Comus Elliott)*

Rodmell [TQ4106]

Abergavenny Arms [back rd Lewes—Newhaven]: Open-plan with small no-smoking section, some interesting bric-a-brac inc shaving equipment, good range of food, seasonal ale and Wadworths 6X; dogs on leads welcome *(Tony and Wendy Hobden)*

Rogate [SU8023]

☆ *Wyndham Arms* [A272 E of Petersfield]: Small welcoming open-plan village local, half no smoking, with low beams, parquet floor, well kept Ballards, King & Barnes, Ringwood and a guest ale tapped from the cask, decent wines, good home-cooked food using fresh local ingredients, helpful staff, no piped music; pool; dogs and well behaved children welcome; bedrooms good value *(Lynn Sharpless, Bob Eardley, Tony and Wendy Hobden, Gwen and Peter Andrews, David Cullen, Emma Stent)*

Rowhook [TQ1234]

☆ *Chequers* [off A29 NW of Horsham]: Attractive 16th-c pub, unpretentious beamed and flagstoned front bar with inglenook fire, step up to low-ceilinged lounge, quick friendly service, well kept Boddingtons, Flowers Original, Fullers London Pride and Whitbreads Fuggles, good wine choice, traditional games, food from baguettes and baked potatoes up inc children's, restaurant; piped music, live Sun lunchtime; tables out on terraces and in pretty garden with good play area, attractive surroundings *(Elizabeth and Alan Walker, Mrs Romey Heaton, DWAJ, LYM)*

Runcton [SU8802]

Walnut Tree [towards N Mundham]: Good choice of ale, smart welcoming staff, open fires and flagstones, good food choice in bar and restaurant; dogs welcome *(Keith Stevens)*

Rusper [TQ2037]

☆ *Plough* [signed from A24 and A264 N and NE of Horsham]: Padded very low beams, panelling and big inglenook, huge range of good value food, attractive dining area, well kept ales such as Courage Directors, local Dorking, Fullers London Pride and King & Barnes, lovely log fire, bar billiards and darts in raftered room upstairs; fountain in back garden, pretty front terrace, occasional live music; children welcome *(Tony Scott, LYM, LM)*

Rye [TQ9220]

Globe [Military Rd]: Almost more like a club than a pub; deep easy chairs in lounge bar by charming dining room, french doors to

attractive garden with barbecue, adventurous menu *(Jeremy Wallington)*

Grist Mill [The Strand]: Flagstones, beams, real oil lamps, decent reasonably priced food in big helpings, excellent local fresh fish and seafood, welcoming staff, piped jazz and blues; open 10am-midnight *(Miss T Devitt)*

Olde Standard [The Mint]: Welcoming cosy atmosphere and lots of beams in small interesting local with nice choice of well kept local beers, good basic food, open fires; enjoyable piped music, open all day *(Pat and Baz Turvill, Tony Scott)*

Ship [The Strand]: Lots of space, wooden tables on bare boards, well kept Harveys and King & Barnes *(Kerry Law, Simon Smith)*

Selmeston [TQ5006]

Barley Mow [A27]: Homely pub with lots of prints and play bills, home-made food in bar and restaurant, Harveys Best, friendly service; small garden *(Val and Alan Green)*

Shipley [TQ1422]

George & Dragon: Good atmosphere, service, and reasonable choice of food; well kept King & Barnes *(Tony Scott)*

Shoreham by Sea [TQ2105]

Airport Bar [signed off A27, A259]: Not a pub, but this small bar in a 1930s art deco airport building has good beers brewed for it by local Brewery on Sea; relaxed atmosphere, friendly obliging staff, well presented cheap simple food, tables on terrace, uninterrupted views all round (plenty of light aircraft action); children welcome, small airport museum *(John Beeken, Tony and Wendy Hobden)*

Marlipins [High St]: Planked ceilings giving nautical feel, bric-a-brac, old local photographs, welcoming licensee, good choice of tasty bar food, well kept Bass, Worthington BB, Fullers London Pride and Harveys Best; piped music, can get busy w/e; back terrace *(Anne Cutler, Tony Scott)*

☆ *Red Lion* [Upper Shoreham Rd]: Dim-lit low-beamed and timbered 16th-c pub with settles in snug alcoves, good value well presented food, well kept Arundel Old Scrooge, Courage Directors, Oakhill Mendip Gold, Harveys Sussex and other guest beers, decent wines, farm cider, log fire in unusual fireplace, no-smoking dining room, pretty sheltered garden; piped music may obtrude; good walks and South Downs views *(John Beeken, Jackie and Alan Moody)*

Sidlesham [SZ8598]

☆ *Crab & Lobster* [Mill Lane; off B2145 S of Chichester]: Individualistic old country local, log fire in chatty traditional bar, no-smoking plusher side dining lounge, charming back garden looking over to the bird reserve of silted Pagham Harbour; limited choice of good fresh food (not Sun evening, starts at 7 other evenings), well kept Archers Village and Gales Best and BBB, decent wines, country wines, traditional games; dogs welcome, no children, music or machines *(Mark Blackburn, Tracey and Stephen Groves, J V Dadswell, David R Crafts, Mr and Mrs K Sandiford, LYM)*

Singleton [SU8713]

Fox & Hounds [off A286]: Two small relaxed

bars dating from 16th c, painted panelling, polished wooden floor, log fire, good food choice from open sandwiches up, Bass, Hancocks, and Wadworths 6X, welcoming service; attractive small back terrace and big garden with colourful flowerbeds, handy for Weald & Downland Open Air Museum *(Martin and Karen Wake, Ann and Colin Hunt)*

Horse & Groom [A286]: Friendly staff, well kept Ballards and Cheriton Pots, generous promptly served reasonably priced home-made food, quiet piped classical music, no-smoking restaurant, garden; open all day Sun *(Dr J B Ainscough, Ann and Colin Hunt, Peter and Susan Maguire, Klaus and Elizabeth Leist)*

Slaugham [TQ2528]

Chequers: Plushly extended dining pub with good food with emphasis on wide choice of seafood, also cheaper lunchtime bar snacks, well kept King & Barnes, enormous wine list; tables on front terrace opp church among pretty cottages by bridleway to Handcross; good-sized comfortable bedrooms *(Mrs J Hilditch)*

Slindon [SU9708]

Newburgh Arms: Congenial, comfortable and relaxed, with pleasantly homey furnishings, sizeable dining area with rows of tables for good value food from good ploughman's up, well kept Badger Best, lots of country wines; piped music; good area for downs walks *(Ron Gentry, Mark Matthewman, Ann and Colin Hunt)*

☆ *Spur* [Slindon Common; A29 towards Bognor]: Popular, roomy and attractive 17th-c pub, good choice of good value food changing daily inc vegetarian, two big log fires, good choice of well kept Scottish Courage and other beers, welcoming efficient staff, friendly dogs; children welcome, games room with darts and pool, sizeable restaurant, pretty garden *(Tony and Wendy Hobden, John Davis, Jill Silversides, Barry Brown)*

South Harting [SU7819]

Ship [B2146]: Welcoming 17th-c local, informal and unspoilt, with dimly lit bar, roaring log fire, old photographs, well kept Mansfield Old Baily, Palmers and Ushers, good wine by the glass, good choice of good value food from toasties up at rather close-set tables, unobtrusive piped music, friendly staff and dogs, simpler public bar (dominoes, maybe chestnuts to roast by its log fire); nice setting in pretty village *(John Evans, E A Froggatt, Gwen and Peter Andrews)*

☆ *White Hart* [B2146 SE of Petersfield]: Attractive unspoilt pub with good generous home cooking inc vegetarian and sandwiches, lots of polished wood, hundreds of keys, big log fire in cosy snug, good service with cheerful long-serving licensees, well kept Tetleys-related ales, good coffee, restaurant, separate public bar; well behaved dogs allowed, children welcome (toys in well integrated games/family room); good garden behind for them too, with spectacular downs views *(Ann and Colin Hunt, Tony and Wendy Hobden)*

Southbourne [SU7806]

Travellers Joy [A259]: Comfortable Gales pub, lounge popular for food – wide range inc Sun roasts and lots of puddings, reasonable prices; friendly service, locals' bar *(Ann and Colin Hunt)*

Southwater [TQ1427]

Bax Castle [Two Mile Ash, a mile or so NW]: Simple and relaxing early 19th-c flagstoned pub pleasantly extended with ex-barn no-smoking restaurant, big fireplace in back room, well kept low-priced beer brewed for them by North Downs and others such as Bass, Brakspears, Fullers London Pride, good bar food inc children's helpings and good Sun lunch (best to book), no music, tables and chairs on pleasant lawns with play area; Downs Link Way for cyclists and walkers on former rail track *(David and Carole Chapman, Tony Scott, Gerald Karn, Bruce Bird)*

Staplefield [TQ2728]

Jolly Tanners [Handcross Rd, just off A23]: Spotless, quiet and comfortable, good reasonably priced varied home cooking, well kept Fullers Chiswick and London Pride, Harveys Best and a Mild such as Thwaites, friendly prompt service even under pressure, lots of china, brasses and old photographs, no-smoking room; attractive garden with lots of space for children; by green, quite handy for Nymans (NT) *(Bruce Bird, Tony Scott, Ron Shelton)*

Victory [Warninglid Rd]: Unpretentious whitewashed pub, dovecote in roof, picnic-sets and play area in garden overlooking cricket green; well kept Courage Best, Harveys and Wadworths 6X, decent wines, vast choice of good value food, welcoming staff, log fire, games area, decorative plates and horsebrasses; popular, get there early *(Brian and Anna Marsden, Bernard and Marjorie Parkin, LM)*

Steyning [TQ1711]

Anchor: Good service, well prepared food, good range of well kept ales *(M G Horne)*

Stone Cross [TQ6104]

Red Lion [the one nr Pevensey; Lion Hill]: Good value food and Harveys ales in big pub with skittle alley *(Tony Scott)*

Stoughton [SU8011]

☆ *Hare & Hounds* [signed off B2146 Petersfield—Emsworth]: Friendly and leisurely much modernised pub below downs with reliably good home-made food (can take a while) in airy pine-clad bar, big open fires, half a dozen changing well kept ales such as Cottage Southern, Ringwood Best and Timothy Taylor Landlord, restaurant, back darts room; children in eating areas, tables on pretty front terrace and in back garden; nr Saxon church, good walks nearby *(LYM, Prof and Mrs S Barnett, Bruce Bird, Ann and Colin Hunt, G B Lungden, Dodie Buchanan)*

Sutton [SU9715]

☆ *White Horse* [nr Bignor Roman Villa]: Traditional country pub in attractive little hamlet nr Bignor Roman villa, island servery separating bare-boards bar from two-room dining area, simple décor and furnishings, interesting choice of good food from good sandwiches to local game and fish, Brewery on Sea, Courage Best, Youngs and guest beers, log fire, friendly staff; tables in garden, good value bedrooms, comfortable and well equipped *(Tony and Wendy Hobden, LM, BB, David Dimock, R D and S R Knight, C L Kauffmann)*

Ticehurst [TQ6830]

Bull [Three Legged Cross; off B2099 towards Wadhurst]: Attractive 14th-c hall house with two big log fires in very heavy-beamed old-fashioned simple bar, light and airy dining extension, real ales such as Harveys Best and Pale Ale, Morlands Old Speckled Hen and local Rother Valley Level Best, darts, bar billiards and other traditional games, maybe piped music; charming garden with fish pond, outside summer bar and barbecue, two boules pitches, maybe w/e bouncy castle *(LYM, Peter Meister, Comus Elliott, Bob and Maggie Atherton)*

Turners Hill [TQ3435]

Crown: Spacious dining pub, different levels (one with pitched rafters), good choice inc Sun lunch, log fire, pleasant décor with pictures etc, well kept ales such as Morlands Old Speckled Hen, Tetleys and Weltons (from Lancing), decent wines, helpful service, soft piped music, tables outside, pleasant valley views from back garden; children welcome; two bedrooms *(Michael and Jenny Back, BB)*

Red Lion [Lion Lane]: Simple pub with well kept Harveys, good value food (no cooking Sun), friendly staff, wonderful fireplace, pretty garden *(W Ruxton, K and E Leist)*

Udimore [TQ8619]

Plough [B2089 W of Rye]: Friendly local with rustic bric-a-brac hanging from ceiling, wide range of food from pies and puddings to Asian and cajun dishes, Harveys and Fullers London Pride *(Conrad and Alison Freezer)*

Upper Beeding [TQ1910]

Rising Sun [A2037]: Fairly old pub just off South Downs Way, well laid out inside, with cosy nooks and crannies and soft lighting; well kept Whitbreads-related ales, bar food inc good ploughman's, welcoming staff, unobtrusive piped music, pleasant garden *(Gerald Karn)*

Wadhurst [TQ6131]

☆ *Best Beech* [Mayfield Lane (B2100 a mile W)]: Well run dining pub, pleasant dim-lit bar on left with wall seats, quiet but individual décor and coal fire, cosy eating area with lots of pictures and china on right, well done fresh bar food (not Sun evening) from sandwiches to particularly good steaks, well kept Harveys and other ales, decent wines, quick friendly service; back restaurant, good value bedrooms, good breakfast; has been cl Mon *(Joe and Mary Stachura, BB, Anon, Comus Elliott, Paul S McPherson, Jill Bickerton, Gwen and Peter Andrews)*

Rock Robin [B2099 NW, opp stn]: Friendly between-wars pub opp country station, recently reopened after being pleasantly brightened up, tempting range of real ales inc a local brew, generous bar lunches from big ploughman's and baguettes up, tables out in front *(Joe and Mary Stachura)*

Walberton [SU9705]

Royal Oak [Yapton Lane (B2132, just off A27 Arundel—Chichester)]: Good choice of good generous fresh food in neat, roomy open-plan bar and restaurant, polite attentive service, Arundel real ale, good range of wines at good prices, designs for film sets; piped classical music; garden with play area *(Tony and Wendy Hobden)*

Walderton [SU7810]

Barley Mow [Stoughton rd, just off B2146 Chichester—Petersfield]: Spacious flagstoned U-shaped bar with country bric-a-brac, well kept ales such as Ringwood Old Thumper, Ruddles Best and Wadworths 6X, good choice of good generous food inc vegetarian, two log fires, quick cheerful service on packed w/e, no music; children welcome, nice furniture in big pleasant garden with fish pond, aviary and swings, good walks, handy for Stansted House *(G B Lungden, Mrs Romey Heaton, Bruce Bird, Ann and Colin Hunt, N E Bushby, W Atkins)*

Waldron [TQ5419]

Star [Blackboys—Horam side road]: Lively modest local with big inglenook log fire in panelled bar, fair range of standard pub food with some interesting specials, real ales inc Bass and Harveys, no music, friendly helpful staff; restaurant, pleasant garden, seats out in front overlooking pretty village *(Mr and Mrs R Illingworth, BB)*

Warnham [TQ1533]

☆ *Greets* [Friday St]: 15th-c beamed pub, concentration on good interesting food (not Sun evening) from filled rolls to ambitious upmarket main dishes, uneven flagstones and inglenook log fire, lots of nooks and corners, well kept Whitbreads-related ales, decent wines, friendly attentive staff; convivial locals' side bar, tables in garden *(Peter and Giff Bennett, G W Stevenson)*

West Chiltington [TQ0918]

☆ *Elephant & Castle* [off A283 or B2139 E of Pulborough; Church St]: Open-plan turkey-carpeted local with stripped stone, dark wood furniture, coal-effect gas fire, good value generous freshly made straightforward food, well kept King & Barnes ales, fresh flowers, helpful service, no music; public bar with darts, children welcome, good terraced garden with play area, aviary, ducks and geese, behind ancient church in attractive village *(Penny and Martin Fletcher, BB, D and J Tapper, Keith Stevens, Peter Lewis, I S Wilson)*

☆ *Five Bells* [Smock Alley, off B2139 SE]: Consistently good reasonably priced fresh food, well kept King & Barnes and other ales from small breweries inc a Mild, annual beer festival, enthusiastic landlord, big sun lounge, pleasant garden *(Prof and Mrs S Barnett, Ian and Carol McPherson)*

West Dean [SU8512]

Selsey Arms [A286 Midhurst—Chichester]: Two large bars, smart dining lounge, tasty good value food inc interesting vegetarian dishes, well kept good value Brewery on Sea beer, decent good value wine, good service, log fire, lots of horse-racing pictures and memorabilia *(Ann and Colin Hunt)*

West Hoathly [TQ3632]

☆ *Cat* [signed from A22 and B2028 S of E Grinstead; North Lane]: Relaxing polished pub/restaurant, fresh flowers and candles, beams and panelling, two roaring log fires, piped classical music, good but pricy home-made food, well kept Harveys Best and Hardy Royal Oak, tables out on small terrace with quiet view of church; no children *(Ian and Carol McPherson, P R Morgan, G Simpson, David H T Dimock, Derek Harvey-Piper, S G N Bennett, LYM, B J Harding, Tony Scott, Mr Grantling)*

West Itchenor [SU8001]

Ship: Large panelled pub in good spot nr Chichester Harbour, cheery welcome and service, well kept Courage Directors, Morlands Old Speckled Hen and a beer brewed for the pub, two roaring fires, lots of bric-a-brac inc many chamber-pots, children in eating area, wide range of food in bar and restaurant, tables outside; said to be able to get supplies for yachtsmen (nearest shop is two miles away) *(Bruce Bird)*

West Marden [SU7713]

Victoria Arms [B2146 2 miles S of Uppark]: Good value home-made food inc interesting dishes and good sandwiches in pleasant rustic surroundings, well kept real ales, decent house wines, quick service, restaurant *(G B Longden)*

West Wittering [SZ8099]

☆ *Lamb* [Chichester Rd; B2179/A286 towards Birdham]: Immaculate 18th-c country pub, several rooms neatly knocked through with tidy furnishings, rugs on tiles, well kept Badger ales, decent wines, wide choice of reasonably priced food from separate servery, friendly staff; dogs on leads allowed, tables out in front and in small sheltered back garden – good for children, with outside salad bar on fine days; busy in summer *(BB, David Dimock, P R and S A White)*

Winchelsea [TQ9017]

☆ *New Inn* [German St; just off A259]: Variety of solid comfortable furnishings in bustling rambling beamed rooms, Georgian décor, some emphasis on food inc good fresh fish (sandwiches too), well kept changing ales such as Beards, Harveys, Greene King Triumph and one brewed for them by Adnams, decent wines and malt whiskies, friendly service, log fire; separate public bar with darts, children in eating area, pretty bedrooms (some sharing bathrooms), delightful setting *(LYM, Betzy*

Dinesen, R and M Bishop, Quentin Williamson, Paul S McPherson)

Wisborough Green [TQ0526]

Three Crowns: Big clean and polished open-plan bar stretching into dining room, stripped bricks and beams, good reasonably priced food inc big ploughman's and popular Sun lunch, well kept ales such as Greene King Abbot, quick attentive service, sizeable back garden *(E A Froggatt, David and Carole Chapman)*

Woodmancote [SU7707]

Woodmancote Arms [the one nr Emsworth]: Comfortable village local with friendly landlord, three well kept real ales, log fire, straightforward reasonably priced food; large games room for pool and darts *(Ann and Colin Hunt)*

Worthing [TQ1504]

Cricketers [Broadwater Green (A24)]: Quiet, clean and friendly extended panelled local with lower restaurant, well kept Bass, Fullers London Pride, Greene King IPA, Harveys and a guest beer, good value food, good staff; garden *(R T and J C Moggridge, Bruce Bird)*

Hare & Hounds [Portland Rd, just N of Marks & Spencer]: Friendly bustling busy extended pub with well kept Whitbreads-related ales and guests such as King & Barnes and Morlands Old Speckled Hen, good choice of reasonably priced straightforward food, wide range of customers, pleasant staff, tented courtyard; no car park but three multi-storeys nearby *(Tony and Wendy Hobden)*

Royal Oak [A259 nr Beach House Park]: Bass, Courage Directors and Morlands Old Speckled Hen, reasonably priced generous food inc local fish, pleasant staff; picnic-sets on sunny front terrace with showy hanging baskets *(John Beeken)*

Vine [High St, W Tarring]: Traditional neatly kept local in nice spot away from the day trippers, well kept King & Barnes, farm cider, good home-made lunchtime food; tables in back courtyard with bird cage (and maybe attentive cat) *(Anna and Martyn Carey, Simon Collett-Jones)*

Yapton [SU9704]

Maypole [signed off B2132 Arundel rd; Maypole Lane]: Friendly country pub with two log fires in lounge, good lunchtime food, well kept Ringwood Best and up to five guests from small brewers like Itchen Valley, Cottage and Frog Island, occasional weekends with all beers from one brewer, farm cider, amusing dog called Sid; seats outside, skittle alley *(Bruce Bird, R T and J C Moggridge)*

Warwickshire (including Birmingham and West Midlands)

This area has an excellent variety of pubs, including some really unusual ones such as the enthusiastic Fiddle & Bone in Birmingham (top-drawer live music), the Castle on Edge Hill (an extraordinary Gothick folly), the Case is Altered at Five Ways (an absolutely classic unspoilt pub), the Crooked House in Himley (so squint you can scarcely believe your eyes – good value, too), and the Little Dry Dock in Netherton (nautical décor taken to hilarious extremes). Some interesting newcomers are the Kings Head at Aston Cantlow (civilised food in charming Tudor surroundings), the Beacon in Sedgley (carefully updated classic traditional layout, brewing its own cheap, very individual and remarkably potent full-flavoured Mild Ale) and the Rose & Crown in Warwick (a very good town pub with a lot of character). Other pubs on top form here include the Bell at Alderminster (a smart and roomy dining pub), the Fox & Hounds at Great Wolford (friendly local atmosphere, imaginative food, very good real ales), and the Navigation at Lapworth (a good value happily pubby canalside pub). Other pubs for a good meal out are the Bear in Berkswell (an outstanding Chef & Brewer), the Howard Arms at Ilmington (promising new licensees) and the Chequers at Ettington (restauranty mediterranean-style food). For its winning combination of good food with all the virtues of a real country pub, the Fox & Hounds at Great Wolford is, for the second year running, Warwickshire Dining Pub of the Year. Drinks prices in the area are cheaper than average, with generally low prices in pubs tied to the regional brewer Banks's (who have now taken over Marstons); the cheapest beer we found was in the Vine in Brierley Hill, tied to the local Bathams. Holdens is another good value local Black Country brewer, and down in the south of the county beers from Donnington and Hook Norton in neighbouring counties are also low-priced. In the Lucky Dip section at the end of the chapter, pubs to note particularly are the Golden Cross at Ardens Grafton, Falcon at Hatton, Greyhound in Hawkesbury, Butchers Arms at Priors Hardwick, Black Swan in Stratford, Blue Boar at Temple Grafton, M A D O'Rourkes Pie Factory in Tipton, Tudor House and Zetland Arms in Warwick, Bell at Welford on Avon, Pheasant at Withybrook and Bulls Head at Wootton Wawen.

You are now allowed 20 minutes after 'time, please' to finish your drink – half an hour if you bought it in conjunction with a meal.

ALDERMINSTER SP2348 Map 4
Bell 🍴 ♀
A3400 Oxford—Stratford

There's a genuinely friendly welcome from the hardworking licensees at this fairly smart and well liked dining pub. It's only four miles from Stratford, so handy for supper before the theatre, but it is a good idea to book. The imaginative menu changes monthly and dishes are produced as far as possible from fresh ingredients. There might be tomato, red lentil and basil soup (£3.25), home-made pâté (£5.25), tomato stuffed with prawns (£5.95), sausages and mash (£6.75), tagliatelle with pesto and parmesan (£6.95), fish pie with watercress mash (£8.95), lemon and ginger chicken (£9.50), roast duck breast (£9.95), and daily specials like Loch Fyne smoked fish platter (£6.95) and grilled swordfish with lemon and dill sauce (£9.50); good value weekday two course lunch (£6.50). The communicating areas of the neatly kept spacious bar have plenty of stripped slatback chairs around wooden tables on the flagstones and wooden floors, little vases of flowers, small landscape prints and swan's-neck brass-and-globe lamps on the cream walls, and a solid fuel stove in a stripped brick inglenook; apart from the small entrance bar the whole pub is no smoking. Greene King Abbot and IPA under light blanket pressure, a good range of wines by the glass, freshly squeezed juice and a cocktail of the month. Readers with children have felt particularly welcome here – they have high chairs but no children's menu. A conservatory and terrace overlook the garden and Stour Valley. There is an extensive programme of parties, food festivals, classical and light music evenings throughout the year. *(Recommended by Brian Skelcher, John Bowdler, John Bramley, Michael and Jeanne Shillington, Jack Houghton, David and Ruth Shillitoe, Janet Arter, John Kane, Maysie Thompson, Roy Bromell, Robert N Burtsal, P and D Carpenter, Roger Braithwaite, P Lloyd)*

Free house ~ Licensee Keith Brewer ~ Real ale ~ Bar food ~ Restaurant ~ (01789) 450414 ~ Children welcome ~ Open 12-2.30, 7-11(10.30 Sun) ~ Bedrooms: £25(£30B)/£35(£55B)

ASTON CANTLOW SP1359 Map 4
Kings Head
Village signposted just off A3400 NW of Stratford

This carefully restored black and white Tudor pub is beautifully timbered: a charming sight, with its wisteria and colourful hanging baskets. Inside, the clean and comfortable village bar on the right has wooden settles around its massive inglenook log fireplace, flagstones, and an old-fashioned snug – a nice mix of rustic surroundings with a civilised gently upmarket atmosphere. There's increasing emphasis on good often inventive food in the carpeted main room, with its attractive window seats, windsor chairs, oak tables and corner longcase clock. The food, freshly prepared and from a menu that changes every three months, might include interesting light dishes such as soup (£3.25), Moroccan chicken kebabs with date, apple and fig chutney (£4.45), fried herring roes with red onion and parsley on a toasted brioche (£4.95), crispy oriental duck salad with sesame and blackberry dressing (£5.45), pork, apricot and sage sausages with cheesy leek mash (£7.95), salmon, cod and chive fishcakes with celeriac tartare (£8.45), braised lamb shank with rosemary jus (£9.45) and grilled sirloin with shallot and garlic confit and thyme jus (£9.95); most people would find their plate of mixed vegetables (£1.75 extra) ample for two, and their duck suppers – good value at £10.95 – are very popular; puddings might include chocolate bread and butter pudding or caramelised cranberry and orange brûlée (£3.95). Prices are the same in the bar and the restaurant. Good cheerful service, well kept Flowers IPA and Marstons Pedigree on handpump, decent wines; darts, dominoes, and cribbage. The pub is not far from Mary Arden's house in Wilmcote – well worth a visit. *(Recommended by Roy Bromell, Nigel and Sue Foster, Lord Sandhurst, Mr and Mrs D Shier, Carol and David Harard)*

Whitbreads ~ Tenants Catherine Shepherd and Paul Hales ~ Real ale ~ Bar food (12-2.30, 7-10(9 Sun)) ~ Restaurant ~ (01789) 488242 ~ Children welcome if eating ~ Open 11-11; 12-10.30 Sun; 11-3, 5.30-11 Mon-Fri winter; closed 25 Dec evening

BERKSWELL SP2479 Map 4

Bear

Spencers Lane; village signposted from A452 W of Coventry

This picturesque 16th-c timbered pub successfully combines a traditional relaxed atmosphere with a very wide choice of good value food happily showing that the Chef & Brewer formula can work well. Inside there are comfortably snug low-beamed areas, alcoves, nooks and crannies, panelling, a longcase clock, bric-a-brac and prints, and roaring log fires in winter; in one place the heavy timbers show the slope of the cat-slide eaves. All food is cooked to order, and besides well served doorstep sandwiches (from £2.75), filled ciabattas or baked potatoes (from £3.85) and ploughman's (from £4.05), a dozen or so daily specials might include fish and chips (£5.55), steak and kidney pudding (£6.20), wild mushroom penne (£6.55), lasagne (£6.50), turkey, ham and pork pie (£7.70), full rack of barbecue ribs (£12.75) and puddings such as apple and pecan pie (from £2.95). Well kept Courage Directors, Theakstons Best and a couple of guests like Ash Vine England Expects and Weltons Summer Special; decent house wines and unusually for this chain quite a few by the glass; piped music. There are tables behind on a tree-sheltered back lawn. The village church is well worth a visit. *(Recommended by John Bramley, B T Smith, Stephen G Brown, Brian Skelcher, Peter Burton, Ted George, Susan and John Douglas)*

Scottish Courage ~ Manager Ian Robinson ~ Real ale ~ Bar food (11-10 Mon-Sat, 12-9 Sun) ~ (01676) 533202 ~ Children welcome ~ Open 11-11; 12-10.30 Sun

BIRMINGHAM SP0586 Map 4

Fiddle & Bone

4 Sheepcote Street; opposite National Indoor Arena South car park

Winner of our Newcomer of the Year Award last year, this remarkably converted airy schoolhouse was set up by two members of the City of Birmingham Symphony Orchestra who couldn't find a pub in Birmingham they liked, so thought they'd start their own. There's a tremendously cheerful lively atmosphere, with live bands on the big stage at the end of the lofty main bar most sessions (see below) – mostly jazz, but also blues, soul, classical, and folk. They have activities you can join in, with a weekly choir practice, and salsa lessons for beginners and intermediates (there's a charge for these). They've hit exactly the right fun note with the decorations, with various musical instruments hanging from the ceiling or the walls, and along the bar counter trombones have been ingeniously converted into lights. Spotless varnished light pine tables with cushioned benches form little booths along each side of the bare-boards room, and a staircase in the middle leads down to the restaurant and a flagstoned bar area with a lighter café-bar feel. There are lots of picnic-sets outside here, but you get a better view of the boats on the adjacent canal through the windows of another bar upstairs. Well kept Marstons Pedigree, Theakstons Best and Old Peculier, and Fiddlers Pluck, a beer named for them by Theakstons, on handpump, a short but good choice of wines by the glass, and unusual schnapps; efficient helpful staff. Good bar food, with most things available all day, includes bread with taramasalata or houmous (£2.10), soup (£2.60), filled baguettes (from £4.05), fish and chips or spinach lasagne (£6.35), wiener schnitzel, roast leg of lamb or hungarian goulash (£7.75), tuna steak marinated in lime (£8.95), and apple strudel (£3.75); there may be a slight wait at busy times. Their website (www.fiddle-bone.co.uk) has a list of gigs coming up over the next month; there's usually good piped jazz when there isn't live music. Next door is a developing craft centre, and a waterbus stops just outside. It's handy for the National Sea Life Centre. *(Recommended by C J Fletcher, SLC, Stephen, Julie and Hayley Brown, Jean and Richard Phillips, Rob and Gill Weeks, Jack Barnwell, Maggie and Peter Shapland, John Dwane)*

Free house ~ Licensee Werner Koder ~ Real ale ~ Bar food (12-10) ~ Restaurant ~ (0121) 200 2223 ~ Children in eating area of bar and restaurant ~ Live music every night and four lunchtimes a week ~ Open 11-11; 12-10.30 Sun; closed 25, 26 Dec

BRIERLEY HILL SO9187 Map 4
Vine ◼ £

Delph Rd; B4172 between A461 and A4100, near A4100

You can get a very good value lunchtime snack at this warmly welcoming no-nonsense pub which is also the tap for the next-door Batham brewery – so the Bitter and Mild, and Delph Strong in winter, are well kept and also very reasonably priced. It's a popular place, full of local characters, so it can get crowded in the warmly welcoming front bar which has wall benches and simple leatherette-topped oak stools; the extended and refurbished snug on the left has solidly built red plush seats, and the back bar has brass chandeliers as well as darts, dominoes and fruit machine. Good fresh lunchtime snacks include samosas (65p), sandwiches (£1.10), pasta bake and salad (£2) and curry, faggots and peas, or steak and kidney pie (£2.75). The pub is known in the Black Country as the Bull & Bladder, from the good stained glass bull's heads and very approximate bunches of grapes in the front bow windows. *(Recommended by JP, PP, Theo, Anne and Jane Gaskin, Ian Phillips, the Didler)*

Bathams ~ Manager Melvyn Wood ~ Real ale ~ Bar food (lunchtimes Mon-Fri only) ~ (01384) 78293 ~ Children in children's room ~ Blues Sun evening ~ Open 12-11; 12-10.30 Sun

COVENTRY SP3379 Map 4
Old Windmill £

Spon Street

Known locally as Ma Brown's after a former landlady and as the friendliest pub in Coventry, this unpretentious timber-framed 15th-c inn, unlike the rest of the buildings in the street which are an interesting collection of transplanted survivors from the blitz, stands on its original site. The nicely battered interior is full of character: one of the rambling series of tiny cosy old rooms is little more than the stub of a corridor, another has carved oak seats on flagstones and a woodburner in a fine ancient inglenook fireplace, and another has carpet and more conventionally comfortable seats. There are exposed beams in the uneven ceilings, and a back room preserves some of the equipment used when Ma Brown brewed here. Well kept Courage Directors, Marstons Pedigree, Morlands Old Speckled Hen and a couple of guests like Banks's all kept under light blanket pressure; fruit machine, juke box and TV. Straightforward good value food passed out straight from the kitchen door includes filled batches (from £1.50), faggots and mushy peas (£3.50), home-made cottage pie or ploughman's (£3.50), cheesy cauliflower and broccoli bake or sausage and chips (£3.60) and gammon steak or steak pie (£3.75); no-smoking dining area. The pub is popular with students, extremely busy on Friday and Saturday evenings, and handy for the Belgrade Theatre. *(Recommended by John Brightley, G Washington, Thomas and Audrey Nott, Dorsan Baker)*

Scottish Courage ~ Tenant Lynne Ingram ~ Real ale ~ Bar food (12-2.30) ~ Restaurant ~ (0124) 7625 2183 ~ Children in restaurant ~ Folk first Tues of month ~ Open 11-11; 12-3, 7-10.30 Sun

DUNCHURCH SP4871 Map 4
Dun Cow

1⅓ miles from M45 junction 1: on junction of A45 and A426

The interior of this extensive mainly Georgian coaching inn, in the centre of the village, has been quite well preserved with lots of traditional features like welcoming open fires, rugs on the wooden and flagstone floors, exposed oak beams and country pictures, farmhouse furniture and bric-a-brac; it's all spotlessly kept and the staff are friendly and attentive. Bass and Worthingtons on handpump and a reasonable choice of wines by the glass; no-smoking area; piped music. The reasonably priced food is very popular so you may have to queue to order from the shortish menu which includes soup (£1.95), sandwiches and chips (from £3.60), liver and bacon (£4.95), beef and ale pie or fish and chips (£5.95), spinach and rice bake (£6.95), sirloin steak with mushrooms and mushroom sauce (£8.50); Sunday roast (£5.95). Outside there are tables in the pretty coachyard and on a sheltered side lawn. *(Recommended by Roy Bromell, John Brightley, Michael Betton, George Atkinson, Patrick Tailyour)*

Bass ~ Manager Florrie D'Arcy ~ Real ale ~ Bar food (all day) ~ (01788) 810305 ~ Children in eating area of bar and restaurant ~ Open 11-11; 12-10.30 Sun

EDGE HILL SP3747 Map 4
Castle
Off A422

Not to be missed, this beautifully positioned crenellated octagon tower is a folly built in 1749 by an 18th-c Gothic Revival fanatic to mark the spot where Charles I raised his standard at the start of the Battle of Edge Hill. The big attractive garden has splendid views across the battlefield, and it's said that after closing time you can hear ghostly sounds of the battle, and there's even been the apparition of a cavalry officer galloping by in search of his severed hand. There are arched doorways and the walls of the warm and cosy lounge bar have the same eight sides as the rest of the main tower and are decorated with maps, pictures and a lovely collection of Civil War memorabilia. In the public bar there are old farming implements as well as darts, pool, cribbage, dominoes, a fruit machine, Aunt Sally and piped music. Very well kept Hook Norton ales and a guest like Shepherd Neame on handpump, country wines and around 30 malt whiskies. Bar food includes sandwiches (from £2.50), ploughman's (£4.50), chicken curry or vegetarian pasta dishes (£5.50), cod and broccoli bake (£6.50), leek and mushroom crumble (£6.75), steak and kidney pudding, cajun chicken or mixed grill (£6.95), lamb tagine (£7.25) and steaks (£8.95). The bedrooms are in a separate tower, with Upton House nearby on the A422, and Compton Wynyates, one of the most beautiful houses in this part of England, not far beyond. *(Recommended by Brian and Anna Marsden, Susan and John Douglas, M Joyner, Prof A Black, Allan and Philippa Wright, Francis Johnston)*

Hook Norton ~ Lease: N J and G A Blann ~ Real ale ~ Bar food (12-2, 6.30-9) ~ (01295) 670255 ~ Children in eating area of bar till 9pm ~ Open 11.30(12 Sun)-2.30, 6.15-11 ~ Bedrooms: £32.50B/£52.50B

ETTINGTON SP2749 Map 4
Chequers
A422 Banbury—Stratford

The emphasis at this delightfully welcoming pub is very much on the imaginative food. Served by charmingly attentive bow-tied waiters, Mediterranean influenced dishes might include filled french bread (from £3.75), chicken club sandwich (£5.50), spinach, bacon and crouton salad or sausage and mash (£5.75), green-lipped mussels (£6.25), pesto pasta with salmon (£6.50), vegetable Thai curry (£7.75), chargrilled peppers with couscous (£8), wild boar (£10.50), Thai monkfish (£11.75) and steaks (from £13.50); puddings include home-made Baileys brûlée and summer pudding (£4). The carpeted lounge bar is decorated with comic hunting scenes, and has Adnams, Fullers London Pride and Hook Norton Best on handpump as well as an extensive wine list, piped music and no-smoking area. There's a spacious conservatory and in summer there are window boxes and flower tubs in front and tables under cocktail parasols in the neat back garden. *(Recommended by Miss H S Carthew, Gordon Hewitt, Miss A Aronica, Roger Braithwaite)*

Free house ~ Licensee R P Russell ~ Real ale ~ Bar food ~ Restaurant ~ (01789) 740387 ~ Children welcome ~ Open 12-2, 6.30-11; 12-3 Sun; closed Sun evenings

FIVE WAYS SP2270 Map 4
Case is Altered 🍺

Follow Rowington signposts at junction roundabout off A4177/A4141 N of Warwick, then
right into Case Lane

It's the feeling that nothing ever changes here which is the real charm of this
delightful white cottage which has been licensed to sell beer for over three centuries.
There's no food, no children or dogs, and no noisy games machines or piped music –
but you can be sure of a delightfully warm welcome from the cheery staff and
regulars. The small, unspoilt simple main bar is decorated with a fine old poster
showing the Lucas Blackwell & Arkwright brewery (now flats) and a clock with its
hours spelling out Thornleys Ale, another defunct brewery; there are just a few
sturdy old-fashioned tables, with a couple of stout leather-covered settles facing each
other over the spotless tiles. From this room you reach the homely lounge (usually
open only weekend evenings and Sunday lunchtime) through a door lit up on either
side. A door at the back of the building leads into a modest little room, usually
empty on weekday lunchtimes, with a rug on its tiled floor and an antique bar
billiards table protected by an ancient leather cover (it takes pre-decimal sixpences).
Well kept and very reasonably priced Ansells Mild, Flowers Original, Greene King
IPA and guest ales at weekends served by rare beer engine pumps mounted on the
casks that are stilled behind the counter. Behind a wrought-iron gate is a little brick-
paved courtyard with a stone table under a chestnut tree. *(Recommended by Jack and
Philip Paxton, Mayur Shah, Pete Baker, Pat and Tony Martin, Brian Skelcher, the Didler)*

*Free house ~ Licensee Jackie Willacy ~ Real ale ~ (01926) 484206 ~ Open 12(11.30
Sat)-2.30, 6-11; 12-2, 7-10.30 Sun*

GREAT WOLFORD SP2434 Map 4
Fox & Hounds ★ 🍽 🍺

Village signposted on right on A3400 3 miles S of Shipston on Stour

Warwickshire Dining Pub of the Year
Doing really well at the moment, this inviting 16th-c stone pub is possibly readers'
favourite pub in Warwickshire. What particularly appeals is its good all round
approach, so alongside its main draw, the imaginative bar food, there's a really
friendly welcome, locals pop in for a drink and they keep seven weekly changing real
ales. The cosy low-beamed old-fashioned bar has a nice collection of chairs and
candlelit old tables on spotless flagstones, old hunting prints on the walls, and a
roaring log fire in the inglenook fireplace with its fine old bread oven. A small tap
room serves the changing beers which might include Adnams, Black Sheep, Fullers
London Pride, Hook Norton Best, Jennings, Shepherd Neame Spitfire and
Wychwood Dog's Bollocks on handpump, and over 200 malt whiskies. Alongside
more straightforward meals like sandwiches, soup and ploughman's, imaginative
specials might include fresh sardines stuffed with onions and basil with provençal
sauce (£3.75), smoked salmon terrine (£3.75), pork fillet wrapped in bacon and
spinach with light green peppercorn sauce (£10.50), lamb kleftico (£9.95), grilled red
snapper with provençal butter, capers and lemon (£11) and puddings like sticky
toffee pudding (£3.50) and chocolate terrine or coconut parfait with an apricot
coulis (£3.75). There's a well on the terrace outside. *(Recommended by Dave and
Deborah Irving, H O Dickinson, R H Davies, M A and C R Starling, John Bowdler, John
Robertson, G Calcott, Sheila Keene, Martin Jones, Mike and June Coleman, Ann and Bob
Westbrook, K H Frostick, P J Hanson, Walter Reid, Mr and Mrs M F Norton, John Bramley, J H
Kane, Bernard Stradling, Pam Adsley, Robert N Burtsal, N, C and P Aston, A Ford, Jerry and
Alison Oakes)*

*Free house ~ Licensees Graham and Ann Seddon ~ Real ale ~ Bar food ~ (01608)
674220 ~ Well behaved children ~ Open 12-3, 7-11; 12-3 Sun; closed Sun evening,
Mon ~ Bedrooms: £35B/£70B*

HIMLEY SO8791 Map 4

Crooked House ★ £

Pub signposted from B4176 Gornalwood—Himley, OS Sheet 139 map reference 896908; readers have got so used to thinking of the pub as being near Kingswinford in the Midlands (though Himley is actually in Staffs) that we still include it in this chapter – the pub itself is virtually smack on the county boundary

Another eccentric building that's not to be missed, this is a pub that really does live up to its name – you'll really lose all sense of balance as you walk into this remotely set wonky old brick house. When subsidence caused by the mine workings underneath threw the pub 15 degrees out of true they propped it up, rehung the doors and straightened the floors. The result leaves your perceptions spinning in a way the landlord suggests is akin to being at sea. Inside on one table a bottle on its side actually rolls 'upwards' against the apparent direction of the slope, and for a 10p donation you can get a big ball-bearing from the bar to roll 'uphill' along a wainscot. There's a friendly atmosphere in the characterful old rooms, and at the back is a large, level and more modern extension with local antiques. Very reasonably priced Banks's Bitter and Marstons Pedigree and maybe Banks's seasonal ales on hand or electric pump; dominoes, fruit machine and piped music. Good value bar food includes sandwiches (from £1.45), soup (£1.55), chip butty (£1.99), chilli (£3.75), battered haddock (£4.40), vegetable tikka rosti (£4.60), beef and ale casserole (£4.75), chicken and mushroom pie (£4.99), and puddings like apple pie (£2.10). The conservatory is no smoking at food times, and there's a spacious outside terrace. It can get busy here with summer coach trips. *(Recommended by Ian Phillips, M Borthwick, Dr S J Shepherd, JP, PP, Mr and Mrs D Lawson)*

Banks's ~ Manager Gary Ensor ~ Real ale ~ Bar food ~ (01384) 238583 ~ Children in conservatory during food times ~ Morris men in summer ~ Open 11-11; 12-10.30 Sun; 11.30-3, 6.30-11 Mon-Fri winter

ILMINGTON SP2143 Map 4

Howard Arms

Village signposted with Wimpstone off A34 S of Stratford

New licensees at this smart golden-stone dining inn seem to be doing very well, with readers quite happy with the improvements they've made to the menu. It changes all the time but there might be soup (£3.25), sardines with garlic and lemon or smoked chicken with spring onion and watercress tart (£4.75), pear, melon and parma ham with rocket salad (£4.95), spaghetti with roasted peppers, tomato, basil and parmesan or twice baked wensleydale soufflé with celery and apple salad (£7.95), battered cod (£8.25), chicken supreme with tarragon cream sauce (£8.50), salmon fillet baked with horseradish and spring onion crust (£9.95), fried duck breast with orange and redcurrant sauce (£11.50), and puddings like toffee meringue, apple cake and custard or brandy snap basket with lemon cream and oranges (£3.95). There's a cosy atmosphere in the friendly heavy-beamed bar (possibly full of shooting gents on Saturday) which has rugs on lovely polished flagstones, comfortable seats, highly polished brass, and open fires, a couple of tables in a big inglenook, screened from the door by an old-fashioned built-in settle). A snug area off here is no smoking. Well kept Everards Tiger, North Cotswold Genesis and a guest like Marstons Pedigree under light blanket pressure, and organic juices; shove-ha'penny. The garden is lovely in summer with fruit trees sheltering the lawn, a colourful herbaceous border and well spaced picnic-sets, with more tables on a neat gravel terrace behind. It's nicely set beside the village green, and there are lovely walks on the nearby hills (as well as strolls around the village outskirts). *(Recommended by Martin Jones, G R Braithwaite, John Bowdler, John Robertson, June and Mike Coleman, Richard Sanders, John Bramley, Martin and Catherine Snelling, David Shillitoe, Maysie Thompson, Graham Tayar, Catherine Raeburn, K Frostick, N, C and P Aston, A Ford, Robert N Burtsal, Richard Fendick, Pam Adsley, J H Kane, Marvadene B Eves, Michael and Jeanne Shillington, Andrew Shore)*

Free house ~ Licensees Robert Greenstock and Martin Devereux ~ Real ale ~ Bar food ~ Restaurant ~ (01608) 682226 ~ Children in eating area of bar ~ Open 11-2.30, 6-11; 12-3, 7-10.30 Sun ~ Bedrooms: £35B/£55B

LAPWORTH SP1670 Map 4

Navigation

Old Warwick Rd (B4439 Warwick—Hockley Heath)

A fun place to be in the summer, this bustling local is prettily set by the canal with canal-users and locals sitting on a back terrace where they have barbecues, jazz, Morris dancers or even travelling theatre companies; outside hatch service, and it's all prettily lit at night. There's a good atmosphere in the friendly flagstoned bar too. It's decorated with some brightly painted canal ware and cases of stuffed fish, and has high-backed winged settles, seats built around its window bay and a coal fire in its high-mantled inglenook. Another quieter room has tables on its board-and-carpet floor, and a modern extension is nicely done with rugs on oak floors, cast-iron tables and bentwood chairs; delightful views over the sheltered flower-edged lawn, and on down to the busy canal behind. Bar food in big helpings includes lunchtime sandwiches (from £2.75), scampi (£6.25), beef in Guinness pie (£6.50), and daily specials like stilton and broccoli quiche (£6.95), venison steak (£8.50) or chicken stuffed with brie (£8.95), and puddings like passion cake or strawberry torte (£2.50). Service is cheery and efficient even when it's busy. Very well kept Bass, M&B Brew XI and a guest like Timothy Taylor Landlord on handpump, farm cider and lots of malt whiskies; cribbage, dominoes, fruit machine and TV. *(Recommended by Pat and Tony Martin, Tony Hobden, Pat and Clive Sherriff, Mike and Mary Carter, Dr Oscar Puls, Mrs G Sharman, Michael and Hazel Duncombe, Robert N Burtsal, Tom McLean)*

Bass ~ Lease Andrew Kimber ~ Bar food (12-2(2.30 Sun), 6(7 Sat)-9) ~ (01564) 783337 ~ Children in eating area of bar ~ Open 11-2.30, 5.30-11; 11-11 Sat; 11-10.30 Sun

LITTLE COMPTON SP2630 Map 4

Red Lion ♀

Off A44 Moreton in Marsh—Chipping Norton

The simple but civilised and comfortable low-beamed lounge at this attractive 16th-c stone inn has snug alcoves and a couple of little tables by the log fire. The plainer public bar has another log fire, and darts, pool, cribbage, fruit machine and juke box. Donnington BB and SBA under light blanket pressure and an extensive wine list; good service; maybe piped music. The good bar food here is popular so you may need to book (especially at weekends). As well as soup (£2.50), chicken liver pâté (£3.75), filled french sticks (from £2.95), ploughman's (£4.25), filled baked potatoes (from £3.75), plaice (£5.25), lasagne or tagliatelle niçoise (£6.25), seafood pie (£6.95), daily specials might include breaded brie and cumberland sauce (£3.75), chicken korma (£6.95), grilled marinated swordfish steak (£7.95) and poached salmon fillet with prawn and scallop sauce (£8.25); no-smoking dining area. No dogs – even in the garden where there are tables and a children's play area. Conveniently positioned for exploring the Cotswolds. *(Recommended by NWN, Pam Adsley, K H Frostick, R Huggins, D Irving, T McLean, E McCall, M G Swift, R C Watkins, Dr A Drummond, Mr and Mrs H Quick, Tim and Linda Collins, Robert N Burtsal, Gordon, D M and M C Watkinson, Tim Brierly)*

Donnington ~ Tenant David Smith ~ Real ale ~ Bar food ~ Restaurant ~ (01608) 674397 ~ Children in restaurant and eating area of bar, must be over eight to stay ~ Open 11-2.30, 6-11; 12-3, 7-10.30 Sun ~ Bedrooms: £25/£38

LOWSONFORD SP1868 Map 4

Fleur de Lys

Village signposted off B4439 Hockley Heath—Warwick; can be reached too from B4095 via Preston Bagot

In summer it's pleasant to sit outside on the picnic-sets among tall weeping willows by the canal at this attractively set pub. In winter the big comfortable spreading bar is warmed by a log fire, has lots of low black beams in the butter-coloured ceiling, brocade-cushioned mate's, wheelback and dining chairs around the well spaced tables, and rugs on the flagstones and antique tiles. Flowers Original, Fullers London Pride and Wadworths 6X under light blanket pressure. Bar food includes pasta with roasted vegetables and sun-dried tomatoes or dressed crab salad (£6.95), sizzling cajun platters or steak and ale pie (from £7.95), rack of lamb (£9.25), beef wellington (£10.95). Children are welcome in the no-smoking family area and there's a good play area outside; no dogs. *(Recommended by George Little, M G Swift, John Bramley, Brian Skelcher, D A Norman, Paul and Judith Booth, Roy Bromell, Sue Rowland, Paul Mallett, Barbara and Alan Mence, Robert N Burtsal, Simon Hulme, Patricia M Holcroft)*

Whitbreads ~ Managers Ian and Maria Blackman ~ Real ale ~ (01564) 782431 ~ Children in family room ~ Open 11.30-11; 12-10.30 Sun

MONKS KIRBY SP4683 Map 4
Bell 🍴 ♀

Just off B4027 (former A427) W of Pailton; Bell Lane

This timbered and flagstoned old pub is a bit of a favourite with us for its warmly comfortable and informal southern European atmosphere generated by the chatty Spanish landlord. That's not to mention the enjoyable extensive tapas board (£3.75-4.25) and the broadly based printed menu with its hugely tempting (though not especially cheap) range of Spanish and fish dishes such as chorizo cooked in garlic and white wine (£3.95), king prawns in garlic and chilli sauce (£4.95), Spanish omelette (£5.95), loin of pork with chilli and garlic sauce (£8.75), chicken with chorizo (£10.50), paella (£10.90), speciality steak grills (from £10.75), monkfish cooked in a clay dish with red peppers, herbs, garlic and white wine (£11.95), sea bass in a white wine and shellfish sauce (£15.25), as well as more traditional dishes like soup (£2.95), moules marinières (£3.75), vegetable curry (£6.50), mixed grill (£9.75) and beef wellington (£11.50). The interior although old is fairly straightforward with a no-smoking dining area and piped music. As well as well kept Boddingtons and Flowers Original on handpump there's a very good wine list, ports for sale by the bottle and a healthy range of brandies and malt whiskies. The plain little back terrace has rough-and-ready rustic woodwork, geese and chickens and a pretty little view across a stream to a buttercup meadow. *(Recommended by Brian Smart, Eric and June Heley, John Bramley, Dave and Deborah Irving, Roy Bromell, Susan and John Douglas, Brian and Anna Marsden)*

Free house ~ Licensee Paco Garcia Maures ~ Real ale ~ Bar food ~ Restaurant ~ (01788) 832352 ~ Children welcome ~ Open 12-2.30, 7-10.30; closed Mon lunchtime, 26 Dec, 1 Jan

NETHERTON SO9387 Map 4
Little Dry Dock £

Windmill End, Bumble Hole; you really need an A-Z street map to find it – or OS Sheet 139 map reference 953881

This lively red, white and blue painted, rather eccentric canalside pub began life as a boatyard. Not much was changed during its conversion – Ushers Best, Founders and a guest on handpump are served from an entire narrowboat which is squeezed into the right-hand bar (its engine is in the room on the left), and there's also a huge model boat in one front transom-style window, winches and barge rudders flanking the door, marine windows, and lots of brightly coloured bargees' water pots, lanterns, jugs and lifebuoys; fruit machines and piped music. Still keeping it pubby, the new licensee plans to make minor improvements to what has always been a fairly simple good value menu including soup (£1.75), sandwiches (from £1.95), faggots and peas (£4.50), gammon and egg (£5.25), minted lamb or beef pie (£5.50), with daily specials like prawn cocktail (£2.50), fried herby mushrooms (£2.95), seafood crumble (£4.95), chicken and mushroom pie (£5) or pork fillet in mustard sauce (£5.50), and traditional puddings and gateaux (£2). There are pleasant towpath walks nearby. *(Recommended by Ian Phillips)*

Ushers ~ Lease: Chris Baggus ~ Real ale ~ Bar food (11-2.30, 6-10) ~ (01384) 235369 ~ Children in eating area of bar ~ Open 11-3, 6-11; 11-11 Sat; 11-10.30 Sun

SAMBOURNE SP0561 Map 4
Green Dragon
A435 N of Alcester, then left fork onto A448 just before Studley; village signposted on left soon after

A reliable place, this welcoming village-green pub with its shuttered and timbered facade is handy to know for its friendly welcome and tasty bar food which includes sandwiches (from £1.95), soup (£2.50), devilled whitebait (£2.95), mussels in white wine, garlic and cream (£4.95), ploughman's, sausages with bubble and squeak, steak and Guinness pie, lasagne or curry (£5.50), tomato and mozzarella in an oregano and white wine sauce or vegetable and nut strudel in tomato and basil sauce (£5.95), scampi or stir-fried chicken (£6.50), marinated chicken with mint yoghurt (£9.50) and 8oz sirloin (£10.95); there are far more elaborate dishes in the restaurant menu. The cheery modernised communicating rooms have low beamed ceilings, rugs on flagstoned floors, little armed seats and more upright ones, some small settles, and open fires; maybe piped music. Well kept Bass, Hancocks and M & B Brew XI on handpump; friendly, attentive service. There are picnic-sets and teak seats among flowering cherries on a side courtyard, by the car park; bowls. The bedrooms are neatly decorated and well equipped. prettily bedecked with colourful hanging baskets in summer. *(Recommended by Pat and Clive Sherriff, B T Smith, Tom Gondris, Kay Neville-Rolfe, E A Froggatt, J H Kane, Christopher Turner)*

Bass ~ Lease: Phil Burke ~ Real ale ~ Bar food ~ Restaurant (12-2, 6.30-10) ~ (01527) 892465 ~ Children in eating area of bar and restaurant ~ Open 11-3, 6-11; 12-5, 7-10.30 Sun ~ Bedrooms: £48S/£60S

SEDGLEY SO9193 Map 4
Beacon ★ ◧
129 Bilston Street (no pub sign on our visit, but by Beacon Lane); A463, off A4123 Wolverhampton—Dudley

The Original Victorian layout of this delightful own-brew brick pub means you'll probably encounter a couple of locals lingering on the stairs and along the quarry-tiled drinking corridor chatting to the waistcoated barman who leans in the doorway of the little central servery. The front door opens into this plain corridor, you can easily imagine a Victorian traveller tucked up in the little room on the left by the imposing green tiled marble fireplace with its big misty mirror, the door closed for privacy and warmth, the pub cat (Sam) asleep under the wall settle, with a drink received through the little glazed serving hatch. The dark painted wood, turkey carpet, velvet and net curtains, heavy mahogany tables, old piano and little landscape prints all seem unchanged since those times. In an even simpler room on the right, with a black kettle and embroidered mantle over a blackened range an old man sits on a stripped wooden bench. The corridor runs round into a very big dark panelled smoking room with particularly long red leather wall settles down each side, gilt-based cast-iron tables, a big blue carpet on the lino floor and dramatic sea prints. Round a corner, the plant filled conservatory has genuinely horticultural intentions with no seats at all. Perhaps the best thing about this atmospheric old place is the wonderfully aromatic award winning Sarah Hughes beers which are brewed in a room at the back and include Sarah Hughes Dark Ruby, Pale Amber and Surprise Bitter; they also keep a guest like Shepherd Neame Masterbrew. The only food they serve is cheese and onion cobs (80p). There's a children's play area in the garden. *(Recommended by Mr and Mrs I Rispin)*

Free house ~ Licensee John Hughes ~ Real ale ~ (01902) 883380 ~ Children in family room ~ Open 12-2.30, 5.30-10.45; 12-3, 5.30-11 Sat; 12-3, 7-10.30 Sun; closed 25 Dec evening

---

Though we don't usually mention it in the text, most pubs will now make coffee – always worth asking. And many – particularly in the North – will do tea.

SHUSTOKE SP2290 Map 4
Griffin 🍺

5 miles from M6, junction 4; A446 towards Tamworth, then right on to B4114 and go
straight through Coleshill; pub is at Furnace End, a mile E of village

There's always a good mixed crowd, even mid-week, at this charmingly
unpretentious country local. The very friendly low-beamed L-shaped bar has a nice
old-fashioned settle and cushioned café seats (some quite closely packed), sturdily
elm-topped sewing trestles, lots of old jugs on the beams, beer mats on the ceiling,
and warming log fires in both stone fireplaces (one's a big inglenook); the
conservatory is popular with families; fruit machine. An outstanding feature here is a
range of up to ten real ales, with one or two from their own microbrewery which
produces the very palatable Church End, Choir Boy, Cuthberts, Old Pal, Vicar's
Ruin or perhaps Pew's Porter, which are served alongside Marstons Pedigree and
Highgate Mild and interesting guests such as Bathams, Exmoor Gold, Holdens,
Otter Bright, Theakstons Mild and Old Peculier, Timothy Taylor Landlord, all from
a servery under a very low, thick beam; country wine, mulled wine and hot punch
also. Good lunchtime bar food includes lasagne or steak pie with chips and mushy
peas (£4.75) and cod and chips (£6); you may need to arrive early to get a table.
There are old-fashioned seats and tables on the back grass, a children's play area,
and a large terrace with plants in raised beds. *(Recommended by JP, PP, John Dinane,
John Dwane, Ian Phillips, Paul Cleaver)*

*Free house ~ Licensee Michael Pugh ~ Real ale ~ Bar food (12-2 only, not Sun) ~
(01675) 481205 ~ Children in the conservatory ~ Open 12-2.30, 7-11; 12-3, 7-10.30
Sun*

WARMINGTON SP4147 Map 4
Plough £

Village just off B4100 N of Banbury

An understated little local this, but well placed in a delightful village a few yards up
a quiet lane from a broad sloping green with duck pond and ducks, and it looks
especially pretty in the autumn, when the creeper over the front of the building turns
a striking crimson colour. There's a nicely relaxed and cheery atmosphere in the
warmly cosy bar which has old photographs of the village and locals, an old high-
backed winged settle, cushioned wall seats and lots of comfortable Deco small armed
chairs and library chairs, and good winter log fires. Well kept Hook Norton Best,
Marstons Pedigree and a guest on handpump, and several malt whiskies; darts,
dominoes, cribbage and piped pop music. Unambitious but good food includes
cottage pie or chilli (£4.50) and flavoursome home-baked ham, egg and chips
(£5.50), and a popular Sunday lunch (although readers report that there may not be
a choice of roasts). Very friendly licensee and staff. *(Recommended by John Bowdler, M
Joyner, J H Bell, George Atkinson, K and A Moncreiffe, John Robertson, B T Smith, Kerry Law,
Simon Smith, CMW, JJW)*

*Free house ~ Licensee Denise Linda Willson ~ Real ale ~ Bar food (12-2, 6.30-8.30) ~
(01295) 690666 ~ Children in eating area of bar ~ Open 12-3, 5.30-11; 12-3, 7-10.30
Sun; closed 25 Dec evening*

WARWICK SP2865 Map 4
Rose & Crown 🍺

30 Market Place

The jovial barman, firmly stanced in front of the mirrored gantry at this cheery town
square pub with its magnificent etched glass windows, extends a warm welcome to
visitors and locals alike. The relaxing main bar is light-heartedly decorated with
painted wooden models - hot air balloons, clowns and airships hanging from the
ceiling, and a wooden dog curled up asleep by the fire (not lit when we inspected). A
couple of polished little round tables with black and gold cast iron bases are set in
the big front windows, and there's a fruit machine and TV. The piped nostalgic pop

music is fairly loud. A cosy snug behind the bar has red leatherette banquettes, framed cigarette cards and an interesting collection of local 1940s automobile industry photographs. And leading back to the front bar the high ceilinged no-smoking lounge with dark green walls above a dark green dado surprised us with its interesting red streaked stone-effect paint finish. As well as Bass, M&B Brew XI and Highgate Dark Mild, well kept, there might be a guest cider like Bounds Brand; darts, cribbage, dominoes and board games. Bar food is pretty good value anyway but if you pick the joker out of the pack you're offered when you place your order you get to eat for free – otherwise sandwiches (from £1.75), soup (£2.50), steak and kidney pie (£4.95), all day breakfast, minted lamb cutlets or cauliflower cheese (£4.95) and traditional sponge puddings. *(Recommended by Pete Baker, B and J Perrett)*

Bass ~ Lease: Brian Parker ~ Real ale ~ Bar food (12-3(5.30 Sat, Sun)) ~ (01926) 492876 ~ Live entertainment Mon, Fri ~ Open 11-11; 12-10.30 Sun

---

Lucky Dip

Besides the fully inspected pubs, you might like to try these Lucky Dips recommended to us and described by readers (if you do, please send us reports):

Alcester [SP0857]
Roebuck [A435]: Old but much altered, with Theakstons Best and XB, friendly service, wide choice of good value generous food inc OAP lunches and pleasant conservatory restaurant; well equipped bedrooms *(June and Mike Coleman)*
Allesley [SP2981]
Rainbow [Birmingham Rd]: Basic busy local in lopsided ancient building, a pub from the early 1950s, brewing its own ales, also Courage; good value food, friendly service, sunny garden; open all day, can be crowded with young people at night *(Edward Norris, John Bramley)*
Ansty [SP3983]
☆ *Rose & Castle* [B4065 NE of Coventry]: Popular low-beamed pub with cheerful friendly service, wide choice of good value food, well kept Bass and other ales inc a rotating guest beer, some canal-theme decoration; not big, fills up quickly and can get a bit smoky; children welcome, lovely canalside garden with play area *(Roy Y Bromell, Ray Crabtree, Tony Hobden, John Brightley)*
Ardens Grafton [SP1153]
☆ *Golden Cross* [off A46 or B439 W of Stratford; Wixford rd]: Friendly L-shaped bar with Shakespearean murals, good choice of food in its small rooms or in dining room with remarkable collection of world-wide and antique dolls, and no-smoking room with teddy bear collection; good choice of well kept more or less local beers such as Barrows 4Bs, Black Knight and Judges, very welcoming efficient service, photographic magazines (local society meets here); unobtrusive piped music, fruit machine; tables in charming garden, nice views *(June and Mike Coleman, Dr B and Mrs P B Baker)*
Armscote [SP2444]
Armscote Inn [off A3400 Stratford—Shipston]: Spotless family-run pub in picturesque Cotswold stone village, cheery family service, good choice of food in bar and restaurant, well kept Greene King Abbot, Hook Norton Best and a guest, decent coffee *(John Kane, Alan Jennings, Mike and Barbara Donaldson)*
Austrey [SK2906]
Bird in Hand [Church Lane]: Thatch and beams, extended and done up; bar meals weekday lunchtimes, evening restaurant, Marstons Pedigree and a guest beer; quiet village *(Robin Shrives, Nick Dowson)*
Barston [SP2078]
Bulls Head [from M42 junction 5, A4141 towards Warwick, first left, then signed down Barston Lane]: Attractive partly Tudor village local, oak-beamed bar with log fires and Buddy Holly memorabilia, comfortable lounge with pictures and plates, dining room, friendly relaxed service, good value basic food inc good fresh fish, well kept Bass, M&B Brew XI and Tetleys, secluded garden, hay barn behind *(Pete Baker, Brian Skelcher, Roy Y Bromell)*
Bearley [SP1760]
Golden Cross [Bearley Cross, A3400 N of Stratford]: Popular and friendly pub/restaurant, lovely old timbered bar with open fireplaces, soft lighting, good generous food in bar and small restaurant, well kept Whitbreads-related ales, helpful staff *(Dave Braisted, David Green)*
Birmingham [SP0786]
Anchor [Bradford St, Digbeth]: Perfectly preserved three-room Edwardian corner pub, carefully restored art nouveau windows, long high-ceilinged bar with basic seating, well kept Ansells Mild, Everards Tiger and Tetleys, interesting quickly changing guest beers, festivals with lots of beers from single brewery, lots of bottled beers; well priced simple food all day inc huge chip butties, friendly staff, back games room with pool, TV, juke box; tables outside, handy for coach stn *(Tony Hobden, John Dwane, Richard Lewis, SLC)*
☆ *Bellefield* [Winson St, Winson Green]: Unspoilt friendly sidestreet local with beautiful Victorian tile pictures, ornate ceiling, Georgian smoking room; Everards Mild, Tiger and Old Bill and guest beers, interesting bottled beers and occasional beer festivals; good value traditional West Indian home cooking, pub games, music; open all day, terrace for children *(the Didler)*

Black Eagle [Factory Rd, Hockley]: Four-room character late 19th-c pub, nicely furnished, with good varied low-priced home-cooked food, good friendly service, well kept Ansells, Marstons and a guest beer such as Beowulf, small back restaurant *(John Dwane)*

Covered Waggon [Yardley Wood Rd, Moseley]: Tastefully extended, good range of usual food with OAP discounts, Bass, welcoming staff and long-serving landlord *(Jack Barnwell)*

Crown [Corporation St]: Ornate city pub with well kept real ales *(Dr and Mrs A K Clarke)*

Factotum & Firkin [Bennetts Hill]: Lively conversion of building society banking hall with balcony, side bar, bare boards, lots of artefacts, red telephone box, friendly staff; good value food, well kept beers, good service, games machines, theme nights, stage for live music; open all day *(Richard Lewis, Paul and Sue Merrick, Ted George)*

Figure of Eight [Broad St]: Large friendly open-plan Wetherspoons pub with raised side area, nicely decorated and furnished, no-smoking areas, lots of old books, good staff, good value food from baguettes up all day, no music, good range of Scottish Courage and other well kept beers, sensible prices *(SLC)*

Lamp [Barford St, Digbeth]: Two small well furnished rooms, cosy and friendly, lunchtime food, well kept ales such as Batemans Mild, Boddingtons, Stanway Stanway and Wadworths 6X; open 12-11 (cl Sun afternoon), live music some nights *(SLC, John Dwane)*

Merchant Stores [Broad St]: Well lit café-bar with bare boards, pine and big windows, Banks's Bitter, food from sandwiches up, piped music (can be loud), fruit machine *(SLC)*

Old Contemptibles [Edmund St]: Spacious and comfortable Edwardian pub with lofty ceiling and lots of woodwork, well kept Bass, M&B Brew XI, Highgate Dark Mild and changing guest beers, friendly attentive staff, food lunchtime and early evening (not Sat eve or Sun); open all day, cl Sun, handy for central attractions *(R Michael Richards, SLC, LYM, Sue Holland, Dave Webster)*

Old Crown [High St, Digbeth]: Said to date from 1368, reopened after many years' closure; Banks's beers, attractive décor, candles on tables; restaurant *(John Dwane)*

Pavilions [Alcester Rd, Kings Heath]: Tastefully converted big Victorian pub, well kept Banks's and other ales such as Marstons, straightforward food *(Jack Barnwell)*

Square Peg [Corporation St]: Roomy Wetherspoons pub in former department store, high ceilings, two levels, no-smoking end, lots of old local prints, good choice of well kept ales inc guests from nearly 30-metre bar (could sometimes do with more staff), farm cider, decent wines, good mix of people, no music; open all day, wholesome good value food 11-10, sensible prices *(Richard Lewis, Daren Haines, G Coates, SLC, Mrs G Sharman)*

☆ *Tap & Spile* [Brindley Wharf/Gas St]: Nice canalside position opp Gas St Basin, authentic wharfside feel, three levels, small interconnecting rooms, stripped brickwork and reclaimed timber, old pine pews and settles, lots of prints, friendly staff, good choice of well kept ales, good menu *(Susan and John Douglas, Sue Demont)*

White Swan [Bradford St, Digbeth]: Unfussy but clean and comfortable friendly local with serving hatch to corridor, big bar, fire in small back lounge, ornate tilework, charming staff, lovely fresh rolls, well kept Ansells Bitter and Mild and Tetleys *(Pete Baker, SLC, Ted George, PB)*

Woodman [Albert St]: Fine little-changed Victorian pub with unusual juke box (mainly 60s and Irish) in friendly and lively L-shaped main bar, hatch service to relaxing back smoke room with superb tiling and coal fire, particularly good fresh warm baguettes, well kept Ansells Mild, Tetleys and a guest beer, friendly unhurried service *(Pete Baker)*

Bishops Tachbrook [SP3161]

Leopard [nr M40 junction 13, via A452]: Friendly country pub with reasonably priced food, well kept ales Flowers, Greene King and guest beers; children welcome away from bar *(Nigel and Sue Foster)*

Bodymoor Heath [SP2096]

Dog & Doublet [Dog Lane]: Cosy canalside pub right by lock, with well kept Bass, Stones and M&B Mild, good value food inc good mixed grill, dark-panelled rooms both sides of bar, beams, brasses, bargees' painted ware, several open fires, tables in pleasant garden; popular with businessmen at lunch, can get a bit crowded at w/e; bedrooms, nr Kingsbury Water Park *(Charles and Pauline Stride, Roger and Pauline Pearce)*

Brinklow [SP4379]

Bulls Head [A427, fairly handy for M6 junction 2]: Taken over by licensees who did well at (main entry) White Lion at Arreton, Isle of Wight; good family atmosphere, decent food from fresh sandwiches up inc plenty of vegetarian and children's dishes, well kept ales such as Brains SA, Flowers Original, Hook Norton Best and Marstons Pedigree; collection of old pub signs, no-smoking area, shove-ha'penny and table skittles; new indoor play area as well as outdoor one *(anon)*

Broom [SP0853]

☆ *Broom Tavern* [High St; off B439 in Bidford]: Attractive and popular 16th-c timber-framed pub, comfortable and relaxing for a drink though emphasis on wide choice of good food, cooked by Polish landlord, in bar and two restaurant rooms (tables can be booked), Bass, Boddingtons, Flowers IPA and Hook Norton, good value choice of wines, big log fire, hunting and country life cartoons, good service; children welcome *(Martin Jones, June and Mike Coleman, Gordon)*

Bubbenhall [SP3672]

Malt Shovel [off A445 S of Coventry; Lower End]: Attractive inside and out, small bar and larger L-shaped lounge rather geared to food (reasonably priced), beams, brass and copper, comfortable banquettes, quiet piped music, fresh flowers, play area with basketball net,

Ansells, Bass, Tetleys and Marstons Pedigree, kindly staff; delightful village *(John Brightley)*
Three Horseshoes: Unspoilt old village local, plenty of character *(John Brightley)*

Church Lawford [SP4576]
Old Smithy [Green Lane]: Much extended thatched and beamed 16th-c dining pub with dark woodwork in L-shaped lounge on various levels, good range of food cooked to order from separate servery, quite a few well kept ales, good friendly service; games room, conservatory; no dogs, children welcome, garden with slide *(Richard Houghton)*

Claverdon [SP1964]
Red Lion [Station Rd; B4095 towards Warwick]: Tasteful dining pub with rooms partly opened together, hop-hung beams, good home-cooked food, well kept Whitbreads-related ales and Marstons Pedigree, log fire, conscientious service, no-smoking back dining area with country views over sheltered terrace and gardens; piped music *(Mr and Mrs D Boynton, John Bowdler, BB)*

Corley [SP2985]
Saracens Head [B4098 Coventry—Tamworth]: Well kept Banks's Mild, Boddingtons, Flowers Original and Wadworths 6X, food inc good Sun lunch, attentive friendly landlord *(Roger Wain-Heapy)*

Coughton [SP0760]
Throckmorton Arms: Enjoyable food inc adventurous specials *(Dave Braisted)*

Coventry [SP3379]
Browns [Jordan Well, between Council House and Herbert Art Gallery]: Exceptional range of freshly cooked low-priced food at one reasonable price all day in big dramatic modern café-bar, many different types of seating area inc terrace, well kept real ales, very wide appeal; live music upstairs some nights, open 9am-11pm (1am Fri/Sat, 10-7 Sun) *(John Brightley)*
Malt Shovel [Spon End; B4101 just W of centre]: Cosy old-fashioned pub in terrace of preserved ancient buildings, log fires, good choice of real ales inc Donnington SBA, occasional music evenings in marquee-covered back courtyard; tables outside *(John Brightley)*

Dudley [SO9390]
☆ *Bottle & Glass* [Black Country Museum]: Splendid reconstruction of old Black Country alehouse in extensive open-air working Black Country Museum (well worth a visit for its re-created assortment of shops, gaslit cinema with Charlie Chaplin shorts, fairground, school, barge wharf and tram system); friendly staff in period clothes, two roaring fires, well kept Holdens ('Lager? We don't sell any of that modern stuff!'), good filled rolls and smokies, children welcome in two separate rooms off passage *(LM)*

Ettington [SP2550]
Houndshill House [A422 towards Stratford; aka Mucky Mongrel]: Recently decorated dining pub with welcoming landlord and good value traditional food in pleasant surroundings, very popular with families and OAPs; Scottish Courage ales, stripped stone and beams, good

service, tables in big attractive garden with play area well away from buildings, good views from front; children welcome, good well equipped bedrooms *(Maureen O'Neill, Roy Bromell)*

Farnborough [SP4349]
☆ *Butchers Arms* [off A423 N of Banbury]: Attractive country pub with period oak furniture to suit its old-fashioned layout and flagstone floor, most of the tables devoted to the generous food from sandwiches up, Bass, Hook Norton Best and Wardens Best, decent wine list, good log fire, countrified dining extension, darts in front public bar; garden liked by children for its rabbits, chickens, hamsters and aviary *(LYM, Dave Braisted, Sheila Keene, Mike Gorton, David Toulson)*

Fenny Compton [SP4152]
Merrie Lion [High St]: Friendly little neatly divided local, old and very clean; quick friendly service, well kept beers inc Banks's and Bass, reasonably priced usual food inc good sandwiches; handy for Burton Dassett country park *(Joan and Tony Walker)*

Flecknoe [SP5164]
Old Olive Bush [off A425 W of Daventry]: Unspoilt Edwardian pub in quiet photogenic village, no piped music – just conversation; attractive garden *(John Brightley)*

Frankton [SP4270]
Friendly [about 1¼ miles S of B4453 Leamington Spa—Rugby]: Hard-working new landlord in friendly old low-ceilinged village pub with good value food, well kept Greene King IPA, Hook Norton and local Judges Grey Wig, wooden settles in dark-wood rooms, coal fire *(George Atkinson)*

Gaydon [SP3654]
Malt Shovel [just off M40 junction 12, across B4100 nr church]: Unusual panelled bar with big stained-glass window at one raised end, small lounge area with sofas and easy chairs, open bar with beams, barrels, stone jars and fish tank with shubunkins, good value standard food, Flowers IPA, filter coffee, welcoming service; maybe loud piped heavy metal *(George Atkinson)*

Grandborough [SP4966]
Shoulder of Mutton [off A45 E of Dunchurch]: Well refurbished creeper-covered pub with attractive pine furnishings in beamed and panelled lounge, good well priced fresh food (should book Fri/Sat evening and Sun lunch), friendly staff, Marstons Pedigree and Whitbreads-related ales, good coffee, no music; garden with play area, cl Mon *(Roy Bromell)*

Halesowen [SO9683]
Waggon & Horses [Stourbridge Rd]: Welcoming local, recently refurbished but still entirely unpretentious, with well kept Bathams, a house beer and up to a dozen or so interesting changing ales from small independent brewers – staff well informed about them; no food *(Paul Kelly, Richard Houghton, the Didler)*

Hampton in Arden [SP2081]
White Lion [High St; fairly handy for M42 junction 6]: Unpretentious inn with unfussy beamed lounge, real fire, nautical décor inc

navigation lights, welcoming staff, quick food (not Sun) from sandwiches to steaks inc children's, well kept Bass, M&B Brew XI and John Smiths, decent wine, public bar with cribbage and dominoes, back dining room; bedrooms, attractive village, handy for NEC (*LYM, Dr S J Shepherd*)

Hampton Lucy [SP2557]

☆ *Boars Head* [E of Stratford]: Friendly beamed local, traditional décor, log fire, lots of brasses, well kept ales inc Theakstons and Youngers, prompt friendly service, well presented straightforward food; small enclosed garden, pretty village nr Charlcote House (*Brian Skelcher, Tony Walker*)

Harbury [SP3759]

Dog: Long bare-boards simply furnished public bar with coal fire and darts, small carpeted lounge, Ansells, Bass and interesting guest beers such as Beowulf and Warden, wide choice of food from good pork batch or nachos to steak and even lobster in bar or sizeable restaurant; good disabled access, tables out under arbour by car park (*Dave Braisted, Graham Coates*)

Shakespeare [just off B4451/B4452 S of A425 Leamington Spa—Southam; Mill St]: Popular and comfortable dining pub with good hospitable service and good choice of freshly cooked food (not Sun evening); linked beamed rooms, stripped stonework, well kept Whitbreads-related ales with guests such as Fullers London Pride and Timothy Taylor Landlord, inglenook log fire, horsebrasses, pleasant conservatory, separate pool room; children welcome; tables in back garden with aviaries (*Roy Bromell, Robert N Burtsal*)

Hatton [SP2467]

☆ *Falcon* [Birmingham Rd, Haseley (A4177)]: Roadside pub you might easily pass, but tastefully reworked inside, with five calm and relaxing rooms around island bar, lots of stripped brickwork and low beams, tiled and oak-planked floors, prints, old photographs, fresh flowers, nice mix of stripped tables and various chairs; well separated games room, no-smoking back dining area, quick friendly service, well kept Banks's Bitter and Mild, Hook Norton Best, Lindridge, M&B Brew XI and Marstons Pedigree, decent wines, wide choice of interesting food; picnic-sets out on lawns at side and behind (*BB, Brian Skelcher, Andy and Sarah Gillett*)

Waterman [A4177]: Well placed next to Hatton flight of locks on Grand Union Canal, with huge garden, and currently doing well; friendly service, good generous food inc vegetarian and children's, Greenalls beers; children welcome (*Alistair Forsyth*)

Hawkesbury [SP3684]

☆ *Greyhound* [Sutton Stop, off Black Horse Rd/Grange Rd; jnctn Coventry and N Oxford canals]: Cosy unpretentious pub brimming with bric-a-brac, well kept Banks's Bitter and Mild and Marstons Pedigree, attentive staff, coal-fired stove, unusual tiny snug; booking essential for the Pie Parlour – lots of canalia and quite private olde-worlde atmosphere; children welcome, tables on attractive terrace with safe

play area by junction of Coventry and N Oxford Canals; wonderful spot if you don't mind pylons – like a prime piece of the Black Country transported 20 miles to Coventry suburbs (*Sam Samuells, Lynda Payton, P J Rowland, Dave Braisted*)

Henley in Arden [SP1466]

Bird in Hand [A34]: Wide choice of good value food inc bargain two-course lunches, well kept beer, friendly attentive service; pretty conservation town with good churches (*June and Mike Coleman*)

Blue Bell [High St]: Impressive timber-framed building with fine coach entrance; more modestly modern inside (despite the beams), with small bar, split dining area, good straightforward food, well kept ales such as Boddingtons and Wadworths 6X; some tables in courtyard (*George Atkinson, Dr D Walker*)

White Swan [High St]: Originally two 16th-c cottages, large low-beamed rambling lounge bar, cosy seats in bay windows overlooking street, four real ales, wide choice of good value food from hot filled freshly baked baguettes to steaks, restaurant; piped music, games machines; bedrooms (*P J Keen*)

Hunningham [SP3768]

Red Lion [off B4455 E of Leamington]: Recently rebuilt, wide choice of good value food, three real ales; nice country spot by river (*Ray Crabtree*)

Kenilworth [SP2871]

Clarendon House [High St]: Comfortable and civilised, with partly panelled bar, antique maps, prints, copper, china and armour, well kept Greene King IPA, Abbot, Triumph and guest beers, decent wines, friendly helpful bar staff, good value simple bar food, interesting restaurant specials; for sale by administrative receivers spring 1999 (*Joan and Tony Walker, Alain and Rose Foote*)

Queen & Castle [Castle Green]: Old ivy-covered chain dining pub opp castle, lots of knick-knacks, attentive staff, quaint corners, beams and pictures, good coffee, quick cheapish food from sandwiches and baked potatoes up; maybe piped music; extensive lawns, good play area (*G R Braithwaite, George Atkinson*)

Knowle [SP1876]

Black Boy [off A4177 about 1½ miles S]: Wide choice of modestly priced food in much extended M&B alehouse dining pub, friendly staff, plenty of seats outside (*Ian Blackwell*)

Herons Nest [Warwick Rd S]: Attractive canalside pub, wide choice of good food inc children's helpings, Bass, plenty of tables in waterside gardens with moorings; bedrooms (*Jack Barnwell*)

Ladbroke [SP4158]

Bell [signed off A423 S of Southam]: Rambling Greenalls pub, comfortable, clean and friendly, with wide choice of well prepared good value food, well kept Bass and Tetleys, attentive staff; tables in garden, pleasant surroundings – very busy w/e (*John A Foord, Dave Braisted*)

Lapworth [SP1670]

☆ *Boot* [B4439, by Warwickshire Canal]: Well

run busy waterside pub with two small attractive bars, good atmosphere, good if not cheap food inc imaginative dishes, also good filled baguettes, well kept beers, decent wines (big glasses); refurbished restaurant upstairs, nice garden, pleasant walks *(P R and S A White, T R and B C Jenkins, Steve and Sarah Pleasance, Mrs D Rawlings)*

Leamington Spa [SP3165]

Hogshead [Warwick St]: Exceptional range of well kept changing ales, good value food, good atmosphere and bric-a-brac in character small open-plan pub *(John Brightley, Joan and Michel Hooper-Immins)*

Leek Wootton [SP2868]

☆ *Anchor* [Warwick Rd]: Busy all week, comfortable and very popular (esp with older people) for wide choice of good value generous food (all day Sat, not Sun) in bookable dining lounge and smaller bar, friendly efficient service, particularly well kept Bass and a guest ale, decent wine; picnic-sets in pleasant garden behind *(Dr Oscar Puls, Robert N Burtsal, E V Walder, John Bramley, Keith and Margaret Kettell, Roy Y Bromell)*

Long Itchington [SP4165]

☆ *Harvester* [off A423 S of Coventry; Church Rd]: Unpretentious welcoming two-bar village local with 60s feel, quiet, neat and tidy (nothing to do with the chain of the same name), with efficiently served very cheap food from sandwiches to good steaks, three well kept Hook Norton brews and a guest ale, friendly landlord, fish tank in lounge bar, cosy relaxed restaurant *(Pete Baker, Ted George)*

Long Lawford [SP4776]

Sheaf & Sickle [Coventry Rd (A428)]: Small cosy lounge, good value straightforward freshly made lunchtime bar food (so may be a wait), more extensive restaurant choice, biggish bar with darts and dominoes, well kept Ansells Bitter and Mild, Tetleys and one or two guest beers, friendly staff; tables in garden by cricket ground, open all day Sat *(Alain and Rose Foote)*

Lower Brailes [SP3039]

☆ *George* [B4035 Shipston—Banbury]: Good freshly made food in fine old inn, attractively refurbished roomy flagstoned front bar with dark oak tables, nice curtains and inglenook log fire, darts, panelled oak-beamed back bar with soft lighting and green décor, well kept Hook Norton, ales, smart country-style flagstoned restaurant; provision for children, renovated bedrooms, sizeable neatly kept sheltered garden with terrace, lovely village *(John Bowdler, George Atkinson)*

Lower Quinton [SP1847]

College Arms [off A46 Stratford—Broadway]: Not cheap, but wide range of good fresh food, well kept Whitbreads-related ales, welcoming efficient service, cosy well furnished eating area, spacious open-plan lounge with stripped stone and heavy beams, unusual highly polished tables inc one in former fireplace, leather seats, partly carpeted parquet floor, bric-a-brac; piped music, games in roomy public bar; on green of pretty village *(Ted George, Brian Skelcher)*

Loxley [SP2552]

☆ *Fox* [signed off A422 Stratford—Banbury]: Cheerful pub in sleepy village, very neat and clean, with friendly landlord and cat, five well kept ales inc Bass, Greene King Abbot and Hook Norton, wide range of good value fresh homely cooking (very popular evening); panelling, a few pictures and plates, settles, brocaded banquettes, pleasant dining area; piped music; tables in good-sized garden behind, handy for Stratford *(Nigel and Sue Foster, George Atkinson)*

Meer End [SP2474]

Tipperary [A4177 SW of Coventry]: Low-ceilinged pub pleasantly refurbished by Greenalls, good popular fresh food, reasonable prices, four real ales, friendly service, children welcome; quiet piped music; picnic-sets in garden *(Michael and Hazel Lyons, Brian Skelcher, LYM)*

Middleton [SP1798]

Green Man [Church Lane]: Busy pleasantly refurbished dining pub, decent food all day inc fine vegetarian dishes (may be a wait when busy), well kept Bass and guest beer, plenty of atmosphere *(James Nunns)*

Moreton Morrell [SP3356]

Black Horse [off B4455 Fosse Way]: Traditional village local (but no dogs) with two real ales, lunchtime rolls, pool, juke box and fruit machine; seats outside *(CMW, JJW)*

Newbold on Stour [SP2446]

White Hart [A3400 S of Stratford]: Chain dining pub popular for wide range of generous reasonably priced food (not Sun evening), long and airy beamed and tiled bar divided by stub walls and big stone fireplace (good log fire), big bay windows, roomy back bar with pool and so forth, well kept Bass and M&B Brew XI; dining room; picnic-sets and boules out in front, giant draughts at the back; children welcome, open all day Sat *(LYM, P R and S A White, June and Mike Coleman, Ted George, K Frostick, Roy Bromell)*

Norton Lindsey [SP2263]

New Inn: Clean and comfortable modern village pub doing well under newish licensees, now a good choice of generous good food cooked by landlady *(Pat and Clive Sherriff, David Green)*

Nuneaton [SP3592]

Felix Holt: Wetherspoons conversion with good cheap beer and wine, nice surroundings, reasonable food; exemplary lavatories *(Ian and Joan Blackwell)*

Offchurch [SP3565]

Stags Head [Welsh Rd, off A425 at Radford Semele]: Low-beamed thatched village pub with enjoyable food inc good value two-course lunch, good friendly service, well kept Bass and Flowers Original; quiet piped music; tables in good-sized garden with play area *(George Atkinson, Roy Bromell)*

Old Hill [SO9685]

Waterfall [Waterfall Lane]: Down-to-earth local, very friendly staff, well kept and well priced Bathams, Enville, Hook Norton, Marstons and three or four interesting guest beers, farm cider, country wines, cheap plain home-made food from good filled rolls to Sun lunch and special snacks Fri, tankards and jugs hanging from boarded ceiling; piped music, children welcome, back garden with play area; open all day w/e *(Julian Pearson, Dave Braisted)*

Oldbury [SO9888]

☆ *Waggon & Horses* [Church St, nr Savacentre]: Ornate Victorian tiles, copper ceiling and original windows in busy town pub with well kept changing ales such as Bass, Brains Bitter and SA, Everards Tiger and Nutcracker, Marstons Pedigree and Nailers OBJ, wide choice of generous food inc good value baltis and lots of puddings in bar and bookable upstairs bistro, decent wines, friendly efficient service even when busy, lively comfortable lounge with tie collection, side room with high-backed settles and big old tables, open fire, Black Country memorabilia; opens noon *(Richard Lewis, C J Fletcher, the Didler)*

Pailton [SP4781]

White Lion [B4027 Coventry—Lutterworth]: Biggish nicely furnished 18th-c pub/restaurant popular for wide range of quickly served decent food inc two-sitting Sun lunch and children's dishes, good range of wines, well kept beers; play area in garden; cl Mon; bedrooms *(Dave Braisted)*

Princethorpe [SP4070]

Three Horseshoes [High Town; junction A423/B4453]: Friendly old coaching inn with lots of brass, beams, plates, pictures, comfortable settles and chairs; Judges Barristers, Marstons Pedigree, Ruddles County and John Smiths, country wines, good value freshly prepared food inc children's, vegetarian and Sun lunch, good service, no-smoking eating area, open fire; pleasant big garden with play equipment *(Robert N Burtsal)*

Priors Hardwick [SP4756]

☆ *Butchers Arms* [off A423 via Wormleighton or A361 via Boddington, N of Banbury]: Dark medieval oak beams, flagstones, panelling and antiques, huge choice of very well cooked and presented food (not cheap but worth it) in small welcoming bar with inglenook log fire, and in restaurant – arrive early for a table; keg beer, very welcoming licensee, good service, country garden *(Hugh Spottiswoode, H W Clayton)*

Priors Marston [SP4857]

☆ *Holly Bush* [follow Shuckburgh sign, then first right by phone box]: Golden stone pub, small rambling rooms, beams and stripped stone, old-fashioned pub seats, up to three fires in winter, friendly helpful service, well kept Bass, Hook Norton Best, Marstons Pedigree and guest beers, friendly elderly dogs, food from good range of baguettes to steaks inc children's and Sun roasts, large restaurant; darts, pool, games machines, juke box, piped music; children welcome, tables in sheltered garden, bedrooms *(LYM, Mr and Mrs C R Little, Robert N Burtsal, George Atkinson)*

Red Hill [SP1355]

Stag [Alcester Rd]: Relaxed atmosphere, friendly staff, nice furnishings inc pine tables,

good standard food from ploughman's and baguettes up, pleasant front terrace; attractively refurbished bedrooms, one with old-fashioned sofa down spiral stairs *(Wendy Pennington)*

Ryton on Dunsmore [SP3874]

Blacksmiths Arms [High St]: Friendly village local, good menu, Bass and M&B, no-smoking area *(D Marsh, Shirley Fletcher)*

Shilton [SP4084]

Shilton Arms [B4065 NE of Coventry]: Pleasant village pub with good range of good value food, enormous helpings, decent house wine; no-smoking section *(Roy Y Bromell)*

Shipston on Stour [SP2540]

☆ *Black Horse* [Station Rd (off A3400)]: 16th-c thatched pub with interesting ornaments and inglenook coal fire in atmospheric low-beamed bar, decent range of interesting food inc small but tasty filled rolls and weekday OAP bargain lunches, well kept Chadwicks Best, Marstons Pedigree and Ruddles, friendly staff and locals, small dining room, back garden with terrace and barbecue *(Dr A Y Drummond, George Atkinson)*

Horseshoe [Church St]: Pretty timbered inn with open-plan largely modern bar, lots of maroon plush, generous well presented straightforward food inc hefty mixed grill, nice log fire in big fireplace with copper pans above, enjoyable chintzy evening restaurant; Courage-related ales with a guest such as Butcombe, decent coffee, darts, no piped music; small flower-decked back terrace; bedrooms pretty, bright and clean *(BB, Dennis D'Vigne, K Frostick)*

White Bear [High St]: Massive settles and cheerful atmosphere in traditional front bar with good log fire, well kept Bass and Marstons Pedigree, friendly staff; back bistro with live music Sun; tables in small back yard and benches on street; bedrooms simple but clean, with huge breakfast *(Jim Sargeant, LYM, John Bramley)*

Shirley [SP1078]

Drawbridge [Haslucks Green Rd]: Roomy Greenalls pub by canal drawbridge worked by boatmen, waterside terrace, well kept Banks's, Greenalls Bitter and Original and a guest beer, good choice of food inc fish and OAP specials; open all day *(Jack Barnwell)*

Shustoke [SP2290]

Plough [B4114 Nuneaton—Coleshill]: Rambling local done up in olde-worlde style with brass galore, cheap lunchtime snacks and good value straightforward meals, good service, Bass-related and a guest beer *(John and Liz Soden, Dave Braisted)*

Snitterfield [SP2159]

Fox Hunter [Smiths Lane/School Rd; off A46 N of Stratford]: Attractive and comfortable, with banquettes and hunting pictures in L-shaped bar/lounge, wide range of well presented and reasonably priced standard food inc Sun roasts, Bass, M&B Brew XI and Hook Norton Old Hooky; piped music (turned down on request), fruit machine, children allowed; tables outside *(Ian and Joan Blackwell)*

Southam [SP4161]

☆ *Old Mint* [A423 towards Banbury]: Impressive

14th-c pub with two character heavy-beamed rooms, some concentration on good reasonably priced food, well kept ales such as Adnams Broadside, Bass, Hook Norton Old Hooky and Wadworths 6X, friendly service, log fire; small garden *(John A Foord, Kerry Law, Simon Smith, LYM)*

Wharf [A423 towards Banbury]: Pleasantly refurbished canalside pub with good cheap food in nice eating area, games in large long public bar, waterside garden; space for caravans *(Ted George)*

Stonnall [SK0703]

Old Swann [off A452]: Wide choice of home-made lunchtime food from sandwiches up inc bargain OAP meals, big dining extension (booking advised Sun), cold Bass, M&B Brew XI and Worthington *(Dr S J Shepherd, Jack Barnwell)*

Plough: Comfortable, with changing ales such as Courage Directors, Theakstons and Timothy Taylor, good copious cheap food *(Dr S J Shepherd)*

Royal Oak [just off A452 N of Brownhills]: Popular refurbished beamed local, real ales such as Bass, Morlands Old Speckled Hen, Ruddles County, Charles Wells Bombardier and Wadworths 6X, farm cider, jovial attentive landlord, varied food esp fish in bar and evening restaurant, also Sun lunch; no music *(Cliff Blakemore)*

Stourbridge [SO8984]

Seven Stars [Brook Rd, nr stn]: Large Victorian pub with impressive high ceiling, decorative tiles and ornate carving, good generous food inc all-day cold snacks in second bar's eating area or restaurant on left, well kept changing ales such as Bathams, Courage Directors and Theakstons Best; comfortably bustling atmosphere, friendly regulars, nice staff; open all day *(Kerry Law, Simon Smith, G Coates)*

Stratford upon Avon [SP2055]

Arden [Waterside]: Hotel not pub, but closest bar to Memorial Theatre, Courage Best and Directors, good baguettes and other bar food, smart evening bouncer; very popular, get there early; bedrooms good, not cheap *(B T Smith, Sue Holland, Dave Webster)*

☆ *Black Swan* [Southern Way]: Great atmosphere in very popular 16th-c pub nr Memorial Theatre – still attracts actors, lots of signed RSC photographs; wide choice of good plain wholesome food at moderate prices, Flowers (that brewing family firmly supporting the RSC before Whitbreads bought them out) and other Whitbreads-related ales, quick service, open fire, bustling public bar (little lounge seating for drinkers), children allowed in small dining area, no piped music; attractive little terrace looking over riverside public gardens – which tend to act as summer overflow; known as the Dirty Duck *(LYM, F J Robinson, Brian Skelcher, B T Smith, Peter and Audrey Dowsett, Sue Holland, Dave Webster)*

☆ *Garrick* [High St]: Attractive ancient building with lots of beams and timbers, stripped stone, bare boards, lively evening theatrical character, cosy front bar, busier back one, central open

fire, well kept Whitbreads-related ales with guests such as Bass, Greene King Abbot and Wadworths 6X, generous sensibly priced food in air-conditioned eating area, friendly efficient service, thoughtfully chosen piped music; children allowed away from bar *(Bett and Brian Cox, Ted George, Bill Sykes, BB, Kevin Blake)*

Lamplighter [Rother St, opp United Reform Church; handy for Friday Market]: Civilised and spacious, with nice mix of wooden chairs and settles around oblong and round tables, square central bar, alcoves and pillars, lots of show business pictures, guns on walls and beams, good cheap food, well kept Marstons and other beers, homely atmosphere, friendly staff *(Ted George)*

Pen & Parchment [Bridgefoot, by canal basin]: L-shaped split-level lounge and snug, now a Whitbreads Hogshead, with wide choice of changing ales and ciders, a dozen wines by the glass, Shakespeare theme, big open fire, decent food; tables in garden, good canal basin views, pretty hanging baskets; busy road *(Rob and Gill Weeks)*

Queens Head [Ely St]: Tastefully refurbished L-shaped bar, tidy and clean, log fire, good lunchtime food, well kept beers inc Highgate, cheerful long-serving staff, no piped music *(Ted George)*

☆ *Slug & Lettuce* [Guild St/Union St]: Lively friendly bustle in open-plan bar with zebra-print sofas and light wood tables and chairs on rugs and flagstones, period prints on stripped panelling, popular enterprising bar food, well kept Tetleys-related and guest beers, decent wines, daily papers, helpful staff, solid fuel fire; good lunchtime atmosphere, can get crowded with young people later, TV, piped music; floodlit two-level back terrace, children welcome, open all day Thurs-Sun *(Dr A Sutton, LYM, Julia Hiscock, Ted George, Nigel Wilkinson)*

Windmill [Church St]: Cosy old pub with town's oldest licence, beyond the attractive Guild Chapel; low beams, quarry-tiled front bar, bare boards in main one, wide choice of good value food inc vegetarian, well kept Whitbreads-related and interesting guest ales, friendly efficient staff, good civilised mix of customers, carpeted dining area; tables outside *(Sue Holland, Dave Webster, Ted George, Ian and Jane Irving)*

Studley [SP0763]

☆ *Old Washford Mill* [Icknield St Drive; left turn off A435, going N from B4093 roundabout]: Attractive ivy-covered converted watermill, different levels, quiet alcoves, good value bar snacks and three different restaurants in varying styles, provision for children, real ales tapped from the cask (some brewed on the premises), country wines, internal millstream and interesting old mill machinery inc waterwheel; pretty waterside gardens with good play area, ducks and black swan *(LYM, Dave Braisted)*

Royal Oak [Alcester Rd]: Good cheap lunchtime food inc faggots and chips, Tetleys-related beers with a cheap guest such as Wyre Piddle *(Dave Braisted)*

Swan [High St]: Friendly refurbished pub, Whitbreads and other beers such as Highgate Mild, food inc tasty sandwiches; quiz night Weds *(Dave Braisted)*

Tanworth in Arden [SP1170]

Bell [The Green]: Roomy lounge with villagey atmosphere, well kept Whitbreads-related ales, good bar food, outlook on peaceful green and lovely 14th-c church; children in eating area and restaurant *(Dave Braisted, LYM)*

Temple Grafton [SP1255]

☆ *Blue Boar* [a mile E, towards Binton; off A422 W of Stratford]: Country dining pub with beams and log fires, cheerful staff, well kept Courage Directors, Hook Norton Best and Theakstons XB, usual bar food from baked potatoes up, more elaborate dishes in comfortable stripped-stone restaurant (past glass-top well with golden carp) with no-smoking section, good wine choice, traditional games in flagstoned stripped-stone side room; children welcome, open all day summer w/e, picnic-sets outside; comfortable well equipped bedrooms *(June and Mike Coleman, J H Kane, Duncan Cloud, George Little, Pat and Clive Sherriff, JCW, Peter Burton, William R Cuncliffe, LYM)*

Tipton [SO9592]

☆ *M A D O'Rourkes Pie Factory* [Hurst Lane, Dudley Rd towards Wednesbury; A457/A4037]: Exuberantly eccentric, full of esoteric ancient meat-processing equipment, strings of model hams, sausages, pigs' heads and so forth; good value hearty food inc children's and lots of pies, well kept Ansells Mild, Greene King Abbot, Marstons Pedigree and Tetleys, piped music, live Irish folk Sun lunchtime, jazz some evenings; children welcome, open all day, food all day Sun, can get packed esp Fri/Sat night *(LYM, Edward Leetham, Stephen and Julie Brown, Charles and Pauline Stride, G P Kernan)*

Upper Gornal [SO9291]

Jolly Crispin [Clarence St]: Little old local, once a cobbler's shop, doing well under new landlord, with interesting particularly well kept changing ales such as Courage Directors, Holdens Special and Church End Sunshine *(Kerry Law, Simon Smith)*

Warwick [SP2865]

Millwrights Arms [Coten End; A445 towards Leamington]: Comfortable well run old pub, very welcoming, with well kept beer that might include one brewed on the premises *(Richard Houghton)*

Saxon Mill [Guy's Cliffe, A429 just N]: Converted mill with long history, wheel turning slowly behind glass, mill race under glass floor-panel, tables in lovely setting by broad green wooded river, delightful views; inside is straightforward Harvester family eating pub, with early supper bargains and OAP discount card, beams and flagstones, well kept Scottish Courage ales, summer weekend barbecues, good play area; open all day *(Roger Braithwaite, LYM)*

Tilted Wig [Market Pl]: Roomy and airy, somewhere between tearoom and pub, big windows on square, stone-effect floor on left, bare boards on right, carpet behind, brocaded banquettes and kitchen chairs around pine tables, some stripped stone and panelling, well kept Ansells, Tetleys and a guest ale, good range of wines, wide choice of good reasonably priced home-made food (not Sun evening), lively bustle, quick friendly service; SkyTV; tables in garden, live jazz and folk Sun evening, open all day Fri/Sat and summer *(M Joyner, BB, Ted George, John A Foord)*

☆ *Tudor House* [West St]: Heavily timbered and jettied Tudor inn opp castle car park, lots of black wood, tiles and parquet floor, leaded lights, lofty pitched ceiling, massive stone fireplace, galleried landing, solid furnishings and Tudoresque décor, rather pricy food, Courage Directors, John Smiths, Websters Yorkshire and a guest such as Shepherd Neame Spitfire, decent wine; piped music; tables in front and on back terrace; bedrooms with own bathrooms, opens noon *(Joan and Michel Hooper-Immins, George Atkinson, BB)*

☆ *Zetland Arms* [Church St]: Pleasant and cosy town pub with short choice of cheap but good bar food (not weekend evenings), well kept Bass, decent wine in generous glasses, friendly quick service, neat but relaxing small panelled front bar with toby jug collection, comfortable larger eating area; small conservatory, interestingly planted sheltered garden; children may be allowed; bedrooms, sharing bathroom *(John Bramley, Ted George, LYM, Graham Tayar, Catherine Raeburn)*

Welford on Avon [SP1452]

☆ *Bell* [off B439 W of Stratford; High St]: Good imaginative food from generous sandwiches up inc good pasta, fish and vegetarian range in dim-lit dark-timbered low-beamed lounge with open fire and polished copper, friendly keen staff, well kept Whitbreads-related ales, comfortable restaurant and dining conservatory (children allowed here), flagstoned public bar with darts, pool and so forth; piped music; tables in pretty garden and back courtyard; attractive riverside village *(Tim and Linda Collins, LYM, Michael Gittins, Mick and Jeanne Shillington)*

Willoughby [SP5267]

Rose [just off A45 E of Dunchurch]: Friendly small partly thatched beamed pub with emphasis on good value straightforward food inc tender Sun carvery joints and OAP lunches Tues and Thurs, low panelled bar, evening restaurant, Scottish Courage ales, cheerful staff, games room, garden with play area; cl Mon and Weds lunchtimes, Tues music night *(Charles and Pauline Stride)*

Wilmcote [SP1657]

Masons Arms [Aston Cantlow Rd]: Attractive ivy-clad local, neat and snug, with good generous food in bar or conservatory restaurant, well kept Hook Norton and Whitbreads-related ales *(Dave Braisted)*

Wishaw [SP1794]

Cock [Bulls Lane]: Partly Tudor country pub, good range of appetising well presented food, prompt cheerful young staff; children welcome

(Mr and Mrs D Wood)
Withybrook [SP4384]

☆ *Pheasant* [B4112 NE of Coventry, not far from M6, junction 2]: Big busy dining pub with lots of dark tables, plush-cushioned chairs, prompt friendly service, wide choice of generous food inc good value specials and good vegetarian choice, Scottish Courage ales under light carbon dioxide blanket, good coffee, blazing log fires; piped music; children welcome, tables under lanterns on brookside terrace *(David Peakall, LYM, Chris and Ann Garnett, Roy Bromell, Roger Braithwaite, Janet Pickles)*

Wixford [SP0954]
Fish [B4085 Alcester—Bidford]: Roomy L-shaped bar and snug, beams, polished panelling, carpets over flagstones, stuffed fish, reasonably priced bar food; corridor to lavatories is quite an art gallery *(Dave Braisted)*

☆ *Three Horseshoes* [off A46 S of Redditch, via A422/A435 Alcester roundabout, or B439 at Bidford]: Roomy and nicely furnished, with consistently good generous food inc fresh fish, interesting choice (esp w/e, when it can get crowded), nice puddings, charming landlord and staff, good range of well kept mainly Whitbreads-related ales, bric-a-brac from blowtorches to garden gnomes *(Dave Braisted, P Lloyd)*

Wolverhampton [SO9198]
Great Western [Sun St, behind BR station – left down subway under railway, turn right at end]: Vibrantly popular, with particularly well kept Bathams and Holdens, many old railway photographs and other memorabilia, traditional front bar, other rooms inc newer separate no-smoking bar, very promptly served good inexpensive unpretentious lunchtime food (not Sun) from hot and cold cobs up, warm friendly atmosphere; SkyTV; open all day, roomy back conservatory, tables in yard with good barbecues *(DAV, Pete Baker)*
Kearneys [Tettenhall Rd (A41)]: Former Combermere, and the Irishing hasn't been enough to spoil what's still essentially a friendly local; three small rooms, Banks's and a guest beer, very friendly service, food inc good value Sun lunch, bare boards, bar billiards, small garden; quiz Tues *(Ian and Elizabeth Rispin)*

Wootton Wawen [SP1563]

☆ *Bulls Head* [just off A3400 Birmingham—Stratford]: Smart, attractive and expensive black and white Elizabethan dining pub with low beams and timbers, rugs setting off good flagstones, well kept Banks's, Bass, Marstons Pedigree and Wychwood, good wines, good choice of somewhat pricy food inc several fresh fish and unusual vegetarian dishes (beware, they charge extra for veg); pews in more austere tap room with dominoes, shove-ha'penny; children welcome, open all day Sun, tables on pleasant terrace – handy for Stratford Canal walks *(David and Ruth Shillitoe, P R and S A White, Barbara and Alan Mence, Roy Bromell, June and Mike Coleman, George Little, Maysie Thompson, Robert N Burtsal, LYM, Karen Eliot, M G Hart, James Nunn, William R Cuncliffe, Mike Gorton)*

'Children welcome' means the pubs says it lets children inside without any special restriction. If it allows them in, but to restricted areas such as an eating area or family room, we specify this. Places with separate restaurants usually let children use them, hotels usually let them into public areas such as lounges. Some pubs impose an evening time limit – let us know if you find this.

Wiltshire

Many of this county's pubs are in particularly attractive settings, such as the
Quarrymans Arms near Box, the Horseshoe at Ebbesbourne Wake (a
charming country pub, doing very well these days), the White Hart at Ford
(flourishing under its new management), the Woodbridge with its huge
riverside garden at North Newnton, the George in the delightful village of
Lacock (another pub that's on really fine form), the canalside Barge at Seend
and the Benett Arms at Semley. Other pubs which in recent months have been
earning specially high praise are the Crown at Alvediston (good food and
bedrooms, pleasant relaxed service), the Red Lion at Axford (good reasonably
priced food and wine), the Three Crowns at Brinkworth (very much a dining
pub), the enjoyably individual Two Pigs in Corsham (good beer), the Angel at
Heytesbury (earning a Food Award this year, good service too), the snug and
cheerful little Linnet at Great Hinton (a newcomer to the Guide), the
welcoming Red Lion at Kilmington, the Hop Pole at Limpley Stoke (good
balance between dining and drinking), the Owl at Little Cheverell (very good
all round), the Hatchet at Lower Chute (quite a charmer, good food and
atmosphere), the Vine Tree at Norton (interesting food, interesting décor), the
Raven at Poulshot (very popular food, good beers), the George & Dragon at
Rowde (the food, especially the fresh fish, is very well liked in this neat and
friendly pub), the ancient New Inn in Salisbury (entirely no smoking – people
love the atmosphere), the Rattlebone at Sherston (good all round), the Pear
Tree at Whitley (another new entry, coming straight in with a Food Award –
nice atmosphere, too), and the Seven Stars near Woodborough (great
atmosphere, excellent Anglo-French food, good beers and wines). From
among all these, the Three Crowns, George & Dragon, Pear Tree and Seven
Stars have most to offer for a special meal out: it's the George & Dragon at
Rowde which is our final choice as Wiltshire Dining Pub of the Year. In the
Lucky Dip section at the end of the chapter, current front-runners include the
Waggon & Horses at Beckhampton, White Horse at Biddestone, Horse &
Groom at Charlton, Black Dog at Chilmark, Dove at Corton, Bell at Great
Cheverell, Calley Arms at Hodson, reopened Harrow at Little Bedwyn, Bear
in Marlborough, Radnor Arms at Nunton, Old Mill on the edge of Salisbury,
Lamb at Semington, Cross Keys at Upper Chute, Golden Swan at Wilcot and
Royal Oak at Wootton Rivers. Drinks prices in the area are close to the
national average. The main local brewer is Wadworths of Devizes, and beer in
pubs tied to them tends to be relatively very cheap. Other good local beers we
found some pubs here offering as their cheapest were Archers, Moles, Bunces
and Hop Back, and Tisbury beers are quite widely available here too.

ALVEDISTON ST9723 Map 2

Crown 🏠

Village signposted on left off A30 about 12 miles W of Salisbury

There's an increasing emphasis on good imaginative bar food at this lovely old
thatched inn, peacefully set in a quiet spot. As well as soup (£2.95) and sandwiches

(from £3.25), a daily changing blackboard menu includes lots of fish and game in season with starters such as smoked mackerel (£3.50) and home-made crab cakes (£5.25), and main courses including vegetable stir fry or steak and kidney pie (£7.50), venison faggots (£7.95), game pie (£8.25), poached salmon with hollandaise sauce (£9.50), wild mallard with Cointreau sauce (£9.95), whole lemon sole (£10.50), red snapper with champagne sauce (£12.50), monkfish thermidor (£12.95), Scotch fillet steak (£13.50) and lobster (£19.50); puddings (£3.50) might include sticky toffee pudding, home-made apple pie or chocolate fudge cake. The three charming low-beamed wood panelled rooms are cosily painted deep terracotta, and have two inglenook fireplaces, dark oak furniture and shelves crowded with bric-a-brac and antiques. Well kept Courage Best and Wadworths 6X and guests such as Morlands Old Speckled Hen and Shepherd Neame Spitfire on handpump; darts and piped music. On different levels around a thatched white well, the attractive garden is nicely broken up with shrubs and rockeries among neatly kept lawns; it faces a farmyard with ponies and other animals, and there's a children's play area; good value bedrooms. *(Recommended by C N R Bateman, Martin and Karen Wake, Jerry and Alison Oakes, Mrs J Morton, Clive Bonner, Dr and Mrs N Holmes)*

Free house ~ Licensees Nickolas Shaw and Colin Jordan ~ Real ale ~ Bar food ~ Restaurant ~ (01722) 780335 ~ Children in restaurant ~ Live music on Sun evenings ~ Open 12-3, 7-11 ~ Bedrooms: £20(£25B)/£45B

AXFORD SU2370 Map 2
Red Lion
Off A4 E of Marlborough; on back road Mildenhall—Ramsbury

There are fine views over a valley from picture windows in the bustling beamed and pine-panelled bar of this pretty flint-and-brick pub. Although the emphasis here is mainly on the good food, drinkers are made to feel just as welcome as diners. From a menu available both in the bar and restaurant, you can expect sandwiches (from £1.75), soup (£2.50), pâté and toast with rhubarb and tomato chutney (£3.25), ploughman's (from £3.75), home-cooked Wiltshire ham, lasagne, stilton and pasta bake, haddock or plaice (£4.95), home-made steak and kidney pie (£5.95), beef and venison pie (£10.75), crevette platter or sirloin steak (£11.50) and roast duck with orange sauce (£12.50), with daily specials such as crab fishcakes (£4.25), Dorset mussels (£4.50), chicken breast filled with cream cheese and leeks (£9.75), pork roulade (£11.50), rack of lamb (£11.75) and several fresh fish dishes such as skate (£11.50), sea bass (£14.50) and lobster (£24.50); puddings (£3.50). The bar has a pleasant mix of comfortable cask seats and other solid chairs on a spotless parquet floor, and you can buy the paintings by local artists which hang on the walls; no-smoking restaurant. Well kept Hook Norton and Wadworths 6X and an occasional guest such as Badger Best on handpump, and a good choice of sensibly priced wines by the glass. The sheltered garden has picnic-sets under cocktail parasols, swings, and lovely views. *(Recommended by Ian Phillips, Dr and Mrs Morley, Sheila and Robert Robinson, David Gittins, Trevor Owen, D M and M C Watkinson, June and Tony Baldwin, Paul and Ursula Randall, John and Deborah Luck)*

Free house ~ Licensees Mel and Daphne Evans ~ Real ale ~ Bar food (12-2, 7-10) ~ Restaurant ~ (01672) 520271 ~ Children welcome ~ Open 11-3, 6.30-11; 12-3.30, 7-10.30 Sun ~ Bedrooms: £35B/£50B

BERWICK ST JOHN ST9422 Map 2
Talbot
Village signposted from A30 E of Shaftesbury

Unchanging and with friendly attentive licensees, this old village pub offers a warm welcome for locals and visitors alike. The single long, heavy-beamed bar is simply furnished with cushioned solid wall and window seats, spindleback chairs, a high-backed built-in settle at one end, and tables that are candlelit in the evenings. There's a huge inglenook fireplace with a good iron fireback and bread ovens and nicely shaped heavy black beams and cross-beams with bevelled corners. Freshly prepared bar food includes soup (£3.50), ploughman's (£4.95), pasta dishes (from £5.95), ham and eggs or vegetarian macaroni (£7.50), steak and kidney pie, madras beef curry or chicken tikka masala (£8.50), rainbow trout (£8.95), 14oz gammon (£12.95) and steaks (£14.95); home-made puddings include treacle tart and bread and butter pudding. Adnams Best and Broadside, Bass, and Wadworths 6X on handpump, farm cider, fresh juices and good wines; cribbage and dominoes. There are some tables on the back lawn; be warned, they lock the car park when the pub is closed, so check with the licensee if you wish to leave your car and walk in the Ebble Valley. *(Recommended by Phyl and Jack Street, DP, Bill and June Howard)*

Free house ~ Licensees Roy and Wendy Rigby ~ Real ale ~ Bar food (not Sun) ~ Restaurant ~ (01747) 828222 ~ Children in eating area of bar at lunchtime ~ Open 12(11.30 Sat)-2.30, 7(6.30 Fri, Sat)-11; 12-2.30 Sun; closed Sun evening, and Mon except bank holidays

BOX ST8369 Map 2
Quarrymans Arms

Box Hill; coming from Bath on A4 turn right into Bargates 50 yds before railway bridge, then at T-junction turn left up Quarry Hill, turning left again near the top at grassy triangle; from Corsham, turn left after Rudloe Park Hotel into Beech Rd, then third left onto Barnetts Hill, and finally right at the top of the hill

This low stone building tucked away down a warren of lanes is ideally situated for cavers, potholers and walkers, and while some readers have noted that a spot of housekeeping wouldn't go amiss, its sweeping valley views make it well worth the sinuous drive. Although there's quite some emphasis on the imaginative food, one pleasant modernised room with an open fire, interesting quarry photographs and memorabilia covering the walls, is set aside just for drinking the well kept Butcombe, Moles and Wadworths 6X on handpump, and a guest or two such as Eccleshalls Top Totty or Moles Barley Mole tapped straight from the cask, good wines, over sixty malt whiskies, and ten or so vintage cognacs. As well as soup and sandwiches (both £2.50), enjoyable bar food might include stilton and asparagus pancake (£3.50/£5.95), moules marinières or macaroni cheese (£5.25), ploughman's (£5.50), lamb or beef burgers, local spicy sausages and chips or scampi (£5.75), home-made lasagne, various stir fries or penne tossed in a rich pomadori sauce with black olives, garlic and hot chilli (£6.95), tuna niçoise (£7.25), chicken breast with brandy, cream and mushrooms or tuna steak (£8.95), pork medallions in a rich cream and dijon mustard sauce (£9.25) rib-eye steak (£11.50) and puddings (from £3.50) such as ginger sponge or chocolate amaretti torte; good prompt service. Darts, cribbage, dominoes, fruit machine, football, boules, cricket, and piped music; an attractive outside terrace has picnic-sets. The pub runs interesting guided trips down the local Bath stone mine. *(Recommended by Brian P Beedham, Pat and Roger Fereday, Peter and Audrey Dowsett, Steven M Gent, Peter Burton, Lyn and Geoff Hallchurch, Mrs Laura Gustine, Jenny and Roger Huggins)*

Free house ~ Licensees John and Ginny Arundel ~ Real ale ~ Bar food (12-3, 6.45-10) ~ Restaurant ~ (01225) 743569 ~ Children in eating area of bar and restaurant ~ Open 11-11; 12-10.30 Sun; 11-4, 6-11 Mon-Weds in winter ~ Bedrooms: £25/£45

BRADFORD ON AVON ST8060 Map 2
Cross Guns

Avoncliff; pub is across footbridge from Avoncliff Station (road signposted Turleigh turning left off A363 heading uphill N from river in Bradford centre, and keep bearing left), and can also be reached down very steep and eventually unmade road signposted Avoncliff – keep straight on rather than turning left into village centre – from Westwood (which is signposted from B3109 and from A366, W of Trowbridge)

Passengers on the Bristol to Weymouth railway line may be tempted to alight at the platform opposite this marvellously situated country pub: just a short walk across an aqueduct leads to an enjoyable pubby atmosphere and reasonably priced food. The new licensee has added more tables to the floodlit terraced gardens which command fabulous views over the wide river Avon, with its maze of bridges, aqueducts (the

Kennet & Avon Canal) and railway tracks that wind through this quite narrow gorge. There's a pleasant old-fashioned feel to the bar, with its core of low 17th-c, rush-seated chairs around plain sturdy oak tables (most of which are set for diners, and many of them reserved), stone walls, and a 16th-c inglenook with a smoking chamber behind it. Well kept Courage Directors, Millworkers (brewed for the pub), Ruddles Best and a guest such as Wadworths 6X on handpump, about 100 malt whiskies and over twenty country wines; piped music. Generously served dishes might include hearty sandwiches (from £1.80), home-made soup (£3), ploughman's (from £3.75), steak and ale (£5.95), battered cod or mediterranean avocado bake (£6.50), steaks (from £6.50) and kangaroo steak in red wine sauce (£8.95); puddings include banoffee pie or treacle tart (£3.50); a Tannoy system announces meal orders from outside tables. Walkers are very welcome, but not their muddy boots. The pub gets very busy, especially at weekends and summer lunchtimes, so if you want to eat it's probably best to book. *(Recommended by Nigel Spence, Kim Greek, R C Fendick, Meg and Colin Hamilton, Jane Kingsbury, Neil Spink, D M and M C Watkinson, Daren Haines, Paul and Judith Booth, P and S White, Alison and Mick Coates)*

Free house ~ Licensees Jenny and Ken Roberts ~ Real ale ~ Bar food ~ (01225) 862335 ~ Children in eating area of bar ~ Open 10.30-11; 10.30-3.30, 6-11 winter ~ Bedrooms: £40B/£55B

Dandy Lion

35 Market St

Depending on the time of day, you will find an interesting and varied mix of customers in this particularly friendly place. The local poets and artists enjoy their morning cappuccino, local businessmen come for lunch, visitors and regulars flock in for evening meals, and drinkers congregate a little later than that – it's all very relaxed. The long main bar has big windows on either side of the door with a table and cushioned wooden armchairs by each, nice high-backed farmhouse chairs, old-fashioned dining chairs, and a brocade-cushioned long settle on the stripped wooden floor (a couple of rugs too), sentimental and gently erotic pictures on the panelled walls, an over-mantle with Brussels horses, fairy-lit hops over the bar counter, newspapers to read, and a daily saying chalked on a board; nostalgic piped pop music. At the back and up a few steps in a snug little bare-boarded room with a lovely high-backed settle and other small ones around sturdy tables, a big mirror on the mulberry walls, and a piano. Very well liked and reasonably priced bar food at lunchtime includes sandwiches or filled french bread (from £2.50), home-made soup or home-made liver pâté (£3.25), seven pasta dishes (from £3.50), filled baked potatoes (£3.95), ploughman's (£4.50), popular stuffed mushrooms or grilled gammon (£4.95), fresh local trout (£5.50), and sirloin steak (£7.95); in the evening there might be brie wedges with a sour cream and chive dip (£3.50), home-made gravadlax (£4.25), moules and frites or a pastry basket filled with roasted vegetables in a garlic cheese sauce (£6.50), kleftico (£8.25), chicken breast with a sauce of honey and mustard or lemon, prawn and fresh dill (£8.75), tuna steak on a bed of peppers with roast pepper sauce (£8.95), and speciality 'hot stone' dishes you cook yourself (from £8.95); daily specials, and puddings like home-made treacle coconut tart or sticky toffee pudding (from £3.10). Well kept Butcombe Bitter, and Wadworths IPA, 6X and seasonal ales on handpump, and good coffee. The upstairs restaurant is candlelit at night and has an area with antique toys and baskets of flowers. *(Recommended by Susan and Nigel Wilson)*

Wadworths ~ Tenant Jennifer Joseph ~ Real ale ~ Bar food ~ Restaurant ~ (01225) 863433 ~ Well behaved children in eating area of bar and restaurant ~ Open 10.30-3, 6-11; 11-3, 7-10.30 Sun

BRINKWORTH SU0184 Map 2
Three Crowns 🍽 ♀

The Street; B4042 Wootton Bassett—Malmesbury

We continue to hear very favourable reports about the extremely popular bar food at this friendly village pub, nicely set across a lane from a church. The menu (which covers an entire wall) is highly imaginative and changes regularly, and while it is not cheap, the generous helpings certainly offer good value for money: as well as filled rolls (lunchtime only, from £3.65), meals might include filled baked potatoes (from £6.40), steak and kidney pie (£9.45), vegetarian tagliatelle (£9.95), chicken breast wrapped in filo and stuffed with prawns, boursin and fresh basil with a madeira, mushroom and cream sauce (£12.85), tuna en croûte (£13.50), roast sliced duck with marsala and cream sauce (£13.85), guinea fowl wrapped in bacon with apple, rosemary and sausagemeat stuffing (£14.30), rack of lamb or king scallops (£14.95), seabass filled with a mushroom duxelle or halibut poached in white wine with sweet coconut milk and fresh lime juice or 8oz fillet of Scotch beef (£15.95) and marinated crocodile strips sautéed with onions and pink peppercorns and flamed in whisky on a bed of angel hair pasta (£16.45); all dishes are served with half a dozen fresh vegetables. Puddings might include fruits of the forest crème brûlée, strawberry shortbread, chocolate and Grand Marnier mousse or sticky toffee pudding (from £4.20); most people choose to eat in the elegant no-smoking conservatory. Although food is certainly the priority here (most people come to dine rather than drink), there's a good range of real ales such as Archers Village, Boddingtons, Castle Eden, Flowers Original and Wadworths 6X kept under light blanket pressure, just under 80 wines, with at least ten by the glass, and mulled wine in winter. There's a lovely traditional feel in all its little enclaves, as well as big landscape prints and other pictures on the walls, some horsebrasses on the dark beams, a dresser with a collection of old bottles, tables of stripped deal (and a couple made from gigantic forge bellows), big tapestry-upholstered pews and blond chairs, and log fires; sensibly placed darts, shove-ha'penny, dominoes, cribbage, chess, fruit machine, piped music. A terrace has a pond and fountain, and outdoor heating. The garden stretches around the side and back, with well spaced tables, and looks over a side lane to the village church, and out over rolling prosperous farmland. *(Recommended by Janet Pickles, Evelyn and Derek Walter, Alan and Paula McCully, Andrew Shore, Tom Rees, Susan and Nigel Wilson, D Irving, E McCall, R Huggins, T McLean, Peter Mueller, Pat and Robert Watt)*

Whitbreads ~ Lease: Anthony Windle ~ Real ale ~ Bar food (12-2, 6-9.30) ~ Restaurant ~ (01666) 510366 ~ Children welcome ~ Open 10-3(3.30 Sat), 6-11; 12-4.30, 6-10.30 Sun

CHICKSGROVE ST9629 Map 2

Compasses ♀ 🍺

From A30 5½ miles W of B3089 junction, take lane on N side signposted Sutton Mandeville, Sutton Row, then first left fork (small signs point the way to the pub, in Lower Chicksgrove; look out for the car park)

There are friendly new licensees for the second year running at this lovely timeless old thatched house which readers believe is well worth seeking out. We hadn't received any reports on the new regime when we went to press, but the new landlord told us that he had made no changes to the atmospheric bar where old bottles and jugs are suspended from the beams above the roughly timbered bar counter, farm tools, traps and brasses hang on the partly stripped stone walls, and high-backed wooden settles form snug booths around tables on the mainly flagstone floor. Indeed the only innovations he had planned were for the menu, which he hoped to make more eclectic. Changing on a regular basis it might include sandwiches (£2.50), soup (£2.95), bacon and avocado salad (£4.25), moules marinières (£4.95), scallops in filo pastry (£5.25), steak and kidney pie or interesting vegetarian meals such as mille feuille of sautéed vegetables with a blue cheese sauce or Moroccan vegetable bake (£7.95), guinea fowl braised in red wine and garlic or tuna steak with lemon and lime-infused couscous (£9.95), rack of lamb with a herb crust or 8oz sirloin steak (£11.95), sea bass with a caper and pine kernel risotto (£13.95) and puddings such as ginger and advocaat alexander or chocolate and orange brûlée (£3.25). Well kept Bass, Tisbury Stonehenge and Wadworths IPA and 6X on handpump. The quiet garden or flagstoned farm courtyard are very pleasant places to sit, and there's a nice walk to Sutton Mandeville church and back via Wadder Valley. Be warned, they close on Tuesdays after bank holiday Mondays. *(Recommended by Phyl and Jack Street,*

Jenny and Michael Back, Jill Bickerton, C and A Moncreiffe, Jerry and Alison Oakes, M Mackay,
Dr and Mrs Nigel Holmes, Roger Byrne, Jan R Watts, Brad W Morley, John Hayter`)

*Free house ~ Licensee Jonathan Bold ~ Real ale ~ Bar food (not Sun evenings or all
day Mon) ~ Restaurant ~ (01722) 714318 ~ Well behaved children in restaurant and
garden ~ Open 11-3, 6-11; 12-3, 7-10.30 Sun; closed Mon except bank holidays ~
Bedrooms: £35S/£45S*

CORSHAM ST8670 Map 2
Two Pigs 🍺
A4, Pickwick

A pub in the true sense of the word, this old-fashioned and charismatic roadside
drinking house is a rarity these days – under 21s aren't allowed, the emphasis is
firmly on drinking, the only piped music is the blues (with live blues Mon evenings),
and they don't serve any food whatsoever. An unusual range of beers, mostly from
smaller independent breweries, includes Bunces Pigswill and four changing guest ales
such as Church End Tamworth Two Pigs, Hop Back Summer Lightning, Moors
Merlins Magic and Woods Shropshire Lad; also a range of country wines. The very
narrow long dimly lit bar with stone floors, wood-clad walls and long dark wood
tables and benches, is crammed with zany décor including enamel advertising signs,
pig-theme ornaments, old radios, a bicycle and a canoe. The country atmosphere is
kept lively and chatty by the entertaining landlord (he's been here over a decade
now), friendly staff and good mix of customers. A covered yard outside is called the
Sty. Beware of their opening times – the pub is closed every lunchtime, except on
Sunday. *(Recommended by Susan and Nigel Wilson, Mrs Laura Gustine, Andrew and Eileen
Abbess, Dr and Mrs A K Clarke)*

*Free house ~ Licensees Dickie and Ann Doyle ~ Real ale ~ (01249) 712515 ~ Blues
Mon evenings ~ Open 7-11; 12-2.30, 7-10.30 Sun*

DEVIZES SU0061 Map 2
Bear 🍺 🛏
Market Place

Although local annals reveal that the first landlord was granted a licence in 1599,
rumour has it that this imposing ex-coaching inn existed under another name for a
long time before. Boasting a colourful history to complement its age, it has provided
shelter to distinguished guests as diverse as King George III and Dr Johnson, and at
one time was home to the portrait painter Thomas Lawrence, whose father ran the
establishment in the 1770s. The big main bar gives the striking impression of having
been the centre of the town for three hundred years, yet is imbued with a calm and
comfortable atmosphere with roaring winter log fires, black winged wall settles and
muted red button-back cloth-upholstered bucket armchairs around oak tripod
tables. Separated from the main bar by some steps and an old-fashioned glazed
screen, the traditionally-styled Lawrence Room has dark oak-panelled walls, a
parquet floor, shining copper pans on the mantlepiece above the big open fireplace,
and plates around the walls; part of this room is no smoking. Straightforward good
value bar food includes sandwiches (from £2.50), filled rolls (from £2.75), home-
made soup (£2.75), filled baked potatoes (from £3.75), ploughman's (from £3.75),
ham, egg and chips (£4.25), omelettes (from £4.50), sausage and mash (£4.75), roast
of the day (£4.95), scampi (£5.95) and home-made puddings (£2.50); there are
buffet meals in the Lawrence Room – you can eat these in the bar too. On Saturday
nights they have a good value set menu. Well kept Wadworths IPA and 6X and
maybe a guest beer such as Youngs Bitter on handpump, wines by the glass and
freshly squeezed juices are served from an old-fashioned bar counter with shiny
black woodwork and small panes of glass, along with a good choice of malt
whiskies. Wadworths brewery where you can buy beer in splendid old-fashioned
half-gallon earthenware jars is within sight of the hotel. *(Recommended by the Didler,
Gwen and Peter Andrews, Martin and Barbara Rantzen, Ian Phillips, Alan and Paula McCully,
Francis Johnston, E J and M W Corrin, Mike and Mo Clifford)*

Wadworths ~ Tenant Keith Dickenson ~ Real ale ~ Bar food (11-2.30, 7-9.15) ~ Restaurant ~ (01380) 722444 ~ Children in eating area of bar ~ Open 9.30am-11pm; 10.30am-10.30pm Sun ~ Bedrooms: £54B/£80B

EBBESBOURNE WAKE ST9824 Map 2

Horseshoe 🍺 🛏

On A354 S of Salisbury, right at signpost at Coombe Bissett; village is around 8 miles further on

Over the last year we've had nothing but glowing reports about this charming old country pub, delightfully set off the beaten track in fine hilly downland. In warm weather, the pretty little garden makes a lovely place to eat, with seats that look out over the steep sleepy valley of the River Ebble, and a paddock at the bottom with three goats. The very cheerful welcoming landlord also has a couple of playful dogs. There are fresh flowers from the garden on the tables in the beautifully kept bar, which also has lanterns, farm tools and other bric-a-brac crowded along its beams, and an open fire; a new conservatory extension seats 10 people. Enjoyable home-made bar food is served by caring efficient staff and might include soup (£3.25), sandwiches (from £3.25), a hearty ploughman's (£4.50), oak smoked trout salad (£5.95), watercress and mushroom lasagne or locally made faggots (£6.95), liver and bacon casserole or venison or steak and kidney pie (£7.25), fresh fish bake (£7.50), beef in red wine (£8.95), honey-roast duck (£12.95), local fillet steak (£14.95) and excellent home-made puddings such as sticky toffee meringue, bread and butter pudding, gooseberry crumble and blackberry and apple pie (£3.25); good breakfasts and three course Sunday lunch. Well kept Adnams Broadside, Ringwood Best, Shepherd Neame and Wadworths 6X tapped from the row of casks behind the bar, farm cider, country wines, and several malt whiskies. Booking is advisable for the small no-smoking restaurant, especially at weekends when they can fill up quite quickly. The barn opposite is used as a pool room, with darts and a fruit machine; good walks nearby. *(Recommended by the Didler, Phyl and Jack Street, Richard Gibbs, Paul S McPherson, Dr D E Granger, Jerry and Alison Oakes, John Hayter, Dr D Twyman, Tom and Rosemary Hall, JP, PP, Eddie Edwards, Mrs Margaret Ross, Michael Hill, Tim Barrow, Sue Demont)*

Free house ~ Licensees Anthony and Patricia Bath ~ Real ale ~ Bar food (not Sun or Mon evenings) ~ Restaurant ~ (01722) 780474 ~ Children in eating area of bar ~ Open 12-3, 6.30-11; 12-4, 7-10.30 Sun ~ Bedrooms: /£50B

FONTHILL GIFFORD ST9232 Map 2

Beckford Arms 🛏

Off B3089 W of Wilton at Fonthill Bishop

The friendly new licensees have settled in well at this pleasant old inn, where they have refurbished all the rooms, stripping back furnishings to bare wood to create a light and airy interior with a parquet floor and a pleasant mix of wood tables with church candles. In winter a big log fire burns in the lounge bar which leads into a light and airy back garden room with a high pitched plank ceiling and picture windows looking on to a terrace. Popular with locals, the straightforward public bar has darts, fruit machine, pool, TV and piped music. Four changing well kept ales might include Hampshire Pride of Romsey, Hop Back Summer Lightning, Morlands Old Speckled Hen and Tisbury Best. The landlady told us that they try to use as much local produce as possible to prepare the well liked reasonably priced food, with some fruit and vegetables picked fresh from the garden. The bar food menu includes soup (£2.95), sandwiches (from £2.95), ham and eggs (£5.95), ploughman's (from £5.95), cajun chicken (£7.95) and Scotch rump steak (£9.95) with specials such as Irish stew or steak and kidney pudding (£6.95), stir-fried vegetables with mozzarella (£7.95), skate, bream or Thai king prawns (£8.95), and home-made puddings such as apple pie, rhubarb crumble or treacle pudding (£3.75). Friendly staff; good value bedrooms. *(Recommended by Pat and Richard, Alan and Ros)*

Free house ~ Licensees Karen and Eddie Costello ~ Real ale ~ Bar food (12-2.30, 7-9.30(till 9 Sun and 10 Fri, Sat)) ~ (01747) 870385 ~ Children in restaurant, eating

area of bar, garden room and garden ~ Open 11-11; 12-10.30 Sun ~ Bedrooms:
£35S/£65B

FORD NT9538 Map 2
White Hart ★ ⓦ ⓨ ◀ ⌁

A420 Chippenham—Bristol; follow Colerne sign at E side of village to find pub

New managers took over this fine stone country inn (which more than one reader has described as a 'gem') last November, and according to reports, are running it along the same lines as their predecessors. Set in stunning countryside, the grounds are wonderful in summer, when peacocks strut around the garden and you can sit on the terrace by the trout stream that babbles under a little stone bridge. Despite the number of people who come for the splendid food (for which you will need to book), a bustling atmosphere and an impressive range of real ales make the bar a pleasant place to come for just a drink. There are heavy black beams supporting the white-painted boards of the ceiling, tub armchairs around polished wooden tables, small pictures and a few advertising mirrors on the walls, and an ancient fireplace (inscribed 1553). They keep fine wines, farm ciders and a dozen malt whiskies, and up to ten well kept real ales might include Badger Tanglefoot, Flowers Original, Fullers London Pride, Hop Back Summer Lightning, Marstons Pedigree, Smiles Best and Theakstons XB on handpump or tapped from the cask; friendly staff; pool on a circular table and piped music. Generous helpings of palatable food from a daily-changing menu might include lunchtime carrot and coriander soup (£1.95), lunchtime baguettes (from £3.95), ploughman's (from £4.25), green bean salad with smoked bacon, lardons, garlic croutons and blue cheese dressing or pasta neapolitan with pesto and shaved parmesan (£4.95), pan-fried lamb's kidneys with a mustard and caper sauce and mash (£5.50) or beef stroganoff (£6.95). There are no bar snacks in the evening, but you can eat from the more elaborate restaurant menu at lunchtime and in the evening in the bar: ceviche of salmon with avocado salsa and cured red onions (£5.75), roast chicken breast with courgette fritters, chickpea mash and thyme juices (£10.50), roast duck breast with honey and black peppercorns, celeriac dauphinoise, caramelised apple, braised fennel and calvados sauce or roast monkfish wrapped in smoked bacon on creamed potatoes with buttered spinach and a chive cream sauce (£13.95); puddings include steamed chocolate pudding, glazed lemon tart with raspberry sauce or crème brûlée (from £3.75); excellent breakfasts; there's a secluded swimming pool for residents. *(Recommended by Mr and Mrs J Evans, Cliff Blakemore, Susan and Nigel Wilson, Bernard Stradling, John and Christine Simpson, B J Harding, Mr and Mrs A H Young, Nick and Meriel Cox, Alan J Morton, Simon Penny, Lyn and Geoff Hallchurch, Mr and Mrs J Brown, David and Nina Pugsley, Comus Elliott, Dr and Mrs A K Clarke, Ann and Colin Hunt, Mrs Laura Gustine, Adrian White, D Parkhurst, Mike and Mo Clifford, Carol and Steve Spence, Dr D Twyman, Pam and David Bailey, J Sheldon, Pat and John Millward, KC)*

Lionheart ~ Managers Peter and Kate Miller ~ Real ale ~ Bar food ~ Restaurant ~ (01249) 782213 ~ Children in eating area of bar ~ Open 11-3, 5-11; 12-3, 7-10.30 Sun ~ Bedrooms: £59B/£79B

GREAT HINTON ST9059 Map 2
Linnet

3½ miles E of Trowbridge; village signposted off A361 opp Lamb at Semington

In summer, the flowering tubs and window boxes at the front of this attractive old brick pub are quite a sight and there are seats dotted amongst them. Inside, you'll get a warm welcome from the friendly licensees, and the little bar to the right of the door has lots of photographs of the pub and the brewery, dogs, and little hunting plates on the green walls, brass pistols and horsebrasses on the beams, and blue patterned wall banquettes and wheelback chairs with matching seats on the blue-green carpet. The biggish, rather smart dining area has lots of decorative china and bird pictures (including linnets) on the pink ragged walls, bric-a-brac on window shelves, plenty of dark wheelback chairs and pub tables, and a snug end part with bookshelves and a cabinet with china. Well kept Wadworths IPA and 6X on handpump, 25 malt whiskies, and summer pimms. Good lunchtime food includes sandwiches (from £2.25), soup and a sandwich (£3.95), ploughman's (from £4), and home-made steak and kidney pie or lasagne (£5.95), with evening dishes like ham and asparagus crêpes (£3.40), pasta with coriander and pecan nut pesto (£6.75), chicken in a tarragon, mushroom, brandy and white wine sauce or salmon in a véronique grape sauce (£7.75), beef stroganoff (£9.25), and home-made puddings (£2.75). The landlord is a keen golfer and is the reigning Wadworths landlords champion, and they have a labrador and a labrador-cross. *(Recommended by Colin and Joyce Laffan)*

Wadworths ~ Tenants Brian and Anne Clanahan ~ Real ale ~ Bar food (lunchtime) ~ (01380) 870354 ~ Children in eating area of bar and restaurant ~ Open 11-2.30, 6.30-11; 12-3, 7-10.30 Sun; closed Mon except bank holidays

HEYTESBURY ST9242 Map 2
Angel 🍴 🍷 🍺 🛏

High St; just off A36 E of Warminster

Readers have been very impressed by the high standard of food and the friendly service from young staff at this 16th-c inn, set in a quiet village street just below Salisbury Plain. The varied and interesting bar food includes a good choice of fish dishes (delivered fresh on Tuesday and Friday) such as popular salmon fishcakes with dill mayonnaise (£6.75), dressed crab (£7.50), grilled turbot fillet with a fresh herb butter sauce or sautéed salmon fillet on a wild mushroom and leek stroganoff (£8.95) and lobster salad with basil mayonnaise (£14.95). Other very well prepared meals, served with perfectly cooked vegetables, might include soup (£3.50), filled baguettes – made with authentic flour flown in from France – (£4), ploughman's (from £4.25), a vegetarian tart such as spinach and wild mushroom (£6.25), venison sausages (£6.75), chicken breast stuffed with feta cheese, sun-dried tomatoes and basil (£8.95) and honey and ginger-glazed duck breast (£10.50); puddings include tarts such as pear and almond or treacle and sticky toffee pudding (£3.50); cappuccino. As well as about a dozen wines by the glass and freshly squeezed orange juice there's well kept Marstons Pedigree, Ringwood Best, Timothy Taylor Landlord and a guest such as Hop Back Summer Lightning on handpump. The cosy and homely lounge on the right, with well used overstuffed armchairs and sofas, flower and Japanese prints and a good fire, opens into a charming back dining room which is simple but smart with a blue carpet, blue-cushioned chairs and lots more flower prints on the white-painted brick walls. On the left is a long beamed bar with quite a buoyant atmosphere, a woodburner, some attractive prints and old photographs on the terracotta-coloured walls, and straightforward tables and chairs. The dining room opens on to an attractive secluded courtyard garden; hot nuts, maybe piped Phil Collins; cribbage. This is a nice place to stay. *(Recommended by Gwen and Peter Andrews, Jason Caulkin, Hugh Roberts, Chris and Ann Garnett, Barry and Anne, Jenny and Chris Wilson, Richard Fendick, John and Deborah Luck, P J and J E F Caunt)*

Free house ~ Licensees Sue and T Smith and Philip Roose-Francis ~ Real ale ~ Restaurant ~ (01985) 840330 ~ Children welcome ~ Open 11.30-3, 6.30-11; 12-3, 7-10.30 Sun; closed 25 Dec ~ Bedrooms: £37.50B/£49B

HINDON ST9132 Map 2
Lamb

B3089 Wilton—Mere

Apart from the arrival of a new manager last December, nothing has changed at this solid old hotel (dating back in part to the 13th c), prettily set near Fonthill Park and Lake, and very usefully open all day. Perhaps the nicest parts of the roomy long bar, split into several areas, are the two lower sections with a slate floor. There's a long polished table with wall benches and chairs, and a big inglenook fireplace, and at one end a window seat with a big waxed circular table, spindleback chairs with tapestried cushions, a high-backed settle and brass jugs on the mantelpiece above the small fireplace; there are lots of tables and chairs up some steps in a third bigger area. Bar food includes soup (£3.95), ploughman's (£4.50), lasagne or pork, asparagus and mushroom pie, vegetable and cheese bake or spinach and cottage cheese lasagne (£6.95), lamb curry (£7.50), liver and bacon, pork loin and mustard, well liked seafood, spinach and leek au gratin, steak and game casserole with dumplings or garlic and lemon tiger prawns (£7.95), balsamic baby chicken stir fry, grilled tuna steak with garlic butter or smoked salmon with wild mushroom tagliatelle (£8.95), pan-fried sirloin steak (£9.95), and a well liked good value Sunday roast; the restaurant is no smoking. They usually serve cream teas throughout the afternoon. Four real ales include Ash Vine and Wadworths 6X alongside two constantly changing guests such as Exmoor Gold and Slaters Original; there are just under a dozen wines by the glass, and a range of whiskies includes all the malts from the Isle of Islay; service can become slow when they get busy. There are picnic-sets across the road (which is a good alternative to the main routes west); limited parking. No dogs. *(Recommended by Phyl and Jack Street, John Evans, Peter and Audrey Dowsett, DP, Tony Gayfer, John and Christine Vittoe, Lynn Sharpless, Bob Eardley, Michael Hill, Peter and Joan Elbra, David and Ruth Shillitoe, Howard Clutterbuck, Shaun Flook, Mayur Shah, C P Scott-Malden, K H Frostick, Mr W W Burke, Gwen and Peter Andrews, Brad W Morley, Colin Laffan, Mrs J Lang, Julie and Bill Ryan, Paul and Ursula Randall, L C Rorke)*

Free house ~ Licensees John Croft and Cora Scott ~ Real ale ~ Bar food (12-2, 7-10) ~ Restaurant ~ (01747) 820573 ~ Children welcome ~ Open 11-11; 12-10.30 Sun ~ Bedrooms: £43B/£65B

KILMINGTON ST7736 Map 2
Red Lion 🍺

Pub on B3092 Mere—Frome, 2½ miles S of Maiden Bradley; 3 miles from A303 Mere turn-off

Without any of the distractions of modern life to bother you, this homely and welcoming 400-year-old local (originally a drover's inn and post house) is a good place to unwind. While the ivy covered exterior is rather inconspicuous, the comfortably cosy low ceilinged bar is pleasantly individual, with a curved high-backed settle and red leatherette wall and window seats on the flagstones, photographs on the beams, and a couple of big fireplaces (one with a fine old iron fireback) with log fires in winter. A newer no-smoking eating area has a large window and is decorated with brasses, a large leather horse collar, and hanging plates. Simple reasonably priced bar food is served at lunchtime only and includes home-made soup (£1.20), sandwiches (from £2.20, toasted £2.70), filled baked potatoes (from £2.50), cornish pasties (from £3.10), game pie or ploughman's (from £3.95), steak and kidney or lamb and apricot pie (£4.05), meat or vegetable lasagne (£5.25), and two daily specials such as home-made chicken casserole (£3.95) or very good home-cooked ham and egg (£4.25); last orders for food at 1.50pm. Well kept Butcombe and two guests such as Butts Barbus Barbus and Jester on handpump; also farm cider, various pressés such as elderflower, citrus, limeflower and lemongrass and ginger, and monthly changing wines. Sensibly placed darts, dominoes, shove-ha'penny and cribbage. There are picnic-sets in the big attractive garden, where Kim the labrador is often to be found. It's popular with walkers – you can buy the locally made walking sticks, and a gate leads on to the lane which leads to White Sheet Hill, where there is riding, hang gliding and radio-controlled gliders. Stourhead Gardens are only a mile away. *(Recommended by Mayur Shah, Michael Hill, Drs R A and B F Matthews, Alan and Paula McCully, Peter C B Craske, Mrs Stevens, Stephen, Julie and Hayley Brown)*

Free house ~ Licensee Chris Gibbs ~ Real ale ~ Bar food (lunchtime) ~ (01985) 844263 ~ Children in eating area of bar till 8.30pm ~ Open 11.30-2.30, 6.30-11; 12-3, 7-10.30 Sun

LACOCK ST9168 Map 2
George 🍺

The reader who found an uncanny physical resemblance between Basil Fawlty and the landlord of this lovely homely old pub is evidently not alone in doing so, as a sign up at the Glass's farm (where you can stay) bears the name of John Cleese's calamitous hotel! However, similarities between the two hosts go no further than the physical, as the welcome John Glass and his staff offer their customers is unfailingly friendly. Very popular with readers, the pub has been licensed continuously since the 17th c, and run by Mr Glass for well over a decade. One of the talking points has long been the three-foot treadwheel set into the outer breast of the magnificent central fireplace. This used to turn a spit for roasting, and was worked by a specially bred dog called, with great imagination, a turnspit. Often very busy indeed, the comfortably welcoming bar has a low beamed ceiling, upright timbers in the place of knocked-through walls making cosy corners, candles on tables even at lunchtime, armchairs and windsor chairs, seats in the stone-mullioned windows and flagstones just by the bar. The well kept Wadworths IPA, 6X, and seasonal ale such as Farmers Glory are very reasonably priced, and there's a decent choice of wines by the bottle. It's a good idea to book for the generous helpings of good value tasty bar food (served with fresh vegetables and real chips) which might include sandwiches (from £1.95), home-made soup (£2.50), filled french stick (from £3.75), goat's cheese salad (£3.95), ploughman's (from £4.50), home-made lasagne or steak and kidney pie, lamb and mint sausages or home-made spinach, mushroom, nut and blue cheese crumble (£6.25), chicken breast stuffed with stilton in a leek sauce (£8.50), Scotch salmon fillet with hollandaise sauce or 8oz sirloin (£8.95), and home-made puddings such as raspberry and hazelnut crumble, bread and butter pudding or treacle sponge (£3.95); prompt and friendly service; no-smoking barn restaurant; darts. There are picnic-sets with umbrellas in the back garden, as well as a play area with swings, and a bench in front that looks over the main street. The bedrooms (very highly praised by readers) are up at the landlord's farmhouse with free transport to and from the pub. It's a nice area for walking. *(Recommended by Mike and Mo Clifford, W W Burke, P and S White, Hugh Spottiswoode, Meg and Colin Hamilton, Lawrence Pearse, John and Christine Vittoe, Dr and Mrs B D Smith, Lyn and Geoff Hallchurch, Miss Veronica Brown, Paul and Sandra Embleton, Janet Pickles, David Heath, Comus Elliott, Paul Cleaver, Alan and Paula McCully, Carol and Steve Spence, Ann and Colin Hunt, Mrs Laura Gustine, J A Woolmore, Sheila Keene, Mrs N W Neill, John Hayter, M G Hart, Joan and Michel Hooper-Immins, Monica Shelley, Peter and Audrey Dowsett)*

Wadworths ~ Tenant John Glass ~ Real ale ~ Bar food (12-2, 6-9.30) ~ Restaurant ~ (01249) 730263 ~ Children welcome ~ Open 10-2.30, 5-11; 11-11 Sat; 12-10.30 Sun ~ Bedrooms: £25B/£40B

Red Lion

High Street; village signposted off A350 S of Chippenham

Life at this Georgian inn, the other main entry in this lovely National Trust village, remains unchanged under its new manager. A modest frontage belies the nicely spacious and welcoming inside, where the comfortable long bar is divided into separate areas by cart shafts, yokes and other old farm implements, and old-fashioned furnishings including a mix of tables and comfortable chairs, turkey rugs on the partly flagstoned floor, and a fine old log fire at one end. Plates, paintings and tools cover the walls, and stuffed birds, animals and branding irons hang from the ceiling. Bar food includes soup (£2.50), sandwiches (from £2.85), pâté (£3.10), ploughman's (from £5.50), scampi (£7.95) salmon with hollandaise sauce or 8oz rump steak (£9.50) and daily specials such as pie of the day (£5.95); puddings including cheesecake, trifle and sticky toffee pudding (£2.75); part of the pub is no smoking. Well kept and priced Wadworths IPA, 6X and seasonal beer on handpump, and several malt whiskies; darts, shove ha'penny, table skittles, dominoes and fruit machine. It can get busy, and towards the latter half of the evening is popular with younger people. Close to Lacock Abbey and the Fox Talbot Museum. *(Recommended by Janet Pickles, Alan and Paula McCully, Ann and Colin Hunt, Richard and Ann Higgs)*

Wadworths ~ Manager Alban Joseph ~ Real ale ~ Bar food (12-2.30, 6-9) ~ Restaurant ~ (01249) 730456 ~ Children in eating area of bar ~ Open 11(11.30 Sat)-11; 12-10.30 Sun; 11-3 Mon-Fri in winter ~ Bedrooms: £55B/£75B

Rising Sun

Bewley Common, Bowden Hill – out towards Sandy Lane, up hill past Abbey; OS Sheet 173 map reference 935679

Friendly unpretentious pub, blessed with one of the most splendid views we know. Seats on the two-level terrace look out right over the Avon valley, some 25 miles or so away; it's a particularly attractive sight around sunset. Inside, the three little rooms have been knocked together to form one simply furnished and characterful area, with a mix of old chairs and basic kitchen tables on stone floors, stuffed animals and birds, country pictures, and open fires. The friendly and helpful licensees and cook have been here two years now, and have built up a reputation for good, generously served home-made bar food. Particularly popular with readers are spicy dishes (all around £7.50) such as red Thai chicken curry, sizzling chilli, stir fries and pork steaks with various sauces, but from the changing blackboards other food might include sandwiches (from £2.50, filled french bread from £3), soup (£3), ham, egg and chips (£5), ploughman's (£5.25), nut loaf or macaroni cheese with bacon (£6.50) and steak and kidney pie (£7); Sunday roast (£6). Very well kept Moles Best, Brew 97 and Tap Bitter plus one of their seasonal ales and a guest such as Bass on handpump; friendly service. Darts, shove-ha'penny, dominoes, cribbage, table skittles and piped music. The surrounding countryside is lovely. *(Recommended by Miss D Drinkwater, Roger and Valerie Hill, Mrs Mary Walters, Roger and Jenny Huggins)*

Free house ~ Licensees Mr and Mrs Sturdy ~ Real ale ~ Bar food (not Sun evening or Mon lunchtime) ~ (01249) 730363 ~ Children away from bar ~ Live music every Weds and every other Sun evening ~ Open 11.30-3, 6-11; 12-10.30 Sun; closed Mon lunchtime

LIMPLEY STOKE ST7861 Map 2

Hop Pole

Coming S from Bath on A36 take B3108 at traffic lights signed Bradford on Avon, turn right of main road at sharp left-hand bend before the railway bridge, pub is 100 yds on right (car park just before on left)

Heaving with locals and visitors alike, this idyllic cream stone monks' wine lodge (with its name deeply incised on the front wall) is a traditional pub which manages to keep a respectable balance between eating and drinking. Most of the latter is done in the welcoming and atmospheric cosy dark-panelled room on the right, with red velvet cushions for the settles in its alcoves, some slat-back and captain's chairs on its turkey carpet, lantern lighting, and a log fire – this can get very crowded when the pub is busy. The roomier left-hand lounge (with an arch to a cream-walled inner room) is mostly laid for diners, and also has dark wood panelling and a log-effect gas fire. Well cooked and presented home-made bar food (you may need to book) includes filled baps (from £1.90), local smoked trout pâté (£2.50), a choice of ten ploughman's or salads (from £3.75), a daily pie such as steak and ale (from £5.50), local trout (£6.95), Scotch salmon or 8oz sirloin steak (£7.95), sea bass (£8.55), duck breast in black cherry sauce (£8.95) and local game in season. Puddings (from £2.50) include ice creams made at a local farm (£2.95); children's meals (from £2.50), and Sunday roast (from £5.50); friendly, courteous service. Part of the restaurant is no-smoking. Bass, Butcombe, Courage Best and a changing guest such as Morlands Old Speckled Hen on handpump, with a range of malt whiskies; darts, shove ha'penny, cribbage, dominoes and piped music. An attractive enclosed garden behind has rustic benches, a terrace and pond; boules. Just a few minutes' walk to the Kennet & Avon canal, the pub makes a good base for waterside walks. *(Recommended by Brad W Morley, Dr and Mrs A K Clarke, Dr M E Wilson, Susan and Nigel Wilson, Charles Bardswell, Keith and Janet Eaton, Janet Pickles, JDM, KM)*

Free house ~ Licensees Bob and Mich Williams ~ Real ale ~ Bar food ~ Restaurant ~ (01225) 723134 ~ Well behaved children in restaurant ~ Open 11-3, 6-11; 12-3, 7-10.30 Sun

LITTLE CHEVERELL ST9853 Map 2

Owl ◖ £

Low Rd; just off B3098 Westbury—Upavon, W of A360

This splendidly cosy little village local, delightfully set in a peaceful spot, offers an infallibly warm welcome to customers, many of whom come for their very good value lunchtime special offer of two courses for £4.50 or three courses for £4.95. Other reasonably priced good value food includes soup (winter only, £2.30), ploughman's (from £3.95), filled baked potatoes (from £4), summer salads (from £4.50), breaded haddock (£5.50), poached salmon steak (£5.95), 8oz rump (£6.50), sea bass poached in white wine (£7.50) and puddings such as caramel and apple crumble or cheesecake (£1.25-£2.50). The peaceful and neatly traditional bar has a comfortably relaxing atmosphere and seems a lot bigger than it really is thanks to plenty of chairs, stools, high-backed settles and tables; a piano separates the main area from a snugger room at the back. There are fresh flowers on the tables, local papers and guides to read, a gently ticking clock, two or three stuffed owls behind the bar, a few agricultural tools on the walls, and noticeboards advertising local events and activities. Alongside well kept Wadworths 6X there are three changing real ales such as Bunces Pigswill, Hambleton Bitter or Oakhill Mendip Gold; a blackboard lists forthcoming brews, and there's usually a beer festival the last weekend in April and in early September. They also have country wines, maybe farm cider and jugs of pimms in summer; friendly smiling service; the Stable is no smoking. At the back, the lovely tall ash and willow lined garden reverberates with the sound of wood pigeons cooing, and has rustic picnic-sets on a long lawn that runs down over two levels to a brook; there's a terrace above here with plastic tables and chairs. A pergola with climbers and hanging baskets across the front of the pub makes another lovely area of tranquil seating. They have a springer spaniel called Toby, and fellow canines are welcome. *(Recommended by N Rushton, Glen Armstrong, Lyn and Geoff Hallchurch, Susan and Nigel Wilson, Colin and Joyce Laffan, Mr and Mrs A H Young, David and Kay Ross, Brian and Anna Marsden)*

Free house ~ Licensee Mike Hardham ~ Real ale ~ Bar food ~ (01380) 812263 ~ Children in eating area of bar ~ Open 12-2.30(3 Sat, Sun), 7-(10.30 Sun)11; closed Mon, 25 Dec and Sunday evenings in winter

LOWER CHUTE SU3153 Map 2

Hatchet

The Chutes well signposted via Appleshaw off A342, 2½ miles W of Andover

It's easy to see why several readers have donned this timeless 16th-c thatched cottage their favourite pub: its enchanted appearance ranks it alongside some of the country's most attractive pubs, and inside it has the atmosphere of a traditional village local. Especially low beams look down over a lovely mix of captain's chairs and cushioned wheelbacks set around oak tables. There's a splendid 17th-c fireback in the huge fireplace, with a big winter log fire in front. Good bar food includes sandwiches (toasted or plain from £2.25, steak in french bread £4.95), home-made soup (£2.75), stuffed green-lipped mussels (£3.75), ploughman's (£4.25), battered cod, tortillas filled with chilli, giant filled yorkshire pudding, half a roast chicken or liver and bacon (£5.25), vegetable lasagne or home-made steak and stout pie (£5.45), and gingered seafood stir fry or salmon, halibut and prawn wellington (£6.95). The restaurant menu has a few more dishes such as chicken breast filled with stilton (£9.95), lemon sole (£10.95) and peppered steak (£11.95); tasty puddings include two daily gateaux (one fruit, one chocolate) and a couple of sponges such as ginger and lemon (£2.50). Well kept real ales on handpump served by the friendly barmaid include Adnams, Bass and Greene King IPA and Triumph, and there's a range of country wines. Shove-ha'penny, dominoes, cribbage, and maybe piped music. There are seats out on a terrace by the front car park, or on the side grass, as well as a children's sandpit. *(Recommended by Lynn Sharpless, Bob Eardley, Jenny and Michael Back, R R Winn, John and Joan Calvert, Dr Alan Green, Phyl and Jack Street, Mrs Pat Crabb, Mrs J Lang)*

Free house ~ Licensee Jeremy McKay ~ Real ale ~ Bar food ~ Restaurant ~ (01264) 730229 ~ Chidren in restaurant and eating area of bar till 9pm ~ Open 11.30-3(4 Sat), 6-11; 12-4, 7-10.30 Sun; closed evening 25 Dec ~ Bedrooms: /£45B

LOWER WOODFORD SU1136 Map 2
Wheatsheaf

Leaving Salisbury northwards on A360, The Woodfords signposted first right after end of speed limit; then bear left

There are lots of lovely walks around this 18th-c farm prettily set in the Avon valley a few miles from Salisbury. The inside – part of which was originally the barn and stables – has a rather cosy feel, and though most of it is laid for dining there are a couple of tables by the front bar which are still used by drinkers. At the heart of the bar there's an unusual indoor pond with goldfish, and to get from one part of the pub to another you have to cross a miniature footbridge. The very wide choice of well liked food includes home-made soups such as spinach and broccoli (£2.25), filled baguettes with chips (£3.95), ploughman's or baked potatoes with tasty fillings such as chicken tikka mayonnaise (£4.55), ham and eggs, sweet and sour chicken, courgette, pepper and mushroom lasagne or seafood pasta (£5.95), pies such as steak and mushroom or chicken, stilton and bacon (£6.35), filo wrapped prawns (£6.50), barnsley lamb chops or chicken breast with various sauces (£7.45), sirloin steak (£10.95) with daily specials including lamb and mint pie (£6.50) and salmon steak with stilton and herb sauce (£8.95); puddings include treacle sponge or meringue with chocolate and liqueur (from £2.95); children's meals (from £2.50); most of the pub is no smoking. Well kept Badger Best, Tanglefoot and a guest beer from the brewery are promptly served on handpump by helpful efficient staff; darts, dominoes, cribbage and piped music; Sunday evening quiz. Good disabled access, and baby-changing facilities. The big walled garden has picnic-sets, a climber and swings, and is surrounded by tall trees; it's handy for Old Sarum. *(Recommended by C Smith, JCW, Betsy and Peter Little, Susan and Nigel Wilson, Mara Kurtz, A Lock, Glen and Nola Armstrong, Phyl and Jack Street)*

Badger ~ Managers Ron and Anne May ~ Real ale ~ Bar food (12-2, 6.30-9.30) ~ (01722) 782203 ~ Children in eating area of bar ~ Open 11-2.30(3 Sat), 6.30(6 Sat)-11; 12-3, 7-10.30 Sun; closed 25 Dec

MARLBOROUGH SU1869 Map 2
Sun

High Street

Cardinal Wolsey was inducted in the church adjacent to this lively little 15th-c inn, whose heavy sloping beams and wonky floors give a charming sense of busy old time Marlborough. The cheery gregarious landlord instils a warm atmosphere in the attractively furnished and dimly lit characterful bar, with brasses and harness hanging above the log fire, benches built into the black panelling, an antique high backed settle, and newspapers. Bar food includes chicken liver pâté or popular fish soup (£3.25), smoked salmon and prawn open sandwich (£4.75), very tasty fresh battered haddock or various home-made pies (£6.25), moules marinières or sizzling chicken in mushroom and black bean sauce (£7.25) and steaks (from £9.50); no-smoking dining area. Well kept Bass and Courage Directors on handpump, and several reasonably priced wines; fruit machine and TV. Although bedrooms are simple and could be neater they are characterfully positioned, one is in a garret with a lovely view of the High Street. You can sit outside in a small sheltered back courtyard. *(Recommended by Trevor Owen, Michael and Jean Wilby, John Faby, Tina and David Woods-Taylor, Meg and Colin Hamilton, Mrs Kay Neville-Rolfe, Howard and Margaret Buchanan, Ian Phillips, Sheila and Robert Robinson)*

Scottish Courage ~ Manager Peter Brown ~ Real ale ~ Bar food ~ Restaurant ~ (01672) 512081 ~ Children in eating area of bar and restaurant ~ Open 11-11; 12-10.30 Sun ~ Bedrooms: £35S/£45S

NETHERHAMPTON SU1029 Map 2
Victoria & Albert 🍺

Just off A3094 W of Salisbury

In the summer they have live music in the garden at least one weekend every month at this charmingly traditional thatched cottage. The black beamed bar now resembles the photograph over the fireplace (which shows it as it was a decade ago) and is filled with gleaming brassware, a good mix of individual tables, nicely cushioned old-fashioned wall settles and some attractive small armed chairs on the ancient polished floor tiles; darts, fruit machine and piped music. As well as Courage Best and Directors and a beer from Wychwood they keep a guest such as Hampshire Brewery Ironside on handpump. Straightforward bar food includes soup (£2.75), filled baguettes (£3.75), battered cod and chips or macaroni cheese (£4.95), ploughman's (£5.25), steak and ale pie (£5.35), sausages, mash and onion gravy in a yorkshire pudding (£5.95), cajun chicken breast (£6.95), and rump steak or locally smoked trout (£7.95), along with puddings including blackberry and apple crumble and sticky toffee pudding (from £2.95). There's hatch service for the sizeable garden behind, with well spaced picnic-sets, a fountain and a big weeping willow. Handy for Wilton House (and Nadder Valley walks). *(Recommended by Rose Magrath, Stephen G Brown, Anne Viney, Mike and Mary Carter)*

Free house ~ Licensees Harriet Allison and Pam Bourne ~ Real ale ~ Bar food ~ (01722) 743174 ~ Children in restaurant ~ Usually jazz first Fri of month ~ Open 11-3, 5.30(6 Sat)-11; 12-3, 7-10.30 Sun

NORTH NEWNTON SU1257 Map 2
Woodbridge 🍷

A345 Upavon—Pewsey

Perfectly placed for the keen angler, this friendly pub has an expansive garden that backs on to the River Avon, and offers a day's fly fishing pass at £25. Apart from painting the walls bluey-green, the licensees who arrived last December have kept things pretty much as they were with a blazing log fire, prints on the walls, flowery cushions and curtains, daily papers and magazines to read and quite a collection of old wine bottles. A wide choice of bar food includes home-made soup (£2.50), open sandwiches (from £3.95), Thai seafood dim sum (£4.25), a good range of Mexican dishes (£4.25-£8.25), home-cooked ham or local pork sausages with egg and chips (from £4.60), steak and ale pie (£5.95), stuffed sweet pepper (£6.95), applewood and dill chicken (£8.25), salmon fillet with cracked black peppers (£8.95), pork, honey and ginger stir fry (£9.25), red snapper with a tangy orange hollandaise sauce (£9.75), guinea fowl supreme with a mushroom, smoked bacon and red wine sauce (£11.25), 8oz fillet steak (£12.95) and honey roast half duckling (£13.95); puddings (£3.50) and children's meals (from £2.95). It's worth booking for Sunday lunch (£6.95). Well kept Wadworths IPA, 6X, Farmers Glory and a seasonal guest beer, country wines, helpful friendly service; piped music. Three of the four pleasantly furnished bedrooms have their own bathroom. The garden has plenty of tables and a play area, and they have space for a few tents or caravans; no dogs inside. *(Recommended by John Hayter, Kevin Flack, Joe and Mary Stachura, TRS, Helen Pickering, James Owen)*

Wadworths ~ Managers Charles and Rebecca Meldrum ~ Real ale ~ Bar food (12-10(9.30 Sun)) ~ Restaurant ~ (01980) 630266 ~ Children in eating area of bar and restaurant ~ Open 12-11; 12-10.30 Sun; closed 25/26 Dec ~ Bedrooms: /£45B

NORTON ST8884 Map 2
Vine Tree

4 miles from M4 junction 17; A429 towards Malmesbury, then left at Hullavington, Sherston signpost, then follow Norton signposts; in village turn right at Foxley signpost, which takes you into Honey Lane

Seeming much more remote than its proximity to the motorway would suggest, this civilised dining pub – popular with readers for its good food and efficient service – is housed in an attractively converted 18th-c mill house. A lively atmosphere fills the three smallish rooms which open together with plates, small sporting prints, carvings, hop bines, a mock-up mounted pig's mask (used for a game that involves knocking coins off its nose and ears), lots of stripped pine, candles in bottles on the tables (the lighting's very gentle), and some old settles. From a seasonally changing menu, a wide range of enjoyable food might include soup (£2.95), filled french bread (from £3.50), crab cakes or seafood linguine (£4.75), pigeon, venison and Guinness terrine with red berry and tarragon dressing (£4.95), fish and chips (£7.25), leek, parmesan and potato ravioli with rocket pesto and toasted pine kernels (£7.95), chicken wrapped in prosciuto ham stuffed with a tapenade of olives, sun-dried tomatoes and mozzarella (£8.75), pork marinated in ginger, honey and soy sauce on a bed of Chinese vegetables (£8.95), panachet of fried fish with ciboulette sauce and wild rice (£9.25), 8oz rump steak with peppercorn sauce (£9.95), crispy duck breast with summer berry sauce (£13.95) and puddings such as french chocolate tart with white chocolate ice cream, summer pudding with cornish clotted cream or bread and butter pudding (£3.50); children's meals (£2.95); two course Sunday lunch (£9). Best to book, especially at weekends; one dining area is no smoking. Well kept Archers Vine Tree with a couple of guest beers such as Bunces Pigswill and Fullers London Pride; piped music. There are picnic-sets under cocktail parasols in a vine-trellised garden with young trees and tubs of flowers, and a well fenced separate play area with a fine thatched fortress and so forth. *(Recommended by Stephen Alexander, Betsy and Peter Little, F C Johnston, S H Godsell, D Irving, E McCall, R Huggins, T McLean, M G Hart, Richard and Stephanie Foskett, Comus Elliott, G W Bernard)*

Free house ~ Licensee Helen Johnson-Greening ~ Real ale ~ Bar food ~ (01666) 837654 ~ Children welcome ~ Open 11.30-2.30, 6-11; 12-10.30 Sun

PITTON SU2131 Map 2
Silver Plough ♀

Village signposted from A30 E of Salisbury (follow brown tourist signs)

Readers continue to praise the well prepared imaginative food at this civilised country dining pub which was a farmhouse until WWII. As well as home-made soup (£2.95) and hearty sandwiches (from £3.95), a wide range of food might include generously served tagliatelle with avocado and cream or chicken liver and fresh mushroom terrine (£4.50), ploughman's (£5.25), omelette, stir-fried chicken breast with chinese vegetables, smoked trout and avocado gratin or yorkshire pudding filled with cumberland sausage (£5.95), smoked pork sausage with sweet peppers (£7.75), sautéed lamb's kidneys (£9.25), pork fillet with tomato, basil and mozzarella sauce (£10.50), chargrilled sirloin steak with brandy and peppercorn sauce (£12.95) and daily specials such as roast aubergine filled with ratatouille on a bed of mange tout (£6.95), whole lemon sole with herb butter (£8.95) or ostrich and kangaroo steaks (£11.95-£12.95), with home-made puddings including treacle tart, banoffee pie and cheesecake (£3.50); no-smoking area in the restaurant. Old jugs, glass rolling pins and other assorted curios hang from the beamed ceilings of the main bar with comfortable oak settles and paintings and prints on the walls. Well kept Badger Best, IPA and Tanglefoot and Wadworths 6X under light blanket pressure, a fine wine list including 10 by the glass and some well priced and carefully chosen bottles, a good range of country wines, and a worthy choice of spirits. There's a skittle alley next to the snug bar; cribbage, dominoes and piped music; efficient service. A quiet lawn with an old pear tree has picnic-sets and other tables under cocktail parasols, and there are good downland and woodland walks nearby. *(Recommended by Ian and Jacqui Ross, Mrs B Nickson, Charles Gray, Richard Fendick, Phyl and Jack Street, Mr and Mrs K Flawn, Dr D Twyman, Val and Alan Green, John Hayter, Jerry and Alison Oakes, John Bowdler)*

Badger ~ Manager Adrian Clifton ~ Real ale ~ Bar food (12-2.30, 7-9.30(till 10 Sat, Sun)) ~ (01722) 712266 ~ Children in eating area of bar ~ Open 11-3, 6-11; 11-11 Sat; 12-10.30 Sun

POULSHOT ST9559 Map 2

Raven ⚑

Village signposted off A361 Devizes—Seend

Faultlessly kept Wadworths IPA, 6X and seasonal brews are tapped straight from the cask at this splendidly tucked-away pub, prettily set across from the village green with a nice country welcome, thriving chatty atmosphere (no piped music here) and smiling helpful service. The two cosy and intimate rooms of the black-beamed bar are well furnished with sturdy tables and chairs and comfortable banquettes, and there's an attractive no-smoking dining room. An enjoyable menu of tasty generously served food is prepared by the friendly landlord and along with sandwiches (from £2.45) and home-made soup such as cream of broccoli (£2.50), there might be hot roast beef granary roll (£3.25), ploughman's (from £3.25), prawn curry (£4.15), breaded plaice or ham and double egg and chips (£6.20), vegetable bake with a cheese and yoghurt topping (£6.25), home-made pies such as chicken and vegetable or steak and kidney, grilled pork chasseur with mushroom and white wine sauce or minted lamb meat balls on a bed of tagliatelle with tomato sauce (£6.80), grilled chicken breast topped with smoked bacon and melted gruyère (£7.35), poached salmon supreme with tarragon and dill sauce with pasta (£8.15), sirloin steak with a peppercorn sauce (£10.10), mixed grill and puddings such as home-made raspberry cheesecake, apple and blackberry crumble or sticky toffee pudding with cream (from £2.10). The gents' are outside. A classic country pub. *(Recommended by June and Tony Baldwin, Lady Palmer, Gwen and Peter Andrews, G Washington, John Hayter, Hazel and Michael Duncombe, JEB, Mr and Mrs Peter Smith, Colin Laffan, George Atkinson, Mrs Laura Gustine, Ron Gentry, MRSM)*

Wadworths ~ Tenants Philip and Susan Henshaw ~ Real ale ~ Bar food ~ Restaurant ~ (01380) 828271 ~ Children in restaurant ~ Open 11-2.30, 6.30-11; 12-3, 7-10.30 Sun

RAMSBURY SU2771 Map 2

Bell

Village signposted off B4192 (still shown as A419 on many maps) NW of Hungerford, or from A4 W of Hungerford

Since arriving last October, the new licensee has been gradually refurbishing and modernising several parts of this comfortably civilised pub, nicely positioned in a smartly attractive village. When we went to press, the frontage had just been re-plastered and given a fresh coat of paint, and they were hoping to begin work on smartening up the restaurant area. The stylishly relaxed and chatty bar areas are divided by a big chimney breast with a woodburning stove, and remain nicely furnished with fresh flowers on the polished tables. Victorian stained-glass panels in one of the two sunny bay windows look out onto the quiet village street where, in summer, you can sometimes see Morris dancing; there's a new conference room at the back. Bar food (not cheap) includes lunchtime sandwiches (from £2.50), soup (£3.20), smoked duck and mango platter with a passion fruit vinaigrette (£5.65), spinach and chard dumplings topped with parmesan cheese with a cherry tomato compôte (£7.35), baby clams, linguini and sun-dried tomato casserole (£9.95), honey-roast lamb with celeriac mash with a lemon and rosemary jus (£12.85), roast beef fillet with roquefort cheese (£14.95) and daily specials such as cumberland sausages and smoked bacon with mash (£6.95), poached salmon (£7.50) and grilled whole sea bass (£15); puddings such as coffee, date and apricot pudding with toffee sauce or poached pears in red wine with calvados cream (£3.95); there's a more elaborate à la carte menu. Tables can be reserved in the restaurant, though the same meals can be had in the bar; one section is no smoking. Butts, Fullers London Pride, Wadworths IPA and 6X and an occasional guest beer on handpump, and over 25 types of schnapps; evening piped music. There are picnic-sets on the raised lawn. Roads lead from this quiet village into the downland on all sides. *(Recommended by Peter Burton, Tom Evans, Yavuz and Shirley Mutlu, John Hayter, M G Hart, Mr and Mrs Peter Smith, D M and M C Watkinson, Nigel Clifton, Gordon, P Neate, John Fahy)*

Free house ~ Licensee Andrew Fitton ~ Real ale ~ Bar food (12-2.30, 6.30-10) ~
Restaurant ~ (01672) 520230 ~ Children in restaurant ~ Open 12-3, 6-11(10.30 Sun)

ROWDE ST9762 Map 2
George & Dragon 🍴 ♀
A342 Devizes—Chippenham

Wiltshire Dining Pub of the Year

Readers really enjoy the extremely well cooked food served by friendly courteous
staff at this warmly welcoming old dining pub. A special highlight of the shrewdly
inspired seasonally changing menu is the fresh Cornish fish, with dishes such as fried
squid with lemon, garlic and parsley or pan-fried scallops in a bacon and shallot
sauce (£7/£12 large helping), red gurnard baked with cider and cheese (£9), cod in
beer batter with chilli soy sauce or Thai fish curry (£10), roast hake with aioli and
peppers (£12), seared tuna steak with tomatoes and balsamic vinegar or pan-fried
swordfish with lemon and butter (£14) and whole grilled lobster with garlic or herb
butter (£25). Other palatable meals made from well chosen fresh ingredients might
be new potato and lovage soup (£3), aubergine caviar with yoghurt, mint and garlic
(£4.50), half a dozen oysters or carpaccio of tuna, rocket, olive oil and balsamic
vinegar (£5), English cheese with bread, salad and home-made pickles (£6.50), gratin
of chicken savoyarde (£8.50), picchiatelle with ham and mushroom sauce (£9),
lamb's sweetbreads with tomato salsa (£10) and puddings such as rhubarb crumble,
chocolate St Emilion or iced lime soufflé (from £4.50); no-smoking dining room.
Tastefully furnished with plenty of dark wood, the bar has a log fire with a fine
collection of brass keys by it, while the bare-floored dining room has quite plain and
traditional feeling tables and chairs, and is close enough to the bar to retain a
pleasant pubby atmosphere. Three changing well kept real ales on handpump might
be from brewers such as Ash Vine, Butcombe, Goffs, Hop Back and Tisbury, and
there are also local farm cider and continental beers and lagers; friendly and efficient
service; shove ha'penny, cribbage, dominoes and trivia. There are lovely walks along
the nearby Kennet and Avon Canal. *(Recommended by Lyn and Geoff Hallchurch, Peter
and Audrey Dowsett, Gwen and Peter Andrews, Mrs Laura Gustine, Susan and Nigel Wilson,
Marvadene B Eves, Andrew and Rosemary Reeves, Tony Beaulah, Dr D Twyman, Comus Elliott,
Ron Gentry, F J and A Parmenter, John Hayter, Phyl and Jack Street, Sheila Keene, Ruth Warner,
Tina and David Woods-Taylor, Dr Michael Smith, Trevor Owen, W Burke)*

Free house ~ Licensees Tim and Helen Withers ~ Real ale ~ Bar food (12-2, 7-10; not
Sun, Mon) ~ Restaurant ~ (01380) 723053 ~ Children welcome ~ Open 12-3, 7-
(10.30 Sun)11; closed Mon lunchtime

SALISBURY SU1429 Map 2
Haunch of Venison ★
1 Minster Street, opposite Market Cross

Readers find it difficult to tear themselves away from the vibrant atmosphere at this
marvellous old building, constructed some 650 years ago as the church house for St
Thomas's, just behind. Worth seeking out if you're in the city, it has massive beams
in the ochre ceiling, stout red cushioned oak benches built into its timbered walls,
genuinely old pictures, a black and white tiled floor, and an open fire; a tiny snug
opens off the entrance lobby. A quiet and cosy upper panelled room has a small
paned window looking down onto the main bar, antique leather-seat settles, a nice
carved oak chair nearly three centuries old, and a splendid fireplace that dates back
to the building's early years; behind glass in a small wall slit is the smoke-preserved
mummified hand of an unfortunate 18th-c card player. Well kept Courage Best and
Directors and a guest such as Wadworths 6X on handpump from a unique pewter
bar counter, with a rare set of antique taps for gravity-fed spirits and liqueurs; over
70 malt whiskies, decent wines (including a wine of the week), and a range of
brandies; chess. Bar food includes filled ciabatta (£4.25), soup with a sandwich
(£4.50), baked potato filled with panchetta and brie mesclun salad (£4.95), venison
sausages and mash, aubergine caviar and mushroom ragoût with baked potato or

pork tenderloin with apple and calvados cream sauce (£8.50), salmon fillet with spinach and potato galette and a basil, white wine and cream sauce (£9.50) and pan-fried wild haunch of venison with juniper berry jus (£11.95); puddings (from £2.95). The pub can get a little smoky, and at times service can veer towards the inattentive. *(Recommended by the Didler, Jerry and Alison Oakes, Sheila Keene, Mr and Mrs Jon Corelis, Mr and Mrs Buckler, Dr C C S Wilson, Dr and Mrs R E S Tanner, Phyl and Jack Street, Colin and Ann Hunt, M Gardner, Dr Alan Green, W Burke, Mr and Mrs A P Reeves, Roger and Pauline Pearce, Simon Penny, David Yandle, John Robertson, Veronica Brown, JP, PP, Tracey and Stephen Groves, Mrs A Chesher)*

Scottish Courage ~ Lease: Antony and Victoria Leroy ~ Real ale ~ Bar food (lunchtime only) ~ Restaurant ~ (01722) 322024 ~ Children in restaurant ~ Open 11-11; 12-3, 7-10.30 Sun

New Inn

New Street

One reader described this ancient and creaky timbered town centre pub as the archetypal old-fashioned inn, and a number of laudatory reports show that it's still as popular as ever. It's completely no-smoking throughout, and an inglenook fire in the largest room creates a warm cosy atmosphere; there are heavy old beams, horsebrasses, timbered walls, and a panelled dining room, with quiet cosy alcoves. A good range of well presented home-made food served throughout the pub includes soup (£2.45), sandwiches (from £3.25), Dorset liver pâté or filled baked potatoes (£3.95), ploughman's or broccoli and cauliflower bake (£4.95), beef and mushroom pie, lamb casserole or lamb's liver with bacon and onions (£6.95), salmon steak with hollandaise and dill sauce (£7.95), chicken breast cooked with mushrooms in white wine and cream sauce (£8.95), pork tenderloin done in cider and apricots (£9.95), duck breast cooked in honey with chestnut stuffing (£10.95) and good sturdy puddings (from £3.25); friendly helpful licensees and staff, well kept Badger Dorset Best and Tanglefoot and Charles Wells Eagle on handpump, decent house wines; maybe piped Radio 2. Tables out in the sizeable pretty walled garden look up to the spire of the nearby cathedral. The back bedrooms are quieter; no cooked breakfast. *(Recommended by Neil Spink, John and Christine Vittoe, Mrs Margaret Ross, Colin and Ann Hunt, DMT, David and Kay Ross, Brian and Anna Marsden, Lucy Bloomfield)*

Badger ~ Tenants J F and M G Spicer ~ Real ale ~ Bar food ~ (01722) 327679 ~ Children in eating area of bar and restaurant ~ Open 11-3, 6(7 Sun)-11; 11-11 Sat; closed 25, 26 Dec ~ Bedrooms: £39.50B/£49.50B

SEEND ST9461 Map 2
Barge

Seend Cleeve; signposted off A361 Devizes—Trowbridge, between Seend village and signpost to Seend Head

It's little wonder that this canalside pub gets very busy in summer, as the neatly kept waterside garden with its old streetlamps makes a perfect spot to watch the comings and goings of boats and barges on the Kennet & Avon Canal – there are moorings by the humpy bridge. Inside there's a friendly and relaxed atmosphere in the bar with an unusual barge theme décor – perhaps at its best in the intricately painted Victorian flowers which cover the ceilings and run in a waist-high band above the deep green lower walls. A distinctive mix of attractive seats includes milkchurns and the occasional small oak settle among the rugs on the parquet floor, while the walls have big sentimental engravings. The watery theme continues with a well stocked aquarium, and there's also a pretty Victorian fireplace, big bunches of dried flowers, and red velvet curtains for the big windows. A lengthy range of good bar food generously served by cheery uniformed staff includes soup (£2.50), sandwiches (from £3.50), pancakes filled with spinach and mushrooms with nutmeg (£4.50/£7.25 large helping), ploughman's (£5.25), 10oz gammon steak (£6.95), chicken and ham or steak and kidney pie (£6.95), chicken curry or scampi (£7.95), salmon in hollandaise sauce (£8.25), roasted pork loin wrapped in bacon with black pepper, herbs and a madeira-peppercorn sauce (£8.95), 8oz sirloin (£9.95), rack of lamb with a redcurrant sauce (£11.50), and specials such as steamed vegetables topped with cheese sauce (£6.25) or cod in a beer batter with chips (£7.25). In the evening dishes are served with fresh vegetables and a couple of additional dishes are a bit more restauranty; the restaurant extension is no smoking. They recommend booking for meals, especially at weekends. Well kept Badger Tanglefoot, Wadworths IPA and 6X, and a guest beer (usually from the brewery) such as Summer Sault on handpump, lots of malts and mulled wine in winter; trivia, fruit machine and piped music. Barbecues outside on summer Sundays. At the busiest times you may find queues to get in the car park, and service can slow down. Dogs are welcome. *(Recommended by Mr and Mrs Peter Smith, Jerry and Alison Oakes, R M Sparkes, Michael and Hazel Duncombe, R H Rowley, P and S White, Alan and Paula McCully, Tracey Hamond, Lyn and Geoff Hallchurch, Meg and Colin Hamilton)*

Wadworths ~ Tenant Christopher Moorley Long ~ Real ale ~ Bar food ~ Restaurant ~ (01380) 828230 ~ Children welcome ~ Open 11-2.30(3 Sat), 6-11; 12-4, 7-10.30 Sun)

SEMLEY ST8926 Map 2
Benett Arms ♀

Turn off A350 N of Shaftesbury at Semley Ind Estate signpost, then turn right at Semley signpost

Set in a lovely spot just across the green from a church right on the Dorset border, this delightful village inn gains much of its atmosphere from the cordial and helpful landlord Joe Duthie, now in his 23rd year at the pub. Since last year's edition, an old York stone floor has been laid in the bottom bar and most of the walls here have been stripped to bare stone. Friendly and welcoming, the two cosy and hospitable rooms are separated by three carpeted steps, and have one or two settles and pews, a deep leather sofa and chairs, hunting prints, carriage lamps for lighting, a pendulum wall clock, and ornaments on the mantlepiece over the log fire; there's a thatched-roof bar servery and in the carpeted upstairs area, there's a dark panelling dado. Freshly prepared bar food includes sandwiches (from £1.80), very good home-made soup (£2.95), ploughman's, moules marinières or duck liver pâté (£4.95), steak and kidney pie or leek and cheese bake (£5.95), scampi (£6.95), stincotto (half a roasted Italian pork shank with soya and ginger sauce), two springwater trout, gammon in cider or chicken in cream and white wine sauce with peppers and mushrooms (£9.95), and beef stroganoff (£13.95); puddings include several ice creams such as grapes and red wine or lemon sorbet, and hot bananas cooked in rum sauce or treacle and walnut tart (from £2.95). Four changing real ales might include Brains SA, Brakspears, Wadworths 6X and a guest such as Courage Directors on handpump, kept under light blanket pressure; farm cider, four chilled vodkas, 18 malt whiskies, lots of liqueurs, and a thoughtfully chosen wine list, including a good few by the glass; friendly chatty staff. Dominoes and cribbage, but no machines or music. There are seats outside. Well behaved dogs welcome. We have not yet heard from readers who have stayed here, but would expect this to be a pleasant place to stay in. *(Recommended by John A Barker, W Burke, WHBM, Phyl and Jack Street, Mr and Mrs D E Powell)*

Enterprise ~ Tenant Joe Duthie ~ Real ale ~ Bar food ~ Restaurant ~ East Knoyle (01747) 830221 ~ Children welcome ~ Open 11-11; 12-10.30 Sun; closed 25, 26 Dec ~ Bedrooms: £31B/£48B

SHERSTON ST8585 Map 2
Rattlebone

Church St; B4040 Malmesbury—Chipping Sodbury

Although chef Roger Payne has been at this lively old inn for 10 years now, he continues to add new and interesting dishes to the menu of unpretentious bar food, which some readers think is going from strength to strength. A lighter choice of snacks is served at lunchtime only, and includes filled jumbo baps (from £2.95), filled baked potatoes (from £3.50), ploughman's (from £3.95), cauliflower cheese with garlic bread (£4.50) and ham, egg and chips (£5.25). Another more sophisticated menu is always available and includes home-made soup (£2.75), creamy leek and smoked cheese pancake (£4.25), slices of duck breast with toasted almonds and mango chutney or smoked salmon with a dill and mustard sauce (£4.75), deep-fried plaice (£5.50), steak and kidney pie or mediterranean vegetables au gratin (£6.95), salmon fillet topped with roasted parmesan on a tomato coulis (£9.50), roast chicken breast wrapped in bacon with a rich tarragon mustard sauce (£9.75), prime Scotch rib-eye steak with a hot red chilli and garlic butter (£11.50) with daily specials such as tender lamb cooked with apricots and sage and ginger sauce (£7.95) or fresh cod fillet with a fennel and courgette sauce (£8.95) and puddings such as home-made crème brûlée or pecan nut and treacle pie (from £2.75); three course Sunday roast and coffee (£9.95); part of the dining area is no smoking. As we went to press, plans to serve meals all day had not yet been realised. Regardless of the notable emphasis on food, there's still a good pubby atmosphere in the several rambling rooms: nooks and crannies have pink walls, pews and settles, country kitchen chairs around a mix of tables, big dried flower arrangements, lots of jugs and bottles hanging from the low beams, and plenty of little cuttings and printed anecdotes. In the public bar there's a hexagonal pool table, darts, table football, connect four, shove ha'penny, fruit machine, cribbage, dominoes and juke box; also table and alley skittles. Well kept Smiles Best and Golden and up to three guests such as Everards Tiger, Greene King Abbot and Youngs Bitter on handpump, over 70 malt whiskies, more than 20 liqueurs and fruit wines, 12 rums, decent wines, and friendly service from well trained staff. The smallish garden is very pretty with flowerbeds, a gravel terrace, and picnic-sets under umbrellas. There are four boules pitches, and the Sherston carnival week concludes with a festival of boules at the pub on the second Saturday in July. It's handy for the M4 and Westonbirt Arboretum. *(Recommended by Pat and Roger Fereday, Ian, Roger, Tom, Ewan, Susan and Nigel Wilson, John Fahy, Jacquie and Jim Jones, Mrs Pat Crabb, Peter and Audrey Dowsett, Mr and Mrs M Clifford, Comus Elliott, Derek and Sylvia Stephenson, Martin and Karen Wake, Peter Neate, Janet Pickles, Andrew Shore, Nicholas and Kedrun Martyn, D Godden, Keith and Margaret Kettell, B T Smith, Deborah and David Rees)*

Smiles ~ Manager David Baker ~ Real ale ~ Bar food (12-2, 7-9; 12-7 Sun) ~ Restaurant ~ (01666) 840871 ~ Children away from main bar servery ~ Open 10(10.30 Sun)-11; closed evening 25 Dec

WHITLEY ST8866 Map 2
Pear Tree 🍴 ♀

Off B3353 S of Corsham, at Atworth 1½, Purlpit 1 signpost; or from A350 Chippenham—Melksham in Beanacre turn off on Westlands Lane at Whitley 1 signpost, then left and right at B3353

This is Debbie and Martin Still's first pub and they are already winning awards for their excellent imaginative food. It's an attractive honey-coloured stone farmhouse with a civilised, friendly and chatty atmosphere and a good mix of locals and visitors. The front bar has cushioned window seats, some stripped shutters, a mix of dining chairs around good solid tables, a variety of country pictures and a Wiltshire regiment sampler on the walls, a little fireplace on the left, and a lovely old stripped stone one on the right. The popular big back restaurant has green dining chairs, quite a mix of tables, and a pitched ceiling at one end with a quirky farmyard theme – wrought-iron cockerels and white scythe sculpture. Served by first class staff, the enticing food at lunchtime might include soup (£2.95), cheese ploughman's (£5.50), roast leek, baby sweetcorn and cheese tart with a grained mustard dressing and mixed leaf salad (£5.95), flaked lamb salad with a curried onion and rosemary marmalade in foccacia bread (£6.25), venison, prune and sherry pâté on sweet and sour savoy cabbage with a redcurrant and rosemary dressing (£6.95), wild mushroom, roast artichoke and toasted pine nut lasagne with a tomato salad and smoked applewood cheese sauce (£7.50), and super roasted scallops with roasted cherry tomatoes on a rocket leaf salad and a balsamic and lemon oil dressing (£11.50); in the evening, there might be poached quail eggs and smoked bacon salad with a balsamic and shallot dressing (£4.75), warm monkfish salad with a lemongrass and black olive tapenade dressing or prawn and pimento spring roll on an avocado salsa (£5.25), calf's liver on a sweet potato mash with a curried onion marmalade or loin of pork marinated in cider and sage with a caramelised apple and juniper berry tart and red wine gravy (£9.50), roast chicken breast glazed with an orange and oriental sauce on egg noodles (£9.75), and chargrilled salmon with a saffron and sorrel risotto on a sun-dried tomato and coriander pesto (£10.50). Puddings such as rhubarb and roast hazelnut cheesecake with a mixed berry compôte, banana and lavender brûlée, and steamed pear and ginger sponge with a caramel and vanilla anglaise (£4.25), with a set lunch menu (2 courses £8.95, 3 courses £10.95). Well kept Bass, Oakhill Best Bitter, and Wadworths 6X on handpump, and a good wine list with around 10 by the generous glass. It's best to book a table in the evening. There are picnic-sets on the terrace, and boules. *(Recommended by Mrs G Roberts, Alan and Janice Curry, Pete and Rosie Flower, Andrew Shore, J A Barker)*

Free house ~ Licensees Martin and Debbie Still ~ Real ale ~ Bar food ~ Restaurant ~ (01225) 709131 ~ Children in restaurant ~ Open 11-3, 6-11; 12-3, 7-11 Sun; closed evenings 25, 26 and 31 Dec and all day 1 Jan

WOODBOROUGH SU1159 Map 2
Seven Stars 🍴 🍷

Off A345 S of Marlborough: from Pewsey follow Woodborough signposts, then in Woodborough bear left following Bottlesford signposts

Described by one reader as 'Anglo-French and thoroughly fantastic', this red brick thatched house has a civilised yet friendly and unpretentious atmosphere and an interesting menu of well liked good food. At first, most of the furnishings appear to follow a traditional style: polished bricks by the bar counter, hunting prints, attractively moulded panelling, a hot coal fire in the old range at one end, a big log fire at the other, a pleasant mix of antique settles and country furniture, cast-iron-framed tables and cosy nooks here and there. It's when you notice the strings of onions and shallots by one fireplace, and then the bounty of retired wine bottles on delft shelves – and perhaps the gingham tablecloths and decidedly non-standard art up steps in the attractive back dining area – that you sense a Gallic influence, equally discernible in the menu. Changing daily, this might include french onion soup (£2.75), filled baguettes (from £3.25), ploughman's (from £4.25), moules farcies, provençale or marinières or croque monsieur (£4.75), crayfish tails (£5.75/£10.75 large helping), vegetable curry (£6.25), beef bourguignon, salmon fishcakes, venison and mushroom casserole or navarin of lamb (£7.95), roast duck with orange sauce (£8.75), bream fillets with hollandaise sauce (£9.75), pan-fried pheasant breasts with mushrooms and sherry sauce (£10.75), tournedos of fillet steak with celery and stilton in port sauce (£13.75), Brittany seafood platter (£21.75), and puddings such as tarte tartin, raspberry crème brûlée or home-made sorbets (£3.95); they receive regular deliveries from France, and smaller helpings are available for children. Well kept Badger Dorset Best, Bunces Pigswill, Wadworths 6X and an occasional guest such as the disconcertingly green Bunces Sign of Spring on handpump. An exemplary wine list has about ten (including plenty of French) by the glass in the £1.90ish range, and interesting bin ends; helpful chatty bar staff. There's an attractive restaurant with handsome Victorian pictures; maybe sophisticated piped music. Seven acres of riverside gardens. An alsatian, a white west highland terrier and a black cat constitute the friendly menagerie. *(Recommended by Nick Lawless, TRS, Martin and Karen Wake, Dr Paul Khan, Jenny and Brian Seller, Howard and Margaret Buchanan, Jim Bush, Bill Cooper, Gordon)*

Free house ~ Licensees Philippe Cheminade and Kate Lister ~ Real ale ~ Bar food ~ Restaurant ~ (01672) 851325 ~ Well behaved children in restaurant and garden ~ Open 12-3, 6-11; 12-3 Sun; closed Sun evening and all day Mon except lunchtimes on bank holidays

You can send us reports through our web site: www.goodguides.com

Lucky Dip

Besides the fully inspected pubs, you might like to try these Lucky Dips recommended to us and described by readers (if you do, please send us reports):

Aldbourne [SU2675]
☆ *Blue Boar* [The Green (off B4192)]: Friendly, relaxed and nicely furnished, with homely feel and boar's head in Tudor bar, blazing log fire, extensive more modern lounge/dining area popular for good choice of inexpensive food from generous sandwiches up, fresh veg; well kept Archers Village, Wadworths IPA and 6X, decent wine, quick service; quiet piped music; children welcome, neatly kept small back country garden, seats out facing pretty village green nr church (*John Hayter, Trevor Owen, Peter and Audrey Dowsett, B T Smith*)
Crown: Unpretentious village pub with oak bar furnishings in two-part beamed lounge, unusual huge log fireplace linking to public bar, well presented generous food, small nicely laid out dining room; friendly quick service, pleasant atmosphere, well kept Ushers, interesting bric-a-brac, quiet piped music; tables under cocktail parasols in neat courtyard (*Trevor Owen*)
Ashton Keynes [SU0494]
Horse & Jockey: Friendly and chatty newish landlord in lively local with several real ales (*D Irving, R Huggins, T McLean, E McCall*)
White Hart [High Rd]: Roomy and friendly village pub with beams and stripped stone, interesting well priced home cooking, well kept Brakspears and Wadworths, prompt service, good log fire; maybe piped music; garden, delightful Thameside village nr Cotswold Water Park (*Jenny and Brian Seller*)
Avebury [SU0969]
☆ *Red Lion* [A361]: Much-modernised and substantially extended thatched wayside pub in touristy village, in the heart of the stone circles; pleasant original core, quick friendly service, well kept Boddingtons, Gales HSB, Morlands Old Speckled Hen and Wadworths 6X, open fires, food bar, no-smoking area and unpubby restaurant extension; maybe piped classical music (*LYM, Dr M Owton, Peter and Audrey Dowsett, George Atkinson*)
Stones: Good reasonably priced vegetarian restaurant in converted barn, not a pub but atmosphere not entirely unpubby – and they have a local organic real ale and cider tapped from the cask, country wines and home-made soft drinks; cold food all day, home-made hot lunches, not Nov-Mar (*Mrs Pat Crabb, JJW, CMW, June and Tony Baldwin*)
Barford St Martin [SU0531]
Barford Inn [junction A30/B3098 W of Salisbury]: Pleasantly old-fashioned panelled bar with big log fire, chatty interlinking rooms, Badger Best and Tanglefoot, lots of Israeli wines, ambitious food (not cheap) with Mediterranean influences inc Friday evening Israeli barbecues, no-smoking restaurant; maybe piped music; disabled facilities, tables out on terrace and in garden; small but comfortable, well equipped and nicely refurbished bedrooms (*P Draper, LYM, Lisette Collingridge*)

Beckhampton [SU0868]
☆ *Waggon & Horses* [A4 Marlborough—Calne]: Friendly stone-and-thatch pub handy for Avebury and open all day, full range of Wadworths ales and a guest beer kept well, good coffee, old-fashioned unassuming bare-boards bar, understated Dickens connections, log fires, wide choice of popular good value bar food, all home-made, inc children's and imaginative dishes, teas, dining lounge, family room; side room with pool and machines, CD juke box, pleasant garden with good play area; parking over road, no dogs; disabled access possible despite a few steps and cobbles, bedrooms (*D M and M C Watkinson, Janet Pickles, Paul and Diane Edwards, LYM, Lyn and Geoff Hallchurch, Trevor Owen, Chris Mawson, Neil Spink, G W A Pearce*)
Berwick St James [SU0639]
Boot: Well prepared food inc plenty of good interesting snacks and light dishes, good choice of well kept if cold beers inc Wadworths 6X, welcoming atmosphere (*Charles and Ann Moncreiffe, J Monk*)
Biddestone [ST8773]
Biddestone Arms [off A420 W of Chippenham; The Green]: Well kept roomy village pub, mostly set out for eating – simple choice of tasty generous food; good welcoming service, Wadworths 6X, games in cosy public bar, swings in small fairylit garden; attractive village with lovely pond (*George Atkinson, BB*)
☆ *White Horse* [The Green]: Busy 16th-c village local, wide choice of sensibly priced well cooked food and filled rolls in unusual stencilled lounge and partly no-smoking dining area, well kept Courage and Wadworths 6X, quick friendly service, small hatch-served bar with shove-ha'penny, darts and table skittles, games machine; children welcome; overlooks duck pond in picturesque village, tables in good garden with play area, aviary and rabbits; bedrooms (*Trevor Owen, Colin and Peggy Wilshire, Alan Kirkpatrick, Lyn and Geoff Hallchurch, Alan and Paula McCully, Ann and Colin Hunt*)
Bishops Cannings [SU0364]
☆ *Crown* [off A361 NE of Devizes]: Welcoming and unassuming refurbished two-bar village local with wide choice of good value generous food, well kept Wadworths IPA and 6X, decent wines, upstairs dining room; dogs welcome, tables outside, next to handsome old church in pretty village, walk to Kennet & Avon Canal (*John and Christine Simpson, Marjorie and David Lamb, Lyn and Geoff Hallchurch*)
Bishopstone [SU2483]
Royal Oak [the one nr Swindon]: Recently refurbished two-bar local, some beams and oak panelling, wood floors, settles, bookshelves, prints on striped wallpaper; warm and friendly, with Arkells Bitter, 2B and 3B, good food inc organic meat and burgers, cribbage, darts and chess, garden; quiz and murder mystery nights;

beautiful village *(Sam Samuells, Lynda Payton, Richard and Catherine Preston)*

White Hart [the one nr Salisbury]: New landlord doing good food from grilled goat's cheese to steak with stilton and port sauce, fresh veg, proper trifle, Flowers Original and Wadworths 6X (not cheap), attentive staff and pleasant atmosphere *(Dr and Mrs Nigel Holmes)*

Bradford Leigh [ST8362]

Plough [B2109 N of Bradford]: Good service from efficient smartly dressed staff, good choice of well cooked food, Wadworths 6X and Worthington, decent cider; nice seats outside *(Lyn and Geoff Hallchurch)*

Bradford on Avon [ST8261]

Beehive [Trowbridge Rd, Widmore]: Small very welcoming old-fashioned pub on outskirts nr Kennet & Avon Canal, old playbills, cricketing prints and cigarette cards, well kept Butcombe, Wadworths and changing guest beers inc some from abroad, good value generous home-made food inc baked potatoes with unusual fillings, good range of wines; resident cats, children and dogs welcome, tables in large waterside back garden, barbecues *(Dave Jones, Trevor Owen, JEB)*

☆ *Bunch of Grapes* [Silver St]: Dim-lit wine-bar style décor though definitely a pub, with cask seats in small front room with rugs on bare boards, bigger tables on composition floor of roomier main bar, well kept Smiles Best and Golden and guests such as Batemans XXXB and Youngs Special, good range of wines and malt whiskies, good choice of reasonably priced food in bar and upstairs eating area (pub recently taken over by chef) *(Dr M Owton, Susan and Nigel Wilson, BB)*

Kings Arms [Silver St]: Dim lighting, bare boards and rugs, ceiling loaded with fishing gear, smiling service, big open fire, popular dining area (some interesting dishes), well kept Greene King IPA, Abbot, Smiles Best and Theakstons Best, good choice of spirits; piped music, one side very popular with young people *(Nick Lawless)*

Swan [Church St; car park off A363 Trowbridge rd, beside central bridge]: Large civilised bar, well kept Butcombe and Courage Directors, good choice of food, friendly staff, huge fireplace; good bedrooms, nice breakfast *(LYM, Nick Lawless)*

Bratton [ST9052]

☆ *Duke* [B3098 E of Westbury]: Warmly welcoming, clean and civilised, well refurbished, with comfortable lounge bar, public bar and nice small dining room, very good generous food inc lunchtime bargains, Moles ales (tied to them), experienced licensees and quick pleasant service, well behaved labrador called Wellington, exemplary lavatories; ancient whalebone arch to garden; bedrooms *(Colin and Joyce Laffan, Lyn and Geoff Hallchurch, Alan and Janice Curry)*

Broad Chalke [SU0325]

☆ *Queens Head* [Ebble Valley SW of Salisbury; North St]: Roomy and friendly, with heavy beams, inglenook with woodburner, padded settles and chairs, some stripped brickwork, wide range of home-made food from sandwiches up (very long-serving chef), welcoming service, well

kept ales inc Ringwood Best and Wadworths 6X, decent wines, farm ciders and country wines, good coffee; maybe piped music; wheelchair access from back car park, tables in pretty courtyard overlooked by comfortable well equipped bedrooms in newish separate block *(Neil Spink, Paul McPherson)*

Broad Hinton [SU1076]

☆ *Crown* [off A4361 about 5 miles S of Swindon; High St]: Light and airy open-plan bar, plush and roomy eating area, good home-cooked food inc vegetarian, friendly licensees and uniformed waitresses, well kept Arkells BB, BBB, Kingsdown and Mild, good range of wines, no-smoking area, interesting bric-a-brac, unobtrusive piped music; unusual gilded inn sign, attractive spacious garden with fish pond and play area; bedrooms *(LYM, G W A Pearce, Trevor Owen)*

Brokerswood [ST8352]

Kicking Donkey: Good sensibly priced food, fine range of beer such as Ash Vine, Ushers, Wadworths 6X, Wychwood and one brewed for them by Bunces, good service even on a busy Sun, several bars and various nooks, log fires; picnic-sets in pretty garden opp, lovely rural setting with woodland walks *(Derek and Sylvia Stephenson, Ian Phillips, Colin Laffan)*

Bromham [ST9665]

Oliver Cromwell [A342]: Good value quickly served home-made bar food (should book for lunch – you can even order lobster), Sun lunch in restaurant, attractively priced real ales, decent wines, friendly landlord; fine view over Roundway Down Civil War battlefield – good small museum in bar *(Richard Pierce)*

Bulford [SU1643]

Rose & Crown [Crown St]: Friendly pub with reasonably priced food inc sizzler dishes, Greene King ales *(James Nunns)*

Castle Combe [ST8477]

☆ *Castle*: Old-world country hotel in beautiful village, clean and attractive, with good elaborate food in nicely furnished bars and restaurant (starters can be ordered as main courses), welcoming helpful service, cellar games room, tables out on terrace; good value bedrooms *(Alison Keys)*

☆ *Salutation* [The Gibb; B4039 Acton Turville—Chippenham, nr Nettleton]: Surprisingly large old pub with choice of beamed seating areas inc comfortable lounge and locals' bar, huge handsome fireplace, separate raftered thatched and timbered restaurant; jovial landlord, Whitbread-related ales, good choice of wines, good food inc fresh Cornish fish and Aberdeen Angus steaks; open all day, pretty garden with pergola *(MRSM, John Knighton, Alan and Paula McCully)*

White Hart [signed off B4039 Chippenham—Chipping Sodbury]: Attractive ancient stonebuilt pub, beams, panelling, flagstones, seats in stone-mullioned window, lots of old photographs; Wadworths IPA, Farmers Glory and 6X and a guest such as Adnams, smaller lounge, family room, games room; they may make you pay in advance if you're eating, walkers welcome, tables in sheltered courtyard *(George Atkinson,*

Andrew and Eileen Abbess, Barry and Anne)

Charlton [ST9588]

☆ *Horse & Groom* [B4040 toward Cricklade]:
Wide choice of good generous food in carefully
refurbished pub's civilised and relaxing bar, old
firearms, farm tools and log fire, simpler right-
hand bar with hops on beams, friendly staff, well
kept Archers and Wadworths, farm cider, decent
wines; restaurant (good value Sun lunch), tables
outside; dogs welcome, comfortable bedrooms
*(John and Pat Smyth, J and M de Nordwall, D
Irving, E McCall, R Huggins, T McLean, Gwen
and Peter Andrews, LYM, Mike and Heather
Watson)*

Chilmark [ST9632]

☆ *Black Dog* [B3089 Salisbury—Hindon]:
Interesting food from imaginative baguettes and
burgers with blue cheese to enticing main dishes
(different blackboards lunchtime and evening),
well kept ales such as Bass, Hook Norton and
Wadworths 6X, good value house wines, Irish
landlord, friendly staff and good local
atmosphere (regulars turn up on horseback) in
comfortably modernised 15th-c beamed pub
with armchairs by lounge log fire, fossil
ammonites in the stone of the attractive dining
room; dogs welcome *(KN-R, Julie and Bill Ryan,
Mr and Mrs C Moncreiffe, Mr and Mrs T Bryan,
Ian Bradshaw, LYM)*

Chippenham [ST9173]

Porter Blacks [Borough Parade]: New Irish
theme pub with tables out by River Avon
(Richard Pierce)

Chitterne [ST9843]

Kings Head: Cheerful newish licensees, varied
food, bedrooms; pretty village, good walks
(J W G Nunns, Pat and Robert Watt)

Cholderton [SU2242]

Crown [A338 Tidworth—Salisbury]: Cosy
thatched low-beamed cottage with welcoming
licensees, simple choice of very generous
reasonably priced food cooked to order (so may
be a wait), well kept Boddingtons, efficient
service; L-shaped bar with nice open fire, bar
billiards one end; seats outside *(D M Brumfit,
David and Ruth Shillitoe)*

Christian Malford [ST9678]

☆ *Mermaid* [B4069 Lyneham—Chippenham, 3½
miles from M4 junction 17]: Long bar pleasantly
divided into areas, good food inc some
interesting dishes, well kept Bass, Courage Best,
Wadworths 6X and Worthington BB, decent
whiskies and wines, some attractive pictures, bar
billiards, darts, fruit machine, piped music (live
Thurs), tables in garden; bedrooms *(BB, Patrick
Godfrey)*

Collingbourne Ducis [SU2453]

Blue Lion: Comfortable and popular, with wide
choice of reasonably priced food, Flowers IPA,
Ringwood and Wadworths 6X, decent wines, no
piped music, quick friendly service, big log fires;
back garden, pretty village *(SLC)*

Corsley Heath [ST8245]

Royal Oak [A362 Frome—Warminster]:
Comfortable 19th-c pub very popular lunchtime
for generous reasonably priced home-made food
inc vegetarian and some unusual dishes, helpful
friendly service, ales such as Marstons Pedigree

and Wadworths 6X, roomy two-part beamed
bar, big pleasant back children's room, big
garden, restaurant; handy for Longleat *(Cliff
Blakemore, K R Harris)*

Corton [ST9340]

☆ *Dove* [off A36 Warminster—Wilton]:
Welcoming and attractive homely country pub
with daily papers, well kept local beers maybe
inc Wylye Valley own-brew, good wine list, good
food in restaurant; bedrooms *(Colin McKerrow,
LYM, Lyn and Geoff Hallchurch)*

Cricklade [SU0993]

Vale: Very friendly local atmosphere in pleasant,
comfortable bar adjoining Georgian hotel; well
kept ales such as Archers and Wadworths 6X,
good guest beers, popular food; bedrooms *(D
Irving, E McCall, R Huggins, T McLean, R T
and J C Moggridge)*

White Hart [High St]: Large airy bar on several
levels, Arkells real ale, good bar food, friendly
service *(John and Joan Wyatt)*

Crudwell [ST9592]

Plough [A429 N of Malmesbury]: Nice local
feel, quiet lounge, dining area with comfortable
well padded seats and more in elevated part;
remarkably wide range of promptly served
reasonably priced food, well kept ales such as
Bass, Boddingtons, local Foxley, Morlands Old
Speckled Hen and Wadworths 6X, maybe open
fires, bar with darts and juke box, pool room;
pleasant side garden *(P and D Carpenter, D
Irving, E McCall, R Huggins, T McLean, Laura
and Stuart Ballantyne)*

Devizes [SU0061]

☆ *Black Swan* [Market Pl]: Comfortable and
spotless two-bar town-centre pub with friendly
atmosphere, local and military memorabilia,
wide choice of good value food in bar and
upstairs restaurant, well kept Wadworths; good
bedrooms, open all day *(Alan and Paula
McCully, John and Christine Simpson)*

Castle [New Park St]: Tastefully refurbished,
with medley of polished old tables, comfortable
carver chairs and settles, pewter candlesticks,
well kept Wadworths ales and a choice of malts
and brandies, interesting freshly prepared good
value specials; unobtrusive piped music;
bedrooms *(Alan and Paula McCully)*

Elm Tree [Long St]: Heavy-beamed local with
authentic spicy Italian food esp pizzas, well kept
Wadworths, decent house wines, jolly landlord,
no-smoking area; piped music; restaurant, clean
and tidy bedrooms *(Dr and Mrs A K Clarke, N
Rushton, Alan and Paula McCully, Michael and
Hazel Duncombe)*

Lamb [St Johns St]: Basic bare-boards local with
Wadworths 6X and guest beers; open all day
(the Didler)

White Bear [Monday Mkt St]: Pleasant 16th-c
pub with dark beams, panelling, antiques,
relaxing atmosphere, foreign banknotes on
ceiling, well kept Wadworths IPA and 6X,
limited choice of good value food inc good
lunchtime pies, welcoming prompt service,
restaurant; good big bedrooms *(Alan and Paula
McCully, David E Daniel)*

Donhead St Andrew [ST9124]

Forester [off A30 E of Shaftesbury, just E of

Ludwell; Lower St]: Small traditional thatched pub with plenty of character, very friendly new owners, good food, well kept beers inc Ringwood Best, Greene King and Smiles, inglenook fireplace; garden with nice views, lovely village *(K Bouch)*

East Knoyle [ST8830]

Bell & Crown [A350]: Local with very cheap good plain food in large separate dining area, well kept beer *(K H Frostick)*

☆ *Seymour Arms* [just off A350 S of Warminster]: Pretty 17th-c pub, quiet and comfortable, with immaculately polished tables, good food from huge granary baguettes to properly presented freshly made hot dishes, plenty of fresh veg and real chips, eating area on left, china display, quotations on beams, well kept Wadworths ales, friendly Welsh landlady, two well behaved dogs, efficient service; tables in garden with play area; bedrooms good value *(M A and C R Starling, John and Joan Nash, Colin Fisher, Mrs W Dillon)*

Easterton [SU0155]

Royal Oak [B3098]: Attractive thatched Wadworths pub, comfortably renovated and hospitable, spotlessly clean with interesting nooks in low-beamed rambling bars and two dining areas, friendly landlord, well kept ales, maybe potent home-made country wine, log fires; tables in small front garden *(Gordon)*

Enford [SU1351]

Swan [off A345]: Village dining pub with enjoyable food from moules marinières to game pie, sole and Thai dishes, well kept local beers *(Howard and Margaret Buchanan)*

Erlestoke [ST9654]

George & Dragon: Welcoming atmosphere, log fire, good food; upstairs dining room *(Lyn and Geoff Hallchurch)*

Farleigh Wick [ST8064]

☆ *Fox & Hounds* [A363 Bath—Bradford]: Good fresh food served quickly by friendly helpful staff in welcoming low-beamed rambling bar (the extension has now blended in well), highly polished old oak tables and chairs, gently rural decorations; attractive garden; can get packed w/e *(Andrew and Eileen Abbess, MRSM, Meg and Colin Hamilton, Lyn and Geoff Hallchurch)*

Fonthill Bishop [ST9333]

Kings Arms: Welcoming open-plan bar with interesting décor and bric-a-brac, quiet side room, interesting reasonably priced food inc huge club sandwich and good warm bacon salad, entertaining staff; children welcome *(Lyn and Geoff Hallchurch)*

Fovant [SU0128]

Pembroke Arms [A30 W of Salisbury]: Two-roomed pub with three fires, interesting WWI museum in saloon bar, also pig bric-a-brac (landlady's an aficionado – there's a live one outside); good food with ironic emphasis on sausages, several vegetarian choices, well kept Flowers and Ringwood, friendly staff, room with revolving hexagonal pool table; neat and tidy side garden, close to WWI regimental badges cut into the hillside *(Neil Spink, Grahame McNulty, John Hayter)*

Froxfield [SU2968]

Pelican [A4]: Relaxed atmosphere, good welcome and service, some emphasis on tasty good value food; pleasant streamside garden behind with pond and ducks *(JEB, Michael Inskip)*

Gastard [ST8868]

Harp & Crown: Good friendly service, nice furnishings, decent food *(Lyn and Geoff Hallchurch)*

Great Cheverell [ST9754]

☆ *Bell* [off B3098 Westbury—Mkt Lavington]: Well run recently reorganised dining pub in same hands as Cross Guns nr Bradford on Avon (see main entries), very popular for wide choice of good food with lots of trimmings; comfortable chairs and settles, cosy little alcoves, well kept Courage Best and Marstons Pedigree, upstairs dining room, friendly attentive service, attractive village *(Colin and Joyce Laffan)*

Highworth [SU2092]

☆ *Saracens Head* [Market Pl]: Comfortable and relaxed rambling bar, good-humoured licensees, friendly service, several distinct interesting areas around great central chimney block, wide choice of good value straightforward bar food (limited Sun) inc OAP bargains, vegetarian and children's, well kept Arkells BB and BBB; piped music, public bar with TV; children in eating area, tables in sheltered courtyard, open all day weekdays; comfortable bedrooms *(Trevor Owen, LYM)*

Hindon [ST9132]

☆ *Grosvenor Arms* [High St]: Newish management doing well in recently refurbished 18th-c coaching inn, some concentration on the good food inc unusual and exotic dishes, good light choice and midweek bargain suppers, log fire in tastefully spare flagstoned main bar, tapestried second room, softly furnished lounge, well kept Bass, good house wines, good service; decent bedrooms, good breakfast *(Miss P J Simpson, John Evans, A and G Evans, Mr and Mrs C Moncreiffe, W W Burke, Dr Michael Smith)*

Hodson [SU1780]

☆ *Calley Arms* [not far from M4 junction 15, via Chiseldon; off B4005 S of Swindon]: Well run, relaxed and welcoming big bar with raised no-smoking dining area, interesting choice of good well priced food (not Sun/Mon evenings) inc vegetarian, good range of well kept Wadworths ales with a guest, dozens of malt whiskies, farm ciders, country wines, darts and open fire one end; picnic-sets in garden with dovecote, children welcome, pleasant walk from Coate Water country park and on downs *(Richard Burton, Brenda Hawkins, Jeff Davies, Andy Larter, CMW, JJW, R Mattick)*

Honeystreet [SU1061]

Barge: Unspoilt pub by Kennet & Avon Canal, charming almost 18th-c atmosphere in bar, well kept ales, pleasant pictures, wide range of home-made food from sandwiches to fresh trout, good prices, log fires; garden, bedrooms – nice setting, good downland walks *(K R Harris, Jenny and Brian Seller)*

Hullavington [ST8982]

Star: Seems little changed since the 1960s, decent

food, friendly staff *(F C Johnston)*

Kington Langley [ST9277]

Hit or Miss [handy for M4 junction 17; Days Lane]: Welcoming pub with well kept Marstons Pedigree, food from good baguettes up, cricket-theme bar with no-smoking area, darts and pool in room off, busy restaurant with good log fire; attractive village *(Meg and Colin Hamilton, J E Hobley)*

Plough [handy for M4 junction 17]: Spacious and comfortable, welcoming landlord, good food, well kept Archers and Butcombe, big back conservatory *(Meg and Colin Hamilton)*

Kington St Michael [ST9077]

Jolly Huntsman [handy for M4 junction 17]: Roomy, with scrubbed tables, old-fashioned settees, pleasant rather dark décor, good range of well kept changing ales (friendly landlord interested in them), good value promptly served fresh-cooked food inc vegetarian, open fire; maybe sports on TV; two cheap bedrooms *(Lyn and Geoff Hallchurch, Dave and Deborah Irving)*

Lacock [ST9367]

Bell [back rd, bottom of Bowden Hill]: Wide choice of food from sandwiches to steaks (game or lobster if ordered), well priced Smiles ale, good wine list, lots of malt whiskies; garden and pets corner for children *(Richard Pierce)*

Langley Burrell [ST9375]

Brewery Arms: Recently refurbished local with imaginative choice of good food, good coffee *(Lyn and Geoff Hallchurch)*

Little Bedwyn [SU2966]

☆ *Harrow* [Village signposted off A4 W of Hungerford; OS Sheet 174 map ref 294657]: Reopened 1999, better thought of now as a restaurant with pub surroundings than as a pub – though the friendly new licensees do keep good real ale; the emphasis is now on very good food elegantly presented in the middle of big plates, excellent fresh fish, stunning puddings; good service *(Mrs D E Parkinson, Gill Rowlands, LYM, John H Smith)*

Lockeridge [SU1467]

Who'd A Thought It [signed off A4 Marlborough—Calne just W of Fyfield]: Welcoming village pub particularly popular with older people at lunchtime for good sensibly priced well presented food, well kept Wadworths, good wine choice, log fire, family room; pleasant back garden with play area, delightful scenery, lovely walks *(June and Tony Baldwin, G J Gibbs, Pat Crabb, Nigel Norman, Jenny and Brian Seller, Mrs Laura Gustine)*

Longbridge Deverill [ST8740]

George [A350/B3095]: Newly extended village pub, spacious and relaxed even when busy, good reasonably priced food, well kept Gales, good service, restaurant *(Dave Braisted, Richard Tabor)*

Malmesbury [ST9287]

Kings Arms [High St]: Popular well worn in 16th-c town pub with two bars, low prices, quick friendly service, good value specials and lots of puddings, Flowers IPA and a guest such as Mighty Oak, pleasant restaurant; good courtyard garden, jazz last Sat of month;

comfortable bedrooms *(Eric and Margarette Sibbit, Mrs Heather March, John Fahy, Peter and Audrey Dowsett)*

☆ *Smoking Dog* [High St]: Cosy beamed and stripped stone local, big stripped pine tables on bare boards, friendly efficient service, a beer brewed for the pub and changing well kept ales from casks behind bar, farm ciders, decent wines, good coffee, good value food, log fires, daily papers, board games, reference books, soft piped music; back bistro, garden; children welcome, open all day, bedrooms *(Mrs Margaret Ross, Tom Rees, Dave and Deborah Irving)*

☆ *Suffolk Arms* [Tetbury Hill, S of junction with B4014]: Cheerful efficient service in knocked-through bar and big no-smoking panelled dining room, well kept Wadworths IPA and 6X and a changing guest beer, log fire, usual food well prepared; children welcome *(LYM, Mike and Grete Turner, D Irving, E McCall, R Huggins, T McLean)*

Manton [SU1668]

Oddfellows Arms [High St]: Good village local, for both drinkers and diners alike; roomy bar with lots of nooks and crannies, imaginative menu; well kept Wadworths inc a seasonal beer, country wines; big garden *(Jenny and Brian Seller)*

Marlborough [SU1869]

☆ *Bear* [High St]: Rambling well worn in Victorian inn with jovial ex-Navy landlord, impressive central log fire, main bar and lounges on separate levels, well kept Arkells ales, generous interesting food inc huge baguettes and good fish (intriguing biographical menu) in old-fashioned side bar, small front lunchtime tapas bar (evening restaurant), medieval-style banqueting hall for special occasions, skittle alley, tables in small back courtyard *(Lyn and Geoff Hallchurch, Bruce Pennell, HNJ, PEJ, Graham Fogelman)*

Marshfield [ST7773]

☆ *Catherine Wheel* [High St; signed off A420 Bristol—Chippenham]: Interesting inside, with plates and prints on stripped stone walls, medley of settles, chairs and stripped tables, open fire in impressive fireplace, cottagey back family bar, charming no-smoking Georgian dining room, flower-decked back yard; cheerful service, wide choice of good if not cheap food inc imaginative dishes, generous fresh veg and Thurs fresh fish (not Sun), well kept Theakstons Old Peculier and Wadworths IPA and 6X, farm cider, decent wines; golden labrador called Elmer, darts, dominoes; provision for children, unspoilt village *(LYM, Susan and John Douglas, Keith and Norma Bloomfield, Andrew Shore)*

Marston Meysey [SU1297]

Masons Arms: Pleasant pub with comfortable atmosphere and well kept beers *(Dave Irving, Ewan McCall, Roger Huggins, Tom McLean)*

Netheravon [SU1449]

Dog & Gun: Comfortable and friendly, large pleasant beamed lounge, plenty of tables, good reasonably priced menu, good choice of well kept ales; unobtrusive piped music *(G W A Pearce)*

Newton Tony [SU2140]

☆ *Malet Arms* [off A338 Swindon—Salisbury]:
Very popular nicely placed local opp footbridge
over chalk stream, good food in cosy bar and
separate side restaurant, well kept Badger, Bass,
Butcombe and Hampshire King Alfred, pleasant
mix of customers, efficient cheerful staff;
attractive village *(Kim and Nigel Spence)*

Nunton [SU1526]

☆ *Radnor Arms* [off A338 S of Salisbury]: Good
interesting food esp fish and local game in lovely
ivy-clad village pub with friendly helpful staff,
well kept Badger inc Tanglefoot; three pleasantly
decorated and furnished linked rooms inc
cheerfully busy yet relaxing bar and staider
restaurant; log fires, very friendly labrador; can
get rather crowded; attractive garden popular
with children *(Dr D Twyman, W W Burke)*

Pewsey [SU1560]

French Horn [A345 towards Marlborough;
Pewsey Wharf]: Old pub on Kennet & Avon
Canal, two bars separated by fireplace open on
both sides, one dominated by single big chatty
round table, good reasonably priced food inc
regional dishes, well kept Wadworths 6X, log
fire, good welcoming service; interesting village
(Jenny and Brian Seller)

Potterne [ST9958]

☆ *George & Dragon* [High St (A360)]: Steep steps
up to homely take-us-as-you-find-us traditional
beamed bar, pool and darts in games room,
usual food, well kept Wadworths 6X, friendly
licensees and cat; small collection of antique farm
tools, unique indoor .22 shooting range (can be
booked by groups), skittle alley, pleasant garden
and suntrap yard; well behaved children in
eating area, cl Mon lunchtime; bedrooms *(Mrs
Laura Gustine, LYM, Peter and Audrey
Dowsett, W W Burke, Lyn and Geoff
Hallchurch)*

Ramsbury [SU2771]

Crown & Anchor [Crowood Lane/Whittonditch
Rd]: Friendly and relaxed beamed village pub,
good value food, well kept Bass, Tetleys and
usually a guest beer, open fires, pool in public
bar; no piped music, children welcome, garden
with terrace *(Mr and Mrs Peter Smith)*

Salisbury [SU1429]

Market [Market Pl]: Comfortable and handy for
shops, with straightforward bar food, well kept
Wadworths 6X, pictures *(Colin and Ann Hunt)*
Old Ale House: Marvellous choice of well kept
changing ales *(C Smith, Veronica Brown)*

☆ *Old Mill* [Tow Path, W Harnham]: 17th-c
former mill building in lovely setting, with
floodlit garden by duck-filled millpond, a stroll
across meadows from cathedral with classic view
of it; simple but comfortable beamed bars (can
get rather crowded), over 500 china and other
ducks, well kept Boddingtons, Flowers Original,
Hop Back GFB and Summer Lightning and a
guest beer, decent malt whiskies and wines,
friendly helpful staff, bar food inc good
sandwiches choice, imaginative hot dishes and
good seafood, restaurant; children welcome,
comfortable bedrooms, good breakfast *(C Smith,
LYM, Dr D Twyman, Adrian Littleton, Ian and
Jacqui Ross, Mr and Mrs P Spencer)*

Town House [Bridge St]: Opulently restored
early 19th-c building, well divided tables by huge
windows, taller stools and tables at back,
balcony seating, imposing light fitting,
reasonably priced food, real ales such as Flowers
Original and Wadworths 6X (more choice in
Spire bar next door – this is a Whitbreads
Hogshead hotel), wheelchair access; bedrooms
comfortable and fairly priced *(G Coates)*

Sandy Lane [ST9668]

George [A342 Devizes—Chippenham]: Neat
stonebuilt pub with wide choice of decent food
from doorstep sandwiches to unusual main
dishes, well kept Wadworths, decent wines,
pleasant efficient service, interesting décor, bons
mots chalked on beams, attractive back bar-
restaurant; car park on dodgy bend; tables on
front terrace, more in back garden with play area
*(LYM, June and Tony Baldwin, Karen Hogarth,
John and Vivienne Rice)*

Seend [ST9460]

Bell [Bell Hill (A361)]: Four-room refurbished
pub with cosy lounge, attentive cheerful service,
well kept Wadworths IPA and 6X, good food
from sandwiches to steaks in bar and tasteful
upstairs restaurant (with good views), no music
*(Dr and Mrs A K Clarke, Lyn and Geoff
Hallchurch, Dennis Heatley)*

Three Magpies [Sells Green – A365 towards
Melksham]: Unspoilt partly 18th-c pub with well
kept Wadworths IPA and 6X, Stowford Press
cider, wide range of food from good value
ploughman's to exotic main dishes, good
vegetarian choice; big garden with play area
(Tess Powderham)

Semington [ST9259]

☆ *Lamb* [The Strand, Keevil; A361 Devizes—
Trowbridge]: Cheerfully pubby and busy series
of rooms with helpful service, good choice of
popular food inc some interesting dishes, well
kept Butcombe, Ringwood Best and Shepherd
Neame Spitfire, decent wines, good coffee,
woodburner and log fire, children in eating area,
tables out in colourful walled garden; helpful to
wheelchairs, cl Sun evening *(Pat and Robert
Watt, Peter Neate, Mr and Mrs Broadhurst, Lyn
and Geoff Hallchurch, Mike Brearley, LYM, Dr
and Mrs A K Clarke, A C Curry)*

Somerset Arms [A350 2 miles S of Melksham]:
Welcoming and cosy 16th-c coaching inn with
heavy-beamed long bar, real and flame-effect
fires, high-backed settles, plenty of tables, lots of
prints and brassware, good value food in bar and
restaurant inc imaginative dishes, helpful service,
real ales, good coffee; piped music; garden
behind, nr Kennet & Avon Canal *(Lyn and
Geoff Hallchurch, A S Lowe, Mrs C Wilkes)*

South Marston [SU1987]

Carpenters Arms [just off A420 E of Swindon]:
Spaciously extended in olde-worlde style, with
lots of seating areas, good value generous food,
well kept Arkells and Marstons, friendly
landlord and staff, blazing coal fire, old Swindon
photographs; quiet piped music, quiz night Mon;
play area and animals in big back garden *(Peter
and Audrey Dowsett)*

South Wraxall [ST8364]

Longs Arms [off B3109 N of Bradford on

Avon]: Busy cosily refurbished country local with welcoming landlord, wide-ranging good reasonably priced food inc good Sun lunch, well kept Bass and Wadworths, log fire, pretty garden *(Lyn and Geoff Hallchurch, A G Chesterton)*

Staverton [ST8560]

Old Bear [B3105 Trowbridge—Bradford on Avon]: Wide choice of good food inc fish, vegetarian and sizzler dishes in stone pub's long bar divided into four sections, Bass and Wadworths 6X, nice mix of seats inc some high-backed settles, stone fireplaces (biggest in end dining area, another with teddy bears on mantlepiece), lots of flower arrangements (fresh and faux), back restaurant (booking recommended Sun lunchtime); village dominated by huge Nestlé factory *(Meg and Colin Hamilton, Mrs V Rixon, Colin and Joyce Laffan, BB)*

Stockton [ST9738]

Carriers [just off A36 Salisbury—Warminster, nr A303]: Another new landlord, very experienced, doing good food at reasonable prices inc award-winning steak and kidney pie, interesting veg and fresh fish from Brixham and Poole, well worn in bar, pretty dining extension, coureously old-fashioned service, Ringwood, Stonehenge and Wadworths 6X, decent wine; pretty village pub in Wylye valley *(Pat and Robert Watt, Michael Doswell)*

Stoford [SU0835]

Swan [A36 Salisbury—Warminster]: Clean and pleasant country pub over rd from river, interesting food inc delicious puddings, excellent friendly service, good choice of well kept ales *(Mr and Mrs N D Buckland)*

Stourton [ST7734]

☆ *Spread Eagle* [Stourhead signpost off B3092 N of junction with A303 just W of Mere]: NT pub in lovely setting at head of Stourhead lake (though views from pub itself not special), front bar with open fire, settles and country décor, cool and spacious civilised back dining rooms popular with older people; standard food, Ash Vine, Bass and Wadworths 6X, friendly waitress service, tables in back courtyard; bedrooms *(Meg and Colin Hamilton, LYM, John Roots)*

Swallowcliffe [ST9627]

Royal Oak [Common Lane]: Attractively and comfortably converted 18th-c thatched tannery, relaxed atmosphere, wide choice of good food inc fresh fish, popular Weds steak and kidney pudding day, pleasant staff, log fires, quiz night; tables under cocktail parasols in big garden, good walks *(Dr and Mrs P Watson, Patrick James)*

Swindon [SU1086]

Footplate & Firkin [Bridge St]: Usual Firkin style and well kept beers, lots of railway memorabilia, upstairs bar too; generous food, friendly efficient staff, open all day *(Richard Lewis)*

Friary [Elstree Way, Abbey Meads]: Comfortable new family pub with lots for children inc special eating areas, outdoor and indoor adventure play areas; real ales inc Morlands Old Speckled Hen and Tetleys, good range of quickly served cheap food; shame about

the piped music *(Peter and Audrey Dowsett)*

Glue Pot [Emlyn Sq]: Bare-boards tap for Archers Brewery, with their Village, Best, Golden and Headbanger kept well, and a guest such as Brains; high-backed settles, lunchtime snacks, friendly locals, pub games, tables on terrace – in Brunel's Railway Village; open all day (cl Sun afternoon) *(Richard Lewis)*

Litten Tree [Bridge St]: Large comfortable bar with well divided areas, chilled Courage and Wadworths ales, California house wines, usual traditional and modern bar food from filled baguettes up, friendly staff; open all day *(Richard Lewis)*

Manor Farm [Haydon Wick]: Very civilised, comfortable, light and airy, with wide choice of good value food, two or three real ales, attentive service, no piped music *(Peter and Audrey Dowsett)*

Savoy [Regent St]: Wide choice of real ales and of affordable food in excellently converted cinema, a Wetherspoons; split-level seating areas, books and film memorabilia, comfortable atmosphere, decent wine, quick friendly service; popular with all ages, no music, no-smoking areas *(Peter and Audrey Dowsett)*

Tilshead [SU0348]

Rose & Crown [A360 Salisbury—Devizes]: Well cared for, with welcoming attentive family service, well kept beer, good value simple wholesome food inc some unusual dishes *(Lyn and Geoff Hallchurch)*

Upper Chute [SU2954]

☆ *Cross Keys*: Very welcoming, good value varied food using good fresh ingredients, from beautifully presented ploughman's up (proper butter and mustard pots), pleasant old-fashioned bar (very quiet at lunchtime), well kept beers, friendly service; rustic views from proper tables on charming shady south-facing terrace, interesting area for walking *(Mrs Margaret Ross)*

Upper Woodford [SU1237]

Bridge: Roomy softly lit pub in delightful setting, friendly staff, well presented food inc good vegetarian choice, ploughman's with lots of bread (handy for ducks in riverside garden across road), well kept beers *(Lyn and Geoff Hallchurch)*

Upton Scudamore [ST8647]

Angel: Recently refurbished old whitewashed village pub liked by its regulars for food in bar and restaurant, cheerful attentive staff, decent wine; tables outside, comfortable well equipped bedrooms *(Pat and Robert Watt)*

Wanborough [SU2083]

Black Horse [2 miles from M4 junction 15; Callas Hill (former B4507 towards Bishopstone)]: Delightfully unspoilt country local with lovely downland views, beams and tiled floor, open fires in both bars, small aquarium, longcase clock, lunchtime food inc good value Sun lunch, well kept competitively priced Arkells Bitter, 3B and seasonal ales, good generous coffee, no piped music, darts; picnic-sets in informal elevated garden with play area *(Andy Larter, CMW, JJW)*

Shepherds Rest [Foxhill, out towards Baydon; from A419 through Wanborough turn right]:

Remote and unassuming Ridgeway pub popular with local racing people (decorations to match), friendly licensees, long lounge and dining extension, half a dozen well kept ales such as Badger and Flowers IPA, reasonably priced food, log fire, lots of pictures, pool room, restaurant; piped music; picnic-sets and play area outside; children and walkers welcome, very busy in summer, camping behind with shower etc *(Jenny and Brian Seller, JJW, CMW, Giles Francis)*

West Lavington [SU0053]

Bridge [Church St]: Long dim-lit and relaxing pink family dining bar, big log fire, pleasant country pictures and the like, well kept Gibbs Mew ales, decent wines, welcoming service, wide choice of good value home-cooked food in bar and restaurant inc interesting fish and vegetarian; piped music; pretty flower-filled garden *(James Morrell, Lyn and Geoff Hallchurch)*

Stage Post [High St (A360)]: Two-room comfortably refurbished pub with big glazed front dining area, short but imaginative food choice, well kept Ushers beers, good wine choice inc bin ends, friendly young staff; pool room with TV *(Dr and Mrs A Newton, Colin Laffan, Dr and Mrs A K Clarke, Trevor Owen)*

West Overton [SU1368]

Bell [A4 Marlboro—Calne]: Pleasant and homely, with cosy well used furnishings, Wadworths and guest beers such as Shepherd Neame Canterbury Jack, very reasonably priced good straightforward food, prompt cheerful service; popular with older people *(June and Tony Baldwin)*

Whaddon [SU5711]

Three Crowns [off A36 SE of Salisbury]: Pleasant friendly bar, well kept Ruddles, appealing menu; lovely downland walks with fine views *(Phyl and Jack Street)*

Wilcot [SU1360]

☆ *Golden Swan* [signed off A345 N of Pewsey, and in Pewsey itself]: Very pretty old steeply thatched pub nr Kennet & Avon Canal, unpretentiously welcoming and well worn in, lots of china hanging from beams of two small rooms, well kept Wadworths IPA and 6X and in winter Old Timer, friendly licensees, retriever and playful cats, limited good value home-made bar food (not Sun evening or Mon), dining room, games room with bar billiards; rustic tables on pretty front lawn, field with camping, occasional folk and barbecue weekends, children welcome; good value simple bedrooms, not smart but big and airy *(LYM, Mark Brock, Roger and Jenny Huggins)*

Wilton [SU2661]

Swan [the village S of Gt Bedwyn]: Warm and friendly simple pub with bright unusual décor, wide variety of enjoyable cheap food all day from doorstep sandwiches to Thai and Indian dishes – good for family lunches; well kept changing ales such as Fullers London Pride, Thwaites and Wadworths 6X, pool; children welcome, garden with small play area, picturesque village with windmill, handy for Crofton Beam Engines *(Nick Holmes, S Tait, S Lonie, Paul Fleckney, Brian and Anna Marsden)*

Wingfield [ST8256]

☆ *Poplars*: Attractive and friendly country local with decent food inc fine steak sandwich and good value hot dishes, well kept Wadworths, quick pleasant service, enjoyable atmosphere, no juke box or machines, no children; own cricket pitch – landlord a keen cricketer *(Susan and Nigel Wilson, LYM, Steven Bertram, Lyn and Geoff Hallchurch)*

Winterbourne Bassett [SU0975]

☆ *White Horse* [off A4361 S of Swindon]: Attractively restored 1920s pub in lovely countryside, pleasant dining conservatory, well kept Wadworths and occasional guest beers, limited choice of decent freshly made food (so may be a wait if busy) inc several fish dishes, cheerful friendly service, huge goldfish in tank on bar; seats outside *(Colin and Joyce Laffan, June and Tony Baldwin, CMW, JJW, Mr and Mrs Peter Smith)*

Woodfalls [SU1920]

Woodfalls [The Ridge]: L-shaped bar, small dining room, conservatory, imaginative food from lobster bisque to mixed grill, well kept beers such as Courage Best and Directors, Fullers Summer Ale, Gales HSB and Youngers Tavern, friendly staff; bedrooms, nr New Forest *(W W Burke)*

Wootton Bassett [SU1082]

Sally Pusseys [A420 just off M4 junction 16]: Named for former landlady; good choice of generous tasty unpretentious food at sensible prices from filled rolls to super puddings, helpful friendly staff, busy main bar, lower restaurant; mainly dining, but well kept Arkells, good coffee; maybe piped 10cc, James Taylor etc *(Lyn and Geoff Hallchurch, Mrs B Sugarman)*

Woodshaw [Garraways, Woodshaw; handy for M4 junction 16]: Good value food cooked by landlord, Arkells ales, good wines *(D and M T Ayres-Regan)*

Wootton Rivers [SU1963]

☆ *Royal Oak* [signed off A345, A346 and B3087 S of Marlborough]: Extended 16th-c thatched pub in attractive village, wide choice of popular food in pleasantly furnished L-shaped dining lounge, games in area off timbered bar, well kept Boddingtons and Wadworths 6X tapped from the cask and a guest ale on handpump, farm cider, interesting whiskies, particularly good wines, restaurant, fresh flowers; children welcome, tables under cocktail parasols in pretty back courtyard, bedrooms in adjoining house *(S Tait, S Lonie, Dr Paul Khan, Paul and Ursula Randall, Steve and Carolyn Harvey, A C Curry, Mrs Laura Gustine, Jenny and Brian Seller, Trevor Owen, Pat Crabb, Gordon)*

Wylye [SU0037]

Bell [just off A303/A36 junction]: Nicely set in peaceful village, dark beams, timbering, stripped masonry, three log fires, sturdy rustic furnishings, Badger and Smiles beers, wide choice of food inc some good puddings, no-smoking area, side eating area; may be piped music; children welcome, fine downland walks; bedrooms *(D and A Hayden, LYM)*

Worcestershire

This is the first time we have treated Worcestershire as a separate chapter in the Guide, instead of coupling it with Herefordshire. Doing this has shown how cheap pub drinks prices tend to be here. During our price survey the proudly traditional King & Castle in Kidderminster was even selling beer for under £1 a pint. Ruling that out as a special exception, beer prices here are still on average nearly 20p a pint lower than the national norm, with the local-ingredients beer brewed by the Talbot at Knightwick, called Teme Valley, particularly cheap. Two other local brews which we found as a pub's cheapest offering were Hobsons and Wyre Piddle. Worcestershire pubs doing particularly well these days include the good value Farmers Arms at Birtsmorton, the comfortable Fox & Hounds at Bredon (good food, impressive service), the Peacock at Forhill (an attractive and well run rather foody pub – a newcomer to the Guide), the Walter de Cantelupe at Kempsey (very promising food, which gains it a Food Award this year), the Talbot at Knightwick (good food here too, in attractive surroundings), the Anchor at Welland (another new entry, a pretty pub, good all round) and the Cardinals Hat in Worcester (an interesting and welcoming ancient town pub – yet another new entry). The Walter de Cantelupe at Kempsey is our choice as Worcestershire Dining Pub of the Year. Many of the pubs we've mentioned are most attractive buildings – rather a speciality of this county's pubs. The Fleece at Bretforton (owned by the National Trust) deserves a special mention in this respect. Another pub to pick out is the unusual Monkey House at Defford: this basic cider house is a really unexpected throwback. Some pubs to highlight in the Lucky Dip section at the end of the chapter are the Little Pack Horse in Bewdley, Crown & Trumpet in Broadway, Boot at Flyford Flavell, Old Bull at Inkberrow, Crown at Kemerton, Sun & Slipper at Mamble, Brandy Cask in Pershore, Peacock near Tenbury Wells, Coventry Arms at Upton Snodsbury, and, for food, the Bear & Ragged Staff at Bransford, Chequers at Fladbury and Fox & Hounds at Lulsley.

BIRTSMORTON SO7935 Map 4

Farmers Arms 🍺 £

Birts Street, off B4208 W of Birtsmorton

Visitors and locals are made to feel equally at home at this neatly kept black and white timbered local run by a friendly mother and daughter team. On the right a big room rambles away under low dark beams, with some standing timbers, and flowery-panelled cushioned settles as well as spindleback chairs; on the left an even lower-beamed room seems even snugger, and in both the white walls have black timbering. Good value straightforward home-made bar food includes sandwiches (from £1.45), soup (£1.70), ploughman's (from £2.60), macaroni cheese (£3.10), chicken and vegetable curry (£4.25), fish and chips (£4.30), lasagne (£4.70), steak and kidney pie (£5.25), gammon steak (£6.50) and mixed grill (£8); puddings such as apple pie or steamed treacle pudding (from £1.90); they do a good Sunday lunch in winter (£5.50). Well kept Hook Norton Best and Old Hooky with weekly guest ales from breweries such as Cannon Royall, Cottage, Ledbury or Queens Head on handpump; darts in a good tiled area, shove-ha'penny, cribbage, and dominoes. There are seats out on the grass. If custom demands, the pub may stay open until 4pm on Saturday afternoons. There are plenty of good walks nearby. *(Recommended by Simon Watkins, John Teign, Dave Braisted, Derek and Sylvia Stephenson, Ted George, Tim and Linda Collins)*

Free house ~ Licensees Jill and Julie Moor ~ Real ale ~ Bar food (11-2, 6-10; 12-2, 7-9.30 Sun) ~ (01684) 833308 ~ Children in eating area of bar ~ Open 11-2.30(3 Sat), 6-11; 12-4, 7-10.30 Sun

BREDON SO9236 Map 4
Fox & Hounds

4½ miles from M5 junction 9; A438 to Northway, left at B4079, then in Bredon follow To church and river signpost on right

This warm and welcoming thatched pub, attractively set next to a church down a lane leading to a river, is at its prettiest in summer when adorned with colourful hanging baskets. Over the years it has built up a reputation for good food, and a seasonally changing menu served by friendly efficient staff might include home-made soup (£2.95), ploughman's (from £4.50), black pudding with crispy bacon and dijon mustard sauce (£4.50), melon with prawns (£5.25), lasagne (£6.95), vegetable stir fry (£7.95), coq au vin (£8.95), 8oz sirloin steak (£9.95), lamb noisettes with redcurrant sauce (£10.50), beef and bacon stroganoff (£11.95) with daily specials such as cajun-style chicken with spicy tomato sauce (£7.75) and plaice filled with prawns, lemon and dill (£10.95); Sunday roast (£6.95); puddings (from £2.50). There's a friendly atmosphere in the comfortable and well modernised carpeted bar with dressed stone pillars and stripped timbers, a central wood burning stove, upholstered settles, wheelback, tub, and kitchen chairs around attractive mahogany and cast-iron-framed tables, dried grasses and flowers, a toy fox dressed in hunting scarlet, and elegant wall lamps. A smaller side bar has an open fire at each end. Well kept Banks's Bitter, Marstons Pedigree and Morlands Old Speckled Hen on handpump, several malt whiskies and wines by the glass; dominoes, shove-ha'penny, cribbage and piped music. No smoking in the restaurant and part of the bar; some of the picnic-sets are under Perspex. *(Recommended by Marvadene B Eves, F J Robinson, W W Burke, David and Nina Pugsley, Ian Phillips, Mrs K Neville-Rolfe)*

Whitbreads ~ Lease: Mike Hardwick ~ Real ale ~ Bar food ~ Restaurant ~ (01684) 772377 ~ Children welcome ~ Open 11.30-3, 6.30-11; 12-10.30 Sun; 12-3.30, 6.30-10.30 Sun in winter

BRETFORTON SP0943 Map 4
Fleece ★★ £

B4035 E of Evesham: turn S off this road into village; pub is in centre square by church; there's a sizeable car park at one side of the church

The main reason for coming to this lovely medieval building, bequeathed in 1977 to the National Trust by the great granddaughter of the original landlord, is to sit and gaze in wonder at the original antique furnishings that fill the fine country rooms. Before it became a pub in 1848 it was a farm owned by one family for nearly 500 years, and many of the furnishings are heirlooms such as the great oak dresser that holds a priceless 48-piece set of Stuart pewter. Elsewhere there's a fine grandfather clock, ancient kitchen chairs, curved high-backed settles, a rocking chair, and a rack of heavy pointed iron shafts, probably for spit roasting, in one of the huge inglenook fireplaces. There are massive beams and exposed timbers, worn and crazed flagstones (scored with marks to keep out demons), and plenty of oddities such as a great cheese-press and set of cheese moulds, and a rare dough-proving table; a leaflet details the more bizarre items, and there are three warming winter fires. The room with the pewter is no smoking. Simple generously served bar food (which may be a bit slow on busy days owing to limited kitchen facilities) is ordered through a hatch and includes sandwiches (from £1.90), ploughman's (from £3.75), chilli (£4.10), broccoli and cheese quiche (£4.25), lasagne (£4.50), steak and kidney or chicken and leek pie (£4.75), locally cured gammon (£5.50), and mixed grill (£6.95); puddings such as apple pie and cream or lemon meringue pie (from £2). Cannon Royall Buckshot, M & B Brew XI, Highgate Fox's Nob, Hook Norton Bitter, Uley Old Spot and Wyre Piddle on handpump, over a dozen country wines and farm cider; friendly staff. Darts, cribbage, dominoes, shove-ha'penny. In summer, when it gets very busy, they make the most of the extensive orchard, with seats on the goat-cropped grass that spreads around the beautifully restored thatched and timbered barn, among the fruit trees, and at the front by the stone pump-trough. There's also an adventure playground, an aviary, and an enclosure with geese and goats; there are more picnic-sets in the front courtyard. There may be Morris dancing and they hold the village fete and annual asparagus auctions at the end of May, an annual beer festival in July and the village Silver Band fete on August bank holiday Monday. *(Recommended by June and Mike Coleman, Jason Reynolds, JP, PP, Andy and Jill Kassube, K H Frostick, Gwen and Peter Andrews, David Crafts, Ted George, Greg Kilminster, Kerry Law, Simon Smith, Susan and John Douglas, Mrs G Connell, Peter and Giff Bennett, Colin and Ann Hunt, the Didler, Peter and Audrey Dowsett, Marvadene B Eves, LM, Joan and Michel Hooper-Immins, KN-R)*

Free house ~ Licensee Graham Brown ~ Real ale ~ Bar food (12-2 (11.45-2.30 Sat/Sun), 6.30-9) ~ (01386) 831173 ~ Children welcome ~ Open 11-3, 6-11; 11-11 Sat; 12-10.30 Sun

DEFFORD SO9143 Map 4
Monkey House

A4104 towards Upton – immediately after passing Oak public house on right, there's a small group of cottages, of which this is the last

The name of this pretty black and white thatched cottage – one of the few remaining absolutely traditional cider-houses – is taken from the story of a drunken customer who, some years ago, fell into bramble bushes and swore that he was attacked by monkeys. It has been run by a member of the landlord's wife's family for the last 140 years, and readers love its unapologetic simplicity: from the outside the only hint that it is actually a pub is a notice by the door saying 'Licensed to sell cider and tobacco'. Very cheap Bulmer's Medium or Special Dry cider is tapped from barrels and poured by jug into pottery mugs (some locals have their own) and served from a hatch beside the door. As a concession to modern tastes, beer is sold in cans. They don't do food (except crisps and nuts), but allow you to bring your own. In good weather, you can stand outside in the garden with Anna the bull terrier and Tapper the jack russell, and hens and cockerels that wander in from an adjacent collection of caravans and sheds; there's also a pony called Mandy. Alternatively you can retreat to a small and spartan side outbuilding with a couple of plain tables, a settle and an open fire; darts and dominoes. *(Recommended by Derek and Sylvia Stephenson, Pete Baker, the Didler, Joe Rafferty, JP, PP, Chris Raisin, Ivan and Sarah Osborne)*

Free house ~ Licensee Graham Collins ~ (01386) 750234 ~ Children welcome in one room ~ Open 11-2.30, 6-10.30; 12-2, 7-10.30 Sun; closed Mon evening, all day Tues, and possibly Weds and Thurs lunchtimes outside summer

FORHILL SP0575 Map 4
Peacock

2 miles from M42 Junction 2; A441 towards Birmingham; after roundabout 1st right (sharp) into Ash Lane just before garage by highish canal bridge, left into Stonehouse Lane, left at T junction, right at next T junction (into Lea End Lane); pub at junction Lea End Lane and Icknield St. Can also be reached from Junction 3

There's a particularly relaxed atmosphere in the spacious knocked-through beamed rooms of this hard-to-find pub with its especially cheery bar staff. There's an attractive mix of country chairs, pews and tables on flagstone and quarry-tiled floors, standing timbers, cream or stripped brick walls simply decorated with a couple of prints, fresh blue curtains in big leaded windows and a couple of fires including a woodburning stove in a big inglenook. The dining area, with a big serving hatch showing the working kitchen, has some attractive decorations including a striking peacock print and a big stone greyhound by its fireplace. Very generous helpings of good value tasty food might include soup (£2.50), sandwiches (from £3.25), filled french sticks (from £3.95), seafood terrine (£4.95), steak and kidney pudding (£5.25), chilli or feta and pepper salad (£5.95) fish casserole or beef in red wine and mushrooms (£6.95), steamed plaice with tomato coulis or braised minted half shoulder of lamb with redcurrant and rosemary jus (£9.95), and puddings like banoffee pie and bread and butter pudding (£3.25). Well kept Banks's Bitter and Mild, Greene King Abbot, Hobsons, Marstons Pedigree and Woods Special on handpump. There are picnic-sets on a back terrace, and more on front grass under a striking Scots pine and other trees; fruit machine, bar billiards. *(Recommended by Dave Braisted, John A Barker, Jack Barnwell, Michael and Hazel Lyons, Richard Houghton)*

Scottish Courage ~ Manager Stephan Wakeman ~ Real ale ~ Bar food (12-6 only) ~ Restaurant (evening) ~ (01564) 823232 ~ Children in eating area of bar and restaurant ~ Jazz last Tues of month ~ Open 12-11(10.30 Sun)

KEMPSEY SO8548 Map 4

Walter de Cantelupe 🍽 ♀

Main Road; 3¾ miles from M5 junction 7: A44 towards Worcester, left on to A4440, then left on to A38 at roundabout

Warwickshire Dining Pub of the Year

Readers continue to praise the good food at this roadside pub run by an assiduous and friendly young landlord. The imaginative well thought-out bar food menu incorporates as much local produce as possible: as well as tasty home-made soup with locally baked bread (£2.35) and sandwiches (from £3), you might find smooth chicken liver pâté spiked with brandy and served with redcurrant jelly and hot toast (£3.85), ploughman's including local cheese, locally baked bread and home-made chutneys (£4.20), smoked salmon cornets filled with prawns (£4.75), steak and Guinness pie (£5.80), home-made chicken curry (£6.25), jalapeno peppers, capsicum and root vegetable stir fry with fresh coriander or roasted half shoulder of lamb marinated in mint and garlic (£7.50), 6oz beef fillet tartare (£7.80), baked sea bass on sliced tomatoes and mozzarella (£8.20) and tempting puddings such as mango and lime cheesecake, hot filled pancakes or chocolate and almond cake (£3); good value Sunday lunch (£7.20 for 2 courses, £9.70 for 3); no-smoking dining area; the friendly service can get rather slow at times. Boldly decorated in red and gold, the interior comprises a friendly and relaxed bar area with an informal mix of furniture, a couple of steps up to a carpeted area, an old wind-up HMV gramophone and a good big fireplace, and a dining area pleasantly furnished with a mix of plush or yellow leather dining chairs, an old settle, a sonorous clock and candles and flowers on the tables. Well kept ales on handpump include Black Pear from the nearby Malvern Hills brewery, Marstons Bitter, Timothy Taylor and frequently changing guest beers such as Cannon Royall Arrowhead on handpump, good choice of wines by the glass (they import direct from Italy and have regularly changing bin ends as well as English wines from a local vineyard); no music or games machines; cribbage and table skittles. You can sit out in the pretty walled garden at the back; the friendly labrador is called Monti. *(Recommended by G Braithwaite, Michael Coates, Keith and Margaret Kettell, John and Vivienne Rice, June and Mike Coleman, Mike and Mary Carter, Mike Green, Dave Braisted, M Joyner, Alan and Paula McCully, Denys Gueroult)*

Free house ~ Licensee Martin Lloyd Morris ~ Real ale ~ Bar food (12-2, 7-9(till 10 Fri and Sat); not Mon or winter Sun evenings) ~ Restaurant ~ (01905) 820572 ~ Children welcome till 8.15pm in eating area ~ Open 11.30-2.30, 6-11; 12-3, 7-10.30 Sun; closed Mon except bank holidays

Post Office address codings confusingly give the impression that some pubs are in Worcestershire, when they're really in the West Midlands or Gloucestershire (which is where we list them).

KIDDERMINSTER SO8376 Map 4
King & Castle £
Railway Station, Comberton Hill

Set on the terminus of Britain's most lively private steam railway, and perfectly conjuring up the feel of a better-class Edwardian establishment that has relaxed a little to embrace the more informal ways of the late 20th c, this intriguing re-creation of a classic station refreshment room offers a cheery welcome to its many customers. The good humoured landlady and her friendly staff cope well with the bustle of bank holidays and railway gala days (when it can be very difficult to find a seat). Furnishings are solid and in character (even to the occasional obvious need for a touch of reupholstery), and there is the railway memorabilia that you would expect. The atmosphere is lively and sometimes noisily good-humoured (and again in character can sometimes be rather smoky). With steam trains right outside, some railway-buff readers are quite content to start and end their journeys right here; others have used a Rover ticket to shuttle happily between here and the Railwaymans Arms in Bridgnorth (see Shropshire chapter). Either way you can take your pint outside on to the platform and watch the trains steam by. Very well kept Bathams, Tetleys and two guests such as Berrow, Cottage or Wyre Piddle on handpump, Addlestones farm cider. A wide choice of simple good value bar food includes filled rolls (£1.50), filled baked potatoes (from £2.30), ploughman's, omelettes or vegetable curry (£4.50), scampi or breaded plaice (£4.75), cajun chicken (£4.95) and weekend specials such as lasagne (£4.50) and beef and beer pie (£4.95); children's meals (from £2.25). *(Recommended by Phil Putwain, John C Baker, Ian Phillips, John Teign, Pat and Tony Martin)*

Free house ~ Licensee Rosemary Hyde ~ Real ale ~ Bar food (lunchtime Mon-Thurs, plus 6-8 Fri, Sat and Sun) ~ (01562) 747505 ~ Children in eating area of bar and on station platform till 9pm ~ Open 11-3, 5-11; 11-11 Sat; 12-10.30 Sun

KNIGHTWICK SO7355 Map 4
Talbot ♀ 🍽
Knightsford Bridge; B4197 just off A44 Worcester—Bromyard

The good food and ales at this 14th-c coaching inn have a distinctly domestic flavour: the well kept This, That, Wot and T'other ales (they also have Hobsons Bitter) on handpump are brewed locally from hops grown on the licensees' own small farm, and many of the ingredients for the almost completely home-made food are also grown there or in the pub's organic garden. Besides lunchtime sandwiches (from £1.50) and ploughman's (£4.25), meals (often of award standard) are priced according to the number of courses you have (at lunchtime 1 course £8.95, 2 courses £11.95, 3 courses £14.95, more in the evenings), although there is room for flexibility within this. Starters might include saffron fish soup, stir-fried squid, lentil cake or devilled kidneys, main courses such as lobster ravioli, roast wild boar loin with rosemary and chilli, beef ali aziz, whole lemon sole or timbale of garden vegetables, and puddings such as rice pudding with toasted almonds, sultanas and lemon peel with cinnamon shortcake, Danish chocolate terrine, spiced pear or sticky date and toffee pudding; three course Sunday lunch (£14.95); over 25 wines by the glass. The heavily beamed lounge bar with a warming log fire has humorous Cecil Aldin coaching prints and Jorrocks paintings by John Leech on its butter-coloured walls, a variety of interesting seats from small carved or leatherette armchairs to the winged settles by the tall bow windows, and a vast stove which squats in the big central stone hearth. The well furnished back public bar has pool on a raised side area, darts, fruit machine, video game and juke box; dominoes and cribbage. In front of the pub there are some old-fashioned seats, with more on a good-sized lawn over the lane by the river (they serve out here too); boules. Some of the bedrooms are above the bar. *(Recommended by Dr Stephen Feast, PS, Stephen and Tracey Groves, R F Grieve, Marvadene B Eves, Mr Mann, Eddie Walder, Rob Whittle, John Teign)*

Own brew ~ Wiz and Annie Clift ~ Real ale ~ Bar food ~ Restaurant ~ (01886) 821235 ~ Children in eating area of bar ~ Open 11-11; 12-10 Sun; closed evening 25 Dec ~ Bedrooms: £37B/£62.50B

OMBERSLEY SO8463 Map 4
Crown & Sandys Arms ♀ ⇌

Coming into the village from the A4133, turn left at the roundabout in middle of village, and pub is on the left

As we went to press, the arrival of new licensees was imminent at this pretty Dutch-gabled white inn, popular for food. The departing landlord could neither tell us who would be taking it over, nor the kind of food and ales they might be serving, but in the past food has included sandwiches, soup, ploughman's, home-cooked ham, steak and kidney pie, vegetarian quiche, steaks and daily specials such as grilled tuna with pine nut sauce or wild boar casserole with apricot. On the beer front, they used to rotate two to four well kept real ales from breweries such as Beowulf, Hancocks, Hook Norton or Woods, and they also offered around six wines by the glass, litre or half-litre, and country wines. The warm, comfortable and cosy lounge bar has a relaxing atmosphere, black beams and some flagstones, comfortable windsor armchairs, antique settles, a couple of easy chairs, old prints and maps on its timbered walls, log fires, and daily newspapers; half is no smoking. There are picnic-sets in the garden behind the building; no dogs; the comfortable bedrooms are no smoking. It's worth phoning to check that the opening hours have not changed under the new licensees. More reports please. *(Recommended by Neil Townend, Chris and Pascale Worth, Dennis Stevens, M Joyner, B T Smith, Francis Johnston, Mike Gorton, Richard and Robyn Wain, Brian Borwick, GSB, Joan and Michel Hooper-Immins, John Whitehead, Ian and Jacqui Ross, Mrs Ursula Hofheinz, Denys Gueroult, Richard and Margaret Peers, Ron Fletcher, John Bramley, W H and E Thomas)*

Free house ~ Real ale ~ Bar food (12-2, 6-9.45) ~ Restaurant ~ (01905) 620252 ~ Well behaved children welcome till 7pm ~ Open 11-3, 5.30-11; 12-3, 7-10.30 Sun; closed 25 Dec and evenings 26 Dec and 1 Jan ~ Bedrooms: £35S/£55S

Kings Arms 🍴

One room at this friendly big black-beamed and timbered Tudor pub has Charles II's coat of arms moulded into its decorated plaster ceiling – a trophy from his reputed stop here in 1651. They try to change the very good varied bar food menu seasonally, and alongside home-made soup (£2.50) and sandwiches (from £3.50) meals might include grilled goat's cheese on toasted ciabatta with chargrilled sweet peppers (£4.25), linguini with baby onions, cherry tomatoes, rocket and grated parmesan (£7.25), somerset brie, broccoli and leek strudel with mixed leaves (£7.75), pancetta wrapped ham with baby spinach and avocado salad (£8.25), 8oz sirloin steak (£10.50), roast lamb rump with a port glaze on a bed of bubble and squeak (£11.50) and daily specials including fresh fish such as chargrilled grey mullet on a mediterranean salad (£12) or roast sea bass with cajun mash and crispy sugar snap peas (£14); all snacks pleasantly served with linen napkins. A mellow atmosphere pervades the comfortably informal rambling rooms, and the various cosy nooks and crannies are full of stuffed animals and birds and a collection of rustic bric-a-brac, and have four open fires. Well kept Banks's Bitter, Bass, Marstons Pedigree and Morrells Varsity on handpump; no piped music. A tree-sheltered courtyard has tables under cocktail parasols, and colourful hanging baskets and tubs in summer, and there's also a terrace. *(Recommended by John Bramley, June and Mike Coleman, D A Norman, Alan and Paula McCully, Mike and Mary Carter, G Neighbour, Martin and Karen Wake, Jack Barnwell, Joy and Peter Heatherley, G and E Dorey, Mrs C Fielder, John Whitehead, P Neate)*

Free house ~ Licensee D Pendry ~ Real ale ~ Bar food (12-2.15, 6-10; 12-10 Sun) ~ (01905) 620142 ~ Well behaved children over 8 years old away from bar ~ Open 11-3, 5.30-11; 12-10.30 Sun

PENSAX SO7269 Map 4
Bell 🍺

B4202 Abberley—Clows Top, S of village

'Probably the happiest pub I know' is how one enamoured reader described this homely and welcoming roadside mock-Tudor place. The immaculately kept beers are certainly conducive to such merriment, and the friendly landlord, Graham Titcombe, is more than happy to chat about his enthusiasm for real ale: alongside Archers Golden and Enville Best, the three other handpumps quickly rotate around 500 well kept beers a year including many from small and local breweries; also farmhouse cider. However, this is by no means exclusively a pub for real-ale fans. The mostly home-made food is served with an impressive range of vegetables, and besides sandwiches (from £1.95) might include filled baked potatoes (from £2.95), omelettes (from £3.25), home honey-cured ham and egg (£4.25), lasagne or cheese, onion and potato pie (£4.95), chicken, ham and leek pie, steak and ale pie, scampi or pork with orange and ginger casserole (£5.75), lamb, mint and coriander balti or smoked haddock and prawns in a cream sauce with pasta (£5.95), gammon steak with egg and pineapple or grilled plaice with watercress sauce (£6.50), beef stroganoff (£6.95) and steaks (from £6.95). The L-shaped main bar has a restrained traditional décor, with long cushioned pews on its bare boards, good solid pub tables, and a woodburning stove. Beyond a small carpeted area on the left with a couple more tables is a more airy dining room added in the late 1980s, with french windows opening on to a wooden deck that on hot days can give a slightly Californian feel; it has a log fire for more British weather; cribbage, dominoes and piped music; no-smoking restaurant. In the back garden, picnic-sets look out over rolling fields and copses to the Wyre Forest. *(Recommended by John Bowdler, Joy and Peter Heatherley, John Whitehead, Mrs S Bull, Brian and Genie Krakowska Smart, Mike and Mary Carter)*

Free house ~ Licensee Graham Titcombe ~ Real ale ~ Bar food ~ Restaurant ~ (01299) 896677 ~ Children in restaurant, snug bar and garden ~ Open 12-2.30, 5-11; 12-10.30 Sun; closed Mon lunchtime except bank holidays

WELLAND SO7940 Map 4
Anchor
Drake Street; A4104 towards Upton

The L-shaped bar of this pretty extended fairy-lit cottage has country prints on the walls, some armchairs around chatty low tables, and more sitting-up chairs around eating-height tables. Beyond is a spreading comfortably furnished dining area, attractively furnished and nicely set, with candles, pink tablecloths and napkins. Besides garlic bread (£2.25), filled baked potatoes (from £3.50) and a variety of ploughman's and filled french bread (from £3.99), a very wide choice of good changing food on the blackboards might include chilli con carne (£3.99), baked eggs or mushrooms and bacon with black pudding (£4.10), vegetable stroganoff or tagliatelle (£6.25), tuna in tarragon sauce (£7.20), Thai chicken curry (£7.95), lamb cutlets done with honey and mint (£9.99) and steaks (from £10.05). Six well kept changing beers such as Black Sheep, Malvern Hills, Smiles, St Georges, Woods Shropshire Lad and a beer brewed for the pub on handpump, good friendly service; shove-ha'penny, cribbage, chess, maybe unobtrusive piped music. Outside, there are picnic-sets on the lawn, with flower borders and a big old apple tree; the tiled house has well tended big hanging baskets, with a passion flower and roses climbing its walls. The pub is handy for the Three Counties Showground, and has a field for camping with tents or caravans. *(Recommended by June and Mike Coleman, Bernard Stradling, Alan and Paula McCully)*

Free house ~ Licensees Colin and Caroline Barrett ~ Real ale ~ Bar food ~ Restaurant ~ (01684) 592317 ~ Children in restaurant ~ Live entertainment Fri evening from 9.30pm ~ Open 11.45-3, 6.45-11; 12-3 Sun; closed Sun evenings (unless custom demands)

WORCESTER SO8555 Map 4
Cardinals Hat 🍺 £
Friar Street; just off A44 near cathedral

Behind its Georgian façade, this ancient place has some nice surprises. It's been licensed since 1518 and had been open as an alehouse several decades earlier. The little beamed and timbered front bar has an elaborate plasterwork cardinal's hat above the big stone fireplace (with a coal-effect gas fire), an interesting collection of antique pewter spoons, a working pianola, and well kept (and priced) Banks's Bitter and Original, Camerons Bitter and Ruby Red, Marstons Pedigree and Banks's seasonal Festival ales on handpump, from a heavily carved counter. Like some other pubs, this has regulars' tankards on the wall – unlike any other we know of, it also has their cushions hanging up. There's a snug little leaded-light side room with a couple of long tables and wall benches. The most striking place is down a short corridor at the back: a wholly oak-panelled room with fine 17th-c carving over its handsome stone fireplace (another coal-effect fire), and built-in wall seats all the way round. Cheap food runs from filled french bread (£2.30, hot fillings £2.65) to rump steak (£5.99, with fresh vegetables) and home-made crumble with custard (£2.10), with their daily roast (£3.99 – or £7 for two) and sausage, mash and yorkshire pudding (£4) among their most popular dishes. Very friendly staff, cribbage, dominoes, piped pop music. The picnic-sets in the back concrete courtyard (not to mention the real ales) are a magnet for the colourful Worcester Militia on bank holidays and other occasions when they meet here during parades and other Civil War re-enactments. The pub has its own car park. *(Recommended by Barry and Anne)*

Banks's ~ Manager Susan Roberts ~ Real ale ~ Bar food (11.30-2.30, 6-9) ~ (01905) 22423 ~ Children in eating area of bar ~ Open 11-11; 12-10.30 Sun; 12-3, 7-10.30 Sun in winter

WYRE PIDDLE SO9647 Map 4
Anchor
B4084 WNW of Evesham

This friendly 17th-c pub is at its most pleasant in summer when you can watch the tranquil comings and goings on the River Avon from seats on the spacious back lawn that runs down to the water. Beyond there are views spreading out over the Vale of Evesham as far as the Cotswolds, the Malverns and Bredon Hill. The friendly and well kept little lounge has a good log fire in its attractively restored inglenook fireplace, comfortably upholstered chairs and settles, and two beams in the shiny ceiling; the big airy back bar affords the same marvellous views as the lawn. The recently refurbished dining area has an open fire, rugs on stripped wood floors and wooden tables and chairs. Generously served and reasonably priced good bar food (as all food is cooked to order service can be a little slow when they are very busy in the summer months) changes every fortnight or so and might include tomato and basil soup (£2.50), sandwiches (from £3.50), crab cakes and chilli salsa (£3.75), macaroni cheese (£4.25), pork and sage sausage and mash (£4.50), smoked haddock, mushroom and leek pie (£4.95), stir-fried chicken and vegetables with oyster sauce (£6.50), deep-fried cod in beer batter (£6.70), duck breast with raspberry jus (£7.95), fillet steak with black pepper sauce (£11.50) and puddings such as bakewell tart, lemon cheesecake or chocolate mousse with bitter coffee sauce (£2.50); children's meals (from £3). Well kept Boddingtons, Banks's Best, Flowers Original and Marstons Pedigree under light blanket pressure, 10 wines by the glass, 10 whiskies, and country wines; fruit machine. *(Recommended by Iona L Thomson, Pat and Tony Martin, IHR, G Braithwaite, Martin Jennings, Alan and Paula McCully, Bronwen and Steve Wrigley, Dr A Y Drummond, Ken and Jeni Black, Brian and Bett Cox, P H Roberts, Michael Bourdeaux, Ian and Jacqui Ross, Mr Mann, Ivor Paul Evans, KN-R)*

Whitbreads ~ Licensee Michael Senior ~ Real ale ~ Bar food ~ (01386) 552799 ~ Children welcome ~ Open 11-2.30, 6-11; 12-11 Sat; 12-10.30 Sun; 12-3, 6-11 Sat, 12-3, 7-10.30 Sun in winter

Bedroom prices normally include full English breakfast, VAT and any inclusive service charge that we know of. Prices before the '/' are for single rooms, after for two people in double or twin (B includes a private bath, S a private shower).

Lucky Dip

Besides the fully inspected pubs, you might like to try these Lucky Dips recommended to us and described by readers (if you do, please send us reports):

Beckford [SO9835]
Beckford Inn [A435]: Wide and interesting food choice, well kept Courage Directors, Theakstons, and guest beers such as Goffs or Marstons Pedigree, old-fashioned feel, good service; bedrooms *(Dave Braisted)*
Belbroughton [SO9277]
Holly Bush: Comfortable beamed pub with food inc Sun roast, Tetleys and Woods Shropshire Lad; no music *(B T Smith, James Nunn)*
Bewdley [SO7875]
☆ *Little Pack Horse* [High St]: Ancient low-beamed heavily timbered building, cosily pubby and bustling, with helpful service, candles and woodburner, masses of intriguing bric-a-brac and old photographs and advertisements, pleasant mix of old furnishings, good value food, well kept ales inc Ind Coope Burton and Ushers; children in eating area, open all day w/e *(LYM, Charles and Pauline Stride)*
Bournheath [SO9474]
Gate [handy for M5 junction 3; Dodford Rd]: Attractive country dining pub with wide choice of food inc vegetarian, Mexican, Caribbean and Asian dishes and lunchtime and early evening bargains, well kept Smiles Best and Heritage and a weekly guest beer, restaurant; nice garden *(David Edwards)*
Bradley Green [SP9862]
Red Lion [Feckenham Rd]: Pleasant staff, good food at reasonable prices, well kept beers;handy for NT Hanbury Hall *(Dave Braisted)*
Bransford [SO7852]
☆ *Bear & Ragged Staff* [off A4103 SW of Worcester; Powick Rd]: Good dining pub, with country views from relaxed interconnecting rooms inc no-smoking restaurant, good service, well kept Boddingtons and Wadworths 6X, good range of other drinks; darts and traditional games in public bar, children welcome *(Marvadene B Eves, LYM, Mr Mann)*
Bredon [SO9236]
Royal Oak [High St]: Roomy and relaxed carpeted bar with open fire, Banks's, Marstons Pedigree and a guest beer, nice choice of well presented food (not Sun evening, Mon/Tues) in bar and dining room inc very good fish and chips (can take away), friendly staff; pool, darts, skittle alley, barbecues *(Derek and Sylvia Stephenson)*
Broadway [SP0739]
☆ *Collin House* [follow Willersey sign off A44 Broadway bypass roundabout, into Collin Lane; marked Gt Collin Farm on OS Sheet 150 map ref 076391]: Wide choice of good interesting freshly done food inc traditional puddings in lovely bar of small country hotel, very relaxed and civilised – good log fires, no machines or piped music (but no sandwiches or ploughman's either), very accommodating newish management; nice restaurant not overpriced (wise to book), good wines, local beers, pleasant staff; tables outside; comfortable bedrooms *(IHR)*

☆ *Crown & Trumpet* [Church St]: Cosy unspoilt beamed and timbered local with dark high-backed settles, stripped stone, big log fire, well kept Boddingtons, Flowers IPA and Original, Morlands Old Speckled Hen, local Stanway and Wadworths 6X, seasonal made drinks, good value home-made food, friendly efficient staff, good range of pub games; fruit machine, piped music, Thurs quiz night, Sat duo; children welcome, open all day Sat, seats on front terrace; bedrooms *(Steven M Gent, BB, Ted George, TBB, Miss Veronica Brown, Meg and Colin Hamilton, David and Nina Pugsley)*
Horse & Hound [Main St]: Spacious bay-windowed bar with plenty of woodwork, open fire, china cabinets, dining end with wide choice of good value food; quick pleasant staff, Whitbreads-related ales with guests such as Hook Norton Old Hooky or Wadworths 6X, Sunday papers; open all day *(Pam Adsley, Miss Veronica Brown)*
Lygon Arms [Main St]: Stately but very expensive Cotswold hotel in strikingly handsome ancient building, interesting old rooms rambling away from the attractive oak-panelled bar; imaginative food in adjoining Goblets wine bar, tables in prettily planted courtyard, well kept gardens; children allowed away from bar; bedrooms smart and comfortable; open all day in summer *(LYM, Bernard Stradling, Wendy Arnold)*
Bromsgrove [SO9570]
Hop Pole [Birmingham Rd]: Homely and welcoming local nr football ground, well kept real ale (one of the few sources of Nailers beers), wide range of reasonably priced sandwiches and other snacks *(Richard Houghton, Dave Braisted)*
Catshill [SO9573]
Plough & Harrow [Stourbridge Rd]: Good value food, well kept Tetleys-related beers *(Dave Braisted)*
Chaddesley Corbett [SO8973]
Fox [off A448 Bromsgrove—Kidderminster]: Spaciously refurbished, with well priced bar food and popular carvery (get there early for a table), friendly staff, well kept Marstons and Worthington, nice dogs *(W H and E Thomas)*
Charlton [SP0145]
Gardeners Arms [the one nr Pershore; Strand]: Straightforward local on green of pretty thatched village, good value generous fresh food, welcoming atmosphere and service, lots of tables in lounge, spartan public bar with darts, Whitbreads-related ales, decent choice of wines; quiet piped music *(June and Mike Coleman)*
Cleeve Prior [SP0849]
Kings Arms [Main St (B4085 Evesham—Bidford)]: Unspoilt 16th-c beamed pub, well run and comfortable, with good imaginative food at reasonable prices, well kept Wadworths 6X and a guest beer, friendly helpful service, no-smoking dining room; no piped music,

children welcome, bedrooms planned *(Alison, Pete and Matty Johnson)*

Clent [SO9279]

Hill: At foot of Clent Hills, good bar food, Courage Directors and Marstons Owd Rodger; skittle alley *(Dave Braisted)*

Clows Top [SO7171]

Colliers Arms [A456 Bewdley—Tenbury]: Roomy and comfortable dining pub, with two log fires in bar – one part a reception area for the spacious no-smoking restaurant, the other part (smoking allowed) with tasty sandwiches and rolls; wide choice of generous well prepared food inc vegetarian, efficient service, well kept Theakstons Best and XB, unobtrusive piped music; children welcome, no dogs, nice countryside *(Mrs S Bull, Theo, Anne and Jane Gaskin)*

Conderton [SO9637]

Yew Tree: Nice old beamed and flagstoned pub on S slope of Bredon Hill, with friendly lively locals, well kept real ales inc a guest such as Badger Tanglefoot, good value food; good walks *(Guy Vowles)*

Crabbs Cross [SP0364]

Crabbs Cross Inn [A448 S of Redditch]: Refurbished cosy local doing well under current landlord, Tetleys, Ansells and Banks's Milds and four changing guest beers, tables outside *(Graham Coates)*

Crowle [SO9256]

☆ *Old Chequers* [2 miles from M5 junction 6, off A4538; Crowle Green]: Big spreading dining pub rambling around island servery, comfortable chairs, coal-effect gas fire one end, lots of pictures for sale, popular generous food (no sandwiches etc, but good value light lunches; no food Sun evening), well kept Banks's, Woods Shropshire Lad and Worthington Best, good house wines, friendly prompt service; picnic-sets on back grass among shrubs and fruit trees, nice spot with pasture behind *(Mike and Mary Carter, BB, Mrs Ursula Hofheinz)*

Cutnall Green [SO8768]

Chequers [Kidderminster Rd]: The people who made the Kings Arms at Ombersley a popular main entry are now here, with a good chef doing interesting food (not cheap, and freshly cooked so may be a wait) in beamed bar and restaurant; well kept Bass, old tables, stylish green and cream décor, picnic-sets out in front; more reports on this promising place please *(anon)*

Dodford [SO9372]

Dodford Inn [Whinfield Rd]: Unpretentious Greenalls country pub in extensive grounds, quiet spot overlooking wooded valley, lots of footpaths; relaxed peaceful atmosphere, very reasonably priced home cooking inc vegetarian menu and plenty of snacks, guest beers, tables on terrace, play area; camp and caravan site *(Jean and Richard Phillips)*

Drakes Broughton [SO9248]

Plough & Harrow [A44 NW of Pershore]: Attractive rambling lounge, well kept ales, friendly efficient service; tables nicely set behind by old orchard *(Sarah and Peter Gooderham)*

Droitwich [SO8861]

Barley Mow: Friendly welcome in attractively refurbished local *(Mike Taylor)*

Railway [Kidderminster Rd]: Small friendly traditional local with railway memorabilia in two-room lounge bar (even a model train running sometimes), canal basin and Vines Park views from big balcony, well kept Banks's Mild, Marstons Pedigree and guest ales, expanding imaginative choice of freshly made food inc vegetarian, friendly landlords and customers, pub games; open all day Fri/Sat *(Ian Colley, Bill and Pam Baker)*

Talbot [High St]: Old-fashioned local with cheap bar food inc huge hot pork sandwiches, Banks's beers, etched glass; very friendly *(Dave Braisted)*

Dunhampstead [SO9160]

☆ *Firs* [just SE of Droitwich, towards Sale Green – OS Sheet 150 map ref 919600]: Pretty dining pub, with flower-filled terrace, small grassy garden, lots of hanging baskets, comfortable conservatory; good food from doorstep sandwiches up (hot dishes freshly made so can be a wait), well kept Banks's and Marstons, welcoming service, friendly dogs, flowers on tables; fairly quiet weekday lunchtimes, booking advised w/e; nice spot not far from canal *(David Edwards, Roger and Pauline Pearce, Jenny and Michael Back, Charles and Pauline Stride, LYM)*

Earls Croome [SO8642]

☆ *Yorkshire Grey*: Cheerful bustling roadhouse doing well under new regime, attractively appointed and efficiently run, with young cheerful competent staff, good food (all day w/e), well kept Bass and good Australian house wines, candlelit restaurant *(Tom Evans, Peter and Sue Davies)*

Eldersfield [SO8131]

Greyhound [signed from B4211; Lime St (don't go into Eldersfield itself), OS Sheet 150 map ref 815314]: Unspoilt two-bar country local with good inexpensive food (not Mon), well kept Ansells, Tetleys, Theakstons and a couple of guest beers such as Butcombe, friendly young licensees, surprisingly modern lavatories with interesting mosaic in gents', pretty garden and room for children to play in *(Derek and Sylvia Stephenson, Dave Braisted)*

Evesham [SP0344]

Green Dragon [Oat St, off High St at Barclays, follow Library signs]: 16th-c coaching inn, formerly part of monastery, brewing own Asum and Gold (glass panel shows brewery); small dining lounge, big comfortable public bar, back pool room and skittle alley, old well in corridor, friendly staff, attractive prints, cheap food, quiet at lunchtime; evening piped music, maybe TV, live music, bouncers; good value bedrooms, good breakfast *(Pete Baker, Dr and Mrs B Baker)*

Royal Oak [Vine St]: Comfortable and attractive old timbered local with Worcs CCC cricket memorabilia, good choice of Whitbreads-related and other ales, good value home-made food, prompt service *(Pam Adsley)*

Fladbury [SO9946]

☆ *Chequers* [Chequers Lane]: Dating from

14th c, reworked over time into cosy, warm and comfortable up-market dining pub, with huge old-fashioned range as centre-piece, lots of local prints, good food not over-priced given the quantities, charming beamed restaurant with carvery, well kept John Smiths, Theakstons XB and other ales, very friendly owners, quick service; large garden with play area being developed, peaceful pretty village; comfortable well equipped bedroom extension *(M G Lavery, Peter and Audrey Dowsett)*

Flyford Flavell [SO9754]

☆ *Boot* [½ mile off A422 Worcester—Alcester; sharp turn into village beside Flyford Arms, then turn left into Radford Rd]: Very wide range of decent food in country pub with heavily beamed medieval core, beamed dining rooms (one no smoking) with open fires and glass-topped well, more dining chairs in conservatory with swagged curtains; attractive little front bar with hunting prints, darts, well lit pool table and inglenook log fire, well kept Boddingtons, an Everards seasonal beer, Marstons Pedigree, Morlands Old Speckled Hen and Wadworths 6X; children welcome to eat, tables and slide in small sheltered garden; bedrooms, one suited to wheelchair *(June and Mike Coleman, Martin Jennings, Ian Shorthouse, BB, Mike and Mary Carter, B T Smith, Peter Williams, Mick and Jeanne Shillington)*

Hadley [SO8664]

Bowling Green [Hadley Heath; off A4133 Droitwich—Ombersley]: Large but cosy bar in pleasantly refurbished 16th-c inn, wide range of good value food inc enterprising filled baguettes, interesting hot dishes and good value Sun carvery; well kept Banks's Bitter and Mild, Marstons Pedigree and Hook Norton, good value wines, big log fire, hops on beams, attractive restaurant, comfortable bedrooms; children welcome, tables outside, has UK's oldest bowling green *(Meg and Colin Hamilton)*

Hallow [SO8258]

Camp [off A443 N of Worcester]: Friendly unspoilt Severnside local with enjoyable atmosphere, Enville White, interesting pictures of floods here, simple good value food *(Ian and Elizabeth Rispin)*

Hanbury [SO9663]

Eagle & Sun [B4090 Droitwich rd]: Spotless recently refurbished pub adjacent by canal marina, good value food, real ales inc Banks's Bitter and Mild and Marstons Pedigree *(W H and E Thomas)*

Gate Hangs Well [Woodgate, nr B4091 towards Stoke Prior]: Much extended dining pub alone in farmland, open-plan but well divided, with conservatory and country views; good value attractively presented generous food inc carvery (bargains some nights), enormous home-made pies and huge cod, well kept Banks's, Bass and Worthington, friendly service; very popular, best to book *(June and Mike Coleman, David and Helen Wilkins)*

Vernon Arms [B4090]: Good value food, Bass, Boddingtons, M&B Brew XI and Worthington; camp site, annual steam fair *(Dave Braisted)*

Hanley Castle [SO8341]

☆ *Three Kings* [Church End, off B4211 N of Upton upon Severn]: Unspoilt friendly country local, well worn in, with huge inglenook and hatch service in little tiled-floor tap room, well kept Butcombe, Thwaites and usually three guest beers from small breweries, farm cider, dozens of malt whiskies, two other larger rooms, low-priced homely food (not Sun evening – singer then; be prepared for a maybe longish wait other times), seats of a sort outside; family room, bedroom *(the Didler, P and M Rudlin, Mr Mann, LYM, JP, PP, Alan and Paula McCully, R J Walden)*

Hanley Swan [SO8142]

Swan [B4209 Malvern—Upton]: Relaxed traditional pub by green with big duck pond, varied reasonably priced food running up to steaks, well kept Theakstons Best and XB, decent wine, prompt friendly service, comfortable spacious lounge with hunting trophies, old guns and cow-bells, nice locals' bar (TV news), small attractive restaurant evenings and Sun lunch; tables on lawn, big play area *(BB, Mr and Mrs M J E Pearson, D A Hughes, Richard and Valerie Wright)*

Harvington [SO8774]

Golden Cross: Unpretentious village local making real efforts on the food side, inc succulent and filling steak baguettes *(John and Moira Cole)*

Himbleton [SO9458]

☆ *Galton Arms*: Friendly old-fashioned country pub, log fires, oak beams, good well presented food inc interesting vegetarian dishes in bar and restaurant, well kept Bass and Banks's, personal service; garden with play area *(Ian Shorthouse, P Gondris)*

Honeybourne [SP1144]

Thatched Tavern: Attractive thatched country local, homely, comfortable and relaxing; bay window seats, leaded lights, beams and flagstones, real fires, attractive and cosy lower room with pool table leading to dining room, Boddingtons and guest beer; tables in garden with hens to feed *(Gordon)*

Inkberrow [SP0157]

☆ *Bulls Head* [A422 Worcester—Alcester]: Handsome Georgian inn with good village atmosphere in much older heavily beamed, timbered and partly flagstoned bar with woodburner in big fireplace, comfortable banquettes and other seats, Banks's, Bass and a beer brewed for the pub by Church End, darts, neat helpful staff; two comfortable dining areas, decent food inc good roasts; picnic-sets and play area behind, bedrooms *(B T Smith, Sarah and Peter Gooderham, Patricia Tovey, BB)*

☆ *Old Bull* [off A422 – note that this is quite different from the nearby Bulls Head]: Photogenic and fascinating Tudor pub with bulging walls, huge inglenooks, flagstones, oak beams and trusses, and some old-fashioned high-backed settles among more modern furnishings; lots of *Archers* memorabilia (it's the model for the Ambridge Bull), friendly service, good simple home-made food inc sandwiches, vegetarian and Sun roast, good range of Whitbreads-related ales with guests such as Banks's and Marstons Pedigree, good value coffee; children allowed in eating area, tables outside *(Gordon, LYM, Alan and Paula McCully)*

Kemerton [SO9437]

☆ *Crown* [back rd Bredon—Beckford]: Welcoming 18th-c pub with refreshingly modern light furnishings in bustling L-shaped lounge bar, consistently good food from sandwiches up inc plenty of fish and enjoyable puddings, well kept Whitbreads-related ales, friendly helpful staff, daily papers; pretty garden, upmarket village, good walks over Bredon Hill *(Mrs A Oakley, John Brightley, Derek and Sylvia Stephenson)*

Long Bank [SO7674]

Running Horse [A456 W of Bewdley]: Large well kept Greenalls Millers Kitchen family dining pub, well kept ales, reasonable prices, pleasant atmosphere; large garden and terrace, very big fenced play area *(Ian Shorthouse)*

Longdon [SO8336]

Hunters Inn [B4211 S, towards Tewkesbury]: Attractive décor and relaxed atmosphere, comfortable furnishings, beams, flagstones, log fires, brass, copper and bric-a-brac; pleasant service, food from sandwiches up inc children's dishes, real ales, decent wines, good views; now owned by a chain – the licensees who previously made this a popular main entry can be found at the Farmers Arms at Wellington Heath (Herefs) *(LYM, John Teign, Mary and David Richards, Bernard Stradling)*

Lulsley [SO7455]

☆ *Fox & Hounds* [signed a mile off A44 Worcester—Bromyard]: Tucked-away country pub with smallish parquet-floored bar stepping down into neat dining lounge, pretty little restaurant on left, good food from unusual soups and excellent steak baguette to interesting main dishes, well kept Bass and a local beer, decent wines, open fire; picnic-sets in quiet and colourful enclosed side rose garden *(Dave Braisted, Dr and Mrs R Rowland, BB, J H Peters)*

Malvern [SO7641]

Malvern Hills Hotel [British Camp, Wynds Point; junction A449/B4232 S]: Half a dozen well kept ales such as Bass and Woods Parish, filling food, friendly service, welcoming panelled plush lounge bar with open fire; good position high in the hills, former owners include Jennie Lind, and the Cadbury brothers; bedrooms small but comfortable *(Miss B Mattocks)*

Mamble [SO6971]

☆ *Sun & Slipper* [just off A456 Bewdley—Tenbury Wells]: Friendly, attractively refurbished and well run 16th-c inn in small village, good imaginative food inc set lunches, well kept Hobsons; village has interesting church and superior craft centre; bedrooms *(BB, R Morgan, Dave Braisted)*

Pershore [SO9445]

☆ *Brandy Cask* [Bridge St]: Own-brewed generously hopped Brandysnapper, John Baker and Whistling Joe, guest beers, Aug beer festival, good freshly made food from sandwiches to steaks inc vegetarian and some

interesting dishes in bar and quaintly decorated no-smoking brasserie, quick friendly service; well behaved children allowed; long attractive garden down to river, with terrace and koi pond *(Graham Reeve, Dr and Mrs B Baker, Pat and Tony Martin, Alan and Paula McCully, Derek and Sylvia Stephenson, Kerry Law, the Didler)*

Pound Green [SO7678]

New Inn [B4194 NW of Bewdley]: Attractive and old (indeed now calling itself Ye Olde New Inn), with friendly staff, good atmosphere, good food in bar and dining room, well kept beer with usually two guests *(Patrick Herratt)*

Rowley Regis [SO9787]

Bell & Bear [Gorsty Hill Rd]: Cosily refurbished old building with good atmosphere, cheerful efficient service, good varied food all day, wide range of well kept beers; Black Country views from hilltop terraced garden *(Dr A Pollock, Mrs P White)*

Shatterford [SO7981]

☆ *Bellmans Cross* [Bridgnorth Rd (A442)]: Big welcoming attractively refurbished pub/restaurant with imaginative beautifully presented French-influenced bar food, good food in tasteful restaurant, Bass and guest beer, thoughtful wine list, courteous service *(Brian and Pat Wardrobe, Neil and Jane Kendrick)*

Red Lion [Bridgnorth Rd (A442)]: Immaculate olde-worlde pub straddling the Shropshire boundary, with gleaming copper and brass, lively coal fire, partly no-smoking dining extension, reasonably priced Banks's Mild and Bitter and local ales such as Herefordshire Classic and Woods Shropshire Lad, wide choice of good generous well presented food inc vegetarian and properly cooked veg, good atmosphere, very friendly staff; fine views *(John Teign, Phil Putwain, W H and E Thomas)*

Stoke Pound [SO9667]

☆ *Queens Head* [Sugarbrook Lane, by Bridge 48, Worcester & Birmingham Canal]: Big plush canalside dining pub with good generous straightforward food inc good value evening carvery, lots of puddings, Scottish Courage ales, quick friendly service, air conditioning, rather close-set tables; Sun lunch very popular (booking advised); waterside terrace, camping site, good walk up the 36 locks of the Tardebigge Steps *(Roger and Pauline Pearce, Charles and Pauline Stride)*

Stoke Prior [SO9468]

☆ *Country Girl* [Hanbury Rd (B4091 S of Bromsgrove)]: Attractive country pub with comfortable lounge, rustic brickwork, light oak beams, farm tools, soft lighting, enterprising choice of specials inc quite a few vegetarian, very friendly efficient service, well kept Whitbreads-related and other ales such as Wadworths 6X, unobtrusive piped music; enclosed garden, walks on Dodderhill Common *(Dave Braisted, Ian Shorthouse, M C Jeanes)*

Ewe & Lamb [Hanbury Rd (B4091)]: Recently refurbished Whitbreads pub, nice layout and décor, beams, tiled floors, food inc adventurous dishes; attractive garden *(Ian Shorthouse, Dave Braisted)*

Stonehall Common [SO8749]

☆ *Fruiterers Arms* [S of Norton, via Hatfield]:
Interesting guest beers from across Great Britain,
good service, good reasonably priced food in
welcoming panelled bar with chesterfields and
open fires, and in extension restaurant inc good
carvery lunchtime and early evening; garden with
big gazebo *(Kerry Law, Simon Smith, W E and
E Thomas, Ivor Paul Evans)*

Tenbury Wells [SO6168]

☆ *Peacock* [A456 about 1½ miles E – so inn
actually in Shrops]: Beautiful 14th-c roadside
inn with relaxed yet buoyant atmosphere in
several separate rooms, heavy black beams, big
log fire in front lounge, comfortable kitchen
chairs and ex-pew settles; good attractively
presented food with lots of fresh veg, good
friendly service, well kept ales, decent wines,
back family room, charming bistro; picnic-sets
on terrace, lovely setting by River Teme; good
bedrooms *(Mr and Mrs Woolnough, Helen
Winter, Mr and Mrs Donald Anderson, LYM,
W H and E Thomas, TOH)*

☆ *Ship* [Teme St]: Small L-shaped bar with lots of
dark wood inc fine Elizabethan beams, little
hunting prints and other pictures, well kept
Ansells and guests such as Exmoor Gold and
Hobsons Best, decent wines, good coffee, good
imaginative generous food inc fresh fish and
Sun lunch, bright no-smoking dining room with
fresh flowers, reasonable prices; piped music;
picnic-sets in coach yard and on neat sheltered
back lawn; comfortable bedrooms *(BB, G
Coates, John and Moira Cole, Peter Lloyd)*

Upton Snodsbury [SO9454]

☆ *Coventry Arms* [A422 Worcester—Stratford]:
Hunting prints, fox masks, horse tack and
racing gossip in welcoming country inn with
cottagey armchairs among other seats, coal fire,
well kept Bass, Boddingtons, Marstons Pedigree
and Morlands Old Speckled Hen, lots of malt
whiskies and ports, good friendly service, good
choice of enjoyable food – two comfortable
dining rooms, back conservatory with well
spaced cane tables; well equipped play area;
bedrooms attractively decorated *(Mrs Ursula
Hofheinz, BB, June and Mike Coleman)*

☆ *French House*: Recently reopened (by the
founder of the entertaining chain of Little
pubs), two roomy bars with over-the-top
French décor, hundreds of wine bottles, French
signs and ornaments, two grandfather clocks,
even a useable mock guillotine; good value
French food, good choice of wines, well kept
Highgate Saddlers, Morlands Old Speckled Hen
and Theakstons Best, French piped music *(Dave
Braisted, June and Mike Coleman)*

Upton upon Severn [SO8540]

Little Upton Muggery [Old St, far end main st]:
Basic pub with thousands of mugs on the
ceiling, simple furnishings, open fires, pool in
third room, unusual beer, good value generous
food, good friendly service *(Joy and Peter
Heatherley, P and M Rudlin, Ted George)*

☆ *Olde Anchor* [High St]: Picturesque rambling
16th-c pub, neat, tidy and chatty, with helpful
service, old-fashioned furnishings, black timbers

propping its low beams, glowing copper, brass
and pewter, good fire in unusual central
fireplace; well kept Scottish Courage ales,
enjoyable low-priced food; open all day
summer, can get crowded evenings then *(LYM,
P and M Rudlin, Ted George, Alan and Paula
McCully, Peter and Audrey Dowsett)*

Swan [Riverside]: Popular straightforward low-
beamed main bar in charming riverside setting,
well kept Banks's and Marstons Pedigree,
friendly staff and young dog, two open fires,
boating memorabilia, fruit machine, games
machines in anteroom; separate cosy smarter and
more hotelish bar with sizeable dining room off,
good value generous interesting food; waterside
garden with summer barbecues *(BB, Alan and
Paula McCully, Michael and Gillian Ford, Neil
Townend, Jo Rees, Peter and Audrey Dowsett)*

Weatheroak Hill [SP0674]

☆ *Coach & Horses* [Icknield St – coming S on
A435 from Wythall roundabout, filter right off
dual carriageway a mile S, then in village turn
left towards Alvechurch; not far from M42,
junction 3]: Roomy country pub notable for
wide choice of interesting well kept ales, most
from small breweries and one brewed for the
landlord; plush-seated low-ceilinged two-level
dining bar, tiled-floor proper public bar, bar
food inc bargain fish and chips, also modern
restaurant with well spaced tables; plenty of
seats out on lawns and upper terrace; piped
music; children allowed in eating area *(Richard
Houghton, W H and E Thomas, LYM)*

Welland [SO7940]

Hawthorne [Upper Welland Rd]: Good bar
food inc interestingly filled baked potatoes, well
kept Marstons *(Dave Braisted)*

Marlbank [Marl Bank (A4104 W)]: Good value
straightforward food, friendly staff, well kept
Banks's *(Dave Braisted)*

Whittington [SO8752]

Swan [just off M5 junction 7]: Brightly painted
country-style bar with lots of pews, friendly
staff, well kept Banks's and Marstons Pedigree,
decent wine, imaginative moderately priced
food, log fire; children welcome, garden with
play area *(M Crabtree)*

Wildmoor [SO9675]

Wildmoor Oak [a mile from M5 junction 4 –
1st left off A491 towards Stourbridge; Top Rd]:
Good value food, M&B and guest ales, good
service, collection of foreign number-plates;
very busy in summer *(Stan and Hazel Allen)*

Worcester [SO8555]

Eagle Vaults [Friar St]: Homely pub with good
atmosphere, good lunchtime food choice inc
bargains for two, well kept Banks's and
Marstons Pedigree *(Revd and Mrs David
Hunter)*

Wychbold [SO9267]

Thatch [A38 towards Bromsgrove]: Not a pub
(part of Webbs Garden Centre, open 10-5, with
wines licence) but useful for good value food
from sandwiches to hot dishes, wine, canned
beer, good coffee and tea, in pleasant
surroundings; new larger restaurant fully into
its stride now *(D Green, David Green)*

Yorkshire

This is always a delightful chapter of the book for us to write. Shining through the Yorkshire pub reports from readers (more than 2,000 for this edition), through the letters we have from licensees when we are checking facts, and through our telephone conversations with them, there is a warm glow of friendliness which vividly takes us back to the joys of our Yorkshire inspection tours, even when we are locked into the final throes of trying to catch up with our publishers' editorial deadlines. There is an excellent choice of pubs here, from the most basic and traditional to the very smart and plush, with some splendid all-rounders, some that win high marks for good value food, many in lovely countryside, and a growing number with really excellent imaginative cooking. Pubs which have been earning the warmest praise in recent months include the Black Bull in Boroughbridge (good all round, nice to stay in), the beautifully placed Red Lion in Burnsall (earning a Food Award this year), the Abbey Inn at Byland Abbey (another to gain its Food Award now), the well run Fox & Hounds at Carthorpe, the well managed Devonshire Arms at Cracoe, the New Inn at Cropton (brews its own beer), the civilised Blue Lion at East Witton (good all round, excellent food), the Plough at Fadmoor (a new entry, run by licensees who were very popular in their days at the Feathers in Helmsley), the pretty Star at Harome (another new entry, good food in nice surroundings), the Angel at Hetton (very good food and service), the friendly and well run Chequers at Ledsham (exemplary all-rounder), Whitelocks in Leeds (great character), the Nags Head at Pickhill (still seems to get better and better, under the brothers who have run it for nearly 30 years now), the Yorke Arms at Ramsgill (imaginative food, great to stay in, very smart but a genuine welcome for all – it earns a Star Award this year), the civilised and aptly named Old Bridge in Ripponden, the immaculate old Sawley Arms in Sawley, the charming Hare at Scawton (a newcomer to the Guide), the Fat Cat in Sheffield (excellent value food, their own fine cheap real ales, and an interesting new brewery centre), the Three Acres in Shelley (more restaurant than pub, but very popular now with readers for its excellent food), the Fox & Hounds at Sinnington (good food at this friendly new entry), the smashing little Fox & Hounds at Starbotton in Upper Wharfedale, the Jefferson Arms at Thorganby, the warm-hearted Buck at Thornton Watlass, the Wombwell Arms at Wass (a top-drawer all-rounder), and the Duke of York in its very special spot in Whitby. For a special meal out, we'd recommend the Blue Lion at East Witton, the Angel at Hetton, the Yorke Arms at Ramsgill, the Boars Head at Ripley and the Three Acres at Shelley; of these, the Three Acres at Shelley is our Yorkshire Dining Pub of the Year. There's no shortage of notable pubs to pick out from the Lucky Dip section at the end of the chapter, too: the Plough at Allerthorpe, Falcon at Arncliffe, Cock & Bottle in Bradford, Farmers at Brafferton, Ferry at Cawood, Kaye Arms on Grange Moor (for food), Royal Oak in Great Ayton, Shears in Halifax, Old Hall in Haworth, Crown in Helmsley, George in Hull, Fountain at Ingbirchworth, Racehorses in Kettlewell, Star & Garter at Kirkby Overblow, Charles Bathurst near Langthwaite and Red Lion in that village, Maypole at Long

*Preston, Black Sheep Brewery in Masham (not exactly a pub, but well worth
visiting), White Swan in Middleham, Cubley Hall in Penistone, White Horse
just outside Rosedale Abbey, Royal in Runswick Bay, Plough at Saxton
(food), Railway at Spofforth, Boat at Sprotbrough, Tan Hill Inn on Tan Hill,
Ring o' Bells in Thornton (food), Wensleydale Heifer at West Witton and
Plough at Wigglesworth. As we have said, there are plenty of bargains on the
food side in Yorkshire; low-price early suppers are also worth looking out for.
Drinks usually cost less in pubs here than in most places elsewhere, too. The
cheapest beer we found was in pubs tied to Sam Smiths of Tadcaster, but pub
prices generally here seem to be held down by strong competition between the
national brewers (notably Scottish Courage with their local John Smiths and
Theakstons brands), the regional brewers Banks's/Camerons and Mansfield
(Wards of Sheffield was closed in 1999 by their owners Swallow), and a very
healthy flush of smaller local brewers. Local firms which we found supplying
at least some of our main entry pubs with their cheapest beers were (in rough
price order, starting with the cheapest) Barnsley, Clarks, Daleside, Black Sheep
(now very widely available) and Hambleton, and there is quite a number of
other good local brewers. Moreover, several pubs here brew their own good
beers, often very cheaply.*

ALDBOROUGH SE4166 Map 7

Ship 🍽

Village signposted from B6265 just S of Boroughbridge, close to A1

Handy for the Roman town with its museum and Roman pavements, this neatly kept
and attractive old pub offers a friendly welcome to both locals and visitors. The
heavily beamed bar has some old-fashioned seats around heavy cast-iron tables,
sentimental engravings and lots of copper and brass on the walls, and a coal fire in the
stone inglenook fireplace. Good bar food includes sandwiches (from £1.95; open ones
from £4.35), home-made soup (£2), garlic mushrooms (£3.60), ploughman's (£4.75),
giant yorkshire pudding with roast beef (£5.25), home-made steak and kidney pie or
lasagne (£5.50), home-made chicken curry (£5.95), battered cod (£6.50), steaks (from
£7.95), and good, often interesting daily specials such as queen scallops (£5.50),
spinach dumplings or wild boar and pheasant pie (£6.50), and cod and prawn
crumble; good breakfasts and friendly brisk service. Well kept Courage Directors,
John Smiths and Tetleys Bitter on handpump, and quite a few malt whiskies; shove-
ha'penny, dominoes, and piped music. There are seats on the front terrace or on the
spacious lawn behind, and an ancient church opposite.
*(Recommended by Paul Fairbrother, Helen Morris, Clifford and Joan Gough, John R Ringrose,
Janet and Peter Race, Mrs P Forrest, Geoffrey and Brenda Wilson, Comus Elliott, Janet Pickles,
Isabel and Robert Hatcher)*

*Free house ~ Licensee Duncan Finch ~ Real ale ~ Bar food (not Sun evening) ~
Restaurant ~ (01423) 322749 ~ Children in eating area of bar ~ Open 12-2.30(3 Sat),
5.30-11; 12-3, 7-10.30 Sun ~ Bedrooms: £32S/£45S*

APPLETREEWICK SE0560 Map 7

Craven Arms 🍷 🍺

Village signposted off B6160 Burnsall—Bolton Abbey

After enjoying one of the many walks around this creeper-covered pub, you can relax
with a pint and enjoy the splendid view from the picnic-sets in front of the building,
which looks south over the green Wharfedale valley to a pine-topped ridge; there are
more seats in the back garden. Inside, the small cosy rooms have roaring fires (one in
an ancient iron range), attractive settles and carved chairs among more usual seats,

beams covered with banknotes, harness, copper kettles and so forth, and a warm atmosphere. Bar food includes home-made soup (£2.10), sandwiches (from £2.20), basket meals (from £3), potted shrimps (£3.30), ploughman's (£4.20), cumberland sausage and onion sauce (£5.30), home-made steak and kidney pie (£5.20), grilled ham and eggs (£6.20), and steaks (from £8.70); the little no-smoking dining room is charming. Well kept Black Sheep Bitter and Special, Tetleys Bitter, and Theakstons Best and Old Peculier on handpump, decent, keenly priced wines, and several malt whiskies; darts, cribbage, and dominoes – no music. They have a self-catering cottage. *(Recommended by Richard and Valerie Wright, B and M Kendall, David Edwards, R V G Brown, K Hogarth, Paul R White, Daryl Gartan, Graeme Guilbert, John and Enid Morris)*

Free house ~ Licensee Linda Nicholson ~ Real ale ~ Bar food (not Tues evening) ~ Restaurant ~ (01756) 720270 ~ Children welcome until 10pm ~ Open 11.30-3, 6.30-11; 12-3, 7-10.30 Sun

ASENBY SE3975 Map 7
Crab & Lobster ♀ ⇔
Village signposted off A168 – handy for A1

There's a lot of character in the rambling, cosily cluttered L-shaped bar here, and an interesting jumble of seats from antique high-backed and other settles through settees and wing armchairs heaped with cushions to tall and rather theatrical corner seats and even a very superannuated dentist's chair; the tables are almost as much of a mix, and the walls and available surfaces are quite a jungle of bric-a-brac, with standard and table lamps and candles keeping even the lighting pleasantly informal. Bar food changes regularly and might include sandwiches, spaghetti with wild mushrooms, ham, and peccorino (£4.50; main course £8.25), salmon fishcakes with chive beurre blanc (£4.95; main course £8.95), Thai seafood salad (£5.50), crispy duck, chorizo, bacon, and pineapple salsa salad (£5.95), lobster and brie spring rolls (£6.95), oriental beef with sesame noodles (£10.50), spring lamb steak with bruschetta of aubergine, peppers and courgettes with mint pesto (£11.95), chargrilled rib steak with béarnaise sauce (£13.50), and puddings like chocolate and orange cake with vanilla sauce, lemon curd tart with citrus mascarpone or sticky toffee pudding with hot butterscotch sauce (£4.25). Bass, Black Sheep, Theakstons Best, and Timothy Taylor Landlord on handpump, and good wines by the glass, with interesting bottles; well reproduced piped music. There's a sizeable garden, and a mediterranean-style terrace in front of the pub for outside eating; wood-stove barbecues every summer Sunday lunchtime with entertainment, weather permitting. A permanent marquee is attached to the no-smoking restaurant. The bedrooms are in the surrounding country house which has three acres of mature gardens, tennis court and 180 metre golf hole with full practice facilities. *(Recommended by David and Ruth Hollands, Liz Bell, Allan Worsley, I R D Ross, Julie Sage, George Green, Nick and Alison Dowson, Susan and John Douglas, Andy & Ali, Walker and Debra Lapthorne, ALC, Simon G S Morton)*

Free house ~ Licensees David and Jackie Barnard ~ Real ale ~ Bar food ~ (01845) 577286 ~ Children welcome ~ Live music Sun lunch, jazz suppers twice a month ~ Open 11.30-3, 6-11; 12-11 Sun ~ Bedrooms: £55B/£75B

AYSGARTH SE0088 Map 10
George & Dragon
Off A684

With plenty to do nearby, including a walk to the Aysgarth Falls and others in the surrounding woodland, this attractive 17th-c coaching inn is a good place to head for. The small, cosy and attractive bar has a warm open fire with a dark wooden mantlepiece, built-in cushioned wooden wall seats and plush stools around a few pubby tables, tankards, jugs, and copper pots hanging from the thick beams, portraits of locals by the landlord on the panelled walls, and high bar stools by the decorative wooden bar; well kept Black Sheep Bitter and Theakstons Best on handpump. There's also a polished hotel lounge with antique china, and a grandfather clock; friendly obliging service. A lot of emphasis is placed on the food which can be eaten in the bar or two other attractive no-smoking dining areas: home-made soup (£2.95), chicken and duck liver pâté or stuffed mushrooms (£4.25), king prawns in garlic butter (£5.75), walnut and sweetcorn tagliatelle (£7.95), steak in ale pie or cod steak with dijon sauce (£8.50), roast lamb with minty gravy or apricot and almond chicken (£8.95), duckling with black cherry sauce (£11.25), oriental beef stir fry (£11.50), sizzling steaks, and children's dishes. Piped music, and a grey and white cat called Smokey. Outside on the gravelled beer garden are some picnic sets and tubs of pretty flowers. *(Recommended by Mrs Y M Lippett, Mrs J Powell, Maurice Thompson, B, M and P Kendall)*

Free house ~ Licensees Nigel and Joan Fawcett ~ Real ale ~ Bar food ~ (01969) 663358 ~ Children welcome ~ Open 10-3, 6-11; 10-11 Fri and Sat; 11-10.30 Sun ~ Bedrooms: £32B/£56B

BECK HOLE NZ8202 Map 10
Birch Hall
Off A169 SW of Whitby, from top of Sleights Moor

It's such fun to come across this delightfully unique and unchanging pub-cum-village shop. There are two rooms, with the shop selling postcards, sweeties and ice creams in between, and hatch service to both sides. Furnishings are simple – built-in cushioned wall seats and wooden tables and chairs on the floor (flagstones in one room, composition in the other), and well kept ales such as Black Sheep Bitter, Theakstons Black Bull, and guests from local breweries on handpump; several malt whiskies. Bar snacks like butties (£1.80), locally made pies (£1.20), and home-made scones and cakes including their lovely beer cake (from 70p); friendly, welcoming staff. Outside, an ancient oil painting hangs on the pub wall, there are benches out in front, and steep steps up to a charming little steeply terraced side garden with an aviary and a nice view. This is a lovely spot with marvellous surrounding walks – you can walk along the disused railway line from Goathland. *(Recommended by Andy and Jill Kassube, SLC, Peter Smith, Bruce Bird, PACW, Martin and Jane Wright, Alison Keys, Nick and Alison Dowson, JP, PP, John Brightley, the Didler)*

Free house ~ Licensee Colin Jackson ~ Real ale ~ Bar food (available during all opening hours) ~ (01947) 896245 ~ Children in small family room ~ Open 11-11; 12-10.30 Sun; 11-3, 7.30-11 in winter, 12-3, 7.30-10.30 winter Sun; closed winter Mon evenings

BEVERLEY TA0340 Map 8
White Horse £
Hengate, close to the imposing Church of St Mary's; runs off North Bar

For those who prefer comfortable modern pubs, this determinedly traditional local (known as 'Nellies') may be a little too spartan – anyone else will quickly feel at home. The basic but very atmospheric little rooms are huddled together around the central bar, with brown leatherette seats (high-backed settles in one little snug) and basic wooden chairs and benches on bare floorboards, antique cartoons and sentimental engravings on the nicotine-stained walls, a gaslit pulley-controlled chandelier, a deeply reverberating chiming clock, and open fires – one with an attractively tiled old fireplace. Well kept and very cheap Sam Smiths OBB on handpump. Cheap, simple food includes sandwiches (from £1.20; toasties £3.25), home-made yorkshire pudding and gravy (£2), home-made steak pie, gammon and egg, a roast of the day or cheese and broccoli bake (all £3.95), daily specials such as home-made chilli (£3.50) or liver, bacon and onions (£3.95), and puddings such as home-made fruit crumble or chocolate sponge (£1.75); Sunday roast (£3.95). A separate games room has pinball, fruit machine, juke box, and two pool tables – these and the no-smoking room behind the bar are the only modern touches *(Recommended by David Carr, Pete Baker, David and Ruth Hollands, Mike and Mary Carter, Paul and Pam Penrose, JP, PP, the Didler)*

Sam Smiths ~ Manager John Etherington ~ Real ale ~ Bar food (lunchtime only) ~ (01482) 861973 ~ Children welcome away from bar until 8pm ~ Live folk Mon, jazz Weds, poetry 1st Thurs of month, free-for-all folk 1st Sun lunchtime of month ~ Open 11-11; 12-10.30 Sun

BLAKEY RIDGE SE6799 Map 10
Lion 🍺 🛏

From A171 Guisborough—Whitby follow Castleton, Hutton le Hole signposts; from A170 Kirkby Moorside—Pickering follow Keldholm, Hutton le Hole, Castleton signposts; OS Sheet 100 map reference 679996

This isolated 16th-c inn is said to be the fourth highest in England (1325 ft up) and the views are stunning – so it's not surprising that there's a good mix of customers from walkers and campers to motorists. The cosy and characterful beamed and rambling bars have a bustling, friendly atmosphere, warm open fires, a few big high-backed rustic settles around cast-iron-framed tables, lots of small dining chairs on the turkey carpet, a nice leather settee, and stripped stone walls hung with some old engravings and photographs of the pub under snow (it can easily get cut off in winter). Reliably good bar food includes lunchtime sandwiches (£2.45) and ploughman's (£4.45), as well as soup or giant yorkshire pudding and gravy (£1.95), smoked salmon and scrambled egg (£3.95), home-cooked ham and egg, pure beef burgers, home-made steak and mushroom pie, home-made vegetable chilli, mushroom balti, and beef curry (all £5.95), deep-fried king prawns (£6.75), home-made game pie or pork fillet with apple and white wine sauce (£6.95), sirloin steak (£8.95), puddings like chocolate sponge, sticky toffee pudding or apple pie (£2.45), and children's menu (£3.25). One of the restaurants is no smoking. Well kept Morlands Old Speckled Hen, John Smiths, Tetleys Bitter, and Theakstons Best, Old Peculier, Black Bull and XB on handpump; dominoes, fruit machine and piped music. *(Recommended by Piotr Chodzko-Zajko, Bernard Stradling, Martin and Jane Wright, M Borthwick, Bronwen and Steve Wrigley, Andy and Jill Kassube)*

Free house ~ Licensee Barry Crossland ~ Real ale ~ Bar food (11.30(10.30 Fri/Sat)-10) ~ Restaurant ~ (01751) 417320 ~ Children welcome ~ Open 10.30-11; 12-10.30 Sun ~ Bedrooms: £17(£24.50B)/£49(£57B)

BOROUGHBRIDGE SE3967 Map 7
Black Bull 🛏

St James Square (B6265, just off A1(M)

This lovely 13th-c inn is a good all-rounder. Readers have very much enjoyed staying here, supping the well kept beers, and eating the good, interesting food – all in a friendly atmosphere. The main bar area, with a big stone fireplace and brown leather seats, is served through an old-fashioned hatch, and there's a cosy and attractive snug with traditional wall settles. The well presented food is totally home-made (bread rolls, pasta, sorbets, ice creams) and is served in the bar and extended dining room: soup (£2.25), lunchtime sandwiches (from £2.75; not Sunday; ciabatta rolls from £4.95), crab and salmon fishcakes in lemon butter sauce (£3.95), omelettes (from £3.95), home-made pork and sage sausages with mustard spiced gravy (£4.75), stir-fried vegetables and noodles with a Thai red curry peanut sauce in a crisp pastry basket (£5.25), yorkshire pudding filled with lamb casserole (£5.75), a pie of the day (£5.95), chargrilled steaks (from £11.95), fresh fish and daily specials listed on boards, and puddings like warm chocolate pecan tart with a whisky fudge sauce or tangy lemon cheesecake with a thick raspberry compôte (from £2.95). Well kept Black Sheep Bitter, John Smiths, and a guest beer on handpump, enjoyable wines (with 10 by the glass), proper coffee – and they do afternoon teas (not on Sunday). Service is friendly and attentive; the fat ginger cat is called Sprocket. Cribbage, dominoes, shove-ha'penny, chess and Captain's Lady; classical piped music in the restaurant. The comfortable bedrooms are in a more modern wing; good breakfasts. *(Recommended by Michael and Hazel Duncombe, Alyson and Andrew Jackson, Roger Byrne, Phil Revell, Marlene and Jim Godfrey, Julie Peters, Malcolm Taylor, Mr and Mrs P Eastwood, Dorothee and Dennis Glover, Neil Ben, P R Morley, John Knighton, Ian Phillips, Richard and Robyn Wain, Stan and Hazel Allen, the Didler)*

Free house ~ Licensee Margaret Chrystal ~ Real ale ~ Bar food (12-2, 7-9 Mon, 12-9 Tues-Sun; not 1 Jan) ~ Restaurant ~ (01423) 322413 ~ Children in eating area of bar until 9pm ~ Open 11-11; 12-10.30 Sun ~ Bedrooms: £37B/£49B

BRADFIELD SK2392 Map 7
Strines Inn

Strines signposted from A616 at head of Underbank Reservoir, W of Stocksbridge; or on A57
heading E of junction with A6013 (Ladybower Reservoir) take first left turn (signposted with
Bradfield) then bear left

Set on the edge of the High Peak National Park, this isolated old place used to be a
manorial farm and is partly 13th c. The main bar has black beams liberally decked
with copper kettles and so forth, quite a menagerie of stuffed animals, homely red-
plush-cushioned traditional wooden wall benches and small chairs, a coal fire in the
rather grand stone fireplace, and a warmly welcoming and relaxed atmosphere;
there's a good mixture of customers. A room off on the right has another coal fire,
hunting photographs and prints, and lots of brass and china, and on the left, a
similarly furnished room is no smoking. Tasty bar food includes home-made soup
(£2.10), sandwiches (from £1.60; toasties from £1.80; hot pork £2.25), filled baked
potatoes (from £3), garlic mushrooms (£3.95), good chilli in a giant yorkshire
pudding (£4.95), ploughman's (£4.95), liver and onions (£5.95), spicy bean casserole
or Thai mushroom noodles (£5.50), steaks (from £8.25), daily specials such as steak
in ale pie (£5.95) or halibut with a parsley sauce (£6.95), and puddings such as hot
pancakes with ice cream or apple crumble (from £2); Sunday roast lunch (£5.95;
children £3). Well kept Mansfield Old Baily and Ridings Bitter, Marstons Pedigree,
and Morlands Old Speckled Hen on handpump, several malt whiskies, and good
espresso or cappuccino coffee; good service, darts, dominoes, cribbage, and piped
radio. The children's playground is safely fenced in (and far enough away from the
pub not to be too noisy), and they have a permanent bouncy castle. From the picnic
sets are fine views, and there are some rescued animals – goats, geese, hens, sheep, and
several free-roaming peacocks; well behaved dogs welcome. The bedrooms have four-
poster beds and two of the ensuite rooms have open log fires; breakfast can be served
in your room. *(Recommended by D Alexander, Michael Butler, Anne and David Robinson, JP,
PP, M Borthwick, RWD, Dave Braisted, Andy and Jill Kassube)*

*Free house ~ Licensee Jeremy Stanish ~ Real ale ~ Bar food (all day Mar-Oct) ~ (0114)
285 1247 ~ Well behaved children welcome until 9pm ~ Open 10.30-11; 12-10.30
Sun; 10.30-3, 6-11 weekdays in winter ~ Bedrooms: £35B/£59.50B*

BREARTON SE3261 Map 7
Malt Shovel 🍴 ♈ 🍺

Village signposted off A61 N of Harrogate

Run by genuinely friendly and helpful licensees, this 16th-c village pub places obvious
emphasis on the enjoyable, good value food – though they also serve well kept Black
Sheep Bitter, Daleside Nightjar, Theakstons Bitter and two guests from small local
breweries such as Durham Magus, Rooster's Special, and Rudgate Battleaxe on
handpump. Several heavily-beamed rooms radiate from the attractive linenfold oak
bar counter with plush-cushioned seats and a mix of tables, an ancient oak partition
wall, tankards and horsebrasses, both real and gas fires, and paintings by local artists
(for sale) and lively hunting prints on the walls. From the menu, the good food might
include sandwiches (from £2.50), cajun bean casserole (£4.95), nut roast with pesto
sauce or ham and asparagus tart (£5.25), rabbit and mushroom pie in red wine and
port or fresh haddock in beer batter (£5.95), liver, bacon and black pudding with red
wine gravy (£6.20), warm chicken salad with a lemon and caper dressing or seafood
gratin (£6.95), chargrilled rib-eye steak with a whisky and green peppercorn sauce
(£8.95), and puddings such as treacle tart, apple and blackberry crumble or fresh lime
tart (£2.50); over 30 malt whiskies, a small but interesting and reasonably priced wine
list (they will serve any wine by the glass), and farm cider; they serve their house
coffee (and a guest coffee) in cafetières. Darts, shove-ha'penny, cribbage, and
dominoes. You can eat outside on the small terrace on all but the coldest days as
they have special heaters. There are more tables on the grass. *(Recommended by Liz Bell,
R F and M K Bishop, Marlene and Jim Godfrey, Vann and Terry Prime, Andrew Low, Nick
Lawless, Janet Lewis, Paul R White, Prof and Mrs S Barnett, Roger Byrne, Anthony Barnes,
Geoffrey and Brenda Wilson, David and Helen Wilkins, John and Enid Morris)*

Free house ~ Licensee Leslie Mitchell ~ Real ale ~ Bar food (not Sun evening, not Mon)
~ (01423) 862929 ~ Children welcome ~ Open 12-3, 6.45(6.30 Sat)-11; 12-3, 7-10.30
Sun; closed Mon

BUCKDEN SD9477 Map 7
Buck ♀

B6160

It makes sense for this attractive creeper-covered stone pub to be open to non
residents for breakfast, morning coffee, bar lunches, afternoon teas and evening
meals, as it is close to so many fine walks, castles, abbeys, and bustling market towns.
The modernised and extended open-plan bar has upholstered built-in wall banquettes
and square stools around shiny dark brown tables on its carpet – though there are still
flagstones in the snug original area by the serving counter – local pictures, hunting
prints, willow-pattern plates on a delft shelf, and the mounted head of a roebuck on
bare stone above the log fire. Helpful uniformed staff quickly serve the popular bar
food which includes home-made soup (£3.25), black pudding parfait (£4.25), home-
made salmon fishcake (£4.50), terrine of pressed bass (£5.25), confit of duck with
oriental vegetables (£9.65), hock of Dales lamb (£8.50), roasted escalope of salmon
with a sorrel and vermouth veloute or sautéed pork medallions in a honey and mead
sauce (£8.85), smoked chicken on slow-roasted mediterranean vegetables with a spicy
tomato sauce (£9.25), goujons of monkfish in tempura batter with rice noodles and
Thai dressing (£12.85), and puddings such as sticky date pudding with hot toffee and
ginger sauce or home-made chocolate truffle cheesecake; the dining area and
restaurant are no-smoking. Well kept John Smiths Magnet, and Theakstons Best, Old
Peculier, Black Bull and XB on handpump, a fair choice of malt whiskies, and decent
wines; dominoes, piped music and fruit machine. Seats on the terrace enjoy good
surrounding moorland views. *(Recommended by Eddie Edwards, L Walker, Greta and
Christopher Wells, David Edwards, Barry and Anne, R Inman)*

Free house ~ Licensee Nigel Hayton ~ Real ale ~ Bar food (12-5, 6.30-9 Sun) ~
Restaurant ~ (01756) 760228 ~ Children welcome away from bar ~ Open 11-11; 12-
10.30 Sun ~ Bedrooms: £36B/£72B

BURNSALL SE0361 Map 7
Red Lion 🍽 ♀ 🛏

B6160 S of Grassington, on Ilkley road; OS Sheet 98, map reference 033613

The bustling main bar in this popular 16th-c former ferryman's inn has been
refurbished this year to make it much lighter and they've panelled the back of the bar
itself to match the attractively panelled walls (which are hung with old photographs
of local fell races); sturdy wall seats, windsor armchairs, oak benches, and rugs on the
newly stripped floor, and steps up past a solid-fuel stove to a no-smoking back area.
The carpeted, no-smoking front lounge bar, served from the same copper-topped
counter through an old-fashioned small-paned glass partition, has a log fire;
dominoes. Praise for their enjoyable and imaginative food has earned them a well
deserved Food Award this year. At lunchtime, there might be sandwiches (from
£3.50; open sandwiches £5.75), parfait of duck and chicken liver pâté (£4), good
Cumbrian air-dried ham cured in molasses and served with their own chutney
(£4.25), ploughman's with home-made chutneys and relishes or ratatouille and blue
wensleydale cheese (£6.95), steak and kidney in ale pie (£7.50), lamb's liver and
bacon with bubble and squeak and onion gravy (£7.75), smoked haddock topped
with welsh rarebit and served on a salad of beef tomatoes and basil (£8.95), and
braised shoulder of Wharfedale lamb stuffed with garlic, rosemary, wild mushrooms
and lemon (£9.50), with evening dishes such as crab and coriander or salmon and dill
fishcakes with a compôte of plum tomatoes and red peppers (£4.75), confit of duck
with red cabbage and black pudding on a potato galette (£4.95), fresh chargrilled
tuna steak salad (£8.95), escalopes of Old Spot pork with a sage and onion polenta
and a light sweet and sour sauce (£9.95), and breast of duckling with red onion
marmalade and apple sauce (£11.50), and puddings like lovely bananas with a rum

and banana ice cream, chocolate sponge with a chocolate and orange sauce and lemon tart. Well kept Morlands Old Speckled Hen, and Theakstons Best, Black Bull, and Old Peculier on handpump, several malt whiskies, and a very good wine list with around 14 by the glass kept fresh on a cruover machine. The back terrace is lit by old gas lamps, and as well as fine views from here, you can also see the River Wharfe from more seats on the front cobbles and from most of the bedrooms (most of which now have large Victorian beds). Lots of fine surrounding walks, and fishing permits for 7 miles of river. *(Recommended by Liz Bell, Stephen and Tracey Groves, Prof and Mrs S Barnett, M A Buchanan, Neil Townend, WAH, R Inman, D Goodger, Walter and Susan Rinaldi-Butcher, Hugh Roberts, Roger and Anne King, Mr and Mrs V G Ogilvie, Richard and Valerie Wright, Gwen and Peter Andrews, J M Law, Alan J Morton)*

Free house ~ Licensee Elizabeth Grayshon ~ Real ale ~ Bar food (12-2.30, 6-9.30) ~ Restaurant ~ (01756) 720204 ~ Children welcome ~ Open 11.30-11.30; 12-10.30 Sun ~ Bedrooms: £45B/£90B

BYLAND ABBEY SE5579 Map 7
Abbey Inn 🍴

The Abbey has a brown tourist-attraction signpost off the A170 Thirsk—Helmsley

It's quite special to be able to sit in the two no-smoking front rooms here looking out at the very large stone end wall of the abbey ruins opposite – which are elegant and floodlit at night. The rambling, characterful rooms have big fireplaces, oak and stripped deal tables, settees, carved oak seats, and Jacobean-style dining chairs on the polished boards and flagstones, various stuffed birds, cooking implements, little etchings, willow-pattern plates and china cabinets, and some discreet stripping back of plaster to show the ex-abbey masonry; the big back room has lots of rustic bygones; piped music. Good lunchtime bar food changes daily but might include home-made soup (£2.50), sandwiches (from £3.25; hot roast beef baguette £5.50), pear, stilton and bacon salad (£6), salmon and prawn tart (£7.25), breast of chicken with apricot sauce or lamb shank with a mint and caper glaze (£8), and grilled tuna with tomato salsa (£9); in the evening (the menu changes monthly) there's a terrine of salmon, sole and scampi (£5.25), cold smoked venison with caramelised onions and sweet peppers (£6), mediterranean vegetables and nut crumble on bubble and squeak (£8), braised saddle of rabbit cooked in apples and calvados (£9.75), half roast duckling with a lime and marmalade sauce (£10.75), and sirloin steak with a diane sauce (£12). Puddings like chocolate bread and butter pudding, Drambuie parfait or a tangy lemon mousse (£3.25); 'fish and fizz' night is popular and Sunday lunch is served until 4pm. Well kept Black Sheep Bitter and Tetleys on handpump, and an interesting wine list with 7 by the glass. The grey tabby cat is called Milly. There's plenty of room outside in the garden and on the terrace. *(Recommended by R Inman, Geoff and Angela Jaques, Mr and Mrs K Hosen, Mr and Mrs G Smallwood, Walter and Susan Rinaldi-Butcher, SS, Tom Johnson, Anthony Barnes, Geoffrey and Brenda Wilson, R E and F C Pick)*

Free house ~ Licensees Jane and Martin Nordli ~ Real ale ~ Bar food ~ (01347) 868204 ~ Children welcome ~ Open 11-3, 6.30-11.30; 12-4 Sun; closed Sun evening and Mon lunch except bank holidays

CARLTON SE0684 Map 10
Foresters Arms 🍴 ♀ 🛏

Off A684 W of Leyburn, just past Wensley; or take Coverdale hill road from Kettlewell, off B6160

Tucked away in Coverdale, this charming inn cleverly manages to offer really delicious, imaginative food while retaining the atmosphere of a village local – and regulars are most welcome to drop in for just a drink. There are open log fires, low beamed ceilings, a good, relaxed feel, and well kept Black Sheep Bitter, Ruddles County, John Smiths, and Theakstons Best on handpump. As well as lots of fish dishes such as smoked fish chowder (£3.95), crab spring rolls with oyster sauce (£5.95), king prawn and smoked bacon salad (£7.50), braised conger eel with herb crust and red wine (£9.50), salmon fillet on potato rosti with asparagus and sun-dried tomato vinaigrette (£10.50), fillet of haddock with parma ham and chive butter sauce (£11.75), and ragoût of monkfish and mussels with coriander (£14.50), there might be light lunch dishes like soup (£3.25), baked sweet onion and coverdale cheese tart (£5.50), grilled goat's cheese with a sun-dried tomato dressing (£5.95), sautéed breast of chicken with honey and dijon mustard (£7.50), ham and eggs (£7.95), and woodland mushroom salad or boar's liver and bacon with onions (£8.95), with evening dishes such as chargrilled pigeon with smoked bacon and roast garlic vinaigrette (£4.25), confit of duckling on orange salad with truffle dressing (£5.50), and baked breast of chicken with wild mushroom and chicken boudin (£11.95). Puddings include hot baked chocolate tart with armagnac cream or sticky toffee pudding (from £3.95). A good restauranty wine list, 46 malt whiskies, freshly squeezed orange, and fruit coulis with sparkling waters. The restaurant is partly no smoking. Darts, dominoes, and piped music. There are some picnic-sets among tubs of flowers. *(Recommended by Bob and Maggie Atherton, Susan and Philip Philcox, Philip Cooper, David Hawkes, Gwen and Peter Andrews, G F Tomlinson, Alan J Morton, K F Mould, M Borthwick, Mrs J Powell, Paul R White)*

Free house ~ Licensee B Higginbotham ~ Real ale ~ Bar food (not Mon, not Tues lunchtime) ~ Restaurant ~ (01969) 640272 ~ Well behaved children in eating area of bar and in restaurant ~ Open 12-3, 6.30-11; 12-3, 7-10.30 Sun; closed all Mon and Tues lunchtime ~ Bedrooms: £40S/£70S

CARTHORPE SE3184 Map 10
Fox & Hounds 🍴 ♀

Village signposted from A1 N of Ripon, via B6285

To be sure of a table in this neatly kept and friendly extended dining pub, it's best to book (particularly at weekends) as customers travel some miles to come here. Served by well trained staff, the very good food might include sandwiches, home-made soup (£2.55), bubble and squeak with a fried egg (£3.95), smoked salmon pâté (£4.45), chicken breast filled with coverdale cheese in a creamy sauce or prawn curry (£8.95), halibut steak with lobster and prawn sauce (£10.95), and half roast duckling with orange sauce, parsley and thyme stuffing and apple sauce (£12.95), with daily specials such as fried brie with cranberry sauce (£3.95), queen scallop and prawn mornay (£4.95), steak and kidney pie (£7.95), lamb's liver with smoked bacon and parsley mash (£8.95), whole dressed large Whitby crab (£9.95), and bass with a soft parsley crust (£11.95); home-made puddings like white chocolate and Irish cream cheesecake with a dark chocolate ice cream, passion fruit tart with their own passion fruit ice cream and fruit coulis or home-made ice creams such as lemon curd or honey and orange (£3.25). 3-course Sunday lunch (£11.95; children £6.95), and 3-course set dinners (£11.95). There is some theatrical memorabilia in the corridors, and the cosy L-shaped bar has quite a few mistily evocative Victorian photographs of Whitby, a couple of nice seats by the larger of its two log fires, plush button-back built-in wall banquettes and chairs, plates on stripped beams, and some limed panelling; piped light classical music. An attractive high-raftered no-smoking restaurant leads off with lots of neatly black-painted farm and smithy tools. Well kept John Smiths Bitter on handpump, and from their extensive list they will open any wine for you just to have a glass. *(Recommended by Clifford and Joan Gough, B H Turner, M J Brooks, M Doswell, R F Grieve, T R Forrest, K F Mould)*

Free house ~ Licensees Howard and Helen Fitzgerald ~ Real ale ~ Bar food (not Mon) ~ Restaurant ~ (01845) 567433 ~ Children welcome ~ Open 12-2.30, 7-11(10.30 Sun); closed Mon; 1st full week of New Year

COXWOLD SE5377 Map 7
Fauconberg Arms ★ ♀

This inn is named after Lord Fauconberg, who married Oliver Cromwell's daughter Mary, and it is set in a pretty village with attractive tubs of flowers on the cobbled verges of the broad street. There's a civilised atmosphere and the two cosy knocked-together rooms of the lounge bar have carefully chosen furniture – most of it is either Mouseman or the work some of the other local craftsmen – or cushioned antique oak settles and windsor high-backed chairs and oak tables; there's a marvellous winter log fire in an unusual arched stone fireplace, and gleaming brass. For those wanting an informal drink and chat, there's also an old-fashioned back locals' bar. Good bar food cooked by Mrs Jaques includes home-made soup (£2.45), sandwiches (from £3.15), filled baked potatoes (£3.45), duck, chicken and ham terrine with orange cumberland sauce and apple salad (£3.75), roast beef and yorkshire pudding (£6.45), home-made chicken curry using authentic Indian spices (£6.75), spinach and mushroom pancakes with a wensleydale cheese and cream sauce (£7.65), fresh salmon, cod and smoked salmon mornay on a julienne of leeks with a watercress mash (£7.75), Moroccan lamb (£7.95), sirloin steak (£9.95), and puddings such as apricot crème brûlée with lemon scented crème fraîche or home-made butterscotch pudding with a fudge sauce (£3.45); children's menu (from £2.50). They run a loyalty card system. Well kept Morlands Old Speckled Hen, John Smiths, Tetleys, and Theakstons Best and Black Bull on handpump and an extensive wine list. Darts, dominoes, cribbage, fruit machine, and piped music. *(Recommended by Nick and Alison Dowson, Peter and Giff Bennett, K F Mould, Richard Cole, David and Helen Wilkins, John Robertson, Mr and Mrs Staples)*

Free house ~ Licensees Robin and Nicky Jaques ~ Real ale ~ Bar food ~ Restaurant ~ (01347) 868214 ~ Children welcome ~ Open 11-2.30, 6.30(6 Sat)-11; 12-3, 7-11 Sun ~ Bedrooms: £30B/£55B

CRACOE SD9760 Map 7
Devonshire Arms

B6265 Skipton—Grassington

Well placed for visitors going up the dales from Skipton, this is an attractive and enjoyable pub. The bar has low shiny black beams supporting creaky white planks, little stable-type partitions to divide the solidly comfortable furnishings into cosier areas, polished flooring tiles with rugs here and there, and gleaming copper pans round the stone fireplace. Above the dark panelled dado are old prints, engravings and photographs, with a big circular large-scale Ordnance Survey map showing the inn as its centre. Good bar food, generously served, includes home-made soup (£2.05), sandwiches (from £2.95; filled french sticks £4.50), mushroom pot (£3.95), popular fishcake with home-made tartare sauce (£4.25), garlic prawns (£5.35), poached egg, bacon and black pudding salad (£5.95), cumberland sausage with bubble and squeak (£6.95), chicken stuffed with apricots in a creamy sauce (£7.25), lamb slowly roasted and served with minted gravy or pork fillet and black pudding topped with creamy mustard sauce (£7.95), rib-eye steak crusted with pepper and chilli with a whisky sauce (£10.95), and puddings; children's helpings (£3.10). Well kept Jennings Bitter, Cumberland, Cockerhoop and Snecklifter, and a guest such as Theakstons on handpump, and several malt whiskies; darts, dominoes, cribbage, and piped music. There are picnic-sets on a terrace flanked by well kept herbaceous borders, with more seating on the lawn; Monty the dog still watches customers coming and going from his position on the roof. *(Recommended by Eddie Edwards, Mr and Mrs Garrett, Ann and Rob Westbrook, Derek and Sylvia Stephenson, Lyn and Geoff Hallchurch, WAH, RJH, K and F Giles, M A Buchanan, Nick Lawless, Andy and Jill Kassube)*

Jennings ~ Manager Christopher Gregson ~ Real ale ~ Bar food (all day Sun) ~ Restaurant ~ (01756) 730237 ~ Children in eating area of bar ~ Open 11.30-11; 12-10.30 Sun ~ Bedrooms: £25.50B/£39.50B

CRAY SD9379 Map 7
White Lion 🍺

B6160, Upper Wharfedale N of Kettlewell

Surrounded by some superb countryside and 1,100 ft up by Buckden Pike, this former drovers' hostelry is the highest pub in Wharfedale; in good weather, you can sit at picnic-sets above the very quiet steep lane or on the great flat limestone slabs in the shallow stream which tumbles down opposite. Inside, the simply furnished bar has a traditional atmosphere, seats around tables on the flagstone floor, shelves of china, iron tools and so forth, a high dark beam-and-plank ceiling, and a warming open fire;

there's also a no-smoking dining room. Bar food includes sandwiches, home-made soup (£2.50), garlic mushrooms (£2.95), home-made chicken liver pâté (£3.10), vegetable lasagne (£6.25), home-made steak and mushroom pie (£7.25), poached local trout with almond butter (£7.95), chicken breast in an orange and tarragon sauce (£8.50), venison casserole (£9.50), and steaks (from £10.95); if you eat very early evening in summer, you get a discount. Well kept Black Sheep, Moorhouses Pendle Witches Brew, Roosters, and John Smiths on handpump; dominoes and ring the bull. *(Recommended by Tracey Hamond, Eddie Edwards, Stephen and Tracey Groves, Lynn Sharpless, Bob Eardley, B and M Kendall)*

Free house ~ Licensees Frank and Barbara Hardy ~ Real ale ~ Bar food ~ (01756) 760262 ~ Children welcome away from main bar area ~ Open 11-11; 12-10.30 Sun ~ Bedrooms: £27.50(£35S)/£40(£50S)

CROPTON SE7588 Map 10
New Inn 🍺 🛏

Village signposted off A170 W of Pickering

Run by friendly, enthusiastic owners, this popular pub brews its own real ales (you can tour the brewery if you ask) and the Cropton Brewery shop sells take-home beers. Well kept on handpump, there's Two Pints, Backwoods, Honey Gold, King Billy, Monkmans Slaughter, Uncle Sams and Scoresby Stout, with a guest like Tetleys; farm cider. The airy lounge has Victorian church panels, terracotta and dark blue plush seats, lots of brass, and a small open fire, and a local artist has designed historical posters all around the no-smoking downstairs conservatory. Bar food includes filled french bread (from £3.50), steak and mushroom in stout pie (£5.95), fish dishes such as tuna provençale or poached salmon (from £6.95), their much loved lamb joint with mint gravy (£7.95 or £9.95), and steaks (from £8.95). The elegant no-smoking restaurant is furnished with genuine Victorian and early Edwardian furniture. Darts, pool, dominoes, fruit machine, and piped music. There's a neat terrace, and a garden with a pond. Comfortable, good value bedrooms – readers have enjoyed staying here. *(Recommended by Bruce Bird, John and Esther Sprinkle, Dr Paul Khan, Walter and Susan Rinaldi-Butcher, Peter and Pat Frogley, Derek and Sylvia Stephenson, SLC, Gwyneth and Salvo Spandaro-Dutturi, Mr and Mrs P Spencer, Martin and Jane Wright, Mrs K L Heath, Richard Lewis, John and Joan Wyatt)*

Own brew ~ Licensee Sandra Lee ~ Real ale ~ Bar food ~ Restaurant ~ (01751) 417330 ~ Children in conservatory and restaurant ~ Open 11-11; 12-3, 6.30-10.30 Sun; maybe 11-3, 6.30-11 midweek in winter ~ Bedrooms: £35B/£58B

DACRE BANKS SE1962 Map 7
Royal Oak

In a village just above the River Nidd, this friendly and peaceful 18th-c stone pub has lovely views from the seats on the terrace and from the big garden; boules. Inside, it's open-plan and the two comfortable lounge areas have interesting old photographs and poems with a drinking theme on the walls, an open fire in the front part, and well kept Black Sheep Bitter, Daleside Old Legover, Tetleys, and Timothy Taylor Landlord on handpump. Under the new licensee, bar food now includes snacks such as sandwiches, filled baked potatoes or ploughman's, plus home-made soup (£2.50), home-made chicken liver pâté (£2.95), mussels in white wine and cream (£3.95), home-made steak and kidney or rabbit, ham and mushroom pies (£5.95), chicken balti or local trout (£6.95), roast rack of lamb (£8.50), and puddings; the restaurant is no smoking. Darts, pool, cribbage, dominoes, and piped music. *(Recommended by Derek Stafford, Paul R White, Richard Lewis, William Foster, Norman Stansfield, Prof and Mrs S Barnett, B and M Kendall)*

Free house ~ Licensee Stephen Cock ~ Real ale ~ Bar food ~ Restaurant ~ (01423) 780200 ~ Children in eating area of bar and restaurant ~ Open 11.30-3, 5-11; 11.30-3, 7-10.30 Sun ~ Bedrooms: £25B/£50B

EAST WITTON SE1586 Map 10

Blue Lion 🍴 🛏

A6108 Leyburn—Ripon

This stylish place is particularly enjoyable and run by welcoming licensees who seem to cope with the crowds – a good mix of locals and visitors – with courteous efficiency. There is still some pubby atmosphere, and it's a super place to stay overnight, but most people do come to it for a civilised meal, and it does pay to get there early as you can't book a table in the busy bar (though you can, of course, in the restaurant). The big squarish bar has high-backed antique settles and old windsor chairs and round tables on the turkey rugs and flagstones, ham-hooks in the high ceiling decorated with dried wheat, teazles and so forth, a delft shelf filled with appropriate bric-a-brac, several prints, sporting caricatures and other pictures on the walls, a log fire, and daily papers; the friendly labradors are called Ben and Archie. Imaginative and very popular, the sandwiches, home-made soup (£2.95), crab Thai fishcake with chilli jam (£3.25), escalope of chicken chargrilled with mediterranean vegetables and pesto (£4), smoked wild boar sausage with bubble and squeak and a red wine sauce (£5), roast king scallops with a lemon risotto and gruyère cheese (£6.50), tagliatelle with leeks and oyster mushrooms toasted with parmesan (£6.75), steamed steak and kidney suet pudding (£9.55), roast fillet of cod with spring onion mash and a chive and tomato butter sauce (£10.60), peppered duck breast with a port and blackberry sauce (£11.25), pork fillet roasted with walnuts and toasted with Swiss cheese and sage (£11.50), chargrilled sirloin of beef with a chasseur sauce and fondant potato (£11.95), chargrilled roe deer cutlet with a juniper and red wine sauce and dauphinoise potatoes (£13.75), and puddings such as dark chocolate pudding with a white chocolate centre, crisp prune tart with Guinness ice cream and caramel sauce or sultana and rum crème caramel with green apple sorbet (from £3.25); good breakfasts; no snacks on Sunday lunchtime. It's always heartening to find a pub offering children's helpings rather than sausage and chips. Well kept Black Sheep Bitter and Theakstons Best on handpump, and decent wines with quite a few by the glass. Picnic sets on the gravel outside look beyond the stone houses on the far side of the village green to Witton Fell, and there's a big pretty back garden. *(Recommended by G F Tomlinson, Vann and Terry Prime, Keith and Jill Wright, Mike and Maggie Betton, John Read, Jane Taylor, David Dutton, B, M and P Kendall, RB, Walter and Susan Rinaldi-Butcher, JP, PP, Matthew Wright, CRJH)*

Free house ~ Licensee Paul Klein ~ Real ale ~ Bar food ~ Restaurant ~ (01969) 624273 ~ Children in eating area of bar and restaurant ~ Open 11-11; 12-10.30 Sun ~ Bedrooms: £52.50B/£75B

EGTON BRIDGE NZ8005 Map 10

Horse Shoe 🛏

Village signposted from A171 W of Whitby; via Grosmont from A169 S of Whitby

There are plenty of good walks surrounding this pleasant inn and comfortable seats on a quiet terrace and lawn beside a little stream with ducks; the attractive gardens have pretty roses, mature redwoods, geese and bantams, and fishing is available on a daily ticket from Egton Estates. Inside, the bar has been redecorated this year and has old oak tables, high-backed built-in winged settles, wall seats and spindleback chairs, a big stuffed trout (caught near here in 1913), pictures on the walls, and a warm log fire. Generous helpings of bar food include lunchtime sandwiches, and dishes such as salmon and dill tart (£3.80), warm salad of duck breast (£4.50), salmon and broccoli fishcakes (£7.50), and corn fed chicken with a wild mushroom sauce (£8.40). Well kept John Smiths and Theakstons Best, and guests from local breweries like Black Dog and Durham on handpump, and malt whiskies; darts, dominoes, and piped music. The bedrooms have been redecorated. A different way to reach this beautifully placed pub is to park by the Roman Catholic church, walk through the village and cross the River Esk by stepping stones. Not to be confused with a similarly named pub up at Egton. *(Recommended by MLR, David Heath, RWD, Anthony Barnes, Ian Phillips, Comus Elliott, K F Mould, John Robertson, Phil and Heidi Cook)*

Free house ~ Licensees Tim and Suzanne Boulton ~ Real ale ~ Bar food ~ Restaurant ~ (01947) 895245 ~ Children in back bar ~ Open 11.30-4(3 in winter), 6-11; 12-4(3 in winter), 7-10.30 Sun; closed 25 Dec ~ Bedrooms: £20(£26B)/£38(£46B)

ELSLACK SD9249 Map 7
Tempest Arms
Just off A56 Earby—Skipton; visible from main road, and warning signs ¼ mile before

A series of quietly decorated areas in this 18th-c stone pub have small chintz armchairs, chintzy cushions on the comfortable built-in wall seats, brocaded stools, and lots of tables, quite a bit of stripped stonework, some decorated plates and brassware, and a log fire in the dividing fireplace. A fair choice of bar food (with prices unchanged since last year) includes home-made soup (£1.95), sandwiches (from £2.95), mushroom and stilton casserole (£3.35), chicken liver or cream cheese and herb pâté with home-made orange and onion chutney (£3.50), black pudding on an apple and parsnip purée mash with mild mustard sauce (£4.25), battered fresh haddock (£5.95), bangers and mash (£6.50), marinated shoulder of lamb with a mint and redcurrant gravy (£7.25), chicken dijon (£7.85), Aberdeen Angus sirloin steak (£9.25), and confit of duck with home-made stuffing (£9.95). Well kept Jennings Bitter, Cumberland, Snecklifter and guest beers on handpump, and quite a few malt whiskies and wines by the glass. Darts, dominoes, and quiz nights. Tables outside are largely screened from the road by a raised bank. *(Recommended by Richard Butcliffe, Prof and Mrs S Barnett, Ed Miller, Paul R White, WAH, M A Buchanan, Norman Stansfield, Richard and Valerie Wright)*

Jennings ~ Managers Carol and Gary Kirkpatrick ~ Real ale ~ Bar food ~ Restaurant ~ (01282) 842450 ~ Children in eating area of bar and restaurant ~ Open 11-11; 12-10.30 Sun

FADMOOR SE6789 Map 10
Plough
Village signposted off A170 in or just W of Kirkbymoorside

The new licenseees at this cream and dark green painted pub did very well in previous editions of the Guide when they ran the Feathers at Helmsley. They've smartened its snug little rooms up considerably in an elegantly simple way with rugs on seagrass matting, lemon walls and richly upholstered furnishings; piped music. It's run in a very genuine way with an extremely hospitable and helpful landlady who is responsible for the ample helpings of beautifully presented bar and restaurant meals which might include soup (£2.95), sandwiches (from £3.75), black pudding with apples and onions or fried brie with cranberry sauce (£4.75), avocado and prawn salad (£5.50), mushroom and stilton tartlets with a mustard and tarragon sauce (£6.75), steak and kidney pudding (£7.50), salmon fishcakes with lemon and dill sauce (£8.50), pork medallions with stilton sauce (£11.75) and puddings like almond meringue roulade or crème brûlée (£3.30), with a few more elaborate evening dishes like oyster mushrooms and bacon on leaves (£5.95), monkfish and scampi in leek, cream and garlic sauce with saffron rice (£12.75). They have a decent wine list, and well kept Black Sheep and Timothy Taylor Landlord. This is a lovely spot overlooking the quiet village green; comfortable bedrooms. *(Recommended by Greta and Christopher Wells, Karen and Andy Hutton, I R D Ross)*

Free house ~ Licensees Andrew and Catherine Feather ~ Real ale ~ Bar food (12-1.30, 6.30-8.45; not Sun evening) ~ Restaurant ~ (01751) 431515 ~ Children welcome at lunchtimes, by prior arrangement evenings ~ Open 12-2.30, 6.30-11(8-10.30 Sun)

FERRENSBY SE3761 Map 7
General Tarleton 🍴 ♀ 🛏
A655 N of Knaresborough

Under new licensees, this smartly refurbished 18th-c coaching inn has a civilised beamed and carpeted bar with brick pillars dividing up the several different areas to create the occasional cosy alcove, some exposed stonework, neatly framed pictures on the white walls, a mix of country kitchen furniture and comfortable banquettes, and a big open fire; a door leads out to a pleasant tree-lined garden with smart green tables. Good, imaginative bar food includes soup (£2.95), crisp tomato tart drizzled with pesto (£4.25), tagliolini with smoked salmon, avocado and pecorino (£4.25; main course £7.50), terrine of ham shank and foie gras (£4.95), tempura of tiger prawns with red chilli and onion pickle (£6.25), sausage and mash with roasted shallots and red wine sauce (£7.85), maple cured loin of free-range local pork with Tuscan vegetables, pesto and parmesan shavings (£9.25), chargrilled Aberdeen Angus minute steak (£8.50), honey glazed confit of duck (£9.95), calf's liver and pancetta (£11.50), and puddings such as chocolate marquise with griottines cherries, sticky toffee pudding with pecan caramel sauce or summer pudding (from £3.95). Well kept Black Sheep Best, Tetleys and Timothy Taylor Landlord on handpump, and 25 good wines by the glass including 3 pudding wines. The courtyard eating area (and restaurant) are no smoking. Good bedrooms with their own separate entrance. *(Recommended by David and Phyllis Chapman, M A Godfrey, Ann and Bob Westbrook, Alistair and Carol Tindle, Alyson and Andrew Jackson, Alan and Janice Curry, Malcolm and Jennifer Perry)*

Free house ~ Licensee John Topham ~ Real ale ~ Bar food ~ Restaurant ~ (01423) 340284 ~ Children welcome ~ Open 12-3, 6-10.30(11 Sat); closed 25 Dec

FLAMBOROUGH TA2270 Map 8
Seabirds ♀
Junction B1255/B1229

Handy for visiting the seabird colonies at Bempton Cliffs, this straightforward village pub has a public bar with quite a shipping theme, and leading off here the comfortable lounge has a whole case of stuffed seabirds along one wall, as well as pictures and paintings of the local landscape, and a woodburning stove. Bar food includes sandwiches (from £1.95; filled french bread £3.95), soup (£1.70), lunchtime dishes like giant yorkshire pudding filled with onion gravy (£2.70), omelettes (from £4.85), leek and mushroom crumble (£5.95), and haddock mornay (£6.15), with evening dishes such deep-fried battered mushrooms with blue cheese dressing (£3.75), gammon and eggs (£6.95), salmon steak mornay (£7.25), pork fillet in creamy peppercorn sauce (£8.25), and steaks (from £10.85), and daily specials like sausage and onion pie, fresh local crab, and roast barbary duck breast on celeriac mash with marmalade sauce; puddings (from £2). Best to book for Sunday lunchtime. Well kept John Smiths and a weekly changing guest on handpump, and a wide range of malt whiskies. Friendly, hardworking staff; dominoes, fruit machine, and piped music. There are seats in the garden. *(Recommended by Trevor Owen, DC, David Carr, JP, PP, Pat and Tony Hinkins)*

Free house ~ Licensee Jean Riding ~ Real ale ~ Bar food ~ Restaurant ~ (01262) 850242 ~ Children in restaurant ~ Open 11.30-3, 7-11; 12-3, 7-10.30 Sun; closed Mon evening in winter

GOOSE EYE SE0340 Map 7
Turkey
High back road Haworth—Sutton in Craven, and signposted from back roads W of Keighley; OS Sheet 104 map reference 028406

Tucked away in a village at the bottom of a steep valley, this pleasant pub has various cosy and snug alcoves, brocaded upholstery, and walls covered with pictures of surrounding areas; the restaurant is no smoking. Generous helpings of decent bar food include home-made soup (£2.10), sandwiches (from £2.40), pâté (£2.50), vegetable lasagne (£5.20), home-made pie or battered cod (£5.80), steaks (from £6.90), and puddings (£2.40); roast Sunday lunch (£5.80). Well kept Greene King Abbot, Ind Coope Burton, Tetleys, a beer named for the pub (Turkey Bitter), and a guest beer on handpump, and 40 malt whiskies; noticeable piped music. A separate games area has pool, fruit machine, and video game. *(Recommended by Margaret and David Watson, WAH)*

Free house ~ Licensees Harry and Monica Brisland ~ Real ale ~ Bar food (not Mon) ~ Restaurant ~ (01535) 681339 ~ Children welcome until 9pm ~ Open 12-3(4 Sat), 6.30(7 Sat)-11; 12-3, 7-10.30 Sun; closed Mon lunch except bank holidays

GREAT OUSEBURN SE4562 Map 7
Crown

Off B6265 SE of Boroughbridge

Notably friendly, this cheery village pub is the sort of place where locals chat to you, and the licensees and staff are obliging. The welcoming carpeted bar has lots of Edwardian prints and pictures on the walls, as well as a hefty old mangle, plenty of hops, flowers and greenery, cushions on the chairs and wall settles, some military badges, and assorted knick-knacks from a pair of china dogs to a model witch hanging beside the fireplace. Two no-smoking eating areas open off, one with plates and an old cooking range, the other with smart tablecloths and stripped stone walls. Beyond a third area laid out for eating is a sunny terrace with green plastic tables and chairs (and maybe summer barbecues) and behind that is a garden with a play area. Well kept Black Sheep, John Smiths, Timothy Taylor Landlord and a changing guest on handpump; dominoes, piped music. Well presented food includes home-made soup such as lamb broth or celery and blue cheese (£1.95), deep-fried haggis with tomato chutney (£3.50), baby rack of barbecued ribs (£3.95), filled french bread (from £3.95; Saturday and Sunday lunchtime only), thai-style red curried vegetables (£5.50), garlic and herb sausages in yorkshire pudding with onion gravy (£5.95), steak, mushroom and Guinness pie (£6.50), 16oz gammon and eggs (£8.95), chicken italiano (£9.95), chargrilled swordfish with chilli sauce and an avocado, tomato and cucumber salsa (£11.95), steaks (from £12.95), and puddings (from £2.95); Sunday roast (from £4.95). The landlord used to play for Leeds United. Note that they don't open weekday lunchtimes. *(Recommended by Malcolm Taylor, Mr and Mrs Allen, Alan Morton)*

Free house ~ Licensees Steve Balcombe and Patricia Grant ~ Real ale ~ Bar food (all day Sun) ~ Restaurant ~ (01423) 330430 ~ Well behaved children welcome ~ Open 5-11; 11-11 Sat; 12-10.30 Sun

HARDEN SE0838 Map 7
Malt Shovel £

Follow Wilsden signpost from B6429

This is a lovely spot by a bridge over Harden Beck and there are seats in the pretty garden. Inside, the three spotlessly clean rooms in this handsome dark stone building have stone mullioned windows, blue plush seats built into the walls, kettles, brass funnels and the like hanging from the black beams, and horsebrasses on leather harness; one room has oak panelling, a beamed ceiling, and an open fire; at lunchtime, there is one room that is no smoking. Good value bar food (with prices unchanged since last year) includes sausage, mustard and onion sandwich (£2.75; the hot beef are £3), giant yorkshire pudding with sausages or beef and gravy (£3.50), omelettes (from £4.75), and home-made steak pie or chilli (£4.95). Well kept Tetleys on handpump, and efficient service; dominoes, Monday quiz nights, and piped music. *(Recommended by JDM, KM, Jason Caulkin, Paul R White)*

Allied Domecq ~ Keith and Lynne Bolton ~ Real ale ~ Bar food (lunchtime (not Sun)) ~ (01535) 272357 ~ Children in eating area of bar ~ Open 12-3, 5.30-11; 12-11(10.30 Sun) summer Thurs/Fri, and Sat

HAROME SE6582 Map 10
Star

Village signposted S of A170, E of Helmsley

This pretty thatched inn is said to be the first pub that 'mousey Thompson' ever populated with his famous dark wood furniture. The current licensees have freshened up the interior with which has a dark bowed beam-and-plank ceiling, well polished tiled kitchen range, plenty of bric-a-brac, two wonderful log fires, daily papers and magazines and a no-smoking dining room. The inventive very good (if not cheap) food is particularly popular. The changing menu might include soup (£2.95), lunchtime sandwiches (from £4.50), terrine of gammon with fried quail eggs, pineapple pickle and mustard dressing (£4.95), ploughman's, wild boar sausages with sage mash and apples, onions and garlic or steak and kidney pudding (£7.95), wild mushroom risotto (£8.95), provençal fish stew (£9.95), roast partridge with black pudding risotto, smoked bacon and thyme juices (£14.50), halibut fillet with red wine butter, celeriac mash and burgundy sauce (£16.50), and puddings like baked ginger parkin with hot spiced treacle and rhubarb ice cream (£3.95), and English cheese board (£5). Well kept Black Sheep, John Smiths and Theakstons Best on handpump and just under a dozen wines by the glass from a fairly extensive wine list. There are some seats and tables on a sheltered front terrace with more in the garden with fruit trees and a big ash behind *(Recommended by Marion Turner, PACW, Bernard Stradling, Nick and Alison Dowson, Stephen Adams, Ann and Bob Westbrook, Pierre and Pat Richterich, I R D Ross, R F Grieve, John and Esther Sprinkle)*

Free house ~ Licensees Andrew and Jacquie Pern ~ Real ale ~ Bar food (11.30-2, 6.30-9; 12.6 Sun; not Mon, not Sun evening) ~ (01439) 770397 ~ Children welcome ~ Open 11.30-3, 6.30-11; 12-10.30 Sun; closed Mon Lunchtime

HEATH SE3519 Map 7
Kings Arms

Village signposted from A655 Wakefield—Normanton – or, more directly, turn off to the left opposite Horse & Groom

A new licensee has taken over this old-fashioned pub which faces the village green and is surrounded by stone merchant's houses of the 19th c. There's quite a bit of atmosphere inside, helped by gas lighting in most parts, and the original bar has a fire burning in the old black range (with a long row of smoothing irons on the mantelpiece), plain elm stools and oak settles built into the walls, and dark panelling. A more comfortable extension has carefully preserved the original style, down to good wood-pegged oak panelling (two embossed with royal arms), and a high shelf of plates; there are also two other small flagstoned rooms, and the conservatory opens onto the garden. Good value bar food includes sandwiches (from £1.75), home-made soup (£1.95), omelettes (from £3.75), home-made lasagne or beef in ale pie, gammon and egg or battered haddock (all £4.75), puddings (£2.75), and children's meals (£2.50). As well as cheap Clarks Bitter, they also serve guests like Tetleys Bitter and Timothy Taylor Landlord on handpump. The pub is in a fine setting with seats along the front of the building facing the green, picnic-sets on a side lawn, and a nice walled flower-filled garden. *(Recommended by JJW, CMW, Ian Phillips, JP, PP, K Frostick, Michael Butler, the Didler, Andy and Jill Kassube)*

Clarks ~ Manager Alan Tate ~ Real ale ~ Bar food ~ Restaurant ~ (01924) 377527 ~ Children in eating area of bar and restaurant ~ Open 11.30-3, 5.30-11; 11-11 Sat; 12-10.30 Sun

HECKMONDWIKE SE2223 Map 7
Old Hall

New North Road; B6117 between A62 and A638; OS Sheet 104, map reference 214244

Built in the 15th c, this interesting building was once the home of nonconformist scientist Joseph Priestley. It has lots of old beams and timbers, latticed mullioned windows with worn stone surrounds, brick or stripped old stone walls hung with pictures of Richard III, Henry VII, Catherine Parr, and Joseph Priestley, and comfortable furnishings. Snug low-ceilinged alcoves lead off the central part with its high ornate plaster ceiling, and an upper gallery room, under the pitched roof, looks down on the main area through timbering 'windows'. Bar food includes filled rolls (from £2.50), a pie of the day, vegetable lasagne, chicken curry or chilli con carne (all £4.95), gammon and egg (£5.95), good beer-battered haddock (£6.25), steaks (from £7.45), and puddings such as fruit crumbles or pies (£2.25). Well kept (and cheap) Sam Smiths OB on handpump; fruit machine, piped music, and maybe sports or music quizzes on Tuesday night and a general knowedge one on Thursday evening. *(Recommended by Sue and Bob Ward, Michael Butler, W W Burke, Derek and Sylvia Stephenson, Andy and Jill Kassube)*

Sam Smiths ~ Manager Robert Green ~ Real ale ~ Bar food (all day Sun) ~ (01924) 404774 ~ Children welcome ~ Open 11-11; 12-10.30 Sun

HETTON SD9558 Map 7
Angel ★ ⑪ ♀
Just off B6265 Skipton—Grassington

The food at this friendly, very well run dining pub is extraordinarily good – and therefore very popular, so to be sure of a table it's best to arrive early early – even during the week. Served by hard-working uniformed staff, there might be home-made soup (£2.95; lovely rustic fish soup with aioli £4.75), parfait of chicken livers and foie gras (£3.95), pasta with mixed mushrooms, spinach, basil and pecorino (£4.25; main course £7.50), eggs benedict or seafood in a crispy pastry bag with lobster sauce (£4.75), fresh salmon marinated with lime juice, chilli and coriander, finished with guacamole, tomato salsa and sour cream (£4.95), tempura of tiger prawns (£6.25), burger with gruyère, pancetta and tomato salsa with crispy fried onions (£7.50), sausage and mash with roasted shallots in red wine sauce (£7.85), steaks (from £8.50), maple cured loin of free-range local pork with chargrilled Tuscan vegetables, pesto and parmesan shavings (£9.25), honey-glazed confit of duck with oriental vegetables and soy dressing (£9.95), grilled calf's liver and pancetta (£11.50), daily specials such as baked queen scallops with gruyère and garlic butter (£4.95; main course £6.95), smoked haddock with buttered spinach and hollandaise sauce or roasted wood pigeon with forrestière sauce (£8.50), and chargrilled leg of lamb (£9.95), with puddings such as lemon tart with raspberry coulis, bramley apple and walnut crumble or sticky toffee pudding with pecan caramel sauce (from £3.75). Well kept Black Sheep Bitter, Tetleys, and Timothy Taylor Landlord on handpump, 300 wines (with around 24 by the glass, including two champagnes), and a good range of malt whiskies. The four timbered and panelled rambling rooms have lots of cosy alcoves, comfortable country-kitchen chairs or button-back green plush seats, Ronald Searle wine snob cartoons and older engravings and photographs, log fires, a solid fuel stove, and in the main bar, a Victorian farmhouse range in the big stone fireplace; the snug and bar lounge are no smoking (as is part of the restaurant). Sturdy wooden benches and tables are built on to the cobbles outside. *(Recommended by Liz Bell, WAH, Neil Townend, Michael Butler, M Kershaw, Gwen and Peter Andrews, GLD, Peter and Giff Bennett, Karen Eliot, Pierre and Pat Richterich, John A Eteson, Vann and Terry Prime, Norman Stansfield, Prof and Mrs S Barnett, David Hawkes, Prof P A Reynolds, B and M Kendall, Malcolm and Jennifer Perry)*

Free house ~ Licensees Denis Watkins and John Topham ~ Real ale ~ Bar food (12-2, 6-9.30) ~ Restaurant ~ (01756) 730263 ~ Children welcome ~ Open 12-3, 6-10.30(11 Sat)

HUBBERHOLME SD9178 Map 7
George
Village signposted from Buckden; about 1 mile NW

Friendly new licensees took over this remote and unspoilt old inn just as we went to press, but were not planning any major changes – though they hoped to upgrade the bedrooms. The two neat and cosy rooms have genuine character: heavy beams supporting the dark ceiling-boards, walls stripped back to bare stone and hung with antique plates and photographs, seats (with covers to match the curtains) around shiny copper-topped tables on the flagstones, and an open stove in the big fireplace. Good, wholesome bar food now includes home-made soup (£2.30), sandwiches (from £2.60), home-made trout pâté (£3.50), cumberland sausage (£5.95), steak and kidney pie (£6.75), gammon and eggs (£6.90), goat's cheese lasagne (£6.95), and puddings such as sticky toffee pudding (£3.25). Very well kept Black Sheep Special, and Tetleys Bitter and Mild on handpump; dominoes. There are seats and tables outside looking over the moors and River Wharfe – where they have fishing rights. The pub is near the ancient church where J B Priestley's ashes are scattered (this was his favourite pub). *(Recommended by Mr and Mrs Staples, MDN, John and Shirley Smith, Greta and Christopher Wells, R Inman, D Goodger, Peter and Ruth Burnstone, T G Brierly, Eddie Edwards, JP, PP, Prof and Mrs S Barnett, Vann and Terry Prime, Mrs Hilarie Taylor, K Frostick, Peter and Giff Bennett, John A Eteson, Gwen and Peter Andrews, Chris and Sue Bax)*

*Free house ~ Licensees Jenny and Terry Browne ~ Real ale ~ Bar food ~ (01756)
760223 ~ Children welcome until 8.30pm ~ Open 11.30-3, 6.30-11; 12-10.30 Sun;
closed 2 wks Jan ~ Bedrooms: £27/£41(£54B)*

HULL TA0927 Map 8
Minerva 🍺

Park at top of pedestrianised area at top of Queen's St and walk over Nelson St or turn off
Queen's St into Wellington St, right into Pier St and pub is at top; no parking restrictions
wknds, 2-hour stay Mon-Fri

More outside seating has been added in front of this handsome pub and on the piers
on each side – it's fun to sit and watch the harbour activity in the bustling marina.
Inside, the several rooms ramble all the way round a central servery, and are filled
with comfortable seats, quite a few interesting photographs and pictures of old Hull
(with two attractive wash drawings by Roger Davis) and a big chart of the Humber;
one room is no smoking during mealtimes. A tiny snug has room for just three
people, and a back room (which looks out to the marina basin) houses a profusion of
varnished woodwork. Good sized helpings of straightforward bar food such as soup
(£1.75), hot or cold filled french bread (from £2.55), filled baked potatoes (from
£2.25), ploughman's (from £4.25), home-made steak in ale pie or lasagne (£4.45),
popular huge battered haddock (£4.85), cajun chicken (£5.25), and puddings (£2.25);
daily specials, Sunday roast (£4.45), and they also hold winter curry nights. Well kept
Tetleys Bitter, Timothy Taylor Landlord and three guests such as Black Sheep,
Caledonian, and Greene King on handpump. They hold four beer festivals during the
year, but have stopped brewing their own ale. The lounge is no smoking when food is
being served. Dominoes, cribbage, fruit machine, trivia, and piped music.
(Recommended by Mike and Mary Carter, JP, PP, Andy and Jill Kassube)

*Allied Domecq ~ Managers Eamon and Kathy Scott ~ Real ale ~ Bar food (not
Fri/Sat/Sun evenings) ~ (01482) 326909 ~ Children in eating area if eating ~ Open 11-
11; 12-10.30 Sun; closed 25 Dec*

Olde White Harte ★ £

Off 25 Silver Street, a continuation of Whitefriargate (see previous entry); pub is up narrow
passage beside the jewellers' Barnby and Rust, and should not be confused with the much
more modern White Hart nearby

Known as Hull's most haunted pub – and on a local ghost walk – this ancient tavern has
some fine features in its six bars. The downstairs one has attractive stained-glass windows
that look out above the bow window seat, carved heavy beams support black ceiling
boards, and there's a big brick inglenook with a frieze of delft tiles. The curved copper-
topped counter serves well kept Courage Directors, McEwans 80/- and Theakstons Old
Peculier and XB on handpump. Decent bar food includes soup (£1.95), sandwiches (from
£1.95), roast of the day (£3.95), Thai chicken (£4.25), beef in ale pie (£4.75), steaks (from
£5.45), and daily specials (from £3.95). It was in the heavily panelled room up the oak
staircase that in 1642 the town's governor Sir John Hotham made the fateful decision to
lock the nearby gate against Charles I, depriving him of Hull's arsenal; it didn't do him
much good, as in the Civil War that followed, Hotham, like the king, was executed by the
parliamentarians. There are seats outside in the courtyard where they've installed outside
heaters. *(Recommended by JP, PP, Andy and Jill Kassube, the Didler)*

*Scottish Courage ~ Managers John Anderson and Stephanie Firth ~ Real ale ~ Bar food
(12-7 wkdys, 12-8 wknds) ~ Restaurant ~ (01482) 326363 ~ Children in restaurant ~
Open 11-11; 12-10.30 Sun*

KIRKBYMOORSIDE SE6987 Map 10
George & Dragon 🛏

Market place

Although new licensees have taken over this civilised 17th-c coaching inn, as we went
to press, most of the staff had stayed on. No major changes are planned, though the

partly no-smoking restaurant is to be refurbished and the bedrooms redecorated. The friendly pubby front bar has leather chesterfields as well as the brass-studded solid dark red leatherette armchairs set around polished wooden tables, dark green walls and panelling stripped back to its original pitch pinè, horse-brasses hung along the beams, and a blazing log fire; piped music. There's also an attractive beamed bistro. Good bar food includes lunchtime sandwiches, soup with home-made bread (£2.50), chicken liver pâté with cumberland sauce (£3.95), venison sausage (£4.95), vegetarian stroganoff (£7.50), seafood hotpot (£8.90), gammon and eggs (£9.50), barbary duck with raspberry jus (£10.90), half rack of Ryedale lamb with a rosemary and madeira sauce (£12.50), and steaks (from £12.90), with daily specials such as strips of chicken in mint, ginger and chilli with a tomato and cucumber salsa (£4.90), scallops sautéed in garlic and white wine (£6.90), lamb's liver and bacon (£8.50), Moroccan lamb (£9.90), pink snapper on softened cabbage with beurre blanc sauce (£10.90), and puddings like brandy and chocolate bread and butter pudding or passion fruit and Malibu brûlée with hazelnut shorts (£3.50). Well kept Black Sheep Bitter, Boddingtons, John Smiths, and Timothy Taylor Landlord on handpump. There are seats under umbrellas in the back courtyard and a surprisingly peaceful walled garden for residents to use. The bedrooms are in a converted cornmill and old vicarage at the back of the pub. Wednesday is Market Day. *(Recommended by O Richardson, Roger and Anne King, Ben and Sheila Walker, IHR, John Robertson, Geoffrey and Brenda Wilson, Mrs K L Heath, Joe and Mary Stachura, Julie and Tony Warneck, Bruce Bird, Vann and Terry Prime, Walter and Susan Rinaldi-Butcher, Brian Wardrobe, Derek and Sylvia Stephenson, R Styles)*

Free house ~ Licensee Elaine Walker ~ Real ale ~ Bar food ~ Restaurant ~ (01751) 431637 ~ Children welcome until 9pm ~ Occasional live bands ~ Open 11.30-3, 6-11; 12-3, 7-10.30 Sun ~ Bedrooms: £49B/£79B

KIRKHAM SE7466 Map 7
Stone Trough
Kirkham Abbey

New licensees were on the point of taking over this attractively set inn as we went to press. There are several beamed and cosy rooms with warm log fires, a friendly atmosphere, and well kept Black Sheep, Tetleys, and Timothy Taylor Landlord on handpump; 8 wines by the large glass. Good bar food includes sandwiches (from £2.25), home-made soup (£2.95), warm salads such as chicken and smoked bacon (£5.25), wild mushroom risotto (£6.25), chicken and leek pie or steak pudding (£6.95), baked cod with parsley sauce and olive oil mash (£7.25), steaks (from £12.95), and puddings such as hot apricot and almond sponge or caramelised banana and toffee fool (£2.95). The no-smoking restaurant has a fire in an old-fashioned kitchen range; the cats are called Cobweb and Crumble. Darts, pool, dominoes, fruit machine and piped music; TV in the pool room. There are seats outside with lovely valley views, and the inn is handy for Kirkham Abbey and Castle Howard. *(Recommended by Patrick Hancock, Pat and Tony Martin, Christopher Turner, Colin and Dot Savill, Chris Gabbitas, Hugh McPhail, Maureen Jacques, Anthony Quinsee, Paul Barnett)*

Free house ~ Licensees Sarah and Adam Richardson ~ Real ale ~ Bar food ~ Restaurant ~ (01653) 618713 ~ Well behaved children welcome ~ Open 12-2.30, 7-11; 12-3, 7-10.30 Sun; closed Mon

LEDSHAM SE4529 Map 7
Chequers
Claypit Lane; a mile W of A1, some 4 miles N of junction M62

Readers enjoy this stone-built village pub very much – and it's a marvellous haven from the nearby A1. The friendly licensee and his helpful staff make everyone welcome, and there's a good bustling atmosphere. The old-fashioned little central panelled-in servery has several small, individually decorated rooms leading off, with low beams, lots of cosy alcoves, newspapers to read, a number of toby jugs, and log fires. Good, well liked straightforward bar food includes home-made soup (£2.45), sandwiches (from £3.25; the steak is excellent, £5.85), ploughman's (£4.85), scrambled eggs and smoked salmon (£5.50), lasagne or vegetable pasta bake (£6.25), home-made steak and mushroom pie (£6.75), generous grilled gammon and two eggs (£7.50), daily specials such as courgette, celery and green pepper gratin (£6.35), mediterranean lamb (£6.45), chicken breast in raspberry sauce (£6.95), grilled fillet of bass (£8.95), and puddings such as sherry trifle, sticky toffee pudding or fruit pie (from £2.95). They brew their own Brown Cow Best Bitter, and also keep John Smiths, Theakstons Best, and Youngers Scotch on handpump. A sheltered two-level terrace behind the house has tables among roses, and the hanging baskets and flowers are very pretty. *(Recommended by Geoffrey and Brenda Wilson, Catherine and Martin Snelling, Pete Yearsley, Tony Gayfer, Lawrence Pearse, Ian Phillips, Kevin Thorpe, Jenny and Chris Wilson, Derek and Sylvia Stephenson, Joy and Peter Heatherley, the Didler, Malcolm and Jennifer Perry, Andy and Jill Kassube)*

Free house ~ Licensee Chris Wraith ~ Real ale ~ Bar food ~ Restaurant ~ (01977) 683135 ~ Children in eating area of bar and restaurant ~ Open 11-3, 5.30-11; 11-11 Sat; closed Sun, some evenings, all day Mon, and Tues-Thurs lunchtimes

LEEDS SE3033 Map 7
Whitelocks ★ £

Turks Head Yard; alley off Briggate, opposite Debenhams and Littlewoods; park in shoppers' car park and walk

'A timeless gem' is how several people describe this marvellously preserved and atmospheric Victorian pub. The long and narrow old-fashioned bar has polychrome tiles on the bar counter, stained-glass windows and grand advertising mirrors, and red button back plush banquettes and heavy copper-topped cast-iron tables squeezed down one side. And although it might be best to get here outside peak times as it does get packed, the friendly staff are quick and efficient. Good, reasonably priced bar food includes yorkshire pudding and gravy (85p), sandwiches (from £1.35), and tasty chilli, home-made steak and potato pie or vegetable or meaty lasagne (£2.35); after 8pm, they only serve sandwiches. Well kept McEwans 80/-, Morlands Old Speckled Hen, John Smiths, Theakstons Best, XB and Old Peculier, and Youngers IPA and Scotch on handpump. At the end of the long narrow yard another bar is done up in Dickensian style. *(Recommended by Allan Worsley, P G Plumridge, Karen Eliot, Reg Nelson, Roy Butler, Alan Morton, JP, PP, K F Mould, the Didler)*

Scottish Courage ~ Manager Simon McCarthy ~ Real ale ~ Bar food (all day) ~ Restaurant ~ (0113) 245 3950 ~ Children in restaurant ~ Open 11-11; 12-10.30 Sun; closed 25-26 Dec, 1 Jan

LEVISHAM SE8391 Map 10
Horseshoe

Pub and village signposted from A169 N of Pickering

Friendly, efficient licensees run this neatly kept, traditional pub – when one reader turned up in a party of 30, they coped speedily and without any fuss. The bar has brocaded seats, a log fire in the stone fireplace, bar billiards, and well kept John Smiths, and Theakstons Best, XB and Old Peculier on handpump, and over 30 malt whiskies. Good bar food includes home-made soup (£2.25), sandwiches (from £2.95), Spanish mushrooms or home-made chicken liver pâté (£3.75), ploughman's (£4.95), sausages with rich red wine and onion gravy, steak and kidney in ale pie or home-made lasagne (£5.95), beef curry (£6.25), Thai vegetable curry (£6.95), gammon and egg (£7.50), tuna loin with a herb and citrus butter (£8.25), steaks (from £10.95), puddings, and children's menu (£3.25); the dining room is no smoking. Bar billiards, dominoes, and piped music. On warm days, the picnic-sets on the attractive village green are a fine place to enjoy a drink, and there are plenty of surrounding walks. *(Recommended by Don and Thelma Anderson, M Borthwick, Comus Elliott, B T Smith, M A Buchanan, Alan J Morton, Mark J Hydes, Martin and Jane Wright, SLC, Jerry and Alison Oakes)*

Free house ~ Licensees Brian and Helen Robshaw ~ Real ale ~ Bar food (not 25 Dec) ~ Restaurant ~ (01751) 460240 ~ Children welcome ~ Open 11-3, 6.30-11(11.30 Sat); 12-3, 6.30-10.30 Sun; closed winter Mon and 25 Dec ~ Bedrooms: £26/£52B

LEYBURN SE1191 Map 10
Sandpiper
Just off Market Pl

The new licensee here is a well respected chef and so there will be more emphasis on dining in this 17th-c little stone cottage. The bar has a couple of black beams in the low ceiling, a stuffed pheasant in a stripped-stone alcove, antlers, and a few tables and chairs; the back room up three steps has attractive dales photographs. Down by the nice linenfold panelled bar counter there are stuffed sandpipers, more photographs and a woodburning stove in the stone fireplace; there's also a spick-and-span dining area on the left. Good bar food includes sandwiches, goat's cheese salad with tomato dressing (£3.25), omelette Arnold Bennet (£3.50), fishcakes in parsley sauce (£3.95), pressed ham and celeriac terrine (£4.50), cannelloni of ricotta and spinach (£7), mixed grill (£8.50), medley of fish in a shellfish sauce or Moroccan spiced lamb with couscous (£8.95), and puddings like lemon tart with marinated red fruits and lime sorbet, chocolate délice with a coffee bean sauce or summer pudding with clotted cream (from £3.25); a good selection of local cheeses (£3.50). Well kept Black Sheep Riggwelter, Dent Bitter, and Theakstons Bitter on handpump, around 100 malt whiskies, and a decent wine list. There are lovely hanging baskets, white cast-iron tables among the honeysuckle, climbing roses, and so forth on the front terrace, with more tables in the back garden. *(Recommended by John and Shirley Smith, Bruce Bird, Alan Morton, Peter A Burnstone, B and M Kendall, Janet and Peter Race)*

Free house ~ Licensees Jonathan and Michael Harrison ~ Real ale ~ Bar food (till 10pm Fri/Sat) ~ (01969) 622206 ~ Children in eating area of bar and restaurant ~ Open 11-2.30, 6-11; 12-2.30, 7-10.30 Sun ~ Bedrooms: £27.50S/£45S

LINTHWAITE SE1014 Map 7
Sair 🍺
Hoyle Ing, off A62; 3½ miles after Huddersfield look out for two water storage tanks (painted with a shepherd scene) on your right – the street is on your left, burrowing very steeply up between works buildings; OS Sheet 110 map reference 101143

A marvellous choice of own-brewed ales on handpump is offered at this unspoilt and old-fashioned pub – and if Mr Crabtree is not too busy, he is glad to show visitors the brewhouse: pleasant and well balanced Linfit Bitter, Dark Mild, Special, Swift, Gold Medal, Old Eli, Leadboiler, Autumn Gold, and the redoubtable Enochs Hammer; occasionally they replace Swift with Ginger Beer, Janet St Porter, Smoke House Ale, Springbok Bier or Xmas Ale. Westons farm cider and a few malt whiskies; weekend sandwiches. The four rooms are furnished with pews or smaller chairs on the rough flagstones or carpet, bottle collections, beermats tacked to beams, and roaring log fires; one room is no smoking. This room on the left has shove-ha'penny, dominoes, cribbage, and juke box; piano players welcome. There are more seats in front of the pub this year, and a striking view down the Colne Valley. The Huddersfield Narrow Canal is being restored, and they hope to re-open the canal in Slaithwaite; in the 3½ miles from Linthwaite to the highest, deepest, and longest tunnel in Britain are 25 working locks and some lovely countryside. *(Recommended by JP, PP, H K Dyson, the Didler)*

Own brew ~ Licensee Ron Crabtree ~ Real ale ~ (01484) 842370 ~ Children welcome in 2 rooms away from bar ~ Open 7-11; 12-11 Sat; 12-10.30 Sun

LINTON SE3946 Map 7
Windmill 🍺
Leaving Wetherby W on A661, fork left just before Hospital and bear left; also signposted from A659, leaving Collingham towards Harewood

In an attractive village, this friendly pub has carefully restored and spotlessly kept small beamed rooms with walls stripped back to bare stone, polished antique oak settles around copper-topped cast-iron tables, pots hanging from the oak beams, a high shelf of plates, and log fires; the conservatory is no smoking. Enjoyable generously served food includes home-made soup (£2.75), yorkshire pudding and onion gravy (£2.80), lunchtime sandwiches (from £2.80; filled french bread from £5.75), fried feta cheese and peppers (£3.15), fresh battered haddock (£6.50), beef and mushroom in ale pie (£6.95), cajun tikka masala (£7.25), steaks (from £9.75), and daily specials such as pigeon breast with rhubarb dressing (£3.75), Thai fishcakes with sweet chilli sauce (£3.95), king scallops with smoked bacon and garlic butter (£4.50), spinach and ricotta cannelloni (£5.95), wild boar sausages with pickled red cabbage (£7.25), red snapper fillet with spring onions and lemon grass (£8.50), and medallions of venison in a cranberry, shallot and red wine sauce (£10.75); they also offer early-bird menus between 5.30 and 7pm during the week: 2 courses £6.95, 3 courses £8.50), 3 courses from the specials board on Sunday, Monday or Tuesday evenings (£11.95 per person), and children's menu (from £3.25). Well kept Ruddles County, John Smiths, Theakstons Best and three weekly guest beers on handpump from breweries such as Daleside, Hambleton, Marston Moor, Rooster's, and Rudgate; piped music. The two black labradors are called Jet and Satchmo. The pear tree outside was planted with seeds brought back from the Napoleonic Wars and there is a secret passage between the pub and the church next door. *(Recommended by GSB, June and Malcolm Farmer)*

Scottish Courage ~ Tenants Geoff and Daron Stoker ~ Real ale ~ Bar food ~ Restaurant ~ (01937) 582938 ~ Children welcome until 9pm ~ Open 11.30-3, 5-10.30; 11-11 Sat; 12-10.30 Sun

LINTON IN CRAVEN SD9962 Map 7
Fountaine

B6265 Skipton—Grassington, forking right

Several changes under the new licensee here will include an extension to house a new bar, large dining room, new kitchen, and new lavatories. The original little rooms are furnished with stools, benches and other seats, and they have well kept Black Sheep Bitter, Tetleys Bitter, and Theakstons Best on handpump. From the new menu, there might be home-made soup (£2.25), sandwiches or filled baked potatoes (from £2.75), steak pie or cumberland sausage (£5.95), chicken supreme (£6.95), knuckle of baked lamb on the bone (£7.25), monkfish and king prawns with garlic (£7.95), steaks (from £10.50), and puddings like sticky toffee pudding (£2.75); one small eating area is no smoking. Darts and dominoes. This pub looks down over the village green to the narrow stream that runs through this delightful hamlet, and is named after the local lad who made his pile in the Great Plague – contracting in London to bury the bodies. *(Recommended by Gwen and Peter Andrews, Mrs Janet Annison, WAH, RJH, Alan Thwaite, Paul R White, Neil Ben, Roger and Christine Mash)*

Free house ~ Licensee Alex Losada ~ Real ale ~ Bar food ~ Restaurant ~ (01756) 752210 ~ Children in eating area of bar and restaurant ~ Open 11-11; 12-10.30 Sun; 11-3, 6-11 Mon-Sat in winter

LITTON SD9074 Map 7
Queens Arms

From B6160 N of Grassington, after Kilnsey take second left fork; can also be reached off B6479 at Stainforth N of Settle, via Halton Gill

Ideally situated for walkers, this attractive white-painted inn has stunning views over the fells from picnic sets in front of the building, and from the two-level garden – a track behind the inn leads over Ackerley Moor to Buckden and the quiet lane through the valley leads on to Pen-y-ghent. Inside, the main bar on the right has a good coal fire, stripped rough stone walls, a brown beam-and-plank ceiling, stools around cast-iron-framed tables on the stone and concrete floor, a seat built into the stone-mullioned window, and signed cricket bats. On the left, the red-carpeted room has another coal fire and more of a family atmosphere with varnished pine for its built-in wall seats, and for the ceiling and walls themselves; one area is no smoking. Decent bar food includes home-made soup (£2.20), sandwiches (from £3.20), filled baked potatoes (from £2.90), meaty or vegetable lasagne (£6.20), home-made pies (£6), gammon and egg (£6.50), daily specials (from £4.95), steaks (from £11.60), puddings (from £2.85), and children's meals (from £3.50). Well kept Tetleys and, in summer, Black Sheep on handpump; darts, dominoes, shove-ha'penny, and cribbage.

(Recommended by MDN, John A Eteson, D Goodger, Geoffrey and Brenda Wilson, Paul R White)

Free house ~ Licensees Tanya and Neil Thompson ~ Real ale ~ Bar food ~ (01756) 770208 ~ Children welcome ~ Open 11.30-3, 6.30-11; 12-3, 7-10.30 Sun; closed Mon and all Jan ~ Bedrooms: £30B/£40(£50B)

LOW CATTON SE7053 Map 7
Gold Cup

Village signposted with High Catton off A166 in Stamford Bridge or A1079 at Kexby Bridge

Neatly kept and friendly, the three comfortable communicating rooms of the lounge in this white rendered house have open fires at each end, plush wall seats and stools around good solid tables, flowery curtains, some decorative plates and brasswork on the walls, and a very relaxed atmosphere. Good bar food includes lunchtime sandwiches, warm goat's cheese on an olive oil croûte or layered salad of mackerel and sweet roasted peppers (£2.95), baked chicken wrapped in bacon with a creamy leek sauce (£8.50), and locally made black pudding between two fried pork fillet medallions with a smoked bacon and port sauce (£8.95); the no-smoking restaurant has pleasant views of the surrounding fields. Well kept John Smiths and Tetleys Bitter on handpump. The back games bar is comfortable, with a well lit pool table, dominoes, fruit machine, and well reproduced music. There's a garden with a timber climing frame and grassed area for children, and the back paddock houses Annie and Billie the goats, Tina and Pony the shetlands, and Kandy the horse; they have fishing rights on the adjoining River Derwent. *(Recommended by B P White, Calum and Jane Maclean)*

Free house ~ Licensees Pat and Ray Hales ~ Real ale ~ Bar food (not Mon lunchtime) ~ (01759) 71354 ~ Children in eating areas and in games room ~ Open 12-2.30, 6-11; 12-11(10.30 Sun) Sat; closed Mon lunch except bank holidays

LUND SE9748 Map 8
Wellington ♀

Off B1248 SW of Driffield

Most people come to this smartly refurbished pub in a delightfully unspoilt village to enjoy the good lunchtime food – in the evening the bar is food-free and the several rooms feel quite different. The most atmospheric part is the cosy Farmers Bar, a small heavily beamed room with an interesting fireplace and some old agricultural equipment; the neatly kept main bar is much brighter, with a brick fireplace and bar counter, well polished wooden banquettes and square tables, dried flowers, and local prints on the textured cream-painted walls; one part is no smoking. Off to one side is a plainer flagstoned room, while at the other a York-stoned walkway leads to a room with a display case showing off the village's Britain in Bloom awards. The short range of well prepared lunchtime food might include soups like cauliflower and almond or lentil and smoked bacon (£2.95; soup plus half any sandwich £4.25), home-made chicken liver parfait with redcurrant and orange sauce (£3.95), sandwiches (from £3.95; tuna with sun-dried tomato £4.95, fresh crab £5.50), smoked haddock fishcakes with mild curried apple sauce and home-made chips (£7.50), fresh asparagus flan, pork and hop sausage with onion gravy or fresh tagliatelle with roasted vegetables in a basil and garlic cream sauce (£7.95), chicken breast with coriander, garlic and orange (£8), and puddings like chocolate sponge with chocolate sauce and vanilla ice cream, lemon and ginger mousse, and vanilla cheesecake with mulled berry compôte (from £2.80). Well kept Batemans Dark Mild, Black Sheep, John Smiths, and Timothy Taylor Landlord on handpump, and a good wine list with a helpfully labelled choice by the glass. Briskly efficient service from uniformed staff; piped music, darts, pool, cribbage, dominoes, and fruit machine. A small courtyard beside the car park has a couple of benches. *(Recommended by Mr and Mrs J Grayson, I R D Ross, Gordon Thornton)*

Free house ~ Licensees Russell Jeffery and Sarah Warburton ~ Real ale ~ Bar food (lunchtimes only) ~ Restaurant ~ (01377) 217294 ~ Children in eating area of bar until 8pm ~ Open 12-3, 7-11(10.30 Sun); closed Mon lunchtime

MASHAM SE2381 Map 10
Kings Head 🛏

Market Square

The new licensees here have refurbished the bedrooms to a high standard and given them individual names. It's a busy, popular place especially on market days (Wednesday, Saturday and bank holidays) when you can sit at the front windows and watch the bustle. The two opened-up bar rooms of the spacious lounge bar are neatly kept (one is carpeted and one has a wooden floor), and there are green plush seats around wooden tables, a big clock (from Masham Station) over the imposing slate and marble fireplace, and a high shelf of Staffordshire and other figurines. The new menu had not quite been finalised as we went to press, but would probably include sandwiches (from £2.95), beef in ale casserole or a daily roast (£6.95), stuffed trout or Whitby cod (£7.95), rack of lamb (£8.95), fillet of wild boar (£13.25), and puddings (from £2.95). Well kept Theakstons Best, XB, and Old Peculier on handpump, and 25 wines (all by the glass); fruit machine, cribbage, dominoes, and piped music. The handsome inn's hanging baskets and window boxes are most attractive, and there are picnic-sets under cocktail parasols in a partly fairy-lit coachyard. *(Recommended by Mrs J Powell, Nick Lawless, Chris Smith, Barry and Anne, Malcolm and Helen Baxter)*

Scottish Courage ~ Manager Philip Capon ~ Real ale ~ Bar food ~ Restaurant ~ (01765) 689295 ~ Children in restaurant ~ Open 11-11; 12-10.30 Sun ~ Bedrooms: £51.95B/£73.90B

White Bear 🍺

Signposted off A6108 opposite turn into town centre

With the Theakstons old stone headquarters buildings being part of this pub and the brewery just the other side of town (tours can be arranged at the Theakstons Brewery Visitor Centre (01765 689057, extension 4317, Weds-Sun), it's not surprising that the Theakstons Best, XB, Old Peculier and seasonal beers are well kept here. The traditionally furnished public bar is packed with bric-a-brac such as copper brewing implements, harness, pottery, foreign banknotes, and stuffed animals – including a huge polar bear behind the bar. A much bigger, more comfortable lounge has a turkey carpet and is partly no smoking. The licensees seem to change frequently, and the food now includes soup (£2.25), filled french bread (from £3.25), beef in ale (£5.25), vegetable pasta (£5.50), shark steak in red wine (£7.95), and steaks (from £9.50). Darts, fruit machine and CD juke box. In summer there are seats out in the yard. *(Recommended by Bill and Kathy Cissna)*

Scottish Courage ~ Tenant Roger Pybus ~ Real ale ~ Bar food (12-3, 6-9) ~ (01765) 689319 ~ Children welcome ~ Live music Fri/Sat ~ Open 11.30-11; 12-10.30 Sun ~ Bedrooms: £25/£37.50

MIDDLEHAM SE1288 Map 10
Black Swan

Market Pl

As we went to press, we heard that this 17th-c stone inn was up for sale. There's usually a good mix of customers with plenty of walkers and lads from the local stables – the pub is in the heart of racing country – and the immaculately kept heavy-beamed bar has high-backed settles built in by the big stone fireplace, racing memorabilia on the stripped stone walls, and horsebrasses and pewter mugs; well kept John Smiths Bitter and Theakstons Best, Old Peculier, and XB on handpump, several malt whiskies and a decent little wine list. Bar food includes lunchtime sandwiches (from £1.95), filled baked potatoes (from £2.75), and ploughman's (from

£3.50), as well as home-made soup (£1.90), egg mayonnaise (£1.95), battered haddock (£4.95), vegetable lasagne (£5.25), lasagne or chicken with a creamy spicy, coconut sauce (£5.50), and evening gammon with pineapple (£7.95), steaks (from £10.25), and children's dishes (£2.95). Darts, dominoes and piped music. There are tables on the cobbles outside and in the sheltered back garden. Good walking country. *(Recommended by Paul R White, Dorothee and Dennis Glover, Graham and Lynn Mason, J and H Coyle, William Cunliffe, Christoper and Jo Barton)*

Free house ~ Licensees George and Susan Munday ~ Real ale ~ Bar food ~ Restaurant ~ (01969) 622221 ~ Children in eating area of bar until 9pm ~ Open 11-3.30, 6-11; 12-3, 6.30-10.30 Sun ~ Bedrooms: £27B/£66B

MOULTON NZ2404 Map 10
Black Bull 🍴

Just E of A1, 1 mile E of Scotch Corner

A haven from the A1, this decidedly civilised place is very much somewhere to come for an enjoyable meal out. The bar has a lot of character – as well as a huge winter log fire, fresh flowers, an antique panelled oak settle and an old elm housekeeper's chair, built-in red-cushioned black settles and pews around the cast-iron tables (one has a heavily beaten copper top), silver-plate Turkish coffee pots and so forth over the red velvet curtained windows, and copper cooking utensils hanging from black beams. A nice side dark-panelled seafood bar has some high seats at the marble-topped counter. Excellent lunchtime bar snacks include lovely smoked salmon in sandwiches (£3.25), on a plate (£5.50), in pâté (£5.75) and in a quiche with asparagus (£5.95); they also do very good home-made soup served in lovely little tureens (£2.75), fresh plump salmon sandwiches (£3.25), walnut, grape and blue cchese salad or warm salad of black pudding, pancetta and apple (£4.25), herb crumbed fishcake with tomato or hollandaise sauce or steak and meaux mustard baguette (£4.95), welsh rarebit and bacon (£5), barbecued spare ribs (£5.50), queenie scallops in garlic with wensleydale and thyme crumb (£5.75), half a dozen oysters (£6.75, and puddings such as slow baked meringue with fruit compôte, dark and white chocolate terrine with gingered custard or hot orange liqueur pancakes (£3.50). In the evening (when people do tend to dress up), you can also eat in the polished brick-tiled conservatory with bentwood cane chairs or in the Brighton Belle dining car – where they also do a three-course Sunday lunch. Good wine, a fine choice of sherries, and around 30 malt whiskies, and 30 liqueurs. There are some seats under trees in the central court. *(Recommended by Jim Bush, K F Mould, B and C Clouting, Chris Brace, I R D Ross, Mr and Mrs A Bull, SS, M Borthwick)*

Free house ~ Licensees Mrs Audrey and Miss S Pagendam ~ Bar food (lunchtime, not Sun) ~ Restaurant (evening) ~ (01325) 377289 ~ Children in eating area of bar and in restaurant if over 7 ~ Open 12-2.30, 6-10.30(11 Sat); closed Sun evening and 24-26 Dec

MUKER SD9198 Map 10
Farmers Arms

B6270 W of Reeth

There are plenty of rewarding walks around this unpretentious pub in grand scenery – as well as interesting drives up over Buttertubs Pass or to the north, to Tan Hill and beyond. The cosy bar has a warm open fire and is simply furnished with stools and settles around copper-topped tables. Straightforward bar food includes lunchtime baps (£1.95) and toasties (£2.25), as well as soup (£1.95), home-made steak pie or chilli con carne (£5.25), broccoli and tomato bake or filled yorkshire pudding (£5.50), roast chicken (£5.95), salmon with dill sauce (£7.75), steaks (from £8.50), puddings (£2.75), and children's meals (from £3). John Smiths Bitter, and Theakstons Best and Old Peculier on handpump; darts and dominoes. They have a self-catering studio flat to rent. *(Recommended by Mary Thompson, Paul R White, Edward and Richard Norris, David and Mary Webb, Vann and Terry Prime)*

Free house ~ Licensees Chris and Marjorie Bellwood ~ Real ale ~ Bar food ~ (01748) 886297 ~ Children welcome ~ Open 11-3, 6.30(7 in winter)-11; 11-11 Sat; 12-10.30 Sun

NEWTON ON OUSE SE5160 Map 7

Dawnay Arms

Village signposted off A19 N of York

In fine weather, one of the obvious draws to this black-shuttered inn is the neat, sloping lawn that runs down to the River Ouse where there are moorings for three or four cruisers; plenty of seats on the terrace. Inside, on the right of the entrance is a comfortable, spacious room with a good deal of beamery and timbering and plush wall settles and chairs around wooden or dimpled copper tables. To the left is another airy room with plush button-back wall banquettes built into bays and a good log fire in the stone fireplace; lots of brass and copper. Good bar food includes sandwiches, soup (£2.50), home-made pâté (£3.25), deep-fried stilton mushrooms (£3.50), beef curry or baked squash filled with courgette provençale (£5.25), beef bourguignon or steak and mushroom in ale pie (£6.25), lamb's liver in red wine sauce (£7.95), fillet of salmon (£9.25), rack of Yorkshire lamb (£10.95), steaks (from £11.25), and home-made puddings (£3.25); the restaurant is no smoking. Well kept Boddingtons, Flowers Original, Morlands Old Speckled Hen and Tetleys on handpump, and over 40 malt whiskies; darts, pool, and fruit machine. Benningbrough Hall (National Trust) is five minutes' walk away. *(Recommended by Clifford and Joan Gough, J C Burley, Marlene and Jim Godfrey, M J Morgan, Malcolm Taylor, Mrs Frances Gray, Geoffrey and Brenda Wilson, Christopher Turner, Derek and Sylvia Stephenson, Janet and Peter Race)*

Free house ~ Licensees Alan and Richard Longley ~ Real ale ~ Bar food ~ Restaurant ~ (01347) 848345 ~ Children welcome ~ Open 12-3, 5.30(6 Sat)-11; 12-3, 7-10.30 Sun

NUNNINGTON SE6779 Map 7

Royal Oak 🍴

Church Street; at back of village, which is signposted from A170 and B1257

It's still the good, enjoyable food that draws people to this spotlessly kept and attractive little dining pub. Served by friendly and efficient staff, there might be sandwiches, home-made vegetable soup with lentils and bacon (£2.75), coronation chicken or spicy mushrooms (£3.95), egg mayonnaise with prawns (£4.75), ploughman's (£6.95), vegetable lasagne (£7.50), chicken curry, ham and mushroom tagliatelle or steak pie (£7.95), fisherman's pot (£8.50), pork fillet in barbecue sauce (£8.95), sirloin steak (£10.95), and daily specials such as toasted goat's cheese with crispy bacon and apple chutney (£3.95), tiger prawns in garlic butter (£5.95), crispy roast duckling with fresh orange sauce (£10.50), and fillet steak au poivre (£13.95). Well kept Black Bull, Tetleys and Theakstons Old Peculier on handpump. The bar has carefully chosen furniture such as kitchen and country dining chairs or a long pew around the sturdy tables on the turkey carpet, and a lectern in one corner; the high black beams are strung with earthenware flagons, copper jugs and lots of antique keys, one of the walls is stripped back to the bare stone to display a fine collection of antique farm tools, and there are open fires. Handy for a visit to Nunnington Hall (National Trust). *(Recommended by Paul and Ursula Randall, I R D Ross, Walter and Susan Rinaldi-Butcher, Trevor and Diane Waite, R Inman, Gethin Lewis, Mrs Frances Gray)*

Free house ~ Licensee Anthony Simpson ~ Real ale ~ Bar food ~ (01439) 748271 ~ Children in dining room if over 8 ~ Open 12-2.30, 6.30-11; 12-3, 7-10.30 Sun; closed Mon

OSMOTHERLEY SE4499 Map 10

Three Tuns 🍴 🛏

South End, off A19 N of Thirsk

The pubby front part of this well liked inn is just the place for a relaxed drink and has hardly been knocked about at all – it's popular with walkers, and with visitors to this lovely village centred around Mount Grace Priory. On the left is a simple small square bar and tap room, which fill quite quickly at weekends, a warm coal fire, and John Smiths Bitter and Theakstons Old Peculier and XB on handpump. There's quite a lot of emphasis on the good food with daily specials such as cream of fresh whiting and lobster soup (£3.25), cod fishcake with tomato and basil sauce (£3.25), various hors d'ouevres (£6.75), chestnut mushroom and stilton parcel with madeira sauce (£8.95), roast mini rack of pork with apricot and sage sauce (£9.50), grilled fresh salmon with creamed leeks (£9.75), grilled whole bass with parsley butter (£10.95), and fresh lobster (£15.45); from the menu, there might be sandwiches (from £2.95), deep-fried camembert with fresh raspberry sauce (£5.25), ploughman's with interesting cheeses from small producers and really good bread (£5.65), home-cooked ham or fresh goujons of Whitby lemon sole (£7.25), chicken breast filled with home-cooked ham and topped with melted cheese and a tomato sauce (£10.25), steaks (from £12.75), and home-made puddings like blueberry and apple crumble or sticky toffee pudding (£3.25). Sunday lunch (4 courses, £11.95); smart courteous and efficient service. The inn has a modest stone facade (with an old-fashioned wooden seat out by the door), and seats in the pleasant back garden with lovely views. The bedrooms are well equipped and comfortable. *(Recommended by Barry and Anne, RB, R F Grieve, Mr and Mrs W B Walker, Charles and Pauline Stride, Janet and Peter Race, Walter and Susan Rinaldi-Butcher)*

Free house ~ Licensee Hugh Dyson ~ Real ale ~ Bar food ~ Restaurant ~ (01609) 883301 ~ Children welcome ~ Open 11.30-3.30, 6.45-11; 12-3.30, 7-10.30 Sun ~ Bedrooms: /£68B

PICKHILL SE3584 Map 10

Nags Head 🍴 ♀

Take the Masham turn-off from A1 both N and S, and village signposted off B6267 in Ainderby Quernhow

This is the sort of place that customers return to regularly: either for the good food, the friendliness of the licensees – who have now been here over 29 years – or the accommodation (including the hearty breakfasts). This year, the no-smoking restaurant has been redesigned with a library theme, a new front verandah has been added, and there are plans for a boules and quoits pitch, and 9-hole putting green. The busy tap room on the left has beams hung with jugs, coach horns, ale-yards and so forth, and masses of ties hanging as a frieze from a rail around the red ceiling. The smarter lounge bar has deep green plush banquettes on the matching carpet, and pictures for sale on its neat cream walls, and another comfortable beamed room (mainly for restaurant users) has red plush button-back built-in wall banquettes around dark tables, and an open fire. Much enjoyed food includes soup (£2.75), sweet potato frittata with a tomato salad (£3.75), chicken liver and walnut pâté or garlic mushrooms with gruyère cheese and bacon (£3.95), hot and spicy prawns (£4.75), cottage pie with leek and mashed potato topping (£5.50), smoked salmon and scrambled egg (£5.75), timbale of Italian vegetables with goat's cheese and sun-dried tomatoes or prawn, salmon and cod fishcake with spinach and tomato salsa (£6.75), Caribbean red fish with ginger, chillis and coconut milk or steak, mushroom and oyster pie (£8.95), suet pudding of English game birds (£9.95), king scallops thermidor (£10.95), roast rack of English lamb with honey and rosemary (£13.95), and puddings like baked apple strudel with home-made plum and cinnamon ice cream, individual banoffee pie or spotted dick with custard sauce (£3.25). Well kept Black Sheep Bitter, Hambleton Bitter, John Smiths, Theakstons Black Bull, and a guest beer on handpump, a good choice of malt whiskies, and good value wines (several by the glass). One table is inset with a chessboard, and they also have cribbage, darts, dominoes, shove-ha'penny, and faint piped music. *(Recommended by Barry and Marie Males, Ian Phillips, Chris and Sue Bax, Julie and Tony Warneck, R Macnaughton, John Knighton, John and Christine Simpson, Walker and Debra Lapthorne, Susan and John Douglas, Isobel Paterson, Ken and Norma Burgess, Brian Abbott, Pat and Tony Martin, Anne Morgan, Susan and Nigel Wilson, Richard and Anne Hollingsworth, Neil Porter; also in the Good Hotel Guide)*

Free house ~ Licensees Edward and Raymond Baynton ~ Real ale ~ Bar food (12-2, 6-9.30) ~ Restaurant ~ (01845) 567391 ~ Well behaved children welcome until 7.30pm ~ Open 11-11; 12-10.30 Sun ~ Bedrooms: £40B/£60B

POOL SE2445 Map 7

White Hart

Just off A658 S of Harrogate, A659 E of Otley

This is a friendly pub with a good relaxing atmosphere and well liked food, usefully served all day. The four rooms have a restrained country décor, a pleasant medley of assorted old farmhouse furniture on the mix of stone flooring and carpet, and two log fires; one area is no smoking. At lunchtime, the good food includes sandwiches (from £3.60; sirloin steak £4.50), savoury bacon and cheddar melt (£2.95), home-roasted mediterranean style vegetables on garlic bread (£3.60), liver and bacon (£4.95), beef in ale pie (£5.95), and spicy grilled chicken breast on pasta with a creamy tomato sauce (£6.95); evening extras such as prawn cocktail (£2.70), rump steak (£7.50), grilled peppered halibut (£7.75), and minted lamb loin with savoury cheese bread and butter pudding (£7.95). Daily specials and puddings. Well kept Bass, Stones, and Worthington Best on handpump, and a good choice of wines with quite a few by the glass; fruit machine and piped music. There are tables outside, and pleasant surrounding walks. *(Recommended by Derek Stafford, Julia Gorham, Walter and Susan Rinaldi-Butcher, Geoffrey and Brenda Wilson, Rachael Ward, Mark Baynham, Michael Gittins, David and Phyllis Chapman, Anne and David Robinson)*

Bass ~ Manager David Britland ~ Real ale ~ Bar food (12-10 weekdays, till 9.30 weekends) ~ (0113) 202 7901 ~ Children welcome away from bar ~ Open 11.30-11; 12-10.30 Sun

RAMSGILL SE1271 Map 7

Yorke Arms ★ ⑪ ♟ 🛏

Take Nidderdale rd off B6265 in Pateley Bridge; or exhilarating but narrow moorland drive off A6108 at N edge of Masham, via Fearby and Lofthouse

One of the things that we particularly like about this creeper-clad former shooting lodge is that although this is a super place to stay with comfortable bedrooms and marvellous breakfasts – and the food is first rate – the courteous and friendly owners genuinely do welcome customers dropping in for just a drink. The bars have fresh flowers and polish smells, two or three heavy carved Jacobean oak chairs, a big oak dresser laden with polished pewter and other antiques, and open log fires. Exceptionally good imaginative food includes home-made soup such as lobster bisque (£3.50), house terrine with toasted brioche (£4.95), sandwiches on home-made bread (from £4.95), crispy duck with roasted fennel and citrus (£5.30), Yorkshire cheeses with home-made relish (£5.25), freshly made pasta with chilli and chargrilled vegetables (£7.95), Yorkshire ham and eggs with sauté potatoes (£8.20), caesar salad with chargrilled tuna (£8.50), venison steak with celeriac, wild mushrooms and a port wine sauce (£9.20), herb-crusted loin of lamb with pestou mash and sweet potato shavings (£10.20), steaks (from £12.50), and daily specials such as avocado, artichoke and prawn mille-feuille or asparagus and tomato tart tatin (£5.20), grilled butternut squash, spinach and goat's cheese (£8.50), fillet of brill, prawns, spinach and vermouth sauce (£9.75), and sautéed calf's liver, duck breast and black pudding with sweet potato mash and greens (£10.50), with puddings like banana and caramel sable, lemon charlotte with raspberries or chocolate tart with apricot sorbet (from £4.20). Well kept Black Sheep Special, John Smiths, and Theakstons Best on handpump, a fine wine list with 10 by the glass, and a good choice of brandies, malt whiskies, liqueurs, and fresh juices. Darts, dominoes, and piped music. They prefer smart dress in the no-smoking restaurant in the evening. You can walk up the magnificent if strenuous moorland road to Masham, or perhaps on the right-of-way track that leads along the hill behind the reservoir, also a bird sanctuary. *(Recommended by Peter and Giff Bennett, Ian Phillips, Lesley, Peter and Alastair Barrett, R Inman, A Longden, B and M Kendall, Julian and Alison Roberts, Caroline Raphael, David Hawkes, Alan and Mandy Maynard, Michael Butler, Geoff Tomlinson)*

Free house ~ Licensees Bill and Frances Atkins ~ Real ale ~ Bar food (not Sun evenings) ~ Restaurant ~ (01423) 755243 ~ Children in eating area of bar ~ Open 11-11; 12-10.30 Sun ~ Bedrooms: £70B/£130B

REDMIRE SE0591 Map 10
Kings Arms ◀

Wensley—Askrigg back road: a good alternative to the A684 through Wensleydale

Now run by the previous licencee's son James, this charming little pub is tucked away in an attractive small village. The simply furnished bar has cloth-covered wall settles and wall seats set around cast-iron tables, and there's a fine oak armchair (its back carved like a mop of hair) and a woodburning stove. Good bar food includes good soup (£2.25), sandwiches (from £2.25), smoked wild boar or salmon goujons (£3.95), vegetarian dishes (from £5.95), home-made lasagne (£6.95), good steak and kidney pie (£7.45), tasty stilton chicken (£8.45), well like duck with black cherry sauce (£11.45), steaks (from £11.45), and Sunday roast (£5.45); the restaurant is no smoking and has local scenes on the wall painted by a local artist. Well kept Black Sheep, John Smiths, Theakstons, and a guest such as Redmire Brew (brewed for the pub by Hambleton Ales) or Hambleton White Boar on handpump kept under light blanket pressure, over 50 malt whiskies, and decent wines. The rather sweet staffordshire bull terrier is called Kim. Pool, dominoes, and cribbage; quoits. From the tables and chairs in the pretty garden here there's a superb view across Wensleydale; fishing nearby. Handy for Castle Bolton where Mary Queen of Scots was imprisoned. *(Recommended by Kevin Thorpe, Jim Bush, DJW, Bruce Bird, B, M and P Kendall, Mr and Mrs P Frost, K F Mould, Vicky and David Sarti, Mary Thompson, Vann and Terry Prime)*

Free house ~ Licensee James Stevens ~ Real ale ~ Bar food ~ Restaurant ~ (01969) 622316 ~ Children welcome ~ Open 11-3, 6-11; 12-3, 7-10.30 Sun ~ Bedrooms: £18/£36

RIPLEY SE2861 Map 7
Boars Head 🍽 � ◀ 🛏

Off A61 Harrogate—Ripon

In a delightful estate village, this is, of course, a comfortable hotel – but it does have a welcoming, very well liked bar with the feel of an upmarket village pub. There's a separate entrance to reach it, though you can walk through the public rooms if you wish; it's a long flagstoned room with green checked tablecloths and olive oil on all the tables, most of which are arranged to form individual booths. The green walls have jolly little drawings of cricketers or huntsmen running along the bottom, as well as a boar's head (part of the family coat of arms), a couple of cricket bats, and well kept Theakstons Best and Old Peculier, and their intriguing Crackshot – brewed to their own 17th-c recipe by Daleside; an excellent wine list (with ten or so by the glass), and a good choice of malt whiskies. The excellent bar food changes weekly and might include sandwiches, home-made soup (£2.50), warm salad of black pudding, chorizo and bacon lardons with a sweet chilli dressing (£3.95), mousseline of smoked salmon on a lemon and lime scented salad (£4), filo parcel of goat's cheese and basil on a fine herb salad with hoisin dressing or with pesto and tomato sauce (£7.95), grilled fillet of seabream with pesto flavoured sauté potatoes and watercress sauce or braised shank of lamb on carrot and turnip purée with rosemary gravy (£8.50), roast chicken breast on a compôte of calvados prunes and port wine jus or lamb's liver with crispy smoked bacon and minted crushed new potatoes with red wine gravy (£8.95), chargrilled rib-eye steak on sweet and sour onions with madeira sauce (£9.95), and puddings such as sticky toffee pudding, chocolate and mint terrine with a compôte of oranges or raspberry and pecan crème brûlée topped with vanilla pod ice cream (£3.50). Part of the bar is no smoking. Some of the furnishings in the hotel came from the attic of next door Ripley Castle, where the Ingilbys have lived for over 650 years. A pleasant little garden has plenty of tables. They are kind to children and dogs. *(Recommended by Peter and Jennifer Sketch, Miss L Hodson, Janet and Peter Race)*

Free house ~ Licensee Sir Thomas Ingilby ~ Real ale ~ Bar food ~ Restaurant ~ (01423) 771888 ~ Children welcome ~ Open 11-11; 12-10.30 Sun ~ Bedrooms: £95B/£115B

RIPPONDEN SE0419 Map 7

Old Bridge ♀

Priest Lane; from A58, best approach is Elland Road (opposite Golden Lion), park opposite
the church in pub's car park and walk back over ancient hump-backed bridge

Set by the medieval pack horse bridge over the little River Ryburn, this rather civilised
14th-c pub has been run by Mr Beaumont since 1963. The three communicating
rooms are each on a slightly different level, and there are oak settles built into the
window recesses of the thick stone walls, antique oak tables, rush-seated chairs, a few
well chosen pictures and prints, a big woodburning stove, and a relaxed atmosphere;
fresh flowers in summer. Good, popular bar food includes a well liked weekday
lunchtime cold meat buffet which always has a joint of rare beef, as well as spiced
ham, quiche, scotch eggs and so on (£8.50 with a bowl of soup and coffee); also,
sandwiches (from £2.50), country-style terrine (£3.25), devilled crab (£3.95), stilton,
mushroom and lentil cannelloni (£4.50), pork, pepper and butterbean stew,
chargrilled vegetable lasagne or fish pie (£4.75), and puddings like banana and toffee
pancakes, lemon cream pie or chocolate and brandy vacherin (£2.50). Well kept
Black Sheep Special, Timothy Taylor Best, Landlord, and Golden, and a beer named
for the pub on handpump, 30 malt whiskies, a good choice of foreign bottled beers,
and interesting wines with at least a dozen by the glass. The popular restaurant is over
the bridge. *(Recommended by Chris and Pascale Worth, ALC, Ian and Nita Cooper, Pat and
Tony Hinkins, Steve Goodchild, Derek and Sylvia Stephenson)*

*Free house ~ Licensees Tim Walker and Ian Beaumont ~ Real ale ~ Bar food (12-2, 6-
9.30; not Sat or Sun evening) ~ Restaurant ~ (01422) 822595 ~ Children in eating area
of bar until 9pm ~ Open 12-3, 5.30-11; 12-11 Sat; 12-10.30 Sun*

ROBIN HOODS BAY NZ9505 Map 10

Laurel ◀

Village signposted off A171 S of Whitby

Just far enough down the hill in this particularly pretty and unspoilt fishing village for
the journey back up again not to be too taxing, you'll find this charming little pub set
in a row of fishermen's cottages. The friendly beamed main bar bustles with locals
and visitors, and is decorated with old local photographs, Victorian prints and
brasses, and lager bottles from all over the world; there's a roaring open fire. Bar food
consists of summer sandwiches and winter soup. Well kept John Smiths and
Theakstons Old Peculier and Black Bull on handpump; darts, shove-ha'penny,
dominoes, cribbage, and piped music. In summer, the hanging baskets and window
boxes are lovely. They have a self-contained apartment for two people. *(Recommended
by Ian Phillips, JP, PP, RWD, John and Esther Sprinkle, Jamie and Sarah Allan, Keith and Janet
Morris, SLC, David Carr, Nick and Alison Dowson)*

*Scottish Courage ~ Tenant Brian Catling ~ Real ale ~ (01947) 880400 ~ Children in
snug bar only ~ Open 12-11; 12-10.30 Sun*

ROSEDALE ABBEY SE7395 Map 10

Milburn Arms ⊕ ♀ ⇚

The easiest road to the village is through Cropton from Wrelton, off the A170 W of Pickering

Surrounded by fine, steep moorland and overlooking the village, this welcoming
18th-c inn is run by a helpful, kind licensee. It's an enjoyable place to spend a couple
of days (the breakfasts are huge), and there's a good atmosphere and log fire in the
neatly kept L-shaped and beamed main bar plus well kept Bass, Black Sheep Special,
and Stones on handpump; lots of malt whiskies and eight good house wines by the
glass. Generous helpings of good food served by smartly dressed waitresses might
include home-made soup (£2.50), good lunchtime sandwiches (from £2.75), chicken
liver and bacon salad (£3.25), wild boar sausage on a leek and mustard mash with
onion gravy (£4.50), confit of duck on braised cabbage and a green peppercorn sauce
(£4.75), mediterranean prawns in garlic butter with bacon and a lemon dressing
(£5.50), grilled gammon with pineapple (£6.50), fresh crab salad (£6.95), halibut with

a balsamic dressing (£7.50), chicken breast with mushroom and tarragon sauce (£7.95), chargrilled fillet of pork with hunter sauce (£8.75), 10oz sirloin steak (£10.95), and home-made puddings (£2.75); huge breakfasts. The restaurant is no smoking. The terrace and garden have plenty of seats. *(Recommended by Barry and Anne, David and Brenda Tew, Pamela and Merlyn Horswell, Peter and Pat Frogley, Gethin Lewis, Barbara Wensworth, Comus Elliott)*

Free house ~ Licensee Terry Bentley ~ Real ale ~ Bar food ~ Restaurant ~ (01751) 417312 ~ Children welcome but must leave bar by 8.30pm ~ Open 11.30-3, 6.30-11; 11-11 Sat; 12-3, 6.30-10.30 Sun ~ Bedrooms: £45B/£76B

SAWLEY SE2568 Map 7
Sawley Arms ♀
Village signposted off B6265 W of Ripon

Neatly kept and welcoming, the series of small turkey-carpeted rooms in this rather smart pub have been firmly run by Mrs Hawes for over 30 years now. There are log fires and comfortable furniture ranging from small softly cushioned armed dining chairs and settees, to the wing armchairs down a couple of steps in a side snug, and maybe daily papers and magazines to read; two small rooms (and the restaurant) are no smoking. Good, genuinely home-made bar food includes lunchtime sandwiches (from £4.10), interesting soups with croutons (£2.60), salmon mousse or stilton, port and celery pâté (£4.50), salads (£7.20), plaice mornay on a bed of leeks (£7.50), steak pie with buttercrust pastry (£8.70), breast of chicken with a mushroom and herb sauce (£8.80), and puddings such as apple pie with cream, madeira surprise or amaretti schokolandentorte – amaretti biscuits with chocolate, cream, rum, brandy and cider – (from £3.25). Good house wines and quiet piped music. The award-winning flowering tubs, baskets and gardens are quite spectacular. Fountains Abbey (the most extensive of the great monastic remains – floodlit on late summer Friday and Saturday evenings, with a live choir on the Saturday) is not far away. *(Recommended by Walker and Debra Lapthorne, Janet and Peter Race, Paul R White, Bill and Kathy Cissna, Gwen and Peter Andrews, Derek Harvey-Piper, M A Buchanan, Ian Phillips, B, M and P Kendall, Geoffrey and Brenda Wilson)*

Free house ~ Licensee Mrs June Hawes ~ Bar food ~ Restaurant ~ (01765) 620642 ~ Well behaved children allowed if over 9 ~ Open 11.30-3, 6.30-10.30; 12-3 Sun; closed Sun and Mon evenings ~ Bedrooms: /£45B

SCAWTON SE5584 Map 10
Hare
Village signposted off A170 Thirsk—Helmsley, just E of Sutton Bank

This low-built red-tiled pub catches the eye, with the roses against its cream walls and green woodwork, and its pair of inn-signs with attractive naïve hare paintings. Inside, the atmosphere is excellent; it's been comfortably modernised without losing its cosy and unspoilt feel. It has rag rugs on flagstones and carpet, stripped pine tables, an old-fashioned range and a woodburner, lots of bric-a-brac, a settee, simple wall settles, a seat in the bow window, a comfortable eating area, and in the innermost area a heavy old beam-and-plank ceiling; new pool room. Sensibly priced good generously served food listed on big blackboards includes soup (£2.50), sandwiches (from £3.50), ploughman's (£4.50), steak and kidney pudding, roasted stuffed peppers with mozzarella, basil and tomatoes or smoked haddock fishcakes (£6.95), roast suckling pig or fried monkfish with tomato and garlic sauce (£10.95), and a good choice of puddings such as trio of chocolate puddings (£4.50). Service is friendly (as are the two dogs); well kept Timothy Taylor Landlord and Black Sheep on handpump; piped music. A big garden behind has tables. The pub, which is said to date back in part to Norman times, is handy for Rievaulx Abbey. *(Recommended by Mr and Mrs R Illingworth, C A Hall, Juliet Short, Richard Cole)*

Free house ~ Licensee Heather Jones ~ Real ale ~ Bar food ~ Restaurant ~ (01845) 597289 ~ Children in eating area ~ Open 12-2.30, 6.30-11(10.30 Sun); closed Mon lunchtime

SETTLE SD8264 Map 7
Golden Lion
B6480, off A65 bypass

There's a good mix of customers in this handsome inn, and the licensee and his staff are friendly and helpful to all. As well as a cheerful atmosphere, the bar has an enormous fireplace, comfortable settles and plush seats, brass, and prints and chinese plates on dark panelling; a surprisingly grand staircase sweeps down into the spacious high-beamed hall bar. Enjoyable bar food includes soup (£2), sandwiches (from £2.95; crispy bacon and egg with tomato and melted cheese £4.15; prawns, banana and pineapple £4.50; chicken tikka £4.55), filled baked potatoes or pasta carbonara (£3.95), good chilli with garlic bread or ploughman's (£5.95), chicken caesar salad (£6.25), and daily specials like slices of black pudding with mustard sauce (£3.10), prawn and egg mayonnaise (£3.75), vegetable tikka (£5.25), steak and kidney pie (£6.25), home-made game casserole (£6.75), curried lamb (£6.95), poached fillet of Shetland salmon topped with shrimp sauce (£7), barbary duckling and chicken breasts on onion marmalade with orange sauce and roasted garlic (£7.75), and 10oz rib-eye steak (£9.95). Well kept Thwaites Bitter, Chairmans, and a guest beer on handpump, decent wines, and country wines. The lively public bar has pool, fruit machine, dominoes, and piped music; the labrador-cross is called Monty, and the black and white cat, Luke. *(Recommended by Joy and Peter Heatherley, Arthur Williams, Lyn and Geoff Hallchurch, RT and JC Moggridge, Walter and Susan Rinaldi-Butcher, Anthony Barnes, Jim Bush, Margaret and Arthur Dickinson, Carol and Dono Leaman)*

Thwaites ~ Tenant Phillip Longrigg ~ Real ale ~ Bar food (12-2.30, 6-10) ~ Restaurant ~ (01729) 822203 ~ Children in eating area of bar until 8pm ~ Open 11-11; 12-10.30 Sun ~ Bedrooms: £23.50(£30.50B)/£47(£59B)

SHEFFIELD SK3687 Map 7
Fat Cat 🍺 £
23 Alma St

They've now opened a new Brewery Visitor's Centre in this friendly, bustling pub and brewery trips can be booked (0114) 249 4805. As well as their own-brewed and cheap Kelham Island Bitter, Pale Rider and another Kelham Island beer, and Timothy Taylor Landlord, there are seven interesting guest beers on handpump from breweries like Iceni, Maypole, Roosters, Rudgate, York, and so forth, plus Belgian bottled beers (and a Belgian draught beer), British bottled beers, fruit gin, country wines, and farm cider. Good bar food (with prices virtually unchanged) includes sandwiches, soup (£1.30), vegetable cobbler, ploughman's, Mexican mince, leek and butter bean casserole, and pork and pepper casserole (all £2.50), and puddings such as apple and rhubarb crumble or jam roly poly (£1); well liked Sunday lunch (£3). The two small downstairs rooms have a good mix of customers, coal fires, simple wooden tables and cushioned seats around the walls, and jugs, bottles, and some advertising mirrors on the walls; the one on the left is no smoking; cribbage and dominoes. Steep steps take you up to another similarly simple room (which may be booked for functions) with some attractive prints of old Sheffield; there are picnic-sets in a fairylit back courtyard. *(Recommended by Richard Lewis, Tony Hobden, David Carr, John McDonald, Ann Bond, Ian Phillips, Geoff and Sylvia Donald, the Didler, JP, PP)*

Own brew ~ Licensee Stephen Fearn ~ Real ale ~ Bar food (lunchtime) ~ (0114) 249 4801 ~ Children in upstairs room lunchtime and early evening (if room not booked) ~ Open 12-3, 5.30-11; 12-3, 7-10.30 Sun; closed 25 and 26 Dec

New Barrack 🍺 £
601 Penistone Rd, Hillsborough

Bustling and friendly, this sizeable pub has a fine choice of nine real ales well kept on handpump, with regulars such as Abbeydale Moonshine, Black Sheep, Barnsley Bitter, and John Smiths Magnet, and five guest beers; also, four continental draught lagers, 30 continental bottled beers, and 50 malt whiskies. The comfortable front lounge has red leather banquettes, old pine floors, an open fire, and collections of decorative plates and of bottles, and there are two smaller rooms behind, one with TV and darts – the family room is no smoking. Darts, cribbage, dominoes, and piped music. The good value simple food is all freshly made and might include sandwiches (from £1.30, bacon or sausage £1.85 with egg £2.25; steak £3.95), home-made pork terrine (£2.75), and ploughman's with home-made chutney, citrus roast chicken, mushroom and leek crumble with hazelnut topping, lamb in red wine or chilli con carne (all £3.95); on the first Wednesday of the month, they hold a vegetarian evening, and on the other three, they have a curry or middle eastern evening (£4.50); good value Sunday lunch. Service is friendly and competent; daily papers and magazines to read; maybe quiet piped radio. There are tables out behind. Local parking is not easy. *(Recommended by CMW, JJW, JP, PP, Terry Barlow, S E Paulley, Stephen and Julie Brown, Richard Lewis, the Didler)*

Free house ~ Licensee James Birkett ~ Real ale ~ Bar food (12-2.30, 5.30-7.30; not Sat or Sun evening) ~ (0114) 234 9148 ~ Children in no-smoking back room ~ Folk Mon evening, quiz Thurs evening, jazz/blues Sat evening ~ Open 12-11; 12-10.30 Sun

SHELLEY SE2112 Map 7
Three Acres 🍴 ♀ 🍺 🛏

Roydhouse; B6116 and turn left just before Pennine Garden Centre; straight on for about 3 miles

Yorkshire Dining Pub of the Year

The range of well kept real ales in this civilised former coaching inn manages to qualify this exceptionally popular place as a pub – but it is certainly the food that most people come to enjoy. The roomy lounge bar has a relaxed, friendly atmosphere, tankards hanging from the main beam, button-back leather sofas, old prints and so forth, and maybe a pianist playing light music. Imaginative and highly enjoyable, the food includes sandwiches like cumberland sausage with fried onions and mild mustard mayonnaise (£3.25), wafer thin smoked ham with brie, plum tomatoes and real ale chutney (£3.50), and open fresh Cornish crab on sun-dried tomato bread with aioli and red chard (£5.95), as well as good soups (from £2.95; a croque of french onion soup £3.25), yorkshire pudding with award winning black pudding, caramelised apple and onion gravy (£4.25), parfait of chicken livers with onion bread and cornichons (£4.95), half a dozen Cuan Irish oysters or a timbale of various prawns with herb salad (£6.95), steak, kidney and mushroom pie or deep-fried cod with home-made chips and minted mushy peas (£8.75), a plate of charcuterie and mixed antipasti with garlic and herb bruschetta (£8.95), and king prawns in Thai dressing (£12.95), with evening dishes like award winning potted shrimps with hot buttered soldiers or foie gras and ham knuckle terrine (£6.95), a noodle bowl with Chinese pork and barbecued duck with pak choi and shi-itake mushrooms (£12.95), and whole roast Cornish plaice on the bone with baby capers and herb oil (£15.95); puddings such as passion fruit tart with raspberry sauce, assiette of chocolate gourmande or apple pie with crème anglaise and gingerbread ice cream (£4.25). There's a popular seafood bar, and they've opened a specialist delicatessen next door. Well kept changing ales such as Adnams Bitter, Mansfield Bitter and Riding, Morlands Old Speckled Hen, and Timothy Taylor Landlord on handpump, a good choice of malt whiskies, and exceptional (if not cheap) choice of wines. This is a nice place to stay and the breakfasts are particularly good. There are fine views across to Emley Moor, occasionally livened up by the local hunt passing. *(Recommended by Neil Townend, GLD, David Hawkes, Peter Marshall, Hugh Roberts, Mr and Mrs G Turner, Mike and Mary Carter, Alan J Morton, Michael Butler)*

Free house ~ Licensees Neil Truelove and Brian Orme ~ Real ale ~ Bar food (not Sat lunch) ~ Restaurant ~ (01484) 602606 ~ Children welcome ~ Open 12-3, 7-11(10.30 Sun) ~ Bedrooms: £50B/£65B

SINNINGTON SE7485 Map 10
Fox & Hounds 🛏

Village signposted just off A170 W of Pickering

Good food is the main draw in this well kept pub which is nicely set in an attractive village with a pretty stream and lots of grass. The clean and welcoming beamed bar has nice pictures and old artefacts, a woodburning stove, and comfortable wall seats and carver chairs around the neat tables on its carpet; winter pool. The curved corner bar counter has well kept Camerons and Black Sheep on handpump and a good choice of malt whiskies. The food, quickly served here and in the sizeable comfortable dining room, includes sandwiches (from £2.40), soup (£2.95), filled french sticks (from £3.95, steak and onion £4.95), steak pie or battered haddock (£6.25), pasta with tomato and spinach sauce (£6.75), scampi (£6.95) and fried chicken supreme with tarragon sauce (£7.45), and more elaborate evening dishes like roasted peppers stuffed with cherry tomatoes and mozzarella (£4.25), shellfish salad (£5.95), broccoli and mushroom tart or cod fillet with salmon and prawn sauce (£8.25), half a roast duck with port and brandy sauce (£10.95) with puddings such as caramelised banana and strawberries in a brandy snap basket with butterscotch sauce, blackberry brûlée, chocolate roulade and honeycomb ice cream (£3.25). There's a separate stables bar. Dogs are welcome, pleasant chatty service and if you're staying, the breakfasts are good (one reader found 1796 graffiti diamond-cut on their window). Outside in front are picnic-sets. *(Recommended by David and Ruth Hollands, I R D Ross, SLC, Vanessa Hatch, Dave Creech, Colin and Dot Savill)*

Free house ~ Licensees Andrew and Catherine Stephens ~ Real ale ~ Bar food (12-2, 6.30-9(8.30 Sun)) ~ (01751) 431577 ~ Well behaved children welcome ~ Open 12-2, 6-11; 12-2, 6.30-10.30 Sun ~ Bedrooms: £44/£64

SNAITH SE6422 Map 7
Brewers Arms 🍺

10 Pontefract Rd

The Old Mill Brewery where the excellent ales here are brewed is just around the corner, and you can arrange a tour. The selection on handpump may include Old Mill Traditional, Mild, Old Curiosity, Black Jack, Nellie Dean and Three Lions; unusually, they also do their own lager as well; quite a few malt whiskies. In the pleasant clean and bright open-plan rooms of the bar there are old local photographs, exposed ceiling joists and a neat brick and timber bar counter. Straightforward bar food includes good steak and kidney pie (£5), roasts (£5.50) and chicken à la crème (£5.95). There are also good value home-cooked restaurant meals in the fresh and airy conservatory-style no-smoking dining area with green plush chairs, a turkey carpet, a pine plank ceiling and lots of plants. Fruit machine and piped music; beware of joining the skeleton at the bottom of the old well. *(Recommended by JP, PP, Tony Hobden, Roger Bellingham, D J Walker)*

Own brew ~ Manager John McCue ~ Real ale ~ Bar food ~ Restaurant ~ (01405) 862404 ~ Children in eating area of bar until 9pm ~ Open 12-3, 6-11(7-10.30 Sun) ~ Bedrooms: £40B/£57B

STARBOTTON SD9574 Map 7
Fox & Hounds 🍽️ 🛏️

B6160 Upper Wharfedale rd N of Kettlewell; OS Sheet 98, map reference 953749

This is a smashing and warmly friendly little pub with very good food and enjoyably well kept real ales. It's notably well run by the helpful licensees, and the bar has traditional solid furniture on the flagstones, a collection of plates on the walls, whisky jugs hanging from the high beams supporting ceiling boards, and a big stone fireplace (with an enormous fire in winter). To be sure of a seat, it's best to get here early as the food is so popular: tomato and basil soup with home-made granary bread (£2.50), black pudding parcels with apple sauce (£3.25), blue cheese soufflé with tomato and onion salad (£3.50), pork and sage burger (£6.25), steak and mushroom pie (£6.50), parsnip and chestnut crumble or picadillo, a Mexican mince dish (£6.75), chicken and leek crumble (£7), moroccan-style lamb (£7.50), daily specials such as bobotie (£6.50), and thai-style green chicken curry or smoked haddock kedgeree (£7), and home-made puddings like rhubarb and ginger pudding, dark chocolate pudding with white chocolate sauce or lemon ice box pie; at lunchtime there are also filled french sticks and ploughman's and yorkshire pudding filled with mince or ratatouille (£5).

The dining area is no smoking. Well kept Black Sheep Bitter, Theakstons Black Bull and Old Peculier, and Timothy Taylor Landlord on handpump, and around 60 malt whiskies. Dominoes, cribbage, and well reproduced, unobtrusive piped music. Seats in a sheltered corner enjoy the view over the hills all around this little hamlet. *(Recommended by Chris Brace, Prof and Mrs S Barnett, P Abbott, Lesley, Peter and Alastair Barrett, Alan Morton, Vann and Terry Prime, Geoffrey and Brenda Wilson, B and M Kendall, Pierre and Pat Richterich, Marlene and Jim Godfrey, Stephen and Tracey Groves, Gwen and Peter Andrews, David Heath, Chris and Elaine Lyon, David Hawkes, WAH, Chris and Sue Bax, Tim and Linda Collins, Malcolm and Jennifer Perry)*

Free house ~ Licensees James and Hilary McFadyen ~ Real ale ~ Bar food ~ (01756) 760269 ~ Children welcome ~ Open 11.30-3, 6.30-11; 12-3, 7-10.30 Sun; closed Mon except bank hol lunchtimes, Jan-mid Feb ~ Bedrooms: £35B/£50B

STUTTON SE4841 Map 7
Hare & Hounds

Particularly at weekends, this friendly stone-built pub tends to fill up quickly, so it's best to get here early then. The cosy low-ceilinged rooms are unusually done out in 1960s style, and they keep Sam Smiths OB on handpump, and decent wine; piped music. Good, helpful service and well liked bar food such as home-made soup (£2.25), sandwiches (from £2.95), chicken liver pâté or spare ribs in a spicy tomato sauce (£3.75), ploughman's (£4.50), home-made steak and mushroom pie, liver and bacon or cumberland sausage with mash and yorkshire pudding (£4.95), roast beef or chicken (£5.50), seafood pie (£5.95), prawn curry (£6.25), steaks (from £7.95), grilled halibut with garlic sauce (£9.50), and puddings (£2.95); traditional Sunday lunch. The lovely long sloping garden is quite a draw for families, and there are toys out here for children. *(Recommended by Janet Pickles, Michael A Butler, Andy and Jill Kassube)*

Sam Smiths ~ Tenant Mike Chiswick ~ Real ale ~ Bar food (11.30-2, 6.30-9.30; not Sun evenings, not Mon) ~ Restaurant ~ (01937) 833164 ~ Well behaved children in eating area of bar and restaurant until 8pm ~ Open 11.30-3, 6.30(6 Fri/Sat)-11; 12-3, 7-10.30 Sun; closed Mon and 26 Dec

SUTTON UPON DERWENT SE7047 Map 7
St Vincent Arms 🏠

B1228 SE of York

A fine choice of well kept real ales on handpump here might include Banks's Bitter, Fullers London Pride, ESB, Chiswick and a seasonal beer, John Smiths, Timothy Taylor Landlord, and Wells Bombardier; also a range of malt whiskies, and very reasonably priced spirits. Bar food includes sandwiches (from £1.80), home-made soup (£1.90), filled baked potatoes (from £1.95), baked goat's cheese or smoked haddock topped with welsh rarebit (£3.75), lasagne (£6.50), steak and kidney pie (£6.80), king prawn provençale (£9), steaks (from £9.50), daily specials like breast of chicken stuffed with mango with a mild curry sauce (£8.50) or scallops with a cream and vermouth sauce (£9.50), and puddings like treacle tart or sticky toffee pudding (£2.35). One eating area is no smoking. The parlour-like, panelled front bar has traditional high-backed settles, a cushioned bow-window seat, windsor chairs and a coal fire; another lounge and separate dining room open off. No games or music. There are seats in the garden. The pub is named after the admiral who was granted the village and lands by the nation as thanks for his successful commands – and for coping with Nelson's infatuation with Lady Hamilton. *(Recommended by Paul and Pam Penrose, DJW, B T Smith, Mr and Mrs A H Young, C A Hall, Mr and Mrs Staples, Peter Marshall, Malcolm Taylor, Derek and Sylvia Stephenson, Roger Bellingham, Margaret and Arthur Dickinson)*

Free house ~ Licensee Phil Hopwood ~ Real ale ~ Bar food ~ Restaurant ~ (01904) 608349 ~ Well behaved children in eating area of bar and in restaurant ~ Open 11.30-3, 6-11; 12-3, 7-10.30 Sun; closed evening 25 Dec

It's very helpful if you let us know up-to-date food prices when you report on pubs.

TERRINGTON SE6571 Map 7
Bay Horse

W of Malton; off B1257 at Hovingham (towards York, eventually signposted left) or Slingsby (towards Castle Howard, then right); can also be reached off A64 via Castle Howard, or via Welburn and Ganthorpe

In an unspoilt village on one of the rolling old coach roads that make the most of the Howardian Hill views, this charming country pub has a peaceful, relaxed atmosphere. The cosy lounge bar has country prints, china on delft shelves, magazines to read, and a good log fire, and a traditional public bar has darts, shove-ha'penny, and dominoes. There's a dining area handsomely furnished in oak, and a back family conservatory has a collection of old farm tools on the walls. Well presented bar food includes lunchtime sandwiches, baps or crusty bread (from £2), filled baked potatoes (£2.35), and ploughman's (£4.95), as well as home-made soup (£2), good potted blue and white wensleydale with port and walnuts (£3.25), garlic mushrooms with a tomato and onion dip (£3.45), crisp fried Whitby king prawns with blue cheese dressing (£3.95), nut, wholemeal and celery croquettes with a sweet and sour sauce (£5.45), lamb's liver and smoked bacon with onion and Guinness gravy (£5.75), home-made steak and kidney pie (£5.95), chicken breast with a mild Thai sauce (£6.95), pork fillet in fine oatmeal on a bed of apple, onion and potato in cream (£7.25), steaks (from £8.50), daily specials, and puddings such as toffee mousse on a biscuit base with toffee coated popcorn, white chocolate, brandy and chestnut terrine on dark chocolate sauce or apple pie (£2.50); children's dishes (from £1.50), and on Tuesday lunchtimes, they only serve soup and sandwiches. Well kept Courage Directors, John Smiths, and Theakstons Black Bull on handpump, and 70 blended and malt whiskies. There are tables out in a small but attractively planted garden. *(Recommended by Greta and Christopher Wells, I R D Ross, Brian Wardrobe, Allan Worsley, Don and Thelma Anderson, Dave Braisted, Pat and Tony Martin)*

Free house ~ Licensees Robert and Jill Snowdon ~ Real ale ~ Bar food (not Sun or Tues evenings) ~ Restaurant ~ (01653) 648416 ~ Children welcome ~ Open 12-3, 6-11(7-10.30 Sun)

THORGANBY SE6942 Map 7
Jefferson Arms ⌨

Off A163 NE of Selby, via Skipwith

Run by two friendly and helpful sisters, this handsome and surprisingly old village inn is well liked for its good food. The spacious main bar is relaxed and stylish, with brick pillars and bar counter, dark wooden cushioned pews, several big mirrors on the green fleur-de-lys pattered walls, and a couple of smart display chairs with huge sunflowers. A delightful little beamed lounge is more comfortable still, full of sofas and armchairs, as well as fresh flowers and potted plants, a fireplace with logs beside it, an antique telephone, and a pile of *Hello!* magazines. A long narrow conservatory is festooned with passion flowers and grape vines. The good food includes a rosti menu prepared by Mrs Rapp's husband who is Swiss. A rosti is a speciality with grated, fried potatoes: bacon, mushrooms and two eggs or spinach, cheese and a fried egg (£4.90), prawns, herbs, green peppercorns and scrambled eggs or ham, tomatoes, mushrooms and mozzarella cheese (£5.20), and ostrich in red wine and cranberry sauce or pork in a cream of mushroom sauce (£5.90). Also, sandwiches (from £2.20), stuffed jalapeno peppers (£4.20), battered haddock with home-made chips (£5.80), Milanese potato gnocchi (£6.60), and poached salmon in a creamy orange sauce (£8.60). Well kept Black Sheep Bitter and John Smiths on handpump and a thoughtful wine list; darts chess, backgammon, and piped music; The restaurant and conservatory are no smoking. There are tables in a porch area, and more in a side garden with roses and a brick barbecue. It's a nice, peaceful place to stay. *(Recommended by P Barnes, Eileen and David Webster, H Bramwell)*

Free house ~ Licensee Margaret Rapp ~ Real ale ~ Bar food ~ Restaurant ~ (01904) 448316 ~ Children in eating area of bar until 9pm ~ Open 12-3, 6-11; 12-10.30 Sun; closed Mon ~ Bedrooms: £35B/£55B

THORNTON WATLASS SE2486 Map 10
Buck 🍴 🍺 🛏

Village signposted off B6268 Bedale—Masham

Even though the warmly friendly licensees have been here 13 years – 11 of which they've been in this Guide – their enthusiasm is as buoyant as ever. It remains a genuine local with their own cricket team (the pub not only borders the village cricket green – one wall is actually the boundary) and quoits team, and regular live music. Readers are quick to tell us, though, that as visitors they are made just as welcome as regulars, and it is a good place from which to base a holiday (they offer golfing, racing and fishing breaks and there are plenty of surrounding walks), and the accommodation is clean and warm, with excellent breakfasts. The pleasantly traditional right-hand bar has upholstered old-fashioned wall settles on the carpet, a fine mahogany bar counter, a high shelf packed with ancient bottles, several mounted fox masks and brushes (the Bedale hunt meets in the village), a brick fireplace, and a relaxed atmosphere; piped music. Good, popular food at lunchtime might include sandwiches, mushrooms in beer batter with a choice of dips or popular Masham rarebit (wensleydale cheese with local ale topped with bacon, £3.75), caesar salad with smoked chicken or Singapore noodles with prawns (£4.25), ploughman's with good cheeses and home-made chutney or a platter with melon, ham, pâté, salad and french bread (£4.50), beef and beer curry (£5.95), steak and kidney pie or Whitby cod (£6.95), and plaice fillet baked with prawns in a cream and wine sauce (£7.25), with lunchtime dishes such as avocado, orange and celery salad (£3.25), chicken livers in garlic (£3.75), chickpea and potato curry (£6.50), salmon fillet with a cream and tarragon sauce (£7.95), rich venison casserole (£8.25), roast breast of spicy duck in honey and soy (£9.75); puddings (from £2.45), well liked Sunday roasts, and there's a new lunch menu for customers with smaller appetites (2 courses £6.50, 3 courses £7.25). Well kept Black Sheep Bitter, John Smiths, Tetleys, Theakstons Best, and a local guest beer on handpump, and around 40 malt whiskies. The beamed and panelled no-smoking dining room is hung with large prints of old Thornton Watlass cricket teams. A bigger bar has darts, pool and dominoes. The sheltered garden has an equipped children's play area and there are summer barbecues – both quite a draw for families. *(Recommended by Miss L Hodson, Mr and Mrs P B Miller, Bruce Bird, Andy and Jill Kassube, RB, Susan and Nigel Wilson, Elizabeth and Alex Rocke, Maggie and Peter Shapland)*

Free house ~ Licensees Michael and Margaret Fox ~ Real ale ~ Bar food (not 25 Dec) ~ Restaurant ~ (01677) 422461 ~ Well behaved children welcome ~ Live country/pop Sat evenings, jazz twice monthly Sun lunchtime ~ Open 11-2.30, 5.30-11; 11-11 Sat; 12-10.30 Sun; may close Sun evening in winter ~ Bedrooms: £34(£38B)/£50(£55B)

THRESHFIELD SD9863 Map 7
Old Hall Inn

B6160/B6265 just outside Grassington

The three communicating rooms at this very well run pub have high beam-and-plank ceilings hung with lots of chamber-pots, unfussy decorations such as old Cadbury's advertisements and decorative plates on a high delft shelf, simple, cushioned pews built into the white walls, a tall well blacked kitchen range, and a good, bustling atmosphere with a mix of locals and visitors. Much liked bar food, using fresh local ingredients, might include soup (£2.25), sandwiches (from £2.65), grilled brie with apple and crispy bacon (£3.95), queen scallops in garlic butter (£4.75), steak and mushroom pie or cumberland sausage and mash (£6.50), battered cod or haddock and chips (£6.95), goat's cheese and roasted vegetables (£7.45), oak smoked salmon with tomato and garlic sauce with dill mash (£8.95), chicken breast stuffed with mozzarella and mushroom and madeira sauce (£9.25) and home-made puddings like sticky toffee pudding or steamed orange and raisin sponge (£2.95). Well kept Timothy Taylor Bitter, Landlord, Golden Best on handpump, and up to 60 malt whiskies; dominoes, and piped music. A neat, partly gravelled side garden has young shrubs and a big sycamore, some seats, and an aviary with cockatiels and zebra finches. This is, of course, a fine base for dales walking; there are two cottages behind the inn for hire. *(Recommended by John Eteson, Claire and Christopher Riddell, Mrs R A Cartwright, WAH, Prof and Mrs S Barnett, Norman Stansfield, Mr and Mrs Garrett)*

Free house ~ Licensees Ian and Amanda Taylor ~ Real ale ~ Bar food (not winter Sun evenings) ~ Restaurant ~ (01756) 752441 ~ Children in family room ~ Open 11.30-3, 6-11; 12-3, 6-10.30 Sun; closed Mon (except bank holidays) ~ Bedrooms: £20/£40

WASS SE5679 Map 7
Wombwell Arms 🍴 ⏟ 🛏

Back road W of Ampleforth; or follow brown tourist-attraction sign for Byland Abbey off A170 Thirsk—Helmsley

'A real all-rounder' says one reader summing up what many of us feel about this bustling pub. There's a warm welcome from the friendly licensee, a good range of real ales and wines, super, reliable food, and well liked bedrooms. The little central bar is spotlessly kept and cosy, and the three low-beamed dining areas are comfortable and inviting and take in an 18th-c former granary. At lunchtime, bar food might include sandwiches (from £2.95; hot or open ones from £4.15; not Sunday), soups such as mushroom and tarragon or celery and stilton (£2.50), goat's cheese with caramelised shallots (£4.10), ragoût of mushrooms and courgettes on wholegrain rice (£5.95), smoked haddock with welsh rarebit topping (£6.45), tagliatelle with chargrilled mediterranean vegetables (£6.50), chargrilled chicken breast with a pesto salad (£6.75), and lamb cooked slowly in red wine, mint and rosemary sauce (£6.95), with evening dishes such as smoked venison with red onion marmalade (£4.10), smoked trout and walnut pâté (£4.15), pheasant with an orange and brandy sauce (£8.65), wok-fried salmon fillet with a lime butter sauce (£8.75), guinea fowl with a port, cream and mushroom sauce (£8.95), and puddings like cherry brandy chocolate pots, lemon posset, and caramelised rice pudding (£3.25). Two no-smoking dining areas. Well kept Black Sheep Bitter, Timothy Taylor Landlord, and guests such as Greene King Triumph, Hambleton Blizzard, Girthstretcher, and Lightning, Malton Double Chance Bitter, and York Yorkshire Terrier on handpump, decent malt whiskies, and around 9 wines by the glass. *(Recommended by PACW, Mr and Mrs A Burge, Chris and Elaine Lyon, John Robertson, F J Robinson, I R D Ross, Neil Townend, Walter and Susan Rinaldi-Butcher, John Lane, Chris Brace, R Inman, Allan Worsley, Geoffrey and Brenda Wilson, Mr and Mrs D Price)*

Free house ~ Licensees Alan and Lynda Evans ~ Real ale ~ Bar food (not Sun evening or Mon except bank holidays) ~ (01374) 868280 ~ Children in eating area of bar but must be over 5 in evening ~ Open 12-2.30, 7-11; 12-3, 7-10.30 Sun; closed Mon except bank holidays, winter Sun evenings and 2 wks Jan ~ Bedrooms: £29.50B/£49B

WATH IN NIDDERDALE SE1467 Map 7
Sportsmans Arms 🍴 ⏟ 🛏

Nidderdale rd off B6265 in Pateley Bridge; village and pub signposted over hump bridge on right after a couple of miles

Over the 20 years that Mr Carter has been running this civilised restaurant-with-rooms, it has remained utterly reliable. Most people do come, of course, to enjoy the marvellous food or stay overnight in the extremely comfortable and well equipped bedrooms – but there is a welcoming bar where locals drop in just for a drink. Using the best local produce – game from the moors, fish delivered daily from Whitby, and Nidderdale lamb, pork and beef – the carefully presented and prepared food might include fillets of smoked trout with creamed horseradish, roast black pudding on creamed potatoes in a spicy chorizo and tomato sauce or tartlet of avocado and prawns in a red pepper coulis, glazed with gruyère (all £4.95), main courses such as crumbed loin of pork on chive mash with a mild creamed curry and sultana sauce, baked Scarborough woof topped with rarebit, tomato and caper sauce, roast Scottish salmon with ginger and spring onions or breast of chicken in a white wine, bacon and creamed mushroom sauce (all £9.50), guinea fowl in a creamed vermouth and grape sauce (£10.50), roast breast of duckling with ginger and almonds (£12.95), and slices of sirloin in a bacon, mushroom and olive sauce (£13.50). The restaurant is no smoking. There's a very sensible and extensive wine list, a good choice of malt whiskies, several Russian vodkas, and attentive service; open fires, dominoes. Benches and tables outside *(Recommended by Ian Phillips, Ian and Jacqui Ross, Sue and David Arnott, Chris and Sue Bax, Anne and David Robinson, Janet and Peter Race; also in the Good Hotel Guide)*

Free house ~ Licensee Ray Carter ~ Real ale ~ Bar food ~ (01423) 711306 ~ Children in eating area of bar ~ Open 12-2.30, 6.30-11; closed 25 Dec ~ Bedrooms: £40(£45B)/£60(£70B)

WHITBY NZ9011 Map 10
Duke of York
Church Street, Harbour East Side

Before attempting the famous nearby 199 steps that lead up to the abbey, it might be an idea to fortify yourself at this bustling, popular pub first. There's a splendid view over the harbour entrance and the western cliff, and the welcoming and comfortable beamed lounge bar has decorations that include quite a bit of fishing memorabilia – though it's the wide choice of good value fresh local fish on the menu itself which appeals most: there might be fresh crab or prawn sandwiches (£2.95), large fillet of fresh cod (£4.95), and fresh crab salad (£5.95), as well as other sandwiches (£2.25), ploughman's or leek and stilton bake (£4.50), steak and mushroom pie (£4.95), puddings (£2.25), and children's meals (from £2.50). Well kept Black Dog Abbey Special (brewed in Whitby), Courage Directors, and John Smiths on handpump, decent wines, lots of malt whiskies, and quick pleasant service even when busy; darts, piped music, and fruit machine. *(Recommended by David and Ruth Hollands, Joan and Michel Hooper-Immins, Martin Jones, Mark Matthewman, C J Fletcher, DJW, Val Stevenson, Rob Holmes, Norma and Keith Bloomfield, David and Carole Chapman, Ian Phillips, Roger and Ann Kine, Ben and Sheila Walker, JP, PP, G Smale, Brian Wardrobe, David Carr, Tony Scott)*

Unique Pub Co ~ Lease: Lawrence Bradley ~ Real ale ~ Bar food (12-9) ~ (01947) 600324 ~ Children welcome until 9.30pm ~ Live entertainment winter Sun and Weds ~ Open 11-11; 12-10.30 Sun ~ Bedrooms: /£30(£45B)

WIDDOP SD9333 Map 7
Pack Horse
The Ridge; from A646 on W side of Hebden Bridge, turn off at Heptonstall signpost (as it's a sharp turn, coming out of Hebden Bridge road signs direct you around a turning circle), then follow Slack and Widdop signposts; can also be reached from Nelson and Colne, on high, pretty road; OS Sheet 103, map reference 952317

After you've been walking on the moorland, this isolated traditional pub with its warm winter fires and friendly welcome is quite a haven. The bar has window seats cut into the partly panelled stripped stone walls that take in the moorland view, sturdy furnishings, and well kept Black Sheep Bitter, Morlands Old Speckled Hen, Theakstons XB, Thwaites Bitter, and a guest beer on handpump, around 130 single malt whiskies, and some Irish ones as well, and decent wines; efficient service. Generous helpings of good bar food includes soup (£1.80), sandwiches (from £1.95), ploughman's (£3.95), home-made steak and kidney pie (£4.50), steaks (from £7.25), and specials such as chicken curry (£4.95), mushroom stroganoff or haddock mornay (£5.95), rack of lamb (£8.95), and puddings such as sticky toffee pudding or apple pie (£2.95). The new restaurant is open only on Saturday evenings at the moment. There are seats outside. *(Recommended by Ian and Nita Cooper)*

Free house ~ Licensee Andrew Hollinrake ~ Real ale ~ Bar food ~ Restaurant ~ (01422) 842803 ~ Children welcome until 8pm ~ Open 12-3, 7-11; 12-11 Sun; closed weekday lunchtimes and Mon from Sept to Easter ~ Bedrooms: £28B/£44B

YORK SE5951 Map 7
Black Swan
Peaseholme Green; inner ring road, E side of centre; the inn has a good car park

It's worth a visit here just to see the splendid timbered and jettied façade and original lead-latticed windows in the twin gables of this interesting building. Inside, the busy black-beamed back bar (liked by locals) has wooden settles along the walls, some cushioned stools, and a throne-like cushioned seat in the vast brick inglenook, where there's a coal fire in a grate with a spit and some copper cooking utensils. The cosy panelled front bar, with its little serving hatch, is similarly furnished but smaller and more restful. The crooked-floored hall that runs along the side of both bars has a fine period staircase (leading up to a room fully panelled in oak, with an antique tiled fireplace); there is provision for non smokers. Decent bar food includes soup (£1.95), filled baked potatoes (from £2.10), filled french sticks (from £2.95), and daily specials such as giant yorkshire pudding with gravy (£2.25; or filled up to £4.95), cumberland sausage or lasagne (£4.25), haddock or scampi (£4.95). Well kept Worthington Best, and guests like Bass, Fullers London Pride, Shepherd Neame Spitfire, and York Yorkshire Terrier on handpump, and several country wines; dominoes, fruit machine, trivia, and piped music. If the car park is full, it's worth knowing that there's a big public one next door. *(Recommended by Roger Bellingham, Paul and Ursula Randall, Chris Gabbitas, Hugh McPhail, Eric Larkham, Ian Phillips, J and P Halfyard, the Didler)*

Bass ~ Manager Ms Pat O'Connell ~ Real ale ~ Bar food (lunchtime) ~ (01904) 686911 ~ Well behaved children in dining area until 7.30pm ~ Folk club Thurs evening ~ Open 11-11; 12-10.30 Sun; closed 25 Dec ~ Bedrooms: /£50B

Olde Starre £

Stonegate; pedestrians-only street in centre, far from car parks

From seats in the flower-filled garden and courtyard here there are minster views across the rooftops. This is the city's oldest licensed pub (1644), though parts of the building date back to 900, and it does get crowded at peak times. The main bar has original panelling, green plush wall seats, a large servery running the length of the room, and a large leaded window with red plush curtains at the far end. Several other little rooms lead off the porch-like square hall – one with its own food servery, one with panelling and some prints, and a third with cream wallpaper and dado; the tap room is no smoking. Well kept John Smiths Bitter and Magnet, and Theakstons Best, XB and Old Peculier on handpump, good coffee, and decent whiskies – most spirits are served in double measures for a single's price; friendly, helpful staff. Obtrusive piped music, fruit machine, and trivia. Decent bar food includes filled rolls, lamb's liver, sausage and onion (£4.50), steak and kidney pie (£4.75), and tipsy beef, cumberland sausage or lamb with rosemary (all £4.80). A 'gallows' signs stretches right across the street (one of York's prettiest); we only know of two or three others as they were generally banned when coach and waggon loads become so high that they were obstructed. *(Recommended by MLR, Ian Phillips, Rona Murdoch, M Borthwick, Colin Draper, Peter Marshall, Eric Larkham, Chris Gabbitas, Hugh McPhail)*

Scottish Courage ~ Managers Bill and Susan Embleton ~ Real ale ~ Bar food (11.30-8.30(till 7 Fri); not Sat evening) ~ (01904) 623063 ~ Children welcome away from bar area ~ Open 11-11; 12-10.30 Sun

Spread Eagle £

98 Walmgate

Just far enough to escape the tourist trail, this friendly pub has a fine choice of ales, and good, enjoyable food. On handpump, there might be Mansfield Riding, Bitter, and Old Baily, Timothy Taylor Landlord, and York Brideshead, Stonewall, and Yorkshire Terrier; they hold a beer festival in October. Decent wines and lots of malt whiskies. Well liked bar food includes filled rolls or hoagies (£2; soup and a sandwich £2.50; hot roast beef with onion gravy £3.10), filled baked potatoes (from £2.50), burgers (from £3.30), steak and kidney pudding or liver and onions(£4), vegetarian moussaka (£4.50), all-day breakfast, cajun chicken, bangers and mash or cod and prawn crumble (all £4.90), combos (enough for two, £7), and puddings like treacle sponge (£2). The main bar is a dark vault with two smaller, cosier rooms leading off – lots of old enamel advertisements and prints on the walls, and a relaxed atmosphere. Fruit machine, trivia and juke box. There are seats in the enclosed back garden.

(Recommended by Paul Fairbrother, Helen Morris, Darly Graton, Graeme Gulibert, Lester Edmonds, Eric Larkham, Roger Bellingham, Marlene and Jim Godfrey, Ian Baillie, Chris Gabbitas, Hugh McPhail, Kerry Law, Simon Smith)

Mansfield ~ Manager Trudy Pilmoor ~ Real ale ~ Bar food (12-8; till 3 Sun) ~ Restaurant ~ (01904) 635868 ~ Children in eating area of bar until 7pm ~ Live rock/blues Sunday from 2pm ~ Open 11-11; 12-10.30 Sun

Tap & Spile ⛏ £

Monkgate

It remains the eight well kept real ales on handpump that draws customers to this traditional pub. Changing almost daily, there might be Ash Vine Giant Leap, Black Sheep Bitter, Butterknowle Banner Bitter, Old Mill Bitter, Phoenix Old Oak Ale, Tap & Spile Premium, Theakstons Old Peculier, and Websters Yorkshire; they also keep wheat beer, farm cider, and country wines. The big split-level bar has bare boards, brown or burgundy cushioned wall settles right around a big bay window, with a smaller upper area with frosted glass and panelling; darts, dominoes, fruit machine, and piped music. Straightforward bar food includes sandwiches or toasties (from £1.50), home-made soup (£1.70), filled baked potatoes (from £1.80), omelettes (£3), chilli con carne (£3.25), vegetable lasagne (£3.75), gammon and egg (£4.25), and mixed grill (£5); daily specials, children's meals, and Sunday roast lunch. The outside terrace has seats under parasols and outside heaters for cooler weather; there are more seats in the garden. *(Recommended by Piotr Chodzko-Zajko, the Didler)*

Century ~ Manager Andy Mackay ~ Real ale ~ Bar food (12-3(2.30 Sun); not evenings) ~ (01904) 656158 ~ Live jazz/blues most Sun evenings ~ Open 11.30-11; 12-10.30 Sun

---

Lucky Dip

Besides the fully inspected pubs, you might like to try these Lucky Dips recommended to us and described by readers (if you do, please send us reports):

Aberford [SE4337]
Swan [best to use A642 junction to leave A1]: Useful high-throughput dining pub, vast choice of good value generous food from sandwiches to carvery and display of puddings, lots of black timber, prints, pistols, cutlasses, stuffed animals and hunting trophies, well kept Boddingtons, Flowers, Tetleys and Timothy Taylor, generous glasses of wine, friendly uniformed staff, upstairs evening restaurant; children welcome, comfortable bedrooms *(William Cunliffe)*

Ainderby Steeple [SE3392]
Wellington Heifer: Long low-ceilinged bar and lounge on two levels, dining room, log fires, good choice of generous fresh food and of beers, quick friendly service; discounts for local B&B visitors *(Mary and David Richards, Carol and Dono Leaman)*

Ainthorpe [NZ7008]
Fox & Hounds: Traditional friendly moorland pub with good freshly made food inc much vegetarian, open fires, well kept Black Sheep and Theakstons *(Janet Foster, Sue Hales)*

Allerthorpe [SE7847]
☆ *Plough* [Main St]: Clean and airy two-room lounge bar with snug alcoves, hunting prints, WWII RAF and RCAF photographs, open fires, wide choice of good sensibly priced food, well kept Theakstons Bitter, XB and Old Peculier, decent house wines, well served coffee, restaurant, games extension with pool, juke box etc; pleasant garden, handy for Burnby Hall

(LYM, Mrs M Hunt, Roger Bellingham)

Ampleforth [SE5878]
White Swan [Main St]: Extensive modern lounge/dining bar in small attractive village, wide choice of generous food from good big filled buns to popular Sun lunch, front country bar with well kept John Smiths and Timothy Taylor Landlord, lots of malt whiskies, log fires, darts, no piped music; no-smoking restaurant, decent wines, good friendly service even on very busy Sat night; back terrace *(Bill and Liz Green, Paul and Ursula Randall)*

Appleton Roebuck [SE5542]
Shoulder of Mutton: Cheerful and attractive pub bar overlooking village green, wide choice of good value food inc cheap steaks in bar and restaurant, well kept Sam Smiths, quick service; can be crowded with caravanners summer; bedrooms *(Mary and David Richards, Beryl and Bill Farmer, Peter and Anne Hollindale)*

Arncliffe [SD9473]
☆ *Falcon* [off B6160 N of Grassington]: Classic old-fashioned haven for walkers, ideal setting on moorland village green, no frills, Youngers tapped from cask to stoneware jugs in central hatch-style servery, generous plain lunchtime and early evening bar snacks, open fire in small bar with elderly furnishings and humorous sporting prints, airy back sunroom (children allowed here lunchtime) looking on to garden; run by same family for generations – they take time to get to know; cl winter Thurs evenings;

bedrooms (not all year), good breakfast and evening meal – real value *(JP, PP, Philip and Ann Board, Vicky and David Sarti, LYM, K H Frostick)*

Askrigg [SD9591]

Crown: Unassuming and neatly kept, several separate areas off the main bar with blazing fires inc old-fashioned range, reasonably priced generous food, Black Sheep and Theakstons XB and Old Peculier, Seabrooks crisps, helpful courteous staff; walkers welcome *(Sue Holland, Dave Webster)*

☆ *Kings Arms* [signed from A684 Leyburn—Sedbergh in Bainbridge]: Early 19th-c coaching inn, three old-fashioned bars with photographs of filming here of James Herriot's *All Creatures Great and Small*, interesting traditional furnishings and décor, good log fires, well kept Dent, Morlands Old Speckled Hen, John Smiths, Theakstons XB and Youngers No 3, good malt whiskies and wines, variety of food from toasted sandwiches to steaks inc no-smoking waitress-served grill room and set-priced restaurant; bedrooms, new independent holiday complex behind, lovely village *(Paul and Sandra Embleton, LYM, C Smith, Bruce Bird, Walter and Susan Rinaldi-Butcher, Sue Holland, Dave Webster, K F Mould, Bob and Maggie Atherton, RWD, Suzy Miller, B Kneale)*

Atwick [TA1950]

Black Horse [B1242 N of Hornsea; The Green]: Two friendly comfortable rooms with old photographs, three well kept ales, straightforward fair-priced food, good landlord; TV, piped music and fruit machines; dogs and children welcome *(Mr and Mrs P Eastwood)*

Austwick [SD7668]

Cross Streets [A65 Settle—Ingleton]: Substantial good value meals in bar and restaurant; Tetleys *(Walter and Susan Rinaldi-Butcher)*

☆ *Game Cock* [just off A65 Settle—Kirkby Lonsdale]: Prettily placed below the Three Peaks, homely old-fashioned beamed back bar with furniture to take wet walkers in its stride, sensibly priced good simple bar food inc vegetarian, well kept Thwaites, good fire, welcoming landlady, smarter no-smoking restaurant, no music, seats outside with good play area; clean bedrooms, good walks all round *(BB, Mrs Hilarie Taylor, Margaret and Arthur Dickinson)*

Bainbridge [SD9390]

☆ *Rose & Crown*: Ancient inn overlooking moorland village green, old-fashioned beamed and panelled front bar with big log fire, busy back extension popular with families (pool, juke box etc), John Smiths and Theakstons, enjoyable food in bar and restaurant; children welcome, open all day, bedrooms *(Gwen and Peter Andrews, Gethin Lewis, LYM)*

Bardsey [SE3643]

☆ *Bingley Arms* [Church Lane]: Ancient pub with décor to match, wide range of good home-made fresh food inc early-supper bargains, spacious lounge divided into separate areas inc no smoking, huge fireplace, well kept Black Sheep, John Smiths and Tetleys, good wines, pleasant speedy service, smaller public bar, picturesque

upstairs brasserie, charming quiet terrace with interesting barbecues inc vegetarian *(Roger Kiddier, LYM)*

Barkston Ash [SE4936]

Ash Tree [A162 Tadcaster—Sherburn]: Good food changing daily, lots of fish, in bar and restaurant, well kept John Smiths and Theakstons *(Edward Leetham)*

Barnby Dun [SE6209]

Gateway [Station Rd]: Hotel with Barnsley and John Smiths ales in large bar, large-screen TV; restaurant *(Tony Hobden)*

Beckwithshaw [SE2853]

Pine Marten [Otley Rd, Beckwith Knowle; B6162 towards Harrogate]: Recent conversion of rambling Victorian house, large rooms, panelling, open fires, good food all day, welcoming service, Bass and Worthington, decent wines; handy for Harlow Carr gardens *(Edward Leetham)*

Beverley [TA0339]

Tap & Spile [Flemingate]: Well done Tap & Spile with friendly laid-back atmosphere, interesting range of ales often from small breweries, huge choice of country wines, decent basic food, no-smoking room; lovely view of Minster *(JP, PP, Tim Barrow, Sue Demont, Wendy Muldoon)*

Tiger [Lairgate]: Small and interesting, with little rooms and alcoves, good choice of beers inc Vaux, friendly atmosphere, very reasonably priced food *(James Chatfield)*

Bilbrough [SE5346]

☆ *Three Hares* [off A64 York—Tadcaster]: New owners in dining pub with Black Sheep, Timothy Taylor Landlord and a guest beer from end bar with sofas and log fire, good value wines, upmarket menu, interesting décor inc old cameras and pocket watches; cl Mon *(M A Buchanan, Mrs M D Jeffries, Alan J Morton, Michael A Butler)*

Bingley [SE1039]

Ferrands Arms [Queen St]: Very lively, warm and friendly, with DJ Fri and weekly karaoke; smartly refurbished, with well priced drinks and lunchtime food *(Miss G Hardy)*

Birstall [SE2126]

Black Bull [from Bradford towards Dewsbury turn right at Parish Church into Church Lane]: Old building opp ancient Norman church, dark panelling and low beams, former upstairs courtroom (now a function room), Whitbreads-related ales, good cheap home-made food inc bargain early meals, old local photographs; recent small extension *(Michael Butler)*

Bolton Abbey [SE0754]

Devonshire Arms: Comfortable and elegant hotel in marvellous position, limited choice of good if pricy food from sandwiches up in brasserie bar, well kept beers, good wines, tables in garden; handy for the priory, walks in the estate and Strid River valley; smart restaurant, helicopter pad; good bedrooms *(Geoffrey and Brenda Wilson, Julia Gorham)*

Boroughbridge [SE3967]

Three Horseshoes [Bridge St]: Spotless traditional pub with character landlord, friendly locals, huge fire in lounge, darts, dominoes and cards in public bar, great atmosphere, good plain home cooking from sandwiches to steaks in bars and restaurant, well kept Black Sheep; bedrooms *(Pete Baker, the Didler)*

Bradfield [SK2692]

Old Horns [High Bradfield]: Friendly old stonebuilt pub with comfortably refurbished divided L-shaped bar, lots of pictures, no-smoking area, good value food, busy but efficient service, ales such as Boddingtons, Courage Directors and John Smiths; quiet piped music, children welcome, picnic-sets and play area outside, hill village with stunning views, interesting church, good walks *(CMW, JJW, David Carr)*

Bradford [SE1633]

Beehive [Westgate]: Renovated Edwardian gaslit pub, pleasant traditional décor, several rooms, wide range of well kept beers, over 70 whiskies; live jazz, summer barbecues *(the Didler)*

Branch [Keighley Rd (A650/A6038)]: Large open-plan bar with well kept real ales inc Black Sheep and Tetleys, also guest beers; decent food *(D W Stokes)*

City Vaults [Hustlergate]: Loud and lively esp at w/e, happy helpful staff, lunchtime food and a good night out; no trainers, good bouncers *(Miss G Hardy)*

☆ *Cock & Bottle* [Barkerend Rd, up Church Bank from centre; on left few hundred yds past cathedral]: Carefully restored Victorian décor, well kept John Smiths and Tetleys, deep-cut and etched windows and mirrors enriched with silver and gold leaves, stained glass, enamel intaglios, heavily carved woodwork and traditional furniture, saloon with a couple of little snugs (one often with Christian counselling) and a rather larger carpeted music room, open fire in public bar; now run by volunteers from Bradford Christian Pub Consortium *(BB, the Didler)*

☆ *Fighting Cock* [Preston St (off B6145)]: Busy bare-floor alehouse by industrial estate, particularly well kept Timothy Taylor Landlord and ten or more changing ales such as Black Sheep, Exmoor Gold, Sam Smiths and Theakstons, also farm ciders, foreign bottled beers, food inc all-day doorstep sandwiches, coal fires, recently re-upholstered seats; low prices *(Reg Nelson, M and J Godfrey, the Didler)*

Freestyle & Firkin [Morley St]: Successful conversion of swimming baths, imaginative swimming theme, old Bradford memorabilia, wooden benches, decent ales *(Reg Nelson)*

McCrorys [Easby Rd, nr univ]: Classic cellar bar reminiscent of late 1950s, a haven for bohemians, great acoustics for Weds/Sun blues bands, cajun or folk music; John Smiths *(Reg Nelson)*

Queens [Apperley Bridge; A658 towards airport]: Good bar food inc fish specialities, Tetleys, restaurant *(M and J Godfrey)*

Brafferton [SE4370]

☆ *Farmers* [between A19 and A168 NW of York]: Friendly unspoilt village pub refurbished with pine country furniture, nice Yorkshire range with glowing fire, subtle lighting, wide choice of good fair-priced food, Black Sheep and Theakstons Best, XB and Old Peculier, cheerful landlady, small restaurant, comfortable games room with fruit machine and darts, tables in garden; bedrooms *(Nick and Alison Dowson, John Knighton, R E and F C Pick)*

Bramhope [SE2543]

Fox & Hounds: Popular two-roomed pub, simply furnished but civilised, with well kept Tetleys Bitter and Mild, lunchtime food, buoyant atmosphere, open fire, corridor with old sports photographs; children welcome, has been open all day *(Michael Butler)*

Brandesburton [TA1247]

☆ *Dacre Arms* [signed off A165 N of Beverley and Hornsea turn-offs]: Brightly modernised comfortable pub popular for wide choice of generous food from lunchtime sandwiches (not w/e) to steaks, inc OAP specials and children's; Black Sheep, Courage Directors, Tetleys and Theakstons Old Peculier tapped from the cask, children welcome, darts, restaurant; open for food all day w/e *(C A Hall, Joan and Michel Hooper-Immins, I Maw, LYM, Jamie and Sarah Allan)*

Bridlington [TA1867]

Beaconsfield Arms [Flamborough Rd]: Well laid out pub with good low-priced food, friendly staff, well kept Bass, decent wine; comfortable lounge, airy lively public bar, nr promenade *(BB, R and E Treasure)*

Hook & Parrot [N Promenade]: Modern pub done out in olde-worlde nautical style, lots of old lamps, snug alcoves, reasonably priced Scottish Courage beers, lunchtime food; pool, TV etc in separate bar *(Kevin Blake)*

Brighouse [SE1323]

Red Rooster [Brookfoot; A6025 towards Elland]: Homely stonebuilt alehouse with quickly changing country-wide interesting well kept real ales and their own Roosters Yankee, no food, no machines, brewery memorabilia, open fire, separate areas inc one with books to read or buy *(the Didler)*

Brockholes [SE1411]

Travellers Rest [A616 S of Huddersfield]: Welcoming local with well kept Mansfield and wide choice of very good value food inc early evening bargains *(Neil Townend)*

Brompton [SE9582]

Cayley Arms [A170 W of Scarborough]: Quiet and welcoming uncluttered pub in pretty village, friendly helpful service, good freshly cooked generous food inc good choice of fish and local shellfish, reasonable prices, well kept ales inc Theakstons; garden *(A M Pring, Peter Burton, Beryl and Bill Farmer)*

Burley in Wharfedale [SE1646]

Hermit [Burley Woodhead; A65 at top of hill]: Small friendly pub with two oak-panelled and beamed rooms, comfortable built-in seats, bay window seat with Wharfedale views, well kept Courage Directors, John Smiths and Magnet, Tetleys and Theakstons Best, simple good food, restaurant; no machines or juke box *(John and Lis Burgess)*

Burnt Yates [SE2561]

New Inn: Good atmosphere in candlelit pub

with lots of antiques, well prepared traditional food, good reasonably priced wines *(Tracey Briggs, Andrew Blakeman)*

Burton Agnes [TA1063]

Blue Bell: Small charming white-fronted pub with limited choice of good food from doorstep sandwiches up, separate dining room, helpful landlord; handy for Burton Agnes Hall and Norman manor house *(Janet Pickles)*

Cadeby [SE5100]

☆ *Cadeby Inn* [Manor Farm, Main St]: Biggish pub locally popular for generous food from good hot beef sandwich to good value carvery, with over 200 malt whiskies, well kept Barnsley, Courage Directors, Sam Smiths OB and Tetleys, prompt cheerful service, local pictures, open fire, quiet front sitting room, no-smoking snug, gleaming brasses and lots of house plants in pleasant back dining lounge, separate games area; children in eating area, tables in garden, open all day Sat *(Peter F Marshall, Michael and Jenny Back, Nigel and Sue Foster)*

Cawood [SE5737]

☆ *Ferry* [King St (B1222 NW of Selby), by Ouse swing bridge]: Unspoilt but neatly kept 16th-c inn, smallish comfortable rooms, massive inglenook, stripped brickwork, bare boards, well kept Marstons, Timothy Taylor Landlord and local guest beers tapped from the cask, good reasonably priced food inc vegetarian, tables out on flagstone terrace and grass by River Ouse swing bridge; cl weekday lunchtimes; good value modest bedrooms with bathrooms *(Bill and Pam Baker)*

Chapel Haddlesey [SE5826]

Jug [quite handy for M62 junction 34; off A19 towards Selby]: Homely little two-roomed village pub, once a blacksmiths' and said to be haunted, copper-topped round tables, comfortable banquettes and stools, jugs hanging from beams, wide choice of cheap food inc filled yorkshire puddings, Marstons and guest beers, garden and play area *(Tony Hobden)*

Chapel le Dale [SD7477]

☆ *Old Hill* [B5655 Ingleton—Hawes, 3 miles N of Ingleton]: Basic stripped-stone moorland bar with potholing pictures and Settle railway memorabilia, roaring log fire in cosy back parlour, well kept Black Sheep, Dent and Theakstons Bitter, XB and Old Peculier, generous simple home-made food in separate room inc good beef sandwiches and pies, plenty of vegetarian, rather alternative staff, flagstones and bare boards – good for boots; juke box; children welcome; wonderful isolated spot, camping possible *(Joy and Peter Heatherley, LYM, Nigel Woolliscroft, Jenny and Brian Seller)*

Chapeltown [SK3596]

Royal Oak [Station Rd; A6135 N of Sheffield]: Comfortable banquettes in 1840s stonebuilt local, real fire, walking sticks and jugs on beams, old tobacco advertisements and banknotes, brass taps on bar, lunchtime food inc OAP bargain Mon-Sat, Barnsley Bitter, friendly obliging service; piped music, machines, SkyTV etc; open all day *(CMW, JJW)*

Clapham [SD7569]

New Inn [off A65 N of Settle]: Riverside pub in

famously pretty village, small comfortable panelled lounge, well kept Dent and other ales, public bar with games room, popular food in bar and restaurant, friendly service; handy for round walk to Ingleborough Cavern; bedrooms *(Jenny and Brian Seller)*

Clifton [SE1622]

☆ *Black Horse* [Towngate/Coalpit Lane; off Brighouse rd from M62 junction 25]: Smart yet cosy dining pub, very popular for wide choice of good generous traditional food in restaurant; comfortable oak-beamed bars, good service, at least four well kept Whitbreads-related beers, friendly service, open fire; bedrooms comfortable *(Michael Butler)*

Cloughton [TA0297]

Hayburn Wyke [N of village]: Great position nr NT Hayburn Wyke, Cleveland Way coastal path and Scarborough—Whitby path/bicycle trail, lots of tables outside; very black and white L-shaped bar, restaurant and eating area beyond, well kept Black Sheep and Tetleys, plentiful reasonably priced food, friendly informal service, well behaved children welcome; can get busy and smoky; bedrooms *(M Borthwick, Keith and Janet Morris, John Brightley)*

Cloughton Newlands [TA0196]

☆ *Bryherstones* [Newlands Rd, off A171 in Cloughton]: Several interconnecting rooms, well kept Timothy Taylor beers, over 50 whiskies, good local atmosphere (dogs seem welcome), good reasonably priced generous food in separate eating area, welcoming service; pool room, quieter room upstairs; children welcome, delightful surroundings *(S E Paulley, Keith and Janet Morris)*

Coley [SE1226]

☆ *Brown Horse* [Lane Ends, Denholme Gate Rd (A644 Brighouse—Keighley, a mile N of Hipperholme)]: Particularly good interesting sensibly priced home cooking (not Sat evening), prompt smart staff, well kept Timothy Taylor Landlord and Theakstons, decent house wines, open fires in three bustling rooms (can be a bit smoky), golfing memorabilia, pictures, delft shelf of china and bottles, no-smoking restaurant and small light bank conservatory overlooking garden *(Mike Ridgway, Sarah Miles, Geoffrey and Brenda Wilson)*

Collingham [SE3946]

Barley Corn [Wetherby Rd (A58)/Jewitt Lane]: Large comfortable Thwaites dining pub, wide choice of good generous food, real ale, three areas; darts, fruit machine and TV one end, piped music; children welcome, high chairs; open all day Fri-Sun, food all day w/e; grass and terrace with picnic-sets *(CMW, JJW)*

Star: Friendly and popular main road pub, flagstones and beams, Black Sheep and Tetleys, good choice of food from lunchtime open sandwiches to restaurant meals *(David and Phyllis Chapman)*

Coneysthorpe [SE7171]

Tiger: Friendly and well worn in, with wholesome simple food, prompt service, Marstons Pedigree *(John Allen)*

Copt Hewick [SE3471]

Oak Tree [off B6265 E of Ripon]: Friendly and

comfortable country pub, good for families, with good choice of beers and of reasonably priced wines, wide choice of individually cooked good food, attentive service; pleasant garden *(Mr and Mrs A R Hawkins, R Buchanan)*

Dalehouse [NZ7818]

Fox & Hounds [Dalehouse Bank, off A174 at Staithes]: Small traditional country pub doing well under new landlady, well kept Marstons Pedigree and John Smiths, busy local front bar, good traditional home-made food in side room *(William Foster, Chris Hales)*

Dalton [NZ1108]

Travellers Rest: Good moderately priced French food in old stone dining pub with pleasant warm atmosphere, friendly service, real ales, mainly French wines; quiet hamlet *(Guy Vowles)*

Danby Wiske [SE3398]

White Swan [off A167 N of Northallerton]: Handy pub for coast-to-coast walk (Wainwright himself signed the visitors' book), friendly and informal, with cosy beamed bar, good value home cooking inc vegetarian and maybe own free range eggs, well kept beer; tables out by green, bedrooms cheap and comfortable, camping in back garden *(Neil and Anita Christopher)*

Darley [SE2059]

Wellington: Well placed extended Nidderdale pub with pleasant service, food in bar and restaurant, ales such as Black Sheep, Morlands Old Speckled Hen, Tetleys and Theakstons; comfortable good value bedrooms with own bathroom, good breakfast *(T M Dobby)*

Deighton [SE6243]

White Swan [A19 N of Escrick]: Good food from sandwiches and ploughman's up inc vegetarian, two very popular comfortable bars, separate restaurant, good choice of wines by the glass; seats outside, but traffic noise *(Janet Pickles)*

Dewsbury [SE2523]

Huntsman [Walker Cottages, Chidswell Lane, Shaw Cross – pub now signposted]: Cosy converted cottages alongside urban-fringe farm, lots of brasses and agricultural bric-a-brac, low ceilings, friendly locals, wide choice of well kept beers inc Black Sheep and John Smiths; no food evening or Sun/Mon lunchtime, busy evenings *(Michael Butler)*

☆ *West Riding Licensed Refreshment Rooms* [Station, Wellington Rd]: Busy three-room early Victorian station bar distinguished by fine choice of three Batemans ales and three interesting guest beers in top condition; farm ciders, good cheap food inc vegetarian, popular midweek curry or pie nights, daily papers, friendly staff, lots of railway memorabilia, coal fire, no-smoking area till 6, disabled access; juke box may be loud, jazz nights; open all day *(JP, PP, the Didler, Richard Lewis, Michael Butler)*

Doncaster [SE5902]

Black Bull [Market Pl]: Quiet and handsomely refurbished pub with lots of comfortable seating in different areas inc large no-smoking part, particularly well kept ales such as Barnsley Bitter and Black Heart Stout, Black Sheep Special, Glentworth Yorkshire Gold, Old Mill, John Smiths and York Last Drop, good well served food all day till late inc bargain Sun roast and early evening bargains Sun-Thurs, friendly efficient staff; Sun live music *(Richard Lewis, Richard Cole)*

Corner Pin [St Sepulchre Gate W, Cleveland St]: Friendly little corner pub not far from stn, good value traditional food from fine hot sandwiches up, well kept Barnsley, local Glentworth and John Smiths, two rooms, lots of local pictures; open all day *(Richard Lewis)*

Dr Browns [Hallgate]: Long comfortable bar with bare boards, prints on panelling, well kept Black Sheep, Boddingtons and Theakstons Best, draught Hoegaarden, lunchtime food; open all day, good live music *(Richard Lewis)*

Horse & Jockey [St Sepulchre Gate W]: Traditional pub with comfortable lounge, games in bar, well kept Black Sheep and Glentworth Light Year, friendly staff; open all day *(Richard Lewis)*

Lakeside [Wilmington Drive, Doncaster Carr]: Popular nicely fitted family Beefeater with racing memorabilia, good choice of generous good food, friendly staff, well kept Boddingtons, Flowers Original and Marstons Pedigree, disabled facilities; restaurant, open all day *(Richard Lewis)*

Leopard [West St]: Lively, with superb tiled frontage, comfortable lounge with juke box, bar area with pool, darts and machine, lunchtime food, friendly staff, well kept John Smiths and a changing guest such as Moorhouses Pendle Witches Brew; open all day, live music upstairs, disabled access *(Richard Lewis)*

Masons Arms [Market Pl]: Friendly and chatty 18th-c local with particularly well kept John Smiths and Tetleys, comfortable without being plush, lots of bric-a-brac inc jugs and bottles, framed papers relating to its long history; tables out in sheltered back garden *(Richard Lewis)*

Paris Gate [St Sepulchre Gate]: Nicely decorated continental bar with stone floor, spiral stairs to upper level, well kept Joshua Baileys and John Smiths, friendly staff; open all day *(Richard Lewis)*

Plough [W Laith Gate]: Traditional local with well kept Barnsley, Bass and John Smiths, old town maps, friendly staff, bustling front room with dominoes and sports TV, quieter back one, tiny garden; open all day Tues, Fri and Sat *(Richard Lewis)*

Queens [Sunny Bar]: Comfortable bare-boards Tetleys Festival Ale House with good choice of well kept ales, lunchtime food, friendly staff, juke box, pool area; open all day, cl Sun lunchtime – busy on market day *(Richard Lewis)*

Railway [West St]: Well kept Barnsley and John Smiths Bitter and Magnet in large corner local with small lounge, railway paintings, games; open all day exc Sun afternoon *(Richard Lewis)*

Regent [Regent Sq]: Bright, colourful and comfortable panelled hotel bar, welcoming and relaxing, with well kept Ind Coope Burton, Marstons Pedigree and Tetleys Bitter and Imperial, lots of books on one side, friendly

staff; comfortable bedrooms *(Richard Lewis)*
Salutation [South Parade]: Welcoming 18th-c
Tetleys Festival Alehouse with good choice of
their other well kept beers, lunchtime food, pub
games, good music, lots of pump clips; games
area, quiet juke box; open all day Thurs-Sat, can
get busy and smoky late evening *(Richard Lewis)*
Tut 'n' Shive [W Laith Gate]: Good choice of
well kept ales such as Black Sheep, Boddingtons,
Brakspears, Marstons, Morlands and Tetleys,
popular food, attractive prices, friendly staff,
bare boards and panelling, good juke box,
games machine; open all day *(Richard Lewis)*
White Swan [Frenchgate, by central pedestrian
precinct]: Front room so far below counter level
that you need a high reach for your well kept
pint, tiled side passage leading to surprisingly
big back bar/eating area – full range of cheap
lunchtime pub food; friendly landlady,
traditional games; open all day *(Richard Lewis,
BB, Tony Hobden)*
Easingwold [SE5270]
George [Market Pl]: Smart bar areas in market
town hotel popular with older people, well kept
Black Sheep Bitter and Special, good food in bar
and restaurant inc Whitby fish and imaginative
dishes, friendly enthusiastic service; bedrooms
(Roger A Bellingham, Dr B and Mrs P B Baker)
Station [Knott Lane]: Victorian former railway
hotel surrounded by housing estate, brewing its
own good appropriately named ales such as
Steamcock and Express, tasteful décor with
local steam railway memorabilia, friendly
landlord, good lunchtime bar food, real fire,
family room; bedrooms comfortable, with own
bathrooms *(Dr B and Mrs P B Baker, Nick and
Alison Dowson, JP, PP, the Didler)*
East Keswick [SE3644]
Travellers Rest [A659 N of Leeds]: Welcoming
pub with good value food inc children's helpings
and good choice of sandwiches; play area,
handy for Harewood House *(Mrs E Sanders)*
Eastby [SE0254]
Masons Arms [Barden Rd; back rd NE of
Skipton past Embsay]: Friendly small pub with
well kept Scottish Courage ales, wide choice of
good reasonably priced food inc nice puddings;
bedrooms *(Eric and Shirley Briggs)*
Eccup [SE2842]
New Inn [off A660 N of Leeds]: Popular pub
with log fire in big comfortable lounge, family
room, small dining area, good value bar meals
and sandwiches, Tetleys Bitter and Dark Mild,
friendly efficient service; children's play area
behind, in open country on Dales Way and nr
Harewood Park *(D Stokes)*
Egton Bridge [NZ8005]
Postgate [signed off A171 W of Whitby]:
Relaxed moorland village local used as Black
Dog in ITV's *Heartbeat*, ochre walls, quarry
tiles, rustic bric-a-brac, simple good value food
inc vegetarian, Whitby fish and children's,
Tetleys; traditional games in public bar, tables
on sunny flagstoned terrace; has been open all
day, bedrooms *(Comus Elliott, LYM, Neil and
Anita Christopher, John Higgins)*
Embsay [SE0053]
☆ *Elm Tree* [Elm Tree Sq]: Popular well

refurbished open-plan beamed village pub with
good honest hearty home-made food inc good-
sized children's helpings, friendly helpful service,
settles and old-fashioned prints, log-effect gas
fire; well kept changing ales such as Fullers
London Pride, Greene King Abbot, Marstons
Pedigree, Timothy Taylor Landlord, Wadworths
6X and one brewed for the pub, no-smoking
dining room, games area; busy weekends esp
evenings; comfortable good value bedrooms;
handy for steam railway *(Karen Eliot, Derek
and Sylvia Stephenson, Dr B and Mrs P B
Baker, SLC)*
Escrick [SE6442]
☆ *Black Bull* [E of A19 York—Selby]: Friendly
licensees and staff in unpretentious village pub
with pleasant open-plan bar/dining area divided
by arches and back-to-back fireplaces, flagstones
on one side, mix of wooden tables with benches,
stools and chairs, wide choice of good value
generous food here and in back dining room inc
early supper bargains, cheap Sun lunch, small
helpings for children and OAPs, well kept John
Smiths, Tetleys and Theakstons (weekday happy
hour 5-7); bedrooms *(P R Morley, Janet Pickles)*
Exelby [SE2987]
Green Dragon [B6285 SE of Bedale]:
Comfortable fireside seats, well kept beer,
particularly good home-made food *(Robert
Gartery)*
Faceby [NZ4903]
Sutton Arms: Dining pub with cosy and
comfortable bar and restaurant, good
reasonably priced food inc Sun lunch, well kept
distinctive local Captain Cook beer, friendly
helpful staff, interesting 30s to 50s bric-a-brac
(Nigel and Anne Cox, Chris and Sue Bax)
Farndale East [SE6697]
☆ *Feversham Arms* [Church Houses], next to
Farndale Nature Reserve]: In lovely daffodil
valley (very busy then), two unspoilt but bright
rooms with flagstone floors, lots of brass, jugs
and plates, fox masks, stuffed stoat, coal fire in
old kitchen range; well kept Tetleys, good value
home-cooked food, smart beamed and stripped-
stone restaurant, friendly service; very popular
w/e; walkers with wet boots and dogs not
welcome; nice small garden, good bedrooms, big
breakfast *(Neil and Anita Christopher)*
Felixkirk [SE4785]
☆ *Carpenters Arms* [off A170 E of Thirsk]:
Comfortable and very welcoming old-world
17th-c dining pub in picturesque small village,
big helpings of well presented good value food
from generous sandwiches to fish, grills and
popular Sun lunch (should book), well kept
John Smiths, cosy bar, smart restaurant where
landlord plays the grand piano *(Bob and Ann
Westbrook)*
Fishlake [SE6513]
Hare & Hounds: Traditional village local, well
kept Mansfield ales, no food *(Tony Hobden)*
Follifoot [SE3352]
Radcliffe Arms [Pannal Rd; off A658 SE of
Harrogate]: Well kept ales, good value food inc
good open sandwiches, friendly efficient service,
Sat barbecue, no music; children welcome,
tables outside *(Bob Ellis)*

Fylingthorpe [NZ9405]
Fylingdales [Thorpe Lane]: Extended stonebuilt pub with good choice of reasonably priced food, well kept beer; children welcome in conservatory with toys, play area on back lawn *(Edward Leetham)*

Gargrave [SD9354]
☆ *Masons Arms* [Church St/Marton Rd (off A65 NW of Skipton)]: Friendly and busy well run local, attractive and homely, well kept Boddingtons, Timothy Taylor Landlord and Tetleys, generous quick bar food inc good vegetarian choice and good sandwiches, copper-canopied log-effect gas fire dividing two open-plan areas; tables in garden, bowling green behind; children if well behaved; in charming village on Pennine Way, between river and church and not far from Leeds & Liverpool Canal *(Roger and Pauline Pearce, Charles and Pauline Stride, Christoper and Jo Barton)*

Giggleswick [SD8164]
Black Horse: Quaint 17th-c village pub crammed between churchyard and pretty row of cottages, smartly done up, with helpful staff, good usual bar food, well kept Timothy Taylor, intimate dining room *(Walter and Susan Rinaldi-Butcher)*
Old Station [A65 Settle bypass]: Handy stop for generous straightforward home-made food inc excellent black pudding in L-shaped bar with brasses, railway prints and dining end, no-smoking restaurant, friendly staff, well kept John Smiths and Tetleys Mild and Bitter; bedrooms *(Lyn and Geoff Hallchurch)*

Gilberdyke [SE8329]
Cross Keys [B1230]: Proper pub with particularly well kept beers inc constantly changing guests, pub games, pool, TV, no food; open all day from noon *(C A Hall)*

Gillamoor [SE6890]
☆ *Royal Oak* [off A170 in Kirkbymoorside]: Well run traditional village inn, clean and comfortable, with roomy old L-shaped beamed and panelled bar, generous genuinely home-made food, well kept beer, reasonable prices, efficient friendly service, no music; comfortable bedrooms, good breakfast, handy for Barnsdale Moor *(Janet and Peter Race)*

Goathland [NZ8301]
Mallyan Spout Hotel [opp church]: More hotel than pub, popular from its use by TV's *Heartbeat* cast, with three spacious lounges (one no smoking), traditional relaxed bar, good open fires, fine views, Malton PA and Double Chance, good malt whiskies and wines; children in eating area, usually open all day, handy for namesake waterfall; comfortable bedrooms *(LYM, DJW)*

Golcar [SE0815]
Golcar Lily [Slades Rd, Bolster Moor]: Attractive and unusual building (former Co-op and manager's house), small pastel-shades bar area with comfortable pink wall seats and stools, swagged curtains, big no-smoking restaurant leading off, fine valley views; interesting food, well kept Mansfield and two guest beers, pleasant atmosphere; Sun quiz night, luxurious lavatories upstairs; has been cl

Mon-Thurs lunchtimes *(Stuart Paulley)*

Grange Moor [SE2215]
☆ *Kaye Arms* [A642 Huddersfield—Wakefield]: Good civilised and busy family-run restaurantry pub with imaginative proper food, courteous efficient staff, exceptional value house wines, hundreds of malt whiskies, no-smoking room; children allowed lunchtime, handy for Yorkshire Mining Museum; cl Mon lunchtime *(LYM, Michael Butler, Norman Stansfield, Neil Townend, Dave Braisted)*

Grassington [SE0064]
☆ *Black Horse* [Garrs Lane]: Comfortable and cheerful open-plan modern bar, very busy in summer, with well kept Black Sheep Bitter and Special, Tetleys and Theakstons Best and Old Peculier, open fires, generous straightforward home-made bar food from good sandwiches up inc children's and vegetarian, darts in back room, sheltered terrace, small attractive restaurant; bedrooms comfortable, well equipped and good value *(BB, Prof and Mrs S Barnett, Barry and Anne)*
☆ *Devonshire* [The Square]: Well kept welcoming hotel, comfortable lounge bar with good window seats overlooking sloping village square, interesting pictures and ornaments, open fires, good range of well presented food inc good Sun lunch in big well furnished dining room, good family room, attentive landlord, full range of Theakstons ales kept well, also Tetleys, tables outside; well appointed good value bedrooms, good breakfast *(LYM, Gwen and Peter Andrews, Dick Brown, Paul R White)*

Great Ayton [NZ5611]
☆ *Royal Oak* [off A173 – follow village signs; High Green]: Wide range of generous good food, well kept Courage Directors and Theakstons, helpful newish licensees, friendly unpretentious bar with open fire in huge inglenook, beam-and-plank ceiling, bulgy old partly panelled stone walls, traditional furnishings inc antique settles, long dining lounge (children welcome); pleasant views of elegant village green from bay windows; comfortable bedrooms *(Edward Leetham, Nancy Cleave, LYM)*

Great Barugh [SE7479]
Golden Lion [off A169 Malton—Pickering]: Interesting and welcoming country pub, good home-made food esp steak pie, well kept John Smiths and Tetleys, helpful staff, separate dining room (must book lunchtime), tables in garden; children allowed in daytime *(Brian Wardrobe)*

Grenoside [SK3394]
☆ *Cow & Calf* [3 miles from M1 junction 35; Skew Hill Lane]: Neatly converted farmhouse, three friendly connected rooms, one no smoking, high-backed settles, stripped stone, brass and copper hanging from beams, plates and pictures, good value hearty freshly made food (not Sun evening) inc sandwiches, children's and vegetarian, well kept Sam Smiths OB, tea and coffee; piped music, music quiz nights; family room in block across walled former farmyard with picnic-sets; splendid views over Sheffield, disabled access, open all day Sat *(CMW, JJW, Don and Shirley Parrish, LYM, Roy Butler)*

Grewelthorpe [SE2376]
☆ *Crown* [back rd NW of Ripon]: Popular local with well kept ales such as Black Sheep, John Smiths, Old Mill and Theakstons, good generous straightforward food inc fresh fish, reasonable prices, whistling landlord, two bar rooms, simple décor, games room with bar billiards, back restaurant; picnic-sets out in front, pleasant small village *(Bill and Kathy Cissna)*

Grinton [SE0598]
☆ *Bridge* [B6270 W of Richmond]: Cosy unpretentious riverside inn in lovely spot opp Cathedral of the Dales, two well used bars, very friendly service, good range of good value simple well prepared food from decent sandwiches to good steaks, ales such as Black Sheep Special, John Smiths, Tetleys Imperial, Theakstons Best, XB and Old Peculier, decent wines, nice restaurant area; attractive tables outside, front and back; bedrooms with own bathrooms; dogs welcome, open all day, good walks *(Philip and Caroline Pennant-Jones, Vann and Terry Prime, Edward and Richard Norris, Richard and Valerie Wright)*

Guiseley [SE1942]
Yorkshire Rose [Leeds Rd]: Well kept beer, good company, popular evening meeting place *(David Naylor)*

Gunnerside [SD9598]
Kings Head [B6270 Swaledale rd]: Small welcoming open-plan flagstoned local in pretty dales village, good value home-made food, well kept changing beers from small breweries inc one brewed for the pub by local Swaledale, old village photographs, children welcome; unobtrusive piped music; seats out by bridge, good walks nearby *(Bruce Bird)*

Halifax [SE0924]
☆ *Shears* [Paris Gates, Boys Lane; OS Sheet 104 map ref 097241]: Hidden down steep cobbled lanes among tall mill buildings, dark unspoilt interior, well kept Timothy Taylor Landlord and Golden Best and a guest beer, welcoming knowledgeable landlord (not Tues), friendly staff; very popular lunchtime for good cheap food from hot-filled sandwiches to home-made pies, curries, casseroles etc; sporting prints, local sports photographs, collection of pump clips and foreign bottles; seats out above the Hebble Brook *(Pat and Tony Martin, the Didler)*
Three Pigeons [Sun Fold, South Parade; off Church St]: Six or seven changing real ales such as Black Sheep, Hop Back, Phoenix, Nick Stafford and Timothy Taylor, simple lunchtime bar food inc burgers, sandwiches and ploughman's, friendly service; handy for Eureka! Museum *(Pat and Tony Martin)*

Harewood [SE3245]
Harewood Arms [A61 opp Harewood House]: Busy hotel, former coaching inn, three attractive, comfortable and spaciously relaxing lounge bars refurbished in dark green, wide choice of good food from sandwiches up (also breakfast and bacon and sausage sandwiches served till 11.30, and afternoon teas), friendly prompt service, well kept ales inc cheap Sam Smiths OB, decent house wines, Harewood family memorabilia; bedrooms *(Janet Pickles, Rachael Ward, Mark Baynham)*

Harpham [TA0961]
St Quintin Arms [Main St]: Lovely old whitewashed village pub, welcoming staff, good value food, well kept John Smiths; attractive garden with lawn and trellis, comfortable good value bedrooms *(Craig Knight)*

Harrogate [SE3155]
Gardeners Arms [Bilton Lane]: Small house converted into good old-fashioned local in lovely peaceful setting – totally unspoilt with tiny bar and three small rooms, flagstones and panelling, tables in spacious garden; well kept very cheap Sam Smiths OB *(the Didler)*
New Inn [B6162 towards Harlow Carr]: Refreshingly down-to-earth, with friendly helpful service, simple food inc good choice of proper sandwiches and ploughman's *(Janet Pickles)*

Hartshead [SE1822]
Gray Ox [not very far from M62 junction 25]: Rustic dining pub with flagstones, farm tools and country pictures, four areas inc no-smoking room, good choice of generous tasty food, Black Sheep, Tetleys and Theakstons, long wine list, pleasant attentive staff; open all day Sun *(Mike Ridgway, Sarah Miles)*

Hawes [SD8789]
Crown [High St]: Traditional market town local with well kept Theakstons Best, XB and Old Peculier, friendly service, coal fire each end; walkers welcome, children allowed away from bar; seats out on cobbled front forecourt *(Adam Garland)*
Fountain [Market Pl]: Bright open bar and lounge, friendly helpful staff, real ales inc Black Sheep, Boddingtons, John Smiths, Theakstons, bar food; bedrooms *(Maurice Thompson)*
White Hart [High St]: Friendly, warm and cosy, busy around bar (esp w/e and Tues market day), quieter on left, wide choice of reasonably priced food in bar and restaurant, real fire, well kept Black Sheep and John Smiths, welcoming service; good value bedrooms *(Maurice Thompson, P A Legon)*

Haworth [SE0337]
☆ *Old Hall* [Sun St]: Friendly and atmospheric open-plan 17th-c beamed and panelled building with several areas off long bar, log fire, stripped stonework, appropriately plain furnishings, good value generous food from baguettes up in bar and restaurant, friendly service, well kept Black Sheep and Tetleys, inoffensive piped music; five mins from centre, open all day Fri, Sat; bedrooms *(MLR)*
Three Sisters [Brow Top Rd, Cross Roads]: Roomy bars and smoking and no-smoking restaurants, varied interesting reasonably priced food from sandwiches to speciality big steaks, well kept ales such as Black Sheep and Theakstons, very helpful staff; open all day; bedrooms *(Norman Stansfield)*
Worth Valley Railway [buffet car on Keighley & Worth Valley steam trains]: Remarkable for its choice of well kept real ales such as Clarks and Timothy Taylor Landlord, as well as

sandwiches and full range of other drinks; occasional White Rose Pullman wine-and-dine trains too *(Dave Braisted)*

Hebden Bridge [SD9927]

Hare & Hounds [Billy Lane, Wadsworth]: Welcoming local licensees, roaring fire, well kept Timothy Taylor Landlord, Best and Golden Best, wide range of generous reasonably priced food (not Mon evening or winter Tues evening) inc vegetarian, various bric-a-brac, well behaved children welcome, no music; some seats outside – lovely hillside scenery with plenty of good walks, handy for Automobile Museum; bedrooms *(Bruce Bird)*

Hedon [TA1928]

Kingstown [A1033]: Comfortable and spacious bar and family restaurant, play areas indoors and out, food to suit, Bass, Stones and Worthington, cheerful staff; bedrooms, open all day *(Paul and Ursula Randall)*

Shakespeare [Baxtergate, off A1033]: Cosy village local with open fire in small L-shaped bar, well kept changing guest beers, decent wine, good value food from sandwiches and toasties up inc decently cooked fresh veg lunchtime and early evening, cheerful welcome, thousands of beermats on beams, old framed brewery advertisements, darts, games machines, small TV; gets very busy; bedrooms *(Paul and Ursula Randall)*

Helmsley [SE6184]

☆ *Black Swan* [Market Pl]: Smart and attractive hotel, not a pub, but pleasant beamed and panelled bar with carved oak settles and windsor armchairs, cosy and gracious lounges with a good deal of character, surprisingly reasonable bar lunch menu, courteous staff, charming sheltered garden; good place to stay – expensive, but comfortable and individual *(W H and E Thomas, John and Esther Sprinkle, BB)*

☆ *Crown* [Market Pl]: Simple but welcoming and pleasantly furnished beamed front bar opening into bigger unpretentious central dining bar, separate no-smoking dining room, good choice of substantial food (sandwiches, puddings and high teas all specially praised), well kept Camerons and Tetleys, good wines by the glass, efficient staff, roaring fires, tables in sheltered garden behind with conservatory area; bedrooms pleasant *(Janet and Peter Race, Mrs Jenny Castle, Keith and Janet Morris, W and E Thomas, Mrs J A Powell, BB, Mr and Mrs J Goodhew)*

☆ *Feathers* [Market Pl]: Sturdy stone inn with heavy medieval beams, dark panelling, oak and walnut tables, big inglenook log fire, bar food from sandwiches to steaks (from £11.75), well kept John Smiths and Theakstons Old Peculier, comfortable separate lounge, no-smoking restaurant; tables in attractive back garden; children in eating area, bedrooms, open all day *(Mr and Mrs A H Young, LYM, Val Stevenson, Rob Holmes, Mrs J E Moffat, John and Esther Sprinkle)*

Royal Oak [Market Pl]: Comfortable and popular, with friendly staff, three well decorated rooms, antiques, good food inc superb roasts and filled yorkshire puddings (worth the wait if busy – no food orders after 8), well kept

Camerons Bitter and a Banks's seasonal beer; pool, piped music, TV; picnic-sets outside, bedrooms good if not cheap *(David and Ruth Hollands, Bruce Bird, SLC, John and Esther Sprinkle)*

Helperby [SE4470]

Golden Lion [Main St]: Quiet and cosy during the week, with well kept Timothy Taylor Landlord and Best and two or three interesting changing ales from smaller often distant brewers, wide choice of food, good fire, friendly staff, no juke box or games; two beer festivals a year; busy Sat, tables out in front *(Nick and Alison Dowson)*

Hepworth [SE1606]

Butchers Arms [off A616 SE of Holmfirth; Towngate]: Friendly L-shaped bar, jovial landlord, dark beams, partly panelled stone walls, pine tables on light wood floor, large log fire in dining room, well kept Marstons Pedigree, Theakstons XB and Timothy Taylor Landlord, lunchtime buffet inc salads, pies, lasagne, good evening meals; pictures for sale, pool and darts at one end, dogs welcome; open all day Fri/Sat, good animal sculpture nearby *(Stephen, Julie and Hayley Brown)*

Hessle [TA0325]

Country Park [Cliff Rd]: Large modernised divided bar, reasonably priced standard food; on foreshore almost under Humber Bridge, tables outside *(Neil and Anita Christopher)*

High Hawsker [NZ9308]

Hare & Hounds [B1447 Whitby—Robin Hoods Bay]: Handy for railway-path walk Whitby—Robin Hood's Bay, pleasant prints, reasonably priced food inc good value Sun carvery, John Smiths and Theakstons on electric pump, pleasant staff, family and games room; open in afternoons *(SLC)*

Holme [SE1006]

☆ *Fleece* [A6024 SW of Holmfirth]: Cosy pleasant L-shaped bar, lots of lifeboat memorabilia, well kept Theakstons with a guest such as Marstons Pedigree, good coffee, popular fresh pub food inc bargain meals, very welcoming landlord, efficient staff, real fire; conservatory with nice flowers, pool/darts room, quiet piped music; attractive village setting below Holme Moss TV mast, great walks *(Bill Sykes)*

Holme on Spalding Moor [SE8038]

Red Lion [Old Rd]: Clean, friendly and comfortable L-shaped bar, good food with fish emphasis in bar and restaurant, attentive staff, sunny terrace with koi carp; comfortable bedrooms in cottages behind *(Roger Bellingham, Michelle Hayles)*

Horbury [SE3018]

Boons [Queen St]: Comfortably basic, with local Clarks and John Smiths kept well, simple décor with some flagstones, bare walls, Rugby League memorabilia, back tap room with pool; very popular, can get crowded *(Michael Butler)*

Horsforth [SE2438]

Bridge [Low Lane]: Welcoming open-plan pub with big stone fireplace and well kept Tetleys beers *(Dr and Mrs A K Clarke)*

Horton in Ribblesdale [SD8172]

☆ *Crown* [B6479 N of Settle]: Clean and pleasant

straightforward low-ceilinged bar with dark woodwork, lots of brass and good fire, good value interesting food inc vegetarian (soups and specials particularly praised), very well kept ales such as Theakstons Old Peculier, welcoming helpful staff, open fire; simple good value bedrooms *(Brian Abbott, Joy and Peter Heatherley, A C and E Johnson)*

Hovingham [SE6775]

Malt Shovel: Nice décor, good old-fashioned small tables and long comfortable banquettes, well kept beers, good house wine, friendly staff, good value food inc interesting dishes in separate dining room; pretty village *(Mrs D Fiddian)*

Huby [SE5766]

☆ *New Inn* [the one nr Easingwold]: Traditional four-bar beamed pub with Victorian range, stripped timbers, bare boards, brasses, old photographs of local RAF base, racing memorabilia, good value bar and restaurant food inc bargain early suppers, pleasant dining conservatory, well kept Tetleys Bitter and Imperial, Theakstons and John Smiths, lots of malt whiskies, helpful staff; quiet piped music, domino and darts teams *(Nick and Alison Dowson, Walter and Susan Rinaldi-Butcher)*

Huddersfield [SE1416]

Head of Steam [Station]: Railway memorabilia, model trains and cars for sale, pies, sandwiches, baked potatoes and good value Sun roasts, friendly staff, coal fire, changing ales such as Boddingtons, Morlands Old Speckled Hen, Ridleys Rumpus and local Kitchen Town, Huddersfield Pride and Wilsons Wobble, lots of bottled beers; open all day *(Pat and Tony Martin, Richard Lewis, R J Bland)*

☆ *Rat & Ratchet* [Chapel Hill]: Bare-boards two-room local brewing its own beer (changing each month) alongside big changing collection of well kept guest ales, two more comfortable rooms up steps, basic well cooked cheap bar food inc outstanding sandwiches and popular Weds curry night; ambiance more pleasant than you might guess from outside, open all day (from 3.30 Mon/Tues) *(JP, PP, Richard Lewis, Patrick Hancock, Derek and Sylvia Stephenson, the Didler)*

Huggate [SE8855]

Wolds: Attractively refurbished small 16th-c pub, mildly upmarket, wide range of good generous food inc good value Sun lunch, friendly staff, well kept John Smiths, Old Mill, Tetleys and Theakstons XB, benches out in front and pleasant garden behind with delightful views; has been cl Mon; bedrooms compact but clean and nicely appointed – lovely village, good easy walks, handy for Wolds Way *(JKW, Paul and Ursula Randall, TRS)*

Hull [TA0927]

Bay Horse [Wincolmlee]: Popular corner local, Batemans' only tied pub here, their beers kept well, good menu; open all day *(the Didler)*

Darley [Boothferry Rd, junction with A164 Beverley rd]: Ample cheap food in large bar and separate restaurant, well kept Vaux Samson and Wards, brisk service *(Tony Gayfer)*

☆ *George* [Land of Green Ginger]: Handsomely preserved traditional long Victorian bar, lots of oak, mahogany and copper, good choice of cheap, generous and tasty freshly cooked lunchtime food at bargain prices inc good fish, well kept Bass and Stones, good service; quiet piped music, fruit machines, can get very busy – get there early; handy for the fine Docks Museum; children allowed in plush upstairs dining room, open all day *(Ian and Nita Cooper, LYM)*

Olde Black Boy [High St, Old Town]: Sympathetically refurbished Tap & Spile in Old Town conservation area, little black-panelled low-ceilinged front smoke room, lofty 18th-c back vaults bar, two rooms upstairs, good value food, friendly service, eight well kept real ales, about 20 country wines, interesting Wilberforce-related posters etc, old jugs and bottles, darts, piano *(BB, the Didler)*

Olde Blue Bell [alley off Lowgate; look out for huge blue bell over pavement]: Friendly traditional three-room 17th-c local with well kept cheap Sam Smiths OB, good value simple lunchtime food, remarkable collection of bells; open all day exc Sun afternoon *(BB, the Didler)*

Sailmakers Arms [High St, Old Town]: Recent conversion of ships' chandlers opp museum in conservation area, nautical theme, cheap lunchtime food from sandwiches up, Morlands Old Speckled Hen and Ruddles; tables outside, lots of plants, birds and chipmunks in run *(Neil and Anita Christopher)*

Hutton Rudby [NZ4706]

Bay Horse: Cosy low-beamed bar and larger main bar, good food inc filled baguettes and children's here and in restaurant, well kept ales inc Morlands Old Speckled Hen, pleasant staff, friendly dog; tables in big garden with lovely views over Leven valley and church, pretty setting on village green *(Chris Pyle)*

Ingbirchworth [SE2205]

☆ *Fountain* [off A629 Shepley—Penistone; Welthorne Lane]: Neat and spacious red plush turkey-carpeted lounge, cosy front bar, comfortable family room, lots of beams, open fires; emphasis on generous good value varied bar food inc exotic salads and superb puddings; well kept Marstons beers, well reproduced pop music, friendly staff, tables in sizeable garden overlooking reservoir; comfortable bedrooms *(RWD, R H Beaumont, BB, Richard Cole, Michael A Butler)*

Ingleton [SD6973]

Bridge [A65]: Pleasant pub with food from good sandwiches to generous hot dishes inc good value Sun roast (eat as much as you like); Black Sheep and Theakstons ales *(Andy and Jill Kassube)*

Goat Gap [A65 towards Clapham]: Welcoming and comfortable 17th-c inn with above-average well presented food, good range of beers, proper coffee, open fire, children welcome; picnic-sets out among trees, play area; bedrooms, also caravan and camp site *(J H and Dr S A Harrop)*

Wheatsheaf: Friendly pub with long bar serving well kept Black Sheep Best and Riggwelter and Moorhouses, changing good value food prepared to order from fresh ingredients, big garden; walkers and children welcome, handy for Ingleborough *(John Plumridge, Andy and Jill Kassube)*

Keighley [SE0641]

Boltmakers Arms [East Parade]: Split-level open-plan local with long-serving licensees, well kept Timothy Taylor Landlord, Best, Golden Best and guest beers; open all day *(the Didler)*

Globe [Parkwood St]: Refurbished local by Worth Valley steam railway track, weekday lunches, Tetleys and Timothy Taylor Landlord, Best and Golden Best; open all day *(the Didler)*

Kelfield [SE5938]

Grey Horse [off B1222 S of York]: Pleasant beamed pub with good choice of freshly made food inc bargain offers for two and good Sun lunch, well kept beer, decent wines *(Janet Pickles)*

Kettlesing [SE2256]

☆ *Queens Head* [signed off A59 W of Harrogate]: Friendly dining pub with nicely presented good value food, popular weekday lunchtimes with older people, lots of quite close-set tables, well kept Black Sheep Riggwelter and Daleside Crackshot, good house wines, quick service, unobtrusive piped music, attractive and interesting decorations; children welcome *(BB, Charles York)*

Kettlewell [SD9772]

☆ *Racehorses* [B6160 N of Skipton]: Comfortable and civilised, with very friendly attentive service, good well presented home-made food from sandwiches to good value Sun roast, well kept ales inc Theakstons XB and Old Peculier, good choice of wines, log fires; tables on attractive terrace; well placed for Wharfedale walks, good bedrooms with own bathrooms *(Dick Brown, BB, MDN, B, M and P Kendall, Malcolm and Jennifer Perry)*

Kilburn [SE5179]

☆ *Forresters Arms* [between A170 and A19 SW of Thirsk]: Next to 'mouseman' Thompson furniture workshops (visitor centre opp), largely furnished by them; big log fire, good home cooking, friendly staff, well kept Hambleton and Tetleys, games and piped music, upper bar mainly for eating; restaurant, well behaved children allowed, open all day; suntrap seats out in front, pleasant village; good value bedrooms, cheerful and bright *(MLR, LYM, Nick and Alison Dowson, Mrs Jenny Castle)*

Kildwick [SE0145]

White Lion [A629 Keighley—Skipton, by Leeds—Liverpool Canal]: Old good value dining pub by Leeds—Liverpool Canal, log fire in dining room, Tetleys and guest beers, friendly attentive service; next to ancient church in attractive village *(M and J Godfrey, D Stokes)*

Killinghall [SE3059]

Greyhound [A61/B6161]: Stonebuilt pub with plush banquettes, bookshelves in lower bar, well kept Sam Smiths, good value food, prompt friendly service *(GSB)*

Kilnsea [TA4015]

Crown & Anchor: Two bars, dining room and family room, Bass Bitter and Mild and Tetleys, horsebrasses and china; front picnic-sets facing Humber estuary, and in back garden; open all day, handy for Spurn Point nature reserve walks *(DC)*

Kirby Hill [NZ1406]

☆ *Shoulder of Mutton* [off A66 NW of Scotch Corner, via Ravensworth]: Friendly and unassuming village inn with green plush wall settles, stone arch to public bar, open fires, good food from lunchtime sandwiches to steaks, vegetarian dishes, good service, Black Sheep Bitter and Riggwelter and John Smiths, quite a few malt whiskies, restaurant; darts, dominoes, cribbage, piped music, Fri quiz night; children in eating area, fine views from picnic-sets in yard behind and from good value bedrooms (you do hear the – tuneful – church bell); cl Mon lunchtime *(LYM, P Abbott, Chris and Ann Garnett, Bruce Bird, B Kneale)*

Kirkby Overblow [SE3249]

☆ *Star & Garter* [off A61 S of Harrogate]: Cosy unspoilt pub, friendly and relaxing, very popular lunchtime with older people for generous good value food inc imaginative specials and good vegetarian choice, outstanding value 3-course Sun lunch, particularly well kept Camerons and Tetleys, two log fires, bluff no-nonsense Yorkshire landlord, first-rate service, dining room for evening meals; open all day, beautiful setting *(Howard and Margaret Buchanan, Robert Gartery, Margaret and Arthut Dickinson)*

Kiveton Park [SK4983]

Station Hotel [B6059 opp stn]: Good helpings of reasonably priced food inc vegetarian and children's, stripped brick dining area through arch off lounge, Stones ale, fruit machine, pool and TV in bar, piped music *(CMW, JJW)*

Knaresborough [SE3557]

☆ *Blind Jacks* [Market Pl]: Former 18th-c shop now a charming multi-floor traditional tavern, with simple but attractive furnishings, brewery posters etc; well kept Black Sheep, Hambleton White Boar and Nightmare Stout and Timothy Taylor Landlord with changing guest beers; farm cider and foreign bottled beers; well behaved children allowed away from bar, open all day, cl Mon till 5.30 *(LYM, the Didler)*

Board: Unpretentious pub with friendly easy-going landlord, well kept Theakstons ales, simple good value food; bedrooms *(Judith Hirst)*

Langthwaite [NY9902]

☆ *Charles Bathurst* [Arkengarthdale, a mile N towards Tan Hill; aka the CB Inn]: Old Dales cottages knocked through to make very popular and friendly long bar with clean and spartan bistro décor, light pine scrubbed tables, country chairs and benches on stripped floors, roaring fire, quick attentive service, well kept Black Sheep, John Smiths and Theakstons from island bar, good imaginative reasonably priced food using local ingredients, frequently changing menu inc good vegetarian choice, fairly short but interesting wine list; walkers and well behaved dogs welcome, bedrooms, attractive spot with wonderful views, open all day *(Chris and Fiona Whitton, Revd J E Cooper, Kevin Thorpe, Richard and Valerie Wright)*

☆ *Red Lion* [just off Reeth—Brough Arkengarthdale rd]: Homely unspoilt 17th-c pub, individual and relaxing, in charming dales village with ancient bridge; basic cheap nourishing lunchtime food, well kept Black Sheep Bitter and Riggwelter and John Smiths, country wines, tea and coffee; well behaved children allowed lunchtime in very low-ceilinged (and sometimes smoky) side snug, quietly friendly service; good walks all around, inc organised circular ones from the pub – maps and guides for sale *(Kevin Thorpe, LYM, Judith Hirst, Richard and Valerie Wright)*

Lastingham [SE7391]

☆ *Blacksmiths Arms* [off A170 W of Pickering]: Attractively old-fashioned village pub opp Saxon church, log fire in oak-beamed bar's open range, traditional furnishings, no-smoking dining area with home-made food from sandwiches to steaks inc vegetarian (breakfasts for campers etc), well kept real ales inc Black Sheep, quite a few malt whiskies, separate games room with pool etc; can get crowded; children welcome, no-smoking bedrooms, lovely countryside *(Mr and Mrs A H Young, Mrs K L Heath, LYM, Barry and Anne, Duncan Hunter)*

Lealholm [NZ7608]

Board [off A171 W of Whitby]: In wonderful moorland village spot by wide pool of River Esk, two tidy refurbished bars, straightforward food, Camerons, big log fire favoured by Billy the monster pub cat; secluded riverside garden *(DJW)*

Ledston [SE4328]

☆ *White Horse*: Spacious beamed and partly flagstoned pub, several rooms, lots of brass, good choice of generous food from fish and chips to Thai curries, well kept ales inc Boddingtons, pleasant service; two flowery terraces, attractive village *(Neil and Anita Christopher)*

Leeds [SE3033]

☆ *Adelphi* [Hunslet Rd]: Well restored handsome Edwardian tiling, woodwork and cut and etched glass, several rooms, impressive stairway; particularly well kept Tetleys Bitter, Mild and Imperial (virtually the brewery tap), prompt friendly service, good spread of cheap food at lunchtime, crowded but convivial then; live jazz Sat *(Reg Nelson, Tony and Wendy Hobden, the Didler)*

Duck & Drake [Kirkgate, between indoor mkt and Parish Church]: No-frills big two-bar pub with a dozen or more well kept reasonably priced ales inc obscure local brews, farm ciders; bare boards, basic furniture and beer posters and mirrors; simple substantial food, friendly staff, quieter locals' back room with coal fire; juke box, live music Sun, Tues and Thurs nights, open all day *(Pete Baker, Martyn and Mary Mullins, the Didler, Richard Lewis)*

Felon & Firkin [Gt George St]: Friendly bustle in former court rooms, with decorated vaulted ceilings, fancy windows and cops' and robbers'' décor along with the usual Firkin benches, barrels and breweriana; upper gallery shows microbrewery producing their good Fuzz, Felon, Bobby, Dogbolter and a chocolate and orange Stout; usual food from big sandwiches up, table footer, games machines, big screen TV, live music and comedy nights, friendly staff, disabled access; open all day *(Richard Lewis, Norma and Keith Bloomfield)*

Fenton [Woodhouse Lane, opp BBC]: Large open-plan panelled pub nr university, old Tetleys advertisements, well kept beer *(Dr and Mrs A K Clarke)*

☆ *Garden Gate* [Whitfield Pl, Hunslet]: Ornate but thoroughly down-to-earth Victorian pub with various rooms off central drinking corridor, well worth a look for its now near-unique style and intricate glass and woodwork; Tetleys Bitter and Mild foaming with freshness, farm cider, no food; open all day, can be boisterous evenings *(BB, Reg Nelson, the Didler)*

Grove [Back Row, Holbeck]: Well preserved 1930s pub, four rooms off drinking corridor, Courage Directors, Ruddles County, John Smiths, Theakstons XB, Youngers No 3 and guest beers; open all day (cl 4-7 w/e) *(the Didler)*

Hogshead [Lower Briggate]: Spacious open-plan Whitbreads pub, bare boards, barrels, partitions, old Leeds prints, some upstairs seating, very wide choice of changing well kept ales inc unusual ones, pub food from filled rolls to pies, friendly efficient staff, relaxing atmosphere; open all day, opp listed Leeds General Infirmary *(Pat and Tony Martin, Richard Lewis)*

Myrtle [Parkside Pl, Meanwood]: Stonebuilt pub with emphasis on food, own cricket pitch, good outside seating areas *(Dr and Mrs A K Clarke)*

Palace [Kirkgate]: Up to ten or so particularly well kept Tetleys-related and changing guest ales, polished wood, good value lunchtime food from sandwiches up inc two-for-one bargains in no-smoking dining area, friendly staff; games end with pool, piped music; tables in attractive yard, open all day *(Richard Lewis)*

Prince of Wales [Mill Hill, nr stn]: Popular refurbished pub with consistently well kept ales such as Barnsley, Black Sheep, John Smiths and Wadworths 6X, lunchtime food, lounge, basic pool and TV room, friendly staff; live music Sat, open all day *(Richard Lewis)*

Roundhay [Roundhay Rd, Oakwood]: Cheap and cheerful Foresters Feast dining pub, well kept Whitbreads-related beers, quick friendly service; handy for Roundhay Park and Tropical World *(Phil and Anne Smithson)*

Scarborough [Bishopgate St, opp stn]: Tetleys Festival Alehouse with ornate art nouveau tiled curved frontage, bare boards, barrel tables, lots of wood, ten or so interesting changing real ales inc Milds in fine condition, farm cider, wide choice of cheap lunchtime food, friendly helpful staff, music-hall posters; machines, TV; open all day exc Sun afternoon *(Richard Lewis)*

Viaduct [Lower Briggate]: Peaceful pub which actively caters for disabled customers; pleasantly furnished long narrow bar, lots of wood, no-smoking area, lunchtime food, good choice of well kept Tetleys and guest ales, friendly helpful staff; back garden, open all day exc Sun afternoon *(Richard Lewis)*

☆ *Victoria* [Gt George St, just behind Town Hall]: Ornate bustling Victorian pub with grand etched mirrors, impressive globe lamps extending from the ornately solid bar, imposing carved beams, booths with working snob-screens, smaller rooms off; well kept Tetleys inc Mild and several well chosen guest beers, friendly smart bar staff, reasonably priced food in luncheon room with end serving hatch, no-smoking room; open all day *(Dr and Mrs A K Clarke, Richard Lewis, Reg Nelson, the Didler)*

Whip [alley off Boar Lane, parallel to Duncan St]: Particularly well kept Ansells Mild, Ind Coope Burton, Tetleys Mild, Bitter and Imperial; traditional feel, friendly helpful staff, lively mixed customers; tables in courtyard *(the Didler)*

Woodies [Otley Rd, Headingley; A660 N, past university]: Several rooms in large welcoming roadside pub, busy friendly atmosphere, bare boards, wooden seats, good changing range of real ales *(Dr and Mrs A K Clarke)*

Linthwaite [SE1014]

Royal Oak [Manchester Rd]: Good local recently tastefully refurbished, relaxed and friendly, good choice of beers inc guests, roaring log fire, traditional games esp darts, good juke box; plans for garden overlooking canal and river; open from 4.30, and Sun lunchtime *(Lorraine Graham, John Plumridge)*

Lockton [SE8490]

Fox & Rabbit [A169 N of Pickering]: Family local nicely placed on moors edge, comfortable plush banquettes, brasses, stuffed foxes and game, well kept Banks's and Camerons, generous good value straightforward food from sandwiches up, friendly helpful young staff, restaurant; darts, two pool tables, machines, family area, seats outside and in sun lounge *(SLC, Colin and Dot Savill, LYM)*

Long Preston [SD8358]

☆ *Maypole* [A65 Settle—Skipton]: Clean and friendly dining pub on village green, spacious beamed dining room and comfortable lounge with copper-topped tables, stag's head, open fires; good choice of good value generous food inc home-made pies, Sun lunch and good fresh veg, well kept Boddingtons, Timothy Taylor and Whitbreads Castle Eden, helpful jolly service; good value bedrooms with own bathrooms, good breakfast *(Andy and Jill Kassube, Gordon Neighbour, M and J Godfrey, E Warburton, John and Sylvia Harrop)*

Low Row [SD9897]

Punch Bowl [B6270 Reeth—Muker]: Cheerful family bar, open all day in summer, with well kept Theakstons Best, XB and Old Peculier and guests, rows of malt whiskies, decent house wines, wide choice of good value generous food, log fire, games room; piped music; fine Swaledale views esp from terrace with quoits pitches below; popular tea room 10-5.30 with home-made cakes, small shop, bicycle and cave lamp hire; folk music Fri; good basic bedrooms, also bunkhouse, big breakfast *(Jane Taylor, David Dutton, Gwen and Peter Andrews, Sue Holland, Dave Webster)*

Malham [SD8963]

Buck [off A65 NW of Skipton]: Big village pub suiting walkers, wide range of quickly served

good value generous home-made food inc vegetarian, well kept Black Sheep, Tetleys, Theakstons Best and a guest beer, big log fire in comfortable lounge, roomy hikers' bar, separate candlelit dining room, picnic-sets in small garden; attractive building, decent well equipped bedrooms, many good walks from the door *(K H Frostick, Ian Phillips, Comus Elliott, Lyn and Geoff Hallchurch, Dave Braisted, Ian Pendlebury)*

☆ *Lister Arms* [off A65 NW of Skipton]: Friendly easy-going open-plan lounge, busy w/e, relaxed attitude to children and dogs, fine choice of very enjoyable good value bar food inc vegetarian, well kept changing ales such as Black Sheep, Ind Coope Burton and Wadworths 6X, growing range of continental draught beers, lots of malt whiskies, well worn-in furnishings and fittings, roaring fire, restaurant famous for steaks (good wine list), games area with pool and maybe loudish piped music; seats outside the substantial creeper-covered stone inn overlooking small green, more in back garden – nice spot by river, ideal for walkers; bedrooms *(Norman Portis, Prof and Mrs S Barnett, Ian Phillips, D W Stokes)*

Malton [SE7972]

Kings Head [Market Pl]: Ivy-covered pub with comfortable café-bar layout, wide choice of good bar food, well kept ales such as Caledonian Deuchars and Marstons Bitter and Pedigree; piped music *(SLC)*

Royal Oak [Town St, Old Malton]: Friendly helpful service, good guest beers, good generous quickly served standard food inc Whitby seafood platter; tables in garden, children welcome *(Tony Hemesley)*

Mankinholes [SD9523]

Top Brink [Lumbutts]: Small lively moorland village pub, quite close to Pennine Way and nice walks to nearby monument on Stoodley Pike, Timothy Taylor Landlord and weekly changing guest beers, good value well cooked food inc good steaks; can get busy *(Dr C C S Wilson)*

Marsden [SE0412]

☆ *Riverhead* [Peel St, next to Co-op; just off A62 Huddersfield—Oldham]: Basic own-brew pub in converted grocer's, spiral stairs down to microbrewery producing good range of interesting beers named after local reservoirs (the higher the reservoir, the higher the strength) inc Mild, Stout and Porter, farm cider, friendly service and locals, unobtrusive piped music, no food (maybe sandwiches) or machines; wheelchair access, cl weekday lunchtimes, open all day w/e, nice stop after walk by canal or on the hills *(Richard Lewis, JP, PP, R J Bland, the Didler)*

Marton [SE7383]

Apple Tree [the one off A174 S of Middlesbrough; The Derby]: Recently refurbished, with helpful service, well kept Black Sheep Special, Camerons, Tetleys and Theakstons Best, good food, open fire, games room with pool; restaurant *(SLC)*

Masham [SE2381]

Bay Horse [Silver St, linking A6168 with Market Sq]: Recently refurbished, comfortable brocaded seats in split-level lounge, good range of good value generous food inc choice of Sun roasts, friendly staff, well kept Theakstons, real fire, darts and fruit machine in separate bar; piped music; children allowed; bedrooms up twisty stairs, good breakfast *(Judith Hirst)*

☆ *Black Sheep Brewery*: Stylish modern bistro-style drinking area on top floor of maltings which now houses the brewery – not a pub, but likely to appeal to Good Pub Guide readers, together with a brewery visit; pleasant functional décor, upper gallery, good imaginative varied food all day, excellent service, some worthwhile beery tourist trinkets, and of course the Baa'r has well kept Black Sheep Bitter, Special and Riggwelter; interesting brewery tour, good family facilities inc play area; can be very busy; cl 5 Mon, and late winter Sun evenings *(Liz Bell, Susan and Nigel Wilson, Richard Lewis, R C Vincent, Sue Holland, Dave Webster)*

Bruce Arms: Very traditional friendly local with attractive menu, particularly well kept Black Sheep; juke box, fruit machine *(Nick Lawless)*

Meltham [SE0910]

Will's o' Nat's [Blackmoorfoot Rd, NW of village off B6107]: A long-standing main entry under its excellent previous landlord Kim Schofield, handy for walkers on Colne Valley and Kirklees circular walks and for Blackmoorfoot reservoir (birdwatching); still has good solid furnishings, log fire, well kept Tetleys Bitter and Mild with Old Mill as a guest, and good value food from lots of hot and cold sandwiches up inc children's meals, with views from slightly raised partly no smoking end dining extension; maybe piped music *(H K Dyson, LYM, Michael A Butler)*

Mexborough [SE4800]

Concertina Band Club [Dolcliffe Rd]: Friendly pubby club welcoming visitors, brewing its own changing ales such as Club, Bengal Tiger and Old Skellow, also well kept John Smiths and Tetleys; bar, lounge with pool, SkyTV and games machine, traditional games, large music room; cl Sun lunchtime *(Richard Lewis)*

Middleham [SE1288]

Richard III [Market Pl]: Big bustling friendly local, horsey pictures, quick service, open fire in front bar, side pool area, back bar with tables for well presented food from good cheap sandwiches to imaginative evening meals; well kept Tetleys, Theakstons and John Smiths; good bedrooms *(R Frank)*

☆ *White Swan* [Market Pl]: Old flagstoned and oak-beamed village inn with open fires, good choice of interesting food in bar and homely dining room inc vegetarian and good cheeses, well kept Black Sheep, Hambleton and John Smiths; comfortable bedrooms, attractive setting *(Mrs Joanna Powell, M G Simpson, Denise Dowd)*

Middlesmoor [SE0874]

Crown [top of Nidderdale rd from Pateley Bridge]: Remote inn with warmly welcoming landlord and family, simple well presented food inc good sandwiches, particularly well kept Black Sheep and Ruddles, blazing log fires in

cosy spotless rooms, homely dining room, beautiful view over stonebuilt hamlet high in upper Nidderdale, tables in small garden; good value simple bedrooms *(Trevor and Diane Waite, Catherine and Richard Preston, R Styles)*

Middleton on the Wolds [SE9449]

Robin Hood: Friendly local with good value home-made food inc good chips; pool *(Susan and Nigel Wilson)*

Mytholmroyd [SE0126]

Shoulder of Mutton [New Rd (B6138)]: Comfortable and friendly stonebuilt streamside local, emphasis on good value very generous home cooking (not Tues evening) inc fish, children's and good range of puddings, OAP lunches and children's helpings, no-smoking and family dining areas; well kept Boddingtons, Castle Eden and Timothy Taylor Landlord, nice display of toby jugs and other china, small no-dining area *(Malcolm Stewart, Ian and Nita Cooper)*

North Grimston [SE8468]

Middleton Arms: Good locally popular dining pub nicely placed on edge of Yorkshire Wolds, lovely garden, well kept Tetleys *(James Nunns)*

Norwood Green [SE1427]

☆ *Olde White Bear* [signed off A641 in Wyke, or A58 just W of Wyke]: Recently successfully renovated and extended, with several attractive rooms, beams, brasses, good personal service, well kept Whitbreads-related and guest beers, good choice of food in bar and handsome restaurant in former barn inc bargain early suppers *(George Little, Geoffrey and Brenda Wilson)*

Nun Monkton [SE5058]

Alice Hawthorn [off A59 York—Harrogate]: Modernised down-to-earth beamed village local with lots of brass etc, big brick inglenook fireplace, Boddingtons, Tetleys and guest ales, recently improved food, keen darts players; on broad village green with pond and lovely avenue to church and Rivers Nidd and Ouse *(BB, Janet and Peter Race, Andy and Jill Kassube)*

Osmotherley [SE4499]

Golden Lion [The Green]: Popular beamed local dining pub with whitewashed stone walls and old pews, good food, well kept beers such as North Yorkshire Golden, John Smiths Magnet and Theakstons XB, pleasant efficient service, fresh flowers, tables out overlooking village green; 44-mile Lyke Wake Walk starts here *(Neil and Anita Christopher, Mike Smith, Donald and Margaret Wood)*

Ossett [SE2719]

☆ *Brewers Pride* [Low Mill Rd/Healey Lane, off B6128; OS Sheet 104 map ref 271191]: Warmly friendly basic local now brewing its own beers in plant designed by landlord, well kept guest beers too, cosy front room and bar both with open fires, brewery memorabilia, small games room, good food choice Fri/Sat, generous Sun bar nibbles, big back garden with local entertainment summer w/e; quiz night Mon, country & western Thurs, open all day w/e; nr Calder & Hebble Canal *(the Didler)*

Victoria [Manor Rd, just off Horbury Rd]: Plain exterior concealing wide range of interesting evening food and popular Sun carvery, small dining room with washroom theme, well kept Tetleys and guest beers, decent wines, cosy bar (piped music may obtrude a bit); cl lunchtime Mon-Thurs, no lunchtime food Fri/Sat *(M Borthwick, Michael Butler)*

Oswaldkirk [SE6279]

☆ *Malt Shovel* [signed off B1363/B1257 S of Helmsley]: Attractive former small 17th-c manor house being revived by hard-working new landlord, heavy beams and flagstones, fine staircase, simple traditional furnishings, huge log fires, two cosy bars (one may be crowded with well heeled locals), family room, interestingly decorated dining room, unusual garden *(LYM, Jenny Cantle)*

Otley [SE2045]

Bay Horse [Boroughgate]: Very old traditional local with low beams and well kept ales *(Reg Nelson)*

Junction [Bondgate (A660)]: Warm and welcoming old-fashioned beamed pub with single small bar, bare boards, wall benches, big fire, well kept Tetleys, Theakstons XB and Old Peculier, Timothy Taylor Landlord and Best, interesting curios from animals to sprockets, usual food *(Reg Nelson, John and Lis Burgess)*

Oulton [SE3628]

Three Horseshoes: Very generous good food, favourable prices, friendly professional staff *(anon)*

Pateley Bridge [SE1666]

Crown [Main St]: Cosy lounge with railed-off dining area alongside, big coal fire, welcoming atmosphere, stripped stonework and horsebrasses, good generous food (separate lunchtime and evening menus) inc children's, well kept John Smiths, public bar with back pool room, restaurant, good chatty service *(Richard Lewis, Ian Phillips)*

Patrington [TA3122]

Hildyard Arms [Market Pl]: Cheerful and friendly old coaching inn, tastefully refurbished, with shelves of decorative teapots, model sailing ship, pictures and old cupboards in main bar's pleasant dining area, wide range of inexpensive food (not Sun evening) inc children's and vegetarian, Tetleys Bitter, Dark Mild and guests such as Greene King Abbot *(Ian and Nita Cooper)*

Penistone [SE2402]

☆ *Cubley Hall* [Mortimer Rd; outskirts, towards Stocksbridge]: Former grand Edwardian country house, panelling, elaborate plasterwork, mosaic tiling, plush furnishings, roomy conservatory, distant views beyond the neat formal gardens (with a good play house and adventure playground), wide choice of good generous imaginative food all day from sandwiches up inc vegetarian and children's, well kept Ind Coope Burton, Tetleys Bitter and Imperial and interesting guest beers, decent wines (wide choice by the glass), efficient good-humoured service, restaurant; piped music, children in restaurant and conservatory; very popular for w/e wedding receptions, comfortable bedrooms *(Derek and Sylvia Stephenson, R T and J C Moggridge, M Payne, L M and C J Clark, C*

Hinchcliffe, LYM, RWD)

Pickering [SE7984]

Bay Horse [Market Pl]: Welcoming heavy-beamed open-plan red plush bar with old-fashioned prints and horsey bric-a-brac, big fire, well kept John Smiths, generous good value food, back public bar with games and inglenook, upstairs restaurant with good w/e carvery (gluten-free gravy) *(BB, Mr and Mrs J Goodhew)*

Black Bull [A169 towards Malton]: Wide choice of remarkably generous well priced food in straightforward roadside pub *(Janet Pickles)*

Station [Park St]: Decent food and well kept Johns Smiths, Tetleys and Theakstons Best on electric pump, big back restaurant *(SLC)*

☆ *White Swan* [Market Pl; off A170]: Attractive small hotel, former coaching inn, with two small panelled bars, good if not cheap food from lunchtime sandwiches to interesting main dishes inc good vegetarian choice, well kept Black Sheep Bitter and Special and Hambleton, open fires, friendly helpful staff, busy but comfortable family room, good no-smoking restaurant with interesting wines esp St Emilion clarets; bedrooms comfortable, good breakfast *(JWGN, SLC, Bruce Bird, Norma and Keith Bloomfield, Janet and Peter Race)*

Rastrick [SE1421]

Globe [Rastrick Common]: High above Brighouse, with good welcoming service, well kept Wards, imaginative food in restaurant (not Tues evening or Mon) *(David Coleman)*

Reeth [SE0499]

☆ *Black Bull* [B6270]: Friendly recently refurbished village pub in fine spot at foot of broad sloping green, traditional dark beamed and flagstoned L-shaped front bar, well kept John Smiths and Theakstons inc Old Peculier tapped from the cask, reasonably priced usual food inc good vegetarian options, open fires, helpful staff, children welcome; piped music in pool room; comfortable bedrooms overlooking dales, good breakfast *(Jane Taylor, David Dutton, LYM, James Nunns)*

Buck: Comfortably refurbished, with good varied food in bar and restaurant, reasonable prices; bedrooms, good breakfast *(R and K Halsey)*

Richmond [NZ1801]

Black Lion [Finkle St]: Bustling local atmosphere in well used coaching inn with well kept ales inc Camerons Strongarm, Flowers and Tetleys, character beamed black-panelled back bar, nice no-smoking lounge, basic locals' bar, lots of regimental shields and badges, log fires, no-frills good value food inc vegetarian, front dining room; bedrooms reasonably priced *(Neil and Anita Christopher, Vann and Terry Prime, B Kneale)*

Ripon [SE3171]

Golden Lion [Allhallow Gate, off Market Sq]: Neatly kept local, brass-topped tables, lots of naval memorabilia, well kept Black Sheep and John Smiths, simple good value food inc lots of sandwiches, friendly staff, airy conservatory; quiet piped music *(Lesley, Peter and Alastair Barrett, Ian Phillips)*

Ripponden [SE0419]
Besom Broom: Well kept Marstons Pedigree
and Tetleys, good home cooking (not w/e) inc
lunchtime and early evening bargains for two,
friendly staff *(Pat and Tony Martin)*

Robin Hoods Bay [NZ9505]
Bay [The Dock, Bay Town]: Unpretentious
hotel with fine sea views from cosy picture-
window two-room bar, very friendly staff, well
kept Courage Directors, Ruddles, John Smiths
and Theakstons, log fires, good value generous
food in bar and separate dining area, welcoming
staff; open all day, tables outside, cosy
bedrooms (not many with own bath) *(JP, PP,
Neil and Anita Christopher, David Heath, John
Brightley)*
☆ *Olde Dolphin* [King St, Bay Town]: Roomy
18th-c inn stepped up above sea front in
attractive little town; unpretentious basic bar
with friendly service, convivial atmosphere,
good range of well kept Scottish Courage ales,
good open fire, good value bar food inc
vegetarian and local seafood, popular back
games room; dogs welcome in bar if well
behaved, piped music, can get crowded w/e,
long walk back up to village car park; Fri folk
club, cheap simple bedrooms *(JP, PP, Neil and
Anita Christopher, John and Liz Soden, John
Higgins)*
Victoria [Station Rd]: Clifftop Victorian hotel
overlooking bay, good views from garden, solid
period décor in bar, large airy green-walled
family room with cheerful wipe-clean
tablecloths, well kept Camerons and Marstons
Pedigree, wide choice of fresh food; bedrooms
(Jamie and Sarah Allan)

Rosedale Abbey [SE7395]
☆ *White Horse* [300 yds up Rosedale Chimney
Bank Rd – entering village, first left after Coach
House Inn]: Cosy and comfortable farm-based
country inn in lovely spot above the village,
character bar with elderly maybe antique
furnishings, lots of stuffed animals and birds,
well kept Black Sheep, Tetleys and Theakstons
Best and Old Peculier, quite a few wines and
good choice of malt whiskies, friendly service,
good generous home-made food from
sandwiches and ploughman's to mixed grill,
great views from terrace (and from restaurant
and bedrooms); children allowed if eating,
occasional jazz nights, open all day Sat;
attractive bedrooms – a nice place to stay, good
walks *(Comus Elliott, SLC, LYM)*

Rotherham [SK4393]
Moulders Rest [Masbrough St]: Large roadside
pub with very cheap weekday lunchtime food,
Stones and a guest ale *(Tony Hobden)*

Runswick Bay [NZ8217]
☆ *Royal* [off A174 NW of Whitby]: Super setting
tucked into cliffs, lovely views over fishing
village and sea from welcoming big-windowed
plain front lounge, limited choice of good value
food inc huge helpings of fresh local fish, well
kept Black Sheep, good service, bustling nautical
back bar, family room with TV and darts;
terrace, bedrooms; steep walk down from top
car park, or use expensive village car park
(Malcolm and Helen Baxter, DJW, BB)

Ryther [SE5539]
Ryther Arms [just off B1223 Selby—Tadcaster]:
Good food from meal-sized starters to speciality
steaks (they hang their own beef) and good fish
in bar and partly no smoking restaurant –
beware, two sittings Sat evening, 7 and 9 *(C A
Hall)*

Saltaire [SE1437]
Boathouse: Devent riverside pub *(Esther and
John Sprinkle)*

Saltburn by the Sea [NZ6722]
☆ *Ship* [A174 towards Whitby]: Beautiful setting
among beached fishing boats, sea views from
tasteful nautical-style black-beamed bars and big
plainer summer dining lounge with handsome
ship model; good range of reasonably priced
food, quick friendly service, evening restaurant
(not Sun), children's room and menu,
Theakstons, seats outside; busy at holiday times,
smuggling exhibition next door *(LYM, Ian
Phillips)*

Saxton [SE4736]
Crooked Billet [B1217 Towton—Garforth
about mile outside Saxton opp Lead church]:
Tidy and well run extended pub very popular
for reasonably priced food inc good sandwiches,
vegetarian, children's and giant yorkshire
puddings, friendly comfortable atmosphere, well
kept John Smiths, decent wine, pleasant efficient
staff, fire in each bar, conservatory dining
extension, tables in garden *(Michael Butler,
Janet Pickles, D M and B K Moores)*
Greyhound [by church in village, 2½ miles from
A1 via B1217]: Charming unchanging local in
attractive quiet village, well kept cheap Sam
Smiths OB tapped from the cask, Victorian
fireplace in chatty tap room (children allowed
here), traditional snug, corridor to games room,
a couple of picnic-sets in side yard; open all day
w/e *(LYM, JP, PP)*
☆ *Plough* [not far from A1, off B1217 towards
Towton; Headwell Lane]: Emphasis on smart
but friendly big dining room off small
straightforward bar with blazing coke fire; huge
changing blackboard choice of good freshly
made food (not Sun evening) from enterprising
lunchtime snacks through carefully prepared
interesting main dishes to beautifully presented
puddings, friendly staff, well kept Theakstons,
good choice of house wines, good coffee; seats
outside, cl Mon; pleasant stone village with
magnificent church *(P R and A M Caley,
Stephen Adams, Guy Vowles)*

Scammonden Reservoir [SE0215]
Brown Cow [A672]: Dramatic views over M62,
reservoir and moors in old-fashioned pub with
long bar, reasonably priced food and interesting
changing guest beers; busy evenings and w/e
(H K Dyson)

Scarborough [TA0489]
Hole in the Wall [Vernon Rd]: Unusual long
pub, refreshing conversation and lively radical
debate, well kept Malton Double Chance,
Theakstons BB, XB and Old Peculier and good
changing guest beers, country wines, no piped
music or machines; cheap basic lunchtime food
(not Sun lunchtime) *(Kevin Blake, Keith and
Janet Morris, Reg Nelson)*

Lord Rosebery [Westborough]: Handsome Wetherspoons in former local Liberal HQ, in traffic-free central shopping area; galleried upper bar, well kept beers inc interesting guests, reasonably priced good food inc Sun roast; open all day, very busy evenings *(Kevin Blake, Simon Orme, Keith and Janet Morris)*

Seamer [TA0284]

Mayfield [the one nr Scarborough]: Varied choice of competitively priced restaurant-quality food, attentive service; children welcome *(Ron and Shirley Richardson)*

Selby [SE6132]

Albion Vaults [The Crescent]: Tied to Old Mill, with their Best, Nellie Dene and Porter, lunchtime food inc excellent value Sun lunch with care taken over ingredients and presentation, friendly welcome, hard-working landlord *(Simon Reynolds)*

Cricketers Arms [Market Pl]: Popular pub handy for abbey, friendly and chatty; long bar with banquettes in bays, cricketing memorabilia, generous good value home-made lunchtime food (not Sun), Sam Smiths OB; games machines, juke box, piped music; quiz nights Sun and Mon; disabled access, open all day exc Tues and Weds *(Tony Hobden)*

Settle [SD8264]

Royal Oak [Market Pl]: Market-town inn with roomy partly divided open-plan panelled bar, comfortable seats around brass-topped tables, well kept Boddingtons, Flowers IPA, Timothy Taylor Landlord and Best, generous bar food all day, restaurant, no-smoking area; children welcome, bedrooms *(LYM, Mr and Mrs P Stainsby, Bruce Bird, Anne and David Robinson)*

Sheffield [SK3687]

Bankers Draft [Market Pl]: Wetherspoons conversion of a former Midland Bank, roomy and well kept, with standard food all day inc bargains, good range of sensibly priced real ales, no-smoking area; open all day *(Richard Lewis, Tony Hobden)*

Cask & Cutler [Henry St; Shalesmoor tram stop right outside]: Well refurbished small corner pub, coal fire in no-smoking bar on left, no juke box or machines, friendly licensees and cat, half a dozen well kept changing beers inc a Mild from small breweries (starting to brew their own), regular beer festivals, farm ciders and perry, appropriate posters, good value home-made food till 6.30 inc popular cheap Sun lunch (booking advised); open all day Fri/Sat, wheelchair access, tables in nice back garden *(Richard Lewis, CMW, JJW, the Didler, JP, PP)*

Frog & Parrot [Division St/Westfield Terr]: Bare boards, lofty ceiling, huge windows, comfortable banquettes up a few steps, lively studenty café-bar atmosphere in evenings, friendly staff, interesting beers brewed on the premises (one fearsomely strong) and beers from parent Whitbreads, lots of malt whiskies and vodkas, good range of food inc pizzas; juke box, games machine; open all day *(LYM, Richard Lewis)*

Gardeners Rest [Neepsend Lane]: Timothy Taylor Landlord, Mild and Porter and two

guest beers, bar billiards, music most nights, quiz Sun; open all day Fri *(the Didler)*

Hillsborough [Langsett Rd/Wood St; by Primrose View tram stop]: Newly reopened, real ales such as Coniston Bluebird, Cotleigh Tawny, Hop Back Summer Lightning, Roosters Yankee and Theakstons Old Peculier at attractive prices in bare-boards bar, no-smoking room with coal fire and newly refurbished lounge, views to ski slope from big back terrace with barbecues, very experienced landlord; bedrooms with own bathrooms *(the Didler)*

Hogshead [Orchard St]: Bare boards, breweriana, ten or more well kept ales inc unusual ones, plenty of Belgian bottled beers, country wines, malt whiskies, farm cider, wide choice of reasonably priced food, daily papers, staff friendly and helpful even when very busy; piped music; also downstairs patisserie; open all day *(Richard Lewis)*

Kings Head [Poole Rd, off Prince of Wales Rd, Darnall; not far from M1 junctions 33/34]: Friendly and chatty new licensee, very wide choice of good value food, three real ales, wide-screen TV in comfortable lounge, no piped music; tables in small back yard *(Patrick Hancock, CMW, JJW)*

Morrisseys Riverside [Mowbray St]: Unspoilt three-room pub, one of small chain, with nice garden overlooking River Don, good choice of well kept interesting beers; folk nights upstairs *(the Didler)*

Noahs Ark [Crookes]: Friendly pub, popular with students, with huge range of simple cheap filling food (not Sun evening) all freshly prepared (so may be a wait) inc early evening bargains, six real ales inc guests; dominoes, pool, TV, quiet piped music; disabled lavatory, open all day exc Sun *(CMW, JJW)*

Old Grindstone [Crookes/Lydgate Lane]: Busy refurbished Victorian pub popular with students, good value food inc choice of Sun roasts, three or four real ales inc a guest, raised no-smoking area, teapot collection, obliging service, friendly black cat, games area with pool, SkyTV etc, piped music; open all day, jazz Mon, quiz Thurs *(CMW, JJW)*

Red House [Solly St]: Small comfortable backstreet pub with panelled front room, back snug, main bar with pool, darts and cards; well kept Wards, good value weekday lunchtime food; occasional folk music *(Pete Baker)*

Red Lion [Duke St]: Welcoming and utterly traditional, central bar serving four separate rooms each with original ornate fireplace and coal fire, attractive panelling and etched glass; cosy and comfortable, well kept real ales, no food *(the Didler, Pete Baker)*

Rutland Arms [Brown St]: Jolly place handy for the station and the Crucible; good wine and beers inc Marstons Pedigree and Stones, plentiful good value food lunchtime and very early evening *(Tony Hobden)*

Sheaf Quay [Victoria Quays, Wharf Rd; off B6073 N of centre]: Tom Cobleigh pub in fine old canal basin building, relaxed atmosphere, good value cheerful bar food inc children's and vegetarian *(David Carr, Tony Hobden)*

Three Cranes [Campo Lane]: Comfortable, with friendly staff and locals, well kept ales such as Black Sheep Special, Stones and Wychwood Mistletoad from central bar, lunchtime food *(Richard Lewis)*

Walkley Cottage [Bole Hill Rd,]: Chatty 1930s pub doing well after refurbishment under jovial new licensees, good choice of good value food (not Sun evening) inc vegetarian and generous Sun roast, up to five real ales, good coffee, friendly black cat; piped music, games room with pool, darts and TV; children welcome, views from garden with swings *(CMW, JJW)*

White Swan [Greenhill Main Rd (not the B6054 bit)]: Friendly four-room local with fair choice of food (not Sun evening, not after 6.45 Sat), freshly cooked so may be a wait, OAP discount, no-smoking tables, four real ales, small aquarium; piped music, pianist Sat, quiz nights; usually open all day *(CMW, JJW)*

Shelf [SE1029]

☆ *Duke of York* [West St; A644 Brighouse—Queensbury]: Popular and welcoming 17th-c beamed dining pub, eating areas off light open bar with lots of antique brass and copper, almost equally vast menu inc daily Scottish fish and seafood, even ostrich and kangaroo; well kept Timothy Taylor Landlord, open fires; booking advised evenings *(K H Frostick, B A Haywood)*

Sicklinghall [SE3648]

☆ *Scotts Arms*: Recently enlarged and attractively refurbished Chef & Brewer, interesting layout keeping old timbers and double-sided fireplaces, good food choice, well kept Theakstons Best, XB and Old Peculier, good coffee, pleasant young staff, daily papers, enthusiastic piped music; big garden with play area *(Janet and Peter Race, LYM, Michael Wadsworth, Roy Bromell)*

Skeeby [NZ1902]

Travellers Rest [Richmond Rd (A6108)]: Sparkling long bar, welcoming new landlord, good service, good food inc vegetarian and children's, Theakstons beers, copper and pewter on beams, coal fire; tables in garden *(Neil and Anita Christopher)*

Skerne [TA0455]

Eagle [Wansford Rd]: Quaint unspoilt village local with two simple rooms either side of hall, coal fire, well kept Camerons from rare Victorian cash-register beer engine in kitchen-style servery, chatty locals, friendly landlord brings drinks to your table; no food, cl weekday lunchtimes *(Pete Baker, JP, PP, the Didler)*

Skipton [SD9852]

Craven Heifer [Grassington Rd (B6265)]: Well run old country, good for families, home-made food, real ales, pleasant staff; good value annexe bedrooms with own bathrooms *(Mr and Mrs B W Twiddy)*

Red Lion [Market Sq]: Cheerful and bustling (next to the market), well furnished, with pleasant self-serve food and Whitbreads ales; open for most of the day on Suns *(Bill and Kathy Cissna)*

Woolly Sheep [Sheep St]: Two beamed bars off flagstoned passage, exposed brickwork, stone fireplace, lots of sheep prints and old photographs, old plates and bottles, well kept Black Sheep, Timothy Taylor Landlord and Tetleys Bitter and Mild, good changing range of food inc good home-made puddings; six bedrooms *(Jim and Maggie Cowell, Jenny and Brian Seller)*

Skipwith [SE6638]

Drovers Arms [follow Escrick sign off A163 NE of Selby]: Comfortably well worn two-room pub with good log fires, very friendly landlord, Boddingtons, Marstons, John Smiths and Theakstons XB, fine range of house wines, good value food from sandwiches to choice of Sun roasts; separate dining room, children given free rein (big toy box in lounge, tables out behind with play area); wheelchair access, open all day Sat, cl Mon lunchtime *(Janet Pickles)*

Slaithwaite [SE0613]

Rose & Crown [Cop Hill, up Nabbs Lane then Holme Lane]: Marvellous Colne Valley and moor views, three refurbished rooms off friendly bar, end restaurant, well kept Tetleys, Timothy Taylor Landlord and a seasonal beer, wide choice of malt whiskies, good food inc enormous puddings and weekday lunchtime bargains – quiet then; good walks *(Robert Gartery, R J Bland)*

Sneaton [NZ8908]

Sneaton Hall [Beacon Way; B1416 S of Whitby]: Comfortable old-fashioned hotel bar with good changing choice of well cooked food, elegant restaurant, good Sun lunch, lovely views to Whitby abbey, very friendly staff, dominoes; tables on terrace, garden with quoits; bedrooms *(M Borthwick)*

Sowerby Bridge [SE0623]

☆ *Moorings* [canal basin]: Spacious multi-level canal warehouse conversion, big windows overlooking boat basin, cast-iron pillars supporting high beams, stripped stone and stencilled plaster, scatter cushions on good solid settles, canal pictures, Tiffany-style lamps, no-smoking family room, Belgian-style grill room; wide choice of food (not Sun evening) from filled cobs to steaks inc children's and vegetarian, welcoming staff, well kept Black Sheep and Theakstons Best and XB, lots of bottled beers, good wine choice; unobtrusive piped music, pub games; tables out on terrace, open all day Sat *(Sam Samuells, Lynda Payton, LYM, S E Paulley)*

Spofforth [SE3650]

King William IV [Church Hill]: Large lounge, small bar, beams, John Smiths, Kelham Island and guest beers, good food from Belgian chef *(Dr B and Mrs P B Baker)*

☆ *Railway* [A661 Harrogate—Wetherby; High St]: Simple little Sam Smiths pub lifted out of the ordinary by friendly hard-working landlord who goes out of his way to make sure everything is right; wide choice of very good value home-made food, straightforward furnishings in basic locals' bar and unfussy lounge, real fires, no juke box; Weds quiz nights; tables and swing in garden behind *(Paul Gray, Geoff Roberts, Geoffrey and Brenda Wilson, BB)*

Sprotbrough [SE5302]

☆ *Boat* [2¾ miles from M18 junction 2; Nursery

Lane]: Interesting roomy stonebuilt ex-farmhouse with lovely courtyard in charming quiet spot by River Don, three individually furnished areas, big stone fireplaces, latticed windows, dark brown beams, very wide choice of good value generous usual food (no sandwiches), well kept Scottish Courage beers, farm cider, helpful staff; piped music, fruit machine, no dogs; big sheltered prettily lit courtyard, river walks; restaurant (Tues-Sat evening, Sun lunch); open all day summer Sats *(Janet Pickles, Pete Yearsley, John and Sylvia Harrop, Barry and Marie Males, LYM, GSB, DC)*

Staithes [NZ7818]

Black Lion [High St]: Small comfortable dining bar with ironwork chairs and tables, good food esp crab and other local seafood, real fire, well kept Theakstons Best, good friendly service; second rather dark traditional bar with TV; unspoilt fishing village *(Mike Ridgway, Sarah Miles)*

☆ *Cod & Lobster* [High St]: Basic pub in superb waterside setting in charming fishing village under sandstone cliff, emerging from massive sea-defences rebuild; well kept Camerons ales, good sandwiches inc crab, friendly service and locals, lovely views from seats outside; quite a steep walk up to top car park *(LYM, Keith and Janet Morris)*

Royal George [High St]: Unassuming old inn nr harbour, with locals' bar on right, three plusher interconnected rooms, straightforward food inc fresh fish, well kept Camerons Bitter and Strongarm, children welcome; piped music, darts; good value bedrooms *(Comus Elliott, Martin and Jane Wright)*

Stamford Bridge [SE7155]

Three Cups [A166 W of town]: Spacious friendly family dining pub done up in timbered country style, interesting food all day, well kept Bass and Tetleys, decent wines; children welcome, good play area behind; bedrooms *(LYM, Ian and Nita Cooper)*

Sutton on the Forest [SE5965]

☆ *Rose & Crown* [B1363 N of York]: Picturesque and comfortable two-room dining pub with relaxed and informal bistro atmosphere, good fresh generous food, imaginative without being too clever, esp steaks, fresh fish and lots of properly cooked veg, Theakstons ales, interesting wines, smart customers, welcoming licensees; charming wide-street village *(Bill and Sheila McLardy, Brian Wardrobe, Marlene and Jim Godfrey, Janet Lewis)*

Sutton under Whitestonecliffe [SE4983]

☆ *Whitestonecliffe Inn* [A170 E of Thirsk]: Friendly and popular beamed roadside pub with very wide choice of good value food from sandwiches to more exotic dishes in bar and restaurant inc good puddings, good service, log fire, well kept John Smiths, separate side bar and back games room with pool; bedrooms *(PACW, Janet Pickles)*

Tadcaster [SE4843]

☆ *Angel & White Horse* [Bridge St]: Tap for Sam Smiths brewery, cheap well kept OB, friendly staff, big helpings of good simple lunchtime

food (not Sat) from separate counter; big often under-used bar with alcoves at one end, fine oak panelling and solid furnishings; restaurant (children allowed there); piped music; the dappled grey dray horses are kept across the coachyard, and brewery tours can be arranged – (01937) 832225; open all day Sat *(John and Esther Sprinkle, LYM)*

Tan Hill [NY8906]

☆ *Tan Hill Inn* [Arkengarthdale rd Reeth—Brough, at junction Keld/W Stonesdale rd]: Wonderfully remote old stone pub on Pennine Way – Britain's highest, nearly five miles from the nearest neighbour, basic, bustling and can get overcrowded, full of bric-a-brac and pictures inc good old photographs, simple sturdy furniture, flagstones, big log fires (with prized stone side seats); well kept Black Sheep Riggwelter and Theakstons Best, XB and Old Peculier (in winter the cellar does chill down – for warmth you might prefer coffee or whisky with hot water), big helpings of warm comforting food served by unstuffy and friendly staff, sandwiches too; children and dogs welcome, open all day at least in summer; bedrooms, inc some with own bathrooms in newish extension; often snowbound, with no mains electricity (juke box powered by generator); Swaledale sheep show here last Thurs in May *(Bronwen and Steve Wrigley, LYM, JP, PP, Judith Hirst, Nigel Woolliscroft, Richard and Valerie Wright)*

Thixendale [SE8461]

Cross Keys [off A166 3 miles N of Fridaythorpe]: Unspoilt welcoming country pub in deep valley below the rolling Wolds, single L-shaped room with fitted wall seats, relaxed atmosphere, four or five well kept ales such as Jennings and Tetleys, sensible home-made food all from blackboard; popular with walkers, pleasant garden behind *(Mr and Mrs J R Ringrose, TRS)*

Thoralby [SE0086]

George: Welcoming down-to-earth dales village local under new licensees, generous good value food, real ales such as Black Sheep and John Smiths, darts, dominoes *(T M Dobby)*

Thornhill [SE2519]

Alma [Combs Hill, off B6117 S of Dewsbury]: Relaxed local, comfortable and friendly, good choice of reasonably priced food, flagstones by counter, carpeting elsewhere, solidly attractive pine furniture and pink banquettes in partitioned rooms, cigarette card collections, well kept Bass, Stones, Theakstons and Worthington BB; small popular restaurant *(Michael Butler)*

Thornton [SE0933]

☆ *Ring o' Bells* [Hill Top Rd, off B6145 W of Bradford]: Spotless 19th-c moortop dining pub very popular for wide choice of well presented good home cooking inc fresh fish, meat and poultry specialities, superb steaks, good puddings, bargain early suppers, pleasant bar, popular air-conditioned no-smoking restaurant and newish conservatory lounge; Black Sheep Bitter and Special and Theakstons ales, friendly helpful staff, wide views towards Shipley and Bingley *(Charles York, Donald and Margaret*

Wood, Geoffrey and Brenda Wilson, Mike Ridgway, Sarah Miles)

Thornton in Lonsdale [SD6976]

☆ *Marton Arms* [just NW of Ingleton]: Big welcoming beamed bar opp attractive church, ancient stripped stone walls festooned with caving pictures, roaring log fire, good relaxed atmosphere, plain pine furniture, up to 15 well kept ales, farm cider, 150 malt whiskies, martinis to make your hair stand on end, good value generous food inc home-made pizzas, enormous gammon and daily specials, efficient friendly service even when busy; bar billiards room; children welcome, marvellous dales views from garden; open all day w/e, cl winter weekdays, pleasant spacious bedrooms in annexe (one equipped for disabled), good breakfast, great fell walking country with Kingsdale caves and Ingleton waterfalls *(Bruce Bird, E G Parish, Kevin and Amanda Earl, Jenny and Brian Seller)*

Thornton le Clay [SE6865]

☆ *White Swan* [Low St]: Comfortable and spotless old-fashioned family-run beamed dining pub with good freshly cooked food inc vegetarian, friendly landlord, well kept ales such as Black Sheep and Youngers Scotch, decent wines, good log fire, shining brasses, tables on terrace; good view from impeccable ladies', attractive countryside nr Castle Howard; cl Mon lunchtime *(O Richardson, Mark Leigh, Sylvia Kitching, A Quinsee)*

Thorpe Hesley [SK3796]

Masons Arms [Thorpe St]: Friendly extended early 19th-c pub with four real ales, good reasonably priced food freshly made Mon-Sat (may be a wait), central coal-effect fire, pictures for sale; live music Tues *(CMW, JJW)*

Travellers [Smithy Wood Rd, just off A629 Cowley Hill at M1 junction 35]: Homely early Victorian two-bar pub with no-smoking dining room/conservatory, well kept Banks's Bitter in lined glasses, decent food (not Sun/Mon evenings) with fresh veg, stuffed birds, brass, pictures and fresh flowers; piped music, high chairs for children; big garden with play area, aviary, rabbits and dogs, woodland walks nearby *(CMW, JJW)*

Thurgoland [SE2901]

Bridge [Old Mill Lane]: Warmly welcoming old stonebuilt local by River Don, wide choice of good value fresh home-made food inc children's and Mon/Tues bargain OAP lunch, well kept Stones and a guest beer such as Marstons Pedigree, cosy and friendly atmosphere; quiet piped music, children and dogs in second room, big garden; handy for Forge Museum, good walks; no food Sun evening *(CMW, JJW, Mr and Mrs Staples)*

Tickton [TA0642]

Tickton Inn [just off A1035 NE of Beverley]: Friendly country pub, well kept Black Sheep and Tetleys Bitter and Dark Mild, good value food all day from sandwiches up *(D L Parkhurst)*

Tong [SE2230]

Greyhound: Traditional low-ceilinged local by village cricket field, open-plan but with distinctive areas inc flagstones, good

atmosphere, well kept Tetleys, popular food in bar and restaurant inc lots of specials; can be very busy w/e *(Michael Butler)*

Upper Poppleton [SE5554]

Red Lion [A59 York—Harrogate]: Good value food in comfortably dark and cosy olde-worlde bars and dining areas, popular with older people and businessmen; pleasant garden, bedroom extension *(Roger A Bellingham)*

Wakefield [SE3315]

Dam [Newmillerdam (A61 S)]: By reservoir dam, attractive walking country; recently refurbished L-shaped stripped-stone bar, good friendly service, generous usual food, busy Toby carvery/restaurant, well kept Bass-related beers, pleasant coffee lounge; very popular in summer *(Michael Butler)*

Henry Boons [Westgate]: Well kept Clarks (from next-door brewery), Black Sheep, Tetleys and Timothy Taylor in two-room bare-boards local, cheap weekday lunchtime food, evening snacks, friendly staff; side pool area, machines, live bands, open all day *(Richard Lewis, the Didler)*

Redoubt [Horbury Rd, Westgate]: Busy traditional city pub, four rooms off long corridor, Rugby League photographs, well kept Tetleys Bitter and Mild and Timothy Taylor Landlord, pub games *(the Didler)*

Talbot & Falcon [Northgate]: Popular Tetleys Festival Alehouse with friendly long bar, back lounge, wide choice of well kept ales largely from small breweries, foreign bottled beers, good choice of reasonably priced food; open all day *(Richard Lewis)*

Wagon [Westgate End]: Busy friendly local specialising in good choice of well kept ales mainly from interesting small breweries usually inc Roosters Yankee, log fire, reasonable prices, pub games, benches outside; open all day *(Richard Lewis, the Didler)*

Waterloo [Westgate End]: Friendly and comfortable open-plan Tetleys Festival Alehouse with lunchtime food, good choice of beers, lots of bric-a-brac, games room; open all day *(Richard Lewis)*

White Hart [Westgate End]: Popular, friendly and comfortable, coal fire, good choice of well kept ales such as Buchanans Original, Ind Coope Burton, Morlands Old Speckled Hen and Youngs Special; open all day *(Richard Lewis)*

Wales [SK4783]

Duke of Leeds [Church St]: Well kept Whitbreads-related ales, good generous inventive food, friendly licensee, no machines etc; not far from M1 junction 31, via A57 W, A618, B6059 *(G P Kernan)*

Walsden [SD9322]

Cross Keys [Rochdale Rd, by Rochdale Canal, S of Todmorden]: Well kept Black Sheep Best, Tetleys and five changing ales mainly from small breweries (often inc a Mild), good generous home cooking (all day Sun) inc vegetarian, helpful friendly service even when busy, friendly cat and locals; conservatory overlooking restored Rochdale Canal, lots of good walks – nr Pennine Way *(Bruce Bird, Norman Stansfield)*

Weaverthorpe [SE9771]
Star [Main St]: Two comfortable bars with log
fires, wide choice of food inc game and
vegetarian, well kept Camerons and guest beers
such as Yorkshire Last Drop, exceptionally
welcoming staff, restaurant; nice bedrooms,
good breakfast, quiet village setting; cl weekday
lunchtimes *(A N Ellis, Revd John Hibberd,
Colin and Dot Savill)*
Welburn [SE7268]
Crown & Cushion: Spaciously refurbished yet
cosy village pub with good home cooking from
enjoyable ploughman's up, friendly staff, decent
wine, Camerons and Tetleys beers, games in
public bar, restaurant, children in eating areas,
amusing pictures in gents'; piped music;
attractive small back garden with terrace *(Peter
and Anne Hollindale)*
West Burton [SE0186]
☆ *Fox & Hounds* [on green, off B6160
Bishopdale—Wharfedale]: Clean and cosy
unpretentious local on long green of idyllic
Dales village, simple generous inexpensive fresh
food inc children's, well kept Black Sheep and
Theakstons ales, friendly labrador and cat,
chatty budgerigar, residents' dining room,
children welcome; nearby caravan park; good
modern bedrooms, lovely walks and waterfalls
nearby *(Sue Holland, Dave Webster)*
West Tanfield [SE2678]
Bruce Arms [A6108 N of Ripon]: Village pub
pub doing well under friendly new management,
good choice of rather upmarket food in bar with
log fire and in restaurant *(LYM, Janet and Peter
Race)*
West Witton [SE0688]
☆ *Wensleydale Heifer* [A684 W of Leyburn]:
Comfortable inn with good generous if not
cheap food from tasty sandwiches to fish and
game, low-ceilinged small interconnecting areas
in genteel front lounge, big attractive bistro,
separate restaurant, good log fire, attractive
prints, pleasant décor, excellent service, no
music; small bar with decent wines, well kept
Black Sheep, John Smiths and Theakstons Best,
and another fire; nice bedrooms (back ones
quietest), good big breakfast *(Ian Pendlebury,
Nick Lawless, Gwen and Peter Andrews)*
Whitby [NZ9011]
Dolphin [Bridge St, just over bridge to E/Old
Whitby]: Basic pub with good straightforward
generous food esp local fish, well kept Tetleys
and Theakstons, quick service; picnic-sets
outside *(Anne and David Robinson, John and
Esther Sprinkle)*
Wigglesworth [SD8157]
☆ *Plough* [B6478, off A65 S of Settle]: Warm and
friendly, with little rooms off bar, some spartan
yet cosy, others smart and plush, inc no-smoking
panelled dining room and snug; consistently good
bar food inc huge sandwiches and children's
dishes, separate conservatory restaurant with
panoramic dales views, well kept Boddingtons
and Tetleys, decent wines and coffee; attractive
garden, pleasant bedrooms *(N Thomas, Mr J and
Dr S Harrop, WAH, K H Frostick)*
Wormald Green [SE3065]
George [A61 Ripon—Harrogate]: Former Cragg

Lodge, renamed after changing hands; now a
smart and stylish restaurant, not a pub, so no
longer eligible for this book despite its very good
food; five well equipped bedrooms *(LYM)*
Wykeham [SE9783]
Downe Arms [A170 nr Scarborough]: Stripped
pine and cottagey furnishings, good choice of
generous food from baguettes up, John Smiths
and Theakstons, good service, family room,
pool; piped music; play area, bedrooms *(SLC)*
York [SE5951]
Acorn [St Martins Lane, Micklegate – now
calling itself the Ackhorne]: Fine range of well
kept ales from small breweries, usually five from
Yorkshire; bare boards, carpeted snug one end,
good value lunchtime food, friendly staff *(Lester
Edmonds, Richard Lewis, the Didler)*
Blue Bell [Fossgate]: Untouched Edwardian pub
with friendly staff and traditional landlady,
corridor linking tiny front bar to back room not
much bigger, well kept Greene King Abbot and
Wards Waggle Dance, good lively flat-cap
atmosphere, lunchtime sandwiches on counter;
open all day, can get very busy *(Eric Larkham,
Kerry Law, Simon Smith, C J Fletcher, Lester
Edmonds, Pete Baker, the Didler)*
Cross Keys [Goodramgate]: Roomy rambling
pub with very friendly staff, well kept beers inc
Bass *(Justin Hulford)*
First Hussar [opp Viking Hotel, North St]: Very
basic stripped-brick décor in three smallish
rooms, well kept changing ales such as Adnams,
Castle Eden, Theakstons and Ridleys, Weston's
Old Rosie cider, cheap lunchtime food inc nice
sandwiches and simple hot dishes, magazines to
read; darts, machines, tables outside, open all
day, Weds music night *(Richard Lewis, Eric
Larkham)*
Fox & Roman [Tadcaster Rd, opp racecourse]:
Large and rambling, with lots of nooks and
crannies, good food inc imaginative dishes and
superb fresh fish and chips, cheerful helpful staff
(Mick and Jeanne Shillington)
Golden Fleece [Pavement]: Long corridor from
bar to back lounge, Courage Directors and John
Smiths, bar food; fruit machine *(SLC)*
Golden Lion [Church St]: Big open-plan T J
Bernards pub done up in stone-floored
Edwardian style (in fact first licensed 1771),
dark with plenty of lamps; friendly efficient
staff, Scottish Courage ales with good guest and
lots of bottled beers, wide choice of generous
food, good choice of wines by the glass; fruit
machine, piped music *(Ian Phillips, SLC, Ann
and Bob Westbrook)*
Golden Slipper [Goodramgate]: Country pub in
the city, dating from 15th c, quaint series of
rooms much favoured by locals, old and young,
inc friendly story-telling regulars, resident dog
and ghost, warm genuine atmosphere, good well
priced food inc OAP bargains, John Smiths,
Morlands Old Speckled Hen and Theakstons
(Tony Eberts)
Kings Arms [King's Staithe, by Clifford St]: Fine
riverside position, bowed black beams,
flagstones, straightforward furnishings, good
lunchtime food from sandwiches up; CD juke
box can be loud, keg beers; open all day, nice

picnic-sets out on cobbled waterside terrace *(John and Esther Sprinkle, LYM)*

Lendal Cellars [Lendal]: Recently refurbished split-level Hogshead ale house down steps in broad-vaulted 17th-c cellars carefully spotlit to show up the stripped brickwork, stone floor, interconnected rooms and alcoves, well kept Whitbreads and guest ales such as Adnams and Castle Eden, farm cider, country wines, foreign bottled beers, friendly staff; good piped music, popular with students; open all day, children allowed while food being served, 11.30-7 (5 Fri/Sat) *(Richard Lewis, Eric Larkham)*

Lowther [King's Staithe, not 50 yds from Kings Arms]: Courage beers, usual food inc steak bargains, quiet by day, lively at night; cheap bedrooms *(Justin Hulford)*

☆ *Maltings* [Tanners Moat/Wellington Row, below Lendal Bridge]: Small pub notable for well kept Black Sheep and half a dozen or more quickly changing esoteric real ales, good choice of continental beers, farm ciders and country wines; tricksy décor (door-panelled ceiling studded with enamel advertisements, corner lavatory, part stripped brickwork), jovial landlord, decent well priced generous weekday lunchtime food, daily papers in gents', traditional games; piped radio, parking virtually impossible; open all day, handy for Rail Museum, jazz or folk Mon/Tues, popular beer festivals in May and October *(Richard Lewis, Richard Houghton, Neil Townend, Eric Larkham, the Didler, Andy and Jill Kassube)*

Masons Arms [Fishergate]: Unchanged 1930s local, good range of beers inc guests, interesting food, friendly service *(Dr Andy Wilkinson)*

Minster Tavern [Marygate]: Four-room pub refurbished by newish landlady, Bass, John Smiths and two guest beers, friendly staff, sandwiches and pickled eggs, no-smoking room; piped music *(Lester Edmonds)*

Old White Swan [Goodramgate]: Split personality pub with Victorian, Georgian and Tudor themed bars, covered courtyard good for families, enjoyable food, Bass, Fullers London Pride and Worthington, friendly staff; juke box, piped music, games machines – can get loudly

busy towards w/e *(Ian Baillie, Ian Phillips)*

Phalanx & Firkin [Micklegate]: Usual bare-boards Firkin style, well kept beers, helpful friendly staff, good value food, good juke box, games and machines; tables outside, open all day *(Richard Lewis)*

Punch Bowl [Stonegate]: Friendly town local with small rooms off corridor, friendly helpful service, good generous lunchtime food from sandwiches up (no-smoking area by food servery), well kept Bass and Worthington, panelled lounge; piped music, games machines; open all day, good value bedrooms *(G Washington, Ian Baillie, Janet Pickles, Rona Murdoch, Ian Phillips)*

Roman Bath [St Sampson Sq]: There are indeed Roman bath remains below the pub (tours can be arranged); John Smiths, bar food *(SLC)*

Snickleway [Goodramgate]: Snug little old-world pub, friendly landlord, well kept Morlands Old Speckled Hen and John Smiths, limited range of good value lunchtime food (not Sun) inc fresh sandwiches, lots of antiques, copper and brass, good coal fires, cosy nooks and crannies, unobtrusive piped music, prompt service, cartoons in gents' *(Paul and Ursula Randall, Kevin Blake)*

Starting Gate [Tadcaster Rd, opp racecourse]: Good Beefeater, friendly staff *(Janet Pickles)*

☆ *York Arms* [High Petergate]: Snug little basic panelled bar (beware the sliding door), big modern no-smoking lounge, cosier partly panelled room full of old bric-a-brac, prints, brown-cushioned wall settles, dimpled copper tables and an open fire; quick friendly service, well kept Sam Smiths OB, good value simple food lunchtime to early evening, no music; by Minster, open all day *(Eric Larkham, BB, Darly Graton, Graeme Gulibert)*

York Brewery Tap [Toft Green, Micklegate]: New upstairs lounge with lots of breweriana, comfortable settees, things to read, and York Brewery's own Brideshead, Stonewall, Terrier and Last Drop in top fresh condition, also bottled beers, friendly staff happy to talk about the beers, shop; small membership fee, brewery tours *(Esther and John Sprinkle, Richard Lewis)*

London
Scotland
Wales
Channel Islands

London

Three new entries here are the well placed Archery Tavern, handy for Hyde Park, O'Hanlons up near Sadlers Wells (a nice proper pub, with good interesting beers brewed by Mr O'Hanlon), and in West London the Atlas – still a proper pub, but with really interesting food under the two brothers who have recently taken it over, it comes straight in with a Food Award in its first year. Other pubs doing well here are (in Central London) the Argyll Arms (efficient service, decent food), the Eagle (good food), the nicely tucked away Grenadier (lots of character), the Jerusalem Tavern (a great all-rounder, gaining its Star this year), the Lamb (new licensee settled in well), the Old Bank of England (an impressive conversion, and scores highly as a well run pub), the striking Olde Cheshire Cheese, the Olde Mitre (a favourite for its timeless character), and the Star (a friendly relaxed local in rather grand surroundings); in North London, the Chapel (very good food), peaceful hidden-away little Compton Arms and the much more touristy Spaniards Inn; in South London, the lively and trendy Fire Station (gains both a Food Award and a Beer Award this year), the George (a great old building), and the busy Market Porter (good beers); and in West London, both Anglesea Armses (great food on Wingate Street, bubbling atmosphere on Selwood Terrace), the lively Churchill Arms, and the pleasantly countrified old Windsor Castle. The pubs with the best food here all tend to be either loud or a bit too popular with trendy young smokers in the evenings: a quieter more traditional London pub that started offering top-quality inventive food to match theirs would have people queuing at its door. Until that happy day, we choose as London Dining Pub of the Year the Fire Station, Waterloo Road, SE1. This year we have reorganised the Lucky Dip section at the end of the chapter, as before listing the pubs in Central, North, South, West and East, but this time with a final section on Outer London, including all the places outside the London postal districts but still within Greater London. Pubs showing specially well recently in this section are, in Central London, the Audley, Buckingham Arms, Chandos, Dirty Dicks, Fox & Hounds, Hamilton Hall, Mortimer, O'Connor Don, Red Lion in Duke of York Street, Salisbury, Victoria and (in Victoria Station) Wetherspoons; Crockers in North London; the Founders Arms in South London; in West London, the Britannia in Allen St, Chelsea Ram, City Barge and Sporting Page; the Sir Alfred Hitchcock in East London; and in Outer London, the Wattenden Arms in Kenley and White Swan in Richmond. Beer prices are high in London – on average just over £2 a pint now. The cheapest beers we found were in pubs tied to Sam Smiths – if this Yorkshire brewer can keep its London pub prices down to little more than £1.50, that's a splendid target for London's two main brewers, Fullers and Youngs, to aim for.

We mention bottled beers and spirits only if there is something unusual about them – imported Belgian real ales, say, or dozens of malt whiskies; so do please let us know about them in your reports.

CENTRAL LONDON Map 13

Covering W1, W2, WC1, WC2, SW1, SW3, EC1, EC2, EC3 and EC4 postal districts

Parking throughout this area is metered throughout the day, and generally in short supply then; we mention difficulty only if evening parking is a problem too. Throughout the chapter we list the nearest Underground or BR stations to each pub; where two are listed it means the walk is the same from either.

Albert

52 Victoria Street, SW1; ✚ St James's Park

One of the great sights of this part of London (if rather dwarfed by the faceless cliffs of dark modern glass around it), this fine Victorian building is handily placed between Westminster and Victoria. Civil servants, tourists, and the odd (as in occasional) MP all add to the wonderfully diverse mix of customers in the huge open-plan bar, which has good solid comfortable furniture, and some gleaming mahogany. There's a surprisingly airy feel thanks to great expanses of heavily cut and etched windows along three sides, but though there's plenty of space, it can be packed on weekday lunchtimes and immediately after work. Service from the big island counter is generally swift and efficient (particularly obliging to overseas visitors), with Courage Best and Directors, Theakstons Best and a couple of well chosen guests on handpump. The separate food servery is good value, with sandwiches (from £1.45), soup (£2), salads (from £3.50) and five home-cooked hot dishes such as shepherd's pie, steak pie, fish and chips, chicken lasagne or a vegetarian dish (all £4.50). The upstairs restaurant does an eat-as-much-as-you-like carvery, better than average (all day inc Sunday, £14.95). The handsome staircase that leads up to it is lined with portraits of former prime ministers. They sound the Division Bell for those MPs who've popped in for a quick drink. Piped music, fruit machine. *(Recommended by George Atkinson, Stephen and Julie Brown, Tony Scott, David Carr)*

Scottish Courage ~ Managers Roger and Gill Wood ~ Real ale ~ Bar food (11-10.30, 12-10) ~ Restaurant ~ (020) 7222 5577 ~ Children in eating area of bar and restaurant ~ Open 11-11; 12-10.30 Sun; closed 25, 26 Dec

Archery Tavern ♟

4 Bathurst St, W2, opposite the Royal Lancaster hotel; ✚ Lancaster Gate

Very handy for Hyde Park, this well positioned and nicely maintained Victorian pub takes its name from an archery range that occupied the site for a while in the early 19th c. A big draw is the range of five well kept real ales that you're unlikely to find very often in this area – Badger Dorset Best, IPA and Tanglefoot, and Gribble Ale and Black Adder II. All sorts of types and ages were chatting quietly on our last visit, and it's a good bet for passing tourists and visitors, with plenty of space in the several comfortably relaxing, pubby areas around the central servery. On the green, pattern-papered walls are a number of archery prints, as well as a history of the pub and the area, other old prints, dried hops, and quite a few plates running along a shelf. A big back room has long tables, bare boards, and a fireplace; darts, a big stack of board games, fruit machine, piped music. Served all day, bar food includes sandwiches, ploughman's (£4.75), fishcakes (£5.95), pies such as steak and ale or chicken and mushroom (£6.25), and daily specials; they do breakfasts some mornings. There's lots more seating in front of the pub, under hanging baskets and elaborate floral displays, and some nicely old-fashioned lamps. A side door leads on to a little mews, where the Hyde Park Riding Stables are based. *(Recommended by Ian Phillips, Stephen and Jean Curtis)*

Badger ~ Tenant Tony O'Neill ~ Real ale ~ Bar food (12-9.30) ~ (020) 7402 4916 ~ Children welcome ~ Open 11-11; 12-10.30 Sun

Argyll Arms ♟

18 Argyll St W1; ✚ Oxford Circus, opp tube side exit

Quite a surprise given its location just off Oxford Street, this bustling and unexpectedly traditional Victorian pub is one of the best pubs in the area, much as it was when built in the 1860s. The most atmospheric and unusual part is the three cubicle rooms at the front; all oddly angular, they're made by wooden partitions with distinctive frosted and engraved glass, with hops trailing above. A good range of changing beers typically includes Brakspears, Marstons Pedigree, Morlands Old Speckled Hen, Tetleys and Timothy Taylor Landlord on handpump, and they may well have one or two more unusual guests; also Addlestone's cider, malt whiskies, and freshly squeezed orange and pineapple juice. A long mirrored corridor leads to the spacious back room, with the food counter in one corner; this area is no smoking at lunchtime. Chalked up on a blackboard (which may also have topical cartoons), the choice of generously served meals includes good, unusual sandwiches like stilton and grape (£2.50), salt beef (£3.25), or roast chicken, bacon and melted cheese (£3.65), and main courses such as salads, steak and kidney pie or chicken curry (£5.95), and traditional roasts (£6.95). Friendly, prompt and efficient staff; two fruit machines, piped music (louder in the evenings than at lunch). Open during busier periods, the quieter upstairs bar overlooks the pedestrianised street, and the Palladium theatre if you can see through the foliage outside the window); divided into several snugs with comfortable plush easy chairs, it has swan's neck lamps, and lots of small theatrical prints along the top of the walls. The gents' has a copy of the day's *Times* or *Financial Times* on the wall. The pub can get very crowded, but there's space for drinking outside. *(Recommended by Andrew and Eileen Abbess, Jasper Sabey, PS, SLC, P J and J E F Caunt, Stephen and Julie Brown, Tony Scott)*

Allied Domecq ~ Managers Mike Tayara and Regina Kennedy ~ Real ale ~ Bar food ~ Restaurant ~ (020) 7734 6117 ~ Children welcome ~ Open 11-11; 12-9 Sun; closed 25 Dec

Bishops Finger ♀

9-10 West Smithfield, EC1; ⊖ Farringdon

In a verdant square beside Smithfield Market, this formerly rather grotty pub has been transformed in the last couple of years into a swish little bar cum restaurant. Laid back but classy (especially in the evenings), the well spaced out room has bright yellow walls (nicely matching the fresh flowers on the elegant tables and behind the bar), big windows, carefully polished bare boards, a few pillars, and comfortably cushioned chairs under a wall lined with framed prints. Distinctive food from an open kitchen beside the bar includes soup (£1.95), tasty ciabatta sandwiches filled with things like goat's cheese, pesto and beef tomato (from £3.25), raw salmon sushi (from £3.25), bangers and mash (£4.75), roasted parsnips and chestnut crumble on bed of bubble and squeak (£5.60), beer battered haddock (£5.95), topside pork teryaki (£6.25), lamb zingara (£7.95), and puddings like apple and cinnamon tart (£2.95). Well kept Shepherd Neame Master Brew, Bishops Finger and Spitfire on handpump, with a wide choice of wines (eight by the glass), and several ports and champagnes; friendly service. Upstairs is another bar, which they hope to develop as an evening restaurant. There are a couple of tables outside. *(Recommended by Tim Barrow, Sue Demont)*

Shepherd Neame ~ Manager Hannah Chalk ~ Real ale ~ Bar food (12-3, 6-9) ~ (020) 7248 2341 ~ Well behaved children welcome ~ Open 11-11; closed Sat, Sun, bank hols, 24 Dec

Black Friar

174 Queen Victoria Street, EC4; ⊖ Blackfriars

Standing out for its unique design and appearance, this busy place is bigger inside than seems possible from the delightfully odd exterior. In the inner back room is some of the best fine Edwardian bronze and marble art-nouveau décor to be found anywhere: big bas-relief friezes of jolly monks set into richly coloured Florentine marble walls, an opulent marble-pillared inglenook fireplace, a low vaulted mosaic ceiling, gleaming mirrors, seats built into rich golden marble recesses, and tongue-in-cheek verbal embellishments such as Silence is Golden and Finery is Foolish. See if you can spot the opium smoking-hints modelled into the fireplace of the front room. You'll see the details more clearly if you come on a Saturday lunchtime, when the pub isn't so crowded as during the week. A limited range of bar food includes filled rolls (from £2.20), baked potatoes, and straightforward daily specials such as sausage and mash (£4.25), and a roast (£5.25), with perhaps fish and chips or scampi (£4.75) in the evenings. Adnams, Fullers London Pride, Marstons Pedigree and Tetleys on handpump; fruit machine. In the evenings lots of people spill out onto the wide forecourt in front, near the approach to Blackfriars Bridge. If you're coming by tube, choose your exit carefully – it's all too easy to emerge from the network of passageways and find yourself on the other side of the street or marooned on a traffic island. *(Recommended by Dr M E Wilson, JP, PP, LM, the Didler)*

Nicholsons (Allied Domecq) ~ Manager Mr Becker ~ Real ale ~ Bar food (12-2.30, 6-9) ~ (020) 7236 5650 ~ Well behaved children away from bar ~ Open 11.30-11; 12-4 Sat; closed Sun

Cittie of Yorke 🍺

22 High Holborn, WC1; find it by looking out for its big black and gold clock; ⊖ Chancery Lane

The main back bar of this unique pub can take your breath away when seen for the first time. It looks rather like a vast baronial hall, with vast thousand-gallon wine vats resting above the gantry, big bulbous lights hanging from the soaring high raftered roof, and its extraordinarily extended bar counter stretching off into the distance. It does get packed in the early evening, particularly with lawyers and judges, but it's at busy times like these when the pub seems most magnificent. Most people tend to congregate in the middle, so you may still be able to bag one of the intimate, old-fashioned and ornately carved cubicles that run along both sides. The triangular Waterloo fireplace, with grates on all three sides and a figure of Peace among laurels, used to stand in the Grays Inn Common Room until barristers stopped dining there. Appealingly priced Sam Smiths OB on handpump (well below the cost of a typical London pint); friendly service from smartly dressed staff, fruit machine and piped music in the cellar bar. A smaller, comfortable wood-panelled room has lots of little prints of York and attractive brass lights, while the ceiling of the entrance hall has medieval-style painted panels and plaster York roses. There's a lunchtime food counter in the main hall with more in the downstairs cellar bar: as well as filled baps, ploughman's and salads, they have several daily specials such as steak and ale pie, lamb braised in red wine, chicken and spinach lasagne, and leek, stilton and mushroom bake (all £4.25). A pub has stood on this site since 1430, though the current building owes more to the 1695 coffee house erected here behind a garden; it was reconstructed in Victorian times using 17th-c materials and parts. *(Recommended by Dr M E Wilson, Ted George, Tracey and Stephen Groves, Sheila and Phil Stubbs, J Fahy, Nigel Wilson, David and Carole Chapman, Greg Kilminster, Susan and Nigel Wilson, Rachael and Mark Baynham, Tony Scott, T Barrow, S Demont, Ian Phillips, the Didler)*

Sam Smiths ~ Manager Stuart Browning ~ Real ale ~ Bar food ~ (020) 7242 7670 ~ Children in eating area of bar ~ Open 11.30-11; closed Sun, 25 Dec

Dog & Duck 🍺

18 Bateman St, on corner with Frith Street, W1; ⊖ Tottenham Court Rd/Leicester Square

A contrast to the ever-changing bars and restaurants all around, this pint-sized corner house is quite a Soho landmark. The chatty main bar really is tiny, though at times it manages to squeeze in a real mix of people; there are some high stools by the ledge along the back wall, and further seats in a slightly roomier area at one end. On the floor by the door is a mosaic of a dog, tongue out in hot pursuit of a duck, and the same theme is embossed on some of the shiny tiles that frame the heavy old advertising mirrors. The unusual little bar counter serves very well kept Tetleys, Timothy Taylor Landlord, and a couple of guests on handpump; they do doorstep sandwiches (from £1.85). Upstairs is a snug bar overlooking the street, where they have a weekly Sunday evening club for deaf people; the assistant manager has been on a sign language course. There's a fire in winter, and newspapers to read; piped music. In good weather especially there tend to be plenty of people spilling onto the bustling street outside. Ronnie Scott's Jazz Club is near by. *(Recommended by Stephen and Julie Brown, Andrew Abbess, Michael McGarry)*

Allied Domecq ~ Manager Gene Bell ~ Real ale ~ (020) 7437 4447 ~ Open 12-11; 6-11 Sat; 7-10.30 Sun; closed Sat, Sun lunchtimes

Eagle 🍴 🍷

159 Farringdon Rd, EC1; opposite Bowling Green Lane car park; ⊖ Farringdon/Old Street

The distinctive Mediterranean-style meals here still rank as some of the very best pub food in London, effortlessly superior to those in the welcome imitators that have sprung up all over the city. Made with the finest quality ingredients, typical dishes might include Portuguese winter vegetable soup with paprika and olive oil (£4), bruschetta with mozzarella, trevisse, punterella and pine nuts, mint, oregano and balsamico, or pasta with tomatoes, aubergines, basil and parmesan (£7.50), pork and bean casserole with chorizo and pancetta, or marinated rump steak sandwich (£8.50), black paella with squid and its ink (£9.50), grilled haunch of venison with mashed potatoes and roasted red onions (£10), and grilled halibut with roast peppers, chillies, almonds, olive oil and sherry vinegar (£11); they also do Spanish and goat's milk cheeses (£6), and Portuguese custard tarts (£1). Note they don't take credit cards. On weekday lunchtimes especially, dishes from the blackboard menu can run out or change fairly quickly, so it really is worth getting here as early as you possibly can if you're hoping to eat. Though the food is out of the ordinary, the atmosphere is still lively, chatty and pubby (particularly in the evenings), so it's not the kind of place you'd go to for a smart night out or a quiet dinner. The open kitchen forms part of the bar, and furnishings in the single room are simple but stylish – school chairs, a random assortment of tables, a couple of sofas on bare boards, and modern paintings on the walls (there's an art gallery upstairs, with direct access from the bar). Quite a mix of customers, but it's fair to say there's a proliferation of media folk (*The Guardian* is based just up the road). Well kept Boddingtons, Flowers Original and Wadworths 6X on handpump, good wines including a dozen by the glass, good coffee, and properly made cocktails; piped music. There are times during the week when the Eagle's success means you may have to wait for a table; it's much quieter at weekends. *(Recommended by Yavuz and Shirley Mutlu, Rachael and Mark Baynham, Dr S J Shepherd, Tracey and Stephen Groves, Greg Kilminster, David Carr, MB)*

Free house ~ Licensee Michael Belben ~ Real ale ~ Bar food (12.30-2.30(3.30 Sat, Sun), 6.30-10.30) ~ (020) 7837 1353 ~ Children welcome ~ Open 12-11(5 Sun); closed Sun evening

Grapes

Shepherd Market, W1; ⊖ Green Park

On sunny days and evenings you'll usually find smart-suited drinkers spilling out from this chatty pub onto the square outside. Bang in the middle of civilised Shepherd Market, its old-fashioned dimly lit bar has a nicely traditional atmosphere, with plenty of stuffed birds and fish in glass display cases, and a snug little alcove at the back. Bar food, lunchtimes only, might include sandwiches (from £2.75), seafood platter or half roast chicken (£4.55), and ploughman's (£5.25); the eating area is no smoking. A good range of six or seven well kept (though fairly pricy) beers on handpump usually takes in Boddingtons, Flowers IPA and Original, Fullers London Pride, Marstons Pedigree, and Wadworths 6X; fruit machine. Service can slow down a little at the busiest times – it's much quieter at lunchtimes. *(Recommended by Mark and Rachael Baynham, Ian Phillips, Gordon, David Carr, Chris Glasson)*

Free house ~ Licensees Gill and Eric Lewis ~ Real ale ~ Bar food (12-2) ~ (020) 7629 4989 ~ Children over 10 if eating ~ Open 11-11; closed Sun

Grenadier

Wilton Row, SW1; the turning off Wilton Crescent looks prohibitive, but the barrier and watchman are there to keep out cars; walk straight past – the pub is just around the corner; ⊖ Knightsbridge

One of London's most special pubs, tucked away in a tranquil part of Knightsbridge, this snugly characterful old place is famous for its bloody marys and well documented poltergeist – it's reckoned to be the capital's most haunted pub. Patriotically painted in red, white and blue, it was used for a while as the mess for the officers of the Duke of Wellington, whose portrait hangs above the fireplace, alongside neat prints of Guardsmen through the ages. The bar is tiny (some might say cramped), but you should be able to plonk yourself on one of the stools or wooden benches, as despite the charms of this engaging little pub it rarely gets too crowded. Well kept Courage Best and Directors, Marstons Pedigree, and Morlands Old Speckled Hen from handpumps at the rare pewter-topped bar counter; service is friendly and chatty, if occasionally a little slow. Bar food runs from bowls of chips and nachos (very popular with after work drinkers), through ploughman's, fishcakes and good sausage and mash (£4.50), to hot steak sandwiches (£5.50); they may do a Sunday roast. The intimate back restaurant is quite pricy, but good for a romantic dinner. There's a single table outside in the peaceful mews, a nice spot to while away a sunny evening dreaming you might eventually be able to afford one of the smart little houses opposite. *(Recommended by Val Stevenson, Rob Holmes, Susan and John Douglas, Ian Phillips, Ted George, Tracey and Stephen Groves, Jasper Sabey, Christopher Wright, P Rome, Guy Consterdine, Gordon)*

Scottish Courage ~ Manager Patricia Smerdon ~ Real ale ~ Bar food (12-3, 6-9.30) ~ Restaurant ~ (020) 7235 3074 ~ Children in eating area of bar and restaurant ~ Open 12-11(10.30 Sun)

Jerusalem Tavern ★ ◧

55 Britton St, EC1; ⊖ Farringdon

One of only a very few pubs belonging to the newish, small Suffolk-based St Peter's Brewery, this carefully restored old coffee house has rapidly become very highly regarded by readers, and deservedly so. Darkly atmospheric and characterful, it's a vivid re-creation of an 18th-c tavern, seeming so genuinely old that you'd never guess the work was done only a few years ago. One of the highlights is the full range of the brewery's rather tasty beers: depending on the season you'll find St Peter's Best, Extra, Fruit beer, Golden Ale, Grapefruit, Mild, Strong, Porter, Wheat beer, and Winter Spiced, all tapped from casks behind the little bar counter. If you develop a taste for them – and they are rather addictive – they also sell them to take away, in rather elegant distinctively shaped bottles (as word gets out, these are starting to creep into supermarkets too). There's been a pub of this name around here for quite some time, but the current building was developed around 1720, originally as a merchant's house, then becoming a clock and watchmaker's. It still has the shop front added in 1810, immediately behind which is a light little room with a couple of wooden tables and benches, a stack of *Country Life* magazines, and some remarkable old tiles on the walls at either side. This leads to the tiny dimly lit bar, which has a couple of unpretentious tables on the bare boards, and another up some stairs on a discreetly precarious balcony; the atmosphere is relaxed and quietly chatty. A plainer back room has a few more tables, as well as a fireplace, and a stuffed fox in a case. There's a very relaxed, chatty feel in the evenings. Blackboards list the simple but well liked lunchtime food: soup, good big sandwiches in various breads (from £4.50), sausages in rolls (£4.95), a couple of changing hot dishes, and carrot cake (£3); they open at 9am for breakfasts and coffee, and generally do toasted sandwiches in the evenings. A couple of tables outside overlook the quiet street. The brewery has another main entry at Wingfield in Suffolk. *(Recommended by David Carr, Rachael and Mark Baynham, Ian Phillips, Michael and Alison Sandy, Val Stevenson, Rob Holmes, C J Fletcher, Tim Barrow, Sue Demont, Tracey and Stephen Groves, John A Barker, Pauline Starley)*

St Peters ~ Bruce Patterson ~ Bar food (12-2.30, 6-10) ~ (020) 7490 4281 ~ Children welcome till 6pm ~ Open 9-11; closed weekends

Lamb ★ ◀

94 Lamb's Conduit Street, WC1; ⊖ Holborn

There's been a change of licensee at this old favourite since our last edition, but nothing else ever alters: a unique and timeless survival, it's long been one of our most popular London pubs. Famous for the cut-glass swivelling 'snob-screens' all the way around the U-shaped bar counter, it feels much as it would have done in Victorian times. Sepia photographs of 1890s actresses on the ochre panelled walls, and traditional cast-iron-framed tables with neat brass rails around the rim very much add to the overall effect, and when you come out you almost expect the streets to be dark and foggy and illuminated by gas lamps. Consistently well kept Youngs Bitter, Special and seasonal brews on handpump, and around 40 different malt whiskies. Lunchtime bar food such as filled rolls or soup (£2.45), lasagne (£4.95), breaded scampi (£5.25), and chicken in a cream and paprika sauce or steak, kidney and mushroom pudding (£5.45); on Sunday lunchtimes the choice is limited to their popular Sunday roast (£5.45). There are slatted wooden seats in a little courtyard beyond the quiet room down a couple of steps at the back; dominoes, cribbage, backgammon. No machines or music. A snug room at the back on the right is no smoking. It can get very crowded, especially in the evenings. Like the street, the pub is named for the Kentish clothmaker William Lamb who brought fresh water to Holborn in 1577. *(Recommended by LM, Rachael and Mark Baynham, Mr and Mrs Jon Corelis, the Didler, Robert Davis, Ian Phillips, Dr M E Wilson, Tracey and Stephen Groves, JP, PP, Richard Lewis, Tony Scott, J R Ringrose, Joel Dobris)*

Youngs ~ Manager David Edward Lipscomb ~ Real ale ~ Bar food (not Sat, Sun evenings) ~ (020) 7405 0713 ~ Children in eating area of bar ~ Open 11-11; 12-4, 7-10.30 Sun

Lamb & Flag ◀

33 Rose Street, WC2; off Garrick Street; ⊖ Leicester Square

Another place that's remained essentially unchanged for as long as we've known it, this busy old pub near Covent Garden attracts a real mix of tourists and after-work drinkers. It can be quite a squeeze some evenings, so even in winter you'll find plenty of people drinking and chatting in the little alleyways outside. It's had an eventful and well documented history: Dryden was nearly beaten to death by hired thugs outside, and Dickens described the Middle Temple lawyers who frequented it when he was working in nearby Catherine Street. The busy low-ceilinged back bar has high-backed black settles and an open fire, and in Regency times was known as the Bucket of Blood from the bare-knuckle prize-fights held here. It fills up quite quickly, though you might be able to find a seat in the upstairs Dryden Room. Well kept Courage Directors, Greene King IPA and Abbot, Youngs Special and maybe a couple of guest beers on handpump; like most pubs round here, the beer isn't cheap, but on weekdays between 11 and 5 you should find at least one at quite an attractive price. Also, a good few malt whiskies. Lunchtime bar food includes a choice of several well kept cheeses and pâtés, served with hot bread or french bread (£2.50), as well as doorstep sandwiches or ploughman's (£3.50), sausage, chips and beans (£3), and, upstairs, hot dishes like vegetable bake (£3.95), beef stroganoff or chicken and mushroom pie (£4.25), and a roast (£5.95). They have jazz on Sunday evenings. *(Recommended by Mick Hitchman, R J Bland, Mark Brock, Dr M E Wilson, T Barrow, S Demont, the Didler, Simon Collett-Jones, Ted George, Neil Brown, Monica Shelley)*

Free house ~ Licensees Terry Archer and Adrian and Sandra Zimmerman ~ Real ale ~ Bar food (11-4) ~ (020) 7497 9504 ~ Children in eating area of bar at lunchtime ~ Jazz Sun evenings ~ Open 11-11(10.45 Sat); 12-10.30 Sun; closed 25 Dec, 1 Jan

Leopard ♀ ◀

33 Seward St, EC1; ⊖ Farringdon

It doesn't look too promising from the outside, but this smartly refurbished pub is actually rather civilised, especially in the unusual conservatory at the back. It's quite a surprise when the more traditional front part suddenly gives way to a soaring atrium – rather like an indoor garden – but it doesn't feel at all out of place. Plants cover the side walls and there are plenty of light wooden tables, with french windows leading to a small but not unappealing terrace. A green wrought-iron spiral staircase leads to another comfortable room, and a small outside drinking area. Back downstairs, the front of the pub has plenty of space and a comfortably relaxed feel, as well as a long dark wooden bar counter, a couple of big mirrors, fading rugs on the bare boards, and a neat tiled fireplace; soft piped music. The choice of beers usually includes well kept Salisbury Best, and three changing guests from independent brewers either around the country (such as Batemans or Ushers), or closer to home (like O'Hanlons); also a dozen wines by the glass. An open kitchen serves good freshly prepared bar meals from a changing blackboard menu, which might include sandwiches, warm spicy chicken and roast pork pepper salad (£5.25), Thai green chicken curry (£5.35), cumberland sausages with cajun mushrooms (£5.50), salmon steak topped with tomato concassé and golden cheese crust (£6.95), and grilled tuna steak on noodles with sweet and sour sauce (£7.25); friendly service. *(Recommended by Richard Lewis)*

Free house ~ Licensee Malcolm Jones ~ Real ale ~ Bar food (12.30-9) ~ (020) 7253 3587 ~ Children welcome ~ Open 11-11; closed weekends

Lord Moon of the Mall

16 Whitehall, SW1; ⊖ Charing Cross

One of the more individual Wetherspoons pubs, this well converted former bank is well placed within easy walking distance of many of central London's most famous sights, making it a useful pitstop for sightseers and visitors. The impressive main room has a very high ceiling and quite an elegant feel, with smart old prints, big arched windows looking out over Whitehall, and a huge painting that seems to show a well-to-do 18th-c gentleman; in fact it's Tim Martin, founder of the Wetherspoons chain. Once through an arch the style is recognisably Wetherspoons, with a couple of neatly tiled areas and nicely lit bookshelves opposite the long bar; fruit machines, trivia. The back doors are now only used in an emergency, but were apparently built as a secret entrance for account holders living in Buckingham Palace (Edward VII had an account here from the age of three); the area by the doors is no smoking. Courage Directors, Fullers London Pride, Theakstons Best and a couple of quickly changing guests such as Charles Wells Bombardier or Smiles on handpump. Bar food, from the standard Wetherspoons menu, is good value and reliable, ranging from soup (£2.50), and filled baguettes (£3), to vegetarian pasta (£4.35), battered fish or steak pie (£4.65), and daily specials such as spicy bean casserole; Sunday roast. The terms of the licence rule out fried food. As you come out of the pub Nelson's Column is immediately to the left, and Big Ben a walk of ten minutes or so to the right. Note they don't allow children. *(Recommended by Val and Alan Green, David Carr, Mayur Shah, Rachael and Mark Baynham, Jill Bickerton, John Fahy, Dr M E Wilson, MS, Tim Barrow, Sue Demont)*

Wetherspoons ~ Manager Russel Vaughan ~ Real ale ~ Bar food (11-10, 12-9.30 Sun) ~ (020) 7839 7701 ~ Open 11-11; 12-10.30 Sun

Moon Under Water ◀

105 Charing Cross Rd, WC2; ⊖ Tottenham Court Rd/Leicester Square

Apart from its size, perhaps the most remarkable thing about this fiercely modern Wetherspoons pub – a breathtaking conversion of the old Marquee club – is the intriguing mix of customers it attracts, from Soho trendies and students to tourists and the local after-work crowd; for people-watching it's hard to beat. The carefully designed main area is what used to be the auditorium, now transformed into a cavernous white-painted room stretching far off into the distance, with seats and tables lining the walls along the way. It effortlessly absorbs the hordes that pour in on Friday and Saturday evenings, and even when it's at its busiest you shouldn't have any trouble traversing the room, or have to wait very long to be served at the bar. Good value food and drinks are the same as at other Wetherspoons pubs (see previous entry), and they have regular real ale festivals and promotions; friendly service. The former stage is the area with most seats, and from here a narrower room leads past another bar to a back door opening on to Greek St (quite a surprise, as the complete lack of windows means you don't realise how far you've walked). A couple of areas – including the small seating area upstairs – are no smoking. Essentially this is a traditional pub that just happens to have a rather innovative design, so it's worth a look just to see the two combined; if you find it's not quite your style, at the very least it's a handy shortcut to Soho. Note they don't allow children. *(Recommended by Chris Parsons, Mark and Rachael Baynham, Andrew Hodges, Stephen and Julie Brown, C A Hall)*

Free house ~ Licensee Lorenzo Verri ~ Real ale ~ Bar food (11-10; 12-9.30 Sun) ~ (020) 7287 6039 ~ Open 11-11; 12-10.30 Sun

Museum Tavern 🍺

Museum Street, WC1; ⊖ Holborn or Tottenham Court Rd

The 19th-c bar and wooden fittings give this quietly civilised pub a genuinely old-fashioned feel, not much changed since Karl Marx is supposed to have had the odd glass here. It's directly opposite the British Museum, which explains why lunchtime tables are sometimes hard to come by, but unlike most other pubs in the area it generally stays pleasantly uncrowded in the evenings. In late afternoons especially there's a nicely peaceful atmosphere, with a good mix of locals and tourists. The single room is simply furnished and decorated, with high-backed benches around traditional cast-iron pub tables, and old advertising mirrors between the wooden pillars behind the bar. A decent choice of well kept beers on handpump usually takes in Courage Best and Directors, Greene King Abbot, Theakstons Best and Old Peculier, and a more unusual guest, but even for this area they're not cheap. They also have several wines by the glass, a choice of malt whiskies, and tea, coffee, cappuccino and hot chocolate. Available all day from a servery at the end of the room, bar food might include pie or quiche with salads (£5.75), ploughman's (£4.85), roasted pepper lasagne (£5.45), sausage and mash in yorkshire pudding (£5.75), and lamb and rosemary hotpot (£6.95); helpful service. It gets a little smoky when busy. There are a couple of tables outside under the gas lamps and 'Egyptian' inn sign. *(Recommended by Gordon Prince, Ted George, Ian Phillips, Tim Barrow, Sue Demont, Mr and Mrs Jon Corelis)*

Scottish Courage ~ Manager Tony Murphy ~ Real ale ~ Bar food (11-11, 12-10.30 Sun) ~ (020) 7242 8987 ~ Children in eating area of bar ~ Open 11-11; 12-12.30 Sun; closed 25 Dec

Nags Head

53 Kinnerton St, SW1; ⊖ Knightsbridge

One of the most unspoilt pubs you're likely to find in the whole of London, let alone so close to the centre, this quaint little gem is hidden away in an attractive and peaceful mews minutes from Harrods. You could be forgiven for thinking you'd been transported to an old-fashioned local somewhere in a sleepy country village, right down to the friendly regulars chatting around the unusual sunken bar counter. Homely and warmly traditional, it's rarely busy, even at weekends, when even in summer there's a snugly relaxed and cosy feel. The small, panelled and low-ceilinged front area has a wood-effect gas fire in an old cooking range (seats by here are generally snapped up pretty quickly), and a narrow passage leads down steps to an even smaller back bar with stools and a mix of comfortable seats. There's a 1930s What-the-butler-saw machine and a one-armed bandit that takes old pennies, as well as rather individual piped music, generally jazz, folk or show tunes. The well kept Adnams and Tetleys are pulled on attractive 19th-c china, pewter and brass handpumps. There are a few seats and a couple of tables outside. Bar food (not really the pub's strength) includes sandwiches (from £3.50), ploughman's or plenty of salads (from £4.75), and sausage, mash and beans, chilli, or steak and mushroom pie (all £4.95); there's a £1.50 surcharge added to all dishes in the evenings, and at weekends. *(Recommended by the Didler, Gordon, PB, Rachael and Mark Baynham, Ted George, Ian Phillips, Peter Baker)*

Free house ~ Licensee Kevin Moran ~ Real ale ~ Bar food (12-10) ~ (020) 7235 1135 ~
Children welcome ~ Open 11-11; 12-10.30 Sun

O'Hanlons 🍺

8 Tysoe St, EC1; ● Angel, but some distance away

Genuinely Irish, and a proper traditional local, this cheerful pub is worth a detour for
the excellent range of beers produced in Mr O'Hanlon's small brewery over the river.
Some of these – notably the delicious Blakeleys Number One – have found their way
into a few other pubs around the south (if you're further away, their award-winning
wheat beer can now be found in Safeway), but this is the finest place to sample the
full range, which varies according to the season. One winter ale, Myrica, is made
from bog myrtle and honey. Highlights are their Maltsters Weiss, Firefly, Red Ale,
and Dry Stout (you won't find Guinness here); they'll generally have between four
and six on at a time, as well as a guest from other independent brewers, such as Wye
Valley Dorothy Goodbody. The friendly, chatty landlord is happy to advise on the
various brews. The long basic bar has bare boards and stained yellow walls, assorted
prints and posters, newspapers to read, a signed rugby ball in a case, and comfortably
cushioned furnishings; there are a couple of cosy armchairs tucked away in an oddly
angular little alcove. The TV is used for rugby, but no other sports. A narrow
corridor with a big mirror lined with yellowing cuttings about the beer or other
London brewers leads to a lighter back room that's open during busy periods. Usually
served only on weekdays, a very short choice of good home-made food includes
things like monkfish, smoked salmon, prawn and dill terrine (£5.50), spring lamb,
fresh mint, and mixed pepper meatloaf (£5.50), and in winter Irish stew (£5.50); in
winter they also do Sunday lunch, with a choice of roasts. The atmosphere is notably
relaxed, and the look of the place fits in with that perfectly – to more particular tastes
it may seem slightly scruffy. Popular with locals, young trendies and visitors who've
tracked it down with their A-Z, the pub is very handy for Sadlers Wells. They take
credit cards. There are a couple of tables outside. *(Recommended by Richard Houghton,
C J Fletcher, Richard Lewis)*

Free house ~ Licensee Barry Roche ~ Real ale ~ Bar food (12-2.20, 6-9; 1-7 Sun; not
Sat, Sun evening) ~ (020) 7837 4112 ~ Well behaved children welcome ~ Live music
Sun evening ~ Open 11-11; 12-10.30 Sun

Old Bank of England ♀

194 Fleet St, EC4; ● Temple

Particularly well liked by readers at the moment, this splendidly converted old
building was until the mid-1970s a subsidiary branch of the Bank of England, built to
service the nearby Law Courts; after that it was a building society before Fullers
transformed it into their flagship pub in 1995. The opulent bar never fails to impress
first and even second time visitors: three gleaming chandeliers hang from the
exquisitely plastered ceiling high above the unusually tall island bar counter, and the
green walls are liberally dotted with old prints, framed bank notes and the like.
Though the room is quite spacious, screens between some of the varied seats and
tables create a surprisingly intimate feel, and there are several cosier areas at the end,
with more seats in a quieter galleried section upstairs. The mural that covers most of
the end wall looks like an 18th-c depiction of Justice, but in fact was commissioned
specially for the pub and features members of the Fuller, Smith and Turner families.
Well kept Fullers Chiswick, ESB and London Pride on handpump, along with a
couple of changing guests, and around 20 wines by the glass; efficient service from
neatly uniformed staff. Good generously served bar food includes soup (£2.50), deep-
filled sandwiches (from £3.50), ploughman's, a pasta special or bean, celery and
coriander chilli (£5.25), battered fish and chips (£5.95), and several pies like leek and
potato, chicken, bacon and spinach, or a good game pie (from £5.25); they do cream
teas in the afternoon. The dining room is no smoking at lunchtime. A rather austere
Italianate structure, the pub is easy to spot by the Olympic-style torches blazing
outside; the entrance is up a flight of stone steps. Note they don't allow children. Pies

have a long if rather dubious pedigree in this area; it was in the vaults and tunnels below the Old Bank and the surrounding buildings that Sweeney Todd butchered the clients destined to provide the fillings in his mistress Mrs Lovett's nearby pie shop. *(Recommended by Walter and Susan Rinaldi-Butcher, Dr and Mrs A K Clarke, the Didler, Mark Brock, Tony Scott, Rachael and Mark Baynham, David Carr, David and Carole Chapman, Christopher Glasson, JP, PP, Simon Collett-Jones, Tim Barrow, Sue Demont, Elizabeth and Klaus Leist, Chris Parsons, J R Ringrose, Tracey and Stephen Groves, Robert Gomme, Neil and Anita Christopher)*

Fullers ~ Manager Peter Briddle ~ Real ale ~ Bar food (12-8) ~ (020) 7430 2255 ~ Open 11-11; closed weekends

Olde Cheshire Cheese

Wine Office Court; off 145 Fleet Street, EC4; ⊖ Blackfriars

One of London's most famous old pubs, this 17th-c former chop house delights readers with its genuinely historic feel and dark, unpretentious little rooms. Over the years Congreve, Pope, Voltaire, Thackeray, Dickens, Conan Doyle, Yeats and perhaps Dr Johnson have called in, a couple of these probably coming across the famous parrot that for over 40 years entertained princes, ambassadors, and other distinguished guests. When she died in 1926 the news was broadcast on the BBC and obituary notices appeared in 200 newspapers all over the world; she's still around today, stuffed and silent. Up and down stairs, the profusion of small bars and rooms have bare wooden benches built in to the walls, sawdust on bare boards, and on the ground floor high beams, crackly old black varnish, Victorian paintings on the dark brown walls, and big open fires in winter. It's been extended in a similar style towards Fleet St. There's plenty of space, so even though it can get busy during the week (it's fairly quiet at weekends) it rarely feels too crowded. Lunchtime bar food includes hot toasted panini (£2.95), ploughman's (£3.95), and shepherd's pie, lasagne or various daily specials (£4.25). Well kept (and, as usual for this brewery, well priced) Sam Smiths OB on handpump; friendly service. Some of the Cellar bar is no smoking at lunchtimes. *(Recommended by Dr M E Wilson, Tony Scott, Jenny and Brian Seller, Nigel Wilson, Val Stevenson, Rob Holmes, Tracey and Stephen Groves, the Didler, Giles Francis, M A and C R Starling, Anthony Longden, Rona Murdoch, JP, PP)*

Sam Smiths ~ Manager Gordon Garrity ~ Real ale ~ Bar food (not weekends) ~ Restaurant ~ (020) 7353 6170/4388 ~ Children in eating area of bar ~ Open 11.30-11; 12-3, 5-11 Sat; 12-3 Sun; closed Sun evening, bank hols

Olde Mitre £

13 Ely Place, EC1; the easiest way to find it is from the narrow passageway beside 8 Hatton Garden; ⊖ Chancery Lane

The iron gates that guard the way to this well hidden, carefully rebuilt little tavern are a reminder of the days when the law in this district was administered by the Bishops of Ely; even today it's still technically part of Cambridgeshire. The pub stands out not just for its distinctive character and history, but also for the really exceptional service and welcome; the landlord clearly loves his job, and works hard to pass that enjoyment on to his customers. The cosy dark panelled small rooms have antique settles and – particularly in the back room, where there are more seats – old local pictures and so forth. It gets good-naturedly packed between 12.30 and 2.15, filling up again in the early evening, but by around nine becomes a good deal more tranquil. An upstairs room, mainly used for functions, may double as an overflow at peak periods. Well kept Friary Meux, Ind Coope Burton and Tetleys on handpump; notably chatty staff; darts. Bar snacks are usually limited to really good value cheese sandwiches with ham, pickle or tomato (£1, including toasted), as well as pork pies or scotch eggs. There are some pot plants and jasmine in the narrow yard between the pub and St Ethelreda's church. *(Recommended by Val Stevenson, Rob Holmes, Anthony Longden, Rachael and Mark Baynham, Tony Scott, Tracey and Stephen Groves, the Didler, R J Bland)*

Allied Domecq ~ Manager Don O'Sullivan ~ Real ale ~ Bar food (11-9.30) ~ (020)

7405 4751 ~ Open 11-11; closed weekends, bank hols

Orange Brewery ◖

37 Pimlico Road, SW1; ⊖ Sloane Square

The little brewery beneath this friendly pub each week produces over 500 gallons of their popular ales – SW1, a stronger SW2, and popular seasonal ales. You may also find a couple of guest beers, plus a good range of foreign bottled beers, including some Trappist brews; welcoming staff. Above the simple wooden chairs, tables and panelling is some vintage brewing equipment and related bric-a-brac, and there's a nicely tiled fireplace; fruit machine, piped music. A viewing area looks down into the brewery, and you can book tours for a closer look. Some readers feel it's like a posh version of a Firkin pub, and it's after-work appeal is such that there may be times when it's hard to find anywhere to sit; a few seats outside face a little concreted-over green beyond the quite busy street. A slight refurbishment was planned as we went to press. The menu typically features pies, various sausages with mash, and fish and chips (all around £4). *(Recommended by Esther and John Sprinkle, Ian Phillips, Rachael and Mark Baynham, Jasper Sabey)*

Own brew ~ Manager Tom McAuley ~ Bar food (11(12 Sun)-10) ~ (020) 7730 5984 ~ Children in eating area of bar ~ Open 11-11; 12-10.30 Sun

Red Lion ◖

Waverton Street, W1; ⊖ Green Park

With something of the atmosphere of a smart country pub, this civilised place is tucked away in one of Mayfair's quietest and prettiest corners; only the presence of so many suited workers reminds you of its city centre setting. The main L-shaped bar has small winged settles on the partly carpeted scrubbed floorboards, and London prints below the high shelf of china on its dark-panelled walls. Well kept Courage Best and Directors, Greene King IPA, and Theakstons Best on handpump, and they do rather good bloody marys (with a daunting very spicy option); also a dozen or so malt whiskies. Bar food, served from a corner at the front, includes sandwiches (from £2.50), cumberland sausage (£4.75), cod and chips or half rack of ribs with barbecue sauce (£6.95) and a couple of daily specials (£5). Unusually for this area, they serve food morning and evening seven days a week. It can get crowded at lunchtime, and immediately after work, when there's a busy, buzzy feel to the place. The gents' has a copy of the day's *Financial Times* at eye level. *(Recommended by David Carr, Mark and Rachael Baynham, Gordon, Ian Phillips, Joel Dobris)*

Scottish Courage ~ Manager Greg Peck ~ Bar food (12-2.30, 6-9.30) ~ Restaurant ~ (020) 7499 1307 ~ Children in eating area of bar ~ Open 11.30-11; 11-3, 6-11 Sat; 12-3, 7-11 Sun; closed 25, 26 Dec, 1 Jan

Seven Stars £

53 Carey St, WC2; ⊖ Holborn (just as handy from Temple or Chancery Lane, but the walk through Lincoln's Inn Fields can be rather pleasant)

Facing the back of the Law Courts, this tranquil little pub has hardly changed in the several hundred years it's stood here. We're not using the word little lightly – it's not just mild temperatures that lead people to stand in the peaceful street outside. The door, underneath a profusion of hanging baskets, is helpfully marked General Counter, as though you couldn't see that the simple counter is pretty much all there is in the tiny old-fashioned bar beyond. Lots of caricatures of barristers and other legal-themed prints on the walls, and quite a collection of toby jugs, some in a display case, the rest mixed up with the drinks behind the bar. Beers such as Courage Best and Directors or Fullers London Pride on handpump, several malt whiskies, and bar snacks such as sandwiches and various hot daily specials (£4.50); you may have to eat standing up, the solitary table and stools are on the left as you go in. A cosy room on the right appears bigger than it is because of its similar lack of furnishings; there are shelves round the walls for drinks or leaning against. Stairs up to the lavatories are very steep – a sign warns that you climb them at your own risk. *(Recommended by David Carr)*

Scottish Courage ~ Lease David and Denise Garland ~ Real ale ~ Bar food (12-11) ~ (020) 7242 8521 ~ Open 11-11; closed weekends, bank hols

Star ◖

Belgrave Mews West – behind the German Embassy, off Belgrave Sq; ⊖ Knightsbridge

A favourite with some readers, this simple and traditional pub is another of those places that seems distinctly un-London, with a pleasantly quiet and restful local feel outside peak times. A highlight in summer is the astonishing array of hanging baskets and flowering tubs outside – though many pubs try hard with such displays, few end up with anything quite so impressive. The small entry room, which also has the food servery, has stools by the counter and tall windows; an arch leads to a side room with swagged curtains, well polished wooden tables and chairs, heavy upholstered settles, globe lighting and raj fans. The back room has button-back built-in wall seats, and there's a an airy room upstairs. Good value straightforward bar food might include sandwiches (from £2.35), sausage, chips and beans (£4.25), and rib-eye steak (£7.95). Very well kept Fullers Chiswick, ESB, London Pride and seasonal beers on handpump. It can get busy at lunchtime and on some evenings, with a nice mix of customers. *(Recommended by Gordon, Bob and Maggie Atherton, Tracey and Stephen Groves, the Didler, David Carr, Rachael and Mark Baynham, David Coleman, Jasper Sabey, Ian Phillips, SLC, LM)*

Fullers ~ Manager T J Connel ~ Real ale ~ Bar food (12-2.30, 6-9) ~ (020) 7235 3019 ~ Open 11.30-11; 11.30-3, 6.30-11 Sat; 12-3, 7-11 Sun

Westminster Arms ◖

Storey's Gate, SW1; ⊖ Westminster

Close to Westminster Abbey and the Houses of Parliament, this unpretentious and friendly Westminster local is usually packed after work with government staff and researchers. The main draw is the choice of real ales, which generally includes Bass, Boddingtons, Brakspears PA, Gales IPA, Greene King Abbot, Theakstons Best, Wadworths 6X, Westminster Best brewed for them by Charringtons, and a monthly changing guest; they also do decent wines. Furnishings in the plain main bar are simple and old-fashioned, with proper tables on the wooden floors and a good deal of panelling; there's not a lot of room, so come early for a seat. Pleasant, courteous service. Most of the food is served in the downstairs wine bar (a good retreat from the ground floor bustle), with some of the tables in cosy booths; typical dishes include filled rolls (from £3), lasagne or steak and kidney pie (£5.50), and fish and chips or scampi (£6). Piped music in this area, and in the more formal upstairs restaurant, but not generally in the main bar; fruit machine. There are a couple of tables and seats by the street outside. *(Recommended by T Barrow, S Demont, the Didler, Janet and Colin Roe, David Carr, Derek and Sylvia Stephenson, Ian Phillips, Rachael and Mark Baynham)*

Free house ~ Licensees Gerry and Marie Dolan ~ Real ale ~ Bar food (all day weekdays, till 5 Sat, Sun) ~ Restaurant (weekday lunchtimes (not Weds)) ~ (020) 7222 8520 ~ Children in restaurant at lunchtime ~ Open 11-11(8 Sat); 12-6 Sun

EAST LONDON Map 12
Grapes

76 Narrow Street, E14; ⊖ Shadwell (some distance away) or Westferry on the Docklands Light Railway; the Limehouse link has made it hard to find by car – turn off Commercial Rd at signs for Rotherhithe tunnel, Tunnel Approach slip-road on left leads to Branch Rd then Narrow St

A favourite with Rex Whistler who came here to paint the river, this 16th-c tavern is one of London's most characterful riverside pubs, in a peaceful spot well off the tourist route. It was used by Charles Dickens as the basis of his 'Six Jolly Fellowship Porters' in *Our Mutual Friend*: 'It had not a straight floor and hardly a straight line, but it had outlasted and would yet outlast many a better-trimmed building, many a sprucer public house.' Not much has changed since, though as far as we know watermen no longer row out drunks from here, drown them, and sell the salvaged bodies to the anatomists as they did in Dickens' day. The back part is the oldest, with the recently refurbished back balcony a fine place for a sheltered waterside drink; steps lead down to the foreshore. The partly panelled bar has lots of prints, mainly of actors, some elaborately etched windows, and newspapers to read. Adnams, Tetleys, Ind Coope Burton and a changing guest on handpump, and a choice of malt whiskies. Bar food such as soup (£2.75), sandwiches (from £2.95), bangers and mash (£4.95), home-made fishcakes with caper sauce (£5.25), dressed crab (£6.95), and a Sunday roast (no other meals then); hard-working bar staff. Booking is recommended for the upstairs fish restaurant, which has fine views of the river. Shove ha'penny, table skittles, cribbage, dominoes, backgammon, maybe piped classical or jazz; no under 14s. *(Recommended by A Hepburn, S Jenner, C J Fletcher)*

Allied Domecq ~ Manager Barbara Haigh ~ Real ale ~ Bar food (not Sat lunchtime or Sun evening) ~ Restaurant ~ (020) 7987 4396 ~ Open 12-3, 5.30-11; 7-11 Sat; 12-3, 7-10.30 Sun; closed Sat lunchtimes, bank hols

Prospect of Whitby

57 Wapping Wall, E1; ⊖ Wapping

Pepys and Dickens were both frequent visitors to this entertaining old pub, Turner came for weeks at a time to study its glorious Thames views, and in the 17th c the notorious Hanging Judge Jeffreys was able to combine two of his interests by enjoying a drink at the back while looking down over the grisly goings-on in Execution Dock. With plenty more stories like these it's no wonder they do rather play upon the pub's pedigree, and it's an established favourite on the evening coach tours (it's usually quieter at lunchtimes). The tourists who flock in lap up the colourful tales of Merrie Olde London, and only the most unromantic of visitors could fail to be carried along by the fun. Plenty of bare beams, bare boards, panelling and flagstones in the L-shaped bar (where the long pewter counter is over 400 years old), while tables in the courtyard look out towards Docklands. Well kept Courage Directors and Morlands Old Speckled Hen on handpump, and quite a few malt whiskies; basic bar meals such as ploughman's (£4.25), steak and ale pie or pasta bolognese (£4.95), with a fuller menu in the upstairs restaurant. One area of the bar is no smoking; fruit machine, trivia. Built in 1520, the pub was for a couple of centuries known as the Devils' Tavern thanks to its popularity with river thieves and smugglers. *(Recommended by Tony Scott, Neil and Anita Christopher, C J Fletcher, A Hepburn, S Jenner, Richard and Valerie Wright)*

Scottish Courage ~ Manager Christopher Reeves ~ Real ale ~ Bar food (12-2.30(3 Sun), 6-9) ~ Restaurant ~ (020) 7481 1095 ~ Children in eating area of bar ~ Open 11.30-3, 5.30-11; 11.30-11 Sat; 12-10.30 Sun; closed 25, 26 Dec

Town of Ramsgate

62 Wapping High St, E1; ⊖ Wapping

Rarely crowded, despite its proximity to the City, this evocative old pub has kept a really unspoilt feel (how many other pubs can boast their own gallows?). It overlooks King Edward's Stairs (also known as Wapping Old Stairs), where the Ramsgate fishermen used to sell their catches. Inside, an enormous fine etched mirror shows Ramsgate harbour as it used to be. The softly lit panelled bar is a fine combination of comfort and good housekeeping on the one hand with plenty of interest on the other: it has masses of bric-a-brac from old pots, pans, pewter and decorative plates to the collection of walking canes criss-crossing the ceiling. There's a fine assortment of old Limehouse prints. At the back, a floodlit flagstoned terrace and wooden platform (with pots of flowers and summer barbecues) peeps out past the stairs and the high wall of Olivers Warehouse to the Thames. Good value bar food includes sandwiches (from £1.85), burgers (from £2.45), all-day breakfast (£2.50), good hot baguettes (from £2.85), vegetable tikka (£3.45), tagliatelle carbonara (£3.75), fish and chips (£3.80), steak and ale pie (£4.35), and daily specials. Service is friendly, but not always fast. Well kept Fullers London Pride and maybe Youngs Special on handpump; darts, fruit machine, video game, trivia, TV for rugby matches, unobtrusive piped music. There's a good sociable mix of customers. *(Recommended by Monica Shelley, Geoff and Sylvia Donald, Ian Phillips, Richard and Valerie Wright)*

Bass ~ Manager Robin Gardner ~ Real ale ~ Bar food (12-2.30, 6-9; 12-6 Sat, 12-4 Sun) ~ (020) 7264 0001 ~ Open 12-11; 12-10.30 Sun

NORTH LONDON Map 13

Parking is not a special problem in this area, unless we say so

Chapel 🍽 ♀

48 Chapel St, NW1; ⊖ Edgware Rd

Good food brings most people to this cosmopolitan, much modernised pub. It's relaxed and civilised at lunchtimes, especially in summer, when tables on the terrace outside can be busy with chic, suited creative folk enjoying a break. Light and spacious, the cream-painted main room is dominated by the open kitchen, which produces unusual soups such as lemon and courgette, and generously served dishes like goat's cheese, tomato and oyster mushroom tart (£8), roast chicken stuffed with sun-dried tomatoes and peppers (£9.50), roasted john dory with artichoke and anchovy sauce (£12), roast guinea fowl breasts with sage (£12.50), and puddings such as an excellent tarte tatin. Prompt and efficient service from helpful staff, who may bring warm walnut bread to your table while you're waiting. Furnishings are smart but simple; there are plenty of wooden tables around the bar, with more in a side room with a big fireplace. It fills up quite quickly, so you may have to wait to eat during busy periods. In the evening trade is more evenly split between diners and drinkers, and the music can be rather loud then, especially at weekends. Fullers London Pride on handpump (rather expensive, even for London), a good range of interesting wines (up to half by the glass), cappuccino and espresso, and a choice of teas such as peppermint or strawberry and vanilla. *(Recommended by Tim Barrow, Sue Demont, Michael and Alison Sandy, Nick Rose, Greg Kilminster)*

Bass ~ Lease: Lakis Hondrogiannis ~ Real ale ~ (020) 7402 9220 ~ Children welcome ~ Open 12-11; 12-3, 7-10.30 Sun

Compton Arms ♀

4 Compton Avenue, off Canonbury Rd, N1; ⊖ Highbury & Islington

With beautiful hanging baskets in front and a delightfully relaxing little crazy-paved terrace behind, this tiny pub is hidden away up a peaceful mews. Well run by friendly staff, the unpretentious low-ceilinged rooms are simply furnished with wooden settles and assorted stools and chairs, with local pictures on the walls; free from games or music, it has a very personable, village local feel. Well kept Greene King Abbot, IPA, and Triumph on handpump, and around 22 wines by the glass. Good value bar food includes sandwiches, soup and the like, but majors on sausages, with half a dozen different types served with mashed potato and home-made gravy (£3.95). At the back are benches and tables among flowers under a big sycamore tree; there's a covered section so you can still sit out if it's raining, and maybe heaters in winter. *(Recommended by Roger and Jenny Huggins, Caroline Wright, Nigel Woolliscroft, Mark and Rachael Baynham)*

Greene King ~ Manager Paul Fairweather ~ Real ale ~ Bar food (12-3, 6-9; not Tues evening) ~ (020) 7359 6883 ~ Children welcome in back room ~ Open 11-11; 12-10.30 Sun

Flask ♀ £

14 Flask Walk, NW3; ⊖ Hampstead

Just around the corner from the tube, but miles away in spirit, this civilised old local still has the distinctive spirit that for many years has made it a popular haunt of Hampstead artists, actors, and local characters. The snuggest and most individual part is the cosy lounge at the front, with plush green seats and banquettes curving round the panelled walls, a unique Victorian screen dividing it from the public bar, an attractive fireplace, and a very laidback and rather villagey atmosphere. A comfortable orange-lit room with period prints and a few further tables leads into a much more recent but rather smart dining conservatory, which with its plants, prominent wine bottles and neat table linen feels a bit like a wine bar. A couple of white iron tables are squeezed into the tiny back yard. Unusual and good value bar food might include sandwiches, good soups such as pumpkin, and daily changing specials like seafood and asparagus lasagne or chicken and mushroom in mustard sauce (£3.90); everything is home-made, including the chips. Well kept Youngs Bitter, Special and seasonal brews on handpump, around 20 wines by the glass, and decent coffees – they have a machine that grinds the beans to order. A plainer public bar (which you can only get into from the street) has leatherette seating, cribbage, backgammon, lots of space for darts, fruit machine, trivia, and SkyTV; this is the favourite part of the resident german shepherd dog, Lady. Friendly service. A noticeboard has news from their darts and cricket teams. There are quite a few tables outside in the alley. The pub's name is a reminder of the days when it was a distributor of the mineral water from Hampstead's springs. *(Recommended by Tony Scott, Mr and Mrs Jon Corelis, Michael and Alison Sandy, Jane and Robert Oswaks, the Didler, P A Legon, Mark and Rachael Baynham)*

Youngs ~ Manager Mr J T Orr ~ Real ale ~ (020) 7435 4580 ~ Children in eating area of bar till 9pm ~ Open 11-11; 12-10.30 Sun

Holly Bush

Holly Mount, NW3; ✆ Hampstead

The stroll up from the tube station to this cheery old local is delightful, along some of Hampstead's most villagey streets. It's the kind of pub that's especially appealing in the evenings, when real Edwardian gas lamps light the atmospheric front bar, and, despite the mix of chatty locals and visitors, there's a timeless feel to the place. Under the dark sagging ceiling are brown and cream panelled walls (decorated with old advertisements and a few hanging plates), open fires, and cosy bays formed by partly glazed partitions. Slightly more intimate, the back room, named after the painter George Romney, has an embossed red ceiling, panelled and etched glass alcoves, and ochre-painted brick walls covered with small prints and plates. Well kept Benskins, Tetleys, and three changing guests. As we went to press no bar food was available, but a new menu was about to come into service. Last year we'd been told the brewery were planning big changes here – happily that's no longer the case. *(Recommended by Mick Hitchman, Mr and Mrs Jon Corelis, Mark and Rachael Baynham)*

Allied Domecq ~ Manager Ellen Roi ~ Real ale ~ (020) 7435 2892 ~ Open 12-3, 5.30-11; 12-11 Sat; 12-10.30 Sun

Olde White Bear

Well Road, NW3; ✆ Hampstead

Friendly and traditional, this villagey and almost clubby neo-Victorian pub pulls off the rare trick of making all sorts of different types of people feel relaxed and at home. The dimly lit main room has lots of Victorian prints and cartoons on the walls, as well as wooden stools, cushioned captain's chairs, a couple of big tasselled armed chairs, a flowery sofa, handsome fireplace and an ornate Edwardian sideboard. A similarly lit small central room has Lloyd Loom furniture, dried flower arrangements and signed photographs of actors and playwrights. In the brighter end room there are elaborate cushioned machine tapestried pews, and dark brown paisley curtains. Beers on handpump usually include Greene King IPA and Abbot, Tetleys, Wadworths 6X and a weekly changing guest; also 15 or so malt whiskies. Bar food is now served all day, with a seasonal menu including things like sandwiches (from £2.35), tomato and basil soup (£2.85), baked aubergine slices (£5.95), Thai chicken curry (£6.50), beef bourguignon (£6.75), and chargrilled tuna steak with spiced lentil salsa (£6.95); they generally have special offers on Tuesday evenings. Darts, cribbage, shove ha'penny, dominoes, fruit machine, piped music. Parking may be a problem – it's mostly residents' permits only nearby. *(Recommended by Jilly and George Little, Ian Phillips, Tony Scott, Mark and Rachael Baynham)*

Allied Domecq ~ Licensees Deborah Finn, Jason Rudolph ~ Real ale ~ Bar food (12-10) ~ Restaurant ~ (020) 7435 3758 ~ Children welcome ~ Jazz Mon evening ~ Open 11-11; 12-11 Sat; 12-10.30 Sun

Spaniards Inn 🍺

Spaniards Lane, NW3; ⊖ Hampstead, but some distance away, or from Golders Green station take 220 bus

Named after the Spanish ambassador to the court of James I (for whom it was built as a private residence), this big, busy former toll house boasts one of London's finest pub gardens. Separated into separate seeming areas by judicious planting of shrubs, it has slatted wooden tables and chairs on a crazy-paved terrace opening on to a flagstoned walk around a small lawn, with roses, a side arbour of wisteria and clematis, and an aviary. Inside, the low-ceilinged oak-panelled rooms of the attractive main bar have open fires, genuinely antique winged settles, candle-shaped lamps in pink shades, and snug little alcoves. Lunchtime bar food includes filled baguettes (£3.75), and changing hot dishes like steak and kidney pie or sausage and mash (£5.25); in the evenings they do a vegetarian pasta dish (£6.95), fish and chips (£7.95), rosemary roasted lamb shanks (£9.45), and steak (£13.45); on Sundays they may just do a roast. The food bar is no smoking. A quieter upstairs bar may be open at busy times. Well kept Bass, Fullers London Pride, and Hancocks BB on handpump – though on warm days in summer you may find the most popular drink is their big jug of pimms; piped classical music, newspapers, fruit machine, trivia. The pub is very handy for Kenwood, and indeed during the 1780 Gordon Riots the then landlord helped save the house from possible disaster, cunningly giving so much free drink to the mob on its way to burn it down that by the time the Horse Guards arrived the rioters were lying drunk and incapable on the floor. Parking can be difficult – especially when people park here to walk their dogs on the heath. The pub will be closed for five weeks around February 2000 for a slight refurbishment. *(Recommended by Mark and Rachael Baynham, Jilly and George Little, Ian Phillips, Tony Scott, Jasper Sabey)*

Bass ~ Manager Mike Bowler ~ Real ale ~ Bar food (12-9) ~ (020) 8731 6571 ~ Children away from main bar ~ Open 11-11; 12-10.30 Sun; closed 25 Dec

Waterside

82 York Way, N1; ⊖ Kings Cross

Over the next few months they plan to add a terraced rooftop garden to this handily positioned pub, a useful place to know about if you're passing through what's not exactly an appealing area for visitors. The building really isn't very old but it's done out in traditional style, with stripped brickwork, latticed windows, genuinely old stripped timbers in white plaster, lots of dimly lit alcoves (one is no smoking), spinning wheels, milkmaids' yokes, and horsebrasses and so on, with plenty of rustic tables and wooden benches. One area is no smoking. There's an unexpectedly calm outside terrace overlooking the Battlebridge Basin. The beers are currently more interesting than you might expect: as well as Boddingtons, they stock changing brews from the Batemans, Caledonian and Rebellion breweries. The new menu is from the Pizza Hut chain, like the pub, owned by Whitbread (expect to see more of this kind of joint venture in the next few months). Pool, pinball, fruit machine, good-sized TV for sports, and sometimes loudish juke box. No dogs inside. *(Recommended by Mr and Mrs A R Hawkins, Rachael and Mark Baynham)*

Whitbreads ~ Manager John Keyes ~ Real ale ~ Bar food (11.30-9) ~ (020) 7837 7118 ~ Children in eating area of bar till 7pm ~ Open 11-11; 12-11 Sat; 12-10.30 Sun

SOUTH LONDON Map 12

Parking is bad on weekday lunchtimes at the inner city pubs here (SE1), but is usually OK everywhere in the evenings – you may again have a bit of a walk if a good band is

on at the Bulls Head in Barnes, or at the Windmill on Clapham Common if it's a fine evening

Alma ♀

499 York Road, SW18; ⊖ Wandsworth Town

Unexpectedly civilised, this stylish local has an air of chattily relaxed bonhomie. It feels rather smart, though the furnishings are mostly quite simple – a mix of chairs and cast-iron-framed tables around the brightly repainted walls, and a couple of sofas, with gilded mosaics of the Battle of the Alma and an ornate mahogany chimney-piece and fireplace adding a touch of elegance. The popular but less pubby dining room has a fine turn-of-the-century frieze of swirly nymphs; there's waitress service in here, and you can book a particular table. Even when it's very full with smart young people – which it often is in the evenings – service is careful and efficient. Youngs Bitter, Special and seasonal brews on handpump from the island bar counter, good house wines (with around 20 by the glass), freshly squeezed juices, good coffee, tea or hot chocolate, newspapers out for customers. Bar food might include sandwiches, toulouse sausages with mash and onion gravy (£6.45), thai-style fishcakes with a sweet chilli mayonnaise (£6.85), grilled blue fin tuna on niçoise salad (£7.85), and steak frites (£8.95); the menu may be limited on Sunday lunchtimes. They've started opening earlier at weekends to serve breakfasts, with everything from muesli and fruit to a full cooked meal. If you're after a quiet drink don't come when there's a rugby match on the television, unless you want a running commentary from the well heeled and voiced young locals. Cribbage, pinball, table football, dominoes, fruit machine. Charge up their 'smart-card' with cash and you can pay with a discount either here or at the management's other pubs, which include the Ship at Wandsworth (see below). Travelling by rail into Waterloo you can see the pub rising above the neighbouring rooftops as you rattle through Wandsworth Town. *(Recommended by David Carr, Richard Gibbs, Jasper Sabey, Ian Phillips)*

Youngs ~ Tenant Charles Gotto ~ Real ale ~ Bar food (12-10) ~ Restaurant ~ (020) 7870 2537 ~ Children in eating area of bar and restaurant ~ Open 11-11; 10.30-11 Sat; 10.30-10.30 Sun; closed 25 Dec

Anchor

34 Park St, Bankside, SE1; Southwark Bridge end; ⊖ London Bridge

About to be extended as we went to press, with bedrooms set to open in late 1999, this atmospheric riverside spot has a hard to beat view of the Thames and the City from its busy front terrace. A warren of dimly lit, creaky little rooms and passageways, the current building dates back to about 1750, when it was built to replace an earlier tavern, possibly the one that Pepys came to during the Great Fire of 1666. 'All over the Thames with one's face in the wind, you were almost burned with a shower of fire drops,' he wrote. 'When we could endure no more upon the water, we to a little ale-house on the Bankside and there staid till it was dark almost, and saw the fire grow.' The main bar has bare boards and beams, black panelling, old-fashioned high-backed settles, and sturdy leatherette chairs, and even when it's invaded by tourists it's usually possible to retreat to one of the smaller rooms. Bass, Flowers Original, and rapidly changing guest beers such as Greene King Abbot on handpump or tapped from the cask; they also do jugs of pimms and sangria, and mulled wine in winter. Cribbage, dominoes, three fruit machines, and fairly loud piped music. Bar food includes filled baguettes (from £2.95), winter soup, baked potatoes (£3.75), and five changing hot dishes like steak and ale pie, or chicken with a mustard and porter sauce (all around £5.50); they do a Sunday roast in the restaurant. The pub can get smoky, and service can be erratic at busy periods. Sword or Morris dancers may pass by on summer evenings, and there's an increasing number of satisfying places to visit nearby; the Clink round the corner is good on the area's murky past. *(Recommended by Rachael and Mark Baynham, Ian Phillips, Tim Barrow, Sue Demont, Susan and John Douglas, Mr and Mrs A R Hawkins, Tony Scott, the Didler)*

Greenalls ~ Manager Stephen Walmsley ~ Real ale ~ Bar food (12-2.30) ~ (020) 7407 1577 ~ Children in eating area of bar and restaurant ~ Open 11-11; 12-10.30 Sun

Bulls Head ♀ £

373 Lonsdale Road, SW13; ⇌ Barnes Bridge

Top class modern jazz groups performing every night are what draw the crowds to this imposing Thameside pub, built in 1684. You can hear the music quite clearly from the lounge bar (and on peaceful Sunday afternoons from the villagey little street as you approach), but for the full effect and genuine jazz club atmosphere it is worth paying the admission to the well equipped music room. Back in the bustling bar, alcoves open off the main area around the island servery, which has Youngs Bitter, Special and seasonal beers on handpump, over 80 malt whiskies, and a good range of decent wines, with 20 by the glass. Around the walls are large photos of the various jazz musicians and bands who have played here; dominoes, cribbage, Scrabble, chess, cards, and fruit machine in the public bar. Home-made bar food might include things like soup (£1.40), sandwiches (from £1.80), steak and kidney pie (£4), pasta (£7.50), rack of lamb (£9.50), fresh fish such as halibut or swordfish (£12.50) and steaks (£13.50); service is efficient and friendly. Bands play 8.30-11 every night plus 2-4.30 Sundays, and depending on who's playing prices generally range from £3.50 to around £6. One reader described his recent morning visit here as 'absolute heaven', enjoying both a river view, and the sound of that night's band rehearsing. *(Recommended by Roger Huggins, David Carr)*

Youngs ~ Tenant Dan Fleming ~ Real ale ~ Bar food (12-3, 7-9) ~ Restaurant ~ (020) 7876 5241 ~ Children welcome in back room ~ Open 11-11; 12-10.30 Sun

Crown & Greyhound

73 Dulwich Village, SE21; ⇌ North Dulwich

Though this grand place does get busy in the evenings, it's so big that there's enough room to absorb everyone without too much difficulty. Readers like the way it caters so well for children, offering Lego and toys to play with as well as children's meals, and never making families feel like second-class citizens. They have baby changing facilities, and an ice cream stall in the very pleasant big two-level back terrace, which also has a play area with sandpit, and a good many picnic-sets under a chestnut tree. The most ornate room inside is on the right, with its elaborate ochre ceiling plasterwork, fancy former gas lamps, Hogarth prints, fine carved and panelled settles and so forth. It opens into the former billiards room, where kitchen tables on a stripped board floor are set for eating. Changing every day, the lunchtime choice of bar meals might include soup (£1.60), toasted sandwiches (from £2.60), enormous doorstep sandwiches, a range of specials like steak and kidney pie, herb fishcakes, vegetable moussaka and chicken and broccoli bake (£5.50), cashew nut paella (£7.65), and pork in a rosemary and tomato sauce with apples, mushroom and onions (£8.95). Best to arrive early for their popular Sunday carvery, they don't take bookings. A central snug leads on the other side to the saloon – brown ragged walls, upholstered and panelled settles, a coal-effect gas fire in the tiled period fireplace, and Victorian prints. Well kept Ind Coope Burton, Tetleys and Youngs on handpump, along with a monthly changing guest like Adnams or Morlands Old Speckled Hen; they have a wine of the month too. Dominoes, fruit machines, trivia, and piped music. The pub was built at the turn of the century to replace two inns that had stood here previously, hence the unusual name. Known locally as the Dog, it's handy for walks through the park. *(Recommended by Comus Elliott, Ian Phillips, Mike Gorton, Dave Braisted)*

Allied Domecq ~ Manager Bernard Maguire ~ Real ale ~ Bar food (12-2.30, 6-10) ~ Restaurant (evenings only) ~ (020) 8693 2466 ~ Children in restaurant and family room ~ Open 11-11; 12-10.30 Sun

Cutty Sark

Ballast quay, off Lassell St, SE10; ⇌ Maze Hill, from London Bridge, or from the river front walk past the Yacht in Crane St and Trinity Hospital

Across the narrow cobbled lane from this attractive late 16th-c white-painted house is a waterside terrace with tables well placed to enjoy good views of the Thames and the

Millennium Dome. You'll see more perhaps from inside, through the big upper bow window, itself striking for the way it jetties out over the pavement. Despite a few recent changes the atmospheric bar still conjures up images of the kind of London we imagine Dickens once knew, with flagstones, rough brick walls, wooden settles, barrel tables, open fires, low lighting and narrow openings to tiny side snugs. Well kept Fullers London Pride, Morlands Old Speckled Hen and Youngs Special on handpump, a good choice of malt whiskies, and a decent wine list. An elaborate central staircase leads to an upstairs area; fruit machine, trivia, juke box. Served in a roomy eating area, bar food includes filled baguettes (from £4.50), roast vegetable lasagne (£5.50), steak and ale pie (£5.95), battered cod or plaice (£6), and cajun chicken (£6.75); staff are helpful, but service can slow down at times. The pub can be very busy with young people on Friday and Saturday evenings, and fine summer evenings are also likely to draw the crowds. *(Recommended by Brian and Anna Marsden, the Didler, Jill Bickerton, David and Carole Chapman, Robert Gomme)*

Free house ~ Licensee Arthur Hughs ~ Real ale ~ (020) 8858 3146 ~ Children upstairs till 9pm ~ Open 11-11; 12-10.30 Sun; closed 25 Dec evening, 11-3 bank hols

Fire Station 🍺 🍴

150 Waterloo Rd, SE1; ⊖ Waterloo

London Dining Pub of the Year

Very handy for the Old Vic, Waterloo Station and the Imperial War Museum a bit further down the road, this remarkable conversion of the former LCC central fire station is reckoned by regular visitors to keep getting better and better. Best known for the imaginative food served from the open kitchen in the back dining room, it's hardly your typical local, but it does a number of traditionally pubby things far better than anyone else nearby, and the two vibrantly chatty rooms at the front certainly seem to be the favoured choice for the area's after-work drinkers. The décor is something like a cross between a warehouse and a schoolroom, with plenty of wooden pews, chairs and long tables (a few spilling onto the street), some mirrors and rather incongruous pieces of dressers, and brightly red-painted doors, shelves and modern hanging lightshades; the determinedly contemporary art round the walls is for sale, and there's a table with newspapers to read. Well kept Adnams, Brakspears, Youngs, a beer brewed for them by Hancocks, and a changing guest on handpump, as well as a number of bottled beers, variously flavoured teas, and a good choice of wines (several by the glass); helpful service. They serve a short range of bar meals between 12.30 and 6, which might include filled ciabattas (from £3.50), leek and fennel soup (£3.50), salads (£5.25), and half a dozen oysters (£6.50), but it's worth paying the extra to eat from the main menu. Changing every lunchtime and evening, this has things like chargrilled smoked cod with parsley mash and tomato and chilli salsa (£9.95), guinea fowl with risotto verde and courgette flowers (£10.50), and puddings such as peach and almond tart with custard sauce (£3.50); they don't take bookings, so there may be a slight wait at busy times. Piped modern jazz and other music fits into the good-natured hubbub. Those with quieter tastes might find bustling weeknights here a little too hectic – it's less busy at lunchtimes and during the day. At the busiest times in the bar, it's a good idea to keep your belongings firmly to hand. *(Recommended by Rachael and Mark Baynham, Comus Elliott, Mayur Shah, Tim Barrow, Sue Demont)*

Free house ~ Licensee Peter Nottage ~ Real ale ~ Bar food (12-2.45, 5.30-11) ~ Restaurant ~ (020) 7620 2226 ~ Children welcome away from bar ~ Open 11-11; 12-10.30 Sun

George ★ 🍴

Off 77 Borough High Street, SE1; ⊖ Borough or London Bridge

Preserved by the National Trust, this splendid looking 17th-c coaching inn is such a London landmark that it's easy to forget it's still a proper working pub. Noted as one of London's 'fair inns for the receipt of travellers' as early as 1598, it was rebuilt on its original plan after the great Southwark fire in 1676, then owned for a while by Guys Hospital next door. It was under the next owners, the Great Northern Railway

Company, that it was 'mercilessly reduced' as E V Lucas put it, when the other wings of the building were demolished. The remaining wing is a unique survival, the tiers of open galleries looking down over a cobbled courtyard with plenty of picnic-sets, and maybe Morris men and even Shakespeare in summer. It's just as unspoilt inside, the row of simple ground-floor rooms and bars all containing square-latticed windows, black beams, bare floorboards, some panelling, plain oak or elm tables and old-fashioned built-in settles, along with a 1797 'Act of Parliament' clock, dimpled glass lantern-lamps and so forth. The snuggest refuge is the simple room nearest the street, where there's an ancient beer engine that looks like a cash register; darts, trivia. A good choice of well kept beers includes Boddingtons, Flowers Original, Fullers London Pride, Greene King Abbot, Morlands Old Speckled Hen, and a beer brewed for them, Restoration; they do mulled wine in winter; darts, trivia. Lunchtime bar food might include club sandwiches or filled baked potatoes (£3), sausage and mash (£4.45), and ploughman's, roast vegetable lasagne, and deep-fried cod (all £4.95). A splendid central staircase goes up to a series of dining rooms and to a gaslit balcony. Service can slow down at busy times. Unless you know where you're going (or you're in one of the many tourist groups that flock here during the day in summer) you may well miss it, as apart from the great gates there's little to indicate that such a gem still exists behind the less auspicious looking buildings on the busy high street.
(Recommended by Ian Phillips, Rachael and Mark Baynham, Richard Lewis, Jasper Sabey, Mr and Mrs Jon Corelis, Tony Scott, Robert Davis, Philip Vernon, Janet and Colin Roe, Tracey and Stephen Groves, the Didler, Dr Oscar Puls)

Whitbreads ~ Manager George Cunningham ~ Real ale ~ Bar food (11-4) ~ Restaurant ~ (020) 7407 2056 ~ Children in eating area of bar and restaurant ~ Open 11-11; 12-10.30 Sun

Horniman

Hays Galleria, Battlebridge Lane, SE13; ⊖ London Bridge

This spacious, gleaming and rather elaborate pub has splendid views of the Thames, HMS *Belfast* and Tower Bridge from the picnic-sets outside. Inside, the area by the sweeping bar counter is a few steps down from the door, with squared black, red and white flooring tiles and lots of polished wood; from here steps lead up to various comfortable carpeted areas, with a few sofas, and the tables well spread out so as to allow for a feeling of roomy relaxation at quiet times but give space for people standing in groups when it's busy. There's a set of clocks made for tea merchant Frederick Horniman's office showing the time in various places around the world. A wide range of beers (rather pricy even for central London) typically takes in Adnams Extra, Fullers London Pride, Morlands Old Speckled Hen, Tetleys, Timothy Taylor Landlord, and Youngs, and a tea bar serves a choice of teas, coffees, and other hot drinks, plus danish pastries and so forth; a hundred-foot frieze shows the travels of the tea. Bar food includes soup (£2.75), big sandwiches (around £4.95), and daily changing hot dishes such as honeyed chicken supreme, battered haddock, or goat's cheese and spinach cannelloni (£6.95). Fruit machine, TVs, trivia, pinball, table football, unobtrusive piped music. The pub is at the end of the visually exciting Hays Galleria development, several storeys high, with a soaring glass curved roof, and supported by elegant thin cast-iron columns; various shops and boutiques open off. It's busy round here in the daytime, but quickly goes quiet as the evening goes on. Note the early closing at weekends.
(Recommended by Mike Ridgway, Sarah Miles, Susan and John Douglas)

Nicholsons (Allied Domecq) ~ Manager David Matthews ~ Real ale ~ Bar food ~ Restaurant ~ (020) 7407 3611 ~ Children welcome till 9pm ~ Open 10-11; 10-5 Sat; 11-5 Sun; closed 25, 26 Dec, 1 Jan, 11-5 bank hols

Market Porter 🍺

9 Stoney Street, SE1; ⊖ London Bridge

Particularly well liked for its range of well kept beers – one of the most varied in London – this busily pubby place is open between 6.30 and 8.30 am for market workers and porters (and anyone else who's passing) to enjoy a drink at the start of the day. The seven ales on handpump usually include a combination of Bunces Pig Swill, Courage Best and Directors, Fullers London Pride, Gales HSB, Harveys Sussex, Thirsty Willey and Youngs Bitter. The main part of the atmospheric long U-shaped bar has rough wooden ceiling beams with beer barrels balanced on them, a heavy wooden bar counter with a beamed gantry, cushioned bar stools, an open fire with stuffed animals in glass cabinets on the mantlepiece, several mounted stags' heads, and 20s-style wall lamps. Sensibly priced simple bar food includes sandwiches, teriyaki chicken (£5.25), seafood crêpe or fish and chips wrapped in newspaper (£5.50), rib-eye steak (£7.95), and Sunday roasts. Obliging service; darts, fruit machine, video game, TV, and piped music. A small partly panelled room has leaded glass windows and a couple of tables. Part of the restaurant is no smoking. The company that own the pub – which can get a little full and smoky – have similar establishments in Reigate and nearby Stamford St. *(Recommended by Greg Kilminster, Rachael and Mark Baynham, Richard Lewis, Tracey and Stephen Groves, the Didler, Tim Barrow, Sue Demont, Mr and Mrs A R Hawkins)*

Free house ~ Licensee Anthony Heddigan ~ Real ale ~ Bar food (12-2.30 only) ~ (020) 7407 2495 ~ Children in eating area of bar at weekends ~ Open 6.30-8.30, then 11-11; 12-10.30 Sun

Phoenix & Firkin

5 Windsor Walk, SE5; ⇌ Denmark Hill

The glory day of the Firkin pubs may be over, but this busy place is still worth a look for its unusual décor and lively atmosphere. At times quite loud, and crowded with young people in the evenings, it's an interesting conversion of a palatial Victorian railway hall, with a model railway train running back and forth above the bar, paintings of steam trains, old-fashioned station name signs, a huge double-faced station clock (originally from Llandudno Junction in Wales), solid wooden furniture on the stripped wooden floor, plants, and old seaside posters and Bovril advertisements. At one end there's a similarly furnished gallery, reached by a spiral staircase, and at the other arches lead into a food room; chess, dominoes, Twister, fruit machines, video game, pinball, satellite TV, and juke box. Firkin Ale and Dogbolter on handpump, with maybe a couple of changing guests. Straightforward food includes big filled baps (usually available all day), a good cold buffet with pork pies, salads, quiche and so forth, and daily hot dishes like vegetable chilli (£3.95) or beef and Dogbolter pie (£4.50); they do a Sunday roast (£4.95). The pub can get smoky at times, and though the piped music can be noisy later in the day, it's much quieter at lunchtimes. There are a couple of long benches outside, and the steps which follow the slope of the road are a popular place to sit. Recent reports suggest the service impresses less than the surroundings. *(Recommended by the Didler)*

Allied Domecq ~ Manager Francis Evans ~ Real ale ~ Bar food (12-10) ~ Restaurant ~ (020) 8701 8282 ~ Children in eating area of bar and restaurant ~ Open 11-11; 12-10.30 Sun

Ship ♀

41 Jews Row, SW18; ⇌ Wandsworth Town

Some pubs are at their best on cosy winter evenings, but this smartly bustling place comes into its own in summer, when, weather permitting, there's a barbecue every day on the extensive two-level riverside, with home-made burgers and sausages, marinated lamb steaks, goat's cheese quesidillas, cajun chicken and lobster. There are lots of picnic-sets, pretty hanging baskets and brightly coloured flower-beds, small trees, and an outside bar, with a Thames barge moored alongside. Inside, only a small part of the original ceiling is left in the main bar – the rest is in a light and airy conservatory style; wooden tables, a medley of stools, and old church chairs on the wooden floorboards, and a relaxed, chatty atmosphere. One part has a Victorian fireplace, a huge clock surrounded by barge prints, and part of a milking machine on a table, and there's a rather battered harmonium, old-fashioned bagatelle, and jugs of flowers around the window sills. The basic public bar has plain wooden furniture, a black kitchen range in the fireplace and darts, pinball and a juke box. Well kept Youngs Bitter, Special and Winter Warmer on handpump, freshly squeezed orange and other fruit juices, a wide range of wines (a dozen or more by the glass) and good choice of teas and coffees. Relying heavily on free-range produce, the main bar menu might include sandwiches (not weekends), rabbit terrine with sweet pepper and ginger pickle (£4.25), home-made pork sausages with chive mash or lamb and spinach curry (£6.50), mussel and squid stew (£7), roast cod with clams (£8.40), pan-fried duck breast (£9.50), daily specials, and puddings like blueberry bread and butter pudding (£3.50). Service is friendly and helpful. The pub's annual firework display draws huge crowds of young people, and they also celebrate the last night of the Proms. Barbecues and spit roasts every weekend in summer, when the adjacent car park can get full pretty quickly. *(Recommended by Christopher Wright, Tim Barrow, Sue Demont, David Carr)*

Youngs ~ Tenants C Gotto and Rupert Green ~ Real ale ~ Bar food (12-3, 7-10.30; 12-5, 7-10.30 Sun) ~ Restaurant ~ (020) 8870 9667 ~ Children welcome ~ Open 11-11; 12-10.30 Sun

White Cross ♀

Water Lane; ⊖/⇌ Richmond

This busy old pub enjoys a perfect riverside position, delightful in summer, and with a certain wistful charm in winter as well. The best part is the paved garden in front, which on a sunny day feels a little like a cosmopolitan seaside resort; the plentiful tables are sheltered by a big fairy-lit tree (not so long ago identified by Kew Gardens as a rare Greek Whitebeam), and in summer there's an outside bar. Inside, the two chatty main rooms have something of the air of the hotel this once was, as well as comfortable long banquettes curving round the tables in the deep bay windows, local prints and photographs, an old-fashioned wooden island servery, and a good mix of variously aged customers. Two of three log fires have mirrors above them – unusually, the third is underneath a window. A bright and airy upstairs room has lots more tables and a number of plates on a shelf running round the walls; a couple of tables are squeezed onto a little balcony. Youngs Bitter, Special and seasonal beers on handpump, and a good range of 15 or so carefully chosen wines by the glass. From a servery at the foot of the stairs, lunchtime bar food includes sandwiches, and a variety of hot dishes such as home-made sausages or sweet potato and cream cheese bake (£5.95), and game pie or kangaroo in port sauce (£6.60). No music or machines – the only games are backgammon and chess. Boats leave from immediately outside to Kingston or Hampton Court. Make sure when leaving your car outside that you know the tide times – it's not unknown for the water to rise right up the steps into the bar, completely covering anything that gets in the way. *(Recommended by Val Stevenson, Rob Holmes, B J Harding, David and Carole Chapman, Nigel Williamson, Comus Elliott, Ian Phillips, David and Nina Pugsley, Tony Scott)*

Youngs ~ Licensees Ian and Phyl Heggie ~ Real ale ~ Bar food (12-4 only) ~ (020) 8940 6844 ~ Children in upstairs room ~ Open 11-11; 12-10.30 Sun

Windmill ♀

Clapham Common South Side, SW4; ⊖ Clapham Common/Clapham South

Big and bustling, this Victorian pub at times seems to serve all the visitors to neighbouring Clapham Common, yet it's spacious enough to mean that however busy it gets you should be able to find a quiet corner. A painting in the Tate by J P Herring has the Windmill in the background, shown behind local turn-of-the-century characters returning from the Derby Day festivities; it hasn't changed that much since. The comfortable and smartly civilised main bar has plenty of prints and pictures on the walls, real fires, and a mix of tables and seating. Bar food such as sandwiches and baguettes (from £3.50), steak and ale pie, chargrilled burgers and salads (£5.50); service is prompt and friendly. The Youngs Bitter, Special and seasonal beers are reckoned by one reader to taste better here than just about anywhere else in London; also a good choice of wines by the glass and plenty more by the bottle. Bar billiards, cribbage, dominoes, fruit machine, trivia, piped music. We imagine the bedrooms would merit a stay award, though we rarely hear from anyone who's used them. *(Recommended by Ian Phillips, Susan and John Douglas, P A Legon)*

Youngs ~ Managers James and Rachel Watt ~ Real ale ~ Bar food ~ Restaurant ~ (020) 8673 4578 ~ Children in eating area of bar and conservatory till 9pm ~ Open 11-11; 12-10.30 Sun; closed 12-2.30, 7-10; 12-10 Sat, Sun ~ Bedrooms: £90B/£100B

WEST LONDON Map 13

During weekdays or Saturday daytime you may not be able to find a meter very close to either of the two Anglesea Arms or to the Windsor Castle, and parking very near in the evening may sometimes be tricky for all of these, but there shouldn't otherwise be problems in this area

Anglesea Arms

15 Selwood Terrace, SW7; ✪ South Kensington

Genuinely old-fashioned and delightfully chatty, this old favourite is going from strength to strength at the moment. Despite the surrounding affluence the pub has always been friendly and unpretentious, managing to feel both smart and cosy at the same time. The elegantly characterful bar has central elbow tables, a mix of cast-iron tables on the bare wood-strip floor, wood panelling, and big windows with attractive swagged curtains; at one end several booths with partly glazed screens have cushioned pews and spindleback chairs. The smaller area down some steps has in the last few months been transformed into a separate eating area, in recognition perhaps of the pub's growing popularity for good food; it still has its Victorian fireplace. The traditional mood is heightened by some heavy portraits, prints of London, a big station clock, bits of brass and pottery, and large brass chandeliers. On busy evenings customers spill out onto the terrace and pavement. A very good choice of real ales might include Adnams Broadside, Brakspears, Fullers London Pride, Harveys Sussex, Wadworths 6X, and Youngs; they also keep a few bottled Belgian beers (the landlord is quite a fan), and several malt and Irish whiskies. The lunchtime menu includes filled baguettes, salmon fishcakes (£5.30), and rib-eye steak (£6.50), while in the evening you'll find things like dressed crab (£4) and brochettes of duck (£9); they do Sunday roasts. Service is notably friendly and helpful. The pub is very popular with well heeled young people, but is well liked by locals too; perhaps that's because many of the locals are well heeled young people. *(Recommended by T Barrow, S Demont, David Carr, Mrs Thomas Pierpont Grose, Mick Hitchman, Tony Scott)*

Scottish Courage ~ Licensees Andrew Ford, T W Simpson, Milan Kolundzic ~ Real ale ~ Bar food (12-3, 6-10) ~ Restaurant ~ (020) 7373 7960 ~ Children in eating area of bar and restaurant ~ Open 11-11; 12-10.30 Sun

Anglesea Arms ⊕ ♀

35 Wingate St, W6; ✪ Ravenscourt Park

One reader tells us that on his regular visits here he enjoys sitting right by the kitchen, taking great pleasure from watching what really is top-notch food being prepared from scratch. A number of smart locals come here just for a drink, but it's the meals that encourage most people to seek it out. Changing every lunchtime and evening, the inventive menu might include several starters like Catalan-style chorizo, garlic and eel gratin (£4.75), sautéed lamb sweetbreads, with pappardelle, pancetta, button onions and mushrooms (£4.75), deep-fried stuffed courgette flowers with wild goat's curd (£5), and pigeon and foie gras terrine (£5.25), and half a dozen or so main courses such as risotto primavera with shaved parmesan and salsa rossa (£7.50), stuffed saddle of rabbit with caramelised shallots (£9), chargrilled chump of lamb (£9.75), and toasted scallops with minted green split peas, bacon and tarragon (£10); good puddings, and some unusual farmhouse cheeses (£4.50). The eating area leads off the bar but feels quite separate, with skylights creating a brighter feel, closely packed tables, and a big modern mural along one wall; directly opposite is the kitchen, with several chefs frantically working on the meals. You can't book, so best to get there early for a table. It feels a lot more restauranty than, say, the Eagle, and they clearly have their own way of doing things; service can be a little inflexible, and efficient rather than friendly. The bar is rather plainly decorated, but cosy in winter when the roaring fire casts long flickering shadows on the dark panelling. Neatly stacked piles of wood guard either side of the fireplace (which has a stopped clock above it), and there are some well worn green leatherette chairs and stools. Courage Best and Directors, Marstons Pedigree and Theakstons XB on handpump, and a good range of carefully chosen wines listed above the bar. A couple of readers find the place a bit smoky. Several tables outside overlook the quiet street (not the easiest place to find a parking space). Despite its out of the way location, this busy place is one of the best-known of London's gastro-pubs. *(Recommended by John A Barker, Richard Siebert)*

Scottish Courage ~ Lease: Dan and Fiona Evans ~ Real ale ~ Bar food (12.30-2.45, 7.30-10.45) ~ (020) 8749 1291 ~ Children welcome ~ Open 11-11; 12-10.30 Sun; closed one week over Christmas and New Year

Atlas 🍴 ♀

16 Seagrave Rd, SW6; ⊖ West Brompton

Not so long ago the Atlas was the kind of pub that merited a fleeting visit at best (particularly galling when your Associate Editor lived directly across the road), so it was quite a surprise when we heard about its dramatic transformation. It's now run by two brothers, one of whom used to be a chef at the Eagle, which should give an idea of the quality of the food. Listed on a blackboard above the brick fireplace, and changing every day, the shortish choice of excellent meals might include soup, substantial ciabatta sandwiches (£7), roast chicken piri-piri or grilled Tuscan sausage with spicy black beans (£8), Spanish rabbit stew or grilled tenderloin of pork (£9), and whole baked bass or roast rainbow trout (£10); no puddings, but good cheeses. The long knocked-together bar has been nicely renovated without removing the original features; there's plenty of panelling and dark wooden wall benches, with a mix of school chairs and well spaced tables. The atmosphere is relaxed, chatty, and friendly; smart young folk figure prominently in the mix, but there are plenty of locals too, as well as visitors to the Exhibition Centre at Earls Court (one of the biggest car parks is next door). Charles Wells Bombardier, Theakstons Best and Wadworths 6X on handpump, and a well chosen wine list, with a changing range of around ten by the glass; friendly service. The piped music is unusual – one reader hated the salsa, but on our balmy summer evening inspection it seemed to fit rather well (there was jazz too); down at the end is a TV, by a hatch to the kitchen. At the side is a narrow yard with lots of tables and colourful plants; they plan to extend this, and add heaters for winter. *(Recommended by Dr Lyn Webb, Stuart Cotton)*

Free house ~ Licensees Richard and George Manners ~ Real ale ~ Bar food ~ (020) 7385 9129 ~ Children lunchtimes only ~ Open 12-11(10.30 Sun)

Bulls Head

Strand-on-the-Green, W4; ⊖ Kew Bridge

Strand-on-the-Green is a delight for those who enjoy Thameside pubs, and it can be hard choosing between this well worn old place and its even older neighbour the City Barge. The pleasant little rooms ramble through black-panelled alcoves and up and down steps, and the traditional furnishings include benches built into the simple panelling and so forth. Small windows look past attractively planted hanging flower baskets to the river just beyond the narrow towpath. Well kept Courage Directors, Greene King IPA, Theakstons Best, Wadworths 6X and a guest on handpump. Well liked bar food, served all day, includes filled baguettes (£4.95), spinach and ricotta cannelloni (£5.50), chicken tikka (£5.95), a roast (£5.99), rack of ribs (£7.50), and 10 oz rump steak (£8.50); the food area is no smoking. A games room at the back has darts, fruit machine and trivia. The pub isn't too crowded even on fine evenings, though it can get busy at weekends, especially when they have a raft race on the river. The original building on this spot served as Cromwell's HQ several times during the Civil War, and it was here that Moll Cutpurse overheard Cromwell talking to Fairfax about the troops' pay money coming by horse from Hounslow, and got her gang to capture the moneybags; they were later recovered at Turnham Green. *(Recommended by*

Jenny and Brian Seller, Gordon, David and Carole Chapman, David Carr, Simon Collett-Jones, Brian Higgins, Ana Kolkowska)

Scottish Courage ~ Manager Bob McPhee ~ Real ale ~ Bar food (12-10) ~ (020) 8994 1204 ~ Children in conservatory ~ Open 11-11; 12-10.30 Sun

Churchill Arms ◀

119 Kensington Church St, W8; ⊖ Notting Hill Gate/Kensington High St

Whether it be Halloween, St Patrick's Day or even Churchill's birthday (November 30th), they like to celebrate at this bustling, cheery place, which on any day feels very much like a busy village local. The vibrant atmosphere owes a lot to the notably friendly (and chatty) Irish landlord, who works hard and enthusiastically to give visitors an individual welcome. One of his hobbies is collecting butterflies, so you'll see a variety of prints and books on the subject dotted around the bar. There are also countless lamps, miners' lights, horse tack, bedpans and brasses hanging from the ceiling, a couple of interesting carved figures and statuettes behind the central bar counter, prints of American presidents, and lots of Churchill memorabilia. Well kept Fullers Chiswick, ESB, London Pride, and seasonal beers on handpump. The pub can get crowded in the evenings, so even early in the week it's not really a place to come for a quiet pint; it can get a bit smoky too. The spacious and rather smart plant-filled dining conservatory may be used for hatching butterflies, but is better known for its big choice of really excellent Thai food, such as a very good, proper Thai curry, or duck with noodles (£5.25). Service in this part – run separately from the pub – isn't always as friendly as in the pub. They also do things like lunchtime sandwiches (from £1.50), ploughman's (£2.25), home-made steak and kidney pie (£2.75), and Sunday lunch. Shove-ha'penny, fruit machine, and unobtrusive piped music; they have their own cricket and football teams. *(Recommended by LM, David Peakall, Susan and John Douglas, George and Jill Little, Klaus and Elizabeth Leist, John Knighton, Tony Scott)*

Fullers ~ Manager Jerry O'Brien ~ Real ale ~ Bar food (12-2.30, 6-10) ~ Restaurant ~ (020) 7727 4242 ~ Children in eating area of bar and restaurant ~ Open 11-11; 12-10.30 Sun

Dove

19 Upper Mall, W6; ⊖ Ravenscourt Park

Said to be where 'Rule Britannia' was composed, this old-fashioned Thameside tavern is the nicest of the clutch of pubs punctuating this stretch of the river. Its best feature is the very pleasant tiny back terrace, where the main flagstoned area, down some steps, has a few highly prized teak tables and white metal and teak chairs looking over the low river wall to the Thames reach just above Hammersmith Bridge. If you're able to bag a spot out here in the evenings, you'll often see rowing crews practising their strokes. By the entrance from the quiet alley, the main bar has black wood panelling, red leatherette cushioned built-in wall settles and stools around dimpled copper tables, old framed advertisements, and photographs of the pub; well kept Fullers London Pride and ESB on handpump. Bar food includes satay chicken (£4.50), lasagne (£4.95), lamb burger, cod and chips or steak and kidney pudding (£5.95), and nut roast provençal (£6.95). No games machines or piped music. It's not quite so crowded at lunchtimes as it is in the evenings. A plaque marks the level of the highest-ever tide in 1928. Note they don't allow children. *(Recommended by Jasper Sabey, Mick Hitchman, Alison McCarthy, Greg Kilminster, D J and P M Taylor, Tony Scott, David Carr, Brian Higgins, Ana Kolkowska, the Didier, Gordon, Jestyn Thirkell-White)*

Fullers ~ Manager M L Delves ~ Real ale ~ Bar food (12-2.30, 6.30-9; not Sun lunchtime) ~ Restaurant ~ (020) 8748 9474 ~ Open 11-11; 12-10.30 Sun; closed 26 Dec

Ladbroke Arms

54 Ladbroke Rd, W11; ⊖ Holland Park

A good bet for a well above average meal, this popular food pub is handy for Holland

Park and Notting Hill. There's a warm red hue to its neatly kept bar (especially up in the slightly raised area with fireplace), as well as simple wooden tables and chairs, comfortable red-cushioned wall-seats, several colonial-style fans on the ceiling, some striking moulding on the dado, colourful flowers on the bar, newspapers and *Country Life* back numbers, and a broad mix of customers and age-groups; soft piped jazz blends in with the smartly chatty atmosphere. The landlord deals in art so the interesting prints can change on each visit. Well kept beers are rotated from a range that takes in Adnams Broadside, Courage Best and Directors, Everards Tiger and Greene King Abbot; also a dozen malt whiskies, and a good wine list. Chalked up on a couple of blackboards on the right hand side of the central servery, the imaginative range of home-made bar meals might typically include soup (£3.25), rabbit and chorizo terrine with tomato and coriander chutney (£4.95), and good main courses between around £7 and £14, such as salt cod fishcakes with red pepper relish and aioli or grilled brochette of lamb with couscous. Lots of picnic-sets in front, overlooking the quiet street. *(Recommended by Mick Hitchman, Jilly and George Little, Ian Phillips, Jill Bickerton, Evelyn and Derek Walter)*

Courage (S & N) ~ Tenant Ian McKenzie ~ Real ale ~ Bar food (12-2.30, 6.30-10) ~ Restaurant ~ (020) 7727 6648 ~ Children in eating area of bar ~ Open 11-11; 12-10.30 Sun; closed 25 Dec

White Horse ♀ ◖

1 Parsons Green, SW6; ⊖ Parsons Green

As we went to press this meticulously run pub was about to close for refurbishment, though it should have reopened by the time the book hits the shops. The main attraction is the eclectic range of drinks, which as well as particularly well kept Adnams Extra, Bass, Harveys Sussex, and perhaps an unusual guest (with some helpful tasting notes), takes in 15 Trappist beers and a good few other foreign bottled beers, a dozen malt whiskies, and good, interesting and not overpriced wines. It's usually busy (sometimes very much so), but there are enough smiling, helpful staff behind the solid panelled central servery to ensure you'll rarely have to wait to be served. Food is well liked and often inventive; their weekend brunch is especially popular (£5.25), and in winter they do a very good Sunday lunch. The spacious U-shaped bar has big leather chesterfields on the wood plank floor, and huge windows with slatted wooden blinds; the area to one side has a marble fireplace. It's a favourite with smart young people, so earning the pub its well known soubriquet 'the Sloaney Pony'; many locals never refer to it at all by its proper name. On summer evenings the front terrace overlooking the green has something of a continental feel, with crowds of people drinking al fresco at the white cast-iron tables and chairs; there may be imaginative Sunday barbecues. They have regular beer festivals (often spotlighting regional breweries), as well as lively celebrations on American Independence Day or Thanksgiving. *(Recommended by D P and J A Sweeney, A Hepburn, S Jenner, Tracey and Stephen Groves, ALC, H Flaherty)*

Bass ~ Managers Mark Dorber and Rupert Reeves ~ Real ale ~ Bar food (12-3, 5.30-10) ~ Restaurant ~ (020) 7736 2115 ~ Open 11-11; 12-10.30 Sun; closed 24-27 Dec

White Swan

Riverside; ⇌ Twickenham

Reassuringly traditional, this 17th-c riverside house is built on a platform well above ground level, with steep steps leading up to the door and to a sheltered terrace, full of tubs and baskets of flowers. Even the cellar is raised above ground, as insurance against the flood tides which wash right up to the house. Across the peaceful almost rural lane is a little riverside lawn, where tables look across a quiet stretch of the Thames to country meadows on its far bank past the top of Eel Pie Island. The friendly unspoilt bar has bare boards, big rustic tables and other simple wooden furnishings, and blazing winter fires. The photographs on the walls are of regulars and staff as children, while a back room reflects the landlord's devotion to rugby, with lots of ties, shorts, balls and pictures. Readers like the weekday lunchtime buffet, which in summer might include everything from cheese and ham to trout and smoked salmon; other bar food includes sandwiches (from £2), soup (£2), and winter lancashire hotpot or calf's liver (£5). Well kept Charles Wells Bombardier, Courage Best, Marstons Pedigree, Morlands Old Speckled Hen and Websters on handpump, with around 10 wines by the glass; backgammon, cribbage, piped blues or jazz. They have an annual raft race on the river the last Saturday in July, and there's an equally enthusiastic Burns Night celebration. The pub can get busy at weekends and some evenings. It's a short stroll to the imposing Palladian Marble Hill House in its grand Thameside park (built for a mistress of George II). *(Recommended by Dr and Mrs A K Clarke)*

Scottish Courage ~ Managers Steve and Kirsten Roy ~ Real ale ~ Bar food (12-3, 7-9) ~ (020) 8892 2166 ~ Children welcome ~ Live entertainment some winter Weds ~ Open 11-11; 12-10.30 Sun; 11-3, 5.30-11 Mon-Thurs winter

Windsor Castle

114 Campden Hill Road, W8; ⊖ Holland Park/Notting Hill Gate

The big tree-shaded area at the back of this unchanging old place is a real draw in summer (it's closed in winter). There are lots of sturdy teak seats and tables on flagstones – you'll have to move fast to bag one on a sunny day – as well as a brick garden bar, and quite a secluded feel thanks to the high ivy-covered sheltering walls. The series of unspoilt and small rooms inside all have to be entered through separate doors, so it can be quite a challenge finding the people you've arranged to meet – more often than not they'll be hidden behind the high backs of the sturdy built-in elm benches. Time-smoked ceilings and soft lighting characterise the bar, and a cosy pre-war-style dining room opens off. Bar food includes filled ciabattas (£5), home-made salmon and haddock fishcakes (£6.50), and steamed mussels and oysters, good fish and chips, or often unusual sausages with mash and onion gravy (all £6.95). Bass and Fullers London Pride on handpump, along with decent house wines, various malt whiskies, and maybe mulled wine in winter; a round of drinks can turn out rather expensive. No fruit machines or piped music. Usually fairly quiet at lunchtime (when one room is no smoking), the pub can be packed some evenings, often with smart young people. Some of the mostly young staff can still leave you waiting alone at the bar for quite some time. *(Recommended by Susan and John Douglas, Jasper Sabey, Mick Hitchman, Alison McCarthy, Val Stevenson, Rob Holmes)*

Bass ~ Manager Carole Jabbour ~ Real ale ~ Bar food (12-10.30(10 Sun)) ~ (020) 7243 9551 ~ Children in eating area of bar ~ Open 12-11; 12-10.30 Sun

---

Lucky Dip

Besides the fully inspected pubs, you might like to try these Lucky Dips recommended to us and described by readers (if you do, please send us reports). We have split them into the main areas used for the full reports – Central, North, and so on. Within each area the Lucky Dips are listed by postal district. The entries for pubs in the Greater London suburbs are listed at the end.

CENTRAL LONDON

☆ *Mortimer* [Mortimer St, corner Goodge St/Berners St]: New food pub with good interesting modern food, well kept Adnams, very good wine choice, freshly squeezed orange juice, good coffees, friendly staff, lots of tables in pleasant pavement area; busy on weekdays, very quiet w/e *(BB, Charlie Ballantyne)*

EC1

Britannia [Ironmonger Row]: Comfortable, welcoming and busy, with well kept Boddingtons, Fullers London Pride and ESB and Marstons Pedigree, fairly priced lunchtime food, traditional games; open all day, live music w/e *(Peter Plumridge, Richard Lewis)*

Crown [Clerkenwell Green]: Large friendly neatly kept corner pub with real ales such as

Adnams, Batemans Jollys Jaunt, Jennings Ushers Founders, full menu inc lots of filled baguettes, tables out on square; handy for Marx Memorial Library *(Ian Phillips)*

Melton Mowbray [Holborn]: Large pastiche of Edwardian pub attractively done with lots of woodwork, etched glass, front button-back banquettes (opening in summer on to pavement café tables), back booths, tables on small upstairs gallery; well kept Fullers ales, friendly staff, sandwiches and simple hot dishes, good food service even when packed with lunchtime suits *(Ian Phillips, Greg Kilminster, John Fazakerley, Dr M E Wilson)*

☆ *Pheasant & Firkin* [Goswell Rd]: Genuine local feel (a rare treat for EC1, as is the Sun evening opening), with down-to-earth concentration on good beer (own cheap light Pluckers, also good

value Pheasant and powerful Dogbolter brewed
here), and basic food at very reasonable prices;
bare boards, plenty of bar stools, very friendly
service, daily papers, good cheap CD juke box
(Peter Plumridge, Jane Keeton, LYM)
Sekforde Arms [Sekforde St]: Small corner
Youngs pub with friendly welcome and well kept
beers; pavement tables *(the Didler)*

EC2

51 Gresham Street [Gresham St]: Traditional
City pub and cellar bar done by Fullers in big
modern office block, their beers kept well, food
inc hot and cold sandwiches, filled baps, hot
dishes *(Ian Phillips)*
☆ *Dirty Dicks* [Bishopsgate]: Traditional City cellar
(now a Whitbreads Hogshead) with bare boards,
brick barrel-vaulted ceiling, interesting old prints
inc one of Nathaniel Bentley, the original Dirty
Dick; good choice of real ales, wine racks
overhead, decent food inc open sandwiches,
baguettes and reasonably priced hot dishes,
pleasant service, loads of character – fun for
foreign visitors *(LYM, Francis and Deirdre
Gevers, Ian Phillips, David and Carole
Chapman, Tony Scott)*
☆ *Hamilton Hall* [Bishopsgate; also entrance from
L'pool St Stn]: A Wetherspoons flagship, striking
Victorian baroque décor, plaster nudes and fruit
mouldings, chandeliers, mirrors, upper mezzanine,
good-sized upstairs no-smoking section (not
always open, though – can get crowded and
smoky downstairs), comfortable groups of seats,
reliable food all day from well filled baguettes up,
well kept low-priced Scottish Courage and guest
beers; fruit machine, video game but no piped
music; open all day – and of course the lavatories
are free, unlike Railtrack's extortionate ones
nearby *(Tim Barrow, Sue Demont, J Fahy, Tony
Scott, Paul and Ursula Randall, Anthony Barnes,
LYM, Dr and Mrs A K Clarke)*

EC3

Cheshire Cheese [Crutched Friars, via arch under
Fenchurch St Stn]: Large pub with upstairs
lounge, lots of tables and shelves for plates or
glasses; busy lunchtime (mainly standing then),
with good choice of sandwiches and pies, other
hot dishes, Bass, Fullers London Pride; big screen
sports TV evening *(Ian Phillips)*
Hoop & Grapes [Aldgate High St]: Largely late
17th-c (dismantled and rebuilt 1983), with
Jacobean staircase, carved oak doorposts and
age-blackened oak serving counter; long narrow
beamed and timbered bar, good food, well kept
ales such as Adnams, Fullers and Jennings; cl Sun
evening, open all day weekdays, very popular
(Tony Scott)
Lamb [Grand Ave, Leadenhall Mkt]: Old-
fashioned stand-up market bar with engraved
glass, plenty of ledges and shelves, spiral stairs to
mezzanine with lots of tables, light and airy top-
floor no-smoking carpeted lounge bar
overlooking market's central crossing, with plenty
of seats and corner servery strong on cooked
meats inc hot sandwiches; well kept Bass, Youngs
and a guest beer; also smoky basement bar with
shiny wall tiling and own entrance *(the Didler)*

EC4

Old Bell [Fleet St, nr Ludgate Circus]: Fine old
intimate tavern (rebuilt by Wren as commissariat
for his workers on nearby church), lively
atmosphere, some tables tucked away to give a
sense of privacy; Bass and a guest beer, good
sandwiches *(the Didler, Tony Scott)*
☆ *Punch* [Fleet St]: Warm, comfortable, softly lit
Victorian pub, not too smart despite superb tiled
entrance with mirrored lobby; dozens of *Punch*
cartoons, ornate plaster ceiling with unusual
domed skylight, good bar food, Bass and guest
beers such as Marstons and Wadworths *(the
Didler, Kevin Blake)*

SW1

☆ *Antelope* [Eaton Terr]: Stylish panelled local,
rather superior but friendly; bare boards, lots of
interesting prints and old advertisements, well
kept ales such as Adnams, Fullers London Pride,
Marstons Pedigree and Tetleys, good house
wines, sandwiches, baked potatoes, ploughman's
and one-price hot dishes; quiet and relaxed
upstairs weekday lunchtimes, can get crowded
evenings; open all day, children in eating area
(LYM, the Didler, Ian Phillips, Gordon)
☆ *Buckingham Arms* [Petty France]: Congenial
Youngs local close to Passport Office and
Buckingham Palace, lots of mirrors and
woodwork, unusual long side corridor fitted out
with elbow ledge for drinkers, well kept ales,
decent simple food, reasonable prices, service
friendly and efficient even when busy; SkyTV for
motor sports (open Sat); handy for Westminster
Abbey and St James's Park *(LYM, the Didler,
Rachael and Mark Baynham)*
Cask & Glass [Palace St]: Tiny inviting Shepherd
Neame pub, single room overflowing into street
in summer – colourful flowers then; pleasant
surroundings, good service, limited lunchtime
food, handy for Queen's Gallery *(Jill Bickerton)*
Colonies [Wilfred St]: Friendly and comfortable
open-plan split-level pub with surprisingly local
feel, good typical lunchtime food from good
sandwiches up, Courage Best and Directors and
Theakstons Best, African bric-a-brac; very
popular with Palace St civil servants *(Miss W
Reynolds, Stephen Bonarjee)*
Duke of Wellington [Eaton Terr]: Busy and
friendly, in elegant street not far from house
where Mozart lived; popular reasonably priced
lunchtime food and well kept Shepherd Neame
(M A Hickman)
☆ *Fox & Hounds* [Passmore St/Graham Terr]:
Unchanging unpretentious weekday lunchtime
calm in small cosy single bar with just a beer and
wine licence – well kept ales such as Adnams,
Bass, Greene King IPA and Harveys, also wines,
sherries, vermouths etc; very friendly landlady
and staff, narrow bar with wall benches, big
hunting prints, old sepia photographs of pubs
and customers, some toby jugs, hanging plants
under attractive skylight in back room, coal-
effect gas fire; piano replaced by shorter-
keyboard organ (not such a tight fit – you can
now reach the bottom octave); can be very busy
Fri night, maybe quieter Sat *(Gordon, Robert
Lester, Glynn Davis)*

Molly O'Gradys: Still succeeds in developing Irish atmosphere despite being in a food court over a shopping arcade above a station; good value food with an Irish tinge too *(Dave Braisted)*

☆ *Morpeth Arms* [Millbank]: Roomy Victorian Youngs pub handy for the Tate, some etched and cut glass, old books and prints, photographs, earthenware jars and bottles; busy lunchtimes, quieter evenings – well kept ales inc a seasonal one, good range of food from sandwiches up, good choice of wines, helpful staff; seats outside (a lot of traffic) *(BB, Tim Barrow, Sue Demont, Ian Phillips, Tim and Linda Collins)*

☆ *Paxtons Head* [Knightsbridge]: Peaceful classy Victorian pub, attractive period décor and furnishings inc gas lamps, and Victorian etched glass and mirrors from Paxton's Crystal Palace; large central bar, decent lunchtime food, unobtrusive piped music, real ales such as Adnams and Courage Directors *(the Didler)*

☆ *Red Lion* [Crown Passage, behind St James's St]: Nice unpretentious early Victorian local tucked down narrow passage nr Christies, panelling and leaded lights giving a timeless feel, friendly relaxed atmosphere, decent lunchtime food, unobtrusive piped music, real ales such as Adnams and Courage Directors *(Gordon, James Nunns, BB)*

☆ *Red Lion* [Duke of York St]: Busy little pub, flowers cascading down outside, notable inside for dazzling mirrors, crystal chandeliers and cut and etched windows, gleaming mahogany, ornamental plaster ceiling – architecturally, central London's most perfect small Victorian pub (it is very small indeed); good value proper sandwiches, snacks and hot dishes in minuscule upstairs eating area (recently a few front tables downstairs have had tablecloths and a sign saying diners may require them – a good compromise), well kept Hardy Country and Tetleys, friendly efficient service; can be very crowded at lunchtime, customers spilling out on to pavement *(Dr M E Wilson, J Fahy, LYM, P G Plumridge, Gordon)*

Tattershall Castle [off Victoria Embankment]: Converted paddle steamer – marvellous vantage point for watching river traffic; canopied bar serveries with snacks, barbecues and ice creams too in summer, for both forward and aft decks with picnic-sets; wardroom bar, restaurant and nightclub below decks *(Dave Braisted, BB)*

Walkers of St James [Duke St]: Busy basement pub, friendly welcome, well kept beer, sensible bar food *(Dr and Mrs A K Clarke)*

☆ *Wetherspoons* [Victoria Station]: Warm, comfortable and individual, a (relatively) calm haven above the station's bustle, with very cheap ever-changing real ales inc interesting guest beers, wide choice of reasonably priced decent food all day, prompt friendly service, good furnishings and housekeeping – and great for people-watchers, with glass walls and tables outside overlooking the main concourse and platform indicators *(Tony and Wendy Hobden, George Atkinson, Tim Barrow, Sue Demont, Stephen Bonarjee)*

Wilton Arms [Kinnerton St]: Pleasant and comfortable civilised local with friendly atmosphere, Whitbreads-related ales, bar food; open all day *(Tony Scott)*

SW3

☆ *Front Page* [Old Church St]: Civilised local with good interesting bistro food, heavy wooden furnishings, white-painted panelling, huge windows and big ceiling fans for airy feel, good wines, well kept real ales; big-screen sports TV; open all day *(LYM, James Nunns, Jasper Sabey)*

W1

☆ *Audley* [Mount St]: Solid opulence, all red plush and cornices, with High Victorian woodwork, clock hanging from ornate ceiling in lovely carved wood bracket, well kept Courage Best and Directors from long polished bar, good food and service, good coffee, upstairs panelled dining room; open all day *(LYM, Ian Phillips, Tony Scott)*

Beehive [Homer St, just off Edgware Rd]: Small hidden-away country-feel pub with unfussy décor, wonderful pictures of Victorian London, friendly helpful landlady *(Dan Wilson)*

Carpenters Arms [Seymour Pl]: Bare boards, friendly staff, wide choice of well kept ales inc various Harveys; can get very busy early evening *(Dan Wilson)*

Champion [Wells St]: Good value Sam Smiths pub with upstairs dining area; very handy for shopping *(Rachael and Mark Baynham, Tim Barrow, Sue Demont, Mick Hitchman)*

Clachan [Kingly St]: Wide changing range of ales and above-average food in comfortable well kept pub behind Libertys, ornate plaster ceiling supported by two large fluted and decorated pillars, smaller drinking alcove up three or four steps; can get very busy *(Tim Barrow, Sue Demont, DC)*

Cock [Great Portland St]: Large corner local with enormous lamps over picnic-sets outside, Victorian tiled floor, lots of wood inc good carving, some cut and etched glass, high tiled ceiling, ornate plasterwork, velvet curtains, coal-effect gas fire; popular lunchtime food in upstairs lounge with coal-effect gas fire each end, full Sam Smiths range kept well at bargain prices *(Rachael and Mark Baynham, Rob)*

Devonshire Arms [Denman St]: Small bustling wood-and-sawdust bar downstairs, small lounge up, food all day, welcoming friendly staff, well kept Courage Best and Directors, interesting mix of customers *(Christopher Glasson)*

Dover Castle [Weymouth Mews]: Quiet, simple and cosy, some panelling and old prints, snug back area, cheap Sam Smiths OB; quiet at w/e *(Tim Barrow, Sue Demont)*

Fanfare & Firkin [Gt Marlborough St]: Typical bare-boards Firkin, split-level back room, their own ales kept well, hot baps etc, piped music; lavatories down stairs *(SLC)*

Fitz & Firkin [Gt Portland St]: Usual Firkin style, well kept Fitz, Great Titchfield, DOA and Dogbolter, good menu, lots of friendly efficient staff (can be very busy); open all day, some live music *(Richard Lewis)*

Guinea [Bruton Pl]: Well kept Youngs, bar food inc good steak and kidney pudding and ciabatta-bread sandwiches, decent wines, lunchtime suits spilling out into mews; separate restaurant *(Richard Gibbs, LYM, Thomas Shortt, Andy and Jill Kassube)*

King & Queen [Foley St]: Rare Adnams pub, their beers kept well, friendly landlord; quiet w/e *(Tim Barrow, Sue Demont)*

Masons Arms [Seymour Pl]: Roomy pub with convincing flame-effect fires, a few little private nooks, Badger ales *(Dan Wilson)*

☆ *O'Connor Don* [Marylebone Lane]: Enjoyable and civilised, Irish (genuinely and unobtrusively so, unlike the usual new so-called Irish pubs), with good sandwiches and other freshly made bar food, waitress drinks service (to make sure the Guinness has settled properly), warm bustling atmosphere; good upstairs restaurant with daily fresh Galway oysters, folk music Sat *(Jill Bickerton, BB)*

☆ *Old Coffee House* [Beak St]: Masses of interesting bric-a-brac, unusually wide choice of decent lunchtime food (not Sun) in upstairs food room full of prints and pictures, well kept Courage Best and Directors and Marstons Pedigree; fruit machine, piped music; children allowed upstairs 12-3, open all day exc Sun afternoon *(Tony Hobden, LYM, Dr M E Wilson, Ian Phillips, Simon Collett-Jones)*

Red Lion [Kingly St]: Friendly, solidly modernised without being spoilt, with well kept Sam Smiths at a sensible price, reasonably priced food upstairs; video juke box *(Susan and Nigel Wilson, BB)*

Toucan [Carlisle St]: Small Guinness pub, five taps for it in relaxed dark and cosy basement bar with toucan paintings and Guinness advertisements, Irish whiskey and good Irish piped music, enjoyable food such as Guinness pie, Irish stew, Galway oysters; lighter upstairs bar overflows on to pavement when busy; quiet TV in both bars *(Andrew Abbess, Michael McGarry)*

William Wallace [Blandford St]: Good choice of Scottish beers and foods *(David Atkinson)*

W2

☆ *Victoria* [Strathearn Pl]: Interesting corner local, lots of Victorian Royal and other memorabilia, *Vanity Fair* cartoons and unusual little military paintings, two cast-iron fireplaces, wonderful gilded mirrors and mahogany panelling, bare boards and banquettes, friendly managers, Fullers ales, well priced food counter; quiet piped music, pavement picnic-sets; upstairs (not always open) replica of Gaiety Theatre bar, all gilt and red plush, with piano Sat *(Dan Wilson, Ian Phillips, LYM, James Nunns)*

WC1

Calthorpe Arms [Grays Inn Rd]: Consistently well kept Youngs Bitter, Special and seasonal beer at sensible prices in relaxed and unpretentious corner pub with plush wall seats, big helpings of popular food upstairs lunchtime and evening; nice pavement tables *(the Didler)*

Enterprise [Red Lion St]: No-frills pub, bare boards and high ceiling give a spartan feel at quiet times, with tiled walls and big mirrors, well kept Bass and Fullers London Pride, wide range of reasonably priced food, small back garden; gets busy evening *(Dr M E Wilson, Greg Kilminster)*

Pakenham Arms [Pakenham St]: Relaxed unspoilt split-level local, generally quiet at lunchtime and w/e; well kept ales such as

Adnams, Brakspears and unusual guest beers, big helpings of good value simple food *(Tim Barrow, Sue Demont)*

☆ *Princess Louise* [High Holborn]: Etched and gilt mirrors, brightly coloured and fruity-shaped tiles, slender Portland stone columns, lofty and elaborately colourful ceiling, attractively priced Sam Smiths from the long counter (no longer the wide range of real ales they used to have), quieter plush-seated corners, simple bar snacks, upstairs lunchtime buffet; even the Victorian gents' has its own preservation order; crowded and lively during the week, usually quieter late evening, or Sat lunchtime; all day, cl Sun *(the Didler, Dr Oscar Puls, LYM, Tony Scott, Rachael and Mark Baynham)*

Rugby [Rugby St]: Well kept Fullers ales and good service in fairly big one-bar corner pub with good atmosphere, muted beige décor, a few cartoons *(JP, PP)*

Skinners Arms [Judd St]: Greene King pub, refurbished with side bar replacing the traditional central one, lunchtime food, two back rooms, well kept IPA and Abbot, tables outside; open all day *(Richard Lewis)*

WC2

Champagne Charlies [The Arches, off Villiers St]: Down in the vaults, Davys bar in busy but relaxing series of knocked-through rooms, their usual food, champagne by the glass, real ales such as their Old Wallop and Hardys Royal Oak (in half-gallon copper jugs if you like), interesting triptych on walls, quick friendly service *(Rona Murdoch)*

☆ *Chandos* [St Martins Lane]: Open all day from 9 (for breakfast), very busy downstairs bare-boards bar, quieter more comfortable upstairs with alcoves and opera photographs, low wooden tables, panelling, leather sofas, orange, red and yellow leaded windows; generally enjoyable food from sandwiches to Sunday roasts, well kept cheap Sam Smiths Mild, Stout and OB, air conditioning (but can get packed and smoky early evening), prompt cheerful mainly antipodean service; children upstairs till 6, darts, pinball, fruit machines, video game, trivia and piped music; note the automaton on the roof (working 10-2 and 4-9) *(Susan and Nigel Wilson, John Fazakerley, Tony and Wendy Hobden, Dr S J Shepherd, Jim Bush, Mick Hitchman, LYM, Peter and Pat Frogley, SLC)*

Griffin [Villiers St]: Recently refurbished, decent food, well kept beer, pleasant service and décor *(M R D Foot, P A Legon)*

☆ *Salisbury* [St Martins Lane]: Floridly Victorian, theatrical sweeps of red velvet, huge sparkling mirrors and cut glass, glossy brass and mahogany; wide food choice from simple snacks to long-running smoked salmon lunches and salad bar (even doing Sun lunches over Christmas/New Year), well kept Tetleys-related ales, decent house wines, no-smoking back room, friendly service; shame about the piped music and games machines *(BB, the Didler)*

Sherlock Holmes [Northumberland St; aka Northumberland Arms]: Well appointed pub decorated with particularly fine collection of Holmes memorabilia, inc complete model of his apartment; good choice of well kept ales, comfortable plush booths, friendly staff, upstairs restaurant; busy lunchtime *(M Hickman, BB, Robert Lester)*

Ship & Shovell [Craven Passage]: Recently reopened by Badger, with their Best, Champion and Tanglefoot kept well, reasonably priced food, pleasant décor inc interesting prints, mainly naval *(John A Barker)*

EAST LONDON
E1
Captain Kidd [Wapping High St]: Thames views from enormous rooms of newish nautical-theme pub in renovated Docklands warehouse, good choice of hot and cold food all day inc several puddings, Sam Smiths keg beers, obliging bow-tied staff, chunky tables on roomy back waterside terrace *(Tony Scott, Richard and Valerie Wright)*

Dickens Inn [St Katharines Way]: Splendid position above smart Docklands marina, oddly Swiss-chalet look from outside with its balconies and window boxes, interesting stripped-down bare boards, baulks and timbers interior, several floors inc big pricy restaurant extension, well kept Theakstons Old Peculier; popular with overseas visitors, seats outside *(A Hepburn, S Jenner, Mike Ridgway, Sarah Miles, the Didler, LYM, Ian Phillips)*

Lord Rodneys Head [Whitechapel Rd]: Long and narrow, with rickety bentwood chairs on bare boards, matchboard walls, old clocks and photographs, lively atmosphere, well kept B&T beers – one price regardless of strength; regular live music, tables outside *(C J Fletcher)*

Pride of Spitalfields [Heneage St]: One-bar comfortable local with varying well kept ales such as Fullers London Pride and Woodhams IPA, mixed customers, very crowded Fri/Sat evenings *(Mark Brock)*

E4
Coppermill [Old Church Rd]: Pleasant and friendly open-plan pub with books and bric-a-brac, Courage Best and Directors; piped music *(Robert Lester)*

E9
☆ *Royal Inn on the Park* [Lauriston Rd]: Substantial Victorian building overlooking Hackney's Victoria Park, rejuvenated by current young management – friendly and relaxed, with daily papers, Sun seafood nibbles, casual furniture (bar hooks for dog leads), six real ales, German beers, restaurant-standard food in bar and small dining room *(Maurice Healy)*

E11
Cuckfield [High St Wanstead]: Highly refurbished partitioned pub, lots of light-coloured wood, prominent lamps and lanterns – comfortable and smart; Bass and Charrington, good lunchtime food inc Sun, real fire, good friendly atmosphere, conservatory; smart dress, no under-21s, bouncers Fri/Sat *(J Fahy, Ian Phillips, Robert Lester)*

☆ *Sir Alfred Hitchcock* [off Whipps Cross Rd, 15 mins from Leytonstone tube stn]: Good rather countrified atmosphere, with well kept ales such as Boddingtons, Flowers, Fullers ESB, enthusiastic Irish landlord, big inglenook open fires, good Chinese bar meals and restaurant, reasonable prices; TV in bar; dogs welcome, sunny back courtyard; bedrooms *(M Matson, Rachael and Mark Baynham)*

E14
Barley Mow [Narrow St]: Former dockmaster's house, clean and comfortable, with big heaters for spacious if breezy terrace overlooking swing-bridge entrance to Limehouse Basin, mouth of Regents Canal and two Thames reaches, still has electric windlass used for hauling barges through; lots of sepia Whitby photographs, food, Ind Coope Burton and Tetleys-related, conservatory *(Ian Phillips)*

George [Glengall Gr]: Cheery and pleasant East End pub, good food in bar and restaurant inc good value specials and market-fresh fish, Courage-related and Tetleys ales, conservatory dining room *(Ian Phillips)*

E17
Nags Head [Orford Rd]: Friendly open-plan pub in handsome building, Ruddles County, Websters Yorkshire, darts, pool, good juke box *(Robert Lester)*

Village [Orford Rd]: Popular open-plan pub opened 1989, camera collection, Boddingtons and Fullers London Pride, children's room; garden *(Robert Lester)*

NORTH LONDON
N1
Duke of Cambridge [St Peters St]: London's first organic pub with appropriate beers and wines and interesting, varied carefully prepared food changing seasonally; large no-smoking area *(Rachel Boulton)*

N5
Highbury Barn [Highbury Pk]: Particularly well kept beers, good value food; recently refurbished, handy for Arsenal FC *(Nigel Woolliscroft)*

N6
☆ *Flask* [Highgate West Hill]: Comfortable Georgian pub, mostly modernised but still has intriguing up-and-down layout, sash-windowed bar hatch, panelling and high-backed carved settle tucked away in snug lower area (but this nice original core open only w/e and summer); usual food all day inc salad bar, good barman, changing beers such as Adnams, Ind Coope Burton, Greene King Abbot, Morlands Old Speckled Hen, Tetleys and Youngs, coal fire; very busy Sat lunchtime, well behaved children allowed, close-set picnic-sets out in attractive front courtyard with big gas heater-lamps *(Ian Phillips, LYM, J S M Sheldon, the Didler)*

N10
Fantail & Firkin [Muswell Hill Broadway]: Usual Firkin beers in unusual surroundings of converted church *(anon)*

N18

Angel [opp Angel tube stn]: Now a light and airy Wetherspoons with feel of a comfortable continental bar, relaxing atmosphere, good choice of beers (some real bargains); no-smoking areas, silenced games machines, no music, open all day *(Richard Lewis)*

NW1

☆ *Euston Flyer* [Euston Rd, opp British Library]: Spacious and comfortable, handy for British Library across rd, full Fullers range kept well with a guest beer such as Coniston Bluebird, decent food inc vast baps with chips, friendly service – still quick and attentive when it's crowded; open plan, with tile and wood floors, smaller more private raised areas, flying machines with Latin tags as décor; unobtrusive piped music, open all day *(Richard Lewis, M R D Foot, George Atkinson)*

Feathers [Linhope St]: Tiny bar with well kept Boddingtons and Flowers, friendly staff, sensibly priced food in variety, good-sized helpings *(Nigel and Sue Foster)*

Friar & Firkin [Euston Rd]: Usual Firkin décor, bare boards, barrels, lots of wood and breweriana, their usual menu, well kept beers brewed on the spot, friendly staff; games machines; open all day, happy hour, quiz or live music nights *(Richard Lewis)*

Green Man [Euston Rd]: Neat and clean if big and busy open-plan pub, with well kept Courage Directors, Theakstons Best and a guest beer, good food choice esp pies and good fish and chips, very friendly helpful staff; handy for the Royal College of Physicians, open all day *(Richard Lewis)*

Head of Steam [Eversholt St]: Large busy bar up stairs from bus terminus and overlooking it, fun for train/rail buffs with lots of memorabilia, also Corgi collection, unusual model trains and buses and magazines for sale; interesting well kept ales (also take-away), most from little-known small breweries (esp Northern and Scottish), Biddenham farm cider and lots of bottled beers and vodkas; TV, bar billiards, downstairs restaurant; open all day, security-coded basement lavatories *(Richard Lewis, C J Fletcher, Tony Scott, SLC, BB, T Barrow, S Demont)*

Victoria [Mornington Terr]: Five well kept ales and good daily-changing food in curved bar with photographs and other memorabilia; reasonably priced well chosen wines, pleasant atmosphere; piped music *(Lorna and Howard Lambert)*

NW3

Hamilton [along from Olde White Bear]: Undemanding family-run Fullers pub with London Pride, ESB and a seasonal beer; suntrap terrace *(Mark and Rachael Baynham)*

Horse & Groom [Heath St]: Quiet cosy Youngs pub with lots of wood, big windows overlooking steep street, their beers kept well, wonderfully friendly barman, atmosphere to match; reasonably priced home-made food *(the Didler, LYM, Mark and Rachael Baynham)*

Nags Head [Heath St]: Long narrow local, sawdust floor, nice brewing photographs, good beer choice *(BB, the Didler)*

☆ *Old Bull & Bush* [North End Way]: Attractively decorated in Victorian style, comfortable sofa and easy chairs, nooks and crannies, side library bar with lots of bookshelves and pictures and mementoes of Florrie Ford who made the song about the pub famous (but did you know that before that the song found fame in the US as Under the Anheuser Bush?); friendly landlord, prompt attentive service, good food bar inc tender filled bagels and good Sun specials, decent wines and mulled wine, good provision for families *(BB, G S B G Dudley)*

Sir Richard Steele [Haverstock Hill]: Cosy, with lots of atmosphere, unusual bric-a-brac, fine stained glass, bare boards, snug rooms candlelit at night, laid-back bar staff, well kept real ales, Bud on tap; live music (especially good on Sun) *(BB, Dr and Mrs A K Clarke)*

Three Horseshoes [Heath St]: Pleasant Wetherspoons in nice spot, usual solid décor, well kept sensibly priced beers, good staff, food all day, no-smoking area *(Mark and Rachael Baynham)*

NW5

☆ *Lord Palmerston* [Dartmouth Park Hill]: Reliably good cheapish contemporary food, not too noisy, well planted conservatory and prize-winning garden *(D M Thomas, Rachel Boulton)*

NW8

☆ *Crockers* [Aberdeen Pl]: Magnificent original Victorian interior, full of showy marble, decorated plaster and opulent woodwork; relaxing and comfortable, with well kept Bass and wide range of other sensibly priced ales, friendly service, decent food inc vegetarian and good Sun roasts, tables outside *(T Barrow, S Demont, the Didler, LYM)*

NW10

William IV [Harrow Rd]: Spacious, with good food, good wine choice, two real ales *(A Jennings)*

SOUTH LONDON
SE1

☆ *Barrow Boy & Banker* [Borough High St]: Tasteful banking hall conversion, good value food, good welcoming service *(Charles Gysin)*

Coopers [Waterloo Stn]: Typical of the new breed of much-improved station pubs, grand staircase down to spacious Victorian-style bar with sepia décor, pastel carpet, prints, brass and light washed wood; lively and noisy, nine wines by the glass, interesting changing real ales *(Eddie Edwards)*

☆ *Founders Arms* [Hopton St (Bankside)]: Sparkling view of Thames and St Paul's from spacious glass-walled plush-seat modern bar and big waterside terrace; well kept Youngs Bitter and Special, good value food inc vegetarian, good service, genuine feel; fairly handy for the Globe *(DJW, David and Carole Chapman, Val and Alan Green, LYM, T Barrow, S Demont)*

Globe [Bedale St/Green Dragon Ct]: Dark Victorian interior in heart of Borough Market, good choice of real ales *(the Didler)*

Kings Head [Borough High St]: Down-to-earth local with basic sensibly priced food, big-screen sports TV *(Rachael and Mark Baynham)*

Liams Og [Jamaica Rd]: Busy lunchtime pub nr Tower Bridge, reasonably priced food, Courage ales *(anon)*

Mad Hatter [Stamford St—Blackfriars Rd end]: New but traditional Fullers pub with interesting hat collection, helpful staff, good range of food, their usual beers and fine range of wines by the glass *(John A Barker)*

Old Dispensary [Leman St]: Cleverly recycled building – works well; friendly staff, well kept beer *(Dr and Mrs A K Clarke)*

☆ *Old Thameside* [St Mary Overy Wharf, Clink St]: Good pastiche of ancient tavern, two floors – hefty beams and timbers, pews, flagstones, candles; splendid river view upstairs and from charming waterside terrace by schooner docked in landlocked inlet; good choice of well kept ales such as Adnams Broadside, Bass and Marstons Pedigree, friendly staff, all-day salad bar, lunchtime hot buffet *(Richard Lewis, LYM, M Hickman)*

Paper Moon [Blackfriars Rd]: Recently refurbished, bright, airy and modern, with real ales such as Fullers London Pride, Greene King and Harveys and lots of continental lagers on tap; Sun seafood bar *(Rachael and Mark Baynham)*

Ship [Borough Rd]: Busy, long and narrow, with good atmosphere, well kept Fullers, good food, friendly staff; a local for the RPO *(the Didler)*

Shipwrights Arms [Tooley St]: Handy for HMS *Belfast*, with nautical theme, well kept changing beers such as Bishops, Cottage Broad Gauge and Crouch Vale SAS, good choice of very reasonably priced food, comfortable seats, friendly landlady and staff; open all day *(Richard Lewis)*

Wheatsheaf [Stoney St]: Two-bar local on Borough Market, dark-panelled and basic, with wholesome cheap food, Courage and several guest beers such as Adnams, Fullers, O'Hanlons Red and Uley Old Spot, farm cider, friendly staff; open all day exc Sun, under threat of closure (railway track widening) but for now seems reprieved *(the Didler, Richard Lewis)*

SE8

Dog & Bell [Prince St]: Remarkably well kept beer, particularly good service, reasonable prices *(Steve Cox)*

SE10

Ashburnham Arms [Ashburnham Grove]: Friendly Shepherd Neame local with good pasta and other food (not Mon evenings), quiz night Tues; pleasant garden with barbecues *(the Didler)*

Pilot [River Way, Blackwall Lane]: Busy, with brisk friendly service, well kept Bass, Courage Best and Youngs Special, wide range of sandwiches, baked potatoes and hot dishes at very reasonable prices; handy for Millennium Dome *(D P and J A Sweeney, Tony Gayfer)*

Richard I [Royal Hill]: Quiet and friendly no-nonsense traditional two-bar local with well kept Youngs, bare boards, panelling, good range of traditional food inc outstanding sausages, good staff, no piped music; tables in pleasant back garden with barbecues, busy summer w/e and evenings *(the Didler, M Chaloner)*

☆ *Trafalgar* [Park Row]: Attractive and substantial Regency building with splendid river view, fine panelled rooms, friendly efficient staff, good atmosphere, well prepared usual food, good house wines; children given free rein; handy for Maritime Museum, may have live jazz weekends *(Jill Bickerton)*

SE11

Doghouse [Kennington Cross]: Large and bright, with reasonably priced food, maybe loud music; quieter side bar for locals and diners *(S Hayre)*

SE13

Watch House [High St]: Usual Wetherspoons style, good value special offers *(A M Pring)*

SE16

☆ *Mayflower* [Rotherhithe St]: Friendly and cosy riverside local with black beams, high-backed settles and open fire, good views from upstairs and atmospheric wooden jetty, well kept Bass and Greene King IPA, Abbot and Rayments, decent bar food (not Sun night), friendly staff; children welcome, open all day; in unusual street with lovely Wren church *(LYM, the Didler, Kevin Flack, Tim Barrow, Sue Demont)*

SE17

☆ *Beehive* [Carter St]: Surprising find for the area, unpretentious but stylishly run pub/bistro with charming island bar, pictures ranging from former prime minister photographs to modern art in surrounding seating areas, excellent choice of home-made food all day from sandwiches to steaks inc imaginative dishes, well kept Courage Best and Directors, Fullers London Pride and guest beers, good whisky choice and remarkably wide range of wines; friendly laid-back service *(Pete Baker)*

SE20

Moon & Stars [High St Penge]: Wetherspoons pub in former cinema, nice little alcoves, food all day inc good filled baked potatoes and maybe bargain meals for two, very low-priced beer, immaculate lavatories, life-size image of Dorothy from *Wizard of Oz* hanging from high ceiling; sheltered back terrace *(A M Pring)*

SW2

Crown & Sceptre [Streatham Hill/South Circular junction]: Wetherspoons at their best, imposing and ornate yet warm and friendly, good traditional décor, sensible-sized areas inc no smoking, well kept reasonably priced ales inc some unusual ones, good value well organised food, good service *(Dr and Mrs A K Clarke)*

SW4

Bread & Roses [Clapham Manor St]: Food pub owned by Workers Beer Co, with its own Workers Ale brewed for it, good wine list, various leftish cultural events; piped music can be rather loud *(Tim Barrow, Sue Demont)*

Goose & Granite [Clapham High St]: Large well furnished chain pub with well kept Fullers, good sensibly priced food all day *(P A Legon)*

SW8

☆ *Rebatos* [South Lambeth Rd]: Lots of Spanish customers, real Spanish feel, consistently good authentic food in front tapas bar and pink-lit mirrored back restaurant – great atmosphere, frequent evening live music *(Tim Barrow, Sue Demont, BB)*

SW11

Eagle [Chatham Rd]: Attractive old side-street pub, Whitbreads-related and interesting guest ales, helpful landlord, paved back garden and seats in front; peaceful and relaxed unless big-screen sports TV on *(Tim Barrow, Sue Demont)*

SW13

Sun [Church Rd]: Several areas around central servery, interesting pictures and decorations, Victorian-style wallpaper, pleasant atmosphere, six Tetleys-related and guest ales, usual home-cooked food, benches and tables over road overlooking duck pond; very popular in summer, no under-21s *(Roger Huggins, Mayur Shah, Susan and John Douglas)*

SW14

Hare & Hounds [Upper Richmond Rd]: Well run classic panelled Youngs pub with well kept beers, friendly atmosphere, full-sized snooker table, pleasant garden *(Dr and Mrs A K Clarke)*
Plough [Christ Church Rd]: Relaxing pub dating from 17th c, real ales, home-made food, well kept Courage Directors, courteous and very helpful landlord and staff , tables out on terrace; four comfortable well equipped bedrooms – a good place to stay *(Joe and Mary Stachura)*

SW15

☆ *Dukes Head* [Lower Richmond Rd]: Classic Youngs pub, spacious and grand yet friendly, in great spot by Thames, well kept ales, 20 wines by the glass; main bar light and airy with big ceiling fans, very civilised feel, tables by window with great river view, smaller more basic locals' bar, good fresh lunchtime food; plastic glasses for outside *(Tony Eberts, BB)*
Prince of Wales [Upper Richmond Rd]: Nicely refurbished, lively and welcoming, with well kept real ales, interesting skylight in back room *(Dr and Mrs A K Clarke)*
Spotted Horse [High St]: Comfortably carpeted open-plan bar with island servery, well kept Youngs, good service, lunchtime food, relaxing evening atmosphere *(Tony Eberts)*

SW19

Crooked Billet [Wimbledon Common]: Popular olde-worlde pub by common, lovely spot for summer drinking, open all day; full Youngs range kept well, well cooked generous food, pleasant helpful service, good relevant décor, restaurant in 16th-c barn behind *(Tony Scott, Colin McKerrow, Jenny and Brian Seller)*
Fox & Grapes [Camp Rd]: By common, with good friendly service, Scottish Courage ales with a guest such as Wadworths 6X, soft lighting, attractive mural behind food servery, hearty food; piped music, big screen sports TV; open all

day, children welcome till 7, pleasant on summer evenings when you can sit out on the grass *(David Peakall, BB, Susan and John Douglas)*
Prince of Wales [Hartfield Rd]: Large handsome pub with good reasonably priced food inc all-day snacks, well kept ales such as Ridleys, Smiles and Theakstons Old Peculier, German beer on draught, good range of bottled beers *(Dave Braisted)*
Rose & Crown [Wimbledon High St]: Comfortably modernised old local with well kept Youngs Bitter and Special, friendly service, decent generous food from back servery at sensible prices, open fires, set of Hogarth's proverb engravings, roomy U-shaped bar with open fire and green plush seats in alcoves; conservatory, tables in former coachyard *(LYM, Roger and Jenny Huggins)*
Swan [The Ridgeway]: Helpful welcoming licensees, good range of real ales and of decent wines, reasonable choice of good food; wonderful three-dimensional inn sign *(Dr and Mrs A K Clarke)*

WEST LONDON
SW10

☆ *Chelsea Ram* [Burnaby St]: Lively yet relaxed feel in unusually winebar-like Youngs pub with pleasant golden walls, shutters, books, pine tables, lovely fire, amusing mix of yuppies, arty types, locals and usually at least one dog, some emphasis on good if not cheap food changing daily, inc vegetarian, pasta, fish and Smithfield meat; helpful friendly service, well kept Youngs, interesting wines inc good choice by the glass, outstanding bloody mary, good Pimms, no music, quiet back part; open all day Fri *(Nicole Belmont, BB, Mrs C Scrutton)*
☆ *Ferret & Firkin* [Lots Rd, opp entrance to Chelsea Harbour]: Unusually curved corner house with pews radiating out to big windows, basic bare-boards style, quiet at lunchtime but lively with youngish people in the evenings; brews its own Ferret, Firkin Best and Dogbolter, good value food counter, good juke box, chess, backgammon, bar billiards, table football, fruit machine and video game; open all day *(Giles Francis, Gordon, LYM)*
☆ *Sporting Page* [Camera Pl]: Unusual civilised and upmarket local off Kings Rd, quietly smart, plenty of polished wood and brass, genuinely good interesting home-made food, well kept Scottish Courage and a guest ale, decent house wines, efficient friendly service, downstairs overflow; one or two seats outside *(Richard Osborne, LYM)*

W4

Bell & Crown [Strand on the Green]: Big busy pub with several comfortable areas, very friendly feel, local paintings and photographs, simple good value food inc lunchtime hot dishes, sharing platters, Sun lunches and lots of sandwiches, well kept Fullers, log fire, no piped music or machines; good views esp from conservatory and picnic-sets out by towpath; open all day, good towpath walks *(Piotr Chodzko-Zajko, Warren Elliott, Ian Phillips, Tony Scott, David and Carole Chapman)*

☆ *City Barge* [Strand on the Green]: Small panelled riverside bars in picturesque partly 15th-c pub (this original part reserved for diners lunchtime), also airy newer back part done out with maritime signs and bird prints; good atmosphere, usual bar food (not Sun), well kept Courage Directors and Wadworths 6X, back conservatory, winter fires, some tables on towpath – lovely spot to watch sun set over Kew Bridge *(Chris Glasson, Piotr Chodzko-Zajko, B J Harding, David Carr, Val Stevenson, Rob Holmes)*

George & Devonshire [Burlington Lane/Hogarth Corner, A4]: Spacious and popular old-style local with well kept Fullers ales from the nearby brewery, good low-priced lunchtime food, realistic coal-effect gas fire *(Susan and Nigel Wilson)*

W5

Duffys [Pitshanger Lane]: Attractive and civilised pub/bar/bistro with local feel but good value seriousish food, soft lighting, stripped floor, chess tables, well kept Brakspears, Fullers London Pride and Wadworths 6X, good friendly staff, TV one end, quiet the other; slightly separate small restaurant *(Louise Lemieux, T Manning, Greg Kilminster)*

Fox & Goose [Hanger Lane]: Smart Fullers pub, good range of their beers, reasonable choice of bar food and wines; bedrooms comfortable and well priced *(Andy and Jill Kassube, Piotr Chodzko-Zajko)*

Rose & Crown [Church Pl, off St Marys Rd]: Good value food, well kept Fullers ales and good atmosphere, well refurbished, with dining area opening into secluded garden; friendly efficient staff, small public bar with machines, maybe unobtrusive piped country music, Sun quiz night *(Dr M Owton, Val Stevenson, Rob Holmes, Piotr Chodzko-Zajko)*

Wheatsheaf [Haven Lane]: Pleasant flower-decked Fullers pub with their full range, wide choice of good Thai food, enormous log fire in back room, pictures for sale, maybe even a small antiques auction Sun lunchtime; maybe piped Capital Radio *(Val Stevenson, Rob Holmes, Ian Phillips)*

W6

Andover Arms [Cardross St/Aldensley Rd]: Small intimate unspoilt local, particularly well kept Fullers Chiswick, London Pride, ESB and seasonal beers, good wines, freshly cooked Thai food; unobtrusive SkyTV *(Louise Lemieux, T Manning, Giles Francis)*

Brook Green [Shepherds Bush Rd]: Large unpretentious Victorian pub with much of its original character inc noble high ceilings, ornate plaster, chandeliers, coal fire; good choice of reasonably priced home-made food with proper veg, well kept Youngs, friendly atmosphere, good mix of customers *(Pete Baker)*

Queens Head [Brook Green]: Pleasantly placed Chef & Brewer on green by tennis courts, lots of cosy rooms, beams, candlelight, fires, country furniture and bric-a-brac, consistently good hearty food inc imaginative specials, well kept Courage Directors, no music, secret garden *(Patrick Renouf, Susan and John Douglas)*

Thatched House [Dalling Rd]: Youngs pub with

their full range, and emphasis on particularly good food – though local drinkers still come; no music *(Stephen King)*

W8

☆ *Britannia* [Allen St, off Kensington High St]: Peaceful and very friendly two-bar local little changed since the 60s, good value fresh home-cooked lunches, well kept Youngs, helpful long-serving landlady, no music; attractive indoor back 'garden' (no smoking at lunchtime), friendly dog and cat; open all day *(the Didler)*

W9

Truscott Arms [55 Shirland Rd]: Pleasant local, splendid row of ten handpumps, guest beers, jazz nights *(the Didler)*

Warrington [Warrington Cres]: Handsome and comfortable Victorian gin palace with decorative woodwork and tiles, luscious mirrors, arches and alcoves (said once to have been a brothel – hence the murals); well kept full Fullers range with a guest such as Brakspears, good pub food, small coal fire, imposing staircase up to Thai restaurant; good tables on big back terrace, nr Little Venice *(the Didler)*

W12

Crown & Sceptre [Melina Rd]: Busy quite big backstreet local, proper public bar, lounge free of noise and fruit machines, efficient friendly staff, well kept Fullers, weekday lunchtime food; popular with QPR football and Wasps rugby fans, open all day *(the Didler)*

W13

☆ *Drayton Court* [The Avenue, opp West Ealing stn]: Big Edwardian turreted stone building with two bars, friendly staff, lots of locals of all ages, full Fullers range kept well, good choice of homely fresh-tasting food inc vegetarian and good Sun roasts, sensible prices; barbecues on terrace, balcony overlooking big garden with unobtrusive play area; downstairs theatre *(Val and Alan Green, Val Stevenson, Rob Holmes)*

W14

Britannia Tap [Warwick Rd]: Small narrow Youngs pub, kept well (as are the beers), with welcoming landlord, sensible food, Sun bar nibbles *(the Didler)*

☆ *Colton Arms* [Greyhound Rd]: Villagey U-shaped bar, almost an upmarket country feel, with lots of dark carved wood, gleaming brass, even carved settles; good housekeeping, log fire, well kept Scottish Courage ales, two tiny back rooms with own counter – ring bell for service; pretty back terrace with rose arbour, next to Queens Club *(Susan and John Douglas)*

Frigate & Firkin [Blythe Rd, Olympia]: Typical Firkin – lots of wood, brewing memorabilia, bare boards, good choice of reasonably priced food, friendly staff, well kept ales in variety; open all day, tables outside, maybe live music *(Richard Lewis)*

Kensington Tavern [Russell Rd]: Well kept beers, good food; tables outside *(Chris Leonnard)*

Warwick Arms [Warwick Rd]: Early 19th-c,

with lots of old woodwork, comfortable atmosphere, friendly regulars (some playing darts or bridge), good service, well kept Fullers beers from elegant Wedgwood handpumps, limited tasty food (not Sun evening), sensible prices, no piped music; open all day, tables outside, handy for Earls Court and Olympia *(the Didler)*

OUTER LONDON
BARKING
Britannia [Tanner St]: Large dimly lit yet airy Youngs pub with Bitter, Light and Special, good value Sun lunches, pool, tables outside; occasional live music *(Mark and Rachael Baynham)*

BARNET
☆ *King William IV* [Hadley Highstone, towards Potters Bar]: Cosy and well tended small local, old-fashioned inside and out, with good atmosphere, nooks and corners, some antique Wedgwood plates over fireplaces (real fires), good home-made lunchtime food inc good fresh fish Fri, well kept ales, friendly staff; new back restaurant, flower-framed front terrace *(David Shillitoe, Kevin Macey)*
Monken Holt [High St]: Well run, with good home-made food all day, well kept Courage Best and Directors, friendly landlord, pleasing olde-worlde interior; nice setting, handy for Hadley Wood Common *(Kevin Macey)*
☆ *Olde Mitre* [High St]: Small early 17th-c local, bay windows in low-ceilinged panelled front bar with fruit machines, three-quarter panelled back area on two slightly different levels, bare boards, lots of dark wood, dark floral wallpaper, open fire, pleasant atmosphere, friendly service, well kept McMullens and other ales; cl afternoon *(LYM)*

BECKENHAM
Bricklayers Arms [High St]: Decent well run local, well kept beers, quick service, good mix of customers; darts *(A Pring)*

CHESSINGTON
[TQ1763]
☆ *North Star* [Hook Rd (A243)]: Refurbished as Bass family dining pub, popular with older people weekday lunchtime for reasonably priced food from sandwiches and baked potatoes to bargain steak or mixed grill; several areas, good log fire, quiet piped music, good friendly service and atmosphere *(DWAJ)*

CHISLEHURST
Bulls Head [Royal Par]: Two big lively bars, one with high-backed armchairs and big winter fire; pleasant staff, generous straightforward bar food (no snacks Sun), spacious back carvery, well kept Youngs; tables in garden, nr pleasant nature reserve *(anon)*
Olde Stationmaster [Chislehurst Rd]: Recently tastefully refurbished with fine old railway posters etc, good range of amazingly cheap food, friendly helpful family service; tables in garden with play area; beside Chislehurst Caves *(Tony and Dorothy Eberts)*
Queens Head [High St]: Comfortable and

friendly local dating from 16th c, by attractive pond on green; pleasantly laid out with separate areas, bookshelves, food inc superb value ploughman's (Sun roasts – no snacks then), well kept ales inc Ind Coope Burton, efficient jolly service; tables in garden *(Jenny and Brian Seller)*
Sydney Arms [Old Perry St]: Pleasant quick service even when busy, good range of good value food inc vegetarian even on Sun (good bar nibbles then too), well kept ales inc Morlands Old Speckled Hen, friendly atmosphere, big conservatory and pleasant garden – good for children; almost opp entrance to Scadbury Park – lovely country walks *(Jenny and Brian Seller, B J Harding)*
Tigers Head [Watts Lane/Manor Park Rd, opp St Nicholas Church]: 18th-c, now pleasantly airy Chef & Brewer, overlooking church and common, wide food choice inc variety of fish and quite good value Sun lunch, considerable wine list, beers inc Trafalgar; efficient even when quite busy; smart casual dress code an obstacle to muddy walkers *(Jenny and Brian Seller, B and M Kendall)*

COCKFOSTERS
Cock & Dragon [Chalk Lane/Games Rd]: Comfortable well run traditional pub combined with Thai restaurant, plentiful good English bar food too *(Kevin Macey)*

COWLEY
Paddington Packet Boat [Packet Boat La]: Modern but caring Fullers pub with well thought out no-smoking room, one bar calm even with World Cup on in the other, wide choice of food, tremendous staff, good terrace *(Piotr Chodzko-Zajko)*

CRANHAM
Thatched House [St Marys Rd (B187, not far from M25 junction 29)]: Large beamed olde-worlde 19th-c Vintage Inn with good choice of beers and well priced food, good friendly service *(Eddie Edwards)*

CROYDON
Princess Royal [Longley Rd]: A Croydon oasis, like a small country pub, with particularly well kept Greene King IPA, Abbot, Dark Mild and a seasonal or guest ale, home-cooked food throughout opening hours, log fire; piped music *(Martin Hill)*

CUDHAM
☆ *Blacksmiths Arms* [Cudham Lane]: Warm welcome, decent generous reasonably priced food inc interesting soups, good ploughman's, well kept Courage, Fullers London Pride and Morlands Old Speckled Hen, good coffee, quick friendly service; nearly always busy yet plenty of tables, with cheerful cottagey atmosphere, soft lighting, blazing log fires, low ceiling; big garden, pretty window boxes, handy for good walks *(John and Elspeth Howell)*

DOWNE
Queens Head [High St]: Quaint and civilised refurbished village pub, open all day and very

comfortable, with friendly helpful service, good value food, well kept ales, log fire, well equipped children's room; small back courtyard with aviary, handy for Darwin's Down House *(Klaus and Elizabeth Leist)*

GREENFORD
[TQ1382]
Black Horse [Oldfield Lane]: Good food, well kept Fullers, good atmosphere; overlooks canal *(Adam Harris)*

HAMPTON
White Hart [High St, by Kingston Bridge]: Well kept Boddingtons, Flowers, Greene King Abbot and changing guest ales, helpful knowledgeable staff, usual decent lunchtime food, warm log fire and quiet relaxed atmosphere; subdued lighting, good staff, small front terrace *(R Houghton, Dr M Owton, Alain and Rose Foote)*

HAMPTON COURT
☆ *Kings Arms* [Hampton Court Rd, next to Lion Gate]: Oak panels and beams, stripped-brick lounge with bric-a-brac and open fire one end, public bar the other end with stripped pine food servery beyond (eat where you like, food all day from 8.30); pleasant relaxed atmosphere, well kept Badger ales, upstairs restaurant; unobtrusive piped music, children welcome; open all day, picnic-sets on new terrace with camellias in tubs *(LYM, B T Smith, Ian Phillips, Val and Alan Green, John Crafts)*

HARROW
Castle [West St]: Unspoilt Fullers pub in picturesque old part, doing well under current management, with vast choice of good food from generous sandwiches and starters to steaks, very friendly staff, classic lively traditional bar, sedate and civilised lounge with open fires, wall seats, variety of prints; nice garden *(Ron and Val Broom)*

HILLINGDON
Red Lion [Royal Lane, Hillingdon Hill (A4006 towards Uxbridge)]: Large rambling old Fullers pub, low ceilings, cosy welcoming traditional atmosphere, well kept beers, good bar food, real fires; staff cope easily with the large numbers *(Anthony Longden)*

ILFORD
Bell [Ley St, nr A123]: Massive but friendly two-bar John Barras pub, very spacious and atmospheric; Greene King Abbot and Scottish Courage beers, cheap food, big-screen TV; darts and pool in public bar *(Robert Lester)*

ISLEWORTH
Town Wharf: Well appointed modern pub worth knowing for riverside position, splendid views from spacious upstairs bar with seats around high tables, also leather chesterfields, small alcoves, lunchtime hot food and good range of beers; good waterside seating area; can be crowded, esp summer Fri lunchtimes *(Steve Power, Mayur Shah)*

KENLEY
CR8 [TQ3259]
☆ *Wattenden Arms* [Old Lodge Lane; left (coming from London) off A23 by Reedham Stn, then keep on]: Popular dark-panelled traditional 18th-c country local nr glider aerodrome, well kept Bass and Hancocks HB, straightforward lunchtime food from good sandwiches and steak sandwiches up, friendly prompt service, lots of interesting patriotic and WWII memorabilia; a welcome for walkers, seats on small side lawn *(Jenny and Brian Seller, LYM)*

KEW
[TQ1874]
Coach & Horses [Kew Green]: Typical Youngs pub in nice setting, well kept beers *(Dr and Mrs A K Clarke)*

KINGSTON
Bishop out of Residence [Bishops Hall, off Thames St – down alley by Superdrug]: Riverside Youngs pub with pleasant Thames views, big bar and eating area, impressive service, lunchtime emphasis on wide range of good value quick food, well kept ales, decent house wines, customers of all ages; tables out on balcony *(Jill Bickerton, Mayur Shah, GP)*
Bricklayers Arms [Hawks Rd]: Simple bareboards pub with baseball caps hanging from beams, wide choice of food, well kept Morlands, vintage jazz on juke box, hard-working licensees, considerate staff *(LM)*
Gazebo [Kings Passage; alley off Thames St by Superdrug – or from Kingston Bridge]: Comfortable and uncrowded, with terrific river view upstairs, cheap Sam Smiths beer, leather chesterfields and low tables, reasonable range of usual food; lots of seats on balcony and terrace *(Sue and Mike Todd)*
Norbiton Dragon [Clifton Rd]: Atmospheric and lively, esp w/e, with good Thai restaurant *(S Hayre)*

LOCKS BOTTOM
BR6 [TQ4364]
British Queen [Crofton Rd]: Useful for very cheap lunchtime food, popular then with older people; more a young person's pub evenings, with juke box, TV, machines, football memorabilia *(A M Pring)*

OSTERLEY
TW7 [TQ1477]
☆ *Hare & Hounds* [Windmill Lane (B454, off A4 – called Syon Lane at that point)]: Well kept Fullers in light and airy suburban pub, recently extended and completely refurbished, some emphasis now on wide choice of good food, prompt very friendly service; spacious terrace and good mature garden, nice setting opp beautiful Osterley Park *(D P and J A Sweeney, Adam Harris, Steve Power)*

PINNER
[TQ1289]
Queens Head [High St]: Traditional pub dating from 16th c, good value fresh food inc

sandwiches and vegetarian, well kept changing ales such as Marstons Pedigree and Youngs Special, very friendly staff and landlord, no music or machines; welcome car park *(Chris Glasson)*

PURLEY

Foxley Hatch [Russell Hill Rd]: Smart modern Wetherspoons pub converted from bathroom centre, warmly friendly local atmosphere, Theakstons Best and other well kept ales inc at least two changing guests, decent food all day, low prices, good staff, no music; no-smoking area, disabled lavatory *(Jim Bush)*

RICHMOND

Britannia [Brewers Lane]: Good atmosphere, food inc excellent chips; nice upstairs room *(Bill and Vera Burton, Peter Burton)*

Princes Head [The Green]: Large friendly open-plan pub nr theatre, good traditional areas off big island bar, good lunchtime food cooked to order, Fullers Chiswick and London Pride, open fire, seats outside – fine spot *(Tony and Wendy Hobden)*

White Horse [Worple Way, off Sheen Rd]: Fashionable gastropub, bare boards, scrubbed tables, long aluminium bar, imaginative if pricy modern cooking with Mediterranean influences, superb cheeseboard from nearby Vivians, well kept beer, excellent wine choice; spoilt by strident piped music, at least after 9 *(anon)*

☆ *White Swan* [Old Palace Lane]: Charming respite from busy Richmond, welcoming dark-beamed open-plan bar, well kept Courage beers and Marstons Pedigree, good freshly cooked bar lunches, coal-effect gas fires; children allowed in conservatory; pretty paved garden, barbecues, pretty setting *(Ian Phillips, LYM, Jill Bickerton)*

ST PAULS CRAY

[TQ4769]

Bull [Main Rd, junction with A223 towards Bexley]: Two-bar pub with pleasant service, nice range of reasonably priced food inc good sandwiches, generous ploughman's and some hot dishes, decent wines, garden; games machines, quiz night *(AMP, A E Brace)*

STANMORE

Vine [Stanmore Hill]: Friendly and quiet pub, handy for good walks (and welcoming to walkers, and children); huge helpings of good reasonably priced food esp burgers and steaks, also vegetarian, well kept beer, garden *(Piotr Chodzko-Zajko)*

Vintry [Church St]: Huge open-plan modern bar with sectioned-off seating over on right, pictures, machines, SkyTV; useful for area *(MS)*

SURBITON

Victoria [Victoria Rd]: Character Victorian Youngs pub, four distinct areas (one no smoking) around central bar, friendly staff, daytime food inc good value hot dishes, well kept beers; secluded back terrace, open all day *(Mr and Mrs M Ashton)*

Waggon & Horses [Surbiton Hill Rd]: Roomy traditional family local, very friendly staff inc full-time potboy, well kept Youngs, good value home cooking, four bar areas and mezzanine eating area leading to grapevine terrace with barbecues and Sun roasts *(Jonathon Bromley, Robin Boss)*

TEDDINGTON

Abercorn Arms [Church Rd]: Good traditional pub food, good local atmosphere; jazz Mon *(Melanie Bennett)*

Adelaide [Park Rd]: Good friendly corner local with Adnams Bitter and Broadside, Hardy Country and Popes, good home-made food inc filled baguettes, pretty creeper-clad back yard; popular lunchtime *(Ian Phillips, LM)*

TWICKENHAM

Barmy Arms [riverside]: Pleasant riverside pub with good beer choice, generous food in restaurant area, tables on terrace *(Eddie Edwards)*

Cabbage Patch [London Rd]: Recently well refurbished, variety of furniture in several rooms inc no-smoking area, Fullers London Pride, Wadworths 6X and Charles Wells Bombardier, decent simple food, raised central fire, comfortable seating in quieter areas, games room; very busy on rugby days *(Jonathan Gibbs)*

Turks Head [Winchester Rd, St Margarets; behind roundabout on A316]: Friendly civilsed local with full Fullers range kept well, home-cooked food changing daily; manic on rugby days; stand-up comics Mon/Sat in hall behind *(Ian Phillips, BB)*

White Swan [Riverside]: Easy-going country-style pub tucked away in very quiet spot by Thames, pleasant balcony overlooking it and tables outside right down to the water's edge; reasonably priced lunchtime buffet, real ales, big rustic tables, walls packed with rugby memorabilia (other sports banned on TV), blazing fire; very busy Sun lunchtime and for events such as barbecues, raft races *(Dr and Mrs A K Clarke, LYM)*

UPMINSTER

Thatched House [St Marys Lane]: Attractive olde-worlde décor, well spaced tables in extended alcovey dining area, well presented food inc light lunches such as giant sandwiches and filled mushrooms, also generous main meals inc choice of fish and vegetarian, fresh veg, quick friendly service; picnic-sets outside *(M A and C R Starling)*

UXBRIDGE

☆ *Load of Hay* [Villiers St, off Clevedon Rd opp Brunel University]: Small local popular for wide choice of good value freshly made generous food, well kept Scottish Courage and interesting guest beers, thoughtful choice of teas, impressive fireplace in no-smoking back part used by diners, more public-bar atmosphere nearer serving bar, another separate bar, local paintings; dogs welcome, attractive back garden *(R Houghton, Anthony Longden)*

Scotland

There's a splendid choice of good pubs and bars in both Edinburgh (particularly the Guildford Arms) and Glasgow. Outside here, especially in the least populated places, it's often hotels and inns that are the local counterparts of England's good pubs. Places doing particularly well currently include the welcoming Village Inn at Arrochar (good food, and it gains its Beer Award this year), the civilised Riverside Inn at Canonbie, the Tigh an Truish on its small island at Clachan Seil (enjoyable food), the very well run Creebridge House Hotel at Creebridge (nice place to stay, good food), the well placed Tormaukin in Glendevon (excellent bedrooms), the very remote Glenelg Inn (good all round), the cheerful Fox & Hounds in Houston (back in the Guide after a break – and brewing its own good beers now), the Traquair Arms in Innerleithen (food much enjoyed), the Kilberry Inn (very good food, good bedrooms, warm welcome), the friendly Cross Keys at Kippen, the harbourside Anchor at Kippford (on fine form these days – many years since it was last a main entry), the Glenisla Hotel at Kirkton of Glenisla (a good all-rounder, nice to find here), Burts Hotel in Melrose, the nicely pubby Moulin in Pitlochry (good food, great beer), the delightfully placed Plockton Hotel in Plockton, the Wheatsheaf at Swinton (excellent food), and the Ailean Chraggan at Weem (good all round, especially food). Perhaps unsurprisingly, we don't hear much from readers about it – but we'd add to this shortlist the friendly and gloriously set Applecross Inn, with its excellent seafood. It's another pub that entails a long but extremely worthwhile coastal drive which we name as Scottish Dining Pub of the Year: the Kilberry Inn at Kilberry. Some pubs and inns to draw special attention to in the Lucky Dip section at the end of the chapter are the Allanton Inn at Allanton, Cobbles in Kelso and Tibbie Shiels on St Marys Loch (Borders); Stag at Falkland (Fife); Royal in Kingussie and Ferry Boat in Ullapool (Highland); Milnes and Standing Order in Edinburgh, and Bridge just outside at Ratho (Lothian); Cask & Still in Glasgow and Oban Inn in Oban (Strathclyde); Castleton House at Eassie and Kenmore Hotel at Kenmore (Tayside); and Stein Inn and Flodigarry Hotel on Skye. In general beer costs more in Scottish pubs than in English ones; we found it cheapest in the Counting House, the showy Wetherspoons pub in Glasgow, with the Riverside Inn in Canonbie, Bow Bar in Edinburgh and Prince of Wales in Aberdeen also cheaper than most.

ABERDEEN NJ9305 Map 11
Prince of Wales 🍺 £

7 St Nicholas Lane

Standing in the narrow cobbled lane outside this cheery old tavern it would be easy to forget that this is the very heart of the city's shopping centre, with Union Street almost literally overhead. The cosy flagstoned area at the heart of the pub has the city's longest bar counter, and it's a good job too; some lunchtimes there's standing room only, with a real mix of locals and visitors creating a friendly bustling feel. It's furnished with pews and other wooden furniture in screened booths, while a smarter main lounge has some panelling and a fruit machine. A fine range of particularly well kept beers includes Bass, Caledonian 80/-, Courage Directors, Tomintoul XXX and guest ales on handpump or tall fount air pressure; good choice of malt whiskies. Popular and generously served home-made lunchtime food includes filled french bread (£2.70), filled baked potatoes (£3), macaroni cheese (£3.70), and steak and ale pie or fresh breaded haddock (£4); cheery staff. On Sunday evening fiddlers provide traditional music. *(Recommended by Ian and Nita Cooper)*

Free house ~ Licensees Peter and Anne Birnie ~ Real ale ~ Bar food (lunchtime only) ~ (01224) 640597 ~ Fiddlers Sun evening ~ Open 11-12; 11-11 Sun

APPLECROSS NG7144 Map 11
Applecross Inn 🍴
Off A896 S of Shieldaig

Reached by a breathtaking drive over the 'pass of the cattle' (one of the highest in Britain), this friendly, compact inn is wonderfully placed in a beautiful bay. More popular than you might expect from the loneliness of the setting, you'll usually find a number of cheerful locals in the simple but comfortable bar, and it's particularly well regarded for its meals. Usually available all day, the bar menu includes sandwiches (from £1.50), home-made vegetable soup (£1.95), nice venison or cheeseburgers (£2.50), ploughman's or vegetable samosas (£4.95), half a dozen oysters or fresh deep-fried cod or haddock (£5.95), dressed local crab salad (£7.50), squat lobster curry or delicious queen scallops in a cream, wine and mushroom sauce (£7.95), sirloin steak (£10.95), and puddings like home-baked apple crumble (£2.50); children's helpings. You must book for the no-smoking restaurant. Darts, dominoes, pool (winter only) and juke box (unless there are musicians in the pub); a good choice of around 50 malt whiskies, and efficient, welcoming service. There's a nice garden by the shore with tables. Bedrooms are small and simple but adequate, all with a sea view; marvellous breakfasts. They may warm food for babies, and highchairs are available. You can hire mountain bikes. As we went to press they were carrying out various improvements, which among other things will see a traditional woodburning stove added to the bar. *(Recommended by Joan and Tony Walker, Steve Radley, Paula Williams, K M Crook, Mr and Mrs Archibald)*

Free house ~ Licensees Judith and Bernie Fish ~ Bar food (12-9) ~ Restaurant ~ (01520) 744262 ~ Children welcome until 8.30pm ~ Open 11-11(12 Fri); 11-11.30 Sat; 12.30-11(7 Nov-Mar) Sun ~ Bedrooms: £25/£50(£57B)

ARDFERN NM8004 Map 11
Galley of Lorne
B8002; village and inn signposted off A816 Lochgilphead—Oban

Ideally placed across from Loch Craignish, this relaxing inn has seats on a sheltered terrace enjoying marvellous views over the sea and yacht anchorage; on a cooler day you can appreciate the same outlook from the cosy main bar. There's a log fire, as well as old Highland dress prints and other pictures, big navigation lamps by the bar counter, an unfussy assortment of furniture, including little winged settles and upholstered window seats on its lino tiles, and a good mix of customers. Good bar food includes home-made soup (£2; soup and a sandwich £4.25), haggis with whisky and cream (£3.50), lunchtime open sandwiches (from £3.95), ploughman's or burgers (from £4.95), good moules marinières (£5.75; large £8.95), spicy vegetable pakora (£5.75), home-made steak, ale and mushroom pie (£6.25), fresh battered sole fillets (£7.95), daily specials like haunch of local venison in port or Loch Craignish langoustines, and puddings such as home-made sticky ginger pudding (£3); children's menu; spacious restaurant. Quite a few malt whiskies; darts, pool, dominoes, fruit machine, piped music. They can get busy on Friday and Saturday evenings. Count on a good breakfast if you're staying. *(Recommended by Richard Gibbs, Mike and Penny Sanders, Chris and Ann Garnett)*

Free house ~ Licensee Susana Garland ~ Bar food ~ Restaurant ~ (01852) 500284 ~ Children welcome ~ Open 11-2.30, 5-11.30; 11-11.30 Sat; 12-11 Sun; closed 25 Dec ~ Bedrooms: £43.50B/£67.50B

ARDUAINE NM7910 Map 11
Loch Melfort Hotel 🛏

On A816 S of Oban and overlooking Asknish Bay

Quite a few changes at this comfortable cream-washed Edwardian hotel since our last edition, particularly in the airy, modern bar, now known as the Skerry Café Bistro. All the old furnishings have gone, and they've added three big decorative panels by a local artist, as well as big picture windows looking out over the small rocky outcrops from which the room takes its name. Lunchtime meals include sandwiches (from £2.75), soup (£2.95), ploughman's (£5.25), half pint of prawns (£5.50), pasta with tomato, basil, mushrooms and crème fraîche (£6.50), rice balls with diced pork, nuts, smoked bacon and herbs in a spiced tomato sauce (£6.95), half a dozen oysters (£7.25), salmon and prawn fishcakes with cucumber and watercress sauce (£7.50), lamb cutlets or cassoulet (£8.50), grilled langoustines with herb butter (£10.50) and half lobster (£12.95); children's menu (£3.50). The main restaurant is no smoking; good wine list and selection of malt whiskies. Wooden seats on the front terrace have a magnificent view over the wilderness of the loch and its islands; they have a pair of powerful marine glasses which you can use to search for birds and seals on the islets and the coasts of the bigger islands beyond. The comfortable bedrooms also enjoy sea views, and breakfasts are good. Passing yachtsmen are welcome to use the mooring and drying facilities, and hot showers. It's a short stroll from the hotel through grass and wild flowers to the rocky foreshore, where the licensees keep their own lobster pots and nets. From late April to early June the walks through the neighbouring Arduaine woodland gardens are lovely. *(Recommended by Colin Thompson, Peter F Marshall, Neil and Karen Dignan, also in the Good Hotel Guide)*

Free house ~ Licensees Philip and Rosalind Lewis ~ Bar food (12-2.30, 6-9) ~ (01852) 200233 ~ Children in eating area of bar ~ Open 10.30-11.30; closed 4 Jan–12 Feb ~ Bedrooms: £53B/£106B

ARDVASAR NG6203 Map 11
Ardvasar Hotel 🛏

A851 at S of island; just past Armadale pier where the summer car ferries from Mallaig dock

On the edge of the Sound of Sleat, with fine views across the water to the dramatic mountains of Knoydart, this friendly and comfortably modernised white stone inn is a good place for a meal. Served all day in summer, the home-made bar food might include country-style lamb and vegetable broth (£2.50), lentil and cheese bake with provençale sauce (£6.30), roast prime rib of Scottish beef with bordelaise sauce (£6.80), fresh dressed local crab (£8), roasted local pheasant breast with venison and apple and calvados sauce (£12.90), large baked scallops with grapes, cheese, mustard and wine sauce (£13.90), and puddings like warm apricot and marmalade almond flan or blueberry cheesecake (from £2.25). The simple public bar has stripped pews and kitchen chairs, while the smartly modern cocktail bar is furnished with plush wall seats and stools around dimpled copper coffee tables on the patterned carpet, and Highland dress prints on the cream hessian-and-wood walls. A room off the comfortable hotel lounge has armchairs around an attractive coal-effect gas fire; darts, pool, juke box, fruit machine, and background music. Well kept Tennents 80/- and a weekly guest like Isle of Skye Red Cuillin tapped from the cask, and lots of malt whiskies. The hotel is handy for the Clan Donald Centre. *(Recommended by Walter and Susan Rinaldi-Butcher, Barry and Marie Males, Colin Draper, G D K Fraser)*

Free house ~ Licensee Michael Cass ~ Real ale ~ Restaurant ~ (01471) 844223 ~ Children in restaurant ~ Open 11-12 ~ Bedrooms: £55B/£90B

ARROCHAR NN2904 Map 11
Village Inn 🍺

A814, just off A83 W of Loch Lomond

A welcome stop close to the main tourist routes, this notably friendly pub was built as a manse for the local church in the last century, but it's the more recent informal dining area that readers consider the real heart of the place. It's very comfortable and atmospheric, with a candle on each table, lots of bare wood, a big open fire, soft traditional piped music, and lovely views (over the shore road) of the head of Loch Long, and the hills around The Cobbler, the main peak opposite. Steps lead down to the bar, which has an open fire. Well liked lunchtime bar food, served until 5, includes soup (£1.95), steamed mussels (£3.75), sandwiches (from £3.95), home-made lasagne or beef and ale pie (£4.95), and cajun grilled chicken breast (£5.95); evening extras might include haggis, neeps and tatties (£6.25), venison, honey and mushroom pie (£7.55), and various specials including good fresh fish; children's meals (from £3.50). Service is efficient and chatty. Well kept Orkney Dark Island, Wallace IPA, and two weekly changing guest beers on handpump, and 42 malt whiskies; piped music, juke box. Booking is recommended for the restaurant in the evenings. *(Recommended by Geoffrey and Brenda Wilson, Mrs Angela Power, Dave Braisted, Peter F Marshall, Sarah and Brian Fox, Martyn and Katie Alderton)*

Maclays ~ Manager Jose Andrade ~ Real ale ~ Bar food (11-5) ~ Restaurant (11-9.30) ~ (01301) 702279 ~ Children in eating area of bar and restaurant ~ Open 11-12(1am Fri, Sat)

BRIG O TURK NN5306 Map 11
Byre

A821 Callander—Trossachs, just outside village

The setting of this carefully converted pub is delightful, on the edge of a network of forest and lochside tracks in the Queen Elizabeth Forest Park – lots of walking, cycling, and fishing. The name byre means cowshed, so the place has come a long way since it was built in the 18th c; it's now a lovely secluded spot for a relaxed, tranquil meal. Using fresh local produce, the good bar food includes home-made soup (£2.10), sandwiches (from £2.75), haggis, neeps and tatties (£2.95), filled baked potatoes (£3.25), mushroom stroganoff (£4.95), deep-fried haddock or wild game casserole (£5.95), chicken, bacon and haggis with a whisky and grain mustard sauce (£6.50), and puddings (£2.95); service is prompt and friendly. The more elaborate menu in the no-smoking restaurant is popular in the evenings – it's worth booking then. No bar food on Saturday evenings, though you can eat the restaurant menu in the beamed bar. Cosy and spotless, this has prints and old photographs of the area, some decorative plates, stuffed wildlife, comfortable brass-studded black dining chairs, an open fire, and rugs on the stone and composition floor. Well kept Maclays 70/- and Wallace IPA and guests on handpump, maybe under light blanket pressure, and 20 malt whiskies; traditional Scottish piped music. There are tables under parasols outside. Note the winter opening times. *(Recommended by PACW, Susan and John Douglas, A Muir, E A Froggatt, Roger and Christine Mash)*

Free house ~ Licensees Elizabeth and Eugene Maxwell ~ Real ale ~ Bar food (not Sat evening) ~ Restaurant ~ (01877) 376292 ~ Children in eating area of bar and restaurant ~ Open 12-11; 12-12 Sat; 12.30-11 Sun; closed Mon-Thurs in winter

BROUGHTY FERRY NO4630 Map 11
Fishermans Tavern ◪ £

12 Fort St; turning off shore road

On summer evenings they might have barbecues at this unspoilt, bustling and friendly town pub – you can come by boat, to the nearby jetty. The impressive range of well kept real ales is one of the main attractions; it can change every day, but typically includes Belhaven 80/-, Sandy Hunters and St Andrews, Fraoch Heather Ale, Maclays 80/-, and guests, all on handpump or tall fount air pressure. There's also a good choice of malt whiskies, some local country wines, and a draught wheat beer. The little brown-carpeted snug on the right with its nautical details, light pink soft fabric seating, basket-weave wall panels and beige lamps is the more lively bar, and on the left is a secluded lounge area. The carpeted back bar (popular with diners) has a Victorian fireplace; dominoes and fruit machine, and an open coal fire. Lunchtime bar food includes filled rolls (from £1.30), soup (£1.45), pasta of the day (£3.20), filled jacket potatoes (£3.25), hot Mexican tortilla with spicy chicken, chilli and tomato filling (£4.75), seafood hotpot or steak and ale pie (£5.50), and specials like haunch of venison in red wine sauce (£5.50); children's helpings (£3.75). Disabled lavatories, and baby changing facilities. The breakfast room is no smoking. The landlord also runs the well preserved Speedwell Bar in Dundee. The nearby seafront gives a good view of the two long, low Tay bridges. *(Recommended by Susan and John Douglas, R M Macnaughton)*

Free house ~ Licensee Jonathan Stewart ~ Real ale ~ (01382) 775941 ~ Children in eating area of bar ~ Folk music Thurs night ~ Open 11am-midnight(1am Sat); 12.30-midnight Sun ~ Bedrooms: £21(£45B)/£38(£55B)

CANONBIE NY3976 Map 9
Riverside Inn 🍽 ♉ 🛏

Village signposted from A7

Most of the very good food at this civilised little inn is free range and local; breads are organic, cheeses unpasteurised, and fresh fish delivered three times a week. Tables are usually laid for dining, and the varied bar menu, on two blackboards, might include soups such as mushroom and bacon or carrot and sage (£2.20), with home-made breads like tomato and courgette or Guinness and treacle loaf, home-made pork and venison terrine (£4.25), moules marinières (£4.95), salads such as fresh dressed crab (£5.75), plenty of fresh fish like medallions of cod in beer batter (£6.55), poached fillet of sea tout with chive sauce (£7.55), grilled sea bream with red peppers (£7.95), and fillet of wild salmon with watercress hollandaise (£7.95), thick barnsley chop or marinated guinea fowl (£8.95), and fine puddings such as prune and apple crumble or rhubarb and ginger fool (£3.50). They do a three course Sunday lunch. Well kept Yates Bitter on handpump, along with maybe a guest beer like Caledonian IPA; also, a dozen or so malt whiskies, an organic lager, and a carefully made choice of properly kept and served wines, with quite a few by the glass or half bottle. The communicating rooms of the bar have a mix of chintzy furnishings and dining chairs, pictures on the walls for sale, and some stuffed wildlife; the dining room and half the bar area are no smoking. In summer – when it can get very busy – there are tables under the trees on the front grass. The bedrooms aren't cheap, but have several nice little extras. Over the quiet road, a public playground runs down to the Border Esk (the inn can arrange fishing permits), and there are lovely walks nearby. *(Recommended by K F Mould, R Macnaughton, Dr Michael Allen, K M Crook, Vann and Terry Prime, Christopher Beade, John Plumridge, Peter Marshall, Bonnie Bird, Michael Collins, Paul S McPherson; also in the Good Hotel Guide)*

Free house ~ Licensee Robert Phillips ~ Real ale ~ Bar food ~ Restaurant ~ (01387) 371512 ~ Children in eating area of bar ~ Open 11(12 Sun)-2.30, 6.30-11; closed last two weeks Feb, two weeks in Nov ~ Bedrooms: £55B/£78B

CARBOST NG3732 Map 11
Old Inn

This is the Carbost on the B8009, in the W of the central part of the island

One of the most traditionally pubby places on Skye (though watch out, there isn't an obvious sign), this straightforward old stone house is useful for walkers and climbers, in a nice spot beside Loch Harport. From the terrace, there are fine views of the loch and the harsh craggy peaks of the Cuillin Hills. The three simple areas of the main bare-boards bar are knocked through into one, and furnished with red leatherette settles, benches and seats, amusing cartoons on the part-whitewashed and part-stripped stone walls, and a peat fire; darts, pool, cribbage, dominoes, and piped traditional music. A small selection of bar meals includes cock-a-leekie soup (£1.70), sandwiches, chestnut and stilton pâté with highland oatcakes (£2.25), haggis, neeps and tatties (£5.50), spinach and cashew nut strudel (£5.65), and fresh cod in beer batter (£6.45); readers have enjoyed their Scottish cheeses. Several malt whiskies – including Talisker, from the distillery just 100 yards from the pub (in summer – except on Saturdays – there are guided tours, with samples). Children's play area. Non-residents can come for the breakfasts if they book the night before, and the bedrooms in a separate annexe have sea views. They recently added a new bunkhouse and shower block for the loch's increasing number of yachtsmen. Note the reduced opening in winter. *(Recommended by Steve Radley, Jenny and Brian Seller, Nigel Woolliscroft, E J Locker)*

Free house ~ Licensee Deirdre Morrison ~ Bar food (6-10) ~ (01478) 640205 ~ Children in eating area of bar till 8 ~ Open 11-12(11.30 Sat); 12.30-11 Sun; 12-2.30, 5.30-11 winter ~ Bedrooms: £24.50B/£49B

CAWDOR NH8450 Map 11
Cawdor Tavern

Just off B9090 in Cawdor village; follow signs for post office and village centre

This friendly Highland village pub looks rather modern from the outside, so the elegant fittings inside are quite a surprise. Most impressive is the beautiful oak panelling in the substantial rather clubby lounge, gifted to the tavern by a former Lord Cawdor and salvaged from the nearby castle; more recent panelling is incorporated into an impressive new ceiling. The public bar on the right has a brick fireplace housing an old cast-iron stove, as well as elaborate wrought-iron wall lamps, chandeliers laced with bric-a-brac, and an imposing pillared serving counter. Popular dishes this year have included fresh mussels steamed with garlic, shallots, cream and white wine, oak smoked chicken and chorizo sausage salad (£3.25), warm crab tart with chive cream sauce (£3.95), fillet of pork on grain mustard mash with a thyme jus or chicken filled with haggis and served with a drambuie cream sauce (£8.95), and puddings like Belgian chocolate tart with a heather honey cream (£3.95); the restaurant is partly no smoking. They usually serve snacks all day in summer. Caledonian 80/- and Orkney Dark Island on handpump, and over a hundred malt whiskies; darts, pool, cribbage, dominoes, table skittles, board games, cards, fruit machine, video games, juke box, piped music. There are tables on the front terrace, with tubs of flowers, roses, and creepers climbing the supports of a big awning. *(Recommended by Nigel Wilkinson, Neil Townend, Ian and Villy White)*

Free house ~ Licensee Norman Sinclair ~ Real ale ~ Bar food (12-2, 5.30-9) ~ Restaurant ~ (01667) 404777 ~ Children welcome away from public bar ~ Open 11-11(12.30 Fri, Sat); 12.30-11 Sun; 11-3, 5-11(12.30 Fri, Sat) winter; closed 25 Dec, 1 Jan

CLACHAN SEIL NM7718 Map 11
Tigh an Truish

Island linked by bridge via B844, off A816 S of Oban

Near a lovely anchorage and set next to the attractive old bridge which joins Seil Island to the mainland, this 18th-c inn is very much a traditional local, but with good food that readers very much enjoy. The unpretentious and informal L-shaped bar has pine-clad walls and ceiling, some fixed wall benches along with the wheelback and other chairs, tartan curtains for the bay windows overlooking the inlet, prints and oil paintings, and a woodburning stove in one room, with open fires in the others; pleasant service. The good bar food might include excellent home-made soup (£1.90), scallops and salmon in cheese and leek sauce (£3.50), moules marinières (£4.25), spicy bean casserole or chicken curry (£4.95), smoked haddock mornay (£6.50), steak and ale pie (£6.75), venison in a pepper, cream and drambuie sauce (£6.95), half a lobster (£7.50), and puddings such as syrup sponge or chocolate pudding with Mars bar sauce (£1.90); the dining room is no smoking. Well kept McEwans 80/- and a summer guest on handpump, and a good choice of malt whiskies; darts, dominoes, TV, piped music. There are some seats in the small garden, and they have their own filling station just opposite. There's a rather jolly story about the origin of the pub's name. *(Recommended by Pamela and Merlyn Horswell, M A Buchanan, M Mason, D Thompson, Paul Cleaver, Mike and Penny Sanders)*

Free house ~ Licensee Miranda Brunner ~ Real ale ~ Bar food (12-2, 6-8.30) ~ Restaurant ~ (01852) 300242 ~ Children in restaurant ~ Open 11(12 Sun)-11.30; 11-2.30, 5-11 winter; closed 25 Dec ~ Bedrooms: /£45B

CREEBRIDGE NX4165 Map 9

Creebridge House Hotel 🛏

Minnigaff, just E of Newton Stewart

Very popular with readers at the moment (several of whom come back every year), this sizeable country house hotel is a fine place to stay with lots to do nearby. Tables under cocktail parasols out on the front terrace look across a pleasantly planted lawn, where you can play croquet. The welcoming and neatly kept carpeted bar has well kept Marstons Pedigree, Orkney Dark Island and Timothy Taylor Landlord on handpump, as well as about 40 malt whiskies, and that great rarity for Scotland, a bar billiards table. Enjoyable brasserie-style food includes home-made soup (£2.10), lunchtime sandwiches (from £1.95; elaborate baguettes and filled rolls from £3.95), cullen skink (£2.75), chicken liver pâté or warm crispy duck salad (£3.95), goat's cheese and leek pancakes with a coconut and coriander dressing (£6.75), filo parcels of wild mushrooms with madeira cream (£6.95), chargrilled loin of pork on an apricot caramel topped with apple and black pudding compôte (£7.75), beef stroganoff with wild mushrooms and brandy (£8.95), steaks (from £10.95), and good puddings; daily specials, excellent fresh fish, and Sunday lunchtime carvery in the comfortable restaurant. Meats are local and well hung, presentation careful with good attention to detail, and service cheerful and helpful. Fruit machine, comfortably pubby furniture, and maybe unobtrusive piped music. The garden restaurant is no smoking. The hotel is set in three acres of gardens and woodland, and they can arrange fishing, walking, pony-trekking, and complimentary golf at the local golf course. *(Recommended by Neil Townend, Brenda Crossley, John Plumridge, Walter and Susan Rinaldi-Butcher, Stan and Hazel Allen, John and Joan Wyatt)*

Free house ~ Licensee Chris Walker ~ Real ale ~ Bar food ~ Restaurant ~ (01671) 402121 ~ Children welcome ~ Open 12-2.30, 6-11.30 ~ Bedrooms: £59B/£98B

CRINAN NR7894 Map 11

Crinan Hotel 🍴 🛏

A816 NE from Lochgilphead, then left on to B841, which terminates at the village

Picture windows in this beautifully positioned hotel's two stylish upstairs bars make the most of the marvellous views of the busy entrance basin of the Crinan Canal, with its fishing boats and yachts wandering out towards the Hebrides. The simpler wooden-floored public bar (opening onto a side terrace) has a cosy stove and kilims on the seats, and the cocktail bar has a nautical theme with wooden floors, oak and walnut panelling, antique tables and chairs, and sailing pictures and classic yachts framed in walnut on a paper background of rust and green paisley, matching the tartan upholstery. The Gallery bar is done in pale terracotta and creams and has a central bar with stools, Lloyd Loom tables and chairs, and lots of plants. Good bar food (lunchtimes only) might include home-made soup (£3.25), Isle of Jura clams with smoked bacon and parmesan salad (£7.50), grilled Arbroath smokie (£8.50), braised sausages with chive mash and onion gravy (£9.50), locally smoked wild salmon or a substantial seafood stew (£12.50), and a pudding such as lemon tart or chocolate roulade (£3.95), or Scottish farmhouse cheddar (from a 75lb cheese) with oatcakes (£4.25). You can get sandwiches and so forth from their coffee shop. Theakstons Best, a good wine list, a good few malt whiskies, and freshly squeezed orange juice. The restaurants are very formal. Breakfasts can be outstanding. Many of the paintings are by the landlord's wife, artist Frances Macdonald. *(Recommended by Nigel Woolliscroft, Walter Reid)*

Free house ~ Licensee Nicholas Ryan ~ Real ale ~ Bar food (12-2.30 only) ~ Restaurant ~ (01546) 830261 ~ Children in cocktail bar and lounges ~ Open 11-12 ~ Bedrooms: /£105B

CROMARTY NH7867 Map 11

Royal 🛏

Marine Terrace

Pretty much the centre of things in this beautifully restored sleepy village at the tip of the Black Isle, this friendly old-fashioned seaside hotel is a wonderfully peaceful and relaxing place to stay. Most of the rooms and a long covered porch area look out over the sea, and a couple of picnic-sets outside enjoy the same tranquil view. The comfortable lounge has quite a bright feel, as well as pink painted walls, cushioned wall seats and leatherette armchairs, small curtained alcoves with model ships, and old local photos; piped Scottish music. A room to the right with a fireplace is rather like a cosy sitting room; it leads into an elegant lounge for residents. The basic public bar, popular with locals, has a separate entrance; pool, darts, cribbage, dominoes, TV, juke box. Good bar food includes deep-fried haggis balls (£3.95), local mussels with pâté and tomato sauce (£4.40), smoked salmon and prawn tagliatelle or vegetable risotto (£6.50), various crêpes such as chicken with spicy rice, curry sauce and coconut (£6.60), scampi, mussels and prawns sautéed with onions and bacon (£9.25), and daily specials such as venison in red wine or huge prawns (£9.95); children's menu. Around three dozen malt whiskies, and very friendly, chatty service. The porch (a nice bit to eat in) is no smoking. It's hard to believe Cromarty was once a thriving port; a little museum a short stroll away sparkily illustrates its heritage. You can get boat trips out to see the local bottlenose dolphins, and maybe whales too in summer. *(Recommended by Neil Townend)*

Free house ~ Licensee J A Shearer ~ Real ale ~ Bar food (12-2, 5.30-9) ~ Restaurant ~ (01381) 600217 ~ Children welcome ~ Open 11-12 ~ Bedrooms: £35.40B/£55.65B

EAST LINTON NT5977 Map 11
Drovers 🍺

5 Bridge St (B1407), just off A1, Haddington—Dunbar

With a good range of six real ales and some excellent food, this comfortable old inn has much more of a genuinely pubby feel than most places in the area. The atmospheric main bar feels a bit like a welcoming living room as you enter from the pretty village street, with faded rugs on the wooden floor, a basket of logs in front of the woodburning stove, and comfortable armchairs and nostalgic piped jazz creating a very relaxed air. There's a goat's head on a pillar in the middle of the room, plenty of hops around the bar counter, fresh flowers and newspapers, and a mix of prints and pictures (most of which are for sale) on the half panelled, half red-painted walls. Changing every week, the choice of beers might include brews like Deuchars IPA, Elgoods Black Dog, Flowers Original, Nethergate Old Growler, Smiles Mayfly, and Tomintoul Wild Cat; friendly, helpful service from the two sisters in charge and their smartly dressed staff. A similar room leads off, and a door opens onto a walled lawn with tables and maybe summer barbecues. Relying on fresh local ingredients delivered daily (their local meats are excellent), the very good food might include soups such as a traditional Scotch broth (£2.45), seafood bisque finished with cream and brandy (£3.50), vegetarian lasagne (£4), good, substantial sandwiches (from £4.95), yorkshire pudding filled with braised sausages (£6), whole baked peppers or fondue of aubergines, mushrooms and tomatoes (£6.95), mint glazed leg of lamb with cumberland sauce (£7), and game casserole with sweet red cabbage (£7.95). Part of the upstairs restaurant is no smoking. The gents' has a copy of the day's *Scotsman* newspaper on the wall. *(Recommended by R M Corlett, Christine and Malcolm Ingram)*

Free house ~ Licensees Michelle and Nicola Findlay ~ Real ale ~ Bar food (11.30-2(12.30-2.30 Sun), 6-9.30(10 Sat)) ~ Restaurant ~ (01620) 860298 ~ Children welcome ~ Folk and other music Weds night ~ Open 11.30-2.30, 5-11(1 Sat); 12.30-11 Sun; closed 25 Dec, 1 Jan

EDINBURGH NT2574 Map 11
Abbotsford

Rose St; E end, beside South St David St

Something of a long-standing institution for city folk, this small and gently formal single bar pub (originally built for Jenners department store) has a notably pleasant, friendly atmosphere. Rarely too busy, it has dark wooden half panelled walls, a highly polished Victorian island bar counter, long wooden tables and leatherette benches, and a welcoming log effect gas fire; there are prints on the walls and a rather handsome ornate plaster-moulded high ceiling. The range of well kept beers changes every week, but there are usually a couple of guests like Aviemore Red Murdoch, Flowers Original, or Inveralmond Ossians alongside the Caledonian 80/- and Deuchars IPA, served in the true Scottish fashion from a set of air pressure tall founts. Good, reasonably priced lunchtime food might include sandwiches, soup (£1.30), haggis, neeps and tatties (£4.95; locals reckon it's amongst the best in town), curry (£4.95), a roast of the day (£4.95), breaded haddock (£5.25), and sirloin steak (£6.50). Around 72 malt whiskies, efficient service from dark-uniformed or white shirted staff, piped music. *(Recommended by Colin Draper, Monica Shelley, A Jones, Mr and Mrs Jon Corelis, D Parkhurst)*

Free house ~ Licensee Colin Grant ~ Real ale ~ Bar food (11.45-3) ~ Restaurant (evening) ~ (0131) 225 5276 ~ Children in eating area of bar and restaurant ~ Open 11-11; closed Sun

Bannermans 🍺 £

212 Cowgate

In the evenings this busy city centre pub is aimed very much at the younger end of the market, with DJs, discos, live music and karaoke, but it's rather different in tone earlier in the day which is when readers really love it. Used to store oysters before it became a pub, it's set underneath some of the tallest buildings in the Old Town, and has a unique warren of simple crypt-like flagstoned rooms with barrel-vaulted ceilings, bare stone walls, wood panelling and pillars at the front, and quite a mixture of wrought-iron and wooden tables and chairs. There may a big screen during sporting events. Well kept Caledonian 80/- and Deuchars IPA, with guests like Maclay Wallace and Heather Fraoch, and around 30 malt whiskies; dominoes, fruit machine, piped music. Popular Sunday breakfasts, and the usual lunchtime bar snacks. *(Recommended by Eric Larkham, Mr and Mrs Jon Corelis, Roger and Jenny Huggins)*

Caledonian ~ Manager Paul D Hastie ~ Real ale ~ (0131) 5563254 ~ Children welcome till 6pm ~ Live entertainment every night ~ Open 12(11 Sun)-1

Bow Bar ★ 🍺 £

80 West Bow

The range of up to a dozen very well kept real ales is one of the main draws at this chatty and traditional drinking pub, handily placed just below the castle. Served from impressive antique tall founts made by Aitkens, Mackie & Carnegie, Gaskell & Chambers, and McGlashan, a typical choice would take in Caledonian 80/- and Deuchars IPA, Dent Aviator, Fullers London Pride, Timothy Taylor Landlord, and various changing guests. The grand carved mahogany gantry has quite an array of malts (over 140) including lots of Macallan variants and cask strength whiskies, as well as a good collection of vodkas (nine) and gins (eight), and, particularly, rums (24); they're an exclusive supplier of Scottish Still Spirit. Basic, but busy and friendly, the spartan rectangular bar has a fine collection of appropriate enamel advertising signs and handsome antique trade mirrors, sturdy leatherette wall seats and heavy narrow tables on its lino floor, café-style bar seats, an umbrella stand by the period gas fire, a (silent) prewar radio, a big pendulum clock, and a working barograph. Look out for the antiqued photograph of the bar staff in old-fashioned clothes (and moustaches). Simple, cheap bar snacks such as steak and mince pies (£1.20). Cheery and knowledgeable service, and no games or music – just relaxed chat, and the clink of glasses. *(Recommended by Andy and Jill Kassube, the Didler, D Parkhurst, Dennis Dickinson, Peter Marshall, A Jones, Eric Larkham, Steve and Carolyn Harvey, Vann and Terry Prime)*

Free house ~ Licensee Lee Thorbers ~ Real ale ~ Bar food (12-4 (not Sun)) ~ (0131) 226 7667 ~ Open 11-11.30; 12.30-11 Sun; closed 25, 26 Dec, 1, 2 Jan

Guildford Arms 🍺

West Register St

Easily the most popular of our Edinburgh main entries with readers, this most enjoyable Victorian city pub stands out for its friendly, bustling atmosphere and exquisite décor – though the range of beers is quite a draw as well. They keep a very fine choice of up to eleven real ales on handpump, most of which are usually Scottish, with Belhaven 60/-, Caledonian Deuchers IPA and 80/-, Harviestoun 70/- and Ptarmigan, Orkney Dark Island, and changing guests (three of which are always English). During the Edinburgh Festival they usually hold a beer and folk festival. The main bar has lots of mahogany, glorious colourfully painted plasterwork and ceilings, big original advertising mirrors, and heavy swagged velvet curtains at the arched windows. Refurbished after some recent flooding, the snug little upstairs gallery restaurant gives a dress-circle view of the main bar (notice the lovely old mirror decorated with two tigers on the way up), and under this gallery a little cavern of arched alcoves leads off the bar. Good choice of malt whiskies; fruit machine, lunchtime piped jazz and classical music. Lunchtime bar food includes chargrilled steak burger (£5.10), home-made steak pie (£5.70), breaded haddock (£5.65), and daily specials; on Sundays they only do filled rolls. It is very popular, but even at its busiest you shouldn't have to wait to be served. No children. *(Recommended by Eric Larkham, the Didler, Neil Townend, Stephen and Jean Curtis, Simon and Amanda Southwell, B, M and P Kendall, Roger Huggins, A Jones, Susan and John Douglas, Andy and Jill Kassube, Steve and Carolyn Harvey, Mr and Mrs Jon Corelis)*

Free house ~ Licensee David Stewart ~ Real ale ~ Bar food (12-2) ~ Restaurant ~ (0131) 556 4312 ~ Open 11-12; 12.30-11 Sun

Kays Bar £

39 Jamaica St West; off India St

Prices never seem to alter at this cosy and atmospheric little back street pub, which is bigger than you might think from the outside and well loved by readers. John Kay was the original owner selling whisky and wine; wine barrels were hoisted up to the first floor and dispensed through pipes attached to nipples which can still be seen around the light rose. As well as various casks and vats there are old wine and spirits merchant notices, gas-type lamps, well worn red plush wall banquettes and stools around cast-iron tables, and red pillars supporting a red ceiling. A quiet panelled back room leads off, with a narrow plank-panelled pitched ceiling; very warm open coal fire in winter. A good range of eight constantly changing interesting real ales might include well kept Belhaven 80/-, Boddingtons, Exe Valley Devon Glory, Exmoor Ale, McEwans 80/-, St Peters Well, Theakstons Best and XB, and Youngers No 3 on handpump; up to 70 malts, between eight and 40 years old, and 10 blended whiskies. Simple, good value lunchtime bar food includes soup (£1), haggis, neaps and tatties, chilli or steak pie (£2.60), filled baked potatoes (£2.75) and chicken balti, lasagne or mince and tatties (£3); dominoes and cribbage. *(Recommended by Roger and Jenny Huggins, Steve and Carolyn Harvey, the Didler, Ian Phillips)*

Scottish Courage ~ Tenant David Mackenzie ~ Real ale ~ Bar food (12-2) ~ (0131) 225 1858 ~ Quiet children in back room till 5pm ~ Open 11-12(1 Fri, Sat); 11-11 Sun

Ship on the Shore

26 The Shore, Leith (A199)

In the heyday of Leith's docks (well represented in a reproduction engraving in the dining room) the Ship was a hotel that enjoyed a somewhat bawdy reputation; these days it's well regarded for its very good meals, with quite an emphasis on locally caught fish and seafood. Easy to spot by the delightfully intricate ship model that serves as a sign, it's right in the heart of what in recent years has become a really rather appealing part of town. At lunchtime they do a bargain three-course meal for £6.50, as well as soup (£1.95), sandwiches (from £4) and fish and chips (£5.95), while the evening menu might include things like rainbow trout with almond butter (£10.50), stir-fried medallions of monkfish with walnut oil and tomato and courgette brunoise, and grilled black bream on a bed of Chinese leaves (£13.95); popular Sunday breakfasts (£5.25). The atmospheric bar has a number of old painted signs for companies like the East India Bay Co, or Podgie Mullen, fishmonger and greengrocer, as well as wooden chairs, floors and wall benches, ships' lanterns, and compasses and other nautical equipment; cribbage, dominoes, cards, Jenga, draughts, piped music. Well kept Courage Directors, Deuchars IPA and McEwan 80/- on handpump, and a dozen or so malt whiskies. Oars and fishing nets hang from the ceiling of the nicely panelled dining room. Tables outside are well placed for the late evening sun. *(Recommended by Monica Shelley, A Muir, Heather Martin)*

Free house ~ Licensee Roy West ~ Real ale ~ Bar food (not Fri lunchtime or Sat evening) ~ Restaurant ~ (0131) 555 0409 ~ Children over 8 ~ Open 12-11; 11-1 Sat; 11-11 Sun

Starbank ♀ ◀ £

67 Laverockbank Road, off Starbank Road; on main road Granton—Leith

Well regarded by readers for its friendly atmosphere and excellent choice of properly kept beers, this comfortably elegant pub has marvellous views over the Firth of Forth from the picture windows in the neat and airy bar. The range of beers changes all the time, but might include Belhaven 80/-, St Andrews and Sandy Hunters, Broughton Special, Harviestoun, Marstons Pedigree, Thwaites, and Timothy Taylor Landlord. A good choice of wines too (all 30 are served by the glass), and 25 malt whiskies. Well presented and tasty home-made bar food (with prices unchanged for the third year running) includes soup (£1.20), madeira herring salad (£2.50), a daily vegetarian dish (£4.25), lasagne or sausage casserole (£4.50), ploughman's (£4.75), baked haddock mornay (£5.25), mixed seafood salad or roast lamb (£5.50), and poached salmon with lemon and herb butter (£6.50). Service is helpful, the conservatory restaurant is no smoking, and there are no noisy games machines or piped music; sheltered back terrace. *(Recommended by Ian Phillips, Roger Huggins, Neil Townend, M A Buchanan, Andy and Jill Kassube, Neil Ben)*

Free house ~ Licensee Valerie West ~ Real ale ~ Bar food (12-2.30, 6-9.30; 12-9.30 Sat, Sun) ~ Restaurant ~ (0131) 552 4141 ~ Children welcome till 8pm ~ Monthly jazz ~ Open 11-11(12 Thurs-Sat); 12.30-11 Sun

ELIE NO4900 Map 11
Ship

Harbour

Tables on the terrace behind this welcoming harbourside pub look directly over Elie's broad sands and along the bay. It's a setting that's hard to beat if you like the seaside, and a fine spot for watching the Sunday matches of the pub's successful cricket team, who use the beach as their pitch (as do the rugby team in winter). Tables in the restaurant enjoy the same view. The villagey, unspoilt beamed bar has a lively nautical feel, as well as friendly locals and staff, coal fires, and partly panelled walls studded with old prints and maps; there's a simple carpeted back room. Good bar food includes dishes such as soup (£1.50), sandwiches (from £3.25), grilled haggis with onion sauce (£3.50), vegetable curry or fresh local haddock and chips (£6.50), steak pie (£7), poached salmon with lime mayonnaise (£7.50), Scottish steaks (from £12), and puddings (£3.50); children's menu (£3.95). They do a good Sunday lunch, and maybe barbecues in summer, and have nice home-made cakes if you pop in during the afternoon. Well kept Belhaven Best and 80/-, and Theakstons Best; darts, dominoes, captain's mistress, cribbage and shut the box. Bedrooms are next door, in a guesthouse run by the same family. *(Recommended by Eric Locker, Mike and Penny Sanders, Sue and John Woodward)*

Free house ~ Licensees Richard and Jill Philip ~ Real ale ~ Bar food ~ Restaurant ~ (01333) 330246 ~ Children welcome away from front bar ~ Open 11-12(1 Fri, Sat); 12.30-11 Sun; closed 25 Dec ~ Bedrooms: £30B/£50B

FORT AUGUSTUS NH3709 Map 11
Lock

Well placed at the foot of Loch Ness, this former village post office is right by the first lock of the flight of five that start the Caledonian Canal's climb to Loch Oich. It's a proper pub, full of locals and characters, and with a welcoming and amusing landlord. The atmosphere is lively and cheerful, especially in summer when it can be packed in the evenings with a good mix of regulars and boating people; they have folk music evenings then (Mon-Weds). Good value substantial food, with generous helpings of chips, includes lunchtime toasted sandwiches and filled rolls (from £2.50), soup (£1.85), a pint of Loch Fyne mussels (£4.65), stir fry vegetable and stilton bake (£5.50), fresh haddock (£5.95), venison casserole (£6.95), seafood stew (£8.95), steaks (from £11.75), and daily specials, including a catch of the day; quite a bit of the space is set aside for people eating – one part is no smoking. The fish dishes – particularly good in the upstairs restaurant – are very fresh indeed, and no wonder: Mr MacLennen has his own fishmonger's shop nearby. The bar is homely and comfortable, with a gently faded décor and some stripped stone, a new flagstone floor, big open fire, and unobtrusive piped music; Caledonian 80/-, Deuchars IPA and maybe Orkney Dark Island on handpump, and a fine choice of about 100 malt whiskies (in generous measures). The restaurant is no smoking (the rest of the pub can get smoky during busy periods). *(Recommended by Neil Townend, Mrs Kay Neville-Rolfe, Simon and Amanda Southwell)*

Free house ~ Licensee James MacLennen ~ Real ale ~ Bar food (12-3, 6-10) ~ Restaurant ~ (01320) 366302 ~ Children welcome ~ Folk music Mon-Weds June-Aug ~ Open 11-12(11.45 Sat); 12.30-11 Sun; closed 25 Dec, 1 Jan

GIFFORD NT5368 Map 11
Tweeddale Arms 🛏

High St

Looking across a peaceful green to the 300-year-old avenue of lime trees leading to the former home of the Marquesses of Tweeddale, this efficiently run hotel is probably the oldest building in this quiet Borders village. Comfortable and relaxed, the modernised lounge bar has cushioned wall seats, chairs and bar chairs, dried flowers in baskets, Impressionist prints on the apricot coloured walls, and a big curtain that divides off the eating area. Well liked lunchtime bar food typically includes very good soups (£1.70), deep-fried Japanese prawns with sweet and sour sauce (£3.75), battered haddock (£5.50), broccoli and haddie bake under cheese sauce or pork fillet in cider and mango chutney sauce (£5.95), poached salmon with prawn and parsley sauce (£6), pan-fried noisettes of lamb with mushrooms and tomato (£6.25), pan-fried Aberdeen Angus steak (£9), and puddings (£2.60); sandwiches are available all day (except Sundays). In the evening you may be able to order dishes in the bar from the restaurant. The well kept Belhaven Best and guest beers such as Borders SOB, Broughton Black Douglas, and Morlands Old Speckled Hen are usually rather cheaper in the public bar than in the lounge; cheerful service. Quite a few malt whiskies, including the local Glenkinchie, and charming, efficient and friendly service; dominoes, fruit machine, video game, cribbage, and piped music. If you're staying, the tranquil hotel lounge is especially comfortable, with antique tables and paintings, chinoiserie chairs and chintzy easy chairs, an oriental rug on one wall, a splendid corner sofa and magazines on a table. *(Recommended by Neil Townend, Nick and Meriel Cox, R Macnaughton, Comus Elliott)*

Free house ~ Licensee Wilda Crook ~ Real ale ~ Bar food ~ Restaurant ~ (01620) 810240 ~ Children welcome ~ Open 11-11(12 Sat, Sun) ~ Bedrooms: £42.50B/£65B

GLASGOW NS5865 Map 11
Auctioneers £

6 North Ct, St Vincent Pl

Walking past you might not instantly realise that these former auction rooms have been splendidly converted into a pub: the windows look like a shop front, replete with junk and a shop dummy. Inside, the valuation booths around the edges of the main high-ceilinged, stone-flagged room have been transformed into intimate little booths, and there are plenty of antiques and more junk dotted about as if they were for sale, with lot numbers clearly displayed. You'd probably be most tempted to bid for the goods in the smarter red-painted side room, which rather than the old lamps, radios, furnishings and golf clubs elsewhere has framed paintings, statues, and even an old rocking horse, as well as comfortable leather sofas, unusual lamp fittings, a big fireplace, and an elegant old dresser with incongruous china figures. There's quite a bustling feel in the bar (especially in the evenings), which has lots of old sporting photos, programmes and shirts along one of the panelled walls. Well kept Caledonian 80/- and Deuchars IPA, Orkney Dark Island and a changing guest on handpump, and over 30 malt whiskies; friendly, helpful service, big screen TV (popular for big sporting events), fruit machine, video game, trivia, piped music. Served most of the day, bar food includes soup (£1.45), potato wedges with haggis (£2.75), lasagne or haggis, neeps and tatties (£3.95), fish and chips or chicken tikka (£4.45), and rib-eye steaks or Louisiana chicken (£4.95). The pub was about to undergo a slight facelift as we went to press, with fresh paint on the walls, and new furnishings. Sir Winston Churchill and William Burrell are just two of the figures who passed through when the place was still serving its original purpose, the latter returning a painting because he couldn't afford it. Another impressive conversion, the Counting House (see below), is just around the corner. *(Recommended by Richard Lewis, SLC, Ian Baillie, A Muir)*

Bass ~ Manager Michael Rogerson ~ Real ale ~ Bar food (11(12.30 Sun)- 8.45 (9.45 Fri, Sat)) ~ (0141) 229 5851 ~ Children till 8 ~ Open 11(12.30 Sun)-12; closed 25 Dec, 1 Jan

Babbity Bowster ⑪ ♀ £

16-18 Blackfriars St

Named after an 18th-c dance, this lively but stylish 18th-c town house feels rather like a continental café bar, and is one of our favourite Glasgow pubs. Welcoming and cosmopolitan, the simply decorated light interior has fine tall windows, well lit photographs and big pen-and-wash drawings in modern frames of Glasgow and its people and musicians, dark grey stools and wall seats around dark grey tables on the stripped wooden boards, and an open peat fire. The bar opens on to a terrace, extended this year, which has tables under cocktail parasols, trellised vines and shrubs, and adjacent boules; there may be barbecues out here in summer. They've jazzed up the menus a bit this year, and there's usually food available all day, starting with good value breakfasts from 8am to 10.30 (till 11.45 Sun). Popular dishes include several hearty home-made soups in three sizes (from £1.75), ratatouille (£3.50), croque monsieur (£3.65), haggis, neeps and tatties (£4.25; they also do a vegetarian version), stovies (£4.95), good daily specials, more elaborate treats like foie gras (£8.75), and evening tapas (from £2.50). There are more elaborate meals in the airy upstairs restaurant – watch out for special offers on food and drinks at various times of the day. Well kept Maclays 70/- and 80/-, and well chosen changing guest beers on air pressure tall fount, a remarkably sound collection of wines, malt whiskies, cask conditioned cider, freshly squeezed orange juice and good tea and coffee. Enthusiastic service is consistently efficient and friendly, taking its example from the energetic landlord. They have live Celtic music at weekends (and maybe spontaneously at other times too); dominoes. Car park. The bedrooms aren't huge. *(Recommended by Nigel Woolliscroft, Mark Percy, Lesley Mayoh, A Muir, M Hyde, Eric Larkham, Dodie Buchanan, Vann and Terry Prime, Walter Reid, SLC, Monica Shelley, Mike and Penny Sanders, Ian Phillips, Richard Lewis)*

Free house ~ Licensee Fraser Laurie ~ Real ale ~ Bar food (12-12) ~ Restaurant ~ (0141) 552 5055 ~ Children welcome ~ Celtic music at weekends ~ Open 11(12.30 Sun)-12; closed 25 Dec ~ Bedrooms: £50B/£70B

Blackfriars £

36 Bell Street

With its newspaper rack, candles on tables, and big shop-front windows looking over the street, the vibrant bare-boards bar of this relaxed and cosmopolitan cornerhouse manages to combine the atmosphere of a traditional pub with a younger café-like buzz. It's definitely somewhere students feel at home (there's the usual city centre array of posters for plays and arts events), but you'll usually find a real range of types and ages scattered about the spacious room. The main draw is the imaginative range of drinks, which has something for everyone: as well as five real ales, often from smaller independent breweries, they have 10 wines by the glass, 30 or so malt whiskies, a couple of draught Belgian beers, and, more unusually, a blackboard menu listing a dozen different coffees, from Brazilian Santos to Colombian supremo, all with helpful tasting notes. Changing regularly, the well kept beers might include Belhaven 60/-, Caledonian Deuchars IPA, Houston Killellan, Ind Coope Burton and Tetleys; they have a good range of European bottled beers too, and farm cider. Opposite the long bar is a big interestingly framed mirror above a cushioned wallseat, while elsewhere are a couple of tables fashioned from barrels, and up by the coffee menu a section with green cloths on all the tables; piped music, loudish some evenings. Lunchtime bar food such as sandwiches, a vegetarian pasta dish (from £3.50), sausages in red wine gravy with mustard mash (£3.95), and steak and ale pie (£4.95); in the evening they have pizzas (from £3.50), and a snackier 'tapas' menu with nachos, dips and the like; popular Sunday brunch menu. Friendly service, fruit machine, TV. In the basement is a long established Sunday night comedy club, with jazz on a Thursday (cover charge for these); on weekend evenings they might have free jazz in the bar as well. *(Recommended by Richard Lewis, Eric Larkham)*

Free house ~ Licensee Alan Cunningham ~ Real ale ~ Bar food (12-6, snacks only 6-12) ~ (0141) 552 5924 ~ Children in eating area of bar ~ Comedy Sun evening, jazz Thurs, Sun evenings ~ Open 11.30-12; 12.30-12 Sun

Counting House 🍺 £

24 George Square

Astonishingly roomy, this imposing place is a remarkable conversion by Wetherspoons of what was formerly a premier branch of the Royal Bank of Scotland. It's a perfect antidote for those who get a slight feeling of claustrophobia in some other Glasgow pubs. A lofty richly decorated coffered ceiling culminates in a great central dome, with well lit nubile caryatids doing a fine supporting job in the corners. There's the sort of decorative glasswork that nowadays seems more appropriate to a landmark pub than to a bank, as well as wall-safes, plenty of prints and local history, and big windows overlooking George Square. As soon as it opens there's a steady stream of people coming for coffee or early lunches, but there's endless space to absorb them; away from the bar are several carpeted areas (some no smoking) with solidly comfortable seating, while a series of smaller rooms, once the managers' offices, lead around the perimeter of the building. Some of these are surprisingly cosy, one is like a well stocked library, and a few are themed with pictures and prints of historical characters like Walter Scott or Mary, Queen of Scots. The central island servery has a good range of well kept ales on handpump, such as Caledonian 80/- and Deuchars IPA, Courage Directors, Theakstons Best, and a couple of guests such as Hop Back Summer Lightning or Stillmans 80/-, with a good choice of bottled beers and malt whiskies, and 12 wines by the glass. The usual Wetherspoons menu includes soup (£2.10), filled rolls (from £2.55), burgers (from £3.75), ploughman's (£4.25), mushroom stroganoff (£4.95), chicken and vegetable pie (£5.15), evening steaks (£8.95), daily specials, and puddings like chocolate truffle tart (£2.20). Fruit machine, video game. Several readers have detected a slight drop in standards in recent months: there seem to be less staff than previously, making service less efficient. *(Recommended by Isabel and Robert Hatcher, Richard Lewis, SLC, Mark Percy, Lesley Mayoh, Simon and Amanda Southwell, A Abbess, M McGarry, M Fryer, Eric Larkham)*

Free house ~ Licensee Philip Annett ~ Real ale ~ Bar food (11-10 (12.30-9.30 Sun)) ~ (0141) 248 9568 ~ Open 11(12.30 Sun)-12

GLENDEVON NN9904 Map 11
Tormaukin ♀ 🛏

A823

Readers have particularly enjoyed staying at this remote but well run hotel over the last year. A popular stop on one of the most attractive north-south routes through this part of Scotland, it still fulfills much the same role as it did when first built as a drovers' inn. Comfortable and neatly kept, the softly lit bar has plush seats against stripped stone and partly panelled walls, ceiling joists, log firs, and maybe gentle piped music. Good imaginative bar food includes soup (£2.20), chicken liver and herb pâté (£3.85), lunchtime ploughman's (£4.75), fresh haddock (£6.95), good salads (from £7.25), pork and pineapple casserole or stir-fried vegetables wrapped in a Mexican enchilada (£7.50), venison and mushroom sausages (£7.85), chicken breast with olive and sun-dried tomato tapenade, fish casserole (£9.50), good steaks (from £9.95), and puddings like sticky gingerbread pudding (£3.65); children's menu (from £2.75), good breakfasts. Three well kept real ales on handpump such as Harviestoun 80/- and Bitter and Twisted, and Ind Coope Burton, a decent wine list, quite a few malt whiskies, and several vintage ports and brandies; attentive service, even when they're busy. Some of the bedrooms are in a converted stable block, and they've recently added a self-catering chalet for weekly lets. Loch and river fishing can be arranged, and there are plenty of good walks over the nearby Ochils or along the River Devon – plus over 100 golf courses (including St Andrews) within an hour's drive. *(Recommended by Jean and George Dundas, John T Ames, Andrew Low, Grant Thoburn, Colin Draper, Basil J S Minson, IHR, Vicky and David Sarti)*

Free house ~ Licensee Marianne Worthy ~ Real ale ~ Bar food (12-2, 5.30-9.30) ~ Restaurant ~ (01259) 781252 ~ Children welcome ~ Open 11(12 Sun)-11; closed ten days in Jan ~ Bedrooms: £55B/£78B

GLENELG NG8119 Map 11
Glenelg Inn 🛏

Unmarked road from Shiel Bridge (A87) towards Skye

Getting to this unique and atmospheric old inn is quite an adventure, the single-track road climbing dramatically past heather-strewn fields and mountains with spectacular views to the lochs below. Glenelg is the closest place on the mainland to Skye (there's a little car ferry across in summer) and on a sunny day tables in the inn's beautifully kept garden have lovely views across the water. Instantly welcoming, the unspoilt red-carpeted bar gives an overwhelming impression of dark wood, with lots of logs dotted about, and a big fireplace – it feels a bit like a mountain cabin; there are only a very few tables and cushioned wall benches, but crates and fish boxes serve as extra seating. Black and white photos line the walls at the far end around the pool table, and there are various jokey articles and local information elsewhere; darts, fruit machine. A blackboard lists the very short range of good bar meals such as soup (£2), hoagies (£2.50), locally smoked haddock kedgeree (£6), or pan-fried fillet of lamb with orange sauce (£7); in the evening they do an excellent three course meal in the no-smoking dining room (£24), making very good use of fresh local ingredients. A good choice of malt and cask strength whiskies; enthusiastic service. They may occasionally have fiddlers playing in the bar; if not, the piped music is in keeping with that theme. They can organise local activities, and there are plenty of excellent walks nearby. The bedrooms are excellent, and certainly much improved since Dr Johnson wrote 'We did not express much satisfaction' after staying here in 1773. *(Recommended by Jenny and Brian Seller, Guy Vowles; also in the Good Hotel Guide)*

Free house ~ Licensee Christopher Main ~ Bar food (not Nov-March) ~ Restaurant ~ (01599) 522273 ~ Children until 8 ~ Open 12-2.30, 5-11(11.30 Sat); closed lunchtimes Nov-March (not Sat) winter; closed Sun ~ Bedrooms: £67B/£134B

HADDINGTON NT5174 Map 11
Waterside

Waterside; just off A6093 at E end of Town

The tables outside this long two-storey white house enjoy a perfect view across the water to the church and narrow little bridge; on a sunny summer's day it really is a beautiful spot, and on Sundays then there may be a jazz band playing on the side terrace. The scene is captured rather well on an unusual glass engraving in the comfortably plush carpeted bar, which also has tied back curtains around little windows, lampshades on the window sills beside square wooden tables, a woodburning stove, and quite a mix of decorations on the walls (among the prints and pictures is a CD presented to them by the singer Fish). Across the hall a similar room has bigger tables and long cushioned benches, and there's a more formal stone-walled conservatory. Most people come here to eat (several tables have reserved signs), with the good bistro menu taking in soup (£2.25), smoked haddock and leek fishcakes or deep-fried haggis in whisky sauce (£3.50), mussels done in a variety of ways (£3.95), chicken in pepper sauce (£6.95), usually five vegetarian dishes, steak and Guinness pie, chicken and asparagus tagliatelle or salmon with puff pastry and a white wine sauce (all £6.95), pork cutlet with apple and cider sauce (£7.95), and steaks (from £10.95). Adnams Broadside, Belhaven 80/- 32, Caledonian Deuchars IPA and Timothy Taylor Landlord on handpump, and a good range of wines. There's a family connection with another new entry, the Drovers at East Linton. If you're driving, the gap under the adjacent bridge is very small; it's much nicer to park a short distance away and walk. *(Recommended by R M Corlett)*

Free house ~ Licensee Jim Findlay ~ Real ale ~ Bar food (all day Sun) ~ Restaurant ~ (01620) 825674 ~ Children welcome ~ Open 11.30-3, 5-12; 11.30-12 Sat, Sun

HOUSTON NS4166 Map 11
Fox & Hounds 🍺
Main St (B790 E of Bridge of Weir)

The friendly landlord at this cheerful village pub is also the brewer of the four Houston beers – Barachon, Formakin, Killellan and St Peters Well – that are well kept on handpump alongside two interesting guests like Harviestoun Schiehallion and Timothy Taylor Landlord (they also have occasional beer festivals); half a dozen wines by the glass and around 100 malt whiskies. A lively downstairs bar has pool, a fruit machine and a juke box and is popular with a younger crowd, and the clean plush hunting-theme lounge has comfortable seats by a fire and polished brass and copper. A wide range of food might include sesame chicken goujons with spicy tomato sauce or deep-fried mushrooms stuffed with red peppers and pesto with garlic mayonnaise (£2.95), grilled scallops provençale (£3.50), fresh mussels (£4.50), home-baked ham salad (£5.50), home-made steak, mushroom and ale pie (£5.95), apple, celery and mushroom stroganoff with calvados and rice or fresh batterd scampi (£6.50), and puddings like chocolate mousse with cream, caramelised bananas and fruit coulis (£3.50). There's a more elaborate menu in the upstairs restaurant; no-smoking areas in lounge and restaurant. *(Recommended by Walter Reid, Geoffrey and Brenda Wilson, O K Smyth, K M Crook)*

Free house ~ Licensee Carl Wengel ~ Real ale ~ Bar food (12-10) ~ Restaurant ~ (01505) 612448 ~ Children in restaurant and lounge bar till 8pm ~ Open 11-12; 11-1 Fri, Sat; 12.30-12 Sun

INNERLEITHEN NT3336 Map 9
Traquair Arms 🛏
Traquair Rd (B709, just off A72 Peebles—Galashiels; follow signs for Traquair House)

Highly praised again this year for its very good food, this pleasantly modernised inn is a hospitable and welcoming place, popular with locals and visitors alike. Making good use of fresh local ingredients, and served pretty much all day, the enjoyable meals might include home-made soups (£1.95), filled baked potatoes (from £3), omelettes (from £4), sweet potato and french bean pasty or beans bourguignon (£5.40), venison in port and hazelnut sauce or salmon baked in red wine with button mushroom and shallot sauce (£5.95), lamb cutlets in a lemon and ginger sauce (£7.95), pan-fried duckling (£10.95), steaks (from £11.75), and traditional puddings. The simple little bar has a warm open fire, a relaxed atmosphere, and well kept Broughton Black Douglas, Greenmantle and (from nearby Traquair House) Traquair Bear on handpump; several malt whiskies and draught cider, friendly staff. A pleasant and spacious dining room has an open fire and high chairs for children if needed; all the dining areas are no smoking. No music or machines. *(Recommended by John*

Knighton, R M Macnaughton, Christine and Malcolm Ingram, June and Tony Baldwin, Ian and Villy White, Gill and Maurice McMahon, Colin Thompson, Andy and Jill Kassube, Mel and Jan Chapman, Colin Draper, Ian and Nita Cooper)

Free house ~ Licensee Hugh Anderson ~ Real ale ~ Bar food (12-9) ~ Restaurant ~ (01896) 830229 ~ Children welcome ~ Open 11(12 Sun)-12 ~ Bedrooms: £45B/£58B

INVERARAY NN0908 Map 11
George £
Main Street East

A central part of the little Georgian town that's stretched along the shores of Loch Fyne in front of Inveraray Castle, this atmospheric and comfortably modernised hotel has been run by the same family for over 130 years. Often busy, the friendly stone-flagged bar has a nicely traditional feel, particularly on a dark winter's evening, with exposed joists, old tiles and bared stone walls, some antique settles, cushioned stone slabs along the walls, nicely grained wooden-topped cast-iron tables, lots of curling club and ships' badges, and a cosy log fire. The landlord went to some trouble tracking down and refitting the original flagstones. Lunchtime bar food (with prices unchanged from last year) includes soup (£1.80), ploughman's (from £3.25), sweet pickled herring (£3.95), fried haddock (£4.50), home-made steak pie (£4.95), and daily specials like Irish stew (£4.50) or cod in filo pastry and mornay sauce (£6.50), with evening dishes such as grilled Loch Fyne salmon (£7.50), and steaks (from £10.75); good local cheeses, and a choice of coffees. The two real ales are rotated from a range of ten, and might typically include Caledonian Deuchars IPA or Houston St Peter's Well on handpump; they keep over 80 malt whiskies. Friendly, helpful service, darts, pool, dominoes, and juke box. The bar can get a little smoky at busy times. The inn is well placed for the great Argyll woodland gardens – the rhododendrons are at their best in May and early June – and there are good walks nearby. The bedrooms have been individually redecorated, some with antique furnishings and big bathrooms. *(Recommended by Neil Townend, Dave Braisted, David Hoult, David and Carole Chapman)*

Free house ~ Licensee Donald Clark ~ Real ale ~ Bar food (12-9) ~ Restaurant ~ (01499) 302111 ~ Children welcome ~ Open 11(12 Sun)-12.30; closed 25 Dec, 1 Jan ~ Bedrooms: £30B/£65B

INVERARNAN NN3118 Map 11
Inverarnan Inn £
A82 N of Loch Lomond

Lots of tartan, stuffed animals and whisky galore – this friendly and atmospheric old drovers' inn feels very Scottish indeed (or so its English visitors tell us). The staff wear kilts to serve, accompanied by piped traditional Scottish music, and the long bar feels a little like a small baronial hall, unchanged for at least the last hundred years (some of the fusty furnishings and fittings look as if they could have been around even longer). Log fires burn in big fireplaces at each end, and there are green tartan cushions and deerskins on the black winged settles, Highland paintings and bagpipes on the walls, and a stuffed golden eagle on the bar counter. Lots of sporting trophies (such as a harpooned gaping shark), horns and so forth hang on the high walls of the central hall, where there's a stuffed badger curled on a table, and a full suit of armour. A wide range of good malts – 60 in the gantry and 60 more in stock, and farm cider. Bar food includes good broth (£1.75), toasted sandwiches (£1.80), pâté (£2.35), steak and Guinness pie (£4.50), pork chop (£5.25), and grilled trout (£6.95). Tables outside on a back terrace, with more in a field alongside – where you might come across a couple of ponies and geese. A stream runs behind. The bedrooms were about to be refurbished as we went to press. *(Recommended by Nigel Woolliscroft, Richard Gibbs, Susan and John Douglas, Tim Robbins)*

Free house ~ Licensee Stephen Muirhead ~ Real ale ~ Bar food (12-8.15) ~ (01301) 704234 ~ Children in eating area of bar ~ Open 11(12 Sun)-11(12 Fri, Sat); closed 25 Dec ~ Bedrooms: £21B/£21B

ISLE OF WHITHORN NX4736 Map 9
Steam Packet £

Harbour Row

The big picture windows of this friendly modernised inn have good views of the picturesque natural working harbour – there's usually quite a bustle of yachts and inshore fishing boats. Inside, the homely low-ceilinged bar is split into two: on the right, plush button-back banquettes and boat pictures, and on the left, green leatherette stools around cast-iron-framed tables on big stone tiles, and a wood-burning stove in the bare stone wall. Bar food can be served in the lower-beamed dining room, which has a big model steam packet boat on the white wall, excellent colour wildlife photographs, rugs on its wooden floor, and a solid fuel stove, and there's also a small eating area off the lounge bar. Good value bar meals might include soup (£1.50), filled rolls, sausage and thyme casserole or fish and chips (£4.50), and twice baked spinach and gruyère soufflé (£5.25), with evening dishes like salmon tail fillet wrapped in filo pastry on a root vegetable mash with honey dressing (£6.95), pork medallions layered with parma ham and parmesan cheese with a sage cream sauce (£7.95) and venison steak topped with pâté in puff pastry with a mushroom and leek sauce (£9.95); they do a good seafood platter (£8.95). Local cheeses, children's menu. Unusually, you can take food away. Well kept Theakstons XB on handpump, with a guest such as Black Sheep, Batemans XB or Caledonian Deuchars IPA; two dozen malt whiskies; pool, dominoes and piped music. Dogs welcome. White tables and chairs in the garden. The back bar and conservatory are no smoking (the main bar can be smoky at times). Every 1½ to 4 hours there are boat trips from the harbour; the remains of St Ninian's Kirk are on a headland behind the village. *(Recommended by John Plumridge, M Mason, D Thompson, Anthony Longden, Mrs Mary Walters, Brenda Crossley, Neil Townend, John and Joan Wyatt, Joyce McKimm, Mr and Mrs D Price)*

Free house ~ Licensee John Scoular ~ Real ale ~ Bar food ~ Restaurant ~ (01988) 500334 ~ Children welcome ~ Open 11(12 Sun)-11; closed Mon-Thurs 3-6 winter ~ Bedrooms: £25B/£50B

ISLE ORNSAY NG6912 Map 11
Eilean Iarmain ♀ 🛏

Signposted off A851 Broadford—Armadale

A particularly nice place to stay, this civilised little inn is attractively positioned overlooking the sea in a picturesque part of Skye. Gaelic is truly the first language of the charming staff, many of whom have worked here for some years; even the menus are bilingual. Friendly and relaxed, the cheerfully busy bar has a swooping stable-stall-like wooden divider that gives a two-room feel: good tongue-and-groove panelling on the walls and ceiling, leatherette wall seats, brass lamps, a brass-mounted ceiling fan, and a huge mirror over the open fire. There are about 34 local brands of blended and vatted malt whisky (including their own blend, Te Bheag, and a splendid vatted malt, Poit Dhubh Green Label, bottled for them but available elsewhere), and an excellent wine list; darts, dominoes, cribbage, and piped music. Bar food might include home-made soup (£1.75), lunchtime sandwiches, local mussels in whisky (£3.50), herring in oatmeal (£5.50), pork, fennel and mushroom casserole (£5.75), local crab with mozzarella (£6), grilled sea bass with lime and fennel (£8.50), and puddings like baked lemon tart (£2.50); children's menu (£3.50). They have their own oyster beds and every day send a diver to collect fresh scallops. The pretty, no-smoking dining room has a lovely sea view past the little island of Ornsay and the lighthouse on Sionnach (you can walk over the sands at low tide). Some of the bedrooms are in a cottage opposite. The most popular room has a canopied bed from Armadale Castle. *(Recommended by Don and Shirley Parrish, Mrs J H S Lang, Colin Draper, Myra Johnson, Jamie and Ruth Lyons, Eric Locker, Guy Vowles)*

Free house ~ Licensee Sir Iain Noble ~ Bar food (12-2.30, 6.30-9.30) ~ Restaurant ~ (01471) 833332 ~ Children in bar till 8.30 ~ Live entertainment Thurs, occasionally Fri and Sat ~ Open 12(12.30 Sun)-2.30, 5(6.30 Sun)-11.30 ~ Bedrooms: £80B/£105B

KELSO NT7334 Map 10
Queens Head ◖ £

Bridge Street (A699)

Tables at this Georgian coaching inn fill quickly at lunchtime for the wide choice of good generously served home-made food, which might include soup (£1.50), sandwiches (from £1.95), ploughman's (£3.75), fried haddock (£4.55), steak and ale pie (£4.65), and daily specials such as duck stir fry or a vegetarian dish (from £4); evening dishes like pan-fried medallions of pork with dijon mustard and red pepper sauce (£7.25), and breaded chicken stuffed with haggis with a whisky cream sauce (£7.40); children's meals (from £1.50). Service is by courteous waitresses, with very helpful and efficient licensees. With its comfortable mix of modern and traditional, the roomy and attractive back lounge has a very pleasant atmosphere; there's also a small simpler traditional streetside front bar, with a lively local feel. Well kept Courage Directors, Morlands Old Speckled Hen, Marstons Pedigree, and Whitbreads Castle Eden on handpump; darts, pool, dominoes, fruit machine, video game, and piped music; they can arrange golf, fishing and horse riding. *(Recommended by Andy, Julie and Stuart Hawkins, Nigel Woolliscroft, L Walker, Mike and Penny Sanders, B, M and P Kendall, J H and Dr S A Harrop)*

Free house ~ Licensee Ian Flannigan ~ Real ale ~ Bar food (12-2, 6-9) ~ Restaurant ~ (01573) 224636 ~ Children if eating ~ Open 11-12(1 Sat) ~ Bedrooms: £37B/£50B

KILBERRY NR7164 Map 11
Kilberry Inn ⑪ ⇌

B8024

Scotland's Dining Pub of the Year

The landlady at this whitewashed former post office must spend all her time cooking: as well as the inventive meals – easily among the best of any pub in Scotland – she makes all their own breads, muesli, pickles and chutney. You can buy some of these to take away, and indeed one reader seems to treat each visit like a trip to the supermarket, stocking up on jams and cakes each time he leaves. This is all the more remarkable given the pub's remote location – local produce often arrives by taxi. Particular favourites on the menu this year have included home-made malted granary garlic bread, soup with home-made bread, their award-winning country sausage pie (£7.95), Tobemory trout stuffed with mushroom pâté (£10.95), and good puddings accompanied by their own ice creams (including one made with genuine Blackpool rock). They appreciate booking if you want an evening meal. The small relaxed dining bar is tastefully and simply furnished but warmly friendly, with a good log fire. No real ale, but a good range of bottled beers and plenty of malt whiskies; the family room is no smoking. It's a lovely place to stay with neat, cosy bedrooms, and particularly attentive and welcoming service. Breakfasts are hearty, with a different home-made marmalade each day. The pub is on a delightful slow winding and hilly circular drive over Knapdale, from the A83 S of Lochgilphead, with breathtaking views over the rich coastal pastures to the sea and the island of Gigha beyond. Note it isn't open in winter (or on Sundays). *(Recommended by Dr G E Martin, Mike and Penny Sanders, R and T Kilby, C Johnson, A Maclean, Dr M Allen)*

Free house ~ Licensee John Leadbeater ~ Bar food ~ (01880) 770223 ~ Children in family room ~ Open 11-2.30, 5-10; 11-2.30, 5-10 Sat; closed Sun, mid Oct-Easter ~ Bedrooms: £38.50B/£67B

KILMAHOG NN6108 Map 11
Lade ♀

A84 just NW of Callander, by A821 junction

Set in the beautiful richly wooded surroundings of the Pass of Leny, with high hills all around and the Trossachs not far off, this well run place feels like a proper pub rather than the hotel bars more prevalent around here. The wide range of bar food is all freshly made, with no frozen things at all, not even peas. The choice takes in soup (£1.99), lunchtime sandwiches (from £3.95), local herring marinaded in sweet dill sauce (£3.80), haggis, neeps and tatties, steak pie or vegetable pancake (£6.85), fish pie or game casserole (£7.85), grilled whole trout with lime butter (£8.95), rack of lamb (£14.95), daily specials, and puddings like crannachan (a rich mousse with whisky) or bread and butter pudding (£2.99); children's menu (£3.99). Well kept Broughton Greenmantle, Heather Fraoch Ale, and Orkney Red MacGregor on handpump, and a wine list strong on New World ones; friendly informal service, piped Scottish music, dogs allowed. The main carpeted dining bar has blond wood chairs around pine tables, with beams, some panelling, stripped stone and Highland prints; a no-smoking room opens on to the terrace and attractive garden, where they have three ponds stocked with fish, and hold summer evening barbecues. *(Recommended by PACW, Isabel and Robert Hatcher, Ian Baillie, Neil and Karen Dignan)*

Free house ~ Licensee Paul Roebuck ~ Real ale ~ Bar food ~ (01877) 330152 ~ Children in eating area of bar until 9 ~ Open 12-3, 5.30-11(12 Sat); 12.30-2.30, 5.30-11 Sun; closed 1 Jan

KIPPEN NS6594 Map 11
Cross Keys 🛏
Main Street; village signposted off A811 W of Stirling

Relaxed and comfortable, this friendly 18th-c inn is the kind of place where the licensees work hard to make you feel at home. Popular with locals, the straightforward but welcoming lounge has a good log fire, and there's a coal fire in the attractive family dining room. Good generously served food, using fresh local produce, includes home-made soup (£1.85), haggis filo parcels with whisky sauce (£3.65), omelettes (from £3.30), lamb stovies (£4.95), venison burgers (£5.95), chicken and apricot casserole (£6.75), steak pie (£6.85), salmon with a ginger and lime sauce (£6.95), and puddings like bread and butter pudding (£2.95) and clootie dumpling (£3.10); smaller helpings for children. Well kept Broughton Greenmantle on handpump, and quite a few malt whiskies; dominoes, shove-ha'penny, fruit machine, and juke box, with darts, pool and TV in the separate public bar. The garden has tables and a children's play area. Booking is essential for the well regarded restaurant. The bedrooms were about to be upgraded as we went to press. *(Recommended by Neil Townend, Neil Ben, Ian Jones, Graham and Lynn Mason, Mr and Mrs George Dundas, R M Macnaughton)*

Free house ~ Licensees Angus and Sandra Watt ~ Real ale ~ Bar food (12-2, 5.30-9.30; 12.30-2, 5.15-9.30 Sun) ~ Restaurant ~ (01786) 870293 ~ Children welcome ~ Open 12-2, 5.30-11(5.15-12 Sat); 12.30-11.30 Sun; closed 1 Jan, 25 Dec evening ~ Bedrooms: £19.50/£39(£42B)

KIPPFORD NX8355 Map 9
Anchor
Off A710 S of Dalbeattie

Overlooking the big natural harbour and the peaceful hills beyond, this waterfront inn has a good bustling summer atmosphere and friendly, helpful staff. The traditional back bar has built-in red plush seats, panelled walls hung with nautical prints, and a coal fire. The no-smoking lounge bar, more used for eating, has comfortable plush banquettes and stools and lots of prints and plates on the local granite walls. Tasty bar food includes home-made soup (£1.80), sandwiches (from £1.80), lunchtime dishes like fresh breaded haddock (£5.75), pies like steak (£5.95) or fish (£6.50), and daily specials like pasta (£5.95) or chicken with parma ham (£7.95); evening extras such as chicken in cashew nuts (£7.95), fajitas (£8.50), and steaks (from £11.50). Well kept Boddingtons, Marstons Pedigree, and Theakstons Best on handpump, and lots of malt whiskies. The games room has a juke box, TV, football table, fruit machine, video game, and board games. There are plenty of surrounding walks and the area is good for bird watching. Seats outside. *(Recommended by Stan and Hazel Allen, Andrew and Rachel Ratcliffe)*

Scottish Courage ~ Lease: Mark Charlloner ~ Real ale ~ Bar food (12-2.30, 5-9.30) ~ Restaurant ~ (01556) 620205 ~ Children welcome ~ Open 11-midnight; 11-3, 5-11 in winter ~ Bedrooms: £24B/£52.50B

KIRKTON OF GLENISLA NO2160 Map 11

Glenisla Hotel 🛏

B951 N of Kirriemuir and Alyth

Surrounded by the good walking country of one of the prettiest Angus Glens, this friendly 17th-c former posting inn is a very welcoming place to stay, but still feels like it's at the heart of the community. The licensees are keen to promote local produce, with the beers, wines, and cheeses all coming from nearby suppliers. The real ales Independence, Lia Fail, and Ossians – from the small Inveralmond brewery in Perth – are proving especially popular. The simple but cosy carpeted pubby bar has beams and ceiling joists, a roaring log fire (sometimes even in summer), wooden tables and chairs, decent prints, and a rather jolly thriving atmosphere; a garden opens off it. The lounge is comfortable and sunny, and the elegant high-ceilinged dining room has rugs on the wooden floor, pretty curtains, candles and fresh flowers, and crisp cream tablecloths. Carefully prepared bar food at lunchtime might include soup (£2.50), popular home-made farmhouse pâté (£3.85), good haggis, neeps and tatties with a whisky sauce (£5.95), and a big mixed grill (£6.85), with evening dishes such as tomato and basil risotto (£5.95), steak and pigeon pie (£6.95), and free-range duck breast with a seasonal sauce (£9.95). The landlord has a keen interest in whiskies (he used to work for a distiller) so can advise on their 60 or so malts; also local fruit wines. A refurbished stable block has darts, pool, alley skittles, dominoes, cribbage, and a TV and video for children. The bedrooms are attractively individual, and they can arrange fishing in local lochs. No smoking in the restaurant. *(Recommended by Chris and Sue Bax, Susan and John Douglas, Gregg Davies, Jan and Corrie Wagenaar, Bob and Marilyn Fordham, Russell and Carole George, Grant Thoburn, Carole Smart, Andrew Jeeves)*

Free house ~ Licensee Shona Carrie ~ Real ale ~ Bar food (12.30-2.30, 6.30-8.30; 12-8 Sun) ~ Restaurant ~ (01575) 582223 ~ Children in eating area of bar ~ Open 11-11(11.45 Sat); 12-11 Sun; 11-2.30, 6-11 Mon-Fri Oct-June winter; closed 25, 26 Dec ~ Bedrooms: £40B/£66B

LINLITHGOW NS9976 Map 11

Four Marys 🍺 £

65 High St; 2 miles from M9 junction 3 (and little further from junction 4) – town signposted

Mary Queen of Scots was born at nearby Linlithgow Palace, and this atmospheric and welcoming pub is named after her four ladies-in-waiting. There are masses of mementoes of the ill-fated queen, such as pictures and written records, a piece of bed curtain said to be hers, part of a 16th-c cloth and swansdown vest of the type she'd be likely to have worn, and a facsimile of her death-mask. The L-shaped bar also has mahogany dining chairs around stripped period and antique tables, a couple of attractive antique corner cupboards, and an elaborate Victorian dresser serving as a bar gantry. The walls are mainly stripped stone, including some remarkable masonry in the inner area; piped music. A good choice of around eight constantly changing well kept real ales on handpump might take in Adnams Broadside, Belhaven 70/-, 80/- and St Andrews, Broughton Greenmantle, Caledonian Deuchars IPA, Fullers London Pride, Harviestoun Schiehallion, Orkney Dark Island and Shepherd Neame Spitfire; readers have found the reception at the bar very friendly. Bar food might include sandwiches, home-made chicken liver pâté (£2.25), haggis, neeps and tatties (£3.95), fresh smoked or fried haddock (£4.95), and good steamed puddings; the eating area is no smoking. When the building was an apothecary's shop, David Waldie experimented in it with chloroform – its first use as an anaesthetic. Parking can be difficult. *(Recommended by John T Ames)*

Belhaven ~ Manager Eve Forrest ~ Real ale ~ Restaurant ~ (01506) 842171 ~ Children in restaurant ~ Open 12-11(11.45 Thurs-Sat); 12.30-11 Sun; closed 1 Jan

---

'Children welcome' means the pubs says it lets children inside without any special restriction; readers have found that some may impose an evening time limit – please tell us if you find this.

LYBSTER ND2436 Map 11
Portland Arms 🛏

A9 S of Wick

Under new ownership since our last edition, this staunch old granite hotel is our most northerly main entry. It's a good base for the area, renowned for its spectacular cliffs and stacks. Extensively refurbished in recent months, the knocked-through open-plan bar is comfortable and attractively furnished, with winter open fires; there's also a small but cosy panelled cocktail bar. Lunchtime bar food includes home-made soup (£1.95), sandwiches (from £1.95), filled baked potatoes (£3.50), macaroni cheese (£5.45), fish and chips (£5.95), chicken with oatmeal stuffing and bacon (£6.95), several daily specials, and various steaks (from £10.50), with evening extras like king prawns fried in tempura batter on a sweet plum sauce (£9.75), or roast fillet of beef with a herb and cheese crust on a shallot red wine glaze (£11.50). They keep 40 or more malt whiskies (beers are keg); dominoes, trivia, piped music. They can arrange fishing and so forth. *(Recommended by Chris and Ann Garnett, Mr and Mrs Dewhurst, Sarah Markham, Neil Townend)*

Free house ~ Licensee Mark Stevens ~ Bar food (12-3, 5-9) ~ Restaurant ~ (01593) 721721 ~ Children welcome ~ Open 12-12(11.45 Sun) ~ Bedrooms: £45B/£68B

MELROSE NT5434 Map 9
Burts Hotel 🍽 🛏

A6091

The licensees of this comfortable and rather smart hotel have been here more than 25 years now, and in that time attracted a good few loyal devotees; we know of people who've made a 240-mile trip just for lunch. It's a civilised place to stop for a reliably good meal, but best to get there early – it can get very busy indeed. Promptly served by professional, hard-working staff, the menu might include lunchtime sandwiches, soup (£2), parfait of ostrich with quail on a hazelnut and passion fruit salad (£3.95), smoked haddock and scallop tartlet with leek and orange (£3.95), deep fried haddock (£6.75), vegetable lasagne (£6.95), and imaginative specials such as chicken breast with wild mushroom and asparagus risotto drizzled with Thai chilli dressing, braised shank of lamb with apricot, rosemary and root vegetables, or roast fillet of ling with salmon mousse and a shellfish salad (all £7.95); puddings such as pecan pie with maple walnut ice cream or baked croissant stuffed with ice cream on a bed of marinaded fruits (£3.95). Extremely good breakfasts. Recently renovated, the comfortable and friendly L-shaped lounge bar has lots of cushioned wall seats and windsor armchairs on its turkey carpet, and Scottish prints on the walls; the Tweed Room and the restaurant are no smoking. Well kept Bass and Belhaven 80/- and Sandy Hunters on handpump, 80 malt whiskies, and a good wine list; dominoes. There's a well tended garden (with tables in summer). Melrose with its striking ruined abbey is probably the most villagey of the Border towns; an alternative if distant way to view the abbey ruins is from the top of the tower at Smailholm. *(Recommended by Andy, Julie and Stuart Hawkins, Mr and Mrs R M Macnaughton, Mrs J Lang, K F Mould, Ian and Nita Cooper, Gill and Maurice McMahon, George and Jean Dundas, Ray and Chris Watson, Prof A Black, Comus Elliott, Vicky and David Sarti, Pamela and Merlyn Horswell, M Mason, D Thompson, Alan J Morton)*

Free house ~ Licensee Graham Henderson ~ Real ale ~ Bar food ~ Restaurant ~ (01896) 822285 ~ Children welcome ~ Open 11(12 Sun)-2.30, 5(6 Sun)-11; closed 26 Dec ~ Bedrooms: £50B/£88B

MOUNTBENGER NT3125 Map 9
Gordon Arms

Junction A708/B709

A cheery sight amidst splendid empty moorlands, this remotely set inn has its own petrol station, and in addition to the hotel bedrooms has a bunkhouse providing cheap accommodation for hill walkers, cyclists and fishermen, all of whom should find the surrounding area particularly appealing. Sir Walter Scott and James Hogg used to meet here, and letters from both are displayed on the walls of the comfortable public bar, along with an interesting set of period photographs of the neighbourhood (one dated 1865), and some well illustrated poems. Well kept Broughton Greenmantle and Ghillie and maybe summer guest beers on handpump, 56 malt whiskies, and a fair wine list. Bar food includes sandwiches (lunchtime only), vegetarian dishes, and things like home-made steak pie (£5.50), roast beef and yorkshire pudding (£5.95), and lamb chops (£7.50); children's dishes. Winter fire; pool, dominoes, and trivia. *(Recommended by Mike and Penny Sanders, Neil Townend)*

Free house ~ Licensee Harry Mitchell ~ Real ale ~ Bar food ~ Restaurant ~ (01750) 82232 ~ Children in eating areas till 8pm ~ Accordian and fiddle club third Weds every month ~ Open 11-11(12 Sat); 12.30-11 Sun; closed Mon, Tues Oct-Easter ~ Bedrooms: £26/£42

PITLOCHRY NN9162 Map 11
Killiecrankie Hotel 🍽 🛏

Killiecrankie signposted from A9 N of Pitlochry

Well run by warmly welcoming licensees, this smart but relaxed country hotel has dramatic views of the mountain pass from the lovely peaceful grounds. Unfailingly good bar food is served by friendly staff and might at lunchtime include soup (£2.50), sweet cured herrings (£4.50), ploughman's and salads (from £6.25), vegetable and bean cassoulet (£6.95), deep-fried fresh haddock in beer batter or popular cumberland sausage with hot onion chutney (£7.50), and oak-smoked chicken breast with minted mango and papaya compôte (£8.95); evening extras such as tagliatelle with salmon, mussels and prawns (£8.50). The attractively furnished bar has some panelling, upholstered seating and mahogany tables and chairs, as well as stuffed animals and some rather fine wildlife paintings; in the airy conservatory extension (which overlooks the pretty garden) there are light beech tables and upholstered chairs, with discreetly placed plants and flowers. The restaurant – rather formal – is no smoking. Decent wines and lots of malt whiskies, coffee and a choice of teas. The grounds have a putting course, a croquet lawn – and sometimes roe deer and red squirrels. *(Recommended by Chris and Sue Bax, J and H Coyle, BKA, Roger and Christine Mash, Dr D Twyman, J F M West; also in the Good Hotel Guide)*

Free house ~ Licensees Colin and Carole Anderson ~ Bar food (12.30-2, 6.30-9.15(8.30 winter)) ~ Restaurant ~ (01796) 473220 ~ Children in eating area of bar ~ Open 11-2.30, 5.30-11; 12-2.30, 6.30-11 Sun; till 10pm in winter ~ Bedrooms: £58B/£116B

Moulin 🍺 🛏

11 Kirkmichael Rd, Moulin; A924 NE of Pitlochry centre

Probably the closest thing to a traditional pub in the area, this impressive white-painted 17th-c inn is especially worth a visit for the delicious real ales made in their little stables brewery across the street: Braveheart, Ale of Atholl and the stronger Old Remedial. The pub has been much extended over the years, but the bar (in the oldest part of the building) still seems an entity in itself rather than just a part of the hotel. Above the fireplace in the smaller room is an interesting painting of the village before the road was built (Moulin used to be a bustling market town, far busier than Pitlochry), while the bigger carpeted area has a good few tables and cushioned banquettes in little booths divided by stained-glass country scenes, another big fireplace, some exposed stonework, fresh flowers, and local prints and golf clubs around the walls; bar billiards, shove ha'penny, dominoes, fruit machine. A wide choice of popular bar food includes soup (£1.95), lunchtime sandwiches and baked potatoes (from £3.50), steak and ale pie (£5.75), root vegetable and lentil bake or leek and sweet pepper pasta (£5.95), venison casserole (£6.50), minute steak stuffed with haggis (£6.95), and daily specials such as grilled rainbow trout with garlic and parsley butter (£6.95) or Isle of Skye langoustines (£9.95); prompt friendly service. They keep around 40 malt whiskies. Picnic-sets outside are surrounded by tubs of flowers, and look across to the village kirk. Groups can tour the brewery by arrangement, and they have good value three night breaks out of season. Rewarding walks nearby. *(Recommended by David Potts, Dave Braisted, Kate and Robert Hodkinson, Pauline and Jim Welch, Neil Ben)*

Free house ~ Licensee Heather Reeves ~ Real ale ~ Bar food (12-9.30) ~ Restaurant (6-9) ~ (01796) 472196 ~ Children welcome ~ Live entertainment Fri ~ Open 12-11(11.45 Sat) ~ Bedrooms: £45B/£50B

PLOCKTON NG8033 Map 11
Plockton Hotel
Village signposted from A87 near Kyle of Lochalsh

The setting of this friendly little hotel is lovely, in a delightful National Trust village, looking out past the palm trees and colourfully flowering shrub-lined shore, and across the sheltered anchorage to the rugged mountainous surrounds of Loch Carron. The comfortably furnished, bustling lounge bar has window seats looking out to the boats on the water, as well as antiqued dark red leather seating around neat Regency-style tables on a tartan carpet, three model ships set into the woodwork, and partly panelled stone walls. The separate public bar has pool, darts, shove-ha'penny, dominoes, and piped music. Good, promptly served bar food includes home-made soup (£1.95, with their own bread), lunchtime sandwiches and filled baked potatoes, chicken liver and whisky pâté (£3.50), a vegetarian dish of the day (£5.95), poached smoked fillet of haddock (£6.75), venison casserole (£6.95), prawns fresh from the bay (starter £6.25, main course £12.50), grilled blue trout (£8.50), monkfish and prawns provençal (£10.95), local scallops (£11.25), and steaks (from £11.50); children's menu (from £2.25). It's worth booking, as they do get busy. Good breakfasts; small no-smoking dining room. Caledonian Deuchars IPA on tall fount air pressure, a good collection of malt whiskies, and a short wine list. Further bedrooms are planned for the recently acquired building next door. A hotel nearby has recently changed its name to the Plockton Inn, so if this is where you're headed don't get the two confused. *(Recommended by Andy, Julie and Stuart Hawkins, Nigel Woolliscroft, Chris and Sue Bax, Mr and Mrs Archibald, T M Dobby, Paula Williams, E J Locker, Guy Vowles, M Mason, D Thompson, K M Crook, Mr and Mrs J E Murphy, Chris and Ann Garnett, Dave Braisted)*

Free house ~ Licensee Tom Pearson ~ Real ale ~ Bar food (12-2.30, 6-9.30) ~ Restaurant ~ (01599) 544274 ~ Children welcome away from public bar ~ Live entertainment Thurs evening summer ~ Open 11-12(11.30 Sat); 12.30-11 Sun; closed 1 Jan ~ Bedrooms: £30B/£55B

PORTPATRICK NX0154 Map 9
Crown ★ 🛏
Welcoming and efficient even at its busiest, this bustling and atmospheric harbourside inn has lots of little nooks, crannies and alcoves in its rambling old-fashioned bar. Tucked amongst them are interesting furnishings such as a carved settle with barking dogs as its arms, and an antique wicker-backed armchair, as well as a stag's head over the coal fire, and shelves of old bottles above the bar counter. The partly panelled butter-coloured walls are decorated with old mirrors with landscapes painted in their side panels. Served by obliging staff, good bar food includes sandwiches (from £1.70; toasties from £1.90), soup (£2), and extremely fresh seafood such as local prawns, lobster, and monkfish tails and scallops; good breakfasts. Carefully chosen wine list, and over 250 malt whiskies; maybe piped music. An airy and very attractively decorated early 20th-c, half no-smoking dining room opens through a quiet no-smoking conservatory area into a sheltered back garden, and you can sit outside on seats served by a hatch in the front lobby and make the most of the evening sun. *(Recommended by Christine and Malcolm Ingram, Pamela and Merlyn Horswell, Neil Townend, Nigel Woolliscroft, Stan and Hazel Allen, Ian Potter, John and Joan Wyatt)*

Free house ~ Licensee Bernard Wilson ~ Bar food (till 10) ~ Restaurant ~ (01776) 810261 ~ Children welcome ~ Open 11-11.30; 12-11 Sun ~ Bedrooms: £48B/£72B

We accept no free drinks or payment for inclusion. We take no advertising, and are not sponsored by the brewing industry – or by anyone else. So all reports are independent.

SHERIFFMUIR NN8202 Map 6
Sheriffmuir Inn

Signposted off A9 just S of Blackford; and off A9 at Dunblane roundabout, just N of end of M9; also signposted from Bridge of Allan; OS Sheet 57 map reference 827022

The wonderful lonely moorland views from this remotely set drovers' inn haven't dramatically changed since it was built in 1715, the same year as the Battle of Sheriffmuir commemorated in a couple of the prints on the walls inside. The welcoming L-shaped bar is basic but comfortable, with pink plush stools and button-back built-in wall banquettes on a pink patterned carpet, polished tables, olde-worlde coaching prints on its white walls, and a woodburning stove in a stone fireplace; there's a separate no-smoking room. Well kept Marstons Pedigree on handpump, along with three weekly changing guests like Inveralmond Independence, and a good choice of whiskies; piped music. Promptly served by particularly friendly and efficient staff, lunchtime bar food includes home-made soup (£1.95), steak pie or broccoli and mushroom pie (£6.50), and battered haddock or chicken korma (£6.95); they can get busy at lunchtimes so it's worth getting there early. There are tables and a children's play area outside. *(Recommended by K M Crook, Paula Williams, Neil and Karen Dignan)*

Free house ~ Licensee Roger Lee ~ Real ale ~ Bar food ~ Restaurant ~ (01786) 823285 ~ Children welcome ~ Open 11.30-2.30, 5.30-11; 11.30-11 Sat; 12-11 Sun; closed Mon, Tues Oct-Feb

SHIELDAIG NG8154 Map 11
Tigh an Eilean Hotel

Village signposted just off A896 Lochcarron—Gairloch

Very much a hotel with a tiny locals' bar attached, but worth a visit for its delightful waterside setting, looking out over the Shieldaig Island – a sanctuary for a stand of ancient Caledonian pines – to Loch Torridon, and then out to the sea beyond. It's a comfortable place to stay, with easy chairs, books and a well stocked help-yourself bar in the neat and prettily decorated two-room lounge, and an attractively modern dining room specialising in tasty and good value local shellfish, fish and game. The bar is very simple, with red brocaded button-back banquettes in little bays, and picture windows looking out to sea; winter darts, juke box. Simple quickly served bar food includes home-made soup (£1.75), sandwiches, crab with lemon mayonnaise (£4.50), beef in Guinness casserole (£6.25), fresh local turbot or halibut (£6.75), and puddings such as mango mousse (£2). A sheltered front courtyard has three picnic-sets. The National Trust Torridon estate and the Beinn Eighe nature reserve aren't too far away. *(Recommended by Ian Jones, Anthony Barnes; also in the Good Hotel Guide)*

Free house ~ Licensee Elizabeth Stewart ~ Bar food (12-2.15, 6-8.30) ~ Restaurant ~ (01520) 755251 ~ Children until 8 ~ Open 11-11; 12.30-2.30 Sun; 11-2.30, 5-11 Mon-Fri, Sat 11-11, closed Sun winter ~ Bedrooms: £46.25B/£102.50B

SKEABOST NG4148 Map 11
Skeabost House Hotel ★

A850 NW of Portree, 1½ miles past junction with A856

Splendidly grand-looking, this civilised hotel is set in twelve acres of secluded woodland and gardens, with glorious views over Loch Snizort, said to have some of the best salmon fishing on the island. One of the draws is the excellent evening and Sunday lunch buffet (£7.95) served in the spacious and airy conservatory, with a very wide choice of cold meats and fresh salmon; they also do home-made soup (£2), good filled baked potatoes (£3.50), haggis with oatcakes (£3.90), several substantial hot sandwiches with home-made bread such as medallions of chicken with plum tomatoes, basil, sweet red onion and pesto mayonnaise (£5.90), good lunchtime salads (from £7.95), and in the evening a big seafood platter. Children's meals are better than usual (from £2.60). All the eating areas are no smoking; best to dress fairly smartly in the main dining room. The bustling high-ceilinged bar has a pine counter and red brocade seats on its thick red carpet, and a fine panelled billiards room leads off the stately hall; there's a wholly separate public bar with darts, pool, fruit machine, trivia, juke box, piped music (and even its own car park). They serve the unique Snizort ale from the Isle of Skye Brewery, plus a fine choice of over 100 single malt whiskies, including their own and some very rare vintages. *(Recommended by Mrs J Lang, Joan and Tony Walker)*

Free house ~ Licensee Iain McNab ~ Real ale ~ Bar food ~ Restaurant ~ (01470) 532202 ~ Children in eating area of bar ~ Open 11-2, 5-11; 12.30-11 Sun; closed 1 Jan ~ Bedrooms: £50(£65B)/£79(£85B)

ST MONANCE SO5202 Map 11
Seafood Restaurant and Bar 🍽

16 West End; just off A917

It's changed its name since our last edition (it used to be called the Cabin), but though the food is very much the centre of attention you're still welcome to come just for a drink – you may find local sea salts in their waterproofs and wellies in the public bar. The excellent seafood in the back restaurant isn't cheap, but it's among the finest in the area – quite a surprise unless you're in the know, as from the outside you'd think the place quite ordinary. The snug front bar is immaculate yet warmly cosy, the well polished light wooden panelling and fittings and lack of windows creating something of a below-decks feel. On the mantelpiece above a smart tiled fireplace is a gleaming ship's bell, and there are a few seafaring models and mementoes on illuminated shelves, as well as turn-of-the-century photos of local life. Well kept Belhaven 80/- and St Andrews and a changing guest like Wadworths 6X on handpump; also a wide range of wines, around 30 malt whiskies (including a malt of the month), and freshly squeezed fruit juices. Very friendly service. Lunchtime bar food such as soup (from £2.50), half a dozen oysters (£6), pan-seared tuna steak (£9.95), and grilled langoustines (£11.95); they do a two course lunch for £13. In the evenings they only do food in the airy restaurant (except in summer when you can generally eat outside on the terrace), with its big windows overlooking the harbour and the Firth of Forth; meals then might include cullen skink (£2.85), pan-seared hand-dived scallops with a basil purée and orange, cardamom and vanilla reduction (£14.50), grilled fillet of halibut masked in garlic and herb butter with baby vegetables (£12.95), and roast breast of gressingham duck with sweet blackcurrant sauce (£13.95). *(Recommended by E J Locker, Paul and Ursula Randall, Sue and John Woodward)*

Free house ~ Licensee Tim Butler ~ Real ale ~ Bar food ~ Restaurant ~ (01333) 730327 ~ Children in restaurant till 8pm ~ Open 11-11; 12.30-11 Sun; 11-3, 6-11; 12.30-3, 7-11 Sun winter; closed Mon, three weeks in Jan

STONEHAVEN NO8493 Map 11
Lairhillock ♀

Netherley; 6 miles N of Stonehaven, 6 miles S of Aberdeen, take the Durris turn-off from the A90

There are panoramic views from the conservatory at this smart but relaxed and friendly extended country pub, but what draws most visitors here is the unusual freshly prepared food. In the bar, this might include soup (£2.25), cullen skink (£3.75), a changing terrine or pâté (£4.15), filled baguettes (£4.65), lunchtime ploughman's (£5.45), steak and kidney pie (£7.25), baked salmon with ginger and tomato chutney or vegetable risotto (£7.50), seafood crêpes (£7.95), roast local wild boar or grilled venison with tagliatelle and a wild mushroom sauce (£8.95), monkfish and king prawn stir fry (£9.45), chicken stuffed with haggis in a whisky sauce (£9.50), and ostrich steaks (£9.75); Sunday buffet lunch. The cheerful beamed bar has panelled wall benches, a mixture of old seats, dark woodwork, harness and brass lamps on the walls, a good open fire, and countryside views from the bay window. The spacious separate lounge has an unusual central fire; the traditional atmosphere is always welcoming, even at the pub's busiest. Well kept Boddingtons, Courage Directors, Flowers IPA, McEwans 80/-, and a changing guest beer on handpump, over 50 malt whiskies, and an extensive wine list; cheery efficient staff, darts, cribbage, dominoes, shove-ha'penny, trivia, and piped music. The cosy restaurant – reckoned by some readers to be one of the finest in the Aberdeen area – is in a converted raftered barn behind. *(Recommended by Jean and George Dundas, John Poulter, Steven Bertram)*

Free house ~ Licensee Frank Budd ~ Real ale ~ Bar food (12-2, 6-9.30(10 Fri, Sat)) ~ Restaurant ~ (01569) 730001 ~ Children in eating area of bar and restaurant ~ Open 11-2.30, 5-11(12 Sat); 12-2.30, 6-11 Sun; closed 25-26 Dec, 1-2 Jan

SWINTON NT8448 Map 10
Wheatsheaf 🍽 🛏

A6112 N of Coldstream

The exceptional food and service at this extremely well run and rather civilised place continue to delight. At lunchtime the daily changing menu might include sandwiches, soups such as parsnip and curried apple (£2.35), deep-fried squid with garlic mayonnaise (£4.25), breast of wood pigeon with black pudding and puy lentils (£4.50), smoked fish and potato pie or stir-fried broccoli and oyster mushroom with noodles (£5.90), sautéed lamb's liver with bacon and shallots (£6.45), seared fillet of codling on parsley mash (£6.80), and delicious puddings, with evening dishes like corn-fed chicken filled with parma ham and St Andrews cheese (£10.85), escalopes of veal with wild mushrooms and spring onion (£13.90), and roasted fillet of venison on whisky scented skirlie with spiced redcurrant sauce (£14.75). Booking is advisable, particularly from Thursday to Saturday evening. Well kept Arrols 80/- and Caledonian 80/- and Greenmantle on handpump, a decent range of malt whiskies and brandies, good choice of wines, and cocktails. Service is helpful, unhurried and genuinely welcoming. The carefully thought out main bar area has an attractive long oak settle and some green-cushioned window seats, as well as wheelback chairs around tables, a stuffed pheasant and partridge over the log fire, and sporting prints and plates on the bottle-green wall covering; a small lower-ceilinged part by the counter has pubbier furnishings, and small agricultural prints on the walls – especially sheep. The front conservatory has a vaulted pine ceiling and walls of local stone, while at the side is a separate locals' bar; dominoes. The garden has a play area for children. The dining areas are no smoking. Bedrooms are simple but comfortable, and, not surprisingly, they do very good breakfasts. The pub is in a pretty village surrounded by rolling countryside. *(Recommended by Ian S Morley, W K Wood, Anthony Barnes, Christopher Beadle, Mrs M Wood, Alan Morton, Comus Elliott, Andrew Low, Nick and Meriel Cox, B, M and P Kendall, John and Kathleen Potter, Bill Wood, David Hawkes, Mike Doupe; also in the Good Hotel Guide)*

Free house ~ Licensee Alan Reid ~ Real ale ~ Bar food (12-2, 6-9) ~ Restaurant ~ (01890) 860257 ~ Children in eating area of bar ~ Open 11-2.30, 6-11; 12.30-2.30, 6.30-10.30 Sun; closed Sun evening winter; closed Mon ~ Bedrooms: £48B/£76B

TAYVALLICH NR7386 Map 11
Tayvallich Inn 🍽

B8025, off A816 1 mile S of Kilmartin; or take B841 turn-off from A816 two miles N of Lochgilphead

Plenty to watch while you eat at this simply furnished café/bar, as there are lovely views over the yacht anchorage and loch from the terrace. Under the new owners fresh seafood continues to be the highlight of the menu, brought in by local fishermen from the bay of Loch Sween just across the lane. The choice typically includes sandwiches, soup (£2), chicken liver pâté or moules marinières (£3.65), home-made burgers (from £4.95), baked goat's cheese with roasted peppers (£5.10), beef curry (£5.70), warm salad of smoked haddock and prawns (£6.25), cajun salmon with black butter (£10), pan-fried local scallops (£13), and puddings (£3.10); children's helpings. All the whiskies are Islay malt. Service is friendly, and people with children are very much at home here. The small bar has local nautical charts on the cream walls, exposed ceiling joists, and pale pine upright chairs, benches and tables on its quarry-tiled floor; darts, dominoes, cards. It leads into a no-smoking (during meal times) dining conservatory, from where sliding glass doors open on to the terrace;

there's a garden, too. *(Recommended by Nigel Woolliscroft, Colin Thompson, Neil Townend, Mr and Mrs D Lee, Mike and Penny Sanders)*

Free house ~ Licensee Andrew Wilson ~ Bar food (12-2, 6-8) ~ Restaurant ~ (01546) 870282 ~ Children welcome during meal times ~ Open 11-12(1 Sat); 11-3, 6-11(1 Fri, Sat; 12 Sun) winter; closed Mon Nov-March

THORNHILL NS6699 Map 11
Lion & Unicorn
A873

Some parts of this pleasant inn date back to 1635, and in the restaurant you can see the original massive fireplace, six feet high and five feet wide. It's changed hands since our last edition, but it's still the same chef, so you'll find the same consistently good food. The constantly changing bar menu might at lunchtime include soup such as carrot and coriander (£1.95), baked potatoes (from £3.50), open sandwiches (from £3.75), warm brie salad with peach and chilli jam (£3.95), steak pie (£4.75), scampi (£5.25), chicken in tarragon and white wine sauce (£5.75), and Aberdeen Angus steaks on big sizzling platters (from £11); you can eat from the restaurant menu in the bar, and they're fairly flexible with what's on the menu. Recently refurbished, the open-plan front room has a warm fire, beams and stone walls, and comfortable seats on the wooden floors, while the beamed public bar has stone walls and floors, and darts, cribbage, and dominoes. The restaurant is no smoking. They weren't doing real ale as we went to press, but hoped to reintroduce it soon. Very nice in summer, the garden has a children's play area, and maybe barbecues in summer. A couple of readers have found the pub closed at unexpected times in winter – it may be best to check first then. *(Recommended by Justin Hulford, Neil Townend)*

Free house ~ Licensee Robert Stephenson ~ Bar food (12-10) ~ Restaurant ~ (01786) 850204 ~ Children welcome ~ Open 12-12(1 Fri, Sat); 12.30-12 Sun ~ Bedrooms: £40B/£60B

TUSHIELAW NT3018 Map 9
Tushielaw Inn ⛺
Ettrick Valley, B709/B7009 Lockerbie—Selkirk

New owners at this friendly and traditional country inn since our last edition. In a pleasantly remote setting by Ettrick Water, it's a good base for walkers or for touring, with its own fishing on Clearburn Loch up the B711. The unpretentious but comfortable little bar has decent house wines, a good few malts, an open fire, local prints and photos, and an antique brass till; it opens on to an outside terrace with tables. Darts, cribbage, dominoes, and piped music. Bar food includes soup (£2.50), filled baguettes (from £4), ploughman's (£4.50), deep-fried haddock (£5), lasagne (£5.50), chilli (£6), poached salmon with turmeric sauce (£6.50), and Aberdeen Angus sirloin steak (£11). The dining room is no smoking. *(Recommended by Andy, Julie and Stuart Hawkins, Bob Ellis, Dave Braisted, A N Ellis)*

Free house ~ Licensee Gordon Harrison ~ Real ale ~ Bar food ~ (01750) 62205 ~ Children welcome ~ Open 12-3, 6(7 Sun)-11; only open 7-11 Fri, 12-3, 7-11 Sat and Sun winter ~ Bedrooms: £25B/£42B

ULLAPOOL NH1294 Map 11
Ceilidh Place
West Argyle St

In a quiet side street above the small town, this pretty, rose-draped white house is rather like a stylish arty café/bar – but with a distinctly Celtic character. There's always plenty going on, with an art gallery, bookshop and coffee shop, and regular jazz, folk, ceilidh and classical music. The eclectic furnishings and décor include bentwood chairs and one or two cushioned wall benches among the rugs on the varnished concrete floor, spotlighting from the dark planked ceiling, attractive modern prints and a big sampler on the textured white walls, magazines to read, venetian blinds, and houseplants; there's a woodburning stove, and plenty of mainly young upmarket customers. The side food bar – you queue for service at lunchtime – does good food from fresh ingredients, such as varied and original salads, home-made soups and breads (from £2), baked potato (£3.25), and various hot dishes like venison mince (£4.95); there's always a good choice for vegetarians (£3.95). Decent wines by the glass, an interesting range of high-proof malt whiskies, and a choice of cognac and armagnac that's unmatched around here; dominoes, piped music. There's an attractive no-smoking conservatory dining room, where the appealing menu has quite a few fish dishes. Tables on a terrace in front look over other houses to the distant hills beyond the natural harbour. The bedrooms are comfortable and pleasantly decorated. *(Recommended by Mrs Jean Dundas, G D K Fraser, Paula Williams; also in the Good Hotel Guide)*

Free house ~ Licensee Jean Urquhart ~ Bar food (12-9 summer, 12-6 winter) ~ Restaurant ~ (01854) 612103 ~ Children welcome ~ Open 11(12.30 Sun)-11 Bedrooms ~ £45(£60B)/£90 (£120B)

Morefield Motel 🍴

North Rd

The owners here have changed since last year, but the management and staff are the same, so you can expect the same high standards of fresh fish and seafood. Depending on availability, the generously served meals might include oak-roasted smoked salmon (£5.75), a basket of prawns (£6.25), battered haddock (£6.95), moules marinières (£8.95), seafood thermidor (£8.75), scallops with bacon (£9.50), a marvellous seafood platter (£16.75), and daily specials such as monkfish, red snapper, turbot, fresh dressed brown crab, bass with fresh ginger, and giant langoustines with garlic or herb butter. Non-fishy dishes also feature, such as soup (£2.50), fillet steak with haggis and Drambuie sauce (£14.50), and various vegetarian and vegan meals. The smarter Mariners restaurant has a slightly more elaborate menu. In winter the diners tend to yield to local people playing darts or pool. Well kept Orkney Dark Island and Worthingtons Best on handpump, and a wide range of malt whiskies, some nearly 30 years old; decent wines and friendly tartan-skirted waitresses. The L-shaped lounge is mostly no smoking and the restaurant is totally no smoking. There are tables on a terrace. The bedrooms remain popular with hill-walking parties; enjoyable breakfasts. *(Recommended by Neil Townend, Ian Baillie, R F and M K Bishop, Russell and Carole George, H Dickinson)*

Free house ~ Licensee David Caulfield ~ Real ale ~ Bar food (12-2, 5.30-9.30) ~ Restaurant ~ (01854) 612161 ~ Children welcome ~ Open 11-11 ~ Bedrooms: £25B/£50B

WEEM NN8449 Map 11
Ailean Chraggan 🛏

B846

The very good food is a huge draw to this family-run hotel, but it's an enjoyable place to stay too – small and friendly and set in two acres with a lovely view to the mountains beyond the Tay, sweeping up to Ben Lawers (the highest in this part of Scotland). The changing menu typically includes sandwiches (from £2.45), soup (£2.45), excellent cullen skink (£4.15), moules marinières (£4.45), leek and parmesan risotto with poached egg (£7.50), mediterranean vegetable parcels (£7.95), fresh cod au gratin (£8.25), grilled lamb chops or beef and ale pie (£8.50), venison casserole or fillet of salmon with lime and tarragon butter (£8.75), and puddings such as spiced raisin cream pie or sweet carrot tart (£3.50); children's menu (£3.50). Readers very much enjoy their good fresh seafood platter (£15) – the barman apparently drives over to Loch Etive every week and buys up the entire catch of prawns. The main part of the dining room is no smoking. Very good wine list, around 100 malt whiskies, and separate children's menu. The modern lounge has new carpets and striped wallpaper; a dining room shares the same menu, and there are two outside terraces (one with an awning) to enjoy the view. Winter darts and dominoes. *(Recommended by Arthur Williams, Anthony Barnes, Ken and Norma Burgess, D S and J M Jackson, Mr and Mrs P Spencer, Andrew Low, Susan and John Douglas, Ron and Sheila Corbett, Roger and Christine Mash, Chris and Ann Garnett)*

Free house ~ Licensee Alastair Gillespie ~ Bar food ~ Restaurant ~ (01887) 820346 ~ Children welcome ~ Open 11(12.30 Sun)-11; closed 25, 26 Dec, 1, 2 Jan ~ Bedrooms: £38.50B/

Lucky Dip

Besides the fully inspected pubs, you might like to try these Lucky Dips recommended to us and described by readers (if you do, please send us reports):

BORDERS

Allanton [NT8755]
☆ *Allanton Inn* [B6347 S of Chirnside]: Comfortable and traditional stone terraced inn with creaky swinging sign, changing beer choice such as Belhaven 80/-, Charles Wells Bombardier and Greene King IPA, good enterprising food from daily changing menu in side dining room, children's menu; attentive and friendly smartly dressed staff, brick fireplace in homely front bar, local honey for sale, public bar with darts and pool, tables in garden behind; occasional beer and folk festivals; bedrooms, open all day w/e *(Bob Ellis, BB)*

Ancrum [NT6325]
Cross Keys [off A68 Jedburgh—Edinburgh]: Lovely village green setting, friendly staff, well kept Caledonian Deuchars IPA and 80/-, fresh local produce inc good well priced Aberdeen Angus steaks; games room, nice back garden *(Tony Bruce)*

Auchencrow [NT8661]
Craw [B6438 NE of Duns; pub signed off A1]: Sadly this attractive cottagey pub, very popular with readers for its good fresh fish and other virtues, closed recently, and may be converted to a private house *(BB)*

Blyth Bridge [NT1345]
Old Mill [A6094 Edinburgh—Galashiels]: Ex watermill with beams, open fires, good value food inc interesting Sun lunch, well kept ales, restaurant; pleasant gardens, open all day Sun *(Mike and Maggie Betton)*

Carlops [NT1656]
Allan Ramsay: Welcoming late 18th-c pub, several interconnecting beamed rooms, eating areas each end (wide choice of good generous food all day), two fires, lots of bric-a-brac, fresh flowers, witches' sabbath mural recalling local legend; well kept Belhaven, good coffee; piped pop music, fruit machine and TV; children welcome *(Pat and Robert Watt)*

Jedburgh [NT6521]
Pheasant [High St, lower end]: Welcoming and efficient service, good range of good value food inc local game in season, McEwans, decent wines *(G Neighbour)*

Kelso [NT7334]
☆ *Cobbles* [Beaumont St]: Small two-room dining pub with wall banquettes, some panelling, warm log and coal fires, wide choice of good value food inc interesting dishes; very courteous quick service, real ales such as Caledonian Deuchars

and McEwans 70/- and 80/-, decent wines and malt whiskies; piped music; disabled lavatory *(Pamela and Merlyn Horswell, B, M and P Kendall)*

Ednam House [Bridge St]: Old-fashioned fishing hotel with good food, bedrooms *(Mrs J Lang)*

Kirk Yetholm [NT8328]
Border: Welcoming end to 256-mile Pennine Way walk (Pennine Way souvenirs for sale), consistently well cooked generous bar lunches and evening meals, well kept Belhaven, pleasant service, very friendly locals; prominent red décor *(Mark Percy, Lesley Mayoh)*

Melrose [NT5434]
Kings Arms [High St]: Late 18th-c inn with French landlord, cosy log fire in recently refurbished beamed bar, well kept Tetleys-related and other ales, good choice of malt whiskies, wide choice of good value generous food inc some local dishes and good fish soup, good children's menu (they're welcome); attentive friendly service even when busy; bedrooms *(Mike and Penny Sanders, Kit Ballantyne, Mark Percy, Lesley Mayoh, Gill and Maurice McMahon)*

Paxton [NT9453]
Hoolits Nest [pub signed off B6460 W of Berwick]: Comfortable bar, partly modern panelling, full of namesake owl models and prints, simple food range inc good vegetarian, well kept changing ales such as Broughton Ghillie, Help Ma Bowb and Orkney Dark Island, malt whiskies, reasonable prices, friendly landlord and locals; unobtrusive piped music, children welcome in dining room *(Ian and Nita Cooper)*

Peebles [NT2540]
Bridge [Tweed Bridge]: Small single-room pub by river, well kept Caledonian Deuchars and Courage Directors, fair prices *(J Harrison)*
Green Tree [Innerleithen Rd]: Small hotel with very well kept Caledonian 80/- and two guest beers such as Bass, Jennings, Orkney; reasonably priced food; well equipped bedrooms *(J Harrison)*

St Marys Loch [NT2422]
☆ *Tibbie Shiels* [A708 SW of Selkirk]: Down-to-earth inn with interesting literary history in wonderful peaceful setting by a beautiful loch, handy for Southern Upland Way and Grey Mares Tail waterfall – quite a few caravans and tents in summer; stone back bar, no-smoking lounge bar, straightforward waitress-served

lunchtime bar food, well kept Belhaven 80/- and Greenmantle, several dozen malt whiskies, traditional games; children welcome, restaurant, open all day (cl Mon/Tues Nov-Mar); bedrooms *(John Knighton, Andy, Julie and Stuart Hawkins, Mike and Penny Sanders, Vicky and David Sarti, Ian S Morley, Jane Keeton, LYM, Richard Gibbs)*

CENTRAL
Aberfoyle [NN5201]
Inverard: Friendly staff, small helpings of decent bar food, Heather ale; separate restaurant, bedrooms *(PACW)*
Fintry [NS6186]
Clachan [Main St]: Cosy bar with plentiful cheap food, attractive garden *(Isabel and Robert Hatcher)*
Gartmore [NS5297]
Black Bull: Refurbished 17th-c drovers' inn on edge of Trossachs with good choice of well cooked food in bar and restaurant, also quite separate tap room; garden, bedrooms *(PACW)*
Stirling [NS7993]
Settle [St Mary's Wynd; from Wallace Memorial in centre go up Baker St, keep right at top]: Early 18th-c, restored to show beams, stonework, great arched fireplace and barrel-vaulted upper room; cosier than this all sounds, with bar games, Belhaven 70/- and 80/- and Maclays, friendly staff; piped music, open all day *(Andy, Julie and Stuart Hawkins, LYM)*
Whistlebinkies [St Mary's Wynd]: Former 16th-c castle stables, looking old outside, but quite modern inside – three comfortable levels linked by wooden staircase, some bargain dishes on mostly standard menu, quite a few mirrors, lots of posters and leaflets for local and student events; friendly staff, Morlands Old Speckled Hen, newspapers, piped pop music, weekly quiz night; tables on slightly scruffy sloping garden behind, handy for castle and old town *(Andy, Julie and Stuart Hawkins)*

DUMFRIES & GALLOWAY
Annan [NY1966]
Queensberry Arms [High St]: Pleasant surroundings, quick service, good value food – lunchtime sandwiches, baguettes, baked potatoes and basket meals, more choice evening; McEwans 70/-, Theakstons Best *(Christopher and Jo Barton)*
Auchencairn [NX8249]
☆ *Balcary Bay* [about 2½ miles off A711]: A hotel (and a good one), but also has honest reasonably priced food from soup and open sandwiches up (inc huge child's helpings) in civilised but friendly bar, good service even when busy; lovely spot for eating outside, terrace and gardens in peaceful seaside surroundings, idyllic views over Solway Firth; keg beers; comfortable bedrooms, cl Oct-Mar *(David and Ruth Hollands)*
Bladnoch [NX4254]
Bladnoch Inn: Good small fairly plain bar and dining area with dog pictures, well kept Theakstons, limited good value lunchtime food, friendly service; children and dogs welcome;

distillery across river *(Mr and Mrs S Hussey)*
Eaglesfield [NY2374]
Courtyard [B722 just off junction 20 of A74(M) E of Ecclefechan]: Hotel not pub, but warmly welcoming, with good choice of food and wines, Scottish Courage beers; good well equipped bedrooms on far side of courtyard *(Gordon Neighbour)*
Gatehouse of Fleet [NX5956]
☆ *Murray Arms* [B727 NW of Kirkcudbright]: Pleasantly casual inn with wide choice of good honest food all day inc good buffet with seafood, meats, lots of salads, cheeses and puddings, well kept ale such as Theakstons XB, lots of malt whiskies, decent reasonably priced wines, interesting layout of mainly old-fashioned comfortable seating areas inc one with soft easy chairs, friendly staff, games in quite separate public bar, rather upmarket restaurant; children welcome; big comfortable bedrooms *(Andy, Julie and Stuart Hawkins, Canon David Baxter, LYM)*
Kingholm Quay [NX9773]
☆ *Swan* [signed off B725 Dumfries—Glencaple]: Small dining pub in quiet spot on River Nith overlooking old fishing jetty, well kept dining lounge (children welcome), comfortable newly decorated public bar, very friendly staff, Theakstons and Youngers, wide choice of good value food esp fish, good puddings, also high teas; restaurant, quiet piped music, children welcome, tables in small garden; bedrooms – handy for Caerlaverock nature reserve *(Christine and Malcolm Ingram, M A Buchanan, Gordon Neighbour)*
Moffat [NT0905]
Balmoral [High St]: Well kept ale, good simple plentiful food, quick friendly service, comfortable bar, peaceful at lunchtime *(PACW)*
Moniaive [NX7790]
☆ *George* [Main St]: 17th-c inn with interesting no-frills old-fashioned flagstoned bar of considerable character; well kept beer, decent wine, friendly staff and locals; most days except at quietest times of year have reasonably priced lunchtime food; simple bedrooms *(Stan and Hazel Allen)*

FIFE
Anstruther [NO5704]
☆ *Craws Nest* [Bankwell Rd]: Well run popular hotel with good value bar meals inc outstanding fresh haddock in attractive light long lounge with comfortable banquettes, photographs, paintings for sale, maybe a real ale such as Crusoe, good service; comfortable bedrooms in modern wing *(Paul and Ursula Randall)*
☆ *Dreel* [High St]: Cosy ancient building in attractive spot with garden overlooking Dreel Burn, plenty of timbers, small two-room bar, back pool room, open fire and stripped stone in atmospheric dining room, good helpings of traditional bar food, well kept Orkney Dark Island, friendly staff, biscuits for dogs; popular with locals, open all day *(Neil Spink, E J Locker)*
☆ *Smugglers* [High St]: Old inn overlooking harbour, with big windows in comfortable upstairs bar the best place to enjoy the view;

wide range of good value straightforward bar food, cheerful décor and service, pleasant cocktail lounge with winter fires, sofas, ship's wheel and other nautical memorabilia; summer barbecues on pretty terrace, children allowed in eating area; bedrooms *(BB)*

Ceres [NO4011]

Meldrums [Main St]: Small hotel's cottagey parlour bar, pleasant atmosphere, clean and attractive beamed dining lounge with good choice of well prepared and presented reasonably priced bar lunches, prompt friendly service even when busy; bedrooms *(Susan and John Douglas)*

Crail [NO6108]

Marine [Nethergate]: Sea-view bar, great views too from tables in upper garden, food from soup to Aberdeen Angus steaks, Caledonian 80/-; comfortable recently refurbished bedrooms, lovely old fishing village *(Paul and Ursula Randall)*

Crossgates [NT1588]

Coaledge Tavern [B925, Coaledge]: Well kept ales inc Belhaven 80/-, horseshoe bar with TV above, panelling, real fire; run by ex-footballer Alex Smith *(Roger and Jenny Huggins and family)*

Falkland [NO2507]

Hunters Lodge: Chatty low-ceilinged inn opp Falkland Palace (NTS); neatly kept brightly lit roomy bar, friendly local feel, Maclays Liberty, back eating area with good value straightforward food from sandwiches and baguettes to steaks; fruit machine, piped pop music *(Deborah and Ian Carrington, BB)*

☆ *Stag* [Mill Wynd]: Cosy long low white-painted 17th-c house in delightful setting opp charming green, round corner from medieval village square; dimly lit and pubby, with dark wooden pews and stools, exposed stone, copper-topped tables, stone fireplace, antlers and line drawings on wall, and some stained glass above bar; friendly helpful staff, Ind Coope Burton, coffee cocktails, decent food (not Tues or Sun eve), toasted sandwiches and take-away pizzas available most of day, helpful service, dining room with masses of posters; bar billiards, fruit machine, TV, unobtrusive piped music, children welcome *(Mike and Penny Sanders, Susan and John Douglas)*

Lathones [NO4708]

Inn at Lathones [A915 Leven—St Andrews, just S of B940]: Comfortable bar with bare bricks, beams and open fire, light and airy cheerful decorated restaurant area, imaginative nicely presented fresh food, courteous helpful staff, well kept Belhaven 80/-; children's helpings, two well equipped playrooms, outdoor play area; well equipped bedrooms *(Paul and Ursula Randall)*

North Queensferry [NT1380]

Queensferry Lodge: Useful motorway break with good views of Forth bridges and the Firth from modern hotel lounge, McEwans real ale, good value bar food inc good buffet 12-2.30, 5-10; bedrooms good *(Neil Townend)*

St Andrews [NO5114]

Grange [Grange Rd (off A917 S)]: More

restaurant than pub, good choice of enjoyable food inc attractive puddings in spotless small beamed and flagstoned bar too, polite friendly service, good range of malt whiskies, decent wines (but keg beers), good coffee, furniture in keeping with the age of the building, two open fires, lovely views to sea; cl Mon/Tues Nov-Mar *(George and Jean Dundas)*

Ma Bells [The Scores]: By golf course, open all day, with big lively basement café/bistro bar brimming with students during term-time, well kept Caledonian Deuchars IPA, Theakstons XB and guest beers, interesting bottled beers and malt whiskies, popular food, friendly service; no-smoking raised back area, bar mirrors, old enamel signs; well reproduced piped music, pleasant seafront views from outside *(Paul and Ursula Randall)*

Ogstons [South St]: Café-bar/bistro, marble tables in vestibule and gallery over main bar, real ales such as Bass and Caledonian, good espresso coffee etc, daily papers, friendly willing service, more or less continental snacks most of the day, pleasant airy conservatory dining area, evening Italian restaurant *(Paul and Ursula Randall)*

Westport [South St]: Cosmopolitan atmosphere, with European newspapers, board games, bagels and croissants as well as good lunchtime sandwiches, good vegetarian choice, good range of coffees all day; friendly staff, live music Sun night *(Madeira Faye)*

Wormit [NO4026]

☆ *Sandford* [Newton Hill]: Golfing hotel's cosy and attractive bar with Highland paintings and bay window seat overlooking the handsome former mansion's grounds, good inventive bar lunches and suppers (inc children's helpings) served till late, helpful service; bedrooms good *(Susan and John Douglas)*

GRAMPIAN

Aberdeen [NJ9305]

Illicit Still [Guest Row, Broad St]: Cellar bar with bits of stills, food all day till early evening inc no-holds-barred breakfast (comes with free drink w/e); usual keg beers *(Dave Braisted)*

Ballater [NO3695]

Deeside: One well kept changing ale such as Harviestoun, Tomintoul or even Shepherd Neame from down in Kent; good food *(Gregg Davies)*

Glenlivet [NJ2127]

Croft: Former almshouse, small intimate and cosy, with very welcoming atmosphere, interesting choice of good home-cooked food, reasonable prices; open all day in summer *(Revd John E Cooper)*

Knockandhu [NJ2123]

Pole: Character stand-up wooden bar like 1930s time-warp in beautiful Highland setting, meteorologically minded landlord mounts weather records in long strip; this reader reports particularly well kept Charles Wells *(Colin Lavery)*

Monymusk [NJ6815]

Grant Arms [signed from B993 SW of Kemnay]: Comfortable well kept inn with good Don fishing, log fire dividing dark-panelled lounge bar, lots of malt whiskies, well kept McEwans 80/-, games in simpler public bar, wide choice of good food inc vegetarian in bar and restaurant, good service; children welcome, open all day w/e; bedrooms *(A Williams, LYM, Neil Townend)*

Pennan [NJ8465]

Pennan [just off B9031 Banff—Fraserburgh]: Marvellous spot right by sea at foot of steep single street, tables out by the seagulls; good imaginative food inc fantastic fish soup – may stop bar food 6.30pm to concentrate on restaurant; bedrooms *(MJVK)*

Potarch [NO6097]

Potarch Hotel [B993, just off A93 5 miles W of Banchory]: Tartan-carpeted bar beautifully placed by River Dee, with copper-topped tables, good friendly service, real ales, good bar meals, fresh salmon and steaks in restaurant; bedrooms *(IHR)*

St Cyrus [NO7465]

The Hotel [Main Rd (A92)]: Good range of good inventive food in bar and large adjacent dining room; new place in old hotel, old-fashioned village; bedrooms *(George and Jean Dundas)*

HIGHLAND

Aviemore [NH8912]

Olde Bridge [Coylumbridge Rd]: Well kept extended inn with stripped stone and wood, good value food inc four-course meals (whisky for the haggis), cheerful mainly antipodean waitresses, changing real ales such as Caledonian and Lairds, Tues ceilidh; pleasant surroundings *(Eric Locker, EJL, Vicky and David Sarti, BKA, Isabel and Robert Hatcher)*

Badachro [NG7773]

☆ *Badachro Inn* [B8056 by Loch Gairloch]: Energetic new young local licensees in welcoming understated pub in superb waterside setting, relaxing atmosphere – locals and yachtsmen (two moorings, shower available); enjoyable food inc good fresh fish, well kept beers, simple comfortable public bar with big log fire, children welcome; Nov-Mar has been open only Weds and Fri evenings, Sat lunch and evening; nice garden and tables on terrace over loch; homely bedrooms *(Philip Hastain, Dawn Baddeley, Tim Robbins)*

Ballachulish [NN0858]

Ballachulish Hotel [Oban Rd, S]: Wonderful position and views, pleasant lounge bar, very friendly staff, good food inc vegetarian and children's, wide range of malt whiskies, McEwans 80/- and Theakstons ales; basic public bar; comfortable bedrooms *(Isabel and Robert Hatcher)*

Loch Leven Hotel [North Ballachulish]: Friendly, with good food and very attentive staff *(Gordon Theaker)*

Carrbridge [NH9022]

☆ *Dalrachney Lodge* [nr junction A9/A95 S of Inverness]: Consistently good reasonably priced food and friendly staff in pleasantly relaxed traditional shooting-lodge-type hotel with simple bar, comfortable lounge with books and

log fire in ornate inglenook, plenty of malt whiskies, well kept McEwans 70/-, old-fashioned dining room; very busy with locals w/e; children welcome, bedrooms, most with mountain and river views; open all year *(Neil Townend, R F and M K Bishop)*

Dornie [NG8827]

Dornie Hotel: Hotel's friendly and lively bar, keg Caledonian 80/-, good food inc haggis, local langoustines, queen scallops, fresh veg, good service; bedrooms *(Jenny and Brian Seller)*

Dornoch [NH8089]

Mallin House [Church Rd]: Good well priced food (limited Sun) esp local fish and langoustines in welcoming lounge or restaurant, well kept Theakstons Best and other Scottish Courage beers, good range of malt whiskies, friendly service, interesting collections of whisky-water jugs and golf balls; comfortable bedrooms *(Mike and Penny Sanders, Mick Hitchman)*

Fort William [NN1174]

Grog & Gruel [High St]: Done out in cosy traditional alehouse style, barrel tables, changing well kept ales such as Arrols 80/-, Orkney Dark Island and Raven, wide range of good value usual pub food inc vegetarian, chilli, nachos etc, upstairs restaurant with helpful waiters; children welcome; in pedestrian part *(Adrian Bulley, Mike Jones)*

Inverie [NG7600]

Old Forge: Utterly remote waterside pub with fabulous views, good warm atmosphere, open fire, good reasonably priced bar food, new restaurant extension; open all day, late w/e, occasional live music and ceilidhs; the snag's getting there – Mallaig ferry three days a week, or 15-mile walk through Knoydart from nearest road *(Alan Bellis)*

Inverness [NH6645]

Finlays [A82 just before river]: Typical Scottish town bar with exceptional value lunchtime food *(Dave Braisted)*

Harlequin [Old Edinburgh Rd, just beyond castle]: Downstairs bar with good restaurant upstairs – venison chateaubriand and salmon stir fry recommended *(Dave Braisted)*

Sleepers [Station]: Decent sensibly priced food, waitress service, reasonable décor; keg beers *(Jenny and Brian Seller)*

Kentallen [NN0057]

☆ *Holly Tree* [A828 SW of Ballachulish]: Comfortable hotel converted from Edwardian railway station and much extended since, in lovely quiet setting by Loch Linnhe, with pleasant grounds stretching a mile inc grassy pier and slipway; neat little carpeted bar, some railway prints and photographs, good fish and game in modern dining room looking out over water; bedrooms all have loch views *(BB, Mrs I Foster)*

Kingussie [NH7501]

☆ *Royal* [High St]: Big former coaching inn brewing half a dozen or so interesting Iris Rose real ales and lager in the former stables; also 200 malt whiskies, spacious open-plan bar with plush banquettes and stage for evening entertainment, standard well priced food inc good baguettes, friendly helpful staff, no-smoking area; juke box; children welcome, open all day; bedrooms *(Steven and Tracey Groves, M Mason, D Thompson, BB, G Neighbour)*

Kinlochewe [NH0262]

Kinlochewe Hotel: Welcoming old-fashioned public bar and lounge, good food from toasties and ploughman's up, open fire, piped classical music, Tennents 80/-; stupendous scenery all around, esp Loch Maree and Torridon mountains; attractive bedrooms, also bunkhouse *(Dave Braisted)*

Lochinver [NC0923]

Culag: Down-to-earth hotel bar next to harbour, always full of trawlermen from all over Europe *(Vicky and David Sarti)*

Inver Lodge: Large modern hotel, no public bar, but readers still recommend their bar lunches and service; nice spot on hill overlooking harbour and sea *(June and Tony Baldwin)*

Mallaig [NM6797]

Marine: Comfortable hotel bar overlooking harbour, good lunchtime bar food, enjoyable evening restaurant; bedrooms, in centre of fishing village *(Mr and Mrs Archibald)*

Melvich [NC8765]

Melvich Hotel [A836]: Food from simple sandwiches to fresh wild salmon in civilised bar, relaxed atmosphere and friendly service, peat or log fire, lovely spot, beautiful sea and coast views; bedrooms *(Neil Townend, Chris and Ann Garnett, June and Tony Baldwin)*

Muir of Ord [NH5250]

Ord Arms [A9 N of centre]: Welcoming pub with friendly landlord and locals, good range of beer and food; bedrooms with own bathrooms *(Gordon Theaker)*

Onich [NN0261]

Nether Lochaber Hotel [A82]: Well kept Bass and good value food in side bar of friendly little hotel; bedrooms, with good value set dinner *(Guy Vowles)*

Onich Hotel: Good bar food in pleasant open lounge overlooking Loch Linnhe; wonderful garden, bedrooms *(Isabel and Robert Hatcher)*

Poolewe [NB8580]

Pool House: Hotel in lovely setting on Loch Ewe, nr Inverewe Gardens, spacious and comfortable bar, good reasonably priced food esp fish, McEwans beer, good service; tables out by water, bedrooms *(June and Tony Baldwin)*

Shiel Bridge [NG9318]

Kintail Lodge: Good food inc local game, wild salmon and own smokings, also children's helpings, in simple front bar or attractive conservatory restaurant with magnificent loch views; well kept Theakstons Best, plenty of malt whiskies, decent wines; good value big bedrooms *(Guy Vowles)*

Spean Bridge [NN2491]

☆ *Letterfinlay Lodge* [A82 7 miles N]: Well established hotel, lovely view over Loch Lochy from big picture-window main bar with popular lunchtime buffet and usual games, small smart cocktail bar, no-smoking restaurant; good malt whiskies, friendly service, children and dogs welcome, pleasant lochside grounds, own boats for fishing; clean and comfortable bedrooms,

good breakfast, dog baskets available; gents' have good showers and hairdryers – handy for Caledonian Canal sailors *(K M Crook, LYM, George and Jean Dundas, Mike Jones, Colin Draper, Chris and Sue Bax)*

Tain [NH7484]

Dornoch Bridge [Meikle Ferry, A836 W of bridge]: Old station converted into pub/restaurant, good reasonably priced food inc choice of Sun roasts, wide range of real ales, friendly staff, cosy atmosphere *(Ron and Marjorie Bishop, Freda Andrews)*

Tongue [NC5957]

Ben Loyal [A836]: Hotel with lovely views up to Ben Loyal and out over Kyle of Tongue, good bar food, small but imaginative choice of restaurant food using local (even home-grown) produce, friendly owners; keg Tennents; traditional live music in lounge bar in summer; comfortable good value bedrooms in annexe (hotel itself more pricy) *(June and Tony Baldwin, Margaret Mason, David Thompson, Mr and Mrs A Dewhurst)*

Ullapool [NH1294]

☆ *Ferry Boat* [Shore St]: Simple, friendly and busy pubby bar, harbour and sea views, well kept changing ales such as Greenmantle, Isle of Skye Red Cuillin and Black Cuillin, Orkney Dark Island, coal fire in quieter inner room, honest lunchtime bar food from sandwiches up, no-smoking evening restaurant; open all day, children in eating areas, Thurs folk night, good value bedrooms *(LYM, Ian Baillie, Mike and Penny Sanders)*

LOTHIAN

Balerno [NT1666]

Grey Horse [Main St (off A70)]: Small late 18th-c stonebuilt pub with unspoilt panelled bar, friendly lounge, Belhaven, Boddingtons and Caledonian Deuchars, dominoes, cards; open all day *(the Didler)*

Johnsburn House [Johnsburn Rd]: Lovely old-fashioned beamed bar in 18th-c former mansion with masterpiece 1911 ceiling by Robert Lorimer; Caledonian Deuchars, Orkney Dark Raven and guest beers, good food inc shellfish, game and vegetarian, more formal evening dining rooms; children welcome, open all day w/e, cl Mon *(the Didler)*

Cramond [NT1876]

☆ *Cramond Inn* [Cramond Glebe Rd (off A90 W of Edinburgh)]: Softly lit little rooms with generally good well priced food inc interesting snacks, comfortable brown-and-brass décor, traditional English-style pub furnishing but Scottish bric-a-brac, two good coal and log fires, prompt friendly service by extraordinarily long-serving barman and other staff, Sam Smiths OB; very popular with retired couples at lunchtime (babies welcome too); in picturesque waterside village *(LYM, Lynn Sharpless, Bob Eardley, Neil Townend, Ian and Villy White, Gregg Davies)*

Dunbar [NT6878]

☆ *Starfish* [Old Harbour]: Brightly redecorated bar/bistro with good waitress-served food esp

good chowder, paella and (expensive) fresh fish
and lobster specials, good chowder; changing
wines, malt whiskies, bottled beer only; nice
wood fittings, orange-painted walls and ceiling,
friendly staff, relaxed atmosphere *(BB, Peter
O'Malley)*

Edinburgh [NT2574]

☆ *Athletic Arms* [Angle Park Terr]: Unpretentious
pub famous for its perfectly kept McEwans 80/-
from an impressive row of tall founts – up to 15
red-jacketed barmen keep it flowing on
Tynecastle and Murrayfield football and rugby
days; also guest beers, good value all-day
snacks, dominoes in a side room, cribbage,
darts, glossy grey cubicles off island servery; no
children *(LYM, Neil Townend, the Didler)*

Balmoral [Princes St; the former North British
Hotel]: Big hotel, not pub, but this corner lobby
of the landmark former North British Hotel is a
relaxing refuge in its comfortable clubby
armchairy way (despite the piped music);
welcoming staff, canapés with the expensive
cocktails, good hot rolls filled with daily roast
(not cheap either); also good value champagne
by the glass in the Palm Court, and very good
teas; bedrooms *(Stephen and Jean Curtis)*

☆ *Bennets* [Leven St]: Elaborate Victorian bar with
wonderfully ornate original glass, mirrors,
arcades, panelling and tiles, well kept
Caledonian Deuchars and other ales from tall
founts (even the rare low-strength Caledonian
60/-), lots of uncommon malt whiskies, bar
snacks and simple lunchtime hot dishes; children
allowed in eating area lunchtime, open all day,
cl Sun lunchtime *(LYM, the Didler)*

Bests [Raeburn Pl, Stockbridge]: Spit and
sawdust style but good Australian and South
African wines as well as well kept Caledonian
Deuchars IPA and 80/-, Ind Coope Burton and
great guest beers from Harviestoun and other
small breweries; food from hot pies to steaks,
very broad mix of customers *(Gregg Davies)*

Brecks [Rose St]: Lots of hanging baskets, well
kept McEwans 80/-, good value food in back
part *(R T and J C Moggridge)*

☆ *Cafe Royal* [W Register St]: Can be noisy and
crowded – go at a quiet time to take in the
superb Doulton tilework portraits of 19th-c
innovators, showy island bar counter and other
Victorian details; well kept Caledonian
Deuchars, McEwans 80/-, Morlands Old
Speckled Hen and Theakstons Best, lunchtime
carvery (not Sun) with hot sandwiches carved to
order, daily papers, gents' with some fine
original fittings; children allowed in restaurant,
open all day *(LYM, Roger Huggins, Andy
Jones, Eric Larkham, Steve and Carolyn
Harvey, the Didler)*

Caledonian Ale House [Haymarket, by Stn]:
Good range of food, good service, well kept
beers *(Stephen and Jean Curtis)*

Cask & Barrel [Broughton St]: Bare-boards
traditional drinkers' pub, half a dozen beers inc
Caledonian Deuchars from U-shaped bar,
helpful service, good value bar food esp stovies
Mon-Fri, Thai lunch Fri *(Roger Huggins, BB)*

Cloisters [Broughton St]: Parsonage turned
alehouse, mixing church pews and gantry

recycled from redundant church with bare
boards and lots of brewery mirrors; Caledonian
Deuchars and 80/-, guests such as Courage
Directors, Flying Firkin Aviator, Inveralmond
Lia Fail and Village White Boar, friendly
atmosphere, lunchtime toasties; open all day,
folk music Fri/Sat *(the Didler)*

Coopers [Waverley Stn]: Busy but well kept
station bar, warm welcome, good choice of
enjoyable well presented fresh food from
sandwiches up; tables outside *(G Cameron)*

Cumberland [Cumberland St]: Classic
unpretentious old-fashioned bar, seven real ales
such as Bass, Caledonian 80/-, Fullers London
Pride, and Hopback Summer Lightning, lots of
malt whiskies, busy chatty feel, good service,
daily papers, lunchtime food; leather seating,
brewery memorabilia and period
advertisements, cosy side room, bright lighting,
plain modern back extension; space in front for
outside drinking *(BB, Dennis Dickinson, Vann
and Terry Prime, Andy and Jill Kassube)*

Dirty Dicks [Rose St]: Carefully remodelled
unusual decorations inc clock in floor, very
friendly humorous staff, good range of real ale,
decent food *(Tony Eberts)*

☆ *Dome* [St Georges Sq/George St]: Opulent
Italianate former bank, huge main bar with
magnificent dome, elaborate plasterwork and
stained glass; central servery, pillars, lots of
greenery, mix of wood and cushioned wicker
chairs, Caledonian Deuchars IPA and 80/-,
smart dining area with interesting food; smaller
and quieter art deco Frasers bar (may be cl some
afternoons and evenings early in week) has
atmospheric period feel, striking woodwork,
unusual lights, red curtains, lots of good period
advertisements, piped jazz, daily papers, same
beers – also wines (rather pricy) and cocktails;
complex includes hotel bedrooms *(W D
Christian, BB)*

Jolly Judge [James Court, by 495 Lawnmarket]:
Interesting and comfortable basement of 16th-c
tenement with traditional fruit-and-flower-
painted wooden ceiling, friendly service,
Caledonian 80/- and a guest beer, changing malt
whiskies, hot drinks, lovely fire, quickly served
lunchtime bar meals (children allowed then) and
afternoon snacks; piped music, games machine;
cl Sun lunchtime; space outside in summer
*(Roger Huggins, LYM, Lynn Sharpless, Bob
Eardley)*

Kenilworth [Rose St]: Friendly Edwardian pub
with ornate high ceiling, carved woodwork,
huge etched brewery mirrors and windows, red
leather seating around tiled wall; central bar
with Tetleys-related and a guest ale, hot drinks
inc espresso, good generous bar food lunchtime
and evening, quick friendly service, back family
room; piped music, discreetly placed games
machines, TV; space outside in summer, open
all day *(Roger Huggins)*

Last Drop [Grassmarket]: Crowded friendly
pub in old area where public hangings ('the last
drop'), took place; lots of atmosphere, good
food, well kept beer, good reasonably priced
house wine *(R T and J C Moggridge)*

Leith Oyster Bar [The Shore, Leith]:

Comfortable pub overlooking water in restored docks, short choice of reliable simple good value meals, inc breakfasts; pleasant candlelit bar with wooden floors, real ales, decent wines *(Walter Reid, BB)*

☆ *Milnes* [Rose St, corner of Hanover St]: Well reworked and extended in 1992 as traditional city pub, rambling layout taking in several areas below street level and even in yard; busy old-fashioned bare-boards feel, dark wood furnishings and panelling, cask tables, lots of old photographs and mementoes of poets who used the 'Little Kremlin' room here, wide choice of well kept mostly Scottish Courage beers with unusual guest and bottled ones, open fire, good value lunches inc various pies charged by size; cheerful staff, lively atmosphere, esp evening *(Monica Shelley, Roger and Jenny Huggins, Mr and Mrs Jon Corelis, Peter and Jeremy Lowater, Steve and Carolyn Harvey, Nick and Meriel Cox, BB, the Didler)*

Old Hundred [Rose St]: Friendly lively bar with good cheap filling food in pleasant upstairs eating area *(R T and J C Moggridge)*

Peacock [Lindsay Rd, Newhaven]: Good straightforward food esp fresh seafood in neat plushly comfortable pub with conservatory-style back room leading to garden, McEwans 80/- and a guest such as Orkney Dark Island; very popular, best to book evenings and Sun lunchtime; children welcome, open all day *(M A Buchanan, LYM, Ian and Villy White)*

☆ *Rose Street Brewery* [Rose St]: Brewing their own good beers (malt extract, though you'd never guess), mild-flavoured though quite potent Auld Reekie 80/- and stronger sticky 90/-, also Brewhouse Reserve and AGM 80/-; tiny brewery can be seen from upstairs lounge (cl at quiet times), comfortably bustling back-to-basics downstairs bar with wood and slab floor open all day, well reproduced (maybe loud) pop music from its CD juke box, machines; reasonably priced food inc haggis in upstairs restaurant, good friendly service, tea and coffee, live music some evenings *(BB, Steve and Carolyn Harvey, Andy Jones, Roger Huggins, R T and J C Moggridge, the Didler)*

Ryans [West End]: Busy noisy central bar with good street views from pavement tables and terrace eating area, good food, well kept McEwans; popular evening meeting place for the under-30s *(R T and J C Moggridge)*

☆ *Sheep Heid* [The Causeway, Duddingston]: Friendly former coaching inn in lovely spot nr King Arthur's Seat, relaxed pubby atmosphere, interesting pictures and fine rounded bar counter in main room, well kept Bass and Caledonian 80/-, daily papers, decent food in bar and restaurant, children allowed; piped music; pretty garden with summer barbecues, skittle alley; open all day, can get crowded *(Dennis Dickinson, LYM)*

☆ *Standing Order* [George St]: Former bank in three elegant Georgian houses, well converted by Wetherspoons in grand mansion style, enormous main room with splendidly colourful and elaborate high ceiling, lots of tables, smaller side booths, other rooms inc no-smoking room with floor to ceiling bookshelves, comfortable green sofa and chairs, Adam fireplace and portraits; good value food, coffee and pastries, decent choice of beers; civilised atmosphere, extremely popular Sat night *(W D Christian, Andy and Jill Kassube, BB, Susan and John Douglas)*

Steading [Hill End, Biggar Rd (A702)]: Popular modern pub, several cottages knocked together at foot of dry ski slope, a dozen well kept Scottish and English real ales inc Timothy Taylor Landlord, reliably good varied generous food 10-10, relatively cheap, in bar, restaurant and conservatory – dining pub atmosphere evening; friendly staff *(M A Buchanan)*

Linlithgow [NS9976]

Old Hole in the Wa' [High St]: Pleasant service, well kept beer, very cheap good food; handy for the Palace *(R T and J C Moggridge)*

Musselburgh [NT3472]

Volunteer Arms [N High St; aka Staggs]: Same family since 1858, unspoilt busy bar, dark panelling, old brewery mirrors, great gantry with ancient casks, Caledonian Deuchars, 60/- and 80/- and guest beers; open all day (not Tues/Weds, cl Sun) *(the Didler)*

Queensferry [NT1278]

☆ *Hawes* [Newhalls Rd]: Featured famously in *Kidnapped*, now comfortably modernised, in great spot for tourists with fine views of the Forth bridges (one rail bridge support in car park), friendly staff, well kept Arrols 80/-, Ind Coope Burton and guest beers such as Caledonian Deuchars from tall founts, decent usual food from efficient servery, games in small public bar, no-smoking family room, restaurant, children welcome; tables on back lawn with play area; good bedrooms, esp Duke of Argyll suite *(D Parkhurst, Heather Martin, LYM)*

Ratho [NT1470]

☆ *Bridge* [Baird Rd]: Very welcoming extended 18th-c pub enjoyed by all ages (esp children), good food all day inc fresh veg and vegetarian, good children's dishes and tactful range of food for those with smaller appetites, choice between quick Pop Inn menu and more expensive things, well kept Belhaven 80/- and Summer Ale, pleasant helpful and chatty staff; garden by partly restored Union Canal, good well stocked play area, wandering ducks and geese, own canal boats (doing trips for the disabled, among others); open all day from noon, very busy in summer *(Neil Townend, Ken and Norma Burgess)*

STRATHCLYDE

Ardrishaig [NM8485]

Barge: Nice range of bar food, very friendly; usual beers *(Justin Hulford)*

Balloch [NS3881]

Balloch Hotel [just N of A811]: Pleasantly pubby big bar broken up by pillars, helpful young staff, four particularly well kept ales such as Caledonian Deuchars, Ind Coope Burton and Timothy Taylor Landlord, good value food all day inc good haggis; many small tables, scattering of fish tackle, restaurant area; bedrooms, nice spot by River Leven's exit from Loch Lomond

(Gill and Maurice McMahon, E A Froggatt)
Blanefield [NS5579]
Carbeth Inn [A809 Glasgow—Drymen, just S of B821]: Low whitewashed pub with good choice of generous bar food inc some less usual dishes, well kept real ale, unusual pine-panelled bar with high fringe of tartan curtains, woodburner one end, log fire the other; fires in smarter lounge and family room too; lots of tables outside, open all day; bedrooms *(LYM)*
Bridge of Orchy [NN2939]
Bridge of Orchy Hotel [A82 Tyndrum—Glencoe]: Comfortable bar with nice views, good food and service, warm atmosphere, particularly well kept Caledonian 80/-, interesting mountain photographs; bedrooms *(Ian Baillie)*
Bridgend [NR8492]
Horseshoe [A816 N of Lochgilphead]: Good value food esp surprising prawn cocktail, two bars, recently refurbished restaurant *(Justin Hulford)*
Colintraive [NS0374]
Colintraive Hotel [opp the Maids of Bute]: Clean, bright and friendly small family-run hotel in lovely spot by ferry to Rhubodach on Bute; straightforward food inc nice puddings; bedrooms immaculate and attractive, with huge baths and good breakfast *(Nigel Woolliscroft)*
Connel [NM9134]
☆ *Lochnell Arms* [North Connel]: Attractive hotel with cosy public bar, small lounge, conservatory extension; good value generous food inc good seafood, friendly service, bric-a-brac, plants, beautiful views over Loch Etive; waterside garden; bedrooms *(Andrew Low, Adrian Bulley)*
Glasgow [NS5865]
Aragon [Byres Rd]: Comfortable L-shaped bar, an institution for students, with well kept Broughton Ghillie, Caledonian Deuchars IPA, Elgoods Pageant, Marstons Pedigree, McEwans 80/- and Theakstons Best, quite a few whiskies, lunchtime food; quite small and friendly, open all day *(Richard Lewis)*
☆ *Bon Accord* [North St]: Attractively done up in Victorian kitchen style, busy and friendly, with Marstons Pedigree, McEwans 80/-, Theakstons Best and Old Peculier, Youngers No 3 and several guest beers, good choice of malt whiskies and wines, good value simple bar food through the day (maybe not midweek evenings), traditional games; restaurant, Weds quiz night, open all day *(Mike and Penny Sanders, LYM)*
Canal [Bearsden Rd]: New American-style brewpub producing all its own beers, wide choice of interesting food *(Ian Baillie)*
☆ *Cask & Still* [Hope St]: Comfortable and welcoming, with shelves and shelves of interesting malt whiskies, bare boards and panelling, big carpets, raised back leather seating area, reasonably priced food all day (menu limited evenings), well kept ales such as Caledonian, Theakstons Best and Orkney Dark Island, lots of unusual bottled beers, Bulmer's cider, decent wines, friendly helpful staff, interesting prints, good piped music; open all day (cl lunchtime Sun) *(BB, SLC, Richard Lewis)*

Clutha Vaults [Stockwell St]: Popular Clydeside local, big beams and panelling, well kept Caledonian Deuchars on tall fount from central bar, good choice of malt whiskies, friendly landlord; folk and blues nights, open all day *(Richard Lewis)*
Fitter & Firkin [Partick]: Large recent conversion in usual Firkin style with Firkin beers, wide choice of food inc some interesting specials, friendly staff, pool and games machines, tourist leaflets; open all day *(Richard Lewis)*
Fruitmarket & Firkin [Wilson St/Hutcheson St]: Large airy open-plan pub brewing four real ales, bare boards, pool and games machines, food from sandwiches to cheap hot dishes, some live music; open all day *(SLC, Richard Lewis)*
Hogshead [Queen St Stn]: Two-floor combination of Costa coffee-bar and comfortable real ale tavern (the shape of things to come?), up to 11 well kept beers, good food choice, lots of prints, daily papers, friendly efficient staff *(Richard Lewis)*
Hogshead [Argyle St, by Kelvin Hall arena]: Half a dozen well kept changing ales, appropriate artefacts, good value simple bar food, good comfortable atmosphere, good service, well reproduced piped blues music, games machines, quiz nights, beer festivals; opp art galleries, open all day *(David Potts)*
☆ *Horseshoe* [Drury St, nr Central Stn]: Classic high-ceilinged pub with enormous island bar, gleaming mahogany and mirrors, snob screens and all sorts of other Victorian features – well worth a good look round; friendly service, well kept Bass, Greenmantle and Caledonian 80/-, lots of malt whiskies, good service even when very busy; games machines, piped music; amazingly cheap food in plainer upstairs bar, no-smoking restaurant (where children allowed); open all day *(Richard Lewis, SLC, A Muir, LYM)*
Mitre [Brunswick St]: Tiny unspoilt Victorian pub with horseshoe bar and coffin gantry, well kept Belhaven and guest beers, also unusual Belgian and other bottled beers; friendly sports-loving staff, football scarves and pennants on ceiling and walls, wholesome cheap food, upstairs restaurant; open all day, cl Sun *(Richard Lewis, SLC)*
Pipers Tryst [McPhater St, Cowcaddens]: Small bright upstairs bar/brasserie of Piping Centre, with bagpipe museum etc; appropriate pictures and quiet piped music, good food all day inc lots of traditional Scottish dishes, also coffee and cakes, traditional bottled beers, a couple on tap; bedrooms *(Andrew and Eileen Abbess)*
☆ *Rab Has* [Hutcheson St]: Sensitively converted Georgian town house, well cooked seafood in delightfully informal ground floor bar and basement restaurant, intermittent robust live music but otherwise relatively quiet; good service; same family as Babbity Bowster – see main entries; bedrooms elegant and immaculate *(BB, SLC, Ian Phillips)*
Rogano [Exchange Pl]: Elegant restaurant with smart downstairs front bar area popular for a discreet drink – good cocktails and wines; piped

jazz, sophisticated atmosphere, bar menu less expensive than the good restaurant (mostly seafood), but still not cheap; cushioned seats in booths, big ceiling fan; outstanding 1930s art deco décor echoes the Clyde-built liner *Queen Mary* (Walter Reid, BB)

Scotia [Stockwell St]: Low ceiling, panelling, events posters old and new, cosy seating around island bar, service friendly even when very busy; half a dozen well kept ales inc interesting guests such as Maclays 80/- and Broadsword, lunchtime food; popular for folk music, also promotes poetry and writers' groups; open all day (Richard Lewis)

Station Bar [Port Dundas Rd]: Recently refurbished, with two or three changing Caledonian ales such as Deuchars IPA, Waverley and Double Amber kept well, welcoming helpful staff, lunchtime food inc popular pie and baked beans; open all day (Richard Lewis)

Tap & Spile [Airport]: Well done in the style of a traditional pub, with plenty of seats and good service even when packed; well kept beers such as Caledonian 80/-, Greenmantle, Greene King Abbot and Theakstons Best and XB, decent malt whiskies, good lunchtime snacks inc fresh sandwiches, no-smoking area (Monica Shelley, Mike and Penny Sanders, Ian Phillips)

Tennents [Byres Rd]: Big lively high-ceilinged pub with ornate plasterwork, panelling, paintings, well kept Caledonian Deuchars IPA, 80/- and Golden Promise, Broughton Greenmantle and Old Jack and several interesting changing guest ales, also several dozen good malt whiskies, decent house wine, quick good-humoured service, cheap usual lunchtime food; open all day (Mike and Penny Sanders, Richard Lewis, Monica Shelley)

Three Judges [Dumbarton Rd, Kelvinhall]: Open-plan leather-seat local with Maclays 80/- and Broadsword and excellent choice of quickly changing real ales from small breweries far and wide – they run through several hundred a year; farm cider, basic food, friendly staff and locals (with their dogs); open all day (Richard Lewis, Walter Reid, Eric Larkham)

☆ *Ubiquitous Chip* [Ashton Lane]: Well placed mirrors giving feeling of space, striking raftered roof, bustling chatty atmosphere, minimal decoration except for some stained glass and carefully carved wooden chests and pews, Caledonian 80/- and Deuchars, 120 malt whiskies, excellent choice of wines by the glass, chilled vodkas, farm cider, helpful service; good bistro menu in adjacent rooms or on pleasant balcony overlooking well known downstairs restaurant; very popular, can be packed with university people (Walter Reid, BB, Monica Shelley)

Victoria [Bridgegate]: Comfortably worn in long narrow bar with basic wooden décor, very warm and friendly, plenty of old panelling, lots of musical events posters, well kept Maclays 70/-, 80/-, Kanes Amber and Wallace on tall fount, lounge on left popular with folk musicians, back bar with wonderful historic bottled beer collection; open all day, cheap food

till 6, friendly staff and locals (Richard Lewis)

Glencoe [NN1058]

Clachaig [old Glencoe rd, behind NTS Visitor Centre]: Spectacular setting, surrounded by soaring mountains, extended inn doubling as mountain rescue post and cheerfully crowded with outdoors people in season, with walkers' bar (two woodburners and pool), pine-panelled snug, big modern-feeling lounge bar; snacks all day, wider evening choice, lots of malt whiskies, well kept ales such as Arrols 80/-, Maclays 80/-, Marstons Pedigree, Theakstons Old Peculier, Tetleys and Youngers No 3; children in no-smoking restaurant; frequent live music; simple bedrooms, good breakfast (LYM, Andrew and Eileen Abbess, T M Dobby, B and C Clouting, Robert Stephenson)

Kilmelford [NM8412]

☆ *Cuilfail* [A816 S of Oban]: Former coaching inn in attractive setting, cheerful stripped-stone pubby bar with light wood furnishings in inner eating area, welcoming family service, good food in bar and restaurant, well kept McEwans and Youngers No 3, good range of malt whiskies, charming garden across road; bedrooms (Nigel Woolliscroft, LYM)

Kilwinning [NS3043]

Claremont [Byres Rd]: Busy hotel with attractive pubby bar, interesting and tasty reasonably priced home-made food, cheerful service, usually a real ale; happy hours, special offers, nightclub, karaoke; bedrooms in quiet house next door (Margaret Mason, David Thompson)

Luss [NS3593]

☆ *Inverbeg* [A82 about 3 miles N]: Useful lunch stop across road from Loch Lomond with tables overlooking it, lounge often crowded for straightforward waitress-served food inc several haggis dishes (also restaurant), well kept real ales, friendly staff, games in simple public bar, private jetty with boat trips; bedrooms inc quiet water's-edge lodges with bathrooms suiting disabled – great views (LYM, Bronwen and Steve Wrigley, Andy, Julie and Stuart Hawkins)

Milngavie [NS5574]

Talbot Arms [Main St]: Pleasantly refurbished, wide choice of good value lunchtime food from substantial sandwiches up, Caledonian 80/-, Marstons Pedigree and guest ales, frequent beer festivals; handy for start or finish of West Highland Way; two TVs (Bronwen and Steve Wrigley, Ian Baillie)

Milton [NS4274]

Milton [Dumbarton Rd]: Pleasant pub popular with families, food most of the day, well kept beers, friendly helpful staff; piped music (Geoffrey and Brenda Wilson)

Oban [NM8630]

☆ *Oban Inn* [Stafford St, nr North Pier]: Friendly bustling traditional pub, beams and slate floor downstairs, quieter upstairs with banquettes, panelling and stained glass, no-smoking family area; hard-working staff, well kept McEwans 70/- and 80/-, lots of whiskies, sandwiches downstairs, cheap food upstairs 11-9 inc vegetarian and good fish and chips, traditional and modern games, juke box or piped music;

open all day, folk Sun, singer most w/e *(Nigel Woolliscroft, LYM, David and Carole Chapman, Andrew and Eileen Abbess, Chris and Ann Garnett)*

Old Kilpatrick [NS4673]
Ettrick [Dumbarton Rd]: Warmly welcoming and comfortable, good cheap food from pies and toasties to steaks and fish, well kept ales such as Bass, Caledonian Deuchars, Orkney Dark Island, weekend live music; in picturesque Clyde village *(Geoffrey and Brenda Wilson)*

Symington [NS3831]
☆ *Wheatsheaf* [Main St; just off A77 Ayr—Kilmarnock]: Busy 18th-c pub in quiet pretty village, charming and cosy, popular lunchtime for wide blackboard choice of consistently good original food esp fish and local produce, Belhaven beers, friendly quick service; must book w/e, tables in garden *(Christine and Malcolm Ingram, Roy Y Bromell)*

Tweedsmuir [NT0924]
Crook [A701 a mile N]: Unusual mix of 17th c (as in simple flagstoned back bar) with 1930s art deco (airy lounge, classic lavatories); log fires, decent bar food, well kept Greenmantle, good choice of malt whiskies, restaurant, traditional games, tables outside, play area, garden over road; craft centre behind, children welcome, open all day, bedrooms, Tweed trout fishing and lamping *(Grant Thoburn, LYM)*

TAYSIDE

Abernethy [NO1816]
☆ *Crees*: Comfortably refurbished, with open fire in snug, four well kept ales, good whiskies, good home-made lunches inc vegetarian, children's and scrumptious puddings, evening pizzas (restaurant planned in adjoining barn); monthly folk music, handy for Pictish tower nearby *(Dallas Seawright, Catherine Lloyd)*

Blair Atholl [NN8765]
Atholl Arms: Friendly, with well priced good food – and the singing gets better as the beers go down; bedrooms *(Anthony Barnes)*

Broughty Ferry [NO4630]
☆ *Ship* [Shore Terr/Fishers St]: Small busy local by lifeboat station, handsomely refurbished in burgundy and dark wood, stately model sailing ship and other mainly local nautical items; open all day for enjoyable food inc massive good value seafood platter, good service, pleasant upstairs dining room with lovely waterfront view, friendly staff; keg beer *(Susan and John Douglas)*

Colliston [NO6045]
Colliston Inn [A933 N of Arbroath]: Popular for bar meals and suppers inc local fish, Arbroath smokies and good Angus meat; genial service, pleasant furnishings, open fire in bar/dining area, some fashionably dim lighting *(George and Jean Dundas)*

Crieff [NN8562]
Glenturret Distillery [N, signed off A85, A822]: Not a pub, but good adjunct to one of the best whisky-distillery tours; good value whiskies in big plain bar/dining area with tasty sandwiches, good generous Highland soups, stews, pies, salmon and venison, and knock-out ice cream,

from self-service food counter; open Mar-Dec Mon-Fri till 5.30, also Apr-Oct Sat till 4 *(Susan and John Douglas)*

Dundee [NO4030]
Royal Oak [Brook St]: Pubby bar with stripped stone, old furniture, well kept Ind Coope Burton and several other changing ales, open fire; more like Indian restaurant behind, with sombre dark green décor, tasty curries, also wide choice of more general food; weekday food may stop around 8ish, can be very busy w/e *(Neil Townend, Susan and John Douglas)*

Eassie [NO3547]
☆ *Castleton House* [A94 Coupar Angus—Forfar]: Country-house hotel with elegant high-ceilinged armchair bar, very pleasant service, big log fire, consistently good modern food at most attractive prices in spacious candlelit L-shaped conservatory restaurant and separate no-smoking dining room; beautiful grounds, bedrooms; fairly handy for Glamis Castle *(Susan and John Douglas, Jean and George Dundas)*

Errol [NO2523]
Old Smiddy [The Cross, High St (B958 E of Perth)]: Attractive heavy-beamed bar with assorted old country furniture, good food inc fresh local ingredients and interesting recipes, well kept interesting local Ossian ale, lots of country wines, decent coffee, good welcoming service, rather dark décor with farm and smithy tools inc massive bellows; pleasant village setting, open all day Sun, cl Mon/Tues lunchtime *(Mr and Mrs R M Macnaughton, Susan and John Douglas)*

Glamis [NO3846]
Strathmore Arms: Smart hotel with warm and bustling pub bar, unusual semi-modern décor with stripped stone and fairy-lit twig arrangements, vast choice of enjoyable food inc interesting dishes (people eat early here), charming helpful staff; keg beers; bedrooms *(Susan and John Douglas, Mr and Mrs R M Macnaughton)*

Kenmore [NN7745]
☆ *Kenmore Hotel*: Civilised and quietly old-fashioned small hotel beautifully set in pretty 18th-c village by Loch Tay; main front bar with long poem pencilled by Burns himself on the chimney-breast ('Admiring Nature in her wildest grace'), also old fishing photographs, china, panelling, tartan furnishings; good helpful service, enjoyable food from good sandwiches up, cosily old-fashioned upmarket feel; children welcome, back garden with great Tay views; bedrooms, elegant residents' rooms and back dining room, own fishing *(LYM, Susan and John Douglas, R M Macnaughton, David Atkinson, Neil Townend, Anthony Barnes)*

Kinloch Rannoch [NN6658]
Bunrannoch House: Hotel not pub, but like other hotels in these parts does duty as one – with friendly and unoppressive feeling here of being in someone's home; delicious food with simple ingredients beautifully prepared, inc particularly good breakfast; bedrooms *(Anthony Barnes, Bob Ellis)*

Kinlochleven [NN1861]
McDonald Hotel: Simple public bar with good

attractively priced home-made food; good bedrooms *(Justin Hulford)*
Kinnesswood [NO1703]
☆ *Lomond* [A911 Glenrothes—Milnathort, not far from M90 junctions 7/8]: Well appointed and friendly small inn with lovely sunset views over Loch Leven, good reasonably priced food choice in bar and restaurant, fresh local produce, delicious puddings, well kept Belhaven, Jennings and guest beers such as Greene King Abbot, quick thoughtful service, log fire; comfortable bedrooms *(R M Macnaughton, R F and M K Bishop)*
Meikleour [NO1539]
☆ *Meikleour Hotel* [A984 W of Coupar Angus]: Two lounges, one with stripped stone, flagstones and armour, another more chintzy, both with open fires, helpful friendly service, good bar food inc fine range of open sandwiches and lunchtime snacks, well kept Maclays 70/-; fruit machines, back public bar; pretty building, charming garden with tall pines and distant Highland view; nr famous 250-yr-old beech hedge over 30 m (100 ft) high *(Susan and John Douglas)*
Perth [NO1123]
Greyfriars [South St]: Prettily refurbished by new owners, with cheap lunchtime food from baguettes and baked potatoes up, well kept real ales; small restaurant upstairs *(Catherine Lloyd)*
Huntingtower House Hotel [off A85 W]: Plush decoration – even the conservatory overlooking streamside hotel gardens; good reasonably priced bar food, small range of beers; bedrooms *(IHR, Ray Watson, Neil Townend)*
St Fillans [NN6924]
Achray House [12 miles W of Crieff]: Hotel in stunning lochside position, good friendly service, good varied reasonably priced food esp puddings, extensive wine list; good value bedrooms *(Andy, Julie and Stuart Hawkins, IHR)*

SCOTTISH ISLANDS

ISLE OF ARRAN
Brodick [NS0136]
Brodick Bars [Alma Rd]: Tucked away off seafront rd, wide choice of food, McEwans beers *(John Knighton)*

ISLE OF BARRA
Castlebay [NL6698]
Castlebay Hotel: Great view, good food; decent bedrooms *(Nigel Woolliscroft)*

ISLE OF MULL
Craignure [NM7136]
Ceilidh Place [by Oban ferry pier]: Good food such as Moroccan lamb stew in rather spare bar/dining area *(C J Bromage)*

ISLE OF NORTH UIST
Lochmaddy [NF9168]
Lochmaddy Hotel: Clean and smart, with helpful pleasant staff, good genuinely home-made bar lunches *(Walter and Susan Rinaldi-Butcher)*

ISLE OF ORKNEY
Stromness [HY2509]
Houton Hotel: New hotel by ferry for Hoy, plenty of seals and birds – haunt for divers amateur and professional; decent reasonably priced food inc local fish, McEwans and Orkney Dark Island beer; good bedrooms *(Gordon Neighbour)*

ISLE OF SKYE
Flodigarry [NG4572]
☆ *Flodigarry Hotel* [nr Staffin]: 1895 turreted mansion with stunning views of sea and highlands, Moorish former billiard room now bar open all day for wide range of reasonably priced food, also coffee and afternoon teas, conservatory, Theakstons; some live music, bedrooms, Flora MacDonald connections – you can stay in her cottage *(Eric Locker, Jack and Heather Coyle)*
Portree [NG4843]
Pier Hotel [Quay St]: Down-to-earth boatmen's bar, language to match sometimes, welcoming landlord, interesting murals, occasional live music, pipers during Skye games week; keg beers; harbour-view bedrooms good value *(Nigel Woolliscroft)*
Stein [NG2556]
☆ *Stein Inn* [end of B886 N of Dunvegan]: Down-to-earth small inn delightfully set above quiet sea inlet, tables out looking over sea to Hebrides (great sunsets), peat fire in flagstoned and stripped-stone public bar, really welcoming licensees and locals, well kept Isle of Skye Cuillin Red, good malt whiskies, good value bar food (in winter only for people staying) inc huge three-cheese ploughman's; recently renovated bedrooms *(D Prodham, E J Locker)*
Uig [NG3963]
Ferry: Tiny, friendly and unpretentious lounge bar, warm welcome, good value food from soup and toasties to good fresh fish; clean and comfortable bedrooms overlooking pier and water, same great view from garden tables *(BB, Chris and Ann Garnett, Christopher Beade)*

ISLE OF SOUTH UIST
Loch Carnan [NF8044]
Orasay Inn [signed off A865 S of Creagorry]: Friendly service and wide choice of home-made food inc good local seafood and puddings in comfortable modern lounge and conservatory, open all day; bedrooms with own bathrooms *(Jack and Heather Coyle)*
Pollachar [NF7414]
☆ *Polachar Hotel* [S end of B888]: Comfortably modernised and extended 17th-c shoreside inn with glorious views across Sound of Barra to Barra and Eriskay, dolphins, porpoises and seals; big public bar, separate dining room, good bar meals running up to Aberdeen Angus steaks; very helpful friendly staff and locals (all Gaelic speaking); 11 well renovated bedrooms with own bathrooms, good breakfast *(Jack and Heather Coyle, Nigel Woolliscroft)*

Wales

Besides a lot of newly inspected places swelling the upper ranks of the Lucky Dip section at the end of the chapter, there are several interesting new main entries here this year: the Nags Head at Abercych (nice setting and atmosphere, good food and good beer), the Castle in Llandeilo (with its own good Tomos Watkin beers), the Sloop by the sea in the interesting little village of Porthgain, the very popular King Arthur in Reynoldston on the Gower, and the friendly Nags Head in Usk (decent food, good beer). Other Welsh pubs really making their mark these days are the Ty Gwyn in Betws-y-Coed (good stylish atmosphere and food, especially fish), the very popular Bear in Crickhowell (a fine all-rounder), just outside Crickhowell the Nantyffin Cider Mill (a very good dining pub, but this year it gains a Beer Award as well), the truly ancient Blue Anchor at East Aberthaw (good beer, food and service), the Pant-yr-Ochain in Gresford (good food), the attractive and magnificently set Pen-y-Gwryd high above Llanberis, the Walnut Tree at Llandewi Skirrid (excellent food), the White Swan at Llanfrynach (good food and service), the Crown at Llwyndafydd (good food and beer, well laid out play area), the Griffin at Llyswen (friendly and efficient service, good food), the ancient Plough & Harrow at Monknash (well kept beers, lots of atmosphere), the friendly Ferry Inn at Pembroke Ferry (good fresh fish), the Clytha Arms near Raglan (good food, service and atmosphere), the waterside Ship on Red Wharf Bay (the landlord's been here nearly 30 years, but the food side has livened up a lot this year – who said you can't teach an old dog new tricks?) and the Armstrong Arms at Stackpole (the new people are doing good food). As we've said, quite a few of these pubs have good food; our choice as Welsh Dining Pub of the Year is the Nantyffin Cider Mill near Crickhowell. We have divided the Lucky Dip section at the end of the chapter into the former county areas (more useful in terms of areas, at least for visitors, than the new smaller unitary authority ones). Here, pubs doing well these days are, on Anglesey the Liverpool Arms in Menai Bridge; in Clwyd, the West Arms at Llanarmon Dyffryn Ceiriog and (for food) Cross Foxes at Overton Bridge; in Dyfed, the Druidstone Hotel at Broad Haven, Brunant Arms at Caio, Dyffryn Arms at Cwm Gwaun, White Hart at Llanddarog and Royal Oak in Saundersfoot; in Glamorgan, the Joiners Arms in Bishopston (West), Goose & Cuckoo at Rhyd-y-Meirch and Travellers Rest at Thornhill (both Mid); in Gwent, the Abbey Hotel at Llanthony, Village Green at trelleck and Fountain at Trelleck Grange; in Gwynedd, the Royal Oak in Betws-y-Coed and Kings Head in Llandudno; and in Powys, the Trout at Beulah, Hundred House at Bleddfa, Farmers Arms at Cwmdu, Vine Tree at Llangattock, Neuadd Arms in Llanwrtyd Wells, Radnor Arms at Llowes and Harp at Old Radnor. Drinks prices in Welsh pubs are a little lower than the national average. The cheapest pub we found was the attractive Old House at Llangynwyd (tied to Whitbreads – the national brewers dominate beer supply in Wales), with the Castle in Llandeilo (the tap for the Tomos Watkin brewery) and Olde Bull at Llanbedr-y-Cennin (tied to Lees of Manchester, who supply other pubs in North Wales too) running it close.

ABERCYCH SN2441 Map 6

Nags Head 🍺

Off B4332 Cenarth—Boncath

Wrong turnings and muddle-headed navigation almost caused us to abandon our expedition to this cheery place, but perseverance eventually led us to what turned out to be the highlight of this year's Welsh inspection tour. Remarkably lively given the size of the village, it's a busily traditional ivy-covered pub in a lovely riverside setting, worth a detour for its food and particularly good choice of beers. The landlord stocks mostly Welsh brews, which on our visit included Dyffryn Clwyd Pedwar Bawd, Wye Valley Dorothy Goodbody, Summer of 69 and Total Blackout, as well as their own Old Emrys, named after one of the regulars. The dimly lit beamed and stone-flagged bar has a real mix of ages and accents, as well as a comfortable old sofa in front of its big fireplace, clocks showing the time around the world, stripped wooden tables, a piano, photos and postcards of locals, and hundreds of bottles of beer displayed around the brick and stone walls; piped music. A plainer small room leads down to a couple of big dining areas (one of which is no smoking), and there's another little room behind the bar. Bar food includes sandwiches (from £1.75), soup (£2.95), home-made pies like Welsh lamb and leek or steak and ale (£6.95), local salmon or crab (£7.95), and seabass (£11); Sunday lunch (£5.50). No credit cards. Across the peaceful road outside are tables under cocktail parasols looking over the water, as well as a number of nicely arranged benches, and a children's play area. It's an attractive spot on a summer's day, or in the evening when the pub is lit by fairy lights. There may be barbecues out here in summer. *(Recommended by Howard James)*

Free house ~ Licensee Steven Jamieson ~ Real ale ~ Bar food ~ (01239) 841200 ~ Children welcome ~ Open 11-11; 11-3, 6-11 winter

ABERDOVEY SN6296 Map 6

Penhelig Arms 🍽 🍷 🛏

Opp Penhelig railway station

Very good fresh fish continues to be one of the main draws to this nicely set mainly 18th-c hotel – it's delivered daily by the local fishmonger. Well prepared and generously served, there might be fresh sardines grilled with peppers, tomato and garlic (£4.50), delicious fish pie (£6.95), salmon seared with basil and mint in a vanilla hollandaise sauce or spiced cod baked with spring onion and peppers with chilli relish and sour cream (£7.50), roast fillet of hake wrapped in bacon (£7.95), halibut grilled with prawns and cheese in a tomato and orange sauce (£9.50), and whole lemon sole in tarragon butter (£9.75). They also do soup (£1.95), filled baguettes (from £2.75), beef goulash (£6.75), grilled Mexican spiced chicken or lamb's kidneys braised in a red wine sauce (£7.50); readers have particularly praised the vegetables over the last few months. Puddings such as apricot mousse or chocolate torte (£2.95), and they're great supporters of British cheeses. The excellent wine list has over 40 half bottles (not to mention 250 whole ones), and about 14 by the glass; they also have two dozen malt whiskies, fruit or peppermint teas, and various coffees. The small original beamed bar has a cosy feel with winter fires, and changing real ales such as Bass, Brains SA, Greene King Abbott, Morlands Old Speckled Hen and Tetleys on handpump; dominoes. Service is friendly and concerned. Completely redecorated in the last year, the separate restaurant is no smoking. In summer you can eat out on a terrace by the harbour wall while you take in the lovely views across the Dyfi estuary – the comfortable bedrooms share the same views. *(Recommended by J Sheldon, J H Jones, Sue and Bob Ward, E Holland, Betty Petheram)*

Free house ~ Licensees Robert and Sally Hughes ~ Real ale ~ Bar food ~ Restaurant ~ (01654) 767215 ~ Children welcome ~ Open 11-4, 5.30-11(all day bank hols and Aug) ~ Bedrooms: £39.50B/£69B

Pubs with particularly interesting histories, or in unusually interesting buildings, are listed at the back of the book.

ABERYSTWYTH SN6777 Map 6
Halfway Inn

Pisgah (not the Pisgah near Cardigan); A4120 towards Devil's Bridge, 5¾ miles E of junction with A487

Busy in summer thanks to its panoramic views down over the wooded hills and pastures of the Rheidol Valley, this enchanting old place has a genuinely old-fashioned and peaceful charm. Readers who arrived on a damp, blustery day were delighted when the landlord offered to put the heating on for them. The atmospheric beamed and flagstoned bar has stripped deal tables and settles and bare stone walls, as well as darts, pool, dominoes, trivia and piped music (classical at lunchtimes, popular folk and country in the evenings), and a well kept beer from Badger alongside Felinfoel Double Dragon, Hancocks HB and maybe a weekly guest on handpump. There might be up to four draught ciders, and a few malt whiskies. Generously served with fresh vegetables, bar food includes soup (£1.50), filled baked potatoes (from £2.25), sandwiches (from £2.50), ploughman's or chicken, mushroom and ham pie (£5.50), breaded scampi (£5.75), steak and ale pie (£5.95), 8oz sirloin (£9.95), daily specials like saucy jerk chicken (£5.75), home-made puddings, and children's meals (£2.75). Note they don't do lunches on winter weekdays except by prior arrangement. Tables can be reserved in the dining room/restaurant area, part of which is no smoking. Outside are picnic-sets under cocktail parasols, a very simple play area, a new nursery, and a baling rail for pony-trekkers; there's free overnight camping for customers. *(Recommended by Dr Oscar Puls, Joan and Michel Hooper-Immins, Dorothy and Leslie Pilson)*

Free house ~ Licensee David Roberts ~ Real ale ~ Bar food ~ Restaurant ~ (01970) 880631 ~ Children welcome ~ Open 12-2.30, 6.30-11(10.30 Sun); closed weekday lunchtimes in winter unless prior arrangement is made ~ Bedrooms: £25B/£38B

BEAUMARIS SH6076 Map 6
Olde Bulls Head ★ ♀

Castle Street

Perhaps especially nice for a winter break, this smartly cosy old hotel has plenty of reminders of its long and interesting past, particularly in the quaintly old-fashioned rambling bar. Amidst the low beams and snug alcoves are a rare 17th-c brass water clock, a bloodthirsty crew of cutlasses, and even the town's oak ducking stool, as well as lots of copper and china jugs, comfortable low-seated settles, leather-cushioned window seats and a good open fire. Very well kept Bass, Worthington Best and a guest like Hancocks HB on handpump, a good comprehensive list of over 220 wines (with plenty of half bottles), and freshly squeezed orange juice; cheerful, friendly service; chess and cards. The entrance to the pretty courtyard is closed by the biggest simple hinged door in Britain. They don't do food in the bar any more, but there's a good choice in the new brasserie they've built behind; the menu includes home-made soup (£2.50), sandwiches (from £3.20), ploughman's (£4.50), confit of duck with kumquat marmalade and toasted almond salad (£4.95), several pasta dishes such as potato gnocchi with baked goat's cheese, leeks and cream (£5), grilled mullet with melted onions and tapenade (£5.95), pan-fried pork schnitzel with couscous and lemon and caper butter (£6.25), braised Welsh lamb with root vegetables and mint gravy (£7.25), and puddings such as almond and Amaretto parfait or bara brith and butter pudding with ginger ice cream (£2.95). There's also a smart no-smoking restaurant. The simple but charming bedrooms (with lots of nice little extras) are named after characters in Dickens's novels. *(Recommended by Pamela and Merlyn Horswell, A J Bowen, J H Jones, G C Hackemer, Anthony Bowen, Anne P Heaton)*

Free house ~ Licensee David Robertson ~ Real ale ~ Bar food ~ Restaurant ~ (01248) 810329 ~ Children welcome, must be over seven in restaurant ~ Open 11-11; 12-10.30 Sun; closed 25, 26 Dec ~ Bedrooms: £51B/£81B

By law pubs must show a price list of their drinks. Let us know if you are inconvenienced by any breach of this law.

Sailors Return

Church Street

Service at this bright and cheerful pub is very friendly and helpful, and you really get the feeling the landlord enjoys his calling. More or less open-plan, it's often packed with happy diners of all ages, especially in the evenings (lunchtimes tend to be quieter); the tables in the dining area on the left can be booked. The good value bar food includes sandwiches, soup (£2.25), garlic mushrooms or prawn cocktail (£3.95), ploughman's (£5.95), brie, potato, courgette and almond crumble (£5.85), chicken curry (£6.25), grilled plaice (£6.50), gammon steak with egg and pineapple (£6.95), sirloin steak (£9.45), and daily specials like salmon and smoked haddock fishcakes with parsley sauce (£5.85) or chicken in leek and smoked bacon sauce (£6.50); children's menu (from £2.65). Furnishings include comfortable richly coloured banquettes, with an open fire in winter. There's a quaint collection of china teapots, and maps of Cheshire among the old prints and naval memorabilia betray the landlord's origins; the Green Room to the left of the bar is no smoking. Well kept Morlands Old Speckled Hen and Tetleys on handpump; maybe unobtrusive piped music. *(Recommended by Stephen Hughes, Jill Bickerton, Chris and Shirley Machin)*

Free house ~ Licensee Peter Ogan ~ Real ale ~ Bar food ~ (01248) 811314 ~ Children welcome ~ Open 11.30-3, 6-11; 12-3, 7-10.30 Sun; closed 25 Dec

BETWS-Y-COED SH7956 Map 6

Ty Gwyn

A5 just S of bridge to village

Reports on this cottagey coaching inn have been consistently enthusiastic this year; you can't just pop in for a drink, as the terms of the licence are such that you must eat or stay overnight to be served alcohol. Neither condition is a major hardship – if you stay it's well placed for the area's multitude of attractions, and it's definitely worth a visit for the generously served tasty meals. Very good fresh fish features heavily on the menu, with perhaps herring fillets marinated in madeira (£3.25), green-lip mussels with garlic butter (£3.75), battered cod or deep-fried king prawns in filo pastry (£6.50), trout with lobster and prawn sauce or baked fillet of conger eel with prawns, mushrooms and peppers (£7.95), salmon with Dubonnet and dill sauce (£8.95), king scallops Brazilian (£11.95) and whole lobster thermidor (£13.95); other dishes might include good soup (£2.75), chicken liver, hazelnut and port pâté (£3.50), black pudding and toffee apple with coarse mustard and cheddar volute (£3.75), mushroom and nut fettucine (£5.95), Thai chicken curry (£7.50), chargrilled Welsh lamb steak (£8.95), and various steaks (£11.95). There's a nice personally welcoming atmosphere in the beamed lounge bar, which has an ancient cooking range worked in well at one end, and rugs and comfortable chintz easy chairs on its oak parquet floor. The interesting clutter of unusual old prints and bric-a-brac reflects the owners' interest in antiques (they used to run an antique shop next door); highchair and toys available. Flowers IPA on handpump, welcoming and efficient staff, and maybe two friendly cats; piped music. Part of the restaurant is no smoking. Breakfasts are well sized. *(Recommended by Colin McKerrow, R J Bland, Mike and Penny Sanders, J H Jones, Keith and Margaret Kettell, KC, Jack and Gemima Valiant, Jill Bickerton)*

Free house ~ Licensees Jim and Shelagh Ratcliffe ~ Real ale ~ Bar food ~ Restaurant ~ (01690) 710383/787 ~ Children welcome ~ Open 12-2, 7(8.30 winter weekdays)-9; closed Mon-Wed in Jan ~ Bedrooms: £17(£40B)/£35(£52B)

BODFARI SJ0970 Map 6

Dinorben Arms ♀

From A541 in village, follow Tremeirchion 3 signpost

In a pretty spot beside a church, and clinging to the side of the mountain, this attractive black and white inn is well known for its incredible range of over 250 malt whiskies (including the full Macallan range and a good few from the Islay distilleries). They also have plenty of good wines (with several classed growth clarets), vintage ports and cognacs, and quite a few unusual coffee liqueurs. As well as a glassed-over old well, the three warmly welcoming neat flagstoned rooms which open off the heart of this carefully extended building have plenty of character, with beams hung with tankards and flagons, high shelves of china, old-fashioned settles and other seats, and three open fires; there's also a light and airy garden room. Well kept Aylesbury Best, Tetleys and a weekly changing guest on handpump; occasional piped classical music. There are lots of tables outside on the prettily landscaped and planted brick-floored terraces, with attractive sheltered corners and charming views, and there's a grassy play area which – like the car park – is neatly sculpted into the slope of the hills. Bar food includes home-made steak and kidney pie or chicken, ham and mushroom pie (£4.85), broccoli and cream bake or scampi (£5.25), lasagne (£6.50), seafood mornay (£6.75), sirloin steak (from £7.95), and daily specials such as local lamb or salmon. One child can eat free if both parents are dining (except on Saturday nights and bank holidays). On Sunday lunchtimes you'll find their very well liked smorgasbord which includes a changing range of hot soups, main courses and puddings (£8.95); there's no other choice of bar snacks then, and it's advisable to book. A no-smoking area in the upstairs Badger Suite has a carvery on Friday and Saturday (£12.95) and a good help-yourself farmhouse buffet on Wednesday and Thursday, and Sunday evenings (£9.95). *(Recommended by KC, Gill and Maurice McMahon, Norman Stansfield, Pete Richards, W C M Jones)*

Free house ~ Licensee David Rowlands ~ Real ale ~ Bar food (12-3, 6-10) ~ Restaurant ~ (01745) 710309 ~ Children welcome ~ Open 12-3.30, 6-11; 12-11 Sat

BOSHERSTON SR9694 Map 6
St Govans Inn
Village signed from B4319 S of Pembroke

The south wall of the bar of this usefully placed, comfortably modernised inn is decorated with murals of local beauty spots painted by a local artist, W S Heaton, and there are certainly enough to choose from. It's a lovely area: quite close by there's a many-fingered inlet from the sea, now fairly land-locked and full of water-lilies in summer, while some way down the road terrific cliffs plunge to the sea. Not surprisingly the pub is very popular with walkers and climbers comparing climbs, and there are lots of very good climbing photographs. Stone pillars support the black and white timbered ceiling of the spacious bar which has a woodburning stove in a large stone fireplace, plenty of button-back red leatherette wall banquettes and armed chairs around dimpled copper tables, and stags' antlers; pool, dominoes, fruit machine, juke box and board games. A small but useful choice of mostly home-made bar food might include sandwiches, their speciality cawl, cumberland sausage (£3.85), scampi (£5.85), crab salad (£6.50), gammon (£7.50), and 10oz sirloin steak (£10.75). The dining area is no smoking. In season they usually have five well kept real ales on handpump at once (there may only be one at quiet times in winter), from a range including Bass, Brains SA, Crown Buckley Reverend James, Everards Tiger, Fullers London Pride, Hancocks HB and Thwaites Daniels Hammer; also about a dozen malt whiskies. There are a few picnic-sets on the small front terrace. *(Recommended by Richard and Ann Higgs)*

Free house ~ Licensee Sheila Webster ~ Real ale ~ Bar food ~ (01646) 661311 ~ Children welcome ~ Open 12-3(2.30 winter), 6(7 winter)-11.30(10.30 Sun); closed Mon lunchtime Jan, Feb ~ Bedrooms: £19S/£38S

CAPEL CURIG SH7258 Map 6
Bryn Tyrch
A4086 W of village

This comfortable Snowdonian country inn is very much a place for walkers and climbers, and in fact on our inspection visit we found the polite barman offering advice on local climbs – and explaining how he fitted climbing in around his work schedule. Big picture windows run the length of one wall, with views across the road to picnic-sets on a floodlit patch of grass by a stream running down to a couple of lakes; in the distance is the Snowdon Horseshoe. There are several easy chairs round low tables, some by a coal fire with magazines and outdoor equipment catalogues piled to one side, and a pool table in the plainer hikers' bar; several areas are no smoking. Wholesome food, with an emphasis on vegetarian and vegan dishes, is generously served to meet the healthy appetite of anyone enjoying the local outdoor attractions – or you could try one of the many coffee blends (listed on a blackboard) or Twinings teas with a piece of vegan fruit cake. The seasonally changing menu might include interestingly filled ciabatta sandwiches (from £3.95), zucchini dippers with teriyaki dip or prawns in a garlic, lime and yoghurt dressing (£3.65), breakfast (meat, vegetarian or vegan, £5.95), butterbean and vegetable curry, or carrot, courgette and lentil cottage pie (£6.45), broccoli, cauliflower and stilton crumble (£6.95), chicken, leek and bacon cobbler or traditional Welsh lamb lobscouse (£7.95), smoked haddock dauphinoise (£7.95), merguez sausages with mushroom gravy (£8.25), and puddings like rhubarb crumble or a vegan chocolate sponge (£3.25); some sort of food most of the day, with nice range of cakes for afternoon tea. Well kept Flowers IPA, Wadworths 6X and Whitbreads Castle Eden, with possibly a summer guest; also country wines, and lots of malt whiskies. Shove-ha'penny, dominoes. There are tables on a steep little garden at the side. *(Recommended by J Porter, J and J Hoppitt)*

Free house ~ Licensee Rita Davis ~ Real ale ~ Bar food (all day) ~ Restaurant ~ (01690) 720223/352 ~ Children welcome ~ Open 12-11(10.30 Sun); closed 25, 26 Dec ~ Bedrooms: £24.50(£27.50B)/£41(£49B)

CAREW SN0403 Map 6
Carew Inn
A4075, just off A477

Delightfully set just opposite the imposing ruins of Carew Castle, this simple old inn is a positively friendly place with a good deal of character. It's now so popular that in summer they put a marquee in the garden to help accommodate the summer crowds; they also have live music in it on Thursday and Sunday nights. There's a notably cheery welcome in the very characterful little panelled public bar and comfortable lounge, as well as old-fashioned settles and scrubbed pine furniture, and interesting prints and china hanging from the beams. The no-smoking upstairs dining room has an elegant china cabinet, a mirror over the tiled fireplace and sturdy chairs around the well spaced tables. Generously served, reasonably priced bar food includes sandwiches (from £2.25), ploughman's (£3.95), mussels in white wine with garlic and herbs (£4.95), vegetable tikka (£6.50), chicken, leek and mushroom pie (£6.95), local dressed crab (£7.95), gammon steak (£8.95), and specials such as Greek lamb with mint and yoghurt dressing (£8.95) or pork tenderloin in mustard suce (£9.50); children's meals (from £2.95). Local mackerel and sea bass can be caught and served within two hours. The menu may be more limited on Sunday, when thy have a choice of roasts. Changing beers on handpump might include well kept Boddingtons, Brains Reverend James, Worthington Best and Wye Valley; sensibly placed darts, dominoes, cribbage, piped music. Dogs in the public bar only. The back garden has a wheelchair ramp and is safely enclosed, with a sandpit, climbing frame, slide and other toys, as well as a remarkable 9th-century Celtic cross. Seats in a pretty little flowery front garden at this popular and unchanging inn look down to the river where a tidal watermill is open for afternoon summer visits; it's also opposite the imposing ruins of Carew Castle. *(Recommended by Graham Baker, IHR, Ben and Sheila Walker, JP, PP, Chris Brace, Dr M Owton, the Didler, John and Enid Morris)*

Free house ~ Licensees Rob and Mandy Hinchcliffe ~ Bar food (12-2.30, 5.30-9.30(12-2, 7-9 winter)) ~ Restaurant ~ (01646) 651267 ~ Childrewn welcome away from public bar ~ Live music Thurs evening, and Sun evening in summer ~ Open 11-11; 12-10.30 Sun; 11.45-2.30, 4.30-11 Mon-Fri, 11-11 Sat, 12-3, 7-10.30 Sun winter; closed 25 Dec

COLWYN BAY SH8578 Map 6
Mountain View
Mochdre; take service-road into village off link road to A470, S from roundabout at start of new A55 dual carriageway to Conwy; OS Sheet 116 map reference 825785

Since our last edition they've had a major refurbishment at this neatly kept pub, and the result is rather smart, with new flooring, and antique pine tables and chairs. But it's still the big helpings of good value bar food that draw people in, with a fairly extensive choice that might include soups such as stilton and broccoli (£2.25), whole plaice (£6.95), strips of chicken and gammon in diane sauce (£7.75), peppered pork steak on a bed of mushrooms and onions (£7.50), crispy duck in port and redcurrant sauce (£8.50), and devilled rack of Welsh lamb (£9.95); readers have praised the vegetables, but service can slow down when they're particularly busy. The bar is divided into different areas by arched walls, and there are plenty of houseplants (and bright window boxes in the large windows). Despite the emphasis on food, you'll still find locals who've popped in for a chat. Friendly and efficient service, well kept real ales such as Burtonwood Bitter, Buccaneer, James Forshaws and Top Hat on handpump, and around 30 malt whiskies (the landlord is very knowledgeable on this topic); darts, pool, dominoes, fruit machine, table football and juke box. The raised seating area is no smoking. There are a few tables on the front patio. *(Recommended by KC, Bob and Marg Griffiths, Paul and Margaret Baker)*

Burtonwood ~ Tenant Malcolm Robert Gray ~ Real ale ~ Bar food ~ (01492) 544724 ~ Children in eating area of bar ~ Open 11.30-3, 6-11; 12-5, 7-10.30 Sun

CRESSWELL QUAY SN0406 Map 6
Cresselly Arms
Village signposted from A4075

If the tides are right you can get to this marvellously traditional old Welsh-speaking creeper-covered local by boat, an approach that adds to its uniquely timeless appeal. There's a relaxed and jaunty feel in the two simple comfortably unchanging communicating rooms, which have red and black flooring tiles, built-in wall benches, kitchen chairs and plain tables, an open fire in one room, a working Aga in the other, and a high beam-and-plank ceiling hung with lots of pictorial china. A third red-carpeted room is more conventionally furnished, with red-cushioned mate's chairs around neat tables. Well kept Worthington BB is tapped straight from the cask into glass jugs by the landlord, whose presence is a key ingredient of the atmosphere; fruit machine and winter darts. Seats outside face the tidal creek of the Cresswell River. *(Recommended by John and Enid Morris, JP, PP, Pete Baker, the Didler)*

Free house ~ Licensees Maurice and Janet Cole ~ Real ale ~ (01646) 651210 ~ Children welcome in back room ~ Open 12-3, 5-11; 11-11 Sat; 12-3, 6-10.30 Sun

CRICKHOWELL SO2118 Map 6
Bear ★ ⑪ ♀ ◧ 🛏
Brecon Road; A40

Always busy, whatever the season, this faultlessly run old coaching inn has once again pleased a great many readers over the last year. There's a calmly civilised atmosphere in the comfortably decorated, heavily beamed lounge, which has lots of little plush-seated bentwood armchairs and handsome cushioned antique settles, and a window seat looking down on the market square. Up by the great roaring log fire, a big sofa and leather easy chairs are spread among the rugs on the oak parquet floor; antiques include a fine oak dresser filled with pewter and brass, a longcase clock and interesting prints. Making very good use of local ingredients, the changing range of beautifully presented freshly cooked bar meals might include soup (£2.75), sandwiches (from £2.50), welsh rarebit on olive bread with bacon (£4.20), smoked haddock tartlet (£4.50), spinach and stilton soufflé with parmesan and pickled pears (£4.95), chicken, ham and leek pie (£5.95), venison burger or salmon wrapped in basil leaves and baked in filo pastry (£7.95), steamed lamb and leek suet pudding with rosemary jus (£8.25), local game hotpot (£8.50), and steaks (from £10.95); delicious puddings such as bread and butter pudding made with rum and bananas, served with brown bread ice cream (£3.50), and a good range of Welsh cheeses. Their Sunday lunch is well liked. The family bar is partly no smoking. Well kept Bass, Hancocks HB and Ruddles County on handpump; malt whiskies, vintage and late-bottled ports, and unusual wines (with about a dozen by the glass) and liqueurs, with some hops tucked in among the bottles. Apple juice comes from a mountainside orchard a few miles away. Even at the busiest times service generally remains prompt and friendly. The back bedrooms – particularly in the quieter new block – are the most highly recommended, though there are three more bedrooms in the pretty cottage at the end of the garden. Lovely window boxes, and you can eat in the garden in summer; disabled lavatories, piped music. *(Recommended by David and Nina Pugsley, Mrs S Bull, Dr and Mrs A Newton, Gordon Tong, B T Smith, Ian Phillips, Derek and Margaret Underwood, Rona Murdoch, DJW, Roy Smylie, Kim and Nigel Spence, R C Morgan, Jackie Orme, RKP, D and N Pugsley, D and L Berry, Dr and Mrs Cottrell, J H Jones, Christoper and Jo Barton, Pamela and Merlyn Horswell, Peter Meister, R Michael Richards; also in the Good Hotel Guide)*

Free house ~ Licensee Judy Hindmarsh ~ Real ale ~ Bar food (till 10pm(9.30 Sun)) ~ Restaurant ~ (01873) 810408 ~ Children in eating area of bar ~ Open 11-3, 6-11; 12-3, 7-10.30 Sun; closed 25 Dec evening ~ Bedrooms: £49B/£61B

Nantyffin Cider Mill 🍽 ♉ 🍺

1½ miles NW, by junction A40/A479

Wales Dining Pub of the Year

Facing an attractive stretch of the River Usk, this handsome pink-washed inn is a favourite for its inventive food – easily of restaurant standard. Relying wherever possible on local and organic meat and vegetables (quite a lot comes from a relative's nearby farm), the thoughtfully prepared menu changes constantly but might include starters such as home-made soup (£2.95), baked field mushrooms on sautéed black pudding, spinach and melted stilton glaze (£5.25), and marinated local goat's cheese with leeks on griddled bruschetta (£5.50), and main courses like leek and thyme burger (£6.95), spinach and ricotta tart with herb crumb topping (£8.95), orange glazed roast pork tenderloin with spiced sweet potatoes or skate wings with steamed fennel and deep-fried anchovies (£10.95), rack of Welsh lamb with celeriac purée and a herb crust (£14.95), and grilled lobster with oregano butter (£21.50). Excellent puddings like tart au citron, or coconut parfait with apricot coulis and rum ice cream (from £3.50), and children's meals or smaller helpings. Some dishes may be a pound or so more expensive in the evenings. Service is excellent and very well organised. The look of the place is smartly traditional – almost brasserie style, with a woodburner in a fine broad fireplace, warm grey stonework, cheerful bunches of fresh and dried flowers, and good solid comfortable tables and chairs. The bar at one end of the main open-plan area has three very well kept real ales on handpump, rotated from a range that includes Brains SA, Marstons Pedigree, Morlands Old Speckled Hen, Tomas Watkins Old Style Bitter, and Uley Old Spot, and three draught ciders like Dunkertons, Mendip Magic and Thatchers Dry, well chosen New World wines (a few by the glass or half bottle), popular home-made lemonade and pimms in summer, and hot punch and mulled wine in winter. A raftered barn with a big cider press has been converted into quite a striking no-smoking restaurant. The river is on the other side of a fairly busy road, but there are charming views from the tables out on the lawn above the pub's neat car park. A ramp makes disabled access easy. *(Recommended by N H E Lewis, E Holland, R R Winn, J Goodrich, Gethin Lewis, Pat and John Millward, Dr Oscar Puls, Mary and David Richards, Mr and Mrs Pyper, David and Nina Pugsley, Ian Phillips, Bernard Stradling, Deirdre Goodman, Mrs S Bull, J H Jones)*

Free house ~ Licensees Glyn Bridgeman and Sean Gerrard ~ Real ale ~ Bar food ~ (01873) 810775 ~ Children welcome ~ Open 12-3, 6-11; 12-3, 7-10.30 Sun; closed Mon

White Hart

Brecon Rd (A40 W)

Now tied to Brains, and with a chatty new landlord, this friendly pub remains a quieter, more homely alternative to the often busy Bear. They've put in a new bar, changed the carpets and furniture and given things a fresh coat of paint, but the cosy little bar is essentially unchanged, with its stripped stone, beams and flagstones. It's flanked by an eating area on one side (with TV) and sizeable no-smoking restaurant on the other. Well kept Brains Bitter, Best and Reverend James on handpump, and enjoyable home-made bar food (much the same as under the previous regime) such as sandwiches (from £1.95), soup (£2.75), their speciality roast leg of Welsh lamb in local honey (£5.95), and goose in sloe gin sauce (£11.25); the choice is wider in the evening. On Sunday they do a choice of roasts (£5.95); cribbage, dominoes, trivia, fruit machine, quiz Mon eve, piped classical music. There are tables with parasols on a suntrap terrace above a few parking bays by the road: beware of the blind exit from the small side car park on the other side of the pub. The pub used to be a toll house – as the interesting tariff sign outside shows. *(Recommended by Rev J Hibberd, Christopher and Mary Thomas, Mr and Mrs J Williams)*

Brains ~ Tenants David and July Rees ~ Real ale ~ Bar food (till 9.45) ~ (01873) 810473 ~ Children in eating area of bar and restaurant ~ Open 11-3, 6-11; 12-11 Sat; 12-4, 7-10.30 Sun

EAST ABERTHAW ST0367 Map 6
Blue Anchor ★ ◀
B4265

The centuries-old charm of this enchanting thatched and creeper-covered stone pub never fails to impress; its picture-book exterior is quite a contrast to some of the more modern sights you might see along the way. Dating back in part to 1380, the warren of snug, low-beamed rooms is full of character: nooks and crannies wander through massive stone walls and tiny doorways, and there are open fires everywhere, including one in an inglenook with antique oak seats built into its stripped stonework. Other seats and tables are worked into a series of chatty little alcoves, and the more open front bar still has an ancient lime-ash floor; darts, cribbage, fruit machine and trivia machine. Consistently reliable bar food includes sandwiches (from £2.50), soup (£2.50), filled baked potatoes (from £3.50), cumberland sausage (£5.50), linguini with mediterranean vegetables, baked fillet of salmon on a prawn-crab bisque or cajun-spiced pork chop (£5.75), peppered 8oz rump steak (£7.50), specials like lamb chop or fish pie (£5.75), and puddings such as cointreau and chocolate mousse (£2.75) or Welsh cheeses (£3.25); children's menu (£3.50). They do a three-course roast lunch (£10.75) on Sundays, for which it's best to book. Carefully kept Boddingtons, Buckleys Best, Flowers IPA, Marstons Pedigree, Theakstons Old Peculier, Wadworths 6X and an interesting changing guest on handpump; friendly service from cheerful staff. Rustic seats shelter peacefully among tubs and troughs of flowers outside, with more stone tables on a newer terrace. From here a path leads to the shingly flats of the estuary. The pub can get packed in the evenings and on summer weekends, and it's a shame the front seats are right beside the car park. The lavatories have been upgraded since our last edition. *(Recommended by Mr and Mrs S Thomas, David and Nina Pugsley, John and Joan Nash, David Lewis, Sarah Lart, the Didler, I J and N K Buckmaster)*

Free house ~ Licensee Jeremy Coleman ~ Real ale ~ Bar food (12-2, 6-8 Mon to Fri, Sat evening restaurant only) ~ Restaurant ~ (01446) 750329 ~ Children welcome ~ Open 11-11; 12-10.30 Sun

GLADESTRY SO2355 Map 6
Royal Oak
B4594 W of Kington

This nicely old-fashioned village pub just below the Hergest Ridge is a welcome sight to walkers on the Offa's Dyke Path. It's very much a cheerful local, but very welcoming and helpful to visitors. The simple roomy bar has beams, stripped stone and flagstones, and maybe enthusiastic regulars meticulously laying out a green felt cloth for a game of cribbage; there's also a cosy turkey-carpeted lounge. Locals gather in friendly chatty groups around the bar, where beaming bar staff draw well kept Bass and Hancocks HB from handpump. Our last visit was in dreary weather, but we warmed up nicely at our small table next to the log fire. Bar food might include sandwiches, ploughman's (£3.25), cottage pie (£4.25), broccoli and cheese bake or lasagne (£4.50), mixed grill

(£6) and sirloin steak (£8.50). No-smoking restaurant; darts, pool, cribbage, dominoes, video game, juke box, quoits, piped music; camping available on the helpful licensees' hill farm. *(Recommended by Edward Leetham, Ian Jones, DC)*

Free house ~ Licensees Mel and Chris Hughes ~ Real ale ~ Bar food ~ (01544) 70669 ~ Children welcome ~ Open 12-2(3 Sat, Sun), 7-11(10.30 Sun) ~ Bedrooms: £18.50B/£37B

GRAIANRHYD SJ2156 Map 6
Rose & Crown

B5430 E of Ruthin; village signposted off A494 and A5104

In a remote part of the Clwydian Hills, this simple building is the sort of place you'd almost certainly go straight past if you weren't in on the secret, but hidden inside is a really enjoyable pub. The bar sparkles with carefully chosen eclectic bric a-brac and plentiful locals, and the informal young landlord makes sure strangers don't feel left out. One small room has hundreds of decorative teapots hanging from its beams, the other has steins and other decorative mugs; there are 1950s romantic prints, Marilyn Monroe memorabilia, antlers, china dogs (and a real one called Doris), highly ornamental clocks, a fiddling cherub, cottagey curtains and two warm coal fires. Well kept Boddingtons, Flowers IPA and Marstons Pedigree on handpump, tea and coffee; darts, dominoes, trivia, fruit machine. A wide choice of promptly served tasty bar food includes sandwiches and toasties (from £1.40), soup (£1.95), burgers (from £1.80, including lamb or walnut and cheese), filled baked potatoes (from £2.50), very good salads, stuffed peppers or whitebait (£3.25), lasagne, steak and kidney pie or vegetarian dishes like moussaka or leek and mushroom nut crumble (£4.95), chicken tikka (£5.25), local trout with almonds (£6.25) and 10oz sirloin steak (£8.95). There may occasionally be well reproduced piped pop music, which for once we found a decided plus, though perhaps not everyone would agree; it goes well with the very relaxed chatty atmosphere. Picnic-sets out on a rough terrace by the car park have pretty hill views. *(Recommended by MLR, KC)*

Free house ~ Licensee Tim Ashton ~ Real ale ~ Bar food ~ (01824) 780727 ~ Children welcome ~ Rock band Sun evening ~ Open 12-11(10.30 Sun)

GRESFORD SJ3555 Map 6
Pant-yr-Ochain ♀

Off A483 on N edge of Wrexham: at roundabout take A5156 (A534) towards Nantwich, then first left towards the Flash

Very well liked by readers at the moment for its enterprising food, this spacious old country house stands in its own beautiful grounds with a small lake and some lovely trees – it feels more like a manor house than a typical pub. Its light and airy rooms are stylishly decorated, with a wide range of interesting prints and bric-a-brac on its walls and on shelves, and a good mix of individually chosen country furnishings including comfortable seats for chatting as well as more upright ones for eating. There are good open fires, and the big dining area is set out as a library, with books floor to ceiling. Consistently good, interesting food from a menu that constantly develops might include home-made soup (£2.95), Thai chicken balls with a chilli and coconut dressing (£4.35), ploughman's, fishcakes (£5.95), roasted aubergines stuffed with tomato and vegetable ratatouille or grilled plaice (£8.75), and braised half shoulder of lamb with redcurrant, port and rosemary sauce (£10.95). They have a good range of decent wines, strong on up-front New World ones, as well as Boddingtons, Flowers Original, the tasty locally brewed Plassey, and a changing guest like Wadworths 6X, and a good collection of malt whiskies. Service is friendly and efficient. This is in the same small family of pubs as the Grosvenor Arms at Aldford (see Cheshire main entries), and not dissimilar in style and gently up-market atmosphere; one room is no smoking. *(Recommended by Joy and Peter Heatherley, M Kershaw, Mark Howarth, Robert Dubsky, Mr and Mrs F Carroll, Quentin Williamson, Dr Phil Putwain)*

Free house ~ Licensee Duncan Lochead ~ Real ale ~ Bar food (12-9.30) ~ (01978) 853525 ~ Children in eating area of bar at lunchtime only ~ Open 12-11; 12-10.30 Sun

HALKYN SJ2172 Map 6
Britannia
Britannia Pentre Rd, off A55 for Rhosesmor

On a clear day you may be able to pick out Blackpool Tower and Beeston Castle from the dining conservatory and terrace at this warmly welcoming old farmhouse, and you'll usually find the fabulous views stretching to Liverpool and the Wirral; it's best to book if you want a window table. The cosy unspoilt lounge bar has some very heavy beams, with horsebrasses, harness, jugs, plates and other bric-a-brac; there's also a games room with darts, pool, dominoes, fruit machine, TV, juke box and board games. Good value, generously served bar food includes home-made soup (£1.30), sandwiches served on Rhes-y-Cae bread (from £2.95), black pudding and mustard sauce (£3.05), mushroom and stilton bake (£4.50), cumberland sausage (£4.75), a popular beef and beer pie (£5.50), lamb steak marinated in honey or pork escalopes in pepper sauce (£6.05), daily specials, and children's meals (from £1.70). The conservatory is partly no smoking. Lees Bitter, GB Mild and Moonraker on handpump or tapped from the cask, a dozen or so malt whiskies, and a choice of coffees. In the garden children will enjoy meeting Jacob, a 27-year-old donkey, along with some tame goats, Fleur the oxford sandy and black, several sheep and lambs and various breeds of ducks and chickens – you can usually buy fresh eggs. *(Recommended by MLR, Andy and Jill Kassube, KC, Dave Braisted, Joy and Peter Heatherley, Norman Stansfield, Mr and Mrs P Eastwood, Alan and Paula McCully)*

Lees ~ Tenant Keith R Pollitt ~ Real ale ~ Bar food ~ Restaurant ~ (01352) 780272 ~ Children welcome ~ Open 11-11; 12-10.30 Sun

HAY ON WYE SO2342 Map 6
Kilverts 🛏

Bullring

Locals and visitors all seem happy at this friendly town pub, which stands out not just for its informal relaxed atmosphere, but also for its thoughtful menu. Lunchtime bar food includes french sticks or sandwiches (from £2.75), soup (£2.95), crab and prawn terrine (£4.25), ploughman's (from £5.25), spinach and mushroom roulade filled with cream cheese and chives on a bed of sweet peppers (£7.95) and grilled trout marinated with lime and coriander (£8.95). In the evening there are several weightier dishes like breast of corn-fed chicken with braised pearl barley and lemon and thyme butter cream sauce (£10.95) or half roast duckling on parsnip purée with cranberry and orange sauce (£11.95), and the specials board might include moules marinières (£4.25), skate wing with capers and black butter (£8.25) and braised rack of Welsh lamb (£10.50). The airy high-beamed bar has an understated civilised feel, with some stripped stone walls, *Vanity Fair* caricatures, a couple of standing timbers, candles on well spaced mixed old and new tables, and a pleasant variety of seating. Well kept Bass, Hancocks HB and Highgate Saddlers on handpump, Bulmer's farm cider, local Welsh wines, good cappuccinos, and freshly squeezed orange juice in summer; maybe piped pop radio. Easy-going but efficient service. There are tables out in a small front flagstoned courtyard. *(Recommended by John Hillman, J and B Coles, John Cockell)*

Free house ~ Licensee Colin Thompson ~ Bar food ~ Restaurant ~ (01497) 821042 ~ Children welcome ~ Open 11-11; 12-10.30 Sun; closed 25 Dec ~ Bedrooms: £30S/£66B

Old Black Lion ♀ 🛏

26 Lion St

Oliver Cromwell is reckoned to have stayed at this atmospheric old inn, and it's thought to date back to the 13th c. Still comfortably old-fashioned, the attractive smartly civilised bar is particularly lovely at night when candles on old pine tables cast a cosy inviting glow over the red carpet, black panelling, oak and mahogany bar counter, and two old timber and glass screens. Thoughtfully prepared bar meals might include lunchtime sandwiches, home-made soup (£3.25), ploughman's (from

£5.60), filled baked potatoes (from £5.75), vegetarian dishes such as hungarian vegetable goulash or nut roast (£7.95), tempura battered plaice (£8.25), braised lamb with Indian spices (£8.95), spicy peppered venison (£9.45), 8oz sirloin (£11.95), and a good selection of specials like Loch Fyne langoustines (£5.95) or roast monkfish tail wrapped in bacon with an onion cream sauce (£11.85); puddings such as treacle tart with walnuts and ginger or sticky toffee pudding. They do special breakfasts for fishermen (with Loch Fyne kippers), and a three course lunch on Sundays. The cottagey restaurant, also candlelit, is no smoking. Wadworths 6X, Wye Valley Supreme and their own Black Lion (made for them by the Wye Valley brewery) on handpump – as well as an extensive, good value wine list, several malt whiskies, and decent coffee. Service is good but this is a firmly run place and they do like food orders to be in promptly, and to shut the bar at closing time in the evening. A sheltered back terrace has some tables. The inn has trout and salmon fishing rights on the Wye, and can arrange pony trekking and golf. *(Recommended by Gwen and Peter Andrews, Nicholas Stuart Holmes, Richard Fendick, Brian Seller, Martin Jones, Mr and Mrs A Craig, E A Froggatt, Derek and Margaret Underwood, Chris Mawson, Pam and David Bailey, Paul and Sandra Embleton, Mrs P Goodwyn, Tim Barrow, Sue Demont)*

Free house ~ Licensees John and Joan Collins ~ Real ale ~ Bar food ~ Restaurant ~ (01497) 820841 ~ Children over 5, over 8 in restaurant ~ Open 11-11; 11-3, 6-11 Sun ~ Bedrooms: £28B/£56.90B

LITTLE HAVEN SM8512 Map 6
Swan

Right on the coastal path, and set in one of the prettiest coastal villages in west Wales, this delightful little inn has lovely views across the broad and sandy hill-sheltered cove from seats in its bay window, or from the sea wall outside (just the right height for sitting on). Cooked by the genial landlord (who's now been here over a decade), the compact choice of well liked lunchtime bar food includes sandwiches (from £1.50), home-made soup (£2.95), traditional Welsh lamb and vegetable soup (£3.50 – with cheese on the side £3.75), ploughman's (from £4.25), crab bake (£4.75), sardines grilled with spinach, egg and mozzarella (£4.95), chicken curry (£5.50), locally smoked salmon or fresh local crab (£6.95), and home-made puddings (£2.95); no credit cards. Well kept Greene King Abbott, Wadworths 6X and Worthington BB on handpump from the heavily panelled bar counter, and a good range of wines and whiskies; efficient service. The two communicating rooms have quite a cosily intimate feel, as well as comfortable high-backed settles and windsor chairs, a winter open fire, and old prints on walls that are partly stripped back to the original stonework. No children, dogs or dirty boots. *(Recommended by John and Enid Morris, Paul and Sandra Embleton, Carole Smart, Andrew Jeeves, Martin Jones, Jeremy Brittain-Long, H and D Payne)*

James Williams ~ Tenants Glyn and Beryl Davies ~ Real ale ~ Bar food (lunchtime) ~ Restaurant ~ (01437) 781256 ~ Open 11.30-3, 6.30(7 in winter)-11; 12-3, 7-10.30 Sun; closed evening 25 Dec

LLANBEDR-Y-CENNIN SH7669 Map 6
Olde Bull

Village signposted from B5106

Some of the massive low beams at this delightful little 16th-c drovers' inn were salvaged from a wrecked Spanish Armada ship. Perched on the side of a steep hill, the pub has splendid views over the Vale of Conwy to the mountains beyond, especially from seats in the particularly lovely herb garden, with its big wild area with waterfall and orchard. Inside, the knocked-through rooms have elaborately carved antique settles, a close crowd of cheerfully striped stools, brassware, photographs, Prussian spiked helmets, and good open fires (one in an inglenook); darts, dominoes. Well kept Lees Bitter and Mild on handpump from wooden barrels, and several malt whiskies; friendly service. Generous helpings of home-made bar food include soup (£1.95), big filled french sticks (from £2.50), spring rolls with sweet and sour sauce (£2.50), cumberland sausage (£5.75), mushroom stroganoff or steak and kidney or chicken and mushroom fresh crusty bread pot (£5.95), evening steaks (from £10.95) and old-fashioned puddings like fruit crumble or bread and butter pudding (£2.50); children's menu (£2.50). Recently redecorated, the two restaurants are both no smoking. The pub is popular with walkers. Lavatories are outside. *(Recommended by Roger Byrne, Mike and Wena Stevenson)*

Lees ~ Tenants John and Debbie Turnbull ~ Real food ~ Bar food ~ Restaurant ~ (01492) 660508 ~ Children welcome ~ Open 12-5, 7-11

LLANBERIS SH6655 Map 6
Pen-y-Gwryd 🍺 🛏

Nant Gwynant; at junction of A498 and A4086, ie across mountains from Llanberis – OS Sheet 115 map reference 660558

This magnificently set old climber's inn already doubles as a mountain rescue post, and as we went to press they told us they were adding another string to their bow, building a chapel for the Millennium. It's a very hospitable and welcoming place: one couple we know turned up bedraggled and hungry on a wet afternoon when food service had stopped, but found the friendly staff happy to put together a meal. One snug little room in the homely slate-floored log cabin bar has built-in wall benches and sturdy country chairs to let you contemplate the majestic surrounding mountain countryside – like precipitous Moel-siabod beyond the lake opposite. A smaller room has a collection of illustrious boots from famous climbs, and a cosy panelled smoke room more climbing mementoes and equipment. Like many other mountaineers, the team that first climbed Everest in 1953 used the inn as a training base, leaving their fading signatures scrawled on the ceiling. There's a hatch where you order lunchtime bar meals: good value robust helpings of home-made food such as soup (£1.80), ploughman's using home-baked french bread, quiche lorraine or pâté (£3.50), with pies and casseroles in winter. You will need to book early if you want to stay here. Residents have their own charmingly furnished, panelled sitting room and a sauna out among the trees, and in the evening sit down together for the hearty and promptly served dinner (check on the time when you book); the dining room is no smoking. As well as Bass, and home-made lemonade in summer and mulled wine in winter, they serve sherry from their own solera in Puerto Santa Maria; table tennis, darts, pool, bar billiards, table skittles, and shove-ha'penny. Note the winter opening times. *(Recommended by Roger Byrne, J H Jones, G C Hackemer, Brian and Anna Marsden, Robert Pettigrew, Quentin Williamson, Jack Valiant, Martin Pritchard, Jenny and Brian Seller, Sarah and Peter Gooderham; also in the Good Hotel Guide)*

Free house ~ Licensee Jane Pullee ~ Real ale ~ Bar food (lunchtime, restaurant only in the evenings) ~ Restaurant ~ (01286) 870211 ~ Children in eating area of bar ~ Open 11-11(10.30 Sun); closed Nov-New Year, weekdays Jan, Feb ~ Bedrooms: £22(£27B)/£44(£54B)

LLANDEILO SN6222 Map 6
Castle 🍺

113 Rhosmaen St

This popular town pub is the home of the very successful Tomos Watkin range of beers, which over the last three years have made their way from the little brewery behind to around 40 pubs across Wales. They're now so in demand that the brewery isn't really big enough, so they plan to move production elsewhere and convert the current brewery into a museum; they hope to open bedrooms then as well. Friendly bar staff are good at explaining the different beers, which on our visit included Tomos Watkin Bitter, the heavier Old Style Bitter and seasonal Cwrwhaf, Merlins Stout, and lighter Whoosh. The tiled and partly green-painted back bar is the most atmospheric room, with locals sat round the edge chatting, a big fireplace with stuffed animal heads above it, and dried hops hanging from the ceiling. A more comfortable carpeted bar at the front has smarter furnishings, and there's also a side area with a sofa, bookshelves, old maps and prints, and an elegant red-painted dining room with fresh flowers on the tables. Well presented good value food includes filled baguettes (from £1.80), home-cooked ham (£2.95), ploughman's with Welsh cheeses, steak and ale pie (£4.95), and medallions of beef on a bed of onions with a creamy pepper sauce (£8.95). A noticeboard in the hallway has newspaper cuttings charting the growth of the brewery, and its success in helping promote Welsh real ales; an outside area with tables leads off here. *(Recommended by David Brammer, Joan and Michel Hooper-Immins)*

Free house ~ Licensee Mark Wilby ~ Real ale ~ Bar food ~ Restaurant ~ (01558) 823446 ~ Children in eating areas ~ Jazz Sun afternoons, folk alternate Fri evenings ~ Open 11-11; 12-10.30 Sun

LLANDEWI SKIRRID SO3416 Map 6
Walnut Tree ★ ⑪ ♀
B4521

The excellent, imaginative food has made this restaurant justifiably well known; we continue to include it here for its very relaxed atmosphere, and the caring hands-on approach of the licensees who're quite happy if people just pop in for a glass of wine. The attractive choice of wines is particularly strong in Italian ones (they import their own), and the house wines by the glass are good value. Meals aren't cheap, but combine strong southern European leanings with an almost fanatical pursuit of top-class fresh and often recherché ingredients. The menu might include carefully prepared soups such as asparagus and prawn (£4.95), crispy crab pancakes (£5.45), risotto with spring vegetables (£6.45), smoked haddock fishcake in lobster bisque sauce (£6.95), and main courses like homemade Italian sausage with borlotti beans (£7.95), baked aubergine stuffed with pasta (£10.50), salmon with rhubarb sauce and asparagus (£13.85), roast guinea fowl or duck with celeriac gratin and sweet and sour pumpkin (£14.95), roast monkfish with scallops, prawns and laver bread sauce (£15.85), and mixed fish casserole (£16.85); vegetables are £2.75 extra. There's quite a choice of delicious puddings – the Toulouse chestnut pudding (£5.55) is particularly good. No credit cards, and £1 cover charge. The small white-walled bar has some polished settles and country chairs around the tables on its flagstones, and a log-effect gas fire. It opens into an airy and relaxed dining lounge with rush-seat Italianate chairs around gilt cast-iron-framed tables. There are a few white cast-iron tables outside in front *(Recommended by A C Morrison, A J Bowen, Dr and Mrs Cottrell, I J and N K Buckmaster, Gwen and Peter Andrews, Jackie Orme, RKP, Helen Pickering, James Owen, Bernard Stradling, R C Morgan, Paul and M-T Pumfrey, J H Jones, PS)*

Free house ~ Licensees Ann and Franco Taruschio ~ Bar food (12-3, 7-10) ~ Restaurant ~ (01873) 852797 ~ Children welcome ~ Open 12-4, 7-12; closed Sun, Mon, one week at Christmas and two weeks in Feb

LLANDRINDOD WELLS SO0561 Map 6
Llanerch ◀ £
Waterloo Road; from centre, head for station

A favourite with some readers, this welcoming low-ceilinged 16th-c inn is set in a quiet leafy spot on the edge of this spa town, enjoying peaceful mountain views looking over the Ithon Valley. There's a really cheerful local atmosphere in the busy squarish beamed main bar, which has old-fashioned settles snugly divided by partly glazed partitions, and a big stone fireplace that's richly decorated with copper and glass; there are more orthodox button-back banquettes in communicating lounges (one of which is no smoking for most of the day). Popular lunchtime dishes include soup (£1.95), sandwiches (from £1.95), filled baked potatoes (from £2.50), ploughman's (£3.50), fisherman's pie or vegetable lasagne (£3.50), chicken curry or steak, kidney and mushroom pie (£5.50), daily specials like pork in cream and mustard sauce (£5.95), and evening extras like chicken breast cooked in white wine and cream sauce with grapes (£5.95) or Welsh lamb baked in garlic and redcurrant sauce (£7.50); children's meals. Well kept Hancocks HB and two regularly changing guests on handpump; there may be up to 20 real ales during their late August

Victorian Festival. Service is prompt and generally friendly; piped music. The pub can get busy on Friday and Saturday evenings, with a nice mix of age groups. A separate pool room has a fruit machine, darts and dominoes. A front play area and orchard give it the feel of a country pub, and there are delightful views from the terrace, which leads to a garden (with boules; they have a Monday night league). *(Recommended by Stephanie Smith, Gareth Price, Derek and Margaret Underwood, Joan and Michel Hooper-Immins)*

Free house ~ Licensee John Leach ~ Real ale ~ Bar food ~ Restaurant ~ (01597) 822086 ~ Children welcome ~ Live entertainment every other Thurs evening ~ Open 11.30-3(2.30 in winter), 6-11; 11.30-11 Sat; 12-10.30(12-2.30, 7-10.30 winter) Sun ~ Bedrooms: £29.50B/£49B

LLANDUDNO JUNCTION SH8180 Map 6
Queens Head 🍴 🍷

Glanwydden; heading towards Llandudno on B5115 from Colwyn Bay, turn left into Llanrhos Road at roundabout as you enter the Penrhyn Bay speed limit; Glanwydden is signposted as the first left turn off this

The very good, often imaginative bar food at this modest-looking village pub is so popular that you'll need to book or arrive early to be sure of a table. Fresh local produce is firmly in evidence on the weekly changing menu, which might include carefully prepared and generously served dishes such as soup, celery with brie and apple (£2.15), open rolls (from £3.75), home-made chicken liver pâté (£3.95), grilled goat's cheese with sun-dried tomatoes and walnuts (£4.95), salmon and pasta bake, mussels in garlic butter topped with smoked local cheese, or field mushrooms filled with crab meat (£6.50), pancake with fresh herbs, mushroom and asparagus (£6.95), steak and mushroom pie (£7.25), lamb cutlets with raspberry and amaretto sauce (£8.50), roast loin of pork with leek and whisky cream sauce (£8.95), and pot roasted partridge on a bed of puy lentils with wild mushroom and juniper berry sauce (£11.50). Delicious puddings include chocolate nut fudge pie or fruit crumble (£2.95). Though at first it may seem the place is geared solely for eating, locals do pop in here for a drink; well kept Benskins, Ind Coope Burton and Tetleys on handpump, decent wines including several by the glass, several malts, and good coffee (maybe served with a bowl of whipped cream and home-made fudge or chocolates). The spacious and comfortably modern lounge bar has brown plush wall banquettes and windsor chairs around neat black tables and is partly divided by a white wall of broad arches and wrought-iron screens; there's also a little public bar; the dining area is no smoking, unobtrusive piped music. There are some tables out by the car park. No dogs. *(Recommended by KC, Joy and Peter Heatherley, Bronwen and Steve Wrigley, Jane and Adrian Tierney-Jones, Liz Bell, Mike and Wena Stevenson, Mike Jones, Pamela and Merlyn Horswell, M Meadley)*

Allied Domecq ~ Lease Robert and Sally Cureton ~ Real ale ~ Bar food ~ Restaurant ~ (01492) 546570 ~ Children over 7 welcome ~ Open 11.30-3, 6-11; 12-10.30 Sun; 12-3, 6-11 Sun in winter

LLANFERRES SJ1961 Map 6
Druid 🛏

A494 Mold—Ruthin

Food and service continue to impress at this delightfully set extended 17th-c inn, a real favourite with some readers. Nothing is too much trouble for the friendly staff and licensees, and the interesting range of very good changing bar food is almost up to our Food Award standard. A typical choice might include soups (£2.25), delicious granary baps filled with mozzarella and mushrooms, chicken fillet and lemon mayonnaise or pepperoni and mozzarella (£3.45), good vegetarian dishes like mixed vegetables in a creamy chilli sauce (£7.95), and main courses such as monkfish thermidor, chicken balti or grilled salmon with a lime, local mustard and honey dressing (£8.95); vegetables are fresh and generous. Tables sheltered in a corner by a low wall with rock-plant pockets outside make the most of the view looking down

over the road to the Alyn valley and the Craig Harris mountains beyond, as does the
broad bay window in the civilised and sympathetically refurbished smallish plush
lounge. You can also see the hills from the bigger welcoming beamed back bar, also
carpeted (with quarry tiles by the log fire), with its two handsome antique oak settles
as well as a pleasant mix of more modern furnishings. The attractive dining area is
relatively smoke-free. Well kept Burtonwood Best, Black Parrot and Everards Tiger
on handpump, two dozen or so malt whiskies and wine list; games area with darts
and pool, also dominoes, shove-ha'penny, bagatelle, Jenga and other board games;
maybe unobtrusive piped music. *(Recommended by KC, Maurice and Gill McMahon, Sue and
Bob Ward, Mr and Mrs Archibald, Susan Mullins, P Thomas, Daphne Key, Jack and Pat Manning)*

*Burtonwood ~ Tenant James Dolan ~ Bar food (12-3, 5.30-10; 12-10 Sat, Sun, bank
hols) ~ (01352) 810225 ~ Children welcome ~ Piano sing-along first Sat of month ~
Open 12-3, 5-10(12-10 bank hols); 12-10 Sat; 12-10 Sun ~ Bedrooms: £26.50/£36.50*

LLANFRYNACH SO0725 Map 6
White Swan ◖

Village signposted from B4558, just off A40 E of Brecon bypass

Very much enjoyed by readers for its good food and tranquil atmosphere, this
stylishly done up village pub is a nice retreat in summer, when the rambling bar has
a very cool, calm feel. With its flagstoned floor and partly stripped walls, one reader
likens it to eating in a cloister. There are plenty of well spaced tables – each with a
blue aluminium lamp above – in its series of softly lit alcoves, as well as a roaring log
fire in winter and maybe piped classical music. An idyllically secluded terrace behind
is green and shady with plenty of stone and wood tables, and attractively divided
into sections by low privet hedges, roses and climbing shrubs; it overlooks peaceful
paddocks. A short list of well prepared bar food includes tasty french onion soup
(£2.60), ploughman's (from £4.75), lasagne, ratatouille, or macaroni and broccoli
cheese (£4.75), fisherman's pie or a hot chicken curry (£7), welsh-style grilled trout
with bacon (£8.75), beef and mushroom pie or very good lamb chops marinated in
garlic and herbs (£10.50), well hung steaks (from £11.50), puddings such as sherry
trifle (from £2), children's dishes (£3.90), and maybe weekend specials; the
vegetables are nicely cooked. Service is prompt, welcoming and efficient; well kept
Brains Bitter and Flowers Original on handpump, and good value South African
house white wine. The churchyard is across the very quiet village lane. (*Recommended
by Christoper and Jo Barton, G W Bernard, Mrs S Bull, Jackie Orme, RKP, Mary and David
Richards, Mr and Mrs B Craig, Richard and Stephanie Foskett, A J Bowen)*

*Free house ~ Licensees David and Susan Bell ~ Real ale ~ (01874) 665276 ~ Children
welcome ~ Open 12-3, 7-11; 12-2.30, 7-10.30 Sun; closed Mon (except bank hols)
and first three weeks in Jan*

LLANGEDWYN SJ1924 Map 6
Green

B4396 SW of Oswestry

Just inside Wales, in a lovely spot in the Tanat Valley, this handy country dining pub
is well placed just opposite the village green. In summer this road is well used as a
scenic run from the Midlands to the coast, so the pub sees a lot of business then – and
that's when its attractive garden over the road comes into its own, with lots of picnic-
sets down towards the river. Kept spotless inside, it has a nice layout, with various
snug alcoves, nooks and crannies, a good mix of furnishings including oak settles and
attractively patterned fabrics, and a blazing log fire in winter; there's a pleasant
evening restaurant upstairs. An impressive range of good home-made food includes
lunchtime sandwiches (from £1.50), ploughman's (£4.25), chicken curry, steak and
kidney, chicken and mushroom or cottage pie (£5.25), fresh local trout, and several
home-made daily specials like shepherd's pie (£5.75) or game pie (£6.75), as well as
tasty puddings. Well kept Tetleys and about five guests like Courage Directors,
Fuggles IPA, Morlands Old Speckled Hen, Theakstons Old Peculier and Woods
Special on handpump, farm cider in summer, a good choice of malt whiskies, and a

decent wine list; friendly quick service. Darts, dominoes, and piped music; the restaurant is no smoking. The pub has some fishing available to customers, a permit for the day is £5. *(Recommended by June and Mike Coleman, J H Kane)*

Free house ~ Licensee Gary Greenham ~ Real ale ~ Restaurant ~ (01691) 828234 ~ Children welcome ~ Open 11-3(5 Sat, Sun), 6-11

LLANGYNWYD SS8588 Map 6
Old House

From A4063 S of Maesteg follow signpost Llan ¾ at Maesteg end of village; pub behind church

Dating back to 1147, this lovely thatched pub has an incredible range of over 400 whiskies. Although much modernised, the two cosy rooms of its busy bar still have some comfortably traditional features, high-backed black built-in settles, lots of china and well polished brass around the huge fireplace, shelves of bric-a-brac, and decorative jugs hanging from the beams; piped music. Half the pub is no smoking. Well kept Brains, Flowers Original and IPA on handpump, and a choice of wines by the glass; good service. An attractive conservatory extension leads on to the garden with good views, play area, and a soft ice-cream machine for children. Reasonably priced bar food such as filled rolls (from £1.10), generously served soup (£1.90), pâté (£2.70), prawn cocktail (£3), ploughman's (£3.80), salads (from £4.45), aubergine lasagne (£4.50), steak and kidney pie (£4.60), beef or chicken curry (£4.70), 16oz sirloin (£11.15), daily specials, and fresh fish such as trout and almonds (£6.90), poached salmon (£8.50), and prawn provençale (£10.50 – the landlord regularly goes to the local fish market); children's meals (from £1.25). The Welsh inn sign with a painting of the Mari Lwyd refers to the ancient Mari Lwyd tradition which takes place here at Christmas. *(Recommended by Anne Morris, David Holloway)*

Whitbreads ~ Lease: Richard and Paula David ~ Real ale ~ (01656) 733310 ~ Children welcome ~ Open 11-11(10.30 Sun)

LLANNEFYDD SH9871 Map 6
Hawk & Buckle

Village well signposted from surrounding main roads; one of the least taxing routes is from Henllan at junction of B5382 and B5429 NW of Denbigh

Perched over 200m up in the hills, this welcoming little hotel is a nice place to stay; in clear weather most of the comfortably modern, well equipped bedrooms boast views as far as the Lancashire coast, and you may even be able to spot Blackpool Tower 40 miles away. The long knocked-through black-beamed lounge bar has comfortable modern upholstered settles around its walls and facing each other across the open fire, and a neat red carpet in the centre of its tiled floor. The lively locals' side bar has pool and unobtrusive piped music. Bar food is well above average, with a choice of home-made dishes like toasted sandwiches, ploughman's, vegetarian meals like mushroom and nut fettucine (£5.95), steak and kidney pie or various curries (£6.25), local lamb chops (£6.85), peppered pork (£6.95), steaks (from £9.45), and fresh lemon sole (£9.95); the dining room is no smoking. Good Spanish house wines (the beer is keg). Friendly helpful licensees, two cats and a cheery labrador. There's an attractive mosaic mural on the way through into the back bedroom extension. *(Recommended by Norman Stansfield, EML, Ben Hill, Guy Vowles)*

Free house ~ Licensees Bob and Barbara Pearson ~ Bar food ~ Restaurant ~ (01745) 540249 ~ Children welcome till 8.30pm ~ Open 12-2.30, 7-11(10.30 Sun); closed Mon, lunchtime winter Mon-Fri ~ Bedrooms: £40B/£55B

LLANYNYS SJ1063 Map 6
Cerigllwydion Arms

Village signposted from A525 by Drovers Arms just out of Ruthin, and by garage in Pentre further towards Denbigh

A popular choice for a reasonably priced lunch, this welcoming old place has a delightfully rambling maze of atmospheric little rooms, filled with dark oak beams, a good mix of seats, old stonework, interesting brasses, and a collection of teapots. In addition to well kept Bass and Tetleys on handpump they keep a good choice of malt whiskies, liqueurs and wines; darts, dominoes and unobtrusive piped music. Besides sandwiches and standard bar snacks, bar food includes home-made soup (£1.80), and changing dishes of the day such as asparagus spears rolled in home-made ham in cheese sauce (£5.85), dressed crab salad (£6.40), baked pork chops in apple and cider sauce (£6.60), duck in port and brandy sauce (£8.80), roasted lamb in mint and redcurrant sauce (£8.90), and a big mixed grill (£10.50); the restaurant is no smoking. It may be worth booking at busy times. Across the quiet lane is a neat garden with teak tables among fruit trees looking across the fields to wooded hills. The adjacent 6th-c church has a medieval wall painting of St Christopher which was discovered under layers of whitewash in the 60s. *(Recommended by KC, Tom Gondris, Roger and Christine Mash, Joy and Peter Heatherley, M Mason, D Thompson)*

Free house ~ Licensee Brian Pearson ~ Real ale ~ Bar food (not Mon) ~ Restaurant ~ (01745) 890247 ~ Children in restaurant ~ Open 12-3, 7-11(10.30 Sun); closed Mon lunchtime

LLWYNDAFYDD SN3755 Map 6
Crown

Coming S from New Quay on A486, both the first two right turns eventually lead to the village; the side roads N from A487 between junctions with B4321 and A486 also come within signpost distance; OS Sheet 145 map reference 371555

The pretty, tree-sheltered garden at this attractive white painted 18th-c pub has won several awards, with its delightfully placed picnic-sets on a terrace above a small pond among shrubs and flowers; there's a good play area for children. Service is friendly and efficient, whether you come on your own or, as one reader did, as part of a group of 16. Reliably good home-made bar food might include decent lunchtime sandwiches (from £2), as well as soup, garlic mushrooms (£3.65), vegetarian lasagne or steak and kidney pie (£6.15), Welsh lamb pie (£6.35), salmon fillet (£6.65), chicken supreme with feta cheese (£6.75), and daily specials prepared from local produce; children's meals. They do a roast on Sunday lunchtimes, and the choice of other dishes may be limited then. The friendly, partly stripped-stone bar has red plush button-back banquettes around its copper-topped tables, and a big woodburning stove; piped music. Very well kept Boddingtons, Flowers IPA and Original, Wadworths 6X and maybe a guest on handpump, a range of wines, and good choice of malt whiskies. The side lane leads down to a cove with caves by National Trust cliffs, very pretty at sunset. *(Recommended by Mr and Mrs K Fawcett, Mike and Mary Carter, J H Jones, Michael and Yvonne Owens, K and J Brooks, David and Natasha Toulson)*

Free house ~ Licensee Keith Soar ~ Real ale ~ Bar food ~ Restaurant ~ (01545) 560396 ~ Children in eating area of bar ~ Open 12-3, 6-11(10.30 Sun)

LLYSWEN SO1337 Map 6
Griffin ★ ♀ ⇌

A470, village centre

Readers have once again been delighted by this peaceful well run ivy-covered inn over the last twelve months. It's a charming place to stay, and a soundly imaginative range of very good hearty country cooking relies firmly on local produce, some from their own gardens. Most days after Easter they serve brown trout and salmon, caught by the family or by customers, in the River Wye just over the road, and they're well known for very good seasonal game such as pheasant or jugged hare. In the evenings you may find a range of tapas, and they do regular wine tasting nights. Excellent lunchtime meals from a sensible choice might include delicious home-made soups such as carrot and sweetcorn (£2.95), duck liver pâté (£4.50), cottage pie (£5.35), ploughman's (£5.65), curry and rice (£6.75), ratatouille pasta au gratin (£6.75), pan-fried fillets of trout with bacon and mushrooms (£7.60), and crispy leg of duck on apple and onion compôte with roasted vegetables (£7.25). Evening meals are more elaborate and might include grilled goat's cheese and tapenade en croûte (£5.50), roast knuckle of lamb in garlic and rosemary (£10.80), and sirloin steak in a green peppercorn sauce (£11.50); good puddings like strawberry pavlova or sticky toffee pudding. Service is efficient and friendly: one reader stayed three nights as one of a party of ten, and the group were always served their meals at the same time. Crown Buckley Reverend James, Flowers IPA, and changing guest beers on handpump, and a good varied wine list with around 20 wines by the glass. The Fishermen's Bar is popular with chatty locals; it's decorated with old fishing tackle and has a big stone fireplace with a good log fire, and large windsor armchairs and padded stools around. They have what they describe as an over friendly gordon setter called Carrie; other dogs are allowed. There are a few tables out in front, and the building may be appealingly floodlit at night. Pretty, comfortable bedrooms and great breakfasts; if you're staying they can arrange shooting or fishing – they have a full-time ghillie and keeper. *(Recommended by Chris Brace, Mike and Wena Stevenson, David Gregory, J H Jones, Nigel Clifton, Mike and Sue Loseby, M S Catling, J A Snell, David Cullen, Emma Stent, G Wallace, Dr Oscar Puls, TRS)*

Free house ~ Licensees Richard and Di Stockton ~ Real ale ~ Bar food (not Sun) ~ Restaurant ~ (01874) 754241 ~ Children welcome ~ Open 12-3, 7-11; closed 25, 26 Dec ~ Bedrooms: £45B/£70B

MAENTWROG SH6741 Map 6
Grapes ♀ 🛏

A496; village signposted from A470

From the good-sized sheltered verandah of this rambling old inn you can see trains on the Ffestiniog Railway puffing through the wood, beyond the pleasant back terrace and walled garden (there's a fountain on the lawn). The kind of place that appeals to all sorts of people, it's well geared for families and people out for a decent meal, but at the same time is quite a favourite with Welsh speaking locals here for the lively pubby bar; you may even be addressed in Welsh when they greet you. Hearty bar food includes lunchtime sandwiches, soup (£2.20), lentil, wild mushroom medley (£5.25), good burgers (from £5.50), vegetable korma (£6.25), steak and mushroom pie (£6.50), tandoori buttered chicken (£6.75), gammon steak (£7.95), lamb chops with a creamy leek and stilton sauce (£8), venison with a red wine and juniper berry sauce (£9.25), and good specials tending to concentrate on fresh fish; children's menu (£2.95). It's a popular place, so there may be a wait for meals at busy times. They do a Sunday roast on the verandah. Four changing beers on handpump might include well kept Bass, Dyffryn Clwyd Pedwar Bawd, Greene King Abbott, and Wye Valley; well chosen house wines, over 30 malt whiskies, and good coffee. All three bars are attractively filled with lots of stripped pitch-pine pews, settles, pillars and carvings, mostly salvaged from chapels. Good log fires – there's one in the great hearth of the restaurant, which has been completely redeveloped since our last edition. An interesting juke box in the public bar, where there's also an intriguing collection of brass blowlamps, and cribbage and dominoes; it can get smoky in here at times. The dining room is no smoking; disabled lavatories. Breakfasts on the verandah can be chatty. *(Recommended by Mike and Wena Stevenson, Anthony Bowen, W K Wood, Bob and Marg Griffiths, Pamela and Merlyn Horswell, D Goodger, J H Jones, A J Bowen, George Atkinson, Joan and Michel Hooper-Immins, G Neighbour, Roger Byrne, Keith and Margaret Kettell, Suzy Miller)*

Free house ~ Licensee Brian Tarbox ~ Real ale ~ Bar food (12-2, 6-9.30, 12-9.30 Sat, Sun) ~ Restaurant ~ (01766) 590365/208 ~ Children in restaurant ~ Open 11-11; 12-10.30 Sun ~ Bedrooms: £25B/£50B

MONKNASH SS9270 Map 6
Plough & Harrow ◗

Signposted Marcross, Broughton off B4265 St Brides Major—Llantwit Major – turn left at end of Water Street; OS Sheet 170 map reference 920706

In a peaceful spot not far from the coast near Nash Point, this unspoilt country pub is a delightful find for those who enjoy really old-fashioned traditional pubs. It's a basic place (as is the gents'), and the main bar seems hardly changed over the last 60 or 70 years. It was originally part of a monastic grange and dates from the early 12th c: the stone walls are massively thick. The dark but welcoming main bar (which used to be the scriptures room and mortuary) has a log fire in its huge fireplace with a side bread oven big enough to feed a village, as well as a woodburning stove with polished copper hot water pipes. The heavily black-beamed ceiling has ancient ham hooks, there's an intriguing arched doorway to the back, and on the broad flagstones is a comfortably informal mix of furnishings that includes three fine stripped pine settles. A simple choice of tasty and very good value food includes filled rolls, ploughman's, faggots, chips, peas and gravy or local sausages (£4.95), and half a dozen changing specials such as beef in black bean sauce (£4.95). Up to fourteen well kept ales – inc some unusual ones – might include Bass, Brains, Buckleys, Felinfoel, Greene King Abbot, Shepherd Neame Spitfire, and Worthington on handpump or tapped from the cask; also real cider and country wines. Daily papers, sensibly placed darts. The room on the left has darts, dominoes, and piped music. Very quiet on weekday lunchtimes, the pub can get crowded and lively at weekends; it's popular with families. There are picnic-sets in the small front garden. It's an enjoyable walk from the pub down to the sea, where you can pick up a fine stretch of the coastal path). *(Recommended by David Lewis, Sarah Lart, R T and J C Moggridge, John and Joan Nash, Stephanie Smith, Gareth Price, Mr and Mrs S Thomas, David and Nina Pugsley)*

Free house ~ Licensee Andrew David Davies ~ Real ale ~ Bar food (not Sat, Sun evening) ~ Restaurant ~ (01656) 890209 ~ Children in restaurant ~ Acoustic duo Sun evening ~ Open 12-11(10.30 Sun)

PEMBROKE FERRY SM9603 Map 6
Ferry Inn
Nestled below A477 toll bridge, N of Pembroke

There's still quite a nautical feel to this unaffected and warmly welcoming old sailor's haunt. Good generously served bar food has quite an emphasis on simply served very fresh fish, with maybe cod and chips (£5.25), plaice (£6.50), shell-on prawns, green-lip mussels and crispy fried clams on a platter (£6.95), scallops, prawns and mushrooms in a creamy sauce (£7.25) and dover sole or sea bass (£9.95); other dishes might include cumberland sausage (£4.95), lamb chops marinated in garlic and rosemary, vegetarian lasagne (£5.25), duck breast with a red wine and cranberry sauce, and sirloin steak (£8.95). The bar has a buoyantly pubby atmosphere, plenty of seafaring pictures and memorabilia, a lovely open fire, and good views over the water; fruit machine, unobtrusive piped music. Well kept Bass, Hancocks HB and a weekly changing guest such as Crown Buckley Reverend James or Everards Tiger on handpump, and a decent choice of malt whiskies; friendly knowledgeable staff. There are tables outside on a terrace by the water. *(Recommended by Lynda Payton, Sam Samuells, Maureen and Les Dodd, John and Enid Morris, JP, PP, S Kempson, Dave and Shirley Smith)*

Free house ~ Licensee Colin Williams ~ Real ale ~ Bar food ~ Restaurant ~ (01646) 682947 ~ Children in eating area of bar ~ Open 11.30-2.45, 6.30-11; 12-2.45, 7-10.30 Sun; closed 25, 26 Dec

PENMAENPOOL SH6918 Map 6
George III 🛏
Just off A493, near Dolgellau

The spectacular setting of this popular family-run hotel is hard to beat: the tidal Mawddach estuary stretches away below the well positioned stone terrace, and on a summer evening you can watch the sun go down over the water, catching the heather on the opposite hillside as it slowly disappears from view. Inside, the beamed and partly panelled welcoming upstairs bar opens into a cosy lounge where armchairs face a big log fire in a stone inglenook and there's an interesting collection of George III portraits. The downstairs bar (recently extended to cope with the demand for bar food) has long leatherette seats around plain varnished tables on the flagstones, heavy beams, stripped stone walls, and a good few malt whiskies; darts, dominoes and maybe piped classical music. Well kept John Smiths, Ruddles Best and a changing guest on handpump. Home-made bar food includes soup (£2), chicken liver pâté (£4.50), welsh rarebit (£4.75), ratatouille or crab and salmon fishcakes (£5.95), hake fillet in mild mustard sauce or steak and kidney pie (£6.50), queen scallops in cheese sauce or pork schnitzel with garlic butter and lemon (£7.50), half a roast crispy duckling with bramley apple sauce (£12.50), daily specials, and puddings like apricot and apple crumble or sticky date pudding (£3); children's menu (£2.50). Part of the eating area is no smoking, as is the cellar bar, and the restaurant. They also have baby-changing facilities and a disabled lavatory. Some bedrooms are in a very comfortable award-winning conversion of what used to be an adjacent station (the main building is an amalgamation of the original 17th-c pub and an adjacent chandler's), and most have stunning views over the water. There are fine walks in the forested hills around, such as up the long ridge across the nearby toll bridge. The hotel has fishing rights and can reserve sea-fishing trips from Barmouth, and there's an RSPB reserve next door. *(Recommended by Rob Whittle, John, Karen and Harry Langford, Sarah and Peter Gooderham, Miss J F Reay, Mike and Wena Stevenson, Dr and Mrs C P Kirby, Dr and Mrs Rod Holcombe, Dave Braisted; also in the Good Hotel Guide)*

Free house ~ Licensees John and Julia Cartwright ~ Real ale ~ Bar food ~ Restaurant ~ (01341) 422525 ~ Children welcome in family room ~ Open 11-11(10.30 Sun) ~ Bedrooms: £55B/£94B

PONTYPOOL ST2998 Map 6
Open Hearth ◀

The Wern, Griffithstown; Griffithstown signposted off A4051 S – opposite British Steel main entrance turn up hill, then first right

The splendid range of real ales at this friendly well run local is much better than you'll find anywhere else in the area. They usually have up to nine beers on handpump, typically including Archers Golden, Boddingtons, Felinfoel Double Dragon, Greene King Abbott, Hancocks HB, and three daily changing guests; they also have a good choice of wines and malt whiskies. Reliable good value bar food includes filled rolls (from £1.40), soup (£2.15), filled baked potatoes (from £2.85), various curries (from £4.50), vegetable stir fry (£4.75), scampi or cod (£5.50), steak and ale pie (£5.45), lots of occasionally inventive meat dishes like pork loin glazed in a fresh ginger and orange sweet caramel (£6.95) or lamb chops topped with stilton (£7.95), and sirloin steak cooked in a Mexican sauce (£9). Service is very friendly and efficient – they do their best to try and suit you if you want something not on the menu. The comfortably modernised smallish lounge bar has a turkey carpet and big stone fireplace, and a back bar has leatherette seating; cribbage, dominoes, and piped music. The downstairs no-smoking restaurant is something of a local landmark. You can watch the comings and goings on a stretch of the Monmouthshire & Brecon Canal from seats outside, and the garden has swings, shrubs and picnic-sets, and boules in summer. *(Recommended by David Lewis, Sarah Lart)*

Free house ~ Licensee Gwyn Phillips ~ Real ale ~ Bar food (11.30-2, 6.30-10) ~ Restaurant ~ (01495) 763752 ~ Children in eating area of bar and restaurant ~ Open 11-4, 6-11; 11-11 Sat; 12-4, 7-10.30 Sun

PORTHGAIN SM8132 Map 6
Sloop

Appealingly placed beside a low-key working harbour, opposite a rather fortress-like former granite works, this long, white-painted pub first opened its doors in 1743, and has been run by pretty much the same family ever since. Chatty and relaxed, the plank ceilinged bar has a fair amount of seafaring memorabilia around the walls, from lobster pots and fishing nets, through ships' clocks and lanterns, to relics from wrecks along this stretch of coast. Locals congregate round the bar counter, from which helpful staff serve well kept Brains SA, Felinfoel Double Dragon,

Worthingtons Best and a changing guest. Down a step another room leads round to a decent sized eating area, with simple wooden chairs and tables, cushioned wall seats, a help-yourself salad counter, and a freezer with ice creams for children; one area is no smoking. Popular bar food includes lunchtime sandwiches (the fresh crab ones are especially well liked, £3.25), fried cod (£4.95), steak and kidney pie (£5.95), chilli (£5.80), braised leg of lamb (£8.50), and a couple of fish specials; they hope to expand the fish menu before too long. Rather than having a number for food service, many of the tables are named after a wrecked ship; they take credit cards. A well segregated games room is used mainly by children. An outside terrace has plenty of tables looking over the harbour, with heaters for fresher weather. Owned by the National Parks, Porthgain has an appealingly forgotten feel, like somewhere that knows its busiest days are past, but rather enjoys its peaceful present; there's a small gallery across from the pub, and you can get boat trips from the harbour. Coastal walks lead off from nearby. *(Recommended by Jeff Davies, Mr and Mrs Dalby)*

Free house ~ Licensee Matthew Blakiston ~ Real ale ~ Bar food ~ (01348) 831449 ~ Children welcome ~ Live music alternate Fri or Sat evening ~ Open 12-2.30, 6-9.30

PORTHMADOG SH5639 Map 6
Ship 🍺

Lombard Street; left turn off harbour rd, off High Street (A487) in centre

The oldest pub in town, on a quiet little street near the centre, this roomy well run local is known round here as Y Llong. The two dimly lit bars have an easy-going, relaxed feel, as well as lots of attractive ship prints, photographs and drawings, quite a bit of brass nautical hardware, and candles in bottles. It's sturdily furnished, with pews, mate's chairs and so forth, and there are good fires in winter; TV, silenced fruit machine, dominoes. Well kept Ind Coope Burton, Morlands Old Speckled Hen, Tetleys and a weekly changing guest on handpump (they have a beer festival the first two weeks of March), and over 70 malt whiskies. A wide choice of good value, nicely cooked bar food includes sandwiches, soup (£2.25), port and stilton pâté (£3.25), haddock in batter or beef and ale casserole (£6.85), medallions of lamb with dijon mustard and tarragon (£7.85), 16oz gammon steak (£8.35), fillet of salmon with herb crust or skate wings in black butter (£8.75), and whole sea bass (£12.85); there's also an attractive no-smoking bistro-style back restaurant. Service is friendly and efficient, and helpful to families. The lounge bar is no smoking. It's not a long walk from the Ffestiniog Railway terminus. *(Recommended by Mrs J Hinsliff, B Thomas, Stephen Hughes)*

Allied Domecq ~ Lease: Robert and Nia Jones ~ Real ale ~ Bar food ~ (01766) 512990 ~ Children in eating area of bar ~ Open 11-11; 12-10.30 Sun; 12-6.30 only Sun in winter

PRESTEIGNE SO3265 Map 6
Radnorshire Arms 🛏

High Street; B4355 N of centre

Renovations at this rambling, timbered old inn have revealed secret passages and priest's holes, with one priest's diary showing he was walled up here for two years. Although part of a small chain of hotels, its old-fashioned charm and individuality remain unchanged, and discreet modern furnishings blend in well with venerable dark oak panelling, latticed windows, and elegantly moulded black oak beams, some decorated with horsebrasses. Most areas were enjoying a slight refurbishment as we went to press. Reasonably priced bar food might include good sandwiches (from £2.75), welsh rarebit (£3.95), vegetable korma or prawn and mushroom tagliatelle (£4.95), steak and Guinness pie or fisherman's pie (£5.95), and puddings such as hot lemon sponge (£2.75) or baked cheesecake (£2.95). Every day except Sunday they also do a special two-course lunch for £5. Well kept real ales include Bass, Cains and Peter Yates on handpump, several malt whiskies, local wine, and welcoming attentive service; separate no-smoking restaurant, morning coffee, afternoon tea. There are some well spaced tables on the sheltered flower-bordered lawn, which used to be a bowling green. *(Recommended by Pamela and Merlyn Horswell, E A Froggatt, B T Smith)*

Free house ~ Licensee Philip Smart ~ Real ale ~ Bar food ~ (01544) 267406 ~ Children welcome ~ Open 11-11; 12-10.30 Sun; 11-3, 6-11 Mon-Sat in winter; 12-3, 6-10.30 Sun in winter ~ Bedrooms: £59.50B/£79B

RAGLAN SO3608 Map 6
Clytha Arms ⊘ ◧ ⌁

Clytha, off Abergavenny road – former A40, now declassified

Very well liked by readers for its impressive food, fine beers, and easy gracious comfort, this fine old country inn stands in its own extensive well cared for grounds – a mass of colour in spring. Making good use of fresh local ingredients, the changing choice of very appealing, generously served bar food might include sandwiches (from £2.25), soup (£3.80), leek and laverbread rissoles (£4.45), moules marinières or half a dozen oysters (£4.95), wild boar sausage with potato pancakes (£5.25), salmon burger with tarragon and mayonnaise (£5.45), wild mushroom ragoût with pasta (£5.75), ploughman's (£5.95), grilled mixed shellfish (£7.95), and delicious home-made puddings like lime and mascarpone tart with pecan ice cream (£3.50); they do a good three-course Sunday lunch in the no-smoking restaurant. A well stocked bar serves well kept Bass, Deuchars IPA, Felinfoel Double Dragon and two changing guest beers on handpump, as well as Weston's farm ciders, and home-made perry; the extensive wine list has a dozen or so by the glass. There are generally a few locals in the tastefully refurbished bar which has a good lively atmosphere, solidly comfortable furnishings and a couple of log fires; darts, shove ha'penny, boules, table skittles, cribbage, dominoes, draughts and chess. One reason it's such a nice place to stay is the very pleasant service from the interested licensees and charmingly helpful staff. *(Recommended by Mike and Wena Stevenson, Mr and Mrs I Rispin, GSB, David and Nina Pugsley, Dr W J M Gissane, B T Smith, Jenny and Chris Wilson, Roger White, Brian and Lis, James Morrell, Mike and Sue Loseby)*

Free house ~ Licensees Andrew and Beverley Canning ~ Real ale ~ Bar food (not Sun, Mon evenings and possibly Sat evening) ~ Restaurant ~ (01873) 840206 ~ Children welcome ~ Open 12-3.30, 6-11; 12-11 Sat; 12-4, 7-11 Sun ~ Bedrooms: £45B/£50B

RED WHARF BAY SH5281 Map 6
Ship ◧

Village signposted off B5025 N of Pentraeth

Run by the same family for nearly 30 years, this very popular 18th-c house looks down over ten square miles of treacherous tidal cockle-sands and sea, with low wooded hills sloping down to the broad bay; tables on the front terrace are ideally placed to enjoy the view. Inside is old-fashioned and interesting, with lots of nautical bric-a-brac in big friendly rooms on each side of the busy stone-built bar counter, both with long cushioned varnished pews built around the walls, glossily varnished cast-iron-framed tables and welcoming fires. Since our last edition they've put a great deal of effort into improving the already enterprising bar food, and these days the changing choice of dishes might include sandwiches (from £2.05), soup (£2.80), chicken liver parfait with mustard seed dressing (£4.55), salmon, crab and coriander fishcakes (£4.95), couscous with roasted vegetables and feta cheese (£5.20), braised lamb chops (£5.95), smoked haddock, leek and prawn bake (£6.35), medallions of gammon in a sweet cumberland sauce (£6.55), provençal vegetables with a pesto cream sauce (£6.85), pepperpot beef with ginger (£7.10), chargrilled chicken on buttered cabbage and white beans with a creamy tarragon sauce (£7.15), grilled sea bass (£10.35), and puddings like white chocolate cheesecake on a blackberry coulis (£3.35); children's menu (from £3.10). There may be delays at busy times, and it can be quite crowded on Sundays, when food service stops promptly at 2, and you do need to arrive early for a table. Service is always friendly and smiling. The family room, dining room and cellar room are no smoking. Very well kept Friary Meaux, Ind Coope Burton, Marstons Pedigree, Tetleys and a guest beer on handpump; a wider choice of wines than usual for the area (with a decent choice by the glass), and about 50 malt whiskies. Dominoes, piped music. There are rustic tables and picnic-sets by an ash tree on grass by the side. *(Recommended by Joy and Peter Heatherley, GLD, J H Jones, M Meadley, George Atkinson)*

Free house ~ Licensee Andrew Kenneally ~ Real ale ~ Bar food ~ Restaurant ~ (01248) 852568 ~ Children in eating area of bar ~ Open 11-11; 12-10.30 Sun; 11-3.30, 7-11 weekdays in winter

REYNOLDSTON SS4789 Map 6
King Arthur
Off A4118

Easily the area's most popular place for food, this busy hotel opposite the village green had cars flocking in on the midsummer evening we visited. It's named after the King Arthur stone nearby, which according to legend was transformed from a pebble the mythical monarch found in his shoe. The hotel's rather grand hallway has a splendid sword in a case that's purported to resemble Excalibur, as well as an illustration of various local castles. The various rooms lead off from here, with the big main bar the most appealing; a jumble of guns, plates and fishing equipment lines the walls, and there are old timbers, rugs on floorboards, winter log fires in the big fireplace, and a piano. In winter the back bar has pool and a second fire – in summer it's needed as a family dining area. Most people here do come to eat, and it's the specials that stand out; on a typical day the menu might include filled baguettes, cockles, laverbread and bacon (£2.95), ploughman's (£3.95), a pint of prawns (£4.75), potato, cheese and onion pie (£4.95), curry (£5.45), chicken in a cheese and leek sauce (£5.75), Somerset pork (£5.95), grilled trout (£6.75), salmon in a cream and herb sauce (£7.50), Welsh black rump steak (£8.50), grilled halibut (£8.95), and local seabass (£10.50); Sunday lunch is £6.95 for one course, £8.95 for three. Attentive, friendly staff, well kept Bass, Felinfoel Double Dragon and Worthingtons Best on handpump; piped music. The restaurant is no smoking. There are a couple of tables in front, and more in a garden behind, which also has a play area. Over the next year they plan to add a gym, pool and sauna, and a conservatory. Built as a private house 250 years ago, the hotel is said to be haunted. Good walks nearby. *(Recommended by M M O'Brien, David and Nina Pugsley, Dr Nigel and Mrs Elizabeth Holmes)*

Free house ~ Licensees Len and Kim O'Driscoll ~ Bar food ~ Restaurant ~ (01792) 391099 ~ Open 11-11; 12-10.30 Sun

ROSEBUSH SN0630 Map 6
New Inn ♀ ◖
B4329 Haverfordwest—Cardigan, NW of village

An atmospheric pub in an isolated spot, this attractively restored 17th-c drovers' inn has a quietly relaxed atmosphere in its cosy, cottagey rooms. Relying very much on carefully chosen local ingredients, the short choice of generously served bar food is very highly praised by readers at the moment. A typical choice might include soup (£3), a half pint of prawns (£3.50), crostini of cockles and bacon with a laver pesto or parmesan cake with duck liver pâté and red onion marmalade (£5), grilled aubergine and pepper parmigiana or outstanding Thai red pork curry (£6), stilton and mushroom flan or leg of duck with orange and cardamom (£8.50), tuscan-style beef casserole with chocolate and mushrooms (£11), and puddings such as dark and white chocolate roulade or lemon fudge tart (£3.75); good local cheeses. As meals are freshly prepared there may be a wait, and in season it may be worth booking. The restaurant is no smoking. Very well kept real ales include Wye Valley Bitter, and several guests from smaller breweries around the country; well chosen wines by the bottle or glass, Weston's farm cider and friendly staff; darts, piped music (often Gaelic). The three rooms have interesting stripped stonework, simple antique oak country furniture on handsome slate flagstones or red and black diamond Victorian tiles, and a couple of coal fires – one in a quite cavernous fireplace. There's a small garden room, and tables outside. Plenty of good walks nearby. *(Recommended by John and Enid Morris, Mr and Mrs J J Ferguson, Michael and Yvonne Owens, Richard Siebert, R Mattick, Tom and Rosemary Hall, Guy Vowles)*

Free house ~ Licensee Diana Richards ~ Real ale ~ Bar food ~ Restaurant ~ (01437) 532542 ~ Children welcome ~ Open 12-3.30, 6-11; 12-3.30 only Sun; closed Tues except in Aug, middle week Nov, middle two weeks of Jan, one or two weeks after Easter

SHIRENEWTON ST4894 Map 6
Carpenters Arms 🏮

B4235 Chepstow—Usk

Originally a smithy, this very pleasant country pub has an eye-catching array of hanging baskets outside. Once past these, it's well worth wandering around the hive of small interconnecting rooms before you settle: there's plenty to see, from chamber-pots and a blacksmith's bellows hanging from the planked ceiling of one lower room, which has an attractive Victorian tiled fireplace, to a collection of chromolithographs of antique Royal occasions under another room's pitched ceiling (more chamber-pots here, too). Furnishings run the gamut too, from one very high-backed ancient settle to pews, kitchen chairs, a nice elm table, several sewing-machine trestle tables and so forth. Food includes stilton and vegetable crumble (£4.95), pheasant casserole (£5.45), steak and mushroom pie or beef stroganoff (£5.95) and very good chicken supreme in leek and stilton sauce (£6.75); Sunday lunch is good value. Well kept Brakspears, Flowers IPA, Fullers London Pride, Marstons Pedigree and Owd Rodger, and Timothy Taylor Landlord on handpump, and a good selection of over 50 malt whiskies; cheerful service, darts, shove-ha'penny, cribbage, dominoes, backgammon and piped pop music. The pub is handy for Chepstow. *(Recommended by Ian Phillips, Andy Jones, I J and N K Buckmaster)*

Free house ~ Licensee James Bennett ~ Real ale ~ Bar food (not Sun evening in winter) ~ (01291) 641231 ~ Children welcome in family room ~ Open 11-2.30(3 Sat), 6-11; 12-3, 7-11 Sun

ST HILARY ST0173 Map 6
Bush £

Village signposted from A48 E of Cowbridge

Busy throughout the year, this unpretentious and genuinely old-fashioned 16th-c thatched pub fits in well with its equally charming surroundings. The comfortable and snugly cosy low-beamed lounge bar has a very friendly atmosphere, and a nice mix of locals and visitors, as well as stripped old stone walls, and windsor chairs around copper-topped tables on the carpet; the public bar has old settles and pews on aged flagstones; darts and subdued piped music, and a warming wood fire. Very good, reasonably priced bar food includes sandwiches (from £1.75), soup (£2.20), laverbread and bacon (£2.95), welsh rarebit (£3.35), spinach and cheese crêpe (£3.55), ploughman's (£3.95), trout fillet grilled with bacon or liver with onion gravy (£4.50), chicken curry and rice or steak and ale pie (£4.95), mixed grill (£7.50), and daily specials such as fresh cod or plaice; the restaurant menu is available in the bar in the evenings, with meals like trout fried in sherry (£8.95) or breast of duck in orange (£11.95). They do smaller helpings for children. The restaurant is no smoking, as is the lounge bar at meal times. Well kept Bass, Hancocks HB, and Morlands Old Speckled Hen on hand or electric pump, with a range of malt whiskies and a farm cider; efficient service. There are tables and chairs in front, and more in the back garden. *Recommended by M Joyner, M G Hart, David and Nina Pugsley, N H Lewis, Rob Holt, I and N Buckmaster, C D Jones, Alain and Rose Foote, Marlene and Jim Godfrey, Jeremy Brittain-Long)*

Punch Taverns ~ Tenant Sylvia Murphy ~ Real ale ~ Bar food (till 9.45, not Sun evening) ~ Restaurant ~ (01446) 772745 ~ Children welcome ~ Open 11.30-11; 12-10.30 Sun; closed 25 Dec evening

---

Places with gardens or terraces usually let children sit there – we note in the text the very few exceptions that don't.

STACKPOLE SR9896 Map 6
Armstrong Arms
Village signposted off B4319 S of Pembroke

Hidden away on the Stackpole estate, this warmly welcoming, rather Swiss-looking pub is garnering high praise for its bar food under the current mother and daughter team. Lunchtime meals, served by cheerful black-and-white-uniformed waitresses, change daily, but might include soup (£3.25), lasagne (£4.95), rosti cakes or crêpes filled with spinach and stilton (£5.25), and more elaborate evening dishes like moules marinières (£5.50), beef, Guinness and mushroom pie (£6.95), grilled chicken supreme with garlic and herb butter or cheese sauce (£7.25), rack of Welsh lamb with port, cranberry and orange sauce or leek cream (£8.95) and rib-eye steak. Puddings include crème brûlée or chocolate and raspberry roulade (£3.25). One spacious area has new pine tables and chairs, with winter darts and pool, but the major part of the pub, L-shaped on four different levels, is given over to diners, with neat light oak furnishings, and ash beams and low ceilings to match; piped music. At busy times you may find it hard to grab a table in some parts of the pub if you're not eating. Well kept Brains SA, Buckleys Best and Reverend James, and several malt whiskies. There are tables out in the attractive gardens, with colourful flowerbeds and mature trees around the car park; they take credit cards. Dogs welcome in bar and garden. The estate, maintained by the National Trust, has a couple of sandy beaches and walks through woodland or along craggy clifftops. *Recommended by Miss A G Drake, Patrick Wintour, Jeremy Brittain-Long, H and D Payne, John Coatsworth, Carole Smart, Andrew Jeeves, Deirdre Goodman)*

Free house ~ Licensees Margaret and Valerie Westmore ~ Real ale ~ Bar food ~ Restaurant ~ (01646) 672324 ~ Children welcome till 8.30pm ~ Open 11-3, 6-11; 12-3, 7-10.30 Sun

TALYBONT-ON-USK SO1122 Map 6
Star ♕ £
B4558

A small pub in a small village, but this old-fashioned and unpretentious canalside inn has one of the biggest ranges of real ales we know of – generally twelve at a time. Beers they've served recently include Batemans XB, Bullmastif Best, Felinfoel Double Dragon, Freeminer, Hancocks HB, Shepherd Neame Best, Theakstons Best and Old Peculier, Wadworths 6X, and Wye Valley Dorothy Goodbody. They keep farm cider on handpump too. Several plainly furnished pubby rooms – unashamedly stronger on character than on creature comforts – radiate from the central servery, including a brightly lit games area with pool, fruit machine and juke box; roaring winter fires, one in a splendid stone fireplace. Cheerily served bar food includes sandwiches (from £2), soup (£2), ploughman's (£3.50), lasagne or faggots, peas and chips (£4.50), spinach, leek and pasta bake or chicken curry (£4.95), lamb's liver casserole (£5.25), grilled trout (£6.50), steaks (from £7.95), a daily roast, and various specials; children's meals (£2). You can sit outside at picnic-sets in the sizeable tree-ringed garden or walk along the tow path, and the village, with both the Usk and the Monmouth & Brecon Canal running through, is surrounded by the Brecon Beacons national park. *(Recommended by David Lewis, Sarah Lart, Dr and Mrs A K Clarke, JP, PP, John and Joan Nash, Dr M E Wilson, the Didler, Mary and David Richards)*

Free house ~ Licensee Joan Coakham ~ Real ale ~ Bar food ~ (01874) 676635 ~ Children welcome ~ Open 11-3, 6-11; 11-11 Sat; 12-10.30 Sun ~ Bedrooms: £25B/£45B

TALYCOED SO4115 Map 6
Halfway House
B4233 Monmouth—Abergavenny; though its postal address is Llantilio Crossenny, the inn is actually in Talycoed, a mile or two E

The handsome ancient door of this welcoming and pretty 17th-c country inn is surrounded by a huge wisteria. Inside, a step up on the left takes you into a cosy little dining room with burgundy furnishings and carpet, sporting and other prints, and black kettles around its hearth. The main bar is also snug and cosy: soft lighting, bare boards, polished brasses around a nice old stone fireplace, wall settles, a few red plush bar stools, and a back area with a couple of antique high-backed settles and enormous foresters' saws. Lovers of picturesque old inns will recognise many old friends in their collection of Wills cigarette cards. Carefully presented bar food includes mussels in white wine and garlic (£3.25), avocado and corn bake (£5.80), steak and stout pie (£5.95), chicken breast in port and mushroom sauce (£6.30), venison with red wine and redcurrant sauce (£7.85) and duck in orange and cointreau sauce (£8.40); friendly service; no-smoking area in dining room. Well kept Bass and Felinfoel Bitter and Double Dragon on handpump; darts, maybe quiet piped radio. All is neat and clean, including the outside gents'. There are picnic-sets out on a front terrace with a big barbecue, and in a neatly kept garden; there's a cricket field in front, though the future of the pub's own team was in doubt as we went to press. Surprisingly, we don't hear much from readers about this nice little pub, and unless that changes, we'll have no choice but to drop it. *(Recommended by Chris McCormick)*

Free house ~ Licensees Mr and Mrs L G Stagg ~ Real ale ~ Bar food ~ Restaurant ~ (01600) 780269 ~ Children in eating area of bar and restaurant ~ Open 12-3, 6-11(7-10.30 Sun); closed lunchtime Mon-Fri winter ~ Bedrooms: £25/£37

TALYLLYN SH7209 Map 6
Tynycornel 🛏

B4405, off A487 S of Dolgellau

All you can hear in the evenings around this splendidly restful hotel is birdsong, sheep and wavelets lapping under the moored boats on the lake. Nestling below high mountains – Cadair Idris opposite (splendid walks), Graig Goch behind – it's a charming spot; as soon as you step out of your car here you're enveloped in peace. It's very civilised inside, not at all pubby, but relaxed and friendly, with deep armchairs and sofas to sink into around the low tables, a central log fire, and big picture windows looking out over the water (the serving bar, with keg beer, is tucked away behind); there's floral wallpaper, good big bird prints, local watercolours, and a good range of malt whiskies. Well served food includes sandwiches (from £2.25), ploughman's (£4.95), plenty of fresh fish such as local crab, seabass or their own brown trout (from £5.50), and daily specials such as lamb curry, pheasant or duck. Efficient uniformed staff; no-smoking restaurant and conservatory. An attractively planted side courtyard has good teak seats and tables – a nice spot for afternoon tea. Guests have the use of a sauna and outdoor swimming pool, fishing facilities, and can hire boats on the lake. *(Recommended by M and A Leach, Mr and Mrs B W Twiddy, J Sheldon, Sarah and Peter Gooderham, Miss J F Reay)*

Free house ~ Licensee Thomas Rowlands ~ Bar food ~ Restaurant ~ (01654) 782282 ~ Children in eating area of bar and restaurant ~ Open 11-11; 12-10.30 Sun ~ Bedrooms: £70B/£140B

TYN Y GROES SH7672 Map 6
Groes 🍽 🍷 🛏

B5106 N of village

First licensed in 1573 – and claiming to be the first licensed house in Wales – this very well run inn has magnificent views over the mountains and scenic reaches of the Conwy River, particularly from its good bedrooms (some with terraces or balconies. You can enjoy similar views from the airy verdant conservatory, and from seats on the flower decked roadside. The homely series of rambling, low-beamed and thick-walled rooms are beautifully decorated with antique settles and an old sofa, old clocks, portraits, hats and tins hanging from the walls, and fresh flowers. A fine antique fireback is built into one wall, perhaps originally from the formidable fireplace which houses a collection of stone cats as well as winter log fires. A good range of well presented country cooking, with lots of local produce, might include french onion soup (£2.75), sandwiches (from £3), Welsh cheese board (£4.95), soup and a sandwich (£5.95), lasagne, chicken curry or steak (£6.75), steak and kidney pot with thyme dumplings (£6.95), fillet of poached salmon and grilled plaice with hollandaise sauce (£8.75), daily specials like ham, pork and turkey rolled in bacon or braised marrow provençale (£6.50), crab or local salt marsh lamb braised with honey and rosemary (£8.50) and fresh fish such as Conwy lobster (£18.50); lots of tasty puddings fresh fruit pavlova, treacle tart, bread and butter pudding (£3.30), and tempting home-made ice creams like lemon curd or caramelised pears with maple syrup (£2.95). Well kept Ind Coope Burton and Tetleys, a good few malt whiskies, kir, and a fruity pimms in summer; cribbage, dominoes and light classical piped music at lunchtimes (nostalgic light music at other times). It can get busy, but this shouldn't cause any problems with the efficient friendly service. There are seats in the pretty back garden with its flower-filled hayricks. *(Recommended by Joy and Peter Heatherley, Mrs P Goodwyn, R Davies, E Holland, Bob and Marg Griffiths, Roger and Christine Mash, Tim Harper, Dave Braisted, RJH, Roger Byrne, Liz Bell, Vicky and David Sarti)*

Free house ~ Licensee Dawn Humphreys ~ Real ale ~ Bar food ~ Restaurant ~ (01492) 650545 ~ Children welcome in eating area of bar, must be over 10 in restaurant ~ Open 12-3, 6-11 ~ Bedrooms: £63.25B/£80.50B

USK SO3801 Map 6
Nags Head
The Square

In the last century there have been only three landlords at this well run and relaxing old coaching inn – the current licensees have been here now for over 33 years. Characterful and traditional, the main bar has a huge number of well polished tables and chairs packed under its beams, some with farming tools, lanterns or horsebrasses and harness attached, as well as leatherette wall benches, and various sets of sporting prints and local pictures, amongst which are the original deeds to the pub. Well kept Brains SA, Buckleys Best and Reverend James on handpump, served by polite, friendly staff – it's the sort of place where they greet you as you come in, and say goodbye when you leave. The food enjoys a very good reputation locally, with the most popular choices on the menu usually the home-made rabbit pie (£6.25), and fresh local salmon (£9); they also do sandwiches (from £2), soup (£2.25), and various other game in season – readers have enjoyed pheasant, partridge and excellent duck. You can book tables, some of which may be candlelit at night; piped classical music. Hidden away in a corner at the front is an intimate little corner with some African masks, while on the other side of the room a passageway leads to the pub's own popular coffee bar, open between Easter and autumn. Built in the old entrance to the courtyard, it sells snacks, teas, cakes and ice cream. Tables from here spill out onto the pavement in front, and are rather nice on a sunny day. A simpler room behind the bar has prints for sale, and maybe locals drinking. In summer, the centre of Usk is full of hanging baskets and flowers, and it's the landlord's responsibility to water all the ones in the square; lucky for him his duties don't include the ferociously festooned house in the road that leads to the little town's rather splendid church. *(Recommended by Christopher and Mary Thomas, David and Nina Pugsley)*

Free house ~ Licensees The Key Family ~ Real ale ~ Bar food ~ (01291) 672820 ~ Children welcome ~ Open 11-3, 5.30-11

Post Office address codings confusingly give the impression that some pubs are in Gwent or Powys, Wales when they're really in Gloucestershire or Shropshire (which is where we list them).

Lucky Dip

Besides the fully inspected pubs, you might like to try these Lucky Dips recommended to us
and described by readers (if you do, please send us reports):

ANGLESEY
Brynsiencyn [SH4867]
Mermaid [Foel Ferry]: Good choice of good
food under new landlord in extended pub
overlooking Menai Strait and Snowdonia,
attractive sheltered terrace; handy for Anglesey
Sea Zoo (*Mr and Mrs B Hobden*)
Menai Bridge [SH5572]
☆ *Liverpool Arms* [St Georges Pier]: Unpretentious
old-fashioned four-roomed local with cheerful
relaxed atmosphere, low beams, interesting
mostly maritime photographs and prints,
panelled dining room, conservatory catching
evening sun, one or two tables on terrace; very
popular lunchtime for good value food from
generous sandwiches up, well kept Greenalls
and a guest beer, welcoming landlord, prompt
service; no music (*Dennis Dickinson, D
Goodger, J H Jones, Jeff Davies*)

CLWYD
Broughton [SJ3263]
Spinning Wheel [Old Warren; old main rd
towards Buckley]: Very wide choice of good
freshly made well served food in big eating area,
friendly efficient staff, good choice of beers and
malt whiskies; piped music (*KC*)
Burton Green [SJ3558]
Golden Grove [Llyndir Lane, off B5445 W of
Rossett]: Friendly relaxed timbered pub dating
from 13th c, partly knocked-through rooms
with open fires, comfortable settees and settles,
plates, horsebrasses, figures carved in the beams;
Marstons Best and Pedigree, usual food with
some more unusual specials, children
welcome, piped music; big streamside garden
with play area, open all day w/e in summer (*KC,
LYM*)
Cwm [SJ0677]
Blue Lion [B5429, off A55 at Rhuallt S of
Dyserth]: 16th-c pub in lovely hill setting with
views over Vale of Clwyd towards Snowdonia,
L-shaped bar with inglenook log fires, beams
crowded with chamber-pots, lots of brasses and
china, well kept Marstons, plenty of wines and
spirits; popular meals inc children's, help-
yourself salads, good puddings and Sat evening
carvery in bistro bar, separate candlelit
restaurant, friendly efficient service; restaurant;
garden, just off Offa's Dyke Path (*Mrs D C E
Ryder, Mr and Mrs Archibald, Brian Seller, June
and Mike Coleman*)
Ffrith [SJ2855]
Poachers Cottage [B5101, just off A541
Wrexham—Mold]: Welcoming traditional 18th-
c pub, two bars and restaurant, real ales,
extensive wine list, good reasonably priced
home-cooked food inc imaginative vegetarian
dishes; has been cl lunchtime exc Sun (*Greg
Yates*)
Gwernymynydd [SJ2263]
Swan: Friendly staff, good generous food inc
plenty of vegetarian; can be a bit smoky, but they
will turn down the piped music if you ask (*KC*)

Gwytherin [SH8761]
Lion [B5384 W of Denbigh]: Isolated small
village pub with roaring log fire in attractive
main bar, pleasant small restaurant area with
another log fire; has had wide choice of
interesting food and well kept Marstons
Pedigree, but no news since change of landlord
in spring 1999; good bedrooms (*Guy Vowles*)
Higher Kinnerton [SJ3361]
Royal Oak [off A55/A5104 SW of Chester; also
signed off A483]: Ancient picturesque coaching
inn, log fires, settles, lots of small rooms, low
oak beams hung with jugs, teapots, copper
kettles and chamber-pots, interesting collection
of soda syphons, good interesting food in dining
area; tables in small garden, barbecues and play
area (*Graham and Lynn Mason*)
Knolton [SJ3839]
Trotting Mare [A528 Ellesmere—Overton]:
Well renovated family dining pub, usual food,
Greenalls, friendly landlord, great
welcome for children with climbing frames
indoors and out; tables outside (*Mr and Mrs F
Carroll*)
Llanarmon Dyffryn Ceiriog [SJ1633]
☆ *West Arms* [end of B4500 W of Chirk]: Warm
welcome and roaring log fires in restful 16th-c
beamed and timbered pub that's grown over the
years, picturesque upmarket lounge bar full of
antique settles, sofas, even an elaborately carved
confessional stall, good original food, well kept
Boddingtons, good range of wines and malt
whiskies, Stowford Press cider, more sofas in
old-fashioned entrance hall, comfortable back
bar too; pretty lawn running down to River
Ceiriog (fishing for residents); children welcome;
bedrooms comfortable, lovely surroundings,
good walks (*KC, A J Bowen, LYM*)
Llanarmon-yn-Ial [SJ1956]
☆ *Raven* [B5431 NW of Wrexham]: Friendly
18th-c beamed country local with well kept
Flowers IPA, Marston Pedigree and Tetleys,
good value simple lunchtime food from good
sandwiches up, two stoves, separate dining
room; pleasant seats outside – attractive village,
unspoilt countryside; bedrooms (*Maurice and
Gill McMahon, LYM*)
Llandegla [SJ1952]
Plough [Ruthin Rd]: Well run dining pub, well
kept Robinsons, good generous home-made
food inc good range of fresh fish, interesting
meat dishes and good value puddings; piped
music; nr Offa's Dyke Path (*Richard C Morgan,
Rita and Keith Pollard*)
Llanelidan [SJ1150]
Leyland Arms [signed off A494 S of Ruthin]:
Beautifully set interesting old pub in charming
surroundings, a former popular main entry,
reopened under friendly and enthusiastic new
licensees, with plans to do food again (*LYM*)
Llangollen [SJ2045]
Britannia [Horseshoe Pass, A542 N]: Lovely
Dee Valley views from picturesque though much
extended pub, pleasant pine furniture in two

quiet bars and brightly cheerful dining areas (one no smoking), John Smiths, McEwans and Theakstons, reasonably priced food from sandwiches up inc children's and some OAP bargains; well kept garden with tables on terrace, good value attractive bedrooms *(E G Parish, Mr and Mrs P A King, KC)*

☆ *Sarah Ponsonby* [Mill St; A539, 200 yds E of bridge (N end)]: Large welcoming pub next to canal museum on quieter side of the Dee, good choice of good value generous home-made food, no-smoking eating area, pleasant staff, well kept Theakstons; children welcome, good games range inc dominoes, chess, kerplunk, connect-4, pleasant garden overlooking park *(KC, J Morrell, Mr and Mrs McKay)*

Sun Trevor [Trevor Uchaf, off A539]: Spectacular views over River Dee and canal, decent food from sandwiches up in bar and small restaurant, friendly staff, well kept Courage Directors and Wadworths 6X, fair number of malt whiskies, no piped music; handy for walkers *(MLR, KC)*

Mold [SJ2464]

Bryn Awel [A541 Denbigh rd nr Bailey Hill]: Consistently good value dining pub, good choice of satisfying food inc vegetarian, huge helpings, good service, cheerful bustling atmosphere, attractive décor, good no-smoking area; no piped music *(KC)*

Overton Bridge [SJ3643]

☆ *Cross Foxes* [Overton Bridge; A539 W of Overton, nr Erbistock]: Pleasant and airy 17th-c coaching inn in beautiful spot on Dee, interesting views from large terrace, lawn below; small entrance room, lounge on left, small back bar and games room, relaxed atmosphere, friendly landlord and attentive staff, well kept Marstons Bitter and Pedigree, good choice of wines by the glass, good generous straightforward home cooking with some interesting specials; dogs welcome *(Mr and Mrs P King, Jenny and Michael Back, Pat and Tony Hinkins, Robert Dubsky, Mr and Mrs F Carroll)*

Rhewl [SJ1744]

☆ *Sun* [off A5 or A542 NW of Llangollen]: Unpretentious little cottage in lovely peaceful spot, good walking country just off Horseshoe Pass, relaxing views from terrace and small pretty garden; simple good value generous food from sandwiches to good Sun lunch, well kept Felinfoel Double Dragon, Worthington BB and an interesting guest beer, chatty landlord, old-fashioned hatch service to back room, dark little lounge, portakabin games room – children allowed here and in eating area *(MLR)*

Ruthin [SJ1258]

Olde Anchor [Rhos St]: Black and white timbered former coaching inn, lots of flower baskets; open fire, well kept Bass and Worthington, reasonably priced bar food inc vegetarian, good restaurant using local produce; bedrooms good value, attractive country town *(Kevin Owen, Shirley Scott)*

St Asaph [SJ0374]

Farmers Arms [The Waen; B5429 between A55 and Tremeirchion]: Super little country pub,

cosy lounge with log-effect gas fire, good food inc some local specialities, local beer tapped from the cask and served in a jug, good wine list, friendly landlord (may play piano requests evening), efficient staff *(Guy Vowles)*

St George [SH9576]

Kinmel Arms [off A55 nr Abergele]: Interesting building, clean and comfortable, with short but good choice of freshly made food often using unusual local ingredients (plenty of time needed, as everything cooked for you); good range of real ales with weekly guest; bedrooms, attractive village *(E Holland, KC)*

DYFED

Abergorlech [SN5833]

☆ *Black Lion* [B4310 (a pretty road roughly NE of Carmarthen)]: Old-fashioned house beautifully placed in Cothi valley below Brechfa forest, stripped-stone bar with plain oak tables and chairs, high-backed settles, beams, flagstones and sporting prints, restaurant extension with light oak woodwork, garden over road sloping towards river with Roman bridge (and fishing rights), lots of good walks; decent food inc children's, well kept Worthington Best, friendly service, sensibly placed darts, cribbage, unobtrusive piped music *(Richard Siebert, A J Bowen, Howard G Allen, Mr and Mrs K Fawcett, David Gregory)*

Ammanford [SN6212]

Perrivale : Good value food, attractive separate restaurant *(Lyn and Geoff Hallchurch)*

Broad Haven [SM8614]

☆ *Druidstone Hotel* [N of village on coast rd, bear left for about 1½ miles then follow sign left to Druidstone Haven – inn a sharp left turn after another ½ mile; OS Sheet 157 map ref 862168, marked as Druidston Villa]: Very unusual and a favourite place to stay for many; its club licence means you can't go for just a drink and have to book to eat there (the food is inventively individual home cooking, with fresh ingredients and a leaning towards the organic; restaurant cl Sun evening), a lived-in informal country house alone in a grand spot above the sea, with terrific views, spacious homely bedrooms, erratic plumbing, cellar bar with a strong 1960s folk-club feel, well kept Worthington BB tapped from the cask, good wines, country wines and other drinks, ceilidhs and folk jamborees, chummy dogs (dogs welcomed), all sorts of sporting activities from boules to sand-yachting; cl Nov and Jan; bedrooms *(John and Enid Morris, LYM, Gerald Barnett)*

Caio [SN6739]

☆ *Brunant Arms* [off A482 Llanwrda—Lampeter]: Unspoilt pretty village local covered with flowers; welcoming and chatty, with well kept Hereford and other ales, good layout inc pews, good value generous food (best to book for small eating area), good service, interesting egg cup collection, pool table, quiz nights; bedrooms good value, good walks *(M Joyner, David Gregory)*

Capel Bangor [SN6580]

Tynllidiart Arms [A44]: Quaint roadside cottage, two bars, good friendly landlord, nice atmosphere, limited good well presented food, well kept ales sometimes inc one brewed on the premises; clean outside gents' *(Richard Houghton)*

Carmarthen [SN4120]

Coracle [Market Entrance]: Good atmosphere, well priced beers inc Worthington, good generous food in pleasant spacious upstairs eating area *(M Joyner)*

Drovers Arms [Lammas St]: Small family-run hotel with homely bar where women feel happy, good value standard food, well kept Felinfoel Double Dragon, welcoming service; bedrooms comfortable, good breakfast inc cockles and laverbread *(Mike and Wena Stevenson)*

Cilgerran [SN1943]

☆ *Pendre* [off A478]: Medieval pub with massive stone walls, broad flagstones and high-backed settles in friendly locals' bar, new licensees doing promising interesting food at low prices in comfortable lounge bar, good choice of sandwiches, well kept Bass and Hancocks HB; pool table, fruit machine and juke box in public bar, restaurant; children welcome, tables out in garden, has been open all day Sat; nr romantic riverside fort *(David Keating, LYM)*

Ramp : Cosy and friendly two-room village local, Bass or Worthington BB, woodburner *(the Didler)*

Cwm Gwaun [SN0035]

☆ *Dyffryn Arms* [Cwn Gwaun and Pontfaen signposted off B4313 E of Fishguard]: Classic unspoilt country tavern, very basic and idiosyncratic, run by same family since 1840 – charming landlady Bessie has been here 40 years herself; 1920s front parlour with plain deal furniture inc rocking chair and draughts-boards inlaid into tables, coal fire, well kept Bass and Ind Coope Burton served by jug through a hatch, good sandwiches if you're lucky, Great War prints and posters, very relaxed atmosphere, darts; pretty countryside, open more or less all day (but may close if no customers) *(Kevin Thorpe, the Didler, LYM, JP, PP)*

Cwmann [SN5847]

Ram [A482 SE of Lampeter]: Lively atmosphere in two-bar pub with well kept Bass and guest beers, good value tasty food, welcoming staff, small restaurant *(Keith Arnold)*

Cwmbach [SN4802]

Farriers Arms [B4308 Llanelli—Trimsaran]: High wooden settles in stripped stone bar, plush split level lounge/dining area with wood and dark wallpaper, well kept Bass, Marstons Pedigree and a guest beer, decent food, big informal garden with covered barbecue area, bridge over trout stream to play area and tables well spread in woodland glade *(Michael and Alison Sandy)*

Fishguard [SM9537]

☆ *Fishguard Arms* [Main St, Lower Town]: Tiny traditional front bar with Worthington BB and a couple of guest beers served by jug at unusually high counter, open fire, rugby photographs; cheap snacks, traditional games and impromptu music in back room *(the Didler, LYM)*

☆ *Royal Oak* [The Square, Upper Town]: Busy old inn with pictures and mementoes commemorating defeat here of second-last attempted French invasion in 1797, looks small from outside, but steps lead down from well used beamed front bar through panelled room to big no-smoking picture-window dining extension; stone walls, cushioned wooden wall seats, woodburner, Welsh dragon carved on bar counter, three well kept real ales inc Buckleys, big helpings of mostly standard food with some interesting dishes and children's menu, friendly service, tea, coffee, hot chocolate; bar billiards, fruit machine *(Mike and Mary Carter, Anne Morris, Dr Oscar Puls, BB)*

Laugharne [SN2910]

Browns Hotel [King St, A4066 nr Town Hall]: Sturdy old local not much changed since Dylan Thomas used to drink here, with mementoes of the poet in plainly furnished bar, well kept Buckleys beers, basic food inc good cawl, small garden behind; open all day, handy for Thomas's boathouse, and opp splendid secondhand bookshop; open all day *(Dr B and Mrs P B Baker, BB)*

Letterston [SM9429]

Harp [A40 Haverfordwest rd]: Dining pub with dark wood and careful décor in smart lounge bars and restaurant, good well presented food inc lots of fresh fish, real ales such as Ansells, Morlands Old Speckled Hen and Tetleys; simple, pleasant bar with good food, efficient service, open all day *(Dr B and Mrs P B Baker)*

Little Haven [SM8512]

☆ *St Brides Inn* [in village itself, not St Brides hamlet further W]: A short stroll from the sea, with pews in stripped-stone bar and communicating dining area (children allowed here), welcoming staff, consistently enjoyable freshly made straightforward food, open fire, Worthington BB and guest beers such as Theakstons Old Peculier, no piped music; interesting well in back corner may be partly Roman; big good value bedrooms, some in annexe over rd *(LYM, Mr and Mrs D Gardner)*

Llanarthne [SN5320]

☆ *Golden Grove Arms* [B4300 (good fast alternative to A40)]: Wide choice of good food inc some sophisticated dishes, and very pleasant prompt service, in nicely laid out child-friendly inn with roomy lounge, open fire, well kept Buckleys beers, huge play area; Tues folk night; bedrooms *(Michael and Yvonne Owens, LYM)*

☆ *Paxton* [B4300, 7 miles E of Carmarthen]: Cosy and friendly dimly lit bar with two cats and loads of bric-a-brac, more sober restaurant, helpful service, wide choice of generous bar food, well kept Buckleys, farm cider, decent malt whiskies; folk, jazz and blues nights; opp wood leading to Paxtons Tower (NT); open all day w/e *(Pete Baker)*

Llanddarog [SN5016]

☆ *White Hart* [just off A48; aka Yr Hedd Gwyn]: Friendly thatched stonebuilt dining pub with heavy beams hung with bric-a-brac, 17th-c carved settles, two stone fireplaces (one with motorised spit), L-shaped dining area hung with Welsh tapestries and farm tools; above-average generous food running up to seafood and sizzling venison, well kept real ale (plans to brew their own); piped nostalgic music (even in the garden) *(J Taylor, Lynda Payton, Sam Samuells, A J Bowen)*

Llandovery [SN7634]

Red Lion [Market Sq]: One basic but welcoming room with no bar, well kept Buckleys and guest beers tapped from the cask, friendly and individual landlord; cl Sun, may close early evening if no customers *(the Didler, BB)*

Llandybie [SN6115]

Red Lion [Llandeilo Rd]: Reworked under new management, usual food in family restaurant, Whitbreads-related real ales, spacious sports bar with SkyTV, upstairs Irish/American rock-theme bar; bedrooms *(Howard James, DAV)*

Llangranog [SN3154]

Ship: In pretty fishing village, with tables under canopy by beachside car park giving continental feel in summer; wide choice of interesting generous home-made food inc vegetarian and children's, spacious upstairs eating area, good Sun carvery, well kept Whitbreads-related ales, open fire; can get busy summer, may be cl Mon in winter; bedrooms *(Simon Pyle)*

Marloes [SM7908]

Lobster Pot: Recently reopened, clean and pleasant, with freshly made usual food in bar and restaurant, games area, facilities for children *(Miss A G Drake)*

Narberth [SN1114]

☆ *Angel* [High St]: Interesting guest beers, good food inc local fish, help-yourself salad bar, children's dishes and good value Sun lunch, pleasant furnishings, quick friendly service; pub pianist *(M Joyner, Dr and Mrs B Baker)*

New Cross [SN6377]

New Cross [B4340 SE of Aberystwyth]: Small pub with friendly locals, good reasonably priced generous food from sandwiches up inc children's, Sun lunch and delicious puddings, landlord with keen sense of humour, young well trained staff; restaurant *(John and Ann Colling)*

Newport [SN0539]

Llwyngwair Arms [East St]: Straightforward local with friendly landlord, good food inc smoked local trout from its own smokery and genuine Indian dishes (takeaways too), well kept Worthington and a cheap house beer, coal-effect fire; copes well with the busy holiday season *(R Michael Richards)*

Pelcomb Bridge [SM9317]

Rising Sun: Attractive and welcoming, generous freshly made food particularly good for the area *(Miles P Jervis)*

Pumsaint [SN6540]

Bridgend: Friendly prompt service, good value food inc good Sun lunch in nicely set no-smoking dining room; no dogs *(Lyn and Geoff Hallchurch)*

Red Roses [SN2011]

Sporting Chance [A477 Carmarthen—Pembroke, W of St Clears]: Clean, cheerful and roomy, with wide choice of good value food, friendly staff, separate restaurant area *(anon)*

Rhandirmwyn [SN7843]

Royal Oak: Nicely set 17th-c stone inn with

great potential, in remote and peaceful walking country, plenty of hanging baskets and flowering tubs, good views from tables in front garden, comfortable bar with two changing real ales, big dining area (can book) with decent food (quite a few vegetarian dishes); handy for Brecon Beacons, dogs and children welcome; big bedrooms with hill views *(David Gregory, Lyn and Geoff Hallchurch, David Lewis, Sarah Lart, John and Joan Nash, BB)*

Rosebush [SN0729]

Tafarn Sinc: Unpromising (a big zinc shed) but really interesting inside – reconditioned railway halt, full of local history, with well kept if anonymous beer and cheap cheerful food; platform with life-size dummy passengers and steam sound-effects in big garden *(John and Enid Morris, the Didler, Howard G Allen)*

Saundersfoot [SN1304]

☆ *Royal Oak* [Wogan Terr]: Notably friendly and well cared-for local in bustling seaside town, popular generous bar food, good fresh seafood specials, may be worth booking meals in season; well kept Flowers Original, Morlands Old Speckled Hen and Worthington Best, good pubby atmosphere, small public bar with TV, several other little rooms for eating, no music or machines, tables outside get snapped up quickly in summer, and have overhead heaters for cold days; children welcome *(D Prodham, Brian and Pat Wardrobe, BB)*

Solva [SM8024]

☆ *Cambrian Arms* [Lower Solva; off A487 Haverfordwest—St Davids]: Attractive dining pub popular with older people, clean and warm, good cawl, authentic pasta and popular Sun lunch, decent Italian wines, Tetleys-related ales, efficient service, log fires; piped music, and rather too many 'no' notices inc no dogs or children *(John and Enid Morris, John Coatsworth, Maureen and Les Dodd, Martin Jones, Simon Watkins, Gerald Barnett)*

☆ *Ship* [Main St, Lower Solva]: Welcoming fishermen's pub quaintly set in attractive harbourside village, interesting low-beamed bar with lots of old photographs, nautical artefacts and bric-a-brac; big back family dining room with barn-like village hall atmosphere; well kept Bass, Hancocks HB and guest beers, simple generous reasonably priced food, friendly service, maybe radio; little garden has play area over stream *(Mr and Mrs Dalby)*

St Clears [SN2716]

Butchers Arms [Lower St]: Small and welcoming, with good beautifully presented food inc good value Sun roast, Felinfoel beer, helpful young licensees, log fires with oven for roasting potatoes and chestnuts *(John Coatsworth, Mr and Mrs Cyril Davison)*

St Davids [SM7525]

Farmers Arms [Goat St]: Cheerful and busy genuine pub, good straightforward food, well kept Flowers and Worthington BB, cathedral view from tables in tidy back garden *(N H E Lewis, Stephanie Smith, Gareth Price)*

Talsarn [SN5456]

Red Lion: Old-fashioned typical Welsh local with huge log fire, good value fresh tasty home-

made food (all day Sat) inc Sun lunch, two changing guest beers *(David Miller, Jill Young)*
Tenby [SN1300]
Lifeboat [Tudor Sq]: Atmospheric boat-shaped bar, friendly staff and locals, good food inc children's menu, huge helpings, bargain steaks; tables on back terrace *(Mr and Mrs W Craze)*
White Mill [SN4621]
White Mill [A40 Carmarthen—Llandeilo]: Attractive whitewashed building with shutters and flowers, clean inside with comfortable plush wall seats, beams and tiles, friendly helpful licensees, decent traditional food, well kept Hancocks HB and Worthington; children welcome *(Mr and Mrs G J Garrett, Michael and Alison Sandy)*
Wolfs Castle [SM9526]
☆ *Wolfe* [A40 Haverfordwest—Fishguard]: Good fresh home-made food (not Sun or Mon evenings in winter) in comfortable dining lounge, garden room and conservatory, well kept Worthington and a weekly guest beer, decent wines, obliging service, attractively laid-out garden; simpler public bar with darts, restaurant; children welcome; bedrooms *(LYM, Rob Holt)*

GWENT
Abergavenny [SO3014]
☆ *Greyhound* [Market St]: Warm hospitable dining pub (not a place for just a drink), interesting food cooked and presented with real flair at sensible prices, lots of fresh veg, decent wines, good service; keg beers *(Adrian White)*
Hen & Chickens [Flannel St]: Small well used traditional local, Bass and Brains, basic wholesome cheap lunchtime food (not Sun; shame about all the young smokers), friendly staff, popular darts, cards and dominoes *(Pete Baker)*
Lamb & Flag [B4598, 3 miles E]: Generous good value food inc some unusual dishes, children's meals and fresh veg in roomy and comfortable modern plush lounge bar or two dining rooms, well kept Brains Bitter and SA, good service; children welcome, high chairs; open all day in summer, country views – tables outside with play area *(David Lewis, Steve Thomas, Joan and Michel Hooper-Immins, Sidney and Erna Wells)*
Bassaleg [ST2787]
Tredegar Arms [handy for M4 junction 28; A468 towards Caerphilly]: Vast range of well kept real ales, enthusiastic landlord, good eating area, family and outdoor areas *(David Lewis, Sarah Lart, Dr and Mrs A K Clarke, MRSM)*
Bettws Newydd [SO3606]
☆ *Black Bear* [off B4598 N of Usk]: Cottage-style pub in tranquil village, good food in bar and big formal eating area, enterprising game and seafood dishes, cheaper separate snack menu; tiled floor, big wooden tables, piano, lots of brasses, and well kept changing ales such as Ash Vine and Bath SPA; picnic-sets by road, more in attractive sloping side garden *(Gwyneth and Salvo Spadaro-Dutturi, BB)*
Chepstow [ST5394]
Castle View [Bridge St]: Opp the castle and its

car park, hotel bar with white-painted walls and some exposed stonework, plush chairs and stools, standard bar food inc vegetarian, limited range of drinks from small bar counter; tables in garden, bedrooms *(Gordon Theaker, BB)*
Three Tuns [Bridge St]: A Porters Ale House, well refurbished in a faux-traditional way, with bare boards, yellow walls, old dresser with china plates, newspapers, and a nice wooden bar counter at an unusual angle; three real ales, decent bar food, friendly staff, piped pop music *(GSB, BB)*
Dolwyddelan [SH7353]
Gwydr: Well used pub with wide range of cheap bar food, helpful staff *(Sarah and Peter Gooderham)*
Gilwern [SO2414]
Lion [A4077 W of Abergavenny; Lion Terr]: Small hotel locally popular for wide choice of freshly made mainly authentic Italian food in attractive bar and dining room, knowledgeable courteous service, good value house wines; bedrooms *(Brian and Pat Wardrobe)*
Grosmont [SO4024]
Angel: Friendly ivy-covered 17th-c village pub on attractive steep single street within sight of castle, seats out by ancient market cross beside surprisingly modern little town hall; welcoming local atmosphere, several changing well kept ales from Wye Valley and Watkins, Bulmers cider, usual food with well priced specials, cheery service, big Welsh flag; TV, separate room with pool and darts, a couple of tables and boules pitch behind *(R T and J C Moggridge, LM, BB)*
Gwehelog [SO3904]
☆ *Hall* [old rd Usk—Raglan]: Neatly kept small former coaching inn with beams and log fire, doing well under new licensees, with good choice of unusual fresh food using local ingredients, separate dining and games areas, Bass and Hancocks HB *(Dave and Sharon Holgate)*
Llanfihangel Crucorney [SO3321]
☆ *Skirrid* [signed off A465]: One of Britain's oldest pubs, dating partly from 1110; ancient studded door to high-ceilinged main bar, all stone and flagstones, dark feel accentuated by furniture inc pews (some padded), huge log fire; panelled dining room, good generous bar food from big sandwiches up (may be a wait), fresh veg, full range of Ushers beers; darts, pool and piped music; open all day summer, children welcome, tables on terrace and small sloping back lawn, well equipped bedrooms *(Stephanie Smith, Gareth Price, Pamela and Merlyn Horswell, LYM, Mike and Mary Carter)*
Llantarnam [ST3093]
☆ *Greenhouse* [Newport Rd (A4042 N of M4 junction 26)]: Welcoming and roomy, lots of dark wood, civilised good value dining room (children welcome, very wide choice from good sandwiches up), well kept Scottish Courage ales, beautiful big tree-sheltered garden with terrace and play area *(Christoper and Jo Barton)*
Llanthony [SO2928]
☆ *Abbey Hotel* [Llanthony Priory; off A465, back rd Llanvihangel-Crucorney—Hay]: Enchanting

peaceful setting in border hills, lawns among Norman abbey's graceful ruins; basic dim-lit vaulted flagstoned crypt bar, well kept Bass, Flowers Original, Ruddles County and Wadworths 6X, farm cider in summer, simple lunchtime bar food, no children; occasional live music, open all day Sat (and Sun in summer); in winter cl Sun evening and weekdays exc Fri evening; evening restaurant, bedrooms, great walks all around *(LYM, Stephanie Smith, Gareth Price, A C Morrison)*

Llantrisant Fawr [ST3997]

☆ *Greyhound* [off A449 nr Usk]: Consistently good home cooking at sensible prices in largeish busy country pub, attractive and prettily set, with spacious open-plan rooms, hill views, friendly service; gardens attractive even in winter, good bedrooms in small attached motel *(Janet Pickles)*

Llanvair Discoed [ST4492]

☆ *Woodlands* [off A48 W of Chepstow]: Simple small village pub undergoing extensive refurbishment to restaurant as we went to press – should give more scope to its unusually good interesting food inc excellent puddings; friendly service, good coffee *(Dr Oscar Puls, BB)*

Llanwenarth [SO2714]

☆ *Llanwenarth Arms* [A40 Abergavenny—Crickhowell]: Popular and beautifully placed riverside inn with good food in light and airy modern restaurant, and splendid views from conservatory and terrace down to water and across hills; dates from 16th c, but much modernised since, some dark wood in well stocked bar, very good service, daily papers, children welcome (high chairs available); 18 comfortable bedrooms overlooking Wye *(Steve Thomas, Mrs Heather March, Anne Morris, BB)*

Machen [ST2288]

White Hart [White Hart Lane]: Unusual bar and lounge with ship's panelling and recently restored ceiling painting, at least two weekly-changing real ales, generous bar meals *(Emma Kingdon)*

Michaelston-y-Fedw [ST2484]

Cefn Mably Arms [a mile off A48 at Castleton]: Brightly furnished local with very friendly service, well kept Hancocks HB, enjoyable freshly made food inc fish and vegetarian in bar and restaurant, tables in garden – country setting *(Michael Richards, R T and J C Moggridge, I J and N K Buckmaster)*

Monmouth [SO5009]

☆ *Gockett* [Lydart; B4293 2 miles towards Trelleck]: Extended country pub with light and airy raftered room on left, houseplants, sliding doors to pleasant garden, no-smoking dining room with low beams, some stripped stone, coaching prints and log fire, enjoyable generous efficiently served food inc interesting dishes, well kept Bass and a guest such as Hook Norton; children welcome; bedrooms with own bathrooms, good breakfast *(BB, LM, Dennis Heatley)*

May Hill [May Hill (A4136)]: Marstons Bitter and Pedigree, open all day Sun, quiz night Sun *(Gwyneth and Salvo Spadaro-Dutturi)*

Newport [ST3189]

Red Lion [Stow Hill]: Good choice of well kept changing ales, real fire, real characters *(Robert Davies)*

Pandy [SO3322]

Offas Tavern: Tasteful décor, welcoming helpful licensees, good home cooking inc bargain Sun lunch; play area *(Mr Thomas)*

Penhow [ST4291]

☆ *Rock & Fountain* [Llanvaches Rd]: Big roadside pub doing well under friendly newish owners, shortish choice of interesting home-made food changing daily inc fresh fish and shellfish, low-beamed green-painted main bar with barrel tables, oak benches, comfortable window seats, log fires, Bass, Hancocks HB and Morlands Old Speckled Hen, more formal red-painted eating area, yellow room with TV; piped music, fruit machines in separate area, jazz/folk Fri/Sun; dogs and children welcome *(Mrs Anna Chalkley, BB)*

Rhyd-y-Meirch [SO2907]

☆ *Goose & Cuckoo* [up cul-de-sac off A4042 S of Abergavenny]: Tiny unspoilt country pub in beautiful alpine setting, simple and interesting good value food inc vegetarian, home-made pizzas and ice cream, well kept real ales inc Brains SA, good coffee, lots of whiskies, friendly licensees; dogs on leads allowed, handy for hill walks *(Guy Vowles)*

Shirenewton [ST4893]

☆ *Tredegar Arms* [signed off B4235 just W of Chepstow]: Busy welcoming dining pub with very wide choice of good food from fresh sandwiches up (booking advised w/e), comfortable sofa and chairs in tastefully chintzy lounge bar with big bay window, well kept changing guest beers, good choice of malt whiskies, decent wines, cheerful staff, interesting sugar-tongs collection; games in public bar, seats outside; children in eating area; colourful hanging baskets, small sheltered courtyard, good value bedrooms *(Mike and Mary Carter, C Smith, LYM, Robert Davies, Mrs G Rogers)*

The Narth [SO5026]

Trekkers [off B4293 Trelleck—Monmouth]: Log cabin high in valley, unusual and welcoming, esp for children; lots of wood with central fire, helpful licensee, good value generous food inc vegetarian and fun ice creams (service can slow when they're busy), good range of well kept Felinfoel Double Dragon, Freeminers and a guest such as Hardy Country, skittle alley family room, facilities for the disabled; dogs, long back garden, open all day Sun *(Dr B and Mrs P B Baker, LM)*

Tintern [SO5301]

Cherry Tree [Devauden Rd, off A446 about ¾ mile W of main village]: Quaint unspoilt country pub in quiet spot by tiny stream, steps up to simple front room, well kept Hancocks HB and farm cider, cards and dominoes, bar billiards in second room, charming garden; children welcome *(Pete Baker, Paul and Heather Bettesworth)*

Trelleck [SO5005]

Lion [B4293 6 miles S of Monmouth]: Welcoming and comfortable country pub, unpretentious lounge bar, wide choice of good food inc good value Sun lunch, three well kept ales, good service *(Paul and Heather Bettesworth)*

Village Green [B4293 S of Monmouth]: Comfortable beamed restaurant/bistro in unflashy old building, good freshly made food using local produce, wonderful puddings, friendly service, cosy little front bar, well kept Bass and Worthington, good wines, prints, lots of dried flowers; bedrooms in well converted former stables *(Maureen and Les Dodd, Pamela and Merlyn Horswell)*

Trelleck Grange [SO5001]

Fountain [minor rd Tintern—Llanishen, SE of village]: Tucked away on a back road through quiet countryside, cheerful unassuming inn with well kept Boddingtons and Wadworths 6X in dark-beamed bar, roomy and comfortable dining room, wide range of popular food inc good fresh sandwiches and fish; maybe nostalgic piped pop music, darts, decent malt whiskies and wines; children allowed away from bar, small sheltered garden with summer kids' bar; bedrooms *(BB, J Potter)*

Usk [SO3801]

Castle [The Square]: Useful for generous bar food all day, extended pub with busy dining room, relaxed and jaunty front bar with sofas, locals reading newspapers, interesting carved chair and comfortable window seats; a couple of cosy little alcoves open off the eating areas, big mirrors, lots of dried hops, piped music, Bass tapped from cask and Tetleys on handpump, tables in garden behind *(David and Nina Pugsley, BB)*

Royal Hotel [New Market St]: Pleasant and popular country-town inn with traditional fixtures and fittings, old crockery and pictures on the walls, old-fashioned fireplaces, comfortable wooden chairs and tables, good food (not Sun evening, and may be a wait) inc wider evening choice and popular Sun lunch, well kept real ales, friendly service; piped music; well behaved children welcome, has been cl Mon lunchtime *(LYM, J W Hackett)*

GWYNEDD

Abergynolwyn [SH6807]

Railway [Tywyn—Talyllyn pass]: Old-fashioned village pub neatly upgraded by friendly and helpful new landlord, two bars, big fire in pleasant lounge, good range of well kept beers, good reasonably priced food, no-smoking dining area with piped music; nice outside seating, lovely setting; bedrooms planned *(Mr and Mrs B W Twiddy, Dr R Holcombe)*

Bangor [SH5973]

Nelson [Beach Rd]: 19th-c two-bar corner local overlooking harbour, good choice of usual food inc vegetarian and children's, well kept Tetleys, friendly landlady; machines, pool, juke box *(CJW, JJW)*

Beddgelert [SH5948]

Prince Llewelyn: Plush hotel bar with log fire and raised dining area, simpler summer bar, good atmosphere, wide choice of good value generous bar food, well kept Robinsons, rustic

seats on verandah overlooking village stream and hills – great walking country; piped music, busy at peak holiday times, children allowed at quiet ones; bedrooms pleasant, with good breakfast *(George Atkinson, Stephanie Smith, Gareth Price, BB)*

☆ *Tanronen* [A498 N of Porthmadog]: Comfortably and attractively refurbished hotel bar, good choice of good value bar food, attentive staff, well kept Robinsons, restaurant; walkers welcome, good bedrooms overlooking river across road, or fields and mountains behind *(Paul and Sharon Sneller, BB, Stephanie Smith, Gareth Price)*

Betws-y-Coed [SH7956]

Pont y Par: Decent spread of food, amiable landlord, Tetleys *(A J Bowen)*

☆ *Royal Oak*: Huge well organised tiled-floor Stables Bar with good facilities for family eating (partly no smoking, good disabled access), attractive décor and some interesting pictures, popular food inc good original specials and local fish, very long bar counter with Boddingtons, Flowers IPA and Morlands Old Speckled Hen, decent house wines, espresso machine, friendly helpful service; one end with pool, darts, TV and fruit machine, tables on verandah and big terrace; open all day, jazz Thurs, male voice choir alternate Fri; bedrooms – and the substantial hotel has its own comfortable bar *(E A Froggatt, J F M and M West, BB, Roger Byrne, A J Bowen)*

Waterloo [A5 next to BP garage and Little Chef]: Wide choice of well served generous food, even mountain mutton sometimes, also several vegetarian dishes, good obliging service even when busy, freshly squeezed orange juice, no piped music; bedrooms *(KC)*

Bontddu [SH6719]

Bontddu Hall: Lovely position, great view, good food, friendly atmosphere; comfortable bedrooms *(Mrs D W Jones-Williams)*

Half Way: Good out-of-the-ordinary fresh food esp fish, beautifully served, very welcoming licensees *(D Jones-Williams)*

Capel Curig [SH7258]

Cobdens: Reasonably priced food inc home-made bread and interesting vegetarian dishes, sensible prices, well kept Cambrian and Scottish Courage beers, pleasant staff, bare rock in back bar; lovely river scene across road, good walks all around; bedrooms *(Stan and Hazel Allen)*

Conwy [SH7778]

Mulberry [Marina, Morfa Drive]: New pub nicely decorated with sailing memorabilia, good choice of quality food at reasonable prices, excellent service; heavily booked w/e *(Roland Saussehod)*

Dolgarrog [SH7767]

☆ *Lord Newborough* [Conwy Rd (B5106 just S)]: Small bar, main room with log fire, separate dining room, welcoming landlord and staff, wide choice of good food *(D W Jones-Williams, RJH)*

Ganllwyd [SH7224]

☆ *Tyn-y-groes*: Friendly old inn owned by NT in lovely Snowdonia setting, fine forest views, old-fashioned furnishings in partly panelled beamed lounge, well kept Boddingtons and Flowers, quite a few malt whiskies, cheeerful landlord, wife does good choice of generous straightforward home cooking, woodburner, small pleasant family dining room, separate no-smoking restaurant; may not open till 7 evenings; comfortable well equipped bedrooms, salmon and seatrout fishing, good walks *(M Mason, D Thompson, Mr and Mrs B W Twiddy, LYM)*

Llanbedrog [SH3332]

Ship [Bryn-y-gro, B4413]: Extended refurbished pub with thriving atmosphere, well kept Burtonwood, lively front family lounge, good range of popular straightforward food; good outside seating area *(Norman Revell, LYM)*

Llandudno [SH7883]

Albert [Madoc St]: Friendly pub comfortably refurbished in olde-worlde style, good staff, wide choice of reasonably priced food inc vegetarian, good beer *(Liz and John Soden)*

Cottage Loaf [Market St]: Pleasant atmosphere, good value food, several well kept mainly Courage-related real ales, big log fire, flagstones and bare boards, salvaged ship's timbers, good piped music, some live music; handy for shoppers *(Bob and Marg Griffiths)*

☆ *Kings Head* [Old Rd, behind tram stn]: Rambling pretty pub, much extended around 16th-c flagstoned core, spaciously open-plan, bright and clean, with comfortable traditional furnishings, interesting old local photographs, red wallpaper, dark pine, wide range of generous food inc vegetarian, well kept Tetleys-related ales, good choice of wines in friendly-sized glasses, quick service, huge log fire, smart back dining room up a few steps; children welcome, open all day in summer, seats on front terrace overlooking quaint Victorian tramway's station (water for dogs here) *(LYM, Keith and Margaret Kettell, GLD, Liz and John Soden)*

Llanuwchllyn [SH8731]

Eryrod [aka The Eagles]: Good food (may be a wait), well kept beer, reasonable prices, friendly Welsh-speaking atmosphere, panoramic view of mountains with Lake Bala in distance; no music, no smoking *(KC)*

Rhyd Ddu [SH5753]

Cwellyn Arms [A4085 N of Beddgelert]: More eatery than pub, popular with Snowdon walkers, wide choice, also several real ales inc Bass, flagstones, log fire in huge ancient fireplace, small games bar with pool, darts and TV; children and walkers welcome, fine Snowdon views from garden tables with barbecue, babbling stream just over wall, big adventure playground; open all day Sun at least in summer *(KC)*

Talybont [SH5922]

Ysgethin [A496 N of Barmouth]: No-nonsense pub with wide range of reliable pub food, efficient staff; wet walkers welcome *(Sarah and Peter Gooderham)*

MID GLAMORGAN

Bedwas [ST1689]

Church House [Church St]: Jovial welcoming landlord, well kept beer, excellent value food in popular lounge *(Emma Kingdon)*

Caerphilly [ST1484]

☆ *Black Cock* [Watford; Tongwynlais exit from M4 junction 32, then right just after church]: Big helpings of good value food from cheap snacks up in neat blue-plush bar with open fire in pretty tiled fireplace, and interesting brass-tabled public bar where children allowed; well kept Bass and Hancocks HB, happy atmosphere, friendly staff, sizeable terraced garden among trees with play area and barbecue, restaurant extension; up in the hills, just below Caerphilly Common *(BB, Ian Phillips, I Buckmaster)*

☆ *Courthouse* [Cardiff Rd]: 14th-c pub with splendid castle views from light and airy modern back café/bar and tables on grassy terrace; character original core has rugs on ancient flagstones, stripped stone walls, raftered gallery, generous food all day (not Sun evening, not after 5.30 Mon, Fri or Sat) inc several vegetarian and children's dishes, good choice of ales such as Courage Best, Morlands Old Speckled Hen, Theakstons XB and Wadworths 6X, good coffee, partly no-smoking restaurant; children welcome in eating areas, pub games, piped pop music (can be a bit loud), open all day, virtually no nearby parking *(Dr and Mrs Cottrell, Ian Phillips, LYM, David and Anne Daniel, M G Hart)*

Goodrich [Van Rd]: Big recently refurbished family pub with welcoming landlord, popular cheap food (may need to book Fri lunchtime), well kept Brains and Worthington, locals' bar with games *(Emma Kingdon, Ian Phillips)*

Corntown [SS9277]

Golden Mile [B4524 Ewenny rd, off A48 Cowbridge—Bridgend]: Two-bar pub with well kept Bass, Timothy Taylor and Worthington, good generous meals, sensibly priced wine, friendly service; good Vale of Glamorgan view from tables outside *(M Joyner)*

Creigiau [ST0781]

☆ *Caesars Arms* : Large dining area with fine display of good value fish cooked in open kitchen, tasty starters and tempting puddings; good wine by the glass and coffee, very busy *(Tom and Ruth Rees, J H Jones)*

Kenfig [SS8383]

☆ *Prince of Wales* [2¼ miles from M4 junction 37; A4229 towards Porthcawl, then right at roundabout leaving Cornelly]: Interesting ancient pub among sand dunes, heavy settles, long tables and open fire in stripped stone bar, well kept Bass, Worthington and maybe a guest ale tapped from the cask, good choice of malt whiskies, traditional games, small dining room; handy for nature reserve and walks, children welcome *(John and Joan Nash, the Didler, LYM)*

Llwydcoed [SN9704]

Red Cow [Merthyr Rd (B4276 N of Aberdare)]: Very welcoming neatly kept traditional pub with well kept beer, good value plain food and new carvery, no juke box or machines; large garden *(Nelly Reliat)*

Pontneddfechan [SN9007]

Angel: Welcoming 16th-c inn tastefully opened

up by newish landlord, comfortable, light and airy, with plenty of tables for generous standard food, well kept Bass and Boddingtons, separate flagstoned hikers' bar; lots of flowers in front, tables on terrace; bedrooms, good walks inc the waterfalls *(John and Joan Nash, Jenny and Brian Seller)*

Rudry [ST1986]

☆ *Maenllwyd*: Comfortably furnished olde-worlde lounge in low-beamed Tudor pub with log fires, good reasonably priced food, well kept ales, good choice of wines, friendly staff, spacious restaurant; provision for children, good walks *(Lisa Huish, Mrs B Sugarman, LYM)*

Thornhill [ST1484]

☆ *Travellers Rest* [A469 towards Caerphilly]: Attractive old thatched stone hilltop pub, carefully extended as Vintage Inn dining pub with wide choice of good value popular generous food all day inc vegetarian, good veg, Bass-related and a guest ale, sensibly priced wine, good service, daily papers and magazines; huge fireplace and nooks and crannies in atmospheric low-beamed bar on right, other bars more modernised, with great views over Cardiff; piped music, very busy w/e, no bookings; open all day, tables out on grass, good walks *(G Coates, David and Nina Pugsley, Hugh and Shirley Mortimer, R Michael Richards, I J and N K Buckmaster, Bill and Sheila McLardy)*

POWYS

Aberedw [SO0847]

Seven Stars [just off B4567 SE of Builth Wells]: Cosy attractively refurbished beamed local with butcher landlord, good value generous honest food inc tasty steaks and gammons, three well kept low-priced real ales, efficient friendly service, log fire, bustling restaurant *(Mrs S Parrish, Alan and Sheila Hart, M S Catling)*

Berriew [SJ1801]

Lion [off A483 Welshpool—Newtown]: Neatly kept timber-framed country inn with very friendly efficient staff, good home-cooked food in bar/bistro and restaurant, Bass and Worthington with guest beers such as Greene King and Shepherd Neame, decent house wines, fairly smart atmosphere, separate public bar; well equipped cottage bedrooms, quiet attractive village fairly handy for Powis Castle (NT) *(Paul and Maggie Baker, Leonard and Ann Robinson, E Holland)*

Beulah [SN9351]

Trout [B4358/A483 Llanwrtyd Wells—Builth Wells]: Big friendly Edwardian pub, settees in tidy nicely refurbished front lounge, spacious well lit dining area with wide choice of reasonably priced good home-made food (limited Mon/Tues) inc good puddings, good views from big windows, public bar and pool, Hancocks HB, Youngers IPA and Worthington BB; very busy w/e; six comfortable bedrooms, good walking area *(John Brightley)*

Bleddfa [SO2168]

Hundred House [A488 Knighton—Penybont]: Log fire in small, quiet and relaxed lounge's huge stone fireplace, wall seats in L-shaped public bar with attractively flagstoned lower games area, lacy tablecloths and enjoyable food in little dining room with another vast fireplace, well kept Woods Shropshire Lad and Worthington; tables in garden with barbecue – very quiet spot, dropping steeply behind to small stream, lovely countryside; bedrooms simple but comfortable, good breakfast *(G W A Pearce, Stephanie Smith, Gareth Price, Mrs Heather March, BB)*

Brecon [SO0428]

Camden Arms [Walton]: Gleaming newly refurbished free house with some good furniture inc sofa and dresser with books off main bar, good range of beers, named house wines, wide choice of food, very efficient service *(Anne Morris)*

Bwlch-y-Cibau [SJ1818]

Stumble Inn: Attractive newly refurbished inn in quiet village, comfortable and friendly lounge bar, good food inc children's here or in restaurant, friendly cat; tables in neat garden with swings and play tractor *(Mr and Mrs I Barker)*

Coedway [SJ3415]

☆ *Old Hand & Diamond* [B4393 W of Shrewsbury]: Attractive pub festooned with climbing roses and hanging baskets; roomy, clean and pleasant, with well kept Bass, Worthington BB and guest beers such as Salopian Minsterley and Woods Shropshire Lad, log fire, good reasonably priced food in dining area and restaurant, smaller back bar, friendly service, no music; tables outside *(SLC, Albert and Margaret Horton)*

Cwmdu [SO1823]

☆ *Farmers Arms* [A479 NW of Crickhowell]: Genuine friendly country local, popular with walkers, with helpful welcoming service, unpretentious partly flagstoned bar with attractive prints and stove in big stone fireplace, good range of well kept ales inc Brains and several unusual changing guest beers, good value hearty home cooking, plush restaurant, tables in garden; TV; bedrooms with good breakfast, camp site nearby – handy for pony-trekkers and Black Mountains *(BB, Jenny and Brian Seller, Dr and Mrs A K Clarke, A R Griffith)*

Derwenlas [SN7299]

☆ *Black Lion* [A487 just S of Machynlleth]: Cosy and welcoming 16th-c country pub, heavy black beams, thick walls and black timbering, attractive pictures and lion models, tartan carpet over big slate flagstones, great log fire, popular straightforward food inc vegetarian and good steak and kidney pie, well kept Tetleys, decent wines; piped music; garden up behind with play area and steps up into woods; bedrooms *(Maureen and Les Dodd, BB)*

Hay on Wye [SO2342]

☆ *Blue Boar* [Castle St/Oxford Rd]: Mix of pews and country chairs in attractively individual if sometimes smoky panelled bar, log fire, pleasant relaxed atmosphere with nice mix of customers inc children, well kept Whitbreads-related ales; separate light and airy long dining room with food counter, lots of pictures for sale, bright tablecloths and cheery décor, big sash windows, good choice of generous straightforward home cooking, decent wines, good coffees and teas *(SLC, Tim Barrow, Sue Demont, Nigel Woolliscroft, BB, Rona Murdoch)*

Rose & Crown: Partly no-smoking lounge, flagstone bar, Marstons Pedigree, Theakstons Best and Woods Shropshire Lad, limited food *(SLC)*

Three Tuns [Broad St]: Charming basic and unfussy pub with fireside settle and a few old tables and chairs in tiny dark quarry-tiled bar in one of Hay's oldest buildings, landlady knowledgeable about local history, well kept Worthington tapped from the cask, Edwardian bar fittings, lots of bric-a-brac; no food *(the Didler, JP, PP, Kevin Thorpe)*

Wheatsheaf [Lion St]: Beams strung with hops, bric-a-brac in nooks and crannies, log fire, attractively priced good home-made food, cheerful friendly staff *(John and Esther Sprinkle)*

Knighton [SO2972]

Horse & Jockey [Wilcwm Pl]: Several bars, one with log fire, good brasserie food (all day Sun), good personal service, well kept John Smiths and Tetleys, friendly atmosphere, tables in pleasant courtyard, handy for Offa's Dyke *(Richard C Morgan)*

Llanafan Fawr [SN9655]

Red Lion [B4358 SW of Llandrindod Wells]: Old whitewashed pub, bar in front hall, tables in two separate rooms (but plans for some opening up), friendly landlord, good generous food; adjoining holiday cottage, tables on roadside, very small village *(Stephanie Smith, Gareth Price)*

Llandrindod Wells [SO0561]

Metropole [Temple St (A483)]: Big Edwardian hotel's comfortable front bar with glassed-in terrace, useful for all-day snacks and a hot dish; well kept Brains SA, Flowers Original and Marstons Pedigree; bedrooms *(Joan and Michel Hooper-Immins)*

Llangammarch Wells [SN9346]

Aberceiros: Old but mildly modernised without losing character, welcoming landlord, cosy seating inc armchairs around woodburner, good food, separate dining room; excellent walking country, railway stn nearby *(John Brightley)*

Llangattock [SO2117]

☆ *Vine Tree* [signed from Crickhowell; Legar Rd]: Well run small and simple pub with emphasis on good interesting food in bar and restaurant inc local meat and veg, fresh fish from Cornwall; pleasant service, well kept Boddingtons and Wadworths 6X, coal-effect gas fire; children welcome, tables out under cocktail parasols with lovely view of medieval Usk bridge *(Pat Brown, Connie Fisher, D and N Pugsley, D and L Berry, LYM, Jackie Orme, RKP, Ian Phillips)*

Llangynidr [SO1519]

☆ *Coach & Horses* [Cwm Crawnon Rd (B4558)]: Friendly and spacious, with wide choice of generous uncomplicated food, well kept Bass and Hancocks HB, open fire, pub games, restaurant; service can slow when they're busy; children welcome, safely fenced sloping pretty

waterside garden by lock of Brecon—Monmouth Canal across road; good value bedrooms, lovely views and walks *(Mrs S Bull, Neil Graham, LYM, Jackie Orme, Robert Price, Iorwerth Davies)*

Llanwrtyd Wells [SN8746]

☆ *Neuadd Arms* [The Square]: Comfortably relaxed turkey-carpeted bar with plush seats, big log fire and local pictures, separate tiled public bar with craft tools and splendid row of old service bells, well kept reasonably priced Hancocks HB, Felinfoel Double Dragon and an interesting guest beer, lots of unusual bottled beers, popular food inc vegetarian and theme nights; beer festival Nov, various other events; bedrooms pleasant and well equipped; tables out on front terrace, engaging very small town – good walking area, mountain bike hire *(Joan and Michel Hooper-Immins, BB)*

Stonecroft [Dolecoed Rd]: Very friendly Victorian pub with wholesome simple reasonably priced food, Brains SA and Youngers Scotch (and twice-yearly beer festival), big riverside terrace with barbecues and evening events; bedrooms – dormitory type, popular with walkers *(John Brightley, G Coates)*

Llanyre [SO0462]

Bell [just off A4081]: Old but modernised inn, comfortable and well kept, doing well under current friendly management, with good changing food choice, well kept Hancocks HB, very good choice of wines by the glass; back bar with eating area, separate restaurant, locals' front bar with pool; bedrooms *(Derek and Margaret Underwood, Stephanie Smith, Gareth Price, Eddie Edwards)*

Llowes [SO1941]

☆ *Radnor Arms* [A438 Brecon—Hereford]: Well run and attractive country inn with very wide choice of good food served in local pottery from good filled rolls and inventive soups to fine restaurant-style dishes, with dozens of puddings; ancient cottagey bar with beams and stripped stone, very welcoming, with well kept Felinfoel and log fire, two small dining rooms, tables in imaginatively planted garden looking out over fields towards the Wye; cl Sun pm, Mon; at w/e it's wise to book *(Dr Oscar Puls)*

Llyswen [SO1337]

Bridge End: Friendly genuine village pub with good plain cooking, good service, Hancocks HB, decent house wine, good coffee; lovely flower tubs and window boxes *(T R Phillips, M and A Leach)*

Montgomery [SO2296]

☆ *Dragon* [Market Sq]: 17th-c timbered hotel with attractive prints and china in lively beamed bar, attentive service, well kept Woods Special and guest beer, good coffee, sensibly priced food from sandwiches to steaks inc vegetarian and children's, board games, unobtrusive piped music, restaurant; jazz most Weds, open all day; comfortable well equipped bedrooms, very quiet town below ruined Norman castle *(J H Kane, LYM, E A Froggatt)*

New Radnor [SO2160]

Eagle: Good homely atmosphere, comfortable old armchairs, ploughman's with real spiced

plum pickle and red chilli jam, well kept guest
beers, hospitable licensee *(Nigel and Caroline
Aston)*
Old Radnor [SO2559]
☆ *Harp*: Superb tranquil hilltop position, with
lovely views and good walks nearby; attentive
and hospitable new licensees, fine inglenook and
elderly seats in slate-floored lounge, stripped-
stone public bar with a smaller log fire and old-
fashioned settles, good value home cooking,
well kept Shepherd Neame Early Bird and a
guest beer, character dining room with antique
curved settle and other high-backed seats; seats
outside with play area, pretty bedrooms, good
breakfast (dogs allowed); cl weekday lunchtimes
*(Peter Gooderham, David Edwards, LYM,
Stuart Rusby, Angela and Michael Blagden)*
Pencelli [SO0925]
Royal Oak [B4558 SE of Brecon]: Two small
simple bars, welcoming service, well kept
Boddingtons and Flowers and farm cider, good
home-made food Thurs-Sat pm and w/e
lunchtimes inc half-price children's helpings, log
fires, polished flagstones, simple dining room;
charming terrace backing on to canal and fields,
lovely canal walks and handy for Taff Trail
*(Martin and Alison Stainsby, Donna and Ian
Dyer)*
Pontdolgoch [SO0193]
Talk House: Tastefully refurbished, with
friendly efficient staff, plenty of locals, good
choice of hearty food cooked by licensee *(Sarah
and Peter Gooderham, Graham and Norma
Field)*

SOUTH GLAMORGAN
Barry [ST1068]
Colcott Arms [Colcott Rd]: Good well presented
pub food in refurbished pub with better than
average wine list and good friendly staff *(Risha
Stapleton)*
Cardiff [ST1877]
Cottage [St Marys St, nr Howells]: Proper
down-to-earth pub with well kept Brains SA,
Bitter and Dark Mild and good value generous
home-cooked lunches, long bar with narrow
frontage and back eating area, lots of polished
wood and glass, good cheerful service, relaxed
friendly atmosphere (even Fri/Sat when it's
crowded; quiet other evenings), decent choice of
wines; open all day *(M Joyner, Steve Thomas,
Dave and Deborah Irving, P A Legon)*
Eli Jenkins [Bute St]: Traditional pub well
refurbished, but lots of seating inside and in
attractive courtyard, Hancock HB inc good baguettes,
well kept Hancock HB *(M Joyner)*
Halfway [Cathedral Rd]: Recently refurbished
local, popular with rugby enthusiasts; good
helpings of limited bar food, well kept Brains
SA, Bitter and Dylans; skittle alley *(Derek
Stafford)*
Hollywood Bowl [Cardiff Bay]: Part of new
leisure complex incorporating multi-screen
cinema, cafés and restaurants; primarily a
bowling alley brewing its own beers and lagers
on the premises, also very cheap but good food
– a good family place *(S Bobeldijk)*
Pantmawr [Pantmawr, handy for M4 junction

32]: Small local in 1960s estate, well kept
Hancocks HB, good garden *(I Buckmaster)*
Traders [David St]: Attractive bar with show-
business posters, busy at lunchtime for wide
choice of nicely presented food, charming
landlady; handy for International Arena
(Margaret and Bill Rogers)
Vulcan [Adam St]: Largely untouched Victorian
local with good value lunches (not Sun) in
sedate lounge with some original features inc
ornate fireplace, well kept Brains Bitter and
Dark Mild; maritime pictures in lively sawdust-
floor public bar with darts, dominoes, cards and
juke box – can be a little loud *(Pete Baker)*
Lisvane [ST1883]
Griffin: Pretty and busy, with well kept Brains
SA and a couple of interesting guest beers,
reasonably priced traditional food inc
vegetarian, chairs and settles in long beamed bar
with raised eating area, upstairs children's room;
facilities for disabled, a couple of benches out in
front, open all day *(G Coates, I J and N K
Buckmaster)*
Old Cottage [Cherry Orchard Rd, towards
Thornhill]: Big Steak pub in well converted and
decorated old barn on edge of new housing
estate, Tetleys-related ales, good value food in
bar and restaurant, friendly local bustle, no-
smoking area; quiz night Sun, open all day,
handy for Cefn Onn Park – good walks any
time of year but best in May *(I J and N K
Buckmaster)*
Llancarfan [ST0570]
☆ *Fox & Hounds* [signed off A4226; can also be
reached from A48 from Bonvilston or B4265
via Llancadle]: Popular and prettily set good
value dining pub by interesting church,
streamside tables out behind; neat comfortably
modernised open-plan bar rambling through
arches, traditional settles and plush banquettes,
coal fire, Hancocks HB and guest ale, candlelit
bistro, more sparely furnished end family room;
children welcome, darts, fruit machine,
unobtrusive piped music; open all day w/e, but
may not always open some lunchtimes out of
season *(I J and N K Buckmaster, Mr and Mrs S
Thomas, BB, M G Hart, R Michael Richards,
Dave and Deborah Irving)*
Llandaff [ST1578]
Black Lion: Friendly local with Brains ales;
lovely ancient village, superb cathedral *(I
Buckmaster)*
Morganstown [ST1281]
Ty Nant [Ty Nant Rd, not far from M4
junction 32]: Well run, busy and popular, with
traditional beamed lounge and basic bar, good
generous usual food, well kept Brains, pool
table, seats outside *(I Buckmaster)*
Morriston [SS6698]
Red Lion [Woodfield St]: Impressive décor inc
old bicycles hanging from ceiling, good range of
well prepared food, wide upon shelf of spirits,
esp whiskies, Welsh beers *(T John Nicholson)*
Rhiwbina [ST1581]
Nine Giants [Thornhill Rd]: Now doing
popular bar food; good spot with extensive
gardens – ideal for children, very busy in warm
weather *(I J and N K Buckmaster)*

Sigingstone [SS9771]
Victoria [off B4270 S of Cowbridge]: Spotless neo-Victorian dining pub useful for good value quickly served food, popular upstairs restaurant, well kept Bass (though not the sort of place to go to for just a drink), good service *(C D Jones, David and Nina Pugsley, Margaret and Bill Rogers)*
St Fagans [ST1177]
Plymouth Arms: Attractive and well run, with interesting very generous food; handy for Museum of Welsh Life *(Marlene and Jim Godfrey)*

WEST GLAMORGAN
Bishopston [SS5789]
☆ *Joiners Arms* [Bishopston Rd, just off B4436 SW of Swansea]: Thriving local, clean and welcoming, with quarry-tiled floor, traditional furnishings, local paintings and massive solid-fuel stove; good cheap simple food lunchtime and early evening inc sizzler dishes, also now their own Bishopswood beers, and well kept Theakstons and Marstons Pedigree; children welcome, open all day Thurs-Sat – the rugby club's local on Sat nights; parking can be difficult *(LYM, John and Joan Nash)*
Kittle [SS5789]
☆ *Beaufort Arms* [Pennard Rd (B4436 W of Swansea)]: Good food inc fresh fish (also sandwiches) and well kept Brains SA in attractive old pub below ancient chestnut tree, front bar with low beams, dark walls and comfortably cushioned settles, quick cheery service, small family area; TV in public bar, restaurant *(D Crowle, Ian Phillips, David and Nina Pugsley)*
Llanmadoc [SS4393]
☆ *Britannia* [the Gower, nr Whiteford Burrows – NT]: Almost as far as the roads go on the Gower peninsula, busy summer pub with tables in front, and plenty more behind in neatly kept big back garden with flowers, aviary, lots of play equipment, maybe ducks, goats and donkers – and great estuary views; popular bar food from standard menu, well kept Brains beers, gleaming copper stove in beamed and tiled bar, a few farm tools, separate restaurant, accordionist Sat night; children welcome, open all day Fri/Sat *(Mike and Mary Carter, Michael and Alison Sandy, Dr and Mrs Marriott, BB)*
Parkmill [SS5589]
Gower [A4118, just outside]: Huge chain-like dining pub open all day in summer, useful for families if passing; very busy, lots of room, standard menu, Bass and Hancocks HB, long plush lounge, no-smoking eating area up steps, walkers' bar with pool and boot store, entry dominated by games machines; lots of tables outside, play area, big car park with space for coaches, attractive wooded surroundings *(David and Nina Pugsley, BB)*
Penclawdd [SS5495]
Berthlwyd [Berthlwyd; B4295 towards Gowerton]: Fine estuary views from plush fairly modern popular open-plan local with good value food inc bargain early suppers, Bass, Worthington and Felinfoel Double Dragon, settles in restaurant end, helpful staff, seats on hillside lawn by road *(Dr Nigel and Mrs Elizabeth Holmes)*
Swansea [SS6593]
Bankers Draft [Wind St]: Wetherspoons in huge converted bank, typical beer range and value, smart plusher and quieter panelled lower-ceilinged eating area behind, decent good value food; large back terrace *(Michael and Alison Sandy)*
Builders Arms [Dyffryn Arms]: Friendly clean pub, spacious dining room and gallery, usual food inc home-cooked ham, grilled fish, well kept Buckleys and Brains beers *(Dr B and Mrs P B Baker)*
Potters Wheel [Kingsway]: Extremely long Wetherspoons pub divided by seats and pillars, more tables on raised area; wide range of bar food all day, good choice of reasonably priced beers, decent wines in big glasses *(John and Joan Nash)*
Pub on the Pond [Singleton Park, off Mumbles rd]: Greenalls Ale & Hearty good value family dining pub, packed with bric-a-brac; Greenalls Mild, Marstons Pedigree, Wadworths 6X and Worthington, SkyTV sports; pool and jenga on one side *(Michael and Alison Sandy)*
Three Crosses [SS5694]
Poundffald [NW end]: 17th-c beamed and timbered local with old tables, horse tack, armchair lounge bar, separate dining room, tasty good value food, Ansells Mild, Tetleys and Worthington, coffee inc decaf, welcoming efficient staff, quiz nights, tables on side terrace, small pretty garden *(Dr Nigel and Mrs Elizabeth Holmes)*
Upper Cwmtwrch [SN7511]
George IV [Heol Gwys]: Good atmosphere, friendly service, well kept Boddingtons and Flowers IPA, good freshly made usual food in pleasant large dining area, good house wines *(Dr H R Long, K R Harris)*
West Cross [SS6089]
West Cross [A4067 Mumbles—Swansea]: Comfortably refurbished with great view over Mumbles Bay from glassed back dining extension upstairs, good choice of usual food inc fine fish and chips, well kept Wadworths 6X, decent wines, friendly staff; just above beach, garden below by shoreside ex-railway pedestrian/cycle way *(John and Vivienne Rice, David and Nina Pugsley, Ian Phillips)*

The letters and figures after the name of each town are its Ordnance Survey map reference. 'Using the *Guide*' at the beginning of the book explains how it helps you find a pub, in road atlases or large-scale maps as well as in our own maps.

Channel Isles

Low taxes mean cheap drinks prices here, particularly on Jersey for beers produced by the local Jersey Brewery (undercutting beers from the mainland, with their high transport costs, but even these tend to be significantly cheaper here than back in England). Another difference from the mainland is that even country pubs here all tend to stay open all day – and a change in the law means that on Sundays they can now serve alcohol at least at lunchtime without the food which used to have to go with it. Pubs which have stood out this year are the Hougue du Pommier in Castel (good food), the busy Moulin de Lecq at Greve de Lecq (good atmosphere, pleasant service), the Old Portelet Inn in St Brelade (great for families, generous food), the busy Admiral in St Helier (good value food) and La Pulente on St Ouens Bay (attractive refurbishment, and a good range of fresh fish in its sea-view restaurant). With fish so abundant around these islands, it's a shame more pubs here don't give us a good choice; La Pulente sets a fine example, and is our Channel Islands Dining Pub of the Year. Three Jersey pubs to mention from the Lucky Dip section at the end of the chapter are Chambers and the Original Wine Bar (both in St Helier) and the Star & Tipsy Toad (St Peter, brewing its own real ales).

CASTEL Map 1
Hougue du Pommier 🛏

Route de Hougue du Pommier, off Route de Carteret; just inland from Cobo Bay and Grandes Rocques

Readers appreciate the good bar food at this calmly civilised and well equipped hotel, whose name (Apple Tree Hill) commemorates the fact that a cider mill stood in this pleasant spot in the 18th c. Daily specials might include cod and chips (£5.25), steak and kidney pudding (£5.95), Guernsey plaice with capers and prawn tails (£6.95) and T-bone steak (£10.25), while the bar menu includes sandwiches (from £2.40, filled french bread from £4.20), home-made soup (£2.50), potato skins with garlic cream, field mushrooms, smoked bacon and cheddar melt (£3.50), sun-dried tomato and red onion tart (£4.80), cottage pie (£5.25), chicken, bacon and mushroom casserole (£5.50), spicy Thai crab cakes (£5.95), and 8oz fillet steak (£9.95); seven wines by the glass or bottle; obliging staff. The oak-beamed bar is quite roomy, with leatherette armed chairs around wood tables, old game and sporting prints, guns, sporting trophies and so forth; the oak bar counter is attractively carved with some mellowed oak linenfold panelling. The nicest seats are perhaps those in the snug area by the big stone fireplace with its attendant bellows and copper fire-irons; part of the bar is no smoking; piped music. A conservatory with cane furniture overlooks fruit trees shading tables on the neatly trimmed lawn. There are more by the swimming pool in the sheltered walled garden, and in a shady flower-filled courtyard. Leisure facilities include a pitch-and-putt golf course and a putting green (for visitors as well as residents), and for residents there's free temporary membership to the Guernsey Indoor Green Bowling association (the stadium is next door and rated as one of the best in Europe); daily courtesy bus into town. No dogs. *(Recommended by John and Elspeth Howell, Andy and Jill Kassube)*

Free house ~ Licensee Stephen Bone ~ Bar food (not Sun evening) ~ Restaurant ~ (01481) 256531 ~ Children welcome ~ Open 12-2.30, 6-11.45; 12-2.30 Sun; closed Sun evening ~ Bedrooms: £45B/£90B

GREVE DE LECQ Map 1
Moulin de Lecq

A massive restored waterwheel still turns outside this black-shuttered old mill, with its formidable gears meshing in their stone housing behind the bar. Commandeered by the Germans during the Occupation of Jersey (who used it to generate power for their searchlight batteries in this part of the island), it is now a well liked pub with plenty of local custom and a warm and pleasant atmosphere. There's a good log fire toasting you as you come down the four steps into the cosy bar, as well as plush-cushioned black wooden seats against the white-painted walls; piped music. Decent generously served bar food might include soup (£1.75), breaded mushrooms (£2.75), ploughman's (£3.95), lasagne (£5.25), steak and kidney pudding (£5.45), half a chicken with barbecue sauce (£5.75) and daily specials such as giant yorkshire pudding filled with cumberland sausage and mash (£5.50) or Jersey scallops wrapped in bacon (£6.50); puddings such as tiramisu, apple crumble and treacle pudding (£2). Guernsey Sunbeam Bitter, Tipsy Toad Jimmy's Bitter and occasional guest beers on handpump; TV, cribbage, dominoes and piped music. The terrace has picnic-sets under cocktail parasols, and there's a good children's adventure playground. The road past here leads down to pleasant walks on one of the only north-coast beaches. *(Recommended by John Evans, George Atkinson, Jack Morley)*

Jersey ~ Manager Shaun Lynch ~ Real ale ~ Bar food (12-2.15, 6-8.30; not Sun evenings) ~ (01534) 482818 ~ Children in main bar till 9pm ~ Open 11-11; closed evening 25 Dec

KINGS MILLS Map 1
Fleur du Jardin 🍴 ♀ 🛏

Kings Mills Rd

Flowering cherries, shrubs, colourful borders, bright hanging baskets and flower barrels surround picnic-sets in the two acres of beautiful gardens at this old-fashioned inn. Inside, the cosy and sensitively refurbished rooms have low-beamed ceilings and thick granite walls, a good log fire burns in the refurbished public bar popular with locals, and there are individual country furnishings in the lounge bar on the hotel side. Bar food includes sandwiches (from £1.95, hot chargrilled steak £4.95), soup (£2.50), penne and mushrooms in ricotta sauce, steak, kidney, mushroom and ale pie, seafood pie or cumberland sausage (£4.95), red Thai vegetable curry (£5.25), half a roast chicken or fish and chips (£5.95), 8oz sirloin steak (£9.50) and various imaginative daily specials such as roast sea bream with olive oil and aubergine caviar or braised lamb shanks with haricots and a red wine jus (£8.50) and saddle of rabbit with a lobster tortellini or chicken breast with broad beans and a foie gras sauce (£9.95). Well kept Guernsey Sunbeam and Tipsy Toad Sunbeam on handpump, and maybe other guest beers, decent wines by the glass or bottle; friendly efficient service; unobtrusive piped music. There is a swimming pool for residents. *(Recommended by Gordon Neighbour, Mark Percy, Lesley Mayoh)*

Free house ~ Licensee Keith Read ~ Real ale ~ Bar food ~ Restaurant ~ (01481) 57996 ~ Children in eating area of bar and restaurant ~ Open 11-11.45; 12-3.30, 6.30-10.30 Sun ~ Bedrooms: /£82.70B

ROZEL Map 1
Rozel Bay Inn

On weekend evenings in summer they have barbecues in the attractive steeply terraced hillside gardens behind this pub, set on the edge of a sleepy little fishing village just out of sight of the sea. The bar counter and tables in the snug and cosy small dark-beamed back bar are stripped to their original light wood finish; also an open fire, old prints and local pictures on the cream walls, dark plush wall seats and stools. Leading off is a carpeted area with flowers on big solid square tables; darts, pool, cribbage and dominoes in the games room; piped music. Sensibly priced bar food includes home-made soup (£1.95), sandwiches (from £2), ploughman's (£4.75), vegetarian meals, sausage and mash, beef and Guinness pie or shepherd's pie (£5.95), and daily specials including lots of fresh seafood such as mussels or cod in beer batter (£5.95) or half lobster (from £11); puddings such as roast bananas with butterscotch sauce or sticky toffee pudding (from £3.75). Bass, Courage Directors and an occasional guest such as Marstons Pedigree under light blanket pressure; pool, cribbage, dominoes and TV. *(Recommended by Steve and Carolyn Harvey, Ewan and Moira McCall, Mr and Mrs S Davies, J R Hawkes, George Atkinson)*

Randalls ~ Lease Lorna King ~ Real ale ~ Bar food (12-2.30, 6-8) ~ Restaurant (not Sun evening) ~ (01534) 863438 ~ Children in bar till 9pm ~ Open 11-11; closed evening 25 Dec

ST AUBIN Map 1
Old Court House Inn 🏠

There are wonderful views past St Aubin's fort right across the bay to St Helier from this charming 15th-c inn. The building has a very colourful history: the front part used to be the home of a wealthy merchant, whose cellars stored privateers' plunder alongside more legitimate cargo, while the upstairs restaurant still shows signs of its time as a courtroom. The conservatory, which overlooks the tranquil harbour, now houses the Westward Bar – elegantly constructed from the actual gig of a schooner. The atmospheric main basement bar has cushioned wooden seats built against its stripped granite walls, low black beams and joists in a white ceiling, a turkey carpet and an open fire; it can get crowded and smoky at times. A dimly lantern-lit inner room has an illuminated rather brackish-looking deep well, beyond that is a spacious cellar room open in summer. Bar food includes soup (£2.50), open sandwiches (from £3.50), lasagne (£4.75), vegetable lasagne (£4.95), half a roast chicken, spare ribs and barbecue sauce or scampi (£5.50) with lots of seafood such as moules marinières (£5.75), crab salad (£5.95), six Jersey oysters (£6), Jersey plaice (£8.95), roast seabass with grilled asparagus (£14.95) and a fisherman's platter for two including whole lobster, crab, mussels and prawns (£70). At lunchtime there's a set menu (2 courses £10.50), and in the evening you can eat off the more elaborate à la carte menu throughout the pub. Well kept Marstons Pedigree and a guest such as Courage Directors on handpump; cribbage, dominoes, scrabble, chess, shut the box, piped music, and darts in winter. The small and comfortable bedrooms (some look out over the harbour) are all individually decorated and furnished, and have been refurbished since last year. Parking near the hotel can be difficult. *(Recommended by P J and J E F Caunt, Steve and Carolyn Harvey, George Atkinson, Richard and Robyn Wain)*

Free house ~ Licensee Jonty Sharp ~ Real ale ~ Bar food (not Sun evening) ~ Restaurant ~ (01534) 746433 ~ Children welcome ~ Open 11-11.30 ~ Bedrooms: £50B/£100B

ST BRELADE Map 1
Old Portelet Inn

Portelet Bay

Built as a farmhouse in 1606, this clifftop pub is festooned with flowers during the summer. It's unashamedly aimed at families and beach visitors, and ideally positioned to do so: a sheltered cove right below is reached by a long flight of steps with glorious views across Portelet (Jersey's most southerly bay) on the way down. The atmospheric low-ceilinged, beamed downstairs bar has a stone bar counter on bare oak boards and quarry tiles, a huge open fire, gas lamps, old pictures, etched glass panels from France and a nice mixture of old wooden chairs. It opens into the big timber-ceilinged family dining area, with standing timbers and plenty of highchairs. Generously served bar food includes soup (£1.60), sandwiches (from £1.70), ploughman's or nachos with chilli (£3.95), filled baked potatoes (from £3.80), burgers (from £4), spinach and ricotta cannelloni (£4.50), lasagne or chicken curry (£4.99), seafood risotto or cod and chips (£5.20), half roast duckling with orange sauce (£6.99), 8oz sirloin steak (£7.80); puddings (from £1); children's meals (including baby food), and a large range of liqueur coffees and hot chocolates. Efficient service from friendly and neatly dressed staff. Well kept Boddingtons, Theakstons and either Courage Directors or Marstons Pedigree under light blanket pressure, and reasonably priced house wine; plenty of board games in the wooden-floored loft bar. No-smoking areas, disabled and baby changing facilities, and a superior supervised indoor children's play area (entrance 50p); pool. Outside there's another play area and picnic-sets on the partly covered flower-bower terrace by a wishing well, as well as in a sizeable landscaped garden with lots of scented stocks and other flowers. *(Recommended by John Evans, Steve and Carolyn Harvey, George Atkinson)*

Randalls ~ Manager Tina Lister ~ Real ale ~ Bar food (12-2, 6-9) ~ (01534) 41899 ~ Children in eating area of bar ~ Live music Mon-Fri in summer ~ Open 10(11 Sun)-11

Old Smugglers

Ouaisne Bay; OS map reference 595476

There's a genuinely relaxed, pubby atmosphere at this building which has metamorphosed from old fishermen's cottages – through a stint as a small residential hotel until after World War II – into a popular friendly pub. It's in a pretty position on the road down to the beach, close to some attractive public gardens. Inside, thick walls, black beams, open fires, and cosy black built-in settles make up the bar. Well kept Bass and two guests such as Ringwood Best and Old Thumper on handpump; sensibly placed darts as well as cribbage and dominoes. Well liked bar food includes home-made soup (£1.95; local seafood chowder £2.75), ploughman's (£3.80), filled baked potatoes or burgers (from £4.20), oriental vegetable stir fry or steak, Guinness and mushroom pie (£4.95), grilled lamb chops with rosemary sauce (£5.20), cod in beer batter with chips (£5.65), home-made chicken kiev (£5.95), king prawns cantonese-style with sweet and sour sauce (£7.85) and fresh fish specials; puddings such as white chocolate mousse, apple pie or lemon meringue pie (£2.30); children's meals (£2.95). A room in the restaurant is no smoking. *(Recommended by P Hildick-Smith, J Gaylord, George Atkinson, Mr and Mrs S Davies)*

Free house ~ Licensee Nigel Godfrey ~ Real ale ~ Bar food (12-2, 6-9; not Sun evening Oct-Mar) ~ Restaurant ~ (01534) 41510 ~ Children in bar till 9pm ~ Open 11-11.30

ST HELIER Map 1
Admiral £

St James St

Popular for its very good value food, this impressive candlelit pub can get busy in the evenings, when it is well liked by a younger crowd. Inside, as well as dark wood panelling, attractive solid country furniture, and heavy beams – some of which are inscribed with famous quotations, there is a plethora of interesting memorabilia and curios including old telephones, a clocking-in machine, copper milk churn, enamel advertising signs (many more in the small back courtyard which also has lots of old pub signs) and an old penny 'What the Butler Saw' machine; daily papers to read. Quickly served bar food includes soup (£1.95), filled baked potatoes (from £2.75), half a spit-roast chicken or scampi, steak and kidney pie, battered cod and chips or vegetarian dish of the day (£4.50); four course Sunday lunch (£8.95). Well kept Boddingtons on handpump; dominoes, cribbage and piped music. Outside, the flagged terrace (with plastic tables) is quite a suntrap in summer. *(Recommended by Steve and Carolyn Harvey, Mr and Mrs S Davies, George Atkinson)*

Randalls ~ Manager Joanna Lopes ~ Real ale ~ Bar food (12-2, 6-8) ~ (01534) 30095 ~ Children welcome till 9pm ~ Open 11-11

Tipsy Toad Town House £

New Street

Owned by the Jersey Brewery, this attractive 1930s pub is on two floors; downstairs the traditional bar has old photographs, solid furnishings, some attractive panelling and stained glass, and heavy brass doors between its two main parts to allow in more light; there's wheelchair access and lavatories. Upstairs has at least as much space again and is very well planned with a lot of attention to detail; baby changing facilities and high chairs. Reasonably priced bar food includes soup (£1.80), lunchtime filled french bread (hot or cold from £1.85), filled baked potatoes (from £2), spaghetti bolognese (£3.75), chicken curry (£4.25), pork fillet (£4.75) and deep-fried cod or nachos with spicy beef and melted cheese (£4.95). On their à la carte menu you might find creole crab cakes or moules à la crème (£4.95), cumberland sausage (£5.25), beef burger with bacon, avocado and cheese (£5.95), various popular fajitas (including vegetarian from £6.50) and fillet steak (£10.95); lots of fresh fish and daily specials on the blackboard and children's meals (from £2); two course set lunch (£6.75). There's a no-smoking area in the restaurant. Tipsy Toad Jimmys Bitter and sound house wines; pool, fruit machine, large TV and piped music. It can get busy in the evenings. *(Recommended by Tim and Chris Ford)*

Jersey ~ Manager Denis Murphy ~ Real ale ~ Bar food ~ Restaurant (6.30-10) ~ (01534) 615000 ~ Children in restaurant and eating area of bar till 9pm ~ Live music Sun evenings in summer (maybe winter too) ~ Open 11-11; closed Good Friday and evening 25 Dec

ST JOHN Map 1
Les Fontaines
Le Grand Mourier, Route du Nord

Attractively set on the northernmost tip of the island, where the 300-feet-high granite cliffs face the distant French coast, this pub is where the locals hide out, and where you'll hear the true Jersey patois. To be sure not to miss the best part – the distinctive public bar, and particularly the unusual inglenook by the large 14th-c stone fireplace – look for the worn and unmarked door at the side of the building, or as you go down the main entry lobby towards the bigger main bar, slip through the tiny narrow door on your right. There are very heavy beams in the low dark ochre ceiling, stripped irregular red granite walls, old-fashioned red leatherette cushioned settles and solid black tables on the quarry-tiled floor, and for decoration antique prints and Staffordshire china figurines and dogs; look out for the old smoking chains and oven by the granite columns of the fireplace. The main bar is clean and carpeted, with plenty of wheelback chairs around neat dark tables, and a spiral staircase leading up to a wooden gallery under the high pine-raftered plank ceiling. Bar food includes soup (£1.65), sandwiches (from 1.70), ploughman's (from £4.60), chicken kiev (£4.60), cumberland sausage (£4.95), chicken and ham pie (£5.10), steak and mushroom pie (£5.20), battered cod (£5.60), steaks (from £7.95) and up to 10 daily specials; children's meals (£2). One large area is no smoking; dominoes, cribbage and piped music. Courage Directors under light blanket pressure. For families a particularly popular feature is the supervised play area for children, Pirate Pete's (entry £1), though children are also made welcome in the other rooms of the bar. Seats on a terrace outside, although noisy lorries from the nearby quarry can mar the atmosphere. There are good coastal walks nearby. *(Recommended by Tim and Chris Ford, George Atkinson)*

Randalls ~ Manager Sandra Marie King ~ Real ale ~ Bar food (12-2.30, 6-9) ~ Restaurant ~ (01534) 862707 ~ Children welcome ~ Open 11-11

ST OUENS BAY Map 1
La Pulente
Start of Five Mile Road; OS map reference 562488
Channel Islands Dining Pub of the Year

Just across the road from the southern end of Jersey's longest beach, this comfortably civilised pub makes a superb spot to watch the sun go down. It was totally refurbished a couple of years ago, and now has a fresh modern décor throughout. The public bar has a surfing theme with photographs and prints on the walls, while upstairs, the carpeted restaurant with ragged walls and scrubbed wood tables leads off onto a balcony, where you can enjoy a meal overlooking the bay; there are views of the sea from the restaurant, lounge and conservatory. There's a strong emphasis on fish in the upstairs restaurant, and a weekly changing menu might include marinated king prawns or pan-fried scallops meunière (£4.95), red snapper (£6.95), john dory with a red wine jus or grilled dover sole (£11.95) and seafood platter (£15.95). Other swiftly served good simple bar food includes soup (£1.50), filled french bread and baked potatoes (from £3.75), ploughman's (from £4.75), mediterranean vegetable wellington (£4.95), steak and mushroom pie (£5.50) and daily specials such as Jersey crab salad (£6.50), ostrich with a wild mushroom sauce (£8) and T-bone steak with pepper sauce (£10.50); children's meals. Well kept Bass and Courage Directors on handpump. There are wonderful walks along the miles of curving sand nearby. *(Recommended by Tim and Chris Ford, Steve and Carolyn Harvey)*

Randalls ~ Manager Harry Kasstan ~ Real ale ~ Bar food (12-2.30, 6-8) ~ Restaurant ~ (01534) 44487 ~ Children in eating area of bar and restaurant ~ Live music Weds and Sun evenings in summer ~ Open 11-11

Lucky Dip

Besides the fully inspected pubs, you might like to try these Lucky Dips recommended to us and described by readers (if you do, please send us reports):

ALDERNEY
Newtown
☆ *Harbour Lights*: Welcoming, clean and well run hotel/pub in a quieter part of this quiet island, comfortably refurbished bar with limited choice of good well presented bar food esp fresh local fish and seafood, attractive prices, well kept Guernsey Bitter; caters particularly for families; terrace in pleasant garden, bedrooms *(Mr and Mrs A Craig, Mrs Rosemary Bayliss, Donald Godden)*

GUERNSEY
St Peter Port
☆ *Taylors Bar* [The Arcade; off High St, behind Town Church]: Plush upstairs eating bar with a good range of snacky things, airy Edwardian refurbished downstairs bar with tulip-style brass lamps on the long mahogany counter, pretty Victorian tiles around the fireplace, raj fans; Guernsey Sunbeam, good choice of wines by the glass, quick service; maybe loudish piped music *(LYM, Andy and Jill Kassube, Val and Alan Green)*

JERSEY
St Helier
☆ *Chambers* [Mulcaster St]: Impressive heavy-beamed pub with well done courts theme, separate areas (one with panelling, club chairs and daily papers), imposing paintings, prints and mirrors, candlelit tables, massively long bar counter with well kept Marstons Pedigree, Theakstons XB and Old Peculier and guest beers, decent wines, good generous reasonably priced food, neat staff, separate gallery dining room; children welcome till 8, quiet and civilised at lunchtime, can be very busy evenings; live music – open till 1 am *(Jack*

Morley, Steve and Carolyn Harvey)
☆ *Original Wine Bar* [Bath St]: Informal welcoming environment, with casual décor and comfortable sofas; real ales such as Brains, Jersey Brewery, Tipsy Toad, imported Breda Dutch lager, good wines, coffees and teas, good choice of interesting lunchtime food (not Sun) inc vegetarian, friendly efficient service, relaxing cheerful atmosphere *(Steve and Carolyn Harvey, R J Watson, Basil Cheesenham)*
St Peter
☆ *Star & Tipsy Toad* [St Peters Village]: Brewpub producing Tipsy Toad, Jimmys, Horny Toad and occasional seasonal brews; basic style, with bare boards, stripped stonework, panelling, large viewing window for brewery beyond, small games room with darts, pool etc, family conservatory, bar food from sandwiches to steaks inc children's, friendly staff, disabled facilities; terrace and play area, open all day, live bands Sat (and Fri in summer) *(LYM, Richard and Robyn Wain, Steve and Carolyn Harvey)*

SARK
Dixcart: Granite hotel, originally 16th-c farm, in extensive grounds sloping down lovely wooded valley to sheltered cove; comfortable public bar with log fire, stripped vertical panelling and nautical touches, decent children's room off, reasonably priced bar food, maybe Theakstons, picnic-sets out in front yard; bedrooms comfortable and pleasantly decorated *(Val and Alan Green)*
Petit Champ: Small country hotel in a sheltered wooded valley; small bar, lounge, wide-ranging menu inc fresh lobster and crab and splendid stilton ploughman's, good value keg Guernsey Bitter, pretty garden with seats on side terrace; bedrooms *(Val and Alan Green)*

If a service charge is mentioned prominently on a menu or accommodation terms, you must pay it if service was satisfactory. If service is really bad you are legally entitled to refuse to pay some or all of the service charge as compensation for not getting the service you might reasonably have expected.

Overseas Lucky Dip

We're always interested to hear of good bars and pubs overseas – preferably really good examples of bars that visitors would find memorable, rather than transplanted 'British pubs'. We start with ones in the British Isles (but over the water), then work alphabetically through other countries. A star marks places we can be confident would deserve a main entry. Note that the strong £ currently makes the best bars in foreign capitals (often very pricy) a good deal more accessible than previously.

IRELAND

Belfast

☆ *Crown* [Gt Victoria St, opp Europa Hotel]: Bustling 19th-c gin palace with pillared entrance, opulent tiles outside and in, elaborately coloured windows, almost church-like ceiling, handsome mirrors, individual snug booths with little doors and bells for waiter service, gas lighting, mosaic floor – wonderful atmosphere, very wide range of customers (maybe inc performers in full fig from Opera House opp); good lunchtime meals inc oysters, Hilden real ale, open all day; National Trust *(Dr and Mrs A K Clarke)*

Bunratty

McNamaras [in Castle Folk Park – entry fee]: Enjoyable working pub with lunchtime food at top of 19th-c street in folk park with reconstructed old houses and other buildings, converted old house with piano and lots of bric-a-brac, good lunchtime snacks inc cheap sandwiches, wider choice evening (when entry's free – but park and castle are worth the daytime visit); Guinness and Smithwicks, children until 7pm *(GLD)*

Dublin

Brazen Head [Lower Bridge St]: Charming bar, said to be oldest here, lots of dimly lit cosy unspoilt rooms off attractive red and white tiled passage, with old beams, mirrors, old settles, open fires; lunchtime bar carvery, restaurant; peaceful courtyard, traditional music each night, main bar very busy Sun lunchtime with music too *(David Carr, C J Fletcher, Chris Raisin)*

Bruxelles [Harry St, off Grafton St]: Cosy and friendly upstairs Victorian bar with dark panelling, mirrors and outstanding Guinness; downstairs much more modern, Celtic symbols, grey/black/red décor, seats in alcoves and around central pillars, dim lighting; rock music can be very loud *(Mayur Shah, Chris Raisin)*

Davy Byrnes [Duke St, just off Grafton St]: Classic three-room pub, splendid décor with magnificent Cecil Salkeld murals, good food and stout, friendly efficient service; mentioned in *Ulysses* *(C J Fletcher)*

Doheny & Nesbitt [Lower Baggot St, by the Shelburne just below St Stephens Green]: Friendly traditional pub close to Irish Parliament, Victorian bar fittings, two rooms with marble-topped tables, wooden screens, old whiskey mirrors etc; mainly drink and conversation, but has good value Irish stew *(Chris Raisin, C J Fletcher)*

Fitzsimons [East Essex St, Temple Bar]: Very comfortable and welcoming if not genuine 'old Dublin', highly geared to tourists esp downstairs – free all-day traditional music, periodic dancers; good Guinness and bar food, friendly staff, lots of varnished wood, polished floor and bar counter *(Mayur Shah, Chris Raisin)*

John M Keating [Angel St, off O'Connell St]: Trendily decorated modern bar with unusual features – large mosaic of a phoenix, large metal spiral stair to gallery and more rooms; very welcoming, good Guinness *(Chris Raisin)*

Long Hall [South Great George St]: Victorian bar, mostly original large lounge area, can get very crowded; good Guinness *(Chris Raisin)*

McDaids [Harry St, off Grafton St]: Late 19th-c pub with traditional furnishings and character, lively atmosphere, Irish music most nights – can get busy; was haunt of Brendan Behan and Patrick Kavanagh *(C J Fletcher)*

Mercantile [Dame St, coupled with O'Briens]: One of the best, dim-lit, trendy yet friendly, several rooms on two floors, wall stools and huge barrels on bare boards, ceiling fans, primarily young couples (maybe loud rock music), lovely stairs to gallery over bar; coupled with O'Briens Bar – long side counter, raised end area, big fish tank *(Chris Raisin, Mayur Shah)*

Mulligans [Poolbeg St]: Dark polished woodwork, large Victorian mirrors, gas lighting, old theatre posters, friendly service, fine Guinness; one of the best *(C J Fletcher)*

☆ *O'Donoghues* [Merrion Row, off St Stephens Green]: Small old-fashioned Victorian bar with dark panelling, mirrors, posters and snob screens, musical instruments and other bric-a-brac on ceiling, bank-note collection behind long side counter; superb atmosphere, good friendly service even when busy, popular with musicians – maybe an impromptu riot of Celtic tunes played on anything from spoons to banjo or pipes; fine Guinness, gets packed but long-armed owner ensures quick friendly service; plainer back bar has live music too; open all day *(Mayur Shah, Chris Raisin)*

O'Neills [Suffolk St]: Large early Victorian pub, lots of dark panelling, several rooms off big bar, good lunchtime hot food bar, super thick sandwiches, good Guinness *(David and Ruth Hollands, Chris Raisin)*

Oliver St John Gogarty [Anglesea St, Temple Bar]: Large popular bare-boards bars, bric-a-brac inc bicycle above counter, good Guinness, good if not cheap food in fairly small cosy upper-floor restaurant, very friendly efficient service; live music upstairs *(Mayur Shah, David and Ruth Hollands)*

Palace [Fleet St, Temple Bar]: Splendid original Victorian bar with snob screens, rooms through etched glass doors, tiny snug, plainer back room; good Guinness *(Chris Raisin)*

Porter House [Parliament St, nr Wellington Quay]: Modern vibrant three-storey pub, lots of pine and brass for café-bar feel, brewing own Porter, Stout, Lager and usually a cask-conditioned real ale; high tables and equally high seats, excellent upstairs restaurant, live music *(Chris Raisin, C J Fletcher)*

Ryans [Park Gate St]: Beautifully fitted Victorian pub, dark mahogany around bar with partitions and old mirrors, stained-glass windows, huge mirrors, houseplants, daily papers (even in the gents'), cosy back snugs – seems little changed since 1896; good choice of fair-priced food (not Sun) in bar and restaurant, friendly atmosphere, no piped music, unobtrusive TV; seats around barrels with cocktail parasols outside *(Chris Raisin, CMW, JJW)*

Stags Head [Dame Court, off Dame St]: Imposing frontage for elegant upmarket pub with lofty main bar, lots of carved mahogany, etched mirrors, stained glass, whiskey vats, huge stag's head over marble bar, cosy leather-seat back snug with dark panelling and glass ceiling, downstairs music bar; can get very busy *(Chris Raisin, C J Fletcher)*

Temple Bar [Temple Bar]: Rambling multi-levelled, multi-roomed pub, rather bohemian, usually crowded; good Guinness; tables out in big yard *(Chris Raisin, David and Ruth Hollands)*

Toners [Lower Baggot St]: Traditional high-ceilinged Victorian pub, dark woodwork, gilded mirrors advertising old whiskeys; wooden settles and high stools in snug on left *(C J Fletcher, Chris Raisin)*

Limerick

Thady O'Neils [N18 towards Shannon]: Lots of stripped brick, plaster and tiles, areas with old-fashioned themes and bric-a-brac such as creamery, mill, station, shop, sports bar, good choice of food all day inc some unusual, children's TV room, live Irish music nightly *(CMW, JJW)*

ISLE OF MAN
Glenmaye [SC2480]
Waterfall [just off A27 3 miles S of Peel – OS

Sheet 95 map ref 236798]: Named for the waterfall nearby; very popular, warm and welcoming, with good service, good varied reasonably priced food served piping hot inc sizzlers, well kept Cains, Tetleys and sometimes local Okells ale *(Gill and Maurice McMahon)*

AUSTRALIA
Kangaroo Valley
Friendly Inn: Fascinating 19th-c building in old settlers' town, now craft shops and small eateries, fine day's drive out of Sydney which could include Pacific vistas, mountain circuit, dramatic Fitzroy Falls, bush walks, Bradman Museum at Bowral; large bar, two big eating rooms, basic wooden furniture, cheerful atmosphere, wide range of beers and interesting food inc excellent fish; traditional ironwork balcony, wide back verandah with magnificent hill views, back paddock with play area and beautiful trees; landlord ran pubs in Bristol and Thornbury *(JCW)*

St Albans
Settlers Arms: Standing back from river, tables on wide green, neat iron-posted verandah, very reasonable food, range of beers; built 1836, in settlement overlooking the MacDonald, deep in the bush, nr Old General Cemetery (remarkable historical site, some members of First Fleet buried); fine drive N of Sydney via Wisemans Ferry *(JCW)*

AUSTRIA
Vienna
Ofenloch [Kurrentgasse 8]: Fine early 18th-c pub nr where Mozart lived, five beers on tap, lots of wines and liqueurs, wide food choice, extraordinary horned man creature hanging over bar *(Jane Kingsbury)*

BELGIUM
Antwerp
Het Elfde Gebod [Torfbrug/Blauwmoezelstr]: Ivy-clad pub behind cathedral, overflowing with mix of religious statues and surreal art; good beer range inc Trappist Westmalle from altar-like bar, food inc mussels with frites and good steaks, overflow upper gallery; piped classical music *(Mark Brock)*

Bruges
Hobbit [Kemelstraat 8, SW of centre]: Cluttered bar, lively and bustling, with good choice of local beers and of whiskies, attentive staff, good generous food esp grills, also pasta and seafood, friendly English-speaking staff; candlelit tables, subdued lighting *(Nigel Wilson, Amanda Hill, David Halliwell)*

Brussels
☆ *Mort Subite* [R Montagne aux Herbes Potageres]: A local institution, under same family since 1928, long Belle Epoque room divided by two rows of pillars into nave with two rows of small polished tables and side aisles with single row, huge mirrors on all sides, leather seats, brisk uniformed waiters and waitresses scurrying from busy serving counter on right; their own Gueuze, Faro, Kriek, Peche and Framboise brewed nearby, good

straightforward food inc omelettes and croques monsieur, no piped music *(Joan and Michel Hooper-Immins)*

CANADA
Whistler
Blacks [4270 Mountain Sq, British Columbia]: Excellent atmosphere in very busy upstairs apres-ski pub nr main gondolas, spectacular view from full-length windows, Bass, John Smiths and Guinness on draught, good world-wide bottled beer range, over 20 malt whiskies, interesting good value food inc good soups with hefty sandwiches, usual good Canadian hospitality *(Val Stevenson, Rob Holmes, John and Joan Nash)*
Brewhouse: Large three-room pub brewing its own fine range of beers, real fires, huge helpings of good food – dining area opens into large restaurant with open kitchen *(Val Stevenson, Rob Holmes)*

CHINA
Beijing
Xiyuan Hotel [1 Sanlihe Rd]: Hotel bar with draught local and foreign beers, usual spirits, cocktails, French and New World wines as well as decent Chinese cabernet sauvignon; snacks *(Ian Phillips)*

CYPRUS
Evdhimou Beach
Kyrenia Beach Bar [S coast between Paphos and Limassol]: In beautiful undeveloped beach in Sovereign Base area, family run with no pretentions at Englishness; good mix of very reasonably priced Greek and English food inc fish, meat and vegetarian; tables outside and on verandah *(Brian Skelcher)*
Kathikas
Araouzos: Traditional taverna with long tables, central woodburner, still on one wall, jugs of local wine, Keo beer, olives and cheap food *(J F M and M West)*
Peyia
Kyrenia: By fountain square, excellent salads, dips and mezze, good house red and Keo beer *(J F M and M West)*

CZECH REPUBLIC
Prague
Branicky Sklipek [Vodickova 26, Nove Mesto]: Busy dining bar with Branik Pale and Dark; open all day *(the Didler)*
Bubenicku [Myslikova]: Small many-roomed local, Gambrinus beers, food all day *(the Didler)*
Budvarka [Wuchterlova 22, nr Vitezni Namesti]: Busy two-room pub nr three separate breweries, food inc local carp; open all day *(the Didler)*
Cerneho Vola [Loretanske Namesti 1]: Up steps above castle, beams, leaded lights, long dark benches or small stand-up entrance bar, good Kozel Pale and Dark 12, local snacks; can get very busy, cl 9 *(the Didler)*
Cerny Pivovar [Karlovo 15, Nove Mesto]: Stand-up café with self service, superb prices; restaurant part open from mid-morning, local

beers *(the Didler)*
Europa Café [Vaclavske Namesti, by Europa Hotel off Wenceslas Sq]: Good value food and Radegast beers from waiters and waitresses in time-warp café, small admission charge when nicely dated trio playing; open 7am-midnight *(the Didler)*
☆ *Fleku* [Kremencova 11, Nove Mesto]: Brewing its own strong flavoursome black Flekovsky Dark 13 since 1843 (some say 1499); waiters will try to sell you a schnapps with it – say Ne firmly; huge, with benches and big refectory tables in two big dark-beamed rooms – tourists on right with 10-piece oompah band, more local on left (music here too), also courtyard after courtyard; good basic food – sausages, pork, goulash with dumplings; open early morning to late night, very popular with tourists at w/e *(the Didler)*
Havrana [Halkova 6]: Pleasant bar open 24 hours (night surcharge), with Kozel beers *(the Didler)*
Houdku [Borivojovo 693, Zizkow]: Typical of this working suburb's many basic honest bars, crowded and noisy early evening, Eggenberg Pale and Dark – never an empty glass; open all day till 9 *(the Didler)*
Jama [V Jame 7, Stare Mesto]: Busy studenty local, Elvis Presley posters, Western piped music, Samson Pale 12; open till late, occasional jazz *(the Didler)*
Kocovra [Nerudova 2, Mala Strana]: Long narrow three-room pub behind big black door, quiet and relaxing; Pilsner Urquell 12 *(the Didler)*
Krale Jiriho [Liliova 10, Stare Mesto]: 13th-c stone-arched cellar bar with Hendrix and Clapton pictures, maybe loud piped music; Platen Pale and Dark, can get crowded; open 2pm-midnight *(the Didler)*
Medvidku [Na Perstyne 5, Stare Mesto]: Superb busy old bar in red light district, namesake bears etched in stone over entry, lots of copper in left bar, bigger right room more for eating, excellent Budvar Budweiser *(the Didler)*
Milosrdnych [Milosrdnych 11, Stare Mesto]: Busy three-room local nr St Agnes Convent (now an art gallery), good beers inc Pilsner Urquell, Gambrinus and maybe Primus Pale 10; open all day *(the Didler)*
Molly Malones [Obecniho Dvora 4]: The best of Prague's Irish-theme pubs, rickety furniture on bare boards, Guinness, whiskeys, Irish stews or breakfast etc, also good choice of Czech beers, tea, coffee, fresh orange juice, daily papers, even a real fire; open all day till late, live Irish music Sun night *(the Didler)*
Na Kampe [Na Kampe 15]: Ancient tiled-floor bar in nice spot below Charles Bridge, very popular and friendly, scrubbed furniture, Gambrinus Dark and Pale, excellent food – try skvarky (pork cracklings); open all day *(the Didler)*
Nadrazni Pivnice [Pikovicka 2, Branik]: Very basic early-hours station bar with very cheap beer from nearby Branik Brewery, breakfast dumplings, live music Weds afternoon *(the Didler)*

Novomestsky Pivovar [Vodickova 20, Nove Mesto]: Fine brewpub opened 1994 in unlikely spot off shopping arcade, small long dark bar with copper vessels producing unfiltered Novomestsky Pale, restaurant down steps; open all day *(the Didler)*

Pinkasu [Nove Mesto]: Historic beer hall with white-coated waiters serving armfuls of luscious beers – esp Pilsner Urquell, others constantly changing; low prices, good food, also small back bar and upstairs drinking room; open all day *(the Didler)*

Radegast Pivnice [Templova, Stare Mesto]: Cheap Radegast Pale 10 and 12, excellent value food all day, service quick even when very busy in this low narrow beer hall *(the Didler)*

Snedeneho [1st left over Charles Bridge]: Tiny bar, quiet and friendly, with Budvar Pale and Purkmistr Dark and Pale, lots of old photographs, old record player in window; downstairs restaurant *(the Didler)*

Staropramenu [Nadrazni 102, Smichov]: Tap for nearby Staropramen Brewery, has even their rare Dark; small no-nonsense stand-up bar, or waiter-service dining room with excellent very cheap meat and dumpling dishes; open all day, cl till 3 w/e *(the Didler)*

Svateho Tomase [Letenska 12]: Fascinating arched cellars of ancient Augustine monastic building, very popular with tourists; great beer range inc Budvar, Ferdinand, Krusovice and Radegast, superb menu; not cheap; maybe concerts in adjoining gardens, open all day *(the Didler)*

Vahy [Nadrazni 88, Smichov]: Nice location, good food, Gambrinus Pale; open all day from 6am *(the Didler)*

Zlateho Tygra [Husova 11, Stare Mesto]: Sometimes a queue even before 3pm opening, and no standing allowed, but worth the wait (don't be put off by Reserved signs as the seats aren't usually being used till later); 13th-c cellars with white-coated waiters serving superb Pilsner Urquell 12 and eponymous Golden Tiger *(the Didler)*

FALKLAND ISLANDS
Port Stanley

Denos: Good atmosphere, very popular with cruise ship crew *(John and Enid Morris)*

FRANCE
Antibes

La Tour International [6 Cours Massena, Marche Provencal]: German and Belgian beers, food esp fish and chips, barbecued spare ribs and Texas burger, multilingual staff, jazz; owner cooks, plays piano after 10.30 *(Barry Adams)*

Avorlez

Bar Travaillon [Promenade du Festival]: Dutch, German and French lagers on tap, numerous bottled beers, Belgian and British bar snacks; gets very busy evening *(Ian Phillips)*

Chamonix

Queen Vic: Tasteful re-creation of Victorian pub, three levels inc large bar and pool room, Charles Wells beers inc Bombardier *(Val Stevenson, Rob Holmes)*

Coquelles

Moulin a Biere [1001 Bvd du Kent, Cité Europe]: Single French brew-pub among the faux-British pubs around Cité Europe; their own Blonde, Blanche, Brune and Ambree, wide choice of quick decent food; most staff speak some English *(Joan and Michel Hooper-Immins)*

Thonon Les Bains

Auberge d'Anthy [Anthy sur Leman]: 7 am till late, locals playing cards, drinking a small beer or white wine, buying papers, bread, tobacco; wide range of Swiss and French local wines, restaurant specialising in local lake fish inc pike, family raise own lamb; good place to stay, summer or snow *(Ian Phillips)*

GERMANY
Munich

Altes Hackerhaus [Sendlinger Str]: Sedate and not one of the cheapest, but good value delicious traditional food, Hacker-Pschorr beers, alcoves, attractive Tiffany-style lanterns, tables outside; very Bavarian staff – helps if you speak German *(Tim Barrow, Sue Demont)*

Augustinerbrau [Neuhauser Str]: Classic beer hall with ancient rickety tables, costumed staff, delicious Augustiner beer, good value hearty food; tables out in pedestrianised street *(Tim Barrow, Sue Demont)*

Hirschgarten [Hirschgartenallee]: Huge attractive beer garden under lime trees nr Nymphenburg Castle, good beers, very good cheap food – rather lighter than usual *(Tim Barrow, Sue Demont)*

Hundskugel [Hotterstrasse]: 15th-c, Munich's oldest, long dark trestle tables, traditional blue and white decorations and photographs in classic whitewashed room, delightful attentive staff, some emphasis on beer, also good range of food and interesting German wines *(Tim Barrow, Sue Demont)*

Lowenbraukeller [Nymphenburger Str]: Lowenbrau flagship, with their beers, good value hearty Bavarian food in rustic bar, very cosy and evocative; large beer garden *(Tim Barrow, Sue Demont)*

Nurnburger Bratwurst-Glockl [Frauenplatz]: Dark and atmospheric, with good range of local beers, good value hearty Bavarian food, cheerfull traditionally dressed staff, lively outdoor area in pedestrianised part next to cathedral *(Tim Barrow, Sue Demont)*

Weisses Brauhaus [Im Tal]: Schneider brewery flagship, fairly basic but friendly and lively; good Weissbier *(Tim Barrow, Sue Demont)*

Passau

Heilig Geister Stift Schenke [Heiliggeistgasse 4]: Very interesting old Bavarian pub with own vineyards, wide choice of beers inc one traditionally brewed for the bishop and church, beer mug collection, stained-glass windows; good local cooking *(Jane Kingsbury)*

HONG KONG
Causeway Bay

Brewers Tap [Gloucester Rd]: Nr Victoria Pk, with good range of UK kegs and lagers (some lunchtime discounts), good food choice in bar

and restaurant, happy hour 4-9 *(Alan Bowker)*
Dickens Bar [Excelsior Hotel]: Sports bar with
huge wide-ranging show of memorabilia, live
sports on big screens and other monitors
(Carlsberg discount during late-night FA League
matches), Tetleys keg and changing British
bottled beers *(Alan Bowker)*

ITALY
Florence
Bar La Ribotta [Borgo degli Albizi]: Wide range
of draught beers, simple good food, relaxed
atmosphere, good mix from students to older
people; stays open late *(Tim Barrow, Sue
Demont)*
Fratellini [Via dei Cimatori]: More hole in the
wall than bar, about 70 wines by the glass,
great choice of interesting sandwiches such as
salami with artichoke heart *(Tim Barrow, Sue
Demont)*
Venice
Caravella [Calle Largo XXII, Marco 2397]:
Stylish panelled bar attached to hotel and
expensive intimate seafood restaurant; good
choice of cocktails, good value local sparkling
wine, generous bar nibbles, marine theme *(Val
Stevenson, Rob Holmes)*
Harrys Bar [Calle Valleresso]: Legendary bar,
upmarket and relaxing, fantastic spot by
entrance to Grand Canal (Onassis used to park
his huge yacht outside), wonderful cocktails inc
their famous Bellini (fresh peach juice and
champagne), good spirits range, great value
local sparkling wine; happy hour from 5 *(Val
Stevenson, Rob Holmes)*

MADEIRA
Funchal
Red Lion [Rua do Favila; off main rd W, just
before Reids – on left, coming from town]: Not
the fake-English pub the name suggests, but in
fact a pleasant restaurant and bar, doing good
reasonably priced food esp espada (scabbard
fish) and espatada (skewered beef); friendly
attentive English-speaking service, local Coral
beer, excellent wine choice, not expensive;
children welcome, handy for hotel quarter and
Quinta do Magnolia gardens; open-air tables
(Joanne Morris, George Atkinson)

MAJORCA
Cala D'Or
Hostal Cala Llonga [Carrer d'en Rito 12]:
Exquisitely furnished (remaining stock of
owner's former antique shop), lots of marble
busts, wonderful paintings, oriental rugs, objets,
extravagant flower arrangements, candles
everywhere, glossy magazines, colourful
lanterns; good choice of drinks inc remarkable
range of Spanish brandies, coffee in antique
silver and Wedgwood bone china (with
Bendicks mint), well reproduced opera or jazz (if
landlady not playing operetta on the corner
grand piano); terrace with pretty balcony
overlooking marina, bedrooms and a small s/c
flat *(Susan and John Douglas)*

MONACO
Monte Carlo
Sparco Cafe [Galerie Charles III]: A must for
motor-racing fans, everything made by Sparco,
even a real racing car, and five red lights go off
as you enter; good food, reasonable prices for
Monaco *(JM, PM)*
Tip Top Bar [Ave des Speluges]: Rough-and-
ready hole-in-the-wall bar used by race teams, a
legend; good value simple food at back *(JM, PM)*

NETHERLANDS
Amsterdam
Maximiliaan [Kloveniersburgwal]: Brewpub
with café tables and chairs on bare boards, good
meals and snacks, seven beers piped direct from
the brewery with its traditional copper
equipment – more tables there, with a tiled-floor
tasting room and tours available; plenty of
atmosphere esp evening, mural on stairs to
gallery showing lots of local characters *(Jenny
and Roger Huggins)*

NEW ZEALAND
Christchurch
Oxford on the Avon [opp Victoria Park]: Busy
bar and cafeteria, huge range of excellent value
straightforward food from breakfast on inc
lovely carvery lamb, good range of nicely served
local beers, decent wine by the glass, friendly
helpful service, quite a pub-like atmosphere;
tables out by the river with evening gas heaters
(Mr and Mrs A Albert, Tony and Shirley Albert)
Dunedin
Albert Arms [George St/London St]: English-
style pub furniture inc high-backed booths, very
friendly service, good range of well presented
local beers, hearty cheap pub food inc seafood
and steaks – very popular with families; big
screen TV can be obtrusive (esp when England
is losing) *(Tony and Shirley Albert)*
Geraldine
Village Inn: Popular modern pub with good
range of local beers, back eating area with
outside tables and good food inc steaks and
Pacific Rim seafood *(Tony and Shirley Albert)*
Keri-Keri
Homestead [Homestead Rd]: Huge modern
family dining pub, very popular w/e, with good
beer range and very reasonably priced good
buffet, seafood and steaks, friendly service,
tables outside *(Tony and Shirley Albert)*
Oamaru
Last Post [Thames St]: Locally very popular for
good beer range and reasonably priced food in
bar and restaurant; very friendly *(Tony and
Shirley Albert)*

NORTH CYPRUS
Kyrenia
Harbour Club [Mersin; harbour]: Good bars on
two floors, good local beer and Turkish wines,
great evening atmosphere at verandah tables
overlooking harbour, more by harbourside;
good service, English-educated manager;
attached restaurant, French upstairs, Turkish
down *(Derek Stafford)*

OMAN
Muscat
Al Ghazal [Intercontinental Hotel]: Terrific atmosphere, two pool tables, lots of little booths, Guinness and various keg beers, drinkable wines, long early-evening happy hour, good friendly service, plenty of happy locals *(Mike and Karen England)*

S AFRICA
Stellenbosch
Terrace [Alexander Rd, opp Woolworths]: Overlooking church and green, with lots of tables and benches built into stoep to watch world go by; several local lagers on tap, maybe TV sports – popular with university students and their parents *(anon)*

SRI LANKA
Kandy
Pub Royale [Queens Hotel, opp the artificial lake]: Spacious colonial-style sanctuary from the steamy streets, with magnificent bar, period ceiling fans, huge mirrors and traditional carved furniture, ice-cold local Three Coins pilsner and Lion lager *(Amanda Hill, David Halliwell)*

SWEDEN
Stockholm
Soldaten Svejk [Istgotagatan/Folkungatan]: Friendly but busy Czech bar with good choice of well kept, well served Czech beers on draught, simple pleasant surroundings, home-made food, seats outside; open 5-midnight Sun-Thurs, till 1am Fri/Sat *(Richard Butler)*

SWITZERLAND
Les Pallots
Rosalys [Lac des Joncs]: Bar/restaurant overlooking tiny fairy lake, good local food, Cardinal on draught, bottled foreign beers; cheery skiing place in winter, lovely forest walks summer *(Ian Phillips)*

TENERIFE
Puerto De La Cruz
Molly Malone [harbour]: Irish-theme bar, cl lunchtime, with usual Guinness etc, also much cheaper local beers; very friendly barman/entertainer – a real good sing-along *(Phil and Anne Smithson)*

THAILAND
Bangkok
O'Reillys [Silom Rd]: You've guessed – yet another Irish pub, here of all places; wide food choice, lively atmosphere; open 11 till late *(Bill and Margaret Rogers)*

USA
Birmingham
Lou's [726 29th St South]: Liquor store with every drink imaginable, tables and chairs presided over by friendly and amusing character landlord, happy welcoming staff, very varied customers, good draught beers, good wines *(Simon Keymer, Tannahill Glen)*

Boston
Brew Moon [theatre district]: One of many brewpubs here; very good Porter, food very popular *(Bob and Marg Griffiths)*
Commonwealth Brewing Co [138 Portland St, nr North Stn]: Bare wood and gleaming copper for the counter of the pillared island bar, and no less than five plump old brewing kettles (they still use the one in the window to brew); ten largely British-style beers inc seasonal ales (served at British temperatures, too), one a cold proper lager; can see and tour downstairs brewery; food inc nachos, ribs, fish and chips, very friendly staff; can be very busy w/e *(Mike Gorton)*
Cleveland
Cleveland Chophouse [824 W St Clair]: Downtown bar/restaurant with view of own microbrewery producing good Pilsner, American Pale Ale, Nut Brown Ale and Irish Stout, wide choice of good value food inc plenty of vegetarian; stylish décor in converted warehouse, piped jazz and swing *(Amanda Hill, David Halliwell)*
New York
Barrow Street Ale House [Barrow St]: Busy local with good beer choice inc Black Star Golden Lager *(the Didler)*
Brewskys [41 E 7th St]: Busy, with good beer choice, good food *(the Didler)*
Broome Street Bar [363 W Broadway]: Busy local with good beer range inc Brooklyn Pennant PA *(the Didler)*
Chelsea Brewing Co [Pier 59, Chelsea Piers]: Large friendly waterside brewpub, about six on draught inc Checker Cab Blonde and Sunset Red; restaurant *(the Didler)*
Chelsea Commons [242 10th Ave/W 24th St]: Small very friendly local with great food, four beers inc Pete's Wicked, garden *(the Didler)*
Chumleys [86 Bedford St, between Grove and Barrow Sts]: Great atmosphere, real fire, excellent beer choice, good food *(the Didler)*
Commonwealth Brewing Co [10 Rockefeller Plaza]: Large, very clean and comfortable, massive visible microbrewery producing excellent beers such as Gotham City Gold; excellent food *(the Didler)*
DBA [41 1st Ave, between E 2nd and 3rd Sts]: Even handpumped English ales, also a dozen kegs and 60 bottled beers in excellent narrow dark busy bar *(the Didler)*
Fraunces [Pearl St/Broad St]: Vast array of stuffed animals in very dim-lit comfortable bar, good beer choice inc Robert Norden Dark, good restaurant *(the Didler)*
Greenwich Brewing Co [418 6th Ave]: Roomy alehouse with fine range of local microbrews, superb food range all day *(the Didler)*
Heartland Brewery [35 Union Sq W]: Very friendly, cosy and comfortable, brewing its own India PA, Red Rooster and Harvest wheat beer; excellent food choice *(the Didler)*
Jekyll & Hyde [91 7th Ave S, between Barrow and Grove Sts]: Old Jekyll & Hyde silent movies in dark basic bar with lots of novelty hanging bric-a-brac, good beers, nice food; lavatories hidden through secret bookcase *(the Didler)*

Jeremys [254 Front St]: Large friendly concrete-floor warehouse-style bar, lots of hanging bric-a-brac from hundreds of bras to a bicycle, good beer choice, very good juke box *(the Didler)*

Manhattan Brewing Co [40 Thompson St/Spring St]: Spacious sawdust-floored beer hall with copper-topped tables, live music w/e, and own-brewed City Light, Royal Amber, Rough Draft, Tailspin Brown and bottled Manhattan Gold lager; friendly service, bar snacks, smart restaurant *(Joel Dobris)*

☆ *McSorleys* [15 East 7th St, between 2nd and 3rd Aves]: Oldest Irish bar in town, much quieter and altogether more genuine than most, really original, almost unchanged since 1854 establishment, lots of dark wood, sawdust on old-fashioned concrete floor, close-set chairs around nicely worn pub tables, walls packed with old photographs and framed news clippings, interesting décor (inc model steam train around picture rail), plenty of unusual beers; one reader has been coming here for over 50 years *(the Didler, John Roue, David Carr, Eddie Edwards)*

☆ *North Star* [93 South St Seaport]: Good imitation two-room English pub, busy and lively, with dark green lincrusta ceiling, wall mirrors, oak furniture, handpumps for the Bass, Boddingtons and Fullers ESB, good choice of English bottled beers and Scotch malt whiskies, good shepherd's pie, steak and kidney pie, fish and chips, bangers and mash, obliging friendly staff; attractive pedestrianised location in group of restored warehouses and quays with a couple of full-rigged ships as background *(Graham Reeve, the Didler, Eddie Edwards)*

Olde Stock & Tankard [3rd Ave, between 38th and 39th Sts]: Popular, with good beer and food choice *(the Didler)*

Olde Tripple [263 W 54th St, between Broadway and 8th Ave]: Basic Irish bar with good cheap food lunchtime and early evening, good beers inc Petes Seasonal *(the Didler)*

P J Clarkes [915 3rd Ave, between E 55th and 56th Sts]: Classic dark panelled alehouse (familiar from film *The Lost Weekend*), several good beers inc superb Sierra Nevada PA, good back restaurant *(the Didler)*

Peculiar Pub [145 Bleeker St, between La Guardia and Thompson Sts]: Around 300 world beers inc good choice of Belgians on tap in busy local; good juke box *(the Didler)*

Slaughtered Lamb [182 W 4th St]: Very welcoming long dark bar, beers inc Full Moon *(the Didler)*

Times Square Brewery [160 W 42nd St]: Bustling circular bar with visible microbrewery producing good beers inc Times Square PA, Bock, Pilsner and Highlands 60/- *(the Didler)*

Typhoon Brewery [22 E 54th St]: Large dark brewpub with handsome stainless equipment producing fabulous beers inc Golden and very strong Wee Heavy; free bar nibbles, very friendly atmosphere, upstairs restaurant; cl Sun *(the Didler)*

Village Idiot [355 W 14th St, 9th Ave]: Big basic beer hall with four beers on tap inc excellent Hefe Weizen, landlord Tommy eats beer cans and glasses, superb country juke box, great barmaids; can buy goldfish to feed to the turtles *(the Didler)*

Waterfront [540 2nd Ave]: Great beer choice inc Brooklyn Chocolate Stout, good menu, comfortable *(the Didler)*

West Side Brewing Co [Amsterdam Ave/West 79th]: Visibly brews its own good beer range inc Blonde, Holiday and Porter; good food choice all day *(the Didler)*

White Horse [567 Hudson/W 11th St]: Classic unchanging bare-boards timber-framed bar built 1880, where Dylan Thomas drank his last beer; good food, excellent juke box *(John Roue, the Didler, David Carr)*

Red Bank

Basil Ts [183 Riverside Ave, New Jersey]: Red Bank's first brewpub, multiple brew tanks and barrels out front, at least five handcrafted pale to dark beers, sampler tray available; Italian grill *(RBPC)*

Sals [141 Shrewsbury Ave]: Oldest tavern in town, historic local pictures, old dark wood and brass bar serving new locally brewed Red Bank Ale, light or dark *(RBPC)*

Salt Lake City

Red Rock Brewing Co [254 South 200 West]: Wonderful choice of beers from European-style ones to Mormon fruit beers, real buzz, good food and friendly staff in modern warehouse-style pub and restaurant, free parking *(Jane Kingsbury)*

San Francisco

Gold Dust Lounge [Powell/Geary]: Great jazz bar, local microbrews as well as Samuel Adams etc, showy cocktail shaking – and as with all California bars now, no smoking *(Rachael and Mark Baynham)*

Pig & Whistle [Geary/Wood St]: English pub run by ex-pats, wide choice of kegs inc imports such as Bass, Fullers and Newcastle Brown alongside local microbrews, big helpings of inexpensive pub food (even Heinz baked beans) till 10, darts, pool, pinball and board games; comfortable bar chairs and table seating, young lively very friendly customers *(Robert Barker)*

Steelhead Brewing Co [353 Jefferson]: On Fishermans Wharf (two hours' free parking for customers), with view behind glass of microbrewery producing changing range of beers from stout to wheat beer, inc some cask-conditioned versions on handpump such as excellent dry-hopped Bombay Bomber; also other draught and bottled beers; happy relaxing atmosphere mingling sea air with hops; another branch at Burlingame Station *(Rachael and Mark Baynham)*

Stowe

Shed [Mountain Rd, Vermont]: Very atmospheric, done out like a ranch house, brewing its own good beers, five or six from light gold IPA to dark heavy Bitter; substantial reasonably priced meals, also large popular restaurant *(Mike Gorton)*

Special Interest Lists

Pubs with Good Gardens

The pubs listed here have bigger or more beautiful gardens, grounds or terraces than are usual for their areas. Note that in a town or city this might be very much more modest than the sort of garden that would deserve a listing in the countryside.

Bedfordshire
Milton Bryan, Red Lion
Ridgmont, Rose & Crown
Riseley, Fox & Hounds

Berkshire
Aldworth, Bell
Hamstead Marshall, White Hart
Holyport, Belgian Arms
Hurley, Dew Drop
Marsh Benham, Water Rat
West Ilsley, Harrow
Winterbourne, Winterbourne Arms

Buckinghamshire
Amersham, Queens Head
Bledlow, Lions of Bledlow
Bolter End, Peacock
Fawley, Walnut Tree
Hambleden, Stag & Huntsman
Little Horwood, Shoulder of Mutton
Northend, White Hart
Skirmett, Frog
Waddesdon, Five Arrows
West Wycombe, George & Dragon

Cambridgeshire
Fowlmere, Chequers
Heydon, King William IV
Madingley, Three Horseshoes
Swavesey, Trinity Foot
Wansford, Haycock

Channel Islands
Castel, Hougue du Pommier
Kings Mills, Fleur du Jardin
Rozel, Rozel Bay Inn

Cheshire
Aldford, Grosvenor Arms
Bunbury, Dysart Arms
Faddiley, Thatch
Lower Peover, Bells of Peover
Macclesfield, Sutton Hall Hotel
Weston, White Lion
Whiteley Green, Windmill

Cornwall
Helford, Shipwrights Arms
Philleigh, Roseland
St Agnes, Turks Head
St Ewe, Crown
St Kew, St Kew Inn
St Mawgan, Falcon
Trematon, Crooked Inn
Tresco, New Inn

Cumbria
Barbon, Barbon Inn
Bassenthwaite Lake, Pheasant
Bouth, White Hart
Eskdale Green, Bower House

Derbyshire
Birch Vale, Waltzing Weasel
Buxton, Bull i' th' Thorn
Melbourne, John Thompson
Woolley Moor, White Horse

Devon
Avonwick, Avon
Berrynarbor, Olde Globe
Broadhembury, Drewe Arms
Clyst Hydon, Five Bells
Cornworthy, Hunters Lodge
Dartington, Cott
Exeter, Imperial
Exminster, Turf Hotel
Haytor Vale, Rock
Kingskerswell, Bickley Mill
Lower Ashton, Manor Inn
Lydford, Castle Inn
Sidford, Blue Ball
South Zeal, Oxenham Arms
Westleigh, Westleigh Inn

Dorset
Christchurch, Fishermans Haunt
Corfe Castle, Fox
Kingston, Scott Arms
Marshwood, Bottle
Nettlecombe, Marquis of Lorne
Osmington Mills, Smugglers
Plush, Brace of Pheasants
Shave Cross, Shave Cross Inn

Essex
Castle Hedingham, Bell
Chappel, Swan
Coggeshall, Compasses
Great Yeldham, White Hart
Hastingwood, Rainbow & Dove
High Ongar, Wheatsheaf
Mill Green, Viper
Stock, Hoop
Toot Hill, Green Man

Wendens Ambo, Bell
Woodham Walter, Cats

Gloucestershire
Amberley, Black Horse
Bibury, Catherine Wheel
Blaisdon, Red Hart
Ewen, Wild Duck
Great Rissington, Lamb
Greet, Harvest Home
Gretton, Royal Oak
Kilkenny, Kilkeney Inn
Minchinhampton, Old Lodge
Nailsworth, Egypt Mill
North Nibley, New Inn
Oddington, Horse & Groom
Old Sodbury, Dog
Redbrook, Boat
Tewkesbury, Olde Black Bear
Withington, Mill Inn

Hampshire
Alresford, Globe
Bramdean, Fox
Longparish, Plough
North Gorley, Royal Oak
Owslebury, Ship
Petersfield, White Horse
Steep, Harrow
Tichborne, Tichborne Arms
Whitsbury, Cartwheel
Woodgreen, Horse & Groom

Herefordshire
Aymestrey, Riverside Inn
Much Marcle, Slip Tavern
Sellack, Lough Pool
Ullingswick, Three Crowns
Woolhope, Butchers Arms

Hertfordshire
Ayot St Lawrence, Brocket Arms
Potters Crouch, Holly Bush
Walkern, White Lion

Isle of Wight
Chale, Clarendon (Wight Mouse)
Shorwell, Crown

Kent
Biddenden, Three Chimneys
Bough Beech, Wheatsheaf
Boyden Gate, Gate Inn
Chiddingstone, Castle
Dargate, Dove
Fordcombe, Chafford Arms
Groombridge, Crown
Ickham, Duke William
Linton, Bull
Newnham, George
Penshurst, Bottle House

Ringlestone, Ringlestone
Selling, Rose & Crown
Smarden, Bell
Toys Hill, Fox & Hounds
Ulcombe, Pepper Box

Lancashire
Darwen, Old Rosins
Newton, Parkers Arms
Whitewell, Inn at Whitewell

Leicestershire
Braunston, Old Plough
Exton, Fox & Hounds
Medbourne, Nevill Arms
Old Dalby, Crown

Lincolnshire
Newton, Red Lion
Stamford, George of Stamford

London
East London, Prospect of Whitby
North London, Spaniards Inn, Waterside
South London, Crown & Greyhound, Ship
West London, Dove, White Swan, Windsor Castle

Norfolk
Great Bircham, Kings Head
Sculthorpe, Sculthorpe Mill
Stow Bardolph, Hare Arms
Titchwell, Manor Hotel
Woodbastwick, Fur & Feather

Northamptonshire
East Haddon, Red Lion
Eastcote, Eastcote Arms
Thorpe Mandeville, Three Conies
Wadenhoe, Kings Head

Northumbria
Belford, Blue Bell
Blanchland, Lord Crewe Arms
Diptonmill, Dipton Mill Inn
Greta Bridge, Morritt Arms
Thropton, Three Wheat Heads

Nottinghamshire
Caunton, Caunton Beck
Colston Bassett, Martins Arms
Kimberley, Nelson & Railway
Upton, French Horn

Oxfordshire
Binfield Heath, Bottle & Glass
Broadwell, Five Bells
Burford, Lamb
Chalgrove, Red Lion
Chinnor, Sir Charles Napier
Clifton, Duke of Cumberlands Head

Finstock, Plough
Fyfield, White Hart
Hook Norton, Gate Hangs High, Pear Tree
Kelmscot, Plough
Maidensgrove, Five Horseshoes
South Stoke, Perch & Pike
Stanton St John, Star
Tadpole Bridge, Trout
Watlington, Chequers
Westcott Barton, Fox
Woodstock, Feathers

Scotland
Ardfern, Galley of Lorne
Arduaine, Loch Melfort Hotel
Creebridge, Creebridge House Hotel
Edinburgh, Starbank, Gifford, Tweeddale Arms
Glenelg, Glenelg Inn
Haddington, Waterside
Kilmahog, Lade
Pitlochry, Killiecrankie Hotel
Skeabost, Skeabost House Hotel
Thornhill, Lion & Unicorn

Shropshire
Bishops Castle, Three Tuns
Cressage, Cholmondeley Riverside
Hopton Wafers, Crown
Norton, Hundred House

Somerset
Ashcott, Ashcott Inn
Bristol, Highbury Vaults
Combe Hay, Wheatsheaf
Compton Martin, Ring o' Bells
Freshford, Inn at Freshford
Litton, Kings Arms
Monksilver, Notley Arms
South Stoke, Pack Horse

Staffordshire
Acton Trussell, Moat House
Onecote, Jervis Arms
Salt, Holly Bush

Suffolk
Bildeston, Crown
Brandeston, Queens Head
Dennington, Queens Head
Lavenham, Angel, Swan
Laxfield, Kings Head
Rede, Plough
Walberswick, Bell

Surrey
Coldharbour, Plough
Compton, Withies
Gomshall, Compasses
Hascombe, White Horse
Mickleham, King William IV
Newdigate, Surrey Oaks
Pirbright, Royal Oak
Warlingham, White Lion
Wotton, Wotton Hatch

Sussex
Amberley, Black Horse
Ashurst, Fountain
Barcombe, Anchor
Berwick, Cricketers Arms
Blackboys, Blackboys Inn
Byworth, Black Horse
Coolham, George & Dragon
Elsted, Three Horseshoes
Firle, Ram
Fletching, Griffin
Hammerpot, Woodmans Arms
Heathfield, Star
Kirdford, Half Moon
Oving, Gribble Inn
Rushlake Green, Horse & Groom
Rye, Ypres Castle
Scaynes Hill, Sloop
Seaford, Golden Galleon
Wineham, Royal Oak

Wales
Aberystwyth, Halfway Inn
Bodfari, Dinorben Arms
Crickhowell, Bear, Nantyffin Cider Mill
Llandrindod Wells, Llanerch
Llanfrynach, White Swan
Llangedwyn, Green
Llwyndafydd, Crown
Presteigne, Radnorshire Arms
St Hilary, Bush
Stackpole, Armstrong Arms
Tyn Y Groes, Groes

Warwickshire
Edge Hill, Castle
Ettington, Chequers
Ilmington, Howard Arms
Lowsonford, Fleur de Lys

Wiltshire
Alvediston, Crown
Bradford-on-Avon, Cross Guns
Brinkworth, Three Crowns
Chicksgrove, Compasses
Ebbesbourne Wake, Horseshoe
Lacock, George, Rising Sun
Little Cheverell, Owl
Lower Woodford, Wheatsheaf
Netherhampton, Victoria & Albert
North Newnton, Woodbridge
Norton, Vine Tree
Salisbury, New Inn
Seend, Barge
Woodborough, Seven Stars

Worcestershire
Bretforton, Fleece
Welland, Anchor

Yorkshire
East Witton, Blue Lion
Egton Bridge, Horse Shoe
Heath, Kings Arms

Osmotherley, Three Tuns
Scawton, Hare
Stutton, Hare & Hounds
Sutton upon Derwent, St
  Vincent Arms
Threshfield, Old Hall Inn

Waterside Pubs
*The pubs listed here are right
beside the sea, a sizeable
river, canal, lake or loch that
contributes significantly to
their attraction.*

Bedfordshire
Linslade, Globe
Odell, Bell

Berkshire
Great Shefford, Swan

Cambridgeshire
Cambridge, Anchor
Sutton Gault, Anchor
Wansford, Haycock

Channel Islands
St Aubin, Old Court House
  Inn
St Ouens Bay, La Pulente

Cheshire
Chester, Old Harkers Arms
Wrenbury, Dusty Miller

Cornwall
Bodinnick, Old Ferry
Cremyll, Edgcumbe Arms
Falmouth, Quayside Inn &
  Old Ale House
Helford, Shipwrights Arms
Mousehole, Ship
Mylor Bridge, Pandora
Polkerris, Rashleigh
Polruan, Lugger
Port Isaac, Port Gaverne
  Hotel
Porthallow, Five Pilchards
Porthleven, Ship
St Agnes, Turks Head
St Ives, Sloop
Trebarwith, Port William
Tresco, New Inn

Cumbria
Ulverston, Bay Horse

Derbyshire
Shardlow, Old Crown

Devon
Ashprington, Watermans
  Arms
Avonwick, Avon
Dartmouth, Royal Castle
  Hotel
Exeter, Double Locks
Exminster, Turf Hotel
Instow, Boat House
Plymouth, China House
Torcross, Start Bay
Tuckenhay, Maltsters Arms

Dorset
Chideock, Anchor
Lyme Regis, Pilot Boat

Essex
Burnham-on-Crouch, White
  Harte
Chappel, Swan
Heybridge Basin, Jolly Sailor

Gloucestershire
Ashleworth Quay, Boat
Great Barrington, Fox
Redbrook, Boat
Tewkesbury, Olde Black Bear
Withington, Mill Inn

Hampshire
Alresford, Globe
Bursledon, Jolly Sailor
Langstone, Royal Oak
Portsmouth, Still & West
Wherwell, Mayfly

Herefordshire
Aymestrey, Riverside Inn

Hertfordshire
Berkhamsted, Boat

Isle of Wight
Bembridge, Crab & Lobster
Cowes, Folly
Seaview, Seaview Hotel
Shanklin, Fishermans Cottage
Ventnor, Spyglass

Kent
Deal, Kings Head
Faversham, Albion
Oare, Shipwrights Arms

Lancashire
Garstang, Th'Owd Tithebarn
Liverpool, Baltic Fleet
Manchester, Dukes 92, Mark
  Addy
Whitewell, Inn at Whitewell

Lincolnshire
Brandy Wharf, Cider Centre

London
East London, Grapes,
  Prospect of Whitby, Town
  of Ramsgate
North London, Waterside
South London, Anchor, Bulls
  Head, Cutty Sark,
  Horniman, Ship
West London, Bulls Head,
  Dove, White Swan

Norfolk
Sculthorpe, Sculthorpe Mill

Northamptonshire
Oundle, Mill
Wadenhoe, Kings Head

Oxfordshire
Tadpole Bridge, Trout

Scotland
Ardfern, Galley of Lorne

Arduaine, Loch Melfort Hotel
Carbost, Old Inn
Clachan Seil, Tigh an Truish
Crinan, Crinan Hotel
Edinburgh, Starbank
Elie, Ship
Fort Augustus, Lock
Glenelg, Glenelg Inn
Haddington, Waterside
Isle Of Whithorn, Steam
  Packet
Isle Ornsay, Eilean Iarmain
Kippford, Anchor
Plockton, Plockton Hotel
Portpatrick, Crown
Shieldaig, Tigh an Eilean
  Hotel
Skeabost, Skeabost House
  Hotel
St Monance, Seafood
  Restaurant and Bar
Tayvallich, Tayvallich Inn

Shropshire
Cressage, Cholmondeley
  Riverside
Llanyblodwel, Horseshoe
Ludlow, Unicorn
Shrewsbury, Armoury
Whitchurch, Willey Moor
  Lock

Staffordshire
Acton Trussell, Moat House
Onecote, Jervis Arms

Suffolk
Chelmondiston, Butt &
  Oyster

Sussex
Barcombe, Anchor

Wales
Aberdovey, Penhelig Arms
Cresswell Quay, Cresselly
  Arms
Little Haven, Swan
Llangedwyn, Green
Pembroke Ferry, Ferry Inn
Penmaenpool, George III
Pontypool, Open Hearth
Red Wharf Bay, Ship
Talyllyn, Tynycornel

Warwickshire
Lapworth, Navigation
Lowsonford, Fleur de Lys
Netherton, Little Dry Dock

Wiltshire
Bradford-on-Avon, Cross
  Guns
North Newnton, Woodbridge
Seend, Barge

Worcestershire
Knightwick, Talbot
Wyre Piddle, Anchor

Yorkshire
Hull, Minerva

Newton on Ouse, Dawnay
  Arms
Whitby, Duke of York

Pubs in Attractive Surroundings
These pubs are in unusually attractive or interesting places – lovely countryside, charming villages, occasionally notable town surroundings. Waterside pubs are listed again here only if their other surroundings are special, too.

Bedfordshire
Linslade, Globe

Berkshire
Aldworth, Bell
Frilsham, Pot Kiln
Hurley, Dew Drop

Buckinghamshire
Bledlow, Lions of Bledlow
Brill, Pheasant
Frieth, Prince Albert
Hambleden, Stag &
  Huntsman
Ibstone, Fox
Little Hampden, Rising Sun
Northend, White Hart
Skirmett, Frog
Turville, Bull & Butcher

Channel Islands
St Brelade, Old Portelet Inn,
  Old Smugglers
St John, Les Fontaines

Cheshire
Barthomley, White Lion
Bunbury, Dysart Arms
Langley, Leathers Smithy
Lower Peover, Bells of Peover
Whiteley Green, Windmill
Willington Corner, Boot

Cornwall
Boscastle, Cobweb
Chapel Amble, Maltsters
  Arms
Helston, Halzephron
Lamorna, Lamorna Wink
Porthallow, Five Pilchards
Ruan Lanihorne, Kings Head
St Agnes, Turks Head
St Breward, Old Inn
St Kew, St Kew Inn
St Mawgan, Falcon
Tresco, New Inn

Cumbria
Askham, Punch Bowl
Bassenthwaite Lake, Pheasant
Boot, Burnmoor
Bouth, White Hart
Braithwaite, Coledale Inn
Broughton In Furness,
  Blacksmiths Arms

Buttermere, Bridge Hotel
Caldbeck, Oddfellows Arms
Cartmel, Cavendish Arms
Chapel Stile, Wainwrights
Coniston, Black Bull
Crosthwaite, Punch Bowl
Dent, Sun
Elterwater, Britannia
Garrigill, George & Dragon
Grasmere, Travellers Rest
Hawkshead, Drunken Duck
Ings, Watermill
Langdale, Old Dungeon Ghyll
Little Langdale, Three Shires
Loweswater, Kirkstile Inn
Melmerby, Shepherds
Mungrisdale, Mill Inn
Seathwaite, Newfield Inn
Troutbeck, Mortal Man,
  Queens Head
Ulverston, Bay Horse
Wasdale Head, Wasdale
  Head Inn

Derbyshire
Brassington, Olde Gate
Froggatt Edge, Chequers
Hardwick Hall, Hardwick
  Inn
Kirk Ireton, Barley Mow
Ladybower Reservoir,
  Yorkshire Bridge
Little Hucklow, Old Bulls
  Head
Monsal Head, Monsal Head
  Hotel
Over Haddon, Lathkil
Woolley Moor, White Horse

Devon
Blackawton, Normandy
  Arms
Branscombe, Fountain Head
Broadclyst, Red Lion
Buckland Monachorum,
  Drake Manor
Chagford, Ring o' Bells
Exminster, Turf Hotel
Haytor Vale, Rock
Holbeton, Mildmay Colours
Horndon, Elephants Nest
Horsebridge, Royal
Iddesleigh, Duke of York
Kingston, Dolphin
Knowstone, Masons Arms
Lower Ashton, Manor Inn
Lustleigh, Cleave
Lydford, Castle Inn
Meavy, Royal Oak
Peter Tavy, Peter Tavy Inn
Postbridge, Warren House
Rattery, Church House
Slapton, Tower
Stokenham, Tradesmans Arms
Two Bridges, Two Bridges
  Hotel
Widecombe, Rugglestone
Wonson, Northmore Arms

Dorset
Abbotsbury, Ilchester Arms
Askerswell, Spyway
Corfe Castle, Fox
Corscombe, Fox
East Chaldon, Sailors Return
Kingston, Scott Arms
Loders, Loders Arms
Marshwood, Bottle
Osmington Mills, Smugglers
Plush, Brace of Pheasants
Powerstock, Three Horseshoes
Worth Matravers, Square &
  Compass

Essex
Fuller Street, Square &
  Compasses
Little Dunmow, Flitch of
  Bacon
Mill Green, Viper
North Fambridge, Ferry Boat

Gloucestershire
Amberley, Black Horse
Ashleworth Quay, Boat
Bibury, Catherine Wheel
Bisley, Bear
Bledington, Kings Head
Chedworth, Seven Tuns
Chipping Campden, Eight
  Bells
Cold Aston, Plough
Coln St Aldwyns, New Inn
Great Rissington, Lamb
Guiting Power, Hollow
  Bottom
Minchinhampton, Old
  Lodge
Miserden, Carpenters Arms
North Nibley, New Inn
St Briavels, George
Stanton, Mount

Hampshire
Alresford, Globe
East Tytherley, Star
Fritham, Royal Oak
Hawkley, Hawkley Inn
Micheldever, Dever Arms
North Gorley, Royal Oak
Petersfield, White Horse
Tichborne, Tichborne Arms
Woodgreen, Horse & Groom

Herefordshire
Aymestrey, Riverside Inn
Mathon, Cliffe Arms
Much Marcle, Slip Tavern
Ruckhall, Ancient Camp
Sellack, Lough Pool
Walterstone, Carpenters
  Arms
Weobley, Salutation
Woolhope, Butchers Arms

Hertfordshire
Aldbury, Greyhound
Sarratt, Cock
Westmill, Sword in Hand

Isle of Wight
Chale, Clarendon (Wight Mouse)

Kent
Boughton Aluph, Flying Horse
Brookland, Woolpack
Chiddingstone, Castle
Groombridge, Crown
Newnham, George
Selling, Rose & Crown
Toys Hill, Fox & Hounds

Lancashire
Blackstone Edge, White House
Conder Green, Stork
Downham, Assheton Arms
Entwistle, Strawbury Duck
Fence, Forest
Newton, Parkers Arms
Whitewell, Inn at Whitewell

Leicestershire
Exton, Fox & Hounds
Glooston, Old Barn
Hallaton, Bewicke Arms
Upper Hambleton, Finches Arms

Lincolnshire
Aswarby, Tally Ho

London
Central London, Olde Mitre
North London, Spaniards Inn
South London, Crown & Greyhound, Horniman, Windmill

Norfolk
Blakeney, White Horse
Blickling, Buckinghamshire Arms
Burnham Market, Hoste Arms
Great Bircham, Kings Head
Heydon, Earle Arms
Horsey, Nelson Head
Thornham, Lifeboat
Woodbastwick, Fur & Feather

Northamptonshire
Chapel Brampton, Brampton Halt
Harringworth, White Swan

Northumbria
Allenheads, Allenheads Inn
Blanchland, Lord Crewe Arms
Craster, Jolly Fisherman
Diptonmill, Dipton Mill Inn
Etal, Black Bull
Great Whittington, Queens Head
Haltwhistle, Milecastle Inn, Wallace Arms
Langley on Tyne, Carts Bog Inn
Romaldkirk, Rose & Crown
Stannersburn, Pheasant

Nottinghamshire
Laxton, Dovecote

Oxfordshire
Ardington, Boars Head
Burford, Mermaid
Chalgrove, Red Lion
Checkendon, Black Horse
Chinnor, Sir Charles Napier
Kelmscot, Plough
Maidensgrove, Five Horseshoes
Oxford, Kings Arms, Turf Tavern
Shenington, Bell

Scotland
Applecross, Applecross Inn
Arduaine, Loch Melfort Hotel
Brig O Turk, Byre
Clachan Seil, Tigh an Truish
Crinan, Crinan Hotel
Haddington, Waterside
Kilberry, Kilberry Inn
Kilmahog, Lade
Mountpottinger, Gordon Arms
Pitlochry, Killiecrankie Hotel
Sheriffmuir, Sheriffmuir Inn
Tushielaw, Tushielaw Inn

Shropshire
Bridges, Horseshoe
Cardington, Royal Oak
Wenlock Edge, Wenlock Edge Inn

Somerset
Appley, Globe
Batcombe, Three Horseshoes
Combe Hay, Wheatsheaf
Cranmore, Strode Arms
Farleigh Hungerford, Hungerford Arms
Luxborough, Royal Oak
Stogumber, White Horse
Triscombe, Blue Ball
Wambrook, Cotley
Wells, City Arms
Winsford, Royal Oak

Staffordshire
Alstonefield, George

Suffolk
Dennington, Queens Head
Dunwich, Ship
Lavenham, Angel
Levington, Ship
Snape, Plough & Sail
Walberswick, Bell

Surrey
Abinger Common, Abinger Hatch
Blackbrook, Plough
Cobham, Cricketers
Dunsfold, Sun
Friday Street, Stephan Langton
Mickleham, King William IV
Reigate Heath, Skimmington Castle

Sussex
Amberley, Black Horse
Barcombe, Anchor
Billingshurst, Blue Ship
Brownbread Street, Ash Tree
Burpham, George & Dragon
Burwash, Bell
East Dean, Tiger
Fletching, Griffin
Heathfield, Star
Kirdford, Half Moon
Lurgashall, Noahs Ark
Rye, Mermaid, Ypres Castle
Seaford, Golden Galleon
Wineham, Royal Oak

Wales
Aberystwyth, Halfway Inn
Bosherston, St Govans Inn
Capel Curig, Bryn Tyrch
Carew, Carew Inn
Crickhowell, Nantyffin Cider Mill
Llanbedr-y-Cennin, Olde Bull
Llanberis, Pen-y-Gwryd
Llangedwyn, Green
Maentwrog, Grapes
Penmaenpool, George III
Red Wharf Bay, Ship
Talyllyn, Tynycornel

Warwickshire
Edge Hill, Castle
Himley, Crooked House
Warmington, Plough

Wiltshire
Alvediston, Crown
Axford, Red Lion
Bradford-on-Avon, Cross Guns
Ebbesbourne Wake, Horseshoe
Lacock, Rising Sun

Worcestershire
Kidderminster, King & Castle
Knightwick, Talbot
Pensax, Bell

Yorkshire
Appletreewick, Craven Arms
Beck Hole, Birch Hall
Blakey Ridge, Lion
Bradfield, Strines Inn
Buckden, Buck
Burnsall, Red Lion
Byland Abbey, Abbey Inn
Cray, White Lion
East Witton, Blue Lion
Heath, Kings Arms
Hubberholme, George
Levisham, Horseshoe
Linton in Craven, Fountaine
Litton, Queens Arms
Lund, Wellington
Masham, Kings Head
Middleham, Black Swan
Muker, Farmers Arms
Ramsgill, Yorke Arms

Ripley, Boars Head
Robin Hoods Bay, Laurel
Rosedale Abbey, Milburn
Arms
Shelley, Three Acres
Starbotton, Fox & Hounds
Terrington, Bay Horse
Thornton Watlass, Buck
Wath in Nidderdale,
Sportsmans Arms
Widdop, Pack Horse

Pubs with Good Views

These pubs are listed for their particularly good views, either from inside or from a garden or terrace. Waterside pubs are listed again here only if their view is exceptional in its own right – not just a straightforward sea view for example.

Berkshire
Chieveley, Blue Boar

Buckinghamshire
Brill, Pheasant

Channel Islands
St Aubin, Old Court House
Inn

Cheshire
Higher Burwardsley, Pheasant
Langley, Hanging Gate,
Leathers Smithy
Overton, Ring o' Bells
Willington Corner, Boot

Cornwall
Cremyll, Edgcumbe Arms
Polruan, Lugger
Ruan Lanihorne, Kings Head
St Agnes, Turks Head

Cumbria
Braithwaite, Coledale Inn
Cartmel Fell, Masons Arms
Hawkshead, Drunken Duck
Langdale, Old Dungeon Ghyll
Loweswater, Kirkstile Inn
Mungrisdale, Mill Inn
Troutbeck, Queens Head
Ulverston, Bay Horse
Wasdale Head, Wasdale
Head Inn

Derbyshire
Monsal Head, Monsal Head
Hotel
Over Haddon, Lathkil

Devon
Instow, Boat House
Postbridge, Warren House
Westleigh, Westleigh Inn

Dorset
Kingston, Scott Arms
Worth Matravers, Square &
Compass

Gloucestershire
Amberley, Black Horse
Cranham, Black Horse
Gretton, Royal Oak
Kilkenny, Kilkeney Inn
Sheepscombe, Butchers Arms
Stanton, Mount

Hampshire
Beauworth, Milbury's
Owslebury, Ship

Herefordshire
Ruckhall, Ancient Camp

Isle of Wight
Bembridge, Crab & Lobster
Carisbrooke, Blacksmiths
Arms
Ventnor, Spyglass

Kent
Linton, Bull
Penshurst, Spotted Dog
Tunbridge Wells, Beacon
Ulcombe, Pepper Box

Lancashire
Blackstone Edge, White House
Darwen, Old Rosins
Entwistle, Strawbury Duck

Leicestershire
Saddington, Queens Head

London
South London, Anchor

Northumbria
Haltwhistle, Wallace Arms
Seahouses, Olde Ship
Thropton, Three Wheat Heads

Scotland
Applecross, Applecross Inn
Ardvasar, Ardvasar Hotel
Arrochar, Village Inn
Crinan, Crinan Hotel
Cromarty, Royal
Edinburgh, Starbank
Glenelg, Glenelg Inn
Isle Ornsay, Eilean Iarmain
Kilberry, Kilberry Inn
Pitlochry, Killiecrankie Hotel
Sheriffmuir, Sheriffmuir Inn
Shieldaig, Tigh an Eilean
Hotel
Tushielaw, Tushielaw Inn
Weem, Ailean Chraggan

Shropshire
Cressage, Cholmondeley
Riverside

Suffolk
Erwarton, Queens Head
Hundon, Plough
Levington, Ship

Sussex
Amberley, Sportsmans
Byworth, Black Horse
Elsted, Three Horseshoes
Fletching, Griffin

Icklesham, Queens Head
Rye, Ypres Castle

Wales
Aberdovey, Penhelig Arms
Aberystwyth, Halfway Inn
Bodfari, Dinorben Arms
Capel Curig, Bryn Tyrch
Halkyn, Britannia
Llanbedr-y-Cennin, Olde Bull
Llanberis, Pen-y-Gwryd
Llanferres, Druid
Llangynwyd, Old House
Llannefydd, Hawk & Buckle
Penmaenpool, George III
Talyllyn, Tynycornel
Tyn Y Groes, Groes

Wiltshire
Axford, Red Lion
Box, Quarrymans Arms
Lacock, Rising Sun

Worcestershire
Pensax, Bell
Wyre Piddle, Anchor

Yorkshire
Appletreewick, Craven
Arms
Blakey Ridge, Lion
Bradfield, Strines Inn
Kirkham, Stone Trough
Litton, Queens Arms
Shelley, Three Acres
Whitby, Duke of York

Pubs in Interesting Buildings

Pubs and inns are listed here for the particular interest of their building – something really out of the ordinary to look at, or occasionally a building that has an outstandingly interesting historical background.

Berkshire
Cookham, Bel & the Dragon

Buckinghamshire
Forty Green, Royal Standard
of England

Derbyshire
Buxton, Bull i' th' Thorn

Devon
Dartmouth, Cherub
Harberton, Church House
Rattery, Church House
Sourton, Highwayman
South Zeal, Oxenham Arms

Hampshire
Beauworth, Milbury's

Lancashire
Garstang, Th'Owd Tithebarn
Liverpool, Philharmonic
Dining Rooms

Lincolnshire
Stamford, George of
Stamford

London
Central London, Black Friar,
Cittie of Yorke
South London, George,
Phoenix & Firkin

Northumbria
Blanchland, Lord Crewe
Arms

Nottinghamshire
Nottingham, Olde Trip to
Jerusalem

Oxfordshire
Banbury, Reindeer
Fyfield, White Hart

Scotland
Edinburgh, Guildford Arms

Somerset
Norton St Philip, George

Suffolk
Lavenham, Swan

Sussex
Rye, Mermaid

Warwickshire
Himley, Crooked House

Wiltshire
Salisbury, Haunch of Venison

Worcestershire
Bretforton, Fleece

Yorkshire
Hull, Olde White Harte

Pubs that Brew their Own Beer

*The pubs listed here brew
their own beer on the
premises; many others not
listed have beers brewed for
them specially, sometimes to
an individual recipe (but by a
separate brewer). We mention
these in the text.*

Berkshire
Frilsham, Pot Kiln

Cambridgeshire
Peterborough, Brewery Tap

Channel Islands
St Helier, Tipsy Toad Town
House

Cornwall
Helston, Blue Anchor

Cumbria
Cartmel Fell, Masons Arms
Cockermouth, Bitter End
Coniston, Black Bull
Dent, Sun
Hawkshead, Drunken Duck

Tirril, Queens Head

Derbyshire
Derby, Brunswick
Melbourne, John Thompson

Devon
Branscombe, Fountain Head
Hatherleigh, Tally Ho
Holbeton, Mildmay Colours
Newton St Cyres, Beer Engine
Two Bridges, Two Bridges
Hotel

Gloucestershire
Apperley, Farmers Arms

Hampshire
Cheriton, Flower Pots
Southsea, Wine Vaults

Herefordshire
Aymestrey, Riverside Inn

Hertfordshire
Aldbury, Greyhound

Lancashire
Bispham Green, Eagle &
Child
Manchester, Lass o' Gowrie,
Marble Arch

London
Central London, Orange
Brewery

Norfolk
Reedham, Railway Tavern

Nottinghamshire
Nottingham, Fellows Morton
& Clayton

Scotland
Houston, Fox & Hounds
Pitlochry, Moulin

Shropshire
Bishops Castle, Three Tuns
Munslow, Crown
Wistanstow, Plough

Staffordshire
Burton on Trent, Burton
Bridge Inn
Eccleshall, George

Suffolk
Earl Soham, Victoria

Surrey
Coldharbour, Plough

Sussex
Donnington, Blacksmiths
Arms
Oving, Gribble Inn
Seaford, Golden Galleon

Warwickshire
Birmingham, Fiddle & Bone
Sedgley, Beacon
Shustoke, Griffin

Worcestershire
Knightwick, Talbot

Yorkshire
Cropton, New Inn
Ledsham, Chequers
Linthwaite, Sair
Sheffield, Fat Cat
Snaith, Brewers Arms

Open all Day (at least in summer)

*We list here all the pubs that
have told us they plan to stay
open all day, even if it's only
Saturday. We've included the
few pubs which close just for
half an hour to an hour, and
the many more, chiefly in
holiday areas, which open all
day only in summer. The
individual entries for the pubs
themselves show the actual
details.*

Berkshire
East Ilsley, Crown & Horns
Hare Hatch, Queen Victoria
Inkpen, Swan
Reading, Sweeney & Todd
West Ilsley, Harrow

Buckinghamshire
Brill, Pheasant
Cheddington, Old Swan
Easington, Mole & Chicken
Fawley, Walnut Tree
Long Crendon, Churchill
Arms
Skirmett, Frog
Wheeler End, Chequers
Wooburn Common,
Chequers

Cambridgeshire
Cambridge, Anchor, Eagle
Huntingdon, Old Bridge
Peterborough, Brewery Tap,
Charters
Wansford, Haycock

Channel Islands
Greve de Lecq, Moulin de
Lecq
Kings Mills, Fleur du Jardin
Rozel, Rozel Bay Inn
St Aubin, Old Court House
Inn
St Brelade, Old Portelet Inn,
Old Smugglers
St Helier, Admiral, Tipsy
Toad Town House
St John, Les Fontaines
St Ouens Bay, La Pulente

Cheshire
Aldford, Grosvenor Arms
Barthomley, White Lion
Broxton, Egerton Arms
Bunbury, Dysart Arms
Chester, Old Harkers Arms
Cotebrook, Fox & Barrel
Higher Burwardsley, Pheasant

Langley, Leathers Smithy
Lower Peover, Bells of Peover
Macclesfield, Sutton Hall Hotel
Nantwich, Crown
Plumley, Smoker
Tarporley, Rising Sun
Wettenhall, Boot & Slipper
Whitegate, Plough
Whiteley Green, Windmill
Willington Corner, Boot

Cornwall
Bodinnick, Old Ferry
Boscastle, Cobweb
Cremyll, Edgcumbe Arms
Edmonton, Quarryman
Falmouth, Quayside Inn & Old Ale House
Helston, Blue Anchor
Lamorna, Lamorna Wink
Lostwithiel, Royal Oak
Mithian, Miners Arms
Mousehole, Ship
Mylor Bridge, Pandora
Pelynt, Jubilee
Polperro, Old Mill House
Polruan, Lugger
Port Isaac, Golden Lion
Port Gaverne Hotel
Porthleven, Ship
St Agnes, Turks Head
St Ives, Sloop
St Keverne, White Hart
St Mawes, Victory
St Teath, White Hart
Trebarwith, Port William
Tresco, New Inn
Truro, Old Ale House

Cumbria
Ambleside, Golden Rule
Askham, Punch Bowl
Bowness On Windermere, Hole in t' Wall
Braithwaite, Coledale Inn
Brampton, New Inn
Broughton In Furness, Blacksmiths Arms
Buttermere, Bridge Hotel
Caldbeck, Oddfellows Arms
Cartmel, Cavendish Arms
Cartmel Fell, Masons Arms
Chapel Stile, Wainwrights
Coniston, Black Bull
Crosthwaite, Punch Bowl
Dent, Sun
Elterwater, Britannia
Eskdale Green, Bower House
Garrigill, George & Dragon
Grasmere, Travellers Rest
Heversham, Blue Bell
Keswick, Dog & Gun
Kirkby Lonsdale, Snooty Fox, Sun
Langdale, Old Dungeon Ghyll
Little Langdale, Three Shires
Loweswater, Kirkstile Inn
Mungrisdale, Mill Inn

Penrith, Agricultural
Seathwaite, Newfield Inn
Sedbergh, Dalesman
Threlkeld, Salutation
Tirril, Queens Head
Troutbeck, Mortal Man, Queens Head
Ulverston, Bay Horse
Wasdale Head, Wasdale Head Inn

Derbyshire
Ashbourne, Smiths Tavern
Beeley, Devonshire Arms
Buxton, Bull i' th' Thorn, Old Sun
Buxworth, Navigation
Castleton, Castle Hotel
Derby, Alexandra, Brunswick, Olde Dolphin
Fenny Bentley, Coach & Horses
Froggatt Edge, Chequers
Hardwick Hall, Hardwick Inn
Hope, Cheshire Cheese
Ladybower Reservoir, Yorkshire Bridge
Monsal Head, Monsal Head Hotel
Over Haddon, Lathkil
Wardlow, Three Stags Heads
Whittington Moor, Derby Tup

Devon
Abbotskerswell, Court Farm
Ashprington, Watermans Arms
Branscombe, Masons Arms
Cockwood, Anchor
Dartmouth, Cherub, Royal Castle Hotel
Exeter, Double Locks, Imperial, White Hart
Exminster, Turf Hotel
Hatherleigh, Tally Ho
Haytor Vale, Rock
Iddesleigh, Duke of York
Lustleigh, Cleave
Newton St Cyres, Beer Engine
Plymouth, China House
Postbridge, Warren House
Rackenford, Stag
Stoke Gabriel, Church House
Torcross, Start Bay
Torrington, Black Horse
Tuckenhay, Maltsters Arms
Ugborough, Anchor
Wonson, Northmore Arms
Woodland, Rising Sun

Dorset
Abbotsbury, Ilchester Arms
Bridport, George
Chideock, Anchor
Christchurch, Fishermans Haunt
Corfe Castle, Greyhound

East Chaldon, Sailors Return
Kingston, Scott Arms
Loders, Loders Arms
Lyme Regis, Pilot Boat
Osmington Mills, Smugglers
Worth Matravers, Square & Compass

Essex
Burnham-on-Crouch, White Harte
Dedham, Marlborough Head
Heybridge Basin, Jolly Sailor
High Ongar, Wheatsheaf
North Fambridge, Ferry Boat
Rickling Green, Cricketers Arms
Stock, Hoop
Stow Maries, Prince of Wales

Gloucestershire
Amberley, Black Horse
Awre, Red Hart
Barnsley, Village Pub
Bibury, Catherine Wheel
Bisley, Bear
Blockley, Crown
Brimpsfield, Golden Heart
Chedworth, Seven Tuns
Chipping Campden, Eight Bells, Noel Arms
Coln St Aldwyns, New Inn
Ewen, Wild Duck
Ford, Plough
Great Barrington, Fox
Guiting Power, Hollow Bottom
Littleton-upon-Severn, White Hart
Nailsworth, Egypt Mill
Old Sodbury, Dog
Oldbury-on-Severn, Anchor
Redbrook, Boat
Sheepscombe, Butchers Arms
Stanton, Mount
Tetbury, Gumstool
Withington, Mill Inn
Woodchester, Royal Oak

Hampshire
Bentworth, Sun
Boldre, Red Lion
Bursledon, Jolly Sailor
Droxford, White Horse
Fritham, Royal Oak
Froyle, Hen & Chicken
Ibsley, Old Beams
Langstone, Royal Oak
North Gorley, Royal Oak
Owslebury, Ship
Petersfield, White Horse
Portsmouth, Still & West
Rotherwick, Coach & Horses
Sopley, Woolpack
Southsea, Wine Vaults
Well, Chequers
Wherwell, Mayfly
Winchester, Wykeham Arms

Herefordshire
Ledbury, Feathers
Lugwardine, Crown & Anchor
Walterstone, Carpenters Arms
Weobley, Salutation

Hertfordshire
Aldbury, Greyhound
Ashwell, Three Tuns
Ayot St Lawrence, Brocket Arms
Berkhamsted, Boat
Bricket Wood, Moor Mill
Knebworth, Lytton Arms
Sarratt, Cock
Walkern, White Lion
Watton-at-Stone, George & Dragon

Isle of Wight
Arreton, White Lion
Bembridge, Crab & Lobster
Carisbrooke, Blacksmiths Arms
Chale, Clarendon (Wight Mouse)
Cowes, Folly
Downend, Hare & Hounds
Rookley, Chequers
Shorwell, Crown
Ventnor, Spyglass
Yarmouth, Wheatsheaf

Kent
Bough Beech, Wheatsheaf
Boughton Aluph, Flying Horse
Chiddingstone, Castle
Deal, Kings Head
Fordcombe, Chafford Arms
Groombridge, Crown
Iden Green, Woodcock
Ightham Common, Harrow
Langton Green, Hare
Luddesdown, Cock
Markbeech, Kentish Horse
Oare, Shipwrights Arms
Ringlestone, Ringlestone
Tunbridge Wells, Beacon, Sankeys

Lancashire
Bispham Green, Eagle & Child
Brindle, Cavendish Arms
Chipping, Dog & Partridge
Conder Green, Stork
Croston, Black Horse
Darwen, Old Rosins
Entwistle, Strawbury Duck
Fence, Forest
Garstang, Th'Owd Tithebarn
Liverpool, Baltic Fleet, Philharmonic Dining Rooms
Lytham, Taps
Manchester, Britons Protection, Dukes 92, Lass o' Gowrie, Marble Arch, Mark Addy, Royal Oak
Newton, Parkers Arms

Raby, Wheatsheaf
Ribchester, White Bull
Stalybridge, Station Buffet
Yealand Conyers, New Inn

Leicestershire
Empingham, White Horse
Glaston, Monckton Arms
Loughborough, Swan in the Rushes
Redmile, Peacock
Upper Hambleton, Finches Arms
Wing, Kings Arms

Lincolnshire
Grantham, Beehive
Heckington, Nags Head
Lincoln, Victoria, Wig & Mitre
Stamford, George of Stamford

London
Central London, Albert, Archery Tavern, Argyll Arms, Bishops Finger, Black Friar, Cittie of Yorke, Dog & Duck, Eagle, Grapes, Grenadier, Jerusalem Tavern, Lamb, Lamb & Flag, Leopard, Lord Moon of the Mall, Moon Under Water, Museum Tavern, Nags Head, O'Hanlons, Old Bank of England, Olde Cheshire Cheese, Olde Mitre, Orange Brewery, Red Lion, Seven Stars, Star, Westminster Arms
East London, Prospect of Whitby, Town of Ramsgate
North London, Chapel, Compton Arms, Flask, Holly Bush, Olde White, Bear, Spaniards Inn, Waterside
South London, Alma, Anchor, Bulls Head, Crown & Greyhound, Cutty Sark, Fire Station, George, Horniman, Market Porter, Phoenix & Firkin, Ship, White Cross, Windmill
West London, both Anglesea Arms, Atlas, Bulls Head, Churchill Arms, Dove, Ladbroke Arms, White Horse, White Swan, Windsor Castle

Norfolk
Bawburgh, Kings Head
Blakeney, Kings Arms
Blickling, Buckinghamshire Arms
Brancaster Staithe, White Horse
Burnham Market, Hoste Arms

Fakenham, Wensum Lodge
Garboldisham, Fox
Hunworth, Blue Bell
Kings Lynn, Tudor Rose
Larling, Angel
Mundford, Crown
Norwich, Adam & Eve, Fat Cat
Reedham, Railway Tavern
Reepham, Old Brewery House
Sculthorpe, Sculthorpe Mill
Snettisham, Rose & Crown
Swanton Morley, Darbys
Thornham, Lifeboat
Tivetshall St Mary, Old Ram
Upper Sheringham, Red Lion
Winterton-on-Sea, Fishermans Return

Northamptonshire
Chacombe, George & Dragon
Chapel Brampton, Brampton Halt
Great Brington, Fox & Hounds
Oundle, Mill, Ship

Northumbria
Allendale, Kings Head
Craster, Jolly Fisherman
Etal, Black Bull
Greta Bridge, Morritt Arms
Haltwhistle, Wallace Arms
New York, Shiremoor Farm
Newcastle upon Tyne, Crown Posada
Seaton Sluice, Waterford Arms
Shincliffe, Seven Stars
Thropton, Three Wheat Heads

Nottinghamshire
Beeston, Victoria
Caunton, Caunton Beck
Elkesley, Robin Hood
Kimberley, Nelson & Railway
Nottingham, Fellows Morton & Clayton, Lincolnshire Poacher, Olde Trip to Jerusalem
Upton, French Horn

Oxfordshire
Bampton, Romany
Banbury, Reindeer
Bloxham, Elephant & Castle
Burford, Mermaid
Chipping Norton, Chequers
Clifton Hampden, Plough
Cuddesdon, Bat & Ball
Cumnor, Bear & Ragged Staff
Cuxham, Half Moon
Dorchester, George
East Hendred, Wheatsheaf
Exlade Street, Highwayman
Finstock, Plough
Kelmscot, Plough

Oxford, Kings Arms, Turf
  Tavern
Stanton St John, Talk House
Wytham, White Hart

Scotland
Aberdeen, Prince of Wales
Applecross, Applecross Inn
Ardfern, Galley of Lorne
Arduaine, Loch Melfort Hotel
Ardvasar, Ardvasar Hotel
Arrochar, Village Inn
Brig O Turk, Byre
Broughty Ferry, Fishermans
  Tavern
Carbost, Old Inn
Cawdor, Cawdor Tavern
Clachan Seil, Tigh an Truish
Crinan, Crinan Hotel
Cromarty, Royal
Edinburgh, Abbotsford,
  Bannermans, Bow Bar,
  Guildford Arms, Kays Bar,
  Ship on the Shore, Starbank
Elie, Ship
Fort Augustus, Lock
Gifford, Tweeddale Arms
Glasgow, Auctioneers,
  Babbity Bowster,
  Blackfriars, Counting House
Glendevon, Tormaukin
Haddington, Waterside
Houston, Fox & Hounds
Innerleithen, Traquair Arms
Inveraray, George
Inverarnan, Inverarnan Inn
Isle Of Whithorn, Steam
  Packet
Isle Ornsay, Eilean Iarmain
Kelso, Queens Head
Kippen, Cross Keys
Kippford, Anchor
Kirkton of Glenisla, Glenisla
  Hotel
Linlithgow, Four Marys
Lybster, Portland Arms
Mountbenger, Gordon Arms
Pitlochry, Moulin
Plockton, Plockton Hotel
Portpatrick, Crown
Sheriffmuir, Sheriffmuir Inn
Shieldaig, Tigh an Eilean
  Hotel
St Monance, Seafood
  Restaurant and Bar
Swinton, Wheatsheaf
Tayvallich, Tayvallich Inn
Thornhill, Lion & Unicorn
Ullapool, Ceilidh Place,
  Morefield Motel
Weem, Ailean Chraggan

Shropshire
Bishops Castle, Three Tuns
Cleobury Mortimer, Kings
  Arms
Cressage, Cholmondeley
  Riverside
Nescliffe, Old Three Pigeons

Norton, Hundred House
Shrewsbury, Armoury

Somerset
Ashcott, Ashcott Inn
Bath, Old Green Tree
Beckington, Woolpack
Bristol, Highbury Vaults
Churchill, Crown
Clapton-in-Gordano, Black
  Horse
Farleigh Hungerford,
  Hungerford Arms
Huish Episcopi, Rose &
  Crown
Norton St Philip, George
Rudge, Full Moon
South Stoke, Pack Horse
Sparkford, Sparkford Inn
Stanton Wick, Carpenters
  Arms
Wells, City Arms

Staffordshire
Acton Trussell, Moat House
Alstonefield, George
Eccleshall, George
Onecote, Jervis Arms
Salt, Holly Bush

Suffolk
Butley, Oyster
Chelmondiston, Butt &
  Oyster
Chillesford, Froize
Cotton, Trowel & Hammer
Lavenham, Angel
Laxfield, Kings Head
Walberswick, Bell
Wangford, Angel

Surrey
Abinger Common, Abinger
  Hatch
Betchworth, Dolphin
Coldharbour, Plough
Effingham, Sir Douglas Haig
Friday Street, Stephan
  Langton
Gomshall, Compasses
Hascombe, White Horse
Leigh, Plough
Pirbright, Royal Oak
Reigate Heath, Skimmington
  Castle
Warlingham, White Lion
Wotton, Wotton Hatch

Sussex
Barcombe, Anchor
Barnham, Murrell Arms
Berwick, Cricketers Arms
Brownbread Street, Ash Tree
Burwash, Bell
Chiddingly, Six Bells
Coolham, George & Dragon
East Dean, Tiger
Firle, Ram
Hartfield, Anchor
Horsham, Black Jug

Icklesham, Queens Head
Kingston Near Lewes, Juggs
Lewes, Snowdrop
Oving, Gribble Inn
Pett, Two Sawyers
Playden, Peace & Plenty
Punnetts Town, Three Cups
Rushlake Green, Horse &
  Groom
Rye, Mermaid, Ypres Castle
Seaford, Golden Galleon

Wales
Beaumaris, Olde Bulls Head
Bodfari, Dinorben Arms
Bosherston, St Govans Inn
Capel Curig, Bryn Tyrch
Carew, Carew Inn
Colwyn Bay, Mountain View
Cresswell Quay, Cresselly
  Arms
Crickhowell, White Hart
East Aberthaw, Blue Anchor
Graianrhyd, Rose & Crown
Gresford, Pant-yr-Ochain
Halkyn, Britannia
Hay-on-Wye, Kilverts, Old
  Black Lion
Llanberis, Pen-y-Gwryd
Llandeilo, Castle
Llanferres, Druid
Llangynwyd, Old House
Maentwrog, Grapes
Monknash, Plough &
  Harrow
Penmaenpool, George III
Pontypool, Open Hearth
Porthmadog, Ship
Presteigne, Radnorshire Arms
Raglan, Clytha Arms
Red Wharf Bay, Ship
Reynoldston, King Arthur
St Hilary, Bush
Stackpole, Armstrong Arms
Talybont-on-Usk, Star

Warwickshire
Berkswell, Bear
Birmingham, Fiddle & Bone
Brierley Hill, Vine
Coventry, Old Windmill
Himley, Crooked House
Lapworth, Navigation
Lowsonford, Fleur de Lys
Warwick, Rose & Crown

Wiltshire
Box, Quarrymans Arms
Bradford-on-Avon, Cross
  Guns
Brinkworth, Three Crowns
Devizes, Bear
Fonthill Gifford, Beckford
  Arms
Hindon, Lamb
Lacock, George, Red Lion,
  Rising Sun
Marlborough, Sun
North Newnton, Woodbridge

Norton, Vine Tree
Pitton, Silver Plough
Salisbury, Haunch of
   Venison, New Inn
Semley, Benett Arms
Sherston, Rattlebone

Worcestershire

Bredon, Fox & Hounds
Bretforton, Fleece
Forhill, Peacock
Kidderminster, King &
   Castle
Knightwick, Talbot
Pensax, Bell
Worcester, Cardinals Hat

Yorkshire

Asenby, Crab & Lobster
Aysgarth, George & Dragon
Beck Hole, Birch Hall
Beverley, White Horse
Blakey Ridge, Lion
Boroughbridge, Black Bull
Bradfield, Strines Inn
Buckden, Buck
Burnsall, Red Lion
Cracoe, Devonshire Arms
Cray, White Lion
Cropton, New Inn
East Witton, Blue Lion
Egton Bridge, Horse Shoe
Elslack, Tempest Arms
Ferrensby, General Tarleton
Great Ouseburn, Crown
Harden, Malt Shovel
Harome, Star
Heath, Kings Arms
Heckmondwike, Old Hall
Hubberholme, George
Hull, Minerva, Olde White
   Harte
Ledsham, Chequers
Leeds, Whitelocks
Linthwaite, Sair
Linton, Windmill
Linton in Craven, Fountaine
Low Catton, Gold Cup
Masham, Kings Head, White
   Bear
Muker, Farmers Arms
Pickhill, Nags Head
Pool, White Hart
Ramsgill, Yorke Arms
Ripley, Boars Head
Ripponden, Old Bridge
Robin Hoods Bay, Laurel
Settle, Golden Lion
Sheffield, New Barrack
Thorganby, Jefferson Arms
Thornton Watlass, Buck
Whitby, Duke of York
Widdop, Pack Horse
York, Black Swan, Olde Starre,
   Spread Eagle, Tap & Spile

Pubs with No-smoking Areas

We have listed all the pubs which have told us they do set aside at least some part of the pub as a no-smoking area. Look at the individual entries for the pubs themselves to see just what they do: provision is much more generous in some pubs than in others.

Berkshire

East Ilsley, Crown & Horns
Hare Hatch, Queen Victoria
Inkpen, Swan
Reading, Sweeney & Todd
West Ilsley, Harrow

Buckinghamshire

Brill, Pheasant
Cheddington, Old Swan
Easington, Mole & Chicken
Fawley, Walnut Tree
Long Crendon, Churchill
   Arms
Skirmett, Frog
Wheeler End, Chequers
Wooburn Common,
   Chequers

Cambridgeshire

Cambridge, Anchor, Eagle
Huntingdon, Old Bridge
Peterborough, Brewery Tap,
   Charters
Wansford, Haycock

Channel Islands

Greve de Lecq, Moulin de
   Lecq
Kings Mills, Fleur du Jardin
Rozel, Rozel Bay Inn
St Aubin, Old Court House
   Inn
St Brelade, Old Portelet Inn,
   Old Smugglers
St Helier, Admiral, Tipsy
   Toad Town House
St John, Les Fontaines
St Ouens Bay, La Pulente

Cheshire

Aldford, Grosvenor Arms
Barthomley, White Lion
Broxton, Egerton Arms
Bunbury, Dysart Arms
Chester, Old Harkers Arms
Cotebrook, Fox & Barrel
Higher Burwardsley, Pheasant
Langley, Leathers Smithy
Lower Peover, Bells of Peover
Macclesfield, Sutton Hall
   Hotel
Nantwich, Crown
Plumley, Smoker
Tarporley, Rising Sun
Wettenhall, Boot & Slipper
Whitegate, Plough
Whiteley Green, Windmill

Willington Corner, Boot

Cornwall

Bodinnick, Old Ferry
Boscastle, Cobweb
Cremyll, Edgcumbe Arms
Edmonton, Quarryman
Falmouth, Quayside Inn &
   Old Ale House
Helston, Blue Anchor
Lamorna, Lamorna Wink
Lostwithiel, Royal Oak
Mithian, Miners Arms
Mousehole, Ship
Mylor Bridge, Pandora
Pelynt, Jubilee
Polperro, Old Mill House
Polruan, Lugger
Port Isaac, Golden Lion, Port
   Gaverne Hotel
Porthleven, Ship
St Agnes, Turks Head
St Ives, Sloop
St Keverne, White Hart
St Mawes, Victory
St Teath, White Hart
Trebarwith, Port William
Tresco, New Inn
Truro, Old Ale House

Cumbria

Ambleside, Golden Rule
Askham, Punch Bowl
Bowness On Windermere,
   Hole in t' Wall
Braithwaite, Coledale Inn
Brampton, New Inn
Broughton In Furness,
   Blacksmiths Arms
Buttermere, Bridge Hotel
Caldbeck, Oddfellows Arms
Cartmel, Cavendish Arms
Cartmel Fell, Masons Arms
Chapel Stile, Wainwrights
Coniston, Black Bull
Crosthwaite, Punch Bowl
Dent, Sun
Elterwater, Britannia
Eskdale Green, Bower House
Garrigill, George & Dragon
Grasmere, Travellers Rest
Heversham, Blue Bell
Keswick, Dog & Gun
Kirkby Lonsdale, Snooty Fox,
   Sun
Langdale, Old Dungeon Ghyll
Little Langdale, Three Shires
Loweswater, Kirkstile Inn
Mungrisdale, Mill Inn
Penrith, Agricultural
Seathwaite, Newfield Inn
Sedbergh, Dalesman
Threlkeld, Salutation
Tirril, Queens Head
Troutbeck, Mortal Man,
   Queens Head
Ulverston, Bay Horse
Wasdale Head, Wasdale
   Head Inn

Derbyshire
Ashbourne, Smiths Tavern
Beeley, Devonshire Arms
Buxton, Bull i' th' Thorn, Old
    Sun
Buxworth, Navigation
Castleton, Castle Hotel
Derby, Alexandra,
    Brunswick, Olde Dolphin
Fenny Bentley, Coach &
    Horses
Froggatt Edge, Chequers
Hardwick Hall, Hardwick Inn
Hope, Cheshire Cheese
Ladybower Reservoir,
    Yorkshire Bridge
Monsal Head, Monsal Head
    Hotel
Over Haddon, Lathkil
Wardlow, Three Stags Heads
Whittington Moor, Derby
    Tup

Devon
Abbotskerswell, Court Farm
Ashprington, Watermans
    Arms
Branscombe, Masons Arms
Cockwood, Anchor
Dartmouth, Cherub, Royal
    Castle Hotel
Exeter, Double Locks,
    Imperial, White Hart
Exminster, Turf Hotel
Hatherleigh, Tally Ho
Haytor Vale, Rock
Iddesleigh, Duke of York
Lustleigh, Cleave
Newton St Cyres, Beer Engine
Plymouth, China House
Postbridge, Warren House
Rackenford, Stag
Stoke Gabriel, Church House
Torcross, Start Bay
Torrington, Black Horse
Tuckenhay, Maltsters Arms
Ugborough, Anchor
Wonson, Northmore Arms
Woodland, Rising Sun

Dorset
Abbotsbury, Ilchester Arms
Bridport, George
Chideock, Anchor
Christchurch, Fishermans
    Haunt
Corfe Castle, Greyhound
East Chaldon, Sailors Return
Kingston, Scott Arms
Loders, Loders Arms
Lyme Regis, Pilot Boat
Osmington Mills, Smugglers
Worth Matravers, Square &
    Compass

Essex
Burnham-on-Crouch, White
    Harte
Dedham, Marlborough Head

Heybridge Basin, Jolly Sailor
High Ongar, Wheatsheaf
North Fambridge, Ferry Boat
Rickling Green, Cricketers
    Arms
Stock, Hoop
Stow Maries, Prince of Wales

Gloucestershire
Amberley, Black Horse
Awre, Red Hart
Barnsley, Village Pub
Bibury, Catherine Wheel
Bisley, Bear
Blockley, Crown
Brimpsfield, Golden Heart
Chedworth, Seven Tuns
Chipping Campden, Eight
    Bells, Noel Arms
Coln St Aldwyns, New Inn
Ewen, Wild Duck
Ford, Plough
Great Barrington, Fox
Guiting Power, Hollow
    Bottom
Littleton-upon-Severn, White
    Hart
Nailsworth, Egypt Mill
Old Sodbury, Dog
Oldbury-on-Severn, Anchor
Redbrook, Boat
Sheepscombe, Butchers Arms
Stanton, Mount
Tetbury, Gumstool
Withington, Mill Inn
Woodchester, Royal Oak

Hampshire
Bentworth, Sun
Boldre, Red Lion
Bursledon, Jolly Sailor
Droxford, White Horse
Fritham, Royal Oak
Froyle, Hen & Chicken
Ibsley, Old Beams
Langstone, Royal Oak
North Gorley, Royal Oak
Owslebury, Ship
Petersfield, White Horse
Portsmouth, Still & West
Rotherwick, Coach & Horses
Sopley, Woolpack
Southsea, Wine Vaults
Well, Chequers
Wherwell, Mayfly
Winchester, Wykeham Arms

Herefordshire
Ledbury, Feathers
Lugwardine, Crown &
    Anchor
Walterstone, Carpenters Arms
Weobley, Salutation

Hertfordshire
Aldbury, Greyhound
Ashwell, Three Tuns
Ayot St Lawrence, Brocket
    Arms
Berkhamsted, Boat

Bricket Wood, Moor Mill
Knebworth, Lytton Arms
Sarratt, Cock
Walkern, White Lion
Watton-at-Stone, George &
    Dragon

Isle of Wight
Arreton, White Lion
Bembridge, Crab & Lobster
Carisbrooke, Blacksmiths
    Arms
Chale, Clarendon (Wight
    Mouse)
Cowes, Folly
Downend, Hare & Hounds
Rookley, Chequers
Shorwell, Crown
Ventnor, Spyglass
Yarmouth, Wheatsheaf

Kent
Bough Beech, Wheatsheaf
Boughton Aluph, Flying
    Horse
Chiddingstone, Castle
Deal, Kings Head
Fordcombe, Chafford Arms
Groombridge, Crown
Iden Green, Woodcock
Ightham Common, Harrow
Langton Green, Hare
Luddesdown, Cock
Markbeech, Kentish Horse
Oare, Shipwrights Arms
Ringlestone, Ringlestone
Tunbridge Wells, Beacon,
    Sankeys

Lancashire
Bispham Green, Eagle &
    Child
Brindle, Cavendish Arms
Chipping, Dog & Partridge
Conder Green, Stork
Croston, Black Horse
Darwen, Old Rosins
Entwistle, Strawbury Duck
Fence, Forest
Garstang, Th'Owd Tithebarn
Liverpool, Baltic Fleet,
    Philharmonic Dining
    Rooms
Lytham, Taps
Manchester, Britons
    Protection, Dukes 92, Lass
    o' Gowrie, Marble Arch,
    Mark Addy, Royal Oak
Newton, Parkers Arms
Raby, Wheatsheaf
Ribchester, White Bull
Stalybridge, Station Buffet
Yealand Conyers, New Inn

Leicestershire
Empingham, White Horse
Glaston, Monckton Arms
Loughborough, Swan in the
    Rushes
Redmile, Peacock

Upper Hambleton, Finches Arms

Wing, Kings Arms

Lincolnshire

Grantham, Beehive

Heckington, Nags Head

Lincoln, Victoria, Wig & Mitre

Stamford, George of Stamford

London

Central London, Albert, Archery Tavern, Argyll Arms, Bishops Finger, Black Friar, Cittie of Yorke, Dog & Duck, Eagle, Grapes, Grenadier, Jerusalem Tavern, Lamb, Lamb & Flag, Leopard, Lord Moon of the Mall, Moon Under Water, Museum Tavern, Nags Head, O'Hanlons, Old Bank of England, Olde Cheshire Cheese, Olde Mitre, Orange Brewery, Red Lion, Seven Stars, Star, Westminster Arms

East London, Prospect of Whitby, Town of Ramsgate

North London, Chapel, Compton Arms, Flask, Holly Bush, Olde White Bear, Spaniards Inn, Waterside

South London, Alma, Anchor, Bulls Head, Crown & Greyhound, Cutty Sark, Fire Station, George, Horniman, Market Porter, Phoenix & Firkin, Ship, White Cross, Windmill

West London, both Anglesea Arms, Atlas, Bulls Head, Churchill Arms, Dove, Ladbroke Arms, White Horse, White Swan, Windsor Castle

Norfolk

Bawburgh, Kings Head

Blakeney, Kings Arms

Blickling, Buckinghamshire Arms

Brancaster Staithe, White Horse

Burnham Market, Hoste Arms

Fakenham, Wensum Lodge

Garboldisham, Fox

Hunworth, Blue Bell

Kings Lynn, Tudor Rose

Larling, Angel

Mundford, Crown

Norwich, Adam & Eve, Fat Cat

Reedham, Railway Tavern

Reepham, Old Brewery House

Sculthorpe, Sculthorpe Mill

Snettisham, Rose & Crown

Swanton Morley, Darbys

Thornham, Lifeboat

Tivetshall St Mary, Old Ram

Upper Sheringham, Red Lion

Winterton-on-Sea, Fishermans Return

Northamptonshire

Chacombe, George & Dragon

Chapel Brampton, Brampton Halt

Great Brington, Fox & Hounds

Oundle, Mill, Ship

Northumbria

Allendale, Kings Head

Craster, Jolly Fisherman

Etal, Black Bull

Greta Bridge, Morritt Arms

Haltwhistle, Wallace Arms

New York, Shiremoor Farm

Newcastle upon Tyne, Crown Posada

Seaton Sluice, Waterford Arms

Shincliffe, Seven Stars

Thropton, Three Wheat Heads

Nottinghamshire

Beeston, Victoria

Caunton, Caunton Beck

Elkesley, Robin Hood

Kimberley, Nelson & Railway

Nottingham, Fellows Morton & Clayton, Lincolnshire Poacher, Olde Trip to Jerusalem

Upton, French Horn

Oxfordshire

Bampton, Romany

Banbury, Reindeer

Bloxham, Elephant & Castle

Burford, Mermaid

Chipping Norton, Chequers

Clifton Hampden, Plough

Cuddesdon, Bat & Ball

Cumnor, Bear & Ragged Staff

Cuxham, Half Moon

Dorchester, George

East Hendred, Wheatsheaf

Exlade Street, Highwayman

Finstock, Plough

Kelmscot, Plough

Oxford, Kings Arms, Turf Tavern

Stanton St John, Talk House

Wytham, White Hart

Scotland

Aberdeen, Prince of Wales

Applecross, Applecross Inn

Ardfern, Galley of Lorne

Arduaine, Loch Melfort Hotel

Ardvasar, Ardvasar Hotel

Arrochar, Village Inn

Brig O Turk, Byre

Broughty Ferry, Fishermans Tavern

Carbost, Old Inn

Cawdor, Cawdor Tavern

Clachan Seil, Tigh an Truish

Crinan, Crinan Hotel

Cromarty, Royal

Edinburgh, Abbotsford, Bannermans, Bow Bar, Guildford Arms, Kays Bar, Ship on the Shore, Starbank

Elie, Ship

Fort Augustus, Lock

Gifford, Tweeddale Arms

Glasgow, Auctioneers, Babbity Bowster, Blackfriars, Counting House

Glendevon, Tormaukin

Haddington, Waterside

Houston, Fox & Hounds

Innerleithen, Traquair Arms

Inveraray, George

Inverarnan, Inverarnan Inn

Isle Of Whithorn, Steam Packet

Isle Ornsay, Eilean Iarmain

Kelso, Queens Head

Kippen, Cross Keys

Kippford, Anchor

Kirkton of Glenisla, Glenisla Hotel

Linlithgow, Four Marys

Lybster, Portland Arms

Mountbenger, Gordon Arms

Pitlochry, Moulin

Plockton, Plockton Hotel

Portpatrick, Crown

Sheriffmuir, Sheriffmuir Inn

Shieldaig, Tigh an Eilean Hotel

St Monance, Seafood Restaurant and Bar

Swinton, Wheatsheaf

Tayvallich, Tayvallich Inn

Thornhill, Lion & Unicorn

Ullapool, Ceilidh Place, Morefield Motel

Weem, Ailean Chraggan

Shropshire

Bishops Castle, Three Tuns

Cleobury Mortimer, Kings Arms

Cressage, Cholmondeley Riverside

Nesscliffe, Old Three Pigeons

Norton, Hundred House

Shrewsbury, Armoury

Somerset
Ashcott, Ashcott Inn
Bath, Old Green Tree
Beckington, Woolpack
Bristol, Highbury Vaults
Churchill, Crown
Clapton-in-Gordano, Black Horse
Farleigh Hungerford, Hungerford Arms
Huish Episcopi, Rose & Crown
Norton St Philip, George
Rudge, Full Moon
South Stoke, Pack Horse
Sparkford, Sparkford Inn
Stanton Wick, Carpenters Arms
Wells, City Arms

Staffordshire
Acton Trussell, Moat House
Alstonefield, George
Eccleshall, George
Onecote, Jervis Arms
Salt, Holly Bush

Suffolk
Butley, Oyster
Chelmondiston, Butt & Oyster
Chillesford, Froize
Cotton, Trowel & Hammer
Lavenham, Angel
Laxfield, Kings Head
Walberswick, Bell
Wangford, Angel

Surrey
Abinger Common, Abinger Hatch
Betchworth, Dolphin
Coldharbour, Plough
Effingham, Sir Douglas Haig
Friday Street, Stephan Langton
Gomshall, Compasses
Hascombe, White Horse
Leigh, Plough
Pirbright, Royal Oak
Reigate Heath, Skimmington Castle
Warlingham, White Lion
Wotton, Wotton Hatch

Sussex
Barcombe, Anchor
Barnham, Murrell Arms
Berwick, Cricketers Arms
Brownbread Street, Ash Tree
Burwash, Bell
Chiddingly, Six Bells
Coolham, George & Dragon
East Dean, Tiger
Firle, Ram
Hartfield, Anchor
Horsham, Black Jug
Icklesham, Queens Head
Kingston Near Lewes, Juggs
Lewes, Snowdrop
Oving, Gribble Inn
Pett, Two Sawyers
Playden, Peace & Plenty
Punnetts Town, Three Cups
Rushlake Green, Horse & Groom
Rye, Mermaid, Ypres Castle
Seaford, Golden Galleon

Wales
Beaumaris, Olde Bulls Head
Bodfari, Dinorben Arms
Bosherston, St Govans Inn
Capel Curig, Bryn Tyrch
Carew, Carew Inn
Colwyn Bay, Mountain View
Cresswell Quay, Cresselly Arms
Crickhowell, White Hart
East Aberthaw, Blue Anchor
Graianrhyd, Rose & Crown
Gresford, Pant-yr-Ochain
Halkyn, Britannia
Hay-on-Wye, Kilverts, Old Black Lion
Llanberis, Pen-y-Gwryd
Llandeilo, Castle
Llanferres, Druid
Llangynwyd, Old House
Maentwrog, Grapes
Monknash, Plough & Harrow
Penmaenpool, George III
Pontypool, Open Hearth
Porthmadog, Ship
Presteigne, Radnorshire Arms
Raglan, Clytha Arms
Red Wharf Bay, Ship
Reynoldston, King Arthur
St Hilary, Bush
Stackpole, Armstrong Arms
Talybont-on-Usk, Star

Warwickshire
Berkswell, Bear
Birmingham, Fiddle & Bone
Brierley Hill, Vine
Coventry, Old Windmill
Himley, Crooked House
Lapworth, Navigation
Lowsonford, Fleur de Lys
Warwick, Rose & Crown

Wiltshire
Box, Quarrymans Arms
Bradford-on-Avon, Cross Guns
Brinkworth, Three Crowns
Devizes, Bear
Fonthill Gifford, Beckford Arms
Hindon, Lamb
Lacock, George, Red Lion, Rising Sun
Marlborough, Sun
North Newnton, Woodbridge
Norton, Vine Tree
Pitton, Silver Plough
Salisbury, Haunch of Venison, New Inn
Semley, Benett Arms
Sherston, Rattlebone

Worcestershire
Bredon, Fox & Hounds
Bretforton, Fleece
Forhill, Peacock
Kidderminster, King & Castle
Knightwick, Talbot
Pensax, Bell
Worcester, Cardinals Hat

Yorkshire
Asenby, Crab & Lobster
Aysgarth, George & Dragon
Beck Hole, Birch Hall
Beverley, White Horse
Blakey Ridge, Lion
Boroughbridge, Black Bull
Bradfield, Strines Inn
Buckden, Buck
Burnsall, Red Lion
Cracoe, Devonshire Arms
Cray, White Lion
Cropton, New Inn
East Witton, Blue Lion
Egton Bridge, Horse Shoe
Elslack, Tempest Arms
Ferrensby, General Tarleton
Great Ouseburn, Crown
Harden, Malt Shovel
Harome, Star
Heath, Kings Arms
Heckmondwike, Old Hall
Hubberholme, George
Hull, Minerva, Olde White Harte
Ledsham, Chequers
Leeds, Whitelocks
Linthwaite, Sair
Linton, Windmill
Linton in Craven, Fountaine
Low Catton, Gold Cup
Masham, Kings Head, White Bear
Muker, Farmers Arms
Pickhill, Nags Head
Pool, White Hart
Ramsgill, Yorke Arms
Ripley, Boars Head
Ripponden, Old Bridge
Robin Hoods Bay, Laurel
Settle, Golden Lion
Sheffield, New Barrack
Thorganby, Jefferson Arms
Thornton Watlass, Buck
Whitby, Duke of York
Widdop, Pack Horse
York, Black Swan, Olde Starre, Spread Eagle, Tap & Spile

Pubs close to Motorway Junctions

The number at the start of each line is the number of the junction. Detailed directions are given in the main entry for each pub. In this section, to help you find the pubs quickly before you're past the junction, we give in abbreviated form the name of the chapter where you'll find the text.

M1
6: Bricket Wood, Moor Mill (Herts) 2 miles
13: Ridgmont, Rose & Crown (Beds) 2 miles
14: Moulsoe, Carrington Arms (Beds) 1¼ miles
18: Crick, Red Lion (Northants) 1 mile
24: Kegworth, Cap & Stocking (Leics) under a mile; Shardlow, Old Crown (Derbys) 2¼ miles
26: Kimberley, Nelson & Railway (Notts) 3 miles
29: Hardwick Hall, Hardwick Inn (Derbys) 4 miles

M3
5: Mattingley, Leather Bottle (Hants) 3 miles; Rotherwick, Coach & Horses (Hants) 4 miles
7: Dummer, Queen (Hants) ½ mile

M4
8: Bray, Fish (Berks) 1¾ miles
9: Holyport, Belgian Arms (Berks) 1½ miles
13: Winterbourne, Winterbourne Arms and Blue Boar, Chieveley (Berks) 3½ miles
14: Great Shefford, Swan (Berks) 2 miles; Hare & Hounds, Lambourn (Berks) 5 miles
18: Old Sodbury, Dog (Gloucs) 2 miles
21: Aust, Boars Head (Gloucs) ½ mile

M5
7: Kempsey, Walter de Cantelupe (Worcs) 3¾ miles
9: Bredon, Fox & Hounds (Worcs) 4½ miles
16: Almondsbury, Bowl (Gloucs) 1¼ miles
19: Clapton-in-Gordano, Black Horse (Somerset) 4 miles
28: Broadhembury, Drewe Arms (Devon) 5 miles
30: Woodbury Salterton, Diggers Rest (Devon) 3½ miles; Exeter, White Hart (Devon) 4 slow miles

M6
13: Acton Trussell, Moat House (Staffs) 2 miles
16: Barthomley, White Lion (Cheshire) 1 mile; White Lion, Weston (Cheshire) 3½ miles
19: Plumley, Smoker (Cheshire) 2½ miles
29: Brindle, Cavendish Arms (Lancs) 3 miles
32: Goosnargh, Bushells Arms (Lancs) 4 miles
33: Conder Green, Stork (Lancs) 3 miles
35: Yealand Conyers, New Inn (Lancs) 3 miles
40: Penrith, Agricultural (Cumbria) ¾ mile; Yanwath, Gate Inn (Cumbria) 2¼ miles; Stainton, Kings Arms (Cumbria) 3 miles; Tirril, Queens Head (Cumbria) 3½ miles; Askham, Punch Bowl (Cumbria) 4½ miles

M9
3: Linlithgow, Four Marys (Scotland) 2 miles

M11
7: Hastingwood, Rainbow & Dove (Essex) ¼ mile
10: Hinxton, Red Lion (Cambs) 2 miles; Thriplow, Green Man (Cambs) 3 miles

M25
8: Reigate Heath, Skimmington Castle (Surrey) 3 miles; Betchworth, Dolphin (Surrey) 4 miles
10: Cobham, Cricketers (Surrey) 3¾ miles
18: Chenies, Red Lion (Bucks) 2 miles; Flaunden, Bricklayers Arms (Herts) 4 miles

M27
1: Cadnam, White Hart (Hants) ½ mile; Fritham, Royal Oak (Hants) 4 miles
8: Bursledon, Jolly Sailor (Hants) 2 miles

M40
2: Beaconsfield, Greyhound (Bucks) 2 miles; Forty Green, Royal Standard of England (Bucks) 3½ miles
5: Ibstone, Fox (Bucks) 1 mile; Bolter End, Peacock (Bucks) 4 miles
6: Lewknor, Olde Leathern Bottel (Oxon) ½ mile; Watlington, Chequers (Oxon) 3 miles; Cuxham, Half Moon (Oxon) 4 miles
11: Chacombe, George & Dragon (Northants) 2½ miles

M42
2: Forhill, Peacock (Worcs) 2 miles

M45
1: Dunchurch, Dun Cow (Warwicks) 1⅓ miles

M48
1: Littleton-upon-Severn, White Hart (Gloucs) 3½ miles

M50
3: Upton Bishop, Moody Cow (Herefs) 2 miles

M56
12: Overton, Ring o' Bells (Cheshire) 2 miles

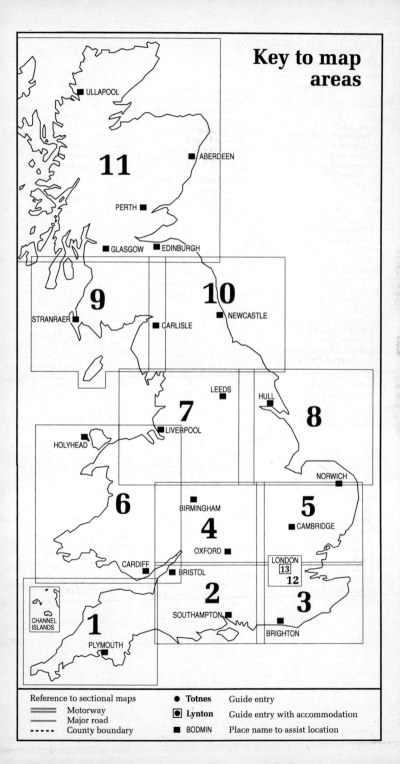

Key to map areas

ULLAPOOL

ABERDEEN

11

PERTH

GLASGOW   EDINBURGH

9

STRANRAER   CARLISLE

10

NEWCASTLE

LEEDS

HULL

7

LIVERPOOL

8

HOLYHEAD

NORWICH

6

BIRMINGHAM

5

CAMBRIDGE

4

OXFORD

LONDON
13
12

CARDIFF

BRISTOL

2

3

CHANNEL
ISLANDS

SOUTHAMPTON

BRIGHTON

1

PLYMOUTH

1

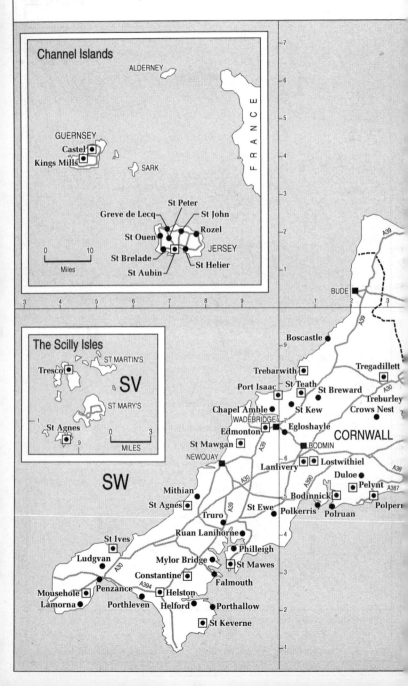

Channel Islands

ALDERNEY

GUERNSEY
Castel ■
Kings Mills ■

SARK

F R A N C E

St Peter
Greve de Lecq ● ● St John
● Rozel
St Ouen ● ●
■ JERSEY
St Brelade ● ● ● St Helier
St Aubin

0   10
Miles

3   4   5   6   7   8   9   1   2   3

BUDE ■

The Scilly Isles

ST MARTIN'S
Tresco ■
SV
ST MARY'S

St Agnes ●

0   3
MILES

SW

Boscastle ●

Trebarwith ● Tregadillett ■
Port Isaac ● St Teath ●
St Breward ● Treburley
Chapel Amble ● St Kew ● Crows Nest
WADEBRIDGE ■ ●
Edmonton ■ Egloshayle **CORNWALL**
St Mawgan ■ ■ BODMIN
NEWQUAY Lanlivery ● ■ Lostwithiel
Duloe ■
Pelynt ■
Mithian ● Bodinnick ■ Polruan ■ Polperro
St Agnes ■ St Ewe ●
Truro Polkerris ●
Ruan Lanihorne ●
St Ives ■ Philleigh ●
Ludgvan ■ Mylor Bridge ● ● St Mawes
Constantine ■
Mousehole ■ Penzance Falmouth
Lamorna ● Porthleven Helston Porthallow ●
Helford ●
St Keverne ■

A39
A30
A38
A387
A390
A394

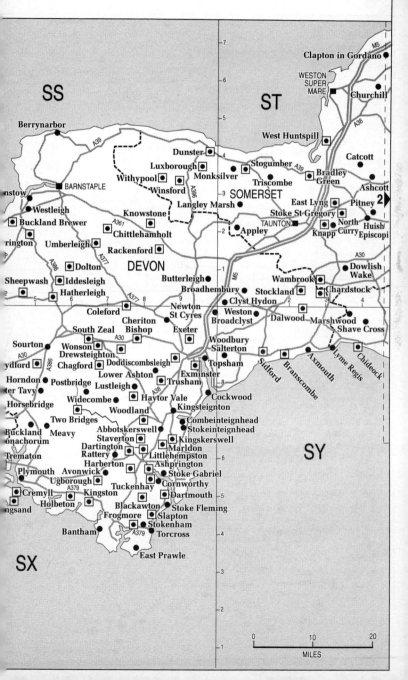

1

SS

ST

SY

SX

Clapton in Gordano

WESTON SUPER MARE

Churchill

Berrynarbor

West Huntspill

Catcott

Dunster

Stogumber

Bradley Green

Ashcott

Luxborough

Monksilver

Withypool

Triscombe

Pitney

2

Winsford

SOMERSET

East Lyng

Huish Episcopi

BARNSTAPLE

Langley Marsh

Stoke St Gregory

nstow

Knowstone

North Curry

Knapp

Westleigh

Buckland Brewer

Chittlehamholt

Appley

Umberleigh

rington

DEVON

Rackenford

Dolton

Butterleigh

Dowlish Wake

Sheepwash

Iddesleigh

Broadhembury

Wambrook

Hatherleigh

Stockland

Chardstock

Coleford

Newton St Cyres

Clyst Hydon

Weston

Dalwood

Marshwood

Cheriton Bishop

Exeter

Broadclyst

Shave Cross

South Zeal

Woodbury Salterton

Chideock

Sourton

Wonson

Axmouth

Lyme Regis

ydford

Drewsteignton

Doddiscombsleigh

Topsham

Sidford

Branscombe

Horndon

Chagford

Exminster

ter Tavy

Postbridge

Lower Ashton

Trusham

Horsebridge

Lustleigh

Haytor Vale

Cockwood

Widecombe

Kingsteignton

Buckland onachorum

Two Bridges

Woodland

Combeinteignhead

Meavy

Abbotskerswell

Stokeinteignhead

Trematon

Staverton

Kingskerswell

Dartington

Marldon

Plymouth

Avonwick

Rattery

Littlehempston

Ashprington

Ugborough

Harberton

Stoke Gabriel

Cremyll

Kingston

Tuckenhay

Cornworthy

Holbeton

Dartmouth

ngsand

Blackawton

Stoke Fleming

Frogmore

Slapton

Bantham

Stokenham

Torcross

East Prawle

0   10   20
MILES

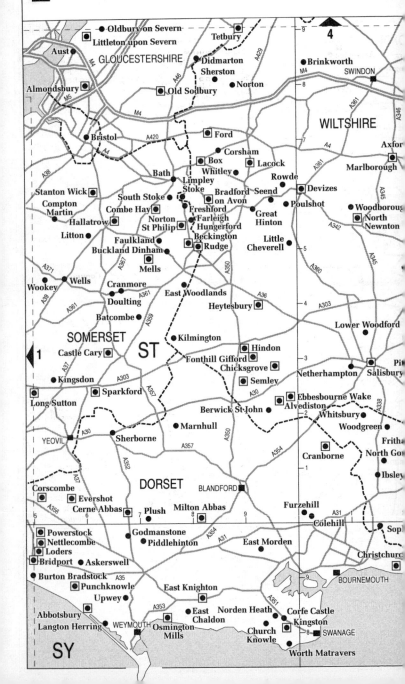

2

4

Oldbury on Severn
Littleton upon Severn
Tetbury
Aust
GLOUCESTERSHIRE
Didmarton
Sherston
Almondsbury
Old Sodbury
Norton
Brinkworth
SWINDON

Bristol
Ford
WILTSHIRE
Axfor

Corsham
Box
Lacock
Marlborough
Bath
Whitley
Limpley
Stoke
Rowde
Stanton Wick
South Stoke
Bradford
on Avon
Seend
Devizes
Compton
Martin
Combe Hay
Freshford
Poulshot
Woodboroug
Hallatrow
Norton
St Philip
Farleigh
Hungerford
Great
Hinton
North
Newnton
Litton
Faulkland
Beckington
Buckland Dinham
Rudge
Little
Cheverell
Mells
Wells
Cranmore
East Woodlands
Wookey
Doulting
Heytesbury
Batcombe
Lower Woodford
SOMERSET
Kilmington
ST
Castle Cary
Hindon
Fonthill Gifford
Chicksgrove
Pi
Kingsdon
Netherhampton
Salisbury
Sparkford
Semley
Long Sutton
Ebbesbourne Wake
Alvediston
Berwick St John
Whitsbury
Marnhull
Woodgreen
YEOVIL
Sherborne
Fritha
North Go
Cranborne
Ibsley
Corscombe
DORSET
BLANDFORD
Evershot
Furzehill
Cerne Abbas
Plush
Milton Abbas
Colehill
Powerstock
Godmanstone
Sop
Nettlecombe
Piddlehinton
East Morden
Loders
Bridport
Askerswell
Christchur
Burton Bradstock
Punchknowle
East Knighton
Upwey
Abbotsbury
East
Chaldon
Norden Heath
Corfe Castle
Langton Herring
WEYMOUTH
Osmington
Mills
Church
Knowle
Kingston
SWANAGE
SY
Worth Matravers
BOURNEMOUTH

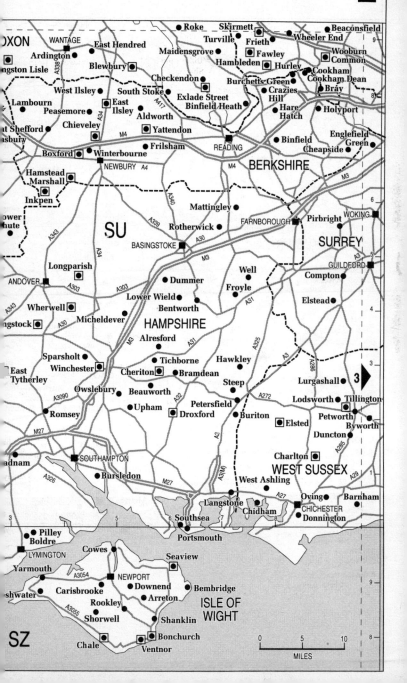

2

OXON
WANTAGE
Ardington ●
ngston Lisle
Blewbury ●
Lambourn
Peasemore ●
at Shefford
sbury
Chieveley
Boxford ● Winterbourne ● Frilsham
Hamstead Marshall ●
Inkpen ●
ower hute
SU
NEWBURY A4
ANDOVER ■
Wherwell ●
ngstock ●
East Tytherley
Sparsholt ●
Winchester ●
Romsey
M27
adnam
SOUTHAMPTON ■
Bursledon ●
LYMINGTON
Yarmouth
shwater
Pilley ● Boldre ●
Cowes
A3054 NEWPORT ■
Carisbrooke ●
Rookley ●
Shorwell ●
Chale ●
SZ

East Hendred ●
West Ilsley ●
South Stoke ●
East Ilsley ●
Aldworth ●
Yattendon ●
Longparish ●
Dummer ●
Lower Wield ●
Bentworth ●
Micheldever ●
HAMPSHIRE
Alresford ●
Tichborne ●
Cheriton ●
Bramdean ●
Owslebury ● Beauworth ●
Upham ●
Droxford ●

Roke ● Skirmett ●
Turville ● Frieth ●
Maidensgrove ● Fawley ●
Hambleden ● Hurley ●
Checkendon ● Burchetts Green
Exlade Street Crazies Hill
Binfield Heath Hare Hatch
READING
BERKSHIRE
Binfield ●
Cheapside ●
Mattingley ●
Rotherwick ●
FARNBOROUGH ■
BASINGSTOKE ■
M3
Well ●
Froyle ●
A31
Hawkley ●
Steep ●
A272
Petersfield ●
Buriton ●
Elsted ●
Charlton ●
WEST SUSSEX
West Ashling ●
Langstone ● Chidham
Southsea
Portsmouth
Seaview ●
Downend ● Bembridge ●
Arreton ●
ISLE OF WIGHT
Shanklin ●
Bonchurch ●
Ventnor

Beaconsfield ●
Wheeler End
Wooburn Common ●
Cookham
Cookham Dean
Bray ●
Holyport ●
Englefield Green
WOKING ■
SURREY
GUILDFORD ■
Compton ●
Elstead ●
Lurgashall ●
Lodsworth ● Tillington ●
Petworth ●
Byworth ●
Duncton ●
Oving ● Barnham ●
CHICHESTER
Donnington

0   5   10
MILES

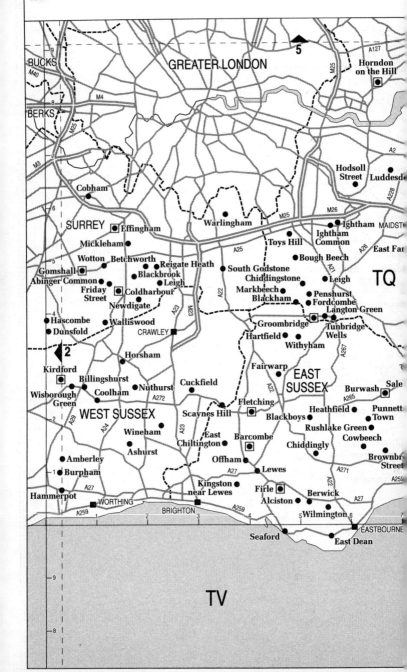

3

BUCKS

BERKS

GREATER LONDON

5

Horndon
on the Hill

Hodsoll
Street

Luddesd

Cobham

SURREY

Effingham

Warlingham

Ightham

Toys Hill

Ightham
Common

MAIDST

East Far

Mickleham

Wotton

Betchworth

Reigate Heath

Bough Beech

Gomshall

Blackbrook

South Godstone

TQ

Abinger Common

Friday
Street

Coldharbour

Chiddingstone

Leigh

Markbeech

Penshurst

Leigh

Newdigate

Blackham

Fordcombe

Hascombe

Walliswood

Langton Green

Dunsfold

CRAWLEY

Groombridge

Tunbridge
Wells

2

Hartfield

Withyham

Kirdford

Horsham

Fairwarp

Billingshurst

EAST
SUSSEX

Wisborough
Green

Coolham

Nuthurst

Cuckfield

Burwash

Sale

Fletching

Heathfield

Punnett
Town

WEST SUSSEX

Scaynes Hill

Blackboys

Wineham

Rushlake Green

Cowbeech

Ashurst

East
Chiltington

Barcombe

Chiddingly

Amberley

Offham

Brownbr
Street

Burpham

Lewes

Hammerpot

WORTHING

Kingston
near Lewes

Firle

Berwick

BRIGHTON

Alciston

Wilmington

EASTBOURNE

Seaford

East Dean

TV

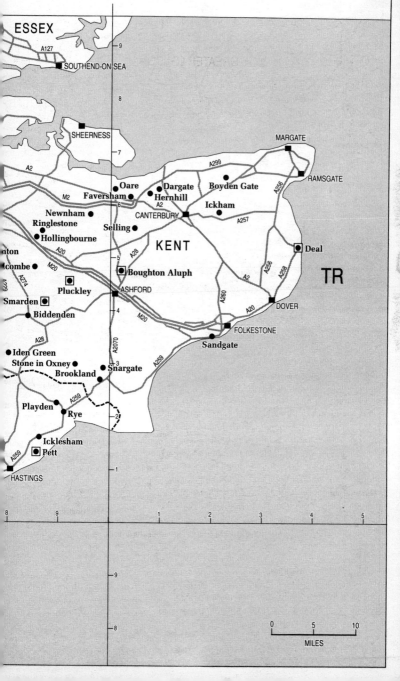

3

ESSEX

A127

SOUTHEND-ON-SEA

SHEERNESS

A2

A299

MARGATE

RAMSGATE

Oare • Dargate • Boyden Gate
Faversham • Hernhill
Newnham • A2
Ringlestone CANTERBURY
Hollingbourne Selling • Ickham A257

A256

Deal

M2

KENT

nton
combe •
A20
M20 A28
Boughton Aluph
A274 Pluckley ASHFORD
Smarden A360 A2 A256 A258 TR
Biddenden M20
A28
Iden Green A2070
Stone in Oxney • A20
Brookland Snargate A259 FOLKESTONE
Playden A259 Sandgate
Rye
Icklesham
Pett
HASTINGS

DOVER

A2

9

8

7

6

5

4

3

2

1

8   9   1   2   3   4   5

9

8

0   5   10
MILES

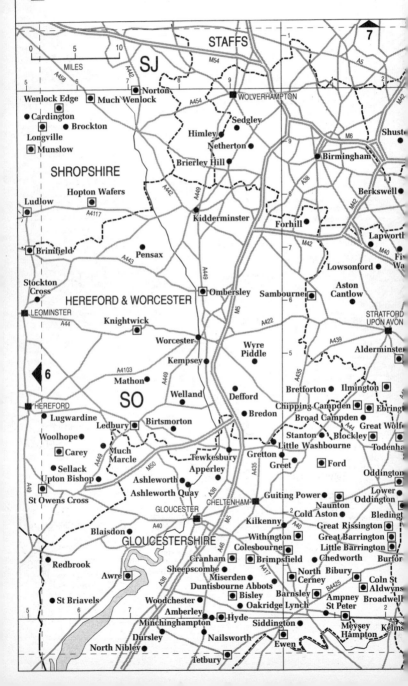

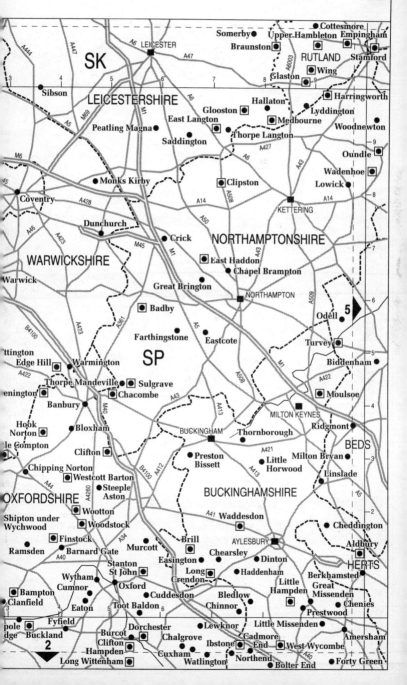

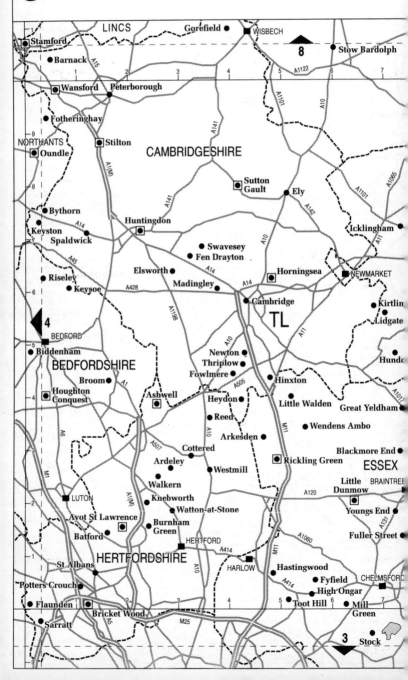

5

LINCS

Stamford
Barnack
Gorefield •
Wisbech
8
Stow Bardolph •

Wansford
Peterborough
A1122

Fotheringhay •

NORTHANTS
Stilton •
CAMBRIDGESHIRE

Oundle •

Bythorn •
Sutton Gault •
Ely •
Icklingham •

Keyston •
Huntingdon
Spaldwick
Swavesey •
Fen Drayton •

Elsworth •
Horningsea •
NEWMARKET

Riseley •
Madingley •

Keysoe •
Cambridge •
Kirtlin •

TL
Lidgate •

4
BEDFORD

Biddenham •
Newton •
Hundo

BEDFORDSHIRE
Thriplow •
Fowlmere •

Broom •
Hinxton •

Houghton
Conquest
Ashwell •
Heydon •
Little Walden •

Reed •
Great Yeldham •

Arkesden •
Wendens Ambo •

Cottered •
Blackmore End •

Ardeley •
Rickling Green •
ESSEX

Westmill •

Walkern •
Little
Dunmow
BRAINTREE

Ayot St Lawrence •
Knebworth •
Watton-at-Stone •
Youngs End •

Burnham
Green
LUTON

Batford •
HERTFORD
Fuller Street •

St Albans •
HERTFORDSHIRE
HARLOW

Potters Crouch •
Hastingwood •
CHELMSFORD

Flaunden •
Fyfield •

Bricket Wood
High Ongar •

Sarratt •
Toot Hill •
Mill
Green •

M25

3
Stock •

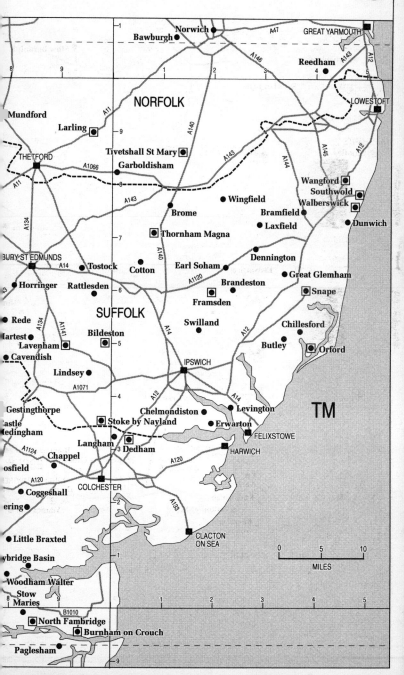

5

Norwich
Bawburgh
A47
GREAT YARMOUTH
A146
A143
Reedham 4
A12

NORFOLK
A11
Mundford
Larling 9
A140
LOWESTOFT
Tivetshall St Mary
THETFORD
A1066
Garboldisham
A143
A11
A143
Wingfield
Brome
Thornham Magna
7
A140
A144
A145
A12
Wangford
Southwold
Walberswick
Bramfield
Laxfield
Dunwich

BURY ST EDMUNDS
A14
Tostock
Cotton
Earl Soham
Dennington
Horringer
Rattlesden
6
A1120
Brandeston
Great Glemham
Rede
A134
A1141
SUFFOLK
Framsden
Snape
artest
Lavenham
Bildeston
5
Swilland
Chillesford
Butley
Orford
Cavendish
Lindsey
A14
A12
A1071
4
IPSWICH
Gestingthorpe
A12
A14
TM
astle
edingham
Stoke by Nayland
Chelmondiston
Levington
Erwarton
A1124
Langham
3 Dedham
FELIXSTOWE
Chappel
HARWICH
osfield
A120
A120
COLCHESTER
Coggeshall
2
A133
ering
Little Braxted
1
0   5   10
ybridge Basin
MILES
Woodham Walter
Stow
Maries
8
CLACTON
ON SEA
B1010
North Fambridge
Burnham on Crouch
Paglesham
9
1   2   3   4   5

8   9

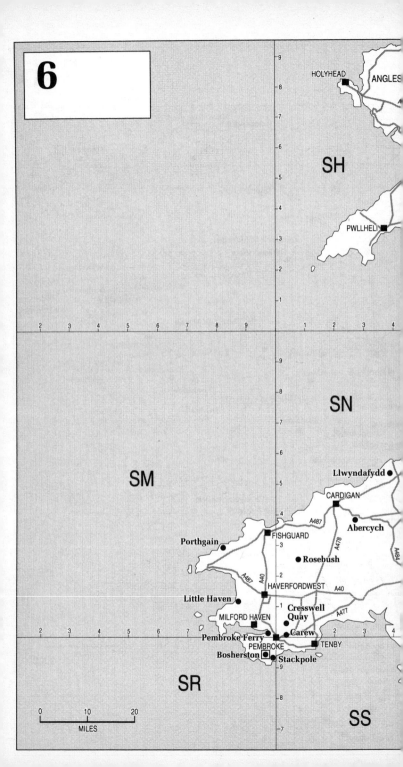

6

HOLYHEAD
ANGLES

SH

PWLLHELI

SN

SM

Llwyndafydd ●

CARDIGAN

Abercych

Porthgain ●

A487

FISHGUARD

A478

A484

● Rosebush

A487   A40

HAVERFORDWEST   A40

Little Haven ●

**Cresswell
Quay**

A477

MILFORD HAVEN

Carew

Pembroke Ferry

● TENBY

PEMBROKE

Bosherston ●

● **Stackpole**

SR

SS

0   10   20
MILES

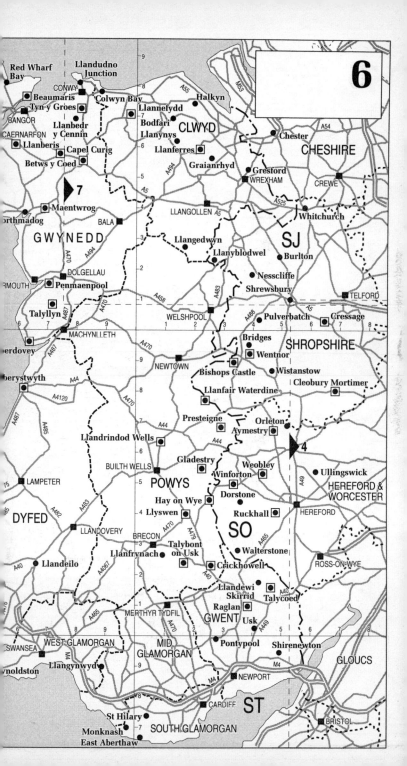

7

9

MILES
0   10   20

Ulverston
Beetham
Casterton
Kirkby Lonsdal
Cartmel
Yealand Conyers
BARROW-IN-FURNESS
Settle
SD
LANCASHIRE
Conder Green
Whitewell
Newton
Downham
Garstang
Chipping
Wharles
Goosnargh
Fen
BLACKPOOL
Ribchester
PRESTON
Lytham
Brindle
Darwen
Entwh
Croston
Belmont
SOUTHPORT
Bispham Green
GREATER
MANCHEST
MERSEYSIDE
Liverpool
Llandudno
Junction
Colwyn Bay
Raby
Overton
CHESHIRE
Lowe
CONWY
Plumley
Peove
Tyn y Groes
Bodfari
Halkyn
Delamere
Over Peover
Pe
Llanbedr y
Cennin
Llannefydd
Willington Corner
Whitegate
He
CLWYD
Chester
Cotebrook
Llanferres
Tarporley
Llanynys
Aldford
Handley
Wettenhall
Betws y Coed
Graianrhyd
Higher Burwardsley
Bunbury
Barthor
Gresford
Broxton
Nantwich
Llanelidan
Faddiley
We
WREXHAM
Bickley Moss
Shraleybrook
GWYNEDD
LLANGOLLEN
SJ
Wrenbury
Aston
BALA
Whitchurch
6
Llanyblodwel
Burlton
Nesscliffe
SHROPSHIRE
Shrewsbury

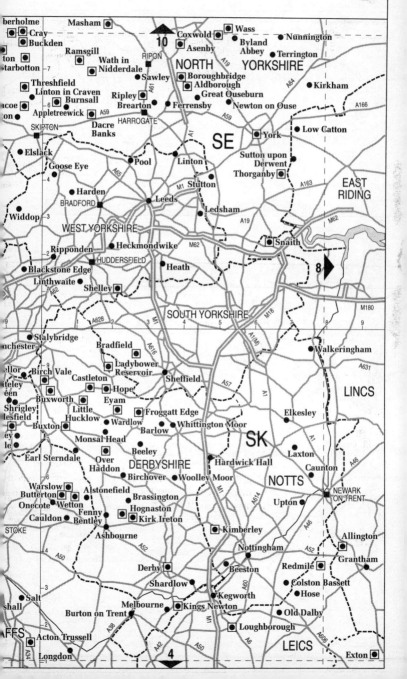

berholme
Masham
Cray
Buckden
ton
Starbotton
Ramsgill
Wath in
Nidderdale
Threshfield
Linton in Craven
Burnsall
acoe
Appletreewick
on
SKIPTON
Dacre
Banks
Elslack
Goose Eye
Harden
BRADFORD
Widdop
WEST YORKSHIRE
Ripponden
Heckmondwike
HUDDERSFIELD
Blackstone Edge
Linthwaite
Shelley
Heath

Coxwold
Asenby
RIPON
NORTH
YORKSHIRE
Sawley
Boroughbridge
Aldborough
Great Ouseburn
Ripley
Brearton
Ferrensby
Newton on Ouse
HARROGATE
Pool
Linton
Stutton
Leeds
Ledsham

Wass
Nunnington
Byland
Abbey
Terrington
Kirkham
A166
Newton on Ouse
York
Low Catton
SE
Sutton upon
Derwent
Thorganby
EAST
RIDING
Snaith
8
M180

Stalybridge
nchester
Bradfield
ellor
Birch Vale
teley
Castleton
een
Hope
Buxworth
Eyam
Shrigley
Little
lesfield
Hucklow
Buxton
Wardlow
Monsal Head
Earl Sterndale
Over
Haddon
Warslow
Butterton
Onecote
Wetton
Cauldon
Fenny
Bentley
Ashbourne
STOKE

Ladybower
Reservoir
Sheffield
Froggatt Edge
Barlow
Whittington Moor
Beeley
Birchover
Woolley Moor
DERBYSHIRE
Hardwick Hall
Brassington
Hognaston
Kirk Ireton
Kimberley
Derby
Shardlow
Melbourne
Kings Newton
Burton on Trent

Walkeringham
A631
LINCS
Elkesley
SK
Laxton
Caunton
NOTTS
NEWARK
ON TRENT
Upton
Allington
Grantham
Nottingham
Beeston
Redmile
Colston Bassett
Hose
Kegworth
Old Dalby
Loughborough
LEICS
Exton

Salt
shall
Acton Trussell
Longdon
FFS

4

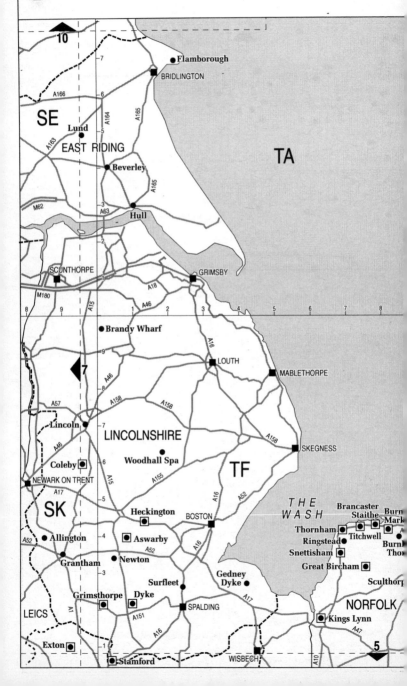

10

Flamborough
BRIDLINGTON

A166

SE

Lund

EAST RIDING

A164   A165

Beverley

A165

M62

A63

Hull

TA

2

SCUNTHORPE

M180   A18   GRIMSBY

A15   A46

M180

8   9   1   A46   2   3   4   5   6   7   8

Brandy Wharf

A16

9

7   LOUTH

A46

MABLETHORPE

8

A158   A158

A57

A46

Lincoln

LINCOLNSHIRE

A158   SKEGNESS

7

Coleby

6   Woodhall Spa

TF

NEWARK ON TRENT

A15   A155

A17

SK

5

A16   A52

THE
WASH

Brancaster
Staithe

Burn

A52

Heckington   BOSTON

Mark

4   Aswarby

Thornham

Burn

A52   Allington

A52

Titchwell

Thor

Newton

Ringstead

Grantham

3   A16

Snettisham

Surfleet   Gedney
Dyke

Great Bircham

Grimsthorpe   Dyke

A17   Sculthorp

LEICS

A1   SPALDING

NORFOLK

A151

A16   Kings Lynn

A47

1   Exton

5

Stamford   WISBECH   A10

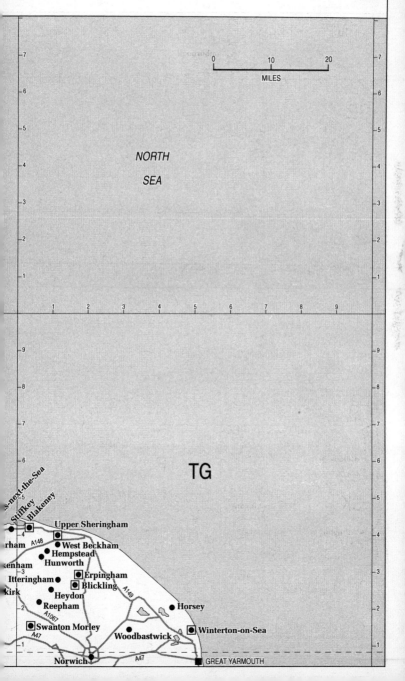

8

0   10   20
MILES

NORTH

SEA

TG

s-next-the-Sea
Stiffkey
Blakeney
Upper Sheringham
ham
A148
West Beckham
Hempstead
Hunworth
kenham
Erpingham
Itteringham
Blickling
kirk
A148
Heydon
Reepham
Horsey
A1067
Swanton Morley
A47
Woodbastwick
Winterton-on-Sea
Norwich
A47
GREAT YARMOUTH

9

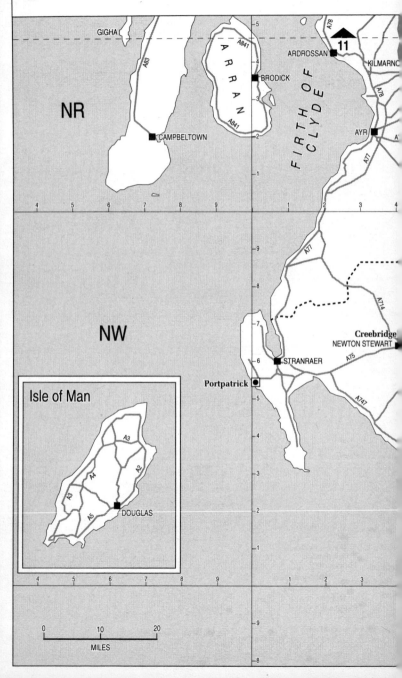

GIGHA

A83

A841

ARRAN

■ BRODICK

■ CAMPBELTOWN

NR

FIRTH OF CLYDE

ARDROSSAN ■

11

KILMARNC

A78

A78

AYR ■

A

A77

A77

A714

Creebridge
NEWTON STEWART ■

STRANRAER ■

A75

Portpatrick ●

A747

NW

Isle of Man

A3

A4

A2

A3

A5

■ DOUGLAS

0   10   20
MILES

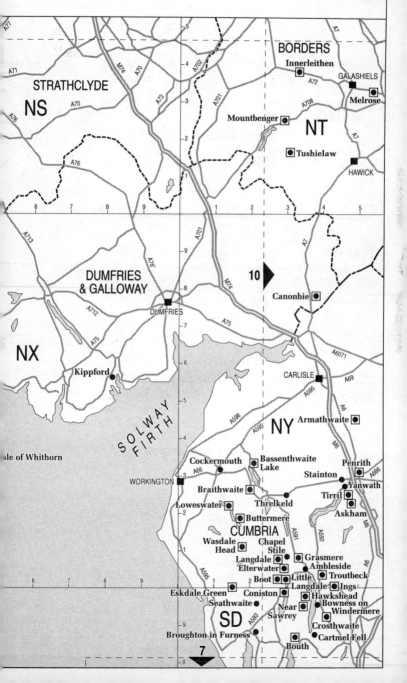

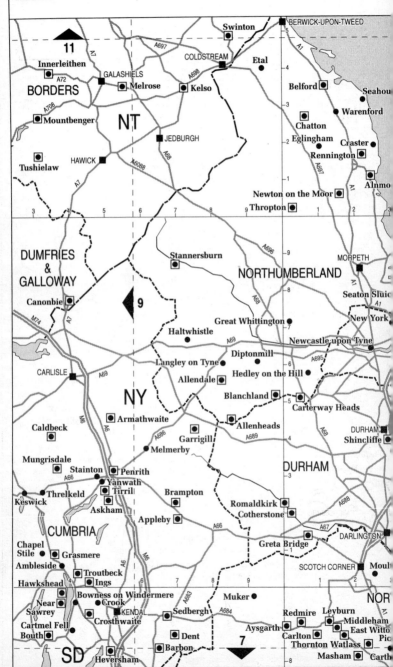

11

Innerleithen

A72

BORDERS

A7

GALASHIELS

Melrose

A708

Mountbenger

Tushielaw

A7

NT

HAWICK

A6088

JEDBURGH

A68

Swinton

A697

COLDSTREAM

A698

Kelso

Etal

BERWICK-UPON-TWEED

A1

4

Belford

Seahou

Warenford

3

Chatton

2

Eglingham

Rennington

Craster

1

Alnmo

Newton on the Moor

Thropton

A697

DUMFRIES & GALLOWAY

Canonbie

M74

A7

9

Stannersburn

A696

MORPETH

NORTHUMBERLAND

A1

Seaton Sluic

A1

New York

9

8

A68

Great Whittington

Haltwhistle

A69

Diptonmill

CARLISLE

A69

Langley on Tyne

Allendale

Newcastle upon Tyne

6

A695

Hedley on the Hill

NY

Blanchland

Carterway Heads

5

Armathwaite

A686

Allenheads

DURHAM

Shincliffe

Caldbeck

Garrigill

A689

4

Melmerby

A68

Mungrisdale

A6

Stainton

Penrith

DURHAM

Yanwath

Tirril

Brampton

3

Keswick

Threlkeld

Askham

Romaldkirk

A688

Cotherstone

Appleby

A66

CUMBRIA

DARLINGTON

Chapel Stile

Grasmere

Greta Bridge

A67

1

Ambleside

Troutbeck

SCOTCH CORNER

Moul

Hawkshead

Ings

A6

M6

7

8

A693

9

1

2

Near Sawrey

Bowness on Windermere

Crook

Muker

Redmire

Leyburn

NOR

Cartmel Fell

KENDAL

Crosthwaite

Sedbergh

A684

Middleham

Bouth

Dent

Barbon

Aysgarth

Carlton

East Witto

Pic

7

Thornton Watlass

Masham

Carth

Heversham

SD

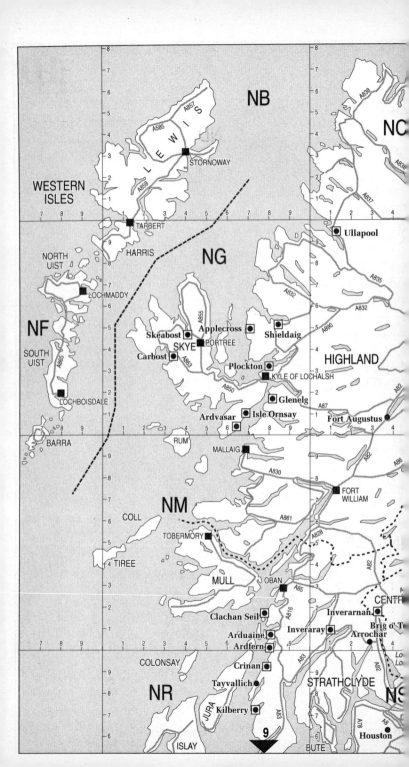

11

THURSO

WICK

ND

Lybster

0   10   20

MILES

A836   A836   A897   A9   A895

6 7 8 9   1 2 3 4 5 6 7 8 9   1 2 3 4

DORNOCH

Cromarty

BANFF   FRASERBURGH

Cawdor

INVERNESS

NK

A96   A95   A97   A98

NJ

GRANTOWN-ON-SPEY   **GRAMPIAN**

A95   A96   A92

NH

A9

Aberdeen

6 7 8 9   1 2 3 4 5 6 7 8 9   1 2 3 4

A93   A93   A90

Stonehaven

Kirkton of
Glenisla

A9   A90   A92

Pitlochry   **TAYSIDE**   MONTROSE

Weem   A827

A94

NO

DUNDEE   Broughty Ferry

PERTH   A90

A85

ST ANDREWS

mahog   Sheriffmuir   M90   A91   **FIFE**   St Monance

hornhill   Glendevon   A92   3

ippen   STIRLING   Elie

M9   M90

A9

NT

East Linton

Linlithgow   Edinburgh   Haddington

M9   A1   Gifford

asgow   M73   M8   M8   **L O T H I A N**   A70   **10**   **BORDERS**   BERWICK UPON TWEED

M74   A70   A1   A68

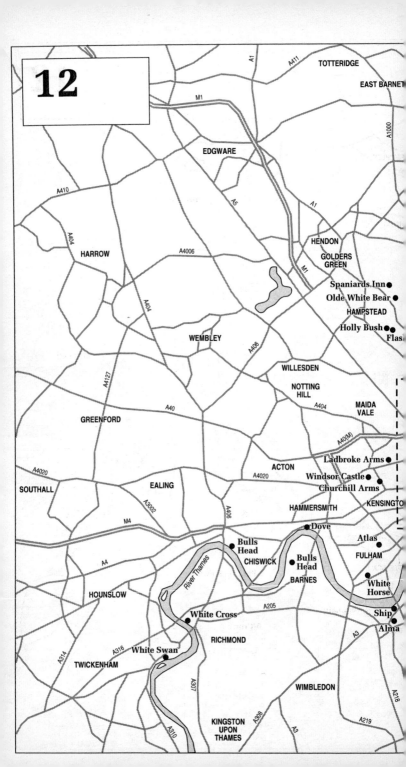

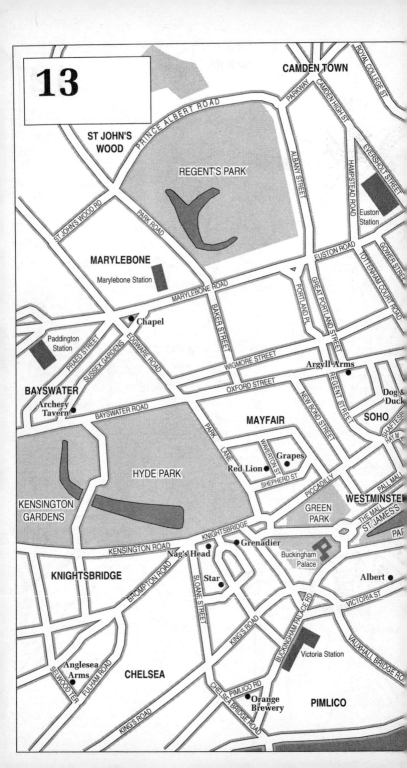

13

CAMDEN TOWN

ROYAL COLLEGE ST

PARKWAY

CAMDEN HIGH ST

ST JOHN'S WOOD

PRINCE ALBERT ROAD

ALBANY STREET

HAMPSTEAD ROAD

EVERSHOLT STREET

REGENT'S PARK

ST JOHN'S WOOD RD

PARK ROAD

Euston Station

EUSTON ROAD

GOWER STREET

MARYLEBONE

Marylebone Station

MARYLEBONE ROAD

BAKER STREET

PORTLAND PL

GREAT PORTLAND STREET

TOTTENHAM COURT ROAD

Paddington Station

PRAED STREET

SUSSEX GARDENS

EDGWARE ROAD

• Chapel

WIGMORE STREET

BAYSWATER

OXFORD STREET

REGENT STREET

Argyll Arms •

Dog & Duck

Archery Tavern •

BAYSWATER ROAD

PARK LANE

MAYFAIR

NEW BOND STREET

SOHO

SHAFTESBURY AV

Grapes •

WAVERTON ST

Red Lion •

SHEPHERD ST

PICCADILLY

PALL MALL

HYDE PARK

WESTMINSTER

KENSINGTON GARDENS

GREEN PARK

THE MALL

ST JAMES'S

PARK

KENSINGTON ROAD

KNIGHTSBRIDGE

Grenadier •

Nag's Head •

Buckingham Palace

KNIGHTSBRIDGE

BROMPTON ROAD

SLOANE STREET

Star •

Albert •

VICTORIA ST

KING'S ROAD

BUCKINGHAM PALACE RD

VAUXHALL BRIDGE RD

Victoria Station

Anglesea Arms •

SELWOOD TER

FULHAM ROAD

CHELSEA

KING'S ROAD

PIMLICO RD

CHELSEA BRIDGE ROAD

• **Orange Brewery**

PIMLICO

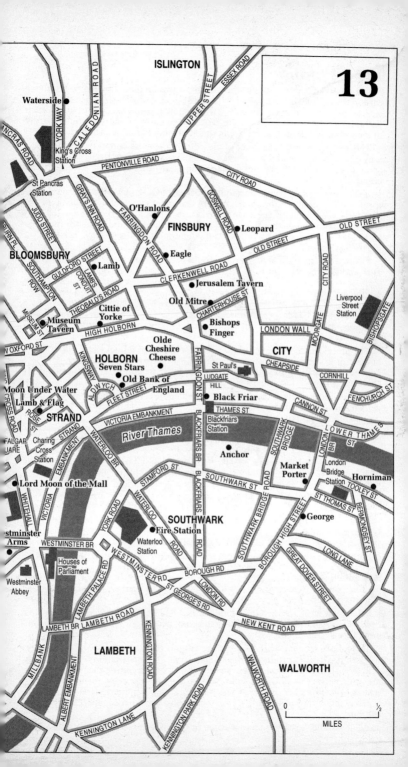

13

ISLINGTON

Waterside

King's Cross Station

St Pancras Station

PENTONVILLE ROAD

CITY ROAD

OLD STREET

O'Hanlons

FINSBURY

Leopard

BLOOMSBURY

Eagle

Lamb

CLERKENWELL ROAD

Jerusalem Tavern

Old Mitre

Liverpool Street Station

Cittie of Yorke

Bishops Finger

LONDON WALL

Museum Tavern

HIGH HOLBORN

CITY

CHEAPSIDE

Olde Cheshire Cheese

St Paul's

CORNHILL

HOLBORN

Seven Stars

Old Bank of England

LUDGATE HILL

Moon Under Water

Black Friar

Lamb & Flag

FLEET STREET

THAMES ST

Blackfriars Station

STRAND

VICTORIA EMBANKMENT

River Thames

Anchor

Market Porter

London Bridge Station

Horniman

Charing Cross Station

Lord Moon of the Mall

STAMFORD ST

SOUTHWARK ST

George

SOUTHWARK

Fire Station

Waterloo Station

stminster Arms

WESTMINSTER BR

Houses of Parliament

WESTMINSTER RD

BOROUGH RD

Westminster Abbey

LAMBETH BR

LAMBETH ROAD

NEW KENT ROAD

LAMBETH

WALWORTH

KENNINGTON LANE

0   ½

MILES

Report forms

Please report to us: you can use the tear-out forms on the following pages, the card in the middle of the book, or just plain paper – whichever's easiest for you – or you can report to our website, www.goodguides.com. We need to know what you think of the pubs in this edition. We need to know about other pubs worthy of inclusion. We need to know about ones that should not be included.

The atmosphere and character of the pub are the most important features – why it would, or would not, appeal to strangers, so please try to describe what is special about it. But the bar food and the drink are important too – please tell us about them.

If the food is really quite outstanding, tick the FOOD AWARD box on the form, and tell us about the special quality that makes it stand out – the more detail, the better. And if you have stayed there, tell us about the standard of accommodation – whether it was comfortable, pleasant, good value for money. Again, if the pub or inn is worth special attention as a place to stay, tick the PLACE-TO-STAY AWARD box.

Please try to gauge whether a pub should be a main entry, or is best as a Lucky Dip (and tick the relevant box). In general, main entries need qualities that would make it worth other readers' while to travel some distance to them; Lucky Dips are the pubs that are worth knowing about if you are nearby. But if a pub is an entirely new recommendation, the Lucky Dip may be the best place for it to start its career in the *Guide* – to encourage other readers to report on it, and gradually build up a dossier on it; it's very rare for a pub to jump straight into the main entries.

The more detail you can put into your description of a Lucky Dip pub that's only scantily decribed in the current edition (or not in at all), the better. This'll help not just us but also your fellow-readers gauge its appeal. A description of its character and even furnishings is a tremendous boon.

It helps enormously if you can give the full address for any new pub – one not yet a main entry, or without a full address in the Lucky Dip sections. In a town, we need the street name; in the country, if it's hard to find, we need directions. Without this, there's little chance of our being able to include the pub. **Even better for us is the postcode.** And with any pub, it always helps to let us know about **prices** of food (and bedrooms, if there are any), and about any lunchtimes or evenings when food is **not** served. We'd also like to have your views on drinks quality – beer, wine, cider and so forth, even coffee and tea – and do let us know if it has bedrooms.

If you know that a Lucky Dip pub is open all day (or even late into the afternoon), please tell us – preferably saying which days.

When you go to a pub, don't tell them you're a reporter for the *Good Pub Guide*; we do make clear that all inspections are anonymous, and if you declare yourself as a reporter you risk getting special treatment – for better or for worse!

Sometimes pubs are dropped from the main entries simply because very few readers have written to us about them – and of course there's a risk that people may not write if they find the pub exactly as described in the entry. You can use the form on the page opposite just to list pubs you've been to, found as described, and can recommend.

When you write to The Good Pub Guide, FREEPOST TN1569, WADHURST, East Sussex TN5 7BR, you don't need a stamp in the UK. We'll gladly send you more forms (free) if you wish.

Though we try to answer letters, there are just the four of us – and with other work to do, besides producing this *Guide*. So please understand if there's a delay. And from June till August, when we are fully extended getting the next edition to the printers, we put all letters and reports aside, not answering them until the rush is over (and after our post-press-day late summer holiday). The end of May is pretty much the cut-off date for reasoned consideration of reports for the next edition.

We'll assume we can print your name or initials as a recommender unless you tell us otherwise.

I have been to the following pubs in *The Good Pub Guide 2000* in the last few months, found them as described, and confirm that they deserve continued inclusion:

Continued overleaf

PLEASE GIVE YOUR NAME AND ADDRESS ON THE BACK OF THIS FORM

Pubs visited continued...

....

Your own name and address *(block capitals please)*

....

Please return to
The Good Pub Guide,
FREEPOST TN1569,
WADHURST,
East Sussex
TN5 7BR

REPORT ON   *(pub's name)*

....

Pub's address

....

☐ **YES MAIN ENTRY**   ☐ **YES** *Lucky Dip*   ☐ **NO don't include**
Please tick one of these boxes to show your verdict, and give reasons and
descriptive comments, prices etc

☐ Deserves FOOD award   ☐ Deserves PLACE-TO-STAY award   2000:1

PLEASE GIVE YOUR NAME AND ADDRESS ON THE BACK OF THIS FORM

--✂

REPORT ON   *(pub's name)*

....

Pub's address

....

☐ **YES MAIN ENTRY**   ☐ **YES** *Lucky Dip*   ☐ **NO don't include**
Please tick one of these boxes to show your verdict, and give reasons and
descriptive comments, prices etc

☐ Deserves FOOD award   ☐ Deserves PLACE-TO-STAY award   2000:2

PLEASE GIVE YOUR NAME AND ADDRESS ON THE BACK OF THIS FORM

Your own name and address *(block capitals please)*

DO NOT USE THIS SIDE OF THE PAGE FOR WRITING ABOUT PUBS

Your own name and address *(block capitals please)*

DO NOT USE THIS SIDE OF THE PAGE FOR WRITING ABOUT PUBS

If you would like to order a copy of *The Good Britain Guide 2000* (£14.99), *The Good Hotel Guide 2000 Great Britain & Ireland* (£12.99) or *The Good Hotel Guide 2000 Continental Europe* (£14.99), direct from Ebury Press (p&p free), please call our credit-card hotline on **01206 256000** or send a cheque/postal order made payable to Ebury Press to **TBS Direct, Frating Distribution Centre, Colchester Road, Frating Green, Essex CO7 7DW**